A PRONOUNCING AND ETYMOLOGICAL DICTIONARY

OF THE

GAELIC LANGUAGE

A PRONOUNCING AND ETYMOLOGICAL DICTIONARY

OF THE

GAELIC LANGUAGE

GAELIC-ENGLISH
ENGLISH-GAELIC

BY

MALCOLM MACLENNAN

PUBLISHED JOINTLY BY

ACAIR

AND

ABERDEEN UNIVERSITY PRESS

This edition, published in 1979,
is a photolithographic reproduction
of the first edition, 1925,
published by John Grant,
Edinburgh
Reprinted 1982, 1984, 1985, 1986, 1988

Acair Ltd is a bilingual publishing company set up by
the Highlands & Islands Development Board, An
Comunn Gaidhealach, and Comhairle nan Eilean to
produce mainly books in Gaelic for children and adults.
The company is based at Cromwell St Quay, Stornoway,
Isle of Lewis, Scotland

British Library Cataloguing in Publication Data
MacLennan, Malcolm
A pronouncing and etymological dictionary
of the Gaelic language
1. Gaelic language—Dictionaries—English
I.Title
491.6'3'321   PB1591

ISBN 0-08-025713-5
ISBN 0-08-025712-7 Pbk

PRINTED IN GREAT BRITAIN
AT THE UNIVERSITY PRESS
ABERDEEN

PREFACE

THIS Dictionary is based on *A Pronouncing Gaelic Dictionary* by Neil MacAlpine which made its first appearance about 1831. In 1903 it reached its twelfth edition, which indicates the useful position it occupied in the study of Gaelic. The work of revision and enlargement was begun with the intention of preserving its distinctive feature as a pronouncing dictionary. Soon it became evident that much more than that was required in order to increase its usefulness, and to meet the needs of the modern student of Gaelic. Since Gaelic became a subject qualifying for graduation in Arts in the Scottish Universities, its study has been arranged on broader lines. In this course a knowledge of Irish in its various stages has long been regarded as essential to a proper understanding of Gaelic literature. In view of this development, it was felt that if the present work was to be in any true sense in advance of its predecessor, it must needs offer assistance in the field of etymology. Accordingly the original scheme has been amplified in this direction, so that the present edition may be described as both a Pronouncing and an Etymological Dictionary.

In preparation for the work the editor read most of the principal literature of modern Gaelic, and from this source a great many words have been added. He has also incorporated a considerable number of words current in common speech, but not recorded in other Dictionaries.

It will be found that the Gaelic-English part of this work contains all the words in MacBain's *Etymological Dictionary* and in MacEachan's *Gaelic-English Dictionary*, as well as all those recorded in MacAlpine's ; and it is estimated that it includes some 13,000 words more than are given in MacBain's, and some 10,000 more than in MacAlpine's twelfth edition.

The etymological element is the result of painstaking research, in the course of which a great variety of sources has been laid under contribution—works in English, Irish, French, German, Danish dealing with Celtic, or with Old Norse, or with the interrelation of these languages, as well as with the indebtedness of Celtic to Latin and Greek.

Valuable help has been rendered by a group of Gaelic scholars, representing different parts of the Gaelic-speaking area : the Rev. Adam

Gunn, D.D., Durness, Sutherland ; the Rev. D. M. MacDonald, M.A., Ness, Lewis ; Mr. Donald MacIver, retired Headmaster, Bayble Public School, Lewis ; Mr. Alexander MacAskill, M.A., Carloway, Lewis; the Rev. Malcolm MacLeod, M.A., Glasgow ; the Rev. Donald MacLean, D.D., Professor of Church History, Free Church College, Edinburgh ; William J. Watson, LL.D., Professor of Celtic Languages, Literature, History and Antiquities, Edinburgh University.

Mr. Bruce Dickins, M.A., Lecturer in English Language, Edinburgh University, kindly gave the benefit of his special knowledge of Old Norse. His notes and criticisms inspired confidence, on the one hand, and contributed to accuracy of form and of matter, on the other.

These friends read all the Proofs and Revise, and it is a pleasure to make grateful acknowledgment of their cheerful service and their valuable suggestions. Special mention must be made here of the personal interest which Professor Watson took in the work, and of the generous way in which he put his expert knowledge at the service of the editor. It only remains to be said that, as a matter of course, the editor accepts all responsibility for the final form of the Work.

MALCOLM MACLENNAN.

EDINBURGH, *January 1925.*

REFERENCES

Anwyl, J. Bodvan: Spurrell's Welsh-English Dictionary: eighth edition.
Armstrong, R. A. : À Gaelic Dictionary in two Parts ; Gaelic-English and English-Gaelic.
Atkinson, Robert : The Passions and the Homilies from Leabhar Breac.

Brachet, Auguste : Dictionnaire étymologique de la langue française : nouvelle édition.

Cameron, Alexander : Scottish Celtic Review. Reliquiae Celticae, edited by MacBain and Kennedy.
Cameron, John : The Gaelic Names of Plants.
Carmichael, Alexander : Carmina Gadelica: two vols., 1900.
Carswell, John : The Book of Common Order, commonly called John Knox's Liturgy, edited by Thomas McLauchlan, LL.D., 1873.
Cleasby, R. : Icelandic-English Dictionary, enlarged and completed by Gudbrand Vigfusson, 1874.
Cormac : Sanas Cormaic : an Old Irish Glossary, compiled by Cormac úa Cuilennáin, edited by Kuno Meyer, 1912.
Curry, Eugene : Cath Mhuighe Léana, edited by Eugene Curry.

Darmesteter, Arsène : A Historical French Grammar. Authorised English edition by Alphonse Hartog, 1907.
Dinneen, Patrick S. : Foclóir Gaedhilge agus Béarla, 1904.
Dottin, G. : Manuel d'irlandais moyen : 1. Grammaire ; 2. Textes et glossaire, 1913.
Dwelly : Faclair Gàidhlig, air son nan Sgoiltean, le Dealbhan : three vols.

Ernault, Émile : Dictionnaire breton-français du dialecte de Vannes, 1904.

Feist, Sigmund : Etymologisches Wörterbuch der gotischen Sprache.
Fowler, H. W. and F. G. : The Concise Oxford Dictionary of Current English.

Gunn, Adam, and Calum MacPhàrlain : Orain agus Dàin le Rob Donn MacAoidh.
Güterbock et Thurneysen : Indices glossarum et vocabulorum Hibernicorum quae in Grammaticae Celticae editione altera explanantur.
Gwynn, Edward : Vols. vii. and viii. in Todd Lecture Series, Royal Irish Academy.

Henderson, George : Fled Bricrend, vol. ii. Irish Texts Society.
Highland Society : Dictionary of the Gaelic Language, two vols. ; Gaelic-English and English-Gaelic.
Hogan, Edmund : Vols. iv. and vi. in Todd Lecture Series, Royal Irish Academy.
Holder, Alfred : Altceltischer Sprachschatz, with Supplement.

Jamieson, John : An Etymological Dictionary of the Scottish Language. New edition in four vols., 1879.
Jones, Sir Morris : A Welsh Grammar, 1913.

Keating, Geoffrey : Trí Bior-ghaoithe an Bháis (Three Shafts of Death), edited by Atkinson. Foras Feasa ar Eirinn : four vols. in Irish Texts Society.
Kluge, Friedrich : Etymologisches Wörterbuch der deutschen Sprache. Siebente Auflage, 1910.

Larsen, A. : Dansk-Norsk-Engelsk Ordbog.
Lhuyd, Edward : Archaeologia Britannica, 1707.

MacBain, Alexander : Etymological Dictionary of the Gaelic Language.
MacCarthy, B. : The Codex Palatino-Vaticanus : vol. iii. of Todd Lecture Series, Royal Irish Academy.
MacEachen, Eoghan : Faclair Gàidhlig is Beurla.
MacLean, Rev. Donald : The Songs of Dugald Buchanan, 1913.
MacLeod and Dewar : A Dictionary of the Gaelic Language, in two Parts : Gaelic-English and English-Gaelic.
MacPhàrlain, P. : Foclair ùr Gàidhlig agus Beurla, 1815.
Marstrander, Carl J. S. : Dictionary of the Irish Language : Fasciculus I., the Royal Irish Academy. Bidrag Til Det Norske Sprogs Historie I Irland, 1915.
Meyer, Kuno : Contributions to Irish Lexicography. Cáin Adamnáin, in Anecdota Oxoniensia, 1905. Hibernica Minora, in Anecdota Oxoniensia, 1894. Vols. xiii., xiv., xvi., xvii. in Todd Lecture Series, Royal Irish Academy.

Noreen, Adolf : Altisländische und altnorwegische Grammatik, 1903. Geschichte der nordischen Sprachen, besonders in altnordischer Zeit, 1913.

O'Donovan, John, LL.D. : Supplement to O'Reilly's Irish-English Dictionary. Leabhar na g-Ceart (The Book of Rights).
O'Grady, Standish H. : Silva Gadelica : two vols.
O'Reilly, Edward : An Irish-English Dictionary.

Pedersen, Holger : Vergleichende Grammatik der keltischen Sprachen : two vols.

Revue Celtique : A number of vols.

Shaw, William : A Gaelic and English Dictionary, 1780.
Skeat, Walter W. : A Concise Etymological Dictionary of the English Language. New edition, 1901.
Stokes, Whitley : The Calendar of Oengus, in the Transactions of the Royal Irish Academy. Lives of Saints from the Book of Lismore. Urkeltischer Sprach-schatz (vol. ii. of the fourth edition of Fick's Vergl. Wörterbuch der indo-germanischen Sprachen, Stokes und Bezzenberger). Martyrology of Gorman.
Stokes and Kuno Meyer : Archiv für celtische Lexicographie : three vols.
Stokes and Strachan : Thesaurus Palaeohibernicus : two vols.
Stokes und Windisch : Irische Texte, vols. i., ii., iii., iv.
Strachan, John : Old Irish Glosses. Old Irish Paradigms.
Stuart, John : The Book of Deer, edited for the Spalding Club.

Todd, James H. : Cogadh Gáedhel re Gallaibh.
Thurneysen, Rudolf : Handbuch des Altirischen : 1. Grammatik ; 2. Texte und Wörterbuch.
Transactions of the Gaelic Society of Inverness.

Vendryes, J. : Grammaire du vieil-irlandais.

Walde : Lateinisches etymologisches Wörterbuch, 1910.
Watson, W. J. : Bàrdachd Ghàidhlig. Rosg Gàidhlig.
Watson, Mrs. W. J. (Miss E. C. Carmichael) : The Celtic Review : ten vols.
Windisch, Ernest : Die altirische Heldensage Táin Bó Cúalgne. Irische Texte mit Wörterbuch. See Stokes und Windisch.

Zeitschrift für celtische Philologie : fifteen vols.
Zeuss, J. C. : Grammatica Celtica, ed. Ebel.

ABBREVIATIONS

(Abbreviations of grammatical terms are sufficiently obvious)

A.M.	Alexander MacDonald (MacMhaighistir Alasdair).	Goth.	Gothic.
		Gr.	Greek.
A.S.	Anglo-Saxon.	Heb.	Hebrew.
Arm.	Armstrong.	Hebr.	Hebrides.
		H.F.B.	Henderson's Fled Bricrend (Irish Texts Society, vol. ii.).
B.D.	Book of Deer.		
Br.	Breton.		
Carm. Gad.	Carmina Gadelica.	Hr.	Alfred Holder.
Car. n. Gl.	Caraid nan Gàidheal.	H.S.	Highland Society's Dictionary.
Carsw.	John Carswell, Bishop of the Isles.		
C.R.	Rev. Charles M. Robertson (in Transactions of Gaelic Society of Inverness).	Icel.	Icelandic.
		I.L.	Iain Lom.
		Ir.	Irish.
Corm.	Sanas Cormaic.	I.T.	Irische Texte, Stokes und Windisch, four vols.
Corn.	Cornish.		
		Ital.	Italian.
Dan.	Danish.		
D.Lis.	Dean of Lismore.	Kl.	Friedrich Kluge.
Dial.	Dialect.	Ktg.	Keating.
Din.	Dinneen's Irish - English Dictionary.		
		Lat.	Latin.
Duan.	An Duanaire, by Donald MacPherson.	L.Br.	Leabhar Breac.
		L. na gC.	Leabhar na g-Ceart, The Book of Rights.
Du.B.	Dugald Buchanan.		
D.B.	Duncan Bàn MacIntyre.	L.S.	Lives of Saints, from The Book of Lismore, Stokes.
Du.	Dutch.		
		Lh.	Lhuyd.
E.Ir.	Early Irish.		
Fél.	Félire Oengusa, Whitley Stokes, LL.D.	McB.	MacBain.
		McCod.	John MacCodrum.
Fern. MS.	Fearnaig Manuscript.	McE.	MacEachen's Gaelic - English Dictionary.
Fr.	French.		
fr.	from.	McF.	P. MacPharlain's Focalair.
		Marstr.	Carl J. S. Marstrander.
Gaul.	Gaulish.	M.H.G.	Middle High German.
Ger.	German.	M.Ir.	Middle Irish.
Gl.	Gloss.	M.G.	Modern Gaelic.

O.Celt.	Old Celtic. This includes conjectural ancient forms.	**Sc.**	Scottish.
		Sh.	Shaw.
O'Dav.	O'Davoren Glossary.	**Tbc.**	Táin Bó Cúalgne.
O'D.	John O'Donovan.	**Thn.**	Thurneysen.
O.Fr.	Old French.	**TSh.**	Three Shafts of Death, by Keating.
O.H.G.	Old High German.		
O.Ir.	Old Irish.	**Td.L.**	Todd Lecture Series.
O.N.	Old Norse.	**T.**	Turner.
O'R.	O'Reilly.		
O.W.	Old Welsh.	**Vendr.**	J. Vendryes.
Phœn.	Phœnician.	**W.**	Welsh.
Rel. Celt.	Reliquiae Celticae.	**Wb.**	The Würzburg Glosses.
R.D.	Rob Donn.	**W.R.**	William Ross.
S.O.	Sar Obair nam Bard Gàidhealach.	**Z².**	Zeuss (Gram. Celt., second edition).

PRONUNCIATION

THE pronunciation recorded here must be regarded as only approximately correct. For that there are two good reasons. On the one hand, there are dialectal variations, of considerable interest and importance, of which a few examples, taken at random, are given :

màthair is pronounced mã:hir, mã:hith, mɛ̃:r ; **leughadh,** le:øgʰ, le:vøgʰ, lja:øgʰ ; **sabhal,** so'øl, sɑvøl, sɑul ; **amhach,** ãvøx, ɔ̃øx, ã̃øx ; **seabhag,** ʃɛvøg, ʃoøg ; **each,** ɛx, jɑx ; **feur,** fɛ:r, fiɑr ; **labhairt,** lɑvørt, lɑurst, lɑurd.

It would not be correct to say that of such variations a certain number must be wrong, but it is obvious that it would overload the text to record them all. For this reason the editor does not claim completeness in each case.

On the other hand, the medium of expression is incomplete. The English alphabet can be so manipulated as to give a great range of sounds, but it has its embarrassment. There are certain sounds in Gaelic for which there are no equivalents in English. So often, too, the same symbol varies in sound, e.g. *ie* in f*ie*, f*ie*ld, f*ie*rce ; or *u* in c*u*p, f*u*neral, s*u*re ; or *ou* in r*ou*t, r*ou*te, r*ou*gh, though. Further, the same sound may be represented by different symbols, e.g. *i* in th*i*rst, *e* in h*e*r, *u* in c*u*r, *ou* in col*ou*r; *o* in the last syllable of mot*o*r and *a* in mort*a*r represent one and the same sound. For this reason one's choice of symbols is materially circumscribed in the endeavour to reproduce the sounds of unfamiliar words.

It is hoped that, in these circumstances, the following table may prove helpful.

PHONETIC SOUNDS

The phonetic symbol represents the sound of the italicised letter in the words printed opposite it.

Broad vowels : long, a, o, u

	Phon. sym.	English	French	German	Gaelic
à	a :	f*a*ther.	p*a*sse.	S*aa*t.	bàrd, brà.
à (flanked by m or n)	ã :		v*i*:n.		màs, àmhailt, ànradh.
ò	ɔ :	m*o*re.	enc*o*re.	T*o*r.	òl, còrr, crò.
ò (flanked by m or n)	ɔ̃ :		r*o*nde.		òmar, mòine, nòs.
ó	o :	t*o*ne.	ch*o*se.	S*oh*n.	có, mór, bó.
ù [1]	u :	s*u*re.	t*ou*r.	M*u*t.	cùlan, ùr, brù.
ù (flanked by m or n)	ũ :				rùn, ùnsa, ùmaidh.

[1] Represented in pronouncing element in the text by **oo.** The presence or absence of the stress accent in the Gaelic word may be taken to indicate whether the **oo** is long or short.

PRONUNCIATION

Broad vowels : short, a, o, u

	Phon. sym.	English	French	German	Gaelic
a	a	p*at*.	p*a*tte.	s*a*tt.	ad, sad, nach.
a	ø	c*u*p.	p*eu*.	K*ö*chin.	stadh.

It is so, as a general rule, when it ends a word (na *art*., balla) ; when it precedes dh or gh (agh, bladh) ; when it precedes dh or gh followed by a vowel (aghaidh, tadhal) ; when it occurs in unstressed syllables—penult, final, or in both, except the dim. -an and -ag (cadøl, cadøløch).

a (flanked by m or n)	ɛ̃		v*i*n.		amh. na (neg.), nathair.
o (open)	ɔ	p*o*t.	h*o*mme.	S*o*nne.	do, conas.
o (preceded by m or n)	õ		b*o*n.		monadh, nochd.
o	o	c*o*at.	s*o*t.		coma, bolla.
u ¹	u	f*oo*l.	t*ou*s.	M*u*tter.	cus, ubag, gu.
u (flanked by m or n)	ũ				mulad, umhail.

Narrow vowels : long, e, i

è	ɛ :	f*a*re.	pr*è*s.	b*ä*te.	dèan, cè.
é	e :	j*a*de.	*é*tais.	B*ee*t.	éigin, féin, dé.
ì	i :	f*ee*l.	p*i*re.	B*ie*ne.	rìgh, sìth.

Narrow vowels : short, e, i

e	ə	h*e*r.	d*e*.	Geb*o*te.	gille, tein*e*.
e	ɛ	f*e*ll.	f*ai*t.	B*e*tt.	le, teth.
i	i	f*i*t.	n*i*.	b*i*n.	ith, glic, fir.
i	ai	b*i*te.	t*ai*ller.	st*ei*f.	tigh, rinn (pret. of dèan).

Vowel combinations : long

ao	ø :		n*eu*ve.	H*ö*hle.	aobhar, saobhaidh.
ao	y :		m*u*se.	f*ü*hle.	caob, faobhar, aon.
ài ²	*a* :	f*a*ther.			àithne, càin, fàilte.
òi ²	o :				fòill, fòir.
ói	ø : i				cóibhneas.
ua	uø				uallach, fuar.
ua (flanked by m or n)	uã :				uan, nuagach, uamha.
ùi ²	u :	mood.		K*u*hle.	cùil, dùin.
uì	ui :				luib, tuinn.
uì (flanked by m or n)	uĩ :				cuimhne, muing.
ià	*ia* :				iadach, siadaire.
ìa	i : ø				iasg, ciatach.
ìo	i : ø				sìol.
iù	ju :				iùl, fiù, iùbhrach.
eò	jo :				ceòl, beò.
eu	e :	f*a*me.	m*é*nage.	N*e*bel.	ceum, seud.

eu often = ja, fjar for feur. In O.Ir. too é often broken into ia, except when arising from compens. lengthening.

¹ See note, p. xi.   ² The i gives a slender quality to the adjacent cons., cf. càl and càil.

	Phon. sym.	English	French	German	Gaelic
eà	ja :	yard.		ja.	deàrrsa, eàrra.
éi	e :	shame.	aime.	beten.	éigin, léigh.
èi	ε :	fair.	tête.	bäte.	sgèith, sèimh.

Vowel combinations : short

		English	French	German	Gaelic
ai	ε	any.	errer.	Tenne.	ainm, aithne, caisean.
ai	a				cais, ait, caithream.
ai	ə		secret.	Gedicht.	airmis, cairbh.
oi [1]	ø		jeudi.	Gölte.	goil, oide.
oi	o	home.	sot.	oder.	boil.
oi	ɔ	'cot.	école.	doch.	sgoil, oil.
ui	u			Hui.	cuid, guidh.
ea	ε	pet.	fait.	Bett.	eas, seas, gead.
ea (close)	e	base.	église.	Feder.	beag, eaglais.
ea	ja				ealag, gealach, cealg.
eo	jɔ				seot, beothail.
ei (close)	e	case.	éclat.	Feder.	ceil, seid, eile, sgeilp.
io [2]	i	skid.	si.	Sinn.	giodar.
io	ju				spiol, siola, iola.
aoi	øi (a common Gaelic pron. of Eng. i).				saoile, aoibhneas.
aoi	y : (freq. rhymes with ee).				gaoil, saoil.

Any vowel, or combination of vowels, short or long, followed immediately by p, t, or c, takes the rough breathing, between itself and the following cons. as ba^ht, co^hp, bui^hc.

Consonants

		English	French	German	Gaelic
b	b	ban.	robe.	Bein.	bobarr.
bh (initial)	v	veil.	vent.	weil.	bheil.
bh (medial)	v or w	gravel.	lavage.	Löwen.	labhairt, abhras.
		towel.	oui.	taufen.	abhras, cabhsair.
bh (final)	silent				lobh.
c (flanked by e or i)	k	king.	car.	Kunst.	cìr, reic.
c (flanked by a, o, u)		cock.	corps.	Chor.	cù, brucach.
ch (flanked by e or i)	ç			gleich.	chì, cìch.
ch (flanked by a, o, u)	x	loch.		ach.	ach, cha.
d	d		dent.	da.	dall, cadal.
d (flanked by e or i) = Eng. j, (dʒ), as in jerk.					dearc, callaid.
dh (flanked by e or i)	j	yea.	yeux.	ja.	dhearc, buidhe.
dh (flanked by a, o, u)	g			Tage.	dha, modh, modhail.
dh (final, and preceded by e or i) silent.					branndaidh.
f	f	fell.	fée.	feil.	fear.
g (flanked by e or i)	ɟ	give.		gilt.	gean, éigin.
g (flanked by a, o, u)	g	good.	gare.	Gunst.	gabh, bog, bagair.

[1] The i gives a slender quality to the adjacent cons., cf. càl and càil.
[2] The o preserves the broad quality of the d.

	Phon. sym.	English	French	German	Gaelic
gh (flanked by e or i), is quite similar to dh (narrow).					oighe, gheibh.
gh (preceded by narrow vowel and followed by a cons.) silent.					oighreachd, maighdeag.
gh (flanked by a, o, u)	g			Ta*g*e.	ghabh, magh.

h is not strictly a letter. Its sound is similar to the Greek breathing, both smooth and rough. Its function is to aspirate cons. (ch, dh, mh, etc.), and also as *punctum delens* (là **fuar**, but **uair fhuar,** *i.e.* **uair uar**).

	Phon. sym.	English	French	German	Gaelic
l	l	*l*ong.	*l*ong.	*l*ieb.	leam, calanas, banail.
l	lh	fu*ll*.			a làmh (his hand).
l	ll				a làmh (her hand), feall.
l	hl (less explosive than the Welsh ll).				leig (*pret.*), leaghta (*adj.*).
m	m	*m*an.	da*m*e.	*m*ein.	mac.
m for mm, therefore long. a$\bar{\text{m}}$, ca$\bar{\text{m}}$.					
mh (nasal)	v	*v*ain.	ri*v*e.	Gewehr.	amh, damh, damhan.
mh (nasal)	au		H*au*s.		Samhradh.
mh (nasal, med. or final) silent.					domh, domhsa.
n	n	*n*ame.	â*n*e.	*n*ein.	ainm, dàn, a nàmh (his enemy).
n and nn	ɲ	a*nn*ual.	ag*n*eau.		a nàmh (her enemy).
So nn when flanked by a slender vowel.					sinne, againn.
ng	ŋ	a*ng*le.			mang.
p	p	a Teutonic letter adopted.			
r	r	fa*r*.	pa*r*.	de*r*.	mar, a ràmh (his oar).
r	R	*r*ich.	*r*auch.		ràn, a ràmh (her oar).
rn		co*rn*.	sou*rn*ois.	Do*rn*.	mórnaich.
s (flanked by a, o, u)	s	*s*un.	*s*i.	wi*ss*e.	sàr, thusa, bus.
s (flanked by e or i)	ʃ	*s*ure.	*ch*at.	a*sch*e.	sian, moisein, cois.
sh	h	*h*ave.		*h*ier.	Shàbaid, sheachdain.
t-s (initial)	t				an t-Sàbaid (=an tabaid).
t (flanked by a, o, u)	t		pa*tt*e.	*T*ier.	tàmh, cotan, cat.
t (flanked by e or i)	tʃ	*ch*in.		ku*tsch*er.	peitean.
th	h				athair, tha.
th (final) practically silent.					math, dath.

THE ACCENT

In Gaelic usage the accent has three different senses. It means the syllabic pitch, and is named the stress accent. In this sense it has no visible sign of its own, save that it coincides with the other two. It is placed on the first syllable of a word, except in the case of hyphenated compounds, when it is placed on the last member; and on the first syllable thereof, if there be two or more syllables: *e.g.* **tòimhseachan**; **corra-mhàg**; **tigh-còmhnuidh**; **gille-cŏmhailteach.**[1]

---

[1] The sign ˅ here indicates the place of the stress accent on a short vowel.

The stress accent plays an important part in the formation of words, in combination of course with the phonetic laws of the language. It may shorten a long vowel and lengthen a short one within the same formation: co + fìr > còir ; ad + rím > O. Ir. áram, now àireamh. It may shorten a long vowel and at the same time syncopate the word: candelārius > O.Ir. caindlóir, now cainnleir. It may telescope a phrase into a word: Ciod e a b'àil leibh > bàilibh or bailidh ; is maith a dh'fha-oidte > smǎithide and even smĕite. It exerts its influence in various other ways also, but it is not necessary to elaborate the point here.

It is important to notice that words borrowed from foreign languages come under the sway of the stress accent in the same way as native words do : Lat. quadrāgēsima became in O. Ir. corgais, now carghas ; scriptūra becomes sgriobtur ; O. N. Grágásvík becomes Gràsǎvǐg.

The stress accent may change the quantity of a vowel, but there is one thing it does not do : it does not change its quality—it does not change a close vowel into an open one, or an open vowel into a close one.

The accent is used, in the second place, to indicate a certain quality of vowel sound. In this sense it is used to distinguish the open and the close sounds of the vowels e and o, reserving the grave accent (`) to mark the open sound and the acute (') to mark the close sound : dèan (dɛːn), féin (feːn) ; òr (ɔːr), mór (moːr). The application of this rule, however, is modified by the dialectal idiosyncrasy of any given writer. At the same time it may be taken as in the main of general value.

Valuable as this rule is, it would have been more serviceable still if it could have been extended to cover unstressed vowels also. There is nothing, for example, to distinguish the close sound of the plural ending -an from the open sound of the diminutive ending -an, e.g. casan (casən), feet, from casan (casan), path ; measan (misən), fruits, from measan (misan), lapdog ; clachan (claxən), stones, from clachan (claxan), a thing made of stone, a stone church.

The accent is used, in the third place, as a mark to indicate the length of a vowel sound. For this purpose both the grave and the acute are employed, and placed on all the vowels. So far as e and o are concerned, the same accent serves to indicate both quality and quantity.

One would wish that some means had been devised to indicate the quantity of long consonants also : e.g. am (time) is often written àm, no doubt under the influence of the Gaelic Scriptures (1826), which is obviously wrong. It is the consonant that is long, and not the vowel. One is familiar with two ways of pronouncing the word, but àm is not one of these. One is aᵘm like aum in Ger. Baum, and the other is am like amb in ambit.

FACLAIR GAIDHLIG AGUS BEURLA

A

a, the first letter of the alphabet, called ailm, the palm tree.

a, *voc. particle*, asp. a dhuine ! man ! *O.Ir.* á, ái.

a, *poss. pr. m.* his. Asp. initial cons.: a mhac, his son ; a bhean, his wife ; *pl.* an, their.

a, *poss. pr. f.* her, does not asp., but requires h- bef. vowels : a h-each, her horse ; a mac, her son ; *pl.* an, their.

a, *rel. pron.* who, which, that. *O.Ir.* a, a n-.

a, *prep.* (1) to (of infinitive) =do. Aspirates : a' dol a chluich, going to play (here a' =ag and a =do). Distinguish : is còir dhuinn a (*pron.*) mheas mar, from is còir dhuinn sin a (*prep.*) mheas mar ; (2) to (a place) =do ; a Dhun-éideann, to Edinburgh.

a, in a rìs is *prep.* do. *E.Ir.* doridisi.

a, *prep.* from, out of. *See* as.

a, *prep.* from ; forms *adv.* a nios, from below ; a nuas, from above ; a null, thither ; a nall, hither.

a, *prep.* in, into ; forms *adv.* a stigh, in (the house) ; a steach, into (the house) ; a muigh, outside ; a mach, outwards ; rach a mach, go out. *O.Ir.* i, i n- ; immach, i n- +mach ; immaig, i n- + mag.

a', *prep.* ag, at, which see.

a, *idiom. part.* used to express the card. numerals. a h-aon, one ; a cóig, five, etc.

a', the *art.* the, for an, which see.

aba, *n. m.* an abbot ; an ni ni an dara h-aba subhach, ni e dubhach an t-aba eile, what makes the one abbot glad, makes the other abbot sad. *Ir.* ab, *O.Ir.* abb. *W. and Br.* abad. *Lat.* abbas.

abab, *int.* fie ! pshaw ! shame : *n. m.* filth, dirt. *Ir.* abab, *M.Ir.* abb, *interj.* of defiance ; and obo, of wonder ; *also* àbh ! àbh ! Cf. *Lat.* babae, *Gr.* βαβαί.

ababach, *a.* filthy, dirty.

ababachd, *n. f.* filthiness, dirt.

ababardaich, *n. f.* a disgusting repetition of abab.

abachd, ab'-achc, *n. f.* contraction of abaidheachd, ripeness.

abachd, *n. f.* an abbey.

abact, *n. f.* ironical joking. Cf. àbhachd.

abadh, *n. m.* a syllable.

abaich, abich, *a.* ripe. *E.Ir.* apaig, ripe ; fr. ad +bongid. *Thn.*

abaid, abej, *n. f.* an abbey.

abaid, *n. f.* a monk's cowl, a hat.

abaideachd, abejuchc, *n. f.* an abbacy.

abaidealachd, abijeluchc, *n. f.* griping.

abaideil, abijel, *n. f.* the colic.

abailt, *n. f.* an abbey.

abair, ab'-ir, *v.* say, affirm, express ; one of the irreg. verbs ; *imper.* abair, *ind. pres.* abraim, deirim, *ind. pret.* thubhairt, *ind. fut.* their, abraidh, *cond.* theirinn, *pr. part.* ag radh. *O.Ir.* atbeir, as-beir, epiur.

abairt, ab'-art, *n. f.* speech, babbling, recrimination, scolding, politeness, an idiom. *O.Ir.* epert.

abaisd, abeshj, *n. m.* a brat.

abalt, *a.* expert, proficient, masterly, very able ; fr. *Eng.* able.

abaltachd, *n. f.* proficiency, dexterity, uncommon skill ; strength.

abaltaiche, abultichu, *n. m.* a proficient man, an adept.

abar, *n.* confluence, estuary (only in place-names). *W.* aber, *O.W.* aper.

abarach, abarrach, 1. *a.* bold ; 2. *n. f.* a bold, brazen woman.

abardair, *n. m.* a dictionary. *Sh.*

abarrachd, *n. f.* indelicacy, as a female, immodesty ; impudence, turbulence.

abartach, abartuch, *a.* talkative.

abartachd, ab'-art-uchc, *n. f.* loquacity, unbecoming boldness.

abartair, ab'-art-er, *n. m.* a babbler.

àbh, āv, *n. m.* a nose net, a hand net ; *also* tàbh, tāv, spoon net, landing net. *O. N.* háfr.

abh, af, *n. f.* the yelp of a terrier.

I

àbhach, āvuch, *a.* sportive, humorous, joyous.

àbhachd, āvachc, *n. f.*, àbhachdas, *n. m.*, sport, diversion, frolic, good-humoured gibing ; ball àbhachdais, a laughing-stock.

àbhachdach, *a.* joyful, merry ; gach creutair a' togail an cinn gu h-àbhachdach, all creatures lifting their heads joyfully.

àbhachdail, āvachcal, *a.* amusing ; sgeula beag àbhachdail, amusing little tale.

abhadh-ciuil, ava-kiool, *n. f.* a musical instrument.

abhag, afug, *n. m.* a terrier, a dwarf. *Ir.* abhach.

abhagail, ăf'-ag-al, *a.* terrier-like ; *n. m.* yelping ; snapping, carping.

àbhagas, *n. f.* a surmise, an evil report.

àbhaich, *n. pl.* the deer. *See* àbhach.

abhainn, avin, *n. f.* river ; *gen. sing.* aibhne and abhann ; srath na h-abhann, strath of the river ; *pl.* aibhnichean. *O.Ir.* aba, *gen.* abann. *O.Celt.* abona, *W.* afon. Cf. *Lat.* amnis, orig. ap-nis.

abhall, av'-ull, *n. f.* 1. an orchard. 2. an apple-tree. 3. a chief, " Craobh a b'àirde dhe'n abhal thu," the tree that was highest in the orchard thou. 4. cabbage run to seed. *O.Ir.* aball, *malus, Gaul.* avallo (gl. poma), *O.W.* afal.

àbhais, āvish, also àbhaist, *n. f.* 1. custom ; behaviour. 2. abode. " An làrach an robh àbhaist do sheanar "— the site on which stood your grandfather's habitation.

abhall-ghort, *n. f.* an orchard. *O.Ir.* aball + gort.

abharr, *n. f.* a silly jest, joke.

abharrach, avuruch, *a.* given to silly jokes, or jesting.

àbharsair, āv'-ar-ser', *n. m.* opponent, enemy, Satan. *Ir.* áidhbheirseoir, *O.Ir.* on adbirseoir = *ab adversario.* fr. *Lat.*

abhcaid, aukej, *n. f.* jest, merriment ; raillery.

abhcaideach, aukejuch, *a.* jocular.

abhlan, āv'-llan, *n. m.* a wafer ; abhlan coisrigte, a consecrated wafer. *O.Ir.* obla, *gen.* oblann. *Lat.* oblationem.

abhra, aura, *n. m.* eyelid. *See* fabhra, *also* abhraid. *E.Ir.* abra, eye-lash.

abhran, auran, *n. m.* a song. *See* òran.

abhras, aurus, *n. m.* spinning ; wool, flax, etc., for spinning ; yarn ; herring net. *Ir.* abhras, *E.Ir.* abras ; abra (maid) + feis (handiwork). *Corm.*

abhrasach, *a.* of or belonging to spinning material, employed about or well supplied with spinning material.

abhrasaiche, āu'-rus-ich-u, *n. m.* a spinner, carder, cloth-worker, cloth manufacturer.

abhsadh, aüsu', *n. m.* a tug at a rope ; slackening sail ; cessation.

abhsporag, aüsporac, *n.m.* cow's throttle ; *also* amhsporag.

ablach, *n. m.* 1. mangled carcase. 2. a brat ; ablach bochd, a poor creature, an object.

Abrach, contraction of Abarach, belonging to Lochaber.

abran, *n. m.* an oar-slip ; *also* aparran, apron.

abraon, *n. m.* April.

abstol, abs'-tull, *n. m.* an apostle. *O.Ir.* apstal, *Ml.W.* ebestyl. *Lat.* apostolus.

abstolachd, abs'-tull-uchc, *n. f.* apostleship.

abuchadh, *vbl. n. m.* act of ripening ; maturing, mellowing, ripening.

abuich, abich, *v.* ripen, mellow, mature ; *a.* ripe, mellow. *See* abaich, which is better form.

abuich, *a.* ripe, mature ; pert ; duine abuich, a pert meddling person.

abuicheachd, ăbichachc, *n. f.* ripeness, maturity ; pertness.

aca, *comp. pron.* of them, with them, in their possession ; their ; as, an tigh aca, their house ; aca siod, in the possession of those ; theid aca air, they can master it ; tha móran aca ag radh, many of them say. *See* ag.

acaid, akaj, *n. f.* a stitch ; a transient lancinating pain.

acaideach, akejuch, *a.* painful, groaning.

acain, aken, *n. f.* a moan, a sigh ; gun och no acain, without sigh, or moan. *E.Ir.* accáine (ad-cóine).

acaineach, akenach, *a.* plaintive, sobbing.

acair, akir, *n. f., gen. s.* acrach ; *pl.* acraichean ; anchor ; stone holding down heather rope protecting thatch. *O.Ir.* ingor. *O.N.* akkeri, *Lat.* ancora.

acair, akir, *n. f., gen. s.* acrach ; *pl.* acraichean, an acre ; a rick of corn ; fr. *Eng.* acre. *A.S.* æcer. Cf. *O.N.* akr ; *M.H.G.* acker ; *Lat.* ager ; *Gr.* ἀγρός. Orig. pasture.

acairpholl, akir-foul, *n. m.* anchorage.

acanaich, akenich, *n. f.* grief, sobbing, plaintive moaning.

acaran, *n. m.* lumber.

acarra, *a.* benefit ; moderate in price, lenient, indulgent ; settled ; *also* acartha, akuru, profit ; acarach, *a.* kindly, gentle. *E.Ir.* accarda, profit.

acarrachd, acurachc, *n. f.* abatement, moderation, indulgence.

acarsaid, acursej, *n. f.* a harbour, an anchorage ; a haven ; roads. *E.Ir.* accarsóit. *O.N.* akkeris-sæti.

acastair, acustur, *n. m.* an axle-tree.

acfhuinn, acinn, *n. f.* 1. apparatus, implements ; acfhuinn an t-saoir, carpenter's tools ; **acfhuinn an eich,** horse's harness ; **acfhuinn iasgaich,** tackling of the fishing-rod ; **acfhuinn thogalach,** apparatus for distilling. 2. salve ; **acfhuinn shùla,** eye-salve. *E.Ir.*

accmaing, *O.Ir.* cumang, power.

acfhuinneach, etc., *a.* well equipped, well furnished with apparatus ; **duine acfhuinneach,** a well-endowed man, a resourceful man.

ach, *interj.* oh ! alas !

ach, *conj.* but, except, save ; if only ; **ach do làmhansa bhi leinn,** if only your hands were with us ; **ach beag,** almost ; **theid mi ach am faic mi,** I shall go that I may see. *O.Ir.* act, acht, provided that, if only ; equates etym. with *Gr.* ἐκτός. *Thn.*

ach, *n. m.* field.

achadh, *n. m. pl.* achannan, and *also* achaidhean, field. *E.Ir.* achad.

achain, ach'-en', *n. f.* a supplication ; dial. for athchuinge, āching. *E.Ir.* achain, egg, incite.

achanach, *a.* supplicatory.

achanaich, ăchenich, *n. f.* an earnest entreaty, supplication, a solemn appeal or prayer ; *v. i.* entreat, beseech earnestly ; **tha mi 'g achanaich ort,** I solemnly entreat of you.

acharradh, achara, *n. m.* dwarf ; sprite.

achd, achk, *n. m.* 1. statute, act, **achd pàrlamaid,** an act of Parliament. 2. manner, **air an achd so,** in this way. 3. case, **air aon achd,** in any case. *Lat.* actum.

achdaidh, achki, *a.* actual ; *adv.* gu h-achdaidh, assuredly.

achlaid, achlej, *n. f.* chase, pursuit.

achlais, ach'-lesh, *n. f.* the arm-pit, hollow, or bosom ; **ràimh 'g an snìomh an achlais nan àrd thonn,** oars twisting in the trough of lofty waves ; **leabhar fo achlais,** a book under his arm. *O.Ir.* ascall, ochsal ; *Lat.* axilla. *O. N.* öxl, *Ger.* achsel, *Fr.* aisselle.

achlan, *n. m.* lamentation.

achlasan, *n. m.* anything carried under the arm.

achlasan Challum chille, *n. m.* St. John's wort.

achmhasan, ăchusan, *n. m.* a reproof, a reprimand, a reprehension, rebuke. *E.Ir.* athchomsán.

achmhasanach, *a.* reprehensive ; prone to rebuke ; reproachful.

achmhasanaich, *v.* reprove, rebuke, chide, reprimand, reprehend.

achmhasanaiche, *n. m.* reprover, a rebuker, a reprimander.

achrannach, *a.* intricate ; *v. tr.* achran-naich, entangle, entwine.

achuinge, achinge, *n. f.* supplication ; for

athchuinge : ath + cuinge, intensive request. *O.Ir.* cuintgim, *peto.*

acrach, *a.* hungry. *Ir.* ocrach.

acraich, acrich, *v.* drop anchor, moor, come to anchor.

acras, *n. m.* hunger ; appetite. *Ir.* ocrus, *E.Ir.* accorus and ocras.

acrasach, *a.* hungry-looking, bespeaking poverty.

acuinn. *See* acfhuinn.

ad, *n. f.* a hat ; **ad mholach,** a beaver hat.

adag, *n. f.* a shock of corn ; stook.

adag, *n. f.* haddock, fr. the *Eng.*

adagaich, adagich, *v.* gather into stooks, make stooks ; **ag adagachadh,** making stooks ; stooking.

adha, a'u, *n. f.* liver. *O.Ir.* óa, ae.

adha-geir, ā-ger, *n. f.* 1. fat of liver. 2. fish or train oil.

adhal, *n. m.* flesh hook. *O. Ir.* áel, *fuscina.*

adhal, u'ul, *n. m.* udder (of cow).

adhaltrach, u'ultruch, *a.* adulterous.

adhaltranach, u'ultranuch, *a.* adulterous, guilty of adultery.

adhaltranas, *n. m.* adultery. *O.Ir.* adaltras, *Lat.* adulterium.

adhan, ă'-un, *n. m.* a byword, a proverb ; **man d' thuirt an t-adhan,** as the proverb says ; *recte* athan.

adhar, a'ur, *n. m.* sky, air. *O.Ir.* áer ; fr. *Lat.* aër.

adharc, u'urc, *n. f.* a horn. *O.Ir.* adarc, *cornu.*

adharcach, *a.* horned.

adharcan, *n. m.* peewit, or lapwing ; *also* adharcan-luachrach.

adhart, *n. m.* pillow ; **ceann-adhairt,** the head of a bed. *E.Ir.* adart, pillow.

adhart, u'urt, *n. m.* progress ; **air adhart,** forward. *O.Ir.* arairt.

adhartan, *n. m.* a pillow.

adhastar, u'ustur, *n. m.* halter. *O.Ir.* adastar.

adhbhal, aval, *a.* vast, awful. *O.Ir.* adbul, adbol, adbal, very great.

adhlacadh, aulaca, *vbl. n. m.* act of burying ; burying ; burial, interment. *O.Ir.* adnacul, *sepulcrum.*

adhlaic, aulic, *v.* bury, inter.

adhmhol, avoll, *v.* magnify.

adhna, ana, *n. m.* advocate. *E.Ir.* aignid, pleader.

adhrach, ŭrach, *a.* reverent, worshipping.

adhradh, ūra, *n. m.* worship ; *also* aoradh. *O.Ir.* adraim = *Lat.* adoro ; adrád, *adoratio.*

afoinn, *n. f.* predicament, distress. *See* amhain.

afraighe, afryu, *n. m.* a rising ; preparation for battle.

ag, *n. m.* refusal, doubt, hesitation ; **gun aga sam bith,** without any doubt. *O.Ir.* acc, no !

4   AG—AIDHMHILLTEACH

ag, *prep.* at ; sign of the *present participle* : as, ag ràdh, saying ; ag iarruidh, seeking ; ag òl, drinking. *O.Ir.* oc, occ ; uc, ucc.

ag, *prep.* at, with ; joined to *pers. pron.*, and signifying possession : 1. *sing.* agam, *pl.* againn ; an tigh agam =mo thigh, my house ; an tigh againn =our house. 2. *sing.* agad, *pl.* agaibh ; an cù agad =do chu, your dog. 3. *m. sing.* aige, *f. sing.* aice, *pl.* aca ; an duine aice =a duine, her man ; am baile aca =their town ; but, tha tigh againn =we have a house ; tha bàta aca = they have a boat.

agadh, agu, *n. m.* hesitancy in speech.

àgadh, àgu, *n. m.* ox, bull ; =òg-agh.

agail, *a.* doubtful, sceptical.

agair, ag'-ur, *v. n.* plead, accuse, tha choguis 'g a agairt, his conscience accuses him ; crave, tha e 'g agairt orm, he craves me ; prosecute, tha e 'g agairt, he prosecutes. *O.Ir.* acre, *reprobatio.*

agairt, ag'-urt, *n. m.* prosecution ; accusation ; pursuing, craving ; prosecuting ; blaming.

agalachd, ăg'-al-uchc, *n. m.* doubtfulness.

agallamh, ag'-al-uv, *n. m.* conversation ; *also* agalladh. *O.Ir.* acaltam (=ad-glad-ma), address.

agam, ag'-um, *prep.* and *pron. See* ag.

agarrach, ag'-urr-uch, *n. m.* pretender.

agartach, agurtuch, *a.* litigious, vindictive, revengeful.

agartachd, agurtuchc, *n. f.* litigation, litigiousness.

agartas, ăg'-urt-us, *n. m.* a suit at law, a plea, a suit.

agh, *n. f.* a heifer, hind. *O.Ir.* ag.

àgh, *n. m.* happiness, luck ; success ; Is fearr àgh na ealain, luck is better than skill ; an ainm an àigh, in the name of goodness. *E.Ir.* àd, luck.

àghach, *a.* warlike. *E.Ir.* àg, war.

aghaib, u'eb, *n. f.* an attempt, an essay, trial (a syn. of oidhirp).

aghaibeach, u'ebuch, *a.* persevering, industrious, indefatigable.

aghaibeachd, u'ebuchc, *n. f.* industry, perseverance, indefatigability.

aghaidh, u'ee, *n. f.* face, countenance, visage ; chuir e an aghaidh air, he faced him ; theirig air t'aghaidh, go forward ; cuir 'n a aghaidh, oppose, thwart him. *O.Ir* aged, aiged, face.

àghann, à'un, *n. m.* frying-pan ; a goblet, a pan of any kind. *O.Ir.* aigen.

aghastar, u'ustur, *n. m.* a horse halter. *See* adhastar.

àghmhor, àghvor, *a.* prosperous, happy. *E.Ir.* àdmar, lucky, *I.T.* iv. 1.

àghmhorachd, *n. m.* prosperity, joyfulness.

agus, *conj.* and. *O.Ir.* acus, ocus.

ah, *interj.* oh !

aha, *interj.* aha !

aibheis, āy-vish, *n. f.* the deep, the sea ; a great quantity ; the great void, the atmosphere ; an aibheis uile làn bhòchdan, the whole atmosphere full of goblins. *O.Ir.* abís, abyss, *Lat.* abyssus.

aibheis, *n. f.* boasting.

aibheiseach, āy-vishuch, *a.* ethereal, vast, incredible, enormous. *E.Ir.* aibsech, awful, terrible.

aibheiseachadh, āy-vishuchu, *vbl. n. m.* act of exaggerating from envious motives ; an exaggeration.

aibheiseachd, *n. f.* enormity, incredibility, exaggeration.

aibhist, āy-visht, *n. m.* an old ruin ; " cha b'aibhist fhuar e mar a nochd," it was not a cold ruin as (it is) to-night.

aibhistear, āy-vishter, *n. m.* the devil ; a form of àbharsair.

aibhistearachd, ay-vishteruchc, *n. f.* demonism, the conduct of a devil.

aibhlitir, ayv-litur, *n. f.* the alphabet, an A, B, C. *O.Ir.* abbgitir, apgitir, *abecedarium.*

aibhse, ayshu, *n. f.* a spectre, goblin ; *also* taibhse. *O.Ir.* taidbsiu, *demonstratio.*

aibhsich, *v.* exaggerate from envious motives.

aibidil, āy-bijel, *n. f.* the alphabet.

aibidileach, *a.* alphabetical.

aice, aice-se, *prep.* and *pron. suf. fem.* her, or hers. *See* ag.

aice, ecke, *n. f.* proximity. *See* taice. *E.Ir.* aicce, nearness.

aice, *n. f.* lobster's hole, crab hole ; *also* faiche.

aiceachd, eckachk, *n. f.* a leading, guidance ; lesson. *E.Ir.* acept, a lesson.

àicheadh, āchay, *n. m.* denial, refusal ; is e an t-àicheadh maith dara puing as fhearr 'san lagh, a strenuous denial is the next best point in law.

aicheamhail, ĕch'-uv-al, *n. f.* vengeance, reprisals. ath + gabhail, *McB.*

àicheidh, āchey, *v.* deny, refuse, disavow, renounce. Cf. *O.Ir.* atchúad, *exposui.*

aicme, eckma, *n. f.* race, tribe. *O.Ir.* aicmae, *genus.*

aideachadh, ejuchu, *n. m.* confession, acknowledgment, avowal ; acknowledging, confessing, avowing. *O.Ir.* ad-daimim, attaimim, ataimim, I confess, I admit. *W.* addef.

aideachail, ej-ach-al, *a.* affirmatory, penitent, confessing.

aidheam, īyem, *n. f.* joyous carol.

aidhmhillteach, ay-veeltiuch, *n. m.* a

spendthritt ; a beast that steals from the pasture to feed on the growing corn. *E.Ir.* ad-millim, I destroy.

aidich, ejich, *v.* confess, acknowledge, avow.

aidichte, ejichtu, *vbl. a.* confessed, acknowledged, owned, admitted, allowed.

aidmheil, ăj'-val, *n. f.* confession, profession, persuasion, religious belief.

aidmheileach, ejvelach, *a.* acquiescent, forthcoming ; bithidh mise aidmheileach dhuitse, I will be responsible to you.

aidmheileachd, *n. f.* acquiescence, responsibility ; acknowledgment.

aidmheiliche, aj'-vall-ich-u, *n. m.* a professor, one that follows some creed.

aifrionn, eff-runn, erin, *n. m.* mass. *E.Ir.* oifrend, *Lat.* offerenda.

aig, egg, *prep.* at, near, near to, close by, aig baile, at home ; on account of, for ; aig meud aigheir, on account of his excessive joy ; in possession ; bha aig duine àraidh dithis mhac, a certain man had two sons. *O.Ir.* oc.

àigeach, āgeach, *n. m.* stallion. *Also* òigeach, young horse.

aigeal, eggal, *n. m.* hard, shingly, bottom of the sea, the deep ; thuit m' aigne 'san aigeal, my mind sank to the bottom. A by-form of aigean.

aigealach, ĕg'-al-ach, *n. m.* a sounder.

aigeallaidh. *See* agallamh.

aigean, eg'-en', *n. m.* an abyss ; the sea ; grunnd an aigein, the bottom of the deep. *E.Ir.* oician, *Lat.* oceanus.

aigeannach, ĕg'-unn-uch, *n. f.* a self-willed boisterous female.

aigeannach, egunuch, *a.* spirited, mettlesome ; "is aigeannach fear aotrom," sprightly is the free man. *Also* aigeanta. *E.Ir.* aignech, sprightly ; agile.

aigeannachd, egunuchc, *n. f.* stubbornness ; a turbulent disposition. *Is.*

aigeantach, ĕg'-annt-uch, *n. f.* a turbulent female ; *a.* stubborn, mulish.

aigeantachd, *n. f.* courage, hilarity.

aigheab, ăyeb. *See* aghaib.

aighear, ăyur, *n. m.* joy ; exultation, gladness, mirth, happiness. *O.Ir.* airer, aerer, satisfaction, pleasure.

aighearach, ăyuruch, *a.* exulting, joyous, gay, happy ; odd, òlach aighearach, an odd fellow. *Ir.* aiereach, merry, aerial ; áer, air.

aighearachd, ayuruchc, *n. f.* gladness, merriment, mirthfulness ; oddness.

aigilean, ĕg'-ill-en, *n. f.* a tag or horn, earring, tassel.

aigne, egna, and aigneadh, *n. m.* mind, spirit. *O.Ir.* aicned, nature, reason.

aigneach, ĕg'-nuch, *a.* lively, brisk.

àil, āl, *n. f.* desire, will. *O.Ir.* áil, desirable ; áilim, I beg.

àil, àileadh, àilt, *n. m.* mark, impression.

ail, *n. f.* rock. *O.Ir.* ail, rock.

ailbhe, *n. f.*, poverty. beò air an ailbhe, living in poverty ; an ailbhe ghorm, next to nothing.

ailbheag, elvag, *n. f.* ring ; an ear-ring.

ailbhinn, elvin, *n. f.* flint ; the firm rock ; a projecting rock, a projection ; precipice. Cf. *E.Ir.* ailbech.

àile, āla, *n. m.* air, scent.

aile, for eile. *Lat.* alius.

aileag, alag, *n. f.* hiccup. *Ir.* fail.

ailean for oilean.

ailean, alen, *n. m.* a green, a plain.

àilear, alir, *n. m.* a porch; *also*, sgàththigh.

àilgheas, ālyes, *n. m.* will, desire ; fastidiousness, pride ; imperiousness ; ailgheas dhaoine, the pride of men. *O.Ir.* áil + geiss (request) ; fr. guidim.

àilgheasach, alyesach, *a.* fastidious ; proud, haughty ; imperious, arrogant.

àilgheasachd, *n. f.* fastidiousness, haughtiness ; arrogance.

ailis, āl'-ish, *n. f.* imitation, mockery ; reproach, blemish ; rivalling ; " ag ailis air Oscar nam beuman trice," rivalling Oscar of the deft blows ; a form of aithris.

àill, *n. f.* will, desire, pleasure ; ciod is àill leibh ? what is your will ? an àill leat ? do you prefer ? *See* àil.

aill-bhill, alvil, *n. m.* bridle-bit.

àille, āliu, *n. f.* beauty, sublimity, glory, dignity ; àille thalmhaidh, earthly beauty; *comp. deg.* of àlainn, handsome.

àille, *a.* beautiful; as àille, most beautiful.

àilleachd, ālachc, *n. f.* beautifulness, handsomeness, sublimity.

àillead, āliud, *abstr. n. m.* beauty.

àilleagan, āliugan, *n. m.* a jewel, darling, a toy. Cf. *O.Ir.* áilgen, gentle, tender.

ailleagan, eliugan, *n. m.* root of the ear.

aillealachd, elulachc, *n. f.* modesty.

aillean, *n. f.* shyness ; air an aillein, among strangers. *E.Ir.* ail, bashful.

ailleanach, elenuch, *a.* bashful, shy.

ailleanachd, *n. m.* bashfulness.

ailleann, ĕll'-unn, *n. f.* the herb elecampane ; a young beau ; a minion.

ailleanta, elantu, *a.* delicate.

ailleantachd, *n. f.* delicacy, bashfulness ; is e ailleantachd maise nam ban, modesty is the ornament of women.

àilleort, āylort, *a.* high-rocked.

àillidh, āli, *a.* charming.

aillionair, *n. m.* a caterer.

aillse, āylshu, *n. m.* diminutive creature ; a fairy.

aillse, *n. m.* cancer. *O.Ir.* ailsin, cancerem.

aillseag, āylshag, *n. f.* a caterpillar.

aillsich, ailsich, *v. a.* exaggerate; *also* aibhsich.

ailm, elm, *n.f.* the letter a, elm. *Ir.* ailm, palm tree, *Lat.* ulmus, *O. N.* álmr.

ailm, *n. f.* helm; "an ailm an uchd na glaic," the helm against the palm.

ailmse, elmshu, *n. f.* mistake, error.

àilt, *a.* noble, stately, high. *Lat.* altus.

aim-, aimh-, *privative prefix*, as, aimbeart, aimhleas.

aimbeairteach, *a.* poor; aim + beartach.

aimbeart, āym-erst, *n. f.* poverty.

aimheal, ev'-al, *n. m.* mortification, pique, great vexation; aith + méala. *E.Ir.* méla, sorrow, reproach, *O.Ir.* mebul, *dedecus.*

aimhealach, ev'-al-uch, *a.* galling, vexing to the utmost; mortifying.

aimhealachd, ev'-al-uchc, *n. f.* the greatest mortification, or vexation.

aimhealaich, ĕvilich, *v.* gall, pique, mortify; vex.

aimhealtach, evaltach, *a.* vexed, galled.

aimhealtas, *n. m.* home-sickness.

aimhfheoil, evyol, *n. f.* proud flesh. *Also* ainfheoil, aimh + feòil.

aimhleas, āylus, *n. m.* destruction, ruination, ruin; b'e sin car t'aimhleis, that would be your ruination; harm, mischief; am + leas. *E.Ir.* am-less, disadvantage; hurt. *W.* af les.

aimhleasach, āylusuch, *a.* destructive, hurtful, ruinous, injurious.

aimhleasachd, *n. f.* ruinousness, destructiveness; mischievousness.

aimhleathan, āy-lehun, *a.* strait, narrow; am (*priv.*) + leathan (broad).

aimhreidh, āy-rēy, *a.* disordered, confused; am (*priv.*) + réidh, plain.

aimhreit, ayrēt, *n. f.* entanglement, disorder, confusion, disagreement.

aimhreiteach, *a.* confused, entangled; contentious; duine aimhreiteach, a contentious person.

aimhreiteachd, *n. f.* degree of confusion, or disorder; quarrelsomeness.

aimhreitich, āy-retich, *v.* entangle, disorder, entwine as thread, put in confusion.

aimhriar, āy-riur, *n. f.* mismanagement.

aimhriochd, āy-riuchc, *n. f.* disguise.

aimid. *See* amaid.

aimideach. *See* amaideach.

aimlisg, amalishc, *n. f.* confusion, quarrel, calamity, mischief; mishap; "Conan, aimlisg na Féinne," Conan, the evil genius of the Fiann; *also* ailmisg.

aimlisgeach, emliscach, *a.* quarrelsome, mischievous.

aimrid, emrij, *a.* barren, sterile. *O.Ir.* am-brit, aimbritt, barren; an + beir.

aimrideach, emrijach, *n.f.* a barren woman.

aimrideachd, *n. f.* barrenness.

aimsichte, emshichtu, *a.* bold, resolute.

aimsir, emshir, *n. f.* time; season; weather; a réir na h-aimsir a bhios ann, according to the weather we may have. *O.Ir.* aimser, aimmser, *O.W.* amser.

aimsireil, *a.* temporal; oft. op. of spiritual.

aimsith, emshi, *n. m.* mischance, missing of aim.

àin, *n. f.* splendour, heat, broad daylight, noon. *O.Ir.* áne.

ain-, same as aimh-, *priv. prefix* for an.

ainbheach, envuch, *n. m.* a debt, an obligation; fo ainbheach dhuitse, under obligations to you; from an (*intens.*) and fiach (debt).

ainbheil, en-vel, *n. f.* impertinence, rudeness.

ainbhfhiach, enev-yuch, *n. m.* a debt.

ainbhios, en-vis, *n. m.* ignorance; an ainbhios duit, unknown to thee (an and fios). *E.Ir.* ainbhfeasach, *ignoratus.*

ainbhiosach, en-visuch, *a.* ignorant of; unknown to.

ainbhte, *n. f* a heifer.

ainbhtheach, ene-fuch, *a.* stormy. *O.Ir.* anbthech, tempestuous.

ainbi, ainbith, enbi, *a.* odd, unusual; an (*priv.*) + bith (*vb.* to be).

aincheard, én-chyard, *n. f.* a witticism, a jest.

aincheardach, *a.* jocose, sportive, witty, merry.

aincheas, enches, *n. m.* danger; doubt, dilemma. *E.Ir.* ánces, aingcess, difficulty, distress. *Wi.*

aincheist, en-chesht, *n. f.* dilemma.

ainchis, en'-chish, *n. f.* fury, rage, curse. *E.Ir.* aingcis.

aindeoin, enyon, *n. m.* compulsion, reluctance; defiance; a dh' aindeoin có theireadh e, in defiance of all that would oppose it; a dheòin no dh' aindeoin, willy-nilly = an + deòin. *E.Ir.* am-deón, ill-will, displeasure.

aindeoineach, *a.* reluctant.

aindeoineachd, enyonuchc, *n. f.* reluctancy; obstinacy; unwillingness.

aindeiseal, ainjeshal, *a.* unprepared = an + deas.

aindreann, an'-drenn, *n. m.* fretfulness.

àine, ā'-nu, *n. f.* the liver of fish; àinean nam piocach, the liver of coal-fish; dissyl. form of ae.

aineamh, en'-uv, *n. f.* a flaw, blemish, defect; ceilidh seirc aineamh, charity conceals faults or blemishes. *O.Ir.* anim; *Gr.* ὄνομαι, blame, censure.

aineartaich, āy-nertich, *n. f.* act of yawning.

aineas, aynas, *n. f.* passion, fury.

aineasach, *a.* furious, passionate.

aineol, ĕnol, *n. m.* unacquaintance ; an tìr m' aineoil, in the country where I am unacquainted ; is trom geum bà air a h-aineol, deep is the low of a cow on strange pasture.

aineolach, *a.* ignorant, illiterate, unintelligent, rude.

aineolas, *n. m.* ignorance ; is trom an t-eallach an t-aineolas, ignorance is a heavy burden ; boorishness.

ainfheoil, āynol, *n. f.* proud flesh.

aingeal, engul, *n. m.* light, fire.

aingeal, eng′-ul, *n. m.* an angel. *O.Ir.* angel. *Lat.* angelus ; *Gr.* ἄγγελος.

aingealach, eng′-ul-uch, *a.* angelic.

aingealachd, *n. f.* numbness, tingling with cold ; *also* aingealaich.

aingealag, *n. f.* angelica.

aingealta, eng′-alt-u, *a.* perverse, wicked.

aingealtachd, eng′-alt-achc, *n. f.* perverseness, wickedness.

aingeanta, engant, *a.* malicious.

aingidh, eng′-i, *a.* perverse, wicked. *O.Ir.* andgid, andgaid, angid, andaid, *nequam.* Z².

aingidheachd, engy-achc, *n. f.* perverseness, wickedness, sin, viciousness.

ainglidh, eng-ly, *a.* angelic.

àinich, ānich, *n. f.* panting, gasping.

ainid, en′-ij, *a.* vexing, galling.

ainis, *n. f.* anise, caraway ; fr. *Eng.*

ainleag, en′-lyag, *n. f.* a swallow ; ainleag mhara, a sea-martin. *Ir.* áinle, ainléog.

ainm, en′-um, *n. m.*, *pl.* ainmeannan, a name ; an t-ainm gun an tairbhe, the name without the benefit ; character ; is fhasa deagh ainm a chall na chosnadh, it is easier to lose a good name than to gain one. *O.Ir.* ainmm, ainm ; *O.W.* anu ; *Lat.* nomen ; *Gr.* ὄνομα.

ainmeachadh, en′-um-uch-u, *vbl. n. m.* act of naming, appointing, denominating. *E.Ir.* ainmnigud, naming.

ainmeachas, en′-um-uch-us, *n. m.* a bare name ; a nominal thing ; a trifle.

ainmealachd, en′-um-aluchc, *n. m.* celebrity, fame, reputation ; notoriety.

ainmeannach, én′-um-ann-uch, *n. m.* a nominative, a denominator.

ainmeil, en′-um-al, *a.* namely, celebrated, renowned ; dh' fhàs iad sin 'nan daoine ainmeil, those became men of renown.

ainmeinn, enemenn, *n. f.* bad temper, fury, rage ; pride, arrogance ; an + méinn (disposition).

ainmeinneach, *a.* perverse, full of rage.

ainmhid, *n. f.* a heifer.

ainmhide, envide, *n. m.* a rash fool.

ainmhidh, envy, *n. m.* a brute ; a beast.

ainmhidheachd, envy-achc, *n. m.* brutality.

ainmich, en′-um-ich, *v.* name ; mention,

fix upon ; denominate ; *vbl. a.* ainmichte, named, etc. *E.Ir.* ainmnigim.

ainmig, en′-um-ig, *a.* rare, scarce, seldom ; is ainmig a thig e, he seldom comes ; an (*priv.*) + minig (often).

àinne, *n. f.* splendour, noon-day. *O.Ir.* áne.

ainneal, en′-yal, *n. m.* a common fire.

ainneamh. *See* annamh.

ainneamhag, en′-uv-ag, *n. f.* a phœnix.

ainneart, én′-nyert, *n. m.* force, violence ; an (*intens.*) + neart.

ainneartach, *a.* oppressive.

ainneartachd, *n. f.* force, violence, oppression.

ainnighte, aynitu, *vbl. a.* made tame or patient.

ainnir, enir, *n. f.* a virgin. *E.Ir.* ander, ainder.

ainnis, enish, *a.* poor, needy.

ainniseach, enishuch, *a.* poor.

ainniseachd, en′-nish-achc, *n. f.* poverty.

àinniuigh, *n. m.* a sigh, a sob.

ainsgean, en′-sken, *n. f.* fury, rage.

ainsheasgair, *a.* inhospitable, rude, violent = an (not) + seasgair (cosy).

ainsrianta, an-sriùnt′-u, *a.* unbridled, debauched, obstinate.

ainteas, ayn-tes, *n. m.* inflammation, great heat, zeal ; an (*intens.*) + teas.

ainteasach, *a.* inflammatory, hot, violent.

ainteist, āyn-tesht, *n. m.* bad report, bad character.

ainteisteanas, āyn-teshtunus, *n. m.* a bad character, false testimony.

ainteisteil, ayn-teshtal, *a.* discreditable, ill-famed.

ainteth, ayn-te, *a.* very hot, scorching.

aintighearna, *n. m.* a tyrant.

aintighearnas, ayn-ti-y-urnus, *n. m.* tyranny, oppression.

air, ar′, *prep.* upon, on, of, concerning. 1. = *O.Ir.* ar. This asp., air chùl, behind ; rejected ; air chéilidh, on a visit ; air bheagan céille, of little sense or wit ; muin air mhuin, in a heap (lit. back on back) ; cóig air fhichead, five on twenty = twenty-five. 2. = *O.Ir.* for, upon ; air barr a' bhalla, on the top of the wall ; air caolas, on a channel ; air druim eich, on the back of a horse. 3. = *O.Ir.* iar n-, after ; air sgur, finished (after finishing) ; tha e air briseadh, it is broken (lit. after breaking). But, air dhuinn sgur, when we had finished ; this air = ar. Idiom : air sgàth, for the sake of ; air ainm, by name ; air mo shonsa dheth, as for me ; air éigin, "touch and go" ; air seachran, astray ; air chor, so that ; leabhar air choireigin, some book or other.

air, *prep.* + *pron. m.* on him. *See* orm.

àir, v. tr. plough. See àr.
airbhinneach, ervinuch, a. noble, honourable.
airc, erc, n. f. strait, predicament, poverty ; is mairg a shineadh làmh na h-airce do chridhe na circe, woe to him who stretches poverty's hand to the hen's heart. E.Ir. airc, a strait, difficulty. Cf. Lat. parcus.
àirc, ārc, n. f. an ark, a chest. O.Ir. árc, gen. árcae, áirc. Lat. arca.
airceas, ĕrk'-us, n. f. poverty.
airceil, erkel, a. poor, needy.
airchealla, n. m. 1. sacrilege. 2. theft. O.Ir. arcelim, aufero.
aircheas, erchis, n. m. kindness, for oircheas, charity. O.Ir. airches, proper ; airchissecht, gratia.
aircill, erkil, v. a. lie in wait ; listen secretly. See faircill.
aircinneach, erkinach, n. m. a chief ; a head man of a monastery. E.Ir. airchindeach, a vicar, a lay superintendent of church lands. Satan is "airchindech iffirn," L.Br. M.W. arbennic, ar+penn-ic.
airciseach, erkishach, a. difficult, hungry.
aircleach, erkluch, n. f. a cripple ; an dall air muin an aircleich, the blind on the back of the cripple ; fr. airc.
àird, ārj, n. f. 1. airt, point (of the compass) ; an àird a deas, the south. 2. promonotory (not necessarily high). 3. condition, state ; ciod e an àird a tha air ? what condition is he in ? 4. height ; àird nan sliabh, the height of the hills. 5. plan, expedient ; gun dèanadh e àird air a chur am charaibh, that he would devise an expedient to put it into my possession ; cuir àird ort, prepare ; an àird, upwards, aloft ; os àird, public, above-board. E.Ir. áird, a point and limit. See ard.
àirde, ārj'-u, n. f. height, stature, highness ; deg. more, or most high.
àirdeachd, ārj'-ăchc, n. f. highness.
àirdead, ārj'-ud, abstr. n. f. height.
àirdeanna, ārj'-un-u, n. pl. a constellation.
àirdeil, ārj'-al, a. ingenious.
airdhean, eryen, n. f. a symptom. E.Ir. airden, sign, symptom.
aire, eru, n. f. attention, heed, notice ; thoir an aire ! pay attention ! chan e bha air m' aire=that was far from my thoughts. O.Ir. airim, I watch.
àireach, ār-uch, n. m. a dairyman, keeper of cattle.
aireachail, ăr-ach-al, a. attentive.
àireachas, ār-uch-us, n. f. the business of dairymen, summer pasture.
àireamh, ar'-uv, n. m. number ; v. count, number, compute. O.Ir. ad-rímim, I reckon. W. rhif.

àireamhach, a. numeral, relating to numbers ; n. f. numerator, an accountant.
àireamhachd, āruvachc, n. f. numeration, computation ; counting, numbering.
àirean, āren, n. m. a ploughman. E.Ir. ar, tillage ; airim, I plough. See àr.
àireanach, a. agricultural.
àireanachd, ārenuchc, n. f. agriculture.
airfid, ăr'-fij, n. f. harmony. See oirfid. E.Ir. airfitiud, to play.
airfideach, arfijuch, a. harmonious ; n. m. a musician.
airfideachd, arfijuchc, n. f. harmoniousness, melodiousness.
airgbhraiteach, ergvratach, a. in stately robes ; airg+brat. O.Ir. airegde, a. noble.
airgiod, er'-gyud', n. m., gen. s. airgid, money, silver ; airgiod beò, quicksilver, mercury ; airgiod caguilt, hearth money ; airgiod cinn, reward money, poll money ; airgiod ullamh, ready money ; airgiod caorrach, slate diamond ; airgiod ruadh, copper money. O.Ir. argat and arget, O.W. aryant, Lat. argentum.
airgiodach, a. rich, silvery.
airidh, ery, a. worthy, deserving, meritorious ; n. f. desert, merit ; is maith an airidh e, he richly deserves it ; is olc an airidh, it is a pity. O.Ir. aire, lord ; aire=general term for a degree. O'D.
àirigh, āry, n. f. shieling ; hill pasture in summer ; bothan àirigh, a shieling booth, or hut. E.Ir. airge, áirge, place where cows are milked, herd of cattle ; airgech, herdswoman.
àirigheach, āryach, a. rich in shielings.
airilleach, ăr''-il-ach, n. m. a sleepy person. E.Ir. airél, a bed.
airleag, v. t. lend. O.Ir. airlicim, I lend.
airleagadh, n. m. loan.
airleig, arlig, n. f. strait ; tha mi an airleig, I am in a strait. E.Ir. airlech, gen. airlig, slaughter, wound.
airleigeach, arliguch, a. urgent.
airleis, ar'-lèsh, n. f. earnest-penny, pledge ; fr. Sc., arles.
airm, erm, n. m. place. Ir. (not in use in M.G.).
airmis, ermish, v. a. hit upon, find (one's way). See eirmis. M.Ir. airmaisim, I hit upon.
àirne, ārnu, n. f. a sloe, a damson ; a kidney, reins (Bible). M.Ir. airne, sloe, E.Ir. áru, kidney.
àirneach, ārnuch, a. full of sloes, kidneyed, valiant.
àirneach, ārnach, n. f. murrain in cattle.
àirneag, ārnag, n. f. a sloe.
àirneis, ārnesh, n. f. household furniture, moveables ; household stuff. M Ir. airnéis, cattle, goods, furniture.

air-neo, ar-nyŏ, *ad.* else, otherwise ; **air-neo an t-sleagh mu bheil do làmh,** otherwise the spear your hand grasps.

airr-ais = come back ! (shepherd thus directs his dog) ; for **air d'ais, d** *assim.* with r. *See* **ais.**

airsid, arshij, *n. f.* unanimity.

airsideach, *a.* unanimous.

airsneal, ărs'-nyal, *n. m.* weariness ; drowsiness ; languor, depression of spirits ; sadness ; heaviness.

airsnealach, *a.* heavy, sad, drowsy, depressed, melancholy.

airsnealachd, ars-nyal-uchc, *n. f.* drowsiness, sadness, melancholy sadness.

air son, ar-son', *prep.* for, on account of, for the sake of ; **air son nam fìrean,** for the sake of the righteous ; **air mo shonsa,** for me.

airtein, airtine, arten, *n. m.* a pebble, flint. *O.Ir.* **artene,** *dim.* form of **art,** a stone.

airther. *See* **là.**

airtneal. *See* **airsneal.** *Ir.* **airtnéal.**

ais, ash, *n. m.* back ; **air ais,** backwards ; **cum air t'ais,** keep back ! **thig air t'ais,** come back ! *E.Ir.* **ais,** back.

aischeimich, eshchemich, *v.* retire, withdraw, back, go backwards = **ais** + **ceum.**

aisde, eshju, *prep.* + *pron.* out of her, or it. **as** (ex) + *pron. suf.* 3. s. *f.*

aiseag, àsh'-ug, *n. m.* ferry ; passage ; **thar an aiseag,** across the ferry. *M.Ir.* **aissec.**

aiseal, ash'-ul, *n. f.* an axle-tree ; *Ir.* **ais,** axis, *Km.* ; *W.* **echel.** *Cf. O.N.* **öxull.**

aiseal, *n. f.* jollity ; fun.

aiseal, eshul, *n. f.* an ass. *See* **asal.**

aisean, *n. f.* a rib. *See* **asann.**

aisearan, esharan, *n. m.* a weanling.

aiseirigh, ash'-ery, *n. f.* resurrection ; **aiseirigh nam marbh,** the resurrection of the dead. *Ir.* **aisi,** death. *Lh. O.Ir.* **esséirge,** resurrection = **es** (ex) + **érig** (rising).

aisg, ashc, *n. f.* a request. *E.Ir.* **ascid.**

aisg, *n. f.* a spot, a blemish. *E.Ir.* **aisc,** reproach.

àisgeir, àshcer, *n. f.* a rocky mountain, a ridge of high mountains. *Ir.* **áisgeir,** a mountain. *Lh.*

aisig, ash'-ig, *v.* restore, ferry over, transfer ; **aisigte,** ferried ; restored. *E.Ir.* **aissec,** restitution.

aisinnleachd, ash-eenluchc, *n. f.* a wicked contrivance, a wicked stratagem.

aisinnleachdach, *a.* crafty, plotting, mischievous.

aisir, ash'-ir, *a.* defile, a path.

aisith, *n. f.* strife = **as** (priv.) + **sìth.**

aislear, ash'-lyar, *n. m.* spring-tide.

aisling, ashlig, *n. f.* a dream. *O.Ir.* **aislinge,** a vision.

aislingeach, *a.* visionary.

aislingiche, ashligichu, *a.* dreamer.

aisneach, ash'-nyuch, *a.* ribbed.

aisneis, ashnesh, *n. f.* rehearsing, narration, tattle. *E.Ir.* **aisneisim,** I speak.

aisridh. *See* **aisir.**

aisteach, ashtach, *n. m.* a diverting fellow.

ait, *a.* glad, happy, joyful ; odd, funny ; **òlach ait,** an odd, or funny fellow. *E.Ir.* **aitt,** pleasant.

àite, àtiu, *n. m.* a place, a situation ; **àite còmhnuidh,** a dwelling-place ; **àite suidhe,** a seat. *E.Ir.* **áitt,** place, site.

àiteach, *n. m.* 1. agriculture, farming, cultivation of the land ; **ri àiteach,** cultivating, farming. 2. an inhabitant; **tha àitich Innse-torrain fo gheilt,** the inhabitants of Inistore are in terror. 3. a habitation.

àiteachadh, àtiuch-u, *vbl. n. m.* act of cultivating, improving ; **ag àiteachadh an fhearainn,** improving, or cultivating the land.

àiteachas, àtiuch-us, *n. m.* a colony ; colonising ; **ri àiteachas,** improving waste land.

áiteag, àtiag, *n. f.* a shy girl. *See* **fàiteach.**

aiteag, aytag, *n. f.* a plumb-line.

aiteal, ăytal, *n. m.* a glimpse, **fhuair mi aiteal dheth,** I got a glimpse of him ; **aiteal de 'n calg,** a glimpse of their hair ; a sprinkling, **aiteal mine,** a sprinkling of meal ; a slight breeze, **aiteal an earraich,** the fanning breeze of spring ; a tinge, **aiteal an òir,** the tinge of gold. *Cf. E.Ir.* **atal,** calmness, fair (after storm).

aiteal, *n. m.* juniper; **dearcan aiteil,** juniper berries ; **craobh aiteil,** a juniper tree ; *also* **craobh iubhair.**

aitealach, *a.* in glimpses ; in slight breezes.

aitealach, *a.* relating to juniper, abounding in juniper.

aiteam, aytum, *n. f.* a tribe, a people.

aiteamh, aytuv, *n. m.* a thaw ; *v.* thaw ; **tha e ag aiteamh,** it is thawing.

aiteann, aytun, *n. m.* juniper. *O.Ir.* **aittenn.** *Also* **aitionn.**

àitear, àter, *n. m.* a husbandman.

àitearachd, aturuchc, *n. f.* agriculture.

aiteas, aytus, *n. m.* joy ; gladness ; fun, oddness ; **t'aiteas,** your oddness ; **a chuireas aiteas orm,** which will make me glad.

aitgheal, aityal, *a.* bright, joyous.

aith-, an *iterative prefix. See* **ath.**

aitheach, ahach, *n. m.* a sow. *Lh.*

aitheamh, e-huv, *a.* fathom. *O.W.* **etem,** *O.Celt.* (p)étemâ, (p)atemâ.

aitheornach, a-hurnuch, *n. m.* land where barley was the last crop; repeated crop.

aithghearr, a-yar, *a.* soon, brief ; short ; short-tempered ; **tha e aithghearr,** he is short-tempered ; **sgaoil sinn cho aithghearr**, we dispersed so soon ; *n. f.* short time, or way ; **an aithghearr**, in a short time ; **so an aithghearr**, this is the short way, or road ; short method, or abridgement. *M.Ir.* **aith** (*intens.*) + **gerr**, very short.

aithinne, a-hin, *n. m.* fire-brand. *O.Ir.* **athinne**, gl. *torris, fax,* = **aith** + **tene**.

aithis, a-hish, *n. f.* a reproach, check ; a fit means to do evil. *O.Ir.* **aithisim**, I revile.

aithlis, a-lish, *v.* imitate, mimic, *n f.* mimicry ; reproach, disgrace ; *vid.* **aithris**.

aithliseach, al′-èsh-ach, *a.* imitative.

àithn, ā-in, *v.* command, order, bid, enjoin. *O.Ir.* **àithne**.

àithne, ā′-nyu, *n. f., pl.* **àithntean**, commandment, injunction, charge. Often **fàithne**.

aithne, enu, *n. f.* knowledge, acquaintance ; **an aithne dhuit**, do you know ? **chan aithne dhomh**, I know not. *O.Ir.* **aithgne, aidgne**, *cognitio, recognitio* ; **adgénsa**, *gl.* cognosco ; **ath** (re) + **gen** (= *Gr.-Lat.* rt. gno). Cf. *Lat.* cognosco, *Gr.* γιγνώσκω.

aithneach, enuch, *a.* 1. discerning, considerate, attentive ; **tha i glè aithneach**, she is considerate enough. 2. *a.* used as noun ; acquaintance, or a guest ; **leis nach dragh aithnichean**, by whom acquaintances, or guests, were not counted a trouble.

aithneach, *n. m.* woodrush, or wild leeks.

aithneachadh, *n. m.* a slight degree ; what is discernible : **cuir aithneachadh an taobh so e**, put it a slight degree this way ; *vbl. n. m.* act of knowing, recognising, discerning ; **a dh′ aithneachadh gliocais**, to know wisdom.

aithneachd, èn′-achc, *n. f.* discernment, knowledge ; humanity.

aithneil, enol, *a.* knowing ; *also* **aithneachail**.

aithnich, èn′-ich, *v.* know, recognise, discern, perceive ; **dh′ aithnich mi**, I knew or recognised. *O.Ir.* **aithgnim**, I perceive, know.

aithnichte, enichta, *vbl. a.* 1. known. 2. manifest ; **duine aithnichte**, remarkable man ; **aithnichte maith**, remarkably good.

aithre, *n. m.* repentance. Uncom. in *M.G. O. Ir.* **athirge, athrige**, *f.*

aithreach, eruch, *a.* giving cause to regret ; **chan aithreach leam**, I do not regret it ; repentant. *O.Ir.* **aithrech**.

aithreachail, *a.* penitent ; regretful.

aithreachas, *n. m.* repentance, regret, penitence ; **is amaideach a bhi cur a mach airgid a cheannach aithreachais**,

it is foolish to expend money on the purchasing of repentance ; **cha leighis aithreachas breamas**, regret does not remedy a blunder. *O.Ir.* **aithrige**, *f.* poenitentia.

aithridh, eri, *n. m.* a penitent one ; **diol déirc agus aithridh**, a mendicant and a penitent.

aithrinn, *n. m.* sharp point. *Lh. See* **ath** ; **aith** + **rinne**.

aithris, erish, *n. f.* imitation, mimicry ; report, rehearsal ; *v.* imitate ; mimic ; **ag aithris ormsa**, imitating or mimicking me ; rehearse, report, affirm ; **agus dh′ aithris e na nithe sin uile**, and he told all those things. *E.Ir.* **aithrisim**, re-tell ; **ath** + **ris** (*gl.* scél).

aithriseach, erishuch, *a.* imitative ; traditionary, widely celebrated.

àitich, ātich, *v.* cultivate, till, improve ; **ag àiteachadh an fhearainn**, cultivating the land ; dwell, inhabit ; **gach neach a dh′ àitich colunn riamh**, every one that ever dwelt in a body ; drop anchor, moor ; **dh′ àitich an long**, the ship anchored ; *vbl. a.* **àitichte**, cultivated, improved ; inhabited. *E.Ir.*, **àittigim**, I inhabit.

àitidh, āty, *a.* damp, moist, wet.

àitidheachd, āty-achc, *n. f.* moistness, dampness ; moisture.

aitim, *n. f. See* **aiteam**.

aitionn, *n. m.* juniper (so named from its pointed leaves) ; *also* **aiteann**.

aitreabh, aytruv, *n. f.* premises, steading ; **tigh is aitreabh**, mansion-house and premises ; **théid an aitreabh sios**, their buildings shall decay. *O.Ir.* **aittreb**, dwelling, **atreba**, *habitat. See* **treabh**.

aitreabhach, *a.* domestic, belonging to premises ; *n. m.* an inhabitant.

aitreabhail, aytruval, *a.* domestic.

àl, *n. m.* brood, offspring, young ; generation ; **a solar dhearc da cuid àil**, gathering berries for her young ; **trà thig an sealgair gun fhios air àl**, when the hunter comes unexpectedly on a covey ; **a′ mhuc ′s a cuid àil**, the sow and her litter. *M.W.* ael, litter.

àlach, āluch, *n. m.* 1. brood ; covey ; litter ; tribe ; generation. 2. a set, a group, a collection ; **àlach ràmh**, bank of oars and rowers ; **àlach bhur biodag**, your complement of dirks ; **àlach thairngean**, set of nails in a boat. 3. activity (*Sh.*). 4. request (*Sh.*). 5. **àlach nan ràmh**, space between a boat and the shore to allow easy rowing, an oar-length from the shore ; fr. **àl**, a brood.

alachag, *n. f.* peg, hook.

alachuinn, *n. m.* repository. *Ir.* **ealachuing**, a rack.

àladh, *n. m.* 1. nursing. 2. skill, craft.

àladh, *n. m.* 1. a lie ; malice. 2. a wound ; scar ; often an imprecation, àladh oirbh ! = " plague " on you ! *E.Ir.* álad, a wound. *M.W.* aeled, ailment.

alag, *n. f.* hiccup, hard task.

àlaich, āl'-ich, *v.* breed ; fall to, commence, attack ; dh' àlaich iad air, they fell to ; they attacked him ; is luath a dh' àlaich iad, soon have they multiplied.

àlainn, allin, *a.* beautiful. *O.Ir.* álaind, *formosus,* beautiful.

Alba, *n. f.* Scotland ; *gen.* Albann, *dat.* Albainn.

Albannach, Albunuch, *n. m.* a Scot, a Scotsman ; *a.* Scottish.

all-, over. *See* thall.

alla, *a.* wild, fierce. *See* allta.

allaban, *n. m.* wandering, astray ; perhaps leaning on all- (over).

alla-bhuadhach, ala-voou-uch, *a.* victorious, but in disgrace.

alladh, all'-à, *n. f.* fame, reputation— good or bad ; " ma's àil leat alladh tha fiùghail," if you wish honourable fame. *O.Ir.* allud, fame.

allaidh, alli, *a.* wild, fierce ; madadh allaidh, a wolf. *O.Ir.* allaid, wild.

allail, *a.* illustrious, noble. *O.Ir.* all, noble.

allamharach, all'-var-ach, *n. m.* a foreigner ; a straggler ; *a.* foreign, strange ; all- (over) and muir (sea).

allamharachd, *n. m.* straggling, loitering, wandering ; savageness.

allsadh, all'-su, *n. m.* a jerk, a sudden inclination of the body. *See* abhsadh.

allsaich, all'-sich, *v.* jerk ; suspend ; lean to one side.

allsmuain, *n. f.* great buoy, a float.

allsporag, *n. f.* the throttle of a cow, or any brute. *See* abhsporag.

allt, ault, *n. m., gen. s.* and *n. pl.* uillt, a river with precipitous banks ; stream, a brook.

allta, *a.* savage. *M.Ir.* allta, wild.

alltachd, aultachc, *n. f.* savageness.

alltan, *n. m.* a rill, a brook ; dim. of allt.

alm, *n. m.* alum ; fr. the *Eng.*

alp, *v.* ingraft ; dovetail. *See* ealp.

alt, *n. m.* a joint ; as an alt, out of the joint. *E.Ir.* alt, a joint.

alt, *n. m.* 1. *n.* a method ; ni sinn alt eile air, we shall use another method. 2. condition ; air na h-uile alt, at all events. 3. bent, aptitude ; tha alt aige air, he has a bent for it. *E.Ir.* alt.

alt, *n. m.* a height, a cliff. *W.* allt. *Lat.* altus.

altachadh, alt'-ach-u, *n. m.* thanksgiving ; grace before or after meat ; altachadh beatha, welcoming, saluting ; dh' alt-

aich iad beath a chéile, they saluted each other. *O.Ir.* atlugud.

altachadh, *vbl. n. m.* act of articulating joints ; act of moving to exercise one's self (after being in a cramped position).

altaich, alt'-ich, *v.* salute, join, ease one's joints ; (by taking a walk).

altair, altir, *n. f.* an altar, *gen.* altrach. *O.Ir.* altóir ; *W.* allor ; fr. *Lat.* altãre.

altcheangal, *n. m.* articulation, inosculation, act of jointing.

altrum, *n. m.* nursing, rearing, fostering ; *v. t.* nurse, foster, rear ; cajole. *O.Ir.* altram, *nutritio* ; fr. alim. *Lat.* alo.

altrumachadh, *vbl. n. m.* act of nursing.

altrumaich, *v.* nurse, cherish.

alt-shligeach, alt'-hlig-uch, *a.* crustaceous, crusty ; like shells.

àluinn, āl'-inn, *a.* handsome, very beautiful, elegant, superb ; *prefer* àlainn. *O.Ir.* álaind, *formosus.*

àluinneachd, *n. f.* handsomeness, beauty, elegance, superbness.

am, *pers. pron.* their. *See* an.

am, *art. sing. See* an.

am, often needlessly written a' m', contraction of ann mo ; as, am thigh, in my house.

am, *intens. part. See* an.

am-, *privative prefix. See* an.

am (the m is long and pronounced aum or amm), *n. m., pl.* amannan, time, season ; opportunity ; fit time ; 'se so an t-am, this is the time ; gabh am air sin, watch an opportunity to do that ; tha an t-am ann, it is high time ; am iomchuidh, fit, or proper time, or season. *O.Ir.* am, amm.

amach, *n. f.* a vulture.

amadan, *n. m.* a foolish man, a simpleton ; am + ment = non-minded. *McB.*

amadanach, *a.* foolish, silly-looking ; aodann amadanach, a silly expression of countenance.

amadanachd, *n. f.* silliness ; foolishness ; the conduct of a fool.

amadan-mòintich, *n. m.* a dotterel ; leth-amadan, half-fool.

amaid, am'-ij, *n. f.* a foolish woman. *E.Ir.* ammit, *m.* and *f.* witch, wizard. Cf. *Lat.* amita.

amaideach, *a.* foolish, silly.

amaideachd, amijuchc, *n. f.* foolishness, folly, silliness. *E.Ir.* ammaitecht, witchcraft.

amail, am'-al, *a.* seasonable, timely.

amail, amil, *n. f.* evil, mischief. *E.Ir.* admillim, I destroy.

amail, *n. f.* hindrance ; *v. t.* hinder, obstruct ; ad + mall. *McB.*

amaill, am'-ill, *v.* entangle ; dh'amaill thu an lion, you have entangled the

net ; obstruct, thwart, hinder. *E.Ir.*
amaill, sporting.
amais, am′-ish, *v. i.* hit ; meet, dh'amais
sinn, we met ; find, light upon ; an
d'amais thu air, did you find it ? is sona
an duine a dh′ amaiseas air gliocas,
happy is the man that finds (that lights
upon) wisdom. *O.Ir.* ammus, *temp-
tatio*, lying in wait, attack.
amaiseach, *a.* of sure aim, unerring.
amal, *n. m.* a swingle-tree. *See* cuibh.
amalachd, am′-al-ăchc, *n. f.* seasonableness, timeousness, due time.
amaladh, *n. m.* hindrance ; fr. amail.
amar, *n. m.* bed (of a river) ; amar na
h-aibhne, the bed of the river ; a
trough, a mill-lead ; amar na muilne
(or a′ mhuilinn), water channel leading
to the mill. *E.Ir.*ammor, amor, a trough.
amarlaid, am′-ar-laj, *n. f.* a blustering
female, a careless woman.
amarlaideach, *a.* careless ; blustering.
amas, am′-us, *n. m.* power of hitting,
aim ; chaill thu t'amas, you have lost
your aim, or mark. *See* amais.
amasguidh, *a.* 1. profane ; obscene.
2. confused, disorderly. 3. mischievous ; duine amasguidh, a light-headed
person.
àmh, *n. f.* kiln, nasalised form of àth.
amh, av, *a.* raw, unsodden, unboiled, un-
roasted, boorish ; duine amh, boorish
person ; *n. f.* a fool, simpleton. *Ir.*
amh. *E.Ir.* om, raw.
amhach, *n. f.* the neck.
amhaidh, avy, *a.* sour, lowering
(weather) ; gloomy.
amhaidheachd, avyachc, *n. f.* rawness,
gloominess, sulkiness.
àmhailt, āvilt, *n. f.* trick, cunning.
àmhailteach, *a.* full of cunning.
amhain, aven, *n. m.* predicament ; lying
on the back without power of moving,
as a horse or a sheep ; *also,* afoinn,
tafoinn. *O.Ir.* athboingid, wresting,
compelling. *Wi.*
amhainn, avin, *n. f.* river. Proper form
is abhainn, *q.v.*
amhairc, avirc, *v.* look, see, behold,
observe, regard, attend ; am fear
nach amhairc roimh, amhaircidh e 'na
dhéidh, he that will not look before
him will look behind him.
amharc, av′-ark, *n. m.* look, appearance ;
is bochd an t-amharc tha air, he has
a miserable appearance ; view, sight ;
'san amharc, in view, in sight ; a′ dol
as an amharc, getting out of sight ;
the vizzy of a gun ; inspection. *M.Ir.*
amarc.
amharcach, *a.* considerate, attentive,
humane ; bha sin amharcach uaith,
that was very considerate of him.

amharcaiche, av′-ărk-ich-u, *n. m.* a
spectator.
amhartan, *n.m.* luck; fortune; prosperity.
amhartanach, *a.* lucky, prosperous.
amharus, av′-ur-us, suspicion, doubt ; is
mór m′ amharus, I very much suspect ;
thà, gun amharus, yes, undoubtedly ;
O.Ir. amires, amaires, amiress = am
(neg) + iress (*fides*) ; *infidelitas*, distrust.
amharusach, *a.* suspicious, doubtful ;
distrustful, ambiguous. *O.Ir.* amires-
sach, *infidelis*.
amharusachd, avurusuchc, *n. f.* distrust-·
fulness, suspiciousness, ambiguousness.
amhas, amhasg, avas, *n. m.* a wild man,
madman, idiot, a blundering fool.
E.Ir. amos, a mercenary soldier, a wild,
ungovernable man.
amhchunn, *n. f.* holes of a button.
àmhghar, ā′-ghur, *n. m.* affliction, tribulation, anguish, dismay, distress. *E.Ir.*
amgar. 1. unpleasant. 2. misery.
àmhgharach, *a.* afflicted.
amhlair, auler, *n. m.* a fool, boor. *O.Ir.*
amlabar, mute (am + labar), *op.* of
suilbhir = su + labar.
amhlaireachd, auleruchc, *n. f.* fooling
away one's time ; trifling conduct,
silly play.
amhlaisg, *n. f.* bad beer.
amhluadh, aulu′, *n. m.* confusion, dismay.
amhluidh, *adv.* as, like as. *E.Ir.* amlaid.
amh-nàrach, *a.* shameless.
amhran, auran, *n. m.* song, sonnet. *E.Ir.*
amrán, a song, dim. of amor, singing,
a song.
amhsan, ausan, *n. m.* solan goose.
amhuil, av′-ul, *adv.* as, like as, even as ;
is amhuil sin, just so, or even so ; *n. f.*
attention, regard ; air an amhuil
cheudna, in like manner. *O.Ir.* amail,
amal.
àmhuilt, āvilt, *n. f.* a trick or stratagem ;
deceit.
àmhuilteach, *a.* full of bad tricks, deceitful, wicked ; full of stratagems.
àmhuilteachd, *n. f.* extreme deceit,
deceitfulness ; degree of deceit.
àmhuiltear, āvilter, *n. m.* a strategist, a
cunning fellow.
àmhuiltearachd, āvilteruchc, *n.f.* a trick ;
extreme deceitfulness.
àmhuinn, āvinn, *n. f.* a furnace, oven.
Ir. óigheann, pan, cauldron. *Lh.*
amlach, *a.* curled. *E.Ir.* amlach, curling.
amladh, amlu, *n. m.* impediment, obstruction, entanglement ; *vbl. n.* act
of entwining, entangling, retarding ;
fr. amail.
amladh, *vbl. n. m.* act of tonguing and
grooving..
amlag, *n. f.* a curl, a ringlet.
amlagach, *a.* curled, in ringlets.

amlagaich, am'-lag-ich, *v. trans.* curl, make into ringlets.

amraidh, *n. m.* cupboard. *Sc.* ambry.

an, an, *def. art. sing.* the. Asp. initial cons. : 1. *fem. n.* in *nom. ac. dat.* exc. dentals and *l, n, r*; 2. *masc. n.* in *gen.* and *dat.* exc. dentals and *l, n, r.* In construction it takes foll. forms : *masc. s. nom.* and *ac.* an bef. cons. exc. *b, p, f, m* ; an cù, the dog ; an duine, the man ; am bef. *b, p, f, m* ; am balach, the boy ; am fiadh, the deer ; an t- bef. vowels ; an t- athair, the father : *gen.* and *dat.*, an before vowels, dentals, and *fh* ; an òir, of the gold ; an daraich, of the oak ; an fheòir, of the grass ; a' bef. cons. (exc. dentals) which it asp. ; a' bhrathar, of the brother ; an t- bef. *s* + vowel, *s* + *l*, *s* + *n*, *s* + *r* ; an t- sàil, of the sea ; an t- sléibhe, of the hill ; an t-snàth, of the thread; an t- srath, of the strath. *Fem. s., nom.* and *ac.* an bef. vowels, dentals, *f.* asp. ; an abhainn, the river ; an dùthaich, the country ; an fhìrinn, the truth ; a' bef. cons. (exc. dentals), a' chearc, the hen ; a' chuileag, the fly ; an t- bef. *s* + vowel, *s* + *l*, *s* + *n*, *s* + *r* ; an t- sùil, the eye ; an t- slige, the shell ; an t- snàthad, the needle ; an t- sràid, the street : *gen.* na bef. cons. (does not asp.) ; na circe, of the hen ; na mathar, of the mother ; na h- bef. vowels ; na h- eala, of the swan ; *m.* and *f. pl., nom.* and *ac.* na bef. cons. ; na h- bef. vowels : *gen.* nan bef. vowels and cons. (exc. labials) ; nam bef. labials. The article is used without being translated into English : 1. when the noun is followed by so, siod, sin ; as, an cù so, this dog ; am bealach so, this breach, or gate-way ; 2. before a noun preceded by an adjective ; as, is mòr an duine e, is maith an duine e, he is a great man, he is a good man ; 3. before names of certain places ; as, ann san Asia, in Asia ; ann san Fhraing, in France. *See O.Ir.* article.

an, *poss. pron.* their ; as, an cuid, their property : used before all letters, except *b, f, m, p.* Before these an becomes am : am baile, their town ; am fearann, their land ; am màthair, their mother.

an, *rel. pron.*, as, leis an d'fhàg mi e, with whom I left it ; leis an d'fhalbh e, with whom he went : contracted after prepositions 'n ; as, o'n d'thàinig e, from whom he is descended.

an, *infixed pron.* 3rd *pl.* them. It becomes am bef. verbs beginning with *p, b, f,* or *m* ; as, 'g am moladh ;

'g am fuadach ; 'g am bronnadh ; 'g am bogadh.

an, *interrog. pron.*, as, an tu tha so ? is this you ? used before all letters, except *b, f, m, p,* before which an becomes am ; as, am faca tu ? did you see ? Eclipsis is seen in a bheil which = an feil > a bhfeil, now, a bheil. Cf. gu bheil ; gun feil > gu bhfeil, now, gu bheil.

an, *prep.* in. *See* ann.

an, *neg. prefix,* an-iochd, cruelty ; ànrath, distress : becomes am- (asp. amh-) bef. labials and *l, r,* and ain-, aim-, aimh-, when next syll. begins with *e* or *i* ; aineolach, aimbeart, aimhleas

an, *intens. pref.* ainteas, inflammation ; ainneart, violence.

ana-, *intens. pref.* like an.

ana-, *neg. pref.* like an.

anabarr, *n. m.* excess, superfluity. Sometimes written anabharr.

anabarrach, *a.* exceeding, excessive, desperate, indispensable ; anabarrach feumail, indispensably or very necessary ; used as an *adverb.* Cf. *E.Ir.* anbhail, very great.

anabas, *n. m.* dregs, refuse.

anabasach, *a.* muddy.

ana-beachdail, *a.* inattentive, haughty. 2. not recollecting, not punctual.

anabhiorach, an'-a-veer-uch, *n. m.* centipede, whitlow, rabbit-heap.

anabhuil, anavool, *n. m.* misapplication.

anablach, an-ab-lach, *n. m.* coarse flesh.

anablas, *n. m.* insipidity, a bad or bitter taste, tastelessness.

ana-blasda, *a.* insipid, tasteless, of a bad taste.

ana-blasdachd, *n. f.* tastelessness, insipidity, insipidness.

anabrais, an'-a-brash, *n. m.* lust.

anabuich, an-ăb'-ich, anabuidh, an'-a-bi, *a.* unripe, immature.

anabuidheachd, *n. f.* unripeness, immaturity, abortiveness. *Is.*

anabuirt, an'-a-bŭrt, *n. m.* frenzy.

anacail, *v.* defend, manage. *E.Ir.* anacul, inf. of angim, I protect.

anacainnt, ana-caynt, *n. f.* abusive language, reproach, ribaldry.

anacainnteach, *a.* abusive in language, reproachful.

anacair, anakir, *n. f.* sickness, disease, = an + socair.

ana-caith, ana-keh, *v.* squander, waste, be profuse or prodigal.

ana-caitheamh, ana-kehoo, *n. m.* extravagance, prodigality, waste, profusion, squandering.

ana-caithteach, ana-catuch, *a.* prodigal.

anaceart, an-a-cyärt', *a.* unjust, partial.

anaceartas, *n. m.* injustice, unfairness.

anachaoin, *v.* deplore.

anacladh, anaclu, *vbl. n.*, fr. anacail.
ana-cleachd, ana-clechc, *v.* discontinue the practice of.
ana-cleachdainn, ana-clechcin, *n. f.* want of practice, want of custom.
ana-cneasda, ana-cnesdu, *a.* inhuman, cruel, barbarous, horrid.
ana-cneasdachd, ana-cnesdachc, *n. f.* barbarity, inhumanity, cruelty.
anacothrom, anacorum, *n. m.* violence, oppression, unfairness, distress.
anacothromach, anacorumuch,*a.* uneven; unjust.
anacrach, *a.* sick; unwell.
ana-creidmheach, ana-credvach, *n. m.* an unbeliever, infidel; *a.* unbelieving, irreligious.
anacriosd, anacrist, *n. m.* antichrist.
ana-crìosdachd, ana-crisdachc,*n. f.* paganism, heathenism, infidelity.
ana-crìosdail, *a.* unchristian, inhuman, cruel, barbarous.
ana-crìosduidh, ana-crisdy, *n. m.* infidel, a pagan, a heathen.
ana-cuibheas, ana-cooyis,*n. m.* immensity, vastness, enormity; a thing incredible.
ana-cuibheasach, *a.* enormous, desperate; anacuibheasach aingidh, desperately wicked; used as an adverb.
ana-cuibheaseachd, ana-cooyisuchc, *n. m.* enormousness, immoderateness, terribleness.
ana-cùimhne, anacuinu, *n. f.* forgetfulness, negligence, want of memory.
ana-cuimhneach, *a.* forgetful, negligent, inattentive.
ana-cuimhnich, *v.* forget, disremember, neglect.
ana-cuimse, *n. f.* vastness, immensity, immoderateness, terribleness.
ana-cuimseach, *a.* vast, exaggerated, exorbitant, enormous.
ana-cuimseachd, *n. f.* exaggeration, immenseness, vastness.
ana-cuimsich, *v.* exaggerate, make exorbitant.
ana-cùram, *n. m.* negligence, carelessness, inattention.
ana-cùramach, *a.* inattentive, regardless, negligent.
ana-gealtach, ana-gyaltuch, *a.* fearless.
ana-ghleusta, *a.* spiritless.
ana-ghnàth, *n. m.* an ill habit, bad practice, or custom.
ana-ghnàthach, *a.* bad, irregular, unusual.
ana-ghneitheil, *a.* pernicious, destructive, mischievous.
ana-ghoireasach, *a.* very needful, requisite; inconvenient, incommodious.
ana-ghràdh, *n. m.* doating, love.
ana-ghràdhach, *a.* loving excessively.
ana-ghrinn, *a.* unkind, inelegant.
anagrach, *a.* quarrelsome.

anail, anel, *n. f., gen. s.* analach, breath, breeze, rest; anail na beatha, the breath of life; anail nan speur, the breath of the skies, *i.e.* the breeze; leig t'anail, rest, take your rest; leigibh bhur n-anail, rest yourselves; is blàth anail na màthar, warm is the breath of the mother. *E.Ir.* anál. *W.* anadl.
anaimsir, an'-ém-shir', *n. f.* unseasonable storm, bad weather, tempest.
anaimsireil, *a.* unseasonable, stormy, tempestuous.
anainn, *n. f.* eaves; projecting roof.
analaich, an'-al-ich, *v. t.* breathe.
analtra, *n. m.* a fosterer; " analtra e is oide ar sgoil," fosterer and patron of our schools.
an-am, *n. m.* unseasonable time.
anam, *n. m.* soul, spirit, breath. *O.Ir.* anim.
anamadach, *a.* lively.
anamadaich, an-am'-ad-èch, *n. f.* convulsions.
ana-measarra, *a.* intemperate, immoderate, lewd.
ana-measarrachd, *n. f.* intemperance, immoderateness.
ana-meidheachd, *n. f.* prematurity, abortiveness.
ana-meidhidh, *a.* premature, abortive.
anameinn, *n f.* perverseness, bad temper.
anameinneach, *a.* perverse, short-tempered.
an-amharus, *n. m.* extreme distrust. *See* amharus.
an-amhrusach, *a.* very distrustful, extremely jealous, very suspicious.
ana-miann, *n. m.* inordinate desire; sensuality. *M.Ir.* an-mían, passion, lust.
ana-miannach, *a.* lustful.
ana-minig, *a.* infrequent. *E.Ir.* an-menic, unfrequented.
anamoch, an'-am-uch, *a.* late, unseasonable; *n. m.* the evening; 'san anamoch, in the evening. an (*priv.*) + moch.
an-aoibhinn, *a.* joyless; woeful. *E.Ir.* an-áebda, distressful.
an-aoibhneas, *n. m.* woe, sorrow.
ànart, *n. m.* pride.
anart, *n. m.* linen. *E.Ir.* anart, linen cloth, fine linen; usu. lín-anart.
anasta, *a.* boisterous, stormy.
anastachd, *n. f.* toil in bad weather; bad usage; boisterousness.
an-dàna, *a.* presumptuous. an (*intens.*) + dàn.
an-dànadas, *n. f.* presumption.
an-diadhachd, *n. f.* ungodliness; for an-diadhaidheachd.
an-diadhaidh, *a.* ungodly, unholy, wicked, perverse.
an-diadhaidheachd, *n. f.* ungodliness, unholiness, wickedness.

an-dligĥe, *n. m.* unjustness, undutifulness. *O.Ir.* **in-dligad,** illegality.

an-dligheach, *a.* unjust, not due.

an-dòchas, *n. m.* despondency, distrust,
despair. *Ir.* **an-dóchas,** presumption.
Ktg.

an-dòchasach, *a.* despondent, mistrustful, distrustful, despairing.

an-dòigh, *n. f.* bad condition.

an-dòlas, *n. m.* sadness, discomfort,
distress, unhappiness.

an-dùchasach, *a.* not hereditary. In *E.Ir.*
=of foreign extraction.

an-duine, *n.m.* a decrepit person; a wicked
man. So *E.Ir.* a nobody. *W.* **adyn.**

an-eagal, *n. m.* fearlessness.

an-eagalach, *a.* fearless.

an-ealamh, *a.* inexpert.

an-ealanta, *a.* unskilful.

an-earb, *v.* distrust, despair ; mistrust,
doubt, suspect.

an-earbsa, *n. f.* despair, distrust.

an-earbsach, *a.* distrustful, despairing,
despondent.

an-earbsachd, *n. f.* distrustfulness, suspiciousness.

an-éibhinn, *a.* woeful, sad, depressed in
spirits.

an-éibhneas, *n. m.* discomfort, unhappiness, grief, misery.

an-éifeachd, *n. m.* inefficacy.

an-éifeachdach, *a.* ineffectual, inefficient,
inefficacious, weak.

an-eireachdail, *a.* indecent, unseemly,
unbecoming.

an-eireachdas, *n. m.* indecency.

anfadh, *n. m.* storm. *E.Ir.* **anfud,** tempest. *See* **onfhadh.**

an-fhaidhidinn, *n. m.* impatience. *See*
foidhidinn.

anfhainneachd, *n.f.* weakness, feebleness,
infirmity, debility. *Ir.* **anbhfainne.** *Ktg.*

anfhann, **an'-ann,** *a.* weak, feeble, infirm,
debilitated, enfeebled. **an** (*intens.*) +
fann. *Ir.* **anbhfann.**

anfhannaich, **ananich,** *v.* weaken, enfeeble, debilitate.

an-fharsuing, **an'-ârs-ing,** *a.* narrow,
strait, tight, circumscribed.

an-fhiachail, *a.* unworthy.

an-fhios, *n. m.* ignorance ; **tha sin an
an-fhios ormsa,** I am unaware of that.
E.Ir. **an-fiss,** ignorance.

an-fhiosrach, *a.* ignorant, unaware.

an-fhois, *n. m.* restlessness. *E.Ir.* **an-
foiss,** unsteady.

an-fhuras, *n. m.* impatience.

an-fhurasach, *a.* impatient, discontented,
fretful.

anghnath, *n.m.* bad habit. *M.Ir.* **an-gnás,**
an arbitrary or unwonted proceeding.

anglonn, *a.* brave, powerful ; *n. m.*
adversity, distress.

an-iochd, *n.f.* cruelty, oppression. *M.Ir.*
an-icht, unkindness.

an-iochdaire, *n. m.* a tyrant.

an-iochdmhoireachd, *n. f.* unmercifulness, cruelty, oppression, tyranny.

an-iochdmhor, *a.* merciless, cruel, oppressive, tyrannical, pitiless.

an-iùl, *n. m.* want of guidance.

anlamh, **annlamh,** *n. m.* misfortune.

ann, *adv.* there ; **a bheil thu ann ?** are
you there ? is **ann a tha tìde bhi falbh,**
it is time to be going. *O.Ir.* **and.**

ann, *prep.* in ; often needlessly doubled :
ann an, **ann an tigh,** in a house ; **ann
am baile,** in a town. *O.Ir.* **in, ind**
(indium, in me).

ann, *prep.+pers. pron., 3rd sing. m.* in
him, in it ; **ann,** combines with *pers.
pron.* thus : **annam,** in me ; **annad,** in
thee ; **ann,** in him ; **innte,** in her ;
annainn, in us ; **annaibh,** in you ;
annta, in them.

annaid, *n. f.* a church. *Ir.* **annóit,**
andoóit, a patron saint's church.

annaladh, *n. m.* era, calendar. *E.Ir.*
annálaim, I chronicle, *Lat.* annulia.

annamh, **ann'-uv,** *a.* rare, scarce ; **is
annamh a leithid,** his match is seldom
met with ; **gnothuch annamh,** a rare
thing ; seldom ; **is annamh a thig thu,**
you seldom come. *E.Ir.* **andam.** *Also*
ainneamh.

annamhachd, *n. f.* rareness, fewness ;
rareness of occurrence ; scarceness.

annas, *n. m.* a rarity, a novelty, a
dainty.

annasach, *a.* novel, dainty, new, uncommon.

annasachd, *n. f.* rareness, novelty,
scarceness, fewness, uncommonness.

annlag-fairge, *n. f.* sea-martin.

annlamh, **ann'-lav,** *n. f.* misfortune ;
perplexity, vexation.

annlan, **ann'-lan,** *n. m.* condiment ;
kitchen. *E.Ir.* **annlann.** *O'D.S.*

annrach. *See* **ànrach.**

annrath. *See* **ànradh.**

anns, *prep.* in, used always before the
article and relative ; **anns a' bhaile,**
in the town ; often contracted **'san,**
'sa, **'sa' bhaile,** in the town ; **'san arm,**
in the army ; for **ann san.**

annsa, the *compar.* and *superl.* of **toigh,**
beloved ; **is toigh leam thusa ach is
annsa leam esan,** I love *you,* but *he* is
more dear to me ; **cò is annsa leat ?**
whom do you like above all others ?
M.Ir. **andsa.**

annsachd, *n. f.* the greatest attachment ;
best beloved object ; **is tu m' annsachd,**
thou art my best beloved.

ann-saoghalta, *a.* covetous, greedy.

ann-saoghaltachd, *n.f.* worldliness, greed.

annsgairt, annsgarst, *n. f.* loud shout.
annsgairteach, *a.* loud shouting.
annspiorad, *n. m.* the devil.
anntlachd, ann'-tlachc, *n. f.* nuisance, disgust, displeasure; indecency; quarrel, dispeace.
ann-tlachdmhor, *a.* disagreeable, disgusting; unpleasant.
ànrach, ān'-rach, *n. m.* a wanderer; stranger; subject of misfortune; a fuller form is ànrathach, contracted through infl. of the accent; **tha dorus Fhinn do'n ànrach fial,** Fionn's door is open (liberal) to the wanderer; *a.* wandering, toiling in vain, disordered.
ànradh, ān'-ră, *n. m.* disorder, distress, disaster; for an + rath; **tha thu ruith air t'ànradh,** you are courting disaster. *E.Ir.* andró, misery.
an-riaghailt, *n. f.* disorder, confusion, uproar, tumult, riot.
an-riaghailteach, *a.* disorderly, confused, riotous, tumultuous.
an-sheasgair, *a.* uncomfortable, restless.
an-sheasgaireachd, *n. f.* restlessness; rudeness, violence.
anshocair, *a.* not properly fixed, unsettled, uneasy; *n. f.* discomfort; sickness, restlessness; **uair anshoca'r,** unsettled weather.
an-shògh, *n. m.* discomfort, misery.
an-shòghail, *a.* miserable, adverse.
anstruidh, ann-strüy, *v.* waste, spend, squander.
anstruidhear, an-struyer, *n. m.* a prodigal, a spendthrift, a squanderer.
anstruidheas, ann-strüy'-as, *n. m.* prodigality, squandering.
an-struidheasach, *a.* wasteful, prodigal, profuse.
an-struidheasachd, *n.f.* prodigality, wastefulness, extravagance.
antighearn, ann-tee'-urn, *n. m.* a tyrant, an oppressor, a despot.
an-tighearnail, ann-tee'-urn-al, *a.* oppressive, tyrannical, cruel.
antighearnas, *n. m.* oppression, tyranny, cruelty.
an-tiorrail, *a.* uncomfortable; cold, unsympathetic.
an-tiorralachd, *n. f.* discomfort, badness of climate, want of snugness.
an-togair, *v.* lust after.
an-togradh, *n. m.* lust, concupiscence; a criminal propensity; a keen desire.
antoil, *n. m.* self-will; lust, against one's will.
an-toilich, *v.* lust after.
antrath, *a.* unseasonable; *n. m.* an unseasonable time.
an-tròcair, *n. f.* cruelty.
an-tròcaireach, *a.* cruel, merciless, unmerciful.

an-tròcaireachd, *n. f.* cruelty, unmercifulness.
antrom, *a.* grievous to be borne, very heavy.
an-tromachadh, *n. m.* aggravation, aggrieving, aggravating.
an-tromaich, *v.* aggravate, oppress, overload.
an-truacanta, *a.* merciless.
an-truacantachd, *n. f.* want of feeling, or compassion.
an-truas, *n. m.* want of pity.
antruime, *n. f.* oppression, tyranny.
an-uabhar, *n. m.* excessive pride; **luchd an an-uabhair,** the excessively proud.
an-uaibhreach, *a.* excessively proud—gentle, kind.
an-uaill, *n. f.* excessive pride; **air mhór an-uaile is air bheag céille,** excessively proud and senseless; humility.
an-uailse, *n. f.* meanness, baseness.
an-uair, *n.f.* an unseasonable storm; bad weather in summer. *E.Ir.* an-úair, an evil hour.
an-uallach, *a.* indifferent; not haughty; *n. f.* an oppressive burden.
a nuas, from above; for an-uas.
anuasal, *a.* low, mean.
ao-, eu-, *neg. pref.* for an-, not.
aobhach, ūvuch. *See* aoibheach and aoibheil.
aobhar, ūvur, *n. m.* material; cause, reason; **aobhar bròin,** cause of grief; **air an aobhar sin,** for that reason; **aobhar còta,** material for making a coat; **aobhar bhròg,** material for making shoes. *O.Ir.* adbar, adbur, material, cause. **adbar ríg** = crown prince.
aobharach, *a.* causing, giving rise to.
aobharach, material; *n.m.* **aobharach mnà tighe,** suitable house-wife; a young person, or beast, of good or bad promise; **is maith an t-aobharach an gamhainn sin,** that stirk promises well; **is tu an t-aobharach ciatach,** you are a youth that promises well indeed.
aobrunn, ūbrun, *n. m.* ankle. *O.Ir.* odbrann, udbronn, fodbrond. *W.* uffarn.
ao-coltach, *a.* unlike, dissimilar, unlikely, not like.
ao-coltas, *n. m.* dissimilarity, improbability, unlikelihood.
ao-cosamhlachd, *n. m.* unlikelihood, improbability.
ao-cosmhail, *a.* improbable, unlikely, dissimilar.
aodach, ūduch, *n. m.* cloth, clothes; **cuir ort t'aodach,** put on your clothes; **aodach leapa,** bed-clothes, bedding; *v.* aodaich, clothe. *O.Ir.* étach, *vestitus.*
aodann, ūdun, *n. m.* face, visage, countenance; **an cron a bhios san aodann, chan fhaodar a chleith,** the blemish

in the face cannot be hid. *O.Ir.* étan, *frons.*

aodannach, *n. m.* the front of a bridle.

aodion, *n. m.* a leak.

aodionach, *a.* leaky.

ao-dòcha, *a.* less probable, less likely.

ao-dòchas, *n. m.* despair, despondency, distrust. *Also* eu-dòchas.

ao-dòchasach, *a.* hopeless, despairing, despondent, distrustful.

ao-dòchasachd, *n. f.* hopelessness.

aodraman, *n. m.* bladder. *See* aotrom.

aog, ŭg, *n. m.* death ; a skeleton ; a spectre ; is tu an t-aog duainidh, you are a miserable-looking skeleton ; a' dol aog, getting useless, getting vapid as liquor ; rotting. *O.Ir.* éc, death.

aogachadh, uguchu, *vb. n. m.* act of getting lean, withering, fading, dying by inches.

aogail, ūgal, *a.* death-looking.

aogas, ūgus, *n. m.* appearance ; likeness, face. *Also* aogasg. *O.Ir.* écosc, appearance, *habitus.*

aoghaire, ūghiru, *n. m.* shepherd, pastor. *O.Ir.* augaire, shepherd.

aoghaireachd, *n. f.* work of shepherd.

aognachadh, ùgnacha, *n. m.* nervous sensation ; alarmed feeling ; creeps, disgrace.

aognaich, ūgnich, *v.* fade, wither ; shame.

aognaidh, ūgny, *a.* pale, frightful, ugly, shelterless.

aoibh, ūyv, *n. f.* a cheerful countenance.

aoibhealachd, āyalachc, *n. f.* cheerfulness, politeness.

aoibheil, āy-val, *a.* cheerful, in good humour.

aoibhinn, āy-vin, *a.* pleasant. *O.Ir.* óibind, áebind, bright, beautiful.

aoibhneach, oyv-nuch, *a.* glad, happy, joyous.

aoibhneas, oyv-nus, *n. m.* gladness ; joyfulness.

aoigh, ūy, *n. m.* a guest. *Also* aoidh. *Ir.* aoidhe. *O.Ir.* óegi, guest.

aoigh, ūy. *See* aoibh.

aoigheachd, ūyachc, *n. f.* hospitality ; óigedachd, *hospitalitas.*

aoigheil, ūyal. *See* aoibheil.

aoil, ū-il, *v.* lime, plaster ; manure with lime.

aoin, ūn, *v.* unite, join.

aoine, ūnu, *n. f.* a fast, *Ir.* ; di h-aoine, Friday ; aoine na ceusta, Good Friday. *L.Lat.* jejūnium. *Fél.*

aoineadh, ūnu', *n. m.* a steep promontory, a steep brae with rocks.

aoineagan, *n. m.* wallowing. *Also* aonagraich.

aoir, ūr, *v.* satirise, lampoon ; *n.f.* a satire, a lampoon ; ribaldry. *O.Ir.* áer, áir.

aoir, *n. f.* sheet- or bolt-rope of a sail ;

fear gealtach 'san aoir, a timorous person holding the sheet-rope.

aoireachas, ūrachas, *n. f.* satire.

aoireachd, *n. f.* calumniation, a libel.

aoireadh, ūra, *vbl. n. m.* act of satirising, cursing.

aoirean, ùren, *n. m.* farmer, herd.

aoirneagain, *v.* wallow, welter.

aoirneagan, ūrnugan, *n. m.* wallowing, weltering. *See* aoineagan.

aois, ūsh, *n. f.* 1. age ; old age, antiquity ; ciod e an aois a tha thu ? what is your age ? is mairg a dh'iarradh an aois, woe to him that wishes extreme old age ; an làn aois, in full age. 2. *coll. n. m.* people : aois-dàna, artists, bards ; aois-ciùil, musicians. So *O.Ir.* ais, ois. Cf. *Lat.* aevum.

aol, ūl, *n. m.* lime ; àth aoil, a lime-kiln ; aol gun bhàthadh, quicklime, un-slackened lime. *O.Ir.* áel, chalk, lime.

aolach, *n. m.* dung, manure.

aoladair, ūluder, *n. m.* a plasterer.

aoladaireachd, *n. f.* plastering, burning lime.

aolais, ūlish, *n. f.* indolence.

aolaisdeach, ūleshjuch, *a.* lazy, sluggish.

aolar, *a.* abounding in lime.

aolmann, *n. m.* ointment.

aom, ūm, *v.* incline, bend ; lean ; be seduced by ; dh' aom i leis, she was seduced by him.

aomach, *a.* inclining, tending, bending.

aomadh, ūmu, *n. m.* inclination, or the act or state of inclining, bending, bulging, etc. ; tendency.

aomta, ūmtu, *vbl. a.* inclined, bent, bulged.

aon, ūn, *a.* 1. one ; alone, same, only, single ; aon bhean, one woman ; aon eile, another one, another ; aon sam bith, any one ; aon seach aon, neither ; gach aon, every one ; 'san aon luing, in the same ship ; do aon seach a chéile, to the one no more than to the others. 2. about, more or less : tha aon dà cheud ann, there are about two hundred—not less than two hundred ; aon cheithir cheud, about four hundred. *T.* Cf. *O.N.* usage. *Also* aonan. *O.Ir.* oín, óen, óenán. *W.* un. *Lat.* ūnus.

aonach, ūn'-ach, *n. m.* 1. a green plain near the shore on a stony bottom, a green beach. 2. a meeting ; a market-place ; aonach na samhna, the meeting of Martinmas. 3. moor, hill, steep slope. *O.Ir.* óenach, assembly, a fair.

aonach, *n. m.* galloping, panting.

aonachadh, ūn'-ach-u, *pt.* uniting ; *f. m.* union ; galloping.

aonachd, ūn'-ăchc, *n. f.* unity, concord ; aonachd an spioraid, the unity of the spirit ; còmhnuidh a ghabhail cuideachd an aonachd, to dwell together in unity.

aonadh, ūn'-u, *vbl. n. m.* union ; act of uniting ; air an aonadh, united. *O.Ir.* oínugud.

aon-adharcach, ūn-u'urcuch, *n. m.* a unicorn.

aonagail, *vbl. n. f.* act of wallowing.

aonaghurag, *n. f.* snipe. *See* eun-ghobhrag.

aonagraich, *vbl. n. f.* another form of aonagail.

aonaich, ūnich, *v. t.* unite, join into one, add.

aonaichte, ūn'-icht-u, *vbl. a.* united, joined.

aonairt. *See* aoirneagan.

aonais, unish, *prep.* awanting, without ; as aonais, without it.

aonar, ūn'-urr, *a.* alone, solitary, singular ; duine 'na aonar, a man all alone ; chan 'eil thu ad aonar mar sin, you are not singular in that respect. *O.Ir.* oínar, óenur, áenar.

aonarach, *a.* solitary, lonely ; forsaken.

aonarachd, *n. f.* solitude, solitariness.

aonaran, *n. m.* a solitary person ; a hermit, a recluse, a person left alone, or forsaken ; aonaran liath nan creag, the hoary hermit of the rocks.

aonaranach, *a.* solitary, like a hermit, lonely, forsaken, in solitude ; biodh an oidhche sin aonaranach, let that night be solitary.

aonaranachd, *n. f.* solitude, solitariness, loneliness.

aon-bhith, ūn'-vee, *n. f.* unity of being.

aon-bhitheach, ūn-vee-huch, *a.* co-essential ; co-substantial, of the same nature.

aon-chaithreach, *n. m.* a fellow-citizen ; luchd aon-chaithreach, fellow-citizens.

aonchasach, *a.* having a single stalk or stem, as an herb ; species of seaweed.

aon-chridheach, *a.* having like sentiments, unanimous.

aon-dathach, *a.* of one colour.

aon deug, ūn-jiug, *a.* eleven.

aonfhillte, ūn-eeltu, *a.* of a single ply ; simple, sincere, foolish ; a' dèanamh an duine aonfhillte glic, making the simple wise.

aonfhillteachd, sincerity ; *n. f.* le aonfhillteachd, with simplicity.

aonghin, *n. m.* an only child ; mar aonghin mic, like an only-begotten son.

aon-ghnèitheach, *a.* of one nature, of one kind ; homogeneous.

aon-ghnèitheachd, *n. f.* homogeneousness.

aon-ghràdh, *n. m.* one object of love, the best beloved object.

aon-ghuthach, *a.* having one voice or vote ; consonous, unanimous.

aon-inntinneach, *a.* unanimous, of one mind or intention.

aon-mhaide, *n. m.* a simultaneous pull in rowing.

aonragan, *n. m.* a solitary.

aonraganach, *a.* solitary.

aonsgeulach, *a.* unanimous, of one mind.

aonsgoch, ūn'-scŏch, *n. f.* swallow wort.

aont, ūnt, *n. m.* assent, admission, acquiescence ; tha mi a' toirt aont do na tha thu ag ràdh, I yield assent to what you say.

aonta, ūn'-tu, *n. f.* a lease, licence, indenture ; fo aonta, indentured.

aontachadh, ūn'-tuch-u', *vbl. n. m.* act of acceding, admitting, consenting ; tha mi ag aontachadh, I accede, I admit, or allow.

aontachd, ūn'-tachc, *n. f.* acquiescence, agreement ; admission.

aontaich, ūnt'-ich, *v.* agree, yield, consent, admit ; dh' aontaich i leis, she yielded to him ; na aontich thusa leò, consent or acquiesce thou not ; ma dh' aontaicheas tu aon uair, once you consent.

aorabh, ūruv, *n. m.* constitution, mental or bodily ; tha galar 'na aorabh, there is a disease in his constitution.

aoradh, ūru, *vbl. n. m.* act of worship, adoration, adoring ; ag aoradh dha, worshipping him; *recte,* adhradh. *O.Ir.* adraim, *L.* adoro.

aosar for aosmhor.

aosda, ūsdu, *a.* somewhat aged, old, aged, ancient, antiquated ; an déidh dhomh fàs aosda, after I have become old.

aosdachd, ūsd'-achc, *n. f.* agedness.

aos-dàna, *coll. n. m.* poets ; aos (people) + dán (art).

aosmhoireachd, ūsvoruchc, *n. f.* agedness ; great age, properties of old age.

aosmhor, ūsvor, *a.* old ; aged.

aotrom, ūtrum, *a.* light ; giddy ; creutair aotrom, a giddy creature. *Also* eutrom. *O.Ir.* étromm = an (*priv.*) + trom.

aotromachadh, *vbl. n. m.* ease, respite, as of a fever; alleviation, abatement, as of rain ; tha 'n t-uisge ag aotromachadh, the rain abates ; fhuair e aotromachadh o'n fhiabhrus, he got a slight respite, or crisis, or ease from the fever.

aotromaich, ūtrumich, *v.* lighten ; ease ; abate, as rain ; alleviate, as disease.

aotroman, *n. m.* a bladder ; a giddy person.

ap, *n. f.* an ape.

aparr, *a.* expert.

aparran, *n. m.* an apron.

aparsaig, *n. f.* knapsack ; fr. *Eng.* haversack.

àpas, *n. f.* a silly vain woman; based on ape.

ar, seems ; ar leam, seems to me. *E.Ir.* indar simm ; *also* dar or in dar.

ar, *pron. poss. pl.* ; our ; **ar fearann**, our land ; takes **n-** before a vowel ; **ar n-each**, our horse ; **ar n-athair**, our father. *O.Ir.* **arn**, ante vocales et medias, alias **ar**. *Z²*. *See* **mo**.

àr, *n. m.* ploughing ; **àr meadhonach**, second ploughing. *E.Ir.* **ar**. *W.* **âr,** tilth. *Lat.* arāre, *Gr.* ἀρόω. *O.N.* erja. *Goth.* arjan, to plough.

àr, *n. m.* slaughter ; **dàn an àir**, the song of the battle-field ; **'san àr**, in the slaughter. So *O.Ir.*

àr, *n. m.* a kidney ; **geir nan àr**, the fat of the kidneys.

ara, *n. pl.* **airnean**, kidneys. *M.Ir.* **áru**.

arabhaig, ar'-a-veg, *n. f.* strife. *O.Ir.* **ar-bág, ir-bág**, contention.

àrach, *n. m.* a tie, stall-tie for a cow, a collar ; blame, help ; **chan 'eil àrach air**, there is no help for it ; **cha robh àrach agamsa air**, I did not blame him ; **na bi 'g a àrach ormsa**, do not blame me for it. *E.Ir.* **árech** = bond ; security.

àrach, *n. m.* field of slaughter, a battle-field ; " **mun do chaisgeadh an t-àrach**," ere the battle was finished. *T. E.Ir.* **ár** + **mag**.

àrach, *n. m.* rearing, maintenance.

àrachas, *n. m.* insurance. *E.Ir.* **árach**, bail, contract.

àradair, *n. m.* an agriculturist.

àradh, **àru**, *n. m.* ladder.

araiceil, **arikel**, *a.* valiant ; important. Cf. *E.Ir.* **argg**, champion.

àraich, ar'-ich, *v.* rear, maintain, support.

araichd, **arichc**, *n. f.* treasure, or wealth in clothing ; a lady or gentleman's clothes given to servants, a present, a perquisite.

araichdeil, *a.* precious ; **gnothuch araichdeil**, a precious or important affair.

àraid, àr'-èj, *a.* particular, peculiar, special ; **duine àraid**, a notable person ; **gu h-àraid**, especially, particularly ; **gnothuch àraid**, an important affair.

àraideach, *a.* joyous, glad.

àraideachd, *n. f.* importance, singularity, particularity, peculiarity.

àraidh, àry, *a.* certain ; **duine àraidh**, a certain man ; **là àraidh**, a certain day. Cf. *Lat. quidam, O.Ir.* **àirithe**, *quidam*.

aralachd, *n. f.* niceness, fine quality.

ar-amach, *n. m.* rebellion, insurrection, mutiny, treason, conspiracy. *O.Ir.* **éirghe a mach**, a rising.

aran, *n. m.* bread ; **aran làthail**, daily bread ; livelihood ; **a tha cumail t'arain riut**, who gives you your livelihood ; **cha bhi thu gun aran**, you shall not want a livelihood ; **aran taisbeanta**, shew-bread.

aranach, *n. f.* bridle-rein.

aranaid, ar'-ăn-ăj, *n. f.* bread basket.

araon, ar-ūn, *ad.* both together ; **araon thusa agus esan**, both you and he.

arbhar, arv''-ur, *n. m.* sheaf-corn, standing corn, growing corn ; **tha an crodh 's an arbhar**, the cattle are in the corn. *E.Ir.* **arbar**, *O.Ir.* **arbe**. *Wb.* 10ᵈ.

arbharach, *a.* fertile in corn.

arbharrachd, *n. f.* forming into line, embattling.

arbhartaich, ar'-vărt-ich, *v.* dispossess, disinherit, forfeit, confiscate ; **am fearann arbhartaichte**, the confiscated or forfeited estates ; *vbl. a.* **arbhartaichte**, forfeited.

àrbhuidh, ār-vooy, *a.* auburn ; for **òr** + **buidhe**.

àrc, *n. f.* the cork-tree.

àrca, *n. m.* cork ; a cork or stopple.

àr-chu, ār-choo, *n. m.* a war-hound, blood-hound ; a chained dog.

archuisg, **archooshc**, *n. f.* experiment.

arcuinn, ark'-inn, *n. m.* a cow's udder.

àrd, *a.* high, lofty ; supreme ; tall ; **beinn àrd**, a lofty hill ; answers to arch-as a prefix in English ; **àrd-easpuig**, an archbishop ; before an adjective as a prefix, supplies the place of an adverb ; **àrd-shona**, supremely blessed ; **àrd-aoibhneach**, ecstatic, exulting in the highest degree. *Lat.* arduus.

àrdachadh, ārd'-ach-u, *vbl. n. m.* augmentation, increase ; **àrdachadh tuarasdail**, increase of salary ; promotion, elevation, exaltation ; **àrdachadh nan amadan**, the promotion of fools ; exalting, promoting, raising, extolling, praising.

àrdaich, ārd-ich, *v.* exalt, extol, raise, promote ; elevate ; increase.

àrd-aigneach, ārd-egnuch, *a.* mettlesome, magnanimous.

àrd-aingeal, ārd-engul, *n. f.* an archangel, a supreme angel.

àrdamas, *n. m.* high aim, ambition.

àrdan, *n. m.* 1. an eminence, or rising ground ; **'na shuidhe air àrdan**, sitting on an eminence. 2. pride, haughtiness, arrogance ; **dh' at àrdan 'na chridhe**, pride swelled in his breast ; **uabhar is àrdan**, pride and arrogance.

àrdanach, *a.* high-minded, haughty, arrogant, prone to take offence ; **spiorad àrdanach**, a haughty spirit, irritable, irascible.

àrdanachd, ārd-an-ăchc, *n. f.* haughtiness, arrogance, pride.

àrd-athair,* *n. m.* a patriarch.

àrd-bhaile, *n. m.* a metropolis, a city ; **esan a ghlacas àrd-bhaile**, he that takes a city.

* For pronunciation of compounds see the separate words.

àrd-bhreitheamh, *n. m.* a supreme judge ; a chief justice.
àrd-cheannabhard *n. m.* a commander-in-chief, a supreme ruler or governor.
àrd-cheannard, *n. m.* a chief, a supreme head.
àrd-cheannas, *n. m.* superiority ; dominion, pre-eminence, command.
àrd-chlachair, *n. m.* an architect, a master mason.
àrd-chlachaireachd, *n. f.* architecture, business of a master mason.
àrd-chomas, *n. m.* discretionary power, despotic power, despotism.
àrd-chomhairle, *n. m.* supreme council, parliament, a synod.
àrd-chomhairliche, *n. m.* a chief counsellor, a consul.
àrd-chuan, *n. m.* the high sea.
àrd-chumhachd, *n. f.* supreme power or authority.
àrd-chumhachdach, *a.* of high dignity and authority.
àrd-dhrùidh, *n. m.* an arch-druid.
àrddorus, *n. f.* a lintel.
àrd-easpuig, *n. m.* archbishop.
àrd-easpuigeachd, *n. f.* archbishopric, office of a bishop.
àrd-fheamanach, *n. m.* a high steward.
àrd-fhéill, *n. f.* a festival.
àrd-fhiosachd, *n. f.* vaticination, prophesying, predicting.
àrd-fhlaitheas, *n. m.* supreme dominion.
àrd-fhlath, *n. m.* supreme lord; a monarch.
àrd-fhuaim, *n. f.* bombulation.
àrd-ghleadhraich, *n. f.* bombulation, loud noise.
àrd-ghlonn, *n. m.* a feat.
àrd-ghnìomh, *n. m.* a feat, exploit, achievement ; treubhas.
àrd-ghuailleach, *a.* high-bowed (ship).
àrd-ghuthach, *n. m.* clamorous, shouting loudly.
àrd-iarla, *n. m.* first earl.
àrd-inbhe, *n. f.* eminence, excellence, high rank.
àrd-inbheach, *a.* eminent, excellent, in high rank or office.
àrd-inntinneach, *a.* high-minded.
àrd-iolach, *n. f.* loud shout, acclamation.
àrd-mhaighstireachd, *n. f.* supreme command or authority.
àrd-mhaor, *n. m.* a herald ; **ard-mhaor righ**, a pursuivant.
àrd-mharaiche, *n. m.* an admiral ; **priomh àrd-mharaiche**, lord high admiral.
àrd-mhìlidh, *n. m.* a heroic chief.
àrd-mhoirear, *n. m.* an admiral, a lord president.
àrd-mhol, *v.* magnify, highly praise.
àrd-ollamh, *n. m.* chief doctor (lit.).

àrdrach, ārd-ruch, *n. f.* a ferry-boat, a transport ; a boat. *Also* **àrdroch.** *M.Ir.* **arthrach**, *id.*
àrd-sgoil, *n. f.* classical education, philosophy ; a high-school.
àrd-sgoilear, *n. m.* an excellent scholar, a philosopher, a student.
àrd-sgoilearachd, *n. f.* choice education, philosophy.
àrd-shagart, *n. m.* a high priest.
àrd-shagartachd, *n. f.* high priesthood.
àrd-sheanadh, *n. m.* a general assembly; parliament.
àrd-sheanair, *n. m.* a member of a general assembly ; a member of any supreme council.
àrd-shona, *a.* supremely happy.
àrd-shonas, *n. m.* supreme bliss.
àrd-thainistear, *n. m.* lord-regent.
àrd-thriath, *n. m.* a high-lord, sovereign, a supreme ruler or lord, chief or hero.
àrd-uachdran, *n. m.* a chief ruler or sovereign.
àrd-uachdranachd, *n. f.* supreme ruler or authority.
àrd-ùghdarras, *n. m.* full authority, discretionary power.
arfuntaich, ār'-funt-ich, *v.* disinherit, dispossess, forfeit.
argarrach, arg-ruch, *n. m.* claimant.
argnachadh, *vbl. n. m.* act of plundering ; applied to a fishing-ground that is overdone ; **tha an t-àite sin air argnachadh**, that place is plundered. *O.Ir.* **orgun**, killing, raiding.
argumaid, ărg'-um-ej, *n. f.* an argument, a motive, a reason.
argumaideach, ărg'-um-ej-ăch, *a.* argumentative, fond of arguments, prone to argue.
argumaidich, ărg'-um-ej-ich, *v.* argue, reason, debate ; foil.
a rithist, u-rìsd, a rìs, *ad.* again, a second time. *E.Ir.* **doridisi.**
àrlas, *n. m.* a chimney. *E.Ir.* **forlés.**
arlogh, ar-lo', *n. m.* harvest-home ; **féisd an arloigh**, feast of harvest.
arm, *n. m., gen. s.* and *n. pl.* ; **airm**, a weapon ; the army ; **sgian, arm a bu mhiann leis**, knife, a weapon he was fond of ; **tha e 'san arm**, he is in the army ; **ghabh e 'san arm**, he joined the army. *Lat.* **arma.**
armach, *a.* mailed, covered with armour ; **gach gaisgeach armach**, every mailed hero ; a warrior ; **labhair an dubh armach**, the dark warrior spoke.
armachd, *n. f.* armour ; arms ; **armachd an t-soluis**, the armour of light.
armadh, arm'-u', *n. m.* oil or grease for anointing wool ; *vbl. n. m.* act of anointing or greasing wool.
armaich, ărm'-ich, *v.* clothe with armour ;

gird on arms ; *vbl. a.* **armaichte,** armed, clothed with armour. *M.Ir.* **armda.**

armail, *a.* stately, soldierly.

armailt, armelt, *n. m.* an army.

armailteach, *a.* belonging to an army ; having great armies.

arm-chaismeachd, *n.f.* an alarm of battle.

armchleasach, *a.* expert in military exercise.

armchliseach, *a.* expert in arms.

arm-coise, *n. m.* infantry.

armoilean, *n. m.* military discipline ; drilling.

armta, arm'-tyà, *vbl. a.* oiled, greased as wool.

armthaisg, arm-heshc, *n. m.* an armoury ; a military magazine. **arm + taisg.**

àrmunn, *n. m.* a hero, a warrior ; a gentleman ; **air slios an àrmuinn,** on the warrior's side. *O.N.* **ármaᵭr,** a steward, esp. of roy. estates.

aroch, *n.m.* a hamlet, dwelling.

àros, *n. m.* habitation, house. *M.Ir.* **àrus.**

àrosach, *a.* habitable.

arpag, *n. f.* a harpy.

arpag, *n. f.* a triangular cake.

arraban, *n. m.* distress.

arrabanach, *a.* sorrowful.

arrabhalach, ărr'-ă-văll-uch, *n. m.* a traitor ; a treacherous fellow ; a person that conceals himself in a house to bear away tidings. *See* **farbhalach.**

arrach, *n. m.* dwarf, spectre. *Also* **garrach.**

arrachar, *n. m.* rowing, steering.

arrachd, arr'-achc, *n. m.* spectre, a contemptible person. *M.Ir.* **arracht** (*f.*).

arrachogaidh, ara-choky, *n. m.* the first hound that gets wind of the deer.

arraghaideach, *a.* careless.

arraid, àrr'-ej, *n. f.* toiling in vain.

arraideach, *a.* toiling and wandering to no purpose, erratic. *M.Ir.* **arritech.**

arraideachd, *n. f.* toil, fatigue ; wandering to no purpose.

arraing, aruig, *n. m.* a stitch, convulsions.

arral, *n. m.* fastidiousness. *Also* **moit, moinig,** foolish pride.

arralach, *a.* fastidious. *Also* **moiteil, moinigeil.**

arronnach, arr'-on-uch, *a.* fit, decent.

arronta, *a.* bold. *See* **farranta.**

arrusg, *n. m.* indecency.

arsa, *v.* said, quoth ; **arsa mise,** said I ; **arsa esan,** said he = ar (quoth) + se or si (he or she). *E.Ir.* **bar,** for, or, *inquit, O.Ir.* **ol,** and *somet,* **ar.**

àrsachd, *n. f.* antiquity. *E.Ir.* **ársacht.**

àrsachd, *n. f.* noisy play (of children), horse-play ; *also* **àrsaidheachd.**

àrsadair, ār'-sa-der', *n. m.* antiquarian.

àrsaidh, ār'-sy, *a.* old, decrepit, ancient. *O.Ir.* **arsid,** *vetus.*

àrsaidheachd, *n. f.* antiquity.

àrsaireachd, ārsherachc, *n. f.* antiquarianism.

arseap, ăr'shep, *n. f.* retreat.

arsmachd, *n. f.* strife, overwhelming odds. **àr + smachd.**

arspag, *n. f.* largest sea-gull. *O. N.* svartbakr.

artan, *n. f.* a pebble ; stone ; *dim.* of **art,** stone. *O.Ir.* **art.**

artlaich, artlich, *v.* baffle. *See* **fairtlich.**

artrach, *n. f.* a ship's boat ; a vessel. *Also* **ardrach.**

artreud, ar-trēd, *n. m.* retreat ; transposed for **ratreud.**

art-theine, art-henu, *n. f.* a flint. *E.Ir.* **artéine,** *O.Ir.* **art,** a stone.

àruinn, ār'inn, *n. f.* kidney. *O.Ir.* **áru,** *d. pl.* **áirnib.**

àruinn, ārinn, *n. f.* neighbourhood, precincts, proximity ; **féidh air a h-àruinn,** deer in its vicinity. *I.L. E.Ir.* **àirrand,** front (of a house).

as, á, *prep.* out, out of, from ; **as a' mhachair,** out of the field ; **tha an solus air dol as,** the light is gone out ; **cuir as da,** kill him ; **chaidh e as,** he escaped ; **leig as,** let go ; **a** is used for **as** before consonants ; **a tigh na daorsa,** out of the house of bondage ; **dubh as,** blot out ; **as a chéile,** loosened, disjoined, asunder. **as + pers. pron. :** *sing.* **asam,** out of me, **asad,** out of thee, **as,** out of him, **aisde,** out of her ; *pl.* **asainn,** out of us, **asaibh,** out of you, **asda,** out of them. *Lat.* ex., e.

as-, a *priv. pref. O.Ir.* ess-, es-. *W.* eh-, ech-. *Lat.* ex.

as, *n. f.* an ass. *M.Ir.* **asan,** a she-ass.

asad, es-ud'. *See* **as.**

àsag, *n. m.* plug for draining hole in a boat. *Also* **tùc.**

asaibh, asiv. *See* **as.**

asaid, ăs-ej, *n. f.* childbirth ; delivery ; *v.* deliver, be delivered ; **dh' asaideadh, air mac i,** she was delivered of a son. *E.Ir.* **assait, adsaitim,** parturition.

asainn. *See* **as.**

asair, as'-ur, *n. f.* an herb, *asara bacca. Ir.* **asair,** heather, bedding for cattle.

asair, *n.* harness, shoemaker. *Ir.* **asaire,** shoemaker. *Lh. M.Ir.* ass, shoe ; **atat di assa . . . imbe,** two shoes are on him.

asal, *n. f.* an ass. *Lat. dim.* asellus.

asam. *See* **as.**

asann, *n. f.* (*pl.* **asnaichean** ; *gen. s.* **asainn, aisne**), a rib. *Ir.* **asna.**

asbhuan, asvin, *n. f.* stubble.

ascain, as'-ken', *v.* ascend.

ascairt, *n. m.* tow, refuse, coarse lint. *O.Ir.* as (ex) + scar- (separate).

ascall, *n. m.* loss, damage ; **ascall earraich,** loss of cattle in spring. *M.Ir.* escal.

ascaoin, askin, *a.* 1. harsh, inclement. 2. wrong side of cloth. 3. *v.* curse, excommunicate.

asgaidh, askee, *n. m.* present, boon, only in *phr.*, an asgaidh, as a gift. *O.Ir.* ascid, a gift.

asgaill, ăsk'-ill, asgailt, askelt, *n. f.* armpit; retreat, the embrace. *E.Ir.* ascall, ochsal.

asgan, *n. m.* a grig; a merry creature; dwarf.

asgnadh, *n. m.* ascending.

asgnadh. *See* fasgnadh.

aslach, *n. m.* request. *E.Ir.* aslach, *inf.* of adsligim.

aslachadh, asluchu, *vbl. n. m.* supplication, entreaty; act of entreating, supplicating.

aslaich, as'-llich, *v.* entreat, supplicate. *E.Ir.* adsligim, I entice, solicit.

aslomairt, *n. m.* a plain, battle-field. *Also* faslomairt.

aslonnach, *a.* prone to tell. *E.Ir.* aslonnud, making known.

as-onoir, *n. m.* dishonour; dishonest.

asp, *n. f.* an asp. *Also* nathair.

àsradh, *n. m.* disease in sheep; àsradh giollain, a dwining boy.

àsran, *n. m.* a forlorn object.

àsruidh, *n. m.* puny creature, pining.

astail, astil, *n. m.* a contemptible fellow.

astail, *n. m.* a dwelling; a building.

astairich, ăst'-ur-ich, *v.* go, get under way, as a ship or boat.

astar, *n. m.* a journey; distance; astar mór, a great distance; astar thrì làithean, three days' journey; fad air astar, far away; speed, as a ship; a' dol fo astar, going under way; a' gearradh a h-astair, cutting her way. *M.Ir.* astur: 1. toil; 2. travel.

astaraiche, ast'-ur-ich-u, *n. m.* traveller.

àsuing, àsuinn, àsuig, *n. m.* apparatus, weapon.

at, *n. m.* a swelling, a boil; *v.* swell, suppurate. *E.Ir.* att. *id.*

atach, *n. m. pl.* ataichean, worn-out boots. *Sc.* bauchles; shabby clothes. For ath + aodach. *E.Ir.* ath-étach, a cast-off dress.

ataich, at-ich, *v.* entreat, request. So *E.Ir.*

ataig, *n. m.* a stake, a palisade.

ataireachd, aturachc, *n. m.* swelling, blustering; noise of breaking billows.

atamach, *a.* fondling, indulgent, caressing, lenient, partial.

atamachd, *n. f.* fondling an unreasonable person; lenity, indulgence, partiality; gun atamachd do dhuine seach duine, without partiality to any one.

atamaich, at-ăm-ich, *v.* fondle an unreasonable person, caress, fondle, indulge.

atar, *a.* swelling. *M.Ir.* attmar. *See* atmhor.

at-cuisle, *n. m.* aneurism, a disease of the arteries.

àth, *n. m.* a ford; àth na sùla, the corner of the eye; is fhearr tilleadh am meadhon an àth, na bàthadh uile, it is better to turn in the middle of the ford than be quite drowned. So *M.Ir.*

àth, *n. f.* a kiln; air son mo chuidse de'n ghràn gabhadh an àth teine, for my part of the grain, the kiln may take fire. *Also* àmh. *E.Ir.* áith.

ath, ă, *a.* next, the next; an ath uair, the next time; over again.

ath, *v.* flinch; na seòid nach athadh an cruadal, the heroes that would not flinch in time of danger.

ath-, **aith-**, re- and ex- prefix of varying force: iterative, intensive, depreciative, out of date.

athach, ahuch, *n. m.* a giant. *E.Ir.* athach, a boor; a giant.

athach, *a.* bashful, blushing; modest; duine athach, a person easily abashed.

athach, *n. m.* a breeze, a blast. So *E.Ir.*

athadh, ahu, *n. m.* a daunt, blush; duine gun nàire gun athadh, a man without shame or confusion of face.

athailt, ahelt, *n. m.* a scar, mark; for ath + fail. *Also* fail, sliochd.

athailteach, *a.* full of scars.

athainne, *n. f.* embers, brand. *E.Ir.* aithinne, *m.* a firebrand.

athair, ahur, *n. m.* a father, an ancestor; athair - mhort, parricide, murdering one's father. *O.Ir.* athir, *L.* pater.

athair-ainmeach, *a.* patronymical.

athair-céile, ahur-kela, *n. m.* father-in-law.

athairealachd, ahuralachc, *n. f.* fatherliness, affectionateness, humanity, kindness.

athaireil, ahiral, *a.* fatherly, paternal. *O.Ir.* athramil = athar + samil.

athairich, *v.* father, adopt.

athair-lus, *n. f.* ground-ivy.

athair-mhort, ahurvort, *n. m.* parricide.

athair-mhortach, *a.* parricidal.

athair-mhortair, *n. m.* one who kills his father, parricide.

athair-neimh, *n. m.* serpent.

athair-thalmhain, *n. m.* yarrow, milfoil. *See* cair-thalmhainn.

athais, ahish, *n. f.* leisure, ease, rest, opportunity; air t' athais, at leisure, stop. ath (*intens.*) + fois.

athais, *n. f.* shame, ignominy. *O.Ir.* áthis, opprobrium.

athaiseach, *a.* slow, tardy, dilatory, leisurely.

athaiseachd, *n. f.* slowness, tardiness, dilatoriness, sluggishness, laziness.

athaisich, ahishich, *v.* get calmer ; abate, as rain ; get ease.

athar, ahur, *n. m.* evil effects, evil consequence ; **bithidh tu an athar sin ri do bheò**, you shall feel the evil effects of that during your lifetime ; **athar na grìobhaich**, the dregs or evil effects of the measles ; **athar òil**, the dregs of a debauch, or drink.

athar, a-ur, *n. m.* the air, atmosphere, the firmament ; *also*, **adhar** ; **c'àit' an robh e fo 'n adhar**, where was he under the sky. *I.Lom. O.Ir.* **aer** = *Lat.* aër ; **inàer** = in aërae. *Wb.* 12ᵈ. issinnaíar, in the air. *Wb.* 25ᵇ.

atharail, à'-ur-al, *a.* atmospheric, ethereal, relating to the air.

athar-amharc, *n. m.* aëroscopy, the observation of the air.

athar-eòlas, *n. m.* aëromancy, the art of divining by the air.

athar-iùl, a-ur-yool, *n. m.* aërology.

atharla, à'-ur-la, *n. f.* a heifer, a quey. *E.Ir.* aithirne, a calf.

athar-mheidh, a-ur-vey, *n. f.* a barometer.

atharnach, *gen.* -aich, *n. f.* repeated crop. See **aitheornach**.

atharrach, ă'-hur-ach, *a.* droll, strange.

atharrach, ă'-hur-ach, *n. m.* alternative, change, alteration ; another ; a fairy changeling ; **cha d' thàinig atharrach riamh**, another never came ; **chan e maith an atharraich tha air aire**, it is not the interest of another he has in view ; **tha e air an atharrach**, he has to toil for his bread. *O.Ir.* atherrach.

atharrachadh, ahuracha, *n. m.* change, removal, alteration ; **is mór an t-atharrachadh a thàinig air**, there is a great change on him ; changing, moving.

atharrachail, a'-hărr-ăch-ăl, *a.* changeable, changing, unsteady, given to change.

atharraich, ahurich, *v.* change, alter, translate, move, make an alteration ; *vbl. a.* atharraichte, changed, translated. *O.Ir.* aitherraigim, I change.

atharrais, *v.* and *n. m.* mimic, imitate. For **ath-aithris**.

athar-thomhas, *n. m.* aërometry.

athbhach, a'-vach, *n. m.* strength.

ath-bharr, *n. m.* a second crop.

ath-bheachd,* *n. m.* retrospect, a second thought, an after-thought, reconsideration, consideration.

ath-bheachdaich, *v.* look steadfastly a second time ; reconsider.

ath-bheothachadh, *vbl. n. m.* reviving, rekindling ; refreshing, reanimating, rekindling.

ath-bheothachail, *a.* refreshing, causing to revive.

* For pronunciation of compounds see separate members elsewhere.

ath-bheothaich, *v.* revive, refresh, reanimate, quicken ; rekindle.

ath-bhliochd, a-vluchc, *n. m.* second month after calving.

ath-bhreith, *n. f.* re-birth ; regeneration.

ath-bhriathar, *n. m.* a repetition, tautology, saying the same thing twice.

ath-bhriathrach, *a.* tautological, repeating the same thing.

ath-bhriathrachas, *n. m.* tautology, repetition.

ath-bhrosnachadh, *n. m.* rallying or re-inspiring with courage.

ath-bhrosnaich, *v.* re-inspire, re-encourage, resume courage.

ath-bhuail, *v.* re-strike, strike again, rethrash.

athbhualadh, *vbl. n. m.* repercussion ; act of striking or thrashing a second time.

ath-bhuannaich, *v.* regain, recover, gain a second time.

ath-bhuidhinn, *v.* regain, recover, retrieve, repossess, gain a second time ; *n. m.* a second gaining or retrieving.

ath-chagainn, *v.* chew, or ruminate a second time.

ath-chagnadh, *vbl. n. m.* rumination, chewing again, chewing the cud.

ath-chàirich, *v.* re-mend.

ath-chaithte, *vbl. a.* greatly worn out.

ath-chas, *v.* retwist, retwine.

athcheangal, *n. m.* rebinding, renewal of an agreement.

ath-cheangail, *v.* rebind, bind again, renew an agreement.

ath-cheannaich, *v.* repurchase, redeem.

ath-cheannsaich, *v.* reconquer, subdue a second time ; retrieve.

ath-cheasnachadh, *vbl. n. m.* re-examination ; act of re-examining.

ath-cheasnaich, *v.* re-examine, examine or interrogate again.

ath-cheumaich, *v.* retrace, repace, pace a second time.

ath-cheumnachadh, *n. m.* retracing ; recapitulating.

ath-chlaon, *v.* relapse into error, deviate a second time.

ath-chlaonadh, *vbl. n. m.* relapsing into error, a second deviation.

ath-chog, *v.* rebel.

ath-choisich, *v.* travel again, retrace, repass.

ath-chomain, *n. f.* a second obligation ; recompense, retaliation, requital.

ath-chomhairle, *n. f.* a second thought, a second advice.

ath-chomhairlich, *v.* re-advise, re-admonish.

ath-chomhairlichte, *vbl. a.* re-advised, re-admonished.

ath-chostus, *n. m.* after-cost.

ath-chronaich, *v.* rebuke a second time.

ath-chruinnich, *v.* re-gather, re-assemble, re-unite, rally as an army.
ath-chruinnichte, *vbl. a.* re-assembled, gathered again, rallied.
athchruth, *n. f.* change of form or appearance, transformation.
ath-chruthachadh, *vbl. n. m.* regeneration, transformation ; act of recreating, regenerating, transforming.
ath-chruthaich, *v.* recreate, transform, regenerate.
athchuimhne, *n. f.* recollection, remembrance.
ath-chuimhnich, *v.* recollect, remember, put in mind a second time.
ath-chuimirich, *v.* pare a second time, pare minutely.
athchuinge, *n. f.* a request, supplication, prayer ; ath- (iterative) + cuinge (entreaty). *O.Ir.* cuintgim, peto. *Wb.* 14ᶜ.
ath-chum, *v.* shape a second time ; keep a second time.
ath-chumadh, *vbl. n. f.* transformation ; act of transforming, reshaping.
ath-chunn, *v.* reshape, shape anew ; transform.
ath-dhealbh, *v.* transform.
ath-dhealbhadh, *vbl. n. m.* transformation, changing the shape.
ath-dhèanadach, *a.* itinerant, circumlocutory.
ath-dhioghail, *v.* retaliate, revenge, recompense evil for evil.
ath-dhioghaltach, *a.* revengeful, vindictive ; retributive.
ath-dhioghladh, *n. m.* retaliation, retribution, evil for evil ; revenging.
ath-dhìol, *v.* repay.
ath-dhìoladh, *n. m.* requital.
ath-dhruid, *v.* reshut.
ath-dhùblachadh, *vb. n. m.* redoubling, reduplication.
ath-dhùblaich, *v.* redouble.
ath-dhùin, *v.* reshut.
atheo, *n. m.* hemlock.
ath-fhàs, ahās, *n. m.* aftergrowth.
ath-fhuaraich, *v.* recool.
ath-fhuasgladh, *vbl. n. m.* releasing or untying a second time ; ransom.
ath-ghamhnach, *n. f.* a cow two years without a calf.
ath-ghin, *v.* regenerate, produce a second time.
ath-ghineamhainn, *n. f.* regeneration, reproduction.
ath-ghlac, *v.* retake, apprehend a second time.
ath-ghlan, *v.* recleanse, polish, purify ; ath-ghlanta, recleansed.
athghoirid, a-ghurij, *n. f.* a short road, way, or method ; *a.* short-tempered ; tha e athghoirid, he is short-tempered.

ath-iarr, *v.* seek or search a second time.
ath-iarrtas, *n. m.* a repetition in prayer ; a second searching or seeking.
ath-lathachadh, *n. m.* procrastinating ; procrastination ; *v.* athlathaich, procrastinate.
ath-leagh, *v.* remelt.
ath-leasachdadh, *vbl. n. m.* reformation, amendment ; second dunging.
ath-leasaich, *v.* remend, reform, ameliorate, correct ; re-dung.
ath-loisg, *v.* re-burn.
ath-lorgaich, *v.* retrace.
ath-mhalairt, *v.* re-exchange ; *n. f.* a second exchange or bargain.
ath-neartachadh, *n. m.* re-strengthening, recruiting strength, reinforcing.
ath-neartaich, *v.* re-strengthen, recruit, get new strength.
ath-nuadhachadh, *n. m.* renovation, renewal.
ath-nuadhaich, *v.* renew. *M.Ir.* ath-núaidigim.
ath-réitich, *v.* disentangle.
ath-roinn, *v.* subdivide.
athsgeul, *n. m.* a tale at second hand, twice-told tale.
ath-sgrìobh, *v.* transcribe, copy.
ath-sgrìobhadair, *n. m.* a transcriber, one that copies.
ath-sgrìobhadh, *n. m.* transcript, a copy ; act of transcribing. *O.Ir.* ath-scríbend, a rescript.
ath-shealbhachadh, *n. m.* re-inheriting, re-possessing.
ath-shealbhaich, *v.* re-inherit, re-possess.
ath-sheall, *v.* look again.
athshealladh, *n. m.* the second sight, retrospect.
ath-smaoineachadh, *vbl. n. m.* reflection, meditation.
ath-smaoinich, *v.* think again, meditate. *Also* ath-smaointich.
ath-stiùir, *v.* reconduct, steer again.
ath-theòidh, *v.* warm, or simmer again.
ath-thill, *v.* return, come back.
ath-thog, *v.* rebuild, lift again.
ath-thòisich, *v.* recommence.
ath-threòraich, *v.* reconduct.
ath-thuislich, *v.* relapse.
ath-thuit, *v.* fall again, relapse.
athtoirt, *n. m.* strippings.
ath-ùrachadh, *vbl. n. m.* refreshment ; reviving, refreshing, renovating.
ath-ùraich, *v.* refresh, revive; *vbl. a.* ath-ùraichte, refreshed, revived, renovated.
atmhor, *a.* swelled, turgid. *M.Ir.* attmar.
atmhoireachd, *n. f.* swelling; atmhoireachd Iordain, the swelling of Jordan.
atuinn, *n. m.* a rafter ; a wicket.

B

b, the second letter of the Gaelic alphabet, **beith**, the birch-tree.

b', for bu ; used before an initial vowel, or f aspirated ; as, **b' fhearr leam,** I would prefer ; **b' eòlach mise air,** well did I know him.

ba! ba! bâ bâ, *int.* a lullaby ; **bà! bà! mo leanabh,** sleep, sleep, my child.

bà, *a.* foolish, simple. *Also* **bàth.**

bab, *n. m.* a child's excrement ; hence **abab** ; some parts of Perthshire, **biob** ; **dèan do bhab.**

babach, *a.* filthy, abominable.

babachd, băb'-ăchc, *n. f.* filthiness, abomination.

babag, *n. f.* a filthy female ; confounded sometimes with **pabag,** a tassel.

baban, *n. m.* a bobbin.

babhaid, bav'-ĕj, *n. f.* a tassel.

babhaideach, băv'-aj-ach, *a.* tufted.

babhd, baud, *n. m.* a surmise, a rumour, a quirk.

babhdach, băud-ăch, *a.* spreading a surmise or rumour.

babhdaire, *n. m.* a tale-bearer ; useless person.

babhdaireachd, băud-ăr'-ăchc, *n. f.* spreading rumours.

babhdaireachd, *n. f.* surmising, puzzling.

babhsgach, bausgach, *a.* easily scared.

babhsgaire, bausgere, *n. m. a.* bladderskite.

babhsgannta, bausgantu, *a.* boastful, blustering, but easily frightened ; cowardly.

babhsganntachd, bausgantachc, *n. f.* cowardice ; fright from false alarm.

bàbhunn, bâ'vunn, *n. m.* bulwark, rampart ; a fold, enclosure for cattle. Better, **bàdhun.** *M.Ir.* bódhún. **bó** +**dún.**

bàbhunnach, băv'-unn-ach, *a.* well fenced with bulwarks, secure.

bac, *v.* hinder, restrain, obstruct ; forbid ; **na bac e,** do not hinder him. *E.Ir.*

baccaim, I lame, obstruct ; **bacc,** a shackle, a hindrance.

bac, *n. m.* a bend ; a rowlock ; the notch of a spindle : **bac an righe,** the bend of the arm ; **bac na h-easgaid,** the hough ; **bac a' chruachainn,** the haunch. *O.Ir.* **bacc,** a crook, a hollow.

bac, *n. m.* a bank ; **baca-mòna,** a peat-bank ; **gu bac,** to the full. *O. N.* bakki, a bank.

bacach, băc'-ăch, *a.* lame, cripple. *E.Ir.* **baccach.**

bacadh, bac'-ā, *vbl. n. m.* act of hindering, restraining.

bacag, *n. f.* a trip (in wrestling) ; **cuir cas bhacaig air,** trip him.

bacaiche, băc'-ich-u, *n. f.* lameness.

bacaichead, băc'-ich-ud, *abstr. n. f.* lameness, degree of lameness.

bacaid, bacej, *n. f.* ash-holder, ash-bucket.

bacail, băc'-al, *n. f.* a stop, hindrance, obstacle, interruption ; act of stopping.

bacaladh, *n. m.* an oven ; fr. *Eng* bake.

bacan, *n. f.* a tether-stake, a hinge ; **gamhuinn bacain,** tethered heifer ; a balcony, a notch.

bacastair, *n. m.* a baker ; fr. *Eng.* bake, **baxter.**

bacbhord, bacvord, *n. m.* windward, weather side. *O.N.* bakborði, *id.*

bach, *n. m.* drunkenness ; **bach thinneas,** sickness occasioned by drinking. So *E.Ir.* Cf. *Lat.* Bacchus.

bachall, *n. f.* an old shoe, a slipper. *Sc.* bauchle, bachle.

bachall, *n. f.* staff, a crosier. *Lat.* **baculum.** *O.Ir.* bachall=bishop's crook.

bachar, *n. m.* an acorn. Cf. *Lat.* baccar, nard.

bachlabh, *n. m.* a small creel, a dim. creel. **ba,** under +**cliabh,** creel.

bachlach, *a.* curled, in ringlets ; **cùl bachlach,** wavy, curly tresses.

bachlag, *n. f.* a shoot, as that of lint, turnip, etc. ; fr. **bachall.**

bachoid, băch'-oj, *n. f.* the boss of a shield. *E.Ir.* **boccoit,** hump, boss, *Lat.* buccatus.

bàchruidh, *col. n.* cattle, cows.

baclamh, baclav, *n. m.* hand-cuff. *O.Ir.* bacc-lám, lame or crooked hand.

bad, *n. m.* a tuft, a bunch, a cluster ; a grove, clump, thicket ; **bad coille,** a clump of trees ; a flock ; **bad chaorach,** a flock of sheep ; garment ; **bad aodaich,** an article of clothing (used disparagingly) ; a plain, a spot ; **as a' bhad,** on the spot, at once ; a sheaf ; **bad coirce,** a sheaf of oats ; hair, beard ; **bad mullaich,** hair on top of the head ; **am mullach nam bad,** free fight. It is common in place-names.

badach, *a.* tufted.

badag, *n. f.* small cluster.

badagach, *a.* full of tufts.

badan, *n. m.* Same as **badag.**

badhal, *n. m.* a wandering. *Also* **bàdharan.**

badhar, *n. f.* after-birth of a cow.

bag, *a.* a bag, a big belly.

bagaid, băg'-ăj, *n. f.* a cluster, a corpulent female ; **bagaidean searbh,** sour clusters.

bagaideach, bagejach, *a.* clustered, full of clusters ; corpulent.

bagailt, bagelt, *n. f.* a cluster.

bagair, bag'-ur', *v. n.* threaten, denounce evil, terrify ; **tha e bagairt an uisge,** it threatens rain. *E.Ir.* **bacraim,** threaten.

bagaire, băg'-ur'-u, *n. m.* a corpulent man; a glutton.

bagairt, bag'-ărt, *n. m.* a threat ; act of threatening, denouncing ; **cha téid plàst air bagairt,** no plaster is applied to a threat.

bagan, *n. m.* a little bag ; diminutive fellow.

baganach, *a.* small corpulent fellow.

baganta, *a.* corpulent ; neat, tight.

bagantachd, *n. f.* corpulency.

bagarrach, *a.* prone to threaten, threatening, denouncing evil. *Also* **bagairteach.**

bagarrachd, bàg'-urr-ăchc, *n. f.* a habit of threatening, denouncing evil.

bàgh, *n. m.* a bay. *Fr.* baie. *L.Lat.* baia, harbour.

bàgh, *n. m.* purpose ; **a dh' aon bhàgh,** of set purpose. *O.Ir.* bágu, *promitto,* vow.

baghaire, bu-yiru, *n. m.* fool, a dolt.

baghan, *n. f.* a stomach. Cf. *O.H.G.* mago. *O.N.* magi. *E.* maw.

bàghan, *n. m.* a churchyard, a cemetery.

bagradh, bagru, *vbl. n. m.* a threat ; act of threatening, denouncing evil.

bàibeil, by'-bal, *a.* terrible, enormous ; lying, given to fables.

bàibh, byv, *n. m.* a terrible sight ; an incredible thing ; a fairy, a goblin. *See* **baobh.**

bàibhealachd, byvuluchc, *n. f.* enormousness, terribleness ; exaggeration.

bàibheil, byval, *a.* incredible, enormous, terrible, exaggerated ; **pris bhàibheil,** an exorbitant price.

baideal, băj'-ăll, *n. m.* a pillar ; a cloud ; **baideal neòil,** a pillar of cloud ; a tower ; **mo bhaideal àrd,** my high tower.

baidealach, băj'-all-ach, *a.* like a pillar, a tower; full of pillars of cloud, bannered.

baidean, *n.m.* a flock of sheep ; *dim.* of **bad.**

bàidh, bāy, *n. f.* attachment, fondness, partiality, affection ; **dh' fheòraich i le bàidh,** she inquired affectionately ; improp. **bàigh.** *E.Ir.* **báid,** fond, affectionate, *O.Celt.* **bâdi-s.**

bàidheach, bāy'-ăch, *a.* kind ; *n. m.* a favourite.

bàidhealachd, bāy'-all-uchc, *n. f.* favour, partiality, kindness; benignity, fondness.

bàidheil, bāy'-yal, *a.* favourable ; **bha thusa bàidheil,** thou hast been favourable.

baidreag, bedrag, *n. f.* a ragged garment. *Also* **paidreag.**

baidreagach, bejraguch, *a.* ragged.

bàidse, bājshu, *n. m.* a musician's fee. *Eng.* **wage.**

bàidse, bājshu, *n. f.* a voyage ; an enormous load or cargo.

bàidsire, bājsheru, *n. m.* a voyager, an adventurer.

bàidsireachd, bājeruchc, *n. f.* adventuring, cruising, sea-faring life.

baigear, beg'-er', *n. m.* a beggar, a mendicant, a pauper ; fr. the *Eng.*

baigearachd, beg'-er'-uchc, *n. f.* begging, beggary, pauperism ; indigence ; begging ; pleading.

bail, bă'l, *n. f.* economy ; thrift ; the allowance in a mill to the poor. *Ir.* **bail,** success.

bailbhe, belevu, *n. f.* dumbness, muteness ; *a.* more or most dumb.

bailbheag, belvag, *n. f.* corn, poppy.

bailc, belk, *n. f.* seasonable rain ; genial showers ; a shower that comes suddenly, a plump of rain.

bailc, *n. f.* a ridge, a beam.

bailceach, belkach, *a.* in seasonable showers ; a strong, robust man. *E.Ir.* **balc,** strong. *Fél.* Feb. 1.

bailcean, belken, *n. m.* a round thick-set person ; dialect, **boilcean.**

bailceanta, belkanta, *a.* stout, strong.

baile, balu, *n. m., pl.* **bailtean,** a town ; a village ; a township; **baile mór,** a city ; **baile-puirt,** a sea-port town ; home ; **a bheil t' athair aig baile ?** is your father at home ? **chaidh e o'n bhaile,** he went from home ; **fear a'bhaile,** the gentleman or proprietor of the farm ; a farm ; **tha baile aige,** he has a whole farm ; **baile-mòid,** a court town. *E.Ir.* **baile, bale,** a place, a village. *O.Celt.* **bali-s, baljo-s,** a dwelling, a place. *O.N.* **ból,** a farm, abode.

baileach, bă'-l-uch, *a.* economical, *Arm.* ; also used for **buileach** ; **glanaidh e gu ro bhaileach,** he will purge thoroughly ; **na tréig mi gu baileach,** do not forsake me utterly.

bailgeann, bal'-ĕg-unn, *a.* pie-bald, spotted, white-bellied ; sometimes **bailgfhionn.**

bailich, balich, and **builich,** bulich, *v.* grant, bestow ; to use well, or ill.

bàilidh, bă'-ly, *n. m.* a magistrate ; a factor for an estate. *Sc.* bailzie, bailiff.

bàilidheachd, bālyachc, *n. f.* magistracy.

bailisdeir, bal'-ishj-ar', *n. m.* a babbler.

bailteachas, bal'-tyach-us, *n. f.* planting towns ; colonising.

bainbh, bán'-uv, *n. f.* a young pig. *See* **banbh.**

baindeachd, bendachc, *n. f.* modesty.

baindidh, bendi, *a.* modest. *E.Ir.* banda, womanly, feminine.

bàine, bā-nyà, *n. f.* paleness, whiteness ; *comp. deg.* of bàn ; more or most pale or white.

bàineasg, ban'-äsk, *n. f.* a ferret ; bàn + neas, white weasel.

bàinidh, bàn-è, *n. f.* fury, rage ; tha e air bàinidh, he is raging, he is quite furious.

bainionn, banun, *n. f.* a female.

bainisg, ban-eeshg, *n. f.* a little old woman.

bainne, ban-nyu, *n. m.* milk ; crodh bainne, milk cattle ; bó bhainne, a milk cow ; bainne milis, sweet milk ; bainne nùis, biestings ; bainne binn-dichte, curdled milk ; bainne lom, skimmed milk ; bainne goirt, sour milk ; bainne togalach, skimmed milk ; bainne-cruinnich, whisked milk. *Also* boinne. *E.Ir.* banne : 1. a drop ; 2. milk.

bainneach, ba-nyach, *a.* milky, lacteal.

bainneachas, ba-nyǎch-us, *n. m.* milkiness.

bainnear, ba'-nyur, *a.* milky, abounding in milk ; *n. f.* fold for milking sheep, *rectius* mainnir.

bainneardaich, ban-ǎrt-ich, *n. m.* lazy, drops of rain falling now and then. *Also* boinnealaich.

bainnseachas, bén-shǎch-us, *n. f.* feasting at weddings ; banqueting.

bainnsich, bén-sheech, *v.* waste.

baintighearna, ben'-tyurn-à, *n. f.* a lady ; a proprietor's lady.

baintighearnachd, bén-tyurn-achc, *n. f.* ladyship ; acting the part of a lady.

baintighearnas, bén-tyurn-us, *n. m.* the rule or sway of a lady ; petticoat government.

bàir, *n. f., gen.* bàrach, goal ; ràinig iad a' bhàir, they reached the goal ; game at shinty ; bhuidhinn iad bàir, they won a goal ; strife. *E.Ir.* báire, a goal ; fr. ancient times báire = game of " ball and hurleys," applied also to any contest, or battle. *O'Curry.*

bàir, *n. f.* a road, path through snow.

baircinn, bǎr-keenn, *n. m.* side timbers of a house. *Also* taobhain (*n. pl.*).

bairghin, baryin, *n. m.* bread, cake. *O.Ir.* bargen, bread.

bàirich, bǎr-ich, *n. f.* lowing of cattle.

bàirig, bǎr''-ig, *v.* bestow.

bàirisg, *n. m.* a wreck ; nach b'e bhàirisg e! what a wreck he is !

bàirleigeadh, bǎr-ligu, *n. m.* warning, summons, from *Eng.* warning. *Also* bàirnigeadh.

bàirlinn, bǎrling, *n. f.* summons, warning.

bàirlinn, *n. f.* an enormous wave, rolling billow. *O.N.* bára, wave, billow.

bàirlinnich, *v.* serve with summons of removal.

bàirneach, bǎrnuch, *n. f.* a limpet ; from bairenn, rock. *K.M. O.Celt.* barennîkâ.

bàirneachd, bǎrnachc, *n. f.* judgment.

bairnigeadh, barnigu. *See* bairleigeadh.

bàirseag, bǎrshag, *n. f.* a scold, shrew. *M.Ir.* bàirsecha, foolish talk.

baisceall, bashcal, *n. m.* a wild person. *E.Ir.* bascall, a lunatic.

bàiseach, bāshach, *n. f.* a heavy shower.

baist, basht, *v.* baptize. *O.Ir.* baitsim, fr. *Gr.* βαπτίζω.

baisteach, basht'-ach, *n. m.* a baptist ; *a.* baptismal, relating to baptism.

baisteadh, basht'-u, *vbl. n. m.* baptism ; act of baptizing ; 'ga bhaisteadh, baptizing him. *O.Ir.* baitsid, baithsid.

bàite, bā'-tyu, *vbl. a.* drowned ; quenched, extinguished ; *fig.* overwhelmed. *See* bàth.

baiteal, bateal, *n. m.* battle.

baith, bah, *n. f.* a lure, a decoy.

balach, *n. m.* a fellow, a boor, a young man ; a boy ; now used often in praise of prowess ; nach b'e am balach e ! what a heroic, noble fellow ! *Ir.* balach, a clown, churl. Cf. *E.Ir.* bachlach, a shepherd, a rustic, a clown.

balachail, *a.* clownish, boyish.

balachan, *n. m.* a boy, a little boy.

balachanas, *n. m.* boyhood.

balaist, *n. m.* ballast ; fr. the *Eng.*

balbh, bǎl'-uv, *a.* dumb, mute, quiet, still ; bha mi balbh tosdach, I was mute and silent. *M.Ir.* balb, dumb ; stammering ; *Lat.* balbus.

balbhachd, bǎl'-uv-ǎchg, *n. f.* dumbness.

balbhan, bǎl'-uv-ǎn, *n. m.* a dumb person, a deaf mute.

balbhanachd, bǎl'-uv-ǎn-uchc, *n. f.* interpretation, or communication of ideas by signs, dumb show ; ri balbhanachd, communicating ideas by signs.

balc, *n. m.* balk, landmark, ridge.

balcach, *a.* splay-footed.

balcanta, balk'-ǎnt-u, *a.* stout; firm. *E.Ir.* balcc, strong, stout, *O.Celt.* balko-s.

balg, *n. m.* a bag, belly, womb ; *gen. sing.* and *n. pl.* builg. Compds. : balg-abhrais, wool bag ; balg-béice, balgan-beice, furze ball, the sponge mushroom ; balgchasach, bandy - legged ; balg-losguinn, mushroom ; balg - saighid, quiver ; balg-séididh, bellows ; balg-shuileach, having prominent eyes ; balg-snàmh, air-bladder in fish ; balg-uisge, blister ; bubble ; balgan-peas-rach, a pea-bellied fat boy. *O.Ir.* bolg, bolc, *O.Celt.* bolgo-s.

balgaire, balguru, *n. m.* a fox, a dog ; a mean man.

balgum, *n. m.* mouthful.
ball, baul, *n. m., gen. sing.* and *n. pl.*
buill. 1. member (of family, of a
society, of the body) ; **ball comuinn,**
member of a society ; **buill a' chuirp,**
members of the body. 2. an article
(of clothing) ; **ball aodaich,** an article
of clothing. 3. a spot ; **ball dubh,**
black spot ; **ball-dóbhrain,** a mole,
spot on the skin ; **ball-seirce,** beauty
spot, " love-spot " ; **air ball,** on the
spot, immediately. 4. an object ;
ball-àbhacais, object of fun ; **ball-fanoid,** laughing-stock ; **ball-sampuill,**
disgraceful person ; **droch bhall,** mis-
chievous person, an imp. 5. stripe (in
cloth or tartan) ; " **luchd nam breacan
ballbhreac,**" men of the variegated
tartans. *O.Ir.* ball, *membrum.*
ball, baul, *n. m., gen.* and *n. pl.*
buill, a ball ; **ball-coise,** football ; **ball-iomaineach,** shinty ball ; **céis-ball,**
" dog and spell " ball ; fr. *Eng.*
ball, baul, *n. m., gen. sing.* and *n. pl.*
buill, a rope, cable.
ball, baul, *n. m., gen. sing.* and *n. pl.*
buill, membrum virile (specialised
meaning of **ball,** membrum). *O.Ir.* ball,
O.Celt. ballo-s, *Gr.* φαλλós.
balla, *n. m.* a wall, a fence ; *pl.* **ballachan.**
ballach, *n. m.* spotted, speckled ; **laogh
ballach,** a spotted or speckled calf.
ballaire, băll'-ur'-u, *n. m.* a cormorant.
ballan, băll'-an, *n. m.* a teat ; a dug ;
ballan na bà, the cow's teat ; a tub, a
vessel ; **ballan binndeachaidh,** a cheese
vat ; **ballan stiallach,** a sort of pillory
used of old in the Highlands ; " **air
ballan stiallach 'g ad sparradh,**" fastening thee to the pillory ; **balm** : **ballan
ath-bheothachaidh,** reviving cordial ;
ballan no sàbh, balm nor salve ; cup :
chuir iad ballan air, they cupped him.
O.Ir. ballán, drinking-vessel, *O.Celt.*
ballano-.
ballart, *n. m.* noise, fuss about one's
family ; boasting. Cf. *O.N.* ballra,
strepere.
ballartach, *a.* boastful.
balt, *n. m.* the welt of a shoe ; border,
belt ; *pl.* built, baltan.
baltach, *a.* bordered, belted.
baltag, *n. f.* a soaking (from rain).
ban, compositional form of **bean,** woman,
wife ; it is used principally to indicate
fem. gender ; as, **ban-fhàidh,** a prophetess ; **bancharaid,** a female friend.
bàn, *a.* pale, white, fair-haired ; cpd. **bàn-chur,** a degree of sea-sickness, squeamishness. *O.Ir.* bán, *O.Celt.* bâno-s.
bàn, *n. m.* left side of furrow—right side
is dearg ; each a'bhàin is each an deirg,
the near and off horse in ploughing.

bàn, *a.* vacant, waste (land), untilled ;
talamh **bàn,** untilled land ; tha an
sgìre **bàn,** the parish is vacant. *E.Ir.*
bán, *a.* pale ; *n.* blank space, unploughed field.
ban-aba, băn-ab'-ă, *n. f.* an abbess.
ban-bharan, banavaran, *n. f.* a baroness.
bana-bhàrd, bana-vārd, *n. f.* a poetess.
bana-bhreabadair, bana-vrebader, *n. f.*
a woman weaver.
bana-bhuidseach, bana-vujshech, *n. f.*
a witch.
bànachadh, bān'-ăch-u, *vbl. n. m.* whiten-
ing, growing pale or wan. *E.Ir.*
bánaigim.
banachagach, *n. f.* smallpox.
banachaig, *n. f.* dairy-maid.
banacharaid, băn'-a-chăr-èj, *n. f.* a female
friend, a female relation.
banachdach, *n. f.* vaccination.
banacheard, ban'-a-chyărd', *n. f.* a gipsy,
a tinker's wife.
bana-cheileadair, *n. f.* an executrix, a
female guardian.
bana-chìobair, *n. f.* a shepherdess.
banachocair, *n. f.* a cook, " female cook."
bana-choigreach, *n. f.* a female stranger.
banachomdhalta, *n. f.* foster sister.
bana-chompanach, *n. f.* a female companion.
bana-chompanas, *n. m.* female companionship.
bana-chruitear, *n. f.* a female harper, a
female minstrel.
banachuisleanaiche, *n. f.* a female performer on a wind instrument.
bana-churadair, *n. f.* an executrix, a
female guardian.
ban-adhaltrannach, *n. f.* an adulteress.
bànag, *n. f.* a grilse. *Also* gealag.
banag, *n. f.* a little woman.
bana-ghaisge, *n. f.* surprising feats or
exploits of a female.
bana-ghaisgeach, *n. f.* a heroine, an
amazon, female warrior.
banaghoistidh, *n. f.* a god-mother.
bana-ghrùdair, *n. f.* the landlady of an
inn ; a female brewer, a hostess ;
cagar na banaghrùdair, the ale-wife's
whisper (soon turns loud).
ban-àibhistear, *n. f.* a she-devil, a fury, a
virago.
bànaich, bān'-ich, *v.* to whiten, grow pale.
banail, băn'-al, *a.* womanly, modest,
becoming a female, comely. = ban +
samail.
banair, baner, *n. m.* sheep-fold. *See*
mainnir.
banais, băn'-èsh, *n. f., gen.* bainnse, a
wedding ; fear na bainnse, the bridegroom ; bean na bainnse, the bride.
M.Ir. bainfheis = ban + féis.
banalachd, băn'-ăl-ăchc, *n. f.* womanli-

ness, modesty, behaviour becoming a female.

banaltrachd, ban'-altruchc, *n. f.* nursing, fostering, cajoling, the business of a nurse ; **mach air bhanaltrachd,** out a-nursing.

banaltradh, băn'-alt-tru, *n. f.* a nursing.

banaltraich, băn'-ălt-rich, *v.* nurse.

banaltruim, băn'-ălt-rŭm, *v.* nurse.

banaltrum, băn'-altrum, *n. f.* a nurse.

banaltrumas, *n. f.* nursing ; cajoling.

banamhaighstir, bana-veshtir, *n. f.* a mistress, **female** master.

bana-mharcaiche, *n. f.* a female rider.

bana-mharcas, bana-varcus, *n. f.* a marchioness.

bana-mharsanta, *n. f.* a female merchant.

banamhoirear, *n. f.* a noblewoman, the wife of a lord ; **ban** must be prefixed almost in every case, when speaking of a female's nationality ; **ban-Alban-nach,** Scotswoman ; **ban-Sasunnach,** an Englishwoman ; **ban-Fhrangach,** a Frenchwoman.

banamhortair, *n. f.* a female that commits murder.

bana-phrionnsa, *n. f.* a princess, a king's daughter.

banarach, *n. f.* a dairy-maid. **ban** + **àireach.**

banarachas, *n. f.* the office of a dairy-maid or milk-maid.

banas-tighe, banus-tyu, *n. m.* house-wifery ; house-keeping.

banbh, băn'-uv, *n. m.* land unploughed for a year. *E.Ir.* **banb,** *O.Celt.* **banvo-s.**

banbh, *n. m.* a pig. *E.Ir.* **banb,** a sucking-pig.

Banbha, poetic name for Ireland. *O'R.*

banc, *n. m.* a balk, a bank ; fr. *Eng.*

bànchruthach, bān-chroohach, *a.* pale, wan, pale-complexioned.

bandaidh, bănd-ĕ, *a.* modest, delicate, feminine. *See* **baindidh.**

ban-dalta, *n. f.* a foster daughter.

ban-dia, ban'-jeeu, *n. f.* a goddess.

ban-diùchd, ban-diooc, *n. f.* a duchess, a duke's wife.

ban-drùidh, ban-drooy', *n. f.* a sorceress.

ban-fhàidh, *n. f.* a prophetess ; **Miriam, a'bhan-fhàidh,** Miriam, the prophetess.

ban-fhiosaiche, *n. f.* a fortune-teller, a gipsy.

ban-fhlath, *n. f.* a chief's lady.

ban-fhuaighliche, *n. f.* a sempstress, a milliner, a mantua-maker.

banfhuasglach, ban-oousg'-lach, *a.* menstrual ; **banfhuasgladh,** menstrual courses. *H.S.*

ban-fhuineadair, *n. f.* a female baker, a woman that bakes bread.

bang, *n. f.* a drum ; **a' toirt fuaim air banga,** making a drum beat.

bangadh, *n. m.* a binding, promise. **Cf.** *Lat.* pango.

bangaid, bang'-ej, *n. f.* a feast at the christening of a child ; a feast, fr. *Eng.* banquet, < *Fr.* and *Ital.*

ban-iarla, *n. f.* a countess.

ban-ifrionnach, *n. f.* a she-devil ; a fury ; a furious female, a virago.

ban-laoch, *n. f.* a heroine, an amazon.

ban-léigh, *n. f.* a female skilled in medicine. *M.Ir.* **ban-liaig,** a female physician.

ban-leómhann, *n. f.* a lioness ; more commonly **leómhann bhoirionn,** female lion.

ban-lighiche, *n. f.* a female physician.

bann, *n. m.* (*pl.* **boinn, banntan**), a hinge ; **bann an doruis,** the hinge of the door ; **théid mise am bannaibh dhuit,** I can assure you ; a chain, a tie, a cord ; a key-stone : **cuir boinn anns a' bhalla,** put key-stones in the wall ; *v.* bind, tie, make firm with key-stones : **balla air a dheagh bhannadh,** a wall well secured with key-stones ; **bann-làmh,** a hand-cuff, a manacle ; **bann-dùirn,** a wrist-band. *E.Ir.* **bann,** *O.Celt.* **banno-.**

bann, *n. m., pl.* **boinn, banntan,** *d.* **bann-aibh,** a deed ; a bond ; fr. *Eng.* band.

bannag, *n. f.* Christmas Eve, or the night before the 25th December ; a present or treat given at Christmas ; **oidhche nam bannag,** night of the (Christmas) cakes. *Sc.* bannock.

bannag, *n. f.* a corn-fan. *Lat.* vannus.

bannal, *n. m.* a bevy, a gang, a band, a troop ; a covey ; **bannal uchd ruadh,** the red-breasted covey. *Also* **pannal.** *E.Ir.* **ban-dál** : 1. tryst with a woman. 2. assembly of women.

bannalach, *a.* in companies, in troops, in gangs, in crowds.

ban-naomh, *n. f.* a female saint, a nun.

bann-ceirde, bann'-kerj-a, *n. m.* a deed of indenture. *Also* **aonta. fo aonta** = indentured.

bann-cheangal, baun-chengul, *n. m.* a bond, a cautionary bond.

banndalach, *a.* foppish.

bann-dìdein, baun-jeejen, *n. m.* safe conduct.

bann-dùirn, bann-doorn, *n. m.* wrist band.

bann-làmh, *n. m.* a cubit. So *Ir.*

bann-làmh, *n. m.* a manacle, a handcuff. *Also* **glas làmh** = lock for hands.

bann-seilbhe, bănn'-shelvu, *n. m.* a deed of infeftment ; **bann taisbeanaidh,** a bail-bond.

bann-shaor, *v.* free, license.

banntach, *n. f.* a bond or obligation.

banntach, *n. f.* a hinge.

banntair, *n. m.* a drawer of bonds.

banntairean, *n. m. pl.* covenanters. *I. Lom.*
banoglach, *n. f.* a servant, maid, a hand-maiden.
ban-oighre, ban-oyru, *n. f.* an heiress.
ban-ridire, baun-reejiru, *n. f.* a baroness, the wife of a knight.
banrigh, baunri, *n. f.* a queen.
banrighinn, bānrinn, *n. f.* a queen.
ban-sealgair, baun-shalger, *n. f.* a huntress.
bansgal, *n. f.* female, hussy. *O. Ir.*
ban-scál, *pl.* banscala, *servae*; cf. scoloca, *servi. See* sgalag.
ban-solairiche, baun-solarichu, *n. f.* a cateress.
ban-stiubhart, baun-steward, *n. f.* a housekeeper, a stewardess.
bantrach, bauntrach, *n. f.* a widow, a widower. *E. Ir.* bantrebthach, landlady, a widow.
bantrachas, bauntruchus, *n. m.* widowhood.
ban-tràill, *n. f.* a bond-maid, a female slave, mean woman.
ban-tuathanach, baun-tuahanach, *n. f.* a farmer's wife ; a woman holding a farm.
baobach, bū'-bach, *n. f.* panic ; a terrible fright ; a female easily frightened ; *a.* panic-struck, terribly afraid.
baobaire, būb'-ur-u, *n. m.* a panic-struck man, a man easily frightened.
baobh, būv, *n. f.* a wicked mischievous person, a fury, a witch ; càineam is aoiream a' bhaobh, a rinn an t-òran, let me satirise and lampoon the furious woman that made the song. *E. Ir.* badb and bodb, a scald-crow, rook.
baobhachd, *n. f.* the conduct of a foolish woman.
baobhaidh, būvy, *a.* fierce.
baodhaisteachadh, bū'-āsht-ach-u, *n. m.* drenching and fatigue in bad weather.
baodhaistich, bu-eshtich, *v.* drench, give a miserable appearance ; spoil one's clothes in bad weather.
baogaid, būg'-äj, *n. f.* a whim, caprice.
baogaideach, būgejuch, *a.* whimsical, capricious, odd, fanciful ; *n. f.* a fanciful whimsical female.
baogaideachd, būgejuchc, *n. f.* whimsicality, fancifulness, oddity ; capriciousness.
baogh, *n. f.* a she-spirit. *See* baobh.
baoghal, bū'-all, *n. m.* danger, peril. *O. Ir.* baigul, baegul, risk, chance, peril.
baoghalach, bū'-ul-uch, *a.* dangerous, furious ; destruction, dangerous, perilous.
baoghalta, bū'-ultu, *a.* simple, foolish.
.baoghan, bū'an, *n. m.* a calf, anything jolly.
baogram, bū-gram, *n. m.* a flighty emotion.

baoileag, boylag, *n. f.* blaeberry. Same as braoileag.
baoireadh, boyru', *n. m.* foolish talk.
baois, būsh, *n. f.* lust, lewdness, madness. *E. Ir.* baes, bais, *O. Celt.* baisso-.
baoiseach, būsh'-ach, lewd, lustful.
baoit, byt, *n. f.* a foolish, giddy female.
baoiteag, bytag, *n. f.* small white maggot ; fish-worm ; ground-worm.
baol, *n. m.* approximation, nearness in doing anything ; *v.* approach or come near doing anything ; cha bhaol e air, it will not come near it.
baolastair, būlaster, *n. m.* a dolt, blockhead.
baoth, bū, *a.* foolish, silly ; baoth bheus, immorality, folly ; baoth chreideamh, superstition ; baoth shùgradh, foolish and profane jesting ; baoth smaointinn, a foolish thought ; baothchleasachd, immodest play. *O. Ir.* báith, " báith no amhirissig " idiotae aut infidiles. *Wb.* 12ᵈ.
baothaire, bū-hiru, *n. m.* simpleton, a fool.
baothaireachd, *n. f.* folly, stupidity.
baothan, bū-han, *n. m.* blockhead.
bara, *n. m.* a barrow ; bara roth, a wheelbarrow ; bara làimhe, a hand-barrow ; a tumble, or inclination : chuir e bara dheth féin, he turned somersault. *E. Ir.* bara.
barail, băr'-ăl, *n. m., gen.* baralach, opinion, belief, conjecture, supposition ; tha mi 'm barail, I suppose ; ma 's math mo bharail-sa, if I judge aright ; *pl.* baralaichean. *O. Ir.* bar (a sage) + samail.
baraille, barilu, *n. m.* a barrel. *Also* barailte. *E. Ir.* barille.
baraisd, bareshj, *n. f.* the herb borage. *Also* barraisd ; fr. the *Eng.*
baralach, *a.* hypothetical, conjectural.
baralachadh, bar'-al-ach-u, *vbl. n. m.* act of guessing, supposing, conjecturing.
baralaich, bar'-al-ich, *v.* guess, suppose, conjecture.
baran, *n. m.* a baron, a baronet.
baranachd, bar'-un-ăchc, *n. f.* a barony.
barant, *n. m.* a surety, or reliance, warrant.
barantach, *a.* confident, assured.
barantaich, bar'-ant-ich, *v.* warrant.
barantail, *a.* warrantable.
barantas, *n. m.* warrant, commission, power, authority ; barantas glacaidh, a warrant to secure or apprehend.
barbair, bărb'-er', *n. m.* a barber. *Fr.* barbe, *Lat.* barba. *Also* borbair.
barbarra, *a.* barbarous. *Lat.* barbarus.
bar-bhrigein, b-vrigen, *n. m.* silver-weed. *Also* brisgean.
barbrag, *n. m.* tangle tops, barberry. *Also* bragaire.

bàrc, *n. f.* a boat, a skiff ; chunnacas bàrc, a boat was seen. *E.Ir.* bárc, *L.Lat.* barca.

bàrc, *n. m.* breaking billow ; muir mhór a' bàrcadh, heavy sea breaking (fiercely).

bàrcaideach, *a.* flowing, torrential.

bàrd, *n. m.* 1. an enclosed field, paddock. *Sc.* calf's ward. 2. a garrison. *Ir.* a ward, guard.

bàrd, *n. m., pl.* bàird, a poet, bard, a rhymer ; sheinn am bàrd, the bard sang. *E.Ir.* bárd = inferior poet or rhymer : bárd bélghach, prattling bard. *L. na gC. W.* bardd. *O.Celt.* bardo-s.

bàrdachd, bārd-ăchc, *n. f.* poetry ; term for poetry in general, and applies to satire, elegy, epic, etc.

bàrdail, *a.* poetical.

bàrdainn, bārd'-een, *n. f.* summons of removal. *Also* bàirlinn. .

bàrdalachd, bārd'-al-uchc, *n. f.* satire, ribaldry ; unseemly language. *E.Ir.*

bargan, *n. f.* a bargain, a good penny-worth ; fr. *Eng. O.F.* bargaignier.

barganaich, bărg'-an'-ich, *v.* bargain, buy.

bàrlag, *n. f.* a rag, a tatter. Cf. *Ir.* barlin, sheet.

bàrlagach, *a.* ragged, tattered, full of rags or tatters.

bàrluadh, bār'-loou, *n. m.* a term in pipe music. *Eng.* bar + *G.* luath. *McB.*

bàrnaig, *n. m.* summons, warning.

barp, *n. f.* a conical heap of stones, sepulchral cairn ; memorial of the dead.

bàrr, *n. m.* top, point, tip, end, extremity : barr na craoibhe, top of the tree ; barr a' bhalla, the top of the wall ; barr na slaite, point, or tip of the rod ; barr na cluaise, tip of the ear ; crest ; barr nan tonn, crest of the waves ; cream ; crop ; barr buntàta, potato top ; a season's crop ; barr maith, a good crop ; *adv.* a bharr, etc., moreover ; *v.* cut off the surface, crop, top : a' barradh na mòna, paring the peat bank ; a' barradh a' bhuntata, cropping the potatoes ; a' barradh nan craobh, pruning the trees. *E.Ir.* barr.

barra, *n. m.* spike, bar.

barrabhall, bărr'-ă-văll, *n. m.* bartisan, battlement ; embrasure.

barrabhard, barr'-a-vărd, *n. m.* a chief poet ; a poet laureate, a graduate in poetry.

barrabhord, barr'-a-vŏrd, *n. m.* the deck of a vessel ; barr (top) + bòrd (*q.v.*).

barracaid, barucej, *n. f.* pride, loud talk.

barracaideach, barracajach, *adj.* saucy.

barrach, *n. m.* tow ; hards of flax or hemp. *Sc.* brairds ; *a.* heaped up as a load ; excessive.

barrach, *n. m.* top branches of trees, brushwood ; loppings of birch.

barrachd, bărr'-ăchc, *n. f.* superiority, excellence ; " thaobh barrachd do ghnìomh," because of the excellence of your deed ; surplus ; advantage ; *adv. phr.* a bharrachd, moreover.

barrachdail, bărr'-ăchc-al, *a.* surpassing.

barradh, bărr'-u, *vbl. n. m.* 1. act of cropping ; act of skinning peat-bank. 2. clinching (nails) ; òrd-barraidh, clinching hammer.

barrag, *n. f.* scum, froth ; " cha tig barrag air cuid cait," scum will not come on a cat's portion.

barraiche, *n. m.* overlord ; superior ; proud race. *Ir.* barraidhe, a proud, tall, aspiring fellow.

barraichte, bărr'-ech-tyà, *vbl. a.* surpassing, excellent.

barraidh, *n. m.* baron-bailie.

barrail, bârr'-al, *a.* excellent.

bàrraisg, bārishc, *n. m.* boaster ; a braggadocio.

barrall, *n. m.* a shoe-tie. *Also* barriall.

barran, *n. m.* any kind of coping on a fence : thorns, flags, etc.

barrasach, *a.* topped, excellent.

barr-bhuidhe, bărr'-a-vooy, *a.* yellow-topped, yellow-haired.

barr-chaol, baru-chūl, *n. m.* a pyramid ; *a.* pyramidal, conical, tapering. *Ir.* barr-chael, tapering.

barr-dhias, *n. f.* point of a sword.

barr-dhriopair, bar-ghriper, *n. m.* a butler.

barrfhionn, barr'-unn, *a.* fair-haired. *Also* written barrunn.

barr-ghnìomh, bar-ghreev, *n. m.* a work of supererogation, a transcendent exploit.

barr-ghnìomhach, *a.* superfluous.

barr-guc, *n. m.* potato blossom ; bloom.

barriall, bar-ul, *n. m.* shoe-tie, boot-lace.

barrmais, bărr-măsh', *n. m.* a cornice. barr + maise.

barrmaisich, barr-măsh'-ich, *v.* ornament.

barr-roc, *n. m.* broad-bladed tangle. *Also* bragaire.

bas, *n. f., pl.* basaibh, basan., the palm of the hand ; buailibh bhur basaibh, clap your hands. *Also* bois. *O.Ir.* bass, *d.* boiss, *O.Celt.* bostà.

bas, *n. f.* a spoke.

bas, *n. m.* hollow or concave side of a club.

bàs, *n. m.* death ; faigh bàs, die ; gheibh gach ni bàs, everything shall die ; ri uchd bàis, at the point of death. *O.Ir.* bás ; *abstr.* of baa, may die.

bàsaich, bās'-ich, *v. i.* die.

basaidh, basi, *n. f.* basin.

bàsail, bās'-al, *a.* mortal, deadly.

bàsalachd, bās'-ăl-ăchd, *n. f.* mortality.

basardaich, bass'-ard'-ich, *n. m.* clapping of hands with joy, acclamation, rejoicing.

bàsarm, *n. m.* a deadly weapon.

basbaire, bas'-bur'-u, *n. m.* a fencer ; " bha thu 'n ad bhasbaire còir," you were a bonny fencer.

bascaid, bask'-ej, *n. f.* a basket ; fr. the *Eng.*

basdal, *n. f.* noise, glitter, merriment.

basdalach, *a.* cheering, gay ; 'nuair thig a' ghloine bhasdalach, when the cheering glass comes round.

basgair, basg'-ăr', *n. f.* clapping of hands (expressive of intense feeling) ; bas + gàire, " palm-noise.' So *E.Ir.*

basganta, *a.* warbling, melodious.

basgluath, basc-loo-.u, *n. f.* vermilion. *E.Ir.* basc, red, and luath, ashes.

bàshruth, *n. m.* a calm stream.

baslach, *n. m.* a handful.

bàsmhor, bās'-vur, *a.* mortal, deadly, fatal, subject or liable to death.

bàsmhorachd, bās'-vur-àchc, *n. f.* mortality, deadliness ; fatality.

basraich, băs'-rich, *n. f.* mournful clapping of hands.

bata, *n. m.*, *pl.* bataichean, a staff.

bàta, *n. m.*, *pl.* bàtaichean, a boat. *O. N.* bátr.

batail, batal, *n. m.* a battle. *Also* batailt.

batair, bat'-ur', *n. m.* a cudgeller.

bàtannach, *a.* rich in boats.

bàth, *a.* simple. Same as baoth. *Also* bà.

bàth, bā, *v.* drown, quench, extinguish ; bhàthadh e, he was drowned ; bhàth i an gealbhan, she extinguished the fire ; bhàth e phathadh, he quenched his thirst. *Ir.* bàthaim, *O.Ir.* bádud *naufragium*. *Wb.* 17ᵈ. bàth, sea. *O'Dav. O.Celt.* bâdiô.

bàthach, bā'-hăch, *n. f.*, *pl.* bàthaichean, cow-house, byre ; sloth. bó + tigh, cow-house.

bàthadh, bahu', *vbl. n. m.* a drowning, quenching, slaking, smothering, extinguishing ; aspiration (of consonants).

bathais, ba-hish, *n. f.* forehead, front, impudence ; nach ann aige a bha bhathais, what impudence the fellow had. *O.Ir.* baithes, the head.

bathar, bă'-ür, *n. m.* merchandise, goods, wares ; droch bhathar, bad goods (applied to a worthless, tricky person).

bathar, *n. f.* after-birth (of a cow).

batharbhord, bă'-ür-vörd, *n. m.* a counter.

batharnach, bă'-ur-nach, *n. m.* a warehouse, a shop, a storehouse.

bàthghiullan, bā-yoolan, *n. m.* a simple lad. *O.Ir.* báith (foolish) + giullan (byform of gille).

bàthlaoch, bā-luch, *n. m.* simple fellow.

b'e for bu e. *See* bu.

beach, beăch, *n. m.* a bee. *O.Ir.* bech.

beachach, *a.* waspish, abounding with bees.

beachaid, bech'-ăj, *n. f.* a bee-hive.

beachan, bech'-un, *n. m.* a wasp ; beachan each, a horse-fly.

beachd, bechc, *n. m.* opinion, idea, keen observation, judgment ; distinct recollection ; as a bheachd, out of his opinion ; ma 's math mo bheachdsa, if I have distinct conception or recollection ; mór 'na bheachd, having high ideas, or haughty ; aim or mark ; geur shaighde laoich is ro-chinntiche beachd, the arrows of the hero of surest aim ; gabh beachd air, pay particular attention, mark well ; cum sin ann do bheachd, keep that steadily in view ; *adv. phr.* gu beachd, fully, surely. *E.Ir.* becht, precise, certain, complete.

beachdachadh, bechc'-ăch-u, *vbl. n. m.* meditation, contemplation ; paying close attention ; act of meditating, contemplating.

beachdaich, bechk'-ich, *v.* attend, look steadfastly, perceive, observe ; review, criticise.

beachdaid, bechk'-ej, *n. f.* an observatory, a watch-tower.

beachdaidh, bechk'-y, *a.* sure, certain, positive ; gu beachdaidh, most assuredly, most decidedly so.

beachdail, bechc'-al, *a.* keenly observant, attentive ; sure in aim ; nach beachdail an t-sùil a tha aige, how keenly observant his eye is ; conceited.

beachdair, bechc'-urr, *n. m.* a keen observer, a reviewer or critic.

beachdaireachd, bechc'-ar'-achc, *n. f.* criticising ; reviewing ; spying.

beachdalachd, bechc-ăl-uchc, *n. f.* keenness and sureness of perception, great punctuality in observing, sureness of aim.

beach-eòlais, *n. m.* queen bee, leading bee.

beadach, bedach, *a.* impertinent, pert, petulant, pettish. *E.Ir.* bedeach, skittish.

beadachd, *n. m.* impertinence, pertness, petulance ; for beadaidheachd.

beadag, bedag, *n. f.* a petulant female.

beadagan, bedagan, *n. m.* petulant man. *Cf. M.Ir.* betán, saucy fellow.

beadaidh, bedi, *a.* impertinent, petulant, pert, capricious, fastidious. *Ir.* beadaidhean, a scoffer. *Lh.*

beadair, bedur, *v.* fondle, caress, indulge ; cajole, coax.

beadarrach, běd'-urr-ăch, *a.* sportive, fondled, caressed, spoiled as a child ; fond of ; pampered.

beadradh, bĕd'-ru, *vb. n. m.* act of fondling, toying, caressing ; flirting ; **a' beadradh r'a leannan,** flirting with his sweetheart. *O.Ir.* **medrach,** merry.

beag, beg, *a.* little ; short ; diminutive ; disagreeable ; trifling ; **gnothuch beag,** a trifling business or affair ; **is beag orm thu,** you are disagreeable to me, I hate you ; **iadsan air am beag sibh,** they who hate you ; **is beag so,** this is a light thing ; **is beag an dolaidh,** it is no great harm, he or she richly deserves it ; *n. m.* little, nothing, any, the least, the young ; **cha d'fhuair thu a bheag,** thou hast found nothing ; **a bheil a bheag de mhaith air ?** is it worth anything ? **am beag is am mór,** both great and small ; **chan fhaigh a bheag bàs,** nothing shall die ; **a bheag a dh' aon ni as leatsa,** the least particle of what is thine ; **is beag,** almost ; **is beag nach do mharbh e mi,** he almost killed me ; **rud a chì na big, is e nì na big,** what the young see, the young do. *O.Ir.* becc, *O.Celt.* bekko-s, bekkano-s.

beagaich, begich, *v.* lessen ; diminish.

beagan, began, *n. m.* a little, a few ; a **lìon beagan is beagan,** by little and little ; **ni sinn e a lìon beagan is beagan,** we will do it by degrees ; **air bheagan tuaireim,** possessing little sense.

beag-eagalach, beg-egalach, *a.* fearless, bold, intrepid, undaunted.

beag-nàrach, beg-nāruch, *a.* shameless, impudent, impertinent.

beag-nàrachd, *n. f.* shamelessness, impudence.

bealach, byăl''-uch, *n. m.* a gap, a pass, mountain gorge ; a breach in a wall or fence ; a gateway, a gate ; **tog am bealach,** build the breach or gap ; a road. *E.Ir.* belach, gap ; pass, road.

bealaidh, byăl'-y, *n. m.* broom. *See* mealaich ; **bad mealaich,** a tuft of broom.

bealamas, byal'-am-us, *n. m.* the refuses of a feast, the crumbs that fall from the table.

bealbhach, *n. m.* a bit ; fr. beul, mouth.

bealbhan - ruadh, *n. m.* a species of hawk.

bealltainn, byaul'-tinn, *n. f.* May Day. *E.Ir.* beltene, *O.Celt.* belo-te(p)niâ.

bean, ben, *v.* touch, handle. *O.Ir.* benaim.

bean, ben, *n. f.* (*gen.* mnà, *dat.* mnaoi, *pl.* mnathan) ; a woman, a female, wife ; **bean ghlùin,** a midwife ; **bean shiùbhlaidh,** a woman in child-bed ; **beantighe,** a housewife, a landlady ; **bean òsda,** the landlady of an inn ; **bean baile,** the lady or proprietress of a farm;

bean chinnidh, a kinswoman ; **bean chìche,** a wet nurse ; **bean choimhideachd,** a bridesmaid, a maid of honour ; **bean nigheadaireachd,** a washer-woman ; **bean uasal,** a lady, a gentlewoman ; **bean brathar athar,** a paternal uncle's wife ; **bean brathar màthar,** a maternal uncle's wife ; **bean brathar,** a brother's wife ; **bean bhochd,** a female mendicant, pauper or beggar ; **bean mic,** a daughter-in-law ; **bean shith,** a female fairy. *O.Ir.* ben, *O.Celt.* benâ.

beanas-tighe, benus-tehu, *n. f.* duties of housewife.

bean - chomhailteach, *n. f.* bridesmaid. *M.Ir.* bean-chomalta, foster sister.

beann, byann, *n. f., pl.* beannaibh, beanntan, *gen. pl.* beann, horn, peak ; **tìr nam beann,** land of the bens ; **ceithir beannaibh,** four peaks, or corners. *O.Ir.* benn, a horn. *W.* bann, a peak.

beann, *n. f.* attention, regard ; **na toir beann air ciod a their e,** pay no attention to what he says. *Ir.* benn, regard.

beannach, *a.* horned, pointed, peaked.

beannachadh, byann-uch-u, *vbl. n. m.* a blessing, benediction, grace ; **iarr beannachadh,** say grace.

beannachd, byann'-ăchc, *n. m.* a benediction, a blessing ; **beannachd Dhé leat,** may the blessing of God attend you ; **tha mo bheannachd-sa agad,** you have my benediction ; compliments, respects ; **thoir mo bheannachd,** bring my compliments ; farewell ; **beannachd leat,** farewell, adieu ; **fàg beannachd aige,** bid him adieu ; **beannachd a sheud is a shiubhail leis,** may he fare as he deserves. *O.Ir.* bendacht, *Lat.* benedictio.

beannachdail, byănn'-ăchc - ăl, *a.* valedictory. *Also* beannachdach.

beannachdan, byann'-àchc-an, *n. m.* a beetle, an insect that strikes one's finger when holding it. *Also* òrdalan.

beannag, byanag, *n. f.* corner, skirt, pointed coif (worn under mutch, as a sign of marriage).

beannaich, byann'-ich, *v.* bless, salute, hail, invoke a blessing. *O.Ir.* bendachaim, *Lat.* benedico.

beannaichte, byann'-ich-tyà, *vbl. a.* happy, holy, blessed ; **is beannaichte an duine sin,** blessed is that man.

beanntach, byannt'-ach, *a.* mountainous, hilly ; pinnacled, rocky.

beanntachd, byannt'-achc, *n. f.* a mountainousness, hilliness, steepness.

beanntainn, *n. m.* an herb, mint.

beanntaire, byannt'-ir'-u, *n. f.* mountaineer.

beantag, byant'-ag, *n. f.* a corn-fan. *Also* **bannag.**

beantainn, bent'-hin', *vbl. n. m.* act of touching.

bearach, beer'-uch, *n. f.* dog-fish. *Also* **gobag** and **biorach.** *O.Ir.* **berach,** pointed, snouted, the " snouted one "; verutus (veru).

bearachd, *n. f.* judgment.

bearbhain, bervin, *n. f.* vervain. *Lat.* verbena.

beàrn, bjãrn, *n. f.* a small gap or breach, a fissure ; *v.* notch, hack. *E.Ir.* **berna.**

beàrnach, bjãrn'-ăch, *a.* notched, hacked, full of gaps ; having broken teeth ; *n. f.* a female with broken teeth.

beàrnan-brìde, byarnan-breedu, *n. m.* the dandelion.

bearr, byarr, *v.* shave, crop ; taunt, gibe, jeer. *O.Ir.* **berraim,** shear, clip, *W.* **byrr,** short, *O.Celt.* **berso-s,** short.

bearradair, byarr'-u-der, *n. m.* a barber ; giber, a taunting fellow.

bearradaireachd, byărr-u-der'-uchc, *n. m.* the occupation of a barber ; gibing, jeering, taunting, criticising.

bearradh, byărr'-u, *n. m.* the brow of a hill ; edge of a precipice.

bearradh, *vbl. n. m.* act of cutting, clipping, shaving.

bearraideach, byărr'-ej-uch, *a.* flighty, light-headed, giddy ; nimble ; sharp-tongued.

bearraideachd, byarr'-ej-uchc, *n. f.* flightiness, giddiness ; light-headedness.

bearras, biãrus, *n. m.* sharpness (of tongue), satire.

beart, byart, *n. m.* deed, act. *M.Ir.* **bert,** a deed, a task.

beart, *n. m.* engine, instrument ; a loom ; a plough ; harness ; fishing - tackle ; sword sheath ; ship's rigging ; gear ; **cais-bheart,** foot-gear ; **ceann-bheart,** head-dress. *E.Ir.* **bert** (*f.*), clothes.

beartach, biãrstuch, *a.* well-rigged ; rich ; wealthy.

beartadh, *vbl. n. m.* act of adjusting, trimming.

beartaich, *v.* equip, repair, harness. *M.Ir.* **bertaigim,** I poise, adjust.

beartas, *n. m.* wealth, riches, abundance.

beart-chunnairt, *n. m.* matter of doubt.

beatha, béh'-à, *n. f.* life, food, livelihood ; welcome, salutation ; biography ; **is amhuil ar beatha is aisling,** our life is like a dream ; **gheibh e bheatha,** he will get his livelihood ; **bhur beathasa, a ghaisgich,** you are welcome, O heroes ! **dèan a bheatha,** welcome him ; **làn tì do bheatha,** you're quite welcome to it ; **bhur beatha an dùthaich,** you are welcome to the country, you are welcome home ; **bheir duine beatha air**

éigin ach cha toir e rath air éigin, a man may force a livelihood, but cannot force prosperity. *O.Ir.* **bethu,** life.

beathach, be-huch, *n. m.* an animal, a beast, a brute ; term of contempt for a person. *M.Ir.* **bethadach.**

beathachadh, be-huchu, *vbl. n. m.* livelihood, sustenance, maintenance ; a benefice ; **fhuair am ministir òg beathachadh,** the young clergyman got a benefice ; act of supporting, maintaining, feeding.

beathaich, be-hich, *v.* feed, support, cherish ; **bheathaich e chuid eile,** he fed the rest. *E.Ir.* **bethaigim.** 1. I animate. 2. I nourish.

beathaichte, be-hichtu, *vbl. a.* fed, nourished, supported, maintained.

beathail, be'-hal, *a.* vital, living, pertaining to life.

beathalachd, be'-hal-achc, *n. f.* vitality.

beathannan, be'-hann-un, *pl.* victuals.

beic, *n. m.* curtsy, obeisance ; *v.* curtsy ; **dean do bheic,** make a curtsy. *Sc.* beck.

beiceadaich, beikudich, *vbl. n. f.* act of curtsying.

beiceasach, beckesach, *a.* fond of hopping, bobbing ; frisky.

beiceil, beckel, *n. f.* act of curtsying, hopping, frisking, prancing.

beiceis, beckesh, *n. f.* hopping, bobbing, skipping, frisking ; **beic leumnach,** prancing.

béignoid, bēgnej, *n. f.* bayonet. *Also* **beuglaid.**

beil, *v.* grind. *See* **meil.**

beil. *See* **is.**

beilbheag, bel'-uv-ăg, *n. f.* a corn poppy.

béile, bēlu, *n. m.* bit of bridle. *E.Ir.* **bellic,** bridle-bit.

béileach, *n. m.* a muzzle. *Also* **méileag.** *Ir.* **beulmhach,** bridle-bit, *E.Ir.* **bélbach,** mouth.

béileach, *a.* thick-lipped.

béileag, bēlag, *n. f.* a muzzle.

béilean, bēlen, *n. m.* a prating mouth, a little mouth.

béileanach, *a.* prating ; *n. f.* a prating, garrulous female ; loquacious, talkative. *M.Ir.* **bélghach,** prattling.

béileanachd, *n. f.* half-impertinent prattle or prating.

béilich, bēlich, *v.* muzzle, stop impertinent talk.

béill, *n. f.* a thick hanging lip.

beilleach, beiluch, *a.* blubber-lipped, having thick lips. *Also* **borrach.** *M.Ir.* **bélach,** big-lipped.

beilleag, *n. f.* outer coating of birch, rind.

béim-cheap, bēm-chiäp, *n. f.* a whipping stock.

being, bēnc, *n. f.* a bench plank of a bed,

sitting-bench. *N.* bekkr, long sitting-bench.

beingidh, bēngy, *n. f.* the front plank of a bed ; a bank.

beinn, bēyn, *n. f.* (*pl.* beanntan, beannaibh ; *gen. pl.* beann), a mountain, a hill, a pinnacle. *E.Ir.* benn, peak.

beinneal, beynal, *n. m.* binding of a sheaf of corn, bundle. *Also* bann, band.

beir, ber, *v. i. irreg.* bear ; lay hold of, capture, overtake, get out of sight with ; agus beiridh tu mac, and thou shalt bear a son ; agus rug e air an sliabh Ghilead, and he overtook him in the mount of Gilead ; beir uam e ! away with him ! beir air an uan, catch. or lay hold of the lamb ; rug sinn orra mu leth na slighe, we overtook them about half way. *See irreg. vb. O.Ir.* berim, *W.* adfer, *O.Celt.* berô, *Lat.* fero.

beirm, berum, *n. f.* barm, yeast. *M.E.* berme ; *Lat.* fermentum.

beirte, bertu, *vbl. a.,* born, brought forth.

béist, bēsht, *n. f.* a beast, a brute, a beastly person ; béist dubh, béist donn, an otter ; beist mhaol, a sea-calf. *O.Ir.* béist, *Lat.* bestia. *Also* biast.

béistealachd, bēshtaluchc, *n. f.* beastliness, brutality, brutishness.

béisteag, bēshtag, *n. f.* a worm, an earth worm. *Also* biastag.

béisteil, bēshtal, *n.* beastly, brutish.

beith, be, *n. f.* birch. *O.Ir.* bethe, *O Celt.* betva.

beithir, be-hir, *n. f.* 1. a prodigiously large serpent. 2. thunderbolt. 3. a very large skate. 4. a bear.

beitir, beytir, *a.* tidy, neat, clean.

beò, biō, *a.* lively, active ; tha e gu math beò, he is pretty lively or brisk ; living, alive ; ma bhitheas mi beò, if I live : *n. m.* lifetime, the living ; ri do bheò, during your lifetime ; chan fhaic thu ri do bheò e, you shall never see him ; gum bu fada beò an rìgh, long live the king ! ; an tìr nam beò, in the land of the living ; thoir beò, bring alive ; beò-leatromach, quick with child ; beò-dhùil, a living creature ; beò-iobairt, a living sacrifice ; beò-ghlac, take alive.

beò, *n. f.* life, a living ; cha toir e bheò as, 1. he will not make his living out of it ; 2. he will not survive it. *E.Ir.* beó, *gen.* bí.

beòdha, *a.* active, sprightly ; fuileachd-ach, beòdha, bloody and lively.

beòir, byōer, *n. f.* beer ; beòir làidir, strong beer ; beòir chaol, small beer. So *M.Ir. A.S.* beór, *N.* bjórr.

beòlach, byō'-llăch, *n. f.* ashes with living embers, hot ashes. beò + luathach, live ashes.

beòlach, *n. m.* lively youth; beòlaoch, hero.

beòladas, beuladas, *n. m.* tradition.

beòshlainte, beō-hlantu, *n. f.* lifetime ; tha a beòshlainte aice dheth, she has a life-rent of it ; livelihood.

beòtachd, *n. f.* sustenance, means of living.

beothach, beo-huch, *n. m.* a beast, a brute. *Dial. form* of beathach.

beothachadh, *vbl. n. m.* reanimation, refreshment ; act of reanimating ; act of kindling as a fire ; enlivening ; quickening.

beothachail, *a.* having a reanimating or quickening influence.

beothachan, beohachan, *n. m.* a little fire. *Also* written beòchan.

beothaich, beo-ich, *v.* kindle ; reanimate, revive, quicken.

beothail, byō'-al, *a.* lively, active, brisk.

beothalachd, byō'-all-achc, *n. f.* liveliness, smartness, briskness ; agility, activity. *Ir.* beó-ghalachd = beò (living) + gail (valour).

beuban, bēban, *n. m.* anything mangled.

beubanaich, *v.* mangle ; slander.

beuc, bēk, *v.* yell, bellow ; *n. m.* a yell, an outcry, a bellow. *O.Ir.* béccim, *O.Celt.* baikkiô, beikkiô.

beucail, bēcal, *vbl. n. m.* act of yelling, bellowing ; roaring.

beud, bēd, *n. m.* harm, hurt, mischief, calamity ; chan 'eil beud air, there is no *hurt* on him ; there's nothing the matter with him ; is mór am beud e, it is a great calamity, a great pity ; cha bhi beud dhuit, you will be quite well. *E.Ir.* bét, a deed ; harm, calamity, crime.

beudach, bēduch, *a.* hurtful, blemished. guilty ; fatal ; am fear a bhios beudach, cha sguir e dh' éigneachadh chàich, he that is guilty himself, tries to involve others.

beudachd, bēdachc, *n. f.* harm, hurt.

beul, biäl, *n. m.* ; (*gen. s.* bheòil, *n. pl.* beòil), a mouth ; air bheul a bhi deas, nearly prepared, or ready ; beul an latha, dawn of day ; beul na h-oidhche, dusk of the evening ; an taobh bheòil, the fore-part, or front ; beul ri trì mìosan, about three months ; beul tana, thin-lipped ; " beul sios ort ! " form of imprecation = may you be dead ! *O.Ir.* bél, a lip.

beulach, biä'-lach, *a.* fawning, fairspoken, plausible, prating.

beulachas, bial'-ăch-us, *n. f.* fawning, flattering, artful speaking.

beulag, biälag, *n. f.* a gap, a little opening, a fissure, a fore tooth.

beulag, *n. f.* a person mounted in front of a rider ; one riding behind is cùlag.

beulaibh, bialiv, *n. m.* front, foreside,

presence ; **air a beulaibh**, in front of her ; wrongly spelt **beulaobh**, as if for **beul + thaobh**. *O.Ir.* **bélib**, *d. pl.* of **bél**, mouth, front.

beul-aithris, bial-erish, *n. f.* tradition ; **beul-aithris nan seanar**, the tradition of the elders.

beulan, *n. m.* small mouth ; **a beulan binn**, her musical little mouth.

beulanach, *n. m.* approaching waves ; the first of a series of towering waves.

beulanaich, *v.* allure with words.

beul-àtha, *n. m.* a ford.

beul-chràbhadh, *n. m.* lip-devotion, cant.

beul-ghràdh, *n. m.* lip-love, flattery, dissimulation.

beul-maothain, *n. m.* the slot of the breast.

beul-mòr, *n. m.* gunwale.

beulradh, *n. m.* speech, phrase. *See* **beurla**.

beul-snaip, *n. m.* flint-socket of a gun, the dog-head.

beulstoc, bial-stoc, *n. m.* a gunwale. *See* **stoc**.

beum, bēm, *n. m.* a stroke, a cut, a gash, a sarcasm or taunt ; **cha ruig thu leas beum a thoirt**, you need not taunt ; *v.* strike ; taunt ; ring. *O.Ir.* **béimm** (fr. **benim**), a blow, reproach.

beum, *n. m., pl.* **beumannan**, a sheaf of barley (a sheaf of oats is **bad**).

beumach, bēm′-ăch, *a.* given to blows, sarcastic, bitter, destructive ; **mar theine beumach**, like a destructive fire ; **aineolach beumach**, ignorant and sarcastic.

beumnach, bēm′-nach, *a.* sarcastic, reproachful ; **bilean beumnach**, reproachful lips ; destructive ; **buillean cothromach beumnach**, well-aimed destructive blows. *O.Ir.* **béimnech**.

beum-sgéithe, bēm-sgēha, *n. m.* a striking the shield, the usual mode of giving challenge, or of sounding an alarm among the old Gaels ; **le beum sgéithe ghlaodh iad còmhrag**, with a blow on the shield they called to battle ; a severe sarcasm, a sly insinuation.

beum-sléibhe, bēm-shlēvu, *n. m.* a mountain torrent.

beum-soluis, bēm-soluish, *n. m.* a beam of light.

beum-sùl, bēm′-sool, *n. m.* a blasting of the eye, an optical delusion.

beur, bēr, *n. m.* a point, a pinnacle ; **beur àrd**, a lofty pinnacle.

beur, *a.* sharp, pointed, clear, incisive.

beuradh-theine, bēra-hena, *n. f.* a meteor, a falling star.

beurla, bērla, *n. f.* speech, language ; the English tongue ; **gnàth-bheurla na h-Eirionn**, the vernacular dialect of the

Irish ; **beurla Albannach**, the Anglo-Scottish ; **a' bheurla leathan**, **a' bheurla mhór**, the broad Scotch ; **a' bheurla Shasunnach**, pure English. *O.Ir.* **bélre**, language (now usually = English language).

beurlach, *a.* well versed in the English language, belonging to the English language.

beurra, bērr′-à, *a.* eloquent and witty, well-spoken ; genteel.

beurrach, bērr′-ach, *a.* witty, eloquent ; *n. f.* prating female.

beurrachd, bērr′-ăchc; *n. f.* eloquence, wit, waggery.

beurradair, bērr′-u′der′, *n. m.* a wit, a wag ; a satirist.

beurran, bērr′-an, *n. m.* a witty, prating, garrulous little fellow.

beurtha. *See* **beurra**.

beus, bēs, *n. m.* habit, custom, manner ; conduct, behaviour ; conduct, doings ; **aithneachar leanabh air a bheus**, a child is known by his manners ; **deagh bheus**, good behaviour ; practice, use and wont ; **beus is gnàth na dùthcha**, the use and wont of the country ; **beus an àite anns am bitear 's e nitear**, the custom of the place you dwell in must be conformed to ; moral character. *O.Ir.* **bés**.

beus, *n. m.* bass (in music) ; " **mo chearc féin 'g am bheus air stocan**," my own hen singing my bass on a twig ; fr. *Eng.*, after *Ital.* **basso**.

beusach, *a.* virtuous, of good manners.

beusachd, bēs′-achc, *n. f.* manners, moral rectitude, modesty ; morals : inoffensive conduct.

beusadh, *vbl. n. m.* tuning pipes for playing ; fr. **beus**, manner.

beusadh, *vbl. n. m.* act of singing bass.

beusaichead, bēs′-ich-ud, *n. m.* degree of moral purity or modesty.

beusail, bēs′-al, *a.* *See* **beusach**.

beusalachd, *n. f.* good conduct.

beusan, *n. m.* manners, morals ; **deagh bheusan**, good morals.

beutal, bēt′-al, *a.* a cow ; kine.

b'fhearr, byàrr (for **bu fheàrr**), it were better, it is preferable ; **b'fhearr leam**, I would prefer.

bha, vā, *pret. ind.* of **bi**, was, were, wert ; **an duine a bha**, the man who was. *See* **is**.

bhàn, vàn, *adv.* down ; **thig a bhàn**, come down ; for **bhfan**. *O.Ir.* **fán**, a slope.

bharr, varr, *prep.* off, from off ; **bhàrr na talmhainn**, from off the earth.

bheil, *v.* is, for eclip. **fuil** = **bhfuil**. *O.Ir.* **fail**, **fil**, **feil**.

bheir, *ver. fut.* of **thoir**, to give, grant, bestow ; " **an làmh a bheir is i a**

gheibh," 'tis the hand that gives that gets.

bho, vō, *prep.* from. *Also* o. *O.Ir.* ó, úa, joined with *pers. pron.* both o and ua in use, commonly with bh : bhom, bhuam, from me ; bhot, bhuat, from thee ; bhoidhe, bhuaidhe, from him ; bhoithe, bhuaithe, from her, etc.

bhobh, vov, *int.* O dear ! strange ; O bhobh, O dear ! strange.

bhos, vos, *prep.* this side, on this side ; better a bhos ; thall 's a bhos, here and there, hither and thither. *O.Ir.* foss, rest ; i foss, here. bhos = bh-fos.

bhur, vur, *poss. pron.* your. *O.Ir.* far.

bi, the *verb* to be, be thou or you ; *pres.* tha ; tha gu dearbh, yes, indeed ; *past.* bha ; bha lach air an loch, a duck was on the lake ; *fut.* bidh ; bithidh (emph.), shall be ; bithidh iad an sin, they shall be there ; *cond.* bhithinn, I would be ; bhiodh e, bhitheadh e (emph.), he would be ; bithibh, be ye or you. (*See* Gram.) ; bidh cron duine cho mór ri beinn mun léir dha féin e, a man's fault will be as huge as a mountain before he himself can perceive it ; bidh na gobhair bodhar 'san fhogharadh, the goats are deaf in harvest ; am bi thu an so aig an uair ? Bithidh, will you be here at the hour ? Yes, without fail. *O.Ir.* bíu, sum, *Lat.* fio, *O.Celt.* bivo-s.

b'i, *v.* for bu i, it was she ; am b'i bha siod, was it she that was yonder ?

bì, *n. f.* tar, pitch. *O.Ir.* bí, *pix*, *O.Celt.* bei-, resinous wood.

b' iad, for bu iad, it was they.

biadh, bee-u', *v.* feed, nourish, maintain ; biadh orra e, dole it out to them, as short provision.

biadh, bee-u', *n. m., gen.* bidh, food, provision, meat ; biadh is aodach, food and clothing. *O.Ir.* bíad, *O.Celt.* bivoto-n.

biadhaid, bee-u'-ăj, *n. f.* a pantry.

biadhaidh, *n. f.* lugworm for fishing.

biadhchar, biachur, *a.* productive ; siol biadhchar, substantial, or productive corn, corn that produces a good deal of meal, rich in food.

biadhcharachd, biacharuchc, *n. f.* productive quality, substance.

biadhta, biata, *vbl. a.* fed, fattened.

biadhtach, *n. m.* 1. a provider, a victualler, farmer. 2. a kitchen. *E.Ir.* bíatach, a farmer who held his land free of rent. In return for this he had to entertain his chief, and his soldiers at certain seasons ; baile biataigh, a farm of twelve plough-lands and pasture for 300 cows. *CML.*[107.]

biadhtachd, biatachc, *n. f.* hospitality,

entertainment ; 's bochd a' bhiadhtachd so, this is a poor entertainment.

biadhtaich, beeut'-ich, *v. t.* feed, share.

biadhtaiche, beeut''-ich-a, *n. m.* an entertainer, a host, or hostess.

bian, beeun, *n. m.* a wild animal's skin : often applied in poetry to human skin.

bianadair, beeun'-ud'-er', *n. m.* a currier.

biasgach, beeusg'-uch, *n.* niggardly.

biast, beeust, *n. m.* a beast. *Also* béist, *v.* abuse, revile.

biastalachd, *n. f.* beastliness, meanness.

biatach, *n. m.* raven.

biatas, *n. m.* betony, beet.

biathadh, *vbl. n. m.* feeding, rationing, doling out food ; bait ; baiting a fishing-line, enticing. *E.Ir.* biathaim.

biathainne, biū-hinn, *n. m.* earth-worm ; hook-bait. *Also* biathaidh.

biatsadh, *n. m.* viaticum, provisions for a journey.

bibhidh, beevy, *n. m.* a very large fire.

biceas, *n. m.* viscount.

bicein, *n. m.* a single grain.

bicein-càil, *n. m.* a species of wren. *St. Kilda.*

biceir, beeker, *n. f.* a small wooden dish.

bicheanta, beechanta, *a.* common, frequent, general ; properly bitheanta.

bicheantachd, beechantachc, *n. f.* frequency, generality, commonness.

bid, bēj, *n. f.* a chirp ; a nip ; *v.* pinch, nip.

bideach, beej'-ach, *a.* little, small.

bìdeachd, beej'-achc, *n. f.* littleness, smallness.

bìdeag, beej'-ag, *n. f.* a bite, a small portion of anything.

bidean, beej'-an', *n. m.* a point, a tip, a pinnacle ; a hedge, a fence.

bìdearra, *n. m.* a biter ; a cow or heifer that eats the hair off another.

bideil, beej'-el, *n. f.* chirping. *Also* biogal.

bidhis, *n. f.* a vice, screw.

bididh, a name for the devil.

bidse, beej'-shu, *n. f.* a bad woman ; fr. the *Eng.*

big, big, *v.* chirp, be bickering.

big, *n. m.* a chirp ; *interj.* mode of calling to chickens, big ! big ! *n. pl.* of beag, little, small, the young ; na big, the little ones ; "an rud a chì na big is e nì na big," what the little ones see is just what the little ones do.

bìgeil, beegul, *n. f.* chirping.

bigeire, *n. m.* a chicken.

bìgh, bee, *n. m.* a post ; a pillar ; eadar dà bhìgh an doruis, between the posts of the door. *E.Ir.* bí, threshold.

bil, *n. m.* a lip ; a margin ; a rim, brim, edge ; bil nan sruthan uaigneach, the margin of the lonely brooks; **bil na h-aide**, the brim of the hat; **bil na lobhta**, the front of the gallery. *E.Ir.*

bil, *O.Celt.* bili-, bilio-.

bile, *n. m.* a great tree a champion. *E.Ir.* bile, large, or old tree.

bile, *n. m.* a blade, a fibre, filament, a hair; **bile feòir**, a blade of grass; **bile fuilt**, a hair; **bheil bile aodaich agad?** have you *any* clothes?

bileach, beel'-uch, *a.* bordered, edged, having a margin; **bileach choigeach**, marigold.

bileag, beel'-ag, *n. f.* a blade, a leaflet; **bileag fheòir**, a blade of grass; **bileag bhàite**, water-lily. *E.Ir.* billeóc, leaflet.

bileanach, same as bilearach.

bilearach, beel'-ăr-uch, *n. f.* sweet, or sea grass.

bileil, beel'-al, *a.* labial, belonging to the lips.

bilistear, beelisht-er', *n. m.* 1. a mean fellow; a glutton. 2. rancid butter or tallow.

bilisteireachd, *n. f.* mean hankering for food.

billeachd, beel-achc, *n. f.* poverty. *E.Ir.* bill, a leper, a wretch.

binealta, been-altu, *a.* fine, elegant.

binid, *n. f.* rennet, stomach.

binideach, *a.* like rennet.

binn, beeyn, *a.* melodious, harmonious, musical. *O.Ir.* bind.

binn, *n. f.* sentence, decision; verdict; **b' i sin a' bhinn a thug e mach**, that was the decision he gave.

binnbheul, *n. m.* sweet mouth or voice.

binndeach, beenj'-ăch, *a.* coagulation.

binndeachadh, beenj'-ăch-u, *vbl. n. m.* act of curdling; coagulating; making cheese.

binndeal, beenjal, *n. m.* a head dress.

binndich, beenjich, *v.* curdle, coagulate, make cheese.

binne, beenye, *n. f.* melody, music.

binneach, beenuch, *a.* pointed, pinnacled, high-topped, light-headed.

binnead, beenud, *n. f.* degree of melody.

binnean, binen, *n. m.* pinnacle, point; **binnean an teampuill**, the pinnacle of the temple.

binneas, *n. m.* music, melody. *O.Ir.* bindius, *euphonia sonoritas*.

binnteach, *a.* coagulative.

bìobull, beeb'-ull, *n. m.* the Bible. *Also* píobull. *Gr.* Βίβλος, inner rind of the papyrus anciently used for writings, a roll, volume, *Lat.* biblia.

bìobullach, beeb'-ull-uch, *a.* Biblical.

biod, beed, *v. n.* pique, gall, vex; *n. m.* pointed top; **air a chorra-biod**, on tip-toes.

biod, *v.* bicker; canker.

biodach, *a.* sharp-pointed.

biodach, *a.* very small; **creutar beag, biodach**, a tiny little creature.

biodag, bidag, *n. f.* a dirk, a dagger.

biodag, *n. f.* a baby girl; fr. **biodach**, small.

biodan, *n. m.* a baby boy.

biodan, bidan, *n. m.* bickering fellow.

biodanach, *a.* bickering, cankering; *n. f.* a bickering, eternally scolding, or complaining female.

biod-cheann, *n. m.* a pointed head.

biog, *n. m.* a chirp.

biog, big, *v.* gripe; *n. m.* start. *E.Ir.* bidcim, fright, I startle, leap.

biogach, *a.* small, contemptible.

biogadh, bigu, *vbl. n. m.* a griping; a starting, a sudden emotion, a whim.

biogail, beegul, *a.* lively, active, smart, chirping.

bioganta, bigantu, *a.* sprightly.

biogaran, *n. m.* small wooden dish.

biogarra, biguru, *a.* mean, churlish.

biogarrachd, biguruchc, *n. f.* meanness, churlishness, inhospitality.

biolagach, *a.* melodious.

biolair, byool'-ur', *n. f.* cresses, water-cresses. *E.Ir.* biror, water-cress (bir =water), *O.Celt.* beruro-.

biolaireach, *a.* rich in water-cresses.

biolar, *a.* dainty, spruce.

biolasgach, *a.* prattling (*rel.* to bil, lip).

bior, bir, *n. m.* a pointed small stick, a thorn, a prickle; *v.* prick; gall, vex. *E.Ir.* bir, a spit, a spear, *O.Celt.* beru-, *Lat.* veru.

biorach, beeruch, *a.* pointed; sharp; *n. f.* a heifer; a colt; an instrument to prevent calves from suckling; dog-fish. *See* bearach. *O.Ir.* berach.

bioradh, *n. m.* stinging, pricking.

bioraich, beerich, *v. n.* make sharp; look steadfastly, stare.

bioraichead, beerichud, *n. m.* pointedness, degree of sharpness or pointedness.

bioran, beeran, *n. m.* a little stick; *dim.* of bior.

bioranach, *a.* full of little sticks, prickled, full of prickles.

bioran deamhainn, beeran-devin, *n. m.* a pink, a minnow. *Also* **breac deamhainn**.

bioras, beeras, *n. f.* water-lily; connected with *O.Ir.* bir, water.

biorchluasach, beer-chloo-usuch, *a.* sharp-eared, keen-eared, intent.

biorg, beerg, *v.* tingle, thrill, twitch, feel a tingling sensation.

biorgadaich, beergejich, *n. f.* a thrilling or tingling sensation or feeling.

biorgadh, *v. n.* a sudden start; **is tu chuir am biorgadh annam**, what a start you gave me!

biorganta, beergantu, *a.* thrilling.
biorgantachd, *n. f.* degree of thrilling or tingling sensation ; entanglement.
biorguinn, beer-goon, *n. f.* rending pain.
biorraid, byúrr'-aj, *n. f.* a cap with a scoop on it, a head-piece, a helmet ; an osier twig. *L. Lat.* birretum.
biorraideach, beerejuch, *a.* scooped, conical.
bior-ròstaidh, beer-ròsty, *n. m.* a spit.
biorsadh, bir-su', *n. m.* eager desire ; goading.
biorsamaid, byúr'-sa-măj, *n. f.* a Roman balance for weighing small quantities ; a steel-yard. *Sc.* bismar, bysmer, *O.N.* bismari.
biorshuileach, beer-hooluch, *a.* sharp-sighted.
bior-snaois, beer-snūis, *n. m.* top of stem of a boat (*Lewis*), bowsprit (*Lochaber*).
biortaich, beerstich, *v. a.* poke, stir up ; goad; biortaichan teine,poke up thefire.
biota, beetu, *n. m.* a churn, a wooden pail ; biota bhùrn, water-pail. *O.N.* bytta.
biotailt, beetelt, *n. f.* victuals. *E.Ir.* bitáill, *Lat.* victualia.
biotais. *See* biatas.
biothuntach, bee-huntuch, *a.* glutinous, viscous, tenacious, ropy.
bir, *n. m.* the alarm note of the solan geese when attacked. *Martin.*
birlinn, beerlin, *n. f.* a barge or pleasure boat, a galley ; equated with *O.N.* byrðingr, but Marstrander thinks the equation erroneous.
bith, bee, *n. f.* existence, being, world, spirit, temper. *O.Ir.* bith, *mundus.*
bith, bee, *n.m.* gum, tar. *O.Ir.* bíde. *See* bì.
bith, *a.* quiet ; bi cho bith ri uan, be as quiet as a lamb.
bith-, ever ; constant. *O.Ir.* bith, bid ; bith-beó, *semper vivus* ; bith-bethu, the eternal life.
bith-bhuan, bee-vooun', *a.* eternal, everlasting.
bithbhuantachd, beevuntachc, *n. f.* eternity, perpetuity.
bitheanta, bee-hantu, *a.* frequent, general, common.
bitheantachd, *n. m.* frequency.
bith-fhuaim, bee-ooum, unceasing noise.
bithis, bee-ish, *n. f.* vice, screw.
biùg, bioog, *n. m.* slight sound ; chan 'eil biùg aice, she lost her voice, she has not a note.
biùthaidh, *n. m.* hero. *E.Ir.* bidbu, bidba, culprit, enemy.
biùthas,. byu-as, *n. m.* fame.
biùthasach, *a.* famous.
blabaran, *n. m.* stammerer. Cf. *M.E.* blabbe.
blabhdair, blaud-ir', *n. m.* a babbler ; howling, babbling, clumsy simpleton.

blad, *n. m.* an enormous mouth.
bladach, *a.* wide-mouthed ; *n. f.* a female with a large mouth.
bladaidh, blady, *n. m.* Same as bladaire.
bladaire, blăd'-ur-à, *n. m.* a wide mouth, a babbler ; flatterer. *M.Ir.* bladar, dissembling, flattery.
bladairt, blăd''-ărt, *n. f.* babbling.
bladh, blu-gh', *n. f.* renown, fame ; substance, meaning, pith, energy. *E.Ir.* blad.
bladhail, *a.* pithy, substantial, strong.
bladhar, blughur, *a.* substantial, full of meaning, substance, or importance. *E.Ir.* bladmar, renowned, famous.
bladhm, blūm, *n. m.* a boast. *See* blaomadh. *E.Ir.* bladmann, boasting, bragging.
blad-shronach, blad-hrōnach, *a.* flatnosed.
blad-spagach, *a.* flat-footed.
blàidhealtrach, blā-yealtruch, warm and dewy. blàth + dealt.
blaigh, blai, *n. f.* a part, a portion, a fragment, a small share ; properly bloigh, *q.v.*
blaighdeach, blaijach, *n. f.* part, a portion, an instalment ; *a.* in pieces, in portions. *See* bloighdeach.
blaighdeachadh, blaijuchu', *vbl. n. m.* act of cutting asunder, or into fragments or small portions.
blaighdeachas, blaijachus, *n. f.* the act or state of being cut into small portions.
blaighdich, blaijich, *v.* cut asunder or into small portions ; bloighdich.
blàilin, *n. m.* a sheet.
blais, blash, *v.* taste, try ; 'nuair a bhlais e air an fhìon, when he tasted the wine.
blaisbheum, blash-vem, *n. f.* blasphemy.
blaiseamachd, blăsh'-am-ăchc, *n. f.* smacking with the lips.
blaiseamaich, *v.* smack with the lips ; taste, try.
blàithe, blāye, *deg.* of blàth, warm, affectionate, kind ; na 's blaithe, more warm, more affectionate.
blàitheachadh, blāhacha', *vbl. n. m.* act of warming ; feeling affection for.
blàithich, blāhich, *v.* warm, heat.
blanndaidh, blaundi, *a.* stale (as milk), rotten, addled. *O.N.* blanda, mix, blend.
blanndar, blaund'-ur, *n. f.* dissimulation, flattery. *Lat.* blandior.
blaodh, *n. f.* shout, noise. *E.Ir.* bláed.
blaodhag, blu'ag, *n. f.* a noisy girl.
blaodhan, *n. m.* a fawn's cry.
blaom, blūm, *v. n.* stare with the greatest surprise, as when taken unawares, start.
blaomadh, blūmu, *vbl. n. m.* a wondering stare ; act of staring, starting ; foolish excitement ; loud talking.

blaomag, blūmag, *n. f.* a silly woman.
blaomaire, blūmiru, *n. m.* a fellow that stares like a fool; a fellow easily frightened; nonsensical talk.
blaomaireachd, blūmiruchc, *n. f.* a habit of staring foolishly; starting.
blaomannach, blūmunuch, *a.* inconstant, variable, talking inconsistently.
blaomastair, blumuster, *n. m.* a blusterer; witless fellow.
blaosg. *See* plaosg.
blàr, *n. m.* moor, clear level space, a plain; battlefield; a battle; **a' cheud bhlàr a chuir iad**, the first battle they fought; **fraoch nam blàr**, the rage of battle; **a muigh air a' bhlàr**, out on the field; **sgeadaichear na blàir**, the plains shall be covered or clothed; **thoir am blàr ort**, away! go about your business; **blàr mòna**, a peat-moss.
blàr, *a.* white-faced, having a white spot in the face; **an t-each blàr**, the white-faced horse. *M.W.* blawr, grey.
blàrag, *n. f.* a white-faced cow.
blàran, *n. m.* a little moss or field.
blas, *n. m.* taste, savour, relish; a particle, the least part; **cia milis leam blas do bhriathran**, how sweet are thy words unto my taste! **chan 'eil blas deth an so**, there is not a particle of it here. *O.Ir.* mlass, savour; zest.
blasachd, *n. f.* a tasting.
blasad, *n. m.* taste, a tasting; **gun am blasad**, without tasting them.
blasadh, blās'-u, *vbl. n. m.* act of tasting; the act of tasting.
blasardaich, *n. f.* smacking the lips, tasting with relish. *E.Ir.* blassachtach, smacking the lips.
blasda, *a.* delicious, sweet, savoury, tasteful; agreeable: eloquent; **agus dèan domh biadh blasda**, and make unto me savoury meat; **briathran blasda**, agreeable or eloquent words. *E.Ir.* blasta, tasty.
blasdachd, blasdachc, *n. f.* deliciousness, sweetness, savouriness, agreeableness.
blasdagraich, blast-agrich, *n. f.* smacking, relishing. *Also* blasagraich.
blasmhor, blăss'-vur, *a. See* blasda.
blasphòg, blass'-ffŏg, *n. f.* a sweet kiss.
blàth, blā, *n. m.* bloom, blossom; flowers; **ged nach toir an crann-fige uaith blàth**, although the fig-tree shall not blossom; **fo làn bhlàth**, in full bloom; **thig e mach mar bhlàth**, he shall come forth as a flower; consequence; effects; **bidh a bhlàth ort**, the consequence will be seen in your case; **tha bhlàth 's a bhuil**, its bloom and its "fruit" is to be seen = the result is obvious. *E.Ir.* bláth (*m.*) a blossom. *M.W.* blawt.
blàth, *a.* warm, affectionate, tender; is

blàth anail na màthar, affectionate is the breath of a mother; **tha e glé bhlàth**, it is very warm (of weather).
blàthach, blāhach, *n. f.* buttermilk. So *E.Ir.*
blàthaich, blāhich, *v.* warm, heat.
blàthan, blā-han, *n. m.* a small flower.
blàthas, blā'-hus, *n. m.* warmth, kindliness, affectionate disposition.
blàth-chainnteach and blàth-bhriathrach,* *a.* kind in speaking.
blàth-fhleasg, *n. f.* a garland of flowers. blàth + fleasg.
blàthmhaiseach, blā-veshach, *a.* in the bloom of youth.
blàthobair, blā-hobir, *n. f.* embroidery; *v. t.* blàthoibrich, embroider.
bleachdair, blechc'-ur', *n. m.* a flattering fellow; fr. bliochd, milk = cowmilker.
bleadraig, *v.* to blether with nonsense, to bore; fr. the *Eng. O.N.* blaðra.
bleagain, *n. m.* peeled or shelled grain.
bleagh, *v.* milk. *Ir.* blighim, I milk.
bleaghan, *n. m.* a dibble (for digging shell-fish), a worthless tool.
bleathghluineach, ble-ghloon-uch, *a.* in-kneed, knock-kneed.
bleid, blej, *n. f. a.* importunity, sly kind of impertinent begging.
bleideag, *n. f.* large snow-flake; cf. *O.N.* blað. *A.S.* blad. *Ger.* blatt, a leaf.
bleideil, blejal, *a.* intrusive, begging in a sly way, troublesome.
bleidir, blejir, *v.* beg in a genteel way, tease, importune, trouble.
bleidire, blejiru, *n. m.* genteel beggar, a mean obtrusive fellow, a coward. *O.N.* bleyði, cowardice.
bleidireachd, *n. f.* importunity; genteel begging.
bleith, ble, *v.* grind; *n. f.* grinding; **gabh na clacha muilinn agus bleith min**, take the millstones and grind meal; **fuaim na bleith**, the sound of grinding. *E.Ir.* bleith. *O.Ir.* melim, *inf.* mlith. *Lat.* molo, I grind.
bleithte, blehte, *vbl. a.* ground.
bleodhan, bloyan, *n. m.* a wheel-barrow.
bleoghainn, bloïn, *v.* milk, squeeze out of. *See* bligh.
bleoghan, bloün, *vbl. n. m.* milking, the act of milking cattle. *E.Ir.* blegon, inf. of bligim (for mligim).
bliadhna, bliana, *n. f., pl.* bliadhnachan, a year; **is buaine bliadhna na nollaig**, a year is more lasting than Christmas. With numerals from eleven to nineteen often bleidhinn; **cóig bleidhinn deug**, fifteen years. *O.Ir.* blíadain. *O.Celt.* bleidni-.

* For pronunciation of compounds see separate members elsewhere.

bliadhnach, *n. m., pl.* bliadhnaich, a year old, a yearling.
bliadhnachd, blianachc, *n. f.* an annuity.
bliadhnail, blianal, *a.* yearly.
blialum, *n. m.* confused talk.
blian, blee-an, *n. m.* the groin, the belly ; air a bhlian, prone. *Also* fish's basking (the a is open). *O.Ir.* blén, mlén.
blian, *a.* (the a is dull), meagre, lean ; searmon blian, a lean sermon.
blianach, *n. f.* very lean, under-fed mutton, a pithless man. *E.Ir.* blin.
bligh, blee, *v.* milk ; is ann as a ceann a bhlighear a' bhó, the cow is milked from her head, *i.e.* flow of milk depends on feeding. *O.Ir.* mligim. *W.* blith.
bliochan, bleuch'-an, *n. f.* marigold.
bliochd, bleuchc, *n. m.* milk. strippings =athtoirt. *E.Ir.* blicht. *O.Ir.* mlicht.
bliochdas, *n. m.* tendency to milk.
bliochdmhorachd, *n. f.* milkiness.
blìon. *See* blian.
blìonach. *See* blianach.
blìonadh, *vbl. n. m.* act of basking.
bliosan, blisan, *n. m.* artichoke.
blob, *n. m.* blubber lip.
blobach, *a.* blubber-lipped.
blobaran, *n. m.* stammerer.
blocan, *n. m.* a little block, a mallet.
bloigh, bloi, *n. f.* a part, a fragment. *E.Ir.* blog. *O.Celt.* blogâ.
bloighdich, bloidich, *v.* cut into pieces.
bloinig, *n. f.* lard ; suet.
bloinigeach, blŏn'-ig-ach, *a.* plump, fat, soft.
bloinigean, blŏn''-ig-an, *n. m.* a fat child.
bloinigean-gàraidh, *n. m.* spinage.
blomas, *n. m.* ostentation.
blonag, *n.f.* lard, fat. *M.Ir.* blonac, blonoc.
blosg, *v.* sound, sound a horn. *M.Ir.* blosc, noise, report. *O.Celt.* blusko-s.
blotrach, *n. m.* a marsh, a bog.
blubach, *a.* stammering.
bo, *interj.* exclamation to frighten children ; *a.* strange.
bó, *n. f.* a cow ; *gen. sing.* bà ; *dat. sing.,* also *dual,* boinn ; *pl.* ba ; bó shamhna, a cow claimed, lifted, at Hallowe'en. *O.Ir.* bó. *O.Celt.* bóv-s, bovi-. *L.* bōs.
bobaidh, *n. m.* a father.
boban, *n. m.* term of affection for a boy, and also for a father ; a god-father ; also a term of contempt. *E.Ir.* bobba, master. popa, from *Lat.* papa.
bobhstair, bouster, *n. m.* a bolster.
bobug, *n. m.* a fellow, a boy ; once a term of affection, now often used ironically.
boc, *n. m., gen. s.* and *n. pl.* buic, a he-goat, a roe-buck ; *v.* leap, skip, as a buck. *O.Ir.* bocc. Cf. *O.N.* bukkr. *A.S.* bucca.
bòc, *v.* swell, inflame. *See* tòc.

bòcadh, *vbl. n. m.* act of swelling ; a blister.
bocaidh-fhàileag, *n. f.* hip, fruit of the dog-rose or briar. *Also* muca-fàileag.
bòcam ort ! *interj.* threat to children.
bòcan, *n. m.* hobgoblin, a bogle ; *pl.* bòcain. *E.Ir.* boccánach.
bòcan, *n. m.* a pimple, pustule ; *pl.* bòcain.
bocan, *n. m.* a little buck ; *pl.* bocain.
boc-earba, *n. m.* a roe-buck.
boc-gaibhre, *n. m.* a he-goat.
boch, *n. m.* ecstasy, great happiness, joy, rejoicing.
bochail, *a.* happy, overjoyed.
bochalachd, bŏch'-ăl-uchc, *n. f.* extreme happiness or joy ; *a.* liveliness.
bochd, bŏchc, *a.* poor, needy, necessitous ; ni làmh na leisg bochd, the hand of laziness maketh poor ; is fearr a bhi bochd na bhi breugach, it is better to be poor than a liar ; sad, melancholy ; is bochd an gnothuch e, it is a sad affair ; is bochd nach d' fhuair sinn e, it is a pity we did not get it ; dear, an duine bochd, the dear creature ; tha e gu bochd, he is not well, he is sick ; lean, lank ; crodh bochd, lean cattle ; *n. m.* a pauper, the parish poor ; a' roinn airgiod nam bochd, distributing the poor's funds ; am bochd 's an nochd, the poor and naked. *E.Ir.* bocht.
bòchd, *v.* swell, puff, get turgid. *See* bòc.
bochdainn, bŏchc'-inn, *n. f.* extreme poverty, poverty, distress, affliction, trouble, mischief, mishap ; 's ann air a tha blàth na bochdainn, he has every sign of extreme poverty about him ; ciod e a' bhochdainn a rug ort, what mischief came over you ! *E.Ir.* bochtaine.
bòchdan, bŏchc'-an, *n. m.* a· hobgoblin, scare-crow, an apparition. *Also* bòcan.
boc-ròin, *n. m.* a prawn, a shrimp.
boc-ruadh, *n. m.* the roebuck.
bocsa, *n. m.* a box (from the *Eng.*).
bòc-thonn, *n. f.* a large billow, swelling-wave.
bod, *n. m.* the pęnis. *E.Ir.* bot.
bòd, *n. m.* an offer, a bid at sale, a pledge, wager. *Sc.* bode, bod. Cf. *O.N.* bjóða, offer.
bodach, *n. m.* an old man, a churl or niggardly fellow ; chan 'eil e 'na bhodach, he is not a churl ; a mutchkin ; bodach uisge bheatha, a mutchkin of whisky ; bodach ruadh, a codling ; a hobgoblin, a spectre ; beiridh na bodaich ort, the goblins will catch you ; churlishness, meanness of spirit, niggardliness ; 's e chuireadh am bodach á fear a bhiodh teann, it

42   BODACHAIL—BOICIONNACH

(whisky) would drive niggardliness out of a miser.

bodachail, *a.* churlish : aged (as an old man, carle).

bodachan, *n. m.* a little old man.

bodach-beag, bodach-beg, *n. m.* a codling.

bodach-fleasgaich, b.-flesgich, *n. m.* an old bachelor.

bodach-ruadh, b.-roou, *n. m.* a codling.

bòdadh, bōda', *m.* pledging, bargaining.

bodag, *n. f.* anger, rage.

bodagach, *a.* angry, enraged.

bod-chrann, *n. m.* a kind of crupper.

bodha, bo-a, *n. m.* a rock over which the sea breaks ; a rock visible only at low tide, and often not visible at all ; the wave called a heaver. *O.N.* boði, a breaker, boding a sunken rock or bank.

bòdhag, bō'-hăg, *n. f.* a sea-lark.

bodhaig, bo-ig, *n. f.* the human body, the trunk of a living person, the " body "-part of dress.

bodhair, bo-ir, *v.* deafen, stun with noise ; cha mhór nach do bhodhair an t-òlach mi le raibheiceil, the fellow almost stunned me with his roaring. *E.Ir.* bodraim.

bòdhan, bō'-han, *n. m.* the ham, thigh.

bodhar, bo-ar, *a.* deaf, dull of hearing ; the deaf ; tha na bodhair a' cluinntinn, the deaf hear ; cluinnidh am bodhar fuaim an airgid, even the deaf hear the clink of silver (money) ; bodhar fhead, a dull, heavy sound, as of whistling wind ; bodhar fhuaim, a dull, heavy, hollow sound. *O.Ir.* bodar, *surdus.*

bodhbh, bobh, bòv, *n. m.* a fright. *E.Ir.* bódbda, fierce, fatal.

bódhradh, bōh'-ră, *vbl. n. m.* act of deafening ; tha thu air mo bhódhradh, you have deafened me.

bog, *a.* soft, miry, moist, damp ; àite bog, a place where a person or beast is apt to sink ; soft, timid, spiritless ; chan 'eil ann ach duine bog, he is only a simple, timid, chicken-hearted, spiritless fellow. *O.Ir.* bocc.

bog, *v. tr.* steep, soak ; wag, bob, shake ; bhogainn anns an allt e, I would steep him in the stream ; tha 'n cù a' bogadh earbaill, the dog wags his tail ; is fhearr an cù a bhogas earball na cù a chuireas dreang air, the dog that wags his tail is better than the one that snarls ; move or excite ; 'nuair bhogadh an dram air, when the whisky would excite him. *E.Ir.* bocaim, bocaigim, soften, shake, vibrate, toss.

bogachadh, bŏg'-ach-ă, *vbl. n. m.* act of softening ; steeping ; moistening ; getting more soft.

bogadaich, bògg'-ad-ich, *n. f.* waving, tremor from heat or passion, up and down motion.

bogadan, bògg'-ad-an, *n. m.* waving, wagging, heaving ; tha chraobh a' bogadan, the tree waves ; wagging, bobbing ; a quagmire.

bogadanaich, *n. f.* continued bobbing.

bogadh, *vbl. n. m.* act of moistening, softening ; the state of sticking fast in the mire ; chaidh a' bhó am bogadh, the cow stuck fast in the mire ; act of casting a line (in fishing).

bogaich, bogg'-ich, *v.* soften, soak, steep ; bogaich an leathar, steep the leather.

bogaichte, bogg'-ich-tya, *vbl. a.* softened, moistened.

bogainn, *n. m.* a marsh.

bogalach, *n. m.* a marsh, a soft place.

bogan, *n. m.* anything soft, quagmire.

boganach, *n. m.* a soft, simple, booby-like fellow.

bogarsaich, bòg'-ar-ssich, *n. f.* waving ; wagging ; bobbing.

bogbhuine, bog-vuna, *n. f.* a bulrush.

bog - chridheach, bog - chree - uch, *a.* chicken-hearted, faint-hearted.

bogha, bò'-ha, *n. m.* a bow, a bend, an arch ; bogha shaighead, an archer's bow ; tha bogha air, it has a bend or bow ; bogha na drochaid, the arch of the bridge ; tha bogha mór air a' bhalla, the wall has a great bow or bulge ; fear bogha, an archer ; bogha na fiodhlach, the fiddle-bow ; bogha braoin, bogha frois, *n. m.* a rainbow ; mar bhogha braoin a' soillseachadh, as a rainbow shining ; *v.* bow, bend, bulge ; tha e a' boghadh a mach, it bulges out. *E.Ir.* boga. *A.S.* boga.

bogha-catha, *n. m.* a battle-bow.

boghadair, bo'-adair, *n. m.* an archer.

boghadaireachd, bo - aderachc, *n. f.* archery.

boghainn, bo'in, *n. m.* the human body, person ; is ciatach a' bhoghainn duine e, he is a handsome person ; nach ann aig a tha bhoghainn, what a handsome body he has. *See* bodhaig.

bó ghamhna or ghamhnach, bō-ghàv'-na *n. f.* a farrow cow.

boghan, bo-han, *n. m.* the calf of the leg, the ham.

boglach, *n. m.* a marsh, a quagmire, any place where a beast is apt to stick fast.

bogluachair, *n. f.* bulrush.

bogluasgach, *a.* waving, floating ; softly moving.

bógus, *n. f.* a bug, timber moth.

boicionn, boicunn, *n. m.* a goat-skin, a skin. *O.Ir.* ceinn, *gl.* testa. *O.Celt.* kenni-, skin, hide. *Fick.*

boicionnach, boicunach, *n. f.* the small-

pox, the shingles or herpes. *Also*
boicineach.

boicneachadh, bo-yc-nuchu', *vbl. n. m.*
act of belabouring most furiously ;
beating till the skin blisters.

boicnich, *v.* belabour till the skin blisters ;
beat with all your might.

bòid, bōj, *n. f., pl.* **bòidean**, a solemn
vow ; **bòidean baistidh**, baptismal
vows. *M.Ir.* **móit**. Cf. *Lat.* võtum.

bòideach, bōj'-ăch, *a.* pertaining to a vow.

bòidhchead, boychud, *n. f.* beauty, degree
of beauty, extreme beauty ; **'s e do
bhoidhchead a leòn mi**, it is thy excessive beauty that has wounded me.

bòidheach, boyach, *a.* pretty, beautiful,
comely, handsome, neat ; *compar.*
boidhiche, more beautiful, more
comely ; from **buaidh**. *McB.*

bòidheachd, boyachc, *n. f.* beautifulness,
handsomeness, elegance.

bòidheam, bōyem, *n. m.* fawning, flattery.

bòidheanachd, boyenachc, *n. m.* petting
(a dog).

boidhre, buira, *compar.* of **bodhar**, more
or most deaf or dull of hearing, more
commonly **buidhre**.

boidhread, buirud, *abstr. n. f.* deafness ;
degree of deafness.

bòidich, bōj'-ich, *v.* vow, promise ; forswear solemnly ; **bhòidich thu bòid**,
thou hast vowed a vow.

boidsear, bojsh-er', *n. m.* a blockhead, a
stupid fellow. *Eng.* botcher.

boidsearachd, bòjsh'-er-uchc, *n. f.* stupidity, the conduct of a blockhead ;
clumsy workmanship, badly made
article.

boigear, boiger, *n. m.* puffin, ducker.
Also **budhaigir** and **budhaide**.

boil, bol, *n. f.* madness in the extreme,
rage, fury ; highest degree of passion,
frenzy ; **a chridhe laiste le boil chatha**,
his soul highly inflamed with the fury
of battle ; **tha e air bhoil**, he is in a
frenzy ; **is ann a tha thu air bhoil**, you
are quite mad ; **boil a' bhàis**, delirium
of death. *E.Ir.* **baile**.

boileis, bolesh, *n. f.* panic, excitement.

bòilich, bōlich, *n. f.* ostentation, boasting,
romancing ; gasconading ; telling fibs ;
**tha e cho làn de bhòilich is a tha 'n
t-ugh de'n bhiadh**, he is so full of
romancing as the egg is of meat ;
thoir thairis do bhòilich, be done of your
romancing ; delirium of fever ; noise.

boilisg, bolisg, *n. f.* prattling, delirium.

boillsg, boisg, *v.* flash, gleam, shine with
great lustre or glitter ; *n. f.* effulgence,
glitter. Cf. *Lat.* fulgeo ; *Gr.* φλέγω.

boillsgeach, boisgach, *a.* flashing, gleaming, shining with effulgence.

boillsgeadh, boisgu', *vbl. n. m.* effulgence ;

act of gleaming, shining ; beaming, a
glimpse ; **cha d'fhuair mi ach boillsgeadh dheth**, I got only a glimpse of
him.

boillsgean, buysh-cen, *n. m.* middle (of the
fire), the middle. *Also* **buillsgean**. *Ir.*

boillsceann, the very middle : the
navel.

boillsgeanta, boisgantu, *n. f.* gleaming,
flashy, gaudy ; fond of dress.

boillsgeantachd, boisgantachc, *n. f.* effulgence, flash, gaudiness.

boillsgeil, boisgel, *a.* flashing, gleaming,
effulgent, gaudy.

boineid, bonej, *n. f.* a bonnet.

boinne, *n. m.* a drop ; a current ; **boinne
taig**, bonu-teg, quick succession of
very large drops. *O.Ir.* **banne, banda**.
O.Celt. bannjâ.

boinnealaich, bòin'-nyal-ich, *n. f.* dropping of rain before a shower. *Also*
boinneartaich.

boinneanta, boinanta, *a.* mild, gentle ;
stout, handsome, well-built.

boinneantachd, boin'-nyant-àchc, *n. f.*
mildness, gentleness, handsomeness.

boir, *n. m.* an elephant.

bòirc, *n. f.* thatch used as manure.

boirche, borchu, *n. m.* an elk, a buffalo ;
Ir. " **borr agh, no agh mór**, a large
hind." *Lh.*

bòireal, boral, *n. m.* a joiner's brace.

boiream, borum, *n. m.* a rumour, a surmise, creating a hubbub.

boireamail, bòr'-um-al, *a.* spreading as a
rumour or surmise ; creating great
interest.

boirg, borig, *n. m.* a little screwed-up
mouth.

boirgeach, bòr'-èg-ach, *a.* having a little
prating mouth ; *n. f.* a prating female.

boirgire, bòr'-èg-èr-à, a fellow with a
little screwed mouth, a tattler.

boiriche, borichu, *n. m.* rising ground, a
bank (root as in *Ger.* berg). *McB.*

boirionn, bòr''-unn, *a.* female, feminine
gender. *M.Ir.* **boinenn, boinenda**,
female.

boirionnach, bòr-unn-àch, *n. m.* a female ;
boirionnach bòidheach, a pretty
female ; **firionnach is boirionnach**, a
male and a female, a man and a
woman.

bois, bosh, *n. f.* the palm of the hand.
Same as **bas**.

boisceal, boysh-kel, *n. m.* a savage man
or woman. *E.Ir.* **bascell, boisgell**, a
lunatic, a panic-stricken person.

boiseag, bosh'-àg, *n. f.* a palm full of
water ; a blow with the palm or on the
palm ; *dim.* of **bois**.

boiseid, bosh'-èj, *n. f.* a budget, a belt, a
girdle ; soldier's purse.

boiteadh, bŏytu, *n. f.* 1. a cauldron. 2. boiled food (for horses).

boiteag, boytag, *n. f.* a maggot, a white worm in dung, earth-worm for bait.

boiteal, *n. m.* pride.

boitean, bŏyten, *n. m.* a bundle or truss of straw or hay. *Also* **boiteal.**

boiteanaich, *v.* make into bundles or trusses.

boitidh, bŏyty, *n. m.* a sow; *interj.* **boitidh ! boitidh !** the call to a pig. *Also* **duradh ! duradh !**

ból, bóla, póla, *n. m.* a bowl.

boladh, bolu, *n. m.* smell, stink; **boladh gràineil,** an abominable smell. *O.Ir.* **bolad.**

bolannta, *a.* excellent.

bó-laoigh, bo-lūy, *n. f.* a cow with a calf, a milch cow.

bolb, *n. f.* a sort of worm.

bolg, *n. m.* bag, sack; womb, the belly; **bolg na maidne,** womb of the morning; cpds. **bolg - saighid,** a quiver; **bolg-séididh,** bellows; **bolg - uisge,** water blister, bubble. *Also* **balg.** For Fir-bolg *see* Keating I.¹⁹⁴. *E.Ir.* **bolg.**

bolgach, *a.* bulging, jutting, having a large belly; blistered, full of bubbles. *M.Ir.* **bolgach,** blistered, bubbling; *n.* boils, smallpox.

bolgaire, bolgera, *n. m.* a man with a big belly; a glutton.

bolgam, *n. m.* a mouthful of any liquid; **bolgam bainne,** a mouthful of milk; **bolgam uisge,** a mouthful of water. *Also* **balgam.** *E.Ir.* **bolgam.**

bolgan, *n. m.* the calf of the leg; a little blister.

bolgan-beucan, bolgan-bēcan, *n. m.* a fuzz-ball.

bolg-fheadan, *n. m.* poet. descrip. of the pipes: **bolg - fheadan meur - thollach,** bagpipes with finger-holes.

bolg-losgainn, bolg-losgin, *n. m.* a mushroom; a " paddock-stool."

bolg-solair, *n. m.* a magazine; "sack of provisions."

bolla, *n. m., pl.* **bollachan,** a net- or anchor-buoy.

bolla, *n. m.* a dry measure of sixteen pecks; a boll; **bolla mine,** a boll of meal; **bolla buntata,** a boll of potatoes; fr. *Eng.* Cf. *Sc.* **bow.**

bollsg, *v.* bluster, babble.

bollsgach, bolsgach, *a.* blustering, boasting; *n. f.* a blustering curious female.

bollsgaire, bolsg'-ur-u, *n. m.* blustering, swaggering, bullying fellow.

bollsgaireachd, bolsgiruchc, *n. f.* a habit of blustering or swaggering.

bollsganta, bolsgantu, *a.* blustering, swaggering; bullying.

bolt, *n. m.* a welt. *Also* **balt.** *Ir.* **balta.** *L.* **balteus,** a girdle.

boltrach, *n. f.* smell, perfume. *E.Ir.* **boltanugud**; a volume or bolt of smoke and fire, ashes, etc.

boltrachas, *n. f.* 1. perfumery, fragrance. 2. a scent-bottle, a nosegay.

bomanach, *a.* blustering.

bonn, bounn, *n. m., gen. sing.* and *n. pl.* **buinn** and **bonnan.** 1. sole; **bonn na coise,** the sole of the foot; **thug e na buinn as,** he ran off at full speed. 2. base; **aig bonn na beinne,** at the base of the mountain. 3. purpose, object; **ciod e am bonn air an d'fhalbh iad ?** what was the object of their journey ? 4. ground, warrant; **bonn an dòchais,** the ground of their confidence. 5. **bonn an tighe,** foundation of the house. Idiom : **cuir craicionn a' bhuinn air a' bhathais,** face it with courage, be not thin-skinned. *O.Ir.* **bond.** *L.* **fundus.**

bonn, *n. m., gen. sing.* and *n. pl.* **buinn,** a coin; **bonn òir,** a gold coin; **chan 'eil mi bonn 'n a eisimeil,** I am not a whit in his reverence; **bonn crùin,** a five-shilling piece.

bonnach, *n. m.* a cake. *Also* **bannach.** *Sc.* bannock

bonnachair, bonn'-ach-ur, *n. m.* a wandering greedy beggar.

bonnachan, *n. m.* a little cake.

bonnacharach, *a.* solid, steady, sensible.

bonnach-brathainn, bonuch-brainn, *n. m.* quern-bannock.

bonnach-iomanach, *n. m.* cow-herd's cake (in special reward for good herding at calving time).

bonnanta, *a.* firm, stout.

bonn-a-sia, boun-u-shiä, *n. m., pl.* **bonn-acha-sia,** halfpenny.

bonnchart, boun-chärt, *n. m.* balk, a ridge left unploughed, a landmark. *Also,* **cnàimh criche.**

bonntach, bountuch, *n. f.* the thickest part of a hide for soles.

borb, *v.* inflame ; get enraged ; **bhorb a chas,** his foot inflamed; **bhorb i 'na aghaidh,** she got enraged against him.

borb, *a., compar.* **buirbe,** turbulent; of a turbulent disposition; fierce, savage, cruel, boisterous; **o'n iorghuill bhorb,** from the fierce contest; **an geamhradh borb,** the boisterous winter; **is borb an duine e,** he is a passionate man; rude, unlettered; more or most fierce or furious. *O.Ir.* **borp,** *stultus. Lat.* barbarus.

borbachd, borbachc, *n. f.* turbulence, savageness, cruelty, fierceness.

borbadh, bŏrb'-u, *vbl. n. m.* act of inflaming, as a limb ; enraging, getting furious.

borbas, *n. f.* strictness, rigour.

borb-bhriathrach, b.-vriarach, *a.* fierce speaking ; furious.

borbhan, borvan, *n. m.* a murmur ; the purling of a streamlet ; more often morbhan.

borbhanaich, borv-anich, *n. f.* murmuring ; gurgling ; muttering.

borbnaich, borbnich, *v.* enrage, heave with anger. *See* borb.

borb-smachdail, *a.* imperious, arbitrary.

bòrc, *v.* blossom, sprout.

bòrcach, *a.* swelling, strutting.

bòrd, *n. m., gen. sing.* and *n. pl.* bùird : 1. a table, a board (of any description) : air a' bhòrd, on the table ; aig bòrd, at table. 2. food ; a bhòrd 's a leabaidh, his board and bed. 3. board ; bòrd daraich, an oak board ; bòrd na leapa, front side of the bed. 4. embarking ; chaidh e air bòrd, he went on board. Idioms : tha e fo'n bhòrd, he is dead ; tha e air a' bhòrd, he is on the parish. Compds. : bòrd nam bochd, the parish council ; bòrd-fasgaidh, lee side ; bòrd mór, a fault in the design on either side affecting sailing qualities ; bòrd - fuaraidh, weather side ; bòrd na sgoile, school board ; bòrd-slios, front side of a bed ; bòrd-uachdair, a lid ; bòrd-urchair, and bòrd-urchrainn, the mould board of a plough. *E.Ir.* bordd, board, table.

bòrd, *n. m.* bank edge ; bòrd an loch, bank or edge of the lake. *E.Ir.* bórdd, edge, rim.

bòrd, *v.* board ; bhord iad an long, they boarded the ship ; tack in sailing.

borganta, *a.* fierce.

borgh, *n. m.* a fortification. It survives only in *pl.* names. *O.N.* borg. *M.Ir.* borgg, a castle.

bòrlanachd, *n. f.* compulsory labour, service due by tenant to proprietor.

bòrlum, *n. m.* a sudden flux or vomiting.

bòrlum, *n. m.* a ridge of arable land.

borr, *n. m.* a curled upper lip, a blubber-lip ; pout ; pride, arrogance ; *v.* scent as a dog. *E.Ir.* borr, puffed, bloated, proud. *O.Celt.* borso-s.

borrach, *a.* blubber-lipped ; haughty ; *n. m.* a haughty man ; mountain grass ; protruding bank.

borradh, *n. m.* 1. scent, smell. 2. inciting.

borran, *n. m.* little blubber-lip.

borran, *n. m.* moor grass. *Also* morran.

borras, *n. m.* blubber-lip.

borrghanta, boranta, *a.* turgid, fierce.

borrshuileach, bor-hulach, *a.* large-eyed.

bos, *n. f.* palm of the hand. *Also* bas.

bòsd, *v.* boast, vaunt ; *n. m.* boasting, vaunting, vain-glory.

bòsdail, *a.* boastful, vain, vaunting, boasting, inclined to boast.

bòsdair, *n. m.* a swaggerer.

bòsdalachd, bōsd'-ăl-uchc, *n. f.* boastfulness, vain-glory ; romance, swaggering.

bòsdan, *n. m.* a small trunk or box ; a small box (for trinkets) ; a child's coffin. Cf. *E.Ir.* bossán, a small bag or purse.

bosgaire, *n. f.* applause. bos + gàir.

bòt, *n. f.* a vote ; *v.* vote.

bot, *n. f.* a mound, a bothy, a house, bank of a river.

bòtach, *a.* stout-legged.

botaidh, boty, *n. m.* a chamber vessel.

botal, *n. m.* a bottle.

botalaich, botulich, *v.* put in bottles.

both, bo, *n. m.* a plash, agitation.

both, bo, *n. m.* a hut ; bothie, shieling. *E.Ir.* both, *f.* a hut.

bothag, *n. f.* a booth, a cottage, a doll's house.

bothag, *n. f.* ringed plover.

bothan, bŏ'-han, *n. m.* a hut, a booth, a tent ; bothan am fasgadh nam fuar bheann, a hut in the shelter of the bleak mountains. *E.Ir.* bothán.

bothar, *n. m.* a lane, street. *E.Ir.* bóthar, a road for cattle.

botrachan, *n. m., pl.* botrachain, part of horse's harness ; a stick used as a crupper. *Also* bodchrann.

botramaid, bot'-ram-ăj, *n. f.* a slattern.

bòtuinn, bōt''-inn, *n. f.* a boot.

bòtuinneach, *a.* booted.

botus, *n. m.* a belly worm.

brà, *n. f.* eyelid, eyebrow. So *E.Ir.*

brà. *See* bràth.

brabhd, braud, *n. f.* a bandy leg.

brabhdach, *a.* bandy-legged ; *n. f.* a bandy-legged female.

brabhdadh, brauda', *n. m.* bravado.

brabhdair, *n. m.* a bandy-legged man ; a boaster.

brabhtalachd, brautalachc, *n. m.* haughtiness.

bracach, *a.* grayish.

brach, *v.* malt, ferment.

brach, *n. m.* a bear.

brachadair, brăch'u-der', *n. m.* a maltman. *Ir.* brachadóir, a maltster.

brachadh, brăch'-u, *vbl. n. m.* act of malting ; fermenting, putrefying.

brachag, *n. f.* 1. a squat shapeless thing or female. 2. a pustule.

brachaidh, *a.* brackish. *Sc.* brak. *Dan.* brak.

brachan, *n. m.* anything rotten, leaven.

brachd, *n. m.* anything fermented, rubbish.

brà-cheo, *n. m.* stupefaction, bewilderment.

braclach, *n. f.* brake ; a place full of fallen broken trees ; a fox's lair.

bradach, *a.* thievish, stolen, roguish ; tha thu cho breugach is a tha luch cho bradach, you lie as the mouse pilfers. *E.Ir.* broit, *gen.* braite.

bradag, *n. f.* a thievish female.

bradaidh, brăd'-y, *n. m.* a thief ; the devil. *Also* braidean.

bradaidheachd, *n. f.* theft, trickiness.

bradalach, *a.* haughty, thievish.

bradan, *n. m.* a salmon ; a swelling in a person's skin. *E.Ir.* bratán.

bradhadair, bră'-ăd-er', *n. m.* a large fire.

brag, *n. m.* 1. a burst, explosion. 2. boast. *O.Ir.* braigim, *pedo. L.* fragor.

brag, *n. m.* a herd of deer ; brag, *v. intr.* be infected, come by contagion.

bragadaich, bragadich, *n. f.* crackling.

bragadair, bragadar, *n. m.* a boaster.

bragail, bragul, *n. f.* crackling.

bragaire, *n. m.* tangle tops.

bragaireachd, bragirachc, *n. f.* vain, boasting.

bràghad, brā-ud (also *gen.* of bràighe, neck), *n. m.* neck, throat, the upper part of the neck ; losgadh-bràghad, the heartburn. *O.Ir.* bráge.

bràghadach, *a.* belonging to the neck.

braghadh, *n. m.* noise, explosion.

bragoil, bragol, *a.* boasting, challenging, bullying.

bragsaidh, brăg'-sy, *n. m.* disease in sheep, braxy.

braich, brăich, *n. f.* malt ; *gen.* bracha. *O.Ir.* mraich.

braicnich. *See* breacnaich.

bràid, brāj, *n. f.* a horse collar ; bràid-chluaisean, a pair of hems.

braid, brāj, *n. f.* theft ; luchd braid, thieves, rogues. *E.Ir.* brat, booty ; brataim, I rob, plunder.

braidean, *n. m.* a sneak, the evil one.

braidseal, brajshal, *n. m.* a great fire, a bonfire.

braigh, bray, *v.* give a crackling sound, as wood burning ; crackle ; explode. *O.Ir.* braigim, *v.* I fart. *Sg. gl.* pedo.

braigh, *n. f.* a hostage, a pledge. *E.Ir.* bráge, *f. gen.* bragad, hostage.

bràigh-chrann, brāy-chran, *n. m.* a top-mast.

braighde, braighdean, *n. m.* captives, hostages, pledges. *E.Ir.* braig, a chain.

bràighdeach, *n. m.* a horse collar.

bràighdean, bryden, *n. m.* a calf's collar, a tether.

bràighdeanas, brydenus, *n. m.* bondage, captivity. *E.Ir.* braigdenus, imprisonment.

bràighe, brāyu, *n. m.* neck, throat ; the upper part (of places) ; bràighe na

beinne, upper part of the ben ; bràighe a' chrainn, mast-head. *O.Ir.* bráge, the neck, throat. *O.Celt.* bragnt-.

bràighe, brā-yu, *n. m.* a rope, anchoring cable ; rope to which is attached the buoy of a fishing line, or nets.

bràigheach, bryuch, *n. m.* a mountaineer, one that inhabits the mountains ; *a.* belonging to the braes.

braigheachd, *n. f.* imprisonment, constraint, confinement.

braigheadh, brayu, *n. m.* report, an explosion, crackling ; a blow ; a sudden jerk.

braigheardaich, bry'-ărt-ich, *n. f.* crackling ; blustering ; swaggering.

bràigh-ghill, bry-eel, *n. f.* the goal, the ascendant, or pre-eminence ; thug thu bràigh-ghill air na chualadh mi riamh, you surpass everything I have ever heard ; fhuair e braigh-ghill ort, gun taing dhuit, he got the ascendant or pre-eminence, in defiance of you.

bràighid, bryij, *n. f.* a pair of hems ; a collar about a thief's neck.

braighleab, bryleb, *n. m.* wood-roof of a house ; sarking.

bràighleach, brāylich, *n. m.* the breast.

braighlich, brylich, *n. f.* noise, crackling ; blustering, swaggering ; jumping and struggling to get free ; *v.* make noise, crackle ; bluster, swagger.

bràigh-lìn, *n. m.* top part of a net ; strong top meshes of a net.

bràigh-sheol, bry-hol, *n. m.* a topsail.

bràigh-shlat, bry-hlat, *n. f.* a topsail-yard.

bràight, bryt, *n. f.* an enormous large fire ; a bonfire ; in old times, the fire that the Druids had on the top of mountains.

bràightseal, bryt-shal, *n. m.* a fire on the top of a hill, as a beacon, now used for a large fire of any kind, particularly in time of rejoicing ; a volley ; a broadside ; a billingsgate, or a terrible scolding of ladies ; is ann agaibh a tha am bràightseal ciatach, what a fine blazing fire you have ; a' cheud bhràightseal a leig iad, the first broadside or volley they fired ; is iad siod a thug am bràightseal, what a billingsgate those (ladies) had.

brailis, brăl'-ish, *n. f.* wort of ale or beer. *Ir.* braithlis, braichlis. *IT.* iv.[1].

braim, brym, *n. m., pl.* bramannan, *crepitus ventris. O.Ir.* braigim, I fart. *Also* broimm. *O.Celt.* bragsmen-.

brainn, *n. f., gen.* branna, the belly ; a bulging. *Also* broinn. *O.Ir.* brú *d.* broind.

brais, bresh, *n. f.* a fit, a convulsion ; tha na braisean tric, the fits return often ; *a.* active, rash ; duine brais, quick-tempered man. *E.Ir.* **brass**, great, quick.

bràisd, brēshj, *n. m.* a brooch ; fr. the *Eng.*

braise, bresh'-u, *n. f.* impetuosity ; keenness ; rashness ; sudden sickness.

braisead, bresh'-ud, *n. f.* degree of impetuosity ; rashness ; impetuosity, fervour, ardour ; wantonness ; forwardness.

braiseil, bresh'-al, *a.* keen, impetuous, forward.

braisgeul, brash-gal', *n. m.* a romance. *M.Ir.* **bras-scélach**, *n. m.* a great storyteller.

braisiche, bresicha, *n. m.* a man in middle life ; a sprightly middle-aged man.

braisleach, brashlach, *n. m.* a full-formed, bulky man ; based on *E.Ir.* **bras**, great.

bràithlin, brīlin, *n. f.* linen sheet, a winding-sheet.

bràithreachas, brāruchus, *n. m.* brotherhood, friendship, partiality.

bramaire, *n. m.* a noisy fellow. *E.Ir.* **brammaire**, a blusterer.

braman, *n. m.* misadventure, the devil. *Also* **broman**. *Ir.* **bromán**, boor, rustic. *O'R.* and *Lh.*

bramanach, *n. m.* an awkward fellow, a blusterer, a bungler.

bramas, *n. m.* misfortune, blunder.

bramasag, *n. f.* a clot-bur, the prickly head of a thistle.

bran, *n. m.* a raven ; used much in personal and river names. *McB. Also* **bran-én**. *O.Ir.* **bran** ; " so called from his great voraciousness." *Corm. Gl.*

bran, *n. m.* bran, chaff. So *Ir.*

brang, *n. m.* a horse's collar ; a small stick in the headstall of horse's halter.

brangach, *a.* snarling, grinning, growling.

brangas, *n. m.* pillory. *Sc.* **branks**, head pillory.

brang-shronach, *a.* wrinkled, grinning nose.

brannach, *a.* corpulent, having a big belly ; *n. f.* a corpulent female. *O.Ir.* **brann**, a woman.

brannaire, brann-ăr'-u, *n. m.* a corpulent man.

brannamh, bran'-uv, *n. m.* a coat of mail.

branndaidh, braundy, *n. m.* brandy, fr. *Eng.*

branndair, braund'-ăr', *n. m.* a sort of a gridiron ; fr. *Sc.* **brander**. Cf. *M.Ir.* **brann**, firebrand, embers.

braodhlach, brūlach, *n. f.* loud noise, brawling. *Also* **braoileadh**.

braoileag, broylag, *a.* whortleberry.

braoisg, brūshg, *n. f.* a grin, a distortion of the mouth, as in contempt, grimace.

braoisgeach, *a.* grinning, gaping ; having

broken teeth, notched ; *n. f.* a female with broken teeth ; a grinning female.

braoisgeil, *n. f.* prating, prattling.

braoisgein, brushcen, *n. m.* a grinning person.

braoisgire, brūshgiru, *n. m.* a grinning fellow, one that distorts his mouth in contempt.

braolaid, *n. f.* raving, dreaming.

braon, brūn, *n. m.* drop ; dew ; **gach braon de fhuil**, every drop of his blood ; drizzling rain ; **le braonaibh na h-oidhche**, with the dew of night ; light shower ; **braon fallais**, pouring perspiration. *O.Ir.* **bróen**, rain.

braonach, *a.* showery, drizzling ; rainy ; dewy ; **'sa mhadainn bhraonaich**, in the dewy morning ; **an duibhre bhraonach**, the dewy gloom ; falling in gentle showers.

braonachd, *n. f.* drizzling rain ; genial showers ; showery weather.

braonan, *n. m.* an earth-nut; **braonan nan con**, dog carmillion ; **braonan-fraoich**, *n. m.* tormentil. *Also* **praonan**.

bras, *a.* keen, rash, impetuous, fervent, ardent, incautious ; inconsiderate ; **bras le do bheul**, rash with thy tongue ; **sruth bras**, an impetuous current or torrent ; **each bras**, a mettlesome horse. *See* **brais**. Compds. : **bras-bhuilleach**, ready in dealing blows ; **bras-bhuinne**, a torrent ; **bras-chaoin**, quick and pleasant ; **bras-chomhrag**, a tournament ; **bras-phort**, fast reel (music). *E.Ir.* **brass**, quick, brisk.

brasailt, braselt, *n. m.* a panegyric, eulogy. *O.Ir.* **bras**, great, large.

brat, *n. m.* a mantle, a covering, a veil ; hair-cloth for a kiln, an apron ; **crochaidh tu am brat**, thou shalt hang the veil. Compds. : **brat - bròin**, mortcloth, funeral pall ; **bratchrann**, flagstaff ; **brat-gnùise**, a veil ; **bratlong**, flag-ship ; **brat-nasc**, a clasp ; **bratspéillidh**, a swaddling cloth ; **bratùrlair**, a carpet. *O.Ir.* **brat**, mantle. *W.* **brethyn**. *O.Celt.* **bratto-s**.

bratach, *a.* banner, flag, colours, ensign ; **chuir iad suas a' bhratach**, they unfurled the flag. *M.Ir.* **bratach**.

bratag, *n. f.* the rough, or grass caterpillar. *Ir.* **bratóg** = " the mantled one."

brataich, brăt'-ich, *v.* kindle.

bràth, brā, *n. f.* quern, hand-mill ; " is fheàirde bràth a breacadh gun a briseadh," a quern is the better of sharpening without being broken, *i.e.* too much of a good thing. *O.Ir.* **broo**, *gen.* **broon** (mola trusatilis). *Z².* *W.* **breuan**. *Corn.* **brou**. *O.Celt.* **brevon-**.

brath, bra, *n. m.* knowledge, information ; pursuit of information ; advantage by unfair means ; **ghabh e brath orm**, he took the advantage of me ; **a bheil brath agad c'àit' a bheil e ?** have you any idea where he is ? ; **is ann aig Dia tha brath**, God alone knows ; **a' brath tighinn**, intending or meaning to come ; **bha e a' brath mo bhualadh**, he was on the point of striking me ; **cha bhi brath air a' bhàrd**, the bard shall not be found. *M.Ir.* braithim, I conceive, think.

brath, brah, *v.* betray, deceive, inform against ; **esan a bhrath e**, he that betrayed him ; **tha miann air do bhrath**, he wants to betray you. *O.Ir.* mrath, betrayal, spying.

bràth, bràch, *n. m.* judgment ; **là bhràth**, day of judgment ; **seachd bliadhna roimh'n bhràth, thig muir thar Eirinn re aon trà**, seven years before the last day, the sea at one tide shall cover Ireland ; *adv.* **gu bràth**, for ever (till judgment) ; **na tréig mi gu buileach no gu bràth**, do not forsake me utterly or for ever. *O.Ir.* bráth, *iudicium.* **dia brátha** gl. *in diem Christi.*

bràthadair, *n. m.* a great fire.

brathadair, brahuder, *n. m.* an informer, a traitor, a betrayer, a knave.

brathadh, brahu, *vbl. n. m.* act of betraying, informing ; treachery, deceit.

bràthair, bràhir, *n. m.* a brother ; **brathair-athar**, a paternal uncle ; **brathair-màthar**, a maternal uncle ; **brathair-céile**, a brother-in-law ; **bràthair bochd**, a friar. *O.Ir.* bráthir. *W.* brawd. *O.Celt.* brâtêr. *L.* fráter. *Goth.* brōþar.

bràthaireachas, bràruchus, *n. m.* brotherhood, fraternity ; partnership.

bràthairealachd, bràralachc, *n. f.* brotherhood, brotherly attachment, fraternity, unanimity, harmony.

bràthaireil, bràhirol, *a.* brotherly, affectionate.

bràthair-mhort, *n. m.* fratricide.

brath-foille, bra-foylu, *n. f.* disguise, deceit.

brath-mhionn, bra-viùnn, *n. m.* an oath of extermination.

breab, breb, *v.* kick, stamp with the foot ; *n. m.* a kick, a prance, a start.

breabadair, brebuder, *n. m.* a weaver.

breabadair-ladhrach, brebuder-lūrach, *n. m.* the spider.

breabadh, brebu', *vbl. n. m.* act of stamping, kicking.

breabail, brebil, *n. f.* kicking.

breaban, breban, *n. m.* 1. a heelpiece. 2. a patch of leather.

breabardaich, breburtich, *n. f.* kicking, prancing, stamping, raging.

breac, breck, *a.* piebald ; spotted ; **each** breac, a piebald horse ; **bó bhreac**, a parti-coloured cow ; pock-mark ; **a'bhreac**, smallpox ; **breac le neòn-ainibh**, chequered with daisies. *O.Ir.* brec, variegated, freckled.

breac, brec, *v.* variegate, bespangle, chequer, speckle ; *n. f.* the smallpox ; **breac nam bó, breac a' chruidh**, the cow-pox ; **breac a' mhuiltein**, that modification of cloud called cirro-cumulus ; **breac òtrach**, the shingles or herpes (**deilginneach** is another name for it) ; **breac an t-sìl**, the white and grey wagtail ; **breac beadaidh**, the fish called loach (*Fr.* loche). *E.Ir.* breccaim, I variegate.

breac, *v. tr.* pick, sharpen a millstone. *E.Ir.* breccaim, I carve.

breac, breck, *n. m., gen. s.* and *n. pl.* **bric**, a trout ; **breac-geal**, salmon trout. *E.Ir.* brecc.

breacadh, brecku', *vbl. n. m.* act of getting freckled ; getting black and white ; picking a millstone ; **breacadh teine**, shin-freckles ; **breac-luirgneach**, shin-freckled ; **breac shìth**, livid spots on the shin, hives ; **breacadh rionnaich**, a dapple sky ; **breacadh-sianain**, ("weather-spots") freckles ; **breac-mhìnidh**, freckles. *E.Ir.* brechtrad.

breacag, breckag, *n. f.* a pancake ; *syn.* **bonnach**, a bannock.

breacair, *n. m.* the engraver's tool. *So Ir.*

breacan, breckan, *n. m.* tartan, tartan plaid, a Highland plaid ; a parti-coloured dress, used by the Celts from the earliest times ; **breacan an fhéilidh**, the belted plaid (consisting of twelve yards of tartan, worn round the waist, obliquely across the breast and over the left shoulder, and partly depending backwards). According to Keating it was the custom in ancient time to have *one* colour in the dress of a slave, *two* in the dress of a peasant, *three* in the dress of a soldier or young lord, *four* in the dress of a **brughaidh** (land-holder), *five* in the dress of a district chief, *six* in the dress of an *ollamh*, and in that of a king and queen. *Hist. II.* 122.

breacan, breachdan, breckan, *n. m.* a custard. *M.Ir.* brechtán.

breacarsaich, breckarsich, *n. f.* twilight ; middle state, particularly of health.

breac-lìon, *n. m.* a trout net.

breac-luirgneach, *a.* shin-freckled.

breacnaich, *v.* chequer, mix ; make spotted ; variegate. *O.Ir.* mrechtnigim.

breacta, *vbl. a.* picked as a millstone ; spotted ; carved.

brèagh, bria, *a.* handsome, beautiful, fine ; **nighean bhreagha**, a handsome girl ; surprising ; **is breagh nach d' thàinig thu dhachaidh an am**, it is surprising you did not come home in time.

brèaghachd, breea'-ăchc, *n. f.* handsomeness ; beauty, elegance ; degree of beauty.

brèaghad, breea'-ud, *abstr. n. f.* beauty, superiority in beauty.

brèaghaich, breea'-ich, *v.* adorn, decorate.

breall, *n. m.* knob, lump ; the glans penis. *E.Ir.* **brell.**

breallach, brialuch, *n. m.* a kind of shell-fish ; fr. **breall.**

breaman, breman, *n. m.* tail, train.

breamanach, bremanach, *a.* tailed, as a tail or train.

breamas, bremus, *n. m.* a blunder, mishap ; misfortune ; **cha leighis aithreachas breamas**, repentance cannot remedy a blunder.

breamasach, *a.* unfortunate, unlucky ; blundering ; bungling.

breamasachd, *n. f.* unfortunate state or condition, fatality, misfortune.

breamhainn, *n. m.* a wheelbarrow.

breannach. *See* **brionnach.**

breanndalach. *See* **brionndal.**

breath, bre, *n. f.* a row, a rank, a layer.

breath, bre, *n. f.* sentence ; judgment. *recte* **breith.** *O.Ir.* breth (*gen.* brith), *iudicium.*

breathal, brehal, *n. f.* raving, confusion of mind, terror, flurry.

breathanas, brehanus, *n. m.* judgment, decision, retributive justice. *See* **breith.**

breathas, brehus, *n. m.* fury, frenzy.

breathnachadh, brenuchu, *n. m.* apprehension ; conception, imagination.

breathnaich, bren'-nich, *v.* conceive, apprehend, suppose. *See* **breithnich.**

Breatunn, *n. m.* Britain.

Breatunnach, *a.* British ; *n. m.* a Briton.

brèid, brēj, *n. m.* a piece of cloth, a kerchief, a napkin, a woman's coif, consisting of a square of fine linen, folded diagonally into a triangle. Is called also **beannag** and **brèid beannach** (the peaked thing, the pointed cloth), and used to be worn as a badge of marriage ; sail of a boat (*poet.*) ; **do loingeas brèidgheal**, your white-sailed fleet. *E.Ir.* **brét**, a fragment.

brèideach, brējuch, *a.* like a kerchief, ragged, patched ; *n. f.* a woman wearing the **brèid** or badge of marriage ; **is iomadh gruagach is brèideach**, many were the maidens and the married women.

brèideag, *n. f.* the kerchiefed one ; a wife.

brèigchiabh, brēg-chiuv, *n. f.* a wig. gruag.

brèigchiabhadair, brēg-chiuvadar, *n. m.* a wig-maker.

brèig-riochdaich, brēg-richcach, *v.* disguise, disfigure.

breilleis, brelish, *n. f.* confusion of mind, raving, delirium.

brèine, brēnu, *n. f.* turbulence, a turbulent disposition ; stink, stench ; stinginess. **cho breun ris a' chù**, as stingy as the dog, is a common expression. *E.Ir.* **brén**, rotten.

brèinead, brēnud, *abstr. n. f.* degree of turbulence, turbulence ; rottenness, stench, stinginess.

brèineag, brēnag, *n. f.* a turbulent female ; dirty, sulky woman.

brèinean, brēnen, *n. m.* a turbulent man ; sulky, inhospitable man.

breisleach, breshluch, *n. f.* raving, delirium, confusion of mind ; **chaidh mi am bhreislich**, I got quite bewildered ; distraction of mind.

breisleach, *n. f.* oats and barley mixed and growing together.

breisleachail, breshluchal, *a.* confusing, confounding ; delirious, causing delirium.

breislich, breshlich, *v.* confuse, confound, rave, talk inconsistently or incoherently. *E.Ir.* **bressim**, uproar, din.

breith, bre, *n. f.* judgment, decision, sentence ; **breith air a' phobull bheir thu**, thou shalt judge the people ; **breith luath lochdach**, a rash judgment or opinion (is) unfair ; interpretation, meaning, signification ; **thoir breith air mo bhruadar**, interpret my dream ; violence. *O.Ir.* **breth**, *iudicium.*

breith, bre, *vbl. n. m.* act of bearing, seizing, carrying away, catching ; **a' breith air làimh orm**, seizing me by the hand ; **cha b' fhada bha sinn a' breith orra**, we soon overtook them ; **a' breith air a chéile**, laying hold of each other ; **a' breith uighean**, laying eggs ; **a' breith laoigh**, calving ; **a' breith uain**, yeaning ; **a' breith oircean**, farrowing ; **a' breith chuileanan**, whelping ; **a' breith phiseag**, kittening. *O.Ir.* **berim** bear, carry, take, and various other meanings.

breith-buidheachas, *n. f.* thanksgiving.

breith-dhìtidh, bre-yīti, *n. f.* sentence of condemnation.

breitheach, brehuch, *a.* judicial, exact.

breitheal, brehal, *n. f.* raving, delirium. *Also* **breathal.**

breitheamh, brihuv, *n. m.* a judge ; an umpire ; **britheamh** is better form. *O.Ir.* **brithem.**

breitheanas, brehonas, *n. m.* a judgment ; decision, sentence ; a just retribution

for one's sins ; thàinig breitheanas ort, a judgment came upon you. *O.Ir.*
brethemnas, brithemnas, sentence, judgment.

breitheanasach, brehonusach, *a.* retributive, as a just judgment.

breithneachadh, brenachu', *n. m.* apprehension, idea ; sound sense.

breithnich, brenich, *v.* conceive, explain, interpret.

breitich, bretich, *v.* swear.

breò, bryô, *n. m.* a fire, a flame. *E.Ir.* bréo, flame.

breò, *v.* rot, corrupt.

breoc, brioc, *v.* patch.

breòchaid, *n. m.* any tender or fragile thing.

breòchdail, briōchcil, *v.* patch, mend.

breòchdlair, briōchcler, *n. m.* a mender, a botcher.

breòcladh, breōclu, *n. m.* clumsy patching.

breòclaid, breōclej, *n. f.* sickly person.

breòite, briōtu, *a.* decayed, rotten ; frail, weak, feeble, infirm, sickly, indisposed.

breòiteachd, briōtachc, *n. f.* infirmity, weakness, debility, frailty, feebleness.

breòlaid, briōlej, *n. m.* dotage.

breòth, briō, *v.* putrify, rot, corrupt.

breothadh, brio-u', *vbl. n. m.* corruption, beginning to corrupt, or get useless : rotting.

breug, brēg ; *also* briag, *gen.* bréige, *n. f.* a lie, a falsehood, an untruth ; bilean nam breug, lying lips ; fhuaradh 'sa' bhréig e, he was found out in a lie ; *v.* entice, pacify, lull, flatter ; breug am pàisde, pacify, lull, or soothe the child ; breug leat e, flatter or cajole him away with you ; 'ga bhreugadh mar gum biodh leanabh ann, cajoling, soothing, or caressing him as if he was a child. *O.Ir.* bréc, brécaim, lie, decoy, beguile. *O.Celt.* brenkâ.

breug, usu. in pl., breugan, open-work near top of a creel.

breugach, breg'-ach, *a.* lying, false, deceitful ; cha e cho breugach is a tha an cat cho bradach, he is as great a liar as the cat is a thief ; *n.f.* a lying female

breugadair, brēguder, *n. m.* a liar.

breugadaireachd, *n. f.* lying.

breugadh, brēg'-u, *vbl. n. m.* act of cajoling, flattering, lulling, pacifying, soothing, caressing. *E.Ir.* brécad, deception.

breugag, *n. f.* a fib ; a lying little female.

breugaich, brēg'-ich, *v.* belie, falsify, give the lie, disprove, gainsay ; deceive, beguile ; bhreugaich e mi, he belied me ; breugaich e, belie him.

breugaire, brēgire, *also* briagaire, *n. m.* a liar ; is fearr duine bochd na breugaire, a poor man is better than a liar ; is

feairrde breugaire fianuis, a liar requires a voucher.

breugaireachd, brēgirachc, *n. f.* the habit or vice of telling lies ; the practice of belying or contradicting.

breug-chràbhadh, brēg-chrāva', *n. m.* hypocrisy, pretensions to religion ; breug-chràbhach, hypocritical, deceitful.

breuglaich, brēglich, *v.* foreswear, perjure, gainsay.

breugnachadh, brēgnacha', *vbl. n. m.* act of belying, falsifying, contradicting ; " cha bhreugnaichear an sean-fhacal," the proverb shall not be falsified.

breugnaichte, brēgnichte, *vbl. a.* belied, falsified, contradicted.

breug-riochd, brēg-ruchc, *n. f.* disguise.

breug - riochdaire, b. - ruchker, *n. m.* a disguiser, a pretender, a traitor.

breun, brēn, *a.* putrid, filthy ; of a turbulent, boisterous disposition ; bold indelicate ; inhospitable. *O.Ir.* brén-aim, I putrify, rot. *O.Celt.* bregno-s.

breunach, brēnach, *n. f.* a turbulent, indelicate, or immodest female.

breunachd, brēnachc, *n. f.* rottenness, putridness, turbulence, indelicacy.

breunadh, brēnu', *vbl. n. m.* act of becoming putrid.

breunag, *n. f.* a wild, mean woman.

breunain, *n. m.* a mean character, the devil.

breunair, brēner, *n. m.* a turbulent man.

briaghachd, bria-achc, *n. f.* beauty, finery.

Brian, the name Brian.

briathar, breeuhar, *n. m.* a word, a verb ; a saying, an assertion ; dh'iarr an searmonaiche briathra taitneach fhaotainn, the preacher sought out acceptable words. *O.Ir.* briathar, verbum.

briathrach, breeur'-uch, *a.* wordy, talkative, verbose, loquacious.

briathrachas, breeur'-ruch-us, *n. m.* wordiness, wit, eloquence, verbosity.

briathradair, breeur'-ud-er, *n. m.* a dictionary, a lexicon.

briathradaireachd, breeur'-ud-er-uchc, *n.f.* lexicography ; a lexicographer's work.

briathradan, breeur'-ud-an, *n. f.* a vocabulary. *Also* briathrachan.

briathraich, breeur'-rich, *v.* affirm, assert, maintain.

briathrail, breeur'-al, *a.* verbal, in a word.

brìb, breeb, *n. m.* a small sum of money, a dribblet, an item ; a bheil thu brath am brìb sin a phàidheadh ? are you going to pay that trifling sum ? a bribe ; brìb nach do ghabh, who has not accepted a bribe.

brìb, breeb, *v.* bribe, corrupt, fr. *Eng.*

brìbeadh, breebu, *vbl. n. m.* act of bribing.

bribearachd, breeb'-ar'-ăchc, *n. f.* payment in small sums, trifling sums of money.

bribide, bribija, *n. m.* a trifling sum ; chosg e bribide, it cost a trifle (meaning, it cost a great deal). Cf. *E.Ir.* brib, short. *Lat.* brevis.

bricean, bricen, *n. m.* a sprat, or small trout ; bricean baintighearn, a wagtail ; bricean beithe, a linnet ; fr. breac.

bride, breeju, contraction of brighide ; Brighit, latha fhèill Bride, Candlemas, St. Bridget's day.

brideach, breejach, *a.* a dwarf ; cha bhrideach air an fhaich e, he is not a dwarf on the battlefield.

brideag, breejag, *n. f.* the jaws of a brute.

bridean, breejen, *n. m.* the sea-piet ; cho luath ris a' bhridean 'san traigh, as swift as the sea-piet on the sea-shore.

brig, breeg, *n. f.* a heap, a pile ; *v.* pile, build, as a pile of peats, etc. ; a' brigeadh na mòna, piling the peat-stack. Cf. *O.N.* brik ; *Eng.* brick.

brigh, bree, *n. f.* substance, essence, elixir, juice, sap ; chaill na h-ùbhlan am brigh, the apples lost their juice ; feòil gun bhrigh, beef without substance ; meaning, interpretation ; briathran gun bhrigh, words without meaning ; a' caitheamh mo bhrigh, dissolving my substance ; do bhrigh, a bhrigh, by virtue of, because ; pith, energy ; thuirt triath Eirinn bu mhór brigh, said Ireland's chief of mighty energy. *O.Ir.* bríg (with sim. var. of meaning). *O.Celt.* brigâ, brigo-.

brighealachd, bree-alachc, *n. f.* substance, vigorousness, juiciness, pithiness.

brigheil, bree-al, *a.* substantial, juicy, pithy, full of meaning, sap or energy. *O.Ir.* brígach.

brighinn, bree-in, *n. f.* seasoning, any fat ; delicacies, dainties.

brighinneachadh, bree-inachu, *vbl. n. m.* the act of seasoning ; the act of feeding with dainties or delicacies.

brigis, brigish, *n. f.* breeches. *Also* briogais. *Sc.* breeks.

brilleanach, brilenach, *a.* lewd.

brimin, *n. m.* related to braman (which see) ; brimin bodaich, a shabby carle.

briob, brib, *v. a.* wink.

briobadh, *vbl. n. m.* act of winking.

briodal, breedul, *n. m.* caressing. Cf. brionnal, brionndal. *E.Ir.* brionn = dream, lie.

briog, brig, *v.* stab, thrust ; cut round ; *n. m.* confinement, restraint.

briogach, *a.* mean, miserly, spiritless, avaricious, sordid.

briogachd, *n. f.* sordidness, meanness, want of spirit, shabbiness.

briogadaich, brigudich, *n. m.* sordidness, avarice, meanness ; ludicrous capering.

briogadh, *vbl. n. m.* act of pricking ; act of cultivating, cleaning (growing potatoes).

briogaid, brigej, *n. f.* a little, elderly, morose, miserly female.

briogaideach, brigejach, *a.* elderly, little and mean.

briogaire, brigira, *n. m.* a sordid, shabby fellow ; a miser ; a churl.

briogaireachd, brigirachc, *n. m.* sordidness, meanness, avarice, want of spirit.

briogais, *n. m.* breeches. *Ir.* brigis. *Sc.* breeks. *A.S.* brēc (*pl.*). *O.N.* brækr (*pl.*).

brioghas, briyus, *n. f.* fervour of passion, dalliance ; fondness.

brioghasach, briyusach, *a.* fond.

brioghmhoireachd, breevorachc, *n. f.* substantiality ; the state of being full of meaning.

brioghmhor, breevor, *a.* full of substance, or meaning, or energy. *O.Ir.* brígmar, powerful.

briollag, bryoolag, *n. f.* an illusion.

briollaire, *n. m.* a lewd person ; fr. breall.

briollan, *n. m.* a chamber pot ; fr. breall.

brionglaid, bringlej, *n. f.* a bickering sort of squabble ; wrangling, disagreement.

brionglaid, brioonglej, *n. f.* confusion, dream. *E.Ir.* brionglóid, a vision, dream, based on brinda, a vision.

brionglaideach, bryung'-llăj-uch, *a.* squabbling, bickering, wrangling, quarrelsome.

brionn, briun, *n. f.* prettiness.

brionnach, bryunn'-ăch, *a.* parti-coloured and shining, or glittering ; pretty ; flattering ; lying.

brionnachd, bryunn'-ăchc, *n. m.* variety of colours, glitter ; flattery, falsehood.

brionnal, bryunn'-al, *n. f.* flattery, fawning ; toying, caressing, flirting. *Also* brionndal.

brionnalachd, *n. f.* flattery, fawning.

brionshuileach, bryunn'-hooluch, *a.* having a bright shining quick eye.

brios, brees, *n. m.* the state of being half intoxicated ; mockery. *Eng.* breeze.

briosaid, brisej, *n. f.* a girdle, a belt ; a witch, a sorceress.

briosaideach, brisejach, *a.* belted.

briosg, brisg, *v.* start, jerk ; crumble.

briosgadh, brisgu', *vbl. n. m.* act of jerking, starting.

briosgaid, *n. f.* a biscuit.

briosgail, brisgul, *n. f.* sudden start or movement.

briosganta, brisgantu, *a.* apt to start, move, jerk.

briosgardaich, brisgardich, *n. f.* starting or jerking movement ; starting, moving. *Ir.* briscurnach, crackling. *O'R.*

52 BRIOSUIRNEACH—BRÒDAIL

briosuirneach, brees'-urn-ach, a. ludicrous.
briot, breet, briotal, brihtul, n. m. the
language of birds, a flock of wild fowls,
in pursuit of the fry of fish ; a meeting
or company where every one is speaking ; nonsensical talk; chit-chat, tattle,
chattering ; flattery. E.Ir. briotach,
chirping, chitter-chatter ; briotaire,
stammerer (Lh.).
briotas, n. m. chattering, lisping.
bris, breesh, v. break, fracture. O.Ir.
brissim, I break, rout (in battle).
brisd, breesht, v. break, fracture, become
insolvent, or a bankrupt ; splinter.
brisdeach, bristeach, breeshtach, a. apt to
break, brittle, interrupted, confused,
unsettled, as weather ; uair bhrisdeach,
unsettled weather.
brisdeadh, breeshtu', vbl. n. m. a break, a
breach, a fracture ; an eruption ; an
outbreaking ; act of breaking, fractur-
ing ; brisdeadh cridhe, a heart-break ;
brisdeadh céile, derangement ; brisdeadh a mach, an eruption, an outbreaking, an insurrection.
brisg, breeshc, a. brittle, apt to break ;
as flesh — tender, fine. E.Ir. brisc,
brittle, tender, fragile. Corm. " ab
eo quod est priscus, ar is brisc gach
. . . n-arsaid."
brisg, a. lively, mettlesome, active,
brisk ; from the Eng.
brisge, breeshcu, n.f. brittleness; tenderness ; readiness, aptness, activity.
brisgeachd, breeshcachc, n.f. brittleness,
readiness, aptness ; tenderness, activity, cleverness.
brisgead, breeshcud, n. f. brittleness,
degree of brittleness, tenderness ;
briskness, etc.
brisgean, breeshcen, n. m. the part of
tripe called the brisket or gristle ; the
root of wild tansy or silver-weed ;
moor grass. E.Ir. briscean, wild tansy.
Archiv. I.338.
brisgein, n. m. cartilage (as of the nose).
brislean, breeshlen, n. m. wild tansy.
brist, brisht, v. break, fracture.
briste, breeshtu, vbl. a. broken, made a
bankrupt, insolvent, bruised ; tha mo
chridhe briste, my heart is broken ;
is iad iobairtean Dhé spiorad briste,
the sacrifices of God are a broken spirit.
britheagach, bree-haguch, a. sensible,
becoming.
britheamh, breev, n. m., pl. -nan, a
judge. O.Ir. brithem.
britinneas, breetinus, n. f. the measles.
brobh, bròv, a. round-rooted, bastard
cypress.
brobht, brout, n. m., a large piece of bread.
broc, n. m. a badger ; gen. sing. and n. pl.
bruic. E.Ir. brocc. Cf. Lat. broc-

cus, having projecting teeth. O.Celt.
brokko-s.
brocach, a. marked with the smallpox ;
speckled in the face ; greyish like a
badger ; parti-coloured (Lh.).
brocail, v. mangle.
brocair, broker, n. m. a fox-hunter, a
destroyer of vermin.
brocaireachd, brokerachc, n. f. the
occupation of fox-hunter, etc.
brochail, brochul, v. mangle, spoil. Cf.
brochan for root.
brochaill, n. f. the name of the Banner
of Goll, the son of Morna.
brochan, n. m. gruel ; porridge, pottage ;
deoch brochain ; sodar brochan, thick
gruel ; generally, brochan is gruel, and
lite is porridge, but there are places
where brochan = porridge ; brochan
balgum, very thick gruel ; brochan
bàn, thin gruel ; stiùireag, gruel made
with a pinch of oaten flour (very thin) ;
brochan bainne, gruel made with milk
instead of water ; brochan lòm, very
thin gruel ; brochan bùrn, water gruel.
O.Ir. brothchán, pottage.
brochanach, a. well supplied with porridge or pottage ; bi gu curaiceach,
brògach, brochanach 'sa gheamhradh,
be thou well capped, well shod, and
well supplied with gruel in winter.
brochlach, n. f. a woman.
brochlaid, brochlej, n. m. trash ; farrago,
confused broken mass.
brochlainn, broch'-llinn, n. f. a badger's
den ; any stinking place.
broclach, n. m. a badger's or fox's den.
Also braclach.
bròcladh, vbl. n. m. spoiling, mangling. See
breòcladh.
brod, n. m. the choice part of anything,
choice quality of anything ; brod an
t-sil, the best of oats, choice oats.
Also brad.
brod, v. t. poke, probe, level, smooth (as
land after plough).
brod, n. m. a pot-lid. Sc. brod.
brod, n. m. land. E.Ir. brogach, full of
lands. K.M.
brod, n. m. a box ladle for receiving the
people's offering in church ; the collection itself.
brod, n. m. a goad, prickle. E.Ir. brott.
O.Celt. brotto-s. O.N. broddr, a sting.
bròd, n. m. a crowd, a brood.
bròd, n. m. pride, arrogance, haughtiness.
bròdach, a. in crowds.
brodadh, brodu', vbl. n. m. act of levelling
land, poking ; v. goad, sting, excite.
bròdail, bròd'-al, a. proud, haughty,
arrogant ; tha e cho bhròdail ris a'
mhac-mhallachd, he is as proud as
Lucifer.

bròdalachd, brod'-al-uchc, *n. f.* arrogancy, haughtiness, extreme pride.

brodann, *n. m.* a goad, a staff.

brod-iasg, bröd'-eeusg, *n. m.* needle-fish.

brog, *n. m.* a probe, a poker ; *v. i.* poke, probe, stir, stimulate ; bestir yourself.

bròg, brōg', *n. f., gen.* bròige, sròn na bròige, the toe of the shoe. 1. a shoe. 2. hoof (of horse) ; bròg an eich, the hoof of the horse. 3. challenge ; " bualadh nam bròg 'g an teumadh," challenges stinging them. 4. misfortune ; bhuail an t-earrach so bròg oirnn, this spring brought us misfortune ; buailidh sud bròg ort fhathast, that will be your misfortune yet. *E.Ir.* bróc, greaves, shoe, hoof. *O.N.* brókr.

broga, *n. m.* an awl, a prod. Cf. *Sc.* brog.

brògach, *a.* well shod ; strong-hoofed.

brògach, *a.* black-faced ; caora bhrògach, a black-faced sheep. *Also* brocach.

brogach, brog'-ăch, *n. m.* a boy, a lad. Cf. brogail, active, lively.

brògag, *n. f.* a little shoe.

brògaich, *v.* shoe ; provide footwear.

brògaich, *v.* approach, draw near.

brogail, *a.* lively (applied to a sprightly old man). *Also* frogail, fr. brog, stimulate.

brògaire, brōguru, *n. m.* a cobbler, a shoe-mender.

brògaireachd, brōg''-ur-uchc, *n. f.* shoe-mending, cobbling.

broganach, *n. m.* a little boy.

broganta, *a.* sturdy, lively, hale.

bròg na cuthaig, *n. m.* wild violet.

bròid, bröj, *v.* embroider.

bròidireachd, brōjeruchc, embroidering.

broidneireachd, brojneruchc, *n. f.* embroidery, fr. the *Eng.*

broigealachd, brōgialuchc, *n. f.* activity, liveliness, as an old man or woman.

broigeanta, broiganta, *a.* active, lively, spirited, sturdy.

broigeantachd, broigantachc, *n. f.* liveliness, activity, sturdiness, alacrity.

broigeil, broigal, *a.* stout, lively, and active ; hale, hearty, applied to old people always. *Also* sbroigeil.

broigheal, broyal, *n. m.* a cormorant. *Ir.* broighioll.

broighleadh, broylu', *n. m.* bustle, dangling.

broighleag, broylag, *n. f.* whortleberry.

broighlich, broylich, *n. f.* for braighlich. 1. the crackling of wood on fire; swaggering. 2. struggling for freedom (as an animal bound or in a person's grip).

broigileineach, brogilenach, *a.* substantial. By-form of broigeil.

broilean, bröl'-en', *n. m.* manyplies or king's hood in an animal ; pig's snout.

broileanach, bröl'-en'-uch, *a.* manyplied.

broilleach, broilach, *n. m.* the breast, the bosom ; front ; a broilleach mar chòbhar nan stuadh, her bosom like the foam of the waves. *See* brollach.

broineach, brŏn'-uch, *n. f.* a ragged woman, a ragged garment or vesture ; *a.* ragged, tattered. *E.Ir.* brainech, edged, fringed.

broineag, bron'-ăg, *n. f.* a rag, a tatter, a shred.

broineagach, bron'-ăg-uch, *a.* ragged, tattered.

bròinein, *n. m.* sorry-looking man, pitiable object ; often used in tenderness, to sympathise, or comfort.

broinn, *n. f.* a belly. *See* brù.

broinndeargan, broyn-dergan, *n. m.* robin red-breast. *Also* brù-dearg.

broisde, brosju, *n. m.* a brooch.

broisg, broshg, *v.* excite, stir up.

broit, brŏët, *n. f.* bosom ; cuir ad bhroit e, put it in thy bosom ; the breast covering (a *fem.* form of brot). *O.Ir.*

broiténe, Sg. gl. on *palliolum.*

brolachan, *n. m.* a ragged person.

brolaich, brolich, *n. m.* incoherent talk, unintelligible speech.

brolasg, brolusc, *n. m.* garrulity.

brollach, *n. m.* breast, bosom. *E.Ir.* brollach, bosom.

brollach, *n. m.* a mess. *E.Ir.* brothlach, cooking-pit of the Fiann. *See* Fiann.

brollachan, *n. m.* anything entangled or entwined.

brolluinn, bröll'-inn, *n. m.* steam, stench ; meeting of currents. *Also* brothluinn, boiling, tide-boiling ; fr. broth.

bromach, *n. m.* a colt. *E.Ir.* brommach, a colt, foal.

bròn, *n. m.* mourning, sorrow, wailing, weeping ; grief, lamentation ; mourning dress or habiliments ; is e so fàth mo bhròin, this is the cause of my sorrow ; fo bhròn, sorrowing, lamenting ; ola aoibhnis an àite bròin, the oil of joy for mourning ; tha iad am bròn, they are wearing mournings. *O.Ir.* brón. *O.Celt.* brugno-s.

brònach, *a.* sad, mournful, melancholy, grievous, sorrowful ; mean, pathetic ; sealladh brònach, pathetic sight ; very small ; bean bheag bhrònach, a puny little woman.

brònag, *n. f.* a sorrowful woman, a pitiable woman ; often used in tenderness ; bronag bhochd ! poor soul !

brònbhrat, bròn'-vrat, *n. m.* a mort-cloth.

bronn, *v.* grant, distribute. *E.Ir.* bronnaim, I bestow, spend.

bronnach, *n. f.* a girth, a belt ; *a.* swagbellied.

bronnag, *n. f.* a gudgeon.

brosdaich, v. incite, stimulate. E.Ir. brostaim and brostaigim, I incite, stir up, provoke.

brosdan, n. m. a spunk, little sticks to kindle the fire. E.Ir. brosna, a faggot.

brosgadh, brŏsg'-u, vbl. n. m. an exhortation, an excitement, stimulation.

brosglach, a. lively, active, brisk; given to flattery.

brosglaich, brŏsg'-llich, v. excite, bestir yourself; flatter, coax, cajole.

brosguil, brosg'-il, v. flatter, coax.

brosgul, brosg'-ul, n. m. flattery.

brosluinn, broslin, n. m. stirring sound (as of song).

brosnachadh, bros'-nach-u, vbl. n. m. incitement, provocation, exhortation; also a piece of Highland music; encouragement; act of spurring, exciting. See brosdaich. E.Ir. brostudach, inciting.

brosnachail, bross'-nach-al, a. instigating, encouraging.

brosnaich, bross'-nich, v. excite, provoke, bestir, encourage.

brot, n. m. broth. Cf. O.Ir. broth, corn; an ear of corn.

brot, n. m. a veil, upper garment; a form of brat. O.Ir. broiténe, palliolum.

brotaich, brotich, v. thrive, grow fat.

broth, broh, n. m. 1. an eruption on the skin; itch. 2. a lunar halo. E.Ir. broth, flesh.

brothach, bro-huch, adj. having an eruption on skin. E.Ir. eruptive, scabby.

brothag, bro-hag, n. f. the bosom, a fold of the breast clothes. E.Ir. broth, a mantle.

brothair, n. m. flesher, butcher; " am brothair gun naire," the shameless butcher. I.Lom. E.Ir. broth, flesh.

brothas, brohus, n. m. farrago, brose; Athole brose, heather honey and whisky. Ir. brothas, mixture, medley. O'R.

brothlainn, brohlinn, n. f. heat and stink; disagreeable heat; cross - current; swelling sound (of pipes). See brolluinn. Ir. broth, fire.

brù, n. f. (gen. bronn, pl. bronnan), a belly; a big belly, a bulge; tha brù air a' bhalla, the wall bulges; a womb. O.Ir. brú, gen. bronn, dat. and ac. broinn.

bruach, n. m. a bank, a border, edge, brim, a steep; bruach an uillt, the bank of the stream; air na bruachan so, about these borders; bruach dhuine, a boor of a fellow, a stupid fellow; a small rising ground. So O.Ir. Also brú, brink, border, bank.

bruachaire, bruach'-ir'-u, n. m. a hoverer; a sullen fellow.

bruachaireachd, bruachiruchc, n. f. act of hovering, dawdling about (with a sinister purpose). So E.Ir.

bruadair, brooud'-dir, v. dream, see a vision; bhruadair mi an raoir, I dreamed last night; bhruadair mi gum faca mi, I dreamed that I saw.

bruadar, n. m. a dream, a vision. Also bruadal.

bruadaraiche, brooud'-ar-ich-u, n. m. a dreamer.

bruadrach, a. visionary; given to dreaming.

bruaillean, brooulen, n. m. trouble, disturbance, noise, tumult, offence; mental confusion, or trouble; có a tha cur bruaillean ort, who is troubling or offending you; duine gun bhruaillean, an inoffensive man; is mór am bruaillean a dhùisg thu, you have created a tumult; mar bhruaillean thonn air druim a' chuain, as the tumult of waves on the height of the ocean—tha bruaillean air aghaidh nan tom, there is boding gloom on the face of the bushes. Ir. bruaidleann, sorrow, woe. O'R.

bruailleanach, brooulenach, a. troublesome, riotous, tumultuous; noisy, disturbing; causing disturbance; annoying, grieved, vexed.

bruailleanachd, brooulenuchc, n. f. troublesomeness, the state of giving trouble or being troubled; restlessness.

bruais, v. crush, gnash.

bruan, n. m. a crumb; a morsel; shortbread, a cake made with butter, etc., to keep children quiet; v. crumble, pulverise, crush, maul. E.Ir. brúan, a fragment.

bruan, v. thrust, wound.

bruanachd, broooun'-ăchc, n. f. continued breaking or smashing; fragments.

bruanadh, vbl. n. m. act of mauling.

bruanag, broooun'-ag, n. f. a little cake, a crumb.

bruanagach, a. full of crumbs.

bruanan, n. m. a small morsel.

bruansgadh, bruanscu, vbl. n. m. crunching, crushing.

bruansgail, broooun'-scul, v. make a deep crashing, crushing noise; make a grating noise; crumble, break into fragments.

bruansgal, broooun'-scal, n. f. a crumbling noise; a grating noise.

bruanspealt, broooun'-spiălt, n. m. splinter; v. smash, hack, hew.

brùc, brook, n. f. sea-ware cast ashore in a storm. Cf. O.N. brúk, dried heaps of sea-weed.

brucach, a. speckled in the face, as a sheep; gloomy, lowering, as weather;

latha brucach, a gloomy lowering day ; caora bhrucach, a speckled sheep, a black-faced sheep ; " black and blue " (from a fall or blow). *Also* brocach.

brucachd, brooc'-uchc, *n. f.* gloominess.

brucag and bruchag, *n. f.* a chink, eyelet ; dim candle light.

brucanaich, brookanich, *n. f.* peep of day, the dawn ; bi an so 'sa bhrucanaich, be here at peep of day.

bruchag, *n. f.* a leaky boat ; a little untidy woman.

brùchd, broochc, *n. m.* a sudden rushing forth, a belch ; a disruption, or rushing forth,as a multitude ; a bulge ; rinn e brùchd, he belched ; thàinig brùchd de na daoine a mach, a rush of the people came forth ; a heap, or great quantity ; thuit brùchd de 'n mhòine, a great quantity of the peats fell ; a rush, a gush ; thàinig brùchd de 'n uisge a mach, a gush of the water came forth. *E.Ir.* brúcht, burst, belch.

brùchd, broochc, *v.* belch, rush forth, sally, bulge ; bhrùchd na daoine a mach, the men rushed forth ; tha e brùchdail, he is belching, or rifting ; gush ; bhrùchd fhuil a mach, his blood gushed or poured out. *E.Ir.* brúchtaim.

brùchdadh, broochcu, *vbl. n. m.* rushing ; bulging ; belching ; rifting ; gushing.

brùchdail, broochcul, *n. m.* belching ; rifting ; rushing ; a gush.

bruchlag, broochlag, *n. f.* a mean hovel ; a bad boat.

bruchlas, broochlas, *n. f.* fluttering of birds.

bruchorc, broo-chorc, bruth-chorcan, *n. m.* stool-bent, or dirk grass.

bruchshuil, brooch - hool, *n. f.* a bird-eye.

brùdhearg, brooyèrg, *n. m.* robin red-breast. *E.Ir.* bruinne-derg.

brugan, *n. m.* a small conical rising in the ground. *E.Ir.* brug, a lump.

brugh, *n. m.* a large house, a tumulus, a dwelling of fairies. *O.Ir.* mruig, later bruig, *gen.* broga, a palace ; manor ; sìth-brug, a fairy dwelling.

brùgh, broo, *v.* bruise, crush. *Also* brùth.

bruich, brich, *v.* boil, seethe, simmer, sod ; mellow ; *a.* boiled, seethed, simmered ; *n. f.* boiling ; the state of being boiled ; the act of boiling ; bruich e, boil it ; tha e bruich, it is boiled ; act of boiling ; tha e 'ga bhruich, he is boiling it. *E.Ir.* bruith, cooked, boiled.

bruichealachd, brichaluchc, *n. f.* warmth, sultriness.

bruicheil, brichal, *a.* sultry, warm.

bruid, brooj, *n. f.* captivity ; anguish ; great anxiety ; tha thu 'gam chumail ann am bruid, you keep me in great anxiety. *E.Ir.* broit, *gen.* broite, spoil, booty.

bruid, *v.* poke, probe ; give the hint, by touching, nudge ; bhruid e mi, he gave me the hint,—he touched me ; a' bruideadh fo'n bhruaich, probing under the bank. *Ir.* brod, goad.

brùid, brooj, *n. m.* a brute, a beast, a brutal person ; fr. the *Eng.* brute.

bruideadh, brooju, *vbl. n. m.* poking ; probing ; nudging ; a hint ; stabbing, thrusting.

bruideag, broojag, *n. f.* a little stab, prod.

brùideag, *n. f.* a little brute, or beast.

brùidealachd, broojaluchc, *n. f.* brutality ; brutishness, beastliness ; coarseness.

brùideil, broojal, *a.* brutal, beastly.

bruidhinn, bruyinn, *n. f., gen. s.* bruidhne, talk, speech, report ; conversation ; tha mi a' cluinntinn bruidhinn, I hear a talk or conversation ; tha leithid sin de bhruidhinn a measg dhaoine, there is such a report among people ; *v. i.* speak, say, talk ; bruidhinn ris, speak to him ; chan 'eil agad ach a bhi bruidhinn, you have only your talk for it ; talking, speaking.

bruidhneach, bruynach, *a.* talkative, blabbing ; loquacious ; is e siod am fear bruidhneach, what a garrulous talkative fellow he is.

bruidhneachd, bruynachc, *n. f.* talkative-ness, garrulity, loquaciousness.

bruidlich, brujlich, *v.* stir up.

brùill, brool, *v.* crumble, bruise, crush ; brùillidh mi do chnàmhan, I will crush your bones to atoms ; squeeze ; fr. brùth.

brùilleadh, broolu, *vbl. n. m.* bruising, crushing ; a squeezing, a bruising.

bruillidh, brooly, *n. m.* a man of clumsy figure, and of awkward unwieldy motion.

brùillig, broolig, *n. m.* a person of clumsy figure and gait.

bruimfheur, *n. m.* switch-grass. braim + feur.

bruinard, broonard, *a.* high-chested.

brùinidh, broony, *n. m.* the Brownie.

bruinne, brooniu, *n. f.* breast, waist.

bruinneadh, brooniu, *n. m.* the front. *O.Ir.* bruinne, breast. *O.Celt.* brondâ, brondjo-.

bruinngheal, broon-yal, *a.* white-bellied.

brùite, brootu, *vbl. a.* bruised, broken, oppressed, sad, crushed ; daoine brùite truagh, poor oppressed men ; iadsan a tha brùite 'n an spiorad, they who are contrite in their spirit ; fuil bhrùite, extravasated blood. *E.Ir.* brúim, crush, break.

bruiteach, *a.* warm, sultry. *O.Ir.* bruth,

heat, fever, fervour, glowing metal. *O.Celt.* brutu-.

bruith, *v.* boil, cook. So *Ir.*

brunsgal, broonscul, *n. m.* rumbling noise ; fr. brù. *McB.*

brusg, broosc, *n. m.* a crumb ; a particle of food. *E.Ir.* brus, refuse of corn, loppings of trees ; brusgar, crumbs.

brusgach, *a.* diminutive, trifling.

brusgach, *a.* shaggy, unkempt. *E.Ir.* brosc, gross, stout, large.

brutach, brootuch, *n. m.* the act of digging.

brutag, *n. f.* a worm.

bruth, broo, *n. m.* the dwelling of fairies in a hill ; a house half under the surface ; a cave. *See* brugh.

brùth, broo, *v.* bruise, crush, pulverise ; pound ; bruthaidh esan do cheann agus bruthaidh tusa a shàil-san, it shall bruise thy head, and thou shalt bruise his heel. *E.Ir.* brúim, I smash, bruise.

bruthach, broohuch, *n. m.* and *f.* an acclivity, ascent, a steep, a hill-side, a bank ; a' dol suas am bruthach, ascending the acclivity or ascent ; thug e a' bhruthach air, he took to his heels ; le bruthach, downwards ; ri bruthach, ascending, upwards ; fo chreig a' bhruthaich, under the rock of the steep ; ruithidh an taigeas féin le bruthach, the haggis itself will run downwards. *Cf. E.Ir.* brúach (dissyl.) edge, brink, bank.

bruthachail, broo-uchol, *a.* steep, full of rising grounds or eminences.

bruthadair, broo-uder, *n. m.* a pounder, a pestle ; a bruiser or crusher.

bruthadh, broo-u, *vbl. n. m.* a contusion, a bruise ; act of bruising, crushing ; pounding. *E.Ir.* brúim.

bruthainn, broohinn, *n. f.* sultry heat, sultriness. *See* bruiteach. *Cf. E.Ir.* brothal, heat, sultriness.

bruthainneach, broohinnuch, *a.* sultry ; warm ; aimsir bhruthainneach, sultry weather.

bruthainneachd, *n. f.* sultriness.

bruthais, broo-hish, and bruthaist, broo-hesht, *n. f.* brose.

bu ! *int.* a sound to excite fear in children.

bu, *pret. indic.* of the verb to be ; bu i, bu e, bu iad, contracted b'i, b'e, b'iad, it was he, it was she, it was they ; it is always contracted before f aspirated ; as, b' fhearr leam, b' fhasa, I would prefer, it would be easier; b, g, m, p, are aspirated after bu ; as, ged bu bhàrd e, though he was a bard. nach bu gheur e, how sharp it was, etc. ; bu mhiosa e, it was worse, he was

worse ; bu phailt 1ad, they were plentiful. *O.Ir.* bu.

buabhall, boouvul, *n. f.* a cow-stall. *Also* bualla.

buabhall, boouvul, *n. m.* a unicorn, a buffalo ; buabhall, horns. *E.Ir.* búaball, wild ox ; bugle-horn, cornet, a wind instrument, a trumpet. *Lat.* būbalus.

buac, *v.* work lime and gravel into mortar ; work clay, etc.

buacadh, *vbl. n. m.* working lime, clay, etc.

buachaille, boouchilu, *n. m.* a cowherd, a herd, a shepherd. *O.Ir.* bóchaill, gl. *bobulcus. W.* bugail. *Gr.* βουκόλος, a cowherd. *O.Celt.* bou-kali-, boukaljo-.

buachailleachd, boouchiluchc, *n. f.* herding, tending cattle, the occupation of a herd.

buachaillich, boouchilich, *v.* tend, herd, watch, or keep cattle.

buachair, *v.* bedaub with dung.

buachar, *n. m.* cow-dung, dung. *E.Ir.* bóchar.

buadh, *n. f.* an attribute, quality, virtue, power, faculty. *See* buaidh.

buadhach, *a.* victorious, triumphant ; highly gifted; having inherent qualities; efficient, talented ; pleasant ; profitable ; là buadhach, a pleasant day ; leasan buadhach, a profitable lesson. *E.Ir.* búadach, victorious, prevailing.

buadhachadh, *vbl. n. m.* the act of gaining the ascendant ; succeeding well in anything ; conquering, overcoming, winning, gaining ground.

buadhachail, *a.* triumphant, victorious, overcoming, subduing.

buadhachas, *n. m.* the ascendancy, superiority ; success, victory.

buadhaich, *v.* overcome, gain the victory, prevail, subdue, overthrow, subject, triumph.

buadhaiche, *n. m.* a victor.

buadhail, boughal, *a.* victorious, triumphant.

buadhalachd, *n.* superiority, ascendant, mastery.

buadhmhoireachd, *n. f.* the mastery, ascendant, superiority ; victoriousness.

buadhmhor, *a.* triumphant, victorious, successful, gaining the ascendant.

buaghair, *n. m.* a herd ; thachair orra buaghair bhó, a cowherd met them ; fr. bu + aoghair.

buaghallan, *n. m.* groundsel, ragwort, or ragweed ; stinking ragwort, buaghallan buidhe. *Also* buadhghallan. *Ir.* buathbhallan, " virtue-wort " (?) *E.Ir.* buafallán, toad-wort ; buaf = toad (*Lh.*).

buagharra, *a.* sulky, boisterous.

buaic, *n. f.* the wick of a candle or lamp, a greased rag, fr. the *Eng.*

buaic, *n. f.* cow dung, with which green linens are steeped preparatory to bleaching; bleaching lees; conglomerate mass; a coarse person.

buaiceach, *a.* giddy.

buaicean, *n. m.* a little wick.

buaicean-iall, *n. m.* tallow to rub a thong for sewing.

buaicneach, *n. f.* smallpox.

buaidh, boo-ay, *n. f. (gen. s.* buadha, *n. pl.* buadhan), victory, conquest, success, palm; endowments, qualifications, talents, accomplishments; deagh bhuadhan nàduir, excellent, natural endowments or talents; virtue, attribute; tha buaidh air an uisge bheatha, whisky has a virtue in it; fear nam buadh, the man of talents or accomplishments. *O.Ir.* búaid. *Also* bóid (later búad), victory, prize, grace (gift). *See Z².* *O.Celt.* boudi-.

buaidh-chaithream, *n. f.* shout of victory.

buaidhfhacal, *n. m.* an adjective.

buaidh-ghàir, *n. f.* shout of victory.

buaidhghuth, *n. m.* shout of victory.

buaidh-làrach, *n. m.* decisive victory.

buaidh-shìthne, *n. f.* victorious peace.

buaidheam, *n. f.* fits of inconstancy.

buaidhear, bua-yer, *n. m.* a conqueror, a victor.

buaidhearachd, buayerachc, *n. f.* triumph, victory; coming off victoriously.

buaigheal, booa-yal, *n. f.* a cow-stall.

buail, booul, *v. t.* strike, beat, smite; bhuail e mi, he struck; thrash, as sheaf corn; beetle, as lint; tha iad a' bualadh 'san t-sabhal, they are thrashing in the barn; tha iad a' bualadh an lìn, they are beetling the lint; attack, fall to, belabour; bhuail iad oirnn, they attacked us; bhuail chuige Deargo, Dargo rushed towards him; buailibh clàrsach, strike up the harp; bhuail e tìr, he touched land; knock; buail an dorus, knock at the door. *E.Ir.* bualaim.

buaile, booulu, *n. f., pl.* buailtean, a circle; a fold for black cattle; a' bhó as miosa a tha 'sa' bhuaile is i as àirde geum, the worst cow in the fold gives the loudest low; buailtean spréidhe, herds of cattle. *O.Ir.* búale, enclosure, cattlefold; kine. *Lat.* bovile.

buaileach, booul'-uch, *a.* belonging to a fold.

buaileag, *n. f.* a small circle.

buailte, booultiu, *vbl. a.* struck, thrashed.

buailteach, *a.* subject to, liable to; buailteach do iomadh cunnart, subject to, or liable to many dangers; apt to strike, or quarrelsome.

buailteach, *n. m.* 1. booth, or huts for shielings. 2. *a.* rich in cattle-folds.

buailtean, booulten, *n. m.* that part of a flail that strikes the corn.

buailtear, booulter, *n. m.* a thrasher.

buain, boo-uin, *n. f., gen. s.* buana, reaping, harvest; a' dol thun na buana, going to the reaping or harvest; a' bhuain eòrna, barley harvest; am na buana, harvest-time, or reaping-time; cut, pull; a' buain na mòna, cutting the peats; a' buain shlat, cutting twigs; a' buain chnù, pulling or gathering nuts. *O.Ir.* búain, *inf.* of bongaim, reap.

buain, *v.* reap, shear, cut, hew, pluck, pull; am fear nach dean cur ri là fuar, cha dean e buain ri là teth, he that will not sow on a cold day, will not reap on a warm one.

buaine, boo-uniu, *compar.* of buan, lasting, durable; lasting; is buaine na gach nì an nàire, shame is more lasting than anything else; *n. f.* durability, durableness. *E.Ir.* búane, lastingness.

buainead, boo-uniud, *abstr. n. m.* degree of durability or lastingness; durability.

buainte, boountu, *vbl. a.* shorn, reaped, cut, pulled.

buair, boo'-ur, *v.* trouble or make muddy, as water; bhuair thu an t-uisge, you have made the water muddy; tempt, allure, provoke, annoy, tease, disturb; an uair a bhuair bhur n-aithrichean mi, when your fathers tempted me. *O.Ir.* búadraim, *turbo,* din t-sruth búadarthu, *turbatus;* gl. de turbulento rivo.

buaireadair, boo'uruder, *n. m.* a tempter. *E.Ir.* búaidertóir, a jangler.

buaireadh, boo'uru, *vbl. n. m.* provocation, disturbance, annoyance; severe trial; a temptation, a quarrel; scolding match.

buaireanta, boour-ant-u, *a.* given to tempting; causing trouble, quarrelling.

buaireas, boour'-as, *n. m.* tumult, an uproar, confusion, disturbance, trouble, ferment; fo bhuaireas, troubled, annoyed; a' cur buaireas am measg nan daoine, creating a disturbance or tumult among the people.

buaireasach, boo-urasuch, *a.* annoying, disturbing, creating a tumult; inflaming the passions, tumultuous, provoking; deoch bhuaireasach, drink that inflames, or maddens.

buaireasachd, *n. f.* turbulence of temper or disposition; tumultuousness; turbulence, boisterousness; storminess.

buairte, boo'urtiu, *vbl. a.* disturbed, confused; troubled or made muddy, as water; tempted, enraged, provoked.

bualachd, booul'-ăchc, *n.f.* a drove. *O.Ir.* búale, kine.
bualadh, booul'-u, *vbl. n. m.* thrashing, beetling ; striking, beating, knocking.
bualaidh, booul'-y, *n. f.* cow-stall ; *deriv.* fr. búale, kine.
bualan. *See* buaghallan.
bualla, *n. m.* cow-stall.
bualtrach, *n. f.* cow dung. Cf. *E.Ir.* búalta, excrement.
buamasdair, boo'umusder, *n. m.* a blockhead, a turbulent fellow, a noisy fool ; " dh'fhàgadh tu buamasdair treubhach," you would put mettle in a blockhead. Cf. buath, madness, mad frolic.
buamasdaireachd, *n. f.* stupidity ; turbulence ; boasting ; clumsy half-wit ; blundering conduct.
buan, *a.* lasting, durable ; cruaidh mar am fraoch, buan mar an darach, hard as the oak, lasting as the pine ; tedious ; rathad buan, a tedious road or way. *E.Ir.* búan, lasting constant.
buan-chuimhne,* *n. f.* lasting remembrance.
buan-mhaireannach, *a.* lasting, durable.
buan-mhaireannachd, *n. f.* durability.
buan-sheas, *v.* persevere.
buan-sheasamh, *n. m.* perseverance.
buanachadh, buan'-ăch-u, *vbl. n. m.* perseverance, continuing, persevering ; lasting.
buanaich, booun'-ich, *v.* continue, abide, endure, last, persevere. *E.Ir.* búanaigim, I persevere.
buanaiche, booun'-ich-u, *n. m.* a shearer, a reaper.
buanas, *n. m.* durability, perseverance.
buanna, *n. m., pl.* buannachan, a billeted soldier, champions billeted on the people at will ; a mercenary developed into a parasite ; an idler, a straggler ; sè buannachan deug Mhic Domhnaill, MacDonald's sixteen " bullies."
buannachail, booun'-năch-al, *a.* beneficial, useful, advantageous.
buannachas, booun'-năch-us, *n. f.* free quarters of soldiers, in place of rent.
buannachd, booun'-năchd, *n. f.* benefit, profit, gain, emolument.
buannachdach, booun'-năchc-uch, *a.* profitable, beneficial, useful.
buannachdail, booun'-nuchc-al, *a.* beneficial, profitable, useful.
buannaich, booun'-ich, *v.* gain, profit, acquire, win, reap benefit from.
buantas, *n. f.* duration.
buar, *n. m.* cattle, kine. *E.Ir.* búar. *Lat.* bovarius, boarius.

* For pronunciation of compounds see separate members elsewhere.

buarach, *n. f.* cow's fetters ; shackles on the hind legs of a cow while milking. So *E.Ir.* bu (cow) + àrach (spancel).
buarach na baoibhe, *n. f.* lamprey, an eel supposed to possess magical powers.
buath, boou, *n. m.* madness, rage.
buathadh, *n. m.* a rushing, a fit of rage.
buatham, boo-uhum, *n. m.* deaf person's guess, often ludicrous (leaning on buath).
bùb, *v.* blubber, as a child ; weep in a most melancholy way ; *n. m.* a roar, a yell.
bùbail, boobil, *n. f.* blubbering.
bùbaire, boobiru, *n. m.* a person that blubbers.
bùbaireachd, boob'-ir'-uchc, *n. f.* blubbering.
bùban, booban, *n. m., pl.* bùbain, a coxcomb.
bùbanachd, *n. f.* a pimple, pustule, a bucket.
bùbarsaich, boobursich, *n. f.* blubbering.
bucach, bookuch, *n. m.* a boy. Founded on *Lat.* bucca. *McB.*
bucaid, bookej, *n. f.* a pimple ; a boil ; a bucket. *E.Ir.* boccóit, spot, boss of shield. *Lat. buccatus,* fr. bucca. *McB.*
bucaideach, booc'-ej-uch, *a.* full of pimples.
bucall, bookul, *n. m., pl.* bucaill, a buckle.
bucallach, *a.* abounding in buckles.
bùchainn, boochin, *a.* melodious.
bùchallach, boochuluch, *a.* nestling, melodious.
bùchd, boochc, *n. m.* bulk, size ; the cover of a book.
buchdail, boochcal, *a.* bulky.
buclaich, booc-lich, *v.* buckle on.
bucsa, boocsu, *n. m.* boxwood. So *Ir.*
budagochd, boodugok, *n. m.* snipe ; woodcock.
budhag, boo'ag, *n. f.* a bundle of straw.
budhaigir, boo'ugir, *n. m.* a puffin ; coulter-neb. *Also* bùigire, budhaid.
budhailt, boo'elt, *n. f.* recess in a wall ; a wall press in a cottage.
bugarnach, boogurnuch, *n. m.* a sturdy well-fared lump of a boy. *Also* bugalach.
bughall, boo'ul, *n. m.* a pot-hook. *Also* bùlais, bùileasg.
buicean, booiken, *n. m.* a pimple, a pustule ; a little buck, roe ; *transf.* small bundle or load.
buiceanach, booikenuch, *a.* full of pimples or pustules ; breaking out in pimples.
buiceis, booikesh, *n. f.* sporting like a buck. *Also* buicil, sporting of lambs, etc. *See* boc.
buideal, boojal, *n. m.* a cask, an anker, a bottle ; a fat person ; mar bhuideal anns an toit, as a bottle in the smoke. *E.Ir.* buidél.

buidealaich, boojalich, *n. f.* a conflagration ; a blaze ; topsy-turvy ; is ann an sin a tha bhuidealaich, what a conflagration is there ; chaidh e 'na bhuidealaich, it blazed ; boiling with rage. *Ir.* buite, fire ; buitelach, big fire. *Lh. O.Ir.* bótt, fire. *O.Celt.* bouzdo-.

buidhe, booyu, *a.* yellow ; falt buidhe, yellow hair. *O.Ir.* buide. *O.Celt.* bodio-s. *Lat. badius. Eng.* bay.

buidhe, *n. m.* a buoy, a float.

buidhe, *a.* grateful, pleasing ; bu bhuidhe leis na rùisg itheadh, he would fain eat the husks or peelings ; ged bu bhuidhe leat, in spite of you, *i.e.* " though it should please you." *O.Ir.* bude, buide, thanks, pleasure ; buidigim, to thank, be pleased.

buidheach, booyuch, *a.* pleased, satisfied, contented ; grateful, thankful ; chan 'eil e buidheach, he is displeased ; bi buidheach, be grateful or thankful ; tha mi buidheach, I am satisfied ; tha e buidheach, he has eaten his fill. *O.Ir.* buidech, Ml. gl. *contentus.*

buidheach, *n. f.* the jaundice. *E.Ir.* budechar.

buidheachas, booyuchus, *n. m.* thanksgiving, gratitude ; thanks ; thoir buidheachas, return thanks, express your gratitude ; the state of being bought, but the bargain not concluded ; abeyance ; fo bhuidheachas, or am buidheachas, in abeyance. *E.Ir.* budechas.

buidhead, booyud, *abstr. n. f.* yellowness.

buidheag, booyag, *n. f.* anything yellow ; the yellow-hammer ; a goldfinch ; a buttercup. (*E.Ir.* budén.)

buidheagan, booyagan, *n. m.* the yolk of an egg.

buidheann, booyun, *n. f.* a company, a troop, a gang, band, a party; buidheann shaighdearan, a company or party of soldiers ; *gen. s.* buidhne ; *pl.* buidhnean, buidhnichean, parties, etc. *O.Ir.* buden, troop, band ; *pl.* buidne.

buidhe-ruadh, *a.* of a bay colour, auburn.

buidhinn, booyinn, *n. m.* gain, profit, emolument ; quarrying stones ; is dona a' bhuidhinn a tha air na clachan sin, these stones are not properly quarried. *E.Ir.* buidne, profit.

buidhinn, *v. t.* gain, win, acquire, get the better of ; bhuidhinn sinn bàir, we gained a goal ; quarry. Related to *Sc. win ; winning* hay.

buidhinneach, *n. f.* a quarry.

buidhneach, booynach, *a.* in troops or companies ; numerous ; na laoich bhuidhneach, mhór, the high-minded, numerous heroes; victorious.

buidhnich, booynich, *v.* arrange into companies.

buidhre, booiru, *compar.* of bodhar, more or most deaf; *n. f.* deafness, degree of deafness. *E.Ir.* buidre. (*O.Ir.* bodar, *surdus.*) *O.W.* bydderi.

buidileir, boojiler, *n. m.* a butler. fr. *Eng.*

buidileireachd, boojileruchc, *n. m.* work of a butler.

buidseach, boojsh'-uch, *n. f.* a witch, a wizard ; is buidseach i, she is a witch ; is buidseach e, he is a wizard ; fr. *Eng.* witch.

buidseachas, boojsh'-uch-us, *n. m.* witchcraft, sorcery.

buidseachd, boojsh'ăchc, *n. f.* witchcraft, sorcery. *Also* buisneachd.

buige, boogiu, *n. f.* softness ; humidity ; effeminacy ; flatness in music ; *compar.* of bog ; ni's buige, softer, more effeminate. *E.Ir.* buce.

buigead, boogiud, *abstr. n. f.* degree of softness, softness.

buigean, boogen, *n. m.* soft, effeminate fellow.

buigeanag, booginag, *n. f.* any soft lump ; a soft crab ; an egg with undeveloped shell ; a soft, cowardly fellow. *Also* buigearnach. *R.D.*

buigileag, boogilag, *n. f.* a crab after casting the shell ; a soft unmanly person ; a quagmire.

buiginn, *n. f.* morass, marshy ground.

buil, bool, *n. f.* consequence, effect, result ; is léir a bhuil, the result is obvious ; tha a' bhuil sin air, the effect of that is obvious on him or it ; an rud a nithear gu ceart chìtear a bhuil, when a thing is properly done, the result must tell ; use, application, completion, end ; a thoirt fhacail gu buil, to complete or fulfil his word ; make good use of it, apply it properly ; buil cheart a dheanamh dheth, to make proper improvement or application of it. *Ir.* boil, issue, success, use. *E.Ir.* bail, excellence, success.

buileach, booluch, *a.* complete, whole, total, entire ; the word has the force of *superl. deg.* ; tha e buileach dona, he is thoroughly bad ; tha sin buileach nàr, that is most shameful ; is buileach a chaill thu air, you lost completely on it ; *adv.* entirely, completely, wholly ; gu buileach is gu bràth, wholly and for ever ; thrifty ; bean bhuileach, a thrifty wife, who lets nothing to waste ; stingy ; economy degenerating into stinginess. *Ir.* bailech, prosperous ; bailigim, I husband.

buileachadh, *vbl. n. m.* act of bestowing ; granting ; improving ; finishing completely ; **a' buileachadh ort,** bestowing on you.

buileastair, boolaster, *n. m.* a bullace, sloe ; fr. the *Eng.*

builg, boolig, *v.* bubble, blister ; rise, as a fish in the water ; rise to the fly ; **a' builgeadh,** bubbling ; distemper in cattle.

builg, *n. m., gen. s.* and *n. pl.* of **bolg,** a sack, bag.

builgeadh, boolgu, *vbl. n. m.* act of bubbling, blistering.

builgeag, boolgiag, *n. f.* a blister, a bubble.

builgeagach, boolgiaguch, blistered.

builgean, boolgen, *n. m.* a blister, a little bag, a globule on liquid.

builgeanach, boolgenuch, *a.* full of blisters ; of bubbles.

builgeasach, *a.* spotted, blistered.

builich, boolich, *v. t.* grant, bestow, improve ; **gach ni a bhuilich Dia ort,** everything God hath bestowed on thee ; finish completely ; **builich an latha,** finish the day completely.

builionn, booliun, *n. f.* a loaf.

builionnaiche, booliunichu, *n. m.* a baker.

buillbheirt, *n. m.* tackle, instruments.

buillceasach, *a. See* builgeasach. *R.D.*

buille, booliu, *n. m.* a stroke, blow, a knock ; **buille air a' bhuille,** blow for blow. *E.Ir.* buille. *O.Celt.* boldjâ.

builleach, booliuch, *a.* apt to strike, given to dealing blows.

builleachas, booliuchus, *n. f.* striking ; hesitating ; on the point of deciding.

buille-choilleig, *n. f.* stroke in shinty.

buille-trot, *n. m.* compulsion, cowed (obedience at the expense of a whipping).

buillsgean, bool-shgen, *n. m.* the middle, the centre ; **am buillsgean an teine,** in the centre of the fire ; *Ir.* buillsgéin, middle, midriff, and also **boilscéan,** the navel (*O'R.*) ; **bolsgen,** middle, centre. *K.M.*

buin, booin, *v. t.* touch, handle, be related to, belong to ; meddle ; **na buin da sin,** do not touch that ; **buinidh iad da chéile,** they are related to each other ; **is ann do Dhia a bhuineas slàinte,** to God belongs salvation ; deal with ; tear from ; **buin gu coibhneil ri mo ghaol,** deal gently with my love ; **cò dha a bhuineas so ?** to whom does this belong ? **cha bhuin e dhuitse,** it does not belong to you ; **comhairle clag Sgàin :** " **an rud nach buin duit na buin dà,**" the advice of the bell of Scone, —the thing that does not belong to you, meddle not with. *See* bean, to touch.

buinne, booniu, *n. m., pl.* buinneachan,

a rapid current ; a tidal current ; a current in a river ; " **snàmh air buinne sruith fior-uisg,**" swimming in the current of a crystal stream ; confluence ; a pool in a river ; **air buinne réidh,** on a smooth pool. *E.Ir.* buinne, a wave ; a rapid river.

bùinne, *n. m.* a statue, a bust ; one that stands stock-still ; **is tu am bùinne,** you stand stock-still, like a statue.

buinneach, *n. f.* a flux ; a diarrhœa, dysentery ; *a.* contemptible, abominable ; **duine buinneach,** a contemptible person ; fr. **buinne.** So *Ir.*

buinneag, boonug, *n. f.* dockan, twig ; a maid ; *Ir.* **buinneog,** sapling, twig. *O'R.*

buinnig, *v.* win. *See* buidhinn. **buingim,** I arrive, profit. So *O'R.*

buinnire, booniru, *n. m.* a footman.

buinnteach, bùinnt'-tyach, *n. f.* leather for soles ; the thickest part of a hide ; fr. bonn.

bùir, boor, *v.* bellow, as a bull ; roar. *E.Ir.* bùirim.

buirbe, boorbu, *n. f.* turbulence, a fierce, boisterous temper ; boisterousness ; rage, fury, ferocity, barbarity ; fr. borb.

buirbeachd, boorbachc, *n. f.* turbulence, extreme degree of rage or wrath, boisterousness, savageness.

buirbein, boorben, *n. m.* a cancer ; a savage.

bùird, boorj, *n. f.* mockery ; **cuis-bhùird,** object of ridicule, a butt. *See* bùrt.

buirdeiseach, boorjesh-uch, *n. m.* a boarder, an idler ; a burgess, a citizen ; an inhabitant ; **buirdeisich sgiathach nan speur,** the winged inhabitants of the sky. *M.Ir.* buirgéisech.

bùire, buireadh, booru, *n. m.* act of roaring ; a rutting-place of deer ; burst of grief, a wailing. *E.Ir.* **bùir-fedach,** roaring.

bùireineach, boorenuch, *a.* bellowing.

bùirich, boorich, *n. f.* roaring as a bull, bellowing ; wailing.

buirleadh, boorlu', *n. m.* language of folly and ridicule.

bùirseach, boorshuch, *n. m.* deluge of rain ; rousing fire.

buiseal, *n. m.* a bushel ; fr. the *Eng.*

buisean, booshen, *n. m.* a little mouth.

buisinn-iall, *n. m.* a horn for holding tallow.

bùit, booit, *a.* bashful.

bùiteach, bootiuch, *n. f.* a threat.

buitseach, bootshuch, *n. f.* a witch.

bùla, *n. m.* a pot-hook. *Also* **bùlais.**

bùlas, *n. m.* pot-hook ; fr. *Sc.* bools.

bulg, *pl.* **builg,** *n. m.* a belly, a lump ; a form of bolg.

bulgach, *a.* convex ; blistered.

bulla, *n. m.* a bowl, ball.

bumailear, *n. m.* a booby, blockhead, a clumsy fellow, bungler ; fr. *Sc.* **bummeler,** bungler. *McB.*

bun, boon, *n. m.* 1. root. 2. a stock. 3. bottom. 4. a stump ; **bun na craoibhe,** the root or stump of the tree ; **spìon as a bhun e,** root it out ; **bun na beinne,** the bottom of the hill ; **bun an earbaill,** the rump ; **bun na h-àltrach,** the foot of the altar ; dependance, trust, confidence ; **na dèan bun á gàirdean feòla,** place no dependence or confidence in an arm of flesh ; **cha 'n fhàg e bun no barr,** he will leave neither root nor branch ; **bun os cionn,** upside down, topsy-turvy ; **am bun an tighe,** taking care of the house ; **bun eich,** an old stump of a horse. *E.Ir.* bun. *O.Celt.* bonu-.

bunabhas, boonavas, *n. m.* an element ; buttock ; fr. **bun.**

bunach, boonuch, *n. m.* coarse tow. *See* **barrach,** *a.* of or belonging to roots.

bunachainnt, boonuchent, *n. f.* etymology.

bunachar, *n. m.* dependence, confidence, trust ; **na dèan bunachar sam bith á sin,** place no dependence on that ; **chan 'eil bunachar eile agam,** I have nothing else to depend on. Cf. *E.Ir.* **bun-chor** ; **bunchar,** root, foundation.

bunachas, boonuchus, *n. f.* principle, foundation.

bunachasach, *a.* radical, fundamental.

bunadas, boonudus, *n. m.* origin, foundation, stock. *O.Ir.* **bunud,** inclainnd **bunid,** the original clan. *Wb.* 5[b]. *O.Celt.* bonuto-.

bunadh, boonu, *n. m.* a stump, a stub ; survivor ; **an aona bhunadh,** the only one left (and poor at that).

bunaich, boonich, *v. i.* depend on ; found, establish.

bunailt, boonelt, *n. f.* constancy, steadiness, inflexibility ; firmness.

bunailteach, booneltuch, *a.* stationary, fixed in one place ; established, sure, steady ; **a bheil e bunailteach 'san àite sin,** is he stationary or established in that place ? attentive ; **bunailteach aig a ghnothuch,** attentive to his business.

bunailteachd, booneltuchc, *n. f.* constancy, firmness, steadiness ; fixedness ; inflexibility.

bunait, boonej, *n. f.* foundation, a basis.

bunaiteach, boon'-äj-ach, *a.* stationary, fixed, steadfast, immovable.

bunaiteachd, boonejuchc. *See* **bunailteachd.**

bunaitich, boonejich, *v.* settle, fix your abode, inherit, inhabit.

bunamas, boonumus, *n. m.* discernment, sense.

bunamhas, *n. m.* a principle, a fundamental.

bunan, *n. m.* a little root.

bunanta, boonantu, *a.* strong, stout, firm, well set, having a good foundation.

bunantachd, boonantuchc, *n. f.* sturdiness, firmness.

bunasach, boonasuch, *a.* steady, firm.

bun-chiall, boon-chiul, *n. m.* root meaning ; a moral meaning.

bun-chùis, *n. f.,* a principle ; a first cause.

bundàidh, boondāy, *n. f.* kind of weaving.

bun-dubh, *n. m.* root underground ; fern root, root of barley cut off for thatch.

bungaid, boongej, *n. f.* a clumsy fat woman, a sullen dour person, a hussy.

bun-luchd, boon-loochc, *n. m.* original inhabitants ; aborigines. So *O'R.*

bunndaist, boondesht, *n. f.* a perquisite, a bounty ; grassum, fee, wages ; payment in kind ; " **liuthad poca bunndaist,**" the many bags of perquisites. *R.D.* **choisinn le bunndaist am pàidheadh,** deserved payment in kind. *I.Lom.* fr. the *Eng.* poundage ; *Eng.* -age becomes -aist in Gaelic.

bunnlum, boonlum, *n. m.* steadiness.

bunnsach, boonsuch, *n. m.* a rod, twig. *E.Ir.* bunsach, rod, playing-pole.

bunnsach, *n. m.* a sudden rush ; fr. **buinne,** current.

bunnsaidh, boonsy, *a.* firm, steady.

bunntainn, boontin, *n. f.* dealing, belonging to, taking away, touching (fr. **bean).**

bunntam, boontam, *n. f.* solidity, firmness.

bunntamas, boontumus, *n. m.* sense, solidity. Cf. *Ir.* **buntomhas.**

buntàta, *n. m.* potato.

burabhuachaill, burrabhuchaill, boorravuchil, *n. m.* the sea-bird called the Holland auk, northern diver ; for **muir + buachaill,** " sea-lad."

bùrach, booruch, *n. m.* searching or turning up the earth ; delving, digging. Cf. *Eng.* burrow.

buragadair, *n. m.* purgatory. *See* **purgadair.**

bùraich, boorich, *v.* howk, dig lightly and irregularly.

bùraiche, boorichu, *n. m.* a delver, a digger, a hoe, a mattock.

bùraidh, boory, *a.* mouldy, as land ; easily dug or delved.

bùraidheachd, booryachc, *n. f.* mouldiness.

burban, boorban, *n. m.* wormwood, leaning on **borb.**

bùrd, boord, *n. m.* a hum.

bùrdan, *n. m.* a humming noise, grumbling, muttering ; a gibe, sing-song. *Sh.*

bùrdanach, *a.* humming, grumbling, muttering, prone to grumble.

burgaid, boorgaj, *n. f.* a purge, physic. *Lat.* purgo.

burgaid, boorgej, *n. m.* an awkward or noisy fellow ; a fit of temper.

burgaideach, boorgejuch, *a.* clownish.

burgaidich, *v.* purge.

burmaid, boormej, *n. m.* wormwood ; fr. the *Eng.*

bùrn, boorn, *n. m.* fresh water ; sàl is bùrn, salt water and fresh water ; ni bùrn salach làmhan glan, foul water makes clean hands.

bùrnach, *a.* watery.

bùrnlam, boornlam, *n. m.* a flood, a downpour.

burracaid, boorrukej, *n. f.* a stupid female ; a silly woman.

burrach, *a.* heavily mouthed. *E.Ir.* borr, bloated, large.

burradh, booru', *n. m.* a bout, a nasty attack (of illness). Cf. **purradh.**

burraidh, boory, *n. m.* a bully ; a fool. *E.Ir.* burr, a clown, a boor.

burrail, booral, *v.* romp, as children ; play rudely.

burral, *n. m.* a deep-toned howl, or weeping ; wailing, burst of grief.

burralach, *a.* crying ; apt to whine or howl.

burraladh, booralu, *vbl. n. m.* romping ; rude play, noisy play.

burralaich, booralich, *n. f.* continued howling, wailing, or lamentation.

burras, booras, *n. m.* caterpillar.

burrasgadh, boorasgu', *n. m.* a fit of rage.

burrasgaireachd, boorasgirachc, *n. f.* rage, brutality.

burrghlas, boorughlas, *n. f.* a torrent of brutal rage.

burrghlasach, *a.* brutally passionate.

bùrsach, boorsuch, *n. m.* a torrent of rain ; a stormy fellow.

bursaid, boorsej, *n. f.* worsted.

bùrt, boorst, *n. m.* mockery, sport, ridicule. *Sc.* bourd. fr. *Fr.* bourde, a game.

bururas, *n. m.* a harsh or gurgling noise, infant purling.

bururasach, *a.* harsh, grating, purling.

bus, *n. m.* a mouth, especially that of a beast ; a mouth with very protruding pouting lips. *E.Ir.* buss, lip. *O.Celt.* bussu.

busach, boosuch, *a.* pouting-lipped ; having protruding lips ; sulky.

busachd, boosachc, *n. f.* the deformity of blubber-lips.

busag, boosag, *n. f.* a smacking kiss ; blow on the lips.

busaire, boosiru, *n. m.* a man having pouting-lips ; a sullen fellow.

bus-dubh, *n. m.* a black mouth, or snout ; black as to the muzzle. Name of common terrier.

busg, boosc, *v.* thread a fishing-hook. *Sc. Eng.* busk. Also **reidhleadh.**

busgadh, booscu, *n. m.* threading or splicing a hook to fishing line.

busgaid, boosgej, *n. m.* bustle.

bustail, boostal, *n. f.* puffing, blowing.

buta, bootu, *n. m.* difference in price ; difference, surplus ; boot, fr. *M.E.*

butadh, bootu, *n. m.* a push, nudge. *See* putadh.

butag, *n. f.* oar pin. *See* putag.

butarrais, booturesh, *n. f.* confused mixture, hotch-potch ; mess.

bùth, boo, *n. m., pl.* bùithean, and bùitean, a tent ; a cot ; a shop ; shuidhich e bhùth, he pitched his tent ; sròl as a' bhùth, satin from the shop ; an ant-hill. *Eng.* booth. *O.N.* búð.

bùthach, boo-hach, *n. f.* snare for birds and rabbits.

buthailt, bu-elt, *n. f.* a nook, private keeping-place ; poor bowels.

buthainn, boo-hin, *n. m.* long straw used for thatch ; *v.* thump, beat lustily.

buthainnich, boo-hinich, *v.* thrash, bang, thump.

C

c, the third letter of the alphabet ; called call, or calltuinn, the hazel-tree.

c' for cia, ca, *pron. interr.* ; thus, c'àite for cia àite, c' ainm a thoirt ? what is your name ? for cia ainm ——

cà, ca, where ? com. in gl. as by-form of cia ; as also co, ce.

cab, *v.* notch ; hack, indent ; chab thu an sgian, you have notched the knife.

cab, *n. m.* a mouth with broken teeth, or ill set with teeth ; a notch, a gap. Cf. *Eng.* gap, gab.

cabach, *a.* having broken teeth ; notched, gapped ; given to tattling, tell-tale.

càbach, *a.* abounding in gaps, toothless.

cabadair, cabuder, *n. m.* a man who keeps no secret.

cabadh, cabu', *vbl. n. m.* act of indenting, notching ; indenting the edge.

càbag, *n. f.* a cheese ; kebboch.
cabag, *n. f.* a female with broken teeth ; a hacked instrument, as a knife, etc. ; a tattling, prating female.
cabaire, cabiru, *n. m.* a fellow with broken teeth ; tattler ; a prating fellow.
cabaireachd, cabiruchc, *n. f.* the practice of tattling or prating.
cabais, cabesh, *n. f.* the prating, prattling, or babbling ; fr. cab.
cabaist, cabesht, *n. m.* cabbage ; fr. the *Eng.*
càball, cāb'-ull, *pl.* càbaill, *n. m.* a cable ; fr. the *Eng. Ir.* cábla.
cabar, *n. m.* a pole ; rafter on the roof of a house ; an antler or a deer's horn ; cabar fèidh, the antler of a deer.
cabarach, *a.* well supplied with antlers or rafters ; gu cabarach, well supplied with antlers ; *n. pl.* deer ; an déidh chabarach, in pursuit of deer ; a thicket ; mar astar doill an cabarach, as a blind man's progress through a thicket.
cabar-coille, *n. m.* wood - grouse, the capercailzie.
cabasdar, cabstar, *n. m.* a bit, a curb. Cf. *Lat.* capistrum, a halter.
cabh, cav, *v. n.* drift ; tha cur is cabhadh ann, it is snowing and drifting ; dial. form of caith, cast.
cabhachan, cavachan, *n. m.* the bird, cuckoo-titterer.
cabhadh, cava, *vbl. n. m.* act of throwing, casting ; a driving snow-storm ; drifting ; cabhadh-làir, light snow swept into a blinding storm by strong wind ; dial. for caitheadh.
cabhag, cafag, *n. f.* haste, hurry, speed, strait, difficulty.
cabhagach, cafagach, *a.* hasty ; fast-speaking ; hurried, impatient, abrupt, sudden.
cabhagachd, cafagach, *n. f.* hastiness.
cabharnach, cavarnach, *n. f.* a wicket, a bar-gate, gateway.
cabhlach, cav'-lach, *n. m.* and *f.* a fleet ; 'na chabhlach dhorcha, in his dark fleet. *E.Ir.* coblach, a fleet. *O'Dav.* has, cobluth = curach, no long beg fora mbi imram, five- or seven-seated rowing-boat.
cabhlaiche, cavlichu, *n. m.* an admiral.
cabhruich, caürich, *n. f.* flummery ; in *Scotch*, sowens. *Also* làghan. *Ir.* cáth-bhruith. *O'R.*
cabhsaidh, causy, *a.* snug, comfortable. Cf. *Eng.* cosy.
cabhsaidheachd, causyachc, *n. f.* snugness, too much fondness for comfort.
cabhsair, causer, *n. m.* pavement, a causeway, paved path or walk. *Eng.* causeway.
cabhsaireachd, causerachc, *n. m.* the business of making pavements or causeways.
cabhsairiche, causerichu, *n. m.* a paver.
cabhsanta, causanta, *f.* fond of comfort, effeminate, unmanly.
cabhtair, cauter, *n. f.* an issue in the body.
cabhull, cav'-ul, *n. m.* a creel for catching fish, a hose net.
càblach, *a.* supplied with cables.
cablaid, cablej, *n. f.* turmoil, tumult.
cablaideach, cablejach, *a.* tumultuous.
càbon, *n. m.* a species of shellfish.
cabrach, *n. f.* a bold masculine female : a thicket.
cabrach, *n. m.* a deer ; cabrach nan cnoc, the deer of the hill.
cabstair, *n. m.* a curb, a bridle bit.
cac, *n. m.* excrement, ordure ; *v.* void, go to stool ; *a.* filthy, dirty. *E.Ir.* cacc. *O.Celt.* kakko-. *Lat.* caco.
cach, *a. pron.* ; cach aon, each one ; cach là, each day ; cacha chèile, each other. *O.Ir.* cach, cech, each.
càch, *pron.* the rest ; thoir do chàch e, give it to the rest ; thàinig e roimh chàch, he arrived before the rest. *O.Ir.* cách, every one else, the rest.
cachaileith, cachliadh, *n. f.* a barred gate ; bó mhór na cachaileith, a cow that stands in the gate in the way of the rest. *See* atuinn. co + cliath. *McB.*
cachdan, *n. m.* disgust through disappointment, vexation. *E.Ir.* cachtaim, enslave, fetter.
càdadh, kādu, *n. m.* tartan for hose : còta de chàdadh nam ball, a coat of the striped tartan.
càdaidh, cādi, *n. m.* an errand boy, caddie.
cadal, *n. m.* sleep, slumber ; tha e 'na chadal, he is sleeping ; as mo chadal, in my sleep (as here has the force of ex) ; chaidh iad a chadal, they went to bed ; cha do chaidil mi neul, I have not slept a wink ; cadal-deilgneach, tingling sensation in a torpid limb ; " pins and needles " ; cadal-ceàrnach, a nap ; a siesta. *O.Ir.* cotlud.
cadalan, *n. m.* a little sleep, nap.
cadalan tràghad, *n. m.* sea bait; " whelk's eggs."
cadaltach, *a.* sleepy.
cadaltachd, cǎd''-ult-uchc, sleepiness.
cadaltaiche, cad''-ult-ich-u, *n. m.* a dormant creature, such as the serpent ; cadaltigh, a sleeping-place.
cadha, ca-u, *n. m.* a pass, a narrow, an entry. *E.Ir.* cái and cói, way, path.
cadhag, ca'-ăg, *n. f.* a wedge.
cadhag, *n. f.* jackdaw. *Ir.* cabhóg. *Lh. E.Ir.* cáec.

cadhan, *n. m.* wild goose, barnacle goose. *E.Ir.* cadan.

cadh-luibh, *n. m.* the cud-weed.

cadhmus, *n. m.* mould for casting bullets.

cafach, *a.* peppery, tasting *high*, as " high " fish.

cagail, kag′-il′, *v.* cover fire, to keep it from extinguishing ; cagail an teine, secure the fire. *Also* taisg.

cagailt, kagilt, *n. f.* the hearth ; corra-chagailt, the sulphurous hue seen in ashes on a frosty night.

cagailt, *n. f.* a roll of chewed grass in a horse's mouth.

cagainn, kăg′-inn, *v.* chew, champ, gnaw, masticate. *E.Ir.* cocnaim, I chew ; con-cnáim, gnaw.

cagair, *v.* whisper, listen. *E.Ir.* cocur, whisper, secret talk, council.

cagar, *n. m.* a whisper, secret.

cagaran, *n. m.* a pet, a darling.

cagarsaich, kag′-ar-sich, *n. f.* whispering.

caglachan, *n. m.* a chewed mass ; pulp.

cagnadh, kag′-nă, *vbl. n. m.* mastication ; act of chewing, champing, gnawing.

caibe, keba, *n. m.* a mattock, a spade, shoe of " cas-chrom " ; caibe-làir, turfing-spade. *Ir.* coibe, cuibe.

caibeal, kebal, *n. m.* a chapel, a tomb ; a family burying-place. *Lat.* capella.

caibheis, kavesh, *n. f.* prattling, tittering.

caibhtinn, keftin, *n. m.* a captain.

caibideal, kĕb′-ij-al, *n. m.* a chapter. *O.Ir.* caiptel ; fr. *Lat.* capitulum.

caidil, kăj′-ĕl, *v.* sleep, repose. *O.Ir.* cotlaim, contulim.

caidir, kaj′-ir,*v.* embrace, hug; indulge in, fondle, caress, cherish ; olc ni 'n caidir thu, thou shalt not indulge in iniquity.

caidreabh, kaj′-ruv, *n. m.* fellowship, affection, the embrace, familiarity. Also *improperly* caidreamh.

caidreabhas, kajruvas, *n. m.* intimacy, friendship.

caidreach, kajrach, *a.* embracing, familiar, social ; *n. m.* and *f.* a friend, a companion, a bosom friend.

caidrich, kajrich, *v.* cherish.

caig, keg, *n. f.* rush of conversation ; caig air an leanabh, take notice of the child, make winning signs to the infant.

caigeadh, kegu, *n. m.* nodding ; caigeadh air a chéile, noticing each other (of opposing armies).

caigeann, kegun, *n. f.* a brace, two tied together, a couple, a pair ; a group.

caigeann, kegun, *n. m.* rough mountain pass.

caigneachadh, caigneadh, kegnacha, *n. m.* coupling, crossing, *e.g.* swords.

caignich, kegnich, *v.* join two and two.

càil, *n. m.* constitution, energy, strength. pith, taste, appetite ; tha a chàil air

falbh, his constitution wears away ; gun chàil, without strength or energy ; 's an tigh chaol gun chàil, in the narrow house, without power ; lifeless ; chaill iad càil an claisteachd, they lost their sense of hearing ; chan 'eil càil do bhiadh agam, I have no appetite for food. *E.Ir.* cáil, quality, condition.

càil, kāl, *n. m.* a trifle, husk ; chan 'eil càil an so, there is nothing here ; chan 'eil càil agamsa, I have absolutely nothing ; a bheil cail ann a nì mi? anything I can do ?

cailbh, keluv, *n. m.* partition wall. *Also* caileadh ; fr. calbh.

cailbhean, *n. m., dim.* of colbh, a small pillar ; cailbhean corrach, an unstable little pillar, or pedestal.

cailc, kelk, *n. f.* chalk ; *v.* chalk, line. *E.Ir.* cailc, chalk, lime. *W.* calch, lime.

caile, ka′l-à, *n. f.* a girl ; caile-bhalach, a romp. *E.Ir.* cale ; gl. *rustica.*

caileach, caluch, *n. m.* cock. So *E.Ir. O.Celt.* kaljâko-s.

càileach, căluch, *n. m.* husks. *Ir.* càithleach.

càileachd, că′l′-ăchc, *n. f.* endowments, energy, ability.

càileachdach, călachcach, *a.* strong, able, powerful.

caileadair, caluder, *n. m.* star-gazer, philosopher. *Eng.* calendar.

caileag, cal-ăg, *n. f.* a girl, a lassie.

càilean, cālen, *n. m.* a husk. *See* càithlean.

càileanta, cālanta, *a.* hard, firm.

càileiginn, cà′l′-è-ginn, *n. m.* some, somewhat, something, a small matter ; in some measure ; tha càileiginn de mhaith air, it is worth something.

caileil, căl′-ăl, *a.* quean-like, girlish.

càilghuth, căl-ghu, *n. f.* musical talent.

cailidear, ca′l′-ij-er, *n. m.* snot ; rheum. *Also* cailidhir. *Ir.* cailidéar. *O′R.*

cailin, ca′l′-in, *n. f.* a damsel, a maid ; cailin ro mhaiseach, a very handsome damsel. *Ir.* cailin.

cailis, calish, *n. f.* chalice. *Ir.* cailis. *E.Ir.* cailech, a cup ; fr. *Lat.* calix, cup.

cailise, *n. f.* kails, ninepins.

caill, cyle, *v.* lose, suffer loss ; forfeit.

cailleach, keluch, *n. f.* a veiled one ; a nun, an old woman ; the last handful of standing corn in a farm ; the circular wisp on the top of a cornstalk; cailleach oidhche, an owl, a spiritless fellow ; cailleach dhubh, a nun. *O.Ir.* caillech ; fr. caille, veil, a veiled one =nun ; an old woman. *W.* pall ; *Lat.* pallium.

cailleachail, keluchol, *a.* old - wifish, cowardly.

cailleachanta, keluchantu, *a.* old-wifish.

cailleachas, keliuchus, *n. f.* old-wifish conduct.

cailleag, coilag, *n. f.* a cockle, husk of lint. *Also* **coilleag.**

caillte, kylta, *vbl. a.* lost, ruined ; fr. **call.**

caillteach, kyltach, *a.* ruinous, losing ; causing loss.

caillteachd, kyltachc, *n. f.* ruination ; degree of loss or detriment, loss.

caillteanach, kyltenuch, *n. m.* a eunuch.

caimdeal, kymjal, *n. f.* tedious way of speaking ; an objection.

caimdealach, kymjaluch, *a.* tedious, drawling, prolix.

caime, kymu, *n. m.* crookedness, degree of crookedness ; blindness of an eye ; **tha am bata ni's caime,** the staff is more crooked ; fr. **cam.**

caimean, kymen, *n. f.* a mote.

caimleid, kymlej, *n. f.* worsted cloth.

càin, cān, *v.* traduce, revile, dispraise, backbite, slander, satirise ; **càineam is aoiream a' bhaobh rinn an t-òran,** let me revile, lampoon, or satirise the fury that composed the song. *O.Ir.* **cáned,** slander. *O.Celt.* **kâkniô.**

càin, *gen.* **cànach,** *n. f.* tribute, tax, fine ; **chuir iad càin air,** they fined him ; **dh'òladh e chàin a bh'aig Pàdruig air Eirinn,** he would drink the tribute that Ireland owed St. Patrick. *E.Ir.* **càin,** law, statute.

càin, *a.* white, fair ; **cù càin,** a white dog. *Lat.* cānus.

cainb, kenab, *n. f.* hemp, canvas ; rope. *Ir.* cnáibe (*Keat.*) ; cnáip (*KM.*). *Lat.* cannabis.

cainb-aodach, *n. m.* sackcloth.

cainbeach, kenapuch, *n. f.* rope-yarn.

càineachd, cānachc, *n. f.* taxation.

càineadh, cāna, *vbl. n. m.* traducing, slandering ; scolding, backbiting.

caineal, canal, *n. m.* cinnamon. *Lat.* canella.

caingeann, kengun, *n. f.* a fine. *Also* **ceadhann.**

caingis, kyngish, *n. f.* Pentecost, Whitsuntide. *E.Ir.* **cingciges, cingices, cinquagisima.** *Corm. Lat.* quinquagesima.

càinich, *v.* impose a tax.

cainichean, *n. m.* cotton grass. *Also* **canach.**

cainneag, kĕn'-ăg, *n. f.* a hamper ; mote.

cainneal, *n. f.* a candle. *E.Ir.* **caindel.** *W.* cannwyll. *Lat.* candēla. *See* **coinneal.**

càinnealachadh, cānialuchu, *n. m.* act of shining ; daybreak, first dawn. Cf. *E.Ir.* caindleóracht ; fr. *O.Ir.* caindloir, *candelarius.*

cainnean, kenen, *n. m.* a live speck of fire ; a spark.

cainnt, kynt, *n. f.* talk, language ; speech ; conversation, discourse ; act of saying, speaking, talking ; conversing ; discoursing. *E.Ir.* caint. *O.Celt.* kan(s)ti. *See* **can.**

cainnteach, kyntach, *a.* loquacious, talkative.

cainnteachd, kyntachc, *n. f.* talkativeness.

cainnteal, kyntal, *n. m.* a press, a crowd.

cainntear, kynter, *n. m.* a speaker, an orator.

cainntearachd, kaynteruchc, *n. f.* eloquence, oratory, conversation, reciting tales.

caiptein, *n. m.* a captain ; fr. the *Eng.*

càir, *n. f.* a blaze ; breaking crest of wave ; a grin. Same as **caoir.**

càir, *n. f.* the gum ; the teeth ; an image.

càir, *n. f.* a peat moss ; "**tha muineal bàn mar chanach càir,**" her neck, fair as the cotton grass of the moss. *O.N.* kjarr. *Dan.* kjær. (fem.). *Yorks.* carr, marsh.

càir, form of **còir,** fitting ; **ciod e'n t-àite 'n càra dhi bhi fàs, na air a' cheann ?** what place more fitting for it (a horn) than on his head ? **còir càir e !** ironical exclamation = what impertinence !

cairb, *n. m.* bent ridge of a pack saddle. Cf. *Ir.* corb, a coach.

cairbh, curuv, *n. f.* carcase, a dead body ; **cairbh spréidhe neòghloinn,** the carcases of unclean cattle.

cairbhinn, curvinn, *n. f.* the carcase of a person ; **cairbhinn an righrean,** the carcases of their kings.

cairbhinneach, curvinuch, *a.* full of carcases.

cairbhinneachd, *n. f.* slaughter, massacre.

cairbhist, curvisht, *n. f.* baggage, luggage ; rent-service due by sub-tenant to tacksman (*see* **borlanachd**) ; flogging.

cairbinn, *n. f.* a carabine.

cairbinneach, *n. m.* a toothless person ; fr. **cairb,** gum, jaw.

cairc, cerc, *n. f.* strait, predicament ; **is e bha 'na chairc,** he was in a serious predicament ; hurry-burry.

càird, cārj, *n. f.* delay, respite ; **gun chàird,** without partiality ; without delay ; kindness ; **fasgadh is càird,** shelter and kindness. *E.Ir.* cáirdde, truce, respite.

càirde, *n. m.* friendship, a relation.

càirdeach, cārjuch, *a.* related, connected ; **tha iad càirdeach da chéile,** they are connected or related to each other.

càirdeachas, cārdachus, *n. m.* relation, friendliness.

càirdealachd, cārjalachc, *n. f.* friendliness, benevolence, kindness, goodness, goodwill.

càirdeas, cārjus, *n. m.* friendship, relationship, connection, fellowship. *O.Ir.* cáirdes.

càirdeil, cārjol, *a.* friendly, kind, tender ; related, connected ; gu càirdeil, kindly. càirde + samail.

càirdich, *v.* befriend.

caire, *n. m.* blame, fault. So *E.Ir.* See coire.

caireachd, *n. f.* wrestling.

càireag, *n. f.* a prating girl.

caireal, *n. m.* noise. *Also* coirioll.

càirean, cārun, *n. m.* the gum, palate ; tha caithlean am chàirean, there is a seedling in my teeth.

càireanach, cārenuch, *a.* having gums.

cairfhiadh, car-iagh, *n. m.* a hart, stag.

cairgein, *n. m.* sea moss, Irish moss, carrageen ; fr. carraig.

càirgheal, *a.* white-foaming (as a wave).

càirich, cārich, *v.* mend, repair, order, soothe ; lay deliberately to one's charge ; lay out the dead, inter, bury ; càirich an altair, repair their altar ; càirich an leabaidh, " make " the bed ; na càirich am peacadh òirnne, lay not their sins to our charge ; càirich r' an taobh e, place it beside them. *O.Ir.* cóir, gl. *congruus.*

cairidh, carry, *n. f.* a weir. *See* caraidh.

cairis, *n. m.* corpse, carcase ; a wake. Cf. *Eng.* cors.

cairmeal, car-mil, *n. m.* wild liquorice. *Also* carra-mille.

càirneach, cārnuch, *n. f.* a place which abounds in boulders, heaped together ; a quarry.

càirnean, cārnan, *n. m.* egg-shell.

cairt, carst, *n. f., gen.* cartach, *pl.* cairtean : a cart ; roth na cartach, the cart wheel ; fr. *Eng.* cart.

cairt, *n. f.* a chart ; cairt-iùl, a mariner's chart. *Lat.* charta.

cairt, *n. f.* bark of a tree ; cairt dharaich, the bark of an oak tree ; *Lat.* cortex ; *v.* tan ; cairt an lion, tan the net.

cairt, *v.* cleanse, oust, clean ; tha a' bhathach air a cairteadh, the byre is cleaned ; cairteadh, act of cleaning out. *E.Ir.* cartaim, I cleanse.

cairt, *n. f.* a card ; ag cluich air chairtean, playing at cards. *Lat.* charta, paper.

càirte, *vbl. a.* of càirich, mended, etc.

cairteadh, *vbl. n. m.* act of tanning ; lion air a chairteadh, a tanned net.

cairteadh, *vbl. n. m.* act of carting.

cairteal, carstal, *n. m.* a quarter ; cairteal a' mhile, quarter of a mile ; cairteal na h-uarach, quarter of an hour. *L.Lat.* quartellus. *Lat.* quartus.

cairtealan, carstalun, *n. pl.* quarters ; lodgings ; places for temporary residence ; hospitality.

cairtear, carster, *n. m.* a carter, a waggoner.

cairtearachd, carsteruchc, *n. f.* a carter's trade.

cair-thalmhainn, car-halavinn, *n. f.* mill-foil, yarrow.

cairtidh, carsti, *a.* tanned, swarthy, tawny, bark-coloured ; " aois chairtidh as olc greann," swarthy old age of boding mien.

cairtidheachd, carsti-achc, *n. f.* swarthiness.

cairt-iùil, *n. f.* a mariner's chart.

cairt-làir, *n. f.* tormentil.

cais, cash, *v.* twist, twine ; cais an t-sreang, twist the string ; *a.* caiste, twisted, twined.

càis, kāsh, *n. m.* .cheese ; pailteas de im is de chàis, plenty of butter and cheese. *Lat.* cāseus.

caisbheart, kash'-art, *n. m.* foot-wear ; shoes, stockings, boots, together. cas + beart = " foot-gear."

caisd, cusht, *v.* hark ! listen. *Ir.* coisteachd, listening. *E.Ir.* coistim. *O.Ir.* coitsea, *auscultet* = co + étsim, listen. *McB.*

caisdeachd, *n. f.* listening.

caise, kāsh'-u, *n. f.* steepness ; caise na brúthach, the steepness of the ascent ; shortness of temper ; is e do chaise féin as coireach, it is your own crossness that is the cause ; impetuosity, rapidity ; caise an t-srutha, the impetuosity of the current ; shortness of time, haste ; cha tig e an caise, he will not come in a hurry ; *cpv.* of cas, more or most rapid, passionate, etc. ; tha an sruth na's caise, the stream or current is more or most rapid ; wrinkle ; gun chaise am aodann, without a wrinkle on my face.

càiseach, kāsh'-uch, *a.* well supplied with cheese.

caisead, kash'-ud, *n. m.* degree of rapidity ; passion ; steepness, impetuosity, etc.

caiseal, kāsh'-al, *n. m.* castle, bulwark. *Ir.* caiseal, a circular stone fort. *O'Don.* *E.Ir.* caisel. *Lat.* castellum.

caiseal, *n. m.* a ford.

caisean, keshen, *n. m.* a short-tempered person ; a curl, dewlap ; caisean uchd, breast-stripe of a sheep, roasted at Christmas, and smelled by all in the house, to keep away fairies for the rest of the year.

caiseanach, keshenuch, *a.* short-tempered.

caiseanachd, keshenuchc, *n. f.* fretfulness, peevishness, bickering, shortness of temper.

caisearbhain, keshervon, *n. m.* the herb dandelion. *Also* breunan-brothaich.

caisfhionn, kăsh'-un, *a.* white-footed ; cas + fionn.

càisg, cāshc, *n. f.* Easter, the passover ; Di-dòmhnaich na càsg, Easter Sunday ; a feast. *E.Ir.* cásc. *W.* pasc. *Lat.* pascha.

caisg, ceshc, *v.* restrain, check, stop, still, quiet ; caisg an cù, stop or restrain the dog ; staunch ; caisg an fhuil, staunch the blood. *O.Ir.* cosc, restraint, discipline. *W.* cosp.

caisial, cash'-al, *n. m.* shoemaker's strap.

caisil-chrò, cashil-chrō, *n. f.* a bier, a coffin, hearse. *E.Ir.* cossair, litter ; cossair-cró =litter of gore.

caisionn, cashun. *See* caisfhionn.

caisleach, kăsh'-lyăch, *n. m.* a ford, a footpath, a smooth place ; cas + lach.

caisleachadh, kash'-lyăchu, *vbl. n. m.* act of stirring up a feather bed, shaking ; dubbing ; bedding stock.

caislich, kăsh'-lich, *v.* shake, stir, rouse ; " bed " cattle. *E.Ir.* caislechta, polished, smooth (*pass. part.* of consligim, cut, hew).

caislinn, kashlin, *gen.* of caiseal, a ford. *R.D.*

caismeachd, kash'-măchc, *n. f.* the quick part of a tune on the bagpipes ; an alarm to battle ; a war-song ; irritable excitement. Cf. *M.Ir.* caismert. *E.Ir.* cosmert, war-whoop, signal.

caisnich, *v.* crush, shake roughly.

caisreabhachd, kăsh'-ruv-ăchc, *n. f.* juggling ; leger de main. *Lh.*

caisreag, kăsh'-răg, *n. f.* a ringlet, a curl, entanglement.

caisreagach, kăsh'-răg-uch, *a.* curled.

caisrig, *v.* consecrate. *See* coisrig.

caiste, kăsh'-tyà, *vbl. a.* twisted, curled, twined ; snath caiste, sewing thread.

caisteal, kăsh'-tyàl, *n. m.* a castle, a garrison, a tower ; a turreted mansion. *Lat.* castellum.

c'àite, cātu, *ad.* where, in what place ; c'àit an robh thu? where have you been ? c'àite a bheil e ? where is he ? =cia + àite.

càiteach, catiuch, *n. f.* a winnowing-sheet, rush-mat for measuring corn ; fr. càth, husks.

caiteag, catyag, *n. f.* a basket for trouts ; a leather pot ; a small bit ; a place to hold barley, etc., in a barn. *Also* cat eòrna, cat sìl, cat buntata, etc.

caitean, catyan, *n. m.* shag, or nap of cloth ; tha caitean air an aodach, the cloth is shaggy ; the ripple of the sea ; a ruffled surface. *Ir.* caitin, (1) shag, (2) blossom of osier, (3) nap. *O'R.*

caiteanach, catyanuch, *a.* nappy, shaggy, ruffled, rough with a slight breeze.

caiteas, ca-chus, *n. m.* caddice ; scrapings of linen applied to wounds.

caith, ca, *v.* spend, waste, wear, consume, exhaust ; squander ; caitheamh a' chuain, speeding over the sea ; chaith e a shaoibhreas, he squandered his wealth ; chaith e a aodach, he has worn his clothes ; casting, shooting, putting ; an am caitheadh na cloiche, when putting the stone ; a' caitheadh chlach, casting stones at ; a' caitheadh air comharra, shooting or aiming at a mark. *O.Ir.* caithim : nad chaithi gl. qui non edit.

caith, *v.* winnow corn ; more often cath.

caitheach. *See* caithteach, prodigal, wasteful.

caitheadh, cahagh, *vbl. n. m.* act of spending, wearing ; consumption, wasting, dying by inches.

caitheamh, kehuv, *n. m.* consumption.

caitheamh-aimsir, kehu-amshir, *n. m.* pastime, sport.

caitheamh-beatha, kyhu-behu, *n. m.* conduct, mode of living, moral conduct, conversation ; behaviour.

caithear, kaher, *a.* well bestowed, just, right. *Ir.* caithear, caithfidh, it behooveth. *Lh.*

càithleach, cāleach, *a.* husks, chaff ; fr. càth.

càithlean, cā-len, *n. m.* seedling ; càithlean 'na fhiacail, a seedling between his teeth.

càithleanach, cālenuch, *a.* seedy, husky ; min chàithleanach, meal full of seedlings.

caithream, căr'-um, *n. f.* a noise, a shout ; beating, as a drum ; joyful sound, shout of triumph and rejoicing ; chum caithream a dhèanamh ann ad chliù, to rejoice in thy praise ; is caithream bròin am beul ar bàird, and the shout of sorrow in the mouth of our bards. *O.Ir.* cath + réim, battle shout, triumph. *Ir.* réim curadh, hero's shout. *Lh.* Cf. osnadh milidh, warrior's groan. *C.M.L*[136].

caithreamach, carumuch, *a.* shouting for grief or joy ; beating at regular intervals.

càithrinn, cārinn, *n. f.* refuse of straw taken out of corn after being thrashed.

càithrinnich, cārinich, *v.* shake straw before bundling it, or making it into trusses.

caithris, kerish, *n. f.* watching (at night) ; excessive fatigue from watching incessantly ; the state of being exhausted and worn out by watching.

caithriseach, kerishuch, *a.* wakeful ; fatigued by continual watching ; restless ; wanting regular rest.

caithte, cahtu, *vbl. a.* spent, worn out, consumed, exhausted, lean, lank.

caithteach, ka-tyàch, *a.* apt to wear or waste one's strength ; **caithteach air duine,** apt to exhaust or wear one down soon ; wasteful, lavish, prodigal, profuse ; **duine caithteach,** a wasteful or prodigal person.

caithteachd, ka-tyachc, *n. f.* waste, prodigality, profusion ; liability to be worn out; state of wearing or exhausting.

caithtiche, ka-tich-u, *n. m.* a spendthrift.

càl, *n. m.* cole-wort, greens, cabbage ; kail ; **càl ceannan,** a dish of potatoes and greens mashed together ; **càl ceairsleach,** cabbage ; **càl colaig,** cauliflower. *Sc.* kail. *A.S.* cawl. *Lat.* caulis. *O.N.* kál.

cala, caladh, *n. m.* the " hard," " firm " beach ; a landing place ; a harbour, a haven, a port ; **cha d'thug thu do long gu cala fhathast,** you have not brought your ship into harbour yet ; this is the *adj.* **calad,** hard, used as a noun ; " the hard." *Watson. E.Ir.* **calath, calad.** *O.Celt.* kaleto-s, hard.

caladair, *n. m.* a calendar.

cala-dhìreach, *a. recte* **calg-dhireach,** " sword-straight " ; **tha e cala-dhìreach mar a thuirt thu,** it is just exactly as you said.

caladh-phort, cala-forst, *n. m.* a haven, a harbour.

calaich, kàl'-ich, *v.* moor, anchor.

calaman, *n. m.* a dove, a pigeon. *Lat.* columba.

calanas, *n. m.* spinning ; working at wool, flax, hemp, etc., manufacturing.

calbh, kàl'-uv, *n. m.* a twig, an osier, headland ; gushing of water. *See* **colbh.**

calbhar, kal'-uv-er, *a.* greedy of food. *R.D.*

calc, *v.* caulk, drive, ram, push violently. *Lat.* **calco.**

calcadh, kalk'-ă, *vbl. n. m.* act of caulking, cramming.

calcaire, kàlk'-ir-à, *n. m.* a caulker, a rammer.

calg, *n. m.* awn, beard of barley ; refuses of lint ; a spear ; bristles of pigs. *Ir.* **calg, colg.** *E.Ir.* colgg, old name for sword ; a prickle ; bristle ; an awn. *O.Celt.* kalgo, kolgo.

calgach, *a.* prickly, bristly.

calg-dhireach, calg-yeerach, *adv.* straight. *E.Ir.* colg + dìreach, straight like a sword.

call, caul, *n. m.* loss, detriment, damage, privation ; **is mór mo chall ris,** great is my loss by it ; *vbl. n.* act of losing,

dropping ; **a' call air,** losing by it. *E.Ir.* coll, destruction, loss. *W.* coll. *O.Celt.* kolda.

callag, *n. f.* the bird called the diver ; the guillemot. *Also* **colltag.**

càllaich, kàll'-ich, *v.* tame, domesticate.

callaid, calej, *n. f.* a partition ; a hedge, a fence. *W.* **clawdd.** Cf. **tallaid.**

callaid, calej, *n. f.* a wig, cap. *E.Ir.* **callad,** a woman's cap.

callaideach, calejuch, *a.* surrounded, fenced.

càllaidh, càly, *a.* domesticated, tame ; **beathaichan càllaidh,** domesticated animals ; benumbed, weak. *Also* **callda** and **calla.**

càllaidheachd, càly-achc, *n. f.* tameness.

callaidheachd, caly-achc, *n. f.* amorous conduct ; fr. **collaidh,** sensual.

callan, càll'-ăn, *n. m.* noise, absurd hammering at anything ; hardness of the hands from working with spades, oars, etc. ; callosity ; a corn.

callda, same as **callaidh.**

calldach, caulduch, *a.* losing, ruinous; *n. f.* loss, damage, detriment; fr. **call.**

calldachd, cauldachc, *n. f.* loss, damage.

calltuinn, caultin, *n. m.* hazel. *E.Ir.* coll, *corylus. W.* coll.

Calluinn, callin, *n. f.* New Year's Day. *E.Ir.* calann, kalends. *Lat.* kalendae.

calma, cal'-mu, *n. m.* a pillar, a thick-set stout-built person ; a prop. *E.Ir.* coloman = *Lat.* columna.

calma, *a.* thick-set, brawny, powerful, strong.

calmachd, calm-ăchc, *n. f.* stoutness.

calman, *n. m.* a dove. *Also* **columan.**

calmar, *n. m.* a kind of fish, hake. *Also* **falmar.**

calmarra, cal'-um-arr-a, *a.* brawny, thick-set, well-made.

calmnach, *a.* rich in doves.

calpa, *n. m., pl.* **calpannan,** the calf of the leg ; the shaft of an arrow ; a rivet nail ; the principal at interest ; **calp is riadh,** principal and interest ; a halyard. *E.Ir.* colpa. *O.N.* kálfi.

calpach, and **calpannach,** *a.* stout-legged.

calum, *n. m.* hardness on the skin. *Lat.* callum, callus.

cam, *a.* crooked, bent ; **maide cam,** a crooked stick ; blind of an eye ; **tha e cam,** he is blind of an eye, or squinteyed. *v.* bend ; curve ; **cham thu am maide,** you bent the stick ; make crooked. *O.Ir.* camm, camb. *W.* cam, crooked, one-eyed. *Gaul.* **Cambo-.**

camacach, *a.* crooked.

camacag, *n. f.* a trip. *Also* **cas-bhacaig.**

camachag, *n. f.* a small bay.

camachasach, *a.* bow-legged.

camadh, *n. m.* a bend, crook, curve ;

camadh 's a' chrannchur, crook in the lot.

camadhubh, *n. f.* the arm, or thigh bone.

camag, *n. f.* a curl, a ringlet, a crook, clasp ; the temple ; bhuail e 'sa chamaig e, he struck in the temple ; a comma in writing ; a club.

camagach, *a.* crooked, bending, curled.

camag-gharaidh, *n. f.* the hollow above the temple ; the temple. *Ir.* camóg-ara. *O.Ir.* aire (temple).

caman, *n. m.* a shinty, a club for golf or cricket ; golf club. *E.Ir.* cammán, hurley stick.

camanachd, *n. f.* playing at golf or shinty.

camart, *n. f.* a wry-neck.

camas, *n. m.* a bay, a creek ; the groin. *E.Ir.* cammas, bend of a river, a bay.

camh, *căv, n. m.* the dawn. *E.Ir.* camáir, dawn, twilight.

camhach, cavach, *a.* talkative.

càmhal, cāvul, *n. m.* a camel.

camhan, cavan, *n. m.* a hollow plain. *Lat.* cavus.

camhanach, cav'-an-ach, *n. m.* the dawn. " 's a' chamhanaich 's tu 'g éirigh," at dawn as you dress.

cam-luirgneach, *a.* bow-legged.

càmp, *n.m., pl.* -annan, a camp ; fr. *Lat.*

campachadh, camp'-ach-u, *vbl. n. m.* act of encamping.

campaich, camp'-ich, *v.* encamp, surround.

campair, *n. m.* camp - master. *E.Ir.* camper, a champion. *O'Dav.*

campar, *n. m.* vexation, uneasiness, grief ; na cuireadh sin campar ort, let not that vex you. *E.Ir.* campar, contention, quarrel.

camparach, *a.* galling, vexing, sad.

camparaid, *n. f.* bustle ; a slight quarrel.

camshron, cam'-hrŏn, *n. f.* crooked nose.

camshronach, kam'-hron-ach, *a.* having a crooked nose ; *n. m.* and *a.* Cameron, Cameronian.

camshuil, *n. f.* squint eye.

càmus, *n. m.* mould for making bullets. *Also* cadhmus.

can, *v.* say, affirm, speak, express, sing ; canaibh òran, sing a song. *O.Ir.* canim, I sing, I recite, say. *W.* canu. *Lat.* cano. *O.Celt.* kanô.

cana, *căn'-u, n. f., pl.* canachan, a little whale ; a porpoise.

canabhas, can'-a-vas, *n. m.* canvas, sack-cloth ; fr. the *Eng. Lat.-Gr.* cannabis.

canach, *a.* cunning. *Sc.* canny, orig. = know.

canach, *n. m.* cotton-grass ; mountain-down. *O.Ir.* canach, gl. *lanugo.*

canach, *n. m., pl.* canaichean, porpoise, sturgeon ; " Caol Muile nan canach," Sound of Mull of the porpoises. *I.Lom.*

cànain, cānan, *n. f.* language, speech, dialect.

cànainiche, cānanichu, *n. m.* a linguist.

canal, *n. m.* cinnamon.

canan, *n. m.* cannon ; ult. fr. *Lat.* canna.

canas for conas. *R.D.*

canastair, *n. m.* a canister.

cangairnich, *n. m.* gangrene. *Sc.* canker.

cangaruich, *v.* fret, vex, agitate, suppurate.

cangluinn, *căng'-llun', n. f.* vexation, angry words ; *syn.* aimhil. *Sc.* cangle.

cangluinneachd, *n. f.* turbulent words. Cf. *Sc.* cangle.

cangrachadh, *vbl. n. m.* suppurating.

cànmhuin, *n. m.* language.

canna, *n. m.* a can. *E.Ir.* cann.

cannach, *n. m.* sweet-willow, myrtle.

cannach, *a.* pretty, kind, tender ; " na puirt a b'fhìor channaich rainn," the reels of the sweetest strains.

cannlach. See connlach. *R.D.*

canntair, *n. m.* a chanter, a singer. *E.Ir.* cantaire, singer. *Corm.*

canntaireachd, caund'-ar'-ăchc, *n. f.* humming a tune ; chanting, singing ; warbling ; " greis air canntaireachd is ceòl," a while at chanting and song. *E.Ir.* cantairecht.

cànran, *n. m.* bickering, scolding, and reflecting incessantly ; grumbling.

cànranach, *a.* bickering, fretful.

cantal, *n. m.* grief, weeping. *E.Ir.* cantlam, moaning, sorrow.

caob, cūb, *n. m.* a lump, as in thread ; a bite, and also a nip ; *v.* bite ; nip, clod. *E.Ir.* cáeb. *O.Ir.* caip, clot, lump, mass. *W.* cyfan.

caoch, *a.* void, hollow ; blind. *O.Ir.* caich. *W.* coeg. *O.Celt.* kaiko-s, one-eyed. *Lat.* caecus. *Goth.* haihs.

caoch, for cuthach, *n. m.* rage, madness ; duine fo'n chaoch, a man in a rage ; ghabh an t-each an caoch, the horse ran away—got wild.

caochag, *n. f.* a nut without the kernel ; blind man's buff.

caochail, *v.* change, alter ; putrefy ; chaochail e a ghnùis, he changed his countenance ; expire, die, give up the ghost ; chaochail e, he yielded up the ghost. *O.Ir.* con-imchláim, alter, exchange (fr. clóim, overthrow, destroy, muto).

caochan, *n. m.* the little blind one ; a streamlet hidden by herbage ; a gurgling streamlet ; a purling rill, purling noise, like worts fermenting ; caochan nan allt, the purling noise of the brooks ; fermented worts ; in *Sc.* wash ; togsaid chaochain, wash vat.

caochlach, *a.* changeable.

caochladh, kăoch′-llă. *vbl. n. m.* change, alteration ; act of changing, putrefying. *O.Ir.* cóimchlód, cáemchlód.

caochlaideach, cūchlejach, *a.* changeable, variable ; uair chaochlaideach, changeable or variable weather ; fickle, inconstant, whimsical ; duine caochlaideach, a fickle or inconstant person.

caochlaideachd, cūchlejach, *n. f.* changeableness, variableness ; inconstancy, mutability, fickleness.

caod Chalum chille, *n. m.* St. John's wort.

caog, cūg, *v.* wink, connive, cock (the eye).

caogach, cūguch, *a.* squint-eyed.

caogad, cūgud, *n. f.* fifty. *O.Ir.* cóica, cóicat.

caogadh, *vbl. n. m.* a wink ; act of winking.

caogshuil, cūg-hool, *n. f.* a winking eye, a squint eye.

caogshuileach, *a.* squint-eyed.

caoibean, *n. m.* the few inches that are not woven at the beginning of a web.

caoidh, cūy, *v.* lament, weep, wail for loss of ; *vbl. n. m.* lamentation, wailing, weeping ; act of lamenting, wailing, weeping. *E.Ir.* cói, cái. *O.Ir.* cíit, *plorant. O.Celt.* keiô, keô.

caoidh-chòmhradh, mournful expressions.

caoidheach, cūyuch, *a.* mournful.

caoidhearan, cūyuran, *n. m.* a wailing, mournful voice.

caoidhearnach, *a.* plaintive, mournful.

caoile, cūla, leanness, dearth ; *n. f.* want of fodder for cattle ; bhàsaich an crodh leis a' chaoile, the cattle starved for want of fodder ; narrowness, straitness, slenderness. *E.Ir.* cóile. *O.Celt.* koiljâ.

caoilead, cūlud, *abstr. n. f.* degree of narrowness, smallness ; fineness, as linen, yarn, etc.

caoilean, cūlen, *n. m.* a twig, slatag.

caoilich, cūlich, *v.* attenuate.

caoimheach, cūiv′-ach, *a.* kind ; *n. m.* a friend, a bedfellow.

caoimhnealachd, coynaluchc, *n. f.* kindness ; courteousness ; agreeableness to the touch. *Properly* coibhnealachd.

caoimhneas, coynas, *n. m.* kindness, mildness ; affability ; a kind turn. *Prop.* coibhneas. *O.Ir.* coibnius, *affinitas.*

caoimhneil, coynal, *a.* kind, mild, affable, courteous, benevolent. *Prop.* coibhneil.

caoin, cūin, *v.* weep, lament, mourn, deplore, wail ; regret. *O.Ir.* cóinim, cáinim. *W.* cwyno, lament.

caoin, *a.* kind, tender ; seasoned, as hay, sheaf-corn, fish, etc. *O.Ir.* cáin, *bonus.*

caoin, *n. f.* the face, right side of cloth ; caoin is ascaoin, the right and the wrong side ; rhind ; surface skin ; bhrisd e caoin an leathrach, he broke the rhind of the leather ; sward ; caoin uaine, a green sward. *E.Ir.* cáin, the smooth part.

caoineachadh, cūin′-ăch-ā, *n. m.* seasoning or drying hay, fish, etc. ; exposure to the sun's heat for the purpose of drying.

caoineachas, cūinachus, *n. m.* mildness, tranquillity.

caoineadh, cūniu, *vbl. n. m.* act of weeping, wailing, mourning ; lamenting, lamentation. So *O'R. See* coineadh.

caoinear, cūner, *n. m.* sheer indifference.

caoinearach, *a.* indifferent, careless.

caoineis, cúnesh, *n. m.* taking off, gibing, jeering.

caoineiseach, *a.* indifferent, apt to gibe, jeer, or take off.

caoineiseachd, *n. f.* assumed indifference ; fastidiousness ; foolish pride.

caoinich, cūnich, *v.* dry, season, expose to dry, as hay, fish.

caoin-shuarach, *a.* indifferent, careless. caoin is *intensive* here, and = very, or *sim.* word ; caoin-shuarach mun chùis, quite indifferent about the matter. Cf. *Ir.* cáin - duthracht, " good " + goodwill ; cáin - fhuairrech, "very" clement.

caoin-shuarachd, *n. f.* indifference.

caointeach, cūntiuch, *n. f.* a female fairy or water-kelpie, whose particular province it was to forewarn her favourite clans of the approach of death in the family, by weeping and wailing opposite the kitchen door ; *a.* weeping, mourning.

caointeachan, *n. m.* a mourner.

caoir, cūr, *n f.* a blaze, stream of sparks ; sparks from clashing steel ; brightly burning ember ; a fiery flame, great haste, rush (of foaming stream in spate). *R.D. E.Ir.* caer.

caoireach, curiuch, *a.* blazing, sparkling, flashing.

caoireall, coiral, *n. m.* loud and continual speaking.

caoirean, cūren, *n. m.* a plaintive song. *Also* caoi-ràn, moaning.

caoirgheal, cūryal, *a.* bright, flaming.

caoirlasair, cūr-lasir, *n. f.* a bright or sparkling flame.

caoirnean, cūrnen, *n. m.* drop of sheep or goat's dung. Cf. *Ir.* caoirín, a little berry.

caoirneinean, *pl.* angry squalls. *R.D.*

caoirruith, *n. f.* hot haste. *R.D.*

caoirsholus, cūr-holus, *n. f.* a gleaming light.

caoirtheach, cūr-hach, *a.* flaming, fiery ; sruth caoirtheach, a stream in spate.

caoir-theine, *n. f.* a fire-brand ; a meteor, a thunderbolt.

caol, *a.. compar. deg.* caoile, slender, thin ; lean, lank, attenuated ; narrow ; *n. m., pl.* caoil and caoiltean, a narrow ; a sound, a strait, a frith ; an caol Muileach, the sound of Mull ; the small parts of body and limbs ; caol an droma, the small of the back ; caol an dùirn, the wrist ; caol na coise, the ankle ; ceangal nan cóig chaoil, the binding of the five " smalls," *i.e.* two wrists, two ankles brought together and tied to the waist ; an tigh caol, the narrow house, the grave ; osier ; cliabh caoil, a creel made of osier. *E.Ir.* cóel, cóil. *O.Celt.* kailo-s.

caolchasach,* *a.* slender-limbed.

caol-chòmhnuidh, *n. f.* narrow abode, the grave.

caolchruth, *n. m.* slender form.

caol-chruthach, *a.* of slender form.

caol-dhearrsa, *n. f.* the name of a star.

caoldruim, *n. m.* the small of the back.

caol-earra, *a.* with narrow butt.

caolmhala, *n. f.* well-shaped eyebrow.

caolmhuingeach, *a.* narrow-maned.

caolruith, *n. f.* a narrow course (straight).

caolshrath, *n. m.* a narrow strath.

caolach, cūluch, *n. m.* the worst part of corn ; fairy flax.

caolaich, cūlich, *v.* make narrow, taper.

caolan, *n. m., pl.* caolain and caolanan, gut, tripe ; entrail. *E.Ir.* coelán. *O.Celt.* koilo-, entrails.

caolas, kūlas, *n. m.* a sound, a strait.

caomh, kūv, *a.* kind, mild, beloved, meek, gentle ; labhair e gu caomh ris a' ghruagaich, he spoke kindly to the damsel ; cha chaomh leam e, I do not like him ; a dearly beloved person ; kindness, hospitality ; caomh mo theach, the hospitality of my house. *O.Ir.* cóim, handsome, dear, gentle. *O.W.* cum. *O.Celt.* koimo-s, dear.

caomhach, kūv'-ăch, *n. m.* a friend.

caomhachas, kūv'-ach-us, *n. m.* chambering ; sensuality, dalliance.

caomhachd, cūvachc, *n. f.* kindness, affection.

caomhag, kūvag, *n. f.* a mild or kind woman ; an ironical term applied to a woman or she-animal.

caomhaidh, kūvy, *a.* protecting, sheltering.

caomhail, kūv'-al, *a.* kind, friendly.

caomhainn, kūv'-inn, *v.* spare, save, economise, reserve ; caomhainn e gus a màireach, reserve it till to-morrow ; na caomhainn e, do not spare it.

caomhalachd, kūv'-ăl-ăchc, *n. f.* kindness of disposition ; kindness ; urbanity.

caomhan, kūvan, *n. m.* a kind or friendly man ; an ironical term.

caomhantach, kūv'-ant-ach, *a.* sparing, economical, frugal, saving ; stingy.

caomhantachd, kūv'-ant'-ăchc, *n. f.* economy, frugality ; a saving disposition, parsimony.

caomh-chridheach, *a.* kind-hearted.

caomhnach, *a.* frugal, sparing.

caomhnadh, kūv'-nu, *vbl. n. m.* economy, frugality, parsimony ; act of saving, sparing, reserving.

caonag, caoineag, *n. f.* the " weeper," the naiad who foretells the death of, and weeps for, those slain in battle. *Carm. Gad.* " Is lìonmhor . . . caonag air an duine thapaidh," calamity often befalls the brave.

caonnag, cūnag, *n. f.* bustle, tumult, strife, fight.

caonnagach, *a.* given to strife ; contentious.

caor, cūr, *n. f.* a berry ; rowan ; the berry of the mountain ash ; caora bada miann, the stone brambles ; caora feullain, ivy berry ; caora madaidh, dog berry ; caora-fiadhag, also caora-fithich, crow-berries ; caora dromain, elder berries. *O.Ir.* cáir, berry, a lump.

caora, cūru, *n. f., pl.* caoirich, a sheep ; *gen. s.* and *pl.* caorach ; taobh na caorach, the side of the sheep ; crò nan caorach, sheep-fold. *O.Ir.* caora, gl. on ói (*Corm.*) and curu, *O'D. Sup. Later* cáera.

caorach, cūruch, *a.* plentiful in rowan berries.

caorachd, *n. f.* 1. stock, cattle and sheep. 2. a raid, cattle raid ; cumha na caorachd, the lament of the raid. *Ir.* caoraighecht, professional raiders. *O'R.*

caoran, cūran, *n. m.* a fragment of peat. *See* caor.

caorann, cūrun, *n. m.* mountain ash or rowan tree ; rowan berries ; the wood of the mountain ash. *Ir.* caorthann. *E.Ir.* cáerthenn. *O.Celt.* kairâ.

caorann-cuthaich, cūrun-coo-hich, *n. m.* a species of wild berry.

caorann-thalmhainn, c. halvin, *n. m.* a strawberry.

caornag, cūrnag, *n. f.* a wild hive, a battle, a fray, a squabble.

capall, *n. f.* a mare, in some places a horse, a colt. *E.Ir.* capall. *W.* ceffyl. *Lat.* caballus. *O.Celt.* kaballo-s.

capal-coille, kap'-ull-culiu, *n. m.* the great cock of the wood ; capercailzie.

capall-lìn, *n. m.* a lint-beetle.

---

* For pronunciation of compounds see separate members elsewhere.

car, *n. m.* agreement, bond (in car mo làimhe). *E.Ir.* cor, obligation, surety. *O'Don.*

car, *n. m.* a friend, for caraid.

car, *prep.* during, for the space of ; car tiota, for a moment ; car oidhche, for the space of a night ; car uair, for a time.

car, *n. m., gen. s.* and *n. pl.* cuir and caran, a turn, a twist, a bend ; meandering ; an car a bhios 'san t-seana mhaide is duilich a thoirt as, the twist that is in an old stick is not easily made straight ; trick, fraud, deceit ; gach car a tha ann is cleas, all his wiles and tricks, *Ps.* ; thug e an car asam, he outwitted me ; thug e a char as, he cheated him ; car a' mhuiltean, a somersault ; car air char, topsy-turvy ; chaidh e car mu char leis an leathad, he went rolling down the slope ; contact, direction ; gach ni a thig ad charaibh, everything that comes your way ; an caraibh a chéile, in contact with each other, in mutual contact ; wrestling ; an caraibh a bhrocluinn, in the direction of its den ; motion, movement ; na cuir car dheth, do not move it ; gun aon char a chur deth, without movement, without stirring it ; skill, knack ; a fhuair a char san uisge, that acquired his skill in the water ; a string of beads, pearls, etc. ; car chneap, a string of beads ; car neamhuinn, a string of pearls. *O.Ir.* cur, a vice ; a turn.

càr, *n. m.* a mossy plain, a fen ; mar channach càir, like the moss cotton ; feadh ghlumag a' chàir, through the pools of the moss. *See* càir.

càr, *a.* friendly, related to. *See* caraid. *Ir.* cára, friend. *W.* câr.

càr, *n. m.* "flesh " of seal, whale. *O.Ir.* carna, flesh. *Lat.* car-o, car-nis.

cara, for caraid ; gun cluinn mi mo chara, that I may hear my friend.

càra, *a.* fitting. *See* còir. Cha chàr dhomh a chliù a sheinn, 'tis not fitting that I should sing his praise.

carach, *a.* deceiving, deceitful ; tha an soaghal so carach, this world is deceitful ; fear carach, a cunning person ; cho carach ris a' mhadadh ruadh, as wily as a fox ; whirling, circling.

carachadh, *vbl. n. m.* act of moving, stirring.

carachd, *căr'-ăchc, n. f.* wrestling, sparring ; deceitfulness ; carachd an t-saoghail so, the deceitfulness of this world.

càradh, *căr'-ă, vbl. n. m.* act of adjusting, mending, dressing ; càradh, "making" a bed, dressing a corpse ; usage, treatment ; condition ; is truagh mo

chàradh, sad is my condition ; air dhroch càradh, badly used, treated. *E.Ir.* córaigim, cóirigim, I adjust, arrange.

caradh, *căr'-u, vbl. n. m.* act of turning, cheating, deceiving ; caradh fodha, diving (of bird).

caraich, carich, *v.* move, stir, turn ; na caraich e, do not stir it ; cha charaich thu as an so, you shall not move hence. *E.Ir.* coraigim, I stir.

caraid, carij, *n. m., pl.* càirdean, a male friend or relation ; banacharaid, a female friend or relation. *O.Ir.* cara, *d.* carait ; carim, I love. *W.* câr, kinsman. *O.Celt.* karaô, I love. *Lat.* carus.

càraid, cărej, *n. f.* a pair, a brace, a couple, a married couple ; *a.* càraideach, paired, coupled. *E.Ir.* córait, a brace, a yoke.

caraidh, *n. f.* a weir ; " caraidh gu caradh an éisg," a *weir* to deceive the fish. *Ir.* cora. *W.* cored. *O.Celt.* korajat.

càraidich, cărejich, *v.* join together in pairs or couples.

carainnean, carinun, *pl.* refuse of threshed barley.

caraist, caresht, *n. m.* catechism. *Sc.* carritch.

caramasg, *n. m.* confusion, contest.

caramh, *prep.* beside. *See sub* car.

càramh, *n. m.* state, condition. *Prop.* càradh.

càran, *n. m.* a beloved one, darling ; *dim.* of càr, friend.

carathaisd. *See* cairbhist.

carbad, *n. f.* a chariot ; araon carbad is marc-shluagh, both chariot and horsemen ; a bier. *O.Ir.* carpat. *W.* cerbyd. *O.Celt.* karbanto-n, karbito-n.

carbad, *n. m.* a jaw bone ; the teeth ; " buail am balach air a' charbad is buail am balgair air an t-sròin," strike the clown on the jaw, and the dog on the nose. *O.Ir.* carpat.

carbadair, *n. m.* a charioteer.

carbard, *n. m. See* carbad.

carbh, *cărv, n. f.* a ship or boat, built after a particular fashion (*carvel* built). *O.N.* karfi. *Mid.Lat.* carabus.

carbh, carv, *v.* engrave, fr. the *Eng.*

carbhaidh, carvi, *n. f.* caraway.

carbhair, *n. m.* a carver, engraver.

carbhaireachd, carveruchc, *n. f.* carving, mangling.

carbhanach, *n. m.* a carp. *O.N.* karfi.

carcair, kark'-ur, *n. m.* a prison, a sink, or sewer (in a cow house). *E.Ir.* carcair. *W.* carchar. *Lat.* carcer.

carcair, *n. m.* skinned top of peat bank, ready for cutting the peat.

carcais, carcesh, *n. m.* a carcase.

càrd, *n. f.* a card ; *v.* card wool, etc.
càrd, *n. m.* an English gallon, or two Scotch pints ; a quarter of a yard.
càrdair, carder, *n. m.* carder.
càrdaireachd, carderuchc, *n. f.* carding.
carfhacal, *n. m.* quibble, pun.
car-fhaclaiche, *n. m.* a quibbler.
carghus, *n. m.* Lent, torment. *E.Ir.* corgais. *W.* garawys. *Lat.* quadragesima.
càrla, *n. m.* a wool-card.
carlach, *n. m.* a cart-load.
càrlag, *n. f.* a lock of wool.
càrlas, kār'-lus, *n. f.* excellence.
càrn, kārn, *n. m., pl.* cùirn and carnaichean, a heap of stones ; a rocky hill or mountain ; *cairn* raised over the tombs of heroes ; cuiridh mise clach ad chàrn-sa, I will put a stone in your *cairn* ; I will not forget you ; *v.* heap, pile, Accumulate ; a' càrnadh airgid, accumulating silver or wealth. *E.Ir.* cárn.
càrn, *n. m.* a cart ; càrn-slaoid, a sledge ; carn-féinidh, a rung-cart.
càrn, *n. m.* a horning ; fo chàrn, at the horn, outlawed.
càrnach, *n. f.* a stony place, *a.* rocky.
càrnadh, cārn'-u, *vbl. n. m.* heaping, piling.
càrnag, *n. f.* a small fish, a sea eel ; a she terrier.
càrnaichte, *vbl. a.* heaped on.
càrnaid, cārnej, *n. f.* flesh colour, a red colour. *Eng.* carnation.
càrnan, *n. m.* a small heap of stones.
càrn-cuimhne, cārn-cooynu, *n. m.* a monument. A rude heap of stones is still built on the spot where any one is found dead. To this heap the passer-by reverently adds a stone.
càrn-eaglais, cārn-eglish, *n. m.* excommunication.
càrr, *n. m.* the scurvy, scab, mange ; scall or leprosy ; plàigh na càrra, the plague of the leprosy, *Bible. E.Ir.* carr ; carr-matrad, a mangy cur.
carr, *n. m.* a dray, a sledge ; each anns a' chàrr, a horse in the dray or sledge. *See* càrn. *O.Ir.* carr ; fén nó carr nó carpat (*Corm.*). *O.Celt.* karso-s, karre.
carr, *n. m.* the udder. *Carm. Gad.*
carracaig, *n. f.* a pancake.
carrach, *a.* scorbutic, itchy, mangy ; having an uneven surface ; am fear a bhios carrach 'sa bhaile so, bithidh e carrach 'sa bhaile ud thall, he that is scabby in this town, will be mangy in that town ; crustaceous, as potatoes ; " sùileagan de bhuntàta carrach," " marbles " of scabby potatoes. So *E.Ir. O.Celt.* karsâko-s.
carrachan, *n. m.* a little, old-fashioned fellow ; the fish called the lump, frog-

fish, or chub ; carrachan cnuacach, rock fish or conger-eel. *E.Ir.* carra, stone.
carragh, cărr'-u, *n. m.* an erect stone, raised as a monument ; a monument ; a pillar ; far an d'ung thu an carragh, where thou didst anoint the pillar. *Bible. E.Ir.* corthe.
carraid, carej, *n. f.* strife, conflict, trouble ; le carraid ghéir, with sore distress ; fatigue and anguish from watching a sick person dear to one.
carraideach, carejuch, *a.* troublesome ; afflicting ; quarrelsome ; fatigued and sorely distressed from watching a sick person ; grieved and fatigued.
carraideachd, carejuchc, *n. f.* fatigue.
carraig, carig, *n. f.* a rock, a cliff, a rock jutting into the sea, serving as a quay or fishing station ; a headland ; carraig mo neart, the rock of my strength ; carraig an uchd, the centre of the chest. *O.Ir.* carric (saxum). *W.* carreg. *O.Celt.* karsakki-.
carraigeach, cariguch, *a.* rocky, full of cliffs ; gnarled.
carraigean, *n. f.* knot in wood, root of tangle ; short curly sea-weed ; "Irish moss."
carraigeanach, *a.* rocky, knotty.
carra-meille, *n. m., pl.* carrcha-meille, wild liquorice, wood pease. *Ir.* carramhilis.
carran, *n. m.* scurvy grass ; a dwarf ; an irritable *creature.*
carran, *n. m.* a shrimp.
carran-creige, carran-cregu, *n. m.* fish called the lump ; the sea porcupine.
carrasan, cār-asan, *n. m.* a wheezing in the throat, catarrh.
carrs, *n. m.* a buttercup.
carrsanach, *a.* catarrhal ; wheezing, hoarse. *Ir.* carsán.
cars, *n. f.* a plain, a fertile tract. *Sc.* carse.
carshuil, *n. f.* a rolling eye.
c'arson, car-son', *adv.* why, wherefore ; for ce-ar-son. *Cf.* c'ainm = ce-ainm.
càrt, cārt, *n. m.* a quart, a quarter, a lippy. *Lat.* quartus.
cart, carst, *v.* clean, as stable, etc. *E.Ir.* cartaim, cleanse, oust.
cart, *n. f.* bark ; root of water-lily ; tanning material ; *v. tr.* tan. *Lat.* cortex, bark, rind.
cartadh, carsta', *vbl. n. m.* act of cleaning a stable, byre, sty, etc.
cartadh, *vbl. n. m.* act of tanning.
cartair, *a.* pirouetting (as in a dance) ; applied to the neat movements of birds.
cartan, *n. m.* a heath-mite, flesh-worm.
cartaran, *n. m.* a fourth part of a stone.

carthannach, car-hanach, *a.* kind, polite, charitable. *E.Ir.* **carthanach**, loving. *Lat.* caritas.

carthannachd, car-hanachc, *n. f.* charity, politeness.

carthanta, car-hantu, *a.* kind, polite.

carthantachd, car-hantachc, *n. f.* politeness.

carthuinnich, car-hunich, *v. i.* dwell apart (as in a cave) ; separate.

cart-làir, *n. f.* tormentil.

car-tuathal, car-toou-hul, *n. m.* a wrong turn ; unprosperous course ; **car** + **tuathal** (*a.* of **tuath**, the left).

caruinnean, *coll. n.* refuse of threshed corn.

caruinnich, *v. t.* separate, winnow.

cas, *a.* curled, twisted. *E.Ir.* **cass.**

cas, *v. i.* and *t.* curl, twist, wreathe. So *Ir.* **cas**, wreathed, twisted. (*Lh.*)

cas, *a.* steep, sudden ; **leathad cas,** a steep brae ; **sruth cas,** rapid stream. *E.Ir.* **cass.** *O.Celt.* **kasto-s.**

cas, *a.* hasty, passionate, irritable ; **duine cas,** an irritable man ; *v. i.* grin, girn, snarl, be enraged. *O.Celt.* **kassi-,** hate.

cas, *n. f., gen.* **coise,** *pl.* **casan,** foot, leg, stem, haft, handle, shaft ; **cas na sgine,** the haft of the knife ; **cas an ùird,** the shaft of the hammer ; **aig cois na beinne,** at the foot of the hill ; **cas mu sheach,** heads and thraws. *E.Ir.* **coss.**

càs, *n. m.* dilemma, predicament ; hardship ; distress, difficulty, emergency ; **anns gach càs,** in every emergency ; **chan e an càs,** it is not the difficulty ; **is ann dhuit as léir mo chàs,** thou seest my distress. *E.Ir.* **càs,** *a.* hard, cruel ; *n. m.* a case, predicament. *Lat.* casus.

casa-carrach, *n. f.* stilts.

casa-cearbain, *n. f.* " legs " from the sun. *Also* **casan-cainbe.**

casach, *n. f.* part of tackle attached to the hook ; a hook line. *Also* **snòt.**

casach, *n. m.* an ascent. So *O'R.*

casach, *n. f.* the outlet of a lake, a ford.

casachdaich, *n. f.* cough, coughing.

casad, *n. f.* a cough ; *v.* cough. *Also* **casd, casdaich.** *W.* **pas,** a cough.

casadaich, cas'-ăd-èch, *n. f.* colic ; gripes in cattle, making them strike the belly with their feet.

casadh, căs'-u, *vbl. n. m.* act of grinning, twisting, approaching ; gnashing ; snarling ; gaping ; **a' casadh fhiacal,** showing his teeth, snarling.

casa-feannaig, casa-fyaneg, *pl. n.* crow's-foot stitching.

casag, *n. f.* a long coat. *Eng.* cassock. Cf. *It.* casacca.

casaid, cas'-ej, *n. f.* complaint, accusation ; *v.* accuse, complain, lodge a

complaint ; **chasaid e orm,** he lodged a complaint against me ; **a' casaid,** lodging a complaint. *E.Ir.* **cossáit.** *Wi.* **cosáit** = **cogad.** *O'Don. Lat.* causatio.

casaideach, cas'-ej-uch, *a.* prone, or apt to complain.

casaidich, casejuch, *v.* accuse, arraign.

casair, casir, *n. f.* sea drift. *E.Ir.* **casar,** hail. *KM.* **casir.** *Wi.*

casaire, *n. m.* a hammer.

càsairean, căserun, *n.,* *pl.* of **càsair,** causeway, street.

casan, *n. m.* a foot-path, a walk, a treadle, a post in the inside of a wall. *E.Ir.* **cassán,** fr. **cos.**

casan-ceangail, *pl. n.* couples in roofing.

cas-aodannach, *a.* having wrinkled face.

casbhrat, cas'-vrat, *n. m.* a carpet.

cas-chairbeil, *n. f.* a roof-couple.

caschiabh, *n. f.* curled lock ; *a.* **caschiabhach.**

cas-chrom, *n. f.* a long-handled delving-crook ; a crooked spade.

cas-dhìreach, *n. f.* straight spade.

cas fa chrann, *n. f.* honeysuckle.

casg, *v. tr.* stop, quench ; staunch, prevent, silence. *E. Ir.* **cosc,** a checking, quenching.

casgadh, cascu, *vbl. n. m.* stopping, staunching ; **a' casgadh na fola,** staunching the blood ; **an fhuil a ruith gun luibh g'a casgadh,** the blood flowing without an herb to staunch it.

casgair, cascir, *v. tr.* butcher, slaughter. *O.Ir.* coscram, coscrad, destroy.

casgairt, casgurt, *n. m.* massacre, slaughter ; **casgairt ort féin,** may death take you.

càsgoil, căscol, *n. f.* dilemma, predicament ; **an càsgoil,** in a dilemma.

casgradh, cascru, *n. f.* slaughter ; *a.* **casgrach.**

caslach, *n. f.* children, a clan, a tribe.

cas-maighich, cas-myich, *n. f.* hare's foot clover.

casnaid, cas'-nej, *n.f.* split wood, chips.

cas na tonnaig, *n. f.* wild mustard.

caspanach, *a.* parallel. *Ir.* cospanach.

casruisgt, căs'-rŭsht, *a.* barefooted.

castan, *n. f.* chestnut. *Lat.* castanea.

castaran, *n. m.* a measure for butter = ¼ stone. *Eng.* castor.

cast-earbhain, *n. f.* the herb, succory, dandelion.

castreaghainn, castreyin, *n. f.* the straw below the grain on a kiln. *Also* **sràbhag** and **streadhaig.**

casurlach, *a.* curly-locked. *O.Ir.* **cass,** curly, and **urla,** long hair.

cat, *n. m.* and *f.* a cat ; heap of potatoes, corn, etc. *Lat.* cattus. *O.Celt.* **kattâ, katto-s.**

cata, càta, *n. m.* a sheep-cot, pen.

catadh (both a's open), *vbl. n. m.* act of gently calming a crying infant; taming. *Also* càtadh and catachadh.

catag, *n. f.* potato cellar.

cataich, cât'-ich, *v.* tame. Cf. tataich.

catanach, *a.* hairy, rough. Cf. *W.* casnach.

catas, *n. m.* refuse (at wool-carding).

cat-fiadhaich, cat-fia-ich, *n. m.* wild cat.

cath, ca, *n. m.* a battle, a fight; struggle; chuir iad cath ris, they struggled against him. *O.Ir.* cath. I. a battle. 2. a battalion. *W.* cad. *O.Celt.* katu-.

càth, cā, *v.* winnow, fan; a' càthadh san t-sabhal, winnowing in the barn; *n. m.* husks of grain. *Also* fasgnadh. *O.Ir.* cáith.

catha. *See* cadha.

cathach, ca-huch, *n. m.* a warrior; name of St. Columba's notable Psalter. *E.Ir.* cathach. I. warlike. 2. a reliquary taken to battle. *O.Celt.* katâkos.

cathachadh, ca-huchu, *vbl. n. m.* act of fighting, struggling; a' cathachadh riut, struggling against you. *O.Ir.* cathugud.

cathadh, *n. m.* drifting (snow); cathadh-fairge, sea-drifting; cathadh-làir, snow-drifting; sea-drifting is also marcach-sìne.

cathag, că'-hag, *n. f.* a daw, a jackdaw.

cathaich, ca-hich, *v.* fight, contend, struggle.

cathair, ca-hir, *n. f., gen.* cathrach, a city. *O.Ir.* cathir. *W.* caer. *Lat.* castrum. *O.Celt.* kastro-.

cathair, *n. f.* a chair, a throne. *E.Ir.* catháir, *civitas. W.* cadair. *Lat.* cathedra.

cathair-breitheanais, *n. f.* a throne of judgment; the bench; a tribunal.

cathair-easbuig, *n. f.* Episcopal chair.

cathair-rìoghail, *n. f.* a throne.

cathan, *n. m.* wild goose.

cathan, kăh'-ăn, *n. m.* yarn on the warping machine.

cathan-aodaich, *n. m.* a web.

càthar, *n. m.* mossy ground. *See* càir.

cathardha, catharra, *a.* brave; militant. *Ir.* an creideamh cathardha, the reformed religion.

catharrachd, *n. f.* valour, bravery.

cathlabhar, *n. m.* an inciting speech.

cathlunn, *n. m.* a corn. Cf. *Lat.* callum.

càthmhor, cā-hur, *a.* husky, chaffy; is e am fogharadh gaothmhor a ni an coirce càthmhor, it is the windy harvest that makes the oats husky.

catluch, c-looch, *n. m.* a mouse-trap. *M.Ir.* fidchat, wooden cat, mouse trap.

catluibh, *n. f.* cudwort. *Also* cadhluibh.

catran, cat'-ran, *n. m.* the fourth of a stone of cheese, butter, wool, etc.

c'è, kē, *int. pron.* who, which, what;

c'è do làmh, show me your hand, give me your hand. *For* cia e.

cé, kē, *n. m.* and *f.* the earth; an cruinne cè, the globe, the earth, the world. So in *Ir.* cruinne + cé (this here); am bith-cé, the present world. *O.Celt.* kei, this.

cé, kéath, *n. m.* cream. *Ir.* ceó, milk.

ceaba, keibe, *n. m.* the iron part of spade.

céabhar, kēv'-ur, *n. m.* gentle breeze, the state of being slightly intoxicated.

céabharan, *n. m.* slight breeze.

ceach, kech, *interj.* expression of dislike.

ceachail, *v.* dig, excavate. *Ir.* cechlad, hack, cut. *O.Ir.* cechladatar. *Wb.* gl. *suffoderunt.*

ceacharra, *a.* dirty, mean, sordid. *M.Ir.* cecharda, *a.* miry, stingy; cechair, *n. f.* quagmire.

ceachladh, *n. m.* digging.

cead, ked, *n. m.* leave, permission, license, liberty; farewell, adieu; iarr cead, ask leave; cead cothrom, fair play; full freedom; gun do chead a ghabhail, without asking your permission; an d' fhuair thu cead? have you got liberty?; thoir dhomh cead, give me leave; le'r cead, with your permission; thà, le'r cead, yes, sir or madam, or with your permission; le cead na cuideachd, with the company's leave; thoir a chead da, set him about his business. *O.Ir.* cet, is cet duit, licet tibi.

ceadachail, kedachol, *a.* allowable, permissible, permissive.

ceadaich, kedich, *v.* permit, allow, grant, give permission; na ceadaich dha, do not permit him; *vbl. a.* ceadaichte, permitted, granted, permissive.

ceadalach, kedalach, *a.* crazy; subject to fits of sickness.

ceadan, *n. m.* a bunch of wool; a lock of hair; a burden.

ceadha, ke-u, *n. m.* quay; part of a plough, on which the share is fixed.

ceafan, *n. m.* part of a plough; a frivolous person.

ceaird, kiărj and kiŭrj, *n. f.* trade, occupation, handicraft, employment; ciod e as ceaird duit, what is your occupation? *See* ceard. *E.Ir.* cerd.

ceairdealachd, kyùrj'-ăl-ăchc, *n. f.* skilfulness; tradesman-like manner.

ceairdeil, kyùrj'-al, *a.* mechanical, tradesman-like, business-like. *E.Ir.* cerd-damail, skilful. cerd + samail.

ceairsle, kyărsh'-llà, *n. f.* a clew; a ball of yarn or of heather rope. *Also* ceirthle. *E.Ir.* certle, a ball of thread.

ceairsleach, kyărsh'-lyach, *a.* like a clew.

ceairslich, kyarsh'-llich, *v.* make clews, wind, form into clews, coil.

céal, kyè'll, *n. m.* hue of the countenance; is bochd an céal a tha ort, you have a miserable expression of countenance.

céal, *n. m.* a nook, a cranny; step for the mast in a boat.

ceal, *n. m.* stupor, forgetfulness. *E.Ir.* cel, death.

cealach, *n. m.* the fireplace of a kiln.

céalaich, kēlich, *v.* eat. *Kirk.*

céalaideach, kēlejuch, *n. m.* a miserable-looking person.

cealg, kiălug, *n. f., gen.* ceilge, hypocrisy. *E.Ir.* celg, deceit, treachery. *O.Celt.* kelgâ.

cealgach, kiăluguch, *a.* deceitful, hypocritical, treacherous, cunning, crafty, wily.

cealgaire, kiălugiru, *n. m.* a hypocrite, a cheat, a rogue, a deceiver.

cealgaireachd, kiălugiruchc, *n. f.* hypocrisy, treachery, deceit, dissimulation; bàsaichidh dòchas a' chealgaire, the hope of the hypocrite shall perish.

ceall, kial, *n. f., gen.* cille, dependent monastery; monastic cell; a church; a churchyard. *O.Ir.* cell. *Lat.* cella.

ceallaire, kialiru, *n. m.* head or superior of a church or monastery.

cealltair, kialter, *n. m.* coarse grey cloth. *E.Ir.* celtar, cloak; celt, hair garment; common in Irish tales in phrase cealltar draoidheachta, an enchanted covering, a spell of invisibility. *Hyde.*

cean, *n. m.* love, favour. *Ir.* cen, affection.

ceana, *interog.* whither? *Ir.* cá h-ionad.

ceanal, *n. m., gen.* ceanail, pleasantry, kindliness, merriment; fhir a dh'ionnsuich an ceanal, you who drank in kindliness.

ceanalta, ken-ălt-u, *a.* docile, tractable, amiable, kind, mild, pleasant, urbane, polite.

ceanaltachd, kén-alt-achc, *n. f.* docility, tractableness; mildness of disposition, urbanity, politeness.

ceanaltas, ken-alt-us, *n. m.* Same as ceanaltachd.

ceangail, kengil, *v.* tie, bind, fetter, fasten, restrain; ceangailte, bound; restrained; tied, fastened.

ceangal, kengul, *n. m., pl.* ceanglaichean, tie; fastening; a tether; obligation, a bond, a knot; ceangal pòsaidh, betrothment; fo cheangal aig duine sam bith, under restraint to any one; am fear a cheanglas is e a shiùbhlas, he that ties (his bundle) is he that speeds. *E.Ir.* cengal. *Lat.* cingulum.

ceangaltas, kengultus, *n. m.* obligation; *a.* ceangaltach.

ceanglachan, *n. m.* a bundle, a truss.

ceanglaiche, keng'-lichu, *n. m.* a binder.

ceann, kyănn, *n. m., gen. s.* and *n. pl.* cinn, a head, point; end, beginning, limit; period, expiration; extremity; genius, ingenuity; chief, master, commander, attention; headland; hilt; subject of discourse; thog tuinn an cinn, waves reared their head; ceann nan laoch, the chief of the heroes; an ceann bliadhna, at the expiration of a year; "ceann goimh air madainn earraich," surly beginning on a spring morning; mu cheannaibh nan crann, about the top of the trees; bi ad cheann mhath dha, be kind to him (be good to him); ghabh i droch ceann da, she took a dislike to him; bha e 'na dhroch cheann da, he used him badly; a' dol air cheann gnothuich, going on business; chan 'eil an droch cheann aige, he is not destitute of brains; an ceann a chéile, mixed, assembled; na cuir ceann 'na leithid sin, do not attempt such a thing; ceann na ciche, the nipple; liath thu mo cheann, your conduct has made my head grey; ghabh e an saoghal fo a cheann, he went forth into the wide world; os cionn an athair, above the firmament. *O.Ir.* cenn. *W.* penn.

ceannabhard, kyann'-a-vărd, *n. m.* commander-in-chief, commander, a leader.

ceannabharr, *n. m.* head-dress, cap, hat.

ceannabheirt, *n. m.* head-gear, a helmet.

ceannabhiorach, *a.* conical.

ceannabhrat, *n. m.* canopy, head-dress.

ceannach, kyănn'-ach, *n. m.* a present, a reward, compensation; a bribe; ceannach geal an uair thig an sneachd, a white present when the snow comes; is ceannach air an ugh an gog, the egg is dearly bought at the price of the cackling; *vbl. n. m.* act of purchasing, buying; a cheannach fiodha, to purchase timber. *O.Ir.* cennige. *Gl.* lixa.

ceannachd, kyann'-ăchc, *n. f.* merchandise, commerce, traffic; agus ni sibh ceannachd 'san tìr, and ye shall trade in the land.

ceannachnap, *n. m.* the knee-piece that joins the bench to the gunwale. *Also* ceannachraidh.

ceann-adhairt, *n. m.* the head of a bed. *E.Ir.* cenn-adart.

ceannag, *n. f.* a head-rig, a bottle of hay or straw.

ceann-aghaidh, *n. m.* the forehead, the face.

ceannaich, kyann'-ich, *v.* purchase, buy, redeem; traffic; a cheannaich sinn cho daor, which we so dearly purchased. *Ir.* cennaigim, I buy.

ceannaiche, kyann'-ichu, *n. m.* a buyer, a merchant.

ceann-aimsir,* *n. m.* term, period ; epoch, date, era.

ceannairc, kyann'ĕrk, *n. f.* rebellion, sedition, mutiny, insubordination.

ceannairceach, kyann'-ĕrk-ach, *a.* rebellious, seditious, mutinous ; perverse ; stubborn.

ceannaire, kyanneru, *n. m.* a horse-driver, a horse-leader (when ploughing), a guide. *Ir.* a hammer ; a wedge (to drive hoops).

ceannaireachd, cianerachc, *n. f.* a goodsman's office.

ceannan, cianan, *n. m.* a small wooden vessel, a bank.

ceann-aobhair, kyann-ūvir, *n. f.* a prime or first cause.

ceannaodach, *n. m.* head-dress.

ceannard, *n. f.* a commander, a leader, a chief. *Ir.* ceannphort. *W.* pennaeth.

ceann-àrd, *a.* high-headed.

ceannardach, *a.* high-headed.

ceannardachd, *n. f.* arrogance ; superiority, chieftainship.

ceann-armailt, also ceann-airm, *n. m.* a general.

ceannpholag, *n. f.* a tadpole. *W.* penbwl.

ceannas, *n. f.* superiority, pride ; *also* disobedience. *E.Ir.* cendas, headship.

ceannasach, *a.* proud, aspiring, headstrong. *E.Ir.* cendasach, haughty.

ceannasachd, kyănn'-as-ăchc, *n. f.* ambition, pride.

ceannas-feadhna, *n. m.* leadership of a clan.

ceannasg, kyann'-ăsg, *n. f.* hair-lace.

ceannbheirt, ciana-verst, *n. f.* headgear, helmet.

ceann-buidhne, *n. m.* head of a company ; a captain.

ceann-céille, *n. m.* an adviser ; ceann na céille, a wise head ; a shrewd person.

ceann-cinnidh, *n. m.* a chieftain. *Also* ceann-fine.

ceann-còmhraidh, *n. m.* subject of conversation.

ceann-cònspaid, *n. m.* subject of debate.

ceann-éideadh, *n. m.* a head-dress.

ceann-fàth, *n. m.* cause, reason. *Also* cion-fàth.

ceann-feachd, *n. m.* a general.

ceann-feadhna, *n. m.* leader of a host.

ceannfhionn, *a.* white-headed, white-faced. *Ir.* ceanann. *Lh. O.Ir.* cenn + fin, find (white).

ceann-fine, *n. m.* head of a clan, chief.

ceannghalair, *n. m.* dandruff. *Also* scealpaich.

ceannghlas, *a.* grey-headed.

* For pronunciation of compounds see separate members elsewhere.

ceann-Ileach, *n. m.* a sword-hilt—esp. of sword made in Islay.

ceann-iùil, *n. m.* a guide.

ceann-làidir, *a.* strong-headed ; mulish, stubborn, self-willed.

ceann-litir, *n. m.* a capital letter.

ceann-mathain, *n. f.* name of a star.

ceann-òrdaig, *n. m.* a diminutive person, a Tom-Thumb.

ceannphort, *n. m.* chief, chief leader ; same as ceannard, and ceannbhard.

ceannrach, *n. m.* head-tie, horse's halter. *Also* ceannraig, a bridle. *E.Ir.* cendrach. *W.* penffestr.

ceann-riabhach, *a.* with brindled head.

cennsa, *n. f.* gentleness. *O.Ir.* cendsa, clemency, *mansuetudo.*

ceannsachadh, kyănn'-săch-u, *vbl. n. m.* act of subduing ; subjecting ; keeping under authority.

ceannsachd, kyann'-ssăchc, *n. f.* subordination, authority, government ; temperance.

ceannsaich, kyann-sich, *v.* subdue ; conquer, quell, train ; *vbl. a.* ceann-saichte, subdued, quelled. *E.Ir.* cennsaigim, I grow gentle, I appease.

ceannsal, kyănn'-sal, *n. f.* rule, government, authority. *M.Ir.* cendsal, pre-eminence, emulation.

ceannsalach, *a.* authoritative.

ceannsalachd, kyann'-săl-ăchc, *n. f.* sway, rule.

ceann-seanachais, *n. m.* source of information.

ceannsgal, *n. m.* command, authority. *See* ceannsal.

ceannsgalach, *a.* masterful, authoritative.

ceann-sgrìobhaidh, *n. m.* subject of writing.

ceann-sgur, *n. m.* period, full stop.

ceann - simid, kyann - shim'- ij, *n. m.* tadpole.

ceann-sithe, *n. m.* peace-maker, a pacifier.

ceann-slaite, *n. m.* the man at the yard of a boat.

ceann-suidhe, *n. m.* president.

ceann-taice, *n. m.* chief support.

ceann-tàla, *n. m.* a bard.

ceann-teagasg, *n. m.* a text (for sermon).

ceann-tighe, *n. m.* head of a family.

ceann-tìre, kyann-tiĕru, *n. m.* a peninsula, headland, promontory, land's end ; Kintyre.

ceann-tobhta, *n. m.* bench-piece, wooden knee fixing boat bench to the gunwale.

ceann-uidhe, *n. m.* journey's end, destination ; hospitable landlord. *O.Ir.* cend + ude, end of journey.

ceap, ciap, *n. m.* a last ; a clog or stumbling-block on a beast's foot ; the stocks ; a snare ; do leag iad ceap, they laid a snare ; *v.* intercept, stop, obstruct ; **ceap e**, intercept or stop him ; carp. *E.Ir.* **cepp.**

ceap, kepp, *n. m.* a cap ; fr. the *Eng.*

ceapach, *n. f.* plot of land ; *a.* full of lasts, trunks of trees. *E.Ir.* **ceppach**, a plot of land for tillage ; a village (of one tribe). *O.Celt.* **keppo-s**, a garden.

ceapadh, kep'-ă, *vbl. n. m.* act of intercepting, catching, carping ; **a' ceapadh chuileag**, catching flies. *Sc.* kep, kepp, catch, intercept.

ceapag, *n. f.* a small turf, sod ; a barrow wheel.

ceapag, *n. f.* impromptu verse. *E.Ir.* **cepóc**, *f.* a song, chorus.

ceapaire, kep'-ur'-à, *n. m.* bread covered with butter and overlaid with cheese ; usage varies : *McL.D., MacE.* 2nd ed., *H.S.D.*, and perhaps *McB.*, as here ; but *Arm., McFarl., Shaw., MacE.* 1st ed., say " bread covered with butter."

ceapan, *n. m.* a little last, or stock ; *a.* ceapanach.

ceapanta, kep'-ant-á, *a.* snatching, carping. *Ir.* ceppánta, stiff, stubborn.

ceap-shuileach, *a.* having eyes with a tendency to meet.

cearb, kerb, *n. f.* a tatter, corner, a skirt ; **rug e air chirb**, he laid hold of a skirt ; a defect, a blemish ; **òran gun chearb**, a song without blemish or defect. *M.Ir.* cerbb, a rag, skirt of a garment. *O.Ir.* cerp, cut ; small piece. *O.Celt.* kerbo-. Cf. *W.* **crybibion**, tatters.

cearbach, *a.* ragged, imperfect, unfortunate ; **is cearbach nach robh thu so**, it is a pity you were not here.

cearbaiche, *n. f.* awkwardness, raggedness.

cearbaire, *n. m.* an awkward person.

cearban, kerban, *n. m.* the sail-fish ; **cearban feòir**, the *plant* crow-foot.

cearc, kiarc, *n. f., gen. s.* circe, *n. pl.* cearcan, a hen ; **cearc fhrangach**, a turkey hen, and also a species of the common hen ; **cearc fhraoich**, moor hen ; **cearc thomain**, a partridge. *Ir.* cerc.

cearcag, *n. f.* a little hen.

cearcall, kiarcul, *n. m.* a circle ; a hoop ; circumference ; **ged chuireadh tu cearcall air Albainn**, though you should encircle Scotland. *E.Ir.* **cercal**. *Lat.* circulus.

cearcallach, kiarculuch, *a.* hooped.

cearchaill, *n. f.* pillow, unwieldy person.

ceard, kyârd', *n. m.* an artificer ; tinker ; **ceard airgid**, silversmith ; **ceard òir**, goldsmith ; **ceard staoin**, tinsmith ; **ceard umha**, coppersmith. *O.Ir.* cert, gl. *Wb.* aerarius, artisan. *O.Celt.* kerdâ, art.

ceardach, kyârd'-ach, *n. f.* a smithy ;

forge. *E.Ir.* **cerddcha.** cerd + cái (house) ; unde dicitur ; cerdcha, *i.e.* **tech cerda.** *Corm.*

ceardachd, *n. f.* trade, craft ; trade of a tinker.

ceardail, kyârd'-al, *a.* tinker-like.

ceardalachd, kyard'-al'ăchc, *n. m.* ingenuity, handicraft ; shameful conduct.

ceardaman, kyârd'-am-an, *n. m.* a hornet ; a dung-beetle.

ceard-dubhan, *n. m.* a dung-beetle ; hornet ; *scarabaeus. Also* **òrdlan.**

cearmanta, *a.* tidy.

ceàrn, kyârn, *n. m.* corner ; quarter ; region ; **ceàrnan iomallach**, remote corners ; **sluagh bho gach ceàrn**, people from every quarter. *E.Ir.* cern.

ceàrnabhan, *n. m.* a hornet, a beetle.

cearnach, kyârn'-ach, *a.* angular, cornered, square ; *n. m.* a pane of glass. *Also* **lòsan.** *Ir.* cernach, four square.

ceàrnag, *n. f.* a little corner ; a short stout person.

cearnan, *n. m.* a square, a quadrangle.

cearr, kyărr, *a.* left, wrong, awkward ; **an taobh cearr**, the left side ; the wrong side ; **chaidh e cearr**, he went wrong ; *adv.* improperly ; **is cearr a fhreagair thu**, you answered very improperly. *E.Ir.* cerr, maimed, awkward, left-handed. *O.Celt.* kerso-s, left.

cearrach, kyârr'-ach, *a.* dexterous ; *n. m.* a gamester, a gambler. *Ir.* cearrbhach, a professional gambler, plunder.

cearrachas, kerachus, *n. m.* gaming, gambling. So *O'R.*

cearrbhag, and **cearrag**, *n. f.* left hand ; **air a' chearraig**, left-handed.

cearrlamhach, kĕr-lavach, *a.* left-handed, awkward.

ceart, kyart, *a.* right, just, upright, proper, fair, correct ; **tha thu ceart**, you are quite correct ; exact, precise ; very, identical ; **a cheart duine**, the very man ; **an ceart ni a bha dhìth orm**, the very thing I wanted ; **cuir ceart**, put to rights, rectify, correct, adjust ; **an ceart uair**, this moment ; in certain parts, **an ceart uair** means, in a little while, presently ; *adv.* equally, just ; exactly, precisely ; **cheart cho math**, equally well ; **ceart mar thuirt thu**, exactly as you said ; *n. m.* justice, propriety ; **is rinn se an ceart**, and he executed justice. *E.Ir.* cert. *O.Celt.* kerto-. *Lat.* certus.

ceartachadh, kyărt'-ach-ă, *vbl. n. m.* amendment ; act of rectifying, correcting, amending, putting to rights ; adjusting, trimming ; **ceartaichean**, little domestic jobs, chores.

ceartachail, kyărt'-ach-al, *a.* rectifiable.

ceartachair, kyart'-ăch-er', *n. m.* a rectifier, adjuster, corrector, regulator.
ceartaich, kyart'-ich, *v.* rectify, adjust, amend, put in order, or to rights.
ceartaiche, kyart'-ėch-à, *n. m.* a corrector.
ceartas, kyărt'-us, *n. m.* justice, equity ; dèan ceartas, decide impartially ; is iad ceartas agus breitheanas àite tàimh do rìgh chaithreach, justice and judgment are the habitation of thy throne.
ceart-bheart, kerst-verst, *n. f.* a good deed, a good turn.
ceart-bhreith, kerst-vre, *n. f.* a just judgment.
ceart-bhreitheach, *a.* righteous in judgment.
ceart-bhreitheanas, kerst-vre-honus, *n. m.* a just judgment.
ceart-chreideamh, kyart'-chreju, *n. m.* soundness of faith, orthodoxy ; ceart-chreidmheach, orthodox, sound in the faith.
ceart-sgrìobhadh, kerst-sgreevu, *n. m.* orthography.
ceart-tarnach, *a.* musical term, correct pitch.
céas, kes, *n. m.* coarse, matted wool. *Ir.* cés, hair, coarse wool on legs of sheep. *KM.*
ceasach, kesuch, *a.* temporary bridge or footpath over bogs.
ceasad, kes'-ad, *n. m.* repining, grumble at one's lot or one's share of anything ; discontent ; a' ceasad, repining, grumbling. *E.Ir.* cess, gloom, cessim, sadness, I grumble. *Lat.* questus.
ceasadach, kĕs'-ăd-ach, *a.* repining, whining, discontented, displeased with one's share.
ceasnachadh, kesnachu, *vbl. n. m.* an examination ; act of examining, interrogating, catechising.
ceasnachail, kesnachol, *a.* interrogatory ; inquisitive ; impertinent.
ceasnaich, kesnich, *v.* examine ; catechise, interrogate, question ; *vbl. a.* ceasnaichte, catechised. *O.Ir.* cestaigim, cestnigim.
ceathach, ke-hach, *n. m.* mist, fog ; an ceathach a' seòladh, the mist gliding ; mar cheathach air beanntaibh, as mist on the hills.
ceathachail, kĕ-hachal, *a.* misty, foggy. *E.Ir.* citheach, showery. Also ceth, a shower.
ceathairne, kya-harna, *coll. n.* yeomanry, men fit for war ; peasantry. *Also* tuath.
ceathairneach, kya-harnach, *n. m.* a freebooter, a robber ; a hero, a sturdy fellow.
ceathairneachd, kya-harnachc, *n. f.* heroism.

ceatharn, *n. f.* a troop of stout men. *E.Ir.* cethern, company of foot-soldiers. Cf. *Lat.* caterva. *O.Celt.* katernâ.
ceatharn-choille, *n. f.* outlaws, freebooters.
ceatharnach, *n. m.* an able-bodied man. *E.Ir.* cethernach, a foot-soldier.
ceatharnachd, *n. f.* valour, heroism.
ceathramh, ker'-ruv, *a.* the fourth ; a quarter ; an ceathramh bliadhna, the fourth year ; ceathramh mairt, a quarter of beef. *O.Ir.* cethramad (Z^2).
ceathramhan, ke-ruvan, *n. m., pl.* ceathramhain, a quadrant, a cube.
ceathramhanach, *a.* like a quadrant.
ceathrar, kĕrr'-ur, *n. m. a.* four ; ceathrar mhac, four sons ; ceathrar nighean, four daughters ; *n. m.* *O.Ir.* cethrar.
ceidhe, ke-u, *n. m., pl.* ceidheachan, a pier, a quay, caulter-holder ; fr. *Eng.*
ceig, *n. m.* a kick ; fr. the *Eng.* McB.
ceig, *n. m.* a lump, bunch, clot, mass of shag. *O.N.* kaggi, a keg. *Swed.* kagga.
ceigeach, keguch, *a.* lumpish, matted (hair), shaggy.
ceigean, kĕgen, *n. m.* a tuft ; a fat man ; a squat fellow ; a turd.
ceigeanachd, kegenuchc, *n. f.* squatness.
ceigeil, kegil, *vbl. n. m.* kicking, stirring. *O.N.* kvikna, to stir. *Sc.* kicky. Cf. spruce and *kicky* with frogail is ceigeil, smart and frisky.
ceil, kel, *v. t.* conceal, hide, screen, shelter ; ma cheileas sinn fhuil, if we conceal his blood. *O.Ir.* celim. *Lat.* celo, ni ceil som, *non celat ipse* (Z^2). *W.* celu, to hide. *O.Celt.* kelô.
céile, kēla, *n. m.* a fellow ; a spouse ; a match ; husband ; a wife ; céile a h-òige, the husband of her youth ; a céile, her husband, her spouse ; as *match* it is never used but with *per. pronouns* ; as a chéile, asunder, disjoined ; a chum a chéile, towards each other ; chaidh iad am badaibh a chéile, they came to grips. *O.Ir.* céle, maritus, socius, sóirmug = sóirchéle, gl. *Wb.* 10ª. *O.Celt.* keiljo-.
ceileach, keluch, *a.* martial. *M.Ir.* cellach, contention.
ceilear, kelar, *n. m.* warble, warbling. *E.Ir.* celebraim. 1. celebrate. 2. warble.
ceilearach, kelaruch, *a.* warbling.
ceileir, keler, *v.* warble, sing sweetly ; mar smeòrach a' ceilearadh, warbling like a mavis. *O.Ir.* gl. lase celebirsimme, cum valefecissemus. $(Z^2.)$
ceileireach, keleruch, *a.* chirping, musical.
ceileiriche, kelerichu, *n. m.* a warbler.
céilich, kĕ'-lėch, *v.* participate, eat ; a chéilich m'aran, who partook of my bread.

céilidh, kēli, *n. f.* visit ; air chéilidh, on a visit ; gossiping; pilgrimage, sojourning ; fhad 's a bhios tu an céilidh an t-saoghail, while your earthly pilgrimage lasts. *E.Ir.* célide, a visit.
céillidh, kēyly, *a.* wise, sober, prudent; from ciall, sense.
ceilp, *n. f.* kelp ; fr. the *Eng.*
ceilte, keltu, *vbl. a.* concealed, hid, secret.
ceilteach, *a.* 1. concealing. 2. penurious. 3. reserved.
céilteach, kēltuch, *a.* fond of gossiping or visiting ; " cha robh céilteach nach robh bradach," there was no gossip who was not thievish ; *n. f.* a gossiping female.
Ceiltich, keltich, *n. p.* Celts.
céiltidh, kēlty, *a.* wise, sober.
ceiltinn, keltin, *vbl. n. f.* concealing, hiding.
céin, kēn, *a.* distant ; tìr chéin, foreign land. By-form of cian, *q.v.*
céir, kēr, *n. m.* wax ; *v.* seal, wax ; céir an litir, seal or wax the letter So *E.Ir.* *W.* cŵyr. *Lat.* cēra.
céir, *n. f.* a deer's buttock. *See* péire.
céir-bheach, *n. f.* honey-comb.
céir-chuachag, *n. f.* cup, waxen-cell.
céireach, keruch, *a.* waxen, full of wax.
céirean, kēren, *n. m.* a wafer. *Also* abhlan.
ceirean, *n. f.* a plaster, poultice ; *v. t.* ceireanaich, fondle, pet. *M.Ir.* ceirin.
céirgheal, *a.* white-buttocked. *Also* cileach.
céirseach, kērshuch, *n. f.* the thrush.
ceirsle, *n. f.* a clew. *See* ceirtle.
ceirsleag, kerslag, *n. f.* a small clew.
ceirslich, kerslich, *v.* make into clews. *Also* tachrais.
céirte, kértū, *vbl. a.* sealed, waxed.
ceirtle, kertlu, *n. f., pl.* ceirtlean, clew, ball of yarn. *O.Ir.* certle. *O.Celt.* kertiliá.
céis, kēsh, *n. m.* a case, hamper. *M.Ir.* cess (*f.*), a basket.
céis, *n. f.* a frame, sash, a picture frame. *O.Celt.* keissi-.
céischrann, kēsh'-chrann, *n. m.* herb, polypody.
ceisd, kesj, *n. f.* a question, doubt, anxiety ; thà, gun cheisd, yes, undoubtedly, yes, indeed ; a beloved object, darling ; thà, a cheisd, yes, darling ; " is mór mo cheisd air a' ghruagaich," great is my fancy for the lass. *O.Ir.* ceist, gl. *Wb., pl.* ceisti, gl. *contendere.* *Lat.* quaestio.
ceisdeil, kesjal, *a.* questionable ; beloved, modest, of a good character. *Also* teisteil.
ceisdealachd, kesjalachc, *n. f.* questionableness.
ceisdleabhar, kesj-lo-ar, *n. m.* catechism.

céiseach, kēshuch, *n. f.* a large, corpulent woman. *See* céis, a frame ; nach ann air tha chéis, used with reference to a man of unusual size.
céiseag, *n. f.* a small case, small creel.
ceistean, *n. m.* a lover, sweetheart.
ceistear, *n. m.* a catechist.
ceistich, *v.* examine.
céiteanach, kētanuch, *n. m.* the size larger than a cuddy of the coal-fish.
céiteil, keytel, *a.* noisy, fussy ; " bu chéiteil cinneadh t-athar ann," noisy, was your father's clan there ? Cf. *E.Ir.* cétal, singing, song.
céitein, kēchen, *n. m.* month of May, beginning of summer ; fair weather, a favourable season; céitein na h-òinsich, from April 19 to May 12 ; *a.* belonging to May. *O.Ir.* cétsoman=cét-sámsin, *i.e.* first " weather " of summer. *Corn.* gl. Cf. cétam, *gen.* cétaman, mensis Maius (*Z*²). *Also* cétain.
ceithir, ke-hir, *a.* four. *O.Ir.* cethir. *W.* pedair.
ceithirchasach, ke-hir-chasuch, *a.* four-footed, quadruped ; *n. m.* a quadruped, or four-footed animal.
ceithir-cheàrnach, ke-hir-chyārnuch, *a.* quadrangular, quadratic.
ceithir-deug, kiu-hir-diūg, *n. m.* fourteen.
ceithir-fillte, ke-hir-feelt, *a.* fourfold.
ceithir-oisinneach, ke-hir-oshinuch, *a.* square, quadrangular, having four angles.
ceithir-ràmhach, ko-hir-ravuch, *n. f.* a four-oared boat, a quadreme.
ceithir-shlisneach, ke-hir-hlishnuch, *a.* four-sided, quadrilateral.
ceò, kyo, *n. m.* and *f.* mist, fog ; amazement ; chaidh e 'na cheò, he got quite amazed ; " duathar a' cheò," the murk of the mist. *E.Ir.* ceó, *gen.* ciach. *O.Celt.* kjâvak-s, a cloud.
ceòb, *n. m.* a dark nook, corner.
ceòb, kyôb, *n. m.* drizzly rain.
ceòban, kyôb'-an, *n. m.* drizzly rain.
ceòbanach, kyôb'-an-ach, *a.* drizzling ; misty.
ceòbhainne, kyō-vainu, *n. m.* drizzling rain. ceò + boinne = mist-drop.
ceòdhar, kyō-ur, *a.* misty, foggy, obscure.
ceò-éideadh, *n. m.* shroud of mist.
ceòl, kyoll, *n. m., gen.* ciùil, music, melody, harmony. So *E.Ir.* *O.Ir.* cél, *gen.* ciúil, *acc.* céol.
ceòlach, *a.* musical, melodious, abounding in music.
ceòlan, kyôl'-an, *n. m.* a hum-drum of a person ; one quite bewildered. *E.Ir.* ceolán, *n. m.* a little bell.
ceòl-cadail, *n. m.* a lullaby.
ceòlchuirm, kyôll'-chūrm, *n. m.* a concert. *Ir.* féis-ciùil.

ceòl-cluaise, *n. m.* music or singing learned by ear only.

ceol-gàire, *n. m.* mirth, ludicrous object.

ceòlmhoireachd, kyôl'-vŭr-achc, *n. f.* melodiousness, harmony, harmoniousness.

ceòlmhor, kyôl'-vur, *a.* tuneful, harmonious, melodious. *Also* funny, amusing. *E.Ir.* céolmar.

ceòlraidh, kyōl-ri, *n. f.* the muses.

ceòs, *n. m.* podex, hip. *Also* cias.

ceòsach, *a.* broad-skirted, bulky, clumsy.

ceòsan, *n. m.* burr; light down (of feathers).

ceòthaireachd, kyō-heruchc, *n. f.* mistiness.

ceòthanach, *a.* misty; " geamhradh ceòthanach, earrach reòthanach, samhradh breac-riabhach, foghar geal grianach," these are ideal seasons.

ceòthmhor, kyō-vor, *a.* misty, foggy. *E.Ir.* céomar.

ceòthmhorachd, *n. f.* mistiness.

ceòthragach, *a.* drizzling; misty.

ceòthran, *n. m.* slight drizzle.

ceòthranach, *a.* drizzling. *Also* ciuthranaich, *n. f.* warm drizzle.

ceud, kēd, *n. m.* a hundred; ceud fear, a hundred men. *O.Ir.* cét. *W.* cant. *Lat.* centum. *Goth.* hund. *O.H.G.* hunt.

ceud, *num. a.* first; an ceud fhear (*masc.*), the first man; a' cheud àithne (*fem.*), the first commandment. *O.Ir.* cét. *W.* cynt. *O.Celt.* kentu-, first.

ceudach, kēd'-uch, *a.* centuple, in hundreds.

ceudamh, kēd'-uv, *a.* the hundredth. *O.Ir.* cétmad.

ceudbhileach, kēd'-vill-ach, *a.* the herb centuary.

ceudchathach, *a.* of a hundred battles.

ceudfadh, *n. f.* sense, faculty. *O.Ir.* cétbaid, *sensus, sententia* (*Z²*); cét + buith (be).

ceudna, kēd'-na, and kee-andu, *adv.* also; mar an ceudna, also; the one formerly mentioned, the same; an duine ceudna, the same man, the identical man. *O.Ir.* cétne fer, the *first* man, but in fogur cétne, the *same* sound.

ceudnachd, kēd'-nachc, sameness, identity.

ceudtarruing, ki-ad-tarin, *n. m.* first drawing, singlings.

ceud-thoiseach, kēd'-hosh-ach, *n. m.* first principles, commencement.

ceum, kēm, *n. m., pl.* ceumannan, a step, a pace, a degree; *v.* step, walk, pace; move; trì cheumannan, three paces; cheum e gu mór mun cuairt, he walked majestically about; tha e ceum na's

fhaide mach, he is a degree farther removed; deich ceuman air ais, ten degrees backwards. *O.Ir.* céim; *v. i.* céimnigim, step, proceed. *O.Celt.* kengmen-.

ceumach, kēmach, *a.* a stately gait.

ceum-inbhe, *n. m.* dignity, rank.

ceum-tuislidh, *n. m.* a false step.

ceus, *n.* ham; the lower part of the body.

ceus, *n.* the coarse wool on sheep's legs. *See* céas.

ceus, kās, *v. t.* crucify, torture. *O.Ir.* cessaim, I suffer. *O.Celt.* kentsô.

ceusach, *a.* torturing.

ceusadair, kēs'-ad-er', *n. m.* a tormentor.

ceusadaireachd, kēs'-ad-er'-achg, *n. f.* crucifying.

ceutach, *a.* becoming. *Also* ciatach.

cha, chan, *neg. part.* not; cha bhuail mi, I shall not strike; cha dèan mi, I will not do; cha d'éisd mi, I did not listen. Takes n before a vowel and f aspirated; chan fhaod thu, you must not; chan 'eil eadar an t-amadan agus an duine glic ach tairgse mhaith a ghabhail, 'nuair a gheibh e i, there is no difference between the wise man and the fool, but to accept a good offer when he gets it; cha tig fuachd gu 'n tig earrach, cold comes not till spring. *O.Ir.* is nicon; nicon fitir, knows not.

chaidh, chay, *pret.* of theirig, go; theirig dhachaidh, go home; chaidh e dhachaidh, he went home; théid e dhachaidh, he shall go home. *Also* chuaidh. *O.Ir.* dochóid.

chaoidh, *adv.* for ever. *Ir.* choidhche. *E.Ir.* caidche and coidche. 1. till night. 2. ever, always. co + oidche = till night.

cheana, chena, *adv.* already, before, now; am fear a mharbh a mhàthair cheana, bheireadh e beò a nis i, he who killed his mother a little ago, would fain have her alive now. *O.Ir.* cene, now, while. *W.* gynneu.

chì, *fut.* of faic, will see. *O.Ir.* atchí, ad-ciu. *O.Celt.* kesiô, I see.

chiall and chiallach, *voc.* darling, exclamation of surprise.

chiaramh and chianaibh, *adv.* a moment ago.

chionn, chyúṇṇ, *conj.* because, as; chionn gun do bhuin e ruinn gu fial, because he dealt bountifully with us.

chìteadh, *pret. subj.* of chì, might be seen. *Also* chìtist.

cho, *adv.* so, as; cho dalma, so presumptuous; cho cruaidh ris an stàilinnn, as hard as steel.

choidhche, chooy'-chà, *adv.* for ever, never; cha till e choidhche, he shall never return. So *Ir.* *See* chaoidh.

chon, *prep.* to ; chon a' bhaile, to town. *Also* thun.

chuala. *See* cluinn.

chugad, *prep.* + *pron.* towards thee. *O.Ir.* chucut.

chugam, *prep.* + *pron.* towards me. *Also* thugad, thugam.

chum, *prep.* to, towards ; chum a' bhaile, to the town ; chum an duine, to or towards the man ; *conj.* for the purpose of, in order that ; a chum mo sgrios, for the purpose of destroying me. *O.Ir.* do chum.

chun, *prep.* to, until. *See* chon.

chunnaic, *pret.* of faic (see), saw. *O.Ir.* con-acca, *pref.* of ad-ciu, con + faic.

cì, *inter.* + *pron.* let me have it (*fem.*) ; cidhì, "show" it ; cì dhomh fhéin an sgian, let *me* have the knife. *O.Ir.* cé + si.

cia, *inter. adj.* with *masc.* " what is it ? " cia, show it ; cia dhòmhsa sin, show me that, let me have that. *O.Ir.* cé + hé.

cia, kā, *int. pron.* who ? what ? how ? cia as duit, whence art thou ? cia minig, how often ? cia mheud, how many ? cia mheud a tha ann, how many are there of them ? c'ainm a tha ort ? what is your name ? *O.Ir.* cia, cé. *Lat.* qui.

ciaban, *n. m.* gizzard, fowl's stomach. *Also* giaban and geuban.

ciabh, kee-uv, *n. f.* lock of hair, tress ; *v.* tease, gall, vex ; tha e 'gam chiabhadh, he is teasing me. *O.Ir.* ciab, a lock of hair.

ciabhach, *a.* having ringlets, tressy.

ciabhag, *n. f.* a lock, or tress of hair (that part in front of the ear).

ciabhag-choille, *n. f.* wood-lark.

ciad, *n. m.* opinion, impression. *O.Ir.* cét-, in cetbaid, *sensus.*

ciadaoin, *n. f.* Wednesday. *O.Ir.* cétáin, first fast ; Di-ciadaoin, the day of the first fast.

ciadlomadh, *n. m.* breakfast.

ciagach, *a.* sly - humoured, goose - like walking.

cial *n. f.* side or brim of a vessel.

ciàl, *n. f.* cùil is ciàl, nook and cranny.

ciall, *n. m.*, *gen.* céille, sense ; meaning ; prudence ; as a chéill, out of his senses, mad, deranged ; duine gun chiall, a madman, a senseless fellow ; ceann na céille, the prudent man ; *a.* darling ; a chiall mo chridhe, my darling ; a chiall de na fearaibh, my beloved of all men : glac ciall, be easy, do not forget yourself ; ciod is ciall duit ? what do you mean ? understanding, wisdom ; tha e dhìth céille, he lacks understanding ; is e an ciall ceannaichte as fhearr, bought wisdom is best. *O.Ir.* cíall, *gen.* céille. *W.* pwyll.

ciallach, *a.* sensible, sedate, prudent, rational ; ceilidh duine ciallach masladh, a prudent man covereth shame.

ciallachail, kee-ul-ach-al, *a.* significant.

ciallaich, kee-ul-ich, *v.* signify, mean ; ciod e tha sin a' ciallachadh ? what does that mean ?

ciallan, *n. m.* a pet, darling.

ciallradh, kee-ul-rǎ, *n. m.* a full sentence.

cialtach, *a.* easy-going.

ciamar, *interrog.* how ?

ciamh. *See* ciabh.

ciamhadh, *v.* pulling by the hair.

ciamhair, *a.* sad. *M.Ir.* cíamar, sad, sorrowful.

cian, *n. m.* long time ; is ioma cian o nach robh e an so, it is a long time since he was here ; gu cian nan cian, for ever ; *a.* tedious, long, dreary ; is cian an oidhche, tedious is the night ; bu chian leinn guin am buillean, painful was the wound of their blows ; *adv.* as long as, while, whilst ; cian a bhios mi beò, while I live. *O.Ir.* cían, cén.

cianail, ki-unal, *a.* solitary, dreary, tedious, forlorn ; sad, lamentable, mournful. *Ir.* cianamhuil.

cianalachd, kee-un-ǎl-ǎchg, *n. f.* tediousness, dreariness, loneliness ; solitariness ; sadness.

cianalas, *n. m.* dreariness, sadness, melancholy ; a' cur dhinn a' chianalais, banishing dreariness, or melancholy, or sadness ; home-sickness. *M.Ir.* cianamlas.

cianog, *n. f.* a small measure of arable land. *Ir.* cianóg, half a farthing.

ciar, *a.* dun, sable ; roan ; dusky, dark, brown ; sléibhte nan earba ciar, the hills of the dusky roes ; *n. m.* the dusk, gloominess ; ciar nan càrn, the gloom of the rocks ; *v.* grow dusky ; am feasgar a' ciaradh, the evening getting dusky ; *cpds.* ciar-dhubh, *a.* dark-brown ; ciar-mhonadh, *n. m.* dark-coloured hill ; ciar-shuil, *n. f.* dark-eyed, scowling eye ; *adj.* is ciarshuileach. *E.Ir.* cíar. *O.Celt.* kíro-s.

ciaradh, kiur'-u, *vbl. n. m.* dusk of the evening, growing dusky ; 'sa chiaradh, in the dusk.

ciarag, *n. f.* a little dark woman.

ciaralach, kee-ur-ǎl-ach, *a.* quarrelsome.

ciaran, *n. m.* a swarthy man.

ciarsach, *n. m.* thrush. *Also* smeòrach.

cias, *gen.* ceòis, *n. m.* hip, buttock ; *adj.* is ciasach, squat (*see* ceòsach).

cias, *n. m.*, *gen.* ceòis, border, skirt, fringe.

ciasan, *n. m.* chafing (between the buttocks).

ciaslach, *n. m.* coarser part of wool ; coarse wool on sheep's legs. *See* céas.

ciat, *n. m.* pleasure, love ; ciatmhor, great pleasure or love.

ciata, *n. m.* esteem, regard, admire.

ciatach, kee-utuch, *a.* handsome, goodly, seemly ; personable ; beautiful ; luach chiatach, goodly price ; duine ciatach, a handsome person. *E.Ir.* cétach, possessing hundreds ; well-endowed.

ciataich, kee-utich, *n. f.* love ; delight ; pleasure ; chan 'eil ciataich sam bith aige dheth, he has no great affection for him or it.

ciataichead, kee-utich-ud, *n. f.* handsomeness, degree of beauty, elegance, or beauty ; a' dol an ciataichead, improving in elegance, beauty, etc.

ciatalach, *a.* sensible.

cibein, *n. m.* rump of a bird. *Also* gibean. *Ir.* ciben. *O'R.*

cibeir, *n. m.* shepherd. *Eng.* keeper.

cibh, ki, *n. m.* a wreath of snow. *Also* cuidhe.

cibhear, kiver, *n. m.* drizzle, drizzling rain.

cibhearg, kiverg, *n. f.* a rag ; a little ragged woman.

cibhlean, *n. pl.* jaws ; *pl.* of ciobhal, *q.v.*

cibhrinn, keev'-rinn, *n. m.* counterpane, coverlet. *Also* ciobhraig and cuibhrig.

cidhì. *See* cì ; cé + dh (syll. divider) + sí.

cidhis, kee-yish, *n. m.* a mask ; luchdcidhis, masqueraders ; fr. *Sc.* gyis, a mask ; gysars, masqueraders. *McB.*

cigil, *v.* tickle. *Also* ciogail, diogail.

cìleach, *a.* having white posterior like deer, *esp.* with reference to sheep.

cìleag, kee-lag, *n. f.* a frail old woman ; a weak, unmanly fellow.

cìlean, kee-len, *n. m.* a large cod. *Also* cilig. *O.N.* keila, " long cod."

cill, *n. f., gen.* cille, *pl.* cilltean, a cell, a church ; a churchyard, a burying ground ; frequent in place-names, as : Cill-Mhoire, Kilmuir ; Cill-Mhìcheil, Kirkmichael ; Cill-Donnain, Kildonan. *See* ceall.

cillein, *n. m.* repository, concealed heap. *Ir.* cillín, purse, hoard.

cineal, *n. m.* offspring ; clan. *O.Ir.* cenéle, race. *W.* cenedl. *O.Celt.* kenetlo-n.

cinn, keenn, *v.* grow, increase ; vegetate, multiply ; result from, happen, grow taller. *E.Ir.* cinim, am born, spring from. *O.Celt.* keniô.

cinneabhag, *n. f.* a young woman who prides herself on her family.

cinneach, kènn'-ach, *n. m.* a nation ; *pl.* cinnich.

cinneachadh, *n. m.* growth.

cinneadail, kin'-ad-al, *a.* clannish.

cinneadalachd, kin'-ad-al-ăchc, *n. f.* clannishness, attachment to one's clan.

cinneadh, kin'-niu, *n. m.* clan, kin, tribe ; surname ; kindred ; fear-cinnidh, clansman ; bean-chinnidh, clanswoman. *E.Ir.* ciniud.

cinneag, *n. f.* a spindle ; small barley ear ; *dim.* of ceann.

cinneas, kènn'-as, *n. m.* growth ; vegetation ; produce, crop, production ; increase ; fruit ; tumour.

cinneasach, *a.* productive, germinative ; vegetative ; fruitful.

cinneasachd, *n. f.* fruitfulness, vegetativeness ; vegetation, growth.

cinnseal, keenshal, *n. m.* origin, commencement ; contact ; facing, undertaking ; a' dol an cinnseal gàbhaidh, facing danger ; is coma leam dol 'na chinnseil, I do not like to undertake it ; fr. *E.Ir.* cinim.

cinnseal, *n. m.* need ; hardship ; want ; desire. *O.Ir.* cene. *O.Celt.* keno-s, empty.

cinnte, keentu, *n. f.* assurance, certainty ; chan 'eil cinnte 'nam beul, there is no certainty in their lips ; air chinnte, certainly, decidedly so. *O.Ir.* cinnim, determine, decree.

cinnteach, *a.* certain, positive, assured, confident ; unerring ; exact ; plain, evident, obvious ; cho cinnteach ris a' bhàs, as sure as death ; nach cinnteach a làmh ! how unerring his hand is ! a bheil thu cinnteach ? are you quite sure ?

cinnteachd, *n. f.* unquestionableness, sureness of aim ; positiveness ; assurance ; demonstration ; confidence, reliance.

cinntealas, keentalus, *n. f.* certainty.

cinntich, *v.* hit the " bull's eye," take sure aim. *E.Ir.* cinntigim, I fix, settle.

cinntinn, keentin, *vbl. n. m.* act of growing, increasing.

cìob, keeb, *n. m.* moor-grass ; tow ; sponge ; *a.* spongy, porous ; mòine chìob, spongy or porous peats. *Also* mòine phlòiteanach. *M.Ir.* cíp, reeds, wickers.

cìob, keeb, *v.* bite, wound.

cìobair, keeber, *n. m.* a shepherd.

cìobaireachd, *n. f.* herding sheep.

ciobhal, keevul, *n. m., pl.* ciobhlan and cibhlean, jaw-bone. *Also* giall.

cìoch, cìach, *n. f.* pap, breast of a woman ; nave ; hub (of a wheel) ; *cpds.* cìochbhraghad, cìoch-mhuineil, cìoch-shlugain, the uvula. *E.Ir.* cích. *O.Celt.* kîkâ

cìocharan, keechuran, *n. m.* a suckling an infant.

cìocharanachd, keechuranuchc, *n. f.* at the stage of infancy.

cìocrach, keecruch, *a.* longing, greedy, voracious.

cìocras, keecrus, *n. m.* hunger; earnest longing; greediness.
ciod, kud, *int. pron.* what. *O.Ir.* cate, cote. ced = cé + hed (quid est).
ciogail, kigel, *v.* tickle. *Also* diogail. *Ir.* cicil.
ciogailteach, kigeltuch, *a.* ticklish, critical; gnothuch ciogailteach, a critical affair. *Also* cuglaidh, *q.v.*
ciogaladh, *n. m.* tickling. *Also* diogaladh.
ciolam, kilum, *n. f.* an Irish vessel.
cìom, kēm, *n. f.* a wool card.
ciomach, kim'-ach, *n. m.* a prisoner, a captive. *O.Ir.* cimbid. *Wb.* gl. *anathema* (*captivus* was anathema when offered to the gods).
ciomachas, kim'-ach-us, *n. m.* captivity.
ciombal, kimb'-al, *n. m.* a cymbal, a bell. *Lat.* cymbalum.
ciomboll, kiumbul, *n. m.* a bundle of straw or of heather; a certain measure. *O.N.* kimbill, a bundle.
cion, kin, *n. m.* want, defect; cion léirsinn, want of sight, defect of vision; cion faobhair, bluntness. *O.Ir.* cene, awanting it. *O.Celt.* keno-s, empty. *Gr.* κενός.
cion, *n. m.* love, esteem. *M.Ir.* cen, cin. Cf. *O.Ir.* fochen, welcome.
cion. *See* cionta.
cionag, *n. f.* small measure of land; ¼ of cleitig; ⅛ of " farthing " land. *Ir.* cionóg.
cionar, *n. m.* music. *Also* cionthar.
cion-fàth, kyun-fâ', *n. m.* cause, reason.
cionn, kyunn, old, *dative* of ceann; air mo chionn, waiting me; air chionn da tighinn dachaidh, waiting him when he comes home; os do chionn, over your head.
cionnarra, *a.* identical. *Also* cionda for ceudna.
cionnas, kyunn'-us, *inter. adv.* how? by what means? for cia-ionnus. *O.Ir.* cindas (cia + indas).
cionta, kyunt, *n. m.* fault, guilt, crime. *O.Ir.* cin, *delictum*; *ac. pl.* cinta.
ciontach, kyunt'-ach, *a.* guilty, criminal, at fault, sinful; gun chionta, blameless.
ciontach, kyunt'-ach, *n. m.* a defaulter.
ciontachadh, kyunt'-ach-ă, *vbl. n. m.* transgressing, sinning; le ciontachadh am aghaidh, by trespassing against me.
ciontachd, kyunt'-ăchc, *n. f.* degree of guilt, guiltiness; sinfulness.
ciontaich, kyunt'-ich, *v.* sin, transgress; chiontaich iad am aghaidh, they sinned against me.
cìopadh, *m.* ill-using, mauling. *M.Ir.* cíp, rods.
ciora, kiru, *n. f.* a pet sheep. *Also*

cireag, ciridh; ultimately derived from caora; ciora and ciridh are pet names by which sheep are called to one.
cioralta, kiraltu, *a.* cheerful.
ciorbail, *a.* snug.
ciorram, kyur'-um, *n. m.* a maim, a defect in a person's body. *E.Ir.* cirpaim, hack; later, cirrbaim.
ciorramach, kyurr'-am-ach, *a.* maimed, deformed, mutilated; painful.
ciorrbhadh, keirvu, *n. m.* maiming, mangling. *Also* ciurradh. *See* ciorram.
ciosan, kisan, *n. m.* large bowl-shaped basket made of bent; bread basket, corn-skep. *M.Ir.* cess, basket, hamper.
ciosanach, ciosnach, *a.* tiresome, subdued.
ciosnachadh, keesnuchu, *vbl. n. m.* subduing, conquering; appeasing; oppressing.
ciosnachail, keesnuchal, *a.* made to pay tribute, overpowering.
ciosnaich, keesnich, *v.* subdue; overpower, conquer. *Also* cìoslaich; fr. cìs, tax. *E.Ir.* cìs, tribute, tax.
ciotach, *a.* left-handed, sinister, defective, awkward: So *E.Ir. W.* chwith.
ciotachd, *n. f.* left-handedness.
ciotag, keetag, *n. f.* the left hand.
ciotag, *n. f.* a little plaid, a shawl. *O.Ir.* cétaig.
ciotaireachd, keetiruchc, *n. f.* left-handedness, clumsiness, ineffective toil; trickiness, dishonesty.
cipean, keepen, *n. m.* a peg; a pin; a tether-stake.
cìr, keer, *n. f.* a comb; part of a key; cìr-mheala, honeycomb; *v.* comb; curry; tease, as wool. *O.Ir.* cír. *O.Celt.* kênsrâ.
cìr, *n. f.* cud. *E.Ir.* oc cocnam a cire. Corm. *Gl.*
circ-fheoil, *n. f.* flesh of a hen.
cìreag, *n. f.* a little comb.
cìrean, keeren, *n. m.* crest, cock's comb.
cìreanach, *a.* crested; feamainn chìreanach, curly seaweed.
ciridh, *int.* call to a sheep. *See* ciora.
cìs, keesh, *n. f.* tax, tribute; impost; subjection; fo chìs, under tribute, in subjection. *O.Ir.* cís. *Lat.* census.
cisd, *n. f.* a chest. *M.Ir.* ciste. *Lat.* cista.
cisde-laighe, *n. f.* a coffin.
cisean, kishen, *n. m.* a hamper. *See* ciosan.
cisire, keeshira, *n. m.* tax-gatherer.
cìsireachd, *n. f.* tax-gathering.
cìs-leagadair, *n. m.* an assessor.
cìs-mhaor, *n. m.* a tax-gatherer.
ciste, kishtu, *n. f., pl.* cisteachan, a chest; a coffin. *E.Ir.* ciste, a chest, store. *Lat.* cista.
ciste-chlàraich, *n. f.* a coffin.

ciste-mhairbh, *n. f.* coffin.
cith, kee, *n.* fury, rage ; ardour.
cith, *n. f.* a shower. So *E.Ir.*
cith-chatha, *n. m.* ardour of battle.
citheach, ki-huch, *a.* furious.
cithean, ki-hen, *n. m.* a complaining,
bemoaning. *See* caoineadh.
cithill, *n. m.* act of bemoaning, grousing.
cithris - chaithris, kirish - cherish, *n. f.*
hurly-burly, confusion.
ciùbhran, kiooran, ciùran, ciùrach, *n. m.*
mist ; drizzle. *Ir.* ceobhrán (ceò +
braon). *M.Ir.* ciabor, mist, haze.
ciùchair, kioochir, *a.* beautiful, dimpling.
ciùcharan, kioocharan, *n. m.* a low-
voiced lamentation ; plaintive moaning. *O.N.* kjökra, whine.
ciùin, kioon, *a., comp.* ciùine, mild, gentle;
amiable, meek ; agus bha an duine
Maois ro-chiùin, and the man Moses
was very meek ; still, calm, quiet ;
feasgar ciuin, a still or calm evening ;
smooth, agreeable to the touch ; *v.*
calm. *M.Ir.* ciúin, quiet, calm, gentle.
McB. suggests *N.* hyrr (with its Teut.
cog.).
ciùine, kioonu, *n. f.* mildness, meekness,
gentleness.
ciùineachadh, *vbl. n. m.* calming, appeasing, pacifying, quieting.
ciùineachd, *n. f.* mildness, etc. ; calm.
ciùineas, kioonus, *n. m.* mildness, meekness, gentleness.
ciùinich, kioonich, *v.* pacify, appease,
assuage, still, calm ; chiùinich e, he
stilled or calmed ; *vbl. a.* ciùinichte,
stilled, calmed, appeased.
ciùirteach, kioortuch, *a.* extremely painful, agonizing ; torturing the mind.
ciùrr, kioor, *v.* torture, agonize; hurt.
Ir. ciorrbhaim, I mangle. *E.Ir.* cirpaim, I cut, lacerate.
ciùrradair, kiooruder, *n. m.* tormentor.
ciùrradh, *n. m.* a hurt, a sore.
ciùrrail, kiooral, *a.* painful in the extreme.
clab, *n. m.* an enormous mouth ; dùin
do chlab ! shut your big mouth ! tha
an dorus air a chlab, the door is wide
open.
clabach, *a.* having a large mouth ; *n. f.*
a large-mouthed female.
clabag, *n. f.* a garrulous female, thick-
lipped female.
clabaire, klabiru, *n. m.* a babbler, a prater.
claban, *n. m.* mill-clapper ; fr. clab.
claban, *n. m.* brain-pan ; top of the head.
clabar, *n. m.* a mill-clapper.
clàbar, klāb'-ur, *n. m.* filth, mire, dirt,
clay, a puddle.
clabastair, *n. m.* a brawler.
clabastair-cìocharain, *n. m.* the frog-fish
or angler.
clàbhinn, *n. m.* loud incessant talking.

clàbhadh, *vbl. n. m.* act of tossing about ;
blowing into confusion by draughts.
clabog, *n. f.* a good bargain,
clach, *n. f.* a stone ; a stone weight ;
gen. cloiche ; *dat.* chloich ; *v.* stone,
punish by stoning ; *cpds.* clachbhalg,
a rattle ; clach-chinn, a head grave-
stone ; clach - fhaobhrachaidh, *also*
clach-ghleusaidh, a hone, a sharping
or whetstone ; clachan-meallain, hail.
O.Ir. cloch. *O.Celt.* klukâ. *O.N.* hella.
Goth. halla.
clachach, *a.* stony, rocky, pebbly.
clachair, clach'-er, *n. m.* a mason.
clachaireachd, clach'- er'- achc, *n. f.*
masonry, mason-work, architecture.
clachan, *n. m.* stepping-stones, a village,
a hamlet, where a church is ; a kirk
town.
clacharan, *n. m.* a wagtail ; a stone-
chatterer ; stepping-stones.
clachbhalg,* *n. m.* a rattle.
clach-bhleith, *n. f.* a grindstone.
clach-bhrath, *n. f.* rocking-stone.
clach-bhuaidh, *n. f.* an amulet, a charm ;
a gem. *Also* clach-bhuadhach.
clach-cheangail, *n. f.* a keystone.
clach-chinn, *n. f.* a headstone (at grave) ;
a corner-stone.
clach-chnotain, *n. f.* a mortar ; hollowed
stone where corn is beaten.
clach-chriadha, *n. f.* brick.
clach-chrìch, *n. f.* march-stone. *Also*
cnaimh, cnaimh-crich.
clach-chuimhneachain, *n. f.* a monument.
clach-dhearg, *n. f.* a keel.
clach-fhuail, *n. f.* gravel-stone ; clach +
fual (bual), water.
clach-ghaireil, *n. f.* freestone.
clach-gheurachaidh, *n. f.* a hone, a whetstone, sharping-stone.
clach-ghlùin, *n. f.* an amulet.
clach-ghuiteir, *n. f.* kennel-stone.
clach-inne, *n. f.* a kennel-stone.
clach-iùil, *n. f.* a loadstone.
clach-léig, *n. f.* a precious stone.
clach-lianraidh, *n. f.* grindstone.
clach-liathra, *n. f.* the rolling, revolving
stone ; a grindstone. *See* liathra.
O.Ir. liathraim, I roll. *Z*² Cf. *O.Ir.*
liathróit.
clach-liomhaidh, *n. f.* whetstone, a
polishing-stone.
clach-mheallain, *n. f.* hailstone.
clach-mhìle, *n. f.* a milestone.
clach-mhuilinn, *n. f.* millstone.
clach-mhullaich, *n. f.* topstone.
clach-na-cineamhuinn, *n. f.* stone of
destiny, the stone on which the ancient
Caledonians inaugurated their kings.
clach-na-sùla, *n. f.* the apple of the eye.

* For pronunciation of compounds see separate
members elsewhere.

clach-neirt, *n. f.* putting-stone ; cur na claiche, putting the stone ; cur air a' chlaich, playing at putting the stone.
clach-oisinn, *n. f.* corner-stone.
clach-smior, *n. f.* emery.
clach-theine, *n. f.* flint.
clach-thomhais, *n. f.* weighing-stone, a weight.
clach-uasal, *n. f.* a precious stone.
clàd, klăd, *n. m.* a wool-card ; *v.* card wool.
cladach, kladuch, *n. m., pl.* cladaichean, shore, beach, stony shore, or beach ; anything scattered ; cha shuaicheantas còrr air cladach, a heron on the shore is no badge ; channel of a river.
clàdan, *n. m.* a flake of snow ; burr. So *Ir.*
clàdanach, *a.* flaky, like burrs.
cladh, klu'-gh', *v.* spawn, as fish ; tha na bradain a' cladh, the salmon are spawning ; *n. m.* the act of spawning.
cladh, *n. m.* a trench ; churchyard. *O.Ir.* clad. 1. a dyke. 2. a ditch. *W.* cladd.
cladhach, clu'-uch, *vbl. n. m.* digging, delving.
cladhaich, clu-ich, *v.* dig, delve, poke. *O.Ir.* cladim, rocechladatar, gl. *suffoderunt. O.Celt.* kladô, *fodio.*
cladhaire, clu-yire, *n. m.* a coward ; a poltroon ; cladh, "clod-hopper." *E.Ir.* cladaire, rogue, villain.
cladhaireachd, clu-ir-achc, *n.f.* cowardice.
cladh-dùdaidh, clu'-doodi, *n. m.* a roaring billow.
cladrach, cladruch, *n. m.* anything scattered.
cladraich, cladrich, *v.* scatter.
clag, *n. m., gen. s.,* and *n. pl.* cluig, a bell, a crash, a noise. *E.Ir.* cloc, a bell, a blister, a bubble.
clagan, *n. m.* a small bell.
claganach, *a.* full of bells.
clagarsaich, *n. f.* crashing, crashing noise ; dangling, waving.
clag-thigh, *n. m.* a belfry, steeple. *E.Ir.* cloicc-thech. *O.Celt.* klukko-tego-s.
clàibhean, clyven, *n. m.* slip-bolt of a door.
clàideag, clăjag, *n. f.* a lock, ringlet.
claidean, clajen, *n. m.* an absurd hammering at anything ; dangling.
clàidheag, clă-yag, *n. f.* last handful of corn cut.
claidheamh, clyiv, *n. m., pl.* claidhean, claidhrean, a sword ; claidheamh mór, a broad sword ; claidheamh crom, a sabre ; claidheamh caol, a small sword ; chan 'eil fhios ciod an claidheamh a bhios 'san truaill gus an tàirnear e, it is not known what sword is in the sheath till it is drawn. *O.Ir.* claideb. *W.* cleddyf. *Lat.* gladius. *O.Celt.* kladebo-s.

claidheamhair, clyver, *n. m.* swordsman, a fencer. *E.Ir.* claidbech, a swordsman.
clàidhean, clyen, *n. m.* slip-bolt of a door.
clàidhmhaireachd, clyver-uchc, *n. f.* swordsmanship ; playing of two cows with their horns, sparring.
claidreach, clăj'-rach, *a.* fatiguing, damaging.
claidrich, *v.* fatigue, shatter, deafen.
claigeach, clycuch, *n. m.* a steeple. *E.Ir.* cloc-thech, bell-tower, belfry.
claigionn, clycun, *n. m.* a skull, scalp ; the best field of arable land in a farm. *Also* claigeann. *O.Ir.* cloccenn. *M.Ir.* cloicend.
claigionnach, clyc'-unn-ach, *a.* head-stall of a bridle, halter, etc. ; best arable land of a district.
claimh, clev, *n. f.* scab, leprosy. *E.Ir.* clam, leprous. *W.* clafr, mange, leprosy. *O.Celt.* klamo-s, ill.
clais, clash, *n. f.* a furrow, a trench. *E.Ir.* class, trench, pit, groove.
clàisdeachd, clăshj'-achk, *n. f.* sense of hearing, hearing ; ann am chlàisdeachd, in my hearing ; chaill e a chlàisdeachd, he lost his sense of hearing. *Also* clàisneachd.
claiseach, clash-ach, *a.* furrowed, trenched, fluted (sword).
claisghorm, *a.* blue-fluted.
claisire, clasheru, *n. m.* trencher.
clàisneachd, clashnachc, *n. f.* hearing ; mo chlàisneachd, my hearing.
clàistinn, clăshtin, *vbl. n. m.* hearing, listening.
clàiteachd, clătiachc, *n. f.* gentle rain.
clambar, *n. m.* litigiousness, wrangling ; evil report, private slander. *Lat.* clamor. Cf. *M.Ir.* clámar, satire.
clambrach, *a.* litigious, fond of law ; wrangling, slandering.
clamhair, clavir, *v.* scratch, shrug.
clamhan, clavan, *n. m.* buzzard ; hawk.
clamhas, clav'-us, *n. m.* clamour, unfounded report, clatter ; brawling.
clamhasail, clavusal, *a.* brawling, clattering.
clamhradh, clavru, *vbl. n. m.* scratching, shrugging.
clàmhuinn, clăvin, *n. m.* sleet. *Also* flinne, and flion.
clann, *n. f.* children, offspring, descendants ; a clan ; a chlann nan sonn, ye descendants of heroes ; clann an Tòisich, the Mackintoshes ; clann Dòmhnaill, the MacDonalds ; clann an cloinne, their children's children. *O.Ir.* cland, 1. plant, 2. offspring ; clandaim, 1. I plant, 2. I beget, gl. *obsero,* I plant. *W.* plant, children. *Lat.* planta.
clann, *n. f.* a lock of hair, a ringlet, a

curi ; 'na clannaibh, in curls, in ringlets. *Lat.* planta, a sprout.

clannach, klann'-ach, *a.* fruitful ; curled,
in ringlets ; **Anna chlannach,** Anna,
with the many ringlets ; hairy, leafy.

clannaich, klann'-ich, *v. n.* beget children. *W.* planta.

clanna-speura, *n. pl.* the heavenly hosts.

clannfhalt, *n. m.* clustering hair, hair in
ringlets.

claoidh, kloo-y, *v.* cloy, exhaust, over-
fatigue ; fag ; overcome with fatigue ;
mar chlaoidheas teine coillteach, as
fire overcomes wood ; *vbl. n. m.* fatigue,
excessive fatigue ; act of fagging,
fainting; mortifying; **claoidhibh bhur
buill,** mortify your members. *O.Ir.*
clóim, overcome, prostrate.

claoidhte, klooytu, *vbl. a.* exhausted with
fatigue.

claoidhteach, klooytuch, *a.* exhausting
one's strength ; fatiguing, fagging,
fainting, overcoming ; spending.

claoidhteachd, klooytachc, *n. f.* exhaustion, fagging or exhausting ; fatigue.

claoine, klūnu, *n. f.* inclination, squint-
ness. *O.Ir.* clóine, gl. *iniquitas.*

claon, klūn, *v.* incline, go aside, rebel ;
chlaon iad uile, they have all gone
aside ; move aslant or obliquely ;
squint, oblique, slanting ; meandering ;
squint-eyed ; **fear claon,** a man that
squints. *O.Ir.* clóin, cloen, gl. iniquus,
inclined, perverse. *O.Celt.* kloino-s.
Lat. clino.

claonadh, klūna', *vbl. n. m.* squinting,
slanting, meandering, inclining, bending ; **mar sgàile a' claonadh sìos,** like
a shadow declining ; *a.* inclination ;
oblique motion.

claonaireachd, klun-iruchc, *n. f.* inclination, partiality.

claonbhàigh, *n. f.* partiality ; **claon +
bàigh,** "oblique regard."

claonbhord, *n. f.* desk, inclined plane, a
sloping table.

claonbhreith, *n. f.* partiality, an unfair
judgment or decision.

claonbhreitheach, *a.* unjust, partial.

claonshuil, *n. f.* squint-eye.

claothaire. *See* cladhaire.

clap, *n. m.* clap, clapping, noise made by
clapping ; **dhùin an dorus le clap,** the
door shut with a bang ; flapping of
wings ; fr. the *Eng.*

clapartaich, *n. f.* clapping, banging.

clàr, *n. m.* plank, table, board ; bottom
of a chest ; stave of a cask, harp, etc. ;
chuir e 'n a clàran i, he broke it into
pieces ; **clàr na ciste,** bottom of the
chest (inside) ; **chan 'eil grainne air
a clàr,** not a dust on its bottom ; a
wooden dish (oblong and hollowed out

of one block) ; **clàr buntàta,** wooden
dish for potatoes ; a chess-board ;
board of a coffin. *O.Ir.* **claar,** gl.
tabula. O.Celt. **klàro-s.**

clàr, *v. tr.* maintain, fasten on one,
oppose, contradict.

clàrach, *n. f.* clumsy female ; *a.* belonging to staves, of staves.

clàradh, *n. f.* a floor of boards ; **seòmar
clàraidh,** room with wooden floor.

clàradh, *vbl. n. m.* act of insisting, fastening blame ; act of persisting in
attributing to one.

clàrag, *n. f.* a fore or front tooth ; frame
of a fishing-line ; **clàrag-duirgh,** frame
for fishing-line. *E.Ir.* **clàr-fhiacail,**
front tooth.

clàraich, klār'-ich, *n. f.* wooden partition ;
wooden floor.

clàrainm,* clar-innsidh, *n. m.* catalogue.

clàranach, *a.* flat-faced ; broad, squat.
M.Ir. clàr-enech, flat-faced. *O.W.* enep.

clàr-aodainn, *n. m.* the forehead.

clàr-buideil, *n. m.* stave of a cask.

clàrchas, *n. m.* splay-foot.

clàrchasach, *a.* splay-footed.

clàr-feòirne, *n. m.* chess-board, draughts-
board.

clàr-fuine, *n. m.* kneading trough.

clàr-iomairt, *n. m.* chess or draughts-
board.

clàr-mìneachaidh, *n. m.* a glossary.

clàrsach, *n. m.* a harp ; **cho caoin ri
clarsach,** as melodious as a harp.
E.Ir. **clàirseach.**

clàrsach-ùrlair, *n. f.* an old woman in
gentlemen's families, kept for the
purpose of telling stories ; a witch.

clàrsaid, clārsej, *n. f.* floored chamber ;
ad chlàrsaid is ad chlòsaid, in your
"drawing"-room and closet.

clàrsair, klàr'-ser, *n. m.* a harper, minstrel.

clàrsaireachd, klār'-ser'-uchc, *n. f.* harping, music.

clàr-tomhais, *n. m.* a scale, a measure.

clàr-uachdair, *n. m.* lid of a chest.

claspa, *n. m.* a clasp.

clath-nàire, *n. f.* bashfulness.

cleachd, *n. f.* a curl, ringlet, a fillet of
wool. *E.Ir.* clecht, a plait.

cleachd, klechc, *v.* practise, accustom,
inure, habituate, use ; **chleachd mi a
bhi,** I was accustomed to be. *E.Ir.*
clechtaim, I am wont, I practise.

cleachdach, klechg'-ach, *a.* customary,
practised ; habitual.

cleachdach, *a.* curled.

cleachdadh, *vbl. n. m.* habit, custom, use
and wont.

cleachdta, klechg'-tya, *vbl. a.* accustomed,
practised, inured ; trained ; used ;

---

* For pronunciation of compounds see separate
members elsewhere.

cleachdta ri olc, accustomed to do evil.

cleachduinn, klechc'-inn, *n. f.* habit, practice, custom ; is dona a' chleachduinn sin, that is a bad practice or custom.

cleamhnas, kleaw'-nus, *n. m.* affinity, sexual intercourse.

clearc, klerck, *n. f.* a curl, a ringlet, a lock of hair ; *v.* curl, make into ringlets, arrange.

clearcach, klerk'-ach, *a.* curled, in ringlets.

cleas, cles, *n. m.* trick, craft, feat, gambol ; a stratagem ; Cuchulainn nan cleas, Cuchulainn of the feats ; rinn e cleas chàich, he behaved just like the rest. *E.Ir.* cless, a feat, trick ; clessim, perform. Cf. clissim, I leap.

cleasach, clesuch, *a.* playful, full of tricks.

cleasachd, clesachc, *n. f.* play, sport, diversion, as jugglery, legerdemain, sleights ; ri cleasachd, playing, sporting ; dh' éirich iad gu cleasachd, they rose up to play ; cleasachd dhaoine, the sleights of men.

cleasaiche, clesichu, *n. m.* a trickster, a juggler, a cunning fellow ; a conjuror.

cleasanta, cles'-ănt-u, *a.* tricky, playful.

cleasantachd, clesantuchc, *n. f.* frolicsomeness.

cleath, cle, *n. f.* concealment, hiding. *Also* cleith.

cleatha, cle-hu, *n. m.* a club or clumsy stick, a goad, a rib, a stake.

cleibe, clebu, *n. m.* hooked instrument (for laying hold of fish). *Ir.* clipe. *Eng.* clip. *O.N.* klypa, to pinch.

cleid, clej, *n. f.* a flake, a clot.

cleideach, clejuch, *a.* clotted, shaggy.

cleideag, klej'-ag, *a.* clot, a flake. *Also* bleideag.

cleideagach, klej'-ăg-ach, *a.* clotted, shaggy, ragged, full of clots or tatters.

cléir, klăr', *n. f.* a company, the clergy ; a presbytery (in Scotland). *E.Ir.* cléir, a chorus, a band. *Lat.* clerus. *See* cliar.

cléireach, klēr''- uch, *n. m.* a cleric ; a clerk ; a beadle or church officer. *Lat.* clericus. *O.G.* clérec ; iarnéré nagleréc, for refusing the clerics. *E.Ir.* ciérech, a cleric

cleireanach, klăr'-ăn-ăch, *a.* sword.

cleit, *n. m.* an oar cleat.

cleit, *n. m.* a ridge or reef of sunk rocks ; eaves ; a rocky eminence ; a beehive bothy, built of stone, and so constructed as to let the wind blow through freely, yet water - tight (*St. Kilda*). *O.N.* klettr, rock, cliff, crag.

cléit, cleyt, *n. f.* a quill, a flake of snow.

cléiteag, *dim.* of cléit.

cleith, cle, *v.* conceal, hide ; *n. m.* concealment, secrecy ; chan 'eil cleith air

an olc ach gun a dhèanadh, the best way to conceal evil is not to commit it. *O.Ir.* cleith, inf. of celim.

cleith, cle, *n. f.* a stake, concealment.

cleitheach, cle-huch, *a.* concealing.

cleitheachd, cle-huchc, *n. f.* concealment.

cleith-inntinn, *n. f.* dissimulation, mental reservation.

cleitig, clitig, *n. f.* one-eighth of pennyland. *See* cionag.

cleitinn. *See* clitig.

cleòc, clōc, *n. m.* a cloak, a mantle ; fr. *Eng.*

cleòcan, *n. m.* a little cloak, a mantle ; *a.* cleòcanach.

clì, clee, *n. m.* strength, energy ; locomotion, vigour, pith ; gun chlì, without power of motion ; duine gun chlì, a man without vigour ; force.

clì, clee, *a.* left, left-handed ; slow, awkward ; feeble ; an taobh clì, the left side ; a dh' ionnsaigh na làimhe clì, to the left side ; clì anns a' chòmhrag, lame or feeble in the strife. *E.Ir.* clí and clé. *W.* cledd. *O.Celt.* klijó-s.

cliabh, clee-uv, *n. m.*, *gen.* cléibh, a basket, a hamper, a creel ; a straitjacket, a strait-vest of wicker-work, for a madman ; hence, is ann a tha 'n t-òlach an cliabh, the fellow is mad, said to people who have bad Gaelic ; the chest, the breast ; a' taomadh m'a chliabh, pouring it on his breast ; cliabh guthainn, bodice of a gown. *O.Ir.* cliab, corbis ; clébene gl. sportam.

cliabhach, clee-uv-uch, *a.* like baskets, chested, belonging to the chest.

cliabh-sgeithreach, *n. m.* a vomit.

cliadan, *n. m.* a burr. Cf. clàdan.

clia-lu, *n. m.* all the fingers in motion playing on the bagpipes.

cliamhuinn, clia-vin, *n. m.* a son-in-law, a brother - in - law. *E.Ir.* cliamain, relation by marriage, father-in-law, brother-in-law, son-in-law.

cliamhuinneas, clia-vin-us, *n. m.* relationship by marriage ; consanguinity, friendship. *See* cleamhnas.

cliar, clear, *n. m.* a poet ; a brave man ; fuil nan cliar, the blood of the brave ; *coll. n. f.* poets, bards ; cliar Sheanchain, the bardic company of Senchan, referred to in Folk Tales. *E.Ir.* cliar, *clerus*, band, train ; clergy. *W.* y glêr, the bards. *Lat.* clerus. *Gr.* κλῆρος, a lot.

cliarachas, *n. m.* bardism, poetry, feats of valour.

cliarachd, *n. f.* wandering ; singing ; feats.

cliaradh, *n. m.* singing.

cliaraiche, kliur'-ich-u, *n. m.* a singer.

cliaranach, *n. m.* a bard ; swordsman.

cliata, kleeut'-a, *n. m.* a meadow; a burr. *See* cliathta.

cliatan, *n. m.* a level patch of ground. *Also* cléiteag.

cliath, clia, *n. f.* a harrow, a hurdle, as when fulling cloth; a lattice or casement; a worm in distillation; stann cléith, worm vat; a shoal of fish; cliath sgadan, a shoal of herrings; darning of stockings; weir for salmon; a set of oars; a body of fishers; in piping, cliath = all the fingers. *E.Ir.* clíath, hurdle, raft, phalanx, side; also a spear, an oar. *W.* clwyd, hurdle. *O.Celt.* kleitokleitâ.

cliath, cli-u, *v.* harrow; tread, as the male, in poultry; a' cliathadh nan cearc, treading the hens; darn.

cliathach, cliu-huch, *n.f., pl.* cliathaichean, the side of anything; ri cliathach na luinge, at the side of the ship; ri do chliathaich, by your side.

cliathag, clia-hag, *n. f.* a small harrow or hurdle.

cliathair, *n. m.* a harrower.

cliathan, clia-han, *n. m.* the chest, breast.

cliath-chliata, *n. f.* a harrow.

cliath-chòmhraig, *n. m.* a champion.

cliath-làimhe, *n. f.* a hand harrow.

cliath-luaidh, *n. f.* a fuller's hurdle.

cliath-ràmh, *n. f.* a bank of oars; cliath-fhuaraidh, rowers on windward side; cliath-leis, rowers on lee side.

cliath-sheanchais, *n. f.* a genealogical table.

cliathta, cliata; *in phr.* lothagan cliata, brood mares.

clib, *v.* stumble, slip awkwardly.

clib, *n. m.* an excrescence.

clibeadh, *n. m.* stumbling; also, nibbling.

clibeag, *n. f.* a trick, wile; filly.

clibealachd, *n.f.* awkwardness, clumsiness.

clibean, *n. m.* an excrescence; an appendage, a dangling end.

clibid, *n. m.* stammering.

clibis, *n. f.* a misadventure.

clibiste, *n. m.* an awkward fellow.

clibisteach, klib'-isht-ach, *a.* awkward.

clìchd, kleek, *n. m.* a hook. *Sc.* kliek.

clìchd, *n. m.* a plot, sly plan. *Fr.* clique.

clìchdeach, *a.* cunning, artful.

cli-lamhach, *a.* left-handed.

cliob, clib, *n. m.* 1. an excrescence. 2. stumble.

cliobach, *a.* stumbling, awkward.

cliobag, *n. f.* a filly.

cliobain, cliban, *n. m.* an excrescence, a dew-lap; anything dangling.

cliobaire, clibiru, *n. m.* a clumsy person; a simpleton.

cliopach, *a.* halt (in speech).

cliopad, *n. f.* lisping, stammering.

cliospach, klisp'-ach, *a.* lame, not active.

clìostar, *n. m.* a clyster; fr. the *Eng.*

clìostradh, *n. m.* thorough purging.

clip, *n. m.* 1. a large hook, a hand-hook, for taking large fish, too heavy for the line, into a boat. 2. a stratagem, deceit, cunning; *v. t.* hook, pilfer; snatch, steal.

clip-làmhachas, *n. f.* unhandiness.

clis, klish, *a.* quick, active; lively, nimble, agile, speedy, clever, handy; *v.* leap; na fir chlis, the merry dancers. *E.Ir.* clissim, I leap.

clisbeach, *a.* unsteady; cripple. *Also* clisneach.

cliseach, *n. f.* a wicket.

clisg, klishg, *v.* start, leap through fear; chlisg e, he took a start.

clisgeach, klishg'-ach, *a.* skittish, apt to be startled, timid, fearful.

clisgeadh, clishcu, *vbl. n. m.* a startle, a start; starting, leaping; bi an so an clisgeadh, be here instantly; chlisgeadh féidh is earba 'san fhraoch, deer and roe were startled in the heath.

clisneach, clishnuch, *n. f.* 1. a wicket, a bar gate. 2. a mouth never at rest. 3. the human body, outward appearance.

cliù, clew, *n. f.* fame, good name, reputation; praise, renown; character; fo dheagh chliù, under good reputation. *O.Ir.* clú; gl. rumour, fame, reputation. *O.Celt.* klevos.

cliùchd, clooc, *n.f.* a stratagem, a cunning trick, deceit; *v.* mend nets.

cliùchdach, *a.* deceitful, cunning; *n. f.* a deceitful female.

cliùchdaire, cloociru, *n. m.* 1. a strategist, a cunning fellow. 2. mender of nets.

cliùchdaireachd, *n. f.* deceitfulness, cunningness; mending nets.

cliùd, cloot, *n. f.* a small, trifling hand.

cliùdan, *n. m.* a trifling stroke or blow.

cliùiteach, clootuch, *a.* famous, celebrated, renowned, extolled; praiseworthy, laudable, commendable; praised; is cliùitiche an onair na 'n t-òr, honour is more commendable than gold.

cliùmhor, cloovor, *a.* praiseworthy. Same as cliùiteach.

cliùmhorachd, *n. f.* renown, celebrity.

cliùthachadh, cloo-huchu, *vbl. n. m.* praising, extolling, celebrating, lauding, exalting.

cliùthaich, cloo-hich, *v.* praise, laud, extol, commend, exalt; celebrate.

cliu-thoillteanach, *a.* praiseworthy, commendable.

clò, *n. m.* cloth, home-made cloth. *Also* clòth.

clò, *n. m.* a slumber, dozing, lethargy; clò-cadail, slumber, dozing.

clò, *n. m.* a print, printing-press. *Also* clòdh. *Ir.* clódh, mould, type. *Ktg.*
clò, *n. m.* a nail. *O. Celt.* klovo-s, a nail.
clobha, clow, *n. m.* a pair of tongs. *N.* klofi.
clobhdach, clouduch, *a.* clumsy ; ragged.
clobhsa, clousu, *n. m.* close, lane, farm-yard. *Ir.* clamhsa.
clò-bhuail, *v.* print.
clò-bhuailtear, *n. m.* a printer.
clò-bhualadh, *vbl. n. m.* printing.
clòca, *n. m.* a cloak, mantle; *fr.* Eng.
clòcaire, clōciru, *n. m.* a rogue, a deceitful fellow, a dissembler ; pretender.
clòcaireachd, clōciruchc, *n. f.* dissimulation.
cloch, *n. f.* a goggle-eye.
clochar, *n. m.* wheezing in the throat.
clocharra, *a.* goggle-eyed.
clochranaich, *n. m.* a wheezing in the throat.
cloch-sniaraidh, *n. f.* a grindstone. *Also* clach-lianraidh. *See* clach-liathra.
clod, *n. m., pl.* clodan and cluid, a clod ; thuit e 'n a chlod, he fell in a heap ; *v.* pelt with clods. *M. E.* clot, clotte.
clodach, *a.* full of clods.
clodaire, clodiru, *n. m.* a pelter ; a dull person. *E. Ir.* cladaire, a rogue.
clodaireachd, *n. f.* pelting (with clods).
clodan, *n. m.* a little clod. *Also* plodan.
clodcheann, *n. m.* a dull, heavy head ; *a.* clod-cheannach.
clodhadair, klo'-ad-ăr', *n. f.* printer.
clodhadaireachd, klo'-ad-ar'-achg, *n. f.* printing.
clog, *n. m., pl.* cluig, a ball, a clock. *See* clag. *E. Ir.* cloc, a bell, a bubble.
clogad, *n. m.* a helmet, a cap, a head-piece ; a cone, a pyramid. In some parts, clogard. *E. Ir.* clocat (.i. bell-hat), helmet.
clogais, klog'-ash, *n. f.* a wooden shoe.
clogmheur, *n. f.* hour hand.
clogshnathad, *n. f.* gnomon of a dial.
cloilein, *n. m.* a little web of cloth.
cloimh, cloif, *n. f.* scab, mange, itch. *See* claimh. *E. Ir.* clam. 1. scurvy. 2. a leper. *Lat.* leprosus.
clòimh, klò'-ee, *n. f.* down, feathers, plumage ; in some places, wool. *Also* clùimh. *E. Ir.* clúm, clúim. *W.* plu. *Lat.* pluma.
clòimhdich, *v.* rub, scratch (as itch), shrug. *Also* clàmhradh.
clòimheach, *a.* woolly.
clòimheag, *n. f.* small eel. *Also* clài-mheag.
clòimhein, *n. m.* icicle, snot.
clòimheinich, *v.* flutter, as flakes, down.
clòimh-gharrain, *n. f.* down (on birds).
clòimhneag, *n. f.* flake of snow. *Also* bleideag.

clòimhneagach, *a.* flaky.
clòimhteach, klò'-tyach, *n. f.* down, feathers. *Also* clùimhteach.
clois, klŏsh, *n. f.* march weed.
cloitheag, *n. f.* shrimp, prawn.
clomhach, *a.* scabbed.
clomhais, *coll. n.* cloves.
clòmhar, *v.* scratch by shrugging. *Also* clàmhar.
clomhrachan, *n. m.* a fledgling.
clos, *n. m.* rest, repose, stillness, quietness ; gabh clos, rest, be still ; *v.* be quiet.
closach, *n. f.* a carcass, carrion.
closaich, klos'-ich, *v.* get lank or gaunt, as a half-starved brute.
clòsaid, *n. f.* a closet, a study.
clò-suaine, *n. f.* slumber.
clòth, *v.* mitigate, restrain, stop. *O. Ir.* clóim, overcome.
clòthadh, *vbl. n. m.* gadding, roving.
cluaimh, *Ross.* and *Suth.* ; form of clòimh, wool ; clùimh, in *Lewis.*
cluain, cloo-ain, *n. f.* intriguing ; pacification, quietness ; cuir cluain air an leanabh, pacify the child. *M. Ir.* clúain, dissimulation, flattery. *O. Celt.* klo(p)ni, intrigue.
cluain, *n. f., pl.* cluaintean, a green plain ; a bower ; a pasture. *E. Ir.* clúain, meadow. *O. Celt.* klo(p)ni, meadow.
cluaineag, *n. f.* a lawn, a patch of green.
cluaineagach, *a.* full of lawns, fields.
cluainearachd, *n. f.* deceit, fraud.
cluaineas, *n. m.* deceit, intrigue.
cluaineis, *n. m.* basking ; a' mire 's a' cluaineis, making merry and basking.
cluainlin, *n. f.* corn-spurry.
cluaintear, klu-ainter, *n. m.* a flatterer, a cajoler, a hypocrite, a cunning fellow. *E. Ir.* clúanaire, beguiler. *O' Dav.*
cluaintearachd, cloo-ainter-uchc, *n. f.* fawning ; cajoling, flattery, hypocrisy, intrigue.
cluaisean, kluăsh'-an, *n. m.* a blow on the ear ; " ear " of a pot ; porringer, a shoe latchet.
cluanag, *n. f.* an islet in a river, a small piece of choice pasture, a meadow.
cluar, *n. f.* a rag, tatter ; cluaran bhròg, boots very much worn and shapeless. *(Sc.)* bauchles ; chaidh i 'n a cluar chlar, it fell to pieces.
cluaran, *n. m.* a thistle, fountain ; a sponge.
cluaranach, *a.* thistly, fungous.
cluas, klooăs, *n. f.* an ear ; handle of a dish (.i. " ear "-like handle). *O. Ir.* clúas. *W.* clust. *O. Celt.* kloustâ.
cluasach, *a.* eared, having handles, large-eared.

cluasag, *n. f.* pillow, pincushion. *M.Ir.* clúaschan. *W.* clustog.
cluas-bhiorach, *a.* sharp-eared, pointed ears.
cluas-chiùil, *n. m.* a musical ear.
cluas-fhàinne and cluas-fhàil, *n. f.* an earring.
cluas-liath, *n. f.* herb, colt's foot.
clùd, clood, *n. m.* patch, a rag, clout ; *v.* patch ; *a.* clùdach, clouted ; fr. *Eng.*
clùdadh, cloodu, *vbl. n. m.* patching, mending. *M.Ir.* act of covering, clothing.
clùdag, *n. f.*, and clùdan, *n. m.*, a little clout.
clùdair, clooder, *n. m.* patcher, cobbler.
cluich, cloo-ich, *n. m.* play, sport, game, school vacation ; *v.* play, sport. *O.Ir.* cluche, cluichech ; gl. ludibundus. *O.Celt.* klokjâ.
cluicheadair, cloo-ich-uder, *n. m.* a player.
cluicheag, cloo-ichag, *n. f.* children's sport ; a toy.
cluichealachd, cloo-ich-aluchc, *n. f.* playfulness.
cluicheil, clooichal, *a.* playful, sportive.
cluigean, cloogen, *n. m.* an earring or pendant, a cluster; anything dangling; fr. clag.
cluigeanach, *a.* full of bells, appendages.
clùimh. *See* cluaimh, clòimh.
cluinn, *v.* hear, listen, hearken, attend ; nach cluinn e ? shall he not hear ? chuala mi, I heard. *O.Ir.* ro-cluniur ; " dochách rodchluinethar," to every one who hears it. *Wb.* gl. *W.* clyw, hearing. *O.Celt.* klunêmi.
cluinnte, cloo-intu, *vbl. a.* heard, attended to.
cluinntear, *n. m.* a hearer.
cluinntearachd, *n. f.* hearing.
cluinntinn, *inf.* of cluinn, hearing.
cluip, klwip, *n. f.* deceit. *See* cuip ; *v.* cheat.
cluipearachd, *n. f.* fraud, deception.
clù-nead, *n. m.* warm or sheltered rest.
clupaid, cloopej, *n. f.* swollen throat in cattle. *Also* am pluc.
clùthaich, *v.* cover, warm. *Ir.* cluthaighim.
clùthaich, *v.* chase.
clùthmhor, *a.* cosy. *M.Ir.* cluthmar = clithmar, sheltered.
clùthmhorachd, *n. f.* warmth, shelter.
cnab, *v.* pull, haul.
cnàbaire, *n. m.* instrument for dressing flax. *Ir.* cnáib, hemp.
cnac, *v.* crack ; *n. f.* a sound ; fissure.
cnag, krág, *n. f.* a peg, a pin, a knob, thole-pin of a boat ; *v.* thump, knock, rap. So *Ir.*

cnag, *v.* crack ; *n. f.* snap of the fingers, knock.
cnagach, *a.* knotty, knobby.
cnagachd, knag'-achc, *n. f.* knobbiness, knottiness.
cnagaid, krăg'-ăj, *n. f.* an old maid ; an old cow with stumps of horns.
cnagaire, krag'-ŭr-ă, *n. f.* a gill, a noggin. *Also* frangach (*Lewis*).
cnagaire, *n. m.* knocker.
cnagan, *n. m.* a little pin or peg ; an earthen jar (for oil).
cnàid, kréj, *v.* scoff ; *n. f.* a jeer, a scoff. *Also* magadh. *Ir.* cnáid, tattle, jeer.
cnàimh, crêv, *n. m., pl.* cnàmhan, *gen. pl.* cnàmh, a bone ; cnàimh an droma, the spine, the backbone ; cnàimh, cnàimh criche, a balk, or landmark. *Is. O.Ir.* cnáim, *pl.* cnámai. *O.Celt.* knâmi-s, a bone.
cnàimh-bhristeach, *n. m.* the ossifrage.
cnàimheach, cryv-uch, *n. m.* a rook. *Also* ròcaideach.
cnàimhgheadh, *n. m.* a fowl between a goose and a duck.
cnàimhgheal, *a.* white-boned.
cnàimhseag, crăyshag, *n. f.* the bearberry ; a pimple on the face (blackhead).
cnàimhseagach, *a.* pimply ; full of bearberries.
cnàimhteach, crăv-tuch, *a.* digestive, corrosive.
cnàmh, krăv, *v.* chew, ruminate, digest ; a' cnàmh a chìr, chewing the cud ; corrode, consume ; chnàmh an t-iarrunn, the iron corroded ; chnàmh an gealbhan, the fire consumed. *E.Ir.* cnáim, I gnaw, consume, languish.
cnàmhach, krăv'-uch, *a.* bony, having large bones.
cnàmhach, *a.* corrosive, consuming.
cnàmhag, krăv'-ăg, *n. f.* refuse of anything, anything deprived of its substance ; corn spoiled by cattle.
cnàmhairneach, krăv'-ăr'-nuch, *n. f.* sprats of the mackerel ; a skeleton ; a raw-boned fellow.
cnàmhan, krăv'-an, *n. m.* unceasing bickering, corroding words, gnawing pain (the last a has an open sound).
cnàmhanach, *a.* corroding, vexatious.
cnàmharlach, krăv'-ar-lach, *n. m.* a hardboned, cadaverous person ; a stalk. *Also* cnàmhlach.
cnàmhuin, *n. m.* gangrene.
cnap, krápp, *n. m.* a lump, a knob, a thump ; *v.* thump ; 'gam chnapadh, thumping me. *O.N.* knappr, a knob, button.
cnap, *n. m.* a rope made of bent. tether.
cnapach, kráp'-ach, *a.* lumpy, knobby ; *n. m.* a youngster.

cnapach, *a.* rattling.

cnapadair, *n. m.* a thumper.

cnapag, *n. f.* a block, little stool ; a shinty-ball.

cnapaich, *v.* gather into lumps.

cnapaire, kráp'-ur-à, *n. m.* a thumper ; a stout article ; a stout fellow.

cnapan, kráp'-an, *n. m.* a little lump ; a little block.

cnapanach, kráp'-an-ach, *a.* lumpy.

cnapanach, *n. m.* a strong lump of a boy.

cnaparra, krap'-ărr-u, *a.* stout, sturdy ; falling with a thumping noise.

cnapraich, *n. f.* act of rattling.

cnap-starra, krap'-starr-à, *n. m.* obstruction ; ball on the end of a spear.

cnarra, *n. f.* a ship. *E.Ir.* cnarr. *O.N.* knörr, *gen.* knarrar.

cnatan, *n. m.* a cold, cough ; *a.* cnatanach.

cnead, kréd, *n. f.* a sudden sigh or moan ; chan 'eil cnead air, nothing is wrong with him ; *v.* sigh, moan. *O.Ir.* cnetaim.

cneadail, kréd'-ul, *vbl. n. m.* act of sighing and moaning heavily and quickly.

cneadh, *n. f.* a wound, a sore. *E.Ir.* cned. *O.Celt.* knidâ.

cneadraich, credrich, *n. f.* a sighing, moaning, sobbing.

cneamh, krev, *n. m.* wild garlick. *See* creamh.

cneap, krepp, *n. m., pl.* cneapan, a button ; a bead ; a pebble.

cneapadair, krepp'-a-dăr, *n. m.* buttonmaker.

cneas, kress, *n. m.* skin ; bosom, breast, waist. *E.Ir.* cnes.

cneasaich, *v.* beautify ; shape.

cneas-Chuchulainn, *n. m.* meadow-sweet.

cneasda, kres'-d-u, *a.* humane ; moderate ; meek. *E.Ir.* cnesta, honest, seemly.

cneasdachd, kres'-dăchc, *n. f.* humanity ; piety ; meekness.

cneasgheal, *a.* white-skinned.

cneasmhor, *a.* pretty, comely.

cneasnaich, kres'-nich, *v.* squeeze and shake a person.

cneasnaidh, kres'-ni, *a.* delicate, slender.

cneasnaidheachd, cresny - achc, *n. f.* delicacy.

cneatan, cretan, *n. m.* a cold, coughing.

cneatas. *See* cneidsinn.

cneatraich, *m.* groaning. *M.Ir.* cnetnach, sobbing, groaning.

cnèbilt, *n. m.* garter. *O.N.* kné + belt, garter. *Also* crèapaild.

cnéid. *See* cnàid.

cneidh, cney, *n. f.* wound, hurt.

cneidsinn, cnej-shin, *n. m.* knitting, tape.

cneisne, *a.* slender.

cniadaich, *v.* caress, stroke.

cniadaiche, *n. m.* caresser.

cniopanach, cnipanuch, *n. m.* a shrunken fellow.

cnò, for cnù, *n. f., pl.* cnothan, a nut, a filbert. *O.Ir.* cnú. *W.* cneuen. *O.Celt.* knovâ. Cf. *O.N.* hnot.

cnò-bhainne, *n. f.* the milk-nut ; nutshaped wooden vessel for carrying home milk from the milking place.

cnoc, *n. m.* a knoll, an eminence. *O.Ir.* cnocc. *W.* cnwc, bump, hillock. *O.Celt.* knokko-. Cf. *O.N.* hnakki, nape.

cnocach, *a.* hilly, rugged.

cnocach, *a.* sensible ; duine cnocach, a sensible man.

cnòcaid, crocaj, *n. f.* a landmark, balk, woman's hair bound in a fillet.

cnocaire, crociru, *n. m.* a loiterer, saunterer.

cnocaireachd, crocirachc, *n. f.* loitering on hills.

cnocan, crocan, *n. m.* a hillock, a knoll. *E.Ir.* cnoccán.

cnocan, *n. m.* small ball (of yarn).

cnoc-faire, *n. m.* an alarm post.

cnòd, krŏd, *n. m.* a patch ; a knot ; *v.* patch.

cnòdach, *n. m.* a covering.

cnòdach, *a.* industrious ; clouted.

cnòdaich, *v.* acquire, lay up. ˙

cnòdan, *n. m.* the gurnet.

cnoid, krŏj, *n. m.* a splendid present.

cnoimh, cruiy, *n. f.* a maggot. *Also* cnuimh.

cnoimheag, knó'-àg, *n. f.* a maggot ; niggardly female. *Also* cnuimheag.

cnomhagag, *n. f.* (conachag, a conch). *Also* guth-le-gug.

cnomhagan, *n. m.* large whelk, buckie

cnot, krótt, *v.* husk barley ; *n. m.* oar-slip.

cnotag, krott'-ăg, *n. f.* husking mortar.

cnù, croo, *n. f.* a nut, a filbert ; cnù-fhrangach, a walnut : cnù-dharaich, an acorn ; cnù-bhachair, a Molucca nut. Same as cnò.

cnuac, croo-ac, *n. f.* a lump, a head, brow, temple.

cnuacach, *a.* lumpy ; shrewd, shy.

cnuacarra, *a.* deep ; shrewd.

cnuachdaire, croo-aciru, *n. m.* shrewd man.

cnuaic, *n. f.* heaping full ; a bheil e làn ? thà, agus cnuaic, is it full ? yes, heaping full.

cnuas, croo-as, *v.* gather, ponder, chew. *M.Ir.* cnúas, nuts ; gathering harvest.

cnuasachd, croo-asachc, *n. f.* gathering, chewing, pondering, reflection.

cnuasaich, croo-asich, *v.* gather, ponder, chew. *M.Ir.* cnúasaim, cnúasaigim.

cnuasaiche, *n. m.* a searcher.

cnuasmhor, *a.* fruitful, fertile.

cnùcach, *a.* dehorned.

cnùcag, *n. f.* a hornless cow.

cnùdan. *See* cnòdan.

cnùicean, *n. m.* short stubby horn.

cnuimh, *n. f.* a worm, maggot ; toothache ; tha a' chnuimh orm, I have the toothache.

cnuimheagach, *a.* wormy, maggoty.

cnuimhfhiacal, *n. f.* toothache.

cnumhag, *n. f.* snap of fingers.

cnumhagan, *n. m.* a handful.

có, *int. pron.* who ; cò e, who is he ? cò i, who is she ? cò iad ? who are they ? *O.Ir.* cote, cate.

co, *adv. See* cho.

co-, com-, con-, *prefix,* used to form cpds. =similar, equal.

co-aigne,* *n. f.* a similar turn of mind.

co-aigneach, *a.* of the same mind.

co-aimsireachd, *n. f.* concurrence of events.

co-aontachadh, *vbl. n. m.* consent, acquiescence, agreement ; act of consenting, agreeing.

co-aontaich, *v.* acquiesce, yield.

còb, *n. m.* plenty. *Lat.* copia. Cf. *E.Ir.* cob, a victory.

cobhair, co-ir, *n. f.* relief ; *v.* relieve, aid, help. *O.Ir.* cobir.

cobhan, koff'-an, *n. m.* a chest, coffin ; *a.* cobhanach ; fr. the *Eng.*

còbhar, kó'-ur, *n. m.* froth, foam. *Also* sillabub. *E.Ir.* cobur.

cobhartach, kòv'-art-ach, *n. m.* booty, spoil.

cobharthach, *n. m.* a helper ; better use *cpd.* fear-cobhair.

co-bhrìghich, *v.* consubstantiate.

coc, *v.* cock ; hold up in defiance ; coc do bhonnaid, cock your bonnet.

coca, *conj.* or *pron.* whether, which of the two ; còca a dh' fhalbhas no dh' fhanas tu, whether you go or stay. For co aca.

còcaire, cōciru, *n. m.* and *f.* a cook ; is math an còcaire an t-acras, hunger is a good cook. So *Ir. Lat.* coquo.

co-cheangail, *v.* bind together in a bond, covenant.

co-cheangal, *n. m.* compact, league, bond.

co-cheòl, *n. m.* symphony.

cochlaich, *n.f.* 1. a rattling, throat-rattle, death-rattle ; cochlaich a chléibh, the rattle of his chest. 2. a tangled skein.

co-chomhairle, *n. f.* consultation.

co-chomunn, *n. m.* fellowship.

co-chreutar, *n. m.* a fellow-creature.

co-chruinnich, *v.* gather, collect.

cochull, *n. m.* husk, hood, cowl ; cochull a' chridhe, the pericardium ; skin of a snake. So *O.Ir. Lat.* culcullus.

cochullach, *a.* capsular, husky.

* For pronunciation of compounds see separate members elsewhere.

cocontachd, *n. f.* smartness.

codach, *gen.* of cuid, *q.v.*

codaich, *v.* share, divide.

còdhail, *n. f.* meeting, reproach ; am chòdhail, to meet me ; thoir còdhail da, face him. *See* còmhdhail.

co-dhùin, *v.* conclude.

co-éignich, *v.* compel, constrain.

co-fharpuis, *n. f.* rivalry.

co-fhoghlumaiche, *n. m.* a school-fellow.

co-fhreagair, *v.* correspond.

co-fhreagartas, *n. m.* symmetry, correspondence.

co-fhreagrach, *a.* answering, corresponding.

co-fhreagrachd, *n. f.* symmetry, conformity.

co-fhulangas, *n. m.* sympathy, fellow-feeling.

co-fhurtachd, *n. f.* comfort, consolation.

co-fhurtair, *n. m.* comforter.

cog, *v. t.* war, fight ; jibe, jeer ; chog iad, they warred ; tha e a' cogadh air, he jibes or jeers him.

cogach, *a.* warlike.

cogadh, kògg'-ă, *vbl. n. m.* war, warfare ; warring ; jibing ; thun cogaidh, for war. *E.Ir.* cocad, warfare (=con+cath).

cogais, cogosh, *n. f.* a prodigious large, red, carbuncled nose ; the cog of a wheel ; a large pinch of snuff ; the nasal canal ; the cork of a bottle ; a huge frog ; the throttle.

cogais, *n. f.* conscience. *O.Ir.* cúbus, cubus, cocubus, gl. *conscientia.* cubus =con+fius. (*Z²*.)

cogall, *n. m.* cockle, tares. *Also* peasair chapull. *E.Ir.* cocal.

cogan, *n. m.* a loose husk, a small vessel. *M.Ir.* cocán, blossom.

cogar, *n. m.* a whisper. *E.Ir.* cocraim, whisper, conspire.

cogarsaich, cogursich, *n. f.* whispering.

co-gheall, *v.* fulfil a promise.

co-ghleachd, *n. f.* struggling, wrestling.

co-ghlòir, *n. f.* equal glory.

co-ghné, *n. f.* a similar nature.

co-ghuil, *v.* weep with, condole.

cograich, *n. f.* whispering.

cogull, *n. m.* cockle, tares.

coibhneas, *n. f.* kindness. *O.Ir.* coibnes, *affinitas* ; coibnesta, affinis. co+fine.

coibhseachd, *n. f.* propriety, sufficiency. *Also* cuidheasachd. *M.Ir.* cuibdius, fitness, harmony.

coiceig, *n. f.* trouble, hindrance.

coicheid, cochej, *n. f.* an objection, obstruction, doubt, suspicion ; cò chuir coicheid, who objected ?

coicheideach, cochejuch, *a.* objecting, hindering, suspicious.

coidheas, coyesh, *a.* equally ready, ready for either ; frequently written coingeis, tha mi coingeis, I do not care which ; *prop*. coimdheas.

coidhirp, *n. f.* competition, rivalry.

cóig, *a.* five ; cóig-deug, fifteen. *O.Ir.* cóic. *O.W.* pimp. *Lat.* quinque.

cóigeach, *n. f.* a hand. From cóig.

cóigead, cōgid, *n. m.* fifty ; *a.* fifty. *O.Ir.* cóica, *gen.* cóicat.

cóigeamh, cōgiv, *a.* the fifth. *O.Ir.* cóiced.

cóigear, cōgir, *n. m.* and *f.* five persons.

coigil, *v.* spare. *E.Ir.* coiclim, coicill.

cóignear, cōgnur, *n.* five persons. *O.Ir.* cóicer.

coigreach, coigruch, *n. m., pl.* coigrich, stranger, foreigner ; air choigrich, in a strange place, among strangers. *Ir.* coigcrich, *n. f.* foreign country ; *a.* strange. *Ktg.*

coigreachail, coigruchal, *a.* strange, foreign.

cóig-shlisneach, *a.* pentilateral.

coilbean, *n. m.* a small rope (for carrying a burden).

coilce, *n. f.* a bed.

coilceadha, col-ceya, *n. m.* bed materials (put under sheets or blankets). *Ir.* coilce, a bed.

coilchean, *n. m.* a little cock ; water spouting.

coilchinn, *a.* stunted (of cereals).

coileach, culuch and caluch, *n. m.* a cock ; coileach frangach, a turkey - cock ; coileach - coille, woodcock ; coileach dubh, a blackcock ; coileach fraoich, heath-cock ; coileach tomain, a cock partridge ; coileach ruadh, a red grouse cock ; a gush of water ; rapids ; an coileach an t-srutha, in the rapids ; tha coileach air a' ghaoith, a half-gale ; tha coileach air an loch, white-heads on the lake. *O.Ir.* cailech. *W.* ceiliog.

coileachan, culuchan, *n. m.* a little cock.

coileach - gaoith, culach - gooy, *n. m.* weathercock, a vane.

coileag, coylag, *n. f.* a cole of hay ; a knoll.

coileagaich, *v.* gather into cocks.

coileid, colej, *n. f.* noise, stir, hubbub.

coileir, coler, *n. m.* a collar, neck.

coilìobhar, coleever, *n. m.* kind of gun. *See* cuilbheir.

coilionn, culiun, *n. f.* candle. *See* coinneal.

coille, culu, *n. f.* wood, forest ; *pl.* coilltean, woods ; fo'n choill, outlawed. *O.Ir.* caill. *O.Celt.* kaldet.

coilleag, culiag, *n. f.* a cockle.

coilleag, *n. f.* a rural song ; young potato ; smart blow.

coilleagach, *a.* full of sprouts ; musical ; *n. f.* a song.

coilleannach, *n. m.* truant, poltroon.

coilleanta, culantu, *a.* tall, straight, and slender.

coillearnach, culy'-ar-nach, *n. f. a.* shrubbery.

coillteach, cuiltuch, *n. f.* woods, forest, wilds, woodland.

coillteachail, cuiltuchol, *a.* woody ; savage, wild ; sylvan ; uninhabited.

coilltear, cuilter, *n. m.* a saunterer, wanderer.

coilltearachd, coylteruchc, *n. f.* state of a fugitive.

coillteil, cuiltol, *a.* wild, woodland.

coilpeachadh, *n. m.* equalising cattle stock.

coilpein, *n. m.* a rope.

coimeas, koym'-us, *n. m.* comparison, parable, an equal, a match ; gun a choimeas ann, without his equal or match ; *a.* like. Cf. *E.Ir.* cobés, equal amount.

coimeas, *v. t.* compare, liken.

coimeasach, coymisuch, *a.* co-equal.

coimeasg, koym'-isg, *v.* mix, mingle.

coimeata, *a.* co-mate.

coimh-, a prefix, answering *con* and *com* in English.

coimhcheangal, co-chengul, *n. m.* treaty, covenant.

coimheach, kóy'-ach, *a.* foreign, strange, shy, unkind ; duine coimheach, a strange person, or a shy person ; terrible ; gnothuch coimheach, a terrible affair ; *n.* a stranger ; aig na coimhich, with strangers. *M.Ir.* comaithchech. *O.Ir.* comaightech, strange, a stranger.

coimheachas, coyuchus, *n. f.* estrangement, want of hospitality, sourness of disposition. *E.Ir.* comaithchęs, hostility.

coimhead, coyud, *v.* see, look ; preserve, keep ; watch ; *vbl. n. m.* preserving, inspection. *O.Ir.* comét, *servatio.*

coimhearsnach, coyarsnuch, *n. m.* a neighbour. *E.Ir.* comarse (= com + ursainn). *Zim.*

coimhearsnachd, kŏy'-ar-snăchc, *n. f.* neighbourhood, vicinity ; vicinage ; neighbourly conduct.

coimheart, co-art, *n. m.* a comparison. *Also* comhard. Cf. *Lat.* confero.

coimheirbse, *n. m.* wrangling (for con + farpuis).

coimhgheall, co-yal, *v.* fulfil an engagement, perform your promise.

coimhghealladh, co-yala, *n. m.* performance of one's promise, fulfilment.

coimhideachd, coyidachc, *n. f.* accompanying, escorting ; attending ; luchd coimhideachd, an escort, a suite, a levee, a retinue. *E.Ir.* coimtecht.

coimhirp, coyirp, *n. f.* rivalry, competition (con + oidhirp).

coimhleapach, coylapuch, *n. m.* and *f.*
a bedfellow. *E.Ir.* com-lepaid, joint-
bed, cohabiting.
coimhling, coyling, *n. f.* a race, competition, contest (con + lingim, leap).
coimhlion, colin, *v.* fulfil, fill up, accomplish, perform a promise. *O.Ir.*
comalnaim.
coimhlion, co-leen, *a.* and *adv.* as often
as, as many as ; equal in number.
E.Ir. comlín.
coimhlionta, colintu, *a.* perfect, complete.
coimhliontachd, colintachc, *n. f.* perfection.
coimhseas, coy-shas, *n. f.* conscience.
See cogais.
coimhseasach, coy-shasach, *a.* conscientious, conscionable.
coimhseasachd, coyshasuchc, *n. f.* consciousness.
coimhthional, co-hinal, *n. m.* assembly,
gathering, collecting ; collection. *O.Ir.*
comthinol.
coimirce, *n. f.* protection, mercy, quarter.
Ir. comairce, coimirce, protection, care.
coimpire, co-impiru, *n. m.* an equal in
rank.
coimpireachd, co-impirachc, *n. f.* equality
in rank, a commonwealth, common-
weal.
coimrig, cuimrig, *n. f.* trouble, interruption.
coimseach, *a.* indifferent, careless.
coimsich, *v.* perceive.
cóin, *v.* weep. *See* caoin. *M.Ir.* cóinim,
complain, wail. *O.Celt.* koinio.
coin-bhraghad, *n. pl.* king's evil.
coin-chrìch, *n. m., pl.* eye-teeth, gag-
teeth.
coindean, coynen, *n. m.* a kit, small
tub.
cóineadh, *vbl. n. m.* act of weeping.
còineag, cōniag, *n. f.* a nest of wild bees.
coinean, conyan, *n. m.* a rabbit, a coney ;
a. coineanach.
coingeis, *a.* indifferent, quite careless ;
tha mi coingeis, I am quite indifferent,
I do not care ; is coingeis còca, it is
no matter which ; co + deas.
coingheal, congal, *n. f.* a whirlpool.
coingheall, conu-yul, *n. m.* a loan. con
+ giall.
coingheallach, conu-yulach, *a.* accommodating, lending, helping, kind, ready
to lend.
coingheallaich, conu-yulich, *v.* lend,
accommodate.
coingir, *n. f.* a pair.
coinigin, conigin, *n. f.* a rabbit warren.
coinlein, *n. m.* a nostril. *Also* cuinlein ;
and cuinnein.
coinn, *n. f.* a fit of coughing.
coinne, co-nyà, *n. f.* 1. meeting, assigna-

tion ; chan fhaigh mi coinne air son
m' athar, I will never be faced on
account of my father. 2. picnic party,
a party to which each brings his provisions ; *v.* imitate, follow the example
of ; an ann a' coinne riumsa a tha thu,
is it imitating me you are ? *E.Ir.*
conne, coinne.
còinneach, cō'-nyach, *n. f.* bog, moss.
Also còinnteach. *E.Ir.* coennich.
coinneal, cuniul, *n. f.* a candle ; *pl.*
coinnlean. *E.Ir.* candel. *Lat.* candela.
coinnealaich, cuniulich, *v.* brandish,
flourish ; coinnealaich bata, brandish
a stick.
coinneal-bhàth, *v.* excommunicate.
coinnealta, cunialtu, *a.* bright, brilliant.
E.Ir. caindelta.
coinneamh, cu-niuv, *n. f.* meeting,
assembly. *E.Ir.* conne.
coinneas, *n. f.* a ferret.
coinnich, *v.* meet, assemble, oppose.
coinnleach, cuyluch, *a.* full of candles.
coinnleag, cuylag, *n. f.* oily surface
(broth).
coinnlean bianain, *n. pl., also* teine-
shionnachain, phosphorescence.
coinnlein, coylen, *n. m.* a stalk of corn.
O.Ir. connall.
coinnleir, cayler, *n. m.* a candlestick.
Lat. candelarius.
coinnseas, coy-shas, *n. f.* conscience.
See cogais.
coinnspeach, coyspiach, *n. m., pl.* coinn-
speich, a wasp.
co-inntinneach, *a.* agreeable.
co-iomlan, *a.* equally complete.
co-ionann, *a.* alike, equal.
coip, koyp, *n. f.* a heap of foam or froth.
còir, *a.* decent ; pious-minded, worthy ;
duine còir, a decent or pious man ;
kind, generous. *O.Ir.* cóir, *congruus.*
còir, kôêr, *n. f., pl.* còraichean, right,
equity, justice, integrity, honesty ;
propriety ; a' cumail na còrach rium,
doing justice to me ; rinn thu chòir,
you have acted with propriety ; air
chòir, properly, comfortably ; charter ;
còraichean an fhearainn, the charter of
the land ; proximity, nearness, contiguity ; air chòir a' bhaile, near the
town ; na tig am chòir, don't come
near me. *O.Ir.* cóir (two syl.), co + fhir.
W. cywir. *O.Celt.* ko-vero-s, true, right.
coirb, curb, *v.* corrupt ; coirbte, abandoned. *E.Ir.* corpte, wicked. *Lat.*
corruptus.
coirbidh, *a.* curby, corrupt, corruptible.
coirce, corcu, *n. m.* oats. So *E.Ir. See*
corc.
coirceag, *n. f.* a beehive. *Also* caornag.
coire, kur''-à, *n. m., pl.* coireannan, blame,
fault, defect, wrong, hurt, harm ; sin,

guilt, crime. *O.Ir.* **caire**, gl. *accusatio.*
W. **caredd.** *O.Celt.* **karjâ-**, blame.

coire, coru, *n. m., pl.* **coireachan**, a
cauldron, kettle, a circular place
resembling a cauldron ; a dell, a corrie,
whirlpool ; **coire-bhreacain**, the Jura-
Scarba whirlpool. *E.Ir.* **core, coire**, a
cauldron. *W.* **pair.** *O.N.* **hverr**, a
kettle.

coireach, keruch, *a.* in fault, blameable ; *n. m.* a defaulter ; **criomachair
an coireach**, blame the defaulter ; the
guilty.

coireal, cural, *n. m.* coral; fr. the *Eng.*

coireal, *n. m.* loud tones (as scolding or
in passion).

coireall, *n. m.* a quarry.

coireaman, kuraman, *n. m.* coriander.
Lat. coriandrum.

coirean, *n. m.* a little hollow, little corrie.

coirich, *v. t.* blame, reprove. *O.Ir.*
cairigim, rebuke, censure.

coirilidh, coryly, *a.* alert, nimble, vigorous.

coirill, *n. f.* chirping of birds.

coirioll, corul, *n. m.* a carol.

coirneach, cŏrnuch, *n. m.* the kingfisher.

còirneal, cŏrnal, *n. m.* colonel.

coirpileir, corpler, *n. m.* corporal ; fr.
the *Eng.*

coisbheart, keshort, *n. m.* foot-gear.

coisbheart, *n. m.* greaves ; cos+beart.

coiseachd, kòsh'-ăchc, *n. f.* pedestrianism,
walking ; travelling on foot.

coiseunaich, coshenich, *v.* bless (con +
sian).

coisg, kŏshc, *v.* staunch ; quiet, still.
See **caisg.**

coisich, kòsh'-ich, *v.* walk, travel on foot.

coisiche, kòsh'-ich-u, *n. m.* a traveller,
pedestrian.

coisinn, kòsh'-inn, *v.* gain, earn, win ;
deserve.

còisir, cŏshir, *n. f.* choir.

còisridh, **còisreadh**, cŏshry, *n. f.* a festive
party, chorus.

coisridh, cŏshry, *n. f.* infantry.

coisrig, kòsh'-rig, *v.* consecrate, sanctify ;
coisrigte, consecrated ; **uisge coisrigte**,
holy water. *E.Ir.* **coisecraim.** *Lat.*
consecro.

coiste, coshtu, *vbl. a.* spent, exhausted,
worn.

coit, *n. f.* abuse, hard usage. *O.Ir.*
coit=calad, coitti, hardness. *O'Dav.*

coit, *n. f.* a hut ; a cottage. *E.Ir.* **coite.**
Lat. cotta.

coit, cohtu, *n. f.* a punt, or small boat ;
dh' éigh iad port, 's gun d'fhuair iad
coit, they cried the ferry and they got
a boat. *O.Ir.* coit, wood. *O.W.* coit.

coitcheann, *a.* public, common, general.
So *O.Ir.* coitchonn.

coitcheannas, coit-chyann-as, *n. f.* that
which is common, general ; **anns a'
choitcheannas**, in general, generally.
E.Ir. coitchindus, common property.

coite, *a.* hard, cruel ; " a' bhean choite,"
the cruel woman.

coiteach, co-tiach, *a.* abounding in small
boats.

coiteachadh, coituchu, *vbl. a.* pressing to
accept anything ; coaxing ; contend-
ing, as in an argument.

coitear, coter, *n. m.* a cottager, cotter.
E.Ir. coite, a cot. *Lat.* cotta. *Eng*
cottar.

coitich, cotich, *v.* press, contend, argue,
maintain.

coitidh, coty, *a.* common, general.

col, *v.* restrain, hinder, impede.

col, *n. m.* incest, sin. *O.Ir.* col, crime.
W. **cŵl.** *Bret.* **col-.** *O.Celt.* **kulo-.**

colag, *n. f.* collop, small steak, a cutlet.

colainn, *n. f.* the body, the trunk. *O.Ir.*
colinn, *gen.* colno, flesh.

colaiste, colesht, *n. f.* college ; fr. *Eng.*

colamor, *n. m.* the hake, coal-fish. *Also*
falamor.

còlan, *n. m.* fellow-soldier, companion.
Cf. **còmhlan**, a company, a band of
people.

colbh, colv, *n. m., pl.* cuilbh, plank ; front
of a bed ; pillar ; a reed ; " chuir
colbh 'n a làimh mar rìgh," put a reed
in his hand as if king. *Du.B.* *E.Ir.*
colbh, coloma. *Lat.* columna.

colbh-mhàsach, *a.* having stout hips.

colc, *n. f.* eider-duck. *Also* alc.

colg, *n. m., pl.* and *gen. sing.* **cuilg**,
1. a point, a bristle, a prickle. 2. a
pointed blade. 3. hackles of a dog.
4. anger, wrath. 5. fierce eye, a
threatening aspect. *See* calg, awn.
Ir. calg and colg, a sword, bristle.

colgag, *n. f.* the fore-finger. *Also* sgealbag.

colgaiche, *n. f.* wildness, fierceness,
ferocity.

colgail, *a.* fierce, angry, threatening look.

colganta, *a.* bristling, fierce, angry.

colgantachd, colgantuchc, *n. f.* fierceness.

colgantas, *n. m.* wildness.

colgarra, kolg'-urr-u, *a.* bristling, fierce-
looking, stern, " looking daggers."

colgarrachd, kŏllg'-urr-achc, *n. f.* fierceness, sternness.

coll, coul, *n. m.* a hazel-tree. *See* **calltuinn.** So *E.Ir.* *O.Celt.* koslo-, hazel.

collach, *n. m.* a boar. *See* cullach.

collachail, *a.* boarish.

collachd, *n. f.* lewdness.

collaid, colej, *n. f.* clamour, scolding ;
a. collaideach. *See* coileid.

collaidh, coly, *a.* carnal, lewd. *E.Ir.*
collaide, fleshly, carnal.

collaidin, *n. m.* white poppy. *Also*
codalan.

collainn, colin, *n. f.* a smart stroke. *Also* coilleag.

colman, *n. m.* dove. *See* calman. *O.Ir.* colum, colomb. *O.Celt.* kolombo-s; fr. *Lat.* columba.

colnach, *a.* incestuous.

colpach, *n. f.* heifer. *E.Ir.* colpthach.

coltach, *a.* like, probable, likely.

coltar, *n. m.* a coulter. So *E.Ir.* 'coltas, *n. m.* appearance, resemblance.

com, *n. m.* the trunk of the body, chest, the region of the viscera. *M.Ir.* comm, cumm. *O.Ir.* a hollow, nook, dell.

com-, *prefix. See* co-.

coma, *a.* indifferent, not caring; disagreeable, hateful ; nach coma leatsa ? what is that to you ? is coma leis an righ Eóghan, is coma le Eóghan co dhiùbh, the king hates Ewen, and Ewen does not care a straw for that. *O.Ir.* cumme, gl. aequalis, idem ; indifferent.

comain, comen, *n. f.* obligation, favour received ; tha mi móran ad chomain, I am much obliged to you ; cha b'e do chomain e, I did not deserve that at your hand ; comain do làimh fèin, tit for tat. *O.Ir.* commáin, com + máin, gift for gift, gl. *Wb. Sc.* common, obligation. Cf. *W.* cymwynas, favour.

comairc, comerk, *n. f.* protection. *See* comraich.

comaith, comy, *n. f.* messing, mess ; eating out of the same dish. *E.Ir.* commaid, partnership. *O.Celt.* kombuti-s, connection.

comanachadh, kòm'-ăn-uch-u, *n. m.* sacrament ; communion ; celebration of the Lord's Supper ; luchd comanachaidh, communicants. *E.Ir.* comann, *n. f. Lat.* communio.

comanaich, kòm'-an-ich, *v. i.* communicate; cpds. : fear-comanaich, *n. m.* a male communicant; bean-chomanaich, *n. f.* a female communicant.

comannd, *n. m.* command, authority.

comanndair, *n. m.* commander.

comar, *n. f.* a confluence.

comaradh, kŏm'-ar-u, *n. m.* anything thrown on the shore ; booty.

comaradh, *n. m.* aid, assistance. *See* comradh.

comas, *n. m.* ability, capability, permission ; authority, power ; virility ; orra-chomais, an amulet to deprive a person of his virility ; power, licence. *O.Ir.* comus.

comasach, *a.* able, capable, powerful ; in good worldly circumstances ; garadh comasach, thorough warming in front of a good fire (the skirt knee high).

comasachd, kòm'-as-achc, *n. f.* capability.

combach, *n. m.* a companion, for companach.

combaiste, compaiste, coumbesht, *n. m.* a compass ; fr. the *Eng.*

comeirce, kom'-erk-u, *n. m.* dedication.

comh-, kó, for *con.* and *com.* in English ; written often co, and signifies equality, fellowship ; comh-aigne, fellow-feeling.

comhach, co'uch, *n. f.* prize, prey.

comhachag, *n. f.* the owl. *Also* cailleach-oidhche.

comhad, co'ad, *n. m.* 1. a comparison. 2. second couplet of a quatrain.

comhaib, co'eb, *n. f.* a contention (about rights) ; *v.* contend for rights.

comhaich, co'ich, *v.* contend, assert, dispute, be able ; cha do chomhaich mi a dhol, I did not manage to go.

còmhail, cō'el (for còmhdhail), *n. f.* a meeting ; thug e còmhdhail dha, he kept an appointment with him ; droch còmhdhail dha, bad luck to him.

comhailteachd, cō'iltuchc, *n. f.* a convoy ; cpds. : bean-chomhailteachd, bridesmaid ; fear-comhailteachd, best man.

comh-aimsireach, *a.* at the same time ; contemporary ; *n. m.* a contemporary.

comh-aimsireil, *a.* contemporary.

comh-ainm, co-enm, *n. m.* surname, anniversary. *E.Ir.* comainm, *cognomen.*

comhair, co'-ir, *n. m.* direction, tendency; an comhair a chinn, headlong ; thuit e an comhair a bheòil, he fell forwards ; an comhair a chùil, backwards.

comhair, co'ir, *n. f.* presence, view ; thainig e fa mo chomhair, it occurred to me. com + air.

comhairc, co'erc, *n. f.* an outcry, an appeal, forewarning. *E.Ir.* comaircim, I ask. com + arc (desire).

co-mhairionn, *a.* equally lasting.

comhairle, co'urlu, *n. f.* advice, counsel ; a council, a convocation. *O.Ir.* airle, counsel. com + airle.

comhairlich, *v.* advise, counsel, admonish, put on one's guard.

comhairliche, co'urlichu, *n. m.* an adviser, admonisher, monitor, counsellor.

comhais, *v.* guess ; feuch an comhais thu, see if you can guess. co + meas.

comhal, coäl, *n. f.* a joining.

comhalta, coältu, *n. m.* foster-brother. *E.Ir.* comalta, *collactaneus. Lat.* alo.

comhaltas, *n. m.* fosterage. *E.Ir.* comaltas

comhan, coän, *n. m.* a shrine.

comhaois, co-ūsh, *n. f.* a contemporary. one of the same age. *E.Ir.* com + aes. *O.Celt.* kóm-aivestu-s.

comh-aontaich, *v.* yield assent, agree, accede, accord.

comhard, co'ard, *n. f.* comparison ; chan 'eil comhard air bith aca ri chéile, there is no comparison between them. *O.Ir.* comarde.

comhardach, *a.* comparable.

comharra, co-huru, *n. m.* mark, sign, token, symptom. *O.Ir.* comarde, com + airde (gl. sign).

comharraich, co-hurich, *v.* mark, observe, point out ; *vbl. a.* comharraichte, singular, noted.

comhart, co-hurt, *n. m.* the bark of a dog.

comhartaich, co-hurtich, *n. f.* barking. *Also* tabhunn.

comh-bhann,* *n. m.* bond.

comh-bhuail, *v.* strike mutually.

comh-chomunn, *n. m.* fellowship.

comh-chruinneachadh, *n. m.* collection, assembly, congregation.

comh-chruinnich, *v.* gather, assemble, collect, congregate.

comh-chudthrom, *n. m.* equiponderance, equilibrium, equal weight.

còmhdach, cō-duch, *n. m.* clothing, covering, dress, shelter. *Ir.* cùmhdach, veil, protection, cover of a book. " shrine." *O.Ir.* cùmtach, a cover, a case, " shrine."

còmhdach, cō-duch, *n. m.* proof, evidence. *Ir.* cómhdachadh, quotation, proof. *O'R.*

còmhdaich, cōdich, *v. t.* allege, prove.

còmhdaich, *v. t.* cover, protect, shelter.

còmhdhail, cō-al, *n. f.* a meeting ; droch còmhdhail, bad luck. com + dàil.

comhdhalta, có'-ălt-u, *n. m.* foster-brother or sister. *See* comhalta.

comhdhaltas, có'-alt-us, *n. m.* relationship of fosterage ; sucking the same breast. *E.Ir.* comalta = *collactaneus.* *Wi. O.Celt.* kóm-altjo-s.

comh-dheuchainn, *n. f.* competition, rivalry, trial of valour.

comh-dhosguinn, *n. m.* mutual misfortune.

comh-dhùin, *v.* conclude, close, end.

comh-dhùnadh, *n. m.* conclusion.

comh-éignich, *v.* force, compel.

comh-fharpais, *n. f.* competition, emulation ; gibing, jeering, taking off.

comh-fharpaiseach, *a.* imitative.

comh-fhoghar, *n. m.* a consonant ; mutual stroke and sound, resound.

comh-fhreagair, *v.* suit, re-echo ; chomh-fhreagair gach tulm is cnoc, every hill and knoll re-echoed.

comh-fhreagairt, *n. f.* a re-echo, correspondence, uniformity, agreement.

comh-fhreagarrach, *a.* correspondent.

comh-fhuiling, *v.* sympathise.

comh-fhulangas, *n. m.* fellow - feeling, sympathy, fellow-suffering.

comhfhurtachd, *n. m.* comfort, consolation ; aid, help.

* See note on compounds, p. 19.

comhfhurtaich, *v.* comfort, aid.

comhfhurtair, *n. m.* a comforter.

comh-ghàir, *n. f.* conclamation.

comh-ghàirdeachas, *n. f.* congratulation, mutual joy.

comh-iomlaid, *n. f.* commutation.

comh-ionnan, *a.* equal, same.

comh-ionnanas, *n. f.* equality.

còmhla, *ad.* together, along with, in company ; thigibh còmhla, come together ; falbh còmhla riumsa, come along with me. *Ir.* comhlamh, together. com + làmh.

còmhla, cōlu, *n. f.* door, door-leaf. *E.Ir.* comla, door-valve, a gate.

còmhlaich, cōlich, *v.* meet, intercept.

còmhlan, *n. m.* 1. a company. 2. a companion. *See* cònlan.

còmhlann, cō-lann, *n. f.* duel, combat. *E.Ir.* comlond, a contest, combat.

comh-lorg, *n. m.* result, effort.

comhluadar, co'-lŭd-er, *n. m.* conversation, fellowship. *Ir.* comhluadar, conversation, company. *M.Ir.* comlúadar.

comh-mhothaich, *v.* sympathise ; comh-mhothachadh, sympathy, sympathising. *Also* comh-fhairich.

còmhnadail, cō'-nŭ-dull, *n. m.* conversation, conference, dialogue, talking together.

còmhnadalach, cōnudaluch, *a.* conversable ; duine còir còmhnadalach, a decent conversable man.

còmhnadh, cō'-nu, *n. m.* help, assistance. *O.Ir.* congniu, *inf.* congnam (co-operatio), gl. *Wb.* con + gni = " co-doing."

còmhnard, cōnurd, *a.* level, plain, even ; rathad còmhnard, a level or even road or surface ; *n. m.* a plain. com + ard.

còmhnuich, *v.* dwell, inhabit, reside.

còmhnuidh, kō-ny, *n. m.* habitation, a residence ; an còmhnuidh, habitually. *E.Ir.* comnaide, a dwelling, abiding ; comnaidim, I dwell.

comh-obair, *n. f.* same employment.

comh-oibrich, *v.* co-operate.

comh-oibriche, *n. m.* co-operator, coadjutor ; fellow-labourer.

comh-oighre, *n. m.* co-heir.

comh-òl, *n. m.* a banquet.

comholcas, *n. m.* offence, keen disappointment. com + olcas. *Also* comholc.

còmhradh, cō'-ră, *n. m.* conversation, dialogue. com + radh.

còmhrag, cō'-rag, *n. m.* fight ; conflict ; battle. *O.Ir.* comracc, meeting, encounter.

còmhraideach, cōrejuch, *a.* talkative.

còmhraidiche, *n. m.* a talker.

còmhraig, cōreg, *v.* fight.

comhruith, co-ree, *n. f.* a race, act of racing.
comh-sgoilear, *n. m.* school-fellow.
comh-sheasamh, *n. m.* constancy ; consisting.
comh-sheinn, *n. f.* harmony.
comh-sheirm, *n. m.* harmony.
comh-sheòmraiche, *n. m.* a room companion or chum.
comh-shinte, *a.* parallel, consonant with.
comh-shìorruidh, *a.* coeternal.
comh-shruth, *n. m.* confluence.
comh-shuiriche, *n. m.* a rival.
comh-spàirn, *n. f.* emulation.
còmhstach, cō'-stach, *a.* obliging, accommodating, useful, convenient ; *n. f.* a concubine, a whore.
còmhstath, cō'-sta, *n. m.* a loan, an accommodation, obligation, favour.
còmhstri, cōstry, *n. f.* strife ; emulation, rivalry, mutual striving.
comh-thruas, *n. m.* sympathy, pity.
comh-thulgadh, *n. m.* agitation.
com-pàirt, *n. f.* partnership.
com-pàirteach, *a.* participating, partaking.
com-pàirteachd, *n. f.* participation.
com-pàirtich, *v.* participate, partake, share.
companach, *n. m.* companion.
companachd, comp'-an-uchc, *n. f.* companionship.
companas, *n. f.* partnership, society, friendship, fellowship ; intercourse.
comradh, *n. f.* aid, help.
comraich, comrich, *n. f.* protection, place of refuge, a sanctuary. *M.Ir.* comairce.
comunn, kòm'-unn, *n. m.* society, club, company ; fellowship, intercourse, association. *Lat.* communio.
comunnaich, com'-unn'-ich, *v.* associate.
con-, *prefix*, with.
cona, *n. m.* moss crops ; cat's tail.
conablach, *n. m.* anything mangled. So *Ir.*
conablaich, conablich, *v.* mangle, disfigure, lacerate ; conablachadh, mangling, etc.
conach, *n. m.* affluence. So *Ir.*
conachag, *n. f.* a conch. *Also* conacag.
conachair, con'-ăch-ĕr, *n. m.* a sick person who gets neither better nor worse in health ; uproar.
conachlonn, *n. m.* an equal, a fellow, a mate. *Ir.* conclann, a grasp, a link, comparison. *Lh.*
conachshuil, conach-hool, *n. f.* prominent eyes.
conachuileag, cona-choolag, *n. f.* a sort of fly.
conadal, *n. m.* conversation.
conadal, *n. m.* a stray sheep.
conaidh, *a.* ravenous ; *gen.* of confadh, used as an *adj.*

conaig, *n. f.* foot, leg. *Also* root joints of the fingers.
conair, *n. m.* a path, way. *O.Ir.* conar, *via.*
conair, *n. f.* help, a crown, set of beads.
conaire, *n. f.* the herb " loose-strife."
conairt, cŏnurt, *n. f.* barking of many dogs ; scolding on a high key. *E.Ir.* a pack of hounds.
conalach, *n. f.* brandishing, swinging.
conaltrach, kon'-alt-rŭch, *a.* conversable, congenial fellowship.
conaltradh, cŏnaltru, *n. m.* conversation, talk, fellowship.
Conan, *n. m.* one of the Fian ; peevish person.
conanachd, *n. f.* venery.
conas, *n. m.* 1. furze, whins. 2. strife, wrangling.
conasach, *a.* fretful, peevish, short-tempered, apt to take offence.
conasg, *n. m.* whins, furze.
condasach, *a.* furious ; mad. Cf. *O.Ir.* gl. dásacht (insania). *Wb.*
condrachd, countrachc, *n. f.* mischief, mishap ; condrachd ort, mischief take you. *Also* contrachd. *E.Ir.* contracht, a curse, imprecation. *Lat.* contractus.
condual, *n. m.* embroidery.
confhach, *a.* raging, furious. *M.Ir.* confadach.
confhadh, cona-hu, *n. m.* the raging of the sea ; fury, the greatest rage. *M.Ir.* confad, canine rabies, fury.
conghair, connyar, *n. f.* uproar, fury.
conghlas, conalas, *n. m.* head bandage (on the dead).
cònlan, *n. m.* an assembly, conclave. So in *Lh.*
conn, coun, *n. m.* water-band of a hank of yarn ; dà-chonn, heer-band, band for two cuts of yarn ; principle, sense, reason ; duine gun chonn, a man without sense. *E.Ir.* cond. *O.Celt.* kondo-s, sense.
connadh, conna, *n. m.* fuel, firewood ; cuall chonnaidh, a faggot of firewood. *O.Ir.* condud. *W.* cynnud. *Lat.* candeo, incendo.
connan, *n. m.* lust.
connlach, counlach, *n. f.* straw, stubble, brushwood. *O.Ir.* connall, gl. stipula. *Lat.* cannula, canna, a reed. *O.Celt.* kano-, konnallo-.
connsaich, cŏnsich, *v.* quarrel, dispute, contend. *O.Ir.* sagim, gl. adeo. con + saigim.
connspair, cŏnsper, *n. m.* a disputant. Cf. deasbàir. con + deasbair.
connspeach, counspiuch, *n. f.* a wasp. For conàsbeach, " wrangling or dog-bee." *McB.*
connspoid, cŏnspej, *n. f.* a dispute. *Ir.* conspóid. Cf. deasbud (disputo).

connspunn, cònspun, *n. m.* a hero.
conntrachd, countrachc, *n. f.* curse, imprecation ; " ceud conntrachd orra, nach calbhar iad," curse them, but they are greedy. So *E.Ir. Lat.* contractus.
conntraigh, cuntrai, *n. f.* neap tide. *O.Ir.* contracht, contractus maris. *Z²*.
connuibh, connuv, *n. m.* hornet. *Also* ceardaman.
cònsach, *vbl. n. m.* act of overcoming. *E.Ir.* consníu, contend, wrest.
cònsmunn, *n. m.* hero.
cònsmunnach, *a.* heroic, warlike.
conspull, *n. m.* hero.
conspullach, *a.* heroic.
constabal, *n. m.* a township bailiff.
contaod, *n. m.* a dog-leash.
contran, *n. m.* wild angelica.
conuiche, *n. m.* a hornet. Cf. conas.
cop, *v.* capsize. *Sc.* coup, overset.
cop, *n. m.* a cup.
cop, *n. m.* foam ; froth. *E.Ir.* copp.
còp, *v.* force, press, insist ; coin 'g a còpadh, dogs in hot chase.
còpadh, *vbl. n. m.* act of pressing, forcing ; flooding (of sunshine).
copadh, *vbl. n. m.* foaming, raging ; dashing of angry billows.
copadh, kop'ă, *vbl. n. m.* capsizing (as discharging a cart). *Sc.* coup.
copag, *n. f.* the herb dock, docken ; *a.* copagach. *Also* copag-bhàite.
copan, *n. m.* anything curved ; a cup ; the pan of the head ; the boss of a shield ; *a.* copanach. *O.N.* koppr, cup. *Lat.* cupa.
copar, *n. m.* copper, copperas.
cor, *n. m.* condition, state, situation ; is truagh mo chor, sad is my condition ; ciod is cor da ? what is become of him ? air a' h-uile cor, by all means ; air chor, so that ; custom ; cor na talmhainn, the custom of the land ; cha dèan mi e air chor sam bith, I will not do it on any account. *O.Ir.* cor, case, condition.
còra, *a. compar.* more befitting ; bu chòra dhuit dol dachaidh, it is more befitting that you should go home.
còrach, *gen.* of còir, *q.v.*
corachd, *n. f.* duty, obligation. *E.Ir.* coraigecht, stipulation.
corag, *n.f.* left-hand stilt. *See* lamhairc.
coraisge, *a.* unsafe, risky ; *n.* cross currents.
còram, *n. m.* a faction, a bad set ; fr. the *Eng.* quorum.
corb, *v.* corrupt, spoil.
corbadh, *vbl. n. m.* act of spoiling.
corc, *n. f., gen.* cuirce, a butcher's and fisherman's cleaver or knife. *Scotch,* whittle.

corc, *n. m.* a fairy bull, a water bull ; laogh corcach, a calf having small ears (ominous of evil). *Also* torc-chluasach.
corca, *n. m.* oats. *O.Ir.* corca. *O.Celt.* korkjo-, oats. *Also* coirce.
còrcach, *n. f.* hemp. *Also* còcrach.
corcag, *n. f.* a little knife.
corcan-coille, *n. m.* bullfinch.
corc-chluasach, *a.* purple-eared ; knife-eared.
corcur, *n. m.* crimson, purple. *O.Ir.* corcur. *W.* pwrpur. *Lat.* purpura.
còrd, *v.* agree, settle, accord, adjust, arrange ; *rel.* to *Lat.* cor, heart.
còrd, *n. m., gen. s.* and *n. pl.* cuird, a rope. *Lat.* corda.
còrdadh, còrdu, *vbl. n. m.* agreement, settlement, good terms or understanding.
còrdaidhe, *n. pl.* spasms (*Sh.*) ; " twistings " ; fr. còrd. *McB.*
corghail, *n. f.* gurgling. Cf. coingeal.
còrlach, *n. m.* bran, refuse of grain. *See* corrlach.
cormach, *n. m.* a brewer. *E.Ir.* coirm, ale.
còrn, *n. m.* a drinking-horn, and also a musical instrument. So *E.Ir. Lat.* cornu. *O.Celt.* korno-, drinking-horn.
còrn, *n. m., gen. s., n. pl.* cùirn, a bale of cloth ; *v.* fold cloth. *M.Ir.* corn, a roll.
còrnadh, còrn'-u, *vbl. n. m.* folding cloth.
còrnaire, corneru, *n. m.* a folder.
còrncaisil, *n. m.* wall pennywort.
còrnuil, *n. f.* retching ; violent coughing.
coron, *n. m.* a crown, a chaplet. *E.Ir.* coróin = *Lat.* corona.
coronach, *a.* rich in chaplets, crowns.
coron-Mhoire, conair-Mhoire, *n. m.* a rosary of Mary.
corp, *n. m.* corpse, the body. *O.Ir.* corp. *W.* corff. *Lat.* corpus.
corpach, *a.* corpulent.
corpag, *n. f.* tiptoe.
corpaich, *v.* be disgusted at, revolt from.
corpan, *n. m.* a small body.
corpanta, *a.* corpulent, bulky.
corpantachd, còrp'-ănt-uchc, *n. f.* corpulence.
corparra, còrp'-urr-a, *a.* corporeal ; *adv.* gu corparra, bodily.
corpsgian, *n. f.* a scalpel, or a doctor or dissector's knife.
corp-sgianadair, *n. m.* a dissector, an anatomist.
corpshnasair, *n. m.* a body polisher ; a statuary ; anatomist.
còrr, *n. m.* odds, excess, surplus, overplus, remainder ; thoir dhomhsa an còrr, give me the surplus ; *adj.* singular, extraordinary, odd ; few ; corra fhear, one here and there, very few ; bliadhna chòrr, an extraordinary

year ; **duine còrr,** a singular person, eminent or otherwise ; **còrr òinseach,** veritable fool of a lass.

corr, *a.* 1. tapering, peaked, pointed. 2. uneven, odd ; **corr-chnoc,** peaked hill.

còrr, *n. f.* a heron, crane, stork ; " **còrr air cladach,**" a heron on a shore. So *E.Ir. O.Celt.* korgsà, korgjo-s.

corra-beaga, *n. pl.* tiptoe. *Also* **corra-biod.** *E.Ir.* **corr.**

corra-bhàn, *n. f.* heron.

corra-bheinn, *n. f.* a pointed hill, a steep hill.

corra-biod, *n. m.* tiptoe.

corrach, *a.* steep, precipitous ; **àite corrach,** a steep place, an unsteady seat ; passionate ; unsteady ; " **am fear a bhios a mhana air falbh suidhidh e air cailbhein corrach,**" the man who is bent on leaving sits on an unsteady "stake."

corrach, *n. f.* fetters.

corra-chagailt, *n. f.* sulphureous hue in dying embers, salamander ; *pl.* **corracha-cagailt.**

corrachasach, *a.* with odd feet.

corracheann, *n. m.* a giddy head. *M.Ir.* having a pointed head.

corracheannach, *a.* light-headed, giddy, inconstant.

corra-cheòsach, *n. f.* cheslip.

corra-chodal, *n. m.* sleeping on one's elbow.

corra-chòsag, *n. f.* a small insect ; stone-lice ; a cheslip.

corra-chritheach, *n. f.* a stork.

corra-cnàmh, *n. m.* tiptoe ; sitting on one's heels.

corradhuil, *n. f.* gurgling (of infant).

corrag, *n. f.* the pointing one ; forefinger ; left-hand stilt of a plough.

corragaich, *v.* finger, handle.

corragheal, *a.* having white pinnacles.

corra-ghlas, *n. f.* heron. So *M.Ir.*

corra-ghleus, *n. m.* prime, good condition, impetuous.

corra-ghrian, *n. f.* stork. So *M.Ir.*

corra-ghridheach, *n.f.* crane ; " **a' chorra-ghridheach is bat' aice 's i cur a steach nan caorach,**" the crane with a staff driving the sheep (into the fold).

corra-maothar, *n. m.* the sea-pike.

corra-margaidh, *coll. n.* the rabble, the offscouring of the people.

corra-meille, cora-milu, *n. m.* wild liquorice. *Also* **carra-meille.**

corramheur, *n.* finger pointing. = **corr** + **meur.** *M.Ir.* forefinger.

corran, *n. m.* a shearing-hook or sickle ; a tapering point of land. *M.Ir.* 1. corner, angle. 2. sickle.

corranach, coranach, *n. f.* name of a type of metre used in boat-chant, and lament ; hence, a dirge, a lament, a funeral-cry. (*Watson.*)

corra-riobhach, *n. f.* a heron.

corra-shìomain, *n. f.* a thraw crook.

corra-shùgain, *n. f.* a thraw crook ; instrument for twisting straw ropes.

corra-thulchainn, cora-huluchuin, *n. f.* the central pole reaching from the top of the end-wall (of a thatched house) to the ridge pole.

corrbheann, *a.* taper-peaked, pointed ; " **nan seòl corrbheann,**" of the pointed sails.

corrbheinn, *n. f.* a high pointed hill ; " **nan corrbheann cas,**" of the steep tapering hills ; a stately hill.

corrfhad, *n. m.* first or outside peat (in course of cutting). ; **corr-fhòd,** the concluding furrow of a field. *M.Ir.*

corr-fhòt, smooth sod.

corrfhiacail, *n. f.* pointed tooth, the eye-tooth.

còrrlach, *n. m.* remainder, excess, surplus, overplus, odds.

corruich, korr'-ich, *n. f.* offence, rage, anger, ire, wrath ; **tha corruich air,** he is in wrath ; **na gabh corruich,** be not angry.

corruil, *n. f.* chirping of birds.

còrsa, *n. m.* coast ; **air còrsa na Frainge,** on the coast of France ; the part of a sail above the reefs ; **tha i fo'n chòrsa,** she has all reefs in.

còrsair, kor'-ser, *n. f.* a coaster, cruiser.

còrsaireachd, cōrseruchc, *n. f.* coasting, cruising.

cor-shìomain, cor-heemen, *n. f.* twist-handle (for twisting straw rope).

cos, *n. f.* a foot. *See* **cas.** *O.Ir.* **cos.**

còs, *n. m.* 1. a sponge, crevice, hole. 2. a cave, a crevice. *M.Ir.* **cúass,** a hollow, cavity. Cf. *Lat.* **cavus.**

còsach, *a.* spongy, porous.

còsachd, *n. f.* sponginess, porousness.

còsag, *n. f.* a small cavern, crevice.

còsaiche, kōs'-ich-u, *n. f.* degree of sponginess, etc.

cosail, *a.* likely, like, similar. Better, **cosmhail,** *q.v.*

cosalachd, kŏs'-al-achc, *n. f.* likeliness, similarity. Better, **cosmhlachd.**

cosanta, *a.* industrious ; fr. **cosnadh.**

cosd, *v.* spend, waste, wear ; fr. the *Eng.*

cosdail, *a.* expensive, extravagant.

cosdalachd, kŏsd'-ăl-uchc, *n.f.* expensiveness.

cosdas, *n. f.* expense, expenditure, cost ; waste, profuseness.

cosg. *See* **cosd.**

cosgairt, cosgurt, slaughtering, massacring. *See* **casgairt.**

cosgarach, *n. m.* a kite ; a slaughterer.
cosgoradh, *vbl. n. m.* (in a crofting township) the act of summing stock, allowed to each crofter on common pasture.
cosguis, coscish. *See* cosdas.
coslach, *a.* like.
coslas, *n. m.* appearance, likeness.
cosmal, *n. f.* refuse of meat, straw, etc.
cosmhail, *a.* similar, like. *O.Ir.* cosmal. con + samail. *W.* cyfal = cy-hafal, co-equal.
cosnàbuidh, *n. m.* walking companion.
cosnach, *n. m.* a labourer, hired servant. Better, cosnàiche.
cosnadh, cos'-nu, *vbl. n. m.* act of earning, winning. *M.Ir.* cosnam, contending, maintaining. *O.Ir.* cosnam, effort.
còsshruth, *n. m.* stream underground.
costag, *n. f.* costmary, wild chervil.
còta, *n. m., pl.* còtaichean, coat, petticoat ; còta air bhioran, a knitted petticoat.
còta-bàn, *n. m.* groat, fourpence ; fourpence land ; leirtheas, two of them ; ochdamh, four ; ceithrea, eight.
còta-iochdair, *n. m.* under-petticoat.
còta-mór, *n. m.* a greatcoat.
cotan, *n. m.* cotton ; fr. the *Eng.*
cotan, *n. m.* a small roofless cot (for calf) ; fr. cot, hut.
cothaich, co-hich, *v.* maintain, contend, strive, earn, support. So *M.Ir.* cothugud. *O.Ir.* cathugud ; fr. coth, battle.
cothan, co-han, *n. m.* pulp, froth, foam. *Also* ómhan.
cothanachd, co-hanuchc, *n. f.* frothiness.
cothanta, *a.* helpful.
cothar, cohur, *n. m.* a coffer. *Ir.* cófra ; fr. the *Eng.*
còthar, *n. m. See* còbhar.
cothlam, colam, *v.* mix different sorts of wool, as black and white. *Also* cuthaig.
cothlamadh, colamu, *vbl. n. m.* mixture of wools. *Also* cuthaigeadh.
cothonnach, co-honuch, *n. f.* froth, spray, foam ; comh-thonn, beating of waves together.
cothrom, cor'-um, *n. m.* a balance ; justice, fair play ; opportunity ; a' cheud chothrom a gheibh mi, the first opportunity I get ; thoir cothrom na Féinne dhomh, give me fair play ; cead cothrom, full liberty ; tha cead cothrom agad air, do what you like with it ; comfortable circumstances ; tha e ann an cothrom math, he is in comfortable circumstances ; he is in good form ; scales ; a weight ; means, help ; chan 'eil cothrom air, there is no help for it. *E.Ir.* comthrom = com + trom.

cothromach, cor'-um-ach, *a.* just, honest ; parallel, even with, of the same size ; rich, wealthy ; duine cothromach, a just man, or a man in easy circumstances.
cothromaich, cor'-um-ich, *v.* make even with ; make of the same size ; a' cothromachadh nan sclèata, sizing the slates ; weigh on scales or balance.
crabhach, *coll. n.* crabhaichean, implements, tools, small wares, pudenda.
cràbhach, crav'-uch, *a.* very religious, very devout, very pious, pietistic, pharisaic.
cràbhadair, cràv-u-der', *n. m.* an austere religionist, devotee, formalist.
cràbhadh, crav'-u, *n. m.* piety ; fìor chràbhadh, true piety. *O.Ir.* crabud.
crabhat, cra-vat, *n. m.* a cravat ; fr. *Eng.*
cracaire, crack-iru, *n. m.* a talker.
cracaireachd, crackiruchc, *n. f.* conversation.
cracas, *n. m.* conversation.
cràdh, crā, *n. m.* torment, torture ; *v.* torture. *E.Ir.* craidim.
cràdhearg, *a.* blood-red.
cràdhgheadh, crā - yiagh, *n. m.* shell-drake, a shell-duck, barnacle goose.
cràdhlot, *n. m.* a painful wound ; agony.
cràdhshlat, crà'-hlat, *n. f.* a sort of pillory or treadmill, used by the old Gael ; anguish, torment ; O, mo chràdhshlat ! alas, my torment !
cràg, *n. f.* a large hand. *Also* cròg.
crag, crac, *n. m.* a fissure.
crag, *n. f.* a knock.
cràgair, *v.* handle awkwardly.
cràgaire, *n. m.* botcher ; a man with large hands.
cragan, *n. m.* an earthen jar, generally used for oil ; blas a' chragain, disgust. *E.Ir.* crocan. *O. Celt.* krokko-, a jar.
cràg-chasach, *a.* in-footed.
cràiceanach, *n. m.* squat fellow.
craiceann, cracun, *n. m.* skin, hide. *Also* craicionn. *O.Ir.* crocenn. *W.* croen. *O. Celt.* krokkenno-s, krokno-s, skin.
craidhleag, craylag, *n. f.* skull ; basket.
craidhneach, craynuch, *n. f.* skeleton ; gaunt figure ; anything about to fall to pieces : as a boot, chest, person, etc.
craidhneach, *a.* painful and raw (of a wound or burn).
craidhneag, *n. f.* dried peat ; *a.* craidhneagach.
cràigean, cràgen, *n. m.* a frog ; fr. cràg, cròg, a paw.
cràimhinn, cràvin, *n. m.* cancer ; fr. cnàmh, waste, decay.
crainnte, crainntidh, *a.* parching, withering, pinching ; piercing, sour-tempered.

cràin, crān, *n. f.* the queen of the hive ; an ugly old woman ; a sow. So *Ir.*

cràiteach, crātiuch, *a.* intensely painful, torturing, tormenting ; causing great pain.

cràiteachd, crātiachc, *n. m.* painfulness.

cràiteag, crātiag, *n. f.* a niggardly woman.

cràlad, *n. m.* torment. For **cràdh-lot.**

cràlaidh, cràly, *v.* crawl, sprawl ; *vbl. n. m.* cràladh, crawling, sprawling.

cràleaba, *n. f.* a bier, a hearse.

cramaist, *n. f.* a crease, a fold in cloth.

cramb, *n. f.* a cramp-iron.

cramb, *v.* squeeze, press.

crambaid, kramb'-ăj, *n. m.* a cramp ; objection ; the metal point of a scabbard.

crampadh, *m.* 1. versification. 2. an impression. *Sc.* **crambo.**

crann, *n. m.* a tree ; **Lebanon nan crann,** L. of the trees ; wood ; **cranntarrunn,** a " wooden nail," or spike ; a plough ; **cuir na h-eich anns a' chrann,** yoke the horses in the plough ; bar, bolt ; **cuir an crann air an dorus,** bolt the door ; a mast ; **crann na luinge,** the ship's mast ; a flagstaff ; a cran (= a barrel), standard measure of fresh herring ; a lot ; a ballot ; **thàinig an crann air,** he was chosen by ballot ; acting the part of a friend ; interest ; **cò bhios air do chrann?** who shall be your friend ? **gabh cuid do chrainn,** take your chance ; a shaft ; an arrow ; a coffin ; drone of a pipe. *O.Ir.* **crann,** a tree. *W.* **pren,** tree, wood ; **hwyl-bren,** a mast.

crann, *v.* bar, bolt, barricade ; **crann an dorus,** bolt or bar the door.

crann, *v.* wither, decay, wear off ; wind ; **a' crannadh,** withering. *See* **cranndaidh.**

crannach, *a.* full of masts, trees, etc.

crannach, *n. m., pl.* **crannachoin,** a lap-dog.

crannachan, *n. m.* a churn ; a dasher (of a churn) ; half-churned cream (a Hallowe'en treat).

crannadh, *n. m.* withering, shrivelling ; **fuachd is crannadh an earraich,** the cold and shrivelling of spring. *Ir.*

crannda, wooden, decrepit.

crann-adhair, *n. m.* the constellation called the Bear ; the seven stars in it. *Also* **crann-arair.**

crannag, *n. f.* pulpit ; a ship, a boat ; cross-trees (of ship) ; a lake-dwelling. *M.Ir.* **crannóc,** wooden structure, a vessel, pulpit.

crannaich, cran-ich, *v.* bolt, bar.

crannalach, *n. f.* wood ; broken timber ; a wreck ; **chaidh i 'na crannalaich,** she was wrecked ; ruins of anything ; gone to sticks.

crannanach, *n. m.* a ploughman.

cranna-pheasan, *n. m.* a puny, delicate youngster.

crann-àrain, *n. m.* a plough. *Also* **crann-treabhaidh.**

crann-àrcain, *n. m.* cork-tree.

crann-céille, *n. m.* helm, rudder, wise guide.

crann-ceusaidh, *n. m.* tree of suffering, the Cross.

crannchur, crann'-ach-ur, *n. m.* a ballot ; fate, destiny ; choosing by ballot ; **mo chrannchur,** my lot (in life). *O.Ir.* **crann-chor. crann** + **cor.**

crann-cothromachaidh, *n. m.* balance. *Also* **meidh.**

cranndaidh, craundy, *a.* excessively cold and withering, as weather in the spring of the year, withered. *Ir.*

crannda, decrepit, bowed. *O'R.*

cranndaidheachd, *n. f.* cold, withering weather, the withering blast.

crann-deilbhe, craun-jelvu, *n. m.* warping frame.

crann-deiridh, *n. m.* mizzen-mast.

crann-doruis, *n. m.* door bolt.

crann-druididh, *n. m.* a noble.

crann-fìge, *n. m.* a fig-tree.

crann-fiona, *n. m.* a vine.

crann-fuine, *n. m.* baker's rolling-pin.

crannghail, *n. f.* wood ; drones of bag-pipe ; disparaging name for a bagpipe ; **crannghail bhreòite is breun,** decayed and rotten lumber ; poetic term for a bow. *M.Ir.* **crann-gal,** wood, timber (*KM.*) ; **crannghal-leapa,** a bedstead (*O'R.*) ; **crann caingil,** lattices before the altar (*Lh.*) ; the abandoned Ark is " **crannghaill** " (*I.T.S.* 1).

crannlach, *n. f.* boughs ; branches.

crannlach, *n. f.* teal duck (**crann** + **lach**).

crann-laoicinn, *n. m.* a tulchan, a false calf.

crann-meadhoin, *n. m.* the main-mast. *Also* **crann-mór.**

crann-ola, *n. m.* the olive tree.

crann-reothadh, *n. m.* a light frost, hoar-frost. *Also* **crion - reothadh,** small frost. *Cf. Sc.* **crainroch,** " small frost " ; **cranreugh,** rime, and **cranreuch,** " an' *cranreuch* cauld!" *Burns.*

crann-ristil, *n. m.* a cutting plough.

crann-sgòid, *n. m.* a boom (of a ship).

crann-sìthe, *n. m.* a peacemaker.

crann-spreòid, *n. m.* a bowsprit.

crann-tabhaill, *n. m.* a sling.

cranntachan, *n. m.* a churn piston.

crann-tachrais, *n. m.* a winding wheel.

crann-tàra, *n. m.* the " fiery cross."

cranntarrunn, kraun'-tarr-unn, *n. f.* a tree-nail, or the wooden pegs in ship-building ; " wooden nail."

crann-tarsuinn, *n. m.* diameter.

crann-teannachaidh, *n. m.* a bookbinder's press.

crann-togalach, *n. m.* a crane.

crann-toisich, *n. m.* fore-mast.

craobh, crūv, *n. f.* a tree ; globules or bells on whisky, or any other liquid ; *v.* spread, gush out and ramify at the same time ; fhuil a' craobhadh mu thalamh, his blood gushing and ramifying ; propagate, shoot forth ; a scion. *E.Ir.* cráeb, cróeb.

craobhach, *a.* full of trees ; in ramifying gushes, as blood ; fhuil chraobhach, his streaming blood.

craobhachd, cruv-achc, *n. f.* nervousness, tenderness.

craobhag, cruvag, *n. f.* small tree.

craobhaidh, crūvy, *a.* tender, nervous, shivering.

craobharnach, crūv'-aɼn-ach, *coll. n. m.* a shrubbery, a hedge of thorn, whins, etc.

craobh-chòmhraig, *n. f.* a champion.

craobh-chosgair, *n. f.* 1. laurel. 2. fierce warrior.

craobhdhearg, *a.* red-streaming.

craobh-dhruididh, *n. f.* a noble. Cf. crann-druididh.

craobh-ealp, *v.* ingraft, graft.

craobh-ealpaire, *n. m.* an ingrafter ; fear ealpaidh chraobh, an ingrafter of trees.

craobh-fheirge, *n. f.* a mantling flush of wrath.

craobh-ghinealaich, *n. f.* genealogical tree.

craobh-sgaoil, *v.* branch, ramify, spread, propagate.

craobh-sgaoileadh, *vbl. n. m.* propagation, publishing, spreading.

craobh - shìochainte, *n. f.* peacemaker, peace-keeper.

craoiseach, crūshuch, *n. f.* a spear. *E.Ir.* cróisech.

craoisean, crūshen, *n. m.* a glutton.

craoit, cruit, *n. f.* a croft.

craos, crūs, *n. m.* an enormous mouth. *O.Ir.* cróis, maw, gluttony. *Wb.*

craosach, *a.* wide-mouthed ; voracious ; *n. f.* a wide-mouthed female.

craosachd, crūsachc, *n. f.* gluttony.

craosaire, crūsiru, *n. m.* wide-mouthed fellow.

craosnach, crūsnuch, *n. f.* particular kind of spear, a dart.

crasg, *n. f.* a stilt. *E.Ir.* cross, hilt.

crasg, *n. m.* a crossing ; a crossing over a ridge ; an crasg, the cross-roads.

crasgach, *a.* crawling or walking, as a person feeling torturing pain ; branching, as stamped cloth ; cross-ways.

crasgach, *a.* corpulent. *O.Ir.* cras, a body.

cràsgan, *n. m.* anything cruciform.

cràsgail, crāscul, *v.* spread hands and feet, as a person feeling torturing pain ; *n. f.* sprawling, crawling ; torture.

crasg-shuileach, *a.* cross-eyed.

crath, crā, *v.* shake, agitate ; crath do cheann, shake your head ; tremble, quiver, brandish, flourish : chrath e a bhata, he flourished his staff ; besprinkle, sprinkle, wave ; crath uisge air, besprinkle it with water ; wave ; crath ris, wave to him ; a' crathadh, shaking, brandishing, waving. *O.Ir.* crothim.

cré, *n. m.* clay ; the body ; keel. *O.Ir.* cré, *gen.* criad. *Also* crí. *O.Celt.* kreivo-, flesh, body.

creabhaichean, crevichen, *n. m.* a bandy.

creabhaire, *n. m.* gadfly. *E.Ir.* crebar.

creabhall, crev-ul, *n. m.* a slouching, clumsy fellow.

creach, krech, *v.* pillage, plunder ; harrow a nest, rob birds of their young ; despoil, rob, ruin ; chreach thu mi, you have ruined me ; *n. f.* pillage, spoil, plunder, ruination, devastation ; mo chreach, my complete ruination ! alas ! ; creach air at, premature lancing. *E.Ir.* crech, raid, plunder.

creachadair, crachuder, *n. m.* despoiler, pillager, freebooter, depredator, robber.

creachadaireachd, crachuderuchc, *n. f.* plundering, robbing.

creachag, crechag, *n. f.* a cockle.

creachan, crech'-an, *n. m.* a large ribbed shell-fish, a clam, a drinking shell ; far an nall an t-slige chreachain, hand over the drinking shell ; clam shell. *Ir.* scollop shell.

creachan, crechan, *n. m.* pudding made with a calf's entrails.

creachann, crechun, *n. m. and f.* bare summit of a hill.

crèadh, cre, *n. f.* clay ; *v.* plaster with clay. *O.Ir.* cré, *gen.* criad.

creadhonadh, cre-ghonu, *n. m.* a twitching, piercing pain. cned + gon = " wounding a wound."

creag, *n. f., gen.* creige, a rock, a cliff ; precipice. *E.Ir.* crec, a crag.

creaga, *n. m.* a small hamlet. *Lewis.* Cf. *O.N.* kriki, a nook.

creagach, creguch, *a.* rocky, craggy, rough, cliffy.

creagach, *vbl. n. m.* act of scaling the rocks and precipices for birds or birds' nests ; act of fishing with rods off the rocks.

creagag, *n. f.* sea perch ; creagag uisge, a water perch.

creagan, *n. m.* a little rock, a rocky hillock.

creamh, crev, *n. m.* garlic, leeks. *M.Ir.* crem. *O.Celt.* kremo-, kramo-.

créamhach, crēvuch, *n. m.* a crow, a rook.

creamhachd, crevachc, *n. f.* stock, stump.

crean, cren, *v.* suffer for; có a chreanas air sin, who shall suffer for that ? ; *vbl. a.* creante, dearly bought or suffered for. *O.Ir.* crenim, I buy.

creanaich, crenich, *v.* tremble, shiver, start, feel a tremor or thrilling. *See* crithnich.

creanair, *n. f.* sedition.

creanas, *n. m.* whetting, or hacking of sticks.

creangan, crengan, *n. m.* a deep wound.

crèapailt, *n. m.* garter. *See* cnèbilt.

creapall, *n. m.* a lump; entanglement, hindrance.

creat, *n. m.* framework of a roof. *Eng.* crate. *E.Ir.* crett; body of anything, framework of chariot, or boat.

creathach, *n. f.* underwood, firewood.

creathall, cre-hal, *n. f.* a cradle.

creathall, cre-hal, *n. f.* a lamprey.

creatrach, cretruch, *n. f.* wilderness.

creic, *v.* sell, dispose of; trade. *E.Ir.* creicc, used as *inf.* of *O.Ir.* crenim, I buy. *W.* prynaf. *See* reic.

creid, crej, *v.* believe, rely ; be convinced. *O.Ir.* cretim. *W.* credaf, I believe. *O.Celt.* kreddiô. *Lat.* credo.

creideach, crejach. Better, creidmheach, *q.v.*

creideamh, crejiv, *n. m.* faith, belief, persuasion, religious tenets. *E.Ir.* crédem. *O.Ir.* cretem, crettem.

creideas, crejas, *n. m.* credit, esteem.

creideasach, crejasuch, *a.* respectable ; responsible, creditable ; in good repute, credible.

creidmheach, *n. m.* a believer. *O.Ir.* cretmech.

creidte, crej-tu, *vbl. a.* believed ; confirmed.

creigeir, creger, *n. m.* a grapple.

créim, *v.* pick, nip, nibble, gnaw. *Also* creidhm. *M.Ir.* créim. *W.* cnofain.

creimeadh, cremu, *n. m.* nibbling.

creimeadh-chìre, *n. f.* chewing the cud. *Also* cnàmh-cìre.

creimeartaich, cremartich, *vbl. n. f.* picking ; act of picking.

creimneach, crēmnuch, *a.* knotty, rough.

créis, crēsh, *v.* grease ; *n. f.* grease, fat ; *a.* créiseach ; créiseagan, refuse of melted fat.

creithleag, *n. f.* gadfly ; *a.* creithleagach.

creònadh, *n. m.* paining, torturing.

creòithtiche, creō-tichu, *n. m.* an invalid or sick person, getting well one day, and worse the next.

creòth, creō, *n.* hurt, wound. *Ir.* creó, a wound.

creothar, cro'-ar, *n. m.* a woodcock.

creòthluinn, crōlin, *n. f.* a bier ; sickly person.

creubh, crēu, *n. m.* body. *See* creubhag.

creubh, *v.* dun, crave ; fr. the *Eng.*

creubhach, crēvuch, *n. m.* withered wood or branches ; firewood ; dry sticks.

creubhach, *a.* frail, unwell, poorly.

creubhachan, crē-vuchan, *n. m.* sort of pudding.

creubhag, crēvag, *n. f.* a little body ; a beloved little female ; mo chreubhag ! an exclamation of mixed fear and wonder. *M.Ir.* crefóg, dust, earth.

creubhaidh, *a.* delicate health.

creuchd, crēchc, *n. m.* wound ; *v.* hurt. *E.Ir.* crécht. *W.* craith, scar. *O.Celt.* krekto-s, a wound.

creuchdach, crēchcuch, *a.* full of sores, wounded, hurtful, sore distressed.

creuchdaire, crēchciru, *n. m.* an invalid.

creud, crēd, *n. m.* a creed, belief ; tha barrachd air a chreud is a phaidir aige, he knows more than his creed and "pater." *E.Ir.* crét. *Lat.* credo.

creud, *inter. pr.* what ? For cia rud.

creutair, crētur, *n. m.* a creature, a being. *Lat.* creatura.

criachadh, *n. m.* proposing to oneself; fr. crioch, purpose, end.

criadh, *n. f.* clay. Really the *gen.* of cré.

criathair, criu-hir, *v.* sift, sieve ; examine. *E.Ir.* criathram, pierce with holes, riddle.

criathar, criu-hur, *n. m.* a sieve. *O.Ir.* críathar, sieve. *O.Celt.* kreitro-. *O.W.* cruitr. Cf. *Lat.* cribrum.

criathrach, criurach, *n. f.* marshy ground. *E.Ir.* críathrach, morass, waste.

criathrachail, criurachal, *a.* marshy.

criathradh, criuru, *n. m.* act of piercing, riddling ; the process of sifting ; sifting ; shrugging ; hinching.

cridhe, cree, *n. m.* heart ; cridhe gun cheilg, a heart without guile ; chan 'eil a chridhe agad, you dare not ; dear ; a mhic chridhe, my dear Sir ! a n'ic cridhe, my dear Madam ! fhir mo chridhe, my dear fellow ; Alasdair cridhe nan gleann, beloved A. of the glens ; cha dèan cridhe misgeach breug, the drunken soul tells no lies ; bha e mar a chridhe, he was very keen for it ; centre ; cridhe na talmhainn, the centre of the earth. *O.Ir.* cride.

cridhealas, cree-alus, *n. m.* heartiness, kindliness, kind or hearty reception, as a host ; state of being touched with drink.

cridhean, cri-en, *n. m.* a gallant favourite.

cridheil, cri-al, *a.* hearty, kind, cheerful.

crilein, creelen, *n. m.* a small creel ; a box ; a small coffer. *E.Ir.* criol, a casket.

crinbhriathrach, creen-vriäruch, *a.* silly.

crìne, creenu, *n. m.* excessive littleness, meanness; also, more or most trifling or diminutive. *O.Ir.* **crín**, dead, dry. *O.Celt.* **crino-s.** *W.* **crin**, withered.

crinein, creenen, *n. m.* a miser.

crinlein, creenlen, *n. m.* small writing-desk.

crìoch, cree-uch, *n. f.* boundary, frontier, landmark ; **mu na crìochan**, about the borders or boundaries ; end, conclusion, close ; **cuir crìoch air**, finish it, kill him ; **tha an latha a' tighinn gu crìch**, the day comes to a close ; intention, design ; the *pl.* **crìochan** means not only boundaries but also all the territory within them ; furrow ; territory. *O.Ir.* **crích**, *finis.* *O.Celt.* *kriqâ, frontier.

crìochnach, cree-uch-nuch, *a.* come to the years of maturity or discretion. *Is.*

crìochnaich, cree-uch-nich, *v.* finish, close; expire, die ; **chrìochnaich e an raoir,** he expired last night ; conclude.

crìodhdaich, cree-udich, *v.* pat or stroke affectionately. *See* cniadaich.

criogag, *n. f.* very slight knock.

criom, crim, *v.* nip, pick, nibble. *E.Ir.* **creimm**, a gnawing.

criomadh, *n. m.* act of picking, nibbling.

criomag, crimag, *n. f.* a very small bit.

criomagaich, crimagich, *v. tr.* make very small bits ; nip, nibble, tease, gall.

criomaire, crimiru, *n. m.* a miser, churl.

crioman, criman, *n. m.* small portion.

criomanta, crimantu, *a.* niggardly, mean.

criomantachd, *n. f.* meanness, niggardliness, want of spirit.

crìon, creen, *a.* very little or diminutive, very trifling ; *v.* wither, fade ; **chrìon e**, it faded. *O.Ir.* **crín, crinim**, I am exhausted. *See* crìne.

crìonach, creenuch, *n. m.* withered branches, firewood ; **cual chrìonaich**, faggot of firewood.

crion-cànachd, *n. f.* a strife, quarrelsomeness.

crìonna, cree-unu, **crìonda**, *a.* minute ; penurious ; attentive to the minutest articles of gain ; wise, prudent. *E.Ir.* **crínda**, prudent.

crìonnachd, creeun'-achc, **crìondachd**, cree-undachc, *n. f.* wisdom, prudence, minuteness, sagacity.

crìonntag, creentag, *n. f.* sorry or parsimonious female.

criopag, creepag, *n. f.* a clew of yarn ; a wrinkle. *Also* cnépog.

crioplach, *n. m.* a decrepit person, a cripple. *Also* cripleach.

crioplachd, cripleachd, *n. f.* lameness.

crioplaich, criplich, *v.* cripple, make lame.

crios, cris, *n. m.* girdle, belt, strap, zone ; the waist ; *v.* gird, belt. *O.Ir.* **criss**, a girdle, a circle. *O.Celt.* **krisso-**, girdle .

criosadair, crisuder, *n. m.* belt-maker.

criosan, *n. m.* small belt.

Crìosd, creesd, *n. m.* Christ, our Saviour.

crìosdachd, creesdachc, *n. f.* christianity, christendom ; **feadh na crìosdachd,** throughout christendom ; benignity.

crìosdail, creesdal, *a.* christian-like.

crìosdalachd, creesdalachc, *n. f.* christian behaviour and disposition.

crìosduidh, creesdy, *n. m.* a christian.

crios-guailne, *n. m.* shoulder-belt.

crioslach, cris-luch, *n. m.* a girdle, belt. *O.Ir.* **crislach**, lap, apron.

crioslaich, cris-lich, *v.* gird, tighten, bind. *Also* criosraich.

crios-meadhoin an t-saoghail, *n. m.* the equator.

crios-muineil, *n. m.* necklace.

crios na gréine, grianchrios, *n. m.* the zodiac.

crios-nèimhe, *n. m.* the zodiac.

criostal, cristal, *n. m.* crystal; fr. the *Eng.*

criot, crit, *n. m.* an earthen vessel.

criotaich. *See* cniadaich.

crisgein-cràisgein, cruisgein-craisgein, *n. m.* starfish. *Also* crasgag-thràghad.

crith, cri, *v.* tremble, be in a tremor ; *n. f.* a tremor, ague : trembling. So *E.Ir.* **echryd.** *O.Celt.* **kritu-.**

crith-chiùil, *n. f.* trilling, quavering.

critheach, critheann, *n. m.* aspen tree, poplar.

critheanach, cri-hen-uch, *a.* tremulous, trembling ; **am fiabhrus critheanach,** the ague ; **an galar-critheanach,** paralysis.

crithghalair, *n. m.* palsy, ague.

crithich, *v.* quake, tremble.

crithlàmh, *n. f.* trembling hand ; *a.* **crith-làmhach.** *E.Ir.* **crithlam**, palsy.

crithnich, *v.* tremble ; **chrithnich an tigh,** the house trembled (on its foundation). *E.Ir.* **crithnaigim.** *W.* **crynu.**

crithreothadh, *n. m.* frost that makes blossoms shake and fall ; blighting frost ; **crithreothadh Céitein**, blighting frost of May. *Du.B.* uses this word to express the blight of old age. *See* reothadh.

crith-thalmhainn, *n. f.* earthquake.

crò, *n. m.* a circle ; a fold ; **crò-chaorach,** a sheepfold ; a hut. *M.Ir.* **cró**, a fold, pen (for sheep, cattle, pigs, etc.), a cell. *O.Celt.* **krô(p)o-s.** *O.N.* **kró**, pen (for lambs).

crò, *n. f.* the eye of a needle.

crò, *n. f.* blood, gore ; *metaph.* death. *O.Ir.* **crú.** *O.Celt.* **krovo-s.** *W.* **crau.**

crobhcan, croucan, *n. m.* anything crooked, or bent into ill-formed letter S ; a dry broken bit of peat. *O.Ir.* **crob**, hand, claw.

cròc, *n. f.* antler of deer. *O.N.* krókr.

cròc, *v.* beat, pound.

cròcach, *n. f.* spiked muzzle (to prevent calves from sucking).

cròcach, *a.* antlered ; *n. f.* " the antlered one " ; a stag.

cròcan, *n. m.* a crook ; a long pole with hook at the end, used for pulling down withered branches of trees. *O.N.* krókr, a hook, anything crooked.

cròc-cheannach, *a.* antlered.

cròch, *n. m.* saffron red. *Lat.* crocus.

croch, *v.* hang, suspend ; depend ; an crochadh ris, depending on it. *O.Ir.* croch, cross. *Lat.* crux.

crochadair, krŏch'-a-dăr, *n. m.* a hangman.

crochadan, *n. m.* a pendulum.

crochaire, krŏch-ir'-à, *n. m.* a villain, rogue. *E.Ir.* crochaire, a hangman ; one crucified or hanged.

crochbhrat, *n. m.* hanging tapestry.

crodh, król, *n. m.* cattle, kine. *M.Ir.* crod, cattle, chattels, wealth.

cròdha, krò'-à, *a.* valiant, gaisgeil. *E.Ir.* cróda, bloody, cruel, hardy.

crodhan, król'-an, *n. m.* parted hoof ; *a.* crodhanach. *Ir.* crobhan. *O.Ir.* crob, hand, a claw.

cròdhearg, *a.* blood-red.

crog, *n. m.* earthen vessel ; *a.* crogach.

crog, *n. f.* an aged ewe. *Sc.* crock. *Also* crogais.

cròg, *n. f.* a large hand ; a paw. Cf. *O.N.* krókr.

crògach, *a.* having large hands or paws ; *n. f.* a female having large hands.

crogaid, krogij, *n. f.* a beast having small horns.

crògair, krŏg'-ir, *v.* handle awkwardly ; bungle.

crògaire, krŏg'-ir'-u, *n. m.* a man having large hands ; a bungler.

crògaireachd, *n. f.* handling awkwardly ; clumsily finished job.

crògairsich, krŏg'-ar-sich, *n. f.* rough handling ; bungling, spoiling.

crogan, *n. m.* a little dish ; a pitcher.

crogan, *n. f.* a little horn.

crogan, *n. m.* shrunk person ; shrivelled branch.

cròglach, *n. m.* a handful, a large handful.

cròic, *n. f.* difficulty, hardships, a hard task ; cha chròic sin air, that is no task to him ; rage ; foam, froth ; bell on liquor ; cast seaweed.

cròic, *n. f.* a deer's antler. See cròc.

cròiceach, *a.* of cròic.

croich, kroych, *n. f.* a gibbet, gallows, cross. *O.Ir.* croch. *W.* crog. *Lat.* crux.

croicionn, *n. m.* skin, hide, fleece (skin with wool). So *E.Ir.* croccend.

cròid, cról, *n. m.* a handsome present. *Also* cnòid.

croidhfhionn, croyun, *a.* white-hoofed.

croidhleag, croylag, *n. f.* a basket, a small creel.

cròidhlean, crōlen, *n. m.* a ring or circle of children ; game of touch.

cròileaba, crō-leb'-u, *n. f.* a bier to carry a wounded person.

cròileagan, crōlagun, *n. m.* ring of people or children. Cf. crò, a circle, fold.

cròinneach, crōnuch, *n. f.* an old wornout animal. See craidhneach.

crois, crōsh, *n. f.* a cross, cross-tree of a ship ; a yarn reel ; crois-iarna, a cross for winding yarn into skeins ; a nuisance ; tha thu 'n a do chrois, you are a hindrance ; a misfortune, a mishap ; an affliction ; " crois is creach," affliction and loss ; *v.* reel or wind yarn. *W.* croes. *A.S.* cross. *O.N.* kross. *Lat.* crux.

croisgileid, crosh-gilej, *n. f.* child's head-dress.

croislin, crosh-lin, *n. f.* the line that measures a circle across ; diameter.

crois-tàra, *n. m.* the fiery cross ; a signal of alarm, mobilisation, before commencing battle. *Also* crann-tàra.

croit, croit, *n. f.* a hump : eminence.

croit, *n. f.* a croft, a pendicle of land.

croiteag, *n. f.* a little hump ; eminence.

croitear, *n. m.* crofter.

cròlot, *v.* wound dangerously.

crom, *v.* bend, stoop, decline ; descend, bow ; tha a' ghrian a' cromadh, the sun descends. *O.Ir.* cromm, crumb. *W.* crwm. *O.Celt.* krumbo-s, krumm. *a.* bent, crooked, sloping, curved, not straight ; base (in a moral sense).

crom, *n. m.* a circle ; ridge.

cromachas, *n. f.* bandy-leg.

cromadh, crom-u, *n. m.* roof ; fo chromadh an tighe, under the roof of the house ; act of bending, stooping, bowing ; a measure of length equal to the full length of the middle finger. *E.Ir.* crumma.

cromag, *n. f.* anything bent ; a peg or catch, a tache, a hook to hang on, a fish-hook.

cromaichean, cromichun, *n. pl.* the aged.

cromaisinn, cròm-ash-inn, *n. f.* little rib.

croman, *n. m.* a hawk ; kite ; the hook of a plough ; hip-bone ; hoe ; crom an donais, a bungler, dolt. *E.Ir.* cromán, sickle.

croman-lòin, *n. m.* snipe.

croman-luatha, *n. m.* rake for ashes.

croman-luch, *n. m.* a kite.

cromcheannach, *a.* bent-headed ; sad.

cromghluineach, *a.* in-kneed.

cròmghobach, *a.* curve-billed.
cròmleac, *n. f.* ancient standing-stone.
cròm-nan-gad, crom-nang-ad, *n. m.* a sort of lazy plough.
cròm-shlinneineach, *a.* round-shouldered.
cròmshrònach, *a.* hook-nosed.
cròmshuileach, *a.* bent-eyed.
cron, *n. m.* fault, defect, harm, blame, imputation of wrong. So *E.Ir.* cron.
cronaich, kròn'-ich, *v.* hurt with an evil eye ; reprove, chide, check, reprimand ; chronaich e mi, he reprimanded me.
cronail, *a.* offensive, hurtful.
cronalachd, kron'-al-achc, *n. f.* offensiveness, hurtfulness ; perniciousness.
crònan, *n. m.* murmuring noise ; purling of a streamlet ; purring of a cat ; a croon, a dirge.
crònanach, *a.* purring, purling.
crònanaich, kròn'-an-ich, *n. f.* a continued slow, gurgling, humming, buzzing, purring sound ; a dirge ; a bass.
cron-seanachais, *n. m.* anachronism, error in words.
cron-sgrìobhaidh, *n. m.* a mistake in writing.
cros, *v.* forbid ; go across ; air a' chrosadh, forbidden, set round.
crosach, *a.* thwarting.
crosadh, *n. m.* hindrance, obstruction.
crosag, *n. f.* frame of a fishing-line.
crosan, *n. m.* a peevish man. In *O.Ir.* crosán = cross-bearer in religious processions ; one who also practises the profession of singing satirical poems against persons under Church censure or otherwise obnoxious ; *scurra.*
crosanach, *a.* perverse ; cross ; peevish, fretful.
crosanachd, kross'-ăn-ăchc, *n. f.* bickering, picking a quarrel, as children.
crosanachd, *n. f.* a kind of poetry (*orig. satir.*). *E.Ir.* crosantachd, lewd rhyming ; art of the prof. crosán, often cast in snedbairdne, *i.e.* 2 (8² + 4²) with alliteration, and *ll.* 2 and 4 in rhyme. *See* crosan.
crosda, *a.* perverse, fretful ; froward, peevish, ill-natured, cankering.
crosdachd, krosd'-ăchc, *n. f.* fretfulness, perverseness, ill-nature ; bad behaviour.
crosdan, *n. m.* a peevish fellow, a cross person.
crosg, crasg, *n. m.* a cross, a crossing over a ridge.
crosgach, *a.* traverse, across, diagonal, put cross-ways.
crosgag, *n. f.* a starfish.
crosshuileach, *a.* squint-eyed. *Also* giorcach.
crot, *n. m.* oar-slip ; knot (bow). Cf. *O.N.* knöttr, a ball.
crotach, *a.* hump-backed.
crotag, *n. f.* a crooked woman; a sixpence.

crotaiche, *n. f.* hump-backedness.
crotal, *n. m.* lichen ; cudbear.
cròthadh, *vbl. n. m.* 1. act of leading in corn ; cròthadh an arbhair, housing the corn. 2. act of gathering sheep to a fank ; cròthadh nan caorach, fanking the sheep ; *based on* crò, an enclosure.
cròthaibh, crō-hiv, *n. pl.* in companies.
crothbhach, crovuch, *n.* chores, odds and ends.
cruach, cruǎch, *n. f.* heap ; a stack of hay or peats ; heap above the brim of a vessel ; *v.* pile, heap ; 'ga chruachadh, heaping it, making into stacks. So *E.Ir. W.* crug. *O.Celt.* kroukâ, a heap.
cruachag, *n. f.* small stack.
cruachainn, *n. f.* the hip. *E.Ir.* crúachait.
cruachan, krŭǎch'-an, *n. m.* the hip ; os cionn a' chruachain, above the hip; a conical hill. *E.Ir.* crúachán, crúachíne, small rick or hill.
cruadal, cruadal, *n. f.* hardship, distress, difficulty ; hardihood.
cruadalach, *a.* hardy, capable of enduring hardship or pain ; duine cruadalach, a hardy, energetic person ; distressing, moving. *E.Ir.* crúadach, hard.
cruadalachd, cruǎdaluchc, *n. f.* hardship, hardihood ; endurance, bravery.
cruadhag, cruǎyag, *n. f.* distress.
cruadhaich, cruǎ-ich, *v.* harden, dry ; a' cruadhachadh, hardening, drying.
cruadhas, cruǎs, *n. m.* hardness, rigour. *E.Ir.* crúadas, mettle, temper.
cruadhlach, cruǎluch, *n. m.* hard bottom (boglach, soft bottom) ; rocky place.
cruaidh, cruǎy, *a.* hard, firm ; àite cruaidh, a hard or firm place ; distressing, woeful, painful ; nì cruaidh, a distressing thing; scarce, hard; bliadhna chruaidh, a scarce year ; narrow-minded, niggardly, parsimonious; duine cruaidh, a niggardly, parsimonious, or narrow-minded person. *O.Ir.* cruaid. *O.Celt.* kroudi-s, hard. *Lat.* crudus.
cruaidh, *n. f., gen.* cruadhach, steel, anchor ; cruaidh agus cridhe, steel and fire, straw and fire used to light a torch.
cruaidhbheum, *n. m.* severe blow.
cruaidhchàs, *n. m.* distress, hardship.
cruaidh-cheangal, *n. m.* hard and fast bond.
cruaidhcheist, *n. f.* a hard question.
cruaidh-chuing, *n. f.* bondage, slavery.
cruaidhchuis, *n. f.* 1. a great difficulty. 2. hardihood.
cruaidhfhortan, *n. m.* misfortune ; *a.* cruaidh-fhortanach.
cruaidhghleachd, *n. f.* agony, hard struggle.
cruaidhreothadh, *n. m.* hard frost.

cruaidh-ruith, *n. m.* swift-running, running at full speed.
cruaidhshnaim, *n. m.* hard and fast knot.
cruaidh-theinn, *n. f.* straits, severe affliction.
cruailinn, *n. m.* hard, rocky place.
cruas, *n. m.* hardness; niggardliness; hardship; difficulty. *See* cruadhas.
crùb, *v.* crouch, cringe, squat, sit; *n. f.* a lame foot; nave; part of a mill; a halt. *O.N.* krjúpa, crouch. *A.S.* creõpan.
crùbach, *a.* lame of a leg, cripple.
crùbag, *n. f.* a crab; a lame woman.
crùbaiche, croob'-ich-à, *n. f.* lameness; a halt.
crùban, *n. m.* a crab-fish; cringing or crouching attitude.
crùbh, *n. m.* horse's hoof; a claw. *E.Ir.* crú. *O.Ir.* crob. *O.Celt.* kruvo-.
cruchaill, croochil, *n. f.* a disorderly heap; a bulky, shapeless person.
crùdan. *See* cnòdan.
crùdha, croo-u, *n. f.* hoof, horse-shoe.
crùib, *n. f.* a bend, a bent back as in lifting a heavy weight; doubled with pain; *obl. case* of cròb. *W.* crwb.
crùidein, croojen, *n. m.* the kingfisher.
crùidh, cruee, *v.* shoe, as a horse or wheel of a cart; *n. m.* a horse-shoe; heel-plate, toe-plate (for boots).
crùidheach, cru-yach, *a.* shod; provided with claws.
crùidhte, crootu, *vbl. a.* shod as a horse.
cruime, cruïmu, *n. f.* a bend, curvation, crookedness; more or most bent; *comp.* of crom.
cruimeal, croom'-al, *n. m.* a tall bent person.
cruimh, crŭ-y, *n. f.* a worm, maggot. *O.Ir.* cruim; *W.* pryf, worm.
cruinn, cruïn, *a.* round, globular, circular, rotund; maide cruinn, a round stick; assembled, collected, gathered, as people; tha am pobull cruinn, the people are assembled; scant, somewhat scant or short; tha am bàrr gu math cruinn, the crop is somewhat scant or short. *O.Ir.* cruind. 1. round, exact, complete. 2. niggardly. *W.* crwn. *O.Celt.* krundi-s.
cruinne, crunu, *n. m.* and *f.* roundness, rotundity, circularity; the globe, the world; gu crich na cruinne, to the ends of the earth. *O.Ir.* cruinda, *rotunditas Z²*., the globe.
cruinnead, *n. f.* roundness; air a chruinnead, however round it may be.
cruinne-cé, krun-nya-kã', *n. c.* the globe, this world, this universe. *O.Ir.* cruinda (globe) +cé (this). *See* cé.
cruinneachadh, kruniuchu, *vbl. n. m.*

an assembly, a gathering; act of gathering, collecting, adding.
cruinneadair, crunuder, *n. m.* a geometrician, fear tohmhais a' chruinne.
cruinneadaireachd, *n. f.* geometry, spherics, geography.
cruinneag, crunyag, *n. f.* a neat, tidy female.
cruinnealas, crunyalus, *n. m.* tidiness, economy.
cruinnean, krŭn'-nyan, *n. m.* all the fingers put together; the quantity the fingers can hold.
cruinneil, crun-yal, *a.* tidy, economical.
cruinneineach, crunenuch, *n. m.* anything round; a stout boy.
cruinnich, crun-yich, *v.* gather, collect; assemble, accumulate, convene, draw close, round.
cruinnichte, crun-yichtu, *vbl. a.* collected.
cruinnire, crun-yiru, *n. m.* a turner. *Also* tuairnear.
cruinnleum, cruï-lem, *n. m.* a bound; a standing jump.
crùinte, croontu, *vbl. a.* crowned; finished.
crùisgean, crooshcen, *n. m.* a lamp, fish-oil lamp. *Ir.* crúistin, a lamp. *Lh.*
crùisle, crooshlu, *n. m.* a mausoleum; a burial-vault. *Also* crùist and crùidse; t' uaigh 's a' chrùist, your grave in the vault.
crùisleach, *n. m.* a recluse; a sluggard.
cruit, cruït, *n. f.* a harp; hunchback, a cringing attitude; cruit chiùil, musical instrument. *Ir.* cruit, a bunch on the back. *O.Ir.* crot, crott. 1. harp. 2. hump. *W.* crwth. *O.Celt.* krottâ, krotto-, a harp.
cruiteag, crui-chag, *n. f.* a little harp.
cruitealachd, crootaluchc, *n. f.* pleasantness.
cruiteil, *a.* pleasant, sprightly, lively.
cruitein, *n. m.* a diminutive humpbacked person.
cruiteir, crooter, *n. m.* a harper.
cruiteireachd, *n. f.* performance on harp.
cruitire, krüit'-ir-u, *n. m.* a hunchbacked person; a harper, musician. *E.Ir.* cruittire, *n. m.* a harpist; cruittechán, a hunchback.
cruitheachd, krui-achc, *n. m.* the creation; the universe, the exact figure, the identity of a person. *O.Ir.* cruth.
cruithear, krooy'-ar, *n. m.* a creator. *M.Ir.* cruthaigtheóir.
cruithneach, krŭn'-ach, *n. m.* a Pict. *M.Ir.* cruthen, a Pict; *pl.* cruthni, cruthnech, Pictish, a Pict; in *O.G.* = a Briton, in Scotland =Pict.
cruithneachd, cruineachd, cri-nechc, *n. m.* wheat. *O.Ir.* cruithnecht.
crùlaist, croo-lesht, *n. m.* a rocky hill.
crumag, *n. f.* the plant skirret.

cruman, *n. m.* the hip bone ; a bent surgical instrument.

crumpa, *n. f.* an instrument for making snuff of tobacco.

crùn, croon, *n. m.* a crown, five-shilling piece, crown of the head ; a garland of flowers. *Lat.* corona.

crùnadh, croonu, *vbl. n. m.* coronation ; crùnadh an righ, coronation of the king ; act of crowning.

crùnair, *n. m.* a crowner.

crùn-easbuig, croon-esbig, *n. m.* a mitre.

crunluath, croon-lua, *n. m.* a quick measure in highland music, final measure of a pibroch ; a seal. *Also* crunnluath.

crup, *v.* contract, shrink.

crupadh, croopu, *vbl. n. m.* contraction ; contracting ; crupadh-feithe, a spasm.

crùsach, croosuch, *collective n.* small fry, pigmy race. *R.D.*

cruscladh, crooschu, *n. m.* wrinkling.

cruth, croo, *n. m., pl.* cruthannan, shape, form, appearance, expression of countenance. *O.Ir.* cruth, form. *W.* pryd.

cruthach, croo-huch, *a.* shapely, handsome ; identical, exactly, like, resembling ; cho chruthach, so identical ; adaptable to varying shapes.

cruthach, *n. m.* placenta of a mare. *Carm. G.*

cruthachadh, croo-huchu, *vbl. n. m.* the creation, the universe ; act of creating.

cruthadair, croo-huder, *n. m.* a creator.

crùthag, *n. f.* hardship ; " gun a chosnadh tre chrùthaig," without winning it through hardship. *R.D.*

cruthaich, cru-hich, *v.* create, form. *E.Ir.* cruthaigim.

cruthail, cru-hal, *a.* shapely, elegant.

cruthalachd, *n. f.* comeliness, shapeliness.

cruth-atharraich, *v.* change shape, transform, transfigure ; cruth-atharrachadh, transformation, transfiguration.

cruthlach, crooluch, *n. m.* a tall bent person ; a ghost, a fairy.

cù, coo, *n. m.* a dog ; *gen. s.* and *n. pl.* coin ; cù eunaich, a pointer or spaniel ; cù luirge, a bloodhound, a beagle ; cù uisge, a Newfoundland dog. *O.Ir.* cú. *O.Celt.* kuô, *gen.* kuno-s, a dog. *W.* cî, *pl.* cŵn. *Gr.* κύων. *Goth.* hunds.

cuach, *n. f.* a wooden cup ; a drinking cup ; quoich, bowl of a nest ; a fold, plait ; *v.* plait, fold, curl. So *M.Ir.*

cuach, *n. f.* a cuckoo. *O.Ir.* coí, *gen.* cuach. *W.* cog. *O.Celt.* kouko-s, kukâ. *Lat.* cucûlus.

cuachach, *a.* curled, plaited.

cuachag, *n. f.* a little plait, curl.

cuachag, *n. f., dim.* of cuach (cuckoo), poetical for a neat, melodious-voiced young girl.

cuach-bhleoghan, *n. f.* a milking dish.

cuach-phàdraig, *n. f.* plantain.

cuag, cuàg, *n. f.* an awkward bend.

cuagach, *a.* awkwardly bent ; limping, lame.

cuagaire, cuàg-iru, *n. m.* an awkward, clump-footed man.

cuagaireachd, *n. f.* awkwardness, clumsiness.

cuaichein, cuàchen, *n. m.* a seam, a curl, a nest.

cuaichnich, *v.* plait, curl.

cuaigein, *n. m.* a splay-footed man.

cuailean, koo-ul-en, *n. m.* a cue, plaited hair, a curl. *O.Celt.* kogleno-, lock of hair.

cuaille, cuàlu. *n. m.* a pole, a stake ; a club, bludgeon. *O.Ir.* cúaille, a stake. *O.Celt.* kaullio-.

cuain, *n. f.* a litter of pigs, whelps, etc. *M.Ir.* cúane, cúan-lacht. *Also* cúan.

cuairsg, cuàrsc, *v.* roll, wrap, fold. *M.Ir.* cuairsce, a bundle, volume, a folding.

cuairsgeach, *n. f.* a wrapper ; *a.* coiled, rolled.

cuairt, cuàrst, *n. f.* a circuit, a round, a circle, a circumference ; a' cheud chuairt, the first round ; chuir mi cuairt air a' bhaile, I made a circuit round the town, I visited every house in the town ; pilgrimage, sojourn ; luchd cuairt air thalamh, sojourners on the earth ; fear-cuairt, sojourner, a pilgrim ; a trip, a tour, an excursion ; chaidh sinn air chuairt, we went on an excursion ; circumlocution ; cainnt gun chuairt, language without circumlocution ; circulation ; cuairt na fola, the circulation of the blood ; theirig mun cuairt, get round about ; mun cuairt do dheich bliadhna, about ten years ; a tier, a course (in building house, boat, or in knitting). *E.Ir.* cúairt, a circle, a ring.

cuairteach, cuàrstuch, *a.* surrounding ; circuitous, circulating, *n. f.* a fever.

cuairtear, cuàrster, *n. m.* a sojourner, a pilgrim, a tourist.

cuairtghaoth, *n. f.* whirlwind.

cuairtich, *v.* surround, go about, go over (the houses) ; cuairtich dleasdanas, do duty ; conduct (religious) service.

cuairtiche, *n. m.* a shepherd boy (for a township).

cuairtlinn, cuàrstlin, *n. f.* a whirlpool.

cuairtradh, cuàrst-ra, *n. f.* circumlocution.

cual, *n. m.* a faggot ; cual chonnaidh, a faggot of firewood ; a burden. *M.Ir.* a faggot, a bundle, a heap.

cuala. *See* cluinn.

cualach, *n. m., pl.* cualaichean, a great burden (of sticks). So *M.Ir.*

cualag, cuälag, *n. f.* a hard task, a burden : cha chualag sin air, that is no task to him ; burden.

cuallach, kŭäll'-ach, *n. f.* herding ; agus e a' cuallach na spréidhe, and he tending or herding the cattle.

cuallach, *n. m.* society, family, corporation. *Ir.* cuallaidhe, a companion.

cuallan, cuamhlan, *n. m.* a company ; a band.

cuan, *n. m., pl.* cuaintean, an ocean ; narrow sea, inlet. *M.Ir.* cúan, a haven. haven.

cuanal, *n. m.* a social band ; a group of children living on the best of terms ; a choir. *Also* cuannal, cuantal.

cuanlong, *n. m.* a harbour.

cuanna, *a.* snug, comfortable, trim, handsome. *E.Ir.* cúanna.

cuanta, *a.* robust, able, handsome, fine. *M.Ir.* cúarán. *Also* cuannar.

cuantach, *n. m.* seafaring man ; sea-bred.

cuantaiche, coo-antichu, *n. m.* a rover, sea-bred.

cuar, *a.* crooked, perverse. *E.Ir.* cúar, crooked, bent.

cuar, *v.* torment, pain.

cuaradh, *n. m.* torment ; distress.

cuaran, *n. m.* a wrinkle ; a crinkle ; 'n an cuarain mu chasan, (stockings) in wrinkles on his legs. *E.Ir.* cúar, (*a.*) crooked ; (*n. m.*) a hoop, a circle.

cuaran, *n. m.* a sandal, a brogue (made of untanned skin, and worn with the hairy side outwards), sock, footwear made of cloth (sewn on to a stocking) ; a bandage ; a finger-stall. *E.Ir.* cúarán, *id.* *O.Celt.* kourano-.

cuarsgag, kuarsk'-ag, *n. f.* an eddy ; a curl.

cuartag, kŭärst'-ag, *n. f.* an eddy, curl.

cuartagach, *a.* eddying, circular.

cuartaich, cuärstich, *v.* surround, enclose, encompass, environ, go about, circumnavigate ; a' cuartachadh, surrounding, encircling ; cuir cuairt air tighean a' bhaile, make a circuit of the houses of the town.

cuartalan, *n. m.* a circuit, a circuitous route.

cuartan, *n. m.* a maze, a labyrinth.

cuas, *n. m.* a cave. Cf. cós. *M.Ir.* cúass, a hollow, cavity.

cùb, coob, *v. i.* feel the utmost torment of mind ; coop, cringe ; fit a head in a barrel.

cùb, *n. f.* a pannier, a box-cart.

cùba, *n. m.* a bed ; cùba-chuil, bedroom. *M.Ir.* cub, a cell, a booth ; cubachal, bed, chamber.

cùbadh, coobu, *n. m.* packing around spindle in nether millstone. *M.Ir.* cúp (cúb), *id.*

cùbaid, koob'-äj, *n. f.* a precentor's desk ; a pulpit. *Also* cùbaidh and crannag ; ultimately from *Lat.* pulpitum. *McB.*

cùbair, coober, *n. m.* a cooper.

cùbaire, *n. m.* a shabby mean fellow.

cùbaireachd, cooberuchc, *n. f.* coopering.

cubhag, kŭ'-ag, *n. f.* a cuckoo. *O.Ir.* cúach.

cubhaidh, coovy, *a.* fit, seemly, proper. *O.Ir.* cubaid, *a.* agreeable ; *adv.* inchobaid, gl. concinnenter, *compar.* as chubaithiu.

cùbhrag, coorug, *n. f.* an infant's flannel shawl.

cùbhraidh, coory, *a.* fragrant ; fàile cùbhraidh, a fragrant flavour. *M.Ir.* cumra.

cùbhraidheachd, kû'-rė-ăchc, *n. f.* fragrance.

cùbhraig, coo-rig, cùbhrainn, coo-rin, *n. f.* a coverlet. Cf. *Eng.* cover.

cuchailte, coocheltu, *n. m.* residence.

cuchair, coocher, *n. m.* a hunter. *Also* sealgair.

cudag, cudaige, coodigu, *n. m.* a young coalfish.

cudainn, coodin, *n. f.* sprat of coalfish six months old.

cùdainn, coodin, *n. f.* a large tub. *O.N.* kútr, cask.

cudthrom, coodrum, *n. m.* weight, heaviness, importance. *Also* cudrom and cuideam. *O.Ir.* cutrumma, equal, proportionate.

cudthromach, *a.* weighty, important, momentous ; gnothach cudthromach, a momentous affair.

cudthromachd, *n. f.* the importance.

cugann, coogun, *n. m.* rich milk ; delicacy ; cha tig cé air cugann cait, cream will not rise on a cat's milk. *O.Ir.* cucann, cucan, gl. pistrinum, cocina, culina, penus. Z^2/69. *W.* cegin.

cuglaidh, coogly, *a.* wobbly, unsteady, applied to a difficult kind of work—work requiring delicate and steady handling. *E.Ir.* cuclige (*inf.* of conclichim), a shaking, swerving.

cuibh, quiv, *a.* muzzle-bar or splinter ; cuibh-mhór, one for four horses ; gearrchuibh, one for two horses. *Also* amall.

cuibhe, *compar.* of cubhaidh.

cuibheas, quivus, *n. m.* moderation, competency.

cuibheasach, cooyusuch, *a.* easily dealt with ; middling, tolerable ; fr. cubhaidh. *O.Ir* cuibsech, conscientious.

cuibhle, queelu, cuibhill, cuibheall, cooyul, *n. f.* a wheel.

cuibhlich, v. wheel, turn the wheel.
cuibhne, queenu, n. f., pl. cuibhnean, cuibhnichean, deer's horn.
cuibhreach, cooyruch, n. m. bondage, trammels ; harness of a plough horse. O.Ir. cuimrech, bond, chain. Also cuibrech. Fel.
cuibhrich, cui-rich, v. trammel, entangle, put in bonds or irons ; discommode.
cuibhrig, cuyric, n. m. heavy bed-quilt, a covering, coverlet ; v. cover.
cuicheanachd, cuchenuchc, n. f. hobnobbing.
cuibhrionn, cuyrun, n. f. a lot of land ; a portion, share ; allotment. E.Ir. cuibrend, a share, a portion. W. cyfran.
cuid, cuj, n. f., gen. codach, part, portion ; property, share ; is e so mo chuidse, this is mine ; cuid oidhche, a night's lodging ; cuid an tràth, what serves for a meal ; air son mo chodachsa dheth, for my part of it ; cha toir muir no monadh a chuid o dhuine sona, dangers by sea or land cannot deprive a fortunate man of his lot ; cuid fir, a man's share ; used for his, her : a chuid mhac, his sons ; a cuid mac, her sons ; mo chuid bìdh, my food ; used as an indef. pro. : cuid de na daoine, some of the men ; a' chuid eile, the rest ; privates. O.Ir. cuit, gen. cota. W. peth. = Lat. quota.
cuideachadh, coojuchu, vbl. n. m. assistance, aid, succour, help ; vbl. assisting, aiding, succouring, relieving.
cuideachail, cujuchal, a. aiding, supporting.
cuideachd, coojuchc, n. f. company, society ; am chuideachd, in my company or society ; intercourse ; a company, a society ; cuideachd shaighdearan, a company of soldiers.
cuideachd, coojuchc, adv. also, likewise ; thàinig esan cuideachd, he came also ; adv. in company, accompanying ; cuide rium, along with me.
cuideachdail, coojuchcal, a. social, sociable.
cuideag, cujag, n. f. small effects.
cuideag, n. f. a spider.
cuidealas, coojalus, n. m. conceitedness, pride. Also cuideal.
cuideam, dial. for cudthrom.
cuideil, coojal, a. conceited, prim.
cuidh, cuith, n. f. an enclosure. Cf. O.N. kví.
cuidhe, n. f. a wreath of snow. See cuithe.
cuidheal, cooyul, n. f. a wheel, coil.
cuidhill, cooyil, v. wheel, lash lustily ; coil, roll, make a coil.
cùidhte, cooytu, a. quits, rid of.

cùidhteag, n. f. a whiting.
cùidhtich, cooytich, v. quit, abandon.
cùidhtichte, cooytichtu, vbl. a. forsaken, quit of.
cuidich, coojich, v. assist, aid, help, succour ; cuidichte, helped, assisted, aided.
cuidreach, coojruch, a. in partnership ; powerful.
cuidridh, cujry, a. common.
cuid-roinn, n. f. a share, lot.
cuidseal, n. m. Eng. cudgel.
cuifein, quifen, n. m. wad of a gun.
cuigeal, coogial, a. distaff ; cuigeal is fearsaid, distaff and spindle ; cuigeal nan losgan, or nam ban sìth, the herb, reed-mace. E.Ir. cuicel ; gl. colus.
cuigealach, n. m. reed-grass.
cuigse, n. pl. Whigs.
cùil, cool, n. f., pl. cùiltean, a corner, a recess ; a nook, niche. O.Ir. cúil. O.Celt. kûlî-.
cuilbheart, culu-verst, n. f. wile, deceit.
cuilbheartach, a. wily.
cuilbheartachd, n. f. wiliness.
cuilbheir, coolver, n. f. a gun, fowlingpiece. Eng. culverin.
cuilc, coolc, n. f. reed, cane.
cuilcearnach, coolkernuch, n. f. a place overgrown with reed or bulrushes.
cuile, coolu, n. f., pl. cuilichean, a storeroom, cellar. So E.Ir., gl. colina ; cuile fínda, gl. vinaria cella. O.Celt. koliâ.
cuileachan, kool'-ach-an, n. m. basket.
cuileag, kool'-ag, n. f. a fly ; fishing fly ; a husk ; a trifle. So in E.Ir. O.Ir. cuil, gl. culex. O.Celt. kuli-s, kuliâno-s.
cùileagan, n. m. a private feast.
cuilean, kool'-an', n. m. whelp, cub, pup ; a darling. E.Ir. culén, gl. catulus. O.Celt. kuleino-.
cuilgean, coolgen, n. m. particle of awn.
cuilgeanach, a. prickly.
cuilidh, cooly, n. f. a press, a lockfast place ; cellar ; a treasury ; a secret haunt ; cuilidh nan agh maol, the secret haunts of the hinds. See cuile.
cuilionn, cooliun, n. m. holly ; craobh chuilinn, a holly tree ; cuilionn mara, sea-holly. E.Ir. culenn.
cùilireachd, n. f. intriguing, " hole and corner " business. M.Ir. cúlaidhe, a dodger.
cuillidh, cooly, n. m. a horse ; cuir an cuillidh 'san fheun, yoke the horse in the cart.
cuilm, n. f. a feast. See cuirm.
cuilmeach, a. hospitable.
cùilteach, cooltiuch, a. dark, dismal, full of ugly nooks ; n. f. a skulking female ; a bed, a bakehouse.

cùiltear, coolter, *n. m.* smuggler, skulker.
cùiltearachd, *n. f.* skulking, smuggling.
cuime, quimu, *int. pro.* of whom ? about whom ? respecting whom ? about what ? For co + uime, *see* uime.
cuimein, *n. f.* cumin. *Lat.* cuminum.
cùimhne, queenu, *n. f.* memory, recollection, remembrance ; an cùimhne leat ? do you recollect ? ma's cùimhne leat, if you recollect ; ma's math mo chùimhne, if I recollect aright. *O.Ir.* cuman, cumne, remembrance; co + men (mind). *W.* cof.
cùimhneach, *a.* mindful, of retentive memory. *O.Ir.* cuimnech, mindful.
cùimhneachail, *a.* keeping in mind ; mindful.
cùimhneachair, queenucher, *n. m.* a recorder ; chronicler.
cùimhneachan, queenuchan, *n. m.* a memorial ; token of respect or gratitude.
cùimhnich, queenich, *v. i.* remember, bear in mind, recollect, be mindful. *O.Ir.* cuimnigim. *W.* coffa. *M.W.* cofein.
cùimhniche, quinichu, *n. m.* a remembrancer, a recorder, a chronicler.
cuimir, quimir, *a.* tidy, trim, neat, as a female ; equally filling, exactly of the same size, well proportioned ; short, concise. *E.Ir.* cumbair, short, brief. *O.Ir.* cuimre, brevity; con + berr.
cuimireachd, quimirachc, *n. f.* neatness, symmetry ; proportion, same size.
cuimrich, quimrich, *v.* size, as slate ; make of the same size ; pair, as shoes.
cuimrig, *n.f.* trouble, difficulty, handicap. Cf. *O.Ir.* con-rigim, I bind.
cuimrigeach, cumriguch, *a.* difficult, full of obstacles.
cuimrigeadh, *n. m.* pains, hindrance.
cuimse, cumshu, *n. f.* moderation ; nì gun chuimse, a thing without moderation ; sufficiency, enough ; tha cuimse agamsa, I have enough or sufficiency ; aim ; measurements (for suit) ; gabh mo chuimse, take my measurements.
cuimseach, kŭm'-shach, *a.* moderate, indifferent ; befitting, suitable to one's case ; is cuimseach dhuit sin, it is but proper that you should be so.
cuimsich, cumsich, *v.* aim, hit ; a' cuimseachadh air comharra, aiming or shooting at a mark.
cuimte, coomtu, *a.* neat, tight.
cuin, coo-in, *adv.* when ? at what time ? *E.Ir.* cuin.
cuing, *n. f.* strait, restraint, bondage ; a yoke, the asthma ; tha e làn cuing, he is quite asthmatic ; tyranny ; fa chuing agadsa, under your tyrannical sway.

cuing, *n. f.* a very narrow pass, through which a stream flows ; *obliq.* c. of cong.
cuinge, cuingead, *n. f.* narrowness. *O.Ir.* cumce, cumcigim ; gl. ango.
cuinge, kŭing'-u, *a.* more or most narrow or narrow-minded ; *n. f.* exceeding narrowness ; cuing-fhuail or -uisge, strangury.
cuingeach, kuing'-uch, asthmatic.
cuingead, kŭing-ud, *n. m.* narrowness.
cuingeil, kŭing'-al, *a.* tyrannical, arbitrary, strait ; àite cuingeil, tight corner.
cuingich, kŭing'-ich, *v.* tyrannise, straiten.
cuingire, cuïngiru, *n. m.* a despot.
cùinn, cooin, *v.* coin ; shape.
cùinneadh, cooniu, *vbl. n. m.* a coin ; act of coining.
cuinneag, cuniag, *n. f.* water-pitcher ; a water-stoup ; a milk pail ; a churn. *E.Ir.* cuindeog, churn ; gl. *mulctrella.*
cuinnean, cunean, *n. m.* nostril. *Also* cuinnlean.
cuinnlean, kŭinn'-len', *n. m.* stalk of corn ; stubble ; *a.* cuinnleanach. *E.Ir.* connline, stalks, rushes, stubble.
cuinnse, cuïnshu, *n. f.* a quince.
cuinnsear, cuïnsher, *n. m.* a whinger, a sword, dagger.
cùinnte, coo'ntu, *vbl. a.* coined.
cuip, coop, *v.* whip, lash ; *n. f.* a whip, a stratagem, or trick, deceit ; fr. *Eng.* whip.
cuir, coor, *v.* put, place, lay ; cuir an sin e, put it there ; sow, snow ; tha iàd a' cur, they are sowing ; tha e a' cur, it is snowing ; send, despatch ; cuir fios, send word ; cuir seachad, or cuir mu seach, lay by, hoard ; cuir an cèill, declare, profess ; cuir air falbh, send away ; cuir as da, kill him ; cuir as, extinguish ; cuir umad, dress yourself ; molest, trouble (when foll. by air) ; cha chuir e air, it will not annoy him ; ciod e tha cur ort ? what is bothering you ? tha am muir a' cur air, he is seasick ; cur na mara, sea-sickness ; cur na cloiche, putting the stone ; cur a mach, vomiting ; a' cur a' chuilg, shedding the hair ; a' cur nan itean, moulting ; cuir 'sna casan e, take to your heels ; cuir, invite ; thoir cuireadh dha, invite him. *O.Ir.* cuirim (inf. cor). *O.Celt.* korjô.
cuir, *gen.* of car, *q.v.*
cuircinn, coorcin, *n. m.* head-dress.
cuireadh, cooru, *n. m.* an invitation ; thig gun chuireadh, come without invitation ; thoir cuireadh dhaibh, invite them.
cuireall, cooral, *n. m.* a kind of packsaddle.

cuireid, coorej, *n. m.* a wile, stratagem, as a girl ; coquettish conduct ; fr. **car.**

cuireideach, coorejuch, *a.* coquettish, wily; *n. f.* a coquette ; a flirt or wily girl.

cuireideachd, *n. f.* flirtation.

cuirein, cooren, *n. m.* a little turn ; wile ; fr. **car,** a turn.

cuirinnein, coorinen, *n. m.* the white water-lily.

cuirm, coorm, *n. f.* a feast, banquet. *E.Ir.* cuirm, *gen.* cormma, ale, an ale-feast. *W.* cwrwf. *O.Celt.* kurmên.

cuirmire, coormiru, *n. m.* an entertainer, a host, or one that gives a feast.

cùirneachadh, coornuchu, *n. m.* an envelope, a cover ; act of covering.

cùirnean, coornan, *n. m.* the head of a pin ; a dewdrop, a heap   *a.* **cuir-neineach.**

cùirnich, coornich, *v.* cover, envelop.

cuirpidh, coorpy, *a.* wicked, corrupt. *See* **coirb, coirbte.**

cuirplinn, *n. m.* trappings (of a horse).

cùirt, coorst, *n. f.* a court, palace, honour, favour ; **fhuair e cùirt air,** he has gained favour ; area, yard ; **cùirt mu choinneamh an tighe,** an area opposite the house.

cuirte, coortiu, *vbl. a.* planted, sowed, set.

cùirtealachd, coorstaluchc, *n. f.* courtliness.

cùirtear, coorster, *n. m.* a courtier.

cùirteas, coorstesh, *n. f.* currying favour, ceremony, gallantry.

cùirteil, coorstal, *a.* courtly ; petted.

cùirtein, coorsten, *n. f.* a curtain.

cùirteir, *n. m.*   1. plaiding.   2. a courtier.

cùirteiseach, *a.* ceremonious.

cùis, coosh, *n. f.* case, cause, matter, point or subject of dispute ; **chan e sin a' chùis,** that is not the point ; **millidh tu a' chùis,** you will spoil the business ; **cùis a h-aisling,** the subject of her dream ; lot, portion ; **bu chùis dhomh anart is uaigh,** my lot would be the winding-sheet and the grave ; **cùis-dhìtidh,** ground of condemnation ; **cùis ghearain,** ground of complaint ; **cuis-thruais,** object of pity ; **cùis ghràin,** object of disgust ; **cùis fharmaid,** an object of envy, an enviable object ; **cùis-lagha,** a law-suit. *O.Ir.* cóis. *W.* achaws. *Lat.* causa.

cuis, *n. f.* a narrow sea-stream ; jet from vein.

cuisdeag, *n. f.* the little finger.

cùiseach, *a.* business-like, careful, reliable, shrewd.

cuiseach, coosh'-ach, *n. m.* rye-grass.

cùiseag, *n. f.* a careful little body.

cuiseag, coosh'-ag, *n. f.* a stalk of rye-grass ; stalk of dock.

cùiseil, *a.* punctilious, scrupulous.

cùisire, cooshiru, *n. m.* a client ; one that employs a lawyer ; casuist.

cuisle, cooshlu, *n. f.* a vein, a layer of ore, as in a mine ; an artery ; a blood-vessel ; rapid stream or current in the sea. *E.Ir.* 1. a vein.   2. a stalk.   3. a flute ; **cuislennach,** a flute-player. *O.Ir.* cusle (vena).

cuisleach, *n. f.* a lancet, lance.

cuisleag, *n. f.* a little vein.

cuisleanach, cooshlenuch, *n. m.* an Irish piper. *See* sub. **cuisle**

cuisnich, cooshnich, *v.* freeze.   *Also* reòdh. *M.Ir.* cuisne, ice, frost.

cuiste, *n. f.* a couch ; fr. the *Eng.*

cuithe, cooyu, *n. m.* a wreath of snow ; pit. *E.Ir.* cuthe. *Lat.* puteus.

cùitich. *See* **cuidhtich,** quit, requite.

cùl, cool, *n. m.* the back of anything ; tresses ; **cùl buidh dualach,** yellow curled tresses ; **air do chùl,** behind you ; **air chùl sin,** more than that ; **gu cùl,** thoroughly, completely ; protection, support.   *O.Ir.* cúl has similar variety of meanings (**er cúl,** on behalf of, *Thes.* II. 289¹⁸). *W.* cil. *O.Celt.* kûla. *Lat.* cūlus.

culach, coolach, *a.* fat, plump, in good condition.

culadh, culaidh, cooly, *n. m.* a good condition of body ; flesh, fatness.

cùlag, coolag, *n. f.* the "back one" ; grinder or back tooth, a peat, a turf (for the back of the fire). *See* **beulag.**

culag, *n. f.* a slice, a collop. *Ir.* culóg, a collop.

cùlaibh, *d. pl.* of **cùl,** back ; **air do chùlaibh,** behind you.

cùlaich, *v.* turn the back on ; "**chùlaich thu sannt,**" you scorned greed.

culaidh, cooly, *n. f.* materials, apparatus ; **nam biodh a' chulaidh agam,** were I to have the materials ; condition ; clothes (Bible) ; subject, object ; **culaidh mhagaidh,** an object of sport ; **culaidh bhùird,** a butt ; **culaidh-bhàis,** *poet.* for coffin. *E.Ir.* culaid, a suit, robe ; instrument ; furniture.

culaidh, *n. f.* a boat. *M.Ir.* culad.

cùlaist, coolesht, *n. f.* recess, wall-press ; ben (the house).

cùlan, *n. m.* tresses, hair ; black stripe behind lamb's neck ; a crust.

cùlanach, *a.* behind, coming behind ; a certain billow ; the hindermost (and the angriest) of a rhythmic series of billows in a raging sea.

cularan, cooluran, *n. m.* a cucumber.

cùlbheum, *n. m.* back-stroke.

cùlbhuidhe, *a.* yellow-tressed. *E.Ir.* cùlbuide, *id.*

cùl-chàin, *v.* backbite, detract, slander ; **cùl-chàineadh,** detraction, calumny.

cùlchainnt, *n. f.* calumny; *a.* cùl-
chainnteach.
cùl-cheumnaich, *v.* ġo backwards.
cùl-choimhead, *n. m.* a retrospect.
cùl-chuideachd, cool-chujuchc, *n. m.* rear-
guard, reserve, company to assist.
cùldaich, *n. m.* a back house, a cellar.
cullach, coolach, *n. m.* a boar; the male
of the larger seal; polecat; a stirk,
eunuch. *O.Ir.* callach, caullach; gl.
porcus. *Also* cullach, a stallion, a
boar, a hero. *KM.*
cullachas, *n. m.* impotence.
cullaich, coolich, *v.* line, as a boar.
culm, coolm, *n. m.* 1. broken bits, chaff.
2. misty cloud, filmy cloudlets darkening the sky; gloom, haze. Cf. *E.Ir.*
coll, destruction, ruin.
culm, *n. m.* energy, push.
cùlmhaiseach, *a.* fair-tressed.
cùl-raonaidh, *n. m.* a goalkeeper.
cùl-sgrìobh, cool-sgreev, *v.* direct, address,
as a letter; cùl-sgrìobhadh, direction.
cùl-shleamhnaich, *v.* backslide, apostatise.
cùl-taic, *n. m.* support, prop, a patron;
patronage, support.
cùltharruing, *n. f.* a sly insinuation;
retraction.
cù-luirge, *n. m.* a bloodhound.
cum, coom, *v. n.* keep, hold; cum so,
hold or keep this; contain, as a dish;
cumaidh an soitheach so e, this dish
will contain it; refrain; cum air do
làimh, restrain thy hand; cum a mach,
maintain. contend; cum ris, keep up
to him, do not yield to him. *O.Ir.*
congabim, I hold, keep.
cum, *v.* shape, form. *E.Ir.* cummaim,
I shape, devise, pretend.
cuma, cumadh, *n. m.* shape, form, figure,
pattern. *Also* cunna. *E.Ir.* cumma
(=cumbe, *inf.* of con-benim). *KM.*
shaping, fashioning.
cumachdail, coomachcal, *a.* well-shaped.
cumadalachd, coomudaluchc, *n. f.* symmetry, shapeliness.
cumail, coomel, *n. f.*, *gen.* cumalach,
detention, maintenance; keeping;
celebrating. *Also* conbhail, " rosg glan
a' conbhail dìon orr'," healthy eye-
lids protecting them (eyes). *M.Ir.*
congmhail.
cumaltachd, cumaltuchc, *n. f.* grit,
tenacity.
cuman, cooman, *n. m.* milking pail.
cumanta, *a.* common; fr. the *Eng.*
cumantachd, cumantas, *n. f.* generality.
cumasg, *n. f.* a tumult, a fray. *O.Ir.*
cummasc (con-mescaim), mix up, confuse. *O.Celt.* kóm-misko-, mix.
cumasgach, *a.* given to tumult.
cumha, *n. m.* stipulation. *E.Ir.* coma,
gift, boon, condition.

cumha, coo-u, *n. m.* an elegy, eulogy
or poem in praise of the dead, mourning, lamentation; cumha Shir Domhnall, the elegy of Sir Donald. *E.Ir.*
cuma, grief, sorrow.
cumhachd, coo-achc, *n. m.* power, might,
strength, energy, ability, authority,
commission, permission, influence.
O.Ir. cumachtae, gl. potestas. *O.Celt.*
kóm-akto-, power.
cumhachdach, coo-achc-uch, *a.* powerful,
having great sway or influence; duine
cumhachdach, a man of great influence
or sway; mighty, strong, able.
cumhachdair, *n. m.* a commissioner, a
delegate, agent.
cumhaingich, *v.* make narrow. *E.Ir.*
cumngaigim, I straighten.
cumhang, coo-ung, *n. m.* a defile. *O.Ir.*
cumang cumung. angustus. *O.Celt.*
kóm-ango-s.
cumhang, coo-un, *a.* narrow, strait,
narrow-minded; contracted; *n.* strait;
compar. cuinge. *Also* cumhann. *O.Ir.*
cumang. *W.* cyfyng.
cumhasag, kuv'-as-ag, *n. f.* an owl. *Also*
cailleach oidhche. *See* comhachag.
cùmhdach, cooduch, *n. m.* defence, preservation. *O.Ir.* cumtach, a case,
covering.
cùmhdaidh, coody, *a.* inlaid. *O.Ir.*
cumtach, gl. *ornatio.*
cùmhlait, coolaj, *n. m.* a strait, a pass.
cùmhnant, coo-nant, *n. m.* a covenant,
a league, bargain, contract; an engagement; compact, agreement; a réir
ceannaibh a' chùmhnant, agreeable to
the terms of engagement. *See* cumha.
cùmhnantach, *n. m.* a covenanter.
cùmhnantach, *a.* stingy, unaccommo-
dating; duine cruaidh cumhnantach,
a niggardly, stingy fellow. *See* caomhantach.
cùmhnantaich, coo-nantich, *v.* covenant.
cùmhradh, *n. m.* a good bargain. *See*
cunnradh.
cùmpach, *a.* well-shaped, sturdy.
cumraich, *v.* cumber; fr. *Eng.*
cunbhalach, coonvaluch, *a.* constant,
steady. Cf. *O.Ir.* congabim, I hold,
keep.
cunbhalachd, cunbhalas, *n. f.* sense,
judgment, constancy.
cung, coong, *n. f.* a medicine, drug;
droch chungan, bad medicine.
cungaidh, coongy, *a.* medicine, materials;
cungaidh-leighis, a healing preparation: medicine; nam biodh a' chungaidh agam, if I had the materials;
ingredients; means.
cungaisich, coongeshich, *v.* subdue, conquer, subjugate, overcome, provide
with tools.

cungbhail. *See* **cumail.**

cunglach, coonglach, *n. m.* narrow place or range, a narrow defile ; fr. **cong.**

cunn, coon, *v.* shape, frame, count ; **cunn an còta,** shape the coat.

cunna, *n. f.* shape, form, figure ; construction.

cunnarach, coonaruch, *n. m.* cheap bargain.

cunnart, coonard, *n. m.* danger, risk, jeopardy ; **cuir an cunnart,** risk. *Ir.* **cuntabhairt,** doubt. *O.Ir.* **cuntubart, cumtubart, cundubart,** *dubium. Wb.* gl. *Also* **cuntart** (freq. in *Turner*).

cunnartach, *a.* dangerous.

cunnbhalach, coon-valuch, *a.* steady, constant, precise, well-shaped, well-formed, well-proportioned as a person ; affording means of support ; kind. *Ir.* **cundail, cunnail,** steady ; kindly ; discreet.

cunnbhalachd, coon-valuchc, *n. f.* steadiness, constancy, correctness ; proportion of limbs ; handsomeness.

cùnnradh, coonra, *n. m.* bargain ; a covenant. *Also* **cùnradh.** *M.Ir.* **cundrad,** merchandise, trading. *O.Ir.* **cunnrath,** contract, **cundrad,** gl. *merx.*

cunnt, coont, *v.* count, enumerate.

cunntair, coonter, *n. m.* counter, an arithmetician ; enumerator, accountant.

cunntaireachd, *n. f.* counting, reckoning.

cunntas, coontus, *n. m.* number, arithmetic ; **tha e cunntas,** he is working at arithmetic ; an account ; **pàidh do chunntas,** pay your account ; fr. *Eng.*

cunnuil, coonil, *n. f.* an objection. So *O'R.*

cup, *n. m.* cup. *Lat.* cūpa. *Also* **copan.**

cùp, *n. f.* a box-cart.

cupaill, *n. m.* the shrouds of a ship.

cùpar, *n. m.* a hawk.

cuplach, *a.* full of ship's shrouds.

cuplaich, cooplich, *v.* couple, etc.

cupull, coopul, *n. f.* a pair ; fr. *Eng.*

cur, coor, *n. m.* sowing ; snowing ; **cur an t-sìl,** sowing the seed ; **cur an t-sneachda,** snowing ; **cur na cloiche,** putting the stone ; **tha iad a' cur air a' chloich,** they are playing at putting the stone. *See* **cuir.**

cùra, cooru, *n. m.* a protector, a guardian ; setting, putting, throwing ; protection, guardianship ; **bithidh e 'na chùra orra,** he will be a protector to them. *Lat.* cura.

cura, *n. m.* the woof ; **dlùth is cura,** weft and woof ; fr. **cur.**

curach, cooruch, *n. m.* a canoe, coracle. *E.Ir.* **curach.** *O.Celt.* **kuruko-.**

curach, *n. m.* body (man or beast) ;

cha mhór a curach, tiny is her body. So *E.Ir.*

curachan, *n. m.* diminutive person, baby.

curachd, coorachc, *n. f.* sowing ; the quantity sown, or to be sown.

curadach, *a.* brave, heroic.

curadair, cooruder, *n. m.* curator ; a sower.

cùradh, curabh, *n. m.* affliction ; obstacle.

curaideach, correjuch, *a.* frisky, cunning. *See* **cuireid.**

curaidh, coory, *n. m.* a hero, champion. *E.Ir.* **caur, coraid.** *W.* **cawr.** *O.Celt.* **kavaro-s,** hero.

cùrainn, coorin, *n. f.* plaiding, a coverlet, coarse woollen cloth.

cùrainnich, coorinich, *v.* cover, set a table.

curaisde, *n. f.* a bog.

cùram, coorum, *n. m.* care, anxiety, charge, responsibility ; **air mo chùram-sa,** under my charge ; **na biodh cùram ort,** never you mind ; **bithidh iad fo chùram,** they will feel anxious. So *M.Ir.* *Lat.* cūra.

cùramach, cōōrumuch, *a.* careful, solicitous, anxious ; attentive.

curanta, coorantu, *a.* bold, heroic. *M.Ir.* **curata.**

curantachd, *n. f.* bravery.

curcais, coorcesh, *n. f.* bulrush ; flags ; hair. *M.Ir.* **curchas,** reed, hair.

cùrnaich, coornich, *v.* cover, envelop.

cùrr, coor, *n. m.* corner, site, pit. So *Ir.*

currac, *n. m.* a cap ; woman's cap or head-dress ; froth on glass of stout ; *pl.* **curraicean** ; **currac na cuthaig,** harebell, blue-bottle.

curracag, coorucag, *n. f.* a little heap ; a small stack of corn ; peat heap, cock of hay, a bubble ; a. **curracagach.**

curracag, coorucag, *n. m.* lapwing or pee-wit, sandpiper.

curradh, *n. m.* a crowding together.

curraidh, *a.* exhausting, difficult.

curran, cooran, *n. m.* a carrot ; **currain bhuidhe is currain gheala** ; carrots and parsnips ; horse panniers for corn, etc.

currasan, *n. m.* a pail ; a large deep vessel.

curtha, *a.* wearied ; same as **curraidh.**

currucadh, *n. m.* cooing (of pigeons).

cùrsa, coorsu, *n. m.* course ; **seòl do chùrsa,** steer your course ; career, layer.

cùrsachd, *n. f.* coursing.

cùrsaich, *v.* arrange in courses.

cùrsair, *n. m.* a courser, racer.

cùrsaireachd, *n. f.* coursing.

curta, cursta, *a.* infamous, shocking, wicked, impious.

cus, coos, *n. m.* too much ; enough ; superfluity ; many ; great quantity ;

tha sin cus, that is too much ; an d' fhuair thu iasg ? did you get fish ? cha d' fhuair cus, not " too much," *i.e.* not much ; chan 'eil i cus na's fhearr, she is not " too much " better, *i.e.* doubtful if she is any better.

cusag, *n. f.* wild mustard.

cusp, coosp, *n. f.* a kibe, chilblain, callosity (of the heel). So *Ir.*

cuspach, coospuch, *a.* kibed, as a heel.

cuspadh, *vbl. n. m.* act of driving off, shooing.

cuspair, coosper, *n. m.* a mark to aim at, an object of any kind. *M.Ir.* cuspóir, a bowshot ; target, aim ; theme.

cuspaireachd, coosperuchc, *n. f.* intermeddling, officiousness ; aiming, marking, throwing stones at an object.

cuspairich, coosperich, *v.* meddle, aim.

cuspunn, coospin, *n. f.* custom, tribute, import ; tigh-cuspuinn, custom house. *Also* cusmunn.

cut, coot, *v.* gut (as fish), dock.

cuta, cootu, *n. m., pl.* cutachan, a short log ; a cut of yarn.

cutach, cootuch, *a.* bob-tailed, curtailed, docked ; *n. f.* little woman. *W.* cwta.

cutag, cootag, *n. f.* 1. a little dumpy girl. 2. a short spoon. 3. a cutty pipe. 4. a gutting knife.

cutag, cootag, *n. f.* a circular kiln.

cutaich, cootich, *v.* curtail, dock.

cuthach, kŭ'-ach, *n. m.* fury, rage, hydrophobia ; tigh-cuthaich, a madhouse, *M.Ir.* cuthach. *See* caothach.

cuthag, coo-ag, *n. f.* cuckoo.

cuthaigeadh, coo-higu. *See* cothlam.

cutharlan, coo-hurlan, *n. m.* an earthnut, an onion.

D

d, the fourth letter of the Gaelic alphabet, denominated by the Irish dair, the oak tree.

d', for do, thy, or your, used before words beginning with a vowel or fh- ; as, d' each, thy horse ; d' fhear, thy husband. *See* do.

dà, *prep. +p. pron.* to him ; thoir dà e, give it to him ; da, to his ; da chù, to his dog.

dà, *num. adj.* two ; dà bhean, two women. *O.Ir.* dá (*m.*) ; dí (*f.*) ; dá n- (*n.*).

dabhach, dăv'-uch, *n. f.* a mashing-tun, or vat ; a huge lady ; urchair an doill m' an dabhaich, a throw, or blow at a venture ; a measure of land = four ploughgates—480 acres (*Skene*) ; 1½ miles sq. ; 416 acres ; land suf. to produce 48 bolls (*Jamieson*) ; measure varied with the quality of land.   Appears in placenames as Doch-. *O.Ir.* dabach, *amphora.* B. of D. dabach, land-measure.

dabhan, dăv'-an, *n. m.* pitcher.

dabhasg, dav'-usg, *n. m.* a deer.

dabhd, daud, *n. m.* sauntering.

dabhdail, daudul, *vbl. n. m.* act of sauntering, prowling, loitering.

dàbhliadhnach, *n. m.* a two-year-old beast (used of cattle). *Also* dòbhliadhnach.

dàcha, *a.* more likely, for dòcha.

dachaidh, dăch'-i, *n. f.* a home, dwellingplace ; residence, domicile ; *adv.* homewards ; a' dol dachaidh, going homewards. *Also* dathigh. *M.Ir.* diatig.

dà-chasach, dā'-chăs-uch, *a.* two-footed ; *n. m.* a biped ; gach dàchasach a tha agam, every biped I have.

dad, dadum, *n. m.* anything, aught, tittle ; ciod e th' ort ? what is wrong with you ? chan 'eil dad, nothing is wrong with me. *Ir.* dadadh, dadamh, a jot.

dadhas, dă'-us, *n. m.* a fallow deer.

dadmun, *n. m.* a mote.

dà-fhaobharach, dà-uvarach, *a.* twoedged.

daga, *n. f.* a pistol ; daga diollaid, a holster, a blunderbuss ; *pl.* dagachan.

daibh, dyv, to them ; thoir dhaibh, give them ; *prep.* do+*pron. suf.* 3 *pl.*

daibheid, dyvej, *n. m.* self-command, circumspection ; daibheideach, selfdenying.

daibhir, dyvir, *adj.* adverse, destitute ; daibhir no saoibhir, poor or rich ; *n. m.* the common, or worst pasture of a farm ; innis, the best pasture. *M.Ir.* dáidber, poor ; *opp.* sáidber.

daibhreas, dyvrus, *n. m.* poverty. *M.Ir.* dáidbre, poverty.

daiceall, *n. m.* shyness, modesty. *See* doicheall.

dàichealachd, dāchaluchc, *n. f.* stateliness, gracefulness (in appearance).

dàicheil, dāchal, *a.* graceful, stately, handsome ; likely ; strenuous, strong ; is ann bòidheach is chan ann dàicheil, it is pretty rather than handsome ; is minig a bha an donas dàicheil, often has the devil been handsome.

daidein, *n. m.* daddy, papa.

daigeil, dagel, *a.* firm, strong, well-built.

dail, dăl, *n. f.* a field, a plain, dale. *O.N.* dalr. Cf. *A.S.* dæl. *M.E.* dale.

dàil, dāl, *n. f.* delay ; respite ; interval ; thig gun dàil, come without delay ; dàil eadar an dà làmhnain, the intermediate space of the couples ; trust, credit ; dàil shè mìosan, credit for six months. *M.Ir.* dál, respite.

dail, *n. f.* a wooden collar (for cattle), a stall halter.

dàil, *n. f., gen.* dàlach, a meeting ; contact ; thàinig e 'n am dhàil, he came to meet me ; an dàil a chéile, in grips, come to blows ; an dàil an dòmhnaich, in view of Sunday. *O.Ir.* dál, a meeting, a court. *O.Celt.* datlâ.

dàil, *n. f.* portion, a tribe. *O.Ir.* dál, *O.Celt.* dâliô

dail-chuaich, *n. f.* an herb, violet.

dàilich, *v.* delay, defer, distribute.

daille, *n. f.* blindness. *Also* doille. *E.Ir.* daille.

dàimh, .dyv, *n. f.* connexion, affinity, relationship ; dlùth an dàimh, closely connected. *E.Ir.* dám, company, retinue. tribe. *O.Celt.* dâmâ. *Gr.* δῆμος, δᾶμος.

dàimheach, dyvach, *n. m.* a relation, friend ; *pl.* dàimhich.

dàimhealachd, dyvalachc, *n. f.* relationship, kindred spirit, habits, and disposition.

dàimheil, dyvol, *a.* kindred, fond of relations, affectionate ; closely related.

daimsear, dymsher, *n. m.* the rutting of deer.

daingeann, dainnionn, dyngun, *adj.* firm, strong, unmovable, tight. *O.Ir.* daigen, firm, strong. *O.Celt.* dangeno-s, firm.

daingneach, dynuch, *n. f.* a fortress, a fort, castle. *E.Ir.* daingen, fort.

daingneachas, dyngnuchas, *n. m.* assurance, confirmation, perfect security.

daingnich, dyngnich, *v.* fortify, confirm, establish, tighten. *O.Ir.* dindgne.

dàir, dār, *n. m.* the state of being lined, rutting (of cattle and deer) ; air dàir, a-bulling.

dàir, *v.* line, as a bull ; *vbl. a.* dàirte, lined, in calf. *E.Ir.* dáir, dairim, *inire vaccam vel ovem. O.Celt.* darô.

dair-chruaidh, dur-chroo-ay, *a.* oak-firm.

daire, *n. m.* oak ; hull of boat. *See* doire.

dairireach, durirach, *n. f.* a shot.

dairirich, *n. f.* loud rattling noise. *Also* stairearaich.

dais, dăsh, *n. m.* a mow in a barn of sheaf corn, or a pile of seasoned fish, or peats ; *v.* mow, pile as seasoned fish. *O.Ir.* dais, a heap. *O.Celt.* dasti-. Cf. *Sc.* dass. *O.N.* des, hayrick.

dais, dois, dash, *n. m.* a blockhead, a fool ; *pl.* daiseachan.

daiseachan, dashuchan, *n. m.* insipid rhymer.

daiseireachd, *n. f.* fooling.

dàite, dātiu, *a.* singed, burned.

daite, dătiu, *a.* coloured, dyed.

daithead, déhad, *n. f.* a diet, a meal.

dàl, *n. f.* lot, fate. *See* dail = portion.

dala, one of two. *See* dara.

dall, daül, *a.* blind ; blind person ; *v.* blind, dazzle ; 'gam dhalladh, blinding me. *E.Ir.* dall, gl. caecus. *O.Celt.* dvalno-s.

dallachran, *n. m.* ignorance, blindness.

dallag, *n. f.* a shrew-mouse, a leech ; kingfish, spotted dogfish.

dallan, *n. m.* a corn fan ; a hide corn-sieve, without holes. So in *Ir.*

dallanach, *n. f.* a large fan ; a volley or broadside ; blindness from excessive drinking ; air an dallanaich (blin' fu') completely intoxicated ; leig iad dall-anach, they fired a volley or broadside.

dallan-dà, *n. m.* blind-man's buff.

dallaran, *n.* a bewildered person. *Ir.* a purblind person.

dallaranachd, *n. f.* blindness, groping.

dallbhrat, daulvrat, *n. m.* blinding-wrap ; -na h-oidhche, the dark mantle of night.

dallchur, *n. m.* snowstorm, drifting snow.

dallta, *n. m.* the very same case, or way, or method ; *adv.* in the way, very same manner ; dallta Sheumais, just as James would have acted.

dalma, *adj.* audacious, bold, obstinate.

dalmachd, *n. f.* audacity, presumption, impertinence, forwardness.

dalta, *n. m.* a foster-child, stepson, stepdaughter, godson. *O.Ir.* dalte, pupil ; *alumnus.*

dam, *n. m.* mill-dam, reservoir.

damain, *v.* damn, curse ; *vbl. a.* damainte, accursed, most abandoned. *Lat.* damnare.

dàmais, damesh, *n. m.* draughts ; bòrd-dàmais, a draught-board.

damh, dáv, *n. m.* an ox, bullock ; stag. *O.Ir.* dam, an ox, a champion, a hero. *O.Celt.* damo-s.

damh, *n. m.* a mast ; a joist.

dàmhair, dāvir, *n. f.* 1. the rutting of deer. 2. high time ; dàmhair dùsgadh, time to awake. 3. keen, earnest. *M.Ir.* dam-gaire, stag-roaring.

damhais, dáv'-èsh, *v.* dance, caper.

damhan-allaidh, *n. m.* a spider. So *M.Ir.*

damhsa, dausu, dancing, a ball. *M.Ir.* damsa, a dancing ; a dancer, caperer.

damh-sùirne, *n. m.* ridge-pole over the " cave " of a corn-kiln.

damnadh, dăm'-nă, *n. m.* damnation ; *vbl. n.* act of damning ; damnar e, he shall be damned. *Lat.* damnatio.

dàn, *adj.* resolute, intrepid ; presumptuous ; cha dàna leam innseadh dhuit, I dare not tell you ; cho dàn is a chaidh e air aghaidh, he went forward so resolutely. *O.Ir.* dána, dáne, *audax.*

dàn, *n. m.* what is given, destiny, fate; ma tha sin an dàn, if that be ordained. Cf. *Lat.* donum, gift. *O.Ir.* dán, a gift, endowment. *O.Celt.* dâno-, gift.

dàn, *n. m.* poem, song, ditty. *O.Ir.* dán, craft, art, science. *Wb. 18ᶜ. Gl.* medicus. "Is ionann dán is ceárd"; dán is the same as art, craft; dándíreach, old metrical system practised by the trained Irish bards.

danach, *interj.* a strong negation; an danach ceum, the "divil" a step.

dànach, *a.* poetical, of poetry.

dànachd, dàn'-achc, *n. f.* poetry.

dànachd, *n. f.* boldness. *E.Ir.* dánaigecht, boldness, familiarity.

dànadas, dānudus, *n. m.* presumption, familiarity; audacity, boldness, assurance. *M.Ir.* dánatus, boldness (used in a good and also a bad sense).

dànaich, dàn'-ich, *v.* defy, dare.

dannarra, *a.* mulish, stubborn, obstinate, contumacious, opinionative.

dannarrachd, danuruchc, *n. f.* stubbornness, obstinacy, boldness, resolution.

danns, daus, *v.* dance; dannsa, *n. m.* a dance. *O.F.* danser. *O.H.G.* dans.

dàntachd, dànt'-ăchc, *n. f.* fatalism.

dao, *a.* obstinate. *O.Ir.* doe, *gen.* doi, *tardus.*

daobhaidh, dūvy, *a.* wicked, perverse.

daoch, *n. f.* disgust; horror.

daochan, dūchan, *n. m.* anger.

daoi, duï, *a.* wicked; foolish; an daoi, the devil.

daoidhear, dūyer, *n. m.* wicked man, a fraud (of a man).

daoimean, dymon, *n. m.* diamond; fr. *Eng.*

daoineachd, dūnachc, *n. f.* population, humanity. *O.Ir.* dóinacht.

daoire, dū-ru, *a.* more or most dear; *n.* extreme dearness; na's daoire, dearer.

daol, dūl, *n. f.* a chafer, beetle. *E.Ir.* dael.

daolag, *n. f.* little chafer, a beetle.

daolair, dūlir, *n. m.* a lazy man, a niggard, slow, creeping fellow. So *Ir.*

daolaireachd, *n. f.* playing the sluggard.

daonna, *a.* human; humane; an cinne daonna, mankind.

daonnachd, *n. f.* humanity; fear na daonnachd, the humane man. *See* daoineachd.

daonnan, *adv.* always, continually, habitually, at all times. *Also* daondan.

daor, *a.* servile, high-priced, dear, costly; scant, scarce; bliadhna dhaor, a year of scarcity; abandoned; complete, corrupted; daor shlaoightire, a most abandoned rascal; daor bhodach, a

complete churl; daor bhalach, a complete boor. *O.Ir.* dóire, slavery, *captivitas.*

daorach, dūruch, *n. f.* drunkenness.

daoranach, dūranuch, *n. m.* a slave.

daormunn, dūrmun, *n. m.* miser, diminutive creature.

daorsa, *n. f.* famine, dearth; bondage, captivity.

dà-pheighinn, dā-feyin, *n. f.* two pence Scots; ancient coin.

d'ar, *prep.* and *pron.*; do ar, into our; d'ar cloinn, to our children.

dara, *a.* second; the second; an dara uair, the second time; an dara fear, either one. *O.Ir.* indara, indarna, indala-n.

darach, *n. m.* oak timber, hull of a boat. *E.Ir.* dair. *O.Ir.* daur, *gen.* darach. *W.* dâr. *O.Celt.* daru-.

darag, *n. f.* stump of a tree, an oak.

dararach, *n. f.* a volley; stunning noise.

dara-tomain, *a.* bounding; le ruith dara-tomain, with a bounding race.

darcan, *n. m.* the hollow of the hand.

darcan, *n. m.* a teal.

da rireabh, *adv.* in truth, really, in earnest. *M.Ir.* daríríb, doríríb, *id. prep.* (de + fíre, truth). *Marstr.*

darna, *a.* second; either the one or the other; an darna cuid, either of the two. *Also* an dala = *O.Ir.* indala (ind + aile).

das, *n. f.* a horn.

dàsachd, *n. f.* fury, rage, madness. *O.Ir.* dásact, madness. *O.Celt.* dvâstajô, I make mad.

dàsan, *prep.* and *pron.* to him; thoir dásan e, give it to him.

dàsunnach, *a.* cunning.

dàth, *v.* singe. *E.Ir.* dóthim.

dath, dă, *v.* colour, tinge, dye; *n. m.* dye, colour, tinge. So *E.Ir.*

dathadair, dahader, *n. m.* dyer.

dathadaireachd, da-huderuchc, *n. f.* the process of colouring; trade of a dyer.

dathail, da-hal, *a.* well-coloured.

dathas, dahas, *n. f.* fallow deer. *Also* damhasg, dabhasg.

dé, *int. pron.* what? dè b'aille leat, what is your will? For ciod e.

dé, *gen.* of Dia, God.

dé, *adv.* an dè, yesterday. *O.Ir.* indé, ané.

de, je, *prep.* of. With *pers. pron.: sing.* 1. diom, of or from me. 2. diot, of thee. 3. de (*m.*), of him; di (*f.*), of her. *pl.* 1. dinn. 2. dibh. 3. diubh. *O.Ir. sing.* 1. díim. 2. díit. 3. de (dí-e), dí. *pl.* 1. díin. 2. díib. 3. díib. *O.Ir.* dé.

dèabh, jiav, *v.* drain, dry up, shrink; dhèabh e, he died (from loss of blood).

dèabhadh, jiāvu, *n. m.* a shrinking, drying; small trickling of water, last few drops; a soft place between two lochs.

deabhaidh, deabhadh, *n. m.* dispute, skirmish, battle.

deacaid, jacej, *n. f.* bodice, jacket.

deacair, jacir, *a.* difficult, sore. *O.Ir.* deccair, difficult, hard.

deacaireachd, *n. f.* difficulty.

deach, dyech, deachaidh, *pret.* of *v.* theirig ; an deach e dhachaigh, has he gone home ? *E.Ir.* dechaid.

deachamh, dyêch'-uv, *n. m.* 1. tithe, tenth. 2. decimation. *O.Ir.* dechmad, tenth, tithe, space of ten days.

deachd, jechc, *v.* indite, dictate, inspire ; make completely certain ; assure positively. *Lat.* dicto ; early loan from *Lat.* dictare.

deachdadh, *vbl. n. m.* inditing, composing, inspiring. *M.Ir.* dechtad.

deachdair, *n. f.* dictator. *Ir.* dechtoir, dictator, teacher (*Lh.*), lawgiver, *O'R.*

deadh, diü, *a.* prop; deagh, *q.v.*

deadhan, de'an, *n. m.* a dean, a deacon. *Ir.* deaganach (*Lh.*).

deagal, *n. m.* twilight.

deagh, *a.* good, excellent ; deagh bheus, good conduct ; deagh ghean, goodwill, kindness ; deagh ainm, good name ; deagh always stands before the noun it qualifies. *O.Ir.* deg-, dag-, best-. *W.* da. *O.Celt.* dago-s, good. *Lat.* decus.

deaghad, *n. m.* diet, living, morals.

deaghrach, *n. m.* stinging tingling pain.

deal, jal, *a.* keen, eager : more properly deil ; cho deal is a tha e aig a ghnothuch, so enthusiastic at his business.

deal, jal, *a.* friendly, relative.

deal, jal, *n. f.* a leech. *Also* geal. *Ir.* deal, bloodsucker ; deala, leech. *O'R.* *O.Ir.* del, a teat. *W.* gêl. *O.Celt.* dilo-.

dealachadh, jaluchu, *vbl. n. m.* separation, divorce ; a division ; act of separating, divorcing.

dealachail, jaluchol, *a.* causing separation ; that may be separated, separable.

dealaich, jalich, *v. n.* separate, divide, part with ; cha dealaich mi ris, I will not part with it. *E.Ir.* " deil .i. delugud." *O'Dav.*

dealaidh, jaly, *a.* relative, friendly.

dealair, jalir, *v.* shine, beam, gleam.

dealan, jalan, *n. m.* cross-bar on a door.

dealanach, *n. m.* lightning. *O.Ir.* gellan.

dealan-dé, jalan-jay, *n. m.* 1. a butterfly. 2. fiery circle (made by swinging a firebrand).

dealann. *See* deileann.

dealas, jalas, *n. m.* keenness, zeal, loyalty.

dealasach, *a.* keen, eager, zealous.

dealbh, jalv, *n. m., pl.* deilbh, figure, image, form ; order, arrangement ; gnothuch gun dealbh, an absurd thing. *O.Ir.* delb. *O.Celt.* delvâ.

dealbh, *v.* form, shape ; devise, plot, contrive ; set a warp. tha i a' deilbh, she is warping or setting a warp.

dealbhach, jalvach, *a.* handsome, well-shaped ; likely, probable.

dealbhadair, jalvader, *n. m.* deviser, framer, former ; warper ; a portrait painter.

dealbhadaireachd, *n. f.* warping ; delineation, framing, shaping.

dealbhadan, jalvudan, *n. m.* a mould, frame.

dealbhadh, *vbl. n. m.* act of delineating, forming, shaping, contriving.

dealbhaich, jalvich, *v.* shape, form, mould.

dealbhchluich, jalv-, *n. f.* play, stage-play, drama.

deal-each, *n. f.* horse-leech.

dealg, jalg, *n. f., gen. s.* deilg ; *pl.* deilgne, a thorn, prickle, a skewer, a bodkin, a hairpin, a stocking-wire. *O.Ir.* delg, a thorn.

dealgach, jalgach, *a.* prickly, thorny.

dealgan, jalgan, *n. m.* collar-bone ; spindle. *Also* fearsaid.

dealg-guailne, *n. f.* shoulder-brooch.

dealrach, jalruch, *a.* shining, brilliant, refulgent, resplendent, radiant, bright.

dealradh, jalru, *vbl. n. m.* effulgence, refulgence, splendour, lustre, radiance ; act of gleaming, shining, beaming. *E.Ir.* dellrad.

dealraich, jalrich, *v.* shine, beam, gleam, glitter, flash, emit rays.

dealt, jalt, *n. m.* dew, rain glittering on the grass ; drizzle.

dealtair, jalter, *v.* glitter, gild.

dealtradh, *vbl. n. m.* glitter, besprinkling ; bedropping ; varnishing.

dèam, jaum, *n. m.* sound ; chan 'eil déam aige, he cannot utter a sound ; he is stunned.

deamhais, deimhis, devish, *n. m.* sheep-shears. *E.Ir.* demes = dá scín, two blades. *Corm. Gl.* mes, cut.

deamhan, joün, *n. m.* devil, demon. *O.Ir.* demon. *Gr.* δαίμων.

deamhnuidh, *a.* devilish, malicious.

dèan, jiän, *v.* make, do, act, perform, dèan urnuigh, pray ; dèan deifir, hasten ; dèan gàirdeachas, rejoice ; dèan uaill, boast, brag. *O.Ir.* dogníu, dénim (facio), *imperat.* déne.

dèanachdach, jēnuchcuch, *v.* vehement, keen, incessant ; uisge dèanachdach, vehement rain ; as speech, emphatic ;

labhair e gu dèanachdach, he spoke emphatically.

dèanadach, jēnuduch, *a.* industrious, persevering, laborious, diligent; tha e dèanadaich, it is raining.

dèanadas, jēnudus, *n. m.* industry, diligence, perseverance, activity.

dèanadh, jēnu, *cond.* of *v.* dèan, would make; *imper. 3rd sing.* let him make, do.

dèanamh, jēnuv, *inf.* of dèan; a' dèanamh, a-doing. *O.Ir.* dénum.

dèanas, jēnus, *n. m.* an act, result of one's industry or labour.

dèanasach, jēnusuch, *a.* industrious.

dèanasachd, *n. f.* industry.

deann, jaun, *n. f.* a small quantity of anything, like meal, snuff; chan 'eil deann snaoisean agam, I have not a particle of snuff.

deann, *n. f.* a rush, a race; thàinig e steach 'na dheann, he came in at full speed; an t-each 'na dheann, the horse at full speed. *E.Ir.* deinmne. *Corm. Gl.*

deannag, janag, *n. f.* a very small quantity of snuff, meal, etc. *Also* deannan.

deannal, janal, *n. m.* a spell or a little while at anything with all one's might, —conflict; shot; hurry.

deanntag, jauntag, *n. f.* nettle. *Ir.* neantóg. *E.Ir.* nenaid.

deanntrach, jauntruch, *n. f.* flashing, sparkling.

dèanta, jēnta, *vbl. a.* done, made.

dèantanas, *n. m.* an act.

dèarail, jēral, *a.* poor, wretched. *O.Ir.* deróil, *penuria.*

dearbadan-dé, jarbadan-jay, *n. m.* butter-fly.

dearbh, jarv, *v.* prove, confirm, try; dearbh sin, prove that; *adj.* sure, certain, very identical; an dearbh ni, the very thing; *adv.* gu dearbh, yes, indeed; truly, really, certainly. *O.Ir.* derb.

dearbhachd, jarvachc, *n. f.* demonstration.

dearbhadas, jarvudus, *n. m.* capability of proof; way of leading a proof.

dearbhadh, jarvu, *vbl. n. m.* proof, confirmation; evidence; proving, confirming, demonstrating; mar dhearbhadh air sin, as a proof of that. *O.Ir.* derbid.

dearbhann, jarvun, *n. m.* axiom.

dearbhas, jarvus, *n. m.* a proof.

dearbh-bheachd, *n. m.* certainty.

dearbh-bhràthair, *n. m.* true brother. *Ir.* full brother.

dearbh-chinnte, *n. f.* full certainty.

dearbhta, *vbl. a.* proved, established; confirmed, demonstrated.

dearc, dearcag, jarc, *n. f.* a berry; a grape. *O.Ir.* derc. *O.Celt.* derko-s.

dearc, jarc, *v.* see, behold. *O.Ir.* dercim. *Gr.* δέρκομαι.

dearc, *n. f.* 1. an eye; dearc lìonta, a full, beautifully shaped eye. 2. a cave, a hole. *O.Ir.* derc. *O.Celt.* derkô, I see.

dearc-aitinn, *n. f.* a juniper berry (*also* dearc iùbhair); dearc dharaich, an acorn; dearc fhrangach, a currant; dearc fhìona, a grape; dearc-ola, an olive.

dearc-luachrach, *n. f.* a lizard or asp. *Also* dearc. *Ir.* earc-luachra.

dearcnach, *a.* handsome.

dearcnachadh, *n. m.* marking or criticising, scrutinising keenly.

dearcnaich, jarcnich, *v.* criticise, look steadfastly and keenly.

dearg, jarg. 1. *adj.* red. 2. *superl. adj.* in a bad sense; dearg-amadan, perfect fool; dearg-mheirleach, notorious thief; dearg-nàmhaid, sworn enemy. *O.Ir.* derg.

dearg, *n. m.* red colour, crimson; *v.* redden, make red, make an impression; cha do dhearg e air, he did not *redden* it (much less draw blood), he made no impression on it; cha dearg mi air, I cannot manage it; plough.

dearg, *n. m.* 1. red deer; "fiadhach nan dearg," stalking the deer. 2. ploughed land.

deargadh, *vbl. n. m.* act of reddening; a red mark; a slight impression (*i.e.* reddening of the skin by teeth or a blow or sharp instrument); an d'fhuair sibh iasg? Cha d'fhuair sinn deargadh, did you get any fish? No, not even one (*lit.* we did not get a reddening). *O.Ir.* dergaim, I redden.

deargan, *n. m.* red stain; a nebula.

dearganach, jarganuch, *n. m.* a soldier, a red-coat.

deargan-allt, *n. m.* a kestrel-hawk.

deargan-doirionn, *n. m.* a nebula.

deargann, *n. f.* a flea. *Also* deargad.

dearg-fhraoich, *n. m.* a goldfinch.

dearg-las, *v.* blaze, burn intensely.

deargnaidh, *a.* unlearned.

deargshuil, *n. f.* a red or bloodshot eye.

dèarlan, *a.* brimful. *See* earlàn = derlán, der (intens.), làn (full).

dearmad, jarmud, *n. m.* an omission, neglect. *O.Ir.* dermet, *oblivio.*

dearmadach, *adj.* forgetful; negligent, careless. *O.Ir.* dermatach, oblivious.

dearmadachd, *n. f.* extreme forgetfulness or negligence.

dearmaid, jarmid, *v.* omit, forget. *O.Ir.* dermatim, I forget.

dearmail, jarmal, *n. f.* anxiety, solicitude, worldliness.

deàrn, jarn, *v.* do ; a by-form of **dèan.** *O.Ir.* derninn, facerem ; a conj. form of dogníu.

deàrn, jārn, *n. f.* palm of the hand. *O.Ir.* derna.

dearnadair, jārnuder, *n. m.* a palmist.

dearnadaireachd, *n. f.* palmistry, divination by the palm of the hand.

deàrnagan, jārnagan, *n. m.* a cake.

deàrnan, jārnan, *n. m.* a shoemaker's waxed thread. *Also* streangan.

dearras, jaras, *n. m.* keenness, enthusiasm.

dearrasach, *a.* keen, eager.

dearrasan, jarusan, *n. m.* a crackling, buzzing, rustling. *Ir.* dearrasán, hurry, snarling.

deàrrs, jārs, *v.* shine, beam, emit rays ; gleam, radiate, burnish.

deàrrsach, jārsach, *a.* shining, radiant, flushed. So *Ir.*

deàrrsadh, *n. m.* a gleam, a ray ; radiance, effulgence, a flush (of anger).

deàrrsaich, jārsich, *v.* shine. *Ir.* dearsaim, I shine, beam.

deàrrsanta, jārsantu, *a.* radiant, effulgent, gleaming, beaming.

deàrrsgnaich, *v.* polish. So *Ir.*

deàrrsgnaidh, *a.* burnished, brilliant, excellent.

deàrrsnaich, jārsnich, *v.* polish, gild.

deàrrsnaiche, *n. m.* a polisher.

deas, jes, *n. m.* the right (hand) ; the south ; **bho 'n deas,** from the south ; *adj.* right ; south ; **gaoth deas,** south wind ; proper ; **rinn thu sin gu deas,** you have done that properly ; well-shaped, handsome ; **duine deas,** a well-shaped, personable individual ; ready, prepared ; **a bheil thu deas,** are you prepared ; easily accomplished ; **bu deas domh sin a dhèanamh,** I could easily accomplish that ; **an làmh dheas,** the right hand. *O.Ir.* dess, right, south. *W.* deheu. *O.Celt.* dekso-s.

deasach, jesuch, *n. m.* southerner.

deasachadh, jesuchu, *vbl. n. m.* the act of baking ; a baking, preparing.

deasad, *n. m.* readiness.

deasaich, jesich, *v.* prepare, bake, gird ; **deasaich do chlaidheamh,** gird your sword.

deasbair, jesbir, *v.* argue, dispute.

deasbaire, *n. m.* a disputant.

deasbaireachd, jesbirachc, *n. f.* disputation, dispute, wrangling, reasoning.

deasbud, jesbud, *n. m.* a dispute, a debate.

deaschainnt, jes-chynt, *n. f.* eloquence.

deaschainnteach, *a.* eloquent, witty, ready in replying.

deasfhacal, jes-acul, *n. m.* ready word, smart reply.

deasgadh, *n. f.* lees, yeast.

deasgainn, jesgin, *n. f.* barm, rennet. *O.Ir.* descad, leaven.

deas-ghnàth, *n. m.* ceremony.

deasgraich, *n. m.* heterogeneous mess.

deas-làmhach, jeslavuch, *a.* dexterous.

deasmaireas, jesmirus, *n. f.* curiosity. So *Ir.*

deasoireach, *a.* spicy.

deat, jet, *n. m.* a year-old unshorn sheep ; **cosmhail ri deata,** like an unfleeced year-old sheep, or wedder.

deatach, jetuch, *n. f.* smoke. *See* deathach.

deatam, jetum, *n. m.* keenness, eagerness, anxiety. *O.Ir.* dethitiu, care. *Wi.*

deatamach, jetumuch, *a.* necessary ; needed ; eager, keen for the world.

deatamas, *n. m.* a requisite ; a family necessary or want.

deathach, jehach, *n. f.* smoke. *O.Ir.* dé, *gen.* diad. *Later,* dethach and detfadach.

deathadach, je-huduch, *a.* disappointed, disappointing. *O.Ir.* dethiden, dethidnech.

deathaid, *n. f.* a sucking one. *See* deat.

dee, jay, *n. pl.* gods. *Also* diathan.

déibhleid, *n. f.* an awkward or feeble person. *E.Ir.* dedblén, weakling.

deibhtear, *n. m.* debtor ; fr. *Eng.*

deic, *a.* fit, convenient ; "cha deic dhomh," I have more than enough of it.

deich, jech, *n. f.* ten ; *a.* ten. *O.Ir.* dech. *W.* deg. *Lat.* decem. *O.Celt.* dékn.

deicheamh, jechiv, *num.* tenth, tenth part. *O.Ir.* dechmad.

deich-fillte, *a.* tenfold.

deichnear, jechnur, *n. m.* ten persons ; dechenbar, dechnebar, decem viri (Z^2).

deichroinn, jech-ryn, *n. m.* a decimal.

deichshlisneach, jech-lisnuch ; deich-thaobhach, jech-huv-uch, *n. m.* a decagon.

déideadh, jēju, *n. m.* the toothache. *Also* a' chruimh.

déideag, jējag, *n. f.* a pebble, toy ; a darling.

déideag, *n. f.* rib-wort. *Also* slàn-lus.

déidh, jēy, *n. f.* keen desire, wish, longing.

déidh, an déidh, jey, *prep.* after. *O.Ir.* déad, *finis* ; **macc in-déad a athar,** the son after his father. *See* deòidh.

déidhealachd, jeyaluchc, *n. f.* extreme or degree of desire or propensity.

déidheil, jēyol, *a.* very fond of, or addicted to ; **déidheil air an uisge** bheatha, fond of, or addicted to, whisky.

déidhinn, jeyin, *prep.* concerning, of ; ciod mu dhéidhinn ? what about it ?

déidh-làimh, jey-lyv, *adv.* too late, afterwards.

deifir, jefir, *n. f.* speed, expedition ; haste, hurry. *E.Ir.* deithbhir, necessary, fit ; as *n.* haste.

deifreach, *a.* requiring expedition ; gnothuch deifreach, an affair requiring the utmost expedition ; hasty, hurried.

deifrich, jefrich, *v. i.* hasten, expedite ; deifrich ort, be quick, or clever.

deigh, *n. f.* ice ; *a.* deigheach. *Ir.* oighear. *O.Ir.* aig, ind aig, the ice.

déighlean, jēlen, *n. m.* quire of paper.

deil, jel, *n. m.* an axle, lathe, sharp iron rod. *O.Ir.* rod. *O.Celt.* deli-, deljo-.

deil, *a.* enthusiastic, keen ; cho deil aig a gnothuch, so keen or enthusiastic at her business ; indefatigable, persevering, industrious ; frenzy.

deil. See deal, leech.

deilbh, jelv, *n. f.* warping (for weaving) ; a forming, sketching.

deilbh, *v.* form, warp ; sketch. *O.Ir.* delbaim, I form, shape.

deilbhein, jelven, *n. m.* little image, a little web.

deile, jelu, *n. f.* enthusiasm, industry.

déile, jāl'-à, *n. f.* a deal, plank.

déileadair, jēluder, *n. m.* a sawyer.

deileann, jelun, *n. m.* loud, sharp barkings. *E.Ir.* deilm, noise.

deileas, jelus, *n. m.* eagerness, a grudging. See dealas.

déile-bhogadain, jēlu-voguden, *n. f.* seesaw.

deilginneach, jelginuch, *n. f.* herpes, shingles.

deilgne, *pl.* of dealg, *q.v.*

deilgneach, jelgnuch, *a.* prickly ; cadal-deilgneach, cadal deilgeanach, prickly sensation in a numbed limb ; " pins and needles."

deilich, jelich, *v.* separate, part. Cf. dealaich.

déilig, jēlig, *v.* deal with ; from the *Eng.*

deilleanachd, jeylenuchc, *n. f.* act of honey-gathering (by bee).

déillseag, déiseag, jēlshag, *n. f.* slap with open hand (on buttock).

deiltreadh, jeltru, *n. m.* gilding, lacquering ; *a.* deiltreach.

deimhinn, jevin, *a.* certain, sure, of a truth ; gu deimhinn, verily. *O.Ir.* demin.

deimhinneachd, jevinachc, *n. f.* complete certainty or proof.

deimhinnich, jevinich, *v.* verify, confirm, ascertain, demonstrate.

déine, jēna, *a.* more keen, more certain ; *n. f.* eagerness, keenness ; *v.* dian.

déineachd, jēnachc, *n. f.* ardour.

déineis, jēnesh, *n. f.* faint attempt to be diligent or eager ; keenness.

deir, jer, *v.* say, affirm ; a deirim, I say ; a deir esan, says he. *O.Ir.* adber, *dicit.*

deir, *n. f.* shingles. *Also* an ruaidh.

déirc, jērc, *n. f.* alms, charity. *O.Ir.* dearc, *amor* ; dérc, déserc, gním desercce, *actus amoris.*

déirceach, *a.* beggarly, poor.

déirceag, *n. f.* a penurious woman.

déirceil, *a.* charitable.

déircire, *n. m.* beggar ; an almoner.

deireadh, jera', *n. m.* end, conclusion ; stern of a boat ; deireadh na luinge, the stern of the ship ; deireadh cuaich, a round stern ; rear ; deireadh poite, lees ; air deireadh, behind, in the rear ; mu dheireadh, at last ; toiseach tighinn is deireadh falbh, first to come and last to go ; deireadh linn, the last-born of a family. *O.Ir.* dered. *BD.* derad.

deireannach, jeranach, *a.* last, hindermost, hindmost, latter ; 'sna làithean deireannach, in the latter days ; last. *O.Ir.* dédenach, *finalis.*

deireas, jeras, *n. m.* requisite, a convenience ; dearasan, domestic necessaries or convenience ; tha mi gun deireas, I am quite well ; injury, loss, want.

deireasach, *a.* very requisite, needful, defective.

deirge, jergu, *n. f.* redness, red ; *a.* more or most red. *Also* deirgead ; fr. dearg.

déis, jēsh, *adv.* an déis, after. *O.Ir.* di éis. *BD.* daneis ; fr. éis, footstep, track.

déis, *v.* skelp the breech.

déisbeid, jēsh-bej, *n. f.* a boil.

deisciobul, jeshcibul, *n. m.* a disciple. *Lat.* discipulus.

deise, *n. f.* suit of clothes ; symmetry of the body ; shapeliness ; proportionable parts ; *compar.* of deas ; more or most fit ; shapely, proportioned. See deas.

deisead, jeshud, *abstr. n. f.* degree of symmetry ; handsomeness, elegance of person, etc.

déiseag, jēshag, *n. f.* a little skelp on the breech. *Also* stéiseag.

deisealachd, jeshaluchc, *n. f.* readiness, convenience ; ni e deisealachd, it will come in handy.

deisealan, jeshalan, *n. m.* slap on the cheek, box on the ear.

deisearach, jesharuch, *a.* 1. conveniently situated, applicable ; deisearach air

an sgoil, near the school, etc. 2. sunny, southern exposure ; fr. **deas.**

deisearachd, *n. f.* convenience in point of situation, applicability.

deiseil, *a.* sun-wise, toward the south, southward ; ready. *O.Ir.* **dessel,** *id.*

déisg, jĕshc, *v.* crack, split, dry up.

déisinn, jēshin, **déistinn,** *n. f.* disgust, abhorrence ; poor appetite ; " edge " ; **tha déisinn air fhiaclan,** his teeth are on edge.

deisir, jĕshir, *n. f.* southern exposure ; **deisir a' ghlinne,** the southern exposure of the glen.

deismireach, jĕshmiruch, *a.* curious.

déistinneach, dēshtinuch, *a.* disgusting, causing squeamishness.

déistinneachd, jēshtinachc, *n. f.* disgustfulness, extreme disgustfulness.

deitheasach, je-hesach, *a.* scarce (food and fodder).

deithneamhach, jenevach, *a.* worldly.

deithneas, jenes, *n. f.* haste, speed ; fr. **déine,** *abstr.* fr. **dian.** *McB.*

deò, *n. f.* inver, where water runs into the sea.

deò, jō, *n. m.* and *f.* breath, the vital spark, the ghost ; spark of fire ; ray of light ; **gun deò,** breathless ; **tha e an impis an deò a chall,** he is on the eve of giving up the ghost ; **chan 'eil deò ghaoith ann,** there is not a breath of wind ; **deò gealbhain,** a spark of fire ; **deò soluis,** a ray of light ; **gun deò léirsinn,** without a ray of vision, stone-blind ; **deò-gréine,** sunbeam, Fionn's banner.

deoc, *v.* suck.

deocadh, *vbl. n. m.* act of sucking.

deocan, jocan, *n. m.* noise made in sucking.

deoch, joch, *n. f., pl.* **deochannan,** a drink, draught, liquor ; **deoch-eiridinn,** a potion ; **deoch an doruis,** a stirrup-cup ; **deoch slàinte,** a toast, a health ; spirits, all sorts of drinks, liquors ; **deoch-eòlais,** the first glass drunk to a stranger ; **deoch m' eolais ort,** may we be better acquainted. *O.Ir.* **deug,** *gen.* **dig.** *O.Celt.* **degu-.**

deòdhas, deòthas, jō-has, *n. m.* eagerness, desire. So *O'R.*

deoghail, *v.* suck. *Ir.* **deobhal,** sucking.

deòidh, jōy, *as adv.* ; **fa dheòidh,** at last. *O.Ir.* **fo diud** (*dat.* of **déad,** end). *O.Celt.* **de-vedo-n.**

deòin, jōïn, *n. f.* will, pleasure, acquiescence, assent ; **a dheòin no dh' aindeoin,** whether he wishes it or not. So *E.Ir.*

deòir, jōr, *n. pl.* of **deur,** a tear, *q.v.*

deòirid, *n. m.* a broken-hearted, tearful person. *Also* **deoirideach.**

deòiridh, deòraidh, jōry, *n. m.* an exile, a pilgrim, stranger, destitute person. *M.Ir.* **deorad** ; " **deòrain** is dileach-dain," destitute and orphaned ones.

deònach, jōnuch, *a.* willing ; *adv.* most willingly, voluntarily ; **is deònach a dhèanainnse e,** most willingly would I do it.

deònaich, jōnich, *v.* grant, give consent, vouchsafe ; **deònaich dhuinn gàird-eachas do shlàinte,** vouchsafe unto us the joys of thy salvation. *Ir.* **deónaighim.**

deòrachd, *n. f.* affliction.

deòthas, jōhus, *n. m.* longing or eagerness of a calf for its mother ; lust. So *Ir.*

deòthasach, *a.* keen (as a calf) ; very lustful (as a person).

deth, je (*prep.* et *pron.*) of him, of it, off ; **thoir dheth a' phoit,** take off the pot.

de-theine, je-hénu, *n. f.* a heated boring-iron. *Also* **de-theallaidh.**

detheode, *n.* henbane.

detiach, deteigheach, *n. f.* the weasand, gullet. *Also* **it-igheach.**

deubh, jĕv, *n. f.* fetters for the fore feet of a horse. *Also* **deubh-leum, deubh-ann.**

deubh, jav, *v.* leak, chink, as a dish. *See* **dèabh.**

deubhoil, jēvol, *n. f.* enthusiasm, eagerness ; *adj.* keen, enthusiastic (**dee-bhoil**).

deuch, *v.* taste, try, sort.

deuchainn, jēchin, *n. f.* trial, taste, experiment, essay, distress ; **fhuair mi deuchainn deth,** I got a taste or trial of it.

deuchainnach, jēchinuch, *a.* trying, difficult.

deud, jēd, *n. m.* a tooth ; *coll.* the teeth. *O.Ir.* **det.** *O.W.* **dant.** *Lat.* **dens** ; *gl.* **dentis.**

deudach, *coll. n. f.* teeth.

deudach, *n. f.* toothbrush.

deud-gheal, jēd-yal, *a.* white-toothed.

deug, jēg, *n. pl.* teens ; used only in composition ; **coig-deug,** fifteen. *O.Ir.* **déac, déc,** ten.

deugachadh, *vbl. n. m.* act of going into " -teens " ; **tha e air deugachadh,** it is thirteen or more ; it has gone into -teens.

deur, jĕrr, *n. m.* a drop, a tear ; **a' sileadh nan deur,** shedding tears ; **chan 'eil deur an so,** there is not a drop here. *Also* **diar.** *O.Ir.* **dér.** *W.* **dagr.** *O.Celt.* **dakrû,** tear. *Cf. Gr.* δάκρυ.

deurach, *a.* tearful, sorrowful ; *n. f.* a burning pain. *Also* **diarach.**

deurshuileach, jēr-huluch, *a.* blear-eyed.

dh', aspirated form of d' for do ; sign of the *past*, used before fh and before a vowel ; as, dh' fhàg e i, he abandoned her, he left her ; dh' aithnich mi, I understood, I recognised.

dhà, *asp*. of dà, *q.v.*

dh'aindeoin, yenon, *adv*. in defiance, spite of ; in spite of ; against one's will. do + an + deòin-.

dhi, *prep*. do + *pron*. i, to her ; thoir dhi, give her. *See* dà.

dhomh, *prep*. do (to) + *pron. suf*. I *pers. s*., to me ; innis dhomh, tell me ; thoir dhomh, give me ; dèan dhomh, do for me, or to me.

di-, ji, *n. m*. a day ; di-luain, Monday ; di-màirt, Tuesday ; di-ciadaoin, Wednesday ; diar-daoin, Thursday ; di-haoine, Friday ; di-sathurn, Saturday; di-dòmhnuich, Sunday. *O.Ir*. dia ; *die*. *O.Celt*. dijas.

di-, *neg. prefix*. *Ir*. di, dio. *O.Ir*. di. *O.Celt*. dê. *Also intens. pref*. *O.Ir*. dí, dí-mar, very great ; dí-nert = vast strength.

dia, jia, *n. m*. a god, God, the Almighty ; *pl*. dee, diathan. *O.Ir*. día. *W*. duw. *O.Celt*. deivo-s, dîvo-s.

diabhluidh, jiävly and jialy, *a*. devilish, hellish.

diabhluidheachd, *n. f*. devilishness.

diabhol, jiavul, *n. m*. Satan ; devil. *O.Ir*. diabul. *Lat*. diabolus. *Gr*. διάβολος.

diachadaich, jiachudich, *adv*. especially.

diadhachd, jiayachc, *n. f*. godliness, divinity, theology. *Also* diadhaidheachd. *O.Ir*. díadacht, diade.

diadhaich, jiayich, *v*. deify, adore.

diadhaidh, jiayi, *a*. godly, holy. *O.Ir*. díade, *divinus*.

diadhair, jiayer, *n. m*. a divine.

diadhaireachd, *n. f*. divinity.

diadhalachd, *n. f*. godliness.

diall, jial, *n. m*. attachment, fondness, continuance ; is mór an diall a tha aige air an uisge, there is a great continuance of rain ; *v*. attach, get fond of, as a child, dog, etc.

diallaid, jialij, *n. f*. saddle. *Also* diollaid. Cf. *O.Ir*. dillat, clothes.

dialtag, jialtag, *n. f*. a bat, by-form of ialtag.

diamhair, jiavir, *a*. secret. *O.Ir*. diamair, dimair.

dia-mhaslach, jia-vasluch, *a*. blasphemous.

dia-mhasladh, *n. m*. blasphemy.

dian, jeeun, *a*. keen, impetuous, eager, vehement, violent, furious ; nimble ; often used before the noun qualified : dian fhearg, fiery indignation ; dian theth, intensely hot ; *compar*. déine,

diana. So *O.Ir*. dían (gl. *celer* ; *creber*, *pernix*).

dianach, *a*. Same as dian.

dianag, *n. f*. two-year-old sheep. *See* dionag.

diardan, *n. m*. anger ; fr. dì (intens.) + ardan (pride).

Diar-daoin, *n. m*. Thursday ; etym. doubtful.

diarras, diorras, jeerus, *n. m*. vehemence, stubbornness ; diarrais ort, a form of imprecation.

dias, jeeus, *n. f*. an ear of corn ; point of a blade ; a sword ; dias-fhada, long sword ; " dìas chuimir de 'n stàilinn," a well-shaped blade of steel. *O.Ir*. días, spica.

diasach, *a*. luxuriant as a crop.

diasag, jeeusag, *n. f*. ludicrous name for a carper, or satirist's tongue.

diasair, jeeusir, *v*. glean.

diasanach, *n. f*. lank and thriftless person ; diasanach caileig, a thriftless slip of a lass.

di-beatha, *n. m*. a welcome ; greeting ; is e do bheatha, you are welcome ; is e làn dì do bheatha, you are heartily welcome. di-(*intens*.) + beatha = best of life. *See* dí-.

dibh, jiv, *dat*. of deoch, *q.v.*

dibhe, jivu, *gen*. of deoch, *q.v.*

dibheach, jivech, *n. m*. an ant. *Also* seangan.

dibhfhearg, jiverg, *n. f*. vengeance, wrath. *E.Ir*. díbérg, anger. *Mod.Ir*. revenge.

dibhirceach, jivircuch, *a*. diligent.

dibir, *v*. forsake, abandon, yield. *See* diobair. *E.Ir*. díbirim, banish, exile.

diblidh, jeebly, *a*. very mean or abject. *O.Ir*. díblide, decay (of old age). *Lat*. debilis.

diblidheachd, *n. f*. abjectness.

dibrigh, dimbrigh, *n. f*. contempt, disrespect.

dicheann, jee - chian, *v*. behead. *M.Ir*. díchennaim, *id*. *O.Celt*. dê-qennô.

dichioll, jeechul, *n. m*. utmost endeavour ; effort ; diligence. *Ir*. dícheall, effort. *M.Ir*. díchill.

dichiollach, *a*. struggling with disadvantages ; diligent, endeavouring.

di-chrannaich, jeechranich, *v*. dismast.

Di-ciadaoin, ji-ciadin, *n. m*. Wednesday.

did, dideag, jeej, jeejag, *n. f*. a peep.

did, *a*. worse ; is beag as dìd thu sin, you are little the worse for that.

dideadh, *vbl. n. m*. act of peeping.

dideann, jeejun, *n. m*. rampart, protection, refuge. *O.Ir*. dítiu, protection, shelter.

Di-dòmhnuich, *n. m*. Sunday, Lord's Day.

difir, *n. m*. difference. *Ir*. difir. *M.Ir*. dethfir. *Lat*. differo.

dìg, jeeg, *n. f.* a fen, a ditch, a drain ; wall of loose stones ; *v.* dress or trench, as potatoes ; furrow, drain.

digh, ji, *n. f.* a conical mound ; a rampart ; an abode of fairies ; **digh mhór Thallanta**, a noted fairy abode in Islay.

dìgire, deegiru, *n. m.* a ditcher.

dil, jil, *a.* diligent, persevering, zealous. *O.Ir.* díl, agreeable, beloved. *O.Celt.* dili-s.

dìl, *v.* digest food. *Ir.* díl, digest. *Ktg.*

dìle, jeelu, *n. f.* flood, deluge ; **an dìle ruadh**, the general flood, or deluge. *Also* dìlinn. *E.Ir.* díle, *gen.* dílenn ; *Lat.* diluvium.

dìle, *a.* more or most diligent or persevering ; *n. m.* love ; an herb ; dill.

dìleab, jeelub, *n. f.* a legacy, a bequest.

dìleabach, jeelubuch, *n. m.* a legatee, a beneficiary.

dìleabaiche, dìleabair, jeelubiche, *n. m.* a testator. *Also* fear-tiomnaidh.

dìleadh, *vbl. n. m.* act of digesting. So in *Ktg.*

dìleag, jeelag, *n. f.* a flower, a blossom.

dileag, jilag, *n. f.* a small quantity, a few drops, of any liquor ; a by-form of sileag.

dìleanta, jeelantu, *a.* deep, steadfast (as a rock).

dìleas, jeelus, *a.* loyal, favourable, faithful ; nearly connected or related ; **bi dìleas do'n rìgh**, be loyal or faithful to the king. *O.Ir.* díles, one's own ; special.

di-leum, jilēm, *n. f.* a shackle (stress on last syll.).

dìlinn, jeelin, *n. f.* deluge, eternity, age ; **gu dìlinn**, ever, never ; *adv.* never, ever ; **cha dìlinn a thig e**, he shall never come.

dìlinn, jeelin, *n. f.* the natural rock ; **leac dhìlinn**, " living " rock, rock appearing above ground.

dilinn, *v.* propitiate. *Ir.* díl, díol. *O'R.*

dìlleachdan, jeelachcan, *n. m.* an orphan ; **dìleachdach**, fatherless. *O.Ir.* dilechtu, orphan ; " derelict " ; fr. **dì + leig**, " let go." *McB.*

dìlse, jeelshu, *n. f.* relationship, faithfulness ; more or most nearly related. *O.Ir.* dílse, *proprietas.*

dìlseachd, *n. f.* degree of kindred ; faithfulness, connection.

Di-luain, ji-luan, *n. m.* Monday.

Di-màirt, ji-mārst, *n. m.* Tuesday.

dìmbrigh, jeemry, *n. f.* contempt. *See* dìbrigh.

dìmeas, jeemus, *n. m.* disrespect, contempt, reproach (dì + meas). *O.Ir.* dímess.

dìmeasach, *a.* disrespectful, contemptible, despicable, mean.

dìmeasail, *a.* disrespectful.

dì-mill, *v.* destroy ; dì (*intens.*) + mill.

dì-millteach, jeemeeltiuch, *n. m.* a destroyer ; a miserable person ; an animal that breaks through fences

ding, jeeng, *n. f.* a wedge. *Also* geinn. Cf. *O.N.* tengja.

dinn, jin, *v.* press down, ram, stuff.

dinneadh, *vbl. n. m.* act of pressing down, cramming, stuffing.

dìnnear, jeener, *n. f.* dinner ; fr. *Eng.*

dinnein, jinen, *n. m.* small heap, small quantity.

dinneir, jiner, *n. m.* a presser, wedge.

dinnire, *n. m.* ramrod.

dinnsear, jinsher, *n. m.* ginger ; wedge.

dinnte, *vbl. a.* packed, pressed ; closely packed or stuffed ; crammed.

dìobair, jìbir, *v.* extirpate, root out ; **dhìobair mi an fheanntagach**, I have extirpated the nettle ; depopulate, banish ; forsake, abandon ; for dì (intens.) + iobair. *See* dìbir.

dìobairt, jeeburt, *n. f.* extirpation, depopulation ; act of forsaking, leaving ; giving way, failing.

dìobarach, jeebarach, *n. m.* an outcast ; a deserted person ; an exile.

dìobhail, jeevil, *n. f.* want ; loss. *O.Ir.* dígbail, *diminutio, inf.* of dígabim.

dìobhair, jeevir, *v.* vomit, puke.

dìobhairt, jeevurt, *n. f.* vomiting.

dìobhargach, *a.* fierce, keen.

dìobhargadh, *n. m.* persecution. *See* dibhfhearg.

dìobhlach, *n. m.* a prodigal.

dìocail, jeecal, *v.* abate, lower, extinguish.

dìochaisg, *a.* implacable.

dìochd, juchc, *n. f.* small matter ; **cha diochd dhuinn**, no trifle for us.

dìochra, jeechra, *a.* intense. *M.Ir.* díchra, fervent.

dìochuimhn, jiachun, *n. f.* forgetfulness ;

dìochuimhneach, *a.* forgetful.

dìocla, jeeclu, *n. m.* abatement of rain ; **uisge gun dìocla**, incessant rain.

diod, jid, *n. f.* a drop, spark.

diog, jig, *n. m.* a word, a syllable ; **na h-abair diog**, say not a word ; the tick of a timepiece.

dìogaich, *v. i.* stir, move, budge ; **cha diogaich an fhiacail ud**, that tooth will not move — *i.e.* it is hard and fast.

dìogail, jigle, *v.* tickle ; *vbl. n.* diogailt, tickling ; **cuir diogailt ann**, tickle him.

diogailteach, *a.* ticklish.

dìogair, jeeger, *a.* eager.

dìogan, jeegan, *n. m.* revenge, spite.

dìoghail, jeeyul, *v. t.* revenge, retaliate. *O.Ir.* dígal, revenge. *O.Celt.* dê-galâ.

dìoghailte, *vbl. a.* revenged, avenged.

dìoghaltach, jeeyultuch, *a.* vindictive, revengeful, requiring much.

dìoghaltair, *n. m.* an avenger.

dìoghaltas, *n. m.* vengeance.

dìoghluim, *v.* glean after shearers ; cull, gather minutely ; *n. m.* dìoghlum, gleanings, the thing gathered.

dìol, *v.* recompense, requite ; dhìol thu sin, you have recompensed that : *n. m.* condition, state ; is bòidheach a dhìol, he is in a pretty condition ; satiety, satisfaction, abundance ; tha mo dhìol agamsa, I have my satisfaction or abundance ; a dhìol ùine aige, he has plenty of time ; complement, proportion ; clach chàis le a dìol de dh'ìm, a stone of cheese with its complement of butter. *O.Ir.* dígal. *See* dìoghail.

dìolain, *a.* illegitimate ; mac dìolain, an illegitimate son.

dìolanas, jee-ulanus, *n. f.* bastardy, illegitimacy, fornication ; rugadh an dìolanas e, he was born in fornication.

dìol-déirc, *n. m.* beggar, object of charity.

dìolladair, *n. m.* saddler ; dìolladaireachd, saddler's business.

dìollaid, jee-ulij, *n. f.* a saddle. *Cf.* *O.Ir.* dillat, clothing.

dìomadh, *n. m.* discontent, pain.

dìomarag, *n. f.* clover seed.

dìomasach, jimusuch, *a.* proud. *M.Ir.* díumus, pride.

dìomb, jūm, *n. f.* indignation, offence, resentment, displeasure ; na toill dìomb duine 'sam bith, incur not the displeasure of any person.

dìombach, jūmuch, *a.* indignant, dissatisfied, offended at, displeased ; tha mi dìombach dhìot, I am displeased with you. *E.Ir.* dimdach.

dìombachd, *n. f.* indignation.

dìombas, jimus, *n. m.* lasciviousness.

dìom-bhrìoghail, *a.* without substance.

dìombuain, jimon, *a.* fading, transitory, short-lived. *Also* dìomain. dim + buan.

dìombuanachd, jimanachc, *n. f.* transitoriness, evanescence, short duration.

dìombuil, jimul, *n. f.* misapplication.

dìomhain, jeev-on, *a.* idle. *O.Ir.* dímain.

dìomhair, jeevir, *a.* secret, mysterious, private ; gnothach dìomhair, a private affair ; lonely, solitary. *See* diamhair.

dìomhaireachd, *n. f.* privacy, mystery ; solitude.

dìomhala, *a.* noble, courageous.

dìomhanach, jeevonuch, *a.* idle, lazy ; in vain ; vain ; is dìomhanach dhuit teannadh ris, it is idle, it is in vain for you to attempt such.

dìomhanas, jivanus, *n. f.* idleness, laziness ; labour in vain ; emptiness, vanity. *E.Ir.* dímaines, *vanitas.*

dìomol, jimol, *v.* dispraise, libel, depreciate, undervalue, disparage. di + mol.

dìomoladh, *vbl. n. m.* dispraise, disparagement ; abuse ; act of dispraising, undervaluing, abusing.

dìon, jee-un, *n. m.* shelter, covert, defence ; state of being wind- and water-tight ; tha dìon san tigh, the house is wind- and water-tight ; *v.* protect, defend, shield, save ; shelter, guard ; dìon thu fhèin, defend yourself. *E.Ir.* dín, protect.

dìonach, *a.* water-tight, air-tight ; not leaky as a vessel ; tigh dìonach, water-tight house ; musical term which means flawless, fluent fingering on chanter ; fixity of tenure ; dìonach 'n a fhearann, secure in his holding.

dìonachadh, *n. m.* security, caution, bail.

dìonachd, jeenachc, *n. m.* security.

dìonadair, jeenader, *n. m.* a fender, a defender, protector.

dìonag, jeeun'-ag, *n. f.* a two-year-old sheep or goat. *Also* tearainneach.

dìonaich, *v.* secure.

dìonbhreid, jeen-vrej, *n. m.* apron.

dìong, jeeng, *v.* join, match, concur, equal, pay. *E.Ir.* dingbaim.

dìong, jeeng, *a.* worthy, unmovable.

dìong, *v.* squeeze, press. *O.Ir.* dingim, oppress. *W.* dygn. *O.Celt.* dengô, press.

dìong, *n. m.* a hillock. *M.Ir.* dindgna, hill, fort, dwelling.

dìonganta, *a.* pressing, impetuous.

dìongmhalta, jeeng'-alt-à, *a.* firm, secure, efficient, completely certain (= dìong (worthy) + mol (praise). *Cf.* *O.G.* dingbala.

dìongmhaltas, jeeng'-ãlt-us, *n. f.* security, complete certainty, efficiency, sufficiency, tightness. *Also* dìongaltachd.

dìonnal. *See* deannal.

dìorachd, jirachc, *n. f.* ability.

dìorr, jeerr, *n. m.* spark of life.

dìorras, jeerr'-as, *n. m.* tenacity, pertinacity ; childish efforts. *E.Ir.* dígar, intent, vehement.

dìorrasach, jeerr'-as-ach, *a.* tenacious, pertinacious ; opinionative, striving in vain ; with clenched teeth.

dìorrasachd, jeerr'-as-achg, *n. f.* extreme pertinacity or tenacity.

dìosd, jist, *n. m.* 1. a jump, kick with heels. 2. *v.* spank (a child).

dìosg, jeesg, *v.* creak as hinges, gnash as teeth.

dìosg, jeesc, *a.* barren, dry ; tha bhó dìosg, the cow is dry—off her milk. *Ir.* díosc, dry. *Lh.*

diosg, *n. m.* 1. a dish. *Lat.* discus. 2. any quantity of water in a dish.

diosg, *n. m.* a flaw, a crack.

diosgadh, jeescu, *n. m.* barrenness; not giving milk, dry. *M.Ir.* díoscadh, a running dry (as well, or cow).

diosgail, jeesgul, *vbl. n. m.* act of creaking.

díosganach, jee-usganuch, *n. m.* a ne'er-do-weel, a boarded-out dipsomaniac.

diot, jeet, *n. f.* diet, meal. *E.Ir.* díthait. *Lat.* diaeta.

dìpinn, jeepin, *n. f.* deepening of a net, a certain quantity of net.

dìreach, jeeruch, *a.* straight; upright; *adv.* directly, exactly so; dìreach mar thuirt thu, just as you said; dìreach ! dìreach ! just so ! just so ! *M.Ir.* dír, fit, lawful. *O.Ir.* dírech.

dìreachan, *n. f.* perpendicular.

dìreadh, jeeru, *vbl. n. m.* act of ascending; ceò a' dìreadh aonaich, mist ascending a hill; act of exacting a fine.

dìrich, *v.* make straight, mount, climb, erect. *E.Ir.* dírgim, straighten.

dis, jish, *a.* fond of the fire; susceptible of, or not capable of bearing cold. *E.Ir.* dis, diss, weak.

Di-sathurn, ji-sahurn, *n. m.* Saturday.

discir, jishcir, *a.* nimble, sudden, fierce; cruel. *E.Ir.* fierce. *O.Ir.* nimble.

disearr, jishur, *a.* chilly (in oneself).

dìsinn, jeesin, *n. m.,* gen. dìsne, a die, dice; ag iomairt air dìsnean, playing at backgammon; a cube, a wedge, as in the shaft of anything.

dìsle, *n. f.* another form of dillse, more nearly connected.

dìsleach, jeesluch, *a.* stormy, straggling, uncouth.

dìsneach, *a.* diced.

dìt, jeet, *v.* condemn, sentence, reproach, despise; na dìt mi airson sin, reproach me not for that.

dìteadh, jeetu, *vbl. n. m.* condemnation.

dìth, jee, *n. f.* want, deficiency; dìth cèille, want of sense; ciod e tha a dhìth ort, what do you want ? chuir thu dhìth orm, you deprived me of this. *O.Ir.* díth, end, death. *O.Celt.* dêto-.

dith, jēe, *n. f.* a layer, a course, a streak; dith mu seach, a layer about; a vein, as in a mine; ditheanan luaidhe is airgid, veins of lead and silver ore.

dìth, jee, *v.* press, squeeze.

dìth, *v.* die, perish, wither away. *O.Ir.* death.

dìth-bìdh, *n. f.* annihilation; dìth-bìdh ort ! starvation to you ! (an imprecation).

dìtheach, jee-huch, *n. m.* a beggar.

dìthean, jee-en, *n. m.* the darnel. *Also* sìthean.

dìthich, jee-hich, *v.* extirpate, root out.

dithis, ji-ish, two; a brace; pair; thàinig dithis, two came.

dith-làthraich, jilárich, *v.* utterly destroy, annihilate.

dìthreabh, jeeruv, *n. f.* waste, wilderness; higher grounds. *O.Ir.* dithrub, waste, *desertum.* dì (*neg.*) + treb. *O.Celt.* dê-trebo-.

diù, joo, *a.* worth, value; cha bu diù leam, not worth my while, I scorned.

diù, joo, *n. m.* refuse; the worst; roghainn is diù, pick and choice.

diu, joo, *adv.* diugh, an diu, to-day. *Ir.* andiu, aniu. *O.Ir.* indiu, *hodie.*

diùbh, joo, *prep.* and *pron. suf.* 3 *pl.* of them; cuid diùbh, some of them; aon diùbh, one of them. *Also* diùbhsan.

diùbhaidh, joo'y, diùgha, *n. m.* refuse, the worst; "diùghaidh nam fear," the worst of the lot; *opp.* of rogha.

diùbhail, joov'-al, *n. f.* calamity, distress; destruction, ruin; is mór an diùbhail, it is a thousand pities.

diùbhalach, joo'-al-ach, *a.* calamitous, distressing; heartrending, hurtful.

diùbhalaich, joo'-al-èch, *v.* recompense, compensate; make up deficiencies.

diùbhras, jooras, diùbhar, *n. m.* difference.

diuc, joog, *n. f.* the pip, sickness of fowls.

diùc, *n. m.* duke. *Lat.* dux.

diùcair, jooker, *n. m.* a ducker; bladder for keeping nets at proper depth.

diuchaidh, joochy, *a.* addled; worthless.

diùchair, joocher, *v. t.* ward off; drive away.

diuchd, *vbl. a.* appeared, presented (oneself).

diùdan, joodan, *n. m.* giddiness, a giddy person.

diug, *interj.* chuck; call to hens.

diugan, joogan, *n. m.* mischance.

diugh, joo, *adv.* an diugh, to-day; an diugh fhéin, this very day. *E.Ir.* in-diu, *hodie.* *O.Celt.* divo-.

diùid, jooj, *a.* timid, diffident, fearful, bashful, awkward, sheepish. *O.Ir.* diuit, simplex.

diùide, jooju, *n. f.* timidity, diffidence, sheepishness; *a. compar.* of diùid, more or most timid.

diùideachd, joojachk, *n. f.* extreme diffidence; backwardness, timidity.

diùlanach, joolanuch, *n. m.* a brave man. *Ir.* diolmhaineach, soldier; fr. dìol, pay. *E.Ir.* dílamnach.

diùlanas, joolanus, *n. m.* bravery.

diùlnach, joolnuch, *n. m.* a hero; a handsome brave man. *Also* diùnlach.

diùlt, joolt, *v.* refuse, reject. *O.Ir.* díltuch, refusing.

diùltadh, jooltu, *vbl. n. m.* refusal, denial,

act of refusing, rejecting, denying. *O.Ir.* díltud.

diùmb, joom, *n. m.* hatred, displeasure.

diùmbach, diùmach, *a.* displeased, angry. *M.Ir.* dímdach, dim-buidech.

diùnanaich, joonanich, *v.* wallop, drub ; 'ga dhiùnanachadh, walloping or drubbing him.

diùnlach, joonluch, *n. m.* handsome man. *Also* diùlnach.

diùrr, jùrr, *n. f.* vital spark ; chan 'eil diùrr ann, he is quite dead. *See* diorr.

diùrrais, jūresh, *n. f.* a secret, a mystery ; an diùrrais, as a secret. *E.Ir.* dígrus, secret.

diùrraiseach, jūrresh - uch, *a.* secret, private ; requiring secrecy.

diùthadh, joohu, *n. m.* scruple ; " na dèan diùthadh mu d' shoitheach," be not particular as to your dish.

dlagh, *n. m.* a wisp, what the hand can grasp in shearing corn ; natural order ; as a dhlagh, out of its natural order or arrangement. *Also* dlogh. *Ir.* dlaoigh, a lock of hair, etc. *E.Ir.* dlai.

dleas, dles, *n. m.* right, due, merit, desert ; mo dhleas fhéin, my own due or right ; *adj.* due, deserved, merited ; is dleas sin da, that is due to him ; incumbent ; in duty bound ; an dleas dhomh sin a dhèanamh ? is it incumbent on me to do that ? *v.* owe, extort, procure ; na dleas nì do dhuine sam bith, owe no man anything (*Bible*). *O.Ir.* dles, owe.

dleasnach, dlesnach, *a.* dutiful.

dleasnas, *n. m.* duty ; filial duty ; affection ; rinn mi mo dhleasnas, I did my duty ; obligation. *Also* dleasdanas. *E.Ir.* dlestanas.

dlighe, dlee-u, *n. m.* duty ; right ; due ; is e so mo dhlighe, this is my due. *O.Ir.* dliged, debt. *O.W.* dlêd, dylêd. *O.Celt.* dlgeto-*debitum*.

dligheach, dlee-uch, *a.* rightful, lawful, legitimate ; oighre dhligheach, rightful heir ; clann dligheach, lawful children ; due ; ma's dligheach dhuit sin, if that be due you.

dligheachas, dlee-uchus, *n. m.* duty, right.

dligheir, dlee-er, *n. m.* lawyer, creditor.

dlighim, dlee-im, *v.* owe ; ma dhligheas mi ni sam bith, if I owe anything. *O.Ir.* **dligim**, I claim as a right.

dlò, *n. f.* handful of corn.

dlò, *adv.* alone ; air a dhlò, all alone.

dlogh, dlo, *n. m.* a wart ; handful of half-thrashed corn. *See* dlagh.

dloghainn, dlo-in, *n. f.* sheaf-corn half-thrashed, given to cattle when fodder is scarce.

dluigheil, dlooyel, *a.* active, handy.

dlùith, dlooy, *v.* approach, draw near.

dlùth, *a.* near, nigh, close to ; dlùth air an latha, near daylight. *O.Ir.* dlútai.

dlùth, dloo, *n. m.* warp of cloth ; na 's leòir de dhlùth is fuidheall innich, abundance of warp, and remainder of woof ; enough and to spare. *O.Ir.* dlúth, stamen ; dlúthaim, I make thick, close.

dlùthadh, dloo-hu, *vbl. n. m.* approaching, nearing, drawing near. *Also* dlùthachadh.

dlùthaich, dloo-hich, *v.* Same as dlùith.

dlùth-lean, dloo-len, *v.* stick close to.

dlùth-theann, dloo-hiaun, *v.* press ; near, close.

do, *prep.* to ; do 'n duine, to the man. With *pers. pron.* : *sing.* 1. domh, to me. 2. duit. 3. da (*m.*), di (*f.*). *pl.* 1. duinn. 2. duibh. 3. daibh. *O.Ir. sing.* 1. dom, dam. 2. duit, dait, deit, det. 3. dáu, dó, dí (*f.*). *pl.* 1. dún. 2. dúib. 3. dóib, doaib. do is idiom. employed in various constructions, such as : *dat. of interest*, is buidhe dhuit, you are fortunate ; *dat. of poss.* cha charaide dhòmhsa e, he is no friend of mine ; mac do Ioseph, a son of Joseph's ; *dat. of purpose*, tha mi dol a (=do) chluich, I am going to play ; *dat.* with force of *abl. abs.*, air suidhe dha, when he had sat. For a full description see a good grammar.

do-, du-, *neg. pref.* So *O.Ir.* W. dy-. *Gr.* δυσ-.

dò, *num.* two. *O.Ir.* a dau, a dó.

do, *pron.* thy ; *asp.* do mhàthair, thy mother ; becomes t' (d' still common in the Heb.) before vowels. Frequently in *Ir.* th', and even h'. *W.* dy, 'th.

do-àireamh, do-āruv, *a.* difficult to count, innumerable. *O.Ir.* dírim.

dobair, *n. m.* a plasterer. *Eng.* dauber.

dòbhaidh, dōvy, *a.* boisterous ; oidhche dhòbhaidh, a boisterous night ; terrible.

dobhar, do-ur, *n. m.* water ; dobharchu, " water-dog." *E.Ir.* dobur. *O.W.* dwfr. *O.Celt.* dubro-n.

dobharlus, *n. m.* water-cress.

dòbheart, dō-viarst, *n. f.* vice, evil design, evil plan.

dòbheus, *n. m.* vice, bad habit.

dòbhliadhnach, *n. m.* a two-year old beast.

dóbhrach, dōruch, *n. f.* water-cress.

dóbhran, dōr'-an, *n. m.* an otter ; ball-dóbhrain, a freckle on the skin, mole.

dóbhranach, *a.* abounding in otters.

do-bhrìgh, *adv.* for, because.

do-bhròn, *n. m.* dejection, deep sorrow.

docair, docur, *n. f.* uneasiness, trouble, annoyance ; *a.* uneasy, not settled ; àite-suidhe docair, an uneasy seat ; socair no docair, either easy or uneasy. *E.Ir.* doccair.

docha, dŏch'-a, *a. compar.* of toigh ; is toigh leam thusa ach is docha leam esan, I like you, but I prefer him. *O.Ir.* tochu, compar. of toich, acceptable, like.

dòcha, dôch'-à, *a. compar.* of dòigh; is e so as dòcha, this is more probable. *O.Ir.* dóchu, *compar.* of dóig, *verisimilius.*

dochainn, doch'-inn, *v.* injure, hurt.

dochair, dŏch'-ur, *n. m.* hurt ; *v.* hurt. *E.Ir.* dochor. do (difficult) + cor (state).

dochann, doch'-unn, *n. m.* hurt, harm, damage, mischief ; agony ; a thrashing ; á dochann bàis, from the agony of death ; fhuair e dochann, he got hurt. *M.Ir.* dochond.

dochannach, *a.* hurtful, injurious, noxious.

docharach, *a.* uneasy. *See* dochair.

do-charachadh, *a.* not easily moved, unmovable.

dòchas, *n. m.* expectation, hope, trust, confidence ; do dhòchas, your expectation. *M.Ir.* dóchus.

dòchasach, *a.* hoping, confident, confiding.

dòchasachd, dôch'-as-achc, *n. f.* confidence, hopefulness, reliance.

do-chasgadh, *a.* unquenchable.

do-cheannsachadh, *a.* not easily managed, invincible.

do-chìosnachadh, do-chīsnuchu, *a.* unconquerable, invincible.

do-chlaoidh, *a.* indefatigable.

do-chlaoidhteachd, *n. f.* invincibility, insuperability.

do-chomhairleachadh, *a.* incorrigible, untamable.

do-chreidsinn, do-chreijshin, *a.* incredible, unbelievable.

docran, *n. m.* anguish, *based* on cor ; cf. dochair.

dod, *n. m.* a huff ; tantrum. *Sc.* dod, pet.

dodach, *a.* pettish, peevish.

do-dhèanamh, do-yenu, *a.* impossible.

dog, *n. m.* a junk ; a short thick piece of anything ; thickset person ; dog bùill, a junk of a rope. Cf. *Eng.* dock.

dogail, *a.* cynical.

dogan, *n. m.* a stot, steer.

dogan, *n. m.* a game with bat and ball.

dògan, *n. m.* a sort of oath.

doganta, *a.* thickset, stumpish ; fierce.

dògh, dô, *n. m.* opinion ; mo dhòghsa gu bheil, in my opinion it is so ; *a.* like, probable ; is dògh nach 'eil, it is probably not so.

dogha, do'-u, *n. m.* a burdock. *Also* meacan-dogha.

do ghnàth, *adv.* always. *W.* gnawd.

doibh, for daibh, to them. *See* do.

doibhear, doy-ver, *a.* rude, uncivil.

doibheas, doy-vus, *n. m.* vice. do + beus.

doicheall, do-chial, *vbl. n. m.* act of grudging ; inhospitality ; sensitiveness (with respect to proffered hospitality). *M. Ir.* dochell, niggardliness. *Km.*

doicheallach, *a.* churlish, grudging, inhospitable, sensitive, shy.

doichill, dochil, *v.* begrudge, grudge ; chan ann 'ga dhoicheall a tha mi, I am not grudging it to you ; be churlish ; decline hospitality (through shyness).

dòid, dôj, *n. f.* a croft, a pendicle.

dòid, *n. f.* the hand ; grasp. *E.Ir.* dóit, hand, wrist.

dòideach, dôjuch, *a.* frizzled ; shrunk (singed hair).

dòideach, *a.* strong-handed.

dòideag, dôjag, *n. f.* a celebrated Mull witch. She is supposed to have caused the destruction of the Spanish Armada!

dòidire, dôjiru, *n. m.* a crofter, a cottager.

dòidgheal, dôj-yal, *a.* white-handed.

dòigh, dôy, *n. f.* method, manner, way, means ; air an dòigh so, in this manner ; condition, state ; ciod e an dòigh a tha ort ? how are you ? confidence, trust ; cuiridh mi mo dhòigh annad, I will put confidence in thee. *O.Ir.* dóig, likely.

dòighealachd, dō-yal-uchc, *n. f.* excellent arrangement, capability of adjustment.

dòigheigin, dôy-egin, *adv.* somehow or other, somehow.

dòigheil, dôyal, *a.* well-arranged, in good condition ; in comfort ; systematic, in proper train.

doilbh, dulv, *a.* difficult ; dark. *Ir.* gloomy, obscure. *O'R.*

dòileas, dól'-as, *n. f.* difficulty, hardship, injury (do + leas). *See* dòlas.

doilgheas, dolyès, *n. m.* sorrow, affliction.

doilgheasach, *a.* sorrowful.

doilisg, dolishc, *n. m.* vexation.

doille, *n. f.* blindness, darkness, stupidity ; *a.* more blind or stupid, ignorant. *Also* doillead ; fr. dall.

doillearachd, *n. f.* stupidity, darkness, obscurity.

doilleir, du-ler, *a.* dark, stupid ; duine doilleir, a stupid person ; do + léir.

doilleirich, du-lerich, *v.* obscure, dim.

dòimeach, doymuch, *a.* disconsolate.

doimeag, *n. f.* a slattern.

doimh, dŏyv, *a.* galling, vexing ; gross, clumsy ; gu dùmhail, doimh, mar bhios màthair fhir an tighe an rathad na cloinne, bulky and clumsy, as the husband's mother is in the way of the children.

doimheadach, dŏy-aduch, *a.* vexing, galling ; is doimheadach an nì e, it is a vexing thing ; disappointing.

DOIMHEADAS—DOLTRAM 131

doimheadas, *n. m.* vexation, grief.
doimheal, doyvil, *a.* stormy.
doimheamh, dŏyiv, *a.* vexed, grieved.
doimhne, dūina, *n. f.* depth, the deep, the ocean ; *a.* na's doimhne, deeper, more profound ; fr. domhain.
doimhneachd, dūinachc, *n. f.* depth, deepness, profundity ; deep water ; 'san doimhneachd, in the depth, in deep water ; 'san tanalaich, in the shallow.
doimhnead, dūinud, *n. m.* degree of depth, deepness, profundity. *W.* dyfnedd.
doimhnich, dūinich, *v.* deepen, hollow.
dòineach, dōniuch, *a.* sad, sorrowful.
doinead, *abs. n.* (fr. dona), badness, wretchedness.
dòinidh, dōny, *a.* pitiful, miserable.
doinionn, doniun, *n. f.* storm, wild weather. *E.Ir.* donend, *opp.* sonend. *Wi.*
do-innse, do-eenshu, *a.* that cannot be told ; unaccountable, unutterable.
do-iomchair, do-imcher, *a.* intolerable.
do-iompachadh, dó-ēmp'-uch-u, *a.* perverse.
doirb, dorb, *n. f.* a minnow ; a worm, a reptile, a frog ; a small creature.
doirbeag, *n. f.* minnow ; tadpole.
doirbh, durv, *a.* difficult ; ceisd dhoirbh, a difficult question ; stormy, boisterous ; oidhche dhoirbh, a boisterous night ; wild, ungovernable ; duine doirbh, a turbulent incorrigible person ; grievous, intolerable. *O.Ir.* doirb, *difficilis.* (do + reb), *opp.* of soirbh (so + reb).
doirbhe, durvu, *a.* more difficult, etc. ; *n. f.* difficulty, boisterousness, indocility, etc.
doirbheachd, durvachc, *n. f.* difficulty.
doirbhead, durvud, *n. f.* degree of difficulty, boisterousness, storminess, hardship.
doirbheadas, durvudus, *n. f.* ungovernableness, peevishness, turbulence.
doirbheag, durvag, *n. f.* a peevish woman, a stingy woman.
doirbheas, durvus, *n. f.* difficulty ; grief, anguish, distress, boisterousness ; latha an doirbheis, the day of adversity ; a' dol gu doirbheas, getting obstreperous.
doirbhein, durven, *n. m.* a churl.
doirbheineachd, *n. f.* churlishness.
doirch, *v.* get dark ; dhoirch an oidhche dhuinn, we were benighted, the night got dark on us.
doirche, darker, *n. f.* extreme darkness.
doire, duru, *n. m., pl.* doireachan, *originally,* an oak copse ; a grove, a thicket, a species of tangle ; gach coille is gach doire, every wood and grove. *O.Ir.* daur, dair (*gen.* darach),

quercus. W. dâr. *O.Celt.* dari-, darik-oak.
doireach, dōrach, *a.* woody, wild.
doireagan, durugan, *n. m.* a peewit. *Also* adharcan.
doireannachd, *n. f.* storminess.
doirionn, durun, *n. f.* inclemency, stormy weather ; thàinig doirionn a' gheamhraidh, the inclemency of winter has come ; storminess. *Also* doireann.
doirionnach, *a.* stormy.
doirionta, duruntu, *a.* sullen.
dòirlinn, dōrlin, *n. m.* an islet to which one can wade at low water ; pebbly or stony part of a shore ; an isthmus.
dòirneag, dōrnag, *n. f.* a stone that makes a handful ; a pebble ; *dim.* of dorn.
dòirneagach, *a.* shingly, pebbled.
dòirt, dōrst, *v.* pour, spill, shed, rush forth ; stream, gush ; scatter ; dhòirt e fhuil, he shed his blood. *E.Ir.*
dóirtim, spill, shed.
dòirteach, dōrstach, *a.* apt to spill ; *n. f.* flood, a sudden pour of rain.
dòirteall, dōrstal, *n. m.* a sink, a drain.
doit, *a.* foul, dark.
dòit, *n. f.* small coin (less than farthing), a twelfth of a penny. *Sc.* a doit.
dòite, dō'-tu, *vbl. a.* singed, seared.
dòiteachan, dō'-tyach-an, *n. m.* a miserable singed-looking person.
doitheamh, doy-hev. *See* doimheamh.
doithearra, doy-huru, *a.* swarthy, deformed, ill-humoured. So *O'R.*
dol, *n. m.* condition, state ; dol an t-saoghail, the state of the world.
dol, *inf.* of rach ; a' dol dachaidh, going home ; dol fodha na gréine, the going down of the sun ; an dol sìos, the attack, charge ; dol a mach, going out, but also *idm.* = behaviour. *O.Ir.* dul, *inf.* of doluid, went.
do-labhairt, *a.* unspeakable.
dòlach, *a.* indifferent ; duine dona dòlach, an indifferent person ; destructive, grievous.
dolaidh, doly, *n. f.* harm, ruination, mischief ; cuir a dholaidh, ruin, destroy ; is beag an dolaidh, it is no great harm ; chaidh e dholaidh, it went bad, it rotted. *O.Ir.* dolod = loss.
dòlamhach, dàlamhach, *a.* using both hands with equal facility, ambidexter.
dòlas, *n. m.* harm ; grief ; *opp.* of sòlas.
dòlasach, *a.* grieved, hurtful.
dòlasair, *n. f., pl.* dòlasraichean, a destructive flame.
do-leasach, do-lesach, *a.* irreparable.
do-leigheas, do-lu-us, *a.* irremediable.
do-leughadh, do-lēvu, *a.* illegible, inexplicable, ill to explain.
doltram, doltrom, doltrum, *n. m.* gloom, anguish, terror.

do-lùbadh, a. inflexible.
dòlum, n. m. meanness, wretchedness, poverty, murmuring.
dòlumach, a. wretched, mean, surly.
dòm, n. m. gall-bladder.
domail, n. m. injury, harm, damage, particularly damage by cattle (as corn). Cf. Lat. damnum.
domblas, dōm'-las, n. m. gall; bile; gall-bladder. M.Ir. domblas = do + mblas, " ill-taste," bitterness.
domblas-àighe, n. m. gall-bladder.
domhach, n. m. a savage person.
dòmhail, a. bulky. Also dùmhail.
domhain, do-in, a. deep. O.Ir. domain. W. dwfn. O.Celt. dubno - s. Goth. diups.
domhan, doün, n. m. the universe, the globe, the whole world; an domhan mun iadh grian, the globe which the sun surrounds. O.Ir. domun, gen. domain. Gaul. dubno-, dumno-.
Domhnach, dōnach, n. m. Sunday, the Sabbath; dòmhnach càisg, Paschal Sunday, Easter. E.Ir. domnach. Lat. dominica.
Dòmhnall - dubh, dòn'-all-doo, n. m. euphemism for the Devil.
do-mhùinte, a. untractable, unlearned.
don, n. m. want; evil, badness; don bìdh ort, ill betide thee; don-mathais, a bad requital of good.
dona, a. bad, evil, vile; compar. na 's miosa, worse; superl. as miosa, the worst; opp. to sona. M.Ir. dona, wretched.
donadas, n. m. evil, badness; a' dol an donadas, deteriorating. Also donad.
donadh, dŏn'-u, n. m. evil, injury.
donas, n. m. evil, mischief; harm, hurt, badness; the Devil.
dongaidh, a. moist, humid, dank. Sc. donk.
donn, doun, a. compar. duinne, brown, dun, sable, brown-haired; Diarmad donn, brown-haired Diarmad; voc. a ghille dhuinn, brown-haired lad; indifferent, bad; chan 'eil ann ach duine donn, he is only a man so and so, an indifferent man; v. make brown, imbrown, bronze; an uair a dhonnadh na speuran, when the heavens were darkened. Ossian. O.Ir. donn. O.Celt. donno-s.
donnadh, vbl. n. m. act of browning; " an dornchur a' donnadh làmh," the hilt (of the sword) making brown (the palms of) the hands.
donnag, n. f. a young ling.
donnal, n. m. a howl, bawl, plaint.
donnalaich, n. f. continued howling, or slow drawling barking; barking.
donn-ruadh, a. chestnut-coloured.

dòrainn, dòruinn, n. f. pain, torment; a. dòrainneach. E.Ir. dogra, dógra, lamenting, anguish.
dòraman, n. m. a hermit, morose man.
do-rannsaichte, vbl. a. inscrutable.
dorbh, dorgh, n. m., pl. and gen. s. duirbh, duirgh, hand-line (for deep-sea fishing). Also drogha. Ir. dorga, fishing-net. O'R.; and N. dorg, fishing-tackle, mod. use = fishing through hole in the ice.
dorch, a. dark, somewhat dark; obscure, mysterious. Compar. duirche. O.Ir. dorche, obscuritas.
dorchadas, n. m. darkness. O.Ir. dorchadus; dorchatu.
dorchadh, dor'chu, vbl. n. m. getting dark or obscure, mystifying.
dorchaich, v. darken.
do-réir, do rēr, prep. according to; do rèir t'iarrtais, according to your request. O.Ir. do réir, ad voluntatem, dat. of riar, voluntas.
dorgh, n. m. hand-line. See dorbh and drogha.
dorghach, vbl. n. m. act of fishing with a hand-line.
dòrlach, dôr-llàch, n. m. handful; considerable quantity; a measure of corn; dòrlach eòrna, sixty sheaves of barley. dòrn + lach, " fistful."
dòrn, n. m., pl. dùirn, a fist, a box, the hold of an oar; a hilt; v. box; dorn e, box him. dorn = measure; " traigh is dorn," a foot + fist. O.Ir. dorn. W. dwrn. O.Celt. durno-, fist. Cf. Gr. δῶρον, palm.
dòrnadair, n. m. boxer, pugilist.
dòrnadaireachd, dorn'-ad-ăr'-achc, n. f: boxing, pugilism, thumping.
dòrnag, n. f. gauntlet, a putting-stone; fr. dorn, fist.
dòrnan, n. m. a " fistful "; a " fist-length "; handful of lint; the neck-piece of a tether.
dòrnchrann, n. m. sword-hilt; " iomadh claidheamh dornchrann òir," many a gold-hilted sword. Also dòrnchur.
dòrngheal, dōrn-yal, a. white-fisted (indicating strong grip). Watson.
dòrnlach, n. f. 1. handful. 2. quiver. 3. hilt of a sword; " iubhar is dòrlach," bow and quiver.
dorra, a. more difficult. M.Ir. dorr, rough. O.Ir. doraid, for do + réid, uneven, difficult; opp. soraid, easy, so + réid. Thn.
dorradas, n. m. difficulty, hardship.
dorraman, n. m. a person alone, a hermit, a recluse.
dorramanachd, n. f. hermitage, living or dandering alone, seclusion.
dorran, n. m. offence at a trifling cause;

vexation, slight offence. *M.Ir.* **dorr,** rough. *O.Celt.* dorso-s.

dorranach, doranuch, *a.* vexing, galling.

dorsach, *a.* exposed to the blast, as a house, a field of corn, etc.

dorsaiche, *n. f.* exposure to the blast ; exposed situation.

dorsair, dŏrr'-săr', *n. m.* a door-keeper, porter ; fr. **dorus.**

dorsaireachd, dŏrs'-ăr'-achc, *n. f.* office of a door-keeper, porterage.

dòrtach, *a.* apt to spill, not tight, or keeping, or retaining.

dòrtadh, dōrt'-ǎ, *vbl. n. m.* act of shedding, spilling ; **dòrtadh fola,** bloodshed.

do-ruigsinn, do-rig-shin, *a.* unattainable.

dòruinn, dŏr'-inn, *n. f.* pain, anguish. *See* **dòrainn.**

doruinneach, dōrinuch, *a.* painful, excruciating, tormenting ; much pained.

doruinneachd, dōrinuchc, *n. f.* painfulness ; extreme painfulness.

dorus, *n. m., pl.* **dorsan,** door-way ; an opening, or orifice, as of a wound ; **neasgaid làn dhorsan,** an ulcer full of orifices. *O.Ir.* **dorus,** *limen.* *W.* **dôr,** **drws.** *O.Celt.* dvorestu-. Cf. *Lat.* foris. *Gr.* θύρα. *O.H.G.* Tor.

dorus-iadht, *n. m.* back door. On a shieling there were two doors of which the one on windward side was kept shut, hence **dorus-iadht,** the *closed* door, the door facing the wind.

dos, *n. m., pl.* and *gen. s.* **duis,** a plume or cockade ; a thicket ; one of the drones of a bagpipe ; a hunting-horn ; a tassel ; a forelock ; a bush ; **dos de'n t-sìoda,** a tassel of silk. *O.Ir.* **dos, doss,** a bush.

dosach, *a.* tufted.

dosan, *n. m.* little tuft, forelock.

dosdan, *n. m.* food for horses.

dosgach, *a.* calamitous ; liable to accidents or damage ; unfortunate.

dosgadh, doscu, *n. f.* misfortune.

dosgaich, *n. f.* misfortune ; loss of cattle ; accident ; damage ; liability to damage or misfortunes.

dosgainn, doscin, *n. f.* misfortune.

do-sgaradh, *a.* inseparable.

do-sgrùdadh, *a.* unsearchable.

do-sheachanntach, *a.* inevitable, unavoidable.

do-smachdach, *a.* incorrigible, untractable, obstinate.

dosrach, *a.* tufted, bushy ; luxuriant, flourishing, as corn, trees, etc. ; **a' cinntinn gu dosrach,** growing or flourishing luxuriantly ; plumed.

dosraich, *n. f.* luxuriance, branching appearance.

dotarra, *a.* sulky. *See* **dod.**

doth, *vbl. n.* doating on one.

doth, dath, *v.* singe, scorch. *M.Ir.*

dóthim, dóithim, I burn. *O.Celt.* daviô.

dothadh, dathadh, do-hu, *n. m.* singeing, scorching.

do-thraoghadh, *a.* inexhaustible.

do-thuigsinn, do-hig-shin, *a.* unintelligible.

dràb, *n. f.* a slattern, a slut.

dràbach, *a.* dirty, nasty, slovenly.

dràbag, *n. f.* a dirty woman. So *Ir.*

dràbaire, drāb'-ir-u, *n. m.* a sloven.

drabasda, drǎb'-usd-à, *a.* filthy, obscene, smutty ; indecent in words.

drabasdachd, drab'-usd-achc, *n. f.* obscenity of language ; smuttiness.

drabh, drǎv, *n. m.* draff ; grain. *E.Ir.* **drabh.** *O.Celt.* drabo-. *Fk.* *O.N.* draf.

dràbh, drâv, *v.* dissolve ; scatter, as a multitude ; bulge, as a wall.

dràbh, *n. m.* ruination, ruin ; **chaidh e dhràibh,** it or he has gone to pigs and whistles.

dràbhadh, drâv'-u, separating, as a crowd ; bulging, as a wall.

dràbhag, drâv'-ag, *n. f.* a market thinly attended ; a scattered multitude.

dràbhag, *n. f.* dregs.

dràbhan, *n. m.* poor measure, small quantity.

drabhas, drǎv'-as, *n. m.* filth, foul weather.

drabhasach, dravasuch, *a.* dirty, foul.

drabhc, drouc, *n. m.* an awkward fellow.

drabhcar, *n. m.* a goodly measure (as catch of fish).

drabhloinn, draulin, *n. f.* absurdity, sheer nonsense.

drabhloinneach, draulinuch, *a.* absurd ; very nonsensical ; an absurd person.

drabhloinneachd, draulinuchc, *n. f.* sheer absurdity ; absurd conduct.

dràc, dràchd, *n. m.* a drake.

dragh, drugh, *n. m.* trouble, annoyance ; **na cuir dragh air,** don't trouble him. Cf. *O.N.* trega, to grieve ; *AS.* tregjan.

dragh, drū, *v.* pull, draw, drag. *Eng.* drag. *O.N.* draga. *AS.* dragan. *Goth.* dragan ; cf. *Gr.* τρέχω.

draghadh, *n. m.* act of dragging, pulling.

draghail, drughal, *a.* troublesome.

draghaire, dru-iru, *n. m.* a dray.

draghaistich, dru-isht-ich, *v.* drag, in an absurd or childish way.

draghalachd, dru-al-uchc, *n. f.* troublesomeness ; annoyance.

dràgon, *n. m.* a dragon. *E.Ir.* **drac, draic.** *Lat.* draco. *Gr.* δράκων.

dràic, dryk, **dràichd,** *n. f.* slattern ; *a.* **dràichdeil.**

draighearnach, dry-urnuch, *n. f.* a hedge of thorn ; thicket of thorn.

draighionn, dryun, *n. m.* blackthorn,

wood of the thorn generally. *O.Ir.*
draigen. *W.* draen. *O.Celt.* dragino-.
draighlichd, drylichc, *n. f.* a trollop ; a
draggle-tail.
draighneach, drynuch, *n. f.* blackthorn
thicket, lumber ; absurd detention.
draillsein, drylshen, *n. m.* a sparkling
light. *See* drillsein.
draimheas, drevus, *n. m.* a foul mouth.
draing, dréng, *n. f.* a snarl ; grin.
draingeis, dréng'-äsh, *n. f.* snarling,
carping ; childish bickering.
draingeiseach, dreng'-ash-uch, *a.* girning,
snarling ; bickering.
dram, dràm, *n. m.* a dram. *Eng.*
dramaig, *n. f.* 1. foul mixture. 2.
crowdie. *Sc.* dramock.
drann, draun, *n. m.* a hum ; a word ; a
syllable ; cha d' fhuair sinn drann, we
have not got a word. *Also* drannd.
M.Ir. drantaigim.
drannadh, *n. m.* word.
dranndail, *n. f.* grumbling, snarling.
dranndan, draundan, *n. m.* a hum ; buzzing of bees; a bickering, querulous complaint ; grumbling, teasing, growling.
O.Ir. drenn, quarrel. *O.Celt.* drinno-
dranndanach, draundanuch, *a.* querulous ;
humming ; buzzing.
dranndanachd, *n. f.* querulousness ; gurgling noise.
draoch, *n. m.* fretful, ghastly look (hair-
raising). *Ir.* driuch.
draoganta, *a.* strong, gritty.
draogh, drū, *v.* pull, drag.
draoi, draoidh, druidh, *n. m.* magician,
druid. *E.Ir.* drui, drai ; *gen.* druad
=dru-vides, "very learned," *savant.*
W. derwydd. *O.Celt.* drúi-s, drúid-os.
draoidheachd, drui-achc, *n. f.* enchantment ; state of being spellbound ;
bewitched.
draghlainn, drūlin, *n. f.* a slovenly person,
a mess.
draolainn, drūlin, *n. f.* delay, tediousness,
drawling.
draos, drūs, *n. m.* trash, filth. *See* drùis.
draosda, drūsda, *a.* obscene, smutty ;
ugly.
draosdachd, drūsdachc, *n. f.* obscenity ;
smuttiness ; lewdness ; filthiness of
speech.
draosdail, drūsdal, *a.* obscene, smutty.
draoth, drū, *n. m.* a good-for-nothing
person; a humdrum. *E.Ir.* drúth, a fool.
drapuinn, drapin, *n. f.* tape.
dràsda, an dràsda, *adv.* now =an tràth-sa.
E.Ir. cos trásta (=tráth-sa), till now.
O'Don.
drathais, drǎ'-ish, *n. f.* an old pair of
trousers, patched one ; drawers, from
the *Eng.*
dreach, drech, *n. m.* face, aspect, colour

or hue of the complexion ; form,
image, probability, seemliness ; *v.*
colour, paint, adorn. *E.Ir.* drech,
mien, face. *W.* drych. *O.Celt.* drko-.
dreachadair, drech'-ud-er', *n. m.* painter.
dreachadan, drechudan, *n. m.* a mould.
dreachail, drech'-al, *a.* handsome, good-
looking ; comely, personable.
dreachalachd, drech'-al-achg, *n. f.* comeliness, handsomeness, personableness.
drèachd, dreuchd, *n. f.* office, duty. *O.Ir.*
drecht, drect, pars, dreecht, portio.
dreachdan, *pl.* plots, tricks. Cf. *Sc.*
draucht, an artful scheme.
dreachmhor, drech'-ur, *a.* good-looking,
handsome.
drèag, drēg, *n. f.* a meteor, supposed to
portend the death of a great personage,
particularly the Laird. *Also* driùg.
drèagan, *n. m.* dragon, champion.
dreaganta, drūgantu, *a.* fierce, captious,
peevish. 2. strong, great power of
endurance.
drealainn, drelin, *n. f.* rabble.
dreall, drell, *n. m.* a blaze ; a torch.
dreall, dreoll, *n. m.* door, bar.
dreallag, drelag, *n. f.* a swing (for play),
swinging machine ; swingle-tree.
dreallaire, dreliru, *n. m.* loiterer. *O.N.*
drolla.
dreallan-doininn, *n. m.* stormy petrel.
dreallsach, drelsuch, *n. f.* a blazing fire ;
the face blazing with liquor.
drèam, drèm, *n. m.* race of people ; a
tribe. *E.Ir.* dremm, a multitude,
crowd.
dream, *n. f.* a snarl. *E.Ir.* dremne,
rage.
dreamach, dremuch, *a.* peevish, snarling,
grinning. *E.Ir.* dremne, fierceness.
dreamag, dremag, *n. f.* handful of sheaf-
corn, used as a decoy for a horse ; a
little sheaf-corn.
dream-chraos, *n. m.* distorted mouth.
dreamlainn, for drabhloinn, *vbl. n. m.*
snarling.
dreamsgal, dramascul, *n. m.* a heterogeneous mass ; refuse.
dreang, dréng, *n. f.* a snarl, girn ; a
girning expression of countenance ; *v.*
snarl, grin. *E.Ir.* dreng, a fight. Cf.
drenn.
dreangaire, dreng'-ir'-u, *n. m.* a snarler.
dreangais, dreng'-ash, *n. f.* snarling.
dreangan, drengan, *n. m.* a snarler.
dreas, *n. f.* a bramble, brier. *Also* dris.
dreasail, dresal, *a.* prickly.
dreasarnach, dresarnuch, *n. f.* a thicket
of brambles or briers.
dreathan, dre'-an, *n. m.* a wren. *Also*
dreathan-donn and dreothan-donn.
W. dryw.
dréibh, drēv, *n.* grips, vigour.

dreigeas, dregas, *n. m.* a grin, peevish face. *E.Ir.* dric, wrathful.
dreigeasach, *a.* pertinacious.
dreimire, dremiru, *n. m.* a ladder. *E.Ir.* dréimm, ascent. *O.Celt.* drengô.
dréin, drēn, *n. f.* a grin, grimace ; dèan dréin is cum ort, grin and bear it.
dréineag, drēnag, *n. f.* a grinning girl.
dreingein, drengen, *n. m.* a peevish, fretful, discontented person.
dréisde, drēshtu, *a.* ironed, dressed (linen).
dreòchdam, drōch-cam, *n. m.* purring ; crying of the deer.
dreòdan, drōdan, *n. m.* a little louse.
dreòlan, drōlan, *n. m.* a wren.
dreòlan, *n. m.* a silly person, a dwarf.
Dreòllunn, drôlun, *n. m.* an old name for the island of Mull.
dreòs, dryôss, *n. m.* a blaze.
drèosgach, *a.* coarse, loosely woven.
driachan, *n. m.* plodding, drudgery.
driachanachd, *n. f.* plodding, botching.
driamanach, *a.* intricate, troublesome, as work, etc.
driamlach, dre-um-luch, *n. m.* a fishing-line ; tackle for fishing-rod ; tall, ugly fellow.
drifeag, *n. f.* hurry. *See* drip.
dril, *n. m.* a drop of dew ; state of being slightly drunk ; spark, a sparkle. *M.Ir.* drithle.
drileanach, *a.* shining, sparkling.
drilleachan, dree-luchan, *n. m.* the sandpiper.
drillseach, dreelshuch, *a.* glimmering, radiant.
drillsean, dreellshen, *n. m.* a glimmer ; glimmering fire ; rush-wick ; rush-light.
drillseanach, dreelshenuch, *a.* glimmering, sparkling as fire.
drimneach, dreemnuch, *a.* striped, streaked ; parti-coloured ; piebald.
drine, dreenu, *n. f.* choice bit ; poet's portion of sheep.
driobhail-drabhail, driv'-ul-drav'-ul, *adv.* hurly-burly.
driochan, drichan, *n. m.* screed.
driodar, dridur, *n. m.* lees, dregs.
driodart, dridurt, *n. m.* scandalous event.
driod-fhortan, drid-orstan, *n. m.* a mishap ; an anecdote ; ag innseadh dhrìod-fhortan, relating anecdotes.
driodshuileach, drid-huluch, *a.* having a twinkling eye.
driog, *n. m.* a drop. Cf. *O.N.* dregg, lees.
driogaid, drigej, *n. m.* dregs.
driogaire, drigiru, *n. m.* a distiller.
drioganach, *a.* dropping, tardy, slow ; bó dhrioganach, cow giving milk in driblets.
driongan, dringan, *n. m.* slowness.
drionganachd, *n. f.* slowness, tardiness.

driothlag, drill'-ag, *n. f.* a glimmering fire.
driothlunn, dri-lin, *n. f.* a ray of light.
drip, dreep, *n. m.* predicament ; a trap ; snare meant for another, but ensnaring the author of it ; thuit e fhéin anns an drip, he himself fell into the snare.
drip, *n. f.* hurry, sense of urgency to overtake a piece of work. Cf. *E.Ir.* grip, speed.
dripeil, drēp''-al, *a.* hurried, embarrassed ; confused ; busy, hard at work.
dris, drish, *n. f.* a thorn, a bramble, a brier. *O.Ir.* driss (*gl.* uepres). *O.Celt.* dresso-, dressi-.
driseag, drishag, *n. f.* a little thorn.
drisearnach, drisharnuch, *n. f.* a place where thorns grow.
drithleam, drilem, *n. f.* a sparkle.
drithlean, drilen, *n. m.* a rivet.
driubhlach, drooluch, *n. m.* a cowl.
driùcan, droocan, *n. m.* beak ; an incision under one of the toes.
driuch, drooch, *n. m.* activity, energy ; cuir driuch ort, bestir yourself.
driuchail, droochal, *adj.* active, lively.
driuchan, droochan, *n. m.* a stripe, as in cloth ; driuchean geal is dubh, a white and black stripe.
driuchanach, droochanach, *a.* striped.
driùchd, droochc, *n. m.* dew ; *recte* druchd.
driùchdan, *n. m.* a dewdrop.
driùg, *n. f.* a meteor. *See* drèag.
dròbh, drōv, *n. m.* a drove ; a market ; a crowd ; fr. *Eng.*
drobhailt, drovelt, *n. f.* a hopper.
dròbhair, drôv'-er', *n. m.* a drover, cattle-dealer ; a man at a market.
dròbhaireachd, drōver-uchc, *n. f.* cattle-dealing ; sauntering at market.
drobhlas, droulas, *n. m.* profusion.
droch, drōch, *a.* bad, evil ; droch là, a bad day ; droch dhuine, a bad man ; used always before the noun. *O.Ir.* droch, drog. *W.* drwg. *O.Celt.* druko-.
droch-àbhaist, *n. f.* a bad custom.
drochaid, drōch'-äj, *n. f.* a bridge. *O.Ir.* drochet, a bridge.
droch-bharail, droch-varal *n. f.* a bad opinion ; a prejudice.
drochbheart, *n. f.* bad conduct.
droch-chreideamh, droch-chreju, *n. m.* " bad " faith ; poor faith.
drochmheinn, *n. f.* ill-will, malice.
drog, *n. m.* a wave's impact on a rock.
drògaid, drōgej, *n. f.* drugget ; cloth of wool and linen ; anything spoiled by being mixed.
drògha, drō'-à, *n. m.* a hand fishing-line. *See* dorbh, dorgh. *O.N.* dorg, an angler's tackle.
droigheann, drŏyun, *n. m.* a bramble, a thorn. *O.Ir.* draigen. *W.* draen. *See* draigheann, a copse.

droighneach, droynuch, *n. f.* a heap of thorns or sticks.

droighnein, droynen, *n. m.* a thorny place.

droillse, drylshu, *n. m.* a flame, radiance.

droineach, drŏn'-uch, *n. f.* a ragged garment.

droineap, drŏn'-ap, *n. f.* a ragged person; anything ragged; a hump.

droing, drŏing, *n. f. See* **drong**.

droinip, dronip, *n. f.* canvas, sails, ships' tackle, rag. *See* **droineap**.

drol, *n. f.* a loop, a link. So *Ir.*

drola, drŏl'-à, *n. m., pl.* drolachan, pothook. *Also* bughall.

drolabhaid, drol'-a-vaj, *n. m.* lumber.

drolabhan, drol'-a-vin, *n. m.* a good-for-nothing fellow.

drolag, *n. f.* a chain-link, a swing.

droll, *n. m.* back of a beast; rump; high dudgeon, door bar, sluggard.

drollach, *a.* apt to take great offence.

drollaire, *n. m.* a lazy fellow, a sluggard.

droma, *gen.* of **druim**, *q.v.*

dromach, *n. f.* backbone.

dromach - air - shearrach, dromuch - er - hiaruch, *a.* topsy-turvy.

droman, *n. m.* for **druman**. 1. alder. 2. a ridge, little hill.

dromannan, *pl.* of **druim**, *q.v.*

drong, *n. f.* people, race, tribe. *E.Ir.* drong, troop. *O.Celt.* drungo-.

drongair, droonger, *n. m.* a drunkard.

dronn, *n. f., gen.* druinne, back, rump.

dronnag, *n. f.* a hunch; small height; small of the back; a cushion for the back when under a creel; a small burden.

drothanach, dro-han-uch, *n. m.* a light breeze, a gentle breeze.

druabag, drooubag, *n. f.* small drop.

druablaich, **druablas**, droo'ublich, *n. f.* muddy water, lees. *Also* **druabras**.

druaip, droo-up, *n. f.* debauchery, drinking in bad company; a debauchee, lees, dregs.

druaipeil, droo-upal, *a.* debauched.

druaipire, droo-upiru, *n. m.* a tippler.

drùb, droob, *n. f.* a wink (of sleep).

drùbag, *n. f.* a mouthful of liquid.

drùbanta, *a.* drowsy.

drùbshuileach, *a.* sleepy-eyed.

drùchd, droochc, *n. m.* moisture; dew, tear; *v.* ooze, emit drops. *E.Ir.* **drúcht**, dew. *O.Celt.* druptu-.

drùdhadh, droo-u, *vbl. n. m.* oozing, dripping, penetrating, drooking; impression, influence (as by speech); **cha do rinn e an drùdhadh a bu lugha air**, it has not made the smallest impression on him; pouring out the last drop.

drùdhag, droo'-ag, *n. f.* a small drop, a dram.

drugair, *n. m.* a drudge, a mean swiller.

druid, drooj, *v.* shut, close, draw near.

druid, drooj, *n. f., pl.* **druidean**, a starling. *E.Ir.* truid.

druideadh, drooju, *vbl. n. m.* closing, shutting.

drùidh, drooy, *v.* ooze; penetrate to the skin, impress, make an impression, influence; **dhrùidh e orm**, the rain has penetrated to my skin; **is ann mar sin a dhrùidh e air**, that is the way it impressed him, or he felt it; *v. n.* pour forth the last drop; " 'n uair a dhrùidheadh iad na botail," when they would drain the bottles.

drùidh, druy, *n. m.* a magician, a sorcerer, a philosopher; **dh'innis e sin do na drùidhean**, he told that to the magicians. *See* **draoi**.

drùidheach, drooy-achc, *a.* oozing, penetrating.

drùidheachd, druyachc, *n. f.* magic, sorcery, witchcraft.

drùidhteach, drūtyach, *a.* impressive, emphatic, penetrating; **cainnt dhrùidhteach**, impressive language.

druidte, drooj-tu, *vbl. a.* shut, closed.

druim, *n. m., gen.* **droma**, *pl.* **dromannan**, back, keel, ridge; **cnàimh an droma**, the backbone. *O.Ir.* druimm. *W.* drum. *Lat.* dorsum. *O.Celt.* drotsmen.

druimionn, drimun, *a.* for **druimfhionn**, white-backed.

druimneach, drimnuch, *a.* furrowed, ridged, a series of eminences.

druin, *v.* shut, close.

druineach, drineich, *n. m.* a skilled artificer, embroiderer. *E.Ir.* drunech, **druinech** (*f.*), embroideress.

druinnean, droonen, *n. m.* the lowest part of the back, a little back.

drùis, drush, *n. m.* lust. *E.Ir.* drúth, lewdness, harlot. *M.W.* drud, reckless, mad.

drùis, *n. m.* exudation.

drùiseach, drooshuch, *a.* lecherous.

drùisealachd, drooshaluchc, *n. f.* moisture, perspiration.

drùisealachd, *n. f.* lewdness.

drùiseil, droosh'-al, *a.* lustful.

drùisire, droosh'-ur-a, *n. m.* fornicator.

druma, *n. f.* a drum; *pl.* drumachan.

drumach, *n. f.* ridge-band of a cart-horse, etc. *Also* **drumanach**.

drumair, *n. m.* a drummer.

drumaireachd, droomeruchc, *n. f.* drumming; absurd hammering; noise.

druman, *n. m.* elder or bourtree; a little back.

drunadh, droonu, *vbl. n. m.* shutting, closing; conclusion.

drùth, droo, *n. f.* a harlot. *E.Ir.* drúth. *O.Celt.* drouto-, drûto-.

dù, *a.* meet, proper, hereditary. *See* dùth. *E.Ir.* dú.

du-, do-, *prefix* denoting badness. *O.Ir.* du-, do-. *O.Celt.* dus-. *Gr.* δυς-.

duabharaich, doo-arich, *v.* obscure.

duaichneachd, du-ech-nachc, *n. f.* ugliness, deformity.

duaichnich, *v.* make ugly.

duaichnidh, du-ech-ni, *a.* ugly, gloomy, anything but pretty (du + aithne, obscure). *Also* duainidh.

duaidh, du-ay, *n. f.* a horrid scene, a battle.

duailisg, du-elishc, *n. f.* fraud.

duaineil, du-ayn-al, *a.* ugly sight, unseemly.

duairc, du-erc, *n. f.* surliness, a vice, a rude person. du + serc ; *opp.* suairc.

duairceil, du-erc-al, *a.* unamiable.

duaireachas, du-ay-ruchus, *n. m.* a slander, a squabble.

duairidh, dubharaidh, du-ary, *n. f.* dowry ; fr. *Eng.*

duais, du-esh, *n. f.* a reward, premium, present ; wages, fees. *E.Ir.* duass.

duaisire, du-esh-iru, *n. m.* a rewarder.

dual, doo-ul, *n. m.* a fold, or ply of a rope, or anything twisted ; a plait ; *v.* plait, fold, ply. *E.Ir.* dual. *O.Celt.* doklo-. Cf. *O.N.* tagl, horse's tail.

dual, *a.* right, hereditary. *M.Ir.* right, proper.

dualach, *a.* plaited (as hair).

dualachas, *n. m.* hereditary disposition.

dualtach, *a. adj.* fr. dual.

duan, *n. f.* a poem, song. *E.Ir.* dúan. *O.Celt.* dugnâ.

duanachd, *n. f.* poetry, versification, making poems.

duanag, *n. f.* a sonnet, a ditty, a catch, a canto, a little poem.

duanaire, du-an-iru, *n. m.* a songster, a bard ; a book of poems, or ballads.

duanaireachd, *n. f.* chanting, rhyming.

duarman, doo'urman, *n. m.* a murmur. Cf. torman.

duarmanaich, *n. f.* grumbling, murmuring.

duatharachd, *n. f.* 1. murkiness, obscurity. 2. mystery. Cf. *O.N.* dumbr, the misty.

dub, doob, *n. f.* the smallest measure ; " cha d' thainig dub air," he has not grown the least bit.

dubadh, *n. m.* a slight pull, a jerk.

dùbailte, doo-biltu, *vbl. a.* double, doubleminded ; duine dubailte, a doubleminded person ; fr. *Eng.*

dùbailteachd, doobiltuchc, *n. f.* dissimulation, double-dealing ; deceit.

dubh, doo, *a.* black, dark, lamentable, disastrous ; *v.* blacken, blot out. *O.Ir.* dub. *W.* du. *O.Celt.* dubo-s.

dubh, *n. m.* blackness, darkness, the pupil of the eye, ink.

dubhach, doo-uch, *n. m.* blackening ; dubhach bhròg, shoe blacking ; dubhach cobhain, lamp-black.

dubhach, *a.* gloomy, very sad, very sorrowful, melancholy, disastrous, mournful.

dubhachas, doo-uchus, *n. m.* gloom, melancholy, sorrow, sadness.

dubhadan, doo'-ud-an, *n. f.* ink-holder.

dubhag, *n. f.* a deep or dark pool.

dubhag, *n. f.* a kidney.

dubhaigean, du-egin, *n. m.* abyss.

dubhailc, du-elc, *n. f.* vice ; *E.Ir.* dualig, *vitium.* du (bad) + álaig (behaviour) ; *opp.* of subhailc.

dubhailteach, doo-eltuch, *a.* sad, sorrowful.

dubhair, doo-er, *v.* darken, shade.

dubhairidh, doo-ary, *n. f.* dowry.

dubhais, doo-esh, *n. f.* a hardship.

dùbhaith, doo-vy, *n. f.* a pudding.

dubhan, doo'-an, *n. m.* 1. a hook, particularly a fishing - hook, a claw, a clutch ; ad dhubhain, in thy clutches. 2. kidney.

dubhar, doo-ar, *n. m.* shade ; mar dhubhar na h-uaighe, like the shade of the grave ; darkness.

dubharach, doo-ar-uch, *a.* shady, shadowy, opaque, dusky.

dubharachd, du-ar-uchc, *n. f.* the darkening ; the dusk ; a shady or dusky place ; opacity, an eclipse of the sun or moon.

dubharaich, du-ar-ich, *v.* shade, eclipse.

dubhbhlianach, doo-vliunuch, *n. f.* lean flesh.

dubh-bhreac, doo-vrac, *a.* black and white.

dubh-bhròn, doo-vrōn, *n. m.* overwhelming grief ; dubh-bhrònach, disconsolate.

dubhbreac, doo-breck, *n. m., pl.* dubhbric, black trout.

dubhchaile, doo-chal'-u, *n. f.* a trollop, a scullion.

dubhchasach, doo-chas'-uch, *n. f.* maidenhair fern.

dubh-chìs, doo-cheesh, *n. f.* blackmail.

dubh-chlèin, doo-chlen, *n. f.* the flank, spleen. *Also* lochlèin.

dùbhdan, doodan, *n. m.* a smoke, straw cinders, soot, dust from grinding grain ; mill dust.

dùbhdhearg, doo-yerg, *a.* dark red.

dùbhdhonn, doo-youn, *a.* dark-brown, drab, dun.

dubhfhacal, doo-acul, *n. m.* an obscure saying, a riddle, a parable.

dubhghalar, *n. m.* disease in cattle.

dubhghall, *n. m.* dark stranger, a foreigner.

dubhghlaic, *n. f.* a dark valley or hollow.

dùbhghlas, *a.* dark grey; also the surname Douglas. *O.Ir.* dubglass, *caeruleus. O.Celt.* dubo-glasto-s.

dùbhghorm, *a.* dark blue.

dubhlà, *n. m.* a dark day, day of trial, of temptation.

dùbhlachd, doo-lachc, *n. f.* the dark (season) ; cold and storm in season ; wintry weather, depth of winter. *Also* dùldachd.

dùbhlachdail, doo'-lachc-al, *a.* wintry.

dùbhlaidh, doolly, *a.* darkish ; gloomy ; wintry.

dùbhlaidheachd, dooly-achc, *n. f.* darkishness, lowering sky.

dùbhlan, doo-lan, *n. m.* defiance, challenge ; hardihood, capability of bearing cold, hardship and want ; the quick ; **cuir gu a dhùbhlan e,** touch him to the quick, defy, challenge ; fr. dubh + slàn (defiance), **dùbhshlan.**

dùbhlanach, doolanuch, *a.* defying, challenging, capable of bearing cold and fatigue, hardy ; brave.

dùbhlanachd, *n. f.* hardihood, degree of bravery, fearlessness.

dùbhlanaich, doolanich, *v.* challenge, defy.

dubh-liath, *n. f., gen.* dubh-léithe, the spleen.

dùbhloisg, *v.* burn to a cinder.

dubh-loisgte, *vbl. a.* burnt to a cinder.

dubh-losgadh, *n. m.* great burning.

dubh-neul, *n. m., pl.* d.-neòil, a dark cloud.

dubhobair, *n. f.* unskilled labour.

dubhogha, doo'o, *n. m.* the great-grandson's grandson. *See* glùn.

dùbhrach, dooruch, *n. f.* for **dobhrach,** water-cress.

dùbhradan, doorudan, *n. m.* a mote.

dùbhradh, dooru, *n. m.* darkness, shadow, a dark object in the distance.

dùbh-ruadh, *a.* dark red, auburn.

dubh-shiubhlach, *n. f.* a strolling female or gipsy.

dubhshuileach, *a.* black-eyed.

dùbhthrath, *n. m.* the dusk.

dubhthuil, *n. m.* artillery. *W.R.*

dùblachadh, doobluchu, *vbl. n. m.* act of doubling, distilling the second time.

dùblaich, dooblich, *v.* double, distil.

dùc, dook, *n. m.* a heap.

dùchas, doochus, for **dùthchas,** *n. m.* 1. native land. 2. hereditary right. *E.Ir.* duthchus, duchus, heritage, *patria.*

dùd, dood, *n. m.* a hollow sound, a word, a sound.

dud, *n. m.* a small lump.

dùdach, *n. f.* a trumpet, a bugle, a war-horn ; *pl.* dùdaichean.

dùdaire, doodiru, *n. m.* trumpeter.

dùdan, doodan. *See* dùbhdan.

dùdlachd, doodlachc, *n. f.* depth of winter.

dùgharra, *a.* stubborn.

dù-ghràin, *n. f.* complete disgust.

dù-ghràinich, doo-ghrā-nich, *v.* detest.

duibh, dŭěv, to you. *See* do.

duibhe, dooyu, *n. m.* blackness ; *a.* more or most black ; na's duibhe, blacker.

duibh-leum, *n. f.* a wiid leap.

duibh-lias, *n. m.* torch ; " a' sireadh an éisg le duibh-liasaibh," fishing—searching for fish—with torches.

duibhre, duira, *n. f.* darkness, shade.

duibh-ruith, *n. f.* furious running.

duibhse, *prep.* do (to) + *emph. pers. pron.* 2 *pl.* sibhse, to you.

duibreac, doobrec, *n. m.* a spirling.

dùil, dool, *n. f.* expectation, hope, belief ; supposition ; tha dùil againn, we expect ; tha mi 'n dùil, I hope, I suppose ; thug sinn ar dùil deth, we lost all expectation of his recovery.

dùil, *n. f.* a creature, an element ; gach dùil bheò, every living creature. *O.Ir.* dúil, element, *creatura.*

dùil, dool, *v.* hoop or thread as a hook.

dùile, doolu, *n. m.* a poor creature, a little or diminutive person. *Also* dùileag.

dùileach, dooluch, *a.* expectant, covetous.

dùileach, *a.* elemental, belonging to nature. *E.Ir.* dulech.

dùileachd, doolachc, *n. f.* doubt, suspicion, as of a child ; 'ga chur an dùileachd, suspecting that the child is not one's own.

duileann, doolun, *n. m.* a perquisite, a present ; móran dhuileannan eile, a great number of other perquisites ; a tribute.

duileasg, doolusc, *n. m.* dulse ; " màthair an duilisg " = carrageen.

duileum, du-lēm, *n. m.* a bound, leap.

duilghe, doolyu, **duilgheadas,** doolyudus, *n. m.* sadness, difficulty ; *fr.* duilich.

duilich, doolich, *a.* difficult, hard ; sorry, grievous ; is duilich leam, I am sorry ; is duilich leam gur fior, I am sorry it is too true ; *compar.* duile ; na's duile, more difficult. *E.Ir.* dolig, *compar.* doilghi, difficult, doleful.

duilichinn, doolichin, *n. f.* sorrow, grief, vexation.

duille, dooliu, *n. f.* a leaf of any kind. *M.Ir.* duille. *O.Celt.* dulâ.

duille, *n. f.* sheath ; " bheireadh claidheamh á duille," who would unsheathe a sword.

duilleach, dooliuch, *n. m.* foliage.

duilleachan, *n. m.* a pamphlet.

duilleag, dooliag, *n. f.* a leaflet ; a leaf of any kind ; taobh duilleig, a page ; duilleag còmhla, leaf of a door.
duilleagach, *a.* leafy.
duilleag-bhàite, *n. f.* white water-lily.
duillich, dooilich, *v.* sprout, flourish.
duillinnean, *pl.* customs, taxes.
dùin, dûên, *v. i. t.* shut, enclose, close, button, lace, darken, obscure. *O.Ir.* dúnaim, I barricade, shut.
duine, doonu, *n. m., pl.* daoine, a person ; a man ; an individual ; an duine, the landlord ; an duine agamsa, my husband ; a bheil duine stigh, is there anybody in ? *O.Ir.* duine. *O.Celt.* dunjó-s. *W.* dŷn.
duineachan, doonuchan, *n. m.* a manikin.
duinealachd, doonalachc, duinealas, *n. m.* manliness ; decision of character.
duineil, doonal, *a.* manly ; like a man. dune + samail.
duinn, dooyn, to us. do + sinn. *See* do.
duinne, *a.*, *compar.* of donn, more or most brown.
duinnead, dooynud, *n. f.* brownness ; fr. donn, brown.
dùinte, doontiu, *vbl. a.* shut ; closed.
duirc, doorc, *n. m.* pine cone, acorn.
duirceach, doorcuch, *n. f.* a dirk.
duirceall, doorciul, *n. f.* a rusty knife.
duircein, doorcen, *n. m., dim.* of duirc, a cone of the fir. *O.Ir.* derucc, glans.
dùire, dooru, *a., compar.* of dùr, *q.v.* ; *n. f.* obstinacy, stiffness, indocility.
dùis, doosh, *n. f.* gloom, mist.
duiseal, dooshal, *n. f.* a whip.
dùiseal, dùsal, dooshal, *n. m.* slumber, drowsiness. Cf. *O.N.* dúsa, doze.
dùisealan, dooshulan, dùisleannan, *n. pl.* freaks, ill-natured pretences.
dùisg, dooshc, *v.* awake ; rouse, stir up. *M.Ir.* dúiscim.
duit, doot, *prep.* do + 2 *pers. pron. s.* tu, to you. *See* do.
dul, dool, *n. m.* a noose ; slipping noose, loop, swivel.
dùl, dool, *gen. pl.* of dùil ; leaghar na dùil, the elements shall melt ; Dia nan dùl, God of nature.
dul, *adv.* once upon a time, when.
dula, *n. f.* a pin, a peg.
dùldachd, dooldachc, *n. f.* misty gloom.
dùldaidh. *See* dùbhlaidh.
dùmhail, doo'-ul, *a.* bulky ; thick ; " packed " (audience).
dùmhlachadh, dooluchu, *vbl. n. m.* crowding ; growing more dense ; thickening.
dùmhladas, dooludus, *n. m.* bulk, bulkiness, crowdedness, clumsiness, denseness.
dùmhlaich, doolich, *v.* crowd ; get more dense ; press as a multitude.
dùn, doon, *n. m., pl.* dùintean, a fort,

a fortress, a castle, a fortification, a heap. *O.Ir.* dún, *castrum, arx. W.* dîn. Cf. *Ag.S.* and *O.N.* tún. *Ger.* zaun. *Eng.* town.
dùnadh, doonu, *vbl. n. m.* shutting, closing ; conclusion ; close.
dunaich, doon-ech, *n. f.* mishap, mischief ; ciod e an dunaich a thàinig ort, what mischief came over you ? *Also* dunaidh.
dùnan, doon-an, *n. m.* a heap ; a dunghill.
Dùn-éideann, dun-ējunn, Edinburgh.
dùnlios, doon-lis, *n. m.* palace-yard.
dunt, doont, *n. m.* a thump, a thud.
duntag, *n. f.* a plump little article or person.
duntail, doontal, *vbl. n. f.* thumping.
dùr, door, *a.* stubborn, stiff ; indocile, untractable. *E.Ir.* dúr, hard. *O.Celt.* dûro-. *Sc.* dour, hard, obstinate.
dùrachd, doorachc, *n. f.* sincere intention or wish ; sincerity, earnestness ; luckpenny ; a bheil e an dùrachd mhath dhuit, has he good intentions towards you ? *O.Ir.* dúthracht, desire.
dùrachdach, doorachcuch, *a.* sincere ; very sincere or earnest.
dùradan, doorudan, *n. m.* a mote ; particle of dust ; chaidh dùradan am shùil, a mote stuck in mine eye.
dùraig, dùirig, *v.* desire, wish, have courage ; " na'm b'urrainn mi dhùraiginn," if I could I would wish (attempt) ; *v.* sincerely hope ; fain hope ; sincerely wish. *O.Ir.* dúthracim, I desire, wish.
dùranta, *a.* stiff, obstinate.
dùrantachd, *n. f.* obstinacy.
durc, *n. m.* a lump, shapeless piece.
durcais, *n. f.* pincers, nippers. *Sc.* turkas.
dùrchluasach, *a.* dull of hearing.
dùrchridheach, *a.* hard-hearted.
dùrd, doord, *n. m.* a hum, buzz ; a word, syllable, sound ; *v.* hum, buzz. *O.Ir.* dórd, *mugio.* *O.Celt.* dordô, to low.
dùrdail, doordal, *vbl. n. m.* buzzing, humming ; continued buzzing, murmuring ; blackcock's note.
dùrdan, doordan, *n. m.* grumbling, teasing, humming noise.
dùrdanach, doordanuch, *a.* querulous.
dùrdanaich, doordanich, *n. f.* querulousness.
durga, doorgu, durganta, *a.* surly, sour. *O.N.* durgr, a sulky fellow.
durlus, doorloos, *n. m.* water-cress. = dobhar-lus.
durradh, dooru, *n. f.* a pig, sow ; durradh ! durradh ! grumphy ! grumphy !
durrag, doorag, *n. f.* worm ; a little pig.
durrghail, *n. f.* cooing of dove.
durrghan, *n. m.* snarling of a dog.

dursann, doorsun, *n. m.* mishap, bad luck.

dus, doos, *n. m.* lute.

dus, doos, *n. m.* dust, smithy ashes.

dùsal, doosal, *n. m.* slumber. Cf. *N.* dús, a lull.

dusan, *n. m.* a dozen.

dùsgadh, doosgu, *vbl. n. m.* awakening ; excitement ; act of rousing, exciting.

duslach, doosluch, *n. m.* dust ; mill-dust.

duslachail, doosluchal, *a.* dusty.

duslinn, doos-lin, *n. m.* dust ; dark place.

dùth, doo, *a.* due, hereditary, fit ; what circumstances warrant ; befitting one's case ; **cha dùth dha sin**, that cannot be expected from him.

dùth, *n. m.* complement, due proportion ; equitable share ; proportionate quantity or number ; **clach ime le a dùth de chàis**, a stone of butter, with its complement of cheese. *See* **dù.**

dùthaich, dooich, *n. f.* country ; a district ; **air an dùthaich**, on the country ; **muinntir mo dhùthcha**, my country folk. *O.Ir.* duthoig, hereditary.

dùthaich, *n. f.* large gut ; the *anus.*

dùthail, doohal, *a.* hereditary ; giving just grounds to anticipate or expect ; quite natural ; reasonable.

dùthchas, doochus, *n. m.* 1. native land, native district. 2. hereditary right, an old form of land tenure. 3. heredity.

dùthchasach, *a.* hereditary ; **bu dùthchasach sin dà**, that was hereditary in his family ; *n. m.* a native ; an aboriginal ; **an uair a thrèigeas na dùthchasaich Ila, beannachd le sìth Albann**, when the natives forsake Islay, farewell to the peace of Scotland.

dùthchasachd, *n. f.* hereditary right, or privilege, or failing ; nativity.

dùthrachd, doorachc, *n. m.* earnestness, good wish, diligence. *O.Ir.* dúthracht, *voluntas.*

dùthrachdach, *a.* earnest, well-wishing, sincere, devoted. *O.Ir.* dúthrachtach, diligent, urgent.

duthuil, doohool, *n. m. fluxus alvi.* Same as **dubhghalar.**

E

e, the fifth letter of the alphabet, named eubh, the aspen tree.

e, *pers. pron.*, he, him, and it, both accusative and nominative.

e ! *inter.* ay !

ea-, èa-, eu-, *neg. prefix.*

eabair, ebir, *v.* make slimy, as mud, by continual trampling ; roll in the mud.

eabar, ebur, *n. m.* slimy mud, mire. *Ir.* ebor.

Eabhra, yauru, *n. f.* Hebrew, the Hebrew language or tongue.

Eabhrach, yauruch, *n. m.* a Hebrew, a Jew ; *adj.* Hebrew, Jewish ; **na h-Eabhraich**, the Hebrews ; **a chainnt Eabhrach**, Hebrew language.

eabon, *n. m.* ebony.

eabrach, ebruch, *a.* miry, slimy.

eabradh, ebru, *vbl. n. m.* a wallowing, etc.; **a chum a h-eabradh 'san làthaich**, to her wallowing in the mire. *Bible.*

eabur, *n. m.* ivory. *Lat.* ebur.

each, ech, *n. m., pl.* eich, a horse, a brute ; **eich mheanmnach**, mettlesome horses ; **each marcachd**, a riding horse ; **each ceannaich**, a post horse ; **each breac**, a piebald horse ; **each saibhd, each fuadain**, a stray horse ; **each cartach, each féin**, a cart horse ; **nach bu tu an t-each !** what a brute you are ! *E.Ir.* ech. *W.* ebol, a colt. *O.Celt.* ekvo-s. *Gaul.* epo-s.

eachach, echuch, *a.* well supplied with horses.

eachalachd, echaluchc, *n. f.* brutality.

eachan, *n. m.* a little horse, a winding horse.

eachan, *n. m.* swifts ; smooth cockle.

eachaodach, echuduch, *n. m.* caparison.

eacharnach, echarnuch, *n. f.* park for horses. *Islay.*

eachdair, ech-dur, *n. f.* history.

eachdaire, ech-diru, *n. m.* a historian, a chronicler, a recorder.

eachdaireachd, *n. f.* historiography, history, chronicles.

eachdaran, echcuran, eachdra, *n. m.* a pen for strayed sheep ; fr. *E.Ir.* echtra.

eachdraiche, echdricha, *n. m.* a historian.

eachdraidh, echdri, *n. f.* history. *E.Ir.* echtra, adventures. *E.Ir. prep.* echtar, without. *Lat.* extra, *externus. O.Celt.* ekstero, eksterno.

eachdraidheachd, echdry-achc, *n. f.* historiography, chronicles, history.

eachdranach, echdranuchc, *n. m.* a foreigner. *O.Ir.* echtrann, exter.

eachlair, echler, *n. m.* a brutish fellow, a hostler.

eachlaireachd, *n. f.* brutish conduct.

eachlais, echlesh, *n. f.* a passage, entry.

each-leigh, *n. m.* a farrier.

each-leigheas, *n. m.* the veterinary art.

eachraidh, *coll. n.* horses, cavalry.

eachrais, ech-resh, *n. f.* bustle, confusion, mess. In *Ir.* a fair. *E.Ir.* echtress, a horse-fight.

éad, *n. m.* jealousy, zeal. *See* eud.

éadail, *a.* wealth in cattle ; m' fheudail, my treasure. *See* eudail.

Eadailt, Italy ; 's an Eadailt, in Italy.

eadar, *prep., asp.* when it means, both . . . and, between ; eadar mise agus thusa, between me and you ; among ; eadaruibh fhèin, among yourselves ; both ; eadar bheag is mhór, both great and small ; eadar long is lamraig, between the cup and the lip, lit. between the ship and the quay ; eadar fheala-dhà is dha-rìreadh, between jest and earnest ; eadar am bogha is an t-sreang, with much ado ; making both ends meet with great difficulty ; eadar + *pers. pron.* eadarainn, between us ; eadaraibh, between you ; eatorra, between them. *O.Ir.* eter, iter, etar. *W.* ithr. *Bret.* étré. *Lat.* inter. *O.Celt.* en-ter.

eadar - dhealachadh, *n. m.* distinction, difference ; distinguishing ; separating.

eadar-dhealaich, adur-yalich, *v.* distinguish, separate, divide.

eadar - ghearradh, *n. m.* separation, divorce.

eadar-ghuidh, adur-ghuy, *v.* intercede, make intercession.

eadar-ghuidhe, adur-ghuya, *n. f.* intercession, mediatory prayer.

eadar-ghuidhear, adur-ghuyer, *n. m.* an intercessor, a mediator.

eadar-mheadhonach, adurviänach, *a.* intercessory ; indifferent, middling.

eadar-mheadhonaich, adur-viänich, *n. f.* middling state ; tha e 'san eadarmheadhonaich, he is but very indifferent.

eadar-mheadhonair, adur-viäner, *n. m.* an intercessor, a mediator, an arbiter ; eadar-mheadhonaireachd, mediation, intercession.

eadar-mhìneachadh, adur-veenacha, *n. m.* annotation, interpretation, explanation.

eadar-mhìneachair, adurveenucher, *n. m.* interpreter, annotator, explainer.

eadar-mhìnich, adurveenich, *v.* explain.

eadarra-bhì, aduravee, *n. m.* the doorway.

eadarra-lionn, aduraliùn, *a.* submerged, between the surface and the bottom, in water.

eadarra - sholus, aduraholus, *n. m.* the twilight ; for eadar-da-, the d. being assim.

eadar - sgar, *v.* separate. *O.Ir.* eterscaraim.

eadar-sgarachdainn, adur-sgaruchcin, *n. f.* separation, divorce ; act of divorcing.

eadar-shoillse, adur-hyl-shu, *n. f.* dawn.

eadar-shoillsich, adur-hylshich, *v.* dawn.

eadar-theangachadh, adur-henguchu, *vbl. n. m.* translation, interpretation ; act of translating, interpreting.

eadar-theangaich, adur-hengich, *v.* translate.

eadar-theangair, adur-henger, *n. m.* translator.

eadh, used with *assert. vb.* an eadh ? is it so ? chan eadh, ni h-eadh, it is not so. *O.Ir.* ed = 3 *pers. pron. neut.* it.

eadh, *n. m.* space ; air (f)eadh an tighe, (all) over the house. *E.Ir.* ed, space.

eadha, *n. f.* letter e ; an aspen tree.

eadhal, *n. f.* a burning coal ; a brand. *See* éibheall.

eadhon, *adv.* to wit, namely ; bheir mise, eadhon mise, I, even I, will bring. *O.Ir.* idón, namely.

eadradh, edra, *n. m.* noon ; mu eadradh, about noon ; time of day for milking cattle ; place of milking ; " tha an crodh anns an eadradh," the cows are at the milking-place. *O.Ir.* etsruth, medónlái no etsruth, mid-day or etsruth, 3rd of the eight canonical hours. *Wi.*

eadraig, edrig, *v.* interpose, rescue ; " mur h-eadraig d'fhìor-fhuil féin thu," if your own kin will not rescue you.

eadraiginn, edrigin, *n. f.* interposition to separate two combatants ; act of separating ; is minig a fhuair fear na h-eadraiginn buille, often has the peacemaker been struck ; interference. *O.Ir.* tetar-cor, *interpositio.*

eadrochd, plain, manifest, clear. So *Ir.*

eadruinn, adrin, *prep. +pron. suf.* between us ; a' cur eadrainn, causing us to disagree, eadar + sinn. *See* eadar.

eag, ec, *n. f.* a nick, notch, or hack.

eagach, ecach, *a.* notched, indented.

eagachadh, *vbl. n. m.* act of indenting, hacking.

eagaich, ecich, *v.* indent, notch, imbed, dove-tail.

eagair, ugir, *v.* build, put in order.

eagal, ecall, *n. m.* fear, dread, terror ; tha eagal orm, I am afraid ; tha eagal a chridh air, he is terrified out of his wits ; na gabh eagal, do not be afraid ; ghabh mi eagal roimhe, I got afraid of him ; chuir e eagal orm, he frightened me. *Also* feagal. *O.Ir.* ecal, é (*neg.*) +gal (valour) ; " egal .i. gin gal aige." *Corm.* gl.

eagalach, *a.* fearful, dreadful ; nì eagalach, a dreadful thing ; duine eagalach, a terrible person.

eagalachd, *n. f.* terribleness, dreadfulness.

eagan, *adv.* perhaps, possibly.

eagar, egur, *n. m.* regular building, as peats, hewn stone ; order, rank ; cuir an **eagar**, put in order, build. *E.Ir.* ecor.

eagarra, uguru, *a.* exact, precise, methodical.

éagasg, ēgusc. *See* aogasg.

eaglais, eglish, *n. f.* a church, temple ; an eaglais chléireach, the Presbyterian Church ; eaglais nèamhaidh, church triumphant ; eaglais na Roimhe, Church of Rome. *O.Ir.* eclais. *Lat.* ecclēsia. *Gr.* ἐκκλησία.

eaglaisear, *n. m.* a churchman.

eaglaiseil, *a.* ecclesiastical.

éagmhais. *See* eugmhais.

eagna, ecna, *n. f.* wisdom. *O.Ir.* écne, *savant* ; fr. **asagninim**, *sapio.*

eagnach, egnach, *a.* prudent ; careful about little things, as a housewife.

eagnachd, egnachc, *n. f.* wisdom, prudence.

eagnaidh, egni, *a.* wise, prudent ; attentive to duty ; extremely careful.

eagnaidheachd, *n. f.* prudence, exactness, wisdom.

eairleig, ee-ārlig, *n. f.* strait for want of money.

eàirleigeach, ee-ārligeach, *a.* urgent.

eairleis, ee-ārlesh, *n. f.* earnest-penny.

eàirlinn, ee-ārlin, *n. m.* keel ; bottom, end.

eàirneis, ee-arnesh. *See* airneis.

eala, *n. f., pl.* ealachan, a swan ; Tighearn Loch nan eala, the proprietor of Lochnell. *M.Ir.* ela. *O.Celt.* elaio, elérko-s.

ealabhi, St. John's wort, hypericum perforatum. *Also* ealabhuidhe.

ealacarach, ee-alacuruchc, *a.* artistic, masterly.

ealach, ealachainn, *n. f.* a peg (to hang things on) ; a stand for guns ; rack for weapons ; armoury. So *Ir.* ealachuing.

ealachain, ee-alachen, *n. f.* the furnace, particularly of a distillery ; a hearth ; a gauntree, fulcrum.

ealadh, ee-alu, *n. f.* learning, skill. *E.Ir.* elatha.

ealadh, *n. f.* a tomb ; the place in Iona where the dead were placed on landing. *Ir.* elad, ailad, and ulad. fert = ulad cumdachta, covered tomb. *O'Dav.* ulad = stone tomb, or penitential station in shape of stone altar. *See Wi.*

eàladh, euladh, *n. m.* a creeping along, stalking. *O.Ir.* élud, *inf.* of éláim, escape, elope.

ealag, ialag, *n. f.* a hacking stock, a block.

ealaidh, *n. f.* an ode, a song ; *vide* ealadh.

ealain, ialen, *n. f.* trade, profession, occupation ; ciod e an ealain a tha e leantainn ? what trade does he follow ?

ealamh, ialav, *a.* quick, expert. *E.Ir.* athlom, expert.

ealamhachd, *n. f.* expertness, quickness. *E.Ir.* athlaimecht.

ealanta, ialanta, *a.* ingenious.

ealantachd, *n. f.* ingenuity.

ealbh, ialv, *n. m.* a bit, a little.

ealbhar, yalvur, *n. m.* a good-for-nothing fellow. Cf. *O.N.* álfr, elf.

ealbhuidh, ialvi, *n. f.* St. John's wort. *Also* seud Challum chille.

ealchainn. *See* ealachainn.

ealg, ialg, *a.* noble, expert. *Ir.* ealga, noble, excellent. *O'R. E.Ir.* elg.

ealghrìs, *n. f.* horror, deadly paleness, death pallor.

ealla, *n.* watching ; gabh ealla ris, gabh iolla ris, look at it ; take stock of him.

eallach, *n. m., pl.* eallaichean, burden, charge. Cf. *Ir.* eallach. *O.Ir.* ellach, *conjunctio.* Z².

eallach, ialuch, *n. m.* cattle, gear, a herd, dowry ; " ni àill leam gun eallach i," I like her not without dowry. *Ir.* eallach, cattle.

eallachail, *a.* hard, grievous.

eallsg, ialsg, *n. f.* a scald, a shrew.

ealt, ialt, *n. m.* flight of birds, flock, covey. *E.Ir.* elta.

ealtainn, ialtinn, *n. m.* razor ; *O.Ir.* altan. aith amail altain, keen like a razor. *O'Dav.*

ealtainn, *n. m.* a flock of birds.

ealtraidh, ialtry, *n. f.* mischance.

eaman. *See* feaman.

eàn, *n. m.* a bird. *See* eun.

eanach, iänach, *n. f.* dandriff, scurf ; down, wool.

eanach, enuch, *n. m.* a marsh, a moor.

eanach-gàrraidh, *n. f.* endive.

eanadas, *n. m.* provocation, vexation.

èanaidh, ēny, *n. m.* legs. *R.D.*

eanasg, *n. m.* a tie, engagement.

eanbhruich, envrich, *n. f.* flesh soup, chicken soup. *Ir.* enbruithe, broth. en (water) + bruith = uisce feòla (fleshwater). *Corm.*

eanchainn, enchin, *n. f.* brains, impudence, audacity, ingenuity. *E.Ir.* inchind (in + ceann). *O.Celt.* eni-qenni-.

eandagach. *See* feandagach, nettle, full of nettles.

eang, *n. m.* a gusset, a corner ; mesh of a net ; the twelfth of an inch.

eang, *n. f.* foot, footstep, track, bound. *E.Ir.* eng, track.

eangach, eng'-ach, *n. f.* a large fishing-net ; a chain of nets ; snare, fetter.

eangach, *a.* pointed ; nimble-footed.

eangarra, *a.* cross-tempered.

eangbhaidh, engvy, *a.* hard to tame, high-mettled.

eanghlas, *n. f.* gruel, milk and water,

wish-wash. *E.Ir.* **englas. en** (water) +glas.

eangladh, englu, *n. m.* entanglement.

eangladhrach, *a.* having angular, or pointed, hoofs.

eanntag, deanntag, jaüntag, feanntag, *n. f.* nettles.

eanraich. *See* eanbhruich.

ear, er, *n. f.* the east ; an ear, from the east ; gaoth an ear, east wind. *Ir.* soir. *O.Ir.* an-air, from the east.

earachall, earchall, erachul. *n. m.* misfortune, loss of cattle, mischief.

earail, err'-al, *n. f.* exhortation, guard ; *v. t.* caution ; dh' earail mi air, I cautioned him. *E.Ir.* eráilim, order, command.

earailt, erelt, *n. f.* exhortation ; caution.

earailteach, ereltach, *a.* circumspect.

earailteachd, ereltachc, *n. f.* cautiousness.

earair, erar, *v.* parch corn, as in a pot.

earalachadh, eraluchu, *vbl. n. m.* cautioning, exhorting, putting on one's guard.

earalaich, err'-al-èch, *v.* caution, warn, guard against ; exhort, entreat.

earalas, eralus, *n. m.* provision, caution.

earar, err'-ur, *n. m.* in *comp.* an earar, the day after to-morrow. *See* earthar.

eararadh, er'-ar-u, *n. m.* parched corn ; parching of corn in a pot for the mill.

eararais, eruresh, *adv.* second day after to-morrow. *Also* an iarais.

earasaid, erusej, *n. f.* 1. a square of tartan cloth, worn over the shoulders by women, and fastened by a brooch, a shawl. 2. a robe, a petticoat, an ornament.

earb, erb, *v. n.* entrust, confide, rely, depend, hope ; earb ris, entrust to him ; earb as, trust in him. *O.Ir.* erbaim, erbaid, gl. credit. *O.Celt.* erbiô.

earb, erb, *n. f., pl.* earbachan, a roe. *E.Ir.* erb. *O.Ir.* heirp, *dama, capra. O.Celt.* erbo-s, erbi-s.

earbach, er'-bach, *a.* full of roes.

earbag, *n. f.* a little roe.

earbail, erb'-ull, *n. f.* a trust.

earbais, erb'-ash, *n. f.* inhibition.

earball, erb'-all, *n. m.* a tail, train. *E.Ir.* erball.

earblach, *n. m.* a timid unheroic man ; (a) " dh' fhàgadh earblaich creuchdach," that would leave the timid (mercilessly) wounded. *Also* eirbleach.

earbsa, erb'-sa, *n. f.* complete trust, dependence, reliance, or confidence.

earbsach, erb'-sach, *a.* fully depending, confident, relying, trusting, trusty ; làmh earbsach, a reliable hand.

earbsachd, erb'-sachc, *n. f.* complete confidence fullest assurance or trust.

earbsalachd, erbsaluchc, *n. f.* confidence, trust.

earc, *n. f.* cow, heifer. *Carm. G.*

earca-iucna, *n. pl.* white cows with red ears, fairy cattle.

earc-dhrùchd, *n. f.* mildew.

earchall, *n. f.* a horse spancel. *E.Ir.* aircholl, airchaill, hob-shackle. *O.Ir.* aur-chomal, ur-chomal.

earchall. *See* earachall, loss, calamity ; " bhuin an t-earchall ruinn gort," the spring loss hit us hard. air +call, great loss. *W.* archoll, a wound.

eargnaich, erg'-nich, *v.* inflame ; enrage.

eàrlachadh, iàrluchu, *n. m.* for ullachadh, preparation (of food). *E.Ir.* erlam, *a.* ready.

eàrlaid, iàrlej, *n.f.* trust, expectation, land.

eàrlaidh, iàrly, *a.* for ullamh, ready.

earlas, iàrlus, *n. m.* an earnest, arles, earnest penny.

earnach, ērnach, *n. f.* murrain ; bloody flux in cattle.

earnaid-shìth, iarnej-hee, *n. m.* fairy wort.

eàrnais, *n. f.* property, furniture ; mo nì is m'eàrnais, my cattle and my stock.

eàrr, iàr, *n. m.* tail ; lowest extremity ; glac air a h-eàrr i, catch her by the tail ; chime of a barrel. *E.Ir.* err (*fem.*), tail. *O.Celt.* ersâ. Cf. *O.N.* ars ; podex. *Ag.S.* ears. *Ger.* arsch.

earracais, iaracish, *n. f.* a distress, scarcity of food or fodder.

eàrracn, iàrach, *n. m.* the chink of a dish, where the edge of the bottom enters ; lower extremity ; the chime ; hollow water-course in a ship's deck ; scarred.

earrach, iarach, *n. m.* the spring. *O.Ir.* errech. *O.Celt.* (p)ersâko-.

earrachail, *a.* spring-like.

earradh, eàrr'-u, *n. m.* dress. *E.Ir.* errad, dress, armour.

eàrradh, iàru, *n. m.* a mark, a groove ; a scar, mark of a wound ; groove in staves of a barrel into which the head fits.

earradhris, iaraghrish, *n. f.* dog-brier.

earradhubh, iarghu, *n. m.* wane ; gealach earradhuibh, the waning moon.

earrag, iarag, *n. f.* a taunt, a blow.

earraid, iarej, *n. m.* king's messenger. 1. sheriff officer, a tipstaff.

earraid, iàrej, *n. f.* fault, mistake.

earraig, iarig, *n. f.* the last shift ; great deal, ado ; greatest strait, attempt.

earraigeach, iarigach, *a.* straitened, making brave attempt.

earraigh, iaree, *n. m.* a captain. Cf. urra.

earrann, err'-ann, *n. f.* share ; section of land ; division ; portion ; a paragraph. *E.Ir.* errand = er +rand (portion).

earrannach, iarunuch, *n. f.* fleece, wool.
earrannaich, iarinich, *v.* share, divide.
earras, iarus, *n. m.* goods ; portion ; wealth ; Helen 'sa h-earras théid dhachaidh, Helen and her marriage-portion shall go home ; the person secured, or the principal ; chan fheàrr an t-urras na 'n t-earras, the security is not a whit better than the borrower ; property ; gun òr gun earras, without gold, without property ; wealth, treasure.
earrasach, iarasach, *a.* wealthy, rich.
earr-fhighe, iar-iya, *n. m.* weaver, tenter.
earrgheal, iarayal, *n. m.* "white-tailed" kind of bird.
earrghloir, iara-ghlor, *n. f.* gibberish, vainglory, taunting.
eàrrghóbhlach, *a.* fork-tailed.
eàrrite, iàr-itu, *n. f.* a tail feather.
eàrrlann, *n. f.* bottom or bilge of a ship ; eàrrlaig.
eàrr-thalmhuinn, iar-halvin, *n. f.* yarrow, milfoil.
earthar, in *phr.* an earthar, the eastern part, the front; hence day after, or in front of, to-morrow. *M.Ir.* airther, front.
eas, es, *n. m.* a waterfall, cataract, cascade ; gach coille, gach doire is gach eas, every wood, grove, and waterfall. *O.Ir.* ess. *O.Celt.* (p)esti-.
eas-, es, *priv. prefix*, signifying in, un, etc. *Ir.* eas-. *O.Ir.* es-. *Lat.* ex-. *Gaul,* ex-. *O.Celt.* eks.
easach, esach, *a.* full of cascades ; *n. f.* a cascade.
easach, esuch, *n. m.* water-gruel.
easag, *n. f.* a pheasant, squirrel.
easan, *n. m.* a little cascade, water-gruel.
easaontachd, esantachc, *n. f.* discord, factiousness, disagreement, disobedience.
eas-aontaich, esantich, *v.* disagree ; secede.
easaontas, esantas, *n. m.* transgression.
easaraich, esarich, *n. f.* boiling of a pool where a cascade falls ; tumult, noise ; state of requiring much attendance and service without moving from your seat.
easar-chasain, *n. m.* a thoroughfare.
easbalair, esbaler, *n. m.* a trifling, tall, slender, good-for-nothing fellow.
easbaloid, *n.f.* absolution. *Lat.* absolutio.
easbhuidh, esvi, *n. m.* want, defect ; tha easbhuidh air, he has a want, mental defect. *O.Ir.* esbuith, defect.
easbuig, esbig, *n. m.* a bishop. *O.Ir.* espoc, epscop. *Lat.* episcopus.
easbuigeach, *a.* episcopal.
easbuigeachd, *n. f.* bishopric.
eascain, escin, *n. f.* imprecation.

eascairdeach, *a.* inimical, hostile.
eascairdeas, escardus, *n. f.* enmity, hostility.
eascaoin, escin, *n. m.* unsoundness, as meal, grain ; *a.* unsound, as grain.
eascaraid, escarij, *n. m.* an enemy. *O.Ir.* es-cara, æs cara, *inimicus.* Z^2 ; eter carit et escarit, both friend and foe. *Wb.* 30.
easg, esc, *n.f.* a ditch formed by nature ; a fen, a bog. *E.Ir.* esc, water, fen-water.
easg, easgann, *n. f.* eel. *O.Ir.* escung. *Lat.* anguis.
easga, *n. f.* the moon. *O.Ir.* ésca, ésce.
easgach, *a.* full of ditches.
easgach, *n. f.* a fen ; a bog.
easgaid, iscij, *n. f.* the hough ; the ham. *Also* iosgaid.
easgaideach, *a.* having a slender hough ; *n. m.* term of contempt for a slender, tall person.
èasgaidh, iàsci, *a.* willing to serve, quick, nimble to do a thing. *O.Ir.* éscid. é + scith.
èasgaidheachd, iàsgi-achc, *n. f.* officiousness, excessive readiness.
easgann, escun, *n. f.* an eel ; compd. easgann-bheag, grig ; easgann-bhreac, lamprey ; easgann-faragaidh, eel ; easgann-mhara, conger eel. *O.Ir.* escung, *gen.* escongan.
easgannach, *a.* eel-like, supple, lively.
easgraich, escrich, *n. f.* a torrent ; coarse mixture.
eas-ionracas, es-iunracas, *n. m.* dishonesty.
eas-ionraic, *a.* dishonest, bad.
easlaine, eslanu, *n. f.* infirmity, sickness.
easlaint, eslaint, *n. f.* sickness ; luchd easlaint, invalids, sick people.
easlainteach, *a.* sickly, infirm.
easlan, eslan, *a.* sickly, invalided.
eas-onar, esónor, *n. f.* dishonour, dishonesty.
eas-onaraich, *v.* dishonour.
eas-òrdugh, esórdu, *n. m.* anarchy.
easrach, *n. f.* sowans.
easradh, esra, *n. m.* bedding for cattle; ferns. *E.Ir.* esrad, strewing.
easraich, esrich, *n. f.* boiling water of cascade.
eas-umhail, es-ooïl, *a.* disobedient, irreverent.
eas-umhlachd, es-oolachc, *n. f.* disobedience, insubordination, disloyalty, rebelliousness, irreverence.
eas-urram, es-urum, *n. f.* disrespect, contempt.
eas-urramach, *a.* disrespectful.
eas-urramaich, *v.* contemn.
eathar, e-hur, *n. m., pl.* eathraichean, eh-rich-un, a boat, a skiff. *O.Ir.* ethar, a boat.

eatorra, ett'-urr-a, between or among them, *i.e.* eadar + *pron. suf.* 3 *pl.*

eatorras, ett'-urr-as, *n. f.* mediocrity, middle state of health ; ciamar tha thu ? how do you do ? ; tha mi an eatorras, I am tolerably well.

éibeantach, ĕbantuch, *a.* inopportune, faulty.

éibeantas, *n. m.* awkwardness, timidity.

éibh, ēv, *n. f.* the death-watch, a tingling noise in the ear, portending sudden death ; tha an éibh am chluais, gun gleidheadh Dia na 's caomh leam, the death-watch is in my ear, may God watch over all who are dear to me ; a long-continued cry, as when women hear of some disastrous catastrophe ; éibh nam ban Muileach is iad a' caoineadh 'sa' tuireadh, the lamentation of the Mull women mourning for the dead ; *dial.* form of éigh, *q.v.* ; gh intervoc. not infreq. becomes bh.

eibheadh, ĕvu, *n. f.* the aspen, the letter e.

éibheall, éibhill, ĕvil, *n. f.*, *pl.* eibhlean, live coal. *O.G.* and *E.Ir*, óibell, spark, fire.

éibhinn, ēvin, *a.* very happy, ecstatic. overjoyed, odd, funny, curious ; is éibhinn thu fhéin, you are an odd fellow.

éibhleag, ēwlag, *n. f.* a small ember.

éibhneach, īvnach, *a.* in raptures, in transports of joy, rapturous.

éibhneas, *n. m.* ecstasy, raptures.

éibhrionnach, éirionnach, ĕrunuch, *n. m.* a young gelded goat.

éiceart, ĕcyarst, *n. f.* injustice ; *a.* unjust. é + cert.

éid, ĕj, *v.* accoutre, put on your uniform. dress ; mount, as with silver, or as swingles ; 'ga èideadh fhéin, putting on his accoutrements, dressing.

éidbheann, ejvian, *n. f.* gorge, wild peak.

éideadh, ēja, *n. m.* clothing, a suit ; uniform, armour ; éideadh cuirp, body garments ; gun éideadh gun each, without horse or armour ; éideadh calpa, greaves ; éideadh uchd, breastplate ; éideadh bròin, mournings ; éideadh muineil, a gorget ; éideadh Gàidhealach, Highland garb ; éideadh droma, back-piece. *O.Ir.* étach, dress, clothing.

éideann, ejun, *n. f.* a suit, equipment.

eidheann, e-unn, *n. m.* ivy. *E.Ir.* edenn. *O.Celt.* (p)edenno-, (p)edjevo-.

eidheannach, e-unnuch, eidheantach, *in Islay* = ice, *in Arran* = ivy.

éididh, ējy, *n. f.*, *obliq.* c. of éideadh.

eididh, *n. f.* a web. *Arm.*

éifeachd, ēfachc, *n.* effect, avail, consequence ; gun éifeachd, without effect. *Lat.* effectus.

eifeachdach, ēfachduch, *a.* effectual.

eige, egu, *n. f.* a web ; *pl.* eigeachan, webs.

eigeach, eguch, *n. f.* abb, warp ready for weaver.

éigeannach, ēgunach, *a.* difficult, distressing, requiring every kind of shift, indispensable.

éigeantas, ēgantas, *n. m.* necessity, miserable shifts.

eigh, ey, *n. f.* ice. *Also* deigh.

éigh, *v.* cry, shout. *O.Ir.* égim. *O.Celt.* eig.

éigh, *n. f.* a cry, a shout. *O.Ir.* égem.

eighe, e-u, *n. f.* a file, peat - cutter. *Ir.* oighe.

éigheach, *vbl. n. m.* act of shouting.

eighre, eru, *n. f.* ice, frost ; *a.* éighreach, eighreadail, eireadail, frosty, icy. *E.Ir.* aigred, ice. *W.* eiry, snow.

eighreag, eyrag, *n. f.* a cloudberry. *See* oighreag.

éigin, *a.* some ; cuideigin, some person ; rudaiginn, something.

éiginn, ēgin, *n. f.* rape, violence ; distress, difficulty, strait ; tha e 'na éiginn, he is distressed ; thog e a shùil air éiginn, he raised his eye with difficulty ; beò air éiginn, alive barely; poor livelihood. *O.Ir.* écen. *O.Celt.* enknâ.

éiginneach, ēginach, *a.* violent, difficult, indispensable.

éigne, *n. f.* salmon.

éignich, ēgnich, *v.* force, ravish ; ag éigneachadh, forcing, ravishing, violating.

'eil, el. *See* bheil.

éildeach, ēljach, *a.* abounding in hinds.

éildeag, ēljag, *n. f.* a young hind, roe.

éildeir, ēljer, *n. m.* an elder of the church.

eile, ele, *pron. indef.* another, other ; duine eile, another person ; ni eile, another thing. *O.Ir.* aile. *Lat.* alius.

eileach, eluch, *n. m.* mill-lade, the conduit which leads the water to the mill ; mill-race. *Ir.* eileach, mill-dam. Used to be of stone slabs (ailech).

éileadh, ēlu', *n. m.*, *pl.* éilidhean, ēlyun. 1. a kilt. *Also* féile and feabhladh. 2. folding, plaiting.

eilean, *n. m.* training. *See* oilean.

eilean, elan, *n. m.* an island. *E.Ir.* ailén, oiléan. *O.N.* eyland, island. *Zim., Cr., McB.*, but *Marstr.* says "untenable."

eileanach, *a.* insular ; *n. m.* an islander.

eileanachd, *n. f.* insularity.

eilear, elar, *n. f.* a deer's walk, desert.

eileir, eler, *n. f.* notch in staves of cask where bottom fits.

eileir, *n. f.* sequestered region ; seashore, coast-land. *See* eilthir.

eileircg, eilerig, *n. m.*, a V-shaped deer-trap.

eilgneadh, elya, *n. m.* first ploughing.

eilid, elij, *n. f.* a hind ; laigh an eilid

air an fhuaran, the hind lay on the green. *O.Ir.* elit. *O.Celt.* elinti-s, elanî.

eilidriom, eledrum, *n. f.* a bier, hearse. *Also* snaoimh. *Lat.* feretrum.

eilig, *n. f.* willow-herb.

eilleabanachd, eliubanuchc, *n. f.* ill-usage, mauling.

eilteachadh, eltiuchu, *n. m.* act of rejoicing.

eilthir, el-heer, *n. f.* foreign land. *See* eileir. *E.Ir.* ailithir.

eilthireach, elhirach, *n. m.* pilgrim ; foreigner. *E.Ir.* ailithir, pilgrim, exile.

eiltich, *v.* rejoice, exult.

eineach, enuch, *n. m.* bounty, honour, goodness ; air ghràdh t'einich na ceil orm, on your honour do not hide from me. *Ir.* oineach. *E.Ir.* enech, honour.

eineachlann, enuchlan, *n. f.* protection, safeguard. *O.Ir.* eneclann, " honour-price," fine for an insult.

einneach, *n. f.* stocks of heather (used for fire).

eirbheirt, ervert, *n. m.* locomotion, power of motion ; tha comas eirbheirt aice, she is able to move about ; excessive use ; seeking. *E.Ir.* airbert, use.

eirbhir, erver, *v.* seek in an indirect way ; có a tha ag eirbheirt sin ort, who insinuates that ? indirect blame, hinting ; tha eirbhir nan corp air a cheann, he was indirectly blamed for the dead.

eirbleach, erpliuch, *a.* crippled, infirm.

eirc-chòmhla, erc-chōlu, *n. f.* portcullis.

eire, era, *n. f.* burden. *O.Ir.* aire.

Éire, Éirin, *gen.* Éireann, *d.* Éirinn, Ireland.

eireachd, erachc, *n. m.* an assembly. *O.Ir.* airecht, oirecht, a gathering.

eireachd, erachc, *n. f.* beauty, elegance.

eireachdail, eruchcal, *a.* handsome, fine, beauteous, graceful ; pious ; fit to appear in company with, as dress. *See* eireachd.

eireachdas, eruchcus, *n. m.* decency, seemliness, handsomeness.

eireachdas, eruchcus, *n. m.* company, assembly. *Ir.* oireachtas.

eireag, erag, *n. f.* a pullet, a young hen.

eireallach, eryaluch, *n. m.* monster, a clumsy old carle.

eirearaich, erarich, *n. f.* parched corn hastily dried for the hand-mill.

eiriceach, ericiuch, *n. m.* a heretic. *O.Ir.* heretic. *Gr.* αἱρετικός.

eiriceachd, *n. f.* heresy.

éirich, ērich, *v.* rise, get up ; éirich moch 'sa mhaidinn, rise early in the morning. *O.Ir.* éirge, érge. *O.Celt.* eks-regô.

eiridinn, erijin, *n. f.* nursing a sick person ; *v.* nurse or attend a sick person or patient ; deoch eiridinn, a

potion ; tigh - eiridinn, a hospital. *O.Ir.* airitiu, g. airiten, reception.

eiridinneach, erijinach, *n. m.* a patient.

eiridnich, erijnich, *v.* nurse the sick.

éirig, ērig, *n. f.* ransom, mulct for bloodshed, reparation ; an éirig m' anama, in ransom for my soul. *O.Ir.* éric, éiricc ; is olc indéiricc, evil is the retaliation. *Wb.*25ᶜ.

éirigeach, ērigach, *a.* as a ransom ; *n. m.* a captive, a bondsman.

éirigh, ēri, *n. f.* rebellion, rising. *O.Ir.* érge, *surrectio* (*Z*²).

eirionnach, *n. m.* a churn.

Éirionnach, ērunach, *n. m.* an Irishman ; *adj.* Irish.

éirionnach. *See* éibhrionnach.

eirir. *See* eirbhir.

éiris, *n. f.* mistrust, heresy. é (*priv.*) +iris (faith).

éirisg, *n. f.* scheming, double-minded woman.

eirmis, *v.* find, hit upon. *O.Ir.* ermaissiu, attaining.

eirmseach, ermshuch, *a.* of ready wit.

eirmseachd, *n. f.* act of hitting upon.

eirplich, *v.* limp, hobble.

eirthir, erhir, *n. m.* sea coast ; links. *Also* dialect. eilthir. *Ir.* oirthir.

éis, ēsh, *n. f.* want, hindrance, delay ; finish ; *a.* éiseil, awanting. *O.Ir.* éis, track. *M.Ir.* dá éis, in his stead. *Tbc.*

éisd, ēsht, *v.* listen, hear, hearken, hark. *O.Ir.* étsim, listen.

éisdeachd, eshtachc, *n. f.* hearing, listening, hearkening ; attention ; luchd éisdeachd, hearers, auditory, audience.

éiseach, ēshach, *n. f.* a crupper.

eiseamplair, esempler, *n. m.* example, pattern, ensample, model ; eiseamplaireach, exemplary. *M.Ir.* esimplair. *Lat.* exemplar.

eisearadh, eshuru', *n. m.* destitution, evil plight.

éisfheoil, ēshyol, *n. f.* venison.

éisg, ēshc, éisgear, ēshcer, a satirist ; èisgearachd, satire, a satirical turn. *E.Ir.* écess, learned man. *McB.*

éisgeil, ēshcel, satirical, flippant.

éisglinn, ēshclin, *n. f.* fish pond.

eisimeil, eshimel, *n. f.* reverence, dependence, power ; chan 'eil mi bonn 'n a d' eisimeil, I am not a whit in your reverence. *E.Ir.* esimul, esimol. *Ir.*

eisiomaileach, eshimelach, a dependent.

eisiomaileachd, eshimelachc, *n. f.* dependence, state of dependence, poverty.

eisir, eshir, *n. f., pl.* eisirean, an oyster. So *Ir.*

eisleach, eshliuch, *n. f.* crupper ; the withe that ties the tail-beam to the pack-saddle.

éislean, ēshlen, *n. m.* grief, drowsiness, hindrance.
éisleanach, *a.* dull, drowsy. *E.Ir.* eslinn, weak.
eislinn, eshlin, *n. f.* a shroud ; anns an eislinn, dressed in the shroud. *E.Ir.* aisléne, eisléne, a shroud. *KM.* Cf. ais = death. *Lh. Also* eislig.
eistreadh, eshtru, *n. m.* clothing, vesture.
éite, *n. f.* clach-éite, quartz.
éite, éiteadh, *vbl. n. m.* stretching, extending.
eite, *n. f.* unhusked ear of corn.
éiteach, ēchach, *n. f.* burnt heath.
éiteag, ētiag, *n. f.* a white pebble, precious stone, fair maid.
eitean, echen, *n. m.* kernel ; eitean chnù, kernel of nuts.
eitheach, ehach, *a.* false, perjured ; thug e mionnan eithich, he perjured himself. *O.Ir.* ethech *perjurium.*
eithear, ehir, *n. m.* and *f.* a boat, barge.
éitich, ētich, *v.* refuse, deny.
éitigh, ēti, *a.* dismal, ugly. *O.Ir.* étig, turpe.
eitig, *n. f.* consumption, wasting disease.
eitimeireachd, *n. f.* abuse, rough handling, cowardly conduct towards a helpless one. Cf. *O.Ir.* timthirecht, service.
eitreach, etruch, *n. m.* storm, sorrow.
éitridh, ētri, *n. f.* for sèitrich.
eòin, yōin, *gen. s.* and *n. pl.* of eun.
eòin-bhùchain, *n. f. pl.* melodious birds.
eòisle, *n. f.* a charm.
eòl, yōl, *n. m.* knowledge ; is eòl dhomh, I know ; " chan eòl do'n amhlair e," the brutish man knoweth it not.
eòlach, yòluch, *a.* acquainted, knowing, intelligent, expert, skilful ; duine eòlach, a man well informed, an intelligent man, an experienced hand. *O.Ir.* éula, éola (*peritus*).
eòlan, yòlan, *n. m.* oil, oil for wool.
eòlas, yōlus, *n. f.* acquaintance, intelligence, knowledge ; cuir eòlas air, get acquainted with him ; skill, science, an enchantment or spell ; eòlas nan sùl, a spell to get free of a mote in the eye. *O.Ir.* eolas, heulas (*peritia*) Z^2.
eòrlan, yòrlan, *n. f.* the bottom of a glen ; " air eòrlain a' ghlinne," on the bottom of the glen. *Carm. G.* for ùrlar.
eòrna, yōrnu, *n. m.* barley ; eòrna agus lìon, barley and flax ; a' cur eòrna, sowing barley. So *E.Ir.*
eòrnach, yōrnuch, *n. f.* barley-land.
Eòrpa, yōrpu, *n. f.* Europe.
eothanaich, yohanich, *v.* languish, decay.
erard, *n. f.* height. *E.Ir.* aur-ard, very high.
esan, ess'-un, *emph. pron.* he, him, himself.

eu-, *neg. pref. O.Ir.* é.
eubh. *See* éibh, éigh.
eucail, ēcal, *n. f.* disease, distemper ; gach eucail 'na aoraibh, every disease in his constitution ; for *O.Ir.* é (neg.) + gal (vigour).
eucaileach, ēcalach, *a.* diseased, distempered.
eucaileachd, ēcalachc, *n. f.* state of disease ; infectiousness, distemper.
eucairdeas, *n. m.* unfriendliness, enmity.
eucairdeil, *a.* inimical.
euceart, *n. m.* injustice, evil ; for *O.Ir.* é (neg.) + cert (right).
eu-céillidh, *a.* a foolish person ; blundering. *E.Ir.* an-céllide, senseless.
euchd, ēchc, *n. f.* exploit or achievement ; a feat. *E.Ir.* écht, murder.
euchdach, ēchcach, euchdail, echcal, *a.* heroic, chivalrous, brave, daring ; daoine treubhach euchdail, heroic, chivalrous people ; euchdalachd, degree of heroism, bravery.
euchdag, *n. f.* a fair maid, a charmer ; a pea hen. *Also* eucag.
eucoir, *n. f.* injustice, wrong. *O.Ir.* écoir.
eucoireachd, *n. f.* injustice.
eucorach, *n. m.* a wicked person ; *a.* unjust.
eud, ēd, *n. m.* jealousy ; malice at another's success ; zeal ; trì nithe gun iarraidh, eud, is eagal, is gaol, three things that come without seeking, jealousy, fear, and love. *O.Ir.* ét.
eudach, iädach, *n. m.* jealousy between man and wife ; tha e ag eudach rithe, he is jealous of her.
eudach, *n. m.* cloth, clothes, dress. *See* aodach. *E.Ir.* étim, I clothe.
eudachail, iädachal, *adj.* jealous.
eudaich, iädich, *v.* watch zealously.
eudail, *n. f.* cattle, a treasure, a darling. *Also* feudail. *E.Ir.* étail, treasure, booty.
eudaire, *n. m.* a jealous man.
eudann, ēdun, *n. m.* face. *See* aodann. *E.Ir.* étan, *frons.*
eudar, ēdur, *v.* needs be ; " is cruaidh an càs nach eudar fhulang," one must needs endure the sorest plight. *See* feudar.
eudmhor, ēdvor, *a.* jealous, zealous.
eudmhorachd, ēdvorachc, *n. f.* jealousy ; degree of jealousy, zeal.
eu-dochas, ē-dōchus, *n. m.* despair, despondency, dejection.
eudomhain, aodomhain, *n. f.* a shallow.
eug, ēg, *n. m.* death ; suain an éig, sound sleep of death ; *v.* die, perish ; dh' eug i, she died. *O.Ir.* éc. *O.Celt.* enku-s, enkabi-, enkevo-.
eugach, ēgach, *a.* death-like ; deadly ;

buille eagalach eugach, a terrible deadly blow.

eugais, eugmhais, as eugais, without. So *Ir*. *E.Ir*. écmais, " non-power."

eugas, ēgus, *n. m.* likeness. *See* aogmhais, aogais.

eugnaich, ēgnich, *v.* die, perish, decay.

eugnaidh, ēgny, *a.* pale, death-like ; stale (of food). *Also* aognaidh.

eug-samhlachd, ēgsaülachc, *n. f.* variety.

eug-samhluich, ēg-saülich, *v.* vary, change.

eug-samhuil, ēg-saül, *a.* various, different; dathan eug-samhuil, various colours. *O.Ir*. écsamil = é (neg.) + con-samil.

euladh. *See* èaladh.

eumhann, *n. f.* a pearl. *O.Ir*. (initial n lost) = ném, *gen*. némann. *KM*.

eun, ēn, *n. m., pl.* eòin, a bird, chicken ; an t-eun-fionn, the hen-harrier ; eun-siubhail, a bird of passage, a straggler ; cù-eunaich, a pointer. *O.Ir*. én. *O.Celt*. (p)etno-s, (p)eteno-s.

eunach, *a.* rich in birds.

eunachd, *n. f.* fowling, hunting.

eunadair, iänaden, *n. m.* fowler, game-keeper, bird-catcher ; eunadaireachd, game-keeping.

eunadan, iänadan, *n. m.* a bird-cage. *Also* èanadan.

eunan, èn'-an, *n. m.* a humming-bird.

eunbhrigh, ēn-vry, eunruith, ēnry, soup ; chicken-broth. *See* eanbhruith.

eun-dhraoidheachd, ēn-dhruyachc, *n. f.* augury.

eun-fhiosachd, *n. f.* auspices.

eunghobhrag, *n. f.* a snipe. *Also* aonaghurag, meannan-adhair, gobhar-adhair, eunarag.

eunlaidh, iänli, *v. i.* creep ; sneak as a bird-catcher or fowler.

eunlaith, iänli, *n. f.* fowls ; birds. *Also* eunlann. *E.Ir*. énlaith.

eun-lion, *n. m.* fowler's net.

eun-uisge, *n. m.* water-fowl.

eur, euradh, èr, *v. i.* refuse.

eu-torach, *a.* barren, unfruitful.

eu-treòir, *n. f.* weakness, imbecility.

eu-tròcaireach, *a.* unmerciful.

eutrom, ētrum, *a.* light. *See* aotrom. *O.Ir*. étromm.

F

f, styled fearn by the Irish, is the sixth letter of the alphabet.

fa, *prep*. on account, upon ; fa-dheòidh, at last ; fa-leith, apart.

fa, *prep*. under.

fa, *v.* was. *M.Ir*. fa h-. *E.Ir*. ba h-.

fabh, fav, fabhachd, favachc, *n. m.* a thick cake ; thick bread.

fàbhair, fāvir, *v.* favour, oblige. *Eng*.

fabhairt, fadhairt, fu-urt, *n. m.* forging, moulding ; "tempering." Founded on *Lat*. faber, smith. *McB*.

fàbhairt, *n. m.* delay.

fàbhanadh, fāvanu', *vbl. n. m.* delaying, dallying, trifling with.

fàbhar, fâv'-ur, *n. m.* favour, interest, friendship. *Lat*. favor.

fàbharach, fav'-ur-ach, *a.* favourable, kind.

fàbharachd, fav'-ur-achc. *n. f.* favourableness ; a friendly disposition ; kindliness.

fàbharnadh, *vbl. n. m.* *See sub* fàbhanadh.

fabhd, faud, *n. m.* fault, blame.

fabhra, fav'-ra, *n. m.* an eyelid ; a fringe ; a flounce. *Also* fabhrad, abhra, arabhalg.

facal, *n. m.* word ; solemn oath ; thoir t' fhacal, give your word (of honour) ; swear, make oath. *O.Ir*. focul. *Lat*. vocabulum.

fachach, *n. m.* a puffin, a manikin ; "cha b'iad na fachaich gun rùm," *they* were not the puny men, void of capacity.

fachail, *n. f.* strife.

fachaint, fachent, *n. f.* scoffing, ridicule.

fachant, *a.* despicable, puny.

fa-chomhair, fa-chó'-èr, *prep*. before, in view of ; fa-chomhair m'inntinn, before my mind ; thainig e fa mo chomhair, it occurred to me ; tha e an sin fa do chomhair, he is there in front of you ; fa-chomhair an là màireach, in view of to-morrow.

faclach, faclach, *a.* wordy, verbose.

faclair, facler, *n. m.* a vocabulary.

fad, *n. m.* length, distance, tallness ; bho chionn fada, long ago ; fad finn foinneach an latha, the live-long day ; *prep*. during, over, throughout ; fad an t-saoghail, throughout the world ; *adv*. air fad, altogether, wholly ; air fhad, lengthways, longitudinally. *O.Ir*. fot, fat.

fàd, *n. m.* a peat. *See* fòd.

fada, *adj*. long, distant ; o thir fhada, from a distant country ; rathad fada, a long way ; *adv*. long, tediously ; is fada leam a dh' fhan thu, you stayed too long. *O.Ir*. fota, fada, *longus*.

fadachadh, *n. m.* lengthening, extending.

fadadh, fad'-ă, *n. m.* fireplace of a kiln ; pan of a gun ; *vbl. n.* inflaming, kindling a fire; **fadadh a' ghealbhain**, the kindling of the fire. *M.Ir.* **fatód.** *E.Ir.* **átúd.**

fadadh-cruaidh, *n. m.* rudimentary rainbow, a " dog-tooth."

fadaich, fadich, **fadaidh**, fadey, *v.* kindle, inflame, lengthen; *vbl. a.* **fadaichte**, kindled.

fadal, *n. m.* longing, thinking it tedious; lateness, delay; **na gabh fadal**, do not think it too long; **tha fadal orm**, I think it long. *Also* **fadachd.**

fadalach, *a.* longsome, dreary, tedious; **oidhcheachan fadalach**, dreary or tedious nights; slow, tardy; late, behind appointed time.

fadalachd, fadaluchc, *n. f.* tediousness, prolixity; lateness.

fad-anaileach, *a.* long-winded.

fadcheannach, fad'-chyann-ach, *adj.* longheaded, sagacious, shrewd.

fadcheumach, fad-chēmach, *a.* striding, bounding, bouncing.

fadchluasach, fad'-chloo-us-ach, *a.* longeared.

fad-fhoidhidinn, *n. m.* patience, longwaiting.

fad-fhulang, fad-ool'-ung, *n. m.* longsuffering, forbearing.

fad-fhulangach, fad-ooll'-ung-ach, *a.* longsuffering, forbearing, patient.

fad-fhulangas, *n. m.* long-suffering, patience.

fadgheugach, *a.* long-branched.

fadhail, fu'il, *n. f.* flood, tidal current.

fadhairt, fü-art, *n. f.* temper of a knife, hatchet, etc.; **gun fhadhairt**, blunt.

fadhairtich, *v.* temper.

fadhar. *See* **faghar.**

fadharsach, fagharsach, *a.* trifling, paltry.

fadhbhag, fuvag, *n. m.* cuttle-fish.

fa-dheireadh, *adv.* at last.

fa-dhèòidh, fa yŏy, *adv.* at last, ultimately. *O.Ir.* **fo diud**, *postremo*, **fó deóid**, at last; **deód**, **déad** (*finis*).

fadlamhach, fad'-láv-ach, *a.* long-handed; disposed to pilfer, thievish.

fad-shaoghalach, fad'-hāol-ach, *a.* longlived; living a long life.

fadsheallach, *a.* long-sighted, prospective.

fadtharruing, fad'-harr-ing, *n. f.* dilatoriness, procrastination, drawling; **fadtharruinneach**, dilatory, procrastinating.

fadtheangach, *a.* long-tongued.

fafan, *n. m.* gentle breeze. *Also* **fathan** and **ceabharan.**

fàg, *v.* leave, quit, abandon, forsake, relinquish; outrun, outstrip; **dh' fhàg an darna bàta an tè eile**, the one boat outstripped the other; render, make, effect; " dh' fhàgadh tu am buamas-

dair treubhach," thou wouldst render the blockhead heroic; father upon, accuse of, lay to the charge; **dh' fhàg iad sin air**, they fathered that upon him; **dh' fhàg iad am pàisde air**, they fathered the child on him. *O.Ir.* **fácbaim**, **foácbaim**, *relinquo.* **foácbat**, gl. *deponunt*=foath-gabat. *Z²*.

fàgail, fâg'-al, *vbl. n. f.* act of leaving, forsaking, rendering, abandoning; a curse, a fatality, destiny; **tha fhàgail fhéin aig gach neach**, every one has his own peculiar destiny; a failing, a want; **tha fhàgail fhéin air gach neach**, each one has his own failing. *O.Ir.* **fácbáil.**

fàgaire, fâg'-ir-u, *n. m.* a wag; a conceited wit, a witling; **fàgaireachd**, waggery or witticisms of a person from whom nothing of the kind is to be expected.

fàgannta, fâg'-annt-u, *adj.* slow, drawling, yet witty and waggish.

faghaid, fu'ij, *n. f.* a hunt, a chase, a hunting party.

faghail, *a.* slow. *Ir.* **fóill.**

faghailt, *vbl. n. f.* starting of **game**, hunting.

faghar, fu'ur, *n. m.* a sound, a noise, a whack. *O.Ir.* **fogur.**

faguisgeachd, fagishcachc, *n. f.* nearness.

fagus, fagusd, *a.* near, nigh, near hand, nearly related; **fagus oirnn**, near us; **fagus air bhi deas**, nearly ready; **na 's fhaisge**, nearer. *E.Ir.* **focus**, **ocus.** *O.Ir.* **accus.**

faibhle, fyvla, *n. m.* beech-wood.

faic, *v.* see, behold, observe; **faiceam do làmh gheal**, let me see your fair hand; *inter.* see! behold! lo! *O.Ir.* **accat**, see: **ad-cíu**, **accíu**, **atchíu.**

faiceant, *a.* sharp-eyed, fierce-eyed.

faich, fych, *n. f.* a field where soldiers are reviewed; a green; a plain, a meadow. *E.Ir.* **faidche, faithche.**

faichd, fychc, *n. f.* hiding-place, den.

faiche, fychu, *n. f.* the burrow of shellfish; **faiche giomaich**, a lobster's burrow; a lair.

faicheachd fychachc, *n. f.* training, drilling of soldiers, parading. Cf. *E.Ir.* **faidche**, a green, or lawn.

faicheil, fychal, *a.* neat, trim; tidily and cleanly dressed as soldiers; stately in gait, showy.

faichein, fychen, *n. m.* a wrapper, a baby's napkin. *Also* **foichein.**

faichilleach, **faicilleach**, *adj.* cautious, circumspect, watchful.

faichilleachd, *n. f.* chariness, cautiousness, circumspection, watchfulness, observance.

faicill, fecil, **faichill**, fechil, *n. f.* caution,

precaution ; **faichill ort,** take care, be on your guard ; be upon the watch. *E.Ir.* accill.

faicinn, fecin, *vbl. n. f.* observation ; seeing, observing, viewing, attending to. *See* **faic.**

faicsinneach, fecshinach, *adj.* visible, conspicuous, notorious ; **an eaglais fhaicsinneach,** the visible church ; very observant.

faicsinneachd, *n. f.* visibleness, conspicuousness, clearness.

faide, feju, *deg.* longer, longest ; **is fhaide gu mòr,** longer by far ; length. *Also* **faidead.**

fàidh, fā-i, *n. m., pl.* **fàidhean,** a prophet, seer. *O.Ir.* fáith, a poet. *O.Celt.* vâti-s. *Lat.* vates.

faidhbhile, fyvilu, *n. f.* a beech.

fàidheadaireachd, prophecy. *Also* **fàisneachd, fàidheachd.**

fàidheil, fāyal, *a.* prophetic.

faidhir, fī'-àr, *n. f., gen.* **faidhreach,** *pl.* **faidhrichean,** market, fair. *Eng.* fair. *Lat.* feria.

faidhreachail, fēruchal, *a.* fit, showy, attractive.

faidhrean, *n. m.* a fairing, a present.

faidhreil, *a.* same as last word.

fàidse, fajshu, *n. m., pl.* **faidseachan,** lump of bread ; "a piece." *Also* **ceapaire.**

fàidseach, fājshuch, *n. f.* a lump of a girl.

faigh, fy, *v.* get, acquire, obtain, find ; **gheibh sinn,** we shall get ; **fhuair sinn,** we have found ; **faigh a mach,** find out. *O.Ir.* fagbaim.

faighe, fyu, *n. f. See* **faoighe,** begging.

faighneach, fynuch, **faighneachail,** *a.* inquisitive.

faighnich, *v.* ask ; inquire. *O.Ir.* fagim, I ask.

faighreag, fyrag, *n. f.* a cloud-berry.

faigse, fygshu, *n. m.* nearness ; *deg.* more or most near ; **is fhaigse,** is nearer. *Also* **faisge.** *See* **fagus.**

fail, fal, *n. f.* mark, print, trace ; **fail do làimhe,** the mark of your hand.

fail, fal, *n. f.* a peat-spade.

fail, foil, fal, *v.* corrupt, putrefy, parboil. Cf. *O.N.* vella, to boil. *McB.*

fail, foil, *n. f.* sty ; **fail-chon,** dog-kennel ; **fail-mhuc,** pig-sty. *O.Ir.* foil. *O.Celt.* vali-, or voli-.

fail, fàil, *n. f.* a ring ; ouch ; jewel. *O.Ir.* foil.

fail, *adv.* where. *E.Ir* fail, nearness.

failbhe, felvu, for **failmhe,** *n. f.* emptiness, the aerial expanse ; the firmament.

failbheachan, felvuchan, *n. m.* an ear-ring.

failbheag, felvag, *n. f.* a ring, a bolt-

ring for a rope ; **fàilbheagan òir,** gold rings. *Also* **ailbheag.**

failc, felc, and falc, *v. i.* bathe, lave. *Also* **fairc, fairig.** *O.Ir.* folcaim, *lavo* (*Z²*). *O.Celt.* volko, volkiô.

failceach, *n. f.* a bath, bathing ; **failceach do iubhar beinne,** bath of the juice of juniper. *O.Ir.* folcaim.

failcean, felcen, *n. m.* the patella or knee-pan ; pot-lid. *Arm.*

fail-chuaich, *n. f.* a violet.

fàile, fàileadh, fālu, *n. m.* smell, flavour ; **droch fhàileadh,** bad smell ; the air, the draught ; **tha 'm fàileadh fuar,** the air is cold.

faileadh, falv, *vbl. n. m.* rotting, loosening (of wool from skin) ; moulting.

faileag, falag, *n. f.* hiccup ; **tha 'n an fhaileag orm,** I have the hiccup. *See* **aileag.**

fàileag, fālag, *n. f.* dog-brier berry. *Also* **mucag, muca-fàileag.**

fàileanta, fālanta, *a.* smelling, airy. *Also* **fàileach, fàileanach.**

faileas, falas, *n. m.* shadow, reflected image ; **mar fhaileas ar làithean,** our days are like a shadow, spectre, sheen.

faileasach, falasach, *a.* shadowy.

fàilinn, fālin, *n. m.* failing ; fainting fit ; **thàinig fàilinn air,** he fainted. *E.Ir.* faill, negligence, failure.

fàilinneach, fàilneach, *a.* faint, delicate, wanting ; fallible, frail.

failleagan, faligan, **ailleagan, faillean, aillean,** *n. m.* hollow immediately below the lobe of the ear.

faillean, falen, *n. m.* a branch, a sucker.

fàilling, fāling, *v.* fail.

fàillingeadh, *vbl. n. m.* a failing, weakness, both physical and mental.

failm, felm, ailm, *n. f.* helm. *Also* **falmadair.** *O.N.* hjálm.

failmean, felmen, *n. m.* pan of the knee.

failmhe, felvu, *n. f.* firmament, a void, space; *fr.* falamh.

failms', for "**far a bheil mise,**" where I am (*Rob. Donn*).

failmse, felmshu, *n. f.* blunder, mistake ; *a.* **failmseach.**

fàilnich, fālnich, *v.* fail, faint, decay, fall off ; **a' fàilneachadh,** failing, fainting, wearing away.

fàilte, fāltu, *n. f.* salutation, welcome, a salute, hail ; **chuirinn fàilte,** I would hail or salute ; **cuir fàilte air,** salute him. *O.Ir.* fáelte, fàilte, *gaudium.* *O.Celt.* vâletiâ.

fàilteach, *a.* kind, hospitable.

fàilteachail. *See* **fàilteach,** hospitable.

fàilteachas, fāltachus, *n. f.* hospitality ; kind reception, salutation.

fàilteam, *n. f.* blemish, deficiency. Cf. **fàiling.**

fàiltich, fāltich, v. salute, hail.
fainich, fenich. *See* aithnich, recognise, know.
fàinleag, àinleag, fānlag, n. f. a swallow. *Ir.* áinleóg. *O.Ir.* fannall. *W.* gwennol. *O.Celt.* vannello-.
fainne, n. f. noon. *See* ainne.
fàinne, fānu, n. m., pl. fàinneachan, a ring.
fàinneach, a. in ringlets, in curls ; a cùl fàinneach, her curly locks.
fàinneag, n. f. a little ring, a curl ; a. fainneagach, curly.
fair, v. fetch. *See* far.
fàir, n. f. dawn. *E.Ir.* fáir, sunrise. *W.* gwawr. *O.Celt.* vâsri-.
fair, fer, v. watch at night, keep guard, keep awake ; fair thusa an nochd, keep you guard to-night.
fairc, ferc, n. f. a link, or land sometimes covered by the sea ; hole. *Also* fidean.
fairc, ferc, v. bathe. *See* fathrig.
fairceall, fercal, n. m. lid (brod).
fairche, ferchu, fairchean, ferchen, n. m. mallet, rammer, hammer. *E.Ir.* forcha.
fairchill, ferchil, n. f. a lyre.
fairdeas = farraideas. *See* farraid.
fàirdin, fārdin, n. f. a farthing ; bonn a sè is fàirdin, a halfpenny and a farthing.
faire ! faire ! fera, fera, *inter.* ay ! ay ! my conscience ! what a pother !
faire, feru, n. f. a watch, a guard, a wake, carefulness ; fear-faire, a watchman ; tigh-faire, a wake-house. *E.Ir.* faire, a watch, guard.
fàire, fāru, n. f. a ridge seen in the distance ; sky-line.
faireach, ferach, a. watchful.
faireachadh, feracha, vbl. n. m. act of waking, feeling ; a bheil thu t' fhaireachadh, are you awake ? ; eadar cadal is faireachadh, between sleeping and waking.
faireachail, ferachal, a. attentive, sensitive, wakeful senses.
faireachdan, n. m. pl. feelings.
fàireag, fārag, n. f. a gland. *Ir.* fáireóg.
faireagan, faragan, n. m. a scare, startling experience.
faireagan, *interj.* bravo ! fie !
fairge, fargu, n. f., pl. fairgeachan, the sea, an ocean ; thar fairge, across the sea ; sea-wave, a wave breaking over a ship. *O.Ir.* fairgge, farrce.
fairgneadh, n. m. hacking, sacking, hitting ; " fairgne na druma," playing the drum.
fairich, ferich, v. watch, feel, perceive ; hear ; ciod a dh' fhairich thu, what do you feel ? what do you mean ? what did you hear ? *O.Ir.* airigur, *sentio,* airigim, notice.

fairig, feric, v. bathe. *Also* fairc, failc. *O.Ir.* fothraicim, I bathe. *O.Celt.* vo-tronkatu-, to bathe.
fàirleas, fārlus, n. m. an object on the sky-line.
fairsing, farshing, a. wide. *O.Ir.* fairsing, *amplus.*
fairslich, fairtlich, farslich, v. t. defy, worst ; dh' fhairslich e ormsa, it defied me. *Also* dh' fhailich.
fàisg, fāshc, v. press, wring, squeeze by twisting ; 'ga fhàsgadh eadar a làmhan, compressing it in his hands ; n. m. cheese-press, chesit ; also fiodhan ; fàisgte, vbl. a. wrung, squeezed, pressed, compressed. *E.Ir.* fáiscim, I squeeze. *O.Celt.* vaksko.
faisg, feshc, a. near = fagus.
faisg, v. pick off vermin.
faisge, feshcu, n. f. nearness, proximity ; deg. of fagus, nearest, nearer ; is esan as fhaisge, he is the nearest or nearer.
fàisgeach, fāshcach, n. f. spunge, a press.
faisgead, n. m. nearness.
fàisne, n. f. a pimple, a weal.
fàisneachd, fāshnachc, n. f. prophecy, soothsaying ; a. fàisneach, prophetic. *Also* fàistine. *O.Ir.* fáitsine, and fáissine, *prophetia* ; gl. *Wb., Ml.*
faisneas, fàsh'-nas, n. m. a friendly or secret hint ; secret intelligence.
faisneis, fashnesh, n. m. speaking, whispering. *Ir.* rehearsal. *E.Ir.* aisnéis, aisnéisim, I speak.
fàisnich, fāshnich, v. prophesy, foretell, divine, forebode ; a' fàisneachadh, aislingean brèige, prophesying, false dreams.
faist, fasht, n. f. at anchor.
faitcheas, faiteas, fatchus, n. m. caution, delicacy of sentiment, timidness, shyness ; cha ruig thu leas faitcheas sam bith a bhi ort, you need not feel the least delicacy ; " biodh faitcheas oirnn," let us fear. *O.Ir.* faitches, caution.
fàite, n. f. a smile. *O.Ir.* fáitbim, I laugh.
fàiteach, fātuch, a. delicate, timid, shy. *O.Ir.* fáitech, gl. *cautus.* Z².
faiteal, aiteal, fytal, n. m. breeze ; " faiteal do bheòil," the breath of your mouth.
fàitheam, fē-hum, n. m. a hem ; a stitched border ; " beul gun fhàitheam," unguarded mouth, mouth that cannot keep a secret ; poetic for garrulous person ; a' fuaigheal is a' faitheam, sewing and hemming.
faithiltear, fahilter, n. m. broker.
fàl, n. f. 1. a fold, a circle. 2. a wall, a hedge. 3. turf, a sod (employed in building a wall or hedge). *E.Ir.* fál,

152   FÀL—FAMH-BHUAL

hedge, fold. *W.* **gwawl**, wall. *Pict.* penn-fahel (*caput valli*). *O.Celt.* vâlo-.

fàl, *n. f.* 1. a scythe. 2. a spade, a peat spade. *W.* **pâl**. *Also* **speal.**

falach, *n. m.* concealment, a place of concealment; **tha e am falach**, it is concealed; a veil, covering. *E.Ir.* **folach.**

falachan, *n. m.* anything hidden, a treasure.

falachasan, *n. m.* the hidden thing, a treasure.

falachd, *n. f.* a feud, a family quarrel or grudge; **fuath is falachd**, hate and feud. *Also* **folachd**, *q.v.*

falach - fead, *n. m.* game of high - spy, bo-peep, hide-and-seek. Other names for this game are: **falach-cuain, car mu chnoc.**

fàladair, fāluder, *n. m.* a mower, a scythe, turf cutter. *W.* **paladur.**

fàladair, *n. m.* waste (of straw or hay), litter.

fàladair, fāluder, *n. m.* the "mown" place, bare pasture, turf-land.

fàladaireach, *a.* belonging to scythes.

fàladaireachd, *n. f.* 1. mowing. 2. yarning, fiction.

fàladh, *n. m.* enclosing with sods.

fala-dhà, *n. f.* jest, fun, irony. *See* **fealla-dhà.**

falaich, fal'-èch, *v.* hide, veil, conceal. *See* **folaich.**

falair, alair, *n. f.* funeral, funeral feast. *See* **farair.**

fàlaire, fàl'-ur-à, *n. m.* an ambler, prancing horse. *Also* **àlaire**, brood mare.

fàlaireachd, *n. f.* prancing.

falamh, fal'-uv, *a.* empty, void; in want, unoccupied; **is fhearr fuine thana na bhi uile falamh**, a thin batch is better than to want bread altogether. *E.Ir.* **folom, folomm.**

falamhachd, fal'-uv-ǎchc, *n. f.* void, gap, space.

falasg, falaisg, *n. m.* heath - burning. **fal + loisg.**

falasgair, *n. m.* heath-burning. *M.Ir.* **foloiscim, fallsce, follscaide**, burnt. *Tbc.*

falbh, falv, *v.* go, begone, depart, retire, away with you; **falbh romhad**, go about your business; *n. m.* gait, motion, going.

falbhaiche, falvichu, *n. m.* a walker.

falbhair, falver, *n. m.* young animal (following its mother).

falbhan, *n. m.* continual motion, walking, waving. *O.Ir.* **fuluman**, *volubilis.*

falbhanach, *n. m.* a wanderer.

falbheart, *n. f.* guile, deceit.

fàl-fuinn, *n. m.* a hoe.

falc, *v.* bathe; **a' falcadh**, bathing. *O.Ir.* **folcaim.** *W.* **golchi, ymolchi.**

falc, falcag, *n. f.* common auk. *N.* **álka.**

fallaid, fāll'-èj, *n. f.* sprinkling of meal (on cakes).

fallain, *a.* healthy, sound.

fallaine, falena, *a. deg.* more or most healthy; **is esan as fallaine**, he is more healthy. *Also* **healthiness, soundness.**

fallaineachd, falenachc, *n. f.* soundness, healthiness, wholesomeness, salubriousness.

fallaing. *See* **falluing.**

fallan, *a.* healthy, sound; **duine fallan**, a healthy man; wholesome; **biadh fallan**, wholesome food; **fàileadh fallan**, salubrious air. *E.Ir.* **follan** (fo + slàn). *M'B.*

falloisg, falisc, *n. f.* moor-burn—burnt heath. *See sub* **falasgair.**

fallsa, *adj.* false, deceitful, treacherous; **measg bhràithrean fallsa**, among false brethren. *Lat.* **falsus.**

fallsachd, fall'-sachc, *n. f.* falseness, treacherousness; false philosophy, sophistry.

fallsail, fall'-sǎl, *a.* false, deceitful.

fallsaire, fall'-ser'-u, *n. m.* a sophist, false philosopher; **fallsaireachd**, sophistry.

fallsanach, fall'-san-ach, *n. m.* sophist.

fallsanachd, fall'-san-achg, *n. f.* sophistry.

falluing, fall'-inn, *n. f.* mantle, cloak.

fallus, *n. m.* sweat, perspiration; **tha mi am lòn falluis**, I am just melting. *O.Ir.* **allas.**

fallusach, *a.* sudorific.

falm, *n. m.* alum. *Also* **alm.**

falm, *n. f.* helm, rudder; elm tree; the letter a; **mucaga failm**, elm berries; **glac an fhalm**, take your turn at the helm, steer. *Also* **alm**; "**an alm an aghaidh na glaice**," the helm in sturdy grasp; **air an uilm**, at the helm. *O.N.* **hjálm.**

falmadair, falmuder, *n. m.* a tiller.

falmair, falmor, *n. m.* herring-hake.

falman, *n. m.* knee-pan.

falmarra, *a.* exacting, bitter.

falmhaich, fala-ich, *v.* empty, drain.

falt, *n. m.* hair of the head; *gen.* **fuilt, fuiltean**, a single hair of the head. *O.Ir.* **folt.** *W.* **gwallt.** *O.Celt.* valto-s.

faltan, *n. m.* a snood, hair-belt, a welt; tendon = altan; fr. **alt.**

famh, fáv, *n. m.* a mole. *Also* **famh-thalmhainn** and **fath**; *dial.* **ath-thalmhainn.** *Ir.* **fadhbh.**

famhair, favir, *n. m.* 1. a giant. 2. a mole - catcher. *Cf. E.Ir.* **fomór, fomorach**, sea-demon, pirate.

famhaireachd, favirachc, *n. f.* giganticness; prowess of a giant.

famh-bhual, fav-vual, *n. m.* water-vole. **famh + bual** (water).

fan, *v. i.* wait, stay, stop, continue, remain ; **fan an so**, remain here ; **dh' fhan sinn**, we stayed ; **fanaidh na mnathan**, wives shall stay ; **fan agad fhéin**, keep your distance. *O.Ir.* **anaim**, I rest.

fàn, *n. m.* a gentle slope, declivity ; a level ; lower reach. *O.Ir.* **fán**, slope ; prone ; **etir fán et árdd**, both valley and height. *C.M.L.* 140.

fanachd, fanachc, *n. f.* waiting ; staying, tarrying, remaining, residing.

fànadh, *n. m.* declivity, slope, respite ; "**fànadh is fàth furtachd**," = a fighting chance.

fanaid, fǎn'-ǎj, *n. f.* mockery, ridicule. *E.Ir.* **fonomat**.

fanaideach, fan'ej-uch,*a.* mocking. *Arran:* fanaiseach, farraideach.

fanaigse, fanegshu, *n. f.* dog-violet.

fanarach, *a.* fond of paying court.

fànas, *n. m.* 1. an opportunity. 2. a void. *Lat.* **vanus**.

fa-near, fa-ner, *adv.* under consideration ; "**thoir fa-near**," consider, observe.

fang, *n. f.* a vulture ; **sùil na fainge**, the vulture's eye.

fang, *n. m.* a fank, enclosure, durance, custody ; **ann am fang**, in durance, in custody. *Sc.* **fank**.

fangaich, fangich, *v.* enclose, put into a fold.

fann, faun, *a.* weak, feeble, faint ; **duine fann**, a feeble person. *O.Ir.* **fann**. *W.* **gwan**. *O.Celt.* vanno-s.

fannachadh, fannadh, *n. m.* fainting ; "**air fannachadh, gun leus aithne 'n a sùilean**," having fainted, without a blink in her eyes.

fannadh, *n. m.* gentle rowing of boat while fishing with fly, trolling. *E.Ir.* fonnamh = fogluasacht, motion. *Archiv.*², 338.

fannaich, fanich, *v.* get faint, debilitate, make feeble ; **tha e a' fannachadh**, he is getting more feeble.

fannaidh, fanay, *v.* fish while boat is being rowed slowly, or while stationary.

fannal, fannan, *n. m.* a gentle breeze.

fannanta, *a.* feeble, faint, languid.

fanngheal, faun-yal, *a.* pale, whitish.

fannsholus, faun - holus, *n. m.* weak light.

fanntalach, *a.* faintish.

fantainn, fant'-inn, *vbl. n. f.* waiting. *Also* fantail.

fantalach, *a.* dilatory.

faob, fùbb, *n. m.* a lump ; a knot. *M.Ir.* **ádb**, lump. *O.Ir.* **odb**, *obex*.

faobairneach, fūb'-ur'-nach, *n. m.* a large one of anything.

faobh, fūv, *n. m.* spoil, booty. *O.Ir.* **fodb**, spoils of war.

faobhachadh, fūvuchu, *n. m.* act of despoiling.

faobhadach, fūvuduch, *n. m.* carcass of a sheep (having perished). Cf. *O.Ir.* *sub* faobh.

faobhag, fūvag, *n. f.* common cuttle-fish.

faobhaich, fūvich, *v.* despoil, plunder.

faobhar, *n. m.* edge of a tool, as knife ; air fhaobhar, edgewise. *O.Ir.* **fáibur**, fáebur, edge.

faobhraich, fūvrich, *v.* edge, sharpen, whet, hone ; **faobhraich an sgian**, whet the knife ; *vbl. a.* faobhraichte, whetted, sharpened.

faoch, *a.* periwinkle, whirlpool.

faochag, *n. f.* a little wilk or whirlpool. *M.Ir.* faechóg.

faochag, *n. f.* the centre of the forehead ; **a steach air faochaig do chlaiginn**, in through the centre of your forehead.

faochadh, *n. m.* a favourable crisis of a disease ; alleviation ; **fhuair i faochadh**, she got the crisis—the turn.

faochainn, *v.* entreat most earnestly ; urge earnestly.

faochaistean, *n. pl.* a row of holes near the top of a creel. *Also* briagan.

faochnach, *adj.* urgent, earnest in requesting ; **nì faochnach**, an urgent affair.

faochnadh, *vbl. n. m.* a most urgent request or petition ; urging ; **a' faochnadh orm dol leis**, vehemently urging me to go along with him.

faochnaich, *v.* urge, entreat perseveringly ; be not refused ; insist.

faod, feud, *v.* may, can, must. *E.Ir.* fétaim.

faodail, fūdal, *n. f.* goods found by chance ; waif, foundling. *O.Ir.* **étaim**, I find. (*KM.* suggests étail.)

faodhail, fu-il, *n. f.* a strait or narrow, through which one can wade at low water ; a ford. *O.Ir.* **fodil** (= fo + dáil), a division ; fr. **dálim**, I divide, separate. Cf. *N.* vaðill, fordable water.

faoghaid, fu-ij, *n. f.* a chase, a hunt ; *properly* faghaid, *q.v.*

faoghailt, faodhailt, fū'ilt, *n. f.* See faghailt.

faoighe, faidhe, fyu, *n. f.* begging, begging (wool, corn). *O.Ir.* **foigde**, *mendicatio*, for fo + guide, begging.

faoil, *n. m.* profuse hospitality, generosity.

faoileann, *n. f.* sea-gull, mew. *Also* faoileag. *O.Ir.* foilenn, *alcedo*.

faoileas, fūlas, *n. m.* sparkle, rich colour ; for fo + leus, gentle sheen. Cf. faileas ; "**fìon bu taitniche faoileas**," wine of charming sparkle.

faoilidh, *a.* profusely liberal, hospitable. *O.Ir.* **fáilid**, fáelid, glad, blithe. *O.Celt.* vâleti-s.

faoilleach, faoilteach, *n. m.* the storm-days, first fortnight in spring and last in winter ; from middle of Jan. to middle of Feb., the "wolf month" ; the opposite of iuchar, the worm-month ; smeuran dubha 'san fhaoil-teach, ripe bramble berries in the storm-days, *i.e.* a great rarity.

faoilteachd, *n. f.* hospitality, kindliness. *See sub* **fàilte**.

faoilteas, fūltius, *n. m.* kind welcome, gladness.

faoiltich, *v.* receive kindly and heartily.

faoin, *a.* silly, trifling, light, idle ; nì **faoin**, a trifling affair ; **is faoin duit**, it is idle for you ; **duine faoin**, a silly fellow. *M.Ir.* fáen, weak.

faoincheann, *n. m.* a vain, empty head.

faoineachd, *n. f.* extreme silliness or vanity ; silly manner.

faoinealachd, fūmaluchc, *n. f.* vanity, folly.

faoineis, *n. f.* trifling consideration or conduct ; vanity, idleness.

faoinsgeul, *n. m.* an idle tale ; *a.* **faoin-sgeulach**.

faoisg, fāoĕshg, *v.* chink, as a dish ; unhusk, as nuts.

faoisgeag, *n. f.* a filbert.

faoisgnich, *v.* chink, gape, as a dish ; **tha chuinneag air faoisgneadh**, the water-pitcher chinks or leaks. *Also* **sgréidh-eadh**.

faol, *n. m.* wolf. *Also* **madadh allaidh** (wild dog). *E.Ir.* **fael**. *O.Celt.* vailo-s.

faolaide, fūliju, *n. m.* an amateur.

faolmunn, *n. m.* culture, civilisation ; "measg Thurcach gun fhaolmunn," among uncivilised Turks.

faolum. *See* **foghlum**.

faomadh. *See* **aomadh**.

faondrach, *a.* astray, neglected.

faondradh, *n. m.* wandering, straying ; neglect, unsettled state.

faontraigh, *n. f.* the open shore.

faor, *n. m.* a blade of grass.

faosad, faoisid, faosaid, *n. m.* 1. confession (to a priest). 2. pressing invitation. *Ir.* **faoisidin**. *O.Ir.* fóisitiu, *confessio.*

faosaidnich, *v.* confess.

faosgadh, *vbl. n. m.* lousing. *R.D.*

faotail, *n. f. See* **faodail**.

faotainn, *vbl. n. m.* getting, finding ; **a' faotainn**, getting.

faotalaiche, *n. m.* a foundling.

faothachadh, *m.* relief, crisis (in illness, fever).

faothaich, *v.* relieve.

far, *adv.* where ; **far a bheil e**, where he is ; *also* **fail a bheil e**.

far, *prep.* with ; **far rium**, with me.

far, *v.* freight (a ship).

far, *v.* fetch, bring ; **far am furm**, fetch

the stool ; "**far a nall mo phìob**," fetch hither my pipe.

far-, *prep.* over, upon. *O.Ir.* for, *super.*

farabhradan, *n. m.* spent salmon.

farachan, *n. m.* a mallet, death-watch, beetle.

farach-dubh, *n. m.* figwort.

fàradh, faradh, *n. m.* a ladder ; shrouds.

faradh, *n. m.* freight, fare ; **pàidh am faradh**, pay the fare or freight ; hen-roost or cock-loft ; **air an fharadh**, on the cock-loft.

faraghaol, *n. m.* false love.

faraich, *n. f.* cooper's wedge.

farail, *n. m.* a visit, inquiry for health.

farainm, *n. m.* nickname. **far + ainm**, by-name.

faraire, *n. f.* watching a corpse, a leek-wake, entertainment. *Also* **foraire**.

faral, *vbl. n.* quick energetic action ; endeavour (under pressure of time or force) ; "tilgeadh dhiùbh nan casagan, gu faral as," flinging away their cloaks in the endeavour to escape.

faran, *n. m.* 1. garlic. 2. turtle-dove.

far-aon, *adv.* both, together, also.

farasda, *a.* merry, solid, solemn, softly ; **gu farasda fòil**, solemnly and softly.

farasdachd, *n. f.* composure.

farasg, *n. m.* fish found dead on shore or on sea. **far + iasg**.

farbairneach, *a.* lonely, sad, friendless. Cf. *Ir.* forbach, a funeral entertainment.

farbhach, *n. m.* stranger, foreigner, clown.

farbhail, farvil, *n. f.* a lid. **far + bél**.

farbhailteach, *a.* affable, hospitable.

farbhalach, *n. m.* a stranger, foreigner.

farbhas, *n. m.* a surmise.

farbhonn, *n. m., gen.* and *pl.* **farbhuinn**, the inner sole of a shoe. **far + bonn**.

farbhuille, *n. f.* a back-stroke.

farch, *n. f.* lyre, or lute.

farchachan, far'-ach-an, *n. m.* a mallet.

farchluais, farchlush, *n. f.* eaves-dropping, listening thievishly, overhearing.

fàrdach, *n. f.* house ; lodging ; **fardach oidhche**, night's lodgings.

fàrdadh. *See* **fàrdath**, alder bark (for dyeing).

fàrdal, *n. m.* delay, detention. *E.Ir.* for-dul.

fàrdath, fard'-dă, *n. m.* lye, or any colour in liquid ; **fàrdath gorm**, liquid blue.

fardhruim, *n. m.* false keel.

fàrdorus, àrd-dorus, *n. m.* lintel of a door.

farfhuadach, *vbl. n. m.* driving out of bounds, banishment.

farfonadh, *m.* a warning.

fargradh, *n. m.* a bathing, floundering.

fargradh, *n. m.* a report.

fàrlus, *n. m.* sky-light, chimney, hole in

thatch (for letting out smoke). *E.Ir.*
forlés, loophole, skylight.
farmachan, *n. m.* a sand lark.
farmad, *n. m.* envy ; cùis fharmaid, an
enviable object ; a grudge at another's
success ; malice. *O.Ir.* format, *invidia.*
W. gorfynt, envy. *O.Celt.* ver-mento.
farmadach, *a.* envious.
farmail, *n. f.* large water-pitcher.
farpas, *n. m.* refuse of straw or hay.
farpuis, *n. f.* strife, contest. *Also*
co-fharpuis.
fàrr, *interj.* off ! be off !
farrach, *n. m.* violence, force.
farrad, *adv.* near.
farradh, *n. m.* company, vicinity. *O.Ir.*
in arrad, company.
fàrradh, *n. m.* litter in a boat.
farragan, *n. m.* a ledge.
farraid, farr'-èj, *v.* inquire ; *n. f.* inquiry.
farran, *n. m.* slight offence, anger. *Also*
farral. *E.Ir.* forran, strength, anger.
farranachd, *n. f.* vexation.
farranaich, *v.* vex, anger.
farranta, *a.* neat, stout, stately.
farruinn, *n. f.* a pinnacle. =far + rinn.
farrusg, farrushc, *n. m.* inner rind, or
skin ; peeling (for + rúsg).
fàrsan, fàrsanach, *a.* given to wandering.
farspach, farspag, arspag, *n. f.* a sea-gull
(of the largest type). *See* arspag.
farsuing, *a.* wide, capacious. *O.Ir.* fairsing, *amplus,* wide.
farsuingeachd, farshinachc, *n. f.* wide-
ness.
farsuingich, farshinich, *v.* widen.
farum, *n. m.* a noise, sound of the trampling of horses ; clangour, clashing,
rustling ; farum an stàilinn, the
clangour of their steel ; merry. *Also*
fothrum. *E.Ir.* fothrom. Cf. fothrond,
noise as of thunder, rumbling noise.
farumach, *a.* noisy, merry.
fàs, *n. m.* growth, vegetation, increase,
produce ; fàs an fhuinn, the produce
or increase of the land ; *vbl. n. m.*
growing, increasing. *O.Ir.* fásaim,
ásaim.
fàs, *adj.* unoccupied, uncultivated, vacant,
hollow, void ; tigh fàs, an unoccupied
house ; fearann fàs, waste or uncultivated land ; false, hollow ; thug
e ceum fàs, he gave a false step. *O.Ir.*
fás, fáas, empty. *O.Celt.* vàsto-s.
Lat. vàstus. *O.H.G.* wuosti.
fàs, *v.* grow, increase, become, rise. *O.Ir.*
ásaim, I grow.
fàsach, *n. m.* a grassy place.
fàsach, *n. f.* an empty place ; wilderness,
desert, desolation ; *idiom :* " cha b'e
fàsach e," 'twas not an easy job.
fàsag, àsag, *n. f.* plug-hole (in a boat),
plug.

fàsaich, fāsich, *v.* desolate, lay waste,
depopulate ; dh' fhàsaich e an dùthaich, he depopulated the country.
fàsail, *adj.* desolate, solitary ; sruthan
fàsail, a lonely brook, dry brook.
fasair, *n. f.* harness, girth-saddle.
fàsair, *n. m.* boat plug ; toll an fhàsair,
plug-hole.
fàsalach, *n. m.* a void.
fàsalachd, *n. f.* a state of lying waste.
fàsan, *n. m.* refuse of grain.
fasan, *n. m.* fashion ; as an fhasan, out
of fashion ; fr. the *Eng.*
fàsanadh, *n. m.* luxuriant pasture, an
hour's pasture for milch cows on grass
beside growing crops.
fasanta, fas'-annt-à, *a.* fashionable.
fasantachd, fas'-ant-achc, *n. f.* fashion-
ableness, adherence to custom or
fashion.
fasbhuain, fasvuin, *n. f.* stubble. *Also*
asbhuain.
fàschoill, *n. f., pl.* -tean, young grove,
wilderness.
fasdadh, *vbl. n. m.* hiring, engagement,
as a servant; binding. *Ir.* fastuighim,
I agree to. *E.Ir.* fastaim, astaim, I
hold fast.
fasdaidh, fasdy, *v.* hire, engage.
fasdail, astail, *n. m.* a dwelling, a
wretched house. For rt. *see* suidhe.
fasg, *v.* search for vermin.
fasgach, *a.* sheltered ; àite fasgach, a
sheltered place.
fasgadh, fàsg'-u, *n. m.* search for vermin.
fasgadh, fasg'-à, *n. m.* shelter, refuge,
lee side of boat. *O.Ir.* foscad, *umbra.*
W. gwasgod. *O.Celt.* vo-skàto-.
fasgaidh, fasgay, *v.* clean off vermin. *Ir.*
fasgnaim, I purge.
fasgain, fasgun, *v.* winnow.
fasgnadh, *vbl. n. m.* winnowing, purging.
fasgnag, *n. f.* winnowing fan.
fàslach, *n. f.* a hollow, a void.
faslomairt, aslomairt, fas-lomurt, *n. f.*
a hasty meal, preparation of food in
the open air, a temporary habitation.
fàsmhor, fasvor, *a.* growing.
fàsmhorachd, *n. f.* growth.
faspan, *n. m.* difficulty, embarrassment.
fàsrach, *n. f., pl.* fàsraichean, luxuriant
pasture.
fàsruith, *a.* poetic description of a gun.
fàt. *Sc.* faut, fault.
fàth, fâ, *n. m.* cause, reason ; fàth mo
dhuilichinn, the cause of my sorrow ;
opportunity, seasonable time ; gabh
fàth air, watch an opportunity. So
E.Ir.
fath, fa, *n. f.* mole. *See* famh.
fàth-fith or fìth-fàth, occult power which
rendered a person invisible to mortal
eyes. It also transformed men into

156 FATHACH—FEALLSAIMH

horses, bulls, stags, and women into cats, hares, hinds. *Carm. Gad.*

fathach, *n. m.* a giant, monster, genius. *E.Ir.* **aithech, athech,** champion, farmer, vassal. *Wi.*

fathainm, *n. m.* a nickname.

fathamas, fahamas, *n. m.* indulgence, lenity, partiality ; **gun fhathamas do dhuine seach duine,** without partiality to one man more than another ; mitigation, occasion, opportunity.

fathamas, fa-humus, *n. m.* fear, awe, a warning.

fathan, athan, *făhan, n. m.* coltsfoot.

fàthan, fāhan, *n. m.* noiseless movement, creeping so as not to surprise or startle game or prey, stalking.

fathan, *n. m.* 1. a journey. 2. light breeze.

fathanach, *a.* trifling, silly, mean-looking.

fathast, fa'-ăst, *adv.* yet, still. *Also* **fathastaich.** *E.Ir.* fodesta, fodechtsa.

fathbhan, *n. m.* a mole-hill.

fàthlaidh, *a.* gentle, noiseless. Cf. **fàthan.**

fathraig, fothraig, *v.* bathe. *O.Ir.* fo-thraicim, I bathe ; **fothrucud,** a bath.

fathunn, fahun, *n. m.* sort of report, a floating rumour. *Also* **babhd.**

fè, feath, fiath, *n. f.* dead, calm. *E.Ir.* féth.

feabhas, fio-us, see **feobhas,** superiority, degree of goodness. *O.Ir.* febas, beauty, superiority.

feacadh, fiacu, *n. m.* act of bending, bowing, yielding ; " ceannard nach feacadh," a captain that would not yield ; a mark (as made by sharp point), impression, **cha d'thug e feacadh as,** he made no impression on it. *E.Ir.* fec, a tooth.

feachd, fiāchc, *n. m.* a host, an army, expedition, forces, troops, warfare ; **feachd nan sonn,** the battle of the brave ; **tinneas an fheachda,** malingering ; **deireadh feachda,** the unfit, the rejected. *O.Ir.* fecht, a journey, a time, warfare. *O.Celt.* vektâ.

feachd-dùthcha, *coll. n.* militia.

feachdaire, *n. m.* a warrior.

fead, fed, *n. f.* whistle ; hissing noise as of wind ; **fead an aonaich,** the hissing of the wind on the heath. *E.Ir.* fét, a whistle, music.

feada-coille, *n. m.* the wood-sorrel.

feadag, fedag, *n. f.* 1. flute, a whistle. 2. a plover. 3. the third week of February.

feadaire, fediru, *n. m.* a whistler.

feadailich, fedulich, feadaireachd, fedurachc, *n. f.* continued whistling or hissing. *Also* **feadarsaich.**

Feadailt, fedelt, *n. f.* Italy ; *adj.* **feadailteach,** belonging to Italy ; also an Italian man.

feadan, fedan, *n. m.* an oaten-pipe, fife, discharge of a still, a spout ; water-pipe ; **feadan taomaidh,** a pump ; chanter of bagpipes ; aqueduct, small waterfall, small stream. *Ir.* fedán, a pipe.

feadanach, fedanuch, *a.* piped, well supplied with fifes, flageolets, etc.

feadh, *n. m.* space, length, extent ; **feadh ghleanntan fàsail,** through desert valleys ; **feadh gach tìr,** throughout every land ; **feadh an làtha,** during the daytime. *E.Ir.* ed, space, space of time.

féadhachan, fe'-ăch-an, *n. m.* gentle breeze.

feadhainn, feu-in, *coll. n.* folk, people ; some, others ; those ; **feadhainn eile,** others ; **an fheadhainn a dh' fhàg sinn,** those we left ; **cuid na feadhnach so,** the property of those ; **ceann-feadhna,** a leader. *E.Ir.* fedan, a team, procession. *W.* gwedd, a team.

fèadhan, fē'an, *n. m.* wild goose leader.

feadraich, fedrich, *n. f.* whistling ; **feadarsaich,** whistling, noise made by missile through air.

feàirde, fiārju, *degree* of **math** and **maith,** better ; **is fheàird thu sin,** you are the better for that ; **is fheàirde brà breacadh, gun a briseadh,** a quern is the better of sharpening, without breaking it.

feàirdeachd, fiārjachc, *n. f.* improvement, convalescence ; superiority, excellence ; **chan fhaic mi fhéin feàirdeachd sam bith air,** I don't see any symptom of convalescence or improvement.

feairt, fiarst, *n. f.* attention, answer, notice ; **na toir feairt air,** don't answer, pay no attention to him.

feall, fiaool, *n. f.* deceit ; treachery. *E.Ir.* fell. *O.N.* vél (wile).

feall, fiaool, *a.* deceitful, false.

feallachd, *n. f.* desertion.

fealladh, *n. m.* deceit.

fealla-dhà, *n. f.* a joke ; **thèid an fhealla-dhà gu fealla-trì,** joking will end in serious earnest.

feallan, fyal'-an, *n. f.* itch ; hives. *Also* **sgeallan, sgrìobach.**

feallan, *n. m.* a traitor, a felon.

feall-chùinneadh, *n. m.* forgery, counterfeit.

feall-fhalach, *n. m.* ambuscade.

feall-ghnàthachd, *n. f.* affectation.

feall-lighiche, fiaul-li-ichu, *n. m.* a quack.

feallsa, *a.* deceitful, mendacious.

feallsachd, *n. f.* mendacity, deceit.

feallsaimh, fyall'-sév, feallsanach, fyall'-san-ach, *n. m.* a sophist ; philosopher ; quack. *O.Ir.* felsub, fellsube, philosopher. *Lat.* philosophus.

feallsanachd, fyall'-san-ăchc, *n. f.* sophistry; false philosophy or learning.
fealltach, fiaultach, *a.* false.
fealltair, fyall'-tar', *n. m.* a quack.
fealltanach, *n. m.* a villain, a traitor.
feam, fem, feamain, femen, *n. m.* a dirty tail or train; dirt, filth.
feamach, femuch, *a.* gross, dirty.
feamachas, *n. m.* silliness, dirtiness.
feamainn, fem'-inn, *n. f.* seaweed of all kinds; *v.* manure with seaweed; **a' feamnadh an fhearainn,** manuring the land. *E.Ir.* femnach, femmuin. *O.Celt.* vemmâni-.
feaman, eaman, feman, *n. m.* a tail. So *Ir.*
feann, fyănn, *v. t.* skin, flay; **a' feannadh,** flaying, or skinning a beast; **feannadh builg,** stripping off the skin whole.
feannadh, fianu, *n. m.* skinning; excessive cold; *a.* feannaidh. *O.Ir.* fennaim; gl. *carnifico.*
feannag, fyann'-ag, *n. f.* a royston or hooded crow.
feannag, fianag, *n. f.* a lazy bed. *Also* talamh-taomadh.
feanndagach, fiandagach, *n. f.* nettle; place where nettles grow.
fear, fer, *n. m., pl.* fir, and fearaibh, a man, a husband, a goodman. *O.Ir.* fer. *O.W.* gur. *Lat.* vir. *O.Celt.* viro-s. *Cpds.:*—
fear-aisig, a ferryman.
fear-amharc, an overseer.
fear an tighe, the man of the house, the goodman.
fear-baile, a tenant of a farm, a tacksman.
fear-bainnse, a bridegroom.
fear-beairte, man who attends the gear, member of boat's crew.
fear-bogha, an archer.
fear-brataich, an ensign.
fear-buidseachd, a wizard.
fear-cèirde, fear-ciùird, a tradesman.
fear-cinnidh, a clansman.
fear-ciùil, a musician.
fear-cogaidh, a warrior.
fear-coimhid, a watchman.
fear-cuairt, a sojourner.
fear-cuideachd, a companion, a buffoon.
fear-cùirn, an outlaw.
fear-dàna, a poet.
fear-eadraiginn, a reconciler, an arbiter.
fear-ealaidh, a poet, a man of song.
fear-faire, a watchman.
fear-feòirne, a die, chessman.
fear-fuadain, a fugitive.
fear-ghleus, manly achievement; " bha thu teòm air gach fear-ghleus," you were adept at every manly deed.
fear-labhairt, a speaker.
fear-lagha, a lawyer.
fear-leughaidh, a reader. *E.Ir.* fer legind (*Lector*).

fear-oibre, a workman.
fear-pòsda, married man, husband.
fear-rùin, a confidant; **fear mo rùin,** my loved one (*m.*); **bean-rùin,** confidante; **bean mo rùin,** my loved one (*f.*).
fear-saoraidh, deliverer, saviour.
fear-sàrachaidh, oppressor.
fear-seòlaidh, director.
fear-siubhail, a traveller.
fear-sodail, flatterer.
fear-stiùiridh, a steersman.
fear-suabairt, a spare man in a boat.
fear-tagraidh, pleader, advocate, intercessor.
fear-turuis, a traveller, messenger.
fearachas, fer'-ach-as, fearachdain, fer'-achc-inn, *a.* act of claiming kindred, or siding with; following a chief, kindred, manhood.
fearail, fer'-al, *a.* manly, masculine.
fearaim, *v.* I give, render; " fearfad a chluithe caointe," I shall recite— *R.C.*², 454.
fearalachd, fer'-al-achc, *n. f.* manliness, hardihood, courage.
fearan, *n. m.* a little man.
fearann, fer'-unn, *n. m.* land, earth, ground, country; **fearann tioram,** dry land.
fearas, *n. m.* manliness, vigour. *Ir.* fearamhas. *Cpds.:*—fearas-bheairte, expert seamanship; **fearas-bhogha,** archery; **fearas-chuideachd,** diversion, sport; **fearas-mhór,** conceit; **fearas-tighe,** domestic economy.
fearbhuilleach, *a.* wielding manly blows.
feardha, *a.* brave, manly; male; **ball feardha,** the male member. *E.Ir.* ferda, ferrda.
fearg, ferg, *n. m.* anger, wrath, fury, passion; **am feirg,** in a passion, furious; **nuair a thraoghas fhearg,** when his passion subsides. *O.Ir.* ferc, ferg. *O.Celt.* vergâ.
feargach, ferg'-ach, *a.* passionate, angry, furious, enraged, irritated, outrageous, raging.
feargachd, ferg'-achc, *n. f.* passionateness.
feargaich, ferg'-ich, *v.* enrage, fret, vex, gall, get outrageous, provoke.
feargnadh, fergnu, *n. m.* provocation.
fearn, fiãrn, *n. m.* the alder tree; letter f; alder wood; a shield. *E.Ir.* fern, fernog. *W.* gwern. *O.Celt.* verno-.
feàrr, fiãr, *deg.* of math and maith, better, best, preferable; **is fheàrr dhuit falbh,** you had better go; **b'fheàrr leam,** I would prefer. *O.Ir.* ferr.
fearrasaid, *n. f.* for earrasaid, mantle.
fearrdhris, earradhris, *n. f.* red wild rose, dog rose.
fearsaid, fyarrs'-sèj, *n. f.* a spindle. *M.Ir.* fersaid, a club.

feart, fiarst, *n. f.* a virtue, an attribute ; a virtue to effect something ; wonderful quality ; **feartan buairidh,** tempting qualities ; miracle ; **Dia nam feart,** God of wonderful deeds ; substantial ; **toradh feartach,** substantial or productive crops. *O.Ir.* firt, *gen.* ferto, "miracle." *W.* gwyrth. *Lat.* virtus.

feart, fiarst, *n. f.* attention, notice, heed ; **thoir feart ormsa,** answer me, obey me ; **na toir feart air,** do not heed him.

feart, *n. m.* a grave, a tomb. *O.Ir.* fert, *tumulus.*

feartail, fyart'-al, *a.* having good qualities. *Ir.* feartamhuil ; **feart + samail.**

feartbhriathar, fyarst-vriahar, *n. m.* an adjective.

fearthuinn, fer'-hunn, *n. m.* rain. *E.Ir.* ferthain, *inf.* of feraim, pour ; give.

fearttarnach, *a.* a musical term—proper quality of sound, timbre (?).

feas, feis, *n. f.* carnal communication. *O.Ir.* feiss, sleep ; vid. *Wi.*

feascradh, *n. m.* shrivelling.

feasd, fesd, *adv.* never ; ever, for ever ; **cha tig e am feasd,** he shall never come. *E.Ir.* festa, ifesta, henceforth.

feasgar, fesg'-ur, *n. m., pl.* feasgraichean, evening, afternoon. *O.Ir.* fescor. *W.* ucher. *Lat.* vesper. *Gr.* ἔσπερος.

feasgaran, fesguran, *n. m.* vespers, evening song.

fèath, fĕă, *n. f.* calm weather ; dead calm ; **fèath Faoillich is gaoth Iuchair,** February calm, and wind in dog-days (these do not last). *E.Ir.* féith, a calm. *O'Don.*

fèathachan, fia-huchan, *n. m.* zephyr, very gentle breeze.

fèathail, fèh'-al, *a.* calm, quiet, still.

feathalachd, fè'-al-achg, *n. m.* calmness.

fèath-ghàire, *n. m.* a smile. *Also* fiamh-ghàire.

féicheamh, fēchuv, *n. m.* a debt. *O.Ir.* fechem, *debitor.*

féicheanas, fēchunus, *n. m.* argument (almost hot).

féicheannach, *n. m.* a debtor.

féidh, fēy, *gen. s.* and *n. pl.* of fiadh, deer.

féidhm, féim, *n. f.* use, employment, service due from a vassal. *E.Ir.* feidm, effort, service.

féild, fēlj, *n. m.* philosopher. *Irish.*

féile, fēla, *n. f.* generosity, hospitality ; **cridhe na fèile,** the liberal soul. *E.Ir.* féle ; fr. fíal, *velum.*

féile, fēlu, *n. f.* a charm, incantation. *Ir.* éle, héle.

féileadh, fēla, *n. m.* kilt ; **feile-beag,** the kilt in its modern shape ; *pl.* féilichean.

féileaganaich, fēluganich, *n. f.* trifling with, or playing at, work ; pastime of children.

féill, *n. f.* market day ; holiday ; **a' cumail là féille,** observing or holding a holiday or festival ; a feast ; an **fhéill-Brìde,** Candlemas ; an **fhéill-Màrtainn,** Martinmas ; **féill-Micheil,** Michaelmas ; **féill Bearchain,** St. Berchan's Fair held on 4th Aug. *O.Ir.* féil. *Lat.* vigilia. *O.Celt.* vegli-.

féillire, fēiliru, *n. f.* an almanack. *O.Ir.* félire, calendar of sacred feasts.

féillteachd, fēltiuchc, *n. f.* the keeping of feasts.

féin, " self," -self ; own ; very or self-same. With *pers. pron.* mi féin, myself ; **mise mi féin,** I myself ; *prep.* + *pron.* tha e aca féin, they have it themselves. With *n. def. by art.* an **tigh féin,** the house itself ; *def. by pos. pron.* mo thigh féin, my own house ; *def. by dem. pron.* an tigh sin féin, that very house. Usage varies as to aspir. **thu fhéin, iad fhéin,** etc. ; **sibh fhéin** often pron. si-péin. With *vb.* **dèan fhéin e,** do it yourself. *O.Ir.* féin, fesin, feisne, fadéin, fadesin, cesin, and other forms.

féin-àicheadh, *n. f.* self-denial.

féineachas, fēnuchus, *n. f.* selfishness.

féinealachd, fēn'-al-achg, *n. f.* selfishness, conceit.

féineil, fēn'-al, *a.* selfish, self-interested.

féin-fhiosrach, fēn-isruch, *a.* experimental, conscious.

féin-fhiosrachadh, fēn-isracha, *a.* experience, personal knowledge, consciousness.

féin-fhoghainteach, *a.* self-confident.

féin-ghluasadach, self-moving or automatical.

féin-irioslachd, *n. f.* condescension.

féin-iriseil, *a.* condescending.

féin-mhort, *n. f.* self-murder ; suicide.

féin-mhortail, *a.* suicidal.

féin-mhortair, *n. m.* a suicide.

féinn, oblique c. of fiann, *q.v.*

féinnidh, fēny, *n. m.* a member of a fiann ; a warrior, a champion.

féin-spéis, fēn-spēsh', *n. f.* self-respect ; self-conceit, conceit.

féin-spéiséil, fēn'-spēsh-ol, *a.* respectful to oneself ; self-conceited.

féin-thoil, *n. f.* self-will.

feirm, ferm, *n. m.* a farm. *Ir.* feilm.

féis, *n. f.* a banquet, feast. *O.Ir.* fess. *Lat.* festia.

féisd, fēshj, *n. f.* festival, banquet ; a feast ; an entertainment ; better feusd.

feisd, fēsht, *n. f., pl.* feisdeachan, a tether.

féisdire, fēshjiru, *n. m.* an entertainer.

feith, fe, *v. i.* wait upon, wait ; **feith ris,** wait for him ; **feith air,** attend him. *M.Ir.* féthim.

fèith, *n. f.* a calm, stillness ; a short respite or crisis of a disease ; **fhuair e fèith,** the fever abated a little. *E.Ir.* **féth,** a calm.

fèith, fē, *n. f.* a sinew, a tendon ; a vein ; a blood-vessel; **an fhèith a chrup,** the sinew which shrank. *O.Ir.* **féith,** *fibra.*

féith, *n. f.* a bog, a fen, a morass.

féitheach, *a.* boggy.

fèitheach, fēhach, *a.* sinewy, muscular.

feitheadh, feitheamh, feitheamh, fehuv, *vbl. n. m.* act of waiting, attending ; **a' feitheadh ortsa,** attending you.

feitheid, fehej, *n. m.* a bird or beast of prey, a vulture.

feitheideach, fehejach, *a.* like a bird or beast of prey ; *n. m.* a person ready to pounce on anything, like a vulture or bird of prey.

feithfeoir, *n. m.* looker - on, overseer ; " **Cuchulann feithfeoir na fodla,**" Cuchulann the guardian of Fodla. *RC²*, 222.

féith-ghàire, fe-gharu, *n. m.* a smile. *Also* **fiamh-ghàire.**

feobhas, fio-us, *n.f.* excellence, superiority, improvement ; **an duine d'a fheobhas,** man in his best estate. *Also* **feabhas.**

feochadan, *n. m.* thistle, corn-thistle.

feòcullan, *n. m.* polecat.

feòdaire, *n. m.* a pewterer.

feòdar, *n. m.* pewter.

feodhaich, feo'ich, *v.* decay, wither ; **fuar feodhaich,** cold (and) withering. *M.Ir.*

feodaigim, wither, blight, of fruit.

feòil, *n. f., gen. s.* **feòla,** flesh ; **muiltfheoil,** mutton ; **féidhfheoil,** " deerflesh " ; **martfheoil,** beef ; **feòildhathach,** carnation colour. *O.Ir.* **feúil, feóil, ind feúil.** *Z².*

feòilitheach, *a.* carnivorous.

feòirlig, *n. f.* farthing land. *Also* **feòirligin.**

feòirling, fiòrling, *n. f.* a mite, a farthing ; fr. *A.S.* feorþling.

feòirne, fiōrnu, *n. m.* chess.

feòirnean, fiòrnen, *n. f.* blade of grass ; *a.* **feòirneineach.**

feòlach, *n. m.* carnage, slaughter.

feòladair, fyōl'-ad-ār', *n. m.* a flesher ; a butcher.

feòlan, *n. m.* proud flesh.

feòlmhoireachd, fyōl'-vur-achc, *n. f.* lust, carnality.

feòlmhor, fyōl'-vhur, *a.* fleshy ; according to the flesh, lustful.

feòrag, *n. f.* squirrel. *W.* **gwiwer.**

feòraich, fyōr'-ich, *v.* inquire, ask ; *n. f.* an inquiry ; asking, inquiring. *Also* **fiafraich.** *O.Ir.* iarfaigim = iar + fagim, I ask ; íarfaigid, *gen.* íarfaigtho, a question.

feòran, *n. m.* a green grassy spot.

feòrlan, *n. m.* a firlot, four pecks.

feòthachan, *n. m.* a gentle breeze.

feucantachd, *n. f.* peacockishness ; brilliance, splendour, colour effects ; " **cha robh Bhènus am measg leugaibh dh' aindeoin feucantachd cho bòidheach,**" not so beautiful was Venus, among precious gems, in spite of its variegated splendour.

feuch, fēch, *v. i.* see, try, taste, show ; *inter.* behold ! lo ! see ! ; **feucham, fiacham e !** let me see it, let me try it (handle it) ; **feuch car,** try a wrestle. *E.Ir.* **féchaim.** *O.Ir.* **fégaim,** I see.

feuchadair, fēchuder, *n. m.* a tester, competitor, rival ; witch, wizard.

feuchainn, fēchin or fiachin, *vbl. n. f.* trial, taste ; trying, tasting ; striving, competing ; **a' feuchainn a chéile,** competing with each other.

feuchainneach, *a.* trying.

feud, fèd, *v.* may, can, must. *E.Ir.* **fétaim, étaim ;** can. *O.Celt.* (p)entô.

feudail, fēdal, *n. f.* treasure, dearest object ; wealth in cattle ; **m' fheudail,** my dear one !

feudar, fēdur, I must ; **is fheudar domh,** I must ; **ma's fheudar duit,** if you must ; but, **chan fheudar nach tig mi =** I *may* come.

feum, fēm, *v.* it behoves, requires, must, must needs ; **feumaidh mi falbh,** I must needs go ; *n. f.* service ; need ; necessity, worth, use, occasion ; **tha feum orm,** I am in need ; **tha feum agam dha,** I have use for it ; **duine feumach,** a man in want, a poor man ; **duine gun fheum,** a useless fellow, thriftless creature. *E.Ir.* feidm, effort.

feumach, fēmuch, *a.* needy ; *n. m.* a needy person.

feumail, fēm'-al, *a.* needful, requisite, useful.

feumalachd, fēmaluchc, *n. f.* what occasion requires, what serves one's purpose ; **fhuair mi m' fheumalachd,** I have got what serves my purpose ; utility ; **feumalachd an ni so,** the utility of this thing.

feumannach, fēmanuch, *n. m.* the needy, the poor, the destitute, the beggar; overseer ; **cuid an fheumannaich,** the portion of the poor.

feun, fēn, *n. f.* cart, wain ; **feunadair,** waggoner. *O.Ir.* **fén.** *O.Celt.* vegno-.

feur, fēr, *n. m., gen.* **feòir,** grass, pasture, herbage, hay ; **feur tioram,** hay ; **cruach fheòir,** hay-rick ; *v.* pasture, feed cattle in choice pasture ; **dh' fheur e an t-each,** he grazed the horse. *Also* **fiar.** *O.Ir.* **fér.** *W.* **gwair,** hay.

feurach, fēruch, *a.* grassy ; *n. m.* pasture.

feuraich, fērich, *v.* feed, graze.

feuran, fēran, *n. m.* chives, a wild plant of the onion kind.

feur-itheach, fēr-ich-uch, *a.* graminivorous; beathaichean feur - itheach, beathaichean nach ith ach feur, graminivorous beasts.

feurlochan, fer-lochan, *n. m.* a grassy little loch; morass, marsh. *Also* breun-loch.

feursa, fērsu, *n. m.* a canker.

feursaidh, *n. m.* a horse disease.

feursann, feursnan, fērsun, *n. m.* a worm in the hide of cattle.

feur-saoidhe, feur-saoibhe, feur-saidhe, *n. m.* hay.

feursnach, *a.* subject to worms.

feusag, fes'-ag, *n. f.* beard. *E.Ir.* fésóc.

feusagach, fès-ag-uch, *a.* bearded, hairy.

feusd, fēst, *n. f.* a feast, banqueting. *E.Ir.* feiss. *Lat.* festia.

feusgan, fiascan, *n. m.* a mussel; better fiasgan.

feutantachd, fētantuchc, *n. f. See* feucantachd.

fhuair, hoo-ur, *pret.* of faigh, get. *O.Ir.* fúar.

fiabhras, feeuv'-rus, *n. m.* a fever. *Lat.* febris.

fiabhrasach, feeuv'-rus-uch, *a.* feverish.

fiacail, fiacil, *n. f., pl.* fiaclan, a tooth, a jag, as in a saw, file, rasp, comb, or any other dentated instrument. *O.Ir.* fiacail, *dens.* *Z².* *E.Ir.* fec, a tooth.

fiach, fee-uch, *n. m.* (*pl.* fiachan, fiachaibh), worth, value, debt; fear nam fiach, the creditor; c'uime am b' fhiach leat labhairt ris, why would you condescend to speak to him? a bheil sin mar fhiachaibh ormsa? am I under obligations to do that? *O.Ir.* fiach, *pl.* féich, *debitum.*

fiach, *a.* worth, worthy, respectable, important, valuable; an fhiach dhuit do shaothair? is it worth your trouble? ma 's fhiach an teachdaire, is fhiach an gnothuch, if the bearer is respectable, the message is important; ma 's fhiach leat, if you condescend to such (ironically).

fiachail, *a.* worthy, respectable, valuable, important; duine fiachail, a respectable or worthy man.

fiaclach, *a.* toothed, jagged, pronged.

fiaclaich, *v.* girn, bicker, and gape; indent, notch, make jags.

fiadh, *n. m.* deer; *pl.* féidh, deer. *O.Ir.* fíad, game. *O.Celt.* veido-s.

fiadhach, *a.* full of deer; *n. m.* stalking; venison; deer forest. *Also* frìth. *O.Ir.* fíadach, a hunt. *O.Celt.* veidáko-.

fiadhachd, *n. f.* deer-hunt.

fiadhaich, fiadhaidh, *a.* wild, terrible, savage, as weather, boisterous.

fiadhaichneachd, *n. f.* terribleness, savageness.

fiadhain, fiūdhen, *a.* wild; muc fhiadhain, a wild boar.

fiadhair, *n. m.* ley-land.

fiadhantachd, *n. f.* wildness.

fiadhbheathach, *n. m.* a wild beast.

fiadhdhuine, *n. m.* a savage.

fiadhta, fiūtu, *a.* cruel; cold; surly.

fial, *a.* kind, generous, liberal. *Also* fialaidh; *n. m., gen.* féile, bounty, hospitality. *E.Ir.* fíal, modest. *O.Celt.* veilo-.

fialachd, for fialaidheachd.

fialaidh, fee-ūly, *a.* profusely liberal.

fialaidheachd, *n. f.* hospitality, liberality, generosity.

fialchridheach, *a.* open-hearted, hospitable disposition.

fiallannach, *a.* restless, wandering.

fiamh, fěáv, *n. f.* a tinge, tincture, hue; fiamh dhearg, a tinge of red; fiamh ghorm, a tincture or hue of blue; a degree or tinge of fear, slight fear; fiamh ghàire, a smile, literally, a tinge of a laugh; awe, reverence.

fiamhachd, fiuvachc, *n. f.* modesty; awe; resemblance.

fiamh-ghàire, a smile. *See* fèath-ghàire.

fianach, *n. m.* moor grass, deer-hair grass.

fiann, feeunn, *n. m., gen.* féinn, *pl.* fianntachan. 1. "regular standing armies of the ancient monarchs, and provincial kings of Eire." *Curry.* 2. "buannadha' (hired warriors) of the kings of Ireland" acting also as a military police force. *Ktg.* 3. "a band of warriors on the warpath." *KM.* The earlier form was fían, *gen.* féine, *pl.* fíana.

fiannaidh, *n. m.* a member of a fian; a champion.

fiantag, *n. f.* a black heath berry.

fianuis, fianish, *n. f.* testimony, record, evidence; thog iad fianuis, they bore testimony; mar fhianuis air sin, as evidence of that; a witness; aon de na fianuisean, one of the witnesses; presence; mach as m' fhianuis! get out of my presence! tog fianuis, bear record, give evidence. *O.Ir.* fiadnisse. *O.Celt.* veidôn.

fianuiseach, fianìshach, *a.* capable of bearing testimony; *n. m.* a witness; is fianuiseach thusa air sin, you are able to give evidence in this instance; aon de na fianuisich, one of the witnesses.

fiar, fear, *adj.* and *adv.* oblique, aslant, awry, cross, inclining, meandering, fluctuating; cuir fiar e, place it obliquely; mar bhogha fiar, as a biassed bow; an gleanntaibh fiar, in meandering valleys. *E.Ir.* fiar. *W.* gwyro, to slant. *O.Celt.* veiro-.

fiar, feeur, *v.* pervert ; a' fiaradh na firinn, perverting the truth ; sheer, go obliquely, as a ship, beat against the wind ; squint.

fiarachdail, *a.* coy, captivating, cunning.

fiaras, *n. m.* crookedness, excuse.

fiarshuileach, fear-hulach, *a.* squint-eyed. *Also* siarshuileach.

fiata, fiadhta, fiūtu, *a.* wild ; shy.

fiatachd, *n. f.* wildness. From fiadh.

fich ! fuich ! *interj.* fy ! bad smell ; strong expression of disgust. *O.N.* fúi.

fichead, fich'-ud, *num. adj.* twenty ; cóig ar fhichead, twenty - five ; cóig duine fichead, twenty-five men. *O.Ir.* fiche.

ficheadamh, fich'-ud-uv, *a.* twentieth. *O.Ir.* fichatmad.

fideadh, fiju, *n. m.* a hint, a notice ; *rt.* vid., as *Lat.* vid-eo. *Gr.* εἶδον. *O.H.G.* viz-an. *O.N.* vita.

fideag, feejag, *n. f.* fife, whistle, reed ; fox-tail grass. *Also* feadag.

fidealachadh, fijaluchu, *n. m.* interlacing, intertwining, entangling.

fidean, fijun, fideach, fijuch, *pl. n.* green patch of land covered by the sea when the tide is in ; links. *Also* fighdean, gabht ; mormhaich = muir + magh, sea-plain. *O.N.* fit, meadow beside water.

fidheall, fee-yul, *n. f.* (*gen.* fidhle, *pl.* fidhlean), a fiddle, a violin. *E.Ir.* fidil, *rt.* fid, wood.

fidhleadh, *vbl. n. m.* act of fiddling, fidgeting, restlessness.

fidhleir, feeler, *n. m.* a fiddler.

fidhleireachd, feeleruchc, *n. f.* discoursing on the violin.

fidileir, fidiler, *n. m.* a bad fiddler, a fidgety person.

fidir, fijir, *v.* weigh, consider well, inquire minutely ; chan fhidir an sàthach an seang, the satiated will not consider the starveling ; " ciod a dh' fhidir thu ? " what did you hear ? sympathise. *O.Ir.* fetar, fitir, *scio.*

fidreachdainn, fijruchcin, *vbl. n. m.* act of perceiving.

fidrich, fijrich, *v.* consider, hear, perceive ; inquire into minutely.

fige, figis, *n. f.* a fig.

figeach, *a.* abounding in figs.

figearach, feegeruch, *n. m.* a fiend.

figh, fee, *v.* weave, plait, knit ; figh an eige, weave the web ; figh an t-sreang, plait the cord. *E.Ir.* figim. *O.Celt.* vegio.

fighe, fiyu, *vbl. n. f.* the act of weaving, plaiting ; woven or knitted article.

figheachan, fee-uchan, *n. m.* anything

plaited ; a plait, plaited hair, cord, etc.

figheadh, fi-u, *vbl. n. m.* weaving, knitting.

figheadair, fi-der, *n. m.* weaver, knitter.

figheagach, *a.* belonging to the wild fig tree. (Young women used to wear a sprig of this in their corset as protection from the evil eye.)

fighte, feetu, *vbl. a.* woven, plaited, knitted.

fileanta, filantu, *a.* eloquent, fluent.

fileantachd, fileantachc, *n. f.* eloquence, flow of language, fluency.

filidh, feely, *n. m.* a poet, a bard. *O.Ir.* fili. *O.Celt.* velet-.

filidheachd, feelee-achc, poetry ; art of poetry.

fill, feel, *v.* fold, imply, plait ; fill an t-aodach, fold the cloth ; tha sin a' filleadh a stigh, that implies. *E.Ir.* fillim. *O.Celt.* velvo-.

filleadh, filu, *vbl. n. m.* folding, implying ; a fold, a ply ; trì fillidhean, three plies or folds.

filleag, fillein, filag, *n. f.* a small fold, small plaid. *Also* pilleag.

fillein, *n. m.* a collop, a " roll."

fillte, feeltu, *vbl. a.* folded ; in plies ; implied.

fillteachadh, feeltuchu, *vbl. n. m.* a folding.

filltiche, *n. m.* a multiplier.

fine, finu, *n. f.,* *pl.* fineachan, a tribe, a clan-name ; a clan, kindred ; na fineachan Gàidhealach, the Gadelic clans ; an fhine againne, our clan. *O.Ir.* fine, relationship. *O.Celt.* venjâ.

fineachas, fin'-ach-us, *n. f.* kindred, relationship.

fineag, feenag, *n. f.* a cheese-mite, a miser ; is lìonmhor fineag a tha beartach, there are many misers who are rich.

fineagach, feenaguch, *a.* full of mites.

finealta, feenaltu, *a.* fine, polite, of clean-cut features. *M.Ir.* fin-(fair).

finealtachd, feenaltuchc, *n. f.* fineness, polished manners, politeness.

finichd, feenichc, finiche, feenichu, *n. f.* jet ; cho dubh ri finichd, as black as jet.

finid, feenij, *n. f.* end, finale ; cuir ceann finid air, bring it to a close, finish it. *Lat.* finit.

finideach, *a.* wise.

finn, *a.* fair, white ; finn fhèath, white calm (on sea), dead calm ; "fad finn foinneach an latha," the live-long day.

finne, finn'-à, *n. f.* a maid, a maiden.

finnean, finn'-an', *n. m.* a buzzard.

fioch, *n. m.* wrath. *E.Ir.* fích, feud.

fiochda, *a.* fierce.

fiodh, fiugh, *n. m.* wood, timber ; an t-sail as an fhiodh, the log out of the timber. *O.Ir.* **fid**, *arbor* ; **fid-chat**, mouse-trap. *O.W.* guid. *O.Celt.* vidu-.

fiodhag, fiyag, *n. f.* a fig, bird-cherry.

fiodhan, *n. m.* a cheese-vat.

fiodh-ghual, *n. m.* charcoal.

fiodhrach, fiyrach, *n. m.* timber ; **fiodh-rach a thoirt do Loch-abar**, " bringing coals to Newcastle."

fiodhrach-tarsuinn, *n. m.* timbers of a boat ; general term for ribs of a boat.

fiodhradh, fiūru, *n. m.* an impetuous rush.

fiodhull, fi'-ull, *n. f.* fiddle, violin. *E.Ir.* **fidil.** *Low Lat.* vitula.

fiogag, feegag, *n. f.* a fig-tree.

fioghair. *See* **fiughair.**

fioghuir, *n. f.* a figure. *M.Ir.* **figur.**

fioguis, feegish, *n. f.* a fig.

fiòlagan, *n. m.* a field-mouse. *Also* **feòrlagan ; fiurrlagan.**

fiolair, fiulir, *n. f.* an eagle. *Also* **iolaire.**

fiolan, fiulan, *n. f.* an earwig. *Also* **gòbhlachan.**

fiomhalach, *n. m.* a giant.

fion, fin, *n. m.* wine ; **òl fion**, drink wine. *O.Ir.* **fín.** *W.* **gwin.** *Lat.* vīnum. *See* **fineag.**

fionag, *n. f. See* **fineag.**

fionamar, *n. m.* wine-press.

fionan, fīnan, *n. m.* vine, vineyard, vinery ; **gàrradh-fiona**, **fionlios**, a vineyard ; **fiondhearc**, a grape. *Also* **fion-chaor.**

fionchrann, *n. m.* a vine.

fiondhuille, *n. f.* a vine leaf.

fion-fhàsgaire, feenāsgira, *n. m.* wine-press ; literally, a wine squeezer.

fionfhuil, *n. f.* pure blood.

fionghalach, *a.* fratricidal ; *n. m.* one who murders a relative. *E.Ir.* **fin-galach**, a fratricide.

fionghart, fion-gharradh, *n. m.* vineyard.

fionlios, *n. m.* a vineyard.

fionn-, to, against. *O.Ir.* **ind-.**

fionn, fyúnn, *n. m.* cataract on the eye ; *adj.* pale, lilac, wan, a degree of cold. *O.Ir.* **find.**

fionn, *v.* flay, skin. *See* **feann.**

fionn, *a.* white. *O.Ir.* **find.** *O.Celt.* vindo-s. *M.W.* gwynn, white.

fionna, fionnadh, fiunn'-u, *n. m.* fur, pile in beasts, hair, the grain ; **'ga tharruing an aghaidh an fhionna**, pulling it against the grain. *O.Ir.* **findfad**, and **finda**, hair. *O.Ir.* **fionnae**, pilorum.

fionnachd, fiunn'-achc, *n. m.* cool, coolness ; **am fionnachd an fheasgair**, in the cool of the evening.

fionnag, fiunn'-ag, *n. f.* the fish whiting.

fionn-àirc, *n. f.* suber album, fungus on tree.

fionnairidh, fiunn'ar'-è, *n. f.* watching ; evening.

fionnan-feòir, *n. m.* grasshopper.

fionnar, fionnfhuar, fiunar, *a.* coldish, cool, cold.

fionnarachd, féünn'-ar-achc, *n. f.* coolness. *Also* **feannarachd.**

fionnaraich, feunn'-ar-èch, *v.* cool.

fionnas-gàrraidh, *n. m.* parsley.

fionndairneach, *n. m.* rank grass, downy beard.

fionndruinne. *E.Ir.* **findruine**, white bronze.

Fionnghall, a Gaelicised Norseman—native of the Hebrides ; *opp.* to **Dubhghall**, a Teuton. *See* **Gall.**

fionnogha, fiun-o-u, *n. m.* great-great-grandchild. *See* **ionnogh.**

fionnrach, *n. f.* daylight.

fionnsgeul, *n. m., gen.* -**sgeòil**, a fable ; *pl.* **f.-sgeulachdan**, a romance.

fionnsgeulaiche, fiun-sgelichu, *n. m.* a romancer.

fionntach, fiuntuch, *n. m.* the pile on the body, a pelt ; from **fionnadh.**

fìor, fīr, *a.* true, genuine, real, just, upright ; sterling ; **fìor ghrund an locha**, the very bottom of the lake ; **duine fìor**, a just man ; **fìor shlaoigh-tire**, a complete villain, a sloucher. *O.Ir.* **fír.** *W.* **gwīr.** *Lat.* verus. *O.Celt.* vêro-s.

fìor-aithris, *n. f.* a true recital.

fìor-chinnteach, *a.* quite certain.

fìorchrann, *n. m.* a sycamore tree.

fìor-dhìleas, feer-yeelus, *a.* very faithful, near akin.

fìoreun, *n. m.* an eagle.

fìorfhuil, feer-ool, *n. f.* noble blood.

fìorghlan, fīr'-ghlăn, *a.* transparent, pure.

fìoriasg, *n. m.* salmon. So *E.Ir.*

fìoruisg, fīr'-ŭshg, *n. m.* spring-water ; flowing water.

fios, fis, *n. m.* knowledge ; word, information, message, invitation, intelligence, notice ; **fhuair mi fios**, I got notice ; **tha fios agam**, I know ; **gun fhios nach tig e**, not knowing but he may come ; **gun fhios c'arson**, not knowing why or wherefore ; **fios fuadain**, a flying report ; **fios air an fhios**, repeated information. *O.Ir.* **fius, fiss** (*inf.* of **fetar**, *scio*). *W.* **gwŷs**, summons.

fiosachd, fis'-achc, *n. f.* fortune-telling, divination, augury, sorcery, soothsaying.

fiosaiche, fisichu, *n. m.* " man of knowledge " ; soothsayer, wizard. *O.Ir.* **fissid**, *savant.*

fiosrach, fis-rach, *a.* intelligent, conscious ; **is fiosrach mi**, I am fully aware ; **duine fiosrach**, an intelligent man.

fiosrachadh, fisruchu, *vbl. n. m.* inquiring, experience ; **o m' fhèin fhiosrachadh**, from my own experience.

fiosrachail, fis'-rach-al, *a.* intelligent, informed.

fiosraich, fisrich, *v.* inquire, ask, inquire into, inquire after, ask after, examine.

fir, *gen. s.* and *n. pl.* of fear, man.

fir-bhréige, fir-vrēgu, *n. m.* puppets ; standing stones seen on the sky-line.

Fir-Bolg, *n. prop.* Name of a people who held the sovereignty of Ireland immediately before the **Tuatha Dé ;** " men of the bags." *See Ktg. Hist.*

fir-chlis, fir-chleesh, **fir-chlisneach,** fir-chlis-nyach, *n. pl.* streamers, Northern lights, aurora borealis ; merry dancers ; **fir** (men) and **clis** (nimble in action).

fir-chneatain, fir-chreten, *n. pl.* back-gammon men.

fire faire, firu-feru, *interj.* what ! " what a pother ! "

fireach, fir-uch, *n. m., pl.* **firichean,** moor, hill-land.

fireachail, *a.* manly, cheerful, of good address.

firead, firut, *n. f.* a ferret.

firean, feeren, *n. m.* the righteous, the just man. *O.Ir.* **firén, firian,** *justus.* *Z²*. *O.Celt.* vêriâno-s.

firean, *v. t.* preen, plume, as bird.

fireanachadh, feerenuchu, *n. m.* justification, act of justifying.

fireanaich, *v.* justify.

fireantachd, feerantuchc, *n. f.* righteousness, integrity.

firein, firen, *n. m.* a manikin.

fireun, feer-én, *n. m.* the eagle. *Ir.* **fír-én,** the " true bird."

firinn, feer'-inn, *n. f.* the truth, a truth ; **firinn shuidhichte,** a fact, an aphorism.

firinn, feer'-inn, *a.* girl, maiden ; **an fhirinn,** the girl. Same as **irbhinn, irghinn.**

firinneach, feer'-inn-uch, *a.* true, righteous.

firinnich, feer'-inn-ich, *v.* justify, excuse.

firinnteachd, feer'-innt-tyachc, *n. f.* righteousness. *See* **fireantachd.** *O.Ir.* **firinne** = fír + inne (sense, mind), *justitia. Thn.*

firionn, feer''-unn, *a.* male, masculine. *E.Ir.* **firend.**

firionnach, feer'-unn-ach, *n. m.* a male, a man.

firionnachd, feer'-unn-achd, *n. f.* manhood.

firum forum, hurry-scurry, bustle.

fise faise, *interj.* noise of things breaking ; crashing ; crickle-crackle.

fitheach, fee'-uch, *n. m.* a raven, vulture. *O.Ir.* **fíach.** *O.Celt.* veiko-s.

fithreach, feeruch, *n. m.* dulse. *Also* **duileasg.**

fiù, fjoo, *a.* worthy, estimable ; *n. m.* knowledge, value ; **is beag t' fhiù,** you are worth little , **mar is fhiù is mar is fhiosrach mi,** to the best of

my knowledge and belief. *O.Ir.* **fíu,** *dignus,* **ni fíu,** *non decet.*

fiuchair, *v.* search (by handling).

fiùchd, fioochc, *n. m.* a conspiracy, clique. Cf. **fioch,** anger. *Ir.* **fích.**

fiùdhaidh, fiooy, *n. m.* : 1. a wood. 2. timber. 3. an arrow. 4. a wooden cup. 5. a plank, ship's timber. 6. a chief, prince. 7. a gun, rifle. *Ir.* **fiodhbhadh.** *O.Ir.* **fidbaid,** wood, a wood.

fiùghail, fioo-al, *a.* worthy.

fiughair, fioo'-ur, *n. m.* earnest expectation, hope ; **chan 'eil fiughair ris,** there is no expectation of it. Cf. *O.Ir.* **fiugrad,** figured. *Wb.* 13ª. *Lat.* figura.

fiùghantach, fū'-annt-ach, *a.* worthy ; liberal, benevolent, giving profusely ; brave.

fiùghantachd, fioo'-annt-achc, *n. f.* worthiness ; liberality, generosity, benevolence, bravery.

fiùghantas, fū'-annt-as, *n. f.* worthiness ; liberality.

fiùrach, fiooruch, *n. f.* a barge, a skiff, a rod. *See* **iùbhrach.**

fiùran, fioor'-an, *n. m.* a sapling, stripling, a handsome young man.

flagach, *a.* loose, flaccid, loose-jointed.

flagaiche, *n. f.* looseness, a want, said of a simpleton.

flaiche, *n. m.* gust of wind. *Also* **plathadh.**

flaitheas, flahas, **flaitheanas,** flahunus, *n. m.* sovereignty, dominion ; heaven, region of bliss. *Ir.* **flaithemnas,** *gloria* ; fr. **flaithem,** a chief.

flann, *a.* red, blood-red. *E.Ir.* **fland,** red, blood.

flannbhuineach, flan-vunuch, *n. f.* flux.

flath, fla, *n. m.* a prince, a hero, a chief. *O.Ir.* **flaith** and **flaithem,** chief, dominion. *W.* **gwlad,** region. *O.Celt.* vlato-s.

flathail, flahal, *a.* stately, princely, gay.

flathalachd, *n. f.* stateliness, gracefulness.

flathasach, fla-husuch, *a.* princely, majestic.

fleachdail, flechcal, *a.* curly, flowing in ringlets. Cf. *Lat.* **plecto.**

fleadh, flugh, *n. f.* a banquet, feast. *O.Ir.* **fled.** *W.* **gwledd,** feast.

fleadhachas, *n. m.* a banqueting. *E.Ir.* **fledugud,** feasting.

fleadhadh, *n. m.* a brandishing, a wielding.

fleasg, flesc, *n. m.* a rod, crown, chaplet, wreath ; a rod ; **fleasg òir,** a crown of gold. *O.Ir.* **flesc** (*fem.*). *O.Celt.* vleskâ.

fleasgach, flesg'-ach, *n. m.* a bachelor, a hero, a youth ; fr. **fleasg.**

fleasgairt, flescurt, *n. f.* a barge, or boat (hung with festoons) ; " **air fleasgairt**

bhig chaoil nan trì seòl," on a small, narrow boat of the three sails. *I. Lom.*

fleisdear, fleshjer, *n. m.* an arrow-maker ; Mac an fhleisdeir, the surname Fletcher or Leslie.

fleòdar, flõdur, *n. m.* pewter ; *a.* fleòdrach.

fleodradh, flodru, *n. m.* floating.

fleodruinn, flodrin, *n. m.* a buoy. *O.N.* fljóta.

fleog, flog, *n. m.* a sole, halibut. *Also* bradan leathan.

fleogan, flogan, *n. m.* a flabby person, a flat fish ; *a.* fleoganach.

fleòidhte, flõtu, *a.* flaccid.

fliche, flich'-u, *n. f.* moisture. *Also* flichead, fluiche. *E.Ir.* flechud, wetness.

flichne, flich'-nu, *n. f.* sleet. *Also* slinnteach.

flichneach, flich'-nach, *a.* sleety.

flichneachd, flich'-nachc, **flinneachd,** flinn'-achc, sleety weather ; cold raw weather.

flinne, flinu, *n. m.* sleet. *Also* flion.

fliodh, flugh, *n. m.* chicken-weed ; wen.

fliodhan, *n. m.* a small wen.

flion, *n. m.* snowstorm (of fine small flakes).

fliuch, flooch, *v.* wet, make wet ; fliuch e, wet it ; *adj.* wet, rainy. So *O.Ir.* Compar. fliche. *W.* gwlyb, wet. *Lat.* liqueo.

fliuchadh, floochu, *n. m.* a wetting.

fliuchalachd, floo-chaluchc, *n. f.* wetness.

fliuchan, *n. m.* a wet spot.

fliuchbhord, flooch-vord, *n. m.* keel-board, plank next the keel. *See* eàrrlaig.

fliuiche, flichu, *n. m.* wetness ; more wet.

flò, *n. f.* hallucination, infatuation ; a host ; flò chadail, slumber.

flod, *a.* afloat ; air flod, barely floating (in shallow water) ; fleet of boats. *O.N.* floti, a raft.

flodach, *a.* lukewarm, tepid.

flùr, floor, *n. m.* flour ; a flower.

flùran, flooran, *n. m.* a small flower ; *a.* flùranach.

fo, *prep.* under, beneath, below, at the foot of ; fo chìs, under tribute ; fo bhròn, mournful ; fodham, under me ; tha tighinn fodham, I feel inclined. *O.Ir.* fo. *O.W.* guo. *O.Celt.* vo-.

fòbar, *v.* wish, like, intend. *E.Ir.* fóbairim, I assay, I undertake.

fobhaile, fo'-val-u, *n. m.* a suburb.

fobhannan, *n. m.* a thistle. *Also* gìogan.

focal. *See* facal. *E.Ir.* focul.

fòcal, *n. m.* a pole-cat ; faghaid an fhòcail, chase of the pole-cat.

fòcalan, *n. m.* pole-cat's kitten.

fochaid, fŏch'-aj, *n. f.* mocking, scoffing. *E.Ir.* fochuitbiud = *O.Ir.* fo-con-tibiud, to laugh at, tibiud = *inf.* of tibim, I laugh.

fochaideach, fŏch'-ajj-ach, *a.* derisive.

fochann, *n. m.* blade ; corn in the blade ; fo fhochann, in blade.

fochannachd, fochaireachd, *n. f.* making fun of, teasing, ' drawing one's leg.'

fochar, *n. m.* contact, presence, conjunction ; dithis 'nam fochair, two in contact with them, near them. *E.Ir.* fochair, with, near.

fochlasach, *a.* rich in brook lime.

focladair, facladair, *n. m.* lexicographer.

foclaiche, faclaiche, *n. m.* speaker.

foclair, faclair, *n. m.* dictionary.

fòd, *n. m.* a turf, a peat. *Also* fàd. *O.Ir.* fót, sod, clod.

fodar, *n. m.* fodder, provender ; fr. *Eng.*

fodraich, fod'-rich, *v.* give provender.

fògair, fõg'-ir', *v.* banish, expel. *O.Ir.* fócarim, fúacraim (= fo-od-garim), proclaim ; banish.

fògairt, fõg'-art, *vbl. n. m.* banishment, expulsion ; act of driving away, expelling. *O.Ir.* fócre (*inf.* of focarim), monitio.

fògarrach, fõg'-urr-ach', *n. m.* an exile, a vagabond, an outlaw, a fugitive.

fogh, *a.* quiet, careless.

fogha, *n. f.* a dart, an attack, a blast (of wind).

foghail, *n. f.* robbery, plunder, invasion ; fr. fo + gal (valour, war), depredation.

foghail, fo-ul, noise, bustle, merriment ; gun àrdan gun fhoghail, without pride or blustering. *See* othail.

foghainn, fo'-inn, *v. i.* be sufficient, suffice ; fóghnuidh so, this will suffice ; finish, kill ; fóghnuidh mi dhuit, I will do for you. *Ir.* foghnamh. *O.Ir.* fognam, service ; fr. fo + gníu, I serve.

foghainteach, fo-intuch, *a.* sufficient, fit ; brave, valorous ; duine foghainteach, a brave, valorous person.

foghannan. *See* fobhannan.

foghannas, fó'-unn-us, **foghantas,** fó'-unnt-us, *n. f.* sufficiency, quite enough ; tha m' fhoghantas agamsa, I have quite enough, I have sufficiency.

foghar, *n. m.* a resound, a re-echo ; a blow that causes a sound; vowel. *O.Ir.* fogur, *sonus.*

foghar, fu'-ur, *n. m.* autumn, harvest ; meadhon an fhoghair, mid-autumn ; *dial.* fobhar. *E.Ir.* fogamur (gamur, sameroot with geamradh = 'sub heimem.' *McB.*).

fogharadh, fobharadh, faov'-urr-u, *n. m.* autumn, harvest ; toiseach an' fhogharraidh, beginning of autumn.

fòghlach, fõ-lach, *n. m.* rank grass,

manured grass, grass growing on dung-hill. See **fòlach.**

fòghladh, fō-lu, *n. m.* robbery, trespass ; **luchd-fòghladh,** plunderers, marauders. *See* **foghail,** plunder.

fóghlaide, fū-liju, *n. m.* an apprenticed hand, an amateur.

fóghlainteach, fūlintuch, *n. m.* an apprentice. *O.Ir.* fo-gliunn, I learn. *Z².*

fóghluim, fūlum, *v.* learn, educate.

fóghlum, *vbl. n. m.* act of acquiring intelligence ; learning ; **a' fóghlum gliocais,** learning wisdom. *O.Ir.* fo-glaimm.

fóghlumach, fūlumuch, *n. m.* learner, novice.

fóghlumaid, fūl'-um-aj, *n. f.* a college, a university ; (foghlum + àite), a place of learning.

foghmharach, *n. m.* a pirate, a sea-robber. *M.Ir.* fomórach.

foghmhorachd, *n. f.* piracy.

fóghnadh, fōnu, *n. m.* enough ; use, service ; **air fóghnadh,** *lit.* past service ; passed away ; **fóghnaidh na dh' fhógh-nas,** enough is as good as a feast. *See* **foghainn.**

fògrach, *n. m.* an exile, fugitive.

fògradh, *vbl. n. m.* banishing, exiling.

foicheall, foich'-al, *n. m.* day's hire.

foicheallan, *n. m.* a lout, a useless fellow.

foichearain, fo-cheren, *n. m.* rank growth of the dunghill.

foichein, faichein, *n. m.* a wrapper, a baby's napkin.

foichlean, fo-chlen, *n. m.* a sprout, young corn. Cf. **fochann.**

fòid, foj, *n. m.* a turf, a sod, clod, a peat. *O.Ir.* fót. *Also* fàd.

fòidein, fōjen, *n. m.* a small peat.

foidheam, foy-em, *n. f.* inference ; substance, sense ; **mar nì gun fhoidheam,** as a senseless thing. *See* **oidheam.**

foidhearach, foi-ruch, *a.* naked.

foidhid. *See* **foidhidinn.**

foidhidinn, fu-ijin, **faidhidinn,** fy-ijin, *n. f.* patience, forbearance, long-suffering. *O.Ir.* foditiu, *toleratio* ; fod-aimim, *patior.* *Z².* *O.Celt.* vo-damjô.

foidhidinneach, faidhidinneach, *a.* patient ; **fuirich gu faighidinneach.** wait patiently.

foidhneal, foy-nel, *n. m.* a gleam. *Ir.* **foineul, fo + neul,** cloud, but also colour.

fóigheach, *n. m.* a beggar. *See* **faoighe.**

foighneachd, foinachc, *n. f.* inquiry, inquiring, asking, questioning.

foighnich, foinich, *v.* inquire, ask. *See* **faighnich.**

foighteag ! fytag, *interj.* exclamation on

being burnt, or in case of piercing cold. *Also* **foit.**

foil, fol, *v.* roast or broil hurriedly on embers ; **a' foileadh bonnaich,** toasting a cake in a hurried manner ; **foileachan,** the cake so toasted or roasted.

fòil, fōl, *a.* solemn in gait, slow, stately.

fòil, *a.* soft, gentle.

foileadh, *vbl. n. m.* 1. act of developing slowly. 2. eating or removing something on the sly.

foileag, falag, *n. f.* hastily - made cake (imperfectly toasted).

foill, foil, *n. f.* deceit, treachery. *See* **feall.** *O.Ir.* foile.

fòill, fóill, *n. m.* composure, ease. *O.Ir.* co fóill, slowly.

foillealachd, foilalachc, *n. f.* falsehood, deceitfulness, treachery.

foilleil, fuilal, *a.* false, treacherous, unfair, fraudulent, deceitful.

foilleir, fuler, *n. m.* a cheat, a rogue.

foillseachadh, fylshuchu, *n. m.* a revelation, a declaration.

foillsich, fylshich, *v.* reveal, publish, disclose, discover, manifest, lay open, declare ; **a' foillseachadh,** manifesting, declaring. One often hears **fóislich** for this word. *O.Ir.* foillsigim, I show.

foineasach, fynasuch, *a.* alert, sensitive, inquisitive ; a development of **faigh-nich,** ask.

foinne, fuina, *n. m.* a wart. *Also* **foin-neamh** and **fuinne.** *Ir.* faine.

fòinneach, *a.* straggling, rambling, dragging. *See* **finn.** Cf. *O.Ir.* **foíndel,** ramble, rove.

foinneamh, foniv, foinnidh, *a.* handsome, genteel, neat. Cf. **foinnich.**

foinnich, fuinich, *v.* temper (metal).

fòir, fōr, *v.* help, aid ; succour. *O.Ir.* **fòir,** help ; fr. fo-reith, I run.

foir-, *prefix, super* = for.

foirbheach, furvach, *a.* come to years of discretion or maturity ; *n. m.* one come to years of discretion ; an elder in the church. *Also* incorrectly **for-bhidheach.** *O.Ir.* forbe (*inf.* of for-benim, -fenim), *perfectio* ; **foirbthe,** *perfectus.*

foirbheachd, furvachc, *n. f.* man's estate ; eldership ; **tha e aig foirbheachd,** he is come to man's estate.

foirbhidh, furvi, *a.* come to man's estate ; come to years of maturity ; **duine foirbhidh,** a full-grown man, complete.

foirbhillidh, for-vili, *a.* acceptable.

foir-bhriathar, fur-vriahar, *n.* adverb.

foirceadal, foircheadal, forcudul, *n. m.* instruction, catechism. *O.Ir.* **forcital,** instruction.

foirche, forchu, *n. f.* a reef ; " sorchair

orm gach foirche, is fonn," show me
every reef, and shoal. *Carm. G.*

foirdhealbh, fur-yalv, *n. f.* scheme.

foireag, forag, *n. f.* a small patch of land
allowed a child or a poor person for
planting.

foireann, forun, foirionn, *n. f., gen.* fòirne,
a band, a crew, a troop, a brigade.
Ir. fuireann. *O.Ir.* foirinn. *O.Celt.*
vorênâ, vorinni-.

foir-éiginn, *vbl. n. f.* for-ecin, force,
violence; tyranny; *v.* force, oppress,
tyrannise.

foir-éignich, for-ēcnich, *v.* force, extort.

foirfe, furfa, complete, perfect. *O.Ir.*
foirbthe, *perfectus*, foirbe, *perfectio. See*
foirbheach.

fòirichean, furichun, *n. pl.* borders,
suburbs; mu na fòirichean so, about
these borders; fòirichean a' bhaile,
the suburbs of the city.

fòirin, fōrin, *n. f.* help, assistance. *E.Ir.*
foirithin.

fòiriomal, *n. f.* limit, boundary, frontier.

foirlion, forlin, *n.* crew. *Also* sgioba.

foirm, furm, *n. f.* pomp, ostentation,
display; thàinig e steach le foirm, he
came in with pomp, with ostentation.

foirmealachd, furmalachc, *n. f.* pomposity, formality, formalism.

foirmeil, *a.* pompous, forward, brisk.

fòirn, *v.* intrude, press.

fòirne, fōrnu, *n. m.* a troop, a brigade;
gen. of foireann.

fòirneadh, fōrnu, *n. m.* hosting, act of
gathering a host, act of forcing,
intruding.

fòirneart, fōrnarst, *n. m.* violence, force,
tyranny, oppression, fraud.

foirneartach, fōrnartach, *a.* violent.

foirneata, *a.* conspicuously brave; for,
super, and niata (courageous).

fòirneis, fōrnesh, for fùirneis, *n. f.* a
furnace.

foirtreun, *a.* very bold; from for +
treun.

fois, fosh, *n. f.* rest, respite, quietness,
leisure. *O.Ir.* foss, remaining; rest.
W. gwas, abode.

foisdin, foshdin, *n. f.* quietness.

foisdinneach, fósh'-jin-uch, *a.* at rest.

foisgeul, *n. m.* a little story; " foisgel
agam ar Choin cculuinn," I have a
little tale about Cu-Chulainn.

foisich, fosh'-ich, *v.* rest, remain.

foisteadh, foshtu, *n. m.* wages, hire.
O.Ir. foss, servant. *O.W.* guas, a
vassal.

foistinneach, foshtinuch, *a.* calm, restful,
peaceful.

folach, *a. See* falach.

fòlach, *n. m.* rank grass.

folachd, fol'-achc, *n. f.* a feud, bloodiness,

grudge, extraction; àrd am folachd,
of noble extraction; from fuil, blood.

folachdain, *n. m.* water-parsnip.

folaich, *v. tr.* hide, conceal. *E.Ir.* fol-
aigim. *O.Ir.* fullugaimm, *abdo. O.Celt.*
vo-lugô-.

follais, fol'-ash, *n. f.* publicity, public
view; a thoirt gu follais, to give it
publicity; state of being well known.
O.Ir. follus, clear.

follaiseach, fol'-ash-ach, *a.* public, exposed to public view; quite public.

follaiseachd, fol'-ash-achc, *n. f.* publicity,
state of being public; clearness.

folt, *n. m.* hair. *See* falt.

fonn, foun, *n. m., gen. s.* and *n. pl.* fuinn,
land, region; chan 'eil a leithid 's an
fhonn, his match is not in the land.
Ir. fond. *O.W.* guoun. *Lat.* fundus.

fonn, foun, *n. m.* air, tune; tha fonn
ciatach air, frame of mind; he is in a grand key. *M.Ir.* fonn,
tune, song. Cf. *Lat.* sonus.

fonnar, fonnmhor, fownar, *a.* cheerful,
gay, gleesome, musical; àite fonnar,
a cheerful situation; inclined.

fonnarachd, fonnmhorachd, fownurachc,
n. f. cheerfulness, gaiety, hilarity.

fonnsair, fownser, *n. m.* trooper.

fonntan, fowntan, *n. m.* a thistle.

for-, super-. *O.Ir.* for. *See* far and air.

for, *n. m.* sight, visibility; chan 'eil for
air, there is no trace of it, he is gone
out of sight.

forabuidh, for'-ab-y, *adj.* premature.

forach, *n. m.* 1. projection, swelling.
2. rock, reef (in sea). 3. dispute,
controversy.

foragan, *n. m.* rustling sound, swelling
noise.

forail, for'-al, *n. m.* command. *Ir.*
foráilim. Cf. earail.

forainm, *n. m.* nickname. *Also* farainm.

forair, forer, *n. f.* a watching, a wake.
for + aire.

foras, *n. m.* 1. assumed importance, or
airs of a trifling person; a denomination. 2. information, inquiry. *E.Ir.*
forus, foras, true knowledge; from
for + fios.

forasach, *a.* assuming airs.

forasda, *a.* sedate. Cf. farasda (staid).

forbhas, forvas, *n. m.* ambush. *E.Ir.*
forbas, siege.

forc, *v. t.* push with the feet, as a mule
dragged against its will; *also* fork
(*Lat.* furca); pitch with a fork. *E.Ir.*
forgam, blow, thrust.

forc, *n. f., gen.* fuirc, *pl.* forcannan, a
fork; cramp. *E.Ir.* forc. *Lat.* furca.

forc, *n. f.* a pole, a punting pole, an oar
or boat-hook used by a man in a boat
in pushing the craft from or to the

shore. *Lat.* furca. *O.N.* forkr, a fork, a punting pole.

forchinnteach, *n. f.* predestination.

forchraicionn, for-chrycun, *n. m.* foreskin.

fordhorus, *n. m.* a porch, a vestibule.

fordhruim, *n. m.* "false" keel. for (*super*) +druim.

forfhais, fora-ish, *n. f.* inquiry, information. *See* **foras.**

forgan, *n. m.* keenness, anger. Cf. **fearg.**

forgnadh, *n. m.* sudden commotion (seen in disturbed ant heap).

fòrladh, *n. m.* leave of absence to a soldier; furlough, a pass; fr. the *Eng.*

fòrluinn, *n. f.* spite, hatred, grudge; from **for** +**lonn** (fierce). *M.Ir.* **forlonn.**

forman, *n. m.* a mould. *Lat.* forma.

fòrn, *n. m.* furnace; shop-work. *E.Ir.* sornn = *Lat.* fornus, an oven, bakehouse.

fòrnadh. *See* **foirneadh.**

for-òrdachadh, *n. m.* predestination.

forradh, *n. m.* gain, shift, excrescence.

forsair, forser, *n. m.* a forester; fr. *Eng.*

fortail, forst'-al, *a.* strong, hardy, brave.

fortan, forst'-an, *n. m.* fortune. So *E.Ir., O.F.* fortune; *Lat.* fortuna.

fortanach, forst'-an-ach, *a.* fortunate.

fortanachd, forst'-an-achc, *n. f.* extreme good luck, or good fortune.

fortas, *n. m.* litter, refuse of cattle's food; orts.

forthan, *n. m.* a stud of horses.

fòs, *adv.* moreover, yet, still, also; **fòs tamul beag,** yet a little while. *M.Ir.* fós, beós. *O.Ir.* beus.

fos, *v.* rest, respite. *O.Ir.* **foss.** *O.Celt.* vosso-.

fosadh, *n. m.* a respite; a check; **fosadh còmhraig,** cessation of arms.

fosair, fosir, *v.* labour (in dressing food), pound bark. *O.Ir.* **foss,** a servant. *O.W.* guas. *O.Celt.* vasso-s, a subject, vassal.

fo-scrìobh, fo-sgreev, *v.* subscribe.

fo-scrìobhadh, *n. f.* postscript.

fosgail, *v.* open, unbolt, disclose, unlock; *vbl. a.* fosgailte, opened, unbolted, unbarred. *E.Ir.* oslaicim. *O.Ir.* arosailcim, I open.

fosgailteachd, fosciltach, *n. f.* openness, candour, fairness.

fosgarrach, *a.* open, frank.

fosghair, *a.* energetic, strong.

fosgladh, fos-glu, *vbl. n. m.* an opening, act of opening; discharging.

fosglan, *n. m.* a porch; fr. **fosgail.**

foslong, *n. m.* a mansion, a dwelling.

foslongphort, *n. m.* a camp.

foslongphortaiche, *n. m.* a defender of a camp or fortress.

fos-near. *See* **fa-near.** *Dial.*

fosradh, *n. m.* pounded bark, or anything to stop a leak.

fosradh, *n. m.* hand-feeding of cattle.

fòt, *n. m.* rotten earth.

fòtas, *n. m.* rotten pus, refuse.

fothach, fo-huch, *n. m.* glanders in horses.

fothrom, *n. f.* heavy noise, noise such as that from feet of a horse on the run. *Ir.* **fothrom,** noise, *Lh.* *M.Ir.* **fotham.** Cf. *E.Ir.* **fothrond.** **fo** +**torand.**

frabhas, fravus, *n. m.* refuse, small potatoes.

fracas, fracus, *n. m.* a waste, broken remainder. Cf. *Lat.* frango.

frachd, *n. m.* freight. *Sc.* fraught.

fradharc, fru'-urk, *n. m.* eyesight, vision, sight, view. *Ir.* **radharc.** *E.Ir.* **rodarc.**

frag, *n. f.* a hand; a woman; a wife; shield, a buckler. *O.Ir.* **fracc,** *mulier.* *W.* gwrâch, hag, witch.

fraigeasach, *a.* smart, lively; *n. m.* a lively little man.

fraigeil, *a.* bragging of personal strength.

fraigein, fragen, *n. m.* a brisk, warlike fellow.

fraigh, fry, *n. f.* partition (wattled); a roof, a shelf; **fraigh shnighe,** rain oozing through a wall; **is duilich beanas taighe a dhèanadh air na fraighibh fàsa,** it is hard to keep house with empty cupboards; a border of a country. *Also* **fraidh.** *E.Ir.* **fraig.** *O.Celt.* vragi-.

fraighnich, frynach, *n. f.* moisture oozing through the wall of a house.

fraileach, freluch, *n. f.* sea-weed.

fraingealas, freng'-a-las, *n. f.* tansy; **lus na Fraing,** the French herb.

Fraing, frénc, *n. f.* France.

Fraingeis, frénc'-ish, *n. f.* French language.

Frangach, *adj.* French; *n. m.* a Frenchman, a Frank; gill.

fraoch, *n. m.* heath, heather; bristles; anger, a girning expression of countenance. *E.Ir.* **fráech, fróech,** *brucus,* mane, bristles. *W.* grug. *O.Celt.* vroiko-s.

fraochag, *n. f.* whortle-berry. *M.Ir.* fraochóga, bilberries.

fraochail, *a.* furious, fretful, angry, passionate. *Also* **fraochaidh.**

fraochan, *n. m.* shoe toe-cap.

fraochanach, *a.* angry, fretful.

fraocharnach, *n. f.* a heathy hill.

fraoch-badain, *n. m.* fived-leaved heath.

fraoch-frangach, fràoch'-franc-ach, *n. m.* cat-heather. *Also* **mionfhraoch,** fraoch meangain.

fraoch-sgriachain, *n. m.* crackling heath.

fraoidh, fry, *n. f.* border, border of a country.

fraoidhneadh, frynu, *n. m.* embroidery.

fraoidhneis, froinis, frynus, *n. m.* a fringe embroidery.

fraoidhneiseach, frynusuch, *a.* full of fringes, of embroidery.

fraoighlich, frylich, *n. f.* blustering, as one in liquor. *Also* **fraoileadh.**

fraon, *n. m.* shelter in a hill.

fras, *n. f.* a shower ; *n. m.* seed, small shot ; **fras feòir,** grass seed ; **fras 'sa ghunna,** small shot in the gun ; *v. t.* shower, scatter, dash, attack ; **'ga fhrasadh m'a chluasan,** dashing or scattering it about his ears. *E.Ir.* frass. *O.Celt.* vrastâ.

frasach, *a.* showery.

frasachd, fras'-achc, *n. f.* showery weather.

freagair, fre'-gur, *v.* answer, reply ; **freagair an duine,** answer the man ; suit, fit ; **am freagair an còta,** will the coat suit ? *E.Ir.* frecraim (= frith- garim. *Wi.*). *O.Ir.* frisgart, *respondit.*

freagairt, fregurt, *vbl. n. f.* an answer, a reply ; act of answering, suiting, fitting.

freagarrach, fregarach, *adj.* answering, answerable, suitable, fitting.

freagarrachd, freg'-arr-achc, *n. f.* answer- ableness, suitableness, fitness.

freagarraich, freg'-arr-ich, *v.* suit, fit.

freagradh, *vbl. n. m.* act of replying ; an answer. *O.Ir.* frecr(a)e.

freasdail, fresdil, *v.* attend, wait on ; **freasdail do 'n bhord,** attend the table ; assist, relieve ; **cò a fhreasdail,** who relieved, helped, aided, attended ? *O.Ir.* frestal, fresdel.

freasdal, fresdul, *n. m.* attendance, service ; visitation, charge ; provid- ence ; **freasdal Dé,** God's providence ; **cha bhi mi 'n a fhreasdal,** I shall not be depending on him.

freasdalach, fresduluch, *a.* attentive, serviceable, providential.

freasgair, fresgir, *v.* attend, seize oppor- tunity, serve.

freiceadan, freicudan, *n. m.* a watch, a guard ; from **coimhead.** frith + comét.

freiceadanach, freicudanuch, *a.* watching narrowly, and very attentively, guard- ing.

freimiseanta, frem'-ish-ant-a, *adj.* hale, hearty, though very old.

freimseadh, frem-shu, *n. m.* a great huff, or offence, for no or slight cause, a fuss, a pother.

freimseil, frem'-shell, *a.* hale, hearty, though an old person, jolly.

freiteach, freitach, *n. m.* a vow to refrain from anything, interdictory resolution, vow of abstinence. *E.Ir.* fretech, re- pudiation, restitution.

freitich, freitich, *v.* vow, resolve to keep

from something, take a vow of self- denial. *E.Ir.* fretech.

freòine, fronu, *n. f.* rage, fury.

freothainn, fro-hin, *n. f.* bent-grass.

freumh, frēv, *n. m.* root, stock, stem, lineage ; *v.* take root, establish. *E.Ir.* frém.

freumhach, frēv'-uch, *n. m.* root, fibre.

freumhach, frēv'-uch, *a.* fibrous, full of roots.

freumhachd, frēv'-achc, *n. f.* an original cause ; etymology.

freumhaich, frēv'-ich, *v.* take root.

freumhail, frēv'-al, *a.* radical.

fri, fri, frid, freej, *prep.* through ; **air m' anam gun deach e frìd a' bhealaich, mhóir,** 'pon conscience he took leg- bail, he took to his heels.

frìd, freej, *n. f.* a mote ; " **nach fhaic frìd an sùil brìdein,**" who sees not a mote in an oyster-catcher's eye.

frìde, frij, **frìdeag,** freejag, *n. f.* ringworm, flesh-mite, a tetter. *E.Ir.* frigit.

frìdeam, freejem, *n. f.* support, attention.

frìdiomb, freejum, *n. m.* the use of another man's house for a limited time, as one's own ; kindliest hospitality.

frìdiombach, freejimach, *a.* quite at home, under no restraint in another man's house.

frin, freen, *n. m.* a bristle. *Ir.* frìdhean.

frinn, *a.* steeve, stiff, firm.

friochd, friuchc, *v.* lance, prick, pierce, or probe quickly as with an awl, pin.

friochd, *n. m.* a second dram, a half-glass whisky after a bumper.

friochdadh, frichc, *vbl. n. m.* a quick stab ; stabbing quickly and painfully.

friochdan, *n. m.* a frying-pan.

friogant, *a.* lively, sportive.

friogh, *n. m.* 1. a bristle, a hackle. 2. anger ; " **fearg is friogh an gnùis nan treun-fhear,**" wrath and rage in the faces of the heroes.

frioghail, *a.* keen, sharp, bristly.

frioghan, frighan, *n. m.* sows' bristles ; edge, gloom, frown ; *syn.* of **fearg.** *Ir.* frighan.

frioghanach, fri-gh'-an-ach, *a.* bristly.

frioghlanach, *a.* bristling, rough, frown- ing, wintry ; " **là frioghlanach fuar- raidh,**" a wintry, cold day.

frionas, frìnas, *n. m.* fretfulness, anger.

frionasach, *a.* fretful, nervy.

frionasachd, *n. f.* fretfulness, peevishness, cholericness, impatience.

friosg, frisk, *n. f.* earthworm.

friotach, *a.* fretful.

frioth-, free, *prefix,* small, slender.

friothailt, fri-helt, *n. f.* attendance ; service.

frioth-ainbheach, fri-henvuch, *n. m.*

arrears, trifling debts, remainder of a debt.

friothbhuail, fri - vuäl, v. palpitate, vibrate.

friothgharradh, free-gharu, n. m. an old or small fence ; aig taobh an fhriothgharraidh, aside the old fence ; traces of an old fence ; shaky, unstable wall.

friothlunn, n. m. earwig.

friothnamhach, a. of fierce enmity.

friothraineach, free-renuch, n. f. dwarf fern.

friothrathad, fri'-rād, n. m. a footpath, a by-path.

frith, fri, a. little ; prefix = side-, bye, sub.

frith, fri, n. f. an incantation to find whether people at a great distance or at sea be in life ; gain, profit, part of.

frith, n. f. sour or angry look.

frith, n. f., pl. fritheannan, a deer forest. Ir. frith, wild mountainous place.

frith, n. f. service.

frithainm, n. m. a nickname.

frithbhac, n. m. the barb of a hook. Also riobhag.

frithbhacach, a. barbed.

frithbhaile, n. m. a suburb.

frithbhuille, n. f. a back-stroke, a slight stroke.

frithcheum, n. m. a by-road.

frithealadh, fri-halu, vbl. n.m. attendance, act of serving, attending, ministering ; bean fhrithealaidh, a midwife ; fearfrithealaidh, an attendant a servitor. O.Ir. frith + alim, I attend.

frithear, free-her, n. m. gamekeeper.

frithear, fri-her, a. peevish, whimsical.

fritheil, fri-hel, v. attend, serve, minister.

fritheilean, fri-helan, n. m. a small island.

fritheilt, frè-helt, n. f. attendance.

fritheilteach, fri-heltuch, a. attentive, assiduous.

frithiasg, fri-asc, n. m. small fry (of fish), bait (shellfish used as bait).

frithir, fri-hir, a. earnest, eager, fretful. Cf. E.Ir. frith-airech, vigilant.

frithlean, frilen, n. m. fringe, border : frithleanaibh nan neul, the fringe of the clouds.

frithleum, n. m. a leap, a skip. Also cruinnleum.

frithleumraich, n. f. dancing, trilling (play of fingers on chanter).

frithmhaighistir, n. m. an under-master, an usher.

frò, for prò, a. hoarse, bass ; guth prò, deep voice.

fròg, n. f. a dark dismal hole or crevice, an ugly place or cranny, den, fen. Also ròg.

frog, a. active, energetic, quick (at a job), lively.

frògach, a. full of ugly crannies, having ugly sunk eyes.

frogail, a. blithe, cheerful ; from frog, lively. Sc. frack. See brogail.

frogan, n. m. liveliness ; degree of tipsiness, fit of humour.

froganta, a. merry, lively.

frogshuil, a. surly-eyed.

froineach, frenuch, n. f. ferns.

froineadh, n. m. a rushing, sudden tugging, a shake, a drubbing.

froinse, n. f. fringe.

frois, frŏsh, v. " shake," as standing corn ; come off as thread, untwine yarn from a clew, scatter, run out a stocking.

frois, n. f. a shower (of articles, grains).

froiseach, frŏsh'-uch, a. apt to " shake " (as corn), scattering, shaking.

froisein, n. m. a grain of seed.

fròmh, fròv, n. m. hoarseness, a cold.

fròmhaidh, fròv'-e, adj. hoarse ; rough ; guth fròmhaidh, a hoarse voice, deeptoned.

fròn, n. m. a nose. W. ffroeni.

fruan, n. m. wold, a steep.

fruchag, n. f. a cranny.

fuachd, foo-ūchc, n. m. a cold, coldness. O.Ir. uacht, ócht.

fuadach, fooud'-uch, vbl. n. m. driving away, the driving a vessel out of her course ; estrangement of affections, as a person, abalienation ; air am fuadach as an tir, driven out of the country ; 'ga fhuadach air an tigh, scaring him from the house. E.Ir. running away with. See fuadaich.

fuadachd, foo-ūd-uchc, n.f. estrangement, abalienation, banishment.

fuadaich, fooud'-ich, v. t. expel, banish, drive out of the proper course or channel ; estrange the affections, drive off (sheep). E.Ir. fúataigim, I take away, plunder.

fuadan, fooud'-an, n. m. carrying clandestinely, as a horse ; state of straggling ; naidheachd fuadain, a side-wind story ; air fuadan, astray ; cù-fuadain, a stray dog.

fuadarach, a. hasty, in a hurry.

fuadhaiche, foou-yichu, n. m. a bogle, a scarecrow.

fuagarthach, foou-garuch, n. m. exiled. See fògair.

fuagradh, vbl. n. m. act of banishing. E.Ir. fúacru.

fuaidne, n. m. a peg, the pins of a warping frame. Also fuaithne. E.Ir. úatne, úaitne, a wooden pin, a pillar.

fuaidreag, fooujrag, n. f. the eel or natural fly used in fishing.

fuaigh, foouy. v. sew, stitch, seam or nail,

as planks in boat-building; *vbl. a.*
fuaighte, sewed, seamed, nailed, pegged.
E.Ir. fúagaim. *O.Ir.* úagim and
úaimm, I sew.

fuaigheal, foou-yal, *vbl. n. m.* sewing,
stitching.

fuaigheil, foou-yil, *v.* sew a seam, nail a
peg.

fuaim, fooum, *n. m. f.* a noise, echo;
rumour, report, *fama*; *v.* sound, give
a sound, re-echo. *E.Ir.* fúaimm.
O.Celt. vokmen-.

fuaimearra, fooumura, *a.* resounding;
from fuaim, sound.

fuaimeil, *a.* resounding.

fuaimneach, fooum-nuch, *a.* sonorous.

fuaimnich, fooumnich, *n. f.* a great noise.

fuaimnich, *v.* make a noise, sound.

fuain, *n. m., pl.* fuaineachan, pegs used
in warping cloth. *See* fuaidne.

fuaire, *a. deg.* colder, coldest.

fuairead, foourud, *n. f.* degree of coldness.

fuaithntean, *pl. n.* a loom, the posts of
the loom.

fual, *n. m.* urine; galar-fuail, the stone.
O.Ir. fúal, búal, *urina. O.Celt.* voglo-.

fuamhair. *See* famhair.

fuar, *a.* cold, cool, stingy; *v.* get ahead;
get before the wind of another ship
or boat; get to windward of a point;
feuch am fuar thu a charraig, see and
weather the point. *Also* feuch an
cuir thu fothad an rudha, try and
weather the point. *O.Ir.* úar (later
fúar). *W.* oer. *O.Celt.* ugro-s, or ogro.

fuarachadh, foouruchu, *vbl. n. m.* relief;
act of cooling.

fuarachd, *n.f.* coldness; damp, mustiness.

fuaradh, *n. m.* the weather-gage, the
weather side; air fuaradh ort, on your
weather side; leis ort, on your lee
side. *Also* air taobh an fhuaraidh and
air an taobh leis; act of weathering,
beating, as a ship; anticipation of
foreboding evil.

fuaradh-cluaise, *n. m.* a ship's ear-ring.

fuaradh-froise, *n. m.* strong wind driven
by an imminent shower.

fuarag, *n. f.* mixture of cold water, or
cold milk and meal; hasty pudding;
brose made with cold water; " fuarag
eòrna á sàil mo bhròige," cold barley
brose out of the heel of my boot, a case
of " hunger is the best sauce." *Also*
stapag.

fuaraich, foour'-ich, *v.* cool, become cool,
become sober, as a drunk man.

fuaran, *n. m.* 1. a perennial spring.
2. a green spot (such as found near
a spring). *E.Ir.* úarán, *fons vivus.*
O'Don.

fuaranta, *a.* cold, chilly.

fuarbheann, *n. f.* a cold ben.

fuar-chràbhadh, *n. m.* hypocrisy, pietism.

fuar-chràbhadair, *n. m.* a hypocrite; a
pietist.

fuar-chridheach, *a.* cold-hearted.

fuardhealt, *n. f.* mildew.

fuarghreann, *n. f.* a scowl, a cold look.

fuarlit, *n. m.* cataplasm, poultice.

fuarlorg, *n. f., gen.* -luirg, cold scent,
a cold tracing.

fuarrachd, foour'-achc, *n. f.* dampness,
chill, mustiness.

fuarraidh, foourr'-y, *adj.* dampish, damp,
musty.

fuarshuich, *n. m.* soot-drip (this drips
when there is no rain—dif. from
sileadh or snighe).

fuasgail, fua-sgil, *v.* loose, untie; unriddle, guess; fuasgail an toimhseachan,
guess the meaning of the riddle; relieve, aid, assist; fuasgail air, relieve
him. *E.Ir.* fuaslaicim.

fuasgailte, fua-sgiltu, *vbl. adj.* loose,
untied, free; unrestrained, active,
nimble, loosed, loose in morals.

fuasgailteach, fua-sgiltuch, *a.* loose,
active; immoral.

fuasgailteachd, fua-sgiltuchc, *n. f.* nimbleness; freedom, activity, unconstraint,
free use of limbs.

fuasgladh, fua-sglu, *vbl. n. m.* act of
loosing, freeing; relieving; a'
fuasgladh air, relieving him; relief,
redemption; fuasgladh na cèisd, the
answer of the riddle or dark question.

fuasnadh, fua-snu, *n. m.* astonishment,
driving forward, tumult.

fuath, foo-u, *n. m.* hatred, aversion, hate.
E.Ir. fúath, hate. *O.Ir.* úath, terror.

fuath, *n. m.* a spectre. *O.Ir.* fúath,
forma, figura. Z².

fuathach, fua-huch, *n. m.* a spectre, a
monster.

fuathach, fua-huch, *a.* hating, loathing,
hateful.

fuathachail, fua-huchal, *a.* loathsome.

fuathachd, fua-hachc, *n. f.* loathsomeness.

fuathaich, fua-hich, *v.* hate, loathe, detest.

fuathas, fua-has, *n. m.* a prodigy, a
spectre, terrible sight; chunna iad
fuathas, they saw an apparition or
spectre; great number or quantity;
fuathas dhaoine, a vast number of
people; fuathas éisg, a vast quantity
of fish.

fuathasach, fua-hasuch, *adj.* terrible,
horrid, prodigious, wonderful, astonish-
ing.

fuathlaisg, *n. m.* hatred.

fuathmhor, fua-vur, *a.* horrifying; hateful.

fuathshlat, *n. f.* a temporary hoop.

fùc, v. t. press against, full cloth.

fùcadair, n. m. fuller.

fùcadh, foocu, n. m. fulling cloth, a waulking.

fudaidh, fudy, a. mean, low, vile; a vile and worthless fellow; euphemism for Satan.

fùdar, foodur, n. m. powder, gunpowder; fr. Eng.

fùdaraich, foodurich, v. powder; urge on to mischief; instigate; is tusa a dh' fhùdaraich e, it is you that instigated him.

fùdradh, foodru, n. m. mixing, tossing; turning hay to dry it.

fùdraic, foodric, a. smart, in good condition.

fuich! fooich! interj. fie! fie! pshaw! exclamation of disgust (as at a vile smell).

fuidh, for fo, prep. under.

fuidheag, fuigheag, foo-yag, n. f. a thrum. Ir. fughóg.

fuidheall, fuigheall, foo-yul, n. m. leavings; remainder, a remnant. Also fiudhall. E.Ir. fuidell, and fuigell, leavings. W. gweddillion.

fuidir, v. fumble, besprinkle, stir about.

fuidir, foojir, n. m. 1. fugitive or migratory husbandman, a stranger tenant. 2. fool, lout, clown.

fùidreadh, foojru, vbl. n. m. sprinkling; fumbling, commixing, stirring about.

fùidse, foojshu, n. m. craven; poltroon; one who flees, a cock that will not fight. Also fùididh.

fùidsidh, foojshy, n. f. putting an opponent to flight; fr. Lat. fugio, Sc. fugie.

fuifean, fooiff'-an, n. m. a blister on the breech.

fuigheall, foo-yal, n. m. remainder, refuse. See fuidheall.

fuighleach, fooyluch, n. m. remains.

fuil, fool, n. f., gen. fala, fola: blood; blood extraction; dhòrt iad fuil, they made bloodshed; o'n fhuil rìoghail, from the royal extraction; gu fuil is gu bàs, to bloodshed and death. O.Ir. fuil, gen. fola.

fuilchiont, fool-chiunt, n. f. blood-guiltiness.

fuileach, fooluch, a. bloody, sanguinary, cruel; comhrag fuileach, a bloody battle.

fuileachadh, vbl. n. m. act of drawing blood—barely bleeding.

fuileachd, foolachc, n. f. bloodiness. Also falachd.

fuileachd, n. m. extraction, descent.

fuileachdach, foolachcuch, adj. bloody, sanguinary, ravenous; duine fuileachdach, a bloody man.

fuileamain, foolmen, n. m. a blister on the toe; a bleeding toe (struck against anything); a blister on the breech. Also fuifean.

fuilear, foolar, adv. too much; chan fhuilear dha, not too much for him— i.e. he needs that at least. Ir. fuláir, for furáil = must. O.Ir. foráil (= for + áil, excessive injunction). KM.

fuilich, foolich, v. bleed; let blood.

fuiling, fooling, fuilig, foolig, v. suffer, permit, bear, admit; fuiling domh, permit me. O.Ir. fuloing, sustinet. fo (prep.) + loing (sustinet).

fuilteach, fooltuch, a. bloody, cruel.

fuilteachas, fooltuchus, n. f. bloodiness, slaughter, cruelty; extreme cruelty.

fuiltean, foolten, n. m. a single hair of the head. O.Ir. fuiltín.

fuin, v. bake, knead, make bread. E.Ir. fuinim, I cook, bake.

fuine, n. f. a batch, a baking, kneading; vbl. a. fuinte, baked, kneaded.

fuineadair, foonuder, n. m. a baker.

fuinne, foonu, n. f. a wart. Also foinne.

fuirbidh, foorby, fuirbirneach, foorbirnuch, n. m. a strong man; pl. fuirbidhnean.

fuireach, fooruch, vbl. n. m. a stay; act of staying.

fuireachd, foorachc, n. f. a staying.

fuirich, foorich, v. i. stay, remain, reside, abide, stop, reside; take up your abode. O.Ir. fuirigim, I stay, tarry. fui + rig. Thn.

fuirleach, foorlach, n. f. a parchment or skin to cover a milk dish. Also iomaideal.

fuirm, foorm, gen. s. and n. pl. of furm, a form.

fùirneis, foorn'-esh, n. f. furnace; household furniture.

fùirneisich, foorneshich, v. furnish.

fuithein, fuy-hen, n. m. galling by riding, blistering. Also liasan.

fulachd, n. f. a carcass.

fulag, ulag, n. f. a block, a pulley.

fulang, fulag, foolug, vbl. n. m. suffering, capability of suffering; forbearance, patience, hardihood. See fuiling.

fulaisg, v. i. rock, toss, swing; fr. fo + luaisg.

fulangach, fool'-ann-uch, adj. hardy, patient, enduring.

fulangachd, fool'-unn-uchc, n. f. passiveness, suffering, endurance.

fulangas, fulannas, fooll'-unn-us, n. f. endurance, suffering.

fulasgach, a. moving, rocking. fo + luasc. Also turaman, turaban.

fulasgadh, n. m. rocking, tossing, swinging motion. See luaisg.

fulbh, n. f. gloom.

fulmair, n. m. the grey petrel, fulmar.

fulpanachd, *n. f.* joining, articulation.

funntachadh, funntainn, *n. m.* excessive cold.

furachail, *adj.* attentive ; carefully observing ; looking keenly.

furachar, *a.* quality of waiting ; watching, watchful, attentive ; *syn.* furachail. *See* fuirich.

furacharas, *n. f.* vigilance ; extreme attention to the business in hand.

furail, *adj.* command ; offering. *E.Ir.* furáil, uráil. *O.Ir.* iráil. Same as earail.

furailteach, fooreltuch, *a.* hospitable, kind.

fur, furan, *n. m.* a welcome, salutation ; joy at meeting, fawning, courtesy, courteous reception. Cf. *E.Ir.* ur-áin, excess.

furanach, *a.* joyful at meeting.

furanachd, *n. f.* complacency.

furas, *n. m.* patience ; leisure ; a bheil furas ort, have you leisure ? a' cheud fhuras a bhios orm, the first leisure I get.

furas, furasda, *a.* easy ; easily accomplished. *E.Ir.* urusa.

furasdachd, *n. f.* facility ; ease in doing or accomplishing.

furbaidh, furban, foorby, *n. m.* wrath.

furbhailt, foor-velt, *n. f.* kindly reception, complacency, urbanity. *Also* furailt and furmailt.

furbhailteach, foorveltuch, *adj.* courteous, complaisant, polite, affable.

furbhailteachd, *a.* courteousness, affability ; extreme complacency ; a Highland welcome.

fùrlaich, foorlich, *v.* hate, detest.

furm, *n. m.* a stool, seat.

furmailt, foormelt. *See* furbhailt.

furtach, *a.* helpful, relief-giving.

furtachail, *a.* giving relief.

furtachd, *n. f.* comfort, relief, aid, consolation. *O.Ir.* fortacht, *auxilium.* *O.Celt.* ver-tekton-. Cf. *W.* cysur.

furus, *n. m.* patience, testing.

fùsban, *n. m.* a bungler.

fusgan, *n. m.* a heather brush.

futhar, foo-har, *n. m.* dog-days ; for iuchar.

G

g, the seventh letter of the Gaelic alphabet, named gort or gart, a garden or vineyard (obsolete except in names of farms, in this sense) ; it has the same sound as in English, except before *e* and *i.* *See* gh.

'g, for ag ; as, tha mi 'g iarraidh (ag iarraidh), I seek.

g'a, gă (for gu a), to him, to her, to it ; g'a leadairt, to drub him.

gab, *n. m.* a mouth ; a tattling mouth. *O.N.* gabb, mockery.

gabach, *a.* garrulous ; *n. f.* tattling female.

gabag, *n. f.* a garrulous woman.

gabaire, gabiru, *n. m.* a garrulous fellow.

gabh, gav, *v. n.* accept, receive, take, accept of, gabh so, take this ; kindle, burn, ghabh an t-ainneul, the fire kindled ; conceive, be in the family way, ghabh i ri cloinn, she conceived ; adopt, act the part of a parent, ghabh i ris, she adopted it, she " took " to him ; assume, pretend, gabh ort gum fac thu mise, pretend that you saw me ; betake, repair, gabh thun a' mhonaidh, repair to the hill ; go, proceed, gabh air t'aghaidh, proceed ; gabh romham, lead the way ; gabh romhad, take your own course, *i.e.* 1. be off. 2. take warning ; enlist, engage, ghabh e 'san arm, he enlisted in the army ; gabh agamsa, engage with me ; accept, gabh mo leithsgeul, excuse me ; contain, hold, gabhaidh so tuilleadh, this will hold more ; beat, belabour, gabh air, beat or belabour him, skelp him ; gabh òran, sing a song, gabh rann, recite a verse ; ghabh e aithreachas, he repented ; gabh ris a' phàisde, father the child ; ferment, an caochan a' gabhail, the wash fermenting. *O.Ir.* gabaim. *W.* gafaelu. *O.Celt.* gabô.

gàbhadh, gāv'-u, *n. m.* a jeopardy, peril ; gàbhadh cuain, perils by sea. *E.Ir.* gába, gábud.

gabhagan, gavugan, *n. m.* the titlark.

gàbhaidh, gāvy, *a., gen. s.* of gàbhadh, perilous, dangerous, amannan gàbhaidh, perilous times ; dreadful, austere, stern, tyrannical, duine gàbhaidh, an austere tyrannical fellow ; boisterous, inclement, uair ghàbhaidh, inclement or boisterous weather. *E.Ir.* gáibthech, dangerous.

gàbhaidheachd, gāvy-achc, *n. f.* danger, dreadfulness ; austerity, tyranny ; inclemency, boisterousness.

gabhail, gavel, *vbl. n. f.* of gabh (in its various meanings), *pl.* gabhalaichean, act of taking, receiving : *idiom. :* carriage, bearing, demeanour ; is grinn

do ghabhail, noble is your bearing;
a farm, a lease, gabhail - fearainn,
leasing of land, a tack; colonisation;
invasion, conquest, spoil, booty; kindling, flaming, fermenting; the course
of a ship, tack, bearing, air a' ghabhail so, on this tack; singing, a'
gabhail amhrain, singing a song; protecting, a' gabhail mun tigh, making
the house secure (against a storm);
etc. See gabh.

gabhal, n. m. a fork. gobhal.

gabhal, n. f., pl. gabhla, a descendant,
a branch.

gabhaltach, gav'-ălt-uch, a. infectious,
contagious; galar gabhaltach, an
infectious or contagious disease, contagion.

gabhaltachd, găv'-ălt-uchc, n. f. con-
tagiousness, infectiousness, capaciousness.

gabhaltaiche, găv'-alt-ich-à, n. m. a
renter, farmer; a., deg. more or most
infectious or contagious.

gabhaltas, găv'-alt-us, n. m. a tenement,
leasehold, a farm; conquest.

gabhann, n.m. flattery, adulation; gossip.

gabhar, ga'-ar, n. f. a she-goat; gen.
goibhre. Also gobhar, gen. goibhre;
gabhar-adhair, a snipe; gabhar-bhreac,
a buck-snail, shell-snail. O.Ir. gabor,
gabhar, caper.

gabhd, gaud, n. f. a hellish stratagem,
a crafty trick. Sc. gaud.

gabhdach, gaudach, a. hellishly crafty
or cunning; n. f. a shrew, a coquette.

gabhdaire, gaudiru, n. m. a hellish
strategist.

gabhdaireachd, gaudirachd, n. f. low
stratagem, mean artifice, low cunning.

gabhlan, gavlan, n. m. a wandering,
a man devoid of care.

gabhlanachd, n. f. idle roving.

gabht, gowt, n. m. links. Also mormhaich, and fidean.

gach, adj. every, all, each. O.Ir. cach,
cech.

gad, conj. although, though; for ged.

gad, n. m., pl. goid, a withe, a switch;
gad éisg, a string of fish. E.Ir. gat.
O.Celt. gazdo-.

gàd, gàt, n. m. a bar of iron, or other
metal.

gadachd, gad'-achc, n. f. theft, roguery.

gadair, v. tie the forefeet (of a horse),
hobble.

gadarnas, n. m. 1. the state of being
hobbled. 2. restraint, control.

gadhar, gu-ur, n. m. a hound, a lurcher-
dog. Also gaothar.

gadharanachd, n. f. working with dogs.

gadluinne, n. m. a slender feeble fellow;
a salmon after spawning.

gadmunn, n. m. a nit, mote, insect.

gadraisg, n. f. tumult, confusion.

gaduiche, gadichu, n. m. a thief, robber.
E.Ir. gataige.

gafann, n. m. henbane.

gàg, n. f. a chink; a hack in the skin; v.
chink, cleave.

gagach, a. stuttering, stammering; n. f.
a stuttering or stammering female.

gagachd, gag'-achc, gagaiche, găg'-ich-a,
n. f. impediment of speech; a stammer,
a stutter; gagaire, a stammerer.

gàgail, n. m. cackling (of hens).

gagan, n. m. a cluster.

gaibhneachd, goibhneachd, goi-nachc,
n. f. smith's trade.

gaibhteach, gav-tuch, n. m. a person in
want, a craver. Also gaibheach (I.Lom.).

gaid, gaj (goid), v. steal.

Gàidheal, gayal, n. m. a Gael. O.Ir.
góidel. W. gwyddyl. O.Celt. goidelos.

Gàidhealach, gáyalach, adj. Gadelic.

Gàidhealtachd, gáyaltachc, n.f. Gaeldom;
feadh na Gàidhealtachd, throughout
Gaeldom.

Gàidhlig, gālic, n. f. the Gaelic language.

gailbheach, gelvach, a. boisterous, as
weather; enormous, as price; austere,
as a person; terrible. M.Ir. gailbech
(recte gaillmech).

gailbhinn, gelvin, n. f. a great rough hill.

gàill, n. f. surly look; storm.

gàill, n. f. a large cheek.

gàilleach, gáliuch, n. m. 1. gills. 2.
seam of shoe - uppers. 3. disease of
the gums in cattle. 4. joining of the
outer and inner bark.

gailleag, n. f. a blow on the cheek. Cf.
sgailleog; caper; gearradh ghailleag,
cutting capers; also snapping the
fingers.

gailleart, gailart, n. f. masculine woman.

gaillionn, galiun, n. f. storm, tempest.
M.Ir. gaillim, a storm.

gaillionnach, galiunuch, a. wintry.

gaillseach, goilshuch, n. f. earwig. Also
friothlunn.

gaillseach, n. f. a large mouthful which
makes the cheeks bulge out.

gaineamh, ganuv, gainmheach, ganvuch,
n. f. fine sand; gainmheach-shùigh
and gainmheach-bheò, quicksands.
E.Ir. ganem, sand; ganmech, sandy.

gaineamhan, gán'-uv-an, n. m. sand-
bottom (sea).

gainne, goinn, n. f. scarcity; more
scarce. O.Ir. gainne, hardship.

gàinne, n. f. the tip of an arrow; a dart.

gainneanach, n. m. a scrub, a miser.

gainntir, gointer, n. m. a prison, jail.

gainntireachd, n. f. imprisonment.

gàir, gār, v. laugh; n. f. a din of many

voices ; gàir na mara, the roar of the sea. *E.Ir.* gáir. *O.Celt.* gâri.

gair, *n. f.* nearness, proximity.

gair, *v.* crow, cry. *O.Ir.* gairim.

gairbh, gurv, *n. m.* a greedy stomach, deer's stomach, a paunch or intestines of a deer.

gàir-bhàite, *n. f.* a drowning cry.

gairbhe, gurve, *n. f.* roughness ; *a., deg.* of garbh ; na's gairbhe, more rough, most rough.

gairbhead, gurvud, *abstr. n. f.* roughness.

gairbheal, gaireal, gural, *n. m.* freestone.

gairbheil, gurel, *adj.* rough tempered.

gairbhtheann, gurv-hian, *n. m.* a species of wild grass.

gàirthonn, gār-houn, *n. f.* a roaring wave.

gàirdeachail, gārjachal, *a.* joyous, joyful, glad, congratulatory.

gàirdeachas, garjachas, *n. m.* joy, rejoicing, gladness, congratulation, *fr.* gàir, laugh.

gàirdean, gārjen, *n. m.* an arm. *Also* gaoirdean.

gàirdeanach, gārjenach, *adj.* brawny.

gàirdich, gārjich, *v.* rejoice.

gàire, gāru, *n. m.* a laugh. *E.Ir.* gáire.

gàireach, gārach, *a.* laughing.

gàireachdaich, gārachcich, *n. f.* laughter ; continued bursts of laughter.

gaireas, guras, *n. f.* convenience.

gaireasach, gur''-as-ach, *a.* convenient.

gairge, gurge, *n. m.* tartness ; fierceness ; *a. compar.* of garg, more tart.

gairgean, gurgen, *n. m.* garlic.

gairgein, *n. m.* stale wine.

gairgeanach, *a.* full of garlic.

gàirich, gārich, *n. f.* continued shout.

gairisinn, gurishin, *n. f.* disgust, horror.

gairisneach, gairsinneach, gurishnach, *a.* disgusting, horrible, detestable.

gairm, gurm, *v.* call, cry, proclaim banns in church ; crow as a cock ; call on beasts, as hens, etc. ; *n. f.* a call ; act of calling, a " calling " in the sense of occupation, business, office ; proclamation of banns ; a call to do something. *O.Ir.* gairm. *W.* garm. *O.Celt.* garsmen-.

gairmeadair, gurmuder, *n. m.* proclaimer.

gàirneal, gārnel, *n. f.* a large chest (for meal). *Sc.* garnel, a granary.

gàirnealair, gārn'-al-er', *n. m.* gardener.

gairtleam, *v. tr.* to weed.

gais, gash, *v.* daunt ; shrivel up, blast.

gàis, gāsh, *n. f.* a surfeit ; torrent.

gaisde, *n. m.* 1. a wisp of straw. 2. a trap, snare. *O.Ir.* goisde, halter (to hang).

gaise, gesh'-u, *n. f.* daunt ; cha do chuir e gaise air, it did not daunt him in the least ; boldness.

gaiseadh, *n. m.* a blight, a shrivelling, withering, blasting of crop.

gaisge, geshc'-u, *n. f.* heroism, valour, feats, achievements ; do ghaisge féin, your own valour. *E.Ir.* gasced, gaisced, bravery.

gaisgeach, gashc'-ach, *n. m.* a hero, a champion. *E.Ir.* gascedach, a warrior.

gaisgeachd, gashc'-achc, *n. f.* heroism.

gaisgealachd, gashc'al-achg, *n. f.* heroism.

gaisgeant, gàshc'-annt, *adj.* heroic.

gaisgeil, gashc'-al, *a.* heroic, brave.

gaisinn, gashin, *n. m.* a stalk, a hair. *E.Ir.* gasne, a sprout.

gaisreadh, gashru, *coll.* from gas, a trim lad ; *n. m.* warlike troops.

gaithein, ga-hen, *n. m.* a little dart.

gal, *n. f.* valour, bravery, brave lad.

gal, *n. m., gen.* guil, wailing ; *v.* wail ; wailing ; a' gal is a' caoineadh, wailing and weeping.

galad, *n. f.* a brave lass. Cf. *M.Ir.* galgad, a hero. *E.Ir.* gal, valour.

galan, *n. m.* a gallon measure.

galan, *n. m.* a sudden blast, noise ; galan gadhair, bay of a hound.

galanach, *a.* noisy, tumultuous.

galar, *n. m.* disease, distemper. *O.Ir.* galar, *morbus.* *O.Celt.* galro-n.

galarach, *a.* sickly, diseased. *O.Ir.* galrach, sick.

galc, *v. t.* full cloth. *Also* fùc and luaidh ; fr. *Eng.* waulk.

galcadair, galcuder, *n. m.* a fuller of cloth.

galcanta, *a.* thick, strong, stout.

Gall, gaül, *n. m.* 1. a Gaul. 2. a stranger. 3. a Norseman. 4. a Saxon. *E.Ir.* gall, a foreigner. *O.Celt.* gallo-s.

galla, *n. f.* a bitch.

gallachrann, *n. m., pl.* -chrainn, a Low country plough.

gallan, *n. m.* wild rhubarb ; monk's rhubarb ; dock.

gallan, *n. m.* a straight young tree, a branch, handsome youth.

gallanach, *a.* full of young trees.

gallan-greannach, g.-granuch, *n. m.* colt's foot ; gallan mór, butterwort.

gallchnu, gaül-chro, *n. f.* walnut.

gallda, gaüldu, *a.* foreign, Lowland.

Galldachd, *n. f.* the Low country of Scotland ; air a' Ghalldachd, in the Low country.

galldruma, gaül-drumu, *n. f.* kettle-drum.

gallsheileach, gaul-heluch, *n. m.* cooper's willow.

gall-sheilistir, *n. m.* sedges.

galluran, *n. m.* wood angelica.

galuban, *n. m.* band on the dugs of a mare to prevent the foal sucking.

gàmag, *n. f.* 1. a stride, a span. 2. a

bite (out of anything) ; **thug e gàmag as**, he took a bite out of it.

gamhainn, gáv'-inn, *n. m., pl.* **gamhna**, stirk, year-old calf ; a stupid fellow ; **gamhainn tairbh**, year-old bull ; a yearling. *E.Ir.* **gamuin** ; fr. **gam**, winter, " winter-old." *Wi.*

gamhlanach, *a.* silly, foolish, stupid ; strutting with vain conceit. *Ir.* **gamal**, *n. m.* a fool, a stupid person.

gamhlas, gaülus, *n. m.* malice, grudge. *Also* **gannlas**.

gamhlasach, gáu'-las-ach, *a.* vindictive.

gamhnach, gáu'-nach, *a.* farrow ; *n. f.* a farrow cow ; a stripper ; **tha i 'n a gamhnaich**, she is farrow ; **gamhnach agus trioghamhnach**, one- and three-year stripper.

ganail, *n. m.* a rail, a fold.

gangaid, gang'-ej, *n. f.* deceit, giddy girl ; *a.* **gangaideach**.

gann, gaun, *a. compar.* **gainne**, scarce, scant, limited ; **blidahna ghann**, a year of scarcity ; *adv.* scarcely, hardly, scarce ; **is gann a ni e feum**, it will hardly do ; rare, few, small ; **ni gann**, a scarce thing. *O.Ir.* **gann, gand**. *O.Celt.* gando-s.

ganntachd, gauntachc, *n. f.* scarcity.

ganntar, *n. m.* scarcity ; want, distress.

gànradh, gàn'-ru, *n. m.* (*gen.* **gànraidh**, *pl.* **gànraidhean**), a gander. *Ir.* **gandal**.

gànraich, gàn'-rich, *vbl. n. m.* romping, screeching, loud noise (as of birds or waves).

gaog, *n. m.* lump, as in cloth, or on yarn.

gaoid, gūj, *n. f.* blemish, flaw, particularly in cattle ; defect ; **gun ghaoid gun ghalair**, without blemish or disease. *E.Ir.* **góet**, wound.

gaoilean, gūlen, *n. m.* a darling.

gaoir, gūr, *n. f.* noise ; a cry of pain or alarm ; buzzing of liquors fermenting, or of bees swarming ; shiver of horror ; **chuir e gaoir am fheòil**, it made my flesh creep ; **gaoir chatha**, the din of arms ; **gaoir theas**, a flickering sheet of cobwebs, seen on the grass in autumn, portending rain ; fr. **gáir**, a shout.

gaoir, *n. f.* a spigot ; **thoir a' ghaoir as a' bhuideal**, take the spigot out of the cask.

gaoirean, gūren, *n. m.* a noisy fellow.

gaoirnean, gūrnen, *n. m.* a dung globule.

gaoiseach, goishach, *n. f.* a gun-bolt.

gaoisid, gūshij, *n. f.* coarse hair, horse-hair. *Also* **gaoisd**.

gaoisideach, gūshijach, *a.* hairy. *E.Ir.* **gáesitech**.

gaoisneach, gūshnach, *a.* hairy, rough.

gaoisnean, gūshnen, *n. m.* a single hair.

gaoistean, gūshten, *n. m.* a crafty fellow.

gaoith, gūi, *n. f., obliq. c.* of **gaoth**, wind,

proximity ; **triall 'n ad ghaoith**, going in your proximity, going near you.

gaoithean, guï-hen, *n. m.* a fop, an empty-headed fellow, a wind-bag ; fr. **gaoth**.

gaoithreanachd (*R.Donn*). *See* **gadharanachd**.

gaoithseach, gūshach, *n. f.* a sheaf put as thatch on a little stook.

gaol, gūl, *n. m.* love, affection, fondness, a darling ; **a mhic mo ghaoil**, my beloved son ; **clann mo mhàthar ghaoil**, the children of my beloved mother. *E.Ir.* **gáel**.

gaolach, gūlach, *n. m.* beloved person, a darling ; *adj.* beloved, affectionate, dearly beloved ; **thà, a ghaolaich**, yes, my darling ! yes, my good fellow !

gaorr, *n. m.* gore ; filth ; *v.* tap, gore ; squeeze, crush. Cf. *Eng.* gore. *A.S.* gor, filth.

gaorran, *n. m.* big-belly, a glutton.

gaorrtachd, *n. f.* filth ; **gaorrtachd beoil**, filthy talking.

gaorsach, gūrsach, *n. f.* a most abandoned strumpet, a bawd, a slut.

gaorsachd, gursachc, *n. m.* prostitution.

gaort, gurt, *n. m.* saddle-girth.

gaoth, gū, *n. f.* the wind, flatulency ; **gaoth tuath**, north wind. *O.Ir.* **gáith**, gáeth, *ventus*.

gaothach, *a.* windy, blowy.

gaothail, *a.* windy.

gaothaire, gūhar, *n. f.* mouthpiece of a bagpipe.

gaothar, gaothmhor, gūhur, *adj.* windy ; flatulent. *O.Ir.* **gáethmar**, *ventosus*.

gaotharachd, gaothmorachd, gūharachc, *n. f.* windiness, flatulency.

gaoth-chuairtein, *n. f.* whirlwind.

gaothran, gūhran, *n. m.* a giddy fellow.

gar, *v.* warm ; **gar thu fhéin**, warm yourself. *O.Ir.* **gorim**. **gor** =fire. *O'Dav.* W. **gori**, to incubate. *O.Celt.* garô.

gar, gair, gaire, *n. f.* proximity, nearness ; **am ghair**, near me. Cf. **goirid**.

gar, although, not ; for **ge + ro**, the verbal particle.

'gar, for ag ar, *prep.* and *pron.* ; **'gar toirt**, bringing us.

garadh, găru, *vbl. n. m.* act of warming ; **dèan do gharadh**, warm yourself.

gàradh, gāru, *n. m.* a garden, any dyke, a yard. *Also* **gàrradh**, *q.v.*

garadh, garaidh, gar'-u, *n. m.* den of quadrupeds ; a copse. Cf. **garan**, a thicket.

garail, *a.* snug, comfortable.

garalachd, găr'-al-achc, *n. f.* snugness.

garan, *n. m.* a grove, a thicket, underwood.

garbh, gărv, *adj., compar.* **gairbhe**, rough, thick, rugged ; harsh ; brawny ; **maide garbh**, a thick stick ; **duine garbh**, a harsh man, a brawny man ; hoarse ;

stormy, boisterous; coarse; **guth garbh**, hoarse voice; **anart garbh**, coarse linen; used as *n. m.* the thick; **an garbh is an caol**, the thick and thin. *Cpds.*: **garbh-chrìochan**, *pl. n.* rough bounds, hilly regions; **garbh-fhras**, a heavy shower; **garbh-ghrinneal**, coarse gravel; **garbh-shìon**, rough weather; **garbh-shlios**, rough slope; **garbh-thonn**, an angry wave. *O.Ir.* garb. *W.* garw. *O.Celt.* garvo-.

garbhag, garv'-ag, *n. f.* the plaice, or spotted kind of flounder; sprats; garvie.

garbhag an t-sléibhe, *n. f.* club-moss.

garbhan, *n. m.* gills of fish. *See* **giùran**.

garbhan, garv'-an, *n. m.* coarse ground meal.

garbhanach, *a.* rugged, full of orts.

garbhanach, *n. m.* the sea-bream.

garbhbhallach, gar-val-uch, *a.* brawny.

garbhchnamhach, garv'-chràv-uch, *a.* raw-boned.

garbhghucag, garv-ghoocag, *n. f.* fore-shot, or what comes first from the still.

garbhlach, gara-luch, *n. m.* rank moor-grass; rugged country.

garbhlaoch, *n. m.* a warrior, a hero.

gàrcan, *n. m.* the plaint of a hen, a hen' complaint. *Also* **gàrcail**.

garg, *a.*, *compar.* **gairge**, fierce, harsh, turbulent; **duine garg**, a turbulent person; tart, bitter, acrid, pungent; **blas garg**, a pungent or tart taste; **is gairge**, more tart. *E.Ir.* **gorg**. *O.Celt.* gorgo-s.

gàrlach, gàr-luch, *a.* spoiled child; a most impertinent fellow; a dwarf.

gàrluch, gàr-looch, *n. f.* a mole.

garmainn, garm'-inn, *n. f.* weaver's beam; **garmainn bhall**, a windlass.

garmaisg, *n. m.* a sprite. *Carm. Gad.*

garr, *n. f.* a gorbelly, the belly of a spoiled child, or starveling.

garrach, *n. m.* a gorbellied child, a most impertinent fellow, a wretch, a little glutton, a contemptible manikin.

gàrradair, gàruder, *n. m.* a gardener.

gàrradh, gàrr'-u, *n. m.* an enclosure, a garden, a fence or dyke, a yard. *O.N.* garðr. *Goth.* garda. *A.S.* geard. *O.H.G.* gart.

garrag, *n. f.* young crow.

garrag, *n. f.* a sudden yell. *Ir.* **gartha**, clamour.

garra-gart, garu-garst, *n. m.* corn-crake. *Also* **garra-gartan, garra-ghartan.**

gàrraich, *v.* befilth.

gart, garst, *n. m.* surly aspect, gloom.

gart, *n. m.* standing corn; growing corn (when past the **fochann** stage); vine-yard. *O.Ir.* gort, *seges.* *W.* garth. Cf. *Lat.* hortus. *Gr.* χόρτος.

gartan, *n. m.* garter, heather-tic.

garteun, gart-èn', *n. m.* a quail.

gartghlain, gartlain, gart-lin, *v.* weed, free from noxious weeds.

gartghlan, gartlain, gart'-lann, *n. m.* weeds.

gàrthaich, *n. f.* shouting, crying.

gartlann, *n. m.* a corn-yard.

gas, *n. m.*, *gen.* **gois**, stalk, stem, particle, a broom; **gas a sguabadh an tighe**, a broom to sweep the house; **gas càil**, a stock of coleworts; **gach gas**, every particle. *E.Ir.* gas. *O.Celt.* gastâ.

gasach, *a.* bushy, branchy, tufted.

gasag, *n. f.* a little stalk.

gasair, gas'-èr, *v.* line as a bitch.

gasan, *n. m.* a little stalk, a neat youth. *Ir.* gasán, "gosoon."

gasanta, *a.* tall and handsome.

gasar, *n. m.* pert fellow.

gasda, *adj.* well-shaped, comely; fine; **nì gasda**, a fine thing; **duine gasda**, handsome person; a decent man; a wise and skilful man; fr. **gas**. *E.Ir.* **gasta**, neat, brisk, ingenious.

gasdachd, *n. f.* fineness, handsomeness, goodness, kindliness.

gasg, *n. m.* tail.

gasgag, *n. f.* a step, a stride.

gasgan, *n. m.* a small tail, a tapering ridge running down from a plateau.

gasradh, gasru, *n. m.* salacity in female dogs.

gasradh, *coll. n. m.* a company of young men, a crew (fr. **gas**, a scion).

gasraidh, gasry, *n. m.* a rabble, mercenary soldiers; fr. **gas**, military servant.

gàt, *n. m.* bar of iron; a stalk; **gàt siabuinn**, a bar or stalk of soap; **gàt siùcair duibh**, a stalk of black sugar.

gath, gă, *n. m.*, *pl.* **gathan, gathannan**, a sting, a dart, a beam, or ray; **gath an t-seillein**, the sting of the bee; **gath na gréine**, sunbeam; **deo-gréine**, Fionn's banner; inner row of sheaves in a corn stack; **gath dubh**, foundation sheaves. *E.Ir.* gai, gae. *O.Celt.* gaiso-n. Cf. *O.N.* geirr.

gathan, ga-han, *n. m.* a little sting, a little dart, a small flagstaff, a beam (of light).

gathbholg, ga-volg, *n. m.* a quiver.

gath-cuip, gă'-kwip, *n. m.* medical tent.

gath-dubh, ga-doo, *n. m.* beard of oats, a weed.

gath-muing, gă'-mwing, *n. m.* a mane.

ge, whatever, whoever; **ge b'e neach**, whatever person. *E.Ir.* cé bé.

ge, though. *Ir.* gidh. *O.Ir.* ce, ci, cia.

geacach, giacuch, *a.* pert, sententious.

gead, ged, *n. f.* a noticeable spot; a bed in a garden or small ridge of land; star in a horse's head; *v.* clip.

gead, ged, *n. f.* a lock of hair.

geadach, geadagach, *a.* abounding in spots ; full of lazy-beds.

geadag, gedag, *n. f.* a small spot ; a patch of arable land ; a small tuft of hair.

geadag, *n. f.* a grilse, a large trout, a young salmon.

geadas, *n. m.* the pike. *O.N.* gedda, *id.*

geadas, *n. m.* coquetry ; a tufty head.

geadasach, gedasuch, *a.* coquettish, flirting.

gèadh, giagh, *n. m.* a goose, lump of the finest part of meal, made by children, tailor's goose. *E.Ir.* géd. *W.* gŵydd. Cf. *N.* gagl, a wild goose.

geadh, gé, *v.* pole or shove a boat by means of a boat-hook or pole.

geadha, gé-à, *n. m.* a pole, a boat-hook. *Also* **forc.**

geadhach, gia-uch, *n. f.* goose quill.

geadhachail, gia-uch-al, *n. pl.* domestic jobs or messages.

geadhail, ge-ul, *n.f.* a ploughed field, park.

geadris. *See* **geadas.**

geal, gyal, *adj.* white, fond of, clear, bright ; **chan 'eil e geal da**, he has no great affection for him ; used as *n. m.* white of anything ; **geal na sùla**, the white of the eye. *E.Ir.* gel. *O.Celt.* gelo-s.

geal, giäl, *n. f.* a leech. *E.Ir.* gel.

gealach, gyäl'-uch, *n. f.* the moon.

gealachadh, gialucha, *vbl. n. m.* bleaching, a bleach ; **blàr gealachaidh**, bleach-field. *Also* **todhar.**

gealag, gialag, *n. f.* a white trout. *Also* **bànag** ; **gealag bhuachair**, a bunting.

gealagan, gialugan, *n. m.* the white of an egg.

gealaich, gialich, *v.* bleach, whiten.

gealan, *n. m.* a linnet. *Also* **gealan-lin.**

gealbhan, gialvan, *n. m.* a common fire.

gealbhonn, gialvon, *n. m.* a sparrow. *Ir.* gelbund. *W.* golfan.

geall, gia-ool, *n. m., gen. s.* and *n. pl.* **gill**, a pledge, bet, or wager, mortgage ; **thoir dhomh geall**, give me a pledge ; **mo gheallsa nach faic thu e**, I pledge that you shall not see him ; **an am rùsgadh a' ghill**, when " stripping the pledge," *i.e.* making a clean sweep. *Watson.* **cuiridh mi geall ort**, I wager you ; **cuiridh mi mo chluas air a' gheall**, I shall wager you my ear ; great fondness ; **tha e an geall oirre**, he is excessively fond of her ; *v.* promise, pledge, vow ; **tha e an geall na's fhiach e**, everything he has is at stake. *O.Ir.* gellaim. *O.Celt.* geldô.

geallachas, gialuchus, *n. m.* prospect, success.

gealladh, gialu, *n. m.* a promise, a vow, a mortgage ; **gealladh gun a cho-**ghealladh, a promise without performance ; **gealladh-pòsaidh**, betrothment.

geall-cinnidh, *n. m.* a fine paid to the kinsman of a person killed. *Sc. Law*, kelchyn.

geall-daighnich, *n. m.* a pledge, earnest.

geallmhor, *a.* fond, desirous.

geallshuil, gia-ool-hul, *n. f.* moon-eye.

geallshuileach, *a.* moon-eyed.

gealltainn, gia-ooltin, *vbl. n. f.* promising.

gealltanach, gia-oolt'-unn-ach, *a.* promising, auguring well, promissory, hopeful.

gealltanas, gia-ooltunus, *n. m.* pledge.

gealtach, gialtuch, *a.* cowardly, timid.

gealtachd, gialtachc, *n. f.* cowardice. In *Ir.* =insanity.

gealtaire, gialtiru, *n. m.* a coward. *Ir.* gealt = madman.

geambairn, *n. m.* bondage, fetter, stocks.

geamha, gevu, *n. m.* pledge, compensation ; **cha bu gheamha leam**, it would be no compensation to me ; **cha bu gheamh leam e air not**, I would rather have forfeited a pound note.

geamhail, gevul, *n. m.* a fetter, a chain.

geamhd, gevd, **geamhta**, gevtu, *n. m.* a chunk, thick-set person.

geamhlag, gevlag, *n. f.* a crowbar, lever.

geamhrach, geu-ruch, *n. f.* a winter park.

geamhrachail, geu-ruchal, **geamhradail**, geu-rudal, *a.* wintry, stormy, cold.

geamhradh, geu-ru, *n. m.* winter. *E.Ir.* gemred. *O.Ir.* gaimred (gam or geim + red), **gam** = November. *L.nagC.* *O.Celt.* gaiamo-, gaimo-.

geamhraich, geu-rich, *v.* winter ; feed during winter, furnish provender ; *vbl. a.* **geamhraichte**, wintered.

geamhrail, geu-ral, *adj.* wintry, cold.

geamnaidh, gemny, *a.* chaste.

gean, gen, *n. m.* good humour, mood, keenness. *E.Ir.* gen, a smile.

geanachan, *pl. n.* jaws. *D.B.*

geanachas, genuchus, *n. m.* mirth.

geanail, gen'-al, *adj.* cheerful, gay.

geanalachd, genaluchc, *n. f.* cheerfulness, good humour.

geangach, genguch, *a.* crooked, a dumpy person.

geanm, génum, *n. f.* chastity.

geanmchno, genm-chro, *n. f.* a chestnut.

geanmnaidh, genmny, *adj.* chaste. *E.Ir.* genmnaid. *O.Ir.* genas (*castitas*).

geann, *n. m.* a sword.

> " gean agas colg . . .
> dà shean ainm claidhimh curadh."

" ' gean' and ' colg' . . .
two ancient names of a champion's sword."

geannaire, gyann'-ăr-u, *n. m.* a hammer, a kind of wedge, rammer ; **ri geannaireachd**, hammering.

geanta, ge'nt'-u, *a.* abstemious ; modest, chaste.

geantachd, gentachd, *n. f.* abstinence, modesty, self-command, continence ; **geantachd na faolainn,** the abstinence of the sea-mew—which bolts a full-grown fish at a gulp, and makes three portions of the sprat.

gearain, ger'-ėn, *v.* complain, appeal.

gearan, ger'-an, *n. m.* complaint, appeal, accusation, supplication, application for redress ; **dèan do ghearan ris,** apply for redress ; **rinn iad gearan,** they murmured ; **ri gearan,** complaining ; wailing, moaning ; **bha e a' gearan feadh na h-oidhche,** he was moaning through the night ; indifferent health. *M.Ir.* geran, complaint.

gearanach, ger'-an-uch, *a.* plaintive, sad, apt to complain, querulous.

gearasdan, *n. m.* a garrison ; fr. the *Eng.*

geàrr, gyârr, *v.* cut, geld, satirise, describe as a circle ; **geàrr fead ris,** whistle to him ; **gearr leum,** make a leap ; **gearradh astair,** making speed ; *adj.* short, of short continuance ; **ann an ùine gheàrr,** in a short time ; *n. m.* an abridgement ; **geàrr a' ghnothuich,** the abridged statement of the affair ; **an còrr 's an geàrr,** the short and the long of it ; the odds and ends—the two extremes ; **gearracainnt,** satire. *E.Ir.* gerraim, I cut, shorten ; **gerr,** short. *O.Celt.* gerso-s.

geàrr, *n. f.* a hare. *See* gearr-fhiadh.

gearra-breac, *n. m.* the guillemot.

geàrrach, gyârr'-uch, *n. f.* flux, dysentery.

gearrachuibh, *n. f.* a muzzle-bar for two horses ; **cuibh-mhòr,** for four horses.

gearradair, gyărr'-ud-ĕr, *n. m.* castrater.

gearradh, gyarr'-u, *n. m.* a cut, shape ; a severe taunt, or sarcasm.

gearradh-arm, *n. m.* coat of arms, an engraving of arms, heraldry.

gearrag, *n. f.* a young hare, leveret.

gearraghobach, *n. m.* a wit, banterer.

gearra-gort, *n. m.* a quail, a corn-crake.

gearraidh, giary, *n. m.* a hare = gearr + fiadh.

geàrraidh, *n. m.* home pasture ; shieling. *N.* gerði.

gearraiseach, gerr'-esh-uch, *n. f.* swingle-chain, the chain from the swingle-tree to the horses.

gearraiseach, *n. f.* a hare (= gearr-fhiadh-seach).

gearran, *n. m.* a gelding ; **an uair a dhìt iad an gearran 's a' mhòd,** when they condemned the horse at court ; time from 15th March to April 11th, inclusive. *M.Ir.* a workhorse.

gearrbhodach, gyarr'-a-vŏd-uch, *n. m.* a young middle-sized cod.

gearrbhonn, *n. m.* a half sole.

gearr-fhiadh, giār-ia, *n. m.* 'short deer,' a hare.

gearrsgian, gyarr'-skin, *n. m.* a dirk, biodag.

gearr-shaoghlach, gyărr'-hul-ach, *a.* short-lived.

gearsum, gyar'-sum, *n. m.* a sum paid to a superior, by a tenant, at entry of a lease, or by an heir on succeeding to a lease or feu. *Sc.* gersome, grassum.

geartach, gyărt'-ach, *n. f.* a short time ; a trip, an excursion ; **geartach do 'n Ghalldachd,** a trip or excursion to the Low country.

geas, ges, *n. f.* spell, taboo, charm ; **nighean rìgh fo gheasaibh,** a princess spell-bound ; **tha mi a' cur mar gheasaibh ort,** I put you under a ban. *E.Ir.* geis, ban, tabu.

geasadair, gesader, *n. m.* an enchanter, a charmer ; **geasadaireachd,** enchantment, sorcery, witchcraft.

geata, geta, *n. m.* a gate ; sort of play, a stick.

geathadaich, ge-hadich, *n. f.* hopping, jogging.

ged, *conj.* though, although.

géibhinn, *n. f.* fetters, prison. *M.Ir.* **geibenn.** *W.* gefyn, fetter.

geibnigh, *a.* lively, tripping (music).

geil, *n. f.* fount ; **geil ar slàinte,** fount of our health.

geilb, gilb, *n. f.* chisel. *Also* **sgeilb.**

géill, gēl, *v.* pledge, yield assent, admit, submit ; **tha mi a' gèilleachdainn da sin,** I admit that ; yield—in the sense of breaking or showing signs of giving way under strain ; *n. f.* submission, homage, concession, admission ; **na géill da leithid sin,** yield assent to no such thing. *O.Ir.* gíallaim 3 fut = **geillfit** ; "ro giallsad uile do Chonn," they all submitted to Conn. *C.M.L.*

géillean, gēlen, *n. m.* a jaw. [**géill** =gen. of giall.]

géilligean, gēligun, *n. pl.* fat flabby jaws, tufts on fowl's head.

geilt, geylt, *n. f.* terror, dread, awe. *E.Ir.* geilt, mad. Cf. *O.N.* gjalti, an old dat. of göltr, verða at gjalti, to be turned into a hog=go mad with terror. *Cl.*

geiltreadh, geiltrigeadh, geltru, *n. m.* gilding, enamelling.

geimheal, gév'-ul, *n. f.* chain, fetter, sense of fear. *E.Ir.* geimel, gemel. *O.Celt.* gemelo-.

geimhleadh, gevlu, *n. m.* binding, chaining.

geimhleag, gev-lag, *n. f.* crowbar, lever.

geimhlich, gevlich, *v.* chain, fetter.

geinide, *compar.* of geamnaidh.

geinn, geyn, *n. f.* often ; *m.* a wedge,

anything firm. *E.Ir.* **geind.** *O.Celt.* geni-.

geinn, *v.* wedge.

geinneach, *a.* wedge-like ; **duine geinneach,** a thick-set man.

geinneadh, geynu, *vbl. n. m.* act of wedging.

geinneag, geynag, *n. f.* a short stout woman.

geinneanta, geynantu, *adj.* firm, stout.

geinneil, geynel, *a.* stout, firm, compact.

geinnte, *n. m.* a form of **geinn.**

geintileach, geintleach, *n. m.* a heathen, a gentile ; fr. *Lat.* gens, gentilis. *O.Ir.* gentilecht.

geir, *n. f.* tallow, grease, suet. *E.Ir.* geir, suet, tallow.

géire, gēru, *adj. compar.* of **geur,** more sharp, etc., sharpness ; sharpness (in music). *Also* **geòire.**

géiread, gērud, *n. f.* degree of sharpness, or acuteness. *Also* **geòiread.**

géireas, gēras, *n. f.* witticisms.

géireanachd, gēranachc, *n. f.* a satirical turn, bickering sort of wit. *Also* **geòireanachd.**

géis, gēsh, *n. f.* a roar. *M.Ir.* **géisim,** I resound.

géisg. *See* **giosg,** creaking.

géisgeil, géisgeadh, geshgil, *n. f.* a roaring, a gurgling noise.

géisgeadh, gēshgu, *n. m.* deaving, plaguing ; " gu bheil mi air mo ghéisgeadh le réicil an daimh Charrannaich," but I am plagued with the roaring of the Carron stag. *M.Ir.* **géisecht,** bellowing.

geòb, gyōb, *n. m.* a gaping mouth, a wry mouth ; *v.* gape with the mouth, as fish when losing the vital spark.

geòbail, gyōb′-al, *vbl. n. m.* a gape ; act of gaping.

geòbaire, *n. m.* a babbler.

geòbraich, *n. f.* idle talk.

geòc, gyōc, *n. f.* gluttony.

geòcach, gyōc′-uch, *n. m.* a glutton, gormandiser.

geòcair, gyōc′-al, *a.* gluttonous.

geòcair, gyōc′-ir′, *n. m.* a glutton, a gormandiser ; **geòcaireachd,** gluttony, gormandising.

geodha, gyò′-u, *n. m.* a narrow creek, or cove between impending rocks. *Norse* gjá, a chasm.

geoic, goic, *n. f.* a wry neck. *See* **goic.**

geòireanachd, *n. f. See* **geuranachd.**

geòla, gyōl′-u, *n. f.* a yawl, a small boat.

geòlach, gyōl′-uch, *n. f.* a bier, shoulderbands of the dead.

geolan, *n. m.* a fan.

geon, *n. m.* avidity, keenness. *E.Ir.* geóin, uproar.

geonail, gyòn′-al, *a.* keen, with avidity.

geòp, *n. m.* fast talk mostly unintelligible.

geòpraich, *n. f.* a torrent of idle talk. *Also* **copraich,** frothing.

geosgail, gyŏsg′-ul, *n. f.* blustering talk.

geòtan, gyŏt′an, *n. m.* a driblet, or trifling sum or debt, an item, a small quantity ; a′ cruinneachadh gheòtan, collecting trifling debts ; a pendicle ; a strip of arable land.

geuban, giaban, gēban, *n. m.* the crop of a bird, the gizzard.

geug, gēg, *n. f., gen.* **géige,** a branch, a sapling ; a young female ; a nymph ; **barr-geug,** a belle. (lasdaire, a beau.) *M.Ir.* **gésca,** branch. *E.Ir.* **géc,** a bough. *W.* **cainc.** *O.Celt.* kankâ, kankî.

geugach, gēg′-uch, *a.* branchy, ramifying.

geugag, gēgag, *n. f.* a little branch, a girl.

geum, gēm, *n. m.* a " low " ; lowing of cows, calves, etc. ; *v.* low. *E.Ir.* **géim.**

geumnaich, gēmnich, *n. f.* continuous lowing.

geur, giar, gēr and giär, *a. compar.* **géire,** and **geòire,** sharp, sharp-pointed, sharp-edged ; mentally acute, shrewd, ingenious ; acute of vision ; **sgian gheur,** sharp knife ; **duine geur,** a shrewd man ; **sùil gheur,** a keen eye ; acrid, bitter, tart ; **blas geur,** acrid, bitter, or tart taste ; severe, harsh, keen ; **tha e tuilleadh is geur,** he is too severe ; **bainne geur,** milk of an acrid taste ; **fion geur,** sour wine. *O.Ir.* **gér.**

geurach, gēruch and giäruch, *n. f.* the herb agrimony.

geurad, *abst. n.* from **geur,** sharpness. *Also* **géiread** and **geòiread.**

geuraich, gērich, giàrich, *v.* sharpen, hone, whet ; sour ; **am bainne a′ geurachadh,** the milk turning sour.

geuramharc, *n. f.* gazing, looking intently.

geuranachd, geoireanachd, *n. f.* subtlety, repartee.

geurchluas, *n. f.* quick hearing.

geurchluasach, *a.* quick of hearing.

geurchuis, gēr′-choosh, *n. f.* acuteness, penetration, ingenuity, mental energy.

geurchuiseachd, gēr′-choosh-achc, *adj.* acute, penetrating, sharp, ingenious, subtle, inventive.

geurfhaclach, gēr - acluch, *a.* witty, satirical.

geurlann, *n. f.* the sheep louse.

geur-lean, gēr′-llen, *v.* persecute, harass.

geur-leanmhuinn, gèr′-len-vin, *n. f.* persecution.

gheibh, yo and yev, *fut.* of **faigh** ; **gheibh mi,** I shall get.

gheibheadh, yovu, *f. cond.* of **faigh,** would get.

gheibhear, yevur, *impers. f.* of **faigh,** shall or will be got.

gheibhinn, yo-in, 1. *pl.* of *f. cond.* faigh, I would get.

gial, giall, *n. m.* 1. jaw, cheek, jowl. 2. gill of a fish. *E.Ir.* giall.

giall, *n. m.* a hostage, a pledge; a' gabhail gill dhiubh, forcing them into submission, tyrannising over them. *O.Ir.* giall. *O.Celt.* geislo-s, geistlo-s.

giamh, giomh, *n. f.* a blemish, a fault; a churaidh gun ghiamh, thou hero without blemish.

gibeach, gibuch, *a.* hairy, ragged.

gibeach, *a.* neat, tight; for sgibeach.

gibeag, giobag, gibag, *n. f.* a bundle, a rag, a fringe, a sheaf (of bent or rushes).

gibeagach, gibaguch, *a.* ragged, tattered.

gibean, *n. m.* grease, from solan goose's stomach.

gibein, *n. m.* a piece of flesh.

giblean, geeblen, *n. m.* April.

giblion, *n. m.* entrails of a goose.

gibneach, gibnuch, *n. m.* cuttle-fish.

gidheadh, ge-yugh, *conj.* yet, nevertheless; for cid + ed.

gigean, geegen, *n. m.* a dwarf; said too of a naked child.

gighis, giyish, *n. m.* a masquerade; fr. *Sc.* gyis, a mask.

gilb, *n. f.* a chisel. *See* geilb.

gil, *n. f.* a small narrow glen (often with a stream along the bed). *Norse,* gil.

gile, gilu, *n. f.* whiteness, clearness, fairness; *a. compar.* of geal; na's gile, whiter, fairer. *Also* gilead.

gille, gillu, *n. m.* a lad; a young man; servant man. *Cpds.:* gille-each, a groom; gille - coise, footman; gille-ruith, a courier; gille - fionn and -fiondrain, a small white periwinkle; gille-greasaidh, a postilion; a cooper's drift; gille-marcachd; gille-gnothuich, one that runs messages; gille-mirein, a tee-totum, a whirligig; gille-guirminn, corn - scabious; gille - sguain, train-bearer; gille-copain, cup-bearer; leanabh-gille, a male child, a man child; gille-bride, the oyster-catcher; gille suirghe, a lover's spokesman; gille-martuinn, a fox; gille-feadaig, a plover. *E.Ir.* gilla. Cf. *O.N.* gildr, the word, however, antedates the Norse period. *Marstr.* Zcp. xiii.

gilleachas, *n. m.* young manhood. *O.Ir.* gillacht, third stage of a man's life. *See* naoidheanachd. *Corm.*

gilm, *n. m.* a buzzard.

gilmean, *n. m.* a fop, a flatterer, a sycophant.

gimleid, *n. f.* a gimlet; fr. the *Eng.*

gin, *v.* beget, gender, conceive, produce; o'n a ghineadh e, since he was conceived; *pron. indef.* one, individual,

any; a' h-uile gin, every one, all; chan 'eil gin agam, I do not possess a single one. *O.Ir.* gein, birth; ad-gainemmar. *W.* geni. *O.Celt.* genô, *nascor.*

gineadair, *n. m.* a parent.

gineadh, *n. m.* begetting.

gineal, ginol, *n. f.* offspring, race, lineage; do ghineal, your offspring; growth of corn in the stack or shock.

ginealach, ginalach, *n. f.* a race, generation. *M.Ir.* genelach. *Lat.* genealogia.

ginealachadh, *n. m.* act of quickening (life); an embryo.

ginealaich, ginn'-al-ich, *v.* engender, grow, sprout (of corn in the stooks).

gineamhuinn, ginuvin, *n. m.* conception.

gingein, *n. m.* a cask, a barrel, a thick-set person.

gintear, *n. m.* progenitor, parent.

giob, gib, *n. f.* shag, hairiness.

giobach, gib'-uch, *adj.* shaggy, hairy. *See* gibeach.

giobach, *a.* active, spry. Cf. sgiobalta.

giobag, *n. f.* a handful of lint, a little sheaf, a rag, a fringe.

giobaiche, gibichu, *n. f.* shagginess.

gioball, gibul, *n. m.* mantle, shawl; a rag, cast-off clothes.

gioball, *n. m.* an odd person.

giobarnach, gib'-àr-nach, *n. m.* cuttle-fish. *Also* gibneach.

giobarsaich, gib'-ars-ich, *n. f.* shagginess.

giodal, *n. f.* flattery; " luchd-giodail, a' falbh bhuainn," flatterers leaving us.

giodar, gidar, *n. m.* dung, ordure, soft dirt (as on stable floor).

giodhran, gee-ran, *n. m.* a barnacle, barnacle goose. *Ir.* giodhran. *Lh. O.Ir.* giugrann. *O.Celt.* gegurannâ.

giog, geeg, *v.* peep, steal a look at; cringe, crouch, fawn; ghiog e steach air an uinneig, he peeped in at the window; cha ghiogainn do dhuine, I would not cringe to any man.

giog, *n. f.* shank, slender bit in yarn; " giog chaol no sliasaid reamhar," nor slender shank nor thick thigh, *i.e.* yarn of even thickness.

giogach, giùgach, *a.* cringing, stammering.

giogadh, *n. m.* act of cringing.

giogaire, geegiru, *n. m.* a cringer, fawner.

giogan, *n. m.* a thistle.

giol, giul, *n. f.* a leech; giol-tholl, horse-leech.

giolam, gioleim, *n. m.* talking, prattling.

giolaman, *n. m.* a prattling fellow.

giolc, giulc, *v.* bend, stoop, aim at; giolcom ort, let me try to hit you; make a sudden movement.

giolcair, *n. m.* a flippant fellow.

giolcam-daobhram, *n. m.* animalcule.

gioll, *n. m.* a teat. *See* deal.

giolla, giulu, *n. m.* a lad. *Also* giollan.

giollachd, giulachc, *n. f.* manufacturing, preparing, dressing, improving ; a' giollachd leathair, dressing or manufacturing leather ; a' giollachd buntàta, dressing potatoes in the fields.

giollaichd, geull'-ichg, *v.* dress, manufacture, as leather, etc. ; a' giollachd lìn, dressing or manufacturing lint.

giomach, gim'-ach, *n. m.* a lobster.

giomanach, gim'-an-ach, *n. m.* a hunter, gamekeeper.

gìomh, giamh, gee-uv, *n. m.* a fault, a blemish.

giomlaid, *n. f.* gimlet. *See* gimleid.

gion, gin, *n. m.* excessive love or desire ; appetite ; tha mo ghion ort, I am excessively fond of you. *See* cion, love.

gionach, ginach, *adj.* appetised, keen, greedy (in eating). *O.Ir.* gin, mouth.

gionair, giner, *n. m.* a glutton.

giorag, girag, *n. m.* panic, great fear, start (of sudden fear).

gioragach, giragach, *a.* panic-struck.

giorcach, gircuch, *a.* squint-eyed.

giornalair, girneileir, girnuler, *n. m.* granary, hutch.

giorra, giru, *n. f.* shortness, fewness ; giorra làithean, or giorra shaoghail, fewness of days or shortness of life ; abridgment ; *a. compar.* of geàrr and goirid, na's giorra, shorter, more limited.

giorrach, girach, *n. f.* short heath or hair.

giorrachd, girachc, *n. f.* shortness, abridgment, compendium, abbreviation.

giorradan, gir-udan, *n. m.* an abbreviation.

giorraich, girich, *v.* shorten, abbreviate, abridge, curtail, epitomise.

giorra-shaoghail, giru-hū-il, *n. f.* short life ; giorra-shaoghail ort, shortness of life ; a form of malediction.

giorruinn, girun, *n. f.* a barnacle, a bird of passage. *See* giodhran.

giorsadh, girsu, *n. m.* a pinching of the skin (with salt water, or with cold).

giort, gìrt, *n. f.* a girth.

giortag, *n. f.* a small girth.

gìosg, geesg, *v.* creak ; a' gìosgail, creaking ; *n. m.* a creak ; gìosg fhiaclan, gnashing of teeth. *Also* dìosg.

gìosgan, geesgan, *n. m.* a creaking noise, gnashing (of teeth). *Also* diosgan. *Ir.* díoscán. *M.Ir.* gioscán.

girlinn, girlin, *n. f.* a barnacle : a bird of passage. *See* giorruinn.

gis, gish, *n. m.* enchantment.

giseag, gishag, *n. f.* a charm or spell. *Also* gisreag.

gisgein, gishgen, *n. m.* a nickname applied to a trifler. *Also* gigean and geigean.

gisreagach, gishraguch, *a.* superstitious, fond of charms or enchantment.

gith, gi, *n. f.* a shower, a blast. *E.Ir.*

gith, way of motion. *McB.*

githeilis, gi-helish, *n. f.* idle running to and fro. *Also* giodalais.

githir, gidhir, gi-ur, *n. m.* corn reaper's wrist-pain.

giùd, giùide, *n. m.* a wile, a cheat, deceit. a filthy person.

giùgach, gyūg'-ach, *a.* cringing, drooping the neck in a cringing position ; (from giuig).

giùig, *n. f.* a crouch ; cringing, drooping position of the head, as a person sheltering himself from rain ; *v.* cringe, droop.

giùigire, gioogiru, *n. m.* cringer, a coward.

giùir, gioor, *n. f.* same as giuig.

giùirideach, gioorijuch, *n. m.* a cringing, drooping, miserable-looking person.

giùlain, gioolen, *v.* carry, behave, conduct ; giùlain an gunna so, carry this gun ; giùlain thu féin, conduct or behave yourself ; bear, suffer, permit.

giùlan, giool'-an, *n. m,* behaviour, conduct ; do ghiùlan fhéin, your own conduct or behaviour ; carrying, permitting, enduring, tolerating, a bier or carriage and corpse, a funeral.

giùlanta, *a.* well-behaved, long-suffering.

giulla, giooll'-u, giullan, *n. m.* a lad, a boy. *Ir.* giolla, servant, footman ; cf. gille. *E.Ir.* gillacht = third stage in life. There were six : náidendacht, macdacht, gillacht, óclachus, séndacht, díblidecht. *Wi. i.e.* infancy, boyhood, young manhood, military service age, old age, decay.

giullaich, gioolich, *v.* prepare, manage well ; fr. giulla, *i.e.* serve as giulla, *q.v.*

giùmsgal, gioom-sgal, *n. m.* flattery.

giùraid, gioor. *See* giùran.

giùram, *n. m.* complaining, mournful noise.

giùran, giooran, *n. m.* gills of fish ; *poet.* the throat.

giùran, *n. m.* a barnacle goose. *See* giodhran.

giùran, *n. m.* the cow-parsnip.

giùras, *n. m.* duress, violence.

giùrnaich, gioor-nich, *n. f.* constant motion.

giùsach, *n. f., pl.* giùsaichean, a fir forest.

giuthas, giubhas, geoo'-us, *n. m.* fir, pine ; the banner or armorial ensign of the Macalpines. *E.Ir.* gíus, *pinus.*

glabhcadair, glaw-cu-der, *n. m.* nonsensical talker, a bladderskite.

glabhcas, *n. m.* nonsense, folly, foolery.

glac, *v.* seize, lay hold of, catch, grasp, embrace, take prisoner ; ghlac iad a' phoit ruadh, they seized the still ;

ghlac iad e, they took him prisoner.
M.Ir. glacaim, grasp, take ; glac, the hand.
glac, glaic, *n. f.* palm of the hand, hand-ful ; embrace ; a hollow ; an glaic a làimhe, in the hollow of his hand ; a valley, a defile, a dell ; 'sa ghlaic so, in this hollow ; glac na beinne, the defile of the mountain ; fuar ghlac a' bhàis, the cold embrace or grasp of death. *E.Ir.* glac, hand, palm of the hand.
glacach, glacuch, *n. f.* swelling in the hollow of the hand ; palmful ; *adj.* full of dells.
glacach braghad, *n. f.* asthma.
glacadair, glacuder, *n. m.* catcher, seizer.
glacadan, *n. m.* a receptacle, a gin.
glacadh, *vbl. n. m.* a seizing, a taking, a catching.
glacag, *n. f.* a little hollow or valley.
glacaiche-cleibh, *n. m.* rickets, bronchitis.
glacaid, *n. f.* a handful.
glacail, glacadh, glacu, *vbl. n. f.* seizure ; seizing, catching.
glacaireachd, glacadaireachd, glaciruchc, *n. f.* a seizure.
glacmhor, glacvor, *a.* seizing, fit to catch.
glag, *n. m.* a bell, a noise, a crash ; glag gàire, sgal gàire, a horse-laugh ; thug sud an teanga as a' ghlag, that took the tongue out of the bell, *i.e.* silenced the bore.
glagach, *a.* noisy, clumsy ; loose (of joints). Cf. gliogach.
glagadaich, glagudich, *n. f.* a noise ; a noise like that of hammering ; tapping noise as of a loose bolt in an engine ; boring noise, continuous knocking, boring talk.
glagaid, glag'-ij, *n. f.* blustering female, noisy woman.
glagaire, glagiru, *n. m.* a babbler, a blusterer.
glagaireachd, *n. f.* loud, foolish talk.
glagais, glagesh, *n. f.* loquacity, babbling.
glagan, *n. m.* clapper of a mill, a door-knocker, a loose joint.
glaganach, *a.* noisy, rattling.
glagarra, *a.* noisy, dull, slow.
glagarsaich, glag'-ur-sich, *n. f.* crashing, clangour, blustering, horse-laughter.
glàib, glyb, *n. f.* mire, a puddle.
glàim, gláém, *n. f.* a large mouthful ; *v.* seize upon voraciously ; usurp.
glàim, glym, *n. f.* complaint, howling. *E.Ir.* gláimm, great noise.
glàimhein, glyven, *n. m.* a glutton.
glàimseach, glym-shuch, *n. f.* a glutton-ous woman.
glàimsear, gláém'-shèr, *n. m.* a fellow that wishes to monopolise booty ; a usurper.

glaine, glynu, *n. f.* cleanness, purity.
glaine, glainne, glynu, *n. f.* a glass. *Also* gloine.
glainead, *abstr. n.* cleanness, pureness.
glais, glàsh, *v.* lock, embrace, secure.
glaisdidh, glash-dy, *a.* pale, wan.
glaise, glàsh'-u, *n. f.* greyness, a greenness.
glaiseach, glash'-uch, *n. f.* foam. *Also* còthar.
glaiseach, *n. f.* lockfast place.
glaisean, glàsh'-èn, *n. m.* a coal-fish.
glaisean, glashen, *n. m.* a sparrow.
glaisean-crille, *n. m.* a cage sparrow.
glaisean-daraich, *n. m.* a grey finch.
glaisean-seilich, *n. m.* a water-wagtail.
glaislig, glaisligeach, glashlig, *n. m.* pale and emaciated person, a fairy.
glaisleun, glash'-lèn, *n. f.* spearwort.
glaisneulach, glash'-néll-uch, *adj.* pale, wan.
glaisrig, glash-rig, *n. f.* a female fairy, half-human, half-beast ; a gorgon. *Also* glaistig.
glaiste, glasht'-u, *vbl. a.* locked, secure.
glam, *v.* handle awkwardly ; lay hold of voraciously.
glamair, glam'-ir, glam'-us, glam-us, *n. m.* smith's vice ; chasm. *Also* glamradh. *O.N.* klömbr. *M.H.G.* klammer, ' vice.'
glamarsaich, *n. m.* noisy lapping as of a hungry dog.
glamasair, glamsher, *n. m.* voracious eater, a glutton.
glamhadh, *vbl. n. m.* act of snapping, as of an angry dog ; hence, the sudden snarl of a man in anger.
glamhsa, glawsu, *n. m.* a snap (of a dog).
glan, *v.* clean, wipe, cleanse, wash, purify.
glan, *adj.* clean, cleansed, purged or freed from scandal ; pure, radiant, clear ; *adv.* thoroughly, wholly, com-pletely ; glan marbh, completely dead ; glan ruisgte, wholly bare. *O.Ir.* glan. *W.* glân. *O.Celt.* glano-s.
glanadair, glanuder, *n. m.* a cleanser, purifier.
glanadh, glanu, *vbl. n. m.* cleansing, purifying.
glang, *n. m.* a ringing sound (of metal). Cf. gliong.
glaodh, *n. m.* glue, gutta-percha ; bird-lime ; *v.* adhere. *E.Ir.* gláed. *Lat.* gluten.
glaodh, glu, *n. m.* a cry, a shout. *M.Ir.* gloed, *O.Ir.* adgládur. *W.* bloedd.
glaodh, *v. n.* cry, bawl, shout, proclaim, call ; glaoidh air, call to him.
glaodhaich, glào'-èch, *n. f.* incessant crying.
glaodhan, *n. m.* pith of wood, core of

potato (being cut for seed). *See* laoghan.

glaomar, gleumur, *n. m.* a foolish person.

glaoran, gleuran, *n. m.* blossom of wood-sorrel.

glas, *n. f.* a lock ; glas-chrochta, padlock ; glas-ghuib, a muzzle, a gag ; a' ghlas-mheur, a masterpiece of bagpipe playing. *O.Ir.* glass.

glas, *a. comp.* glaise, pale, wan, grey, green (of grass) ; lèana ghlas, a green plain ; aodach glas, grey tweed ; glas-neulach, pale-faced (of a person) ; transferred meaning : young, fresh. *Cpds. :* glasbheinn, a green mountain ; glaschiabh, grey hairs ; glaschoire, green corry ; glasfheur, glaisfheur, green grass ; glasghèadh, grey goose ; glasghille, a young lad ; glasiasg, a coal-fish, white fish ; glastalamh, ley-land ; Gàidheal glas, young Gael. *E.Ir.* glass, livid, green, blue, yellow. *O.Celt.* glasto-.

glasach, glasuch, *n. f.* ley-land, a green field.

glasadh, glas'-u, *vbl. n. m.* locking, securing.

glasadh, glasu, *n. m.* turning grey ; glasadh an là, grey dawn.

glasag, *n. f.* a small lock.

glasag, *n. f.* water-wagtail ; coal-fish ; female salmon , edible seaweed.

glasdaidh, glasdy, *adj.* greyish.

glas-làmh, glass'-làv, *n. f.* handcuff, manacles.

glasrach, glasruch, *n. f.* woad.

glasradh, glasru, *n. m.* lea, ley-land. *Ir.* glasraidh = glas (green) + radh (*coll.* force), greens.

glasraich, glas'-rich, *v.* convert into meadow.

glastalamh, glas'-tal-uv, *n. m.* unploughed or pasture land.

glastarruing, glas'-tarr-inn, *v.* remove sheaf-corn when cut ; *n. f.* act of removing corn.

glé, *adv.* very. *Ir.* glé, very, pure. *O.Ir.* glé, bright. *O.Celt.* gleivo-.

gleac, glec, *vbl. n. f.* act of sparring, sparring-match ; a struggle, a conflict ; agony ; a fight ; struggling, striving, endeavouring. *E.Ir.* glec.

gleac, *v.* strive ; wrestle.

gleacair, gleciru, *n. m.* a sparrer, wrestler.

gleadh, *n. m.* an onset, exploit. Cf. *Ir.* gleó, *gen.* gliadh, combat.

gleadh, gleadhna, gleu, *pl.* tricks, sham, humour. So *O'R.*

gleadhar, glu'-ur, *n. m.* a noisy fall, a thud, a severe shaking with a fall.

gleadhrach, *n. m.* seaweed.

gleadhraich, gleu-rich, *n. f.* clangour ; a

rattling rustling noise, a hubbub. Cf. *O.N.* gleði, merriment.

gleadhran, gleuran, *n. m.* a rattle.

gleang. *See* gliong.

gleann, gla-un, *n. m., pl.* glinn, gleann-tan, *g. sing.* glinne, a valley, a dell, a dale. *E.Ir.* glenn, glend. *O.Celt.* glennos.

gleannan, glann'-an, *n. m.* a dale.

gleannach, glann'-ach, *a.* full of dales.

gleanntail, glauntal, *adj.* haunting or fond of roaming in glens ; full of glens.

gléidh, glē, *v.* keep, preserve, retain, hold, protect. *E.Ir.* gléim, make clear, set in order.

gléidheadh, gleyü, *vbl. n. m.* preserving, keeping ; preservation ; a good turn.

gléidhteach, gley-tuch, *a.* careful, frugal ; in safe custody or keeping ; duine gléidhteach, a careful man, a selfish man.

gléidhteachd, gleytuchc, *n. f.* safe custody ; state of preservation or keeping ; frugality.

gleithir, *n. m.* a gadfly. *Also* creithleag, creibhire. Cf. *O.N.* kleggi, horse-fly.

gleò, *n. m.* a dazzling kind of haziness about the eyes, as a person threatened with a cataract, a ghost of a person.

gleò, *n. m.* combat, uproar, tumult ; *gen.* gliadh. So *Ir.* ; "mer a mheanma air ghort ghliadh," "fierce in spirit on field of battle " ; "chuireas an gleò reachdmhor," who fight a bonny battle. *E.Ir.* gleó, a fight.

gleodhadh, gleo-ugh, *n. m.* tipsiness.

gleòdhaman, gleo-uman, *a.* silly man. *Also* gleòman.

gleodhartaich, *n. f.* clinking noise, clashing noise.

gleog, gleog, *n. f.* a blow, a slap. *Also* sgleog.

gleogach, *a.* silly, dull, lazy.

gleogaire, gleogire, *n. m.* stupid fellow, a lazy fellow.

gleogaireachd, gleogiruchc, *n. f.* sloth.

gleòid, gleōj, *n. m.* a sloven. *See* sgleòid.

gleòideil, glōjal, *a.* slovenly, silly.

gleòidseach, gleōjshuch, *n. f.* stupid woman.

gleòidsear, gleoj-sher, *n. m.* a stupid man.

gleòisg, glōshc, *n. f.* a slut ; *a.* gleòisgeil.

gleòmanachd, gleòdhamanachd, *n. f.* dulness, stupidity.

gleòramas, gleōrumas, *n. m.* foolish boasting, vain talk. *E.Ir.* glórach, noisy. *See* glòir.

gleòrann, gleo'-rann, *n. m.* cresses. *Also* biolair.

gleòsg, gleòsgaid, gleōsgej, *n. f.* a silly blustering humdrum of a female.

gleòsgaire, gleōsgiru, *n. m.* a silly man.

gleòsgaireachd, *n. f.* silliness.

gleòthaisg, gleō-hishc, *n. f.* a dull or silly woman.

gleus, glēs and gliäs, *v.* tune, attune, put in trim, prepare ; **gleus an fhiodhull**, tune the fiddle or violin ; **gleusaibh bhur cridheachan gu ceòl**, attune your hearts to music ; **ghleus iad na h-eich**, they trimmed or harnessed the horses ; **gleus an sgian**, sharpen the knife.

gleus, glēs, *n. m.* order, trim, tune ; condition ; lock of a gun ; screw of a spinning-wheel ; gamut in music ; preparation ; **ciod e an gleus a th'ort**, how do you do, how are you ? readiness for action ; **tha iad air ghleus**, they are in trim, in readiness for action ; **cuir air ghleus**, prepare, make ready ; **chaidh e air ghleus**, he put himself in preparation. *E.Ir.* glés.

gleusadair, glēsuder, *n. m.* tuner, trimmer.

gleusadh, glēsu, *vbl. n. m.* act of tuning, trimming, sharpening (tools).

gleusda, glēsdu, *vbl. a.* in trim, ready, clever, well exercised ; well accomplished ; **is gleusda a gheibhear e**, he does well, he is clever ; keen.

gleusdachd, glēsd'-achg, *n. f.* expertness, cleverness ; attention and success in business.

glìb, gleeb, *n. f.* weather in which showers of sleet and hail prevail alternately ; raw weather ; **glìbshleamhuinn**, slippery with sleet.

glìb, *n. f.* a shock of hair. So *Ir.*

glìbeil, *a.* sleety and showery, with hail now and then.

glìbheid, gleevej, *n. f.* weather in which a curious mixture of rain, sleet, and hail prevails ; **glìbheid shneàchda**, soft flakes of snow. *Also* **glìbhinn**. *E.Ir.* glifid, outcry.

glìbheideach, gleevejuch, *a.* rainy, sleety, thawing. *Also* **glìobhaid**.

glic, *a.* wise, prudent ; *compar.* glice, na's glice, wiser, or most wise, or prudent, or sagacious. *O.Ir.* glicc.

glidich, glijich, *v.* move, stir.

glideachadh, glijuchu, *n. m.* act of moving, impressing. *Also* clideachadh.

glinn, *n. m.* stamina, extraordinary misfit ; when a thin person is in clothes fit for a stout person, one says : "**cha dèan e glinn annta.**" *E.Ir.* glinn, plain, manifest.

glinn, *a.* pretty ; *dial.* for grinn.

gliocas, glicus, *n. m.* wisdom, prudence.

gliocaire, glicire, **gliocasair**, glicuser, *n. m.* a wise man, a philosopher, a sage.

gliog, glig, *n. m.* motion ; a clink, a tinkling.

gliogach, gliguch, *a.* staggering, pithless, clinking, clumsy.

gliogadaich, gligudich, *vbl. n. f.* clinking.

gliogaid, gligej, *n. f.* a sluggish woman, a thin clumsy man.

gliogaideach, gligejuch, *a.* clumsy about the knees, staggering ; loose-jointed.

gliogaire, gligire, *n. m.* a skeleton of a creature.

gliogar, gligur, *n. m.* a tinkling noise.

gliogarsaich, gligursich, *n. m.* dangling and tingling. *Also* **gliogartaich**.

gliogradh, gligru, *n. m.* rattling ; " **gliogradh nan cas,**" walking with great difficulty.

gliogram, gligrum, *n. m.* staggering ; fr. gliogar.

gliom, gleem, *n. m.* a fling off, sudden motion.

gliomach, *n. m.* a stalwart fellow, a long-limbed fellow ; *a.* slovenly ; drabbish.

gliong, gleung, *n. m.* clang, tingle, jingle ; *v.* tingle, jingle, clash, as metals.

gliongarsaich, glin-gar-sich, **gliongartaich**, glin-gar-tich, *n. f.* a continuous tingling, ringing noise.

gliostar, cleestur, *n. m.* a clyster ; from *Eng.*

glis, glish, nimble step. *See* **clis**. *Ir.* clisim, I skip, jump.

gliùchd, glioochc, *n. m.* a bumper, a gulf ; a blubbering and sobbing.

gliugach, *a.* with drooping wings, sheepish. *Also* **gliughach**.

gloc, *n. m.* a large wide throat or mouth ; the bung of a cask ; clucking of hens ; **a' glocail**, clucking ; a laugh ; **glocgàire**, a loud chuckling laugh.

glocadaich, *vbl. n. f.* laughter.

glocaireachd, glociruchc, *n. f.* a cackling noise.

glocan, *n. m.* a bird cherry ; bung ; angle where branches meet ; notes of a bird.

gloc-gàire, *n. m.* a guffaw.

glochar, *n. m.* a wheezing, gurgling.

gloc-nid, *n. m.* a morning dram (taken in bed).

glog, *a.* sudden, hazy ; *n. m.* a soft lump.

glogach, *a.* soft, lubberly.

glogag, *n. f.* dull or stupid woman.

glogaid, glogij, *n. f.* a lubberly female.

glogainn, glog'-inn, *n. f.* a sudden, hazy kind of calm, with sometimes puffs of soft wind ; stupor, dozing slumber.

glogaire, glogiru, *n. m.* a lubber, a stupid fellow.

glogluinn, gloglin, *n. f.* rolling of the sea ; rolling billows under a calm surface ; noise of water.

glogshuil, *n. f.* hollow slow eye, a lifeless eye.

gloichd, glychc, *n. f.* a stupid blunderer, a half-wit ; an idiot. *Sc.* glaik.

gloichdeil, glychcal, *a.* idiotical, as a female, stupid, senseless.

glòigeach, *n. f.* the mumps.

glòin, *a.* squint-eyed.

gloine, *n. m.* glass, drinking glass, a bumper, a pane of glass. *Also* **glaine.**

glòir, *n. f.* noise, voice, speech ; warbling of birds ; noisy clamour mingled with strong language. *E.Ir.* **glór,** noise, speech.

glòir, *n. f.* glory, state of bliss. *E.Ir.* **glóir.** *Lat.* gloria.

glòir-dhìomhain, glor-yeevon, *n. f.* vainglory.

glòireim, glorem, *n. m.* pomp, pageantry.

glòireis, glōresh, *n. f.* prating nonsense.

glòirionn, glōr'-unn, *adj.* of an ugly drab colour ; spotted face.

glòmag, *n. f.* mouthful of dry oatmeal.

glómainn, glōmin, *n. f.* twilight, dawn.

glomhan, *n. m.* substance covering a calf at birth.

glomhar, glov'-ar, *n. m.* a gag for beasts ; prevent sucking ; **thàinig an glomhar as,** he is ungagged. *E.Ir.* **glomar,** a bridle. *O.Celt.* glomaro.

glomhas, glôv'-us, *n. m.* a horrible chasm.

glomhraich, glovrich, *v.* gag.

glòmnaich, glôm'-nich, *v.* dawn.

glong, *n. m.* a slimy substance, snot. *Also* **sglongaid.**

glongaire, glongiru, *n. m.* a dull, weak fellow.

glonn, gloun, *n. m.* feat, exploit. *E.Ir.* **glond,** a deed.

glòraich, *v.* glorify, praise.

glòramas, *n. m.* boasting.

glòrmhor, glôr'-vur, *a.* glorious.

glothagach, glo-haguch, *n. m.* frog's spawn.

glóthar, *n. m.* noise in the throat ; death-rattle.

gluais, gloo-ash, *v.* move, bestir, stir, make a motion, get up ; **an nì nach cluinn cluas cha ghluais e cridhe,** what does not reach the ear cannot affect the heart. *E.Ir.* **gluais,** move.

gluasachd, *n. f.* moving, mobility.

gluasad, gloo-usud, *n. m.* motion, movement, agitation, conduct, behaviour ; **tha gluasad mnà uaillse aice,** she has the gait of a lady ; *vbl. n.* act of moving, stirring.

gluc, *n. m.* socket of the eye.

gludaranaich, *n. f.* glugging, rippling noise of water in motion, as an underground rill, or a keg.

glug, *n. m.* rumbling noise, as fluids ; a rumbling stutter or stammer ; a swallow-hole ; *v.* stammer ; **glug a' ghuil,** suppressed sobbing. *Eng.* cluck.

glugach, *a.* rumbling, stammering ; *n. f.* stammering, stuttering.

glugaiche, glugaireachd, gloogichu, *n. f.* stammering.

glugaire, gloogiru, *n. m.* a stammerer ; rumbler.

glugan, gloogan, *n. m.* a faint noise of a fluid (in a vessel when moved).

glugraich, gloogrich, *n. f.* rumbling of fluid in a vessel.

gluig, *n. f.*: 1. a slut. 2. addled (egg).

glùineach, gloonuch, *a.* in-kneed, having joints, as reeds ; jointed ; *n. f.* in-kneed person ; large-kneed person ; a weed ; knot-grass.

glùineag, gloonag, *n. f.* a blow with the knee.

glùinean, gloonen, *n. m.* a garter. *Also* **cnèabailt.**

glùm, *n. f.* large mouthful of liquids. *Also* **glumadh.**

glumag, gloomag, *n. f.* a deep pool.

glùn, gloon, *n. m., pl.* **glùinean, glùintean,** a knee, a joint in reeds ; a generation ; **an seachdamh glùn,** the seventh generation ; **bean ghlùine,** midwife ; **glùn-lùbadh,** genuflexion. *O.Ir.* **glún.** *W.* **glin.** *O.Celt.* glûnos.

glùnachan, gloonuchan, *n. m.* a cap or socket to protect the knee.

glùn-bhleitheach, *a.* in-kneed.

glùn-ginealaich, gloon-gin-alich, *n. m.* pedigree, a degree in relationship.

glut, gloot, *n. m.* a gulp, a glut ; voracity ; *v.* gulp, glut. *W.* glwth.

glutadh, glootu, *n. m.* drinking voraciously.

glutaire, glootiru, *n. m.* glutton.

glutaranaich, *vbl. n.* gentle noise (of water).

glutaranaich, glootarnich, *n. m.* packing in stone wall.

gnàithseach, grà'-shach, *n. f.* arable land under crop. *Better* **gràinseach.**

gnàmhan, grāvan, *n. m.* periwinkle.

gnàth, grà, *n. m.* custom, habit, manner, practice ; **mar bu gnàth leis,** as his manner was ; *adv.* **do ghnàth, a ghnàth,** always, habitually ; *adj.* **gnàth obair,** constant work ; **gnàth chleachdainn,** habitual practice. *O.Ir.* **gnáth,** *solitus. W.* gnawd. *O. Celt.* gnâto-s.

gnàthach, grā-huch, *a.* customary.

gnàthachadh, grā-huchu, *n. m.* behaviour, conduct, custom, practice ; **do dhroch ghnàthachadh,** your own bad behaviour.

gnàthaich, grā-hich, *v. n.* use, make a practice of, behave.

gnàth-eòlas, grā-yōlus, *n. f.* experience.

gnàthfhacal, gnā-hacul, *n. m.* a proverb, an aphorism, a wise saying.

gnàths, gnàs, *n. f.* custom, habit. *O Ir.* **gnás,** *consuetudo.*

gnàthsalachd, gnās-aluchc, *n. f.* usual condition.

gnàthta, gnātu, *adj.* arable ; **talamh gnàthta,** arable land.

gnè, grè, *n. f.* nature, quality ; expression of countenance, complexion ; a slight degree of the nature of anything ; a tinge, or tincture ; species, kind, sort ; **is dona a' ghnè a tha air,** his expression of countenance does not bespeak anything good ; **gnè chreadha,** a slight degree of clay—clayish (as soil) ; **gnè dheirge,** a tinge, or tincture of red. *O.Ir.* gné, *ratio, forma, species.*

gnèithealachd, grē - haluchc, *n. f.* "natural," good nature, tenderness ; state of having much of the milk of human kindness.

gnèitheil, grē-hal, *adj.* humane, kindly, tender, urbane.

gnìomh, greev, *n. m., pl.* gnìomharan, action, a deed ; work, office ; the seventh sheaf as payment to the hinds that work the farm of tenants or landlords ; the building of a peat stack, or hewn stones ; **droch ghnìomh,** bad deed ; **gnìomh bean-ghlùine,** the office of a midwife ; **gnìomh duine,** the office or work of any man, an exploit. *O.Ir.* gním, *actio,* a deed.

gnìomhach, greevuch, *adj.* active, busy, making great or good deeds.

gnìomhachas, greevuchus, *n. f.* industry ; office of an overseer.

gnìomhadh, greevu, *n. m.* action.

gnò, gnù, *a.* surly, parsimonious, envious, gruff. *E.Ir.* gnó, derision.

gnob, *n. m.* a knoll, a tumour. *Eng.* knob.

gnoban, *n. m.* a little hill, knoll.

gnocsach, *a.* huffy.

gnog, grog, *v.* knock down, kill ; knock against ; **a' gnogadh an cinn,** knocking their heads against each other ; nodding.

gnogach, grŏg'-uch, *a.* sulky, peevish, pettish, shy.

gnoig, groig, *n. f.* a nose, snout ; a surly old-fashioned face on a young person ; sulks ; a head.

gnoigeag, groigag, *n. f.* a sulky female.

gnoigean, groigen, *n. m.* a ball put on point of horns of vicious cattle ; a kind of game played by children.

gnoigeanan-cinn, groigenun-ceen, *pl.* carle-doddies.

gnoigeas, *n. m.* ugly nose, gross features (spoken in scorn).

gnoigeis, grŏig'-esh, *n. f.* grin, peevishness, sulks, surliness.

gnoigeisach, groigeshuch, *adj.* grim ; peevish, sulky as a young person.

gnoimh, groiv, *n. f.* a grin, greann.

gnoin, groin, *v. t.* shake and scold a person at the same time.

gnomh, grov, *v.* grunt like a pig.

gnòmhan, grōvan, gnùmhan, groo-an, *n. m.* humming of a tune ; a moan ; grunting.

gnos, gros, *n. m.* snout of a beast. So *Ir.*

gnosach, *a.* sullen, grumpy, surly.

gnosail, gròs'-al, *n. f.* a grunt ; *pt.* grunting.

gnosaireachd, grosiruchc, *n. f.* muttering, blubbering.

gnòsd, gnosad, gnùsd, *n.m.* lowing of cattle.

gnothach, gnothuch, gró'-uch, *n. m.* business, message, matter ; an errand. *Ir.* gnothuigh.

gnù, gnò, *a.* surly, parsimonious.

gnùgach, grooguch, *a.* surly, sulky.

gnùgag, groogag, *n. f.* sulky female.

gnùgaire, groogere, *n. m.* a surly fellow.

gnùig, groo-ig, *n. f.* a surly lowering expression of countenance ; a scowl.

gnùis, groosh, *n. f.* countenance, face. *O.Ir.* gnúis, *facies.*

gnùisbhrat, groosh-vrat, *n. f.* a veil.

gnùisfhionn, grooshun, *a.* white-faced.

gnùis-fhiosachd, groosh-isachc, *n. f.* physiognomy.

gnùsad, groosud, *n. m.* a lowing (of a cow). *Also* gnòsad, gnùsd.

gnùsadaich, *vbl. n.* a continuous lowing.

gnùsgul, groosgul, *n. f.* grunting, grumbling.

gnùth, groo, *n. f.* a frowning look, a frown.

gò, *n. m.* guile, deceit ; **duine gun ghò,** a guileless man. *O.Ir.* gó, gáo, gáu. *O.Celt.* gavo-.

gob, *n. m.* a bill or beak of a bird. *E.Ir.* gop. *O.Celt.* goppo-s.

gobach, *a.* beaked ; *n. f.* a scold, fault-finding ; a " clash " ; the hawfinch.

gobag, *n. f.* a dog-fish, a kind of bird.

gobaire, gobiru, *n. m.* trifling prater.

goban, guibein, *n. m.* little bill.

gobha, gobhainn, go-u, *n. m., pl.* goibh-nean, blacksmith. *O.Ir.* goba, *gen.* gobann. *W.* gofan. *O.Celt.* gobân.

gobha dubh, *n. m.* water ousel. *Also* gobha uisge.

gobhal, go'-ull, *n. f.* an angle, a fork ; pair of compasses ; space between the legs ; prop, support. *O.Ir.* gabul. *W.* gafl. *O.Celt.* gabalu-.

gobhalroinn, go-ul-ryn, *n. f.* a pair of compasses.

gobhar, *n. f.* a branching river.

gobhar, gŏ'-ur, *n. f.* (*gen.* gaibhre, *pl.* gobhair), a goat. *O.Ir.* gabar. *W.* gafr. *O.Celt.* gabro-s.

gobhar-adhair, *n. m.* a snipe.

gobharraidh, gō-ry, *n. m.* a pair of compasses. = gobhal + rann.

gòbhlach, gŏll'-ach, *adj.* forked, pronged, long-legged ; *adv.* astride. *E.Ir.* gablach, peaked, horned.

gòbhlachan, *n. m.* an earwig.
gòbhlag, go-lag, *n. f.* a dung fork ; a graip.
gòbhlagan, *n. m.* a little two-pronged fork ; cross-trees for drying nets.
gòbhlaisgeach, gō-lishg-uch, *n. m.* a long-legged person.
gòbhlan, gōlan, *n. m.* a fork.
gòbhlanach, *a.* forked.
gòbhlan-gainmheach, gōlan-genvuch, *n. m.* a sand-martin.
gòbhlan-gaoithe, gōlan-gooy, *n. m.* swallow.
goc, *n. m., pl.* gocachan, a faucet ; *v.* bristle.
gocaich, gocich, *v.* cock, bristle.
gocaireachd, *n. f.* playing the ' fool ' on 1st April. *Sc.* gowk, simpleton.
gocaman, gocuman, *n. m.* a domestic sentinel, one on the look-out in a mast, an attendant, usher.
gocam-gò, *n. m.* a spy, scout, a fellow perched on any place.
gocan, *n. m.* a little attendant, a pert little person.
god, in the *phr.* air ghod, very keen.
god, *v.* toss the head ; chan e godadh nan ceann a ni an t-iomramh, tossing the head will not make the rowing.
god, *a.* stunted, withered ; fochann a' godadh ris an talamh, young corn stunted to the ground.
gòdach, *a.* giddy, coquettish. *See* gabhd.
gòdag, *n. f.* a coquette.
gog, *v.* cackle as a hen.
gogaid, gogej, *n. f.* light-headed girl, coquette.
gogaideach, gogejuch, *a.* light-headed ; loafing, standing idle.
gogaideachd, *n. f.* giddiness.
gogail, *n. f.* cackling, noise of liquor issuing from a bottle.
gogaireachd, gogiruchc, *n. f.* loitering.
gogan, *n. m.* wooden dish (without handles). *Sc.* cogue, cog. Cf. *O.N.* kuggr, small ship. *Eng.* and *Du.* cog.
goganach, *a.* light-headed, stiff-necked.
gogcheannach, gog'-chyann-uch, *a.* light-headed.
gogshuil, gog-hul, *n. f.* a goggle-eye.
goibhlean, goy-lun, a *pl.* form of gabhal, roof-trees, props, supports. *Also* casan-ceangail.
goibhneachd, goy-nachc, *abstr. n. f.* blacksmith's trade ; fr. gobha.
goic, goychc, *n. f.* a wry-neck, in despite.
goiceil, goychcal, *adj.* disdainful.
goid, guj, *v.* steal, pilfer ; sneak, slip ; goid a steach, slip in ; *vbl. n. f.* stealing. *E.Ir.* gataim, I take away, steal.
goidein, gojen, *n. m.* a little withe.
goigean, gogen, *n. m.* a bit of fat meat, cluster, kink or tangle (in thread).

goil, gul, *v.* boil as liquid ; *vbl. n. f.* boiling ; air ghoil, at the boiling point.
goile, gul'-a, *n. m., pl.* goileachan, stomach, appetite. *E.Ir.* gaile, stomach. Cf. *O.Ir.* gelim, I consume. *McB.*
goileach, gul'-uch, *a.* boiling as liquids, hot, at the boiling point. *Ir.* goilim. *O'R.*
goileadair, gul'-ud-ar', *n. m.* a kettle.
gòileag, goylag, *n. f.* a haycock, cole. *Also* còileag.
goileam, gŏl'-um, *n. m.* incessant, high-toned chattering or prattle. *Also* gothlam ; fr. guth, voice. So *Ir., O'R.*
goileamach, gŏl'-um-uch, *adj.* prating.
goill, *n. f.* blubber-cheek, expression of discontent, or sullenness in the face.
goilleach, goluch, *adj.* blubber-cheeked.
goilleag, *n. f.* slap on the cheek. *Also* sgailleag.
goillire, *n. m.* blubber-cheeked fellow ; petrel ; in *Lewis*, a sea bird that comes ashore only in January.
goimh, gŏĕv, *n. f.* a pang ; malice, grudge. So *Ir. W.* gofid. *Lat.* gemo.
goimheagach, *a.* vexing, disappointing.
goimheil, gŏĕv'-al, *adj.* venomous ; in-flicting pangs ; bearing a grudge or malice.
gòineach, gōnuch, *n. m.* a pithless, defective-looking object ; fr. gò, fault, defect.
goineideach, gonejuch, *n. m.* person hurt with an evil eye, or bewitched ; *a.* venomous ; fr. gon.
gòinein, *n. m.* very thin if not transparent breeches.
goinollann, gŏn'-ŏl-unn, *n. f.* bad kind of wool next the skin of a sheep.
goinshuileach, gon-huluch, *a.* having a fascinating eye.
gointe, go-intu, *vbl. a.* hurt with an evil eye, piqued, galled to the core.
goir, gur, *v.* crow as a cock ; sing as the cuckoo. *Also* gair. *O.Ir.* adgaur.
goireal, gural, *n. f.* dregs, refuse ; " goireal na blianaich," the refuse of leanness.
goireas, guras, *n. m.* a convenience ; a tool, apparatus ; gear, merchandise ; supplies for family. *Also* gaireas.
goireasach, gurasuch, *adj.* useful, need-ful.
goirid, gurij, *a.* short. *O.Ir.* garit. *Compar.* giorra.
goirsinn, gur-shin, *vbl. n. f.* cock-crowing, singing as a cuckoo ; crowing, etc.
goirt, gorst, *adj.* sore, painful ; severe, sour, acid ; salt ; bainne goirt, sour milk ; sgait ghort, skate on the turn. *E.Ir.* goirt, bitter.
goirtead, gorstud, *abstr. n. m.* soreness ; degree of soreness.

188 GOIRTEAN—GRADAG

goirtean, gorsten, *n. m.* a field of arable land, an enclosure, a park. *O.Ir.* gort, *seges* (sown field).

goirteas, gorstus, *n. m.* soreness; saltness, painfulness; sourness, acidity.

goirtich, gorstich, *v.* hurt, pain, ferment.

goisdeachd, gosh-jachc, *n. f.* office, or duty of a godfather; ri goisdeachd, assuming the office of a godfather.

goisdidh, goshjy, *n. m.* gossip; godfather. *M.Ir.* goistibe, godfather.

gòisinn, gōsh'-inn, *n. m.* a trap, a gin. *O.Ir.* góiste, a gin.

gòisneach, gōshnuch, *a.* hairy, downy; scattered thinly growing down, a budding moustache.

goisridh, goshry, *coll. n.* company, people. *See* gasraidh, and còisridh.

golag, *n. f.* a budget.

gol-ghàire, *n. f.* loud lamentation. *E.Ir.* gol-gáire, " loud weeping."

golum, *n. m.* a trifling flattery.

gòmadh, *n. m.* nausea.

gomag, *n. f.* a nip, a pinch; criomag, miogag. Cf. gamag.

gon, *n. m.* a blemish; tha aon ghon air, it has one fault.

gon, *v.* hurt with an evil eye; pique or gall to the core; *n. m.* severe wound. *E.Ir.* gonim. *W.* gwanu, to stab. Cf. *O.N.* gunnr, battle. *McB.*

gonach, *a.* sharp, wounding, bewitching.

gonadh, *n. m.* act of paining, stabbing, bewitching; a term of imprecation; gonadh ort! piercing pain be on you!

gonag, *n. f.* a witch, a miserable woman, a spell, a shriek.

gòrach, goruch, *a.* silly, foolish.

gòrag, *n. f.* silly female; young she-crow; gòracan, a young he-one, or silly fellow.

gòraich, gōrich, *n. f.* folly; mo ghòraich as coireach rium, my own folly is my fault.

gòraileis, gōr-ul-esh, gòraichead, *n. f.* folly.

gorglais, gorg-lesh, *n. f.* croaking (of frogs).

gòrlais. *See* gòraileis.

gorm, *adj.* blue, azure; also green, as grass; feur gorm, green grass; each gorm, dark-grey horse; aodach gorm, blue cloth; *v.* dye blue, make blue; a' gormadh, dyeing blue; *n. m.* blue colour; an gorm is an dubh, the blue and black. *E.Ir.* gorm, blue. *W.* gwrm. *O.Celt.* gorsmo-s.

gorman, *n. m.* a wood, a plant.

gormghlas, *a.* sea-green.

gormshuil, gorm-hul, *n. f.* a blue eye; *a.* gorm-shuileach.

gorn, *n. m.* an ember. *Also* éibhleag.

gorracail, goru-cul, *n. f.* tomfoolery.

gòrradaireachd, gōru-der-uchc, *n. f.* swaying, foolish daring, peering dangerously near precipice. *Also* gorradaireachd.

gòrsaid, *n. f.* a cuirass, gorget; fr. *Eng.* gorget.

gort, gart, *n. m.* standing corn, a field, an enclosure. *O.Ir.* gort, *seges.* *O.Celt.* gorto-s. Cf. *Lat.* hortus. *Gr.* χόρτος.

gort, gorst, *n. f.* famine, starvation, letter g. *O.Ir.* gorta, hunger, famine.

gortach, gorstuch, *a.* hungry; miserly.

gortachadh, gorstuchu, *n. m.* starving; hurting; turning sour, bitter.

gortachd, gorstachc, *n. f.* starvation, extreme degree of famine or hunger.

gortag, gorstag, *n. f.* a penurious or starving woman.

gorta-gleòis, *n. m.* poverty of wit, of mental equipment; fr. gorta + gleus.

gortaich, gorstich, *v.* hurt, get sour.

gortan, *n. m.* penurious or starving man.

gos-sheobhag, glas-sheabhag, g.-hio-ug, *n. f.* a goshawk.

goth, gŏ, *v.* toss the head contemptuously, or giddily; *adj.* gothail, airy, giddy.

gothadh, go-hu, *n. m.* a stately gait.

gothadh, *n. m.* a slant, a bend; gothadh gu chùlaibh, a slant backwards.

gothaiche, go-hichu, *n. m.* a bagpipe drone-reed.

gòthanach, go-hanuch, *a.* envious, malicious.

gothar, go-har, *n. m.* stopper in a bagpipe, reed made of green corn.

gothlam, *n. m.* prating noise. *See* goileam.

grab, *v.* obstruct, restrain, intercept, hinder, prevent, impede, stop, molest.

grabadh, grab'-u, *vbl. n. m.* obstruction, hindrance, impediment; act of hindering, detaining, meddling.

grabaire, grabiru, *n. m.* obstructor.

gràbh, gràv, *v.* engrave.

grabh, grav, *n. m.* a horrid thing, abhorrence; *a.* grabhail.

gràbhadh, gràbhaladh, gràvu, *n. m.* engraving.

gràbhailt, gravelt, *n. f.* a steel head-piece.

gràbhaltaiche, gràveltichu, *n. m.* an engraver.

gràbhaltair, gràv'-alt-er', *n. m.* engraver.

gràc, *v.* frighten a child with frowns. *Also* gròic.

gràcan, gràchdan, *n. m.* the note of a hen.

grad, *adj.* quick, nimble; irascible, irritable, very quick in motion; *adv.* uncommonly quick or agile; cho grad is a dh' èirich e, he rose so suddenly; ghrad chlisg e, he made a sudden start. *Ir.* grad, grod.

gradag, *n. f.* hurry, extreme haste, jiffy; bi an so an gradaig, be here instantly.

gradain, v. parch corn (in a pot).

gradan, n. m. gradanachd, n. f. parched corn. See greadan.

gradanadh, n. m. act of parching corn.

gradbheartach, a. quick, clever.

gradcharach, grad-charuch, a. very agile.

gradcharachd, grad-charachc, n. f. agility.

gràdh, grâ-gh', n. m. love or affection ; a dear ; a ghràidh, my dear, my darling. E.Ir. grád. Lat. gratus. O.Celt. gràto-n.

gràdhach, grāgh-uch, adj. loving, dear.

gràdhadair, n. m. a lover.

gràdhag, grā-dhag, n. f. a loved, a dear little one, pet.

gràdhaich, grâgh'-ich, v. love, esteem.

gràdhan, n. m. a little darling.

gràdhmhor, grâ-gh''-var, a. greatly beloved.

gràdharachd, n. f. loveliness.

gràdhran, gràdran, n. m. complaining noise of hens.

gràg, n. m. cawing, croaking of crows.

gràg, v. croak, caw.

gragair, gragir, n. m. a glutton.

graide, graju, abstr. n.f. quickness, compar. of grad, quicker.

graideachd, grajachc, n. f. degree of quickness.

gràidhean, grā-yen, n. m. a beloved person.

gràigh, grāy, a stud, flock of horses. See greigh.

graimpidh, grympy, a. trusty, unyielding ; fr. gréim, graim, grip, hold.

gràin, grā-in, n.f. disgust, loathing. E.Ir. gráin, deformity, loathing. O.Celt. gragni-.

gràinde, gràndachd, n. f. ugliness.

gràineag, grā-niag, n. f. a hedgehog. Ir. gráineóg.

gràinealachd, grā-nialuchc, n.f. abomination, abominableness, detestableness, loathsomeness.

gràineil, grā-nial, a. disgusting.

gràing. See sgraing, dreang.

gràinich, grā-nich, v. intrans. and trans. detest, loathe, impress with disgust ; aversion or loathing ; ghràinich thu air an tigh e, you gave him a dislike for the house.

gràinne, grā-niu, grainnean, grā-nen, n. f. a grain ; a pellet of shot ; a small number or quantity of anything, particularly granulated substances. O.Ir. gráinne. O.Celt. grâno-n. Lat. granum.

gràinneanaich, grā-nenich, v. granulate ; make into small grains.

gràinnich, grā-nich, v. granulate.

gràinnseach, grā-inshach, n. f. a granary, a grange, corn, a farm ; fr. Eng.

gràinnseag, grā-shag, n. f. bear-berry, cracknel.

gràinnsear, grā-sher, n. m. a farmer ; " grainger."

grainnsearachd, grā-sheruchc, n. f. farming, overseeing, bossing.

gràis, n. m. prosperity, blessing.

gràisg, grāshc, n. f. rabble, mob, low people. Ir. gráisg, gramaisg, as to meaning cf. Lat. grex.

gràisgealachd, grashc-aluchc, n. f. vulgarity, blackguardism, turbulence.

gràisgeil, gràshg'-al, a. vulgar, low, mean, blackguardish.

gramaich, for greimich, v. hold, keep, cling to.

gramaiche, greimiche, gramichu, n. m. a holder, nippers, smith's vice, a fork.

gramaisean, gramishen, pl. n. gaiters.

gramalas, gramalus, n. m., gramalachd, n. f. power, vigour, grit.

gramasgar, n. m. crowd, herd (of rather insig. indiv.), fry.

gramur, n. m. refuse of grain, very small potatoes.

gràn, n. m. grain, kiln-dried grain. O.Ir. grán. W. grawn. Lat. granum.

granabhall, gran'-a-vull, n. f. pomegranate.

granna, adj. ugly, shameful ; causing shame. Also grànnda. E.Ir. gránde, gránna.

grànnachd, grànn'-achc, n. f. ugliness.

gràpa, n. m., pl. grapachan, dung-fork.

gràs, n. m. grace, favour ; grace in the soul ; unmerited love. Lat. gratia.

gràsail, adj. gracious.

gràsalachd, grāsaluchc, n. f. graciousness.

gràsmhor, gràs'-vur, adj. gracious.

gràsmhorachd, gràs'-vur-uchc, n. f. graciousness, benignity, gloriousness.

grath, grā, adj. fearful, ugly. Also grathail, gra-hal ; tha e grathail fuar, it is terribly cold.

grathunn, gra-hun, n. f. a long or considerable time ; a while — short while.

gread, gred, v. drub, whip lustily ; dry, burn, scorch. Ir. greadaim, I whip.

greadadh, gredu, n. m. drubbing, whipping lustily ; act of drubbing.

greadan, n. m. a burning ; a whipping which " burns " ; gheibh am màs agad greadanadh, you will get a sound skelping.

greadan, gred'-an, n. m. a considerable time with all one's might at anything.

greadan, n. m. parched corn dried in a pot over a low burning fire. Ir. greadán, id. greadaim, I burn, parch.

greadh, greu, n. f. joy, happiness.

greadhan, gre-yen, n. m. a convivial party, happy band.

greadhnach, greŭ-nuch, *adj*. joyful, cheerful, merry ; fr. greadhuinn.

greadhnachas, greu-nuchus, *n. m*. joy, festivity, pomp ; august appearance, magnificence.

greadhainn, greu-dhun, *n. f*. a convivial party, a festive group, a happy company.

greaghlain, greu-lin, *n. m*. an old starved horse ; a donkey ; an old sword.

greallach, gryall'-ach, *n. f*. entrails ; *a*. dirty. *Ir*. greallach, *id*.

greallag, gryăll'-ag, *n.f*. a swing, swingle ; an greallaig, in a swing ; greallagan a' chroinn, the plough's swingles. So *Ir*.

greann, gryann, *n. f*. hair ; a bristling of hair, as on an angry dog ; a grim, angry, fierce look ; appearance of rage ; a look as if badly chilled ; ripple on the surface of water ; tha greann air an fhairge, the sea has a rippled, scowling aspect. *Ir*. greann, rough hair, beard. *E.Ir*. grend, beard. *O.Celt*. grendâ. *O.N*. grön, moustache.

greannach, gryann'-uch, *adj*. having bristled hair ; claigionn greannach cruaidh, a hard hairy scalp ; of a person, crabbed-looking, irascible ; duine greannach, an irascible or sullen person ; of weather, lowering and gloomy ; feasgar greannach, a lowering chilly evening ; threatening evening. *E.Ir*. grennach, bristly.

greannag, grianag, *n. f*. a few straggling hairs.

greannaich, gryánn'-ich, *v*. bristle, get angry with ; ghreannaich e rium, he bristled, he enraged against me.

greannan, grianan, *n. m*. a shrivelled, ill-favoured creature.

greannar, greannmhor, gryánn'-vur, *adj*. lively, active, pleasantly droll, or facetious.

greann-ghaoth, *n. f*. a cold piercing wind.

greannmhorachd, grian-vor-uchc, greanntachd, grauntachc, *n. f*. neatness.

greanntaidh, graunty, *a*. ruffled, surly.

greanta, *a*. neat, beautiful ; fr. greanaim, engrave.

greas, gres, *v. i*. hasten, urge, drive on, mend your pace ; greas ort, make haste. *M.Ir*. gressim, I urge, stimulate.

greasachd, gresachc, *n. f*. hastening, quickening, urging. *Also* greasadh. *E.Ir*. gressacht, inciting.

greasad, gres'-ud, *n. m*. act of hastening.

greideal, grejul, *n. m*. a griddle (for baking). *Ir*. greadóg, greidéal.

gréidh, gre-iy, *v*. toast as bread ; prepare, dress, whip, winnow ; a' gréidheadh an arain, toasting bread ; cure, as fish ; a' gréidheadh an éisg, curing the fish ; a' gréidheadh san t-sàbhal, winnowing in the barn. *Also* a' càthadh.

gréidheadh, gre-yu, *vbl. n. m*. act of dressing, curing, toasting, winnowing ; act of curing or state of being cured, toasting, etc. ; a handling, treatment ; fhuair e droch ghréidheadh, he has been badly treated ; grèidhte, *vbl. a*. cured, toasted, winnowed.

greidlean, grejlen, *n. m*. a kind of poker, stick for turning bannocks ; in baking, bread-stick ; scimitar ; " an àm rusgadh nan greidlein tana," at time of baring the thin blades.

greigh, grey, *n. f*. uncommon heat of the sun after bursting out from under a cloud. *Also* greighinn.

greigh, gre-iy, *n. f*. a stud of horses, a flock, a herd. *O.Ir*. graig, gl. *equitium*. *O.Celt*. gragi-. *Lat*. grex.

gréighear, gréidhear, greyer, *n. m*. a farm grieve.

greighire, gre-yiru, *n. m*. gnat, gadfly. *See* creibhire.

gréim, grēm, *n. m*. a morsel ; stitch in sewing ; a stitch, or pain ; a bit, or bite ; a hold, custody ; gréim bidh, a morsel of food ; gréim san aodach, a stitch in the cloth ; tha e an gréim, he is in custody. *O.Ir*. greimm. *O.Celt*. gresmen-.

greimeadas, grem'-ad-us, *n. m*. a hold, tenement.

greimealas, grem'-al-us, *n. m*. firmness of hold, or capability of holding well.

greimich, grem'-ich, *v. n*. hold fast, cleave to, cling to ; *n. m*. a flesh-hook ; vice. *Also* glamus.

greimir, grem'-ir', *n. m*. pincers, turcais.

greis, gresh, *n. f*. a while, space of time. *Also* dreis. *O.Ir*. do grés, do gress, *semper*.

greis, gresh, *n. m*. an onset, prowess, slaughter. *E.Ir*. gréss, attack.

gréis, grēsh, *n. f*. embroidery ; *v*. embroider. *Also* greus. *E.Ir*. gress, gréss, work of art.

greòs, *n. f*. expansion of the thighs.

greòsgach, *a*. grinning, chapped, scruffy.

greusaich, grēsich, and griasaich, *n. m*. a shoemaker ; frog-fish, or chub, or lump.

greusachd, griaschc, *n. f*. shoemaking.

griamach, griomach, greemuch, *a*. dark-featured, grim, surly.

grian, *n. f., gen*. gréine, the sun. *O.Ir*. grian, *sol*.

grianach, *a*. sunny, warm. *O.Ir*. grianda, sunny.

grianachd, grëăn'-achc, *n. f*. sunshine.

grianag, *n. f*. a small green.

grianair, grianer, *v*. bask in the sun ; 'ga grianradh fhèin, basking himself in the sun. *Also* grianaich.

grianan, *n. m.* a sunny spot, a drying-place for anything, particularly peats. *M.Ir.* grianán, a sunny spot, a resort for lovers. *Curry.*

Is mairid an grianán grinn,
A gcluinti an tiompán téad-binn.

The pleasant *grianan* also remains,
Where the sweet-stringed *timpan* was heard.

grianchrios, grian-chris, *n. m.* zodiac.

griandheathach, gree-un-ye-huch, *n. f.* exhalations.

griangheal, gree-un-yal, *a.* sun-bright.

griasaich. *See* greusaich.

grìd, greej, *n. f.* quality, substance; a very keen penurious female.

grìdeil, greejal, *adj.* very keen or industrious, hardy. *Eng.* grit. *McB.*

grigirean, grioglachan, *n. m.* pleiades, the seven stars.

grìleag, greelag, *n. f.* a grain of salt, any small matter, a small potato.

grìmeach, greemuch, *a.* grim, surly, thin-haired and dark. *Eng.* grim. *Norse* grimmr, stern, savage.

grimeil, greemel, *a.* valiant, warlike.

grìne, greenu, *n. f., pl.* grìneachan, for *Eng.* a green place.

grinn, *adj.* elegant, beautiful, neat, symmetrical; very kind, very polite; fine as linen, etc.; duine grinn, a very kind person; anart grinn, very fine linen; *adv.* very kindly or politely. *Note :* All the meanings have a moral as well as a physical significance. *E.Ir.* grind, lovely, elegant, pleasant.

grinn, *n. f.* a girning expression of countenance.

grinneach, greenuch, *n. m.* stripling.

grinneal, grinal, *n. m.* bottom of the sea, gravel. *M.Ir.* grinnell. *E.Ir.* grìan (gravel).

grinneas, grinus, *n. m.* fineness, neatness; kindness, extreme kindness or politeness.

grinnich, grinich, *v.* polish, finish.

grinnich, *v.* fasten, grip, seize, relapse in fever.

grìob, greeb, *v.* nibble. *Also* moibeil.

grìobh, greev, *n. m.* a pimple, guirean.

grìobhach, greevuch, *n. f.* the measles. *Also* griùrach, griùlach, driùrach.

grìobhag, greevag, *n. f.* hurry-burry in a neat manner; genteel hurry, a pother.

grìobhagach, greevaguch, *a.* in a hurry-burry about trifles, or nothing at all.

grìobharsgaich, greev-arsgich, *n. f.* a rush of pimples through the skin; lichen, or a kind of scum on water.

grìobhlach, grùl'-ach, *n. f.* measles.

grìobhrach, grur'-ach, *n. f.* measles; really the same as the last word.

grìobon, *n. m.* a brat, a small impertinent boy.

grìoch, gree-uch, *n. m.* a lean deer, a hind.

grìochaire, greech'-ur-u, *n. m.* an invalid, a mean person.

grìochan, greechan, *n. m.* consumption.

grìogag, greegag, *n. f.* a bead or pebble, a small cheese. *Ir.* grígeog, *id.*

grìogan, *n. m.* a bead, a bell on liquor.

grioglachan, grig'-luch-an. *n. m.* constellation of seven stars. *Also* grigirean.

grioglaich, griglich, *v.* cluster.

griogshuil, grig-hul, *n. f.* little lively eye; *a.* griog-shuileach.

grìomacach, greemacuch, *a.* thin-haired.

grìomach, greemuch, *a.* *See* grìmeach.

grìomagach, *a.* shrivelled grass.

grìoman, greeman, *n. m.* lichen, malt bud.

grìos, grees, *v.* incite, beseech; entreat by everything that is holy; blaspheme. *E.Ir.* grísaim, I light a fire; incite; fr. grís, fire.

grìosadair, greesuder, *n. m.* a blasphemer; ri griosadaireachd, blaspheming.

grìosach, greesuch, *n. f.* fire of embers, hot embers mixed with ashes; a hot fight. *E.Ir.* grís, fire.

grioth, gri, *n. f.* a gravel pit, pebble.

griothalach, gri-haluch, *n. f.* gravel.

grìs, greesh, *n. f.* perspiration produced by the idea of horror; great horror; horrified expression or appearance; the horrors; thug e grìs orm, he put me in the horrors; a cold shiver; heat, skin eruption (from heat).

grisdhearg, *a.* red mixed with white, roan-coloured, ruddy, fine-spotted.

griseach, greeshuch, *adj.* shivering, fond of the fire, " goose flesh." *Also* disearr.

grìsfhionn, greeshun, *adj.* brindled.

griùragan, grioo-rugan, *n. m.* a mote, particle, pustules on the skin.

griuthach, for griurach, griulach. *See* griobhach.

gròb, *v.* groove, join; sew awkwardly, cobble; *n. m.* a groove; a' gròbadh, tonging and grooving.

gròbag, *n. f.* a broken tooth, a little female with broken teeth, a niggardly woman.

groban, *n. m.* top, or point of a rock, hillock. So *Ir.*

gròban, *n. m.* mugwort.

gròc, *v.* threaten in order to frighten children; croak; gròcail, croaking.

grod, *adj.* rotten, putrid; *v.* rot, get putrid, become putrid, cause to rot; a' grodadh, becoming putrid, rotting.

grodag, *n. f.* a depraved woman.

grodair, groder, *n. m.* a stinking fellow, or a putrid fish.

grodlach, *n. f.* a rotten tree, a mass of rottenness.

grogach, groguch, *adj.* awkward, coarse.

grogaire, grogiru, *n. m.* a bungler, awkward fellow.

groganach, *a.* wrinkled (heather), stunted.

gròig, *v.* bungle, botch ; *a.* gròigeil ; *n. m.* awkward man.

gròigealais, grōg'-al-esh, *n. f.* unhandiness.

gròigean. *See* grogaire.

gròigeil, grōgel, *adj.* awkward, unhandy.

gròiseid, groshej, *n. f.* a gooseberry. *Scotch* groset.

grolamas, *n. m.* rabble.

gròmhan, grō-an, *n. m.* groaning, growling ; for gnòmhan, gnùmhan.

gros, *n. m.* snout. *Also* gnos. So *Ir.*

gròta, *n. m.* a groat, a silver coin worth 4d.

grothlach, groh-lach, *n. m.* a gravel-pit.

grotonach, *a.* corpulent.

gruag, groo-ug, *n. f.* hair of the head, wig. So *Ir.*

gruagach, groo-uguch, *n.f.* and *m.* damsel, a bride's maid of honour; a supposed household goddess ; a brownie ; *adj.* having a beautiful head of hair.

gruagaire, groo-ug-iru, *n. m.* wig-maker.

gruaidh, groo-ay, *n. f.* cheek, the profile. *E.Ir.* grúad. *W.* grudd. *O.Celt.* groudos-.

gruaigean, groo-egen, *n. m.* birses ; a species of seaweed.

gruaim, groo-aym, *n.f.* gloom, sullenness, surly look, melancholy. *Ir.* gruaim. *O.Celt.* greusmen-.

gruamach, groo-umuch, *adj.* gloomy, sulky, morose, sullen ; forbidding (face). *O.Ir.* gruamda, *acer.*

gruamachd, *n. f.* gloominess, sullenness, surliness ; unhappy temper.

gruamag, *n. f.* a morose woman.

gruaman, *n. m.* gloom, sadness.

grùan, groo-an (a *di-syll.*), *n. m.* liver of a person, or four-footed beast. *Also* grùthan. *Ir.* grúbhan.

grùdaire, groo-diru, *n. m.* brewer, distiller, mashman, a publican, a mean drinker. So *Ir.* Cf. *M.H.G.* grütze, water-gruel. *A.S.* grȳt. *O.N.* grautr. *Du.* grut, groats.

grùdaireachd, groodiruchc, *n. f.* brewing, distilling.

grùgach, grooguch, *adj.* sullen, having a gloomy surly face ; *n.f.* a surly female. Cf. *E.Ir.* grúc, wrinkle.

grùgaire, grooigru, *n. m.* morose man.

grùid, grooj, *n. f.* lees, dregs, grounds. *Ir.* grúid, malt. *Also* druid.

grùig, groo-ig, *n. f.* a morose, cast-down, sullen countenance, a sullen look or expression. *Ir.* id. churlishness.

gruigh, grooy, *n. m.* a dish of curds dressed with butter.

gruilleamach, groolemuch, *a.* prancing, leaping suddenly.

gruitheam, grooyem, *n. m.* curds, crowdie.

grullagan, groolagan, *n. m.* constellation or circle ; a ring of people.

grunn, groon, *n. m.* a crowd, a group ; grunn dhaoine, a crowd of people ; grunnan, a little group or crowd. *O.Ir.* grinne, a bunch, bundle of sticks.

grunnachadh, *n. m.* sounding a depth ; touching bottom, grounding.

grunnaich, groonich, *v.* sound the bottom ; touch the bottom, as of the sea.

grunnaiche, *n. m.* a sinker, a weight for a fishing-line.

grunnasg, groonn'-usg, *n. m.* groundsel.

grunnd, groon, *n. m.* bottom, ground, attention, economy, decision of character ; duine gun ghrunnd, a man without decision of character. *Sc.* grund. *O.N.* grunnr, bottom (of sea).

grunndail, groondal, *adj.* very attentive and punctual ; economical.

grunndalachd, groondaluchc, *n. f.* attention to business ; decisive character.

grùnsgul, *n. f.* grunting ; *a.* grùnsgulach.

gruth, groo, *n. m.* curds, crowdie. *M.Ir.* gruth. *O.Celt.* grutu-.

gu, go, *prep.* to ; gu fichead, to twenty ; with, *plur.* còig gu leth, five and a half ; bliadhna gu leth, a year and a half ; *prefix* to *adj.* to form *adv.*—in which case it prefixes h- to words beginning with a vowel ; gu h-àraidh, especially ; gu h-obann, suddenly ; gu fìor, truly ; gu suthainn, for ever ; gu minig, often ; gu léir, altogether. *O.Ir.* co, cu.

guag, *a.* splay-footed ; light-headed ; guagaire, splay-footed fellow, coarse.

guaigean, *n. m.* a thick, little and round object.

guailisg, *n. m.* falsity.

guailleach, goo-aluch, goo-alinuch, *n. f.* shoulder-chain or strop of a horse.

guailleachan, goo-ayluchan, *n. m.* a small plaid, a home-made tartan shawl worn usually by the older women ; a shoulder plaid ; shoulder strap.

guaillean, goo-alen, *n. m.* a cinder, a coal of fire.

guaillfhionn, goo - alun, *a.* white-shouldered.

guaillich, *v.* go hand in hand, " shoulder to shoulder."

guaim, goo-aym, *n. f.* economy ; attention to minute articles of gain ; prudence.

guaimeas, *n. f.* comfort, quietness.

guain, goo-ayn, *n. f.* giddiness, lightness.

guaineas, *n. f.* briskness, liveliness, easy-going. Cf. guanach.

guaineiseach, *a.* brisk, of stately movements.

guairdean, *n. m.* vertigo. *Ir.* gúairdean, whirlwind.

guairne, goo-arnu, *n. f.* an unshapely, unmannerly female.

guairsgeach, *a.* curled, hairy. *Ir.* gúaire, hair of the head.

guais, *n. f.* danger. *O.Ir.* gúassacht ; gúas, peril.

guaiseach, *a.* dangerous.

guait, *v.* leave ; guait am mart, leave the cow. Cf. *Eng.* quit.

gual, *v.* gall, pain, torture intensely ; a ghuail 's a chràidh thu, who tortured and tormented you.

gual, *n. m.* coal ; *v.* blacken with coal, burn to coal. So *M.I. O.N.* kol, coals. *M.H.G.* kole. *Eng.* coal.

gual, cogs of a loom. *Carm. Gad.*

guala, gualainn, *n. f.* shoulder ; *gen. s.* guailne, *pl.* guaillean ; na Gàidhil an guaillibh a chéile, Gaels shoulder to shoulder, but cf. *E.Ir.* gúalaind fri gúalaind. *O.Ir.* gúala, *gen.* gualand.

gualadh, goo-ulu, *vbl. n. m.* act of torturing, torture ; greatest pain, tormenting.

gualainn, goo-ulin, *n. f.* shoulder, mountain projection ; stamina. *E.Ir.* gúalu, *gen.* gualand.

guamach, *a.* economical, snug, smirking.

guamachd, *n. f.* degree of economy.

guamag, *n. f.* a neat woman.

guamaiseach, *a.* quiet, snug, neat.

guanach, *a.* giddy, light-headed.

guanag, *n. f.* light-headed girl, a coquette.

guanalais, goon'-al-ash, *n. f.* giddiness.

gubarnach-meurach, *n. m.* the cuttle-fish.

gucag, *n. f.* a bud, bell, a corolla, a bumper, an egg shell ; *a.* gucagach.

gùda, goodu, *n. m.*, *pl.* gùdachan, a gudgeon.

guda-leum, *n. f.* a bound, a sudden leap. *Also* duda-leum.

gug, goog, *v. i.* cluck as poultry.

guga, *n. m.* young solan goose ; a fat silly fellow.

gugail, *vbl. n. m.* clucking of poultry.

gugairneach, googirnuch, *n. m.* a fledgling bird. *Also* bugairneach.

gùgan, *n. m.* a daisy.

gugarlach, googurluch, *n. m.* a lumpish fellow. bugarnach.

guidh, gooy, *v.* pray, entreat, beseech, wish earnestly ; imprecate. *O.Ir.* guidiu, gude, guide, *precatio.* *W.* gweddi.

guidhe, *n. f.* entreaty ; a curse, an imprecation ; *vbl. n.* act of beseeching.

guidhidinn, gooyijin, *n. f.* an injunction ; a strict injunction or entreaty ; *v.* enjoin ; tha mi a' cur mar ghuidhidinn ort, I enjoin, I adjure you.

guil, gool, *v.* weep, wail ; *vbl. n.* act of weeping. *E.Ir.* guilim. Cf. gol.

guilbearnach, guilbneach, *n. f.* a curlew. *O.Ir.* gulban, gulpan, beak ; gulbnech

=" beaked one." *O.W.* gilbin. *O.Celt.* gulbano-s, beak.

guileag, goolag, *n. m.* a drawling screech, a swan's note, warbling.

guin, goon, *n. f.* a pang, dart ; *oblique c.* of gon ; *v.* pain. *O.Ir.* guin, *vulnus.*

guineach, goonuch, *adj.* venomous, fierce.

guineideach, goonejuch, *a.* ready to gore (as a bull).

guir, goor, *v.* hatch ; watch strictly. *E.Ir.* guirim, heat, burn ; *O.Ir.* goraim. *W.* gori. *Bret.* gorein.

guirean, gooren, *n. m.* a pimple ; pustule. *O.Ir.* gur, *pus.* *W.* gôr. *Bret.* gor.

guirme, goormu, *compar.* of gorm, blue, *degree* of gorm ; n'as guirme, bluer ; *n. f.* blueness.

guirmean, goormen, *n. m.* indigo.

guirmeanaich, goormenich, *v.* tinge with blue, as linen ; give a blue hue or tinge.

guiseid, gooshej, *n. f.* a gusset of a shirt ; a triangular bit of land. *O.F.* gousset.

guit, gooyt, *n. f.* a corn-fan. *Also* fasgnag.

guitear, *n. m.* kennel, sewer, gutter ; fr. *Eng.*

gul, gool, *n. m.* weeping ; *vbl. n.* act of wailing. *Also* gal ; *a.* galach. *E.Ir.* gol.

gulam, *n. m.* fragments, leavings ; a form of culm.

gulbann, *gen.* of guilb, a beak ; troigh is dorn gulbann, a foot and a fist from the toe. *See* guilbearnach.

gulm, *n. m.* gloom, forbidding look.

gulmag, *n. f.* sea-lark.

gu'n for co (*prep.*) +an (*infix. pron.*), " to their " ; gu'n cùl, to their back, to their utmost.

gun, gun, *prep.* without ; gun eòlas, ignorant. *Ir.* gan. *O.Ir.* cen.

gun, *conj.* that, in order that, until ; takes the form gum *bef. lab.* *O.Ir.* con, *i.e. prep.* co +*rel.* n-(an), con- ; *neg.* co na. *Also* conna, connach. *J. Vendr.*

gùn, *n. m.*, *pl.* gùintean, gùntaichean, a gown ; fr. the *Eng.*

gunna, goonu, *n. f.* gun ; gunna - mór, a cannon ; gunna - glaic, a fusee ; gunna caol, a fowling-piece ; gunna barraich, or sgailc, a pop-gun ; gunna-diollaid, a holster ; gunna - spùt, a syringe.

gunnair, *n. m.* a gunner.

gur, *n. m.* a brood, a hatch, or an incubation ; mar chearc a ni gur, as a hen that hatcheth. *See* guir.

gur, goor, *n. m.* a festering, abscess ; mathair-ghuire, core of an abscess. *Sc.* dottle. *O.Ir.* gur, *pus.* *O.Celt.* goru-.

gur, gurab, *s.vb.* that he is ; rb =dependent

form of **is**, when in combination with particles ; as, **gu-rb** (with helping vowel, **gurab**). *O.Ir.* **co-rb** ; **gur** = **gu-r** (b elided) ; is mise an duine, I am the man ; gur mise an duine, that I am the man.

guraiceach, goorecuch, *n. m.* a blockhead.

gurpan, goorpan, *n. m.* a crupper.

gurraban, **gurradan**, *n. m.* a crouching posture, sitting on one's heels.

gurracag, *n. f.* gurgle, froth bells ; a cole of hay.

gurrach, goorach, *n. m.* a crouching posture ; tha e an sud 'n a ghurrach, he is yonder sitting alone (and lonely).

gurraiceach, goorecuch, *n. m.* a big awkward fellow, a callow young bird, a dotterel.

gurraidh, goory, *n. m.* one in crouching position.

gurt, goorst, *n. m.* sadness, pain, fierceness, sternness of look. *Also* **gart**.

gus, goos, *adv. conj.* and *prep.* until, till, into, to, in order that, as far as, so that ; gus an till iad, until they return ; a sheachdainn gus an dè, yesterday se'ennight ; gus nach cluinnte e, so that he could not be heard ; gus am b'fhearra dhomh, so that it was better for me. *O.Ir.* **co** (*prep.*) + s (frag. of *art.*).

gusair, gooser, *a.* sharp, keen, strong ; fr. **gus**, force, smartness. *E.Ir.* **gus**, weight, force ; **gusmar**, strong.

gusg, *n. m.* a bumper.

gusgan, *n. m.* a swig, a draught.

gusgul, *n. m.* husks, refuse, dirt, idle words, roaring ; *a.* **gusgulach**.

guth, goo, *n. m.*, *pl.* **guthan**, **guthannan**, a voice, a word, a syllable, a mention, report ; chuala e guth, he heard a voice ; dèan guth rium, speak a word ; cha chuala mi guth air a riamh, I never heard the slightest mention of it ; guth caointeach, a plaintive voice ; a warning, or secret hint from the dead ; thàinig guth da ionnsaigh, a voice came to him ; gu bràth na toill ort féin guth, never deserve a word of reproach. *O.Ir.* **guth**. *O.Celt.* gutu-s.

guthach, goo-huch, *a.* vocal ; wordy, noisy.

guthaid, goo-haj, *n. f.* place of an oracle ; an *oraculum*. *Also* **guth-àite**. *Bible*.

H

h : this letter is not acknowledged in the Gàidhlig alphabet. It has certain gram. functions. It is used as the sign of aspiration of cons., corresponding to the "*point*" in Irish. It is retained initially in foreign words. It stands before words beginning with a vowel, in certain circumstances, such as : after the *art.* na (*gen. s., f.*), **na h-òighe**, of the maiden ; and **na** (*n. pl.*), **na h-éildean**, the hinds ; after the *pos. pron. f.*, **a, a h-ainm**, her name ; after the *advbl.* **gu, gu h-àraidh**, especially.

I

i, the eighth letter of the Gaelic alphabet ; styled **iubhar**, the yew tree.

i, *pers. pro.* 3rd (*fem.*) she, her, it.

I, name of Iona.

iach, *n. f.* a cry, a yell ; fr. **éig**, cry. *O.Ir.* **iachtaim**, I yell.

iach, *n. f.* a salmon. *E.Ir.* **eó**, *gen.* iach.

iad, *pers. pron.* 3rd *pl.* they ; iad fhéin, they themselves.

iadach, *n. m.* jealousy. *Ir.* **éad**.

iadh, *v.* surround ; enclose, hover ; an dorus iadht', the closed door (the windward door of a bothy) ; an saoghal mun iadh grian, world about which the sun encircles. *Ir.* i-adaim. *O.Celt.* (p)adâô.

iadhshlat, iu-hlat, *n. f.* honeysuckle, woodbine. *Also* **an t-eidheann, an fheulainn**.

iadsan, èd'-sun, *pers. pron.* 3rd *pl.* (emphatic), they, themselves.

ial, *n. f.* moment ; gach ial, every moment ; gleam of sunshine ; a season.

iall, *n. f.* a thong, leather strop, a leash ; "mar choin air éill ri h-am na seilg," like dogs on a leash at time of the chase. *E.Ir.* **íall**, a thong.

iall, *n. f.* a flock of birds. Cf. **ealta, eallach**. *E.Ir.* **íall**, a flock.

iallach, *adj.* in strings, full of thongs.

ialtag, *n. f.* a bat. *Ir.* ialtóg. *E.Ir.* iatlu.

ian, *n. m.* a bird. *See* **eun**.

iar, *prep.* after.

iar, *n. f.* the back, as one faces the rising

sun, hence the west ; an iar, westward ;
an iar is an iar-dheas, *also* iarras
(the d *assim.* with r), west by south ;
adv. westerly. *Also* siar. *O.Ir.* aniar,
from behind, from the west.

iarais. *See* là.

iarbhail, *n. f.* anger, ferocity (air + boile).

iarbhail, *n. f.* consequence, remains of
a disease. Cf. *Ir.* iarmairt.

iardath, *n. m.* what remains in dyeing-
pot after the wool or cloth is taken out.

iargail, *n. f.* the west, evening twilight.
Ir. iargúl, remote district (iar + cúl).

iargail, *n. f.* strife, contest, bustle.
O.Ir. iargal (air + gal), fight, valour.

iargain, eeurgen, *n. f.* the evil effects of
anything ; lees of whisky. So *E.Ir.*

iargain, *n. f.* bewailing, grief (air + gon).
E.Ir. iargnó, anguish.

iargaineach, iur-genuch, *adj.* afflictive.

iargalta, *adj.* turbulent, uncouth ; ugly ;
frowning ; **tha coltas iargalta air na
speuran**, the sky has a frowning look.

iargaltachd, *n. f.* turbulence, a turbulent
disposition. *Also* iargaltas, *n. m.*

iarghuil, *n. f.* sound, noise. *See* uirghioll.

iarla, *n. m.* an earl. *M.Ir.* iarla. *O.N.* jarl
(older form, earl). *A.S.* eorl.

iarlachd, *n. f.* earldom.

iarmad, *n. m.* offspring, remnant. *O.Ir.*
iarm-ue, descendant.

iarmailt, *n. f.* the sky, the firmament.
Ir. firmeint ; fr. *Lat.* firmamentum.

iarna, *n. f.*, *pl.* iarnachan, hank (of yarn).

iarnag, *n. f.* a little hank.

iarnaich, *v.* iron, smooth with a hot iron
as linen ; **ag iarnachadh**, smoothing,
ironing as linen. *Also* iarnaig.

iarnaich, *v.* make into skeins.

iarnaidh, *adj.* iron-like, very forbidding
in features, hard, miserly.

iarogh, ee-ur-o, *n. m.* great-grandchild.
O.Ir. iarm-aue, iarm-ua, *pronepos.*

iarr, *v.* seek, ask ; search for ; search as
medicine ; probe. *E.Ir.* iarraim. *O.Ir.*
íar-faigim, íarma-faigim, I ask.

iarraidh, *n. f.* a search, petition, request.

iarrtas, *n. f.* petition, request.

iarrtasach, *adj.* soliciting, frequently
asking or seeking.

iar-thuath, iür-hoo, *n. f.* the north-west.

iarunn, *n. m.* iron, an iron. *O.Ir.* iarn,
iarand, iarund, *ferrum.* *W.* haearn.
O.Celt. eisarno-, eiserno-.

iasachd, iasad, *n. f.* a loan. *E.Ir.*
iasacht.

iasg, *n. m.*, *gen. s.* and *n. pl.* éisg, a fish.
O.Ir. iasc, aesc, *gen.* éisc. *W.* pysc.
O.Celt. (p)eisko-s. *Lat.* piscis.

iasgach, iasgachd, *n. m.* fishing, a take
of fish ; act or art of fishing.

iasgaich, *v.* fish, angle.

iasgair, *n. m.* fisher, fisherman.

ibh, *v.* drink ; *n. f.* a drink. *O.Ir.* ibim,
I drink. *O.W.* iben, *W.* yfed. *Lat.* bibo.

ic, *v.* affix ; *n. f.* an affix, appendix.

ic, *v.* cure, heal. *See* ioc.

idir, ijir, *adv.* at all ; **chan 'eil idir**, not
at all ; **chan e idir**, that is not it at all.
O.Ir. itir, etir, *omnino.*

ifrinn, ifrin, *n. m.* hell. *O.Ir.* ifern,
iffern ; *dat.* iffurn ; fr. *Lat.* infernum.

ifrinneach, ifrionnach, ifrin-uch, *adj.*
hellish, fiendlike ; *n. m.* a fiend,
demon.

igh, eey, *n. f.* tallow ; *a.* ìgheil, eeyul.

igh, *n. f.* a burn, a small stream ; properly aoidh, same as ùidh, *q.v.*

ighean, iyun, *n. f.* a daughter, girl.

ilbhinn, ilvin, *n. f.* a craggy mountain ;
ial (many) + beann (peak).

Ile, eelu, *n. m.* Islay, an island of Argyle.

Ileach, eeluch, *a.* belonging to Islay ;
an Islayman ; **ceann-Ileach**, particular
kind of sword made by smiths of the
name of MacEachern ; variegated, neat.

illse, *n. f.* lowness ; *deg.* lower ; for ìsle.

illsich, *v.* lower, abase ; for ìslich.

im, eem, *n. m.*, *gen. s.* ime, butter.
E.Ir. imb. *O.Celt.* emben-.

im-, about ; an intensive prefix. *O.Ir.*
im-, imm-. *W.* ym-. *O.Celt.* embi.

im-chéin, im-chēn, *a.* far, remote, distant
(im + cian).

imcheist, eem-chesht, *n. f.* perplexity,
anxiety, distraction ; **an imcheist**,
perplexed. *O.Ir.* imchesti.

imcheisteach, eem-cheshtuch, *adj.* per-
plexing, perplexed, distracting, distracted.

imeachd, eemachc, *n. f.* travelling,
departure, the very spot, distinction ;
mun imeachd so, hereabouts ; **ciod e
an imeachd mun d' fhàg thu e ?** where-
abouts did you leave it ? *Ir.* im-
theacht. *O.Ir.* immthecht (im + techt),
ambulatio. *O.Celt.* embi-teikto-.

imfhios, im-is, *n. f.* hesitation, eve ; **an
imfhios dol fodha**, almost sinking ;
an imfhios teicheadh, on the eve of
scampering ; **an imfhios a chiall a
chall**, on the eve of losing his senses.

imich, *v.* go. *O.Ir.* immthigim, I go.
= imm (*prep.*) + tíagaim (go).

imideal, *n. m.* (skin) covering of pail of
milk. *E.Ir.* imm-degail, protection ;
but *C.R.* suggests = iombhuideal. *See*
iolaman.

imir, *v.* behove, need ; **imiridh mi falbh**,
I must go, it behoves me to go, I must
be off. *Also* fimir.

imir-chuimir, imir-chuymir, *adv.* wholly
and solely, most completely or
thoroughly ; **tha iad mar sin imir-
chuimir**, they are so wholly and solely,
thoroughly.

imire, im-iru, *n. m.* a ridge of land ; arable land. *E.Ir.* ire, land.

imireachadh, imiruchu, *vbl. n. m.* act of walking in ranks, or procession ; a procession ; imireachadh an tòrraidh, the funeral procession.

imirich, imirich, *v.* march, walk in ranks or procession. *E.Ir.* immirge, journey.

imisg, imishc, *n. f.* sarcasm, scandal. Cf. inisg.

imleach, eemluch, *n. m.* a licking.

imleag, imlag, *n. f.* navel. *E.Ir.* imbliu, *ac.* imblind. *Lat.* umbilicus. *O.Celt.* embiliôn-, embilenko-.

imlich, eemlich, *v.* lick with the tongue. *O.Ir.* lígim, *lingo.*

imnidh, imny, *n. f.* care, diligence. *O.Ir.* imned, *tribulatio.*

impich, iompaich, eoompich, *v.* turn about, convert, change. *O.Ir.* impóim, I turn about = imb + soim (I turn).

impidh, eempy, *n. f.* prayer, persuasion, supplication. *O.Ir.* impude = imb + sude, a " sitting about," a siege.

impidheach, eempy-uch, *a.* inciting, beseeching.

impis, eempish ; same as imfhios. *Also* imis.

imreasan, imresan, *n. m.* dispute, controversy. *O.Ir.* imbresan, imfresan, dispute, quarrel.

imrich, *n. f.* flitting, removing from one residence to another ; *v.* remove residence. *E.Ir.* immirge, immirce (im + éirge), go about, depart.

in-, ion-, ionn-, *prep.* in, used as prefix. Cf. *Lat.* in-.

inbhe, *n. f.* condition, rank, perfection, maturity as a person, state of advancement, progression, progress ; ciod e an inbhe a bheil thu ? how far have you advanced ? what progress have you made ? tha mi an inbhe mhath, I have made a considerable progress ; bha mi an inbhe is an dorus a dhùnadh, I was on the eve of shutting the door.

inbheach, invuch, *a.* mature, ripe, of a mature age ; of rank.

inbhidh, invy, *a.* mature, ripe, of a mature age ; duine inbhidh, a man come to the age of discretion ; *n. f.* set time, time due; perfection; inbhidh na bà, due to calve. *O.Ir.* inbaid, inbuid, particular period of time.

inbhidheachd, invvy-achc, *n. f.* perfection, maturity, years of discretion.

inbhir, invir, *n. m.* a cove or creek at the mouth of a river ; meeting of a stream with the sea or with another stream, confluence. *E.Ir.* indber, inbir, inber. *O.Celt.* eni-bero-s.

ineach, inuch, *n. m.* a chopping-block. *Also* ealag.

ineach, *n. f.* generosity, hospitality. *See* eineach and oineach.

ineachail, *a.* generous, hospitable.

ingealtas, ing - altus, *n. m.* pasture - ground. *See* inghilt.

inghar, *n. m.* plumb-line.

ingharach, *a.* level, perpendicular.

inghean, inyin, *n. f.* daughter, girl. *O.Ir.* ingen, *filia.*

inghilt, *v. tr.* to devour, to pasture. *Ir.* ingilim. *O.Ir.* gelim, I devour. *W.* gwellt, grass.

inich, *a.* neat, tidy.

inichead, *n. m.* neatness.

inid, inij, *n. f.* Shrove-tide. *E.Ir.* init. *Lat.* initium, beginning (of Lent).

inilt, *n. f.* a girl. *O.Ir.* inailt, innilt, a bondmaid, handmaid.

inisg, inishc, *n. f.* reproach, bad name. *O.Ir.* insce, speech.

inn-, ionn-, innt- (bef. s), *prefix,* against, to ; of similar force to frith, ri.

inne, eenu, *n. f.* finger-nail. *O.Ir.* ingen, *ungula. W.* ewin. *O.Celt.* enguînâ.

inne, *n. f.* the kennel, the gutter, a common sewer.

inne, *d. pl.* innibh, *n. f.* bowels, entrails. *O.Ir.* inna, *d. pl.* innib, *viscus.*

inneabhag, *n. f.* a young woman given to borrowing.

inneach, *adj.* black, dirty, having nails.

inneach, *n. m.* woof. *Also* cura, snàth-cura. *E.Ir.* innech.

inneachas, eenuchus, *n. m.* a scramble.

inneadh, *n. m.* want, need.

inneal, inul, *n. m.* machine, an engine, instrument, means, apparatus ; inneal-ciuil, musical instrument ; inneal-coise, footstep of a spinning-wheel ; inneal-stoith, or toitlinn, steam engine ; inneal-tarruing, a capstan ; inneal-buill, a windlass ; inneal-séididh (balg-séididh), a bellows. *E.Ir.* indell, an instrument, preparation.

innealadh, *n. m.* preparations, furnishing.

innealta, inyaltu, *a.* ingenious.

innealtachd, *n. f.* ingeniousness, ingenuity, fitness, aptness.

innean, inyon, *n. f.* smith's anvil. *O.Ir.* indéin.

inneanadh, inyunu, *n. m.* deficiency of yarn in weaving.

innear, inyur, *n. f.* cattle's dung. *M.Ir.* indebar.

inneas, *n. m.* narration, a tale, account. Cf. *Ir.* aisneis. *O.Ir.* aisnaís.

innich, *v. i.* scramble, struggle.

innidh, in-yi, *adj.* expert, clever, smart ; gille innidh, a clever, active young man. *O.Ir.* inne, mind, sense.

innidheachd, in-yi-achc, *n. f.* expertness.

innil, inyil, v. prepare, equip. *E.Ir.* indlim, get ready.

innis, inyish, *n. f.*, *pl.* innseachan. 1. an island. 2. a river-side meadow, haugh, inch. 3. milking place, a resting place. 4. a green spot; innis nam bó laogh 's nam fiadh, choice pasture for milk cows and deer. *O.Ir.* inis. *O.Celt.* inissî. *W.* ynys. *Lat.* insula.

innis, inyish, v. n. relate, tell, inform. *E.Ir.* innisim, indisim, say, describe.

innisg, inyishc, *n. f.* a libel, calumny, defamation, reproach; a' tilgeadh innisgean, defaming, reproaching, libelling. *See* inisg.

innisgeach, inyishcuch, *adj.* reproachful, defamatory, disgraceful.

innleachd, eenluchc, *n. f.* device, invention, a stratagem; ingenuity, contrivance, power of invention, expedient; ni airc innleachd, a strait is the mother of invention; a bheil e ad innleachd? is it within the compass of your invention? *Ir.* inntleachd. Cf. *O.Ir.* intliucht, sense; fr. *Lat.* intellectus.

innleachdach, eenluchcuch, *adj.* inventive, ingenious, fit to devise ways and means.

innleachdair, eenluchc-er, *n. m.* inventor.

innleag, eenlag, *n. f.* a child's doll.

innlich, v. aim, desire.

innlinn, eenlin, *n. f.* the third part of the straw left by the tenant removing for the one entering a farm, for bedding to the cattle to help manure; provender, forage, fodder.

innse, eenshu, *n. f.* information, intelligence, report, sign; is dona an innse ort, it is a very bad sign of you.

innseach, eenshuch, *adj.* insular; prone to inform against, tattling.

innseag, eenshag, *n. f.* an eyot or islet in a river; an isle, a little haugh, green spot.

Innsean, eenshun, and Innseachan, *n. pl.* the Indies; Innsean na h-aird' an ear, the East Indies.

Innseanach, eenshenuch, *n. m.* an Indian; *adj.* belonging to India.

Innse-Gall, *n. pl.* islands of the foreigner ; the Hebrides.

innsgin, *n. m.* mind, courage.

innte, eentu, *prep.* (in) +*pron. suf.* 3 *sing. f.* within her or it.

innteart, eentiart, *n. f.* entry, beginning. *Also* inntreadh, inntreachduinn, commencement.

inntinn, eentin, *n. f.* mind, intellect, intention, intent, purpose, will, pleasure. Cf. *O.Ir.* inne, sense.

inntinneach, eentinuch, *adj.* sprightly, lively, animated, elevated, elated, jolly, intellectual, sportive, merry, hearty, high-minded, willing.

inntir, eentir, v. enter, introduce.

intrinn, eentrin, v. enter. *Also* inntrig.

iob, eeb, *n. m.* lump of dough; ioba, a very stout person.

iobair, eebir, v. sacrifice; dh' iobair iad uan, they sacrificed a lamb. *O.Ir.* idpraim, *offero.*

iobairt, eeburt, *n. f.* sacrifice, offering. *O.Ir.* edpart, edbart; idpart, idbart, sacrifice.

iobartan, eeburtan, *n.* means to do evil.

iobradh, eebru, *vbl. n. m.* act of sacrificing.

ioc, v. pay; fulfil; iocaim mo bhóid, let me pay my vow. *O.Ir.* ícaim, I pay, indemnify.

ioc, eec, v. heal, make whole; *n. m.* medicine, remedy. *O.Ir.* íccaim, heal. *W.* iachau. *O.Celt.* jêkkâ.

iochd, ee-uchc, *n. m.* mercy, clemency, kindness, humanity, generosity, compassion. *M.Ir.* icht, clemency; icht urraid, a gentleman's clemency. *Tbc.*

iochdar, eech-cir, *n. m.* the bottom, the lowest part; iochdar is uachdar, top and bottom. *O.Ir.* ichtar, the lower part.

iochdaran, eech-curan, *n. m.* a subject, an underling, an inferior.

iochdmhor, eechc-vor, *adj.* humane; merciful, compassionate.

iochdmhorachd, eechc-voruchc, *n. f.* mercifulness, kindness, humanity, compassionate regard.

iochdrach, eech-cruch, *adj.* nether, lowest, lowermost, nethermost; a' chlach mhuillinn iochdrach, the nether millstone; ifrinn iochdrach, the lowest hell.

ioclus, eec-loos, *n. f.* medicinal herb. íc + lus.

iocshlaint, eec-hlaynt, *n. f.* balm, medicine, cordial, balsam = ic + sláinte.

iocshlainteach, *a.* balsamic, cordial as medicine; soothing, alleviating, salutary.

iod, *interj.* alas!

iodhal, ee-ghol, *n. m.* an idol, image. *O.Ir.* idal. *Lat.* idolum.

iodhal-aoraidh, *n. m.* idolatry.

iodhan, iodhnadh, *n. m.*, *pl.* iodhannan, pain, pains of child-birth. *E.Ir.* idu, *gen.* idan, a smart, pain.

iodhlann, yoolun, *n. f.* a corn-yard. *O.Ir.* ithla (*gen.* ithland), area, = ith (corn) +lann (area). *W.* yd, corn.

iodhon. *See* eidheann.

iogan, eegan, *n. m.* deceit, guile; *a.* ioganach, deceitful.

ioghnadh, ee-nu, *n. m.* cause of surprise, curiosity, wonder; an exhibition of curiosities; show, play; surprise; cha bhiodh ioghnadh orm, I would not be surprised. *See* iongnadh.

iol, many. *O.Ir.* il, many. *O.Celt.*

(p)elu-. *Cpds.* : **iol-bheusach**, inconstant ; **iol-cheard**, jack of all trades ; **iol-chearnach**, many-cornered ; **iolchasach**, having many feet ; **iolchruthach**, multiform ; **iol-dhathach**, many-coloured ; **iol-dhealbhach**, multiform ; **iol-ghuthach**, many-voiced ; **iol-ghnétheach**, heterogeneous ; **iolghniomhach**, ingenious.

iola, yoolu, *n. f.* 1. trolling (the boat going the while at moderate speed). 2. fishing ground.

iolach, yooluch, *n. f.*, *pl.* iolaichean, a shout, cry, roar ; huzza. *O.Ir.* ilach, gl. *paean.*

iolair, yulir, *n. f.* an eagle. *O.Ir.* ilur.

iolaman, yooluman, *n. m.* skin covering for a wooden vessel carrying milk. *See* imideal.

iolar, yoolar, *adv.* downwards.

iolbheist, yool-vesht, *n. f.* a wild beast, a snake. *See* uilebheist.

iolla, yoolu, *n. f.* sight, view ; gabh iolla, just look at it ! *Also* ealla.

iollag, yoolag, *n. f.* a skip, trip ; gu h-iollagach, on the light fantastic toe. *See* iullagach.

iollain, yoolen, **iollan**, yoolan, *a.* expert ; fr. ealaidh.

iolmaid, iolmej. *See* iomlaid.

iom-, *prefix.* 1. *intensive.* 2. about, *circum* ; used before broad vowels (a, o, u) ; im before e and i.

iomach, imuch, *adj.* various in colours ; parti-coloured ; various ; of various kinds.

iomachagar, imu-chagur, *n. f.* regards, compliments.

iomachain, imu-chen, *n. f.* anxiety, solicitude.

iomachaineach, imchenuch, *a.* anxious.

iomachomhairle, imu-cho-url, *n. f.* perplexity, doubt, suspense.

iomachruthach, imu-chroo-uch, *a.* having many forms or shapes ; various, multiform.

iomachuimhn, imchuyn, *n. f.* anxiety, solicitude ; tha e fo iomachuimhn, he is anxious or solicitous.

iomachuimhneach, *adj.* very anxious, very solicitous.

iomachuinge, im-chyngu, *n. f.* narrowness, extreme narrow-mindedness.

iomachumhann, im-choo-un, *adj.* very narrow ; very narrow-minded, or niggardly.

iomad, imud, *a.* many, various, divers ; iomad seòl, various ways, divers manners. *O.Ir.* imbed, immad, *copia.* *O.Celt.* imbeto-.

iomadach, imuduch, *a.* many ; iomadach uair, often ; iomadach tè, many a female ; iomadach fear, many a man.

iomadaich, imudich, *v.* multiply.

iomadaidh, imudy, *n. f.* many ; great number.

iomadail, imudal, *adj.* multiplicable.

iomadalachd, *n. f.* multiplicity, plurality ; oir thig aislingean le iomadalachd ghnothaichean, for dreams come through multitude of business.

iomadan, imudan, *n. m.* moving, flitting, sadness, concurrence of disasters, a mourning. Cf. *E.Ir.* immada, ruin (used with *verb* of motion).

iomadanach, *a.* unsettled, sad.

iomadathach, imu-da-huch, *a.* of many colours.

iomadh, imu, *n. m.* various, many, divers. *Also* ioma. *See* iomad.

iomagain, iomaguin, imugen, *n. f.* anxiety, great solicitude ; fo iomagain, solicitous. *E.Ir.* imm + gon.

iomagaineach, imugenuch, *adj.* solicitous.

iomaghaoith, iomaghaoth, imu-ghu, *n. f.* eddy-wind ; whirlwind.

iomain, imen, *vbl. n. f.* act of driving ; a drove of cattle ; fear - iomain, a driver ; play at golf, or cricket, or shinty ; *v.* drive, play at shinty ; ag iomain, playing at shinty. *O.Ir.* im-máin, drive ; imm + áin, driving ; oc immain na m-bó, a-driving the herd.

iomair, imir, *v.* drive, lead ; play at cards, at backgammon ; ag iomairt air chairtean, playing at cards. *O.Ir.* imbrim (=imb + berim), I drive about ; *idiom :* working with a sword, playing at a game, etc.

iomair, imir, *n. f.* ridge of land, a strip of arable land. *E.Ir.* immaire, imbaire, gl. on *actus* =measure, a day's ploughing. *O'Dav.*

iomair, *v.* need, behove, must. *O.Ir.* timm-thirim, I serve.

iomairc, imirc, *n. f.* removal ; *v.* remove. *See* imrich.

iomairt, imurt, *n. f.* play, game, conflict, danger, hurry-burry, confusion ; act of playing, gaming, betting.

iomairteach, imurtuch, *adj.* betting, laying wagers ; lavish.

iomal, imul, *n. m.* outskirts, limit, border, refuse, remainder ; an iomal na dùthcha, in the outskirts of the country. *E.Ir.* imbel (=imb + bil), a border. *W.* ymyl, hem, border.

iomalach, imuluch, *adj.* remote, distant ; àitean iomalach, remote or distant places.

iomarbhaidh, imurvy, *n. f.* struggle ; hesitation ; confusion about what to do, or how to proceed. *O.Ir.* im-marbág, emulation, strife. *O.N.* bágr (strife).

iomarcach, imurcuch, *adj.* in many straits ; in distress, distressed, very

numerous, superfluous. *M.Ir.* imar-
craid, superfluity ; immarchor, tossing
about.
iomarchur, imurchoor, *n. f.* a rowing,
tumbling, straying. *E.Ir.* immarchor,
straying.
iomartach, imurtuch, *a.* thrifty.
iomartas, imurtus, *n. m.* sufficiency,
competency.
iomas, imus, *n. m.* confusion, trouble,
pother.
iomasgaoil, imusgul, *v.* slack, slacken,
loosen, untighten.
iomasgaoilte, *vbl. a.* loose, slack, slack-
ened, loosened.
iomasgaoilteachd, *n. f.* slackness, looseness, freedom.
iomchair, imucher, *v.* bear, carry.
iomchan, *n. m.* carriage, behaviour.
iomchar, *n. f.* bearing, carrying, behaviour (im + cur).
iomcharag, *n. f.* compliments, regards.
iomchoir, imchor, *n. f.* reflection ; a' cur
iomchoir ormsa, reflecting on me ; fr.
iom + coire.
iomchoirich, *v.* blame, censure.
iomchorc, iomchomharc, *n. f.* regards,
salutation, petition. *O.Ir.* imchomarc,
interrogatio, salutatio.
iomchuidh, imuchy, *a.* proper, fit, befitting ; mar chì thusa iomchuidh, as
you see proper (im + cubhaidh).
iomchuidheachd, imuchyachc, *n. f.* fitness, suitableness, propriety.
iomdhorus, *n. m.* a back door, a lintel.
iom-dhruid, imu-ghruj, *v.* inclose.
iom - fhuasgail, im - oousgul, *v.* trade,
relieve ; loosen, slacken.
iom-fhuasgladh, *vbl. n. m.* traffic, trade,
something to trade with.
iomhaigh, eevay, *n. f.* image, likeness,
similitude, statute, expression of countenance. *M.Ir.* imáig. *Lat.* imago.
iomhaigheachd, eevay-uchc, *n.f.* imagery,
imagination. *Also* ìmheachd, features
(of face).
iomla, *a.* changeable.
iomlag, *n. f.* navel, nave. *See* imleag.
E.Ir. immlecan. Cf. imbliu.
iomlaid, imlej, *n. f.* exchange, course,
duration ; *v.* exchange ; dèan iomlaid
exchange, barter ; an iomlaid dà latha,
in the course of two days ; change (in
money) ; iomlaidich not, change a
pound note.
iomlaideach, *adj.* fluctuating, tossing as
a sick person, restless, tossing, unsteady, unreliable ; tha e cho iomlaideach ris a' ghaoith, he is as changeable
as the wind.
iomlaideachd, *n. f.* unsteadiness, fickleness, changeableness.
iomlaine, imlanyu, *compar. deg.* of iomlan.

iomlan, im-lan, *adj.* perfect, complete,
full, sound ; duine iomlan, a perfect
man. (im + slàn.)
iomlanachd, iomlaineachd, *n. f.* perfection, integrity, maturity, completeness.
iomluaisg, im-luäshc, *v.* disorder, confuse,
toss, tumble.
iomluasgadh, *vbl. n. f.* confusion, commotion ; putting out of order, de-
ranging. *E.Ir.* imm + luascad.
iom-oiseanach, im-oshen-uch, *a.* multangular.
iompachadh, yoompuchu, *vbl. n. m.* con-
verting, persuading ; conversion, persuasion.
iompaich, yoompich, *v.* change, convert.
See impich.
iompaidh, yoompy, *n. f.* means, medium,
instrumentality, of a person, to do
good ; turning, conversion. *O.Ir.* im-
púd ; fr. imb (about) + sóim, turn.
Gl. στροφή.
iomrachadh, imruchu, *n. m.* bearing,
humouring.
iomradh, eemra, *n. m.* report, fame, renown, mention ; tha t' iomradh feadh
na tìre, your fame is spread throughout the land (im + ràdh). *O.Ir.* im-
mrádud. *O.Celt.* embi-râdo-.
iomraich, imrich, *v.* tell, bear.
iomraiteach, eem-ratiuch, *a.* notorious,
public, far spread ; nì iomraiteach, a
notorious thing ; eminent, far-famed,
renowned. *O.Ir.* imrádad.
iomrall, imrull, *n. m.* an error, entanglement, entwining ; chaidh e iomrall
orm, I missed it. *E.Ir.* imroll, mistake, aberration.
iomram, iomramh, imrum, *n. m.* rowing
(im + ràmh). iomradh (a *vbl. n.*) is
the form in *Lewis*, as if from the *O.Ir.*
imbrim. *E.Ir.* immram.
ion, in, *adv.* having great or fit reason or
cause ; *adj.* fit, befitting ; is ion duit
teicheadh, you have great reason to
scamper ; a *prefix,* signifying worthy,
befitting ; *cpds. :* ion-ghràdh, worthy
to be loved ; ion-mholta, praiseworthy.
ionad, inud, *n. m.* place, situation ; ionad
naomh, a holy place, a sanctuary.
O.Ir. inad, *locus.*
ionadh—c'iona, c'ionadh, whither ; for
co + ionad, what place.
ionaghlais. *See* eanaghlas.
ionaltair, inaltir, *v.* graze, pasture, as
cattle.
ionaltradh, inaltru, *vbl. n. m.* pasture,
pasturage ; act of pasturing, feeding,
grazing. *Also* inilt.
ionann, inun, *adv.* and *adj.* just so, all the
same, equally well, in like manner, in
a suitable manner ; is ionann sin is

mar a thachras dhuit, just so shall it
happen you ; is ionann sin, that is all
the same ; chan ionann a fhreagras
dà latha margaidh, two market days
do not correspond ; chan ionann a thig
an còta fada do na h-uile fear, the long
coat does not suit every one equally
well. *Also* ionnan. *O.Ir.* inonn, innon,
inon, inunn, " the same."
ionannachd, *n. f.* equality ; identity,
similarity, sameness ; equalisation.
ionannas, inanus, *n. m.* mediocrity.
ionar, *n. m.* coat, mantle. *O.Ir.* inar,
tunic.
ionbhruich, in-vrich. *See* eanraich.
ionchaibh, inchiv, *n. f.* entreaty, protection ; *dat. pl.* of *O.Ir.* inech ; " i n-
ionchaibh duine," for a person's sake,
protection.
iondraichinn, eendruchin, *n. m.* act of
engaging in battle. Cf. inntrinn.
ionga, ingu, *n. f., pl.* ìngnean, ìnean, the
nail, a claw, a hoof. *Also* ingne, *pl.*
ingnean, ìnean. *O.Ir.* inga, (finger)
nail. *Lat.* unguis.
iongantach, ing-untuch, *adj.* wonderful,
surprising, strange, extraordinary.
iongantas, iig-untus, *n. m.* wonder, surprise, miracle, astonishment, marvellousness.
iongar, ing-ur, *n. m.* pus, purulent
matter. *Also* ioghar, for in + gur
(*pus*).
iongarach, *a.* purulent.
iongarachadh, *vbl. n. m.* suppurating,
getting purulent ; act of suppuration.
iongaraich, *v.* suppurate ; dh'iongaraich
a chas, his foot suppurated. *Also*
iongraich.
ionghnadh, iongnadh, ee-unu, *n. m.* surprise, astonishment ; chan ionghnadh
leam, I am not at all surprised. *O.Ir.*
ingnád, ingnáth (" unwonted ").
ionmhainn, inu-vin, *a.* dearly beloved ;
is iomhuinn le gach neach a choslas,
every one is fond of his equal, birds of
a feather flock together. *O.Ir.* inmain,
dear, beloved.
ionmhas, inuvas, *n. m.* treasure, riches.
O.Ir. indmass, treasure.
ionmhasach, *a.* wealthy, rich.
ionmhasair, *n. m.* a treasurer.
ionmholta, in-voltu, *a.* praiseworthy.
ionnairidh, yunary, *n. f.* a watch, night-
watching ; space between sunset and
midnight.
ionnal, yoonul. *See* ionnlaid, wash, bathe.
Ir. indalim, I wash hands and feet.
P.H.
ionnaltoir, iunaltor, *n. f.* a bath. *See*
ionnlaid.
ionnas, ionns, yunus, *conj.* and *adv.* so
that, insomuch ; so much so ; ionnus

gun do theich e, so much so, that he
decamped. *O.Ir.* indas, *status, habitus.*
ionndas, yoondas, *n. m.* treasure ; " a
h-òr 's a h-ionndas," her gold and her
treasure. *O.Ir.* indmas, indbas, wealth.
ionndrainn, yoon-tren, *v.* miss ; *n. f.* act
of missing ; the thing amissing ;
object amissing ; am faca tu m' ionndrainn ? saw you the object amissing ?
tha mi 'g a ionndrainn, I am missing
him ; sometimes ionndraichinn ; có
tha thu ag ionndraichinn ? whom do
you miss ?
ionnlad, yoonlij, *n. m.* bathing. *O.Ir.*
indlat, washing.
ionnlaid, yoon-lij, *v.* bathe, wash.
ionnsachadh, yoonsuchu, *vbl. n. m.* learning, scholarship, education ; act of
learning, educating, teaching.
ionnsaich, yoonsich, *v.* learn, teach.
E.Ir. insaigim, I seek out, investigate.
=in + saigim (seek).
ionnsaigh, yoonsy, *n. f.* attack, assault,
a rush or dash ; thug e ionnsaigh orm,
he assaulted me ; thug mi an ionnsaigh, I made the attempt ; a dh'
ionnsaigh, *prep.* to. *O.Ir.* in + saigid,
sue, reach, attain ; ionnsaighim, I sue
for damages. *O'D.*
ionntag, yoontag, *n. f.* nettle. *See*
deanntag.
ionntlas, yoontlas, *n. m.* delight.
ionntraich, yoontrich, *v.* miss ; for ionn-
druinn.
ionracan, inrucan, *n. m.* the just, the
righteous, the honest man ; 'nuair a
throideas na meirlich thig an t-ion-
racan g'a chuid, when the thieves fall
out, the honest man gets his own.
ionracas, inrucas, *n. m.* innocence,
righteousness, sincerity. *O.Ir.* inrucus,
dignitas.
ionraic, inrig, *adj.* honest, just, upright ;
duine ionraic, an honest man. *O.Ir.*
inricc, *dignus.*
ioraltach, iraltuch, *a.* ingenious.
ioras, *adv.* below, down ; *opp.* of urad,
above.
iorball, irbul, *n. m.* a tail. *See* earball.
iorcallach, irculuch, *n. m.* a robust man,
Herculean.
iorgaill, irgul, *n. f.* a fray, a quarrel ;
uproar, skirmish. *Also* iorghuill.
O.Ir. irgal (air + gal), aur-gal.
iorgailleach, *a.* uproarious, quarrelsome,
fond of battles.
ìorna, ee-urnu, *n. m.* hank, skein.
iornalais, ee-urnalish, *n. f.* lumber.
iorpais, irpish, *n. f.* fidgeting.
iorrach, irach, *a.* quiet, undisturbed.
iorram, yoorem, *n. f.* an oar-song ; boat-
song, lament ; a plaintive monotonous
repetition.

ios, ees, *adv.* down ; **a nios**, from below ; **sios**, downwards. *O.Ir.* **iss, is,** *infra.* *O.Celt.* endsô-.

Iosa, ee-usu, *n. m.* our Saviour Jesus.

iosal, ēss'-ul, *a.* low, mean, humble ; **os iosal,** secretly. *O.Ir.* ísel.

iosgaid, isgij, *n. f.* the back of the kneejoint, hough, *poples. M.Ir.* iscait.

iosop, isop, *n. f.* hyssop. Phenician word.

iosp, isp, *n. m.* a tool used by a tinsmith. *Sc.* hesp.

iotadh, eetu, *n. m.* thirst. *O.Ir.* ítu, *gen.* itad. *O.Celt.* (p)êntotât. *Gr.* ἰότης.

iothlann. *See* iodhlann.

irbhinn, irvin, *n. f.* ; for **irghinn,** by *dissim.* fr. inghinn.

ire, eeru, *n. m.* earth, land, field ; " sguab de 'n ire fhìorghlan chruithneachd."

ire, eeru, *n. f.* progress, state ; **nach duilich leat m' ire !** do you not commiserate my plight ! ; **gu ire bhig,** nearly, almost ; or degree of growth, of completion ; *idiom :* 1. justify, " is tu chuireadh an ire do chainnt," 'tis you who would justify your word. 2. use, purpose, (min) " nach deach 's an ire chòir," meal that was used to no honourable purpose ; assurance, " cur an ire gur h-e bhiodh ann," assuring that it would be he ; declaring, proving, " cha chuir mi 'n ire e 'n dràsda," I shall not insist on it just now ; stimulating, " chuir thusa do nimh an ire," as for *you,* you plied your poison ; taunt, reproach, **cur an ire dha,** taunting him, reproaching him. *O.Ir.* hire, ire, *ulterior.*

ireachd, eerachc, *n. f.* maturity, completion.

ireapais, irapish, *n. f.* fidgets, nervous excitement, " stage fright."

iriosal, irisul, *a.* humble, unpresuming, unpretending. *M.Ir.* airísel, érbairt o guth airísil, he said in a low voice. *O.Ir.* air +ísel (*inferus*).

irioslaich, irus-lich, *v.* humble.

iris, irish, *n. f.* hamper-strap ; creel-strap ; braces. *M.Ir.* iris, strap. *Lism.L.*

iris, *n. f.* hen-roost. *Also* spiris.

iriseal, irishal, *a.* humble, retiring, unpretending, unostentatious.

irisleachadh, *n. m.* humiliation, debasement, degradation.

irislich, *v.* debase, humble, lower, degrade, humiliate.

irrinn. *See* irbhinn.

is, *conj.* and. *E.Ir.* is.

is, the indep. form of the assertive verb, pres. tense. It gives emphasis to the word next to it ; **tha an là blàth,** the day is warm ; **Is blàth an là,** the day is warm.

isbean, eeshben, *n. f.* sausage. *Also*

samhsair ; fr. *O.N.* íspen, sausage = í + spen ; fr. speni, a teat. *McB.*

ise, ishu, *pron.* emphatic form, she ; she (in particular).

iseal, eeshal, *adj.* low, humble. *O.Ir.* íssel, *inferus.*

isean, ishen, *n. m.* chick (of any bird) ; young seal, a kitten (*Suth.*) ; a brat.

isle, *n. f.* lowness, meanness, degree ; *compar.* of iosal, more or most humble or low.

isleachadh, eeshluchu, *vbl. n. m.* lowering, abasing, degrading ; humiliation.

isleachd, eeshluchc, *n.f.* degree of lowness.

islead, eeshlud, *n. f.* degree of lowness.

islean, ēsh'-lyan, *n. pl.* lower classes.

islear, *n. m.* the stormy petrel (?). Cf. aisleag.

islich, eeshlich, *v.* lower, humble.

isneach, eeshnuch, *n. f.* rifle, gun.

ist, isht, *inter.* hush ! hist !

ite, ih-tu, *n. f., pl.* **itean,** quill, feather ; fin ; **itean èisg,** fins of fish ; **itean geòidh,** goose-quills. *O.Ir.* ette, *pinna.*

iteach, ituch, *n. f.* plumage, fins.

iteachan, ituchan, *n. m.* bobbin.

iteag, *n. f.* a little feather ; act of flying ; **air iteig,** flying.

iteagaich, itaguch, *v.* fly like a bird.

itealaich, itulich, *n. f.* fluttering.

iteodha, *n. m.* hemlock.

ith, ich, *v.* eat, corrode. *O.Ir.* ithim, mando. *O.Celt.* (p)itô.

ith, corn. So *O.Ir. ceres ;* used only in *cpd. See* iodhlann.

itheanaich, ichunich, *n. f.* something to eat, feeding ; damage done by cattle.

ithte, ichtu, *vbl. a.* eaten, consumed.

iubhar, yoo-ur, *n. m.* yew-tree. *O.Ir.* ibar, *taxus,* yew.

iùbhrach, yooruch, *n. f.* a thing made of yew ; wherry, a barge, a stately woman.

iuchair, yoochir, *n. f., gen.* iuchrach, *pl.* iuchraichean, key ; part of spinningwheel. *E.Ir.* eochuir, eochraib écsi, keys of knowledge.

iuchair, yoochir, *n. f.* roe of fish, spawn. *Ir.* iuchair.

iuchar, yoochar, *n. m.* dog-days ; warmmonth. *Also* uthar, and iuthar.

iudmhail, yood-val, *n. m.* a fugitive.

iugh, *n. f.* a particular posture in which the dead are placed.

iùl, yool, *n. m.* guidance, land-mark, way, art. Cf. eòlas.

iùlchairt, yool-charst, *n. f.* ship's compass, a chart.

iullag, yoolag, *n. f.* a sprightly female ; *a.* iullagach.

iullagaiche, yoolagiche, *n. f.* lightness, airiness, sprightliness.

iùlmhor, yoolvur, *adj.* learned, wise.

iùlmhorachd, yool-voruchc, *n. f.* wisdom, art, sagacity.

iùnais, yoonesh, *n. f.* want. *Also* aonais. *O.Ir.* ingnáis, absence.

iunnrais, yoonresh, *n. m.* a stormy sky ; *a.* iunnraiseach.

iunntas, yoontus, *n. m.* wealth. *See* ionndas.

iurpais, yoorpesh, *n. f.* fidgeting, wrestling. Cf. farpuis. *Also* ireapais.

iursach, *n. f.* black, dark, suspensory.

iùthaidh, yoo-hi, *n. f.* arrow, gun. *See* fiùthaidh.

iutharn, yoo-hurn, *n. f.* hell. *Also* iurna (in *Suth.*). *M.Ir.* ithfern. *W.* uffern. *See* ifrinn.

L

The ninth letter of the Gaelic alphabet, named luis, the quicken-tree.

là, *n. m.* a day ; an là màrach, the morrow ; an là roimhe, the former day, " the other day." *O.Ir.* lae, laithe, lathe.

làb, *n. m.* day's labour. *Also* laib.

làbaire, làbiru, *n. m.* labourer.

làban, *n. m.* mire, dirt ; *a.* làbanach, labanta.

làbanach, *n. m.* a slovenly fellow, a drudge, a day-labourer.

labanachadh, *n. m.* act of drenching.

labh, llav, *n. m.* word, lip (rare).

labhair, lavir, *v.* speak, say on. *O.Ir.* labraim, I speak.

labhairt, lavurt, *vbl. n. f.* speech, delivery, or style of language ; is math an labhairt a tha aige, he has an excellent delivery or style of language ; speaking. *Ir.* labrae. *O.Celt.* (p)labro-.

labh-allan, *n. m.* a mythical animal, larger than a rat and very noxious, lives in deep pools.

labhar, *a.* loud, loquacious ; common in stream names. *W.* llafar, vocal.

labharra, lavuru, *adj.* boastful, noisy, loquacious, talkative.

labharrachd, *n. f.* loquacity, noisy boasting ; in poetry, contracted labhrachd.

labhra, laüru, labhrach, laüruch, *adj.* loquacious, speechifying, boastful ; cho labhra ris a' ghaoith, as noisy in speech as the wind.

labhrad, laü-rad, *n.m.* loudness, loquacity. *O.Ir.* labrad, speech.

labhradair, laüruder, labhraiche, laürichu, *n. m.* orator, speaker ; labhradair pongail, distinct orator.

labhras, laürus, *n. f.* laurel-tree.

lach, *n. f.* a wild duck, a widgeon ; lach-bheag, teal ; lach-bhinn, long-tailed duck ; lach-bhlàir, white-headed coot ; lach-bhreac, golden eye, a mallard ; lach-crann, teal ; lach dhubh, velvet scoter ; lach-eigir, dwarf duck ; lach-fhiacailleach, goosander ; lach-ghlas, gadwall ; lach-liath, long-tailed duck ; lach Lochlannach, lach mhór, eider duck ; a dunter-goose ; lach-sgumanach, crested duck ; lach uaine, a mallard. *E.Ir.* lacha, duck.

lach, *n. m.* a reckoning (at a tavern), expense.

lach, *n. f.* a laugh, a sudden loud laugh.

lachag, *n. f.* a little wild duck.

lachan, *n. m.* a hearty laugh ; thug e lachan gàire as, he burst into hearty laughter.

lachan, *n. m.* the common reed.

lachan nan damh, *n. m.* jointed rush, *juncus articulatus.*

lachar, *n. m.* a vulture ; any large bird of prey.

lachardaich, llach'-ard-ich, ·*n. f.* a loud continued laughter or repeated bursts of laughter. *Also* lachanaich.

lachdunn, lach-cun, *adj.* dun, swarthy. *E.Ir.* lachtna.

làd, *n. m.* a load, a burden ; làd bùrn, as much water as one can carry in two pails at a time.

lad, *n. m.* a mill lead ; fr. *Eng.* lead, lade.

làdach, *n. m., pl.* làdaichean, a volley.

ladar, *n. m.* a ladle ; fr. the *Eng.*

ladar-miot, *n. m.* scrimmage, a mêlée.

ladarna, *adj.* audacious, bold. *M.Ir.* latrand, robber. *O.W.* lleidr, a thief. *Lat.* latro, -onis.

ladarnachd, ladurnuchc, *n. f.* audacity.

ladarnas, ladurnus, *n. m.* audacity.

ladhar, lu-ur, *n. f.* toe, prong, claw, a hoof. *E.Ir.* ladar, toes, fork.

ladhrach, lur-uch, *a.* pronged, clawed, hooved.

lag, *adj.* feeble, faint ; *v. n.* faint, weaken ; lag air, he failed ; lag-mhisneachail, lag - chridheach, faint-hearted, chicken-hearted. *O.Ir.* lacc, weak. *O.Celt.* lakko-s.

lag (*gen.* luig), *n. m.* a cavity, hollow, any depression in landscape.

lagaich, lagich, *v.* faint, weaken.

lagan, *n. m.* little hollow, a dimple ; meal-receiver in a mill. *Also* leubhann.

làgan, làghan, *n. f.* flummery. *Also* cabhruich.

lagbheart, lag-viarst, *n. f.* a weak performance ; *a.* lag-bheartach.

lagchridheach, lag - chriyuch, *a.* fainthearted.

lagchuiseach, lag-chushuch, *a.* frail, weak.

lagh, *v.* forgive. *Ir.* laghadh, remittance. *O'R. E.Ir.* laaim, I throw, send. Cf. *Lat.* remitto. *Gr.* ἀφίημι.

lagh, *n. m.* law, right, order, method ; air lagh, a bow set for shooting.

laghach, lu-uch, *a.* fine, decent, kind ; duine laghach, a decent, kind man ; is laghach a fhuaradh e, he did pretty well ; is laghach an duine e, he is a fine or kindly man. Cf. *Lat.* lectus (chosen).

laghadair, lu-uder, *n. m.* spoon-mould. *Also* laphaid.

laghadh, *vbl. n. m.* act of bending, shaping, *e.g.* a plank for the bow of a boat ; act of setting a bow for shooting.

laghail, *a.* lawful, litigious ; nì laghail, a lawful thing ; duine laghail, a litigious person.

laghalachd, *n. f.* lawfulness, legality ; litigiousness.

làghan, *n. m.* sowens.

laghan, lu-an, *n. m.* a little ruler ; a guiding-stick used in making a net, to keep the meshes uniform in size. Cf. lagh, law.

laglamhach, lag-lavuch, *a.* weak-handed.

làib, lyb, *n. f.* mire ; slimy mud or clay.

làibeil, lybal, *adj.* miry, dirty, filthy.

laibhir, la-vir, *compar.* of labhar, noisy ; " bu laibhir na fuaim tuinne," more noisy than the roar of a billow.

laic, lyc, *n. m.* a moment ; " chan fhaigh mi laic chadail," not a wink of sleep do I get.

laidh, ly, *v. i. See* laigh.

Laidinnich, *v.* Latinise.

Laidionn, lajun, *n. f.* the Latin.

làidir, lājir, *adj.* compar. treasa, treise, strong, robust, powerful, fortified ; potent, ardent, intoxicating ; duine làidir, a strong man ; deoch laidir, intoxicating liquor. *E.Ir.* láidir, *robustus.*

laidireachd, lājiruchc, *n. f.* strength.

làidrich, lajrich, *v.* strengthen.

laige, lagu, *adj.* weaker.

laigh, ly, *v.* lie down, subside ; laigh e orm, he begged me ; laigh a' ghrian, the sun set ; laigh a' ghaoth, the wind subsided ; nach brèagha laigheas am bàta ! how beautifully the boat leans (to the breeze) ! *E.Ir.* laigim. *O.Ir.* lige, bed.

laighe, *n. f.* reclining, lying ; laighe-siùl, lying-in, child-bed ; laighe-chuige, lying-to (of a ship).

laight, lyt, *n. f.* shape, mould ; tha m' ad as a laight, my hat is out of its shape ; natural order, method ; cuir 'na laight e, put it in its natural order ; bogha air laight, a bow on the stretch.

laigse, lygshu, *n. f.* weakness, debility, feebleness, infirmity ; a fainting fit ; chaidh e an laigse, he fainted.

laimh, *v.* attempt, accomplish, venture.

laimhrig, laimrig, lamrig, *n. f.* landing-place, natural quay, or pier. *Also* lamraig. *O.N.* hlaδ-berg, and hlaδ-hamarr.

làimhseachadh, lyshuchu, *vbl. n. m.* handling ; trade, management ; làimhseachadh an nì sin, the management of that affair ; discussion, treatment of an argument.

làimhsich, lyshich, *v.* handle, manage, finger, treat, deal.

làine, lānyu, làinead, lānyud, *n. f.* fullness, degree of fullness, or completeness. *O.Celt.* (p)lānjā. *See* làn.

làinn, *n. f.* a corn-yard. *Also* lann.

lainnir, *n. f.* glitter, brightness, polish, sheen, fish - scales. *E.Ir.* lainderda. *O.Celt.* (p)lāndi-s. *See* lannair.

laipheid, lafaj, *n. f.* spoon-mould (for shaping horn spoons).

làir, *n. f., gen.* làrach, *pl.* làraichean, a mare. *O.Ir.* láir. *O.Celt.* (p)lārek-s.

lairceach, larciuch, *a.* stout, short-legged, fat.

lairceag, larciag, *n. f.* a short, fat woman.

làirig, lārig, *n. f.* pass between hills.

laisde, lashju, *a.* easy, in good circumstances.

laisgeanta, lashc - antu, *a.* fiery, fierce. So *Ir.*

laithilt, ly-hilt, *n. m.* a weighing (on scales).

lamarag, *n. m.* an awkward or cowardly fellow ; *a.* lamaragach.

lamban, *n. m.* milk curdled by rennet. *Also* slaman.

làmh, *v.* able, dare. *E.Ir.* lámaim. *O.Ir.* ro-laumur, ru-laimur, *audeo.*

làmh, làv, *n. f.* a hand, a handle, an attempt, or attack ; thug e làmh air, he attacked him ; tha e làimh rium, he is beside me ; mo làmhsa dhuitse, there is my hand, I can assure you ; làmh air làimh, " hand in glove " ; rug se air làimh oirre, he shook hands with her ; a' cumail làimh rithe, paying his addresses to her, *Sc.* in hands wi' ; dèan as do làimh e, do it at once, *Sc.* fra hand ; tha e an làimh, he is in custody ; gabh os làimh, undertake, assume ; tha iad ag iomairt an làmhan a chéile, they understand each other, there is a collusion between them. *O.Ir.* lám. *W.* llaw. *O.Celt.* (p)lāmâ.

làmhach, làv'-uch, *adj.* dexterous, masterly.

làmhach, *n. m.* 1. casting; volley of guns. 2. gleaning. *E.Ir.* lámach, casting.

làmhachair, lāvucher, *a.* ready-handed, handy.

làmhachas, lāvuchus, *n. m.* readiness to finger, snappishness; làmhachas-làidir, violence.

làmhachdradh, lāvach-cru, *n. m.* pawing, needless handling.

làmhag, *n. f.* a small hatchet. *Also* làmhadh, for làmh-thuagh.

làmhagan, *n. m.* fingering, handling; light work, odds and ends.

làmhaich, lāvich, *v.* finger, handle. So *Ir.*

làmhaidh, lāvy. *See* làmhag.

làmhaidh, *n. m.* the razor-bill, guillemot.

làmhainn, làv'-inn, *n. f.* a glove. *E.Ir.* lámind, glove.

lamhainnear, lāviner, *n. m.* a glover.

làmhairc, lāverc, *n. f.* right-hand stilt of a plough; corag, the left-hand stilt.

làmhanart, lāv-anurt, *n. f.* hand-towel. *Also* searbhadair.

làmhcharach, lā-chur-uch, *adj.* dexterous, ingenious.

làmhcheird, *n. f.* trade, handicraft.

làmhchlag, làv'-chlag, *n. m.* a hand-bell.

làmh-choille, *n. f.* a cubit.

làmhchrann, lā-chran, *n. f.* hand-staff of a flail. *Also* làmhcharan. *Ir.* lámhchara.

làmhfhail, lāv-al, *n. f.* a bracelet.

làmhghlais, làv'-ghlash, *v.* handcuff.

làmh-làidir, lāv-lājir, *n. f.* oppression.

làmhlorg, *n. f.* the handstaff of a flail.

làmhnain, lāv-nen, *n. f.* couple of a house, a pair; làmhnain phòsda, a married couple.

làmhrag, lāvrag, *n. f.* a slut, awkward woman.

làmhragan, *n. m.* awkward handling.

làmhraich, lāvrich, *v.* handle awkwardly.

làmh-sgrìobhaidh, lav-screevy, *n. m.* one's handwriting.

làmhspeic, *n. f.* hand-spike.

làmhuisge, làv-ushg'-à, *n. f.* sluice-handle.

lamraig, *n. f. See* laimhrig.

làn, *adj.* full, perfect; satiated; *n. m.* a full, fullness, repletion; the tide, flood-tide; rug an làn oirnn, the tide overtook us; pique; cha ruig thu leas a leithid de làn a ghabail as, you need not pique yourself as much on that; *adv.* completely, wholly, quite; tha làn fhios agam air sin, I know that quite well; làn cheart, quite right; làn-ùghdaras, full authority, plenipotentiary's authority; làn dhearbh, demonstrate; làn fhiosrach, fully certain; làn damh, a full-grown stag or hart; làn chothrom, ample justice, best opportûnity; làn chumhachd,

discretionary power, full authority; làn fhoighinteach, fully equal to, or capable of, fully competent. *O.Ir.* lán, *plenus. W.* llawn. *O.Celt.* (p)lāno-s.

lànachd, *n. f.* fullness, full.

lànadair, *n. m.* smith's mould-piece.

lànain, *n. m.* a married couple. *O.Ir.* lánamnas, *conjugium.*

lànan, *n. m.* roof couple.

langa, *n. f.* a ling. *O.N.* langa.

langadar, *n. m.* long red seaweed. *O.N.* lang + tre, long tree.

langaid, lang'-ăj, *n. f.* a fetter; a fetter which reaches from a fore to a hind foot. Cf. *Ir.* langpheitir. *Corm.*

langaid, langej, *n. f.* the guillemot.

langan, *n. m.* drawling bellowing, or lowing of deer or cattle.

langanaich, láng'-an-ich, *n. f.* continued bellowing or lowing of deer, etc.

langan-bràghad, l.-brā-ud, *n. m.* the windpipe, the weasand.

langar, *n. m.* a sofa, fetters; langar ileach, a lamprey.

langasaid, langusej, *n. f.* a couch, a settee.

langrach, *a.* fettered

làn-mara, *n. m.* flood-tide; seòl-mara, the tide.

lann, *n. f.* an inclosure, land. *See* iodhlann. *E.Ir.* land, area. *W.* llan, enclosure, church. *O.Celt.* landâ.

lann, laun, *n. f.* a blade, a sword, scales of fish; lannan is itean an èisg, the scales and fins of the fish; lann na sgine, the blade of the knife (or sword); lann-smig, a razor; lann-chuisle, a lancet. *O.Ir.* lann, *scama. O.Celt.* lamnâ.

lannach, *a.* full of blades; of scales of fish. *O.Ir.* laindech, scaly.

lannadh, *n. m.* putting to the sword, act of scraping (scales).

lannair, lanir, *n. f.* radiance, gleam; the phosphoric glitter of scales of fish in the dark, glitter of swords, etc.

lannrach, lanruch, *a.* gleaming, shining. *E.Ir.* lainderda, shining.

lannsa, laünsu, *n. f.* a lance; fr. the *Eng.*

lannsaiche, laünsichu, *n. m.* a lancer, a pikeman.

lanntair, launter, *n. m.* a landscape, beautiful side of country full of wood and arable land facing the sea; a lantern.

laoch, *n. m.* a hero, a champion. *O.Ir.* láech, a hero. *Lat.* laicus.

laochalachd, laochmhorachd, *n. f.* heroism.

laochan, *n. m.* a little hero, a term of endearment to a boy.

laochraidh, *coll. n. f.* a band of heroes; corps of reserve for emergencies. *O.Ir.* laíchrad, láechrad.

laodhan, *n. m.* pulp, as of potatoes or wood, a glutinous substance ; pith of wood. *Also* glaodhan. *Ir.* laodhan.

laogh, *n. m.* a calf ; a friend. *E.Ir.* lóeg, lóig. *O.Celt.* loigo-s.

laoidh, looy, *n. f.* a lay ; a hymn, an anthem. *O.Ir.* láed, lóid.

laoighcionn, lyciun, *n. m.* a calf-skin ; tulchan-calf, a stuffed calf-skin. Used also in a general sense of skin of any animal of the cow kind. *See* boicionn.

laoim. *See* laom.

laoineach, *a.* handsome, elegant. *See* loinn.

laoineach, *a.* handsome, elegant.

laoir, luir, *v.* drub most lustily.

laoireadh, luyru, *n. m.* *See* loireadh.

laom, *v.* lodge, fall (as corn). *M.Ir.* loem.

laom, *n. f.* a crowd, a multitude.

laom, *n. f.* a blaze. *O.N.* ljómi, ray.

laom-chrann, *n. m.* a main-beam or rafter.

laomsgair, *a.* 1. great, vast. 2. fierce, fiery. 3. abundant crop.

laoran, *n. m.* a person too fond of the fireside.

laosboc, laos-bock, *n. f.* gelded he-goat. *Also* eibhreann.

lapach, *a.* slim ; weak, benumbed, stammering, faltering.

lapachas, lapuchus, *n. m.* flabbiness, pliability, a faltering.

lapaich, làp'-ich, *v.* become benumbed ; weaken, discourage.

làr, *n. m.* a floor, ground floor, ground ; centre, gun éitein 'n a làr, without a kernel in its centre ; air làr, on the ground ; dol mu làr, going to nought ; *adj.* complete ; làr bhurraidh, a complete blockhead. *O.Ir.* lár. *W.* llawr. *O.Celt.* (p)lâro-.

làrach, *n. f.* stand or site of a building ; a building in ruins, a ruin ; battle-field ; a scar, an impression ; làrach fhiacal, mark of teeth. *O.Ir.* láthrach.

las, *v.* kindle, enrage, flash, sparkle. *E.Ir.* lassaim, flame.

las, *a.* loose, slack. Cf. *Lat.* laxus.

lasag, *n. f.* little flame, or blaze.

lasaich, làs'-ich, *v.* flag, lag, slacken.

lasail, lasal, *a.* inflammable.

lasair, làs'-ir, *n. f.*, *gen.* lasrach, a flame, a flash. *Ir.* lassar. *W.* llachar. *O.Celt.* laksar-.

lasanta, *a.* fiery, passionate.

lasantachd, làs-ant-uchc, *n. f.* fierceness.

làsdail, làsdal, *a.* imperious, boastful, saucy, lordly. So *Ir.*

lasdaire, lasdiru, lasgaire, lasgiru, *n. m.* a beau, a spark, a fop, a dandy, a young man. *Ir.* lasgaire.

lasganta, *a.* ardent, loud-voiced through anger.

lasgar, *n. m.* sudden noise.

lasgarra, *adj.* beauish, brave, fiery.

lasrach, *adj.* flaming, blazing. *E.Ir.* lassrach, flaming. *W.* llachar, gleaming.

lasraich, las'-rich, *n. f.* conflagration.

lath, lah, *v.* benumb, get benumbed. *Also* leith, tha thu air do leitheadh, you are quite chilled.

latha, la-u, *n. m.* a day. *See* là. *O.Ir.* láthe, laithe.

làthach, lā-huch, *n. f.* mire, clay. *E.Ir.* làthach. Cf. *W.* llaca. *O.Celt.* latâkâ.

lathailt, la-elt, *n. f.* mould, shape, way.

làthair, lā-hir, *n. f.* presence, existence, company, sight ; mach as mo làthair, get out of my presence ! ; a bheil e a làthair ? is he alive ? ; an làthair a chéile, face to face ; cum as an làthair, keep out of sight ; *adj.* present, living, remaining ; *n. f.* làithreachd, presence ; uile-làithreachd, omnipresence. *O.Ir.* láthar, lathair.

lathaisd, *n. f.* lath, lathing. Based on the *Eng.*

le, *prep.* with, by means of, in company ; in the interest of ; bhuail e i le cloich, he struck her with a stone ; tha e le ar càirdean, he is along with, in the interest of, or belongs to our friends. With *pers. pron.* : *sing.* 1. leam, with me ; 2. leat, with thee ; 3. *m.* leis, with him ; 4. *f.* leatha, with her. *Pl.* 1. leinn, with us ; 2. leibh, with you ; 3. leo, with them. *O.Ir.* la.

leaba, lab'-u, *n. f.* a bed, couch ; *gen.* leapa, of a bed ; *pl.* leapaichean, beds. *E.Ir.* lebaid, lepad, *lectus.*

lèabag, leubag, liabag, *n. f.* a flounder. *Also* leòbag.

leabaidh, liaby, *n. f.* a bed.

leabhar, lyō'-ur, *n. m.* a book, volume. *O.Ir.* lebor, lebur. *W.* llyfr. *Lat.* liber.

leabhar, *a.* long, clumsy. *O.Ir.* lebor, long.

leabharlann, lyō'-ur-lann, *n. f.* library ; *n. m.* a bookseller, a retailer of books.

leabhrach, lyō'-ruch, *n. f.* a library ; *adj.* bookish.

leabhradair, lyōr'-ud-er, *n. m.* a publisher, an editor, an author.

leabhraiche, lyōrichu, *n. m.* a librarian, a bookseller.

leabhran, lyōr'-an, *n. m.* a pamphlet. *O.Ir.* lebrán, *libellus.*

leac, *n. f.* a flag, slate, slab, tombstone. *Cpds. :* leac-lighe, a grave-stone ; leac-oighre, a slab of ice ; leac-shuaine, a tile ; leac-theallaich, a hearth-stone ; leac-ùrlair, pavement, floor. *O.Ir.* lie (later lia), *gen.* liac, a stone. *W.* llech.

leac, *n. f.* a grave. *E.Ir.* lecht. *Lat.* lectus.

leac, *n. f.* a cheek. *E.Ir.* lecc, *g.* leccan.

leacach, *a.* having large cheeks.

leacach, *a.* granite, in flags, flat; *n. f.* the bare summit of a hill; **teanga leacach,** a smooth tongue—beguiling tongue.

leacag, *n. f.* a little slab.

leacaich, leckich, *v.* pave with flags.

leacaid, leckej, *n. f.* slap on the cheek; an easy-osy woman.

leacainn, *n. f.* cheeks, forehead; **fo leacainn aoidheil,** under a friendly brow.

leacanaich, liack-anuch, *v.* get inseparably fond of, as a child to a nurse, etc.

leacann, lyechk′-unn, *n. f.* a sloping side of a hill or country. *Also* **leacainn.**

leacanta, lackantu, *adj.* stiff, formal, punctilious.

leachd, *n. f.* a grave, a tomb. *See* **leac.**

leaclach, liack-luch, *n. f.* granite.

lead, led, *n. m.* beautiful head of hair.

leadair, ledir, *v.* drub; mangle, abuse. *Ir.* letraim.

leadairt, ledart, **liodairt,** lidart, act of mangling, of severe mauling; tormenting. *Also* **leadraigeadh.**

leadan, *n. m.* sound thrashing.

leadan, ledan, *n. m.* a little pretty head of hair, locks of hair; a note in music; litany; the herb teazle.

leadanach, ledanuch, *adj.* adorned with beautiful locks; melodious; full of teazles.

leadarra, ledura, *a.* melodious.

leadarrachd, ledaruchc, *n. f.* harmoniousness.

leag, lyug, *v.* place or lay; put or throw down as a wrestler; pull down, fell; **leag e an tigh,** he pulled down the house; **leag e a′ chlach stéidh,** he laid the foundation-stone.

leagadh, lyugu, *vbl. n. m.* a fall; putting down, pulling down. *Also* **leagail.**

leagarra, *a.* smug, plausible, self-satisfied.

leagh, lyu, *v.* melt, liquefy. *O.Ir.* legaim, legad. *O.Celt.* legô. Cf. *O.N.* leka, drip. (*McB.*)

leaghach, *adj.* soluble.

leaghadair, lyu-ud-er, *n. m.* smelter.

leam, le-ŏom, *prep.* + *pron.,* 1st p., with me, having property in; **is leamsa so,** this is mine; with me; **falbh leamsa,** come with me; by my means, by me; **rinneadh leamsa sin,** that was made by me; in my interest, on my side; **agus thuirt e cò tha leamsa,** and he said, who is on my side? **is mór leam,** I think it too much; **is duilich leam,** I am sorry; **is math leam sin,** I am glad of that, in the opinion of; **ar leam,** I should suppose, I think.

leamh, lev, *a.* vexing, galling; **bu leamh leam,** I thought it galling; impudent, pertinacious, foolish, insipid, importunate; sarcastic.

leamhadas, lev′-ud-us, *n. m.* vexation.

leamhan, levan, *n. m.* the elm; elm-tree. *M.Ir.* lem.

leamhnach, levnach, *n. f.* tormenting.

leamhnach, *n. f.* common tormentil; blood-root, potentil.

leamhragan, lev′-rag-an, *n. m.* a stye. *Also* **leamhnagan** and **leamhnad.**

leam-leat, loom-let, *a.* pliable, pleasing everybody. "With me—with you."

lean, len, *v.* follow, pursue, chase; **lean sinn iad,** we followed them; stick to, adhere to, cleave to, continue, persevere; **lean e ri mo làmhan,** it adhered to my hands; **leanadh mo theanga ri mo chiobhall,** let my tongue cleave to the roof of my mouth; **ma leanas an uair tioram,** if the weather continue fair; **lean mar sin,** persevere like that; **na lean orm na′s fhaide,** don't importune me farther. *O.Ir* lenim.

lèana, lianu, *n. f.* a plain; green lawn, meadow. *Ir.* lian. *O.Celt.* leino-s.

leanabachd, len′-ab-achc, *n. m.* childhood, childishness, dotage.

leanabaidh, len′-ub-i, *adj.* childish, silly; **′na aois leanabaidh,** in his dotage.

leanabail, len′-ab-al, *adj.* child-like, spoiled.

leanaban, lenaban, *n. m.* an infant.

leanabanachd, *n. f.* childishness.

leanabanta, *adj.* puerile.

leanabantachd, *n. f.* puerility.

leanabh, len′-uv, *n. m.* a child; infant. *E.Ir.* lenab.

leanachd, len′-achc, *n. f.* pursuit, following, consequence.

leanailteach, leneltyuch, *a.* persevering, adhering. *See* **leantalach.**

leanmhuinn, lenu-vin, *vbl. n. f.* act of following a person, of a chief, claiming kindred; pursuing; kindred, clanship, bond of connection or tie of friendship; **tha leanmhuinn a thaobheigin eatorra,** there is some bond of connection or clan between them; **luchd-leanmhuin,** followers or kindred, vassals, minions. *O.Ir.* lenamain.

leanmhuinneach, lenvinuch, *adj.* following, consequent, adhering, having kindred claims; persistent.

leann, lyann, *n. m.* ale, beer; **leanntan,** humours of the body; **droch leanntan,** bad humours. *See* **lionn.**

leannaich, lănn′-ich, *v.* suppurate; more often **lionnaich.**

leannan, lann′-an, *n. m.* a lover, sweetheart. *E.Ir.* lennan, lendan.

leannanach, lann′-an-uch, *a.* amorous.

leannanachd, lann′-an-uchc, *n. f.* courtship, gallantry, blandishments, dalliance.

leann-dubh, lun′-dŭ, *n. m.* a settled

melancholy, or depression of spirits ; sadness, lowness of spirits.

lèantach, lēnt'-uch, *n. f.* country of plains ; a place abounding in plains ; an extensive plain. *Also* **leuntach**.

leantail, lent'-al, *vbl. adj.* sticking, following.

leantalach, len'-tal-uch, *adj.* adhesive, cohesive, persevering ; **leantalach air obair**, persevering at his work ; **tha 'n glaodh leantalach**, the glue is adhesive ; **leantalach air an uisge**, raining incessantly.

leantalachd, len'-t-al-uchc, *n. f.* adhesiveness, adherence ; ability to persevere unremittingly.

leapachan, lepuchan, *n. m.* a bed-fellow.

leapachas, lep'-uch-us, *n. m.* lodgement.

leapaich, lep'-ich, *v.* imbed ; lodge, as water, etc. ; **tha an t-uisge a' leapachadh an so**, the water is lodging here.

lear, *n. f.* the sea. *O.Ir.* ler, sea, ocean. *O.Celt.* lero-s.

learach, *n. f.* larch-tree. *Also* **learag**, làrag, and **lèireag**. *Sc.* larick.

learg, lerg, *n. f.* sloping face of a hill, or sloping place exposed to the sun and sea ; **learg an locha**, the slope which borders the loch ; *g.* and *d.* **leirg**. *E.Ir.* lerg.

learg, *n. m.* the black-throated diver.

leargainn, lergin, oblique case of **learg**.

leargan, *n. m.* slope of a hill.

leas, *n. m.* interest, advantage ; profit, need ; **cha ruig e a leas**, he need not trouble. *O.Ir.* less. *O.Celt.* (p)lesso-.

leas, less, (*a.*), *n. f.* thigh ; *gen.* leis ; **deasaich do chlaidheamh air do leis**, gird your sword on your thigh.

leas-, les, *prefix*, step-, by- ; **leas-ainm**, nickname. Cf. *O.Ir.* les-mac, *privignus. O.Celt.* lesso-makvo-s.

leasach, *n. m.* manure ; *a.* trifling, sheep-shanked.

leasachadh, lyās'-uch-u, *vbl. n. m.* act of manuring, improving ; **a' leasachadh an fhearainn**, manuring the land ; dung manure ; **a' cur amach an leasachaidh**, carting dung, or laying out manure ; improvement, increase ; **leasachadh tràth**, increase or addition of days ; **chan 'eil leasachadh air**, there is no help for it ; melioration, amends, reparation. *E.Ir.* lessaigim, I redress, reform.

leasachail, lesuchal, *adj.* making amends, ameliorating, repairing.

leasaich, lesich, *v.* improve, repair, make up deficiencies ; **leasaich an nì sin**, improve or amend that thing ; manure, dung, cultivate ; **leasaich am fearann**, manure the land.

leasainm, les-enum, *n. m.* a nickname.

leasan, lesan, *n. m.* a lesson.

leasathair, *n. m.* a stepfather. *Also* **oide**.

leasdair, lesder, *n. m.* a vessel ; a lamp.

leasg, *a.* lazy. *O.Ir.* lesc, *piger. W.* llesg. *O.Celt.* lasko-s. *O.N.* löskr, weak, idle. (*McB.*)

leasmhac, *n. m.* a stepson.

leasmhàthair, *n. f.* stepmother. *Also* **muime**.

leasnighean, *n. f.* a stepdaughter.

leasphiuthar, *n. f.* stepsister.

leasraidh, *n. pl.* the loins.

leastar, *n. m.* a cup, vessel, boat. *O.Ir.* lestar. *W.* llestr. *O.Celt.* lestro-.

leat, let, *prep.* le + *pron. suf.* 2 *sing. m.* in thee, with thee, in your company, in your opinion. *See* **le**.

leatach, *a.* remote, isolated = **leth** + **taobhach**.

leath, le, *n. m.* half. *See* **leth**.

leatha, la, *prep.* le + *pron. suf.* 3 *sing. f.* along with her ; with her. *See* **le**.

leathach, *a.* half ; **leathach slighe**, half-way ; **leathach làn**, half-full.

leathachas, le-huchus, *n.m.* partiality, unfairness, injustice ; **na dèan leathachas sam bith air**, show him no partiality.

leathad, lya-ud, *n. m., gen.* **leothaid**, *pl.* **leothaidean**, a slope, a declivity ; **a' dol le leathad**, declining, descending, falling down hill.

leathag, le-hag, *n. f.* a plaice, a flounder. *E.Ir.* lethech, flounder.

leathan, le-hun, *adj.* broad. *Compar.* na's **leithne**, na's **leatha**, broader. *O.Ir.* **lethan**. *O.W.* litan. *O.Celt.* letano-s.

lèathanach, *n. m.* hoar-frost.

leathar, le-hur, *n. m.* leather. *E.Ir.* lethar, leather. *Also* human skin (*P.H.*). *W.* lledr. *O.Celt.* létro-. *O.N.* leðr. *A.S.* leðer. *M.H.G.* lëder.

leathnaich, *v.* spread, flatten. *E.Ir.* lethnaigim.

leathoir, le-hor, *n. f.* suburb, border ; a leaning to one side.

leathoireach, le-horuch, *a.* remote, lonely, handicapped.

leathrach, le-ruch, *n. m.* tanned leather.

leathtaobh, le-tuv, *n. m.* one side ; **chaidh e leathtaobh**, he went aside.

leatrom, leh-trum, *n. m.* pregnancy, state of being pregnant, a burden, a disadvantage.

leatromach, leh-trumuch, *adj.* pregnant, with child, in the family way ; burdensome.

leibh, *prep.* le + *pron. suf.* 2 *pl.* along with you, by means of you. *See* **le**.

léibh, lēv, *v.* levy, lift ; fr. the *Eng.*

léibhidh, lēvy, *n. f.* a race, a swarm, multitude, levy.

leibid, lebij, *n. m.* a trifle, dirt, bad luck ; a dwarfish fellow.

leibideach, lebijuch, *adj.* paltry, trifling, bungling.

leibideachd, *n. f.* paltriness, a bungling.

leid, lej, *n. m.* 1. a green nook, or patch. 2. a shakedown, a temporary bed (made on the floor).

leideach, lejuch, *a.* strong, shaggy. *O.Ir.* létenach, *audax*.

léidigeadh, lējigu, *n. m.* act of convoying. Cf. "leading" (of corn), fr. *Eng.*

leidir, lejir, *v.* drub most lustily.

leig, lig, *v.* permit, allow, let be, let run ; incite a dog to the chase, broach, fire ; lance, commence raining ; leig dhà falbh, permit him to go ; leig dhomh, let me alone ; lay, join as in joiner-work ; leig fuil, let blood ; leig urchair, fire with the gun ; leig an lionnachadh, lance the tumour ; milk ; leig an crodh, milk the cattle ; tha an latha a' brath leigeil fodha, the day is likely to rain (*Lewis* = the day is about to improve) ; leig am buideal, broach the cask ; leig na coin ann, set the dogs on him ; leig ort, pretend. *O.Ir.* léiccim, lécim. *O.Celt.* leinqio. *Lat.* linquo.

léig, lēg, *n. f.* a muddy puddle.

léig, *n. f.* a gem, precious stone. Cf. leogan, a pebble. *See* leug.

leigeadh, ligu, *vbl. n. m.* act of permitting, urging, etc.

léigeard, léigheart, lēgart, *n. f.* leaguer, a siege.

leigeas, *n. m.* cheek, an abnormal jaw-bone, jaw (in contempt). *O.Ir.* lecco, maxilla. *O.Celt.* likkòn-.

leigeil, ligel, *vbl. n. f.* act of letting, permitting, etc.

léigh, lēy, *n. f.* medicine.

léigh, *n. m.* a physician, surgeon, doctor. *O.Ir.* liaig, *medicus*.

léigheann, leyun, *n. m.* reading, learning. *O.Ir.* fer legind, a reader, a professional " reader." *Lat.* lego, legendum.

leigheas, lyu-us, *vbl. n. m.* a cure, remedy, medicine ; act of healing, curing, remedying. *E.Ir.* leges, healing.

leigheasach, leigheasail, lyu-usuch, *adj.* medicinal, curing, remedial.

leighis, lyu-ish, *v.* cure, heal, remedy.

leighiste, *vbl. a.* healed, cured.

léigh-loisg, ley-loshc, *v.* cauterise.

leigte, *vbl. a.* lanced, running, etc.

léine, lēnu, *n. f., pl.* léintean, a shirt ; shroud ; leine-bhàis, léine-mhairbh, shroud, winding-sheet ; léine chaol, a white shirt ; leine-chreis, a privy counsellor, a confidant ; a chief's body-guard, for léine-chneas, shirt next the skin. *E.Ir.* léne. *O.Celt.* laknet-. *Lat.* linum.

leinn, leyn, *prep.* le + *pron. suf.* 1 *pl.* along with us, in our company ; leig leinn, let us alone ; thalla leinn, come along with us. *See* le.

léinteach, lēntyuch, *n. f.* shirting.

léir, lēr, *adj.* obvious, evident ; *imp. v.* see, behold, perceive, understand ; cha léir domh, I cannot see, it is not obvious to me ; is léir a bhuil, the result is obvious. *O.Ir.* léir, conspicuous.

léir, *adj.* whole, all, every ; gu léir, wholly, altogether, completely, utterly. *M.Ir.* léir (complete). *W.* llwyr. *O.Celt.* leiri-s.

léir, *v.* hurt, torment, suffer.

léirchreach, *n. f.* utter devastation, calamity.

léireadh, lēru, *vbl. n. m.* tormenting, torturing ; act of the severest mental pain, inward torture.

leirg. *See* learg.

léirist, *n. f.* an awkward person, foolish person, slut. *Also* leithrist.

léirsgrios, lēr - sgris, *v.* utterly ruin ; *n. f.* utter destruction, utter ruination, devastation.

léirsinn, lēr-sin, *n. m.* eye-sight, vision, sight, perception, clear conception ; act of perceiving, understanding, seeing.

leirsinneach, *adj.* capable of perceiving, sharp sighted, discerning.

leirsinneachd, *n. f.* perfection of vision, quick perception, intelligence.

leirtheas. *See* cota-bàn.

leis, lesh, *n. f.* thigh. *O.Ir.* less.

leis, *adj.* lee, leeward, larboard ; air an taobh leis, on the larboard side ; am fearann leis, the land to leewards, lee land, leeward land ; leig leis ! slack sheet ! leis oirnn, to leeward of us ; cum leis oirnn, keep to leeward of us.

leis, lesh, *prep.* le + *pron. suf.* 3 *sing. m.* along with him, with it, in his company, being his property or right ; by means of, with what, down hill, down the stream ; a' dol leis, going along with him ; leis fhéin, by himself ; leis an t-sruth, down the stream ; cò leis thu ? whose son or daughter are you ? cò leis a nì thu e, with what (means) shall you do it ? on account of ; leis a' chabhaig, on account of the hurry ; is aithreach leis, he regrets ; leis a' bhruthaich, down the hill. *See* le.

leisbheirt, lesh-verst, *n. f.* armour of the thigh.

leiscioball, lesh-ciubul, *n. m.* a minion, vassal ; a creature.

leisdear, leshjer, *n. m.* an arrow-maker.

leisg, leshc, *adj.* lazy, indolent, slothful ; loath, reluctant, unwilling ; is leisg leam, I am loath ; *n. f.* laziness, sheer indolence, sloth, slothfulness ; cha dèan làmh na leisge beairteas, the hand of sloth maketh not rich. *See* leasg.

leisgear, lesh-cer, leisgean, *n. m.* a sluggard ; imich chum an t-seangain, a leisgein, go to the ant, thou sluggard.

leisgeul, leshc-al, *n. m.* excuse, apology ; gabh mo leisgeul, pardon me ; pretence ; chan 'eil ann ach leisgeul, it is only a pretence. leth + sgeul, a half-story, a lame story.

leisgeulach, *adj.* shuffling, evasive, pretending ; excusable.

leisgeulachd, *n. f.* habits of pretending or evading ; evasiveness.

leith, leh, *n. f.* the half (*see* leth) ; side, share, interest, charge ; air leith, apart, separately ; leith slighe, leitheach slighe, half-way ; troigh gu leith, a foot and a half ; an leith as mò, the majority, the greater part ; somewhat ; leith chruinn, somewhat round. *O.Ir.*

ledmarb, half-dead ; *gl.* emortuum.

leitheadh. *See* lathadh.

leithid, le-hij, *n. m.* match, equal, like, compeer, a fellow ; is annamh a leithid, his match is seldom met with ; leithidean a chéile, the very patterns of each other. *E.Ir.* lethet, the like.

leithne, leh-nu, lethe, *degree* of leathan ; na's leithne, broader ; broadness.

leitir, leytir, *n. f.*, *gen.* leitreach, side of a hill, an extensive slope or declivity, regularly sloping to water. *E.Ir.* lettir. *O.Celt.* lettrek-.

lén, *n. m.* woe, misfortune. *Also* leun. *E.Ir.* lén.

leò, lyō, *prep.* + *pron.* along with them ; ar leò, they thought, they were of opinion.

leòb, liòb, *n. f.* an ugly slice or piece of anything ; a patch of cultivated land ; *v.* tear unmercifully into shreds. *M.Ir.* ledb.

leobhar, lyō'-ur, *adj.* long, clumsy. *See* leabhar.

leòcach, *a.* sneaking, low ; proud, disdainful.

leòdag, *n. f.* a slut, prude, flirt.

leòg, leōg, *v.* fag on the stomach ; *n. f.* a marsh. *Also* leòig, a ditch, morass.

leògach, lyōg-uch, *adj.* marshy.

leogach, *a.* hanging loosely, slovenly ; affected ; affected in speech.

leogan, *n. m.* a pebble, a small stone. *O.Ir.* lecán, a pebble, *lapillus.*

leóghann, leómhann, lyō-unn, *n. m. f.* lion ; ban-leóghann, lioness ; *oftener* leómhann bhoireann, "female lion." *E.Ir.* léu, léo. *W.* llew. *Lat.* leōnem. *O.Celt.* leô.

leoghar-lonn, *a.* fierce-spirited, haughty and heroic.

leòinte, liōntu, *vbl. a.* wounded, painful.

leòir, liōr, *n. f.* sufficiency, enough, a

bellyful ; fhuair mi mo leòr, I have got enough. *O.Ir.* lór, leór, lour ; *gl. sufficiens.* Z^2.

leòlach, *n. m., pl.* leòlaichean, the globe flower. *Cameron.*

leòm, liōm, *n. f.* drawling pronunciation.

leòmach, *adj.* drawling in talk.

leòmann, lūmun, *n. f.* a moth.

leòn, liōn, *v.* wound, gall, pique, grieve ; *n. m.* wound, grief, vexation.

leòr. Same as leòir.

leòra, *interj.* expr. of asseveration (perhaps for leabhar, swearing by " the book ").

le-san, le-sun, *prep. pron.* (for le + esan), along with him, accompanying him, in his opinion ; is leòr lesan, he thinks it enough ; is beag lesan, he thinks it too little.

leth, llé, *n. m.* side, half ; leth ris, next his skin (of clothing) ; tha léine shìoda leth ris, he has a silk shirt next his skin. *O.Ir.* leth. *O.Celt.* lctos-. *Lat.* latus.

leth-amadan, *n. m.* half-fool (male).

leth-amaid, *n. f.* half-fool (female).

lethbhodach, *n. m.* half a mutchkin.

lethbhreac, *n. m.* match, copy, facsimile.

lethcheann, *n. m.* the cheek.

lethlamh, *n. f.* one hand ; air leth-laimh, on one hand. *Ir.* fer lethlamha, one's right-hand man. *C.C.*

lethlinn, *n. m.* halfling, a half-wit.

lethoin, *n.* twins. *Also* leth-aoin.

lethoir, *n. m.* border, side, a slant.

lethoireach, *a.* lop-sided, lonely, remote, handicapped.

leubh, lēv, dial. for leugh.

leubhaidh, *coll. n.* total stock on a village.

leubhann, *n. m.* meal-floor of mill, platform for quern. *E.Ir.* lebend, deck, or scaffold.

leud, lēd, liad, *n. m.* breadth ; leud ròine, hair's-breadth ; air fad is air leud, in length and breadth. Cf. *O.Ir.* leithne, *latitudo.* *O.Celt.* letanjâ.

leudaich, *v. n.* widen, expatiate.

leug, lēg, *n. f.* lye, or ashes and water for bleaching.

leug, *n. f.* a precious stone. *Ir.* leug, a diamond. *O.Ir.* lia, *gen.* liacc.

leug, *n. f.* a lily. *Carm.G.*

leugach, *a.* drawling, sleugach.

leuganach, *a.* gleaming.

leugh, *v.* read, lecture, explain ; chan 'eil math dhomh a bhi leughadh sin duitse, it serves no end to read that to you ; a' leughadh a chall is a chunnart, expatiating on his loss and danger ; a' leughadh an eagail, anticipating dread. *Lat.* lego.

leughadair, lēvuder, *n. m.* reader.

leughadh, lĕvu, *n. m.* reading, lecturing; reading, explaining, expounding, expatiating.

leug-thàlaidh, *n. f.* loadstone.

leum, lĕm, *v. i.* jump, spring, leap, frisk, skip, start, fight, quarrel; **leum iad air a chéile**, they fought, they quarrelled; *n. m.* a jump, leap, spring; a spate; animal semen, an emission. *O.Ir.* **léimm**, *saltus*; fr. **lingim**, *salio.* *W.* **llamu**. *O.Celt.* lengmen-.

leum (an **éisg**), *n. f.* skin eruption caused by eating fish.

leumachan, *n. m.* a frog.

leumadair, lemuder, *n. m.* the size of salmon between the grilse and fullgrown salmon; dolphin; a small whale; **leumadair feòir**, a grasshopper. *Also* **leumadair uaine**.

leum-chrann, *n. m.* honeysuckle. *See* **iadhshlat**.

leumhann, lĕv′-ānn, *n. m.* *See* **leubhann**.

leumraich, lĕmrich, *n. f.* frisking, skipping. *Also* **leumnaich**.

leum-uisge, lĕm-ushcu, *n. m.* waterfall.

leus, lias, *n. m.* blink, glimmer, ray of light; **chan ′eil leus soluis an so**, there is not a ray of light here; a torch used in fishing salmon at night; a blister. *O.Ir.* **léss**, light; **fer brithe lésboiri**, man who carries a taper. *Wb.* 25.

leus, *n. m.* chafing, blister; **mil air do bheul ged robh leus air do theanga**, honey on your lips, though there should be a blister on your tongue; a cataract or speck on the eye.

leusaich, lĕsich, *v.* blister, raise blisters.

leus-teine, lĕs-tenu, *n. m.* firebrand.

lì, *n. f.* colour, tinge, hue, gloss, gloss of oil on surface of water. *O.Ir.* **lí, líi**. *W.* **lliw**. *O.Celt.* lìvos-.

lia-, *n. f.* a stone; used only in composition. *O.Ir.* **lia**, *gen.* **liacc**. *O.Celt.* lêvink-.

liabhach, lee-avuch, *a.* wide-open horns (**gròbach** is narrow, close-set horns).

liabhadh, lee-avu, *n. m.* spreading out, as benumbed fingers.

liacradh, lee-acru, *n. m.* act of rough plastering.

lia-fàil, *n. f.* stone of fate, of destiny (now in seat of coronation chair).

liagh, lee-u, *n. f., gen.* **léigh**, a ladle, an oar-blade, a baking-board. *O.Ir.* **liag**. *O.Celt.* leigâ. *Lat.* ligula.

liagh, *n. m.* physician. *O.Ir.* **liaig**, *medicus*.

liaghag, *n. f.* broad top of tangle.

liath, lee-uh, *a.* grey, grey-haired, greyheaded, mouldy; *v. i.* become grey, turn grey, mould, get mouldy; **liath e**, his head got grey. *W.* lwyt. *E.Ir.* **liath**. *O.Celt.* (p)leito-s.

liathag, lee-u-hag, *n. f.* a salmon trout.

lia-thàil, lee-u-hāl, *n. m.* loadstone.

liathanach, lee-u-hanuch, **liath-cheannach**, *n. m.* grey-headed man.

liathchearc, lee-u-cherc, *n. f.* a heath hen, female of the black grouse or blackcock.

liathghlas, *adj.* greyish.

liathghorm, *adj.* light blue, lilac.

liathlus, lee-u-loos, *n. m.* mugwort.

liathnach, lee-u-nuch, *n. m.* hare- or hoar-frost. *Also* **liath-reothadh**.

liathra, *n. m.* a rotating machine for winding skeins of yarn. *O.Ir.* **liathraim**, I roll, revolve. *See* **clach-liathra**.

liath-reodh, "grey frost" = *E.Ir.* **liath** +**réod**. *O.Ir.* **reo, réud**.

liathrosg, lia-rosc, *n. m.* the bird fieldfare; *pl.* **liath-ruisgean**. Cf. *W.* **socan lwyd**.

liathruisgean, *coll. n.* months of March and April; season of scarcity of food and fodder.

lid, lij, *n. m.* a word, syllable.

ligeach, leeguch, *a.* sly, slow, deliberate (of walk, or movement). *Also* **lìogach**.

lighe, leeyu, *n. f.* flood. *O.Ir.* **lie**.

lighe, *n. f.* in *cpd.* **leac-lighe**, a bed, a grave. *O.Ir.* **lighe**, grave. *O.Celt.* legio-.

lighich, lee-ich, *v.* doctor, lance, let blood.

lighiche, *n. m.* a physician, a doctor, a surgeon; *pl.* **lighichean**, doctors. *O.Ir.* **líaig**, *pl.* lege. *O.Celt.* liagi-.

lìghlais, *a.* pale-coloured; fr. **lì**, sheen.

lìnig, leenig, *n. f.* a lining; fr. *Eng.*

lìnig, *v.* line clothes.

linn, leen, *n. f.* a generation, age, ministration, incumbency or time in office, race, offspring; family; **ri linn do sheanmhair**, during the time of your grandmother, *i.e.* long, long ago; **is iomadh linn a chuir thu romhad**, you sent many a generation before you; **deireadh linn**, youngest, last of a family; **anns na linntean deireanach**, in the latter days; **o linn gu linn**, from generation to generation. *O.Ir.* **lind**, period, time; **rem linn**, in my time.

linne, lĕenu, *n. f., pl.* **linneachan**, a pool, a mill-dam, a lake, a sound, a channel, a bay; **a′ dol thar na linne**, crossing the channel; **an linne rosach**, the Sound of Jura; lit. the channel of disappointment, it being very ill to navigate. *O.Ir.* **lind**, liquid. *W.* llynn. *O.Celt.* lendu-.

linnean, *n. m.* shoemaker's thread.

lìnnich, leenich, *v.* line, as clothes; sheath, as a vessel; *n. f.* layer; a lining, sheathing; a line, a note, a card in writing; **a′ lìnnich phòsaidh**, marriage-line; **cuir lìnnich da ionn-**

saigh, drop him a card; linnich mu
seach, layer about; a brood or dozen
of eggs. *Also* linig.
linnseach, lēēnshuch, *n. f.* shrouds,
canvas.
liob, lib, *n. f.* a blubber-lip. *See* sliop.
liobach, libuch, *a.* protruding lips.
liobarnach, liburnuch, *a.* slovenly, awkward.
liobasta, libustu, *a.* slovenly, clumsy. *See*
sliobasta.
liobh, leev, *n. f.* slimy substance like
blood on the surface of water. *Also*
lith.
liobhair, leever, *v.* deliver, hand over,
resign.
liobhairt, livart, *n. f.* delivery, resignation.
liòbhan, liōvan, *v.* fawn upon one (as a
dog).
liobharra, leevara. *See* liomharra.
liobhragach, leevraguch, *n. f.* kind of sea-
lichen, or seaweed of a greenish
colour.
liobhraigeadh, leerigu, *vbl. n. m.* act of
delivering, deliverance, fr. the *Eng.*
liod, lid, *n. m.* a lisp, stammer.
liodach, liduch, *adj.* stammering.
liodaiche, lidichu, *n. m.* stammerer,
stutterer, lisper; impediment of
speech.
liogadh, leegu, *vbl. n. m.* act of sharpening.
liomh, leev, *v.* put to the grinding-stone,
polish, burnish; clach liomhaidh or
liomhain, a grindstone. *E.Ir.* limtha.
liomhaidh, leevay, *a.* polished, shining.
liomhan, leevan, *n. m.* a file. Cf. *Lat.*
lima, a file.
liomharra, leevuru, *a.* glossy, polished.
liomhta, *vbl. a.* polished.
lion, lee-un, *n. m.* lint, flax; a net, a
snare; lion làn èisg, net full of fish.
O.Ir. lín. *O.Celt.* līnu-. *O.W.* llin.
lion, *n. m.* a quantity, a portion, a
number; a lion cuid is cuid, by
degrees; biadh le lion de annlan, food
with its share of condiments. *O.Ir.*
lín, *pars, numerus.*
lion, *v.* fill, satiate, replenish, completely
please or satisfy; flow as the tide;
lion an soitheach, fill the dish; tha e
lionadh, the tide is coming in. *O.Ir.*
línaim. *O.Celt.* (p)lênô.
lionachan, leenuchan, *n. m.* a filler, a
funnel.
lionadair, liunuder, *n. m.* filler.
lionadh, liunu, *vbl. n. m.* act of filling,
flowing, answering expectations, re-
plenishing, satiating; the reflux of
the tide.
lionanaich, leenenich, *n. m.* green slimy
grass growing in still water.

lionmhor, leenvur, *a.* numerous.
lionmhorachd, *n. f.* numerousness, multiplicity, great abundance.
lionn, lyunn, *n. m.* humour (in the
system).
lionn, leann, *n. m.* liquor, ale, beer;
eadarra-lionn, submerged, but not on
the bottom; " between two liquors,"
i.e. the top and bottom. *O.Ir.* lionn,
lindu, liquid.
lionnachadh, *n. m.* act of suppurating.
lionnaich, *v.* fester, suppurate. *O.Celt.*
linno-s.
lionn-dubh, *n. m.* melancholy, dejection,
sadness.
lionn-tàthaidh, *n. m.* cement, the animal
spirits.
lionobair, *n. f.* network.
lionradh, *n. m.* gravy, juice, washy
liquid.
lionrath, *n. m.* sharpening by grinding.
Also clach‑liarath, c.‑riarath, c.‑
sniarath. *See* liathra.
liontach, liuntuch, *a.* satiating.
liontachd, *n. m.* satiety; fullness;
quality of filling by eating but little.
liop, leep, *n. f.* a lip; *a.* liopach. *Eng.*
liopaire, leepiru, *n. m.* a person with
thick lips.
lios, lis, *n. m.* enclosure, garden; fionlios, vineyard. *Also* leas. *E.Ir.* liss
and less, enclosure, habitation, whose
grounds were enclosed by a fortified
wall. *W.* llys, hall, court.
lios, *n. m.* a press; a fuller or a printer's
press; a mangle.
liosadair, *n. m.* gardener; a printer, a
pressman.
liosair, lisir, *v.* press, as cloth; print,
mangle, drub most heartily; liosairte,
smoothed, pressed.
liosda, lisdu, *adj.* slow, lingering, importunate, getting more intrusive the
more one gets of bounty. *E.Ir.* lista,
slow.
liosdachd, *n. f.* importunity, greed;
tediousness, slowness.
liosraig, *v.* smooth (with an iron), press
(cloth).
liotachd, leetachc, *n. f.* lisping, stammering; *a.* liotach.
lip, leep, *n. m.* lip. *Eng.*
lipin, leepin, *n. m.* a lippie, one-fourth of
a peck.
lir, *coll. n.* a litter, whelps, pigs. *E.Ir.*
lir, *a.* much, numerous.
lireagach, leeraguch, *n. f.* green weed
growing in stagnant water.
lirean, *n. m.* marine fungus, green stuff
growing in stagnant water.
lit, leet, *n. f.* porridge; fuairlit, cataplasm. *E.Ir.* littiu. *O.Celt.* littiôn-.
litir, leetir, *n. f.* (*gen.* litreach, *pl.* litrich-

ean), a letter ; an epistle. *O.Ir.* liter. *Lat.* littera.

litrich, leetrich, *v.* letter, print.

liubhair, liuvir, *v.* deliver. *Lat.* libero.

liubhairt, liùbhradh, liuvurt, *n. m.* delivery.

liùg, lioog, *n. f.* a lame hand, foot ; *v.* crouch (hiding or stalking), creep, sneak, bend.

liùgach, *a.* lame of hand ; *n. f.* an unhandy female ; a drab.

liugach, *a.* whipped-cur look, drooping ears, " hang-tail."

liùgaire, lioogiru, *n. m.* an unhandy fellow ; one with a lame hand ; a sneak.

liugaire, *n. m.* a soft, cowardly fellow.

liùgha, lioou, *n. f.* a lythe.

liùghag, *n. f.* a doll ; leanabh-liùghaig, a doll, a "false" baby. *Ir.* luag. *O.N.* ljúga, to lie ; ljügr, a liar.

liùnastainn. *See* lunasd.

liu-ruaig, *n. f.* a bounding chase, utter rout. liu (intens.) + ruaig (rout).

liutha, liuthad, *a.* several, many a, often ; a liuthad uair, how often ; a liuthad fear, the number of men (severally). *O.Ir.* lia, the many.

liuthail, *v.* bathe.

lò. *See* là, day.

lòb, *n. m., pl.* lòban, a puddle.

lobair, lobir, *v.* draggle in the mire.

lòban, *n. m.* a hurdle, a creel for drying corn, wooden frame inside corn stack ; basket peat-cart. *O.N.* laupr, creel, frame.

lòbanach, *a.* draggled ; fr. lòb, puddle.

lobh, lò, *v.* rot, putrify. *O.Ir.* lobaim, I decay ; *also* logaim.

lobhadh, *vbl. n. m.* act of decaying, rotting. *O.Ir.* lobad, to rot.

lobhar, lò'-ur, *n. m.* a weakling, sickly person, a leper. *O.Ir.* lobar, lobur, *infirmus. O.Celt.* lobro-s. *O.W.* lobur-.

lobhta, *vbl. a.* putrid, smelling.

lobhta, lòt'-u, *n. f.* loft, gallery. *O.N.* lopt.

lòbrachan, *n. m.* a draggle-tail.

lobrogan, *n. m.* a drenched, smeared fellow.

locair, lockir, *n. f.* a plane ; *v.* plane. *O.N.* lokarr. *A.S.* locer.

loch, *n. f.* a lake ; arm of the sea. *E.Ir.* loch, *lacus. O.Celt.* laku-. *Lat.* lacus.

lochan, *n. m.* a pool ; pond.

lochd, *n. m.* harm, hurt, mischief, crime, evil, fault ; a momentary sleep. *O.Ir.* locht, *crimen.*

lochdaich, *v.* hurt, harm, blame.

lochdan, *n. m.* a short sleep ; a nap. So *Ir.*

Lochlann, lochlin, *n. f.* Norway, Scandinavia ; righ Lochlainn, the king of Norway.

lochlannach, loch'-llann-uch, *adj.* Danish ; *n. m.* a Dane ; *n. f.* a widgeon.

loch-léin, lochlen, *n. f.* the groin ; flank of a beast. *Also* loch-bhléin.

lochraidh, *n. pl.* cattle ; eachraidh is lochraidh, horses and cattle.

lòchran, *n. m.* a torch, a light, a lantern. *O.Ir.* lócharn, a light, lamp. *O.Celt.* loukarnâ.

locradh, lockru, *vbl. n. m.* planing.

lod, *n. m.* a puddle.

lòd, *n. m.* a load, a broadside, a volley ; cargo, lading, burden.

lòdaich, lòd'-ich, *v.* lade, burden.

lòdail, *a.* clumsy, bulky, proud, haughty.

lòdalachd, *n. f.* haughtiness, bulkiness.

lodan, *n. m.* a puddle, a pool ; water in one's shoe. *Also* ludan. *Ir.* lodan.

lodrach, lodraich, *n. f.* baggage, luggage ; a great company.

lodragan, *n. m.* a clumsy old man, a plump boy.

logairt, logurt, *n. f.* 1. abuse, bad treatment. 2. wallowing.

logais, logesh, *n. f.* a slipper ; patched shoe, a bauchle ; a big clumsy man ; *a.* logaiseach.

logamail, *n. f.* celebration rejoicings, festivities.

logh, lo, *v.* pardon. *E.Ir.* logaim. *O.Ir.* do-luigim, I forgive.

lòghmhor, *a.* excellent, majestic, bright, valuable. *O.Ir.* lógmar, precious.

loguid, *n. f.* a varlet, a ghost, a soft fellow, rascal.

loibean, *n. m.* one who works in all weathers and places.

loibeanachd, *n. f.* working in mire, or dirt.

loibheach, *a.* dirty, fetid.

loibheachas, *n. m.* dirtiness, fetidness.

loibht, lòyt, *a.* rotten ; fr. lobh.

loiceil, *a.* foolishly fond, doting.

loigear, *n. m.* an untidy person.

loincreadh, *n. m.* ill-usage, wallowing (in mire, dirt).

lòine, lònu, *n. f.* a lock of wool, a flake of snow. Cf. *E.Ir.* ló, wool.

lóineag, lònag, *n. f.* a snowflake, fleece of very fine wool.

loinean, *n. m.* a greedy gut.

loineid, lonij, *n. f.* a froth-stick.

loineis, lonesh, *n. f.* fast-speaking.

loingear, luinger, *n. m.* a mariner, a sailor.

loingeas, luingus, *n. f.* shipping, ships ; loingeas chogaidh, ships of war ; loingeas mharsantachd, merchant ships ; loingeas-spùinnidh, pirates, privateers. *E.Ir.* loinges, longas, a fleet, a voyage.

loinid, lonij, *n. f.* a churn staff, a whisk.

lòinidh, *n. f.* rheumatism.

loinn, lòyn, *n. f.* propriety, ornament,

decorum, elegance, grace, joy ; **cha
bhi loinn ach far am bi thu**, there is no
elegance but where thou art. *M.Ir.*
loinde, joy.

loinn, *n. f.* glade, area ; *obl. c.* of **lann.**

loinn, *n. f.* a badge. *See* **sloinn.**

loinnear, *a.* bright, elegant. *O.Ir.* **lainderda**, glittering, bright, shining.

loinneas, *n. f.* art, skill, dexterity ; a
wavering.

loinneil, **lynal**, *adj.* handsome, elegant,
fine, splendid ; **duine loinneil**, a splendid fellow ; **ceòl loinneil**, fine music ;
tigh loinneil, an elegant house.

loir, **lor**, *v.* roll in the mire ; drub.

loirc, *v. n.* wallow.

loirc, **lorc**, *n. f.* wonderfully short foot,
deformed foot.

loirceach, *adj.* short-footed ; *n. f.* a
woman whose feet can hardly keep
her body from the mire ; deformed
legs.

loircire, **lorciru**, *n. m.* a short-footed man,
one whose body is almost on the
ground. *Also* **loircean.**

loireach, *a.* shaggy, untidy.

loireag, **lorag**, *n. f.* a little stout girl ; a
comely, hairy cow ; a pancake.

loireanach, **lorenuch**, *n. m.* a bespattered
dirty little fellow, a male child just
about to begin walking.

lois, **loiseunn**, *n. f.* the groin.

loisdean, **losh-jen**, *n. m.* primrose.

lòisdean, *n. f.* lodgings, a tent.

lòiseam, *n. m.* show, pomp ; *a.* **lòiseamach.**

loiseam, **loshem**, *n. m.* assumed pomp.

loisg, **loshg**, *v.* burn, consume, fire. *O.Ir.*
loscaim. *W.* llosc-i. *O.Celt.* lo(p)skô.

loisgeach, *a.* inflaming, fiery.

loisgeanta, **loshcantu**, *adj.* very keen,
fiery ; **loisgeantachd**, fieriness.

loisgneag, **losh-cnag**, *n. f.* a puny sheep.

loisneach, **losh-nuch**, *a.* cunning, " foxey."
O.Ir. **loisi**, **los**, a fox. *See Lh.*

loit, *v.* sting as a bee or snake.

loite, *a.* stang, stung, bit.

lom, *a.* bare, ill-clad, thin, lean, defenceless ; **brochan lom**, thin gruel ; **buntàta lom**, (a meal on) potatoes only ;
cnàmhan lom, bare bones = " skinny ";
muir lom, smooth sea ; *v. tr.* bare,
clip, pillage, make bare, shave. *O.Ir.*
lomm. *W.* llwm. *O.Celt.* lummo-s.

lomadair, **lomuder**, *n. m.* a shaver, parer.

lomadh, *vbl. n. m.* act of baring, pillaging ;
ruin, devastation ; shearing sheep.

lomair, **lomir**, *v.* shear sheep, fleece.

lomairt, **lomurt**, *n. f.* a fleece ; act of
fleecing.

loman, **lomanach**, *n. m.* a miser, a person
alone ; **'n am loman aonrachd**, absolutely alone by myself.

lomarra, *a.* neat, clean ; describes skilful
fingering on the chanter.

lomartach, **lomartuch**, *a.* bare, naked.

lomartair, *n. m.* sheep-shearer.

lombar, *n. m.* a bare plain, a common.
O.Ir. **lommar.** *O.Celt.* lombro-s.

lomchar, *n. m.* a bare place.

lomhainn, **lo-inn**, *n. m.* a leash ; pack of
hounds. *O.Ir.* **loman**, a rope, a line.
O.Celt. lomanâ.

lomhair, *a.* shining, bright, brilliant.

lom-làn, **lòm'-u-làn**, *adv.* quite full.
E.Ir. **lommnán**, full to the brim.

lom-luath, **lōm-looa**, *adv.* immediately ;
cho loma-luath 's a chì thu e, as soon
as you behold him (or it).

lomnochd, *a.* bare ; *n. m.* nakedness.
O.Ir. **lommnocht**, stark naked.

lompair, *n. f.* *See* **lombar.**

lompais, *n. m.* penury, niggardliness.

lomrach, *a.* fleecy.

lomradh, *n. m.* act of fleecing, a fleece.
O.Ir. **lommraim**, I make bare.

lomsgarr, *a.* fiery, impetuous.

lom-sgriob, *v.* destroy utterly.

lom-sgriob, *n. f.* a bare sweep, devastation.

lon, *n. m.* voracity, as dogs ; **lon-chraois**,
gluttony.

lòn, *n. f.* a dub, a marsh, morass ; a pond.

lòn, *n. m.* food, provisions. *O.Ir.* **loun**
(=**lóon**, loon, gl. *adeps*). (Z², 33.)

lon, *n. m.* an elk, moose deer.

lon, *n. m.* the blackbird, the ousel. *O.Ir.*
lon.

lon, *n. m.* a rope of raw hides.

lon, *n. m.* a prattle, forwardness.

lonach, *a.* voracious ; *n. f.* a garrulous,
voracious person.

lonaid, *n. f.* churn staff.

lonaig, *n. f.* a path, road, a path through
grass. *Also* **lonaidh.**

lonaire, *n. m.* a voracious man.

lonan, **lon**, *n. m.* prattle, noise.

long, **loong**, *n. f.* a three-masted vessel,
ship ; **long mharsantachd**, a merchant
ship ; **long chogaidh**, a convoy, guardship ; **long dhìon**, a convoy, guardship. *E.Ir.* **long.** *W.* llong. *O.Celt.*
longâ.

longadh, **loongu**, *n. m.* supper. *O.Ir.*
longud, act of eating.

longag, **loongag**, *n. f.* a sling (for slinging
stones). *Ir.* **longadh**, casting, throwing.

longphort, *n. m.* a harbour, haven ; a
palace, royal seat ; a fort, a garrison,
a camp ; =**lùchairt.**

lonn, *a.* strong, powerful, fierce, angry.
O.Ir. **lond**, wild.

lonn, **loon**, *n. m.* 1. a roller (put under
a boat in launching). 2. the part of
an oar between the handle and the

"plate." *O.N.* hlunnr, a roller for launching.

lonnach, *a.* wild ; "air pìob lonnaich," on the wild pipes (*see* **lonn**).

lonnrach, *a.* glittering.

lopan, *n. m.* soft, muddy place. *See* **làban.**

lorc, *n. m.* splay-foot.

lorcach, *a.* mis-shapen, lame, crawling.

lorg, *n. f.* staff ; haft of a spear. *O.Ir.* lorg, *clava.* *O.Celt.* lorgo-s.

lorg, *n. f.* a mark, a footprint, a trace in links, the sand, etc. ; **thog mi air luirg e,** I followed his track ; consequence, footsteps ; **an lorg a' ghnothaich so,** consequent on this affair ; *v.* search for information, forage, trace ; **a' lorg lòin,** foraging provision. *O.Ir.* lorg, *trames*, track. *O.Celt.* lorgo-s.

lorgaich, lorg'-ich, *v.* trace out, track.

lorgaire, *n. m.* a tracer, spy. *E.Ir.* lorgaire, a "tracker."

lorg-iomain, lorg-eemen, *n.f.* a goad, a rod.

los, *n. m.* purpose, sake, control. *E.Ir.* los, sake, part ; **asa los,** on their part.

losaid, losej, *n. f.* a kneading-trough. *E.Ir.* lossat.

losaid, *n. f.* the hip of an animal, a sirloin of beef. Cf. *E.Ir.* loss, tail. *W.* llost.

lòsan, *n. m.* a pane of glass.

losgadh, losg'-u, *n. m.* burning, firing; act of burning. *E.Ir.* loscud.

losgann, *n. m.* a frog, a toad ; a wretch (spoken in contempt). *E.Ir.* loscann.

losgann, *n. f.* a sort of drag, a sledge.

lot, *v.* wound, hurt ; *n. m.* a wound. So *E.Ir.*

lot, *n.f.* a share ; a croft. *N.* hlutr, a lot.

loth, lŏ, *n. f.* a colt, a foal, a filly.

loth, *n. f.* a marsh. *O.Ir.* loth, mud.

lothail, lo-hal, *n. m.* the brooklime.

luach, *n. m.* worth, value. *O.Ir.* lóg, lúag, lúach, reward, *pretium.*

luachair, *n. f., gen.* luachrach, rushes ; **luachair bhog,** bulrushes. So *E.Ir.*

luacha-peighinn, loochu-peyin, *n. m.* barter ; a bargain.

luachmhor, lŏŏ-uch-vor, *a.* precious, valuable. *E.Ir.* lógmar, precious.

luachmhorachd, *n. f.* preciousness, valuableness, worthiness.

luachrach, loo-uch-ruch, *a.* full of rushes.

luach-saoithreach, *n. m.* hire, wages.

luach-saoraidh, *n. m.* ransom, payment.

luadh, loo-ugh, *vbl. n. m.* act of mentioning, laying to the charge. *O.Ir.* lúad, news, speech. *Lat.* laus.

luadh, *vbl. n. m.* waulking, fulling ; the act of waulking or fulling cloth. *E.Ir.* lúadáil, movement, motion ; lúadid, to urge forward, to work.

luadhadair, loo-ughuder, *n. m.* fuller, waulk-miller.

luagha, *n.f.* the lesser paunch. *Ir. id.* less.

luaidh, *v.* speak, mention ; **na luaidh air,** do not so much as mention it.

luaidh, *n. m.* a loved one, a darling. *O.Ir.* lúad. *Lat.* laus, laudis. *O.Celt.* laudo.

luaidh, loo-uy, *v. n.* full, or waulk cloth ; **luaidh an t-aodach,** full the cloth.

luaidhe, looaye, *n. f.* lead, shot, plummet for sounding or sinking ; **stàilinn is luaidhe,** steel and lead. *O.Ir.* luaide, *plumbum. O.Celt.* loudiâ.

luaim, loo-em, *n. f.* restlessness, giddiness. *E.Ir.* lúaim, I stir, move.

luaimear, loo-umer, *n. m.* a prattler.

luaimneach, lŏŏ-emnuch, *adj.* restless. *E.Ir.* lúamnach, leaping, fickle.

luain, loo-en, *n. f.* restlessness, giddiness.

luaineach, *adj.* giddy, restless, changeable, inconstant, volatile ; rambling, roving.

luaineachd, *n. f.* changeableness, volatility, inconstancy, fickleness.

luaineis, *n. f.* fickle conduct.

luaireagan, loo-uragan, *n. m.* one that loves the fire, a grovelling person ; fr. **luaith,** ashes.

luairean, loo-uren, *n. f.* dizziness, vertigo.

luaisg, loo-ushc, *v.* wave, swing, rock. *E.Ir.* luascaim. *O.Celt.* louskô.

luaithe, loo-ayu, *compar. deg.* of **luath,** faster.

luaithead, loo-urud, *n. m.* quickness, speed. *E.Ir.* lúathe, swiftness.

luaithir, loo-ahir, *v.* toss in the ashes.

luaithre, loo-aru, *n. f.* ashes. *E.Ir.* lúath-red, ashes. *See* **luath.**

luaithreach, *adj.* early, as seed ; **sìol luaithreach,** early oats, or seeds ; **fogharadh luaithreach,** an early harvest.

luaithreachd, *n. f.* earliness.

luaithreadh, *vbl. n. m.* act of tossing in ashes.

luaithrich, *v.* make earlier, hasten, expedite.

luamh, loo-av, *n. f.* the lesser paunch.

luan, loo-an, *n. m.* moon, Monday ; **là luan,** Doomsday. So *O.Ir.*

luan, *n. m.* paunch. In *Ir.* woman's breast.

luaran, *n. f.* dizziness, faint. *See* **luairean.**

luas. *See* **luathas.**

lùasaich, for **lughasaich,** allow.

luasgach, *a.* waving, undulating, oscillating, rocking hither and thither.

luasgadh, *vbl. n. m.* tossing, rocking, tumbling, waving, oscillation. *M.Ir.* luascad.

luasgan, *n. m.* tossing, heaving, thinking.

luasganaich, *n. f.* tossing, rocking.

luath, loo-u, *adj.* fast, swift, fleet, nimble, quick, speedy, early ; **each luath,** a fleet horse. *O.Ir.* lúath.

luath, *n. f., gen.* luatha, ashes. *E.Ir.*
lúath. *O.Celt.* loutvi-.
luathad, *n. m.* speed.
luathaich, loo-uhich, *v.* hasten, quicken.
luathair, loo-uher, *n. f.* speed ; air luathair, speedily ; cha tachair e air
luathair, it will not happen in a hurry.
luathair-bheòil, *n. f.* gossip, fond of
blabbing, tattling.
luathaireach, *a.* early, quick (ripening) ;
buntata luathaireach, quickly maturing potatoes, early potatoes.
luatharan, *n. f.* a sea-lark.
luathas, loo-uhus, *n. f.* fleetness, speed,
fastness, quickness, swiftness of foot ;
earliness ; luathas an fhoghair, the
earliness of the harvest. *E.Ir.* luas.
O.Celt. (p)luo, root-form, *plouto-s.*
luathbheulach, loo-uvialuch, *adj.* blabbing, fond of gossiping stories.
luathcheumach, loo-uchemuch, *a.* swift,
nimble.
luathghair. *See* lùthghair.
luathlamhach, loo-ulavuch, *adj.* thievish,
tar-fingered ; apt to strike.
lùb, loob, *n. f.* a bend, fold, curvature,
loop, noose, cunningness, trick ;
meander, maze ; *v.* yield, meander,
assert, be deceived by ; lùb an t-slat,
bend the switch ; tha an abhainn a'
lùbadh, the river meanders ; lùb i leis,
she was deceived by him ; an lùib an
domhnaich, in contact with the Sabbath, in preparation for the Sabbath.
E.Ir. lúpaim.
luba, loobu, *n. f.* a dub, marsh, pool.
lùbach, loobuch, *a.* deceitful, meandering ; a loop, a hinge.
lubach, *a.* marshy, full of pools.
luba-dubha, *n. f.* black puddings.
lùbag, loobag, *n. f.* a little loop, a hank
of yarn ; a little twist or meander ;
lùbag cas laoigh, half-hitch knot.
lùbair, loobir, *v.* paddle, draggle.
lùbaire, *n. m.* a deceitful person.
lùbairneach, loobernuch, *n. m.* a clumsy,
ill-formed man.
lubairt, looburt, *n. f.* paddling, draggling.
lùban, *n. m.* a bow, a hoop.
lùbarsaich, loobursich, *n. f.* contortions,
serpentine motion, as eels, etc.
lùb-ruith, loob-ree, *n. f.* a running knot,
a noose.
luch, looch, *n. f., gen. s.* and *n. pl.*
luchainn, a mouse. *O.Ir.* luch. *W.* llyg.
O.Celt. lukot-.
lùchairt, loocharst, *n. f.* palace, castle,
an establishment. Cf. longphort.
luch-àrmunn, looch-ārmun, *n. m.* a
pigmy, a dwarf.
luchd, loochc, *n. m.* cargo, load ; luchd
an t-soithich, the ship's cargo. *O.Ir.*
lucht. *O.Celt.* lukto-.

luchd, loochc, *coll. n.* folk, people.
Cpds. are formed as follows : luchd-
aiteachaidh, inhabitants ; luchd-eòlais,
acquaintances ; the literati ; luchd-
éisdeachd, hearers ; luchd-leanmhainn,
followers ; luchd - turuis, travellers.
O.Ir. lucht, luct, folk, set of people,
luct inna aecolsa, *qui sunt in ecclesia* =
churchfolk. *Wb.* 12ᵇ. *W.* llwyth.
luchdaich, looch-cich, *v.* load, lade.
luchdail, looch-cal, luchdmhor, looch-cor,
adj. capacious, capable of containing
much, heavy laden.
luch-fheòir, looch-yōr, *n. f.* field-mouse.
lùdag, loodag, *n. f.* the little finger.
O.Ir. lúta.
lùdag, lùdan, lùdnan, *pl.* lùdanan, a
hinge. *Also* lùdagan and lùdallan, a
pivot. *Ir.* lúdrach and lúndrach.
ludair, *v.* mess about in water or dirty
puddle (as ducks), wallow.
ludair, loodir, *n. m.* a slovenly person.
ludaireachd, loodiruchc, *n. f.* indolence,
laziness.
ludar, *n. m.* a heavy, slovenly person.
ludarna, ludarra, *a.* heavy, clumsy,
stupid.
ludarnachd, *n. f.* clumsiness, a drawling
gait.
ludhaig, loo-ig, *v. tr.* permit, allow ;
ludhaiginn, I would fain.
ludhasachadh, *vbl. n.* ordaining, decreeing, allowing.
ludhasaich, *v.* allow, permit, advise,
decree.
ludragan, *n. m.* a heavy, dull person.
ludraig, *v.* bespatter with mud.
lug, loog, *n. f.* a bandy-leg. *Also* brabhd.
luga, *n. f.* sea sand-worm, big worm.
lùgach, *adj.* bandy-legged.
lugaist, *n. f.* quantity of bilge water.
lugh, loogh, *v.* swear ; blaspheme. *O.Ir.*
luige, oath. *W.* llw. *O.Celt.* lugio-n.
lugha, lu-u, *deg.* of beag, little, less, least ;
is lugha, less, least ; more or most
disagreeable. *O.Ir.* lugu, *compar.* of
lau, lú (small). *O.Celt.* legú-s, *compar.*
legiô-s. *Lat.* levis ; lau, lu, *appar.*
borrowed from *W., Fick.*
lughad, lu-ud, *n. f.* littleness, degree of
littleness. *O.Ir.* laiget, littleness.
lùghadair, looghuder, *n. m.* blasphemer.
lùghadaireachd, *n. f.* blasphemy ; ri
lùghadaireachd, blaspheming ; blasphemy.
lùghadh, loo-u, *vbl. n. m.* blaspheming ;
blasphemy, profanation, swearing, profaning.
lùghadrach, loogh'-ad-rach, *a.* blasphemous.
lughaide, lu-iju, *adv.* ; also *deg.* of beag ;
cha lughaide e sin, it is not the less
for that ; cha lughaide, perhaps.

lùghdachadh, lūd′-ach-u, *vbl. n. m.* lessening, diminishing ; diminution, subtraction, decrease.

lùghdaich, lūd′-ich, *v.* diminish, lessen, decrease, subtract, undervalue.

lùib, *n. f.* a fold, corner ; a bay, creek.

lùibeach, *adj.* meandering, serpentine ; full of creeks or corners.

luibh, looy, *n. f.* an herb, a plant ; luibh na nacraidh, wild thyme ; luibh nan trì beann, trefoil. *O.Ir.* lub, *frutex* ; lubgort, herb-garden. *O.Celt.* lubi-.

luibheanachd, *n. f.* botany.

luibheannach, loo-yunuch, *coll. n.* weeds.

lùibhre, looyru, *n. f.* leprosy. *O.Ir.* lobre (*debilitas*), lubhra (*lepra*). *O.Celt.* lobrajâ.

luid, luj, *n. f.* a rag, a tatter, a ragged untidy person.

luideach, lujuch, *adj.* ragged, tattered, slovenly.

luideag, lujag, *n. f.* a rag, tatter.

luideagach, *adj.* ragged ; is màirg a bheireadh droch mheas air gille luideagach is air loth pheallagach, a ragged boy and shaggy colt should never be despised.

luidealach, lujaluch, *n. m.* a ragged person, or shaggy beast ; lazy fellow, big slovenly fellow.

luidh, *v. See* laigh.

luidhe, lyu, *n. f.* lying, perching. *See* laighe.

luidhear, looyer, *n. m.* a vent, chimney.

luidir, lujir, *v.* roll in the mire or mud ; paddle through water, besmear, bedaub.

luidreach, lujruch, *n. f.* a ragged garment ; ragged, clumsy person.

luidreadh, lujru, *vbl. n. m.* rolling in the mire, puddling ; act of rolling, puddling, besmearing.

luidse, luidseach, lujshu, and -shach, *n. f.* a clumsy, awkward, dull, stupid person.

luig, *n. m., obl. c.* of lag, a hollow ; thun an luig, towards the hollow.

lùigean, *n. m.* a weak person. *See* lùgach.

luigheachd, loo-yachc, *n. f.* requital, reward ; fr. *O.Ir.* lóg, a reward.

luighean, loo-yen, *n. m.* an ankle, a foot, leg (of deer). *O.Ir.* lue, heel.

lùim, looym, *n. f.* shift, resource, invention ; leig g′a lùim fhéin e, leave him to his own resources.

lùim, *n. f.* bilge water. Cf. *E.Ir.* loimm, wave.

luime, looymu, *n. f.* sheer poverty, bareness, smoothness ; is i an luime a thug air a dhèanadh, sheer poverty forced him to it. *Also compar.* of lom, na′s luime, barer, more or most bare.

luimean, looymen, *n. m.* a barren place, a miser ; fr. lom.

luimneach, looym-nuch, *a.* active.

luimneachd, *n. f.* shift, barrenness.

luingearachd, *n. f.* seamanship, sailing.

luingeas, *n. f.* a fleet, ships ; a voyage. *E.Ir.* longes, a fleet ; voyage, banishment. *W.* llynges.

luinneag, loonyag, *n. m.* a ditty, sonnet ; mournful voice or sound ; a chorus. *M.Ir.* luindiuc.

luinneanachd, loonyenuchc, *n. f.* paddling ; sailing for pleasure about quays. *Also* luingeanaich ; fr. long.

luinneas. *See* loingeas, luingeas.

luinnseach, looyshuch, *n. m.* a very tall, slim, bowed-down fellow, a sluggard.

luinnsear, *n. m.* a sluggard, a lounger.

luir, *v.* torture, torment ; give most acute pain, drub most lustily ; ′gam luireadh, drubbing me.

lùireach, loo-ruch, *n. f.* a coat of mail, a patched garment, clumsy old footwear, an untidy female. *E.Ir.* lúirech. *Lat.* lorica.

luirgneach, loorignuch, *a.* sheep-shanked.

lùirist, loorisht, *n. m.* a tall, slender, slovenly, pithless, good-for-nothing person.

lùis, *coll. n.* a swarm, a great many.

luisreadh, *n. m.* wealth of herbage.

luitheach, *coll. n.* sinews. *Ir.* lùthach, a sinew.

luitig, *n. f.* bilge water, old rotten bilge water ; for luibhtig. *See* loibht.

luman, *n. m.* a covering, a greatcoat ; a beating, a " dressing."

lunaisd, *n. f.* a slut.

lùnasda, loon′-usd-a, lùnasdal, loon′-usdal, *n. m.* Lammas, 1st of August. *E.Ir.* lúgnasad, fair of Lug mac Ethlend. *Corm. gl.*

lunn, loon, *n. m.* a heaving billow ; a heaver that does not break.

lunn, *n. m.* a round block of wood, a roller for hauling or launching a boat, a staff, lever, part of an oar (between handle and where it enters the rowlock), handle of a bier. *O.N.* hlunnr, a roller.

lunn, *v. tr.* invade, pressing on.

lunna, *n. f.* bilge water. *Also* lùim.

lunnadh, *vbl. n. m.* invasion.

lunnaid, loonej, *n. f.* pin of a cow fetter ; from lunn.

Lunnainneach, *n. m.* a Cockney ; *adj.* Cockney.

lunndach, loon-duch, *a.* very indolent.

lunndachd, *n. f.* extreme indolence or laziness ; lounging.

lunndaire, loondiru, *n. m.* a lounger, a lounge ; indolent fellow. So *Ir.*

lunndaireachd, *n. f.* lounging, sheer indolence, sluggishness.

lunndraig, loon-dric, *v. tr.* thump, beat. *Also* plunndraig.

lunntair, loon-tir, *v.* put down and thump ; box and kick vigorously.

lunntairt, loonturt, *n. f.* a most complete thumping, boxing, and kicking.

Lupaid, loopej, *n. f.* St. Patrick's sister.

lur, loor, *n. m.* a gem, a jewel, a treasure, delight ; thà, a lur, yes, my jewel ! my darling !

lurach, *adj.* exquisitely beautiful, neatly pretty ; gem-like, jewel-like, grand, superb.

lurachan, *n. m.* the flower of ramps ; a smart boy.

lurachas, loorichus, *n. f.* surpassing beauty ; elegance, neatness.

luradair, looruder, *n. m.* a jeweller.

lurag, *n. f.* a pretty little girl.

luran, *n. m.* a pretty little boy ; *a.* luranach.

lurc, *n. m.* a crease in cloth, a lame foot.

lurcaiche, loor-ciche, *n. f.* lameness ; fr. lorc ; *a.* lurcach.

lùrdan, *n. m.* a knave ; *a.* lurdanach.

lurga, loorgu, *n. f., gen.* lurgainn, *pl.* luirgnean, shin, shank, stem, or stalk, as of an herb, shaft ; lurg an fheòir, the stem of the grass. *Also* lurgann. *E.Ir.* lurga. *M.W.* llorf, pillar, shank.

lus, loos, *n. m.* an herb, plant ; lus a' bhalla, pellitory ; lus a' bhainne, milkwort ; lus a' choire, coriander ; lus a' chalmain, columbine ; lus a' chorrain, spleenwort ; lus a' chinn, daffodil ; lus a' chrùbain, gentian ; lus an domhnaich, lus an t-sleugaire, laveage ; lus an t-siùcair, succory ; lus bealtainn, marigold ; lus na fola, yarrow, milfoil ; lus féidh, deer-grass ; lus na macraidh, lus-righ, wild thyme ; lus an t-samhraidh, gilly-flower ; lus mhic Cruiminn, cummin ; lus-crè, speedwell ; lus garbh, goose-grass ; lus a' phiobaire, dittany ; lus na mial, scorpion-grass ; lus na fearnaich, sundew ; lus nan cnàmh, samphire ; lus nan dearc, blackberry plant ; lus nan gnàithseag, whortleberry plant ; lus nan meall, mallow ; lus nan laoch, rosewort ; lus nan laogh, golden saxifrage ; lus nan leac, eye-bright ; lusmór, spearwort, foxglove ; lus nan sibhreach, loose-strife ; an tribhileach, lus nan tri-bilean, valerian. *E.Ir.* luss. *W.* llysiau (*coll.*), herbs. *O.Celt.* lussu-.

lusach, *a.* botanical ; full of herbs.

lusadair, loosuder, *n. m.* a botanist, herbalist.

lusadaireachd, *n. f.* botany ; study of botany.

lusan, *n. m.* a little herb ; *a.* lusanach.

lusarnach, loosarnuch, *coll. n. f.* weeds, a place where weeds abound.

luspardan, *n. m.* a dwarf, pigmy, sprite.

lusrach, *adj.* full of herbs ; *n. f.* herbage ; a place well supplied with herbs ; lusrach a' searg air beinn, herbage withering on a hill.

lùth, loo, *n. m.* strength, power, pith. *O.Ir.* lúth, velocity, motion.

lùth, *n. f.* a sinew. *Ir.* lúth, nerve, vein, tendon.

lùthadh, loo-hu, *n. m.* bending (as bow for arrow), a joint ; sgian lùthaidh, a clasp-knife.

lùthchas, loochus, *a.* strong-limbed, agile, nimble.

lùthchleas, loo-chles, *n. m.* valour, agility ; *a.* lùth-chleasach.

lùth-ghàir, *n. f.* great shout of joy. So *E.Ir.*

lùthmhor, *a.* vigorous, strong.

lùths, loos, *n. m.* vigour, strength.

M

m, the tenth letter of the alphabet ; muin, the vine.

'm, for am, the *art.*

m', for mo, my—used before vowels ; as, m' athair, m' anam, my father, my soul.

m'a, for mu a ; as, m'a cheann, about his head ; m'a casan, about her feet. *Ir.* um, im. *O.Ir.* imb, imm, about ; " coroin do spin im a chend," a crown of thorns about his head.

ma, *conj.* if ; ma's e agus—if so be ; ma 's e 's gum bì, if so be that it be ; ma 's urrainn mi, if I can. *O.Ir.* ma, if.

màb, *v.* abuse, vilify, reproach.

mab, *n. m.* a tassel, a stammer, a lisp. *See* pab.

mabach, *adj.* lisping, stuttering ; *n. f.* stuttering or stammering female.

mabachd, *n. f.* stammering.

màbadh, *n. m.* act of abusing, vilifying.

màbaire, màbiru, *n. m.* stammerer.

mac, *n. m.* son, a darling, used for the young of any animal, and in the names of many Gaels ; mac bràthar athar, a paternal cousin ; mac bràthar, nephew, brother's son ; mac peathar, nephew by a sister ; mac bràthar màthar, maternal cousin ; mac bràthar

seanar, a paternal grand-uncle's son ;
mac bràthar seanmhar, a maternal
grand-uncle's son ; mac an dogha,
burdock ; mac an luinn, Fionn's
sword ; mac na praisich, whisky,
"son of the pot " ; mac na bracha,
son of the malt ; mac samhail, match,
like, equal ; mac sgal, an echo ;
bheireadh e mac-sgal as na creagan,
he would make the very rocks re-echo ;
mac-alla, mac-talla, "son of rock,"
an echo ; *also* mac-stallaidh ; mac
mallachd, the evil one ; mac meamna,
a whim, imagination ; mac làmhaich,
sea devil (*also* greusaiche) ; mac-tìre,
a wolf. *O.Ir.* macc. *O.W.* map.
Og. maqva, *gen. s.* maqvi.

macachd, *n.f.* sonship ; uchd-mhacachd,
adoption. *E.Ir.* maccdacht, youth.
See under naoidheanachd.

macail, macal, *adj.* filial.

macamh, macaomh, macuv, *n. m.* a
youth, generous man. *E.Ir.* maccoem,
mac + coem, lad - friend = a goodly
youth. *W.* maccwy, youth.

macan, *n. m.* a little son.

macanta, *adj.* meek.

macantachd, *n. f.* meekness, urbanity ;
na daoine macanta, the meek.

macantas, mac'-ant-us, *n. f.* meekness.

mac-fraoir, *n. m.* a voracious fowl or
person ; the gannet. *Also* sùlaire.

mach, *adv.* outside, without, out ; thugaibh a mach, take out ; a mach 's a
mach, wholly, thoroughly ; mach air
a chèile, at variance ; *interj.* out ! get
out ! *conj.* except, but ; mach o h-aon,
but one, except one ; a mach, out,
outwards (place whither) ; chaidh e
mach, he went out ; a muigh, out,
outside (place where). *E.Ir.* immuig,
" in the plain " =in + muig (*d.* of mag) ;
immach, " into the plain " =in + mach
(*ac.* of mag).

machair, machir, *n. f.* a plain, level or
low land, an extensive beach ; links.
O.Ir. machaire, *tempe.*

machlag, *n. f.* womb, uterus. *Also*
machlach. *M.Ir.* macloc.

mac-làmhaich, *n. m.* the sea-devil. *Also*
cat-mara, griasaiche.

mac-leisg, *n. m.* a lazy fellow, laziness
personified. *Also* mac na leisg.

macnas, mac'-nus, *n. m.* lust, wantonness, sport. *Ir.* macnas, macras.

macnasach, *a.* lustful.

macraidh, macry, *coll. n.* youths, band
of male children. *O.Ir.* maccrad,
young people.

mac-ratha, *n. m.* a promising son ; mac
(son) + rath (grace) = a lad of good
fortune.

mac-samhail, *n. m.* likeness, similitude ;
a mhac-samhail, its perfect image.

mac-talla, mac-alla, *n. m.* echo. *M.Ir.*
macalla =mac + all (cliff).

madachail, mad'-ach-al, *a.* doggish.

madadh, mad'-u, *n. m.* a dog ; a kind
of shell-fish (of the mussel type) ; the
hold for the flint in a gun. *Cpds. :*
madadh-allaidh, a wolf ; madadh-donn,
an otter ; madadh-ruadh, a fox. *M.Ir.*
madrad.

màdar, *n. m.* madder.

madhanta, *a.* valiant, dexterous in use
of arms.

madraidh, madry, *coll. n.* dogs, pack of
dogs ; *a.* madrach.

maduinn, mad'-in, *n. f., gen.* maidne,
morn, morning. *O.Ir.* matin ; fr. *Lat.*
matutina.

maduinneag, mad'-inn-ag, *n. f.* morning
star.

màg, *n. f.* a soft plump hand ; a paw ;
air a mhàgan, on all-fours. *O.Ir.* mác.
(Zcp. i. 360.)

mag, *v.* scoff, deride ; *vbl. n. m.* magadh,
act of deriding, ridiculing, mocking,
scoffing.

màg, *n. f.* arable land ; broad ridge of
land.

màgach, *adj.* having short and broad feet,
as a cow, pawed ; having soft, large,
plump hands ; a frog ; mial-mhàgach,
a toad.

màgach, *a.* abounding in rigs.

magaid, *n. f.* a whim.

magail, *adj.* derisive, mocking.

màgail, *v.* paw.

màgail, *vbl. n. m.* act of pawing.

màgair, màg'-ir, *v.* creep slyly, paw.

magaire, *n. m.* scoffer, mocker.

magairle, magurlu, *n. f.* testicle, scrotum.
Ir. magarl, a testicle. *Lh.*

màgairt, magurt, *n. f.* pawing.

màgan, mial-mhàgain, *n. m.* a toad.

màgaran, *n. m.* crawling.

màgaranachd, *n. f.* creeping, crawling.

magh, *n. f.* a field, plain. *O.Ir.* mag,
field, *campus.* *O.Celt.* mag-os.

maghaire, *n. m.* a fool, a clown.

maghais, *n. f.* loitering in fields.

maghar, mu'ur, *n. m.* shell-fish, bait ;
spawn, young fish ; trolling ; artificial
fly for fishing. *E.Ir.* magar, small fish.

magharach, *a.* abounding in bait, spawn.
Cf. maorach.

maibean, meben, *n. m.* a bunch, or
cluster.

maibeanach, *a.* full of clusters.

maide, meju, *n. m.* a stick. *Cpds. :*
maide-coire, a spirtle ; maide-leigidh,
weaver's turn stick ; maide-lunndaidh,
a lever, handspike ; maide - milis,
liquorice ; maide - séisd, the pack-

saddle stick (that passes under the tail) ; **maide-stiùiridh,** a pot-stick. *E.Ir.* matan, a club. *O.Celt.* mazdjo-s. Cf. *Lat.* malus, a mast.

maidealag, myjulag, *n. f.* a small shell ; part of a spinning-wheel. *Also* **paindeag.**

maideannas, majunus, *n. m.* morning dram ; *also* **gloic-nid sgailc-sheide,** a dram in bed before rising.

màidhean, māyen, *n. m.* delay, slowness.

maidneach, majnuch, *n. f.* morning star. *Also* **maidneag.**

maidnean, majnen, *n. m.* matin.

màidse, mājshu, *n. m.* a shapeless mass ; a turd. *Also* **smàidse.**

màidsear, mājsher, *n. m.* a major in the army. *Eng.*

màigean, māgen, *n. m.* a short little man, a child beginning to walk.

màigeanachd, *n. f.* crawling, creeping. **Màigh,** māy, *n. m.* May. *Lat.* maius.

maighdeag, myjag, *n. f.* shell of the scallop-fish, pillar of spinning-wheel.

maighdeann, myjun, *n. f.* a virgin, a maid, maiden ; the last handful of corn cut in harvesting ; the upright supports of the flyers of a spinning-wheel = **maighdeannan.** *Ir.* maighdin, -dean, *Lh.* Cf. *Ger.* magd. *O.H.G.* magad. *A.S.* maegþ. *Goth.* magaþs, a maiden.

maighdeannas, *n. f.* virginity.

maighdeann-mhara, *n. f.* mermaid.

maigheach, my-uch, *n. m.* a hare. *E.Ir.* míl maige, " beast of the plain."

maighistir, myistir, *n. m.* master. *Ir.* máigister, master. *W.* meistr. *Lat.* magister.

maighistireachd, myistruchc, *n. f.* mastery, superiority ; superintendence ; assumed authority, officiousness, rule.

maighistirealachd, myistraluchc, *n. f.* assumption of undue authority, masterliness.

maighistireil, *adj.* masterful, lordly, authoritative, dogmatical, arbitrary = **maighistir** + **samail.**

maighistir-sgoile, *n. m.* school-master.

màileid, mālej, *n. f.* a bag, a wallet, budget ; a pedlar's pack ; in derision, a gorbelly. *See* **màla.**

màileideach, *adj.* gorbellied.

maille, mellu, *prep.* along with ; **maille ri,** along with ; **maille ris an sin,** together with that. *O.Ir.* malle, immelle, immaille = imm + aⁿ + le, jointly, *simul.* (*Thn.*)

maille, mallu, *n. f.* delay, hindrance ; fr. **mall,** slow. *M.Ir.* maille, moille, delay.

màille, *n. f.* mail armour, coat-of-mail.

màille, *pl.* **màillean, màilleachan,** *n. f.* a ring, the lobe of the ear.

màilleach, māluch, *n. f.* coat-of-mail.

maillead, *abstr. n. f.* slowness, tardiness.

maim, mym, *n. f.* a panic, horror, accident. *See* **maoim.**

mainisdir, manistir, *n. m.* monastery. *O.Ir.* manister. *Lat.* monasterium.

mainne, menyu, *n. f.* delay. Cf. *O.Ir.* **mendat,** residence.

mainnir, manyir, *n. f., gen.* **mainnreach,** sheep-fold, pen. *M.Ir.* maindir. *Lat.* mandra.

mainnireach, *a.* full of sheep-folds.

mair, mer, *v.* last, live, endure ; **fhad 's a mhaireas an ruaig,** while the pursuit lasts. *O.Ir.* maraim. *Lat.* mora, delay.

mairbh, merv. *See* **marbh.**

mairbhe, mairbhead, *n. f.* deadness, dulness.

mairc, merc, *n. f.* objection, subject of regret ; **có chuir mairc ort ?** who objected to you ? **cha do chuir mise mairc sam bith air,** I did not oppose him or it.

màireach, māruch, *n. m.* next day ; **an diugh is a màireach,** to-day and to-morrow ; **a màireach,** to-morrow ; **là-air-na-mhàireach,** "the morrow," the next day. *Ir.* **a màrach.** *E.Ir.* imbárach, lá iarnabárach, day after to-morrow. *W.* bore, *O.W.* more.

maireachdainn, mairsinn, meruchcin, marsin, *vbl. n. f.* act of enduring, lasting, continuing.

maireann, merun, *n. m.* lasting, enduring, life-time ; *adj.* enduring, living, in the land of the living ; **cha mhaireann e,** he is not living ; **am fear nach maireann,** he that is no more. *O.Ir.* maraim, I remain, live.

maireannach, merunuch, *adj.* everlasting, eternal ; **a' bheatha mhaireannach,** everlasting life.

mairg, merg, *n. m.* woe, foul fall, alas for ; **is mairg tè a fhuair e,** woe to the woman who got him ; deplorable, pitiable ; **is mairg a loisgeadh a thiompan duit,** pity the man who would burn his harp for you. Cf. *Sc.* " Eh ! mergie me ! " = expr. of surprise. *O.Ir.* moircc, " bith moircc domsa," vae mihi est. *Wb.* 10ᵈ **m-oirc** = *interfectio mea.* *Z².* 61. *O.Celt.* margi-.

mairiste, marishtu, *n. m.* match, marriage ; **fhuair i an deagh mhairiste,** she got an excellent match = *Eng.* marriage.

mairisteach, *adj.* marriageable.

màirneal, mārnal, *n. m.* detention ; slow, drawling manner, dilatoriness ; procrastination.

màirnealach, *n. m.* a man on the " look-

out " on board ship. *E.Ir.* **mairnim,**
I spy, inform, betray.

màirnealach, *adj.* dilatory, tardy, tedious,
drawling in manner ; procrastinating.

màirnealachd, *n. f.* procrastination,
dilatoriness, dilatory manner.

mairsinn, marshin, *adj.* lasting, living.

mairtfheoil, marst-yol, =mart (cow,
" beef ") +feòil (flesh), beef.

mairtir, *n. m.* a martyr. *E.Ir.* **martir.**
W. merthyr. *Gr.* μάρτυς, -υρος. *Lat.*
martyr ; *orig.* a witness, came to mean
one who testified by his death.

mairtireach, martiruch, *n. m.* martyr.
one who suffered martyrdom.

maise, măsh'-u, *n. f.* ornament, great
beauty, elegance ; **chuireadh tu maise
air baile,** you would prove an ornament to a city. *E.Ir.* **maisse,** comeliness ; fr. mass, stately. *Wi.*

maiseach, măsh'-ach, *adj.* ornamental ;
very elegant or handsome ; fair.

maiseachd, *n. f.* superiority in beauty,
handsomeness, elegance, fairness.

maiseag, meshag, *n. f.* a pretty woman.

maisealachd, *n. f.* elegance, comeliness.

maiseil, măsh'-al, *adj.* ornamental.

maistir, mystir, *n. m.* stale urine. *Also*
maighistir.

maistir, maistrich, mash'-trich, *v.* churn,
agitate as liquids.

maistreadh, *vbl. n. m.* act of churning,
agitating ; the quantity of butter
made at one churning. *Also* **miosradh.**
E.Ir. **maistred.**

maiteach, mytuch, *adj.* ready to forgive.

maith, math, *a.* good, well. *O.Ir.* maith,
and **maid.** *W.* da, good. *O.Celt.* mati-s,
mato-s, good.

maith, math, *v.* forgive, pardon. *See*
math.

maithean, my-hun, *n. p.* nobles, magistrates, aldermen. So *O.Ir.*

maitheas, my-hus, *n. m.* mercy, goodness,
bounty of God.

màl, *n. m.* rent, tribute. *Ir.* **mál,** a
tribute-tax. *Lh.* So *M.Ir.* *A.S.* mál,
tribute. *M.E.* mail. *Sc.* mail.

màla, *n. f.* a bag ; bag of a pipe ; budget.
M.E. and *O.F.* male. *O.H.G.* mala-
ha, wallet.

mala, *n. f., pl.* **mailghean, malaichean,**
dat. **malaidh,** eyebrow, the grassy edge
of a rig. *O.Ir.* mala, *pl.* malgea, *d.* mal-
aig, *supercilium. Z².* *O.Celt.* malaks.

malach, *adj.* having large brows ; surly,
sulky, forbidding.

màladair, măludir, *n. m.* a sub-tenant
who pays rent in kind ; renter, tenant.

malairt, malart, *n. f.* exchange, barter,
space ; *v.* exchange, barter, traffic,
trade. *Ir.* alteration, change. *O.Ir.*
malart =destruction.

malairteach, malartuch, *a.* exchangeable,
mutual, reciprocal ; fit to exchange.

malairtear, *n. m.* barterer.

malairtich, malartich, *v.* barter.

malc, *v.* begin to rot or putrify. *Ir.*
malcaim, I rot. *O.Celt.* malqô.

màlda, maüldu, *adj.* modest, gentle.
O.Ir. **meld,** pleasant.

màldachd, *n. f.* gentleness, diffidence.

mall, maül, *adj.* slow, tardy, late, calm.
So *O.Ir.*

mallachadh, maluchu, moluchu, *vbl. n.:*
m. act of cursing.

mallachd, mŏll'-achc, *n. f.* malediction ;
thug e mhallachd air, he cursed him.
O.Ir. **maldacht.** *Lat.* maledictio.

mallaich, mŏll'-ich, *v.* curse, imprecate.

màm, *n. m.* 1. a boil in the armpit, or
palm of the hand. 2. a round steep
hill (probably shaped like a woman's
breast) ; an extensive moor. *Ir.*
màm, mountain. *M.Ir.* **mamm,** pap.

màm, *n. m.* a handful (of meal). So *M.Ir.*
O.Celt. mâmmâ. *Lat.* mamma.

mamaidh, mamy, *n. f.* mamma.

màm-sic, mām-sheeck, *n. m.* rupture,
hernia.

man, măn, *conj.* +*neg.* if not, unless.
=ma (if) + ni (not) ; **man biodh,**
(=ma ni b.) were it not ; **ma ni biodh
dhòmhsa** =if it were not for my
handicap. *O.Ir.* mani (if not).

manach, *n. m.* monk. *E.Ir.* **manach.**
W. mynach. *Lat.* monachus.

manach, *n. m.* the angel fish.

manachainn, *n. f.* a convent, a monastery.

manachan, *n. m.* the buttock. *Also*
meanachan.

manadh, măn'-u, *n. m.* omen, sign,
apparition, enchantment ; **chunnaic e
manadh,** he saw an apparition ; **tha
e cur air mhanadh dhomh,** he pro-
phesies to me.

mànas, màn'-us, *n. m.* a cultivated piece
of ground, a farm, a farm in the
natural possession of a proprietor,
the part of an estate farmed by owner ;
fr. *Sc.* mains.

mandrag, maündrag, *n. f.* mandrake.

mang, *n. f.* a fawn, of a year old. So *E.Ir.*

mang, mangnus, *n. f.* craftiness, deceit.

mangan, *n. m.* a bear.

mannas, *n. m.* the gum. *E.Ir.* **mant,** gum.
W. mant, jaw. *O.Celt.* mant, jaw.

mannd, maünd, *n. m.* a lisp, stammer.

mannda, manntach, *a.* lisping, stammering.

manndach, maünduch, *a.* lisping. *E.Ir.*
mant, gum. *O.W.* mantach, toothless
jaw.

mànrain, *v.* hum, croon a love ditty.

mànrain, *v.* dander, saunter ; **manrain
thusa air t' aghaidh,** dander you ahead.

mànran, *n. m.* dandering.
mànran, *n. m.* humming, cooing, tuneful sound ; love song ; amorous discourse.
maodal, *n. f.* paunch, maw. *M.Ir.* medhal.
maodalach, *a.* having a large belly, clumsy ; a clumsy corpulent person.
maoidh, mooy, *v. t.* threaten, cast up favours bestowed, upbraid ; tha e maoidheadh orm, he threatens me ; tha e maoidheadh gun do rinn e siod is so dhomh, he casts up that he did this and that for me. *Ir.* maoidhim, upbraid, brag. *O.Ir.* móidem, to praise.
maoidheadh, mooyu, *vbl. n. m.* a threat, upbraiding ; casting up favours bestowed, reproaching.
maoidhean, mooyen, *n. m.* supplication, personal influence, interest, a threat.
maoidhseig, *n. f.* fastidiousness.
maoile, mūlu, *n. f.* baldness, brow of a hill. *E.Ir.* máile, baldness. *O.Celt.* mailjâ.
maoilead, mŭlud, *abstr. n. f.* baldness. *W.* moeledd, baldness.
maoilean, mūlen, *n. m.* a bald man.
maoim, moym, *n. f.* a burst, an eruption ; panic, wild expression of countenance ; biodh maoim air do naimhdean, let your enemies be in a panic ; a terrible crime ; expressions of fear ; *v.* be horrified, terrified ; *a.* maoimeach. *Ir.* maidhm, sally, breach, defeat. *E.Ir.* maidm, a loud report, a clap (as of thunder). Inf. of maidim, break.
maoim-sléibhe, moym-shlēvu, *n. f.* a landslip ; a water-spout or plump of rain all of a sudden.
maoin, *n. m.* goods ; a hoard, hoarded wealth ; chan 'eil maoin fhallaineachd, there is not a particle of soundness. Cf. *idm.* use of cus (too much), chan 'eil cus, not too much=little or nothing ; mór (great), is mór d' fhios, much you know ; beag (little), is beag m' fhios, what do I know ? *Ger.* viel, ich weiss viel, much I know ; and *Eng.* much, much I care. *O.Ir.* máin, móin, máen. *W.* mwyn, mine. *Lat.* moenia, munia. *Thurn.* *O.Celt.* maini-.
maoineas, *n. m.* slowness. *See* màidhean.
maoirne, moyrnu, *n. m.* a little one, as potatoes ; a bait.
maoirnean, *n. m.* little potato, a kind of cockle.
maois, mūsh, *n. m.* hamper, a heap of seaweed on the shore ; five hundred fresh herrings in time of fishing. *Ir.* maois, a hamper, five hundred fish. *O.N.* meiss, wicker basket. *O.H.G.* meisa.
maoiseach, mushuch, maoisleach, mushluch, *n. f.* a roe or doe, a she-deer = maolsech, " hornless one."

maoisgeag, *n. f.* a small creel, a scolding woman.
maol, mul, *n. f.* 1. bald, bare, tonsured ; ceann maol, a bald head, a head closely cropped ; Maol-Caluim, tonsured one of Columba = Columba's attendant (Malcolm). 2. polled, hornless ; bó mhaol, a polled cow. 3. blunt, pointless ; sgian mhaol, a dull knife ; biodag mhaol, a pointless dagger. 4. a bluff, a high rounded headland ; A' Mhaoil, the Mull. 5. a dull-witted, stupid person (So *M.Ir.*). *O.Ir.* máel, máil, *calvus.* *E.W.* moel. *O.Celt.* mailo, mael-o.
maolachadh, *vbl. n. m.* act of blunting, laying down the ears as a horse.
maolag, mūlag, *n. f.* a bald woman, a hornless cow ; stocking wanting the head ; a dish for milk. *Also* osan.
maolaich, mūlich, *v.* blunt, deprive of edge ; mhaolaich an sgian, the knife got blunt ; lay down the ears as horses, hares, or does.
maolan, maolanach, maoilean, *n. m.* a bald man, a dull, stupid man.
maolchair, mūl-char, *n. f.* space between the eye-brows.
maolchluasach, mūl'-chloo-us-ach, *adj.* blunt, dull, stupid, dull of hearing.
maolchluasaich, *n. f.* stupidity, dulness, lifelessness.
maol-ciaran, *n. m.* a forlorn person.
maoloisean, mūl-oshen, *n. m.* hightemple, bare temple.
maol-oiseanach, *a.* high-templed, as a person.
maol-snaotha, *n. f.* mental vacancy, suspended perception.
maol-snéimheil, m.-snēvel, *a.* careless, indifferent, lazy.
maor, *n. m.*, *pl.* and *gen. sing.* maoir, constable, an officer, messenger ; maorbaile, an under bailiff ; maor-coille, a wood-ranger ; maor-siorraim, a sheriff-officer ; maor-rìgh, king's messenger ; maor-cise, a tax-gatherer, assessor ; maor-striopach, a pimp, pander ; maorrinndeal, a ground-officer—a great man formerly. *O.G.* maer, máir. *W.* maer. *Lat.* maior. The maer was a king's officer in charge of crown land.
maorach, *n. m.* shell-fish ; a bait for fishing. *See* magharach.
maorsainneachd, mūrshinuchc, *n. f.* office of a messenger ; officiousness, meddling.
maoth, mū, *adj.* tender, soft ; of a tender age ; delicate ; muirichinn mhaoth, family of a tender age. *E.Ir.* móeth. *O.Ir.* móith, *tener.* *O.Celt.* moiti-s. *Lat.* mitis. Cf. *W.* mwyn.
maothag, mū-hag, *n. f.* the soft thing, premature egg ; soft crab.

maothaich, mū-hich, *v.* soften, alleviate.

maothail, mū-hal, *adj.* emollient.

maothain, *n. m.* abdomen ; a disease of young persons arising from lifting burdens.

maothais. *See* **maghais.**

maothalachd, mū-hal-achc, *n.f.* delicacy, tenderness, softness ; **a thaobh mùirn agus maothalachd,** on account of tenderness and delicacy.

maothan, mū-han, *n. m.* the chest, a twig, a bud.

maothar, *coll. n.* the young, the tender ; **maothar na treuda,** the young of the flock.

maoth-bhlàth, *n. m.* a tender twig.

maoth - chlòimh, m. - chlōy, *n. f.* soft down.

maoth-chrith, *n. f.* a quivering, quaking.

maothlus, m.-loos, *n. m.* a tender flower, or herb.

maothran, mūr'-an, *n. m.* an infant, child, a tender twig.

maothranach, *a.* infantile, soft, tender.

maothrosg, *n. m.* soft eyelid or look.

maothshuil, *n. f.* a soft eye ; *a.* **maoth shuileach,** soft-eyed.

mar, *conj.* as, just as, even as, like, in the same manner ; **mar theicheas iad,** as they scamper ; **mar gum b'ann,** just as it were ; **mar cheud,** a hundred times ; **leth mar leth,** half and half. *O.Ir.* **immar,** *quasi.* *O.W.* mor.

mara, *gen.* of **muir,** *q.v.*

màrach. *See* **màireach.**

marachan, *n. m.* calf of the leg.

marachd, *n. f.* seafaring life, navigation ; **ri marachd,** following the sea.

marag, *n. f.* pudding, thick person. *M.Ir.* **maróc.** *E.Ir.* mar, sausage. Cf. *O.N.* mörr, suet.

maraiche, *n. m.* seaman, marine.

mar an ceudna, *adv.* likewise.

marannan, *n. pl.* large billows; fr. **muir,** *q.v.*

mar-aon, mar'-ūn, *adv.* together, in concert.

marasgail, mar'-asg-il, *v.* manage, trade.

marasgal, mar'-asg-ul, *n. m.* managing, a master, a marshal.

marasglachd, măr'-ăsg-luchc, *n. f.* see **marasgail.**

marasgladh, *n. m.* management, superintendence, supervision, traffic.

marasglaich, mar'-asg-lich, *v.* superintend, guide, oversee, rule, trade with.

marbh, marv, *adj.* dead, lifeless, dull ; *v.* kill, slay, slaughter ; used as a *n. m.* **am marbh,** the dead one ; *gen. s.* and *n. pl.* **mairbh ; na beò is na mairbh,** the living and the dead. *O.Ir.* **marb.** *O.W.* marw. *O.Celt.* **marvo-s,** dead.

marbhach, marbhtach, *a.* deadly, murderous.

marbhadh, măr'-u, *n. m.* act of killing.

marbhan, *n. m.* a dead body, deadness, stillness ; **marbhan a' mheadhon-oidhche,** the dead of midnight ; margin of a book.

marbhanach, marv-an-uch, *n. m.* person almost dead, one pretending to be dead ; wool of sheep, killed at Hallowtide.

marbhanta, *adj.* inactive.

marbhantachd, mărv'-ant-uchc, *n. f.* dulness, inactivity, stupor. *Also* **marbhantas.**

marbhchann, mar-chun, *n. f.* wool of sheep killed in autumn or winter.

marbhdheoch, *n. f.* deadly draught, dram at a funeral-dirge.

marbhdhraoi, *n. m.* necromancer.

marbhnach, *n. m.* elegy, epitaph. *E.Ir.* **marbnad,** elegy.

marbhphaisg, maru-feshc, *n. m.* death shroud ; form of imprecation. *Ir.* **marbhfaisg,** bands by which hands and toes of dead persons are tied. *O'R.* *E.Ir.* **faiscim,** bind.

marbhrann, marv'-rănn, *n. f.* an elegy ; a funeral oration. *Also* **rann-mairbh.**

marbhshruth, marv-hroo, *n. m.* slackwater, the turn of the tide.

marc, *n. m.* charger, steed, a horse. So *E.Ir.* *O.W.* march. *O.Celt.* markâ, marko-s.

marcachd, mark'-achc, *n. f.* a ride, act of riding, equestrianism ; from **marc.**

marcaich, mark'-ich, *v.* ride.

marcaiche, *n. m.* rider, equestrian. *Also* **marcair. marclann,** stable.

marcan-sìne, marcach-sìne, *n. m.* spindrift.

marcshluagh, mark-hloo-u, *n. f.* cavalry, horsemen.

marg, *n. m.* a merk, a Scottish silver coin formerly current = 13⅓*d.* sterling ; a certain denomination of land ; **marg fearainn,** mark-land ; fr. *Eng.* mark ; *Sc.* merk ; *O.N.* mörk.

margadalachd, *n. f.* saleableness.

margadh, mărg'-u, *n. m.* market, sale. *E.Ir.* **marggad.** *Lat.* mercatus.

margail, mârg'-al, **margadail,** mârg'ad-al, *adj.* marketable, saleable, disposable.

màrla, *n. m.* the clay, marl. *O.F.* marle. *L.L.* margila.

marmor, *adj.* marble. *Lat.* marmor.

marr, màrr, *v.* obstruct, hinder. *Sc.* marr, an obstruction, an injury.

marrach, *n. f.* a labyrinth ; enchanted castle, entering which, none could find his way back till the spell was removed ; a thicket to catch cattle in.

mar-ri, *prep.* with.

marrì, *interj.* indeed ! in truth ! by Maol-
ruibhe ! for the form cf. Maree (loch),
and as to usage cf. Muire, thà, yes, by
Mary.

marrisd. *See* mairist.

marrum, *n. m.* milk produce.

màrsadh, *n. m.* march of troops ; fr. the
Eng.

marsanta, *n. m.* merchant. *Also* marsan.

marsantachd, *n. f.* merchandise, wares,
trade, traffic, dealing.

màrt, *n. m.* seed-time, March, the
throngest time at anything, pressure
of work ; great haste.

mart, *n. m.* a cow, cow to kill. *E.Ir.*
mart, a beef. *Sc.* mart, a cow or ox
killed for winter provisions.

martair, mart'-ar, *n. m.* a martyr, a
cripple. *Also* martarach.

martan, *n. m.* daddy long-legs.

marthannach. *See* marbhchann.

martradh, *vbl. n. m.* act of maiming,
laming. *O.Ir.* martre, martyrdom.
Gr. μαρτυρέω, I witness.

ma's, if it be ; ma's e agus, if so be that.
ma (if) + is (be).

màs, *n. m.* buttock, bottom of dish ;
màs cuinneig, pitcher's bottom. *E.Ir.*
mass. *O.Celt.* mâsto-s.

màsach, *adj.* large-hipped, having large
hips ; *n. f.* a large-hipped female.

màsag, *n. f.* a small red berry.

màsaire, māsiru, *n. m.* large - hipped
man.

masan, *n. m.* dilatoriness ; delay. *Ir.*
masán, delay. *Lh.*

masanach, *adj.* dilatory.

masanaich, *n.f.* act of playing with, flirting.

masg, *v.* infuse, as tea ; mash, as malt.
Sc. mask. Form of measg, *Lat.* misceo.

masgadh, masg'-u, *vbl. n. m.* act of mashing, infusing ; a mash ; an infusion.

masgaire, masgire, *n. m.* mashman.

masgul, *n. m.* flattery.

masgulaiche, *n. m.* flatterer.

maslach, *adj.* disgraceful, ignominious,
reproachful ; slandering. *Ir.* masluigh-
each, ignominious.

masladh, maslu, *n. m.* disgrace. *Ir.*
masla, reproach, scandal. *Lh.*

maslaich, maslich, *v.* disgrace, taunt,
degrade. *Ir.* maslaighim, I scandalise,
blaspheme. *Lh.*

maslaichte, *vbl. a.* disgraced, slandered.

matà, *interj.* then ! oh ! ; *adv.* and *conj.*
indeed, nevertheless, then, if so, truly,
really = ma (if) + tà (be).

math, *v.* pardon, forgive. *See* maith.
O.Ir. mathim, I remit. *O.W.* maddeu.

math, *n. m.* interest, end, purpose, kindness, wish, inclination ; is ann air do
mhath fhéin a tha mise, it is your own
interest I have in view ; am math is

an t-olc, the good and bad. *O.Ir.*
mathius, the good, excellence.

math, *adj. compar.* is fearr ; good, wholesome, considerable ; happy, glad ; is
math leam sin, I am glad of it ; is
math dhuit, it is happy for you ; valid,
legal, rightful ; is math mo chòir air,
I have a valid claim to it : correct,
accurate ; ma's math mo bheachdsa,
if I form a correct or accurate idea of
it ; ready, expert, dexterous ; tha e
math air na h-uile nì, he is dexterous
at everything ; latha math dhuit,
oidhche mhath dhuit, good day to you,
good night to you. *See* maith. math
is the common form in Gaelic speech.
O.Ir. math, good.

mathachadh, ma-huchu, *vbl. n. m.* act of
cultivating, improving ; improvement,
cultivation ; a' mathachadh an fhearainn, improving the land ; manure,
manuring.

mathaich, ma-hich, *v.* improve, manure,
cultivate. So *Ir.* *O'R.*

màthair, mā-hir, *n. f.* mother, dam ; cause,
source ; màthair aobhair, primary
cause ; màthair chéile, mother-in-law ;
màthair-ghuire, the "core" of an
abscess ; màthair na lùdaig, ring-
finger ; màthairmhort, matricide. *O.Ir.*
máthir. *Lat.* māter. *W.* modr - yb.
O.Celt. mâtêr.

màthairealachd, mā-hir-alachc, *n. f.*
motherliness, kindliness, tenderness.

màthaireil, mā-hir-al, *adj.* motherly, kind.

màthair-uisge, mā-hir-ushcu, *n. f.* source,
spring (of water), reservoir, conduit,
source of a river.

mathalt, *n. m.* a blunt weapon.

mathan, ma-han, *n. m.* a bear. *E.Ir.*
mathgaman, *ursus.*

mathanas, ma-hanus, *n. m.* pardon, forgiveness ; written *also* maitheanas.
O.Ir. mathem (inf. of mathim), a
forgiving.

mathanasach, *adj.* forgiving, lenient,
not harsh.

mathas, ma-hus, *n. m.* benevolence,
charity, humanity ; benefit, bounty ;
maitheas. *O.Ir.* mathius.

mathasach, *adj.* benevolent, humane,
tender, kind, bountiful, beneficial.

mathasachd, *n. f.* bountifulness, charitableness ; munificence, benevolence.

mathghamhainn, mà'-ghav-inn, *n. m.* a
bear. *E.Ir.* math-gaman.

mathroinn, măr'-inn, *n. f.* disposal, risk ;
fàg air a mhathroinn e, leave it to his
risk ; air mo mhathroinn-sa, at my
disposal, at my risk.

meaban, meban, *n. m.* a broken instrument, a stump, a stump of an oar,
a flunkey, a follower, an insignificant

person. *O.Ir.* mebaid, he broke, routed, for memaid. *Vendr.*

meabhal, mevul, *n. m.* treachery, fraud, a plot. *O.Ir.* mebol, mebul, shame, *dedecus.* *O.W.* mefyl, disgrace.

meacan, meck-an, *n. m.* root, a bulb, a turnip, a twig, a shoot, a plant; offspring. *Cpds.:* meacan-rìgh, a parsnip; meacan-ragum, a horse-radish; meacan-sléibhe, black helle-bore; meacan - roibe, sneezewort; meacan buidhe, and m-. raidich, a carrot; meacan uileann, elecampane; meacan-dogha, burdock. *O.Ir.* meccun, mecon, a root, *radix.*

meacan a' chruidh, *n. m.* the cow's plant, cow parsnip.

meacanaich, mec-anich, *n. f.* sobbing.

meach, mech, *adj.* mild, modest. *Ir.* meach, hospitality. *Lh.*

meachainn, *n. f.* mercy, lenity; an abate-ment (as rent), discount, luck-penny.

meachair, mechir, *a.* soft, tender, delicate, very fair, beautiful, ruddy-cheeked, cheerful, sportive.

meachaireachd, mechiruchc, *n. m.* beauti-ful countenance; beautiful mixture of colours in the face; sweetness of expression of countenance.

meachannas, mech'-an-us, *n. m.* lenity, indulgence, mitigation, partiality; gun meachannas do dhuine seach duine, without indulgence or partiality to any one.

meachnasach, mechnusuch, *adj.* in-dulgent, lenient, partial.

meachran, mech'-ran, *n. m.* a hospitable person; officious person.

meachuinn, mechin, *n. f.* abatement, lenity, partiality; discretionary power; is màirg a rachadh fo do mheachuinn, pity him that depends on your will. *See* meachainn.

meadar, medur, *n. m.* small ansated wooden dish; milk-pail. *M.Ir.* metur, medar, a drinking vessel.

meadar, *n. m.* verse, metre. *Lat.* metrum. *Gr.* μέτρον, a measure, esp. metre.

meadha, me-u, *n. f., pl.* meadhannan, hip, pelvis.

meadhail, miü-al, *n. f.* ecstasy, trans-ports, raptures, overjoy; burst of joy; cha robh meadhail mhór riamh gun dubh-bhròn na déidh, there never was an extravagant burst of joy without gloom after it.

meadhair, *n. f.* mirth, joy, cheer; *a.* meadhrach.

meadh-bhlàth, miu-vlā, *a.* "mid-warm," lukewarm. *O.Ir.* med + blàth.

meadhlachd, *n. f.* sport, mirth.

meadhon, mé'-un, *n. m.* the middle, centre, heart; waist; mu do mheadhon,

about your waist; medium, means. *O.Ir.* medón. *M.W.* mywn. *Lat.* medium.

meadhonach, miu-unuch, *adj.* central, intermediate; àite gu math meadhon-ach, a pretty central situation; in-different, in a tolerable or middle state, as of health; ciod é mar tha thu, how are you?; chan 'eil mi ach meadhon-ach, I am only middling. *O.Ir.* medóndae, middling.

meadhonaich, *n. m.* middle state, in point of situation or health.

meadhon - latha, *n. m.* mid-day, noon; déidh mheadhon-latha, the afternoon.

meadhon-oidhche, *n. m.* midnight.

meadhrach, miüruch, *adj.* merry, lustful. *E.Ir.* medrach, glad, merry.

meadhrachas, *n. f.* joy, lust.

meadhradh, *vbl. n. m.* sporting, mirth, ecstasy; drawn into lust.

meadrachd, medruchc, *n. f.* poetry.

mèag, miüg, *n. m.* whey; *gen.* mig, meug; *dial.* meang. *O.Ir.* medg. *W.* maidd. *O.Bret.* meid. *Mid.Lat.* mesga. *Thn.*

meaghal, miä-ul, *n. f.* mewing; bleating; alarm. *Ir.* mélighim, bleat as sheep. As to meaning "mew," the word is onomatopoeic: cf. *W.* mewial. *Fr.* miauler. *Ger.* miauen. *O.N.* mjáma. *Icel.* mjálma.

meal, myal, *v.* enjoy, possess; meal is caith e, may you enjoy and wear it. *M.Ir.* melaim, enjoy.

mealag, *n. f.* matted roots of grass, of bent.

mealag, *n. f.* protuberance, belly.

mealanan, myal'-an-un, *coll. n.* sweet-meats.

mealasg, *n. m.* flattery, fawning, great rejoicing. *See* miolasg.

mealbhac, *n. m.* a melon. *Also* meal-bhucan.

mealbhag, *n. f.* a poppy. *Also* pollan buidhe.

mealg, meilg, *n. f.* the milt of fish.

meall, miawl, *n. m., pl.* mill, a mass; a heavy shower, a bank of clouds, of mist, of fog; a lump, knob, bunch; meall luaidhe, a lump of lead; meall fhìgean, a bunch of figs. *O.Ir.* mell. *O.Celt.* mello-.

meall, *v. tr.* deceive, cheat, entice, de-fraud; mar a meall mo bharail mi, unless I am mistaken; mheall thu mi, you deceived or defrauded me; mheall e steach mi, he enticed me into the house. *E.Ir.* mell, error. *O.Celt.* mellsô, I err.

meallach, miäluch, *adj.* lumpish.

meallach, *a.* deceiving, enticing.

meallach, *a.* beautiful, attractive. *O.Ir.* meldach, agreeable.

mealladh, *vbl. n. m.* act of deceiving,

beguiling, cajoling, enticing, cheating, alluring, or disappointing ; deception ; **mar bheil mi air mo mhealladh**, unless I am deceived, if I am not much mistaken.

meallan, miälan, *n. m.* a small lump ; **clach-mheallain**, hailstone ; *dim.* of **meall**.

meallanach, *a.* lumpy.

meallshuil, miäl-hul, *n. f.* ; **meallshuileach**, having a pleasing eye ; **meall** = *O.Ir.* meld, pleasant, tender. *O.Celt.* meldo-s, tender.

meallta, mia-ooltu, *vbl. a.* cheated, enticed.

mealltach, *adj.* deceptive.

mealltachd, *n. f.* imposture.

mealltair, miä-oolter, *n. m.* impostor, deceiver, a cheat ; fraudulent person ; **mealltaireachd**, *n. f.* imposture, fraudulence, deceitfulness.

mealtainn, myalt-inn, *vbl. n. f.* act of enjoying ; **math a mhealtainn 'na shaothair**, to enjoy good in his labour. *Bible.*

meambrana, mem'-bran-u, *n. m.* parchment. *Lat.* membrana.

meamhair, **meomhair**, miü-ir, *n. f.* memory. *O.Ir.* mebuir. *Lat.* memoria.

meamhraich, *v.* meditate, study. *E.Ir.* mebraigim, I study, remember.

meamna, *n. m.* imagination, whim ; gladness, joy ; mettle ; a sensation about the lip or elbow, supposed to portend a sudden death ; **tha meanmhainn 'n a shròin**, the sensation portending something is in his nose ; etc. *Also* **meanmna**. *O.Ir.* menme. *G.* menman. *Lat.* memini. *O.Celt.* ménmês, mind, sense.

meamnach, *adj.* mettlesome, as a horse ; lustful, courageous, brave, as a person.

meamnachd, *n. f.* courage, mettlesomeness, energy, high spirit.

mean, min, *adj.* little. *Also* **mion**. *See* **meanbh**.

meanachair, menuchir, *n. pl.* small cattle.

meanaidh, miny, *n. m.* shoemaker's awl ; **tha thu cur meanaidh orm**, you provoke me. *Also* **mionaidh**. *E.Ir.* menad, an awl.

mèanan, mēnan, *n. m.* a yawn. *See* **mianan**.

mèananaich, *n. f.* act of yawning, fit of yawning ; fr. *O.Ir.* mén, mouth.

meanbh, men'-uv, *adj.* diminutive, very small, slender or little ; **duine meanbh**, a diminutive person. *E.Ir.* menbach. *Lat.* minus. *O.Celt.* menvo-s.

meanbhaidh, menv'-y, *adj.* slender, diminutive.

meanbhbhith, menuv'-y, *n. m.* animalcule.

meanbhbhreac, menv-vrac, *a.* finely dappled.

meanbhchrodh, men'-uv-chrò, *n. m.* small cattle such as stirks, calves, sheep, goats, etc.

meanbhchuileag, mēnu-chŭil-ag, *n. f.* midge.

meanbhlach, menuv-lach, *n. m.* small potatoes, etc., or the refuse of such.

meanbhluath, menv-luä, *a.* deliberate.

meanbhpheasair, menuv-fesir, *n. f.* millet.

meang, méng, *n. m.* fault, blemish, guile. *See* **miong**, *v.* lop. *E.Ir.* **meng**.

meangach, méng'-uch, *n. m.* the plant *cinquefoil*.

meangail, méng'-al, *adj.* faulty, blemished.

meangalachd, méng'-al-uchc, *n. f.* faultiness.

meangan, méng'-an, *n. m.* a branch, twig ; also used of a cut of fish.

meanganaich, *v.* lop, prune.

meanm, *n. m.* mettle, spirit ; courage ; will, desire. *See* **meamna**. *O.Ir.* menma, *mens.* *W.* menw-yd.

meann, *a.* dumb. *E.Ir.* menn, mute.

meann, *a.* clear, famous. *O.Ir.* menn.

meann, miä-un, *n. m.*, *pl.* minn, a kid, young roe ; *gen. s.* and *n. pl.* minn. *Ir.* menn. *W.* myn. *O.Celt.* mendo-s.

meann-athair, miaun-ahir, *n. f.* snipe. *Ir.* mionán-aiéir. *Lh.*

meanndran, *n. m.* a mean, contemptible creature.

meannt, mioont, *n. m.* mint, cartal.

meantarig, the Gaelic form of *Eng.* venturing. *Also* **meatraig**.

meapaid, *n. f.* a tar-brush.

mear, mer, *adj.* quick, nimble, sudden movement ; sportive (of lambs) ; ready to split (of wood) ; in high glee, joyful, joyous, very joyous ; lustful ; **le sùilibh mear**, with lustful eyes ; **bha sinn glé mhear**, we were in great glee. *E.Ir.* mer, madman ; mear, insane. *See* **mire**.

mearacasach, *a.* active, nimble, vigorous.

mearachd, mer'-achc, *n. m.* mistake, error, wrong ; **tha thu am mearachd**, you are mistaken. *O.Ir.* mer, madman ; meracht, excitement, irritability.

mearachdach, mer'-achc-uch, *adj.* in error, wrong, in fault, erroneous, culpable. *M.Ir.* merugud, wandering.

mearachdachd, *n. f.* erroneousness, faultiness, culpability.

mearachdaich, mer'-achc-ich, *v.* go wrong.

mearadh-sionnachain, *n. m.* phosphorus.

mearaiche, mer'-ich-u, *n. m.* merryAndrew.

mearail, mer'-al, *n. m.* error, mistake, = mer + samail.

mearcach, mer'-kach, *adj.* confident, rash ; fr. **mer.**

mearcaid, mercej, *n. f.* a rash, headstrong person.

mearcasach, mercasuch, *a.* headstrong, rash ; wanton ; vigorous ; proud.

mearchunn, mer'-chun, **mearchunnd**, *v.* miscalculate, cheat by misreckoning.

mearchunnas, mer'-chŭn-us, **mearchunndus**, *n. m.* cheating one with his eyes open, miscalculation, misreckoning.

meardrach, *n. m.* metre ; crambo. *See* **meadar.**

meargadaich, mergadich, *v. intr.* be impatient.

mearganta, merg'-ant-u, *adj.* brisk, sportive, wanton, obstinate ; fr. **mer.**

mearrachdas, miaruchcus, *n. m.* wantonness, indelicate romping, nearly wanton joy.

meàrs, mers, *v.* march ; fr. the *Eng.*

mearsuinn, mersin, *vbl. n. m.* vigour, strength, staying power ; fr. **mair** (remain). *Also* **meartuinn.**

meas, mĕss, *n. m.* respect, respectability, estimation, esteem, public notice ; **le meas is miadh**, with respect and approbation ; **is beag meas a bha agadsa air**, you lightly esteemed him ; valuation, estimate, appraisement ; **meas nan tighean**, the appraisement, or valuation of the houses ; *v.* value, estimate, reckon, count, regard ; *vbl. n. m.* esteeming, regarding ; **tha mi a' meas**, I regard, I esteem. *O.Ir.* **mess**, *judicium* ; *infin.* of **midiur**, I judge, estimate. *Lat.* meditari. *Gr.* μέδομαι, think of.

meas, mes, *n. m.* fruit. *E.Ir.* **mess.** *W.* mes, acorns.

measach, mesuch, *a.* fruitful.

measadair, mesuder, *n. m.* appraiser, valuator.

measadaireachd, *n. f.* estimating, valuing, appraising.

measail, mĕss'-al, *adj.* respectable, worthy ; **duine measail**, a respectable individual : esteemed, valued, respected ; **measail aig uaislibh is ìslibh**, respected by high and low.

measair, misir, *n. f., pl.* **measraichean**, a measure, dish. *See* **miosair.**

measalachd, misaluchc, *n. f.* respectability, merit, dignity, regard, esteem.

measan, misan, *n. m.* a lapdog, puppy. *E.Ir.* mesan ; fr. **mess**, fosterling.

measarra, mĕss'-urr-u, *adj.* temperate, abstemious, sober, moderate, frugal ; " measured." *O.Ir.* mesurda. Cf. *Lat.* mensuratus.

measarrachd, mĕss'-arr-uchc, *n. f.* moderation, sobriety, temperance, frugality ; **ann am measarrachd**, in moderation.

measg, *n. m.* a mixture ; **am measg**, among ; *prep.* among, amidst, midst ;

measg bheannta fàsail, among desert mountains ; **'nam measg**, among them.

measg, *v.* mix, mingle, stir about. *E.Ir.* mescaim. *Lat.* misceo. *W.* mysgu. *O.Celt.* misko, I mix.

measgadh, mis-gu, *vbl. n. m.* act of mixing, mingling ; a mixture, admixture.

measgan, *n. m.* butter-crock. *E.Ir.* mescan (lump of butter).

measgnaich, misg-nich, *v.* mix.

measgta, *vbl. a.* mixed, mingled.

measraich, misrich, *v.* think.

meat, met, **meata**, metu, *adj.* timid, chicken-hearted, easily abashed, cowardly ; **sìol meata**, a timid race ; **cha bhuadhaich am meata gu bràth**, the chicken-hearted shall never conquer. *E.Ir.* **meta**, cowardly.

meatachadh, metuchu, *vbl. n. m.* act of benumbing, daunting, damping the spirits ; **thug sin meatachadh mór air**, that daunted him greatly ; fr. **meta.**

meatachd, metachc, *n. f.* timidity, delicacy of feeling or sentiment; cowardice.

meataich, metich, *v.* damp, daunt, intimidate ; starve of cold, benumb ; **mheataich siod gu mór e**, that daunted or damped his spirits greatly.

meath, me, *v.* 1. fade, decay, fail ; **mheath a' chraobh**, the tree faded. 2. taunt, damp ; **mheath e orm**, he taunted me. *E.Ir.* meth, decay.

meathachan, me-huchan, *n. m.* a decaying or fading man.

meathadh, me-hu, *vbl. n. m.* act of decaying, fading, failing ; damping, discouraging ; taunt, jeer, gibe ; **cha ruig thu leas a bhi toirt meathadh dhòmhsa**, you need not be taunting me.

mèathchalltuinn, mĕ-chaultin, *n. f.* southernwood.

mèathchridheach, *adj.* faint-hearted, chicken-hearted, timid.

mèath-ghàire, mĕ-ghàru, *n. f.* a smile.

mèathionnsaigh, mĕ-yunsy, *n. f.* a feeble attack, or attempt.

meathlaich, *v.* chill, benumb. *See* **meilich.**

mèathshuil, mĕ-hul, *n. f.* a blear-eye.

meidh, mey, *n. f.* a balance ; *v.* weigh. *O.Ir.* med, scale ; *lanx.* **hua meid**, gl. on libra. *Ml.* 82a. Cf. *Lat.* modius, a peck. *Gr.* μέδιμνος.

méidheach, mĕyuch, *a.* mild, affectionate, effeminate, decaying.

meidheadair, meyuder, *n. m.* balancer.

meidhichean, meyichun, *n. pl.* hip-joints ; **na meidhichean**, the hip-joints.

meidhinnean, me-inun, **méigean**, mĕgan, *pl. n.* hip-joints.

méidhis, mĕ-yish, *n. f.* an instalment ; **a' cheud mhéidhis**, the first instalment ; **'na mhéidhisean**, by instalments.

meidhisich, me-yishich, *v.* graduate.
meig, *n. f.* a protuberant chin, the snout
of a goat, a voice, a cry. *Also* smig,
smuig (in contempt).
meigead, me-giud, *n. m.* bleating of a kid
or goat. *Gr.* μηκάομαι, bleat ; μήκας,
a she-goat = " bleater." *McB.*
meigeadaich, megudich, meigeardaich,
megurdich, *n. f.* bleating of goats. *Ir.*
meigiodach (*n. m.*). *O'R.*
meigeil, *v.* bleat as a goat.
mèil, *v.* bleat as a sheep. *Also* miaghal.
Ir. meigiallam, bleat as sheep. *M.Ir.*
meglim.
meil, *v.* grind, meal, mill ; pound, pulverise ; a' chailc air a meileadh, the
chalk pulverised. *Also* beil and bleith.
O.Ir. melim. *W.* malu. *Lat.* molo.
O.Celt. melô.
meilbheag, melveg, *n. f.* the poppy ; *a.*
meilbheagach.
meilc, *n. f.* sweetness.
meilcheart, *n. m.* a chilblain.
meile, melu, *n. m.* mill-staff ; quern
handle.
meileachd, melachc, *n. f.* multure.
meileadair, meluder, *n. m.* grinder.
meileag, melag, muzzle ; for beileag.
meilearach, melurich, *n. m.* long seaside
grass. *O.N.* melr, bent.
meileartan, melurtan, *pl. n.* flesh mites,
generally under the toes.
mèilich, mēlich, *n. f.* bleating of sheep.
querulousness ; mèilich nan caorach,
bleating of sheep. *Also* miaghalaich.
meilich, *v.* benumb, chill with cold.
meiligeag, meligag, *n. f.* pea-husk.
méill, béill, *n. f.* a cheek, blubber lip. *Ir.*
méill, a cheek. *Lh.*
méillchritheach, meyl-chri-huch, *a.* of a
trembling-lip (through fear or nervousness).
meilleach, meyluch, beilleach, *a.* blubber-
lipped.
meilleag, meylag, beilleag, *n. f.* outer
rind of bark.
meiltir, meltir, *n. f., gen.* meiltreach, *pl.*
meiltrichean, grist, multure.
mèin, mēn, *n. f.* ore, metal, bullion ; a
mine ; mèin airgid, silver ore ; mèin
òir, gold metal. *Also* méinn. *E.Ir.*
mìanach, ore. *W.* mŵn, mineral.
O.Celt. meini, meinni.
mèineadair, mēnuder, *n. m.* miner,
mineralogist, student of ores.
mèineadaireachd, *n. f.* mineralogy, the
occupation of a miner.
méineil, *a.* flexible, sappy, substantial.
mèinire, mēniru, *n. m.* mine-sieve.
méinn, *n. f.* disposition, expression, features ; will, desire ; is dona a mhéinn
a tha ort, your looks are bad ; cia
mórdha a mhéinn, how majestic his

countenance ; mercy, clemency, discretion, discretionary power ; fàg aig
a mhéinn fhèin e, leave it to his own
discretion ; am méinn na gaoithe, to
the mercy of the wind ; native energy,
or quality ; talamh a bheir bàrr o a
mhéinn fhéin, land that can produce
crops from its own nature or native
energy. *Ir.* méin, desire, mind, disposition ; méinn, quality. *Lh.*
méinnealachd, *n. f.* productive quality ;
tenderness, as grass, tallow, etc.
méinneil, mēnal, *adj.* tender, productive,
prolific, as a female ; native ; flexible,
as metals ; substantial, sappy.
meirbh, merv, *adj.* slender, delicate,
spiritless. *E.Ir.* meirb, slow, tedious,
weak. *E.W.* merw, flaccid. *O.Celt.*
mervi-s, weak.
meirbh, *v.* digest, concoct in the stomach.
meirbhe, *n. f.* delicacy, slenderness. *Ir.*
meirbhe, weakness, craziness. *Lh.*
meirbhean, merven, *n. m.* indigestion.
meirean nam magh, *n. m.* agrimony. *Ir.*
meirin.
meirg, merg, *n. f.* rust ; *v. intr.* rust,
corrode. *O.Ir.* meirc (gl. *aerugo*).
O.Celt. mergi-, rust.
meirgeach, *adj.* rusty ; of a person,
cadaverous, ill-tempered.
meirgeal, *n. m.* a cadaverous person.
meirghe, mer-yu, *n. m.* a banner. *E.Ir.*
mergge. *O.N.* merki, a banner, a mark.
meirgich, mergich, *v.* grow rusty.
meirglas, *n. m.* jaws ; bidh do mheirglas
sgìth, your jaws will be tired.
mèirle, mērle, meairle, *n. f.* theft. *E.Ir.*
merle.
mèirleach, mērluch, *n. m.* a thief. *E.Ir.*
merlech.
meirneal, mernal, *n. m.* a kind of hawk ;
merlin ; fr. the *Eng.*
meiteal, miotailt, *n. f.* metal. *Lat.*
metallum.
mèith, meath, mē, *a.* fat, sappy. *O.Ir.*
méth.
meoghail, meadhail, miö-ul, *n. f.* mirth,
jollity.
meomhair, mio-ir, *n. f.* memory, recollection ; faigh air do mheomhair, get
by rote, get by heart ; gleus do
mheomhair, excite your memory.
See meamhair. *Lat.* memoria.
meòmhrach, miōr'-uch, *n. f.* memorandum, meditating.
meòrachadh, *vbl. n. m.* meditating, pondering ; observing attentively ; act of
meditation.
meòraich, miōr'-ich, *v.* meditate, ponder, calculate, reconsider, study. *Lat.*
memoria. *E.Ir.* mebraigim, study, con.
meuchd, *n. m.* mixture (dial).
meud, mēd, miad, *n. m.* size, bulk,

dimensions, extent, magnitude, greatness ; **meud an tighe**, the size of the house ; **meud a bhròin**, the magnitude of his grief ; as many as, number, quantity ; **co mheud a tha ann**, how many are there ? **a mheud 's a tha làthair**, as many as are present ; **a' dol am meud**, growing in size or extent. *O.Ir.* mét (*f.*), **méit**, *magnitude. O.W.* meint (maint). *O.Celt.* manti. (*Hr.*)

meudachadh, mēduchu, *vbl. n. m.* increasing, augmenting, multiplying ; act of an enlargement, augmentation, increase, growth. *Also* **miadachadh**. *E.Ir.* métugud.

meudachd, mēdachc, *n. f.* size, stature, magnitude, dimensions, extent, bulk. *Also* **miadachd**.

meudaich, mēdich, *v.* increase, enlarge, multiply, add, abound, grow in size, improve, augment ; **am fear nach meudaich an càrn, gum meudaich e a' chroich**, he that will not add to the *cairn*, may he add to the gibbet. *Also* **miadaich**.

meud-bhronn, mēd-vroun, *n. f.* dropsy.
meug, miūg, *n. m.* whey. *See* **mèag**.
meugach, meugail, *adj.* serous, like whey, of whey.
meunan, mén'-an, *n. m.* a yawn, gape.
meunanaich, mèn'-an-ich, *vbl. n. f.* act of yawning ; **thòisich e air meunanaich**, he began to yawn. *Also* **miaranaich**.

meur, mēr, *g. sing.* meòir, *pl.* meòir and **meuran**, *n. f.* a finger, branch, prong, knot of wood, toe ; **meur a ghràpa**, the prong of the fork ; **meur de'n teaghlach sin**, a branch of that family ; **tha meòir san fhiodh**, the wood is knotty ; a kind ; **meur de'n chaithimh**, a kind of consumption ; **meur a' ghiomaich**, the claw of the lobster. *Also* **miar**. *O.Ir.* mér (*m.*), finger.

meurach, *adj.* fingered, pronged, knotty, branchy. *Also* **miarach**.
meuradan, mērudan, *n. m.* a delicate, slender, weak person. *Also* **miarraide**.
meuradanach, *a.* delicate.
meuradanachd, *n. f.* the conduct of a delicate person ; eating or dealing with, gently.
meurag, *n. f.* little finger, clew of yarn ; *a.* **meuragach**.
meuragaich, mēragich, *v.* finger, fidget. *Also* **meuraganaich** and **meuraich**.
meuragan, *n. m.* a little thimble.
meuraich, mērich, *v.* prong, finger.
meuran, mēran and miàran, *n. m.* a thimble ; a ferrule.
meuran nan cailleacha marbha, *m.* foxglove. *Also* **meuran dearg** ; **meuran sìth**.
meuranach, *a.* full of thimbles.

meuranta, mēr'-annt-u, *a.* delicate.
meurantachd, *n. f.* delicacy of constitution, silliness of person.
mhàin, vāin, *adv.* only, alone ; **chan e sin a mhàin**, that is not all, or alone ; always written, a mhàin. *M.Ir.* amáin, only ; the *O.Ir.* equiv. is nammá, only (lit. " not-more ").
mi, *per. pron.* I ; **is mi**, it is I. *O.Ir.* mé, *Lat.* mê.
mi-, *neg. part.* un-, mis-. *O.Ir.* mi-. It forms cpds. freely, such as : **mì-bheus**, immodesty ; **mì-bhuil**, abuse (of opportunity) ; **mì-chiataibh**, dislike.
miad, miadan, miadar, *n. m.* a meadow, mead ; fr. the *Eng.*
miadh, miä, *n. m.* demand, call ; **chan 'eil miadh sam bith air crodh**, there is no demand for cattle ; honour, approbation ; **meas agus miadh**, respect and approbation. *O.Ir.* míad, dignity.
miadhalachd, mia-dhaluchc, *n. f.* demand, preciousness, respectability, fondness, rareness.
miadhail, miadhal, *adj.* in great demand ; precious, valuable, very fond of ; **tha buntàta miadhail**, the potatoes are in great demand ; **miadhail mu a chloinn**, dotingly fond of his children ; **gnothach miadhail**, precious or valuable thing. *O.Ir.* míathamle = míad (honour) + samail (like).
miag, mēăg, *n. m.* a mew of a cat ; caterwauling ; *v.* mew, caterwaul, as a cat.
miagail, mēăg'-al, *vbl. n. f.* mewing, caterwauling. *See* **meaghal**.
mial, mi-ul, *n. m.* a louse ; **mial-spàgach**, a crab-louse ; **mial-mòna**, peat-louse ; **mial-caorach**, a tick ; *also* seòlann. *O.Ir.* mìl, an animal. *W.* mil. *O.Celt.* mêlo-n.
mialach, *adj.* lousy.
mialachd, miu-lachc, *n. f.* lousiness.
mialchu, miül-choo, *n. m.,* *pl.* mialchoin, greyhound. *E.Ir.* míl - chú, greyhound. *E.W.* mil-gi.
mialta, *a.* pleasant, fair and smoothskinned. *O.Ir.* meld, pleasant.
mi-altrum, mee-altrum, *n. m.* bad nursing ; **cinnidh mac o mhi-altrum ach cha chinn e o'n aog**, a son may grow from bad nursing, but cannot escape the grave.
miamhail, miä-vul, *vbl. n. f.* mewing (of cat) ; *onomatop.* word. Cf. *Fr.* miaulement, *cri du chat. See* **meaghal**.
mianan, miaran, *n. m.* a yawn.
miann, miün, *n. m.* intention, desire, inclination, will, purpose, love, delight, appetite ; **an sàsuich thu miann na leómhainn òig**, wilt thou satisfy the appetite of the young lion ? **tha mhiann**

sin orm, I mean or purpose to do that. *O.Ir.* mían, a desire. *E.W.* mynn-u.

miann, *n. m.* a mole ; tha miann air aodann, there is a mole on his face ; miann fion, a mole of the colour of wine.

miannach, meeūn'-ach, *a.* desirous, keen.

miannachadh, meeūn'-ach-u, *vbl. n. m.* coveting, desiring ; am miannachadh cuid duine eile, coveting another's property.

miannaich, meeūn'-ich, *v.* desire, covet, lust after, fix one's heart on, wish greatly.

miannmhor, miannar, meeun'-ur *adj.* desirous, covetous, greedy.

mi-aogus, mee-ūg'-us, *n. m.* unseemliness.

miapachd, miäp'-achc, *n. f.* cowardice.

miapadh, miäp'-u, *n. m.* bashfulness, cowardice, pusillanimity ; seized with concern. *Also* miap.

miapaidh, miäpy, *adj.* cowardly.

miarraide, *n. m.* a weakling, a delicate child—thin, pale, of poor appetite ; " a shilpit thing." (*Sc.*)

mias, meeus, *n. f., gen.* and *dat.* méis, dish, platter, charger, plate. *E.Ir.* mìas = *Lat.* mensa. *Wi.*

mì-bhàigh, *n. f.* unkindness.

mì-bhail, *n. f.* profusion.

mì-bhanail, *a.* immodest.

mì-bhanalachd, *n. f.* immodesty.

mì-bheus, *n. f.* vice, immorality.

mì-bheusach, *a.* immodest.

mì-bheusachd, *n. f.* immorality, immodesty, unpoliteness, bad manners.

mì-bhlasda, *a.* insipid.

mì-bhlasdachd, *n. f.* insipidity.

mì-bhòidheach, *adj.* unhandsome.

mì-bhreathnaich, *v.* misconceive, misjudge.

mì-bhreith, *n. f.* wrong judgement.

mì-bhuaidh, *n. f.* defeat.

mì-bhuaireasach, *a.* good-tempered.

mì-bhuidheach, *a.* dissatisfied, displeased, discontented.

mì-bhuil, *n. f.* misapplication, profusion ; rinn thu mi-bhuil deth, you misapplied it, you made bad use of it.

mì-bhuilich, *v.* misapply, misimprove, waste, squander ; mhì-bhuilich thu t'ùine, you misapplied your time.

mì-bhunailteach, *adj.* unstationary, inconstant, unsettled.

mì-chaidreach, *a.* unsociable, disaffected, unfriendly.

mì-chàirdeas, *n. m.* unkindness.

mì-chàirdeil, *a.* unfriendly.

mì-chalmarra, *a.* feeble.

mì-chaomhainn, *v.* misspend.

mì-chaomhnadh, *n. m.* profusion.

mìcheart, *adj.* unjust, evil.

mì-cheartas, *n. m.* injustice.

mì-chiall, *n. m.* insanity, folly.

mìchiallach, *a.* mad, insane.

mi-chiataibh, *n. f.* dislike. *E.Ir.* mí-chatu, dishonour, shame.

mì-chinnt, *n. f.* uncertainty.

mì-chinnteach, *a.* uncertain.

mi-chion, *n. m.* aversion.

mì-chiùin, *a.* boisterous.

mì-chleachd, *v.* abrogate, disuse, render obsolete.

mì-chlis, *a.* inactive.

mìchliu, *n. f.* disgrace, infamy, reproach, bad fame or character. *Ir.* mí-chlú, dispraise.

mi-chliùiteach, *a.* disgraceful, infamous, reproachful, dishonourable.

mì-chneasda, *adj.* cruel.

mì-chneasdachd, mē-chrest'-achg, *n. f.* cruelty.

mìcholtach, *a.* improbable, unlikely ; unlike, dissimilar.

mì-choltachd, *n. f.* improbability, dissimilarity, unlikeliness.

mì-chòmhdhail, *n. f.* ill-luck.

mì-chompanta, *adj.* unsocial, unsociable, distant.

mì-chompantachd, *n. m.* unsociableness, distant manner.

mì-chòrd, *v.* disagree, dissent.

mì-chòrdadh, *vbl. n. m.* act of disagreeing, dissenting ; disagreement.

mì-chothrom, *n. m.* unfairness, disadvantage, injustice.

mì-chothromach, *adj.* uneven, rugged ; unfair, unjust.

mì-chreid, *v.* disbelieve.

mì-chreideach, *a.* distrustful ; *n. m.* unbeliever, infidel, heretic.

mì-chreideamh, *n. m.* unbelief, heresy, want of faith ; air son am mì-chreideamh, for their unbelief. *Ir.* mí-chretem, unbelief.

mì-chreideas, *n. m.* want of confidence, disrespect, distrust.

mì-chreideasach, *adj.* disrespectful, distrustful.

mì-chridheil, *a.* heartless.

mì-chruinnealas, *n. f.* untidiness, profusion.

mì-chruinneil, *adj.* untidy, uneconomical, profuse.

mì-chuimhneach, *a.* forgetful.

mì-chumachdail, mì-chunnadail, *adj.* unshapely, ill-shaped.

mì-chùram, *n. f.* negligence.

mì-chùramach, *a.* careless.

mì-dhàichealachd, mì-dhàichealas, *n. f.* absurdity.

mì-dhàicheil, *a.* absurd, improbable, unlikely, nonsensical.

mì-dhealbh, *n. m.* absurdity, unseemliness.
mì-dhealbhach, *a.* absurd, unshapely.
mì-dheas, *a.* unprepared, wrong.
mì-dheòin, *n. f.* reluctance.
mì-dheònach, *a.* reluctant.
mì-dhiadhachd, *n. f.* ungodliness, unholiness, irreligion.
mì-dhiadhaidh, *a.* unholy.
mì-dhìleas, *a.* unfaithful.
mì-dhìlseachd, *n. f.* disloyalty, unfaithfulness, treachery.
mì-dhleasnach, *a.* undutiful, disloyal, unfaithful.
mì-dhleasnas, *n. m.* undutifulness.
mì-dhlighe, *n. f.* unlawfulness.
mì-dhligheach, *a.* not due.
mì-dhligheil, *a.* unlawful.
mi-dhòchas, *n. m.* despair.
mì-dhòchasach, *adj.* despondent ; diffident, unpretending, retiring.
mì-dhòigh, *n. f.* want of method, awkwardness, absurdity.
mì-dhòigheil, *adj.* disarranged, unmethodical, absurd, poor in circumstances.
mì-dhreach, *n. m.* deformity.
mì-dhreachmor, *a.* ugly.
mì-dhùrachd, *n. m.* insincerity.
mì-dhùrachdach, *a.* insincere, indifferent, careless, negligent.
mì-earachdail, *a.* unseemly.
mì-earachdas, *n. m.* ungentility.
mì-earbsa, *n. f.* distrust.
mì-earbsach, *adj.* distrustful, suspicious, despondent, despairing.
mì-éifeachd, *n. f.* inefficacy.
mì-fhaichill, *n. m.* negligence, unguardedness ; mi-fhaichilleach, incautious.
mì-fhaighidinn, *n. f.* impatience, greed, keenness.
mì-fhaighidinneach, *adj.* impatient, too impetuous, too keen.
mì-fheart, *n. f.* negligence, want of attention.
mì-fheum, *n. m.* misapplication, uselessness, bad use.
mi-fhortan, mee-orstan, *n. m.* misfortune.
mi-fhortanach, *adj.* unfortunate, misfortunate, disastrous, unhappy.
mì-fhreagarrach, *a.* unsuitable, unanswerable, unbefitting.
mì-fhreasdalach, *adj.* inattentive, heedless, improvident.
mì-fhurachail, *a.* inattentive, careless, unguarded.
mì-fhurasda, *a.* difficult.
mì-ghiùlan, *n. m.* misconduct.
mì-ghlic, *adj.* unwise.
mì-ghliocas, *n. m.* folly.
mì-ghnàthachadh, *n. m.* abuse, misconduct, misapplication.
mì-ghnàthaich, *a.* abuse.
mì-ghràsail, *a.* reprobate.

mì-ghrunnd, *n. m.* indifference.
mì-ghrunndail, *a.* careless.
mì-iomchuidh, *a.* unfit.
mì-iomchuidheachd, *n. f.* impropriety, unfitness, indecency.
mì-iomradh, *n. m.* evil report.
mì-ionraic, *a.* dishonest.
mil, *n. f., gen.* meala, honey ; cir-mheala, honeycomb. *O.Ir.* mil. *E.W.* mel. *O.Celt.* meli-. *Lat.* mel. *Gr.* μέλι.
mì-labhrach, *a.* taciturn.
mì-laghail, *a.* unlawful, illegal, illicit, prohibited.
mil-cheò, *n. m.* mildew.
mìle, *n. m.* a mile, a thousand ; mìltean, thousands. *O.Ir.* mìle. *Lat.* mille, a thousand ; mille passuum, a mile.
mìleach, *n. m.* a war-horse, a bloodhorse.
mileachadh, *vbl. n. m.* benumbing, starving of cold.
mileag, milag, *n. f.* a melon ; *a.* mileagach.
mìleag, *n. f.* a mean woman.
mileamh, *adj.* thousandth ; fr. mìle.
milean, *n. m.* fawning.
mìleanta, *adj.* heroic, brave, stately ; fr. mìl. (*See below.*)
mìleantachd, *n. f.* feats of valour, bravery ; stateliness.
milearach, *n. m.* sweet grass, sea-grass. mil + feur. *Ir.* milfhearach, a marine weed with a sweet root. *O'Don.*
mileis, *n. f.* fawning, affectionate licking of a dog.
milich, *v.* benumb. *See* meilich.
mìlidh, *n. m.* a warrior, champion. *E.Ir.* mìlid. *O.Ir.* mìl. *E.W.* mil-wr, warrior. *Lat.* miles, militis, a soldier ; warrior.
mì-liosda, *adj.* unobtrusive.
milis, *adj.* sweet, savoury. *O.Ir.* milis.
mill, *v.* spoil, hurt, mar, disarrange ; mhill thu e, you spoiled it ; starve of cold. *O.Ir.* millim, I destroy.
mill, *pl.* of meall, *q.v.*
milleach, *n. m.* tender, sappy grass.
milleadh, *vbl. n. m.* act of spoiling, ruin.
millte, *vbl. a.* spoiled, ruined.
millteach, *adj.* ruinous.
millteach, mìlteach, *n. m.* sweet hill grass, arrow-grass. *Also* milneach.
millteachd, *n. f.* destructiveness.
millteag, *n. f.* a small bunch ; a bottle of thatch ; fr. meall.
milltear, *n. m.* a destroyer, spendthrift ; a prodigal person.
milmheacan, *n. m.* mallows, *malvæ.*
mì-loinn, *n. f.* ungracefulness.
mì-loinneil, *adj.* awkward.
mìlse, *compar.* of milis ; na's mìlse, sweeter. *O.Ir.* millsiu.
mìlseachd, *n. f.* sweetness.
mìlsead, *abstr. n. f.* sweetness.
mìlsich, *v.* sweeten.

mì-mhaise, *n. f.* deformity.
mì-mhaiseil, *a.* deformed.
mì-mheas, *n. m.* disrespect.
mì-mheasail, *a.* disrespectful.
mi-mheasarra, *adj.* intemperate, immoderate, dissolute, incontinent.
mì-mhìnich, *v.* misinterpret, misconstrue, misexpound.
mì-mhisneach, *n. f.* discouragement, irresolution, shyness, diffidence, damp.
mì-mhisneachail, *a.* faint-hearted, disheartening, cowardly, backward.
mì-mhisnich, *v.* discourage, dishearten, dismay ; damp the spirits.
mìmhodh, *n. m.* rudeness.
mì-mhodhail, *a.* rude, unpolite, unmannerly, ungentlemanly.
mìn, *meen, adj.* smooth, agreeable to the touch ; soft, delicate, tender ; small, fine ; mìn bhasan bàna, delicate, soft, fair hands ; aodach mìn, smooth cloth ; clacha mìne o'n t-sruth, smooth stones from the stream ; gentle, mild, quiet, inoffensive ; an gille mìn, an nighean mhìn, the gentle, inoffensive young man—the gentle, inoffensive maid ; pulverised, ground small ; fine ; min mhìn, fine meal. *E.Ir.* mín. *E.W.* mwyn. *O.Celt.* mêno-s.
min, *n. f.* meal ; min eòrna, barley-meal ; min-eararaidh, meal made from corn hastily dried in a pot ; min sheaguil, rye-meal ; min-pheasair, pease-meal ; min phònair, bean-meal. *O.Ir.* men, meal, *farina.*
mì-nadur, *n. m.* inhumanity.
mì-nadurra, *adj.* unnatural, preternatural ; void of natural affection.
mì-nàire, *n. f.* impudence.
mì-naomh, *a.* unholy, profane.
mì-naomhachadh, *vbl. n. m.* act of profaning ; profanation.
mì-naomhachd, *n. f.* profanation, unholiness.
mì-naomhaich, *v.* profane, unhallow.
mìnbhriathar, *n. m.* a soft expression.
mìn-bhrist, *v.* pulverise.
mìne, *meenu, n. f.* softness, smoothness ; *compar.* of mìn, smoother, finer.
mìneach, *meenuch, n. m.* tender grass.
mìneachadh, *meenuchu, vbl. n. m.* act of expounding, interpreting, explaining, simplifying ; exposition, explanation, interpretation.
mìneachd, *meenachc, n. f.* softness, delicacy, fineness ; mìnead, deg. of fineness.
mìnead, *abstr. n. m.* fineness, smoothness.
mìneag, *meenag, n. f.* a mild woman.
mìnear, *meener, n. m.* soft fine grass ; for mìn + feur.
mìngheal, *meen-yal, a.* soft and fair.
mìnich, *meenich, v.* interpret, explain,

illustrate, expound, simplify ; mìnich so dhomh, explain this to me. *Ir.* mínigim. 1. reduce to small pieces. 2. interpret. *P.H.*
mìniche, meenichu, *n. m.* interpreter.
minicionn, miniciun, *n. m.* a kid's skin. meann + cionn (skin).
mìnid, minij, *n. f.* runnet. *Also* binid.
minidh, miny, *n. m.* awl. *E.Ir.* menad. *O.Celt.* minaveto.
minidh-teallaich, *n. m.* hot iron for burning holes in wood.
minig, minig, *adj.* frequent, often. *O.Ir.* menicc. *E.W.* mynych. *O.Celt.* nenekki-s.
minis, minish, *n. f.* a degree or portion ; nì sin air minisibh e, we will do it by degrees ; a cheud mhinis deth, the first portion or part of it.
ministeir, minishter, *n. m.* minister, clergyman. *Lat.* minister.
ministeireachd, minishteruchc, *n. f.* ministry.
ministrealachd, minishtraluchc, *n. f.* ministration, clerical function, incumbency.
ministreil, *a.* ministerial.
minmhear, *n. f.* hemlock.
minnean, min'-èn, *n. m.* kidling (*dim.* of meann).
minnseag, meenshag, *n. f.* a yearling she-goat.
minrosg, *n. m.* soft eyelid, soft eyes.
mìnshuil, meen-hool, *n. f.* a mild eye.
mìo-, a stress accent on the prefix of a compound deletes the hyphen, and brings the compound under the ordinary law. Then mì- and di- become mìo- and dìo- respectively, when the first vowel in the next syllable is broad (a, o, u), as, mìothlachd, for mì-thlachd, dìochuimhn for dì-chuimhn.
mìobhadh, mee-vu, *n. m.* ill-usage (as by weather) ; 'g ar mìobhadh le fuachd, making us pithless with cold ; appar. fr. mì-bhàidh.
mìobhail, meeval, *a.* bad-mannered, impolite ; a form of mì-mhodhail.
mìochuis, mee-choosh, *n. f.* flirtation, pretended indifference, coquetry, jilting, smirking, envy, fancy.

> " Ged tha mi siubhal Galldachd
>   Cha'n ann tha mo mhìochuis."
> " Though I travel the Lowlands
>   'Tis not here my fancy is."

chan 'eil mìochuis agam ris, I have no fancy for it.
mìochuiseach, *adj.* coquettish, flirting, as a prude, leering with the eye ; *n. f.* a coquette, flirt.
mìochuiseachd, mee-choosh-achc, *n. f.* flirtation, coquetry ; assumed indifference.

miodal, midul, *n. m.* flattery. *Ir.* miodal.
miodalach, *a.* fawning, given to flattery
miodar, *n. m.* meadow, good grass or pasture.
miodar, midur, *n. m.* a wooden dish. *See* meadar.
miodhair, mee-ur, *n. m.* churl, niggard ; *adj.* pitiful, paltry, ugly. *Also* mìofoir, miodhoir.
mìog, meeg, *n. f.* a smile, a sly look ; miogshuil, laughing eye. *Ir.* mìog.
mìoghlachadh, *n. m.* suspense, presentiment of evil.
mìogshuileach, meeg-hooluch, *adj.* having a smiling eye.
mìolaire, *n. m.* the pivot of a quern. *E.Ir.* míolaire, the pivot on which the mill-stone turns.
miolaran, miooluran, *n. m.* fawning of a dog, expression of joy, whimpering. *Ir.* miolarán, lamentation. *O'R.*
miolaranaich, mioolur-anich, *n. f.* low barking, whimpering.
miolasg, mioolusg, *n. m.* skittishness, skit (of a horse) ; flattery, fawning (as of a dog). *Ir.* míolasg, fawning. *O'R.*
miolasgach, *adj.* skittish.
miolasgachd, *n. f.* skittishness.
miolcach, *a.* flattering ; clownish.
miolcais, *n. f.* caressing, fondling.
mìomhail, meeval, *adj.* impertinent ; for mi + mhodhail.
mìomhalachd, meevaluchc, *n. f.* impertinence.
mion, min, *adj.* small ; buntàta mion, small potatoes ; *adv.* minutely ; a bheil thu mion-eòlach air, are you minutely acquainted with him ? an do mhion rannsuich thu e, did you search it minutely ? *See* mean, meanbh.
mionach, min-uch, *n. m.* entrails, bowels. *M.Ir.* menach.
mionacrach, min-acruch, *a.* eating but little at a time, but often trying meat, as an invalid, when convalescent (min (small) + acrach).
mionagamaid, minagumej, *n. f.* suppressed anxious whispering.
mionaid, minej, *n. f.* minute, moment ; fr. the *Eng. Lat.* minutus, rt. min-.
mionaideach, *adj.* minute ; iarr gu mionaideach, search minutely.
mionan, minan, *n. m.* sheep or dove dung.
mion-aois, min-ūsh, *n. f.* minority.
mion-chunntas, min-choontus, *n. m.* an accurate reckoning, a minute account.
mion-eòlach, min-yōluch, *a.* thoroughly acquainted.
mion-eòlas, min-yōlus, *n. m.* intimate knowledge.
mion-iasg, *n. m.* small fish, fry.
mionn, mioonn, *n. f.* an oath, a vow, de-

claration on oath, curse ; also crown of the head (obsolete). *E.Ir.* mind, diadem, relic ; oath. *O.Ir.* mind ; gl. insignia. *Z².* *O.Celt.* mindi-, diadem.
mionnaich, mèunn'-ich, *v.* swear, curse, make oath, make a solemn appeal to God ; mionnaichte, *vbl. a.* sworn, bound by an oath.
mìonnt, *n. m.* mint (plant). *Lat.* mentha. *Gr.* μίνθα or -η.
mi-onoraich, mee-onorich, *v.* dishonour.
mion-rosg, *n. m.* a sweet or gentle eye.
miontan, *n. m.* the titmouse.
mìorailt, meer-elt. *See* miorbhuil.
mìorailteach. *See* mìorbhaileach.
mìorailteachd. *See* mìorbhaileachd.
mìorath, mee-ra, *n. m.* ill-luck ; for mì-rath.
mìorbhail, meeurval, *n. f.* a wonder ; miracle. *E.Ir.* mìr-bail. *Lat.* mirabile.
mìorbhaileach, *adj.* marvellous, wonderful, miraculous.
mìorbhaileachd, *n. f.* wonderfulness, marvellousness, miraculousness.
miortal, *n. m.* the myrtle tree.
mìorun, mee-roon, *n. m.* malice, ill-will, spite. mì + rùn.
mìorunach, *a.* malicious, malevolent.
mìorunachd, *n. f.* maliciousness, malevolence, ill-will, spitefulness.
mìos, mee-us, *n. m.* a month. *O.Ir.* mí, *gen.* mís. *Lat.* mensis. *W.* mìs. *O.Celt.* mîns. *Gr.* μήν (Ion), μείς, month.
miosa, misu, *compar.* of olc, bad : worse, worst, inferior. *O.Ir.* messa, *compar.* of olc.
mìosach, meesuch, *adj.* monthly, menstrual ; an galar mìosach, menstrual courses ; *n. f.* herb, the purging flax, the fairy flax. *Ir.* místa, monthly, menstrual. *P.H.*
mìosadair, meesuder, *n. m.* an almanac, calendar.
mìosail, meesal, *a.* monthly.
miosar, misir, *n. m.* a wooden dish (larger than miodar) ; a measure (of meal, of shot). *Lat.* mensura.
mìosdadh, mìasdadh, *n. m.* injury, great damage, mischief. =mì + stà.
miosgan, misgan, *n. m.* butter-kit. *Ir.* miosgán.
miosgan, misgan, *n. m.* butter-kit.
miosguinn, misgin, *n. f.* malice, spite, slander ; *a.* miosguinneach. *O.Ir.* miscais, hate, *odium.*
miotag, meetag, *n. f.* worsted glove ; fr. the *Eng.* mitten.
mìotagach, *a.* gloved, wearing gloves.
mìothaird, mee-harj, *n. f.* unprotection, state of not being looked after.
mìothar, mìothur, mee-har. *See* miodhair.
miothlachd, meeulachc, *n. m.* offence, displeasure, resentment.

miothlachdar, meeulachcur, *adj.* dis-
pleasing, disagreeable, vexing, galling.
mìr, meer, *n. m.* bit, particle ; a piece ;
chan 'eil mìr agam, I haven't a particle ;
mìr mòna, a sub-division of a peat-
stack ; mìr fearainn, a patch of ground.
O.Ir. mír. *O.Celt.* mêsrén-.
mircean, *n. m.* an edible seaweed. *See*
muirichlinn.
mire, miru, *n. m.* sport, sporting,
levity, fury, rage, frenzy ; dh' éirich
iad suas gu mire, they rose up to play ;
mire-chatha, rage or fury of battle.
M.Ir. mire ; *adj. compar.* of mear,
merry, wanton ; na's mire, more merry
or wanton.
mireag, mirag, *n. f.* frisking, skipping ;
a. mireagach ; fr. mear.
mirean, miren, *n.m.* in the cpd. gille-mirein,
the " merry-lad " ; spinning-top.
mireanach, *a.* playful, merry.
mìreannach, meeranuch, *n. m.* bridle-bit.
mì-reuson, *n. m.* want of fairness, un-
reason.
mì-reusonta, *a.* irrational ; duine mì-
reusanta, a man who acts contrary to
common sense.
mì-reusontachd, *n. f.* unreasonableness,
unconscionableness.
mì-riaghail, *v. tr.* misgovern.
mì-riaghailt, *n. f.* misrule, disorder,
quarrel, confusion, turmoil.
mì-riaghailteach, *adj.* unruly, confused,
unreasonable, quarrelsome.
mì-rian, *n. m.* disorder, confusion, mental
disorder ; economic waste ; want of
humour.
mì-rìoghail, *adj.* disloyal ; unbecoming
a king, unprincely.
mirr, *n. m.* myrrh. *E.Ir.* mirr. *Lat.*
myrrha. *Gr.* μύρρα ; fr. *Arab.* murr.
misd, mishj, misde, misju, *compar.* of olc,
cha mhisde mi siod, I am not the worse
for that. *M.Ir.* mes-te = messa de,
" worse of it."
misdeachd, mishjachc, *n. f.* inferiority,
deterioration.
mise, mishu, *emph. pers. pron.* I myself,
me myself.
mìseach, for minnseag, *n. f.* a kid.
misg, mishc, *n.f.* drunkenness, a debauch,
intoxication, inebriety ; air mhisg,
drunk ; là air mhisg, is là air uisge,
one day drunk, and next day drinking
water ; misg-chatha, battle drunkenness. *O.Ir.* mescc, drunk. *O.Celt.*
mesko- (fr. med-sko), closely related to
mid, *gen.* meda, mead (mesce =medce).
E.W. medw. *Gr.* μέθυ.
misgeach, *adj.* drunken, intoxicated ;
cha dèan cridhe misgeach breug, a
drunken heart tells no lie.
misgear, misger, *n. m.* drunkard.

misgearachd, *n. f.* drunkenness, potations ; ri misgearachd, at potations.
misgeil, misg'-al, *adj.* intoxicating.
mì-sgeinm, *n. f.* slovenliness, indecorum,
indecency, untidiness.
mì-sgeinmeil, *a.* untidy.
mì-sgìobalta, *adj.* clumsy, untidy, unwieldy, awkward in dress.
mì-sgìobaltachd, *n. f.* untidiness, awkwardness in gait or dress.
mì-sgoinn, *n. f.* lacking in vigour ; spirit-
lessness, slouchiness, indecency.
mì-sheagh, *n. m.* absurdity.
mì-sheaghail, *a.* absurd ; cowardly.
mì-shealbh, *n. m.* ill-luck.
mì-sheilbh, *n. f.* misfortune.
mì-sheirc, *n. f.* disaffection ; uncharitableness.
mì-sheirceil, *adj.* surly.
mì-sheòl, *v.* mislead, misguide.
mì-sheòlta, *adj.* unhandy.
mì-sheòltachd, *n. f.* unskilfulness, unhandiness, inexpertness.
mì-shìobhalta, *adj.* uncivil.
mì-shìobhaltachd, *n. f.* uncivility, rudeness, unpoliteness, turbulence.
mì-shocair, *a.* uneasy, unsettled, uncomfortable, troubled, disturbed ; *n.f.*
disquietude, unsettled state, or case of.
mì-shona, *adj.* unfortunate ; unhappy.
mì-shonas, *n. f.* bad luck ; lack of happiness.
mì-shuaimhneach, *adj.* restless, dis-
quieted, disturbed, annoyed, distressed.
mì-shuaimhneas, *n. m.* disquiet.
mì-shuairc, *a.* unpolite.
mì-shùghar, *a.* sapless.
mì-shùim, *n. f.* heedlessness, indifference,
inattention, carelessness.
mì-shùimeil, *adj.* careless.
misimean-dearg, *n. m.* bog-mint. *Also*
cairteal. *Ir.* cartal.
mìslean, *n. m.* sweet meadow-grass ; fr.
milis.
misneach, mishnuch, *n. f.* courage,
spirit, manliness, cheer, encouragement ; glac misneach, pluck up
courage ; le dìth misnich, for want
of courage ; thoir misneach mhaith
dha, keep him in spirits ; chaill e
mhisneach, he is quite disheartened.
M.Ir. mesnech ; fr. *O.Ir.* mess,
judicium.
misneachail, mishnuchal, *a.* courageous,
manly, brave, intrepid, undaunted.
misneachd, *n. f. See* misneach.
misnich, mishnich, *v.* encourage, exhort.
mistear, *n. m.* a cunning, designing
person. *See* misd.
mì-stéidhealachd, *n. f.* unsteadiness,
fickleness, giddiness.
mì-stéidheil, *adj.* unsteady.
mì-stiùir, *v.* mislead, misguide.

mì-stiùireadh, *vbl. n. m.* misleading, seducing; act of unmanageableness, seduction.

mi-stiùrrachd, *n. f.* wastefulness, misbehaviour, immorality.

mì-stuama, *adj.* unguarded.

mì-stuamachd, *n. f.* unguardedness, intemperance, immodesty.

mith, *n. m.* one of the lower class, as opposed to the nobility; **gach mith is math**, every inferior and superior.

mì-thàbhachd, *n. f.* inefficiency.

mì-thaing, *n. f.* ingratitude.

mì-thaingeil, *a.* ungrateful.

mì-thairbhe, *n. f.* disadvantage.

mì-thaitinn, *v.* disagree with, displease, give offence, offend.

mì-thaitneach, *a.* disagreeable.

mì-thaitneas, *n. m.* offence.

mì-tharbhach, *adj.* unprofitable, unsubstantial, unproductive.

mì-tharbhachd, *n. f.* unprofitableness, unproductiveness, untrustfulness.

mithear, mi-her, *a.* weak, crazy.

mì-theist, *n. f.* bad report.

mì-theisteil, *adj.* disreputable.

mì-theistneas, *n. f.* ill-repute.

mithich, meeich, *n. f.* fit time, high time, nick of time; **is mithich dhuinn falbh,** " is mithich a bhi bogadh nan gad," it is high time to steep the withes; **chan uair roimh 'n mhithich e**, it is not a moment too soon; it is high time. *O.Ir.* mithich, mithig, opportune time; *tempestivus*; καιρός.

mithlean, milen, *n. m.* 1. sport, playfulness. 2. a trick, greed, bad manners; for mi-oilean.

mì-thlusar, *adj.* cold in affections; of clothes next the skin, uncomfortable.

mì-thlusarachd, *n. m.* coldness of manner; uncomfortableness, as clothes.

mì-thogarrach, *a.* adverse.

mì-thogradh, *n. m.* aversion.

mì-thoil, *n. f.* reluctance.

mì-thoileach, *a.* averse.

mì-thoilich, *v.* displease.

mì-thoilichte, *vbl. a.* displeased, dissatisfied, discontented, unsatisfied.

mì-throcair, *n. f.* cruelty.

mì-thuig, *v.* misunderstand.

mì-thuigseach, *adj.* senseless, stupid, dull, absurd.

mì-uaibhreach, *adj.* humble.

mì-uaisle, *n. f.* meanness.

mì-uasal, *adj.* ignoble, mean.

miùghair, *a.* niggardly; fr. **mì + fiù.** Cf. **mìodhoir.**

mì-umhail, *a.* disobedient.

mì-umhlachd, *n. f.* disobedience, rebelliousness, disloyalty.

mì-urram, *n. f.* disrespect.

mì-urramach, *adj.* disrespectful.

mnà, mrà, *gen.* of bean; **ceann na mnà,** the head of the woman (or of the wife).

mnaoi, mrooy, *dat.* of bean; **do 'n mhnaoi** to the woman. *O.Ir.* mnai.

mnathan, mrà'-un, *pl.* of bean, wives, women. *O.Ir.* mná.

mo, *poss. pron.* my, mine; *reg. asp.* initial conson. of foll. word; takes form **m'** before words beginning with a vowel, as, **m' ainm**, my name. *O.Ir.* mo, mu.

mò, *compar.* of mór (great), greater. *O.Ir.* móa, móo. *O.Celt.* mâgô-s.

mobainn, mobin, *n. m.* maltreating, handling roughly.

mobhsgaideach, mouscejuch, *a.* dilatory, neglectful of duty.

mocais, mocish, *n. f.* a moccasin; Indian foot-wear; very like **cuaran.**

moch, *adj.* early; *compar.* muiche, earlier; *adv.* early, betimes, soon; **éirich moch,** rise early; **moch an dè,** early yesterday; **moch is anamoch,** early and late; **moch am màireach,** early to-morrow; *n. m.* dawn, morn; **o mhoch gu dubh,** from the dawn till the dusk. *O.Ir.* moch. *E.W.* moch, early, soon.

mochd, *v.* yield, move.

mocheirigh, mochiry, *n. f.* waking or rising early; **is tu a rinn a' mhocheirigh,** how early you are afoot! **mocheirigh is ioneirigh,** rising early, and late sitting; for **moch + eirigh.**

mochthrath, mochra, *n. m.* dawn; **'s a' mhochthrath,** in the dawn; *adv.* very early; **bha e so mochthrath,** he was here early; **mochthrath is dùbhthrath,** early and late (in the day). = **moch + tràth.**

mòd, *n. m.* a meeting, an assembly; a court of law; a baron-bailie court, presided over by the nominee of the proprietor, and could enforce payment of rent, and deal with disputes among tenants; " **gun ghearsom, gun mhàl, gun mhòd,**" without fee, or rent or court; **a' dol do 'n mhòd,** going to the court. *O.N.* mót, town-meeting, a court of law. *A.S.* gemot. Cf. *Goth.* mōtastaþs, toll-house.

modh, *n. m.* politeness, good manners, good breeding; **duine gun mhodh,** an ill-bred man. *E.Ir.* mod, respect, honour.

modh, *n. m.* manner, method; **air a' mhodh so,** by this method, in this manner. *O.Ir.* mod. *E.W.* modd. *Lat.* modus.

modhadh, *vbl. n. m.* training, taming horses. *I.Lom.*

modhalachd, *n. f.* good manners, politeness, good breeding, modesty.

modhan, *n. m.* the sound of a musical instrument.

mòdhar, mō'ar, *a.* soft, modest, silly, gentle ; an gleann mòdhar nan sruthan lùbach, in the still vale of the meandering streamlets.

mòg, *n. f.* plump hand. *Also* màg.

mògach, *adj.* soft-handed ; pawed.

mogach, *a.* shaggy, hairy, rough.

mogach, *n. m.* a raw youth, a shaggy fellow.

mogan, *n. m.* oat whisky.

mogan, *n. m.* old stocking ; a stocking without the sole of the foot ; a trousers-leg ; a mitt, mitten ; a glove with thumb only, and the fingers enclosed together.

moghunn, *n. m. See* modhan.

moglaich, moglich, *v.* husk nuts ; knit.

mogul, *n. m.* husk of a nut, mesh of a net. *O.Ir.* mocoll, lín, a mesh of a net.

mogur, *a.* bulky, clumsy.

moibean, moibeal, *n. m.* a mop, a broom. Cf. meapaid, a mop for tarring.

moibill, moy-bil, *v.* gnaw, mumble, mutter, half-chew.

moibleadh, moy-blu, *vbl. n. m.* mumbling, muttering, half-chewing ; act of gnawing, mutter. =" mak a mop of."

moiblich, *v.* gnaw, mumble, half-chew.

moiche, moych'-u, *adj., compar.* of moch, earlier, earliest ; *n. f.* earliness, soonness ; degree of earliness. *Also* muiche.

mòid, mō-ij—two *syll., n. f.* greatness. *M.Ir.* móti.

mòid, mōj, *n. f.* a vow. *See* bòid. *E.Ir.* móit.

mòide, mo-ij-u—three *syll., deg.* of mór, great ; cha mhòide e sin, it is not the greater for that ; bu mhòid' a ghlaoidh e, the more he cried. =moo + de, " greater of it."

moidreag, mojrag, *n. f.* a plump girl, a fat, plump, good-natured female child.

moighre, moyru, *a.* robust, handsome.

moil, *n. m.* matted hair. *See* molach.

moile, *n. m.* a rough swelling, caused by hammering.

moilean, mōylen, *n. m.* fat, plump male child ; a plump man. *Ir.* moileán, a fat comely child. *O'R.* Cf. moil, *môles. Lh.*

moileanach, *n. m.* a plump young man ; *adj.* plump.

moille, moliu, meliu, *n. f.* delay, detention. *See* mall.

mòine, mōniu, *n. f.* peat, moss, morass. *E.Ir.* móin, a fen, bog. *W.* mawn, peat, turf.

moineis, monesh, *n. f.* false delicacy, slowness, laziness. *See* monais.

moineiseach, *adj.* low, diffident, dilatory, fastidious.

moinig, monig, *n. f.* vanity, fastidiousness, nicety, boasting of favours conferred.

moinigeil, monigel, *adj.* fastidious, assuming indifference ; making nice.

mòinteach, mōntiuch, *n. f.* moss-land, moor-land ; *adj.* mossy.

mòinteachail, *adj.* mossy.

mòintidh, mōnty, *adj.* mossy.

moirear. *See* morair.

mòirneas, mōrnesh, *n. f.* great cascade, streams ; volcano ; mar mhòirneas de theine theintich, as a volcano of lava ; melted metal.

moisean, muisean, moshen, *n. m.* a sordid fellow, a mean rascal; the devil; fr. mosach, mean, stingy, dirty. *Ir.* moisin, a mean fellow. *O'R.*

moiseanach, *a.* sordid, dirty.

moiseanachd, *n. f.* sordidness.

moit, *n. f.* pride, conceit, airs ; pretended indifference about a thing one is very keen for ; fastidiousness ; nicety about a thing one is fond of.

moitealachd, motaluchc, *n. f.* a state of pride, state of assuming airs of importance ; fastidiousness.

moiteil, *adj.* proud, conceited ; assuming airs, pretending indifference ; excessively nice. *Ir.* moiteamhuil, pettish, sulky, nice. *O'R.*

mol, *v.* praise, laud, eulogise, exalt, extol, magnify ; recommend, exhort, advise ; mholainn dhuit dol dachaidh, I would recommend to you to go home; moladh càch thu, let others praise you. *O.Ir.* molaim, molfait Dia, they will praise God. *M.W.* molaf, I praise.

mol, mal, *n. m., gen. s.* and *n. pl.* muil, a shingly beach. *O.N.* möl, *gen.* malar, pebbles, worn stones, bed of pebbles on the beach or in a river.

molach, *adj.* rough, hairy.

molachas, *n. f.* hairiness.

moladh, mól'-u, *vbl. n. m.* praising, eulogising, applauding, recommending ; act of praise, applause. *O.Ir.* molad, praise.

moll, moul, *n. m.* chaff ; *gen. s.* mùill ; leaba mhùill, chaff-bed ; tiùrr mùill, a heap of chaff. *Ir.* moll. *O.Celt.* muldo-.

mollachd, *n. f. See* mallachd.

molltair, moultir, *n. m.* multure, mill-dues, a mould ; fr. the *Eng.* moulter.

molt, *n. m., gen. s.* and *n. pl.* muilt, a wedder. *E.Ir.* molt. *O.Celt.* molto-s, a wether. *M.Lat.* multo, *vervex.*

moltach, *adj.* praiseworthy. So *O.Ir.*

monadh, mon'-u, *n. m.* moor, heath ; moor and mountains. *W.* **mynydd,** a mountain.

monadail, mon'-ad-al, *adj.* moorish, hilly.

monais, monesh, *n. f.* slowness, negligence ; **monais is mì-chùram,** negligence and carelessness.

monaghar. *See* **monmhar.**

monar, *n. m.* refuse, contemptible person or object ; **thà, is cha b'e monar e,** yes, and it is not the refuse.

monasg, *n. m.* chaff, dross, refuse.

mongaineach, *a.* maned ; of heather = tufted (*DM.* 1st ed., changed to **mògunach** in later edd.) ; fr. **mong,** a mane.

monmhar, mon'-vur, *n. m.* murmur, a mumbling in subdued voice ; *dial.* form is **morbur.** *Ir.* **monmhar, monbhar.** Cf. *Lat.* murmur.

monognach, *a.* clammy, stale.

mop, mob, *n. m.* a tuft, bush.

mopach, *a.* bushy, tufted, shaggy.

mór, *adj.* great, of great size, tall, and important ; **duine mór,** a great man, a tall man, considerable personage ; great, numerous ; **sluagh mór,** multitude ; important, weighty, considerable ; **nì mór,** an important or weighty affair ; mighty, overbearing, self-important ; **cho mór as fhéin ris a' mhac-mhallachd,** as self-important as Lucifer ; familiar, intimate, much attached, gracious ; **tha iad mór aige a chéile,** they are great chums ; much valued, esteemed much, thought much of ; **bu mhór aca fhéin e,** it was much valued by themselves ; much, great in degree ; **is mór a dh' fhuilingeas cridhe ceart mu'm brist e,** a well-regulated heart suffers much ere it break ; much, many ; **is mór leam sin a dhèanadh,** I think it too much to go that length ; **is mór a dh' fhuiling mi,** greatly did I suffer ! **cha mhór a chì e,** few shall see it ; **cha mhór nach do bhual e mi,** he almost struck me ; used as a *n.,* the great, the mighty, the chivalrous, the renowned, the famous ; **am beag is am mór,** both small and great. *O.Ir.* **mór, már.** *W.* mawr. *O.Celt.* mâro-s.

mórachd, mōr'-achc, *n. f.* greatness, mightiness ; majesty, dignity, rank.

mórail, mōr'-al, *adj.* majestic, magnificent.

morair, morer, *n. m.* a lord, an earl, a law-lord. *O.G.* **mormaer,** a provincial ruler, similar to Norse jarl. *Ir.* high-steward, baron. *O'R.*

móralachd, *n. f.* greatness, majesty.

móramh, mōruv, *n. f.* the full note in music, a quaver.

móran, *n. m.* great deal, great number, many, great quantity ; **móran cuid-eachd,** a great company ; **móran èisg,** great quantity of fish ; *adv.* by a great deal ; **móran na 's fhaisge,** a great deal nearer ; too much ; **tha móran an so,** there is too much here.

morbhach, mor-vuch, *n. f. See* **mormhaich.**

mórchuis, mōr-choosh, *n. f.* ambition, pomp, pageantry, magnificence, pride.

mórchuiseach, *adj.* ambitious, pompous, splendid, high-minded.

mórchuiseachd, *n. f.* ambitiousness, splendour, pomposity.

mórdha, *a.* great, eminent, excellent. *O.Ir.* **mórda,** haughty.

mórdhalach, móralach, *a.* magnificent, haughty.

mórdhalachd, móralachd, *n. f.* magnificence, dignity.

mórdhail, *n. f.* an assembly. **mòr + dàil.**

mórghaise, *n. f.* heroism.

morghan, *n. m.* gravel ; small shingle.

morghath, morgh, *n. m.* a fishing spear. **muir + gath** (spear) ; *dial.* **morgh.**

mòrlanachd, mōr-lanuchc, *n. f.* labour done by tenants for the landlord.

mormhaich, moro-ich, *n. f.* grassy plain so near the sea that the tide frequently covers it. *Also* **fidean.** *M.Ir.* **murmhagh = mor** (sea) + **magh** (plain).

mórnaich, *n. f.* considerable quantity or number ; *dial.* for **móran.**

mòrnan, *n. m.* a small tub. *Ir.* **mórnán,** a small wooden dish. *O'R.*

morran, *n. m.* mountain bent.

mórroinn, *n. f.* province.

mórsheisear, seven persons. *O.Ir.* **mór-fheser,** seven men. *Also M.I.* **moir-sheiser.**

mór-shluagh, *n. m.* a host, a multitude, the public.

mort, morst, *n. m.* murder, massacre ; *v.* murder, slay. *Also* **murt.** *M.Ir.* **martad.** *E.Ir.* **mort-** in **mortchenn =** *morticinum* ; **mortlaith =** *mortalitas.* *Lat.* mors, mortis.

mortach, mortail, *adj.* murderous, murdering.

mortair, morster, *n. m.* murderer, killer, assassin ; **am mortair,** the murderer.

mortaireachd, *n. f.* massacre.

mórthir, mōr-hir, *n. f.* mainland. **= mór + tìr.**

mórthireach, *n. m.* person belonging to the mainland ; *a.* belonging to a continent.

mór-thriath, *n. m.* a great chief.

mór-uaisle, *n. m.* nobility.

mosach, *adj.* filthy, nasty ; **nì mosach,** a filthy thing ; mean, inhospitable ; **là mosach,** a " dirty " day, a raw day with some sleet. *See* **musach.** *M.Ir.*

mosach, filthy. *Tbc. E.W.* mws, stale, stinking.

mosag, *n. f.* filthy, a dirty female; parsimonious, niggardly female.

mosaiche, mosichu, mosraiche, mosrichu, *n. f.* filthiness, niggardliness.

mosg, mosgain, mosguin, *n. m.* dry-rot; *a.* having dry-rot, as wood. *Ir.* mosgán, rotten, decayed.

mosgaideach, *a.* dull, slow. *See* mobh-sgaid.

mosgail, mosgil, *v. intr.* arouse. *M.Ir.* muscail; ro muscail, he awoke.

mosgalach, *adj.* wakeful, watchful.

mosgalachd, *n. f.* vigilance, watchfulness.

mosgladh, mosglu, *vbl. n. m.* act of rousing, awaking; rousing.

mosradh, *n. m.* coarse dalliance. mos + radh.

mosraiche, *n. f.* smuttiness; fr. mos.

mothachadh, mo-huchu, *vbl. n. m.* feeling, sensation; chaill e mhothachadh, he lost all sense of feeling; act of feeling, observing, noticing, attending. *Ir.* mothughadh, feeling. *O'R.*

mothachail, mo-huchal, *adj.* sensible, observant, considerate, kind.

mothaich, mo-hich, *v.* feel, perceive; observe, notice; an do mhothaich thu dha a' dol seachad, did you observe or take notice of him passing? *O.Ir.* mothaigim, perceive; co mothaigid; gl. stupeat.

mòthan, mō-han, *n. m.* bog-violet, a love-philtre, carried by wayfarers for protection.

mòthar, mō-hur, *n. m.* a deep-toned, unearthly voice or sound; thug e mòthar as, he gave a most appalling cry; chuala sinn mòthar, we heard a most unearthly voice or sound; swelling of the sea. *Ir.* a high sea, loud noise. *O'R.*

mòthar, mō-har, *n. m., pl.* mòthraichean. 1. bunch, cluster. 2. tuft of grass. 3. park, enclosure. *E.Ir.* móthar, a park; a cluster. *O'Don.*

mòthar. *See* mòdhar.

mu, *prep.* about. *Ir.* um, im. *O.Ir.* imb, imm. *Lat.* ambi. *Gr.* ἀμφί.

muaicnech, *n. f.* the smallpox.

muc, *n. f.* a sow, a pig, a large ball of snow, a heap; muc-mhara, a whale; muc-steallain, muc-bhiorach, porpoise. *O.Ir.* mucc. *W.* moch, swine. *O.Celt.* mocco-s, muccu-s.

mucach, mucail, *adj.* swinish, dirty, surly, stupid.

mucag, *n. f.* a hip; mucagan is sgeachagan, hips and haws. Cf. *O.Ir.* mucóra, the fruit of the dog-brier.

mucaire, muciru, *n. m.* swine-herd.

muc-alladh. *See* mac-talla.

mucbhlonag, mooc-vlonug, *n. f.* hog's lard.

muc-chreige, *n. f.* a wrasse.

muc-failm, muc-felm, *n. f.* dog-brier berry, or hip; muca-fàileag, dogberry.

mùch, mooch, *v.* smother, quench. *O.Ir.* múchaim, to suffocate. *O.Celt.* mûko-s.

mùchadair, mōōchuder, *n. m.* extinguisher.

mùchadh, moochu, *vbl. n. m.* act of smothering, quenching, extinguishing.

mùchan, *n. m.* a vent, a chimney. *E.Ir.* múch, smoke. *W.* mwg.

muclach, mooclach, *n. f.* a piggery.

mucraidh, moocry, *coll. n.* a herd of swine.

muc-shneachda, mooc-niachcu, *n. f.* a huge snowball.

mùdan, moodan, *n. m.* 1. a cover for a gun. 2. overhanging eyebrows, a frown, sulks.

mug, moog, *n. m.* a snuffle through the nose. *Also* smug.

mùgach, *adj.* snuffling, gloomy; *n. f.* a snuffling voice, surliness.

mùgaiche, moogichu, *n. f.* gloom, snuffle.

mùgaid, moogej, *n. f.* the contents of a dyer's vat.

mùgaire, moogiru, *n. m.* snuffler.

mugairle, *n. f.* a bunch of nuts.

mùganach, *a.* damp, misty, muggy (weather). *O.N.* mugga, mugginess.

mùgh, moo, *v.* change, alter, diversify; shift, turn; mùghadh puinnd, the change of a pound. *See* mùth.

mughadh, moo-u, *vbl. n. m.* destruction, decay; act of destroying, decaying. *M.Ir.* mugud, slaying. Cf. mudugud, destruction.

mughairn, moo-urn, *n. m.* ankle. *Ir.* mudharn, *n. f.* an ankle. *O'R.*

mughairneach, *adj.* large-ankled, having large ankles.

muicfheoil, mooycol, *n. f.* pork.

muidh, mooy, *n. f.* front beam in a weaving-loom.

muidhe, *n. m.* a churn. *E.Ir.* muide, vessel, buide, a churn. *W.* buddai, a churn.

muidheachan, mooy-uchan, *n. m.* a small churn.

muidse, moojshu, *n. f., pl.* muidseachan, a mutch, woman's linen headwear; fr. the *Eng. Also* currag.

mùig, mooig, *n. f.* gloom, a frown; discontented expression of countenance; cuir mùig ort, frown; *v.* frown. *Ir.* múig, surly countenance.

mùig, moo-ig, *v.* smother, become gloomy. Cf. *E.Ir.* múch, smoke.

mùigeachd, moo-giachc, *n. f.* gloominess; *a.* mùigeach.

mùigean, moogen, mùigire, moogiru, *n. m.* a surly dog of a fellow, frowner.

mùigeanachd, moogen-uchc, *n. f.* gloominess.

mùigeis, moogesh, *n. f.* snuffling, surliness.

muigh, *dat.* of magh, a plain ; with *prep.* a(n) it forms *adv.* of *pl.* " where " ; a muigh, out of doors, without, outside. *Lat.* foris. *E.Ir.* immaig =in- (*prep.* in) +mag (plain). *See* mach.

mùighteach, mooytuch, *a.* changeable.

muilceann, mool-cian, *n. m.* fell-wort.

muileach, mool-uch, *a.* dear, beloved.

muileag, moolag, *n. f.* cranberry.

Muileach, mooluch, *n.* Mull-man ; *a.* belonging to Mull.

muileann, moolun, *m.* and *f.*, *pl.* muilnean, grist-mill ; muileann-sàbhaidh, a saw-mill, or machine ; muileann-càrdaidh, carding-machine ; muileann-luaidh, waulking-machine, or mill ; muileann-lìn, lint-mill ; muileann làimh, a hand-mill. *O.Ir.* mulenn, muilend ; gl. pistrinum. *E.W.* melin. *Lat.* molendinum (*Z²*) ; molo, grind. molina ; *Gr.* μύλη, a mill.

muileid, *n. m.* mule ; fr. *Lat.* mulus.

muilichinn, moolichin, *n. m.* sleeve. *Also* muinichill.

muillean, mooylen, *n. m.* particle of chaff, a husk ; fr. moll, chaff. *Ir.* muillain, muilnen.

mùillean, *n. m.* a bundle or truss of straw ; certain measure of straw. *Sc.* windlen, bottle of straw or hay. *O.N.* vöndull, a wisp. *Also* boitean.

muillear, mooyler, *n. m.* miller ; for muilnear (the n assim.). *E.Ir.* muilleóir ; fr. *Lat.* molinarius.

muillearachd, *n. f.* the occupation of a miller.

muillion, mooylon, *n. m.* million.

muilteachd, *n. f.* lovableness, charm.

muilteag, *n. f.* small red berry.

muiltfheoil, mooiltol, *n. f.* mutton.

muime, moo-imu, *n. f.* step-mother ; foster-mother ; nurse. *Also* leasmhathair. *E.Ir.* mumme, a nurse. *W.* llysfam.

mùin, moo-in, *v.* piss, make water. *O.Ir.* mún, *deriv.* doubtful ; moo is en (mu is water) or cf. min- in *mingo*. *Corm.*

muin, *n. m.* back, top ; thog e air a mhuin an laoch, he raised the hero on his back. *Also* muinn. *E.Ir.* back, neck. *E.W.* mwn.

mùin, *v.* teach, instruct. *O.Ir.* múnim.

muinichill, moon-chil, *n. f.* sleeve. *See* muilichinn. *E.Ir.* munchille. *Lat.* manicula, manica, the long sleeve of the tunic.

muineal, moo-niäl, *n. m.* neck of a person. *O.Ir.* muinél. *E.W.* myn-wgyl. *O.Celt.* moniklo-.

muineal, *a.* long-necked.

muing, moo-ing, *n. f.* mane of a horse ; *a.* muingeach. *O.Ir.* mong (*f.*), hair. *W.* mwng. *O.Celt.* mongâ, mongo-.

muinighinn, moon-yin, *n. f.* fort, dependence, fortress, trust, stay, confidence. *E.Ir.* muinigin. *O.N.* munr (love). *Goth.* munan, believe.

muinmhear, moon-ver, *n. m.* hemlock.

muinn, mooin, *n. f.* back, top. *See* muin.

muinne, mooinu, *n. f.* tallow-tripe, a stomach.

muinninn, mooinin, *n. m.* dependence, trust.

muinnte, munnda, *a.* beauteous. Cf. *Lat.* mundus. *McB.*

mùinnteachd, *n. f.* disposition.

muinntearach, moointeruch, *n. m.* a servant ; *a.* clannish, friendly.

muinntearas, *n. m.* service ; tha i air mhuinntearas, she is at service. *O.Ir.* muntaras (*m.*), *communio.*

muinntir, moointir, *n. f.* household, people, inhabitants ; relations ; muinntir a' bhaile so, the inhabitants of this town ; muinntir an tighe so, the inhabitants of this house ; do mhuinntir, your people, your relations ; do mhuinntir chéile, your spouse's people. *O.Ir.* muinter, muntar, people, household, some or all members of a band, or even a country ; eter muntir nime et talman, both the people of heaven and of earth. *Wb.* 26ᵇ· Borrowed from monasterium (*Stokes and others*).

muinntireach, moointiruch, *n. m.* an acquaintance, follower ; seann mhuinntireach, an old acquaintance —servant.

muinntireachd, *n. f.* acquaintance, dealings, correspondence ; sean mhuinntireachd, old acquaintance, or correspondence.

muinntireas, *n. m.* service, correspondence, dealing, communication.

muir, moor, *n. f.*, *gen.* mara, *pl.* marannan (waves, usually big billows) ; sea, ocean, wave ; muir làn, high tide ; ris a' mhuir, seafaring ; cur na mara, sea-sickness. *O.Ir.* muir, *gen.* mora. *E.W.* môr. *O.Celt.* mori. Cf. *O.H.G.* meri. *O.N.* marr. *A.S.* mere. *Fr.* mer.

muir-bhàite, moor-vātu, *n. m.* towering engulfing wave, tidal wave.

muirceann, *n. f.* the ankle. *See* mughairn.

mùire, moor'-u, *n. f.* a dry scab ; scurvy ; leprosy. *Ir.* muireadh, leprosy. *O'R.*

muireardach, *n. f.* an undaunted female, a female champion.

muirgheadh. *See* morghath.

muirichinn, moorichin, *n. f.* a young throng, children, family ; hurry-burry, a hard task or burden ; *rt.* mer, smer. *Lat.* memoria. *Gr.* μέριμνα, care. *McB.*

muirichinneach, *adj.* hurried, hard-pressed ; having a large family, or young, ill-provided-for family.

muirichlinn, moorichlin, **muirlinn,** moor-lin, *n. f.* edible seaweed, called birses ; in some places **gruaigean.** *Also* **mircean.**

mùirn, moorn, *n. f.* joy, affection ; cheerfulness, a respectful, tender reception ; **'s ann rompa a bha mhùirn,** how respectfully and hospitably they were received ! caressing ; **le furbhailt is mùirn,** with complacency and cheerfulness ; delicateness, tenderness ; **le mùirn,** with delicacy. *M.Ir.* **múirn, múirnín,** a darling.

mùirneach, *adj.* dearly beloved, excessively fondled, cheerful, jolly ; tender, delicately received and entertained ; hospitable ; **mac mùirneach,** dearly beloved son ; **mùirneach uime,** caressing him ; **an duin' òg is mùirneach agam,** the young man I so dearly cherish.

mùirneag, moornag, *n. f.* civil or polite woman.

mùirnean, moornen, *n. m.* a polite or pompous man ; a darling.

muir-robainn, moor-robin, *n. f.* piracy. *Also* **muir-spùinneadh.**

muirsgian, moor-scin, *n. m.* razor-fish. *Also* **mursaig.** *Ir.* **muirscionn,** a spout-fish. *O'R.*

muir-spuinneadair, *n. m.* a pirate, sea-robber, plunderer.

muir-thacar, *n. m.* sea-spoil ; *rather* **tacar-mara.**

muir-titheachd, m.-tiàchc, *n. f.* sea-blubber. *Also* **sgeith-ròin.**

mùiseag, mooshag, *n. f.* fear, terror, threat ; *a.* **muiseagach.** Cf. **musach.**

muiseal, mooshal, muzzle of a plough. *Ir.* **muisiall,** a curb ; fr. the *Eng.* See **smuiseall.**

muisean, mooshen, *n. m.* a mean sordid fellow. Cf. **musach.**

mùisean, *n. m.* a primrose. *Ir.* **múiseán.**

muisginn, mooshcin, *n. m.* a mutchkin. *Sc.* mutchkin = an English pint. *Du.* mutsie = a quart. *Jamieson.*

mùiteach, mootuch, *a.* changeable, fickle. See **mùth.**

mul, *n. m.* a conical heap, mound. *E.Ir.* mul, eminence. Cf. *O.N.* múli, jutting crag, a " mull " ; fq. in Icel. pl.-names. *M.H.G.* mûl, mûle, snout, mouth.

mul, mool, *n. m.* an axle. *E.Ir.* mol, shaft.

mulad, moolud, *n. m.* sadness, grief, labour pains (cow).

muladach, mulaideach, moolejuch, *adj.* sad, melancholy ; distressing.

mulaideachd, *n. f.* distressing nature, or circumstances of a case.

mulan, moolan, *n. m.* stack of corn— (never of hay) ; a large conical wave or billow.

mulart, moolart, *n. m.* dwarf-elder. *Ir.* **mulabhur, mulaburd.** *O'R.*

mulc, moolc, *n. m.* a lump, a dive, a duck of the head, bob ; *v.* ram, push suddenly, butt ; dive, duck. *Lat.* mulceo, mulco, a stroke.

mulcach, *adj.* lumpish ; **ceann mulcach,** a " bullet " head.

mulcadh, *vbl. n. m.* act of diving, pushing, butting.

mulchag, *n. f.* and **mulchan,** *n. f.* a cheese. *M.Ir.* **mulchán.**

mullach, mooluch, *n. m.* top, roof, ridge, apex ; summit ; top of the head ; height, eminence ; the very essence ; **mullach na beinne,** the top of the hill ; **air mullach an tighe,** on the roof of the house ; **mullach an t-slaoightire,** a most complete rogue ; **mullach na céille !** wise head ! ; **mo ghràdh air a' mhullach !** my love on the head ! *O.Ir.* mullach, top ; head.

mult, moolt, *n. m.* wedder. *O.Ir.* molt.

mùn, moon, *n. m.* urine, piss ; *vbl. n.* act of pissing, drawing water.

mùn, *v.* instruct, teach, rear. (*Irish.*)

mun, *prep.* + *art.* mu + an, about the ; **a chasan mun teine,** his feet about the fire. *O.Ir.* imb + an, often ; *contract.* to **man.**

mun, *prep.* + *rel.* mu + an, " before that " ; **greas ort mun tig e,** make haste before he comes, or " against " his coming. *O.Ir.* imb + an ; fq. *contract.* to **man.**

mun, *prep.* + *infix. pron.* mu + an ; **mun cuala sinn,** about whom we heard. *O.Ir.* imb + an ; fq. *contract.* to **man.**

muna, *conj.* ma (if) + ni (not) ; fq. = **man a.**

munab, *conj.* ma (if) + ni-b (not, and frag. of *v.* to be), were it not.

mùnadh, moonu, *vbl. n. m.* instructing ; act of teaching ; rearing ; good morals, good manners or breeding.

munadh, *n. m.* See **monadh.**

munar, monar, *n. m.* a trifle, a trifling person, a diminutive person or thing, fact, deed. *Ir.* **munar,** a fact, deed.

munaran, *dim.* of **munar.** So *Ir.*

munganachd, moonganuchc, *n. f.* bullying.

mùnloch, moon-loch, *n. f.* puddle, foul water, mire. So *Ir.* **mún** + **loch.**

mur, *conj.* except ; unless ; **mur dèan thu,** except you do ; **mur bhiodh gun,** were it not that ; **mur** is for **mun,** and used only in some parts ; **man a** (= ma + ni), in general use in some of the islands (as in *M.Ir.*, *P.H.*). *O.Ir.* **mani, ma** (if) +**ni** (not).

mùr, moor, *n. m.* wall of a rampart, bulwark, palace. *E.Ir.* **múr.** *Lat.* murus.

mùr, *coll. n.* a countless number. *E.Ir.* **mur,** abundance.

mura-bhith, mur-vee, *n. f.* excuse, pretence, exception ; **gun mura-bhith sam bith,** without any exception or pretension ; without "were-it-not."

mura-bhuachaill, mooru-voochil, *n. m.* a Holland auk ; the great northern diver. **muir** + **buachaill.** *Also* **burabhuachaill.**

mùrach, *n. f.* a down or sand-hill on the seashore ; **feadh na mùraichean,** through the downs, or sand-hills.

murag, moorag, *n. f.* murex, purple-fish. So *Ir.*

muran, mooran, *n. m.* bent, down-grass. *O.N.* mura, goose-grass. *Ir.* **muríneach,** bent grass, *agrestis.* *O'D.,* *S.*

murcach, moor-cuch, *a.* sad, dark, muddy. *Ir.*

murcan, *n. m.* the lump-fish.

murcas, *n. m.* sadness, muddiness.

mùrla, *n. f.* a coat of mail.

mùrla, *n. f.* a female having an ugly head of hair.

murlach, *n. m.* kingfisher.

murlach, *n. f.* fishing-basket.

mùrlag, *n. f.* canoe-shaped basket for wool. *Also* **mùrluinn ; mùdag.**

mùrlan, moor-lan, *n. m.* an ugly head of hair ; dirty, matted hair. *Ir.* **murlán,** a rough top or head.

murrach, mooruch, *a.* rich ; able, fit. *Ir.* **murrtha,** successful. Cf. *M.Ir.* **muirech,** a prince. *Tbc.*

murrachd, *n. f.* ability.

murraichd, moorechc, *n. f.* handsome present.

murraichd, *n. f.* spoil cast up by the sea.

mursaig, moor-shig, *n. f.* razor-fish.

murt, moorst, *n. m.* murder. *See* **mort.**

murtachd, *n. f.* sultry heat.

mus, *prep.* before, ere. *O.Ir.* **mos,** soon. *Lat.* mox. *O.Celt.* moqsu, used as *prefix* to verbs, and *rel.* to **moch.**

musach. *See* **mosach.**

musag, moosag, *n. f.* *See* **mosag.**

musaiche. *See* **mosaiche.**

musal, moosal, *n. m.* a threat.

mu seach, moo shech, *adv.* alternately, by turns.

mùsg, moosc, *n. m.* eye-rheum ; ugly eye.

musg, *n. f.* a musket ; fr. the *Eng.*

musgach, *n. m.* rheum-eyed.

musgan, moosgan, *n. m.* dry-rot, a rotten tree. *See* **mosg.**

mùsgan, *n. m.* 1. shell-fish, mussel, the horse-fish. 2. pith of wood.

musganach, moosganuch, *a.* full of rotten trees.

mùsuinn, moosin, *n. m.* confusion, tumult.

mutach, *a.* short, thick, and blunt.

mutan, *n. m.* a thickness, a small bulb, such as appears on hand-spun yarn.

mùtan, mootan, *n. m.* stump of a finger ; in some places worsted gloves, fingerless glove. *Also* **mùtag.**

mùth, moo, *v. t.* to change. *Lat.* muto.

mùthach, moo-huch, *n. m.* a herd ; **caillear bò an droch mhùthaich seachd bliadhna roimh an mhithich,** the bad herd's cow is lost seven years before the time ; milk contractor ; for **buthach.**

mùthadh, moo-hu, *n. m.* change, alteration ; **mùthaibh bhur n-aodach,** change your clothes.

N

n, the eleventh letter of the alphabet, called by the Irish, **nùin,** the ashtree.

'n, for 1. the *art.* **an,** after words ending with a vowel : thus, **dh'òl iad de'n fhìon,** they drank of the wine. 2. for *pos. pron.* **an,** their : **le'n làmhan is le'n casan,** with their hands and with their feet. 3. the infixed *pron.* **an,** after *prep.* ending in a vowel : **mu, le, gu** (go), whom ; **mu'n d' thubhairt iad,** of whom they said. 4. for the *prep.* **an** : **'n a tigh,** in her house ; **'n ar feum,** in our need ; idiom : **'n a choigreach,** in his (being)

a stranger. 5. for *interrog. part.* **an** : **'n a thuit thu** ? did you fall ?

n-, *frag.* of case ending carried to foll. word, when beginning with a vowel. Used after *pos. pron.* **ar, bhur** ; **ar n-athair,** our father.

na, *n.* and *d. pl.,* and *gen. s.* of the art. (*fem.*).

na, *comp. conj.* than, as **na's fhearr,** better than. *E.Ir.* **inda, indás.** *O.Ir.* **indás, inda as.**

na, *rel. pron. sing.* and *pl.* in all cases, including often the antecedent in itself ; as, all, all those, what, what number, those who, those which ;

NA—NAOIDHEANACHD

na thàinig, all that came ; **na's urrainn mi,** all that I can. *O.Ir. rel.* an =id quod.

na, *indep. neg. part.* not ; used only with *imper. mood* ; **na dèan e,** do not do it. *O.Ir.* na.

nàbachas. *See* next word.

nàbachd, *n. f.* neighbourhood, community.

nàbaidh, nā-by, *n. m.* neighbour. *O.N.* ná-búi (ná, near ; búi, dweller).

nàbaidheachd, nàby-achc, *n. f.* neighbourhood.

nach. 1. *neg. rel. pron.* who not, whom not, what not, that not : **sùinn nach beò,** heroes that are not living. 2. *interrog.* and *neg. part.*: **nach math e ?** is it not good ? **nach 'eil fhios agad ?** do you not know ? 3. *conj.* and *adv.* that not, in that not : **a chionn nach 'eil an righ a' toirt fògarraich air an ais,** because the king does not restore the banished. *O.Ir.* nách, nach.

nàdur, *n. m.* and *f.* nature ; **obair nàduir,** the work of nature ; disposition, temper, inclination ; **do dhroch nàdur,** your bad temper ; nature. *Lat.* natura.

nàdurra, *adj.* natural, affectionate ; **nighean nàdurra,** an affectionate daughter.

nàdurrachd, nād'-urr-uchc, *n. f.* the course of nature ; natural affection ; bent of inclination ; instinct.

nàdurrail, nād'-urr-al, *adj.* natural, etc.

naid, naj, *n. f.* lamprey. So *Ir.*

naidheachd, nyuchc, *n. m.* news, tidings, intelligence ; fr. nuadh, new. *Ir.* núaidheachd. *W.* newyddion.

nàile, nālu, *inter.* yea! **a naile thà!** indeed ! forsooth, it is so !

nàimhdeach, nyjuch, *a.* virulent, hostile.

nàimhdeil, nyjal, *a.* hostile ; venomous, malicious, inimical, keen, eager to revenge.

nàimhdeas, nyjus, *n. m.* enmity, hostility, malice, vindictiveness, resentment. *O.Ir.* náimtide, *hostilis. Z²*.

nàimhdealachd, nyjaluchc, *n. f.* revengefulness, vindictiveness, resentment.

nàimhdealas, *n. f. See* last word.

'naird, nârj, for an àird, *adv.* aloft, upwards, up ; **chaidh e 'n àird,** he went aloft, he mounted, went up ! *E.Ir.* i n-ardi (*prep.* in +àirde).

nàire, nāru, *n. f.* sense of shame ; modesty, honour, disgrace, ignominy ; **gun nàire gun athadh,** without shame or flinching. *E.Ir.* nár, náire, modesty, shame. *O.Celt.* nagro-s.

naisg, nashc, *v.* bind, pledge, vow, deposit money. *See* nasg. *M.Ir.* naiscim, to bind.

naisgte, nashctu, *vbl. a.* deposited, pledged.

nàisinn, nàistinn, nāshin, *n. f.* a deep and

over-delicate sense of duty ; an excessive sense of gratitude, particularly in matters of hospitality ; hospitality that puts to inconvenience ; **na biodh nàisinn 'sam bith ort air mo shonsa,** don't put yourself to any inconvenience on my account. *O.N.* njósn, spying. *A.S.* neósan, search out.

nàisinn, *n. m.* a native ; **nàisinn an àite,** the natives of the place.

nàisneach, nàistinneach, nashnuch, *adj.* modest ; under obligation ; scrupulous ; showing hospitality and decency to a stranger from a delicate sense of the laws of such. *Also* nòistineach.

nàisneachd, *n. f.* deep sense of duty, hospitality ; keenness at work ; shamefacedness, bashfulness ; **le nàisneachd agus stuaim,** with shamefacedness and sobriety.

naitheas, na-hus, *n. m.* hurt ; harm, mischief.

nall, naul, *adv.* to this side, hither, toward us, in our direction ; **an nunn is a nall,** hither and thither, across and back again ; for **an all,** from beyond. *E.Ir.* anall ; *adv. illinc.*

nam, nan, *conj.* if ; **nam biodh,** if it were ; **nan dèanadh iad,** if they would do—. *E.Ir.* dá n-, día n-. *O.Ir.* dian =di (*prep.*) +an (*rel.*).

'nam, for ann (*prep.*) in +lab. form of **an** (*pers. pron.*), their ; **'nam meadhon,** in the midst of them.

nàmh, nāv, *n. m.* enemy. *See* nàmhaid.

nàmhachas, nāvuchus, *n. m.* malice, hostility.

nàmhaid, nāvij, *n. m., pl.* nàimhdean, enemy, foe, adversary. *O.Ir.* náma, *gen.* námat.

nan, *gen. pl.* of the *art.* an. Lab. form is nam.

'nan, for ann an, in their.

'nann, naun, *interrog. part.* an +ann, **'n ann mar sin ?** is it so ?

naoidh, nooy, *num.* nine ; **an ceann naoidh mìosan,** at the expiration of nine months ; **naoidh fir,** nine men. *Also* naodh. *O.Ir.* nói n-. *E.W.* naw. *Lat.* novem.

naoidh-deug, nooy-jĕg, *num.* nineteen ; **naoidh fir dheug,** nineteen men ; *tmesis* occurs in enumerating objects within the *teens* ; **aon duine deug,** eleven men ; **còig duine deug ar fhichead,** thirty-five men, etc.

naoidheamh, nooy-uv, *num.* ninth.

naoidhean, nooyen, **naoidheachan,** nooy-uchan, *n. m.* a little child, an infant, babe. *O.Ir.* nóidiu, *gen.* nóiden ; *a.* naoidheanach.

naoidheanachd, *n. f.* infancy. So *E.Ir.* A man's life was divided into six stages:

naoidendacht, infancy ; macdacht, boyhood ; gillacht, youth (fr. puberty to majority (?)) ; óglachass, prime, fit to bear arms ; séndatu, old age ; díblideta, debility. *Corm.*

naoidhnear, naoinear, nuynur, nine persons. *O.Ir.* nónbur.

naoimhe, nooy-vu, *compar.* of naomh (holy) ; na's naoimhe, holier.

naomh, nŭv, *adj.* holy, sacred, consecrated, sanctified ; *n. m.* a saint, holy person ; *gen. s.* and *n. pl.* naoimh ; na naoimh, the saints. *E.Ir.* nóem, nóeb. *O.Ir.* nóib. *O.Celt.* noibo-s.

naomhachadh, nùv'-ach-u, *vbl. n. m.* sanctifying, consecrating ; act of sanctification, consecration.

naomhachd, nùv'-achc, *n. f.* holiness, sanctity ; naomhachd na Sàbaid, sanctity of the Sabbath.

naomhaich, nùv'-ich, *v.* consecrate, sanctify, hallow ; gu naoimhaichear t' ainm, hallowed be thy name. *O.Ir.* nóebaim, hallow, sanctify.

naomh-cheannachd, *n. f.* simony, purchasing holy things by money.

naomh-ghoid, *n. f.* sacrilege.

naomh-òran, *n. f.* anthem.

naomh-reachd, *n. m.* divine law, or ordinance.

naomh-thréig, *v.* apostatise.

naomh-thréigire, *n. m.* apostate.

naomh-thréigsinn, *n. f.* apostasy, infidelity, hypocrisy.

naosg, nŭsg, *n. f.* snipe. *Also* meanbhghuthrag ; gabhar-athair.

naosgair, *n. m.* an inconstant man. So *Ir.*

nar, *adv.* may not, let not ; nar leigeadh Dia, God forbid. = *O.Ir.* na (*neg. non*) + ro (*vbl. part.*).

'nar, năr, 'nar cadal, in our sleep ; 'nar meadhon, in the midst of us ; for an (*prep.* in) + ar (*pers. pron.* our).

nàr, *a.* shameful, disgraceful. *Ir.* nár, evil, ill. *E.Ir.* nár, shameful.

nàrach, *a.* nàr'-uch, shameful, disgraceful, ignominious ; nì nàrach, a disgraceful thing.

nàrach, *a.* modest, bashful ; caileag nàrach, a modest lassie ; tha an duine nàrach, the man is bashful. *E.Ir.* nár, noble, modest, pure.

nàrachadh, nàruchu, *vbl. n. m.* act of putting to shame ; abashing, disgracing. *Ir.* nárachadh, affronting.

nàraich, nàrich, *v.* shame, put to shame ; disgrace ; nàraichte, *vbl. a.* disgraced.

narrach, narrail, *a.* cross, ill-tempered, fierce.

nàsag, *n. f.* an empty shell.

nasg, *n. m., pl.* naisg, a ring ; cow-tie, or collar ; a sieve frame. *E.Ir.* nasc, ring, tie. *O.Celt.* nasko-, a ring.

nasg, *n. m.* a pledge, a seal, a deposit ; tha an t-airgead an naisg, the money is left in pledge. *O.Ir.* nascim, I bind, fasten.

nasgadh, năsg'-u, *vbl. n. m.* act of pledging, depositing.

nasgaidh, nascy, nasgaich, nascich, *a.* gratis, free, as a gift ; gift ; thug e dhomh a nasgaidh e, he gave it me as a gift ; for an asgaidh. *E.Ir.* ascad, a present, a gift ; i n-ascid, *gratis.*

nasgaidheachd, *n. f.* freeness, unconditional freeness ; gratuity, gratuitousness.

natar, *n. m.* nitre.

nathair, na-hir, *n. f., gen.* nathrach, *pl.* nathraichean, serpent, viper, snake, adder. *O.Ir.* nathir. *W.* neidr (=*natrī). *Corn.* nader. *Bret.* (Van.) aer (=*nazr). Cf. *Teut. O.N.* naðr. *Got.* nadrs. *A.S.* nädra. *O.H.G.* nätara. *Hr. Thn.* deprec. ref. to *Lat.* natrix.

nathrachan, naruchan, *n. m.* place infested with serpents.

-ne, emph. *pronom. suf.* 1st *pl.*, sinne, we ; an tigh againne, our house ; but with ar the order is ar tigh-ne, our house. *O.Ir.* ni, -ni.

neach, nyach, *indef. pron.* an individual, person, one ; neach sam bith, any one ; neach eile, another person or individual ; gach neach, each one. *O.Ir.* nech. *O.W.* nep. *O.Celt.* ne-qo-.

nead, ned, *n. f.* nest, *pl.* and *gen. s.* nid. *E.Ir.* net. *Lat.* nidus. *O.Celt.* nizdo-s.

neadaich, nedich, *v.* nestle, bed, embed ; a' neadachadh am fheòil, embedding in my flesh.

neagaid, negej, *n. f.* a little sob or sigh, oft repeated, as a person before or after weeping ; suppressed sighing or sobbing.

nèal. *See* neul.

neal, *interj.* term of endearment, dear ! darling !

nèamh, nĕv, *n. m.* the sky, firmament ; Heaven, region of bliss ; nèamh nan speur, the starry heavens. *O.Ir.* nem. *O.W.* nem. *W.* nef. *Bret.* nev. *O.Celt.* nemos. *Lat.* nemus. *Gr.* νέμος, wooded pasture ; *rt.* nem, bend, curve. *Hr.*

nèamhach, nĕvuch, *n. m.* an angel.

nèamhachd, *n. f.* heavenliness.

nèamhaidh, nĕvy, *adj.* heavenly, divine. *O.Ir.* nemde.

nèamhaidheachd, *n. f.* heavenliness, holiness, solemnity, blessedness.

neamhain, neven, neamhnaid, niäoo-nej, *n. f.* a pearl, gem, jewel. *E.Ir.* nemanda. *O.Ir.* nem. *O.Celt.* nemos.

neamhnagan, ne-oo-nugan, *n. m.* a stye on the eyelid. *Also* leamhnad ; leamhnagan.

neamhnaid, *n. f.* a pearl, a gem. *E.Ir.*
nemanda, pearly. *O.Ir.* nem, onyx.
neanntag, nauntag, *n. f.* nettle. *E.Ir.*
nenntai, nettles. *See* deanntag.
neapaiginn, nepugin, *n. m.* napkin ; fr.
the *Eng.*
nèarachd, nerachc, *n. f.* happiness, for-
tunateness ; is nèarachd an duine a
smachdaicheas Dia, happy is the man
whom God correcteth. *Also* meur-
achd.
nearag, *n. f.* a daughter.
neart, niärst, *n. m.* force, pith, power,
might, energy, vigour ; vast quantity ; number, superabundance ; neart
airgid, a vast quantity of money ;
neart buntàta, a vast quantity of
potatoes ; neart éisg, enormous quantum of fish. *O.Ir.* nert. *E.W.* nerth.
O. Celt. nerto-s.
neartaich, niärstich, *v.* strengthen, invigorate ; infuse strength, vigour, or
energy into.
neartalachd, niarstaluchc, *n. f.* vigorousness, pithiness ; energy of character.
neartail, *a.* powerful, robust, vigorous.
Also neartmhor, or neartar.
neartmhoireachd, niarst-vuruchc, *n. f.*
powerfulness, energy, vigorousness.
neas, nes·or nis, *adv.* while, whilst ; for
an fheadh 's a—.
neasg, neasgaid, nisgej, *n. f.* a boil, an
abscess. *E.Ir.* nescoit ; fr. ness, wound.
neimh, nev, *n. f.* poison, venom, a sting
(as keen frost). *O.Ir.* neim, nem,
poison, virus ; nem nathrach, gl.
venenum aspidum.
neimhealachd, nevuluchc, *n. f.* sharpness,
wicked keenness, piercing coldness ;
a. neimheil, neval.
nèip, nēp, turnip. *Sc.* neep. *Also*
snèip ; fr. *Lat.* nâpus. *McB.*
neo, nio, *adv.* or, nor, neither, either, else,
otherwise ; neo is truagh mo chàradh,
else sad is my condition ; thusa neo
mise, either you or I ; neo thèid mi
dhachaidh, otherwise I will go home ;
also *neg. part.* as neo-ghlic, unwise ;
neo-amaideach, anything but foolish.
M.Ir. nem-. *O.Ir.* neph- for ne + su-.
Zcp[14].
neo-abuidh, neo-abuich,* *a.* unripe, premature, abortive.
neo-aire, *n. f.* inattention, unguardedness.
neo-airsnealach, neo-airtnealach, *a.* cheerful, gay.
neo-amhalach, *adj.* slily and without
attention ; gu neo-amhalach, unawares, slily.
neo-amharas, *n. m.* unsuspiciousness ;
want of suspicion.

* For pronunciation of these compounds see
separate forms.

neo-amhrasach, *a.* unsuspicious, undubit-
able, unquestionable.
neo - aoibhneach, *a.* surly, cheerless,
gloomy.
neo-aoibheil, *a.* cheerless.
neo-aoibhneas, *n. f.* gloom.
neo-ar-thaing. 1. in spite of, independent of. 2. supreme confidence ;
" neo-ar-thaing mur coisinn i," I'll
wager she will win.
neo-ascaoin, *a.* not unkind.
neo-bhàigheil, *a.* harsh, unkind.
neo-bheothail, *a.* lifeless.
neobhrigh, *n. f.* inefficacy, no effect ;
chuir sibh an neobhrigh àithne Dhè,
you have made of none effect the command of God.
neo-chaochlaideach, *adj.* unchangeable,
immutable.
neo-chaochlaideachd, *n. f.* unchangeable-
ness, immutability.
neo-charraideach, *adj.* quiet, peaceable,
without toil.
neo-cheadaich, *v.* prohibit.
neo-cheadaichte, *vbl. a.* prohibited.
neo - chealgach, *a.* candid ; void of
deceit.
neo-chealgachd, *n. f.* candour, unfeigned-
ness, fairness.
neo-cheangail, *v.* untie.
neo-cheangailte, *vbl. a.* unbound, free,
disengaged, at liberty.
neo-cheannsuichte, *vbl. a.* unconquered,
unsubdued.
neo-chearbach, *a.* handy, expert, efficient.
neo-cheart, *adj.* not true, unfair, ill-
founded ; unhandsome.
neo-chiallach, *a.* mad.
neo-chinnt, *n. f.* uncertainty, fickleness,
whimsicality.
neo - chinnteach, *adj.* uncertain, problematical, fickle.
neochiont, *n. f.* innocence.
neochiontach, *adj.* innocent, free from
blame, unblameable.
neochiontachd, *n. f.* innocence, innocency,
uprightness.
neo-chlabhsanach, *a.* without warning.
neo-chladharra, *a.* uncowardly, spirited.
neo-chlaon, *a.* upright.
neo-chleachd, *v.* abrogate, discontinue
the practice of.
neo-chleachdainn, *v.* discontinuing the
practice of ; abrogation.
neo-chleachdta, *a.* unaccustomed to, unusual, unpractised.
neo-chléireach, *n. m.* a layman.
neo-choimheach, *adj.* free, not stingy,
not surly ; kind.
neo-choimhicheas, *n. f.* making one's
self at home ; freedom, kindness.
neochoireach, *adj.* unblameable, innocent,
blameless.

neochoireachd, *n. f.* blamelessness, innocence.

neo-chomas, *n. m.* impotence.

neo-chomasach, *adj.* impossible, unable, impotent.

neo-chomasachd, *n. f.* impossibility, incapability.

neo-chompanta, *adj.* unsocial, not companion-like.

neo-chompantas, *n. m.* unsociableness, unamiableness.

neo-chosmhail, *adj.* unlikely, unlike, dissimilar, improbable.

neo-chosmhaileachd, *n. f.* improbability, unlikelihood, dissimilarity.

neo-chothromach, *adj.* uneven, rough ; unfair, unjust.

neo-chràbhach, *adj.* not austere in religious matters.

neo-chreidmheach, *adj.* unbelieving, unholy, infidel.

neo-chrìochnach, *adj.* endless, infinite, everlasting, unlimited.

neo-chronail, *a.* harmless.

neo-chruadalach, *adj.* unhardy, soft, effeminate, lubberly.

neo-chruinnichte, *vbl. a.* uncollected, ungathered ; not gathered.

neo-chruthaichte, *vbl. a.* uncreated.

neo-chubhaidh, *adj.* unfit, improper, unharmonious, unmerited.

neo-chuimhne, *n. f.* forgetfulness, negligence, want of memory.

neo-chuimhneach, *a.* forgetful.

neo-chuimseach, *adj.* immoderate, vast, exorbitant ; of a bad aim.

neo-chùirteil, *a.* uncourtly.

neo-chumanta, *adj.* uncommon, rare, novel, unusual.

neo-chumantachd, *n. f.* uncommonness, rareness, novelty.

neo-churaidh, *a.* gentle, unwearied. *Ir.* neamh-chuirthe, neamh-churtha.

neo-chùram, *n. m.* carelessness, negligence, neglect, indifference.

neo-chùramach, *adj.* careless, negligent, prodigal, indifferent.

neo-dhàicheil, *adj.* unlikely, absurd, nonsensical ; ungenteel.

neo-dhàicheileachd, *n. m.* unlikelihood, absurdity ; ungentility.

neo-dhiadhaidh, *adj.* unholy, profane, ungodly, impious.

neo-dhiadhaidheachd, *n. f.* ungodliness, impiety, irreligion.

neo-dhìleas, *adj.* unfaithful, faithless, disloyal, undutiful.

neo-dhìlse, *n. f.* disloyalty.

neo-dhiongalta, *adj.* insecure, insufficient, precarious, uncertain.

neo-dhiongaltachd, *n. f.* infirmness, insecurity, uncertainty.

neo-dhleasnach, *adj.* undutiful, disobedient to parents ; disaffected.

neo-dhligheach, *a.* unlawful, not hereditary, not rightful ; undue.

neo-dhoitheach, not unshapely, not gloomy.

neo-dhuine, *n. m.* a man of no account, a man of low position ; a decrepit person, a useless person ; ninny.

neo-dhuineil, *adj.* unmanly.

neo-dhùrachd, *n. m.* insincerity, heedlessness, negligence.

neo-dhùrachdach, *adj.* insincere, negligent, careless.

neo-eagalach, *a.* fearless.

neo-ealanta, *adj.* inexpert.

neo-ealantachd, *n. f.* awkwardness, unskilfulness, want of art.

neo-éifeachd, *n. f.* inefficacy.

neo-éifeachdach, *adj.* ineffectual, inefficient, inefficacious.

neo-éisleanach, *a.* healthy, sound.

neo-eòlach, *a.* unacquainted.

neo-fhàbhorach, *a.* unfavourable, unfair ; not fair, as wind ; impartial.

neo-fhaicsinneach, *adj.* not visible, invisible ; not to be seen properly.

neo-fhàilteamach, *a.* without flaw, perfect.

neo-fhallain, *adj.* unsound, unhealthy (as food or air), unwholesome.

neo-fhallsa, *adj.* candid, fair.

neo-fhasanta, *adj.* unfashionable, uncommon, out of fashion.

neo-fhasantachd, *n. f.* unfashionableness, oddness, rareness.

neo-fheumail, *adj.* needless, useless, unavailing, unnecessary.

neo-fhìor, *adj.* untrue, false.

neo-fhios, *n. m.* ignorance.

neo-fhiosrach, *adj.* un-knowing, ignorant of, unacquainted, unconscious.

neo-fhìreanteach, *adj.* unrighteous, unjust, wicked, bad.

neo-fhoghainteach, *adj.* unserviceable, ineffectual, inefficacious, cowardly.

neo-fhoghluimte, *vbl. a.* untaught.

neo-fhoilleil, *a.* without deceit.

neo-fhoillsichte, *vbl. a.* unrevealed.

neo-fhoirbhidh, *a.* in nonage, immature, undeveloped, imperfect.

neo-fhoisneach, *adj.* restless, unquiet, annoyed, disturbed.

neo-fhoisneachd, *n. f.* restlessness, disquietude, disturbance.

neo-fhreagarrach, *a.* unsuitable, unfit, inapplicable.

neo-fhreagarrachd, *n. f.* unfitness, unsuitableness.

neo-fhreasdalach, *adj.* inattentive, careless, improvident.

neo-fhuras, *n. m.* " un-ease," impatience.

neo-fhurasach, *a.* uneasy, impatient.

neo-fhurasda, *adj.* difficult, tough work.
neog, *n. f.* a notch, nock. *M.Du.* nocke.
neo-ghealtach, *adj.* fearless, undaunted.
neo-ghealtachd, *n. f.* fearlessness, intrepidity, boldness.
neo-gheur, *a.* blunt, not sour, dull, stupid.
neo-ghioganach, *a.* without cringing, blithely.
neòghlaine, *n. f.* uncleanness, impurity, moral corruption, immorality.
neòghlan, *a.* impure, unclean, vile, immoral.
neo-ghlic, *adj.* unwise, foolish.
neòghloin, *n. f.* impurity.
neo-ghluaiste, *vbl. a.* unmoved.
neo-ghnàthach, *a.* unaccustomed, uncommon.
neo-ghnàthaichte, *adj.* unaccustomed, unpractised, abrogated, unusual.
neo-ghoireasach, *adj.* inconvenient, unfit, unmeet ; unnecessary.
neo-ghrad, *adj.* sluggish, unapt.
neo-ghràsmhor, *adj.* ungracious, unmerciful, graceless.
neo-ghrinn, *adj.* unkind, coarse, inelegant, unmannerly.
neo-ghrinneas, *n. m.* unkindness.
neo-ghriobhagach, *a.* without fuss or fear ; composed, unconcerned.
neòil, *n. pl.* clouds ; *gen.* of neul, a cloud ; neòil a' seòladh, clouds gliding.
neo-inbhe, minority (as to age), unripe, abortive.
neo-inbheach, *adj.* premature, unripe, abortive ; torraicheas neo-inbheach, a premature or abortive conception ; not come to the years of maturity : tha e neo-inbheach, he is not of age, he is minor.
neo-inbheachd, *n. f.* prematurity, abortiveness, nonage.
neòinean, niōnen, *n. m.* daisy ; "noon" flower. *Ir.* nóinin.
neòineanach, *adj.* bespangled or speckled with daisies.
neo-iochdmhor, *adj.* unmerciful, inhuman, merciless.
neo-iochdmoireachd, *n. f.* unmercifulness, inhumanity, cruelty.
neo-iomchuidh, *adj.* improper, unfit, unmeet, unbecoming.
neo-iomchuidheachd, *n. f.* unfitness, impropriety, unmeetness.
neo-iomlaineachd, *n. f.* imperfection, incompleteness.
neo-iomlan, *a.* imperfect.
neo-iomnach, *a.* peaceful, without worry.
neo-iompaichte, *vbl. a.* unconverted, unpersuaded.
neo-ionmhuinn, *a.* unbeloved.
neo-ionnan, *adj.* dissimilar ; unlike each other.

neo-ionnanachd, *n. f.* dissimilarity, inequality, unlikelihood.
neo-ionnsuichte, *vbl. a.* unlearned, unskilful, ignorant, inexpert.
neo-laghail, *a.* unlawful, illegitimate.
neo-laghalachd, *n. f.* unlawfulness, illegitimacy ; illegality.
neo-leasaichte, *vbl. a.* unmanured, undunged ; unamended.
neo-liotach, *a.* not stammering, glib ; easily sounded.
neo-lochdach, *adj.* harmless, inoffensive, innocent, uncontaminated.
neo-lomarra, *a.* not grudging ; not stingy, liberal.
neo-luaineach, *a.* sedate.
neo-luchdaich, *v.* discharge, unship, unload ; neo-luchdaichte, *vbl. a.* disburdened.
neo-mhaithteach, *adj.* unforgiving, unrelenting.
neo-mheadhonach, *adj.* not central ; awkward in point of situation ; out of place.
neo-mhealltach, *adj.* fair, candid, undisguised, sincere, honest.
neo-mheangail, *a.* unblemished, sound, healthy, whole.
neo-mhearachdach, *adj.* unerring, infallible, true, wise.
neo-mheasail, *adj.* disrespectful.
neo-mheasarra, *adj.* intemperate, immoderate, debauched.
neo-mheasarrachd, *n. f.* intemperance, debauchery, glut.
neo-mheasgte, *vbl. a.* unmixed.
neo-mheata, *adj.* daring.
neo-mhisgealachd, *n. f.* sobriety.
neo-mhisgeil, *adj.* sober.
neo-mhothachail, *adj.* void of sense or feeling, senseless, stupid.
neo-mhothachalachd, *n. f.* want of feeling, insensibility, stupidity.
neònach, niōnuch, *adj.* novel, rare, curious, strange ; nì neònach, a novel or curious thing ; eccentric, droll ; duine neònach, a droll, eccentric, or curious fellow ; strange, unusual, surprising ; is neònach leam, I am surprised, I think it strange ; is neònach leis, he thinks it strange. neònach = neo-ghnàthach.
neònachas, niōnuchus, *n. m.* surprisingness, curiosity ; eccentricity, drollness, strangeness ; tha neònachas orm, I am surprised, it is a matter of curiosity to me.
neoni, niony, *n. m.* nothing, non-entity, a ninny ; thig iad gu neoni, they shall come to nothing ; 'nuair chuala neoni guth a bheòil, when chaos heard the voice of his mouth. *O.Ir.* nephní, neb-ni.

neonitheach, nionyuch, *adj.* trifling, inconsiderable, insignificant.

neonitheachd, *n. f.* nothingness, insignificance, inconsiderableness.

neo-oileanaichte, *vbl. a.* not well bred, unmannerly, impatient.

neo-onarach, *a.* ignoble, dishonourable, mean, low.

neo-phrìs, *n. f.* " un-worth," contempt.

neo-riaghailteach, *adj.* irregular, anomalous, turbulent, quarrelsome.

neo-riaghailteachd, *n. f.* irregularity, anomaly, turbulence.

neo-roghainn, *n.* a thing one would not choose ; an undesirable thing.

neo-sgairte, *a.* infirm, flabby.

neo-sgairteil, *a.* spiritless.

neo - sgaiteach, *a.* lisping (of tongue) ; slovenly ; dull.

neo-sgarta, *a.* inseparable.

neo-sgàthach, *a.* fearless.

neo-sgeadaich, *v.* undress.

neo-sgithichte, *vbl. a.* unfatigued.

neo - sgoinneil, *a.* without address, slovenly in bearing and in work ; not keen ; drabbish.

neo-shalach, *a.* unpolluted.

neo-shannt, *n. m.* indifference, want of desire.

neo-shanntach, *adj.* unambitious, not covetous, indifferent.

neo-shàrachail, *adj.* indefatigable, unconquerable, keen.

neo-shàraichte, *vbl. a.* unoppressed, unfatigued, indefatigable.

neo-sheannsar, *a.* unlucky, ominous ; " is neo-sheannsar a' chulaidh i," 'tis a garment of ill-luck.

neo-sheargte, *vbl. a.* undecayed.

neo-sheasach, *a.* unsteady.

neo-shnasar, *a.* inelegant, unpolished, ill-finished, untidy.

neo-shocair, *a.* uneasy.

neo-shocaireachd, *n. f.* uneasiness, unsettledness, restlessness.

neo-shoilleir, *a.* darkish, indistinct, not clear or evident.

neo-shoirbheachail, *adj.* unsuccessful, unprosperous.

neo-shoirbheachalachd, *n. f.* unsuccessfulness, unpromising state.

neo-shòlasach, *adj.* joyless, discomfortable, uncomfortable.

neo-shuaimhneach, *adj.* restless, anything but quiet or easy.

neo-shubhach, *a.* joyless.

neo-shuidhichte, *adj.* unsettled.

neo-shuilbhir, *a.* cheerless.

neo-shunntach, *adj.* drowsy.

neo-smiorail, *a.* spiritless.

neo-spéiseil, *a.* unloving.

neo-spòrsail, *a.* unsporting, humble.

neo-spraiceil, *a.* unassuming, dull.

neo-stràiceil, *a.* unconceited.

neo-struidheil, *a.* frugal.

neo-thàbhachd, *n. f.* futility.

neo-thàbhachdach, *adj.* futile.

neo-thaitinn, *v.* displease.

neo-thaitneach, *a.* unpleasant.

neo-tharbhach, *a.* unproductive.

neo-theagaiste, *vbl. a.* untaught.

neo-thèaruinte, *a.* insecure.

neo-thearuinteachd, *n. f.* insecurity, incautiousness.

neo-theom, *adj.* inexpert.

neo-thimcheall-ghear, *v.* uncircumcise ; neo-thimcheall-ghearradh, *n. f.* uncircumcision.

neo-thogarrach, *a.* uncheerful, reluctant, as a person ; uninviting, as weather.

neo-thoileach, *a.* unwilling ; reluctant.

neo-thoilealachd, *n. f.* reluctance, disinclination, aversion, disgust.

neo-thoilich, *v.* dissatisfy.

neo-thoilichte, *a.* dissatisfied.

neo-thoilltinneach, *adj.* undeserving, unworthy, unmeriting.

neo-thoilltinneas, *n. f.* unworthiness, demerit, bad desert.

neo-thoinisgeil, *a.* without sense, stupid.

neo-thoirt, *n. f.* indifference.

neo-thoirteil, *a.* indifferent.

neo-thorach, *a.* unfruitful.

neo-thorachd, *n. f.* unproductiveness, unfruitfulness, unsubstantialness.

neo-thorrach, *a.* barren.

neo-thorraicheas, *n. f.* barrenness, infecundity, abortiveness.

neo-thràighteach, *adj.* inexhaustible, unexhausted, infinite.

neo-thràthail, *a.* late.

neo-thròcaireach, *adj.* unmerciful, merciless, cruel, relentless.

neo-thròcaireachd, *n. f.* unmercifulness, relentlessness.

neo-thruacanta, *adj.* pitiless, unrelenting, unfeeling, cruel.

neo-thruacantachd, *n. f.* unfeelingness, uncompassionateness.

neo-thruailichte, *vbl. a.* undefiled, pure, unadulterated.

neo-thruaillidh, *adj.* liberal.

neo-thuigse, *n. f.* stupidity.

neo-thuigseach, *adj.* senseless.

neo-thuisleach, *adj.* infallible.

neo-thuisleachd, *n. f.* steadiness, infallibility, stability, firmness.

neo-thuiteamach, *a.* infallible, unerring, steady, sure.

neo-uasal, *adj.* ignoble.

neo-uidheam, *n. f.* deshabille.

neo-uidheamaichte, *vbl. a.* unprepared, undressed ; in deshabille.

neo-ullamh, *a.* unprepared.

neul, nēl, nial, niäl, *n. m., gen. s., n. pl.* niùil, and neòil, a cloud ; mar a' ghrian

is neul 'ga sgàileadh, as the sun and
a cloud overshadowing it ; a nap or
wink of sleep ; cha d' fhuair mi neul
cadail, I have not got a wink of sleep ;
tinge, hue, slight appearance ; neul
bainne, slight tinge or hue, of the
colour of milk ; tha neul deoch air,
he has a slight appearance of drink ;
neul a' bhàis, the colour of death ;
a trance or swoon ; chaidh e an neul,
he was in a trance, he fainted, he
swooned. O.Ir. nél. W. niwl, mist,
fog. O.Celt. neblo-s. Lat. nebula.
Gr. νεφέλη, cloud, mist. Cf. O.H.G.
nëbul.

neulach, niäluch, a. cloudy, pale-faced,
sickly-looking. W. niwlog.

neuladair, niäluder, n. m. astrologer.

neuladaireachd, n. f. astrology, astronomy ; astrological knowledge.

neulaich, v. darken, become cloudy.

neular, nialur, a. well-coloured.

nì, nee, n. m., pl. nithean, thing, circumstance, affair, matter ; aon ni, one
thing, matter, or affair. O.Ir. ní, a
thing, matter ; res.

nì, fut. of the v. dèan ; dèan so, do this ;
nì mi sin, I will do that. O.Ir. dogní.

nì, coll. n. m. cattle, stock. O.Ir. ní, res.

ni, neg. no, not ; used only in compos.

niag, nĕăg, n. f. squint eye.

niagach, adj. surly, squint-eyed.

niarach, a. happy, lucky.

niarachd, n. f. envy.

niata, a. courageous ; fr. nia, champion.
M.Ir. forniatta, brave.

nic, female patronymic prefix ; for
nighean mhic ; Nic Ailpin, a daughter
of Macalpine.

nic-cridhe, nee-cree-u, n. f. term of endearment to a female ; thà, nic-cridhe,
yĕs, my dear madam ! my dear lassie !

nigh, nee, v. wash, cleanse, purify. E.Ir.
nigim. M.W. nithio. O.Celt. nigô, I
wash.

nigheadair, nee-uder, n. m. washer,
cleanser.

nigheadaireachd, nee-uder-uchc, n. f.
cleansing ; washing of clothes particularly.

nigheadh, nee-u, vbl. n. m. act of washing,
cleansing.

nighean, nee-un, n. f. a daughter, a girl.
M.Ir. ini. O.Ir. ingen. O.Celt. ení-
genâ. Cf. W. geneth, girl.

nighneag, n. f. girlie, lassie, a daughter.
Dim. of nighean.

nighte, neetu, vbl. a. washed, bathed.

nimh, niv, n.f. virus, venom. See neimh.

nimheil, nival, a. venomous, keenly
wicked. Cf. O.Ir. neimnech, nemnech,
virulent.

nimbir, n. f. a serpent.

nìomsa, nee-umsu, for ni mise, I will do.

nior, nir, neg. part. not (with pret.).
E.Ir. nír = ni (not) + ro (vb. part.).

nìos, nees, adv. from below up ; a nìos,
up ; thoir a nìos, bring up, bring to
the top. E.Ir. anís. Ir. aníos.

nios, neas, n. f. weasel. O.Ir. ness.

nis, nish, adv. now, at this time. E.Ir.
innossai. O.Ir. indossa [ind (art) + fois].

ni's, rel. pron. (for ni is) that which is.
Not to be taken for compar. part. na's.

nitear, neetur, nithear, neĕ'-ur, fut. pass.
of dèan, shall be done ; nìtear, nithear
sin, that shall be done.

niùc, niooc, n. f. a corner, nook. Sc. neuk.

niùlag, nioolag, n. f. a stunted horn.

no, conj. or, nor. O.Ir. nó. O.Celt. nev.

nochd, nŏchc, v. reveal, show, present,
discover ; nochdaidh mi dhuit, I will
show you ; n. m. nakedness ; mo
nochd is mo nàire, my nakedness and
shame ; adj. bare ; nochta, naked,
bared. O.Ir. nocht. E.W. noeth.
O.Celt. noqto-s.

nochd, n. f. night ; an nochd, to-night.
O.Ir. innocht (to-night). W. nos. Lat.
nox. O.Celt. nokti-.

nochdadh, nochcu, vbl. n. m. act of showing, uncovering, revealing, discovering.

nochta, nochtu, vbl. a. shown, bare ;
shabby, ill-dressed.

nodan, n. m. short sleep, a nod, a wink.

nodha, no-u, a. new ; ùr nodha, quite
new. Gaul. novios. Lat. novus. Gr.
νέος. See nuadh.

noig, n. f. old-fashioned face ; a podex
or anus.

noigean, nogen, n. m. Scotch noggie, or
wooden dish, with one handle or ear.

noigeanach, a. snuffy.

noigeiseach, nogeshuch, a. snuffy.

nòin, nōn, n. m. orig. afternoon, the
evening ; "Is éasgaidh nòin na mainne,"
evening is preferable to dawn (for
starting on a journey) ; seal mun
tigeadh trath-nòine do'n ghréin, ere
time of sunset come. I.Lom. The
Sc.G. Dicts. give "noon." So, O'R.
but Din. gives "noon ; evening." Lh.
gives "evening." E.Ir. nóin, gen.
nóna. 1. evening ; trath nóna deód lái,
tranōna, the end of the day. 2. The
fourth of the eight canonical hours.
See tràth. Lat. nona (hora), ninth
hour = 3 P.M.

noir, the east. O.Ir. anair.

nòistin, n. f. liking, fancy for.

nollaig, noolig, n. f. Christmas ; latha
nollaig, Christmas Day ; an nollaig
bheag, New Year's Day ; nollaig mhór,
Christmas, Christmas feast. E.Ir.
notlaic. Lat. natalicia (the Nativity).

norra, n. m. a wink of sleep.

norranta, *a*. sleepy, nodding with sleep.

nòs, *n. m.* custom. *E.Ir.* nós. *W.* naws. *O.Celt.* nomso-.

nòs, *n. m.* cow's first milk after calving ; bainne nùis, beastings. *E.Ir.* nús ; fr. nua, new, + ass, milk. *McB.*

nòsara, *a*. juicy, sappy.

nòtair, noter, *n. m.* a notary. *O.Ir.* notire ; fr. *Lat.* notarius.

nothaist, no-hesht, *n. m.* an idiot, a foolish person ; *a*. nothaisteach.

nuadarra, *a*. angry, surly. *See* nuarranta.

nuadh, noo-a, *adj.* new, fresh. *O.Ir.* núe, núa, and also núide, *novus. W.* newydd. *Gaul.* novios. *See* nodha.

nuadhachd, noo-adh-achc, *n. f.* newness.

nuadhail, *a*. spick and span.

nuag, noo-ag, *n. f.* sunk eye.

nuagach, *a*. sunk-eyed, surly.

'nuair, noo-ur, *adv.* when, at the time ; for an uair (the hour).

nuall, noo-alan, *n. m.* lowing ; a long, drawling howl, as a lion or wild-cat ; horrid howl or yell ; nuallan na pìoba, the skirl of the pipe. *E.Ir.* núall and úall. *O.Celt.* nouslo-n.

nuallanach, *adj.* horridly yelling or howling ; drawlingly howling.

nuallanaich, noo-alanich, *n. f.* a continuous, drawling howl, or yelling.

nuar, *n. m.* woe, sorrow ; mo nuar ! alas ! my woe ! So *M.Ir.*

nuarranta, *a*. sad, surly. Cf. nuar.

nuas, noo-as, *adv.* from above ; thig an nuas, come down ; a suas is an nuas, up and down. *O.Ir.* anúas.

nuatharra, noo-ahuru, *a*. surly, gloomy, fierce.

'n uraidh, last year. *E.Ir.* innuraid = ind (the) + uraid (last year). *See* uiridh.

nuig, nooyg, *n. f.* extent ; gu nuig, up to ; = go ruige ; gonice (B. of Deer).

nuimhir, noo-ivir, *n. f.* number. *Lat.* numerus.

nuin, noon, *n. f.* ash tree. *Also* letter n.

null, nool, *n. m.* to the other side ; *adv.* thither, across ; theirig an null, go across, go over, go thither. *Also* nunn. *O.Ir.* inunn (in + sund) "from here."

'nur, *adv.* when, at the time ; contraction of an uair.

nùs, noos, *n. m.* milk, cow's first milk (on calving).

O

o, the twelfth letter of the Gaelic alphabet, called oir, furze (conas or conasg) ; *n. m.* also water, *obs.*

o, *prep.* from ; in *comp.* with *pers. pron.* uam and bhòm, uat and bhot, etc. *Also* bho. *O.Ir.* o, ua.

o, *conj.* since, when ; with *art.* o'n ; o'n là ud, since that day. *O.Ir.* o.

o, *interj.* Oh !

òb, *n. m.* creek, haven. *O.N.* hóp, small land-locked bay.

ob, *v.* refuse, reject, object ; chan obadh e dubhan, it (fish) would not hesitate taking a hook. *O.Ir.* obbaim, refuse, deny.

obadh, *m.* a refusal, shunning.

obag. *See* ob-obagail.

obaidh, oby, *n. f.* a charm. *See* ubag.

obair, ob'-ir, *n. f., gen.* oibre and oibreach, *pl.* oibrichean, labour, work, employment, occupation ; intermeddling, workmanship ; obair do mheuran féin, the workmanship of thy own hands ; obair-uchd, parapet ; obair-theine, firework ; obair-dhìon, rampart, bulwark ; obair-shnàthaid, needlework ; obairlìn, network ; obair-uisge, waterwork ; obair ghloine, glasswork ; a dh' aon obair, purposely, intentionally, on

purpose. *O.Ir.* oipred, opred. *Lat.* opera.

obann, obun, *a*. sudden, rash, unexpected, hasty. *E.Ir.* opond, sudden, quick.

obannachd, *n. f.* suddenness, quickness.

obar, confluence ; only used in place names Aber-. *W.* aber. *O.W.* aper, oper, confluence.

obh, obh, ōv, ōv, *interj.* och ! ay ! O dear ! obhraig, *n. f.* collection (at church) ; fr. offering.

ob-obagail, òb-òb'-ag-ul, *n. f.* flutter.

ocar, *n. f.* interest, usury. *Also* riadh *O.N.* ókr, usury. *O.H.G.* wuohhar. *A.S.* wōcor. *Goth.* wōkrs, fruit, profit.

och, *inter.* alas ! my conscience ! *Also* ochan ! och nan och is och eile ! my conscience, thrice over ! *O.Ir.* uch !

ochanaich, ŏch'-an-ich, *n. f.* sighing, sobbing.

ochd, ochc, *adj.* and *n.* eight ; ochdoisneach, having eight sides or angles. *Also* ochd-shlisneach, rifle, gun. *O.Ir.* ocht n-. *W.* ŵyth. *Lat.* octō. *Gr.* ὀκτώ.

ochdamh, ochcuv, *adj.* the eighth ; *n. m.* eight groats land ; an octave. *See* cota-bàn.

ochdamhach, *adj.* octangular ; *n. f.* an octagon, or figure having eight sides.

ochd-deug, *n. f.* eighteen.
ochdar, ochcur, **ochdnar**, ochcnur, *coll. n.*
eight persons or things.
och-òn, *inter.* O dear ! alas, (for) that !
ochras, *n. m.* the gills of a fish. So *Ir.*
òcrach. *See* òtrach.
ocras, *n. m.* hunger. *See* acras.
od, *interj.* yonder, yon. *See* ud.
od, *inter.* tut ! no ! ay !
od', for o do ; o d' cheann, from thy
head. It is advisable to disreg. unnecessary apostr. Write od in this
and sim. cases.
oda, *n. m.* race, race - course. Cf. *O.N.*
hesta-at, horse-fight. *H's F.B.* 191.
òdan, *n. m.* a finger, esp. finger tip.
odhar, *adj.*, when in *gen.* it becomes
uidhir, drab, dun, dapple, sallow ;
odhar-liath, dapple-coloured ; stiall na
ba uidhir, the dun cow's stall ; leabhar
na h-uidhre, the book of the dun (cow).
E.Ir. odar. *O.Celt.* odro-s.
odharan, *n. m.* cow - parsnip. *Also*
meacan a' chruidh.
odhraich, òr'-ich, *v.* make dun.
ofrail, ofrel, *n. f.* offering, sacrifice.
E.Ir. oifrend. *Lat.* offerendum.
òg, *adj,* young ; *n. m.* the young. *O.Ir.*
óc, óac. *O.W.* iouenc. *Lat.* juven-
cus. *O.Celt.* jovnko-s.
ògan, *n. m.* a youth, a sapling.
òganach, *n. m.* young man.
ogha, o'u, *n. m.* grandchild. *Ir.* ó, ua
(*gen.* ui). *O.Ir.* ua, aue, haue (*gen.* haui).
oghum, *n. f.* "ogam" writing ; occult
sciences.
òglach, *n. m.* young man, lad, a servant.
O.Ir. óclach, *juvenis.*
ogluidh, ogly, *adj.* gloomy, awful, terrible.
ogluidheachd, ogly-achc, *n. f.* dreadfulness, wildness.
ògmhadainn, *n. f.* early morn, dawn.
ògmhios, òg-veeus, *n. m.* June.
oibreachadh, obruchu, *vbl. n. m.* working,
labouring ; fermenting ; an caochan
ag oibreachadh, the wash fermenting,
mixing ; 'ga oibreachadh, mixing it.
oibrich, obrich, *v.* work, ferment, mix.
oibrichte, *vbl. a.* wrought, fermented.
oich, *interj.* an exclamation expressive
of pain or weariness.
oide, uju, *n. m.* foster-father, godfather,
stepfather. *E.Ir.* aite, tutor, stepfather.
oideachd, *n. f.* instruction.
oideas, *n. m.* instruction, tuition, counsel.
oide-mùinte, *n. m.* instructor.
oidhche, oychu, *n. f.* night. *Ir.* oidche.
O.Ir. aidche.
oidheadh, oyu, *m.* tragical death ; not
current in Mdn. G. *Also* incorrectly
oigheadh. *E.Ir.* oided, aided.
oidheam, oyem, perh. a form of ogham,

a secret or hidden meaning, inference ;
an uair a dh' fhosgail e an oidheam,
when he expounded or unriddled the
meaning ; gnothach gun oidheam, a
thing without meaning ; có is urrainn
oidheam sam bith a thoirt as, who
can bring any sense out of it ? *See*
foidheam.
oidheamach, *a.* ideal.
oidhirp, u-irp, *n. f.* attempt, essay,
endeavour.
oidhirpeach, *a.* diligent, industrious, persevering.
oidhirpich, *v.* attempt, essay, endeavour.
oid-ionnsachaidh, oj-yoonsuchy, *n. m.* a
tutor, instructor.
oifig, ofig, *n. f.* office, occupation.
M.Ir. oiffice. *Lat.* officium.
oifigeach, *n. f.* officer.
òige, ogu, *n. f.* youth, youthfulness.
òigeach, òg-yeach, *n. m.* a young horse ;
stallion, an entire horse. *Also* àigeach
(òg + each).
òigead, ògud, *n. f.* youth, degree of youth.
òigealachd, ògaluchc, *n. f.* youthfulness.
òigear, òger, *n. m.* young man.
òigeil, ògal, *adj.* youthful, young-looking.
òighe, òyu, *n. f.* virgin, maiden. *O.Ir.*
óg, úag, *integer,* whole one, perfect
one.
òigheachd, òy-achc, *n. f.* virginity. *O.Ir.*
óige, oge (*n. f.*), *integritas,* virginity,
chastity.
oigheam, oyem, *n. m.* obedience, homage.
oigheannach, oyunuch, *n. f.* thistle.
Also froinneach. *See* fobhannan.
oighneach, *a.* liberal, generous.
oighre, oyru, *n. m.* ice. *E.Ir.* aigred, ice.
oighre, oyru, *n. m.* an heir ; beiridh bean
mac, ach 'se Dia ni òighre, a woman
may bear a son, but God alone can
make an heir. *M.Ir.* oigir.
oighreachd, *n. f.* heirship, inheritance,
possession, freehold, freeland.
oighreag, oyrag, *n. f.* a cloudberry.
òigridh, ògry, *coll. n. f.* youth, young folk.
= òg (a youth) + ridh (*coll. suf.*).
oil, *v.* rear, instruct in politeness. *O.Ir.*
ailim. Cf. altrum.
oil, *n. f.* offence, cause of regret or
offence ; chan oil leamsa ged robh thu
air do chrochadh, it is no offence to me
though you were hanged ; ge b' oil
leis a' chruaidh-fhortan, in spite of the
mischief. *M.Ir.* oil, disgrace. *I.T.*4¹.
oilbheum, òl'-vem, *n. m.* offence, scandal,
blasphemy ; *a.* oilbheumach. *M.Ir.*
ailbéim, ail (rock) + béim (blow),
stumbling-block, *P.H.*
oileamhaid, oluvaj, *n. f.* university.
oilean, elon, *n. m.* instruction, breeding ;
household instruction or discipline ;
droch oilean, bad breeding, want of

politeness. *O.Ir.* oilemain, *inf.* of ailim, I nourish, rear.

oileanach, elanuch, *adj.* polite, well-bred ; a student, pupil.

oileanaich, elanich, *v.* instruct in politeness, bring up well.

oileanta, elantu, *adj.* well-bred, polite.

oileid, ul'-ej, *n. f.* college.

oilearach, eluruch, *n. f.* nursery.

oilire, eliru, *n. m.* instructor, teacher.

oillt, oylt, *n. f.* greatest horror, detestation ; dlùthchrith air gach cnàimh le h-oillt, every bone shaking with horror. *Ir.* oilt, horror. *O'R.*

oillteachadh, oyltuchu, *vbl. n. m.* act of horrifying in the highest degree, horror-struck ; the highest degree of horror or detestation, horrification.

oilltealachd, oyltaluchc, *n. f.* horrific nature or quality ; horrificness, dreadfulness.

oillteil, oyltal, *adj.* horrifying, horrific, terrible in the highest degree ; disgusting in the highest degree. =oilt +samail.

oilltich, oyltich, *v.* horrify.

oilthigh, *n. m.* seminary, college, university.

oilthir, elhir, *n. f.* a foreign land. *See* eilthir. *O.Ir.* ailithir, a foreign land.

oilthireach, *n. m.* stranger, pilgrim ; " amal gach n-oilithrech," like every pilgrim. *O.Ir.* ailithrech, a pilgrim.

oin, *n. f.* agony of death, great mental distress. *Also* omhain.

oineach, eineach, *n. m.* liberality, mercy. So *Ir.*

òinid, *n. m.* a fool. *E.Ir.* ónmit ; fr. ón (foolish) + ment (mind).

òinnseach, ōshuch, *n. f.* idiot ; ón (disgrace) + seach (*fem. suf.*),foolish woman.

òinnseachail, ōn'-shach-al, *a.* foolish, as a female, like a foolish female.

oir, *conj.* since, for, because that ; thog iad teine, oir bha an là fuar, they made a fire since the day was cold. *O.Ir.* hóre, < húar = *Lat.* hōra.

oir, *conj.* for ; introd. co-ord. expl. cl. ; ghabh e an t-aiseag, oir bha am bàta aig caladh, he took the ferry, for the boat was at the pier. *O.Ir.* ar.

oir, *n. f.* hem, border, edge, margin ; oir an aodaich, the hem of the cloth. *O.Ir.* or.

oir, *n. m.* the east.

oir-, *intens. prefix.* *O.Ir.* air-, ar-, ir-, aur-, er-, ur-.

oirbh, orv, *prep. pron.* (air +sibh), on you, owed by you ; the matter with you ; you under the necessity. *See* air.

oirbheart, *n. m.* good deed; fr. oir +beart.

oirbheartach, *a.* glorious, famous.

oirbheas, orbhus, *n. m.* act of charity ;

bu oirbheas dhuit a dhèanadh, it were an act of charity in you to do it ; fr. oir +beus.

oirbheasach, *a.* charitable.

oirbhse, orv-shu, *emph.* of oirbh. *See* air.

oircean, orcen, *n. m.* pigling. *Also* uircean. *E.Ir.* orc =porcus ; orcán, *porcellus.*

oircheas, orchus, *n. f.* act of charity, pity ; clemency ; *a.* oircheasach.

oircheum, *n. m.* slow step (as of one under a burden), languor. =oir +ceum.

òirdhearc, ōr-yerc, *adj.* famous, superb. *O.Ir.* airdirc, erdirc (gl. *celebre*). *Also* aurdairc. *Wi.*

oirdhearcas, *n. f.* superiority, excellency, superbness, pre-eminence.

oirean, *n. m.* selvidge.

oirein, *n. m.* the right-hand horse in a plough.

oirfeid, orfej, *n. m.* music ; melody ; uile oirfeid na crìosdachd, the whole melody of Christendom. *E.Ir.* airfitiud (playing), *inf.* of arbeitim, arpeittim (I play). *Wi.* *M.Ir.* fét, music, whistle.

oirfeideach, *n. m.* musician ; *adj.* musical.

òirinn-oirinn, pianoforte.

òirleach, ōrluch, *n. m.* an inch. *M.Ir.* ordlach, orddu lámae (gl. *pollex*). *Z²*.

òirlis. *See* orrais.

òirnean, *n. pl.* pieces (of blasted rock).

oirnn, ōrn, *prep.* +pron. suf. (for air sinn), on us, upon us, owed by us, matter with us. *See* air.

oirre, on her. *See* air.

oirthir, *n. f.* the east. *O.Ir.* airther, airthir, fr. air, front, east ; gl. *Eous*, the morning star. Of old, Celts and others named the airts from the position of one facing the sun in the morning : front =east, right hand =south, back =west, left =north. *Z²*, 57.

oirthir, or-hir, *n. f.* beach, border, the coast. *M.Ir.* oirear, a district, plain.

oirthireach, *n. m.* borderer ; *adj.* maritime.

oisean, oshen, *n. m.* corner, angle, nook ; *gen.* oisinn, of a corner, nook, etc.

oiseanach, oshenuch, *a.* angular.

óisg, o'isc, a yearling sheep. *O.Ir.* óisc. Cf. *Lat.* ovis.

oisir, *n. f.* an oyster. *See* eisir. *Ir.* oisre. *Lat.* ostrea. *Gr.* ὄστρεον.

oit! foit! *interj.* exclamation expressive of great cold or heat. *O.Ir.* uit.

oiteag, oytag, *n. f.* light squall, gust.

oiteagach, *adj.* squally.

oitir, oytir, *n. f.* reef of sand, or bar in the sea, a shallow, or shoal in the sea, a low promontory.

òl, *vbl. n. m.* drink, potations, drunkenness, inebriety, habitual potations ; tha

e trom air an òl, he is a hard drinker ;
'se an t-òl a chuir an dunach ort,
drunkenness put you to the mischief ;
act of drinking, spirituous liquors,
drinking ; *v.* drink, slacken thirst ; dh'
òladh tu is cha phàidheadh tu, you
would drink but you would not pay ;
sip ; ag òl brochain, sipping gruel ; òl
snaoisean, take snuff ! *E.Ir.* òl, *inf.*
of ibim. *O.Ir.* óul (*dat.* s), ól, *potus.*

ola, *n. f.* oil, ointment for medicinal purposes. *O.Ir.* ola. *W.* olew. *Lat.* oleum.

òlach, *n. m.* an hospitable man, now
often a term of sarcasm ; is éibhinn an
t-òlach thu, you are an odd fellow
indeed. *Ir.* ólach, given to drunkenness ; fr. òl.

òlachas, *n. m.* hospitality, kindness.

òlachd, *n.f.* hospitality, kindness, bounty.

olann, *n. f.* wool ; *gen.* olla. *E.Ir.*
oland. *W.* gwlân. *Lat.* lāna. *O.Celt.*
vlaná, vlano-.

òlar, *adj.* addicted to drink.

olc, *n. m., gen.* uilc, *pl.* na h-uilc, mischief,
evil, wickedness, apparition ; an evil
person, the evil one ; seachainn an
t-olc, shun the evil ; nach b' e an t-olc
e ! is he not an evil one ! *adj. compar.*
miosa, evil, bad, wicked ; *adv.*
wickedly, very ill ; is olc a fhuaras thu,
you behaved very ill ; gu h-olc, sick,
very ill, badly. *O.Ir.* olcc, *gen.* uilc,
huilc.

olcas, olk'-us, *n. m.* badness, naughtiness ;
offence ; air olcas, let it or him be
ever so bad ; ghabh e olcas, he took
offence ; olcad, degree of badness, inferiority, etc.

ollabhar, *n. m.* great army. *Ir.* ollarbhar ;
fr. oll (great) + arbar (host).

ollach, *a.* woolly, fleecy.

ollamh, ŏll'-uv, *n. m.* a learned man,
a doctor. *O.Ir.* ollam.

ollamhrachd, *n. f.* professorship.

ollanachd, *n. f.* teaching, drilling, curing.
=ollamhnachd.

ollanaich, olanich, *v.* teach, drill, cure.
=ollamhnaich.

oll-aodach, ol-uduch, *n. m.* woollen cloth.

olltuagh, *n. f.* battle-axe, great axe ;
fr. oll (great) + tuagh (axe).

òmar, *n. m.* amber, ombar ; fr. the *Eng.*

omhail, o'il, *n. f.* care, attention, feeling.
See umhail.

omhan, o-un, *n. m.* milk froth or froth
of whey. *E.Ir.* úan, froth. *W.* ewyn,
foam.

òmhnasach, *a.* foamy, foamy-white.

on, *conj.* since, since it is so.

onagaid, onugej, *n. f.* confusion, row.

onair, oner, *n. f.* honour, dignity. *E.Ir.*
onór (*d.* onóir) = *Lat.* honor.

ònar. *See* aonar.

onarach, *adj.* honourable. *Lat.* honōr-is.

onaraich, *v.* honour, revere.

ònasach. *See* òmhnasach.

onchonn, on'-chunn, *n. m.* ensign. *E.Ir.*
onchú, leopard, banner.

onfhadh, onu-hu', *n. m.* rage, raging of
the sea ; fury. *See* confhadh. *E.Ir.*
an-feth, unrest, tumult=an (*neg.*) +
feth (a calm). *Also* an-fud, a storm.

ònrachd, *n. f.* solitude, solitariness.

ònrachdach, *a.* solitary.

ònrachdan, *n. m.* hermit, a person left
alone, or deserted person, recluse.

ònrachdanach, *a.* solitary.

ònrachdanachd, *n. f.* loneliness, solitariness, seclusion, solitude.

òpar, *n. m.* mud on trousers-legs or on
bottom of skirt, a bedraggling.

òr, *n. m.* gold ; *v.* gild, burnish ; *a.* òrach,
òrail. *O.Ir.* ór. *W.* aur. *Lat.* aurum.

or-, *prefix,* air-, oir-, *q.v.*

òrachan, òruchan, *n. m. pl.* òraichean,
a jewel, enchantment.

òrachd, òrachc, *n. f.* hoarding gold.

òrachd, *n.f.* fictitious ornament, fantasies,
fantastic dress or ornaments ; tuilleadh
is a' chòir de òrachdan, too many
fantastic ornaments or assumed airs.

òradh, *n. m.* act of gilding.

òrag, *n. f.* a sheaf of corn.

orag, *n. f.* unfledged young cormorant.
Also odharag, the dun little one.

oragan, *n. m.* an organ. *E.Ir.* organ.
Lat. organum.

òraid, òrej, *n. f.* oration, speech. *E.Ir.*
orait, prayer ; fr. *Lat.* oratio, speech.

òraideach, *a.* oratorical.

òraidear, òrejer, *n. m.* orator.

òrail, òr'-al, *adj.* golden.

orair, orer, *n. m.* porch.

òrais, òresh, *n. m.* tumultuous noise.

oraisg, *n. m.* waterbrash ; vomit. *See*
orrais.

òran, *n. m.* song, glee ; a' gabhail òrain,
singing songs ; *properly* amhran.
M.Ir. ambrán.

òranaiche, òranichu, *n. m.* a singer, a
book of songs, a songster, a repertoire.

òrbhuidh, òr-vooy, *a.* golden-coloured ;
nighean òrbhuidh, a golden-haired lass.

òrcheard, òr-cherd, *n. m.* goldsmith.

òrchiabh, òr-chiuv, *n. m.* a golden
lock.

òrchul, *n. m.* yellow or golden tresses.

òrd, *n. m., gen. s., n. pl.* ùird, a hammer ;
òrd-mór, a sledge-hammer ; òrd-
ladhrach, a claw-hammer ; òrd-barraidh, a clinching hammer. *O.Ir.* ordd
(gl. *malleus*). *W.* gordd. *O.Celt.* ordo-s.

òrd, *n. m., pl.* òrdan, a chunk, a piece ; a
cut of fish ; a short length of string ;
gearr 'n a òrdan e, cut it in pieces, in
chunks.

òrdachadh, ord'-uch-u, *vbl. n. m.* ordering, directing ; officiously interfering ; ordaining, decreeing, predestinating.

òrdag, *n. f.* thumb, toe.   *O.Ir.* orddu.

òrdagh, òrdugh, ōrdoo, *n. m.* order, command, injunction, instruction ; decree, edict ; òrdugh o'n tigh-chuspainn, a decree or edict from the custom-house ; cuir an òrdugh, put in order, arrange ; gun òrdugh, without instruction or direction, deranged ; an òrdugh catha, in battle array; ordinance, Sacrament of the Lord's Supper.   *O.Ir.* ord, *ordinatio* ; ordaigim, I order, regulate. *Lat.* ordo.

òrdaich, ord'-ich, *v.* order, direct ; decree, ordain.

òrdail, ord'-al, *a.* well-arranged, orderly, decent, becoming, regular.

òrdha, *a.* golden, shining like gold, gilded, excellent.

òrdhuilleag, *n. f.* a gold leaf.

òrdon, *n. m.* order.   *Lat.* ordo.

òrgan, òrghan, *n. m.* an organ.

òrganach, *a.* with playing of organs.

òrghruag, *n. f.* golden hair.

orm, *prep. pron.* on me, owed by me ; wrong with me ; ciod a tha aig orm ? what do I owe him ? ciod a tha ort ? what is wrong with you ? what ails you ? what is annoying you ? a' cur orm, dressing—dressing myself.   *Also* ormsa.   *See* air.

òrmheinn, *n. f.* a gold mine.

orra, *prep. pron.* on them.   *See* air.

orra, ortha, or, *n. f.* amulet or enchantment, a charm to effect something wonderful ; orra-ghràidh, an amulet to provoke unlawful love; orra-sheamlachais, an amulet to make a cow allow the calf of another cow to suck her ; an imposture of any kind ; orra-chomais, an amulet ; orra-na-h-aoine, an amulet to drown a foe ; orra-an-donais, amulet to send one's foe to the mischief; orra-ghrùdaire, an amulet to make every drop of the wash to overflow the wash-tuns ; an orra-bhalbh, an amulet to prevent one's agent to make defence in a court of justice.   *Ir.* orrtha, ortha, prayer in verse ; fr. *Lat.* oratio.

orradh, *n. m.* shift, exertion, endeavour.

orraganach.   *See* oraganach.

orraghain, *pl.* of orra, *q.v.*

orraichean, *n. pl.* charms.

òrrais, or'-èsh, *n. f.* nausea, water-brash, squeamishness, or gnawing at the stomach ; bha'n òrrais ri m' fhiacail fad an latha, the water-brash was annoying me, the live-long day.

orsa, a common dial. form of arsa, said, *inquit.*

ort, *prep.* +*pron. suf.* on thee, upon thee, owed by thee.   *See* air.

os, *n. f.* an elk ; a deer ; lean thusa an os bhallach, pursue thou the spotted elk.   *E.Ir.* os, oss.

òs, *n. m.* outlet of a lake or river, a sand-bar ; òs an loch, the outlet of the lake.   *O.N* óss, outlet of river or lake. *Cl. Lat.* ostium ; fq. in Norse pl. names.

os, *prep.* above ; os cionn, above.   *O.Ir.* ós, uas.   *O.Celt.* oukso-.

os, orsa, *v.* quoth ; for or, ar (say).   *See* arsa.

osadh, osu', *n. m.* act of desisting.   *E.Ir.* ossad, truce.   *Also* abhsadh.

osag, *n. f.* light squall, a gentle breeze.

os-àird, os-ārd, " above board " ; openly, of common knowledge ; thainig an nì a bh'ann os-àird, that matter is no longer secret—it is common knowledge.

osan, *n. m.* a hose, stocking, the leg of trousers.   *Ir.* asan, stocking, *O'D.* W. hosan ; a Teut. word.   *O.H.G., O.N.* hosa.   *A.S.* hosu ; orig. " covering for the legs reaching from the thigh, or even from the knee only, and often also to stockings and gaiters."   *Kl.*

osanaiche, osanichu, *n. m.* a hosier.

osann, osun, *n. f.* a deep sob or sigh.

osannaich, osnich, *n. f.* continuous sighing or sobbing ; heavy blasts or gusts of wind.

os-barr, *adv.* besides, moreover.

oscach, *a.* eminent, superior.   os+càch. *McB.*

oscarra, *a.* fierce, bold ; famous, august ; intrepid ; loud, clamorous.   *Also* oscarach.   *Ir.* oscartha, fearless, bold.

oscarrachd, *n. m.* fierceness ; boldness, energy, loudness.   *Ir.* Oscar, a champion (?).

os-cionn, above.   =os (*prep.*) + cionn (*d. s.* of ceann, head), "over head," above.

òsd, *n. m.* an inn ; ale-house ; a' bhean òsda, the landlady of the inn ; *a.* òsda. *M.E.* ooste, hóst, hotel, house; through *Fr.* from *Lat.* hospitium.   *McB.*

òsdair, osder, *n. m.* a host, landlord of an lnn.   *Also* fear-òsda, innkeeper.

osgan, *n. m.* a yearling wedder.

os-iosal, *adv.* privately.   *Also* gu dìomhair, an diùbhrais.

osnach, *a.* sighing ; blustering, as wind ; blubbering, as a person.

osnadh, osnu, *n. f., pl.* osnaidhean, a sigh. *O.Ir.* osnad, sigh.

osnaich, osnich, *n. f.* continued sighing, or blustering, or blubbering, etc.

osp, *v. i.* gasp, sob quickly.

ospag, *n. f.* a gasp ; quick, deep sob ; a gust of wind.   *Also* osmag, uspag.

ospagail, ŏsp'-ag-al, ospail, ŏsp'-ul, *n. f.* continuous gasping, or quick sobbing; act of sobbing, sighing.

ospairn, osparn, ospairnich, osparnich, *n. f.* same as above, gasping quickly.

ostal, *n. m.* an apostle; astal, *Fern. MS.*; easpul, *Carsw.*; ostal, *D.Lis. Ir.* abstal, aspal. *Lat. Gr.* apostolus. *Watson.*

othaig, *n. m.* habit, practice, usually in a bad sense. Cf. oifig.

othail, o'ul, *n. f.* hurry-burry; tumult, confusion. *Also* foghail, fòghail.

othaisg, o'isc, *n. f.* a yearling ewe; a soft, lubberly person; a blockhead.

othan. *See* omhan.

othanaich, *n. m.* fuss, excitement, bustle.

othar, *n. m.* ulcer, abscess, an open sore. *O.Ir.* othar, sick. *O.Celt.* (p)utro-s.

òtrach, *n. m.* dung-hill; a drabbish, very fat female. *Also* òcrach. *O.Ir.* dung.

òtrachail, ŏt-ruch-al, *a.* drabbish, filthy.

P

p, the thirteenth letter of the Gaelic alph., named beith-bhog. Not native.

pa, *inter.* and *n. m.* papa.

pab, *int. f.* a tassel, knob; pabanan òir, golden tassels; shag, refuse of flax, woolly hair. *E.Ir.* popp, bunch. *Sc.* pab.

pab, *v. t.* twist, buffet, become shaggy.

pabach, *adj.* tasselled, tufted, shaggy.

pabadh, *m.* shagginess, buffeting.

pabag, *n. f.* little tassel.

pabagach, *adj.* tufted.

pabcheann, *n. m.* shaggy-head.

pabhail, pavul, *n. m.* pavement. *Eng.*

pac, *n. m.* the sheep a shepherd is allowed to rear as part wages. *Sc.* packs.

pac, *v.* pack up, get out of the house, get about your business; *n. m.* a pack, a vile crew or set of people; fr. *Eng.*

pacaid, packej, *n. f.* a packet; a female tell-tale or tattler.

pacaire, packiru, *n. m.* one that packs, a pedlar.

pacarras, packurus, *n. m.* trash, refuse, a mass of confusion.

padhal, *n. m.* a ewer, pail. So *Ir.*; *W.* padell; fr. the *Eng.*

pàg. *See* pòg.

pàgach for pògach.

pàganach, *n. m.* a heathen, a pagan; *adj.* heathenish, pagan. *Lat.* paganus.

pàganachd, *n. f.* heathenism.

pàganta, *adj.* heathenish.

paid, paj, paidir, pajir, *n. m.* cluster, string of beads; Lord's Prayer; the Paternoster. *O.Ir.* pater. *W.* pader. *Lat.* pater.

pàidh, pāy, *v.* pay, suffer for, remunerate, atone, make amends; pàidhidh tu sin fhathast, you shall suffer for that yet. Cf. *Fr.* payer. *Lat.* pacare, appease.

pàidheadh, pāyu, *vbl. n. m.* payment, pay; act of paying, remunerating, suffering for.

pàidhear, pāyer, *n. m.* payer, sufferer.

paidhir, pyr, *n. f., gen.* pàidhreach, *pl.* pàidhrichean, pair, brace, couple; fr. the *Eng.*

paidhneachas, pynuchus, *n. m.* penalty, pledge; ann am paidhneachas fichead punnd Sasannach, under the penalty of twenty pounds sterling. Cf. peanas.

paidhnich, pynich, *v.* bind under penalty.

paidhrich, pyrich, *v.* pair, as birds, etc.

paidhrichte, *vbl. a.* paired.

pàidhte, pā-tu, *vbl. a.* paid, remunerated.

paidreag, pajrag, *n. f.* a patch, a clout.

paidrean, pajren, *n. m.* cluster of grapes, etc.; posy, string of anything, as beads, shells, etc. *Ir.* paidirín, a rosary, or set of beads. *W.* paderau, prayers, beads.

paidrich, pajrich, *v.* say your prayers.

pàigh. *See* pàidh.

pail. *See* peula, a pail.

pail-chlach, *n. m.* a pavement. So in *Ir.*

pàilios, pēlis, *n. f.* palace. *Lat.* palātium.

pailleart, peliart, *n. m.* a box on the ear; a blow with the palm. *Lat.* palma.

pàilliun, pāliun, *n. f.* tent, tabernacle, pavilion; fr. *M.Sc.* palzeon. *Fr.* pavillon.

pailm, pelm, *n. f.* palm tree. *M.Ir.* pailm. *Lat.* palma.

pailt, pelt, *adj.* plentiful, abundant; in all likelihood a Pictish word. *McB.*

pailteachd, *n. f.* plentifulness.

pailteas, *n. m.* plenty, abundance.

paind, penj, paindeag, penjag, *n. f.* pebble. *Also* maidealag.

paindeal, *n. m.* a panther.

paindealach, pénj'-al-uch, *n. m.* a person laced up like a dandy; article of dress too straight.

painneal, *n. m.* a panel. *Ir.* paineul. *W.* panel.

painnse, pensh, *n. f.* tripe, paunch. *Sc.* painch, pench.

painntear, pentir, *n. f.* trap, snare; fr. *M.E.* pantere, "bag-net." *O.Fr.* pantière. *M.Ir.* painntér. *a.* painntearach.

pàipear, *n. m.* paper. *Lat.* papyrus. *Eng.* paper.

paipin, *n. m.* a poppy. *Ir.* paipín. *Lat.* popaver.

paiprich, *v.* cover with paper.

pàirc, pārc, *n. f.* a park. So *Ir. W.* parc ; fr. the *Eng.*

pairilis, *n. m.* palsy. *Lat.-Gr.* paralysis.

pàirt, pārst, *n. f.* part, share, portion, interest, connection, some ; ghabh e phàirt, he took his part. *Lat.* pars.

pàirteach, pārstuch, *a.* liberal, sharing.

pairteachail, *a.* divisible.

pàirtich, pārstich, *v.* participate, share.

pàis, *n. f.* suffering ; a slap, a box on the ear.

pàisde, pāshj'-u, *n. m.* child, a little boy ; fr. *Eng.* page.

pàisdean, pāshjen, *n. m.* a little child.

pàisdeil, *a.* infantile, childish.

paisean, peshan, *n. m.* a fit, a fainting fit, a fit of rage ; chaidh e am paisean, he took a fit ; a fit of temper. *E.Ir.* paiss (*passio*).

paiseanadh, *n. m.* fainting ; *a.* paiseanach.

paisg, pesc, *v.* fold, wrap, imply ; paisg an t-aodach, fold up the cloth. *W.* ffasg, bundle. *Lat.* fasces.

paisgte, *vbl. a.* folded, wrapped.

pait, *n. m.* a bump ; a smart blow on the head, producing a bump ; a hump ; a ford. Cf. *Eng.* pat, small lump.

pàiteach, pātiuch, *adj.* thirsty.

pàiteachd, *n. f.* thirst, a state of thirst.

pàiteag, pātiag, *n. f.* a periwinkle.

pàitean, patien, *n. m.* peat (as it falls from the cutting-iron). *Suth.*

pàlas, *n. m.* a palace ; fr. the *Eng. Lat.* palatium.

palla, *n. m.* a ledge in face of a precipice. Cf. *O.N.* pallr, high step ; bench.

palmair, *n. m.* rudder. *See* falmadair.

paltog, *n. f.* a cloak. *See* pealltag.

pannal, pannan, *n. m.* a band, a band of women. *Also* bannal.

paoinear, pyner, *n. m.* mason's labourer. *Sc.* poiner.

Pàp, *n. m.* the Pope. *O.Ir.* papa. *Lat.* papa.

pàpanach, *n. m.* a papist ; *a.* popish.

pàpanachd, *n. f.* popery.

papar, *n. m.* silt, river deposit.

paracas, *n. m.* rhapsody.

paradh, *m.* pushing, brandishing.

paralais, paralesh, *n. f.* a slight stunning or swoon ; palsy.

pàrant, *n. m.* a parent. *Eng.*

pardag, *n. f.* a pannier.

pàrlamaid, pārlumej, *n. f.* parliament. *M.Ir.* pairlimint ; fr. the *Eng.*

pàrlamaideach, *a.* parliamentary.

parra, *n. m.* ; parra ruadh nan cearc, a hen-harrier or hawk.

parraist, par'-esht, parish. *Also* sgìreachd. *Eng.*

Pàrras, *n. m.* Paradise. *O.Ir.* pardus. *Lat.* paradisus < *Gr.* παράδεισος, park.

partan, *n. m.* crab. *Also* portan.

pasbhin, *n. m.* trimming of gold or silver lace, braid, beads ; passementerie.

pasg, *coll. n. m., gen. s.* pasga, bunch, bundle, parcel, faggot ; pasg iuchraichean, a bunch of keys ; pasg aodaich, a parcel of cloth ; pasg shlat, faggot of twigs.

pasgach, *n. f.* a wrapper.

pasgadh, pāsg'-u, *vbl. n. m.* folding, wrapping.

pasgan, *n. m.* little bundle.

pasmunn, *n. m.* expiring pang, spasm.

pat, *n. m. See* pait.

pathadh, pa'u, *n. m.* thirst ; tha pathadh orm, I am thirsty ; *adj.* pàidhteach, thirsty, a form of pòiteach, drinking. *Lat.* potus, drunk.

peabar, piobar, pebur, *n. m.* pepper. *See* piobar.

peabraich, pebrich, *v.* pepper, season, incite.

peacach, peckuch, *a.* sinful ; *n. m.* sinner.

peacachadh, *vbl. n. m.* act of sinning, erring ; *n. m.* transgression.

peacadh, *n. m.* sin. *O.Ir.* peccad. *W.* pechod. *Lat.* peccatum.

peacaich, peckich, *v.* sin, commit sin.

peacaidheachd, peckyachc, *n.f.* sinfulness.

péacan, *n. m.* a beacon.

peall, pial, *n. m.* a hide, a skin ; bunch of matted hair ; a horse ; *v.* clot, mat, as wool ; tha 'ghruag air pealladh, his hair is clotted or matted. *E.Ir.* pell, peall, horse (*Corm.*). *Lat.* pellis, hide.

peallach, piullach, piäluch, *a.* matted ; paltry, trifling, ragged.

pealladh, *m.* act of clothing ; air a pealladh, clothed.

peallag, piälag, *n. f.* a mat of straw ; a rag, tatter ; bass ; sort of under pack-saddle ; *a.* peallagach.

peallag-buarach, piälag-boo-uruch, *n. f.* mushroom.

peallaid, piälej, *n. f.* a sheepskin ; paltry female. *Sc.* pellet. *Lat.* pellis.

peallan, piälan, *n. m.* a tar-mop. *Also* meapaid.

pealltag, pialtag, *n. f.* patched cloak.

peanachas, penuchus, *n. m.* punishment, pains, penance.

peanas, pen'-as, *n. m.* punishment, penance. *Lat.* poena.

peanasach, pen'-as-uch, *a.* penal ; annoying.

peanasaich, pen'-as-ich, *v.* punish, torture.

peanasaiche, *n. m.* punisher.

peann, pi-äun, *n. m.* a pen. *Lat.* penna.

peanntair, pi-äunter, *v.* scribble, scrawl.

peanntaireachd, *n. f.* a scribbling, scrawling.

pearluinn, perlin, *n. f.* muslin, fine linen. *Ir.* péirlin, fine linen, cambric. *O'R.* Cf. *Sc.* pearlin.

pearsa, pers'-u, *n. f.* person, anybody. *O.Ir.* **persan**. *Lat.* persona.

pearsail, persal, *n. m.* parsley.

pearsanta, pers'-annt-u, *adv.* personally ; *adj.* handsome, personable, portly.

pearsantachd, *n. f.* personality.

pears-eaglais, pers-yuglish, *n. m.* clergyman.

peasair, pesir, *n. f.* pease ; *gen. s.* and *n. pl.* **peasrach**. *Lat.* pisum.

peasan, pesan, *n. m.* impertinent person, a mean fellow, a varlet.

peasanach, *adj.* petulant, impudent.

peasanachd, *n. f.* impertinence, pertness, impudence.

peasanta, *adj.* petulant, pert.

peasg, pesc, *n. f.* a gash, as in the skin ; crevice, as in wood ; *v.* gash, chink, notch ; chop, as hands ; possibly Pictish. *McB.*

peasgach, pescuch, *adj.* gashed, chinked.

peata, petu, *n. m.* (*pl.* **peatachan**), a pet ; spoiled child. *E.Ir.* **petta, peta**.

peatarnachd, petarnuchc, *n. f.* fondling.

peathrachas, peruchus, *n. f.* sisterhood.

peic, *n. f.* a peck ; two gallons.

peidseachas, pejshuchus, properly **peideachas**, *n. m.* music. *M.Ir.* **peiteadh**, music. *E.Ir.* **ar-petim**, I amuse. *Watson.*

peighinn, pe'in, *n. f.* penny, coin, stiver ; chan 'eil peighinn agam, I have not a stiver ; fiscal denomination of land equal to **cota bàn**, groat land ; round bit, or anything like a shilling ; 'ga ghearradh na pheighinnean, cutting it in round bits. *E.Ir.* **pinginn**. *O.N.* **penningr**. *A.S.* pending. *O.H.G.* pfenting.

peighinneach, pe'in-uch, *a.* spotted.

peighinnich, make round bits, as a shilling or sixpence.

peighinn-rioghail, pe'in-ree'ol, *n.f.* pennyroyal ; am bearnan-bride is pheighinn-rioghail, the dandelion and the penny-royal.

péile, *n. m.* sheen, brilliancy.

péileag, pylag, *n. f.* a porpoise.

peileasach, pylasuch, *a.* frivolous.

peileastar, pelustur, *n. m.* a quoit, flat stone. Cf. *Lat.* pila.

peileid, pylej, *n. m.* young porpoise.

peileid, pylej, *n. f.* a cod, husk, bag, a mangled sheep-skin.

peileid, *n. m.* a slap on the head ; a blow. Cf. *Eng.* pelt.

peileid, *n. m.* the skull, the crown of the head. Cf. *Sc.* pallet.

peileir, *n. m.* a bullet, a ball. *Ir.* peiléir.

peileir, peler, *n. m.* hard labour, heavy strain ; aig peileir a bheatha, (working) for dear life.

peillic, pylic, *n. m.* skin ; covering of skins, or coarse cloth. *Ir.* peillic, a hide, a hide-covered hut. *E.Ir.*

pellec, *sportula*, basket of untanned hide. *Lat.* pelliceus.

péin, *n. f.* See **pian**. *M.Ir.* **péinn**, penance.

péinealtachd, pynaltuchc, *n. f.* tyranny, pain.

peinneag, penag, *n. f.* a chip of stone for steadying a large stone in course of building, small stones for filling crevices in wall. *Also* peinig. *Sc.* pinning.

peinngilleachd, pe-ingilachc, *n.f.* tyranny.

peinnt, pent, *n. f.* **peinnteag**, pentag, a small pretty shell or pebble ; in *Lewis*, **maidealag**.

peinnteal, pental, *n. m.* a snare ; a form of painntear.

peinntealach, *n.m.* a slender, tightly laced, dandified person ; a straight article of dress, as coat, trousers.

peirceall, percul, *n. m.* a jawbone, a lantern-jaw, a lean, large, lank jaw. *Ir.* peircioll, a corner, lower part of the face, jaw.

peirceallach, *n. m.* a lean, lank, lantern-jawed person ; *a.* lantern-jawed.

péire, pêru, *n. m., pl.* péirean, the buttocks. See **peursa**.

peirealais, peralus, *n. m.* bewilderment, distraction.

péireid, pêrej, *n. f.* a ferret.

peirigill, perigil, *n. f.* danger, strait, agonies of death, excruciating mental tortures or torment. *Lat.* periculum.

peiriglich, *v.* torture, torment.

péiris, pêrish, *n. pl.* testiculi ; fr. *Fr.* pierre (?). *McB.*

peislear, peshler, *n. m.* a trifling person.

peiteag, petag, *n. f.* 1. a waistcoat, a jacket. 2. a lock of wool. *Sc.* petycot, a short sleeveless tunic, worn by men.

peitean, peten, *n. m.* woollen shirt, jacket, a vest.

peithir, pe-hir, **beithir**, *n. m.* a thunder-bolt.

peithire, peathaire, pe-hiru, *n. m.* a message boy ; a forester ; **peithireachd**, running messages, or making domestic jobs.

peitidh, pety, *n. m.* a woollen overshirt.

peitseag, *n. f.* a peach.

peòdar, *n. m.* pewter. *Also* feòdar, fleòdar.

peuc, pēc, *n. f.* pea-hen. *Also* peucag.

peucail, *a.* trim, neat, cleanly, full of pea-hens.

peucchoileach, pēc-chaluch, *n. m.* peacock.

peula, pelu, *n. m.* milk-pail. *W.* **paeol.**

peur, pēr, *n. f.* a pear.

peur, pēr, *n. f., pl.* **peuraisean**, buttock.

peurd, **peàrd**, piärd, *n. f.* first-card ; a roll of wool when giving the first carding ; carded wool.

peurdag, piartag, *n. f.* a partridge. *Also* **cearc-thomain.**

peurs, pērs, *v.* lente perdere.

peursair, *n. m.* a perchman, a shore herd.

pian, piun, *n. f.* infliction of pain by way of punishment ; torture, torment ; *v.* pain, torture ; **phian e mi**, he tortured me. *O.Ir.* **pian.** *Lat.* **poena.**

pianadair, piunuder, *n. m.* tormentor.

pianail, **piantach**, *adj.* excruciating. *Also* **piantachail.**

piantaiche, *n. m.* overwrought person, an ill-used or distressed person.

pibhinn, pee-vin, *n. m.* the lapwing. *Also* **sadharcan** ; better **adharcan**, the " horned one."

pic, *n. f.* a pike, pike-axe ; a pick, a pick-axe ; fr. the *Eng.*

pic, *n. f.* pitch, bitumen. *Ir.* **pic.** *W.* **pyg.** *Lat.* **pix.**

pic, peek, *n. f.* churlishness, niggardliness.

pìcear, peeker, *n. m.* a niggard, churl.

picil, *n. f.* pickle, brine. So *O'R.*

picil, *v.* pickle.

pige, pigu, **pigidh**, pigy, *n. m.* a jar, earthen jar ; fr. *Sc.* **pig.**

pigean, pigen, *n. m.* gorbelly, or a little gorbellied person. *Sc.* **piggin**, earthen jar.

pighe, peeyu, **pigheann**, peeyun, **pigheid**, pee'ej, *n. m.* magpie.

pigidh, pigy, *n. m.* robin-redbreast. *Also* **brù-dhearg.**

pighinn, piyin, *n. m.* pye.

pill, *n. f.* a sheet, cloth ; the sheet on which corn is winnowed ; **pill-chuir**, a sheet holding seed-corn when sowing ; a fold ; *v.* fold, put one in his winding-sheet. Cf. *Lat.* **pellis.**

pill, *v.* turn. *See* **till.** *O.Ir.* **fillim**, I turn.

pilleag, pilag, *n. f.* a small spread (for a bed). Cf. **filleadh**, a fold, a single blanket.

pilleagach, *a.* shaggy. Cf. **peallagach.**

pillean, pilen, *n. f.* saddle-cloth ; a pillion, a pack-saddle. *Ir.* **pillín**, **pilliún.** *W.* **pilyn.**

pinn, *n. pl.* pens ; *gen.* of **peann**, a pen.

pinne, *n. m.* a pin, a peg.

pinneadh, pinu, *m.* act of piercing.

pinnich, *v.* pin, peg, fasten, pierce.

pinnt, *n. f.* a pint, half a gallon ; fr. *Eng.*

pìob, peeb, *n. f.* pipe, bagpipe ; smoke ; **a bheil thu ris a' phìob ?** do you smoke ? Cf. *A.S.* **pîpe.** *O.N.* **pípa.** *O.H.G.* **pfîfa** ;

ult. fr. *M.Lat.* **pîpa** (allied to **pîpare**). *Kl.*

pìobadair, peebuder, *n. m.* pipe-maker.

pìobaire, peebiru, *n. m.* a piper ; **a' pìobaireachd**, playing on bagpipes.

pìoban, peeban, *n. m.* a small pipe or tube.

pìobanach, *a.* tubular.

pìobanta, *a.* given to piping, fond of playing the bagpipe.

pìobar, pibur, *n. m.* pepper. *Lat.* **piper.** *Gr.* πέπερι.

pìob-mhàla, peeb-vālu, *n. f.* a bagpipe.

pìobrachadh, pibruchu, *m.* act of inciting.

pìob-shionnaich, peeb-hiunich, *n. f.* **pìob-theannaich**, p.-hiänich, *n. f.* Irish pipes, or bellows pipe.

pìob-thaosgaidh, peeb-husgy, *n. f.* pump.

pìob-uisge, *n. f.* conduit pipe.

Pìobull, peebul, **bìobull**, *n. m.* the Bible.

pìoc, peek, *n. m.* a nip, a pick, nibble ; *v.* pick, nibble ; **a' pìocadh**, picking, nibbling, nipping ; fr. the *Eng.*

pìocach, piucach, *n. m.* coal-fish in its third and fourth year ; in its first year, **céiteanach.** *Also* **ucas.**

pìocaid, piucej, *n. f.* pick-axe. *L.Lat.* **pīca.**

pìocaire, piuciru, *n. m.* nibbler.

pìocas, pickus, *n. m.* the shingles.

pìoch, peech, *v.* wheeze.

pìochair, *v.* line, as cats ; **air phìochradh**, salacious as a cat.

pìochan, *n. m.* wheezing. *Also* **sìochadh.**

pìoghaid, pee-'ej, *n. f.* a magpie ; fr. *Sc.* pyat, pyet. *McB.*

pìol, piul, **spìol**, *v.* nibble, pick (a bone).

pìolaid, piulej, *n. f.* a pillory.

pìolaiste, *n. m.* trouble, vexation.

pìollach, piuluch, *a.* fretful, and curious-looking, contemptible.

pìollach, *a.* neat, trim. *See* **pìol.**

pìollach, piuluch, *a.* shaggy, hairy, ragged. *See* **peallach.**

pìoraid, piurej, *n. f.* hat, cap. *See* **biorraid.**

pìorr, *v.* scrape, dig.

pìorr, piur, *v.* stab, make a dash at one in order to probe or stab. *See* **purr.** *Sc.* pirr.

pìorrabhuig, pirwig, *n. f.* periwig, a peruke ; through *Eng.* ; fr. *F.* **perruque.** *O.It.* **perucca.** *L.Lat.* **piluco** ; ult. *Lat.* **pilus.**

pìorradh, *vbl. n. m.* act of dashing at, stabbing quickly.

pìorradh, *n. m.* a squall, a blast ; fr. *L.M.E.* pirry, a squall, a gale. *Sc.* pirr, gentle breeze. *O.N.* byrr. *McB.*

pìos, pees, *n. m.* a piece, patch ; *v.* cut into shreds, lacerate, tear ; fr. the *Eng.*

pìos, pees, *n. m.* a cup, silver vessel. *Lat.* **pyxis.**

pìosag, *n. f., dim.* of **pìos.**

pìosaga, piosagraich, *n. f.* witchcraft, dealing in spells in enchantment.

piosan, *n. m.*, *dim.* of pìos.
piostal, *n. m.* piostal. *Also* daga.
piseach, pishuch, *n. m.* increase, progeny, offspring; prosperity, success; piseach ort, success to you! le piseach a bhilean, by the increase of his lips.
piseachail, pishuchal, *adj.* successful.
piseag, pishag, *n. f.* a kitten.
pit, peet, *n. f.* vulva. *Ir.* pit, pis. *Din.*
pit-, *prefix* in place-names, farm, portion; corresp. to baile. *O.G.* pet, pett; a Pictish word allied to *W.* peth, part. *Gael.* cuid. *McB.*
pithean, pee-hen, *n. m.* magpie.
piùg, pioog, *n. m.* a plaintive note, a sound, chirp of a little bird.
piurna, *n. m.* the pirn, or reel (in a spinning-wheel), a spool (of thread). *Sc.* pirn.
piuthar, pioo-'ur, *n. f.* a sister; *gen.* peathar, *pl.* peathraichean. *O.Ir.* siur, *asp.* form = fiur. *W.* chwaer. *O.Celt.* svésôr. *Lat.* soror.
piuthrag, pioorag, *n. f.* female fellow gossip.
piuthragach, *a.* gossiping.
piuthar-athar, pioor-ahur, *n. f.* paternal aunt.
piuthar-chéile, pioor-chèlu, *n. f.* sister-in-law; piuthar-màthar, maternal aunt; piuthar-seanar, paternal grand-aunt; piuthar-seanmhar, maternal grand-aunt.
plab, *v.* make soft noise (a body falling in water); onomatopœic word.
plabartaich, *n. f.* rumbling noise in speech, whirr of birds' wings.
plabraich, plabrich, *n. f.* noise of fluttering.
placaid, placej, *n. f.* a wooden dish; fat, broad, good-natured female.
plaibean, *n. m.* a lump of raw flesh, a plump boy.
plaid, plaj, *v.* drill potatoes, lay out ground in plots, plant as greens or cole-wort.
plaide, *n. f.* a blanket. Cf. peallaid, a sheep-skin. *Lat.* pellis.
plaide, plaju, *n. f.* a plot of ground. Cf. *E.Ir.* plae, a level place (*Corm.*).
plaideag, plajag, *n. f.* a little blanket.
plaide-laighe, plaju-lyu, *n. f.* an ambush; fr. plaide. *Bible.*
plàigh, plāy, *n. f.* plague, pestilence. *E.Ir.* plág. *W.* pla. *Lat.* plaga, a stroke, a wound.
plàigheil, plā-yal, *a.* pestilential.
plais, plash, *v.* splash (water).
plam, *n. f.* fat blubber-cheek, anything clotted, curdled. *See* slaman.
plamach, *adj.* fat-cheeked, fair-haired, and pale-faced.
plamaic, *v.* fumble, mix, handle awkwardly.

plamraich, plamrich, *v.* curdle milk, make a soft noise.
plang, *n. m.* plack, a Scots coin; fr. *Sc.* plack, a copper coin = 4 pence Scots, or ¼ Eng. penny.
plangaid, plang'-ej, *n. f.* blanket; fr. *Eng.*
plannach, *a.* soft (of fish).
plannt, plaunt, *n. m.* a plant; fr. the *Eng.*
planntaich, *v.* plant. *Eng. W.* plannu.
planntar, *n. m.* choice corn for seed, choice quality of oats.
planntrach, *a.* choice, luxuriant.
plaoisg, plūshc, *v.* husk, peel.
plaosg, *n. m.* husk as of nuts, egg-shell. *O.Ir.* blaesc, a shell, a husk; blaesc uige, an egg-shell. *W.* plisgyn.
plaosg, *n. m.* husk as of nuts, egg-shell.
plaosgach, *a.* husky, shelly.
plaosgadh, *n. m.* act of opening, opening the eyes from sleep, peeling.
plaosgaid, plūsgej, *n. m.* soft, stupid woman.
plaosgaire, plusgiru, *n. m.* soft, stupid fellow.
plàsd, *n. m.* a plaster, cataplasm, poultice; *v.* plaster, daub, spread awkwardly.
plasg, pleasg, *n. m.* a string of beads.
plàt, *n. f.* straw-cloth. *Also* peallag.
plàt, *v.* thrust in, clap upon; phlàt e làmh air, he clapped his hand on it.
plath, plă, *v.* puff, blow upon.
plathadh, plă'-u, *n. m.* puff of wind; thàinig platha oirnn, a puff came on us; glimpse, moment; am platha, in a moment; fhuair sinn platha dheth, we got a glimpse of it.
pleadairt, pledart, *n. f.* an importunate petition, begging earnestly and humbly.
pleadhag, plu-ag, pleadhan, *n. f.* a paddle, dibble, a small leg. *Also* bleaghan, spleadhan.
pleadhanachd, plu'anuchc, *n. f.* paddling.
pleadhart, plu'art, *n. m.* a blow, a buffet.
pleasg, plesg, *n. f.* noise, crack. *M.Ir.* pleascán; guna pleascáin, pop-gun.
pleasg, *n. f.* a string of beads.
pleat, plètt, *v.* patch, mend.
pleat, *v.* plait, braid, fold; *n. f.* a plait, braid, tress, fold.
pleata, *n. m.* a patch, a piece.
pleath, plè, *v.* beg a thing to be paid for.
pleathainn, ple'-inn, *n. f.* the act of begging a thing you are to pay for; act of begging humbly a thing you must pay for, earnestly begging.
pléid, plej, *n. f.* spite, wrangle.
pléid, *n. f.* solicitation, imposing on good nature. *See* bleid.
pléideir, plējir, *v.* plead, or beg importunately, beg humbly and incessantly. Cf. *Fr.* plaider.

pleigh, pley, *n. f.* a quarrel, a fight.
pléisg, plêshc, *v.* revile or abuse with all one's might.
pléisgeadh, *vbl. n. m.* act of reviling ; a scold in a calm, sarcastic manner.
pleod, plod, *v.* make milk-warm, warm slightly, make lukewarm. *Also* flodach.
pleodag, *n. f.* soft, simple female.
pleòdar, *n. m.* pewter. *Also* flòdar.
pleòdhaisg, pleòisg, plïōshc, *n. m.* a booby, a simpleton. *Lat.* blæsus.
pleòiteachadh, *vbl. n. m.* act of exploiting ; fishing salmon with torch and spear.
pliad, *n. m.* plot of ground.
pliadh, plee-a, *n. f.* splay-foot, and bandy-leg ; *v.* swagger.
pliadhach, plee-a'-uch, *n. f.* splay-footed female ; *adj.* splay-footed and bandy-legged.
pliadhair, *n. m.* splay-footed, and bandy-legged man.
pliaram, *n. m.* a babbling. *See* **blialum.** *Sc.* blellum.
pliodair, pleeder, *v.* cajole, seduce by flattery, cradle into acquiescence.
pliodaire, *n. m.* cajoler, a fawner.
pliodairt, pleedart, *n. f.* cajoling, caressing ; act of cajoling, caressing a person, as if a child, in a soothing, fawning manner.
pliut, plioot, *n. f.* a clumsy foot or hand, a small hand ; *a.* **pliutach.**
pliutach, *n. m.* a seal ; fr. **pliut.**
pliutag, *n. f.* a little slap (of the hand).
pliutaire, plïootiru, *n. m.* half-splay-footed fellow.
ploc, *n. m.* any round mass ; chunk of a stick ; potato-masher, large clod, a very large head ; mumps ; *v. tr.* ram against, mash as potatoes, greens, etc. ; **a' plocadh a' bhuntàta,** mashing the potatoes ; **ploicneadh,** mauling.
plocach, *adj.* having a large head, or lumps ; **galar-plocach,** quinsy, the mumps.
plocach, *n. m.* boy.
plocag, *n. f.* a thick woman.
plocan, *n. m.* a little clod ; a masher.
plocanta, *adj.* stout, sturdy.
plod, *n. m.* a clod. *Sc.* plod, a green sod.
plod, *v. tr.* pelt with clods.
plod, *n. m.* a fleet of shipping ; **plod mór loingeas,** a large fleet of vessels. *N.* floti, a fleet.
plod, *n. m.* damage, carnage ; **is iad a rinn am plod,** what a carnage they made !
plod, *v.* float, cause to float ; **air phlod,** afloat ; **tha i air phlod,** she is afloat, launched. *O.N.* flota, to float, launch.
plod, *v.* half scald as a pig, in order to loosen the pile ; **a' plodadh na muice,** scalding the pig. *Sc.* plot, scald.
plod, *n. m.* pool of standing water.

plodach, *a.* lukewarm, or milk-warm. *Also* flodach.
plodach, *n. f., pl.* plodaichean, a lair for burial.
plodadh, *vbl. n. m.* act of parboiling.
plodaiche, *n. f.* lukewarmness.
plodachd, *n. f.* milk-warmness.
plodan, *n. m.* a small clod.
plodanach, *a.* full of small clods.
plodh, plo, *n. m.* anything put temporarily together ; a sick person that dies on getting the slightest cold or injury ; a man or anything hardly hanging together.
plodhaisg, plo'isc, **plodhaman,** plo'-a-man, *n. m.* bumpkin, a booby, a humdrum.
plodraich, *n. f.* carnage, havoc, state of lying here and there uncared for.
ploic, *n. f.* the mumps. *See* **pluic.**
plòiceag, *n. f.* plòicean, *n. m.* a big-cheeked woman ; big-cheeked man.
plòiceanach, *a.* plump-cheeked.
ploicneadh, *vbl. n. m.* mauling.
ploide, ploju, *n. f.* a tartan blanket.
plòideag, plój'-ag, *n. f.* a shawl ; good-natured female ; plump little girl.
plòitean, *n. m.* softish lump ; **plòitean mònach,** lump of half-dried peat.
plosg, *v.* palpitate, throb, pant, sob ; *n. m.* a throb, palpitation, pant ; **gun phlosg air déile,** without a throb on the board. *E.Ir.* blosc.
plosgail, *pt.* throbbing, palpitating.
plosgartaich, *n. f.* throbbing, palpitating, panting, gasping.
plub, ploob, *v.* plump, plunge, make noise as in water ; blubber, or speak indistinctly ; *n. m.* a clumsy lubberly person ; noise made by anything falling into water, plump, plunge, soft lump.
plubach, ploobuch, *adj.* soft and clumsy ; *n. f.* a soft lubberly female.
plubadaich, plumasdaireachd, *n. f.* plunging and splashing about in the water.
plubadh, *n. m.* a plunge.
plubaire, ploobiru, *n. m.* lubber, blubberer.
plubaireachd, *n. f.* speaking indistinctly, thick-tongued speech.
plubairt, *n. f.* plunging, plumping ; act of plunging, blubbering, plumping.
plubartaich, *n. f.* plunging always ; floundering, blubbering.
plubcheann, *n. m.* a lumpish head.
plubraich, ploobrich, *n. f.* gurgling, plunging, spluttering.
pluc, plook, *n. m.* lump, bump, jumble of a sea ; sheep rot ; *v.* lump, thump, jumble.
plucach, *adj.* lumpish, jumbling ; **caora phlucach,** sheep suffering from rot.

plùcadh, *vbl. n. m.* mauling, thumping, fisticuffs. *Also* plugadh.

plucair, *n. m.* a beater, thumper.

plucan, *n. m.* little jumble of a sea; plucanach, with a little jumbling of a sea. *Also* plugan, any small lump.

plucas, *n. m.* the flux.

plùch, plooch, *v.* squeeze slowly, compress slowly and gradually, but tightly.

plùchadh, *vbl. n. m.* squeezing slowly and tightly; *n. m.* a squeeze.

pluic, plooick, *n. f.* a blub-cheek, swollen cheek. So *Ir.*

pluiceach, plooickuch, *adj.* blub-cheeked; *n. f.* the toothache.

pluiceanach, *a.* bluff-cheeked person.

pluideach, ploojuch, *a.* club-footed. *See* pliut.

pluidse, ploojshu, *n. m.* big lumpish fellow or beast.

pluidseach, *n. f.* lumpish female. *Also* scluidseach.

plùirean, plooren, *n. m.* a flower.

plùm, ploom, *n. m.* dead-calm; humdrum; one who sits stock-still.

pluma, plumba, *n. m.* a plummet. *Lat.* plumbum, lead.

plumadh, *n. m.* a plunge.

plumaich, *v.* coagulate without yeast, as milk; stagnate.

plumaideach, ploomijuch, *a.* heavy, unshapely, lethargic.

plumanaich, *n. f.* noise of waves.

plumb, ploom, *n. f.* heavy shower, noise of a plunge.

plumbas, ploomus, plumbais, ploomish, *n. f.* a plum.

plundair, ploondir, *v.* plunder, pillage.

plundrainn, ploondrin, *n. f.* plunder, pillage, spoil; act of plundering, pillaging, spoiling, robbing, rough handling, mauling. *Also* plunndraig = *Eng.* plunder.

plùr, ploor, properly flùr, *n. m.* a flower, flour.

plutadh, plootu, *n. m.* heavy fall of rain.

pobull, *n. m.* people, congregation. *O.Ir.* popul; fr. *Lat.* populus.

pòca, *n. m.* pocket or pouch. *O.N.* poki.

poca, *n. m.* a short bag.

pòcaich, pōcich, *v.* pocket, poke.

pocaich, *v.* bag, put into a bag.

pocan, *n. m.* little bag; a little squat fellow.

pòg, *v.* kiss; *n. f.* a kiss; *pl.* pògan. *O.Ir.* póc, bóc, *osculum.* *E.W.* poc. *Br.* poq, smack, kiss. *Lat.* pâcem.

pògach, *adj.* fond of kisses; *n. f.* a blandishing female, offerer of kisses.

pògadh, *vbl. n. m.* act of kissing. *O.Ir.* poccad.

pògaire, pōgiru, *n. m.* a kisser.

poibleach, pobluch, *a gen. form of* pobull, people.

poibleachd, *n. f.* commonwealth.

poiblidh, *a.* public interest.

poicean, poyken, *n. m.* a short, squat fellow; *a.* poiceanach. Cf. *Swed.* pojke, "boy."

poinneach, ponuch, *n. m.* a lump, a brat (of a boy).

pòit, *n. m.* potations, tippling. *Lat.* potus (drunk).

poit, *n. f.* a pot; poit-ruadh-dhubh, a still; poit fheòla, flesh-pot; poit-mhùin, a jordan, a chamber-pot; fr. the *Eng.* Cf. *A.S.* pott. *O.N.* pottr.

poiteag, *n. f.* a small pot.

poitean, poyten, *n. m.* small truss of hay or straw. *See* boitean.

pòitear, pōter, *n. m.* a tippler, drinker; pòitearachd, habitual drinking, or potations.

poll, poul, *n. m., gen. s.* and *n. pl.* puill, a pit, a hole; a nostril; a pond; mud, mire; poll-iasgaich, fish-pond, fishing-station; poll-mòna, peat trench; poll buntàta, pit for potatoes; chan ann 's a' h-uile poll-mòna a gheibhear a leithid, it is not in every peat-bank the like of him is to be found. *E.Ir.* poll, a pit, a hole. *W.* pwll. *Br.* poull. *O.N.* pollr.

pollachas, *n. m.* lumpishness.

pollcheannach, *a.* lump-headed.

pollag, polag, *n. f.* a little pit, nostril; the fish pollock, lythe.

pollairean, *n. m.* the dunlin, *Polidna alpina,* "bird of the mud pits." *Mc.B.*

ponach, *n. m.* a lad, a boy. *See* poinneach.

pònaidh, pony, *n. m.* a docked horse, a pony; fr. the *Eng. Sc.* pownie.

pònar, *n. f.* bean, beans; *a.* pònarach. *M.Ir.* ponaire. *O.N.* baunir (*Marst.*).

pong, *n. f., gen.* puing, point; a quibble in law; tha e làn phongan, he is full of quirks or quibbles; air a' phuing sin, on that point.

pongaid, pong'-ej, *n. f.* a hellish quirk, quibble, or stratagem; làn de phongaidean, full of quibbles, or quirks, or stratagems.

pongaideach, *adj.* strategistical; full of quirks and quibbles, or tricks.

pongalachd, poongaluchc, *n. f.* pointedness, exactness, punctuality; great attention.

pongail, poongal, *adj.* pointed; particularly punctual; business-like in every thing.

pòr, *n. m.* seed of any sort; spore, grain; a clan, a progeny; droch phòr, bad seed; am pòr dubh, the black set; pòr Dhiarmaid, the race of Diarmid, *i.e.* the Campbells. *Gr.* σπόρος.

pòr, *n. m.* the *Eng.* pore. *Gr.* πόρος, a passage.

pòrach, *adj.* seminal.

pòrsan, porshan, *n. m.* a share, portion ; fr. the *Eng.*

port, porst, *n. m., gen. s.* and *n. pl.* puirt, a port, a haven, harbour ; ri port, ri beul puirt, awaiting a ferry, storm-stayed, windbound ; favourable opportunity ; gabh port air, watch your opportunity. *O.Ir.* port, a place, a haven. *W.* porth. *Lat.* portus.

port, *n. m.* dance music, a reel. *Lat.* porto (carry). *McB.*

portair, porster, *n. m.* a porter, a ferryman.

portaireachd, *n. f.* work of a porter, of a ferryman.

portan, *n. m.* a crab. So *Ir.*

portas, *n. m.* a breviary. *O.E.* portos. *O.Fr.* porte hors.

pòs, *v.* marry, wed, get married. *E.Ir.* pósaim. *Lat.* sponsus < spondeo.

pòsachail, *adj.* marriageable.

pòsadh, pōs'-u, *vbl. n. m.* marrying, wedding ; wedlock, matrimony ; bonds of wedlock.

pòsda, pústa, *vbl. a.* married, wedded.

pòsgheall, pos-yaul, *v.* betroth ; posghealladh, betrothment, promise of marriage; better phrase, gealladh pòsaidh.

post, *v.* tramp, as a woman does clothes in washing ; tread ; post an làthach, tread the clay. Cf. *W.* pystylad.

post, *n. m., gen. s.* and *n. pl.* puist, a post, beam, pillar. *Ir.* posda ; fr. the *Eng. Lat.* postis.

post, *n. m., gen. s.* posta, *n. pl.* postachan, letter-carrier, a postman ; fr. the *Eng.*

postachd, pŏst'-achc, *n. f.* letter-carrying.

postanach, *n. m.* thick-set child that just begins to walk.

prab, *n. f.* rheum on the eye ; *v.* unfit, discompose, ravel.

prabach, prăb'-uch, *adj.* rheum-eyed, contemptible, ragged, dishevelled; *n.f.* contemptible female.

prabadh, *n. m.* botching, bungling, spoiling.

prabaire, prabiru, *n.m.* contemptible man.

pràban, *n. m.* a shebeen.

pràbar, prăb'-ur, *n. m.* rabble ; little people ; refuse of grain.

prabardaich, prăb'-ard-ich, prabarsaich, prăb'-ars-ich, *n. f.* a smattering ; slight knowledge ; prabarsaich leughaidh, smattering of reading.

prabshuil, prab-hool, *n. f.* blear-eye.

prabshuileach, prab'-hool-ach, *a.* blear-eyed.

prac, *n. m.* tithes, vicarage dues ; small tithes paid in kind.

pracas, *n. m.* dispute not easily settled ; nonsensical difference ; idle talk ; hotch-potch. *Also* fracas, scattered fragments. Cf. *Lat.* frango.

pradhainn, pră'-inn, *n. f.* press of business, throng, throngness ; flurry. *Isl.*

pradhainneach, *adj.* hurried, pressed for time, throng, flurried.

pradhaisg, pra'isc, *coll. n.* rabble.

pràib, pryb, *n. m.* rabble, filth, mire.

praidseach, prajshuch, proidseach, *n. m.* a boy.

praingealais, prēng'-ul-ish, *n. f.* gibberish.

pràinn, pràinneach, prynuch, *a.* out of sorts, restless.

prainnseag, pryn'-shag, *n. f.* mince collops, haggis.

prais, prash, *n. f.* brass, pot-metal; a still.

prais, prash or presh, *n. f.* a pot ; cas na praise tighinn an uachdar, the stump or foot of the pot coming on the surface (said Donald, seeing the porpoise tumbling).

praiseach, *n. f.* a stall, a manger. *See* prasach.

praiseach, *n. f.* a whore, or concubine ; meretrix ; athphraiseach, a harridan.

praiseach, prashuch, *n. f.* broth, pottage. *M.Ir.* braissech. *W.* bresych, cabbages. *Lat.* brassica.

pràiseach, *a.* and *n.* brazen, pot-metal.

pràisiche, prāshichu, *n. m.* a brazier.

pràmh, prāv, *n. f.* melancholic dulness ; dosing, slumbering, half-sleeping.

pràmhachd, prāvachc, *n. f.* somnolency, grief.

pràmhail, pràv'-al, *adj.* sad, sleepy.

prann, prawn, pronn, *v.* pound, mash, bray, bruise ; mutter ; ciod e am prannadh a th'ort, what are you muttering about ? hence, praingealais and prainnseag, *q.v.*

pranntair, prauntir, *v.* scribble, mutter.

praonan, prūnan, *n. m.* an earth-nut. *See* braonan.

prap, *a.* clever, quick. *Ir.* prab.

prasach, *n. f.* a stall, a manger.

prasgan, brasgan, *coll. n. m.* a little bunch or group, a flock ; frequently used in contempt. Cf. *Ir.* prosnán.

prat, *n. m.* 1. trick, prank. 2. tantrum.

pratach, *a.* pranky, mischievous.

prèach, prèch, *n. f.* a bog, a marsh, a morass ; chaidh a' bhò phrèach, the cow stuck in the marsh.

preach, *v. tr.* croak ; speak, like a bittern.

preachaire, prèch'-ur-u, *n. m.* a croaking speaker, a miserable orator ; am preachaire granna, the ugly, croaking orator.

preachan, prech'-an, *n. m.* the moss-bittern ; a little peat-pit ; a little fen ; mean orator ; preachan ingneach, a vulture ; preachan gearr, a buzzard ; preachan ceannann, an osprey. *M.Ir.* prechan, a crow.

preachanach, *adj.* querulous croaking ; (of a place) full of little pits.

preas, pres, *n. m., gen.* pris, a press, a cupboard ; fr. the *Eng.*

preas, *n. m.* a wrinkle, a fold ; fr. the *Eng.*

preas, pres, *n. m., gen. s.* and *n. pl.* pris, a bush, shrub, thicket. *M.W.* prys, brushwood ; *McB.* says of Pictish origin.

preas, *v.* wrinkle, corrugate ; air preasadh, corrugated ; gun phreas gun smal, without wrinkles or spot ; fr. the *Eng.*

preasach, *a.* wrinkled, corrugated.

preasach, *a.* abounding in shrubs.

preasadh, *vbl. n. m.* act of wrinkling, corrugating.

preasarnach, presarnuch, *n. f.* a shrubbery, brushwood, thicket.

preathal, pre-hal, *n. m.* a fit, a swoon, dizziness. *Also* breitheal.

preig, *n. f.* the mouth, a mouth that has too much to say=the speaking "organ."

preigeadair, *n. m.* a gabby person, a gossip, tale-bearer. *W.* pregethwr (pregeth + gŵr), preacher. *Lat.* praeceptor.

prìne, preenu, *n. m., pl.* prìneachan, a pin for clothes. *Sc.* prein, prene, prine. Mistakenly equated with *O.N.* prjónn. *Marstr.*

prìnich, *v.* pin, tuck.

priob, prib, *v.* wink ; twinkle as the eye.

priobadh, pribu, *vbl. n. m.* act of winking, twinkling ; a wink, a twinkling, glimpse, moment ; bi an so am priobadh, be here in a twinkling, in a jiffy ; cha do phriob mo shùil, I did not sleep a wink. Cf. *M.Ir.* prapud, a brief space (= a twinkling). *O.Ir.* brothad, moment.

priobaid, pribij, *n. m.* a trifle ; fr. an early form of bribe.

priobair, pribir, *n. m.* a worthless fellow. *M.E.* bribour, rascal, thief. Cf. *O.Fr.* bribeur, beggar.

prìobairteach, *n. f.* meanness, avarice, parsimony, shabbiness.

priobairneach, priburnuch, *n. f.* a rousing.

prioblosgadh, *n. m.* sudden burning.

priobshuil, prib-hool, *n. f.* twinkling eye.

priogadh, pricu, *n.m.* Dutch-hoeing, second round of cultivating growing potatoes.

prioghainn, pree-in, *n. f.* sauce or seasoning in viands ; choice food.

prioghainnich, *v.* season, as viands ; feed with choice food.

prìomh, preev, *a.* first, main, chief, principal. *Cpds.* : prìomhbhaile, capital, metropolis ; prìomhsheòl, mainsail ; prìomhathair, patriarch, progenitor ; prìomhchlèireach, notary, secretary ; prìomhchrann, mainmast ; prìomh easbuig, archbishop ; prìomhlong, first-rate ship, etc. ; thog iad am

prìomhsheòl, they raised the mainsail. *O.Ir.* prim. *W.* prif. *Lat.* primus.

prìomhlaid, preev-lej, *n. m.* a prelate.

prionnsa, prioonsu, *n. m.* a prince. *M.Ir.* prindsa.

prionnsail, *a.* princely.

prìosan, preeson, *n. m.* prison. *M.Ir.* prísún.

prìosanach, *adj.* very confined, within narrow bounds ; *n. m., gen. s.* and *n. pl.* prìosonaich, a prisoner.

prìosanaich, *v.* imprison, incarcerate ; a' prìosanachadh, narrowing, keeping confined, or in bondage.

pris, preesh, *n. f.* price, value, esteem, great demand, estimation ; 'ga chur am pris, raising it in estimation ; tha e am pris, it is in high estimation ; ciod e a' phris a tha e ? what is the price of it ? *Lat.* pretium.

prìsealachd, preeshaluchc, *n. f.* preciousness.

prìseil, *adj.* valuable, precious.

prìsich, preeshich, *v.* price, value.

probhaid, *n. f.* profit ; fr. the *Eng.*

procach, *n. m.* a yearling stag.

procadair, prokuder, *n. m.* law-agent. *Ir.* procadoir, *Lh.* *Sc.* procutor. *Lat.* procurator, man of business.

proghan, *n. m.* dregs, lees.

proinn, pryn, *n. m.* dinner. So *B. of D.* *O.Ir.* proind. *W.* prain. *Lat.* prandium.

pròis, pròsh, *n. f.* pride ; haughtiness ; a neat, punctilious little female; a prude.

pròiseag, *n. f.* a prude.

pròisealachd, proshaluchc, *n. f.* pridefulness, punctilious prudery, neatness.

pròiseil, prōshal, *adj.* proud ; neat, little, and punctilious ; uppish, like a prude.

proitseach, projshuch, *n. m.* a good lump of a fellow, a boy ; stripling. Cf. *Fr.* protégé.

pronn, proun, *n. m.* food. *See* proinn.

pronn, *n. m.* bran, corn ; rough ground.

pronn, proun, *v.* pound, bray mash ; *a.* brocken, pounded ; buntàta pronn, mashed potatoes.

pronnadair, pronuder, *n. m.* masher, a mortar.

pronnadh, *n. m.* pounding ; "fingering" a chanter ; playing the pipe.

pronnag, *n. f.* a crumb.

pronnasg, *n. m.* brimstone. *Also* pronnastan and pronnastail. *Ir.* pronnusc. *Sc.* brunstane. *M.W.* brwnstan. *O.N.* brennisteinn.

pronndal, *n. m.* murmuring, muttering ; *a.* pronndalach.

pronnta, *a.* mashed.

prop, *n. m.* a support, prop ; *v.* support, prop. *Eng.*

propanach, *n. m.* a boy well built, beginning to run about.

prosbaig, *n. m.* spy-glass, telescope.
prosmunn, *n. m.* incitement ; by-form of brosdadh.
prosnaich, brosnaich, *v.* incite.
prosnan, *coll. n.* a company, band. So in *Ir.*
prostan, *coll. n. m.* a band.
protaig, *n. f.* a trick. *Sc.* prattik, a prank. Cf. *Fr.* pratique.
prothaist, pro-hesht, *n. m.* provost.
puball, poob'-ùl, *n. m.* a tent. *O.Ir.* pupall. *W.* pebyll. *Lat.* papilio, butterfly, tent. *See* pàilliun.
pùc, pook, *v.* fumble, ram, cram, push. *Sc.* powk. *M.L.G.* boken. *Ger.* pochen, knock.
pucaid, pookej, *n. f.* a pimple, a boil.
pudhar, poo'ar, *n. m.* harm, injury ; loss, mishap ; a sore, ulcer, septic sore. *E.Ir.* putar. *Lat.* putor, bad smell.
pùic, poo-ic, *n. f.* a bribe ; *v.* bribe, ram secretly ; fhuair e pùic, he has been bribed ; cha d'thug e pùic dheth, he made nothing of him. So *Ir.*
pùiceach, *adj.* giving bribes, bribing ; *n. f.* a female that bribes.
puicean, *n. m.* a veil, covering. *Ir.* púicín. *O'R.*
pùicear, poo-cer, *n. m.* a briber.
puidse, poojshu, *n.m.* a pouch; fr. the *Eng.*
puing. *See* pong.
puinne, *n. f.* for buinne, stream, cataract, tide ; *adj.* puinneach. *R.D.*
puinneach, *n. m.* thumping.
puinneag, *n. f.* sorrel, soft vegetable stem.
puinneanaich, *v.* beat, thump.
puinnse, *n. m.* punch, toddy. *Eng.*
puinsean, poo-ishun, *n. m.* poison, virus ; fr. the *Eng.*
puinseanach, *adj.* poisonous, venomous, vindictive ; revengeful.
puinseanaich, *v.* poison.
puinseantas, poo-ish-antus, *n. m.* poison-ousness, venomousness, vindictive-ness ; resentment.
pùirleag, poorlug, *n. f.* a crest, a tuft. *Ir.* puirleog. *O'R.*
pulag, poolag, *n. f.* large round stone, a ball, a pedestal. Cf. *Fr.* boule.
pulaidh, pooly, *n. m.* a turkey-cock, a bully. *Fr.* poulet. *Lat.* pullus, a young cock.
pùlas, *n. m.* a pot-hook. *See* bùlais.
punc, poonc, *n. f.* a point, a quirk. *O.Ir.* ponc. *W.* pwnc. *Lat.* punctum.
punnan, poonan, *n. m.* a sheaf. *O.N.* bundin, a sheaf ; fr. binda, to bind. *O.H.G.* bintan. *Goth.*, *A.S.* bindan.
punnd, poond, *n.m.* a pound (weight) ; a pound (money).
punnd, *n. m.* a pound, a place for securing stray cattle, or cattle trespassing ; poind-ing ; *v.* secure cattle ; fr. the *Eng.*

punndainn, poondin, *n. f.* bad usage in being confined in a damp place ; starvation, benumbing ; the state of being confined to a cold place. *Ir.* puntuin, benumbing.
purgadair, poorguder, *n. m.* purgatory. *Lat.* purgatorium.
purgaid, poorgej, *n. f.* a purge, a purga-tive ; aperient medicine ; purgaideach, aperient, laxative, purging. *Lat.* purgatio.
pùrlag, poorlag, *n. f.* a rag, a tatter, fragment.
purp, poorp, *n. m.* sense, the faculties of the mind ; full possession of mental powers ; purpose ; chaill e phurp, he lost his faculties, he is under mental aberration ; gun phurp, uncollected. *Also* purpais.
purpaidh. *See* purpur.
purpail, *adj.* collected ; in one's senses ; punctual, pointed, sound in mind.
purpalachd, poorpaluchc, *n. f.* collective-ness ; full possession of faculties ; punctuality.
purpur, poorpur, *n. m.* purple colour. *W.* porffor. *O.F.* porpre. *Lat.* purpura. *Gr.* πορφύρα.
purr, poorr, *v.* stab, thrust, push, jostle ; fr. *Sc.* porr.
purradh, *n. m.* a shove, jostle, dash at, as a bull ; act of pushing, jostling, shoving ; a' purradh le adharcaibh, butting with his horns. So *Ir.*
puis, pish, *n.f.* a cat, "puss." *Also* piseag.
put, *n. m.* the cheek.
put, *n. m.* bruised swelling as from a blow. *See* pat.
put, poot, *v.* push, shove, jostle.
pùt, *n. m.* young moor-fowl.
puta, *n. m.* a trout.
puta, *n. m.* a float made of skin for nets and fishing lines, a buoy. *Cpds.* : put-meadhoin, middle buoy ; put-sàis, buoy placed barely below the surface ; put-suab, the buoy which is on the end of the cable.
putadh, poot'-u, *vbl. n. m.* act of pushing, shoving, jostling, butting ; a push, a shove, a jostle ; check.
puta-fuaraidh, *n.m.* first spadeful in delv-ing.
putag, *n. f.* a hold-pin of an oar ; a row-lock. *Ir.* putóg, *n. f.* a thowl. *O'R.*
putag, *n. f.* a pudding. *I.Lom.*
putag, *n. f.* a ring of land.
putag, *n. f.* handle of a scythe.
putan, pootan, *n. m.* a button.
puth, poo, *n.f.* a puff ; *v.* puff ; chuir e puth as a shròin, he puffed through his nose.
puthar, poo'-ar, *n. m.* power, authority ; fr. *Eng.*
pùthar, *n. m.* a hurt, wound, scar.

R

r, the fourteenth letter of the Gaelic alphabet, named ruis, the alder tree.

'r, 1. for ar (*pron.*) le 'r cinn, with our heads. 2. for bhur, your ; le 'r cead, with your permission.

r', for ri, *prep.* ; r'a taobh, at her side ; r'a cois, at her foot ; r'a chois, at his foot.

ra-, *pref.* too, too much, very, exceeding, quite ; ra-mhór, too large, very great.

ràbach, rāb'-uch, *a.* litigious, bullying. *Ir.* rábach, litigious.

ràbachas, rābuchus, *n. m.* litigiousness.

ràbaire, rāb'-ir-u, *n. m.* quarrelsome fellow.

rabh, rav, *v.* warn, guard.

rabhacaire, ravaciru, *n. m.* a nonsensical rhapsodist, haranguer, or proser.

rabhacaireachd, *n. f.* rhapsody, prosing, haranguing, talking nonsense.

rabhachail, răv'-uch-al, *a.* admonitory.

rabhadair, ravuder, *n. m.* a beacon, a warner, a spy, a scout.

rabhadh, răv'-u, *vbl. n. m.* act of warning ; a friendly hint or information, caution ; thoir rabhadh dha, inform, tell, put him on the alert. *E.Ir.* robuth.

rabhagach, rafaguch, *coll. n. f.* weeds at the bottom of water.

rabhail, rav'-ul, *n. m., n. f.* rhapsody delivered in a drawling manner, mad saying ; drawling in manner or gait.

rabhairt, ro'urt, *n. f.* spring-tide, a person that goes furiously to work. *O.Ir.* robarte, *pl.* robarti, flood tide. *W.* rhyferthi, tempest.

rabhan, *n. m.* rhapsody, repetition.

rabhanaich, rafanich, *n. f.* long stalks of grass growing in water ; long limp sea-weed near the shore.

ràbhart, *n. f.* havering. ra + abart.

rabhd, raüd, *n. f.* nonsensical or idle talk ; unordered, baseless fiction.

rabhdail, raüdul, *n. f.* prosing, coarseness.

rabhdaire, *n. m.* rhapsodist ; a clown.

rabhdaireachd, *n. f.* rhapsody, prosing, verbiage, haranguing ; false report.

ràbul, *n. m.* ; for *Eng.* rabble.

ràc, *n. m.* a drake. *Also* ràcaire, rāciru.

ràc, racan, *n. m.* a rake ; *v. t.* rake. *Ir.* rácadh. *W.* rhac.

rac, *n. m.* a ring which runs freely on a mast to which the yard is attached ; the traveller. *O.N.* rakki.

ràcadal, *n. m.* horse-radish. So *Ir.* racadh. *See* sracadh, tearing.

ràcadh, *vbl. n. m.* raking.

racaid, racej, *n. f.* bustle, noise ; a drawling female.

ràcail, rācul, *n. f.* clamorous noise of ducks.

ràcain, rācen, *n. m.* noise, riot, mischief.

ràcaire, rāciru, *n. m.* "croaker" ; a drake; a drawling, croaking orator or piper.

ràcaireachd, *n. f.* croaking, discordant oratory or music ; loud, lying talk.

ràcan, *n. m.* a bandy or crooked stick, a rake.

racas, *n. m.* sail hoop. *See* rac.

rach, *v. irreg.* go, proceed ; rachaibh dhachaidh, go ye home.

rachd, *n. f.* heavy moan, sob, short spasm after long crying ; vexation, groan.

rachdan, *n. m.* a tartan plaid worn mantle-wise.

racuis, *n. f.* a rack, toasting apparatus ; fr. the *Eng.*

radan, rodan, *n. m.* a rat, cunning person.

radh, râ, *n. m.* saying, assertion, word ; tha 'n ràdh ud fior, that assertion or saying is true ; *vbl. n.* act of saying, asserting, affirming, expressing ; tha mi ag radh, I say, I assert, etc. *O.Ir.* rad. *O.Celt.* râdiô.

radharc, ru'-urk, for fradharc, eyesight. *E.Ir.* radarc = ro + dearc, see.

rag, *n. m.* a wrinkle. *Ir.* rag. *See* roc.

rag, *n. f.* a rag ; fr. the *Eng.*

rag-, used as *intens, adj.* rag-mhéirleach, an arrant thief ; "rag-mhéirleach nan cearc," the sly thief of the hens. Cf. *O.N.* hrak-, used in *cpds.*, hrak-menni, a wretched man, a wretch.

rag, *a.* stiff, benumbed, unwilling. Cf. *Lat.* rigeo.

ragadh, *vbl. n. m.* act of stiffening, being benumbed ; tha mi air mo ragadh, I am stiff with cold.

ragaich, *v.* stiffen, benumb.

ragaichte, *vbl. a.* stark stiff (as if frozen) ; perfectly still.

ragaire, *n. m.* extortioner, a rogue.

ragaireachd, ragiruchc, *n. f.* oppression ; stubbornness, stiff-neckedness.

ragbheartachd, *n. f.* force, violence.

ràgh, *n. m.* a row, a rank ; ràgh shaigh-dearan, rank of soldiers ; a raft of wood.

ragha, ru'u, raghadh, ru'ugh, *n. f.* choice. *See* roghainn.

ràghan, rā'an, *n. m.* churchyard. Cf. rath ; rath-thiodhlaic, a lair. *Also* bàghan.

raghar, radhar, *n. m.* arable but untilled land.

rag-mhuinealach, *adj.* stiff-necked, stubborn ; **rag-mhuinealachd**, contumacy, stubbornness.

raibheic, ryveck, *n. f.* a roar ; the roar that a cow gives when gored by another. *Also* **rèic**.

ràic, *n. f.* loud, idle prattling ; *a.* **ràiceil**.

ràicealachd, răcialuchc, *n. f.* loud prattling.

ràideil, rājil, *a.* inventive, sly.

ràidh, rāy, *n. f.* arbitration, decision, appeal ; good-will ; **leig gu ràidh nan daoine so e**, submit it to the arbitration of these gentlemen ; **fear-ràidh**, an arbiter, arbitrator ; competition ; **a ràidh air a chéile**, competing with each other, trying each other's metal.

ràidhe, rāyu, *n. f.* quarter of the year ; **an raidhe samhraidh**, the summer quarter. *See* **ràith**, which is better form.

ràidhe, *n. f.* advice, entreaty, order ; fr. **ràdh** ; " cha teid e ann air mo ràidhe," he will not go, no matter what I say. *Cf. O.N.* ráð. *Ger.* rath, counsel, advice.

ràidheil, rā-yal, *adj.* challenging, fond of challenging, boasting.

ràidheil, rāyal. *See* **ràitheil**.

ràidhle, *n. f.* a weaver's bobbin-wheel, a reel. *R.D.*

raidhlich, rylich, *n. f.* a rag, cast-off clothes.

ràidse, rājshu, *n. m.* a prating fellow. Cf. **ràdh**.

ràidseach, rājshuch, *n. f.* a chief witch.

ràidseachas, *n. m.* witchery ; enchantment ; prating.

raige, **raigead**, rygu, *n. f.* stiffness, obstinacy.

raignich, ragnich, *v.* stiffen, benumb.

raimhe, **raimhead**, revu, *n. f.* fat, suet, fatness; **raimhe a' bheothaich**, the fatness of the beast ; **raimhe 'sa' phoite**, the suet in the pot ; high-water, or full spring tide ; fr. **reamhar**, fat, thick, corpulent.

raimisg, ramishc, *n. f.* coarse, vulgar person.

raineach, ren'-uch, *n. f.* fern. *Also* **froinneach**. *W.* rheden.

raing ; for *Eng.* rank (of soldiers).

ràinig, rānig, *pret. v.* ruig, reach ; **ràinig sinn**, we reached, we arrived. *O.Ir.* **ránic**, *pret.* of **riccim**, reach = **ro** + **iccim**.

raip, rep, *n. f.* filth ; untidy eating ; food over the lips and chin ; debauchery.

raipeas, *n. m.* foul mouth.

raipleach, *n. f.* a filthy or slovenly woman.

raipleachag, *n. f.* a squalid little woman.

ràisean, rāsh'-in, *n. f.* goat's tail.

ràite, rātiu, *n. f.* saying ; for **ràdhte**.

ràiteach, *v.* verbose ; **mór-ràiteach**, babbling ; **beag-ràiteach**, taciturn, quiet.

ràiteachail, rātiuchal, *adj.* challenging, boasting of feats, or bravery.

ràiteachas, rātiuchus, *n. f.* pride, boasting, arrogance ; competition, emulation, trial of strength ; **a ràiteachas air a chéile**, competing, emulating each other from ostentatious motives.

ràith, *n. f.* quarter of a year. Pagan Irish divided the year into four parts, **samh-ratha**, **foghmhar-ratha**, **geimh-ratha**, and **iar-ratha**, each beginning with a religious festival (*L. na gC.*). *M.Ir.* **ráithe**.

ràith, *n. f.* a threatening.

raith, *n. f.* prating largely.

ràitheil, *a.* quarterly.

raithneach, **raineach**, *n. m.* fern. *O.Ir.* **raith**, **raithnech**. *O.Celt.* (p)rati-s.

ràitinn, rātin, *n. f.* saying.

ralls, *v.* rake, as grass.

rallsa, *n. m.* a rake.

rallsadh, ralls'-u, *vbl. n. m.* act of raking ; rough handling ; the act of raking.

ramachdair, *n. m.* a vulgar fellow.

ramair, ramer, *n. m.* a romp, a vulgar, coarse fellow ; **ramaireachd**, romping.

ramalair, ramuler, *n. m.* a coarse, vulgar humorist, a humorous fellow.

ramalaireachd, *n. f.* clambering, noisy play, climbing and chasing through the house.

ramallag, ramulag, *n. f.* a puddle.

ramasg, *n. m.* sea tangle.

ràmh, rāv, *n. m.* an oar ; *pl.* raimh, oars. *O.Ir.* ráme. *W.* rhwyf. *Lat.* rêmus.

ràmhach, rāv'-uch, *a.* oared ; *n. f.* a galley.

ràmhachd, *n. f.* rowing, pulling.

ràmhaiche, rāvichu, *n. m.* a rower.

ràmhadair, rāvuder, *n. m.* a rower.

ramhar, rav'-ur, *a.* fat, thick, corpulent. *See* **reamhar**.

ramhlair. *See* **ramalair**.

ràmhlong, rāv'-loong, *n. f.* a galley.

ramhraich, rav'-rich, *v.* fatten, come to high water, as spring tide ; beat till one's body swells.

ràn, *n. f.* a drawling, dissonant roar or cry ; melancholy cry ; *v.* roar.

rànach, *n. f.* a cave that gives an echo ; a large, ill-furnished house.

rànaich, rānich, *n.f.* drawling crying.

rànail, rān'-ul, *n. f.* same as above.

rangair, *n. m.* a wrangler.

rann, *n. m.* a part, a division ; a genealogy, pedigree, relationship. *O.Ir.* **rann, rand** (*f.*), *pars. W.* rhann, share. *O.Celt.* (p)rannâ.

rann, *n. m.* a verse, a quatrain, a stanza, a poem. *E.Ir.* **rann**, *m.* a stanza, a strophe, a quatrain ; the first two lines,

and the second two of a quatrain, each
made a **lethrann**, a couplet.
rannach, *a.* belonging to a peninsula.
rannadhail, rann'-a-ghil, *n. f.* rhapsody,
rant, ranting, doggerel.
rannadhaileach, *adj.* rhapsodical ; nonsensical in rhyming.
rannaire, *n. m.* a poet, a maker of verse ;
an orator.
rannaire, raniru, *n. m.* a divider, divisor ;
distributor. *O.Ir.* rannaire, one who
divides, a butler.
rannan, *n. m.* slime as of fish, of serpent.
ranndair, *n.f.* a murmuring, complaining.
rannsachadh, raunsuchu, *vbl. n. m.* act
of searching minutely, inquiring into ;
search, scrutiny.
rannsachair, raunsucher, *n. m.* searcher.
rannsaich, raunsich, *v.* search, scrutinise,
examine minutely, explore. *O.N.* rann-
saka, search a house, ransack.
rannsaiche, raunsichu, *n. m.* searcher.
rannt, raunt, *n. m., pl.* **ranntaidh** and
ranntain. 1. connections, allies ; air
do **ranntainibh farsuing**, on your extensive estates ; fr. **rann.**
rannt, *n. m., pl.* **ranntannan**, a title-deed ;
in *pl.* deeds, chattels. *S.O.*
ranntach, *n. m.* songster.
ranntachd, *n. f.* versification, poetry.
ranntachd, *n. f.* 1. a portion of land,
extent of territory. 2. one's connections, supporters. *Ir.* ranntachd, jurisdiction. *O'R.*
ranntair, raunter, *n. f.* a range, a sphere
or extent of territory ; **a' tighinn a
steach air an ranntair againne**, en-
croaching on our territory ; fr. **rann.**
ranntair, raunter, *n. m.* 1. a poet,
songster. 2. murmuring, complaining.
ranntar-bùth, *n.m.* a confused dance. *S.O.*
ranntrach, rauntruch, *adj.* extensive.
raod, rūd, *n. m.* a diminutive creature,
a weakling ; an emaciated person.
raog, rūg, *n. m.* a rushing. Cf. **ruaig.**
raoic, ryck, *n. f.* a hoarse sound or cry,
a wild roar. *Ir.* raoichd, a shout, a
roar. Cf. **ròc.**
raoid, rūj, *n. f.* a sheaf (of corn).
raoine, *n. f.* a young barren cow that
had calf. *See* **réidhne.** Cf. *Ger.* rind.
O.H.G. hrind, rind, horned cattle.
Sc. rhind, rhind mart, a carcase from
the herd.
raoir, ryr, *n. f.* last night. *O.Ir.* a réir.
raoit, ryt, *n.f.* a rakish female ; drunkenness, indecent mirth. Cf. *Sc.* riot,
indecent mirth.
raoitear, ruiter, *n. m.* drunkard.   Cf.
ruitear.
raon, rūn, *n. m.* plain ; mossy plain ;
cùl-raonaidh, a goalkeeper. *O.Ir.* roe,
rói, a plain.

raonach, *n. f.* plain country.
rap, *n. m.* a bad coin ; fr. *Sc.* rap.
rapach, *a.* dirty-mouthed ; slovenly.
ràpach, ràpal, *a.* noisy ; *rel.* to rabble.
rapaire, rapire, *n. m.* a worthless fellow,
a rhapsodist.
rapaire, *n. m.* a drawling fellow.
ràpaireachd, rāpiruchc, ròpaireachd, *n. f.*
foolish or idle talk, silly yarning.
rapais, rap'-esh, *n. f.* filth, noise, nastiness.
ràpal, *n. f.* nonsensical talk.
rapas, *n. m.* filth, slime ; " rapas na
seilcheig," the slime of the snail.
ras, *n. f.* a shrub. So *Ir.*
ràs, *n. f.* fury, rage.
rasaiche, rasiche, *n. f.* a gipsy, hussy ;
a lewd woman.
ràsan, *n. m.* bickering, or grating noise,
or smell ; war of words. *Ir.* rásan,
harsh, grating sound.
ràsan, *n. m.* a tedious highway.
rasan, *n.m.* underwood, brushwood. So *Ir.*
ràsanach, *a.* 1. tedious, drawling. 2. full
of brushwood.
raschrannach, *a.* abounding in shrubs.
ràsdal, *n. m.* rake. *Also* **rallsa.** *E.Ir.*
rastal. *Lat.* rastellus, rake.
ràsdalach, rāsdaluch, *a.* harrowing.
rasgaich, rasgich, *n. f.* perverse, restive.
See **reasgach.** Cf. *Ir.* rascach, clamorous.
ràsgeul, rā-sgel, *n. m.* exaggeration ;
fr. **ra-** for **ro-,** an old *intens. pref.* and
sgeul. Cf. **ràbhart** (ro + abairt) ; " cha
ràsgeul brèig e," 'tis not a lying over-
statement.
ra-sholuis, for **rath-soluis**, ra-holus, *n. m.*
moonlight, waxing moon ; **rath** (a
period of time) and **solus.**
ra-spars, *n. f.* swagger, showing off.
rath, rā, *n. m.* grace, good fortune ;
prosperity, increase, use, profit, advantage ; **chaidh e bho rath**, he is gone
to pigs and whistles ; **mac ratha**, a
lucky man, a man of grace (spir.
sense). *O.Ir.* rath, *gratia.* *E.W.* rat
(rhad). *O.Celt.* rato-n.
ràth, rā, *n. m.* a raft. *Lat.* ratis.
ràth, rā, *n. m.* and *f.* a fortress, residence.
So *E.Ir.* a residence surrounded by
earthen rampart. *O.Celt.* râtî-s, râto-n.
rathachas, ra-huchus, *n. m.* fortune,
success.
rathad, ra'-ud, *n. m.* a road, method,
highway. *E.Ir.* ramut.
rathaich, ra-hich, *v.* bless, prosper. So
O.Ir.
rathail, ra-hal, *a.* fortunate.
ràthan, rāhan, *n. m.* surety, security ;
théid mise an rathan ort, I'll go
security for you. *O.Ir.* ráth, security
=urra ; *ult.* fr. **ràdh**, word.

ràthan, *n. m.* a small fort ; poet. for a row of teeth.

ràthas, ra-hus, *n. m.* a trail, a track.

rath-dorcha, ră-dŏrch′-à, *n. m.* the dark period, the waning moon.

rath-thìodhlaic, *n. m.* burying-plot, lair.

rati, a by-word for whisky.

ré, *n. f.* time, space ; ré an latha, during the day. So *O.Ir.*

ré, *n. f.* moon ; ré nuadh, the new moon ; fad mo ré is mo là, during my time and day. So *O.Ir.*

reabh, rev, *n. m.* wile, trick.

reabhach, *n. m.* 1. a trickster, a wicked fellow. 2. the devil.

reabhag, *n. f.* linnet, titling.

rèabhair, rēver, *n. m.* a crafty, subtle fellow ; a rover. *Sc.* reaver. *Eng.* reave, rob. < *A.S.* rēaf, to break.

reabhradh, revru, *m.* disporting (as boys). So *Ir.* *E.Ir.* rebrad, sportiveness.

reachd, rechc, *n. m.* law, statute, ordinance ; reachd ùr, a new statute or ordinance. *O.Ir.* recht. *Lat.* rectum. *O.Celt.* rektu-, root reg.

reachd, rechc, *n. m.* a loud sob, deep sense of sorrow, expression of grief, great sorrow ; bhrist reachd air, he broke into sobs of grief. *See* rachd.

reachd, *n. m.* *See* riochd.

reachdach, *a.* stout, strong. *See* riochdach.

reachdaich, rechc′-ich, *v.* enact, legislate.

reachdair, rechcuder, *n. m.* law-giver.

reachdar, reachdmhor, rechcor, *adj.* luxuriant, productive as corn, or crop full of substance as corn ; seachd diasan reachdmhor agus math, seven ears rank and good ; commanding, puissant. *Also* riochdmhor.

reachdmhorachd, *n. f.* rankness, productiveness, as corn.

réamhadh, rēvu, *vbl. n. m.* act of journeying, travelling. *See* rèabhair.

réamhair, rēver, *n. m.* a traveller ; rover.

reamhar, rav′- ar, ramhar, *adj.* fat, plump, fleshy, thick, stout. *E.Ir.* remor, thick, fat. *Cf.* *O.N.* ramr, strong, stark ; fr. stem rem.

reamhas, ravus, *n. m.* time, lifetime. *E.Ir.* remes, a period.

reamhrachd, reu-rachc, *n. f.* fatness. *Also* ruimhreachd, rooyrachc.

reamhrad, *n. f.* fatness. *Also* ruimhread.

reamhraich, raü′-rich, *v.* fatten.

reang, reng, *n. f.* a wrinkle, a fibre, as in one's face.

reang, reng, *n. m.* rank, series ; fr. early *Sc.* renk. *McB.*

reang, *n. f.* a boat rib. *Also* rang, *pl.* rangan. *O.N.* röng, *gen.* rangar.

reang, *v.* kill, starve. *E.Ir.* ringim, tear.

reangach, reng′-uch, *adj.* full of wrinkles

or fibres ; full of strings, lean, ribbed, starved.

reangaich, rengich, *v.* starve. *Ir.* reangaim, I starve.

reangair, renger, *n. m.* a loiterer.

reannach, renuch, *a.* spotted, striped. *See* reannag, star.

reannach, rionnach, *n. m.* a mackerel.

reannag, renag, *n. f.* a star. *O.Ir.* rind, constellation.

rèapach, *a.* untidy, slovenly, tawdry.

rèas, rēs, *n. m.* a head of dry curled hair.

rèasach, *a.* having dry curled hair.

reasach, *a.* prattling, talkative. *Ir.* réaseach.

rèasan, rēsan. *See* reas.

reasgach, resguch, *a.* stubborn, restive, irascible.

reasgshuil, resc-hool, *n. f.* a blear eye.

réic, *v.* roar, howl.

reic, reck, *n. f.* sale, traffic ; *v.* sell, dispose of ; *vbl. n. f.* selling, disposing of ; a' reic, selling. *O.Ir.* recc, a sale.

reic, *v. tr.* deliver a message ; reic mise am fios, I gave the message. *M. Ir.* reic, inform. *Ktg.*

reiceadair, recuder, *n. m.* seller.

réiceil, *n. m.* a roaring.

reicte, rectu, *vbl. a.* sold, disposed of.

rèidh, rē, *adj.* plain, level, cleared ; àite rèidh, a plain or cleared place ; exempt, free from, done of ; tha mi rèidh is e, I am done of it ; reconciled, at peace ; tha iad rèidh a nis, they are at peace now ; they have finished ; ready, prepared ; a bheil thu rèidh ? are you prepared ? gu rèidh, at leisure ! avast ! smooth, plain ; fiodh rèidh, smooth wood ; *n. m.* a plain, a level ; gabh rèidh a bhlàir, betake yourself to the plain, to fair field. *O.Ir.* réid. *E.W.* rwydd, free, clear. *O.Celt.* reidi-s, free.

rèidhbheartach, rē-viarstuch, *a.* equable, fit, cool, and under complete self-control in face of danger.

rèidheachd, rē-achc, *n. f.* smoothness.

rèidheas, rēius, *n. f.* peace ; faigh le rèidheas e, get it in peace, without disturbance.

rèidhlabhairt, rā-lavurt, *n. m.* eloquence.

rèidhleadh, *vbl. n. m.* splicing, busking. *See* rìghleadh.

rèidhlean, rēlen, *n. m.* a plain, a green, a bowling-green ; air an réidhlean, on the plain.

réidhne, rēnu, *n. m.* well-conditioned heifer. *Cf.* *O.H.G.* hrind. *Sc.* rhind. *See* raoine.

réidhneach, rē-nuch, *n. m.* a barren cow.

reilig, relig, *n. f.* a crypt or burying-place under a church ; stone chest where the bones dug out of the graves

are placed ; a lair, a cemetery ;
**bithidh dùil ri fear fairge, ach cha bhi
dùil ri fear reilge,** there may be hopes
of a person at sea, but none of one
in the grave. *O.Ir.* reilic, cemetery.
Lat. reliquiae.
réim, rēm, *n. f.* power, authority. So
Ir. a. **réimeil,** authoritative.
réim, rēm, *n. f.* course, a way, order.
Cf. *O.Ir.* réimm ; *inf.* to rethim, I run.
rèim, *n. f.* the rim of the large wheel
of a spinning-wheel.
rèir, rēr, *n. f.* will, accord, agreement ;
do rèir, according to, like as ; **do rèir a
chèile,** on a friendly footing ; *dat.* of
riar, *q.v.*
rèis, rēsh, *n. f.* a race or running-course ;
a span ; **ruith e rèis,** he ran his course ;
rèis d'a theangaidh, a span of his
tongue. *M.Ir.* réis.
reis, resh, *vbl. n. f.* act of playing, gambolling, as kitten, puppy, lamb ; fr.
the *Eng.* race.
réisd, rēsht, then ; **ciod é réisd ?** what
then ?
réisgeadh, rēshcu, *vbl. n. m.* act of smoke-
curing mutton. *Sc.* reist, smoke-cure.
réisgeadh, *vbl. n. m.* an arrest, lien on
goods.
reisimeid, reshumej, *n. f.* a regiment.
rèite, rētu, *n. f.* harmony, agreement,
reconciliation ; **dèan rèite,** be reconciled, be friends ; atonement, expiation ; fr. **réidh.**
rèiteach, rèiteachadh, rētuch, *vbl. n. m.*
disentanglement, putting in order, as
a house ; a smattering ; act of dis-
entangling, unravelling ; reconciling,
agreeing ; espousals (always celebrated
by a feast on a limited scale—a small
impromptu banquet). *See* **réidh.**
reithe, re-hu, *n. m.* a ram ; **reithe-
cogaidh,** battering-ram. *Also* **reath.**
E.Ir. rethe.
reithich, re-hich, *v.* rut, line, as a ram.
rèitich, rētich, *v.* put in order, adjust ;
rèitich an tigh, put the house in order ;
determine, adjust ; **rèitichear a' chéist,**
the question shall be determined ;
betroth, settle on terms of marriage ;
disentangle ; **rèitich an snàth,** disentangle the thread ; **rèitich an
rathad,** clear the way.
reodh, rio', *v.* freeze. *Ir.* **reó.** *O.Ir.*
réud ; gl. gelu. *O.Celt.* regu- frost.
reodhadh, rio'u, *n. m.* frost ; act of freez-
ing.
reòdhte, reòtu, *vbl. a.* frozen.
reotha, *n. m.* frost. Different names
for *frost* : **crannreotha, crithreothadh,
liathnach, leathnach cranntarach.**
reothart, rio-hurt, *n. m.* spring-tide. *See*
rabhairt.

reub, rēb, *v.* tear, rend ; gore, as a bull ;
lacerate, pain intensely. *E.Ir.* **rébaim.**
O.Celt. reippô.
reubadh, rēbu, *vbl. n. m.* act of tearing,
goring.
reubaire, rēbiru, *n. m.* tearer.
reubalach, rēbeluch, *n. m.* a rebel. *Also*
reubaltach ; fr. the *Eng.*
reudan, raodan, rēdan, *n. m.* wood-moth.
O.Ir. rétan.
reul, rēl, *n. f., pl.* reultan, a star ; a belle.
Ir. reult. *E.Ir.* retla. *O.Ir.* **rétglu** ='
rēt + glē, for its brightness. *Corm.*
reulach, rēluch, *a.* starry, starred.
reuladair, rēluder, *n. m.* an astronomer ;
reuladaireachd, astronomy.
reulbhad, rēl-vad, **reul-bhuidhinn,** rēl-
vooyin, *n. f.* a constellation, a bunch
of stars, literally.
reultach, rēltuch, *adj.* starry.
reultair, rēlter, *n. m.* astrologer.
reultaireachd, *n. f.* astrology.
reum, rēm, *n. f.* way, order. *See* **réim.**
reum, *n. f.* course, a march.
reum, *n. f.* phlegm. *Also* **riam.**
reumail, rēmal, *a.* constant ; fr. **réim,**
a course.
reusan, rēsan, *n. m.* reason, cause.
M.Ir. résún.
reusanaich, *v.* reason, argue.
reusanta, rēs'-ant-u, *adj.* reasonable,
rational, endowed with reason and
sense, just.
reusantachd, resantachc, *n.m.* reasonable-
ness, rationality, justness, just grounds.
reusbaid, *n.f.* groove in keel for first plank.
ri, *prep.* to, into, during, like to, of, concerning ; **cho mìn ri minicionn,** as soft
or smooth as kidskin ; **ri do chluas,**
to your ear ; exposed to ; as, **ri
gréin,** exposed to the sun ; ascending,
going up ; **ri bruthach,** ascending a
declivity ; against, in opposition ; **a'
cogadh ri gaisgeach,** fighting against
a hero ; against, in contact with ;
bhuail e chas ri cloich, he dashed his
foot against a stone ; occupied in,
employed in ; **ri saorsainneachd,** occupied or employed as a house carpenter. *M.Ir.* re. *O.Ir.* fri, ri.
riaba-steallag, riäbu-stiälag, *n. f.* a swing.
See **dreallag.**
riabhach, riuvuch, *adj.* drab, greyish,
brindled, grizzled ; **bó riabhach,** a
grizzled or brindled cow ;
"D'an tig na h-airm gu sgiamhach,
Ge bu riabhach leinn do dhath."
"Right handsomely you set off your armour,
Though we thought your complexion brindled."
n. m. louse-wort. *M.Ir.* riab, stripe.
O.Ir. riabach. *O.Celt.* reibâko-s.
riabhach, *n. m.* grizzled one ; an riabhach, the evil one.

riabhag, *n. f.* a lark, hedge-sparrow. *Ir.* riabhóg, riabhag, a lark.

riabhaich, *v.* swear, curse ; **riabhaich e,** he swore by the evil one, he cursed.

riabhaiche, riuvichu, *n. f.* greyishness.

riach, riuch, *v.* cut the surface, score a line. Cf. **strioch.**

riachadh, *m.* a slight cut, a scratch ; a scoring.

riachaid, riuchej, *n. f.* distributing.

riadh, *n. m.* a snare.

riadh, *n. m.* a drill (of potatoes).

riadh, riu', *n. m.* interest of money, usury ; **tigh-réidh,** a bank ; *v.* lend another's property from house to house, without bringing it back to the owner. *Also* riabh. *McB.* rel. it to *Ir.* ríad, running, a course.

riadhadair, riu'uder, *n. m.* usurer.

riag, riäg, *n. f.* a short race, run, a spurt, a dash.

riagail, *n. f.* gambolling of lambs and calves. Cf. **ruagail.**

riagh, *n. m.* a stripe.

riaghail, riu'il, *v.* rule, govern ; **riagh-alaidh làmh an dìcheallaich,** the hand of the diligent shall govern.

riaghailt, riu'ilt, *n. f.* a rule of any kind ; a law, statute ; sense, judgment ; **chaidh e as a riaghailt,** he lost his senses or judgment ; regulation ; **snàth-riaghailt,** a basting. *O.Ir.* riagul, riagol. *Lat.* regula.

riaghailteach, *adj.* regular, sober, decent, orderly.

riaghailteachd, *n. f.* regularity, orderliness, sobriety, sedateness.

riaghailtear, riu-'ilter, *n. m.* regulator.

riaghailtich, riu'iltich, *v.* arrange, adjust, regulate, put to order.

riaghan, *n. m.* a small water-course ; a temporary channel to lead or divert water ; a swathe of hay turned by rake ; a drill, a swing, a gibbet. *O.Ir.* riag, a coil of hay, a shallow course made for water.

riaghladair, riu-luder, *n. m.* governor, supreme ruler.

riaghlair, riu-er, *n. m.* governor.

rialls, riulls, *v.* handle roughly, or unseemly.

riallsadh, riulsu, *vbl. n. m.* act of handling roughly or improperly ; *n. m.* a rough handling. *Also* **riasladh.**

riam, *n. m.* mucus (rather stringy). *See* reum.

riamh, riuv, *n. f.* a drill of potatoes, turnips ; *v.* drill.

riamh, *adv.* ever, used only of past time ; **an robh riamh,** was there ever ? always ; **bha e riamh mar sin,** he was always so. *O.Ir.* riam. *O.Celt.* (p)reimo.

rian, *m.* sense ; method, order, sobriety ; **tha e dhe rian,** he is out of sorts (physically or mentally) ; **tha e as a rian,** he is of a disordered mind. *E.Ir.* rian, way, manner.

rianadair, *n. m.* a controller.

rianaich, *v.* arrange, put in order, adjust.

rianalachd, *n. f.* regularity, order, system.

riar, riur, *n. m.* will, inclination, pleasure, satisfaction ; **agus nì thu mo riar,** and thou shalt do my desire or will ; pleasure, approbation ; word of honour ; **mo riar fhéin,** upon my word of honour ; **mo riarsa nach tig e nochd,** forsooth, he will not come to-night ; **mo riar-sa nach 'eil,** upon my word it is not so. *O.Ir.* ríar, *voluntas.*

riarachadh, riuruchu, *vbl. n. m.* act of distributing at table, serving, pleasing, satisfying ; satisfaction, pleasure ; **riarachadh bùird,** serving a table ; administering a sacrament ; **riarachadh-inntinn,** mental pleasure, mental satisfaction.

riarachas, riuruchus, riarachd, riurachc, *n. f.* satisfaction ; distribution.

riaraich, riurich, *v.* satisfy, please ; distribute, serve ; **riaraich orra e,** distribute it among them. *E.Ir.* riaraim, satisfy.

riaraichte, riurichtu, *vbl. a.* served, supplied ; satisfied, pleased ; distributed.

riasail, *v.* tear, mangle, tousle, maul.

riasan, riusan, *n. m.* reason ; also written reuson, cause.

riasg, riusc, *n. m.* dirk-grass ; morass with sedge, land covered with dirk-grass ; peat-moss. *E.Ir.* riasc, a morass.

riasg, *n. m.* stubbornness, indocility. Cf. **reasgach.**

riasgach, *a.* turbulent.

riasgail, *a.* that cannot be taught, indocile, intractable, mulish.

riasglach, riuscluch, *n. f.* land that cannot be cultivated.

riasglach, *n. f.* mangled carcase ; same stem as that of **riasail.**

riasglachd, *n. f.* turbulence, indocility, intractableness.

riasgshuil, *n. f.* a blear-eye.

riasladh, *vbl. n. m.* act of mauling, mangling. Cf. *E.Ir.* riastrad, distortion.

riaslaiche, riuslichu, *n. m.* mauler, tyrant.

riaspach, riasplach, *a.* confused, disordered.

riastair, riustir, *v.* wander, entangle.

riastradh, riustru, *m.* turbulence, confusion, wandering, immorality. *E.Ir.* riastrad, distortion.

riatach, riutach, *a.* illegitimate, wanton.

riataiche, *n. m.* an illegitimate child.

riataidheachd, riuty-achc, *n. f.* fornication ; wantonness.

riatanas, riutanus, *n. m.* necessity.

rib, *v.* entangle, ensnare.

rib, *n. m.* a hair, a rag, a blade, a tatter, a snare. *Also* rub.

ribeachas, ribuchus, *n. m.* ensnaring.

ribeag, ribag, *n. f.* a little hair, a fringe, a tassel, rag. *Also* rubag.

ribeir, *n. f.* a duster.

ribh, rooiv, *prep.* ri+*pron. suf.* 2 *pl.* to you, with you, against you; molesting you; mastering you; a' bruidhinn ribh, speaking to you; có tha ribh? who molests you? a' cur ribh, mastering you, sorting you.

ribheid, rivej, *n. f.* reed of a pipe, barb of a hook. *Also* rifeid.

rìbhinn. *See* righinn (which is the *prop.* form).

ribigeadh, ribigu, *m.* act of rubbing, polishing. *Eng.*

ribinn, ribean, *n. m.* ribbon. *Also* ruban; fr. the *Eng.*<*O.F.* riban. *Fr.* ruban.

ribleach, ribluch, *n. f.* fringe, shagginess.

rideal, rijul, *n. f.* a riddle.

-ridh, a *collect. suf.*; an òigridh, the youth; ceòlraidh, the muses. *O.Ir.* -rad, -red.

ridhe, *n. f.* field, bottom of a valley; *prop.* righe. *See* ruighe.

ridil, ruidil, rĕjj'-ėly', *v.* riddle, winnow.

ridire, reediru, *n. m.* a knight; ridire nan spleagh, a knight-errant. *E.Ir.* ritire; fr. *A.S.* ridere, a horseman. *O.N.* riddari, a knight. *M.H.G.* ritter.

rìdireachd, *n. f.* knighthood.

rìdireil, reediral, *a.* knightly.

rìgh, ree, *n. m.,* *pl.* rìghrean, a king, governor. *O.Ir.* rí, *gen.* ríg. *W.* rhī. *O.Bret.* ri. *Gaul.* rīx. *Lat.* rex, regis. *O.Celt.* rēks, rēgos; stem rēg, to rule.

righ, *v.* stretch on a death-bed; dress or shroud as a corpse; nach robh thu air do righeadh, I wish to goodness you were shrouded; used of stretching skins to dry. *E.Ir.* rigim, I stretch.

righann, ree-ghan, *n. f.* a serpent.

rìghich, ree-ich, *v.* reign, rule, govern, lord.

rìghil, reel, *n. m.* a reel, a dance. *See* ruithil.

rìghinn, reeyin, *n. f.* a princess, a nymph, a belle. *Dial.* rìbhinn, *asp.* g *intervoc.* not infrequently becomes *asp.* b. *E.Ir.* rígan; fr. rìgh-. *W.* ri-an, a maiden. *O.Celt.* rêganâ, rêganî.

righinn, ri'un, *adj.* tough; dilatory, slow. *Ir.* rithin, tough, viscid.

rìghle, reelu, *n. m.,* *pl.* rìghleachan, a yarn reel.

rìghleadh, *vbl. n. m.* 1. act of rolling, act of dancing. 2. rolling a wheel or spool, or a circular object on the ground. 3. act of splicing a hook to a fishing-line (by neatly winding a thread round the joint); the strapping of cord by which any splice is fastened. In certain areas it is termed rèidhleadh and in others snàthaclachadh.

rìghleadh, reelu, *vbl. n. m.* reeling, floundering.

rìghmhort, ree-vurst, *n. m.* regicide.

rìghmhortair, ree-vurster, *n. m.* a regicide.

rìgh-nathair, ree-nahir, *n. f.,* *pl.* rìgh-nathraichean, cockatrice.

rìghne, reenu, *compar. deg.* of righinn; or na's ruighne, more tough.

rìghneachas, ree-nuchus, *n. m.* laziness, sluggishness.

rìghnich, *v.* get tougher, toughen, delay.

rìghtheach, *n. m.* a palace. *E.Ir.* rìgthech.

rìgh-theachdaire, *n. m.* an ambassador, an envoy, plenipotentiary.

rinn, reen, *n. f.* a sharp point; a promontory. *Also* ruinn. *O.Ir.* rinnd, rind.

rinn, *past t.* of dèan; did; rinn iad sin, they did that. *O.Ir.* rigni, did (ro + gní)

rinncholg, *n. m.* sharp-pointed sword.

rinndeal, reenjal, *n. m.* sphere, extent, limits, boundaries, territory; leabhar an rinndeal, the rental or stent-book; ciod e an rinndeal fearainn a tha agad? what extent of land do you possess? *Also* ringeal, circle, sphere.

rinniche, rinichu, *n. m.* engraving chisel.

riob, rib, *v.* ensnare. *See* rib.

rioba, ribu, *n. m.* a hair, a snare to catch fish, a double rope to keep a mad bull; shag.

riobach, *a.* hairy, shaggy; cold.

riobachd, ribachc, *n. f.* hairiness.

riobadh, ribu, *m.* act of ensnaring.

riobag, *n. f.* a little hair, lock of wool, lint, or any such thing; a ribbon.

riobagach, *adj.* hairy.

riobalach, ribaluch, *n. m.* hairy, curious-looking ragged person.

rioblach, ribluch, *n. m.* a fringe, anything hairy or entangled.

rioblaich, riblich, *v.* fringe, make hairy or entangled.

rìoch, riuch, *v.* graze, plough along the skin, cut as when flaying a beast; rìoch e air mo chraiceann, it grazed on my skin.

riochd, richc, *n. m.* appearance, shape, form, semblance; chaidh i an riochd gearraidh, she assumed the shape of a hare; interpretation, meaning, exposition; ciod is riochd do m' aisling? what is the interpretation of my dream? an riochd mairbh, in the likeness of a dead man. *O.Ir.* richt. *W.* rith, guise. *O.Celt.* riktu.

riochdaich, richcich, *v.* personate.

riochdail, richcal, *adj.* actual, real, positive ; gu riochdail glan, actually and really so, positively so ; dh' innis e dhomhsa e gu riochdail glan, he told it me as a positive fact. *Also* used in a good sense =shapely, well-conditioned.

riochdainm, *n. m.* pronoun.

riochdair, richcer, *n. m.* a substitute, representative, delegate, plenipotentiary.

riochdal, *n.* skeleton, poor-looking person; **riocail.**

riof, rif, *n. m., pl.* riofachan, the reef of a sail ; fr. the *Eng. O.N.* rif.

riof, *n. f.* a sunken ridge of rock ; fr. the *Eng.*

riof, *n. f.* a level plain, with short grass, near sands.

riofag, *n. f.* a barb. Cf. *O.N.* rifa, a rift.

rìoghachadh, ree-uchu, *vbl. n. m.* act of reigning.

rìoghachd, ree-achc, *n. f.* a kingdom, realm, dominion, empire ; is farsuing do rìoghachd 's gur fial, extensive is thy dominion and hospitable. *O.Ir.* ríge. *O.Celt.* rêgio-n.

rìoghaich, *v. tr.* rule as king.

rìoghaich, ree-ich, *v.* pinion, tie.

rìoghail, ree-ghal, *adj.* loyal, kingly.

rìoghainn,*vbl.n.f.*reaching to; arriving at.

rìoghaire, ree-iru, *n. m.* a loyalist.

rìoghalachd, ree-aluchc, *n. f.* royalty, loyalty, dignity of port and character.

rìoghalaich, *n. pl.* the royal troops.

rìoghann. See **rìbhinn.**

rìoghchrann-sìthe, *n. f.* kingly tree of peace, kingly peace-maker.

rìoghthach, ree-hach, *n. f.* felloe of a wheel.

riolluinn, riulin, *n. m.* cloud.

riomb, reem, *n. m.* a wheel. See **réim.**

riomba, *n. m.* a semicircular bay or beach.

riomball, reembal, *n. m.* a circle, a halo ; riomball mun ghealaich, a halo about the moon ; gearr riomball, describe a circle.

riomballach, *adj.* circular, circuitous, like a circle.

riomballachd, *n. f.* circularity, roundness, circuitousness.

rìomh, reev, *n. m.* a costly jewel. Cf. *O.Ir.* rím, number, a reckoning.

rìomhach, reevach, *a.* fine, costly, handsome.

rìomhachas, reevuchus, *n. f.* beauty, adornment.

rìomhadh, *n. m.* finery.

rìomhair, reever, *n. m.* dandy ; counter.

rìon, reeun, *n. m.* See **rian.**

rìonadair, reeunuder, *n. m.* governor, supercargo, representative, ruler.

rionnach, runuch, *n. m.* a mackerel. See reannach, the " striped one."

rionnag, runag, *n. f.* glimmering starlet ; rionnagach, bespangled or studded with glimmering starlets. *Also* runnag. *See* **reannag.**

riopail, *v.* mangle, tear. *Eng.* rip.

riostal, ristal, *n. m.* a lame plough, surface plough, having sickle-like coulter, drawn by one horse. *Sc.* ristle. *O.N.* ristill, a ploughshare.

riplis, *n. f.* weakness in the back.

rìreadh, da-rìreadh, *adv.* really in earnest, truly.

ris, rish, *prep.* ri (to, at) +s (frag. of *pron.*, 3rd *prs. sing., m.*), to him, to it ; tha e ris, he is at it=doing ; or he is at him =teasing, abusing ; or it is exposed to view =" it is to it " (the light); casan ris, barefooted ; leig ris, expose, divulge, reveal your mind to ; cum ris, do not yield to him or it ; is math a tha thu cumail ris, you wear out well ; you match him well ; na bi ris, do not molest him ; with the *art.* ris an = ri +san ; tha dhruim ris a' bhalla, his back is to the wall ; used idiom. to express a habit ; studying ; apprenticeship ; tha e ris an òl, he is fond of strong drink ; tha e ris a' phìob, he smokes ; tha e ris an sgoil, he is studying ; tha e ris a' chlachaireachd, he is learning to be a mason.

rìs, ree-isht, for **rithisd**, again.

ris-san, rish-sun, *prep. + pron. suf.* emphatic form of ris, to him, etc.

risteal, *n. m.* a surface plough, with a sickle-shaped coulter, drawn by one horse. *O.N.* rísta, to cut, whence ristill, a ploughshare.

rithe, ree-u, *prep.* ri (to, at) +*pron. suf.* 3 *sing., f.* to her, at her, or it ; tha a rithe, he is (working) at it ; or he is molesting her ; na bi rithe, do not molest her ; na h-abair rithe, say not unto her ; cuir rithe, master her.

rithisd, ree-isht, *adv.* again, a second time ; an dràsd is a rithisd, now and then. *O.Ir.* arithissi, afrithissi, again ; for ar-frithissi. *Also* doridisi.

riu, riutha, rioo, *prep.* ri (to, at) +*pron. suf.* 3 *pl.* to them, against them ; cum riu, keep up to them, supply them, do not yield to them ; na bi riu, do not molest them.

rium, rioom, *prep.* ri (to, at) +*pron. suf.* 1 *sing.* to me, at me ; teann rium, come close to me ; na bi rium, " do not be at me " =leave me alone ; thuirt e rium, he said unto me ; cum rium, keep up to me, supply me as I want, hold up to me ; **abair rium**, say to me ; **còmhla rium**, along with me.

riut, rioot, *prep.* **ri** (to, at) +*pron. suf.* 2 *sing., m.* and *f.* to thee, towards thee, with thee; **maille riut**, along with thee; **an tig e riut**, will it please you ? **còmhla riut**, along with thee ; **o iomall na talmhainn**, **éighidh mi riut**, from the ends of the earth, I will cry unto thee.

riutha, rioo-u. *See* riu.

ro, an *intens. part.* very, too ; **ro-bheag**, too little ; **ro-mhath**, very well ; **le ro-aire**, with great care. *O.Ir.* ro-, both a *verbal* and *intens. particle.* *O.W.* ry (rhy), too, very. *Lat.* pro.

rò, *n. m.* romance, gasconading ; **thà e cho làn rò is a theachdas e**, he is as full of romancing as he can hold— he draws a long bow.

rò, *n. m.* path ; **rò réidh**, smooth path. *Carm. Gad.* Cf. *Ir.* **ró**, go, reach a place. *O'R.*

ròb, *n. m.* coarse hair, shag ; crested cormorant.

rob, *v.* rob, steal. *Eng.*

robach, *a.* shaggy and filthy.

robag, *n. f.* a slut, a drab.

robain, *n. f.* towering waves, roaring billows, heavy rains.

robair, rober, *n. m.* robber ; **robaireachd**, robbery, housebreaking ; fr. the *Eng.*

robairneach, roburnuch, *n. m.* smart, or clever boy.

robh, rò, *pret.* of the *v.* **bi** ; **an robh thu**, were you ? **c'àite an robh thu**, where were you ?

robhas, ro-us, *n. m.* notification, information regarding anything lost. *Also* **robhaisg**, sight. *See* **rabhadh**. Cf. *Ir.* **robhaim**, I admonish, warn.

roc, rock, *n. m.* a sunk rock ; anything that entangles a fishing-hook ; an entanglement ; **cuiridh tu do cheann an roc**, you will involve yourself— you will entangle yourself. Cf. *Ir.* **roc**, the tops of seaweed.

roc, *n. m.* a wrinkle, or plait, or corrugation, particularly in cloth waulking ; *v.* wrinkle. *O.N.* hrukka, wrinkle. *Dan.* rynke. *Eng.* ruck. *Lat.* ruga.

ròc, *n. m.* hoarse voice ; a haw, a gurgle in throat. Cf. *O.N.* hrókr, a rook.

ròcaideach, rōcejuch, *n. m.* a rook.

ròcail, rōcul, *v.* tear, mangle ; corrugate.

ròcail, *v.* croak, roar hoarsely.

ròcair, rōcir, *n. m.* one with hoarse voice.

ròcan, *n. m.* a wooden clip for seaweed.

rocan, *n. m.* 1. a plait, a fold. 2. intricacy.

ròcanaich, rōcanich, *n. f.* hawing, hemming. *Also* **ròcail**.

ròcas, rōcais, *n. f.* rook. *Ir.* **rócas**, a rook, crow, *O.N.* hrókr, rook.

rochailt, rochelt, *n. f.* a blustering female.

ròchd, *n. m.* a cough, retching. *See* **ròc**.

ròchoill, ro-choyl, *n. f.* great wood, majestic forest. **rò** (very great) + **coill**, a wood. Cf. *E.Ir.* **ró-fhid**.

ròchrann, *n. m.* great tree. (ro +crann.)

rò-chùram, *n. m.* anxiety.

rocladh, *vbl. n. m.* act of tearing, mangling.

ròd, *n. m.* seaweed, seaweed cast ashore ; foam, foaming sea beating against the shore. Cf. *Ir.* **ród**, a cast, shot. *E.Ir.* **rout** (ro +fhut), cast.

ròd, *n. m.* a way, a road. *E.Ir.* **rót**, a way, a road ; fr. *A.S.* rád. *McB.*

ròd, *n. m.* a rood (of mason work or of land).

ròd, *n. m.* a ditch, a drill of potatoes.

ròd, *v.* scarify ; **a' ròdadh**, scarifying.

rodach, *n. m.* seaweed growing on timber long submerged.

rodaidh, rody, *adj.* ruddy, drumly (of water).

rodaidheachd, rodyachc, *n. f.* ruddiness.

ro-dhéidh, ro-yēy, *n. f.* great desire.

ro-dhùil, *n. f.* eagerness, great desire.

rog, *n. f.* obstinacy, balk, a fit of stubborn ness, as in a horse. Cf. *O.N.* hrökkva, recoil (as if shrinking). *Shet.* rokk.

ròg, *n. m.* roguery, slyness, theft ; fr. the *Eng.*

rògaire, rōgiru, *n. m.* a rogue ; **rogaireachd**, roguery, downright villainy.

rogha, ru-a, *n. m.* choice, the best ; **rogha is tagha gach bidh is dibhe**, pick and choice of eatables and drinkables ; **theirig do rogha bealach**, go where you will ; **rogha céile**, the best of husbands or wives. *O.Ir.* **rogu**, *electio*, choice.

ròghail, rōghal, *adj.* fond of romancing.

ròghalachd, rō-ghaluchc, *n. f.* romancing disposition ; gasconading inclination. *See* **rò**.

roghainn, ru'-in, *n. f.* choice, selection, option ; **gabh do roghainn**, take your choice ; **tha diùgha is roghainn ann**, there is pick and choice among them ; **roghainn an t-sealgair**, the best of marksmen ; **dèan do roghainn ris**, make a kirk or a mill of it. *E.Ir.* rogain. *O.Ir.* **rogu**.

roghnach, rū-nuch, *a.* eligible ; **a' ni as roghnaiche leat**, what you think preferable ? **an roghnaiche leat so**, do you prefer this ?

roghnaich, rū-nich, *v.* choose.

ròib, rōb, **ròibinn**, rōbin, *n. m.* filth, a circle of grease about the lips ; pubes, or circle of hair ; little squalid beard. *Also* **rèib**.

roibhe, royv, *n. m.* sneezewort.

roibhne, royv'-nu, *n. m.* dart, lance.

ròic, *v.* tear.

ròic, *n. f.* sumptuous feasting of boorish people ; superabundance of the good things of life, without any of the refined manners of genteel society.

ròicealachd, rō-cealuchc, *n. f.* luxuriousness, a sort of brutish luxury or gluttony.

ròiceil, rō-ceal, *adj.* luxurious, epicurean.

roid, roj, *n. f.* a race before a leap ; a little while or time ; a rush or bounce ; thug e roid a steach, he bounced in, he rushed or popped in ; a' dol roid do 'n bhaile ud thall, going a little while to yonder town ; leum-roid, a leap after a race ; cruinnleum, a bound, a standing-jump. *Also* ruid. *O.Ir.* roitte, gl. *actus*, motion (roithim, I push).

roid, roideagach, rojaguch, *n. f.* wild or bog myrtle; the sweet-gale. *Ir.* rideog.

roidean, *n. m.* wildfire.

ròideil, *a.* meek, gentle, plausible. *Ir.* ród, great humiliation.

roideis, rojesh, *n. f.* bounding, skipping.

ròig, *n. f.* den or cave. Cf. fròig.

ròig, *n. f.* a scowl ; a frown ; threatening aspect.

roilean, *n. m.* snout of a sow, a disc, a roller ; fr. the *Eng.*

roileasg, ro-leshc, *n. f.*, *gen.* roileisg, confused joy, confused hurry.

roileis, *n. f.* playful or flattering talk.

roilig, rolic, *n. m.* a frolicsome person.

roiligeach, *adj.* frolicsome.

roill, *n. f.* dripping saliva.

roille, *n. f.* a fawning reception. ro + toil.

roimh, roy, *prep.* before ; roimh éirigh na gréine, before sunrise ; in preference to, rather than ; roimh na h-uile ni, in preference to everything. *Ir.* roimh. *O.Ir.* rem- (in compounds).

roimh-bheachd, *n. m.* presentiment.

roimh-bhlas, *n. m.* foretaste.

roimh-chraicionn, *n. m.* foreskin.

roimhe, *prep.*, + *pron. suf.* 3 *sing.*, *m.* before him, or it ; ghabh e eagal roimhe, he was afraid of him.

roimhe, *adv.* previously, before ; chunnaic mi roimhe thu, I saw you before.

roimh-eòlas, *n. m.* foreknowledge.

roimhibh, ro-uv, *prep.* roimh (before + *pron. suf.* 2 *pl.* before you ; tha mise an so roimhibh, I am here before you ; in preference to you ; standing or walking before you ; *pron.* cpds. : *sing.* 1. romham, 2. romhad, 3. *m.* roimhe, 3. *f.* roimpe ; *pl.* 1. romhainn, 2. romhaibh, 3. rompa.

roimh-ràdh, *n. m.* a foreword, preface.

roimh-theachdaire, *n. m.* forerunner.

roimpe, *prep.* roimh + *pron. suf.* 3rd *sing.*, *f.* before her.

ròin, rō-in, *n. f.*, *gen.* ròinne, used as

nom., a hair ; leud ròinne, a hair's-breadth. *Ir.* róin, róinne.

ròineach, rō-niuch, *adj.* full of hairs, hairy.

ròineag, rō-niag, *n. f.* a small hair.

roinn, rōyn, *n. f.*, *gen.* ranna, a share, proportion, distribution, division ; mo roinn fhèin, my own share ; a peninsula ; an Roinn Ileach, the Rinns of Islay ; an ìochdar na Ranna, in the farthest-off parts of the Rinns ; roinn mhic is athar, share of son and father, share and share alike ; *v.* divide, share, distribute, impart ; roinn orra e, distribute or divide it amongst them ; *vbl. n. f.* act of dividing, distributing, sharing, imparting ; a' roinn orra, distributing among them. *See* rann. *E.Ir.* roind, rannaim.

roinn, *n. f.* for rinn, sharp point.

ròinne, *n. f.* a hair, a fibre. *O.Ir.* rón. *O. Celt.* râno.

roinneadair, roynuder, *n. m.* divider.

roinnich, roynich, *v.* sharpen.

roinnte, royntu, *vbl. a.* divided, distributed.

rois, rosh, *a.* equidistant, term in a game of buttons, or quoits.

rois, *v.* shake off grain. *Also* frois.

roiseadh, *m.* shaking off seed. *Also* froiseadh, frasadh. *O.Ir.* roissid, shaking.

roiseag, *n. f.* a small potato.

ròiseal, rōshal, *n. f.* boasting, pomp ; display of ability ; le ròiseal, with an ostentatious display ; *also* ròisealadh ; *v.* display ; make a pompous display. *Sc.* rouse, roose. *N.* rausan, boasting.

ròiseal, rōshal, *n. m.* surge of a wave, an attack, assault, impetus of a boat ; fr. *Sc.* roust. Cf. *O.N.* röst, a tidal current.

ròiseal, *n. m.* a rabble, the basest, lowest.

ròisealach, *a.* attacking.

ròisealach, *adj.* pompous, ostentatious ; fond of displaying one's feats, or ability.

ròisealachd, *n. f.* pomposity, ostentatious display ; ostentation.

roisean, *n. m.* spattering of mud on the hem of a skirt ; fr. rois, shake, scatter. *Also* òpar.

ròiseid, ròsh'-ej, *n. f.* rosin. *Sc.* roset.

ròiseideach, *adj.* resinous.

roisg, roshc, *n. f.* diminutive, dwarfish person.

ròisgeul, rōsgel, *n. m.* a romance ; (ròsgeul) rò. (very, over-) + sgeul (tale).

ròisgeulach, *v.* romancing.

ròist, rōsht, *v.* roast. *Eng.*

ròiste, rōshtu, *a.* roasted.

roithlean, ro-hlen, *n. m.* sheave of a block, or pulley ; fr. roth.

roithlean, *n. f.* gall, wormwood.

roithlear, roler, *n. m.* a roller, a ruler ; fr. the *Eng.*

rol, rola, *n. m.* volume or book ; a roll.

rol, *v.* roll, wheel ; make into rolls.

rolag, *n. f.* swathe of grass ; a roll of carded wool. *Also* peàrd.

rolagan, *n. m., dim.* of rolag.

rolais, rolesh, *n. f.* jumbling speech, often resulting in the ludicrous ; spoonerism ; " an uair a bha mi ag ithe na gealaich 's ann a bha mo shuipeir ag éirigh," 'tis when I was eating the moon that my supper was rising.

ròlaist, *n. m.* romance, exaggeration, rigmarole.

ròm, *n. f.* pudenda, pubes.

ròmach, *adj.* hairy, shaggy.

ròmag, *n. f.* a female with a beard ; the pudenda of a female. *Arm.*

ròmag, *n. f.* oatmeal and whisky.

ròmaiche, rōmichu, *n. f.* hairiness.

romhad, ro'-ud, *prep.* (roimh) +*pron. suf.* 2 *sing.* before thee or you, previous to you, in your contemplation or intention ; at you, of you, or with you ; is beag eagal a th' aige romhad, little does he dread you ; ciod a tha thu a' cur romhad, what do you mean to do ? gabh romhad, go about your business, begone ! ; abair romhad, say on.

romhaibh, ro'-iv, *prep.* (roimh) +*pron. suf.* 2 *pl.* before you, tha romhaibh falbh, you are determined to go ; you must needs go.

romhainn, ró'-inn, *prep.* (roimh) +*pron. suf.* 1 *pl.* before us, tha romhainn, we mean to ; we must.

romham, ro'-um, *prep.* (roimh) +*pron. suf.* 1 *sing.* before me, tha romham, I mean to ; I must.

ròmhan, rō-an, *n. m.* a groan, a snore ; wild talk, raving.

ròmhanaich, *vbl. n. f.* act of groaning, snoring.

ro-mheud, ro-vēd, *n. m.* excessive greatness.

ro-mhiann, *n. m.* great desire.

rompa, romp'-u, *prep.* (roimh) +*pron. suf.* 3rd *pl.* before them.

ròn, *n. m., pl.* ròin, a seal, or sea-calf ; ionad falaich nan ròn slapach, the hiding-place of the splashing seals. *O.Ir.* rón, *phoca. O. Celt.* rôno-s.

ròn, *n. m.* fetters for the fore feet of a horse ; hair ; hair band for cream whisk.

rònach, *n. f.* seal-hunt.

rònanach, *a.* abounding in seals.

rong, *n. f.* a bandy ; hockey stick.

rong, *n. f.* slight noise as of breath in the throat, the vital spark ; chan 'eil rong ann, he is quite dead.

rong, *n. f.* a joining spar, a rung, boat-rib. *A.S.* hrung. *O.N.* röng. *Also* rongais.

rongach, *a.* lounging, cadaverous, languishing.

rongaiche, *n. f.* lounging.

rongaire, rongiru, *n. m.* a lounge, a lean person.

rongaireachd, *n. f.* tedious, drawling, lounging manner, or habits.

rongais, rungish, *n. f.* a bandy, a bludgeon.

rongais, rungais, *n. f.* rung of a ladder, rung in the frame of a chair, strips of board fastened across the ribs of a boat. In this sense rangas is the common form in the *Heb.* ; carn-rungais, a rung-cart, a cart with sides of upright rungs at short intervals.

rongan, *n. m.* discordant rattle, moaning ; slow work.

" Mar rongan bà caoile
'S i faotainn a' bhàis,"

" Like the death-rattle of an emaciated cow."

ronn, *n. f.* a slaver, ropy spittle. *E.Ir.* ronna.

ronnach, *a.* viscous, ropy, glutinous.

ronnaich, *v.* become viscid, slaver.

ronnair, roner, *n. m.* a slavering man.

ronnaireachd, *n. f.* fingering a chanter with wet fingers.

rop, *v.* gore ; let out the viscera with a knife ; tear open a bag with a knife. Cf. *E.Ir.* rop, an animal.

rop, *n. m.* an auction ; *v.* roup.

ròpach, *adj.* viscous, glutinous, slovenly, squalid.

ròpadair, *n. m.* rope-maker.

ròpag, *n. f.* a slut, a slovenly woman. *Also* rapag.

ròpaiche, *n. f.* sluttishness.

ròpaireachd, *n. f.* yarning, nonsensical tale.

ròpal, *n. m.* rhapsody ; *a.* ròpalach.

ròpan, *n. m.* a little cord.

ròram, *n. m.* the quality of dealing out extensively among a family, as provisions ; the quality of being able to stand fatigue ; liberality, with a deal of ostentation ; hospitality.

ròramach, *adj.* liberal, highly liberal ; lasting long, and being capable of dividing well in a family, as provisions.

ròramachd, *n. f.* liberality, extensive usefulness in a family.

ròs, *n. m.* a rose ; erysipelas. *M.Ir.* rós. *W.* rhosyn. *A.S.* rōse. *Lat.* rosa.

ròs, *n. m.* knowledge. *Carm. Gad.*

ros, *v. t.* defeat, miscarry ; ros e orm, it miscarried, I have been disappointed in it ; ros an làr bracha so orm, this floor of malt went wrong, miscarried ; *n. m.* disappointment.

ros, *n. m.* seed ; ros lìn, flax seed ; fras is usual word for small seed. *E.Ir.* ross, seed.

ros, *v. See* rois.

ros, *n. m.* a promontory, a wooded promontory ; enters into place-names in both senses : promontory and woods. *E.Ir.* ross. 1. a wood. 2. a promontory. *W.* rhos, moor.

rosach, *adj.* disappointing, defeating ; an Linne Rosach, the channel of disappointment, the Sound of Jura.

rosad, rosadh, *n. m.* disappointment, misfortune, mischief ; ciod e an rosad a rug ort, what misfortune, or what mischief came over you ?

rosadach, *a.* untoward.

ròsarnach, *n. f.* place where roses grow.

ròscal, *n. m.* joy, gladness ; dh'éirich ròscal ad chridhe, joy sprung up in your heart. *I.Lom.*

ròs-chrann, *n. m.* rose-bush.

rò-seol, *m.* highest sails of a ship, topgallants ; full sails.

rosg, *n. m., gen.* ruisg, an eyelid, eyelash ; an eye. *O.Ir.* rosc. *Also* rasg. *O.Ir.* rosc, *oculus.*

rosg, *n. m.* incitement (to battle), war ode, prose. *E.Ir.* rosc.

rò-sgeul. *See* roisgeul.

rosp, *n. f.* a blear eye.

ròst, *n. m.* a roast ; a roast of beef.

rot, *n. m.* a belch, bursting of waves.

rotacal, *n. m.* horse radish. *Sc.* rotcoll.

rotach, *n. m.* a wild storm with raging sea, synchronising with flood tide.

rotach, *n. m.* a spurt, a spring (at the start).

rotach, *n. m.* a hand-rattle to frighten cattle.

rotach, *n. m.* a circle of filth on one's clothes ; bespattering.

rotadh, *m.* cutting, dividing. *Cf. Sc.* rot.

ròtair, roter, *n. m.* a sloven, a lazy fellow.

rotair, *v. tr.* shove a person into a run.

rotal, *n. m.* ship's wake.

roth, ro, *n. m.* wheel of a cart ; halo ; tha roth mun ghealaich, there is a halo round the moon. *O.Ir.* roth. *W.* rhod. *O.Celt.* roto-s. *O.H.G.* rad. *Lat.* rota.

rótha, rō'-u, *n. m.* a roll of tobacco.

rotha, *n. m.* a screw, a vice.

rothadair, ro-huder, *n. m.* wheelwright. *Also* tuairneir.

róthaich, rō'-ich, *v.* twine, roll, swathe.

rothair, *n. m.* chanter.

ro-thoileach, *a.* very willing, greatly desiring.

rotradh, *vbl. n. m.* act of shoving, taking a boy by the shoulder or scruff of the neck and giving him a vigorous shove so that he has to run. *See* rotair.

ruadh, *a.* red, reddish ; *n. m.* reddish colour, redness ; a hind, deer. *E.Ir.* rúad. *O.W.* rudd. *O.Celt.* roudo-s. *Got.* rauþs. *O.N.* rauðr, red. *Lat.* rūber, rūfus.

ruadhag, *n. f.* young roe.

ruadhaich, *v.* redden, make red.

ruadhan, *n. m.* mineral scurf, greatly overcooked food.

ruadhbhoc, *n. m.* a roe-buck.

ruadhbhuidhe, roo-u-vooyu, *a.* reddishyellow, auburn.

ruadhchailc, roo-u-chelc, *n. f.* ochre.

ruag, *v.* pursue, put to flight. *Ir.* ruagaim, expel, hurl. *Ktg.*

ruagadh, rooug'-u, *vbl. n. m.* act of driving away, pursuing. *Ir.* ruagadh, act of expelling. *Lat.* ruo.

ruagaire, roo-ugiru, *n. m.* pursuer, chaser, hunter ; lock bar ; latch of a door ; an outlaw, a wanderer ; swan-shot.

ruaidh, roo-uy, *n. f.* redness ; the disease called the herpes, or shingles, caused by nausea ; the rose ; erysipelas.

ruaig, *n. f.* a shower of rain.

ruaig, roo-u-ig, *n. f.* pursuit, persecution ; thog iad an ruaig, they took up the pursuit ; defeat, flight, hunt, chase ; chuir sinn an ruaig orra, we put them to flight, we defeated them ; ghabh iad an ruaig, they took to flight ; ruaig an tuirc, the boar-hunt ; *v.* drive away, pursue, chase ; 'ga ruagadh, driving him away, pursuing him. *Ir.* ruaig, rout, victory. *Ktg.*

ruaille, *n. f.* poor, wretched female.

ruaim, *n. f.* a line, a fishing line. So *O'R.*

ruaim, *n. f.* flush of anger ; red scum. *E.Ir.* rúaim, red colour.

ruaimh, *n. f.* a burial place, " a Rome." *E.Ir.* rúam, a burial ground, *Lat.* Roma.

ruaimhseanta, rooa'-shant-a, *adj.* jolly, hale ; hearty, though very old.

ruaimhseantachd, roo-ash-antuchc, *n. f.* an old person's heartiness, vigour.

ruaimill, *v.* rumble ; fr. the *Eng.*

ruaimill, *v. tr.* trouble (water), disturb water so that it becomes muddy.

ruaimle, muddy, drumly water.

ruaimleadh, *vbl. n. m.* act of rumbling.

ruaimleadh, *n. m.* water-lily, fuller's earth.

ruaimneach, roo-umnuch, *a.* strong. *M.Ir.* ruamnach.

ruaineach, ruaidhneach, *a.* strong.

ruais, roo-ush, *n. f.* rhapsody ; a senseless flow of language ; rhapsodist.

ruaiseil, roo-ushal, *adj.* rhapsodical.

ruam, *n. m.* kind of plant used in dying red. *E.Ir.* rúaim, the alder.

ruamh, roo-uv, *n. f.* a spade. *Ir.* ruamh (*m.*) a spade. *O'R.*

ruamhair, *v.* delve, dig (with a spade).
ruamhar, *n. m.* delving, digging.
ruanach, *a.* firm, steadfast; fierce. *E.Ir.* rúanaid, heroic.
ruapais, roo-upish, *n. f.* rigmarole.
ruathar, *n. m.* an attack, an expedition, violent onset; **ruathar tinneis,** a violent attack of illness, an epidemic. *E.Ir.* rúathar, an onset. *W.* rhuthr.
ruba, *n.f.* a fibre, a bit of thread, a shred. *Ir.* ruibe, a single hair, a bristle.
rubail, roobul, *n. f.* a tumult, rumbling.
rubair, *n. m.* a rubber, scraper; fr. *Eng.*
ruban, *n. m.* riband. *M.E.* riban, < *O.F.* riban. *Fr.* ruban. *Also* ribinn.
rùc, rook, *n. m.* a rick of hay, peats, etc.; *v.* make ricks, build peats into small stacks. *Also* ruc, rucan. *Ir.* ruc, a rick. *O.N.* hraukr, a heap. *A.S.* hreâc.
rucas, roocus, *n. m.* jostling kind of fondness, wrestling in play. Cf. *Sc.* rook, boisterous company. *Ir.* rucas (*f.*), frisking, prancing. *E.Ir.* ruth, running.
rùchan, rùcan, *n. m.* the throat, wheezing. *Ir.* rúchán, throat, noise.
rùchd, roochc, *n. m.* a retch, grunt, ructation; *v.* retch groaningly. *M.Ir.* rúcht, roar. *Lat.* ructo.
rùchdail, *vbl. n. f.* retching, belching; act of internal gurgling.
rud, rood, *n. m.* a thing; pudendum; **agus rud eile dheth,** and another thing, moreover. *Also* raod. *O.Ir.* rét, *gen.* réto. *O.Celt.* rentu-s.
rudaidh, *a.* obstinate. *Carm. Gad.*
rudaidh, *n. m.* a trifle, a tiny thing.
rudainnte, roodentu, *vbl. a.* done; particular, somewhat odd.
rùdan, *n. m.* a knuckle, a tendon. *Also* ródan.
rudanach, *a.* particular. *See* rud.
rudanaich, *v.* dress; arrange.
rùdh, *v. tr.* make into small heaps.
rudha, roo'u, *n. m.* a point of land in the sea, promontory; **feuch am fuar thu an rudha,** see, and weather the promontory; a turn; **cuiridh so rudha seachad** this will serve for our turn, it will serve for this time.
rudha, *n. m.* a blush; root allied to ruadh.
rudhag, roo-ag, *n. m.* crab, partan.
rudhagail, *n. f.* thrift, shift; **tha e gu math rudhaglach,** he is pretty thrifty.
rudhaglach, *adj.* thrifty.
rùdhan, *n. m.* a small stack of corn; a small stack of peat. *See* rùghan.
rùdhrach, *v.* search, scrutinise, grope.
rug, *n. f.* a wrinkle, ruck. *O.N.* hrukka, a wrinkle, a fold.
rug, roog, *pret.* of beir, bore; **rug iad clann,** they bore children; **rug i uan,** she yeaned; **rug i meann,** she kidded. *O.Ir.* ro-uic, ro-uc (ro-uccim, I carry),

used as *pret.* of berim, when it means to carry, bring, bear, take. *Thn.*
rug, used as ro- *pret.* of berim, when it means to catch, to overtake, to reach; **rug e air,** he caught him, but also, he caught up to him; **rug e air an aiseag,** he caught the ferry. *O.Ir.* ro +icc, *j'atteins,* I reach, arrive at. *Ven.*
ruga, rugu, *n. m.* rough cloth. *Eng.* rug.
rugadh, *n. m.* greedy, grasping of anything.
rugaid, roogej, *n. f.* an old cow; a. long neck; *a.* rugaideach.
rugaire, roogiru, *n. m.* drunkard.
ruganta, *a.* stout, strong, muscular.
rugha, roo-u, *n. m.* a blush. *See* rudha, which is better form.
rùghan, *n. m.* a small peat heap. *O.N.* hrúga, a heap.
ruic, *n. f.* undesirable fondness.
ruicean, *n. m.* a pimple.
ruid, *n. f.* a sprint, a short fast run. *See* roid.
ruideag, *n. f.* the kittiwake, sea-swallow.
ruideal, roojul, *n.f.* a riddle, coarse sieve; *v.* to riddle; fr. the *Eng.*
ruideis, roojesh, *n. f.* skipping, frisking.
ruideiseach, roojeshuch, *adj.* frisky, lively.
ruidhil, *n. f.* a dance. *See* ruithil.
ruidhil, *n. f.* a yarn reel; fr. the *Eng.*
ruidhtear, *n. m.* a glutton, a riotous liver. *Eng.* rioter.
ruididh, *a.* merry, frisky.
ruidil, *vbl. n. m.* skipping, bounding, frisking about.
ruig, rooig, *v. i.* reach, extend; **ruig air so,** reach at this, extend your hand to this; arrive, come to, attain to; **an ruig e nochd,** shall he arrive to-night? **cha ruig mi air,** I cannot attain to it; need, must needs; **cha ruig thu a leas,** you need not trouble. *O.Ir.* riccim, riccu; ro +iccim (I go, attain, reach). *See* thig.
ruig, gu ruige, *prep.* to, as far as. *B.Deer.* gonice, till thou reach. *E.Ir.* corrici (fr. ro-iccim, I reach)‌.
ruig, roige (*Heb.*), *n. m.* ram (half castrated, or naturally defective), rig, ridgel. *O.N.* hryggr, back. *O.H.G.* rucki and hrukki. *Eng.* rig.
ruighe, rooyu, *n. m.* the arm, the forearm. *E.Ir.* rig, the forearm. *Lat.* rego.
ruighe, *n. f.* outstretched base of a mountain, shieling ground; transf. meaning of ruighe, arm.
ruigheach, *a.* taut, stretched; for righeach;

" Gach gàirdean 'n a ruighich
's gach cridhe 'n a leóghann,"

" Each arm at full tension ('steeled ')
And each heart as a lion."

ruigheachd, rooyachc, *vbl. n. f.* arrival ;
air dhuinn ruigheachd, on our arrival ;
act of reaching, attaining, stretching ;
a' ruigheachd air, stretching his hand
towards it. *Also* ruighinn ; based on
ruig.
ruighean, *n. m.* wool-roll, ready to spin.
Also peàrd.
ruinn, *prep.* (ri) *pron. suf.* 1 *pl.* to us,
against us, meddling with us; thuirt
e ruinn, he said to us.
ruinn, *n. f.* a sharp point, a promontory.
See rinn.
ruinnigil, ruinigil, *n. f.* dangerous navigation.
ruinnse, rooyshu, *n. m.* an enormous tail,
a rump, anything long ; a draggled
skirt. *Also* rùnsan.
ruinnse, *n. m.* a rinsing, rinser; fr. the *Eng.*
ruinnseach, *n. f.* tall vulgar woman.
ruinnsear, *n. m.* scourer.
ruinnsich, rinse, *v. tr.* scour. *Also* sgol.
ruire, *n. m.* lord, knight, champion ;

"Misi ar buile ge bé mé
A Dhé mam ruire 's mam rf."

"As for me, I am distracted whoever I am,
O, God, for my chief and King."

rùisg, rooshc, *v.* peel, make bare, disclose ;
gall, denude, unsheathe ; rùisg am
buntàta, peel the potatoes ; rùisg a'
chraobh, strip the tree ; rùisg do
claidheamh, unsheathe thy sword ;
rùisg e ghàirdean, he made bare his
arm. *See* rùsg.
rùisgte, roosgtu, *vbl. a.* peeled, unsheathed, stript, made bare ; dis-
closed, revealed.
ruit, *n. f.* a rakish female.
ruiteach, rooytuch, **ruidhteach,** *adj.*
florid, ruddy, flushing and blushing ;
apt to blush.
ruitear, rooyter, *n. m.* a rake, abandoned
man. The *Eng.* rioter.
ruith, rooy, *v.* run ; flow as a stream ;
ruith e, he ran ; ruith an fhuil, the
blood flowed ; melt, as lead, or suet ;
speak fast ; chase, distil, flow, overrun, or go over superficially ; ruith e
as mo dhéidh, he chased me ; a' ruith
ceudtarruing, distilling low wines ;
ruith thairis orra, run superficially
over them ; ruith a mach, be exhausted, or expended ; *vbl. n.* act of
chasing, running, distilling, adjusting.
O.Ir. rethim. *W.* rhedu. *O.Celt.* retô.
ruith, *n. f.* a race, a rate, full speed ;
esan 'na ruith, he at full speed ; air
an ruith cheudna, at the same rate ;
dysentery ; fast speaking or talking ;
ruith-fhola, hemorrhoids ; air ruith
an tighe so, in a line with this house,
parallel with this house ; thoir ruith
cladaich dhi, run her aground.

ruithil, *n. m.* a reel, a dance. *Also*
ruidhil and righil ; fr. the *Eng.*
ruithlean, reelen, *n. m.* a sheave in pulley.
See roithlean ; fr. roth.
rùm, room, *n. m.* room, space, place ; fr.
the *Eng.*
rumach, runnach, *n. f.* a slimy tough
kind of marsh or puddle.
rùmail, *adj.* spacious, roomy.
rùmalachd, roomaluchc, *n. f.* spaciousness.
rumpall, *n. m.* the rump, tail ; rumpall,
tigh mhóir, one accustomed to affluence. *Sc.* rumple.
rùn, roon, *n. m.,* *pl.* rùintean, secret
intention, mystery, secret ; inclination,
secret resolution, disposition ; ciod an
rùn 's a bheil e dhuit, how is he disposed towards you ? na innis do rùn
do nàmhaid gòrach na do charaid
glic, disclose not your purpose to a
foolish foe, or a wise (cunning) friend ;
a beloved object ; tha a rùin, yes, my
love ! rùnphairteach, communicating
secrets ; rùnphàirtich, communicate
secrets. *O.Ir.* rún, a secret, *mysterium.*
W. rhin. *O.Celt.* rûnâ. *O.H.G.* rūna.
rùnach, roonuch, *adj.* loved, secret.
rùnaich, roonich, *v.* intend, mean.
rùnaire, rooner, *n. m.* secretary.
rùn-diomhair, roon-jeeuvir, *n. m.* a
personal secret, a dead secret, mystery.
rùnsan, roosan, *n. m.* the rump.
rù-rà, in a jumble, topsy-turvy.
rùrach, rooruch, *n. m.* a search.
rùraich, roorich, *v.* search, explore.
rùsal, *m.* search, scrape, burrow among
things in search of anything.
rùsg, roosc, *n. m.* peeling, rind, skin,
fleece ; *gen. s.* and *n. pl.* rùisg. *O.Ir.*
rúsc. *O.Celt.* rûsko-.
rùsgach, *a.* fleecy, husky.
rùsgadh, rooscu', *vbl. n. m.* act of peeling, stripping, fleecing, making bare ;
removing of thatch.
rùsgaire, roosger, *n. m.* a strong brawny
person, that does a deal of work
coarsely.
rùsgan, rooscan, *n. m.* a large basket
made of bent.
rusp, *n. f.* a large coarse file. Cf. *Eng.* rasp.
rut, roort, *v.* rust, corrode. *W.* rhwd (n).
rùta, rootu, *n. m.* a ram, a ridgling. *Also*
reithe. *O.N.* hrútr, a ram.
rùtachd, *n. f.* rutting.
rutaidh, *a.* surly. *Carm.*
rùtan, *n. m.* the horn of a roebuck.
ruth, *n. f.* desire. *Carm.*
rùthan, roo'an, a group of peat set up
to dry ; rùghan is better form. *O.N.*
hrúga, heap.
rutharach, roo-haruch, *a.* quarrelsome ;
fr. ruathar.

S

s, the fifteenth letter of the Gaelic alphabet; named by the Irish sail, or suil, the willow-tree.

's. 1. for is, agus, and. 2. for anns, in. 3. for is (copula).

-sa, -se, -san, emphatic suffixes; attached to 1. simple *prs. pron.*, as: *sing.* 1. mise, I (and no other); 2. thusa; 3. *m.* esan; 3. *f.* ise: *pl.* 2. sibhse; 3. iadsan. For first *pl.* the *part.* is ne, sinne. 2. cpd. *prs. pron.* ormsa, on me; ortsa, on you; dhàsan, to him; dhaibhsan, to them; dhuibhse, to you. 3. nouns gov. by *poss. pron.*, mo mhac-sa, my son. 4. vb. in imper. mood, dèansa, do thou (in any case); so in cond. mood. *O.Ir.* (with sim. usage) *sg.* 1. -sa, -se; 2. -su, -siu; 3. *m.* -som, *f.* -si: *pl.* 1. -ni; 2. -si; 3. -som.

sabaid, *n. f.* fray, row; a brawl, a fight.

sàbaid, sàbej, *n. f.* the sabbath. *Hebrew*, shabbath; fr. shavath, to desist, rest.

sàbaideach, sābejuch, *adj.* sabbatical.

sàbh, sāv, *v.* saw, cut with a saw; *n. m.* a saw; sàbh-dùirn, hand-saw; sàbh-mòr, whip-saw; fr. the *Eng.*

sàbh, *n. m.* salve, ointment; sàbh-shùl, eye-salve. *Sc.* saw, a salve.

sabh, *n. m.* a strong smell. *E.W.* safr, odour.

sàbhadair, sāvuder, *n. m.* a sawyer; ri sàbhadaireachd, a' sàbhadh, sawing, cutting with a saw.

sàbhail, sāval, *v.* save, preserve; fr. the *Eng.* save. *W.* safio, to save.

sàbhailte, sāveltu, *adj.* safe, preserved.

sàbhailteachd, *n. f.* safety, a saving disposition, safe state or condition.

sabhal, sàv'-ull, *n. m., pl.* saibhlean, a barn. *M.Ir.* saball, a barn, a granary. *Lat.* stabulum, a stall.

sàbhaladh, sāv'-al-u, *vbl. n. m.* act of saving, rescuing; retrenchment; is mòr an sàbhaladh sin, that is a great retrenchment, or saving.

sabhan, *n. m.* a light haze on the sea.

sabhd, saud, *n. m.* straying; cù saibhd, stray dog; each saibhd, stray horse; chaidh e air sabhd, he strayed away; a lie, a fable.

sabhdaire, saudiru, *n. m.* stroller; liar, fabulist.

sabhs, saus, *n. m.* a sauce, fish-sauce; sabhs éisg, fish-soup, gravy, juice of meat; fr. the *Eng. W.* saws.

sabhsair, sauser, *n. m.* a sausage. *Also* marag.

sac, *n. m.* a sack; load; a heavy load; sense of a load in one's chest, laboured

breathing. *E.Ir.* sacc. *A.S.* sacc. *Lat.* saccus. *Gr.* σάκκος. *Hebr.* sak.

sacaich, sackich, *v.* press in a bag, load.

sacan, *n. m.* a little load; may be so spoken as to mean a very large load.

sacanta, sackantu, *adj.* thick-set, squat.

sac-aodach, *n. m.* sackcloth.

sachasan, sachusan, *n. f.* sand-eel. *Also* siol, *pl.* siolan.

sacraidh, sakry, *n. f.* luggage, baggage.

sàcramaid, sācrumej, *n. f.* sacrament. *Lat.* sacramentum.

sad, *v.* dash upon, as dust or spray; 'ga shadadh am shùilean, dashing it in my eyes; *n.* dust, dislike.

sadach, *n. m.* meal-dust.

sadharcan, sagharcan, su'urcan, *n. m.* the lapwing. *See* adharcan, and pibhinn.

sagairteachd, *n. f.* priesthood.

sagairteil, sagurtal, *adj.* priestly.

sagart, sagairt, sagurt, *n. m.* a priest; *O.Ir.* sacart, sacardd. *Lat.* sacerdos.

saibhear, syvir, *n. f.* a common sewer; culvert, a small water-course crossing under a road; = *Eng.* sewer.

saidealtach, sajaltuch, *a.* bashful, shy.

saidealtachd, *n. f.* silliness, bashfulness.

saidealtas, sajaltus, *n. m.* silliness, bashfulness. *See* sodal. *Also* soidealtas.

saidh, *n. f.* a bitch. *M.Ir.* sod, *gen.* saidhi. *See* saigh.

saidh, sy, *n. f.* prow of a ship, a beam, a blade; post; saidh-dheiridh, stern-post; saidh-thoisich, bow-post.

saidhe, syu, *n. f.* hay. *Also* tràthach.

saidhean, sooyen, *n. m.* a coal-fish, saith; fr. *O.N.* seiðr, the *Gadus virens.*

saidse, sajshu, *n. m.* a crash, fall, noise, sound of a falling body.

saidseach, *n. f.* beggar's mantle.

saidsear, sajsher, *n. m.* a heavy clumsy man.

saigean, sagen, *n. m.* squat fellow, a corpulent little man.

saigeanach, *adj.* fat, thick-set, and little; *n. m.* man so conditioned.

saigeantachd, *n. f.* shortness, corpulency.

saigh, sy, *n. f.* a bitch. *Also* galla. *See* saidh. *M.Ir.* sogh, sodh. *E.Ir.* sad.

saighd, syj, *v.* dart, pop, bolt, or dash in, or forward; inflict pain, or pang; thug e saighdeadh ud a steach, he made that dash into the house.

saighdeach, syjuch, *a.* piercing, arrowy.

saighdeadh, sydu', *vbl. n. m.* darting, as an arrow.

saighdear, syjer, *n. m.* soldier, arrower; a hero; saighdear-coise, a foot soldier, an infantryman; saighdear-fairge, a marine. *M.Ir.* **saigdeoir.** *W.* saethwr. *Lat.* sagittarius.

saighdearachd, *n. f.* soldiery ; heroism.

saighdearail, *adj.* military, brave.

saighead, syud, *n. f., gen. s.* **saighde,** *pl.* **saighdean,** an arrow ; a stitch ; a knot in wood. *O.Ir.* **saiget.** *W.* saeth. *Lat.* sagitta.

sail, sal, *n. f.* a beam ; a log of wood, joist ; *gen.* **sailthe,** *pl.* **sailthean.**

sàil, sã'l, *n. m.* salt water. *See* **sàl.**

sàil, *n. f., pl.* **sàiltean,** a heel. *O.Ir.* **sál.**

sail-bhuinn, sal-voo-in, *n. f.* groundsel.

sailche, saluchu, *n. f.* dirtiness ; more dirty ; fr. **salach.**

sail-chuach, *n. f.* the violet.

sàileag, sãl'-ag, *n. f.* a heel-step.

sàileagan, *n. m.* pyrosis, waterbrash.

sailean, *n. m.* a willow. *E.Ir.* **sail.**

sàilean, *n. m.* a little creek or inlet.

sàilghille, sãl-yilu, *n. m.* footman.

saill, syl, *v.* salt, season with salt. *O.Ir.* **saillim,** to salt, pickle.

saill, *n. f.* suet, fat ; **saill nan dubhan,** fat of the kidneys. *E.Ir.* **saill,** fat ; bacon. *O.Celt.* saldi-.

sailleach, *adj.* fat, full of suet.

sailleadair, seluder, *n. m.* salter, curer.

saillear, seler, *n. m.* a salt, salt-dish.

saillte, syltu, *vbl. a.* salted, seasoned.

saillteachd, *n. f.* saltness.

sailm, salum, *n. m.* a decoction, oak bark decoction to staunch blood, a consumption pectoral.

saimh, *n. pl.* twins, a pair.

sàimhe, syv, *n. f.* luxury, ease, sensuality. *E.Ir.* **sáim,** pleasant.

sàimheachd, syvachc, *n. f.* love of pleasure ; gross indulgence.

saimir, *n. f.* trefoil clover. *Ir.* **seamar.** *See* **seamrag.**

sainnseal, *n. m.* a whisper, a hint ; rel. to **sanus.**

sainnseal, seyshal, *n. m.* a handsel ; a drubbing ; fr. *Eng.* handsel.

sàiste, sãshj'-è, *n. m.* the herb sage.

sàith, sã, *n. f.* satiety, belly-full. *See* **sàth.**

saith, *n. f.* the backbone, joint of the neck.

saithe, *n. f.* a swarm. So *Ir. O.Celt.* satjâ.

sàitheachd, *n. f.* satiety.

sàl, **sàil,** **sàile,** *n. m.* the sea, salt-water. So *E.Ir. Lat.* salum. *O.Celt.* svâlos-.

sal, *n. m.* slimy dirt, wax of the ear.

salach, *adj.* dirty, nasty, foul. *O.Ir.* **salach.** *O.Celt.* salvo-.

salachadh, *vbl. n. m.* act of polluting, defiling.

salachar, *n. m.* dirt, filth, ordure.

salaich, sal'-ich, *v.* defile, pollute ; soil. *E.Ir.* **salchaim,** defile, pollute.

salaichte, salichtu, *vbl. a.* defiled, poxed.

salann, *n. m., gen.* **salainn,** salt. *O.Ir.* **saland, salond.** *W.* halen. *Lat.* sãl. *Gr.* äλs.

salannan, *n. m.* a salt-pit, a vault.

salann-dreag, *n. m.* salt that had been in use (as in a curing-house).

salldair, saltir, *n. f., pl.* **salldraichean,** chalder, 16 bolls. *Sc.* chalder.

salm, sal-um, *n. f., pl.* **sailm,** a psalm, anthem. *O.Ir.* **salm** (*m.*). *Lat.* psalmus.

salmach, *adj.* psalm tune.

salmadair, salumuder, *n. m.* psalmist.

salmair, salmer, *n. m.* precentor.

saltair, saltir, *v.* trample, tread. *Lat.* saltare.

saltairt, salturt, *vbl. n. f.* act of treading, or trampling ; treading, trampling, walking upon.

samh, sav, *n. m.* bad smell of any kind. *See* **sabh.**

samh, *n. m.* sorrel ; the seed-bearing part of sorrel ; **ag itheadh saimh,** eating sorrel. So *Ir.*

samh, *n. m.* a clownish person, a " pig " of a man ; a savage.

sàmh, *a.* pleasant, tranquil. So *M.Ir.*

samh, *n. m.* surge, white crest of wave, waves as they break on shore. *O.N.* haf.

samh, *n. m.* a god, a giant, a strong person. *Carm. Gad.*

sàmh, *n. m.* a rest, comfort. *M.Ir.* **sám.**

sàmhach, sãv'-uch, *adj.* quiet, still, calm ; **feasgar sàmhach,** a calm, or still evening ; **fan sàmhach,** keep settled, keep quiet.

samhach, *n. f.* haft, handle of an axe ; an axe, or hatchet. *O.Ir.* **samthach,** *manubrium securis.*

samhail, savul, *n. m.* likeness. *O.Ir.* **samail.** *W.* hafal. *O.Celt.* samali. *Lat.* similis.

samhaircean, savircen, *n. m.* primrose.

samhan, *n. m.* savin bush. *Lat.* sabina.

samhan, *n. m.* a little giant, a dog.

samhanach, sáv'-an-uch, *n. m.* a savage ; **chuireadh tu eagal air na samhanaich,** you would frighten the very savages.

samhan-aithrich, savan-erich, *n. m.* skin rubbed off in one's sleep ; cause, or object of regret.

sàmhchar, sã'-chur, *n. m.* quietness. *E.Ir.* **sáme.**

sàmhcharachd, *n. f.* quietness, pleasantness.

samhlach, saü'-luch, *adj.* typical.

samhlachadh, *vbl. n. m.* act of likening, laying something bad to one's charge ; fr. **samhail.**

samhlachail, saü'-luch-al, *a.* emblematical.

samhlachas, *n. m.* comparison.

samhlachd, saü'-lachc, *n. f.* comparability.

samhladh, saü'-lu, *n. m.* type, form, proverb. *O.Ir.* samlid, samlith.

samhlaich, saü'-llich, *v.* compare, liken ; *v. tr.* lay to one's charge ; na samhlaich a leithid sin riumsa, don't lay such thing to my charge. *O.Ir.* samlaim, I compare.

samhnach, sáv'-nuch, *n. f.* a deer park, a winter-park.

samhnachan, sáv'-nuch-an, samhnan, *n. m.* a large river trout.

samhnag, sav'-nag, samhnach, *n. f.* a bonfire, on the 12th of November. *Also* samhnach.

samhnaich, *v.* to winter.

samhrach, saü'-ruch, samhrachail, saü'-ruch-al, *a.* relating to summer ; summer-like.

samhradh, *n. m.* summer. *O.Ir.* samrad =sam, summer, and rad, *abstr. suff.* *W.* haf. *O. Celt.* samo-.

samhsair, *n. m.* a sausage. *See* isbean.

samhuil. *See* samhail.

samhuinn, sáv'-im, *n. f.* Hallowtide, the feast of All Souls ; o Bhealltainn gu samhuinn, from May day to Hallow-day. *Ir.* samhain. *E.Ir.* samfhuin, samuin, samain. *O. Celt.* samani-. *O'Cl.* suggests sam + fuin = end of summer.

samplair, *n. m.* a copy, a pattern.

sampuill, *n. m.* example ; bidh tu ad bhall-sampuill, you will be an example; fr. the *Eng.*

'san, for anns an ; 'san tigh (for anns an tigh), in the house. =*prep.* ann + *art.* san.

-san. *See* -sa.

sanas, san'-us, *n. m.* a friendly hint, or warning ; bheir e sanas le chois, he will give a hint with his foot. So *E.Ir.*

sanasail, *adj.* giving warning.

sannt, saunt, *n. m.* greed, covetousness, lust ; esan a dh' fhuathaicheas sannt, he that hates covetousness ; inclination, desire ; ma tha shannt sin air, if he has a desire for that. *E.Ir.* sant. *W.* chwant, desire. *O. Celt.* svandetâ-.

sanntach, *a.* greedy, covetous. *O.Ir.* santach, *cupidus.*

sanntachd, *n. f.* covetousness.

sanntaich, sauntich, *v.* covet, lust after, incline ; a' sanntachadh, coveting, lusting after.

sanntaire, saunteru, *n. m.* covetous man.

saobh, súv, *n. m.* hypocrisy ; *v.* err ; saobh shruth, " false " current, a current near one shore (in a strait) and which runs in opposite direction to the main tide ; shaobh iad, they erred ; *adj.* erroneous, eddying. *O.Ir.* sáib,

sóib, sáeb, *falsus, pseudo-,* sáebaim, seduce.

saobhadh, *n. m.* misleading, turning aside.

saobhaidh, *n. f.* den, lair of a fox.

saobhchainnt, *n. f.* impertinent or foolish talk.

saobh-chràbhadh, *m.* hypocrisy, religiosity, pietism.

saobh-chreidmheach, *n. m.* a heretic.

saod, súd, *n. m.* a prosperous train, condition ; good humour ; intention ; cuir saod air, put it in a likely or prosperous train ; gun saod air dol as, without an expedient to escape. *Ir.* saod, a state, condition.

saod, *n. m.* a track, a journey. *Ir.* saod, seud. *O.Ir.* sét. *W.* hynt.

saodadh, *vbl. n. m.* act of driving (cattle).

saodaich, súdich, *v.* drive cattle to pasture ; coax away in good humour.

saodar, súdor, saodmhor, *a.* in good humour, on good terms ; well-planned.

saoghal, sú-'ul, *n. m.* life, lifetime ; the world, universe ; feadh an t-saoghail, throughout the world ; saoghal fada dhuit, long may you live ; mo chuid de'n t-saoghal, my all ! my dearest dear ! *O.Ir.* saigul, saegul. *Lat.* saeculum, life, lifetime.

saoghalach, sú'uluch, *a.* long-lived.

saoghalachd, *n. f.* long life.

saoghalta, *adj.* of the world, worldly-minded. *O.Ir.* sáegulta.

saoghaltachd, *n. f.* worldliness.

saoi, saoidh, súy, *n. f.* a mare.

saoi, saoidh, *n. m.* a good generous man, a warrior, a scholar. *E.Ir.* sái, súi, *gen.* suad, a sage.

saoibh, *a.* foolish, perverse. *See* saobh.

saoibhir, syvir, *a.* rich. *E.Ir.* saidber, rich ; *contra,* daidber, poor. *O.Ir.* su + adbar (material).

saoibhir, syvir, *n. m.* St. Kilda skate.

saoibhneas, syvnus, *n. m.* dulness, peevishness ; fr. saobh.

saoibhreas, *n. m.* wealth. *E.Ir.* saidbre.

saoibhread, *n. m.* the richer (for us).

saoibhrich, *v.* enrich.

saoidhean, sooyen. *See* saigh, a young saith, coal-fish. Cf. *O.N.* seiðr.

saoil, súl, *v.* suppose, think, imagine, seem ; shaoil mi, I thought or imagined ; an saoil thu, think you ? ; shaoileadh duine, one should suppose. *E.Ir.* sáilim.

saoil, syl, *n. m.* mark, seal, impression of a blow ; chuir e saoile ort, he left (his) mark on you—he hit you hard ! *See* seul.

saoilsinn, súlshin, saoiltinn, súltin, *part.* supposing, imagining, thinking, judging.

saoir, *v.* set free, deliver, redeem ; reclaim (land). *E.Ir.* sóeraim, sáeraim, set free.

saoire, sūru, *deg.* of saor, na's saoire, cheaper ; *n.f.* preference in cheapness ; cheapness.

saoiread, sūrud, *abs. n. f.* the cheapness.

saoitear, *n. m.* oversman, a tutor. *See* taoitear.

saoithreach, *gen.* of saothair, *adj.* fatiguing ; at great pains ; gu saoithreach, at pains. *Also* saoithreachail.

saoithrich, sūrich, *v.* toil, be at pains, put yourself to the trouble ; shaoithrich mi a nuas, I put myself to the trouble of coming down ; saoithrich am fearann, cultivate the ground. *O.Ir.* sáithar, sáethar, *labor.*

saonas, sūnus, *n. f.* vexation.

saor, sūr, *adj.* noble ; free, at liberty, not enslaved ; clann na mnà saoire, the children of the free woman ; exempt, free, not guilty ; saor o'n mhionnan, exempt from the oath ; saor o'n àladh sin, free, or clear of that aspersion ; bheir mi dhà gu saor, I shall give him freely ; cheap ; tha sin gu math saor, that is fairly cheap ; *v.* free of aspersion or calumny ; purge ; saor am boireannach so, free or clear this woman from scandal ; *conj.* except, save ; saor o dhithis, except two, save two ; *cpds.* saor-thabhartas, free-offering ; saor-thiodhlac, free gift ; saor-thoil, free-will. *E.Ir.* sáer. *O.Ir.* sóir, sóer. *O.Celt.* su-viro-s, =su ("good") +fer (man), free man.

saor, *n. m.* a carpenter, house-carpenter ; mac an t-saoir, the carpenter's son—the surname Macintyre ; saor bhàtaichean, saor-dubh, a boat-builder ; saor mhuileann, mill-wright ; saor luingeas, ship-carpenter ; saor-geal, a joiner. *O.Ir.* sáir, sáer, *artifex.* *W.* saer. *O.Celt.* sa(p)iros.

saorachd, *n. f.* cheapness.

saoradh, sūru, *vbl. n. m.* act of freeing, exempting ; absolution, freedom, liberation.

saoranach, sūranuch, *n. m.* a freeman.

saorsa, sūrsu, *n. f.* freedom, liberty ; saorsa o'n olc, freedom from the evil ; is mór an t-suim air an do cheannaich mise an t-saorsa so, great is the sum for which I purchased this freedom. *O.Ir.* sóere, sóire, sáire, freedom, nobility, salus.

saorsachd, *n. f.* abatement.

saorsainneachd, sūr-shinuchc, *n. f.* carpenter's trade ; working with carpenter's tools ; joiner-work.

saothair, sū-hir, *n. f.* toil, pains, labour, work ; le móran saoithreach, with great pains or toil ; gabh saothair, bestow

pains, toil for it ; luach saoithreach, what is worth one's while or pains ; chan fhìach dhuit do shaothair, it is not worth your while, worth your pain ; tàileamh mo shaoithreach, the result of my toil ; an saothair, in great travail ; saothair-chlainne, travail, labour of childbed. *E.Ir.* sáethar. *O.Ir.* sáithar, *gen.* sáithir, *labor.*

saothrach, *a.* painstaking, diligent. *E.Ir.* sáethrach, laborious.

saothraiche, sū-rich, *n. m.* labourer.

saiphir, *n. m.* sapphire.

sàr, *a.* used as *n. m.* excellent, surpassing, a true hero, a brave warrior ; cha robh eagal air sàr riamh, a true hero was never afraid ; *adj.* complete, wholly, consummate ; sàr ghaisgeach, a complete hero ; sàr chù, a dog every inch of him ; sàr shlaightire, a most abandoned villain—placed always before the noun. *O.Ir.* sár-, exceeding. *O.Celt.* sagro-s.

sàr, *n. m.* oppression. *O.Ir.* sár, outrage. *O.Celt.* s(p)àro-n.

sar, *n. f.* a tick.

sàrachadh, *vbl. n. m.* act of oppressing, wronging, annoying, distressing, harassing ; tiring, exhaustion ; 'gam shàrachadh, oppressing or harassing me ; oppression. *O.Ir.* sáriged, *contemptus.*

sàrachail, *a.* oppressive, distressing, harassing, burdensome.

sàradh, *n. m.* an arrestment, a distraining ; consumption. *See* sàraich.

sàraich, sārich, *v.* distress, oppress, burden, harass ; overcome, wear out, fatigue, deal unjustly with, do violence to, use ill. *O.Ir.* sáraigim, I offend, overcome. *W.* sarhaet, insult.

sàraichte, sārichtu, *vbl. a.* oppressed, exhausted, over-fatigued, overcome, beat.

sàrdail, sārd'-al, *n. m.* sprat.

sàrdhuine, *n. m.* a true man, a chief man, a big-bodied man.

sàrmhaith, *a.* excellent, fine.

sàs, *n. m.* a grip ; custody, durance ; tha e an sàs, he is in custody ; air dhà a bhi an sàs, having happened to be in durance ; cause, means ; is math an sàs thu fhéin air sin, you are a fit cause or means for that yourself ; *v.* lay hold of ; grip. *E.Ir.* sás, an instrument, a trap.

sàsachd, *n. f.* satiety. *Also* sath.

sàsag, *n. f.* straw-chair.

sàsaich, sāsich, *v. n.* satiate, attack, fix ; a' sàsachadh na feòla, satisfying the lusts of the flesh ; shàsaich e orm, he attacked me tooth and nail. *O.Ir.* sásaim, to satisfy, please.

sàsda, *adj.* saucy, contemptuous.

sàsdachd, *n. f.* sauciness, pride.

Sasunn, sas'-unn, *n. m.* England.
sath, saith, sa, *a.* bad ; math no sath,
good or bad. *E.Ir.* saich, etar maith
ocus saich, both good and bad.
sàth, sā, sàith, *n. f.* plenty, abundance,
enough ; chan ith a shàth ach an cù,
none but a dog eats a bellyful or to
satiety. *E.Ir.* saith. *O.Celt.* sâti-.
sàth, *v.* transfix, fix, thrust ; shàth e
dhubhain annam, he fixed his clutches
in me ; shàth e ann e, he thrust it
into it or him. *M.Ir.* sáthud, a
thrust.
sàthach, sā'-huch, *adj.* satiated, filled.
sàthadh, sā-hu, *vbl. n. m.* a thrust, push,
shove ; thug e sàthadh, he gave a
thrust ; act of thrusting, pushing.
Sathairn, sa-hurn, Saturday.
sb, sc, for words thus beginning, *see* sp, sg.
sbairn, scorr. *See* spàirn, sgòrr.
se, *prs. pron.* he ; tha se, he is.
sé, sia, séa, *num.* six. *O.Ir.* sé. *W.* chwech.
seabh, *v.* stray, wander.
seabhach, shev'-uch, *a.* trim.
seabhag, shevug, *n. m.* and *f.*, orig. *neut.*
hawk. *E.Ir.* sebac, *O.Ir.* sebocc.
O'Dav. has another word—séig (*f.*) =
seabag. *W.* hebauc (hebog) ; fr.
Teut. *A.S.* heafoc. *O.H.G.* habuh.
O.N. haukr. *Kl.*
seabhaid, *n. f.* an error, wandering.
seabhaltrach, siavalruch, *n. m.* straggler.
Also seabhaltaiche.
seabhan, siavan, *n. m.* a-wandering.
seabhdail, seabhdaireachd, *n.f.* wandering
about, astray.
seac, shac, *v.* wither, decay ; sheac-
mharbh e i, he killed her outright ;
tha e air seacadh, it is withered. *E.Ir.*
seccaim, secc. *W.* sych. *Lat.* siccus.
seacachd, shacachc, *n. f.* withered state
or condition of anything.
seacaich, shacich, *v.* wither, fade.
seach, shach, *n. m.* turn ; gach aon mu
seach, each in his turn, each alternately ; *adv. conj.* past, gone by, away,
aside ; rather than, rather than that ;
besides, beyond ; seach an dorus, past
the door ; cha téid e seach so, he
will not pass this ; seach aon eile,
rather than any one else ; do aon
seach aon, to the one more than to
another ; seach a chèile, one from
another ; fear seach fear, one man
more than another, neither ; in preference to ; seach e fhéin a mhilleadh, in
preference to spoiling himself ; chaidh
e mu seach orm, I missed it—it did
not occur to me ; cuir mu seach, lay
by, save. *O.Ir.* sech, *ultra, praeter.*
O.Celt. seqos, seqeso.
seachad, shachud, *adv.* aside, by, out of
the way ; along, onward, forward ;

a' dol seachad, passing by ; an latha
air dol seachad, the day is gone ;
cuir seachad so, lay this by ; seachad
oirnn, by us ; cuir seachad airgead,
hoard money ; beyond, more ; chan'eil
seachad air fichead ann, there is not
beyond twenty in it altogether—more
than twenty ; is math seachad e, it is
good to be done of it ; labhair 'san
dol seachad, speak, when passing.
seachainn, shachin, *v.* avoid, shun, keep
at distance from ; seachainn an t-olc,
avoid evil ; dispense with, spare ; an
seachainn thu so, can you spare, or
dispense with this ? mholainn duit
mise a sheachnadh, I would recommend to you, to keep at arm's-length
from me. *M.Ir.* sechnaim, avoid.
seachanta, shachantu, *adj.* to be avoided ;
latha seachanta, a disagreeable day.
M.Ir. sechanta, *vitandus.*
seachantach, *adj.* avoidable, guarded
against ; seachantach air òl, guarded
against drunkenness or debauchery.
seachantachd, *n. f.* avoidableness ; continual precaution to avoid.
seachd, shachc, *num. adj.* seven. *Cpds.*:
seachd-fillte, seven-fold ; seachd-thaobh-
ach, heptagon, heptagonal ; an t-
seachd-reultach, the pleiades ; seachd-
deug, seventeen ; seachd duine deug,
seventeen men ; seachd-fillte, seven-
fold ; seachdmhiosach, a seventh-
month child ; seachdshlisneach, *n. f.*
a heptagon. *O.Ir.* secht n-. *W.* seith
(saith). *Lat.* septem.
seachdainn, shachcan, *n. f.* a week ;
seachdainn bho 'n diugh, this day
week ; uair 'san t-seachdainn, once
a week ; -gus a nochd, this night last
week. *O.Ir.* sechtman ; fr. *Lat.*
septimana, the Christian week—the
heathen week (dechmad) had ten days.
seachdamh, shachcuv, *adj.* seventh.
seachdar, shachcur, seachdnar, shachcnar,
n. m. a band of seven persons.
seachlach, shachluch, *n. f.* cow that
calves only once in two years. *Also*
uairneach, a barren heifer of age to
have a calf. *O.Ir.* sechmall, *omissio.*
seachlaimh, shachlev, *a.* in store, savings.
seachnach, shachnuch, *adj.* shunning.
seachnadh, shachnu, *vbl. n. m.* act of
avoiding, shunning, sparing. *M.Ir.*
sechna.
seachran, shachran, *n. m.* wandering,
act of going astray ; air seachran,
going astray, getting out of the proper
path. *E.Ir.* sechrán.
seachranach, *adj.* wandering ; reultan
seachranach, wandering stars ; erring,
straying ; causing to err.
seadh, *adv. inter.* yes, yea ? just so, as

you say; **seadh gu dearbh**, just so, indeed ! =is + **ed**.

seagal, *n. m.* rye. *Lat.* secale.

seagh, *n. m.* sense, meaning, interpretation ; import, purport ; **seagh na lice** so, the purport of this tombstone ; **duine seaghail**, a manly man, a man of good sense ; a man who has the courage of his conviction. *M.Ir.* seg, strength. *Gaul.* sego-. Cf. *A.S.* sige. *O.N.* sigr. *O.H.G.* siga. *Ger.* sieg, victory.

seaghach, and **seaghail**, *a.* sagacious, sensible, important, weighty.

seaghachas, *n. m.* meaning, sense.

seaghal, *n. m.* the plug for draining-hole in a boat. *Also* tùc.

seal, shal, *n. m.* a while, glimpse, spot, time. *O.Ir.* sel, time; **sel . . . sel**, one time . . . another time.

sealan, *n. m.* short space of time.

sealbh, *n. m.* Providence ; " an ainm an t-sealbh," " for goodness sake," in the name of Providence.

sealbh, shaluv, *n. m.* possession ; good luck, good fortune, stock. *O.Ir.* selb (*f.*). *W.* helw. *O.Celt.* selvâ.

sealbhach, *adj.* prosperous, lucky.

sealbhachadh, *vbl. n. m.* act of possessing, enjoying, acquiring ; winning.

sealbhadair, shalvuder, *n. m.* possessor, supreme being — the possessor *par excellence.*

sealbhag, *n. f.* sorrel. *Also* samh.

sealbhaich, shalvich, *v.* possess, inherit.

sealbhaichte, shalvichtu, *vbl. a.* possessed, inherited.

sealbhan, *n. m.* a flock of small cattle.

sealbhanaich, shalvanich, *v.* throttle.

sealbhar, shalvur, *adj.* possessing, lucky.

sealg, shalg, *v. n.* hunt, lay wait for, stalk game ; *n. f.* a hunt, a chase. *Also* seilg. *O.Ir.* selg. *O.Celt.* selgâ. *O.W.* hel-a.

sealg, *n. f.* milt, spleen. *Also* meilg. *M.Ir.* selg.

sealgair, shalger, *n. m.* a hunter, a fowler, a sportsman.

sealgaireachd, *n.f.* hunting, stalking game.

sealghan, *n. m.* throat, gullet. *Also* **sealbhan**. *Dan.* svælg (throat). *O.N.* svelgja. *O.H.G.*, *A.S.* swëlgan, swallow.

seall, shaül, *v.* see, behold, look. *E.Ir.* sellaim, I look at ; (sell, the eye).

sealladh, shalu, *n. m.* vision, eyesight ; **chaill e a shealladh**, he lost his eyesight ; view, sight ; **fad mo sheallaidh**, the extent of my view ; spectacle, apparition ; **a leithid de shealladh**, such a spectacle.

seallam, shalum, *v.* I behold, let me see, let me show.

sealltainn, shaültin, *vbl. n. f.* act of seeing, viewing.

seal-mara, *n. m.* the tide (Arran).

sèam, seum, shem, *v.* entreat (to desist); enjoin, forbid ; an earnest petition.

seamadh, *vbl. n. m.* act of forbidding ; of hesitating. *Syn.* sòradh.

seama-guad, shemu-gooud, *n.m.* a quibble.

seamair, shemer, *n. f.* wild clover, shamrock ; **breac le seamair is neòineanan**, chequered with clover and daisies. *Also* seamrag. *E.Ir.* semar, trefoil.

seaman, sheman, *n. m.* a nail, a riveting nail ; a little stout man ; *a.* **seaman-ach**. *E.Ir.* seim, a rivet ; **seimnech**, well riveted ; whence **semend**, warrior.

seamanachd, *n. f.* jollity, inattentiveness.

seamarlan, *n. m.* a chamberlain, a factor on an estate ; fr. the *Eng.*

seamasan, shemusan, *n.m.* stupid evasion, a quibble, or quirk, shuffling, sham.

seamasanach, *a.* evasive, tricky, absurd in the extreme.

seamasanachd, *n. f.* evasiveness, habits of shuffling, or quirking, quibbling, shamming.

seamasanaich, shemusanich, *v.* sham, shuffle, evade, coax one out of his right ; **'gam sheamasanachadh air an doigh sin**, quibbling or shamming me in that style.

sèamh, shēv, *n. f.* an enchantment to make one's friend prosper.

sèamh, shēv, *a.* mild, peaceful, gentle. *See* séimh.

sèamhachd, shēvachc, *n. f.* quietness, calmness.

sèamhaich, shevich, *v.* calm, be quiet.

seamhas, shēvus, *n. m.* good luck, prosperity. *Also* seanns.

seamhsail, shevsal, *a.* lucky, fortunate.

seamhsalachd, *n. f.* luckiness.

seamlach, shemuluch, *n. f.* a cow that allows another cow's calf to suckle her ; one that gives milk without recent calving ; a dupe, silly person. *Also* gamhnach. *Sc.* shamloch.

seamlachas, shemuluchus, *n. m.* an imposture.

seamlaich, shemulich, *v.* dupe, impose on ; **'gam sheamlachadh-sa**, duping me, making a fool of me ; **chuir thu an orra-sheamlachais orm**, you charmed me out of my wits, you duped me.

seamrag, shemrag, *n.f.* the shamrock. *Ir.* seamróg. *M.Ir.* semrach. *E.Ir.* semar.

seamsan, *n. m.* a sham, a quibble (to gain time or ends), silly evasion, hesitation.

sean, seann, shen, *adj.* old, aged, ancient ; **an seann sruthan sin**, that ancient stream ; **o shean**, anciently, of old. *O.Ir.* sen, *compar.* siniu. *O.W.* hên. *Lat.* senex. *Gr.* ἕνος. *O.Celt.* seno-s.

sèan, *n. m.* a charm. *See* seun. *E.Ir.* sén, prosperity. *Lat.* signum.

seanacharrach, shen'-uch-ur-uch, *a.* old-fashioned.

seanachd, shen'-achc, *n. f.* oldness.

seana-chrìonta, *a.* old-fashioned, too wise for one's years.

seanadh, shèn'-u, *n. m.* a synod, senate. *E.Ir.* senod. *Lat.* synodus.

seanagar, shenugur, *a.* knowing, old-fashioned.

seanagarrachd, *n. f.* sagacity.

seanaghille, shenu-yilu, *n. m.* bachelor.

seanair, shen'-er, *n. m.* grandfather, senator, elder ; a sheanairean glic, his wise senators. *O.Ir.* sen-athir, *avus* ; but senóir, *senior.* *W.* hen-wr.

seanaireachd, shen-er-uchc, *n. f.* eldership, presbytery. *E.Ir.* senóire, senóraigh (*nom. pl.*), the ancients.

seanailear, shenuler, *n. m.* a general ; fr. the *Eng.*

sean-aois, shen-ūsh, *n. f.* old age.

seanchaidh, shenuchy, *n. m.* reciter of tales ; recorder ; bha e 'na sheanchaidh, he was a recorder, a historian. *E.Ir.* sencha, an antiquary.

seanchant, *a.* newsy, reminiscent.

seanchas, shen'-uch-us, *n. m.* a tale, saga ; tradition ; conversation, or talk of old stories, or ancient history ; history, ancient history or biography. *O.Ir.* senchas, vetus historia, lex. *Z²*. *W.* hanes. *O.Celt.* seno-kastu-, *historia.*

seanchasach, *a.* conversible, having tales ; traditionary ; relating tales.

seanfhacal, shen-acul, *n. m.* proverb, adage, byword.

seanfhaclach, *a.* proverbial.

seang, sheng, *adj.* slim, slender ; a choin sheang, his slim dogs ; hungry-looking. *E.Ir.* seng, slender. *O.Celt.* svengo-s. *O.N.* svangr, slim. *M.H.G.* swanc, slender, pliant.

seangachd, *n. f.* slenderness.

seangaich, shèng'-ich, *v.* get slender, or lank.

seangan, sheng'-an, *n. m.* pismire, ant, emmet ; an seangan beag, the little pismire, emmet, or ant. *Ir.* sengán, the " slim little one."

seangarra, shéng'-urr-u, *adj.* withered in person.

seanghir, shéng'-ir, *n. m.* child in old age.

seangmhear, *a.* lithe and mettlesome, charger ; seang + mear ; " is gur lìonmhor each seangmhear," and full many a charger.

seanmhair, shenuver, *n. f.* grandmother. *O.Ir.* sen-máthir *avia.*

seanns, *n. m.* luck, chance. *See* seamhas ; fr. the *Eng.*

seannsail, *a.* lucky, prosperous.

seannsgeul, shauscel, *n. m.* legend.

seannsgeulach, *a.* legendary.

seannta, shiūntu, *a.* oldish.

seanntachadh, *m.* grown ancient.

seanntachd, *n. f.* agedness, oldness, aged appearance. *E.Ir.* séndacht, séntatu, old age. *See sub* naoidheanachd.

seanntaidh, shaünty, *a.* oldish, aged.

seanntaidheachd, *n.f.* agedness, oldishness.

seanntalamh, shaun-taluv, *n. m.* waste land, new land.

Seann-Tiomnadh, *n. m.* the Old Testament.

seann-todhar, *n. m.* an old manured field.

seanntur, *n. m.* old acquaintance ; frequenter.

sèap, shiäp, *v.* slink, sneak away, drag off, stealth ; shèap e air falbh, he slank off ; *n. m.* a tail (hanging down) ; skulking or sneaking out of battle ; a " turn tail."

sèapach, *adj.* slinking, sly.

sèapaire, shiäpiru, *n. m.* a sly, sneaking fellow ; a poltroon, deserter, " hangtail."

sèapaireachd, *n. f.* slinking.

sear, sher, *n. m.* the east. *See* soir, ear.

sèarach, shèruch, *n. m.* six-month-old beast (horse).

sèaramhach, shiä-ravuch, *adj.* six-oared ; *n. f.* a six-oared galley, a felucca.

searbaid, sharbej, *n. m.* boat-thwart, tota.

searbh, sharv, *adj.* sour, tart, bitter ; disagreeable, disgusting ; gnothach searbh, a disagreeable business ; tha mi searbh dheth, I am disgusted with it. *O.Ir.* serb. *W.* chwerw. *O.Celt.* svervo-s.

searbhachd, *n. f.* bitterness.

searbhadair, *n. m.* a towel. Cf. *Lat.* servio. *Sc.* serviter.

searbhadas, sharvudus, *n. m.* bitterness, disgust, dislike.

searbhag, sharvag, *n. f.* refuse of liquids, acid, satire.

searbhant, sharvant, *n. f.* servant-maid, fr. the *Eng.*

searbhantachd, *n. f.* service, office of a maid ; better, muinntireas.

searbhdaich, sharvudich, *v.* embitter ; disgust, tease ; shearbhdaich e mi, he teased or disgusted me. *O.Ir.* serbigim.

searbh-ghlòir, *n. f.* wearisome clattering ; vain boasting.

seardair, *n. m.* a drudge ; a' brath seardair a dheanamh dhiom, meaning to make me his slave or drudge.

searg, sharug, *v.* wither, decay, fade, shrivel ; pine away ; shearg na lusan, the flowers or herbs faded ; *n. m.* a shrivelled or decayed person. *O.Ir.* sercim, sergaim, wither, decay ; serg, illness.

seargach, *a.* evanescent, fading.

seargadh, sharugu ; *vbl. n. m.* act of fading ; pining.

seargaire, sharugiru, *n. m.* pining person.

seargte, sharugtu, *vbl. a.* withered, faded.

searmon, sharumon, *n. m.* a sermon, discourse, lecture, pleading. *M.Ir.* sermon. *Lat.* sermo.

searmonaich, *v.* preach, lecture, discourse ; deliver a discourse.

searmonaiche, sharunmonichu, *n. m.* preacher.

searr, *v. intr.* stretch oneself (after sleep).

seàrr, shār, *n. m.* a shearing-hook, sickle. *Also* corran ; *v.* reap, cut, hash. *E.Ir.* serr, a scythe, a sickle.

searrach, sharuch, *n. m.* foal, colt. *E.Ir.* serrach.

searradh, *n. m.* act of stretching oneself (after sleep or from tediousness).

searrag, shyarr'-ag, *n. m.* a bottle = *Eng.* jar. *McB.*

searrag, *n. f.* a long stride ; thug e na searragan as, he sped with strides ; fichead troigh searrag an fhéidh, twenty feet the deer's stride.

searraigh, shary, *n. f.* colewort.

seàrs, *v.* charge, load (gun) ; fr. the *Eng.*

searsanach, seirseanach, *n. m.* sheriff officer, estate overseer. *Eng.* serjeant.

seas, shes, *v.* stand, stop ; maintain, endure, support ; có a sheasas tu, who shall support you ? seas an còir, maintain their rights. *O.Ir.* sessim ; -issem, in tairissem = to - air - sessam. *Thn.*

seasaireachd, shesiruchc, *n. f.* penance in church.

seasamh, shesuv, *n. m.* standing posture ; tha e 'na sheasamh, he is standing ; tha i 'na seasamh, she is standing ; enduring, maintaining, etc. *E.Ir.* sessom, sessam, standing.

seasdar, *n. m.* rest, repose ; pallet, pillow.

seasg, shesc, *adj.* barren, unprolific, dry ; without milk. *O.Ir.* sesc, dry (cow). *W.* hysp. *O.Celt.* sisqo-s.

seasg, *n. m.* sedge, watersedge ; a' buain seasg, cutting sedge. *E.Ir.* sesc.

seasgach, *n. m.* farrow cattle.

seasgair, *a.* sheltered, comfortable.

seasgaire, shesciru, *n. m.* a coddled fellow; lazy person.

seasgaireachd, *n. f.* indulgence in ease ; quietness, peace.

seasgan, *n. m.* handful of corn, shock or truss of corn, gleaned land.

seasganach, *n. m.* a bachelor.

seasgann, *n. m.* a fenny country, marsh. *E.Ir.* sescenn. *Ir.* seisg, sedge.

seasgar, shescur, *adj.* quiet, comfortable,

at ease, as weather, settled ; bi seasgar, be quiet ; fan seasgar, keep quiet ; àite seasgair, a sheltered place.

seasghrian, *n. m.* the solstice.

seasglach, shescluch, *n. f.* a barren cow.

seasmhach, shesvach, *a.* steady, settled. *Also* written seasach.

seasmhachd, *n. f.* firmness, settled state, as of weather ; stability, steadiness.

seasrach, shesruch, *a.* sturdy, good staying quality.

sèathamh, shiä-uv, *adj.* the sixth.

sèathnar, siänar, *coll. n.* six persons (together).

seic, *n. f.* a rack, a manger.

seic, sheck, *n. f.* sack made of straw-rope. *A.S.* sæcc. *O.H.G.* sac. *O.N.* sekkr. *Goth.* sakkus ; through *Lat.* saccus. *Gr.* σάκκος, fr. *Hebr.* and *Phoen.* sak. *Kl.* ; sak (in *Hebr.*) means what is knotted together, coarsely woven.

séic, téic, *n. f.* the flyer of a spinning-wheel.

seic, *n. f.* skin, hide, peritoneum, brain pellicle.

seiceal, shecul, *n. f.* heckle (for flax).

seiceil, sheycel, *v.* dress flax ; beat or scold lustily.

seich, *n. f.* profit ; used in phrase, cha seich dhuit, not worth the candle.

seiche, sheychu, *n. f.* a hide ; a skin. *E.Ir.* seche. Cf. *O.N.* sigg, *callus,* hard skin.

seicheadair, sheychuder, *n. m.* a currier, skinner.

seichearnach, sheychurnuch, *n. f.* tanwork.

seiclear, sheycler, *n. m.* flax-dresser.

séid, sēj, *n. f.* plethora, tympany, swelling in a person from luxurious living and deep potations ; *v.* blow, become a storm ; shéid e, is shéid e, it blew and it blew, it blew into a hurricane ; instigate, prompt to evil, puff ; is tusa a tha 'ga shéideadh, it is you that instigate him ; breathe. *E.Ir.* sétim. *W.* chwythaf.

seid, *n. f.* a complete bellyful, surfeit ; fhuair e a sheid, he got his bellyful.

seid, *n. f.* a truss of hay ; pallet, a bed spread on the floor ; 'na laighe air seid, sleeping, or lounging on a pallet.

séideadh, shēju, *vbl. n. m.* act of blowing, puffing ; a storm. *E.Ir.* sétiud, blowing.

séideag, shējag, *n. f.* a little puff, a little blow (of breath) ; slight inebriation.

sèidhir, sheyr, *n. f.* a chair ; cha bhi sèithir aig Domhnall, Donald has never a chair. *McCod.*

sèidire, shējiru, *n. m.* a swell, puffed fellow.

sèidrich, shējrich, *n. f.* hissing of serpents, etc.

sèidte, shējtu, *vbl. a.* blown, puffed.

seilbh, sheluv, *n. f.* possession, stock (on farm) ; a beast or living creature in possession ; gach seilbh a th' agam, every living creature I possess ; fhuair e seilbh, he has got possession ; fadseilbh, infeoffment. *See* sealbh. *E.Ir.* selb, possession.

seilch, *n. f.* water monster, supposed to inhabit certain lochs. *Ir.* seilighide. *Lh.*

seilcheag, shelchag, *n. f.* snail, slug.

seile, shelu, *n. f.* spittle ; glaise-sheile, water-brash. *E.Ir.* sele. *O.Ir.* saile. *W.* haliw. *Lat.* saliva. *O.Celt.* salivâ.

seile, *n. f.* placenta, after-birth of a hind. *Carm. Gad.*

seileach, *n. m.* the willow. *E.Ir.* sail, *gen.* sailech. *W.* helyg (*pl.*), willows. *Lat.* salix.

séileann, *n. m.* sheep-louse, tick.

seilear, sheler, *n. m.* a cellar ; seilear làir, a vault ; seilear-dibhe, spirit-cellar ; fr. the *Eng.*

seileastar, shelustur, *n. m.* yellow waterflag, yellow iris. *Ir.* soiliostar, flags. *Lh. M.Ir.* ailestar, an iris. *KM.*

seilg, shelig, *n. f.* what is hunted or killed ; *dat.-acc.* of sealg, a hunt, chase.

seillean, shelen, *n. m.* a heath-bee ; a teasing repetition or request. *Also* teillean, tilleag, tainnleag.

seilleanach, *adj.* teasing, in request, importunate ; full of bees.

sèim, *n. f.* a squint.

sèimh, shēv, *a.* mild, gentle, calm, placid ; na 's sèimhe, milder, more placid. *O.Ir.* séim, thin, mild, *exile. O.Celt.* s(p)eimis.

sèimheachd, shēv'-achc, *n. f.* mildness, placidity, gentleness, calmness, docility, good temper.

sèimheanachd, shēvenuchc, *n. f.* indulgence in ease, chambering, effeminate conduct.

sèimhich, shēvich, *v.* become calm, or gentle ; abate as a storm, soothe.

sèimhidh, *a.* mild, calm.

seing, *n. f.* game ; a roebuck ; " gun seing gun sithinn," without game, without venison. *Also* seang. *Carm. Gad.*

seinilear. *See* siomlair, chimney.

seinn, sheyn, *v.* ring, sound ; seinn an clag, ring the bell ; sing, chant, warble ; na h-eòin a' seinn, the birds warbling ; play upon a musical instrument ; sheinn e an fhiodhull, he played upon the violin ; report, propagate a story ; air a sheinn feadh na dùthcha, reported ding - dang through the country ; *vbl. n. m.* singing, art of singing or playing on an instrument, melody, church music. *O.Ir.* sennim, play an instrument ; *n.* senim, senm, a sound.

seipeil, *n. m.* a chapel. *M.Ir.* sépél ; fr. the *Eng.* ; fr. *O.F.* chapele. *L.L.* cappella (cappa), a cloak.

seipinn, shepin, *n. f.* choppin, quart. *Also* seipean ; fr. the *Eng.*

seirbhe, shervu, *deg.* of searbh, more tart or disagreeable ; *n. f.* tartness, bitterness. *Also* seirbhead.

seirbheachd, *n. f.* bitterness, tartness, disagreeableness ; discordance.

seirbhis, shervesh, *n. f.* service, hire, work ; fr. the *Eng.*

seirbhiseach, *n. m.* a servant.

seirbhisich, sherveshich, *v.* serve, attend upon.

seirc, sherc, *n. f.* affection, kindness, love ; ball-seirc, *n. m.* a beauty-spot (winning love). *O.Ir.* serc, love. *W.* serch. *O.Celt.* serkâ, serko-, love.

seircealachd, shercaluchc, *n. f.* kindliness, loveliness, charitableness.

seircean, *n. m.* a burdock.

seirceil, shercal, *a.* affectionate, kind.

seircin, *n. m.* a beloved man.

seircire, sherciru, *n. m.* kindly person.

seirge, *n. f.* decline, witheredness.

seirgean, seirgleach, *n. m.* a withered person.

seirgneach, shergnuch, *n. m.* skeleton.

seirm, sherm, *n. f.* tune, tone ; sound (the bell), tune of church-music ; trim ; cuir air seirm, attune, tune, trim ; a bheil a' chlarsach air seirm, is the harp in tune ? Cf. *O.Ir.* seinm, playing on an instrument ; senim, sound. Occasionally n becomes r.

seirmeil, *a.* in trim, tuned, attuned ; in a business-like manner.

seirsealach, *n. m.* robust. *Ir.* séirsean, robust, sturdy person. *O'R.*

séis, *n. f.* intonation, air, a chanting ; the humming of insects. Cf. *E.Ir.* séssilbe, a chant.

séis, *n. f.* a lounge. *E.Ir.* sess, a bench ; sess ethar, bench of a boat. *Corm. O.Celt.* sed. *O.N.* sess, a seat.

seis, *n. m.* pleasure, anything pleasing to the senses ; a companion. *Ir.* seis.

séisd, shēshj, *v.* besiege ; *n. m.* a siege ; séisde Dhoire, the siege of Londonderry. *Eng.* siege ; ult. fr. *Lat.* sedes.

séisdeadh, shēshju, *vbl. n. m.* act of besieging.

séisdeil, shēshjal, *a.* pleasing to the senses.

seise, shēshu, *n. m.* a match or equal in strength or valour ; tha do sheise an taice riut, you have your match in valour in contact with you ; barrachd 's a sheise, more than his match. Cf. *O.N.* sessi, bench - mate ; fr. sessa, ship's seat. *McB.*

séiseach, *n. f.* a sofa.

seisean, *n. m.* a session, season. *Lat.* sessio.

seisear, sheshur, *n. f.* six persons. *O.Ir.* seser.

seisich, shēishich, *v.* satisfy. *Also* sàthaich.

seisneil, sheshnal, *a.* pleasing, charming.

seisreach, sheshruch, *n. f.* a plough, six-horse plough, a team of horses in a plough. *See* seisear. *E.Ir.* sesrech, a plough team ; a plough-land. *Curry.*

séitreach, *a.* blowing, puffing.

seobhag, shyo'-ag, *n. f.* (*masc.* in some places), a hawk. *See* seabhag.

seoc, shock, *n. f.* plume of a helmet ; veil. *Also* seòcan.

seocail, shockal, *adj.* portly and tall, having the port or gait of a gentleman or lady.

seocair, shocker, *n. f.* portly fellow.

seocalachd, *n. f.* portliness and tallness.

seochlan, *n. m.* a feeble, staggering person ; *a.* seochlanach. *Sc.* shochlin', waddling.

seòd, shōd, *n. m., gen. s.* and *n. pl.* seòid, a hero. *Also* siad. *See* seud.

seòg, *v.* swing to and fro.

seòl, shōl, *v.* direct, guide ; seòl e, direct or guide him ; method, expedient, manner, way ; air sheòl eile, by another method ; tha e air a sheòl, he has things to his mind ; seòl-labhairt, mode of speech, idiom. *E.Ir.* seól, course. *W.* hwyl.

seòl, *n. m., gen. s.* and *n. pl.* siùil, a sail. *Cpds.* : seòl-toisich, foresail ; seòl-meadhoin, seol-mór, mainsail ; seòl-mullaich, top-gallant.

seòl, *v.* sail. *O.Ir.* seól, *gen. s.* siùil.

seòladair, sholuder, *n. m.* sailor, seaman ; seòldair is very common form.

seòladaireachd, *n. f.* navigation, sailing, navigating, seafaring life.

seòladh, shòl'-u, *vbl. n. m.* act of sailing, navigating. directing, guiding ; 'gam sheòladh, directing or leading me.

seòlaid, *n. f.* a harbour, anchorage, pier.

seòlann. *See* mial.

seòllann. *See* uamhag.

seòl-mara, shôl'-mar-u, *n. m.* a tide, tide-period (six hours) ; *gen.* siùilmhara.

seòlta, shòltu, *adj.* ingenious, wise, prudent ; gu seòlta, ingeniously, wisely, prudent.

seòltachd, shòltachc, *n. f.* ingenuity, skill.

seòmar, shōmur, *n. m., pl.* seòmraichean,

apartment, a room, chamber ; seòmar-cùil, back-room ; seòmar-cadail, bed-room ; seòmar - biadhtachd, guest- or dining-room ; seòmar-suidhe, sitting-room, parlour ; seòmar - gnothaich, business-room, office ; seòmar-clainne, nursery. *M.Ir.* seómra ; fr. *Eng.*

seòmradaireachd, *n. f.* rakishness.

seonaidh, shony, *n. m.* a Lewis deity (a conjecture of Martin's).

seòrach, *n. f.* the primrose. *Ir.* sorig. *O'R.*

seòrsa, shōrsu, *n. m.* kind, sort, species.

seòrsaich, shorsich, *v.* sort, classify.

seot, shot, *v.* sprout, as greens ; pick the best ; thrust ; sheot an càl, the greens sprouted.

seot, *n. m.* a short tail, stump ; sheep or lambs of little worth ; the worst beast ; a sprout ; na seotaichean, the worst beasts. *Sc.* shot, rejected sheep. Cf. *O.N.* skott, (fox's) tail. *Eng.* scut.

seotach, *a.* dull, lazy, indolent.

seotaiche, *n. f.* indolence, sloth, laziness.

seotaire, *n. m.* a lazy fellow.

sèramhach, *n. f.* six-oared boat.

sèshlisneach, siä-hlishniuch, sè-thaobh-ach, siä-hüvuch, *a.* hexagonal ; *n. f.* hexagon.

seth (gu seth), *adv.* severally, oft. *neg.* neither.

seub, *v. tr.* let the wind into the back of the sail.

seud, sēd, *n. m.* a jewel, a treasure ; a hero ; idiomatic use : chan 'eil seud mhaith air, it is not worth anything ; gach seud a tha agam, everything I have ; cha bhi seud ort, nothing will be wrong with you. Cf. sim. use of maoin. *O.Ir.* sét, *pl.* séuit, later séotu, a precious thing.

seudachan, *n. m.* a jewel-box.

seudaich, shēdich, *v.* adorn, garnish.

seudaire, sēdiru, *n. m.* jeweller.

seudraidh, *coll. n.* jewelry, a collection of precious things.

seul, sēl, *n. m.* a seal for marking ; *v.* seal. *Also* saoil. *Lat.* sigillum. *M.Ir.* séla.

seum, siam, shèm, *n. f.* an earnest entreaty or injunction ; an earnest petition ; is ioma seum a thug mise air, many an earnest injunction I gave him.

seumadair, siamadair, shēmuder, *n. m.* a petitioner.

seumaich, siamaich, shèm'-ich, *v. i.* entreat, petition earnestly ; charge, enjoin solemnly.

seumalair, shēmuler, *n. m.* chamberlain. *Also* siamarlan.

seun, shen, *n. m.* a charm ; an amulet to render a warrior invulnerable. *Also*

sian. *E.Ir.* sén, blessing, sign. *O.Ir.*
sén. *Lat.* signum (=sign of the
Cross).
seun, *v.* shun, refuse ; cha ghabh mi
seunadh no àicheadh, I will not be
either refused or denied. *O.Ir.* sénaim,
deny, refuse.
seunadair, shênuder, *n. m.* charmer.
seunadh, shênu, *vbl. n. m.* act of refusing ;
refusal.
seunan, sianan, *n. m.* spot, mark ;
breaca-sianain, freckles.
seunas, shèn'-us, *n. m.* beauty-teeth.
seurs, shêrs, *v.* charge, brandish.
seusar, shês'-ur, *n. m.* acme, perfection,
height, or utmost point ; ann an
seusar na cluiche, in the heart-middle
of the game.
seusrach, shêsruch, *adj.* mettlesome, as
a horse ; in high condition.
sgab, *n. f.* the scab, itch ; *a.* sgabach.
Also claimh.
sgab, *v.* to scatter. So *Ir. Lh. See*
sgap.
sgabag, *n. f.* cow killed for winter.
sgabaiste, scabeshtu, *n. f.* anything
pounded or bashed.
sgaball, skab'-all, *n. f.* a helmet, a hood.
So *Ir.*
sgàbard, *n. m.* sheath, scabbard ; fr. the
Eng.
sgabh, *n. m.* sawdust. *Ir.* scabh. *Lat.*
scobis, cuttings, sawdust.
sgad, *n. m.* loss ; mishap, misfortune.
Cf. *O.N.* skaði, scathe. *O.H.G.* skado.
sgadan, *n. m.* a herring. *E.Ir.* scatán.
sgadarlach, sgadarluch, *n. m.* anything
scattered ; fr. the *Eng.*
sgafaire, sgaferu, *n. m.* scolding man ;
bold, hearty man.
sgafart, skaff'-art, *n. f.* a scolding female.
sgafall, skaff'-all, *n. m.* scaffolding. *Ir.*
scafal. *Lh.* Fr. the *Eng.*
sgafanta, skaff'-annt-u, *a.* vigorous,
lively, vehement in speech, venomous
in scolding ; emphatically speaking.
Ir. scafánta, spirited, hearty.
sgafantachd, skaff'-annt-uchc, *n. f.* liveliness ; vehemence of speech ; the
quality of scolding keenly.
sgafarra, *a.* spirited, brave, handsome.
sgag, *v.* chink, chop, crack ; winnow,
filter. *Ir.* sgagam, cleanse, winnow.
sgagach, *adj.* chinked, cracked.
sgagaidh, scagy, *a.* unsavoury, sour, as
fish beginning to turn sour ; scait
sgagaidh, a sour or " high " skate.
sgagaire, *n. m.* a strainer ; a poltroon,
great coward ; one that chinks at the
slightest appearance of danger.
sgagaireachd, scagiruchc, *n. f.* cowardice ;
unfounded fear.
sgaift, scaft, *v.* burst in consequence

of eating too much ; *n. f.* a notorious
bellyful.
sgàig, *n. f.* horror, disgust ; shrinking
feeling.
sgàil, scāl, *a.* cover, veil, sprinkle ;
approach, near ; cha sgàil so air, this
will not come near the thing ; cha
dèan e sgàile air, it will not come near
it ; *n. m.* a cover, shade ; fo sgàil do
sgéith, under the shadow of thy wing.
M.Ir. scáil, shadow. *O.Celt.* skâlî,
shade, shadow.
sgàileadh, scālu, *vbl. n. m.* a sprinkling ;
sgàileadh as lugha, the least sprinkling
or shade.
sgailc, *n. f.* baldness, a bald pate. *See*
sgall.
sgailc, scelc, *n. f.* a resounding blow or
pelt ; a slap, skelp ; *v.* pelt, beat in
a masterly manner. *O.H.G.* scal,
loud sound, whence *Ger.* schallen.
O.N. skjalla, to rattle.
sgailcire, scelciru, *n. m.* a bald-headed
man.
sgailceanta, scelcantu, *a.* smart in giving
blows.
sgailc, *n. f.* a full glass, a dram.
sgailc-sheide, *n. f.* a dram in bed before
rising.
sgàileach, scāluch, *n. f.* a veil, curtain.
sgàileachd, *n. f.* sprinkling, a shading,
a shadowing.
sgàileagan, scālagun, *n. m.* a shade, an
umbrella. *Ir.* scáilean, a fan, umbrella.
sgàileanach, scālenuch, *a.* full of shades.
sgàile-ruidil, scalu-roojil, *n. f.* a sieve.
sgàilleag, scelyag, *n. f.* smart slap on
the cheek.
sgailleagan, sceliugan, *n. m.* squashed
mass ; chaidh an t-ubh 'n a sgailleagan,
the egg was squashed.
sgàin, sgàinn, scā-in, *v.* crack, burst,
burst asunder, cause to burst ; sgàinn
e, he burst asunder. *Ir.* scàinim, I
burst.
sgainneal. *See* sgannal.
sgainneart, sca-niart, *n. f.* 1. dispersion,
scattering. 2. contest, trial of strength.
sgainnir, sca-nir, *v.* stroll, scatter. *Ir.*
scainnear, sudden irruption, unexpected
attack.
sgàinte, *vbl. a.* burst, cracked.
sgàinteach, scāntuch, *n. f.* corroding
pain ; rheumatism.
sgàinteachail, *a.* painful ; rheumatic.
sgaipean, *n. m.* a ninny, a dwarf.
sgair, sgar, *n. f.* a seam, a stitch, a
splice. *O.N.* skör, the joints in a
ship's planking.
sgàird, scārj, *n. f.* flux ; diarrhœa. *Ir.*
scáird, a squirt, flux.
sgàirdean, scārden, *n. m.* a trifling fellow.
sgaireach, sgar-uch, *a.* cold, somewhat

windy, and threatening rain (as weather) ; checked (of colour).

sgaireach, *n. m.* a prodigal. *Ir.* sgairioch.

sgàireag, sgārag, one - year - old gull, young scart. *O.N.* skári, a young seamew.

sgaireap, *n. f.* weather with whistling wind, threatening rain ; a sudden squeal, as bagpipes.

sgaireapail, *adj.* whistling, gusty, and threatening rain, as weather.

sgàirn, scārn, *n.f.* noise of stones, howling of dogs.

sgàirneach, *n. f.* a deserted quarry ; a great number of stones like an old quarry on a hill. So *Ir.* *Also* dial. sgarmach. *McB.*

sgàirseach, *n. f.* a downpour ; a torrent of abuse, a severe whacking.

sgairseach, *n. f.* a feat, a smart action.

sgairt, scarst, *n. f.* energy, business appearance, authority; a smart breeze ; dèan do gnothach le sgairt, do your business with energy ; le sgairt de ghaoth tuath, with a smart breeze of northerly wind.

sgairt, scarst, *n. f.* a loud cry. So *Ir.*

sgairt, *n. f.* variously applied, as midriff ; diaphragm; the pericardium; tha a sgairt briste, he has rupture.

sgairteachd, *n. f.* crying aloud, roaring. So *Ir.*

sgairtealachd, scarstaluchc, *n. f.* liveliness, vigorousness ; half-stormy weather.

sgairte-falaich, *n. f.* a cleft, or cave in which to hide. *Carm. Gad.*

sgairteil, scarstal, *adj.* energetic ; clever, active ; duine sgairteil, an energetic person ; breezy ; an latha sgairteil, the blowy day.

sgait, *n. f.* a skate ; fr. the *Eng. O.N.* skata ("*passim* in mod. usage").

sgaiteach, scatiuch, *adj.* keen ; energetic, sarcastic, or cutting in words. *See* sgath.

sgaiteachd, *n. f.* sharpness.

sgaithte, scatiu, *vbl. a.* lopped off ; pruned.

sgal, *n.f.* sudden, quick cry; a howl, shriek, yell ; sgal gàire, a burst of laughter ; *v.* shriek suddenly, cry suddenly ; squeal. *O.N.* skjalla, clash, clatter. Cf. skelli-hlátr, roaring laughter.

sgal, *n. f.* a good slap ; whack.

sgalach, *adj.* shrill and sharp.

sgalag, *n. m.* a man-servant, a farm servant. *Ir.* sgalóg. *E.Ir.* scolóc, *pl.* scoloca, *servi* and *servae*. *Z²*. Cf. *O.N.* skálkr, a servant. *Goth.* skalks, servant, menial. *Feist* says etym. uncertain ; Celtic orig. not excluded though improb.

sgàlaiche, *n. m.* semblance, competency, ability. *See* sgàil. "ged nach sgàl-

aiche bàird mi," though I am not the semblance of a bard ; a man ready to malign his neighbour.

sgalais, sgăl'-esh, *n. f.* jeering, gibing, continuous jeering.

sgàlain, *n. m.* scales of a balance. *O.N.* skál, scale of a balance.

sgàlan, *n. m.* a hut, shieling ; scaffold. *Ir.* scálán. *O.N.* skáli, hut, shed.

sgalanta, *a.* given to shrieking, yelling.

sgalartaich, sgăl'-art-ich, *n. f.* yelling, or sharp howling. *Also* sgalathartaich.

sgàldach, *a.* scalding.

sgàldadh, *vbl. n. m.* act of burning ; trom sgàldadh, painful affliction, bereavement ; fr. the *Eng.* scald.

sgalgail, *n. f.* howling (of whipped dogs).

sgall, scaül, *v.* scald ; gall, pain ; fr. the *Eng.* scald.

sgall, *n. m.* baldness, bald head. *O.N.* skalli, bald head.

sgalla, *n. f.* an old hat.

sgalla, *n. f.* large wooden dish cut out of a tree.

sgallach, scaluch, *a.* bald ; full of bald spots.

sgallaidh, scăly, *n. f.* the bare rock. Cf. *O.N.* skalli, bald head.

sgallais, scalesh, *n. f.* insult, mockery, loud speaking. So *Ir. O.N.* skjalla, talk loud, swagger.

sgamal, *n. f.* scale, *squama. Lat.* squamula.

sgamh, scav, *n. m.* dross, dust. *See* sgabh.

sgamhainn, sgavin, *v.* build corn ; *syn.* dais an t-arbhar : *n.* a rick of corn.

sgamhan, sgáv'-an, *n. m.* a lung, lights. *M.Ir.* scaman. *W.* ysgyfaint.

sgamhanach, sgav'-an-uch, *adj.* roan, drab, having the colour of lights ; aodach sgamhanach, roan - coloured cloth.

sgamhanaich, sgav'-an-ich, *n. f.* break of day, grey of the morning. *Also* cabhanaich.

sgann, *n. f.* swarm, multitude, drove.

sgann, *n. f.* membrane. *Also* sgannan. So *Ir.* Cf. *O.N.* skán, thin membrane.

sgannal, *n. f.* scandal, calumny. *M.Ir.* scandal. *Lat.* scandalum. *Gr.* σκάνδαλον.

sgannalach, *adj.* scandalous.

sganr, skàrr, *v.* scare ; scatter, as cattle, geese, etc.

sgànradh, skàrr-u, *vbl. n. m.* dispersing, scattering, frightening cattle ; act of dispersion. *M.Ir.* scainnred, a scattering.

sgànraich, *v.* scatter, scare. *M.Ir.* scandraim, I scatter.

sgaog, *n. f.* foolish, giddy female. *Also* sgaothag.

sgaoil, scûl, *v.* spread ; extend, stretch ; dismiss, send away ; sgaoil e an sgoil,

he dismissed the school; expand,
distend, widen, loosen, unite ; **sgaoil
an stocainn**, unravel the stocking ;
divulge, reveal ; **sgaoil e an naidheachd,** he divulged the secret ; *n. m.*
liberty, freedom ; **mu sgaoil,** at liberty.
E.Ir. **scáilim,** spread, scatter. *W.*
chwalu.
sgaoileadh, scūlu, *vbl. n. m.* act of spreading, untying, dismissing ; dispersion,
dismission.
sgaoilte, scūltiu, *vbl. a.* unravelled, dismissed, scattered, spread.
sgaoilteach, scūltiuch, *adj.* widespread,
scattered ; unguarded, imprudent,
loose ; **cainnt sgaoilteach,** imprudent
or unguarded expressions. *Also* as *n. f.*
sgaoilteachd, *n. f.* scattered state.
sgaoim, scūm, *n. f.* terror from false
alarm ; skittishness, as a horse, or a
beast. So *Ir.*
sgaoimealachd, scūmaluchc, *n. f.* terror ;
aptness to take alarm.
sgaoimeil, scūmal, *adj.* skittish, timid,
fearful.
sgaoimireachd, *n. f.* restlessness.
sgaomaire, scūmiru, *n. m.* coward.
sgaorr, *n. m.* very great crowd ; swarm.
sgaoth, scū, *n. m.* a swarm ; great
number. *Ir.* **scaoth.**
sgap, *v.* scatter ; hash, hack ; **a' sgapadh
càise,** hacking down cheese ; distribute
profusely, disperse. *Also* **sgab.** *M.Ir.*
scaipim, scatter.
sgapadair, scapuder, *n. m.* scatterer,
hasher.
sgapadh, scap-u, *vbl. n. m.* act of scattering ; hacking, hashing.
sgar, *v.* separate or disjoin by force
or violence. *O.Ir.* **scaraim.** *W.* ysgar,
to separate. *O.Celt.* skaraô.
sgar, *n. f.* seam, or joint, as in a boat ;
tàirnean-sgair, seaming nails, knot on
the surface of wood. *O.N.* skör, *gen.*
skarar (fr. skara, to clinch), joint in
boat planking.
sgarach, *a.* separating asunder ; apt to
separate.
sgarachdainn, scar-achc-in, *vbl. n. f.*
separating, tearing asunder ; act of
separation by force.
sgaradh, scar-u, *vbl. n. m.* act of tearing
from an object of affection ; ruin,
separation ; **mo sgaradh,** my ruin.
O.Ir. **scaraim,** I separate.
sgarbh, scarv, *n. m.* a cormorant.
a scart. *O.N.* skarfr, a scart.
sgarbhnach, *a.* place where cormorants
congregate.
sgàrlaid, scārl'-ej, *n. f.* scarlet. *M.Ir.*
scarloit.
sgàrnach, *n. f.* mass of boulders and
broken stones on a slope ; scree.

sgarrthach, *n. f.* a blast of foul weather.
Also **rotach.**
sgartach, *n. m.* a set of ragamuffins.
sgarthanaich, scar'-han-ich, *n. f.* dawn,
grey of the morning ; twilight.
sgat, *n. m.* a skate. *See* **sgait.** So *Ir.*
sgàth, scā, *n. m.* shelter ; **sgàth an tighe,**
shelter of the house ; slight fear, or
dread ; shade, protection ; **tha sgàth
orm,** I feel somewhat afraid ; **fo sgàth
do sgéith,** under the covert of thy
wing ; account, sake ; **air sgàth
sgoinne,** for decency's sake ; **na dh'
fhuiling e air mo sgàth-sa,** what he
suffered on my account. *O.Ir.* **scáth,**
shade. *M.W.* **isgaud.** *O.Celt.* skâtos.
Cf. *Gr.* σκότος, *Goth.* skadus. *A.S.*
sceadu.
sgath, sca, *v. t.* lop off ; chop, prune ;
sgath an ceann deth, chop off his head ;
n. m. damage by cattle ; short part of
lint ; a fragment ; **chan fhaigh thu
sgath dheth,** you will not get a bit of
it. *Ir.* **sgathadh,** ashred. *O'R. See*
barrach. *E.Ir.* **scothaim.**
sgàth, *n. f.* a wattled door.
sgàthach, scā-huch, *adj.* skittish ; timid ;
**tha an t-each a bhuailear 'sa cheann
sgàthach,** the horse struck in the head
is ever after easily frightened.
sgàthach, *n. f.* a hurdle or a great bundle
of twigs to serve as a portable door ;
a wattled door. *Ir.* **sgath.**
sgathadair, sca-huder, *n. m.* lopper, cutter.
sgathadh, *vbl. n. m.* act of lopping off,
clean cutting ; damage done by cattle.
sgathaire, sca-hiru, *n. m.* hewer, lopper ;
blacksmith's chisel for cutting iron ;
syn. **sgilb fhuar,** cold chisel.
sgàthan, *n. m.* a mirror. So *M.Ir.*
sgathbhàrd, *n. m.* satirist.
sgàthlann, *n. f.* a shade, a booth.
sgàththigh, scā-hy, *n. m.* a porch.
sgeach, sgitheag, *n. f.* a haw. *See* **mucag.**
E.Ir. **scé,** *gen.* **sciach,** the white thorn.
sgeadach, sced'-uch, *n. f.* ornament.
sgeadachadh, sceduchu, *vbl. n. m.* act of
clothing, dressing, adorning ; clothes,
dress, garments. *Ir.* **scéadachadh.**
sgeadaich, scedich, *v.* clothe, dress, adorn ;
trim.
sgeadaichte, scedichtiu, *vbl. a.* clothed,
dressed, adorned.
sgeadas, *n. m.* gayness of dress, ornament, decoration. *Ir.* **scéadas.**
sgealb, sciälb, *n. f.* a splinter, long piece
of wood ; *v.* splinter, dash to pieces,
split, cut ; **sgealb buntàta,** cut, slice
potatoes. *See* **sgolb.**
sgealbag, *n. f.* small splinter or slice.
sgealbag, *n. f.* a name of the forefinger.
sgeallag, *n. f.* wild mustard. *Ir.* **sceall-
agach.** *Din. Also* **sgiollag.**

sgeallan, skyall'-an, *n. m.* wild mustard; itch.

sgealp, skyalp, *n. m.* a lively tall man.

sgealp, skelp, *n.* a slap. *Sc.* skelp.

sgealpaich, *n. f.* dandruff; chaff (of oats).

sgealpanach, *a.* pinching, biting cold. *Ir.* scealparnach. *Din.*

sgealparachd, *n. f.* activity, shrill sound, elasticity, telling fibs; *a.* sgealparra.

sgeamh, skev, *n. m.* speck on the eye, thin skin, membrane.

sgeamh, *n. f.* yelp, severe language, snapping; thug e sgeamhadh as, he fairly snapped. *E.Ir.* scem, scemdacht, a bark, yelp. Cf. *W.* chwefru, to rage, act violently.

sgeamh, *n. m.* polypody, wall fern.

sgeamh, *n. m.* disgust, making one's gorge rise.

sgeamhag, skef-ăg, *n. f.* small slice; *Also* sgiobhag.

sgeamhaire, skefiru, *n. m.* a satirist.

sgeamhaltrach, skev-alt-ruch, *n. m.* and *f.* a person that does anything furiously.

sgeamhla, skev-lu, *n. m.* keen appetite; alarm.

sgèan, skēn, *n. m.* squint; *v.* squint, look awry.

sgèan, sgian, *n. m.* scare, fright, startled, hunted look; a stare (through fear). *See* sgeun.

sgean, sken, *n. f.* cleanliness, polish. Cf. *O.N.* skin, sheen.

sgèanach, *a.* nervous, easily startled, like birds, deer.

sgeanag, *n. f.* species of edible seaweed.

sgeann, *n. f.* a stare, gazing.

sgeannail, skenal, *a.* neatly clean; brisk, lively.

sgearach, skĕr-ach, *n. m.* anything scattered, gelatine. *See* sgeithreach.

sgearaich, skĕr-ich, *v.* scatter.

sgeap, skep, *n. m.* beehive; a straw basket, used for carrying seed when sowing, and other purposes. *Sc.* skep. *O.N.* skeppa.

sgeig, skeg, *n. f.* mockery, derision, jeering; *v.* mock, deride. *Ir.* scige, mockery.

sgeigeach, skeguch, *a.* having a prominent chin or strong straight beard. *O.N.* skegg, a beard.

sgeigeil, *adj.* jeering, jibing.

sgeigeir, skeger, *n. m.* a scoffer.

sgeigeis, skegesh, *n. f.* buffoonery, waggery.

sgeigire, skegiru, *n. m.* derider, wag.

sgeigireachd, *n. f.* waggery.

sgeilbheag, *n. f.* a thin slice. *Sc.* skelve. *Ir.* scealbog.

sgeilcearra, skelcuru, *a.* supple, active. *See* sgiolcarra.

sgéile, *n. f.* misery, pity, ruin. *Ir.* scéile, grief, pity. *O'R.*

sgeileas, skelas, *n. m.* a beak, thin face, talkativeness.

sgeileid, skelej, *n. f.* small pot or saucepan; skillet; fr. the *Eng.*

sgeilltear, skeylter, *n. m.* flat shell of scallop.

sgeilm, *n. f.* neatness, decency. So in *O'R.*

sgeilm, skėlum, *n. f.* a thin-lipped mouth, a prater's mouth; vain glory. *Also* sgiolam, sgeinm. *Ir.* sgeilm, silly babbling.

sgeilmeach, skėlum'-ach, *adj.* prating; *n. f.* a prating, vain silly person.

sgeilmear, skelmur, *a.* bright, neat.

sgeilmeil, skėlum'-al, *adj.* having a prater's contemptuous mouth; prating.

sgeilmire, skėlum'-ur-à, *n. m.* a prater, boaster.

sgeilmireachd, *n. f.* an impertinent prattle or garrulity.

sgeilmse, skėlum'-shu, *n. f.* surprise, an attack. Cf. *Ir.* sgeimhle, a surprise.

sgeilp, skelp, *n. f.* any kind of shelf, shelf of a precipice. *Sc.* skelf, a shelf.

sgeilpeach, *n. f.* shelvy, cliffy.

sgéimh, skēv, *n. f.* beauty, grace, ornament. So *Ir. See* sgiamh.

sgéimh-dhealbhach, *a.* picturesque.

sgeimhle, skevlu, *n. f.* a skirmish, bickering. *Ir.* sgeimhle.

sgeinm, skén'-um, *n. f.* decency; propriety. *See* sgeilm.

sgeinmeil, sken'-um-al, *n. f.* proper; decent. *Also* sgeilmeil.

sgéinnidh, skeyny, *n. f.* small twine, fisher's line.

sgeir, sker, *n. f.* a rock surrounded by the sea; a skerry; a rock sometimes under the water; peat-bank (Islay). *O.N.* sker, a rock in the sea.

sgeireag, skerag, *n. f.* a small rock (in the sea).

sgeir-liamhraidh, *n. f.* yarn-winder.

sgeirmse, skermshu, *n. f.* panic, skirmish. fr. the *Eng.*

sgeith, ske. *n. m.* matter thrown from the stomach; *v.* vomit, usually of animals; tilgeadh and diobhairt apply to human beings; overflow as a river, spread as water; unravel as cloth; banish; sgeith an tìr thu, the country hounded you out. *E.Ir.* scéim, sceithim, I vomit. *W.* chwydu. *O.Celt.* sqeti-.

sgéith, sgéite, *v.* fit, suit.

sgéitheadh, *m.* fitting.

sgeith-fèith, *n. m.* varicose vein.

sgeith-ròin, *n. m.* the sea-blubber, jellyfish. *Also* mur-tiachd.

sgeithreach, ske'-ruch, *n. f.* a vomit. *Ir.* sgeithrigh.

sgeithte, sketiu, *vbl. a.* vomited, overflowed.

sgeò, *n. f.* reproach. *Carm. Gad.*

sgeò, *n. f., gen.* sgiach, haze, fog, vapour; gealach gun sgeò, a moon without a haze. *Carm. Gad.*

sgeòb, *n. m.* aperture, wry mouth.

sgeòc, *n. m.* long neck, tallness.

sgeòcan, *n. m.* long-necked boy.

sgeòcag, *n. f.* long-necked girl.

sgeòd, skyod, *n. f.* corner, angular piece.

sgeòdach, *n. f.* horned sheep; *a.* ragged.

sgeogaire, skyŏg'-ur-à, *n. m.* silly fellow.

sgeòp, *n. f.* a torrent of foolish words, wry mouth. *Also* sgeòg.

sgeòpaire, *n. m.* a tattler, long-tongued fellow.

sgeul, skēl, *n. m.* news, intelligence ; narrative, narration; sgeul mu'n Fhéinn, a tale about the Fian ; droch sgeul, bad intelligence; information, tidings; bi air sgeul, be in pursuit of information ; a bheil e air sgeula (sgiala), is he or it to be found or forthcoming. *O.Ir.* scél. *W.* chwedl. *O.Celt.* sqetlo-n.

sgeulachd, skēlachc, *n. f.* vague reports, old tale, a saga.

sgeulaiche, skēlichu, *n. m.* relater, narrator. *M.Ir.* scélaige, a historian.

sgeultach, scēltuch, *adj.* fond of telling tales ; running from house to house with reports; *n. f.* a female tell-tale or gossip.

sgeultachd, skēltachc, *n. f.* tradition, legendary lore ; sgeultachd mu'n Fhéinn, a tale concerning the Fian ; sgeultachd nan seanar, tradition of the elders or sages.

sgeultair, skēlter, *n. m.* a narrator.

sgeun, skēn, *n. f.* dread, disgust, look of fear. *M.Ir.* scén, affright. *E.Ir.* scingim, I spring.

sgeunach, *a.* skittish, nervous, timid.

sgiab, *n. m.* start, snatch ; *v.* start, spread out, open wide, as fingers, eyes, legs of compass.

sgiabadh, *m.* sudden motion, flight.

sgiabail, sciäbul, *a.* starting, writhing.

sgiamh, sciäv, *n. f.* a squeal, mew ; *v.* squeal, shriek or mew, caterwaul.

sgiamh, sciuv, *n. f.* wild expression of countenance.

sgiamh, *n. f.* beauty, loveliness, bloom. *O.Ir.* scíam, gl. schema. *O.Celt.* skeimâ. Cf. *O.N.* skími, *Goth.* skeima, *A.S.* scīma, gleam. *Feist.*

sgiamhach, sciuvuch, *adj.* pretty, decent.

sgiamhail, sciävul, *vbl. n. f.* squealing, mewing.

sgiamhail, sciuval, *adj.* seemly, decent.

sgian, sciun, *n. f., gen.* sgine and sgidhinn,

pl. sginean, a knife ; sgian-pheann, penknife ; sgian-lùthaidh, clasp-knife; sgian - bhùird, table knife ; sgian-fhola, a lancet ; sgian-phronnaidh, a chopping-knife. *O.Ir.* scían. *E.W* ysgien, knife, blade. *O.Celt.* skêeno-.

sgianach, *a.* nervous, timid (as deer).

sgiansgar, *n. m.* start, fright ; fr. sgeun.

sgiansgarrach, *a.* scared, startled.

sgiath, *n. f., gen.* sgéith, wing ; shield, buckler, target ; fo do sgéith, under thy wing ; le a sgiath is le a chlogad, with his shield and helmet. *O.Ir.* scíath, *ala.* *W.* ysgwyd. *O.Celt.* skeito-s.

sgiathach, sciū-huch, *a.* winged, white-sided.

sgiathaire, sciu-hiru, *n. m.* flutterer, idler.

sgiathalaich, sciu-hulich, *n. f.* fluttering, flying about.

sgiathalan, *n. m.* the fluttering one ; a swallow.

sgiathan, *n. m.* a wing, a partition.

sgiathanach, *a.* winged.

sgibeach, *a.* neat, rel. to sgiobalta. *See* sgibidh.

sgibeachas, *n. m.* tidiness, neatness.

sgibidh, *a.* neat, handsome; tight, active.

sgid, sgij, *n. m.* little excrement, thin mud ; fr. the *Eng.*

sgidean, scijen, *n. m.* little contemptible man.

sgideil, scijel, *n. f.* a plash of water. *See* sgiodar.

sgil, *n. f.* skill, knowledge, expertness, dexterity ; fr. the *Eng.*

sgil, *v.* husk (corn), shell (shellfish). *O.N.* skilja, separate.

sgilbheag, *n. f.* a thin little slice ; a chip of slate. *Sc.* skelve.

sgileadh, *vbl. n. m.* act of shelling, husking (parched corn).

sgilear, sgileil, *adj.* skilful.

sgilig, *n.* shelled grain ; fr. sgil, *q.v.*

sgillinn, scilin, *n. f.* a penny ; fiscal denomination of land ; sgillinn-Shasunnach, a shilling sterling. *M.Ir.* scilling, scillic. Cf. *O.N.* skillingr, *A.S.* scilling. *O.H.G.* scilling. *Goth.* skilliggs. *Kl.* takes it fr. *O.Teut.* skellan, "to sound," a deriv. wh. *Feist* regards as uncertain and etym. futile.

sgilm, *n. m.* a razor-lipped mouth ; or expression of countenance, indicating a scolding, pert, prating, impertinent disposition.

sgilmeil, scilmal, *adj.* having a pert, prating, officious mouth or expression of countenance.

sgilp, *n. f.* cliff, cleft. *See* sgeilp.

sgimilear, *n. m.* a vagrant parasite, intruder.

sgimileir, scimuler, *n. m.* a pedal of

weaver's loom ; lank, ungainly lad.
Sc. skemmil, tall, thin, ungainly
person.

sgìng, *v.* squeeze, squash. *See* sginn.

sginn, *v.* sginnichd, squeeze or force out
of its skin or socket. *Also* sging.
E.Ir. scendim, spring.

sginneadh, *vbl. n. m.* act of protruding ;
gushing out (as water) ; a drop.

sginnich, *n. f.* cord, twine ; sgiùrsair de
sginnich chaol, a scourge of small
cords ; *v.* cord, tie with twine.

sgiob, scib, *n. f.* a Dutch-built boat ; *v.*
man a boat ; air a sgiobadh le gillean
sgairteil, manned with sturdy fellows ;
fr. *O.N.* skip, ship.

sgioba, scibu, *a.* a ship or boat's crew ;
fo làn sgioba, having full complement
of crew ; *transf.* any band of workers,
as in peat-cutting ; fr. *O.N.* skip.

sgiobag, scibag, *n. f.* light touch, touch
in game of " tig."

sgiobaidh, *a.* tidy, neat, trim.

sgiobailt, scibelt, *n. f.* touch, the play,
touch-and-begone, or " tig."

sgiobair, sciber, *n. m.* a captain, skipper,
shipmaster, commander of a boat.
O.N. skipari, mariner. *Eng.* skipper.

sgiobaireachd, sciberuchc, *n. f.* navigating, navigation ; command of a ship.

sgiobal, scibal, *n. m.* barn, granary. *Ir.*
sgiobol. *W.* ysgubor, *id.*

sgioball, *n. f.* fold or loose part of a garment ; cuir ad sgioball e, put it in the
fold of your coat.

sgiobalta, *a.* tidy ; clever, neat; portable.

sgiobaltachd, *n. f.* tidiness, trimness,
portability ; snugness.

sgiobhag, *n. f.* a thin slice. *O.N.* skífa,
a slice.

sgioblaich, sciblich, *v.* make tidy, trim,
or neat ; tuck up dress.

sgiod, *v. tr.* cut off, at a stroke, lop, clip.
Ir. sciotaim, clip.

sgiodar, scidar, *n. m.* plashing through
mud, diarrhœa, skitter. *Also* giodar.

sgiogair, sciger, *m.* jackanapes. *Ir.*
sgiogaire, a buffoon. *O'R.* Cf. sgeig.

sgiol, sciool, *v.* shell corn, unhusk ; loosen,
as the pile of a beast ; abrase.

sgioladh, scioolu, *vbl. n. m.* act of shelling;
baring ; abrasion.

sgiolam, scioolam, *n. m.* forward talk,
gabbling. *Also* giolam and sgeilm.

sgiolan, *n. m.* date with the husks taken off.

sgiolc, scioolc, *v.* slip in or out ; suilean
sgiolcach, prominent eyes.

sgiolcarra, scioolcuru, *adj.* clever in motion, apt to slip out or in (as an eel).

sgiollag, *n. f. See* sgeallag.

sgiolmag, scioolmag, *n. f.* a lie.

sgiolta, sciooltu, *vbl. a.* shelled ; nimble or
eloquent, as one's tongue.

sgioltachd, sciooltachc, *n. f.* neatness,
tidiness, eloquence.

sgìom, sceem, *n. m.* fat sticking to dishes ;
scum on the surface of water.

sgiomalair, scimiler, *n. m.* an instrument
to take suet off a pot ; a mean person
that steals from pots ; an intruder.

sgiomalaireachd, *n. f.* mean habits of
popping in upon people at meals ;
living (and doing nothing) about
gentlemen's kitchens.

sgionbhagan, *pl. n.* smithereens.

sgionnadh, sciunu, *m.* starting, eyes
starting with fear. *See* sginn.

sgionnshuil, *n. f.* a squint eye.

sgiord, sciurd, *n. f.* a squirt, a purge ;
sciordaim, I squirt, purge.

sgiorr, scirr, *v.* slip in, fall, happen. *Ir.*
sgiorram.

sgiorradh, scirru, *vbl. n. m.* mishap ;
hurtful, disastrous accident ; sgiorradh-
facail, a slip of the tongue, mistake in
a word. *Ir.* sgiorradh.

sgiorrail, scir'-al, *adj.* hurtful, in consequence of an accident ; disastrous.

sgiort, scirt, *n. f.* a skirt, edge or hem of
a garment; fr. the *Eng.* Cf. *O.N.*
skyrta. *M.H.G.* schurz.

sgìos, scees, *n. m.* fatigue, weariness ; leig
do sgìos, rest yourself ; a wearying ;
ag obair gun sgìos, working indefatigably ; toil, lassitude. *See* sgìth, *v.*
sglosaich. *E.Ir.* scís.

sgiot, *v.* scatter, disperse. *O.N.* skjóta,
to shoot.

sgiotadh, *vbl. n. m.* act of scattering.

sgiotaireachd, *n. f.* divided interest,
scattered work ; " chan 'eil e dèanamh
ach sgiotaireachd bhochd," he is only
pottering.

sgipidh, sgibidh, *a.* neat, tidy.

sgìre, sgeeru, *n. f.* a parish ; ministeir-
sgìre, parish minister. *A.S.* scìr,
district, shire. *Also* sgìreachd.

sgireachdail, sceerachcal, *a.* parochial.

sgirtean, *n. m.* a disease in cattle ; the
black spauld.

sgiteal, *n. m.* plash of water.

sgìth, scee, *adj.* tired, fatigued, weary.
O.Ir. scith. *O.Celt.* skito-s.

sgitheach, scee-huch, *n. m.* thorn, hawthorn. *O.Ir.* scé, *gen.* sciach. *W.*
yspyddad. *Lat.* spīna. *O.Celt.* skviját.

sgitheachadh, scee-huchu, *vbl. n. m.* act
of fatiguing.

sgìthich, scee-hich, *v.* weary, fatigue, tire.

sgithiol, *n. m.* a shieling hut. *O.N.* skyli,
a shed.

sgiuch, *n. f.* activity, cleverness.

sgiuchail, *adj.* active, clever.

sgiùchan, sgiùcan, scioochan, *n. m.* moorhen's note.

sgiùgan, scioogan, *n. m.* a whimper.

sgiùird, scioorj, v. squirt ; n. f. the flux. *Also* sgiord.

sgiùirdire, scioorjire, n. m. a syringe.

sgiuirt, sciurt, n. f. skirt, corner.

sgiul, v. abrase. *See* sgiol.

sgiùnach, scioonuch, n. f. 1. a charm or enchantment to enable its possessor to get all the fish about a boat or headland ; amulet to excel in anything. 2. a shameless, bold woman.

sgiùrs, scioors, v. scourge, whip, afflict ; sgiùrsaidh iad sibh, they shall scourge you ; shoo ! chase away (sheep or fowl) ; fr. the *Eng. E.W.* ysgwrs.

sgiùrsach, scioorsuch, n. f. scourge ; a whore ; *com.* siùrsach = *Eng.* scourge.

sgiursachas, n. f. whoredom.

sgiùrsadh, scioorsu, *vbl. n. m.* act of scourging, lashing ; a scourge, or scourging ; pain.

sgiùrsaig, scioorsig, v. lavish, give in abundance.

sgiùrsair, scioorser, n. f. 1. whip. 2. whoremonger.

sgiut, scioot, v. dart, or dash forward ; slip by. Cf. *O.N.* skjóta, shoot.

sgiuthadh, scioo-hu, n. f. a lash, stroke with a whip.

sglabhart, sclaff'-art, n. m. box on the ear. *Sc.* sclaffert.

sglaim, sclym, n. f. a great deal of the good things of life, got in a questionable shape ; booty ; v. to usurp wealth or property ; monopolise, usurp.

sglaimire, sclymiru, sglamaire, sclamiru, n. m. a usurper ; one who is wise to appropriate booty or any such to himself, a usurper.

sglaimireachd, n. f. monopoly, usurpation, voracity, glut.

sglaimsear, sclymsher, n. m. usurper.

sglamh, sclav, v. eat voraciously, glut ; eat, as a hungry dog; scold, of a sudden, or furiously.

sglamhadh, sclavu, *vbl. n. m.* act of eating voraciously ; attacking and scolding at a terrible rate. *Also* glamhadh.

sglamhair, v. claw awkwardly.

sglamhaire, sclaviru, n. m. glutton ; terrible scolder ; a voracious fellow.

sglamhradh, sclavru, clawing or scratching one's skin ferociously ; bad itch.

sglamhruinn, sclavrin, n. f. abusive words, a scolding.

sglèadach, sclēduch, a. dark, frowning.

sgleamacair, sclemacer, n. m. dauber ; a mean, low, worthless fellow.

sgleamaic, sclemick, v. plaster, or flatten awkwardly ; daub filthily.

sgleamaid, sclemej, n. f. horrid snotters.

sglèamas, sclemus, n. m. disgust, annoyance.

sgleamhas, sclevus, n. m. meanness, sordidness.

sgleamhraidh, sclevry, n. m. a stupid or mean fellow.

sglèap, sclēp, v. flatten, spoil the shape; draw down the under-lip, wag the head, and stare at a person most astonishingly ; n. m. sglèapaire, a boorish fellow ; sgleàpaid, a silly, boorish woman ; foolish, boorish starers— applied to silly children.

sglèap, n. f. ostentation, low meanness, under the guise of liberality ; a flood of words.

sglèapaid, sclēpej, n. f. *See* sglèap.

sglèapaire, sclēpiru, n. m. *See* sglèap.

sglèapaireachd, n. f. foolish, unmannerly, staring, or boasting.

sglèat, scliät, v. slate, as a house ; fr. *M.Sc.* sclate.

sglèata, n. f. a slate. *Sc.* sclate.

sglèatach, n. f. granite, slate quarry.

sglèatair, n. m. a slater ; hence *p. n.* Sclater.

sglèataireachd, n. f. slating ; the occupation of a slater, or slate-quarrier.

sgléib, n. f. what one gathers by begging.

sgléibire, n. m. one who lives by begging, a beggar. *E.W.* ysglyf, booty.

sgleò, sclō, n. m. a shade, a film ; a vapour, or mist ; a dimness of the eyes, glare about the eyes ; amazement, misapprehension ; romancing of one who sees imperfectly, and consequently misrepresents facts ; romancing, gasconading ; chuir an donas sgleò ort, the devil has beguiled you.

sgleò, n. m. misery.

sgleòbach, a. sluttish, slovenly.

sgleobht, n. f. a chunk.

sgleog, n. f.: 1. a whack, blow. 2. snot, phlegm.

sgleogaire, n. m. a troublesome prattler, a liar.

sgleòid, sclōj, n. m. silly person ; a slattern. *Ir.* scleóid ; a. sgleòideach.

sgleòthail, sclō-hal, *adj.* romancing.

sgleòthaire, sclo-hiru, n. m. romancer.

sgliamach, a. slippery-faced.

sgliat, n. f. slate. *See* sglèat.

sglìmeach, scleemuch, a. troublesome, uninvited guest.

sglimsear, sclimsher, n. m. a parasite.

sgliobhag, n. f. a slap.

sgliomair. *See* sgiomalair, sliomair.

sgliùrach, scliooruch, n. f. an untidy female ; newly fledged crow or seagull. *Ir.* scliúrach, a slattern.

sglòid, sclōj, n. f. a heavy, clumsy, lifeless female ; filth, dirt.

sglong, n. f. a horrid snotter.

sglongach, *adj.* dirtily viscous.

sglongaid, sclungij, n. f. horrid snot.

sglongaideach, *a.* mucous.

sgnog, *n. f.* a little horn, a bite, a biting word. *See* sgrogag.

sgnog, *v.* biting, nagging, shrivel, do away with, pull down firmly (as cap).

sgob, *v.* snatch, nibble lightly; bite, sting.

sgobadh, *vbl. n. m.* act of snatching, stinging; a short while; **sgobadh bho 'n bhaile,** a little while from home; **sgobadh dheth,** a short while of it.

sgobag, *n. f.* 1. small wound. 2. small dram.

sgobanta, *a.* snatching, given to snatching.

sgoch, *v.* gash, make an incision; sprain; *n. f.* a gash, incision; first-shot from a still; **eòlas sgocha féithe,** charm for a burst artery.

sgòd, *n. m.* 1. corner of cloth; sheet, sheet-rope; **sgòd an t-siuil mheadhoin,** main-sheet; **sgòd an t-siùil thoisich,** the foresail-sheet; **sgòd an t-siùil-chinn,** the jib-sheet. 2. blemish. *Also* **sgòd-lin.** *M.Ir.* **scóti.** *O.N.* skaut, corner of square cloth, sheet-rope.

sgog, *n. m.* a fool, an idler; *a.* **sgogach,** foolish.

sgog, *v.* hesitate, waver, turn against food; **sgog e orm,** I turned against it.

sgogarsaich, scog'-ars-ich, *n. f.* hesitation.

sgòid, scōj, *n. f.* pride, conceit.

sgoid, scuj, *n. f.* a stick, a chunk of wood; **sgoid - chladaich,** anything washed ashore, from a wreck.

sgòideis, scōjesh, *n. f.* vain show, pomp; pageantry.

sgoil, scol, *n. f.* school, seminary, education; **a' bheil sgoil aige,** has he education; **a' dol do 'n sgoil,** going to school; **chan 'eil sgoil agam air,** I have no knowledge of it; **sgoil fhairge,** the science of navigation; **sgoil-speur,** sgoil reul, astronomy; **sgoil mharsantachd,** the science of book - keeping; **sgoil - fhearainn,** the science of land surveying; **sgoil riomball,** spherics; **sgoil-fhionnsaireachd,** the science of fencing; **sgoil-dhorn,** the science of boxing; **sgoil-chlaidheamh,** sword exercise; **sgoil-chruinne,** geography; **sgoil-lusan,** botany; **sgoil-mhulcach,** phrenology; **sgoil-chiùird,** mechanics; **sgoil-dhannsaidh,** dancing-school; **sgoil-chreag,** geology; **sgoil-eun,** ornithology; **sgoil-fhacal,** sgoil-fhreumhachd,** etymology; *also* **faclaire-achd; sgoil-mharcachd,** riding-school; **sgoil-leughaidh,** reading-school; **sgoil-shàbaid,** Sabbath school; **sgoil-shamh-raidh,** a summer school; **sgoil-sgrìobh-aidh,** writing-school; **sgoil-dhiadhair-eachd,** theology; **sgoil-eachdraidh,** his-

toriography; **sgoil-mhiotailt,** mineralogy; **sgoil-chogaidh,** military academy; **sgoil-uisge,** hydrostatics; **sgoil-dhreag,** meteorology; or **dreagaireachd; sgoil-inntinn,** intellectual philosophy; **sgoil-bhùird,** a boarding-school; **sgoil-dhubh,** the black art. *È.Ir.* **scol.** *W.* ysgol. *Lat.* schola. *Gr.* σχολή.

sgoileam, scolem, *n. m.* loquacity.

sgoilear, scoler, *n. m.* scholar, a student, pupil, a learned man, disciple, schoolboy. *M.Ir.* scolaige.

sgoilearach, *adj.* scholastic, learned.

sgoilearachd, *n. f.* scholarship, learning; erudition, education, intelligence.

sgoilm, scolm, *n. f.* razor-bill; mouth or face expressive of scolding disposition; high key in scolding. Cf. *O.N.* skálm, short sword.

sgoilmeach, scolmuch, *adj.* venomous in scolding; *n. f.* a shrew, a scold, or scolding female.

sgoilmeis, scolmesh, *n. f.* a biting scold.

sgoilt, scult, *v. t.* cleave, split, separate. *E.Ir.* scoiltim. *O.Celt.* sqoltô.

sgoilte, scultu, *vbl. a.* cleft, split, chinked.

sgoiltean, sculten, *n. m.* a split, half; half of a square neckerchief; a billet of wood; the parting in the hair of the head.

sgoim, *n. f.* wandering about; skittishness.

sgoinn, scu-in, *n. f.* decency, taste, propriety; neatness, care; **dèan le sgoinn e,** do it tastefully; **air sgàth sgoinne,** for decency's sake; **is beag sgoinn a bhios air do ghnothach,** your business must be done with little propriety; esteem, efficiency, haste, speed.

sgoinn, *n. f.* a pool left by receding tide.

sgoinn, *v. tr.* check, reprove, scold.

sgoinneach, scunuch, *adj.* bitter in scolding.

sgoinneil, scunel, *adj.* decent, tasteful, effective, spirited, purposeful.

sgoinneil, *n. f.* bitter scolding female.

sgoirm, scorm, *n. f.* 1. the throat. 2. brow of a hill; **an draigheann gorm air sgoirm nan càrn,** the brier green on the brow of the hills.

sgoitiche, scotichu, *n. m.* a quack, a mountebank.

sgol, *v.* wash, rinse, scull. *O.N.* skola, wash. *W.* golchi. *Bret.* golhein.

sgoladh, *m.* rinsing, washing, sculling.

sgolb, *n. f.* a wattle, or spray for fastening thatch; splinter, split; thorn. *M.Ir.* scolb, a wattle.

sgolbach, *a.* prickly, thorny.

sgolbanach, *n. m.* a stripling (transf. meaning).

sgolbanta, *a.* sharp, prickly, given to chipping, splitting.

sgolbantachd, *n. f.* tallness, slenderness.

sgoll, *n. m.* ugly scum, as on proud flesh.

sgollachan, *n. m.* an unfledged bird.

sgoltadh, scoltu, *vbl. n. m.* act of splitting, cleaving, riving asunder, chinking ; a cleft, a chink, a rent, a rift ; a' sgoltadh cheann, cleaving heads. ` *E.Ir.* scoltad.

sgonn, scoun, *v. n.* gulp. glut, eat in large mouthfuls ; 'ga sgonnadh air, gulping it up ; *n. f.* a large mouthful, a gulp, or glut.

sgonn, *n. m.* a block of wood ; a huge unshapely person, a dunce.

sgonnabhalach, *n. m.* a lump of a boy, a lumpish boor.

sgonnachu, *n. m.* a surly dog.

sgonnaire, sconiru, *n. m.* a gulper, a boor.

sgonnan, *n. m.* the step of cas-chrom, the step of a peat-knife, the handle of a quern ; fr. sgonn, piece of wood.

sgonnsa, *n. m.* sconce, small fort ; thuit mo sgonnsa, my fort has fallen. *Ir.* sgonsa.

sgonsair, *n. m.* an avaricious rascal.

sgop, *n. m.* foam, froth.

sgor, *n. f.* a slice of fish, a fillet, a slice of bread ; a swathe of hay.

sgor, *v.* fork peats or hay, lay out peats to dry ; gash, hack, scarify ; *n. f.* a fork ; sgian agus sgor, a knife and fork ; a gash, a notch, cleft in a rock.

sgor, *n. f.* chink, cleft, rift (in a rock). *O.N.* skor. 1. notch. 2. rift in a rock.

sgoraban, *n. m.* a small pointed rock.

sgoradh, skŏr'-u, *vbl. n. m.* act of forking ; gashing ; laying out or forking of peats (in the course of cutting).

sgoradh, *n. m.* the " summing " of stock (in a township). *Also* co-sgoradh.

sgorag, *n. f.* scollop, a waving edge, small bit of stone, or turf.

sgoragaich, scoragich, *v.* scollop, cut the edge of cloth, etc., in a waving line.

sgòrnan, scōrnan, *n. m.* the throttle, or gullet, or windpipe. So *Ir.*

sgòrr, *n. f.* a peak, or cliff, sharp point, a conical sharp rock ; a buck-tooth.

sgorrach, *adj.* pronged, peaked, cliffy, conical, having a buck-tooth.

sgorrachadh, *n. m.* act of sitting up ; an expectant attitude ; 'g a sgorrachadh fhéin, sitting up and on the alert. *O.N.* skorða, *v. t.* prop.

sgòrradh, *n. m.* a support, prop, *esp.* a prop to keep a boat on even keel (ashore) or on its side. *O.N.* skorða, *id.*

sgòrrbheinn, scōrr'-vèn, *n. f.* a peaking, cliffy, conical mountain ; a mountain in the island of Islay.

sgot, *n. f.* a piece of land ; a small farm ; a smáli village ; a small flock.

sgot, *n. f.* a spot, a blemish.

sgot, *n. f.* a tax ; a poser, a puzzle. *O.N.* skot, a shot ; a tax. *Eng.* scot, pay one's scot, " scot-free."

sgot, *n. f.* a fragment, a tiny thing ; used only in *phr.* sgot chéille, a fragment of sense ; chan 'eil sgot aige, he is quite mad. Cf. *O.N.* skopt (mod. skott), hair. *Goth.* skufts.

sgòth, *n. f.* a cloud over the sun.

sgoth, *n. f.* a Norway skiff. So *Ir.*

sgothlong, sco-hlung, *n. f.* a yacht. So *Ir.*

sgrabach, *a.* rough, ragged. *Ir.* sgrabach ; fr. *Eng.* scrap.

sgrabaire, skrab'-ur-u, *n. m.* Greenland dove.

sgragall, *n. m.* gold-foil, spangle. So *Ir.*

sgraibhse, scryshu, *n. f.* hand-saw.

sgraid, scraj, *n. f.* a hag, or old mare, or cow.

sgraideag, scrajag, *n. f.* little potato, or anything small ; a diminutive woman. *Ir.* a small morsel, a puny person.

sgraig, *v. tr.* hit one a blow.

sgràill, scràl, *v.* revile, abuse terribly, rail at.

sgràilleadh, scràliu, *vbl. n. m.* act of reviling, scolding terribly ; the greatest abuse, worst language.

sgraing, screng, *n. f.* a scowl ; a scowling or forbidding countenance, or aspect ; niggardliness.

sgraingealachd, screng'-all-uchc, *n. f.* sullenness, surly morosity, or countenance.

sgraingeil, screng'-al, *adj.* scowling, sullen.

sgraingire, screng'-ir-u, *n. m.* a scowler.

sgràist, *n. m.* a sluggard, an indolent person. So *Ir.*

sgrait, *n. f.* a shred, rag. So *Ir.*

sgràl, *coll. n.* a host, a large number of minute things.

sgrath, scrǎ, *n. f.* outer skin, rind ; a thin sod (divot) ; what covers the kiln of grain ; scum. Cf. *O.N.* skrá (dry skin). *Sc.* scra, scraw.

sgrath, *n. f.* horror, dread.

sgrathail, scra-hal, *a.* destructive.

sgrathaire, scra-hiru, *n. m.* skeleton.

sgrathall, scra-hul, *coll. n.* small ones of anything, rubbish, refuse of anything.

sgreab, screb, *n. f.* a scab, blotch, a crust.

sgreabach, screbuch, *adj.* scabbed, blotched.

sgreabaire, screbiru, *n. m.* mean fellow.

sgread, scred, *v.* screech ; scream, yell ; *n. f.* screech, a yell, gnash. *M.Ir.* scret.

sgreadag, scredag, *n. f.* an acid, anything sour. *Ir.* scréadog, sharp or sour drink.

sgreadail, scredul, *n.f.* screeching, crying, screaming, gnashing.

sgreadaire, scrediru, *n. m.* screecher.

sgreag, scrēg, *v.* dry, parch. See sgrèath.

sgreagag, *n.f.* a stingy woman.

sgreamh, *n. f.* thin scum or rind, ugly skin ; an excrescence. *Ir.* sgreamh, thin film, rust, crust.

sgreamh, screv, *n. f.* slight nausea, abhorrence, disgust. *O.N.* skræma, scare away.

sgreamhaich, screv'-ich, *v.* loathe, abhor.

sgreamhail, screv'-al, *adj.* loathsome.

sgreamhladh, screv'-llu, *n. f.* a thick wettish rash through the skin.

sgrèanach, scrēnuch, *a.* inclement, rough, stormy.

sgreang, screng, *n. f.* a wrinkle.

sgreat, scret, *n.f.* great horror or disgust.

sgreatachd, scretachc, *n. f.* horrifying nature or quality of anything ; sgreataidheachd, disgustfulness. *Ir.* sgreatachd, hate, abhorrence.

sgreataich, scretich, *v.* horrify, highly disgust.

sgreataidh, screty, *adj.* horrifying, disgusting. Cf. *O.N.* skratti, a goblin, a monster.

sgréath, scrē, *v.* parch, or dry hurriedly the outside, without entering into the inner part. Cf. *O.N.* skreiδ, dried fish ; skreiδar-garδr, a platform for drying fish.

sgreoth, scro, *v.* parch as cloth.

sgreothainn, scro-hin, *n. f.* straw used in place of haircloth on a kiln— straic.

sgreubh, *v.* dry up ; crack by drought. Cf. *Sc.* scrae, a shrivelled old shoe. See sgréath.

sgreuch, sgriach, scrēch, *v.* and *n. m.* screech, scream. *E.Ir.* screch, screchim, I cry, scream. *W.* ysgrech.

sgreuchail, sgriachail, scrēchul, *n. f.* screeching ; *vbl. n. m.* act of screeching.

sgreuchaire, sgriachaire, scrēchiru, *n. m.* screecher.

sgreunach, scrēnuch, *a.* shivering ; boisterous.

sgrìach. See strìoch.

sgribhinn, screevin, *n. f.* rocky side of a hill ; for sgridhinn. *O.N.* skriδa, landslip on a hill-side.

sgrid, scrij, *v.* breathe, live ; *n. m.* breath, gasp ; chan 'eil sgrid ann, there is not a breath in him.

sgrìob, screeb, *n. f.* a scrape, the rut of a plough, or its swathe of earth ; a trip, an excursion ; sgrìob do 'n ghalldachd, an excursion or trip to the Low country ; stroke of a saw ; sgrìob an t-saibh-mhóir, the stroke of the whipsaw. *E.Ir.* scríb, a scratch, a furrow.

sgrìob, screeb, *v.* scrape, drag, or dredge for fish or oysters ; snatch, or sweep away ; sgrìob leat e, sweep or snatch it away with you. *Lat.* scribo.

sgrìobach, screebuch, *n. f.* itch ; mange.

sgrìobadh, *vbl. n. m.* act of scratching, scraping. *M.Ir.* scripad. *A.S.* screpan, screopan.

sgrìobag, *n.f.* a little stroke, scratch, line.

sgrìobaire, screebiru, *n. m.* a dredge, a scraper, scratcher ; curry-comb, a graving tool.

sgrìoban, screeban, *n. m.* a scraper ; a wool-card ; a curry-comb ; a set of hooks attached to a long line, used by fishermen for finding sunken fishinglines ; a hand-line for still deep-sea fishing.

sgrìobh, screev, *v.* write, compose. *O.Ir.* scríbaim. *Lat.* scribo.

sgrìobhadair, screevuder, *n. m.* writer.

sgrìobhadaireachd, *n. f.* a writer's business ; writing.

sgrìobhadh, screevu, *vbl. n. f.* act of writing, composing ; handwriting, manuscript, writing.

sgrìobhte, screevtu, *vbl. a.* written, composed.

sgrìobtur, scrup'-tur, *n. m.* a writing ; the Scripture.

sgrìobturail, *a.* scriptural.

sgrìodan, screedan, *n. m.* stony ravine, track of mountain torrent, quantity of broken stone spread over a slope.

sgrìogalach, *n.f.* bare mountain-top.

sgrìos, scris, *v.* destroy, ruin, annihilate ; scrape, or sweep off the surface ; a' sgriosadh an leathraich, sweeping off the rind of the leather ; *n. f.* destruction, ruin, ruination ; bheir thu sgrìos oirnn, thou wilt bring destruction upon us ; sweeping away of surface, or scraping rind ; stumble, slip. *M.Ir.* scrisaim, rub, scrape, destroy.

sgrìos, *n. f.* a band of yarn on a clew.

sgriosach, scrisuch, sgriosail, scrisal, *adj.* destructive, ruinous, detrimental, pernicious.

sgriosadair, scrisuder, *n. m.* destroyer, pillager.

sgriot, *n. f.* a haggard woman.

sgriotachan, screetuchan, *n. m.* a pining child ; little squalling infant.

sgrioth, scri, *n. m.* gravel. *Also* sgriothan.

sgriothal, scri-hal, *coll. n.* a crowd of young creatures or small things, a lot of items.

sgriubh, scroo, *n. f.* a screw ; *v.* screw ; fr. the *Eng.*

sgròb, *v.* scratch with the nails, or claws

as a cat. *Ir.* **sgróbaim**, I scratch, scrape.

sgròbadh, *vbl. n. m.* act of scratching.

sgròban, *n. m.* little crop of a bird, craw ; gizzard ; cha téid mìr ad sgròban, not a particle will enter your gizzard. *Ir.* scrobán.

sgrobha, scrou, *n. f.* a screw ; a vice. *Ir.* scrobha (*m.*). *Din.*

sgròblaich, *vbl. n. f.* scrawling ; child's attempt at writing.

sgroch, scroch, *v.* scratch with nails, etc.

sgrochaill, scrochil, *v. tr.* scrawl, scribble.

sgrochladh, scrochlu, *vbl. n. m.* act of scrawling, scribbling ; a scrawl, a scribbling.

sgrog, *v.* bite ; *n. f.* a bite, a mouthful ; sgrog e mi, he bit me.

sgrog, *v.* fasten on, tighten ; sgrog do bhonaid ort, tighten down your cap ; *n. f.* the head (in ridicule). *Also* sgruig.

sgrog, *v.* shrivel.

sgrog, *n. f. See* sgrogag.

sgrogach, *a.* stumpy, short-horned.

sgrogag, *n. f.* anything shrivelled or short, shrivelled old woman, old cow or ewe. Cf. *Sc.* scrog, a stunted bush. *O.N.* skrukka (skrokkr), an old shrimp.

sgrogaid, scrogij, *n. f.* an old hat or cap.

sgrogaire, scrogiru, *n. m.* biter, carper.

sgrogais, *n. f.* stopper of a bottle.

sgroig, *n. f.* the head, the neck of a bottle. *Ir.* scrog, a small, or narrow neck.

sgroill, *n. f.* peeling, or rind ; *a.* sgroilleach.

sgroill, *v.* peel, excoriate.

sgròilleag, scrolag, *n. f.* piece of skin or any peeling scraped off.

sgroinneach, *a.* ragged.

sgroll, *n. f.* large wide piece.

sgrot, *n. m.* a contemptible hut. *Shet.* skrott. Cf. *Goth.* hròt, a roof.

sgrotach, *a.* low, squat, insignificant.

sgroth, scro, *n. f.* large thick sod, a layer of dirt. *See* sgrath.

sgrub, scroob, *v.* hesitate, delay ; fr. *Eng.* scruple.

sgrubail, scroobal, *adj.* hesitating, scrupulous, niggardly, parsimonious.

sgrubaire, scroobiru, *n. m.* a churl, niggard.

sgrubaireachd, *n. f.* niggardliness.

sgrubanta, *adj.* scrupulous ; parsimonious ; sgrubantachd, *n. f.* scrupulosity, niggardliness.

sgrùd, scrood, *v.* scrape thoroughly, search minutely, scrutinise, examine minutely. *O.Ir.* scrutaim. *Lat.* scrutor.

sgrùdadh, scroodu, *vbl. n. m.* act of searching ; utmost scraping of anything in a dish.

sgrùdaire, scroodiru, *n. m.* scrutiniser.

sgrùidte, scroojtu, *vbl. a.* cleared out or wholly searched ; scrutinised, perfectly freed or cleared.

sgruigean, scroogen, *n. m.* neck of a bottle, head of stem and stern posts. *Ir.* scruigén.

sgrùilleadh, *n. m.* refuse. *See* sgroill.

sgruit, scrooj, *n. f.* an old decayed person ; a thin person. *Ir.* scruit, a thin, gaunt person. Cf. *O.N.* skrydda (mod. skrudda), a shrivelled skin.

sgrung, *n. f.* ill-conditioned animal. *R.D.*

sgrùthan, scroo-han, *n. m.* a stook of corn. *O.N.* skrúf, hay-cock, a corn-rick.

sguab, *n. f.* a sheaf of corn ; a besom, broom, brush ; *v.* sweep, sweep away. *E.Ir.* scúap. *O.Ir.* scópthe ; gl. scopata, swept. *Lat.* scōpa.

sguabach, *n. f.* a brush, broom.

sguabadh, *vbl. n. m.* sweeping, cleaning ; act of sweeping or cleaning.

sguabag, *n. f.* a little sheaf ; a little broom ; a smart breeze ; the last three days of spring.

sguabanta, *adj.* portable, trim.

sguablion, *n. f.* a sweep-net.

sguaigeis, *n. f.* coquetry.

sguain, *n. f.* a tail, train of dress.

sguainne, *n. m.* a long stick ; an overgrown lad ; an idler.

sguainseach, *n. f.* a hussy, a boisterous girl.

sguan, *n. m.* a slur, slander, gossip.

sguch, scooch, *v.* strain, sprain ; move, stir. *E.Ir.* scuchim, I yield, go.

sgud, scood, *v.* lop, snatch. *Also* sgid. Cf. *W.* ysgŵd, shake, jerk.

sgùd, scood, *n. m.* a cluster.

sgùd, *n. f.* a style of boat, slow and clumsy but capacious ; often a term of contempt for a boat. *O.N.* skúta, small craft or cutter.

sgudal, scoodul, *n. m.* trash, offals.

sguidilear, scoojiler, *n. m.* a scullion, drudge ; a mean fellow.

sgùg, scoog, *n. m.* crouching posture.

sgùgach, scooguch, *n. m.* a soft boorish fellow. *Also* sguga.

sguids, scoojsh, *v.* dress flax, switch, drive. *Eng.* scutch.

sguidseach, scooj-shuch, *n. m.* a tall, slender, young girl ; stripling.

sguidseadh, scoojshu, *vbl. n. m.* act of dressing, lashing.

sguidseanach, scooj-shenuch, *n. m.* a very tall, slender, very young man.

sgùil, scool, *n. f.* a basket of willow, oval shaped, for holding small fishing-line.

sgùilleach, scooluch, *n. f.* species of sea-weed ; seaweed cast up on the shore.

sgùillear, *n. m.* a rakish person.

sguir, *v.* cease, stop, give over, desist ;

sguir dheth, stop it ; desist, cease, be done of it. *O.Ir.* **scorim.**

sgùird, scoord, *n. f.* lap, front part of skirt (when used to carry anything). *Ir.* sgúird, tunic or shirt.

sguit, *n. m.* a wanderer.

sguit, *n. f.* 1. footboard in a boat : 2. flat " knee " against stem or stern post, level with gunwale. 3. the stern bench. *Dan.* skot, stem or stern.

sgùl, *n. m.* a shelter, a temp. wind-screen at a bothy. *O.N.* skjól, a shelter.

sgùlag, *n. f.* basket for holding the linen.

sgulair, scooler, *n. f.* a large old hat.

sgùlan, scoolan, *n. f.* large basket. Cf. *O.N.* skjóla (a bucket).

sgùm, *n. m.* scoom, scum, foam. Prob. fr. *Eng. Dan.* skum. *O.H.G.* scûm.

sgumalair. *See* sgimileir.

sgùman, scooman, *n. m.* a skirt, tawdry head-dress, corn-rick.

sguman, *n. m.* a dish for baling a boat.

sgumrag, scoomrag, *n. f.* fire shovel, a Cinderella.

sgumragach, *a.* slovenly, untidy.

sgur, scoor, *n. m.* cessation, stop ; buidheachas gun sgur, thanks without ceasing ; *vbl. n.* act of ceasing, desisting, leaving off ; stopping ; mun do sguir sinn, ere we desisted, or ceased, or left off ; gun sgur, unceasingly, incessantly. *See* sguir.

sgùr, scoor, *v.* scour, burnish, rub up ; fr. the *Eng. O.F.* escurer.

sgùrach, scooruch, *n. f.* unfledged cormorant.

sgurachdainn, skoor'-achc-inn, *vbl. n. f.* act of stopping. *See* sgur.

sgùradh, scooru, *vbl. n. m.* 1. burnishing, scouring, cleaning. 2. heavy driving showers of rain. 3. a purging.

sgùrainn, scoor'-inn, *n. f.* lye, or ley ; any trash of liquor ; toplash.

sgùrr, *n. m.* a large conical hill. *See* sgorr.

sgurt, *v.* scud, sweep away. *See* sgiut.

sì, she. *O.Ir.* sí.

sia, shee-a, *num. adj.* six. *Ir.* sé.

siab, shiùb, *v.* swipe, breathe away dust ; wipe, jerk ; siabaibh leibh i, swipe it down, *i.e.* the toast.

siabadh, *vbl. n. m.* act of brushing away ; breathing away, sudden pull, dashing away (as a tear from eye) ; " ri siabadh cheann," jerking off the heads.

siabaire, *n. m.* a sprite ; an evil fellow. *E.Ir.* siabur, an evil spirit.

siaban, *n. m.* light dry sand, slight shower, sea-drift, sand-drift.

siabh, *n.* stewed winkles.

siabhair, shiùv'-ir, *v.* tease, weary out.

siabhaireachd, shiùveruchc, *n. f.* ritual, dandering, unconcern for time in face of duty.

siabhas, *n. m.* idle ceremony.

siabhrach, shiùvruch, *n. f., pl.* siabhraichean, a fairy, a ghost. *Also* siobhrag. *E.Ir.* siabrae, siabur, fairy, demon, phantom.

siabunn, shiub'-unn, *n. m.* soap. *Lat.* sapo.

siach, *v.* sprain, strain a joint.

siachadh, *m.* act of straining ; gun a choguis a shiachadh, without straining his conscience.

siachaire, shiùchiru, *n. m.* a pithless wretch, a crafty creature. *See* sìochaire.

'siad, for is iad, it is they.

siad, sheead, *v.* sheer, go obliquely.

siad, *n. f.* a fusty smell, a stink.

siad, *n. f.* sloth.

siad, *n. m.* a brave sturdy fellow ; bu tu fhéin an siad, you brave fellow ; a form of seud.

siadaidh, *n. m.* a sluggard.

siadaire, shiäd'-ur-u, *n. m.* a sly, skulking fellow ; a shuffler ; stinkard ; *v.* slink. *Also* siapaire.

siadaireachd, *n. f.* slinking, shuffling, sly, roguish conduct.

siadha, *n.* testicle. *Carm. Gad.*

sian, shee-un, *n. f.* a drawling scream, or squeal ; *v.* squeal, cry, scream tediously, raising your voice gradually. So *E.Ir.*

sian. *See* sìon.

sian, *n. m., pl.* siantan, storm of wind and rain, weather ; marcach-sìne, spindrift. *O.Ir.* sín. *O.W.* hîn, *tempestas.* *O.Celt.* sênâ.

sian, *n. m.* a pile of grass. *E.Ir.* sion, foxglove.

sian, *n. m.* a whizzing sound (as of a fast moving object through the air).

sian, siän. *See* seun.

sianail, shiän'-al, *n. f.* drawling, squealing.

sianan, breaca sianain. *See* seunan.

siar, shee-ur, *v.* lurch, go obliquely ; pine.

siar, *adv.* behind ; west, westward ; siar ort, to the westward of you. *O.Ir.* síar, s-iar. *See* iar.

siaradh, *n. m.* oblique line, a wasting ; " tha lionn-dubh air mo shiaradh," I am wasted with melancholia.

siaranachadh, *vbl. n. m.* languishing, melancholia. *Also* siarachd.

siarsag, *n. f.* a large species of sand eel.

siarsalachadh, *m.* swinging, charging.

siasnadh, *n. m.* wasting, decaying, dwining.

siataig, *n. m.* sciatica, rheumatism ; fr. *Lat.* sciaticus. *Gr.* ἰσχιαδικός.

sibh, *pron.* ye or you. *O.Ir.* sib. *W.* chwi.

sibheadh, *m.* aslant ; air a shibheadh, slantwise.

sibhreach, shiv-ruch, *n. m.* a fairy, a spectre. For sìothbhrughach.

sibhreachail, shiv-ruchal, *adj.* fairy-like. *Also* sibhrin.

sibht, shivt, *n. f.* shift, expedient; fr. the *Eng.*

sibhteil, *adj.* inventive, thrifty.

sic, shick, *n. f.* a membrane, pellicle; màm - sic, a rupture, hernia. *Ir.* madhm-sic.

sic, sicean, *n. m.* a particle, a small grain. *Carm. Gad.*

sic-chinn, *n. f.* scalp.

sichd, *n.* dash to lay hold of.

sicir, *adj.* prudent, steady. *Sc.* sicker.

sìd, sheej, *n. f.* abatement of a storm, mood or humour; abatement of rage; 'nuair a ni e sìd, when the storm abates; ciod e an t-sìd a th'ort, in what humour are you? a bheil sìd air a nis, has his rage abated now?

sìdeil, sheejal, *adj.* more moderate, as wind; in good humour, as a person; na's sìdeiliche, more moderate, more calm.

sìdhideach, sheeyijuch, *n. f.* spectre, fairy; person taken by fairies.

sifinn, *n. f.* a trifle, a straw; fiach sifinn, worth a straw. *M.Ir.* sifinn; sifinn luachra, a rush stem. *See* siobhag.

sig, *interj.* used in ordering a dog out of one's way.

sìg, seeg, *n. f.* a large haystack. *Ir.* síog, a rick of corn.

sìgeach, sheeguch, *a.* slim, slimy.

sìgean, sheegen, *n. f.* pleasant countenance, diminutive creature, a silly person.

sìgeanta, *adj.* cheerful, dwarfish.

sìgeantachd, sheegantuchc, *n. f.* cheerfulness, complacency, affability, dwarfishness.

sil, seel, *v.* rain, drop, drip; shil e, the rain has commenced; a' sileadh nan deur, shedding tears; *n. m.* sile, a drop; sile mheòir, a drop from a finger.

silc, *n. m.* a seed; a particle. *See* sic.

sile, sheelu, *n. m.* a spittle, saliva. *O.Ir.* saile. *O.Celt.* salivâ. *Lat.* saliva.

sileadh, shilu, *vbl. n. m.* act of raining, dropping, dripping; dispensation, economy; fo shileadh an t-soisgeil, under the gospel dispensation; drop, drip; gach sileadh, every drop.

silean, sheelen, *n. m.* single grain.

sile-reum, shilu-rēm, *n. m.* salivation.

sìliche, *n. m.* a meagre, pithless creature; a lazy fellow; a mean creature.

sillabub, *n. m.* foam. *See* còbhar.

silshuil, *n. f.* a watery eye.

silt, *n. f.* a drop of liquid.

silteach, shiltuch, *a.* dropping, tearful;

sùil shilteach, tearful eye, often raining; uair shilteach, weather in which rain prevails; *n. f.* an issue, running of an issue, discharge.

silteachd, *n. f.* raininess; state of being subject to issues.

simid, sheemij, *n. m.*, *pl.* simidean, a mallet, beetle; a rolling-pin; potato-masher; rammer; tail half of fish; ceann-simid, beetle. *Ir.* siomaide.

similear, sheemiler, *n. m.* chimney. *Also* luidhear, looyer; fr. the *Eng.*

similidh, sheemily, *a.* cowardly, feeble, dastardly, silly.

simisd, *n. f.* a beam laid across the " cave " of a kiln to support the cross-sticks. *Also* simear.

simleag, *n. f.* a silly woman, a simple-minded woman.

sìmplidh, sheemply, *a.* single-hearted, simple. *Lat.* simplex.

sìmplidheachd, sheemply-achc, *n. f.* simplicity.

sin, *adj. pron.* that, those; na daoine sin, those men; an duine sin, that man; *interj. adv.* well done! there now! sin! sin! enough! enough! sin thu, a laochain, well done, my good fellow! mar sin, in that manner; an sin, on that occasion; there, in that place. *O.Ir.* sin. *E.Ir.* sen.

sìn, sheen, *v.* stretch, reach, hand; sìn dhomh sin, hand me that; sìn do làmh, stretch your hand; pursue, chase, with all your might; shìn sinn orra, we pursued them with all our might; begin; an déidh sìneadh, having commenced. *O.Ir.* sínim.

sine, *n. f.* a teat. *E.Ir.* sine. *O.Celt.* s(p)enio-.

sine, shinu, *deg.* of sean, old; is sine, older, elder; cò dhiubh as sine, which of them is the elder; *n. f.* oldness, agedness; a shine, his agedness. *O.Ir.* siniu, older.

sinead, shinud, *n. m.* seniority, degree of age; air a shinead, let him be ever so old.

sìneadh, sheenu, *vbl. n. m.* act of stretching, reaching; length, stretch; pursuit, pursuing; prolongation; commencing; sìneadh làithean, length of days.

sìneas, *n. m.* present, gift, proffer; often said in sarcasm; b' e an sìneas e! but that *is* a present! fr. sínim.

sineubhar, *n. m.* the juniper tree.

sinn, *pers. pron.* we, us; their sinn, we shall say.

sìnn-seanair, shee-shener, *n. m.* great-grandfather; sìnn-sìnn-sheanair, great-great-grandfather; sinn here = seann, old.

sìnn-seanmhair, shee-shenver, *n. f.* great-grandmother; sìnn - sìnn - seanmhair, great-great-grandmother.

sìnnsear, *n. m.* ancestor; *pl.* sìnnsirean, ancestors, the fathers. *E.Ir.* sinser, elder.

sìnnsearachd, shee-shiruchc, *n. f.* genealogy, forefathers, ancestors, ancestry.

sìnte, sheentu, *vbl. a.* stretched, reached, fetched; sìnte r' a thaobh, stretched by his side.

sìnte, *n. pl.* plough traces.

sìnteach, sheentuch, *n. f.* plough trace; *adj.* straight, extended, prostrate.

sìnteag, *n. f.* a stride, a leap; a skip, a pace; is ann aige bha na sìnteagan! such leaping strides as he had!

sìob, *v.* pull, jerk (as in fishing with bait).

sìob, shiub, *v.* drift, as snow; a' cur is a' sìobadh, snowing and drifting. *See* siab.

sìobag, *n. f.* a puff, a blast of the mouth.

sìobail, shēb'-èl, *v.* fish (and the boat under sail); angle.

sìobhach, shiff'-uch, *n. m.* rye-grass.

sìobhadh, *n. m.* a slant; air a shìobhadh, aslant.

sìobhag, shiff'-ag, *n. f.* straw, pile of rye-grass, candle- or lamp-wick. *E.Ir.* simín, a rush; *also* sifinn, sifinn luachra, a rush stem; peeled rush was in use as lamp wicks quite recently.

sìobhalt, sheevult, *adj.* civil, obliging, affable, kind, urbane, polite, courteous. *E.Ir.* sídamail; cogadh siuvalta, civil war. *I.T.* iv²; fr. *Eng.* *Lat.* civilis.

sìobhaltachd, *n. f.* civility.

sìobhaltas, *n. f.* common civility.

sìoblach, sheebluch, *n. m.* a long streamer; a long person.

sìobladh, sheeblu, *vbl. n. m.* fishing (and the boat under sail); *n. m.* time of tide suiting fishing. *Also* fannadh. *See* fann.

sìoc, shik, chaidh e sìoc, he died. *See* sìog.

sìoch, sheeuch, *v.* strain, sprain, hurt.

sìoch, *n. f.* peace, quiet, repose, comfort.

sìochadh, *vbl. n. m.* act of spraining, a strain, straining, as one's foot, etc.

sìochail, *adj.* peaceful, quiet.

sìochaint, sheechent, *adj.* peace, repose; fr. sìth. *E.Ir.* síthchain.

sìochainteach, *adj.* peaceful, quiet, undisturbed, unmolested.

sìochainteachd, *n. f.* peacefulness, quietude, happy repose, and peace.

sìochaire, sheeuchiru, *n. m.* a fairy-like person; a trifling ninny, a dwarf, a sneak. *M.Ir.* sidhcaire. *E.Ir.* síthchaire.

sìochaireachd, *n. f.* trifling conduct, quantity, or consideration.

sìochalachd, *n. f.* peacefulness.

siod, *dem. pron.* yon, that there; siod an duine, yonder is the man, yonder is the hero; *adv.* an siod is an so, here and there; mar siod is mar so, this way and that way. *Also* sud. *O.Ir.* side, sude, suide.

sìoda, sheedu, *n. m.* silk; *a.* silken. *E.Ir.* síta. *Lat.* seta.

sìodchnuimh, *n. f.* silkworm.

sìog, sheeg, *n. f.* cadaverous appearance.

sìogach, *a.* greasy, slimy, ill-shaped, lazy.

sìogaid, shigej, *n. m.* a starveling, lank person. *Also* sìogaideach.

sìogaire, *n. m.* sneak, wily, mean fellow.

sìogal, *v.* suck (a cow) dry. *Ir.* siuc, dry.

sìol, *v.* *See* sìoladh.

sìol, sheeul, *n. m.* seed; oats; sìolgruind, seed-oats, race, offspring; sìol Dhiarmaid, the race or offspring of Diarmaid; semen; *interj.* mode of calling geese. *O.Ir.* síl (gl. *semen*). *O.Celt.* sêlo-n. *O.W.* hîl.

sìola, shioolu, *n. m.* gill measure; fr. *Eng.*

sìola, shioolu, *n. m., pl.* sìolachan, hames.

sìola, *n. m.* eel's liver, hung up in eel's stomach to melt, then used as lotion.

sìola, *n. m.* a syllable. *E.Ir.* sillab. *Lat.* syllaba.

sìolach, shiuluch, *n. m.* breed, brood, offspring; particularly applied to cattle, birds, etc.

sìolachadh, *vbl. n. m.* act of propagating, engendering, breeding; *n. m.* propagation.

sìolachan, siùluchan, *n. m.* strainer, filterer. *Also* sìoltachan.

sìoladh, shee-ula, *vbl. n. m.* act of subsiding; straining, filtering; a' sìoladh a' bhainne, straining the milk; tha a' ghaoth a' sìoladh, the wind is subsiding; tha an t-uisge a' sìoladh, the sediments in the water are subsiding, the water is filtering; propagation, pure, good breeding. *E.Ir.* sithlad, a filter.

sìolag, shiùlag, *n. f.* sand-eel: *pl.* sìolagan, a minnow. *Also* sìol, *pl.* sìolan.

sìolag, *n. f.* a female pigling; a breeding sow; fr. sìol, seed.

sìolag, *n. f.* a small seed, a small potato.

sìolaich, shiùlich, *v.* breed, propagate, multiply; shìolaich iad, they increased, multiplied.

sìolaich, shiùlich, *v.* subside, strain, filter; shìolaich an soirbheas, the wind subsided.

sìolaiche, *n. m.* propagator; stallion.

sìolc, shoolc, *v.* snatch, seek, slip, bound. *Also* tiolp.

sìolcair, shoolker, *n. m.* a light-fingered fellow; one that skips off. *Also* sìolpair; *a.* sìolpanta.

sìolchur, *n. m.* act of sowing.

siol-cura, shul-cooru, *n. m.* seed corn, seed-potatoes, etc.

siolgach, shooluguch, *a.* lazy, dwarfish.

siolgaire, shoolgiru, *n. m.* a mean, lazy fellow.

sioll, shool, *n. m.* turn, rotation ; sioll mu seach, time about, in rotation, alternately ; is e so mo shiollsa, this is my turn.

siolmhoireachd, shiulvoruchc, *n.f.* fecundity, productiveness, fertility.

siolmhor, *adj.* prolific, fertile ; of corn, productive, substantial. *Also* siolar.

siolta, shiültu, *n. m.* teal, small wild duck.

sioltachan, *n. m.* a strainer. So *Ir.*

sioltaich, *n. m.* bird, goosander.

sioltaiche, shiultichu, *n. m.* stallion, breeder, propagator ; fr. siol, seed. *Ir.* síoluidhe, a stallion.

sioman, shee-uman, *n. m.* rope of straw or heather (made in strands, *Lewis*). *See* sùgan. *O.N.* síma, rope. *Shetl.* simman.

siomanach, sheeumanuch, *n. m.* bounding and twisting in a chase (as a chased deer).

siomlach. *See* seamlach.

siomlachd, shee-umlachc, *n. f.* chicken-heartedness, sheepishness, great cowardice.

siomladh, shimlu', *m.* semblance ; gun siomladh atharraich, without a shade of difference. *E.Ir.* seimle, semle, *id.*

siomlaidh, sheemly, *adj.* chicken-hearted, sheepish, spiritless, heartless.

siomlag, sheemlag, *n. m.* great coward.

siomlair, shimiler, siomlainn, shimlin, *n. m.* a chimney vent ; ceann-siomlainn, chimney-stalk ; siomlainn, through the vent.

sion, sheeun, *n. m.* thing, particle ; chan 'eil sion agam, I have nothing ; chan 'eil sion a mhaith air, it is worth nothing.

sion, *n. m.* blast, drift, bad weather of wind and rain. *See* sian.

sionadh, *n. m.* a meeting, convention ; a synod. *E.Ir.* senod = *Lat.* synodus. *Gr.* σύνοδος.

sionn, *a.* phosphorescent ; solus sionn, phosphorus.

sionnach, shoonuch, *n. m.* pipe-reed ; the wind valve of a smith's bellows, or of an Irish bagpipe ; piob-shionnaich, a bellows bagpipe.

sionnach, *n. m.* a fox. *E.Ir.* sindach. *O.Ir.* sinnchenae, *vulpecula.*

sionnsar, *a.* lucky, prosperous.

sionnsar, shoon'-sàr', *n. m.* pipe-chanter. *Ir.* siunsóir.

siop, *v.* despise ; cuir an siop, turn tail on.

sior, sheer, *adj.* long, continual, perpetual. Cpds. : a' sior-amharc, eter-

nally staring ; sior-bhualadh, eternally striking, thrashing ; sior-iarrtach, importunate ; sior-mhagadh air, continually jeering or gibing him. *Also* sir. *O.Ir.* sir, long, eternal. *O.W.* hîr. *O.Celt.* sêro-s. *Lat.* sērus.

siorr, shoorr, *v.* scud or slip in or out.

siorradh, *vbl. n. m.* act of darting, dashing.

siorram, shooram, *n. m.* a sheriff. *Also* siorra, siorraimh. *Ir.* siorram, *O'R.* *M.Ir.* sirriam.

siorramachd, *n. f.* county, shire ; sheriffdom. *Also* siorrachd.

siorruidh, *adj.* eternal, everlasting ; gu siorruidh, eternally ; sir + rad, red, *abstr.* suf.

siorruidheachd, *n. f.* eternity.

sios, shees, *adv.* down ; a sios, down, downward ; a' dol sios, going down ; an dol sios, charge (in battle). *O.Ir.* sís.

siosar, shisor, *n. m.* pair of scissors ; fr. the *Eng.*

siosacot, siostacot, *n. m.* a doublet, a vest.

siota, *n. m.* a blackguard, a pet.

siothbhrugh, *n. m.* fairy knoll.

sir, sheer, *v.* seek, ask, search ; sir e, seek it ; want ; ciod e tha thu sireadh, what do you want. *E.Ir.* sirim.

sirist, siris, shirish, *n. f.* cherry. So *Ir.* Cf. *Lat.* cerasus.

siristeach, shirishtuch, *n. m.* a shelty, pony.

siteag, sheetag, *n.f.* a dunghill. *See* sitig ; fr. the *Eng.*

sitearn, sheetern, *n. f.* a harp.

sith, shee, *adj.* preternatural ; daoine sith, fairies ; bean, no leannan sith, a familiar spirit.

sith, *n. f.* peace, truce ; cogadh no sith, either war or peace ; quietness, tranquillity ; an sith, in quietness.

sith, shee, *v.i.* skip, dart. *M.Ir.* sith, onset.

sithcheartach, *n. m.* arbitrator, umpire.

sithchridh, *n. f.* the beyond, euphemism for death.

sitheach, shee-huch, *n. m.* a fairy. *Also* sithiche.

sitheadh, *n. m.* a stride, a bound, dart, onset.

sithean, shee-hen, *n. m.* a green, little pointed hill, a fairy hill. *Ir.* siothán, a hillock.

sitheil, shee-hal, *adj.* peaceful, quiet. *E.Ir.* sidamail, peaceful.

sithionn, shee-un, *n. f.* venison. *Also* sitheann. *M.Ir.* sieng, sideng, deer.

sithmhaor, shee-vūr, *n. m.* a herald.

sith-shàimh, shee-hyv, *n.f.* keen pleasure, great peace ; sith (intens.) + sàmh (tranquil).

sitig, sheetig, *n. f.* a rafter placed across the drying part of a kiln. *Also* maide-sùirn.

sitig, *n. f.* a kitchen midden.

sitinn, *n. m.* roller for a boat.

sitir, sheetir, *v.* neigh ; *n. f.* a neigh. *O.N.* þytr, whistling sound as of wind.

sitreach, sheetruch, *adj.* neighing.

sitrich, *n. f.* continuous neighing.

siubhail, shoo-ul, *v.* go, proceed, walk ; die, depart this life ; siùbhlaidh sinn gu lèir, we shall all die.

siubhal, shoo-ul, *vbl. n. m.* act of traversing, perambulating, searching ; a' siubhal a' bhaile, traversing the town ; dying, act of dying ; tha e siubhal, he is dying ; time, course, trip ; so mo siubhalsa, this is my time ; marsantasiubhail, a pedlar, packman, hawker ; luchd siubhail, travellers ; tha an làir air shiubhal, the mare is salacious ; time, trip ; air an t-siubhal so, at this time ; siubhal eile, at another time ; bithidh fios seud do shiubhail agamsa, I shall know the object of your pursuit or journey ; *adv.* once, at a time ; siubhal a chaidh mi do'n ghalldachd, once I went to the Low country. *M.Ir.* siubal.

siubhlach, shooluch, *a.* nimble ; traversing.

siùbhlachas, shooluchus, *n. m.* swiftness.

siuc, shooc, *interj.* way of calling horses.

siùcar, shoocur, *n. m.* sugar. *Eng.*

siuch, shooch, *n. m.* a drain, sewer. *Sc.*

siùd, shood, *v.* fall to ; swing.

siùdadh, shoodu, *n. m.* commencement, swinging.

siùdagan, shoodugan, *n. m.* a-going, a-wagging (one's tongue).

siùdan, shoodan, *n. m.* oscillation, swinging ; a' siùdan a nunn is a nall, oscillating this way and that way ; ri siùdan, vibrating, swinging, oscillating.

siùdanach, shoodanuch, *adj.* swinging, rocking, oscillating, vibrating.

siug, shoog, *interj.* call to a calf.

siugalair, shooguler, *n. m.* a lanky fellow.

siugan, *n. m.* " the sucker " ; a pet calf.

siùl, *n. f.* confinement, child-bed ; leabaidh-shiùl, laighe-siùl, child-bed, confinement ; bean-shiùla, a woman in child-bed ; *gen.* of seòl, a bed ; lying-in. *E.Ir.* seól, bed, lying-in ; seóla mna for mac, lying-in of a woman on a son. *Triads.*

siùnas, shoonas, lovage plant. *Also* sunas.

siup, *n. m.* a tail, appendage. *Also* stiùp.

siùrsach, shoorsuch, *n. f.* a whore. *McB.* says, = whore + seach (*f. termin.*).

sùrsachd, *n. f.* whoredom.

siuthad, shoo'ud, *v.* say away, fall to, commence ; swing.

slabhacan, slaükan, *n. m.* sea edible weed, sloke.

slabhag, slav'-ug, *n. f.* a horn-pith.

slabhcar, *n. m.* a slouching fellow, a taunter. *O.N.* slókr, a slouching fellow.

slabhradair, *n. m.* a chain-maker.

slabhraidh, slaüry, *n. f.* a chain ; slabhraidh òir, gold chain ; pot-hanger. *O.Ir.* slabrad.

slachd, *v.* beat, thrash.

slachdan, *n. m.* a beetle, a mallet, a club. *Also* simide.

slachdanaich, *v.* beetle.

slachdraich, slachc-rich, *n. f.* incessant hammering.

slad, *n. m.* havoc, carnage ; is iad a rinn an t-slad, what havoc they have made ; *v.* cause to fag, fag, deprive of strength ; shlad sin seachad iad, that made them fag ; robbing, rob. *Ir.* slat. *W.* llad, slay. *O.Celt.* stlatto-, rob.

sladachd, *n. f.* theft, robbery.

sladadh, *vbl. n. m.* act of plundering, thieving.

sladhag, *n. f.* a sheaf of corn ready to be thrashed.

slag, *n. f.* a hollow ; a dent ; *dial.* form of lag.

slag, *n. m.* flummery, curdled milk.

slagan, *n. m.* cup-shaped interior of a kiln.

slagan, *n. m.* a little hollow.

slàib, *n. f.* mire, mud ; *a.* slàibeach, slàibeil. *See* làib. So *Ir.*

slaic, *n. f.* a whack, a noisy blow.

slaid, *n. f.* a munificent gift.

slaight, slyt, *n. f.* roguery, knavery, villainy ; *v.* sneak or steal by ; shlaight e seachad, he sneaked or stole by.

slaightearachd, *n. f.* roguery, villainy, sneaking.

slaighteil, slytal, *adj.* roguish, sneakish.

slaightire, slytiru, *n. m.* rogue, villain, knave. *Ir.* slaidtheoir, a robber. *M.Ir.* slataile.

slaim, slym, *n. f.* a heap, great booty.

slàine, slàniu, *compar.* of slàn, healthy, more or most healthy.

slàinte, slàntiu, *n. f.* health, salvation ; toast ; thoir dhuinn slàinte, give us a toast ; dh' òl sinn do dheoch slàinte, we drank to your health ; air do shlàinte, to your good health. *O.Ir.* slántu, health.

slàintealachd, slàntialuchc, *n. f.* healthiness.

slàinteil, slàntal, *a.* healthy, solitary. = slàint + samail.

slais, slash, *v.* lash, drub ; *n. f.* a lash ; great quantity or number ; slais èisg, great number of fish ; fhuair iad slais, they got a great quantity.

slam, *n. m.* jam, jelly.

slam, *n. m.* a lock of wool, or hair. *E.Ir.* slamm.

slaman, *n. m.* curds and cream.

slàn, *adj.* whole, perfect, unbroken; healthy, in good health, sound; **a bheil thu slàn?** art thou in good health? **thoir dhomh slàn e**, give it me whole; **slàn leat**, fare thee well! farewell! **gum bu slàn a chì mi thu**, may I see you well! *O.Ir. salvus, sanus*, gl. *sospes. Z²*.

slàn, *n. m.* a garrison; a defence, a protection.

slànach, *a.* convalescent.

slànaich, slàn'-ich, *v.* make whole, heal. *E.Ir.* slánaigim, make whole.

slànaighear, slānyer, *n. m.* a healer; a saviour.

slànlus, slān-loos, *n. m.* ribwort.

slaod, slūd, *v.* drag, haul, pull along; 'ga shlaodadh, trailing or hauling it; *n. m.* raft, float, a great quantity. *E.Ir.* slaet.

slaodach, *a.* lounging, lazy. *E.Ir.* sláet, a slide.

slaodadh, *vbl. n. m.* act of dragging, trailing.

slaodag, slūdag, *n. f.* a slut, slovenly woman.

slaodaiche, *n. f.* a drawling, a dragging, slovenliness.

slaodail, *adj.* clumsy, lazy.

slaodaire, slūdire, *n. m.* lounger, a lazy fellow; a lout, a slovenly fellow, a sluggard.

slaodaireachd, *n. f.* laziness, slovenliness, awkwardness.

slaodan, *n. m.* a cart-track, a sledge.

slaodanach, slūdanuch, *n.* heavy fellow.

slaodraich, slūdrich, *n. f.* great haul of fish; trailing continually or always, mass of lumber.

slaoightire, slytiru. *See* slaightire.

slaop, slūp, *v.* parboil or boil slowly, as shell-fish for fish-bait; boil slightly.

slaopach, slūpuch, *a.* parboiled, dragging lazily, slovenly. *Ir.* slaopach, *a.* lukewarm, brackish, sordid.

slaopaire, slūpire, *n. m.* a drawler, trailer.

slaopaireachd, *n. f.* drawling, trailing, slovenliness.

slap, *n. m.* a flap, flapping; *v.* flap, fling; a' slapail mu mo chluasan, flapping about my ears.

slapach, slàpach, *a.* slovenly. *O.N.* slápr, a good-for-nothing.

slapachail, slapuchal, *n. m.* spinach.

slapaich, slăp'ich, *v.* get flappish, get soft and pliant, as greens heated.

slapaire, slapiru, *n. m.* dangler. *Ir.* a sloven.

slapaireachd, slapiruchc, *n. f.* slovenliness.

slapraich, *n. f.* din, noise, trampling; fr. *Eng.* slap.

slat, *n. f.* a wand, a switch, rod, or twig; a yard measure; the male organ; **slat air fad**, a yard long; **slat-ghorm**, woody nightshade; **slat-iomain**, a goad; **slat-mharcachd**, rider's whip or switch; **slat-shiùil**, sail-yard; **slat-shuaicheantais**, a sceptre, mace; **slat-dhraoidheachd**, mace, rod of office; **slat-thomhais**, a yard-stick; **slat-sgiùrsaidh**, a lash, scourge; **slat-rìoghail**, a sceptre; **slat-mhara**, tangle; **slat-iasgaich**, fishing-rod; **slat-reul**, an astrolabe; **slat-bheòil** (beul-stoc), gunwale. *M.Ir.* slat. *O.Celt.* slattâ-.

slatag, *n. f.* a small rod, a twig.

slataire, slăt'-ur-a, *n. m.* debauchee, amorist.

sleabhag, *n. f.* a mattock for digging up carrots. *Carm. Gad.*

sleagh, shlu', *n.f.* spear, lance, javelin. *E.Ir.* sleg.

sleaghach, shlughuch, *a.* armed with spears.

sleaghag, *n. f.* a small spear; a spear-pointed stick for digging up roots, or for planting and sowing purposes; dibble.

sleaghaire, shlūghiru, *n. m.* spearman.

sleamacair, *a.* sly person.

sleamhainn, *a.* smooth, slippery. *See* sleamhuinn.

sleamhan, *n. m.* stye in one's eye. *Carm. Gad.*

sleamhna, shlev-nu, *adj. compar.* of sleamhainn, slippery, more slippery.

sleamhnnachadh, sleoo'-nach-u, *vbl. n. m.* act of sliding, slipping; retrograding, getting worse.

sleamhnachan, shlau-nuchan, and sleamh nagan, *n. m.* a stye.

sleamhnag, slev-nag, *n. f.* a slide.

sleamhnaich, shlev-nuch, *v.* slide, slip.

sleamhnan, *n. m.* a sneak, a slide.

sleamhnan, slaünan, *n. m.* a stye.

sleamhainn, slev'-inn, *adj.* slippery, smooth. *O.Ir.* slemon, *lubricus. W.* llyfn. *O.Celt.* slibno-s.

sleathag, sle-hag, *n. f.* the slow-worm, blindworm.

sléibhteach, shlēytuch, *adj.* mountainous; *n. m.* mountaineer.

sléibhteach, *n. f.* lodged corn (after heavy rain).

sléibhtrich, shlētrich, *n. f.* wreckage, things strewn.

sléigeil, *a.* drawling, slow, sly. *Also* leug, laziness. *See* sleugach.

sléisdeach, shlēshjuch, *a.* large-thighed.

sléisneadh, *n. m.* backsliding.

sleog, shlog, *v.* pall on the stomach.

304   SLEOGACH—SLIOS

sleogach, shloguch, *adj.* apt to pall on the stomach ; slimy.

sleuchd, shlēchc, *v.* go on your knees, prostrate ; **sleuchdamaid,** let us kneel, prostrate. *O.Ir.* **sléchtaim.** *Lat.* flecto.

sleuchdadh, shlēchcu, *vbl. n. m.* prostration.

sleug, shlēg, *v.* sneak, drawl.

sleugach, shlēguch, *n. f.* a sneaking, sly, drawling female ; *adj.* sly and slow.

sleugaire, shlēgiru, *n. m.* sly, drawling, sneaking fellow ; a sneaker, drawler.

sliabh, shliuv, *n. m.* moor, mountain ; the face of a hill, a heath ; an extensive tract of dry moorland, a hill ; **sléibhtean,** hills ; bent grass. *O.Ir.* **sliab,** a hill, a range of hills.

sliabhaire, shliuviru, *n. m.* mountaineer.

sliachdair, *v.* daub, plaster, spread by trampling, go slow. *O.N.* slíkr, smooth.

sliachdradh, shliäch-cru', *n. m.* daubing, plastering.

sliadhag. *See* **bleaghan.**

sliasaid, shliusij, *n. f.* a thigh ; *pl.* **sléisdean,** part of a boat near the stern ; a strand of thread, a gigot, a leg of meat. *O.Ir.* **sliassit,** *poples.*

slibist, shlibisht, *adj.* clumsy, unhandy.

slige, shligu, *n. f.* a shell ; **slige chrèadha,** a potsherd ; **slige-chreachainn,** a scollopshell ; hull of a ship or any vessel, the scale of a balance ; **slige a chinn,** the brain-pan. *O.Ir.* slice, *lanx ostrea.*

sligeach, shliguch, *adj.* shelly ; *n. f.* a wreck ; crustaceous surface.

sligeag, *n. f.* a small shell.

sligeas, *n. m.* animal's jaw. *See* **leigeas.**

slighe, shliyu, *n. f.* a way, craft ; journey. *E.Ir.* slige.

sligheach, *a.* crafty, wily, cunning.

sligheadair, shliyuder, *n. m.* one who lives by fraud.

sligire, shligiru, *n. m.* conchologist.

sligireachd, shligiruchc, *n. f.* conchology.

sligneach, *n. f.* a quantity of shells, icicles, fish-scales ; *a.* shelly. Cf. *E.Ir.* **slicre,** *coll.* shells.

slim, *a.* smooth, sleek. *See* **slìom.**

slim, *n.* butterwort. *Carm. Gad.*

slinn, shleen, *n. f.* weaver's reed or sleay. *Also* **slige.** *M.Ir.* **slind,** *pecten.*

slinnchrann, *n. m.* flagstaff.

slinnean, shlinen, *n. m.* shoulder-blade. *E.Ir.* **slindén,** and **slindeóc.** slinn = blade (of oar).

slinneanach, *a.* broad-shouldered.

slinneanachd, *n. f.* a sort of divination by inspecting shoulder-blades of an animal ; or acc. to another version, by eating the flesh without touching the bone with a tooth or nail.

slinn-leumnach, shleen-lēmnuch, *a.* graceful leaping (as of salmon).

slinnseag, shleen-shag, *n. f.* silly, tawdry woman.

slinnteach, shleentuch, *n. f.* house tiles, *O.Ir.* **slind,** *imbrex.*

slinnteach, *coll. n.* the frame-work of wood that supports the straw, etc., on which the grain is placed in a kiln.

slinnteach, *coll. n. f.* sleet.

slìob, shleeb, *v.* stroke gently, rub, lick. *M.Ir.* **slipad,** act of polishing, whetting. *Teut.* root. *O.H.G.* slīfan, to glide, smooth. *A.S.* slīpan. *O.N.* slípa, to whet.

sliob, shlib, *n. m.* slush, soft mud, thawing snow.

sliobach, *a.* soft (as snow, fish), clumsy, awkward.

sliobadh, *vbl. n. m.* act of stroking gently, licking, steeping.

sliobair, *n. m.* clumsy, awkward fellow.

sliobasta, shlibustu, *a.* clumsy. *See* **slibist.**

sliobastachd, *n. f.* clumsiness.

sliochd, shluchc, *n. m.* a track ; offspring, progeny, descendants, posterity ; **sliochd Dhiarmaid,** the offspring of Diarmaid ; print, rut ; **sliochd na roithean,** the track or rut of the wheels ; **sliochd a mheur,** the print of his fingers. *M.Ir.* **slicht.** *O.Ir.* **slict,** *vestigium.* *O.Celt.* slektu-.

sliochdach, sliochdmhor, shluchcor, *a.* prolific.

slìog, shleeg, *v.* stroke gently, cajole.

slìogach, shleeguch, *adj.* sleeky, sly ; emaciated ; slim. *Ir.* **slíogach,** sleek, fawning. *N.* slíkr, sleek. *Eng.* and *Sc.* sleek.

slìogaire, shleegiru, *n. f.* stroker, cajoler.

slìom, shleem, *adj.* sleek, smooth, slim. *Ir.* **slíomaim,** I flatter, gloss over. Cf. *Eng.* slim, crafty. *Sc.* slim, naughty.

slìom, *n.* the buttercup. *Carm. Gad.*

slìomachd, shleemachc, *n. f.* daubing, fawning, sponging upon.

slìomachdair, shleemachcer, *n. m.* a mean parasite, a sponge.

slìomair, shleemer, *n. m.* a mean, low, flattering, fawning fellow.

slìomaireachd, shleemeruchc, *n. f.* mean flattery, deceitful talk, laziness.

slìop, shleep, *n. f.* a hanging under-lip.

slìopach, *adj.* blubber-lipped.

slìopaire, *n. m.* a sulky, surly, blubberlipped fellow.

slìopraich, shleeprich, *n. f.* a swishing noise.

slios, shlees, *n. m.* side ; gentle declivity ; a countryside, district. Cpd. : **bòrdslios,** the side of a bed ; **slios - réidh,** shlis-rē, *a.* smooth-sided. *M.Ir.* **slisbord,** side border. *O.Ir.* **sliss,** a side.

slis, shlish, *v.* slice ; *n. f.* a chip, shave. *E.Ir.* sliss, a chip.
sliseag, shlishag, *n. f.* a small chip. *Also* slisteag. *E.Ir.* slisseóc.
sliseagaich, *v.* chip, cut into slices.
slisneach, *adj.* having sides ; fr. *E.Ir.* sliss, a side.
slisneach, *coll. n. f.* posterity ; transf. mean. fr. sliss, a chip.
slisneadh, shlishnu, *vbl. n. m.* act of whittling.
slisneag, *n. f.* a chip.
sloc, *n. m., gen.* and *pl.* sluic, den, pit, dungeon ; sloc-guail, coal-pit ; sloc-sàbhaidh, saw-pit. So *Ir.*
slocach, *a.* full of pits.
slocaich, *v.* hollow, dig.
slocan, *n. m.* a little hole or pit ; *a.* slocanach.
slòcan, *n. m.* sloke. *See* slabhcan.
slod, *n. m.* a puddle. *See* lod.
sloinn, sloyn, *v.* name, bestow a surname. *O.Ir.* slond, *significatio,* atsluindiu, *appello. O.Celt.* stlondiô, I speak, name.
sloinneadh, sloynu, *vbl. n. m.* act of naming, declaring ; surname.
sloinntear, sloynter, *n. m.* genealogist.
sloinntearachd, *n. f.* tracing genealogy.
sloinnteil, sloyntal, *adj.* genealogical.
sloisir, slosh'-ir, *v.* dash against.
sloisreadh, sloshru, sloistreadh, *vbl. n. m.* act of dashing, swirling of billows.
sluagh, *n.m., gen.* sluaigh, *pl.* slòigh, multitude, people, host. *O.Ir.* slúag, slóg, *agmen. W.* llu. *O.Celt.* slougo-s, host.
sluaghadh, *n. m.* a hosting.
sluaigheach, *n. f.* an expedition, hosting.
sluaisir, sluaistir, sluăshir, *v.* shovel, slubber, mix (lime).
sluaisreadh, *m.* violent stirring, mixing ; " sluaisreadh gainneamh na tràghad," swirling the sand of the shore.
sluaisteach, *a.* of shuffling gait.
sluasaid, sloo-usej, *n. f.* a shovel. *E.Ir.* sluasat.
slug, sloog, *n. f.* a miry puddle.
slugadh, *vbl. n. m.* act of swallowing.
slugag, *n. f.* a small pool.
slugaideachd, *n. f.* voracity.
slugaire, sloogiru, *n. m.* a glutton.
slugan, *n. m.* the throat, gullet, a pit.
slugpholl, *n. f.* "swallow-hole," whirlpool.
sluig, *v.* swallow, devour. *E.Ir.* slucim, slocim. *O.Celt.* slukkô, I swallow ; fr. same root as *M.H.G.* slucken.
sluigte, *vbl. a.* swallowed, devoured.
slupaireachd, sloopiruchc, *n. f.* noisy feeding (as a pig). *Also* slopaireachd.
smachd, *n. m.* authority, control ; correction, discipline ; cuir smachd air, correct him, control him, discipline him. *O.Ir.* smacht, rule, *traditio* ; institute,

ritus legis, sway. *M.Ir.* smacht, fine (penalty). *O'Don. sub* aithghin.
smachdaich, *v.* correct, check, discipline ; keep in order, chastise, reprove.
smachdail, smachcal, *adj.* authoritative.
smachdalachd, *n. f.* authoritativeness, firmness of character.
smad, *n. m.* a particle, a grain. *Also* smod.
smàd, *v.* revile terribly, abuse ; threaten, intimidate.
smàdadh, *vbl. n. m.* abusing ; act of abuse.
smàdail, *adj.* abusive in the extreme ; very abusive.
smàg, *n. f.* a paw, large hand ; fo smàig, under authority. *Also* smóg.
smàgach, *n. m.* a toad.
smàgaich, smāgich, *v.* creep, crawl.
smàgair, *n. m.* one who creeps.
smàglach, smāgluch, *n. m.* a good handful.
smàig, *n. f.* tyranny, the upper hand, the ascendant ; despotism ; tha smàig aige oirre, he has her under his power ; fr. smàg.
smàigealachd, smā-gialuchc, *n. f.* extreme despotism, great degree of tyranny.
smàigean, smāgen, *n. m.* a toad.
smàigeil, smā-gel, *adj.* despotic, arbitrary.
smàigire, smāgiru, *n. f.* tyrant, despot.
smàigireachd, smagiruchc, *n. f.* tyranny, despotism, tyrannical conduct.
smàil, smāl, *v.* thrust.
smàileag, sméileag, *n. f.* smart and powerful stroke, as to a shinty ball or golf ball. *Also* sméileag.
smàl, *v.* snuff a candle, cover ; smàl an teine, cover the fire (for the night) ; *also* taisg an teine ; *n. m.* snuff of a candle, ashes.
smàl, *v.* dash to pieces, smash ; smàl e as a chéile iad, he smashed them to pieces.
smàl, *n. m.* darkness, eclipse.
smal, *n. m.* dust covering anything ; spot ; tha smal air an òr, the gold is tarnished ; stain, spot. *Ir.* smal. *O.Celt.* smalo-.
smàladair, smāluder, *n. m.* pair of snuffers.
smàladh, smālu, *vbl. n. m.* snuffing, smashing, dashing to pieces ; smàlaidh mi an t-eanchainn asad, I will dash out your brains.
smalag, *n. f.* coal-fish ; the *Sc.* sellok. *Also* céiteanach.
smalag, *n. f.* smacking kiss.
smalan, *n. m.* slight melancholy, gloom, sadness ; *a.* smalanach.
smaoin, smu-in, *n. f.* a thought, idea. *Also* smuain.
smaoinich, smaointich, smūnich, *v.* think, imagine, conceive, ponder, meditate.

smaointinn, smūntin, *n. f.* idea, thought ; act of thinking, conceiving, pondering, imagining.

smarach, *n. m., pl.* smaraichean, a large louse ; a growing youth, lad.

smarag, *n.f.* an emerald. *Lat.* smaragdus.

smeach, smech, *v.* make a fillip with the fingers ; *n. m.* smart, quick blow ; a fillip.

smeachan, smech'-an, *n. m.* chin, cheekband of a bridle. *E.Ir.* smech, chin. *O.Celt.* smekâ.

smeachan, *n. m.* step of a peat-cutter.

smeacharra, smech'-urr-u, *adj.* lively, brisk.

smeacharrachd, smech'-urr-uchc, *n. f.* liveliness.

smeachran, smech'-ran, *n. m.* too much liberty with edged tools ; tampering.

smeachranachd, smech'-ran-uchc, *n. f.* bandying civilities with one's betters ; officious interference, using too much liberty with people, or with dangerous weapons.

smeadairneach, smedurnuch, *n. f.* a slumber, a light sleep.

smeadhag, sme-ag, *n. f.* a cow's halter, short neck-rope.

smeagailt, *n. f.* the chin. *E.Ir.* smeget ; fr. smech. *O'Dav.*

smealach, smel'-uch, *a.* having a beautiful eye and engaging countenance. Cf. meallach. *O.Ir.* meldach.

smealach, smeallach, *n. m.* remains, offals, dainties.

smealparra, *a.* spirited, manfully, vivacious.

smèar, smēr, smiùr, smioor, *v.* anoint, smear sheep.

smear. *See* smior.

smearach, smeruch, *n. m.* lad. *See* smarach.

smèaradh, *vbl. n. m.* smearing. *See* smiùradh.

smèaradair, smēruder, *n. m.* a smearer.

smeartan, *n. m.* sweet tangle, seabelt.

smèid, smēj, *v.* beckon, wave to ; aim ; smèid air, wave to him, beckon to him. *M.Ir.* smétim, nod, beckon.

smèideadh, smēju, *vbl. n. m.* act of beckoning, waving ; a wink, or beckoning ; aim ; slight tinge, or degree ; cuir smèideadh mar so e, put it a slight degree this way ; smèideadh eile, another touch.

smeileach, smeluch, *a.* pale, ghastly. Cf. meileach.

sméileag, smēlag, *n. f. See* smàil.

sméilean, smēlen, *n. m.* a puny, pale creature.

smeòirn, smiorn, *n. m.* end of an arrow next the bowstring.

smeòrach, smiōruch, *n. f.* mavis, thrush. *M.Ir.* smolach.

smeur, smèr, *n. f.* a bramble-berry ; a blackberry. *E.Ir.* smér. *W.* mwyar. *Gr.* μόρον. *Lat.* mōrum.

smeuraich, *v.* grope like a blind man.

smiach, *n. f.* feeblest voice, or sound ; chan 'eil smiach aige, said of one so hoarse that he can hardly make himself heard ; or who is choking with quinsy.

smid, smij, *n. f.* syllable ; a word ; na h-abair smid, keep mum ! So *Ir.*

smig, smigead, *n. f.* chin. *M.Ir.* smech, *d.* smeich.

smigeadh, *m.* a smile, smiling. *Ir.* smig, mirth.

smigeal, smig'-ul, *n. f.* smirking, smiling.

smigean, *n. m.* a little chin, a smiling face.

smigid, *n. f.* chin.

smiodam, *n. m.* spirit, mettle, liveliness. *Sc.* smeddum.

smiolamas, smioolumus, *n. m.* refuse of a feast. *See* smolamus. Cf. spiol.

smior, smir, *n. m.* marrow, the best, hero, energy ; smior an t-sìl, the best of the seed ; duine gun smior, a man without energy ; smior-cailleach, the spinal marrow. *Also* smear. *E.Ir.* smir. *O.Ir.* smiur, marrow. *W.* mêr. *O.Celt.* smeru-. Cf. *O.H.G.* smëro. *A.S.* smeoro. *O.N.* smjör, butter.

smiorach, *n. m.* a lively louse.

smiorail, smiral, *adj.* brisk, energetic.

smioralas, smiralus, *n. m.* energy, life.

smiot, smeet, *v.* throw in the air with one hand, and strike with the other ; strike smartly ; a' smiotadh, striking ; a smart blow.

smiotach, smeetuch, *a.* crop-eared. *E.Ir.* smit, ear-lobe.

smiotadh, smeetu, *vbl. n. m.* act of sniffing in disdain ; a snigger.

smiùr, smioor, *v.* smear or grease. *Sc.* smear. *O.N.* smyrja, smear.

smiùradh, *vbl. n. m.* act of smearing.

smod, smodan, *n. m.* a particle, grain of dust ; drizzling rain.

smodal, *n. m.* smattering, refuse, sweepings. *M.Ir.* smot, a scrap.

smodanach, *adj.* drizzling ; full of broken bits, sweepings.

smodanachd, *n. f.* drizzliness.

smòg. *See* smàg, *also* spòg.

smògairneach, smōg'-arn'-uch, *n. m.* a large-pawed squat fellow or beast. So smàgairneach.

smòis, smōsh, by-form of smuais.

smòislich, smōshlich, by-form of smuaislich.

smolamas, smolumus, *n. m.* trash, fragments of food.

smotach, smoⁿttuch, *a.* nasal, speaking

with strong nasal accent, with a twang.
Cf. smutach.
smuain, smoo-ain, *n. f.* thought. *M.Ir.*
smuained.
smuainich, *v.* think, imagine. *O.Ir.*
smúainim. *O.Celt.* smudnió.
smuairean, smoo-aren, *n. m.* slight
offence, dejection, or grief, or melancholy.
smuaireanach, *adj.* grieved, dejected,
somewhat melancholy.
smuais, smoo-ash, *n. f.* substance of
bones, marrow, pith. *E.Ir.* smuas.
smuais, *v.* smash.
smuaislich, *v.* awaken from sleep.
smuaisrich, *n. f.* fragments, splinters.
smùc, smook, *n. f.* a snivel, a nasal sound.
smùch, smooch, *n. f.* nasal sound ; *v.* purr.
smùchail, *adj.* nasal, purring through
the nose ; *vbl. n. f.* act of speaking
through the nose.
smùchan, smoochan, *n. m.* half-smothered
fire. Cf. mùch.
smùd, smood, *n. f.* vapour, fine spray ;
smoke ; 'n a smùid, smoking, in hot
action ; energy in any kind of work ;
tha smùid aige air iomradh, he is
rowing at his hardest. *See* smùid.
smùdan, smood'-an, *n. m.* smoke raised
for signal ; a kiln.
smùdan, *n. m.* music of birds, a ring-dove.
smùdan, smoodan, *n. m.* particle of dust.
smùdan, *n. m.* a small block of wood.
Ir. smután.
smug, smoog, *n. f.* spittle, phlegm, snot.
So *Ir.* *Lat.* muc-us. *Gr.* μύξα,
phlegm.
smugaid, smoogij, *n. f.* spittle, phlegm.
So *Ir.*
smugaideach, smoogijuch, *a.* phlegmatic.
smùid, smooj, *n. f.* column of smoke ;
smoke ; *v.* smash, dash to pieces ;
smùid e as a chéile e, he dashed it
to pieces ; curse. *E.Ir.* smút, cloud ;
i n-a smútcheo, "in a cloud of mist."
smùideadh, smooju, *vbl. n. m.* act of
dashing, smashing ; swearing terribly,
cursing.
smùidreach, smoojruch, *n. f.* bolt of
smoke.
smuig, smoo-ig, *n. f.* a snout, a nose, the
face (ridicule).
smuilc, smoolc, *n. f.* a curled nose. *Ir.*
smulc, a snout.
smuilceach, smoolcuch, *adj.* curl-nosed.
smùirnean, smoornen, *n. m.* a mote, dust.
smùisich, smooshich, *v.* suck, extract the
juice.
smùr, smoor, *n. m.* dust, dross, rubbish,
fragments of peat.
smùr, smoor, *n. m.* depression, sadness,
gloom.
smùrach, *n. m.* dust, dross ; groping

among dust with the hands ; act of
groping.
smùraich, smoorich, *v.* grope in dust.
smùsach, smoosuch, *a.* extracting the
juice from.
smut, smoot, *n. f.* pug-nose, snout ; short
log. *See* smotach. *W.* smwt, snub.
smutach, smootuch, *a.* pug-nosed,
snoutish.
'sna, for is na = and the, anns na = in the.
snag, *n. f.* a smart, little, audible knock ;
snagan-daraich, a woodpecker.
snàgach, snàgail, *a.* creeping, crawling ;
biast-snàgach, a reptile.
snagadaich, *n. f.* audible chattering of the
teeth (as in a chill). *Onomatopœic.*
snàgaire, snàg'-ur'-u, *n. m.* creeping, sly
fellow ; sneaking fellow.
snagaireachd, *n. f.* whittling, cutting
with pocket-knife.
snagan, *n. m.* a deep drink, a clinking
noise.
snàgan, *n. m.* creeping slily.
snagardaich, snagarsaich, *n. f.* chattering
of teeth.
snagarra, *a.* active.
snagarrachd, *n. f.* activity, alertness.
snaidh, sne or sny, *v.* reduce by cutting
with a knife ; sned ; hew stones ;
clachan snaidhte, hewn stones ; pine
away ; tha e a' snaidheadh as, he is
pining away. *Ir.* snaidhim, snoighim.
E.Ir. snaidim, I chip. *O.Celt.* snadô-.
Sc. sned, cut, prune.
snaidheadair, sne-uder or snyuder, *n. m.*
hewer, cutter.
snaidheadaireachd, snyuderuchc, *n. f.*
whittling, hewing.
snaidheadh, sne-u or snyu, *vbl. n. m.* act
of cutting, slicing, hewing, pining away.
snàidhm, snàim, *n. f.* a knot, a tie. *E.Ir.*
snáidm, bond.
snaidhte, *vbl. a.* cut down ; hewn ;
dressed, as a stick.
snàig, *v.* creep, crawl, sneak. *Sc.* snaik.
snàith, snày, *v.* thread a hook.
snàithean, snà-hen, *n. m.* a single thread.
snàithle, *n. m.* long white pudding.
snàmh, snàv, *n. m.* act of swimming ; *v.*
swim ; air snàmh, swimming, afloat,
skim over ; tha m'anam a' snàmh an
ceò, my soul swims in mist ; cuir air
snàmh, cause to swim ; deluging ; a'
cur an tighe air snàmh, deluging the
house ; soaked ; *vbl. n.* act of swimming, floating, soaking, deluging.
E.Ir. snám, snáim. *W.* nawf. *O.Celt.*
snâô- (*v.*), snâmu- (*n.*).
snàmhaiche, snàvichu, *n. m.* a swimmer.
snaoidh, snuy, *v.* move, turn ; chan 'eil
snaoidheadh aige, he cannot even move
(so tightly is he held). *O.N.* snúa, to
turn (oneself).

snaoidh, snuy, snaimh, snyv, *n. f.* a bier ;
air an t-snaoidh, on the bier.
snaoim, snym, *n. f.* a knot, tie ; *v.* tie a
knot ; dial. for snaidhm.
snaois, snūsh, *n. f.* a slice ; bior-snaois,
boat-prow. *E.Ir.* snaisse, cut.
snaoisean, snūsh'-ēn, *n. m.* snuff, pinch ;
thoir dhomh snaoisean, give me a
pinch of snuff ; a huff. *W.* snisin.
snaoiseanach, snūsh'-ēn-uch, *a.* snuffy.
snaomanach, snūmanuch, *n. m.* a robust
fellow.
snaoth, snū, *v.* jerk, twitch. *See* snaoidh.
snaothadh, snū-hu, *vbl. n. m.* act of jerking ; a jerk.
snap, *v.* snap ; *n. m.* trigger ; morsel ;
a. snapach.
snapadh, *vbl. n. m.* act of pulling the
trigger, missing fire.
snas, *n. m.* regularity, elegance, seemly
appearance, decency ; dèan le snas e,
do it decently ; gnothach gun snas, an
absurd thing ; polish ; *v.* polish, ornament. *Also* snasaich. *E.Ir.* snass,
cut ; *abstr. n.* fr. snaidh (*Watson*).
snas, *v.* yield, give in, halt.
snasadh, *vbl. n. m.* act of yielding, cessation ; cur is cathadh gun snasadh,
snowing and drifting without a halt.
snasaich, *v.* perfect, order, ornament.
snasaichte, snasichtu, *vbl. a.* dressed,
sculptured ; snasaichte mar ìomhaigh,
sculptured like a statue.
snasar, snasmhor, *adj.* elegant, polished,
neat.
snasmhorachd, snasvoruchc, *n. f.* elegance.
snasta, *a.* elegant, gallant.
snàth, snā, *n. m.* thread, yarn. *O.Ir.*
snāthe (gl. *filum*). *O.Celt.* snātio-.
snàthad, snā-hud, *n. f.* a needle. *O.Ir.*
snāthat. *W.* nodwydd. *O.Celt.* snātanto-.
snàthain, snàithean, snā-hen, *n.m.* thread.
snàthaineach, sna-henuch, *a.* ropy.
snàth-cur, snā-cur, *n. m.* waft.
sneachd, shnechc, *n. m.* snow. *O.Ir.*
snechta. *Lat.* nix.
sneachdaidh, shnechcy, snowy.
sneachd-gheal, shnechc-yal, snow-white.
sneadh, shne, *n. f.* a nit. *O.Ir.* sned. *W.*
nedd, nits.
sneoghan, shno'an, *n. m.* ant. *Also*
seangan.
sniaraidh, sniäry ; dial. form of (clach)
liathra, grindstone.
snicean, *n. m.* a stitch of clothing.
snichd, shnichc, snichdean, shnichcen, *n.
m.* a stitch of a needle ; a thread ;
gach snichdean a tha agam, every
stitch I have.
snigh, shnee, *v.* drop, shed tears ; bheireadh do ghnàthachadh air na clachan

snidheadh, your conduct would make
the very stones shed tears. *E.Ir.*
snigim. *O.Celt.* snigô.
snigheach, shnee-uch, snidhteach, shnee-
tuch, *adj.* dripping, leaky (as a house) ;
tearful.
snigheadh, shnee-u, *vbl. n. m.* act of
oozing through the roof of a house ;
shedding tears ; a shùil a' snidheadh,
his eye shedding tears.
snìomh, shneev, *v.* spin, twist, twine ;
shnìomh na mnathan, the women spun ;
shnìomh e as mo làimh e, he twisted
it out of my hand ; *vbl. n. m.* act of
spinning ; the art of spinning, or
twisting ; spinning. *M.Ir.* snim. *W.*
nyddaf. *O.Celt.* snêmâ.
snìomhadair, shneevuder, *n. m.* spinner.
snìomhain, shneeven, *a.* winding, curling ;
twisted, spiral ; falt snìomhain, hair in
ringlets.
snìomhair, *n. m.* a wimble, borer, auger.
snìomhte, shneevtu, *vbl. a.* spun, twisted.
snòd, *n. f.* fishing-line, fillet of horse-hair
between the hook and the " cable "
line.
snodan, *n. m.* rapid motion of a boat.
snodha, *n. m.* smirk, faint smile ; snodha
gàire, a sniggering smile.
snodhach, snodhachd, *n. m.* sap of a tree,
blossoms.
snòid, snōj, *v.* hoop or thread a hook.
Sc. snood.
snòidean, snōjen, *n. m.* snuff. Cf. snòt.
snoig, *n. m.* expression of countenance
of a testy or snuffy person.
snoigeis, snoig'-esh, *n. f.* huff, testiness.
Sc. snog.
snoigeiseach, snóég'-esh-uch, *a.* huffy,
testy.
snoigheadh, for snaidheadh, *vbl. n. m.* act
of cleaving, hacking.
snomhach, sno'-uch, *n. f.* foliage, verdure. Cf. snodhach.
snòt, *v.* snuff the wind, suspect.
snòtaireachd, *n. f.* nosing about ; prying ;
poking the nose into, as a dog.
snothach. Same as snodhach.
snuadh, snoo-a, *n. m.* visage, hue, colour
of the face ; beauty, complexion,
aspect ; as gruamaiche snuadh, of the
gloomiest aspect. *M.Ir.* snúad.
snuadhar, snuadmhor, snoo-a-or, *adj.*
good-looking, having a fair complexion ; duine snuadhar, a comely
person.
so, shŏ, *dem. pron.* this, these ; an duine
so, this man ; an nighean so, this girl ;
adv. mar so, in this manner, thus ;
c'arson so, why so ? gluais as an so,
leave this place, be off ! o'n àm so,
henceforward, hence ; so agad e, here
you have him or it. *O.Ir.* seo, so.

so-, *prefix* denoting " good," " easy " ; so-àireamh, easily counted, computable, numerable ; **so-cheannsachadh,** conquerable ; **so - leughadh,** legible, readable, easily read ; **so-aithneachadh,** easily recognised, conspicuous ; **so-lùbadh,** flexible, seducible ; **so-aimsir,** good weather ; *opp.* of **do, do-aimsir,** bad weather.

sòbhaidh, sōvy, *v. t.* turn, prevent. *O.Ir.* sóim, I turn.

sobhrach, sōvruch, *n. f* , **sobhrachan,** *n. m.* primrose ; sort of clover. *E.Ir.* sobrach.

soc, *n. m.* snout, ploughshare ; snout of a pig ; a beak. *E.Ir.* socc. *Lat.* soccus.

socach, *a.* snoutish ; *n. f.* pert female ; certain extent of arable land.

socadh, *n. m.* a depression, a sag.

socair, sockir, *n. f.* ease, quiet, rest, leisure ; gabh socair, take ease ; socair, a dhuine ! at leisure, my dear sir ! settled state of weather, abatement of a storm ; a' cheud socair a thig, the first abatement of the storm ; peace, tranquillity ; gun socair oidhche no latha, without peace night or day ; *adj.* easy, comfortably situated, or seated, at rest ; tranquil, peaceable ; tha mi socair, I am well seated, I am at peace ; mild, well balanced, settled ; tha am feasgar socair, the evening is mild. *M.Ir.* soccair.

sochair, *n. m.* benefit, advantage ; cha sochair 'sam bith sin dhòmhsa, that is no advantage to me ; immunity or privilege. *M.Ir.* sochor (so + cor).

sochar, *n. m.* silliness, pliant mood, shyness ; diffidence.

socharach, sŏch'-ar-uch, *adj.* simple, easily imposed upon, silly ; duine socharach, a weak or simple person ; o'n a bha mi cho socharach, since I was so simple, so silly, diffident. In Lewis and elsewhere sochair, socharach, never suggest simplicity or silliness—rather shyness, diffidence.

socharachd, *n. f.* gullibility, simplicity, silliness, want of suspicion, diffidence ; na bi cho socharach, do not be so shy.

sochd, sochc, silence. *M.Ir.* socht.

socrach, socruch, *adj.* easy, moderate.

socraich, socrich, *v.* settle, establish, fix, appease ; shocraich am feasgar, the evening settled, got moderate ; arrange, adjust ; shocraich e an gnothach sin, he adjusted that business, arranged that affair.

socraichte, socrichtu, *vbl. adj.* settled, arranged ; made level, or even ; established, fixed upon.

sod, *n. m.* steam, noise of boiling water, steam of water in which meat is boiled, boiled meat. Cf. *O.N.* soð (same meaning).

sod, *n. m.* a clumsy, awkward person, a stout person. *Sc.* sod.

sodag, *n. f.* a turf, a pillion.

sodal, *n. m.* flattery, pride. *E.Ir.* sotal, proud, **sotaltus,** pride. *O.Ir.* sotla, pride.

sodalach, *n. m.* a flatterer.

sodalaich, *n. f.* flattery.

sodan, *n. m.* caressing, joy ; complaisance, expression of happiness by gesture at meeting ; air son sodain riutsa, out of sheer complaisance to you ; fawning ; rinn an cù sodan ris, the dog fawned upon him.

sodanach, *adj.* complaisant.

sodar, *n. m.* trotting, trotting horse.

sodar-bhrochan, sod'-ur-vrŏch-an, *n. m.* thick gruel.

sodarnach, *n. m.* a stout person.

so-dhèanta, *a.* possible, practicable.

sodradh, *m.* trotting, galloping.

sog, *n. m.* good humour ; merriment.

sogan, *n. m.* mirth, hilarity, tipsiness.

sògh, *n. m.* luxury, delicious fare. *E.Ir.* súaig, prosperous.

sòghail, *a.* delicious, luxurious.

sòghalachd, *n. m.* luxuriousness, sumptuousness, deliciousness.

sòghar, *adj.* luxurious, delicious.

sòghraidhean, *n. pl.* epicurean rejoicings. Cf. sùgradh.

so-iarraidh, *a.* easily ascertainable, desirable.

soideal, sojal, *n. m.* rudeness, vulgarity.

soidealta, sojaltu, *a.* bashful, ignorant. *See* saidealta.

soidean, sojen, *n. m.* a jolly-looking fellow, a stout person ; *a.* soideanach.

soidh, soy, *n. f.* a dart, a javelin, an arrow.

sòighne, sòighneas, soynu, *n. m.* pleasure, joy, delight. So *Ir.*

soileas, soylas, *n. m.* officiousness, flattery.

soilgheas, solyus, *n. m.* wind, fair wind. Cf. soirbheas, fair wind.

soilleir, suler, *adj.* clear, evident, plain ; tha sin soilleir, that is obvious ; limpid, transparent, conspicuous ; soilleir mar chriostal, clear as crystal ; sruth soilleir, limpid stream ; shrewd, clear-sighted ; so + léir.

soilleireachadh, suleruchu, *vbl. n. m.* act of getting clear or dawning ; elucidating, manifesting ; elucidation, dawn ; anns an t-soillearachadh, about the dawn.

soilleireachd, suleruchc, *n. f.* brightness, shrewdness, conspicuousness, clearness.

soilleirich, sulerich, *v.* elucidate, manifest, make evident, explain.

soillse, sylshu, *n. f.* bright light, flash of light ; a luminary ; light of the sun ; light from heaven. *O.Ir.* soillse, soilse.

soillseach, soylshuch, *a.* bright ; *n. f.* eye-bright.

soillseachadh, *vbl. n. m.* act of enlightening, gleaming ; elucidation, explanation.

soillsich, soylshich, *v.* enlighten, dawn.

soillsire, soylshiru, *n. m.* a lantern.

soimeach, soymuch, *a.* prosperous, quiet, easy in circumstances. *O.Ir.* somme, rich.

soimeach, *a.* good-natured, idle, lazy. Cf. *E.Ir.* somenmnach, good humour.

soimeachd, *n. f.* good nature, idleness.

soimhe, *a.* good-natured ; but *see* sàimhe, luxury.

soin, *n. f.* esteem.

soineann, soinnionn, *n. f.* good weather ; *op.* of doinnionn. *E.Ir.* sonend.

soineanta, *a.* good-natured. *See* soinne.

soineil, soineamhail, *adj.* handsome.

soinne, *n. f.* peace. *O.Ir.* so + inne (sense).

so-iomchar, so-imuchar, *a.* easily borne.

soir, sor, *n. m.* bag, vessel ; a bottle.

soir, *n. m.* east, eastward. *E.Ir.* sair.

soirbh, surv, *adj.* easy ; gentle, good-natured, docile ; easily accomplished ; duine soirbh, tractable, docile, or a good-tempered person ; kind, urbane. *O.Ir.* soirb, *facilis.*

soirbhe, survu, *n. m.* easiness ; *compar.* of soirbh ; *deg.* easier, etc.

soirbheachadh, survuchu, *vbl. n. m.* act of succeeding, prospering ; success, prosperity ; **soirbheachadh math leat,** great success to you.

soirbheachd, survachc, *n. f.* easiness, quietness, calmness.

soirbheas, sur'us, *n. m.* favourable wind ; a fair breeze ; easiness, quietness, gentleness, docility, success.

soirbhich, survich, *v.* succeed, prosper.

soire, suru, *n. m.* vessel, womb, a sack, a dish. *See* soir.

soireann, surun, *n. f.* calm weather. *See* soineann.

soireit, *n. f.* easiness of temper. *E.Ir.* soreid, light, happy. = so + réid.

soireiteach, soireadach, *a.* affable, good-tempered.

sois, sŏsh, *adj.* fond of ease, snug. Cf. *Sc.* sosh, snug.

soise, soshu, *n. f.* a bolis, or ball of fire, moving majestically in the heavens, and often near the earth ; perh. for soillse.

soisealta, sŏsh'-allt-u, *adj.* fond of ease, effeminate, unmanly.

soisealtachd, sŏsh'-allt'-uchc, *n. f.* indulgence in ease or effeminacy.

soisgeul, soshcal, *n. m.* gospel. *O.Ir.* soscéle, *evangelium. Z²*.

soisgeulach, soshcaluch, *a.* evangelical ; bringing good news or tidings ; evangelical.

soisgeulaiche, soshcalichu, *n. m.* evangelist. *M.Ir.* suiscélach = sui + scél.

soisich, soyshich, *v.* flash, gleam, enlighten, explain, elucidate, illustrate.

soisinn, soistinn, soyshin, *n. f.* taste, decency, ease, snugness, complacency.

soitheach, soyuch, se'uch, *n. f.* a dish, vessel ; a ship, vessel. *M.Ir.* soithech, saithech.

soitheamh, soy-huv, *adj.* tractable, docile ; gentle, mild ; **duine soitheamh,** a tractable or docile person ; easily prevailed upon or entreated ; easily done or accomplished.

soitheamheachd, *n. f.* docility ; ease.

sol, *adv.* ere that. *E.Ir.* sul.

sòlach, *adj.* highly delighted.

solair, soler, *v.* cater or provide provisions, purvey ; provide accommodation ; a' solar lòin, purveying provisions.

solar, *n. m.* a provision, purveying, providing, provisions provided.

solarach, *a.* making provision.

sòlas, *n. m.* calm, luscious pleasure or delight, comfort, consolation. *Lat.* solatium.

sòlasach, *adj.* affording calm continued pleasure, highly gratifying or comfortable.

sòlasaich, sŏl'-as-ich, *v.* give continued soothing joy.

solasta, *a.* radiant, brilliant.

so-léirsinn, so-lērsin, *a.* very visible.

so-leughadh, *a.* legible, easy to read.

soll, *n. m.* pounded crab or shell-fish thrown out at a fishing rock to attract fish.

solladh, *m.* crushed shell-fish for attracting fish. *See* sonn.

sollain, *n. f.* a welcome, rejoicing. *E.Ir.* sollamain. *Lat.* sollemne.

solta, *a.* pleasant, comely, vigorous, of calm sweet temper ; rel. to sult.

so-lùbachd, *n. m.* elasticity.

so-lùbadh, *vbl. a.* flexible, elastic.

so-lùghachd, *n. f.* pardonableness.

solus, *n. m.* light of any kind ; moon ; an solus ùr, the new moon. *E.Ir.* solus, bright.

solusach, *a.* luminous.

somalta, *a.* liberal, generous, dull, heavy, careless. *See* soimeach. *M.Ir.* soma, plenty. *O.Ir.* somma, rich.

somaltachd, *n. f.* generosity, bulk, liberality.

somaltachd, *n. f.* negligence, favour ; " nach gabh fiamh no somaltachd," who will show neither fear nor favour.

somh, *v. t.* convert, upset.
sòmhail, *a.* tight ; cuibhrionn shòmhail, scrimp lot or portion.
sòmhlaich, sùmhlaich, *v.* settle, come to order. *See* sùmhail.
son, *n. m.* (only in *cpd. prep.* air son), stead, purpose, account, preparation ; sake, reason ; air mo shonsa, on my account, as for me ; in order to, for, for anything ; air son mo chodach-sa dheth, for my part of it ; air son tighinn dachaidh, for the purpose of coming home ; air son dithis, as for two, for two, for the matter of two ; c'ar son, why ? wherefore ? on what account ? for what reason ? ; air a shon-sa, on his account ; air son sin deth, as to that matter, as for that ; air son falbh, as a reward for going, in order to go ; air mo shon féin, for myself, for my own part, as for me ; air son so uile dheth, for all this ; air a shon sin, nevertheless ; air son sgillinn, for a penny, as to a penny. *E.Ir.* son, word. *McB.*
sona, *adj.* lucky, fortunate ; happy ; is fearr a bhi sona na éirigh moch, luck is better than early rising, luck outstrips industry ; gu sona sòlach, happy and quite contented. So *E.Ir.*
sonas, *n. m.* luck, success, fortune ; happiness, bliss, felicity ; sonas is àdh ort, success and prosperity to you ; sonas no donas, success or mischief.
sonasach, *a.* happy, prosperous, lucky.
sonn, *n. m.* a cudgel, a stake, a beam ; a stout man ; a hero ; poet. applied to a stag. *E.Ir.* sonn, club. *W.* ffonn. *O.Celt.* s(p)undo-s. Cf. *O.N.* spönn.
sonn, *n. m.* a bait (for fish). *See* soll.
sonnadh, *vbl. n. m.* act of smashing, pounding.
sonnag, *n. f.* a bird's nest ; a cosy bed.
sonnalta, *adj.* liberal, handsome, very generous.
sonnaltachd, *n. f.* liberality.
sònrachadh, sōr'-ach-u, *vbl. n. m.* act of particularising, specifying ; pointing out ; appointing.
sònraich, sòrr'-ich, *v.* appoint, ordain ; specify, individualise ; *v. tr.* make a tool or a butt of. *O.Ir.* sain-reth, sain-red, *proprietas, peculiare.* *O.Celt.* saní-.
sònraichte, sōr'-ich-tyà, *vbl. adj.* particular, special ; notable, certain, remarkable ; gnothach sònraichte, a particular business. *O.Ir.* sainredach, *peculiaris.*
sop, *n. m., pl.* suip, a handful of straw ; a wisp of thatch ; sop as gach seid, wisp from every bed—said, *inter alia,*

of those that court every one. *E.Ir.*
sop, sopp, *gen.* suip, a wisp.
sopcheann, *n. m.* a bushy head.
soplach, *n. m.* refuse of straw.
sop-seilbhe, *n. m.* an enfeoffment by delivering a straw.
sòr, *v.* hesitate, pause, grudge.
sòradh, sōr'-u, *vbl. n. m.* act of hesitating, hesitation.
soraidh, sōr'-y, *n. f.* compliments, blessing ; success, farewell ; soraidh slàn do'n Ghàidheil ghasda, success and health to the handsome Gael. *E.Ir.* soreid.
sorch, *n. m.* a pedestal, gauntree.
sorcha, light, bright ; *opp.* of dorcha. *E.Ir.* sorcha =so + ríched (*cælum*).
sorchan, *n. m.* a pedestal ; support, a rest (for gun) ; shuidh e air sorchan, he sat on a boulder ; place for ball or cricket.
sòrn, *n. f.* a kiln ; flue of an oven, hearth ; damh-sùirn, a kiln-joist. *E.Ir.* sornd. *W.* ffwrn. *Lat.* furnus.
sòrn, *n. m.* a snout. So *Ir.*
sòrnach, *a.* having a snout, long-chinned.
sòrnach, *n. m.* a heap of heavy stones ; dornag is a small stone (fist-like).
sòrnan, *n. m.* fish, thorn-back ; young skate ; little chin.
so-roinnte, *a.* divisible.
sos, *n. m.* unseemly mixture of food, a mess ; food for dogs ; a bellyful.
sotal, *n. m.* flattery, fawning.
sotalach, *adj.* flattering.
sotalachd, *n. f.* flattering disposition, or fawning nature or quality.
sotail, *v.* fawn, flatter.
so-thaomadh, so-humu, *vbl. a.* exhaustible.
so-theasgasg, *adj.* docile, teachable.
so-thuigsinn, *a.* very intelligible.
spad, *v.* knock down at a blow ; knock the brains out at a blow ; kill ; *a.* flapping, hanging down.
spad-, flat. *Ir.* spad-.
spadadh, *vbl. n. m.* killing, knocking dead.
spadag, *n. f.* fillip ; light blow, quarter or limb of an animal, ham, a leg ; "chaidh a spadagan thairis air," he was thrown on his back (his legs upwards).
spadaire, *n. m.* a killer, a dull person.
spadaire, *n. m.* a fop ; a dandy, a braggart. Cf. *O.N.* spjátra, behave like a fop.
spadaireachd, spadiruchc, *n. f.* silly pride, vain conceit, foppery.
spadal, *n. m.* a paddle.
spadanta, *a.* dull, heavy, benumbed.
spadchas, *n. f.* splay-foot.
spadchluas, *n. f.* hanging, flapping ear.
spadh, *v.* jerk, twitch.

spadhadh, *vbl. n. m.* jerking, twitching; a jerk, or sudden pull; twitch; the utmost extent of outstretched arms; swathe of grass.

spadthinneas, spad-heenus, *n. m.* apoplexy, epilepsy; *syn.* tinneas-tuiteamach.

spàg, *n. f.* large and misshapen foot, paw, claw.

spàgach, *n. f.* a splay-footed person; *adj.* splay-footed, out-toed.

spagach, *v.* speaking indistinctly.

spàgaire, spàgiru, *n. m.* splay-footed man.

spàglainn, spàg-lin, *n. f.* fools' pride, conceit, bombast, ostentation.

spaglainneach, *a.* conceited.

spaid, spaj, *n.f.* a spade; fr. the *Eng.*

spaidealachd, spajaluchc, *n. f.* foppishness.

spaideil, spadjal, *adj.* conceited, proud, brawly dressed.

spaidhir, spyer, *n. f.* pocket hole of a petticoat; flap of trousers or breeches.

spaidhleireachd, spyleruchc, *f.* fidgeting, unnecessary climbing.

spaidir, spajir, *v.* scatter carelessly.

spaidreach, spajrach, *n.f.* thing scattered, or the state of lying here and there.

spaig, *n. f.* wry mouth, a long chin.

spaillichd, spa-lichc, *n. f.* vainglory.

spailp, spelp, *n. f.* pride, a foppish young man, dignified gait; airs of importance; great consequence in one's own eyes.

spailpeachd, *n. f.* ostentation.

spailpeadh, *m.* strutting.

spailpean, spailpire, *n. m.* a fop, a conceited fellow; the *Irish* spalpeen.

spailpeanachd, spelpenuchc, *n.f.* foppishness.

spailpeil, spe'lp'-al, *adj.* self-conceited.

spailpeis, spelpesh, *n. f.* self-importance, self-conceit.

spailpireachd, spe'lp'-ir-uchc, *n. f.* self-importance; airs of importance of a silly person.

spàin, *n. f.* a spoon; *pl.* spàinnean. *O.N.* spánn, spónn, a spoon.

spàineach, *n. f.* a spoonful; spàineach ime, a spoonful of butter.

Spàineach, spànuch, *adj.* belonging to Spain; *n. f.* rifle, a gun; *n. m.* a Spaniard. *Also* spàinteach.

spàineag, *n. f.* a little spoon.

spairis, spyrish, *n. f.* conceitedness, foppishness.

spairiseach, spairiseil, spyrishuch, *adj.* foppish, beauish, gaudy.

spàirn, spàrn, *n. f.* effort, great exertion, hard task; cha spàirn sin orm, that is no hard task for me. *O.N.* sporna, kick

spàirneag, bàirneach, *n. f.* a limpet.

spàirneil, *a.* requiring struggles or efforts.

spairt, spart, *n. f.* clod, a splash; drop; *v.* spatter, bespatter.

spàirte, spàrtu, *vbl. a.* bolted, thrust, jammed.

spairteach, spartuch, *adj.* thick, as cream.

spairtidh, *a.* tart, acid, alum-like.

spaisd, spashj, *v.* walk. *See* spaisdrich.

spaisdear, *n. m.* one who perambulates.

spaisdir, spashjir, *v.* walk for pleasure.

spaisdreach, spashjruch, *n. f.* a walk; a walk in a garden; promenade.

spaisdreachd, *n.f.* walking for exercise or pleasure; promenade; a march (tune); written sometimes spaidsireachd.

spaisdrich, spashjrich, *v.* walk, saunter. Cf. *Ital.* spaziare, to roam; whence *Ger.* spazieren (13th cent.). *Kl.*; fr. the *Ger.* comes *O.N.* spázera. *Cleas.* *Lat.* spatior, walk, promenade.

spàl, *n. f.* weaver's shuttle. *Ir.* spól, smól. *O.N.* spóla, spool.

spàladair, *n. m.* a maker of shuttles.

spàlag, *n. f.* a bean or pea-pod.

spàlan, *n. m.* pea-cod.

spalpadh, *m.* act of thrusting in, push quickly into a receptacle;

" 'Nuair nìtear do spalpadh
Ann an achlais do chéile."
" When two are thrust under the arm
of your partner."

spalpaire. *See* spailpire.

spalparra, *a.* dignified, neat, spirited.

spang, *n. f.* thin plate of metal, a drop, spangle. Cf. *O.N.* spöng; *gen.* spangar.

spann, *v.* wean, sever, divide; *a.* spannail. *Sc.* spain, spane, spean; wean.

spann, *n. f.* a hinge, hasp. *O.N.* spenna, to clasp. *A.S.* spannan.

spannach, *n. f.* a splinter; spannachanguill, bone of contention.

spannaich, *v.* splinter, dash, kill with one blow, despatch.

spaoil, spéill, spuyl, *v.* tie tightly, swathe. Cpd.: brat-spéillidh, *m.* swaddling bands.

spaoile, *n. m.* a spindle of yarn.

spaoileadh, *vbl. n. m.* staring, gaping.

spaoilte, *vbl. a.* swathed, swaddled.

spàrd, spàrdan, *n. m.* roost; hen-roost. *Also* spiris.

sparr, *v.* thrust in, wedge in, clap upon; spàrr e lamh innte, he thrust his hand into it; a' crannadh is a' sparradh an doruis, bolting and fastening the door; enforce by argument, inculcate; a' sparradh an ni so oirnn, thrusting this thing on us; *n. f.* a cross-beam of a couple; a joist, a large nail, a henroost. *E.Ir.* sparr. *O.N.* sparri, spar. *O.H.G.* sparro, a pole, beam.

sparr, *n. m.* spar, more or less vitreous mineral ; **is daoimean iad gun sparr gun truailleadh,** they are diamonds free from spar or admixture.

sparrach, *n. f.* a sheath, truaill.

sparradh, *vbl. n. m.* act of thrusting ; inculcating, driving in, fixing.

sparrag, *n. f.* bridle-bit, a difficulty.

sparraich, *coll. n.* household furniture, particularly beds, tables, chairs.

sparranan, *pl. n.* spasms.

sparsan, *n. m.* the dewlap of an animal. *Also* **caisean-uchd.** So *Ir.*

spart, *n. m.* essence, quintessence ; **spart an uachdair,** the best of cream ; **spart cabhrach,** the ferina of the sowens without the liquid part, a drop, a plaster.

spathalt, spà'-alt, *n. f.* a limb, a clumsy limb.

speach, *n.* a door-step.

speach, spech, *n. f.* a wasp. Cf. **beach.**

speach, *n. f., pl.* **speachannan,** a thrust, a smart clever blow, a bite ; *v.* bite, strike smartly.

speachadh, *vbl. n. m.* act of stinging, inciting.

speachanta, spech'-ant-a, *adj.* waspish, peevish.

speacharra, spech'-urr-a, *adj.* clever, active, waspish, peevish.

spead, *n. f.* a wonderfully small foot or leg.

speadach, *adj.* sheep-shanked ; *n. f.* sheep-shanked female.

speadaire, spediru, *n. m.* a sheep-shanked man or gentleman.

speal, *n. f.* a scythe ; *v.* scythe, mow. *M.Ir.* **spel.**

spealadair, *n. m.* a mower.

spealadaireachd, *n. f.* mowing.

spealg, *v.* splinter, split ; *n. f., gen.* **speilg,** splinter. *Sc.* spelk. *A.S.* spelc. *O.N.* spjalk, splint.

spealgach, *n. f.* splinter ; *a.* easily split.

spealgadh, *vbl. n. m.* act of splitting, splintering.

spealgaire, *n. m.* a splinterer.

spealp, *n. m.* a notable personage. *See* **spailp.**

spealpaireachd, *n. f.* wielding thrusts (of arms).

spealt, *n. m.* a splint ; a tall person ; *v.* splinter.

spealtag, *n. f.* a small splinter.

spealtaire, *n. m.* cleaver, cutter.

spearrach, *n. f.* a shackle, a fetter for sheep or for goats.

spearralach, *n. f.* hamstring.

spearralaich, *v.* hamstring.

spéic, *n. f.* a spike ; spoke, bar, blow. *O.N.* spík.

spéiceadh, *vbl. n. m.* spiking, striking.

spéid, spēj, *n. f.* expedition ; preparation ; haste ; order ; **cuir spéid ort,** bestir yourself; activity. *Eng.* speed.

spéideil, spejal, *a.* clever, business-like.

speil, *pl. n.* cattle ; herd, or drove. So *Ir.*

spéil, *v.* climb ; skate, slide ; **spéileadaireachd,** climbing, sliding.

speil, *n. f.* a space of time, or turn at work ; **thoir dhomh fhin speil air,** let me have a turn at it. *Eng.* spell.

speil, *n. f.* the " spoon " or lever in a game at ball corresponding to " cat and dog " ; **cluich air céis-ball,** playing at " sow-ball " ; céis = farrow sow ; the bat is called cù, a dog which drives the sow.

spéileanachd, spelenuchc, *n. f.* sliding.

speileanta, spelantu, *adj.* eloquent.

speileantachd, *n. f.* eloquence.

spéilearachd, *n. f.* swearing.

spéilearachd, *n. f.* sliding, skating.

speilearachd, *n. f.* playing a game.

spéilearaich, *v.* slide, skate.

speilg, *n. f.* a sheep-shank.

speilgeach, *adj.* sheep-shanked ; *n. f.* a sheep-shanked lady or female.

speilgire, spelgiru, *n. m.* a sheep-shanked man, a trifling-looking fellow.

spéilleag, *n. f.* curled bark. *See* **beilleag.**

spéillig, *n. f.* marrow ; **beag speillig,** but little marrow (said of any trifle).

speir, sper, *n. f.* hoof, ham ; claw, talon ; **gach speir,** every hoof, hough.

speirbh, sperv, *n. f.* a very slender leg or foot.

speirbheis, spervesh, *n. f.* a sheep-shanked female, grit, capacity (for any deed) ; neatness.

speireach, speruch, *adj.* slender-limbed ; *n. f.* cross-fetters, fetter for goat or sheep. *Also* **spearrach.**

speireag, spearag, *n. f.* sparrow-hawk.

spéirid, spērij, *n. f.* energy ; speed, expedition.

spéirideil, *adj.* active, expeditious.

spéis, spēsh, *n. f.* love, affection, regard, attachment ; **thoir spéis,** have regard ; **tha spéis aige dhi,** he is attached to her. *M.Ir.* sbéis. *Lat.* pensus, prized.

spéisealta, spēshaltu, *adj.* cleanly, as a cook or housewife ; neatly dressed, tasteful.

spéisealtachd, *n. f.* cleanliness, as cook or housewife ; tastefulness.

spéiseil, spēshal, *adj.* fond of, attached to.

speuc, **spiac**, *v.* to diverge, divaricate, branch ; gaping eyes (in surprise).

speucadh, spiacadh, *vbl. n. m.* diverging, tearing ; **air speucadh,** opened out like compasses.

speuclair, *n. m.* pair of spectacles ; an object of surprise or wonder.

speuclaireachd, *n. f.* opticians' trade, speculation or surprise.

speur, *n. m.* the sky, or firmament; climate; the heavens. *Lat.* sphaera.

speur, spēr, *v.* blaspheme, swear by the heavens.

speurach, spēr'-uch, *adj.* celestial, ethereal.

speuradair, spēruder, *n. m.* astrologer.

speuradair, *n. m.* blasphemer.

speuradaireachd, *n. f.* astrology, astronomy, star-gazing; swearing loudly.

speuradh, sper'-u, *n. m.* blasphemy; a horrid oath; *a.* an oath by Heaven.

speurghorm, *a.* azure green.

spìc, *n. f.* a spike; applied to the pointed spurs of precipitous rocks. *O.N.* spík.

spìd, speej, *n. f.* contempt; the utmost contempt; tyranny; spite. *Ir.* spíd.

spìd, *n. f.* speed, haste, liveliness, vigour; fr. the *Eng.*

spideag, *n. f.* the nightingale, a taunt, a little blow.

spideag, *n. f.* a delicate or slender creature.

spideal, *n. m.* a spital or hospital. *M.Ir.* spidél; fr. the *Eng. Lat.* hospitalis.

spìdealachd, speedaluchc, *n. f.* contemptuous conduct or disposition; spitefulness.

spìdeil, speedal, *adj.* very contemptuous.

spìdeil, *a.* vigorous, lively, in good health.

spiligean, *n. m.* single grain, a seedling; a dwarfish person.

spinneag, *n. f.* a kind of boat.

spìoc, speek, *n. f.* niggardliness, meanness.

spìocach, *a.* mean, close-fisted, selfish.

spìocaid, speecej, *n. f.* spigot; a tap.

spìocaire, speekire, *n. m.* mean fellow.

spìocaireachd, *n. f.* dastardliness, meanness, shabbiness, parsimony.

spìochan, speechan, *n. m.* a wheezing.

spiod, spid, *v.* tug or pull slightly.

spiodadh, *vbl. n. m.* act of tugging; quick pull or tug; a hint.

spiol, spiool, *v.* nibble, peel; pluck, tug; pick in a childish way; browse; pick (a bone). *Ir.* spiullaim.

spioladair, spiooluder, *n. m.* picker, plucker.

spioladh, spioolu, *vbl. n. m.* act of tugging; picking, a picking.

spiolag, spioolag, *n. f.* a crumb, a bite, a quid.

spiolainn, spioolin, *n. m.* shelled oats, grain hand-shelled (for eating).

spiolg, spioolg, *v.* unhusk, shell; **spiolgadh nam faochag**, shelling the winkles. *Also* sgiolg. *Sc.* spilk.

spiolgaire, spioolgiru, *n. m.* a husker.

spìon, spee-un, *v.* pull, tug, root, tear from by force or violence; **spìon as**

a bhun e, root it out, pull it by the roots.

spìon, spee-un, *n. m.* moor moss.

spìonach, *n. f.* a plucked or emaciated creature.

spìonnadh, spiunu, *n. m.* strength, vigour. So *Ir.*

spìonndach, spiunduch, *adj.* strong, vigorous.

spìontach, speeuntuch, *n. f.* skin wool. *Also* marbhchan.

spìontachan, speeuntuchan, *n. m.* a person like a plucked fowl.

spìontag, *n. f.* a small worm (seen in decaying fish).

spìontag, speentag, *n. f.* a currant. *Ir.* spiontóg, a gooseberry.

spiorad, spirud, *n. m.* a spirit; an apparition, spectre; heart. *O.Ir.* spiurt, spirut. *Lat.* spiritus.

spioradail, *adj.* spiritual. *Ir.* spioratgha. *Ktg.*

spioradalachd, *n. f.* spirituality, spiritedness, liveliness.

spìos, *v.* and *n. f.* spice, flavour; fr. the *Eng.*

spìosadh, *vbl. n. m.* act of flavouring; spicing.

spìosrach, speesruch, *n. f.* spicery.

spìosraich, speesrich, *v.* spice, season.

spiris, *n. f.* a spire; hen-roost, hammock. So *Ir.* Cf. *Sc.* spire. *Dan.* spir (spar).

spitheag, spee-hag, *n. f.* pebble, small stone, a chip; a small light person. *Ir.* spiothóg.

spiuthair, *n. m.* a robber.

splaidse, splajshu, *v.* fall with a crash, shut with a crash; *n. m.* a crash, noise.

splang, *n. f.* the flank, the groin.

splang, *n. f.* a sparkle; *v.* sparkle. *Ir.* splanc.

splangaid, *n. f.* a snot, mucus. *Ir.* spleangaid.

splèachd, *v.* gaze vacantly, plaster awkwardly.

splèachdach, *a.* staring, squinting, spread out.

splèachdag, *n. f.* squint-eyed woman.

splèachdair, *n. m.* a gazer, a squinter.

splèachdaireachd, *n. f.* staring, plastering awkwardly.

spleadh, splu', *n. m., pl.* **spleadhan**, an enormous splay-foot; **cum a stigh do spleadhan**, keep in your ugly toes, or feet; fr. the *Eng.* splay.

spleadh, *v.* fall with a crash.

spleadh, *n. m.* ostentation, romance, false flattery. So *Ir. O.F.* despleier.

spleadhach, *adj.* romantic, incredible; having enormous feet, having ugly feet.

spleadhachas, splu'uchus, *n. m.* wonder,

surprising nature or quality of anything. *Ir.* spleadhachas, boasting,
hyperbole, fiction.
spleadhadair, *n. m.* teller of tales and
fiction.
spleadhadh, *n. m.* a fall, crash, falling.
spleadhaire, splu'iru, *n. m.* a romancer.
spleadhan, *n. m.* a wooden paddle (to
dig up sand eels).
spleadhnas, splūnus, *n. m.* a fiction.
spleadhrach, splūruch, *adj.* romantic,
incredible, enormous ; gasconading,
romancing.
spleadhraich, splurich, *n. f.* romance.
splèamas, *n. m.* affected surprise, vulgar
show.
splèathard, splià-hard, *n. f.* sprawling
feet.
splèathardaich, *vbl. n. m.* act of sprawling
and kicking out in all directions.
spleòcach, *a.* wry, gaping, gash, blubbery.
See spliugach.
spleuc, splĕchc and spliäck, *v.* flatten
awkwardly, stare (mouth and eyes
gaping).
spleucach, *adj.* flat, ugly as stamped
cloth, or print.
spleucaid, spliäcej, *n. f.* a foolish starer.
spleucair, *n. m.* a foolish gazer.
spleuchd, spliachd, *v.* stare, squint,
spread out by trampling.
spliùc, spli-ook, *n. f.* fluke of an anchor.
spliùcan, spliuchan, *n. m.* a tobacco-
pouch.
spliug, splioog, *n. f.* snot ; icicle ; a
blubber-lipped person's mouth, a most
unmanly phiz or expression of countenance ; *a.* spliugach.
spliùgaid, splioogej, *n. f.* a blubbering
female ; *a.* spliùgail.
spliùgaire, splioogiru, *n. m.* a blubberer,
snotty, slovenly fellow.
spliut, spliŏŏt, *n. f.* a splay foot or hand ;
v. gash. *See* pliut.
spliutaire, spliootiru, *n. m.* splay-footed
man ; a splay-footed female ; *a.*
spliutach, deformed hand.
splogan, *n. m.* a double chin. *Also*
sprogan.
spoch, *n. f.* a sudden attack or assault ;
v. attack angrily. *Ir.* spochaim, I rob,
plunder.
spoch, *v.* speak in sudden anger ; snap.
Ir. spochaim, affront, provoke.
spochanach, *a.* fond of picking quarrels.
spochanachd, *n. f.* picking quarrels, as
a feeble ill-natured person.
spòg, *n. f.* a paw, claw, flat foot.
spògach, *a.* clawed, pawed.
spoinnich, spo·nich, *v.* bristle against.
spoithte, spò'-tya, *vbl. a.* gelded, castrated ; very bare, as a measure.
spoll, *n. f.* a quarter, leg, as of a sheep,

fowl ; *v.* quarter, tear. *Ir.* spódhla, a
piece of meat.
spollachdach, *a.* sottish, stupid. *Also*
spolladach.
spollachdaire, *n. m.* a blockhead, stupid
person.
spòlt, *v.* tear, mangle, quarter, hew down
(in battle), splutter.
spòltadh, *vbl. n. m.* act of tearing, hacking ;
a. spòltach.
spong, *n. m.* a tinder, meanness, pith,
sponge. *E.Ir.* spongc, tinder. *Lat.*
spongia, sponge. Same idea in *Ger.*
Feuerschwamm.
spongaire, *n. m.* churl, niggard.
spongaireachd, *n. f.* churlishness, niggardliness, mean disposition.
spor, spuir, *n. f., pl.* spuirean, a spur,
talon of a cock, claw ; *v.* incite, instigate, spur. *M.Ir.* sbor. *O.N.* spori, a
spur ; spor, a footmark.
spor, *n. f., pl.* spuir, tinder, flint, gun-
flint ; clach-spor, a flint. *Eng.* spar.
sporach, spuireach, *a.* provided with
talons, with spurs.
sporan, *n. m.* a purse, pouch. *M.Ir.*
sboran.
sporan, *n. m.* a dewlap.
sporg, *v.* ruzzle, struggle without effect.
sporghail, *n. f.* ruzzle, ruzzling noise ;
a searching among loose stuff ; act of
ruzzling, struggling without effect.
sporracan, *n. pl.* crumbs.
sporraich, *v.* bristle ; sporraich e rium,
he bristled up to me. *Also* sgorraich.
spòrs, *n. f.* diversion, play, fun ; gheibh
sinn spòrs, we shall get some sport or
fun ; pride, disdain ; is i an spòrs
thug ort sin a dheanamh, sheer pride
made you do that ; fr. the *Eng.* sport.
spòrsail, *a.* proud, disdainful.
spòrsalachd, *n. f.* pridefulness, disdainful-
ness, sheer haughtiness.
spot, *n. m.* a spot ; as an spot =imme-
diately ; injury, loss ; " bhuail an
t-earrach orm spot," the spring has hit
me hard—*i.e.* left its mark ; fr. the
Eng.
spotagach, *a.* spotted, full of small spots.
spoth, *v.* geld, castrate ; fit straw for
thatch, clean grain from refuse of
straw ; a term used in cutting peat ;
spoth am fàd, " cut out " the peat.
M.Ir. spochad. *Lat.* spado, eunuch.
spothadair, *n. m.* gelder.
spothadh, spo-hu, *vbl. n. m.* act of gelding, castrating.
spracadh, *n. m.* strength, sprightliness.
Sc. sprack. Cf. *O.N.* sprækr, lively.
spracalachd, *n. f.* vigour, boasting in
one's powers, ability.
spraidh, *n. f.* shot. *See* spreadh.
spraic, spryc, *n. f.* an angry, authori-

tative tone of voice and attitude ;
cleverness ; a frown, mandate, reproof.
spraiceil, sprycal, *adj.* authoritative,
commanding, lively, active, energetic.
spraidh, spraigh, spry, *v.* burst.
spraigheadh, spraiy-u, *vbl. n. m.* act of
bursting, a bursting, loud blast, report
of a gun.
spreadh, *v.* burst, sound loudly while
bursting, kill. *Ir.* spréidhim. *E.Ir.*
sprédaire, sprinkling brush.
spreadhadh, *vbl. n. m.* act of bursting,
report of a gun, activity, life, a scattering through anything bursting (as a
shell). *M.Ir.* sprethach, a scattering.
spreangan, *n. m.* a split stick, a tweezer,
for closing a wound to stop bleeding.
spréidh, sprey, *n. f.* cattle of all sorts.
E.Ir. spré, spréid, cattle.
spreig, spreg, *v.* speak (with energy) ;
incite, instigate ; blame, reprove ;
play on a musical instrument ; divulge
a secret. So *Ir.* spreagaim. Cf. *A.S.*
sprecan. *M.H.G.* sprechen. *O.H.G.*
sprehhan, speak, say. *See* preig.
spreigeadh, spregu, *n. m.* pith, energy ;
mòine gun spreigeadh, pithless peats.
spreigeadh, *vbl. n. m.* chiding, reproving,
inciting, instigating, blabbing, playing ;
pìob 'g a spreigeadh, piping. *Ir.*
spreagaim, incite, play (on instrument)
spreigearra, *a.* expressive, spirited.
spreigeil, *a.* lively, energetic.
spreigh, *v.* scatter, burst. *See* spreadh.
spreill, *n. f.* the tongue hanging out in
contempt, or from discontent ; blubber-
lipped. *Ir.* spreill, a contemptible set.
spreisneach, *n. f.* the remains of a wreck.
spreòchainn, sprochin, *n. f.* a person or
thing hardly hanging together ; feebleness, want of pith. Cf. breòchaid.
spreòchantachd, *n. f.* weak attempts.
spreòd, *n. m.* sprit ; beam ; crann
spreòid, a bowsprit. *A.S.* sprēot.
spreòd, spreòt, *v.* incite, goad on.
spreòdadh, *n. m.* stirring, inciting, urging
on.
spriolag, *n. f.* an evil genius, a practical
joker, a baffler.
sproc, *n. m.* dejection, sadness, lowness
of spirits, melancholy. *M.Ir.* broc,
sorrow.
sprocalachd, *n. f.* dejection, gloom.
sprod, *n. m.* a stick. *O.N.* sproti, a stick,
a twig. *A.S.* sprota.
sprog, sprogan, *n. m.* dewlap, double
chin. *Also* splogan.
sprogaill, *n. m.* dewlap. So *Ir.*
spronnan, *n. m.* a crumb ; fr. pronn.
spruan, *n. m.* shortbread.
spruan, *n. m.* brushwood, firewood.
So *Ir.*
spruchag, *n. f.* a hoard, savings.

sprùdan, sproodun, *coll. n.* fingers, sprouts.
sprùdhan, *n. m.* fragments, crumbs.
sprùilleach, sprùidhleach, sprooluch, *n. m.*
fragments, crumbs, broken pieces.
M.Ir. sbrúileach.
spruis, *n. f.* a branch, a limb.
spruiseil, sprooshal, *a.* spruce, neat, trim.
spruithean, *n. m.* claw, eagle's claw.
spruthar, *coll. n.* a collection of fragments.
spuacadh, spoo-ucu, *vbl. n. m.* act of
thumping, mauling, daubing awkwardly ; dashing, squashing (into
pulp).
spuaic, *n. f.* (*pl.* spuachdan) a bruise,
a maul, callosity, welt ; crown of the
head, a pinnacle, scab, mole ; a
tumour on the side of the head ;
spuaic theanga, disease in cattle ; *v.*
break, splinter ; maul, bruise ; knock
on the head ; blister ; plaster awkwardly and with force. *E.Ir.* buac,
cap, pinnacle.
spuch, *v.* strike with paw (as a cat).
spuchadh, *vbl. n. m.* act of hitting out,
act of striking with paw.
spùidsear, spoojsher, *n. m.* a baling-dish.
spùill, spooil, *v.* plunder, spoil, prey, rob.
spùilleadh, spoolu, *vbl. n. m.* act of
robbing, plundering. *Sc.* spulye. *Lat.*
spoliare.
spùinn, spooin, *v.* plunder, spoil, rob ;
a form of spuill. *Lat.* spoliare.
spùinneadair, spoo-nuder, *n.m.* plunderer,
spoiler, robber.
spùinneadh, spooniu, *vbl. n. m.* act of
spoiling, plundering.
spùinns, *n. m.* rubber ball (washed
ashore) ; for *Eng.* sponge.
spùinns, *n. f.* a great strain, a mighty
pull.
spuir, spoor, *n. f.* a spur, talon.
spùirse, spoorshu, *n. f.* milk-weed, spurge.
spùill, spool, *n. f.* nail of a cat ; a clutch.
spùllach, *a.* nailed, greedy ; *n. f.* a very
greedy, monopolising female.
spùllaire, spooliru, *n. m.* greedy man.
spursan, *n. m.* a gizzard. *Ir.* spursán.
spurt, *n. f.* enjoyment, entertainment,
sport.
spùt, spoot, *n. f.* a spout ; bad liquor or
toplash ; a flux ; a waterfall ; *v.*
squirt, spout, pour out ; gunna-spùt,
a syringe ; a' spùtadh, squirting. *Sc.*
spoot. *Eng.* spout.
spùtachan, spootuchan, *n. m.* a syringe.
Also stealladair, pìob-steallaidh.
spùtaire, spōōtiru, *n. m.* a bird ; syringe.
spùtan, *n. m.* a small spout or squirt.
sràbh, srāv, *n. m.* a straw ; a' trusadh
nan sràbh is a' leigeil nam boitean leis
an abhainn, gathering straws, and
allowing the trusses to go with the
stream. = *Eng.* straw.

sràbhach, srâv'-uch, a. scattered, strawy.
sràbhard, n. f. strife, uproar. R.D.
srac, v. tear, rend violently, rip ; rob. Ir. sracaim.
sracadh, sracu, vbl. n. m. act of tearing ; a rent.
sracaire, srac'-iru, n. m. render, tearer.
sracanta, adj. turbulent.
srad, n. f. a spark of fire ; quick temper ; v. emit sparks of fire ; sparkle. So Ir.
sradadh, vbl. n. m. act of emitting sparks.
sradag, n. f. a little spark ; temper.
sradanta, adj. given to emitting sparks ; quick-tempered.
sradrach, n. f. sparkle ; half inebriety.
sràibhlean, srā-len, n. m. a small straw.
sràid, srāj, n. f. a street, a row, rank ; tha e gabhail sràid, he is taking a walk. E.Ir. sráit. Lat. strata.
sràideach, srājuch, n. f. a lane ; adj. full of streets.
sràidean, srājen, n. m. the plant, shepherd's purse.
sràidear, srājer, n. m. a saunterer.
sraidheadh, n. m. a roaring noise.
sràidimeachd, srājumachc, n. f. walking for pleasure or exercise ; pacing.
sràidimich, srājumich, v. walk for pleasure or exercise.
sraigh, sry, n. f. the cartilage of the nose ; cuiridh mi car an sraigh do shròine, I will twist the cartilage of your nose ; v. sneeze ; tha e a' sraigheadh, he is sneezing.
sraigheartaich, sry-artich, n. f. sneezing.
sramh, n. m. a jet of milk flowing from a cow's udder. Also striod, striodag.
srann, n. f. a snore, whiz ; v. snore, whiz ; whirr. E.Ir. srand. O.Ir. srennim, sterto.
srann, n. f. a drink as deep as one's breath will permit him ; v. drink deep.
srannadh, srànn'-u, vbl. n. m. act of snoring, buzzing, humming ; a great offence. Also srannail, srannraich.
srannan, srannachan, n. m. a buzzing toy, grasshopper.
sraon, srūn, v. make a false step ; stumble ; slip ; rush. E.Ir. sróenim, overthrow, defeat.
sraonadh, srūnu, n. m. slip, digression, a rush, a great offence.
sraonais, srunesh, n. f. great snuffiness.
sraonaiseach, a. snuffy.
srath, sra, n. m. a plain beside a river ; meadow ; flat part of a valley ; a valley ; luchd-àiteachaidh an t-sratha, the inhabitants of the valley. Sc. strath. O.Ir. srath, israth (in gramine). Lat. stratus. O.Celt. stratu-s.
srathach, sra-huch, adj. full of valleys.
srathail, vbl. n. m. noise of people's feet passing by, trampling of feet.

srathair, sra-hir, n. f. pannier-saddle ; bidh na caidearan a' tighinn air na srathraichean, cadgers talk of pannier-saddles (Prov.), i.e. every one to his "shop." O.Ir. srathar. M.Lat. stratura-, a pack-saddle.
sreabhainn, n. f. a membrane, a film, a gauzy substance. O.Ir. srebann.
sream, sriäm, n. f. rheum, wrinkle.
sreamach, sriämuch, a. blear-eyed.
sreamadh, vbl. n. m. act of wrinkling, act of grinning, curbing by the nose.
sreamaid, sriämej, n. f. a string of slaver, or snotter.
sream-shuileach, sriäm-hooluch, a. blear-eyed.
sreang, sreng, n. f. a string ; a cord, a ridge ; charm to prevent harm from an evil eye. E.Ir. sreng. O.N. strengr.
sreangach, sreng'-uch, adj. capillary, in strings.
sreangaich, sreng'-ich, v. string ; get capillary, draw into strings.
sreangaichte, srengichtu, vbl. a. tied ; capillary.
sreann, sren, n. f. a snore, snort ; whiz, buzz, humming noise ; v. snore, snort ; v. srann.
sreannartaich, srann'-art-ich, n. f. a continuous buzzing, whizzing ; snoring or snorting.
sreannchorr, n. f. a whirlwind.
sreap, v. tr. to climb. See sreap.
sreaphainn, n. f. membrane; membrane which covers newly born calf. O.Ir. srebann, srebhand.
sreat, sreatan, srett'-an, n. m. a screech ; sreatan lùghadaireachd, a screech of blasphemies. See sgread.
sreath, sre, n. f. row, rank, stratum ; sreath-aghaidh, the van ; sreath-chùl, the rear. O.Ir. sreth, series, ordo.
sreathach, sre-huch, adj. in ranks or rows.
sreathaich, sre-hich, v. place in ranks.
sreathainn. See sgreothainn, kiln straw. Also sreathaig.
sreathan, n. m. filmy skin covering unborn calf.
sréighe, srēyu, n. m. favourite ; sréighe ar rìgh, the favourite of our king.
sreinglein, srēng'-lèn, n. f. strangles. Also foghach.
sreothan, sro-han, n. m. semen, film.
sreothart, n. f. a sneeze. Ir. sraoth, sraoth-furtach.
sreothartaich. See sraigheartaich, sneezing.
sreud, srēd, n. m. a procession ; a drove.
sreup, srep, v. tr. for streup, to climb.
srian, n. f. a bridle, restraint ; v. bridle. E.Ir. srian. W. ffrwyn. Lat. frenum.

srian, *n. f.* a stroke, a streak ; a line in tartan.

srianach, *a.* full of lines, or streaks ; *n. m.* the "streaked one," a badger, a brock.

srianach, *a.* bridled, curbed.

sriante, *vbl. a.* bridled, curbed.

sringleoin, *n. m.* the strangles.

sriodach, sriduch, *a.* white streaked with dark.

sriodag, sridag, *n. f.* a drop, a spark.

sriut, sroot, *n. m.* torrent of quick sounds, a tirade. *See* sruit ; Ir. sruth, a stream.

sriutan, *n. m.* a stream of words ; *a.* sriutach. *Also* strutan.

srobadh, *n. m.* a push, small quantity of liquor. *See* sruab.

sroghall, *n. m.* a whip. *E.Ir.* sraigell. *O.Ir.* srogill. *W.* ffrewyll. *Lat.* flagellum.

sròin, sròin, *n. f.* a huff ; tha sròin air, he is huffed, or offended ; *d.* of sròn, used as *nom.*

sròineis, sròin'-esh, *n. f.* snuffling, smelling, snorting.

sròineiseach, sròin'-esh-uch, *adj.* huffy, snuffy.

sròl, *n. m.* satin, gauze, veil, banner, streamer. *Ir.* sròl. *Lat.* stragulus.

sròlach, *a.* gauzy, silken, bannered.

sròn, *n. f.* a nose, promontory or peak, supposed to resemble a nose ; a huff ; tha sròn air, he is huffed, he is offended. *O.Ir.* srón. *W.* ffroen. *O.Celt.* sroknâ.

srònach, *adj.* having a prominent nose ; *n. f.* nose-string.

srònagach, *n. f.* smelling, tracing by scent.

srònail, *adj.* nasal.

sruab, *n. f.* noisy draught, noisy sip, pull hastily out of the water. *See* srùb.

sruan, *n. m.* shortbread cake having five corners.

srùb, sroob, *v.* suck, inhale drink, as far as your breath will permit you ; draw in, imbibe ; *n. m.* spout (of kettle or pot). *Ir.* srúb, snout. *O.Celt.* srubu-. Cf. *O.N.* strjúpi, the spurting (of blood).

srùbadh, sroobu, *vbl. n. m.* act of inhaling, imbibing ; a large mouthful of liquids.

srùbag, sroobag, *n. f.* a little gulp.

srùbaire, sroobiru, *n. m.* a sucker, inhaler.

srùban, *n. m.* a cockle ; clam.

sruil, srool, *v.* rinse, half-cleanse. *See* sruthail ; gulp, drink ; sruil ort e, gulp it up.

sruit, sroot, *n. m.* a torrent of words. *Ir.* sruitean, a long and quick repetition of news or poetry.

srùlach, srooluch, *a.* coming in streams.

srùladh, sroolu, *vbl. n. m.* act of half-washing, rinsing, gulping.

srùladh, *vbl. n. m.* suction of air ; an srùladh a tha bho'n dorus, the suction

or stream of air that comes from the door.

srùllamas, sroolumus, *n. m.* a person that speaks as if his mouth was filled with liquid.

sruth, sroo, *n. m.* current, stream, tide ; saobh-shruth, eddy-tide (*i.e.* a "false" current which runs close to the shore but in the opposite direction to the main stream ; am marbh-sruth, slackwater ; sruth-tràghaidh, ebb tide ; sruth-lìonaidh, flood-tide ; caileach an t-sruth, centre of the current ; le sruth is soirbheas, with current and fair wind ; tha'n sruth leinn, the current is with us ; torrent, a fountain ; sruthannan na beatha, the fountains of life ; confhadh an t-sruth, the rage of the torrent ; a' dol leis an t-sruth, "going to the dogs" (carried off by the stream). *O.Ir.* sruth. *W.* ffrwd. *O.Celt.* srutu-. *Gr.* ῥυτός, flowing. *Jones.*

sruth, *v. intr.* flow, stream, shed, drip.

sruthach, sroo-huch, *adj.* streaming.

sruthadh, sroo-hu, *vbl. n. m.* act of flowing, spending, as corn in the shock.

sruthail, sroo-hul, *v.* rinse with water. *See* sruil.

sruthan, sroo-han, *n. m.* streamlet, rivulet, rill.

sruthanach, sroo-hanuch, *a.* full of rivulets.

sruthchlais, *n. f.* water-channel

sruthladh, *n. m.* rinsing, act of rinsing.

srùthlag, sroolag, *n. f.* a small stream, the discharge of a mill.

stà, *n. f.* advantage, use, profit, avail. *Also* stath, substance.

stàbhach, stàv'-uch, *adj.* off the balance, down by the side (of shoes) ; straddling wide asunder.

stàbhaic, stàv'-ichg, *n. f.* a wry-neck, a sullen, or boorish attitude of the head.

stàblair, stàpler, *n. m.* a stabler.

stàbull, stàpul, *n. m.* a stable. *O.F.* estable. *Lat.* stabulum.

stac, *n. m.* dullness of hearing.

stac, *n. m.* a steep rock, conical hill ; a columnar rock. *M.Ir.* stacc. *McB.* and others say fr. *O.N.* stakkr, stack of hay, but *Marst.* says *M.Eng.*

stacach, *adj.* dull of hearing ; very unready to take fire ; peaky, uneven.

stacachd, *n. f.* deafness ; unaptness to take fire.

stacaiche, stachcichu, *n. f.* degree of deafness.

stacan, *n. m.* a little steep hill, a little precipice.

stachaill, stachil, *n. m.* a bar, a barrier.

stad, *n. m.* a stop, period ; stopping, detention, impediment, pause ; *v.* stop, impede, hinder ; tha stad 'na chainnt, there is an impediment in his speech ; **gun stad**, incessantly, unceasingly ; **dèan stad**, wait, stop, pause, not so fast. So *E.Ir.* Cf. *Lat.* status. Cf. *O.N.* staða, a standing.

stadach, *adj.* ceasing, lisping.

stadachd, *n. f.* impediment, detention ; tendency or proneness to stop.

stadaich, *n. f.* stop, impediment of speech ; **duine aig an robh stadaich 'na chainnt**, a man who had an impediment of speech.

stadh, *n. m.* use, service ; a swathe of grass or corn as it leaves the scythe.

stadhadh, stu'u, *n. m.* a lurch, sudden bend, straightening oneself, stretching oneself.

staga, *n. f.* squat stout woman (applied in contempt). Cf. *O.N.* stakka, a stump.

stagarsaich, stag'-urs-ich, *n. f.* staggering, stammering ; fr. the *Eng.*

stagh, stu', *n. m.* stays ; the rope that sustains the mast ; **dhiùlt i tighinn 'sa' stagh**, she refused stays ; **a' tighinn 'sa' stagh**, putting about, as a ship or boat ; **ar stagh is ar tarrainn, cum fallain**, our stays and haulyards, preserve thou. *O.N.* stag, a stay, *esp.* the rope from the mast to the stem. *A.S.* stæg, whence *Eng.* stay.

staid, staj, *n. f.* state, condition ; is **truagh mo staid**, sad is my condition ; an estate, proprietorship. *M.Ir.* stait. *Lat.* statio ; fr. the *Eng.*

stàid, *n. f.* a furlong. So *Ir.*

stàidealachd, stàjaluchc, *n. f.* sedateness, stateliness. *Ir.* stáideamhlachd.

stàideil, stajel, *adj.* sedate, portly.

staidhir, stayr, *n. f.* a stair, steps ; *pl.* staidhreachan. *Also* staidhre ; fr. the *Eng. Ir.* staighre.

staidhreach, stayruch, *a.* having a stair, or steps.

stail, stal, *n. f.* 1. bandage, strop. 2. still, whisky-pot.

stailc, stēlk, *n. f.* thump ; lash against ; stubbornness, stop. *Ir.* stailc, stop, impediment.

stailc, *v.* ram down, stamp, trample ; " busk " a fishing-hook. Cf. **stalc**.

stailceadh, *n. m.* act of stamping.

stailear, *n. m.*, *pl.* stailearan, a distiller ; fr. *Eng.* still. *Lat.* stillare, to drip.

stailearan, *n. m.* a small spring-balance.

stàilinn, stālin, *n. f.* steel. *O.N.* stál, steel. *O.H.G.* stahal (stâl).

stàilinneach, *a.* like steel.

staimhnte, styntu, for **stainnte**, *a.* confined, narrow.

staiminn, *a.* of taminy ; fr. *Sc.* stammyng ; stemyng, the cloth now called tamine or taminy. *Jamieson.*

staing, *n. f.* a ditch, a moat, a trench.

staing, *n. f.* a peg, a cloak-pin ; a prickle, rib of a creel ; a small pointed rock. *O.N.* stöng, *gen.* stangar, a pole.

staing, *n. f.* a firm well-built person or beast.

staing, *n. f.* a site, a stance, a sacred enclosure, a sanctuary, an impregnable position ; distress, difficulty ; an object not easily got rid of.

staing, *n. f.* a gap in a rock, or mountain.

staingeach, steng'-uch, *adj.* full of ditches.

staingean, *n. m.* an obstinate boorish person. *Ir.* stainc, incivility.

staipeal, *n. f.* a handful of drawn straw, tied at one end for thatching.

staipeal, *n. m.* stopper, cork (of bottle). *Sc.* stappil.

stair, *n. f.* a short but vigorous spell at work ; fr. *Eng.* stir.

stair, star, *n. f.* a temporary bridge for cattle ; stepping-stones.

stairirich, stururich, *n. f.* a noise. *See* stararaich.

stairmeil, *a.* sturdy, plucky.

stàirn, *n. f.* a particle, a small quantity. *Sc.* starn, a particle.

stàirn, stārn, *n. f.* noise, tramping, rumbling noise, brain-swimming (from liquor).

stàirneanach, stārnenuch, *n. m.* a robustious fellow.

stàirneil, stārnal, *a.* conceited, ostentatious, swaggering.

stairseach, star'-shuch, **stairsneach**, starsh'-nyuch, *n. f.* a threshold, stone step, a stepping-stone. *E.Ir.* tairsech, " cross-beam or stone."

stairt, *n. f.* considerable distance, trip.

stàit, *n. m.* the state ; a magistrate, great man of a place or city ; **stàitean na tìre**, the great men of the country ; **stàitean a' bhaile**, the magistrates of the city.

stàiteal, stātial, *adj.* magisterial, portly.

stàitealachd, stātialuchc, *n. f.* magisterial conduct or gait, stateliness.

stal, *n. m.* a bandage, esp. a head-bandage.

stalan, *n. m.* a stallion. *Also* àigeach.

stalc, *n. m.* a stout burly man.

stalc, *v.* dash the foot against ; thread a hook, tap ; stiffen, starch ; gaze, stare ; *n. m.* a dash against, thump.

stalcadh, *vbl. n. m.* act of dashing, thumping, threading or hooping ; stiffening, starching, stalking.

stalcair, stalcir, *n. m.* a dresser of hooks, a stiff walker, fowler, deer-stalker.

stalcaireachd, *n. f.* 1. dressing hooks, a hobbling. 2. deer-stalking ; gazing. So *Ir.*

stalcanta, *adj.* stout, firm, stiff.

stalcantachd, *n. f.* stoutness, firmness, robustness.

stall. *See* **stal.**

stall, *n. m.* the step in the floor down to the level of the byre in the very old thatched houses. *See* **stalla.**

stall, *n. m.* bearing ; proper state ; **cha 'n urrainn mi a thoirt gu stall,** I cannot bring him to a bearing, or proper state or trim.

stall, *v.* dash violently against.

stalla, *n. m.* craggy steep, a sea-rock, over-hanging precipice ; a ledge in the face of a rock ; a peat bank. *O.N.* stallr, pedestal ; step of a mast.

stallacaire, stall'-acuru, *n. m.* a block-head.

stallacaireachd, *n. f.* stupidity.

stallachdach, *a.* stupidly deaf, heedless.

stalladh, *vbl. n. m.* act of dashing, thump-ing ; a smart thump or dash against.

stallag, *n. f.* a big drink (to the limit of one's breath).

stamac, *n. f.* stomach ; fr. the *Eng.*

stamh, stav, *n. m.,* *pl.* **staimh,** a kind of (sea) tangle, an edible seaweed. So *Ir.*

stamhnaich, staü'-nich, *v.* reduce to order ; break a young horse ; drub lustily ; **a' stamhnachadh,** drubbing or breaking, as a horse ; press down, compress.

stàmhor, stàthmhor, stā-vor, *a.* useful, substantial.

stamnadh, *n. m.* act of curbing, control-ling ; **biodh stamnadh ort,** control yourself, be still ! *Ir.* **stamnidh,** *a.* manageable.

stàmp, *v.* trample, stamp, tread ; fr. the *Eng.*

stàn, *adj.* below ; **a stàn,** down below = **a bhàn.**

stàn, *n. m.* tin. So *Ir.* *Lat.* stannum, tin.

stang, *n. m.* a tank, pool, a ditch. So *Ir.*; ult. fr. *Lat.* stagnum.

stang, *n. f.* a peg (for hanging things on), a sting, a prick. *Also* **gath ; stangan a' chnòdain,** the prickles of the gurnet. *Sc.* stang, a sting (of a bee). *O.N.* stanga, to prick, goad.

stangarra, *n. m.* the fish stickleback ; fr. **stang.**

stanna, stanu, *n. f.* a vat or tun ; **stann cléith,** worm-vat or -tun ; a goal ; a stall, stand or stance, as at a market. *Ir.* **stanna,** vat, barrel.

stannart, *n. f.* standard, a gauge ; yard, limit ; fr. the *Eng.*

stannd, *n. m.* a set (of knitting needles).

staoig, stū-ig, *n. f.* a clumsy beefsteak ; collop, steak ; *v.* cut into clumsy steaks or lumps. *M.Ir.* **stáic.** *O.N.* steik, a steak.

staoigheas, *n. f.* stays, corsets; fr. the *Eng.*

staoin, stūin, *n. f.* tin, pewter ; anything worthless.

staoin, *n. f.* laziness ; *a.* shallow ; **duine staoin,** a shallow-minded man.

staoin, *n. f.* juniper ; **caoran staoin,** juniper berries.

staon, *v.* bend, curve.

staonag, *n. f.* saliva, spittle ; *syn.* **ronnan.**

staoram, stūrum, *n. f.* inclination ; bend-ing the body to a side.

stapag, *n. f.* mixture of oatmeal and cold water. *See* **fuarag.** *Sc.* stappack. *O.N.* stappa, to stamp, bray.

staplaich, *n. f.* plashing noise of the sea.

staplannach. *See* **staplaich.**

stapull, *n. m.* a staple, bar, bolt.

starach, *a.* cunning, artful, sly ; sagacious.

starachd, *n. f.* romping, blustering.

stàrachd, *n. f.* pacing the floor, pro-menading.

staran, *n. m.* stepping-stones across a ford or a bog. *See* **stair.**

stararaich, star'-ar-ich, *n. f.* great noise.

starbhanach, starv'-an-uch, *n. m.* a stout fellow, an athletic, well-built person.

starcach, *a.* firm. *O.N.* sterkr, strong. *O.H.G.* starc. *A.S.* stearc.

stard, *n. f.* a moon-eye.

stardshuileach, stârd'-hool-uch, *a.* moon-eyed. Cf. *O.N.* starblindr, blind with cataract.

starn, *n. m.* an upstart.

stàrnaich, *vbl. n. f.* act of making a great noise.

starr, *v.* shove violently, dash.

stàrr, *n. m.* long grass that grows in stagnant water. *O.N.* has störr, *gen.* starar, bent-grass.

starra, *n. m.* a fixed block, as of rock ; **tha thu 'n ad starra anns an rathad,** you are a block in the way.

starrachd, *n. f.* roaming.

starradh, *pl.* **starraidhnean,** *vbl. n. m.* act of pushing violently, dashing ; failing, whim, freak ; **cnap-starraidh,** a stum-bling-block, obstruction, a ball on the end of a spear.

starrag, *n. f.* the hooded crow.

starrag, *n. f.* a wry neck, a stiff neck, a twist. Cf. *M.H.G.* starren, become fixed. *Ger.* starr, stiff, stiff-necked.

starraich, stârr'-ich, *n. f.* complete in-toxication.

starram, *n. m.* noise, din, tramping.

starr-fhiacail, s.-iukil, *n. f.* a tusk, a gag-tooth.

starrs, *n. m.* starch. *Also* **stuthaigeadh.**

starrshuileach, s.-hooluch, *a.* having dis-torted eyes. Cf. *Ger.* starr-auge, fixed or staring eye. *O.N.* starblindr.

starsach, *n. f.* threshold; bar, barrier; **'na starsaich an siod,** as a barrier **yonder.**

starsaich, stărs'-ich, *v. tr.* starch, stiffen.
stàt, *n. f.* pride, haughtiness. *Lat.* status.
stàta, *n. f.* the state, government ; fr. the *Eng.*
stàth, stā, *n. m.* good purpose or end, use, benefit ; gnothach air bheag stàth, a thing worth little ; chan 'eil stàth an sin duit, that serves no end to you. *See* stà.
stàthail, stā-hal, *adj.* useful, profitable.
stàthalachd, stā-haluchc, *n. f.* usefulness.
stàthar, *n. f.* a beaten surface, a beaten path ; stàthar nan caorach, the path of the sheep.
steabhag, shtevag, *n. f.* switch, a cane, slender stick. *See* steafag.
steach, shtach, *adv.* inside, in, within (with idea of motion into) ; 'nuair a thàinig iad a steach, when they came in. *M.Ir.* is tech. *E.Ir.* isa tech, into the house.
steadhainn, shteyin, *n. f.* firm, pointed and punctual mode of pronouncing one's words.
steadhainneach, shteyinuch, *adj.* making a slight pause between every word in speaking or reading ; punctual.
steafag, stefag, *n. f.* a switch, a small stick. *Ir.* steafóg. Cf. *Eng.* staff.
steairdean, *n. m.* sea-swallow, tern.
steairn, *n. f.* a roaring fire.
stealdrach, shtialdruch, *n. f.* a torrent ; state of being a good deal intoxicated.
steall, shtaül, *n. f.* spout, pour out, a plash, gush ; a considerable quantity of any liquid ; a torrent, or heavy shower of rain ; diarrhœa ; *v.* plash, pour out irregularly, spout. *Ir.* steall-aim, squirt. *Lat.* stillo, I drop.
steallach, shtialuch, *a.* plashing, gushing.
stealladair, shtial-uder, *n. m.* a syringe, a squirt. *Also* gunna spùt. *See* spùt.
stealladh, *vbl. n. m.* act of plashing, gushing.
steallaire, shtialiru, *n. m.* a cascade, or cataract ; a watering-can ; a syringe ; glyster, or clyster. *Ir.* steallaire.
stear, *n. m.* a rude blow ; a rod used for stunning birds.
stèara, *n. m., pl.* stèaraichean, a stroke with a rod, a vigorous whack.
steàrnag, *n. f.* tern, sea-swallow. *A.S.* stearn. *O.N.* þerna.
steàrnall, shtiārnal, *n. m.* sea-bird, a bittern ; an innkeeper's sign.
stèic, shtēk, *n. f.* a cow's stake, or stall. *Also* stic, shteeck.
steic-bhràghad, shtek-vrā'ud, *n. f.* wind-pipe, the weasand ; " tha bun-stic ri stéill," the windpipe is to the stakes (of one whose freedom is severely curbed).

stéidh, shtēy, *n. f.* foundation, basis ; stéidh-theagaisg, a text ; *v.* found, build upon ; pile peats. In *Suth.* stéibh. *O.N.* stæða, to establish, stæði, a site.
stéidheadh, shtēyu, *vbl. n. m.* act of building (a wall, a large peat-stack).
stéidhealachd, shtēyaluchc, *n. f.* solidity, steadiness, punctuality, firmness.
stéidheil, shtēyal, *adj.* solid, firm, steady, punctual ; decisive in character.
stéidhich, shtēyich, *v.* found.
stéidhichte, shtēyichtu, *vbl. a.* founded, established.
steill, shteyl, *n. f.* pin or peg, on which something is hung ; a shelf, bracket ; a long fellow.
stéilleach, shtēyluch, *a.* lusty, stout, ruddy. Cf. stéigheil, steady, solid.
steimhleag, shtev-lag, *n. f.* hasp of a lock.
steimin, *a.* used as *n.* kind of coarse woollen cloth ; fr. *Sc.* stemyng, orig. of goat's hair (?). *O.Fr.* estamine. *Lat.* stamen. *Jamieson.*
steing, *n. f.* a hook for hanging things on.
steinle, shteynlu, *n. f.* itch, mange.
stéinn, shtēyn, *v.* stain ; disappoint ; stéinn e orm, he disappointed me, he defeated my purpose ; fading (of colour).
stéinneadh, shtēynu, *vbl. n. m.* act of disappointing, staining ; disappointment ; a stain.
steòc, shtiŏck, *v.* stalk, strut ; *n. m.* idler.
steòcair, styŏchg'-aèr, *n. m.* stalker ; an idler.
steòrn, shtiŏrn, *v.* guide, direct, manage ; *n.* a stare. *O.N.* stjórna, stjórn, steering, rule.
steòrnadh, *vbl. n. m.* act of guiding, leading, directing.
steothag, shtio-hag, *n. f.* switch, cane, light staff ; steothaireachd, sauntering with a switch in hand. *See* steafag.
steud, shtēd, *n. f.* a fine young mare ; a charger ; racehorse ; a stride ; a' dol 'n a steud, going at full speed ; *v.* run a race ; bu luaithe a' steudadh e na ghaoth, he could run swifter than the wind ; a wave. *A.S.* stéda. *M.Ir.* stéd.
steudag, shtēdag, *n. f.* a tidy girl.
steud-shruth, shtēd-hroo, *n. m.* a rapid stream.
stiall, *n. f., gen.* stéill, a post to which a cow is tied in a stable.
stiall, shtiul, *n. f., gen.* stéill, a long streak or stripe of cloth, etc. ; *v.* tear in stripes, mark with stripes. *E.Ir.* stiall, girdle, strap.
stiallach, shtiuluch, *adj.* striped, streaked.

stiallag, shtiulag, *n. f.* a small strip, a shred (of cloth).

stiallaire, shtiäliru, *n. m.* a drawling noise ; a long, ugly fellow ; any large thing.

stic, *n. m.* inclination, leaning.

stic, *n. m.* a stick, a stake, a kiln-rafter. *O.N.* stik, stakes.

stic, shteek, *v.* stick, adhere ; fr. the *Eng.*

stic, *n. m.* a bad pet of a person, blackguard ; **droch stic,** a bad " stick " ; an imp ; blemish, hurt, pain. *Sc.* stick, a bungle, botch.

stic, *n. m.* a ghostly person ; imp.

sticeartach, shteekartuch, *n. m.* a long person ; an apparition that stalks beside houses.

sticil, *coll. n.* the wood which supports grain in a kiln, esp. the main " rafters."

stid, shteej, *v.* peep.

stidean, shteejen, cat ; *interj.* word by which a cat is called. *Also* stididh.

stig, shteeg, *n. m.* a sneaking fellow, a skulking or abject look. *O.N.* styggr, shy, wary ; peevish.

stigeal, *n. f.* a mixed mass.

stigearachd, shteegeruchc, *n. f.* a sneaking, skulking.

stigh, stuy, *adv.* within, in the house ; inside (with notion of rest) ; **a stigh no muigh,** either within or without ; **a bheil duine a stigh ?** is there any one in (the house) ? *E.Ir.* istig, istaig, isintig, in the house.

stil, shtil, *n. f.* a quirk, a twist, contrariness ; usually in *plural* ; " tha e làn stilean," he is full of quirks (said of a baulky horse). Cf. *O.N.* stilli, a trap.

still, *n. f.* swift motion, a splash (of water), speed in water ; **a' dol 'n a still,** going at full speed ; *v.* divide, move swiftly.

stingleag, shteeng-lag, *n. f.* the hinge of a box, a hasp, a hank of yarn. *See* steimhleag.

stiob, shteeb, *v.* steep, soak.

stiobadh, shteebu, *vbl. n. m.* act of steeping, soaking.

stiobull, shteepul, *n. f.* a steeple, spire.

stiocach, shteecuch, *adj.* lame, crippled.

stiocaire, shteeciru, *n. m.* a cripple, a feeble man.

stiocall, shtioocul, *n. m.* buttress.

stiocanta, shteekantu, *adj.* adhesive.

stiodach, shtiduch, *n. f. interj.* puss ! push !

stiog, shteeg, *v.* crouch, lie close to the ground.

stiog, shteeg, *n. f.* a stripe in cloth. *Sc.* steik.

stiogach, *adj.* striped, streaked ; sorry ; *n. f.* a slim, sleeky female.

stiom, shteem, *n. f., pl.* stiomannan, a fillet ; ringlet ; a snood, a hair-lace, beading on wall.

stiom, *n. f.* hard substance in cow's udder after calving.

stiom, *n. f.* a covering ; filmy covering, as oil, fat, on water.

stiomag, shteemag, *n. f.* a head-band, fillet for the hair ; a maiden (*Car. G.*).

stiorap, shteerup, *n. f.* a stirrup.

stiorc, stirk, *v.* stretch, stiffen (as in death) ; **stiorcadh,** stiffening.

stiorlach, shteerluch, *n. f.* sorry long female.

stiorlag, shteerlag, *n. f.* a thin, worn-out rag ; an emaciated woman.

stiorlan, *n. m.* any ugly long thing ; a thin, tall person.

stiornach, shtiürnuch, *n. m.* sturgeon. *Also* stirean. *Lat.* sturio.

stipinn, shteepin, *n. f.* stipend ; fr. the *Eng. Lat.* stīpendium, a tax.

stipinnear, shteepiner, *n. m.* a stipendiary.

stiubhard, shtioo-ard, *n. m.* a steward.

stiubhardachd, shti-oorduchc, *n. f.* stewardship.

stiuir, shtioor, *n. f., gen.* stiurach, rudder ; **fear na stiurach,** the helmsman ; **iarunn stiurach,** rudder-hinge or pivot ; two long feathers in a cock's tail ; the long, elastic tail of a lobster ; *v.* steer, direct, guide, lead ; **stiuir am bàta,** steer the boat. *M.Ir.* stiúrad. *A.S.* steōran. *O.N.* styra. *O.H.G.* stiura.

stiuirbheirt, shti-oor-verst, *n. f.* steering gear.

stiuireag, shti-oorag, *n. f.* very thin gruel (meal and water) ; hot oatmeal drink. *Sc.* sturoch.

stiup, shtioop, *n. m.* a long tail, or train ; a foolish person.

stiuradair, shtiooruder, *n. m.* helmsman, one that steers a vessel.

stiuradh, shtiooru, *vbl. n. m.* act of steering, guiding, directing, managing ; direction, guidance, management.

stob, *n. m., pl.* stuib, a small stick, an upright post ; **tha e an sud 'na stob,** he is there like a post ; a stab ; *v.* thrust, prick.

stobach, *adj.* prickly, thorny.

stobadh, *vbl. n. m.* act of planting potatoes, etc.

stoban, *n. m.* a little stub.

stobanach, *n. m.* a short, stout person.

stòbh, stō, *v.* stew ; **stòbhte,** *vbl. a.* stewed.

stóbh, *v.* stow ; stick to, as a person ; feel affection for.

stoc, *n. m., pl.* and *gen. s.* stuic, stock, trunk of tree, root, capital, store, cravat ; pack of cards ; *v. tr.* object, cast up ; **tha e a' stocadh siod is so** rium, he objects this and that; cha ruig thu leas a bhi stocadh sin riumsa, you need not cast up that to me.

stoc, *n. m.* a trumpet. *E.Ir.* stoc.

stoc, *n. m.* gunwale (of a boat), the side of a bed. *O.N.* stokkr, gunwale; bedside.

stocaich, stokich, *v.* stock a farm; fr. the *Eng.*

stocaidh, stoky, stocainn, stokin, *n. f.* stocking-hose; dealg stocaich, stocking-wire.

stocainn, *n. f.* stocking; fr. the *Eng.*

stocainnich, stocinuch, *v.* season, as a cask.

stocair, *n. m.* a trumpeter.

stocan, *n. m.* small trunk; stocan càil, kail stock.

stod, *n. m.* a huff, pet; sudden fit of peevishness; ghabh e stod, he took the pet, he was quite huffed at it.

stodach, *a.* huffy, pettish; *n. f.* pet.

stodaire, *n. m.* a pettish fellow.

stoileanach, *a.* wanton, lewd, lecherous.

stoim, *n. m.* a particle, whit, faintest glimpse (of anything).

stoipeal, stopal, *n. m.* bung, stopple.

stoirm, storum, *n. f.* storm; a gale; tingling, or ringing sensation in the ear; fr. *Eng. O.N.* stormr, a gale, styrma. *A.S.* styrmian, blow a gale.

stoirmealachd, stormaluchc, *n. f.* storminess.

stoirmeil, stormal, *adj.* stormy, blowy, keen.

stòite, *a.* prominent.

stól, *n. m.* stool, a settle; stòl-coise, footstool. *Also* furm. *A.S.* stol. *O.N.* stóll. *Ger.* stuhl.

stòl, *v.* settle, quieten, calm; fr. stòl, stool; settle.

stòladh, *vbl. n. m.* act of settling.

stòlda, *adj.* sedate; solemn in gait.

stòldachd, *n. f.* solemnity of step; sedateness, staidness, tameness.

stolladh, *n. m.* over-feeding.

stòp, *n. m.* stoup; a measure for liquids; pot for liquors; stòp-pinnt, half-gallon measure; stòp-seipinn, quart-measure; stòp-bodaich, half-quart measure; stòp-leth-bhodaich, a half-pint measure; stòp-ceathra, a gill measure. *Sc.* stoup. *O.N.* staup. *A.S.* stoppa.

stop, *v.* dam up, or prevent from running; stop, bung.

stopadh, *vbl. n. m.* act of stopping, bunging.

stòr, stòr, *n. m. poet.* for stòras.

stòr, *n. m.* a bull—word used to excite a bull, to call him; stòr! stòr! *Perthshire*; in *Islay*, tòraidh! tòraidh!

stòr, *n. m.* steep, high peak, crowded teeth.

stòrach, *a.* of crowded teeth, having broken teeth. *Also* storrach.

stòras, *n. m.* wealth, great riches.

stòrasach, *a.* wealthy, rich.

storban, *n. m.* disturbance; fr. the *Eng.*

storr, *v.* over-feed, surfeit, cloy.

storrfhiacail, stor-iucil, *n. f.* a gag-tooth.

stoth, sto, *n. m.* steam; an stoth a thàinig as a' choire, the steam that came from the cauldron; stench.

stoth, *v.* lop off branches, cut corn high.

stothbhàta, sto-vātu, *n. f.* steam-boat

strabaid, strabej, *n. f.* a whore, harlot; ult. fr. *Lat.* stuprum.

strabaire, strabiru, *n. m.* a whoremonger.

stràbh, *n. m.* a straw. *See* sràbh.

stràbhaig, stra'ig, *v. tr.* lay straw on a kiln for drying corn. *Also* sgreothainn and streabhaig.

stra-bhaille, stra-valiu, *n. m.* staggering blow.

stràc, *n. m.* a drake.

stràc, *n. m.* a stroke, a plank in boat-building; *v.* aim at; a' stràcadh oirre, aiming at her; strike.

stràc, *n. f.* a stroke, a whetstone (for scythe).

stràcadh, *vbl. n. m.* 1. act of measuring (meal) in a dish by stroking off all above the brim by a straight-edge. 2. the quantity so stroked off; any small or indefinite quantity; an d'fhuair sibh iasg? did you get fish? thuair sinn stràcadh, we did, but not much. *Sc.* straik.

stràcair, *n. m.* troublesome fellow, gossip, wanderer. *O.N.* strákr, vagabond.

stràcte, *vbl. a.* sharpened, keen, eager; fr. stràc, a whetstone.

stràic, *n. f.* pride, arrogance; swelling with anger.

stràic, *n. f.* the brim of a measure, the strike or measure-roller; the surplus stroked off in the act of measuring; an d'fhuair thu móran? Fhuair, 'san t-stràic, did you get much? Yes, but only a trifle; *v.* roll or strike a measure in measuring.

straiceil, stracial, *adj.* purse-proud.

straighil, stryil, *v.* thump noisily, scourge. *M.Ir.* sroiglim, I scourge. *O.Ir.* sraiglim, *flagello.* *W.* ffrewyll. *L.Lat.* fragillum.

straighleadh, strylu, *vbl. n. m.* act of thumping noisily; a noisy blow; a thorough whipping.

straighlich, strylich, *n. f.* clangour, clashing, blustering, swaggering; noise, or bustle; a fit of intoxication.

stràille, strā-liu, *n. m.* a carpet, mat, rug. *Lat.* strāgulum.

strailleadh, strylu, *n. m.* act of knocking, a loud knock or blow. *See* straighleadh.

strangair, stranger, *n. m.* a lazy, quarrelsome fellow.

streabhainn, streafainn, strefin, *n. f.* membrane ; membrane which covers calf *in utero* ; filmy tallow. *See* sgann. *See* sreabhainn.

streabhon, *n. f.* a fringe, thin beard. *Also* streafon.

streap, strep, *v.* climb, scale, struggle, or scramble ; *vbl. n. f.* act of climbing, struggling ; scaling, scrambling.

streapadair, strepuder, *n. m.* climber, ladder.

streathan, and **streadhon,** forms of streabhon, *q.v.*

streòdag, *n. f.* a thin streamlet, a " drop " of liquor. *Also* striodag.

streud, *n. f.* a row, a line of things ; for treud.

streup, strēp, strèapaid, strēpej, *n. f.* row, fray, skirmish. *Lat.* strepitus.

streupaideach, strēpejuch, *a.* quarrelsome.

strì, stree, *n. f.* strife, contention, exertion. *A.S.* and *O.N.* strìð. *O.H.G.* strìt.

striall, striul, *n. f.* a long shred, stripe ; *v.* tear in long stripes, as cloth.

striam, striäm, *n. m.* a long shred.

striamalach, *n. f.* anything long and ugly ; long ugly person.

strianach, striunuch, *also* **broc,** *n. m.* badger. *See* srianach.

stringlein, *n. m.* strangles.

strìobh, streev, *v.* strive ; *n. f.* strife ; fr. the *Eng.* Cf. *Ger.* streben. *O.F.* estriver.

striobhaid, *n. f.* strippings, the last streamlets of a milking. *R.D.*

striobhail, streeval, *adj.* emulous, striving.

strìoch, streeuch, *v.* draw a line ; scratch, or score a line. Cf. *O.H.G.* streihhôn, graze, stroke. *A.S.* strîcan ; *n. f.* a line, a streak ; a scoring.

strìochd, streechc, *v.* yield, submit, surrender, strike ; **cha strìochdainn do dhuine,** I would not yield to any one. *Ir.* strìocaim, I submit.

strìochdadh, *vbl. n. m.* act of yielding, submitting, giving up ; submission, obedience.

strìochdte, streechtu, *vbl. a.* yielded, submissive, compliant.

striodag, *n. f.* same as **streòdag.**

strioghach, *a.* prodigal.

strioll, striul, *n. f.* a girth.

striop, streep, *n. f.* whoredom.

strìopach, streepuch, *n. f.* a whore. So *Ir.* ; fr. *O.F.* strupe. *Lat.* stuprum.

strìopachas, *n. f.* whoredom.

strìopaire, streepiru, *n. m.* whoremonger.

stritheil, stree-hal, *a.* contentious, quarrelsome ; energetic.

stròdh, strô, *n. m.* prodigality. *Ir.* stró, strógh ; fr. *A.S.* strēowian. *O.H.G.* strouwen. *Goth.* straujan.

stròic, strōik, *v.* tear asunder, lacerate ; *n. f.* a long rag, or ragged person. *Also* stroic ; fr. srac.

stròiceadh, *vbl. n. m.* act of tearing asunder.

strolamas, *n. m.* a mess.

stropach, *a.* wrinkled.

strùic, strook, *v. tr.* rub lightly, brush against. *O.N.* strjúka, rub, brush, stroke gently.

struidh, strooy, *v.* spend, waste, squander.

struidheas, strooyus, *n. m.* prodigality, squandering.

struidheasach, *a.* prodigal.

struidheasachd, strooyusuchc, *n. f.* extreme extravagance, waste or prodigality.

struidheil, strooyal, *a.* extravagant.

struill, *n. f.* a baton, a cudgel. *O.Ir.* sraigell. *See* sroghall.

strump, *n. m.* spout of a kettle.

strumpaid, stroompej, *n. f.* a strumpet ; fr. the *Eng.*

strùp, stroop, *n. m.* spout of a kettle. *See* srùb.

strùpan, stroopan, *n. m.* a cockle.

strùplaich, *n. f.* the backward suction of spent waves, breaking on the shore ; from **srùb,** noisy drinking with the breath.

strutan. *See* sriutan.

struth, stroo, *n. f.* an ostrich. *Lat.* struthio.

strùthan, *n. m.* St. Michael's Eve cake.

stuacach, stoo-ucuch, *adj.* stupid, boorish.

stuacachd, *n. m.* stupidity.

stuacaire, stoo-uciru, *n. m.* a blockhead.

stuacaireachd, *n. f.* stupidity.

stuagh, stoo-u', *n. f.* pillar, column ; a mountain high wave ; **stuaghaibh deataich,** pillars of smoke. *E.Ir.* stúag, arch. *O.Ir.* tuag, a bow, **tuag nime,** *arcus coeli.*

stuaghach, stoo-u'uch, *a.* having huge waves.

stuaghadh, *vbl. n. m.* act of approaching, approximating ; coming near in excellence.

stuaic, *n. f.* a wry-neck and sullen countenance, expressive of discontent, an extreme boorishness or stupidity ; little hill ; for stùic.

stuaic, *n. f.* a hillock, a round promontory.

stuaigh, stoo-uy, *n. f.* a gable of a house.

stuaigh, *v.* come near, approximate ; **cha stuaigh thu air,** you will not come near him ; **cha stuaigh so air a lionadh,** this will not near fill it. *Also* stuaidh.

stuaim, *n. f.* guardedness ; temperance, prudence, modesty ; **stuaim is mac- antas,** meekness and modesty.

stuama, *adj.* temperate in desire or appetite ; temperate, moderate ; modest.

stùbhach, *a.* bobtailed.

stuc, stook, *n. m.* a lump ; surliness.

stùc, stook, *n. f.* a pinnacle, a conical steep rock ; precipice ; cliff. *Sc.* and *Eng.* stook.

stùcach, *adj.* not apt to burn, not in- flammable ; surly, morose.

stùcach, *adj.* cliffy, prominent ; full of bare rocks.

stùcair, *n. m.* a surly man.

stùcan, *n. m.* a little jutting hill.

stùic, stooik, *n. f.* a projecting crag ; wry-neck, as a bull going to fight ; scowling side-look of a morose person. *Also* stùirc. *See* stùc.

stùiceag, *n. f.* a surly woman.

stuidearra, stujuru, *adj.* studious, steady, glum.

stuidearrachd, *n. f.* study, composure, meditation.

stuig, stooig, *v.* set dogs to ; incite, instigate ; *n. m.* a bad pet or per- son.

stùird, stoord, stùirdean, stoorden, *n. m.* vertigo, a disease in sheep, drunken- ness.

stuirt, stoort, *n. f.* assumed gravity, stateliness ; anger, sulkiness.

stuirtealachd, stoortaluchc, *n. f. See* stuirt.

stuirteil, stoortal, *adj.* morose and dignified, but insignificant.

stùr, stoor, *n. m.* dust, motes ; **lur gun stùr,** pure delight. *Sc.* stour.

stùrd, stoord, stùrdan, stoordan, *n. m.* the herb darnel, the seed of which causes intoxication when mixed with meal ; vertigo in sheep, or the disease which causes them to reel.

stùrr, stoor, *n. m.* rugged top of a hill ; a pinnacle.

stùrraic, stoo-rik, *n. f.* head or cap turned to one side.

sturrail, stooral, **sturranta,** stoorantu, *adj.* of sturr.

stuth, stoo, *n. m.* stuff, thing, camlet, particle ; **cha bhi stuth ort,** nothing will be wrong with you ; **cha dèan e stuth air,** he cannot budge it, he cannot manage it. *Eng.* stuff.

stuthaig, stoo-hic, *v.* dress with starch, stiffen.

suabag, soo-ubag, *n. f.* a sweeping blow, a swipe.

suabharaich, soo-uvurich, *v.* illumine.

suacan, *n. m.* anything wrought together awkwardly, as clay ; an earthen pot ; a basket with kindling hung in chimney.

sùadh, *n. m.* a sage, a discreet man, a scholar ; *gen. pl.* of *M.Ir.* sùi. *See* saoi.

suaicean, *n. m.* bundle of straw ; a deformed person.

suaicheanta, *adj.* curious, novel, new, remarkable, notable.

suaicheantas, *n. m.* novelty, curiosity ; **cha suaicheantas còrr air cladach,** a heron on the shore is no novelty or curiosity ; escutcheon, standard, ar- morial ensign, or crest ; **dha 'm bu shuaicheantas giuthas,** whose armorial ensign or crest was the fir-crop ; **slat- shuaicheantais,** a sceptre. *O.Ir.* su- aichnid (su + aichne), clear.

suail, *adj.* small. *E.Ir.* suail, trifle.

suaimh, soo-yv, *n. m.* luxurious kind of rest.

suaimhneach, soo-yvnuch, *adj.* enjoying a kind of luxury in ease and quiet, as after great danger or fatigue ; very tranquil or quiet.

suaimhneas, soo-yv-nus, *n. m.* luxury of ease and rest ; greatest tranquillity or quiet ; **bheir mise suaimhneas dhuibh,** I will give you rest. *Bible.*

suaimhneasach, *a.* luxuriating in peace and tranquillity.

suain, *n. f.* profound or deep sleep. *O.Ir.* súan. *W.* hun. *Lat.* somnus. *Gr.* ὕπνος. *O.Celt.* su(p)no-s.

Suain, *p. n.* Sweden ; Righ na Suain, the King of Sweden.

suain, *v.* wreathe, wind about, *O.Ir.* suanem, a rope = su + óen.

suaineach, *adj.* narcotic ; sound asleep ; in a profound sleep.

Suaineach, *adj.* Swedish ; *n. m.* a Swede, or inhabitant of Sweden.

suaineadh, *vbl. n. m.* act of entwining, wrapping (cravat or plaid round and round one).

suaip, *n. f.* faint or distant resemblance, as persons ; **tha suaip eatorra,** they resemble somewhat each other ; fr. *Sc.* swamp, cast of face. *O.N.* svipr, a glimpse, look. Svip mannsins, the shadow of a man

suaip, *n. f.* swap, exchange or barter ; **rinn iad suaip,** they have bartered commodities ; *v.* exchange or barter ; **shuaip iad na h-eich,** they have exchanged the horses. *Sc.* swap.

suairce, *a.* civil, meek ; kind, polite ; urbane. *E.Ir.* suarc = su (good) + arc (passion, desire) ; *op.* to duairce.

suairceas, *n. m.* kindness, politeness.

suaiteachan, *n. m.* wagging (tails), shrugging (shoulders).

suaithneas, *n. m.* a badge ; **an s.-bàn,** the white cockade.

sual, *n. m.* tumours.

suanach, soo-anuch, *n. f.* hide, skin, fleece ; a covering or mantle ; a plough-rein, a tail.

suanas, *n. m.* twisting, winding, coiffure. *W.R.*

suarach, soo-aruch, *adj.* indifferent ; **tha mi suarach uime,** I am indifferent about it ; insignificant, paltry, inconsiderable ; **duine suarach,** a paltry person ; **bu shuarach dhuit ged a dhèanadh tu sin,** it were no great thing, though you should do that ; **gnothach suarach,** a paltry or shabby thing. So *Ir. McB.* compares *Ger.* schwach(?).

suarachas, *n. f.* trifling nature or quality, paltriness, naught ; **suarachas a' ni so,** the paltriness of this thing ; **na cuir an suarachas an ni so,** do not make light of this thing ; neglect, contempt.

suaraichead, soo-arichud, *n. f.* degree of indifference, contemptibleness ; **a' dol an suaraichead uime,** getting more indifferent about it.

suas, *adv.* up, upwards ; **thoir suas ort,** up with you ; **chaidh e suas,** he went up ; **chan 'eil suas air fichead ann,** there is not more than twenty. *O.Ir.* súas ; fr. **uas.**

suath, *v.* rub, mix, knead. So *Ir.*

suathadh, *vbl. n. m.* act of rubbing.

suathallas, *n. m.* resemblance ; guess.

sùbailt, soobilt, *a.* supple ; fr. the *Eng.*

subh, soo, *n. m., pl.* **subhan, suibheagan,** a berry, fruit.

subhach, soo'uch, *adj.* happy, merry. *O.Ir.* subach, glad, happy ; fr. suba, joy.

subhachas, soo'uchus, *n. m.* happiness, expression of happiness, mirth, merriment, gladness ; **is màirg a dhèanadh subhachas ri dubhachas fir eile,** he is to be pitied that rejoices in another's woe. *O.Ir.* subachus, *laetilia.*

sùbhag, *n. f.* strawberry, fruit. *Ir.* suibh.

subhailc, soo-elc. *n. f.* virtue. *O.Ir.* sualig, *virtus* =su (good) +alig (behaviour) ; *op.* of **du** +**alig,** vice.

subhailceach, soo-elcuch, *adj.* virtuous, moral. *Also* beusach, deagh-bheusach.

subhchraobh, *n. f.* raspberry.

subh-làir, *n. m.* (same as next word).

subh-thalmhainn, *n. m.* wood strawberry.

sùblaich, sooblich, *v.* make supple.

suchd, soochc, *n. m.* sake, account ; **air suchd a' mhaitheis,** for goodness' sake ; **air suchd nan achd,** for the sake of these objections.

suchta, *a.* filled, saturated, absorbed.

sud, shood, *pron. dem.* that, there, yon. *E.Ir.* sút, siut. *W.* hwnt.

sùdh, soo, *n. m.* seam of a plank. *O.N.* súð, suture, clinching of ship's boards.

sùg, sooc, *v. intr.* to suck, imbibe. *O.Ir.* súgim. *W.* sugno. *Sc.* souk. *A.S.* sucan. *O.H.G.* sûgan. *O.N.* súga, to suck. *Lat.* sūgo.

sùg, *n. m.* merriment, mirth, happiness. *E.Ir.* sucach.

sug, *n. m.* a lamb ; *interj.* mode of calling a lamb. *Argyll.*

sùgach, *adj.* merry, cheerful. So *E.Ir.*

sùgair, soogir, *v.* make merry, sport.

sùgaire, soog'-ur-u, *n. m.* Merry-Andrew.

sùgan, soogan, *n. m.* a straw or heathrope ; hay or straw twisted into a rope (of one strand, *Lewis*) ; horse's collar.

sùgan, corra - shùgain, *n. m.* reflection from a moving luminous body from roof or walls of a house.

sùgh, *n. m.* a wave, a billow ; the motion of the waves.

sùgh, soo, *n. m.* sap, juice, moisture ; soup ; dearest object or darling ; **a shùgh mo chridhe,** my dearest ! my darling ! **sùgh feòla,** juice of beef ; **gnothach gun sùgh,** a sapless or senseless affair. *O.Ir.* súg. *O.Celt.* sūgo-, juice. *Lat.* sūcus.

sùghadh, soo-u, *vbl. n. m.* act of drinking up, or drying up ; seasoning, as wood ; **tha fiodh air sùghadh,** the wood is seasoned ; extract the juice ; absorb ; **a' sùghadh an smior as,** extracting the very marrow from it ; *n. m.* the suction of a spent wave on the shore ; receding wave ; extracting, absorption ; **thug na sùghaidh leis e,** the receding waves carried it away.

sùghail, soo'al, *adj.* juicy, sappy.

sùghair, sùghmhor, soo'or, *adj.* sappy, juicy, pithy, succulent.

sùghaireachd, soo-eruchc, *n. f.* juiciness, sappiness, succulency, solidity.

sùghan, soo'an, *n. m.* extract, liquidflummery ; sowans.

sùgradh, soocru, *n. m.* play, sport, diversion, joke ; **chan e an sùgradh cur ris,** it is no joke to master or manage him. *I.Lom* has **sùgradh searbh,** bitter sport. *See* **sùg.**

suibheag, *n. f.* the stump of a rainbow, " a tooth," " dog's tooth."

suibheag, sooi-yag, *n. f.* a raspberry.

sùibhealas, *abstr. n. m.* imposition, sponging.

sùibhealtan, *n. m.* a parasite, a " sucker."

suibhneas, *n. m.* cheer, gladness. *W.R.* =su (good) +áeb. *O.Ir.* óiph, form, beauty. *Cf.* suaimhneas.

suicean, soo-icken, *n. m.* gag for a calf (to prevent sucking).

suidh, sooy, *v.* sit ; sit down ; incubate ;

dèan suidhe, sit, be seated. *O.Ir.*
sudigim. *Lat.* sedeo.
suidhe, soo-yu, *n. f.* sitting, act or state
of sitting. *O.Ir.* suide, sude. *W.* sedd.
Lat. sedes.
suidhe, *n. m., pl.* suidheachan, the couple
of a house.
sùidhe, *n. m.* soot; lamp-black. *Ir.*
suice. *O.Celt.* sodjâ. *Also* sùiche.
suidheachadh, *vbl. n. m.* act of settling,
laying foundation, making framework;
planting or colonising; arranging
terms of marriage; letting of houses,
farms, etc.; plan, model; air a cheart
shuidheachadh, upon the same plan,
after the same pattern or model, as
cloth.
suidheachan, soo-yuch-an, *n. m.* seat;
turf-sofa; cushion; setting. So *Ir.*
suidhe-làir, sooyu-lā-ïr, *n. m.* framework,
groundwork.
suidhich, sooyich, *v.* let, set; shuidhich
e an tigh, am baile, he has let the
house, the farm; betroth, settle terms
of marriage; shuidhich e a nighean
air, he betrothed his daughter to him;
win, lay, plant, arrange, settle, appoint; shuidhich iad an stéidh, they
laid the foundation; shuidhich e beò-
shlaint oirre, he settled an annuity on
her. *Ir.* suidhim, sit, prove, enforce
an argument.
suidhichte, sooyichtu, *vbl. a.* laid, as
foundation; settled, appointed, pointed
out; tha 'n t-àite suidhichte, the place
is appointed, is determined; tha mi
suidhichte air sin a dhèanadh, I am
determined to do that; sedate;
duine suidhichte, sedate man, a sensible,
reliable man.
sùigean, *n. m.* a circle of straw ropes in
which grain is kept.
suigeart, soo-igart, *n. m.* joy, jollity,
frisking, gladness. *Ir.* suigeort.
sùigh, sooy, *v. i.* evaporate, absorb, dry
up, drink up; season or dry, as wood;
extract; shùigh am fiodh, the wood
seasoned; fiodh sùighte, seasoned
wood; shùigh an t-ombar an dùradan
as mo shùil, the amber extracted the
mote from my eye; shùigh am fallus,
the perspiration absorbed; shùigh a'
phoit, the pot dried up. *See* sùgh.
E.Ir. súgim, suck.
sùighte, sooytu, *vbl. a.* absorbed, dried
up, evaporated, boiled in, seasoned.
sùil, sool, *n. f.* an eye, a mark, a spot (as
resembling an eye); the centre of a
whirlpool; expectation, hope; an
opening, orifice; superintendence,
oversight; glance, sight; thog e a
shùil, he raised his eye; gun sùil r'a
theachd, without any expectation of

his coming; tha sùil againn ris, we
expect him; na biodh sùil no dùil agad
ris, have neither expectation nor hope
of him; biodh sùil agad orra, watch
them; air a shùil, exactly, precisely,
"bull's eye"; fighe suil-eòin, a
pattern in weaving = lozenge-shaped,
with an "eye" in its centre; sùil na
gaoithe = *Eng.* id. the teeth of the wind.
O.Ir. súil. *W.* haul. *O.Celt.* sâvali-s,
sûli-s, sun. *Lat.* sōl. *Gr.* ἥλιos, sun.
suilbh, *n. f.* cheer, hospitality, geniality.
sùilbheum, hurt of an evil eye. *Also*
beum-sùla. *Ir.* súlbheim, bewitching,
an evil eye. *Lh.*
suilbhir, soolvir, *adj.* hearty, cheerful.
O.Ir. sulbir, eloquent = su (good) +
labar, *a.* speaking; *bene loquens.*
O.W. helabar. *Z*².
suilbhireachd, *n. f.* hilarity, cheerfulness.
sùil-chritheach, sùil-chruthaich, *n. f.*
quagmire, quicksand.
sùileach, sooluch, *a.* sharp-sighted, knowing; *n. m.* sùileachan, a warning; a
lesson.
sùileag, soo-lag, *n. f.* a little eye; spot
in cloth; the bell on liquors; small
bubble, a little round wooden vessel, a
small potato.
sùileagach, soo-laguch, *a.* spotted.
sùil-ghorm, *a.* blue-eyed.
sùil-mhala-rìgh, *n. m.* a cockatrice.
sùim, *n. f.* a sum, a summary; substance.
So *M.Ir.* *W.* swm. *Lat.* summa.
sùim, sooim, *n. f., pl.* suimeannan, sum;
attention, regard, consideration; chan
'eil sùim 'sam bith aige do d' ghnothach, he pays no attention to your
business; gabh sùim ris, take pains
to, pay attention, attend to. So *Ir.*
suimealachd, soo-im-aluchc, *n. f.* atten-
tiveness, carefulness.
suimear, swimer, *n. m.* a shin, shank.
D.B.
suimeil, soo-imal, *adj.* attentive; momentous, important, considerable.
sùip, *n. m.* a chimney-sweep; fr. the *Eng.*
suipear, sweeper, *n. f.* supper.
suire, swiru, *n. f.* sea-nymph. *Also*
màighdean mhara.
suirghe, *n. f.* courtship, wooing, improp.
writ. suiridhe. *E.Ir.* suirge, courtship.
suirgheach, suruch, *a.* wooing, courting;
n. m. a courtier, wooer, shuffler; improp. suiridheach.
sùist, soosht, *n. m.* a flail. *M.Ir.* suist.
O.Ir. sust. *W.* ffust, a flail. *Lat.*
fustis, a club.
sùistealadh, soosh-jalu, *vbl. n. m.* act
of drubbing, hard work; working
night and day.
sùith, sùich, *n. f.* soot. *Ir.* súithche.
O.Ir. súidi, súith. *W.* hudd-ygl.

sùitheach, sooyuch, *adj.* sooty ; full of soot.

sul, *n. f.* fat ; gun sul gun saill, without fat, without blubber. *Carm. Gad.*

sul, *n. f.* the sun. *A.M.* So *Ir.*

sul, *prep.* ere, before (*rare*).

sùlag, *n. f.* a V-shaped notch; ear-mark in the very top of a sheep's ear.

sùlaire, sooliru, *n. f.* gannet, the solan goose. *O.N.* súla, súlan.

sulas, soolas, *n. m.* complaisance, over-joy, showing itself by gestures and expression of countenance ; air son sulais riutsa, out of sheer complacency to you ; is e rinn an sulas, how over-joyed he was.

sùlas. *See* sòlas.

sùlasach, soolasuch, *adj.* overjoyed, com-plaisant.

sulchair, soolchir, *a.* overjoyed, cheerful, affable.

sult, soolt, *n. m.* plumpness, fatness, joy. So *E.Ir.*

sultaireachd, sooltiruchc, *n. f.* plumpness.

sultar, sultmhor, sooltor, *adj.* plump, fat, in good condition.

sumag, soomag, *n. f.* saddle-cloth. *Also* pillinn.

sumaich, soomich, *v.* give due number, as cattle at pasture. *Sc.* soum.

sùmaid, soomij, sumainn, soomin, *n. f.* a wave, a billow. So *Ir.*

sùmaid, *n. f.* a loose covering, a wrap.

sumair, soomer, *n. m.* drone of a pipe.

sumaire, *n. m.* a bludgeon, a lethal weapon, a beetle.

sumanadh. *See* sunnanadh.

sùmhail, soo'-il, *adj.* of little bulk ; port-able ; as a person, humble, motionless ; obsequious ; *so* + umal.

sùmhlachadh, soo-luchu, *vbl. n. m.* act of getting less bulky, creeping in ; sitting or lying closer and closer ; *n. m.* lessening, or abridgment of bulk.

sùmhlachd, soolachc, *n. f.* littleness of bulk; obsequiousness, abjectness, little-ness. *Also* sumhlas.

sùmhlaich, soolich, *v.* lie or pack close together ; lessen, abridge, get less bulky. *Ir.* súmplaighim, I pack.

sunais, soonesh, *n. f.* lovage (plant). *Also* siunas.

sunnag, soonag, *n. f.* straw chair. Cf. sonnag, a nest.

sunnailt, soonelt, *n. f.* likeness, com-parison, match, resemblance. *Also* siunnailt.

sunnanadh, soonanu, *vbl. n. m.* a sum-mons, act of serving with summons.

sunnanaich, soonanich, *v.* summon.

sunnt, soont, *n. m.* humour, hilarity, cheerfulness ; ciod é an sunnt a th'ort, how do you do ? *Ir.* sund.

sunntach, soontach, *adj.* lively, joyous, in good health and spirits. *Ir.* sundach.

supail, soopil, *adj.* supple, elastic, nimble ; fr. the *Eng.*

supalachd, soopaluchc, *n. f.* suppleness, elasticity, nimbleness.

sur, soor, *n. m.* a flaw ; gun sal gun sur, stainless and flawless.

sùrd, soord, *n. m.* vigour, energy, eager and willing exertion ; meaning busi-ness ; hilarity ; alacrity, good cheer (in work) ; cuir sùrd ort, bestir your-self ; sùrd coiseachd, liveliness of step ; tha sùrd oibreach oirbh, you mean business. *Ir.* surd, industry, dili-gence.

sùrdag, soordag, *n. m.* a stride, leap ; gearr sùrdag, cut a leap, skip, make a bound ; na bric a' gearradh shùrdag, the salmon leaping.

sùrdail, soordal, *adj.* prompt, business-like, full of spirits.

sùrdalachd, *n. f.* alacrity.

surrag, soorag, *n. f.* vent of a kiln, the cavity below the grain in a kiln.

surram-suain, *n. m.* a sound sleep.

sùsan, sùsdan, soosan, *n. a.* thousand. *O.N.* þúsund.

susbaint, soosbent, *n. f.* substance, strength, pith. *Lat.* substantia.

susdal, soosdal, *n. m.* bustle about nothing, fuss, affected shyness.

suth, soo, *n. m.* anything. *E.Ir.* suth, weather.

suthainn, soo-hin, *adj.* everlasting, eternal, infinite. *E.Ir.* suthain, suthin.

T

t, the sixteenth letter of the Gaelic alphabet, named by the Irish, teine.

t-, part of the old art. see art. an ; an t-each, an t-uan, the horse, the lamb.

t', for d' or do, thy, when before a word beginning with a vowel or asp. f. ; as,

t' athair, thy father ; t' fhear, your husband.

tà, pres. ind. of subst. verb am ; tà mi, tà thu, I am, thou art ; common form atà. *O.Ir.* táu, tó (attá, atá) root in *Lat.* stāre. *Gr.* ἔστην.

tabaid, tabej, *n. f.* a row, a fray, a fight.

tabaideach, tabejuch, *a.* quarrelsome.

tabaideachd, tabejuchc, *n. f.* quarrelsomeness ; quarrelsome disposition and habits.

tàbar, *n. m.* a tabor, timbrel ; fr. *Eng.*

tabh, *n. m.* sea, ocean. *Ir.* taibh, the ocean. *O.N.* haf. *A.S.* hæf.

tàbh, tàv, *n. m.* a spoon net. *O.N.* háfr, a pock-net.

tabhach, *n. m.* act of offering, urging acceptance (of anything). *E.Ir.* tobach, compelling. *O.Ir.* do-aithbiuch, I break ; fr. boingim.

tabhach, *n. m.* a sudden eruption, a forcing, a pull. *E.Ir.* tobach, levying.

tàbhachd, tàv'-achc, *n. f.* profit, benefit, advantage ; chan 'eil tàbhachd sam bith dhómhsa ann, it is no profit or benefit to me ; quantity or number ; ciod é an tàbhachd a th' ann, what quantity is there of it ? mun tàbhachd sin, about that quantity ; substantiality, solidity. So *Ir.*

tàbhachdach, tàvuchcuch, *adj.* beneficial, advantageous, profitable, efficient, efficacious ; buillean tàbhachdach, effectual or efficient blows ; ni tàbhachdach, a profitable or advantageous thing ; solid, substantial. *Also* tabhachdail.

tàbhaidh, tàvy, *a.* strong.

tabhaill, tavil, *n. f.* sense, understanding, wits ; chaidh e dhe a thabhaill. 1. he lost his wits. 2. he is in his dotage ; chur an cùisean gu tabhaill, to direct their affairs to good purpose.

tabhainn, tabhoinn, tafoin, *n. f.* distress, entanglement, plight. *Ir.* tabhong ; *a.* overpowered. *M.Ir.* tafond, a rout.

tabhair, *v.* give, grant. *O.Ir.* tabur = do + biur.

tàbhairn, tàv'-urn, *n. m.* a tavern, an inn ; feast, conviviality. *Lat.* taberna.

tabhairt, tavurt, *v.* to give ; inf. of tabhair.

tabhairteach, tavurtuch, *a.* bountiful, liberal. *E.Ir.* tabartach.

tabhall, tav'-ul, *n. m.* a sling (to cast stones). *E.Ir.* taball. *Lat.* tabella.

tàbhan, *n. m.* a small load of peat, such as a child or an aged person would carry.

tabhann, taff'-un, *n. f.* barking, yelping. *Ir.* tabhthán, snarling or growling of dogs.

tabhannaich, taff'-an-ich, *n. f.* continuous barking.

tàbharnadh, tàvurnu, *n. m.* apparition, a haunting infatuation — said of a child who haunts a dangerous place at the edge of a pool.

tabhartair, tavurter, *n. m.* bestower.

tabhartas, tavurtus, *n. m.* gift, offering.

tàbhastal, tavustul, *n. f.* tedious, nonsense.

tabhbheist, tav-vesht, *n. f.* sea monster.

tàbhoradh, tàvoru'. *See* tàbharnadh.

tac, *n. f.* space, time ; mun tac so an uraidh, about this time last year ; a lease, a tack (farm) ; a tack (in sailing).

taca, *n. m.* 1. a prop, support, leaning against (for support) ; 2. the bolt-rope of a sail ; the hook that attaches the forepart of sail to the gunwale. 3. comparison in phr. an taca ri—compared with, instead of.

tacaid, tacej, *n. f.* a tack ; stitch or pain ; fr. the *Eng.*

tacan, *n. f.* little time, while.

tacar, *n. m.* a considerable quantity, plenty provisions ; "kitchen." *Ir.* tacar, plenty. Cf. *O.Ir.* taccair, *congruus.*

tachair, tachir, *v.* meet, light upon, find ; tachraidh sinn fhathast, we shall meet yet ; happen, come to pass ; thachair e gu math dhuit, it has happened well to you. So *Ir.*

tàchair, tàchir, *n. m.* a water weed.

tachairt, tachurt, *inf.* of tachair, happening, act of meeting, or coming to pass.

tachais, tachish, *v.* scratch the skin.

tàcharan, tàchuran, *n. m.* sprite, a ghost, the yelling of ghosts, trifling person ; orphan. *Ir.* tacharán, an orphan, infant, sprite.

tachas, *n. m.* clawing, scratching ; itch, itchiness. *Ir.* tochas, the itch, mange.

tachasach, *adj.* itchy, mangy.

tachd, *v.* choke, strangle, stop up. *O.Ir.* tachtaim.

tachdadh, tachcu, *vbl. n. m.* act of choking, strangling. *O.Ir.* tachtad, *gl.* aggens. *S.G.*

tachrais, tachresh, *v.* wind yarn. *Also* tacharais. *Ir.* tocharais. *M.Ir.* tochartaim.

tachrasach, *n. f.* windlass.

tàclach, tàc-luch, *n. m.* a good measure.

tacsa, tacas, *n. m.* support, solidity, substance.

tàdh, tà, *n. m.* a ledge, a layer.

tadhal, tu'ul, *n. m.* visiting, frequenting, a resort, a goal. *O.Ir.* tadall, *visitatio,* *inf.* of taidlim.

tafaing. *See* tabhainn.

tag, tagan, *n. m.* private, or hid purse, as that of a wife.

tagach, *a.* pouched, full of pouches.

tagair, tag'-ir, *v.* claim, crave, plead a cause, prosecute ; tha e tagairt orm, he claims of me, he craves me. *See* agair. *O.Ir.* taccraim = to-ad-garim, *argumentor,* argue a case.

tagairt, tagurt, *vbl. n. m.* pleading, craving ; *inf.* of tagair.

tagan, *n. m.* six sheaves of corn.

tagarach, *adj.* litigious ; *n. m.* claimant.

tagartair, tagurter, *n. m.* pleader, agent.

tagartas, tăg'-urtt-us, *n. m.* prosecution, law-plea ; **tha tagartas aige an Inbhir-aora,** he has a law-plea in Inveraray; claim.

tagh, tu, *v.* choose, select, elect, make choice ; **tagh a' chuid as fhearr,** select the best, make choice of the best ; *adj.* choice, select, beloved, dear to. *O.Ir.* togu, *eligo.*

taghadh, tu'u, *vbl. n. m.* act of choosing, electing.

taghadair, tu-uder, *n. m.* elector, chooser, cattle oversman.

taghairm, tu-ghurm, *n. f.* an echo, noise, divination through the medium of demons ; a gathering summons. *Ir.* taghairm, a sort of divination ; echo. *O.Ir.* togairm, *invocatio,* to + gairm.

taghan, tughan, *n. m.* polecat, stinkard, the marten, cat ; somet. improperly written **taoghan.**

taghte, tutiu, *vbl. a.* choice, chosen.

tagradair, tagruder, *n. m.* pleader, agent.

tagradh, tăg'-ru, *vbl. n. m.* act of pleading, craving.

taibeist, tybesht. *See* tabhbheist.

taibh, tyf, taibhean, *n. m.* substance.

taibheanach, tyfenuch, *adj.* substantial.

taibhis, taibhse, tysh, *n. m.* spectre, apparition, second sight ; spirit, ghost, a vision of the second-sight ; a starveling child or young animal. So *Ir.* *O.Ir.* taidbsiu, *demonstratio.*

taibhleach, tyvluch, *n. f.* a smart blow, or box sideways ; smart box.

taibhsear, tysher, *n. m.* a visionary, a silly person ; one gifted with the second-sight.

taibhsearachd, tysheruchc, *n. f.* second-sight ; bewildered, or stupid conduct.

taibid, tybij, *n. f.* taunting speech. *Ir.* taibid, a squib in speech.

taibse, tybshu, *n. f.* propriety of speech.

taibseachd, *n. f.* eloquence.

taic, *n. f.* support, prop, fulcrum ; **cuir taic ris a gheamhlaig,** put a fulcrum to the lever ; contact ; **thàinig e an taic na cartach,** he came in contact with the cart ; nearness, approximation ; **taic ri bliadhna,** near a year ; **an taic a chéile,** in contact with each other ; dependence, preparation ; **an taic an dòmhnuich,** in contact, or in preparation for the Sabbath ; **an taic a bhalla,** leaning on the wall ; in virtue of. *M.Ir.* aicc, a bond. *E.Ir.* aicce, relationship, proximity.

taicealachd, tyculuchc, *n. f.* stoutness, solidity, firmness.

taiceil, tycel, *adj.* stout, firm, strong.

taidhe, ta-ee, *n. f.* care, attention. *See* toidh.

taidhe, taidheach, toyuch, toidheach, todhach, *a.* careful, heedful.

taidheam, tyem, *n. f.* meaning, sense, import. *See* oidheam.

taifeid, tefej, *n. f.* bowstring, sharp noise on ground of great drops of rain.

taig, tyg, *n. f.* great attachment ; custom.

tàigeanach, *n. m.* a squat person.

taigeis, tagesh, *n. f.* Scotch haggis.

taigh, ty. *See* tigh.

taighlich, tylich, *n. f.* chattels, paraphernalia ; tigh + lach. Cf. teaghlach.

tail, tal, *n. m.* substance, fee, wages. Seen in tuaras*dal.* *M.Ir.* taile, *sala-rium.*

tailce, telcu, *n. f.* firmness, strength. *E.Ir.* talce, tailce.

tailceanach, telcenuch, *n. m.* a stout man.

tailceas, talcus, *n. m.* scorn, disdain, contempt. Cf. tarcuis.

tailceasach, talcusuch, *a.* disdainful.

tàileasg, talusc, *n. m.* backgammon. *Ir.* táibhleis. *M.Ir.* taiflis, draughtboard. *Lat.* tabula.

tailgneachd, *n. f.* prophecy ; for tairgneachd.

tailleabart, *n. m.* a halbert, a whacking blow.

tàilleabh, tăliuv, *n. m.* apprentice-fee, premium ; consequence, result ; on account of ; **an do phàidh thu do thàilleabh?** have you paid your apprentice-fee, or premium ? **air tàilleabh a' ghnothaich sin,** in consequence of that affair. *Also* tàille. *E.Ir.* athlad, change, *inf.* of athláim, restore.

tàilleabhach, tăliuvuch, *adj.* consequent, as the result ; *n. m.* an apprentice.

tàilleabhachd, tăliuvuchc, *n. f.* apprenticeship, substantiality.

tàillear, tăler, *n. m.* a tailor; fr. the *Eng.* *O.F.* tailleor. *L.Lat.* tăliăre, cut.

tàillearachd, tăleruchc, *n. f.* tailoring ; sewing.

tailm, *n. m.* tool; a sling, noose. *O.Ir.* tailm, *gen.* telma, a sling. *W.* telm.

tailmrich, tulmrich, *n. f.* noise, bustle, sound of footsteps. *E.Ir.* tairmrith, *transcursus.*

tailp, telp, *n. f.* a bundle, parcel.

tàimh, tyv, *n. m.* death, mortality, fainting. *E.Ir.* tàm, plague.

tàimhleac, tyvlec, *n. f.* tombstone, a cairn over the dead. So *Ir.*

taimhlis, tylis, *v. tr.* contemn, traduce.

tàimhneul, tăv-nel, *n. m.* slumber, a trance, a swoon. So *Ir.*

tàin, tan, *n. f.* a drive ; flocks, cattle, a drove ; wealth in flocks. *E.Ir.* táin, a raid ; cattle-driving.

taine, taniu, *compar. deg.* of **tana,**

thinner, *n. f.* thinness ; **na 's taine,** thinner ; **as taine,** the thinnest.

tainead, tanud, *abstr. n. f.* thinness, degree of thinness, degree of tenuity.

taing, tyng, *n. f.* gratitude, thanks, deep sense of gratitude ; **gun tàing dhuit,** without thanks to you, in spite of you ; **a' nochdadh do thàing,** showing your sense of gratitude; fr. the *Eng.*

taingealachd, tyngeluchc, *n. f.* sentiments of gratitude. *Also* **taingealas.**

taingeil, tyngal, *adj.* grateful, thankful, impressed with a sense of gratitude.

tàinidh, *n. f.* intestinal fat in cows.

tàinistear, tānishter, *n. m.* heir-presumptive ; next oldest son ; one acting for the heir ; regent, governor ; trustee, tutor. *See* tànaiste.

tàinistearachd, tānishteruchc, *n. f.* presumptive heirship, regency, trusteeship.

tainneamh, taniuv, *n. m.* thaw. *Ir.* tionadh, melting. *O.Ir.* tinaim, dissolve, vanish.

tàintean, tānten, *n. pl.* of tàin, talents, faculties, accomplishments ; **is mór na tàintean a bhuilich Dia ort,** great are the talents God has bestowed on you.

taip, typ, *n. f.* a mass, a lump ; great wealth, without any of the refined manners or education of genteel society. So *Ir.*

taiplis, teplish, *n. f.* chessboard. *Ir.* tàiphleisg, táibhleis.

tàir, tar, *n. f.* contempt, reproach ; **na dèan tàir,** do not despise or scorn ; pains, trouble, difficulty ; **fhuair mi tàir mhór rithe,** she gave me the greatest trouble. *E.Ir.* tár.

tàir, *v.* come, get, obtain. So *E.Ir.*

tairbealach, terbyaluch, *n. m.* defile.

tairbeart, teruburt, *n. f.* isthmus ; name of isthmus of Kintyre, and other like places in the Highlands.

tairbeartach, terburtuch, *adj.* superabundant, very abundant, almost superfluous. *E.Ir.* tairbert, munificence.

tairbhe, tervu, *n. f.* advantage, profit, avail ; **an t-ainm gun an tairbhe,** the name without the profit or benefit. *O.Ir.* torbe.

tairbheartas, *n. m.* bounty.

tairbhein, *n. m.* surfeit, bloody flux. *Carm. Gad.*

tàirceach, tārciuch, *a.* despicable.

tàirealachd, tāraluchc, *n. f.* contemptuousness, contemptibility, reproachfulness.

tàireil, tāral, *adj.* contemptuous, disdainful, reproachful, insulting.

tairg, terg, *v.* offer, proffer ; propose ; bid ; **thairg e airgead dhaibh,** he

offered them money ; **tairg air so,** bid for this. *Ir.* tairgim, produce, bring on. *M.Ir.* taircim. *O.Ir.* tergabim, proffer.

tairgir, tergir, *v. tr.* prophesy.

tairgire, tergiru, *n. m.* offerer, bidder.

tairgneachd, tergnuchc, *n. f.* prophecy, divination. *O.Ir.* tairngire, *promissio.*

tairgse, tergshu, *n. f.* offer, proposal.

tairgseach, tergshuch, *adj.* inviting, offering.

tairgsinn, tergshin, *vbl. n. f.* act of offering, bidding, proffering ; an offer.

tairiosg, terusc, *n. m.* a saw. *See* tuireasg.

tairis, terish, *intj.* stand still ! spoken by dairymaid to calm the cow. *Also* stairis. *See* teirisd and teiris. *O.Ir.* tairissem = to + air + sessam, to stand. *Thn.*

tairis, terish, *a.* kind, loving, trusty ; **spàinteach gheur thairis,** a keen trusty (Spanish) blade. *I.Lom. O.Ir.* tairisse, true, loyal.

tairiseach, terishuch, *adj.* loyal, tender, kind.

tairisgean, *n. m.* peat-spade. *See* toirsgian.

tairlearach, tar-leruch, *a.* transmarine. tar + lear, " beyond the sea."

tairleas, *n. m.* a cupboard, aumrie. *Also* turlas.

tairm, terum, *n. f.* necromancy. *See* taghairm.

tàirmeas, tārmas, *n. m.* disdain, contempt.

tàirmeasail, tārmusal, *adj.* disdainful.

tàirn, tārn, *n. f.* necromancy. *Also* iodramanachd.

tàirneach, tārnuch, *n. f.* thunder.

tàirneach, *a.* that can be drawn ; extractive ; *a.* fr. tarruing.

tàirneach, tairgneach, *a.* well-nailed.

tàirneanach, tārnenuch, *n. f.* thunder. *See* torrunn. *M.Ir.* tóirnim, make a loud noise.

tàirng, tarrang, *n. m.* a nail. *E.Ir.* tairnge.

tàirnich, tārnich, *v. tr.* nail, fasten.

tàirsinn, tārshin, *inf.* of tàr, to obtain, win, manage to.

tais, tăsh, *adj.* damp, moist, spiritless, soft. *E.Ir.* taise, tasse, weakness. *O.Celt.* taxi-s.

taisbean, tash-ben, *v. tr.* reveal, show, table, present ; **taisbean an t-airgead,** table the money. *O.Ir.* taispenim, taissfenim, I show ; asfenimm (*testificorn*).

taisbeanadh, tashbenu, *pt.* revealing.

taisdeal, tashjal, *n. f.* a journey, voyage, pilgrimage. So *Ir.*

taisdealach, tash-jaluch, *n. m.* a sojourner,

traveller ; vagabond ; ghost, a contemptible person ; one that scuds or vanishes by.

taise, tesh'-u, *compar. deg.* of tais, softer, more spiritless.

taiseachd, tăsh'-achc, *n. f.* extreme cowardice.

taisead, tash'-ud, *abstr. n. m.* softness, moistness, cowardice.

taiseadach, tashuduch, *n. m.* shroud, winding-sheet ; ciste is taiseadach, coffin and shroud. tais (the dead) + étach.

taisealach, tashaluch, *a.* of fair quantity, bountiful. *Ir.* taibhseach, bulky.

taisealachd, tashaluchc, *n. f.* moistness.

taisealadh, tashalu, *n. m.* fair size, bulk, quantity. *O.Ir.* taisselbaim, torc taiselbtha, a full-grown hog.

taisealan, tashulan, *n. m.* reliquary, a keepsake.

taisean, tashun, *pl. n.* a skeleton, relics of the dead. *E.Ir.* taisse, reliques, ghosts.

taisg, tashc, *v.* deposit, lay up, hoard ; 'g a tasgadh seachad, hoarding it up ; *n. m.* store ; *also* tigh-taisg, a storehouse ; nì sam bith tha'n taisg, anything in store. *E.Ir.* taiscim, I lay up in store.

taisgairm, tashc-erm, *n. f.* armoury.

taisgeach, tashc-uch, *n. f.* a store, storehouse, a deposit.

taisgeadach, tashc-uduch, *n. f.* wardrobe.

taisgeal, tăshg'-al, *n. m.* finding anything that was lost ; reward for returning it. *O.Ir.* taiscelaid, exploration (to + scél).

taisgeal, *n. m.* news.

taisgealach, tashcaluch, *n. m.* a spy, reporter, discoverer.

taisgealadh, tashcalu, *vbl. n. m.* report, discovery, news.

taisgleach, *n. m.* same as taisgealach ; it is used to describe the " Teachdaire Gaidhealach " by " *Car. n. Gl.*"

taisich, tăsh'-ich, *v.* moisten ; daunt ; soften.

taite, taiteadh, tytu, *n. m.* a peep, a glimpse, a moment. Cf. tiota.

taitheach, *a.* cautious, careful ; for taidheach.

taitheasg, ta-husc, *n. m.* a repartee. *O.Ir.* taithesc, answer, aithesc, *admonitio.*

taithireach, *a.* saucy, pert, uppish, particular. Cf. tàireil.

taitinn, tytin, *v.* please, give delight to, satisfy. *E.Ir.* taitnim, I shine. *O.Ir.* taitnem, light.

taitneach, tajtnuch, *adj.* happy, pleasant, agreeable, fascinating, acceptable ; taitneach do 'n t-sealladh, pleasant to the sight ; is taitneach leam t' fhaicinn,

I am happy to see you. *O.Ir.* taitnemach, bright, pleasant.

taitneachd, tytnuch, *n. f.* pleasantness, agreeableness, taste.

taitneadh, tytnu, *vbl. n. m.* act of pleasing.

taitneas, tytnus, *n. m.* delight, pleasure.

tàl, *n. m.* adze. *O.Ir.* tál, axe. *Thn.* suggests equating with *O.H.G.* stahal, steel.

talach, *n. m.* complaining, grumbling ; repining ; chan ion duit a bhi talach, you have no reason to grumble. *Ir.* talach, dissatisfied, murmuring.

tàladh, tă'-la, *vbl. n. m.* act of attracting, winning ; enticing, caressing ; a lullaby, cradle song. *O.N.* tál, allurement.

talaich, tall'-ich, *v.* murmur, repine.

tàlaidh, tālay, *v.* attract, allure, soothe.

talainte, talayntu, *n. m.* partition, dividing wall in a house.

talamh, tal'-uv, *n. m., but f.* in *gen. s.* talmhainn, earth, land ; glastalamh, grassy land ; talamh bàn, uncultivated land ; talamh dubh, black land, *i.e.* loamy soil ; *also* absence of snow in winter. *O.Ir.* talam, *gen.* talman. Cf. *Gr.* ταλαός. *Thn.*

tàlan, *n. m.* chivalry, feats of arms.

talan, *n. m.* partition wall (slimly built). *Sc.* hallan, *id. Also* cailbhe.

tàlann, tāl'-an, *n. m.* talent. *O.Ir.* talland. *Lat.* talentum.

talcuis, talcoosh. For tarcuis.

tàl-fuinn, tāl-fooyn, *n. m.* a hoe.

talla, *n. m.* a hall ; tigh thallaidh, house with halls, stately house. *M.Ir.* all. Cf. *N.* höll ; *gen.* hallar ; allied to ceall. *McB.*

tallaidh, *a. See sub* talla.

talmaich, *n.* honour.

talmhaidh, taluvy, *adj.* earthly, worldly ; nithe talmhaidh, earthly things ; inntinn thalmhaidh, worldly mind ; weighty, substantial ; mighty ; curaidhean talmhaidh, mighty heroes ; min thalmhaidh, substantial meal ; pale, sallow.

talmhaidheachd, taluvyachc, *n. f.* weightiness, substantiality, sallowness, worldliness.

talmhantachadh, taluvantuchu, *vbl. n. m.* act of growing or sticking together, as sods or earth does. *Also* talmhachadh.

talmhantaich, taluvantich, *v.* grow, as earth ; stick together, as sods, etc.

tàmailt, tāmelt, *n. f.* insult, reproach. So *Ir.*

tàmailteach, *adj.* insulting, disparaging, reproachful, taunting ; gnàthfhacal tàmailteach, a taunting proverb ; disgraceful.

tàmailtear, tāmelter, *n. m.* taunter.

tàmh, tāv, *n. m.* rest, quietness, quiet, refuge ; àite tàimh, place of rest or refuge ; abode, habitation ; **c'àite an tàmh dhuit,** where is the place of your abode ? idleness, inactivity ; **tha i 'na tàmh,** she is idle ; **leig tàmh dhomh,** let me alone ; *v.* rest, abide, cease, desist, give over ; **tàmh de do sgeig,** give over your jeering ; **ag obair gun tàmh,** indefatigably working. *E.Ir.* **tám.** *O.Celt.* tamô, *morior.*

tàmhaich, tāv′-ich, *v.* rest, abide.
tamhaiche, tāv′-ich-u, *n. m.* inhabitant.
tàmhaite, *n. m.* habitation ; dwelling.
tàmhanachd, tāvanuchc, *n. f.* idleness, sluggishness.
tamharach, tāv′-ar-uch, *n. m.* a dolt.
tamhasg, tav′-usk, *n. m.* spectre, apparition, ghost ; **b'e do thamhasg a bh' ann,** it was your ghost ; a blockhead. *See* **amhas.**
tamhasgail, tav′-ask-al, *adj.* spectre-like.
tamull, *n. m.* while. *Also* **tacan.**
tàn, *n. m.* time ; **an tàn,** when. *O.Ir.* tan intain, intan. *O.Celt.* tanâ.
tàn, *n. f.* cattle, herd of cattle ; cattle raid. *See* **tàin.**
tana, *adj.* thin, slender, lean, shallow ; **duine tana,** lean person ; **àite tana,** a shallow place ; **talamh tana,** shallow soil ; **brochan tana,** thin gruel. So *O.Ir. W.* teneu, thin. *Corn.* **tanow.** *Lat.* tenuis. *Gr.* ταναός, stretched. *O.Celt.* tanaro-s.
tanachd, *n. f.* thinness, leanness, shallowness.
tanaich, tan′-ich, *v. tr.* and *intrans.* get thin or shallow ; thin or single turnips, etc.
tànaiste, tānishtu, *n. m.* the second in order ; a lieutenant ; next heir ; tanist. *O.Ir.* tánaise, *secundus.*
tanalach, *n. m.* shoal, or shallow water ; thin part of a hide ; **tanalach na seiche,** the thin part of the hide.
tannas, tannasg, *n. m.* ghost.
taobh, tūv, *n. m.* side, direction, cause, account ; **an taobh a muigh,** the outside, the exterior ; **có'n taobh,** which side ? **ri mo thaobh,** beside me ; **air mo thaobh,** on my side = taking my part ; **a thaobh sin,** about that, on that account ; **chan 'eil fhios agam ciod as taobh dha,** I do not know what is become of him,—in what direction he has gone ; *v.* come near, take one's part ; **cha do thaobh e am baile,** he did not come near the town ; **cha taobh e sinne,** he will not take our part. *E.Ir.* **tóeb, táib.** *O.Ir.* **tóib.** *O.Celt.* toibos.
taobhach, tūvuch, *adj.* lateral.
taobhadh, tūvu, *n. m.* siding with, taking one's side, partiality ; **ceapair-taobhaidh,** *n. m.* a bannock contrived to win love of man or of woman.

taobhan, tūvan, *n. m.* side-rafter. *Ir.* a rafter ; wattles laid on rafters under thatch.
taobhcheum, tūv-chem, *n. f.* digression.
taobh-leis, tūv-lesh, *n. m.* lee-side.
taobh-luath, *n. m.* a division of a pipe tune.
taobhshruth, tūv-hroo, *n. m.* eddy tide. *See* **saobh-shruth.**
taod, tūd, *n. m.* halter, rope, cable. *See* **teud.**
taodan, tūdan, *n. m.* a little rope.
taod-aoire, *n. m.* sheet rope of a sail.
taod-frithir, *n. m.* a halyard.
taodhain, tū-iru, *n. m.* an apostate.
taoghain. *See* **taghan.**
taoghas, tu′us, *n. m.* the grave.
taoibhleach, toyvluch, *n. f.* rough push to one side.
taoig, tüig, *n. f.* a fit of passion.
taoilidh, *n. f.* a goal at shinty ; **chuir sinn an t-aoilidh orra,** we won the goal from them. *Sc.* hail ; hail the ball, win the goal.
taoim, tooym, *n. f.* bilge-water. So *Ir.*
taois, tūsh, *n. f.* dough or leaven. *E.Ir.* **toes.** *O.Ir.* táis. *O.Celt.* taisto.
taoiseadair, tūshuder, *n. m.* a baker.
taoisinn, tūshin, **taoisnich,** tūshnich, *v.* knead, leaven, work dough.
taoitear, toyter, *n. m.* tutor, trustee ; oversman, a guardian. *Lat.* tutor.
taom, tūm, *v. n.* bale a boat, pour out ; empty, as a dish or cart ; **taom am bàta,** bale the boat ; **taom air e,** pour it on it ; **taom a' chairt,** empty the cart. *E.Ir.* tóem, a jet, taeim.
taom, tūm, *n. f.* a fit of passion, a plash of liquid.
taomaire, tūmiru, *n. m.* a pump.
taoman, tūman, *n. m.* baling-dish.
taosg, tūsc, *n. m.* a pour, a rush ; exact fill ; in some places, = three-quarters full, more or less. *Ir.* **taosgaim,** pump, drain. *E.Ir.* tóesca, spilling, **taescaire,** a baler.
taosgach, *a.* fickle, uncertain ; **duine taosgach,** fickle person ; **ni taosgach,** an uncertain or precarious thing.
taosgach, *a.* nearly full.
taosgadh, tūscu, *vbl. n. m.* act of pouring out, rushing (of water, rain).
taosgaid, tūscej, *n. f.* fickle female.
taosgaire, tūsgiru, *n. m.* fickle man, a man who pumps.
taosgan, tūscan, *n. m.* a pump.
taosnadh, tūsnu, *vbl. n. m.* act of kneading ; horse-play, rough-handling.
tap, *n. m.* lock of lint on a distaff ; *v.* hoop or thread a fishing-hook.
tapachd, *n. f.* heroism.
tapadh, *n. m.* heroic feat, achievement ;

thanks, success ; **tapadh leat,** thank you.

tapadhcion, tapu-cin, *n. m.* a blunder.

tapag, *n. f.* a slip of a word, a casualty.

tapagail, tăp′-ag-al, *n.f.* a blunder, a slip.

tapaidh, tăpy, *adj.* heroic, brave, clever, bold, successful in business. *E.Ir.* **tapad,** suddenness, alertness.

tapaidheachd, tapyachc. *See* **tapachd.**

tapan, *n. m.* little lock of lint, or wool. *Also* **toban.**

tap-dubh, *vbl. n. m.* act of beating drum (calling to quarters).

taplach, tapluch, *n. m.* a wallet, a repository.

tàr, *n. m.* belly ; **tàrgeal,** white belly ; **tàrleathar,** the hide of the belly. *See* **tarr.**

tàr, *v.* get to, obtain ; **tàr as,** move off. *See* **tàir.**

tarachair, tarucher, *n. m.* an auger, a borer. *O.Ir.* **tarathar,** a borer. *O.Celt.* **taratro-n.**

taradh, *n. m.* premonitory noise.

tarag, *n. m., gen.* **tairig,** a nail. *See* **tàirng.**

taran, *n. m.* ghost of unbaptized child.

tarbh, tărv, *n. m.* a bull ; *pl.* **tairbh.** *O.Ir.* **tarb.** *W.* **tarw.** *Corn.* **tarow.** *O.Celt.* **tarvo-s.** *Lat.-Gr.* **taurus.**

tarbhach, tarv′-uch, *a.* supplied with bulls.

tarbhach, *adj.* profitable, beneficial ; **tarbhach do dhuine,** profitable to man ; substantial, productive ; **bàrr tarbhach,** substantial crop, abundant crop ; **buille tharbhach,** an effectual blow, or pull in rowing ; fr. **tairbhe.** *E.Ir.* **torbach.**

tarbhachd, tarvachc, *n. f.* substantiality, productiveness, gainfulness, profit.

tarbhaichead, tarvichud, *abstr. n. f.* degree of profit, or importance, or substantiality.

tarbhail, târv′-al, *a.* bull-faced, brutish.

tarbharnach, *a.* noisy, garrulous.

tarbh-nathrach, tarv-naruch, *n.* dragon-fly.

tarbh-réidh, tarv-rē, *n. m.* farm bull.

tarbh-tàine, tarv-tāniu, *n. m.* parish bull.

tarbh-uisge, t.-ushcu, *n. m.* water bull.

tarcuis, tarcoosh, *n.f.* contempt, dispute. *E.Ir.* **tarcusul.**

tarcuiseach, tarcooshuch, *a.* contemptuous.

tarcuisich, tarcooshich, *v.* despise, revile.

targadaireachd, *n. f.* aiming, threatening.

targadh, tarugu, *m.* a ruling, a governing, an assembly.

targaid, targej, *n. f.* target, shield.

targair, tărg′-ir, *v.* foretell.

targanach, *n. m.* a prognostication, a pro-

phesying. *O.Ir.* **tairgire, tairngire,** promise, anticipate.

tàrla, to come to pass, to happen. *O.Ir.* **tárla** = do + rala (venit).

tàrladh, târ′-lu, *n. m.* great demand, or tearing from each other, as a scarce commodity.

tàrlaid, tārlej, *n. m.* contemptible person, a slave, a thrall.

tarlaidh, tarly, *v.* tear, or drag away.

tarmach, tarm′-uch, *n. m.* source of a disease. *O.Ir.* **tór-mag,** *auctio.*

tàrmachadh, tārm′-uch-u, *vbl. n. m.* act of gathering, as a tumour ; collecting, as matter in a suppuration ; originating, congregating, or settling.

tarmachan, tārm′-uch-an, *n. m.* the bird, ptarmigan, a butterfly (*Suth′d.*).

tàrmaich, tār′-mich, *v.* originate, settle, produce, gather, increase. *O.Ir.* **tórmagim,** I increase, add to.

tarmus, tār′-mus, *n. m.* dislike of food, scorn for plain fare ; fr. **tàir.**

tàrnach, tārn′-uch, *n. f.* clap of thunder, a sound slap.

tàrnadair, *n. m.* a taverner, an inn-keeper. *Lat.* **tabernator.**

tarp, *n. m.* a clod, a lump. Cf. *O.N.* **torf,** turf.

tarr, *n. m.* lowest part of the belly. *E.Ir.* **tarr.** *O.Celt.* **targsâ.**

tarr, *v.* be clever, be alert, nimble ; **tharr e as,** he managed to escape. *See* **tàr.**

tarrach, *n. m.* girth, belly-thong.

tarrachrann, *n.* the wool on a sheep's udder. *Suth′d.*

tarradheargan, *n. m.* a char.

tarragheal, tarr′-yal, *a.* white-bellied ; **bradan tarragheal,** white-bellied salmon ; *n. f.* white-bellied cow.

tarraid, tarej, *n. m.* sheriff-officer. *Also* **earraid.**

tarraodann, *n. m.* paunch-like face.

tarrfhionn, white-bellied, white buttocks.

tarrghlogach, *a.* loose-bellied, flabby—applied by *R.D.* to salmon in winter.

tarrleathar, *n. m.* the hide of the lower part of the belly.

tarruing, tărr′-inn, *vbl. n. f.* act of drawing or extracting ; act of drawing near ; an extracting plaster ; **cuir tarruing air,** apply an extracting plaster to it ; a haul, pull ; **tarruing-chailleach,** dragging in a slovenly manner ; demand ; *v. tr.* draw, pull, extract, haul ; **tharruing e an iongar,** it extracted the matter (from the tumour) ; **tarruing fuil,** let blood ; a haulyard. *E.Ir.* **tairrngim.** Cf. **reng,** and **ringim,** to tear.

tarrunn, *n. f.* a nail ; **tàirnean,** nails ; **biortharrunn,** coffin-nail : (**calp** = a rivet, and **sgolb** = single floorings).

tarsuinn, tăr'-sinn, *adj.* cross, across, traverse, oblique ; *adv.* across, traversely, obliquely, from side to side ; **cuir tarrsuinn e**, place it traversely, or across, or obliquely. *E.Ir.* **tarsnu**, across = **tar** (across) + **sonn** (a beam).

tarsuinneachd, tăr'-sinn-uchc, *n. f.* obliquely, traverseness, crossness, peevishness.

tarsunnan, *n. m.* a cross-beam or bar, a wheel-spoke. *See* **tarsuinn**.

tarsunnanachd, tăr'-sunn-an-uchc, *n. f.* bickering, satirising, lampooning ; sort of poetry.

tart, tarst, *n. m.* thirst, drought ; costiveness in cattle. *Also* **pathadh**. *O.Ir.* **tart**, *sitis*. *O.Celt.* tar(s)to-. Cf. *Lat.* torreo, burn. *Gr.* τέρσομαι, be dry. *Got.* þaurstei. *A.S.* þyrst. *O.H.G.* durst.

tartach, *adj.* thirsty, droughty, dry.

tartar, *n. f.* noise of tramping.

tartarach, *adj.* noisy in stamping ; making heavy noises.

tartmhor, tarst-vor, *adj.* thirsty, droughty, dry.

tartmhorachd, tarst-vorachc, *n. f.* dry or droughty weather ; great drought.

tàsan, *n. m.* bickering, fretting ; bickering, scolding, discontented person.

tàsanach, *adj.* bickering.

tàsanachd, *n. f.* bickering, fretful disposition or habit, fretfulness.

tasdan, *n. m.* a shilling. *Sc.* testan ; fr. *Fr.* teste (tête) head—going back to time of Louis XII., whose " head " appeared on his coinage.

tàsg, *n. m.* a task, allotted job ; fr. *Eng.*

tàsg, *n. m.* a ghost, an apparition.

tàsg, **tàsc**, *n.m.* fame, character, report, *E.Ir.* **tásc**, report.

tasgaidh, tascy, *n. f.* store, treasure ; **tha, a thasgaidh !** yes, my treasure ! my darling ! smouldering a peat fire for the night. *See* **taisg**.

tasp, *n. m.* severe sarcasm.

taspaire, taspiru, *n. m.* satirist.

taspannach, *adj.* very sarcastic, or petulant.

tataidh, taty, *v.* domesticate, as an animal ; attract to oneself. Cf. **cataidh**.

tàth, *v.* join or soder, cement. So *Ir.*

tàth, *n. m.* pitch, strength ; lionn-tàth, energy.

tathach, ta-huch, *n. m.* a guest, a visitor.

tàthadh, tā-hu, *vbl. n. m.* act of joining ; a joint, seam.

tathaich, ta-hich, *v.* visit, frequent. *M.Ir.* **taithigim**, and **aithigim**, I visit.

tathaich, *n. m.* nausea (after intoxication).

tathaich, ta-hich, *n. m.* ghost, apparition, mysterious sounds (attributed to invisible ghost), sound in general ;
" Is binne an tathaich sud mar cheud
Na gleadhraich éitigh chabhsairean."
" A hundred times sweeter yon sound than
the horrid din of the streets."

tathaiche, ta-hichu, *n. m.* a frequent visitor.

tathasg, *n. f.* shade of the departed.

tathunn, ta-hun, *n.* barking, baying. *Ir.*

tathunn, bay of a deer, bark. *See* **tabhunn**.

té, *n. f.* a female, woman, or any object of the feminine gender. *Ir.* **an ti**, she who ; **an té**, he who. *O.Ir.* **intí**, he who ; **indi**, she who ; **aní**, that which.

tè, **tèa**, *a.* insipid, slightly fermented.

teab, teb, *n.* a flippant person's mouth.

teabad, tebud, *n. m.* a stammer, taunt, repartee. *E.Ir.* **tepe**, a cutting. *O.Ir.* **taipe**, *brevitas*.

teabais, tebesh, *n. f.* flippancy of speech.

teabaiseach, *n. m.* flippant.

teabanta, tebantu, *adj.* carping, captious.

teabantachd, tebantuchc, *n. f.* captiousness, flippancy of speech, captious notice.

tèabhachd, *n. f.* virtue, valour, courage. Cf. **teomachd**.

teach, tech, *n. f.* a house, habitation ; *transf.* **gu teach**, **fo theach**, fulfil, happen. *O.Ir.* **tech**, **teg**, *gen.* tige. *W.* ty. *O.W.* tig. *Lat.* tectum (tego), a roof. So *Gr.* (σ)τέγος. *O.Celt.* tegos-. Cf. *O.H.G.* dah. *A.S.* þæc. *O.N.* þak, a roof. *Eng.*

teachd, *n. m.* arrival ; **air dha teachd**, having arrived ; *vbl. n. f.* act of arriving ; **teachd a mach**, increase, product ; **teachd a steach**, income ; **teachd-an-tir**, provision, livelihood. *O.Ir.* **techt**, *itio, aditus*. *Z*².

teachd, tyechg, *v.* be fit to contain, hold, find room for ; **cha teachd e an so**, it has not sufficient room here ; **an teachd e ann**, can it contain it ? **an teachd e 'san leaba**, has he room in the bed ?

teachd, *a.* legal, lawful, fitting. *O.Ir.* **téchte**, *legalis, lex*. *See* **deic.**

tèachd, *n. f.* silly boasting.

tèachdadh, parching thirst. *See* **teuchd.**

teachdaire, techciru, *n. m.* messenger, courier, ambassador, delegate, envoy, missionary. *O.Ir.* **techtaire**, *legatus*.

teachdaireachd, *n. f.* message, embassy, errand, legation, mission.

teachmhail, *n. f.* affliction, sickness.

teadalach, tedaluch, *adj.* slow, inactive ; uncertain, dilatory.

teadalachd, *n. f.* sickliness, dilatoriness.

teadhair, tiu'ir, *n. f., pl.* **teadhraichean**,

a tether ; fr. *Sc. Eng.* tether. *M.E.* tedir. *O.N.* tjöðr. *McB. Marstr.* excludes tjöðr, and prefers < *M.E.*

teadhraich, tiū'rich, *v.* tether.

teagair, tegir, *v.* gather milk for butter, by stinting the allowance of a family ; economise, provide, shelter. So *Ir.*

teagaisg, tegisg, *v.* instruct, teach ; preach or lecture ; teach by precepts. *E.Ir.* tecoscim, *instruo.*

teagaisgte, *vbl. a.* taught, instructed.

teagamh, tiuguv, *n. m.* doubt, suspense.

teagamhach, tiugvach, *adj.* doubtful ; a theagamh, perhaps.

teagar, *n. m.* gathered gear ; provision.

teagasg, tegusc, *n. f.* instruction ; teaching, doctrine ; *vbl. n. m.* act of teaching, lecturing ; **fear-teagaisg,** a lecturer ; **luchd - teagasg,** instructors. *E.Ir.* tecosc, *instructio.*

tèagbhail, tēg-val, *n. f.* an encounter ; a strife ; revenge ; retribution. *See* teugmhail.

teaghlach, tiūluch, *n. m.* a family, household. *O.Ir.* teglach = teg (house) + slóg (host), *Vendr.* and *Thn.*

teaglach, teglach, *a.* doubtful, uncertain.

teaglachd, *n. f.* uncertainty.

teagmhach, tegvach, *a.* doubtful, suspecting.

teagnadh, tegnu, *n. m.* straining, forcing ; squeezing something through a narrow passage ; a *tenesmus.*

tealbh, *n. m.* corn ; **tàn is tealbh,** herd and corn.

teall, *n. m.* an attack all of a sudden. *O.Ir.* tellaim, take, steal.

teallach, *n. m.* a hearth or fireplace, a smith's fireplace or forge. *E.Ir.* tenlach, tellach (ten + lach).

teallachag, *n. f.* concubine.

teallaid, tiälej, *n. f.* a lusty or bunchy woman.

teallsanach, tiaulsanuch, *n. m.* a philosopher.

teallsanachd, *n. f.* philosophy.

teamhaidh, tevy, *adj.* pleasant. *E.Ir.* temair, a pleasant spot ; an eminence.

teamhair, tevir, *n. f.* time, in season, weather ; shaded walk on a hill. Cf. *Lat.* tempora.

teamhal, tevil, *n. m.* slight swoon or stun. *Also* teimhil. *O.Ir.* temel, *obscuritas. O.Celt.* temelo-s.

teamharra, tevuru, *adj.* very pertly eloquent ; eloquent and flippant, as a young person.

teamhrachd, tevruchc, *n. f.* flippancy ; an impertinent prattle.

teampull, *n. m.* a temple. *O.Ir.* tempul. *Lat.* templum.

teanac, tenuc, *v.* save, deliver from danger.

teanacadh, tenucu, *vbl. n. m.* act of saving, delivering.

teanacas, tenucus, *n. m.* deliverance.

teanal, tenel. *See* **tional,** a gathering, congregation.

teanchair, ten'-uch-ur, *n. f.* smith's tongs. *O.Ir.* tenchor = (ten + cor, a hand).

teanchrach, *a.* vice-like ; **gréim teanchrach,** vice-like grip. *I.Lom.* Cf. gréim bàis, death-grip.

teanga, teng'-u, *n. f.* a tongue, language ; pin of a buckle ; clapper of a bell ; tongue of shoe ; " tongue " of a Jew's harp ; " tongue " of a net-needle. *O.Ir.* tenge. Cf. *Lat.* lingua (dingua). *O.H.G.* zunga. *A.S.* tunge. *N.* tunga. *Goth.* tuggô.

teangach, teng'-uch, *a.* having many tongues.

teangair, tenger, *n. m.* an interpreter, linguist.

teangaireachd, tengiruchd, *n. f.* interpreting languages ; skill in languages or philology, interpreting.

teann, tjaun, *adj.* tight, tense, severe, rigid, near, close ; **tha an t-sreang teann,** the string is tight ; **teann air mìos,** close upon a month ; **duine teann,** a severe or rigid person ; *v. n.* draw near, approach, approximate, fall to, commence, begin to move, go, proceed ; **teann as an rathad,** move out of my way ; **teann an nios,** come hither ; **teannaibh r'a chéile,** sit close ; **theann iad ri treabhadh,** they commenced ploughing ; **teann-** (forms compds. freely) ; **teann-chaoir,** *i.e.* " intense blaze," hot haste. *O.Ir.* tend. *W.* tynn. *Lat.* tendo.

teannachadh, *vbl. n. m.* act of tightening ; squeezing.

teannadh, tjannu, *n. m.* sufficiency, enough ; **an diol 's an teannadh,** their satisfaction and their fill.

teannaich, tyann'-ich, *v.* tighten, squeeze.

teannaichte, *vbl. a.* squeezed.

teannair, tyann'-ur, *n. m.* noise in a cave, an instrument for squeezing.

teannas, tiänus, *n. m.* austerity.

teannsgail, tiaunscul, *n. m.* crisis, time of stress, military engagement.

teannsgalach, *a.* brave, heroic ; **an t-òg teannsgalach,** the courageous youth.

teann-shàth, tenn-hā, *n. m.* full satiety ; a full meal.

teanntachd, tyannt'-achc, *n. f.* strait, difficulty.

tearb, terub, *v.* separate, sever. *E.Ir.* terbaim, I sever.

tearbadh, terubu', *m.* separating ; **tearbadh nan uan,** separating the lambs. *E.Ir.* terbud.

tearc, *adj.* rare, unusual, scarce. *E.Ir.*
terc, few, rare. *O.Celt.* ter(s)go-s,
scarcity.

tearcad, teircead, tercud, *abstr. n. m.*
fewness, scarcity. *E.Ir.* terce.

tearceun, terc-iän, *n. m.* phœnix, rare
bird.

tearmad, termud, *n. m.* safety, security;
a form of tearmann.

tearmann, ter'-munn, *n. m.* a sanctuary
(in the sense of place of safety), refuge,
protection. *M.Ir.* termain, termonn.
L.Lat. termo, termon-is.

tearmasg, tiormasg, *n. m.* a mistake, mischance.

tèarn, *v.* escape, evade; preserve, protect, defend, rescue, save; Dia gar
tèarnadh, may God preserve or
rescue us.

teàrn, *v.* descend. *E.Ir.* tairnim, descend.

tèarnach, *a.* sloping, descending.

tèarnadh, *vbl. n. m.* act of preserving,
rescuing, escaping; preservation,
escape, rescue, after-birth; fr. *E.Ir.*
ternaim, escape.

tèarnadh, *m.* descending; " a' tèarnadh
's a' dìreadh," descending and ascending.

tèarr, *n. m.* tar, pitch; *v.* tar. *O.N.* tjara.

tearrach, *n. m.* a char (fish).

tearrachd, *n. f.* keen sarcasm.

tearradh, tyărr'-u', *vbl. n. m.* act of
tarring, daubing.

tèaruinn, tiärin, *v.* preserve, rescue.
E.Ir. térnaim, ternam, érnaim, I
escape.

tèaruinneach, tèarainneach, tiärinuch,
n. m. a two-year-old sheep (which has
had no lamb); syn. dìonag.

tèaruinte, tiärintu, *vbl. adj.* preserved,
rescued, secured, safe, guarded, cautious.

tèaruinteachd, *n. f.* security or protected
state, precaution, caution.

teas, tes, *n. m.* heat, warmth, too much
of the good things of life, superabundance. *O.Ir.* tess. *O.Celt.* te(p)stu-.

teasach, tesuch, *n. m.* heat, fever; cattle
running from excessive heat; warm
water in milk.

teasaich, tesich, *v.* heat, warm, become
warm.

teasaichte, *vbl. a.* heated, warm.

teasairg, teasruig, tesrig, *v.* save, interpose for the purpose of rescuing;
relieve, afford relief. *O.Ir.* tess-argim
tessurc, *servo.* tess=de-es (out of) +
orcun (killing).

teasd, tesd, *v.* die. *O.Ir.* testa, *deest.*

teasd, *n. m.* tràth teasd, milking-time.

teasdadh, tesda', *m.* dying; gu teasdadh
le gàireachdaich,"dying"withlaughter.

teasg, *v.* cut, cut off. *E.Ir.* tescaim.
Lat. seco.

teasraiginn, tesrigin, *n. f.* relief, preservation, rescue; act of rescuing, relieving, interfering. *O.Ir.* tess-argon,
deliverance. *Also* teasargainn.

teibideach, *a.* irresolute, halting, failing.

teibidh, *a.* smart. *See* teab.

teibnigh, *a.* smart, lively, neat, and with
vigour.

teic, teyck, *adj.* due, lawful, legal; cha
teic na th' ann, all there are, are too
much; cha teic dhuit, that is more
than is due; bheir mise dhuit gus
an abair thu cha teic, I will give you
till you say, it is more than enough.
See teachd.

tèic, *n. f.* flyer (part of spinning-wheel).
Also séic, séicle.

teich, teych, *v.* flee, scamper, be off!
desert; abscond; theich e, he fled,
he deserted the army, he took to his
heels. *E.Ir.* techim. *O.Celt.* teko.

teicheach, teychuch, *adj.* fleeing, fleeting.

teicheadh, teychu, *vbl. n. m.* act of fleeing,
taking to his heels, scampering; fleeing, desertion.

téid, tēj, goes, will go. *See* rach. *O.Ir.*
téit, tét, go.

teididh, tejy, *n. f.* wild, fierce; wildfire;
Also teine sionnachain.

teile, tēlu, *n. f.* lime, or linden tree.

teilg, telig, *n. m.* a fishing-line, a " cast."

teilig, *n. f.* a cord (of a musical instrument).

teilinn, *n. f.* a musical instrument. *W.*
telyn, a harp.

teilleach, teyluch, *n. m.* blub-cheeked
fellow. *Cf.* meilleach. *Also* beilleach.

teillim, teylim, *v. tr.* to harp.

teimhil, tevil. *See* teamhal.

teindire, teynjiru, *n. m.* a fire-grate; fr.
teine.

teindreach, teynjruch, *n. f.* a chain; a
watch chain; fr. teinne, a link.

teine, tenu, *n. m., pl.* teinntean, fire;
teine-aigheir, and teine-éibhinn, bonfire; teine sionnachain, wildfire, phosphoric light from decayed wood or
fish; teine - athair, lightning. *See*
bràight, dreallsach, bràightseal. *O.Ir.*
tene, *gen.* tened. *W.* tàn. *O.Celt.*
tep-n-. *Lat.* tep-eo.

teine-dé, tenu-jē, *n. m.* erysipelas; ringworm; butterfly. *Also* deallandè.

teine-sionnachain, *n. m.* phosphorescent
light. *See* sionn.

teinn, tēyn, *n. f.* predicament, strait,
distress; nach e a bha 'na theinn,
what a predicament he was in!
abstract form fr. teann.

teinndeachd, teynjuchc, *adj.* fieriness.

teinndidh, teynjy, *adj.* fiery, hot, keen.

teinndidheachd. *See* teinnidheachd.

teinne, tyenn'-a, *a. compar.* of teann, *n. f.* degree of tightness ; tightness, rigidness. *O.Ir.* tenne, tension.

teinne, *n. f., pl.* teinneachan, link of chain. *Ir.* teinne. *See* tinne.

teinnead, teynud, *abstr. n. f.* tightness.

teinnteach, *a.* fiery, fierce. *O.Ir.* tentide.

teinntean, tēynten, *n. m.* 1. hearth, hearth-stone, stone used as fire-back. 2. peats laid out to dry (*McE.*).

teinntreach, tēyntruch, *coll. n. f.* flashes of lightning, sparks of fire.

teirbeirt, teyrburt, *a.* harassed, forlorn, melancholy ; glaodh teirbeirt, forlorn cry (as of lost sheep) ; fr. tearb.

teirbeirt, *n. f.* weariness, fatigue. So *Ir.*

teirbeirt, *n. f.* bestowing, distributing ; scattering ; increase, growth.

teirbheirt, *vbl. n. f.* worrying, annoying, harassing.

teirbheirt. *See* toirbheart.

teirbheartaich, teruvyartich, *v.* harass, weary, annoy.

teirce, teyrcu, *adj. compar.* of tearc ; na 's teirce, scarcer ; *n. f.* scarceness, scarcity.

teircead, *abstr. n. f.* scarceness, scarcity.

teirceachd, teyrcachc, *n. f.* fewness, rareness.

teireachdainn, *inf.* of teirig, *q.v. Also* teirigeachdan.

teiridneach, teyrijnuch, *a.* medicinal, curative. Cf. eiridneach.

teirig, teyric, *v. i.* 1. go, us. *imper.* na teirig ann, do not go ; theirig a mach, go out. 2. *ind. pret.* gone, finished ; be exhausted, consumed, be spent, run out ; die ; 'nuair theirigeas gual, teirigidh obair, when coals are done work is at an end ; theirig iad, they are done, they died ; as to this sense, cf. *Lat.* per-eo. *Ir.* tairicim. 1. come. 2. ended. *P.H. M.Ir.* tairic tairc (*pret.* of tair and tarnic), finished, past. *Tbc. O.Ir.* tair (come) = to-air-icc.

teirinn, teyrin, *n. m.* alight, descend. *See* tèarn. *Ir.* teirinim, I descend. *E.Ir.* tairnim. *O.Ir.* tairinnud.

teiris, teirisd, teyrish, *int.* stand still ! stand ! keep quiet ! (said to a cow). *Also* tairis. So *Ir.*

teirm, terum, *n. f.* a thumb.

teirm, *n. f.* a term, a condition ; a season, a while. *Ir.* teirme ; fr. the *Eng.*

teirmeasg, termusc, *n. m.* a mishap, misfortune.

teirmeasgach, *a.* unfortunate.

teirmigil, termigil, *n. m.* undeveloped ram.

teirt, *n. f.* one of the eight canonical hours ; tierce ; trath teirt, morning milking time, grazing before morning milking time. *Ir.* sunrise. *E.Ir.* teirt = *Lat.* (hora) tertia. *See* tràth.

téis, séis, tēsh, *n. f.* musical air, a sound.

teis-meadhon, tesh-miä-un, *n. f.* the exact middle, the centre. *O.Ir.* t-ess (*intens.*) +medon.

teismid, teshmij, *n. f.* last will and testament. *Also* tiomnadh. *Lat.* testamentum.

teist, teysht, *n. f.* reputation, character, respectability. *O.Ir.* teist = *Lat.* testis, *testimonium.*

teistealachd, teysh-jaluchc, *n. f.* respectability, fame, good name, reputation, esteem.

teisteanas, teysh-tunus, *n. m.* testimonial, certificate, reputation, testimony.

teisteas, teyshtus, *n. f.* testimony.

teisteil, teyshtal, *adj.* having a respectable character, respectable, reputable.

tèithidh, tē-hy, *a.* stuffy, close, fusty.

teò, teòdh, *v.* warm, heat, make hot. *Ir.* teighim.

teò-, for teth, hot. *Ir.* teo, warm.

teò-chridheach, tiō-chree-uch, *adj.* warmhearted, affectionate, kind.

teòdhadh, tiō-u', *vbl. n. m.* act of warming, simmering, glowing with love, feeling affection for. *Ir.* teothadh, warming.

teòidh, tiŏy, *v.* warm, simmer, glow with delight or affection ; cha do theòidh mi riamh ris, my heart never glowed with delight or affection towards him.

teòidhte, tiŏytu, *vbl. a.* warmed, simmered.

teòldaidh, tiōldy, *a.* cowardly, easily cowed. *Ir.* teoilt, teoitleach, weak, imbecile.

teòldachd, tiōldachc, *n. f.* cowardice, cowardliness.

teòma, *adj.* expert, dexterous, cute, cunning ; gritty. *Ir.* teóma, dexterous, expert.

teòmachd, *n. f.* expertness, dexterity, skill, proficiency in anything, vigour.

teòthachan, *n. m.* a warming-pan, a chafing-dish. So *Ir.*

teothad, *abstr. n. m.* heat, " hotness."

teth, te, *adj., compar.* teotha, hot, impetuous, keen ; na 's teotha, hotter. *O.Ir.* tee, té. Cf. *Lat.* tepens. *O.Celt.* te(p)ens.

teth, teh, *adj.* rancid, insipid, tasteless.

teuchd, tiächc, *v.* congeal ; wither, dry. *M.Ir.* téchtaim, I congeal ; técht, *a.* jellied. *O.Ir.* coiteichtea, *concretionis* ; tèachdadh, tiächcu, *vbl. n. m.* act of parching, withering ; extreme thirst.

teud, tēd, *n. f.* a string ; harp string, string of fiddle. *O.Ir.* tét, *fides,* a gut-string.

teudach, tēduch, *adj.* stringed.

teudbhinneach, tēd-veeniuch, *a.* of melodious strings.

teudbhuidhe, tēd-vooyu, *a.* yellow as harp cords.

teugair, tēgir, *v.* gather milk on short allowance, to make butter.

teugbhail, tēgvel, *n. f.* 1. a keen contest. 2. danger. 3. disease. 4. agony (of death), *W.R.* t-éc (death) + baile (frenzy). *Also* teugmhail.

teugradh, tēgru, *vbl. n. m.* act of gathering milk economically ; milk or butter so gathered.

teum, tēm, *n. f.* a bite, a sudden snatch, a wound ; temptation, whim, caprice ; *v.* bite as a serpent ; tempt, beguile, draw aside ; theum nathair mi, a serpent bit me ; a serpent beguiled, or enticed me. *O.Ir.* teidm, *gl.* pestis. *E.Ir.* témm. *W.* tam. *O.Celt.* tendmen, bite. Cf. *Gr.* τένδω, to bite, gnaw. *Fick.*

teumadh, tēmu, *vbl. n. m.* act of biting, snatching, tempting, beguiling.

teumnach, tēmnuch, *adj.* capricious, whimsical ; chan 'eil ann ach duine teumnach, he is a capricious or whimsical man ; enticing, inviting, tempting ; chan 'eil e 'n a ni teumnach, it is not an enticing affair.

teumnachd, tēmnuchc, *n. f.* tempting nature or quality ; capriciousness.

teurmnasg, term-nasc, *n. m.* a bandage on the toes and thumbs of a dead person, to prevent his ghost from hurting foes.

teuthachd, tē-hachc, *n. f.* rancidness.

thà, is. *See* tà.

thàinig, hàn'-ig, *pret.* of thig, came. *O.Ir.* tànicc = do-ànicc, *pret.* of iccim.

thairis, herish, *adv.* over, across, abroad ; chaidh e thairis, he went abroad, he left the kingdom ; copan a' cur thairis, a cup running over ; beyond, exceeding the bounds, remaining as a surplus ; chaidh e thairis air sin, he went beyond that ; thairis air móran, beyond many ; thug e thairis, he over-fatigued himself ; tha e 'san toirt thairis, he is almost done out ; thoir thairis, give over, be done of it ; chuir iad thairis am bàta, they capsized it the boat. *O.Ir.* tairis = tar (*trans.*) + se (it).

thairte, hartiu, *prep.* and *pron.* beyond her, over her ; an abhainn a' cur thairte, the river overflowing. *See* thairis. *O.Ir.* tar (*trans.*) + te (her).

thall, hăll, *adv.* over, on the other side, beyond, abroad ; *adj.* yon, yonder ; am baile ud thall, yonder town ; over against. *O.Ir.* thall, tall, yonder (to + all).

thalla, hall'-a, *v.* come, come along ; thalla leamsa, come along with me ; thallaibh, come you ; *interj.* thalla ! thalla ! indeed ! indeed ! well ! well ! ay ! ay ! *O.Ir.* talla, tella, take away.

thallad, hăll'-ad, *adv.* yon, yonder.

thar, har, *prep.* over, beyond, across, more than ; thar fichead, beyond twenty, more than twenty ; thar a chéile, at variance ; chuir thu thar a chéile iad, you set them by the ears ; thar na còrach, beyond what is proper. *O.Ir.* tar, dar.

tharad, hăr'-ud, *prep.* + *pron.* beyond thee.

tharaibh, hăr'-uv, *prep.* + *pron.* over you.

tharainn, hăr'-inn, *prep.* + *pron.* over us.

tharam, hăr'-um, *prep.* + *pron.* beyond or over me ; chaidh i tharam, she capsized on me.

thàrladh, *v.* happened. *E.Ir.* dorala, darla. *O.Ir.* tarla = to-rala (venit).

tharta, hărt'-à, *prep.* + *pron.* beyond them ; chaidh am bàta tharta, the boat capsized on them ; cuir tharta e, put it over them.

theab, heb, *def. v.* just missed ; theab mi, I had almost. *Ir.* theib, " grazed," failed.

theagamh, heguv, *adv.* perhaps ; theagamh gu bheil, perhaps it is so—perhaps so. *O.Ir.* tecmaing, tecmang, *accidit.*

théid, hēj, *fut. v.* theirig or rach, will or shall go. *O.Ir.* téit, *venit, it* ; théid mi, I shall go ; an téid thu, shalt thou go ?

their, her, *fut. v.* abair ; their thu, thou shalt say ; their cuid, some shall say. *See* deir.

theirig, herig, *v.* go, proceed ; theirig thusa, go thou.

thig, hig, *v. i.* come ; *fut.* also thig ; thig thusa leamsa, come you along with me ; become, suit, fit, befit ; is math a thig an còta dhuit, the coat becomes, fits, or suits you well ; agree with one's taste, be pleased with ; cha tig sin gu math ris, that will not please him well ; speak of, reflect upon, speculate about ; thig iad ort gu farsuinn fial, they shall speak of you far and wide, everywhere, and liberally ; bidh iad a' tighinn oirnn, they shall speak of us. *E.Ir.* tic, ticc. *O.Ir.* ticcim = do-iccim, I come.

thoir, ho-ir, *v.* give, deliver, grant ; thoir dhomh, give me ; bring, carry, bear ; thoir so d'a ionnsaigh, bring this to him ; compel, force, constrain ; thoir air so a dhèanadh, make him do this ; thoir thu fhéin as, begone, take to your heels ; thoir as e, swig it off, gulp it up ; **thoir an aire**, take care, beware ; **thoir a steach ort**, away in with you ; **thoir ort**, clear out ; **thoir am baile muigh ort**, get out of the house. *Ir.* tabhair.

thu, oo, *pers. pron. asp. form.* thou ; **thu féin**, thou or thee, thyself.

thubhairt, hoo-irt, *past t.* of abair, say.

thuca, hooku, *prep. +pron. suf.* 3 *pl.* towards them ; a common form of chuca. *O.Ir.* cuccu, *prep.* cu (to) +*pron. suf.* 3rd *pl.*

thud, thut, hoot, *int.* indeed ! tut ! has it come to this pitch ! so much so !

thug, hoog, *past t.* of thoir, give ; **thug e domh e**, he gave, or has given it me ; *imper.* **thugaibh leibh e**, take him with you. *E.Ir.* tuc, fr. uc, ucc.

thugad, hoogud, *prep. + pron. suf.* 2 *s.* towards thee ; *interj.* out of my way ! leave that place ! **thugaibh**, towards you ; common form of chugad. *O.Ir.* cucut, cuccut.

thugam, *prep. + pron. suf.* 1 *s.* to me. *O.Ir.* cuccum.

thuice, *prep. + pron. suf.* 3 *s. f.* to her. *O.Ir.* cuicce, cucae.

thuig, hoo-ig, *past t.* of *v.* tuig, understand.

thuige, *prep. + pron. suf.* 3 *s. m.* to him, to it ; towards to the wind ; **thàinig i thuige**, she came to (as a ship), she revived, she improved ; **a' dol thuige is uaidh**, going hither and thither ; gaining and losing, as in illness ; **thainig e thuige fhéin**, he came to himself, recovered his judgment. *O.Ir.* cuci.

thun, hoon, *prep.* to, toward ; **thun an tighe**, towards the house ; *adv.* near, nearly, almost, on the eve ; **thun teir-igeachdainn**, nearly expended or exhausted ; **thun éirigh**, on the eve of rising ; **thun cogaidh**, for war, for the purpose of war ; **thun mo mhac**, to my son ; for chun, chon.

tì, *v.* hail ! welcome ; used in phrase, **gun tì thu féin**, you are right welcome. *O.Ir.* ti, *venit.*

tì, *n. m.* an individual ; **an tì as àirde**, the one who is highest, the Supreme Being.

tì, *n. f.* set design or earnest wish, determination ; **tha e air tì cur as domh**, he is determined to finish me. So *E.Ir.* tí, intent.

tiachaire, *n. m.* a perverse person, a dwarf, ill-disposed person. *E.Ir.* tiachaire, affliction, peevishness.

tiachdaidh, *a. See* teuchdadh, teachdadh.

tíadhan, *n. m.* a little hill, small stone. *Ir.* tíadhan, small stone, testicle.

tiamhachd, tee-uvachc, *n. f.* dreariness,

gloominess ; melodious heart-melting sound.

tiamhaidh, tee-uvay, *adj.* melancholy, dreary, distressing, dismal ; heart-melting, as music ; **àite tiamhaidh**, a dreary place ; port tiamhaidh, a heart-melting strain or tune. *E.Ir.* tiamda, dark, afraid.

tiamhaidheachd. *See* tiamhachd.

tiarmail, *a.* prudent. Cf. tìorail.

tibeart, *n. f., gen.* tibirt, a well, a fountain.

tìde, teeju, *n. m.* time ; weather ; in the *cpd.* **tìde-mhara** it means tide, the state of the tide at any given moment, and the actual flow or ebb ; **ciod e an tìde-mhara tha ann ?** what is the state of the tide ? **tha an tìde-mhara leinn**, the tidal current is with us. *O.N.* tíð. *A.S.* tíd. *O.H.G.* zîd.

tigh, toy, ty, *n. m., pl.* tighean, a house ; tigh-beag, a necessary, a privy ; tigh-marsantachd, a shop, wareroom ; tigh-chon, dog-kennel ; **tigh-chalman**, a dovecot, or ducket ; tigh - bainne, dairy ; **tigh-chaorach**, sheep-cot ; tigh-airm, an armoury ; **tigh-cise**, and tigh-cusbuinn, custom-house ; tigh-chearc, hen-house ; an tigh-mór, the mansion-house ; tigh-bainnse, the house of the wedding ; tigh-samhraidh, a villa, or summer-house ; **tigh-dìomhaireachd**, jakes ; tigh-eiridinn, an infirmary ; tigh-sgoile, a schoolhouse; tigh-geamh-raidh, a winter-house; the grave ; tigh-móid, court-house, justice-court ; tigh-nigheadaireachd, wash-house ; aig an tigh, at home ; o'n tigh, from home, abroad. *O.Ir.* teg, tech. *O.W.* tig.

tighe, tee-u, *compar.* of tiugh, thicker.

tighead, *abstr. n. m.* thickness.

tigheadas, te-hudus, *n. m.* a household ; air a thigh is air a thigheadas, having a house and household. *O.Ir.* tegdas.

tighealt, tee-helt, *vbl. n. f.* calling when passing.

tighearna, tee-urnu, *n. m.* a lord ; a landlord, proprietor ; superior title of respect. *O.Ir.* tigerne, *dominus.* *W.* teyrn. *O.Celt.* tigerno-s.

tighearnail, *adj.* lordly.

tighearnalachd, tee-urnaluchc, *n. f.* lordliness.

tighearnas, tee-urnus, *n. m.* lordship, rule, sway, dominion, proprietorship.

tighich, tee-huch, *n. f.* state of being subject to callers. *Also* tathaich.

tighil, tee-il, *v.* call when passing. *Also* tadhail.

tighinn, tee-in, *n. f.* coming, speaking (by way of recalling), speaking about one (good or evil) ; **tighinn-fodha**, oozing up of water through the soil.

tighinn, *infin.* of tig, come, coming.

E.Ir. **tiagaim.** *O.Ir.* **tiagu, tichtu,** *adventus.*

tileadh, *n. m.* sewage ; **toll-tilidh,** sewerhole in end of stable wall.

tilg, *v.* throw, cast off, reproach, cast up to ; vomit ; **thilg e,** he threw, vomited ; **thilg i searrach,** she cast a foal ; **thilg e a dheoch,** he vomited his drink ; **thilg e orm e,** he cast it up to me ; strike with an elf-shot, shoot, fire at ; **thilg e an duine,** he shot the man ; **duine tilgte,** a man shot by the fairies, a man that cares not what he does. *O.Ir.* **teilcim,** cast, throw.

tilgeadh, *vbl. n. m.* act of casting, throwing, shooting, vomiting, reproaching, a reproach.

tilgte, tilgtiu, *vbl. a.* thrown, cast ; mad.

till, teel, *v.* return, come back ; relapse ; **thill ris,** he has got a relapse. *Also* **pill.** *Ir.* **tillim, fillim, pillim.**

tilleadh, tilu, *vbl. n. m.* act of returning, relapsing ; a relapse, return, act of turning.

tìm, teem, *n. m., pl.* **tìomannan,** time ; **tha tìm teicheadh,** it is time to flee ; fr. the *Eng.*

timchioll, timchul, *n. m.* circuit, compass ; a tier of planks in building a boat ; *prep. adv.* about, around ; **timchioll fichead,** about twenty ; **chaidh e timchioll,** he went round ; **a' cheud timchioll a rinn iad,** the first circuit they made. *O.Ir.* **timmchell,** a circuit.

timchiollach, *adj.* circuitous, circular, encompassing.

timchiollaich, *v.* surround, environ, enclose, encompass.

timchiollaichte, *vbl. a.* environed, surrounded, encompassed, encircled, gone round.

timchioll-ghearr, timchul-yār, *v.* circumcise.

tìmealachd, teemaluchc, *n. f.* timeliness, time.

tinn, teen, *adj.* unwell, sick. *E.Ir.* **tind.**

tinne, tiniu, *n. f., pl.* **tinneachan,** link of a chain, piece of a column. *E.Ir.* **tinde,** ring, link. *O.Ir.* **tinne,** iron, articles made of iron.

tinneas, tinus, *n. m.* sickness, disease ; **tinneas-cloinne,** travail, labour, childbirth, parturition ; **tinneas-goile,** stomach complaint ; **tinneas-mara,** seasickness; **tinneas-tuiteamach,** epilepsy. *O.Ir.* **tinnes,** sickness.

tinnsgeadail, teens-gedal, *n. m.* bad omen. *Also* **tinnsgeal.**

tioba, *n. f.* a heap.

tiobart, tiburt, *n. f.* a well. *O.G.* (B. of D.) *gen.* **tiprat.** *E.Ir.* **tipra,** *d.* **tiprait.**

tiochdadh, to hold, contain, find room. *Inf.* of **teachd.**

tiodal, *n. m.* a title ; fr. the *Eng.*

tiodhlac, tee-uluc, *n. m.* gift, offering. *E.Ir.* **tidnacul.** *O.Ir.* **tindnacul,** *communicatio.*

tiodhlacadh, tee-ulucu, *vbl. n. m.* act of burying, interring ; giving ; burial, interment.

tiodhlaic, tee-ulic, *v.* bury, inter, bestow a gift.

tiolam, tioolum, *n. m.* snatch, space, a short time ; clever opportunity.

tiolp, tiulp, *v.* steal by snatching, pilfer ; steal one's property, and he almost looking at you ; cavil, carp. *Also* **siolp.** *Ir.* **tiolpam.**

tiolpadair, *n. m.* a thief, pilferer ; a critic.

tiolpadh, *vbl. n. m.* act of stealing, pilfering ; carping, cavilling.

tiom, tim, *adj.* easily abashed or daunted ; tender-hearted, sensitive, timid. *E.Ir.* **tim,** soft, timid.

tioma, *n. f.* delicateness of feeling ; a daunt ; melting into tears ; **thàinig tioma air,** he was daunted, he melted into tears ; softness of disposition, sensitiveness. *E.Ir.* **timme,** fear. *L.* **timeo.**

tiomachd, tiumachc, *n. f.* delicacy of feeling and sentiment ; daunt, damp on the spirits.

tiomadh. *See* **tioma.**

tiomaich, tiumich, *v.* soften or melt into tears, or better feelings ; **laoch nach tiomaich,** a hero that goes forward dauntlessly ; **thiomaich a chridhe,** his heart softened. *See* **tiom.**

tiomain, tiumen, *v.* resign solemnly, bequeath, bestow. *O.Ir.* **timmnaim,** bequeath.

tiomainte, *vbl. a.* bequeathed, religiously determined.

tiomnadair, tiumnuder, *n. m.* testator.

tiomnadh, tiumnu, *n. m.* testament, will ; **an Seann-Tiomnadh,** the Old Testament ; act of committing solemnly, bequeathing. *O.Ir.* **timne, timpne,** bequest, a will.

tiompan, tioompan, *n. m.* timbril, cymbal, tabor, or drum. *E.Ir.* **timpan** = *Lat.* tympanum.

tiomsachadh, tiumsuchu, *n. m.* collecting, a second milking of a cow.

tiomsaich, tiumsich, *v.* collect. *E.Ir.* **timmsugud.**

tionail, teenel, *v.* gather, collect. *O.Ir.* **tinólaim,** I gather.

tional, tyun'-al, *n. m.* collection, collecting.

tionnail, tiunel, *n. f.* a likeness of a person or thing. *M.Ir.* **inntshamail.**

tionndadh, tìoonda, *vbl. n. m.* act of turning. *O.Ir.* **tintuith,** *gen.* tintuda, *interpretatio.*

tionndaidh, tioonday, *v*. turn, alter, convert. *O.Ir*. tintaim = do-ind-shóim, *converto*.

tionnsgainn, tioonscin, *v*. begin ; attack or fall to of a sudden without any cause ; invent, devise ; return ; turn ; *n. f*. a beginning, an element. *O.Ir*. tinscnaim, I begin.

tionnsgal, tioonsgal, *n. m*. ingenuity, art. *Ir*. tionsgadail, device, industry. *O.Ir*. tinscetal, a beginning, undertaking.

tionnsgalach, *a*. ingenious, clever.

tionnsgnadh, tioonscnu, *vbl. n. m*. act of attacking or falling to of a sudden ; sudden attack, commencement ; invention ; a project, device. *O.Ir*. tinscnam, a beginning.

tiop, teep, *v*. steal by little and little ; pilfer.

tiop, *v*. thread a fishing-hook.

tìor, tir, teer, *v*. dry, parch, kiln-dry (grain). *E.Ir*. tir, to dry.

tìoradh, tìreadh, teeru, *vbl. n. m*. act of kiln-drying, the quantity of grain dried at one time. *O.Ir*. tíradh, kilndrying.

tìorail, tiural, *a*. warm, cosy, sheltered.

tìoralachd, *n. f*. warmth, shelter.

tioram, tirum, *adj., compar*. tiorma, dry, seasoned, arid, without moisture ; flippant in speech ; fair, as weather ; uair thioram, fair weather ; feur tioram, hay. *O.Ir*. tírim, tír.

tiorc, tiurk, *v*. save, deliver = *O.Ir*. dí (*priv*.) + orcun (killing). Cf. teasairg.

tiormachadh, tiurmuchu, *vbl. n. m*. act of drying, making fair weather ; seasoning, as hay, fish, etc.

tiormachail, tiurmuchal, *adj*. desiccative.

tiormachd, tiurmachc, *n. f*. fair weather ; continuance of fair weather ; flippancy.

tiormaich, tiurmich, *v*. dry, dry up. *O.Ir*. tírmaigim, dry.

tiorman, tiurman, *n. m*. meal-ball, grain on kiln in course of drying.

tiormasg. *See* tearmasg.

tiorr, *a*. degree of heat in process of brewing grain ; teas-tiorr, developed heat in process of brewing.

tiorradh, *vbl. n. m*. act of pot-drying grain.

tiorraidh. *See* tiorr.

tiort, tiurt, *n. m*. accident, mishap. *Also* driod-thiortan.

tiosan, tisan, *n. m*. ptisan, water-gruel. *Gr*. πτισάνη, barley-water. *Fr*. tisane.

tiot, teet, *v*. dispatch quickly.

tiotadh, teetu, *n. m*. moment, little time. *Also* tiotan.

tìr, teer, *n. f*. land, shore ; air tìr, ashore, on land ; country, region ; tìr-mór, continent ; eadar thìr-mór agus eilean-

an, both the continent and islands. *O.Ir*. tír. *W*. tir. *O.Celt*. têrsos.

tìr, teer, *v*. kiln-dry corn. *Also* croch.

tìreachas, teeruchus, *n. f*. patriotism.

tìreadh, teeru, *vbl. n. m*. act of kiln-drying, the quantity of corn kiln-dried at one time.

tirmean, *n. m*. a pert fellow, a would-be wag.

tirmeanachd, tirmenuchc, *n. f*. flippancy.

tìrte, teertu, *a*. earthed ; tìrte an caolchisd, earthed in a coffin.

tit, *interj*. expressive of wet.

tìtheach, tee-huch, *adj*. bent or determined on, keen for ; tìtheach air mo mharbhadh, bent on my destruction. *See* tì.

tiubhair, tioo-ur, *v*. grant. So *Ir*.

tiùbhradh, tiooru, *n. m*. act of giving.

tiugainn, tioogin, *v*. come along, let us go. *Ir*. tiucfainn, we will come.

tiugh, tioo, *adj., compar*. tighe, thick, stout ; frequent, in quick succession, as drops of rain ; dull, hazy, dense, gross, clumsy. *E.Ir*. tiug, *compar*. tigiu. *O.W*. teu. *O.Celt*. tegu-.

tiughaich, tioo-hich, *v*. thicken, crowd.

tiuighead, tee-ud, *abstr. n. f*. thickness. *E.Ir*. tighead.

tiuigheadas, tee-udus, *n. f*. thickness.

tiunnail, tioonal, *n. f*. match, likeness, comparison. *See* tionnail.

tiùrr, tioor, *n. m*. a heap ; high-water mark, usually heaped-up sand, or shingle, or sea-ware ; broken sea-ware cast up by the tide ; a side form of tòrr, a heap.

tlachd, tlachc, *n. m*. love, attachment ; tha tlachd aige dhith, he is attached to her ; pleasure, satisfaction, degree of satisfaction ; chan fhaigh thu e le tlachd, you shall not get it with any degree of satisfaction ; beauty, liberality, affection ; is beag mo thlachd dhi, I have no great affection for her. *M.Ir*. tlacht.

tlachdaireachd, tlachdmhoireachd, tlachcoruchc, *n. f*. handsomeness, comeliness, pleasantness, blandness.

tlachdar, tlachdmhor, tlach-cur, *adj*. handsome, lovely, liberal, pleasant, comely ; leanabh tlachdmhor, a goodly child.

tlàm, *n. m*. handful of wool ; awkward handling ; *v*. fumble, tease wool. *Ir*. tláim, handful of wool, or flax ; tlàmaim, I tease.

tlàmadh, *vbl. n. m*. act of mixing, fumbling.

tlàth, tlā, *adj*. somewhat moist, humid, tha so tlàth, this is somewhat moist or humid ; balmy, soft, mellow, mild, gentle ; uisge tlàth, balmy or genial rain ; smooth, fine to the touch. *E.Ir.* tláith, soft.

tlàthaich, tlā-hich, *v.* moisten gently, become balmy or gentle, abate gently, as weather ; get into gentle perspiration ; tlàthachadh falluis, gentle perspiration.

tlàths, tlā-hus, *n. f.* balminess, mildness, gentleness.

tligheachd, tlee-achc, *n. f.* inclination.

tligheachd, *n. f.* liquid, spume.

tliochd, tliuchc, *n. m.* beginning. So *Ir.*

tlugh, tliu', *n. m.* pair of tongs. So *Ir.*

tlus, tloos, *n. m.* affection, tenderness of manner, gentleness, as weather ; balminess, or mildness ; comfortable sensation ; labhair le tlus, speak with some degree of affection ; chan'eil tlus sam bith 'san aodach, there is no comfort in the clothes ; thig tlus is blàths, balmy weather and genial warmth shall come. So *E.Ir.*

tlusar, tlusmhor, tloosor, *adj.* affectionate, kind ; nighean thlusar, an affectionate daughter ; agreeable to the touch, comfortable ; aodach tlusar, comfortable clothing ; balmy, genial, mild ; uair thlusar, genial or mild weather.

tlusaireachd, tlusmhoireachd, tloosaruchc, *n. f.* balminess, genial warmth, or comfortable feel or sensation.

tlusalachd, tloosaluchc, *n. f.* tenderness, warmth, compassion.

tnùth, tnoo, *n. f.* envy, malice, grudge, indignation, avarice. So *E.Ir.*

tnùthar, tnoo-hur, *adj.* envious, malicious.

to-, do-, *verbal prefix,* to. So *O.Ir.*

tob, *n. f.* surprise. So *Ir.*

tòb, *n. m., gen.* taib, a cove, creek, bay. *O.N.* hóp. *A.S.* hôp, bay.

toban, *n. m.* a tab ; a roll of wool on a distaff.

tobar, *n. f., pl.* tobraichean, *gen. s.* tobrach, well, spring, fountain ; tobar fìoruisg, a spring-well ; tobar-baistidh, a baptismal font ; tobar - tàirne, a draw-well ; source, origin ; an tobar bho bheil gach buaireadh a' sruthadh, the source whence all temptations flow. *O.Ir.* topur, *fons. Also* tipra, a well.

tobha, to'-u, *n. m.* a rope, a cable; *v.* tow. *Sc.* tow, rope. *O.N.* tog, rope.

tobhair, to'-ir, *v.* give, bestow ; *dial.* form of tabhair.

tobhairt, to-urt, to give ; for tabhairt.

tobhartach, to-urt-uch, *adj.* liberal, munificent, charitable ; duine tobhartach, a liberal or charitable man.

tobhartas, tó'-art-us, *n. m.* a gift, offering, charity.

tobhlair, *n. m.* a mastiff ; fr. *Eng.* towler.

tobhta, to-tu, *n. f., pl.* tobhtaichean,

gen. s. tobhtach, rower's bench, thwart; tobhta-thoisich, stem-thwart ; tobhta-chrainn, mast-thwart ; tobhta-bhraghad, bow-thwart ; tobhta-chléith, mid-thwart ; tobhta-hamarr, stern bow-thwart; tobhta-dheiridh, stern-thwart; fr. *O.N.* þopta.

tobhta, *n. f.* wall of a house, the ruins of a house. *O.N.* toft, topt, *id.*

tòc, *v.* swell up, puff, rise gradually, as a loaf does ; swell, as with rage ; thòc a h-aodann, her face swelled with rage; swell with good eating. *Also* bòc.

tòcadh, tōcu, *vbl. n. m.* act of swelling, puffing.

toch, *n. f.* the hough or ham of a beast ; *v.* hough, or cut off limbs of cattle ; thoch iad an crodh, they houghed the cattle.

tochail, *v.* dig, quarry. *R.C.².* *Ir.* tochlaim.

tochailt, tochelt, *n. f.* a quarry. *E.Ir.* tochailt, a digging, a grave, a cave.

tochar, *n. m.* marriage-portion, dowry. *K.M.* makes tochra *vbl. n.* fr. docrenim (to buy) = bride - price. *K.M.'s* text (*Td.L¹⁷*) suggests marriage contract between husband and wife. *O.Ir.* tochur ; fr. cuir, put, "assign."

tòchd, tōchc, *n. m.* 1. suffocating bad smell. 2. disease of the eye in cattle.

tochmarc, a wooing. So *O.Ir., obs.* in *Sc.G.*

tochradh, *n. m.* dowry. *See* tochar.

tochrais, toch'-rèsh, *v.* reel or wind yarn. *Ir.* tocharais.

tochras, toch'-ras, *n. m.* act of winding, reeling.

tocsaid, *n. f.* a hogshead ; fr. the *Eng.*

todhair, tò'-ir, *v.* manure, bleach clothes.

todhar, tò'-ur, *n. m.* dung dropped by cattle on the field ; manure ; bleaching ; a bleach (clothes) ; air todhar, a-bleaching. *Ir.* tuar, a bleaching-yard. *O.N.* taδ, dung.

tog, *v.* build, raise, lift, stir up, rear, bring up ; brew, distil, exact as tribute ; thog iad tigh, they built a house ; a fear a thog thu, the man that reared you ; togaidh fear fiar aimhreit, a perverse man stirreth up strife ; thog iad cìs, they exacted a tribute ; clear up, cheer ; togaidh an latha, the day will clear up ; tog ri, ascend ; tog air, report ill of ; tog cùis, appeal ; tog ort thun a mhonaidh, betake yourself to the mountains ; thog iad air gun robh e déidheil air an òl, they raised a report that he was addicted to liquor ; hoist, weigh ; tog na siùil, hoist the sails ; thog iad an acair, they weighed anchor ; thog iad a' bhraich, they brewed or distilled the malt ; *idm.*, the range of vision ; **thog sinn fearann**, we came in sight of land ; **cha do thog e ceann o'n là sin**, he was never seen from that day. *O.Ir.* **tócbaim**, I raise ; **co tócband**, *ut tollat. Z².*

togail, tóg'-al, *vbl. n. f.* act of raising, rearing, exacting ; ascending, hoisting, weighing, etc. ; **a' togail a' bhruthaich**, ascending the brae ; **chan 'eil mi 'ga thogail**, I cannot see it—make it out ; **air an togail**, (a cow) so reduced that it needs a lift.

togail, tóg'-al, *n. f., gen.* **togalach**, *pl.* **togalaichean**, structure, superstructure, building.

togair, tóg'-ir, *v.* please, wish, incline, desire ; **ma thogras mi fhéin**, just if I please ; **a' togairt dol dachaidh**, inclining, or feeling disposed to go home ; **ma thogair**, who cares ? *Ir.* **togairim**.

togalaiche, tog'-al-ich-u, *n. m.* builder.

togarrach, *adj.* inviting, enticing ; **chan-'eil an latha so togarrach**, this day is not inviting ; willing, desirous ; **tha e togarrach air falbh**, he is desirous to go.

togbhail, *n. f.* a levying of forces, a rising in arms.

togbhalach, tog-valuch, *a.* haughty.

toghadh, *m.* act of choosing, selecting ; **thoghadh tu sgian mar arm**, you would choose a knife for a weapon ; **toghadh nam fear**, the choice among men. *Also* **taghadh**. *O.Ir.* **togu**, *electio.*

toghaidh, toy, *n. f.* guard, care ; attention. *See* **toidh**.

toghlainn, to-lin, *n. f.* exhalation, fume ; **tha toghlainn ag éirigh**, there is an exhalation rising ; disagreeable heat or fume.

toghnadh = toning (*Eng.*).

tograch ; for **togarrach**, willing.

togradh, *vbl. n. m.* desire, inclination, willingness. *E.Ir.* **tócrad.**

togte, togtu, *vbl. a.* raised, lifted under excitement ; **tha speuran a chinn togte**, he is quite in a frenzy.

toibheum, toy-vem, *n. f.* blasphemy. *E.Ir.* **toibeim** = **to** + **béimm** (beum), calumny.

toibheumach, toy-vemuch, *adj.* blasphemous, offensive, profane.

tòic, tòyc, *n. f.* a swelling in the body or face from good living.

toic, *n. f.* wealth ; wealth that puffs up ; gluttony, luxury ; **toic, toice**, wealth, riches.

tòicealachd, tōycaluchc, *n. f.* purse-pride ; *a.* **tòiceil**, purse-proud.

tòicear, tōycer, *n. m.* purse-proud man.

tòicearachd, tōyceruchc, *n. f.* purse-pride.

tòiceil, toycal, *adj.* purse-proud, swelled up with pride of riches ; disdain.

toichiosdal, toy-chusdal, *n. m.* arrogance, presumption.

toidh, toy, *n. f.* care, regard, doing full justice to ; **thug thu toidh do'n cheartas**, you gave fair play to justice. *M.Ir.* **óid**, notice ; **t'óid** = **do** (thy) + **óid** ; **bar n-óid**, your notice ; **a h-óid**, her notice. *O.Ir.* **óid**, heed, care.

toidheachd, toyachc, *n. f.* coming ; **deòn-ach air toidheachd**, willing—keen—on coming.

toigh, toy, *a.* is **toigh leam**, I like, I am fond of ; agreeable ; *compar.* **docha**, is **docha leam**, I prefer. *O.Ir.* **toich**, *compar.* **tochu**. *O.Celt.* togi-s-.

toil, tol, *n. f.* inclination, desire, will, wish, pleasure. *O.Ir.* **tol**, *gen.* **tuile**.

toileach, tol'-uch, *adj.* willing, voluntary ; **tha mi toileach**, I am willing ; **gach ni as toileach le Dia**, everything God pleases. *O.Ir.* **toltanach**, willing.

toileachadh, toluchu, *vbl. n. m.* act of pleasing, satisfying, giving pleasure ; satisfaction

toileachas, toluchus, *n. m.* contentment ; **toileachas-inntinn**, mental pleasure or satisfaction. Cf. *O.Ir.* **toltanche**, willingness.

toileachd, tolachc, *n. m.* willingness.

toilealachd, tolaluchc, *n. f.* eagerness, extreme willingness or readiness.

toilich, tolich, *v.* satisfy, please, will, wish ; **ma thoilicheas tu**, if you will or wish ; **thoilich mi e**, I satisfied him.

toilichte, tolichtu, *vbl. a.* pleased, satisfied ; **tha mi toilichte**, I am content.

toil-inntinn, tol-eentin, *n. f.* gratification, satisfaction, mental enjoyment.

toill, toyl, *v.* deserve, merit ; **thoill thu sin**, you deserved or merited that. *O.Ir.* **tuillim**, enhance, deserve.

toillteanach ; for **toilltinneach.**

toilltineas, toyltinnas, *n. f.* desert, merit ; **a réir bhur toilltineas**, according to your desert or merit.

toilltinn, toyltin, *vbl. n. f.* act of meriting, deserving ; **ciod a tha thu a' toilltinn**, what do you deserve or merit ?

toilltinneach, toyltinuch, *adj.* deserving, meriting ; **duine toilltinneach air bàs**, a person meriting death.

tòimhseachan, tō-shuchan, **tòimhseagan**, *n. m.* a riddle, an enigma, a guess, a puzzle ; fr. **tomhas**. So *Ir.*

toimhsean, toshein, *n. pl.* weights, scales, balances, measures ; faculties.

toimhseil, toshal, *adj.* sensible, prudent, frugal.

toinisg, tonisc, *n. f.* common sense.

toinisgeil, toniscal, *adj.* sensible.

tòinleagan, tŏn-liugan, *n. m.* moving on the hams (as infants).

tòinleaganaich, tŏnliuganich, *v.* crawl on the hams.

toinn, tūyn, *v.* twist, wreathe ; spin, twine. *O.N.* tvinna, twine, twist.

toinneamh, toynuv, *vbl. n. m.* act of twisting, spinning, twining ; arrangement, train ; **chuir thu as mo thoinneamh mi**, you disappointed me, you deranged my plans.

toinneamh, tuniv, *n. m.* toll paid in meal for grinding ; multure. *Also* **molltair.**

toinntean, tuynten, *n. m.* a thread, a lock of wool.

toir, *v.* give ; for **tobhair, tabhair**. *O.Ir.* **dobiur.**

tòir, *n. f.* pursuit, diligent search ; **teichidh sibh, 'nuair nach bi an tòir oirbh**, ye shall flee when there is none in pursuit of you ; enough ; **is tòir e fhéin air sin**, he is quite enough for that himself ; band of pursuers ; **tha'n tòir ad dhéidh**, there is a band of pursuers after you. *E.Ir.* **tóir**, pursuit ; a body of troops.

toirbheart, turuverst, *n. m.* bounty, efficiency. *M.Ir.* **tairbirt**, a gift. Cf. *O.Ir.* **torbatu**, *utilitas.*

toirbheartach, turuverstuch, *a.* rich in quality ; bountiful.

toircheas, torchus, *n. m.* increase. Cf. **torachas.**

toireasg, for **tuiriasg**, saw. *Also* **sàbh.**

toireann, tŏr'-un, *n. f.* thunder. *E.Ir.* **torand**, thunder.

tòiriasg, *n. m.* dead fish, fish found dead at sea.

tòirleum, tŏr-lēm, *n. m.* a bound, a great leap ; **tar +leum.**

tòirlinn, tŏrlin, *v.* alight, come off a horse. *E.Ir.* **tair-lingim**, leap down, alight.

toirm, turum, *n. f.* noise ; rushing noise, as of people going through a wood ; murmuring ; **toirmghaoth**, a cyclone. *E.Ir.* **toirm, tairm.**

toirmeasg, turumusc, *vbl. n. m.* forbidding ; prohibition or hindrance.

toirmisg, turumishc, *v.* forbid, prohibit. *M.Ir.* **tairmiscim**, hinder, forbid.

toirmisgte, *vbl. a.* prohibited.

tòirn, tòirne, *n. f.* a great noise, sound.

tòirnich. *See* **tarmaich.** *McE.²*

toirnichte, *a.* fœtid, " high."

toirp, torp, *n. f.* a sod, divot ; thick person. *O.N.* **torf**, turf.

toirpeanta, torpantu, *adj.* squat, thick.

toirpsgian, torpscin, *n. f.* an instrument specially made for cutting peat ; peat-spade. *O.N.* **torf** + *G.* **sgian** (*McB.*) ; but **toirbhsger** (*Lewis*) = *O.N.* torfskeri ; in *E.Ross*, **tor(bh)aisg.**

toirrcheas, *n. m.* conception. Cf. **torrachas.**

toirsgian, toirsgir, *n. m.* peat-cutter. *See above.*

toirt, for **tabhairt**, giving.

toirt, *n. f.* taste in matters ; decorum, decency, due regard or attention ; **duine gun toirt**, a person destitute of taste ; **is beag toirt a bhios air do ghnothach**, your business must be done very awkwardly. *M.Ir.* **toirt**, quantity, value.

toirtealachd, torstaluchc, *n. f.* decency, tastefulness, excellent order or arrangement.

toirteil, torstal, *adj.* decent, tasteful ; substantial.

toiseach, tosh'-uch, *n. f.* beginning, origin, source ; van or front, precedence ; **toiseach a' ghnothaich**, the origin of the thing ; **toiseach an airm**, the van or front of the army ; **fhuair e an toiseach orra**, he got precedence of them ; **air thoiseach**, foremost ; bow or prow of a ship ; **toiseach is deireadh 'na luinge**, the stem and stern of the ship. *O.Ir.* **tossach**, *initium.*

tòiseach, *n. m.* a beginning, a chief. *O.Ir.* **tóisech**, a leader. *W.* **tywysog**, a leader. *O.Celt.* to-vessâko-s.

tòiseachadh, tŏsh'-ach-u, *vbl. n. m.* act of commencing, beginning, commencement, origin.

***toiseadrach**, toshudruch, *n. m.* crowner ; the deputy of a *maire of fee*. *Jamieson.*

toisg, toshc, *n. m.* an occasion ; fit time, opportunity, an errand, a proposal. *M.Ir.* **toisc**, business, errand. *O.Ir.* **toisc**, necessity.

toisgeal, toshcal. *See* **taisgeul**, reward.

toisgeal, *n. f.* left, sinister ; **an làmh thoisgeal**, left hand, the unlucky hand. Cf. *O.Ir.* **túascert.**

tòisich, tŏsh'-ich, *v.* begin, commence, fall to.

tòit, *n. f.* mist, wet mist.

toit, *n. f.* smoke, fume, steam, coal. *Ir.* **toit.** *M.Ir.* **tutt.**

toiteach, *adj.* fumy, vapoury. So *Ir.*

toiteal, *n. m.* 1. a fray, a hot battle. 2. splashing.

toitean, toh-ten, *n. m.* collop, steak. So *Ir.*

toitean, *n. m.* a little steam, a " draw " of tobacco pipe.

toitlinn, toht-lin, *n. f.* steam, vapour.

toitlinneach, *n. f.* steamboat.

tòlair, *n. m.* foxhound, beagle. Cf. **tobhlair.**

tòlair-mhaigheach, *n. m.* a harrier.

tolcha, *n. m., gen.* of **tulach**, *q.v.*

tolg, *n. f.* a hollow, as in a kettle ; bulge (inwards) ; *v.* make hollows, as in a kettle or cauldron. *Also* **tulg**. *E.Ir.* **tolc**.

tolg, *n.f.* pride. *E.Ir.* **tolgda**, *a.* haughty.

tolgach, **tolug'-uch**, *adj.* hollowed, freakish.

toll, **toül**, *v.* make holes, bore, perforate.

toll, *n. m., gen. s., n. pl.* **tuill**, a hole, a bore, perforation ; hollow ; *cpds.* : **toll-cluaise**, a touch-hole, the ear ; **toll-guail**, a coalpit ; **toll-tora**, an auger - hole. *O.Ir.* **toll**. *W.* **twll**. *O.Celt.* tukslo-s.

toll, *v.* exhale, emit, vapours.

tolladair, **toluder**, *n. m.* borer. *Ir.* **tollaire**.

tolladh, **tolu**, *vbl. n. m.* act of boring, edging in.

tollainn, **tolin**, *n. f.* exhalation, vapour in damp places in summer ; steam, gas. *See* **tothlainn**.

tollaire, **toliru**, *n. f.* one that edges his way ; a genteel intruder.

tolltach, *a.* full of holes ; cho tolltach ri criathar, as full of holes as a sieve.

tolm, *n. m., gen.* **tuilm**, *pl.* **tolmannan**, hillock of round form. *O.N.* hólmr, islet, " inch."

tom, *n. m., gen.* and *pl.* **tuim**, a bush, thicket, a knoll ; tom ghròiseid, gooseberry-bush ; tom luachrach, a clump of rushes ; thug e car mu thom asam, he gave me the slip, he jilted me, or cheated me ; am bun an tuim, sheltered only by the thicket ; air a thom, at stool ; tom-sealga, a hunting-hillock. *M.Ir.* **tomm**. *W.* tom. *O.Celt.* (s)tombo-s, tumbo-s.

tomach, *adj.* bushy, tufted.

tomad, *n. m.* size, bulk.

tomadach, *a.* weighty, bulky, substantial.

tomadh, *vbl. n. m.* act of dipping ; a form of **tumadh**.

tomalt, *n. m.* bulk. *A.M.* *See* **somalta**.

tombaca, *n. m.* tobacco.

tomh, **tó**, *v.* point with the finger ; offer, attempt ; *vbl. n.* **tomhadh**, pointing at, presenting. *O.Ir.* **tomad**, threatening.

tomhail, *n. f.* terror, fright ; *a.* vast, terrible.

tomhais, *v.* measure, survey, weigh, guess, unriddle, resolve an enigma ; tomhais am fearann, survey the land ; tomhais cò choinnich mi, guess who met me ?

tomhas, **to-üs**, *n. m.* weight, measure, survey ; measurement, dimension ; gabh mo thomhais, take my measure ; slat - tomhais, a yard stick ; thar tomhais, beyond measure ; act of measuring, weighing, surveying, guessing. *O.Ir.* **tomus**, mass, weight, measure.

tomhlachd, tov-lachc, *n. m.* thick milk.

tomult, *n. m.* bulk. *Also* **tomad**. Cf. **somalta**, large, bulky.

tòn, *n. f.* bottom, breech, or fundament ; anus. So *E.Ir.* *W.* **tin**. *O.Celt.* tûkno-.

tònach, *adj.*, *n. f.* large-hipped.

tònag, *n. f.* a clew of yarn ; squat female.

tònaire, tōn'-ur-u, *n. m.* broad-bottomed man.

tònlagan, *n. m.* sliding on the breech ; hobbling.

tònlagain, *v.* hobble, slide on the breech.

tonn, **toùn**, *v.* splash ; 'ga thonnadh mu cheann, splashing it about his head ; pouring out irregularly.

tonn, *n. f., gen.* **tuinne**, *pl.* **tonnan** and **tuinn**, a wave, a splash ; thog tuinn an cinn, waves reared their head ; an tonn bhaistidh, baptism, sacred water ; nuallan nan tonn, the raging noise of waves. *O.Ir.* **tond**, a wave. *O.Celt.* tundâ.

tonnag, *n. f.* a tartan shawl ; transferred meaning, a sail. *Lat.* tunica. *O.Ir.* **tonach**. *O.Celt.* tonakâ.

tonn-luaisg, toun-loo-ashc, *v.* rock to and fro, toss (by waves).

tonn-luasgadh, *vbl. n. m.* act of tossing.

topach, *a.* having a top or tuft ; fr. the *Eng.* top.

topag, *n. f.* a lark.

tor, *n. f.* heavy shower.

tor, *n. m., n. f.* bush, shrub.

tora, *n. m., pl.* **torachan**, auger, wimble. *E.Ir.* **tarathar**. *W.* **taradr**.

torach, *adj.* fruitful, fertile, productive, substantial, rank ; sìol torach, productive corn ; talamh torach, fertile or fruitful land ; efficient, effectual ; buillean torach, efficient or energetic pulls, as in rowing. *O.Ir.* **toirthech**, *frugifer*.

tòrachd, *n. f.* pursuit, chase ; pursuing with hostile intention ; strict inquiry ; tha e a' tòrachd, he is making strict inquiry ; a' tòrachd chaorach, searching for sheep ; luchd-tòrachd, persecutors, pursuers ; revenge ; bheir e mach an tòrachd, he will have his revenge. *Ir.* **tóruigheachd**, pursuing. *E.Ir.* **tóraigecht**, pursuit. Cf. *O.Ir.* **tóracht**, *processus*.

toradh, tŏr'-u, *n. m.* fruit, produce ; consequence, result, effect ; toradh do ghnìomharan, the natural effects or consequence of your conduct or deeds. *O.Ir.* **torad**, fruit.

tòraiche, *n. m.* pursuer ; whence *Eng.* Tory.

toraicheas, **torichus**, *n. m.* conception, pregnancy.

toraicinn, *n. m.* a peat-knife (Arran).

toranach, *n. m.* grub-worm. *Ir.* torain.

torair, tor'-er, *n. m.* grub-worm.

torc, *n. m., gen.* and *pl.* tuirc, boar ; a boar and a whale ; sovereign, a lord. *Ir.* a' tomhas an tuirc, measuring the boar. *O.Ir.* torc, a wild-boar, a lord. *W.* twrch. *O.Celt.* torko-s.

torchar, torchuir, *n. m.* a fall, killing ; *v.* happen, befall. So *O.Ir.*

torchradh, tor'-chra, *n. m.* transfixing.

torganach, *a.* spirited, mettlesome.

torghan, *n. m.* a purling sound, a bass voice or noise of drones of the pipe. So *Ir.*

tòrmachadh, *n. m.* increase, act of growing, multiplying. *O.Ir.* tór - mag, *auctio.* See tàrmachadh.

torman, *n. m.* drone of a bagpipe, murmur ; torman nan allt, purling of the brooks.

tòrr, *n. m.* a mound, large heap ; torr gainmhich, heap or mound of sand ; *v.* heap, hoard ; a' torradh airgid, heaping or hoarding money ; teem ; air torradh le gràisg, teeming with rabble ; tòrr sluaigh, great multitude. *E.Ir.* tor, tuir, *d.* turid, a tower. *W.* twrr.

torrach, *adj.* pregnant ; with child ; in the family way. So *E.Ir. W.* torr, belly.

torradh, *vbl. n. m.* act of heaping up ; embankment of a dam ; payment for keeping up a mill-dam.

tòrradh, *n. m.* burial, interment, funeral ; burial solemnities, or procession. *E.Ir.* torroma, watching. Cf. "wake."

torraich, torr'-ich, *v.* impregnate, teem.

torraicheas, torr'-ich-us, *n. f.* conception, pregnancy.

torran, *n. m.* a knoll, hillock.

torranach, torranan, *n. m.* figwort.

torroichim, *n.* sleep, deep snoring.

torrunnach, torrthunnach, noisy, thundering.

torrunn, *n. f.* loud murmuring noise, thunder. *E.Ir.* torand. *W.* tarann. *O.Celt.* toranno-s. Taranis, Gaulish Jove.

tort, *n. m.* a little loaf or cake. *E.Ir.* tort = *Lat.* torta, a cake. *Corm.*

tòsan, *n. m.* plaintive harangue, slow plaintive verse. *Also* làsan.

tosd, *n. m.* silence ; *v.* be silent ; *a.* silent ; bi ad thosd, be silent. *E.Ir.* tost.

tosdach, *adj.* silent, peaceful.

tosg, *n. m., gen. s.* and *n. pl.* tuisg, journey, embassy, report. *See* toisg.

tosg, *n. m.* a peat-cutter ; fr. *Sc.* tusk. *Shetl.* tushker ; fr. *O.N.* torfskeri.

tosg, tosg, *n. f.* a tusk ; *pl.* tuisg, tusks ; *v.* cut irregularly, tear up.

tosgach, *adj.* cut in an uneven way.

tosgaid, toscej, *n. f.* a hogshead. *Also* togsaid.

tosgair, *n. m.* an ambassador, a messenger, the post. *See* toisg.

tosgaire, tosg'-ur-à, *n. m.* one that cuts irregularly, or botches in cutting.

tosgarra, *a.* "tusked," fierce.

tostal, *n. m.* arrogance. *O.Ir.* tochossol, violation.

tot, *v.* roast or toast hurriedly on the embers ; boil hurriedly.

tota, *n. m. See* tobhta.

total, *n. m.* arrogance.

total, *n. m.* a company, a crowd ; a flock of birds ; fr. the *Eng.*

totarach, *n. m.* contemptible creature ; for tothtarachd ; fr. toth.

toth, tŏh, *n. m.* pudenda, stench, foul blast. *Ir.* toith, a stink.

tòthadh, *n. m.* burning desire, passion for.

tothag, to-hag, *n. f.* short trousers.

tothlainn, to-hlin, *n. f.* damp air, "heavy" atmosphere ; fr. toth, steam.

trà ; for tràth.

tràbhach, tràv'-uch, *n. f.* rubbish of river floods, a kind of grass, hay.

trabhailt, travelt, *n. f.* mill-hopper. *Also* drobhailt. *McB.* suggests *Lat.* trabula.

trabhcar, *n. m.* small quantity of inferior quality, as of fish, potatoes, etc.

trabhsdanach, traüsdanuch, *a.* awkward about the legs.

trachd, *v.* negotiate, propose. So *Ir. Lat.* tracto, to treat.

trachd, *n. m.* a drake. *Also* ràcaire.

trachdadh, *vbl. n. m.* act of negotiating, proposal. *Lat.* tracto, treat.

trachladh, *n. m.* fatigue. *Sc.* trachle.

tradh, *n. f.* a lance, a fishing-spear. So *Ir.*

tradhlaich, *vbl.n. f.* toiling to little purpose.

tràghadh, trà-u, *vbl. n. m.* act of ebbing, ebb. *E.Ir.* trágud.

traibeanach, trēbenuch, *a.* a bedraggled fellow.

traidhtear, trayter, *n. m.* a traitor ; a rogue ; fr. the *Eng.*

tràigh, trày, *v.* ebb, dry up ; *n. f., gen.* tràghad, shore, strand, sands, sand-beach ; reflux ; mar thràigh fhuaimear a' chuain, like the raging reflux of the sea. *E.Ir.* tráig. *O.Celt.* trâgô.

tràighgheadh, trày-yiä, *n. m.* stock-gannet.

tràighleachan, *n. m.* a bird that frequents the shore—even nests there.

tràighte, tràytu, *vbl. a.* ebbed, dry.

tràill, tràl, *n. m.* slave, a drudge. So *M.Ir. O.N.* þræll. *Eng.* thrall.

traille, traliu, *n. m.* the fish tusk.

tràilleach, *n. f.* seaweeds. *Also* stràilleach.

tràillealachd, tràliulachc, *n. f.* slavishness, utmost degradation, servility.

tràilleil, trāliul, *adj.* slavish, servile ; obair thràilleil, servile work.

trainge, treng'-u, *n. f.* throng, pressure of business ; degree more or most throng. *Sc.* thrang. *Eng.* throng.

tràisg, trashc, *v.* parch with thirst ; thràisg mo chridhe, my very heart parched.

traisg, *v.* fast, abstain from food, observe a fast. *Also* troisg. *E.Ir.* troisg.

tràisgte, trashctu, *vbl. a.* parched of thirst.

traiste, *vbl. a.* crumpled, stiff.

trait, tryt, *n. f.* cataplasm, a poultice. *Also* fuar-lit and tròidht. So *Ir.*

tràladh, *vbl. n. m.* act of straining, twisted.

tramailt, tramelt, *n. f.* an unaccountable whim or freak.

tramailteach, *adj.* whimsical, capricious, freakish.

trang, *adj.* throng, very busy, on good terms. *Sc.* thrang.

tra-nòin, tra-nōin, *n. m.* noon, midday. *See* nòin.

traochadh, *m.* exhausted. *Ir.* traochad, draining.

traodadh, *vbl. n. m.* fasting, starving ; wasting. Cf. *O.Ir.* trédenus, three days' fast.

traoghadh, trū-hu, *vbl. n. m.* act of subsiding, abating, as a swelling ; draining ; abatement of a swelling. Cf. *O.Ir.* troethath, *submissio.*

traoigh, trūy, *v.* subside, abate, drain. *E.Ir.* trágim.

traoighte, trūytu, *vbl. a.* subsided, abated, drained.

traon, trūn, *n. m.* a rail, or corn-crake. *Also* gearr-gartan ; and treun-ri-treun. *Ir.* traona. *O.Ir.* tradna.

trap, *n. m.* a trap-stair ; snare ; *v.* take places in a class ; carp.

trapan, *n. m.* a cluster.

trasd, *adv.* across, athwart, obliquely, traverse ; awkwardly placed. *O.Ir.* trost, *trabs.*

trasdair, *n. m.* a diameter.

trasdan, *n. m.* a crutch, a stilt, a cross-beam, a crozier. *Also* trabhsdan.

trasg, *n. f.* fasting ; a fast ; 'na thrasg, in his fasting.

trasgadh, trasg'-u, *vbl. n. m.* fasting. *Ir.* trosgadh. *O.Ir.* troscud.

tràsgadh, *vbl. n. m.* act of parching of thirst.

tràst, dràsda, *adv.* just now.

trat, *n. m.* trick.

tràth, trā, *adj. adv.* early, timeously, betimes ; early in season ; dèan tràth e, do it betimes.

tràth, *n. m.* time, season ; canonical hour ; a meal or diet ; dà thràth 'san latha, two meals a day ; season, daytime ; 'sna tràthaibh ceart, at the proper seasons. So *E.Ir.* In early times the day was divided into eight canonical hours, named prím (6 A.M.), teirt (*tertia hora*), médonlái (noon), or etsruth, nóin (*nona*), fescor (=vesper), coimpleit (9 P.M.), iarmeirge (nocturns), tiugnair (matins). *Wi. Also* antert, tert, sest, noon, fescer, midnoct, maten. *L.S.* xc.

tràthadair, trā-huder, *n. m.* timekeeper.

tràthail, trā-hal, *adj.* early, in time.

tràthalachd, *n. f.* seasonableness.

tre, *prep.* though, by means of. *E.Ir.* tré, tria, tri. *O.Ir.* tre, tri, tré.

treabh, tro, *v.* plough, till. *E.Ir.* trebaim, inhabit, cultivate ; treb, a house. *W.* tref. *O.W.* treb, homestead. *Lat.* trabs, a house.

treabh, tréibh, *n. f.* a thrave. *O.N.* þrefi.

treabhair, trō-ir, *coll. n.* houses, steadings. *Ir.* treabhaire, *id.*

treachail, trechul, *v.* dig a grave. So *Ir.*

treaghaid, tre'-aj, *n. f.* stitch in the side, darting pain, pleurisy. *Ir.* treagh, spear. *E.Ir.* tregat, pain.

trèalabhaid, *n. m.* confusion, a confused mass of odds and ends.

trealaich, *n. pl.* trifles, trash, an assortment of things of little value. *Ir.* treath-laigh. *E.Ir.* trelam, weapons, furniture.

trealamh, trēluv, *n. m.* sickness, indisposition.

trealbhaidh, tralvy, *adj.* come to man or woman's estate, grown up.

treall, triàl, *n. f.* short space of time. *M.Ir.* trell, a while.

treamhlaidh, treabhlaidh, trewly, *n. f.* a lingering sickness. *M.Ir.* trebhlaid. *E.Ir.* tréblait. *Lat.* tribulatio.

tréan-ri-tréan, trēn'-ri-trēn', *n. m.* the bird landrail, or corncrake.

treamsgal, tremsgal, *n. m.* rubbish, trash, worthless mixture.

treas, *n. f.* a battle, a skirmish, a stroke, a bout. *E.Ir.* tress, *id.*

treas, tres, *adj.* the third ; an treas uair, thrice, the third time. *O.Ir.* tress, *tertius.*

treasa, *a., compar.* of làidir ; na's treasa, stronger. *O.Ir.* tressa.

treasd, trest, *n. m.* a long form or seat, as in a school ; *v.* bespeak, engage.

treasdach, *a.* thorough-pacing (of a horse)

treasg, *n. f.* weavers' paste. *See* treisg.

treasg, *n. m.* groats, refuse of brewed malt. *M.Ir.* tresc, refuse, offal.

treastarruing, tres-tarin, *n. f.* spirits of wine ; thrice-distilled whisky.

treath-ghamhnach, tre-ghaünuch, *n. f.* a cow that calved three years ago and has milk ; seachlach, calved two years ago; gamhnach, calved last year.

treathnach, tre-nuch, *n. f.* gimlet.

treibhdhireach, trey-iruch, *adj.* faithful to one's engagement; just, sincere, upright. *O.Ir.* trebar, prudent.

treibhdhireachd, *n. f.* faithfulness, sincerity, punctuality, trustiness, uprightness. *Also* tréibhdhireas. *E.Ir.* treabhaire, treabhaireacht, surety, guarantee.

tréig, trēg, *v.* forsake, leave, abandon, relinquish. *E.Ir.* trécim.

tréigsinn, trēg-shin, *n. f., inf.* of tréigim, a forsaking, abandoning; quitting, relinquishing.

tréigte, trēgtiu, *vbl. a.* forsaken, abandoned.

tréine, trēnu, *compar. deg.* of treun, strong; *n. f.* might, power.

treis, tresh, *n. f.* a while, spell. *Also* greis.

treise, treshu, *deg.* of laidir. *See* ness re treath ghamhnach.

treisead, treshud, *abstr. n. f.* "strongness," strength.

treiseil, treshal, *adj.* powerful in body.

treisg, treshc, *n. f.* weavers' paste; trash.

tréitheach, *a.* accomplished, vigorous, courageous. *Ir.* tréith, good, noble; tréitheach, erudite.

treobh, tryó, *v.* plough, till; same as treabh.

treobhadair, tro-uder, *n. m.* ploughman.

treobhadh, tro-u', *vbl. n. f.* act of ploughing.

treobhaiche, tro-ichu, *n. m.* ploughman.

treodhaire, tro-iru, *n. m.* smith's nail-mould, or shape-iron. So *Ir.*

treòir, trōr, *n. f.* vigour, energy. So *E.Ir.*

treòireach, *a.* vigorous, strong (esp. for an aged person).

treòrachadh, trōruchu, *vbl. n. m.* act of leading, guiding, supporting, directing.

treòraich, trōrich, *v.* guide, give strength to accomplish, strengthen. *M.Ir.* treóraigim.

treòraichte, trōrichtiu, *vbl. a.* led, strengthened.

treosdan. *See* trosdan.

treothaid, tro-hej, *n. f.* pain. *See* treaghaid.

treothail, *n. f.* fit of coughing with the whoop (in whooping-cough).

treubh, trēv, *n. f.* tribe, family, race. *E.Ir.* treb. *Lat.* tribus.

treubhach, trēv'-uch, *adj.* heroic, gallant. *E.Ir.* trabthach, a farmer.

treubhanta, trēv'-annt-u, *adj.* heroic, fond of feats or achievements.

treubhantas, trēv'-annt-us, *n. f.* display of feats or achievements, boasting. *Also* treuthanas.

treubhas, trēvus, *n. f.* feat, exploit.

treubhasach, trēvusuch, *adj.* fond of displaying feats of valour; ostentatious.

treud, trēd, *n. m.* a drove, flock, herd; a procession, a line of cattle or birds. *E.Ir.* trét, a herd.

treudach, trēduch, *adj.* having many flocks or herds; gregarious.

treudaiche, trēdichu, *n. m.* herdsman.

treudaire, trēdiru, *n. m.* a drover.

treun, trēn, *adj.* mighty, vigorous; valorous, brave; surprising; ·is treun a fhuaradh thu, you did surprisingly; is treun leam fhéin a b'urrainn thu, I am surprised that you were able; treun an neart, mighty in strength; *n. m.* a hero, or brave man. *O.Ir.* trén, strong. *W.* tren, strenuous.

treunachd, trēnachc, *n. f.* bravery, might; perseverance and success.

treunad, trēnud, *abstr. n. m.* strength, vigour.

treunadas, trēnudas, *n. f.* exploits.

treunair, trēner, *n. m.* diligent man, a hero. *E.Ir.* trén-fhear, a strong man, a hero.

trì, tree, *num.* three; trì uairean, thrice. *O.Ir.* tri. *Lat.* tres.

trialabhaid, *n. f.* a jumble, a confused assortment.

triall, *n. m.* a flock; stock; procession.

triall, triul, *v.* travel, walk; *n. m.* walking, travel, journey; design. So *E.Ir.*

triallaire, triuliru, *n. m.* traveller.

trian, trian, *n. m., pl.* triantan, third, third part; particle, ray; trian de shoillse, ray of light. So *E.Ir.*

triantach, *adj.* triangular, in thirds.

triantach, *n. f.* a triangle.

triath, treeu, *n. m., gen.* tréith, a personage, lord, chief; coimeas do'n charraig an triath, like the rock is the hero. So *E.Ir.*

triathail, triu-hal, *adj.* mighty, lordly.

tribhileach, tree-viluch, *n. f.* marsh-trefoil.

tribilt, *a.* threefold; fr. the *Eng.* triple.

tribuail, *v. intr.* vibrate, quiver. *See* triobuail.

tric, treeck, *adj.* often, frequent; *adv.* often. *E.Ir.* trice.

tricead, treeckud, *abstr. n. f.* frequency.

trichasach, *a.* three-footed.

trichead, trichud, *adj.* thirty; tricha was a measure of land in Ireland.

trichearnach, *n. m.* a triangle.

trid, treej, *prep.* through, throughout. *E.Ir.* trit, per eum.

trideabac, trijubàk, *n. f.* a mishap, ill-luck.

trideach, *a.* transparent. (*A. McD.*)

trì-deug, tree-jiug, *adj.* thirteen; trì duine deug, thirteen men.

trìdshoilleir, *a.* transparent.

trìdshoillse, *n. f.* transparency.

trìd-shoillseach, *adj.* transparency, limpidness.

trìfhoghair, *n. m.* triphthong.

tri-fichead, tree-fichud, *n. f.* sixty.

trì-ficheadamh, tree-fichuduv, *adj.* sixtieth.

tri-fillte, tree-feeltiu, *adj.* threefold.

trìleanta, *adj.* thirling, trill in music, quavering. *E.Ir.* trilech, song. *O.Ir.* trírech, song of birds.

trilis, trilish, *n. f.* locks of hair. *E.Ir.* triliss.

trilleachan, treeliuchan, *n. m.* oystercatcher; sandpiper, or sea-pyet. *See* drilleachan.

trilsean, treelshen. *See* drillsean.

trinnsear, tree-shur, *n. m.* plate, a trencher; fr. the *Eng. Ir.* truinseir.

trioblaich, triplich, *v.* triple; make threefold.

trioblaid, triblej, *n. f.* trouble, distress, calamity; le trioblaid chruaidh, with sore distress. *E.Ir.* tréblait (masc. in *Td.L.* xvii). *Lat.* tribulatio.

trioblaideach, triblejuch, *adj.* distressing, calamitous; ni trioblaideach, a distressing thing; sore distressed.

triobuail, *v.* vibrate, swing, play.

triobuilte, tripiltiu, *a.* triple, threefold.

triogh, triugh, *n. f.* fit, as of coughing or laughing; the chincough, whooping-cough. *Ir.* trioch. *M.Ir.* trichem, a fit of coughing.

trì-oisinneach, *a.* triangular; *n. f.* a triangle.

triomach air shearrach, topsy-turvy.

trìonaid, tree-unej, *n. f.* trinity. *E.Ir.* trinóit. *O.Ir.* trindóit. *Lat.* trinitas.

trìonaidach, tree-unejuch, *adj.* Trinitarian; *n. m.* a Trinitarian.

triopall, treepul, *n. m.* a bunch. *Also* bad.

trìramhach, tree-ravuch, *adj.* three-oared; *n. f.* three-oared boat, trireme.

trìshiollach, tree-hiuluch, *adj.* having three syllables; *n. m.* word of three syllables.

trìshiolladh, tree-hiulu, *n. m.* trisyllable.

trì-shlisneach, tree-hlishnuch, *adj.* tri-lateral.

trìslig, treeshlig, *v. tr.* work, labour.

tri-thothuinn, tri-hohin, *n.* flurry.

triubhas, troo'ish, *n. f.* breeches and stockings in one piece; pantaloons. *M.Ir.* tribus. *O.Ir.* trebus. *Sc.* trews.

triubhsair, trooser, *n. f.* trousers; fr. the *Eng.*

triucair, trooker, *n. m.* a rascal. *Sc.* truker.

triuchan, *n. m.* stripe of distinguishing colours in tartan. So *Ir.*

triugh, triuch, triuthach, *n. f.* whooping-cough or chincough. *See* triogh.

triùir, troor, *num.* three; three in number.

triuirean, trooren, *n. m.* bowl, or children's play-bullet; ag iomairt air triuireanan, playing at bowls; marbles.

triullainn, *a.* wrong, through other, confused; *n. f.* doggerel.

trò, tròbh, *n. f.* an occasion, a trip.

tròbha, trò'-u, *n. m.* the socket of a mast, the "shoe" in which the mast stands; the mast-step is the gap in the thwart into which the mast fits. (*Lewis.*)

trobhad, *v.* come hither, come away; come along with me; opp. thugad.

tròcair, tròkir, *n. f.* mercy, compassion. *O.Ir.* trócaire and trógcaire. *Z²* 69. *W.* trugaredd.

tròcaireach, *adj.* merciful.

tròcaireachd, *n. f.* mercifulness, compassionate regard, clemency.

troch, *n. m.* a mild imprecation; troch ort! botheration! *Ir.* troch, a short life. *O.Ir.* trú, *gen.* troch, a person doomed to die.

trod, *n. m., gen.* truid, troid, scolding; a scold, reprimand, quarrel, a fight, conflict; *v.* scold, reprove. *M.Ir.* trot, troit, *gen.* troda, strife, fight.

trodaire, trodiru, *n. m.* scolder.

trog, *v.* raise, rear. *O.Ir.* trogaim, bring forth.

trog, tròg, *n. m.* trash, busy dealing. *Also* troc; chan 'eil ann ach troc, nothing there but trash. *Sc.* trock.

trogail, *m.* act of raising, rearing.

trògain, *n. m.* trafficking, "on-goings."

tògbhoil, tròg-vol, trògbhail, *n. f.* grumbling, murmuring, grunting; eternal scold, a quarrel. *Ir.* trogbhail, dispute, wrangle.

tògbhoileach, *adj.* apt to murmur, or grumble gruntingly.

troghad, *a.* soft, full (of eyes).

troich, *n. m.* a dwarf, ninny.

troichealachd, troych'-al-uchc, *n. f.* dwarfishness, triflingness of person.

troicheil, troych'-al, *adj.* dwarfish.

troichilean, *n. m.* a dwarf, a pigmy.

troid, *v.* scold, reprimand; throid mo bhean, my wife scolded.

tròidht, tròyt, *n. f.* poultice, rags, bandages. *See* trait.

troigh, traï, *n. f., gen.* traighe, *pl.* traighean, a foot, the top of the foot; troigh is dòrn gulbann, an athletic feat which consists in standing on the edge of a precipice on one foot, measuring a foot-length in space in front with the other, bending forward and measuring two fist-lengths from the toe of the latter. *O.Ir.* traig. *W.* troed, a foot.

troileis, trolesh, truileis, troolesh, *n. f.* trash, sloppy stuff.

troimh, troy, *prep.* through, through him or it. *O.Ir.* tremi-, *trans-, super-*.

troimhe, troyu, *prep.* and *pron.* through him, through it.

troiteir, *n. m.* a traitor = *Eng.*

trom, *adj., compar.* truime, heavy, weighty, addicted ; trom air an òl, addicted to liquor ; luxuriant, rank ; barr trom, rank or luxuriant crop ; ponderous, sad, melancholy, profound, or deep, as sleep ; eallach trom, a heavy burden ; cadal trom, profound sleep ; enceinte, pregnant ; tha i trom, she is with child ; *n. m.* burden, heavy charge ; nach biodh a throm oirnn, that he would not be a burden to us ; embarrassment, impediment, encumbrance ; cha bhi sin 'na throm ort, that will not be an encumbrance to you ; the embryo. *O.Ir.* tromm.

tromachadh, *vbl. n. m.* act of getting heavier or more addicted or ponderous ; aggravating.

tromaich, tröm'-ich, *v.* get heavier, make more heavy or weighty, get more addicted ; aggravate.

tromalach, *n. f.* the heavier portion.

troman, droman, *n. m.* a dwarf elder. So *Ir. O.Ir.* tromm, *g.* truimm.

tromb, *n. f.* Jew's-harp. *Sc.* trump.

trombaid, troombej, *n. f.* a trumpet.

trombair, troomber, *n. m.* trumpeter.

trombaireachd, troomberuchc, *n. f.* harping, carping, canting.

trombhad, trom-vad, *n. m.* herb vervain. *Ir.* trombhód, vervain mallow.

tromchluasach, *a.* dull of hearing.

trom-chràdh, *m.* grief, melancholy.

trom-dhaite, *a.* vividly coloured.

tromham, 1. *sing. prep.+pers. pron.* through me, etc. 2. tromhad, through you. 3. *m.* troimhe, through him ; 3. *f.* troimhpe, through her ; *pl.* 1. tromhainn, through us. 2. tromhaibh, through you. 3. tromhpa, through them.

trom-inntinn, troum-eentin, *n. f.* dejection.

trom-inntinneach, *adj.* dull, dejected, disconsolate, mournful.

trom-laighe, troum-lyu, *n. f.* nightmare.

trom-lighe, troum-leeyu, *n. f.* nightmare.

tromsanaich, *n. f.* heaviness.

troraid, *n. f.* a spire, a steeple. Cf. *Eng.* turret.

trosd, *n. m.* a dead weight, heavy load.

trosd, *n. m.* a dwarf. So *Ir.*

trosdail, *a.* serious, dull, moody.

trosdan, *n. m.* a crutch, support. *Ir.* trostán, crutch, pilgrim's staff. *O.Ir.* trost, *trabs. Lat.* transtrum (*St.*).

trosg, *n. m., gen.* and *pl.* truisg, cod ; a lubber. *O.N.* þorskr.

trosgadh, *n. m.* fasting, hunger. *O.Ir.* troscud.

trot, *n. f.* a sheep's foot ; *v.* trot.

trotan, *n. m.* trotting, running (with short paces as an aged person) ; fr. the *Eng.*

troth, tro, *n. m.* trip, time.

troth, tröh, *n. m.* a taint. *Ir.* troth, *f.*

trothad, *a.* ; bean nan rasg trothad, woman of the full lively eyes. *See* troghad.

trothail. *See* treothail.

trù, *n. m., gen.* and *pl.* troich, a wretch.

truacanta, troo-ucantu, *adj.* merciful, compassionate ; fr. truagh + can (say). *McB.*

truacantachd, *n. f.* pity ; compassion.

truagh, troo-u', *adj.* sad, miserable, wretched ; is truagh leam thu, I pity you ; nach truagh mo chàradh, how piteous is my case ; miserly ; is truagh an tobhartas e, it is a miserable offering or gift. *E.Ir.* trúag. *O.Ir.* tróg, *miser. O.Celt.* trougo-s, miserable.

truaghan, troo-ughan, *n. m.* miserable person, a pitiful creature.

truaighe, troo-uyu, *n. f.* pity, woe, mischief ; tha an truaighe ortsa, you have gone to the mischief ; mo thruaighe mi, woe's me ! *O.Ir.* tróige, trúaige. *O.Celt.* trougjâ, misery.

truaill, troo-ul, *n. f.* sheath or scabbard ; tharruing e a chlaidheamh as a thruaill, he unsheathed his sword. *E.Ir.* trúaill, a sheath.

truaill, *v.* adulterate ; reduce to a standard, as whisky, etc. ; uisge-beatha truaillte, qualified or reduced whisky ; pollute, corrupt, defile ; thruaill thu am fearann, you have polluted the land. *E.Ir.* trúalnim. *O.Ir.* druáilnithe, *corruptus.*

truailleachan, troo-uliuchan, *n. m.* mean person.

truailleachd, troo-ulachc, *n. f.* mean quantity, consideration, or disposition.

truailleadh, troo-uliu, *vbl. n. m.* act of adulterating ; reducing spirits to a standard ; polluting.

truaillidh, troo-uly, *adj.* polluting, mean, dastardly, very low or shabby.

truaillidheachd, troo-ulyachc, *n. f.* meanness of disposition, niggardliness.

truaillte, troo-ultiu, *vbl. a.* reduced, defiled.

truan, *n. f.* trowel. *Also* spàinn-aoil, lime-spoon.

truas, *n. m.* pity, compassion ; ghabh e truas dith, he pitied her wretchedness. So *Ir.*

truasail, *adj.* compassionate.

trubhais, *n. f.* a fish roe.

trudair, troodur, *n. m.* filthy person, beastly fellow, brutish man. *Also* trusdar. *Ir.* trudaire, a stammerer.

trudaireachd, troodiruchc, *n. f.* filth, mean behaviour.

truid, trooj, *n. f.* (*also* truideag), a starling ; tidy, neat female.

truideach, druideach, *a.* abounding in starlings.

trùileach, trooliuch, *n. f.* a worthless person, dirty person.

truileis, *n. f.* slops.

trùille, trooliu, *n. m.* worthless, dirty person.

truime, trimu, *n. f.* weightiness ; *deg.* trom.

truimid, *abstr. n. m.* the heavier ; cha truimid e sin, it is none the heavier for that ; cha truimide an loch an lach, the duck is no burden to the loch.

truis, troosh, *v.* gather, tuck, gird, truss ; *interj.* gather your tail ! be off ! said to a dog or a person in contempt.

trùis, troosh, *n. f.* lasciviousness.

truisealadh, trooshalu, *n. m.* state of having one's clothes tucked up. *M.Ir.* trustalad, act of girding.

truiseil, trooshal, *adj.* lascivious.

truisich, *v. tr.* tuck up, roll up (sleeves).

truitreach, *n. f.* warbling (of bird).

trùp, troop, *n. m.* a troop = *Eng.*

trùpair, trooper, *n. m.* trooper ; a romp.

trus, troos, *n. m.* a belt, girdle. So *Ir.*

trusadh, troosu, *vbl. n. m.* act of gathering, trussing ; collection, a gathering, rolling up sleeves, tucking. So *Ir.*

trusdaireachd, troosdiruchc, *n. f.* filthiness.

trusdar, troosdur, *n. m.* a debauchee ; filthy fellow.

trusgan, trooscan, *n. m.* suit of clothes, dress. *Ir.* truscan, clothes, furniture.

truthaire, troo-hiru, *n. m.* bankrupt, a villain, a traitor, a dishonest man.

truthaireachd, *n. f.* villainy, low mean conduct.

tu, *pers. pron.* thou. *O.Ir.* tú. *Lat.* tū.

tuagh, too-u', *n. f.* hatchet, axe ; tuagh-airm, tuagh-chatha, a battle-axe, a Lochaber axe ; tuagh-chuisle, tuagh-fhola, a fleam, or cattle-lancet. *M.Ir.* tuag. *E.Ir.* túagach, hitting with an axe.

tuaicheal, dizziness, winding, moving left-wise ; tuath + cell. *See* tuaineal-ach.

tuaileas, too-ulas, *n. m.* libel, calumny, defamation, slander. So *Ir.*

tuaileasach, *adj.* defamatory, calumnious, reproachful, slanderous ; tuaileasachd, calumniousness.

tuailt, tubhailt, *n. f.* towel ; fr. the *Eng.*

tuaimeil, too-amel, *v.* swathe awkwardly ; huddle on clothes.

tuain, *v. tr.* loosen ; set free = du + óen

(disunite), opp. of suain = su + óen unite, wind.

tuaineal, *n. m.* dizziness, stupor. *Ir.* toinéal, a trance, astonishment.

tuainealaich, too-analich, *n. f.* giddiness, dizziness, amazement. stupidity.

tuainig, *v.* unloose ; *a.* loose, worthless ; creutar tuainig, a worthless creature. *See* tualaig.

tuaiream, too-urim, *n. f.* a guess, vicinity; sense, judgement ; chan 'eil dìth tuaireim air, he does not want sense ; quantity or number ; ciod an tuaiream a th'ann, what quantity· or number may there be of it ? direction, pursuit, aim, shot ; thilg e mu thuaiream e, he aimed it at him ; mu thuaiream an aon àite, much about the same place. *M.Ir.* tuairim, about, nearly. *T.Sh.* *O.Ir.* tuirem = do + ad + rim (number), a reckoning.

tuaireamach, *a.* sensible, possible, probable.

tuaireamas, *n. m.* haphazard, a venture.

tuaireap, too-urap, *n. f.* a squabble, fray, ill-fate.

tuaireapach, *a.* ill-fated ; *n. m.* miserable creature.

tuaireapadh, *n. m.* mischief, ruin.

tuairgne, tuairgneadh, too-urcnu, *n. f.* confusion ; a mauling ; violent twisting, as of rigging in storm. *O.Ir.* túarcon (do-fo-arcon), to smash.

tuairisgeul, *n. m.* description, report, made - up story. *M.Ir.* túarascbál, description. *O.Ir.* túarascbaim, portray.

tuairmeachd, too-urmuchc. *See* tuaiream.

tuairmse, too-umshu. *See* tuaiream.

tuairneag, too-urnag, *n. f.* a round wooden dish ; a coble, or punt of a boat ; tidy, neat female.

tuairnear, too-urner, *n. m.* a turner ; a wheelwright.

tuairnearachd, *n. f.* turner's trade ; working at a lathe.

tuairsgeul, too-urscal, *n. m.* defamation ; false report,. calumny, slander. *E.Ir.* túarascbal, description.

tuairsgeulach, *adj.* defamatory, calumnious, slanderous.

tuaisceart, *n. f.* the north. So *Ir.* *O.Ir.* túas-cert, the north.

tuaisd,too-usht, *n. m.* an awkward person, dolt.

tuaisdeach, *adj.* awkward, stupid.

tuaisdeachd, *n. f.* stupidity.

tuaisdear, *n. m.* dolt, awkward fellow.

tuaisdeil, *adj.* stupid, awkward.

tuaith, too-u, *n. f.* lordship, territory.

tuaitheal, too-uhul, *adj.* northward, left-wise, wrong, unfortunate. *M.Ir.* tú-athbel, left-hand-wise.

tualaig, *a.* loose, have flux. *Also* tuanlaig.

tuam, *n. m.* tomb, grave, cave, moat or mound. *O.F.* tumbe. *Gr.* τύμβος, a tumulus.

tuamhsgaoil, too-ascul, *v.* roll in clothes, huddle, endeavour to extricate out of a labyrinth, or great deal of clothes.

tuanag, *n. f.* loosening. *See* tuainig.

tuar, *n. m.* food. *O.Ir.* túare, *cibus.*

tuar, *v.* deserve, merit ; an ni a thuar thu, what you deserved ; *n. m.* merit, desert ; hue, colour, appearance ; deserving, meriting ; ciod e tha thu a' tuar a dhèanamh ort, what do you deserve to be done to you ? tha thu tuar do chrochadh, you deserve to be hanged. *M.Ir.* tuar, an omen, presage.

tuaradh, too-uru, *n. m.* quantity, number; ciod an tuaradh a th' ann, what quantity or number is there ? mun tuaradh sin, about that quantity ; fr. tuar, appearance, but *see* tuaiream.

tuaram, *n. m.* a reckoning. *See* tuaiream.

tuarasdal, too-urustul, *n. m.* fee, wages, reward, salary, stipend ; desert. *M.Ir.* túarustal, wages. *O.Ir.* tale (*impv.*), pay ; tale damsa alog, pay me the price of it, gl. *W.* tâl, *id.* perh. = *Ger.* zahle. *Thn.*

tuargan, *n. m.* discontent, complaining ; *a.* tuarganach.

tuasaid, too-usej, *n. f.* row, fray, fight.

tuasaideach, *adj.* quarrelsome.

tuasgail, *v.* loose, untie. *E.Ir.* túaslaicim (do + ass + lécim), let go, let loose.

tuataidh, *n. m.* mean and contemptible man ; a boor. *O.Ir.* tuati (gl. *qui foris sunt*), gentiles. *Z².*

tuath,too-u, *coll. n. f.* tenantry, peasantry, country people ; the country ; air an tuath, on the country. *O.Ir.* túath, *populus. W.* tud. *O.Celt.* teuts. *Goth.* þiuda. *A.S.* þeōd. *O.H.G.* diota, people.

tuath, *n. f.* the north ; *adj. adv.* north, northern, northward ; gaoth tuath, north wind ; tuath ort, northward of you. *O.Ir.* túath, north, left.

tuathach, too-uhuch, *n. m.* northerner ; *opp.* to deasach, southerner.

tuathag, *n. f.* a patch. *Also* tughag. Cf. tùthag.

tuathair, *n. f.* a northern exposure.

tuathall, *a.* left - handwise, awkward, wrong. *Ir.* tuathall.

tuathallan, *n. m.* vertigo, a disease in sheep—supposed to cause the victim to spin round leftwards.

tuathanach, too-uhanuch, *n. m.* tenant, husbandman, agriculturist.

tuathanachas, tuathanas, *n. f.* husbandry, agriculture, farming ; tenement.

tuathcheathairn, tuathchearn, tenantry.

tuba, *n. m., pl.* tubachan, a tub, vat.

tubaist, toobisht, *n. f.* mischance, mischief, mishap, accident ; is trom na tubaistean air na sliobastan, the clumsy are very liable to mischances ; tubaist ort, mischief take you.

tubaisteach, toobishtiuch, *adj.* unlucky, unfortunate, calamitous, untoward.

tubaisteachd, *n. f.* unfortunateness, liability to accidents.

tuban, *n. m.* a tub ; lock of wool.

tubh, too, *v. tr.* cover, thatch ; properly tugh, *q.v.*

tubh, *v.* back, as a horse ; tubh e, back him in.

tubhailt, too-elt, *n. f.* a tablecloth, towel.

tùc, *n. m.* plug, bung (for draining-hole in a boat).

tùch, tooch, *v.* smother, fumigate, grow hoarse.

tuch, *inter.* tut ! hush !

tùchan, toochan, *n. m.* hoarseness, half-smothered fire. *Also* tùchadh.

tùchanach, *adj.* hoarse.

tud, *inter.* tut ! whist !

tud, tood, *n. m.* a little heap, as dough.

tudaidh, *n. m.* a ninny, a manikin.

tudan, toodan, *n. m.* a little cornstack, small heap of anything.

tug, toog. *See* thug.

tugaidean, *pl. n.* witticisms.

tugh, *v.* thatch, cover ; back.

tugha, too'u, *n. f.* thatch, covering ; tighean tughaidh, thatched houses or cots. *E.Ir.* tuga, tugim. *W.* to, roof. *Lat.* toga. *O.Celt.* togo-. *O.N.* þak.

tughadair, too-uder, *n. m.* thatcher.

tughag, *n. f.* a patch ; fr. tugh, cover.

tuig, tooig, *v.* understand, comprehend, perceive, discern. *O.Ir.* tuiccim, tuccim.

tuigse, tooigshu, *n. f.* understanding, sense, reason, judgment ; a' call a thuigse, losing his senses, or judgment ; skill, knowledge ; is beag tuigse tha agadsa air sin, you have little skill of that. *O.Ir.* tuicse, cland tuicse, *populus electus.*

tuigseach, tooigshuch, *adj.* intelligent, prudent, sensible ; duine tuigseach, a prudent or intelligent man ; skilled, expert ; tuigseach air a leithid sin, expert in such things.

tuigsear, *n. m.* one who understands.

tuigsinn, tooigshin, *vbl. n. m.* understanding, perceiving, discerning.

tuil, tool, *n. f.* a flood, torrent, deluge. *O.Ir.* tuile. *Also O.Ir.* tolam, tóla, flood, tide.

tuilbheum, tool-vēm, *n. f.* torrent.

tuildhorus, *n. m.* flood-gate ; tuildhorsan nèamh, the windows of heaven.

tuilich, toolich, tuilidh, tooly, *n. m.* more,

additional quantity or number ; **thoir dhomh tuilidh**, give me more ; **tuilidh is a choir**, too much, superabundance, superfluity.

tuilidh, tŭ'l'-èch, tuille, tŭ'lly'-a, *adv.* more, any more, any further ; **cha till, cha till mi tuilleadh,** I shall never, never more return ; **a thuille** or **thuilidh air sin,** moreover. *See* **tuilleadh.**

tùilinn, *n. f.* twilled linen ; canvas.

tùilinn, *n. f.* angry sea, shipped wave ; **ri uchd tùilinn,** in face of a heavy " sea." *A.M. a., gen.* based on **dìle.**

tuilis, *n.* overfeeding, overloading the stomach.

tuille, tuilleadh, toolu, *n. m.* more, additional quantity or number. *Ir.* **tuillim,** I increase, enlarge. *Lh. E.Ir.* **tuilled, tuillim (do-fo-illim).**

tuilmean, toolumen, *n. m.* a little knoll. *See* **tolm.**

tuilmeanach, *a.* full of knolls, or tufts.

tuilmhor, tuilear, *a.* stout, robust, full-blooded.

tuil-ruadh, *n. f.* deluge, the flood.

tuilteach, tooltiuch, *n. f.* a torrent ; *adj.* in torrents, inundating, deluging ; **frasan tuilteach,** in inundating or deluging showers. So *Ir.*

tuiltean, tooltin, *pl. n.* floods, deluges.

tuimhnich, *n. f.* confusion, dizziness, as from a staggering blow or word.

tuimhseach, tooivshuch, *a.* beating, thumping.

tuimhseadh, *m.* beating, thumping ; a rush, quick action.

tuimhsich, tooishich, *v.* beat, drub.

tuimpe, twimpu, *n. m.* a turnip.

tuin, *v.* dwell ; *n. m.* dwelling.

tuine, *n. f.* dread, alarm.

tuineach, toonuch, *n. f.* dwelling, lodging.

tuineachadh, *vbl. n. m.* act of gathering into a place for residence ; colonising ; dwelling ; a sojourn.

tuineachas, toonuchus, *n. m.* colony.

tuineadh, toonu, *n. m.* an abode. *E.Ir.* **tunide.**

tuineal, *n. m.* a mournful tale. *Ir.* **toineal,** trance, astonishment.

tuinich, toonich, *v.* settle in a place, plant, or colonise ; gather, as matter in a suppuration ; settle, or fix in a place.

tuinneasach, tooniasuch, *a.* mortal.

tuinnidh, *a.* firm, hard. *Ir.* **tuinidhe,** immovable.

tuinnse, *n. m. (pl.* **tuinnseachan),** a blow, a surge.

tuinntean, *n. m.* a lock of wool.

tuir, *v.* sing or rehearse an elegy ; lament for the dead, deplore. *Ir.* **tuirim.** *E.Ir.* **turthiud,** tale.

tuireadh, tooru, *n. m. (gen.* **tuiridh,** *pl.* **tuiridhean),** an elegy, death-song, a dirge, lamentation for the dead ; mourning, wailing ; **ciod fàth do thuiridh,** what is the cause of your lament ? *Ir.* **tuireamh,** a dirge.

tuireann, toorun, *n. m.* spark from anvil. *Ir.* **tuireann,** *id.*

tuireasg, toorusc, *n. m.* a saw. *E.Ir.* **turesc (teasc**=cut).

tuirl, *v.* alight, dismount. *See* **tuirling.**

tuirleig, toorlig, *n. m.* water-spout.

tuirleum, toor-lēm, *n. m.* a fearful leap ; root. *See* **tuirling** (leum =*inf.* of **lingim**).

tuirlich, toorlich, *n. f.* rumbling noise.

tuirling, toorling, *v. tr.* dismount, alight. *Ir.* **tuirling.** *M.Ir.* **tairbling**=do-air-bling. *O.Ir.* **do-arbling, do-eirbling,** *desiluit* ; fr. **lingim,** I leap.

tuirmeadh, *m.* playing (on instrument) ; " **mise ri tuirmeadh theud,**" and I a playing my harp (strings). Cf. **toirm.**

tùirneileas, *vbl. n. f.* act of boxing (like rams) ; contact, collision.

tùirse, toorshu, *n. f.* sadness, mourning, wailing. *E.Ir.* **toirsi, torsi.** *O.Ir.* **torsi.**

tùirseach, toorshuch, *adj.* sad. *Also* **tùrsach.** *O.Ir.* **toirsech.**

tùis, toosh, *n. f.* incense, frankincense. *E.Ir.* **túis.** *Lat.* **tūs.** *Gr.* θύος, incense.

tùisear, toosher, *n. m.* censer.

tuisill, tooshil, *v.* stumble, stammer.

tuisleach, tooshluch, *adj.* unsteady. *M.Ir.* **tuisledach,** stumbling, offending.

tuisleadh, tooshliu, *vbl. n. m.* act of stumbling ; a stumble, jostle ; delivery. *O.Ir.* **tuisled.**

tuislean, *n. m.* a birthday party.

tuislich, tooshlich, *v.* stumble, jostle, slip, fall.

tuit, tooit, *v. n.* fall, slip, chance, happen, befall, benight, get dark ; be seduced by ; **thuit duinn tachairt,** we met by chance ; **thuit iad,** they fell ; **thuit an oidhche oirnn,** we were benighted ; **thuit i leis,** she was seduced by him ; subside ; **tuitidh a' ghaoth ach mairidh ar cliù,** the wind shall subside, but our fame shall last ; fail, damp ; **thuit a chridhe,** his heart failed him. *O.Ir.* **tuitim,** to fall.

tuiteam, tooitum, *vbl. n. m.* a fall ; dusk ; **fhuair e tuiteam,** he got a fall ; **mu thuiteam na h-oidhche,** about the dusk of the evening ; act of falling, getting dusky. *O.Ir.* **tuitimm,** *inf.* of **tuitim,** to fall.

tùiteam, *n. m.* a badger.

tuiteamach, tooitumuch, *adj.* falling, accidental, casual ; **an tinneas tuiteamach,** the falling sickness, epilepsy, apoplexy ; *n. m.* epilepsy.

tuiteamachd, *n. f.* fallibility, contingency.

tuiteamas, tooitumus, *n. m.* chance, accident ; thachair sinn le tuiteamas, we met by accident or chance ; an event, occurrence ; gach droch thuiteamas, every evil occurrence ; chan'eil ann ach tuiteamas, it is only a chance ; epilepsy.

tul-, *intens. prefix*, entirely, wholly.

tula, *n. m.* a hearth, heap, fire.

tulach, tooluch, *n. m., gen.* tulaich, tolcha (*R.C.*², 222), a knoll ; little green eminence ; mi am shuidhe air an tulaich, I sitting on the knoll ; tomb ; chàirich sinn 'san tulaich an laoch, we interred the hero in the green knoll. *E.Ir.* tulach, a hill, (arched) roof of house. *E.W.* twlch.

tulag, toolag, *n. f.* fish pollock.

tul-bhrèag, absolute falsehood, a barefaced lie ; tul (intens.) + bréc.

tulchan, toolchan, *n. m.* a sham-calf ; a stuffed calf-skin.

tulchann, tooluchin, *n. f.* a gable of a house ; the breech ; a horse's croup. *E.Ir.* tulchinne, *dat. s.* of tulach, the " arch," gable.

tulchuis, toolchoosh, *n. f.* sagacity, penetration, intelligence ; confidence.

tulchuiseach, toolchooshuch, *adj.* intelligent, shrewd ; persevering, plodding, brave.

tul-fhirinn, *n. f.* absolute fact. = tul (*intens. pref.*) + firinn.

tulg, toolg, *v.* rock, toss, roll ; tulg a' chreathall, rock the cradle ; an long a' tulgadh, the ship rolling ; wave, late ; an doire a' tulgadh, the grove waving. *Also* turrc, tulg = a dent, *e.g.* in tin dish. *W.* twlc, toss.

tulgach, tooluguch, *adj.* rocking, tossing ; uneasy, as a seat ; unfixed, or uncertain, as an office or employment.

tulgadh, toolugu, *vbl. n. m.* act of tossing, rocking, lurching ; the initial spring in rowing ; a lurch, toss—used by *Armstrong* for tolg.

tulm, toolum, *n. f.* a knoll, or little mound of turf, etc. ; eminence. *Also* tolm.

tulmach, tŭlum'-uch, *adj.* knolly.

tul-mhagaidh, *n. m.* downright mockery.

tum, toom, *v.* dip, immerse, duck, immerge, plunge. *E.Ir.* tummim. *O.Celt.* tumbô.

tumadair, toomuder, *n. m.* baling-dish.

tumadh, toomu, *vbl. n. m.* act of dipping, ducking ; duck, immersion. *E.Ir.* tummud.

tumaire, toomiru, *n. m.* a ducker.

tum-tam, toom-tam, *n. m.* a humdrum ; great hesitation, stupid conduct.

tumte, toomtu, *vbl. a.* immerged, dipped. *E.Ir.* tomtha.

tung, toong, *n. m.* a family burying-ground inclosed, a tomb, vault (Argyle).

tungaid, toongej, *n. f.* a most notorious lie, or hellish evasion, a stratagem.

tungaideach, toongejuch, *adj.* full of hellish evasions or noted lies.

tunna, toonu, *n. m.* a tun ; a ton. *E.Ir. A.S.* tunne. *N.* tunna. *Ger.* tonne ; fr. *Lat.* tunna, a cask.

tunnadair, toonuder, *n. m.* a tunner, a filler, a funnel.

tunnag, toonag, *n. f.* a duck, a hobbling woman.

tùr, toor, *n. m.* penetration, mental acuteness, genius, intelligence ; cha duine gun tùr a dhèanadh e, it is not a man destitute of genius that could accomplish it ; gliocas is tùr, wisdom and understanding ; *v.* invent, devise, contrive, frame ; air a thùradh le Seumas, invented by James ; a thùras olc, that devises evil. *M.Ir.* túr = iarraidh, seek. *O'Dav. O.Ir.* túirim, I search, investigate (do + fo + sirim).

tùr, toor, *n. m.* a tower, fortification, fort, castle. *O.Ir.* túir, a turret. *W.* tŵr. *Lat.* turris. *O.Celt.* turi-.

tur, toor, *adj.* dry, without condiment (or kitchen) ; greim tur, a dry morsel ; aran tur, bread without butter and cheese. *M.Ir.* tar, dry.

tur, *adj.* most completely, or entirely ; is tur a dh' fhairslich e ort, how completely it has defied you ; *adv.* gu tur ; tha e mar sin gu tur, it is absolutely so. *Ir.* tura, plenty. *E.Ir.* tor, crowd. Cf. tòrr.

tùrach, tooruch, *adj.* towering, turreted.

turach, *a.* cross-grained, bad-humour (as through want of tobacco) ; turach air tharach, topsy-turvy. *W.R.*

turachdach, toorach-cuch, *adj.* without anything else than meal, potatoes, etc.

turadan, *n. m.* a small heap or stack.

turadh, tooru, *n. m.* absence of rain, fair weather ; tha e 'na thuradh, it is fair ; rinn e turadh, it faired, the rain ceased. *E.Ir.* turud, dry weather.

turaideach, *a.* turreted. *M.Ir.* turid, a pillar, column.

tùrail, tooral, *adj.* shrewd, ingenious. acute, inventive, skilful ; gach duine toileach, tùrail, every willing, skilful man.

tùrainn, toorin, *n. f.* a fit of sickness ; fhuair e an droch thùrainn, he has got a very bad fit of sickness.

tùrainneach, dexterous, handy, ingenious.

tùrainneach, toorinuch, *adj.* delicate in health ; liable to sickness.

tùrainniche, toorinichu, *n. m.* invalid.

tùralachd, tooraluchc, *n. m.* shrewdness.

turamaich, toorumich. *See* turraman-aich.

turamanaich, toorumanich, *n. f.* rocking. *Also* turraban.

turaraich, *n. f.* rumbling noise, booming of guns.

Turcach, toorkuch, *a.* Turkish ; *n. m.* a Turk ; turkey hen or cock.

turcaideach, *a.* nodding.

turcais, toorkesh, *n. f.* tweezers, pinchers. *Also* durcaisd.

turchair, *v. intr.* to happen, befall. *E.Ir.* torchar, *id.*

turgain, turguin, *n. m.* destruction. *E.Ir.* tuarcaim, hitting. *O.Ir.* orgun, orcun, *occisio.*

tùrlach, toorluch, *n. m.* a very large fire, having smoke and no flame ; pig, clumsy person ; *n. f.* a monstrous ugly head of hair ; tùrlach na fèisde, banquet fire, a heap, a great quantity. *Ir.* ur, úr, fire.

turloch, toorloch, *n. f.* a lake that dries in summer (tur + loch).

tùrn, toorn, *n. m.* job, feat ; tùrn odhar, a mite or twelfth of a penny ; ni e tùrn, it will do, it will serve the purpose. *Also* turnais.

tùrr, toor, *n. m.* a large heap, tomb. *Also* tiùrr. Cf. tòrr. *W.* twr, a heap.

turraban, turraman, nodding, rocking to and fro in grief or in sleep ; grief.

turra-chadal, tooru-chadil, *n. m.* sleeping and rocking, as a person sitting on a chair ; slumbering, dozing, lethargy.

turradh, *n. m.* a surprise, taking unawares.

turrag, turraing, *n. f.* an accident, a slight turn of illness.

turraid, *n. f.* very fat, shapeless woman, a " heap " of a woman.

turraig, toorig, *n. f.* stool in ridicule ; air do thurraig, at stool.

turraim, toorem, turramain, toorumen, *v. i.* rock or vibrate, as a person lamenting the dead, sitting on a grave.

turraisg, *n. f. See* urraisg ; *syn.* òinseach, a witless female.

turrallach, *n. m.* a big clumsy person.

turram, toorum, turraman, tooruman, *n. m.* tossing hither and thither, as a person lamenting ; vibration, oscillation ; turraban, soft sound.

tùrsa, toorshu, *n. f.* dejection, sadness ; waving the head and lamenting ; sorrow. *See* tùirse. *O.Ir.* tórsa.

tùrsach, toorshuch, *adj.* sad, sorrowful ; gu tùrsach, trom, sad and dejected.

turtur, *n. m.* a turtle. *Lat.* turtur.

turus, toorus, *n. m.* journey, travel. So *E.Ir. O.Ir.* tururas, *incursus.*

turusachd, toorusuchc, *n. f.* pilgrimage.

tùs, toos, *n. m.* beginning, commencement, front, origin ; air tùs an airm, in front or van of the army ; air a thùs is air a thoiseach, first and foremost ; tùsmhuinntir, aborigines. *O.Ir.* túus, tús.

tùs-cléithe, *n. m.* the bow-end of a bank of oars.

tut, *interj.* expression of impatience, slight annoyance.

tùt, toot, *n. m.* a foist, stink ; *v.* foist, stink. *M.Ir.* tútt, stench.

tùtaire, tootiru, *n. m.* foister.

tùthag, too-hag, *n. f.* a patch (on a rent on the hull of a boat), a clout.

U

u, the seventeenth and last letter of the Gaelic alphabet, styled ùr, the yew-tree.

ua, *prep.* from. So *Ir. O.Ir.* ua, hua ; ó became ua, as é became ia. soos > suas.

uabairt, uàburt, *n. f.* expulsion.

uabhar, ooàv'-ur, *n. m.* extreme pride, arrogance, vainglory ; uabhar is àrdan, pride and arrogance ; a green slope ; air uabhar an t-sleibh, on the slope of the hill. *O.Ir.* úabar, vainglory.

uachdar, uàch-cur, *n. m.* surface, top ; air uachdair, on the surface, on the top ; uachdar is iochdar, top and bottom ; cream, upper of a shoe ; gruth is uachdar, curds and cream ; mastery ; fhuair e làmh an uachdair, he got the mastery ; farm stock ; fo uachdair, under stock. *O.Ir.* uachtar, ochtar.

O.Celt. oukteero-s. *W.* uchter, uchtwr, top, height.

uachdarach, uäch-curuch, *adj.* upper, higher, superficial.

uachdarachd, uäch-curuchc, *n. f.* top ; o'n uachdarachd gus an iochdrachd, from top to bottom.

uachdaran, ŭăchc-ar-an, *n. m.* a superior, governor, ruler, chief.

uachdaranachd, uäch-cranuchc, *n. f.* supremacy, dominion, rule ; reign, sovereignty ; biodh uachdaranachd aca, let them have dominion.

uachdrach, *a.* rich in cream.

uachdrachd, uäch-cruchc, *n. f.* surface, top ; o'n uachdrachd, gus an iochdrachd, from first to last, from the top to the bottom.

uadh, *a.* alone, singular (number). *O.Ir.*
úathad, *n.* very small number ; the
singular.

uaibh, uäv (*prep.* ua +*pron.* sibh), from
you, a distance from you ; wanted by
you ; being your duty ; tha uaibh falbh,
you had better be gone, it is your duty to
go ; fada uaibh, far from you. *See* uam.

uaibhreach, uävruch, uaimhreach, *adj.*
arrogant, haughty, self - important,
extremely proud. *O.Ir.* uabrech,
arrogant.

uaibhreachas, uaimhreachas, *n.f.* extreme
degree of pride or vainglory ; great
haughtiness. *Also* uaibhreachd.

uaibh-se, ŭäv'-shu, *emph.* of uaibh.

uaidh, *prep.* +*pron.* from him. *See* uam.

uaigh, *n. f.* a grave, tomb, sepulchre.
M.Ir. uag.

uaigneach, uä-gnuch, *adj.* solitary, remote, retired ; àite uaigneach, a
solitary or remote place ; distant, dull ;
duine uaigneach, a person distant or
reserved in manner. *M.Ir.* uagnech.
O.Ir. huam (cave) + icc (go) + nech
(*adj.* suf.) : as to sense cf. *M.Ir.* disert,
W. diserth < *Lat.* desertum.

uaigneachd, uäig-nuchc, *n. f.* secrecy,
solitariness, etc. ; retired, morose disposition or habits.

uaigneas, *n. m.* solitude, retired manners
or habits ; thug e air uaigneas e, he
took him aside ; secrecy, privacy ; tha
an t-aran a dh' ithear an uaigneas
taitneach, bread eaten in secret is
pleasant. *M.Ir.* úaignes, solitude.
Also uairgneas.

uaignidh, uäigny, *adj. See* uaigneach.

uaill, uä-il, *n. f.* pomp, vanity, vain-
glory, inconsistent boasting. *O.Ir.*
úall, *superbia*, pride.

uailleag, *n. f.* a conceited female.

uaillire, uä-iliru, *n. m.* a fop, spark.
Also uailleagan.

uaill-mhiann, uä-il-viun, *n. f.* ambition.

uaim, *n. f.* notes on harp.

uaim, *n. m.* sound. *Also* fuaim.

uaim, *n. m.* alliteration (in verse).

uaimh, *n. f.* a cave, a den. *E.Ir.* uaimh,
a cave, crypt.

uaimhghealtachd, *n.f.* loneliness, eeriness.

uaimhinn, uä-vin, *n. f.* horror ; great
horror or detestation.

uaimhinneach, uä-vinuch, uaimhneach,
uäv-nuch, *adj.* horrifying.

uaimhneachd, *abstr. n. f.* horrifying
nature or quality ; horridness.

uaincionn, *n. m.* a lamb's skin. uan +
cinn.

uaine, uä-niu, *adj.* green, pallid, wan ;
n. m. green, green colour. *E.Ir.* úane,
green.

uaineachan, uä-niuchan, *n. m.* a wan,

pallid, miserable-looking person. *Also*
uainealach.

uainead, uä-niud, *abstr. n. m.* greenness,
pallidness, wanness ; degree of greenness.

uainean, *n. m.* a little lamb.

uainfheoil, *n. f.* lamb's flesh.

uainich, uä-nich, *v.* get green.

uainidh, *a.* greenish.

uainn, uä-in, *prep.* +*pron.* from us, at a
distance from us, wanted by us,
missing by us ; tha triùir uainn, we
want three, we miss three ; being
necessary for us, or our duty ; tha
uainn falbh, it is our duty to go, we
had better be gone. *See* uam.

uainneart, *n. m.* bustle, tumbling, wallowing. Cf. aonairt, aonagail. *Ir.* únfuirt.

uaip, *v.* bungle, botch.

uaipe, *prep.* +*pron.* 3. *s. f.* from her, etc.
See uam.

uaipear, *n. m.* bungler, botcher.

uair, *n. f. gen.* uarach, an hour, time,
weather ; time of day or night ;
allotted time, rotation ; aon uair, one
hour ; aon uair is gun tòisich e, once
he begins ; bha mi uair 's a' bhaile,
I was once in town ; ciod é an uair a
tha e ? what o'clock is it ? uair 's a'
mhadainn, one o'clock in the morning ;
uair 'sam bith, any time ; a' cheud
uair, the first time ; is e so m' uair-sa,
this is my time, this is my turn ; tha
uair air, he is subject to fits and starts
of good humour or generosity ; air
uairibh, sometimes ; an ceart uair,
presently, immediately, instantly; gach
uair, every time ; rinn e sin uair is
uair, he did that more than once,
repeatedly, over and over ; 'na uair-
eannan, sometimes ; ni mi e air an
uair, I will do instantly, immediately ;
tòisichidh e air an uair, he will begin
sharp on time ; uair mu seach, alternately, in rotation. *O.Ir.* úar, ór.
W. awr. *L.* hora.

uaircheann, *I.Lom. See* uircheann.

uaireadair, uaruder, *n. m.* timepiece,
watch ; uaireadair-gainmhich, sand-
glass ; uaireadair-gréine, sun-dial.

uaireiginn, uairigin, *adv.* sometime ; uair
no uaireiginn, some time or other.

uaireil, uaral, *adj.* hourly.

uairneach, *n. m.* a barren heifer of age
to have a calf. *See* seachlach.

uaisle, uashlu, *n. m.* nobility, high birth,
gentlemanly manners, gentility, liberality ; *pl.* na h-uaisle, the gentry ; *compar. deg.* of uasal, more or most genteel.

uaisleachd, uashliuchc, *n. f.* gentility,
dignity of port or mind.

uaislead, uashliud, *abstr. n. f.* gentility.

uaislich, uashlich, *v.* ennoble, dignify.

uaithe, uayu, *prep.* +*pron.* from her, etc. ; ciod a tha uaithe ? what does she want ? thoir uaithe, take from her. *See* uam.

uaithne, ua-niu, *n. m.* pillar, post, a column. *E.Ir.* úatne, a pillar.

uallach, ualuch, *n. m.* burden, charge ; in a moral sense, hard task ; chan uallach sin air, that is no hard task for him ; an oppressive weight, responsibility ; uallach a' ghnothaich, the responsibility of that affair. *Also* eallach.

uallach, *adj.* airy, light, indifferent as to weight ; thog e gu h-uallach, he raised it so cleverly, or lively ; conceited, light - headed, giddy ; duine uallach, a light-headed person ; " a' ghreigh uallach," the light, mettlesome flock ; " am breacan uallach," the gay, proud tartan ; fr. uaill.

uallach, *n. m.* a spirited fellow, a fop.

uallachag, *n. f.* a coquette.

uallachan, *n. m.* a little burden.

uallachas, uäll'-ach-us, *n. m.* conceitedness, vanity, airiness, cheerfulness.

uallachd, ualachc, *n. m.* extreme conceit, or vanity, or airiness ; cheerfulness.

uallaire, ualiru, *n. m.* coxcomb.

uam, oo-um, *prep.* +*pers. pron.* from me, wanted by me, at a distance from me ; fan uam, keep at a distance from me, keep from me ; gum bu fada sin uam, be that far from me ; emphatic uamsa. The *cpd.* with ua and o still obtain in common speech : *sing.* 1. (bh)uam, (bh)om, from me ; 2. (bh)uat, bhot, from thee ; 3. *m.* (bh)uaidhe, bhoidhe, from him ; 3. *f.* uaithe, uaipe, bhoithe, from her ; *pl.* 1. uainn, bhoinn, from us ; 2. uaibh, bhoibh, from you ; 3. uapa, uatha, bhoth, bhopa, from them. The om in bhom is sounded like om in tom, com ; in certain places the bh sounds like f.

uamh, uá, uäv, *n. f.* a cave, den. *O.Ir.* uam, huam, *specus.*

uamh, *n. m.* a chief of savages, terrible fellow ; chan 'eil ann ach uamh dhuine, he is only a savage of a fellow.

uamhach, uäv'-uch, *adj.* like a cave, abounding in caves.

uamhag, uá'-ag, *n. f.* tick, sheep-louse. *Also* seòllan.

uamhair, *n. m.* cave-man, a giant, a robber. *Also* uamhghair, famhair.

uamhann, *n. m.* horror, dread ; *a.* uamhannach. *O.Ir.* oman, úamun, *timor. W.* ofn. *Gaul.* -obnus, -omnus, fear. *O.Celt.* obno-s, omno-s. *Hr.*

uamharr, oo-av'-urr, *adj.* horrid, horrifying, shocking ; atrocious, heinous. *E.Ir.* úathmar ; fr. úath, fear.

uamharrachd, uäv'-urr-achc, *n. f.* horrifying nature or quality ; atrocity, heinousness.

uamhas, uavas, *n. m.* horrid deed, atrocity, horror, greatest astonishment, enormous quantity ; fhuair iad uamhas éisg, they have got an enormous quantity of fish. *E.Ir.* úathbhás, uath + bás, " dread death."

uamhasachd, ooa'-vàs-uchc, *n. f.* horrification, extreme atrocity ; · dreadfulness, horribleness, abominableness, loathsomeness.

uamhla, *n. f.* the deep sea = an object of dread.

uamhlach, *n. m.* " cave-dweller," a monster ; gach bòcan is uamhlach, each bogy and monster. *Duan.*

uamhraidh, *a.* gloomy, fearful, full of caves ; as *adv.* used to denote excess = " awfully " ; uamhraidh maith, exceedingly good.

uan, *n. m., gen.* and *pl.* uain, a lamb. So *M.Ir. W.* oen. *O.Celt.* ogno-s. *Lat.* agnus.

uanalach, *n. m.* lambs' wool.

uan-càisg, *n. m.* Paschal lamb.

uapa, ooupu, *prep.* +*pron.* from them, distant from them, wanted by them ; ciod a tha bhuapa ? what do they want ? tha bhuapa a bhi falbh, they had better be going. *See* uam.

uar, *n. m.* waterspout, shower, a landslip ; uaran, and fuaran, a spring of fresh water. *E.Ir.* úarán, fresh spring.

uarach, *a.* hourly, temporary, homely. *M.Ir.* temporary.

uas, *n. m.* college cap used when graduating.

uasal, *adj.* noble, descended of a noble family ; high rank ; of noble nature ; proud ; fastidious ; duine-uasal, a gentleman ; bean uasal, a lady, a gentlewoman ; tha e tuilleadh is uasal uime, he is too fastidious about it ; rinn thu do ghnothach gu h-uasal, you have done your business like a gentleman ; tha mi uasal asad, I am proud of you. *O.Ir.* uasal, high. *W.* uchel. *O.Celt.* oukselo-s.

uasal, *n. m., pl.* uaislean, a gentleman, a noble.

uath-, *prefix,* expression of dread. *O.Ir.* úath, frightful.

uatha, vua-hu, *prep.* +*pron.* from them, off their hands ; thoir uatha, deprive them of, bring from them. *See* uam.

uathbheist, *n. f.* monster.

uathchrith, *n. f.* a terror.

ub ! ubub ! *interj.* of aversion, contempt.

ubag, *n. f.* an enchantment, incantation,

charm, superstitious ceremony. *O.Ir.*
uptha, charms, filters.

ubagach, ŭb'-ag-ach, *adj.* skilled in charms, etc.

ubagail, ŭb'-ag-ul, *vbl. n. f.* enchanting.

ubaidh. Same meaning as ubag.

ùbairt, *n. f.* bustle, rummaging among heavy articles.

ùbarraid, oopurej, *n. f.* confusion, fidgeting; lumber, confusion. *Also* ùpraid.

ùbarraideach, ooburejuch, *a.* turbulent, confused, unsettled, romping, childish.

ubh, ubh, ûv, ûv, *inter.* O dear ! O dear ! my conscience ! expression of surprise, incredulity.

ubhal, oo-ul, *n. m.* an apple ; ubhal an sgornain, the ball of the throttle ; ubhal na sùa, pupil of the eye ; boss (of a shield) ; " lann sgriùbhta 'n a h-ubhal," a blade screwed into its boss. *E.Ir.* ubull, uball. *O.Ir.* aball.

ubhalach, u'-al-ach, *adj.* apple-bearing.

ubhladh, oolu, *n. m.* fine in church courts, ecclesiastical fine ; in civil courts, càinn. *See* unlagh.

ucas, ugsa, *n. m.* coal-fish, stenlock.

uchd, oochc, *n. m.* breast, bosom ; point, or very time ; ri uchd bàis, at the point of death ; clemency, mercy, humanity ; fàg gu uchd a' Mhoireir e, refer it to his lordship's clemency or humanity (cf. *Ir.* uacht, a will, testament ; uchd Dé, will of God) ; the face of a hill or ascent ; a' togail an uchd, ascending the face of a hill, steep part of a road ; ri uchd cruadail, facing difficulties, grappling with difficulties ; uchd-éideadh, breastplate. *Also* ochd, breast, bosom, lap. *O.Ir.* ucht. Cf. *Lat.* pectus. *O.Celt.* (p)uptu.

uchdach, *n. f.* an ascent or side of a hill ; a' togail na h-uchdaich, ascending the acclivity ; delivery in speech ; is ann aige tha 'n uchdach, how grand his delivery ! pith, energy ; chan 'eil uchdach aige dha, he has not energy to encounter such difficulty ; a creel-strap ; *adj.* prominent, steep.

uchdan, uchg'-an, *n. m.* the instep of a foot or shoe ; child's bib or pinny ; a little eminence or knoll ; a little terrace in a hillside ; chan 'eil uchdan gun ceann-mu-leathad, there is no ascent without an incline.

uchdardach, oochc-arduch, *adj.* high-crested ; bold, brave ; presumptuous.

uchdardachd, *n. f.* pomposity, presumptuousness, pomp.

uchdmhac, ochc-vac, *n. m.* an adopted son.

uchdmhacachd, ochc-vacachc, *n. f.* adoption ; uchdmhacaich, adopt, take another's son as your own.

uchdshnaidhm, *n. m.* a breast-knot.

ud, that, yon, yonder. *E.Ir.* út.

ùdabac, *n. m.* porch, an out-house, back-house.

udag, *n. f.* fluster, flutter, stew.

ùdail, ood'-al, *adj.* gloomy ; inhospitable, churlish ; *n. m.* churl.

udail, *v.* dangle, shake, rock, swing to and fro. *O.Ir.* utmall, unsteady.

udal, *n. m.* distraction for want of a home ; tossing about ; . dangling, swinging. *Also* uideal.

udalan, oodalan, *n. m.* tether-swivel.

udhachd, *n. f.* will, testament. *See* uthachd.

udhar, ooh'-ur, *n. m.* boil, ulcer, sore. *Also* othar.

ùdlachd, *n. f.* gloom.

ùdlaiche, ood-lichu, *n. m.* a stag, old hart.

ùdlaidh, oodly, *adj.* dark, gloomy. *M'F.*

udmhail, oodval, *n. f.* the state of being tossed from place to place, as a person ejected ; state of being absent, a pensioner on the bounty of others, as a person, once in good circumstances ; tossing from place to place ; chan fhaic mise air udmhail thu, I shall not see you a dependent or gentle beggar. *Also* wrongly udbhoil. *O.Ir.* utmall, restless.

udmhaileach, oodvaluch, *adj.* tossed from place to place, as a person.

ùdrathad, ootraj, *n. m.* free egress and regress to common pasture ; any road leading in from main road. *Also* and commonly ùtraid (*q.v.*).

uga, *n. m.,* gen. ugainn, *pl.* ugannan, collar-bone.

ugan, *n. m.* the fore part of the breast, the neck. *Ir.* ugán, craw of a fowl.

ugh, oo, *n. f.* (*gen.* uighe, *pl.* uighean), egg ; ugh-eireig, pullet's egg ; ugh-nid, a nest-egg ; gealagan uighe, the white of an egg ; buidheagan uighe, the yolk of an egg ; ugh mille fithich, and ugh maola feannaig, a tiny egg sometimes laid by a hen. *Also* ubh. *O.Ir.* og, *gen.* uge. *O.Celt.* ogos-.

ùghdair, oodur, *n. m.* an author. *E.Ir.* ugtar. *O.Ir.* augtor. *Lat.* auctor.

ùghdarrachd, ooduruchc, *n. f.* authorship.

ùghdarras, oodurus, *n. m.* authority, command ; a' teagasg mar neach aig am bheil ughdarras, teaching as one having authority.

ugsa, *n. f.* the largest kind of coal-fish ; *Sc.* stenlock. *Also* ucas.

uibe, wibu, *n. m.* a batch, or a lump of dough ; a block of anything, as marble ; lump of a person ; *a.* uibeach. *See* iob.

uibhir, ooyir, *n. f.* an equal quantity or number ; tha uibhir is uibhir aca, they have share and share alike ; **uibhir eile**, as much again ; **uibhir na circe**, the equivalent, or anything as valuable as a hen ; **na-h-uibhir**, a great number or quantity ; **uibhir ri càch**, as much as the rest ; **is e na h-uibhir e**, it is so much. *E.Ir.* numir, umir, number. *Lat.* numerus.

ùidh, ooy, *n. m.* heed, care ; intention, hope ; **gun ùidh ri sólas**, without hope of consolation. *O.Ir.* óid. Cf. **taidhe**.

ùidh, *n. f.* an isthmus ; a stream joining two lochs ; a stream ; mouth of a river. *O.N.* eið, an isthmus.

uidh, *n. f.* a journey, a way, a distance ; **uidh air an uidh**, by degrees ; **ceann-uidhe**, destination. *E.Ir.* ude. *O.Ir.* huide, *profectio.* *O.Celt.* (p)odio.

uidheam, ooyum, *n. f.* instrument, tools, apparatus ; rigging ; regimentals, uniform, accoutrements, equipage, materials ; **fo làn uidheam**, dressed in his full accoutrements or uniform ; **dhèanainn sin nam biodh uidheam agam**, I would do that, if I had materials, or tools, or apparatus. *E.Ir.* udim, a mechanical device, an article.

uidheamach, uyumuch, *adj.* well-furnished with materials or apparatus.

uidheamachadh, uyumuchu', *vbl. n. m.* act of preparing, arranging matters ; preparation, arrangement.

uidheamaich, uyumich, *v.* prepare, fit, arrange, furnish with necessary accoutrements, materials, or instruments ; equip ; **uidheamaich thu fhèin**, equip yourself, dress yourself.

uidheamaichte, *vbl. a.* equipped, prepared.

uidhir, *gen.* of odhar, dun coloured ; **Port Raghnaill uidhir**, Dun Ronald's tune.

uidil, *gen.* of udal. *A.M.*

ùig, ooig, *n. f.* a cove, a conical steep rock, nook. *O.N.* vík, bay, creek.

ùigean, *n. m.* a wanderer, a fugitive.

uigeanta, oogantu, *a.* awandering. *R.D.*

ùigheil, *a.* pleasant, careful ; from **aoigh** and **ùidh**.

uile, oolu, *adj. adv. n. m.* altogether, all, wholly, quite, every ; **tha iad mar sin uile**, they are all so ; **tha mi uile thoileach**, I am quite willing ; **uile-léirsinneach**, all-seeing ; **na h-uile**, every one, all, the whole ; **uile 's eile**, absolutely ; **chan ann am Bód uile tha an t-olc**, *all* the evil is not in Bute. *O.Ir.* uile, huile, ule. *O.Celt.* oljo-s.

uileann, oolunn, *n. f.* (*gen.* uilne, *pl.* uilnean), corner, angle, the elbow ; **uileann na beinne**, the angle or corner of the mountain ; **'nuair bha e air uilinn**, when he was embarrassed ; on the eve of failing. *M.Ir.* uille. *O.Ir.*

uile, *gen.* uilenn, elbow. *O.Celt.* olên-, olêno-. *W.* elin. *Lat.* ulna.

uilear, oolar, *adj.* too much, redundant, superfluous, unnecessary ; **cha b' uilear dhuit a bhi an so**, you would require to be here, it were not too much for you to be here ; **cha b' uilear dhuit sin**, you would require that, that is necessary ; **cha b' uilear uibhir eile**, as much again is requisite. *See* **fuilear**.

uile-bheannaichte, *adj.* truly blessed, all holy, completely blessed.

uilebheist, *n. m.* monster.

uile-bhuadhach, *adj.* all-victorious, triumphant, victorious.

uile-fhiosrach, *a.* omniscient.

uile-fhiosrachd, *n. m.* omniscience.

uile-fhoghainteach, *a.* all-sufficient.

uile-fhoghainteachd, all-sufficiency.

uile-iomlaineachd, *n. f.* all-sufficiency, full perfection or completeness.

uile-iomlan, *adj.* all-perfect.

uile-làthaireach, *adj.* omnipresent ; **tha Dia uile-làthaireach**, God is omnipresent.

ùill, ool, *v.* oil, grease, besmear.

ùilleadh, oolu, *n. m.* lamp-oil ; act of oiling. *Lat.* oleum.

uilleag, uylag, *n. f.* a jostle, elbowing.

uilleagaich, uylagich, *v.* jostle, elbow.

uilleagan, *n. m.* a petted, spoiled boy.

uilleann, uylun, *n. m.* honeysuckle. *M.Ir.* feithlend, woodbine.

ùillich, oolich, *v.* oil ; **ùillichte**, oiled.

ùillidh, ooly, *adj.* oily, greasy.

uilm, *n.* a coffer. *Carm-Gad.*

uilnich, uilnich, *v. t.* jostle, elbow.

uim-, circum-. *O.Ir.* imm-.

uime, eem'-u, *pre. +pro.* about, or around him, or it ; **agus chuir iad uime aodach purpuir**, and they put on him a purple robe ; of, or concerning him, or it ; **cia uime**, about whom, or concerning which ; **uime sin**, therefore, for that reason. *O.Ir.* uimbi. *See* **umam**.

uimpe, eemp'-à, *pron. +prep.* about her or it. *See* **umam**.

ùine, ooin, *n. f.* time, season, space, or interval, leisure ; **uine thrì laithean**, the space of three days ; **'nuair a bhios ùine agam**, when I have leisure. *E.Ir.* úine. *O.Ir.* úain, leisure, time.

ùinich, oonich, *n. f.* bustle, fumbling.

uinneag, oon'-ag, *n. f.* window. *M.Ir.* fuindeog. Cf. *N.* vindauga, wind-eye.

uinneagachadh, *n. m.* dawn ; act of dawning.

uinneagaich, *v. i.* dawn, begin to dawn ; **'nuair a bha an latha ag uinneagachadh**, when the day began to dawn.

uinnean, oon'-un, *n. m.* an onion. *M.Ir.* uinneamain.

uinnean, *n. m.* the ankle ; corn on the foot.

ùinnleag, *n. f.* a poke, a dig with one's elbow. *R.D.*

uinnse, uinshu, *n. f.* ash-tree ; an ash.

uinnseann, uinshun, *n. m.* wood of the ash - tree. *M.Ir.* fuindseog. *O.Ir.* huinnius, gl. fraxinus. *O.Celt.* onnâ, onnestu-, ash.

uinnsich, uinshich, *v.* manage.

uipear, for uaipear, *n. m.* bungler, botcher.

uipinn, eep'-ènn, *n. f.* hoard, treasure.

ùir, oor, *n. f., gen.* ùrach, mould, dust, earth, transf. meaning—grave-mould ; cáirich 'san ùir, bury, inter ; fo'n ùir, under the soil, in the grave. *E.Ir.* úr. *O.Celt.* urâ.

uircean, oorken, *n. m.* grice, a young pig. *O.Ir.* orc, oircnín (gl. porcellus). *O.Celt.* (p)orko-s. *Lat.* porcus.

uircheann, *n. m.* projecting point, at top end of a box acting as hinge for the lid. *Also* foircheanni. *E.Ir.* forcend. *Wi.*

ùiread, oorud, *abstr. n. f.* newness.

uiread, as much as, much. *O.Ir.* erat, airet, space of time or distance.

uireall, ooral, *n. m.* a ferrule, a ring.

uireallach, ooraluch, *n. m.* a dagger ; dirk.

uireas, ooras, *n. f.* want, necessary, family or domestic necessary ; a maim ; a' dol air son uireasan, going for little family necessaries.

uireasach, *adj.* indispensable, very much wanted ; ni uireasach, a thing very much wanted ; defective, maimed, lame ; duine uireasach, a maimed person.

uireasaich, ooresich, *n. f.* want, necessary ; uireasaich 'sam bith a tha ort, any necessary you want ; defect, maim, deficiency.

uireasuidh, uireasbhuidh, ooresy, *n. f.* want. *M.Ir.* auresbadh (air + easbhuidh).

uiridh, oory, *n. f.* last year ; an uiridh, last year ; am bliadhna 's an uiridh, this and last year. *E.Ir.* inn uraid. *O.Ir.* urid.

uirigh, oory, *n. f.* pallet, couch ; 'na laighe air uirigh, stretched on a pallet.

uirigioll, uirghiol, oor-yul, *n. m.* utterance, speech, eloquence, talk, conversation. *E.Ir.* uirgill.

uirigleadh, *vbl. n. m.* act of speaking, talking, conversing.

uiriollach, oor-yuluch, *n. m.* a precipice, based on ail, rock.

uirlios, oorlis, *n. m.* walled garden.

ùirneis, oornesh, *n. f.* a furnace. *M.Ir.* fòrneis.

ùirneis, *n. f.* tools, implements. *See* àirneis.

ùirneisich, *v.* furnish, adorn.

uirsgeil, *n. m.* a spreading (dung, or hay).

uirsgeuł, oor'-skell, *n. m.* news, intelligence, tale, fable, novel, romance ; blarney ; air (*intens.*) + sgeul (tale).

uirsgeulach, oorsceluch, *a.* fabulous.

ùis, oosh, *n. f.* courteous reception, hospitality carried to excess almost ; unnecessary hurry-burry at one's reception ; 's ann rompa bha an ùis, they met with a most courteous reception.

ùis, *n. f.* use, utility ; *a.* uiseil. *Eng.* use. *Lat.* ūsus.

uiseag, ooshag, *n. f.* a lark, a skylark. *Ir.* uiseóg, fuiseóg. *M.Ir.* fuissi, uissi. *O.Ir.* fuiseóg, alauda.

ùisealachd, ooshaluchc, *n. f.* courtesy, courteousness, highest degree of hospitality ; usefulness ; dignity ; snugness, comfort.

ùiseil, ooshal, *adj.* courteous, kind, hospitable in the highest degree imaginable ; gu h-ùiseil, entertained with the utmost hospitality and courtesy ; useful, snug, dignified. *E.Ir.* uisse, dutiful.

uisge, ooshcu, *n. m.* water, rain ; billow, a wave ; fo'n uisge, under water, immersed ; a river, stream ; mar uisge balbh a' ghlinne, like the still stream of the valley ; uisge-beatha, whisky, aqua vitae ; uisge-coisrig, holy or consecrated water. *O.Ir.* uisce, usce.

uisgeachadh, ooshcuchu, *vbl. n. m.* act of raining, watering ; ag uisgeachadh na talmhainn, watering the earth ; irrigation, or watering of land.

uisgealachd, ooshcaluchc, *n. f.* wateriness.

uisgeil, ooshcal, *adj.* watering, irrigating.

uisgichte, ooscuchtu, *vbl. a.* watered, irrigated.

uisgidh, ooshcy, *adj.* watery, waterish.

uisgidheachd. Same as uisgealachd.

ùisinnich, ooshinich, *v.* use. *Also* cleachd.

uisliginn, ooshligin, *n. f.* confusion, disturbance, fury.

uislinn, ooshlin, *n. f.* sport, diversion. *Ir.* uslainn.

uist, oosht, *inter.* hist ! hold your peace ! not a word !

ula, *n. m., pl.* ulachan, a beard ; heavy curled hair, rank grass, brushwood. *E.Ir.* ulcha, *g.* ulchain.

ula, a mound (over a grave). *E.Ir.* ulad, monument.

ulag, *n. f.* a block, a pulley.

ulag, *n. f.* oatmeal and water made into dry dough, often used as a viaticum. *See* ullag.

ulaich, *oblique c.* of ula, rank grass.

ulaidh, ooly, *n. f.* a hid treasure ; darling.

ulainn, oolin, *n. m.* charnel-house.

ùlamh, *n. m.* choice treasure, something priceless.

ulartaich, oolartich, *n. f.* howling, wailing. *Also* ulfhartaich.

ulbh, oolv, *interj.* you brute! Cf. *O.N.* úlfr, wolf.

ulbhach, oolvuch, *coll. n.* ashes. Cf. *Lat.* pulvis.

ulbhag, oolvag, *n. f.* a boulder larger than one man can handle. *Also* bulbhag.

ullabheist, *n. f.* a monster. *See* uile-bheist.

ullabheisteil, *adj.* monstrous.

ullachadh, ulmhachadh, ooll′ - uch - u, *vbl. n. m.* act of dressing, making ready ; preparation, act of appointing, or making a provision.

ullag. *See* ulag. Ingredients varied : oat-meal + water or milk or whisky ; barley-meal + hot water + salt.

ullag shneachda, snow ball.

ullaich, oolich, *v.* prepare, make ready, provide ; =ullamhich.

ullaid, ulej, *n. f.* the screech owl.

ullamhachd, ooluvachc, *n. m.* preparedness, readiness, proneness, completion.

ullamh, ooluv, *adj.* ready, ambidextrous, prepared ; finished with ; prone ; is ullamh le neach, one is prone or ready ; airgiod ullamh, cash, ready money. *E.Ir.* erlam (air + làmh). *O.Ir.* urlam, irlam.

ullamh, *n. m.* a doctor ; high degree in learning ; a sage ; better ollamh. *Ir.* ullamh, ollamh. *O.Ir.* ollam, chief poet.

ullamhaich, ool′ich, *v.* Same as ùllaich.

ulpag, *n. f.* a somewhat biggish stone.

ultach, ooltuch, *n. m.* an armful of any thing ; as much of a load as one can carry in his arms ; a burden for one's back ; ultach a dhroma, as much as he can carry on his back. *M.Ir.* utlach, lapful.

Ultach, ooltuch, *n. m.* an Ulster man.

ultach, *n. m.* a stag.

ultaiche, *n. m.* a lone traveller.

ultanaich, *n. f.* moor grass, deer's hair grass.

umad, oomud, *prep. + pron.* about thee, concerning thee, in reference to thee ; tilg t′ fhallainn umad, throw or cast your mantle about thee ; a′ labhairt umad, speaking about thee. *See* umam.

umaibh, oomuv, *prep. + pron.* about you, in reference to you, or regarding you ; concerning you ; cuiribh umaibh, put on (clothes) ; labhairt umaibh, speaking concerning you. *See* umam.

ùmaidh, oomy, *n. m.* a dolt, a blockhead, a fool ; a brutish person.

umailt, oomilt, *n. f.* a degrading submission of one's judgment to curry favour ; obsequiousness.

umailteach, oomiltuch, *adj.* meanly submissive to curry favour ; fawning.

umainn, oomin, *prep. + pron.* about us, concerning us, etc. ; dh′ iadh iad umainn, they surrounded us ; ag ràdh umainn, saying in reference to us, or concerning us. *See* umam.

umam, oomum, *prep.* um + *pers. pron.* mi, about or regarding me ; an ann umam-sa ? is it about me ? is it in reference to me ? Cpds. : *sing.* 1. umam, about me, 2. umad, about thee, 3. *m.* uime, about him, 3. *f.* uimpe, about her ; *pl.* 1. umainn, about us, 2. umaibh, about you, 3. umpa, about them.

umarlaid, *n. f.* a vulgar, bulky female.

umbadail, oomudal, *adj.* very stupid.

ùmbaidh, oomy, *n. m.* a blockhead, dolt. *See* ùmaidh.

umha, *n. m.* brass or copper. *O.Ir.* humae, ume, ccpper, brass. *W.* efydd. *O.Celt.* umájo-.

umhadair, oo′-uder, *n. m.* brazier.

umhail, oo′il, *n. f.* heed, attention, consideration ; na biodh umhail agad deth, never mind him ; gun umhail do ′n lot ′na chliabh fèin, regardless of the wound in his own side ; half-suspicion ; chuir mi an umhail, I half-suspected ; ciod umhail a th′agadsa ? what do you care ? what matters it to you ? *O.Ir.* umaldóit. *W.* ufyll. *Lat.* humilitas.

umhail, umha, *adj.* obedient, submissive, lowly, humble. *O.Ir.* umal, *Lat.* humilis.

ùmhaillt. *See* ùmaillt.

ùmhailteas, *n. m.* obedience, humility.

ùmhlachd, oolachc, *n. f.* obeisance, salutation, homage ; dèan t′ ùmhlachd, make your obeisance, make homage ; obedience, submissiveness ; rinn e ùmhlachd dhà, he saluted him, he bowed to him. *O.Ir.* humaldóit, omaldóit, fr. *Lat.* humilitas.

ùmhlaich, oolich, *v.* submit, obey, make humble or submissive to rule.

ùmhlaidh. *See* úbhlaidh.

umpa, oompu, *prep. + pron.* about them, in reference to them, concerning them ; labhair e umpa, he spoke in reference to them. *See* umam.

ùmpaidh, *n. m.* a boor, a clown, idiot. *See* ùmaidh.

ùng, oong, *v.* anoint, oil ; dh′ ùng thu mo cheann, thou hast anointed my head. *O.Ir.* ongim. *Lat.* unguo.

ùnga, *n. m.* ounce-land, twenty-penny land, one-eighth mark-land.

ùnga, *n. m.* brass, copper.

ùngadh, oongu, *n. f.* ointment, unction ; *vbl. n.* act of anointing.
ungaidh, *a.* mouldy, musty. *Also* tung-aidh.
unlagh, *n. m.* a fine, a penalty.
unnsa, oonsu, *n. m.* an ounce. *O.Ir.* unga. *O.F.* unce. *Lat.* uncia.
unntas. *See* iunntas.
ùnradh, *n. m.* adversity. *See* anradh.
untas, oontas, *n. m.* windlass, a winch.
ùp, oop, *v.* push, jostle, shove.
ùpadh, *m.* a push ; *dim.* ùpag.
ùprait, confusion, etc. *See* ùbarraid.
ùr, oor, *adj.* new, fresh, recent ; a' gheal-ach ùr, the new moon ; novel, curious ; ni sam bith ùr, anything novel or curious ; as ùr, a second time, again, anew, afresh ; thòisich iad as ùr, they commenced anew ; oiteag ùr nan sliabh, the fresh breeze of the mountains ; ùr nodha, quite new ; *adv.* afresh, newly, second time ; dh'ùr-thòisich iad, they have newly begun. *E.Ir.* úr. *O.Ir.* húrde.
'ur, for bhur, your ; togaibh 'ur siuil, hoist your sails. *See* ar.
urabhallach, ùr'-a-văllach, *n. f.* the herb devil's bit.
ùrach, ooruch, *n. m.* bottle, pail.
ùrach, *gen.* of ùir, mould, soil, earth ; a' bùrrach na h-ùrach, stirring up the mound or earth.
ùrach, *a.* earthy. *Also gen. s.* of ùir.
ùrachadh, ooruchu, *vbl. n. m.* act of renewing, refreshing ; refreshment, renewal, recommencement.
ùrachd, oorachc, *n. f.* newness, novelty.
urad, oorud. *n. m. adv.* equal quantity, or number ; so much ; urad is urad, equal shares, like quantities ; urad eile, as much again ; urad a bhìdh, so much as a meal of meat.
urad, *adv.* above. *E.Ir.* aur-árd, very high. *Also* thurad.
ùrad, *n. m.* newness.
ùradh, *n. m.* oil, grease (in wool) ; stale urine.
ùraich, oorich, *v.* renew, become fresh or green ; dh' ùraich e mo chràdh, he renewed my torment ; refresh, invigorate ; dh' ùraich an deoch e, the potions refreshed him, invigorated him.
uraidh, *adv.* last year. *O.Ir.* uraid. *O.Celt.* (p)eruti.
uraigleadh, *n. m.* speech, utterance. *Also* uirigleadh.
ùrail, ooral, urair, oorar, *adj.* fresh-looking, as a person ; flourishing, green, gay ; a' choillteach ùrair, the green woodland.
ùraireachd, oorurachc, ùralachd, ooral-uchc, *n. f.* freshness, youthfulness, as an aged person.

uraisg, *n. f.* a brownie, a monster. *Also* urraisg.
ùranach, ooranuch, *n. m.* an upstart.
urball, *n. m.* a tail, a train.
urbhailteach, *a.* cheerful, jolly, jocular. *Also* urfhailteach.
ùr-bheachd, *n. m.* second thought.
ùr-bhlàth, *n. m.* a blossom, a flower.
ùr-bhreith, *n. f.* new birth, the newly born. *See* ath-bhreith.
urcag, *n. f.* a thole pin.
urchaill, uruchill, *n. f.* fetters ; chain ; mould-board of a plough. *Also* ur-chair. *O.Ir.* urchomal, fetter for fore-feet of a horse.
urchair, ooruchar, *n. f., gen.* urchrach, *pl.* urchraichean, a shot ; leig urchair, fire, shoot at ; a throw, cast, violent push or jostle; urchair cloiche, measure of distance, a stone-cast ; thug e urchair dha a mach as an tigh, he "fired" him out of the house. ur, air (*intens. prefix*)+cor (cast). *E.Ir.* urchur, aurchur, erchor. *O.Celt.* (p)arei-koru-.
urchasg, *n. m.* antidote ; physic.
urchoid, oorchoj, *n. f* harm ; calamity. *O.Ir.* erchoit, harm ; mischief.
ùrchoill, *n. f., pl.* -tean, green wood.
urchra, urchradh, *n. m.* great distress, excessive grief. ur (*intens.*) +cràdh (pain).
ùrchrann, *n. m.* fresh green tree.
ùr-fhàs, *n. m.* sprout, bloom, the.
urla, oorla, *n. m.* face or front hair, breast ; cas-urlach, frowzy. *E.Ir.* urla, irla, erla.
urlabhairt, oor-lavurt, *n. f.* eloquence. *O.Ir.* aur-labra, erlabra, urlabra. ur (*intens.*) +labar (speech).
ùrlach, *n. m.* a stag.
ùrlaich, *v.* nauseate, detest, turn away in disgust.
ùrlaim, oorlam, *n. f.* readiness. *O.Ir.* erlam, irlam.
ùrlaimh, *adj.* neat, ready, expert.
ùrlamhachas, ùrlamhas, *n. m.* possession.
ùrlann, oorlan, *n. m.* the butt of a spear, a sort of staff. So *M.Ir.*
ùrlaoidh, *n. f.* a lay of excessive beauty, a charming ballad ; sweet singing.
ùrlar, oorlar, *n. m.* floor ; air an ùrlar, on the floor ; a layer, or course, vein, as in a mine; cuir ùrlar mù seach 'san dùnan, put a layer, or course about in the dunghill. air (*intens.*) +làr.
ùrloinn, oorloyn, *n. f.* beauty. ùr, air (*intens.*) +loinn (grace).
ùrloinn, *n. f.* the face, the prow of a ship.
ùrnais, *n. f.* furniture.
ùrnuigh, oorny, *n. f.* entreaty ; prayer to God ; dèan ùrnuigh, pray ; ag ùrnuigh, praying. *O.Ir.* irnigde, ir-nichte. *B.D.* ernacde.

urr, oor, *n. m.* a child, infant.

urra, ooru, *n. f.* a responsible person, a guarantor ; a personage ; an tigh urra mhóir, in a great personage's house ; author, authority ; có 's urra dhuit, who is your authority ? chan 'eil sgeul gun urra agam, my story is not without authority ; owner, proprietor ; có 's urra dha so ? who is owner or proprietor of this ? cha robh caora riamh gun urra, a sheep never wanted an owner ; capable ; nam b' urra mi, were I capable ; ma's urra mise, cha bhi dìth ortsa, if I am " a fit guarantor " you will not be in want. *Also* urradh, urrainn. *M.Ir.* errudus, responsibility. *Cf.* ràth, ràthan.

urracag, *n. f.* thole pin, timber head.

urrach, ooruch, *n. m.* power, ability.

urrachd, oorachc, *n. m.* dependence, reliance ; cha ruig thu leas urrachd sam bith a dhèanadh as an sin, you need not put any reliance in that ; an urrachd a chosnaidh, depending on his daily labour or industry ; chan 'eil mi urrach, I am not qualified, or capable.

urrad. *See* urad.

urradh, urrainn, oorin, *n.* ability, power, author ; chan 'eil mi am urrainn, I am not fit ; an urrainn iad, are they able ? ni mi na's urrainn mi, I will do all I am capable of doing, all I can.

urrag, *n. f.* an infant, a little girl ; *dim.* of urra.

ùrraic, *a.* excellent, notably good. *R.D.*

urrail, ooral, *adj.* self-sufficient, forward, bold ; fr. urra.

urrainn, *n. m.* a capable person. *See* urra.

urraisg, *n. m.* a monster, a savage, a witless blunderer ; nach bu tu an t-urraisg ! what a monster you are ! what a fool you are !

urralachd, ooraluchc, *n. f.* self-sufficiency.

urram, oorum, *n. f.* and *m.* respect, reverence, deference ; air son urram do t'fhacalsa, out of deference to your word ; dignity, honour ; precedence, superiority, preference ; bheir mi an t-urram dhuit thar na chunnaic mi, I will give you preference above all I ever saw, you excel all I ever saw. *M.Ir.* urraim, homage.

urramach, oorumuch, *adj.* honourable, respectable, reverend, powerful, dignified, worshipful, distinguished ; honorary ; principal ; sibhse as urramaiche de'n treud, you which are the principal of the flock ; respectful, submissive ; tha ainm urramach, his name is reverenced, is distinguished ; rinn e gu h-urramach, he did it masterly, he did it in a respectable manner.

urramachd, oorumuchc, *n. f.* honourableness, reverence, respectability, homage.

urramaich, oorumich, *v.* reverence, distinguish, honour, revere, respect.

urranta, oorantu, *adj.* self-sufficient, self-important ; confident in strength or capacity ; bold.

urrantachd, oorantuchc, *n. f.* self-sufficiency, self-confidence, audacity, presumption.

urras, ooras, *n. m.* surety, security, bail, cautioner, warrant ; có théid an urras ort, who will become security, or cautioner, or bail for you ? chan fheàrr an t-urras na'n t-earras, the security or bail is not a whit better than the principal ; quality, courage ; fr. urra.

urrasach, oorasuch, *adj.* secure, sure.

urrasachd, *n. f.* trustworthiness ; assumption.

urrasaich, oorasich, *v.* insure ; go bail.

urrasail, oorasl, *adj.* confident, secure.

urrasair, ooruser, *n. m.* insurer, guarantor.

urruisge, *n. m.* excess of water ; spate, overflow, inundation.

ursann, oorsun, *n. f.* door-post, pillar of a gate ; door-cheek ; ursannan, door-posts, or pillars of a gate. *E.Ir.* ursa, aursa, irsa, a post, door-post.

ursann-chatha, *n. m.* a champion.

ursgath, *n. m.* excessive shyness, fear.

ursgeul, *n. m.* a tale, a fable, a romantic tale ; ur, air (*intens.*) + sgeul = " some " story.

urstan, *n. m.* birthday feast. *Also* nurstan.

ùruisg, oorushc, *n. f.* a water being, that lives in burns and rivers ; every burn in Breadalbane had an ùruisg once, and their king was Peallaidh, whence Obar-pheallaidh, Aberfeldy. *Watson.*

us, oos, *n. m.* impudence, presumption ; na biodh a dh' us agad, presume not, dare not.

usa, oosu, for asa or fasa ; *deg.* of furasd. *O.Ir.* asse, *facilis,* assu, *facilius.*

usachd, *n. f.* easiness, facility.

usaid, oosej, *n. f.* querulousness ; aptness to complain with any, or for a very slight reason.

usaideach, oosejuch, *adj.* querulous ; too apt to complain ; querimonious.

usaideachd, oosejuchc, *n. f.* querulousness ; aptness to complain, or to weep for little or no reason ; querimoniousness.

usgar, ooscar, *n. f., gen.* usgrach, *pl.* usgraichean, a jewel, gem ; any ornament, necklace, bracelet, bell on liquor.

usgaraiche, ooscarichu, *n. m.* a jeweller.

uspag, *n. f.* a push, a pang, a squall of wind ; a shying of a horse.

uspair, oosper, *n. m.* lumpish fellow.

ùspairn, *n. f.* strife, struggle.

uspairneachd, *n. f.* striving, struggling.

ùspairt, *n. f.* strife, contest (of battle) ; **an àm na h-ùspairt,** at the moment of battle. *Duan.* Same as **uspairn.**

uspan, *n. m.* a shapeless mass.

uspann, *n. f.* argumentation, compelling assent.

ùspunn, noise, strife. (*R.D.*) ; form of **uspairn.**

ut ! ut ! *inter.* tut ! tut ! don't !

ut, oot, *v.* push, shove, jostle ; **dh' ut e bhuaidh e,** he pushed him away from him ; **ut i,** shove her. *Also* **put.**

utag, ootag, *n. f.* shove, push, jostle. *Also* **ùtag.**

utaig, ootig, *n. f.* strife, outrage, hubbub, row ; lumber, confusion.

utaigeach, ootiguch, *adj.* turbulent.

utaigeachd, *n. f.* turbulence.

utan, ootan, *n. m.* knuckle. *Also* **riuidean, ródan.**

ùtarras, ooturas, *n. m.* confused heap or mass ; romping ; lumber, confusion ; annoyance, molestation, fidgeting.

utarrasach, *a.* confused, romping, full of lumber, unsettled.

ùth, oo, *n. m., pl.* **ùthannan,** udder ; **ùth boine,** cow's udder. *E.Ir.* **úth.** *O.Celt.* (p)utu-.

uthachd, oo-hachc, *n. f.* suicide ; **thug e uthachd dha fhéin,** he committed suicide, he was the cause of his own death, manslaughter. *Ir.* **udhacht, uadhacht,** bequest. *E.Ir.* **audacht** = **úath** + **feacht,** death-time. *Corm.*

uthachdail, oo-hachcal, *a.* suicidal.

uthar, *n. m.* the dog-days.

uthard, oo-hard, *adv.* above, on high. *Ir.* **ós árd.**

ùtraid, *n. f.* a side-road, a branch-road serving a village. *O.N.* **útarr** (outer) + **stræti** (street).

ùtrais, *n. f.* fidgeting, restlessness, busy among a mass of stuff ; confused mass ; rubbish.

utras, contraction of **ùtarras,** confusion.

ENGLISH-GAELIC DICTIONARY

A

a, an *art.* not translated, there being no *indef. art.* in Gaelic.

aback, *adv.* air ais ; seub ; na seub i, do not let the wind into back of sail.

abacus, *s.* clàr-cunntais; clach-mhullaich.

abaft, *also* **aft,** *adv.* 'n a deireadh, 's an deireadh (of ship).

abaisance, *s.* umhlachd, urram.

abandon, *v. n.* fàg, dìobair, tréig, fàg air a dhlò ; leig reachad.

abandoned, *part.* tréigte, air a dhlò.

abase, *v. a.* ìslich, leag, irioslaich.

abasement, *s.* ìsleachadh, irioslachadh, leagail sìos ; eas-urram, tàir.

abash, *v. a.* nàraich, athaich.

abashment, *s.* breisleachadh, maslachadh.

abate, *v. tr.* lùghdaich, beagaich, traogh.

abatement, *s.* lùghdachadh, traoghadh, leigeadh fodha (of a storm), ìsleachadh (of price).

abb, *m.* inneach, cura, snàth-cùra.

abba, *s.* athair.

abbacy, *s.* dreuchd aba ; ùghdaras aba.

abbess, *s.* ban-aba ; ban-uachdaran aba.

abbey, *s.* abaid, tigh-mhanach, tigh chailleacha-dubha.

abbot, *s.* aba, ceann-abaid, uachdaran aba.

abbreviate, *v. a.* giorrach, ath-ghiorraich.

abbreviation, *s.* giorrachadh.

abdicate, *v. a.* leig dhìot (do dhreuchd), thoir thairis (do chòir).

abdication, *s.* toirt suas, toirt thairis —.

abdomen, *s.* iochdar a' chuirp, broinn, àite a' mhionaich ; com.

abdominal, *adj.* a bhuineas do'n bhroinn.

abdominous, *adj.* bronnach.

abduct, *v.* thoir leat le fòir-éigin ; goid (duine).

abduction, *s.* toirt air falbh (an-dligheach) gadachd pearsa (le ainneart).

abecedarian, *s.* aineolas ; foghlumaiche (air an a, b, c,) : dàn le rainn fo rian litrichean na h-aibidil, *e.g. Salm* 119.

abed, *adv.* air leabaidh, 'n a laighe.

aberrance, *s.* seachran, iomrall, mearachd claonadh (o'n chòir).

aberrant, *adj.* seachranach ; mearachdach.

abet, *v. a.* brosnaich (gu eucoir) ; cuidich ('s an olc) ; thoir fasgath (do'n eucorach).

abetment, *s.* brosnachadh, cuideachadh, co-chòrdadh ('s an olc).

abettor, *s.* fear-brosnachaidh, fear-cuideachaidh, fear-comhairle ('s an olc).

abeyance, *s.* diomhain, **work is in abeyance,** tha an obair diomhain ; bàn, fàs, **land in abeyance,** talamh bàn.

abhor, *v. a.* sgreataich, fuathaich.

abhorrence, *s.* sgreamh, dù-ghràin.

abhorrent, *adj.* fuathach, gràineil, sgreataidh.

abhorring, *s.* fuathachadh.

abide, *v. a.* and *n.* fan, fuirich, comhnuich, buanaich, mair, feith.

abiding, *v. n.* fuireach, fantainn, tàmh, feitheamh.

ability, *s.* comas, cumhachd, buadh, tàlant.

abilities, *s.* càileachd, comas-inntinn, buadhan, ceudfaidhean.

abject, *adj.* suarach, dìblidh, bochd, truaillidh, tàireil, meallta.

abjection, *s.* tromachas inntinn ; suarachas, tràillealachd.

abjuration, *s.* toirt seachad ; leigeil as (fo mhionnaibh) ; àicheadh : abjuration oath, cùl-mhionnan.

abjure, *v. a.* àicheadh, cuir cùl (ri beachd).

ablation, *s.* tabhairt air falbh (le lannsa) ; bleith, cnàmh (le deigh no uisge).

able, *adj.* comasach, teòma, sgileil, ceudfaidheach.

able-bodied, *adj.* treun, calma, tapaidh, foghainteach, inbhe maraiche.

ablings, ablins, aiblins, *adv.* theagamh, 's dòcha.

ablocation, *s.* suidheachadh, no leigeil a mach air mhàl.

ablution, *s.* ionnlad, glanadh ; nighe, fairceadh, saoradh o chiont.

abnegate, *v. a.* àicheadh, diùlt, seachain, cuir seachad (ort fhéin).

abnegation, *s.* àicheadh, diùltadh, féin-àicheadh.

abnormal, *adj.* neo-àbhaiseach, mì-nàdurach, ainneamh.

aboard, *adv.* air bòrd luinge.

abode, *s.* àite-còmhnaidh, tigh, dachaigh.

abolish, *v. a.* thoir thairis ; cuir as, cur air chùl.

abolishable, *adj.* a dh' fhaodar a chur as, no a sgrios.

abolition, *s.* sgaoileadh, atharrachadh, sgrios, cur as.

abominable, *adj.* gràineil, fuathmhor, sgreamhail, sgreataidh.

abominate, *v. a.* fuathaich, oilltich.

abomination, *s.* gràinealachd, dù-ghràin.

aborigines, *s.* luchd-gné (àite) ; cheud-luchd-àitich.

abortion, *s.* torrachas anabaich.

abortive, *adj.* anabaich, neo-inbheach, gu diomhain.

abound, *v. n.* fas lìonmhor, fàs sìolmhor, siolaich, sìr-bhuanaich (in activity).

about, *prep.* mu, mun cuairt, about ten thousand, mu dheich mìle ; they were speaking about you, bha iad a' bruidhinn mu d' dhéighinn ; about him, uime, mun cuairt da, mu thimchioll, mu dhéidhinn ; about them, umpa, mun cuairt daibh ; about her, uimpe, mun cuairt di, mu déidhinn, mu timchioll ; about whom ? cia uime ? cò mu dhéidhinn ?

about, *adv.* an cuairt, gu cruinn ; ceithir thimchioll, mun cuairt ; fagus air ; air tì, gu ; timchioll, toirt gu crìch ; gu buil, gu teachd ; ag iarraidh.

above, *prep.* os cionn, suas, tuilleadh is—, a bharr.

above, *adv.* shuas, gu h-àrd, a bharrachd.

above all, *adv.* os bàrr, gu h-àraidh.

above-board, *adv.* os cionn bùird, gu follaiseach.

abrade, *v. a.* suath dheth, suath air falbh, sgrìob as ; sgiol.

abreast, *adv.* gualainn ri gualainn.

abridge, *v. a.* giorraich, lughdaich.

abroad, *adv.* mu sgaoil ; a muigh, a mach ; air aineol, an tìr chéin ; an tìr thall, do thìr chéin ; air gach taobh ; an leth muigh.

abrogate, *v. a.* cuir air chùl, cuir a leth-taobh, cur mu làimh, cur as.

abrupt, *adj.* cas, corrach, creagach ; aithghearr, grad, cabhagach, gun uidheamachadh ; briste.

abruption, *s.* gradbhriseadh.

abruptness, *s.* cabhag, caise, corrachas.

abscess, *s.* neasgaid, at, iongrachadh.

abscind, *v. a.* gearr dheth, gearr air falbh.

abscission, *s.* gearradh dheth, sgudadh.

abscond, *v. a.* and *n.* falaich thu féin, teich air fògradh, gabh an saoghal fo do cheann.

absconder, *s.* fògarach, fear-cùirn, fear fo choill.

absence, *s.* neo-làthaireachd ; neo-aire.

absent, *adj.* neo-làthaireach, neo-aireach, smuain-sheachranach.

absent, *v. a.* rach o'n tigh, cùm as an t-sealladh.

absentee, *s.* neach a ta air falbh o dhùthaich.

absinthiated, *part.* searbhaichte.

absinthium, *s.* lus-nam-biast, burmaid.

absolute, *adj.* iomlan, coimhlionta, saor, gun chumha ; os cionn lagh is riaghailt, a muigh 's a mach.

absoluteness, *s.* iomlanachd, dligheachas, àrd-chumhachd.

absolution, *s.* saoradh, mathanas, fuasgladh.

absolutory, *adj.* a shaoras, a dh' fhuasglas, a mhathas.

absolve, *v. a.* saor, math, fuasgail, crìochnaich.

absonant, *adj.* mì-chéillidh, baoth.

absonous, *adj.* neo-bhinn, searbhghuthach, searbhghlòireach.

absorb, *v. a.* sluig, deothail, òl, sùigh.

absorbent, *adj.* a shluigeas, a shùghas, a dh'òlas.

absorbent, *s.* leigheas sùghaidh, acfhuinn tiormachaidh — thiormaicheas leannt-aidhean a' chuirp.

absorption, *s.* tiormachadh, sùghadh, slugadh.

abstain, *v. a.* seachain, seun, fàg ; na gabh, àicheadh thu féin.

abstemious, *adj.* stuama, measarra.

abstemiousness, *s.* stuaim, measarrachd.

abstergent, *a.* and *n.* a ghlanas, stuth glanaidh.

abstinence, *s.* measarrachd, stuamachd.

abstinent, *adj.* stuama, measarra.

abstract, *v. a.* tarruing a bhrìgh as, thoir a shùgh as ; thoir a mach, glan.

abstract, *adj.* eadar-dhealaichte, sgairte ; dorch, deacair r'a thuigsinn ; neo-mheasgaichte, buaidh, neo-fhaicsinneach.

abstract, *s.* suim, brìgh ; sùmhlachadh, aith-ghiorrachadh.

abstraction, *s.* dealachadh, eadar-dheal-achadh, brìgh-tharruing ; neo-aire do nithibh 's an làthair.

abstruse, *adj.* doilleir, falachaidh, do-thuigsinn, deacair.

abstruseness, *s.* doilleireachd, doimh-neachd, deacaireachd.

absurd, *adj.* amaideach, baoth, mì-reusonta, gun tonaisg.

absurdity, *s.* amaideachd, baoghaltas faoinealachd.

ABSURDLY—ACCUMULATE

369

absurdly, adv. gu mì-reusonta, mì-chiall-ach, gòrach.

abundance, s. pailteas, lìonmhorachd.

abundant, adj. pailt, saoibhir, làn.

abundantly, adv. gu pailt, gu saoibhir.

abuse, v. a. mì-ghnàthaich, mì-bhuilich ; meall, gabh brath ; thoir ana-cainnt, maslaich, trod, càin, beum.

abuse, s. mì-ghnàthachadh, mì-bhuil-eachadh, ana-caitheamh ; càineadh, trod, ana-cainnt.

abuser, s. milltear, struidhear ; fear-càinidh, fear ana-cainnt.

abusive, adj. millteach, strùidheil, ana-caithteach ; ana-cainnteach.

abuttal, s. crìoch, garradh-crìch fearainn ; sgrìobhadh anns a bheil crìochan air an ainmeachadh.

abutment, s. co-chrìoch, cul-taic.

abyss, s. doimhneachd gun ìochdar dubh-aigean ; ifrinn, aibhis.

academic, s. fòghlumach, feallsonach, fear òil-thigh.

academic, adj. a bhuineas do òil-thigh, fuar, geòireanach, déidheil air dearbh-adh, — air còmhdach.

academy, s. an lios anns am biodh Plato a' teagasg ; sgoil ard ; comunn litre-achais.

accede, v. n. aontaich, strìochd, còrd.

accelerate, v. a. greas, luathaich, cabhag-aich.

acceleration, s. greasad, luathachadh, cabhag, deifir.

accent, s. fuaim, fonn. blas cainnte, sgiobag ; English accent, blas na Beurla.

accept, v. a. gabh, cuir aonta, creid.

acceptability, s. taitneachd, freagarrachd.

acceptable, adj. taitneach, ciatach, iom-chuidh.

acceptance, s. gabhail le deagh-thoil, tlachd.

access, s. rathad, slighe, fosgladh.

accessible, adj. so-ruigsinn ; fosgarra, fàilteach, càirdeil, faoilidh.

accession, s. meudachadh, cuideachadh, leasachadh ; tighinn an seilbh.

accessory, adj. a mheudaicheas, a chuid-icheas, an co-pàirt.

accessory, s. aontachair, co-pàirtiche an ciont, co-chiontaiche.

accident, s. sgiorradh, tubaist, beud.

accidental, adj. tuiteamach, mar a thachras, an corr uair, air thuairmse.

acclaim, v. n. àrd-mhol, dèan luath-ghair, dèan caithream.

acclaim, s. luath-ghàir, iolach, caithream.

acclamation, s. caithream aoibhneis.

acclamatory, adj. luath-ghaireach, ait, aoibhneach.

acclivity, s. bruthach, uchdach, aonach.

acclivous, adj. bruthachail, uchdachail, cas.

accoil, v. n. dòmhlaich, dùmhlaich.

accommodable, adj. goireasach.

accommodate, v. a. dean coingheall, ceartaich ; réitich ; thoir avigheachd.

accommodating, vbl. n. coingheallach, leam-leat, so-lùbaidh.

accommodation, s. freagarrachd, goireas, ceartachadh, rùm ; uidheam, ullach-adh ; réite, socrachadh, còrdadh.

accompaniment, s. leasachadh, co-chuid-eachd, coimhideachd, companas.

accompany, v. n. rach an cuideachd, thoir coimhideachd.

accomplice, s. fear-comuinn, pàirtiche, co-chiontaiche.

accomplish, v. a. crìochnaich, thoir gu buil, thoir gu crìch ; coimhlion.

accomplished, adj. iomlan, déas, sgiamh-ach, snasail, eireachdail, àlainn.

accomplishment, s. crìochnachadh, coimh-lionadh ; sgéimhealachd, maise ; cos-nadh, faotainn, fòghlum.

accord, v. a. and n. réitich, aontaich, ceadaich, còrd, thoir, builich (air neach).

accord, s. co-chòrdadh, aon rùn, aon inntinn.

accordance, s. còrdadh, co-sheirm, càir-deas.

according, prep. a réir, a thaobh.

accordingly, adv. mar sin, a réir sin.

accost, v. a. cuir fàilte, fàiltich, labhair ri —.

accoucheuse, f. bean-ghlùine.

account, s. cunntas, àireamh ; meas-urram, inbhe, àrd-inbhe, àirde ; sgeul, tuairisgeul ; rannsachadh, dearbhadh ; mìneachadh, soilleireachadh.

account, v. a. and n. meas, baralaich, smuainich ; àireamh, cunnt ; thoir cunntas, aithris, bi freagarrach.

accountable, adj. freagarrach, buailteach (do'n lagh), fo fhiachaibh, dh'fheumas cunntas a thabhairt ; cunntachail.

accountant, s. cunntair, fear-cunntais.

account-book, s. leabhar-cunntais.

accoutre, v. a. uidheamaich, deasaich, sgeadaich (an trusgain airm) beartaich.

accoutrements, s. armachd, uidheam, airneis, acfhuin, éideadh-cogaidh.

accredit, v. a. dèan taobh ri, thoir urram do, thoir teist, thoir creideas ; thoir ùghdaras.

accrescent, adj. a chinneas, fàsmhor.

accrete, v. t. and i. cruinnich ri chéile ; dean cnap.

accrue, v. n. thig gu ìre, buannaich, cinnich.

accruement, s. meudachadh, leasachadh, buannachd, riadh.

accumulate, v. a. càrn suas, cruach, cruinnich, cnuasaich, tionail.

accumulation, *s.* co-chruinneachadh, cur r'a chéile, càrnadh suas, cnuasachadh, trusadh, tionaladh, torradh.

accuracy, *s.* pongalachd, cinnteachd, sicireachd, soilleireachd, freagarrachd.

accurate, *adj.* pongail, neo-chearbach, cinnteach, riaghailteach, cothromach, grinn, fìor-cheart.

accurateness, *s.* pongalachd, eagnaidh-eachd, freagarrachd.

accurse, *v. a.* mallaich, dìt.

accursed, *adj.* mallaichte; a thoill mallachd.

accusable, *adj.* ri choireachadh, ri chron-achadh, a thoill dìteadh.

accusation, *s.* casaid, cùis-dhìtidh.

accusatory, *adj.* a dhìteas, a chasaideas.

accuse, *v. a.* dean casaid, dìt, gearain, coirich, tagair.

accused, *part. adj.* fo chasaid; neach air a thoirt gu cùirt.

accuser, *s.* fear-casaid.

accustom, *v. a.* and *n.* cleachd, gnàthaich.

accustomed, *adj.* a réir cleachdaidh, mar bu ghnàthach.

ace, *s.* ni meanbh, smùirnean, cart-cluiche àraidh.

acerb, *adj.* searbh, geur, goirt.

acerbate, *v. a.* dean searbh, geuraich, goirtich.

acerbity, *s.* blas searbh, no geur, no goirt.

acervation, *s.* tòrradh, càrnadh, trusadh, cnapadh.

acescent, *adj.* goirteach, searbh.

acetosity, *s.* searbhas, geurachd, goirt-eachd, gairgead.

acetous, *adj.* goirt, searbh, garg.

ache, *s.* pian, goirteas, goimh, guin.

achieve, *v. a.* crìochnaich; coimhlion gu buadhach, buinig, coisinn.

achievement, *s.* euchd, gaisge, ceann-crìch.

aching, *s.* pian, goirteas, cràdh, acaid.

acid, *adj.* geur, goirt, searbh, garg.

acidity, *s.* geurachd, searbhachd, losgadh-braghad, binnteachd.

acidulate, *v. a.* dèan searbh, garg.

acidulous, *adj.* goirt, searbh.

acknowledge, *v. a.* aidich, thoir gnùis, gabh ri —.

acknowledgment, *s.* aideachadh; buidhe-achas, fios-freagairt.

acme, *s.* àirde, mullach, barr, iomlan-achd.

acoustic, *adj.* a bhuineas do chlàisdeachd, fuaimneach.

acquaint, *v. a.* innis, thoir fios, cuir eòlas (air cùis).

acquaintance, *s.* eòlas; fear eòlais; *pl.* luchd-eòlais.

acquainted, *adj.* eòlach, fiosrach.

acquest, *s.* buannachd, tairbh, seilbh (air a chosnadh).

acquiesce, *v. n.* co-aontaich, géill.

acquiescence, *s.* aontachadh, géilleadh.

acquiescent, *adj.* a cho-aontaicheas.

acquire, *v. a.* coisinn, buannaich.

acquired, *adj.* coisinnte, buannaichte.

acquirement, *s.* cosnadh, ionnsachadh, oilean.

acquisition, *s.* cosnadh, tairbh, buan-nachd, seilbh.

acquit, *v. a.* fuasgail, gairm neo-chiontach, pàigh, bi duineil.

acquitment, *s.* fuasgladh, saoradh.

acquittal, *s.* saoradh, glanadh o choire.

acquittance, *s.* sgrìobhadh fuasglaidh.

acre, *s.* acair, acair-fearainn, raoin treabhaidh.

acrid, *adj.* teith, searbh, garg, goirt.

acrimonious, *adj.* garg, searbh, teith.

acrimony, *s.* gargalachd, geuralachd, caiseanachd.

acritude, *s.* blas geur, searbh, teith.

acronycal, *adj.* a laigheas, 's a dh' éireas, leis a' ghréin (mar na reultan).

acrospire, *s.* gucag, boinne-bàn.

across, *adv.* tarsuinn, o thaobh gu taobh, coinneachadh.

across, *prep.* thar, thairis air.

acrostic, *s.* dòigh bàrdachd; dàn air a dhèanamh air chor 's gun dèan a' cheud litir anns gach sreath suas aon fhacal no barrachd.

act, *v. a.* and *n.* gluais, caraich; dèan, gnìomhaich; giùlain, iomchair; ao-bharaich, thoir gu buil; gabh ort, cleasaich, cluich, gabh samhla ort; cuir air ghluasad.

act, *s.* gnìomh, tùrn, reachd; euchd, cleas; achd, dèanadas; earrann àraidh cluiche; sgrìobhadh achdannan laghail, reachd breithe.

action, *s.* gnìomh, tùrn, obair; cath, blàr; cùis-lagha.

actionable, *adj.* neo-dhligheach, buailte-ach do chùirt lagha.

active, *adj.* sùrdail, beothail, teòma, gnìomhach tapaidh, ealamh, deas, fuasgailte.

activity, *s.* beothalachd, gnìomhachas.

actor, *s.* cleasaiche.

actress, *s.* bana-chleasaiche.

actual, *adj.* cinnteach, dearbhta, fìor, achdaidh.

actuate, *v. a.* brosnaich, gluais.

acuate, *v. a.* geuraich, cuir air chois.

aculeate, *adj.* biorach, gathach, deal-gach.

acumen, *s.* ruinn, geurachd; géire, tulchuis.

acuminated, *adj.* binneanach.

acumination, *s.* ruinn, binnean.

acute, *adj.* geur-thuigseach, biorach; guineach; bras, dealasach; smiorail, beothail, mion, dian (thinneas).

acuteness, *s.* géire, geurachd ; geurad.
adage, *s.* sean-fhacal ; gnàth-fhacal.
adamant, *s.* leug, clach-luachmhor, ailbhinn.
adamantine, *adj.* cruaidh-leuganta.
Adam's - apple, *s.* meall - an - sgòrnain,
ubhall an sgòrnain.
adapt, *v. a.* dean freagarrach, ceartaich.
adaptability, *s.* freagarrachd.
adaptable, *adj.* freagarrach.
adaptation, *s.* ceartachadh.
add, *v. a.* cuir ris, meudaich, leasaich.
adder, *s.* aithir, beithir, nathair-nimhe.
adder's-grass, *s.* lus-na-nathrach.
adder's-wort, *s.* fliogh-na-nathrach.
addict, *v. a.* thoir suas thu fèin do, dèan
cleachdadh.
addicted, *adj.* air a thoirt suas do-, ro
dhéigheil air.
addition, *s.* cur r'a chéile, meudachadh,
leasachadh.
additional, *adj.* a bharrachd, a thuilleadh.
addle, *adj.* breun, grod, lobhta.
addle, *v. a.* cur troimhe chéile, buair,
lobh.
addle-headed, *adj.* gog-cheannach.
address, *v. a.* labhair, sgrìobh, gabh os
làimh, rach an sàs.
address, *s.* deas-labhairt ; modhalachd ;
sgrìobhadh seòlaidh air cùl litreach.
adduce, *v. a.* thoir air aghaidh, tagair,
thoir mar dhearbhadh.
adducible, *adj.* a ghabhas toirt air
aghaidh.
adept, *s.* fear-làn-ealanta, làmh eòlach.
adept, *adj.* oileanta, lan-eòlach.
adequate, *adj.* iomchuidh, co-ionann ;
freagarrach, làn-chomasach.
adequateness, *s.* freagarrachd, uidheam-
achd.
adhere, *v. n.* fan dìleas, dlùth-lean.
adherence, *s.* dlùth-leanailteachd.
adherent, *adj.* leanailteach.
adherent, *s.* fear-leanmhainn.
adhesion, *s.* leanmhainneachd.
adhesive, *adj.* leanailteach.
adhibit, *v. a.* cuir gu feum, gnàthaich,
fritheil ; cuir d'ainm ris.
adieu, *interj.* là maith leat ! beannachd
leat ! soraidh leat !
adipose, *a.* reamhar ; *n.* blonaig, saill.
adjacent, *adj.* fagus, dlùth, faisg.
adject, *v. a.* cuir ris, leasaich, meudaich.
adjective, *s.* buaidh-fhacal.
adjectively, *adv.* mar bhuaidh-fhacal.
adjoin, *v. a.* tàth, dlùthaich, teann.
adjoin, *v. n.* dlùthaich, thig am fagus.
adjourn, *v. a.* cuir dàil gu àm eile.
adjournment, *s.* dàil gu là eile.
adjudge, *v. a.* thoir còir air ni le breth
laghail, thoir binn, thoir breth.
adjudication, *s.* toirt còir le breth laghail.
adjunctive, *adj.* a thàthas r'a chéile.

adjunctively, *adv.* air mhodh tàthaidh.
adjunctly, *adv.* an ceangal.
adjuration, *s.* mionnan air son riaghailt
a' leantainn.
adjure, *v. a.* cuir air mionnan.
adjurer, *s.* neach a chuireas air mionnan.
adjust, *v. a.* ceartaich, réitich ; suidhich.
adjustment, *s.* ceartachadh, co-throm-
achadh.
adjutancy, *s.* dreuchd, no inbhe oifigich
còmhnaidh ; deagh riaghailt.
adjutant, *s.* oifigeach a ni còmhnadh ri
oifigich eile.
admensuration, *s.* tomhas.
administer, *v. a.* righail, tabhair, fritheil.
administration, *s.* frithealadh, riaghladh,
freasdalachadh ; luchd-comhairle an
rìgh, luchd-riaghlaidh, no stiùraidh na
rìoghachd ; uachdaranachd ; taisbeanadh, tabhairt.
administrative, *adj.* fritheilteach, a
bhuilicheas, a riaghlas.
administrator, *s.* fear - riaghlaidh, ard -
fhear - comhairle ; fear - frithealaidh
dìleab.
administratrix, *s.* ban-riaghladair.
admirable, *adj.* ionmholta, cliùiteach.
admirably, *adv.* gu fior mhaith, gu
ciatach.
admiral, *s.* àrd-mharaiche, ceannard
cabhlaich.
admiralty, *s.* luchd-riaghlaidh na cabhlaich cogaidh, dreuchd ceannard cabhlaich.
admiration, *s.* iongnadh, iongantas, mòr-
mheas, mòr-thlachd.
admire, *v. a.* gabh teachd ; cuir mòr-mheas,
bi uasal as.
admirer, *s.* fear-molaidh, fear-gaoil.
admissible, *adj.* ceadachail, airidh air
creideas.
admission, *s.* leigeadh a steach (do thigh),
géill do argumaid.
admittable, *adj.* a dh' fhaodar a leigeadh
a steach, no fhulang ; a dh'fhaodar a
chreidsinn.
admittance, *s.* cead, leigeadh a steach.
admix, *v. a.* measgaich, co-mheasgaich.
admixture, *s.* co-mheasgadh ; cuthaigeadh.
admonish, *v. a.* caoin-chronaich, earailich.
admonisher, *s.* comhairleach, earalaiche.
admonition, *s.* caoin-chronachadh ; achasan.
ado, *s.* othail, iomairt, saothair.
adolescency, *s.* òige, òigeachd ; ùr-fhàs.
adopt, *v. a.* uchd-mhacaich, gabh ri
comhairle, roghnaich.
adoption, *s.* uchd-mhacachadh.
adorable, *adj.* airidh air aoradh, measail.
adorableness, *s.* ard-urramachd, ion-
mholtachd.
adoration, *s.* aoradh, naomh-urram.

adore, v. a. aor, dean aoradh.
adorer, s. fear-aoraidh, fear-gaoil.
adorn, v. a. sgeadaich, sgèimhich, uidheamaich, maisich (le nithean luachmhor).
adrift, adv. leis an t-sruth ; air iomadan.
adroit, adj. deas, ealanta, ealamh, teòma.
adroitness, s. ealantachd, gleusdachd.
adulate, v. t. brosguil, dean miodal.
adulation, s. sodal, brosgul, miodal.
adulator, s. fear-sodail, fear-brosguil, fear-miodail.
adult, s. neach air teachd gu aois — air làn-fhas.
adult, adj. air teachd gu aois — air fas mòr.
adulterant, s. nì a thruailleas.
adulterate, adj. truaillidh, fo smal (tre dhiolanas) ; v. truaill.
adulterer, s. fear-adhaltranais, adhaltranaiche.
adulteress, s. ban-adhaltranaiche.
adulterine, s. leanabh diolain ; a. diolain.
adulterous, adj. adhaltranach, truaillidh.
adultery, s. adhaltras, adhaltranas, diolanas.
adumbrant, adj. faileasach, sgaileach, fann-choltas.
adumbrate, v. samhlaich, thoir fideadh.
adust, a. air tiormachadh, air sgreidheadh, loisgte, seargte (le teas gréine).
advance, v. a. and n. thoir air aghaidh ; àrdaich, meudaich ; leasaich, luathaich; dlùthaich, thig am fagus, thig air t'aghaidh ; cinn, fàs ; tairg, thoir am follais ; dìol roimh-làimh ; tog suas, rùisg, taisbean.
advance, s. dlùthachadh, teannadh, teachd air aghaidh ; féin-thairgse, cuireadh gràidh ; cinntinn, meudachadh, àrdachadh ; soirbheachadh ; airgead-roimh-làimh.
advancement, s. adhartachd, àrdachadh, àirde ; teachd air aghaidh, soirbheachadh ; adhartas.
advantage, s. buidhinn, tairbhe, buannachd, sochair, leas, math, fàth ; cothrom, làmh-an-uachdar.
advantage, v. a. leasaich, àrdaich.
advantaged, adj. leasaichte, air dheagh chothrom.
advantage-ground, s. ionad-buadha.
advantageous, adj. buannachdail, goireasach, tarbhach.
advantageousness, s. feumalachd, buannachd.
advent, s. teachd, teachd an t-Slànaighear; am mìos roimh Nollaig.
adventitious, adj. tuiteamach, air thuaimse, tighinn 's gun duil ris.
adventual, adj. a bhuineas do dh' àm teachd an t-Slànaighir.
adventure, s. tuiteamas, tubaist ; deuch-

ainn, feuchainn, ionnsaigh : cunnart, cuairt dànachd.
adventure, v. a. and n. feuch ri, thoir deuchainn, thoir ionnsaigh ; gabh misneach.
adventurer, s. fear-deuchainn, fear-iomairt, fear-misnich, fear-fuadain ; feardàna.
adventurous, adj. misneachail, dàna, deuchainneach, gleusda, gaisgeil.
adversary, s. eascaraid, nàmhaid.
adverse, adj. tarsainn, crosda, an aghaidh a chéile, a cur an aghaidh, dìobhalach, àmhgharach, ànrach, calldach, dochannach, nàimhdeil.
adverseness, s. crosdachd, tarsainneachd, nàimhdeas.
adversity, s. fàth-bròin, truaighe, anshocair, doilgheas, cruaidh - chas ; àmhghar, teinn, doilghios.
advert, v. a. and n. thoir fainear, beachdaich, dearc.
advertence, s. aire, beachd.
advertent, adj. aireachail, beachdail.
advertise, v. a. thoir fios follaiseach, thoir rabhadh.
advertisement, s. sanas, gairm.
advertiser, s. fear-naidheachd, fear-sanais.
advice, s. comhairle, seòladh ; earal.
advisable, adj. glic, crionna.
advise, v. a. and n. comhairlich, cuir comhairle ri ; gabh comhairle.
advised, adj. air chomhairle ; le làn bheachd, crìonna.
advisedness, s. comhairleachd, crìonnachd.
adviser, s. comhairleach.
advocacy, s. dian-thagradh.
advocate, s. fear-tagraidh.
advocate, v. a. tagair, gabh taobh, dìon.
advocation, s. tagradh eadar-ghuidhe.
advowee, s. neach aig a bheil beathachadh eaglais r'a thoirt seachad.
advowson, s. còir sgìre thoirt do neach.
adze, s. tàl, croma-sgian.
aegis, s. sgiath-chòmhraig, sgiath dion.
aerial, adj. adharail, iarmailteach.
aerie, s. nead eòin fhuileachdaich, alach seobhaig.
aeriform, adj. mar an t-adhar.
aerology, s. eòlas-adhair.
aeromancy, s. speuradaireachd.
aerometer, s. adhar-mheidh.
aerometry, s. adhar-thomhas.
aeronaut, s. adhar-sheòladair.
aeroscopy, s. speur-choimhead.
aethiop's-mineral, s. cungaidh-leighis de phronnasg agus de airgeadbeò.
afar, adv. fad as, fad air falbh.
affability, s. suairceas, ceanaltas, fosgarrachd.
affable, adj. suairce, ceanalta, aoidheil, aobhach.

affableness, s. suairceachd.
affair, s. gnothach ; cùis ; aobhar.
affear, v. n. daingnich, suidhich.
affect, v. a. drùigh air, thoir air fair-eachdainn ; gabh ort, leig ort ; gabh déigh air ; gluais inntinn, riochdaich.
affectation, s. atharrais; spadaireachd ; baoth-choltas, mòr-chuis.
affected, adj. luaisgte le droch, no le deagh rùn, sgleòthach, pròiseil.
affection, s. gràdh, gaol, càil ; dealas ; galar, eucail, tinneas.
affectionate, adj. gràdhach, gaolach, caidreach ; teò-chridheach.
affectionateness, s. teò-chridheachd.
affectiously, adv. gu dùrachdach, gu déigheil.
affective, adj. tiomachail, blàthcridheach.
affiance, s. còrdadh-pòsaidh, earbsa, muinghin, dòchas.
affiance, v. a. réitich, dean coimh-cheangal pòsaidh ; cuir dòchas.
affidavit, s. mionnan-sgrìobhte.
affile, v. a. dean mìn le eighe.
affiliation, s. uchd-mhacachd, dlùth-dhàimh.
affined, adj. ceangailte le bann dàimhe, càirdeach.
affinity, s. cleamhnas ; dàimh.
affirm, v. a. cuir an céill ; dearbh.
affirmable, adj. daingneachail.
affirmance, s. daingneachadh, suidh-eachadh; dearbhachd; daingneachadh.
affirmant, s. fear-dearbhaidh.
affirmation, s. dearbhadh, daingneach-adh, cur an céill, ràdh, spreigeadh.
affirmative, adj. dearbhte, danarra, dìorrasach, a chòmhdaicheas.
affirmatively, adv. gu dearbhta.
affirmer, s. fear-dearbhaidh.
affix, v. a. co-cheangail, tàth.
afflict, v. a. pian, goirtich, sàraich, claoidh.
afflictedness, s. doilghios, àmhghar.
afflicter, s. fear-sàrachaidh.
afflictingly, adv. gu doilghiosach, àmh-gharach.
affliction, s. amhghar, teinn ; doilghios, bròn.
afflictive, adj. doilghiosach, àmhgharach.
afflictively, adv. gu doilghiosach, gu cràiteach.
affluence, s. tòic, mórmhaoin, beartas, saibhreas.
affluent, adj. saoibhir, beartach, pailt.
affluent, s. allt a tha ruith a steach an abhainn.
afflux, s. cruinneachadh, sruthadh ; sruth, maoin-ruith.
afford, v. a. thoir seachad ; builich tabhair, deònaich ; bi comasach.
affranchise, v. a. saor, dean saor.
affray, v. a. cuir eagal air, geiltich.

affray, s. caonnag, sabaid, carraid.
affright, v. a. cuir eagal, cuir briosgadh.
affright, s. eagal, geilt, giorag.
affrighter, s. bòcan, culaidh-eagail.
affrightful, adj. eagalach, oillteil.
affront, v. a. nàraich, maslaich.
affront, s. nàrachadh, masladh, tàir, tarcuis, tàmailt.
affronting, adj. tarcuiseach, spìdeil, tà-mailteach.
affusion, s. dòrtadh, co-mheasgadh.
afield, adv. a mach do'n raon.
afire, adv. 'na theine, gu teinnteach.
aflat, adv. air làr, ri talamh.
afloat, adv. air uachdar, air snàmh, air bhog.
afoot, adv. a chois ; air chois, air ghluasad.
afore, prep. air thùs.
afore, adv. cheana, roimhe so.
aforehand, adv. roimh-làimh.
aforementioned, adj. roimh-luaidhte.
aforesaid, adj. roimh-ainmichte.
aforetime, adv. 's an àm a chaidh.
afraid, adj. fo eagal.
afresh, adv. as ùr, a rithist.
afront, adv. ri aghaidh.
aft, adv. gu deireadh ; an deireadh.
after, prep. an déidh.
after, adv. 's an àm ri tighinn.
after-ages, s. linntean ri teachd.
after-all, adv. mu dheireadh, an déidh gach cùis.
after-bearing, s. ath-fhàs.
after-crop, s. ath-bhàrr, an darna barr.
after-days, s. làithibh ri teachd.
aftermost, adj. deireannach, am fìor-dheireadh.
afternoon, s. nòine, an deidh mheadhon-là.
after-pains, s. ath-phiantan.
after-proof, s. ath-dhearbhadh, ath-chòmhdach.
after-repentance, s. ath-aithreachas ; aithreachas deidh-làimhe.
after-sting, s. ath-ghath, athghuin.
after-thought, s. athsmuain.
after-tossing, s. athluasgadh.
afterward, adv. an déidh sin, an déidh-làimh.
afterwise, adj. glic an déidh làimh, cearbach.
again, adv. a rithist, uair eile, air an làimh eile, fathast.
against, prep. an aghaidh ; fa-chomhair ; thall.
agarick, s. cungaidh-leighis de bhàrr an daraich, datħ le barr learaig.
agate, adv. air an rathad, a' falbh.
agate, s. agat, clach-luachmhor.
agaze, v. a. seall le ioghnadh, spleuc.
age, s. aois ; linn, ginealach ; àm, beatha ; ùin cheud bliadhna.
aged, adj. sean, aosda.

agency, *s.* dèanadachd ; dreuchd fir-gnothaich air son neach eile.

agent, *s.* fear-ionaid, fear-gnothuich.

agentship, *s.* gnìomh fir-ionaid.

aggerate, *v. a.* cuir an àirde, càrn suas.

aggerose, *adj.* cnocanach, tomanach.

agglomerate, *v. a.* cruinnich, cearslaich, trus r'a chéile.

agglomeration, *s.* meall cruinn, trusadh.

agglutinant, *adj.* glaodhach, tàthach.

agglutinate, *v. a.* glaodhaich, tàthaich, dlùth r'a chéile.

agglutination, *s.* tàthadh, aonadh, dlùth-adh.

aggrandise, *v. a.* àrdaich, tog suas an inbhe, meudaich an urram ; fàs mòr.

aggrandisement, *s.* meudachadh, àrdach-adh, mòrachadh, urramachadh.

aggravate, *v. a.* an-tromaich.

aggravation, *s.* an-tromachadh.

aggregate, *adj.* co-chruinnichte.

aggregate, *s.* an t-iomlan, am meall uile.

aggregate, *v. a.* cruinnich, trus, tòrr.

aggregation, *s.* co-chruinneachadh ; an t-iomlan.

aggress, *v. n.* brosnaich ; tòisich an aimhreit, buail an toiseach.

aggression, *s.* a' cheud bhuille, a cheud teine, a' cheud ionnsaigh.

aggressor, *s.* fear togail na strìthe, an coireach.

aggrievance, *s.* eucoir, sàrachadh.

aggrieve, *v. a.* doilghiosaich, léir ; buair ; dochainn, sàraich.

aghast, *adj.* fo uamhann ; fo gheilt.

agile, *adj.* lùthor, ealamh, clis, grad-charach, fuasgailte, beothail.

agileness, *s.* lùthorachd, sgiobaltachd.

agility, *s.* cliseachd, luathas.

agitate, *v. a.* gluais, caraich, cuir troimh-chéile ; buair ; cnuasaich.

agitation, *s.* carachadh, gluasad, luasgadh inntinn ; iomairt ; cnuasachadh, buair-eas, imcheist.

agitator, *s.* fear - brosnachaidh fear-gluasaid.

agnail, *s.* an galar-iongach.

agnate, *adj.* càirdeach, dìleas.

agnatic, *adj.* cairdeach air taobh athar.

agnation, *s.* sinnsireachd nam mac, o'n aon athair ; càirdeas, cleamhnas.

agnus-castus, *s.* craobh-na-geamnachd.

ago, *adv.* o so, o chian, a chaidh.

agog, *adv.* air bhraise, gu h-iollagach.

agoing, *adj.* a' falbh, air ghluasad.

agone, *adv.* seachad, air falbh.

agonist, *s.* lùthchleasaich ; fear-farpais.

agonise, *v. n.* bi air do gheur chràdh, dèan cruaidh spàirn.

agony, *s.* uspagan a' bhàis, piantan bàis, teinn-chràdh, dòrainn ; cruaidhghleac, spàirn.

agood, *adv.* da-rìreadh.

agraffe, *s.* bràiste.

agrarian, *adj.* fearannach, a bhuineas do 'n fhearann.

agree, *v. n.* còird, aontaich ; réitich.

agreeable, *adj.* freagarrach, taitneach, ciatach.

agreeableness, *s.* freagarrachd, tait-neachd, co-aontachd, samhlachd.

agreed, *adj.* còirdte, suidhichte, réidh.

agreeingly, *adv.* do réir.

agreement, *s.* réite, còrdadh, samhla ; co-cheangal.

agricultural, *adj.* tuathanachail, àite-achail.

agriculture, *s.* tuathanachas, àiteach.

agriculturist, *s.* tuathanach, treabhaiche.

agrimony, *s.* a' gheurag-bhileach.

aground, *adv.* an sàs, air grunnd, air gabhail (a' ghrunna).

ague, *s.* am fiabhras-critheach.

agued, *adj.* crith-bhuailte, critheach.

ague-tree, *s.* a' chraobh chrithinn.

ah ! *interj.* ah ! aha ! mo thruaighe !

ahead, *adv.* air thoiseach.

ahold, *adv.* air fuaradh (an fhearainn).

ahungry, *adj.* acrach, ciorcach.

aid, *s.* cuideachadh, còmhnadh.

aid, *v. a.* cuidich, cùm suas, cobhair.

aidance, *s.* cobhair, còmhnadh.

aide-de-camp, *s.* àrd-theachdair ceann-aird feachd.

aider, *s.* fear-cuideachaidh.

aidless, *adv.* gun chobhair.

aigrette, *s.* a' chorra-ghlas, dos itean ; clòimhteach foghannain ; cuach-Phà-druig.

ail, *v. a.* pian, cràdh ; gearain.

ail, *s.* tinneas, galar, eucail.

ailment, *s.* dòrainn, tinneas, galar.

ailing, *adj.* tinn, euslainteach.

aim, *v. a. and n.* cuimsich, cinntich, thoir ionnsaigh ; comharraich, beachdaich.

aim, *s.* cuimse, cuimseachd, ionnsaigh ; rùn, dùrachd ; barail.

aimless, *adj.* neo-chuimseach ; gun rùn.

air, *s.* adhar, àileadh, iarmailt ; speuran ; gaoth ; fàile, tòc ; fonn, ceòl ; aogas, gnè.

air, *v. a.* cuir ris an àileadh, sgaoil ris a' ghaoith ; teò, blàthaich.

air-borne, *adj.* aotrom, air a ghiùlan leis an àileadh.

air-built, *adj.* faoin, gun bhunachar.

air-hole, *s.* toll-gaoithe.

airing, *s.* spaidseireachd, a' gabhail na gaoithe ; sràidimeachd.

airling, *s.* creutair òg iollagach.

air-gun, *s.* gunna-gaoithe.

air-pump, *s.* pìob thaosgaidh an àilidh.

airy, *adj.* adharail ; àrd 's an adhar ; fosgailte, gaothar ; aotrom, faoin ; fonnmhor, sunntach.

aisle, *s.* trannsa eaglais.

ajar, *adv.* leth-fhosgailte.

akin, *adj.* càirdeach, coltach, dluth an dàimh.

alabaster, *s.* clach-éiteig.

alack, *interj.* mo thruaighe! mo chreach, mo léireadh; mo dhìobhail!

alack-a-day, *interj.* mo chreach an diugh! mo dhunaidh!

alacrity, *s.* beothalachd, sunntachd, smioralachd, suigeart, fonn.

à la mode, *adv.* anns an fhasan.

a-land, *adv.* air tìr, air tràigh.

alarm, *s.* caismeachd, gaoir-chatha, rabhadh; clisgeadh, fuathas, miapadh.

alarm, *v. a.* buail caismeachd; thoir rabhadh, thoir sanas; buair.

alarming, *adj.* eagalach, cunnartach, buaireasach.

alarmist, *s.* fear-caismeachd, sgaomaire.

alarm-post, *s.* crann-tàraidh, crois-tàra.

alas, *interj.* och! mo chreach! mo thruaighe! mo dhuilichinn! mo léireadh!

alas the day, *interj.* och mo thruaighe! mis' an diugh!

alb, *s.* léine-aifrinn, clòca bàn sagairt.

albeit, *adv.* gidheadh, air son sin, ged.

Albion, *s.* Alba, *d.* Albainn.

albugineous, *adj.* geal, coltach ri gealagan uibhe.

album, *s.* leabhar dhealbh.

albumen, *s.* gealagan.

alchemist, *s.* oibriche mhiotailt.

alchemy, *s.* eòlas air gnè mhiotailtean; innleachd air miotailt a thionndadh gu òr.

alcohol, *s.* treas-tarruinn, deoch làidir.

Alcoran, *s.* "Bìobull" Mohamed.

alcove, *s.* cùlaist, àite leapa, cùil-suidhe (an lios).

alder, *s.* feàrna, drumanach.

alderman, *s.* bùirdeiseach, ball de Chomh-airle-riaghlaidh baile (an Sasuinn).

ale, *s.* leann, lionn.

ale-berry, *s.* leann teth.

ale-brewer, *s.* grùdair.

ale-house, *s.* tigh-leanna.

alembic, *s.* poit-thogalach, poit-dubh.

alert, *adj.* furachail, beothail, deas.

alertness, *s.* beothalachd.

ale-vat, *s.* dabhach-leanna.

ale-wife, *s.* bean-tigh-leanna.

alexanders, *s.* lus-nan-gràn-dubh.

Alexandrine, *s.* seòrsa bàrdachd, dusan siola 's an t-sreath (te ghoirid is fhada mu seach).

algebra, *s.* an cunntas aibidileach.

algid, *adj.* fuar, fionnar, reòta (crith na fiabhruis).

alias, *adv.* air dòigh eile.

alibi, *adv.* an àite eile, tagar diona an cùirt.

alien, *adj.* coimheach; allmharach.

alien, *s.* coimheach, coigreach; eilthi-reach, allmharach.

alienate, *v. a.* sgar càirdeas, fuadaich seilbh, tionndaidh air falbh; gràinich.

alienated, *adj.* dealaichte, sgaraichte.

alienation, *s.* dealachadh, dìobradh.

alight, *v. a.* teirinn, tùirlinn.

alike, *adv.* coltach, a réir a chéile.

aliment, *s.* lòn, biadh, teachd-an-tir.

alimental, *adj.* biadhar, brìoghmhor.

alimentary, *adj.* a dh' àraicheas, a bheathaicheas, biadhar.

alimentation, *s.* beathachadh.

alimony, *s.* beathachadh, còir mna am maoin a fir, is i dealaichte ris.

alish, *adj.* leannach, mar leann.

alive, *adj.* beò, beothail, sunntach.

alkali, *s.* salann-na-groide.

alkaline, *adj.* nàdur salann-na-groide.

all, *adj.* uile, iomlan, gu léir, na h-uile; an t-iomlan.

all-abandoned, *adj.* uile-thréigte.

all-abhorred, *adj.* uile-fhuathach.

all-changing, *adj.* uile-chaochlaidheach.

all-cheering, *adj.* uile-bheothachail.

all-conquering, *adj.* uile-bhuadhach.

all-consuming, *adj.* uile-chaithteach.

all-disgraced, *adj.* uile-mhaslaichte.

all-hallows, *s.* an t-samhainn ùr.

all-heal, *s.* slàn-lus.

all-knowing, *adj.* uile-fhiosrach.

all-powerful, *adj.* uile-chumhachdach.

all-praised, *adj.* uile-chliùiteach.

All-saints'-day, *s.* Latha nan uile naomh, cheud là de Nobhimber.

all-seeing, *adj.* uile-léirsinneach.

all-sufficiency, *s.* uile-fhoghainteachd, uile-dhiongmhaltachd.

all-sufficient, *adj.* uile-fhoghainteach, uile-dhiongmhalt.

all-sufficient, *s.* an t-uile-fhoghainteach, an t-uile-dhiongmhalt.

all-triumphing, *adj.* uile-bhuadhach.

allay, *v. a.* caisg, bac, ciùinich.

allayment, *s.* lagachadh, ìsleachadh.

allegation, *s.* aithris, casaid (a tha ri dhearbhadh).

allege, *v. a.* abair, aithris, cuir as leth.

allegeable, *adj.* so-aithriseil.

allegiance, *s.* ùmhlachd, géilleadh, strì-ochdadh, cìs-rìgh.

allegorical, *adj.* samhlachail.

allegorise, *v. n.* samhlaich.

allegory, *s.* samhla, cosamhlachd.

alleluiah, *s.* cliù do Dhia.

alleviate, *v. a.* aotromaich, lùghdaich; maothaich, lagaich.

alleviation, *s.* aotromachadh, lùghdach-adh; lagachadh, faothachadh.

alley, *s.* caol-shràid.

alliance, *s.* càirdeas, cleamhnas; co-cheangal.

alligate, *v. a.* ceangail, snaim.
alligation, *s.* snaimeadh, snaim ; seòrsa cùnntais.
alligature, *s.* ceanglachan, lùbag.
allision, *s.* co-bhualadh.
alliteration, *s.* dòigh bàrdachd, sreath fhacal, 's gach facal a' tòiseachadh air an aon litir.
allocation, *s.* cur r'a chéile, roinn, earrannan.
allodial, *adj.* saor o chìs fearainn.
allodium, *s.* fearann saor o chìs, oighreachd tha saor of gach cìs is sumha.
allot, *v. tr.* roinn le tilgeadh chrann.
allotment, *s.* roinn crannachur, cuid, earrainn, cuibhrionn, crannachur.
allow, *v. a.* ceadaich, deònaich, leig.
allowable, *adj.* ceadaichte, dligheach.
allowance, *s.* cead ; cuibhrionn shuidhichte ; cuibhrionn bliadhna.
alloy, *s.* truailleadh, miotailt truaillidh an òr no an airgid.
allude, *v. n.* ciallaich ; thig air ni fo ainm eile.
allure, *v. a.* meall, tàlaidh, buair.
allurement, *s.* mealladh, tàladh, foillghlacadh, ribe.
allurer, *s.* mealltair, fear-tàlaidh.
alluring, *s.* mealladh, tàladh.
alluringly, *adv.* cluaintearach.
allusion, *s.* sanas, coimeas.
allusive, *adv.* sanasach, sanasail.
alluvion, *s.* salachar-srutha, bristleach a dh'fhàgas tide-mhara.
ally, *v. a.* co-cheangail, dean cleamhnas ri, dlùthaich an càirdeas, dean còrdadh còmhnaidh (eadar rìoghachdan).
ally, *s.* companach, caraid.
almightiness, *s.* uile chumhachd.
almighty, *adj.* uile-chumhachdach.
almond, *s.* cnò-almoin.
almonds, *s.* fàireagan bhun na teanga.
almoner, *s.* fear-roinn déirce.
almonry, *s.* taigh-tasgaidh dhéircean.
almost, *adv.* gu ìre bhig, theab, cha mhòr nach.
alms, *s.* déirc, déircean.
alms-house, *s.* taigh-bhochd.
alnage, *s.* slat-thomhais.
aloes, *s.* àlos, fiodh cùbhraidh.
aloft, *adv.* gu h-àrd, an àirde, shuas.
alone, *adj. adv.* aonarach ; ònarach ; 'n a aonar, gu h-aonaranach.
along, *adv.* air fad ; air fhad ; maille ri, còmhla, le ; air aghaidh, air adhart.
alongside, *adv.* ri taobh na luinge, taobh na lamraig.
aloof, *adv.* air falbh, an céin, air fuaradh ; á sealladh, an cleith ; stand aloof, seas air falbh ; fad as, uamhrach.
alpha, *s.* a cheud litir de'n aibidil Ghreugaich ; a' ciallachadh an ceud ni, no nì as àirde.

alphabet, *s.* aibidil.
already, *adv.* cheana, mu thràth.
also, *adv.* mar an ceudna, cuideachd, a thuilleadh.
altar, *s.* altair, leac-ìobairt, crom-leac.
alter, *v. a.* atharraich, mùth.
alterable, *adj.* so-atharraichte, mùthalach caochlaidheach.
alterant, *adj.* a ni atharrachadh.
alteration, *s.* atharrachadh, tionndadh, mùthadh.
alterative, *s.* locshlaint-ghlanaidh.
altercation, *s.* connsachadh, trod, cònspoid, tuasaid.
alternate, *v. a.* atharraich.
alternately, *adv.* mu seach ; fear mu seach.
alternation, *s.* freagradh mu seach, seinn mu seach.
alternative, *adj.* atharrachadh, roghainn, an dara h-aon ; an seòl mùthaidh.
altitude, *s.* àirde.
altogether, *adv.* gu léir, gu tur, gu buileach, gu h-iomlan ; còmhla.
alum, *s.* alm, clach an datha.
always, *adv.* daonnan, an còmhnaidh, a ghnàth, riamh ; gun atharrachadh.
amain, *adv.* gu dian, le neart, le dian chabhaig.
amalgam, *s.* miotailt agus airgead beò triomh chéile.
amalgamate, *v. a.* co-mheasgaich, aon (sluagh, comunn, smuaintean).
amalgamation, *s.* co-mheasgachadh.
amanuensis, *s.* cléireach, fear-sgriobhaidh bhriathran neach eile.
amaranth, *s.* lus-a'-ghràidh, blàth nach searg, dath purpur.
amass, *v. t.* càrn, cruach, trus, cruinnich, torr.
amassment, *s.* meall, cruach, cruinneachadh, trusadh, torradh.
amateur, *s.* faoghlaide.
amatory, *adj.* gaol-gheanmhuinneach.
amaze, *v. a.* cuir ioghnadh.
amaze, *s.* ioghnadh, amhluadh, eagal.
amazement, *s.* mór ioghnadh.
amazing, *adj.* iongantach, uabhasach.
amazon, *s.* bana-ghaisgeach.
ambages, *s.* cuairt-chaint.
ambassador, *s.* tosgaire ; teachdaire rìgh gu rìgh eile, fear-ionaid rìgh (aig cùirt rìgh eile).
ambassadress, *s.* ban-tosgair.
ambassage, *s.* tosgaireachd, teachdaireachd (rìoghail).
amber, *s.* òmar, leann-soilleir.
ambergris, *s.* seòrsa do chùngaidh leighis chùruidh air dhreach na luaidhe agus a leaghas mar chéir, òmar glas.
ambidexter, *s.* gleus-fhear, deas-fhear, fear deaslamhach, fear deas le dha làimh.

ambidextrous, *adj.* coimhdheis ; ealamh air gach làimh ; mealltach, foilleil, leam leat.
ambiguity, *s.* teagamh ; facal, no radh, a dh'fhaodar a ghabhail an dà sheadh.
ambiguous, *adj.* dà-sheadhach.
ambit, *s.* cuairt, criochan.
ambition, *s.* glòir-mhiann ; miann soirbheachaidh.
ambitious, *adj.* glòir-mhiannach.
amble, *s.* fàlaireachd, spaidsearachd.
ambler, *s.* fàlaire, each-marcachd.
amblingly, *adv.* gu fòill-cheumach.
ambrosial, *adj.* cùbhraidh, millis.
ambulate, *v. a.* spaidsearaich, sràidimich.
ambulation, *s.* gluasad, falbh.
ambulative, *adj.* falbhach.
ambuscade, *s.* feall-fholach.
ambush, *v.* and *s.* feall-fholach, fàth, dean feall-fholach, gabh fàth.
ameliorate, *v. a.* dèan na's fearr, cuir am feabhas.
amen, *adv.* gu 'm bu h-amhlaidh bhios.
amenable, *adj.* freagarrach, buailteach.
amend, *v. a.* and *n.* leasaich, ath-leasaich ; dèan na's fearr, càirich ; fàs na's fearr, rach am feabhas.
amending, *s.* leasachadh.
amendment, *s.* ath-leasachadh.
amends, *s.* dìoladh, luach, éirig.
amenity, *s.* taitneachd, ciatachd, maisealachd.
amercement, *s.* ubhladh ; peanas.
amethyst, *s.* clach luachmhor.
amiable, *adj.* ion-ghràdhach, gaolach, taitneach ; maiseach, àluinn ; càirdeil coibhneil.
amiableness, *s.* so-ghràdhachd, taitneachd.
amicable, *adj.* coibhneil, càirdeil.
amid, amidst, *prep.* am measg.
amiss, *adv.* gu h-olc, gu docharach.
amity, *s.* càirdeas, co-chòrdadh, coibhneas.
ammunition, *s.* uidheam gunnaireachd, àirneis-chogaidh, luaidhe is fùdar.
amnesty, *s.* mathanas coitcheann.
among, *adv.* am measg, còmhla.
amongst, *prep.* am measg, air feadh.
amorist, *s.* suiridheach, leannan.
amorous, *adj.* gaolach ; leannanach brìodalach ; gaol-dhùsgach.
amount, *v. n.* ruig, thig, cuir an àird' an cùnntas ; thig gu suim àraidh.
amount, *s.* an t-àireamh iomlan, suim.
amour, *s.* leannanachd-dhiomhair.
amphibious, *adj.* a thig beò an uisge 's air tìr.
amphibological, *adj.* dubh-fhaclach.
amphibology, *s.* cainnt dhà-sheadhach, cainnt dhorcha, gearra-ghobich.
amphibolous, *adj.* ioma-chiallachd.

amphitheatre, *s.* tigh-cluiche, tigh-cleasachd.
ample, *adj.* mór, farsuing, leudach, fiùghantach, foghainteach, pailt.
ampleness, *s.* lànachd, farsuinneachd, pailteas.
ampliate, *v. a.* meudaich, farsuingich.
ampliation, *s.* meudachadh, farsuingeachadh ; lànachadh, leudachadh.
amplificate, *v. a.* meudaich, leudaich.
amplification, *s.* meudachadh.
amplify, *v. a.* meudaich, leudaich.
amplitude, *s.* meudachd, lànachd, pailteachd.
amputate, *v. a.* gearr air falbh, sgar.
amputation, *s.* gearradh, sgaradh.
amuck, *adv.* ruith air bhoil, — air chaothach.
amulet, *s.* paidirean giosagach, seun.
amuse, *v. a.* toilich, cum o fhadal, thoir ceann-réidh, breugadh na clainne, amusing, diverting, the children.
amusement, *s.* caithe-aimsir, feala-dhà.
amusingly, *adv.* air mhodh taitneach.
amusive, *adj.* taitneach, a thogas sproc.
anaemia, *s.* cion-fala, bochdanas fala.
anaesthesia, *s.* cion-faireachdan.
anaesthetic, *s.* stuth gu marbhadh faireachdan (is neach fo lanns an leighiche).
analeptic, *adj.* and *s.* cungaidh neartachaidh.
analogial, *adj.* samhlachail.
analogous, *adj.* co-choltach, co-chòrdadh, co-fhreagarrach.
analogy, *s.* coltas, samhlachas, co-chòrdadh, fìor choltas r'a chéile.
analysis, *s.* mion-rannsachadh.
analyse, *v. a.* bun-rannsaich.
anarchical, *adj.* àimhreiteach.
anarchist, *s.* fear mì-riaghailt, reubaltach, ceannairceach.
anarchy, *s.* mì-riaghailt, buaireas, ceannairc.
anasarca, *s.* seòrsa meud-bhronn.
anathema, *s.* ascaoin-eaglais; mallachadh.
anathematise, *v. a.* sgar o chomunn nan crìosdaidhean, mallaich.
anatomical, *adj.* bhuineas do mhion-eòlas cuirp.
anatomy, *s.* corp-rannsachadh ; eòlas corp-ghearraidh, mion-eòlas air corp an duine.
ancestor, *s.* priomh-athair, sinnsear.
ancestry, *s.* sinnsearachd.
anchor, *s.* acair luinge.
anchor, *v. a.* and *n.* tilg acair, laigh air acair ; seas air acair.
anchorage, *s.* acarsaid ; càin-acarsaid.
anchored, *adj.* acraichte, air acair, air cruaidh.
anchoress, *s.* bana-mhanach.
anchoret, *s.* manach dìobarach.

ancient, *adj.* àrsaidh, aosda ; o shean.
ancient, *s.* duine o shean, fear dhe 'n t-sean-aimsir.
anciently, *adv.* o shean, an céin.
and, *conj.* agus, is, 's.
anecdote, *s.* ursgeul, mionsgeul, sgeula.
anecdotical, *adj.* ursgeulach.
anemometer, *s.* gaothmheidh, meidh gu tomhais luas na gaoithe.
aneroid, *s.* inneal tomhais aimsir.
anew, *adv.* as ùr, a rithist.
anfractuous, *adj.* lùbach, cam.
angel, *s.* aingeal ; neach aillidh, — glan ; fear-cobhair caomh, bonn òir (eadar 6/8, agus 10/-).
angelic, *adj.* air dhreach aingil.
angelica, *s.* lus-nam-buadh.
angelical, *adj.* coltach ri aingeal.
angelically, *adv.* air mhodh aingil.
anger, *s.* fearg, corruich, mìothlachd.
anger, *v. a.* brosnaich gu feirg.
angle, *s.* gobhal ; uileann.
angle, *v. a.* iasgaich le slait.
angled, *adj.* oisinneach, uilinneach.
angler, *s.* iasgair-slaite.
Anglican, *adj.* Sasunnach.
Anglicism, *s.* dòigh na Beurla.
angling, *s.* iasgach le slait.
angry, *adj.* feargach, corrach, cas.
anguish, *s.* dòrainn, àmhghar.
angular, *adj.* ceàrnach ; oisinneach.
angularity, *s.* cearnachd, oisinneachd.
angusti- *in cpd.* àimhleathan, cumhang.
anhelation, *s.* seitrich, plosgartaich.
animadversion, *s.* cronachadh, rannsachadh.
animadvert, *v. n.* thoir achmhasan, cronaich ; rannsaich.
animal, *s.* ainmhidh, brùid.
animalcule, *s.* meanbh-bheathach.
animate, *v. a.* beothaich ; neartaich.
animate, *adj.* beò, beothail, beathail.
animated, *adj.* beothaichte, beothail.
animation, *s.* beothachadh.
animosity, *s.* gàmhlas, falachd.
anise, *s.* anis, seòrsa luibhe.
anker, *s.* leth-bharaille, buideal.
ankle, *s.* aobronn, caol na coise, muthairne.
ankled, *adj.* aobronnach.
annalist, *s.* seanachaidh, eachdraiche, sgeulaiche.
annals, *s.* eachdraidh bhliadhnail.
annex, *v. a.* ceangail ; snàidhm ; cuir ris.
annihilate, *v. a.* dìthich, cuir as, sgrios.
annihilation, *s.* léir-sgrios.
anniversary, *s.* cuirm bhliadhnail.
annotation, *s.* mìneachadh.
annotator, *s.* fear-mìneachaidh.
announce, *v. a.* cuir an céill, foillsich.
annoy, *v. a.* cuir dragh, no càmpar air.
annoyance, *s.* trioblaid, buaireas.
annoyer, *s.* buaireadair.

annual, *adj.* bliadhnail.
annually, *adv.* gach bliadhna ; o bhliadhna gu bliadhna.
annuity, *s.* suim-bhliadhnail, cur a steach bliadhnail.
annul, *v. a.* cuir as, dubh a mach.
annular, *adj.* fàineach.
annulet, *s.* fàine, ailbheag.
annunciate, *v. a.* aithris, innis.
annunciation, *s.* latha-feill-Muire, sgeula na h-aingil air teachd Chriosd.
anodyne, *adj.* furtachail, faothachail, cungaidh a mharbhas pian.
anoint, *v. a.* ung, suath le ola ; coisrig.
anointing, *s.* ungadh, coisrigeadh.
anon, *adv.* an dràst 's a rithist, air ball, an ceart uair.
anonymous, *adj.* neo-ainmichte, gun urra.
another, *adj.* tuilleadh ; neach eile.
ansated, *adj.* cluasach, làmhach.
answer, *v. a. and n.* freagair, thoir freagairt, thoir freagradh ; toilich, dèan an gnothach ; freagair an àite, no air son —.
answer, *s.* freagradh, freagairt.
answerable, *adj.* freagarrach, cunntachail.
ant, *s.* seangan.
antagonist, *s.* nàmhaid, nàmh, fear comfharpais.
antecedence, *s.* tùs-imeachd, urram toisich.
antechamber, *s.* seòmar-beòil ; fosgalan.
antedate, *v. a.* sgrìobh ùine air ais, cuir ceann-là na's tràithe na 'n fhìor àm.
antediluvian, *adj.* roimh 'n tuil.
antelope, *s.* fiadh-ghobhar.
anthem, *s.* laoidh-naomha.
anthology, *s.* badag-lus ; leabhar laoidhean.
anthropology, *s.* eòlas air seann eachdraidh an duine.
antic, *adj.* neònach, fiadh-chleasach.
antichrist, *s.* anacriosd.
antichristian, *adj.* ana-criosdail.
anticipate, *v. a.* cuir roimh-eòlas, r-bhlais, r-sheilbhich.
anticipation, *s.* an dùil ri —.
antidote, *s.* ìocshlaint, leigheas air puinnsean.
antipathy, *s.* fuath, gràin, sgreamh.
antipoison, *s.* ùrchasg puinnsein.
antiquary, antiquarian, *s.* arsadair, arsair, seann-seanachaidh.
antiquate, *v. a.* cuir á cleachdadh, á fasan.
antique, *adj.* aosda ; seann-ghnàthach.
antiquity, *s.* arsachd, seanachd.
antiscorbutic, *s.* claimh-leigheas.
antitype, *s.* brìgh-shamhla.
antler, *s.* meur cabair féidh.
anus, *s.* tòn, toll tòine.
anvil, *s.* innean gobha.
anxiety, *s.* iomagain, smuairean.

anxious, *adj.* iomagaineach, trioblaideach.

any, *adj.* aon, aon sam bith, cò sam bith.

anywise, *adv.* air dhòigh sam bith.

apace, *adv.* gu grad, gu luath.

apart, *adv.* air leth, gu taobh.

apartment, *s.* seòmar.

apathist, *s.* duine gun fhaireachdainn.

apathy, *s.* cion-mothachaidh, meaghbhlàths, leth-choma.

ape, *s.* apa, apag ; fear-fanaid.

ape, *v. a.* dèan atharrais, dèan fochaid.

aperient, *adj.* math gu fosgladh, cungaidh fuasglaidh.

aperture, *s.* fosgladh, sgoltadh, toll.

apery, *s.* atharrais, spadaireachd.

apex, *s.* binnean, barr, mullach, bidean.

aphasia, *s.* cion còmhraidh (le galair eanchainn).

aphonia, *s.* tùchadh, cion gutha.

aphorism, *s.* gnàthfhacal, geurfhacal, seanfhacal.

apiary, *s.* tigh-sheillein, beachlann.

apiece, *adv.* gach aon, an t-aon.

apish, *adj.* pròiseil, faoin-bheachdail.

apnoea, *s.* cion-analach, mùchadh.

apocalypse, *s.* taisbeanadh.

apocrypha, *s.* leabhraichean nach 'eil fios có a sgrìobh iad, agus a tha gun ùgh-darras 's an eaglais.

apocryphal, *adj.* neo - chinnteach teagmhach.

apologise, *v. a.* aidich coire, iarr maitheanas.

apologue, *s.* sgeulachd, no ursgeul, thoir leisgeul cothromach.

apology, *s.* leisgeul, iarraidh maitheanis ; argumaid dhion ; seasamh na firinn (le reusonachadh).

apophthegm, *s.* geurfhacal.

apoplexy, *s.* an spadthinneas, tinneas tuiteamach.

apostasy, *s.* cùl-shleamhnachadh.

apostate, *adj.* mealltach, neo-dhìleas, claonach.

apostatise, *v. n.* claon o chreidimh, — o bhòidean, — o eaglais.

apostleship, *s.* abstolachd.

apostolical, *adj.* abstolach.

apothecary, *s.* drugaist, fear-reic chungaidhean.

appal, *v. a.* cuir fo eagal.

apparatus, *s.* uidheam, acfhuinn.

apparel, *s.* earradh, trusgan, aodach.

apparent, *adj.* soilleir, a réir coltais.

apparition, *s.* sealladh, tanasg, taibhs.

appeal, *v. a.* and *n.* tog do chùis gu cùirt as àirde ; gairm mar fhianais, cuir impidh, dian ghuidhe.

appeal, *s.* togail cùise o aon chùirt gu cùirt as àirde, tagradh an aghaidh binn.

appear, *v. n.* thig am fradharc.

appearance, *s.* teachd an làthair ; sealladh, coltas, cruth ; taisbeanadh.

appease, *v. a.* réitich, sìthich, ciùinich.

appeasement, *s.* sìothchaint, réite.

appellant, *s.* and *adj.* fear a thog a chùis gu àrd-chùirt.

appellative, *s.* co-ainm, tiodal.

append, *v. a.* cuir ris, leasaich (aig deireadh sgrìobhaidh).

appendix, *s.* sgrìobhadh leudachaidh (aig deireadh leabhair).

appertain, *v. n.* buntain a thaobh còrach, no nàduir.

appertinent, *adj.* dligheach.

appetise, *v. t.* thoir càil, geuraich càil.

appetite, *s.* miann, déigh, togradh, toil ; ana-miann, an-togradh feòlmhor ; fìor-chion ; acras.

applaud, *v. a.* àrd-mhol, cliùthaich ; dèan lùth-ghair.

applause, *s.* ard-mholadh, mòr-chliù.

applausive, *adj.* moltach, cliùiteach.

apple, *s.* ubhall.

applicable, *adj.* freagarrach, iomchuidh.

application, *s.* co-chur, samhlachadh ; dian-smuaineachadh, dìchioll, cleachdadh, cur gu feum — gu buil.

applicative, applicatory, *adj.* dìcheallach, freagarrach.

apply, *v. a.* and *n.* co-chuir, càirich air, cuir plàsd ; cuir air son, builich ; dian-smuainich, leag inntinn air, cleachd dìcheall ; iarr, aslaich.

appoint, *v. a.* suidhich, ainmich, òrduich ; deasaich, uidheamaich.

appointment, *s.* suidheachadh, ainmeachadh, òrdachadh ; deasachadh, gairm, dreuchd.

apportion, *v. a.* dèan roinn chothromach.

apposite, *adj.* iomchuidh, cothromach, co-fhreagrach.

appraise, *v. a.* meas, cuir luach air.

appreciate, *v. a.* meas, tuig luach ni.

apprehend, *v. a.* glac, beir, dèan gréim ; tuig, measraich ; gabh eagal ; thoir fainear.

apprehension, *s.* smuaineachadh, measrachadh ; tuigse, reuson, comas fiosrachaidh ; eagal, faiteachas ; amharus.

apprehensive, *adj.* geur-thuigseach ; eaglach, amharusach ; mothachail.

apprentice, *s.* fòghlumaich céirde.

apprenticeship, *s.* úine - ionnsachaidh céirde, aonta.

apprise, *v.* thoir fios, thoir brath, innis, cuir an céill.

approach, *v. a.* thig am fagus ; dlùthaich, tarruing.

approach, *s.* dlùthachadh, teannadh.

approbation, *s.* dearbhadh, moladh, taitneas.

appropriate, *v.* and *a.* cuir air leth ; gabh

mar do chuid féin, cothromach, freagarrach.

appropriation, s. cur gu feum àraidh.

approvable, adj. cliù-thoillteanach.

approve, v. a. and n. bi toilichte, gabh tlachd ; mol ; dearbh, fìreanaich, thoir gnùis —.

approvement, s. dearbhadh, toil, moladh, taitneachd.

approximate, adj. faisg, dlù.

approximation, s. dlùthachadh, teachd am fagus ; a sìor-dhlùthachadh.

April, s. an Giblean.

apron, s. aparan, criosan.

apropos, adv. a thaobh (so no sud).

apt, adj. deas, ealamh, buailteach.

aptitude, s. freagarrachd, deasachd aomadh, buailteachd, claonadh.

aptly, adv. deas, ealamh, buailteach.

aptness, s. freagarrachd, deasachd ; buailteachd, aomadh.

aqua-fortis, s. uisge teinntidh, a leaghas gach meatailt ach òr agus Platina.

aquatic, adj. a bhuineas do uisge ; a' tighinn beò, no fàs 'san uisge.

aqueduct, s. amar uisge.

aqueous, adj. uisgidh.

aquiline, adj. crom-shronach.

Arabic, s. cainnt nan Arabianach.

arable, adj. so-threabhaidh, talamh treabhaidh.

arbiter, s. fear réiteachaidh cùise, breithimh.

arbitrary, adj. aintighearnail, borb-smachdail, magaideach, reasgach.

arbitrate, v. a. and n. thoir breith réiteachaidh ; suidh am breith.

arbitration, s. breith-réite.

arbitrator, s. àrd-uachdaran, fear meas ; fear réiteachaidh.

arborescent, adj. a craobh-fhàs.

arcade, s. sràid fo dhion.

arch, s. bogha.

arch-, in cpd. priomh, àrd.

archangel, s. àrd-aingeal ; an deanntag mharbh, calman.

archangelic, adj. ard-aingealach.

archbishop, s. ard-easbuig.

arched, adj. crom, air chumadh bogha.

archer, s. boghadair, fear-saighid.

archery, s. boghadaireachd.

archetypal, adj. priomh-shamhlachail.

archetype, s. priomh-shamhla.

architect, s. fear-deilbh thogalaichean, fear-teagasg togalach.

architecture, s. eòlas togail thighean.

archives, s. tasg-thigh sheann sgrìobh-aidhean is chòraichean.

ardent, adj. lasganta ; bras, garg, àrd-inntinneach ; teas-ghràdhach, càir-deil.

ardently, adv. dàimheil, blàth chridheach.

ardour, s. blàthas, teas ; teas-ghràdh.

arduous, adj. ard, cas ; duilich.

area, s. raon, magh ; ionad fosgailte.

argue, v. a. and n. reusonaich ; conn-saich, tagair an aghaidh ; dearbh, còmhdaich, dean a mach.

argument, s. argamaid, reuson ; ceann-aobhair, cùis-thagraidh ; suim-sgrìo-bhaidh, connsachadh, deasbaireachd.

argumental, adj. argumaideach.

argumentation, s. reusonachadh, deasb-aireachd, connsachadh.

argumentative, adj. argamaideach, reus-onta, deagh-thagarrach ; connspaid-each, deasbaireach.

argute, adj. seòlta, carach, geur ; sgrea-dach.

arid, adj. tioram, tartmhor, loisgte.

aridity, s. tiormachd, tartmhorachd ; cruas-cridhe, fuar-chràbhadh.

aright, adj. gu ceart, gun chron.

arise, v. n. éirich suas, dìrich an aird ; mosgail.

arista, s. calg.

aristocracy, s. na h-uaislean, daoine mòra na tìre.

arithmetic, s. cùnntas, eòlas-àireamh.

ark, s. àirc.

arm, s. gàirdean ; loch-mara.

arm, v. a. armaich, cuir ort t' airm.

armada, s. feachd-mara.

armament, s. feachd-mara no tire.

armful, s. làn na h-achlais, achlasan.

armistice, s. sìth ghoirid (eadar airm).

armlet, s. meanbh-ghàirdean ; bàghan-mara ; dìon gàirdean.

armorial, adj. suaicheantach.

armour, s. armachd.

armourer, s. fear-dheanamh arm, oifigeir ris a bheil armachd an earbsa.

armpit, s. lag-na-h-achlais.

arms, s. armachd, beart-chogaidh ; suaicheantas, gearradh-arm.

army, s. armailt, feachd-cogaidh.

aromatic, aromatical, adj. deagh-bholt-rach.

aromatics, s. spìosran.

aromatise, v. a. spìosraich ; dean cùbh-raidh.

around, ad. prep. mun cuairt.

arouse, v. a. dùisg, gluais suas, tog.

arraign, v. a. deasaich cùis, cuir an òrdugh, cuir air seòl ; thoir an làthair ; coirich, dìt, cuir cron às leth.

arraignment, s. coireachadh, dìteadh.

arrange, v. a. cuir an uidheam, réitich.

arrangement, s. réiteachadh.

arrant, adj. fìor, tur, arrant fool, fìor amadan ; arrant scoundrel, fìor shlaigh-tire.

arras, s. obair-ghréis.

array, s. riaghailt, uidheam, òrdugh-catha ; deasachadh, éideadh.

array, v. a. cuir an òrdugh, cuir an
riaghailt, tarruing suas ; sgeadaich.
arrear, s. fiachan.
arrest, s. sàradh ; glacadh, cur an làimh.
arrest, v. a. glac, cuir an làimh, cuir
an sàs, cuir sàradh, cuir an gréim
laghail.
arrival, s. tighinn, teachd, ruigsinn.
arrive, v. a. ruig ; thig.
arrogance, arrogancy, s. ladarnas, dànadas, uaill, ceannardas, àrdan.
arrogant, adj. ladarna, dàna, ceannasach,
àrdanach.
arrogate, v. a. gabh ort gu dàna.
arrow, s. saighead, guin, gath.
arsenal, s. arm-lann.
arsmart, s. lus-an-fhogair.
art, s. eòlas, ìnnleachd ; ealain ; cèard ;
seòltachd ; alt, dòigh.
artery, s. cuisle, fèith.
artful, adj. innleachdach, seòlta, ealanta ;
cuilbheartach, carach ; eòlach teòma,
deas.
artfulness, s. ealantachd, seòltachd.
arthritis, s. tinneas-nan-alt.
artichoke, s. farusgag ; bliosan.
article, s. mion-fhacal ; cumha, pong,
ceann-teagaisg.
article, v. a. and n. cùmhnantaich, réitich,
suidhich ; còrd ri, ceangail.
articular, adj. altach.
articulate, adj. pongail, soilleir, so-thuigsinn ; a bhuineas do altaibh a' chuirp.
articulate, v. a. abair gu soilleir, pongail ;
dean cumhachan, altaich, cuir an altan,
cuir fuaim glan air facal.
articulation, s. ceangal nan alt 's nan
cnàmh, alt-cheangal ; pong-labhairt,
fuam glan (air facail).
artifice, s. car, cuilbheart, dò-bheart,
eòlas, teòmachd.
artificer, s. fear-cèirde (saor, clachair, òr-
cheard).
artificial, adj. dèanta le fear-ceirde.
artificiality, s. ceàrdachd, ceàrdachas.
artillery, s. gunnachan mòra, earrainn
dhe 'n arm.
artisan, s. fear-cèirde ; fear-ealain.
artist, s. dealbhadair, snaidheadair.
artiste, s. seinneadair, dannsair, cleasaiche, etc.
artless, adj. aineolach, neo-chealgach,
neo-sgilear, neo-lochdach, libeasta.
as, conj. 1. cho, co : thainig e cho luath
's a b' urrainn e, he came as fast as he
could ; tha thu cho maith ris-san, you
are as good as he is. 2. mar : dean mar
is toigh leat, do as you like. 3. an
uair : an uair a bha mi tighinn, as I
was coming along. 4. chionn : chionn
nach robh thu làthair, as you were not
present. 5. is : cho maith is gu bheil e,
good as he is. 6. ri, ris : cho luath

ris a' chù, as fast as the dog ; cho
luath ri cu, as fast as a dog.
asbestine, adj. nach cnàmh as.
ascend, v. a. and n. dìrich, streap, tog,
gabh suas, éirich.
ascendancy, s. cumhachd, uachdranachd
smachd.
ascendant, s. àirde ; uachdranachd,
ceannardachd, làmh an uachdair.
ascendant, adj. an uachdar, uachdrach,
ainneartach ; 's an t-sealladh.
ascension, s. éirigh, dìreadh, dol suas.
ascension-day, s. latha dol suas ar
Slànaighir.
ascent, s. éirigh, dol suas, dìreadh, rathad-
dìridh, slighe dhol suas ; bruthach,
uchdach, aonach, àirde.
ascertain, v. a. dean cinnteach, dearbh,
socraich, suidhich ; faigh fios, cuir á
teagamh, faigh a mach.
ascertainable, adj. so dhearbhta, so
fhiosraichte.
ascribe, v. a. cuir as leth.
ascription, s. cur as leth.
ash, s. uinnseann.
ashamed, adj. nàraichte, fo nàire.
ashes, s. luath, luaithre.
ashore, adv. air tìr, air tràigh.
ashy, adj. air dhreach na luaithre.
Asia, s. an Asia.
aside, adv. siar, a thaobh, a lethtaobh,
às an t-slighe ; leis féin.
ask, v. a. and n. iarr, sir, guidh ; ceasnaich, feòraich, faighnaich ; fiosraich.
askance, adv. cam, siar, claon.
asker, s. fear-iarraidh, fear-achanaich,
fear-siridh, fear-rannsachaidh ; arc-
luachrach uisge.
askew, adv. gu claon, gu tàireil, gu
sanntach ; gu cam, a leth-taobh.
asleep, adv. an cadal, an suain.
aslope, adv. le leathad, fiar, cam.
asp, aspic, s. nathair nimhe.
asparagus, s. creamh-mac-fiagh.
aspect, s. snuadh, gnùis, aogas, dreach.
aspen, s. critheann, an critheach.
asper, adj. garbh, geur, doirbh.
asperate, v. a. dean garbh, dean doirbh.
asperation, s. garbhachadh, doirbheach-
adh.
asperity, s. gairbhe, garbh-fhuaim ; gairge,
crosdachd, sglàmhrainn, fiatachd ;
geurachd.
asperse, v. a. cùl-chain, maslaich.
asperser, s. fear-tuaileis.
aspirate, v. a. and n. analaich, séid
bogaich, bàth (litir).
aspiration, s. geur-thogradh, beò-iarraidh ;
miann air ni-eigin mór ; bogachadh,
bàthadh litreach.
aspire, v. a. and n. iarr, miannaich,
bi'n déidh air ; dìrich suas, éirich suas.
aspiring, s. ard-mhiann.

382 ASS—ATHWART

ass, s. asal, ùmaidh ; amhlair ; tamhasg.
assail, v. a. thoir ionnsaigh air, leum
air ; cas ris, connsaich ; aslaich.
assailable, adj. so-bhuailte.
assailant, s. fear-ionnsaigh, nàmhaid.
assailant, adj. a bheir ionnsaigh, a dh'
éireas air, connsachail, strìtheil.
assassin, s. mortair, neach a bheir
ionnsaigh mharbhaidh.
assassinate, v. a. and n. mort, marbh
le foill ; thoir ionnsaigh mharbhaidh
gu h-uaigneach.
assassination, s. mort, marbhadh le foill.
assassinator, s. mortair foille.
assault, s. ionnsaigh, buille, ruathar.
assault, v. a. thoir ionnsaigh, buail.
assay, s. deuchainn, feuchainn dearbhadh;
tòiseachadh, luach.
assemblage, s. cruinneachadh, tional.
assemble, v. a. cruinnich.
assembler, s. fear-cruinneachaidh.
assembling, s. cruinneachadh, tional.
assembly, s. co-chruinneachadh, àrd-
sheanadh.
assent, s. aontachadh, còrdadh, aont,
géill.
assert, v. a. tagair, agair ; saor, teasairg,
seas a' chòir.
assertion, s. tagradh, agairt ; facal,
ceann-dearbhaidh.
assertive, adj. tagrach, dian-bhriathrach,
abartach.
assertor, s. fear-tagraidh, fear-dearbhaidh.
assess, v. a. leag cìs, no càin ; tog cìs,
meas.
assessable, adj. cìs-dhiolach.
assessionary, adj. a bhuineas do luchd-
cìse.
assessment, s. càin ; cìs-leagadh.
assever, asseverate, v. a. dian-bhriath-
raich, mionnaich.
asseveration, s. briathar, mionnan.
assiduity, s. dìchioll, buan-dhùrachd.
assiduous, adj. dìchiollach, dùrachdach,
leanmhainneach.
assign, v. a. òrduich, comharraich, cuir
air leth, sònraich ; suidhich, socraich,
ceartaich ; thoir còir seachad.
assignation, s. ainmeachadh ; toirt seachad còrach ; cur air leth, sònrachadh,
ùghdaras riaghlaidh.
assignment, s. sònrachadh, cur air leth.
assimilate, v. a. dèan coltach ; meirbh,
cnàmh.
assist, v. a. cuidich, fòir, dèan còmhnadh.
assistance, s. cobhair, còmhnadh.
assistant, s. fear-còmhnaidh, fear-cuideachaidh, fear-cobhrach.
assize, s. mòd ; luchd-breith, reachd-
riaghailt.
associate, v. a. and n. dèan companas,
cùm cuideachdas.

associate, s. companach.
association, s. co-aontachadh, co-
chomunn, comunn, co-chuideachd ;
co-chùmhnant, co-réite ; co-phàirt,
co-cheangaltas.
assoil, v. a. fuasgail, freagair, thoir
deagh fhreagairt ; cuir mu sgaoil.
assort, v. a. cuir an òrdugh, réitich.
assortment, s. cur an òrdugh, réiteachadh ;
cruinneachadh dhe gach seòrsa.
assuage, v. a. and n. caisg, lùghdaich,
eutromaich ; sìthich ; traogh, tuit,
laigh.
assuagement, s. faothachadh, lasachadh,
lùghdachadh, socair.
assuager, s. fear-sìtheachaidh, fear-
eutromachaidh.
assuasive, adj. ciùineach, a chiùinicheas,
a dh' aotromaicheas.
assume, v. a. and n. gabh ort, togair ;
tog, glac ; bi ceannasach, uaibhreach.
assuming, s. ladarnas, dànadas.
assuming, adj. uaibhreach, ladarna.
assumption, s. glacadh, gabhail do
t'ionnsaigh féin ; barail gun chòmh-
dachadh; togail suas do nèamh (Muire).
assurance, s. dearbhachd, làn-dearbh-
achd, cinnteachas ; làn-dòchas, beag-
narachd, ladarnachd, peasanachd ;
aobhar-dòchais, meamnadh, smioralachd, tréine.
assure, v. a. dèan cinnteach, cuir á
teagamh.
assured, adj. cinnteach, dearbhte.
assuredly, adv. gun teagamh.
astern, adv. gu deireadh na luinge, an
comhair deiridh.
asthma, s. cuing, mùchadh.
asthmatic, adj. leis a' chuing.
astonish, v. a. iongantaich, cuir ioghnadh.
astonishment, s. ioghnadh.
astound, v. a. uamhunnaich.
astray, adv. air seacharan.
astriction, s. teannachadh, ceangal.
astrictive, adj. teanntach.
astride, adv. casa-gòbhlach.
astringe, v. a. teannaich, crup.
astringent, adj. ceangaltach.
astrologer, s. speuradair.
astrology, s. speuradaireachd.
astronomer, s. reulladair, speuradair.
astronomical, adj. reull-eòlach.
astronomy, s. reull-eòlas.
astro-theology, s. reull-dhiadhachd.
asunder, adv. air leth, o chéile, as a
chéile.
asylum, s. ionad-tèarmainn, tigh caoth-
aich.
atheism, s. aicheadh air bith Dhé.
atheist, s. fear-àicheadh Dhé.
atheistical, adj. neo-chreidmheach.
athletic, adj. làidir, calma, fearail.
athwart, adv. gu tuaitheal, tarsuinn.

atlas, *s.* leabhar dealbha dhùthchannan.
atmosphere, *s.* an t-àileadh, adhar.
atom, atomy, *s.* dadmun, smùirnean, càillean, dùradan, fuilbhean.
atomical, *adj.* smùirneanach, deannanach fuilbheanach.
atomism, *s.* teagasg nan smùirnean.
atone, *v. a.* and *n.* thoir dìol, éirig ; dean réite air son chiontach.
atonement, *s.* réite, còrdadh ; éirig, ìobairt-réite.
atrocious, *adj.* aingidh, an-trom, mallaichte, fuilteach, borb.
atrociously, *adv.* gu h-aingidh.
atrocity, *s.* aingidheachd, buirbe.
attach, *v. a.* glac ; tàlaidh, dlùthaich riut féin.
attachment, *s.* dìlseachd, a leanmhainneachd, dàimh ; gràdh, rùn.
attack, *v. a.* thoir ionnsaigh ; cronaich.
attack, *s.* ionnsaigh nàimhdeil.
attain, *v. a.* and *n.* faigh, buannaich, coisinn ; thig suas ; ruig, gabh seilbh thig a dh' ionnsaigh.
attainable, *adj.* so-ruigheachd.
attainder, *s.* dìteadh lagha, cùirtdhìteadh ; truailleachd, coire.
attainment, *s.* buannachd, ionnsachadh ; ruigsinn.
attaint, *v. a.* maslaich ; salaich, truaill.
attemper, attemperate, *v. a.* measgaich ; bogaich ; dean freagarrach.
attempt, *v. a.* thoir ionnsaigh, thoir oidhirp.
attempt, *s.* ionnsaigh ; oidhirp.
attend, *v. a.* and *n.* feith, fritheil, fan, fuirich ; thoir aire, beachdaich.
attendance, *s.* feitheamh, frithealadh ; aire, seirbhis.
attendant, *adj.* fritheilteach.
attendant, *s.* fear-frithealaidh.
attention, *s.* aire, furachras, faicill.
attentive, *adj.* furachail, faicilleach, cùramach.
attenuate, *v. a.* tanaich ; lùghdaich.
attenuation, *s.* tanachadh, tanachd.
attest, *v. a.* thoir fianais, tog fianais.
attestation, *s.* teisteas, dearbhadh.
attic, *adj.* glan - chainnteach, grinnlabhrach.
attic, *s.* seòmar mullaich.
attire, *v. a.* aodaich, còmhdaich, sgeudaich, sgiamhaich, cuir an uidheam.
attire, *s.* eudach, còmhdach, earradh, culaidh, trusgan.
attitude, *s.* suidheachadh, seasamh.
attorney, *s.* àrd-sgrìobhair lagha, fearlagha.
attract, *v. a.* tarruing, tàlaidh, meall.
attraction, *s.* comas tàlaidh no meallaidh, sùghadh.
attractive, *adj.* tarruingeach, sughach ; tàlaidheach, mealltach.

attribute, *v. a.* cuir as leth.
attribute, *s.* feart, buaidh, cliù.
attribution, *s.* moladh, buaidh-chliù.
attrition, *s.* caitheamh, bleith, mìnshuathadh ; duilichinn ; cràdh-inntinn.
attune, *v. a.* gleus, cuir am fonn.
auburn, *adj.* buidhe-dhonn.
auction, *s.* reic follaiseach, rup.
auctioneer, *s.* fear-reic ; fear-rup.
audacious, *adj.* dàna, ladarna ; beagnàrach, beadaidh.
audaciousness, *s.* dànachd.
audacity, *s.* dànadas, ladarnas.
audible, *adj.* labhrach, a chluinnear.
audience, *s.* éisdeachd ; luchd-éisdeachd, co-thional.
auditor, *s.* fear-éisdeachd, fear-rannsachaidh chunntasan.
auditory, *s.* luchd-éisdeachd ; ionadéisdeachd.
auger, *s.* tora, sniamhaire, boireal.
aught, *n.* and *adv.* ni sam bith, dad.
augment, *v. a.* meudaich.
augmentation, *s.* meudachadh, piseach.
augur, *s.* fiosaiche, eun-dhruidh.
auguration, *s.* eun-dhruidheachd.
augury, *s.* fiosachd le comharraibh.
August, *s.* ceud mìos an Fhoghair.
august, *adj.* mór, urramach, naomha.
aulic, *adj.* cùirteil, rìoghail, flathail.
auln, *s.* slat-thomhais.
aunt, *s.* piuthar athar no mathar.
aurelia, *s.* spiontag, òg-chnuimh.
auricle, *s.* bilean na cluaise ; cluasan a' chridhe.
auricula, *s.* lus-na-bann-rìgh.
auricular, *adj.* a bhuineas do'n chluais.
aurist, *s.* leighiche chluas.
aurora, *s.* luibh-chrodh-an-eich ; reull na maidne, fir-chlis.
aurora australis, *s.* fir-chlis an taobh deas.
aurora borealis, *s.* fir-chlis an taobh tuath.
auscultation, *s.* cluas-aire, cluas-rannsachadh an leighiche.
auspice, *s.* fàidhdearachd pàganach ; spéis ; dùthrachd.
auspicious, *adj.* sealbhach ; gealltanach.
austere, *adj.* cruaidh, gruamach ; searbh, geur.
austerity, *s.* teanntachd, gruamachd ; an-iochd.
austral, *adj.* a deas, deiseal.
authentic, *a.* fìor, cinnteach, dearbhte.
authenticate, *v. a.* dearbh, dèan cinnteach.
authenticity, *v. a.* cinnteachd.
author, *s.* ùghdar, fear sgrìobhaidh leabhair.
authorise, *v. a.* thoir ùghdarras, ceadaich ; fìreanaich, dearbh.
authoritative, *adj.* ùghdarrach, le ùghdarras.
authority, *s.* ùghdarras ; cumhachd.
autography, *s.* dearbh làmh-sgrìobhaidh.

autumn, s. am foghar.
autumnal, adj. fogharach.
auxiliary, s. fear-cuideachaidh.
avail, v. a. buannaich, coisinn, dèan feum, gabh cothrom.
available, adj. buannachail, tarbhach, feumail ; cumhachdach.
avarice, s. sannt, spìocaireachd.
avaricious, adj. sanntach, déidheil, spìocach.
avast, adv. cum air do làimh, stad, sguir ; gu leòir.
avaunt, interj. as mo shealladh ! air falbh ! truis !
Ave Mary, s. Fàilte Muire.
avenge, v. a. dìol, thoir gu peanas.
avengement, s. dìoghaltas, dìoladh.
avenger, s. fear-dìolaidh.
avenue, s. rathad, slighe, sràid eadar chraobhan.
aver, v. a. cuir an céill, abair gu barantach.
average, s. àireamh àraidh ; thairis air a chéile.
averment, s. dearbhadh le fianuis.
averse, adj. fuathach, gràinichte.
aversion, s. fuath, gràin.
avert, v. a. tionndaidh gu taobh.
aviary, s. eun-lann.
avidity, s. gionachd, glamaireachd.
avocation, s. gairm ; dreuchd ; obair.
avoid, v. a. and n. seachainn ; cuibhtich, cuir cùl.
avoidable, adj. so-sheachainte.
avolation, s. itealachadh, fuadach, teich-eadh.

avouch, v. a. abair gu daingeann, cuir an céill gu dian ; thoir dearbhadh.
avouchment, s. aideachadh, fianuis, teisteas.
avow, v. a. cuir an céill, aidich, bòidich.
avowal, s. aideachadh fosgailte.
avulsion, s. spìonadh, reubadh.
await, v. a. fuirich, fan, feith.
awake, v. a. dùisg, mosgail.
award, v. a. thoir dìoladh a réir toillteanais ; duaisich.
award, s. breitheanas, binn, duais.
aware, adj. faicilleach, furachair, fiosrach, away, adv. air falbh, trus air falbh !
awe, s. eagal, urram, giorrag.
awful, adj. eagalach, gealtach ; a dhùisgeas urram ; urramach.
awfulness, s. uabhasachd, eagalachd.
awhile, adv. tacan, car tacain.
awkward, adj. cearbach, neo-sgiobalta, slaodach, slaopach, clobhdach, liobasta.
awkwardly, adv. gu cearbach.
awl, s. minidh bhròg.
awn, s. calg arbhair no feòir.
awning, s. brat-dìona ; brat-dubhair.
awry, adv. cam, claon, fiar-shuileach.
axe, s. tuagh ; lamh-thuagh.
axilla, s. lag na h-achlais, asgail.
axillar, adj. asgaileach.
axiom, s. firinn shoilleir, firinn so-fhaicsinneach ; fìrinn shuidhichte.
axle, axle-tree, s. aiseal, crann-aisil.
ay, adv. seadh, gu dearbh.
aye, adv. do ghnàth, gu bràth.
azure, adj. speur-ghorm, liath-ghorm.

B

baa, s. méilich, méile nan caorach.
baal, s. dia bréige, iodhol.
babble, s. gobaireachd, luath-bheulachd.
babbler, s. glagaire, beul-gun-fhàitheam.
babbling, s. glagaireachd, glogaireachd.
babe, s. naoidhean, naoidheachan, lean-aban.
baboon, s. apa de'n t-seòrsa is mò.
baccāte, adj. cuirneanach, caoireanach ; air chumadh caoirean.
bacchanalian, s. misgear.
bachelor, s. seanaghille.
back, s. cùl, cùlaibh ; druim, croit.
back, adv. air ais ; an coinneamh a chùil.
back, v. a. theirig air muin, marcaich ; tog air muin ; seas taobh neach ; tagair, neartaich, cuidich ; dìon ; rach an urras.
backbite, v. a. cùl-chàin, tog tuaileas.
backbiter, s. fear cùl-chàinnt, fear-tuaileis.
backed, part. cùl-tacaichte.

backgammon, s. tàileasg.
backside, s. leth-deiridh, tòn, taobh-cùil.
backslider, s. fear-cul-sleamhnachaidh.
back-stay, s. stagh-cùil.
backsword, s. claidheamh aon fhaobhair.
backward, adv. an coinneamh a chùil.
backward, adj. neo-thoileach, aindeonach ; mall, leasg, tròm.
bacon, s. muicfheoil réisgte.
bad, adj. olc, dona ; aingidh, crosda cronail, ciurrail, tinn, euslan.
bade, pret. of bid, dh' iarr, dh' àithn.
badge, s. suaicheantas ; comharradh.
badger, s. broc, tùitean, srianach.
baffle, v. a. and n. fairtlich air, rach as o, seachainn, mill ; faigh làmh an uachdar air, thoir an car á ; dean fanaid no sgeig air.
bag, s. poca, balg, sac, màla, màileid.
bagatelle, s. faoineas, nì gun luach.
baggage, s. àirneis, treathlaich feachd ; imrich ; dubh-chaile.

bagnio, s. tigh-faircidh, taigh-siùrsachd.
bagpipe, s. pìob mhór.
bail, v. t. taom ; bail the boat, taom an t-eathar.
bail, s. saorsa, no fuasgladh air urras, fear-urrais, urras ; crìoch frìthe.
bail, v. a. urrasaich, rach an urras air, thoir urras air ; fuasgail air urras.
bailiff, s. bàillidh, fear-riaghlaidh an uachdarain ; maor-fearainn.
bailiwick, s. bàillidheachd ; crìochan bàillidh.
bait, v. a. and n. cuir maghar air dubhan ; biadh, thoir biadh ; sàth ann, thoir ionnsaigh air ; sàraich, mar bheathach 's an stuigear coin ; stad a chum bìdh.
bait, s. maghar ; buaireadh, culaidh-bhuairidh, biadh meallaidh.
baize, s. garbh-chlò fosgailte.
bake, v. a. and n. fuin, taosainn, bruich ann an àmhainn.
bakehouse, s. tigh-fuine.
baker, s. fuineadair.
balance, s. meidh, toimhsean ; dlùth-bheachd ; co-chothromachadh ; barr-achd cudthrom.
balcony, s. foruinneag, foraradh.
bald, adj. maol, sgailceach, lom.
balderdash, s. treamsgal, goileam, earra-ghloir.
baldness, s. maoile, sgailc.
baldpate, s. maolcheann.
bale, s. bathar truiste, sac, ni sam bith truiste chum iomchar ; truaighe.
baleful, adj. truagh, brònach, dóghruinn-each ; millteach, sgriosail.
balk, s. sail, sparr ; balc, bailc, bàn-dhruim eadar dà iomaire ; amladh, dìobradh dòchais.
balk, v. dìobair, tréig.
ball, s. ball, peileir, féis-dannsa.
ballad, s. duanag, òran, luinneag.
ballast, s. balaisd ; leth-luchd ; ciall, tonaisg.
balloon, s. inneal dìridh agus seòlaidh 's na speuraibh.
ballot, s. crann, crannchur ; tilgeadh chrann.
balm, s. ìocshlaint, acfhuinn leighis, comhfhurtachd.
balmy, adj. ìocshlainteach, cùbhraidh, ciùin, leaghasach, tlàth.
balsam, s. ola-leighis. See balm.
balsamic, adj. furtachail.
baluster, s. post beag, rongas.
balustrade, s. sreath phost no rongas.
bamboo, s. cuilc Innseanach.
bamboozle, v. a. meall, cur 'n a bhreislich, thoir a char as.
ban, s. and v. t. gairm fhollaiseach, ascaoin, iomsgaradh, toirmeasg, mall-achadh.

band, s. ceangal, bann ; cuibhreach, slabhraidh ; bann - daingneachaidh ; bannal, còisir, cuideachd, còisir inn-ealan-ciuil.
bandage, s. bann, stìom-cheangail.
band-box, s. bòsdan.
banditti, s. pl. luchd-reubainn, spùill-eadairean.
bandore, s. inneal-ciùil trì-theudach.
bandy, v. a. and n. tilg a null 'sa nall, iomain air ais 's air adhart ; gabh is thoir, co-iomlaidich ; ioma-luaisg.
bandy-leg, s. camachas, cas cham.
bandy-legged, adj. camachasach.
bane, s. nimh ; aimhleas, sgrios, creach.
baneful, adj. nimheil, aimhleasach.
bane-wort, s. lus-na-h-òidhche.
bang, v. slacaich, dòrn, garbh-laimhsich.
bang, s. cnap, dòrn, garbh-bhuille.
banish, v. a. fuadaich (á 'dhùthaich) ; fògair.
banishment, s. fògradh, fògairt.
bank, s. bruach aibhne no uillt ; tòrr, tom, dùn ; tigh-tasgaidh airgid ; cuith (shneachda).
bank, s. tobhta (bàta), cliath (ràmh).
banker, s. fear-malairt-airgid.
bankrupt, s. fear-briste, ceannaiche briste.
bankruptcy, s. briseadh creideis.
banner, s. bratach, suaicheantas, meirghe.
banneret, s. ridire - làraich, fear dhe 'n deanar rìdire am blàr air son a ghaisge.
bannock, s. bonnach, breacag.
banquet, s. cuilm, cuirm, fleadh.
banqueting, s. fleadhachas.
banter, s. magadh, fochaid, sgeig, feala-dhà.
bantling, s. isean, leanabh, leanaban ; peasan.
baptism, s. baisteadh.
baptismal, adj. baistidh, baisteachail.
baptist, baptizer, s. fear-baistidh, baist-each.
bar, s. crann, crann-tarsuinn, crann-doruis ; stad, grabadh, amladh, cnap-starraidh ; oitir, sgeir-bhàite ; ionad-tagraidh an cùirt ; àite roinn na dibhe ; geinn.
bar, v. a. crann, glais, dùin le crann ; bac, grab ; cum a muigh.
barb, s. feusag ; corran, gath, friobhag.
barb, v. a. bearr, lomair ; riobhagaich, thoir calg, thoir corran ; uidheamaich each cogaidh.
barbarian, s. allmharach, duine borb.
barbaric, adj. coimheach, borb, aineolach, gun oilean.
barbarism, s. brùidealachd, an-iochd-mhorachd, buirbe.
barbarous, adj. borb, allmhara, fiadh-aich, neo-oileanta, brùideil ; an-iochdmhor, garg, cruaidh-chridheach.

barbed, *adj.* armaichte, beartaichte, fo làn-uidheam - cogaidh ; riobhagach, corranach, biorach, gathach, calgach.

barbel, *s.* seòrsa éisg, breac-feusagach ; a' mhiol gàilleach.

barber, *s.* bearradair (fuilt no feusaig).

barberry, *s.* preas nan gearr - dhearc, berberry, gearr-dhearcag, gràinnseag.

bard, *s.* bàrd.

bardic, *adj.* bàrdail.

bare, *adj.* lom, lomnochd, rùisgte, nochdta, ris, follaiseach ; falamh.

barefaced, *adj.* bathaiseach ; ladarna, leamh, mi-nàrach.

barefooted, *adj.* casruisgte.

bareheaded, *adj.* ceannruisgte.

barelegged, *adj.* luirgruisgte.

bargain, *s.* còrdadh, cùmhnant ; bathar maith air bheag prìs.

bargain, *v. n.* cùmhnantaich, còrd.

barge, *s.* bàta, bìrlinn.

barilla, *s.* luaithre na celp.

bark, *s.* cairt, rùsg ; bàrca, long trì-chrannach.

bark, *v. a.* and *n.* rùisg, thoir a chairt dheth.

barker, *s.* fear-tathuinn ; dreamaire, fear-rusgaidh chraobh.

barky, *adj.* cairteach, cairtidh.

barley, *s.* eòrna.

barleycorn, *s.* gràinnean-eòrna, spilgean eòrna ; treas earrainn na h-òirleach.

barm, *s.* beirm, deasgainn.

barn, *s.* sabhal, sobhal, sgiobal.

barn-yard, *s.* iothlann.

barnacle, *s.* bàirneach ; an cathan.

barometer, *s.* inneal-tomhas na sìde.

baron, *s.* ridire.

baronage, *s.* baranachd, ridireachd.

baroness, *s.* baintighearn, ban-ridire.

baronet, *s.* ridire beag.

baronical, *adj.* baranach.

barony, *s.* inbhe-barain, fearann ridire.

barrack, *s.* tigh-feachd.

barrel, *s.* baraille, feadan gunna.

barren, *adj.* seasg, aimrid, neo-thorrach, fàs.

barrenness, *s.* aimrideachd, seasgachd.

barricade, *s.* gàradh-bacaidh.

barricade, *v. a.* glais suas, dùin.

barricado, *s.* daingneachd, bàdhun, dìdean.

barrier, *s.* daingneach, dìon, ballabac-aidh, tùr, dùn ; bacadh, amladh, cnapstarraidh ; comharradh - crìche, gàradh-crìche.

barrister, *s.* fear-tagraidh (an cùirtibh Shasuinn).

barrow, *s.* barp ; bara ; carn-cuimhne ('s an t-sean-aimsir).

barter, *s.* malairt, badhar ; luacha-peighinn.

barter, *v. a.* iomlaidich, malairtich, suaip, dèan malairt.

bartram, *s.* lus-a-bhalla.

basalt, *s.* gnè chloiche, clach a bha fo chumhachd teine.

base, *s.* stéidh, bonn, bunait, iochdar, bunchar.

base, *adj.* suarach, neo - luachmhor, truaillidh, gun fhiù ; ìosal, tàireil.

baseness, *s.* suarachas, neo-luachmhor-achd, tàirealachd, truailleachd.

bashful, *adj.* nàrach, athach ; diùid, saidealta.

bashfulness, *s.* nàire, saidealtas.

basilica, *s.* eaglais mhór, eaglais àrd-easbuig.

basin, *s.* soitheach ionnlaid ; port-long, gleannan cruinn, coire ; criochan aibhne.

basis, *s.* stéidh, bunait ; roinn iochdrach puist ; bunchar, bun.

bask, *v. a.* and *n.* grianaich, laigh 's a/ ghréin.

basket, *s.* bascaid, cliabh, sgùlan, craidh-leag.

bass, *s.* casbhrat, glùnbhrat.

bass, *adj.* and *n.* dos-fhuaimneach, torghan, guth prò.

bastard, *s.* neach dìolain ; ni truaillidh.

bastard, *adj.* dìolain ; truaillidh.

bastardise, *v. a.* and *n.* dearbh dìolain ; dèan dìolanas, faigh urra dhìolain.

baste, *v. a.* gabh air le bata ; leagh ìm air.

bastinade, bastinado, *v. a.* slachd le bata, gabh air le bata.

bat, *s.* ialtag, an dialtag.

batch, *s.* uiread arain 'sa dh' fhuinear aig aon àm ; buidheann.

bate, *s.* strìth, caonnag, comh-strith.

bate, *v. a.* and *n.* lùghdaich, leag sìos ; thoir sìos am prìs, leag am prìs, math ; bated breath, fo anail.

bath, *s.* amar-ionnlaid, àite-nighe ; nighe, ionnlad.

bathe, *v. a.* and *n.* ionnlaid, fairig, failc, nigh.

bathos, *s.* sgleò-bhàrdachd, faoineachd (cainnt).

baton, *s.* bata, bata-dreuchd àrd-chinn-iùil ; comharradh-dìolanais ann an gearradh-arm.

battalion, *s.* cuideachd shaighdearan an òrdugh catha.

batten, *v. tr.* and *intr.* dèan reamhar, fàs reamhar.

batten, *s.* maide, stiall fiodha ; fiodh làir.

batter, *v. a.* and *n.* buail sìos, pronn, slachd, tilg sìos, leag sìos ; claoidh le trom sheirbhis.

batter, *s.* coimeasgadh, taois.

battering-ram, *s.* reithe-cogaidh, reithe-slachdaidh, ceann-reithe.

battery, s. bualadh sìos, slacadh ; inn-
ealan slacaidh ; balla ghunnachan
móra ; ionnsaigh nàimhdeil ; feachd
ghunnachan-móra.
battle, s. cath, blàr, còmhrag.
battle-array, s. òrdugh-catha.
battle-axe, s. tuagh-chatha.
battledore, s. stroidhleag ; simid ; liagh.
battlement, s. barrbhalla.
bauble, s. déideag, rud faoin ; suaicheantas amadan cùirte (bata is ceann
aisil air).
bawbee, s. bonna-sia.
bawdy, a. and s. drabast, draosdachd,
tigh-na-nàire.
bawl, v. a. and n. glaodh, ràn, raoic.
bawn, s. bàdhun, buaile (spréidhe) ; buaile
aig dorus caisteil.
bawrel, s. spearag.
bay, adj. donn-ruadh.
bay, s. camus, loch-mara, bàgh.
bay, s. comhart ; tabhunn mialchoin.
bay-salt, s. salann-mara.
bay-tree, s. craobh-laibhreis.
bayonet, s. béigeileid.
bazaar, s. àite-margaidh.
be, v. n. bi ; bi ann, bi beò.
beach, s. mol, tràigh, cladach.
beacon, s. tigh-soluis, teine-rabhaidh.
bead, s. paidirean ; grìogag.
beadle, s. maor ; maor-eaglais.
beagle, s. cù-luirg, tòbhlair ; bàillidh ;
fear-luirg.
beak, s. gob ; sròn ; bior-snaois.
beaker, s. soitheach-gobach, copan òil.
beam, s. sail ; meidh ; cròc, garmainn ;
gath - soluis, gath - gréine, dealradh,
boillsgeadh, dearrsadh.
beam, v. n. dealraich, soillsich, dearrs ;
soillsich air.
bean, s. pònar.
bear, v. a. and n. giùlain, iomchair ; cum
suas, fuiling.
bear, s. math-ghamhainn.
beard, s. feusag ; calg, colg.
beardless, adj. gun fheusag, lom-smigeach.
bearer, s. fear-iomchair ; fear-giùlain.
bearing, s. suidheachadh, sealltainn,
aghaidh ; modh, giùlan ; cùrsa.
beast, s. ainmhidh, beathach; brùid, biast.
beastly, adj. brùideil, biastail.
beat, v. a. and n. buail, thoir buille ;
gabh air, faigh buaidh.
beatific, adj. sona, làn sonais, beannaichte.
beatification, s. beannachadh ; sonas nam
marbh.
beating, s. gabhail air, gréidheadh.
beatitude, s. sonas néamhaidh, beannachd.
beau, s. spalpaire, fear rìomhach ;
leannan.
beauteous, adj. maiseach, àluinn, bòidheach, sgiamhach, grinn.

beauteousness, s. maisealachd.
beautiful, adj. bòidheach, rìomhach.
beautify, v. a. and n. maisich, sgiamhaich,
grinnich.
beauty, s. maise, àillte, sgèimh.
beauty-spot, s. ball-seirce ; ball maise.
beaver, s. dobhar-chu, clàr-aghaidh clog
aid ; ad mholach.
becalm, v. a. sàmhaich, foisich, ciùinich.
because, conj. air son, do-bhrìgh.
beck, s. sméideadh.
beck, s. allt, sruthan.
beckon, v. n. sméid air.
become, v. n. cinn, fàs, freagair.
becoming, adj. iomchuidh, dligheach,
tlachdmhor, ciatach, taitneach, freagarrach.
bed, s. leabaidh.
bedash, v. a. eabraich, beubanaich.
bedding, s. uidheam-leapa, aodach-leapa,
connlach, còineach, etc., fo chrodh 's
an bhàthaich.
bedeck, v. a. sgéimhich, snasaich.
bedehouse, s. tigh-oiriceis.
bedew, v. a. dealtraich, driùchdaich.
bedfellow, s. coimhleapach.
bedlam, s. tigh-cuthaich.
bedrid, adj. air gabhail ri leabaidh, tinn.
bedstead, s. fiodh-leapa.
bee, s. beach, seillean.
beech, s. crann-fàibhile.
beef, s. mairtfheoil ; mart biadhta.
beef-eater, s. saighdear faire ; fear-faire
an Tur Lunnuinn.
beer, s. leann-caol.
beet, s. biotais.
beetle, s. daolag, fairche, ceardaman,
ceard-dubhan.
beetle, s. simist.
beeves, s. pl. crodh, daimh, spréidh.
befall, v. n. tachair, thig gu crìch,—gu
teachd.
befit, v. a. freagair, dèan iomchuidh.
before, prep. roimh ; air beulaibh ; an
làthair, 'san làthair ; mu choinneamh ;
roimhe, a roghainn air ; os cionn.
before, adv. roimhe, roimhe sin ; 'san
àm a chaidh ; gus a nise ; cheana.
beforehand, adv. roimh-làimh, air tùs.
befoul, v. a. salaich, truaill.
befriend, v. a. dèan càirdeas, dèan gniomh
caraid.
beg, v. a. and n. iarr, sir, guidh, thig
beò air déircibh, falbh air déirc.
beget, v. a. gin ; tàrmaich.
beggar, s. déirceach, diol-déirce.
beggarly, adj. bochd, dìblidh, truagh.
beggary, s. bochdainn, aimbeairt.
begin, v. a. and n. tòisich, tionnsgain.
beginner, s. fòghlumaiche, fear 's a' cheud
thòiseachadh.
beginning, s. toiseach, aobhar, prìomh-
aobhar, tòiseachadh.

begird, v. a. crioslaich, cuartaich ; iadh.
begone, interj. air falbh thu ! á m' fhianais ! truis !
begotten, pret. part. v. beget, ginte, air a ghineamhuinn.
beguile, v. a. meall, car, breug.
behalf, s. as leth, air a thaobh, air son.
behave, v. a. giùlain, gluais, gnàthaich, bi stòlda, cneasda, biodh modh ort.
behaviour, s. giùlan, gluasad, cleachdadh, gnàthachadh ; beus, modh.
behead, v. a. thoir an ceann dheth, dìcheann.
behemoth, s. an t-uile-bheist.
behind, prep. air chùl, air deireadh.
behind-hand, adv. an déigh làimhe.
behold, v. a. faic, seall, amhairc, thoir fainear, feuch.
behold, interj. feuch.
beholden, adj. an comain, fo fhiachaibh.
behoof, s. ni tha chum buannachd, math, leas.
behoove, v. n. bi iomchuidh, freagarrach.
being, s. bith ; inbhe, cor, beatha ; creutair, tì, urra, neach.
belabour, v. a. slachd, buail ; leadair.
belch, v. a. and n. brùchd, tog gaoth, dìobhair ; taom a mach.
beldam, s. seana chailleach chrosda.
beleaguer, v. a. iomdhruid.
belfry, s. tigh-cluig ; tùr cluig.
belie, v. a. breugaich, thoir a bhreug dha ; aithris breugan.
believe, v. a. and n. creid, thoir creideas, biodh creideamh agad.
believer, s. creidmheach, criosdaidh.
bell, s. clag, glag ; àrd onoir cùise.
belle, s. boirionnach fior-mhaiseach.
belles-lettres, s. snas-chainnt sgrìobhaidh.
belligerent, adj. bagarach air cogadh, buaireanta ; an sàs an cogadh.
bellow, s. beuc, ràn, geum.
bellowing, s. beucaich, bùirich.
bellows, s. balg-séididh.
belly, s. brù, bolg, broinn.
belong, v. n. buin, bhuineas.
beloved, part. gràdhaichte.
below, prep. fo.
below, adv. shìos, gu h-ìosal.
belt, s. crios, crios-leasraidh.
bemoan, v. a. dèan cumha, caoidh, gearain.
bench, s. being, ionad-suidhe, cathair-bhreitheanais ; luchd-ceartais.
bencher, s. fear - riaghlaidh an cùirt-cheartais ; britheamh.
bend, v. a. crom, lùb ; stiùir, aom ; ceannsaich ; bi claon, bi fiar.
bend, s. cromadh, camadh, fiaradh.
bendable, adj. so-lùbaidh.
beneath, prep. fo, an ìochdar.
benediction, s. beannachadh.
benefaction, s. tiodhlac ; deagh-ghnìomh.

benefactor, s. tabhartair ; fear fuasg-laidh, caraid 's an éigin.
benefice, s. teachd an tìr ministeir sgìre ; stìpinn.
beneficence, s. mathas, oircheas.
beneficent, adj. toirbheartach, seirceil, fiùghantach, còir.
beneficial, adj. tarbhach, luachmhor, feumail.
benefit, s. tiodhlac, deagh-ghnìomh, buannachd.
benevolence, s. mathas, coibhneas, fiùghantachd, deagh-ghean.
benevolent, adj. coibhneil, seirceil, mathasach, fiùghantach.
benight, v. a. dorchaich, duibhrich ; cuartaich le dorchadas ; cum an aineolas.
benign, adj. coibhneil, fiùghantach, fial, mathasach, tròcaireach.
benignity, s. tròcaireachd, mathasachd ; caomhalachd.
benison, s. beannachd, beannachadh.
bent, s. camadh, lùbadh, cromadh ; claonadh, fiaradh ; rùn-suidhichte, toil, togradh.
bent, s. muran.
benumb, v. a. meilich, einglich.
bequeath, v. a. tiomnaich, fàg mar dhìleab.
bequest, s. dìleab.
berberry, s. goirt-dhearc, gràinnseag.
bereave, v. a. buin uaith, creach, rùisg, thoir air falbh.
berry, s. dearc, dearcag.
beryl, s. beril, clach luachmor.
beseeching, s. iarrtas, achanaich, guidhe.
beseem, v. a. bi freagarrach, iomchuidh.
beset, v. a. cuartaich, iadh mu thimchioll ; fàth, feith ; buail air.
beside, besides, prep. làmh ri, ri taobh ; a bharr, a thuilleadh.
besiege, v. a. cuir séisd, iomdhruid, teannaich, cuartaich.
besmear, v. a. salaich, luidrich, smeur.
besom, s. sguab-ùrlair.
besottedness, s. amadanachd, drungair-eachd.
bespangle, v. a. dealraich, lainnirich.
bespatter, v. a. salaich, tilg poll air ; cain, mill cliù.
bespeak, v. a. orduich, iarr roimh-làimh, cuir an céill do.
besprinkle, v. a. uisgich, sriodagaich, crath uisge.
best, adj. as fearr, iomlan, math.
bestial, adj. ainmhidheach, brùideil, feòlmhor.
bestir, v. a. grad ghluais, éirich, mosgail, caraich.
bestow, v. a. thoir seachad, builich.
bestride, v. a. rach casa - gòbhlach, marcaich.

bet, *v. a.* cuir geall.

betake, *v. a.* theirig, tog ort, imich, falbh.

bethink, *v. n.* smuaintich, cuimhnich.

betide, *v. n.* thachras ; dh' éireas ; thàrlas.

betimes, *adv.* 'na am, moch, tràthail ; an ùin ghearr, gu luath.

betoken, *v. a.* ciallaich le, comharraich, samhlaich ; cuir an céill roimh-làimh.

betony, *s.* lus-mhic-bheathaig.

betray, *v. a.* brath ; dèan feall, meall, leig ris rùn-dìomhair caraïd ; nochd a chum a chall ; bi luath-bheulach.

betrayer, *s.* brathadair, mealltair.

betroth, *v. a.* réitich, dèan ceangal pòsaidh.

better, *adj.* as fhearr na ; as fearr.

between, *prep.* eadar, sa' mheadhon.

bevel, *s.* oir air shiobhadh.

beverage, *s.* deoch ; deoch làidir, lionn, etc.

bevy, *s.* total eun ; coisir, còmhlan (eun, fhiadh, bhoirionnach).

bewail, *v. n.* dèan caoidh, guil, dèan tuireadh, dèan bròn.

beware, *v. n.* thoir an air, bi air t' fhaiceall.

bewilder, *v. a.* seachranaich, iomrallaich, cur air bhoil,—am breislich.

bewitch, *v. a.* cuir buidseachd, cuir fo gheasaibh.

beyond, *prep.* thall, air an taobh thall ; ni's faide na ; air nach urrainn e ruigheachd ; air thoiseach air ; thairis air.

bias, *s.* taobh-chudthrom, aomadh, claon-adh toil, togradh, air fhiaradh.

bib, *s.* bréid-uchd, uchdan leinibh.

bibber, *s.* misgear, pòitear.

Bible, *s.* Bìobull, an leabhar naomha.

Biblical, *adj.* Bìobullach, sgriobturail.

bice, *s.* dath buidhe no uaine.

bid, *v. a.* iarr, thoir cuireadh ; òrduich ; thoir tairgse, tairg luach.

bidden, *adj.* cuirte, air a chuireadh ; òrduichte.

bidder, *s.* fear-tairgse.

bidding, *s.* ordugh, earail ; tairgse.

bide, *v. n.* còmhnaich, tàmh, gabh còmhnaidh, fuirich ; feith ri fàth.

bidental, *adj.* dà-fhiaclach.

biding, *s.* tàmhachd, àros, fardoch, dachaigh, asdail, ionad-còmhnaidh.

biennial, *adj.* dà - bhliadhnach, gach darnacha bliadhna.

bier, *s.* carbad adhlacaidh, giùlan, eileatrum, caisil-chrò.

biesting, *s.* nùs, ceud-bhainne.

bifarious, *adj.* dà-fhillte ; dà-sheadhach.

biferous, *adj.* a' giùlan dà bharr 's a' bhliadhna.

biform, *adj.* dà-chruthach.

big, *adj.* mór, dòmhail, tomadach ; leth-tromach, torrach ; làn ; àrdanach.

bigamy, *s.* pòsadh is a' cheud bhean beò.

bigot, *s.* fear dall dhian an creideamh, duine cumhang, duine aig a bheil eud gun eòlas.

bigotry, *s.* dian eud mi-reusanta an creideamh, dall-eud am beachdaibh àraidh.

bilberry, *s.* braoileag.

bilboes, *s.* ceap-chas (air bòrd luinge).

bile, *s.* sùgh searbh, domblas ; leann-achadh.

bilious, *adj.* domblasach.

bilk, *v. a.* thoir an car as, meall.

bill, *s.* gob eòin.

bill, *s.* sgian-sgathaidh.

bill, *s.* sgrìobhadh-geallaidh ; bann iom-laid ; cunntas.

bill, *v. n.* cuir gob ri gob.

billet-doux, *s.* litir-leannanachd.

billion, *s.* deich ceud mìle million.

billow, *s.* tonn, sumain, bairlinn.

bin, *s.* ciste mhór air son gràn, no gual, no fìon.

binary, *adj.* dùbailte, dà-fhillte.

bind, *v. a.* ceangail, cuibhrich, cuir an cuing ; crioslaich, cuir uime ; naisg, teannaich ; cuir fo mhionnaibh ; cum a steach, bac ; cuir fo fhiachaibh.

binder, *s.* fear ceangail ; bann-ceangail.

binding, *s.* ceangal, ceanglachan.

bindweed, *s.* iadhlus.

binnacle, *s.* àite combaist air bòrd luinge.

biographer, *s.* beath'-eachdraiche.

biography, *s.* beath'-eachdraidh.

biparous, *adj.* a bheireas càraid, — leth-oin.

biped, *s.* dà-chasach.

bipennated, *adj.* dà-sgiathach.

bipetalous, *adj.* dà-bhileach.

birch, *s.* beithe ; slat chaoil.

bird, *s.* eun, eunlaith.

bird's-cherry, *s.* fiodhag.

birth, *s.* breith ; sinnsireachd, sìol ; staid-breith, inbhe ; an ni a rugadh.

birthright, *s.* còir-bhreith.

biscuit, *s.* briscaid.

bisect, *v. a.* gearr 's a' mheadhon, dèan dà leth.

bishop, *s.* easbuig.

bishopric, *s.* easbuigeachd.

bishop-weed, *s.* lus-an-easbuig.

bit, *s.* mìr, crioman, criomag, bìdeag ; cabastair sréine, camagan sréine.

bitch, *s.* galla ; cù boirionn ; siùrsach baobh.

bite, *v. a.* thoir gréim as, bìd, teum.

bite, *s.* gréim, làn-beòil ; gearradh.

biting, *s.* teumadh, beumadh, bìdeadh.

bitter, *adj.* goirt, searbh, teth, geur ; garg, sgaiteach, an-iochdmhor ; cràiteach, guineach ; mi-thaitneach.

bittern, s. a chorra-ghràin.
bitterness, s. searbhachd, gamhlas, mì-run ; crosdachd ; doilghios.
bitumen, s. bìgh-thalmhuinn.
bivalve, bivalvular, adj. dàdhuilleach, — chòmhlach, dàshligeach, mar fheusgan no coilleag, etc.
bivouac, v. n. campaich, campaich air chabhaig.
blab, v. a. and n. bi luathbheulach.
black, adj. dubh, dorch, doilleir ; gruamach, nuarranta, neulach ; gràineil, mallaichte, aingidh ; dìomhaireach ; muladach, brònach, tùrsach.
blackamoor, s. duine dubh.
blackbird, s. lon-dubh.
black-cattle, s. crodh, buar, nì, feudail, spréidh, tàn.
blackcock, s. an coileach-dubh.
blacken, v. a. and n. dubh, dubhaich, dèan dubh ; dorchaich ; cùl-chàin, mill cliù ; fàs dorch, bi dubh.
blackguard, s. duine suarach, duine mì-bheusach ; trusdar, salachar, slaightire, crochaire.
blackmail, s. dubhchìs, cìs fòir-eigne.
blackness, s. duibhead, dorchachd.
blacksmith, s. gobha-dubh (gen. gobha, gobhann).
bladder, s. aotroman, balg.
blade, s. bileag-fheòir, no fhochainn ; lann, iarann claidheimh no sgeine ; lasgaire, fear spaideil ; cnàimh an t-slinnean.
blain, s. neasgaid, guirean.
blame, v. a. coirich, faigh cron do.
blame, s. coire ; cionta, lochd, cron.
blameable, adj. coireach, ciontach.
blameableness, s. ciontachd, coireachd.
blameless, adj. neochoireach, neochiontach.
blameworthy, a. ri choireachadh.
blanch, v. a. and n. gealaich, dèan geal no bàn ; rùisg, sgrath ; gabh eagal, uamhunn.
bland, adj. caoin, caomh, mìn, tlàth, séimh, ciùin, fòill.
blandish, v. a. séimhich, dèan caoin bhreug, dèan cainnt thlàth.
blandishment, s. cainnt thlàth, caoin-mholadh, fòill-labhairt, brosgal.
blank, adj. geal, bàn ; gun sgrìobhadh, falamh.
blank, s. àite falamh, mìr pàipeir gun sgrìobhadh ; crannchur gun luach ; cuspair.
blanket, s. plaide, plancaid ; aodach-leapa.
blaspheming, s. toibheumachadh.
blasphemously, adv. gu toibheumach.
blasphemy, s. toibheum.
blast, s. osag, séideag, oiteag ; sgal (pioba).

blast, v. a. seac, searg ; mill, plàigh, sgealb, no bris carraig (le fùdar).
blate, adj. saidealta, nàrach, diùid.
blaze, s. lasair, solus lasarach, leus soluis ; blàradh.
blaze, v. a. and n. cuir am farsuingeachd, craobh-sgaoil ; dealraich, taisbean thu féin ; sgall craobh ; las.
blazon, v. a. dèan soilleir gearradh-arm ; sgeadaich gu maiseach ; seòl gu follaiseach, taisbean, cuir a mach ; àrd-mhol, sgaoil cliù, dean follaiseach, gairm suas.
blazon, s. gearradh-arm ; soillseachadh, taisbeanadh ; moladh, cliùghairm.
bleach, v. a. and n. gealaich, dèan geal; fàs geal, todhair.
bleak, adj. lom, fuar, fuaraidh, nochdaidh. gun tuar—gun mhaise.
blear, adj. reasgshuileach, prabshuileach, mùsgach, deargshuileach, brachshuileach ; doilleir, dorch, neulach.
blear-eyed, a. prabshuileach.
bleat, v. n. méil, dèan méil.
bleed, v. a. and n. leig fuil, thoir fuil, tarruing fuil ; caill fuil, sil fuil.
blemish, v. a. cuir gaoid ann ; salaich, truaill.
blemish, s. ciorram, gaoid, cron, mìchliù, sgainneal.
blench, v. a. and n. bac, cum air ais ; crup, clisg, siap air falbh, meall ort fhéin.
blench, s. clisgeadh, leum grad.
blend, v. a. coimeasgaich, cuir troimhe chéile, cuthaig ; truaill, salaich, mill.
bless, v. a. beannaich, dèan sona ; mol, glòraich, thoir taing.
blessed, blest, adj. beannaichte, sona ; naomha, iomlan sona ; air a bheannachadh.
blessing, s. beannachadh, sonas ; naomhachd ; sonas néamhaidh ; gean-math Dhé, deagh dhùrachd.
blight, s. gaiseadh ; fuardhealt, liathreothadh ; crìonadh, seargadh.
blind, adj. dall, gun fhradharc, dorch ; dall-inntinneach, aineolach.
blind, s. sgàile-shùl, dallbhrat ; neach dall.
blindfold, v. a. cuir sgail air sùilean, còmhdaich sùilean.
blindfold, adj. sùil-chomhdaichte.
blindman's buff, s. dallan-dà.
blindness, s. doille ; aineolas, dorchadas.
blink, v. n. caog, priob ; faic gu doilleir.
blink, s. sealladh grad, plathadh, boillsgeadh.
bliss, s. àrd-shonas ; sonas nam flath.
blissful, adj. làn aoibhneach, làn-shona.
blister, s. leus, bolgan, bòcadh, balg-uisce.
blister, v. a. and n. thoir leus air, thoir

bòcadh craicinn air, tog bolg uisge air a chraicionn.

blithe, *adj.* aoibhinn, ait, sunntach.

bloat, *v. a.* and *n.* séid suas, bòc, at.

bloatedness, *s.* at, bòcadh, séideadh.

blobber-lip, *s.* beill, meill, beul tiugh, borr.

block, *s.* sgonn, òrda-fiodha ; meall, cnap, ploc ; ealag.

block, *v. a.* dùin a steach, cur bacadh.

blockade, *s.* iomdhruideadh.

blockhead, *s.* bumaileir, ùmaidh, baothaire, àmhlar, buamasdair.

block-tin, *s.* staoin neo-mheasgte.

blood, *s.* fuil ; sliochd, sìol, gineal ; luchd-dàimh, càirdean.

blood, *v. a.* salaich le fuil, còmhdaich le fuil, thoir fuil, mar do chù òg ; leig fuil as.

bloodhound, *s.* cù-luirg.

bloodshed, *s.* dòrtadh fala.

bloody, *adj.* fuileach, fuilteach ; fuileachdach.

bloom, *s.* blàth ; ùr-fhàs, snuadh na h-òige, dreach cinneachaidh.

bloomy, *adj.* blàthmhor, ùrar.

blossom, *s.* blàth, bàrr-gùg.

blot, *v. a.* dubh a mach ; salaich, cuir ball dubh air ; duaichnich, dorchaich.

blotch, *s.* leus, guirean, builgean, sgall.

blow, *s.* buille, gleadhar, sgealp ; bualadh, slachdadh ; blàth.

blow, *v. a.* and *n.* séid ; séid suas, lìon le gaoith, cuir gaoth ann ; bi gearranalach, plosg ; thig fo bhlàth, cuir blàth a mach ; at, bòc.

blowze, *s.* caile phluiceach dhearg.

blowzy, *adj.* ruiteach ('s an aghaidh), loisgte leis a' ghréin, grannda, piullagach.

blubber, *s.* saill muice-mara ; muirteuchd.

blubber, *v. a.* bòc (le caoineadh), caoin, còin, guil.

bludgeon, *s.* bata, slacan, cuaille.

blue, *adj.* gorm, liath.

bluebottle, *s.* gille-guirmean, cuileag mhór.

blueness, *s.* guirme, guirmead.

bluff, *a.* and *s.* atmhor, bòcach, gruamach, glagach ; maol, neo-gheur ; cas, corrach, sgorrach, carach, seòlta.

bluff, *v. t.* meall, thoir a char as.

blunder, *v. n.* rach am mearachd, tuislich, tuit an iomrall.

blunder, *s.* mearachd, iomrall, tuisleadh.

blunderbuss, *s.* gunna-craosach, gunnaglaice.

blunt, *adj.* maol, neo-gheur, gun fhaobhar ; neo-thuigseach, aineolach, mìmhodhail ; cruaidh, tiugh.

blunt, *v. a.* maolaich, thoir air falbh am faobhar ; lagaich, cìosnaich.

bluntness, *s.* maoilead, cion faobhair ; cion tuisge, cion tùir.

blur, *s.* ball salach, smal, sal.

blush, *s.* rughadh, gnùis-nàire, deirge, athadh.

bluster, *v. a.* and *n.* beuc, dèan toirm mar an sian ; bagair, bi gleadhrach.

bluster, *s.* collaid, gleadhraich ; àimhreit, bòsd, spaglainn.

blusterer, *s.* glagaire, fear-spaglainn.

blustering, *s.* gleadhraich, stairirich.

blusterous, *adj.* gleadhrach, spaglainneach.

boar, *s.* torc, cullach, ùmaidh.

board, *s.* bòrd, clàr, déile ; cuirm ; bòrd luinge.

board, *v. a.* and *n.* cuir air bhòrd ; bi air bhòrd ; rach air bòrd.

boarish, *adj.* aineolach, brùideil.

boast, *v. n.* dèan uaill, dèan spagluinn ; mol thu féin.

boast, *s.* bòsd, uaill, spaglainn.

boaster, *s.* bòsdair ; fear-ràiteachais, glagaire.

boastful, *adj.* bòsdail, mórchuiseach.

boat, *s.* bàta, eithear, sgoth, birlinn, iùbhrach.

boatman, *s.* fear-bàta, seoldair, maraiche, fear leigeadh a mach bhàtaichean air duais.

boatswain, *s.* fear-acfhuinn luinge, oifigeach an earbsa ri acfhuinn bàta.

bobbin, *s.* iteachan.

bobtailed, *adj.* cutach, gearr-earballach.

bode, *v. a.* cuir air mhanadh ; innis roimh-làimh.

bodement, *s.* comharradh, tuar, manadh.

bodice, *s.* cliabhan-ceangail, aodach-cuim.

bodiless, *adj.* neo-chorporra.

bodily, *adv.* gu corporra.

bodkin, *s.* putag, dealg, brodaiche.

body, *s.* corp, colann, neach, creutar ; meall, buidheann, meadhon feachd ; cuideachd, communn ; spionnadh, treòir, neart.

bog, *s.* féithe, boglach, suil-chrithich.

boggle, *v. n.* clisg, leum, bi an teagamh.

boggler, *s.* gealtaire, cladhaire.

boil, *v. a.* and *n.* dèan teth, bruich ; goil.

boiler, *s.* goileadair ; coire.

boisterous, *adj.* gailbheach ; fuathasach, stoirmeil ; borb.

boisterously, *adv.* gu ro-ghailbheach, gu stoirmeil, gu doireannach.

bold, *adj.* dàna, danara, neo-sgàthach ; gaisgeil, fearail, treubhach ; ladarna, mì-mhodhail.

bolden, *v. a.* cuir misneach ann, misnich.

boldness, *adj.* dànachd, neo-sgàthachd ; tapachd ; neo-shaidealtachd ; ladarnas mi-mhodhalachd.

bole, s. seòrsa talmhainn, tomhas shia feòrlain ; craobh lom.
boll, s. cuinnlein déise, lurga déise.
boll, s. bolla ; tomhas mine, no buntata.
bolster, s. adhartan, cluasag, ceannadhart.
bolster, v. a. adhartaich, càirich cluasag fo cheann ; cum taice.
bolt, s. saighead ; crann, dealanach, beithir, clàibhean, clàidhean, bobht, còrn aodaich.
bolt, v. a. and n. glais, dùin ; daingnich le crann, cum ri chéile ; grad leum, briosg.
bolter, s. criathar ; lìon-glacaidh.
bolt-rope, s. ball-oire, ball-aoire.
boltsprit, s. crann-spreòid, crann-uisge.
bolus, s. cungaidh-leighis, seòrsa talmhainn.
bomb, s. toirm, àrd-fhuaim ; peileir bloighdeil ; urchair-froisidh.
bombard, s. gunna - mór, toirm - shligneach ; soitheach dibhe.
bombardier, s. gunnadair toirm-shligean.
bombardment, s. séisd thoirm-shligean.
bombasin, s. sròl-dubh.
bombast, s. earraghloir, àrd-ghlòir.
bombastic, adj. earra-ghlòireach.
bombulation, s. fuaim, gleadhraich.
bomb-ketch, s. longthoirm-shligneach.
bombyx, s. durrag shìoda.
bonasus, s. damh fiadhaich.
bond, s. ceangal, bann, còrd ; gealladh.
bond, adj. ceangailte, tràilleil, daor, fo bhruid.
bondage, s. braighdeanas, daorsa.
bondmaid, s. ban-tràill, daor inilt.
bondman, s. tràill, daor-òglach.
bonelace, s. obair-lìn.
boneless, adj. gun chnàimh.
bonfire, s. tein aigheir, tein-éibhinn, braight, braidseal, samhnag.
bonhomie, s. suilbhireachd.
bon mot, s. geurfhacal, facal àbhachd.
bonnet, s. boineid, ceannaodach.
bonny, adj. bòidheach, maiseach, àlainn, laghach.
bony, adj. cnàmhach, mórchnàmhach.
booby, s. buimilear, ùmaidh.
book, s. leabhar.
book-keeper, s. fear chumail leabhraichean-cunntais.
book-keeping, s. eolas rian-chunntais.
bookcase, s. preas-leabhraichean.
book-mate, s. companach sgoile.
bookseller, s. ceannaiche leabhraichean.
bookworm, s. reudan, leòmann ; feardian-leughach, fear ro dhéidheil air fòghlum.
boom, s. crann-sgòide ; acarsaid, spàrr-dìona acarsaid.
boon, s. tiodhlac, saor-thabhartas.
boon, adj. cridheil, sunntach, aobhach, ait ; coihneil.

boor, s. peasan, burraidh.
boorish, adj. mì-mhodhail, neo-oileanta.
boorishness, s. mì-mhodhalachd.
boot, s. cosnadh, tairbhe ; barrachd, tuilleadh ; creach, faobh.
boot, s. bòtunn, caisbheart.
booted, adj. bòtunnach.
booth, s. bùth, pàilliun, bothan.
boot-jack, s. ceap gobhlach air son tarruing bhòtan bharr chas.
bootless, adj. neo-tharbhach, diomhain, faoin ; neo-bhuadhach.
boot-tree, s. ceap bhrog.
booty, s. cobhartach, creach, reubainn ; cluich cuilbheartach.
booze, s. prasach mhart ; daorach.
bo-peep, s. falach-fead, dìdeagaich.
borachino, s. misgear, searrag leathair.
borax, s. salann-tàth.
border, s. oir, bile, crìoch, iomall, bruach, taobh, oirthir, còrsa.
borderer, s. fear àiteach nan iomal.
bore, v. a. and n. toll, fosgail le tolladh, cladhaich, dèan toll.
bore, s. toll ; tora, boireal.
Boreas, s. a' ghaoth a Tuath.
borer, s. inneal-tollaidh, tora, boireal.
born, v. beirte.
borne, part. pas. giùlainte, air a ghiùlan.
borough, s. baile mór, baile margaidh, bòrgh.
borrow, v. a. gabh an coingheall ; iarr iasachd ; gabh iasad.
borrower, s. fear-gabhail an coingheall.
boscage, s. coille, doire, coillteach.
bosky, adj. coillteach, preasach, garbh, stobanach.
bosom, s. uchd, broilleach, cridhe ; asgail, cliabh.
bosom, v. a. achlaisich, dlùthaich ri broilleach.
boss, s. copan, cnap, meall, pluc ; maighistir, fear-riaghlaidh.
boss, adj. copanach.
botanic, botanical, adj. luidheach.
botanist, s. lusragan.
botany, s. luibh-eòlas.
botch, s. leus, guirean, plucan.
botch, v. a. clùd ; càirich gu neo-shnasmhor, prab, breòcaich.
botcher, s. prabaire, greòig.
both, adj. le chéile, 'n an dithis, araon.
both, conj. araon, cuideachd, le chéile.
bother, v. a. sàraich, sgìthich, cuir dragh.
bottle, s. searrag, botul.
bottom, s. ìochdar, màs, bonn.
bottomless, adj. gun ìochdar, gun ghrunnd, gun aigeal.
bottomry, s. airgead air fhaotainn an geall air son luinge.
bough, s. meur, geug, meangan, fiùran, faillean.
bought, part. ceannaichte.

bounce, *v. n.* leum, gearr sùrdag; dèan leum-làir; bi dàna, ladarna.

bouncer, *s.* fear-spaglainn.

bound, boundary, *s.* crìoch, comharradh-crìche.

bound, *v. a. and n.* cuir crìoch ri; bac, pill, dùin a steach.

bound, *v. a.* thoir leum, gearr sùrdag.

bound, *adj.* suidhichte air dol, fo rùn dol —.

bound, *adj.* ceangailte; bound to win, buaidh cinnteach (dha).

bound, *s.* leum; cruinnleum.

boundless, *adj.* neo-chrìochnach.

boundstone, *s.* clach - chluich, clach-chleasachd.

bounteous, bountiful, *adj.* fiùghantach, tabhartach, pàirteach, fialaidh, math-asach.

bounty, *s.* toirbheartas, fialachd, pàirt-eachd, mathas.

bourgeon, *v. n.* meanglanaich, faillean-aich.

bourn, *s.* crìoch, iomall, oir, ceann; allt, sruthan.

bouse or boose, *v. a.* òl cus, dèan pòit.

bousy, *adj.* misgeach, froganach, sogan-ach.

boutade, *s.* magaid.

bow, *s.* bogha - saighde; bogha - frois; bogha-fidhle; cuing; bogha dìolaide; gualainn luinge; cromadh, lùbadh, sleuchdadh, ùmhlachd.

bow, *v. a. and n.* crom, lùb, claon; sleuchd, crom, dèan ùmhlachd.

bowels, *s.* mionach, innidh; taobh a stigh; cridhe, com; innidh thròcaire, iochd, truas.

bower, *s.* seòmar, bùth; doire, sgàil-thigh, bothan-sàmhraidh, badan; cart chluiche; acair luinge.

bowery, *adj.* sgàileach, bothanach, fionn-nar, dubharach, doireach, badanach.

bowl, *s.* pòla, cuach; ball cruinn.

bowl, *v. a. and n.* cluich le buill, ruith car mu char.

bow-legged, *adj.* camchasach.

bowling-green, *s.* réidhlean bhall.

bowman, *s.* saighdear bogha, fear-saighid.

bowsprit, *s.* crann-spreòid.

bowstring, *s.* taifeid.

bowyer, *s.* boghadair; saor bhoghachan, saor shaighead.

box, *s.* bocsa, cobhan, ciste; dòrn, buille, gleadhar, cnap.

box, *v. a. and n.* cuir am bosca; dèan dòrnadh, thoir sgailleag do.

boxer, *s.* dòrnaiche, fear-iomairt dhòrn.

boy, *s.* leanabh gille, balach.

boyish, *adj.* balachail; cluicheanta.

boyishness, *s.* leanabaidheachd, faoin-eachd.

brabble, *s.* connsachadh, iorghuill.

brace, *v. a.* crioslaich, teannaich, daing-nich.

brace, *s.* crios, bann, ceangal, teannadan; armachd, uidheam cogaidh; teann-achadh, daingneachadh.

brace, *s.* paidhir, dithis, càraid.

bracelet, *s.* làmh-fhailean; làmh usgar.

bracer, *s.* teannadan, bann-teannachaidh; deoch bheothachaidh.

brach, *s.* galla-thòlair, saidh.

brachial, *adj.* gàirdeanach.

brack, *s.* bealach, bearn, briseadh.

bracken, *s.* raineach, froineach.

bracket, *s.* ealchainn, sgeilp.

brackish, *adj.* air bhlas an t-sàile.

brag, *v. n.* dèan uaill, bi ràiteachail, dèan bòsd, dèan spaglainn, dùlanaich.

brag, *s.* uaill, ràiteachas, bòsd, spaglainn; aobhar-uaill.

braggadocio, *s.* spaga-da-glid, gaothaire.

braggart, bragger, *s.* fear - uaillmhor, -bòsdail, -ràiteachail, -spaglainneach, -bragoil, -sprachdail.

braid, *v. a.* figh, dualaich.

braid, *s.* dual, ni fighte 'na dhualaibh; figheachan; dosan-banntraich.

brails, *s.* buill-tharruing sheòl.

brain, *s.* eanchainn, eanachaill; ceann, tuigse, tùr.

brain, *v. a.* cuir an t-eanchainn as.

brainless, *adj.* baoth, faoin, neo-thuig-seach, neo-thùrail, gun eanchainn.

brain-pan, *s.* copan a' chinn, an claigeann, claban.

brain-sick, *adj.* tuainealach, amaideach.

brake, *s.* droighionnach; raineach; slacan-lìn; làmh pìob-thaosgaidh; amar-fuine.

braky, *adj.* driseach, làn droighnich.

bramble, *s.* dris nan smeur dubha.

bran, *s.* càth, còrlach, garbhan.

branch, *s.* meangan, meanglan, meur, geug, fiùran; earrann, cuid; sliochd, gineal, iarmad.

branch, *v. a.* craobh-sgaoil; sgaoil a mach, meur-sgaoil; bi cabrach, bi cròcach.

brancher, *s.* isean-seabhaig, -speireig.

branchy, *adj.* meanganach, geugach, dosach, cròcach, cabrach.

brand, *s.* aithinne, bioran-teine, bior-dearg, maide connaidh.

brand, *v. a.* maslaich, comharraich le iarann dearg.

brandish, *v. a.* crath, luaisg, tog suas.

brandling, *s.* boiteag-dhrùchda.

brandy, *s.* branndaidh.

brangle, *s.* connsachadh, brionglaid, còmhstri.

branny, *adj.* càthach, garbhanach.

brasier, *s.* ceard-umha; aghann-umha, soitheach beòlach, teine-guail.

brass, *s.* umha; dànachd.

brassy, *adj.* umhach ; dàna, ladarna.

brat, *s.* isean, garrach, droch leanabh, peasan.

bravado, *s.* ¦fear - bòsdail, -bagarach, -maoidheach, -bòilich.

brave, *adj.* misneachail, curanta, dàna, gaisgeil, calma ; fearail.

brave, *v. a.* dùlanaich, tàirg cath, bi duineil.

bravery, *s.* misneach, gaisge, treubhantas, fearalas, curantachd.

bravo, *s.* fear a mhortas air son duais.

brawl, *v. a.* and *n.* dèan ghleadhrach, dèan cànran, dèan còmhstri, trod, dèan stairirich.

brawler, *s.* fear-iorghuilleach.

brawn, *s.* feòil a' chalpa ; cruaidh-fheòil tuirc, féith.

brawniness, *s.* spionnadh, neart, lùth, cruas.

brawny, *adj.* féitheach, làidir, cruaidhghreimeach, calpach, gramail.

bray, *v. a.* pronn, brùth.

bray, *v. n.* beuc, sgreuch, ràn.

bray, *s.* sitir asail ; sgread, sgreuch, ràn, raoichd.

brayer, *s.* sitriche, sgreadaire ; pronnadair, bruthadair.

braze, *v. a.* tàth le umha.

brazen, *adj.* umhach ; ladarna, mìnàrach.

brazen-face, *s.* bathais gun nàire.

brazenness, *s.* air dhreach umha ; mìnàire, ladarnas.

breach, *s.* briseadh, fosgladh, sgàineadh ; bealach, bearn.

bread, *s.* aran ; lòn, teachd-an-tìr.

bread-corn, *s.* arbhar-arain.

breadth, *s.* leud, farsuingeachd.

break, *v. a.* and *n.* bris, sgealb, crac ; fàs lag, breòite.

break, *s.* briseadh, sgealbadh, sgoltadh ; bealach, bearn.

breakers, *s.* sùmainnean, bàrc.

breakfast, *s.* biadh maidne.

breast, *s.* uchd, broilleach, maothan ; cìoch, cliabh.

breastknot, *s.* dos ribeanan air an uchd.

breastplate, *s.* uchd-éideadh.

breastwork, *s.* uchdbhalla.

breath, *s.* anail, deò ; beatha.

breathe, *v. a.* and *n.* analaich, séid, bi beò ; leig anail, tarruing anail.

breathing, *s.* analachadh, séideadh, tarruing analach.

breathless, *adj.* plosgartach, séideagach, sgìth, sàraichte ; gun deò, gun anail, marbh.

breech, *s.* màs, tòn, tulachann, earr, deireadh.

breeches, *s.* brisnean, briogais.

breed, *v. a.* and *n.* gin, sìolaich, tàrmaich ; tog, àraich, ionnsaich, tog suas, àlaich.

breed, *s.* seòrsa, gnè, sìol, sliochd ; àlach, linn.

breeding, *s.* ionnsachadh, fòghlum, oilean, eòlas, togail suas ; modh, beus.

breeze, *s.* creithleag, cuileag-ghathach.

breeze, *s.* sgairt-ghaoth, tlàth-ghaoth, soir-bheas.

breezy, *adj.* sgairt - ghaothach, tlàthghaothach ; osagach, oiteagach.

bret, brit, *s.* seòrsa liabaig.

breviate, *s.* gearr-shuim cùise.

brevity, briefness, *s.* giorrad, aithghiorrad.

brew, *v. a.* and *n.* tog, dèan togail, bi grùdaireachd.

brewer, *s.* grùdaire, fear-togalach.

brewery, brewhouse, *s.* tigh - togalach, tigh-grùide.

bribe, *s.* duais chlaon-bhreith.

bribe, *v. a.* ceannaich le duais.

bribery, *s.* duais na h-euceairt.

brick, *s.* clach-chreadha.

brick-dust, *s.* creadhdhuslach.

brick-kiln, *s.* àth-chreadha.

bridal, *adj.* a bhuineas do bhanais, pòsda.

bride, *s.* bean-bainnse, bean-òg.

bridecake, *s.* bonnach-bainnse.

bridegroom, *s.* fear-bainnse.

bridemaid, *s.* maighdean-phòsaidh, beanchomhailteach.

bridewell, *s.* gainntir, prìosan.

bridge, *s.* drochaid.

bridle, *s.* srian, taod, ceannsal.

bridle, *v. a.* and *n.* srian, stiùir, treòraich, seòl ; ceannsaich.

brief, *adj.* goirid, gearr, aithghearr.

brief, *s.* gearrchunntas, suim cuis-lagha.

briefness, *s.* aithghearrachd.

brier, *s.* dris, preas-mhucag.

briery, *adj.* driseach, deilgneach.

brig, *s.* soitheach dà chroinn.

brigade, *s.* buidheann airm.

brigand, *s.* spùinnear, creachadair.

brigandine, *s.* long chreachaidh, lùireach mhàilleach.

bright, *adj.* soilleir, soillseach, deàrsach, dealrach, lainnireach, boillsgeach ; glan, geur, tuigseach.

brighten, *v. a.* and *n.* soillsich, deàrsaich, soilleirich.

brightness, *s.* soilleireachd.

brilliancy, *s.* lainnearachd.

brilliant, *adj.* soillseach, dearsach, boillsgeach, lainnearach.

brim, *s.* oir, bile, bruach, iomall ; beul.

brimmer, *s.* cuach-stràcte, cuach làn.

brimstone, *s.* pronnasg, pronnastan.

brindled, *adj.* srianach, stiallach, riabhach.

brine, *s.* sàl, uisge saillte.

bring, *v. a.* thoir, tabhair, beir.

brinish, *adj.* saillte, air bhlas an t-sàile.

brink, *s.* oir, bruach, bile.

brisk, *adj.* brisg, beothail, cridheil,

sunntach ; gleuste, smiorail, tapaidh, clis.
brisket, *s.* mìr-uchd, broilleach, caiseanuchd.
briskness, *s.* beothalachd, smioralachd, cliseachd, meamnachd.
brista, *s.* am blàr-aoghan.
bristle, *s.* calg muice, friodhan.
bristle, *v.* tog friodhan air ; cuir colg air.
bristly, *adj.* calgach, colgach, friodhanach, ana-meinneach, cas.
British, *adj.* Breatunnach.
Briton, *s.* Breatunnach.
brittle, *adj.* brisg, furasd a bhriseadh, brisgeanach.
brittleness, *s.* brisgealachd.
brize, *s.* creithleag, speach.
broach, *v. a.* cuir bior ann ; toll, leig ruith le ; labhair, cuir an céill ; tionndaidh ris an t-soirbheas.
broacher, *s.* bior-ròslaidh ; fear-innse.
broad, *adj.* leathan ; mòr, farsuing ; garbh ; drabasta, coma mu chainnt.
broad-cloth, *s.* clò Sasunnach.
broadness, *s.* leud, farsuingeachd.
broadside, *s.* làdach ghunnacha-móra o thaobh luinge.
broadsword, *s.* claidheamh-mór.
brocade, *s.* sìoda gréiste.
brocage, *s.* buannachd, ceannachd ; ceannachd bhaidreagach.
brocket, *s.* dà-bhliadhnach féidh.
brocoli, *s.* seòrsa càil.
brogue, *s.* bròg éille ; cuaran.
brogue, *s.* blas dùthchasach (air cànan)
broidery, *s.* See embroidery.
broil, *v.* ròsd, bruich air na h-èibhlean.
broil, *s.* caonnag, sabaid.
broken, *part.* briste.
broker, *s.* fear-gnothaich, fear-dheanamh ghnothaichean air son neach eile ; ceannaiche shean àirneis.
brokerage, *s.* duais fìr gnothaich.
bronchitis, *s.* galar-cléibh.
bronze, *s.* umha, dealbh umha.
bronze, *v. a.* cruadhaich mar umha.
brooch, *s.* bràist.
brood, *v.* àlaich, àraich ; guir.
brood, *s.* sliochd, àl, sìol, gineal, linn.
brook, *s.* alltan, sruthan, caochan.
brook, *v.* fuiling, giùlain.
broom, *s.* bealaidh ; sguabach, sguabùrlair, sguab-làir.
broomy, *adj.* bealaidheach.
broth, *s.* eanaraich ; brot.
brothel, *s.* tigh-siùrsachd.
brother, *s.* bràthair (*pl.* bràithrean).
brotherhood, *s.* bràithreachas.
brotherly, *adj.* bràithreil.
brow, *s.* mala ; bruach.
browbeat, *v. a.* eagalaich, nàraich, cuir fo sproc, sàraich, éignich.

brown, *adj.* donn.
brownish, *adj.* car donn.
brown-study, *s.* smuairean ; trom smaointinn.
browse, *v.* and *s.* inilt ; créim ; barrach.
bruise, *v. a.* pronn, brùth, mion-phronn.
bruise, *s.* bruthadh, ciùrradh, dochann.
bruit, *v. a.* innis, aithris, cuir an céill.
brumal, *adj.* geamhrachail.
brunette, *s.* bean dhonn-ghnùiseach.
brunt, *s.* garbh-ionnsaigh, teas, strì.
brush, *s.* sguab ; sguab-aodaich.
brush, *v.* sguab, slìob, suath.
brushwood, *s.* frith - choille, barrach, crionach.
brusque, *adj.* borb, mì-mhodhail.
brutal, *adj.* garg, brùideil.
brutality, *s.* brùidealachd.
brute, *s.* ainmhidh, brùid, beathach, creutair gun reusan.
brutish, *adj.* brùideil, feòlmhor, allmhara, fiadhaich, borb, garg, aineolach, neomhothachail.
bubble, *s.* gucag, cop, builgean, splangaid, staonag.
bubble, *v. a.* and *n.* meall, thoir an car as — ; éirich gu gucagach, bi sùileagach ; builgnich.
bubbler, *s.* mealltair, cealgair.
bubbly, *adj.* spliùgach, splangaideach, ronnach, staonagach.
buccaneers, *s.* luchd-spùinnidh air fairge.
buck, *s.* boc, damh féidh, fear spaideil, lasgaire.
buckbeam, *s.* seòrsa do thrì-bhilich.
bucket, *s.* cuinneag, bucaid.
buckle, *s.* bucull, claspa ; casfhalt, cuairteag, cuach, cuachag.
buckler, *s.* sgiath-dhìon, sgiath.
buckram, *s.* aodach-lìn ; garbhaodach.
buckskin, *s.* leathair féidh.
buckthorn, *s.* sgitheach.
bucolics, *s.* oran buachailleachd.
bud, *s.* ùr-fhàs, ùr-ròs, gucag.
budge, *v. n.* caraich, gluais, glidnich, smioglaich.
budget, *s.* balg-solair, poca; màileid.
buff, *s.* leathar-sginneir, dath soilleir buidhe.
buff, buffet, *v. a.* buail dòrn.
buffalo, *s.* mart-allaidh, damh-fiadhaich.
buffet, *s.* còrn-chlar ; àmraidh, dreasair.
buffoon, *s.* baothaire ; baoth-chleasaiche bladhastair.
buffoonery, *s.* baothaireachd ; blabhdaireachd.
bug, *s.* miol fhiodha.
bugbear, *s.* bòcan, culaidh-eagail.
bugle, buglehorn, *s.* dùdach, adharc-fhaghaid.
bugloss, *s.* lus-teang'-an-daimh, boglus.
build, *v.* tog, bi clachaireachd.
builder, *s.* clachair, fear-togail.

building, s. togail, tigh, aitreabh.
bulb, s. bun cruinn, meacan, meallan.
bulbous, adj. meacanach, làn ghlùn.
bulge, v. n. bulgaich, brùchd a mach, tulg.
bulk, s. meudachd, tomad, dòmhlachd ;
a' chuid as mò ; a' mhórchuid.
bulkhead, s. talan (soithich), rùm stòir
(soithich).
bulkiness, s. meudachd, dòmhlachd.
bulky, adj. mór, dòmhail, tomadach.
bull, s. tarbh ; mearachd facail, cainnt
cas mu sheach ; reachd Pàpa ; sgoladh
buideil dibhe.
bull-baiting, s. gleachd chon is tharbh.
bull-dog, s. tarbh-chù, cù feòladair.
bullet, s. peileir ; ruagaire.
bulletin, s. naidheachd cùirt.
bullfinch, s. am buidh-eun-coille.
bullion, s. òr no airgiod gun chùinneadh,
gàd òir no airgid.
bullock, s. damh.
bully, s. ceatharnach dàna, duine ceannasach, an-iochmhor, gealltaire bragail.
bulrush, s. gobhal-luachair, bogbhuine.
bulwark, s. balla - dìdein ;   obair - ard,
fear-taic.
bum-bailiff, s. maor-dubh.
bumboat, s. bàta-luiristeach.
bump, s. at, meall, cnap, pluc ; crònan
nan sgarbh.
bumper, s. sgailc.
bumpkin, s. luiriste, gleòsgaire.
bun, s. aran milis.
bunch, s. bagaid, gagan, croit.
bunchy, adj. bagaideach, gaganach.
bundle, s. pasgan, trusan ; ultach.
bung, s. àrcan buideil.
bungle, v. greòigich, clùd, dèan gu
cearbach.
bungle, s. clùd, bréid, obair sgòdach.
bungler, s. greòig, prabaire.
bunion, s. faob.
bunk, s. leabaidh seòldair.
bunker, s. cùil-guail (luinge).
bunkum, s. ràbhart ; gaoitheanachd.
bunt, s. poca lìn, no siùil.
bunting, s. sròlach, brataichean sgaoilte
agus eugsamhla.
bunter, s. sgonnchaile, caile.
bunting, s. gealag-bhuachair.
buoy, s. fleodruinn, bolla, àrca.
buoy, v. cum an uachdar.
buoyancy, s. aotromachd, fleodradh.
buoyant, adj. aotrom, snàmhach.
burden, s. eallach, uallach, eire.
burden, v. a. uallaich, sacaich, luchdaich.
burdensome, adj. doilghiosach, cudthromach.
burdock, s. macan - dogha, an galan-
greannachair, an seircean-mór.
bureau, s. ciste - dhràraichean, bòrd-
sgrìobhaidh oifis.
burgage, s. gabhaltas baile-margaidh.

burgess, s. buirdeiseach.
burgh, s. baile-mór, bòrgh.
burgher, s. saoranach, fear baile-mhóir.
burglary, s. briseadh thighean, chum
mèirle.
burgomaster, s. bàillidh baile mhóir.
burial, s. adhlacadh, tìodhlacadh.
burin, s. iarann-grabhalaidh.
burlesque, adj. sgeigeil, magail.
burlesque, s. sgeigeireachd, fochaid.
burly, adj. corpanta, dòmhail, dinnte ;
stàirneach.
burn, v. a. loisg ; bi losgadh.
burn, s. losgadh, sgaldadh.
burn, s. allt, sruthan.
burnet, s. a' bhileach-loisgein.
burning, s. losgadh.
burnish, v. a. lìobh, lainnrich.
burnisher, s. fear-lìobhaidh, no inneal
lìobhaidh.
burr, s. faillean na cluaise, buaile gealaich no rionnaig, clach muilne, clach
ghleusaidh.
burrow, v. n. cladhaich fo thalamh.
burst, v. a. sgoilt, sgàin, spreadh-bhrùchd.
burst, s. sgàineadh, sgoltadh, spreadhadh.
burstness, s. màm-sic, beum-sic.
burstwort, s. lus-an-t-sicnich.
burthen, s. See burden, s. and v.
bury, v. a. adhlaic, tìodhlaic.
bush, s. preas, dos ; bad.
bushel, s. tomhas tioram àraidh.
bushy, adj. preasach, dosach, gasach ;
badanach, etc.
business, s. obair, gnothach.
busk, s. pleaghan-teannachaidh.
buskin, s. leth-bhòtunn.
buss, s. pòg, busag ; bàt-iasgaich.
bust, s. dealbh snaidhte ceann is guaillean
duine.
bustard, s. coileach-Frangach.
bustle, s. cabhag, iorghuill, othail, drip,
collaid, càmparaid.
bustler, s. fear cabhagach.
busy, adj. saoithreach, dèanadach ; dripeil.
busybody, s. fear-tuaileis, beadagan.
but, conj. ach, gidheadh.
but, s. crìoch, ceann-crìche.
butcher, s. feòladair.
butcher, v. a. casgair, marbh, mort.
butchery, s. feòladaireachd ;   tigh-
feòladaireachd.
butler, s. buidealair.
butment, s. bonn bogha drochaid.
butt, s. ionad cuimse, àite buill-amais ;
buideal mór, baraille, tocsaid.
butter, s. ìm.
butter, v. a. sgaoil ìm.
butterflower, s. buidheag-an-t-sàmhraidh.
butterfly, s. dearbadan-dé, eunan-dé,
dealan-dé, dealbhan-dé, tormagan-dé,
calaman-dé, teillean-dé.

buttermilk, s. blàthach.
butterwort, s. badan-measgain.
buttery, adj. ìmeach, iomacach; broscalach.
buttery, s. tigh-tasgaidh, biadh-lann.
buttock, s. màs, tòn.
button, s. putan, cnap.
button, v. a. putanaich.
buttonhole, s. toll-putain.
buttress, s. balla-taice.
buttress, v. a. taicich, goibhlich.
buxom, adj. aighearach, beothail, reamhar, dùmhail; maiseach.
buxomness, s. macnasachd, beadarachd, meamnadh.
buy, v. a. ceannaich.

buyer, s. fear-ceannachaidh.
buzz, v. a. aithris os n-ìosal, thoir sanas.
buzz, s. srann, crònan, cagar.
buzzard, s. clamhan; sgonnbhalach, bumailear.
buzzer, s. fear-cogarsaich, fear-tuaileis.
by, prep. le; tre, trid, troimh; fag dlùth, faisg.
by and by, adv. an ùin ghearr, an ceart-uair.
by-law, s. riaghailt comuinn.
by-name, s. frith-ainm, far-ainm, leth-ainm, leas-ainm.
bystander, s. fear amharc.
byword, s. frith-fhacal, sean-fhacal.
byre, s. bàthach.

C

cab, s. tomhas Iudhach a chumas trì pinnt; carbad.
cabal, s. coinneamh dhìomhair; cluaint-earachd, claon chomhairle.
cabal, cabala, s. am beul-aithris Iudhach.
cabalist, s. fear fiosrach mu bheul-aithris nan Iudhach.
cabalistical, adj. dìomhair.
caballer, s. fear-comhairle dhìomhair, cluaintear.
cabbage, s. càl, càl-faobach.
cabbage, v. a. goid fuigheall aodaich.
cabin, s. seòmar luinge; bothan.
cabinet, s. seòmar-comhairle; seòmar tas-gaidh; ionad-dìomhair; àrd-chomhairle Parlamaid.
cabinetmaker, s. saor àirneis; saor geal.
cable, s. càball; ròp-mór.
cache, s. àite-falaich, falachasan.
cachectical, adj. euslan, galarach.
cachexy, s. euslaint (cuirp no inntinn).
cackle, v. n. ràc, bi glocail, goir, gàir.
cacodemon, s. deamhan, anspiorad.
cad, s. duine gun mheas, balgaire (duine), trustar.
cadaverous, adj. cairbheach, tana, air dhroch aogais, glas-neulach.
caddis, s. durrag-chonnlaich.
caddy, s. bocsa-tì, bòsdan.
cade, adj. tlàth, tairis.
cadence, s. fonn; comh-fhuaim; ìsleachadh gutha.
cadet, s. am bràthair as òige; fear a chogas a nasgaidh an dùil ri àrdachadh fhaighinn san arm, foghlumaiche airm.
cadger, s. ceannaiche-siubhail.
cag, s. buideal, soire.
cage, s. eunlann, eunadan.
cajole v. a. breug, meall, ciùinich.
cajoler, s. miodalaiche, fear-sodail.
caitiff, s. slaightire; drochbheartach.

cake, s. breacag, bonnach, dearnagan.
calamine, s. seòrsa méine.
calamitous, adj. truagh, dosgainneach.
calamity, s. truaighe, dosgainn, calldachd, àmhghar; doilghios.
calcareous, adj. cailceach.
calcination, s. losgadh gu luaithre.
calcine, v. a. loisg gu luaithre.
calculate, v. n. cunnt, meas; tomhais.
calculation, s. cunntas; meas.
calculator, s. fear-àireamh.
calculous, adj. clachach, moraghanach.
caldron, s. coire mór.
Caledonian, adj. Albannach.
calefactory, adj. teth, a ni teth.
calefy, v. a. dèan teth, teòidh.
calendar, s. mìosachan.
calender, v. a. liosraich.
calender, s. preas liosrachaidh.
calenderer, s. fear-liosraidh.
calf, s. laogh; calpa na coise.
caliber, calibre, s. leud tuill gunna.
calico, adj. aodach canaich.
calid, adj. teth, loisgeach.
calidity, calidness, s. dian-theas.
caligation, s. dorchadas, gruamachd.
caliginous, adj. dorcha, gruamach.
caligraphy, s. làmh-sgrìobhadh.
caliver, s. cuilibhear, gunna-glaic.
calk, v. a. calc, dìonaich, dùin suas.
calker, s. fear-calcaidh, calcadair.
call, v. a. gairm, goir; glaodh, éigh.
call, s. gairm, cuireadh, glaodh.
callat, callet, s. caile shuarach.
calling, s. gairm, dreuchd; inbhe; aidmheil.
callipers, s. gobhal-roinne.
callosity, s. calunn; callan, calum.
callous, adj. cruaidh, teann, neo mhoth-achail, cruaidh-chridheach.
callow, adj. rùisgte, lom.

calm, *adj.* sàmhach, ciùin, fèitheach sèimh, tosdach, sìothchail.

calm, *s.* fè, ciùine, sìth, sàmhchair.

calmness, *s.* ciùine, sàmhchair.

calomel, *s.* airgead-beò, cungaidh fuasglaidh, burgaid.

calorific, *adj.* teth, a theasaicheas.

caltrop, *s.* an deanndag arbhair.

calve, *v. n.* beir laogh.

calumniate, *v.* cùl-chàin; aithris tuaileas.

calumniation, *s.* cùl-chàineadh, tuaileas.

calumniator, *s.* fear-cùl-chàinidh, fear-casaid.

calumnious, *adj.* tuaileasach, sgainnealach.

calumny, *s.* sgainneal, tuaileas, breug.

cambric, *s.* pèarluinn, anart caol.

came, *pret.* of come, thàinig.

camel, *s.* càmhal.

camelots, *s.* aodach clòimhe is sìoda.

camomile, *s.* lus nan cambhil.

camp, *s.* càmpa, feachd-chòmhnaidh.

campaign, *s.* rèidhlean, còmhnard; cogadh.

campaigner, *s.* seann saighdear.

campestral, *adj.* machrach, fiadhain.

can, *s.* copan, còrn, cuach.

canaille, *s.* gràisg, pràbar, fòtus.

canal, *s.* clais uisge.

canaliculated, *adj.* sruthanach.

cancel, *v. a.* dubh a mach.

cancellation, *s.* dubhadh a mach.

cancer, *s.* partan, crùbag; aon de na comharran 'sa chuairt-ghréin; cnàmhainn, buirbean, cangairnich.

cancerous, *adj.* cnàmhainneach.

cancrine, *adj.* partanach, crùbagach.

candent, *adj.* dian-theth, dearg-theth.

candid, *adj.* saor, neo-chealgach, fosgarra.

candidate, *s.* fear-iarraidh, fear a thairgeas e fhéin air son dreuchd.

candidly, *adv.* gu h-ionraic.

candle, *s.* coinneal.

Candlemas, *s.* feill-Brìde.

candlestick, *s.* coinnlear.

candour, *s.* glaine-inntinn, suairceas, fosgarrachd.

candy, *v. a.* gréidh le siùcar.

cane, *s.* bata, lorg, cuilc.

cane, *v. a.* buail le bata, slacuinn.

canine, *adj.* coltach ri cù.

canister, *s.* canastair.

canker, *s.* cnàmhainn, cnuimh; meirg.

canker, *v. a.* truaill, mill, ith air falbh, cnàmh, caith.

cankerous, *adj.* cnàmhach.

cannibal, *s.* fear ithe feòla dhaoine.

cannon, *s.* gunna mór.

canoe, *s.* curach Innseanach.

canon, *s.* riaghailt, lagh, reachd eaglais.

canonical, *adj.* riaghailteach; c. hours, uairean ùrnuigh; c. books, leabhraichean a'Bhìobuill.

canonisation, *s.* cur air àireamh nan naomh (an eaglais na Ròimh).

canonist, *s.* fear-eòlach air lagh na cléire.

canopy, *s.* sgàilbhrat, còmhdach rìoghail, ceannbhrat.

canopy, *v. n.* còmhdaich le sgàilbhrat.

canorous, *adj.* ceòlbhinn, fonnmhor.

cant, *s.* cealgaireachd; cainnt gun bhrìgh.

cantata, *s.* canntaireachd, còisireachd.

canteen, *s.* canna saighdear, bùth ghoireasan (an camp).

canter, *s.* cealgair, mealltair; trotan eich.

cantharides, *s.* cuileagan Fràngach.

canthus, *s.* oisinn na sùla.

canticle, *s.* òran cràbhach; Dàn Sholaimh.

cantle, *s.* mìr, earrann, bloigh.

canto, *s.* earrann de dhuan.

canton, *s.* mìr fearainn, taobh dùthcha.

cantonise, *v. a.* dean mion-roinn, roinn 'na earrannaibh.

canvas, *s.* aodach cainbe.

canvass, *v. a.* mion-rannsaich, sgrùd, iarr fàbhar.

canzonet, *s.* òran beag, duanag.

cap, *s.* currac, còmhdach cinn.

cap, *v. a.* còmhdaich, cuir currac air.

cap-a-pie, o mhullach gu bonn, bho churraic gu bròig.

capability, *s.* cumhachd, comas.

capable, *adj.* comasach.

capacious, *adj.* mór, farsuing.

capaciousness, *s.* farsuinneachd.

capacitate, *v. a.* dèan comasach, dèan iomchuidh; ullaich, deasaich.

capacity, *s.* urrainn, comas, leud, cumhachd.

caparison, *s.* còmhdach rìmheach eich.

cape, *s.* rudha, ceann-tìre, maol rinn, àrda.

caper, *s.* leum, súrdag; seòrsa peabair.

caper, *v. n.* leum, geàrr sùrdagan.

capillary, *adj.* mar ròineig, ròineagach.

capital, *adj.* prìomh, àrd, mór, àraidh.

capital, *s.* ceann cuilbh, mullach; prìomh-bhaile, àrd-bhaile, àrd-chathair; earras; litir mhór; calpa (air riadh).

capitation, *s.* cunntas-cheann, cìscheann.

capitular, *s.* brìgh-sgrìobhaidh.

capitulate, *v. a.* strìochd (an cath).

capitulation, *s.* cumha-géillidh, cùmhnantan-strìochdaidh.

capon, *s.* coileach air a spoth.

caprice, *s.* sròineas, neònachas, mùiteachd.

capricious, *adj.* neònach, mùiteach.

capsular, capsulary, *adj.* fàs, mar chisteig.

capsulate, capsulated, *adj.* dùinte, ann am bocsa.

captain, *s.* ard-cheannard, ceann-feadhna, ceann-feachd; caiptin.

captation, s. seòrsa argumaid ; miodal.
captive, s. ciomach, braighdeanach.
captivity, s. ciomachas, braighdeanas.
caption, s. glacadh, glacadh laghail.
captious, adj. beumach, connspaideach, corrach, tiolpach, frionasach, crosda.
captor, s. glacadair, fear toirt fo chìs.
capture, s. glacadh, creachadh ; creach, cobhartach.
car, s. càrn, carbad, carbad-cogaidh.
carabine, s. gunna-glaic.
carat, s. tomhas cheithir grainnean ; tomhas òir.
caravan, s. carbad-mór ; buidheann luchd-turuis 's an airde 'n-ear, luchd-siubhail.
caravansary, s. tigh-òsda 's an àirde 'n ear.
caraway, s. lùs-mhic-chuimein.
carbonade, v. a. dòigh ghearraidh feòla.
carbiner, carabiner, s. trùpair aotrom.
carbuncle, s. seud dealrach, leug loinn-reach, carbuncul ; guirean, plucan dearg.
carcass, s. cairbh, closach, corp marbh.
card, s. cairt, cairt-chluiche, cairt-iùil : càrd, sgrìoban.
card, v. a. càrd, cìr ; measgaich.
card-table, s. clàr-chairtean.
cardiac, adj. a bhuineas do 'n chridhe, iocshlaint cridhe.
cardinal, adj. prìomh, àrd, urramach.
cardinal, s. prìomh-easbuig an eaglais na Ròimhe.
care, s. iomagain, cùram, aire, faiceall.
care, v. n. gabh cùram, gabh suim, bi faicilleach.
careen, v. a. calc, dìonaich, càirich.
career, s. rèis, cùrsa, dian-ruith, deann, cùrsa-beatha.
careful, adj. cùramach, iomgaineach, faicilleach, faireachail, furachail.
carefulness, s. iomgaineachd.
careless, adj. mi-chùramach, dearmadach, coma, gun fheart.
carelessness, s. mì-chùramachd, dear-madachd.
caress, v. a. caidrich, gràdhaich, tàlaidh, criodaich.
cargo, s. luchd luinge.
caricature, s. dealbh-magaidh.
caries, cariosity, s. grodachd.
carious, adj. grod, lobhta, malcte.
carle, s. mùigean, bodach.
carlings, s. lunnan-chas air ùrlar luinge no bàta.
carman, s. cairtear.
carminative, s. iocshlaint-lasachaidh.
carmine, s. dearg, corcur.
carnage, s. àr, marbhadh, casgradh, léir-sgrios, feòlach.
carnal, adj. feòlmhor, corporra, collaidh.
carnality, s. feòlmhorachd.

carneous, carnous, adj. reamhar, sult-mhor.
carnival, s. a' chuirm inid.
carnivorous, adj. feòil-itheach.
carnosity, s. ainfheòil.
carol, s. coireal, òran-gàirdeachais.
carol, v. a. mol, seinn cliù, ceileirich.
carousal, s. fleadh, cuirm, (òl is misg).
carouse, v. a. òl, bi air mhisg.
carp, s. carbhanach.
carp, v. n. coirich, tiolp, spreig.
carpenter, s. saor, saor luinge, soar dubh.
carpet, s. brat-ùrlair, stràille.
carping, adj. coireachail, tiolpach.
carriage, s. giùlan, beus, carbad.
carrier, s. fear giùlain, cairtear ; seòrsa calamain.
carrion, s. blìonach, ablach.
carrot, s. miuran-buidhe, curran.
carroty, a. dearg, ruadh.
carry, v. a. giùlain, iomchair, thoir leat, biodh agad.
cart, s. cairt, càrn.
cart, v. a. giùlain le cairt.
carte-blanche, s. paipeir geal, làn chead.
cartel, s. litir chùmhnantan eadar da rìoghachd.
carter, s. cairtear.
cartilage, s. maoth-chnàimh, duileasg (na sroine).
cartilaginous, adj. maothanach.
cartoon, s. dealbh àbhacaich.
cartouch, s. bocsa-peileireach.
cartridge, s. roidhleag-urchrach.
cartwright, s. saor chairtean.
carve, v. a. gearr feoil, fiodh, no clachan, etc., snaidh.
carving, s. gràbhaladh, obair-shnaidhte.
cascade, s. eas, casshruth.
case, s. còmhdach, duille, truaill, cochull ; staid, cor, céis.
case-knife, s. sgian mhór.
cash, s. airgead ullamh, airgead làimhe.
cashier, s. fear-gleidheadh an airgeid, ionmhasair ; pàighear airgid am banca.
cask, s. buideal, baraille.
cask, casque, s. clogaid.
casket, s. bocsachan.
cassia, s. craobh chasia ; seòrsa canail.
cassock, s. casag, cota sagairt.
cast, v. a. tilg, tilg air falbh ; cuir sìos ; leag ; cuir air cùl ; cunnt, aireamh ; leagh, deilbh.
cast, s. tilgeadh, urchair, buille ; sgapadh, crathadh, sgaoileadh ; gluasad, clao-nadh, siaradh ; cumadh, dealbh.
castaway, s. dìobarach, ni air a thilgeadh air falbh.
castellan, s. fear riaghlaidh daingnich.
castellated, adj. dùinte, ann an daing-neach.

castigate, v. a. cronaich, smachdaich, gréidh, sgiùrs.
castigation, s. cronachadh, peanas.
casting-net, s. lion-sgrìobaidh.
castor. See beaver.
castrametation, s. campachadh.
castrate, v. a. spoth ; glan (leabhar).
castration, s. spoth, glanadh.
casual, adj. tuiteamach, tubaisteach, tachartach, air uairean.
casualty, s. tuiteamas ; tubaist, leòn, no marbhadh (an cogadh).
casuist, s. fear fuasglaidh cheistean, fear innleachdach (gu tric a' muchadh coguis).
cat, s. cat.
cataclysm, s. tuilbheam, dìle.
catacombs, s. pl. uamhannan adhlaic.
catalogue, s. clàr-ainm, ainmchlar.
cataphract, s. marcach armaichte.
cataplasm, s. plàsd, fuarlite.
catapult, s. tailm, no clachbhogha, longag.
cataract, s. eas ; sgleò sùla.
catarrh, s. cnatan ; galar-lìnig, carrasan.
catastrophe, s. crìoch, droch dheireadh, tubaist, léir-sgrios.
catch, v. a. glac, greimich, beir, ceap.
catch, s. glacadh, beirsinn, ceapadh, gréim, cothrom ; teum ; luinneag, duanag ; gramaiche, acair bheag.
catechise, v. a. ceasnaich, rannsaich.
catechism, s. leabhar-cheist.
catechist, s. fear-ceasnachaidh, ceistear.
catechumen, s. foghlumaiche an eòlas spioradail.
categorical, adj. cinnteach, còmhnardach (am facal).
category, s. òrdugh, dream, treubh, seòrsa, gnè.
catenarian, adj. coltach ri slabhraidh, lùbagach, ailbheagach.
catenation, s. tinne, dul, slabhraidh.
cater, v. n. solair, ullaich biadh.
caterer, s. fear-solair.
cateress, s. bean-sholair.
caterpillar, s. burras.
caterwaul, v. n. dèan miagail mar chat.
cates, s. biadh math, mias bhlasta.
catgut, s. teud fidhill ; snòta (iasgaich).
cathartic, adj. pùrgaideach.
cathedral, s. ard-eaglais easbuigeach (anns a bheil cathair easbuig).
catholic, adj. coitcheann ; cumanta.
catling, s. sgian-sgaraidh léigh ; teudan.
cattle, s. spréidh, crodh, buar, feudail, tàn.
caudle, s. deoch bhan-shiùbhla.
caught, part. pas. glacte.
caul, s. sreafainn, currac sreafainn (naoidhean) ; bréide an crannaig ; currac-an-rìgh.
cauliferous, adj. cuiseagach, luirgneach.

cauliflower, s. càl-gruthach ; càl-colaig.
causal, adj. aobharach.
cause, s. aobhar, ceann-fàth.
cause, v. a. dèan, thoir gu buil.
causeless, adj. gun aobhar.
causey, causeway, s. cabhsair.
caustic, s. clach-loisgeach.
cautery, s. losgadh le iarunn no le cungaidhean léigh.
caution, s. gliocas, cùram, aire, faicill ; ràthan, urras, comhairle ; rabhadh, sanas.
caution, v. a. thoir rabhadh, cuir air fhaicill.
cautionary, adj. an urras, an geall, sanasach.
cautious, adj. curamach, faicilleach.
cautiousness, s. faicilleachd.
cavalcade, s. marc-shluagh.
cavalier, s. marcach, ridire ; rìoghalach.
cavalier, adj. gaisgeil, treun, uallach, stràiceil.
cavalierness, s. mórchuis, stràicealachd.
cavalry, s. marc-shluagh cogaidh.
cave, s. uamh, brugh, toll fo thalamh.
caveat, s. rabhadh, sanas, bacadh.
cavern, s. sloc, uamha.
caverned, cavernous, adj. uamhach, a' gabhail còmhnaidh an uamhaibh.
cavil, v. faigh faoin-choire.
caviller, s. tiolpaire mì-mhodhail féin-bharalach.
cavity, s. fàslach, còs, lag, sloc, glac.
caw, v. n. ròc, glaodh mar ròcais.
cease, v. a. cuir stad air, cuir crìoch air, caisg ; sguir, leig dhìot ; bàsaich ; dèan tàmh.
ceaseless, adj. buan, gun stad.
cedar, s. seudar, craobh sheudair.
cede, v. thoir suas, leig dhìot ; géill.
ceil, v. a. còmhdaich thairis.
ceiling, s. lobhta ; mullach seòmair.
celature, s. eòlas gràbhalaidh.
celebrate, v. a. mol, dèan iomraiteach ; gléidh, cùm.
celebration, s. cuimhneachan urramach, cumail féille, moladh, cliù.
celebrity, s. greadhnachas, iomraiteachd.
celerity, s. luathas, ealamhachd.
celestial, adj. nèamhaidh ; diadhaidh, naomha.
celestial, s. aon de mhuinntir nèimh.
celibacy, celibate, s. beatha sagairt, manaich, no cailliche-duibhe ; neach nach pòs.
cell, s. cill, còs, fròg, bothan ; balgan, pocan.
cellar, s. seilear, cùil.
Celts, s. Ceiltich ; Gàidheil na h-Albann, Eireann, an Eilein Mhanainnich ; Cuimrich Shasunn agus na Fraince.
cement, s. leann-tàth.
cement, v. a. tath, cuir r'a chéile.

cemetery, s. cladh, ionad-adhlacaidh.

cenotaph, s. fàs-chàrn, carragh-cuimhne (air fear 's a chorp an aite eile).

cense, v. a. ung le tùis, dèan dèagh-bholtrach.

censer, s. tùisear, soitheach tùis.

censor, s. fear-cronaichidh.

censorious, adj. cronachail, achmhasanach, cànranach.

censurable, adj. toilltinneach air achmhasan, ciontach, coireach.

censure, s. coire, achmhasan, cronachadh, ascaoin-eaglais.

censure, v. a. cronaich, coirich ; thoir breith, thoir barail.

census, s. cunntas, sluagh-chunntas.

cent, s. giorrachadh air an fhacal laidinn *centum*, ceud ; bonn-sia.

centage, s. pàidheadh as a' cheud.

centenary, s. uidhe cheud bliadhna.

centennial, adj. ceud-bliadhnail.

centesimal, adj. àireamh air cheudan ; ceud mu seach.

centifolious, adj. ceud-dhuilleagach.

central, adj. meadhonach.

centre, s. meadhon, buillsgean.

centre, v. a. cuir 's a' mheadhon, trus gu meadhon, bi 's a' mheadhon.

centric, adj. suidhichte 's a' mheadhon.

centrifugal, adj. meadhon-sheachnach.

centripetal, adj. meadhon-aomachdail.

centuple, adj. ceud fillte.

centuriate, v. n. roinn 'n a cheudaibh.

centurion, s. ceannard-ceud.

century, s. ceud bliadhna, linn.

cerate, s. ìocshlaint chéire.

cere, v. a. céir, céirich.

cereal, a. and s. de ghné arbhair.

cerebral, a. a bhuineas do eanchainn.

cerebrum, s. an eanchainn.

cerecloth, s. aodach-mairbh.

cerement, s. leine-lighe ; aodach mairbh.

ceremonial, s. deas-ghnàth, dòigh, rian, seòl, riaghailt, modh ; riaghailt-cràbh-aidh.

ceremonious, adj. deas-ghnàthach, òrdail, dòigheil ; làn modhalachd.

ceremony, s. deas-gnàth, riaghailt-chràbhaidh ; modhalachd, dòigh, cleachdadh, modh.

certain, adj. cinnteach, fìrinneach, dearbhta, àraidh.

certainty, certitude, s. cinnteachd, dearbhadh, dearbhachd.

certificate, s. teist, teisteanas.

certify, v. a. thoir fios, dèan cinnteach, dèan dearbhta, thoir teisteanas.

certitude, s. cinnteachd, dearbhachd.

cerulean, ceruleous, adj. gorm, liath-ghorm, speur-ghorm.

cerulific, adj. gorm-dhathach.

cerumen, s. céir na cluaise.

ceruse, s. luaidhe gheal, dath geal.

cess, s. cìs, càin, màl.

cessation, s. stad, socair, sgur, tàmh, clos ; fosadh cogaidh.

cession, s. géilleadh, strìochdadh.

cestus, s. crios-gaoil, crios a' ghràidh.

chafe, v. a. and n. suath, blàthaich, teòth ; teasaich, feargaich, casaich ; bi frionasach, bi crosda, bi feargach ; leusaich.

chafe, s. blàthas, teas ; fearg, boile, corraich, frionas, leusan.

chafer, s. daolag-bhuidhe.

chaff, s. moll, càth ; nì suarach.

chaffer, v. n. malairtich, connsaich mu luach.

chaffinch, s. breac-an-t-sìl.

chaffy, adj. càthach, mollach, aotrom, gun bhrigh.

chafing-dish, s. soitheach gu cumail bidh teth.

chagrin, s. frionas, droch-nàdur, mì-ghean, droch-fhonn, farran.

chagrin, v. a. dèan frionasach, sàraich.

chain, s. slabhraidh, geimheal, ceangal, cuibhreach.

chain, v. a. ceangail, cuibhrich, geimhlich, cuir air slabhraidh ; ceangail r'a chéile.

chain-shot, s. urchair shlabhraidh.

chair, s. cathair, suidheachan, séadhar.

chairman, s. fear cathrach, ceann-sùidhe, fear-iomchair.

chaise, s. carbad eutrom, carbad dà eich.

chaldron, s. salldair, tomhas guail no sìl.

chalice, s. cupan calpach, copan comanachaidh.

chalk, s. cailc.

chalk, v. a. comharraich le cailc.

chalky, adj. cailceach.

challenge, v. a. tairg deas-chòmhrag, dùlanaich, fiadhaich (gu cath).

challenge, s. gairm - chatha, tairgse - còmhraig, dùlan, fiadhachadh.

chalybeate, adj. stailinneach, air bhlas iaruinn.

chamade, s. caismeachd, géillidh.

chamber, s. seòmar, rùm.

chamberlain, s. fear-ionaid uachdarain, seumarlan, fear togail màil.

chambermaid, s. searbhant, searbhant seòmair.

chameleon, s. seòrsa dearc-luachrach.

chamois, s. seòrsa gaibhre.

chamomile, s. a' buidheag chambhil.

champ, v. a. and n. cagainn, teum, gearr, criom.

champaign, s. machair, magh, srath.

champaign, s. seòrsa fìona.

champion, s. treunlaoch, gaisgeach, curaidh, milidh.

chance, s. tuiteamas, dàn, sealbh.

chancel, s. ionad altair an eaglais.

chancre, s. drùisghuirean.

chandelier, s. coinnlear meurach.

chandler, s. fear dèanamh choinnlean ; ceannaiche choinnlean, no siabuinn, no ola, etc.

change, v. a. mùth, atharraich ; caochail.

change, s. mùthadh, atharrachadh, caochladh ; iomlaid.

changeable, changeful, adj. caochlaideach,luaineach,sgaogach,neo-sheasmhach ; so-atharraichte ; iomachruthach, ioma-dhathach.

changeless, adj. neo-chaochlaideach.

changeling, s. tàcharan, amadan, ùmaidh; leanabh air fhàgail, no air a ghabhail an àite leinibh eile ; àmhlar, sgaogan.

changer, s. fear-atharrachaidh, fearmùthaidh, fear-malairt airgeid.

channel, s. amar, clais, leabaidh linne ; caolas.

chant, v. seinn, tog fonn air.

chanter, s. fear-canntaireachd ; siunnsair.

chanticleer, s. coileach, deagh sheinneadair.

chaos, s. an aibhais gun chruth, mìriaghailt, troimhchéile.

chap, s. peasg, fosgladh, sgàineadh ; càirean beathaich.

chape, s. teanga, bucail, crampait claidheimh no bata.

chapel, s. eaglais bheag (Shasunnach) ; seòmar aoraidh ; tigh-clo-bhualaidh.

chaplain, s. ministear teaghlaich, feachd, no luinge.

chapless, adj. caol-pheirceallach.

chaplet, s. blàthfhleasg, luschrun.

chapman, s. ceannaiche-siubhail.

chapped, chapt, part. pass. peasgte, pronnte, gàgach.

chapter, s. caibidil.

chaptrel, s. ceann-mullaich carraigh.

char, s. seòrsa éisg, tarragan.

char, v. a. and n. loisg ('n a ghual).

character, s. comharradh, samhla, coltas ; litir ; iomradh, aithris ; cliù, beusan, alla.

character, v. a. sgrìob, grabhal ; dèan iomradh.

characteristic, adj. fìor-shamlachail, mar chliù.

characterise, v. a. thoir cliù, thoir teisteas, aithris buadhan ; comharraich ; grabhal, sgrìobh.

charcoal, s. gual-fiodha, gual-loisgte.

charge, v. a. earb, thoir comas, earb gnothach, cuir as leth, faigh cron, buail, thoir ionnsaigh.

charge, s. cùram, gleidheadh ; àithne, ìmpidh ; dreuchd ; casaid, coire ; cosgas, cìs ; urchair.

chargeable, adj. daor, cosgail, air a chur as leth.

charger, s. mias-mhór ; steudeach.

chariot, s. carbad.

charioteer, s. carbadair.

charitable, adj. oircheasach, déirceach, carthannach ; seirceil.

charity, s. coibhneas, carthannas, gràdh, seirc ; déirceachd, tabhartachd.

charlatan, s. cleasaiche, léigh-bréige, mealltair.

Charles's-wain, s. an griugadan, an crann-reulltach.

charlock, s. an carran-buidhe.

charm, s. druidheachd, buidseachd, seun ; maise, tlachd, caomhalachd.

charm, v. a. seun, cuir seun air, cuir fo gheasaibh ; gairm le drùidheachd.

charmer, s. druidh, geasadair ; gràidhean ; gràidheag.

charming, adj. taitneach, grinn.

charnel-house, s. tigh-adhlacaidh, seòmar adhlacaidh.

chart, s. cairt-iùil.

charter, s. sgrìobhadh, cùmhnant sgrìobhte, bann sgrìobhte ; còir sgrìobhte, daingneachd sgrìobhte ; dlighe, saorsa.

chary, adj. faicilleach, glic, sicir.

chase, v. a. sealg, ruaig, fuadaich.

chase, s. sealg, faoghaid ; tòir, iarraidh ; frith.

chase, s. grèis, carbhaigeadh ; gunna bàta ; céis.

chasm, s. sgaradh, sgor dhomhain.

chaste, adj. geamnaidh ; glan, fìorghlan.

chasten, chastise, v. a. cronaich, smachdaich, peanasaich, claoidh.

chastisement, s. smachdachadh, peanas.

chastity, chasteness, s. geamnachd.

chat, v. n. dèan còmhradh, dèan gobaireachd, dèan geòlam.

chat, s. gobaireachd, frith-chòmhradh, cracaireachd.

chattel, s. maoin, àirneis.

chatter, s. geòlam, sgeilm.

chawdron, s. mionach beathaich.

cheap, adj. saor ; air bheag prìs.

cheapen, v. a. lughdaich, leag prìs.

cheapness, s. saoiread.

cheat, s. foill, feall, car ; mealltair.

check, v. a. caisg, bac, grab, cuir fo smachd ; cronaich, co-shamhlaich r'a chéile.

checker, chequer, v. a. breac, stiallaich, tarruing stiallan tarsuinn.

cheek, s. gruaidh, lic, lethcheann, leigeas.

cheek-tooth, s. cùlag, fiacaill-chùil.

cheer, s. cuirm, cuilm, caithream, toileachas.

cheer, v. a. misnich, toilich.

cheerful, adj. ait, suilbhir, aoibhinn.

cheerfulness, s. sùrd, suigeart, sunnt ; toil-inntinn, cridhealas.

cheerless, adj. dubhach, trom ; gun tuar.

cheery, adj. ait, aoibhneach, toilichte.

cheese, s. càis.

cheese-monger, s. ceannaiche-càise.
cheese-vat, s. fiodhan.
cherish, v. tr. eiridnich, àraich, caidir.
cherry, s. sirist, craobh-shirist.
cherub, s. spiorad nèamhaidh ; aingeal ;
Cherub ; leanabh tlachdmhor.
cheslip, s. corra-chòsag.
chesnut, chestnut, s. geanm-chnò.
chess, s. taileasg.
chess-player, s. fear-feòirne.
chest, s. ciste, com, cliabh, bodhaig.
chevalier, s. ridire, curaidh.
chew, v. a. cagain, cnàmh ; cnuasaich.
chicane, s. staraidheachd, innleachd.
chick, chicken, s. eireag, isean.
chicken-hearted, adj. gealtach.
chicken-pox, s. a' bhreac-òtraich.
chide, v. a. cronaich, coirich, troid.
chief, adj. priomh, àrd, àraid.
chief, s. ceann-feadhna ; ceann-cinnidh.
chilblain, s. cusp, at-fuachd.
child, s'. leanabh, pàisde.
childhood, s. leanabachd, leanabas.
childish, adj. leanabail, leanabaidh.
childishness, s. leanabachd.
childless, adj. gun sliochd ; aimrid.
chiliarch, s. ceannard-mìle.
chill, adj. fuar, fuaraidh, fionnar.
chill, v. a. fuaraich, fionnfhuaraich.
chilliness, s. crith-fhuachd, girg.
chilly, adj. fionnfhuar, fuar, amh, disearr.
chime, s. co-sheirm, co-chòrdadh.
chimera, s. breisleach, faoin-bheachd.
chimerical, adj. breisleachail.
chimney, s. luidheir, fàrleus, simileir.
chin, s. smig, smigead, smeig.
chincough, s. triuthach.
chine, s. cnàimh an droma, cliathag.
chink, s. sgoltadh, sgàineadh, gàg.
chinky, a. gàgach, sgàinte.
chip, v. a. snaidh, pronn ; sgàin, sgoilt.
chip, chipping, s. sliseag, mìr, sgealb.
chirographer, s. fear-sgrìobhaidh.
chiromancer, s. deàrnadair.
chiromancy, s. deàrnadaireachd.
chirp, v. a. ceilear ; dèan dùrdan.
chirp, s. bìdeil, ceileirean.
chirping, s. ceileireachd.
chisel, s. gilb, sgeilb.
chit, s. pàiste, isean ; ball brice.
chit-chat, s. pronnchainnt, gobaireachd,
gusgal, briot, geòlam.
chitterlings, s. mionach, grealach, caolanan beaga.
chivalry, s. ridireachd ; treubhantas,
marc-shluagh ; modhalachd (ri mnathan uasal).
chives, s. seòrsa luis.
choice, s. roghainn, taghadh ; brod.
choice, adj. taghte.
choiceness, s. luachmhorachd, luach.
choir, s. còisir-chiùil.
choke, v. a. tachd ; mùch.

choler, s. leanntan, frionas ; fearg.
choleric, adj. feargach, lasanta, cas.
choose, v. a. tagh, ròghnaich.
chop, v. a. sgud, gearr le buille ; gearr
'n a òrdan.
chop, s. staoig, sgeanach.
chopin, s. seipin.
choppy, adj. làn tholl, gàgach, cairrceach,
mulcach, tomanach (of sea).
choral, adj. còisireach.
chord, s. teud, tafaid.
chorister, s. fear-còisir.
chorus, s. co-sheirm ; luinneag.
chosen, part. taghte, roghnaichte.
chouse, v. a. meall, thoir·an car as.
christen, v. a. baist.
Christendom, s. Crìosdachd.
christening, s. baisteadh.
christian, s. crìosdaidh.
christian, adj. crìosdail.
christianise, v. a. thoir fo bhuaidh an
t-soisgeil.
Christianity, s. criosdalachd ; an creideamh criosdail.
christian-name, s. ainm-baistidh.
Christmas, s. nollag ; am na Nollag.
chromatic, adj. dathach.
chronic, chronical, adj. leanmhainneach,
leantach, do-leighiseach.
chronicle, s. eachdraidh.
chronicler, s. eachdraiche.
chronological, adj. eachdraidheach.
chronometer, s. uaireadair.
chuck, s. gloc, gràchdan.
chuckle, s. gogail ; gàire os iosal.
chuff, s. ùmaidh, burraidh.
chum, s. companach seòmair, companach
dìl.
chump, s. slacan, fairgean.
church, s. eaglais, cill ; coimhthional.
churchman, s. pears-eaglais, ministear.
churchyard, s. cladh, reilic.
churl, s. mùigean, burraidh, duine
mosach.
churlish, adj. mùgach, gnù, iargalta.
churlishness, s. iargaltas, gruamachd,
doichioll ; crosdachd, mì-shuairceas,
mosaiche.
churme, s. toirm, fuaim, borbhan.
churn, s. muidhe, crannag ; mastradh.
churrworm, s. an t-slat-thomhais.
chyle, s. leann-meirbhidh.
chymist, s. feallsanach-brìghe.
chymistry, feallsanachd-brìghe.
cicatrice, s. làrach, eàrradh ; làrach
duilleig.
cicatrise, v. a. leighis, slànaich.
cicisbeo, s. gille-baintighearn.
cicurate, v. a. càllaich, ceannsaich.
cider, s. leann-ubhall.
cilicious, adj. gaoisideach, molach.
cinder, s. gual, eibhleag.
cinereous, adj. air dhath na luaithre.

cingle, s. crios-tarra, or tarr-iall eich.
cinnamon, s. caineal.
cinque-foil, s. seamrag chùig-bhileach.
cipher, s. neo-ni, sgrìobhadh dìomhair.
circle, s. cuairt, cearcall, buaile, còisir, riomball.
circle, v. a. iadh, cuairtich ; cruinnich.
circlet, s. cuairteag, buaileag, nasg òir, nasg sheudan.
circuit, s. cuairt ; crìochan ; cuairt nam mòrairean-dearga.
circuitous, adj. cuairteach.
circular, adj. cuairteach, cuairteagach.
circulate, v. a. cuir timchioll ; cuir mu'n cuairt.
circulation, s. dol mu'n cuairt.
circumambient, adj. mu thimchioll (as air, fluid).
circumambulate, v. n. coisich mun cuairt.
circumcise, v. a. timchioll-ghearr.
circumcision, s. timchioll-ghearradh.
circumference, s. cearcall ; buaileag.
circumfluent, adj. cuairt-shruthach.
circumfuse, v. a. dòirt mun cuairt.
circumfusion, s. iomadhòrtadh.
circumgyrate, v. a. cuibhlich, paisg gu cruinn.
circumjacent, adj. dlùth, fagus.
circumligation, s. ceangal mun cuairt.
circumlocution, s. cuairtchainnt.
circummured, adj. iomadhùinte.
circumnavigable, adj. cuairteach (mara is tìr).
circumnavigate, v. a. seòl mun cuairt.
circumnavigation, s. cuairtsheòladh.
circumnavigator, s. seòladair-cuairt na cruinne.
circumrotation, s. cuibhleadh mun cuairt.
circumscribe, v. a. iomadhuin.
circumscription, s. iomadhunadh.
circumspection, s. aire, cùram, faicill, furachas, crìonnachd.
circumspective, adj. aireil.
circumstance, s. cùis, càs, gnothach, cor, staid.
circumstantial, adj. mionaideach ; pongail.
circumvallate, v. a. daingnich (le balla no le clais).
circumvallation, s. daingneachadh.
circumvection, s. cuairtghiùlan.
circumvent, v. a. meall ; thoir a char as.
circumvention, s. foill, cealg ; car mu chnoc.
circumvolve, v. a. cuir mun cuairt, cuir car, cuir timchioll.
circumvolution, s. iomaroladh.
cist, s. ciste-laighe àrsaidh (air a cladhach á craoibh no á claich).
cistern, s. amar, tobar, linne.
citadel, s. dùn, daingneach, caisteal.

citation, s. sumonadh ; togail fianuis le ùghdar ainmeachadh mar eisimpleir.
cite, v. a. gairm, tarruing gu cùirt ; thoir ùghdar mar fhianuis.
citizen, s. fear-àiteachaidh baile-mhóir.
citrine, adj. buidhe-dhonn.
city, s. cathair, baile-mór.
civil, adj. cuideachdail, comunnach ; riaghailteach, rianail, dòigheil ; còir, deagh-bheusach, ciùin, modhail, sìobhalta, suairce, a bhuineas do lagh na tìre.
civilise, v. a. ciùinich, teagaisg, cuir fo rian, dèan ciallach.
civility, s. modhalachd, sìobhaltachd, suairceas, grinneas.
civil law, s. lagh na rìoghachd, lagh sìobhalt.
civil war, s. ar-a-mach, cogadh eadar buill rìoghachd.
clack, s. claban muileann.
clack, v. a. dèan glagan, gliong ; glagaireachd.
clad, part. aodaichte, sgeadaichte, còmhdaichte.
claim, v. a. tagair, agair, iarr.
claim, s. agradh, agartas, còir.
claimable, adj. agarach, so-agraidh.
claimant, s. fear-tagar, agarach.
clamber, v. a. streap, dìrich suas.
clammy, adj. glaodhach, leantach, sliamach, riamach.
clamorous, adj. gleadhrach, labhrach.
clamour, s. gàraich, gaoir.
clamp, s. cnot, clabhdan ; glamradh.
clan, s. fine, cinneadh.
clandestine, adj. uaigneach ; falachaidh.
clang, s. gliong, glang, gliogar.
clangour, s. gleadhraich, gliongraich, gliongarsich.
clangous, adj. gliongach, glangach.
clank, s. gleadhraich ; fuaim slabhraidh.
clanship, s. cinneadas.
clap, v. a. buail r'a chéile.
clap, s. buille, farum, bragh ; basghair, iolach.
clapper, s. claban muileann, teanga cluig.
clapper-claw, v. a. sgròb ; troid, càin.
claret, s. fìon dearg.
clarify, v. a. glan ; sìolaidh.
clasp, s. bràiste ; bucall ; cromag-dùnaidh (air leabhar).
class, s. buidheann, dream, cuideachd, seòrsa.
classical, adj. òirdhearc ; ionnsaichte, fòghlumte.
clatter, v. a. bi ri straighlich ; dèan glagadaich.
clatter, s. straighlich, gleadhraich.
clause, s. cuibhrionn ; pong.
clausure, s. dùnadh, druideadh.
claw, s. spòg, cròg, ionga ; màg, dubhan, pliut.

claw, *v. a.* sgrìob sgròb, reub, tachais.
clay, *s* criadh, cré, criadhach.
clean, *adj.* glan ; geamnaidh.
clean, *v. a.* glan, nigh, sgùr, ionnlaid.
cleanliness, cleanness, *s.* glainead, neo-thruailleachd, fìorghlaine.
cleanly, *adv.* glan, grinn, eireachdail.
cleanse, *v. a.* glan, nigh, sgùr, ionnlaid.
clear, *adj.* soilleir, soillseach, deàlrach, deàrsach, lainnreach, glan ; so-thuigsinn ; cinnteach ; neochiontach ; saor, tuigseach.
clear, *v. a.* soilleirich, glan, sgùr, soillsich, dèan lainnreach ; dèan so-thuigsinn, réitich ; saor, fìreanaich ; sìolaidh.
clearance, *s.* barantas-seòlaidh, soilleireachd ; réiteach.
clearness, *s.* soilleireachd.
clear-sighted, *adj.* glan-fhradharcach.
cleave, *v.* sgoilt, spealg, spealt, dlùthlean.
cleaver, *s.* sgian-sgoltaidh, corc, sgian mhór (feòladair).
cleft, *part.* sgoilte, roinnte.
cleft, *s.* sgoltadh, clais, sgàineadh.
cleg, *s.* creithleag-nan-each, creibhire.
clemency, *s.* iochd, bàigh, truas.
clement, *adj.* mìn, ciùin, séimh, bàigheil, caoin, tròcaireach.
clench, clinch, *v.* bàrr (tarann), snàim (ball), gabh gréim cruaidh, cruadhaich (dorn), dearbh (argumaid).
clergy, *s.* cléir.
clergyman, *s.* pears-eaglais.
clerical, *adj.* cléireachail.
clerk, *s.* cléireach, duine fòghluimte ; sgrìobhaiche.
clerkship, *s.* cléirsneachd.
clever, *adj.* tapaidh, deas, eòlach, clis, sgiobalta ; eirmseach.
cleverness, *s.* tapachd, cliseachd.
clew, *s.* ceirsle ; sgòd (siùil), fideadh, (snàth) stiuiridh.
clew, *v. a.* paisg seòl.
click, *v. a.* bi gliongarsnaich.
client, *s.* fear-iarraidh comhairle fir-lagha.
cliff, *s.* creag, sgùr, stùc.
cliffy, *adj.* sgorach, creagach, stùcach.
climate, clime, *s.* earrainn-saoghail, àileadh, sìde.
climax, *s.* dìreadh, éiridh an àirde, fìor mhullach, àirde.
climb, *v. a.* dìrich, streap.
climber, *s.* fear-streapaidh, lus streapach.
climbing, *s.* streap, dìreadh.
clinch, *v. a.* daingnich, teannaich, dìon. *See* clench.
clinch, *s.* gearrfhacal,
clincher, *s.* greimiche, am facal dearbhaidh ; òrd-barraidh.
cling, *v. a.* lean ; dlùth-lean.
clinic, *s.* foghlum leighis (taobh na leapa), leasan (an tigh-eiridinn).

clink, *v. a.* thoir gliong.
clip, *s.* bann ; glamradh beag.
clip, *v. a.* gearr, bearr, lomair, rùisg ; giorraich.
clipper, *s.* gearradair, bearradair ; seòrsa luinge.
clipping, *s.* bearradh, gearradh, lomadh.
cloak, *s.* falluinn, cleòc, brat-falaich, sgàile.
cloak, *v. a.* còmhdaich, falaich, cleith, ceil.
clock, *s.* uaireadair ; daolag.
clockwork, *s.* obair-uaireadair.
clod, *s.* clod, ploc, fòd, sgrath ; clodcheann, ùmaidh.
cloddy, *adj.* clodach, plocach.
clodpate, clodpole, *s.* clodcheann, ùmaidh.
clog, *v. a.* uallaich, luchdaich, sacaich bac, tromaich, cuir maille (air cuibhle).
clog, *s.* eallach, slacan, cudthrom, amaladh, bròg-fhiodha, bròg-glasaidh (air cuibhle).
cloister, *s.* cill-mhanach, tigh chailleacha-dubha.
close, *v. a.* dùin, crìochnaich.
close, *s.* dùnadh ; achadh cluiche ; crìochnachadh ; ceann, crìoch, deireadh, co-dhùnadh.
close, *adj.* dùinte, ceilte, dìomhair, uaigneach ; cumhann ; teann, daingeann, dlùth ; dorch, doilleir, neulach.
closeness, *s.* dùinteachd, cuingead, teanntachd ; dìomhaireachd, uaigneachd, fagusgachd.
closet, *s.* seòmar-uaigneach, clòsaid.
closet, *v. a.* dùin, glais, ceil.
closure, *s.* dùnadh, crìochnachadh, glasadh.
clot, *s.* meall, ploc, clodcheann.
cloth, *s.* aodach, clò, tubhailt.
clothe, *v. a.* aodaich, còmhdaich, sgeadaich.
clothier, *s.* tàillear ; ceannaiche earraidh.
clothing, clothes, *s.* aodach, earradh, trusgan.
clott-burr, *s.* bramasag.
cloud, *s.* neul, dubhar, sgòth, ceò.
cloud, *v. a.* neulaich, dorchaich.
cloud-berry, *s.* oidhreag, foidhreag.
cloud-capt, *adj.* neulach, sgòthach, ceò-churragach.
cloudless, *adj.* neo-sgòthach.
cloudy, *adj.* neulach, neo-shoilleir, dubharrach, doilleir, gruamach.
clough, *s.* gleann cumhang, gleann cas is allt 'n a ùrlar.
clout, *s.* luideag, broineag, clùd ; tuthag, mìr, brèid, giobal.
cloven, *part.* sgoilte.
clover, *s.* seamrag, bileag-chapail, saimir.
clovered, *adj.* seamragach.
clown, *s.* lùiriste, tuasdar, sgonnbhalach, amadan-àbhachd.

clownish, *adj.* tuaisdeach, lùiristeach ; liobasta, mì-mhodhail, mì-chiallach.

cloy, *v. a.* lìon, sàsaich, cuir gràin air.

cloyment, *s.* gràin-bidh, séid.

club, *s.* cuaille, lorg, rongas, caman, slacan, a' chairt-chluiche do'n ainm an "dubh-bhileach," no'n "crasg"; cuideachd, còisir, comunn.

club, *v. a.* buail le cuaille ; cuir an t-eanchainn as, gabh cuid roinn (còmhla ri càch).

club-law, *s.* làmhachas-làidir.

cluck, *v. a.* dèan gogail (mar chirc).

clump, *s.* bad (coille).

clumps, *s.* ùmpaidh, slaodair, glogair.

clumsiness, *s.* slaodaireachd, cearbaiche, luidealachd.

clumsy, *adj.* slaodach, liobasta, trom.

clung, *part.* leanta, greimichte.

cluster, *s.* bagaid, cluigean, dos, gagan ; dòrnlach.

clutch, *v. a.* greimich, glais, glac, teann-aich.

clutch, *s.* greimeachadh, glacadh ; cròg, spòg, màg, dubhan ìne.

clutter, *s.* straighlich, stairirich, gleadh-raich, gàraich.

clyster, *s.* clìostar.

coacervate, *v. a.* cruinnich, càrn ; dèan dùn, tòrr, trùs.

coach, *s.* carbad.

coadjutor, *s.* fear-cuidiche.

co-agent, *s.* co-oibriche.

coagment, *v. a.* co-chruinnich, tàth ri chéile.

coagulate, *v. a.* binndich, tiughaich rìghnich, reòdh.

coagulation, *s.* binndeachadh, reodhadh (fuil, etc.).

coal, *s.* gual.

coal, *v. a.* guail, loisg gu gual ; comh-arraich le gual, gabh gual air bòrd.

coal-fish, *s.* ucsa, ucas.

coalesce, *v. n.* aonaich, tàthaich, meas-gaich.

coalescence, *s.* aonadh, tàthadh.

coalition, *s.* glaodhadh (r'a chéile).

coaly, *adj.* gualach, air dhreach guail.

coarse, *adj.* garbh, neo-fhìnealta ; mì-mhodhail, garg.

coarseness, *s.* gairbhe, drabasdachd.

coast, *s.* oirthir, còrsa, slios.

coast, *v. a.* seòl cois an fhearann.

coat, *s.* còta ; éideadh, eudach.

coax, *v. a.* tàlaidh, cuir ìmpidh, tarruing le coibhneas.

cobble, *s.* clach mhuil.

cobble, *v. a.* càirich, bréidich (brògan).

cobbler, *s.* greusache, fear-càradh bhròg ; crògadair.

coble, *s.* eathar beag ; eathar le ùrlar leathan, sia-ramhach.

cobweb, *s.* lìon an damhain-allaidh.

cochineal, *s.* càrnaid.

cock, *s.* coileach ; molan-feòir.

cock, *v. a.* tog suas ; sgrog, cuir air lagh.

cockade, *s.* ròs leathair 'san aid ; suaicheantas Tigh Hanobher.

cockatrice, *s.* righ-naithreach.

cocker, *v. a.* crìodaich, tàlaidh.

cockerel, *s.* coileach eireig.

cocket, *s.* teisteanas tigh-cuspuinn.

cockle, *s.* coilleag, srùban ; cogull.

cockloft, *s.* lobhta mullaich, spiris.

cockney, *s.* Lunnainneach.

cockpit, *s.* blàr-catha choileach.

cocksure, *adj.* làn-chinnteach.

cocktail, *s.* each stùbhach, fear a fhuair inbhe os cionn a staid, deoch-làidir spìosrach.

cod, *s.* pollach, trosg.

coddle, *v.* coigil, altruim, peataich, dèan uilleagan ; slaop, leth-bhruich.

codicil, *s.* leasachadh tiomnaidh.

codling, *s.* bodach-ruadh.

coefficacy, *s.* co-oibreachadh, co-bhuaidh, co-éifeachd.

coemption, *s.* co-cheannachd.

coequal, *adj.* co-ionann.

coerce, *v. a.* co-éignich, ceannsaich, cuir fo smachd, dèan umhail.

coercible, *adj.* so-cheannsaichte.

coercion, *s.* éigneachadh ; smachd.

coercive, *adj.* ceannsalach, smachdail.

co-essential, *adj.* aon-bhitheach, co-fheumail.

co-eternal, *adj.* co-shuthainn.

coeval, *s.* co-aimsireach.

coeval, coevous, *adj.* co-aosda, co-aimsireil.

co-exist, *v. n.* bi co-bhitheach.

co-existence, *s.* co-bhith.

co-existent, *adj.* co-bhitheach.

coffer, *s.* ciste, còbaraid, ulaidh.

coffin, *s.* ciste-mhairbh, ciste-laighe.

cog, *v. a.* dèan miodal, bi carach, dèan claon char, cog dice, meall ; fiaclaich (cuibhle).

cog, *s.* cogus ratha muilleann, fiacail cuibhle.

cogency, *s.* reusonachadh còmhnard, soilleir, làidir.

cogent, *adj.* làidir, spionnadair.

cogitation, *s.* smuain, beachdachadh.

cognate, *adj.* càirdeach, dàimheil (an càirdeas).

cognation, *s.* càirdeas, dàimh.

coif, *s.* bréid, beannag, ceannbheart.

coil, *v. a.* cruinnich.

coil, *s.* cuairteag, còrd-chearcall.

coin, *s.* cùinneadh, airgead.

coincide, *v. n.* coinnich, co-aontaich.

coincidence, *s.* cò-dhalachadh ; co-fhreagradh.

coincident, *adj.* co-chòrdadh.

coiner, *s.* fear-cùinnidh.

coition, s. mairiste, cliathadh ; modh siolaichidh.
colation, colature, s. siòladh.
cold, adj. fuar, fionnar, fuaraidh.
cold, s. fuachd, fuarachd, fionnfhuarachd ; cnatan.
coldness, s. fuarachd, fuairead, fionnfhuaireachd.
cole, s. seòrsa càil.
cole-wort, s. càl-bloinigein.
colic, s. gréim-mionaich.
collapse, v. n. crùp, tuit, leig roimhe.
collar, s. bràid, coileir ; brang.
collar, v. a. beir air amhaich, glac air sgòrnan.
collar-bone, s. an uga.
collate, v. a. coimeas, coimeas aon (sgrìobhadh) ri fear eile.
collateral, adj. co-shìnte, taobh ri taobh.
collation, s. coimeas ; gréim bidh.
collator, s. fear sgrùdaidh.
colleague, s. companach, coimpire.
collect, v. a. co-chruinnich, tionail.
collect, s. ùrnaigh ghoirid.
collection, s. co-chruinneachadh, tional.
collective, adj. co-chruinnichte.
collector, s. fear-trusaidh, cìs-mhaor.
college, s. òil-thigh, àrd-sgoil, colaisd.
collegian, s. fòghlumach ard-sgoile.
collier, s. gualadair.
colliery, s. méinn guail.
colligation, s. co-cheangal, co-nasgadh.
collision, s. co-bhualadh, bualadh 'n a chéile.
collocate, v. a. suidhich, cairich, socraich.
collocation, s. suidheachadh, socrachadh.
collop, s. toitean, staoig.
colloquial, adj. conaltrach ; coitchionn (a thaobh canain).
colloquy, s. co-labhairt.
collusion, s. cuilbheart ; còrdadh uaigneach ('san olc).
collusive, adj. cuilbheartach.
colon, s. an caolan fada.
colonel, s. cornaileir, còirneal.
colonise, v. a. tìrich, àitich, eilthirich.
colonist, s. fear-àiteachaidh tìr chéin.
colony, s. luchd-imriche, nuadh-threabhachas.
colossal, adj. air leth mór, comharraichte.
colour, s. dath ; neul, tuar, fiamh, dreach ; coltas, riochd ; bratach, suaicheantas.
colour, v. a. dath ; cuir dath air.
colourist, s. dathadair.
colt, s. searrach.
coltsfoot, s. fathan ; cluas-liath.
columbary, s. tigh chalaman.
columbine, s. lus-a'-chalamain.
column, s. colbh, carragh ; sreath.
columnar, adj. colbhach, carraghail.
comb, s. cìr ; cìrean ; cìr-mheala.

combat, s. chòmhrag, cath ; comhlann ; gleachd.
combatant, s. fear-còmhraig ; gaisgeach, saighdear.
combinate, adj. naisgte, ceangailte.
combination, s. co-aontachd, co-cheangal.
combine, v. a. co-cheangail, co-aontaich, co-thàth.
combustible, adj. loisgeach, tioram.
combustion, s. fal-losgadh, ùparait.
come, v. n. thig ; trobhad.
comedian, s. cleasaiche, cleasaiche abhcaideach.
comedy, s. cluich àbhachd.
comeliness, s. eireachdas, ciatachd.
comely, adj. eireachdail, ciatach.
comfit, s. gréim milis, mìlsean.
comfort, s. co-fhurtachd, sòlas.
comfortable, adj. socrach, comhfhurtail.
comfortless, adj. neo-shuaimhneach.
comic, comical, adj. abhachdach, cridheil, sùgach, ait, cleasanta, neònach.
coming, s. teachd, tighinn.
command, v. a. òrduich, iarr, àithn ; ceannsaich.
command, s. uachdranachd, ard-chumhachd, ùghdarras, smachd, ceannas, tighearnas ; riaghladh, òrduchadh, àithne.
commander, s. uachdaran, ceannard.
commandment, s. òrdugh, iarrtas, àithne.
commemorate, v. a. cuimhnich.
commemoration, s. cuimhneachan.
commence, v. a. tòisich, siubhad.
commencement, s. tionnsgnadh, tùs, tòiseachadh.
commend, v. a. mol, cliùthaich.
commendable, adj. cliù-thoillteannach.
commendation, s. cliù, moladh ; teachdaireachd gaoil.
commendatory, adj. cliùiteach.
commensurate, adj. co-thoimhseach.
comment, v. a. mìnich, leudaich.
comment, s. brìgh-mhìneachadh.
commentary, s. mìneachadh.
commentator, s. fear-mìneachaidh.
commerce, s. malart ; co-chomunn.
commerce, v. n. malairtich, cum comunn.
commercial, adj. malairteach.
commination, s. bagradh, maoidheadh.
commingle, v. a. co-mheasgaich.
comminute, v. a. pronn, mìnich.
comminution, s. mion-phronnadh.
commiserable, adj. truagh.
commiseration, s. co-mhothachadh, bàigh, truas.
commiserative, adj. iochdmhor.
commissary, s. fear-ionaid Easbuig ; oifigeir ris an earbar biadh an airm.
commission, s. earbsa, barantas ; ùghdarras ; còir, comunn ; teachdaireachd.
commission, v. a. earb, ùghdarraich.

commissioner, s. fear-ùgdarrais.
commit, v. a. earb, cuir an comas, leig fo chumhachd ; thoir seachad, tiomain ; cuir am prìosan, cuir an làimh ; cuir an gnìomh ; ciontaich.
committee, s. cuideachd-riaghlaidh.
commix, v. a. co-mheasg, measgaich.
commode, s. ciste dhràraichean.
commodious, adj. goireasach, rùmail.
commodiousness, s. goireas ; rùm.
commodity, s. tairbh, bathar, goireas.
commodore, s. ceannard-cabhlaich.
common, adj. coitcheann, suarach.
common, s. ionaltradh coitcheann.
commonalty, s. sluagh ; an tuath.
commoner, s. fear dhe'n t-sluagh.
commonness, s. coitcheanntas.
commons, s. tuath-chomhairle.
commonwealth, s. an sluagh, comh-fhlaitheachd.
commotion, s. buaireas, luasgan, aimhreit, ùparait, troimh-chéile.
commune, v. n. co-labhair.
communicant, s. fear-comanaich, bean-chomanaich.
communicate, v. t. and i. compàirtich, builich, thoir seachad ; aithris, innis, cuir an céill, taisbein, co-labhair, co-roinn ; bi an compairt ; comanaich.
communicate, adj. compàirteach, còmhraideach.
communication, s. compàirteachadh, conaltradh, cur an céill ; slighe-fhosgailte ; co-chaidreamh ; co-chainnt.
communion, s. còmpanas, comanachadh, comunn.
community, s. compàirt, coimhearsnachd.
commutable, adj. iomlaideach.
commutation, s. iomlaid, éirig.
commute, v. a. mùth ; dìol éirig.
compact, s. co-cheangal, cùmhnanta.
compact, adj. teann, daingeann ; dùmhail.
compactness, s. daingneachd, dlùthadas.
companion, s. companach.
company, s. cuideachd, comunn.
company, v. a. comunnaich.
comparable, adj. co-ionann.
comparative, adj. a réir coimeis.
compare, v. a. coimeas, samhlaich.
comparison, s. coimheart, samhla.
compartition, s. compàirteachadh.
compartment, s. roinn, earrann.
compass, v. a. cuairtich, iomadhruid.
compass, s. cuairt, cearcall ; farsuing-eachd, tomhas, meud, leud ; crìochan ; cùmbaist, gobhal-roinn ; gobharraidh.
compassion, s. truas, iochd.
compassionate, adj. truacanta.
compatibility, s. co-chòrdalachd.
compatible, adj. co-chòrdail.
compatriot, s. fear-dùthcha.
compeer, s. companach, coimpir.

compel, v. a. co-éignich.
compendious, adj. geàrr - bhrìgheach, suimeil.
compensate, v. a. dìol, pàidh, ìoc.
compensation, s. làn-dìoladh, éiric.
competency, s. pailteas, fòghnadh, dio-chomas.
competent, adj. iomchuidh, comasach.
competition, s. co-dheuchainn, co-strìth, co-fharpais.
competitor, s. fear co-fharpais.
compile, v. a. co-chruinnich, tionail.
compiler, s. fear-trusaidh.
complacency, s. tlachd, riarachadh.
complacent, adj. riaraichte, air dòigh.
complain, v. n. gearain, talaich ; dèan casaid.
complainant, s. fear-agairt dìolaidh.
complainer, s. fear-gearain, fear-cumha.
complaint, s. gearan, casaid ; galar.
complaisance, s. modhalachd.
complaisant, adj. sìobhalta, modhail, suilbhir, suairce, faoilidh.
complement, s. co-lìonadh.
complete, adj. iomlan, coimhlionta.
complete, v. a. dèan iomlan.
completement, s. coimhlionadh.
completeness, s. iomlanachd.
completion, s. coimhlionadh ; crìoch-nachadh.
complex, adj. ciogailteach, deacair, iom-fhillteach.
complexion, s. tuar, neul, dreach, snuadh, coltas, fiamh.
compliance, s. strìochdadh, géilleadh, co-chòrdadh.
compliant, adj. aontach, suairce, soirbh, soitheamh, modhail.
complicate, adj. co-mheasgach ; duilich.
complicate, v. a. co-fhilltich, codhuail, co-amlaich ; dèan duilich.
complication, s. co-amladh, co-dhualadh.
complier, s. fear-co-aontachaidh.
compliment, s. moladh, miodal.
complimental, adj. miodalach.
complot, s. co-bhann, co-chealg.
complot, v. a. gabh claon-chomhairle.
comply, v. n. co-aontaich, géill.
comport, v. a. giùlain, fuiling.
comport, comportment, s. giùlan, gnàths, beus.
comportable, adj. freagarrach.
compose, v. a. co-dhèan, dèan suas, co-chuir, co-dhlùthaich ; càirich, socraich, leag, suidhich, ceartaich ; sgrìobh ; sìthich, ciùinich, dèan sàmhach.
composed, part. suidhichte, socraichte.
composer, s. ùghdar, sgrìobhair ciùil.
composition, s. sgrìobhadh ; cothlam-adh ; co-shuidheachadh ; suidheach-adh, socrachadh, riaghailt.
compositor, s. fear-deilbh (clo-bhualadh), fear-beartachaidh.

compost, composture, s. mathachadh, leasachadh, aolach.
composure, s. suidheachadh, sàmhchar, riaghailt ; sìthealachd.
compotation, s. co-phòitearachd.
compound, v. a. and n. coimeasg, cuir cuideachd, measg, co-dhèan ; dèan facal dùbailte ; dèan co-chòrdadh ; còrd ri luchd fiachan ; thig gu cumhachan.
compound, adj. coimeasgte, dùbailte.
compound, s. coimeasgadh.
comprehend, v. a. measraich, tuig.
comprehensible, adj. so-mheasraichte.
comprehension, s. tuigse, eòlas.
comprehensive, adj. tuigseach, farsuing, làn.
compress, v. a. dlùthaich, teannaich, dinn, fàisg.
compressible, adj. so-dhinnte.
compression, s. teannachadh.
compressure, s. bruthadh, dinneadh.
comprise, v. a. cum, gabh, gléidh.
compromise, s. cùmhnanta-réitich, còrd adh.
compromise, v. a. and n. co-chòrd.
comptrol, v. a. ceannsaich, smachdaich.
compulsatory, adj. éigineach.
compulsion, s. co-éigneachadh.
compulsive, compulsory, adj. àinneartach, a dh'éignicheas.
compunction, s. agartas-cogais.
compurgation, s. co-dhaingneachadh, saoradh, glanadh cliù, fìreanachadh.
computable, adj. so-àireamh.
computation, s. àireamh, suim.
compute, v. a. meas, cunnt.
comrade, s. companach.
con, v. a. aithnich ; breithnich, smuainich, ionnsaich air do mheaghair.
concatenate, v. a. co-thàth, dean 'na shlabhruidh.
concatenation, s. co-thàthadh.
concave, adj. slagach, tulgach.
concavity, s. còs, slag, tulg.
conceal, v. a. ceil, cleith, falaich.
concealable, adj. so-fhalach, a ghabhas falach.
concealment, s. ionad-falaich, cleith.
concede, v. a. and n. co-cheadaich, leig seachad, aontaich, géill, strìochd, fuiling, deònaich, aidich, leig thairis.
conceit, s. beachd, smuain, barail ; tuigse ; féin-bheachd, féin-spéis féinmheas.
conceited, adj. féin-bheachdail, bòsdail.
conceivable, adj. so-shaoilsinn, so-thuigsinn.
conceive, v. a. cnuasaich, tionnsgainn, breithnich, saoil ; fàs torrach.
concentrate, v. a. co-chruinnich (an aon àite) ; beachdaich air aon ni aig an àm.
concentre, v. a. thoir gu meadhon.

concentric, adj. aon-mheadhonach.
conception, s. gineamhuinn, measrachadh.
concern, v. a. gabh gnothach.
concern, s. gnothach, cùis ; cùram.
concerning, prep. mu thimchioll, mu dhéighinn, a thaobh.
concernment, s. gnothach ; cùram.
concert, v. a. and n. co-shuidhich, corùnaich, gabh comhairle gu dìomhair ; co-shocraich, co-chomhairlich.
concert, s. co-chomhairle, co-shuidheachadh, co-shocrachadh, co-rùn ; cosheirm, còisir-chiùil, féisd-chiùil.
concession, s. strìochdadh, ceadachadh, géilleadh, toirt thairis.
conch, s. slige, faochag.
conciliate, v. a. réitich, buannaich.
conciliation, s. réiteachadh.
conciliator, s. fear-réiteachaidh.
concinnity, s. freagarrachd ; maise cainnt.
concise, adj. goirid, gearr, suimeil.
conciseness, s. aithghiorrad.
concision, s. co-ghearradh, sgudadh.
conclave, s. coinneamh ard-Easbuigean Romanach gu taghadh Pàpa.
conclude, v. co-dhùin, dùin, criochnaich.
conclusion, s. co-dhùnadh.
conclusive, adj. crìochnach ; dearbhta.
concoct, v. a. measgaich (deoch).
concoction, s. deoch no cungaidh mheasgaichte.
concomitant, adj. co-aontach.
concomitant, s. companachadh.
concord, s. co-fhreagairt, co-shéirm, cofhonn, co-chòrdadh.
concordance, s. co-chòrdachd.
concordant, adj. co-chòrdail.
concordat, s. co-bhann, co-ghairm.
concorporate, v. a. co-chruinnich (an aon chuideachd).
concourse, s. co-chruinneachadh (sluaigh).
concrete, s. co-chruinnichte, ni faicsinneach.
concretion, s. meall cruinnichte.
concubine, s. coimhleapach.
concupiscence, s. ana-miann.
concupiscent, adj. collaidh.
concur, v. n. aontaich.
concurrence, s. co-aontachd, co-chuideachadh toil ; aonta.
concurrent, adj. co-aontach, co-leantainn.
concussion, s. criothnachadh, ciùrradh eanchainn.
condemn, v. a. dìt, cronaich.
condemnation, s. dìteadh, binn.
condensate, adj. tiughaichte.
condensation, s. tiughachadh.
condense, v. a. co-dhlùthaich, dèan tiugh.
condensity, s. dinnteachd.
condescend, v. n. ìslich, irioslaich, strìochd, deònaich, ceadaich.

condescension, s. irioslachd.
condign, adj. toillteannach, iomchuidh.
condiment, s. annlann.
condition, s. cor, staid ; cumha, cùmhnanta, inbhe.
conditional, adj. air chumha.
condole, v. n. co-ghuil, dean co-bhròn.
condolence, s. co-ghul, co-bhròn, co-fhaireachadh.
condonation, s. mathadh, gabhail leisgeul.
conduce, v. a. co-chèimnich, treòraich, stiùir, seòl an t-slighe ; co-chuidich.
conducible, adj. comhnachail.
conducive, adj. cuideachail.
conduct, s. rian, dòigh, riaghladh ; stiùradh, treòrachadh ; giùlan, beus, caithe-beatha.
conduct, v. a. treòraich, stiùir, seòl.
conductor, s. fear-iùil, fear-treòrachaidh ; ceannard.
conduit, s. pìob-uisge, guitear, cladhan uisge.
cone, s. bidean, stalla.
confabulate, v. n. co-labhair.
confabulation, s. conaltradh.
confection, s. mìlsean.
confectioner, s. fear-dèanamh mhìlsean.
confederacy, s. cùmhnant, stàitean an co-bhoinn.
confederate, v. a. co-aontaich, co-cheangail.
confederate, s. companach 'san olc.
confederation, s. co-chaidreamh.
confer, v. a. thabhair, builich, bàirig ; cuir comhairle ri (neach).
conference, s. còmhradh, co-chruinneachadh ; comhairle.
confess, v. a. aidich ; faoisidich ; éisd faoisid ; taisbean, cuir an céill ; co-aontaich, ceadaich.
confession, s. aidmheil ; faoisid.
confessor, s. fear-aidmheil a' chreidimh ; sagart-faoisid ; fear-aideachaidh.
confest, adj. aidichte, soilleir.
confidant, confident, s. fear-rùin, caraid dealaidh.
confide, v. a. earb, cuir earbsa.
confidence, s. earbsa, muinghinn, bun ; dòchas, misneach ; dànadas, ladarnas.
confident, adj. cinnteach, dearbhte, earbsach, dearbh-chinnteach, neo-theagmhach ; danarra, teann, dalma ; muinghinneach, dòchasach ; dàna, ladarna.
confidential, adj. càirdeil, dìleas, rùnach.
configuration, s. co-fhreagradh, ìomhachd.
configure, v. a. cuir an cruth.
confine, s. crìoch, iomall, oir.
confine, v. a. cum a stigh, cuir fo chrìochan.
confinement, s. prìosanachadh ; asaid.
confirm, v. a. daingnich, socraich.
confirmable, adj. so-dhearbhte.

confirmation, s. co-dhearbhadh ; togail " fianuis," aideachadh follaiseach ('s an eaglais Shasunnaich).
confiscate, v. a. ar-phuntaich.
confiscation, s. ar-phuntachadh.
confix, v. a. daingnich, suidhich.
conflagration, s. teine mór, losgadh sgriosail.
conflict, v. n. cathaich, dèan strì.
conflict, s. strì, spàirn, còmhrag, sabaid, dòrainn, cràdh.
confluence, s. inbhir, coinneachadh dà abhainn an aon ruith.
confluent, adj. a' co-shruthadh, a ruitheas 's an aon leabaidh.
conflux, s. co-shruth ; aonadh nan allt.
conform, v. co-aontaich, géill.
conformable, adj. co-chòrdail, coltach.
conformation, s. co-chruth, cumadh, dealbh.
conformist, s. fear co-aontachaidh, fear co-chumaidh.
conformity, s. co-fhreagarrachd, coltas, samhlachas.
confound, v. a. aimhreitich, cuir thar a chéile ; coimeasg, cuir an imcheist ; tuairgnich, nàraich ; mill, sgrìos.
confounded, adv. gràineil, fuathach.
confounder, s. buaireadair, blaomaire, fear tuairgnidh.
confraternity, s. co-bhràthaireachas.
confront, v. a. seas mu choinneamh ; cuir aghaidh ri aghaidh, thoir coinneamh.
confronted, part. air an toirt aghaidh ri aghaidh.
confuse, v. a. aimhreitich, breislich, cuir thar a chéile ; mì-riaghailtich, dorchaich ; tuairgnich.
confusion, s. breisleach, tuairgneadh ; àimhreit, buaireas, aimlisg ; aimheal.
confutable, adj. so-àicheadh.
confutation, s. breugnachadh.
confute, v. a. breugnaich.
congeal, v. a. reòdh, ragaich.
congealable, adj. reòdhtachail.
congealment, s. reodhadh, eighneadh.
congenial, adj. co-ghnéitheach, còrdail.
conger, s. easgann mhara.
congest, v. a. dlùthaich, dùmhlaich.
congestion, s. dùmhlachd ; mùchadh ; teasach sgamhain.
conglaciate, v. a. tionndaidh gu eigh.
conglobate, v. a. dean meall cruinn.
conglobate, adj. co-chruinn.
conglomerate, v. a. ceirslich.
conglomerate, adj. ceirslichte.
conglomeration, s. co-thrùsadh.
conglutination, s. aonadh, glaodhadh.
Congou, s. seòrsa do thì.
congratulant, adj. co-ghàirdeachail.
congratulate, v. a. dèan co-ghàirdeachas.
congratulation, s. meal an naidheachd.
congratulatory, adj. co-ghàirdeachail.

congregate, *v. a.* tionail.
congregation, *s.* co-thional.
congress, *s.* coinneamh, comhghairm.
congressive, *adj.* a' coinneachadh.
congruence, congruity, *s.* freagarrachd, co-fhreagarrachd, còrdadh.
congruent, *adj.* co-fhreagarrach.
congruous, *adj.* co-fhreagarrach.
conic, conical, *adj.* bideanach.
conjector, conjecturer, *s.* fear-baralach.
conjectural, *adj.* baralach.
conjecture, *s.* barail, tuaiream.
conjecture, *v. a.* baralaich.
conjoin, *v. a.* and *n.* co-dhlùthaich, aonaich, co-aontaich, co-cheangail, co-thàth ; co-naisg.
conjoint, *adj.* co-cheangailte, co-dhlùithte, co-naisgte.
conjugal, *adj.* pòsachail, pòsta.
conjugate, *v. a.* co-cheangail, co-naisg, co-dhlùthaich.
conjunction, *s.* aonadh, co-cheangal, coinneachadh ; facal aonaidh, càraid.
conjunctive, *adj.* co-cheangailte.
conjuncture, *s.* co-chuideachd, coinneachadh, tachairt, còdhail ; càs, cùis, éigin, àm sònraichte, iomcheist ; co-cheangal, co-nasgadh ; co-chòrdalachd.
conjuration, *s.* mìonnachadh, grìosadh ; drùidheachd ; co-chealg.
conjure, *v. a.* grìos, mionnaich ; co-cheangail fo mhionnaibh ; cuir fo gheasaibh ; gnàthaich drùidheachd.
conjurement, *s.* grìosadh, aslachadh.
conjurer, *s.* drùidh, fiosaiche, cleasaiche.
connascence, *s.* co-bhreith ; aonadh.
connate, *adj.* co-bhreitheach, nàdurach.
connatural, *adj.* co-ghnètheach.
connect, *v. a.* co-naisg, ceangail.
connected, *part.* aonaichte.
connex, *v. a.* co-naisg, snàidhm.
connexion, *s.* aonadh, dàimh.
connivance, *s.* leigeadh seachad, priobadh (mu olc).
connive, *v. n.* caog, smèid ; rach seachad.
connoisseur, *s.* fear fiosrach.
connubial, *adj.* pòsachail, posta.
conquer, *v. a.* buadhaich, ceannsaich ; cìosnaich.
conquerable, *adj.* so-cheannsachadh.
conqueror, *s.* buadhaiche, fear buadha.
conquest, *s.* buaidh-làrach.
consanguinity, *s.* càirdeas, dàimh.
conscience, *s.* cogais, ceartas, còir.
conscientious, *adj.* cogaiseach.
conscionable, *adj.* ceart, reusonta.
conscious, *adj.* féin-fhiosrach.
consciously, *adv.* féin-fhiosrachail.
consciousness, *s.* féin-fhiosrachd.
conscript, *s.* saighdear (a dh'aindeon).
consecrate, *v. a.* coisrig, cuir gu feum naomh.
consecrated, *adj.* coisrigte.

consecration, *s.* coisrigeadh, cur gu feum naomh.
consecution, *s.* leanmhainn.
consecutive, *adj.* leanmhainneach.
conseminate, *v. a.* cuir sìol am measg a chéile.
consent, *v. n.* aontaich, géill, còrd.
consent, *s.* aonta.
consentient, *adj.* a dh'aon bharail.
consequence, *s.* toradh, buaidh.
consequent, *adj.* a leanas.
consequential, *adj.* cudthromach, mòr-bheachdail.
consequently, *adv.* uime sin.
conservation, *s.* gleidheadh, dìon.
conservatory, *s.* tigh bhlàthan.
conserve, *v. a.* taisg, gléidh, dìon.
conserve, *s.* biadh blasta ; mìlsean.
consider, *v. a.* and *n.* smuainich, beachd-smuainich, thoir fainear, sgrùd, rannsaich, cnuasaich ; dìol, duaisich ; cuimhnich.
considerable, *adj.* fiùghail, luachmhor, cudhromach, pailt, taisealach.
considerably, *adv.* fiùghalach ; gu taise-alach.
considerate, *adj.* ciallach, glic, coibhneil.
consideration, *s.* smuaineachadh, beachd-smuaineachadh, toirt fainear, rannsachadh, sgrùdadh ; crìonnachd, gliocas ; geur-bheachd ; meas, urram ; luach, dìoladh ; aobhar, fàth.
consign, *v. a.* thoir seachad ; cuir, tilg ('s an teine, no 's an uisge) ; cuir badhar gu neach.
consignment, *s.* toirt seachad ; ceannachd.
consist, *v. n.* mair, buanaich.
consistence, consistency, *s.* staid, cor, bith ; cumadh, dreach ; seasmhachd, buanachd, maireannachd ; co-chòrd-adh.
consistent, *adj.* co-chòrdach, do réir.
consistory, *s.* sionadh Pàpa.
consociate, *s.* companach.
consociate, *v. a.* companaich ; aonaich.
consociation, *s.* co - chomunn ; com-panachas.
consolable, *adj.* so-fhurtachail.
consolation, *s.* comhfhfhurtachd.
consolatory, *adj.* sòlasach, furtachail.
console, *v. a.* comhfhfhurtaich.
consoler, *s.* comhfhurtair.
consolidate, *v. a.* cruadhaich ; dlùthaich, cruinnich, neartaich.
consolidation, *s.* cruadhachadh.
consonance, *s.* co-sheirm, co-aontachd.
consonant, *adj.* co-fhreagarrach.
consonant, *s.* co-fhòghar.
consonous, *adj.* leadarra, binn.
consort, *s.* céile ; aonachd.
consort, *v.* aonaich, companaich ; pòs ; rach an cuideachd.
conspicuity, *s.* soilleireachd.

conspicuous, *adj.* faicsinneach, soilleir, ainmeil, cliùiteach, inbheach.
conspiracy, *s.* feall, foill ceannairc; droch rùn; clìchd; fiùchd.
conspirator, conspirer, *s.* fealltair, fearfoille, cluaintear.
conspire, *v. a.* suidhich air droch-bheart, dèan co-fheall.
constable, *s.* conastapull.
constableship, *s.* dreuchd conastapuill.
constancy, *s.* seasmhachd, neo-chaochlaidheachd, maireannachd, bunailteachd; dìlseachd.
constant, *adj.* seasmhach, daingeann, maireannach; bunailteach; dìleas.
constellation, *s.* grunnan reult (=grioglachan, etc.).
consternation, *s.* fuathas, uabhas.
constipate, *v. a.* teannaich, cruadhaich, glas com.
constipation, *s.* teannachadh, glasadh cuim.
constituent, *s.* cuid, cuibhrionn de'n iomlan; ball, fear-taghaidh.
constitute, *v. a.* suidhich, tog, stéidhich; socraich; dèan suas.
constitution, *s.* suidheachadh, togail; stéidheadh, socrachadh, càileachd; aorabh; the constitution of man, aorabh an duine.
constitutional, *adj.* càileachdail, freumhail; aorabhail, laghail, reachdail.
constrain, *v. a.* co-éignich.
constraint, *s.* eigin, aindeoin.
constriction, *s.* teannachadh.
constringe, *v. a.* teannaich.
constringent, *adj.* teannachail.
construct, *v. a.* tog, dèan, dealbh, cùm, suidhich.
construction, *s.* togail, deanamh, dealbh, cumadh, suidheachadh.
construe, *v. a.* réitich; mìnich.
consubstantial, *adj.* de'n aon bhrìgh.
consuetude, *s.* gnàths, cleachdadh (aig a bheil ùghdaras laghail).
consul, *s.* ard-chomhairleach; fear-ionaid a' chrùin (an crìochan céin).
consult, *v. a.* cuir comhairle.
consultation, *s.* comhluadair comhairle.
consumable, *adj.* so-chaithte.
consume, *v. a.* searg, caith, sgrios.
consumer, *s.* milltear, struidhear.
consummate, *v. a.* foirfich, crìochnaich, coimhlion.
consummation, *s.* foirfeachadh.
consumption, *s.* caitheamh, éiteach.
consumptive, *adj.* caithteach.
contact, *s.* bualadh 'n a chéile; coinneachadh, tachart (ri chéile).
contagion, *s.* gabhaltachd (plàigh).
contagious, *adj.* gabhaltach.
contain, *v. a.* cùm; gléidh.
contaminate, *adj.* truaillidh.

contamination, *s.* truailleadh.
contemper, contemperate, *v. a.* ciùinich, maothaich.
contemplate, *v. a.* beachd-smuainich; rùnaich.
contemplation, *s.* dlùth-aire; smuain, rùn.
contemplative, *adj.* smuainteachail.
contemplator, *s.* fear-beachdachaidh, fear smuainteachail.
contemporary, *adj.* co-aimsireil, co-aois.
contemporary, *s.* co-aoiseach.
contempt, *s.* tàir, tarcuis, dimeas.
contemptible, *adj.* tàireil, suarach.
contemptuous, *adj.* tarcuiseach.
contend, *v. a.* cathaich, dèan strì.
contender, *s.* fear-comhstrì.
content, *adj.* buidheach, toilichte.
content, *v. a.* toilich, riaraich.
contented, *part.* riaraichte, toilichte.
contention, *s.* strì, connspaid.
contentious, *adj.* connspaideach.
contentment, *s.* toileachas-inntinn.
contents, *s.* clar-innse.
contest, *v. a.* tagair; dèan strì.
contest, *s.* strì, cath, arabhaig.
contestable, *adj.* tagluinneach.
context, *s.* co-theagasg.
contexture, *s.* co-fhilleadh; togail.
contiguity, *s.* fagusachd.
contiguous, *adj.* dlùth do chéile.
continence, or continency, *s.* féin-smachd; stuamachd; measarrachd.
continent, *adj.* geamnaidh, beusach.
continent, *s.* tìr-mór, a' mhórthir.
continental, *adj.* mórthireach.
contingent, *adj.* tuiteamach, an crochadh ri, an earbsa ri.
contingent, *s.* tuiteamas; cuid, còir.
continual, *adj.* sìor, daonnan.
continually, *adv.* do ghnàth, gun sgur.
continuance, *s.* mairsinneachd.
continuation, *s.* buanachadh.
continue, *v. a.* buanaich, mair.
continuity, *s.* dlùth-leanmhuinneachd.
contort, *v. a.* toinn, sniomh, fiar.
contortion, *s.* toinneamh, fiaradh.
contra (facal laidinn), *prep.* an aghaidh, mì-.
contraband, *adj.* mì-laghail, toirmisgte, neo-cheadaichte.
contract, *v. a.* and *n.* giorraich, lughdaich, teannaich, beagaich; réitich, dèan ceangal pòsaidh; crup, preas; cumhnantaich.
contract, *s.* cùmhnant, réiteach, còrdadh.
contractible, *adj.* so-ghiorrachadh.
contraction, *s.* giorrachadh.
contractor, *s.* fear-cùmhnantachaidh.
contradict, *v. a.* cuir an aghaidh.
contradictory, *adj.* neo-chòrdail.
contradistinction, *s.* eadar-dhealachadh.
contrariety, *s.* neo-fhreagarrachd, eascòrdadh.

contrariwise, *adv.* dìreach an aghaidh.
contrary, *adj.* an aghaidh.
contrast, *s.* eadar-dhealachadh.
contrast, *v. a.* cuir taobh ri taobh, nochd an t-eadar-dhealachadh.
contravene, *v. a.* bris (lagh), cuir an teagamh (argumaid), eascord.
contribute, *v. a.* cuidich, thoir seachad, builich (tiodhlac).
contribution, *s.* cuideachadh, tabhartas, tional, comh-roinn ; cìs-airm.
contributory, *adj.* a bheir còmhnadh.
contrite, *adj.* brùite, aithreachail.
contrivance, *s.* innleachd, suidheachadh, gnìomh carach, seòltachd.
contrive, *v. a.* dealbh, faigh innleachd.
control, *s.* smachd, ùghdarras.
control, *v. a.* ceannsaich.
controller, *s.* fear-riaghlaidh.
controversial, *adj.* connsachail.
controversy, *s.* connspaid, strì.
controvert, *v. a.* cuir an teagamh, àicheidh, connsaich.
controvertible, *adj.* teagmhach.
controvertist, *s.* fear-connspaid.
contumacious, *adj.* ceann-laidir, ragmhuinealach, crosda ; eas-umhail.
contumaciousness, contumacy, *s.* eas-ùmhlachd, crosdachd.
contumelious, *adj.* talcuiseach, tàireil, mì-mhodhail.
contumely, *s.* tàir, talcuis, athais.
contuse, *v. a.* brùth, pronn.
contusion, *s.* bruthadh, pronnadh.
conundrum, *s.* tòimhseachan.
convalescence, *s.* dol am feabhas (o thinneas), fàs gu maith.
convalescent, *adj.* air taobh an fheabhais.
convene, *v. a.* tionail, gairm cuideachd, cruinnich.
convenience, *s.* goireas, deisealachd.
convenient, *adj.* goireasach.
convent, *s.* tigh chailleacha dubha.
conventicle, *s.* coinneamh fhalachaidh (a chum aoraidh).
convention, *s.* co-chruinneachadh, co-chòrdadh.
conventional, *adj.* a réir gnàthas, ealaineach.
conventionary, *adj.* a réir cumhnaint.
converge, *v. n.* co-aom, thig gu chéile, coinnich.
convergent, *s.* co-aomach.
conversable, *adj.* fosgarach, conaltrach, còmhraiteach.
conversant, *adj.* fiosrach, mion-eòlach.
conversation, *s.* còmhradh, conaltradh.
converse, *v. n.* labhair, dèan seanachas.
conversion, *s.* iompachadh.
convert, *v. a.* iompaich ; bi air t'iompachadh.
convert, *s.* iompachan.
convertible, *adj.* so-thionndadh.

convex, *adj.* cruinn, dronnach.
convexity, *s.* dronnachd.
convey, *v. a.* giùlain, iomchair.
conveyance, *s.* seòl-iomchair ; còir sgrìobhte, riaghladh diamhair.
conveyancer, *s.* sgrìobhadair chòraichean.
conveyer, *s.* fear-giùlain, fear-iomchair.
convict, *v. a.* còmhdaich, dìt.
convict, *s.* ciontach, ciomach.
conviction, *s.* dearbhadh, dìteadh.
convince, *v. a.* dearbh.
convincible, *adj.* so-dhearbhaidh.
convivial, *adj.* fleadhach.
convocate, *v. a.* co-chruinnich.
convocation, *s.* co-chruinneachadh.
convolution, *s.* co-fhilleadh.
convolve, *v. a.* co-fhill, co-thoinn.
convoy, *v. a.* companaich ; thoir coimh-ideachd.
convulse, *v. a.* grad-chlisg.
convulsion, *s.* an tinneas ospagach.
convulsive, *adj.* grad-chlisgeach, buaireasach, creathneachail.
cony, *s.* coinean.
coo, *v. n.* dèan dùrdail mar chalaman.
cook, *s.* còcaire, fear-deasachaidh.
cook, *v. a.* deasaich, bruich.
cookery, *s.* còcaireachd, deasachadh.
cool, *adj.* fionnar ; fuar, amh.
cool, *v. a.* fuaraich, fionnaraich.
coolness, *s.* fionnarachd.
coom, *s.* sùidhe ; smùr a' ghuail.
coomb, *s.* gleannan.
coop, *s.* baraille ; eunlan.
coop, *v. a.* dùin suas.
cooper, *s.* cùbair.
co-operate, *v. n.* co-oibrich.
co-operation, *s.* co-oibreachadh.
co-ordinate, *adj.* co-inbheach.
coot, *s.* an dubhlach.
cop, *s.* ceann, mullach, bàrr.
coparcenary, coparceny, *s.* co-oighreachas, co-phairteachas.
copartner, *s.* fear-comhpairt.
copartnership, *s.* companas.
cope, *s.* currac-sagairt ; sreath-mhullaich, no clach-mhullaich gàraidh.
cope, *v. a.* connsaich ; ceannsaich.
copier, copyist, *s.* fear ath-sgrìobhaidh.
coping, *s.* sreath-mhullaich balla.
copious, *adj.* làn, pailt, lìonmhor.
copiousness, *s.* pailteas.
copper, *s.* copar.
copperas, *s.* copar dubhaidh.
copperplate, *s.* clò-chlàr copair.
coppersmith, *s.* ceàrd-copair ; gobha.
coppice, cops, *s.* preas-choille.
copulate, *v. a.* càraidich.
copulation, *s.* càraideachadh, maraist.
copy, *s.* leth-bhreac, mac-samhail.
copy, *v. a.* ath-sgrìobh.
coquetry, *s.* guaineas, gogaideachd.
coquette, *s.* gogaid, guanag.

coracle, s. seòrsa bàta ; curach.
coral, s. croimheal, coireal.
coralline, adj. croimhealach.
corant, s. seòrsa dannsa.
corban, s. àite-gleidhidh dhéirc, tiodhlac choisrigte.
cord, s. còrd, sreang, ball, ròp.
cordage, s. buill, acfhuinn-luinge.
cordial, s. deoch-eiridinn.
cordial, adj. eiridneach ; càirdeal.
cordiality, s. blàthghradh, carthannas.
cordovan, cordwain, s. leathar eich.
core, s. cridhe, builsgean.
coriander, s. lus-a'choire.
cork, s. àrc, àrcan.
corky, adj. àrcach, àrcanach.
cormorant, s. sgarbh ; geòcaire.
corn, s. gràn, sìol ; arbhar.
corn-chandler, s. grainsear.
corn-marigold, s. a' bhuidheag-shamhraidh.
cornelian, s. clach luachmhor.
corneous, adj. adharcach.
corner, s. oisinn, cearn ; cùil.
cornet, s. dùdach ; fear brataich eachraidh.
corneter, s. dùdaire.
cornice, s. bàrrmhaise, barrbhile.
cornicle, s. adharcag, sgrogag.
cornigerous, adj. cròcach.
cornucopia, s. adharc-shaibhreis.
coronation, s. crùnadh.
coroner, s. ceann cùirte gu rannsachadh aobhar bàis obann.
coronet, s. crùn beag (air son uaislean).
corporal, s. corpaileir.
corporality, s. corporrachd.
corporate, adj. aonaichte ; corporra.
corporation, s. comunn ; comhairle bailemhóir.
corporeal, corporal, adj. corporra.
corps, s. buidheann airm.
corpse, s. corp marbh.
corpulence, s. sultmhorachd.
corpulent, adj. dòmhail.
corpuscular, adj. smùirneanach.
corrade, v. a. suath, sgrìob r'a chéile.
corradiation, s. co-dhealradh.
correct, v. n. smachdaich, cronaich ; ceartaich.
correct, adj. ceart, poncail.
correction, s. smachdachadh, cronachadh, ceartachadh.
corrective, adj. ceartachail.
correctness, s. ceartachd, eagarachd, pongalachd, snasmhorachd.
correlate, s. co-chàraid, dàimh.
correlative, adj. co-dhàimheach.
correspond, v. n. co-fhreagair, sgrìobh litrichean; comhluadair an sgrìobhadh.
correspondence, s. co-fhreagradh ; co-sgrìobhadh litrichean ; caidreamh, càirdeas, co-chomunn.

correspondent, adj. co-fhreagarrach.
correspondent, s. co-sgrìobhair.
corrigible, adj. so-chronachadh.
corroborant, adj. co-neartachail.
corroborate, v. a. co-neartaich.
corroboration, s. co-dhearbhadh, daingneachadh.
corrode, v. a. cnàmh, caith, meirg.
corrodent, adj. cnàimhteach.
corrosible, adj. so-chnàimhteach.
corrosion, s. cnàmh, meirgeadh.
corrosive, adj. cnàimhteach.
corrosiveness, s. cnàimhteachd.
corrugant, adj. preasach.
corrugation, s. preasadh, casadh.
corrupt, v. grod, lobh, dèan breun ; truaill, salaich, mill, lochdaich, dochuinn ; breò.
corrupt, adj. truaillidh, salach, olc.
corrupter, s. truailleadair.
corruptible, adj. so-thruaillidh.
corruption, s. truailleachd.
corruptive, adj. lobhtach, breothach.
corruptness, s. truailleadh.
còrsair, s. long-spùinnidh.
corse, s. corp, cairbh, closach.
corslet or corselet, s. uchd-éideadh.
cortical, adj. cairtidh, sgrothach.
coruscant, adj. deàlrach, lainnreach.
coruscation, s. deàlradh, deàrsadh.
corymbiated, adj. bagaideach.
cosmetic, s. cungaidh mhaise.
cosmogony, s. eòlas a' chruthachaidh.
cosmography, s. iomradh air a' chruthachadh.
cosmopolite, s. faodalaich, neach dh' an dùthchas an saoghal.
cosset, s. uan-pheat, peat uain.
cost, s. luach, fiach, cosgais.
costal, adj. aisinneach.
costard, s. ceann, cnuac ; ubhall.
costive, adj. ceangailte, teann ('s a' chom).
costliness, s. cosgais, daorad.
costly, adj. cosgail, daor, strùidheil.
costume, s. doigh éididh ; deise dreuchd.
cot, cottage, s. bothan.
cotemporary, adj. co-aoiseach.
coterie, s. bannal, cuideachd, còisir.
cotillion, s. seòrsa dannsa ; ceòl dannsa.
cottager, s. coitear, croitear.
cotton, s. canach, aodach canaich.
couch, v. càirich, cuir a laighe ; cuir air lagh ; crùb, crom, dèan laighe.
couch, s. leabaidh ; uraigh-làir.
couchant, adj. sìnte, 'na laighe.
couch-grass, s. feur-a'-phuint.
cough, s. casad, casadaich.
coulter, s. coltar, sgoiltear.
council, s. comhairle, cùirt eaglais ('s an t-sean aimsir).
counsel, v. a. comhairlich, earalaich.
counsellor, s. comhairleach - lagha (an Eirinn).

count, v. a. àireamh, cunntas.
countenance, s. gnùis, aghaidh, aodann, fiamh, dreach, snuadh ; dìon, tearmunn, dìdeann.
countenance, v. a. dìon, seas.
counter, s. bòrd-malairt.
counter, adv. càlg-dhìreach an aghaidh, dìreach an aghaidh.
counter, s. sàil bròige.
counteract, v. a. grab, bac, amail.
counterbalance, v. a. co-chothromaich ; coinnich (le uidhir eile).
counter-change, s. co-mhalairt.
counter-evidence, s. fianuis coinneachaidh.
counterfeit, adj. mealltach.
counterfeit, s. feall-chùinneadh.
countermand, v. a. tarruing air ais (àithne), bac.
counterpane, s. brat-uachdair leapa.
counterpart, s. leth-bhreac.
counterplot, s. innleachd an aghaidh innleachd.
counterpoise, v. a. co-chothromaich.
countertide, s. saobh-shruth.
countess, s. ban-iarla.
countless, adj. do-àireamh.
country, s. dùthaich, tìr.
countryman, s. fear-dùthcha ; fear-tuatha.
county, s. siorramachd.
couple, s. càraid, dithis ; caigeann.
couple, v. càraidich, ceangail.
couplet, s. càraid shreath ; leth-rann.
courage, s. misneach, cruadal.
courageous, adj. misneachail, cruadalach.
courageousness, s. misneachd ; cruadal.
courier, s. teachdair, gille-ruith.
course, s. slighe ; ionad, iomchar, giùlan, caithe-beatha, seòl, gnàthas riaghailt.
course, v. a. ruag, lorgaich, lean.
court, s. cùirt, lùchairt, lios ; taighmòid ; mòd ; miodal, sodal.
court, v. a. dèan suiridhe.
courteous, adj. cùirteil, aoidheil, suairce.
courteousness, s. cùirtealachd, aoidhealachd, suairceas, coibhnealachd.
courtesan, s. strìopach, siùrsach.
courtesy, s. modhalachd, modh.
courtier, s. cùirtear ; suiridheach.
courtliness, s. cùirtealachd ; flathalachd.
courtly, adj. cùirteil, cuirteiseach.
courtship, s. suiridhe, leannanachd.
cousin, s. mac no nighean brathar-athar no màthar,—no piuthar-athar no màthar.
cove, s. bàgh, lùb, camus ; cùmhann, dìon.
covenant, s. co-cheangal, cùmhnant.
covenant, v. a. cùmhnantaich, daingnich, co-cheangail.
covenanter, s. cùmhnantach.
cover, v. a. còmhdaich ; falaich, ceil.
cover, s. còmhdach ; falach, brat, sgàil.

covering, s. còmhdach, aodach.
coverlet, coverlid, s. brat-uachdair.
covert, s. dìdean, ionad-falaich, dìon, fasgadh ; doire, badan-dlùth.
covert, adj. falaichte, dìomhair.
covertness, s. dìomhaireachd.
covet, v. a. sanntaich, miannaich.
covetable, adj. ion-mhiannaichte.
covetous, adj. sanntach.
covey, s. mathair-ghuir le h-àlach.
cow, s. bó, mart.
cow, v.a. cuir eagal ; cuir fo smachd.
coward, s. cladhaire, gealtaire.
cowardice, s. cladhaireachd, geilt.
cowardly, adj. gealtach, eagalach.
cower, v. n. crùb, dèan crùban.
cowherd, s. buachaille.
cowl, s. currac-manaich ; cuinneag-uisge.
cowled, adj. curraiceach, boineideach.
cowslip, s. bròg-na-cuthaig.
coxcomb, s. cìrean ; sgeamhanach.
coxcomical, adj. pròiseil.
coy, adj. nàrach, màlda, beusach ; sàmhach, saidealt, socharach.
coyness, s. saidealtas, màldachd.
cozen, v. a. meall, thoir an car à.
cozenage, s. ceilg, foill.
cozener, s. cealgaire, mealltair.
crab, s. partan ; duine dreamach.
crabbed, adj. dreamach, dranndanach, frionasach, cas.
crabbedly, adv. gu dreamasach, gu dranndanach, gu frionasach, gu cas.
crack, s. sgàineadh, brag ; bristeadh.
crack, v. a. sgoilt, sgàin ; spreadh.
crack-brained, adj. mì-chéillidh.
cracker, s. fear-spaglainn.
crackle, v. n. dèan cnacail, cnac, dèan bragail.
cradle, s. creathall ; lunn bàta.
craft, s. ceàird, innleachd, seòltachd, teòmachd ; loingeas beaga.
craftiness, s. cluaintearachd, foill.
craftsman, s. fear-cèirde.
crafty, adj. carach, fealltach.
crag, s. creag, sgòrr, sgeir.
cragged, craggy, adj. creagach.
cram, v. a. dinn, glaimsich.
crambo, s. rann-chòmhradh, rannachd, duanaireachd.
cramp, s. iodha ; glamaire-teannachaidh, inneal-dlùthaidh, glamradh.
cramp, v. a. bac, grab, ceangail.
crane, s. còrra-sgriach, corra-ghlas, corra-riabhach ; inneal-togail ; pìobtharr-uinn.
cranium, s. claigeann, cnuac, spuaic.
crank, s. crangaid ; fiar-char, fiaradh.
crank, adj. corrach, guanach.
crankle, v. a. lùb, cam, fiar.
crannied, adj. tolltach, sgàinteach.
cranny, s. gàg, sgàineadh, cùil, peisg.
crape, s. sròl-dubh, dubh-shròl.

crapulence, s. amhdheoch, no tinneas-poit.

crash, s. stairn, stairirich.

cratch, s. prasach, mainnir.

cravat, s. suaineach-muineil.

crave, v. a. iarr, tagair; guidh.

craven, s. fùidsidh, gealtaire.

craving, s. miann, miannachadh.

craw, s. sgròban, goile, giaban.

crawfish, crayfish, s. giomach-uisge.

crawl, v. a. crùb, snàig.

craze, v. a. bris, cuir air mhì-chéill.

craziness, s. breòiteachd ; mì-chéill.

crazy, adj. lag, breòite ; méaranta.

creak, v. n. sgread, dìosgain.

cream, s. uachdar, bàrr, cé.

cream-faced, adj. bàn-neulach.

creamy, adj. uachdarach, barragach.

crease, s. filleadh, preasag.

create, v. a. cruthaich, dèan dealbh.

creation, s. an cruthachadh, a' chruith-eachd.

creative, adj. cruthachail.

Creator, s. Cruthadair ; Cruithear.

creature, s. creutair, dùil, bith.

credence, s. creideas, meas.

credenda, s. pongan-creidimh.

credent, adj. creideach.

credentials, s. litrichean teisteis.

credibility, credibleness, s. creideas, teist-ealachd.

credible, adj. creideasach.

credit, s. creideas ; cliù, meas.

credit, v. a. creid ; thoir dàil.

creditable, adj. teisteil ; measail.

creditor, s. fear-féich.

credulity, s. baoghaltachd.

credulous, adj. baoghhalta.

creed, s. creud, aidmheil, creideamh.

creek, s. bàgh, geodha, camus, cùil.

creep, v. a. snàig, crùb, dèan màgaran, falbh air mhàgan.

creeper, s. an iadh-shlat.

crescent, s. leth-chearcall.

cress, s. biolair an fhuarain.

cresset, s. crann-tàra, gath-soluis.

crest, s. ite-mullaich ; fìor-mhullach.

crested, adj. dosach, cìreanach.

crestfallen, adj. fo thùrsa, fo sproc, fo leann-dubh.

cretaceous, adj. cailceach.

crevice, s. sgoltadh, sgàineadh, còs.

crew, s. sgioba bàta no luinge ; gràisg, pàbar.

crib, s. prasach ; bothan, crùban.

crib, v. a. goid, dùin suas, fàngaich.

crible, s. criathar.

cribration, s. criathradh.

crick, s. gìosgan ; tinneas-muinneil.

cricket, s. greòllan, cuileag-theallaich.

crier, s. fear-éigheachd.

crime, s. ceannairce, eucoir, coire, cron, cionta, lochd.

crimeless, adj. neo-chiontach.

criminal, criminous, adj. coireach, ciont-ach, eucorach.

criminal, s. ceannairceach, fear dòbheirt, ciontach.

crimination, s. coireachadh, dìteadh.

criminatory, adj. coireachail.

crimp, v. a. cas, preas, dualaich.

crimson, adj. craobhdhearg.

cringe, s. crùbadh, strìochdadh tràilleil, bochd-ùmhladh.

cringe, v. a. crùb, strìochd.

crinkle, s. preasag, preasadh, crupadh.

cripple, s. bacach, crùbach, cripleach.

crisis, s. cunnart ; faothachadh.

crisp, crispy, adj. cas, bachlagach, cuachach, brisg, pronn.

crispation, s. toinneamh, dualadh, cuach-adh, preasadh.

crispness, crispitude, s. caise, caisead, preasachd, cuachagachd, brisgead.

criterion, s. comharradh, dearbhadh, tomhais.

critic, s. breitheamh, tìolpaire.

critical, adj. eagnaidh, poncail, teann-bhreitheach, tìolpach ; cunnartach.

criticise, v. a. geur-bhreithnich, sgrùd.

criticism, critique, s. geur-bhreithneach-adh, geur-rannsachadh, mion-sgrùd-adh.

croak, v. n. ròc, dèan ròcail.

crock, s. soitheach-creadha, crogan.

crockery, s. gach seòrsa shoithichean creadha.

crocodile, s. an lonach-sligeach.

crony, s. caraid, fear cagair, dlùth-chompanach.

crook, s. cromag ; camag, cròcan, dubhan, lùb, luìb.

crook, v. a. crom, cam, lùb ; aom.

crooked, adj. cam, crom, fiar, cròcanach, lùbach ; crosta.

crookedness, s. caime, cruime, fiarachd, lùbachd, aingeachd, crosdachd.

crop, s. sgròban eòin ; mullach ; bàrr, arbhar.

crop, v. a. bearr, gearr, buain, lomair.

crop-full, adj. làn sgròbain, sàthaichte.

crosier, s. bachull-easbuig.

croslet, s. croiseag ; suacaň.

cross, s. crasg, crois, crann-ceusaidh.

cross, adj. tarsuinn ; fiar, cam, trasda ; deacair, doirbh, àmhgharach ; aingidh, crosta ; frionasach ; mi-shealbhach, tuaitheal.

cross, v. a. cuir tarsainn ; rach thairis ; seun ; coisrig.

crossbow, s. bogha saigheid.

cross-examine, v. a. ath-cheasnaich, mion-cheasnaich.

cross-grained, adj. gearr-ghràineach, craindidh, crosta, tarsuinn.

crossness, s. crasgachd ; reasgachd.

crotch, s. gobhal, cromag, dubhan, bacan.

crouch, v. n. lùb, crom, crùb ri làr; dèan miodal.

croup, s. breaman, rumpull; rùnsan.

crow, s. feannag; geimhleag; gairm-coilich.

crowd, s. dòmhlachd, gràisg.

crowd, v. a. dòmhlaich, mùch; teann-aich, dinn.

crown, s. coron, crùn; fleasg; mullach a' chinn, bàrr; bonn chòig tasdain.

crown, v. a. crùn; sgeadaich, maisich; crìochnaich.

crucial, adj. crasgach, tarsainn, trasta, fiar, as cruaidhe (ceisd).

crucible, s. suacan, poit-leaghaidh.

crucifix, s. crois-sheunaidh.

crucifixion, s. ceusadh.

cruciform, adj. crasgach, tarsainn, air chumadh crois.

crucify, v. a. ceus, croch ri cram.

crude, adj. amh, anabaich; borb.

crudeness, crudity, s. neo-mheirbhteachd, an-abaichead; buirbeachd.

cruel, adj. an-iochdmhor, cruaidh-chridheach, borb, garg, fuilteach, neo-thruacanta, aingidh, mi-thlùsail.

cruelty, s. an-iochdmhorachd.

cruet, s. céis shearrag spìosraidhean (air bòrd).

cruise, v. n. dèan tòireachd mara, cuir cuairt mara, seòl.

cruiser, s. long-thòireachd.

crumb, s. mìr, pronnag, criomag, bìdeag, sprùileag.

crumble, v. a. pronn, criom; bris.

crumbs, n. plur. sprùileach, fuigheal.

crumby, adj. pronnagach.

crupper, s. cuirpean, bod-chrann, botrachan, beairt-earbaill eich.

crural, adj. luirgneach, cosach.

crusade, croisade, s. cogadh (fo ainm na croise); naomhchogadh.

crush, v. a. brùth, fàisg, pronn, teann-aich; ceannsaich, sàraich.

crush, s. bruthadh, pronnadh, mùchadh, dìnneadh, teannachadh.

crust, s. sgramag; sgrath, rùsg, cochull.

crustaceous, adj. alt-shligeach.

crusty, adj. sligeach; dranndanach.

crutch, s. lorg, treosdan, crasg, cuaille.

cry, v. a. glaodh, éigh, gairm; guil.

cry, s. éigh, iolach, beuc, ràn; gul.

cryptical, adj còsach, uaigheach.

crystal, s. criostal, glaine-shòilleir.

cub, s. cuilean, peasan.

cubation, s. suidhe, laighe sìos.

cube, s. trì-chearnag (ionnan leud is fad is tiuighead).

cubit, s. làmh-choille.

cubital, adj. làmh-choilleach.

cuckold, s. fear ban-adhaltraiche.

cuckold, v. a. dèan adhaltras.

cuckoldy, adj. truagh, dìblidh, adhaltrach.

cuckoo, s. cuach, cuthag.

cucumber, s. cular.

cud, s. cìr; that cheweth the cud, "a chnàmhas a chìr."

cuddle, v. n. laigh sìos, crùb a steach.

cuddy, s. baothaire; cudaige, saoidhean.

cudgel, s. bata, cuaille, rongas.

cudgel, v. a. buail le bata, slac.

cudweed, s. an cnàmhlus.

cue, s. feaman, rumpull, roinns, earball, deireadh; sanas.

cuff, s. dòrn, cnap, bann-dùirn.

cuirass, s. uchd-éideadh, uchd-bheart.

cuirassier, s. saighdear armaichte.

cuish, s. leasbheart, leasdhion.

Culdee, s. cùildeach, céile-dé.

cull, v. tagh, tearbaidh, siotaich, glan (siol).

cully, s. suiridheach socharach, creutar ailleanach, ùmaidh.

culm, s. seòrsa do ghual mìn.

culpable, adj. ciontach, coireach.

culprit, s. ciontach, coireach.

cultivate, v. a. leasaich, àitich, treabh, thoir a steach (fearann).

cultivation, s. àiteach, treabhadh, leasachadh; ionnsachadh.

culture, s. treabhadh, leasachadh, foghlum.

culver, s. an smùdan.

culverin, s. gunna fada, cuilbheir.

cumber, v. a. tromaich, cuir moille, fàsaich.

cumbersome, adj. trom, draghail.

cumbrance, s. uallach, dragh.

cumbrous, adj. trom, sàrachail; draghail.

cumin, s. lus-mhic-chuimein.

cumulate, v. a. tòrr, càrn, cruach.

cumulation, s. càrnadh, torradh.

cuneate, cuneiform, adj. coltach ri géinn.

cunning, adj. seòlta, sgileil; carach, cluainteach, sligheach, cealgach.

cunning, cunningness, s. seòltachd, gliocas; cuilbheartachd, cluaintearachd, cealgaireachd, caraireachd.

cup, s. copan, còrn, cuach.

cup-bearer, s. gille-copain.

cupboard, s. amraidh, preas, asair.

cupidity, s. ana-mhiann, sannt.

cupola, s. cruinn-mhullach.

cur, s. madadh, cù, duine dreamach.

curable, adj. so-leigheas.

curacy, s. dreuchd ministear-cuidich.

curate, s. ministear-cuidich.

curb, s. camagan sréine, cabstar; bacadh, ceannsachadh.

curb, v. a. ceannsaich, bac.

curd, s. gruth, slamban.

curd, curdle, v. a. binndich.

cure, s. leigheas, cungaidh-leighis.

cure, *v. a.* leighis, slànaich ; sàill.
curfew, *s.* clag-smàlaidh.
curiosity, *s.* neònachas, ioghnadh.
curious, *adj.* iongantach, neònach.
curl, *adj.* cutach, gearr, camagach.
curl, *s.* dual, bachlag, camlub.
curl, *v. a.* bachlaich, cas, dualaich.
curled, *adj.* bachlach, dualach.
curlew, *s.* guilbneach.
curmudgeon, *s.* spìocaire.
currant, *s.* dearcag-Fhrangach, crabhsgag.
currency, *s.* sgaoileadh, ruith; ruith-chainnt, deas-bhriatharachd ; airgead ullamh.
current, *adj.* iomruitheach ; measail, coitcheann ; gnàthaichte.
current, *s.* buinne, casshruth.
curricle, *s.* carbad dà rotha.
currier, *s.* fear-gréidhidh leathair.
currish, *adj.* sabaideach, mosach, dranndach.
curry, *s.* seòrsa deasachaidh ; biadh spìosrach.
curry, *v.* cìr (each) ; dean miodal.
curry, *v.* deasaich leathar.
currycomb, *s.* cìr-eich, càrd-eich.
curse, *v. a.* mallaich, mionnaich.
curse, *s.* mallachd, droch guidhe.
cursed, *adj.* mallaichte, aingidh.
cursive, *adj.* seòrsa sgrìobhaidh, sgrìobhadh luath.
cursoriness, *s.* prabadh-thairis.
cursory, *adj.* luath, neo-chùramach, cabhagach.
curtail, *v. a.* giorraich.
curtain, *s.* cùirtein, brat-sgàile.
curvation, *s.* cromadh, camadh.
curvature, *s.* cruime, caime, lùb.
curve, *v. a.* crom, cam, fiar, lùb.

curvet, *v. a.* leum, gearr sùrdag.
curvet, *s.* leum, cruinnleum, sùrdag.
curvilinear, *adj.* cam-sgrìobach.
cushion, *s.* sasag, pillean, cluasag.
cusp, *s.* adharc na gealaich ùir.
cuspated, cuspidated, *adj.* rinneach.
cuspidate, *v. a.* geuraich, bioraich.
custard, *s.* ubhagan, uibheagan.
custody, *s.* an làimh ; cùram, an gréim, am prìoson.
custom, *s.* àbhaist ; gnàthachadh, modh, gnàths ; cuspunn.
customary, customable, *adj.* àbhaisteach, gnàthach, gnàthachail.
customer, *s.* gnàth-cheannaiche.
custom-house, *s.* tigh-cuspuinn.
cut, *v. a.* gearr ; sgath, sgud, bèarr.
cut, *s.* gearradh, sgathadh ; leòn ; mìr, dealbh, cumadh.
cutaneous, *adj.* craicneach.
cuticle, *s.* craicionn-uachdrach.
cutlass, *s.* claidheamh-cutach.
cutler, *s.* gobha lann, ceanniche sginean.
cutlery, *s.* lannan, stàillinn.
cut-throat, *s.* mortair.
cutting, *s.* mìr, sliseag ; gearradh.
cuttle, *s.* fear-tuaileis, draosdaire.
cycle, *s.* cuairt, cuairt tìme.
cygnet, *s.* eala òg, isean eala.
cylinder, *s.* rothlair, rothair.
cylindrical, *adj.* pìobanach.
cymar, *s.* falluing, sgàilean.
cymbal, *s.* tiompan.
cynic, cynical, *adj.* dranndanach, sgaiteach, aoireach.
cynosure, *s.* reull na h-àirde tuath.
cypress, *s.* craobh-bhròin.
cyst, *s.* balgan-iongrach.
Czar, *s.* ainm Iompaire Ruisia.
Czarina, *s.* Ainm ban-iompaire Ruisia.

D

dab, *v. a.* frith-bhuail, dèan ballach le uisge.
dab, *s.* seòrsa liabaig, meall, pluc, buille, fear ceàirde.
dabble, *v. a.* luidir, taisich, crath thairis le uisge, ionnsachadh luideach.
dabbler, *s.* greoigean, fear gun sgil.
dace, *s.* seòrsa de iasg aibhne.
daffodil, daffodilly, *s.* lus a' chrom-chinn.
daft, *adj.* gòrrach, mì-chiallach.
dagger, *s.* cuinnsear ; sgian mhór, sgian dubh.
daggle, *v. a.* eabair, luidir, fliuch.
daggle-tail, *adj.* salach, luidirte.
daily, *adv.* gach là, gu lathail.
dainty, *adj.* blasda, taitneach, milis,

sòghmhor ; grinn, fìnealta, muirneach, moiteil, modhail ; mìn, ciatach.
dairy, *s.* tigh-bainne ; bothan-àiridh.
dairymaid, *s.* banarach, banachaig.
daisied, *adj.* neòineanach.
daisy, *s.* neòinean.
dale, *s.* dail, gleann, glaic.
dalliance, *s.* beadradh, sùgradh ; dìomhanas.
dallop, *s.* fàilean, tòrr, dùn.
dam, *s.* màthair (beathaich).
dam, *s.* garadh-dìon air loch.
damage, *s.* dolaidh, beud, dochann, cron ; luach calla.
damage, *v. a.* dochainn, mill.
damageable, *a.* so-mhilleadh ; cronail, ciùrrail.

damask, s. anart-geug-ghréiste.
dame, s. baintighearna, bean-tighe.
damn, v. a. dìt gu peanas; sgrios; mallaich; dìt.
damnable, adj. mallaichte, sgriosach.
damnation, s. dìteadh; mallachadh.
damned, adj. damainte, mallaichte.
damnify, v. a. dochainn, mill.
damp, adj. tais, àitidh, fliuch, bog.
damp, v. a. taisich, fliuch, bogaich.
damsel, s. caile, caileag, cailin; maighdean, gruagach, ainnir, cruinneag, righinn.
dance, v. n. danns.
dancing, s. dannsa.
dandelion, s. am beàrnan-brìde, caisearbhain.
dandle, v. a. siùd, crath, caidrich, cniadaich, tàlaidh; breug.
dandruff, s. carr, sgealpaich.
dane-wort, s. fliogh-a'-bhalla.
danger, s. cunnart, baoghal, gàbhadh.
dangerless, adj. neo-chunnartach.
dangerous, adj. cunnartach.
dangle, v. n. crath mar chluigean, bi co-bhogadan.
dangler, s. gille-bhan, sliomaire.
dank, adj. àitidh, tungaidh, bog.
dapper, adj. beag, lurach, guamach.
dapperling, s. luspardan, duairc.
dapple, adj. ballabhreac.
dare, v. a. dùbhlanaich, thoir dùbhlan.
daring, adj. dàna, dalma, ladarna, neo-sgàthach.
dark, adj. dorch, doilleir; dubh.
darken, v. a. dorchaich, doilleirich.
darkness, s. dorchadas, duibhre.
darksome, adj. doilleir, dubharach.
darling, s. annsachd, luaidh, mùirninn.
darling, adj. gaolach, gràdhach.
darn, v. a. cnòdaich, càirich.
darnel, s. dìthein, bùidheag.
dart, s. gath, guin, gàinne.
dash, v. a. and n. buail air, tilg le neart, spealg, brist, pronn, spealt, spairt, taom, coimeasg, truaill; nàraich.
dash, s. buille, tilgeil; dubh-sgrìoch.
dastard, s. cladhaire, gealtaire.
dastardly, adj. cladhaireach, gealtach, fiamhach, eagalach.
data, s. firinnean suidhichte, cumhachan dearbhta.
date, s. àm, an latha de'n mhìos.
date, v. a. comharraich àm.
dateless, adj. gun àm ainmichte.
dative, adj. tabhartach.
daub, v. a. smeur, buaic, slìob, liacair.
dauber, s. sgleogaire.
daughter, s. nighean, inghean.
daunt, v. a. geiltich, mì-mhisnich.
dauntless, adj. neo-sgàthach.
daw, s. a' chadhag.
dawn, s. camhanaich, briseadh na fàire, glasadh an latha, càinnealachadh.

day, s. latha, là.
daybook, s. leabhar-lathail, leabhar-cunntas air son gach là.
daybreak, s. briseadh na fàire.
daylight, s. solus an latha.
daystar, s. reull na maidne.
dazzle, v. a. deàrrs, deàrrsaich, soillsich, boillsgich.
deacon, s. oifigeach eaglais, deucon, in certain churches = foirfeach.
dead, adj. marbh, trom; the dead, na mairbh.
deaden, v. a. marbh, lagaich, fannaich.
deadly, adj. marbhtach, bàsmhor.
deadness, s. marbhantachd, laigsinn.
deaf, adj. bodhar, gun chlaisteachd.
deafen, v. a. bodhair, dèan bodhar.
deafness, s. buidhre, boidhre.
deal, s. cuibhrionn; déile, clàr.
deal, v. a. roinn, riaraich.
dealbate, v. a. gealaich, cuir ri todhar.
dealbation, s. gealachadh, todhar.
dealer, s. fear-malairt, ceannaiche; fear roinn chairtean.
dealing, s. gnothach, déilig.
deambulation, s. sràidimeachd.
dean, s. deadhan, fear ionaid easbuig.
deanery, s. dreuchd deadhain.
dear, adj. gaolach, gràdhach, prìseil; daor.
dearth, s. gainne, dìth, gort, airc, teircead.
dearticulate, v. a. thoir as a chéile, sgaoil as a chéile.
death, s. bàs, eug, aog.
deathless, adj. neo-bhàsmhor.
death-like, adj. aog-neulach.
death-watch, s. am biog-ghairm.
debar, v. a. bac, cum air ais, toirmisg.
debark, v. a. cuir air tìr, rach air tìr.
debase, v. a. truaill, ìslich; maslaich.
debasement, s. truailleadh, isleachadh, maslachadh.
debate, s. connsachadh, tagradh, deasbad.
debate, v. a. connsaich, tagair.
debauch, v. a. truaill, salaich.
debauch, s. misg, neo-mheasarrachd.
debauchee, s. geòcaire, misgear.
debauchery, s. mì-gheamnachd, geòcaireachd, pòitearachd.
debenture, s. bann-urrais air airgiod-iasaid; riadh.
debilitate, v. a. fannaich, lagaich.
debility, s. laige, anmhuinneachd.
debonair, adj. finealta, grinn, suairce, méinneil.
debt, s. fiachan, féich, comain.
debtor, s. fear-fhiach.
decade, s. deich nithean; deich bliadhna.
decagon, s. deich-shlisneach.
decamp, v. n. dèan imrich, atharraich campa, triall, imich, goid air falbh, siap as.
decant, v. a. taom as gu fòill.

decanter, s. searrag ghlaine.
decapitate, v. a. dì-cheannaich.
decapitation, s. dì-cheannadh.
decay, v. a. caith, crìon, searg, seac.
decay, s. crìonadh, seargadh, seacadh, caitheamh as.
decease, s. bàs, caochladh, eug ; *idiom for* he died = dh' fhalbh e ; shiubhail e ; chaochail e ; dh'eug e ; bhàsaich e.
decease, v. n. bàsaich, caochail.
deceit, s. iogan, cealg, gò, foill.
deceitful, adj. cealgach, foilleil.
deceive, v. a. meall, car, breug.
deceiver, s. mealltair, cealgaire.
December, s. mìos meadhonach a' gheamhraidh.
decency, s. eireachdas, beusachd, loinn ; modh, stuamachd.
decennial, adj. deich bliadhnail.
decent, adj. eireachdail, ciatach, loinneil, grinn, còir, beusach, ceanalta, modhail, stuama, freagarrach.
deceptible, adj. so-mheallach.
deception, s. mealladh, foill, cealg.
deceptive, adj. meallta, foilleil, cealgach, carach.
decide, v. a. thoir breith, co-dhùin.
decidence, s. malcadh, tuiteam dheth ; seargadh, seacadh.
decider, s. breitheamh, fear-réite.
deciduous, adj. seargach, a thilgeas duilleach.
decimal, adj. deich-roinneach.
decimate, v. a. sgrios an deichimh cuid— fear as an deichnear.
decipher, v. a. dèan a mach sgrìobhadh dorch, comharraich, cuir comharradh air ; mìnich, dèan soilleir.
decision, s. binn, co-dhùnadh ; crìoch.
decisive, adj. co-dhùnach, dearbhach.
decisively, adv. dearbhte, cinnteach.
deck, v. a. còmhdaich, sgiamhaich.
deck, s. clar-uachdair, bòrd-luinge, leubhann.
declaim, v. a. tagair, dean àrd-ghlòir, labhair gu snas-bhriathrach.
declaration, s. cur an céill, daingneachadh cùise.
declarative, adj. foillseachail.
declare, v. a. nochd, taisbean, innis, aithris, cuir an céill ; aidich.
declension, s. ìsleachadh, cromadh, tèarnadh ; dol sìos ; lùbadh, claonadh, aomadh.
declinable, adj. so-aomaidh.
declination, s. ìsleachadh, lagachadh, seargadh ; tèarnadh ; cromadh, lùbadh, camadh, fiaradh ; seacharan, claonadh ; mùthadh.
declinator, s. inneal faotainn a chòmhnaird.
decline, v. a. and n. crom, aom, lùb, cam ; seachainn, diùlt, ob, leig seachad ;

crom. seac ; claon, rach a thaobh ; crìon, searg, caith as.
decline, s. tèarnadh, cromadh, dol sìos, caitheamh, crìonadh, seacadh, seargadh.
declivity, s. tèarnadh, bruthach, leathad, cromadh, fiaradh.
decoct, v. a. bruich, goil ; meirbh.
decoction, s. goil, bruicheadh.
decollate, v. a. cuir an ceann dheth.
decompose, v. a. eadar-dhealaich, cuir as a cheile, grod.
decompound, v. a. ath-mheasgaich, cuir air leth.
decorate, v. a. sgeadaich, maisich, dèan àluinn.
decoration, s. sgeadachadh.
decorous, adj. ciatach, cubhaidh.
decorticate, v. a. rùisg, plaoisg.
decorum, s. deagh-bheus, stuaim, eireachdas.
decoy, v. a. meall, tàlaidh, breug.
decoy, s. culaidh-thàlaidh, buaireadh.
decoy-duck, s. tonnag fhiodha, tonnag tàlaidh (air son sealgair eun).
decrease, v. a. lùghdaich, beagaich.
decree, v. n. roimh-òrduich, suidhich, àithn, socraich, sonraich, dèan reachd.
decree, s. reachd-cheangal ; breith cùise, roimh-òrdugh.
decrepit, adj. breòite, fann.
decrepitude, s. breòiteachd.
decrescent, adj. a' crìonadh.
decretal, adj. reachdach.
decretal, s. leabhar-lagha.
decretory, adj. reachdach, laghail.
decry, v. n. cronaich, coirich, càin.
decumbant, adj. liùgach.
decuple, adj. deich-fillte.
decursion, s. ruith le bruthach.
dedentition, s. tilgeadh nam fiacal.
dedicate, v. a. coisrig, naomhaich ; seun, cuir fo thèarmann.
deduce, v. a. tarruing co-dhùnadh ; tog, tuig (o na thachair) ; cuir sìos an òrdugh.
deducement, s. co-dhùnadh.
deduct, v. a. lùghdaich, beagaich, thoir o àireamh.
deduction, s. co-dhùnadh ; co-ghearradh, lùghdachadh, beagachadh.
deed, s. gnìomh, dèanadas ; euchd ; reachd-dhaingneachaidh.
deem, v. a. meas, co-dhùin ; saoil.
deep, adj. domhain ; trom, eagnaidh, tùrail.
deep, s. an doimhne ; an cuan ; aigeal.
deeply, adv. gu trom, brònach.
deer, s. fiadh.
deface, v. a. dubh a mach, mill.
defacement, s. sgrìobadh as, sgrios.
defalcation, s. lùghdachadh, teachd gearr, as-onoir, meirle airgid, mì-dhìlseachd.

defamation, s. tuaileas, mì-chliù.
defamatory, adj. tuaileasach.
defame, v. a. tuaileasaich, cùl-chàin.
defatigate, v. a. sgìthich, claoidh.
default, s. dearmad, dìochuimhn ; coire,
lochd, cionta, fàilling.
defaulter, s. fear dearmaid còrach, fear
brisidh na còrach, fear a theicheas (o
chùirt).
defeasance, s. briseadh cùmhnainte.
defeasible, adj. nach seas lagh.
defeat, s. ruaig, teicheadh, call-catha.
defeat, v. a. cuir ruaig, buadhaich.
defeature, s. atharrachadh gnùise.
defecate, v. a. glan, sìolaidh ; sgùr.
defecation, s. fìor-ghlanadh.
defect, s. easbhuidh, fàilling, uireasbhuidh, dìth ; coire, gaoid.
defection, s. easbhuidh, fàillneachadh ;
ceannairc.
defective, adj. neo-iomlan, neo-choimhlionta ; ciorramach.
defence, s. dìon, dìdean, tèarmann,
daingneachd ; leithsgeul, fìreanachadh.
defenceless, adj. neo-armaichte, gun
tèarmann, nochdta, lom ; lag, fann.
defend, v. a. dìon, teasraig, tèaruinn.
defendant, s. fear-dìona, fear air a bheil
casaid (an cùirt).
defender, s. fear-tagraidh, fear diona,
fear seasamh na còrach.
defensible, adj. tèarmannach.
defer, v. a. and n. cuir air dàil, dàilich ;
leig gu comhairle neach eile ; fuirich,
dèan moille.
deference, s. meas, urram, ùmhlachd ;
strìochdadh, géilleadh.
defiance, s. dùbhlan ; dùbhlanachadh.
deficiency, s. neo - iomlaineachd, easbhuidh, dìth ; fàilling.
deficient, adj. neo-iomlan, easbhuidheach.
defile, v. a. salaich, truaill.
defile, s. cunglach, caol ghleann.
defilement, s. truailleadh, sal.
defiler, s. truailleadair.
definable, s. so-mhineachaidh.
define, v. a. mìnich, soilleirich.
definite, adj. comharraichte, cinnteach.
definiteness, s. soilleireachd.
definition, s. mìneachadh.
definitive, adj. dearbhte, soilleir.
deflagrable, adj. loisgeach.
deflagrability, s. so-loisgeach.
deflect, v. n. crom, lùb, aom, claon.
deflection, s. lùbadh, claonadh.
deflexure, s. cromadh, lùbadh.
defloration, s. òigh-thruailleadh.
deflower, v. a. éignich, truaill òighe.
defluous, adj. silteach, sruthach.
defluxion, s. tèarnadh leanntan.
deforcement, s. cumail á seilbh.
deform, v. a. duaichnich, mì-chùm.

deformity, s. mì-dhreach, mì-dhealbh,
neo-chumaireachd.
defraud, v. a. meall, car, spùill (le
seoltachd).
defrauder, s. meàlltair, cealgaire.
defray, v. a. dìol, ìoc, pàidh.
deft, adj. sgiamhach, lurach, ealamh.
defunct, adj. marbh.
defunction, s. bàsachadh, eug, aog.
defy, v. a. dùbhlanaich ; dèan tàir.
degeneracy, s. claonadh (on chòir) ;
cùl-sleamhnachadh.
degenerate, v. n. tuit air falbh, rach am
measad.
degenerate, adj. andualach, suarach,
truagh.
degeneration, s. dol am measad, andual-
chas, cùl-sleamhnachadh.
deglutition, s. slugadh.
degradation, s. ìsleachadh ; truailleadh.
degrade, v. a. ìslich, beagaich, truaill.
degree, s. inbhe, àirde, staid, cor, ceum,
glùn ginealaich.
by degrees, adv. uidh air uidh, a chuid 's
a chuid.
dehort, v. a. comhairlich.
dehortation, s. comhairleachadh.
deicide, s. fear-marbhaidh dé.
deification, s. meas mar dhia.
deify, v. a. dèan 'n a dhia.
deign, v. a. deònaich, ceadaich.
deist, s. fear tha meas Dhé a mhàin mar
chruithear.
Deity, s. Dia, diadhachd.
deject, v. a. mì-mhisnich ; tilg sìos.
dejection, s. smuairean, mulad.
dejecture, s. òtrach, salachar, inneir.
delactation, s. cur o'n chìch, casg.
delapsed, adj. a' tuiteam sìos.
delate, v. a. giùlain, iomchair ; casaidich,
dèan casaid air.
delation, s. giùlan, iomchar ; dìteadh,
casaid.
delay, v. a. cuir dàil, cuir maille ; bac,
fuirich, cum an amharus.
delay, s. dàil, càird, moille, màirneal,
seamsan, stad.
delectable, adj. taitneach, sòlasach.
delectation, s. tlachd, sòlas.
delegate, v. a. cuir air theachdaireachd ;
earb ri.
delegate, s. fear-ionaid, teachdaire.
delete, v. a. dubh a mach ; mill.
deleterious, adj. sgriosail ; cronail.
deliberate, v. a. meòraich.
deliberate, adj. smuainteach ; socrach,
cùramach ; a dh'aon rùn.
deliberation, s. faicilleachd, cùram, ro-
aire.
deliberative, adj. faicilleach, meòrachail,
smuainteachail.
delicacy, s. mìlseachd ; mìneachd, màldachd ; fìnealtachd, suairceas, grinneas,

ceanaltachd ; mùirn ; séimhealachd ; meurantachd.

delicate, *adj.* blasda, milis, taitneach ; mìlseanach, sòghail ; fìnealta, grinn, mìn, ceanalta, meuranta ; lag.

delicateness, *s.* mùirn, mìneachd.

delicious, *adj.* milis, blasda, taitneach.

deligation, *s.* ceangal suas, trusadh.

delight, *s.* aighear, aiteas ; tlachd.

delight, *v. a.* and *n.* toilich, taitinn, dèan subhach, dèan aoibhneach ; gabh tlachd, faigh tlachd.

delightful, *adj.* sòlasach, ciatach.

delineate, *v. a.* dealbh, dreach, tarruing, nochd an dathaibh.

delineation, *s.* dealbh, dreach, tarruing, cumadh.

delinquency, *s.* coire, cron, lochd.

delinquent, *s.* coireach, ciontach.

deliquate, *v. a.* leagh.

delirious, *adj.* breisleachail, gòrach.

delirium, *s.* breisleach, mearaichinn.

deliver, *s.* cuir fa-sgaoil, saor ; teasraig ; tiomain, thoir seachad, liubhair.

deliverance, *s.* liùbhradh, saorsa.

deliverer, *s.* fear-saoraidh.

delivery, *s.* liubhairt, tèarnadh.

dell, *s.* coire, glacag, lagan, gleannan.

delude, *v. a.* meall, car.

deluge, *s.* tuil, dìle, lighe.

deluge, *v. a.* tuilich, bàth.

delusion, *s.* mealladh, cealg, feall.

delusive, delusory, *adj.* mealltach, cealgach, carach, fealltach.

delve, *v. a.* ruamhair, àitich.

delve, *s.* dìg, sloc, toll.

delver, *s.* fear ruamhair, inneal ruamhar.

demagogue, *s.* ceannard-gràisge.

demand, *v. a.* iarr, tagair, sir ; feòraich.

demand, *s.* iarruidh, iarrtas, sireadh ; tagradh, tagartas.

demandant, *s.* fear-tagraidh.

demander, *s.* tagradair, fear-tagraidh.

demean, *v. a.* giùlain, ìslich.

demeanour, *s.* giùlan, beus, iomchar, modh.

demerit, *s.* droch thoillteannas.

demi, *s.* leth.

demise, *s.* bàs, caochladh, eug.

demise, *v. a.* tiomain, fàg dìleab.

demission, *s.* ìsleachadh, suarachas, toirt thairis dreuchd.

demit, *v. a.* cuir dhiot do dhreuchd.

demobilise, *v.* leig as, sgaoil (feachd).

democracy, *s.* sluagh air an riaghladh leis an t-sluagh.

democratical, *adj.* a bhuineas do cho-fhlaitheachd.

demolish, *v. a.* sgrios.

demolisher, *s.* sgriosadair.

demolition, *s.* leagadh gu làr.

demon, *s.* deamhan, diabhol.

demoniac, *adj.* deamhnaidh.

demonology, *s.* deamhan-eòlas.

demonstrable, *adj.* so-dhearbhadh.

demonstrate, *v. a.* dhearbh ; dèan cinn-teach.

demonstration, *s.* co-dhearbhadh.

demonstrative, *adj.* dearbh-chinnteach, lan-shoilleir.

demoralisation, *s.* milleadh dheagh-bheusan, truaillèadh.

demulcent, *adj.* maoth, bog.

demur, *v. a.* and *n.* cuir teagamh ann ; dàilich, màirnealaich ; dèan moille ; bi an ioma-chomhairle.

demur, *s.* teagamh, ioma-chomhairle.

demure, *adj.* stuama, socrach.

demurrage, *s.* dìoladh moille luinge.

den, *s.* garaidh, uamh ; còs.

dendrology, *s.* craobh-eòlas.

deniable, *s.* so-àicheadh.

denial, *s.* àicheadh ; diùltadh.

denier, *s.* fear-àicheadh

denigrate, *v. a.* dubh, duaichnich.

denizen, *s.* saoranach, bùirdeiseach.

denominate, *v. a.* ainmich, gairm.

denomination, *s.* ainm.

denominative, *adj.* ainmeannach.

denotation, *s.* comharrachadh.

denote, *v. a.* comharraich, taisbean.

denounce, *v. a.* bagair ; casaidich, innis air, cuir sìos air-.

dense, *adj.* tiugh, dlùth, teann.

density, *s.* tiuighead, dlùthas.

dental, *adj.* fiaclach.

denticulated, *adj.* mion-fhiaclach.

dentifrice, *s.* fùdar - fhiacal, siabunn fhiacal.

dentist, *s.* léigh-fhiacal.

dentition, *s.* fiaclachadh.

denudate, denude, *v. a.* rùisg, lomair, faobhaich, feann.

denunciation, *s.* cronachadh follaiseach.

deny, *v. a.* àicheidh, diùlt, ob.

deobstruct, *v. a.* glan, réitich.

deodand, *s.* naomh-thiodhlac.

depart, *v. n.* fàg, imich, triall, coisich, siubhail ; bàsaich, caochail.

department, *s.* gnothach, dreuchd, earrann, no meur, an riaghladh na rìoghachd.

departure, *s.* falbh, fàgail, triall ; siubhal, caochladh, bàs, eug.

depend, *v. n.* bi am freasdal, earb, cuir muinighinn, cuir ùidh.

dependance, *s.* eisimeileachd.

dependant, *adj.* eisimeileach.

dependant, dependent, depender, *s.* ìochdaran, fear-eisimeil.

dependent, *adj.* an crochadh, an earbsa.

depict, *v. a.* dèan dealbh, dreach, cùm, tarruing deilbh-mìnich, soilleirich, cuir sìos an òrdugh.

depilous, *adj.* maol, lom ; gun fhalt.

depletion, s. falmhachadh.
deplorable, adj. brònach, muladach.
deplore, v. a. caoidh, caoin, dèan tuireadh, dèan cumha, dèan bròn.
deplumation, s. spìonadh itean.
deplume, v. a. spìon iteach.
depone, v. a. mionnaich, thoir fianuis.
deponent, s. fianuis air mhionnan.
depopulate, v. a. fàsaich.
depopulation, s. fàsachadh.
deport, v. a. giùlain, iomchair, gluais, fògair.
deport, deportment, s. giùlan, cleachdadh, caitheamh-beatha.
deportation, s. fògradh.
depose, v. a. and n. leig dhìot ; cuir á dreuchd, islich, tàmailtich, cuir á inbhe ; cuir a thaobh, leig seachad ; fianuisich, thoir fianuis.
deposit, v. a. taisg, cuir an làmhan ; thoir an geall ; cuir air riadh ; cuir a thaobh.
deposition, s. mionnan, fianuis air mhionnaibh ; dì-chathrachadh, easonarachadh ; cur á dreuchd.
depository, s. tigh-tasgaidh.
depravation, s. truailleadh.
deprave, v. a. truaill, mill, salaich.
depravedness, s. truailleachd, aingidheachd.
depravement, depravity, s. truaillidheachd, aingidheachd.
depraver, s. fear-truaillidh, fear-millidh, milltear.
deprecate, v. a. guidh (nach tachair), aslaich (bacadh, saoradh).
deprecation, s. aslachadh, guidhe.
depreciate, v. a. cuir an dimeas.
depredate, v. a. spùinn, goid, creach.
depredation, s. spùinneadh, creach.
depredator, s. spùinneadair.
depress, v. a. brùth sìos, tilg sìos ; leag ; islich, ùmhlaich, cuir fo sproc.
depression, s. dinneadh, cudthrom, cumail fodha ; tuiteam sìos, leagadh, tèarnadh ; isleachadh, mì-mhisneachadh, trom-inntinn, sproc.
depressor, s. fear cumail fodha, fear cruaidh, an-iochdmhor.
deprivation, s. toirt air falbh, dìobradh ; call, creachadh, calldachd.
deprive, v. a. buin uaithe, thoir uaithe.
depth, s. doimhneachd ; tulchuis.
depurate, adj. fìr-ghlan, gun druaip.
depuration, s. glanadh, sìoladh.
deputation, s. neach no buidheann air teachdaireachd.
depute, v. a. sònraich, socraich, cuir teachdaire.
deputy, s. fear-ionaid, fear gnothaich.
deracinate, v. thoir as a riamhaichean, spion le riamhaichean.

derange, v. cuir á òrdugh, cuir air àimhreidh.
derangement, s. eas-òrdugh, troimh chéile.
derelict, adj. air thoirt thairis, gun fheum (long).
dereliction, s. dìobradh, tréigsinn.
deride, v. a. sgeig, fochaidich, mag.
derision, s. sgeig, magadh, fochaid, fanaid ; cùis-mhagaidh.
derisive, adj. sgeigeil, magail.
derivable, adj. air a bheil còir shinnsearach ; ag éiridh o.
derivation, s. tarruing ; facal fhreumhachd, sruth-chlaonadh.
derivative, adj. a teachd o ni eile.
derive, v. a. tarruing, dèan facal-fhreumhachd, sruth a dh'ionnsaigh.
derm, s. craicionn.
dernier, adj. deireannach.
derogate, v. a. lùghdaich, lagaich, dèan beaganas, thoir tàmailt.
derogation, s. cur an suarachas.
derogatory, derogative, adj. tarchuiseach, easonarach, mì-chliùiteach, suarach.
Dervish, Dervise, s. Sagart Mohamedanach.
descant, s. òran, ròlaist.
descant, v. a. dèan canntaireachd, dèan amhran.
descend, v. a. teirinn ; tùirlinn.
descendant, s. gineal, sliochd, sìol, linn, iarmad, pòr, clann.
descendent, adj. a' tèarnadh do shliochd, do shiol.
descension, s. tèarnadh, tùirling, teachd le bruthaich.
descent, s. tèarnadh, dol sìos ; aomadh, leathad, leth-bhruthach ; isleachadh, teachd a nuas.
describe, v. a. thoir tuairisgeul, dèan mion iomradh air —.
description, s. iomradh, tuairisgeul.
descry, v. a. faigh a mach, dearc, faic fad as, beachdaich fad as.
desecration, s. mì-naomhachadh.
desert, s. fàsach, dìthreabh.
desert, v. a. tréig, fàg, dìobair, teich (as an arm).
desert, s. toilteanas, neo-airidheachd.
deserter, s. fear-teichidh (á sgiobadh, as an arm, o dhleasdanas).
desertion, s. tréigsinn, teicheadh.
deserve, v. n. bi fiùghail, airidh, bi toilteanach.
desiccate, v. a. tiormaich, traogh.
desideratum, s. ionndrain, easbhuidh, feum sonruichte.
design, v. a. rùnaich, cuir romhad, sònraich, comharraich ; tionnsgainn.
design, s. rùn, tionnsgnadh, miann, beachd, smuain ; samhlachas.
designation, s. sònrachadh, sloinneadh.

designer, *s.* dreachdadair, fear-dealbh-aidh, fear-tionnsgnaidh, fear-deilbh (luingeas, no thogalaichean).

designing, *adj.* innleachdach, carach, seòlta, cealgach, sligheach.

desirable, *adj.* ion-mhiannaichte.

desire, *s.* toil, iarraidh, miann, togradh, déidh, càil, dùrachd.

desire, *v. a.* miannaich, sanntaich, iarr, tagair, togair air.

desirous, *adj.* miannach, togarrach.

desist, *v. n.* stad, sguir, foisich.

desistance, *s.* stad, sgur, fosadh.

desk, *s.* bòrd-sgrìobhaidh.

desolate, *adj.* neo-àitichte ; fàsail ; aon-aranach.

desolate, *v. a.* fàsaich, dìth-làraich.

desolation, *s.* fàsachadh, fàsalachd.

despair, *s.* an-dòchas, an-earbsa.

despair, *v.* cuir an eu-dòchas ; thoir thairis dùil, bi an eu-dòchas.

despatch, *s.* teachdaireachd, cabhag, luaths, ealamhachd, deifir.

desperate, *adj.* eu-dòchasach, an-earb-sach, gun athadh ; ainmheasach, ainniseach, caillte, truagh.

desperation, *s.* eu-dòchas, gniomh cruaidh-chais.

despicable, *adj.* tàireil, suarach.

despise, *v. a.* dèan tàir, dèan tarcuis.

despite, *s.* gamhlas, fearg, diomb, mì-run, spìd, droch-mhéinn, fuath, tailceas, tàir ; dùbhlan, aindeoin.

despiteful, *adj.* gamhlasach.

despoil, *v. a.* spùinn, creach, slad.

despoliation, *s.* spùinneadh, creachadh.

despond, *v. n.* caill dòchas.

despondency, *s.* an-dòchas, mì-mhisneach, an-earbsa ; truim-inntinn.

despondent, *adj.* eu-dòchasach, muladach, trom-inntinneach.

despot, *s.* aintighearna.

despotic, *adj.* aintighearnail.

despotism, *adj.* aintighearnas, ceann-asachd, smachdalachd.

dessert, *s.* biabh milis, measan (aig crìoch dìnneir).

destinate, *v. a.* sònraich, cuir air leth (gu crìoch àraidh).

destination, *s.* sònrachadh, ceann-uidhe.

destine, *v. a.* òrduich, sònraich.

destiny, *s.* dàn ; crannchur siorruidh.

destitute, *adj.* falamh ; ainniseach, bochd daoibhir.

destitution, *s.* ainnis, airc, dìth.

destroy, *v. a.* sgrios, marbh.

destroyer, *s.* milltear, sgriosadair.

destructible, *adj.* so-sgriosadh.

destruction, *s.* léir-sgrios, milleadh, fàsach-adh, marbhadh, toirt gu neo-ni, dol a dhìth, di-mhilleadh.

destructive, *adj.* sgriosail, millteach.

desuetude, *s.* á cleachdadh.

desultory, *adj.* bristeach, luaineach, neo-bhunailteach, neo-shuidhichte.

detach, *v. a.* dealaich, cuir air leth.

detachment, *s.* cuideachd airm.

detail, *v. a.* innis gu poncail.

detail, *s.* mion-chunntas.

detain, *v. a.* cùm air ais, cùm an làimh, gléidh, bac, cuir grabadh.

detect, *v. a.* faigh a mach, leig ris, rannsaich.

detection, *s.* faotainn a mach, rannsach-adh.

detention, *s.* gleidheadh ; cumail an làimh, amladh, grabadh, bacadh.

deter, *v. a.* mi-mhisnich, bac le eagal.

deterge, *v. a.* siab, glan, nigh.

detergent, *adj.* siabach, glanail.

deterioration, *s.* dol am miosad.

determinable, *adj.* so-dheanamh a mach, so chuir a thaobh.

determinate, *adj.* suidhichte, sonraichte, cinnteach, criochnaichte.

determination, *s.* rùn suidhichte.

determine, *v. a.* sònraich, suidhich.

detersion, *s.* glanadh, siabadh.

detest, *v. a.* fuathaich, gràinich.

detestable, *adj.* fuathach, gràineil.

detestation, *s.* fuath, gràin, sgreamh.

dethrone, *v. a.* dìth-chathairich.

detonation, *s.* tàirn-thoirm.

detract, *v. a.* cùl-chàin, diomol.

detraction, *s.* cùl-chaineadh, tuaileas, diomoladh, sgainneal.

detractory, *adj.* tarcuiseach.

detriment, *s.* dìobhail, call, dolaidh.

detrimental, *adj.* diobhalach.

detrude, *v. a.* pùc sìos, ìslich.

detruncate, *v. a.* gearr, bearr, sgud.

detrusion, *s.* pùcadh sìos.

deuce, *s.* dithis (cairtean) ; an diabhol.

devastate, *v. a.* fàsaich, creach, mill, sgrios as.

devastation, *s.* fàsachadh, sgrios.

develop, *v. a.* foillsich, taisbein, fàs.

devest, *v. a.* faobhaich, rùisg, saor uaithe, thoir air falbh.

deviate, *v. n.* rach am mearachd, rach a thaobh.

deviation, *s.* seachran, faontradh, iomrall, mearachd, claonadh air falbh ; peac-adh, cionta.

device, *s.* innleachd, tionnsgal, tionnsg-nadh, cleas, car, dealbh ; run, comh-airle, smuain ; gearradh-arm ; seòlt-achd, ealantas.

devil, *s.* diabhol, deamhan, donas.

devilish, *adj.* diabhlaidh, deamhnaidh, donasach.

devious, *adj.* iomrallach, seachranach, cuairteach.

devise, *v. a.* suidhich innleachd ; beachd-aich, tionnsgain.

devised, *part.* socraichte, suidhichte.

devoid, *adj.* falamh, fàs, as eugmhais.

devoir, *s.* dleasdanas, aire, seirbhis.

devolve, *v. a.* cuir car mu char, cuir dleasdanas mar fhiachaibh air neach eile.

devote, *v. a.* coisrig ; thoir seachad.

devotee, *s.* saobh-chreidmheach.

devotion, *s.* diadhachd ; cràbhadh, aoradh ; ùrnuigh ; teas-ghràdh, dùrachd, toirt suas a' chridhe.

devour, *v. a.* ith suas, glàm, glut, beubanaich, riasail ; sgrios, mill, cuir as, ith gu glamhach.

devout, *adj.* diadhaidh, cràbhach.

dew, *s.* dealt, drùchd.

dewdrop, *s.* cuirnean, braon.

dewlap, *s.* caisean-uchd, sprogaill.

dewy, *s.* dealtach, drùchdach, braonach, cuirneanach.

dexterity, *s.* deisealachd, tapachd, ealamhachd ; teòmachd, seòltachd.

dexterous, *adj.* deiseil, teòma, seòlta.

dextral, dexter, *adj.* deas, deiseil.

diabetes, *s.* an galair-fuail.

diabolical, *adj.* diabhlaidh.

diacodium, *s.* sùgh a' chadalain.

diadem, *s.* crùn, coron, fleasg.

diagnosis, *s.* rannsachadh air galair.

diagonal, *adj.* trasta, tarsuinn, fìar, bho oisinn gu oisinn (air fiaradh).

diagram, *s.* dealbh.

dial, *s.* uaireadair-gréine, aghaidh uaireadair.

dialect, *s.* cànan, cainnt.

dialing, *s.* tarruing uaireadair gréine.

dialogist, *s.* fear co-labhairt.

dialogue, *s.* co-labhairt, còmhradh (eadar dithis).

diameter, *s.* croislin, strioch-mheadhoin (buaileig).

diametrical, *adj.* croislineach.

diamond, *s.* daoimean.

diaper, *s.* anart-gréiste.

diaphoretic, *adj.* fallasach.

diaphragm, *s.* an sgairt.

diarrhœa, *s.* a' ghearrach, spùt, buinneach.

diary, *s.* leabhar-latha.

dibble, *s.* pleadhag.

dice, *s.* dìsnean.

dictate, *v.* deachd, seòl, òrduich.

dictation, *s.* deachdadh, sgrìobhadh á beul neach ; òrduchadh.

dictator, *s.* ard-uachdaran, riaghladair rìoghachd (mar a chì e fhéin iomchuidh).

dictatorial, *adj.* ceannsalach.

dictatorship, *s.* ceannsalachd, riaghladh aon neach (gun a bhi an comhairle neach air bith).

diction, *s.* labhradh, dòigh labhairt; his diction is good, is glan a labhras e.

dictionary, *s.* facalair.

didactic, didactical, *adj.* seòlach.

die, *s.* dìsne ; molltair (cùinidh).

die, *v. n.* bàsaich, eug, caochail.

diet, *s.* lòn, biadh, deathad ; coinneamh fhlath.

diet, *v. a.* beathaich ; biadh, àraich.

differ, *v. a.* and *n.* eadar - dhealaich, cuir eadar-dhealachadh ; bi air t'eadar-dhealachadh ; connsaich, cuir a mach air ; dealaich am barail.

difference, *s.* eadar-dhealachadh, mùthadh ; atharrachadh, caochladh ; connsachadh, connspaid, cur a mach air a chéile.

different, *adj.* air leth ; de ghnè eile.

difficult, *adj.* deacair, duilich, doirbh, cruaidh, draghail ; docair.

difficulty, *s.* duilgheadas, deacaireachd, docaireachd, dorradas ; cruaidh-chàs teinn, imcheist, airc.

diffidence, *s.* an-amharus, mì-earbsa, doicheall, sochair.

diffident, *adj.* an-amharasach, socharach ; nàrach.

diffluent, *adj.* silteach, fuasgailt.

diffuse, *v. a.* dòirt a mach, taom, sgaoil, tanaich.

diffuse, *adj.* sgaipte, sgaoilte.

diffused, diffusedly, *adj.* sgaoilte.

diffusedness, *s.* sgaoilteachd.

diffusion, *s.* sgaoileadh.

dig, *v. a.* cladhaich, tochail, treachail, bùraich, ruamhair.

digest, *v. a.* eagaraich, cuir an òrdugh ; meirbh, cnàmh ; cnuasaich.

digestible, *adj.* meirbheach.

digestion, *s.* meirbheadh ; dìleadh.

digger, *s.* fear-cladhaich.

digit, *s.* meur, ordag ; leud meòir.

dignified, *part.* urramaichte.

dignify, *v. a.* àrdaich, urramaich.

dignitary, *s.* àrd-shagart; fear an ardinbhe.

dignity, *s.* àirde, urram, inbhe.

digress, *v. n.* claon, rach fiar, cuir cuairt, thoir a steach (seanchus), theirig thairis air do sgeula.

digression, *s.* seacharan seanachais.

dike, *s.* clais, dìg, cam-rath ; gàradh.

dilacerate, *v. a.* riasail, stròic, reub.

dilapidate, *v. a.* dìth-làraich, fàsaich, dèan 'na bhruchag.

dilapidation, *s.* tuiteam sìos, anacaitheamh, dol á òrdugh.

dilate, *v. a.* sgaoil a mach, leudaich ; aithris gu mion.

dilatory, *adj.* mall, màirnealach ; leasg.

dilemma, *s.* argumaid-ribidh, eadarrabharail.

diligence, *s.* dìchioll, dùrachd.

diligent, *adj.* dìchiollach, dèanadach.

dilute, *v. a.* tanaich, lagaich, measgaich.

dilution, *s.* tanachadh.

diluvian, adj. tuilteach, dìleach.
dim, adj. doilleir, dorcha, gruamach.
dim, v. a. doilleirich, dorchaich, neulaich, duibhrich, gruaimich.
dimension, s. tomhas, meud, tomad.
diminish, v. a. lùghdaich, beagaich.
diminution, s. lùghdachadh.
diminutive, adj. beag, meanbh, leibideach, crìon, bìodach.
dimity, seòrsa de aodach canaich.
dimness, s. doilleireachd, dubharachd.
dimple, s. lagan, copan.
dimply, adj. laganach, copanach.
din, s. toirm, fuaim, stairirich.
dine, v. gabh dinneir.
dingey, dinghy, s. geòla, eathar beag.
dingle, s. gleann, glac, lag (anns a bheil coille bheag).
dingy, adj. lachdunn ; rapach, salach.
dinner, s. dìothad, dinneir.
dint, s. buille, gleadhar, stràc, coilleag ; lorg ; neart, spionnadh.
dinumeration, s. cunntas aon an déigh aon, cunntas a lion aon is aon.
diocesan, s. easbuig.
diocese, s. sgìreachd easbuig.
dip, v. a. tùm, bog ; taisich.
diphthong, s. dà-fhòghair.
diploma, s. teisteanas (foghlumaiche).
dire, direful, adj. eagalach, uabhasach, oillteil.
direct, adj. dìreach, soilleir, so-thuigsinn, neo-fhiar.
direct, v. a. cuir dìreach, seòl, stiùir ; cuimsich, treòraich.
direction, s. seòladh, treòrachadh.
directly, adv. air ball, dìreach.
director, s. fear-seòlaidh.
directory, s. leabhar-seòlaidh.
direness, s. uamharrachd.
direption, s. spùinneadh, slad.
dirge, s. tuireadh, cumha, corranach, marbhnadh.
dirk, s. biodag, cuinnsear.
dirt, s. salachar ; inneir, aolach ; mosaiche, poll, clàbar.
dirtiness, s. salacharachd, mosaiche.
dirty, adj. salach, mosach, neòghlan.
dirty, v. a. salaich, truaill ; maslaich.
diruption, s. sgàineadh, sgoltadh.
disability, s. neo-chomas, laige.
disable, v. a. dean neo-chomasach.
disabuse, v. a. cuir ceart.
disadvantage, s. calldachd, call, ana-cothrom ; mì-chothrom.
disadvantageous, adj. ana-cothromach, dìobhalach, caillteach.
disaffect, v. a. dèan mì-thoilichte.
disaffected, adj. mì-thoilichte, diùmbach.
disaffection, s. mì-dhìlseachd, diùmbadh.
disagree, v. n. mì-chòrd, eas-aontaich.
disagreeable, adj. neo-thaitneach, gràineil.

disagreement, s. eas-aonachd, eu-coltas, neo-chòrdadh.
disallow, v. a. toirmisg, bac ; diùlt.
disallowable, adj. neo-cheadaichte.
disanimate, v. a. marbh ; mì-mhisnich, meataich.
disappear, v. n. rach á sealladh, teich.
disappoint, v. a. meall, dìobair.
disappointment, s. mealladh, doithead.
disapprobation, disapproval, s. cronachadh, coireachadh, achmhasan, dìteadh, mì-thaitneadh.
disapprove, v. a. coirich, cronaich, dìt, diomoil.
disarm, v. a. dìth-armaich.
disarray, s. àimhreit, àimhreidh, eas-òrdugh, mì-riaghailt ; rùsgadh.
disaster, s. truaighe, tubaist, sgiorradh, bochduinn, calldachd.
disastrous, adj. mì-shealbhach, sgiorrail, tubaisteach ; truagh, cailtteach.
disavouch, disavow, v. a. aicheidh, na aithnich.
disavowal, disavowment, s. àicheadh, diùltadh.
disband, v. a. leig fa-sgaoil, leig air falbh, sgaoil, sgap.
disbark, v. a. cuir air tìr á luing.
disbelief, s. neo-chreidimh.
disbelieve, v. a. na creid.
disburden, v. a. neo-luchdaich, eutromaich, cuir dheth eallach.
disburse, v. a. cosg, cuir a mach airgead, dèan cosgais.
disbursement, s. cur-a-mach.
discard, v. a. cuir air falbh.
discern, v. a. faic, thoir fainear ; beachdaich, dearc.
discernible, adj. so-fhaicinn, soilleir.
discerning, part. beachdail, tuigseach.
discernment, s. deagh-bhreithneachadh, tuigse, eòlas, géire, tùr.
discerp, v. a. sràc, stròic, thoir as a chéile 'na mhìrean.
discharge, v. a. eutromaich, cuir a mach luchd ; tilg a mach, leig as ; caith urchair ; dìol, ìoc, pàidh, thoir seachad ; saor ; cuir air falbh ; coimhlion.
discharge, s. fuasgladh, sgaoileadh, leigeadh as, no air falbh ; urchair ; taomadh, sruth ; cur á dreuchd ; saoradh, saorsa ; pàidheadh, dìoladh ; litir shaoraidh ; coimhlionadh.
disciple, s. deisciobul, sgoilear, fear leanmhuinn.
discipleship, s. deisciobulachd.
discipline, s. oideas, oilean, teagasg, ionnsachadh, fòghlum, riaghladh, riaghailt ; ùmhlachd, smachd.
discipline, v. a. oileanaich, ionnsaich, teagaisg, fòghluim ; stiùir, seòl, riaghail ; smachdaich, ceannsaich.
disclaim, v. a. àicheidh, cuir cùl ri

disclose, v. a. foillsich, cuir os-àird, leig ris ; innis, nochd.

disclosure, s. leigeadh ris, seòladh, taisbeanadh, nochdadh, foillseachadh.

discolour, v. a. mill dath.

discomfit, v. a. ceannsaich, ruaig.

discomfiture, s. teicheadh, ruaig.

discomfort, s. anshocair, mulad.

discommode, v. a. cuir dragh air.

discompose, v. a. àimhreitich, bi draghail, cuir caisean (air neach).

discomposure, s. àimhreit, tuairgneadh, buaireas ; troimh chéile.

disconcert, v. a. cuir troimh chéile, feargaich, dorranaich ; cuir fa-sgaoil.

disconnect, v. fuasgail, dealaich o chéile.

disconsolate, adj. tùrsach, brònach, dubhach, neo-éibhneach.

discontent, discontented, adj. mì-thoilichte ; neo-thoilichte, mì-shuaimhneach.

discontent, s. mi-thoileachadh, antlachd ; mì-ghean, mì-riarachadh.

discontentedness, discontentment, s. neo-thoileachas-inntinn, neo-thoilealachd.

discontinuance, discontinuation, s. neo-mhairsinneachd, bristeachd ; stad, sgur, leigeadh seachad.

discontinue, v. a. sguir, leig seachad, leig dhìot, teirig.

discord, s. àimhreit, mì-chòrdadh, eascòrdadh, fuam neo-bhinn, scriach.

discordant, adj. neo-fhreagarrach, àimhreiteach ; neo-chòrdail ; eu-coltach, neo-sheasmhach, neo-bhinn.

discount, s. leigeadh sìos ; riadh airgeadiasaid (air a thogail roimh 'n àm).

discount, v. a. leag prìs ; tog leat riadh.

discountenance, v. a. mì-mhisnich, amhairc le anntlachd.

discountenance, s. fuaralachd.

discourage, v. a. mì-mhisnich.

discouragement, s. mì-mhisneachadh.

discourse, s. còmhradh, co-labhairt, conaltradh ; cainnt, searmoin, òraid.

discourteous, adj. neo - aoidheil, mì-mhodhail, neo-shuairce, neo-shìobhalta, dalma, borb, ladarna.

discover, v. a. faigh a mach, foillsich, nochd ; leig fhaicinn, seall, leig ris, dèan aithnichte.

discovery, s. faotainn a mach ; foillseachadh, nochdadh, taisbeanadh.

discredit, s. masladh, tàir, mì-chliu.

discredit, v. a. na creid; cuir an teagamh.

discreet, adj. glic, faicilleach, cùramach ; modhail, sìobhalt.

discrepance, s. eadar-dhealachadh (eadar dà sgeula).

discretion, s. gliocas, ciall, crìonntachd ; saor-inntinneachd, toil.

discretionary, adj. a réir toile, aig a thoil.

discriminate, v. a. eadar-dhealaich.

discrimination, s. eadar - dhealachadh, mùthadh, aithneachadh, comharradh air leth, suaicheantas, ciall, geurchuis.

discursive, adj. luaineach, bith-bhriathrach ; reusonach, luasganach (an labhart).

discuss, v. a. feuch, rannsaich, sgrùd, reusonaich.

discussion, s. feuchainn, deuchainn, rannsachadh, sgrùdadh, cnuasachadh, argumaid, reusonachadh.

disdain, v. a. cuir suarach, tarcuisich, na b' fhiach leat.

disdain, s. tàir, tarcuis, dìmeas, spìd.

disdainful, adj. tarcuiseach, tàireil.

disease, s. tinneas, euslaint, galar.

diseased, adj. tinn, galarach.

disembark, v. a. and n. cuir air tìr ; rach air tìr.

disembogue, v. a. sruth, dòirt, taom ; brùchd, steall.

disenchant, v. a. cuir o gheasaibh, — o mhealladh.

disencumber, v. a. dì-luchdaich, thoir dheth uallach, thoir faothachadh.

disengage, v. a. fuasgail, dealaich, cuir fa-sgaoil, réitich, bi fuasgailte.

disengaged, part. neo-cheangailte, diomhain.

disentangle, v. a. fuasgail, réitich.

disenthral, v. a. saor o thràilleachd.

disentomb, v. thoir á uaigh ; thoir gu solus.

disestablish, v. fuasgail (eaglais) o'n Stàt.

disfavour, s. mì-fhàbhar ; gràinn.

disfiguration, s. mì-mhaise, mì-dhreach.

disfigure, v. a. duaichnich, cuir á cruth.

disfranchise, v. a. cuir á còir, thoir air falbh còir (taghaidh).

disgorge, v. a. dìobhair, sgeith, tilg.

disgrace, s. eas-urram, cion-fàbhair ; masladh, tàmailt, nàire, aobhar nàire.

disgrace, v. a. maslaich, tàmailtich, eas-urramaich ; nàraich ; cuir á fàbhar.

disgraceful, adj. maslach, nàr.

disguise, v. a. cleith, falaich, atharraich cruth, cuir á riochd.

disguise, s. còmhdach meallta, riochd.

disgust, s. gràinn, sgreamh, fuath, déisinn, anntlachd, daoch.

disgust, v. a. gràinich, cuir sgreamh air, cuir déisinn air, sgreataich ; fuathaich, cuir miothlachd air.

disgusting, disgustful, adj. déisinneach, gràineil, fuathach, sgreamhail.

dish, s. soitheach, mias.

dish, v. a. cuir am mèis, cuir (biadh) air bòrd ; thoir a char as.

dishabille, s. neo-uidheam, neo-sgeadachadh.

dishearten, v. a. mì-mhisnich.

disherison, v. a. cuir á oighreachd.

428 DISHEVEL—DISQUALIFICATION

dishevel, *v. a.* cléig falt; leag am falt.
dishonest, *adj.* neo-ionraic, bradach; cealgach, fealltach, eas-onarach.
dishonesty, *s.* eas-ionracas, eas-onoir.
dishonour, *s.* eas-urram, eas-onoir, masladh, tàmailt; mì-chliu.
dishonour, *v. a.* eas-urramaich, maslaich, nàraich; truaill.
dishonourable, *adj.* mì-chliùiteach, maslach, nàr, tàmailteach.
disinclination, *s.* mi-thoil, antoil.
disincline, *v. a.* dèan neo-thoileach, dèan neo-aontachail.
disinclined, *adj.* neo-aontachail, neo-thogarach.
disingenuous, *adj.* carach, lùbach, fealltach, dùbailte.
disinherit, *v. a.* buin air falbh còir-bhreith.
disinter, *v. a.* tog á uaigh.
disinterested, *adj.* neo-fhéineil, glan, fialaidh; coma; air bheag spéis.
disjoin, *v. a.* dealaich, eadar-dhealaich.
disjoint, *v. a.* cuir as an alt; bris.
disjointed, *adj.* as an alt, dealaichte.
disjunct, *adj.* dealaichte.
disjunction, *s.* dealachadh, fuasgladh dàimh.
disk, *s.* peileastair, cruinn-leac.
dislike, *s.* fuath, sgreamh, gràin.
dislike, *v. a.* fuathaich, sgreamhaich.
dislocate, *v. a.* cuir á àite, cur as alt.
dislocation, *s.* carachadh, cur á àite; dol as an alt, cur á alt.
dislodge, *v. a.* cuir á àite.
disloyal, *adj.* neo-dhìleas, mì-dhìleas.
disloyalty, *s.* neo-dhìlseachd.
dismal, *adj.* oillteil, uamharra, eagalach, dubhach, brònach, neo-shuilbhear.
dismantle, *v. a.* rùisg, cuir dheth a chòmhdach; tilg sìos, thoir as a chéile.
dismay, *v. a.* oilltich, clisg, cuir eagal.
dismay, *s.* oillt, eagal, uamhunn.
dismember, *v. a.* spìon as a chéile, thoir ball o bhall, gearr 'n a cheathrannan.
dismiss, *v. a.* cuir air falbh, sgaoil; thoir cead; cuir á dreuchd.
dismission, *s.* cur air falbh, cur air theachdaireachd; ceadachadh falbh.
dismount, *v. a.* teirinn; cuir no tilg sìos; tuirling.
disobedience, *s.* eas-umhlachd.
disobey, *v. a.* na toir ùmhlachd.
disoblige, *v. a.* thoir oilbheum, cuir mìothlachd.
disobliging, *adj.* mì-choingheallach.
disorder, *s.* mi-riaghailt, àimhreit, buaireas, troimh chéile; tinneas, galar.
disorder, *v. a.* mì-riaghailtich, àimh-reitich, cuir thar a chéile.
disorderly, *adj.* mi-riaghailteach.
disorganise, *v. a.* eas-orduich.

disown, *v. a.* àicheidh, na gabh ri.
disparagement, *s.* masladh, tàir, tarcuis, mì-chliu, sgainneal.
disparity, *s.* neo-ionannachd.
dispassionate, *adj.* stòlda, ciùin, socrach, neo-bhuaireasach.
dispel, *v. a.* sgap, sgaoil, fuadaich, fògair, iomruag, iomsgaoil.
dispensary, *s.* tigh ìocshlaintean.
dispensation, *s.* compàirteachadh, riarachadh; buileachadh, dòigh buileachaidh; cead peacachaidh; freasdal.
dispense, *v. a.* roinn, riaraich; dèan suas cungaidh leighis; thig as eugmhais.
dispeople, *v. a.* fàsaich, dìth-làraich.
disperse, *v. n.* crath, sgiot.
disperse, *v. a.* sgap, sgaoil, iomsgaoil.
disperser, *s.* sgapadair.
dispersion, *s.* sgaoileadh, sgapadh.
dispirit, *v. a.* mì-mhisnich, tiomaich, lagaich spiorad; claoidh, cìosnaich.
displace, *v. a.* cuir á àite.
displant, *v. a.* cuir air imrich, fuadaich.
displantation, *s.* imrich; fuadach, cur air imrich, fàsachadh.
display, *v. a.* sgaoil a mach, foillsich, taisbean; fosgail, leig ris.
displease, *v. a.* mì-thoilich, thoir oilbheum, feargaich.
displeasure, *s.* mì-thaitneachd, neo-thoileachas-inntinn; diomb, fearg.
disport, *s.* cluich, mireag, fala-dhà.
disposal, *s.* buileachadh, riarachadh; comas buileachaidh; riaghladh, stiùradh, seòladh; toirt seachad.
dispose, *v. a.* suidhich, cuir an òrdugh, builich, ceartaich, òrduich; giùlain, iomchair; dèan ri, builich.
disposition, *s.* riaghailt, dòigh, seòl, suidheachadh, rian; nàdur, aomadh, gnè, càil; aigne, dùrachd.
dispossess, *v. a.* cuir á seilbh.
dispossession, *s.* cur á seilbh.
dispraise, *s.* diomoladh.
dispraise, *v. a.* diomoil, cronaich.
disproof, *s.* àicheadh, dearbhadh 'n a bhréig, breugnachadh.
disproportion, *s.* neo-ionannachd.
disproportionable, disproportionate, *adj.* mì-fhreagarrach.
disprove, *v. a.* dearbh 'na bhréig, cuir ' clach 'n a chraos.'
disputable, *adj.* tagarach, teagmhach.
disputant, *s.* deasbaire, connspaidiche.
disputation, *s.* connsachadh, reusonachadh, deasbaireachd.
disputatious, disputative, *adj.* connsachail, connspaideach.
dispute, *v.* connsaich, cothaich, cathaich, tagair, reusanaich, bi deasbaireachd.
dispute, *s.* connsachadh, deasbaireachd.
disqualification, *s.* neo-fhreagarrachd, neo-iomchuidheachd.

disqualify, *v. a.* dèan neo-iomchuidh.

disquiet, disquietude, *s.* iomguin, neo-fhoisneachd.

disquiet, *v. a.* trioblaidich, cuir campar air, cuir dragh air.

disquietful, *adj.* mì-shuaimhneach.

disquisition, *s.* rannsachadh, sgrùdadh, deasbaireachd, sgrìobhadh no òraid fhada (air ceann-labhart).

disregard, *s.* dìmeas, tarcuis, beag spéis.

disregard, *v. a.* dèan dìmeas air.

disrelish, *s.* anablas, gràin, sgreamh.

disrelish, *v. a.* sgreamhaich, sgreataich, gràinich, fuathaich, gabh gràin.

disrepair, *a.* air tuiteam ; air dol as a chéile ; am feum air leasachadh.

disreputable, *adj.* neo-mheasail, air dhroch cliù.

disrepute, *s.* mìchliu, droch ainm.

disrespect, *s.* eas-urram, tarcuis.

disrobe, *v. a.* faobhaich, rùisg, thoir dheth fhalluinn.

disruption, *s.* bristeadh, sgàineadh.

dissatisfaction, *s.* mì-thoileachadh, mì-riarachadh.

dissatisfy, *v. a.* mì-thoilich, mì-riaraich.

dissect, *v. a.* cuir as a chéile ; sgrùd ; gearr ('n a mhìrean).

dissemblance, *s.* neo-choltas.

dissemble, *v. a.* cuir an aimhriochd, falaich, ceil, meall, leig ort.

dissembler, *s.* cealgaire, mealltair.

disseminate, *v. a.* craobh-sgaoil.

dissemination, *s.* craobh-sgaoileadh.

disseminator, *s.* fear craobh-sgaoilidh.

dissension, *s.* àimhreit, ceannairc.

dissent, *v. n.* mi-chòrd ; eas-aontaich ; sgar.

dissent, *s.* eas-aontachadh, dealachadh, caochladh barail.

dissenter, *s.* fear-dealachaidh o'n eaglais Shasunnaich.

dissentious, *adj.* eas-aontach.

dissertation, *s.* òraid, searmoin.

disservice, *s.* ciùrradh, dochann, cron, beag-seirbhis.

disserviceable, *adj.* caillteach.

dissever, *v. a.* gearr, sgar.

dissimilar, *adj.* eu-coltach.

dissimilarity, dissimilitude, *s.* eu-coltas, eu-cosmhalachd.

dissimulation, *s.* cealgaireachd, gnùis-mhealladh, cluain, cuilbheart.

dissipate, *v. a.* sgaoil, sgap, caith, ana-caith.

dissipation, *s.* ana-caitheamh.

dissociate, *v. a.* eadar-dhealaich, sgar, na gabh gnothuich ri —.

dissoluble, *adj.* so-leaghadh.

dissolute, *adj.* neo-shuidhichte, neo-gheimnidh, fuasgailte, macnasach, baoiseach, drùiseil, strothail, ana-measarra.

dissoluteness, *s.* fuasgailteachd, stròthalachd, neo-gheamnuidheachd, ana-measarrachd.

dissolution, *s.* leaghadh ; fuasgladh, dol as a chéile ; caochladh, bàs.

dissolve, *v. a.* leagh ; sgaoil, cuir o chéile, fuasgail, cuir fa-sgaoil ; eadar-dhealaich, sgar o chéile.

dissolvent, *adj.* leaghach, a leaghas.

dissonance, *s.* ràcaireachd.

dissonant, *adj.* searbh, neo-fhonnmhor, neo-bhinn.

dissuade, *v. a.* ath-chomhairlich, cuir impidh, thoir (neach) as a bheachd.

dissuasive, *adj.* a' comhairleachadh an aghaidh, earalach.

dissyllable, *s.* facal dà lide.

distaff, *s.* cuigeal.

distance, *s.* astar, céin, uidhe ; ùine.

distance, *v. a.* fàg fad air dheireadh.

distant, *adj.* fad air falbh, fad as ; céin, fada uaithe ; neo-dhàimheil.

distaste, *s.* droch-bhlas, searbhachd, gràin, anntlachd, fuath, déisinn.

distasteful, *adj.* neo-bhlasta, searbh.

distemper, *s.* tinneas, galar, eucail.

distemper, *v. a.* cuir galar ann, dèan tinn, dèan eucaileach ; buair.

distend, *v. a.* leudaich, farsuingich, séid (le gaoth).

distention, *s.* leudachadh, farsuingeachadh, sgaoileadh a mach.

distich, *s.* dà shreath (bàrdachd); leth-rann.

distil, *v. a.* tarruing ; leagh, sruth.

distillation, *s.* tarruing, sruthadh.

distiller, *s.* grùdaire, fear-togalach.

distinct, *adj.* soilleir, poncail.

distinction, *s.* eadar-dhealachadh.

distinctive, *adj.* tuigseach, soilleir, sonruichte.

distinguish, *v. a.* eadar-dhealaich, dèan ainmeil.

distinguished, *adj.* comharraichte, ainmeil.

distort, *v. a.* toinn, snìomh, fiar.

distortion, *s.* sreamadh, casadh, toinn-eamh, fiaradh, snìomh.

distract, *v. a.* roinn, cuir as a chéile ; cuir an imcheist ; cuir air bhreitheal, buair.

distracted, *adj.* buairte, claoidhte, sàraichte ; air a chuthach, air bhoile.

distraction, *s.* eas-aonachd, mì-chòrdadh, mì-riaghailt, iomsgaradh, àimhreit, eas-òrdugh ; buaireadh, bruaillean, imcheist, breathal ; cuthach.

distrain, *v. a.* glac, cuir an gréim, gabh seilbh (air cuid féicheanach).

distress, *s.* anshocair, àmhghar, tinneas ; teanntachd, cruaidh-chàs, teinn, airc ; claoidh, sàrachadh ; glacadh laghail.

distress, *v. a.* sàraich, claoidh.

distressed, *adj.* truagh, àmhgharach, anshocrach.

distribute, *v. a.* roinn, compàirtich.

distribution, *s.* roinn, compàirteachadh, riarachas, comh-roinn.

distributive, *adj.* compàirteach.

district, *s.* cèarn, mór-roinn dùthcha.

distrust, *v. a.* mì-chreid, an-earb.

distrustful, *adj.* mì-chreideasach, an-earbsach.

disturb, *v. a.* buair, cuir dragh ; cuir troimh chéile.

disturbance, *s.* buaireas, tuairgneadh, àimhreit.

disturber, *s.* buaireadair.

disunion, *s.* dealachadh, eadar-sgaradh, eas-aonachd, mì-chòrdadh.

disunite, *v.* eadar-sgar, dealaich.

disunity, *s.* eas-aonachd, eadar-sgarach-dainn, tearbadh.

disuse, disusage, *s.* mì-chleachdadh.

disuse, *v. a.* cuir á cleachdadh.

ditch, *s.* clais, dìg, cladhan.

ditcher, *s.* dìgear.

dithyrambic, *s.* duanag òil.

dittany, *s.* lus-a'-phìobaire.

ditty, *s.* òran, luinneag, duanag.

diuretic, diuretical, *adj.* fual-bhrosnachail.

diurnal, *adj.* lathail, gach latha.

diurnal, *s.* leabhar-latha.

divan, *s.* àrd-chomhairl an Turcaich.

divarication, *s.* caochladh baralach.

dive, *v.* rach fo'n uisge ; rannsaich a steach, rach á sealladh.

diver, *s.* an gobha-uisg ; snàmhaich fo'n uisg ; fear-rannsachaidh.

diverge, *v. n.* iomsgaoil.

divergent, *adj.* a' dol gach rathad.

divers, *adj.* iomadh, iomadach.

diverse, *adj.* eug-samhail, air leth.

diversification, *s.* mùthadh, atharrachadh, caochladh ; eug-samhlachd.

diversify, *v. a.* mùth, atharraich, dèan eug-samhail.

diversion, *s.* cridhealas, aighear, fearas-chuideachd ; claonadh.

diversity, *s.* eu-coltas, iomadachd.

divert, *v. a.* tionndaidh air falbh ; cum o fhadal ; breug, cum cluich ri.

divertisement, *s.* aighear, cluiche.

divertive, *adj.* àbhachdach, sùgach.

divest, *v. a.* rùisg, faobhaich.

divide, *v.* roinn, eadar-sgar, dealaich, cuir dealachadh eadar, cùm o chéile ; pàirtich ; eas-aontaich, mì-chòrd.

dividend, *s.* earrann, roinn, cuid.

divider, *s.* roinneadair.

dividual, *adj.* roinnte, pàirtichte.

divination, *s.* fàisneachd, fiosachd.

divine, *adj.* diadhaidh, nèamhaidh.

divine, *s.* diadhaire, sagart, pears-eaglais ; ministear.

divine, *v. a.* baralaich, smaoinich.

diviner, *s.* fàisniche, fiosaiche.

divinity, *s.* diadhachd ; diadhaireachd.

divisible, *adj.* so-roinn, pàirteachail.

division, *s.* roinn, pàirteachadh ; eadar-dhealachadh ; pàirt, cuid, earrann.

divisor, *s.* àireamh leis an roinnear sùim ; fear-roinne ; roinneadair.

divorce, divorcement, *s.* dealachadh pòsaidh ; litir-dhealachaidh.

divorce, *v. a.* dealaich càraid phòsta ; cuir air falbh.

divulge, *v. a.* foillsich, taisbean, innis gu follaiseach, dèan follaiseach.

dizziness, *s.* tuainealaich, clò-ghalar.

dizzy, *adj.* tuainealach ; aotrom.

do, *v.* dèan, gnàthaich ; cuir an gnìomh ; crìochnaich ; atharraich, mùth ; biodh gnothach agad ri.

docile, *adj.* so-ionnsachadh, soirbh, soith-eamh, callta, solta.

docility, *s.* soirbheachd, séimheachd, soltachd.

dock, *s.* copag ; long-phort.

docket, *s.* sgrìobhadh-seòlaidh air bathar, gearr-sgrìobhadh.

dockyard, *s.* long-lann.

doctor, *s.* ollamh ; lighich ; léigh.

doctorate, *s.* ollamhachd.

doctrinal, *adj.* oileanach, teagasgail.

doctrine, *s.* teagasg, ionnsachadh.

document, *s.* àithne, riaghailt, dearbhadh, sgrìobhte.

dodge, *v. n.* meall, bi ri mì-chleasan, thoir car mu chnoc.

doe, *s.* earb, eilid, maoisleach.

doer, *s.* dèanadair, fear-gnothaich.

doff, *v. a.* cuir dhìot, cùir dàil.

dog, *s.* cù, madadh, balgaire.

dog, *v. a.* lorgaich, lean, srònaich.

dogbrier, *s.* con-dris, fàileag.

dog-days, *s.* an t-iuchar.

doge, *s.* uachdaran baile *Venice*

dogged, *adj.* gnù, breun, coimheach, doirbh, iargalta, reasgach ; rag-mhuin-ealach.

doggerel, *s.* treallain, reòlaist, bàrdachd shuarach.

dogish, *adj.* brùideil, dreamach, crost.

dogma, *s.* barail suidhichte, teagasg gnàthaichte.

dogmatic, dogmatical, *adj.* ùghdarrach, féin-bharalach, dearrasach.

dogmatism, *s.* danarrachd, dearras.

dogmatist, *s.* fear teann 'na bharail.

dog-star, *s.* reull an iuchair.

doings, *s.* dèanadais, gniomharran.

dole, *s.* compàirteachadh, co-roinn, sìneas.

dole, *v. a.* builich, compàirtich, riaraich, roinn.

doleful, *adj.* brònach, dubhach, tùrsach, gearanach, doilghiosach ; déisinneach, aonaranach, cianail, tiamhaidh, trom.

doll, *s.* liùdhag, leanabh-liùdhaig, innleag.

dolorific, *adj.* doilghiosach, trioblaideach, àmhgharach, muladach.

dolorous, *adj.* muladach, brònach, tiamhaidh, piantail, doilghiosach, amhgharach.

dolour, *s.* bròn, doilghios, tùrsa, cràdh, dòghruinn, pian.

dolphin, *s.* an leumadair.

dolt, *s.* burraidh, ùmaidh, gurraiceach, tàmhanach.

doltish, *adj.* pleòisgeach, gurraiceil, tromcheannach, ùmanta.

domain, *s.* uachdranachd, oighreachd ; flaitheachd, crìochan fo riaghladh neach, raon, rùm (air son smuain no gnìomh).

dome, *s.* aitreabh, tigh, àros, teach ; cruinn-mhullach, aghaidh nan speur.

domestic, *adj.* teachail, a bhuineas do'n tigh ; dìomhair, uaigneach ; soirbh, callaichte.

domestic, *s.* fear-muinntir, searbhant, bean-muinntiris.

domesticate, *v. a.* cùm aig an tigh, callaich.

domicile, *s.* dachaidh, àros, fàrdoch, tigh, astail, còmhnaidh.

dominate, *v. a.* riaghail, ceannsaich, cùm fo smachd.

domination, *s.* cumhachd, uachdranachd ; aintighearnas, ceannsalachd, cruaidhsmachd.

domineer, *v.* riaghail, sàraich ; bi aintighearnail.

dominical, *adj.* sàbaideach ; a bhuineas do'n phaidir.

dominion, *s.* uachdranachd, àrd-cheannas; cumhachd, ùghdarras ; iompaireachd, rìoghachd ; lamh-an-uachdar.

don, *s.* duin'-uasal Spàinteach.

donation, *s.* tabhartas, tiodhlac, deaghghean.

donative, *s.* tabhartas, déirc.

done, *part. pass.* of the verb to do, dèanta.

donor, *s.* tabhartaiche, tabhartach.

doom, *v. a.* thoir a mach binn, dìt, thoir breith air ; òrduich, àithn, sònraich, rùnaich.

doom, *s.* breitheanas, binn ; dìteadh ; òrduchadh, crannchur, dàn ; milleadh, sgrìos ; breithneachadh.

doomsday, *s.* latha-luain.

doomsday-book, *s.* an leabhar-dubh.

door, *s.* dorus, còmhla.

doorpost, *s.* ursainn.

dormant, *adj.* cadaltach ; dìomhair, os ìosal, falaichte.

dormitory, *s.* seòmar-cadail.

dormouse, *s.* an dall-luch.

dorn, *s.* dronnag, seòrsa éisg.

dose, *s.* tomhas cungaidh leigis ; balgam searbh ; làn-broinne.

dot, *s.* pong, punc, dùradan.

dot, *v. a.* comharraich, puncaich, dèan puncan.

dotage, *s.* breitheal, breisleach, leanabas, sean aois.

dotard, doter, *s.* leannanach ro ghaolach, seann duine leanabail.

dote, *v. n.* bi 'na d' bhreitheal ; bi an trom-ghaol ; beachdaich air le gràdh.

dotterel, *s.* an t-amadan-mòintich.

double, *adj.* dùbailte, dà-fhillte ; a dhà uibhir ; fealltach, carach, cealgach.

double, *v. a.* dùblaich, cuir dà-fhìllte ; dèan uibhir eile ; bi dùbailte, fàs uibhir eile ; bi carach.

double, *s.* dùbladh, dùblachadh, uibhir eile ; car, cleas ; leth-bhreac.

double-dealer, *s.* cluaintear, cealgair.

doublet, *s.* peiteag, siostacota.

double-tongued, *adj.* cealgach.

doubt, *v. a.* cuir an teagamh, cuir an amharus, cuir an umhail, na h-earb as ; bi'n ioma-chomhairle, bi 'n ioma-cheist.

doubt, *s.* teagamh, ioma-chomhairle, iomacheist ; neo-chinnteachd ; an-amharus, an-earbsa.

doubtful, *adj.* teagmhach, mi-chinnteach, neo-shoilleir; amharasach, an-earbsach, sgàthach.

doubtfulness, *s.* teagamh, mì-chinnteachd doilleireachd ; tuiteamas.

doubtless, *adj.* cinnteach, gun teagamh, gun amharus.

doubtless, *adv.* gu cinnteach, gun teagamh, gun cheist, gun amharus.

dough, *s.* taois.

doughty, *adj.* gaisgeil, euchdail, flathail, calma, smiorail, curanta.

doughy, *adj.* taoiseach, plamacaidh.

douse, *v. n.* tùm, thoir leagadh do.

dove, *s.* calaman.

dovecot, dovehouse, *s.* tùcaid, tighchalaman.

dovetail, *s.* amladh, fiaclachadh.

dowager, *s.* banntrach righ, no diùc.

dowdy, *s.* sgumrag, sgliughaisg, sgliùrach.

dowdy, *adj.* sgumragach, slaopach, sgleòideach, sgliuisgeach.

dower, dowry, *s.* tochradh ; cuibhrionn banntraich (an òighreachd a fìr).

dowerless, *adj.* gun tochradh.

dowlas, *s.* tùlainn, anart asgairt.

down, *s.* réidhleach, clòimh-itean, mìnchlòimh, clòimhteach.

down, *prep.* sìos, le bruthach.

downcast, *adj.* airtnealach, trom, smuaireanach, dubhach.

downfall, *s.* tuiteam, leagadh, ìsleachadh ; sgrios.

downhill, *s.* leathad, leacann.

downright, *adj.* soilleir, fosgailte, saor, dìreach ; calg-dhìreach, treidhireach, neo-chealgach ; follaiseach ; **downright fool**, dearg amadan ; **downright lie**, an tula bhreug ; **downright scoundrel**, fìor thrustar.

downright, *adv.* gu buileach, gun stad ; gu soilleir, gu neo-chealgach.

downward, downwards, *adv.* a nuas, sìos, le bruthach.

downward, *adj.* a' dol le bruthach, a' téarnadh, a' cromadh ; smuaireanach, muladach.

downy, *adj.* clòimheach, tairis ; bog, mìn, maoth, plòiteach.

dowry, *n.* tochradh, buadhan ; tàlantan.

doxy, *s.* strìopach ; aigeannach.

doze, *v. n.* clò-chaidil.

dozen, *s.* dusan. a dhà-dheug.

dozy, *adj.* cadalach ; lunndach.

drab, *s.* garbh-chlò ; siùrsach, strìopach, strapaid ; mosag, caile bhreun.

drachm, *s.* seann chùinneadh Greugach ; an t-ochdamh cuid de unnsa.

draff, *s.* treasg, dràbhag, cnàmhag.

draft, *s.* òrdugh air banc, tarruing airgid, buidheann shaighdeirean.

drag, *v. a.* slaoid, tarruing, spìon.

drag, *s.* lion-tarruing, tarruing ; greimiche ; càrn-slaoid.

draggle, *v. a.* luidir, salaich, slaod tre 'n pholl.

dragnet, *s.* lion-sgrìobaidh.

dragon, *s.* dràgon, nathair-sgiathach.

dragon-fly, *s.* tarbh-nathrach, damhan nathrach.

dragoon, *s.* saighdear eachraidh.

drain, *v. a.* traogh, tarruing, tiormaich, sìolaidh.

drain, *s.* guitear, clais.

drake, *s.* dràc, ràc, ràcaire.

dram, *s.* drama, dràm, drùbhag.

drama, *s.* dàn-chluiche, litreachas cleasachd.

dramatic, *adj.* cluicheach, a bhuineas do dhàn-chluiche.

dramatist, *s.* seòrsa bàird ; bàrd cleasachd.

draper, *s.* ceannaiche aodaich.

drapery, *s.* obair-aodaich ; aodaichean.

draught, *s.* tarruing ; srùbadh, deoch ; uiread 's a dh' òlas neach air aon anail, stallag.

draughts, *s.* tàileasg.

draw, *v. a.* tarruing, draogh, slaod ; spìon, spiod, spiol ; deoghail ; sìn, dean fada ; tàlaidh, meall ; crup ; dealbh.

drawbridge, *s.* drochaid-thogalach.

drawer, *s.* fear-tarruing.

drawing-room, *s.* seòmar suidhe, seòmar conaltraidh.

drawl, *v. n.* màirnealaich, labhair gu slaodach.

drawl, *s.* draoluinn, ràsan.

draw-well, *s.* tobar tharruing.

dray, *s.* cairt-leanna.

dread, *s.* eagal, oillt, geilt, gealtachd, fiamh ; cùis-eagail.

dread, *adj.* eagalach, oillteil.

dread, *v. n.* oilltich, criothnaich.

dreadful, *adj.* eagalach, uamhasach.

dreadless, *adj.* neo-eagalach, neo-sgàthach, gun fhiamh.

dream, *s.* aisling, bruadar ; breisleach.

dream, *v.* bruadair, faic aisling, aislingich ; smuainich gu faoin.

dreamer, *s.* bruadaraiche, aislingiche.

dreamless, *adj.* saor o bhruadaraibh.

drear, dreary, *adj.* muladach, brònach, tiamhaidh ; aonaranach, dorcha, déisinneach.

dreariness, *s.* uamharrachd, dubhachas, uaigneachd.

dredge, *s.* prac, lion-eisearan.

dredge, *v. a.* cuir fathadh, crathadh mine.

dreggy, *adj.* druaipeil, dràbhagach.

dregs, *s.* druaip, dràbhag, salchar ; grùid, grunnd ; fuigheall, sguabadh.

drench, *v. a.* fliuch, bogaich ; taisich ; drùidh ; sgùr, purgaidich.

drench, *s.* purgaideadh (beathaich).

dress, *v. a.* sgeadaich, còmhdaich, breaghaich, sgiamhaich, uidheamaich, ceartaich, deasaich ; gréidh.

dress, *s.* aodach, earradh, sgeadachadh, uidheam ; rìomhadh.

dresser, *s.* fear-sgeadachaidh ; aimridh.

dressing-room, *s.* seòmar-sgeadachaidh.

dribble, *v. n.* srid, sil, braon, fras ; boinnealaich.

drift, *s.* cathadh ; cùrsa, brìgh, ciall.

drift, *v. a.* iomain, cuir le gaoith ; cuir 'na chuithe.

drill, *v. a.* toll ; teagaisg arm.

drill, *s.* caochan ; tora, sniamhaire, gimileid ; teagasg-airm.

drink, *v.* òl, srùb, sùgh, gabh deoch.

drink, *s.* deoch.

drinkable, *adj.* a ghabhas òl.

drinker, *s.* misgear, pòitear.

drip, *v. n.* sil, sruth, snith.

drip, *s.* sileadh, braon, snithe.

dripping-pan, *s.* aghann-shilidh.

drive, *v.* greas, buail air adhairt ; iomain, fuadaich, saodaich, ruag ; cuir an éigin.

drivel, *v. a.* bi sileadh ronn.

drivel, *s.* ronn, sgleog, splangaid, staonag, smugaid.

driveller, *s.* ronnaire, sgleogaire, spliugaire ; amhlar.

driven, droven, *part.* fògairte, fuadaichte, air iomain.

driver, *s.* ceannaire, fear-greasaidh ; iomanaiche.

drizzle, *v.* braon, sil ; snith.

drizzly, *adj.* braonach, ciùrach.

drock, *s.* sgonnan.

droll, *s.* cleasaiche, duine àmhailt.

droll, *adj.* neònach, cleasach.

drollery, s. cleasachd, àbhachd, fearaschuideachd.
dromedary, s. dromadair, droman.
drone, s. seillein dìomhain ; leisgean, lunndaire, rongair ; torman, dos.
dronish, adj. lunndach, cadalach, diomhanach, rongach, slaodach.
droop, v. n. searg, crìon, crom, meath ; fàs lag, caith air falbh ; aom.
drop, s. boinne, braon, driog.
drop, v. a. sil, fras, braon, driog ; leig seachad, leig dhìot ; fras ; tuit.
droplet, s. braon, cùirnean, driog.
dropping, s. sileadh, snithe.
dropsical, adj. meudbhronnach.
dropsy, s. meud-bhronn.
dross, s. salchar miotailt; smùrach, dus, sprùilleach.
drossy, adj. salach, smùrach.
drought, drouth, s. tiormachd, tart, turadh ; pathadh.
droughty, adj. tioram, tartmhor ; pàiteach, teth.
drove, s. treud, greigh, dròbh.
drover, s. dròbhair.
drown, v. bàth ; tuilich ; bi air do bhàthadh.
drowsiness, s. trumadas, cadaltachd, tromsanaich ; lunndaireachd.
drowsy, adj. cadalach, tromsanach, tromcheannach.
drub, v. a. spuac, cnapaich, slacuinn.
drub, s. spuac, cnap, buille, dòrn.
drudge, v. n. dèan sìor-obair, oibrich gun tàmh ; dèan dubhobair, dèan obair thràilleil.
drudge, s. dubh-chosannach, tràill.
drudgery, s. dubh-chosnadh, tràillealachd, obair dhìblidh, saothair.
drug, s. cungaidh leighis; stuth-cadail.
drugget, s. drògaid.
druggist, s. fear-reic chùngaidhean.
druid, s. drùidh, draoidh, drubhaid.
druidical, adj. drùidheil.
druidism, s. drùidheachd.
drum, s. druma.
drummer, s. drumair.
drumstick, s. bioran-druma.
drunk, adj. air mhisg, misgeach.
drunkard, s. misgear, pòitear.
drunkenness, s. misg, pòitearachd.
dry, adj. tioram ; pàiteach, ìotmhor.
dry, v. tiormaich, siab o'n t-sùil ; seac.
dryness, s. tiormachd ; seacadh.
dry-nurse, s. banaltrum-thioram.
dub, v. a. dèan ridire, cuir an inbhe ridire ; thoir ainm, thoir far-ainm.
dub, s. buille, cnap, dòrn.
dubious, adj. neo-chinnteach, teagmhach, neo-shoilleir.
dubitable, adj. teagmhach.
ducal, adj. diùcail.
duchy, s. crìochan diùca.

duck, s. tunnag ; lach ; cromadh-cinn, facal tàlaidh.
duck, v. cuir fo'n uisge, tùm ; rach fo'n uisge ; crùb, cuir fodha.
ducking, s. tumadh ; bogadh.
ducking-stool, s. an stòl-dubh.
duck-legged, adj. clàr-chasach, spàgach, pliùtach, spògach.
duckling, s. isean tonnaig.
duct, s. seòladh ; slighe, pìob-ghiùlain.
ductile, adj. sùbailte, so-lùbadh, sotharruing, so-ghéillidh, maoth.
ductility, s. sùbailteachd, ciùineachd.
dudgeon, s. cuinnsear, biodag ; gruaim, dod, drochmheinn.
due, adj. fiachnaichte, dligheach, iomchuidh, cubhaidh ; dìreach, neomhearachdach.
due, adv. gu dìreach ; due north, còmhnard a tuath ; due west, cridhe na h-airde 'n iar.
due, s. còir, dlighe ; fiachan, càin, màl.
duel, s. còmhrag-dithis.
duellist, s. fear-còmhraig.
duenna, s. seann bhan-oide-foghluim.
duet, s. ceòl-dithis.
dug, s. sine.
duke, s. diùc.
dukedom, s. seilbh diùc.
dulcet, adj. milis, taitneach ; binn, fonnmhor ; ciatach ; tiamhaidh.
dulcify, dulcorate, v. a. mìlsich, dèan milis.
dulcimer, s. seòrsa inneil ciùil.
dull, adj. trom-inntinneach, smuaireanach ; baoghalta, neo-gheur, tromcheannach, pleòisgeach, maol - aigneach ; maol, tiugh ; plubach, luidseach, clodcheannach ; neo-chridheil.
dull, v. a. cuir 'na bhreislich, cuir tuairgneadh air ; maol ; dean trom-inntinneach, mì-mhisnich ; fàs trom-inntinneach.
dullard, s. burraidh, ùmaidh.
dullness, s. neo-thuisge, gloidhcealachd, pleòisgeachd, mì-ghèire ; truime, dùsal tromsanaich, cadaltachd ; moillead, màirnealachd, màidheanachd ; dorchacdh ; maoile.
duly, adv. gu h-iomchuidh, gu freagarrach, gu riaghailteach.
dumb, adj. balbh ; tosdach, sàmhach.
dumbness, s. balbhachd ; tosdachd.
dumpish, adj. trom-inntinneach, dubhach, smuaireanach.
dumps, s. airtneal, leann-dubh, tromsanaich ; tuirtealachd.
dun, adj. ciar, lachdunn, odhar ; duaichnidh, dorcha.
dun, v. a. tagair, tathainn, bodhair.
dun, s. fear-tagraidh fhiach.
dunce, s. ùmaidh, burraidh, maolchluasaich.

dung, s. inneir, buachar, mathachadh, todhar, aolach.
dung, v. a. mathaich, leasaich, inneirich, aolaich ; tothair.
dungeon, s. prìosan, toll-dubh.
dunghill, s. òtrach, dùnan, sitig, dùn-aolaich ; breunan.
dungy, adj. salach, breun, làn òtraich.
dupe, s. maoilean, fear socharach, blaigh-laoghain.
dupe, v. a. thoir an car á, meall, gabh brath air.
duplicate, s. dùblachadh.
duplication, s. dùblachadh ; filleadh.
duplicity, s. dùbailteachd, ceilg.
durability, s. maireannachd, buanas.
durable, adj. maireannach, buan.
durance, s. prìosanachadh, prìosan.
duration, s. maireannachd, buanas, fad ùine, no aimsir.
during, prep. ré.
durst, pret. of to dare, dàna.
dusk, adj. ciar, doilleir, dubharach.
dusk, s. doilleireachd, eadarra-sholus, feasgar, beul na h-oidhche ; duibhre.
duskish, dusky, adj. a leth-char dorcha, no ciar.

dust, s. dus, duslach, ùir, smùr, stùr ; ùir a' bhàis ; an uaigh ; corp duine mhairbh.
dust, v. a. sguab, cuir an stùr dheth ; crath stùr air.
dusty, adj. smùirneach, làn duslaich.
duteous, dutiful, adj. dleasdanach.
duty, s. dleasdanas, dlighe ; càin, cìs.
dwarf, s. duairc, troich, luspardan, luch-armann, fathanach.
dwarfish, adj. duaircceach, crìon, troich-eanta, fachanta, beag.
dwell, v. n. fuirich ; còmhnaich, tuinich, gabh tàmh ; lean air, fan.
dweller, s. fear-àiteachaidh, fear-còmh-naidh, tàmhaidh.
dwelling, s. tigh-còmhnaidh, dachaigh, fàrdach ; astail, ionad-còmhnaidh.
dwindle, v. n. beagaich, lùghdaich, crìon, searg, caith air falbh.
dying, part. bàsachadh ; dath.
dynasty, s. uachdaranachd ; slisnich rioghail.
dyscrasy, s. droch coimeasgadh fala.
dysentery, s. an sgaoilteach, a'ghearrach, an sgàird, an tinneas-gearrach.
dysury, s. éigin-fhuail, galar-fuail.

E

each, pron. gach, gach aon.
eager, adj. dian, dealasach, togarrach, miannach, bras ; dùrachdach.
eagerness, s. déine, miannachd, dùrachd, togairt ; braise, caise.
eagle, s. iolaire, fìr-eun ; a' bhratach Ròmanach.
eagle-eyed, adj. biorshuileach.
eagle-speed, s. luathas na h-iolaire.
eaglet, s. isean iolaire.
ear, s. cluas ; dias.
earl, s. iarla.
earldom, s. iarlachd, oighreachd iarla.
earless, adj. bodhar, maol.
earl-marshal, s. ard-mharasgal.
early, adj. moch, tràth, tràthail, moch-thrathach, madainneach.
earn, v. a. coisinn, buannaich.
earnest, adj. dùrachdach, dealasach, dian, dìchiollach ; suidhichte, leagte, togarr-ach ; cudthromach, àraidh.
earnest, s. earlas ; da-rìreadh.
earning, s. cosnadh, tuarasdal.
ear-ring, s. cluas-fhail.
earth, s. talamh, ùir, cruinne.
earthly, adj. talmhaidh.
earth-nut, s. braonan.
earthquake, s. crith-thalmhuinn.
earth - worm, s. cnuimh - thalmhuinn, neach truagh, dìblidh ; spiocaire.

earwig, s. fiolan, fiolar.
ease, s. fois, tàmh, socair, suaimhneas ; lasachadh, faothachadh.
ease, v. a. faothaich, lasaich, aotromaich, lùghdaich, thoir fois.
easeful, adj. sàmhach, socrach.
easement, s. cobhair, còmhnadh, furt-achd, fuasgladh, faothachadh.
easiness, s. furastachd ; soirbheachd, fois, tàmh, socair, suaimhneas.
east, s. ear, an airde 'n ear.
Easter, s. càisg, a' chàisg.
easterly, adj. and adv. an ear, o'n ear.
eastward, adv. o'n àird an ear, gus an àird an ear.
easy, adj. furasta ; soirbh, socrach, sàmhach, aig fois, foisneach, so-gheilleadh ; saor, fosgailte.
eat, v. ith ; caith ; cnàmh.
eatable, adj. a dh' fhaodar itheadh.
eaves, s. anainn, stìm tughaidh.
eavesdropper, s. fear-farchluaise.
ebb, s. tràghadh ; crìonadh, seargadh.
ebb, v. n. tràigh, traogh ; crìon.
ebon, ebony, s. fiodh cruaidh dubh.
ebriety, s. misg, misgearachd.
ebullition, s. goil.
eccentric, adj. mì-riaghailteach, neònach, seachranach, iomrallach.
eccentricity, s. neònachas.

ecclesiastic, s. sagart, pears-eaglais.
ecclesiastic, adj. eaglaiseil.
echo, s. mac-talla ; ath-ghairm.
eclaircissement, s. soilleireachadh.
éclat, s. greadhnachas, glòir, urram, lùth-ghàir.
eclectic, s. roghainneachadh.
eclipse, s. ball-dubh ; dubhar, sgàile.
ecliptic, s. grian-chrios.
eclogue, s. òran buachailleachd.
economical, adj. gléidhteach, caontach, cùramach, grùndail.
economise, v. a. gléidh, cuir gu deagh bhuil, steòrnaich.
economist, s. fear caomhnach, fear crionna, fear-gléidhteach.
economy, s. banas-taighe, steòrnadh, dòighealachd, deagh-riaghladh teaghlaich ; caontachd, gléidhteachd ; dòigh, rian, seòl.
ecstasy, s. mor-ghàirdeachas, àrd-éibhneas, subhachas.
ecstatic, adj. làn aoibhneis, ro aoibhneach, subhach, sòlasach.
edacious, adj. gionach, geòcach, lonach, glutach, glamach.
edacity, s. glàmhaireachd, geòcaireachd, craosaireachd.
eddy, s. sruth, caochan, caileach an t-sruth.
edentated, adj. cabach, gun fhiaclan.
edge, s. faobhar ; roinn ; oir, bile.
edgeless, adj. maol, gun fhaobhar.
edge-tool, s. faobhar-gearraidh.
edgewise, adv. air oir.
edging, s. oir, fàitheam ; stìm.
edict, s. reachd, òrdugh follaiseach.
edification, s. togail suas, oileanachadh ; teagasg, ionnsachadh, fòghlum.
edifice, s. aitreabh, togail, tigh, àros.
edify, v. a. teagaisg, ionnsaich.
edit, v. a. deasaich air son clò-bhualaidh.
edition, s. clò-bhualadh, cur a mach.
editor, s. fear-deasachaidh, etc., leabhair air son clò-bhualaidh.
educate, v. a. fòghluim, ionnsaich, teagaisg, tog suas.
education, s. fòghlum, ionnsachadh, teagasg, sgoil.
eduction, s. foillseachadh, foghlum.
eek, v. a. cuir ri, meudaich, riaghail, sìn a mach (nì tha gann).
eel, s. easgann.
effable, adj. so chur an céill, so-nochdadh, so-innseadh.
efface, v. a. dubh a mach, mill, duaichnich, cuir mì-dhreach air.
effect, s. éifeachd, buaidh, buil, toradh, crìoch, gnìomh ; co-dhùnadh, deireadh.
effect, v. a. coimhlion, thoir gu crìch ; dèan ; cuir an gnìomh.
effective, adj. foghainteach, buadhach, comasach.

effectively, adv. gu cumhachdach, le éifeachd, gu buadhach.
effectless, adj. neo-eifeachdach.
effectual, adj. eifeachdach.
effectuate, v. a. coimhlion.
effeminacy, s. meatachd, buige, neo-smioralachd ; sòghalachd, macnus.
effeminate, adj. meata, bog, meathchridheach ; macnusach, sòghmhor.
effervescence, s. goil, builgeadh beirme.
efficacious, adj. éifeachdach, buadhach, comasach, foghainteach.
efficacy, s. comas, cumhachd, neart, buaidh, éifeachd.
efficient, adj. éifeachdach, tarbhach, comasach, diongmhalta, treun, foghainteach, buadhach.
effigy, s. ìomhaigh, dealbh, cruth.
efflorescence, s. blàth, teachd fo bhlàth, bristeadh a mach (air pòr).
efflorescent, adj. a' teachd fo bhlàth.
effluence, s. sruthadh.
effluent, adj. a' sruthadh, a' teachd o —.
effluvia, s. tòchd.
effluxion, s. sruthadh, sileadh.
effort, s. ionnsaigh, deuchainn, oidhirp.
effrontery, s. bathaiseachd, ladarnas, dalmachd, mì-nàire.
effulgence, s. dearrsadh, boillsgeadh, lannaireachd, soillseachd.
effulgent, adj. dearrsach, boillsgeach, dealrach, soillseach.
effuse, v. a. dòirt, taom.
effusion, s. dòrtadh, taomadh, taosgadh, cur thairis ; ana-caitheamh ; toirbheartachd, buileachadh, tuil chòmhraidh.
egg, s. ugh.
eglantine, s. preas nan ròs.
egotism, s. féin-iomradh, féin-mholadh, bòstadh, an duine mi fhìn.
egotist, s. fear-féin-mholaidh.
egotistical, adj. féin-mholtach.
egregious, adj. comharraichte, sònraichte, ainmeil ; ana-cuimseach.
egregiously, adv. gu h-ana-cuimseach.
egress, egression, s. dol a mach, triall, imeachd, siubhal.
eight, s. ochd.
eighteen, num. adj. ochd-deug.
eighth, adj. ochdamh.
eighthly, adv. anns an ochdamh àite.
eightscore, num. adj. ochd fichead.
eighty, num. adj. ceithir fichead.
either, pron. an dara h-aon, an darna fear, aon air bith dhiù.
ejaculate, v. a. cuir a mach, tilg.
ejaculation, s. guidhe, achanaich.
ejaculatory, adj. bris a mach le cabhaig, mar ùrnaigh ghoirid ; cabhagach, ealamh.
eject, v. a. tilg a mach, cuir a mach ; fògair, dìobair, cuir air falbh.

ejection, *s.* cur a mach, fògradh, fuadach.

ejectment, *s.* bàirligeadh, bàirlinn ; fògradh, cur air falbh.

ejulation, *s.* cumha, no tuireadh, langanaich ; ulartaich ; caoineadh.

eke, or eek, *v. a.* meudaich, leasaich, cuir ri ; lìon, dèan suas.

elaborate, *adj.* saoithreachail, le cùram ; le cuimrigeadh ; *v.* gabh saoithair ri —.

elaborately, *adv.* le mór-shaothair.

elapse, *v. n.* rach seachad, rach thart, ruith air falbh (tìm).

elastic, *adj.* sùbailte, a shìneas a mach ; lùbach.

elasticity, *s.* sùbailteachd, lùbachd.

elate, *adj.* uaibhreach, àrdanach, air a thogail suas, stràiceil.

elate, *v. a.* tog suas, dèan uaibhreach, dèan stràiceil.

elation, *s.* uaibhreachd, móralachd, àilleas, uaill, àrdan, stràic.

elbow, *s.* uileann ; oisinn, luib.

elder, *adj.* as sine, as aosmhoire.

elder, alder, *s.* craobh fhearna.

elderly, *adj.* sean, aosmhor.

elders, *s.* seann daoine, seanairean, athraichean ; foirfich.

eldership, *s.* seanaireachd, urram na h-aoise ; dreuchd foirfich.

eldest, *adj.* as sine, as aosda.

elecampane, *s.* aillean, searbh lus.

elect, *v. a.* roghnaich, tagh ; roimhthagh, roimh-òrduich.

elect, elected, *part.* taghte, roghnaichte ; roimh-òrduichte, air a roimh-thaghadh.

election, *s.* taghadh, roghnachadh, sònrachadh ; roghainn ; roimh-thaghadh, roimh-shònrachadh ; taghadh fir àird-chomhairle.

elective, *adj.* roghainneach, roghnach, taghach.

elector, *s.* taghadair ; prionnsa aig a bheil facal ann an taghadh iompaire na Gearmailte.

electoral, *adj.* aig a bheil urram fir taghaidh.

electorate, *s.* oighreachd taghadair ; luchd-taghaidh (buill Parlamaid).

electrical, *adj.* le gné dealanaich.

electricity, *s.* gné dealanaich.

eleemosynary, *adj.* déirceach.

elegance, *s.* grinneas, eireachdas, maise, ciatachd, maisealachd, bòidhchead, dreach, àile.

elegant, *adj.* eireachdail, maiseach, grinn, fìnealta, ciatach, àillidh.

elegiac, *adj.* marbhrannach, cianail, marbhnach, cumhach.

elegy, *s.* marbhrann, cumha, tuireadh ; dàn bròin.

element, *s.* ceud-aobhar ; dùil-thionnsgnaidh ; dùil ; na ceithir dùilean, 's iad sin, talamh, gaoth, teine 's uisge,

dòigh ; he is in his element, tha e air a dhòigh.

elemental, elementary, *adj.* dùileach, dùileachail, prìomh, neo-mheasgte.

elephant, *s.* elephant, elebhean ; boir.

elephantine, *adj.* a bhuineas do elephant.

elevate, elevated, *part.* ardaichte.

elevate, *v. a.* tog suas, àrdaich, tog an inbhe, urramaich, séid suas, dèan uaibhreach.

elevation, *s.* àirde, togail suas ; àrdachadh, urramachadh, cur an onoir.

eleven, *adj.* a h-aon-deug.

elf, *s.* sìthiche, duine-sìth, tàcharan, màileachan ; droch spiorad ; gàrlaoch, sìochaire, luspardan.

elicit, *v. a.* thoir a mach, tarruing a mach.

eligible, *adj.* airidh air roghainn.

eliminate, *v. n.* cuir a mach, sgar, fasgainn.

elimination, *s.* fògradh, tilgeadh air falbh.

elision, *s.* gearradh, sgathadh dheth ; eadar-sgaradh, dealachadh.

elixir, *s.* cungaidh-leighis, ìoc-shlaint.

elk, *s.* lon, làn-damh, seòrsa féidh.

ell, *s.* an t-slat-thomhais Albannach ; slat chùig cairteil.

elliptical, *adj.* air chumadh uibhe ; bèarnach an cainnt.

elm, *s.* leamhan.

elocution, *s.* ur-labhairt, deas-chainnt, briathrachas, uirghioll, labhairt.

eloge, elogy, eulogy, *s.* moladh.

elongate, *v. a.* fadaich, tarruing a mach, sìn a mach.

elongation, *s.* sìneadh a mach, fadachadh.

elope, *v. a.* ruith air falbh, teich, rach air fuadan.

elopement, *s.* teicheadh, ruith air falbh, fuadach, dol am fuadach.

eloquence, *s.* ùr-labhairt, deas-chainnt, snas-labhairt, fileantachd.

eloquent, *adj.* ùr-labhairteach, deas-chainnteach, fileanta.

else, *pron.* eile, aon eile.

elsewhere, *adv.* an ait' eile, an àit' eigin eile, an ionad eile.

elucidate, *v. a.* mìnich, dèan so-thuigsinn, soilleirich.

elucidation, *s.* mìneachadh, soilleireachadh.

elude, *v. a.* seachain, faigh as le car ; meall, teich, tàrr as, thoir car mu chnoc.

elusion, *s.* seachnadh, cleas.

elusive, elusory, *adj.* mealltach, carach, cleasach, cuilbheartach.

elvish, *adj.* baobhanta, siachaireil.

elysian, *adj.* mar Phàrras, ro-thaitneach, ro aoibhneach.

Elysium, *s.* Pàrras nan cinneach.

emaciate, *v.* searg, tuit as, fas tana.

emaciation, *s.* reangadh, caitheamh as, seargadh, tuiteam as le gort.

emanant, *adj.* a' sruthadh, a' sileadh o.

emanate, *v. a.* sruth, ruith, brùchd.

emanation, *s.* sruth, sileadh, ruith.

emancipate, *v. a.* fuasgail, saor, thoir saorsa bho chuing.

emancipation, *s.* fuasgladh, toirt o chuing, saorsa (thràillean).

emasculate, *v. a.* spoth ; lagaich, meataich.

embalm, *v. a.* spìosraich, lion le spìosradh, cuir spìosraidh air, gréidh.

embar, *v. a.* dùin a steach.

embargo, *s.* bacadh, grabadh-seòlaidh.

embark, *v.* cuir air bòrd, cuir air luing ; rach air bòrd ; gabh gnothach os làimh.

embarrass, *v. a.* àimhreitich ; cuir an imcheist, cuir fo thrioblaid.

embarrassment, *s.* imcheist, teinn, cuibhreach.

embassage, embassy, *s.* tosgaireachd.

embattle, *v. a.* cuir an òrdugh blàir.

embay, *v. a.* fliuch, nigh, dùin an geotha, druid an camus.

embellish, *v. a.* sgeadaich, maisich, sgiamhaich, breaghaich.

embellishment, *s.* sgèimh, sgeadachadh, breaghachd, rìomhadh.

embers, *s.* grìosach, beò-ghrìosach, eibhlean beò.

embezzle, *v. a.* goid ni a chaidh earbsadh riut ; cosg cuid neach eile.

embezzlement, *s.* goid, cumail cuid neach eile, mì-ghnàthachadh airgid-earbsa.

emblaze, emblazon, *v. a.* òraich, dèan lainnireach ; tarruing gearradh arm ; sgiamhaich le suaicheantas.

emblem, *s.* sàmhla, riochd, coltas, cruth-dhealbh, mac-samhail.

emblematic, emblematical, *adj.* samhlach.

emboss, *v. a.* gràbhal, breac, cnapaich, carbh ; dualaich, dùin a stigh.

embossment, *s.* breac-dhualachadh gràbhaladh, obair-ghréis.

embowel, *v. a.* thoir am mionach as.

embrace, *v. a.* iath 'n ad ghlacaibh, cniadaich, caidrich, pòg ; fàiltich.

embrace, *s.* iathadh an glacaibh, pòg, fàilteachadh, cniadachadh, caidreamh.

embrasure, *s.* barra-bhalla.

embrocate, *v. a.* suath le acainn leighis.

embrocation, *s.* suathadh le acainn leighis, acfhuinn.

embroider, *v. a.* gréis, cuir obair ghréis air.

embroiderer, *s.* gréiseadair.

embroidery, *s.* obair-ghréis.

embroil, *v. a.* àimhreitich, cuir thar a chéile, dèan mì-riaghailt ; cuir an imcheist, buair.

embryo, *s.* ceud-fhàs, torrachas anabaich.

emendation, *s.* leasachadh, càradh, ceartachadh, atharrachadh.

emerald, *s.* smàrag, clach uasal uaine.

emerge, *v. a.* éirich an àirde, thig an uachdar, thig as ; thig am fradharc.

emergency, *s.* éirigh an uachdar ; teachd am fradharc ; tubaist, càs, tachartas.

emergent, *adj.* ag éirigh, a' teachd am follais ; tuiteamach, tubaisteach, cruadalach.

emersion, *s.* éirigh, teachd am fradharc.

emery, *s.* clach-smior.

emetic, *s.* purgaid thilgidh.

emication, *s.* lainnir, dealradh.

emigrant, *s.* céin-thìreach, eilthireach, fear-imrich.

emigrate, *v. n.* dèan imrich gu tìr eile, fàg an dùthaich.

eminence, *s.* àirde, mullach ; mór-inbhe, meas, urram ; mórachd, àrd-onoir.

eminent, *adj.* àrd, mór, urramach ; measail, ainmeil ; sònraichte, comharraichte.

emissary, *s.* fear-brathaidh, teachdaire dìomhair ; fear cur a mach.

emission, *s.* leigeadh a mach, leigeadh fa-sgaoil.

emit, *v. a.* leig a mach, cuir uat.

emmet, *s.* seangan, sneaghan.

emollient, *adj.* tlàth, caomh, maoth, tairis, tlusail.

emollient, *s.* ìocshlaint-thlusail.

emolument, *s.* buannachd, tairbhe.

emotion, *s.* gluasad-inntinn.

empale, *v. a.* daingnich, iomadhruid, ceus, troimh-lot.

empannel, *v. a.* taghadh luchd-breith ann an cùirt.

empassion, *v. a.* cuir fo bhuaireas.

emperor, *s.* ìmpire.

emphasis, *s.* neart a' ghutha (air facal).

emphatic, emphatical, *adj.* làidir, neartmhor, brìoghmhor.

empire, *s.* ard-uachdaranachd, mór-chumhachd ; mór-rioghachd, ìmpire.

empiric, *s.* léigh gun eòlas.

empiric, empirical, *adj.* deuchainneach, teagmhach, a' toirt dheuchainnean ; a réir féin-fhiosrachadh.

emplastic, *adj.* ronnach, glaodhach, plàsdach, righinn.

employ, *v. a.* thoir obair, gnàthaich, cleachd.

employ, employment, *s.* gnothach, obair ; dreuchd, cèaird.

employer, *s.* fear toirt oibreacn, maighistir.

emporium, *s.* baile-margaidh.

empoverish, *v.* dèan bochd, dèan ainniseach.

empower, v. a. thoir comas, thoir ùghdarras ; dèan comasach.

empress, s. ban-ìmpire.

emprise, s. gabhail os-làimh chunnartach, dheacair.

emptiness, s. falamhachd, àite falamh ; aineolas.

empty, adj. falamh ; fàs.

empty, v. falmhaich, tráigh ; fàsaich, fàs falamh.

empurple, v. a. dèan dath purpur.

empuzzle, v. a. cuir an imcheist, cuir am breislich.

empyreal, adj. nèamhaidh, flòrghlan.

empyrean, s. nèamh nan nèamh, na flaitheas as àirde.

empyreum, empyreuma, s. bràthlosgadh.

emulate, v. a. dèan co-fharpais, dèan comh-strì, dean strì.

emulation, s. co-fharpais, strì, spàirn, co-dheuchainn; farmad, eud, còmhstri.

emulative, adj. co-fharpaiseach.

emulator, s. fear-co-fharpais, fearstrìthe.

emulous, adj. co-spàirneach, buaidh-dhéigheil.

enable, v. a. dèan comasach, thoir comas.

enact, v. a. òrduich, sònraich, reachdaich.

enacted, part. òrduichte, socraichte.

enamel, v. a. dealtraich ; bi dealtradh.

enamour, v. a. gràdhaich, cuir an gaol.

encage, v. a. cuir an cuing, cròidh.

encamp, v. campaich.

encampment, s. campachadh.

enchafe, v. a. feargaich, fraochaich, brosnaich.

enchain, v. a. ceangail air slabhraidh.

enchant, v. a. cuir fo gheasaibh ; dèan ro-shòlasach.

enchanter, s. geasadair, drùidh.

enchantment, s. drùidheachd ; àrd-shòlas, aoibhneas.

enchantress, s. bana-bhuidsich, banfhiosaiche ; té mhealladh gràidh, té ro mhaiseach.

enchase, v. a. comhdaich le òr, maisich.

encircle, v. a. cuartaich, iomadhruid.

enclose, v. a. dùin, cuartaich, iomadhruid.

enclosure, s. dùnadh, iathadh, ioma-dhruideadh ; àite dùinte.

encomium, s. moladh, cliù.

encompass, v. a. cuartaich, iadh.

encore, adv. a rithist, uair eile.

encounter, s. còmhrag ; cath ; dian-chòmhradh ; tachairt, coinneamh.

encounter, v. a. coinnich, thoir coinn-eamh, thoir ionnsaigh, thoir aghaidh air ; tachair an cath.

encourage, v. a. misnich, brosnaich, beothaich, thoir misneach, cuir misneach ann.

encouragement, s. misneach, brosnach-adh ; còmhnadh.

encroach, v. n. thig, no rach, thar crìch, gun fhios no gun chòir.

encroachment, s. gabhail gun chòir, tighinn a steach air coir fir eile.

encumber, v. a. luchdaich, grab, cuir trom air, bac, cuir éis air.

encumbrance, s. cudthrom, uallach.

encyclopedia, s. cuairt-fhòghluim, uile-fhòghlum, eòlas gach nì, leabhar 's a bheil eòlas air a' h-uile ni.

end, s. deireadh, crìoch, finid ; ceann, dùnadh, co-dhùnadh, foircheann, bàs.

endamage, v. a. ciùrr, dochainn.

endanger, v. a. cunnartaich, cuir an cunnart, cuir am baoghal.

endear, v. a. tàlaidh, tarruing spéis, dèan gràdhach.

endearment, s. gràdhmhorachd, bead-radh, gràdh, gaol, fàth-gaoil.

endeavour, s. ionnsaigh, deuchainn, dìchioll, spàirn, strì, oidhirp.

endeavour, v. thoir ionnsaigh, thoir deuchainn, dèan dìchioll, feuch ri.

endict, endicte, v. a. coirich, cuir as leth.

endictment, s. casaid ; cùis-dìtidh (aig cùirt).

endless, adj. neo - chrìochnach, gun cheann, maireannach, sìorruidh, bith-bhuan ; a ghnàth.

endorse, v. a. cùl-sgrìobh, cur aonta, rach an urras.

endorsement, s. cùl-sgrìobhadh, aideach-adh, teist.

endow, v. a. thoir tochradh, thoir seilbh, no saoibhreas.

endowment, s. saibhreas, beartas ; tìodh-lac airgid ; càil, tuigse, eòlas.

endue, v. a. builich, bàirig, tìodhlaic.

endurance, s. maireannachd, buantas ; foighidinn, fulang, giùlan le.

endure, v. fuiling, giùlain le ; mair, fuirich.

enemy, s. nàmh, nàmhaid, eascaraid, fear-fuatha, an diabhol.

energetic, adj. làidir, neartmhor ; gnìomhach, dèanadach, éifeachdach, tàbhachdach, dìorrais.

energy, s. neart, spionnadh, tàbhachd, feart, lùth.

enervate, enerve, v. a. lagaich, meataich.

enfeeble, v. a. lagaich, anmhannaich.

enfeoff, v. a. cuir an seilbh, gabh seilbh.

enfetter, v. a. cuibhrich, geimhlich.

enfilade, s. aisir dhìreach réith, ceann sreath.

enforce, v. neartaich, thoir spionnadh, spàrr, fòirn ; earalaich ; dearbh.

enforcement, s. co-éigneachadh, ain-deoin, éigin.

enfranchise, v. a. dèan 'na shaoranach, thoir còir taghaidh (fear Parlamaid).

enfranchisement, s. saorsa baile-margaidh, saoradh.

engage, *v.* gabh os láimh, geall, ceangail, freagair air son ; meall, tàlaidh, gabh muinntearas.

engagement, *s.* gabhail os làimh, gealladh, cùmhnant ; cath, còmhrag, blàr, còmhstrì.

engender, *v. a.* gin ; beir ; bi gintinn.

engine, *s.* inneal, uidheam, beairt.

engineer, *s.* fear cuimseachadh ghunnacha-mora an àm catha ; fear deanamh inneal.

engird, *v. a.* iomadhruid, crioslaich.

English, *adj.* Sasunnach.

englut, *v. a.* sluig suas, glut.

engorge, *v.* sluig, glàm.

engrapple, *v. n.* teann-ghlac, greimich, dèan còmhstri.

engrasp, *v. a.* teann-ghlac, greimich.

engrave, *v. a.* gràbhal ; gearr, snaidh.

engraver, *s.* gràbhalaiche.

engraving, *s.* gràbhaladh, gearradh.

engross, *v. a.* tiughaich, dèan domhail, dèan tomadach, meudaich, dèan reamhar ; glac chugad an t-iomlan ; dèan ath-sgrìobhadh garbh, sgrìobh an t-iomlan (an leabhar).

enhance, *v. a.* àrdaich, tog an luach ; cuir barrachd meas air ; meudaich.

enigma, *s.* tòimhseachan, cruaidhcheist.

enigmatical, *adj.* cruaidh - cheisteach, dorcha ; doirbh r'a thuigsinn.

enjoin, *v. a.* òrduich, earalaich.

enjoinment, *s.* òrduchadh, seòladh.

enjoy, *v. a.* meal, sealbhaich ; gabh tlachd ann ; bi sona.

enjoyment, *s.* toil-inntinn, mealtainn, sonas, suaimhneas.

enkindle, *v. a.* fadaidh, las, beothaich ; dùisg, brosnaich.

enlarge, *v.* meudaich, leudaich, cuir am farsuingeachd ; bi bith-bhriathrach.

enlargement, *s.* meudachd, meudachadh, farsuingeachd ; fuasgladh ; saoradh ; leudachadh.

enlighten, *v. a.* soillsich, soilleirich, thoir fradharc ; teagaisg, ionnsaich.

enlist, *v. a.* rach ri àireamh, gabh 's an arm, gabh 's an luing.

enliven, *v. a.* beothaich, misnich.

enmity, *s.* nàimhdeas, mì-run, gamhlas, fuath, falachd.

ennoble, *v.* uaislich, àrdaich, dèan urramach ; dèan ainmeil, dèan cliùiteach.

ennoblement, *s.* uaisleachadh, àrdachadh, togail an urram.

ennui, *s.* cianalas, airtneul, fadal, sgìos (inntinn).

enormity, *s.* uamhasachd, anabarrachd ; gràinealachd, déisinn.

enormous, *adj.* aingidh, déisinneach ; uabhasach, fuathasach.

enough, *adv.* gu leòir.

enrage, *v. a.* feargaich, fraochaich, cuir corraich air.

enrank, *v. a.* cuir an òrdugh.

enrapture, *v. a.* dèan ro-aoibhneach, dèan ro ait.

enrich, *v. a.* beartaich, dèan beartach, saibhrich ; mathaich, leasaich.

enrobe, *v. a.* sgeadaich, éid, còmhdaich.

enrol, *v. a.* sgrìobh sìos ainm an leabharainmean ; gabh (neach) air àirimh.

enrolment, *s.* ainm-chlàr.

ensanguine, *v. a.* dath le fuil.

enshrine, *v. a.* taisg gu cùramach, cuir an naomh-thasgadh.

ensign, *s.* bratach, meirghe, suaicheantas ; fear-brataich.

enslave, *v. a.* dèan 'na thràill, thoir gu tràilleachd, cuir fo dhaorsa.

enslavement, *s.* tràillealachd.

ensue, *v. a.* lean, thig an lorg, bi leanmhainn.

ensure, *v. a.* dèan cinnteach, cuir á cunnart, rach an urras.

entablature, entablement, *s.* barrabhalla.

entail, *v. a.* cuir fo chòir dhligheach, còir oighreachd (nach fhaodar a bhriseadh).

entail, *s.* suidheachadh, riaghailt, còir dhligheach air oighreachd, mar fhiachaibh (so no sud a dhèanamh, no ghiùlan).

entame, *v. a.* càllaich, dèan soirbh.

entangle, *v. a.* rib, cuir an sàs ; àimhreitich, cuir an imcheist.

entente cordiale, *s.* deagh nàbachd, còrdadh càirdeil (eadar rioghachdan).

enter, *v. a.* inntrinn, rach a steach ; tòisich gnothach.

enteric, *adj.* a bhuineas do 'n mhineach ; enteric fever, fiabhrus minich.

enterprise, *s.* ionnsaigh churanta, misneachd (ri aghaidh gairme).

entertain, *v. a.* thoir cuirm, dèan biatachd ; cum còmhradh ri ; rùnaich, thoir aoidheachd.

entertainment, *s.* cuirm, fleagh, aoidheachd, biadhtachd ; co-labhairt ; fearaschuideachd.

enthrone, *v. a.* cuir rìgh air a chathair ; àrdaich.

enthusiasm, *s.* blàthas - inntinn, eudmhorachd, cridhealachd.

enthusiast, *s.* fear dealasach ; duine eudmhor.

enthusiastic, *adj.* dealasach, dian, blàthaigneach, àrd-inntinneach ; baothchreideach.

entice, *v. a.* meall, tàlaidh, buair, thoir a thaobh.

enticement, *s.* mealladh, tàladh gu olc, buaireadh, culaidh-mheallaidh.

enticer, *s.* fear-tàlaidh, mealltair.

entire, *adj.* iomlan, coimhlionta, slàn, uile, làn ; neo-mheasgte ; neo-thru-aillte.

entirely, *adv.* gu léir.

entitle, *v. a.* thoir còir ; urramaich, thoir tiodal ; sgrìobh tiodal.

entity, *s.* beò-bhith, beò-dhùil.

entomb, *v. a.* adhlaic, tìodhlaic.

entrails, *s.* mionach, grealach, caolain.

entrance, *s.* leigeadh a steach, comas dol a steach ; dol a steach, slighe dhol a steach ; tòiseachadh ; gabhail seilbh.

entrance, *v. a.* rach am platha, cuir am paisean ; giulain an inntinn o nithibh faicsinneach.

entrap, *v. a.* rib, glac, cuir an sàs ; gabh cothrom air.

entreat, *v. a.* guidh, aslaich, grìos, iarr gu dùrachdach.

entreaty, *s.* guidhe, achanaich, iarrtas, aslachadh.

entrée, *s.* " dorus fosgailt " (do charaid), di-bheatha caraide (an uair as toigh leis tadhal).

entre nous, *Fr.* eadarainn fhìn.

entrust, *v.* earb (gnothuich) ri neach.

entry, *s.* dorus ; dol a steach ; gabhail seilbh, inntrinn ; sgrìobhadh, no cur sios an leabhar.

entwine, *v.* suain (le ròp no aodach).

enucleate, *v. a.* sgaoil, réitich.

enumerate, *v. a.* cunnt, àireamh.

enumeration, *s.* cunntas, àireamh.

enunciate, *v. a.* cuir an céill, innis, aithris, gairm, foillsich, fuaimnich gu glan, cothromach.

enunciation, *s.* aithris, nochdadh, cur an céill.

enunciative, *adj.* aithriseach.

envelop, *v. a.* paisg, còmhdaich ; falaich, cuartaich.

envelope, *s.* pasgadh, comhdach.

envenom, *v. a.* puinnseanaich ; truaill ; feargaich, cuir air bhoile.

enviable, *adj.* airidh air farmad, farmad-ach.

envious, *adj.* farmadach.

environ, *v. a.* cuartaich, iomadhruid.

environs, *s.* iomall, coimhearsnachd.

envoy, *s.* teachdaire rìgh gu rìgh eile.

envy, *v. a.* gabh farmad ri sonas neach eile.

envy, *s.* farmad ; tnù, mì-run, fuath, doilghios air son sonas neach eile.

epaulette, *s.* bathag-ghuailne oifigich.

ephemera, *s.* fiabhras nach mair ach aon latha ; cnuimh nach bi beò ach aon latha.

ephemeral, *adj.* neo-mhaireannach, diom-buain.

ephemeris, *s.* leabhar-latha.

ephemerist, *s.* speuradair.

epic, *s.* dàn mór, duan-eachdraidh

epicure, *s.* geòcaire, craosaire, glutaire, garbhbhronnach.

epicurean, *adj.* geòcach, sòghmhor, craos-ach, glutach.

epicurism, *s.* sògh, geòcaireachd, sàimh, ròic ; teagasg Epicuruis.

epidemic, epidemical, *adj.* gabhaltach, sgaoilteach, plàigheach.

epidermis, *s.* craicionn, an craicionn uachdrach.

epiglottis, *s.* claban an sgòrnain.

epigram, *s.* gearr-dhuanag.

epigrammatist, *s.* fear-facail, duanaire, bàrd-rann.

epilepsy, *s.* an tinneas tuiteamach.

epileptic, *adj.* tuiteamach.

epilogue, *s.* òraid-crìch cluiche.

Epiphany, *s.* féill an Taisbeanaidh.

episcopacy, *s.* easbuigeachd.

episcopal, *adj.* easbuigeach.

Episcopalian, *s.* fear do chreidimh an easbuig.

episode, *s.* sgeul am meadhon dàin, gearr-sgeul.

epistle, *s.* litir, teachdaireachd-dhiomhair.

epistolary, *adj.* a bhuineas do litrichibh.

epitaph, *s.* sgrìobhadh air leac-lighe.

epithalamium, *s.* beannachadh - bàird, òran pòsaidh, dàn bainnse.

epithet, *s.* facal-buaidh, foir-ainm.

epitome, *s.* giorradan, brìgh sgeòil.

epitomise, *v. a.* giorraich, coimhgheàrr.

epoch, epocha, *s.* àm o'n cunntar aimsir, àm ainmeil sam bith.

epulary, *adj.* fleadhach ; cuirmeach.

epulation, *s.* cuirm, fleadh, féisd, aighear, subhachas.

equability, *s.* co-ionannachd.

equable, *adj.* ionann, co-chothromach, dìreach, socrach (an inntinn).

equal, *adj.* ionann, co-ionann, coimeas ; comasach ; réidh, còmhnard ; dìreach, ceart, neo-chlaon-bhreitheach.

equal, *s.* coimpire, leth-bhreac, seise.

equal, equalise, *v. a.* coimeas, dèan ionann, dèan coltach.

equality, *s.* ionannachd, co-ionannachd, coimeas, còmhnardachd.

equanimity, *s.* socair-inntinn, fois.

equation, *s.* co-fhreagarrachd.

equator, *s.* cearcall meadhon na talmhainn.

equerry, *s.* fear coimhid each an rìgh.

equestrian, *s.* and *adj.* marcach, air muin eich.

equidistant, *adj.* fhad is fhad (àite), an aon fhad o gach aite.

equilateral, *adj.* an aon fhad 's gach taobh.

equilibrium, *s.* air mheidh, gun bhi null no nall, còmhnard.

equinoctial, *s.* là is oidhche an aon fhad.

equinoctial, *adj.* bhuineas do'n àm 's a bheil oidhche cho fada ris an là.

equip, *v. a.* deasaich, cuir an uidheam, ullamhaich, sgeadaich, beartaich.

equipage, *s.* carbad rìmheach 'na làn uidheam ; coisridh frithealadh ; acfhuinn, àirneis, fasair, acfhuinn agus sgiobadh.

equipment, *s.* deasachadh, uidheamachadh ; acfhuinn, airneis.

equipoise, *s.* co-chudthrom.

equiponderant, *adj.* co-chudthromach, co-chothromach.

equiponderate, *v. n.* co-chudthromaich.

equitable, *adj.* ceart, cothromach.

equity, *s.* ceartas, cothrom ; ceartbhreitheanas.

equivalent, *adj.* co-ionann, co-luachmhor, co-chudthromach.

equivocal, *adj.* teagmhach, dà-sheadhach, neo-chinnteach.

equivocate, *v. a.* dèan teagmhach, dèan dà-sheadhach, dèan cleith-inntinn.

equivocation, *s.* dubh-chainnt.

equivocator, *s.* fear dubh-chainnt.

era, *s.* linn, àm, aimsir.

eradiation, *s.* dèarsadh, deàlradh.

eradicate, *v. a.* spion á bun, spion as a riamhaichean.

eradication, *s.* spionadh á bun, sgrios.

erase, *v. a.* mill, sgrios ; dubh a mach.

erasement, *s.* dubhadh as, sgrios.

ere, *adv.* roimhe, mun, mu's.

erect, *v. a.* tog, tog dìreach ; àrdaich, cuir suas (togail, tigh).

erect, *adj.* dìreach, dìreach air bhonnan.

erection, *s.* éirigh, togail, seasamh.

erectness, *s.* dìrichead.

eremite, *s.* maol-ciaran, aonrach, fearcòmhnaidh am fàsach.

eremitical, *adj.* aonaranach, cianail, dubhach cràbhach.

erenow, *adv.* roimhe so.

erewhile, *adv.* a chianamh.

eringo, *s.* critheann-cladaich, seòrsa luibhe.

ermeline, ermine, *s.* seórsa neas.

erosion, *s.* cnàmhuinn, cnàmh as (le siantan).

err, *v. n.* rach air iomrall no air faontradh, rach air seachran, rach am mearachd.

errable, *adj.* mearachdach, seachranach.

errand, *s.* gnothach, teachdaireachd.

errant, *adj.* iomrallach, seachranach.

errata, *s.* mearachdan clò-bhualaidh.

erratic, *adj.* iomrallach, seachranach, neo-sheasmhach.

erring, *adj.* mearachdach, seachranach.

erroneous, *adj.* mearachdach, neoshuidhichte, iomrallach, faondrach ; neo-fhìor, neo-cheart, breugach.

error, *s.* mearachd ; iomrall, seachran, peacadh.

erst, *adv.* air thùs, roimhe so, uaireigin.

erubescence, *s.* deirge, ruthadh.

eructation, *s.* brùchd.

erudite, *adj.* foghluimte.

erudition, *s.* ionnsachadh, fòghlum.

eruginous, *adj.* méirgeach.

eruption, *s.* brùchdadh, bristeadh a mach ; broth.

eruptive, *adj.* a' bristeadh a mach ; brothach, guireanach.

erysipelas, *s.* an ruadh.

escalade, *s.* streapadh balla.

escape, *v. a.* teich, tàr as ; seachain.

escape, *s.* teicheadh, seachnadh, dol as o chunnart.

eschew, *v. a.* seachain, na gabh gnothach ri, teich uaithe.

escort, *s.* coimheadachd ; dìon, freiceadan.

esculent, *s.* (nì) as fhiach ithe.

escutcheon, *s.* sgiath-teaghlaich, suaicheantas brataich.

especial, *adj.* àraidh, sònraichte.

esplanade, *s.* àilean, liàna baile.

espousals, *s.* ceangal pòsaidh, còrdadh, réiteach pòsaidh.

espouse, *v. a.* dèan ceangal pòsaidh ; pòs ; dìon, teasairg.

espy, *v. a.* faic, beachdaich, comharraich ; gabh sealladh.

esquire, *s.* tiotal duin'uasail as ìsle na ridire.

essay, *v. a.* feuch, thoir ionnsaigh, thoir deuchainn, dèan oidhirp.

essay, *s.* deuchainn, feuchainn, oidhirp litreachais.

essayist, *s.* fear sgrìobhaidh òraidean.

essence, *s.* gnè, brìgh, sùgh, bladh.

essential, *adj.* feumail, nach gabh seachnadh, ro-àraidh, prìomh.

establish, *v. a.* suidhich, stéidhich, socraich, daingnich, leag, riaghailtich.

established, *part.* suidhichte, stéidhichte.

establishment, *s.* suidheachadh, socrachadh, stéidheachadh ; eaglais stàta ; seirbhisich tigh - mhóir ; teaghlach ; feachd is cabhlach ; tigh ceannachd.

estate, *s.* oighreachd, seilbh, fearann ; cor, inbhe.

esteem, *v. a.* meas, cuir luach air ; coimeas ; urramaich, meas luachmhor.

esteem, *s.* meas, urram, onoir, miadh.

estimable, *adj.* luachmhor, prìseil, miadhail ; measail, urramach.

estimableness, *s.* luachmhorachd, miadhalachd.

estimate, *v. a.* meas, cuir luach air.

estimate, *s.* cunntas, àireamh, meas ; prìseachadh.

estimation, *s.* meas, luachmhorachd, urram, onoir ; barail, breth.

estival, *adj.* sàmhrachail ; ni a bhuineas do'n t-sàmhradh.

estrange, *v. a.* cum air falbh, tarruing air falbh, dèan fuathach, dèan 'na choigreach.

estrangement, *s.* fad as, gluasad air falbh, eu-cordadh, ana-càirdeas.

estuary, *s.* beul aibhne, caolas, bàgh, camus, cuan.

etching, *s.* dealbh-sgrìobhaidh.

eternal, *adj.* bìthbhuan, suthainn, sìorruidh, maireannach ; neo-chrìochnach ; gun toiseach.

eternity, *s.* siorruidheachd, bithbhuantachd.

ether, *s.* àile fìor-ghlan, adhar fìnealta.

ethereal, *adj.* adharach, adharail; nèamhaidh, spioradail.

ethic, ethical, *adj.* modhannach, modhail beusach.

ethics, *s. pl.* modhannan, riaghailt nam modhannan, lagh nam beus.

ethnic, *adj.* pàganach.

etiquette, *s.* modh, modhalachd cainnt is giùlan.

etymological, *adj.* a bhuineas do shloinneadh fhacal.

etymology, *s.* eòlas air sinnsireachd bhriathran.

etymon, *s.* freumh-fhacal.

Eucharist, *s.* Comanachadh, Suipeir an Tighearna.

Eucharistical, *adj.* a bhuineas do'n chomanachadh.

eulogical, *adj.* moltach.

eulogise, *v. a.* mol, cliùthaich.

eulogy, *s.* moladh, cliù, òraid mholaidh.

eunuch, *s.* caillteanach, òlach.

euphony, *s.* binnfhuaim, binnead.

eurus, *s.* a' ghaoth an ear.

evacuate, *v. a.* falmhaich, dèan falamh, fàsaich ; fàg, falbh as.

evacuation, *s.* falmhachadh ; glanadh, purgaideachadh ; fàgail, falbh.

evade, *v. a.* seachain, faigh as, tàr as.

evanescence, *s.* diombuanachd, caochlaidheachd, faileas.

evangelical, *adj.* soisgeulach.

evangelsie, *v. a.* searmonaich an soisgeul.

evangelist, *s.* soisgeulaiche.

evaporate, *v. a.* cuir 'na smùid, cuir 'na cheò.

evaporation, *s.* dol 'na smùid ; tiormachadh.

evasion, *s.* leithsgeul, seachnadh ; car, cur seachad (leis na caran).

eve, even, *s.* feasgar, anamoch, àrdfheasgar, eadar-sholus, beul na h-oidhche ; trasg roimh latha féille.

even, *adj.* réidh, còmhnard, co-ionann, neo-chaochlaidheach, co-shìnte, dìreach, neo-chlaon ; ciùin, sèimh , de àireamh a ghabhas roinn gun chorr fhagail.

even, *adv.* eadhon.

even-handed, *adj.* ceart, dìreach, neochlaon-bhreitheach, cothromach.

evening, *s.* feasgar, beul na h-oidhche.

evenness, *s.* còmhnardachd, réidheachd, ionannachd, riaghailteachd ; seimheacnd, ciùine.

even-song, *s.* aoradh feasgair.

event, *s.* cùis, ni, tachartas, tuiteamas ; crìoch, buil, toradh.

eventful, *adj.* cudthromach, tùiteamach, a bheir iomadh nì mun cuairt.

even-tide, *s.* tràth-feasgair

ever, *adv.* aig àm sam bith, idir, riamh ; daonnan, gu bràth, an còmhnaidh, a chaoidh, gu sìorruidh.

evergreen, *s.* luibh no craobh shìor-uaine.

evergreen, *adj.* sìor-uaine.

everlasting, *adj.* sìorruidh, bithbhuan, maireannach.

everlasting, *s.* sìorruidheachd.

everliving, *adj.* neo-bhàsmhor.

evermore, *adv.* gu bràth, o so suas.

every, *adj.* gach, na h-uile, gach aon.

evict, *v. a.* cuir á seilbh, thoir uaith (le còir no le eucoir).

eviction, *s.* cur á seilbh.

evidence, *s.* dearbhachd, dearbhadh ; còmhdach, teisteas ; fianuis.

evident, *adj.* soilleir, dearbhte, cinnteach, follaiseach.

evil, *adj.* olc, dona, droch ; aingidh.

evil, evilness, *s.* olc, aingidheachd, do-bheirt dochann, cron, urchaid ; truaighe, call.

evil-minded, *adj.* droch-inntinneach.

evil-speaking, *s.* cùl-chàineadh, sgainneal, tuaileis.

evince, *v. a.* dearbh, dèan soilleir, còmhdaich, co-dhearbh.

evincible, *adj.* so-dhearbhadh.

evitable, *adj.* so-sheachnadh.

evocation, *s.* éigheach, glaodhaich.

evolation, *s.* itealaich, falbh air iteig.

evolution, *s.* fosgladh, fàs.

evolve, *v. a.* fuasgail, sgaoil, fàs.

evulsion, *s.* spìonadh á bun.

ewe, *s.* othaisg, caora.

ewer, *s.* soitheach air son uisge.

exacerbation, *s.* feargachadh.

exact, *adj.* ceart, dòigheil, pungail, riaghailteach ; freagarrach.

exact, *v. a.* iarr mar chòir, tagair ; àithn, earalaich.

exaction, *s.* iarraidh gu smachdail ; daor-chàin, trom-chìs.

exactness, *s.* pungalachd, dòighealachd, riaghailteachd, ceartas.

exaggerate, *v. a.* meudaich, cuir am meud, cuir ri, dèan na's mo na chòir.

exaggeration, *s.* meudachadh, dol thar fìrinn ; ràbhard.

exagitation, *s.* luasgadh, tulgadh.

exalt, *v. a.* àrdaich, tog an àird, tog gu h-urram ; tog suas.

exaltation, *s.* àrdachadh, togail an àirde ; éiridh gu h-urram ; àirde, urram, inbhe.

examination, *s.* ceasnachadh, rannsachadh, mion-sgrùdadh.

examine, *v. a.* ceasnaich, cuir ceistean, fidir ; rannsaich, sgrùd.

examiner, *s.* fear-sgrùdaidh.

example, *s.* samhla ; eisimpleir, ballsampuill.

exasperate, *v. a.* farranaich, feargaich, buair, brosnaich.

exasperation, *s.* brosnachadh, buaireadh, farranachadh.

excavate, *v. a.* cladhaich, tochail, bùraich.

exceed, *v.* theirig thairis air, thoir barrachd ; rach tuilleadh 's fada, rach thar tomhas.

exceeding, *adj.* anabarrach, ro-mhór.

excel, *v.* thoir barrachd, thoir barr, faigh buaidh, coisinn buaidh ; bi os cionn, bi na's cliùthaichte, bi na's ainmeile.

excellence, excellency, *s.* gasdachd, feothas, mathas ; àirde, àrdachd, mórachd ; òirdheirceas.

excellent, *adj.* òirdheirc, gasda, luachmhor, barrail, math.

except, *v.* fàg a mach, cuir air cùl, diùlt, ob, cuir an leth a muigh.

except, excepting, *prep.* ach, saor o ; mur, mur 'eil.

exception, *s.* cur an taobh a mach, fàgail a mach, diùltadh, obadh ; coire, cron.

exceptionable, *adj.* buailteach do choire.

excerpt, *s.* earrainn (á leabhar), rann, caibdil.

excess, *s.* anabharr, tuilleadh 'sa' chòir ; ana-measarrachd.

excessive, *adj.* anabarrach, fuathasach ; ana-measarra.

exchange, *v. a.* malartaich, iomlaidich.

exchange, *s.* iomlaid, malairt, suaip, cocheannachd ; mùthadh luach airgid rìoghachdan ; ionad-malairt.

exchequer, *s.* cùirt ionmhais a' chrùin ; Chancellor of the Exchequer, Ionmhasair rìoghachd.

excisable, *adj.* buailteach do chìs.

excise, *s.* cìs rìgh, cìs a leagar air cosnadh, no air buannachd, no air marsantachd.

exciseman, *s.* gàidsear, cìs-mhaor.

excision, *s.* gearradh as, sgrios.

excitation, *s.* gluasad, carachadh, brosnachadh, dùsgadh, buaireadh.

excite, *v. a.* dùisg, brosnaich, gluais, misnich.

excitement, *s.* culaidh-bhrosnachaidh.

exclaim, *v. n.* glaodh, éigh, gairm.

exclamation, *s.* glaodh, iolach.

exclamatory, *adj.* gairmeach, ard-ghuthach, labhrach.

exclude, *v. a.* dùin a mach, bac, toirmisg ; cùm air ais.

exclusion, *s.* dùnadh a mach ; diùltadh, bacadh, toirmeasg ; tilgeadh air falbh.

exclusive, *adj.* a' bacadh, a' dùnadh a mach, a' diùltadh, a' toirmeasg.

excogitate, *v.* breithnich, tionnsgain, cnuasaich, beachdaich ; smuaintich.

excogitation, *s.* beachd-smuainteachadh, tionnsgnadh.

excommunicate, *v. a.* cuir á comunn nan criosdaidhean, dèan iomsgaradh.

excommunication, *s.* ascaoin-eaglais, cur á comunn nan criosdaidhean.

excoriate, *v. a.* feann, rùisg, thoir an craicionn deth, faobhaich.

excoriation, *s.* rùsgadh, call craicinn ; creach, spùinneadh.

excrement, *s.* cac, aolach, inneir.

excrescence, *s.* meall, fluth, foinne, plugan.

excruciate, *v. a.* cràidh, pian, claoidh.

excruciation, *s.* cràdh, pian, dòruinn.

exculpate, *v. a.* saor, gabh a leithsgeul, fìreanaich.

excursion, *s.* cuairt, siubhal, sgrìob, turas, astar, falbh.

excursive, *adj.* turasach, falbhach, siùbhlach.

excusable, *adj.* leisgeulach, so-mhathadh.

excuse, *v. a.* gabh leisgeul, math.

excuse, *s.* leisgeul.

execrable, *adj.* fuathach, daochail, gràineil, oillteil ; mallaichte.

execrate, *v. a.* mallaich, guidh olc.

execration, *s.* mallachd, droch ghuidhe.

execute, *v.* dèan, cuir an gnìomh, coimhlion ; marbh.

execution, *s.* cur an gniomh, coimhlionadh ; cur gu bàs, crochadh.

executioner, *s.* crochadair.

executive, *adj.* gnìomhach, gnìomhchomasach, cumhachdach.

executor, *s.* fear-cùraim tiomnaidh, riaghladair tiomnaidh.

executrix, *s.* bean riaghlaidh tiomnaidh.

exemplar, *s.* eisimpleir, sampull.

exemplary, *adj.* eisimpleireach, cliùthoillteannach, deagh-bheusach.

exemplify, *v. a.* mìnich le cosamhlachd, dèan soilleir (le gnìomh).

exempt, *v. a.* saor, leig seachad.

exemption, *s.* saorsa, ceadachadh dol saor.

exercise, *s.* saothair, cleachdadh corporra, sràidimeachd, gluasad, falbh ; iomairt, gnàthachadh, gnìomh ; oileanachadh ; seirbhis an Tighearna.

exercise, *v.* oibrich, gnàthaich, cleachd, dèan, cùm ri saothair, cuir an gnìomh, cleachd saothair chorporra.

exert, *v. a.* feuch ri, dèan spàirn, dèan dìchioll, cuir chuige, saothraich, oibrich, thoir ionnsaigh.

exertion, *s.* ionnsaigh, deuchainn, dìchioll, spàirn.

exfoliate, *v. a.* sgrath, sgar.

exhalation, *s.* éirigh 'na smùid no 'na cheò ; ceò, grian-dheatach, ceathach.

exhaust, *v. a.* tràigh, tiormaich, falmhaich, taosg, thoir thairis, leig roimhe.

exhaustion, *s.* tràghadh, traoghadh, sgìos, dith lùiths.

exhaustless, *adj.* neo-thraoghach.

exhibit, *v. a.* nochd, taisbean, feuch, foillsich, leig ris.

exhibition, *s.* nochdadh, foillseachadh, taisbeanadh, leigeadh ris.

exhilarate, *v. a.* cuir aoibhneas air, dèan cridheil, dèan sunntach.

exhilaration, *s.* cridhealas, sunnt.

exhort, *v. a.* earalaich, comhairlich.

exhortation, *s.* comhairleachadh.

exhumation, *s.* togail as an uaigh.

exigence, exigency, *s.* feum, easbhuidh, dìth, uireasbhuidh ; cruaidhchas, teanntachd, éigin.

exigent, *adj.* éigineach, cruaidh, cruadalach.

exigent, *s.* eigin, teanntachd, cruaidhchàs.

exile, *s.* fògradh, fuadach ; fear-fuadain, fògarach, dìobarach.

exile, *v. a.* fògair, cuir as an tìr.

exist, *v. n.* bi, bi beò, bi làthair.

existence, existency, *s.* bith, beatha.

existent, *adj.* a ta beò, a làthair.

exit, *s.* falbh, triall, siubhal, caochladh.

exodus, *s.* turas á aite no tìr, imrich sluaigh.

exonerate, *v. a.* neo-lochdaich, saor, fìreanaich, glan o sgannail.

exoneration, *s.* eutromachadh, fìreanachadh, glanadh o sgannail.

exorbitance, *s.* ana-cuimse, uamharrachd, anabarrachd.

exorbitant, *adj.* ana-cuimseach, anabarrach, fuathasach, thar tomhas.

exorcise, *v. a.* fògair deamhan, fuadaich droch spiorad, cuir spiorad fo gheasaibh.

exorcist, *s.* fear chur spioradan fo gheasaibh, draoidh, geasadair.

exordium, *s.* roimh-ràdh, tùs-labhairt.

exotic, *adj.* coimheach, a bhuineas do dhùthaich eile.

expand, *v. a.* sgaoil, fosgail a mach ; meudaich, at, leudaich.

expanse, *s.* còmhnard mór, fosgladh farsuing, sìneadh ; an iarmailt.

expansion, *s.* sgaoileadh, fosgladh, sìneadh a mach ; farsuingeachd.

expansive, *adj.* sgaoilteach, so-shìneadh a mach.

expatiate, *v. n.* sìn a mach ; leudaich.

expatriate, *v. tr.* fògair, fuadaich.

expect, *v. a.* bitheadh dùil agad ; amhairc air son, feith.

expectancy, *s.* dùil, dòchas ; earbsa.

expectant, *adj.* dòchasach, an dùil.

expectation, *s.* dùil, dòchas.

expectorate, *v. a.* cuir a mach, casad, tilg smugaid.

expectoration, *s.* cur a mach le casad.

expedience, expediency, *s.* freagarrachd, iomchuidheachd, feumalachd, goireas.

expedient, *adj.* freagarrach, iomchuidh, cothromach, goireasach.

expedite, *v. a.* luathaich, cabhagaich.

expedition, *s.* luathas, cabhag, graide ; ionnsaigh, turas-cogaidh.

expeditious, *adj.* ullamh, ealamh, luath, grad, cabhagach.

expel, *v. a.* tilg a mach, cuir air falbh ; fògair, fuadaich ; cum uat.

expend, *v. a.* caith, cosg.

expense, *s.* cosgais, cur a mach airgid.

expensive, *adj.* cosgail, caithteach, struidheil ; daor, luachmhor.

expensiveness, *s.* cosgalachd, struidhealachd ; luachmhorachd.

experience, *s.* cleachdadh, deuchainn ; féin-fhiosrachadh, gnàth, eòlas, aithne, cleachdadh.

experience, *v. a.* aithnich, fairich, mothaich, faigh fios-faireachdainn ; gnàthaich.

experienced, *part.* gnàthaichte ri, cleachdte, gnàth-eòlach, eòlach.

experiment, *s.* deuchainn dhearbhaidh.

experimental, *adj.* féin-fhiosrachail, a réir dearbh-fhios.

expert, *adj.* ealanta, teòma, seòlta ; deas, ealamh.

expertness, *s.* seòltachd, teòmachd.

expiable, *adj.* so-dhìoladh, so-ìocadh.

expiate, *v. a.* ìoc, thoir éirig, thoir dìoladh air son coire.

expiation, *s.* dìoladh, ìocadh, ath-dhìoladh.

expiatory, *adj.* réiteachail, a ni dìoladh.

expiration, *s.* tarruing na h-analach, séideadh analach ; crìoch, ceann ; call an deò, bàsachadh.

expire, *v.* séid, analaich ; bàsaich, thoir suas an deò ; crìochnaich, thig gu crìch.

explain, *v. a.* dèan so-thuigsinn, soilleirich, foillsich.

explanation, *s.* mìneachadh, soilleireachadh, soillseachadh.

explanatory, *adj.* mìneachail.

explicable, *adj.* so-mhìneachadh.

explicate, *v. a.* fosgail, soilleirich.

explication, *s.* fosgladh, soilleireachadh, mìneachadh, fuasgladh, réiteachadh ; eadar-theangachadh.

explicit, *adj.* soilleir, so-thuigsinn, pung-ail.

explode, *v. a.* spreadh, tilg a mach le spreadhadh ; tilg a mach le tàir, cuir an neo-shuim.

exploit, *s.* euchd, treubhantas, mór-ghnìomh.

explore, *v. a.* feuch, rannsaich, sgrùd, sir, lorgaich.

explosion, *s.* spreadhadh, bragh.

export, *v. a.* cuir do thìr eile, reic (ri cuid an tìr eile), cuir (badhar) a mach as an dùthaich.

exportation, *s.* cur bathar thar muir.

expose, *v. a.* nochd, foillsich, leig ris, rùisg, taisbean ; dèan ball-magaidh dheth ; cuir an cunnart.

exposition, *s.* mìneachadh, soilleireach-adh ; suidheachadh, leigeil ris.

expositor, *s.* fear-mìneachaidh, eadar-theangair.

expostulate, *v. n.* reusonaich ; connsaich, cothaich, thoir achasan.

expostulation, *s.* reusonachadh, deasbair-eachd ; connsachadh, cothachadh ; casaid.

exposure, *s.* foillseachadh, leigeil ris, taisbeanadh ; gàbhadh, cunnart.

expound, *v. a.* mìnich, foillsich, dèan soilleir, leig ris.

expounder, *s.* fear-mineachaidh.

express, *v. a.* cuir an céill, innis, aithris ; nochd, foillsich, taisbean ; fàisg, brùth a mach.

express, *adj.* soilleir, pungail, follaiseach ; a dh' aon ghnothach ; a dh' aon obair.

express, *s.* teachdaire-cabhaig, teachd-aireachd-chabhaig.

expression, *s.* dòigh labhairt, aithris, cainnt ; fàsgadh.

expressive, *adj.* làn seadh, brìoghmhor, seadhach, làidir.

exprobate, *v. a.* cronaich, maslaich.

exprobation, *s.* cronachadh.

expulsion, *s.* fògradh, fuadach, cur a mach.

expulsive, *adj.* a dh' fhògras, a dh' fhuadaicheas.

expunge, *v. a.* dubh a mach, sgrìob as.

expurgation, *s.* glanadh, sgùradh, ionnlad.

expurge, *v. a.* glan, ionnlaid.

exquisite, *adj.* gasda, taghte, òirdheirc, grinn, coimhlionta ; ro mhothachail.

exquisiteness, *s.* òirdheirceas, grinneas, sgiultachd.

extant, *adj.* maireann, follaiseach, a làthair ; beò.

extemporaneous, extemporary, *adj.* bharr làimhe, gun ullachadh.

extempore, *adv.* gun ullachadh roimh làimh.

extemporise, *v. n.* labhair gun ullachadh.

extend, *v. a.* sìn, sgaoil ; leudaich, meudaich, farsuingich ; bàirig, com-pàirtich ; ruig air.

extension, *s.* sìneadh, ruigheachd, sgaoil-eadh, farsuingeachd, leud, meud.

extensive, *adj.* farsuing, leathann, mór.

extensiveness, *s.* farsuingeachd, meud, leud.

extent, *s.* farsuingeachd, meud, leud, fad, dòmhladas.

extenuate, *v. a.* lùghdaich, beagaich, tanaich ; gabh leisgeul, aotromaich coire.

extenuation, *s.* lùghdachadh, beagachadh, gabhail leisgeil ; aotromachadh ; tan-achadh, caolachadh.

exterior, *adj.* air an taobh muigh.

exterminate, *v. a.* spìon á fhreumhaibh, dìthich, sgrios ; thoir as a bhun, fògair.

extermination, *s.* sgrios, milleadh, léir-sgrios.

extern, external, *adj.* a muigh, air an taobh muigh.

externally, exteriorly, *adv.* a muigh, air an taobh muigh.

extinct, *adj.* crìochnaichte, nach 'eil a làthair ; marbh.

extinction, *s.* cur as, smàladh ; dol as, mùchadh ; milleadh, sgrios, fògradh.

extinguish, *v. a.* cuir as, mùch, smàl as ; mill, sgrios, caisg.

extinguisher, *s.* smàladair.

extirpate, *v. a.* spìon á bun, sgrios, dìthich.

extirpation, *s.* toirt á fhreumhaichean, spìonadh á bun, sgrios.

extol, *v. a.* ard-mhol, cliùthaich.

extort, *v. a.* dèan fòirneart, thoir air falbh le ainneart.

extortion, *s.* fòirneart, foir-éigneadh.

extortioner, *s.* fear foir-éignidh.

extract, *v. a.* tarruing á, thoir á:

extract, *s.* astarruing, brigh, sùgh.

extraction, *s.* astarruing ; sloinneadh, taruing a mach.

extradite, *v.* thoir seachad (ciontach).

extradition, *n.* toirt seachad (fear fo choill).

extraneous, *adj.* coimheach, nach buin do —.

extraordinary, *adj.* neo-ghnàthach ; neo-chumanta, sònraichte, àraid, ana-barrach, iongantach.

extravagance, extravagancy, *s.* ana-measarrachd, ana-caitheamh, struidh-ealachd ; mì-riaghailt, dol as an t-slighe ; buaireas.

extravagant, *adj.* strùidheil, ana-caith-teach ; mì-riaghailteach, ana-cuim-seach.

extreme, *adj.* anabarrach, ro-mhór, iom-allach, as faide muigh ; deireannach.

extreme, s. iomall, deireadh, ceann thall, crìoch.
extremity, s. ceann as faide mach, crìoch, iomall, oir; cruaidhchas, teinn, éigin.
extricate, v. a. saor, fuasgail.
extrication, s. saoradh, fuasgladh, toirt á amladh.
extrinsic, extrinsical, adj. air an leth a muigh, a bhuineas do ni eile.
extrinsically, adv. o 'n leth a muigh.
extrusion, s. tilgeadh a mach.
exuberance, s. cus, mór-phailteas.
exuberant, adj. pailt, làn, lìonmhor, tarbhach, a' cur thairis.
exudate, exude, v. n. cuir fallus dhiot.
exudation, s. fallus.
exulcerate, v. a. leannaich, eargnaich; bi 'g iongrachadh.
exult, v. n. dèan uaill, dèan aoibhneas, dèan gàirdeachas; dèan meoghail, bi ri aighear.
exultance, exultation, s. uaill, gàirdeachas, aoibhneas, subhachas, aighear, meoghail.
exundate, v. a. cuir thairis.
exundation, s. ro-phailteas, làn.

exuperable, adj. so-cheannsachadh.
exuscitate, v. a. èirich, dùisg, tog suas.
exustion, s. losgadh, cnàmh, caitheamh as le teìne.
eyas, s. isean seabhaic.
eye, s. sùil; crò (snàthaid).
eye, v. a. beachdaich, faic, seall, cum sùil air, dearc, amhairc.
eyeball, s. ubhall na sùla, clach na sùla.
eyebright, s. lus-nan-leac.
eyebrow, s. mala.
eyelash, s. fabhradh, rasg.
eyeless, adj. gun sùilean.
eyelet, s. toll-fradhairc, dul, drol.
eyelid, s. rosg, rasg.
eyesalve, s. sàbh-shùl.
eyesight, s. sealladh, fradharc, léirsinn, léirsinn-shùl.
eyesore, s. culaidh-ghràin, culaidh-mhì-thlachd, cuis-dhéisinn.
eyetooth, s. fiacaill-chrìche.
eyewitness, s. fianuis-shùl.
eyre, s. mòd ceartais.
eyry, s. nead iolaire, -fithich, -seabhaic, no nead eun-feòil-itheach sam bith eile.

F

fable, s. spleagh, uirsgeul, sgeulachd.
fable, v. innis breugan, innis sgeulachd, labhair faoin-sgeul spleaghach.
fabled, part. iomraiteach an uirsgeulan, ainmeil an sgeul.
fabric, s. togail, aitreabh, tigh.
fabricate, v. a. tog, dealbh, co-thog.
fabulist, s. spleaghaire, sgeulaiche.
fabulous, adj. spleaghach, uirsgeulach, faoinsgeulach, breugach.
face, s. aghaidh, gnùis, aodann tuar, aogas; uachdar, beulaibh; dreach.
face, v. a. cuir aghaidh ri, thoir aghaidh air, tachair, coinnich; seas mu choinneamh; tionndaidh t' aghaidh mun cuairt.
facetious, adj. cridheil, sunntach, àbhachdach, sùgach, suigeartach, ait.
facile, adj. furasda, soirbh, so-dhèanamh, ciùin, fòil.
facilitate, v. a. dèan furasta, dèan soirbh, dèan réidh, réitich.
facility, s. furastachd, ullamhachd, teòm-achd; sùbailteachd, géilleachdainn, socharachd.
facing, s. lìnig, aghaidh, còmhdach.
facinorous, adj. aingidh, olc, dona.
fact, s. gnìomh, gnothach, beart, tùrn; firinn.
faction, s. luchd-tuairgnidh; àimhreit, tuairgneadh, eas-aonachd.

factious, adj. àimhreiteach, buaireasach, easaontach, ceannaireceach.
factor, s. siamarlan, bàilidh.
factory, s. tigh-dhèantaichean, ionad luchd gnothaich; tigh-cèirde.
factotum, s. gille-gach-gnothaich.
faculty, s. comas, cumhachd; càil, buaidh-inntinn; seòltachd, dòigh; comunn luchd-teagaisg àrd-sgoile.
facundity, s. fileantachd.
fade, v. caith, seac; teich á sealladh; caill dath; searg, crìon, meath.
fading, s. crìonadh, seargadh, seacadh, caitheamh as.
fæces, s. òtrach, anabas, aolach, dràbhag.
fag, v. n. fàs sgìth, fannaich.
fag, fag-end, s. ceànn-aodaich, fuigheall, deireadh.
fagot, s. cual chonnaidh, fiodh fadaidh, etc.
fail, v. tréig, dìobair, fàg; fàillingich, bi an easbhuidh; teirig, rach as, sguir; fannaich, fàs lag; thig gearr air.
failing, s. fàilling, fàillneachadh; seargadh, seacadh; uireasbhuidh, tuisleadh, coire.
failure, s. easbhuidh, uireasbhuidh; tuisleadh, coire, fàilling.
fain, adj. sòlasach, sunntach, deònach, toileach, an geall.

fain, *adv.* gu toileach, gu deònach, le làn toil.

faint, *v.* fannaich, rach am paisean, fàs lag, fàs fann, caill do spionnadh, bi fo dhiobhail-misnich.

faint, *adj.* lag, fann, anfhann ; neoshoilleir ; breòite, gun chlì, gealtach, meat, tais, fo dhiobhail-misnich ; neosmiorail, neo-sgairteil, doilleir.

faint-hearted, *adj.* lag-chridheach, gealtach, tais, meat, cladharra.

fainting, *s.* fannachadh, paisean, neul, laigse, tiom-tàisean.

faintish, *adj.* fann, a' fàs fann.

faintness, *s.* laigse, laigsinn, anfhannachd ; neo-smioralachd, marbhantachd ; lag-chridheachd, doilleireachd.

fair, *adj.* maiseach, sgiamhach, bòidheach, àillidh ; geal, fionn ; taitneach, maiseach, ciatach, glan, soilleir ; ceart, cothromach, dìreach, sìobhalta, suairce.

fair, *s.* féill, margadh.

fair, *s.* maise, àille.

fairing, *s.* faidhrean.

fairness, *s.* maise, maisealachd, bòidhchead, àilleachd ; ceartas, onoir, ionracas, treidhireachd ; soilleireachd.

fairy, *s.* sìthiche ; bean-sìth.

fairy, *adj.* a bhuineas do shìthichean.

faith, *s.* creideamh ; muinghinn, dòchas, earbsa ; creideas, barail ; dìlseachd ; onoir, fìrinn ; gealltanas, gealladh.

faithful, *adj.* creidmheach ; dìleas ; ionraic, treidhireach, onorach ; fìreanach, fìreanta.

faithfulness, *s.* treidhireachd, ionracas ; dìlseachd, seasmhachd.

faithless, *adj.* mi-chreidmheach ; mìdhìleas, mealltach, cealgach.

faithlessness, *s.* mì-dhìlseachd.

falchion, *s.* claidheamh crom.

falcon, *s.* seabhac seilge.

falconer, *s.* seabhacair, fear-ionnsachaidh sheabhac.

falconry, *s.* seabhacaireachd.

fall, *v. n.* tuit ; teirinn ; traogh, sìolaidh.

fall, *s.* tuiteam, leagadh, léir-sgrios ; tuiteam sìos, ìsleachadh ; tèarnadh cas, bruthach ; eas, steall.

fallacious, *adj.* mearachdach, mealltach, carach, cealgach.

fallacy, *s.* mealltachd, feallsachd, cealgachd.

fallible, *adj.* tuiteamach, buailteach do mhearachd, fàillingeach.

falling, *s.* tuiteam, peacadh.

falling-sickness, *s.* an tinneas-tuiteamach.

fallow, *adj.* dearg-shoilleir, buidheshoilleir ; talamh bàn, neo-threabhte.

fallow, *s.* treabhadh-sàmhraidh, eilgheadh.

false, *adj.* breugach, fallsa, neo-fhìor ; mearachdach ; meallta, mì-dhìleas.

falsehearted, *adj.* meallta, foilleil, cealgach.

falsehood, falsity, *s.* breug ; mealltaireachd, cealg.

falsify, *v.* dèan breugach, breugnaich, dearbh 'na bhréig ; àicheadh an fhìrinn.

falter, *v. n.* bi liotach, dèan gagail cainnte, bi manntach ; fàs sgìth.

faltering, *s.* teabadaich, laigse, teachd gearr.

fame, *s.* cliù, alla, ainm ; iomradh.

famed, *adj.* ainmeil, allail, cliùiteach, iomraiteach ; measail.

fameless, *adj.* neo-iomraiteach.

familiar, *adj.* aoidheil, saor, ceanalta, furanach, faoilidh ; càirdeil ; eòlach, coitcheann, tric.

familiar, *s.* fear eòlais, companach ; leannan-sìth.

familiarise, *v. a.* dèan eòlach, gnàthaich, cleachd.

familiarity, *s.* eòlas, còmpanas ; saorsa còmhraidh, càirdealachd.

family, *s.* teaghlach ; sliochd, àl, clann, gineal ; cinneadh, fine, dream.

famine, *s.* gort, airc, gainne.

famish, *v.* dol gu bàs le gort.

famous, *adj.* ainmeil, cliùiteach, measail, iomraiteach, sònraichte.

fan, *s.* gaotharan, sgàileagan ; guit, fasgnag, dallanach.

fan, *v. a.* fuaraich, gluais an t-àileadh ; fasgain.

fanatic, *s.* neach air boile le baothchreideamh.

fanatic, fanatical, *adj.* boath-chreidmheach, saobh-chreideach.

fanaticism, *s.* baoth-chreideamh, saobhchreideamh.

fanciful, *adj.* mac-meanmnach, neònach, iongantach, saobh-smuainteach.

fancifulness, *s.* neònachas, iongantas, macmeamnainn.

fancy, *s.* mac-meamna, saobh-smuain ; barail, miann, déidh, tlachd.

fancy, *v.* smuainich, saoil, baralaich, beachdaich ; miannaich, gabh déidh ; bi 'n dùil.

fane, *s.* teampull, eaglais ; coileachgaoithe.

fanfaron, *s.* curaidh, gaisgeach.

fang, *s.* tosg, ionga, dubhan, pliut.

fanged, *adj.* tosgach, iongach, dubhanach, spògach, pliutach.

fangle, *s.* faoin ionnsaigh, faoin innleachd.

fantastic, fantastical, *adj.* mac-meamnach, iongantach, neo-sheasmhach, faoin, neònach, gòrach, gogaideach, guanach.

far, *adv.* fada, fada as, fada air falbh, an céin ; gu mór.
far, *adj.* fada, fada as.
farce, *s.* ealaidh, baoth chluich.
farcical, *adj.* àbhachdach, a bhuineas do chluich bhaoth.
farcy, *s.* galar each.
fare, *v. n.* ith, gabh lòn ; siubhail, imich, gabh turas ; tàrladh dhut, bi an cor.
fare, *s.* airgiod faraidh, dìoladh faraidh ; biadh, lòn, teachd-an-tìr.
farewell, *adj.* soraidh leat, slàn leat, beannachd leat.
farfetched, *adj.* air a tharriung fad as, air teachd o chéin.
farinaceous, *adj.* a bhuineas do mhin, air bhlas mine.
farm, *s.* baile fearainn, gabhail fhearainn, tuathanas.
farmer, *s.* tuathanach, gabhaltaiche.
farmost, *adj.* as fhaide as.
farrago, *s.* brudhaiste, bròthas, brochan, cumasg.
farrier, *s.* marc - lighich, léigh - each ; gobhachruidhean.
farrow, *a.* seasg ; a farrow cow, gamhnach.
farrow, *s.* cuain, àlach muice.
farrow, *v. a.* beir uirceanan.
fart, *s.* bràim, bram.
farther, *adv.* ni's fhaide as, a thuilleadh, a bhàrr.
farther, *adj.* ni's fhaide, ni's iomallaiche ; air taobh thall.
farther, *v. a.* cuir air adhart, cuidich.
fartherance, *s.* cuideachadh, còmhnadh.
farthest, *adj.* as fhaide as ; as iomallaiche.
farthing, *s.* feòirlinn, fàirdein.
farthingale, *s.* cearcall-còta.
fascinate, *v. a.* cuir fo gheasaibh, tàlaidh.
fascination, *s.* buidseachd, mór-thlachd.
fashion, *s.* modh, seòl ; fasan ; cleachdadh, gnàths, cumadh, cruth, dealbh, dèanamh, dreach, samhla, coltas ; dòigh, nòs ; uaisle.
fashion, *v. a.* cùm, dealbh, dreach.
fashionable, *adj.* fasanta, gnàthaichte, nòsail, cleachdail.
fast, *s.* trasg, trasgadh.
fast, *adj.* daingeann, teann, neo-ghluasadach, diongmhalta ; luath.
fasten, *v.* daingnich, teannaich, ceangail ; greimich, gabh gréim.
fastening, *s.* ceangal, daingneachadh.
fastidious, *adj.* àilleasach, moiteil, tarcuiseach, àileanta, arralach.
fasting, *s.* trasgadh, trasg.
fat, *adj.* reamhar, sultmhor, feòlmhor.
fat, *s.* reamhrachd, saill, sult, blonag.
fatal, *adj.* marbhtach, bàsmhor, sgriosail, millteach ; an dàn.

fatalist, *s.* fear creidsinn 's an ni tha an dàn.
fatality, *s.* ni tha an dàn.
fate, *s.* manadh ; bàs ; sgrios.
fated, *adj.* mar a tha an dàn.
father, *s.* athair.
father, *v. a.* gabh (ri urra) mar athair, uchdmhacaich ; aidich mar do ghnìomh no do sgrìobhadh ; cuir as leth, cuir air.
father-in-law, *s.* athair-céile.
fatherless, *adj.* gun athair.
fatherly, *adj.* athaireil.
fathom, *s.* aitheamh.
fathom, *v. a.* tomhais aitheamh ; ruig air, faigh a mach ; tomhais doimhneachd.
fathomless, *adj.* gun ghrunnd, gun ìochdar, gun tomhais.
fatigue, *v. a.* sgìthich, sàraich.
fatigue, *s.* sgìos, saothair, sàrachadh, allaban.
fatling, *s.* beathach reamhar, ainmhidh air a bhiadhadh air son a mhàrbhadh.
fatness, *s.* reamrachd, reamhrad, sultmhorachd ; geir, saill.
fatten, *v.* reamhraich, biadh ; fàs reamhar.
fatuity, *s.* baothaireachd.
fatuous, *adj.* baoth, gòrach, faoin, amaideach ; lag, faileasach.
fault, *s.* coire, cron, lochd, gaoid, cionta.
faultless, *adj.* neo-lochdach, neochiontach, neochoireach ; iomlan, gun mheang.
faulty, *adj.* ciontach, coireach, mearachdach ; olc, dona.
favour, *v. a.* cuidich, bi fàbharach, nochd càirdeas, dèan còmhnadh le, còmhnaich.
favour, *s.* fàbhar, deagh-ghean, bàigh, taobh, càirdeas ; suaicheantas.
favourable, *adj.* fàbharach, bàigheil.
favoured, *part.* a fhuair cothrom no fàbhor, dheth a bheil spéis.
favourite, *s.* annsachd, ceist, luaidh.
fawn, *s.* laogh féidh, fiadh òg ; meann earba.
fawn, *v. n.* dèan miodal, dèan sodal, dèan cùirteas ; strìochd, lùb.
fealty, *s.* ùmhlachd, dlighe iochdarain da uachdaran.
fear, *s.* eagal, geilt, sgàth, fiamh.
fear, *v.* gabh eagal, gabh fiamh ; bi fo eagal, geiltich ; bi am fiamh, bi fo chùram, bi fo iomaguin.
fearful, *adj.* gealtach, meat, lagchridheach, eagalach, fiamhail; oillteil, uamhunnach, uabhasach.
fearfulness, *s.* gealtachd, meatachd, geilt, eagal, fiamh, sgàth, oillt, uabhas.
fearless, *adj.* neo-ghealtach, gun athadh, neo-fhiamhach, neo-sgàthach.

feasible, *adj.* so-dhèanamh, coltach.
feast, *s.* cuirm, fleadh, cuilm.
feast, *v. a.* dèan cuirm, thoir fleadh ; gabh cuirm, gabh fleadh.
feat, *s.* gnìomh, euchd, treubhantas ; cleas, car neònach.
feat, *adj.* ealamh, sgiobalta, deas, teòma ; grinn, snasmhor.
feather, *s.* ite, iteag, cleiteag.
feather, *v. a.* sgeadaich le itean.
feather - bed, *s.* leabaidh chlòimhteach, leabaidh itean.
feathered, *adj.* iteagach, iteach.
feature, *s.* tuar, aogas, cruth, dreach ; cumadh, cruitheachd, dealbh, ìomhachd.
febrile, *adj.* fiabhrasach.
February, *s.* ceud mhìos an earraich.
feculence, *s.* drabhas, grùid, druaip.
feculent, *adj.* drabhasach, druaipeil.
fecund, *adj.* torrach, sìolmhor.
fecundity, *s.* sìolmhorachd.
fed, *prep.* and *part.* of to feed, àraichte.
federal, *adj.* a bhuineas do chùmhnant.
fee, *v. a.* tuarasdalaich, gabh neach air thuarasdal.
fee, *s.* duais, dìoladh, tuarasdal.
feeble, *adj.* lag, fann, anfhann.
feebleness, *s.* laigse, anfhannachd.
feed, *v.* biadh, àraich, beathaich, cùm suas.
feed, *s.* biadh, lòn, ionaltradh.
feeder, *s.* fear-biadhaidh ; fear-ithe.
feel, *v. a.* fairich, mothaich, làimhsich ; feuch, rannsaich.
feeling, *s.* faireachduinn, faireachadh, mothachadh, càileachd.
feign, *v.* gabh ort, leig ort ; aithris gu breugach.
feint, *s.* coltas breugach, gabhail air.
felicitate, *v. a.* dèan sona, fàiltich, cuir " meal an naidheachd."
felicitous, *adj.* sona, sòlasach.
felicity, *s.* sonas, sòlas.
feline, *adj.* mar chat.
fell, *adj.* borb, fiadhaich, allaidh, garg, allamhara.
fell, *s.* seiche, bian, craicionn.
fell, *v. a.* leag gu làr, buail sìos, spad, smàil ; gèarr sìos, mar chraoibh.
fellmonger, *s.* ceannaiche-bhoiceann.
fellow, *s.* companach, coimpire ; lethbhreac ; gille ; dubhbhalach.
fellow, *v. a.* càraidich, paidhrich.
fellowship, *s.* companas, compantas, comunn, co-bhann, caidreamh.
felo de se, *s.* féin-mhortair.
felon, *s.* slaoightire.
felonious, *adj.* aingidh, fealltach, olc, ciontach.
felony, *s.* gnìomh fìor olc.
felt, *s.* aodach gaoisideach ; bian.
felucca, *s.* bàta sè-ràmhach.

female, *s.* bean, boirionnach, bainionnach.
female, *adj.* boirionn, bainionn.
feminality, *s.* nàdur nam ban.
feminine, *adj.* boirionn, bainionnach ; caomh, bog, maoth, mìn, màlda.
femoral, *adj.* sléisneach, màsach.
fen, *s.* boglach, càthar, mòinteach.
fence, *s.* dìon, callaid, dìg, daingneach, bàdhun.
fence, *v.* dùin, iomadhruid, cuairtich.
fenceless, *adj.* gun challaid, fosgailte.
fencer, *s.* basbair, cliaranach.
fencible, *adj.* so-dhìon, ghabhas dìon.
fencing, *s.* basbaireachd, cliaranachd.
fend, *v.* dìon, cum dhìot ; connsaich ; tagair.
fender, *s.* dìonadair.
fennel, *s.* lus-an-t-saoidh.
fenny, *adj.* mòinteachail, bog.
feoff, *v. a.* cuir an seilbh fuinn.
feoffment, *s.* cur an seilbh.
ferine, *adj.* fiadhaich, garg.
ferineness, ferity, *s.* gairge, buirbe, allmharrachd, fiadhaichead.
ferment, *v. a.* cuir fo bhuaireas, tog an àirde ; bi fo bhuaireas, oibrich, goirtich, binntich.
ferment, *s.* buaireas, mì-riaghailt, oibreachadh, troimh-chéile.
fermentation, *s.* buaireas, oibreachadh.
fern, *s.* raineach, froineach.
ferny, *adj.* raineachail, làn roinich.
ferocious, *adj.* fiadhaich, garg, allmharra, an-iochdmhor.
ferocity, *s.* fiadhaichead, gairge, buirbe, an-iochd.
ferret, *s.* feòcullan, coinneas ; stìom.
ferret, *v. a.* cuir á toll.
ferriage, *s.* faradh, airgead-aisig.
ferruginous, *adj.* do ghné iaruinn.
ferry, *v.* aisig ; rach thar aiseag.
ferry, *s.* aiseag.
ferryman, *s.* fear-aiseig, portair.
fertile, *adj.* torach, sìolmhor, biadhchar, pailt, lìonmhor.
fertilise, *v. a.* dèan torach, dèan sìolmhor, leasaich, mathaich.
fertility, *s.* sìolmhoireachd, tarbhachd, toraicheas.
ferula, *s.* slat-sgiùrsaidh, sgiùrsair.
fervency, *s.* dealas, teas-inntinn, dianthogradh, déine, beò-dhùrachd.
fervent, *adj.* teth, air ghoil ; dian, bras, cas, dealasach ; dùrachdach, blàth.
fervid, *adj.* teth, air ghoil, loisgeach ; bras, dian, dealasach, deòthasach.
fervidness, *s.* déine, braise, dealas, deòthas.
fervour, *s.* teas, blàthas ; teas inntinn, dealas, déine, beò-dhùrachd.
festal, *adj.* cuirmeach, fleadhach.
fester, *v. n.* eargnaich, at, iongraich.

festival, *s.* féill, cuirm-bhliadhnail.
festive, *adj.* fleadhach, cuirmeach, féisdeach, aoibhneach.
festivity, *s.* aoibhneas, aighear, subhachas, gàirdeachas.
fetch, *v. a.* thoir leat, sìn chucam ; tarruing (fiul, deòir, anail) ; faigh prìs.
fetch, *s.* tàibhs.
fetid, *adj.* breun, loibht, grod.
fetlock, *s.* luidhean, fiarag.
fetor, *s.* droch bholadh, droch thòchd.
fetter, *s.* cuibhreach, geimheal, buarach.
fetter, *v. a.* geimhlich, cuibhrich.
feu, *s.* gabhail, gabhaltas, làrach togalach (air suim 's a' bhliadhna).
feud, *s.* aimhreit, strì, eas-aonachd, connsachadh, falachd, cogadh.
feudal, *adj.* a bhuineas do shuidheachadh fearainn.
feudatory, *s.* gabhaltaiche.
fever, *s.* fiabhras, cuartach, teasach.
feverish, **feverous**, **fevery**, *adj.* fiabhrasach, teth, loisgeach ; mùiteach, neoshuidhichte.
few, *adj.* tearc, ainneamh, gann.
fewness, *s.* teircead, gainnead.
fiat, *s.* breitheanas, binn.
fib, *s.* breug, frith-bhreug.
fib, *v. n.* innis breugan.
fibber, *s.* breugaire.
fibre, *s.* freumh chaol, teudag, ròinne.
fibula, *s.* cnàimh-caol na lurgainn.
fickle, *adj.* caochlaideach, mùiteach, luasganach, luaineach, neo-shuidhichte, neo bhunailteach.
fickleness, *s.* caochlaideachd, mùiteachd, luasganachd, neo-bhunailteachd, neosheasmhachd.
fiction, *s.* naidheachd bhreugach; uirsgeul, sgeulachd.
fictitious, **fictitiously**, *adj.* feallsach, mealltach, faoin, breugach.
fiddle, *s.* fiodhall.
fiddle, *v. a.* dèan fidhleireachd ; bi dìomhanach.
fiddlefaddle, *s.* babhdaire, beag-seadh, faoineis.
fiddler, *s.* fidhleir.
fiddle-string, *s.* teud fìdhle.
fidelity, *s.* tréidhireas, fìrinn ; dìlseachd, seasmhachd.
fidget, *v. n.* dèan iomairt, bi luaisgeanach.
fie, *interj.* ud ! ud ! mo nàire !
fief, *s.* gabhail fearainn ; fo-uachdaran.
field, *s.* machair, raon, achadh, faiche, magh ; blàr, farsuingeachd.
fieldfare, *s.* an liathruisg, seòrsa smeòraich.
fiend, *s.* diabhol, deamhan.
fierce, *adj.* fiadhaich, drochmheinneach, feargach, garg, borb, buaireasach ; laidir, treun.

fierceness, *s.* fiadhaichead, buirbe, gairge, buaireas, guinideachd, fuilteachd ; ainteas, teinntidheachd ; braise, buaireas.
fiery, *adj.* teinnteach, lasarra, loisgeach ; dian, bras, cabhagach ; feargach, frionasach, garg, drochmheinneach ; dealrach, soillseach.
Fife, *s.* Fìdeag-Ghallda.
Fifer, *s.* fear-fìdeig.
fifteen, *adj.* còig-deug.
fifth, *adj.* còigeamh.
fifthly, *adv.* 's a chòigeadh àite.
fifty, *adj.* caogad, leth-cheud.
fig, *s.* fìgis, crann-fìge.
fight, *s.* cath, còmhrag ; caonnag, tuasaid, sabaid.
fighter, *s.* curaidh, gaisgeach, fearcòmhraig, fear sabaideach.
figurable, *adj.* a ghabhas cumadh, a ghabhas dealbh.
figurative, *adj.* samhlachail.
figure, *s.* dealbh, cumadh, dreach, cruth ; pearsa, aogas, coltas, samhla.
figure, *v. a.* cum, dreach, dealbh ; samhlaich ; smuainich.
figwort, *s.* am farach-dubh.
filament, *s.* sreang chaol, toinntean.
filbert, *s.* cnò, faoisgeag, muc-fàileag.
filch, *v. a.* goid, slad, dean méirle.
file, *s.* eighe, lìomhan.
filial, *adj.* macail, dleasdanach.
filiation, *s.* dàimh mic ri athair ; bann cochòrdaidh.
filings, *s.* smùrach iaruinn ; min eighe.
fill, *v. a.* lìon, luchdaich ; sàsaich, dèan buidheach ; fàs làn.
fill, *s.* làn, sàth, leòir, teann-shàth.
fillet, *s.* stìom, crios ; tiugh na sléisde.
fillet, *v. a.* ceangail le stìom, cuir crios air, cuir cuairteag uime.
fillip, *v. a.* thoir cliùdan.
fillip, *s.* spadag, cliùdan.
filly, *s.* loth, lothag.
film, *s.* sgrath, sgannan, sgàilean.
filmy, *adj.* sgrathach, sgàileanach.
filter, *v. a.* sìolaidh.
filter, *s.* sìolachan, sìoltachan.
filth, *s.* salchar, anabas, druaip.
filthy, *adj.* salach, musach, drabasach ; neòghlan, truaillidh.
filtrate, *v. a.* sìolaidh.
filtration, *s.* sìoladh, glanadh.
fin, *s.* ite éisg.
finable, *adj.* airidh air ùbhladh.
final, *adj.* deireannach.
finance, *s.* teachd a steach, màl, cìs, càin, airgiod.
financier, *s.* fear trusaidh cìs rìgh ; fear eòlach air gréidheadh airgid.
find, *v. a.* faigh ; tachair air ; faigh a mach, amais, fairich, aithnich ; codhùin ; cum suas, beathaich.

fine, *adj.* grinn, fìnealta, caol ; glan, fìorghlan, soilleir ; geur, tana.

fine, *s.* ùbhladh, peanas.

fine, *v. a.* glan, ath-ghlan ; dèan fìnealta ; leag ùbhladh.

fineness, *s.* grinnead, fìnealtachd, grinneas, bòidhchead, maise ; minead, caoilead.

finery, *s.* breaghachd, rìmheadh.

finesse, *s.* seòltachd, cleas, cealg.

finger, *s.* meur, corrag.

finger, *v. a.* meuraich, làimhsich.

finical, *adj.* moiteil, cùirteil, grinn, gogaideach, leòmach, aralach.

fining-pot, *s.* suacan-leaghaidh.

finish, *s.* crìoch, ceann.

finish, *v. a.* crìochnaich ; coimhlion.

finisher, *s.* fear-crìochnachaidh.

finite, *adj.* crìochnach, crìochnaichte.

finiteless, *adj.* neo-chrìochnach.

finny, *adj.* iteach.

fir, *s.* giuthas.

fire, *s.* teine, teas, ainteas.

fire, *v.* cuir ri theine, loisg ; fadaidh, beothaich, bruidich ; tilg.

firearms, *s.* airm-theine.

firebrand, *s.* aithinne ; brathadair.

fire-cross, *s.* crois-tàra, crann-tàra.

firelock, *s.* gunna, musgaid.

fireman, *s.* fear-casgaidh teine.

firepan, *s.* aoghan-theine.

firing, *s.* connadh, gual, mòine.

firkin, *s.* buideal naoi galoin.

firm, *adj.* daingeann, làidir, teann ; seasmhach, diongmhalta, bunailteach, neo-ghluasadach.

firmament, *s.* speur, iarmailt, adhar.

firmamental, *adj.* iarmailteach, adharach, speurach, nèamhaidh.

firmness, *s.* daingneachd, greimealas ; maireannachd, seasmhachd, cinnteas, diongmhaltas, bunailteachd.

first, *adj.* ceud, ceudamh ; an tùs, an tòiseach ; prìomh.

first, *adv.* an tùs, air toiseach, roimh.

firstfruits, *s.* ceud-thoradh.

firstling, *s.* ceudghin ; ceud-fhàs.

fiscal, *s.* ionmhas, tighinn a steach rìoghachd.

fish, *s.* iasg ; *gen.* éisg.

fish, *v.* iasgaich ; bi 'g iasgach.

fisher, fisherman, *s.* iasgair.

fishery, *s.* iasgach.

fish-hook, *s.* dubhan iasgaich.

fishing, *s.* iasgaireachd.

fishmeal, *s.* tràth bìdh de dh' iasg.

fishmonger, *s.* ceannaiche éisg.

fishy, *adj.* mar iasg, sleamhainn, seòlta, carach.

fissile, *adj.* sgoilteach, so-sgoltadh.

fissure, *s.* sgoltadh, sgàineadh, gàg.

fist, *s.* dòrn.

fit, *adj.* iomchuidh, freagarrach ; *s.* paiseanadh, fit of coughing=trothail.

fit, *v.* dèan freagarrach, dèan iomchuidh ; cuir an uidheam, cuir an òrdugh, ceartaich.

fitch, *s.* peasair-luch.

fitchat, fitchew, *s.* feòcullan.

fitful, *adj.* 'na ghreisean, plathach.

fitness, *s.* freagarrachd, deisealachd.

five, *adj.* còig.

fivefold, *adj.* còig-fillte.

fives, *s.* an galair-greidh.

fix, *v.* suidhich, socraich, daingnich, dèan teann, spàrr ; beachdaich ; gabh gu fois.

fixation, fixedness, *s.* suidheachadh, maireachduinn, seasmhachd ; daingneach, dùiread ; bunailteachd, diongmhaltachd.

fixture, *s.* ni tàirngte, no ceangailte.

fizgig, *s.* seòrsa mór-ghath.

flabby, *adj.* bog, maoth ; plamcaidh, neo-ghramail.

flaccid, *adj.* bog, tais, anfhann, maoth, so-lùbaidh.

flaccidity, *s.* anfhainne, laigse.

flag, *v. a.* fannaich, lagaich ; caill treòir, fàs lag.

flag, *s.* seileasdair ; bratach ; leac.

flagelet, *s.* gall-fheadan.

flagellation, *s.* sgiùrsadh.

flaggy, *adj.* lag, anfhann, fuasgailte.

flagitious, *adj.* aingidh, drochmhuinteach olc, ciontach.

flagitiousness, *s.* aingidheachd.

flagon, *s.* cuinneag dhibhe.

flagrancy, *s.* sgannal.

flagrant, *adj.* teth, sgannalach, dealasach; follaiseach, soilleir, anabarra, fuathasach, amasgaidh.

flagship, *s.* long an aird-cheannaird.

flail, *s.* sùiste.

flake, *s.* lòineag, bleideag ; scramag.

flaky, *adj.* lòineagach, tlàmach, bleideagach.

flambeau, *s.* dòrnleus céire.

flame, *s.* lasair ; teas-inntinn, déine.

flamen, *s.* sagart pàganach.

flammability, *s.* lasantachd, teinteachd.

flammation, *s.* lasadh, losgadh.

flammiferous, *adj.* lasrach, loisgeach.

flamy, *adj.* lasrach, lasanta.

flank, *s.* slios, loch-bhléin, taobh.

flannel, *s.* cùrainn-chneas.

flap, *s.* libeag, bad air chrathadh, clib, clibeag, cliban.

flap, *v.* buail air falbh ; crath.

flap-eared, *adj.* spadchluasach.

flare, *v. a.* dealraich, dèarrs, boillsg.

flash, *s.* boillsgeadh, dreòs, dèarsadh, lasadh ; caoir, plathadh.

flash, *v.* deàlraich, dèarrs, boillsg.

flash, *a.* spaideil, rimheach.
flask, *s.* adharc-fhùdair ; searrag-pòcaid.
flat, *adj.* còmhnard, réidh, mìn ; ìosal, sìnte, leagte gu làr ; cianail, neo-chridheil, neo-smiorail.
flat, *s.* còmhnard, réidhlean, lòn, fàn, fearann iosal, lom.
flatness, *s.* còmhnardachd, réidheachd ; marbhantachd, neo-bhrisgead, neo-smioralachd ; neo-fhonnmhorachd, dùrantachd.
flatten, *v.* dèan còmhnard, dèan réidh ; leag sios, leudaich, dèan leathan ; mì-mhisnich, cuir fo sproc.
flatter, *v. a.* dèan miodal, dèan sodal, mol gu breugach.
flatterer, *s.* miodalaich, sodalaich.
flattery, *s.* miodal, sodal, miolasg, gabhann, brosgul.
flattish, *adj.* còmhnard, staoin.
flatulency, *s.* gaothmhorachd ; falamh achd, faoineachd, diomhanas.
flatulent, flatuous, *adj.* gaothmhor, at-mhor, falamh, faoin, gaothach.
flaunt, *s.* basdal, lòiseam.
flavour, *s.* blas, bòladh cùbhraidh.
flavorous, *adj.* blasda ; cùbhraidh.
flaw, *s.* gaoid, sgàineadh, sgoltadh ; ciorram, coire, meang.
flax, *s.* lìon.
flax-dresser, *s.* seiclear-lìn.
flaxen, *adj.* de lìon, lìn ; air dath lìn.
flay, *v. a.* feann, faobhaich.
flea, *s.* deargann.
fleam, *s.* cuisleag cruidh, tuadhfhala.
fledge, fledged, *v. adj.* iteagach, sgiathach.
flee, *v. n.* teich, ruith, tàr as.
fleece, *s.* rùsg, lomradh.
fleece, *v. a.* rùisg, lomair ; creach.
fleeced, *part.* ruisgte, creachte.
fleecy, *adj.* clòimheach, rùsgach.
fleer, *v. n.* mag, sgeig, fochaidich.
fleer, *s.* fochaid, magadh, sgeig, fanaid ; gàire fanaid, dréin fhochaid.
fleet, *s.* cabhlach, loingeas.
fleet, *adj.* luath, siùbhlach, clis.
fleet, *v. n.* siubhail grad.
fleeting, *adj.* siùbhlach, diombuan.
fleetness, *s.* luathas, siùbhlachd.
flesh, *s.* feòil.
fleshly, *adv.* gu corporra, feòlmhor.
fleshy, *adj.* feòlmhor, reamhar, sult-mhor, làn.
fletcher, *s.* leistear, fear dhèanamh shaighead.
flew, *pret.* of to **fly,** dh'itealaich.
flewed, *adj.* spreilleach, craosach.
flexibility, *s.* sùbailteachd.
flexible, flexile, *adj.* sùbailte, so-lùbadh ; so-chomhairleach.
flexion, *s.* cromadh, lùbadh, camadh.
flexuous, *adj.* lùbach, cam, crom.

flexure, *s.* fiaradh, camadh, cromadh, claonadh.
flight, *s.* teicheadh, ruaig ; itealaich, teas-inntinn, àrdsmuain ; ealtainn.
flighty, *adj.* fiadhaich, luaineach, neo-shuidhichte, neo-bhunailteach, mac-meanmnach.
flimsy, *adj.* lag, faoin, neo-ghramail, anfhann, neo-sgoinneil, cearbach, tana.
flinch, *v. n.* sèap, fannaich, crup.
flincher, *s.* cladhaire, gealtaire.
fling, *v.* tilg, thoir urchair ; sgap, sgaoil, crath ; fàs neo-cheannsaichte.
fling, *s.* tilgeadh, urchair ; fochaid, innisg, anaisg, beum-tàire.
flint, *s.* ailbhinn, spor, airtein.
flinty, *adj.* ailbhinneach, clachach.
flippancy, *s.* beulchaireachd, leógaireachd.
flippant, *adj.* luath-bheulach bruidh-neach ; gobach, peasanach, beag-narach, beadaidh.
flirt, *v.* tilg, thoir urchair ghrad ; dèan gobaireachd.
flirt, *s.* grad-char, lùth-chleas, bladhm ; gòdag, gogaid, goileag, leòdag.
flirtation, *s.* gogaideachd, beadradh.
flit, *v.* cuir imrich ; rach air imrich.
flitch, *s.* cliathach shaillte muice.
flitter, *s.* giobal, broineag, lùireach.
float, *v.* snàmh, bi air fleodradh.
flock, *s.* greigh ; treud, ealt, ealta.
flock, *v. n.* trus, tionail, cruinnich.
flood, *s.* tuil, dìle ; lìonadh.
flood, *v. a.* còmhdaich le uisge.
floodgate, *s.* tuil-dhorus.
floodmark, *s.* àirde làin mhara ; dubh-chladach.
flook, or **fluke,** *s.* soc acrach ; leòbag, liabag.
floor, *s.* ùrlar, làr.
floor, *v. a.* cuir ùrlar ann.
flooring, *s.* ùrlar, fiodh-ùrlair.
floral, *adj.* lusach, flùranach.
florid, *adj.* lusach, flùranach ; ùrail, ruiteagach ; sgiamhach.
floridness, *s.* ruiteachas, deirge.
florist, *s.* lusragan, gàirnealair bhlàthan, fear-reic bhlàthan.
flounce, *v.* sgiot, spairt ; siubhail le sraon ann an uisg.
flounce, *s.* froinis ; plub, sgiotadh.
flounder, *s.* leòbag, liabag.
flounder, *v. n.* dèan spàirn, spleathairt.
flour, *s.* min chruineachd, flùr.
flourish, *v.* cuir fo bhlàth ; crath gu fraoidhneasach ; fas suas, soirbhich ; bi àrd-ghlòireach, dèan spagluinn, dèan uaill.
flourish, *s.* mórachd, maise, glòir, uaill, bòsd ; blàth, ùr-fhàs, duilleachadh ; fuaim trompaidean.
flout, *v.* sgeig, mag, fochaidich ; dèan fochaid, dèan fanaid.

flout, s. magadh, tàir, fanaid.

flow, v. ruith, sil ; éirich, at ; bi pailt, bi sgaoilteach.

flow, s. lìonadh, éiridh, sruth, tuil ; pailteas, lànachd ; ard-ghlòir, deas-chainnt.

flower, s. blàth, ùr-fhàs ; a chuid as fèarr, brod.

flower-de-luce, s. seileasdair.

floweret, flowret, s. flùran, plùran.

flowery, adj. flùranach, gucagach.

fluctuant, adj. luaineach, neo-shuidhichte, luasganach, neo-bhunailteach.

fluctuate, v. n. bi air udail, luaisg, tulg ; bi neo-sheasmhach, bi 's an ioma-chomhairle.

fluctuation, s. udal, luasgadh, tulgadh ; iomchomhairle, imcheist ; crathadh, luasgadh, tilgeadh a nùll 's a nall.

flue, s. piob-deataich, sòrn.

fluency, s. ùr-labhairt, deas-chainnt.

fluent, adj. sruthach, silteach, leaghach ; a' gluasad, ruitheach ; deas-labhrach, réidh am bruidhinn.

fluid, adj. uisgidh, sruthach, leaghach.

fluid, s. uisge, staid uisge.

fluidity, s. uisgealachd, tanachd.

flummery, s. làghan ; brosgul.

flurry, s. cabhag, othail ; osag.

flush, v. a. cuir rughadh ann, dèan ruiteach ; fàs dearg; ruith uisge.

flush, s. bladhmadh, dian-ghluasad.

fluster, v. a. cuir sogan air; cuir an chabhaig.

flute, s. duiseal ; feadan.

flutter, v. dèan itealaich.

flutter, s. udal, tulgadh, luasgan, crath-adh ; cabhag, triomhe chéile ; each-arais.

flux, s. sruthadh, ruith, siubhal, dol seachad, dol air falbh ; a' ghèarrach, lìonadh, trusadh.

flux, adj. neo-sheasmhach, siùbhlach.

fluxion, s. sruthadh, sileadh, siubhal ; sruth.

fly, v. seachain, teich, tréig, leig dhìot, fàg, dìobair, cuir cul ri ; falbh air iteig.

fly, s. cuileag ; roth ; carbad faraidh.

flying-fish, s. iasg-sgiathach.

foal, s. searrach.

foam, s. cop, còbhar.

foam, v. n. cuir cop dhiot ; bi feargach.

foamy, adj. còbharach, copach.

fob, s. pòcait bheag.

focus, s. buillsgean, teis-meadhon.

fodder, s. fodar, connlach, innlinn.

foe, s. nàmhaid, nàmh ; eas-caraid.

fœtus, fetus, s. ceud-fhàs, torrachas anabuich.

fog, s. ceò, ceathach ; ath-bharr feòir.

foggy, adj. neulach, ceòthach.

foible, s. fàilling, beag-chionta.

foil, v. a. ruaig, gabh air, faigh làmh an uachdar, fairtlich, claoidh.

foil, s. ruaig, fairtleachadh, claoidh; dealtradh, òradh ; claidheamh-maol.

foin, s. sàthadh, buille-thuige.

fold, s. mainnir, fang, buaile, crò ; treud, buar ; filleadh, pleat.

fold, v. a. fangaich, cuir am mainnir ; fill, paisg, cuir air fhilleadh.

foliage, s. duilleach, duilleagan.

foliate, adj. duilleagach.

foliate, v. a. dean 'na dhuilleagan.

foliation, s. blàth chuairteag.

folk, s. muinntir, sluagh, pobull.

follow, v. lean, ruag ; thig an lorg ; géill ; thig 'na dhéidh.

follower, s. fear-leanmhuinn.

folly, s. amaideachd, gòraich.

foment, v. a. blàthaich, teòth ; nigh ; bruidich, brosnaich, misnich.

fomentation, s. bruideachadh.

fond, adj. amaideach, beadarrach, deò-thasach ; déidheil.

fond, fondle, v. tataidh ; gràdhaich, cniadaich.

fondling, s. annsachd, luaidh.

fondness, s. déidh ; gràdh, gaol.

font, s. soitheach-baistidh.

food, s. biadh, lòn, teachd-an-tìr.

fool, s. amadan, burraidh, baothaire.

fool, v. dèan amadan deth, meall, thoir a chreidsinn air, thoir an car á ; cluich, caith aimsir.

foolery, s. amaideachd ; gòraich, fala-dhà, baothaireachd.

foolhardy, adj. dàna, mi-chiallach.

foolish, adj. gòrach, amaideach.

foolishness, s. amaideachd, gòraich.

foot, s. cas, troidh ; bun, bonn.

foot, v. imich, coisich.

football, s. ball-coise, ball-iomain.

foot-boy, s. gille-ruith, gille-coise.

footing, s. àite-seasaimh, bunait, suidh-eachadh, stéidh, seilbh ; staid, cor.

footman, s. gille duin'-uasail.

footpad, s. spùinneadair rathaid-mhóir.

footpath, s. ceum-coise.

footstep, s. lorg coise ; cas-cheum.

fop, s. spailpean, lasgaire, gaoithean.

foppery, s. amaideachd, spailpeis.

foppish, adj. amaideach, gòrach ; spail-leiceil, spailpeil, farumach.

foppishness, s. spailleic, spailpeis.

for, prep. air son, a chionn, do bhrìgh, a thaobh ; air sgàth ; fa chomhair ; air taobh ; a dh' ionnsaigh.

forage, v. spùill, creach ; solair.

forage, s. biadh, lòn, innlinn.

forasmuch, conj. a chionn, do-bhrìgh a thaobh ; air sgàth.

forbear, v. seachain, ob ; giùlain le, caomhain, fuiling, leig le ; sguir ; dèan maille ; caisg.

forbearance, s. seachnadh, obadh, leig-eadh seachad, sgur, stad ; fad-fhul-angas, deagh-mhèinn ; caomhalachd, bàigh, foighidin.

forbid, v. toirmisg ; caisg, cùm air ais.

forbidden, part. toirmisgte.

forbidding, part. adj. sgreataidh.

force, s. neart, spionnadh ; ainneart ; éifeachd, tàbhachd, feart, brìgh ; armailt, feachd.

force, v. co-éignich, thoir a dh' aindeoin ; gnàthaich ainneart ; spàrr, teannaich.

forceps, s. turcais, ; greimiche-léigh.

forcible, adj. laidir, neartmhor ; éifeachd-ach, tàbhachdach, brìoghmhor ; ain-deonach, éigneach.

ford, s. àth, faoghail.

ford, v. a. coisich tre abhainn.

fordable, adj. tana, eu-domhain.

fore, adj. air tùs, air toiseach, roimhe.

forebode, v. n. innis roimh-làimh, roimh-innis, cuir air mhanadh, fàisnich, thoir rabhadh.

forecast, v. dealbh, tionnsgain ; uidheam-aich ; suidhich innleachd, thoir barail (roimh-làimh).

forecast, s. uidheamachadh, deasachadh, seòladh, innleachd, dealbh, tionnsgal.

forecastle, s. seòmar-toisich luinge.

forecited, part. roimh-ainmichte.

foreclose, v. a. dùin, druid a steach.

foredo, v. a. creach, claoidh.

forefather, foregoer, s. priomhathair, seanair, sinnsear.

forefront, s. clàr-aghaidh, fìor-thoiseach.

foreground, s. réidhlean ; beulaibh.

forehand, adj. roimh-làimh.

forehead, s. clar-aodainn, bathais.

foreign, adj. gallda, coimheach.

foreigner, s. gall, coimheach, allmharach, coigreach, eilthireach, deòraidh.

forejudge, v. a. roimh-bhreithnich.

foreknow, v. a. roimh-aithnich.

foreknowledge, s. roimh-fhiosrachadh.

foreland, s. rudha, roinn, àird, sròn.

forelock, s. dosan, ciabhag.

foreman, s. fear-amhairc-thairis, ceann-ard oibreach ; ceann-suidhe (of Jury).

foremast, s. crann toisich.

forementioned, adj. roimh-luaighte.

foremost, adj. prìomh, air thoiseach.

forenamed, adj. roimh-ainmichte.

forenoon, s. roimh mheadhon latha.

forensic, adj. a bhuineas do mhòd lagha.

fore-ordain, v. a. roimh-òrduich.

forepart, s. toiseach, aghaidh.

forerunner, s. roimh-ruithear.

foresail, s. seol-toisich.

foresee, v. a. faic roimh làimh.

foresight, s. roimh-shealladh, geurchuis.

forest, s. frìdh, coille, fàsach.

forestall, v. a. ceannaich roimh làimh, glac an cothrom, bi air thoiseach (air cach).

forestaller, s. fear-millidh margaidh.

forester, s. forsair, fear-comhnaidh coille; eun coille.

foretaste, s. roimh-bhlasad.

foretell, v. roimh-innis, fàisnich.

forethink, v. a. roimh-smaoinich.

forethought, s. roimh-smuain, cùram ciall, gliocas.

foretoken, s. comharradh, sanas.

foretop, s. dos-mullaich, cìrean.

foreward, s. toiseach, aghaidh.

forewarn, v. a. cuir air earalas.

forfeit, v. arbhartaich arfuintich.

forfeit, s. ùbhladh.

forfeiture, s. arbhartachadh.

forge, s. ceardach, teallach, seòrsa gadachd.

forge, v. a. thoir cumadh, dealbh, dèan goibhneachd ; dealbh gu feallsa.

forgery, s. gnìomh mealltach ; cur ainm fìr eile ri pàipeir.

forget, v. a. dìochuimhnich, dearmaid.

forgetful, adj. dìochuimhneach.

forgetfulness, s. dìochuimhne.

forgive, v. a. math, thoir mathanas.

forgiveness, s. mathanas.

forgo, v. a. dealaich, cuir dhìot, cuibh-tich, tréig, fàg, dìobair.

forgotten, part. air dìochuimhneachadh.

fork, s. gobhal, gobhlag.

fork, v. n. fàs gobhlach, cuir a mach dias, cuir (boinn) an tac, cuir (ràmh) an tac, sàth a thaobh (le cabar).

forked, forky, adj. gòbhlach.

fork-tailed, adj. earra-ghobhlach.

forlorn, adj. aonaranach, truagh.

form, s. cumadh, dreach, dealbh, cruth, aogas, riochd, dòigh ; fasan, cleachd-adh, modh, nòs, seòl, àite-suidhe ; suidheachan.

form, v. a. cruthaich, dealbh, cùm.

formal, adj. riaghailteach, dòigheil.

formality, s. deas-ghnàth, modh, dòigh ; òrdugh, poncalachd.

formation, s. cumadh, dealbh.

former, adj. roimh ; roimh-ainmichte ; a chaidh seachad.

formidable, adj. eagalach, uamhasach, fuathasach, cunnartach, deacair.

formless, adj. gun dealbh, gun chruth.

formula, s. riaghailt shuidhichte, riaghailt seòlaidh.

fornicate, v. n. dèan strìopachas.

fornication, s. strìopachas.

fornicator, s. fear-strìopachais.

fornicatress, s. strìopach, siùrsach.

forsake, v. a. tréig, cuir cùl ri.

forsaken, part. tréigte.

forsooth, adv. gu dearbh, fuich ! ma 's fhìor !

forswear, v. cuir cùl ri, àicheadh fo mhionnaibh ; thoir mionnan-eithich.

fort, s. daingneach, dùn, dìdean.

forth, *adv.* o so suas ; air adhart.
forthcoming, *part.* ullamh gu teachd a làthair.
forthwith, *adv.* gun dàil, gun mhoille.
fortieth, *adj.* dà fhicheadamh.
fortifiable, *adj.* so-dhìonadh, ghabhas dìon.
fortification, *s.* eòlas - daingneachd ; daighneach, dìdean, dìon.
fortify, *v. a.* dìon, daingnich ; neartaich, dèan làidir ; misnich.
fortilage, fortin, fortlet, *s.* daingneach beag.
fortitude, *s.* misneach, cruadal.
fortnight, *s.* ceithir-latha-deug.
fortress, *s.* daingneach, dìdean.
fortuitous, *adj.* tuiteamach, mar a thuiteas.
fortuitousness, *s.* tuiteamas.
fortunate, *adj.* sona, seamhsail, soirbheachail.
fortune, *s.* sealbh, àgh ; crannchur, oighreachd, saibhreas ; tochradh.
fortune-hunter, *s.* fear-tòir air tochradh, fear-tòir air beartas.
fortune-teller, *s.* fiosaiche, dearnadair.
forty, *adj.* dà fhichead.
forum, *s.* àite-coinneamh (Romanach).
forward, *adj.* dian, dùrachdach, iarrtach ; dealasach teth, cas, bras ; obann, ceann-làidir, beadaidh ; luath, tràthail ; grad, ealamh, cabhagach.
forward, *v. a.* greas, cuir air adhart.
forwardness, *s.* togarrachd, déine, braise, dùrachd ; tràthalachd, ladarnas.
foss, *s.* dìg, clais.
fossil, *adj.* tochailteach.
fossil, *s.* tochailt.
foster, *v. a.* altrum, àraich, beathaich, àlaich, tog suas.
fosterage, *s.* altrum, togail, àrach.
foster-brother, *s.* co-dhalta.
foster-child, fosterling, *s.* dalta.
fought, *pret.* and *part.* of to fight, chog, chuir cath.
foul, *adj.* salach, mosach, neòghlan, truaillidh ; gràineil, déisinneach ; duaichnidh ; drabhasach.
foul, *v. a.* salaich, duaichnich.
foulness, *s.* salchar, mosaiche ; truailleachd, gràinealachd ; déisinn, gràinde.
found, *pret.* and *part.* of to find, fhuair.
found, *v. a.* stéidhich, suidhich ; tog suas ; socraich ; tilg, leagh.
foundation, *s.* stéidh, bunait.
founder, *s.* fear-suidheachaidh airgid ; leaghadair.
founder, *v.* dèan crùbach ; theirig fodha.
foundery, foundry, *s.* tigh - leaghaidh (mhiotailtean).
foundling, *s.* faodailiche, faodalach.
fount, fountain, *s.* tobar, fuaran ; màthair-uisge, mathair-aobhair, toiseach, tùs, bun.

fountful, *adj.* fuaranach.
four, *adj.* ceithir.
fourfold, *adj.* ceithir-fillte.
fourfooted, *adj.* ceithir-chasach.
fourscore, *adj.* ceithir-fichead.
fourteen, *adj.* ceithir-deug.
fourteenth, *adj.* ceathramh-deug.
fourth, *adj.* ceathramh.
fourthly, *adv.* 's a' cheathramh àite.
fowl, *s.* eun, ian.
fowler, *s.* eunadair.
fowling, *s.* eunach.
fowling-piece, *s.* gunna-eunaich.
fox, *s.* sionnach, madadh-ruadh.
foxcase, *s.* bian sionnaich.
foxglove, *s.* lus-nam-ban-sìth.
foxhound, *s.* gadhar-sionnaich.
foxhunter, *s.* brocair.
fraction, *s.* bristeadh, mìr, bloigh.
fractional, *adj.* bristeach.
fractious, *adj.* crosda, cas.
fracture, *s.* bristeadh.
fracture, *v. a.* bris, bloighdich.
fragile, *adj.* brisg, bristeach, lag.
fragility, *s.* brisgead, breòiteachd.
fragment, *s.* fuigheall, spruilleach.
fragrance, fragrancy, *s.* cùbhraidheachd, deagh bhòladh.
fragrant, *adj.* cùbhraidh.
frail, *adj.* lag, breòite, gun treòir ; anfhann, so-lùbadh.
frailty, *s.* anmhuinneachd ; laigsinn.
frame, *v. a.* dealbh, cruthaich, cùm.
frame, *s.* cumadair, cumadh, dealbh, dreach, cruth.
franchise, *s.* saorsa ; còir taghaidh.
franchise, *v. a.* saor, thoir còir.
frangible, *adj.* brisgeach, pronn.
franion, *s.* leannan ; companach.
frank, *adj.* faoilidh, saor, furanach.
frank, *s.* litir-shaor ; bonn Fràngach deich sgillinn ; fail-muice.
frank, *v. a.* saor litir ; cuir am fail.
frankincense, *s.* ròsaid chùbhraidh ; tùis.
frankness, *s.* fosgailteachd, saorsa.
frantic, *adj.* air bhoile, air chuthach, mearanach ; feargach, buaireasach.
fraternal, *adj.* bràithreil.
fraternity, *s.* bràithreachas.
fratricide, *s.* mort-bràthar.
fraud, *s.* mealltaireachd, foill.
fraudulence, fraudulency, *s.* mealltaireachd, cealgaireachd.
fraudulent, fraudful, *adj.* carach, cealgach, foilleil, fealltach.
fraught, *part.* luchdaichte, làn.
fray, *s.* cath, còmhrag, caonnag.
freak, *v. a.* breac, ballaich, stialaich.
freakish, *adj.* luaineach, neònach.
freckle, *s.* breacadh-seunain.
freckled, *adj.* breac-bhallach.
free, *adj.* saor, fuasgailte.
free, *v. a.* saor, fuasgail, leig fa sgaoil.

freebooter, s. fear-reubainn.
freedom, s. saorsa, saorsainn, cead.
freehold, s. fearann-saor, oighreachd.
freeholder, s. fear tearainn.
freeman, s. duine saor ; fear-chòraichean, tràill a fhuair a shaorsa.
freeness, s. saorsainn ; fosgailteachd.
freestone, s. gaireal.
freethinker, s. as-creidmheach, fear-àicheadh Dhé.
freeze, v. a. reòdh, meilich.
freight, v. a. luchdaich, cuir air bòrd.
freight, s. luchd ; faradh.
French, s. Fràngaich ; fràingis.
French, adj. fràngach.
frenetic, adj. air bhoile, mearanach.
frenzy, s. boile, bàinidh, mearan.
frequency, s. coitcheanntas.
frequent, adj. tric, minig.
frequent, v. a. taghail, tathaich.
frequenter, s. fear-tathaich.
frequently, adv. gu tric, gu minig.
fresh, adj. fionnar ; ùr, ùrail.
freshen, v. a. ùraich, fàs ùr.
freshness, s. ùralachd, ùrachd.
fret, s. buaireas, iomairt, frionas.
fret, v. luaisg, caraich ; suath, caith as ; feargnaich ; gabh fearg.
fretful, adj. frionasach, cas.
fretfulness, s. frionas, caise.
fretty, adj. cnapach, pluganach.
friable, adj. brisgeach, so-phronnadh.
friar, s. brathair-bochd (aon de chomunn 's an eaglais Phapanaich).
friary, s. crùisle.
fribble, s. spalpaire.
friction, s. suathadh ; eas-còrdadh.
Friday, s. Di-h-aoine.
friend, s. caraid, dàimheach.
friendless, adj. gun charaid.
friendliness, s. dàimhealach.
friendly, adj. càirdeil, dàimheil.
friendship, s. càirdeas, dàimh.
frieze, frize, s. clò molach.
frigate, s. long bheag chogaidh.
fright, frighten, v. a. cuir eagal air, oilltich, clisg, geiltich, sgeunaich.
fright, s. eagal, geilt, oillt, clisgeadh.
frightful, adj. eagalach, oillteil.
frigid, adj. fuar, fuaralach, neo-choibhneil ; neo-bheothail.
frigidity, s. fuaralachd ; marbhantachd.
frigorific, adj. a' deanamh fuar.
fringe, s. fraoidhneas, oir.
fringy, adj. fraoidhneasach.
frippery, s. bàrlagan, ribagan.
frisk, v. n. leum, gèarr sùrdag, dèan mire.
friskful, adj. mireagach, mear.
friskiness, s. mire, mireagachd.
frith, s. caolas mara, beul aibhne (-s a' mhuir).
fritter, s. mìrean, crioman.
fritter, v. a. bris ; pronn, bruan.

frivolity, s. faoineas, faoineachd.
frivolous, adj. faoin, suarach, diblidh.
frizzle, v. a. cuairsg, cas, sniamh.
frizzle, s. camag, caisreag.
fro, adv. air ais, suas.
frock, s. gùn beag ; còta-gearr.
frog, s. losgann, leumnachan, gille-cràigean.
frolic, s. mire, sùgradh, beadradh.
frolic, frolicsome, adj. mireagach, sùgach, cleasanta.
from, prep. o, bho, uaithe ; as.
frond, s. geug-dhuilleagach.
front, s. aghaidh, aodann ; toiseach.
front, v. thoir aghaidh, coinnich ; seas mu choinneamh.
frontier, s. crìoch, oir, iomall.
frontispiece, s. dealbh mór aig toiseach leabhair.
frontless, adj. beag-narach, ladarna.
frost, s. reothadh.
frost-bitten, adj. reota.
frosty, adj. reòta, fuaralach ; liath.
froth, s. cop, còbhar, sgùm.
frothy, adj. copach, còbharach, faoin.
froward, adj. daobhaidh, crosda, danarra, do-cheannsachadh.
frowardness, s. dearras, danarrachd.
frown, v. a. cuir gruaim ort; grean-naich.
frown, s. gruaim, greann, sgraing, mùig.
frowzy, adj. breun, air dhroch fhàileadh ; doilleir.
frozen, part. pass. of to freeze, reòte.
fructiferous, adj. measach, a bheir a mach meas.
fructify, v. a. dèan torach ; giùlain meas, bi sìolmhor.
fructuous, adj. sìolmhor, measach.
frugal, adj. caomhainteach, gléidhteach, cùramach.
frugality, s. caomhnadh, crìontachd, riaghladh (air teachd-an-tìr).
fruit, s. meas ; toradh ; sliochd.
fruitage, s. measach.
fruit-bearing, part. a' giùlan meas.
fruitery, s. lobhta-mheas.
fruitful, adj. torach, sìolmhor.
fruitfulness, s. sìolmhorachd, pailteas.
fruition, s. mealtainn, sealbhachadh.
fruitless, adj. neo-thorach ; neo-tharbh-ach, faoin ; aimrid, seasg.
frumentacious adj. a bhuineas do ghràn.
frumenty, s. brochan-cruithneachd.
frump, v. a. mag, cuir 'na thosd.
frush, v. a. bris, bruan, pronn, brùth.
frustraneous, adj. neo-tharbhach, faoin.
frustrate, v. a. meall, mill dùil ; bac, dìobair, cuir a thaobh.
fry, s. sìol-éisg, gramasgar, gràisg.
fry, v. a. ròist ann an aghainn.
frying-pan, s. aghann ; friochdan.
fub, v. a. cuir dhiot le bréig.

fuddle, v. cuir air mhisg ; bi air mhisg.
fuel, s. connadh.
fugacious, adj. luaineach, siùbhlach.
fugaciousness, fugacity, s. luaineachd, siùbhlachd, luathas, diombuanachd, neo-chinnteachd, neo-sheasmhachd.
fugitive, adj. siùbhlach, faileasach.
fugitive, s. fògarach, dìobarach.
fulcrum, s. cùl-taic, tac.
fulfil, v. a. coimhlion.
fulfilment, s. coimhlionadh.
fulgency, s. dèarsadh, dealradh.
fulgent, fulgid, adj. dèarsach, dealrach, boillsgeach.
fuliginous, adj. smalach, ceothach.
full, adj. làn, lìonta ; sàsaichte.
full, s. làn, làine, iomlaine.
full, adv. gu h-uile, gu h-iomlan.
full, v. a. luaidh, fùc.
full-blown, adj. fo làn-bhlàth.
full-eyed, adj. meallshuileach.
fuller, s. fùcadair.
fuller's-earth, s. criadh-an-fhùcadair.
full-grown, adj. aig làn-fhàs.
fullness, s. lànachd, làine, pailteas.
fulminant, adj. tàirneach.
fulminate, v. dèan tàirnich.
fulmination, s. tàirneanach, toirm ; ascaoin-eaglais.
fulsome, adj. gràineil, breun, salach, miodalach.
fumado, s. iasg tioram cruaidh.
fumage, s. cìs-teallaich.
fumble, v. dèan gu cearbach ; laimhsich gu cèarr ; prab, dèan sporaghail.
fumbler, s. prabaire, fear-cearbach.
fume, s. deathach ; ceò, smùd, ceathach ; toth, corraich.
fumet, s. buachar féidh.
fumid, adj. ceòthach, smùdanach.
fumigate, v. n. cuir smùid, toit ; glan tigh (an déidh fiabhrus).
fumigation, s. deatach, smùd.
fumous, fumy, adj. deatachail, smùideach, toiteach.
fun, s. fearas-chuideachd, fala-dhà.
function, s. dreuchd, cèaird.
fund, s. stoc, stòras, maoin.
fundament, s. tòn, leth-deiridh.
fundamental, adj. bunaiteach, sònraichte.
funeral, s. tiodhlacadh, adhlacadh.
funeral, funereal, adj. a bhuineas do thìodhlacadh ; brònach, dubhach, muladach.
fungous, adj. spongach.

fungus, s. ballag-bhuachair, peallag-buarach.
funk, s. droch bholadh.
funnel, s. lìonadair ; pìob-tharruing.
funny, adj. cridheil, sùgach.
fur, s. bian ; craicionn-dóbhrain, etc.
furacious, adj. bradach.
furacity, s. braid, meirle.
furbelow, s. froinis, fraoidhneas.
furbish, v. a. lìomh, loinnrich.
furious, adj. air a chuthach, air bhàinidh ; mearanach, feargach ; garg, borb, lasanta.
furl, v. a. paisg, trus, fill.
furlong, s. an t-ochdamh cuid do mhìle, dà cheud is dà fhichead slat.
furlough, s. fòrlach saighdear.
furnace, s. fùirneis, àmhuinn, sòrn.
furnish, v. a. uidheamaich ; thoir seachad ; sgiamhaich, maisich, breaghaich.
furniture, s. àirneis, uidheam.
furrier, s. fear-reic bhian.
furrow, s. clais ; sgrìob treabhaidh.
furry, adj. molach, ròmach.
further, v. a. cuidich, cuir air adhart.
furthermore, adv. os bàrr, a bharr.
furthermost, furthest, adj. is fhaide air falbh, is iomalaiche.
fury, s. cuthach, bàinidh, boile ; fearg, corraich, buaireas ; boil inntinn, déine ; baobh chuthaich, ban-ifrinneach.
furze, s. conusg.
furzy, adj. conusgach.
fuse, v. leagh ; gabh leaghadh, bi leaghadh.
fusee, fusil, s. gunna-glaice.
fusible, adj. leaghach, so-leaghadh.
fusibility, s. nàdur leaghach.
fusileer, s. saighdear gunna-glaice.
fusion, s. leaghadh.
fuss, s. ùparaid, fuaim, cabhag.
fustian, s. aodach air a dhèanamh de chanach agus de lion ; àrd-ghlòir.
fustiness, s. bréine, liatas.
fusty, adj. breun, malcaidh, liath.
futile, adj. faoin, dìomhain, gun luach ; bruidhneach, lonach.
futility, s. lon, beilean ; faoineas, dìomhanas ; gòraich.
future, adj. ri teachd, a thig.
future, futurity, s. àm ri teachd ; ni ri teachd no ri tachairt.
fuzz-ball, s. balgan-péiteach.
fy, O fie ! interj. mo nàire !

G

gab, gabble, *v. n.* bi gobaireachd.
gabble, *s.* briot, glocaireachd.
gabbler, *s.* glogair, gobaire.
gabel, *s.* cìs, càin.
gaberdine, *s.* earrasaid (Iudhaich).
gable, *s.* stuadh, tulchann.
gad, *s.* geinn stàilinn.
gad, *v. n.* ruith air chéilidh.
gadder, *s.* fear-ceilidh.
gadding, *s.* céilidh.
gadfly, *s.* gleithir, creithleag, crebhire.
Gaelic, *s.* Gàidhlig.
gag, *v. a.* glomharaich, cuir sparrag.
gag, *s.* glomhar, sparrag, cabstair.
gage, *s.* geall, earlas ; tomhas.
gage, *v. a.* cuir geall.
gaiety, *s.* aiteas, cridhealas, aoibhneas, aigeantas ; sunnt, mire ; breaghas.
gaily, *adv.* gu h-ait, gu cridheil, gu h - aoibhneach, gu sunntach ; gu breagha.
gain, *s.* buannachd, buidhinn.
gain, *v.* buannaich, coisinn ; faigh.
gainer, *s.* fear-buannachd.
gainful, *adj.* buannachdail, tarbhach.
gainsay, *v. a.* cuir an aghaidh, thoir a bhreug do ; àicheadh.
gairish, *adj.* basdalach, lòiseamach.
gait, *s.* slighe ; gluasad, siubhal.
galaxy, *s.* sreath reultan ; cuídeachd uaislean.
gale, *s.* gaoth sgairteil ; gaoth làidir.
gall, *s.* domblas ; gamhlas.
gall, *v. a.* cràidh, ciùrr, rùisg ; claoidh ; feargaich.
gallant, *adj,* basdalach, rìmheach, uallach, spaideil ; curanta, flathail.
gallant, *s.* lasgaire, suiridheach.
gallantry, *s.* basdal, spairiseachd, rìmheachas ; treubhantas ; suiridhe.
gallery, *s.* aisir eadar dà sheòmar ; aradh, lobhta.
galley, *s.* birlinn, iùbhrach.
galley-slave, *s.* traill-iomraimh.
galliard, *s.* lasgaire rìmheach.
galligaskins, *s.* briogais ; osain mhóra.
gallipot, *s.* poit-chreadha.
gallon, *s.* galan.
gallop, *s.* deann (eich) ; dian-ruith.
gallop, *v. n.* marcaich le deann.
galloway, *s.* each nach eil thar ceithir làmhan deug air àirde.
gallows, *s.* croich.
gambadoes, *s.* triubhais-mharcachd.
gamble, *v. n.* cluich air son airgid.
gambler, *s.* fear-cluiche ; mealltair, cearrach.
gambol, *v. a.* thoir riag as ; leum, dèan mireag, dèan ruideis, dèan lùth-chleas.

gambol, *s.* mireag, leumnaich ; lùth-chleas, cleas àbhachdach, reis, riagail.
gambrel, *s.* cas-deiridh eich.
game, *s.* cluiche ; fearas - chuideachd, magadh, culaidh-bhùird ; sealg eòin agus beathaichean seilge.
game, *v. n.* cluich air son airgid.
game-cock, *s.* coileach-catha.
gamekeeper, *s.* peathair-seilge, gìoman- ach.
gamesome, *adj.* sùgach, mireagach.
gamester, *s.* ceàrrach.
gaming, *s.* ceàrrachd.
gammon, *s.* ceithreamh deiridh muice.
gander, *s.* gànradh, gèadh ; amadan.
gang, *s.* buidheann, còisridh, bannal.
ganglion, *s.* màm, snàim, ceanglachan.
gangrene, *s.* buirbein, an-fheòil.
gangrene, *v. a.* lobh, grod, cnàmh.
gangrenous, *adj.* cnàimhteach, grod.
gaol, *s.* gainntir, prìoson.
gaoler, *s.* fear-gleidhidh prìosoin.
gap, *s.* bealach, bearn ; fosgladh.
gape, *v. n.* dèan mèananaich, spleuchd.
gaper, *s.* steòcaire ; miannaiche.
garb, *s.* éideadh, earradh ; aogas.
garbage, garbish, *s.* mionach, grealach.
garble, *v. a.* eadar-dhealaich, tagh, criathair, dèan droch aithris.
garden, *s.* lios, gàradh.
gardener, *s.* gàradair, gàirnealair.
gardening, *s.* gàirnealaireachd.
gargarism, gargle, *s.* balgam-glanaidh beòil is slugain, glug-ghoil.
gargle, *v. a.* nigh, glan ; glug-ghoil.
garland, *s.* blàth-fhleasg, lus-chrùn.
garland, *v. a.* maisich le blàth-fhleasg.
garlic, *s.* creamh, gairgean.
garment, *s.* aodach, earradh.
garner, *s.* ionad-tasgaidh sìl, sabhal.
garnet, *s.* clach-luachmhor, gàirneid.
garnish, *v. a.* maisich, sgiamhaich.
garnish, garniture, *s.* sgeadachadh.
garret, *s.* seòmar-mullaich.
garreteer, *s.* fear-seòmair-mullaich.
garrison, *s.* saighdearan baile dìona ; dùn, tùr, daingneach, freiceadan.
garrison, *v. a.* cuir saighdearan air baile dìon ; dìdeann, daingnich.
garrulity, *s.* gobaireachd, geòileam.
garrulous, *adj.* gobach, luath-bheulach.
garter, *s.* gartan, glùinean, cnébilt.
garth, *s.* dòmhlad, tiughead.
gasconade, *s.* spagluinn, spleadhas.
gash, *s.* gearradh, beum, lot domhain.
gasp, *v. n.* plosg, tarruinn ospag.
gasp, *s.* àinich, plosg, ospag.
gastric, *adj.* meirbheach.
gastrotomy, *s.* gearradh-bronn.

gate, s. geata, dorus, cachaileith.
gather, v. cruinnich, tionail, trus.
gatherer, s. fear-cruinneachaidn.
gathering, s. co-chruinneachadh.
gathers, s. fillidhean, pleatan.
gaude, gaudery, s. basdalachd, breagh-achd, rìmheachd.
gaudy, adj. lòiseamach, basdalach, rìmh-each, breagh.
gauge, v. a. tomhais soitheach.
gauge, s. riaghailt thomhais shoithichean.
gauger, s. fear tomhais shoithichean.
gaunt, adj. tana, lom ; seang.
gauntlet, s. làmh-dhion, dòrn-bheart.
gauntree, s. làir-mhaide.
gauze, s. sròl.
gawk, s. cuthag ; baothaire.
gawky, adj. sgleòbaideach, sgleòideach.
gay, adj. cridheil, sunntach, sùgach, beò ; rìmheach, grinn.
gayety, s. cridhealas, aiteas, basdal.
gaze, v. n. beachdaich, dùr-amhairc.
gazer, s. spleuchdaire.
gazette, s. pàipeir-naidheachd.
gazetteer, s. fear-naidheachd.
gazing-stock, s. culaidh-bhùirst.
gear, geer, s. àirneis, cuid, eudail, maoin ; goireas, uidheam ; beairt.
geese, s. plural of goose, geòidh.
gelatine, gelatinous, adj. tiugh ; righinn.
geld, v. a. spoth ; glan siol..
gelder, s. spothadair.
gelding, s. gearran.
gelid, adj. fuar, reòdhte.
gelidity, s. fuachd mór, reòtachd.
gem, s. seud, neamhnaid ; ùr-fhàs.
gemination, s. dùblachadh.
Gemini, s. na leth-aoin, aon do chomh-arran na cuairt-ghréine.
geminous, adj. dà-fhìllt.
gemmary, adj. seudach, leugach.
gender, s. gné, gin, seòrsa.
gender, v. gin, tàrmaich ; àraich.
genealogical, adj. sloinnteachail.
genealogist, s. sloinntear.
genealogy, s. sloinntearachd.
general, adj. coitcheann, cumanta ; gnàth aichte, farsuing an seadh.
general, s. seanailear ; ceann-feachd.
generalissimo, s. àrd-sheanailear.
generality, s. coitcheanntas, cumantas ; a chuid as mò.
generate, v. a. gin, sìolaich, tàrmaich, thoir a mach.
generation, s. gineamhuinn ; sliochd, àlach, àl, glùn-ginealaich ; linn.
generative, adj. sìolmhor.
generical, adj. gnèitheach.
generosity, s. fiùghantachd, fialachd, toirbheartachd, uaisle ; suairceas.
generous, adj. fiùghantach, faoilidh, flathail, fial, tabhartach, suairce ; uasal, làidir, beothail.

Genesis, s. ceud thòiseachadh, ceud leabh-ar Mhaois.
genet, s. each spàinnteach.
Geneva, s. Sùgh an aitil.
genial, adj. gnèitheach ; tlusail, coibh-neil ; nàdurra, dàimheil ; cridheil.
genitals, s. buill-dhìomhair.
genitive, adj. gineamhuinneach.
genius, s. duine air leth geurchuiseach ; cumhachd inntinn ; nàdur, aomadh inntinn.
genteel, adj. modhail ; spéiseil ; suairce ; eireachdail ; grinn, air cruth na h-uaisleachd.
genteelness, s. modhalachd, suairceas, eireachdas, grinneas.
gentian, s. lus a' chrùbain.
gentile, s. cinneach, geintileach.
gentilism, s. pàganach.
gentility, s. spéisealachd, uaisle.
gentle, adj. uasal, inbheach ; modhail, beusach ; ciùin, sèimh, caomh, màllda ; sìtheil, soitheamh.
gentleman, s. duin'-uasal.
gentlemanlike, adj. mar dhuin'-uasal, flathail.
gentleness, s. uaisle ; ciùine.
gentlewoman, s. bean-uasal.
gentry, s. uaislean, daoine uasal.
genuflexion, s. glùn-lùbadh.
genuine, adj. fior, neo-thruaillte.
genus, s. dream, seòrsa, gnè.
geographer, s. cruinne-eòlaiche.
geography, s. cruinne-eòlas.
geology, s. eòlas air gnè a' chruthachaidh.
geomancer, s. fiosaiche, drùidh.
geomancy, s. fiosachd, drùidheachd.
Georgic, s. Dàn-tuathanachais.
geranium, s. lus-gnà-ghorm.
german, s. bràthair, dàimheach.
germen, germin, s. fiùran, faillean.
germinate, v. n. thoir fàs, thig fo bhlàth.
germination, s. ùr-fhàs, blàth.
gestation, s. tòrrachas, leth-tromachd.
gesticulate, v. n. dèan comharran labhairt (mar ri balbham).
gesticulation, s. lùth-chleasachd, àmhail-tean.
gesture, s. car, carachadh, gluasad (mar chòmhnadh labhairt).
get, v. faigh ; coisinn, solair.
getting, s. faighinn ; cosnadh.
gewgaw, s. rud faoin, ni suarach ; brèaghachd fhaoin.
ghastful, adj. gruamach, oillteil.
ghastly, adv. gu h-aogaidh, oillteil.
ghost, s. tannasg, spiorad ; tàsg.
ghostly, adj. spioradail.
giant, s. famhair, athach.
giantess, s. ban-athach.
giantlike, giantly, adj. athanta.
gibber, v. n. labhair gun seadh.
gibberish, s. goileam, brolaich, giolam.

gibbet, s. croich.
gibbosity, gibbousness, s. bolgachd, pluc-achd.
gibbous, adj. crotach, plucach, meallach.
gibcat, s. cat-luathainn.
gibe, s. fochaid, magadh ; sgeig.
giblets, s. grùdhan, adha, giaban geòidh.
giddily, adv. gu guanach ; gun chùram.
giddiness, s. tuainealaich, guanachd, gogaideachd ; gòraiche.
giddy, a. guanach, tuainealach; sgaog-ach, gaoitheanach, gòrach, faoin.
giddy - brained, adj. sgaog - cheannach, itcheannach.
gier-eagle, s. an iolair-fhionn.
gift, s. tìodhlac, tabhartas, gibht.
gifted, adj. tìodhlaicte, comasach.
gig, s. carbad beag ; bàta-caol.
gigantic, adj. athach, tomadach.
giggle, v. n. dèan frith-ghàire.
gild, v. a. òr, òraich.
gilder, s. fear-òraidh.
gilding, s. òradh.
gill, s. stòp-cairteil, giùran ; sprogaill ; lus-na-staoine, eighean-làir.
gillyflower, s. lus-leth-an-t-sàmhraidh.
gilt, s. òr-dhealt, òradh.
gim, gimmy, s. snasmhor, grinn.
gimlet, s. gimileid.
gin, s. ribe, lìon ; sùgh an aitil.
ginger, s. dinnsear.
gingerbread, s. aran-milis, aran-cridhe.
gingerly, adv. gu socair ; gu sàmhach ; gu faiceallach.
gingival, adj. càireanach.
gingle, v. dèan glìongraich ; gliong.
ginglymus, s. alt-cheangal.
gipsy, s. cèard-fiosachd, ban-fhiosaiche, baobh-shiùbhlach, ceàrd.
gird, v. crioslaich, cuairtich.
girder, s. sail-ùrlair.
girdle, s. crios-leasraidh.
girl, s. caileag, cailin, nìgheanag.
girlish, adj. mar chaileig, mar phàiste.
girt, girth, s. giort-tarra, beart-bhronn dìolta ; dòmhlad, gairbhead, cuairt.
girth, v. a. crioslaich, giortaich.
give, v. a. tabhair, thoir, bàirig, builich, thoir seachad.
giver, s. fear-buileachaidh.
giving, s. buileachadh, tabhairt.
gizzard, s. sgròban, giaban.
glaciation, s. reodhadh, deigh.
glacious, adj. deigheach, eighreadail, reòdhte.
glacis, s. bruach daingnich.
glad, adj. ait, aoibhinn, toilichte.
glad, gladden, v. a. dèan aoibhneach, dean éibhinn, dean ait, sòlasaich.
glade, s. réidhlean, blàr, ruidhe, lòm.
gladiator, s. cliaranach, basbair.
gladness, s. aoibhneas, toil-inntinn.
gladsome, adj. aoibhneach, ait.

glance, s. plathadh, grad-shealladh, seall-adh-sùl, buille-shùl.
glance, v. n. grad amhairc, gabh plathadh dheth ; ruith fiar, thoir siaradh.
gland, s. fàireag.
glanders, s. gràineasadh.
glandulous, glandular, adj. fàireagach.
glare, v. boillsg, dealraich, soillsich, dèarsaich ; seall gu fiadhaich ; dèars, bi loinnreach.
glare, s. boillsgeadh, dealradh, soillse, lannair ; sealladh fiadhaich.
glaring, adj. follaiseach, ro shoillear.
glass, s. glaine ; sgàthan.
glassy, adj. glaineach, réidh, mìn, soilleir.
glave, v. claidheamh mór.
glaze, v. a. còmhdaich le glaine.
glazier, s. glaineadair, fear-oibreachaidh glaine.
gleam, s. boillsgeadh, plathadh, drìls.
gleam, v. n. boillsg, dèars, soillsich.
gleamy, adj. boillsgeach, dèarsach.
glean, v. a. trus ; dioghlum.
gleaner, s. fear dioghluim.
gleaning, s. dioghlum, tional.
glebe, s. fearann ministear; fòd.
glede, s. clamhan gòbhlach.
glee, s. mire, sunnt, aiteas, cridhealas ; luinneag, òran sùgraidh.
gleeful, adj. cridheil, sunntach.
gleet, s. sileadh, iongar.
glefty, adj. silteach, iongarach.
glen, s. gleann.
glib, adj. sleamhainn, mìn, réidh.
glibness, s. sleamhnad, mìnead ; luathas teangaidh.
glide, v. n. gluais eutrom, falbh ciùin.
glimmer, v. n. dèan fann-sholus.
glimmer, glimmering, s. fann-sholus, frith-sholus.
glimpse, s. pladhadh, boillsgeadh, seall-adh grad, aiteal.
glisten, v. n. soillsich, boillsg, dealraich.
glister, v. n. soillsich, dèarrs, boillsg.
glitter, v. n. dèarrs, boillsg, bi lainnearach, bi breagha.
glitter, glittering, s. dèarrsadh, boillsg-eadh, lainnir.
globated, globed, adj. cruinn (mar ball).
globe, s. ball cruinn ; cruinne ; dealbh na cruinne.
globose, globular, globulous, adj. cruinn, cuarsgach.
globosity, s. cruinn-chumadh.
glomerate, v. a. cuairsg, cruinnich.
glomeration, s. cuairsgeadh.
gloom, s. gruaim, duibhre, dubhar ; mìghean, mùig, smalan, truim-inntinn.
gloominess, s. duibhre, doilleireachd ; mùgaich, gruamachd. mì-ghean.
gloomy, adj. doilleir, neulach, dubharach; gruamach, mùgach, trom-inntinneach.

glorification, s. glòrachadh.
glorify, v. a. glòraich, cliùthaich ; thoir aoradh, thoir urram, thoir glòir ; thoir gu glòir, naomhaich.
glorious, adj. glòrmhor, òirdheirc, allail, naomha.
glory, s. glòir, cliù ; sonas nèimh ; urram, àrd-mholadh.
glory, v. a. dean uaill, dèan bòsd.
gloss, s. mìneachadh, lìomh, dealradh.
gloss, v. mìnich, cuir cleòc air, thoir leithsgeul bòidheach ; lìomh, sgeadaich.
glossary, s. sanasan, leabhar-mìneachaidh shean fhacal ; Faclair.
glossiness, s. lìomharrachd.
glossy, adj. lìomharra, mìn.
glout, v. amhairc gruamach.
glove, s. làmhainn, meatag.
glover, s. làmhainnear.
glow, v. dèarrs, soillsich le teas ; dianloisg ; bi teth, bi blàth ; bi feargach, las.
glow, s. caoir dhearg, teas, soillse ; lainnir, ainteas, dian-chorraich.
glow-worm, s. cuileag-shnìomhain.
gloze, v. n. dèan miodal, dèan miolasg.
gloze, s. miodal, sodal, miolasg.
glue, s. glaodh ; slaman-tàth.
glue, v. a. glaodh ; co-thàth.
glum, adj. dorcha, gruamach.
glut, v. a. sàsaich ; glàm, glut.
glut, s. glàmadh, slugadh, làn, sàth.
glutinosity, glutinousness, s. glaoghach, rìghneach, leantach.
glutinous, adj. glaodhach, righinn.
glutton, s. glàimsear, geòcaire, craosaire.
gluttonous, adj. craosach, geòcach.
gluttony, s. geòcaireachd, craos.
gnarled, adj. meallach, plucach, cràiceach.
gnash, v. buail r'a chéile, dèan gìosgan ; cas dréin.
gnashing, s. dìosgan, gìosgan.
gnat, s. meanbh-chuileag.
gnaw, v. a. caith, ith, cnàmh, créim, cagainn, teum.
gnomon, s. dealg uaireadair-gréine.
go, v. n. falbh, imich, theirig, rach, siubhail, coisich, gluais ; tàr as.
goad, s. bior-greasaidh.
goad, v. a. greas le bior greasaidh, spor ; bruidich, stuig, cuir thuige.
goal, s. ceann-crìche, crìoch, deireadh, ceann-thall ; ceann-réise.
goat, s. gobhar.
goatherd, s. buachaille ghobhar.
goatish, adj. macnusach, drùiseil.
gob, v. a. sluig, ith gu lonach.
gobbet, v. a. sluig gun chagnadh.
goblet, s. aghann, copan, cuach.
goblin, s. fuath, bòcan, ùruisg, glaistig, baobh.
God, s. Dia.

godchild, s. dalta.
goddess, s. ban-dia.
godfather, s. oide, goistidh.
godhead, s. diadhachd.
godless, adj. ain-diadhaidh.
godlessness, s. aindiadhachd.
god-like, adj. mar dhia.
godliness, s. diadhachd.
godly, adj. diadhaidh, cràbhach.
godmother, s. muime.
goggle, v. n. spleuchd, seall fiar.
goggle-eyed, adj. fiarshuileach.
going, s. falbh, imeachd.
gold, s. òr.
golden, adj. òrdha, òir, òrach, a dh' òr ; òrbhuidhe, àrbhuidhe.
goldfinch, s. lasair-choille.
goldhammer, s. buidhein-coille.
goldsmith, s. òrcheard.
gondola, s. seòrsa bàta, eithear beag (eadailteach).
gone, part. pret. from to go, air triall, air falbh, thairis, marbh, millte.
gonorrhœa, s. an clap silteach.
good, adj. math, deagh ; fallain.
good, s. math ; leas, tairbhe.
goodliness, s. maise, eireachdas.
goodly, adj. maiseach, sgiamhach, bòidheach, ciatach, eireachdail ; sultmhor, dòmhail, tomadach.
goodness, s. mathas, deagh-bheus.
goods, s. cuid, maoin, badhar.
goodwill, s. deagh-thoil.
goody, s. mo bheanag.
goose, s. gèadh ; iarunn-tàillear.
gooseberry, s. gròiseid.
goosequill, s. gèadhach, ite geòidh.
gorbellied, adj bronnach.
gore, s. fuil, flann-fhuil ; gaorr.
gore, v. a. gaorr, troimh-lot, sàth.
gorge, s. sgòrnan, slugan ; bealach.
gorge, v. a. lìon, sàsaich ; glamhaich ; ith gu geòcach.
gorgeous, adj. rìmheach, lòiseamach, greadhnach.
gorget, s. gòrsaid.
gorgon, s. culaidh-dhéisinn.
gormandise, v. n. glut, ith gu lonach.
gormandiser, s. glaimsear, geòcaire.
gorse, s. conusg, droighneach.
gory, adj. air eabradh le fuil.
goshawk, s. seabhac-mhór.
gosling, s. isean geòidh.
gospel, s. soisgeul.
gossamer, s. lus-chlòimh.
gossip, s. goistidh ; sgimilear ; briot.
gossip, v. n. bi bruidhneach, bi gobaireachd ; bi soganach.
got, gotten, part. pass. of to get, fhuaras, fhuaradh.
gouge, v. sgiolg.
gouge, s. gilb chruinn, sgilb-chlaiseach.
gourd, s. luibh-sgàile.

gout, s. tinneas-nan-alt.
gouty, adj. gu h-olc le tinneas-nan-alt ; a bhuineas do thinneas-nan-alt.
govern, v. riaghail, rìoghaich ; stiùir, seòl, steòrn ; ceannsaich, smachdaich cùm an òrdugh.
governable, adj. so-cheannsachadh.
governess, s. ban-ionnsachaich.
government, s. uachdranachd, riaghladh, flaitheachd ; ceannsachd, ceannsalachd.
governor, s. riaghladair ; oid-ionnsachaidh.
gown, s. gùn, earrasaid.
grace, s. fàbhar, deaghghean tròcair, mathanas ; gràs, subhailc, diadhachd ; maise, eireachdas ; loinn, àilleachd ; altachadh.
grace, v. a. sgeadaich, maisich.
grace-cup, s. a' cheud deoch slàinte.
graceful, adj. àluinn, maiseach, ciatach, grinn.
gracefulness, s. eireachdas, maise.
graceless, adj. gun ghràs, aingidh.
gracious, adj. tròcaireach, gràsmhor, mathasach ; fàbharach, caomh, bàigheil.
graciousness, s. gràsmhorachd, caomhalachd, tròcair, bàigh.
gradation, s. ceum ; éiridh, dìreadh riaghailteach, ceum air cheum.
gradatory, adj. a' dol o cheum gu ceum.
grade, s. inbhe, ceum.
gradual, adj. a chuid 's a chuid.
graduality, **graduation**, s. dol air adhart, ceumnachadh ; buileachadh tiodal ionnsachaidh.
graduate, v. a. thoir tiodal ionnsachaidh ; gabh ceum ionnsachaidh ; àrdaich, dean ni's fèarr ; gluais o cheum gu ceum.
graduate, s. sgoilear tiodail.
graft, **graff**, s. faillean, fiùran.
graft, **graff**, v. a. tàth, alp ; co-thàth ; bi suidheachadh fhaillean.
grain, s. sìlean, gràinne, sìol, gràn ; nàdur, gnè.
grained, adj. calgach, garbh, molach.
grains, s. treasg, drabh.
grainy, adj. grànach ; gràinneanach.
gramineal, **gramineous**, adj. feurach, lusanach.
graminivorous, adj. feur-itheach.
grammar, s. eòlas ceart-chainnt.
grammarian, s. fear ceart-chainnteach, snas-bhriathraiche.
grammatical, adj. ceart - chainnteach, snas-bhriathrach.
grampus, s. cana, puthag.
granary, s. sìol-lann, sgiobal.
granate, **granite**, s. graineal.
grand, adj. urramach, ainmeil ; mór, greadhnach, breagha ; prìomh ; àrd, uasal.

grandchild, s. ogha.
grandee, s. duine cumhachdach ; duine mór ; atharrais na h-uaisleachd.
grandeur, s. mórachd, greadhnachas ; meamnachd, mór-chuis.
grandfather, s. seanair.
grandiloquence, s. mórchuis.
grandmother, s. seanamhair.
grandness, s. mórachd, meudachd.
grandsire, s. priomh-athair.
grandson, s. ogha.
grange, s. grainnseach.
granivorus, adj. gràn-itheach.
grant, v. a. ceadaich, aidich, deònaich ; builich, tiodhlaic, bàirig.
grant, s. buileachadh, tabhairt, tiodhlacadh ; tiodhlac, tabhartas ; ceadachach, aideachadh.
grantor, s. fear tiodhlacaidh, feartabhairt (thiodhlac).
granulary, adj. gràinneach.
granulation, s. pronnadh, gràineanachadh.
granulous, adj. gràinneanach.
grape, s. fìon-dhearc.
graphical, adj. dealbhach.
grapnel, s. greimiche.
grapple, v. greimich, glac, beir air, gleachd, teannaich.
grasp, v. greimich, glac, teannaich ; dèan greim ; theirig an sàs.
grasp, s. greimeachadh, glacadh, gréim ; seilbh, cumail.
grass, s. feur.
grasshopper, s. fionnan-feòir, leumnach uaine, dreòlan-teasbhuidh.
grassy, adj. feurach.
grate, s. cliath-theine, àite-teine.
grate, v. suath, sgrìob, meil ; thoir sgreuch air, dèan fuaim sgreuchach.
grateful, adj. taingeil, buidheach ; taitneach, tlachdmhor, ciatach.
grater, s. sgrìobadair ; sgrìoban.
gratification, s. toileachadh, sòlasachadh, sàsachadh ; toil-inntinn, sòlas.
gratify, v. a. toilich, taitinn ; sàsaich, duaisich, dìol, riaraich.
grating, s. cliath-iaruinn.
grating, part. adj. sgreuchach, sgreadach.
gratis, adv. an asgaidh.
gratitude, **gratefulness**, s. taingealachd, buidheachas.
gratuitous, adj. saor-thiodhlaicte.
gratuity, s. saor-thiodhlac.
gratulation, s. fàilte, fàilteachadh ; co-ghàirdeachas, co-bhuidheachas.
gratulatory, adj. sòlasach, co-ghàirdeachail.
grave, s. uaigh, reilic.
grave, v. gèarr, gràbhal ; tarruing, sgrìobh.
grave, adj. stòlda, suidhichte, sàmhach, cudthromach ; trom, tormanach.

grave-clothes, s. aodach mairbh, lion-aodach.
gravel, s. grinneal ; galar-fuail.
gravel, v. a. còmhdaich le grinneal ; amail, grab, bac.
gravelly, adj. grinnealach.
graver, s. fear-gràbhalaidh ; inneal gràbhalaidh, gilb-ghràbhalaidh.
gravid, a. leth-tromach ; trom.
graving, s. gràbhaladh, obair gràbhalaiche.
gravitate, v. n. tuit, theirig le bruthach.
gravitation, s. tuiteam, tèarnadh.
gravity, graveness, s. cudthrom, truimead ; antromachadh, stòldachd, suidheachadh-inntinn.
gravy, s. sùgh feòla ; eanbhruith.
gray, adj. glas, liath ; ciar.
grayish, adj. liath-ghlas.
graze, v. feuraich, cuir air feur ; ionaltair, ith feur.
graze, v. suath, bean.
grazier, s. àireach, fear spréidhe.
grazing, s. ionaltradh.
grease, s. créis, geir, saill, iòlan.
grease, v. a. buaic, smeur.
greasiness, s. reamhrachd.
greasy, adj. créiseach, geireach.
great, adj. mór, dòmhail ; lìonmhor, fada ; àrd ; uaibhreach, àrdanach ; làn, torrach.
greatness, s. mórachd, meudachd ; móralachd, àrd-inbhe, urram, cumhachd ; uaill, uaibhreachas, àrdan.
greaves, s. casbheairt.
Greece, s. a' Ghréig.
greediness, s. sannt, gionach, lon.
greedy, adj. sanntach, gionach, cìocrach, lonach, glutach, glàmhach.
green, adj. uaine, gorm ; glas ; ùrail, ùr ; àitidh, fliuch, tais ; anabaich.
green, s. dath uaine no gorm ; réidhlean, àilean, lèan, raon.
greenness, s. uainead, guirme ; anabaicheachd, anabaichead ; ùraireachd.
green-sickness, s. an galar-uaine.
greet, v. n. fàiltich, furanaich ; dèan co-ghàirdeachas ; cuir beannachd.
greeting, s. fàilte, furan, beannachd.
gregarious, adj. greigheach, treudach.
grenade, grenado, s. peileir spealgach.
grenadier, s. saighdear àrd.
greyhound, s. miol-chù, gaothar.
grice, s. orcan, uircean.
gridiron, s. branndair, greideal.
grief, s. bròn, doilghios, mulad, bristeadh-cridhe.
grievance, s. dochunn, cruaidhchas.
grieve, v. càidh, dochainn ; dèan tùrsach ; caoidh ; bi fo bhròn.
grievous, adj. doilghiosach, cràidhteach, searbh ; trom, anabarrach.
griffin, griffon, s. leòmhan-sgiathach.

grig, s. easgann bheag ; creutair guanach, mireagach.
grim, adj. gruamach, mùgach, duaichnidh, gnù, neo-aoidheil.
grimace, s. gruaim, mùig.
grimness, s. gruamachd.
grin, v. n. cuir dréin ort.
grin, s. dréin, braoisg.
grind, v. meil, bleith, pronn ; suath, geuraich ; dèan bleith, bi bleith.
grinder, s. muillear, meiltear ; muileann, cùl-fhiacail.
grindstone, s. clach-gheurachaidh, clach liathra ; clach sniathra.
gripe, v. greimich, glac ; cum daingean ; teannaich, fàisg ; cràidh.
gripe, s. gréim ; fàsgadh, teannachadh ; éigin, cruaidhchas ; gréim mionaich.
grisly, adj. déisinneach, oillteil.
grist, s. gràn caoin, gràn tìridh.
gristle, s. maothan, brisgein.
gristly, adj. maothanach.
grit, s. garbhan, còrlach.
grizzled, grizzly, adj. grìsfhionn.
groan, v. n. osnaich, gearain, cnead.
groan, s. acain, osna, gearan, cnead.
groat, s. ceithir sgillinn, gròt.
grocer, s. ceannaiche, fear-reic (gach seòrsa bidh).
grog, s. spiorad as uisge co-mheasgte.
groin, s. loch-bhléin.
groom, s. gille stàpuill ; gille each.
groove, s. uamh, sloc ; clais.
grope, v. n. smeuraich.
gross, adj. garbh, tiugh, dòmhail, reamhar, sultmhor ; déisinneach, neo-cheanalta, neo-thaitneach ; neo-ghlan, neo-fhìnealta ; iomlan, uile.
gross, s. an t-iomlan ; dà dhusan-deug.
grossness, s. gairbhead, tiuighead, dòmhlachd ; reamhrachd ; ùmpadalachd.
grot, grotto, s. sgàil-thigh.
grotesque, adj. mì-dhealbhach, eu-cuanda, mì-nadurach.
ground, s. talamh ; làr, fonn ; fearann, tìr ; dùthaich ; aobhar, bun, bunchar, toiseach.
ground, v. a. suidhich 's an talamh ; socraich air làr ; stéidhich, taic ; bonn-shuidhich.
ground-ivy, s. athair-lus, staoin.
groundless, adj. gun aobhar.
groundsel, grunsel, s. grunnasg.
groundwork, s. bunabhas, stéidh.
group, s. grunnan, dòrlach.
grouse, s. cearc fhraoich.
grove, s. doire, coille, badan.
grovel, v. n. snàig, màg ; bi suarach, bi losal.
grow, v. n. thoir fàs air ; fàs, cinn, meudaich ; at, éirich suas.
growl, v. n. dean grùnsgul, dèan borbhanaich ; talaich.

growling, s. grùnsgul, talach, borbhan.
grown, part. cinnichte, air fàs.
growth, s. fàs, cinneas ; toradh ; meudachadh, teachd air adhart.
grub, v. a. bùraich, cladhaich.
grub, s. cnuimh mhìllteach.
grubble, v. n. smeuraich.
grudge, v. maoidh air, talaich ; gabh
farmad ri ; bi neo-thoileach ; bi
farmadach, bi gamhlasach.
grudge, s. mì-run, gamhlas, tnù ; falachd;
farmad, diomb.
gruel, s. brochan, easach.
gruff, grum, adj. gruamach, mùgach,
doirbh, neo-aoidheil.
grumble, v. n. talaich, dèan duarmanaich,
gearain, dèan grùnsgul.
grumbler, s. fear-talaich.
grumbling, s. gearan, duarmanaich.
grunt, s. gnosail, osna, cnead, acain.
grunt, gruntle, v. n. dèan gnosail, sgiamh
mar mhuic.
gruntling, s. uircean, orcan.
guarantee, s. urras ; dearbhachd.
guard, v. a. dìon, dìdinn, gléidh.
guard, s. freiceadan ; faire, earalas.
guardian, s. fear-gleidhidh, fear-dìona,
athair, oide.
guardian, adj. dìonach, gléidhteach.
guardianship, s. dreuchd fir-diona.
guardless, adj. gun dìon.
guardship, s. long-dhìona.
gudgeon, s. clibist ; bronnag.
guess, v. thoir tuaiream, tomhais ; thoir
barail, baralaich.
guess, s. barail, tuaiream, meas.
guest, s. aoidh, coigreach.
guidance, s. seòladh, steòrnadh, stiùireadh,
treòrachadh, riaghladh.
guide, v. a. seòl, steòrn, treòraich.
guide, s. fear-treòrachaidh, fear-seòlaidh ;
fear-steòrnaidh ; fear-riaghlaidh, stiùir-
eadair.
guideless, adj. seachranach, gun treòir.
guild, s. comunn, buidheann.
guile, s. cealg, foill, cluain.
guileful, adj. cealgach, foilleil.
guileless, adj. neo-chealgach, neo-fhoilleil,
treidhireach, gun ghò.
guillemot, s. eun-a'-chrùbain.
guillotine, s. inneal dìth-cheannaidh.
guilt, s. cionta, cron, easaontas.
guiltiness, s. cionta, aingidheachd.
guiltless, adj. neochiontach.
guilty, adj. ciontach ; aingidh.

guinea, s. bonn òir, sgillinn ar fhichead
Shasunnach.
guise, s. seòl, modh, dòigh ; aogas,
éideadh.
gules, adj. dearg an gearradh-arm.
gulf, s. camus, bàgh ; dubhaigean ; coire-
cuairteig, slugan.
gull, v. a. meall, thoir car á.
gull, s. car, cleas, mì-chleas, cuilbheart ;
baothaire ; faoileag.
gullet, s. sgòrnan, slugan, eit-igheach.
gully, s. clais dhomhain uisge.
gulp, v. a. gloc, glut, sluig.
gum, s. bìth ; càirean, mannas.
gum, v. a. buaic le bìth, dlùthaich le
bìth.
gumminess, s. rìghnead, rìghneachas.
gummy, adj. bìtheanta, righinn.
gun, s. gunna.
gunner, s. gunnair.
gunnery, s. gunnaireachd.
gunpowder, s. fùdar-gunna.
gunshot, s. luaidhe gunna.
gunsmith, s. gobha-ghunnachan.
gunstone, s. peileir gunna mhóir.
gunwale, gunnel, s. beul-mór (bàta no
luinge).
gurgle, v. n. dèan glugan.
gurnet, gurnard, s. cnùdan, cnòdan,
crùdan.
gush, v. n. spùt, sruth, brùchd, taoisg.
gush, s. brùchd, spùt, taosg.
gusset, s. guiseid, eang.
gust, s. blas ; sàth-mhiann, déidh,
taitneachd ; osag, oiteag, cuairtghaoth.
gustation, s. blasad, blasachd.
gustful, adj. blasda, taitneach.
gusto, s. blas, miann, aomadh-inntinn.
gusty, adj. stoirmeil, gaothar.
gut, s. caolan ; geòcaireachd.
gut, v. a. thoir am mionach á ; spùill,
spùinn, creach.
gutter, s. guiteir, fear, bean-sgoltaidh
(éisg).
guttler, s. glutaire, geòcaire.
guttural, adj. tùchanach, a' labhairt
'san sgòrnan.
guzzle, v. a. sluig, òl gu bras.
guzzler, s. geòcaire, pòitear.
gymnasium, s. sgoil lùth-chleas.
gymnastic, adj. lùth-chleasach.
gyration, s. cur mu chuairt, cuir char.
gyre, s. cuairt, cearcall.
gyves, s. geimhlean, glas-chas, ceap.

H

ha ! *interj.* ha !
haberdasher, *s.* ceannaiche-aodaichean, ceannaiche ghoireasan, badan beaga aodaich.
haberdine, *s.* trosg saillt' tioram.
habergeon, *s.* uchd-éideadh.
hạbiliment, *s.* éideadh, earradh.
habit, *s.* cor, staid ; uidheam, earradh, éideadh ; cleachdadh, gnàthachadh.
habitable, *adj.* freagarrach air son còmhnaidh.
habitant, *s.* tàmhaiche, tuathanach beag.
habitation, *s.* ionad-còmhnaidh.
habitual, *adj.* cleachdach, gnàthach, gnàthaichte.
habituate, *v. a.* cleachd, gnàthaich.
habitude, *s.* càirdeas, còrdadh ; gnàthachadh, cleachdadh.
hack, *v. a.* spealg, gearr, eagaich.
hack, *s.* each carbad.
hackle, *v. a.* seicil, cìr.
hackney, *s.* each carbad ; tàrlaid.
haddock, *s.* adag.
haft, *s.* cas, samhach.
hag, *s.* baobh, ban-draoidh, buidseach ; cailleach ghrannda mì-aoigheil.
haggard, haggardly, *adj.* fiadhaich, borb, garg ; duaichnidh, grannda, oillteil.
haggis, *s.* taigeis, marag.
haggish, *adj.* basbhaidh, duaichnidh.
haggle, *v.* gearr, pronn, eagaich.
haggler, *s.* fear gearraidh ; fear righinn an co-cheannachd.
hail ! *interj.* fáilte ! slàinte !
hailstone, *s.* clach-mheallain.
hair, *s.* falt, ròine, fuiltean ; fionnadh, gaoisid, calg.
hairiness, *s.* ròmaiche.
hairy, *adj.* ròmach, molach, ròineach, fionnach.
halberd, *s.* pic-chatha.
halcyon, *adj.* sèimh, ciùin.
hale, *adj.* slàn, cridheil, sùgach.
hale, *v. a.* slaoid, dragh.
half, *s.* leth.
half-blood, *adj.* riataich.
halfpenny, *s.* bonna-sè.
halimass, *s.* latha nan uile naomh.
haling, *s.* draghadh, slaodadh.
hall, *s.* talla ; lùchairt.
hallelujah, *s.* moladh do Dhia.
halloo, *v. a.* stuig, leig, brosnaich, glaodh ; beuc, dean gàir.
hallow, *v. a.* naomhaich, coisrig.
hallucination, *s.* mearachd, mealladh.
halo, *s.* roth *no* cearcal na gréine, no na gealaiche.

halser, hawser, *s.* muir-theud ; taod, còrd ; ball bàta, càbal.
halt, *v. n.* bi crùbach, bi bacach ; stad, seas ; bi 'n imcheist ; bi teabadaich.
halt, *adj.* crùbach, bacach.
halt, *s.* crùbaiche ; stad, seasamh.
halter, *s.* taod, togha na croiche, adhastar.
halve, *v. a.* roinn 'na dhà leth.
ham, *s.* spàg, sliasaid, ceithreamh-deiridh ; sliasaid shaillte, feòil réisgte.
hamlet, *s.* baile beag, clachan.
hammer, *s.* òrd.
hammer, *v.* buail le òrd.
hammock, *s.* leaba chrochta.
hamper, *v. a.* cuibhrich, cuir amladh air ; cuir an sàs, cuir an ribe.
hamstring, *s.* féithe na h-iosgaid.
hand, *s.* làmh ; tomhas cheithir òirleach ; dòigh, seòl.
hand, *v. a.* thoir as do làimh, sìn, thoir, tabhair, thoir seachad.
handbreadth, *s.* leud boise.
handcuff, *s.* glas-làmh.
handful, *s.* làn dùirn, dòrlach.
handicraft, *s.* cèaird.
handiness, *s.* làmhchaireachd.
handkerchief, *s.* neapaicin-pòcaid.
handle, *v. a.* làimhsich.
handle, *s.* làmh, cas, cluas.
handmaid, *s.* banoglach.
hand-saw, *s.* sàbh làimhe.
handsel, hansel, *s.* sainnseal.
handsome, *adj.* maiseach, àillidh, eireachdail, bòidheach ; mór, gasda.
handwriting, *s.* lamh-sgrìobhaidh.
handy, *adj.* làmhchair, deas, ealamh.
hang, *v.* croch ; bi'n imcheist.
hanger, *s.* cuinnsear.
hanging, *adj.* an crochadh, a' crochadh.
hangman, *s.* crochadair.
hank, *s.* iarna.
hanker, *v. n.* bi'n geall air.
hap, *s.* tubaist ; tuiteamas, tachairt.
haphazard, *s.* tuiteamas, tubaist.
hapless, *adj.* mì-shealbhar, mì-shona, neo-sheamhsar.
haply, *adv.* theagamh.
happen, *v. n.* tachair, tuit a mach.
happiness, *s.* sonas, àgh, sealbh.
happy, *adj.* sona, sòlasach, àghmhor, sealbhach, rathail ; deas, ealamh.
harangue, *s.* òraid, seanachas.
harass, *v. a.* claoidh, sàraich, léir.
harbinger, *s.* roimh - ruithear, teachd-aire.
harbour, harbourage, *s.* cala, acarsaid, dìon, dìdeann.
harbour, *v.* gabh ri, thoir fasgadh do ; gabh còmhnaidh, gabh dìon.

hard, *adj.* cruaidh, teann, daingeann ; duilich r'a thuigsinn ; deacair, doirbh ; dòghruinneach, cràidhteach ; an-iochd-mhor, cruadalach, garg ; gann.

hard, *adv.* am fagus, dlùth, teann ; gu dìchiollach, gu dian, gu dùrachdach.

harden, *v. a.* cruadhaich, teannaich, lean ri ; dèan ladarna ; fàs cruaidh, fàs teann.

hard-favoured, *adj.* duaichnidh.

hardihood, *s.* cruadal, danarrachd.

hardiness, *s.* cruadal ; dànachd.

hardness, *s.* cruas ; an-iochd, buirbe.

hards, *s.* ascart.

hardship, *s.* cruaidhchas, teanntachd, fòirneart, teinn ; éigin.

hardware, *s.* badhar cruaidh, ceannachd iaruinn.

hardy, *adj.* dàna, ladarna, danarra ; gaisgeil ; cruadalach, fulangach.

hare, *s.* maigheach, gearr, gearr fhiadh.

harebell, *s.* currac-na-cuthaige, bròg na cuthaig.

hare-brained, *adj.* gaoitheanach, sgaogach.

hark, *interj.* éisd ! cluinn ! tost !

harlequin, *s.* àmhuilteach.

harlot, *s.* strìopach, siùrsach.

harlotry, *s.* strìopachas.

harm, *s.* cron, àimhleas, lochd, coire, ciorram, dolaidh, call, beud, dochair.

harm, *v. a.* ciùrr, dochainn, lochdaich.

harmful, *adj.* cronail, lochdach.

harmless, *adj.* neochiontach, neo-chronail, neo-lochdach.

harmonic, harmonical, *adj.* co-fhuaimneach, co-cheòlach ; binn.

harmonious, *adj.* co-chòrdach ; réidh.

harmonise, *v. a.* dèan co-fhuaimneach ; co-fhreagair.

harmonist, *s.* fear-ciùil.

harmony, *s.* co-sheirm, co-chòrdadh, co-fhreagairt ; co-cheòl ; càirdeas.

harness, *s.* fasair ; armachd, acfhuinn.

harp, *s.* clàrsach, cruit-chiùil.

harp, *v. a.* cluich air clàrsaich.

harper, *s.* clàrsair, cruitear.

harpoon, *s.* mor-ghath muice-mara.

harpooner, *s.* fear tilgidh mor-ghath na muice-mara.

harpsichord, *s.* cruit-chiùil.

harpy, *s.* gionair, glàmair.

harridan, *s.* seann strìopach sheargte.

harrier, *s.* tòlair mhaigheach.

harrow, *s.* cliath-chliata.

harrow, *v. a.* cliath ; buair, claoidh.

harsh, *adj.* searbh, garg, borb, reasgach, frithearra ; neo-bhinn ; coimheach, cruaidh, teann.

harshness, *s.* searbhachd, gairge, gairgead ; neo-fhonnmhorachd ; reasgachd ; buirbe.

hart, *s.* damh féidh.

hartshorn, *s.* sùgh chabar féidh.

harvest, *s.* foghar, toradh, buannachd.

harvest-home, *s.* deireadh buana.

harvesting, *part. v.* fogharadh.

hash, *v. a.* pronn, gèarr, bloighdich.

hash, *s.* feòil phronn ; pronnsgail.

hassock, *s.* cluasag ghlùin.

haste, *s.* cabhag, greasad.

haste, hasten, *v. a.* greas, luathaich, brosnaich, cuir cabhag air ; deifirich, dèan cabhag.

hastiness, *s.* greasachd, deifir, cabhag, luaths ; frionas, crosdachd, conasachd.

hastings, *s.* luath-pheasair.

hasty, *adj.* luath, cabhagach ; deifireach, grad, ealamh ; bras, crosda, dian, lasanta, obann, clis.

hasty-pudding, *s.* mèilean, stapag.

hat, *s.* biorraid, ad ; ceannbheart.

hatch, *v.* guir, thoir a mach àl ; thoir gu crìch ; àlaich, tàrmaich.

hatch, *s.* gur, linn, àlach ; dorus bùird luinge.

hatchet, *s.* làmhthuadh.

hate, *v. a.* fuathaich, gràinich, oilltich, sgreamhaich.

hate, hatred, *s.* fuath, gràin, oillt, sgreamh, gairisinn, gamhlas, mìrun, naimhdeas.

hateful, *adj.* fuathach, gràineil, gairisneach, sgreamhail, sgreataidh, déisinneach.

hatter, *s.* fear-dèanamh adan, ceannaiche adan.

haugh, *s.* lèanan ; srath.

haughtiness, *s.* àrdan, uaibhreachas, uaill, uabhar.

haughty, *adj.* àrdanach, uaibhreach, mórchuiseach, àilleasach, àrd-inntinneach ; stràiceil, meamnach.

haul, *v. a.* tarruing, slaoid.

haulm, haum, *s.* fodar, connlach.

haunch, *s.* sliasaid, cruachann.

haunt, *v. a.* taghail, taghaich.

have, *v. a.* biodh agad ; giùlain, caith ; seilbhich, meal ; iarr, agair.

haven, *s.* cala, acarsaid, seòlait.

having, *s.* sealbh, maoin.

havoc, *s.* àr, milleadh, sgrios.

haw, *s.* sgeachag ; gagail.

haw, *v. n.* bruidhinn gu gagach.

hawk, *s.* seabhac, speireag.

hawk, *v. n.* reic badhar (o dhorus gu dorus) ; sealg le seabhaic ; ròc casadaich.

hawker, *s.* seabhacair ; ceannaiche-màlaid, ceannaiche-siubhail.

hawthorn, *s.* sgitheach, droigheann.

hay, *s.* feur-saidhe, tràthach.

haymaker, *s.* fear caoineachaidh feòir.

hayrick, haystack, *s.* curracag-fheòir, tudan, molan.

hazard, *s.* cunnart ; tuiteamas.

hazard, *v. a.* cuir an cunnart ; ruith cunnart ; feuch ri, feuch cuid tuiteamais.
hazardous, *adj.* cunnartach.
haze, *s.* ceò, ceathach, smùd.
hazel, *s.* calltunn.
hazel, hazelly, *adj.* air dhath calltuinn.
he, *pron.* è, se, esan.
head, *s.* ceann ; ceannard ; toiseach ; tuigse ; mullach ; neach ; barr, uachdar ; àirde, cead, comas, saor-thoil.
head, *v. a.* treòraich, stiùir, riaghail ; cuir ceann air.
headache, *s.* ceann-ghalair, cràdh cinn, ceann goirt.
head-bands, *s.* beannag.
head-dress, *s.* anart-cinn, ceann-bheart.
headland, *s.* ceann-tìre, maol, rudha, ard.
headless, *adj.* gun cheann, gun cheannard ; neo-thùrail, aineolach.
headlong, *adj.* cas, corrach, grad ; bras, obann, cabhagach.
headlong, *adv.* an coinneamh a chinn ; an comhair cinn, gu bras, gu h-obann ; gu neo-smaointeachail.
headpiece, *s.* clogaid, tuigse.
headstall, *s.* adhastar.
headstrong, *adj.* ceann-laidir, reasgach.
heady, *adj.* dian, bras, cas ; cabhagach, ceann-laidir ; a' dol 'sa' cheann.
heal, *v.* leighis, slànaich, dèan gu math ; fàs gu math, fàs slàn.
healing, *part.* leigheasach.
health, *s.* slàinte, fallaineachd.
healthful, healthsome, *adj.* slàn, fallain ; slàinteil.
healthy, *adj.* slàn, fallain ; slàinteil.
heap, *s.* tòrr, dùn, càrn, cruach.
heap, *v. a.* càrn, cruach, cruinnich.
hear, *v.* cluinn, éisd.
hearer, *s.* fear-éisdeachd.
hearing, *s.* clàisneachd ; éisdeachd.
hearken, *v. n.* éisd, cluinn.
hearsay, *s.* iomradh, fathunn.
hearse, *s.* carbad-mhàrbh.
heart, *s.* cridhe ; meadhon.
heartache, *s.* briseadh-cridhe.
heartburning, *s.* losgadh-bràghad.
heart-ease, *s.* socair inntinn.
hearten, *v. a.* misnich, beothaich.
heartfelt, *adj.* a' ruigheachd a' chridhe, drùidhteach.
hearth, *s.* teinntean, cagailt.
hearth-money, *s.* cìs-teallaich.
heartiness, *s.* treidhireas ; cridhealas, sunnt, beathalachd.
heartless, *adj.* lagchridheach, cruaidhchridheach.
heart-strings, *s.* féithean a' chridhe.
hearty, *adj.* dùrachdach, dìleas ; slàn, slàinteil ; cridheil, treòrach, sunntach.
heat, *s.* teas ; blàths, bruthainn ; buaireas, ainteas ; braise.

heat, *v. a.* teasaich, teò ; cuir air bhoile, cuir air ghoil ; blàthaich.
heater, *s.* uidheam teasachaidh, iarunn teinntidh, " clach "-iaruinn.
heath, *s.* fraoch.
heath-cock, *s.* coileach-fraoich.
heathen, *s.* cinneach, geintealach.
heathen, heathenish, *adj.* pàganach ; fiadhaich, allamharra.
heathenism, *s.* pàganachd.
heathy, *adj.* fraochach, làn fraoich.
heave, *s.* togail, ospag, plosg.
heave, *v.* tog suas, luaisg ; bòrc, bòc ; plosg, tarruing osna ; at, éirich suas.
heaven, *s.* nèamh, speur, adhar, iarmailt ; flathanas, flaitheas.
heavenly, *adj.* nèamhaidh, flathail, naomha, diadhaidh.
heaviness, *s.* cudthrom, truime, truimead ; airtneal, cianalas, sproc, mulad, trom-inntinn.
heavy, *adj.* trom, cudthromach ; airtnealach, cianail, trom - inntinneach, neo-shunntach ; leisg, lunndach, cadalach, tromcheannach, pleòisgeach ; neulach, dorcha.
hebdomadal, hebdomadary, *adj.* seachduineil.
hebdomand, *s.* ùine sheachd latha.
Hebrew, *s.* Eabhrach ; Eabhra.
Hebrew, *adj.* Eabhrach.
hecatomb, *s.* ìobairt-cheud (=ceud damh).
hectic, hectical, *adj.* gnàthach, fiabhrasach.
hector, *s.* bagaire, bòsdair.
hedge, *s.* fàl gléidhte, callaid ; garadh.
hedge, *v.* dùin le fàl, druid suas le droighionn, cuairtich le callaid.
hedge-born, *adj.* anuasal.
hedgehog, *s.* cràineag.
hedger, *s.* fear-togail fàil-gléidhte.
heed, *v. a.* thoir fainear, thoir aire.
heed, *s.* cùram, aire, faicill.
heedful, *adj.* cùramach, faicilleach, furachair ; aireachail, aireach.
heedless, *adj.* neo-chùramach.
heedlessness, *s.* dearmadachd.
heel, *s.* sàil ; cas beathaich.
heel, *v.* cuir sàil air bròig ; aom, claon, laigh air aon taobh (mu long).
heft, *s.* cudthrom.
heifer, *s.* agh, atharla.
heigh-ho ! *interj.* Oich O !
height, *s.* àirde, àirdead ; mullach, binnein ; inbhe ; iomlanachd.
heighten, *v. a.* àrdaich, tog suas, meudaich ; leasaich ; antromaich.
heinous, *adj.* uabhasach, amasgaidh, anabarrach, antromach, gràineil.
heinousness, *s.* uabhasachd, uabharrachd, amasgaidheachd, gràinealachd.
heir, *s.* oighre.

heir, *v. a.* seilbhich mar oighre.
heiress, *s.* ban-oighre.
heirless, *adj.* gun oighre.
heirloom, *s.* ball-sinnsireachd.
heirship, *s.* staid oighre.
helioscope, *s.* gloine gréine.
hell, *s.* ifrinn, iutharn.
Hellenic, *adj.* Greugach.
hellish, *adj.* ifrinneach.
helm, *s.* clogaid ; falmadair.
helmed, *adj.* clogaideach.
helmet, *s.* clogaid.
helmsman, *s.* stiùradair.
help, *v.* cuidich, cobhair, fòir, còmhnaich, furtaich ; cuir air adhart ; thoir cobhair, thoir cuideachadh.
help, *s.* cuideachadh, cobhair, còmhnadh, taic ; fuasgladh, furtachd.
helpful, *adj.* cuideachail, cobharach, comhnachail.
helpless, *adj.* bochd, truagh, gun chòmhnadh, gun chobhair.
helpmate, *s.* co-chuidiche, céile.
helter-skelter, *adv.* uathrais air thàrais ; muin air mhuin.
helve, *s.* samhach, cas-tuaidhe.
hem, *s.* fàitheam ; cnead, casad.
hem, *v. a.* cuir fàitheam air, cuir oir ri ; iomdhruid, cuairtich ; cnead, dean casad.
hemisphere, *s.* leth-chruinne.
hemistich, *s.* lethrann.
hemlock, *s.* iteotha, minmhear.
hemorrhage, *s.* a' ghèarrach-fhala, sileadh fala. .
hemorrhoids, *s.* neasgaidean fola.
hemp, *s.* còrcach, cainb.
hempen, *adj.* cainbe, còrcaich, cocrach.
hen, *s.* cearc.
hence ! *interj.* or *adv.* as a' so ! uaithe so ; air falbh, fad as ; o'n aobhar so, air an aobhar sin.
henceforth, henceforward, *adv.* uaithe so a mach.
hencoop, *s.* crò-chearc, tigh-chearc.
henpecked, *adj.* fo smachd mnatha.
hen-roost, *s.* spardan, spiris, iris.
heptagon, *s.* seachdshlisneach.
heptagonal, *adj.* seachdshlisneach.
heptarchy, *s.* riaghladh sheachdnar.
her, *pron.* I, ise.
herald, *s.* àrd-mhaor rìgh ; teachdaire.
heraldry, *s.* dreuchd àrd-mhaoir rìgh; eòlas ghearradh-arm.
herb, *s.* lus, luibh.
herbaceous, *adj.* lusach, luibheach.
herbage, *s.* feur, feurach.
herbal, *s.* clar-ainm luibhean.
herbalist, *s.* lusragan, fear-eòlais luibhean.
herby, *adj.* lusach, luibheach.
herculean, *adj.* mór, làidir.
herd, *s.* greigh, buar, treud.
herd, *v.* buachaillich ; comunnaich.

herdsman, *s.* buachaille.
here, *adv.* an so, 's an àite so.
hereabouts, *adv.* mu thimchioll so, air an aruinn so, mun cuairt da so.
hereafter, *adv.* 'san àm ri teachd ; 'san ath shaoghal, 'san ath bheatha.
hereafter, *s.* ath shaoghal, an déidh so.
hereby, *adv.* le so, leis a' so.
hereditable, *adj.* a' teachd mar oighreachd, sealbhach.
hereditary, *adj.* dùthchasach, a' teachd le còir oighre, dualach.
herein, hereinto, *adv.* an so.
hereof, *adv.* uaithe so.
hereon, hereupon, *adv.* air a' so.
heresy, *s.* saobh-chreideamh.
heretic, *s.* saobh-chreidmheach.
heretical, *adj.* saobh-chreidmheach.
hereto, hereunto, *adv.* gu so.
heretofore, *adv.* roimh so.
hereupon, *adv.* air a' so.
herewith, *adv.* leis a' so, le so.
heriot, *s.* càrbhaist, còir uachdrain (air dìleab iochdrain).
heritage, *s.* oighreachd.
hermaphrodite, *s.* neach firionn-boireann.
hermit, *s.* ònaran, fear-comhnuidh fàsaich.
hermitage, *s.* bothan onarain.
hernia, *s.* màm-sice.
hero, *s.* curaidh, gaisgeach, laoch.
heroic, heroical, *adj.* gaisgeil, treun, foghainteach, buadhach, euchdach.
heroine, *s.* banlaoch, banaghaisgeach, bann-seud.
heroism, *s.* euchd, gaisge, treuntas.
hern, heron, *s.* corra-ghriodhach.
heronry, *s.* aite nead nan còrr.
herring, *s.* sgadan.
herself, *pron.* ise, i-féin.
hesitate, *v. a.* stad, bi 'n imcheist, sòr, ob, seun.
hesitation, *s.* teagamh, amharus.
heterodox, *adj.* saobh-chreidmheach.
heterogeneous, *adj.* iol-ghnèitheach.
hew, *v.* gèarr, sgud, snaidh, sgath ; cùm, dreach.
hexagon, *s.* siashlisneag.
hexameter, *s.* seòrsa bàrdachd.
hexangular, *adj.* siaoisinneach.
hey ! *interj.* il ! il !
heyday, *s.* mire, braise.
hiatus, *s.* bèarn, fosgladh.
hibernal, *adj.* geamhrachail.
hiccius-doccius, *s.* cleasaiche.
hiccough, *s.* aileag.
hid, hidden, *part.* falaichte.
hide, *v. n.* ceil, falaich.
hide, *s.* seiche, seic, boicionn.
hide-and-seek, *s.* falach-fead.
hideous, *adj.* uamharra, oillteil, eagalach, déisinneach ; gairisneach, sgreataidh, gràineil, grannda.

hie, *v. n.* falbh, greas, deifrich, dèan cabhag.
hierarchy, *s.* ministeirean na h-Eaglais Easbuigeach.
hieroglyphic, *s.* dealbh-sgrìobhadh.
high, *adj.* àrd ; mór ; uasal, urramach ; spagluinneach, bòsdail ; àrdanach, uaibhreach, mórchuiseach.
highland, *s.* àrd-thir, braighe, garbh-chriochan.
Highlander, *s.* fear-àiteachaidh gharbh-chriochan.
high-minded, *adj.* àrd-inntinneach.
highness, *s.* àirde ; mórachd.
high-water, *s.* muir-làn.
highway, *s.* rathad-mór, rathad an rìgh.
highwayman, *s.* fear reubainn.
hilarity, *s.* cridhealas.
hill, *s.* beinn, monadh, sliabh, cnoc.
hillock, *s.* cnoc, sìthean, tòrr.
hilly, *adj.* monadail, beanntach.
hilt, *s.* dòrnbheirt claidheimh, dòrnchur.
himself, *pron.* e-féin.
hind, *s.* éilid, agh féigh ; sgalag.
hinder, *v. a.* bac, grab ; cum air ais.
hindermost, hindmost, *adj.* deireannach, air deireadh.
hindrance, *s.* grabadh, bacadh.
hinge, *s.* cùlcheangal, bann, lùdagan.
hint, *v. a.* thoir sanas, thoir rabhadh.
hint, *s.* sanas, rabhadh, fideadh.
hip, *s.* alt na sléisne ; cruachan, muc-fhàileag ; trom-inntinn.
hippopotamus, *s.* an t-each-uisge.
hipshot, *adj.* as an leis.
hire, *v. a.* tuarasdalaich, gabh air thuarasdal ; thoir air son tuarasdail, suidhich, dèan muinntearras.
hire, *s.* tuarasdal, duais, pàidheadh, muinntearras.
hireling, *s.* tuarasdalaiche, sgalag.
hirsute, *adj.* ròmach, molach.
his, *poss. pron. masc. a.*
hist ! *interj.* uist ! eist !
historian, *s.* seanachaidh, fear-each-draidhe.
historical, *adj.* eachdrachail.
historiographer, *s.* eachdraiche.
historiography, *s.* eachdraidheachd.
history, *s.* eachdraidh.
histrionic, *adj.* cluicheach, cleasach.
hit, *v.* buail, cuimsich, amais.
hit, *s.* buille ; tuiteamas, tapas.
hitch, *v. n.* bi'n amladh ; gluais.
hitchel, *s.* seicil, cìr-lìn.
hithe, *s.* geodha, camus.
hithe, *s.* lamraig, seòlait.
hither, *adv.* an so, an taobh so.
hitherto, *adv.* gus a nise, fathast.
hitherward, *adv.* chum an àite so.
hive, *s.* beachlann, sgeap.
ho ! *interj.* O ! ho !
hoard, *s.* tasgaidh, ulaidh.

hoard, *v. a.* càrn, taisg ; trus.
hoar-frost, *s.* liathreodhadh.
hoariness, *s.* léithead.
hoarse, *adj.* tùchanach, garbh.
hoarseness, *s.* tùchadh, rùsgadh cléibh.
hoary, hoar, *adj.* liath, glas.
hoax, *s.* mealladh, fala-dhà, abhcaid.
hobble, *s.* ceum crùbaiche, di-leum, spearrach.
hobby, *s.* seòrsa seabhaic ; eachfiodha.
hobgoblin, *s.* màileachan, bòcan.
hobnail, *s.* tacaid bròige.
hock, *s.* fìon gearmailteach.
hocus-pocus, *s.* cleasaiche, mealltair.
hod, *s.* amar-aoil, soitheach-aoil (paidh neir).
hodgepodge, *s.* brochan-breac.
hoe, *s.* fàl-fuinn, sgrìoban.
hoe, *v. a.* cladhaich le fàl-fuinn, croman-aich.
hog, *s.* torc spothte, muc, obhaisg, trùilleach.
hogcote, hogsty, *s.* fail mhuc.
hoggish, *adj.* gionach, mosach, trùilleach.
hog-herd, *s.* mucair, buachaille mhuc.
hogshead, *s.* togsaid.
hogwash, *s.* biadh mhuc.
hoiden, *s.* caile gun oilean.
hoist, *v. a.* tog suas.
hold, *v.* cùm gréim ; gléidh.
hold, *s.* gréim, greimeachadh ; cumail, gleidheadh ; toll luinge ; daingneach.
holder, *s.* fear-séilbhe.
holdfast, *s.* gramaiche.
hole, *s.* toll ; sloc.
holiday, holyday, *s.* latha-féile.
holiness, *s.* naomhachd, diadhachd.
Holland, *s.* an Olaind.
hollow, *adj.* còsach, fàs, falamh-cealgach, foilleil.
hollow, *s.* còs, cobhan, sloc, lag.
hollowness, *s.* còsaichead, falamhachd ; mealltaireachd, neo-sheasmhachd.
holly, *s.* cuileann.
hollyhock, *s.* an ròs-mall.
holocaust, *s.* iobairt-loisgte.
holograph, *s.* dearbh-sgrìobhadh (tiomnadh) air a sgriobhadh le làimh an tiomnaidhear.
holy, *adj.* naomha ; coisrigte.
homage, *s.* dligheachas, dleasdanas ; urram ; strìochdadh, ùmhlachadh.
home, *s.* dachaigh, teach.
home, *adv.* dhachaigh, gu tìr dùthchais ; gu chogais ; gu ceann.
homebred, *adj.* nàdurra, dualach, dùth-chasach ; neo-fhìnealta, socharach.
homeliness, *s.* neo-ghrinneas, dàimheal-achd.
homely, *adj.* neo-ghrinn, dàimheil, càii-deil, faisg.
homer, *s.* tomhas thrì pinnt.
homespun, *s.* clòth.

homeward, *adv.* dhachaigh.
homicide, *s.* mort ; mortair.
homily, *s.* searmoin, lector ; achasan.
homogeneous, *adj.* co-ghnéitheach.
homologous, *adj.* co-ionann.
hone, *s.* clach-gheurachaidh, clach-ghleusaidh.
honest, *adj.* ionraic, onarach.
honesty, *s.* ionracas, onair.
honey, *s.* mil; *gen.* meala.
honeycomb, *s.* cìr-mheala, céirchuachag.
honeymoon, *s.* ceud mhios a' phòsaidh.
honeysuckle, *s.* lus-a'-chraois.
honied, *adj.* mileach, milis, blasda mealach.
honorary, *adj.* urramach, inbhe urram.
honour, *s.* onair, urram ; meas.
honour, *v. a.* onaraich, cuir urram air ; àrdaich, tog gu urram ; glòraich, urramaich.
honourable, *adj.* òirdheirc, urramach, onarach ; àrd, fiùghantach ; ceart, dìreach.
hood, *s.* ceannabharr, currac.
hoodwink, *v. a.* dall ; meall, falaich.
hoof, *s.* crodhan, ionga, ladhar.
hoofed, *adj.* crodhanach, ladhrach.
hook, *s.* dubhan, cromag ; corran.
hook, *v. a.* glac le dubhan, clic.
hooked, *adj.* dubhanach, cromagach.
hoop, *s.* cearcall, cuairteag.
hoop, *v.* cuir cearcall air ; cuairtich, iomdhruid ; glaodh, éigh, dean ulfhartaich.
hooping-cough, *s.* an triuthach.
hoot, *v. n.* sgànraich, fuadaich ; goir mar chomhachaig ; glaodh, dèan iolach.
hop, *v.* leum, dèan beiceis, falbh air leth chois ; bi bacach, bì crùbach.
hop, *s.* lus-an-leanna ; frith-leum.
hope, *s.* dòchas, dùil.
hope, *v. n.* biodh dùil ri.
hopeful, *adj.* dòchasach, earbsach.
hopeless, *adj.* eu-dòchasach.
hopper, *s.* treabhailt ; fear-beiceis.
hopple, *v. n.* deighnich, spearraich.
horde, *s.* ceathairne.
horizon, *s.* cuairt nan speur, bun-sgò.
horizontal, *adj.* còmhnard, réidh.
horn, *s.* adharc, cabar ; còrn.
hornbook, *s.* leabhar na h-aibidil.
horned, *adj.* adharcach, cròcach.
hornet, *s.* connsbeach.
hornowl, *s.* comhachag adharcach.
hornpipe, *s.* dannsa grad-charach.
horny, *adj.* adharcail ; cruaidh.
horologe, *s.* uaireadair.
horoscope, *s.* suidheachadh nan reull aig àm breith, beachdachadh dàn neach (aig a bhreith).
horrible, *adj.* oillteil, uabhasach.
horrid, *adj.* oillteil, eagalach ; déisinn-

each, sgreataidh; garbh, doirbh; gruamach, dorcha.
horrific, *adj.* oillteil, uamharr, uabhasach, eagalach.
horror, *s.* eagal, uamhunn, oilltchrith, ballchrith ; uamhaltachd.
horse, *s.* each ; marc-shluagh.
horseback, *s.* marcachd.
horsebean, *s.* ponar-nan-each.
horseguards, *s.* freiceadan each.
horsehair, *s.* gaoisideach.
horseman, *s.* marcaiche.
horsemanship, *s.* marcachd.
horseway, *s.* eachshlighe.
hortation, *s.* comhairleachadh.
hortative, *adj.* earalach.
horticulture, *s.* gàradaireachd.
hosanna, *s.* moladh do Dhia.
hose, *s.* osan, osain, mogain ; pìob uisge.
hosier, *s.* fear-reic osan.
hospitable, *adj.* fialaidh, faoilidh, fial, fiùghantach, aoidheil, furanach, fàilteach.
hospital, *s.* tigh-eiridinn.
hospitality, *s.* aoigheachd.
host, *s.* fear-tighe, fear-tigh-òsda ; arm, feachd, armailt.
hostage, *s.* fear-gill, braighde-gill.
hostess, *s.* bean-tighe, bean-tigh-òsda.
hostile, *adj.* nàimhdeil, eascairdeach.
hostility, *s.* nàimhdeas, eascairdeas.
hostler, *s.* gille stàpuill.
hot, *adj.* teth, teinntidh, loisgeach, bras, dian, garg, lasanta ; deònach.
hotbed, *s.* leabaidh-theth.
hotel, *s.* tigh-òsda.
hothouse, *s.* tigh - teth, tigh phlanntraisean.
hotness, *s.* teas, gairgead, àinteas, braise, boile.
hotspur, *s.* fear dian, fear feargach.
hough, *s.* iosgaid, bac-na-h-iosgaid.
hough, *v. a.* gèarr iosgaid.
hound, *s.* tòllair, gaothar, cùiseilge.
hour, *s.* uair, fad thri-fichead mionaid.
hourglass, *s.* glaine-ghainmhich.
hourly, *adv.* gach uair.
house, *s.* tigh, fàrdoch, teach.
house, *v.* cuir a steach, thoir fasgadh ; gabh fasgadh, gabh dìon, dèan còmhnaidh.
housebreaker, *s.* spùinneadair thighean.
housebreaking, *s.* bristeadh agus spùinneadh thighean.
household, *s.* teaghlach.
housekeeping, *s.* banas-tighe.
houseless, *adj.* gun àite-còmhnaidh.
housemaid, *s.* maighdean - sheòmair, searbhant.
housewife, *s.* bean-tighe.
housewifery, *s.* riaghladh teaghlaich.
hovel, *s.* sgàth-thigh, bruchlag, bothan.
hover, *v. n.* itealaich ; croch os cionn ;

iadh timchioll air; bi 'n imcheist, bi 'n iomchomhairle.

how, *adv.* cia mar, cia cho mór; ciod an dòigh, cionnas; c'ar son, ciod an t-aobhar.

howbeit, *adv.* gidheadh.

however, *adv.* ciod air bith an dòigh; cò-dhiù; gidheadh.

howl, *v. n.* dèan ulfhartaich, dèan donnalaich; dèan còineadh, dèan burral.

howl, *s.* donnal, burral, ràn, raoic, còinneadh, sgal.

hoy, *s.* seòrsa bàta.

hubbub, *s.* glaodh, iolach, gàir; othail, mi-riaghailt, aimhreit.

huckster, *s.* ceannaiche-siubhail.

huddle, *v.* cuir umad gun dòigh; cuir thar a chéile, tilg air muin a chéile; dòmhlaich, thig muin air mhuin.

hue, *s.* dath, dreach, neul, tuar; iolach, glaodhaich, ruaig.

huff, *s.* dod, sròineas, stuirt.

huff, *v.* séid, bòc, at le àrdan.

huffish, *adj.* uaibhreach, àrdanach.

hug, *v. a.* glac gu caidreach, fàiltich, cniadaich; glac teann; féin-chaidrich.

huge, *adj.* mór, anabarrach, gailbheach, tomadach.

hugeness, *s.* meudachd, anabarrachd, tomadachd.

hugger-mugger, *s.* cuigeann, tasgaidh diamhair, ionad-falaich.

hulk, *s.* tàrlaid luinge, slige luinge; dreall, sgonn, doire bàta.

hull, *s.* cochull, rùsg, plaosg.

hully, *adj.* cochullach, plaosgach.

hum, *v. n.* dèan torman, dèan dùrdail, dèan crònan; mol.

hum, *s.* srann, dranndan, gàir sheillein, crònan, torman.

human, *adj.* daonna, talmhaidh.

humane, *adj.* bàigheil, caomh, seirceil, truacanta, tròcaireach, coibhneil.

humanity, *s.* daonnachd, nàdur a chinne-daonna; bàighealachd, truacantachd, cneasdachd.

humankind, *s.* cinne-daonna.

humble, *adj.* ùmhail, iriosal, sèimh.

humble, *v. a.* irioslaich, ùmhlaich; cìosnaich, thoir fo smachd; thoir gu strìochdadh.

humdrum, *s.* umaidh, tromcheannach, mì-chàilear, neo-shunntach.

humectation, *s.* fliuchadh, bogachadh.

humid, *adj.* aitidh, fliuch, bog.

humidity, *s.* fliche, aitidheachd.

humiliation, *s.* irioslachadh, umhlachadh.

humility, *s.* irioslachd, ùmhlachd.

humming-bird, *s.* an t-eun dranndanach, am beageun.

humorist, *s.* fear neònach, fear mac-meanmnach, fear gun srian; fear àbhachdach, àmhailteach.

humorous, *adj.* neònach; aighearach, sùgach, àbhachdach, neo-riaghailteach.

humorsome, *adj.* frithearra, conasach; neònach, luasganach.

humour, *s.* càil, nàdur, aomadh-inntinn; àbhachd, fearas-chuideachd, cridh-ealas; leann-tàth.

humour, *v. a.* toilich; géill, strìochd.

hump, *s.* pait, meall, croit.

humpback, *s.* druim crotach, croit.

humpbacked, *adj.* crotach.

hunch, *s.* meall, cnap, pait.

hundred, *adj.* ceud, ciad.

hundredth, *adj.* an ceudamh.

hung, *part.* crochta.

hunger, *s.* acras; cìocras.

hungry, *adj.* acrach, air acras.

hunks, *s.* daormunn, spìocaire.

hunt, *v.* sealg, dèan fiadhach, dèan sealgaireachd; ruag, dlùth-lean; rannsaich; stiùir lothainn chon.

hunt, *s.* faoghaid; ruaig, sealg.

hunter, *s.* sealgair; giomhanach.

hunting, *s.* sealgaireachd, fiadhach.

huntress, *s.* ban-sealgair.

huntsman, *s.* sealgair.

hurdle, *s.* càrn-slaodaidh, cliath.

hurl, *v. a.* tilg sios, cuibhil.

hurl, *s.* iorghuill, tuasaid, sabaid.

hurly, hurlyburly, *s.* buaireas, ùparaid, othail, iomairt.

hurricane, *s.* doinionn, gaillionn, stoirm, iomghaoth, an-uair.

hurry, *v.* greas, luathaich, deifrich; dèan cabhag.

hurry, *s.* cabhag, buaireas, othail.

hurt, *v. a.* ciùrr, dochainn, goirtich, cràidh, leòn, lot, dèan dochair air.

hurt, *s.* dochann, ciurradh, leòn; coire cron, dochair

hurtful, *adj.* cronail, dochannach.

hurtfulness, *s.* cronalachd.

hurtleberry, *s.* dearag-choille.

husband, *s.* fear-pòsda, céile.

husband, *v. a.* caomhain, dèan riaghladh maith (air do chuid).

husbandman, *s.* treabhaiche.

husbandry, *s.* treabhadh, tuathanachas; caomhnadh.

hush, *v.* caisg, cuir sàmhach; mùch; bi sàmhach, bi tosdach.

hush-money, *s.* brìob air son a bhi sàmhach.

husk, *s.* cochull, rùsg, plaosg, mogull, mogunn.

husky, *adj.* cochullach, rùsgach, plaosgach; garbh, reasgach, tùchanach.

hussar, *s.* seòrsa trùpair.

hussy, *s.* dubhchaile, botrumaid.

hustings, *s. pl.* mòd, coinneamh.

hustle, *v. a.* coimeasg, uinnleagaich, dèan cabhag, bi dripeil.

hut, s. bothan, bruchlag.
hutch, s. ciste-shìl; bothag coinein.
huzza ! *interj.* co-ghàir, iolach.
hyacinth, s. seòrsa neòinein ; dath.
hydra, s. uathbheist iomcheannach.
hydraulics, s. *pl.* eòlas air tarruing uisge tre phìoban.
hydrocele, s. meud-bhronn.
hydrocephalus, s. uisge 'sa cheann.
hydrographer, s. fear-tarruing dealbh na mara.
hydrography, s. muir-eòlas.
hydromancy, s. fàisneachd le uisge.
hydrometer, hygrometer, s. meidh-uisge.
hydrophobia, s. cuthach nan con.
hydrostatics, s. *pl.* eòlas tomhais uisge.
hydrus, s. nathair uisge.
hyemal, *adj.* a bhuineas do'n gheamhradh.
hyena, s. seorsa de chù fiadhaich.
hymen, s. dia a' phòsaidh ; maighdeanas.
hymeneal, *adj.* pòsachail.
hymn, s. laoidh, dàn spioradail.

hymn, *v. a.* mol le laoidhibh.
hymnic, *adj.* laoidheach.
hyp, *v. a.* cuir fo sproc.
hyperbole, s. aibheiseachadh, spleadh-achas, spleadh.
hyperbolical, *adj.* spleadhach.
hyperbolise, *v. a.* dèan spleadhachas.
hyperborean, *adj.* tuath ; fuar.
hypermeter, s. ni thar tomhas.
hypnotic, s. ìoc-shlaint chadail.
hypochondriac, s. leann-dubh.
hypocist, s. iocshlainte cheanghail.
hypocrisy, s. cealgaireachd.
hypocrite, s. cealgair, mealltair.
hypocritical, *adj.* cealgach.
hypothesis, s. barail gun dearbhadh.
hypothetical, *adj.* baralach.
hyrst, herst, s. doire, badan-coille.
hyssop, s. hisop, seòrsa luibh.
hysterical, *adj.* ospagach, air a bheil tinneas nan neul, no tinneas builg.
hysterics, s. an tinneas paiseanach.

I

I, *pron.* mi ; *emph.* mise.
iambic, s. cam-dhàn.
iambic, *adj.* cam-dhànach.
ice, s. eigh, deigh, éighre.
icehouse, s. tigh-eighe.
ichor, s. ruith-iongrach.
ichorous, *adj.* silteachail.
ichthyology, s. eòlas nan iasg.
ichthyophagy, s. iasg-itheannaich.
icicle, s. caisean-reòdhta, bioran deighe.
icon, s. ìomhaigh.
icy, *adj.* eigheach, reòdhta.
idea, s. smuain, barail, dealbh-inntinn.
ideal, *adj.* a réir barail, dealbh-inntinn-each, àirdmheinn.
identical, identic, *adj.* ceudna, ionann, ceart cheudna.
identification, s. dearbhadh ionannachd, aithneachadh.
identify, *v. a.* dearbh ionannachd.
identity, s. ionannachd.
idiom, s. gnàths-cainnte.
idiomatic, *adj.* gnàths-chainnteach.
idiotism, s. amadanachd.
idle, *adj.* leasg, monaiseach ; dìomhain, dìomhanach ; gun ghnothach ; neo-éifeachdach ; faoin, suarach, baoth.
idleness, s. dìomhanachd, diomhanas; faoineas, neo-éifeachd.
idler, s. leisgean, lunndaire, dìomhan-aiche, bataire, droll.
idol, s. iomhaigh, iodhol.
idolater, s. fear-iodhol-aoraidh.
idolatrous, *adj.* iodhol-aorach.
idolatry, s. iodhol-aoradh.

idolise, *v.* gabh mar iodhol, dean iodhol (dheth).
idolish, *adj.* iodholach.
if, *conj.* ma, na, mur ; if I can, ma 's urra mi; if I were to say, na 'n abrainn ; if he will not come, mur tig e.
igneous, *adj.* teinntidh, lasarra, lasanta, loisgeach.
ignis-fatuus, s. spiorad-lodain, teine-sionnachain, srada-bianain.
ignite, *v. a.* cuir teine ri, fadaidh ; las, gabh teine.
ignition, s. lasadh, losgadh.
ignoble, *adj.* anuasal, neo-inbheach ; mìothar, suarach, iosal.
ignominious, *adj.* nàr, maslach, dìblidh, tarcuiseach.
ignominy, s. nàire, mìchliù.
ignoramus, s. burraidh, sgonn.
ignorance, s. aineolas, an-fhios.
ignorant, *adj.* aineolach.
iliac, *adj.* caolanach.
ill, *adj.* olc, dona ; tinn, euslan.
ill, s. olc, aingidheachd, cron.
illapse, s. sleamhnachadh ; ionnsaigh, tachartas, tuiteamas.
illegal, *adj.* neo-dhligheach, mì-laghail, neo-cheadaichte.
illegality, s. mì-laghalachd.
illegibility, s. do-leughtachd.
illegible, *adj.* do-leughadh, nach urrainn ear a leughadh.
illegitimacy, s. dìolanas.
illegitimate, *adj.* dìolain.

illiberal, *adj.* neo-uasal, neo-fhialaidh ; spìocach, crìon, gortach.
illiberality, *s.* cruas, spìocaiche.
illimitable, *adj.* neo-chrìochnachail.
illiteracy, *s.* neo-fhòghlumachd.
illiterate, *adj.* neo-fhòghlumach.
illiterateness, *s.* neo-fhoghluimteachd.
ill-nature, *s.* droch-nàdur.
illness, *s.* tinneas, galar, euslaint.
illogical, *adj.* mì-reusonta.
ill-starred, *adj.* neo-shealbhach.
illude, *v. a.* meall, thoir an car á.
illume, illumine, illuminate, *v. a.* soillsich, soilleirich, dealraich.
illumination, *s.* soillseachadh, soilleireachadh, dealradh, dearrsadh.
illuminative, *adj.* soillseach.
illusion, *s.* mealladh, mearachd.
illusive, *adj.* mealltach, faoin.
illusory, *adj.* cealgach, carach.
illustrate, *v. a.* soillsich, mìnich.
illustration, *s.* mìneachadh, soilleireachadh.
illustrative, *adj.* mìneachail.
illustrator, *s.* fear-mìneachaidh.
illustrious, *adj.* uasal, ainmeil.
image, *s.* iomhaigh, samhla.
imagery, *s.* ìomhaighean ; faoin-smuaintean ; samhlaidean.
imaginable, *adj.* a dh' fhaodar a smuaineachadh.
imaginary, *adj.* faoin-bharaileach.
imagination, *s.* mac-meanmainn ; smuaininntinn ; breithneachadh ; faoinbheachd ; innleachd.
imaginative, *adj.* mac-meanmnach.
imagine, *v. a.* smaoinich, beachdaich ; dealbh, tionnsgain.
imbecile, *adj.* lagchuiseach, fann, faoin (inntinn), leithchiallach.
imbecility, *s.* lagchuiseachd ('san inntinn).
imbibe, *v. a.* òl, sùigh, deoghail.
imbitter, *v. a.* searbhaich, dèan searbh ; dèan mì-shona, léir ; buair.
imbody, *v.* corpaich ; co-chorpaich ; co-aonaich.
imbolden, *v. a.* misnich, brosnaich.
imbosom, *v. a.* uchdaich, tàlaidh, caidrich, gràdhaich.
imbound, *v. a.* iomdhruid, cuairtich.
imbow, *v. a.* cuir bogha air.
imbower, *v. a.* sgàilich, còmhdaich.
imbricated, *adj.* eagach, slocach.
imbrication, *s.* eagachadh, sloc.
imbrown, *v. a.* donnaich, dèan donn.
imbrue, *v. a.* dath (am fuil).
imbrute, *v. a.* ìslich, dèan brùideil.
imbue, *v. a.* snuadhaich, dath, fliuch ; bogaich.
imitability, *s.* so-shamhlachd.
imitable, *adj.* so-shamhlachdail.

imitate, *v. a.* co-shamhlaich, aithris, lean eiseamplair, dèan coltach ri.
imitation, *s.* lean-shamhlachadh, atharrais.
imitative, *adj.* aithriseach.
imitator, *s.* fear-aithris, fear-atharrais.
immaculate, *adj.* glan, fìor-ghlan.
immarcessible, *adj.* neo-sheargach.
immartial, *adj.* neo-ghaisgeanta.
immaterial, *adj.* neo-chorporra spioradail; neonitheach, is coma co—.
immateriality, *s.* neo-chorporrachd, spioradalachd, neonitheachd.
immature, *adj.* anabaich.
immaturity, *s.* anabaichead.
immeasurable, *adj.* nach gabh tomhais.
immediate, *adj.* dlùth aig làimh, grad, ealamh, clis.
immediately, *adv.* gu grad, gu luath gun dàil, gun stàd, air ball.
immedicable, *adj.* do-leigheas.
immelodious, *adj.* neo-bhinn.
immemorial, *adj.* cian, o chian.
immense, *adj.* fuathasach mór.
immensity, *s.* anabarrachd.
immensurable, *adj.* nach gabh tomhais.
immerge, immerse, *v. a.* cuir fodha, tùm, bogaich ann an uisge.
immersion, *s.* tumadh, cur fodha, bogadh; dol fodha.
immethodical, *adj.* mi-riaghailteach, mi-dhòigheil, neo-sheòlta.
immethodically, *adv.* gun riaghailt.
immigration, *s.* teachd a nall (do'n tìr).
imminence, *s.* cunnart, gàbhadh.
imminent, *adj.* cunnartach, gàbhaidh.
immix, immingle, *v. a.* co-measgaich, co-mheasg.
immixable, *adj.* gun mheasgadh.
immobility, *s.* neo-ghluasadachd.
immoderate, *adj.* ana-measarra.
immoderation, *s.* ana-measarrachd.
immodest, *adj.* mì-nàrach, beag-nàrach ; mì-stuama, neòghlan.
immodesty, *s.* ladornas ; mì-stuaim.
immolate, *v. a.* thoir ìobairt, ìobair.
immolation, *s.* ìobradh.
immoral, *adj.* mì - bheusach, eucorach, droch-bheartach.
immorality, *s.* mì-bheus, eucoir, droch-bheart ; mì-stiùrrachd.
immortal, *adj.* neo-bhàsmhor.
immortalise, *v. a.* dean neo-bhàsmhor.
immortality, *s.* neo-bhàsmhorachd.
immovable, *adj.* neo-ghluasadach.
immunity, *s.* saorsa ; fuasgladh, cead.
immure, *v. a.* druid, cuir an sàs.
immutability, *s.* neo-chaochlaideachd.
immutable, *adj.* neo-chaochlaideach.
imp, *s.* droch bhall, deamhain, beag-dhonas.
imp, *v. a.* cuir ri, meudaich, neartaich (itealaich).

impact, *v. a.* teannaich, spàrr, dinn.
impair, *v. a.* lughdaich, dìobhailich, mill ; fàs ni's miosa.
impalpable, *adj.* nach gabh làimh-seachadh ; mìn, meanbh, neo-fhaic-sinneach.
imparity, *s.* neo-ionannachd.
impart, *v. a.* tabhair, tìodhlaic, com-pàirtich ; soilleirich ; co-roinn.
impartial, *adj.* ceart-bhreitheach, neo-chlaon, dìreach, cothromach, còir.
impartiality, *s.* neo-leth-bhreitheachd, neo-chlaonachd, cothrom.
impassable, *adj.* do-shiubhal.
impassion, *v. a.* feargaich, brosnaich.
impassioned, *adj.* brosnaichte.
impatience, *s.* mì-fhaighidinn, neo-chruadal ; boile, ainteas, caise, braise.
impatient, *adj.* neo-fhoighidneach ; neo-shocrach, cas, dian.
impawn, *v. a.* thoir an geall.
impeach, *v. a.* casaidich, dìt gu follais-each, cuir as leth ; bac, grab.
impeachment, *s.* casaid, dìteadh, cùis-dhìtidh ; coire, masladh.
impeccability, *s.* neochiontas ; eu-comas peacaidh.
impeccable, *adj.* neochiontach ; eu-comasach air peacadh.
impede, *v. a.* bac, cuir maille air.
impediment, *s.* bacadh, cnap-starraidh.
impel, *v. a.* greas, cuir air aghaidh.
impend, *v. n.* croch os - cionn, bi aig làimh.
impenetrable, *adj.* do - tholladh, do-dhrùigheadh ; dùinte ; do-ghluasad.
impenitence, *s.* neo-aithreachas, cruas.
impenitent, *adj.* neo-aithreachail.
imperative, *adj.* ceannsalach, do-sheach-ainte.
imperceptible, *adj.* neo - fhaicsinneach, neo-léirsinneach, do-mhothachadh.
imperfect, *adj.* neo-fhoirfe, neo-iomlan, neo-choimhlionta.
imperfection, *s.* neo-iomlanachd.
imperforate, *adj.* neo-tholldach.
imperial, *adj.* rìoghail, àrd-urramach, àrd-uachdaranach.
imperious, *adj.* àintighearnail, cruaidh-smachdail, fòirneartach ; ceannsach-ail, smachdail ; uachdaranach ; uaimh-reach.
imperiousness, *s.* ceannasachd, smachdal-achd ; aintighearnas.
imperishable, *adj.* neo-bhàsmhor.
impersonal, *adj.* neo-phearsanta.
imperspicuous, *adj.* neo-shoilleir.
impersuasible, *adj.* nach gabh comhairle.
impertinence, *s.* beadaidheachd ; mì-mhodh, leamhadas, dànadas, gòraich.
impertinent, *adj.* amaideach ; leamh, beadaidh, mì-mhodhail, ladorna, dàna, beag-nàrach.

impervious, *adj.* air nach drùighear, dionach.
impetrate, *v. a.* faigh le achanaich, coisinn.
impetuosity, *s.* braise, caise, déine.
impetuous, *adj.* àinteasach, fiadhaich, feargach ; cas, bras, dian.
impetus, *s.* déine, sitheadh, deann, neart.
impiety, *s.* ain-diadhachd, mì-naomh-achd, aingeachd ; droch-bheart.
impinge, *v. a.* buail, tuit air muin.
impious, *adj.* àin-diadhaidh.
implacable, *adj.* gamhlasach, do-chasg-adh.
implant, *v. a.* suidhich, socraich.
implausible, *adj.* neo-choltach.
implement, *s.* inneal, ball-deise.
implicate, *v. a.* rib, bac, caisg.
implication, *s.* ribeadh, bacadh, seadh, ciall.
implicative, *adj.* fillteach, seadhachail.
implicit, *adj.* fillte, iomfhillte ; seadh-aichte ; earbsach, an crochadh air, ùmhal.
implore, *v. a.* aslaich, guidh, grìos.
imply, *v. a.* fill, ciallaich.
impoison, *v. a.* puinnseanaich.
impolite, *adj.* mì-mhodhail.
impolitic, *adj.* neo-sheòlta.
imponderous, *adj.* aotrom.
imporous, *adj.* neo-chòsach, dionach.
import, *v. a.* thoir o chéin, faigh o chéin ; seadhaich, ciallaich.
import, *s.* cudthrom, brìgh, bladh, seadh, toirt.
importance, *s.* cudthrom, seadh, stà.
important, *adj.* cudthromach, toirteil, brìoghmhor, feumail.
importation, *s.* toirt dhachaigh (ceann-achd á tìr eile).
importunate, *adj.* iarrtachail, liosda.
importune, *v. a.* cuir ìmpidh, aslaich, na gabh diùltadh.
importunity, *s.* sìor-ghuidhe, liosdachd.
impose, *v. a.* leag air ; àithn, cuir mar fhiachaibh air ; meall, thoir an car as.
imposition, *s.* leagail, leagail air ; éigin, ainneart ; mealladh, foill.
impossibility, *s.* neo-chomasachd.
impossible, *adj.* eu-comasach.
impost, *s.* cìs, càin, cuspunn.
imposthume, *s.* iongrachadh.
impostor, *s.* mealltair, slaightire.
imposture, *s.* mealladh, foill, ceilg.
impotence, impotency, *s.* laigse, anfhann-achd, lagchuiseachd, neo-chomas.
impotent, *adj.* lag, anfhann, neo-chomas-ach, fann, lagchuiseach.
impound, *v. a.* dùin ann am punnd.
impracticable, *adj.* do-dhèanamh.
imprecate, *v. a.* guidh olc.
imprecation, *s.* droch ghuidhe.
impregnable, *adj.* do - ghlacadh, do-ghluasadach.

impregnate, *v. a.* dèan torrach.
impress, *v. a.* clò-bhuail ; comharraich ; glac, ceap.
impressible, *adj.* so - chomharrachadh, drùighteach.
impression, *s.* comharradh, athailt ; deargadh, dealbh, cruth, riochd ; clò-bhualadh.
impressive, *adj.* drùighteach.
impressure, *s.* comharradh, lòrg.
imprimis, *adv.* anns a' cheud àite.
imprint, *v. a.* comharraich ; drùigh.
imprison, *v. a.* cuir am prìosan.
imprisonment, *s.* prìosanachadh.
improbability, *s.* mì-choltas.
improbable, *adj.* mì-choltach.
improbation, *s.* toirmeasg.
improbity, *s.* eas-ionracas, foill.
improper, *adj.* neo-iomchuidh, mì-fhreagarach.
impropriety, *s.* neo-fhreagharrachd.
improvable, *adj.* ghabhas leasachadh.
improve, *v.* leasaich ; rach am feabhas.
improvement, *s.* leasachadh ; feabhas, teachd air aghaidh ; ionnsachadh.
improvidence, *s.* neo-fhreasdalachd, ana-caitheamh.
improvident, *adj.* neo - fhreasdalach, sgriosail.
imprudence, *s.* gòraich, amaideachd.
imprudent, *adj.* gòrach, amaideach.
impudence, *s.* dànadas, ladornas.
impudent, *adj.* dàna, ladarna.
impugn, *v. a.* coirich, faigh cron.
impuissance, *s.* anmhuinneachd, eucomas.
impulse, *s.* faireachadh, togradh, iarrtus.
impulsive, *adj.* brosnachail, aithghearr (an nàdur).
impunity, *s.* saor o dhioghaltas, sàbhailteachd.
impure, *adj.* neòghlan, truaillidh.
impurity, *s.* neòghloine ; sal.
imputable, *adj.* so-chur as leth.
imputation, *s.* cur as leth ; casaid.
impute, *v. a.* cuir as leth, meas (do neach).
in, *prep.* ann, an, am, anns, 's.
in, *prefix,* do, neo, eu, as, an.
inability, *s.* neo-chomas, laigse.
inaccessible, *adj.* do-ruigsinn.
inaccuracy, *s.* neo-phoncalachd.
inaccurate, *adj.* mearachdach.
inaction, *s.* tàmh, fois, clos.
inactive, *adj.* neo-ghnìomhach.
inactivity, *s.* neo-ghnìomhachas.
inadequacy, *s.* neo-fhreagarrachd.
inadequate, *adj.* neo-fhreagarrach.
inadvertence, *s.* neo-chùram.
inadvertent, *adj.* neo-chùramach.
inalienable, *adj.* do-dhealaichte.
inane, *adj.* fàs, faoin, falamh.
inanimate, *adj.* marbhanta.

inanity, *s.* faoineachd, fàsachd.
inapplicable, *adj.* neo-fhreagarrach.
inaptitude, *s.* neo-iomchuidheachd.
inarticulate, *adj.* manntach.
inattention, *s.* neo-aire.
inattentive, *adj.* neo-aireil.
inaudible, *adj.* do-chluinntinn.
inaugurate, *v. a.* coisrig.
inauguration, *s.* coisrigeadh.
inauspicious, *adj.* mì-shealbhach.
inborn, *adj.* nàdurra.
incalculable, *adj.* do-àireamh.
incantation, *s.* ubag, ubhaidh, geas.
incantatory, *adj.* ubagach.
incapability, *s.* neo-chomasachd.
incapable, *adj.* neo-urrainneach, neo-chomasach.
incapacitate, *v. a.* dèan mì-chomasach.
incapacity, *s.* neo-chomas.
incarcerate, *v. a.* prìosanaich.
incarceration, *s.* prìosanachadh.
incarnadine, *v. a.* càrnaidich.
incarnate, *v. a.* gabh cruth duine.
incarnate, *adj.* 's an fheòil.
incarnation, *s.* corp-ghabhail.
incase, *v. a.* còmhdaich, dùin.
incautious, *adj.* mì-fhaicilleach.
incautiousness, *s.* mì-fhaicilleachd.
incendiary, *s.* loisgeadair ; brathadair, ceann-àimhreit, buaireadair.
incendiary, *adj.* buaireasach.
incense, *s.* tùis.
incense, *v. a.* buair, feargaich.
incensory, *s.* tùisear.
incentive, *s.* brosnachadh, buaireadh ; cùis-aimhreit ; mathair-aobhair.
incentive, *adj.* brosnachail.
incessant, *adj.* daonnan, sìor.
incest, *s.* col.
incestuous, *adj.* colach.
inch, *s.* òirleach.
inchmeal, *s.* mìr-oirleich.
inchoate, *v. a.* tòisich.
inchoation, *s.* tòiseachadh.
inchoative, *adj.* ceud-cheumach.
incidence, incident, *s.* tuiteamas, tachartas.
incident, incidental, *adj.* tuiteamach, tachartach, buailteach.
incinerate, *v. a.* tur-loisg, dèan luath air.
incineration, *s.* dù-losgadh.
incipient, *adj.* tòiseachail, ceud.
incised, *adj.* gèarrte.
incision, incisure, *s.* gearradh ; tolladh.
incisive, *adj.* gearrtach, geur.
incisor, *s.* a' ghearr-fhiacail.
incitation, incitement, *s.* brosnachadh, misneachadh, beothachadh.
incite, *v. a.* brosnaich, gluais, beothaich, tog, misnich.
incivility, *s.* mì-mhodhalachd.
inclemency, *s.* an-iochd.
inclement, *adj.* an-iochdmhor.

inclinable, *adj.* deònach, togarrach, déidheil, toileach, miannach.
inclination, *s.* aomadh ; toil, togradh ;
déidh, miann, iarrtas, deòin ; gaol,
tòirt, ùidh ; cromadh, camadh, claonadh.
incline, *v.* aom, crom, claon, lùb sleuchd ;
togair, miannaich.
inclose, *v. a.* dùin, iomdhruid.
include, *v. a.* iath ; cùm, gabh a
steach.
inclusion, *s.* cumail, cuairteachadh.
inclusive, *adj.* a' gabhail a steach.
incoagulable, *adj.* do-bhinnteach.
incog, incognito, *adv.* gu falaichte, gu
dìomhair, an-riochd.
incoherence, *s.* neo-leanailteachd, fuasgailteachd ; neo-aontachas, eas-còrdadh, brisgleach.
incoherent, *adj.* fuasgailte, sgaoilte, neo-
cheangailte ; neo-fhreagarrach, neo-
aontachail, baoth.
incombustible, *adj.* neo-loisgeach.
income, *s.* teachd a steach, teachd an tìr.
incommensurable, *adj.* gun tomhas.
incommiscible, *adj.* nach gabh measgadh.
incommode, *v. a.* cuir dragh air.
incommodious, *adj.* neo-ghoireasach,
draghail, neo-fhreagarrach.
incommunicable, *adj.* do-phàirteach, do-
labhairt, do-innseadh.
incommunicated, *adj.* neo-phàirtichte.
incommunicating, *adj.* neo-chompanta.
incommutable, *adj.* do-mhalartach.
incomparable, *adj.* gun choimeas.
incompassionate, *adj.* an-tròcaireach, neo-
thlusail, cruaidh-chridheach.
incompatibility, *s.* neo-fhreagarrachd.
incompatible, *adj.* neo-fhreagarrach.
incompetency, *s.* neo-chomasachd.
incompetent, *adj.* neo-chomasach.
incomplete, *adj.* neo-choimhlionta.
incompliance, *s.* diùltadh, raige.
incomposed, *adj.* neo-shuidhichte.
incomprehensibility, incomprehensible-
ness, *s.* do-thuigsinneachd.
incomprehensible, *adj.* do-thuigsinn.
incompressible, *adj.* do-theannachail.
inconcealable, *adj.* do-chleitheach.
inconceivable, inconceptible, *adj.* do-
smuaineachail, do-bharalach, dothuig-
sinn.
inconclusive, *adj.* neo-chinnteach.
inconclusiveness, *s.* neo-chinnteachd.
inconcoction, *s.* an-abaicheachd.
inconcurring, *adj.* neo-aontachail.
inconcurring, *adj.* neo-chòrdail.
inconcussible, *adj.* do-ghluasadach.
incondite, *adj.* neo-riaghailteach, neo-
mhaiseach (litreachas).
inconformity, *s.* neo-aontachd.
incongruence, incongruity, *s.* neo-fhreagarrachd, eu-coltas.

incongruous, incongruent, *adj.* neo-
fhreagarrach.
inconscionable, *adj.* neo-chogaiseach.
inconsiderable, *adj.* suarach.
inconsiderableness, *s.* suarachas.
inconsiderate, *adj.* neo-chùramach, dearmadach, neo-aireil, coma.
inconsiderateness, *s.* neo - airealachd,
neo-chùramachd.
inconsistency, *s.* mì-chòrdadh, seachran.
inconsistent, *adj.* neo-fhreagarrach, seachranach.
inconsolable, *adj.* dù-bhrònach.
inconsonancy, *s.* neo-aontachd.
inconstancy, *s.* neo-bhunailteachd, neo-
sheasmhachd.
inconstant, *adj.* neo-bhunailteach, neo-
sheasmhach.
incontestable, *adj.* nach gabh àicheadh.
incontiguous, *adj.* neo-dhlùth.
incontinence, *s.* mì-stuamachd.
incontinent, *adj.* mì-stuama.
incontrovertible, *adj.* dearbhta, cinnteach.
inconvenience, *s.* neo-iomchuidheachd,
neo-fhreagarrachd, neo-ghoireasachd,
dragh, duilichinn, ana-cothrom.
inconvenient, *adj.* mi-ghoireasach.
inconvertible, *adj.* do-mhùthach.
inconvincible, *adj.* rag-mhuinealach.
incorporate, *v.* measgaich, co-cheangail,
co-chomunnaich ; cuir cruth air, corpaich ; aonaich.
incorporation, *s.* coimeasgadh ; co-
chomunn ; aonachadh.
incorporeal, incorporate, *adj.* neo-chorporra.
incorporeity, *s.* neo-chorporrachd.
incorrect, *adj.* mearachdach.
incorrectly, *adv.* gu mearachdach.
incorrectness, *s.* docharachd.
incorrigible, *adj.* do - cheannsachail ;
aingidh.
incorrigibleness, *s.* do-cheannsachd, aingidheachd.
incorrupt, *adj.* neo-thruaillte.
incorruptible, *adj.* neo-thruaillidh.
incorruption, *s.* neo-thruailleachd.
incorruptness, *s.* ionracas, tréidhireas.
incrassate, *v. a.* dèan tiugh.
incrassative, *adj.* tiughachail.
increase, *v.* meudaich, cuir am meud,
lìonmhoraich ; fàs lìonmhor, cinn,
rach am meud, fàs mòr.
increase, *s.* fàs, cinntinn, meudachadh ;
teachd a mach, tuilleadh ; toradh,
cinneas ; sìol, sliochd, gineal.
incredibility, *s.* neo-chreidsinneachd.
incredible, *adj.* do-chreidsinn.
incredulity, *s.* neo-chreidimh.
incredulous, *adj.* neo-chreidmheach.
incremable, *adj.* nach gabh losgadh.
increment, *s.* fàs, meudachadh leasachadh ; toradh, piseach .riadh (airgid).

incriminate, *v. a.* casaidich, dìt.
incrust, *v. a.* cuir rùsg air.
incrustation, *s.* rùsg, sgroth.
incubate, *v. n.* guir, laigh air uibhean, thoir a mach àl.
incubation, *s.* gur.
incubus, *s.* an trom-lighe.
inculcate, *v. a.* dian-chomhairlich, àithn.
inculcation, *s.* dian-chomhairleachadh.
incumbency, *s.* laighe, leagail taic ; dreuchd.
incumbent, *adj.* a' leagail taic air, a' laighe ; dligheach, mar fhiachaibh.
incumbent, *s.* ministear sgìre 'san Eaglais Shasunnaich.
incumber, *v. a.* cuir eallach air, fàsaich.
incur, *v. a.* bi buailteach do ; toill.
incurable, *adj.* do-leigheas.
incurious, *adj.* coma, suarach mu ni.
incursion, *s.* ionnsaigh, ruathar.
incurvate, *v. a.* lùb, crom, cam.
incurvation, *s.* lùbadh, cromadh.
incurvity, *s.* lùbadh, cruime, caime.
indart, *v. a.* sàth a steach.
indebted, *adj.* am fiachaibh ; fo chomain, an comain.
indecency, indecorum, *s.* mì-chiatachd, mì-bheus, neo-eireachdas.
indecent, *adj.* neo-eireachdail, neo-chumhaidh.
indeciduous, *adj.* neo-thuiteamach.
indecision, *s.* neo-chinnteachd.
indecisive, *adj.* neo-chinnteach ; eadarra-bharail.
indeclinable, *adj.* neo-atharrachail.
indecorous, *adj.* neo-bheusach, mi-mhodhail, neo-eireachdail, mì-chiatach.
indeed, *adv.* gu fìrinneach, gu dearbh, gu deimhinn.
indefatigable, *adj.* do-sgìtheachail.
indefeasible, *adj.* dearbh-chòireach ; làn-dhligheach ; diorraiseach.
indefectible, *adj.* neo-fhàilneach.
indefensible, *adj.* nach gabh dìon.
indefinable, *adj.* do-ainmeachail.
indefinite, *adj.* neo-chrìochnach, neo-shònraichte, sgaoilteach.
indelible, *adj.* nach gabh milleadh.
indelicacy, *s.* mìomhodh, mì-shuairceas, neo-cheanaltas.
indelicate, *adj.* mì-mhodhail.
indemnification, *s.* ath-dhìoladh.
indemnify, *v. a.* dìon o challdach, dèan suas call.
indemnity, *s.* làn-mhathanas, urras (an aghaidh calla).
indemonstrable, *adj.* nach gabh dearbhadh.
indent, *v.* eagaich, fiaclaich ; cùmhnantaich.
indent, indentation, *s.* eagachadh, fiaclachadh, gròbadh.
indenture, *s.* cèird-chùmhnant, aonta.

independence, independency, *s.* saorsa ; neo-eiseamaileachd.
independent, *adj.* saor ; neo-eiseamaileach.
indescribable, *adj.* do-aithris.
indestructible, *adj.* nach gabh milleadh.
indeterminable, *adj.* do-shònrachadh.
indeterminate, *adj.* neo-shònraichte, neo-mheasraichte.
indetermined, *adj.* neo-shuidhichte.
indevoted, *adj.* neo-dhìleas.
indevotion, *s.* mì-dhiadhachd.
indevout, *adj.* neo-chràbhach.
index, *s.* clàr-innseadh leabhair ; làmh-uaireadair ; comharradh-corraig mar so ☞.
indexterity, *s.* neo-ealantachd.
Indian, *s.* and *adj.* Innseanach.
indicate, *v. a.* taisbean, foillsich, innis, comharraich a mach.
indication, *s.* comharradh, innseadh, foillseachadh ; rabhadh, sanas, fios.
indicative, *adj.* taisbeanach, foillseachail, innseachail.
indiction, *s.* cuir an céill, gairm, rabhadh follaiseach.
indictment, *s.* casaid.
indifference, *s.* neo-shuim, neo-chùram neo-aire.
indifferent, *adj.* neo-aireil, coma, dearmadach ; neo - chlaon - breitheach ; meadhonach, an eatarras.
indigence, *s.* bochdainn, ainniseachd, truaighe, gainne.
indigenous, *adj.* dùthchasach.
indigent, *adj.* bochd, gann, truagh ; falamh, fàs.
indigested, *adj.* mì - riaghailteach ; fua-sgailte, sgaoilte ; neo-mheirbhte.
indigestion, *s.* cion-meirbhidh.
indigitate, *v. a.* nochd, feuch.
indigitation, *s.* nochdadh, feuchainn.
indignant, *adj.* feargach, diombach.
indignation, *s.* fearg, corraich.
indignity, *s.* dìmeas, tàmailt, tàir, tarcuis, masladh.
indigo, *s.* guirmean.
indirect, *adj.* neo-dhìreach, fiar, cam ; mealltach, foilleil.
indirectness, *s.* fiaradh, caime.
indiscernible, *adj.* do-fhaicsinneach.
indiscerptible, *adj.* do-sgarachdainn.
indiscoverable, *adj.* do-rannsachadh.
indiscreet, *adj.* neo-chrìonna.
indiscretion, *s.* neo-chrìonnachd.
indiscriminate, *adj.* feadh a chéile.
indiscussed, *adj.* neo-rannsaichte.
indispensable, *adj.* neo-sheachnach.
indispose, *v. a.* neo-uidheamaich.
indisposition, *s.* euslaint ; fuath.
indisputable, *adj.* cinnteach.
indisputableness, *s.* cinnteachas.

indissoluble, *adj.* do-leaghach ; neo-sgaranta ; buan, maireannach.

indistinct, *adj.* neo-shoilleir.

indistinctness, *s.* neo-shoilleireachd, neo-chinnteachas, doilleireachd.

individual, *adj.* leis féin, an aonar.

individual, *s.* aon, urra, neach.

individuality, *s.* pearsantachd, bith air leth.

individually, *adv.* air leth, fa-leth.

indivisibility, *s.* do-roinnteachd.

indivisible, *adj.* do-sgarach.

indocible, indocile, *adj.* do-ionnsachail, dùr, fiadhaich.

indocility, *s.* do-theagaisgeachd.

indolence, *s.* leisg, dìomhanas.

indolent, *adj.* leasg, dearmadach.

indraught, *s.* camus, bàgh, cala, sruthadh a steach.

indrench, *v. a.* tùm, fliuch, bogaich.

indubitable, *adj.* neo-theagmhach.

induce, *v. a.* gluais neach ; cuir ìmpidh.

inducement, *s.* aobhar brosnachaidh, cuireadh, misneach, comhairle.

induct, *v. a.* cuir an seilbh, thoir a steach, pòs (ri coimhthional).

induction, *s.* pùincean dearbhaidh ; deanamh a mach ; pòsadh ri coimhthional.

inductive, *adj.* earalach, treòrachail ; seadhach.

indue, *v. a.* còmhdaich.

indulge, *v. a.* leig le, toilich ; beadraich, breug ; thoir cead do.

indulgence, *s.* coibhneas, caomhalachd, maoth-chaidreamh ; bàigh, deagh-gean ; saor-thìodhlac ; toileachadh ; cead-peacaidh.

indulgent, *adj.* coibhneil, caidreach, fial ; caomh, bàigheil ; faoin-ghràdhach ; truacanta.

indult, indulto, *s.* ùghdarras (leis a' phàp).

indurate, *v.* cruadhaich, fàs cruaidh.

induration, *s.* cruadhachadh ; cruas ; cruas cridhe.

industrious, *adj.* gnìomhach, dìchiollach, dèanadach, adhartach.

industry, *s.* dìchioll, saothair, deanadachd, gnìomhachas.

indweller, *s.* fear-còmhnaidh.

inebriate, *v.* misgich, cuir air mhisg.

inebriation, *s.* misg, daorach.

ineffability, *s.* do-labhartachd.

ineffable, *adj.* do-luaidh nach gabh innse, no cur am briathran.

ineffective, *adj.* neo-bhuadhach, fann, anns nach 'eil maith air bith.

ineffectual, *adj.* neo-tharbhach, fann.

inefficacious, *adj.* neo-éifeachdach.

inefficacy, *s.* neo-chomasachd.

inelegance, *s.* mì-mhaise, mì-loinn.

inelegant, *adj.* neo-mhaiseach, mì-loinneil, mì-dhreachmhor, mì-eireachdail.

inept, *adj.* neo-fhreagarrach, baoth.

ineptitude, *s.* neo-fhreagarrachd.

inequality, *s.* neo-choimeasachd, neo-ionannachd ; eadar-dhealachadh.

inequitable, *adj.* mìcheart.

inerrable, *adj.* neo-mhearachdail.

inert, *adj.* trom, marbhanta, leisg.

inertness, *s.* marbhantachd.

inestimable, *adj.* os cionn luach.

inevitable, *adj.* do-sheachanta.

inexcusable, *adj.* neo-leithsgeulach.

inexhaustible, *adj.* do-thraoghachail.

inexistent, *adj.* nach 'eil am bith.

inexorable, *adj.* do-lùbadh.

inexpedience, *s.* neo-iomchuidheachd.

inexpedient, *adj.* neo-iomchuidh.

inexperience, *s.* cion-eòlais.

inexperienced, *adj.* neo-chleachdte, ain-eolach.

inexpert, *adj.* neo-ealanta.

inexpiable, *adj.* do nach 'eil éiric.

inexplicable, *adj.* do-mhineachail.

inexplorable, *adj.* do-rannsachail.

inexpressible, *adj.* nach gabh luaidh.

inextinguishable, *adj.* do-mhùchail.

inextirpable, *adj.* nach gabh spìonadh.

inextricable, *adj.* nach gabh fuasgladh.

infallibility, *s.* do-mhearachdail.

infallible, *adj.* foirfe ; neo-thuiteamach.

infamous, *adj.* maslach, olc ; aingidh.

infamy, *s.* masladh, mìchliù, sgainneal.

infancy, *s.* leanabachd ; tùs.

infant, *s.* naoidhean, leanabh, leanaban, pàisde.

infanticide, *s.* naoidh-mhortair.

infantile, infantine, *adj.* leanabaidh, leanabail, leanabanta.

infantry, *s.* saighdearan coise.

infatuate, *v. a.* dall, buair, cuir fo gheasaibh.

infatuated, *adj.* buairte, as a chiall.

infatuation, *s.* dalladh, buaireadh.

infeasible, *adj.* do-dhèanamh.

infect, *v. a.* cuir galar no tinneas air ; truaill, lìon le truailleachd.

infection, *s.* galar-ghabhail.

infectious, *adj.* gabhaltach.

infecund, *adj.* neo-thorach, seasg.

infecundity, *s.* neo-thorachas.

infelicity, *s.* mì-shonas, mì-àgh.

infer, *v. a.* co-dhùin (o aobhar no o shanas).

inference, *s.* co-dhùnadh, seadh.

inferior, *adj.* ìochdrach ; suarach, ni's suaraiche, ni's neo-inbhiche.

inferior, *s.* ìochdaran.

inferiority, *s.* ìochdranachd, neo-inbheachd, ìsleachd.

infernal, *adj.* ifrinneach, dona.

inferrible, *adj.* so-thuigsinn o, a thuig-ear le.

infertile, *adj.* mì-thorach, aimrid.

infertility, *s.* mì-thorachas.

infest, *v. a.* sgaothaich ; forgnaich.

infidel, *s.* ana-creidmheach.

infidelity, *s.* as-creidimh ; anacriosdachd.

infinite, *adj.* neo-chrìochnach, air nach 'eil crìoch.

infinitely, *adv.* gun tomhas, gun chrìoch, gu neo-chrìochnach.

infiniteness, infinitude, infinity, *s.* neo-chrìochnachd, anabarrachd.

infirm, *adj.* euslan, anfhann, breòite ; neo-dhaingeann.

infirmary, *s.* tigh-eiridinn, osbadal.

infirmity, *s.* laigse, anfhannachd, anmhainneachd ; breòiteachd, fàilling, euslaint, tinneas.

infirmness, *s.* laigse, eucail.

infix, *v. a.* sàth a steach ; daingnich.

inflame, *v. a.* loisg, las, cuir r'a theine ; feargaich, buair ; brosnaich ; at, gabh fearg ; iongraich.

inflammable, *adj.* so-loisgeach, lasaireach, lasanta.

inflammation, *s.* cur r'a theine, lasadh, losgadh ; brosnachadh ; iongrachadh, àinteas.

inflammatory, *adj.* lasarra, loisgeach, buaireasach, feargach.

inflate, *v. a.* séid suas, cuir gaoth ann ; dèan àrdanach, dèan moiteil.

inflation, *s.* séideadh, at ; moit, féin-bheachd, féin-spèis.

inflect, *v. a.* lùb, fiar, crom.

inflective, *adj.* a lùbas, a chromas.

inflexibility, inflexibleness, *s.* neo-lùbtachd, raige, raigead ; rag-mhuinealas, reasgaiche.

inflexible, *adj.* nach gabh lùbadh ; rag ; dùr, reasgach, ceann-làidir ; doatharrachail, neo-chaochlaideach.

inflict, *v. a.* leag peanas air, peanasaich, pian, sàraich, goirtich, cràidh.

infliction, *s.* leagadh peanais, peanasaichadh, sàrachadh, peanas.

inflictive, *adj.* peanasail.

influence, *s.* cumhachd, ceannardachd, uachdranachd ; buaidh (air inntinn neach).

influence, *v. a.* lùb, aom, treòraich, earalaich, comhairlich.

influent, *adj.* a' lìonadh, a' sruthadh a steach.

influential, *adj.* cumhachdach, buadhach, uachdranail.

influx, *s.* tighinn a steach, sruth-lìonaidh.

infold, *v. a.* fill, paisg.

infoliate, *v. a.* còmhdaich le duilleach.

inform, *v. a.* teagaisg, thoir eòlas ; casaidich, innis ; thoir brath.

informal, *adj.* mar a thuiteas ; mar a thachras.

informality, *s.* gun bhi aig dragh riaghailt.

informant, *s.* fear-bratha.

information, *s.* naidheachd, sgeul ; rabhadh, brath ; ionnsachadh, oilean, fiosrachadh.

informer, *s.* fear-innsidh.

infraction, *s.* briseadh.

inframundane, *adj.* fo'n t-saoghal.

infrangible, *adj.* do-bhristeadh.

infrequency, *s.* anaminic, corr uair.

infrequent, *adj.* ainmic, ainneamh.

infrigidate, *v. a.* fuaraich, ragaich.

infringe, *v. a.* mill, sgrios, bac, bris a steach (air chòir).

infringement, *s.* bristeadh.

infumate, *v. a.* tiormaich sa' cheò.

infuriate, *v. a.* cuir air bhoile.

infuriated, *adj.* air bhoile, air a' chuthach.

infuse, *v. a.* dòirt ann, dòirt a steach ; bogaich, cuir am bogadh, tarruing (tì).

infusible, *adj.* nach gabh leaghadh.

infusion, *s.* dòrtadh a steach ; teagasg, deachdadh ; bogachadh ; sùgh, deoch.

infusive, *adj.* dòirteach ; leaghtach.

ingemination, *s.* ath-aithris.

ingenious, *adj.* innleachdach, tùrail, geurchuiseach, seòlta, teòma, ealanta, innealta.

ingenuity, *s.* innleachd, tùralachd, teòmachd, seòltachd, ealantachd, innealtachd.

ingenuous, *adj.* fosgarra, fìrinneach, ceart, còir, fialaidh.

inglorious, *adj.* neo-allail, suarach ; dìblidh, air bheag cliù.

ingot, *s.* geinn òir no airgeid.

ingraff, ingraft, *v. a.* alp ; suidhich faillean o aona chraoibh ann an craoibh eile.

ingraftment, *s.* alpadh.

ingrate, *s.* mì-thaingeil.

ingratiate, *v. a.* mol thu féin do ; faigh coibhneas o neach, cuir a steach càirdeas.

ingratitude, *s.* mì-thaingealachd.

ingredient, *s.* earrann-measgachaidh.

ingress, *s.* dol a steach, slighe.

ingulf, *v. a.* tilg sios ann an slugan, cuir fodha.

ingurgitate, *v.* sluig sìos, dèan geòcaireachd.

ingurgitation, *s.* geòcaireachd.

inhabit, *v.* àitich, sealbhaich ; còmhnaich, tàmh, fuirich.

inhabitable, *adj.* so-àiteachail, seasgair.

inhabitant, *s.* fear-àiteachaidh.

inhale, *v. a.* tarruing anail, gabh a steach leis an anail.

inharmonious, *adj.* neo-bhinn.

inherent, *adj.* ann-féin, nàdurra, dualach, neo-ghinte, a bhuineas do fhìor-ghné.

inherit, *v. a.* gabh mar oighreachd, faigh mar oighreachd, sealbhaich.

inheritable, *adj.* oighreachail.

inheritance, *s.* oighreachd, sealbh dlighe, maoin dhligheach.

inheritor, *s.* oighre, sealbhadair.

inheritress, inheritrix, s. ban-oighre, ban-sealbhadair.

inhibit, v. a. bac, cum air ais, grab, cuir stad air ; toirmisg, diùlt.

inhibition, s. bacadh, grabadh, stad, amladh ; toirmeasg, casg.

inhospitable, adj. neo-fhialaidh, iargalta, coimheach, doichiollach.

inhospitality, s. neo-fhialachd, iargalt-achd, coimhiche, doichiollachd, mos-aiche, spìocaiche, crìonachd, cruas, mùgaireachd, doirbheachd.

inhuman, adj. mì-dhaonna, borb, an-iochdmhor, cruaidh-chridheach, mì-nàdurach.

inhumanity, s. mì-dhaonnachd, an-iochd-mhorachd, buirbe.

inhumate, inhume, v. a. adhlaic, tòrr, tiodhlaic.

inhumation, s. adhlacadh, torradh.

inimical, adj. neo-chàirdeil, mì-rùnach.

inimitable, adj. do-shamhlach ; gun choimeas ; nach gabh aithris.

iniquitous, adj. eucorach, peacach, aing-idh, ciontach, olc.

iniquity, s. eucoir, peacadh, aingidheachd, anaceartas, cionta, olc.

initial, adj. 's an dol a mach ; 's a' cheud tòiseachadh.

initiate, v. thoir ceud eòlas teagaisg ; tionnsgain, tòisich.

initiation, s. ceud thòiseachadh.

initiatory, adj. tòiseachail.

inject, v. a. tilg a steach ; steall a steach.

injection, s. tilgeadh a steach ; a' chungaidh a steallar a steach.

injudicious, adj. mì-ghlic ; neo-chrìonna, neo-thùrail.

injunction, s. àithne, earail, dian-iarrtas, òrdugh.

injure, v. a. docharaich, lochdaich, ciùrr, dochannaich, dèan coire do.

injurious, adj. cronail, eucorach, ana-ceart ; coireach, ciontach ; àimhleas-ach, docharach ; tarcuiseach, tàmailt-each.

injury, s. lochd, lethtrom, ciùrradh, ana-cothrom, dochair ; dochunn, dìobhail, call, calldach ; tàir, tarcuis, càineadh.

injustice, s. anaceartas, eucoir, ana-cothrom ; easaontas, olc.

ink, s. dubh, dubh sgrìobhaidh.

inkle, s. stìom, stiall, caolchrios.

inkling, s. sanas, faireachadh, rabhadh.

inky, adj. dubh, dorcha.

inland, adj. a stigh air an duthaich.

inland, s. bràighe-dùthcha.

inlet, s. dorus, fosgladh, rathad, bealach, caolas, aisir.

inly, adj. 's an taobh a stigh ; gu faisg, domhain.

inmate, s. fear-còmhnuidh, (an tigh).

inmost, innermost, adj. as fhaide steach.

inn, s. tigh-òsda, tigh-òil, tigh-leanna.

innate, adj. neo-ghinte, nàdurra gnèith-each, dualach.

innavigable, adj. air nach seol bàta.

inner, adj. as fhaide steach.

innholder, innkeeper, s. òsdair.

innocence, s. neo-chiontachd, neo-chiont-as ; neo-lochdachd, neo-chronalachd ; fìreantachd, ionracas, neochiont ; tréidhireas.

innocent, adj. neochiontach, neochoir-each, glan ; neo-lochdach.

innocuous, adj. neo-chronail, neo-lochd-ach.

innovate, v. a. ùr-ghnàthaich, dèan ùr-chaochla ; atharraich.

innovation, s. ùr-ghnàthachadh.

innovator, s. ùr-ghnàthadair.

innoxious, adj. neo-lochdach, neochoir-each, neo-chiùrrail.

innuendo, s. fiarfhacal, athais fheallta.

innumerable, adj. do-àireamh.

inoculate, v. suidhich ; cuir a' bhreac air.

inoculation, s. suidheachadh, alpadh, cur na brice.

inodorous, adj. gun fhàileadh.

inoffensive, adj. neo-lochdach, soitheamh, ciùin, suairce, neo-bhuaireasach.

inoffensiveness, s. suairceas.

inofficious, adj. mì-riaghailteach, mì-bheusail.

inopportune, adj. an-aimsireil, mì-ghoir-easach.

inordinate, adj. ana-cuimseach, mì-riagh-ailteach, àimhreiteach.

inorganic, adj. nach buin do bhuadhan corparra.

inosculate, v. n. buin r'a chéile, co-cheangail, tàthaich.

inosculation, s. aonadh, dlùthachadh, tàthadh, co-bhuntainn.

inquest, s. sgrùdadh, ceasnachadh, ranns-achadh laghail ; iarraidh, sireadh.

inquietude, s. mì-shuaimhneas, neo-fhoisneachd, anshocair.

inquinate, v. a. truaill, salaich, mill.

inquination, s. truailleadh, salachadh.

inquire, v. feòraich, farraid, iarr, faigh-nich ; rannsaich, sir, dèan sgrùdadh.

inquirer, s. fear-rannsachaidh, fear-ceasnachaidh, fear-sgrùdaidh.

inquiry, s. ceasnachadh, feòraich, rannsachadh, sireadh, sgrùdadh.

inquisition, s. rannsachadh laghail, mion-cheasnachadh, sireadh ; cùirt rannsach (creud), rannsach le for-éigin.

inquisitive, adj. rannsachail, faighneach-dail, fidreachail, ceasnachadh mì-mhodhail.

inquisitiveness, s. faighneachdas, geur-rannsachadh, fidreachadh.

inquisitor, s. fear-ceasnachaidh, fear-rannsachaidh, fear-sgrùdaidh.

inroad, s. ionnsaigh, ruathar, creach.

insalubrious, adj. neo-fhallain.

insalubrity, s. neo-fhallaineachd.

insane, adj. cuthach, mearanach, á rian.

insaneness, insanity, s. cuthach, mearan-céille, boile.

insatiable, insatiate, adj. do-shàsachail, do-riarachail, do-thoileachail ; gionach, geòcach, glutach, lonach, craosach, cìocrach.

insatiableness, s. do-riarachadh.

inscribe, v. a. sgrìobh.

inscription, s. sgrìobhadh, tiodal, gràbhaladh, cuimhne.

inscrutable, adj. do-rannsachail.

insculpture, s. gràbhaladh, snaidheadh.

insect, s. cuileag, cnuimh, biastag.

insecure, adj. neo-thèarainte, neo-chinnteach.

insecurity, s. neo-thèarainteachd.

insensate, adj. neo-thuigseach, brùideil.

insensibility, s. neo-mhothachadh.

insensible, adj. neo-mhothachail, neo-thuigseach ; neo-chaidreach.

inseparable, adj. do-dhealachail, do-sgarach, do-fhuasglach.

insert, v. a. suidhich, gabh a steach.

insertion, s. suidheachadh, cur ann.

inside, s. an taobh a stigh.

insidious, adj. meallta, cealgach, foilleil, carach, cuilbheartach, sligheach.

insidiousness, s. mealltachd, ceilg, foillealachd, cuilbheartachd.

insight, s. fiosrachadh, geurbheachd.

insignia, s. suaicheantas.

insignificance, s. faoineas.

insignificant, adj. faoin, suarach, tàireil, neo-luachmhor.

insincere, adj. neo-fhìrinneach, neo-dhùrachdach, neo-threidhireach, cealgach, claon, foilleil, carach.

insincerity, s. neo-fhìrinneachd, neo-threidhireas, ceilg, foillealachd.

insinuant, s. fear miodalach, brionnalach, seòlta, carach.

insinuate, v. cuir a steach le faicill ; dèan miodal, dèan brosgal ; faigh a steach air ; thoir leth-shanas, lethchiallaich.

insinuation, s. cur a steach, sàthadh ; miodal, sodal, brosgal, brionnal.

insinuative, adj. seòltach, miodalach, sodalach, brosgalach.

insipid, adj. neo-bhlasda, neo-shunntach, neo-sheadhach, marbhanta, tioram, trom, amhaidh.

insipidity, s. neo-bhlasdachd ; marbhantachd, tiormachd truime, amhaidheachd.

insipience, s. neo-ghliocas, gòraiche, baothaltachd, baothaireachd.

insist, v. n. seas air, socraich air, lean air, buanaich air, seas ri, cùm air.

insnare, v. a. rib, glac, cuir an sàs.

insobriety, s. ana-measarrachd, misg.

insolate, v. a. cuir ri gréin.

insolation, s. grianachadh.

insolence, s. uaibhreachas, tàir, àrdan, stràic, beadaidheachd.

insolent, adj. uaibhreach, stràiceil, beadaidh, tarcuiseach.

insolvable, adj. do-fhuasglach, do-mhìneachail, do-réiteachail ; nach gabh dìoladh, nach gabh ìocadh.

insolvency, s. bristeadh creideis.

insolvent, adj. briste, bàithte am fiachan.

insoluble, adj. do-leaghaidh, nach gabh mìneachadh.

insomuch, adv. a mheud agus gu.

inspect, v. a. rannsaich, beachdaich.

inspection, s. amharc, geur-amharc, mion-rannsachadh, sgrùdadh, dearcadh ; cùram, sùl-amharc.

inspector, s. fear-rannsachaidh, fear-sgrùdaidh ; fear ceasnachaidh.

inspiration, s. analachadh, sùghadh analach ; deachdadh an Spioraid, teagasg nèamhaidh.

inspire, v. analaich air ; cuir 's an inntinn ; tarruing a steach, sùigh, tarruing t' anail.

inspirit, v. a. beothaich, dùisg suas, brosnaich, misnich.

inspissate, v. a. tiughaich, dèan tiugh.

inspissated, adj. tiughaichte.

instability, s. neo-bhunailteachd, neo-sheasmhachd.

install, v. a. cuir an dreuchd, suidhich, cuir an sàs.

installation, s. cur an seilbh dreuchd, suidheachadh an dreuchd, dreuchd-shuidheachadh.

instalment, s. earrann-dhìoladh.

instant, adj. dian, éigneach, dùrachdach, cabhagach, bras ealamh, air ball.

instant, s. tìota, àm, tamall, uair.

instantaneous, adj. an gradaig.

instantly, instantaneously, adv. gu grad, gu h-obann, gu h-ealamh, gu clis.

instate, v. a. suidhich, cuir an inbhe.

instauration, s. ath-aiseag.

instead, adv. an àite, air son.

instep, s. uachdar na troighe.

instigate, v. a. brosnaich, buair.

instigation, s. brosnachadh, buaireadh.

instigator, s. buaireadair, fear-brosnachaidh.

instil, v. a. sil, sil a steach ; teagaisg.

instillation, s. sileadh a steach ; teagasg, mion-theagasg.

instinct, adj. beò, beothail, beathail.

instinct, s. aomadh nàdurra, nàdur, ciall, gnè.

instinctive, adj. gnèitheil, nàdurrach.

institute, v. a. suidhich, socraich, cuir air chois.

institute, s. reachd, lagh, rian, òrdugh, seòl suidhichte ; àithnte, fìrinn shuidhichte.

institution, s. suidheachadh, òrduchadh ; lagh, reachd ; oilean, foghlum, tigh foghlum.

institutor, s. fear-suidheachaidh, fear-òrduchaidh ; fear-teagaisg.

instruct, v. a. teagaisg, oileanaich, seòl, comhairlich, ionnsaich.

instruction, s. teagasg, oilean, seòladh, eòlas, comhairle ; ionnsachadh.

instructive, adj. teagasgach.

instructor, s. oid-ionnsachaidh, fear-teagaisg, fear-fòghluim.

instrument, s. inneal, ball, beart, arm ; inneal-ciùil ; bann-sgrìobhte ; meadhon, ball-acuinn.

instrumental, adj. 'na mheadhon air.

insuavity, s. neo-thaitneachd.

insubjection, s. eas-ùmhlachd.

insubordination, s. mi-riaghailt.

insubstantial, adj. neo-bhrìoghmhor.

insufferable, adj. do-fhulangach, do-ghiùlanach, do-iomchar ; dèisinneach.

insufficiency, s. neo-choimhliontachd, neo - dhiongmhaltachd, easbhuidheachd, neo-fhoghainteachd.

insufficient, adj. neo-choimhlionta, neo-dhiongmhalta, neo-fhoghainteach.

insular, adj. eileanach ; 'na aonar, leis féin.

insulated, adj. dealaichte, air leth.

insult, s. tàmailt, masladh, tàir, tarcuis, dimeas, beum, toibheum.

insult, v. a. tàmailtich, thoir tàmailt, maslaich, cuir gu nàire.

insulter, s. fear-tarcuis.

insuperability, s. do-cheannsachd, do-chlaoidhteachd ; do-dhèantachd.

insuperable, adj. do-cheannsachail ; do-chlaoidheach, do-shàrachail ; do-dhèanamh, do-fhairtleach.

insupportable, adj. do-ghiùlanta,

insupportableness, s. do-ghiùlantachd.

insuppressible, adj. do-fhalachail.

insurance, s. urras, airgead urrais.

insure, v. a. faigh no thoir urras air.

insurgent, s. ceannaircach.

insurmountable, adj. thar comas.

insurrection, s. ar-a-mach.

intactible, adj. do-fhaireachail.

intangible, adj. do-làimhseachail.

integer, s. slàn-àireamh, an-t-iomlan.

integral, adj. slàn, iomlan, coimhlionta, neo-bhriste.

integral, s. an t-iomlan.

integrity, s. treidhireas, ionracas ; gloine, neo-chiontas.

integument, s. còmhdach, cochull.

intellect, s. tuigse, toinisg, ciall ; inntinn.

intellective, adj. tuigseach, ciallach ; inntinneil, mothachail,

intellectual, adj. inntinneil, inntinneach ; tuigseach, geurchuiseach.

intelligence, s. fios, fiosrachadh, eòlas, tuigse ; spiorad, tùr.

intelligent, adj. tuigseach, eòlach, fiosrach, fòghluimte, ionnsaichte, tùrail.

intelligible, adj. so-thuigsinneach.

intemperance, s. ana-measarrachd.

intemperate, adj. ana-measarra, mì-stuama ; glutail ; lasanta, feargach.

intend, v. a. cuir romhad sònraich, rùnaich, togair ; thoir fainear.

intendant, s. fear-freasdail.

intense, adj. teann, cruaidh, teannaichte ; dlùth-aireach ; dian.

intenseness, s. teinne, teanntachd ; déinead, déine ; ro-aire, dlùth-aire.

intention, s. rùn, miann, sannt, cur romhad, aire, beachd.

intentional, adj. rùnaichte, le deòin.

intentive, adj. dlùth-aireach, dùrachdach.

intentness, s. ro-aire, geur-aire.

inter, v. a. adhlaic, tìodhlaic.

intercalary, adj. barrachdail (là).

intercede, v. a. dèan eadar-ghuidhe.

intercept, v. a. glac 's an t-slighe, beir air ; cuir bacadh air, coinnich.

intercession, s. eadar-ghuidhe.

intercessor, s. eadar-mheadhonair.

interchain, v. a. co-cheangail.

interchange, v. a. malairtich.

interchange, s. iomlaid, malairt.

interchangeable, adj. co-iomlaideach, co-mhalairteach.

intercision, s. bacadh, amladh.

interclude, v. n. dùin a mach.

interclusion, s. dùnadh a mach.

intercolumniation, s. eadar dhà charragh.

intercostal, adj. eadar dhà aisne.

intercourse, s. co-chomunn.

interdict, v. a. toirmisg, seun, bac.

interdictory, adj. toirmeasgach.

interest, v. cuir fo chùram, cuir fo smuain ; gabh gnothach ri, gabh cùram do ; gluais, drùidh air ; tog déidh.

interest, s. leas, math, buannachd, tairbhe, feum ; comh-roinn, comh-pàirt, leth-phàirt ; ocar, riadh.

interfere, v. n. dèan meachranachd, rach an eadraigin.

interference, s. eadraiginn.

interfulgent, adj. eadar-dhealrach.

interfused, adj. eadar-thaomte.

interim, s. greis, treis.

interior, adj. an leth stigh.

interjacent, adj. eadar-laigheach, 's a' mheadhon.

interject, v. dèan eadraiginn.

interjection, s. guth-fhacal.

interjoin, v. a. eadar-dhlùthaich.

interlace, v. a. figh,

interlard, *v. a.* measgaich le.

interleave, *v. a.* eadar-dhuilleagaich.

interline, *v. a.* eadar-shreathaich.

interlineation, *s.* eadar-shreathadh, eadar sgrìobhadh.

interlink, *v. a.* eadar-theinnich.

interlocation, *s.* eadar-shuidheachadh.

interlocution, *s.* eadar-labhairt.

interlocutor, *s.* eadar-labhairtear.

interlocutory, *adj.* conaltrach.

interlope, *v. n.* gabh gnothaich ri nì nach buin duit.

interloper, *s.* sgimilear.

interlucent, *adj.* eadar-shoillseach.

interlude, *s.* eadar-chluiche.

interlunar, *adj.* eadar dhà sholus.

intermarriage, *s.* co-chleamhnas.

intermeddle, *v. n.* dèan meachranachd, gabh gnothuich ri.

intermedial, intermediate, *adj.* eadar-mheadhònach.

interment, *s.* tìodhlacadh, adhlacadh.

intermention, *v. a.* eadar-ainmich.

intermigration, *s.* iomlaid àite.

interminable, interminate, *adj.* neo-chrìochnach, neo-iomallach, gun chrìoch.

intermination, *s.* bagradh.

intermingle, *v. a.* coimeasgaich.

intermission, *s.* stad, clos, tàmh ; eadarùine ; lasachadh, faothachadh.

intermissive, intermittent, *adj.* neo-bhitheanta, neo-ghnàthach, an dràsd 's a rìs.

intermit, *v.* sguir, stad, leig tàmh dha ; faothaich, lasaich, clos ré ùine.

intermix, *v.* coimeasg.

intermixture, *s.* coimeasgadh.

intermundane, *adj.* eadar dhà shaoghal.

intermural, *adj.* eadar dhà-bhalla.

intermutual, *adj.* eadar-mhalairteach, eadar-iomlaideach.

internal, *adj.* 's an leth a' stigh.

internuncio, *s.* teachdaire a' Phàpa.

interpellation, *s.* bairlin, gairm.

interpoint, *v. a.* eadar-phoncaich.

interpolate, *v. a.* eadar-sgrìobh, spàrr an àite nach buin do.

interpolation, *s.* eadar-sgrìobhadh, eadar-sparradh.

interposal, interposition, *s.* eadraiginn, teachd 's an rathad.

interpose, *v.* eadar-chuir, eadar-shuidhich ; cuir grabadh air, amail ; tairg cuideachadh ; dèan eadraiginn.

interposition, *s.* eadraiginn.

interpret, *v. a.* mìnich, soilleirich ; eadar-theangaich.

interpretable, *adj.* so-mhìneachail, soshoilleireach.

interpretation, *s.* mìneachadh, soilleireachadh, eadar-theangachadh, brìgh, seadh.

interpreter, *s.* fear-mìneachaidh.

interreign, interregnum, *s.* eadar-riaghladh, ùin eadar dhà rìgh.

interrogate, *v.* ceasnaich, rannsaich, fidrich, cuir ceistean.

interrogation, *s.* ceasnachadh, rannsachadh, cur cheistean ; ceist, faighneachd.

interrogative, *adj.* faighneachdach, ceisteach, ceasnachail.

interrogative, *s.* ceistfhacal.

interrogatory, *s.* ceist, ceasnachadh, faighneachd.

interrogatory, *adj.* ceasnachail.

interrupt, *v. a.* cuir stad air, bac.

interrupted, *adj.* bristeach, briste.

interruption, *s.* stad, briseadh, briseadh a steach, stad-chur ; eadar-chur, grabadh, bacadh ; cnap-starraidh ; stad, clos.

intersect, *v. a.* co-ghearr, gearr tarsainn; eadar-chuir, eadar-shuidhich.

intersection, *s.* eadar-ghearradh.

intersperse, *v. a.* sgaoil air feadh, sgap.

interstice, *s.* eadar-fhosgladh.

interstitial, *adj.* eadar-fhosglach.

intertwine, *v. a.* tuain, suain.

interval, *s.* uidhe, ionad ; ùine, àm ; faothachadh.

intervene, *v. n.* thig eadar, rach an eadraigin.

intervenient, *adj.* a thig eadar.

intervention, *s.* tighinn a steach an càs.

interview, *s.* comhluadair ; coinneachadh, chòmhradh.

intervolve, *v. a.* suain 'n a cheile.

interweave, *v. a.* figh.

intestate, *adj.* gun tiomnadh.

intestinal, *adj.* caolanach.

intestine, *adj.* 's an leth a stigh ; corpora ; intestine war, cogadh sìobhalta.

intestine, *s.* a' ghrealach.

inthral, *v. a.* cìosnaich cuir fo dhaorsa.

inthralment, *s.* braighdeanas.

intimacy, *s.* comunn, co-chomunn, dlùth-eòlas, companas, caidreamh.

intimate, *adj.* mion-eòlach, caidreach ; dlùth, fagus, teann air.

intimate, *s.* caraid, còmpanach.

intimate, *v. a.* innis, thoir sanas.

intimation, *s.* fios, rabhadh, sanas.

intimidate, *v. a.* gealtaich, cuir fo eagal.

into, *prep.* a steach, gu ; a steach ann ; a dh' ionnsaigh.

intolerable, *adj.* do-ghiùlanta, dona.

intolerant, *adj.* neo-fhulangach.

intonation, *s.* torrunn, tairnthoirm.

intoxicate, *v. a.* cuir air an daoraich, misgich.

intoxicated, *adj.* air mhisg.

intoxication, *s.* misg, daorach.

intractable, *adj.* do - cheannsachail, ceann-laidir, dùr, reasgach.

intransmutable, *adj.* nach gabh mùthadh, do-atharrachail.

intrap, *v. a.* cuir an sàs, glac, rib.

intrench, *v.* cladhaich, tochail, treachail ; dìon le clais ; bris a steach air.

intrenchment, *s.* clais - dhaingneachd, dìdean threachailte.

intrepid, *adj.* gaisgeil, curanta.

intrepidity, *s.* curantachd gaisge.

intricate, *adj.* deacair, ioma-cheisteach, ioma-lùbach.

intrigue, *s.* rùn - àimhleis, comhairle dhìomhair, cùis - leannanachd ; innleachd meallaidh, feall, cuilbheart.

intrigue, *v. n.* meall, cleasaich, dèan leannanachd dhìomhair.

intrinsic, intrinsical, *adj.* nàdurra, gnèith-eil, ann féin, dlùth-dhàimheil.

introduce, *v. a.* thoir 's an làthair, thoir am fianais, thoir am follais, thoir a steach ; thoir air adhart.

introduction, *s.* treòrachadh, toirt an làthair, toirt am fianais ; roimh-ràdh.

intromission, *s.* meachranachd, buintinn ri cuid neach eile ; cur a steach.

intromit, *v.* cuir a steach, leig a steach ; buin ri cuid neach eile.

introspection, *s.* sealltainn a steach.

intrude, *v. n.* fòirn, spàrr a steach ; thig gun chuireadh ; bris a steach.

intruder, *s.* sgimilear, fear-fòirnidh.

intrusion, *s.* sgimeilearachd, fòirneadh.

intrusive, *adj.* leamh, beag-nàrach.

intrust, *v. a.* earb ri, cuir earbs' ann.

intuition, *s.* beachd-eòlas, grad-eòlas.

intuitive, *adj.* so-thuigsinn ; geur-thuigs-each, grad-thuigseach.

intwine, *v. a.* toinn, fill, figh, snìomh.

inunction, *s.* ungadh, ol'-ùngadh.

inundate, *v.* còmhdaich le uisge, cuir thairis.

inundation, *s.* tuil-chòmhdach.

inurbanity, *s.* neo-shuairceas.

inure, *v. a.* ri cur an cleachdadh, cleachd.

inurement, *s.* cleachdadh.

inurn, *v. a.* adhlaic, tìodhlaic, tòrr.

inustion, *s.* losgadh, lasadh.

inutile, *adj.* neo-fheumail, suarach.

inutility, *s.* neo-fheumalachd.

invade, *v. a.* thoir ionnsaigh air, bris a steach ; leum air, cas ri, buail air.

invader, *s.* fear brisidh a steach, fear-fòirnidh, nàmhaid.

invalid, *adj.* lag, anfhann, neo-threòrach, fann.

invalid, *s.* neach tinn, euslainteach, neach gun chlì.

invalidate, *v. a.* lagaich, dìobhalaich, anfhannaich, bris.

invalidity, *s.* laigse, anfhannachd cuirp.

invaluable, *adj.* os ceann luach.

invariable, *adj.* neo-chaochlaideach.

invariableness, *s.* neo - chaochlaideachd, maireannachd, gnàthachas.

invasion, *s.* briseadh a steach, ionnsaigh nàimhdeil.

invasive, *adj.* ainneartach.

invective, *s.* achmhasan, geur-achmhasan, cronachadh, beum.

invective, *adj.* beumnach, aoireil.

inveigh, *v. a.* càin, faigh cron.

inveigle, *v. a.* meall, thoir a thaobh, mì-chomhairlich, rib.

inveigler, *s.* mealltair, mi-chomhairleach.

invent, *v. a.* faigh ìnnleachd ùr, faigh a mach, tionnsgail ; fealltaich.

invention, *s.* ùr-innleachd, ùr-ghleus, breug-dhealbhadh.

inventive, *adj.* innleachdach, ealanta, tùrail, tionnsgalach.

inventor, *s.* fear a dhealbhas innleachd ùr ; fear deanamh bhreug.

inventory, *s.* maoin-chunntas.

inverse, *adj.* tarsainn, air chaochla dòigh.

inversion, *s.* rian-atharrachadh.

invert, *v. a.* cuir bun-os-ceann.

invest, *v. a.* éid, sgeadaich, còmhdaich ; cuir an seilbh, cuir an dreuchd ; cuair-tich, iomdhruid, séisd ; cuir umad.

investigable, *adj.* so-rannsachadh.

investigate, *v. a.* rannsaich.

investigation, *s.* rannsachadh.

investiture, *s.* còir-sheilbhe.

investment, *s.* éideadh, earradh, aodach, culaidh, trusgan ; leigeadh a mach air riadh.

inveteracy, *s.* danarrachd, cian mhairsinn an olc ; dìorrais.

inveterate, *adj.* sean, buan ; danarra, dìorrasach, dùr, dian, cruadhaichte.

invidious, *adj.* fuath-thogalach, farmad-ach, mì-runach, gamhlasach, naimhd-eil.

invidiousness, *s.* fuath-thogalachd.

invigorate, *v. a.* neartaich, beothaich, brosnaich.

invigoration, *s.* neartachadh.

invincible, *adj.* do-cheannsachail.

inviolable, *adj.* do-thruaillidh.

inviolate, *adj.* neo-chiùrrte, neo-thruaillte, neo-bhriste.

invisibility, *s.* do-fhaicsinneachd.

invisible, *adj.* do-fhaicsinneach.

invitation, *s.* cuireadh, iarraidh.

invite, *v.* iarr, gairm, thoir cuireadh ; tàlaidh.

inviter, *s.* fear-cuiridh, fear-gairme.

invitingly, *adv.* gu tàlaidheach.

invocate, *v. a.* guidh, grìos.

invocation, *s.* ùrnuigh, achanich, asluch-adh.

invoice, *s.* maoin-chlàr, cunntas.

involuntary, *adj.* neo-thoileach.

involution, *s.* filleadh, cuairteachadh ; cochull, cuairt-chòmhdach.

involve, *v. a.* cuairtich, iadh; seadhaich; co-aonaich, co-cheangail; rib; cuir troimh - chéile, àimhreitich, cuir an ceann a chéile.

invulnerable, *adj.* air nach deargar; nach gabh leòn.

inward, inwardly, *adv.* 'san taobh a stigh; gu diamhair.

inwrap, *v. a.* fill, cuairtich, iom-chòmhdaich; dorchaich, doilleirich.

inwreathe, *v. a.* stìom-chuairtich, coronaich.

irascible, *adj.* lasanta, feargach, crosda.

irascibleness, *s.* lasantachd, feargachd, crosdachd.

ire, *s.* fearg, corraich, fraoch, boile.

ireful, *adj.* feargach, lasanta, crosda.

iris, *s.* bogha-frois, bhogha-braoin; cearcall na sùl; seileastair.

irksome, *adj.* sgìth, buaireasach.

iron, *s.* iarunn; cuibhreach.

iron, *adj.* iaruinn, iarnach; cruaidh.

iron, *v. a.* iarnaich; lìostraig.

ironical, *adj.* magail, dà-sheadhach.

ironmonger, *s.* ceannaiche - cruadhach, fear-reic badhar iaruinn.

irony, *s.* sgeigearachd, fochaid.

irradiance, irradiancy, *s.* dealradh, dearsadh, soillse.

irradiate, *v.* dealraich, loinnrich; soillsich, soilleirich; sgiamhaich.

irradiation, *s.* dèarsadh, dealradh; soilleireachadh, soillseachadh.

irrational, *adj.* eu-céillidh.

irrationality, *s.* eu-céillidheachd.

irreclaimable, *adj.* do-leasachail.

irreconcilable, *adj.* do-réiteachail.

irrecoverable, *adj.* caillte, do-fhaotainn air ais; do-leasachail.

irreducible, *adj.* nach gabh briseadh, nach gabh toirt gu dòigh, no cur na's lugha.

irrefragable, *adj.* nach gabh àicheadh, tul-fhìrinneach.

irrefutable, *adj.* nach gabh àicheadh; nach gabh breugnachadh.

irregular, *adj.* mì-riaghailteach.

irregularity, *s.* mì-riaghailt, eas-òrdugh; mì-dhòigh; mì-bheus.

irrelative, *adj.* a mach á dàimh; leis féin.

irrelevant, *adj.* neo-fhreagarrach.

irrelievable, *adj.* do-fhuasglach.

irreligion, *s.* aindiadhachd.

irreligious, *adj.* aindiadhaidh.

irremediable, *adj.* do-shlànachail.

irremissible, *adj.* nach gabh mathadh.

irremovable, *adj.* do-ghluasadach.

irreparable, *adj.* do-leasachail.

irreprehensible, *adj.* neochoireach.

irrepressible, *adj.* do-cheannsachail.

irreproachable, *adj.* neochoireach, neochiontach.

irreprovable, *adj.* neochionteach.

irresistible, *adj.* nach gabh diùltadh.

irresolute, *adj.* neo-bhunailteach, an anamharus.

irresolution, *s.* neo-sheasmhachd.

irretentive, *adj.* aodionach.

irretrievable, *adj.* do-leasachail; tur caillte.

irreverence, *s.* neo-urram, eas-urram.

irreverent, *adj.* mì-mhodhail, dìmeasach, eas-urramach.

irreversible, *adj.* do-atharrachail.

irrevocable, *adj.* do-aisigeach.

irrigate, *v. a.* uisgich, fliuch, bog.

irrigation, *s.* uisgeachadh, bogadh.

irritable, *adj.* dranndanach, crosda.

irritate, *v. a.* brosnaich, feargaich.

irritation, *s.* brosnachadh, frionas.

irruption, *s.* briseadh a steach, ionnsaigh, ruathar.

irruptive, *adj.* brùchdach, ionnsaigheach, ruatharach.

is, *v.* is; it is, is e, thà e, is mì, is tu, etc., no, tha mì, tha thu, etc.

ischury, *s.* casg-uisge; galar-fuail.

isinglass, *s.* glaodh-éisg.

island, isle, *s.* eilean, innis.

islander, *s.* eileanach.

isolated, *adj.* air leth, aonarach.

issue, *s.* ruith, dòrtadh, sruthadh; buil, crìoch, toradh; silteach; gineal, sliochd, clann, sìol.

issue, *v.* thig a mach, bris a mach, thig o, sruth o; cuir a mach.

issueless, *adj.* gun sliochd, aimrid.

isthmus, *s.* doirlinn, tairbeart, aoidh.

itch, *s.* cloimh, sgrìobach, tachas; dianiarrtas, miann, fileadh.

itchy, *adj.* claimheach, clamhach.

item, *s.* ni air leth; leth-shanas.

iterable, *adj.* so-aithris.

iterant, *adj.* aithriseach.

iteration, *s.* ath-aithris.

iterative, *adj.* ath-aithriseach.

itinerant, *adj.* siùbhlach, turasach.

itinerary, *s.* leabhar-siubhail, cuairt fear-siubhail.

itself, *pron.* e-féin, no i-féin.

ivory, *s.* deud elephaint.

ivy, *s.* iadhshlat, eidheann.

J

jabber, *v. n.* bi geòlamach.
jabberer, *s.* geòlamaiche.
jacent, *adj.* sìnteach, 'na shìneadh, 'n a laighe.
jacinth, *s.* clach-luachmhor.
jack, *s.* greimiche-bhòt; geadas; lùireach-mhàilleach; sorchan tuirisg; bratach luinge.
jackal, *s.* fear-solair an leòmhainn, seòrsa de chù fiadhaich.
jackalent, *s.* blaghastair balaich.
jackanapes, *s.* peasan, bùban.
jackass, *s.* asail-fhireann.
jackdaw, *s.* cathag-fhireann.
jacket, *s.* peiteag mhuilichinneach, seacaid.
Jacobin, *s.* Manach glas.
jacobine, *s.* calman cìreanach.
Jacobite, *s.* Fear-leanmhainn teaghlach nan Stiùbhartach.
jactitation, *s.* iom-luasgadh.
jade, *s.* sean each; caile.
jade, *v. a.* sgìthich, claoidh; maslaich, sàraich; géill, sìolaidh.
jadish, *adj.* gun chlì, neo-sheasmhach.
jag, *v. a.* eagaich, fiaclaich.
jag, *s.* eag, bearn, cab.
jaggy, *adj.* eagach, fiaclach, bèarnach, cabach.
jail, *s.* prìosan, carcair, gainntir.
jailer, *s.* fear gleidhidh prìosain.
jalap, *s.* seòrsa purgaid.
jam, *s.* mìlsean-measa.
jam, *v. a.* teannaich, stailc, dinn.
jamb, *s.* ursann, taobh-thaic.
jangle, *v. n.* dèan gobaireachd, dèan gleadhraich.
jangler, *s.* fear-bruidhneach.
janitor, *s.* dorsair.
January, *s.* ceud mhìos na bliadhna.
japan, *s.* obair lìomhaidh.
jar, *v. n.* gliong, buail, co-bhuail; cuir an aghaidh, dean aimhreit.
jar, *s.* gliongadh; mi-chòrdadh; soith-each creadha.
jargon, *s.* brolaich, goileam.
jasper, *s.* seòrsa cloiche, iaspar.
jaundice, *s.* a' bhuidheach.
jaundiced, *adj.* fo 'n bhuidhich.
jaunt, *v. n.* thoir sgrìob, rach air turas.
jaunt, *s.* cuairt, sgrìob, turas.
jaunty, *a.* iollagach, sgeilmeil.
javelin, *s.* gath, lethshleagh.
jaw, *s.* giall, peirceall, carbad.
jawed, *adj.* giallach, peirceallach.
jay, *s.* pigheid, sgreuchan-coille.
jealous, *adj.* eudmhor.
jealousy, *s.* eud, eudmhorachd, iadach.

jeer, *v.* mag, sgeig, fochaidich; dèan magadh, dèan fochaid.
Jehovah, *s.* Iehobhah; ainm Dhé 's a' chainnt Eabhraich.
jejune, *adj.* falamh, neo-tharbhach, faoin; neo-bhlasda.
jejuneness, *s.* falamhachd, fàsachd; tiormachd, neo-bhlasdachd.
jelly, *s.* slaman-milis.
jennet, *s.* each Spàinteach.
jeopardy, *s.* cunnart, gàbhadh.
jerk, *v. a.* buail, thoir dubadh.
jerk, *s.* grad bhuille, grad-thulgadh, dubadh.
jerkin, *s.* peiteag; cota-gearr.
jessamine, *s.* lus cùraidh.
jest, *s.* àbhcaid, fala-dhà.
jester, *s.* cleasaiche, amhlair.
Jesuitical, *adj.* Fealltach, cùilteach, seòlta.
jet, *s.* clach-dhubh; steall, spùtan.
jet, *v. n.* gradshruth, steall.
jettee, *s.* laimhrig.
Jew, *s.* Iùdhach.
jewel, *s.* seud, leug, usgar, àilleagan.
jeweller, *s.* seudair.
Jewess, *s.* Ban-Iùdhach.
jew's harp, *s.* tromp.
jiffy, *s.* tiota, priobadh nan sùl.
jig, *s.* port-cruinn; dannsa-cruinn.
jilt, *s.* bristeadh air gealladh-pòsaidh.
jingle, *v. n.* gliong, gliongan.
job, *s.* gnothach, car-oibre.
job, *v.* sàth, gon; reic is ceannaich.
jobber, *s.* fear-mhion-ghnothach, fear-oibreach.
jockey, *s.* dròbhair each; mealltair.
jockey, *v. a.* thoir an car á, meall.
jocose, jocular, *adj.* àbhcaideach, bead-arrach, mear, aighearach, mireagach.
jocoseness, jocosity, jocularity, *s.* abhcaid-eachd, beadarrachd, cleasantachd, mac-nusachd, aighearachd, mireagachd.
jocund, *adj.* mearr, aighearach, cridheil.
jocundity, *s.* aighearachd, cridhealas.
jog, joggle, *v.* put, purr, crath; dèan bogadaich, crath-ghluais; mall-imich.
jogger, *s.* slaodaire, leisgean.
join, *v.* ceangail, dlùthaich, caignich, cuir r'a chéile; aonaich.
joiner, *s.* saor, saor geal.
joint, *s.* alt; teumadh.
joint, *adj.* coitcheann; co-shealbhach, co-oibreachail, co-phàirteach.
joint, *v. a.* altaich; aonaich, cuir r'a chéile; gearr an altaibh.
jointed, *adj.* altach, lùdnanach.
jointer, *s.* locair-dhlùthaidh.
jointly, *adv.* an cuideachd, le chéile.

jointure, *s.* dìleab banntraich, còir banntraich an seilbh a fir.

joist, *s.* sail, spàrr.

joke, *s.* àbhcaid, fala-dhà.

joking, *s.* fala-dhà, àbhcaid.

jollity, *s.* subhachas, cridhealas, aighear ; fleadhachas ; maise, àileachd.

jolly, *adj.* aotrom, aigeannach, cridheil, subhach, aoibhneach ; beothail, mear, fleadhach, ait ; reamhar, sultmhor, fallain ; maiseach, dreachmhor.

jolt, *v.* crath, crith, luaisg.

jolt, *s.* crathadh, crithneachadh, luasgadh.

jonquil, *s.* lus-a'-chrom-chinn.

jorden, *s.* poit-leapa, poit-fhuail.

jostle, *v. a.* put, utagaich, tulg, uinnleagaich.

jot, jota, *s.* ponc, dad, tiodal.

journal, *s.* cunntas-lathail, leabhar-latha, paipeir-naidheachd.

journalist, *s.* fear-deasachaidh Paipeir-naidheachd, sgriobhadair.

journey, *s.* turas, cuairt, astar.

journeyman, *s.* fear-cèirde air thuarasdal, fear a thug a mach cèard.

joust, *s.* còmhrag (eadar dà rìdire).

jovial, *adj.* fonnmhor, aighearach, ait, suilbhearra, subhach.

jovialness, joviality, *s.* fonnmhorachd, aiteas, suilbhearrachd.

jowl, *s.* ciobhal ; meangan-cinn èisg.

joy, *s.* aoibhneas, gàirdeachas, aiteas, aighear ; subhachas, sòlas.

joy, *v.* dèan ait, guidh math le ; dèan aoibhneach, sòlasaich ; bi ait, dèan gàirdeachas, bi aoibhneach.

joyful, *adj.* aoibhneach, ait, subhach.

joyfulness, *s.* aoibhneas, sonas, subhachas, aiteas.

joyfully, *adv.* gu h-aoibhinn, ait.

joyless, *adj.* neo-aoibhneach, neo-shòlasach, dubhach, trom.

jubilant, *adj.* buaidh-ghàireach, lùth-ghaire.

jubilee, *s.* gàirdeachas, fleadhachas, àrd-fhéill ; bliadhna shaorsa nan Iudhach.

jocundity, *s.* taitneachd, taitneas.

Judaical, *adj.* Iùdhach.

Judaism, *s.* creideamh nan Iùdhach.

judge, *s.* breitheamh.

judge, *v. a.* thoir breth, thoir a mach binn ; meas, thoir barail air ; breithnich, feuch, rannsaich cùis.

judgement, *s.* breitheanas ; breth, barail, tuisge, breithneachadh, ciall, geurbheachd ; binn, dìteadh ; làtha a' bhreitheanais.

judicatory, *s.* mòd laghail.

judicature, *s.* riaghladh-ceartais, cùirt-lagha.

judicial, judiciary, *adj.* laghail, a réir ceartais ; peanasach, dìoghaltach.

judicious, *adj.* tuigseach, crìonna, glic, ciallach, seòlta, geur-chùiseach.

judiciously, *adv.* gu tuigseach.

jug, *s.* soitheach-dibhe, noigean creadha.

juggle, *v. a.* dèan cleasachd ; meall.

juggle, *s.* cleasachd, foill.

juggler, *s.* cleasaiche ; mealltair.

jugular, *adj.* sgòrnanach.

juice, *s.* sùgh, brìgh, blagh.

juiceless, *adj.* neo-bhrìoghmhor, blian.

juiciness, *s.* brìoghmhorachd.

juicy, *adj.* sùghmhòr, brìoghmhor.

julap, *s.* uisge millis.

July, *s.* an seachd-mhìos, mìos deireannach an t-Sàmhraidh.

jumble, *v. a.* cuir troimh chéile, co-measgaich, crath an ceann a' chéile.

jumble, *s.* coimeasgadh, dreamsgal.

jump, *v. a.* leum, gearr sùrdag.

jump, *s.* leum, sùrdag.

juncate, *s.* ceapaire-càise.

juncous, *adj.* riasgach, luachrach.

junction, *s.* ceangal, co-aonadh.

June, an òg mhìos, mìos meadhoin an t-Sàmhraidh.

junior, *adj.* as òige, ìochdrach.

juniper, *s.* aiteann.

junk, *s.* ceap, cnap ; òrd càbaill.

junket, *s.* cuirm fhalaich, bainne air bhinid.

junta, junto, *s.* comhairle, comhairle-riaghlaidh, flath-chomhairle (spàinnteach).

juratory, *adj.* mionnachail.

juridical, *adj.* lagh-ghnàthach.

jurisconsult, *s.* comhairleach lagha.

jurisdiction, *s.* uachdranachd laghail.

jurisprudence, *s.* eòlas lagha.

jurist, *s.* fear lagha, fear-breithe.

juror, juryman, *s. See* **jury.**

jury, *s.* buidheann dhaoine air am mionnachadh, gu toirt a mach binn (an cùirt-lagha).

jurymast, *s.* crann-éigin.

just, *adj.* ceart, dìreach, fìrinneach, ionraic, tréidhireach ; dligheach ; co-thromach, iomlan.

justice, *s.* ceartas, còir, cothrom.

justiceship, *s.* dreuchd brèitheamh.

justiciary, *s.* fear-ceartais.

justifiable, *adj.* a réir ceartais.

justification, *s.* fìreanachadh.

justify, *v. a.* fìreanaich, saor ; dìon.

justle, *v.* put, purr, utagaich.

justly, *s.* gu h-ionraic, gu ceart.

justness, *s.* ceartas, ceartachd.

jut, *v.* seas a mach, tulg a mach.

jutty, *v. a.* sìn a mach, cuir am fad.

juvenile, *adj.* leanabaidh, òg, ògail.

juvenility, *s.* òigealachd.

juxtaposition, *s.* fagusachd.

K

kail, s. càl.
kalendar, s. féillire.
kali, s. seòrsa feamainn.
kaw, v. n. ròc, dèan ròcail.
kaw, s. ròc fithich no feannaig.
kayak, s. geòla craicinn ; curach.
kayle, s. cluich-nan-naodh-toll.
keck, v. a. dìobhair, sgreamhaich.
keckle, v. a. suain càball.
kedge, s. acair bheag, gramaiche.
keel, s. druim luinge, no bàta.
keelfat, s. dabhach-fhuarachaidh.
keelhaul, v. a. leth-bhàth.
keen, adj. geur, faobharach ; sgaiteach, coimheach, nimheil ; dian, togarrach, dùrachdach ; beur.
keenness, s. géire ; fuachd ; beurachd, dùrachd, eudmhorachd ; déine.
keep, v. a. cùm, gléidh ; coimhid dìon, teasraig ; bac, cuir stad air, cùm air ais ; cùm suas, beathaich ; ceil, cùm ort ; mair ; buanaich.
keep, s. daingneach.
keeper, s. fear-gleidhidh, fear-coimhid.
keeping, s. cùram ; coimhid, dìon, gleidh-eadh.
keepsake, s. cuimhneachan.
keg, s. buideal beag, gingean, gòthan.
kelp, s. celp, luath feamnach.
kelson, keelson, s. druim a stigh luinge no bàta.
ken, v. a. aithnich.
ken, s. sealladh, eòlas ; aithne.
kennel, s. tigh-chon ; saobhaidh ; guit-ear, clais-shalachair.
kept, pret. and part. pass. of to keep, gléidhte, cùmta.
kerchief, s. bréid ; neapaicin-pòcaid, beannag.
kern, s. saighdear coise (Eirionnach).
kern, v. cruadhaich ; meallanaich.
kernel, s. eitein, biadh cnothan.
kernelly, adj. eiteineach ; fàireagach.
kersey, s. garbh-chlò.
kestrel, s. coileach seabhaic.
ketch, s. sgùda, long throm.
kettle, s. coire, goileire.
kettledrum, s. gall-druma.
key, s. iuchair ; mìneachadh ; fonn, séis.
keyhole, s. toll-iuchrach.
keystone, s. clach-ceangail bogha.
kibe, s. cusp, peisg, gàg.
kick, v. a. breab, buail le do chois.
kick, s. breab, buile coise.
kickshaw, s. annas, faoineas.
kid, s. meann ; cualag fhraoich.
kidnap, v. a. goid clann no daoine.
kidnapper, s. mèirleach cloinne.

kidney-bean, s. am pònar-àirneach.
kidneys, s. àirnean, dubhagan.
kilderkin, s. leth-bharaille.
kill, v. a. marbh, cuir gu bàs.
killer, s. marbhaiche, fear-casgairt.
killow, s. dubh-smùir ; sùthaidh.
kiln, s. àth, àtha.
kilt, s. féile-beag, feabhladh.
kin, s. cinneadh, fine, dàimh, càirdeas.
kind, adj. còir, coibhneil, mathasach ; bàigheil, carthannach, fialaidh.
kind, s. gnè, gineal ; modh, seòl.
kindle, v. las ; beothaich, cuir chuige ; brosnaich, cuir air bhoil ; gabh teine, gabh.
kindler, s. brathadair, fear-lasaidh ; fear-brosnachaidh, buaireadair.
kindliness, s. deagh-ghean, carthannas, tlus, còiread.
kindly, adj. bàigheil, coibhneil.
kindness, s. caomhalachd, seirc.
kindred, s. càirdeas, dàimh ; cleamhnas ; càirdean, cinneadh, luchd-dàimh.
kindred, adj. aon-ghnèitheach, co-ghnèith-each ; dàimheil, càirdeach.
kine, s. crodh, spréidh, feudail, buar.
king, s. rìgh.
kingcraft, s. eòlas-riaghlaidh, eòlas-rìgheachaidh.
kingdom, s. rìoghachd, dùthaich.
kingfisher, s. an gobha-uisge, an cruiteun.
kingly, adj. rìoghail, flathail, mòrdha.
kings-evil, s. tinneas an rìgh, an easba-bhràghaid.
kingship, s. rìoghalachd.
kinsfolk, s. luchd-dàimh, càirdean.
kinsman, s. fear-dàimh, caraide.
kinswoman, s. bean-dàimhe, banacharaid.
kipper, s. bradan tiormaichte, sgadan-réisgte.
kirk, s. eaglais.
kirtle, s. fallainn, aodach-uachdair.
kiss, v. a. pòg, thoir pòg.
kiss, s. pòg.
kit, s. fiodhall bheag.
kit, s. tuba ; poca-ghoireasan.
kitchen, s. tigh-cócaireachd ; seomar-deasaichidh ; annlann.
kitchen-garden, s. gàradh-càil.
kitchen-maid, s. ban-chòcair.
kite, s. clamhan, clamhan-gòbhlach ; ball-cluich àraidh.
kitten, s. piseag ; nighean sgaomach.
knack, s. làmhchaireachd, ealantachd.
knag, s. saighead (am fiodh), bun géige.
knaggy, adj. snàimeach, plucanach.
knap, s. meall, fluth ; maol, àird,caitean.
knap, v. sgath dheth, sgud, criom ; sgailc, buail.

knapsack, s. abarsgaic, crapsaic.
knare, knur, knurle, s. cruaidhshnaim ; gath.
knave, s. slaightear, mealltair, daoidhear, cladhaire.
knavery, s. slaightearachd, fealltachd.
knavish, adj. cluainteach, mealltach, foilleil, fealltach.
knavishness, s. cluaintearachd.
knead, v. a. taoisinn, oibrich, fuin.
kneading-trough, s. losaid, amar-fuine, clàr-fuine.
knee, s. glùn, lùgh.
knee-deep, adj. gu ruig na glùinean, doimhnachd glùn.
knee-pan, s. falaman.
kneel, v. n. strìochd, lùb do ghlùn.
knell, s. beum-cluig, clag-bàis.
knew, pret. of to know, dh' aithnich.
knife, s. sgian, corc ; cuinnsear.
knight, s. ridire.
knight, v. a. ridirich, dèan 'na ridire.
knighthood, s. ridireachd.
knightly, adj. ridireach.
knit, v. a. figh ; ceangail, dlùthaich.
knitter, s. figheadair.
knob, s. cnap, cnag, snaim.

knobbed, knobby, adj. cnapach, gathach, cairgeach, snaimeach.
knock, s. buille, sgailc, cnap.
knock, v. buail ; cnap, sgailc ; spad, buail sìos ; buail aig dorus.
knocker, s. bas-ri-crann ; glagan-doruis.
knoll, v. beum mar chlag, seirm.
knoll, s. tolm, tolman, tom, toman, dùn.
knot, s. snàim ; ceangal, bann, cobhann ; comunn, buidheann ; bagaid.
knot, v. snàim ; àimhreitich ; aonaich, dlùthaich.
knot-grass, s. a' ghlùineach-dhearg.
knotted, knotty, adj. snàimeach.
know, v. aithnich, fiosraich ; ionnsaich ; comharraich ; tuig ; bi eòlach.
knowing, adj. eòlach, ealanta, seòlta, fiosrach, gleusta ; glic, oileanta.
knowingly, adv. gu h-eòlach.
knowledge, s. eòlas ; aithne, tuigse, fios, fiosrachd ; fòghlum, ionnsachadh, soilleireachd, fiosrachadh, tùr.
knuckle, s. rùdan, alt (meòir), pl. uilt.
knuckle, v. n. strìochd, géill.
knuckled, adj. rùdanach, altach.
Koran, s. Bìoball Mhahomet.

L

la ! interj. feuch ! seall ! faic !
label, s. comharra sgrìobhte.
labial, adj. bil-fhuaimneach.
laboratory, s. tigh-foghluim, seòmar 's a bheil rannsachadh air a dheanamh air cungaidhean.
laborious, adj. saoithreachail, gnìomhach, dìchiollach ; doirbh, deacair, sgìth.
labour, s. saothair ; saothair-chloinne ; obair, dubh-obair.
labour, v. saothraich, oibrich, dèan dìchioll, gabh saothair ri ; dèan spàirn ; bi 'n teanntachd, bi 'n teinn ; bi 'n saothair-chloinne.
labourer, s. fear-oibre, oibriche.
laburnum, s. bealaidh Fràngach.
labyrinth, s. cuairt àimhreidh, ioma-chuairt.
lace, s. sreang, stìom, stiall, iall ; balt air fhighe, obair-ghréis.
lace, v. a. ceangail, sreangaich, iallaich ; rìomhaich, grinnich.
lacerate, v. a. reub, srac, sgoilt.
laceration, s. reubadh, sracadh.
lacerative, adj. sracach, reubach.
lachrymal, adj. deurach, deurachail.
lachrymation, s. gul, caoidh, sileadh dheur.
lack, v. bi am feum ; bi dh' easbhuidh, bi 'n uireasbhuidh.

lack, s. uireasbhuidh, easbhuidh, dìth, gainne, ainnis, aimbeart.
lack-a-day ! interj. O ! mis 'an diugh !
lack-brain, s. baoghaire, ùmaidh.
lacker, s. sùgh lìomhaidh.
lacker, v. a. cuir sùgh-lìomhaidh air.
lackey, s. gille coise.
lackey, v. a. fritheil, feith.
lack-lustre, adj. neo-dhealrach.
laconic, adj. gearr, aithghearr, gearr-chainnteach, gearr-bhriathrach.
laconism, s. gearr-chainnteachd.
lactage, s. toradh bainne.
lactary, s. tigh-bainne ; adj. bainneach.
lactation, s. deoghal, cìoch-thabhairt.
lacteal, s. cuisle-goile.
lacteous, lateal, adj. bainneach.
lactescent, latific, adj. bainneach.
lad, s. òganach, òigear, balachan ; gille, giulan.
ladder, s. fàradh, dreimire.
lade, v. a. luchdaich, lìon ; tilg a mach, taom, falmhaich ; tarruing uisge.
lading, s. luchd, làn.
ladle, s. liagh, ladar, lodar.
lady-bird, lady-cow, s. an daolag dhearg bhreac.
Lady Day, s. Latha Muire naoimh.
ladylike, s. bainndidh, màlda, suairce, sgiamhach.

ladyship, *s.* baintighearnas.
lag, *adj.* deireannach, athaiseach ; màirnealach, leisg, trom, mall ; air deireadh.
lag, *v. n.* dèan màirneal, tuit air deireadh, mall-ghluais, fuirich air deireadh.
laic, laical, *adj.* pobullach, tuathach.
laid, *pret. part.* of **to lay,** càirichte, socraichte, suidhichte.
lain, *pret. part.* of **to lie,** air laighe.
lair, *s.* saobhaidh, brocluinn.
laird, *s.* tighearna, uachdaran.
laity, *s.* am pobull ; an sluagh (air leth o'n chléir), am mall-shluagh, tuath.
lake, *s.* loch-uisge.
lake, *s.* dath ruadh, dùbh-dhearg.
lamb, *s.* uan, uainean.
lambent, *adj.* cluicheach, mireagach (mu lasair).
lambkin, *s.* uanan, uanachan.
lame, *adj.* bacach, crùbach, cuagach, stiocach.
lame, *v. a.* dèan bacach, dèan crùbach.
lameness, *s.* bacaiche, crùbaiche.
lament, *v.* caoidh, guil, dèan bròn ; dèan tuireadh, bi brònach, bi dubhach.
lament, *s.* cumha, caoidh, tuireadh.
lamentable, *adj.* tùrsach, brònach, airsnealach, muladach, dubhach.
lamentation, *s.* tuireadh, cumha.
lamina, *s.* sgrath thana, rùsg tana, sgramag.
laminated, *adj.* sgrathach, leacach.
Lammas, *s.* Lùnasdal.
lamp, *s.* lòchran, crùisgean, lamp.
lamp-black, *s.* sùich-lampa.
lampoon, *s.* aoir, aoireadh, éisg.
lampoon, *v. a.* aoir, càin, màb.
lampooner, *s.* aoireadair.
lamprey, *s.* seòrsa easgainn.
lanarious, *adj.* clòimheach.
lance, *s.* sleagh, lann, gath, pìc.
lance, *v. a.* gon, bruidich ; leig fuil.
lancer, *s.* saighdear sleagha.
lancet, *s.* sgian-fhala, cuisleag.
lancitate, *v. a.* srac, sgoilt, sgàin.
lancitation, *s.* sracadh, reubadh.
land, *s.* tìr, dùthaich, fearann ; talamh, talamh tioram, oighreachd.
land, *v.* cuir air tìr, rach air tìr.
landed, *adj.* fearannach.
land-forces, *s.* feachd-tìre.
landholder, *s.* fear-fearainn.
landing, *s.* ceann staighreach, làimhrig.
landlady, *s.* banuachdaran ; bean-an-tighe.
land-locked, *adj.* tìrdhruidte.
landlord, *s.* uachdaran ; fear-an-tighe.
landmark, *s.* comharradh-crìche.
landscape, *s.* dealbh tìre, aghaidh dùthcha.
land-waiter, *s.* maor-cuspuinn.
landward, *adv.* gu tìr.
lane, *s.* caolshràid, frithrathad.

language, *s.* cainnt, cànan.
languid, *adj.* lag, fann, anfhann ; marbhanta, trom, neo-shunntach.
languidness, *s.* marbhantachd, laige.
languish, *v. n.* fannaich, fàs lag, searg as, caith as, crìon.
languishment, *s.* lagachadh, fannachadh, crìonadh, seargadh as, sìoladh seachad ; tlàthshealladh.
languor, *s.* laigse, sgìos, anfhannachd.
lank, *adj.* seang, neo-chullach, bochd.
lankness, *s.* seangachd, neo-lànachd.
lansquenet, *s.* saighdear-coise ; cluiche àraidh chairtean.
lantern, *s.* trillsean ; lanntair.
lap, *s.* uchd ; glùn.
lap, *v.* fill mun cuairt.
lap-dog, *s.* measan, crann-chù.
lapidary, *s.* leug-ghearradair.
lapper, *s.* filleadair, fear-pasgaidh.
lappet, *s.* beannag-chinn, filleag.
lapse, *s.* aomadh, tuiteam, slaodadh, réidh-shruth ; tapag, mearachd.
lapse, *v. a.* sleamhnaich, tuit ; fàilnich, rach am mearachd ; tuislich ; cùlshleamhnaich, tuit o'n chreideamh.
lapwing, *s.* an t-adharcan-luachrach.
larboard, *s.* taobh-leis luinge.
larceny, *s.* braide, mion-mhèirle.
larch, *s.* giubhas-learaig.
lard, *s.* blonag.
lard, *v. a.* lìon le blonaig ; reamhraich.
larder, *s.* tigh-bìdh.
lardon, *s.* staoig muicfheoil.
large, *adj.* mór, tomadach ; farsuing.
largeness, *s.* meudachd, leud ; farsuinneachd.
largess, *s.* tìodhlac, sineas duin'-uasail.
lark, *s.* uisea ̧r, riabhag.
larum, *s.* clagchaismeachd, maoim.
larynx, *s.* bràigh an sgòrnain.
lascivious, *adj.* macnusach, drùiseil.
lasciviousness, *s.* drùisealachd.
lash, *s.* iall-sgiùrsair ; buille.
lash, *v. a.* sgiùrs, buail le slait ; aoir, ceangail.
lass, *s.* nighean, cailin, òg-bhean, ainnir, finne, gruagach, cruinneag, òigh, maighdean.
lassitude, *s.* sgìos, airtneal, laigse.
last, *adj.* deireannach, air deireadh.
last, *adv.* mu dheireadh ; anns an àite mu dheireadh.
last, *v. a.* mair, buanaich, seas, fan.
last, *s.* ceap bhròg.
lastage, *s.* cuspunn faraidh.
lasting, *adj.* maireannach, buan.
latch, *s.* dealan-doruis, sneic.
latchet, *s.* barriall, iall-bròige.
late, *adj.* anmoch, fadalach, màirnealach ; deireannach ; nach maireann.
late, *adv.* mu dheireadh, gu h-anmoch.
lately, latterly, *adv.* o chionn ghoirid.

lateness, s. anmoichead.
latent, adj. falaichte, dìomhair.
lateral, adj. leth-taobhach.
lath, s. lathus, spealt.
lathe, s. beairt thuairnearachd.
lather, v. dèan cop, tog cobhar.
lather, s. cop, cobhar-shiabuinn.
Latin, s. Laidionn.
Latinise, v. a. tionndaidh gu Laidinn.
latish, adj. leth-anmoch.
latitude, s. leud, farsuinneachd, meud-achd, sgaoilteachd, fuasgailteachd.
latitudinarian, s. saobh-chreideach, baoth chreideach.
latrine, s. tigh fuail (an camp no osbadal).
latten, s. umha, iarann geal.
latter, adj. deireannach.
lattice, s. cliath-uinneag.
laud, s. cliù, moladh, àrdmholadh.
laud, v. a. cliùthaich, àrd-mhol.
laudable, adj. ion-mholta, cliùiteach.
laudanum, s. deoch-chadail.
laudation, s. àrdchliù, moladh.
laudatory, adj. moltach, cliùteach.
laugh, v. dèan gàire.
laughable, adj. neònach, a thogas gàire.
laughing-stock, s. culaidh-mhagaidh.
laughter, s. gàireachdaich, fearas-chuid-eachd, aitiolach.
launch, v. cuir air bhog ; leudaich ; gabh farsuinneachd ; grad thòisich air ; gabh gu fairge.
laundress, s. bean-nighe.
laundry, s. tigh-nighe.
laureate, s. am bàrd rìoghail.
laurel, s. craobh laibhreis.
lave, v. nigh, ionnlaid, fairic, failc.
lavender, s. lus-na-tùise.
laver, s. soitheach-nighe ; saigheach-ionnlaid, amar-nighe.
lavish, adj. struidheil, stròdhail, barr-sgaoilteach ; neo-stéidhichte.
lavish, v. a. struidh, barr-sgaoil, sgap, dean ana-caitheamh.
law, s. lagh, reachd, riaghailt ; stàtunn, òrdugh ; bunait, stéidh.
lawful, adj. laghail, ceadaichte.
lawfulness, s. laghalachd, ceartas.
lawgiver, s. lagh-thabhairtear.
lawless, adj. neo-laghail, mì-laghail, an-dligheach, anaceart.
lawn, s. réidhlean, achadh, faiche eadar-dà-choill ; anart grinn.
lawsuit, s. cùis-lagha.
lawyer, s. fear-lagha.
lax, adj. fuasgailte, saor ; fuasgailteach, neo-cheangailte, neo-theann ; neo-dhiongmhalta, neo-eagnaidh ; lasach, neo-dhaingeann ; fuasgailte 'sa' chorp.
lax, s. a' ghearrach ; seòrs' éisg.
laxation, s. lasachadh, fuasgladh.
laxative, adj. fuasgailteach, purgaideach ; sgaoilteach.

laxity, laxness, s. sgaoilteachd, neo-theanntachd, fuasgailteachd ; fosgailt-eachd.
lay, pret. of to lie, laigh.
lay, v. càirich, cuir ; suidhich ; leag sìos, buail sìos ; sgaoil air ; ciùinich, sìthich, cuir gu fois ; cuir geall ; taisg.
lay, s. òran, duanag, luinneag, fonn.
lay, adj. tuathach ; bhuineas do 'n tuath.
layer, s. sreath, breath ; faillean, mean-glan ; cearc-ghuir.
layman, s. fear dhe'n tuath.
lazar, s. fear fo eucail ghràineil, lobhar.
lazar-house, lazaretto, s. tigh leighis nam mùireach, tigh nan lobhar.
laziness, s. leisg, lunndaireachd, màirneal-achd, dìomhanas.
lazy, adj. leasg, lunndach, dìomhain ; màirnealach, mall.
lea, lee, s. achadh, cluan, raon, faiche, glastalamh, fiadhair.
lead, s. luaidhe.
lead, v. treòraich, stiùr.
leaden, adj. luaidheach ; trom, neo-ghluasadach, marbhanta ; dùr.
leader, s. fear-treòrachaidh ; ceann-feadhna ; fear-toisich.
leading, part. prìomh, àrd, ceud.
leading, s. treòrachadh, stiùradh.
leaf, s. duilleag, duille.
leafless, adj. gun duilleach, lom.
leafy, adj. duilleagach, fo bhlàth.
league, s. comhcheangal, comh-phàirt ; fad thrì mile.
league, v. n. dèan comhcheangal, aonaich.
leak, v. a. leig uisg' a mach, no steach ; bi aodionach, sil, snith, call ; the dish leaks, tha an soitheach a' call.
leakage, s. dioll, calldach, aodion.
leaky, adj. aodionach ; bruidhneach, fosgailte, luath-bheulach.
lean, v. n. leag do thaic ri, leig do chudthrom air ; aom ; crom thu fèin.
lean, adj. bochd, tana, caol, gun fheòil ; neo-shultmhor, tioram, neo-bhrìoghail.
lean, s. blìonach, feòil gun saill.
leanness, s. caoile, tainead ; tiormad.
leap, v. leum ; thoir leum.
leap, s. leum, cruinnleum ; briosgadh.
leap year, s. bliadhna-léim.
learn, v. n. fòghlum, ionnsaich.
learned, adj. fòghlumte, ionnsaichte ; eòlach, fiosrach ; leabhrach.
learner, s. fòghlumaiche, sgoilear.
learning, s. fòghlum, ionnsachadh.
lease, s. gabhail, suidheachadh.
lease, v. n. leig a mach air mhàl.
leash, s. iall, bann, ceanglachan, lobhainn.
leasing, s. breugan, mealltaireachd.
least, adj. as lugha, as bige, as crìona.
at least, adv. air a' chuid as lugha, co-dhiù.
leather, s. leathar, seiche cairtidh.

leathern, *adj.* leathair, mar leathar.
leave, *s.* cead ; comas.
leave, *v.* fàg, tréig, cùlaich.
leaven, *s.* taois ghoirt, beirm ; *v.* fàs goirt ; cuir beirm ann am min.
leaves, *s.*, the *plur.* of leaf, duilleach, duilleagan.
leavings, *s.* fuighleach, fuigheall.
lecher, *s.* fear-siùrsachd.
lecherous, *adj.* drùiseil, collaidh.
lechery, *s.* drùisealachd.
lection, *s.* leughadh.
lecture, *s.* lector ; achmhasan, cronachadh, trod.
lecture, *v. n.* mìnich, cronaich, teagaisg am follais.
lecturer, *s.* fear-teagaisg.
led, *pret. part.* of to lead, treòraichte.
ledge, *s.* stìm, oir, palla, sgeilp.
ledger, *s.* leabhar cunntais.
lee, *s.* làib ; taobh an fhasgadh.
leech, *s.* deal, seil-uisge.
leek, *s.* creamh-gàraidh.
leer, *s.* caogshealladh, fiarshealladh.
leer, *v. n.* amhairc siar, dèan caogshùil.
lees, *s.* làib, dràib, druaip.
leeward, *adj.* air fasgadh.
left, *pret. part.* of to leave, fàgte, tréigte, cùlaichte.
left-handed, *adj.* clìth-lamhach, cearrlamhach, ciotach.
leg, *s.* lurga, cas, calpa.
legacy, *s.* dìleab.
legal, *adj.* laghail, ceadaichte, dligheach.
legality, legalness, *s.* dligheachas, dligheachd.
legalise, *v. a.* dèan laghail, dèan ceadaichte, dèan dligheach.
legate, *s.* teachdaire Pàp na Ròimhe.
legatee, *s.* fear dìlib, dìleabach.
legation, *s.* teachdaireachd.
legend, *s.* seanachas, faoinsgeul, sgeulachd ; seann sgrìobhadh.
legendary, *adj.* seannsgeulach.
legerdemain, *s.* lùth-chleasachd, claonchar.
legged, *adj.* luirgneach.
legibility, *s.* soilleireachd, sgrìobhadh glan.
legible, *adj.* ghabhas leughadh, soilleir.
legion, *s.* feachd Ròmhanach (mu chùig mìle fear).
legislate, *v. a.* dèan lagh, thoir reachd.
legislation, *s.* lagh-thabhartas, dèanamh lagha.
legislative, *adj.* lagh-thabhairteach.
legislator, *s.* lagh-thabhartair.
legislature, *s.* Pàrlamaid.
legitimacy, *s.* dligheachd-breithe, fìorcheartas.
legitimate, *adj.* dligheach.
legitimation, *s.* dlighe-thabhairt, tòirt còir dlighe do dhuine diolainn.

legume, legumen, *s.* sìol cochullach, fras, peasair, pònair.
leguminous, *adj.* cochullach mar pheasair no mar phònair.
leisurable, *adj.* athaiseach, socrach.
leisure, *s.* athais, socair, fois.
leisurely, *adj.* athaiseach, mall.
lemon, *s.* seòrsa meas, liomaid.
lend, *v. a.* thoir an iasad, thoir an coingheall.
lender, *s.* conghiollaich, iasadaiche.
length, *s.* fad, feadh, sìneadh, astar.
lengthen, *v.* cuir am fad, dèan na's faide, sìn a mach.
lengthwise, *adv.* air fhad.
lenient, *adj.* ciùin, caoin, maoth, tlàth, tairis, fuasgailteach.
lenient, *s.* ìocshlaint-thaiseachaidh.
lenify, *v. n.* ciùinich, taisich, maothaich.
lenitive, *adj.* ciùineachail, maothachail.
lenitive, *s.* leigheas-maothachaidh.
lenity, *s.* bàigh, iochd, tròcair, ciùine, caomhalachd, caoimhneas.
lens, *s.* seòrsa do ghlain-amhairc.
lent, *s.* an carghus, àm trasgaidh.
lentil, *s.* peasair-nan-luch.
lentitude, *s.* slaodaireachd, leisg.
lentor, *s.* rìghneachd ; màirnealachd.
lentous, *adj.* righinn, rag, slamach.
leopard, *s.* an liopard.
leper, *s.* lobhar, mùireach.
leperous, leprous, *s.* lobharach, luibhreach, mùireach.
leporean, leporine, *adj.* maigheachail.
leprosy, *s.* a' mhùir, an luibhre.
less, lesser, *adv.* na's lugha, na's bige.
lessee, *s.* fear-gabhalach, tuathanach.
lessen, *v.* lughdaich, cuir an lughad ; ìslich ; fàs na's lugha.
lesson, *s.* earann-leughaidh, leasan, ionnsachadh, teagasg ; trod, achmhasan.
lessor, *s.* fear-suidheachaidh fearainn, etc.
lest, *conj.* mu, air eagal gu.
let, *v. a.* leig, ceadaich ; suidhich, thoir air ghabhail.
let, *s.* bacadh, stad, grabadh, maille.
lethal, *adj.* bàsmhor, fuilteach, millteach, air diochuimhn.
lethargic, *adj.* marbhanta, cadalach, airsnealach, trom.
lethargy, *s.* an suain-ghalar ; leisg.
lethe, *s.* deoch dhìochuimhne.
lethiferous, *adj.* bàsmhor, marbhtach.
letter, *s.* litir.
letters, *s.* fòghlum, litreachas.
levee, *s.* cuideachd cruinn air fiadhachadh righ.
level, *adj.* còmhnard, réidh.
level, *v.* dèan còmhnard, dèan réidh, leag sìos, leag gu làr ; dèan comh-inbheach ; gabh cùimse ; thoir ionnsaigh.

level, s. còmhnard, réidhlean; co-àirde, co-chuimse, co-inbheachd.
leveller, s. fear-islichidh.
levelness, s. còmhnardachd.
lever, s. geimhleag, inneal-togail.
leveret, s. maigheach òg.
leviable, adj. so-thogail mar chìs.
leviathan, s. an cinionnan-crò.
levigate, v. a. lìomh; mìn-mheil, mìn-phronn; suath.
levigation, s. lìomhadh, meileadh, suath-adh.
Levite, s. lebhitheach, neach do threubh Lebhi, sagart.
Levitical, s. Lebhitheach, sagartach.
levity, s. aotruime, aotromachd; gòr-aiche; gogaideachd; dìomhanas, amaid-eachd; neo-stòldacdh.
levy, v. a. tog daoine, dèan suas feachd, leag cìs.
levy, s. togail; feachd, armailt, cruinn-eachadh, buidheann.
lewd, adj. olc, aingidh, mì-bheusach; ana-miannach, drùiseil, draosda, coll-aidh.
lewdness, s. mì-nàire, mì-stuamachd; aingidheachd; ana-miann, draosdachd.
lexicographer, s. fear-dèanamh facalair, facalairiche.
lexicography, s. facladaireachd.
lexicon, s. facalair, leabhar-fhacal.
liable, adj. buailteach, buailteach do.
liar, s. breugadair, breugaire.
libation, s. ìobairt-fhiona.
libel, s. aoir, aoireadh; casaid-sgrìobhte, cùis-chasaid, cùis-dhìtidh.
libel, v. a. aoir; càin; maslaich.
libeller, s. aoireadair, fear-càinidh.
libellous, adj. tàir-chainnteach, maslach-ail, tuaileasach.
liberal, adj. fiùghantach, uasal, flathail, fial, fialaidh; tabhairteach, toirbheart-ach, pailtlamhach, faoilidh.
liberality, s. fialaidheachd, tabhairt-eachd, toirbheartachd, aoidheachd, aoidhealachd.
liberate, v. a. cuir fa sgaoil, saor.
liberation, s. cur fa sgaoil, fuasgladh.
liberator, s. fear-fuasglaidh.
libertine, s. duine gun smachd, fear-àimhreit; ana-creideach, fear neo-mheasarra; saoranach.
libertine, adj. ana-creideach, àin-diadh-aidh.
libertinism, s. ain-diadhachd.
liberty, s. saorsa; cead, sochair, dlighe.
libidinous, adj. connanach, ana-miann-ach, neo-gheamnaidh, collaidh, drùiseil.
librarian, s. fear-gleidhidh leabhraichean, fear-leabhar-lann.
library, s. leabhar-lann, seòmar leabh-raichean.
libration, s. co-chothromachadh.

licence, s. cead; cead reic, comas, cead searmonachaidh.
license, v. a. ceadaich, thoir cead reic seachad.
licentiate, s. fear-barantais, searmon-aiche feitheamh ri gairm.
licentious, adj. mì-bheusach.
licentiousness, s. mì-bheus.
lichen, s. crotal, griaman.
licit, adj. laghail, dligheach.
lick, v. a. ìmlich.
lick, s. buille, cnap, dòrn.
lickerish, adj. sòghmhor, geòcach.
licorice, s. maide-milis, cara-meala, carra-mille, siucar dubh.
lictor, s. maor Ròmanach.
lid, s. brod; fabhradh, rosg.
lie, s. breug, spleagh.
lie, v. n. innis breug, dèan breug; laigh; caidil.
liege, s. uachdaran (o bheil seirbhis dligheach) d'a rìgh, iochdaran d'am buin seirbhis a thoirt do'n uachdaran.
lieu, s. àite, ionad, riochd.
lieutenancy, s. fo-uachdranachd.
lieutenant, s. fo-uachdaran.
life, s. beatha, deò; caithe-beatha; beothalachd, meanmnachd.
lifeguard, s. freiceadan diona rìgh.
lifeless, adj. marbh, gun deò; marbh-anta; neo-bheothail, neo-shunntach, tròm.
lifetime, s. aimsir, ùine, làithean.
lift, v. a. tog; àrdaich, cuir suas.
lift, s. togail; eallach.
lifter, s. fear-togalach; gadaiche, mèirl-each.
ligament, s. ceanglachan, ceangal.
ligature, s. bann-cheangail.
light, s. solus; soillse; eòlas, soilleir-eachd, fòghlum; lòchrann.
light, adj. aotrom, eutrom; lùghor; suarach, beag; neo-shuidhichte, gòr-ach, guanach, gogaideach; soilleir, soillseach.
light, v. las, soillsich, beothaich; thoir solus do; tuit air, amais air; teirinn, thig a nuas.
lighten, v. dealraich, dèars, boillsg, soillsich, soilleirich; aotromaich.
lighter, s. bàta-luchda.
lighterman, s. sgiobair bàta-luchda.
light-fingered, adj. bradach.
light-headed, adj. gogcheannach; sgaog-ach, aotrom, air mhearan-céille.
light-hearted, adj. sunntach, aighearach, suigeartach, cridheil.
lighthouse, s. tigh-soluis.
lightness, s. aotromachd, aotruime; luaineachas, guaineas.
lightning, s. dealanach, tein'-adhair.
lightsome, adj. soilleir, soillseach, deal-rach; sunntach, aighearach, cridheil.

ligneous, *adj.* fiodhach, mar fhiodh.
like, *adj.* coltach ; ionann.
like, *s.* mac-samhail, samhail, samhla.
like, *adv.* ionann agus, amhail, mar ;
coltach.
likelihood, *s.* coltas, cosmhalachd.
likely, *adj.* coltach ; dreachmhor.
liken, *v. a.* samhlaich, coimeas.
likeness, *s.* samhla, coltas, cosamhlachd ;
dealbh ; mac-samhail.
likewise, *adv.* mar an ceudna, fòs.
lily, *s.* lili, lilidh.
lily-livered, *adj.* cladhaireach, gealtach.
limb, *s.* ball, ball-cuirp (làmh no cas).
limber, *adj.* sùbailte, maoth.
limberness, *s.* so-lùbaidheachd, maoth-
achd.
limbo, *s.* gainntir ; ifrinn.
lime, *s.* aol ; *v. a.* aol, aolaich.
limekiln, *s.* àth-aoil.
limit, *s.* crìoch, iomall, ceann-crìche.
limit, *v. a.* cuir crìoch ri, cuir crìoch mu,
suidhich crìochan.
limitary, *adj.* iomallach.
limitation, *s.* crìochchur, bacadh ùine
shuidhichte, iomal.
limn, *v. a.* tarruing dealbh.
limner, *s.* fear-tarruing dhealbh.
limp, *v. n.* bi bacach, bi crùbach.
limp, *s.* crùbaiche, bacaiche.
limpet, *s.* bàirneach.
limpid, *adj.* troimh-shoilleir, glan.
limpidness, *s.* troimh-shoilleireachd.
limy, *adj.* aolach.
linchpin, *s.* tarunn-aisil.
linden, *s.* teile, crann-teile.
line, *s.* sgrìob, fad, sìneadh ; sreang ;
driamlach ; sreath-sgrìobhaidh ; crios-
meadhoin an t-saoghail ; sliochd, sìol,
gineal ; deicheamh-earrann na h-
oirlich.
line, *v. a.* lìnig, cluthaich.
lineage, *s.* linn, sliochd, iarmad, clann,
cinneadh, fine, sìol, teaghlach, gineal.
lineal, *adj.* sìnte, sreathach, tarruinnte ;
dìreach, dligheach, dùthchasach.
lineament, *s.* cruth, dreach, dualachas,
comharradh-gnùise, ìomhachd.
lineation, *s.* stiall, sgrìob, sgriach.
linen, *s.* anart, lionaodach.
linen, *adj.* anartach, mar anart.
linen-draper, *s.* ceannaich'-anairt.
ling, *s.* langa.
ling, *s.* fraoch.
linger, *v. n.* bi fad' am péin, bi fo chràdh-
thinneas ; bi an iom-chomhairle ; cuir
dàil ann, dèan dàil, bi fada ri, gabh
ùine.
lingerer, *s.* slaodaire, màirnealaich, leisgean, lunndaire.
lingo, *s.* cànan, cainnt.
linguacious, *adj.* bruidhneach, cainnteach, gobach, geòpach.

linguist, *s.* cànanaich, teangair.
liniment, *s.* cungaidh-leighis, sàbh.
lining, *s.* lìnig, lìnigeadh.
link, *s.* tinne, dul ; leus, dòrnais.
link, *v.* co-cheangail, tàth, figh 'n a
chéile ; co-dhlùthaich ; aon ; cuir am
bannaibh ; bi'n dlùthachd.
linnet, *s.* am breacan-beithe.
linseed, *s.* fras-lìn.
linsey-woolsey, *s.* drògaid.
lint, *s.* lìon ; caiteas.
lintel, *s.* ard-dorus, for-dhorus.
lion, *s.* leòmhann.
lioness, *s.* leomhann bhoirionn.
lip, *s.* bile, lip, oir.
lipothymy, *s.* paisean, breisleach, neul.
lipped, *adj.* bileach, busach ; oireach.
lippitude, *s.* prabaiche, brach-shuileachd
liquable, *adj.* ghabhas leaghadh.
liquate, *v. n.* leagh, fàs tana.
liquation, *s.* leaghadh.
liquefaction, *s.* leaghadh.
liquefiable, *adj.* ghabhas leaghadh.
liquefy, *v. a.* leagh, fàs tana.
liquescent, *adj.* leaghtach.
liquid, *adj.* tana ; bog, soilleir, mìn.
liquid, *s.* uisge, nì tana sam bith.
liquidate, *v. a.* pàidh fiachan, tionndaidh
badhar gu airgead, cuir crioch air
ceannachd.
liquidity, *s.* tainead, leaghtachd, uisgealachd.
liquor, *s.* deoch làidir.
lisp, *v. n.* dèan liotaiche ; bi liotach, bi
manntach.
list, *s.* clàr-ainm ; togradh, miann, toil ;
aomadh.
list, *v.* tog, cuir an àireamh ; gabh mar
shaighdear ; éisd, thoir an aire do ;
dèan farchluais.
listed, *adj.* stiallach, grianach.
listen, *v. n.* eisd ; dèan farchluais.
listless, *adj.* coma ; neo-chùramach,
neo-mhothachail, gun aire, toirt cluas
bhodhar.
listlessness, *s.* cion-umhaill, co-éiseachd,
neo-mhothachalachd, neo-chùram.
lit, *pret.* of to light, las, bheothaich,
shoillsich.
litany, *s.* an leadan, fuirm ùrnaigh.
literal, *adj.* litireil, litireach.
literary, *adj.* ionnsaichte, fòghluimte,
grinn fhòghluimte, litreachail.
literati, *s.* luchd-fòghluim.
literature, *s.* ionnsachadh, fòghlum,
litreachas.
lithography, *s.* leac-sgrìobhadh.
lithotomist, *s.* léigh fuail-chloich.
litigant, *s.* lagh-thagradair, fear-casaid
aig cùirt.
litigant, *adj.* lagh-thagartach.
litigate, *v. a.* agair lagh air.
litigation, *s.* tagairt-lagha.

litigious, adj. connspaideach.
litigiousness, s. tagluinneachd.
litter, s. cròleabaidh ; connlach ; cuain, lir ; treamsgal.
litter, v. a. beir, beir àl ; sgap mu'n cuairt.
little, adj. beag, bìdeach ; crìon, meanbh, suarach.
little, s. beagan, rud beag.
littleness, s. bige, lughad, crìonad ; mìotharachd, suarachas.
littoral, adj. cladach.
liturgy, s. ùrnaigh choitcheann.
live, v. n. bi beò ; thig beò ; mair beò.
live, adj. beò ; beothail, beathail.
livelihood, s. teachd-an-tìr, lòn.
liveliness, s. beothalachd, sunntachd.
livelong, adj. fadalach, buan, sgìth.
lively, adj. sunntach, beothail ; meanmnach, aighearach, mear.
liver, s. adha, sgòchraich, grùthan.
liver-colour, adj. dùdhearg.
livery, s. éideadh-suaicheantais seirbheisich.
liveryman, s. gille-suaicheantais.
livid, adj. dù-ghorm.
lividity, s. dù-ghuirme.
living, part. adj. beò, beothail.
living, s. teachd-an-tìr, beathachadh.
lixivial, adj. saillt, salannach.
lixiviate, adj. saillteach, salannach.
lixivium, s. uisge làn salainn.
lizard, s. arc-luachrach.
lo ! interj. faic ! feuch ! seall ! amhairc ! amhairc !
load, s. luchd, eallach, éire, cudthrom ; trom, truime, uallach.
load, v. a. luchdaich, eallaich, lìon, cuimrigich, cuir fo éire ; cuir urchair an gunna ; tromaich.
loadstone, s. clach-iùil.
loaf, s. builionn, muilion.
loam, s. trom-thalamh, talamh criadh is duilleach ghrod.
loan, s. iasad, iasachd, coingheall.
loath, adj. aindeonach, neo-thoileach, gràineach.
loathe, v. a. fuathaich, sgreataich roimh ; gabh gràin.
loathful, adj. fuathmhor, deisinneach.
loathing, s. gràin, fuath, sgreat.
loathsome, adj. gràineil, sgreataidh.
loathsomeness, s. sgreamhalachd.
lob, s. slaodaire, liobasdair, buimilear.
lobby, s. foirsheòmar.
lobe, s. duilleag an sgamhain, earrann.
lobster, s. giomach.
local, adj. dùthchail, ionadail.
locality, s. àite, còmhnaidh.
location, s. suidheachadh, àite.
lock, s. glas ; gleus gunna ; bachlag, dual, ciabhag.
lock, v. glais ; druid, dùin ; bi dùinte, bi glaiste.

locker, s. àite-gleidhidh, àite-glaiste.
locket, s. glasag-mhuineil.
lockram, s. anart-asgairt.
locomotion, s. gluasad, siubhal.
locomotive, adj. gluasadach, siùbhlach.
locust, s. locust.
lodge, v. cuir an ionad còmhnaidh ; suidhich, socraich, càirich ; gabh còmhnaidh.
lodge, s. tigh-geata, tigh-fasgaidh.
lodgement, s. cruinneachadh, dòmhlachadh ; seilbh-ghlacaidh, toirt a mach daingnich.
lodger, s. fear-fàrdaich, aoigh.
lodging, s. fàrdach, còmhnaidh dìon, fasgadh.
loft, s. ùrlar, ùrlar-déile, lobhta.
loftiness, s. àirde, àrd-smuainteachd ; mòr-chuis, àrdan, féinbheachd.
lofty, adj. àrd, mór, uasal ; allail, òirdheirc ; mór-chuiseach, àrdanach, féin-bheachdail, uaibhreach.
log, s. sgonn, òrda fiodha ; tomhas Eabhruidheach.
log, s. uidheam tomhas astar luinge.
loggerhead, s. gurraiceach, amhlair, baothaire, ùmaidh.
logic, s. ealain reusonachaidh.
logical, adj. reusanta.
logician, s. fear dian-reusonachaidh.
logwood, s. fiodh an datha.
loin, s. leasraidh, am blian.
loiter, v. a. dèan màirneal, bi dìomhanach, bi ri steòcaireachd.
loiterer, s. steòcaire, leisgean, lunndaire, slaodaire.
loll, v. dèan leth-laighe ri, leag do thaic air.
lone, adj. aonarach ; leis féin.
loneliness, loneness, s. aonaranachd ; dìomhaireachd, uaigneachd.
lonely, lonesome, adj. aonarach, aonaranach ; dìomhair, uaigneach.
long, adj. fada, buan, maireannach.
long, v. n. miannaich, bi miannach, biodh a mhiann ort, gabh fadal.
long-boat, s. bàta-mór luinge.
longevity, s. fad-shaoghalachd.
longimanous, adj. fad-làmhach.
longing, s. miann, togradh, geall, déidh, dian-thogradh.
longitudinal, adj. air fhad.
longsome, adj. fadalach ; sgìtheil.
long-suffering, adj. fad-fhulangach.
long-suffering, s. fad-fhulangas.
longways, adj. air fhad.
long-winded, adj. fad-anaileach ; sgìth, gun ciall sgur (of a speaker), briathrach.
looby, s. burraidh, blaghastair.
loof, luff, v. a. teann ri soirbheas, thoir a dh' ionnsaigh na gaoithe ; fan ri gaoith ; cùm ri fuaradh.

look, v. sir, iarr, rannsaich ; dearc, seall air, amhairc, beachdaich ; feuch, mion-rannsaich.

look ! *interj.* seall ! faic ! feuch !

look, s. snuadh, dreach, aogas, sealladh, tuar, fiamh, neul ; faicinn, amharc.

looking-glass, s. sgàthan.

loom, s. beart, beart-fhigheadair.

loon, s. slaoightear, crochaire.

loop, s. lùb, eag-shùl, lùib.

loophole, s. toll, fosgladh ; dorus-teichidh, cuilbheart, car.

loopholed, adj. sùileach, tolltach, lùb-ach.

loose, v. fuasgail, lasaich ; cuir mu sgaoil, leig fa sgaoil ; thoir cead ; cuir saor ; leig ás.

loosen, v. lasaich, fuasgail ; thoir as a chéile ; bi sgaoilteach.

looseness, s. fuasgailteachd, neo-dhaingneachd ; macnus ; mì-riaghailteachd, buaireasachd ; fuasgladh cuirp, a' ghearrach.

loot, v. creach, spùill.

lop, v. a. gèarr, bèarr, sgud, sgath.

loppings, s. barrach, sgathach.

loquacious, adj. bruidhneach, abartach, beulfhuasgailte, gobach.

loquacity, s. abarachd, gobaireachd.

lord, s. tighearna, uachdaran, triath, morair.

lord, v. n. dèan morair dheth ; bi aintighearnail, bi stràiceil ; dèan cruaidh riaghladh.

lording, lordling, s. tighearna beag.

lordliness, s. flathaileachd, mòrachd, urram, àrd-inbhe ; stràic, stràiceal-achd, mórchuis.

lordship, s. tighearnas, moraireachd.

lore, s. fòghlum, oilean, teagasg, seann sgeulachdas.

lorimer, loriner, s. fear deanamh shrian, srianadair.

lorn, adj. tréigte, caillte, aonaranach.

lose, v. caill ; leig á fradharc.

loser, s. fear-calldaich, am fear a chaill.

loss, s. call ; teagamh.

lost, *pret.* of to lose, caillte.

lot, s. crannchur ; roinn, earrann.

lotion, s. cungaidh-nighe.

lottery, s. crannchur, tuiteamas.

loud, adj. ard-fhuaimneach, tartarach, labhar ; farumach.

loudness, s. labhrachd, toirm, farum.

lounge, v. n. bi dìomhain, bi lunndach.

lounger, s. lunndaire, fear-dìomhain.

louse, s. miol, mial.

lousewort, s. an lus-riabhach.

lousiness, s. mialachas, mosaiche.

lousy, adj. mialach, làn mhial.

lout, s. burraidh, sgonn balaich.

loutish, adj. ludaireach, balachail.

lovage, s. lus-an-liùgaire.

love, v. a. gràdhaich, thoir gaol, thoir gràdh ; gabh tlachd.

love, s. gaol, gràdh, déidh ; miann, suiridhe ; càirdeas, deagh-rùn ; gràidhean, gràidheag ; mo ghràdh, mo ghaol, mo rùn.

love-knot, s. bad-leannanachd.

love-letter, s. litir-leannanachd.

loveliness, s. ionmhuinneachd.

love-lorn, adj. tréigte, cùlaichte.

lovely, adj. caomh, àillidh, maiseil.

lover, s. fear-gaoil, leannan.

love-sick, adj. tinn le gaol, an gaol.

love-song, s. òran-gaoil.

love-suit, s. suiridhe.

love-tale, s. sgeula-gaoil.

loving, part. adj. gràdhach, caoimhneil, caomh ; gràdh-bhriathrach.

loving-kindness, s. caoimhneas-gràidh.

lovingness, s. caomhalachd, gràdhalachd, caoimhneas.

low, adj. ìosal ; domhain ; neo-fhuaimneach, neo-labhar ; muladach, trom-inntinneach, tùrsach ; mosach, mì-othar ; neo-allail, bochd.

low, v. n. dèan géimnich, dèan langanaich.

lower, v. t. ìslich, thoir sìos, ceannsaich ; lùghdaich luach ; v. intr. sìolaidh sìos, bi gruamach, bagarrach.

lower, s. gruaim, mùig, bagradh (stoirm).

lowermost, adj. as iochdraiche, as ìsle.

lowland, s. fonn còmhnard, machair.

lowliness, s. irioslachd, macantas, suairceas ; mìotharachd, tàirealachd.

lowly, adj. iriosal, macanta, stuama, ciùin, soitheamh ; an-uasal, mìothar, suarach ; neo-allail, ìosal.

lowness, s. ìsleachd, suarachas, neo-inbheachd ; ùmhlachd ; trom-inntinn, mulad.

low-spirited, adj. trom-inntinneach, dubh-ach, muladach.

loyal, adj. dìleas ; tairis, fìrinneach, tréidhireach.

loyalist, s. fear-dìleas do'n rìgh.

loyalty, s. dìlseachd, treidhireas.

lubber, lubbard, s. ragbhalach, steòcaire, slaodaire, gurraiceach, boganach, claghaire.

lubberly, adj. slaodach, bog, gealltach, claghaireach.

lubric, lubricous, adj. sleamhain, neo-sheasmhach.

lubricate, v. a. lìomh, dèan sleamhainn, fàg sleamhainn (le ola).

lubricity, s. sleamhnachd, slìomachd, macnus, macnusachd.

luce, s. geadas, gead-iasg.

lucent, adj. lìomhaidh, lainnearach.

lucerne, s. seòrsa feòir.

lucid, adj. lainnearach, deàrsach, deal-rach ; soilleir, glan, troi-shoilleir, trìd-shoilleir.

lucidity, s. lainnearachd, dearsachd.
Lucifer, s. reull na maidne ; an diabhol.
luciferous, lucific, adj. soillseach, soilleir, soills-thabhartach.
luck, s. tuiteamas, tachartas, dàn, tapadh, càs ; crannchur.
luckless, adj. mì-shealbhach, mì-shona.
lucky, adj. sealbhach, sona.
lucrative, adj. buannachdail, airgeadach, tarbhach.
lucre, s. buannachd, cosnadh.
lucubrate, v. n. dèan faire, sgrìobh 's an oidhche, no, le solus coinnle.
lucubration, s. sgrìobhadh oidhche, sgrìobhadh le solus coinnle.
ludicrous, adj. àbhachdach, neònach.
luff, v. n. cùm ris a' ghaoith.
lug, v. a. slaoid, spìon leat.
lug, s. an lugais, am biathain-tràghad.
luggage, s. goireas - turais ; trealaich, imrich.
lukewarm, adj. meagh-bhlàth.
lukewarmness, s. meagh-bhlàths.
lull, v. a. cuir gu cadal, cuir sàmhach, tàlaidh, cataidh.
lullaby, s. òran fulasgaidh, crònan, òran altrumais.
lumbago, s. an leum-droma.
lumber, s. trealaich, sean-àirneis.
lumber, v. dòmhlaich, gluais trom.
luminary, s. solus ; fear-eòlais, fear soillseachaidh ; fear-naidheachd.
luminous, adj. soillseach, dealrach ; soilleir, glan ; dearsach, boillsgeach.
lump, s. meall, sgonn, an t-iomlan.
lumping, lumpish, adj. trom, marbhanta, leasg, tomadach.
lumpishly, adv. gu tròm, gu marbhanta.
lumpy, adj. meallanach, cnapanach.
lunacy, s. cuthach eu-céillidh, mearan-céille.
lunar, lunary, adj. gealachail.
lunated, adj. leth-chruinn.
lunatic, s. fear-cuthaich, fear-mearain, fear-aotromais, duine as a rian.
lunation, s. cuairt na gealaich.
lunch, luncheon, s. biadh meadhoin latha.
lunette, s. leth-ghealach, solus-ùr.

lung, s. sgamhan.
lungwort, s. crotal-coille.
lurch, s. teinn, teanndachd, drip, aomadh obann.
lurch, v. thoir an car á, dèan frith-ghoid, siolc ; dèan ceilg.
lurcher, s. cù-seilg, gaothar.
lure, s. culaidh bhuairidh, mealladh.
lure, v. a. buair, tàlaidh, meall.
lurid, adj. duaichnidh, gruamach.
lurk, v. n. dèan feall-fhalach.
lurker, s. gadaich-chùl-phreas.
luscious, adj. sòghmhor, ro-bhlasda.
lush, adj. trom-dhathach.
lust, s. miann-feòlmhor ; ann-togradh, ana-miann.
lustful, adj. ana-miannach, collaidh.
lustiness, s. spionnadh, sultmhorachd, dòmhalachd.
lustral, adj. ionnladach, a ghlanas.
lustration, s. glanadh le uisge.
lustre, s. dealradh, dearsadh, lainnear, soillse ; mór-chliù, ainmealachd ; ùine chùig bliadhna.
lustring, s. sìoda boillsgeil.
lusty, adj. làidir, calma, neartmhor, sult-mhor, foghanteach, reamhar, garbh.
lute, s. inneal-ciùil àraidh, crèadh-ghlaodh.
lute, v. a. cuir crèadh-ghlaodh air.
lux, luxate, v. a. cuir as an alt.
luxuriance, luxuriancy, s. mórchinneas, ro-phailteas, reamhrachd.
luxuriant, adj. ro-phailt, fàsmhor.
luxurious, adj. sòghail, geòcach ; ròiceal, ana-miannach.
luxuriousness, s. sòghalachd.
luxury, s. sòghalachd ; sògh, anabarra, ana-miann, neòghloine.
lycanthropy, s. an tioma-tàisean.
lying, s. deanamh bhreug ; laidhe.
lymph, s. uisge, sùgh glan.
lymphatic, adj. uisgeach, uisgeil.
lympheduct, s. soitheach-uisge.
lynch, v. t. grad-chrochadh (air duine).
lyre, s. clàrsach, cruit.
lyric, lyrical, adj. fonnmhor, ceòlmhor, cruit-bhinn.
lyrist, s. cruitear, clàrsair.

M

macadamise, v. t. leasaich rathad mór le bristleach chlach.
macaroni, s. sgèamhanach.
macaronic, s. measgachadh.
macaroon, s. aran-millis.
macaw, s. a' pharaid; a' phitheid.
mace, s. suaicheantas inbhe ; bata maol.
mace, s. seòrsa spìosraidh.

mace - bearer, s. fear - iomchair slat - shuaicheantais.
macerate, v. a. cnàmh, caith air falbh ; claoidh, sàraich, pian ; brùth, bogaich, taisich an uisge.
maceration, s. cnàmh, caitheadh as ; sàrachadh, bruthadh ; bogachadh, taiseachadh.

machinal, *adj.* innleachdach.
machinate, *v. a.* dèan innleachd.
machination, *s.* dealbhadh, tionnsgaladh, droch-innleachd.
machine, *s.* beart-innleachd, inneal.
machinery, *s.* beart, beartan ; obair bearta.
machinist, *s.* fear-dhèanamh bheartan, fear-oibreachaidh bheartan.
mackerel, *s.* ronnach, reannach.
macrocosm, *s.* an cruinne-cé, a' chruith-eachd, an domhan, an saoghal.
mactation, *s.* ìobradh ; càsgairt.
macula, *s.* ball dubh (air a' ghréin no air miotailt).
maculate, macle, *v. a.* ballaich, salaich.
maculation, *s.* ballachadh, salachadh.
mad, *adj.* air a' chuthaich, mearanaich.
mad, madden, *v.* cuir air chuthach.
madam, *s.* baintighearna.
mad-brained, *adj.* mearanach, bras.
madcap, *s.* fear-fiadhaich, fear-mearain, fear-cuthaich.
madder, *s.* an ruadh dhath, màdar.
made, *pret.* of **to make,** rinn ; dèante.
madhouse, *s.* tigh-cuthaich.
madness, *s.* cuthach, mearan.
madrigal, *s.* òran dùthcha.
magazine, *s.* tigh-tasgaidh, miosachan.
maggot, *s.* spiantag, cnuimheag ; baoth-smuain, magaid.
maggoty, *adj.* cnuimheach, spiantagach ; baoth-smuainteach.
magi, *s.* speuradairean na h-airde an ear.
magic, *s.* drùidheachd, geasan.
magic, magical, *adj.* drùidheil, geasagach.
magician, *s.* drùidh, fiosaiche.
magisterial, *adj.* tighearnail ; ceannas-ach, làdasach, stràiceil.
magistracy, *s.* uachdranachd.
magistrate, *s.* bàillidh, uachdaran, fear-riaghlaidh, breitheamh.
magnanimity, *s.* mór-inntinneachd.
magnanimous, *adj.* mór-inntinneach, fial-aidh, còir.
magnesia, *s.* gnè do dh' fhùdar purgaide.
magnet, *s.* clach-iùil.
magnetic, magnetical, *adj.* tarruingeach, mar a' chlach iùil.
magnetism, *s.* cumhachd tarruing da ionnsaigh féin, mar a ni a' chlach-iùil.
magnificence, *s.* móralachd.
magnificent, *adj.* òirdheirc, mórchuis-each ; glòrmhor ; àrd.
magnifier, *s.* fear-meudachaidh, fear-àrdachaidh ; gloine-mheudachaidh.
magnify, *v. a.* meudaich ; àrdaich, tog, urramaich.
magnitude, *s.* meudachd, meud.
magpie, *s.* pioghaid.
maid, maiden, *s.* maighdeann, òigh, cailin, caileag, gruagach, nighean, ainnir, cruinneag ; ban-oglach.

maiden, *adj.* òigheach, maighdean-nach ; glan, ùr, fìor-ghlan, neo-thruaillidh.
maidenhair, *s.* an dubhchasach.
maidenhead, maidhood, maidenhood, *s.* maighdeannas.
mail, *s.* lùireach - mhàilleach, deise-chruadhach ; màla, balg-litrichean.
maim, *v. a.* leòn, ciurr, dochainn.
maim, *s.* dochunn, ciurradh ; bacaiche, crùbaiche ; cron, coire ; gaoid.
main, *adj.* prìomh, ceud, àraidh ; mór, àrd, fuathasach ; cudthromach, sòn-raichte.
main, *s.* a' mhór chuid ; tomad ; an lear, an cuan, an fhairge mhór.
mainland, *s.* tìr-mór, a' mhórthir.
mainmast, *s.* crann-mór, an crann-meadhoin.
mainsail, *s.* an seòl-mór, an seòl-meadhoin.
mainsheet, *s.* sgòd an t-siùil mhóir.
maintain, *v.* gléidh, cùm ; daingnich, dèan seasmhach ; dìon, seas, buan-aich, coisinn ; cùm suas, beathaich, thoir teachd-an-tìr do ; tagair, còmh-daich.
maintainable, *adj.* ghabhas dìon, so-ghléidhteach, so-sheasmhach, so-chòmhdachail.
maintenance, *s.* dìon, taic, fasgadh, tèarmann ; teachd-an-tìr, beathach-adh ; seasmhachd, maireannachd, daingneachd.
maintop, *s.* bàrr a' chroinn mhóir.
mainyard, *s.* slat shiùil a chroinn mhóir.
maize, *s.* cruithneachd Innseanach.
majestic, majestical, *adj.* mòrdha, urram-ach, flathail ; àrd.
majesty, *s.* mórachd, mórdhalachd, greadhnachas, òirdheirceas ; àrd-chumhachd ; rìoghalachd.
major, *adj.* as mò, as urramaiche.
major, *s.* ard-oifigeach, màidsear.
majoration, *s.* meudachadh.
majority, *s.* a' mhór chuid ; làn-aois, mòid.
make, *v.* dèan, dèan suas ; dealbh ; thoir air, co-éignich gu ; dèan air, coisinn air ; ruig.
makebate, *s.* ball-aimhleis, ceannbuaireis.
makepeace, *s.* fear-eadraiginn.
maker, *s.* fear - dèanamh, dealbhadair, cumadair ; an Cruthadair.
making, *s.* dèanamh, dealbh.
maladministration, *s.* mì-riaghladh, mì-steòrnadh, mì-bhuileachadh.
malady, *s.* galar, euslaint, tinneas, eucail.
malapert, *adj.* beadaidh, dàna, bathais-each, dalma, leamh, lonach
malapertness, *s.* beadaidheachd, ladarnas, dalmachd.

malcontent, *adj.* mì-thoilichte, neo-riaraichte ; *f.* fear-gearanach, feartalaich.

male, *s.* firionn, firionnach.

malediction, *s.* mallachd.

malefaction, *s.* coire, droch-bheart, lochd, oilbheum, ciont.

malefactor, *s.* fear-droch-bheirt, eucorach, ciontach.

malefic, *adj.* buaireasach, cronail.

malevolence, *s.* mìorun, gamhlas, fuath, nimhealachd, miosgainn.

malevolent, *adj.* mìorunach, gamhlasach, nimheil, miosgainneach.

malice, *s.* mìorun, gamhlas, drochmheinn, nàimhdeas, tnù.

malicious, *adj.* gamhlasach, mìorunach, drochmheinneach, naimhdeil.

maliciousness, *s.* falachd, drochmheinneachd, nimhealachd.

malign, *adj.* gabhaltach, guineach, nimheil, millteach.

malign, *v. a.* fuathaich ; dochainn, ciurr, dèan cron do.

malignancy, malignity, *s.* drochmheinn ; millteachd, sgriosalachd.

malignant, *adj.* millteach, sgriosail.

malkin, *s.* bhreunchaile, dubhchaile.

mall, *s.* simid, òrd.

mall, *v. a.* slaicinn, buaill, bruan.

mallard, *s.* dràc fiadhaich.

malleable, *adj.* so-oibreachadh ; (miotailt) a ghabas oibreachadh le òrd.

malleate, *v. a.* oibrich air innean.

mallet, *s.* fairche, slacan, simid, plocan.

mallows, *s.* lus-nam-meall-móra.

malt, *s.* braich.

malt, *v. n.* brach, gabh brachadh.

maltreat, *v. a.* droch ghréidh.

maltster, *s.* brachadair.

malversation, *s.* mealltaireachd.

mam, mamma, *s.* màthair.

mammon, *s.* beartas, saoibhreas (dhe 'n dèanar iodhol).

man, *s.* duine, fear.

man, *v. a.* cuir sgioba air, etc.

manacles, *s.* glas-làmh, cuibhreach.

manage, *v.* stiùr, riaghail, òrduich ; ceannsaich ; steòrn.

manage, management, managery, *s.* riaghladh, stiùradh ; seòltachd, siciread, innleachd ; iomairt, cleachdadh.

manageable, *adj.* furasd iomairt, ghabhas riaghladh, ghabhas stiùradh, so-cheannsachail.

manager, *s.* fear-riaghlaidh, fear-stiùraidh ; fear-steòrnaidh.

manchet, *s.* aran-milis, aran-cridhe.

mancipate, *v. a.* cuir fo dhaorsa, cuibhrich.

mandamus, *s.* òrdugh rìoghail.

mandate, *s.* àithne, òrdugh, earail.

mandatory, *adj.* àithneil, earalach, mar chorachd.

mandible, *s.* peirceall, gial.

mandibular, *adj.* peirceallach.

mandrake, *s.* carra-mille.

manducate, *v. a.* cagainn, ith.

manducation, *s.* cagnadh, itheadh.

mane, *s.* mong ; gath-muinge.

manège, *s.* sgoil-mharcachd.

manes, *s.* tàsg, spiorad, tannasg.

manful, *adj.* fearail, duineil.

manfulness, *s.* fearalas, duinealas.

mange, *s.* cloimh, galar spréidhe.

manger, *s.* prasach, frasach.

mangle, *v. a.* reub, srac, mill, thoir as a chéile ; dèan ablach dheth ; mìnich anart.

mangle, *s.* beart-iarnaigidh.

mangy, *adj.* cloimheach, clamhrach.

manhood, *s.* làn-aois ; fearalas.

mania, *s.* boile-cuthaich.

maniac, *s.* neach cuthaich, duine as a chiall.

maniacal, *adj.* air bhoile cuthaich.

manifest, *adj.* follaiseach, soilleir.

manifest, *s.* cunntas luchd luinge.

manifest, *v. a.* taisbean, soilleirich, foillsich, nochd, feuch, leig ris.

manifestation, *s.* foillseachadh.

manifestness, *s.* soilleireachd.

manifesto, *s.* gairm-fhollaiseach.

manifold, *adj.* iom-fhillteach, eugsamhla.

manikin, *s.* duairc, luspardan.

maniple, *s.* lan-dùirn ; prasgan.

mankind, *s.* an cinne-daonna.

manlike, manly, *adj.* duineil, fearail, gaisgeil.

manliness, *s.* duinealas, fearalachd.

manna, *s.* mana, aran nèamhaidh, etc.

manner, *s.* modh, seòl, alt, rian, gnàths, cleachdadh, nòs ; gnè, seòrsa ; tuar, snuadh, sealladh, aogas.

mannerly, *adj.* beusach, modhail.

manners, *s.* oilean, modh.

manœuvre, *s.* sicireachd.

manor, *s.* fearann tighearna.

manse, *s.* tigh ministeir.

mansion, *s.* tigh tighearna.

manslaughter, *s.* mort, casgairt.

mantle, *s.* falluinn, aodach-uachdair.

mantua, *s.* gùn baintighearna.

mantua-maker, *s.* ban-tàillear.

manual, *adj.* làmhach, leabhar-sgoile.

manuduction, *s.* làmh - threòrachadh, làmh-stiùradh.

manufactory, *s.* bùth cèirde.

manufacture, *s.* làmhobair.

manufacture, *v. a.* oibrich, dèan.

manufacturer, *s.* fear-làimh-oibre.

manumission, *s.* saoradh tràille.

manumit, *v. a.* saor o dhaorsa.

manurable, *adj.* ghabhas mhathachadh.

manure, *v. a.* leasaich, mathaich, tobhair.

manure, *s.* mathachadh, inneir, tobhar.

manuscript, *s.* leabhar - sgrìobhte (le peann).

many, *adj.* iomadh, lìonmhor.
many-coloured, *adj.* iomdhathach, eug-samhla.
many-cornered, *adj.* iombheannach, beannagach, oisinneach.
many-headed, *adj.* iomcheannach.
many-times, *adv.* iomadh uair, tric.
map, *s.* dealbh dùthcha, no baile, etc.
mar, *v. a.* léir, mill, dochainn, truaill.
marasmus, *s.* an tinneas caitheamh.
marauder, *s.* saighdear-spùinnidh.
marble, *s.* marmor, marbhal.
marble, *v. a.* breacaich, srianaich.
March, *s.* A Mhàrt, mìos na Màirt.
march, *s.* feachd-shiubhal; ceum stòlda; port-siubhail; crìoch, iomall, oir.
march, *v.* màrsail, imich le feachd-cheum; triall, gluais; ceumnaich, gluais gu stàtail; gluais an òrdugh.
marchioness, *s.* bana-mharcus.
marchpane, *s.* seòrs' aran-milis.
marcid, *adj.* caol, seargte, glais-neulach.
mare, *s.* làir.
mareschal, *s.* ard-mharascal.
margarite, margarites, *s.* neamhnaid, déideag.
margent, margin, *s.* oir, bile, iomall, crìoch, beul, lethoir.
marginal, *adj.* iomallach, bileach, oireach.
margrave, *s.* duin-uasal Gearmailteach.
marigold, *s.* a' bhile-bhuidhe.
marine, *adj.* mara, muireach.
mariner, *s.* maraiche, seòladair.
maritime, *adj.* fairgeach, cois mara.
mark, *s.* marg; bonn airgeid thrì tasdain deug as gròt; comharradh; làrach, athailt, lorg; dearbhadh, còmhdach; ball-amais, cuspair.
mark, *v.* comharraich; beachdaich, thoir fainear; seall, amhairc.
market, *s.* féill, margadh, faighir; reic, is ceannachd.
marketable, *adj.* a ghabhas reic.
marksman, *s.* fear-cuspaireachd.
marl, *s.* lagus, criadh-mhathachaidh.
marline, *s.* sreang sgeinnidh, taifeid.
marquis, *s.* oighre diùc, marcus.
marriage, *s.* pòsadh.
marriageable, *adj.* aig aois-pòsaidh.
married, *adj.* pòsta.
marrow, *s.* smior, smear.
marrow-fat, *s.* a' pheasair mhór.
marrowless, *adj.* neo-smiorach.
marry, *v.* pòs; thoir am pòsadh.
marsh, marish, *s.* lòn; boglach, breun-loch, féith, srath.
marshal, *s.* marasgal.
marshal, *v. a.* tarruing suas, cuir an òrdugh; treòraich.
marshalship, *s.* marasgalachd.

marsh-mallow, *s.* lus-nam-meall móra, an cnaplus.
marsh-marigold, *s.* lus-buidhe-bealltainn, lus Muire.
marshy, *adj.* bog, fliuch, féitheach.
mart, *s.* àite margaidh.
marten, *s.* taghan; gobhlan-gaoithe.
martial, *adj.* cathach, gaisgeanta, cur-anta, crodha, treun.
martialist, *s.* curaidh, gaisgeach.
martingal, *s.* srian-cheannsachaidh.
Martinmas, *s.* an Fhéill-Màrtainn.
martyr, *s.* martarach, fear-fianais.
martyrdom, *s.* bàs air son creidimh.
martyrology, *s.* eachdraidh mhartarach.
marvel, *s.* iongantas, iongnadh.
marvel, *v. n.* gabh iongnadh.
marvellous, *adj.* iongantach, neònach.
marvellousness, *s.* neònachas.
masculine, *adj.* firionn; duineil.
mash, *s.* measgan, coimeasgadh, mogul lìn.
mash, *v. a.* pronn, brùth, masg.
mask, *s.* cidhis; leithsgeul, car.
masker, *s.* fear-cidhis.
mason, *s.* clachair.
masonic, *adj.* clachaireach.
masonry, *s.* clachaireachd.
masquerade, *s.* cluiche-chidhis.
masquerader, *s.* fear-cidhis.
mass, *s.* meall, dùn, torr; tomad; a' mhór-chuid.
mass, *s.* aifrionn.
massacre, *s.* casgradh, mort.
massacre, *v. a.* casgair, marbh, mort.
massive, massy, *adj.* cudthromach, trom, tomadach.
massiveness, *s.* cudthrom, tomad, truimead.
mast, *s.* crann; cnò.
master, *s.* maighistear, fear-tighe; fear-riaghlaidh, fear-stiùraidh, uachdaran, tighearna; sgiobair; fear-teagaisg.
master, *v. a.* dèan maighistearachd, riaghail; ceannsaich; bi ealanta, bi gleusda.
masterliness, *s.* àrd-ealantachd.
masterly, *adj.* ealanta, grinn.
masterpiece, *s.* àrd-ghnìomh, euchd.
mastership, mastery, *s.* maighistearachd, uachdranachd, ceannsal; urram, buaidh; ealain, eòlas.
mastication, *s.* cagnadh.
mastich, *s.* bìgh, seòrsa glaoidh.
mastiff, *s.* cù mór, balgaire.
mastless, *adj.* gun chrann.
mastlin, meslin, *s.* prac.
mat, *s.* brat luachrach.
match, *s.* lasadan, brathadair.
match, *s.* mac-samhail, fear-dùbhlain; lethbhreac; pòsadh; comh-strì.
match, *v.* co-fhreagair; pòs, thoir am pòsadh, bi pòsta.
matchable, *adj.* co-ionannach.

matchless, *adj.* gun choimeas.
mate, *s.* céile ; còmpanach.
material, *adj.* corporra ; feumail, sòn-raichte, aobhar.
materialist, *s.* fear-àicheadh spiorad.
materiality, *s.* corporrachd.
materials, *s.* deisealasan.
maternal, *adj.* màithreil.
maternity, *s.* màthaireachd.
mathematician, *s.* fear-eòlais thomhas is àireamh.
mathematics, *s.* eòlas tomhas is àireamh.
matin, *adj.* madainneach, moch.
matins, *s.* aoradh maidne, madainnean, maidnean.
matrice, or matrix, *s.* bolg, machlag ; laghadair, inneal cumaidh, laphaid.
matricide, *s.* mòrt màthar.
matriculate, *v. a.* cuir sìos ainm an oil-thigh, ceud-thòisich 's an oil-thigh.
matrimonial, *adj.* pòsachail.
matrimony, *s.* an dàimh-phòsaidh, pò-sadh.
matron, *s.* bean ; seann bhean ; bean-tighe.
matronly, *adj.* sean ; màithreil.
matter, *s.* ni corporra, ni talmhaidh ; brìgh, ni, rud, stuth ; cùis, gnothach, aobhar, mathair-uilc, cùis-ghearain, cùis-thalaich ; iongar.
mattock, *s.* piocaid, matag.
mattress, *s.* leabaidh-ìochdrach, liteir.
maturation, *s.* abachadh.
maturative, *adj.* abachail.
mature, *adj.* abaich ; deas, ullamh.
maturity, *s.* abaichead, coimhliontachd.
maudlin, *adj.* leth-mhisgeach, froganach, soganach ; *s.* lus àraidh.
maugre, *adv.* a dh' aindeoin.
maul, *s.* fairche, slacan mór, plocan.
maul, *v. a.* buaill, gréidh, spuac, brùth, pronn, slacraich, dochainn, ciurr, bruan.
maund, *s.* sgùlan-laimhe, seòrs' ùird.
maunder, *v. n.* dèan monmhar, dèan bòrbhan.
mausoleum, *s.* tigh adhlacaidh.
maw, *s.* goile ; sgròban eòin.
mawkish, *adj.* sgreamhail, sgreataidh, déisinneach.
mawkishness, *s.* sgreamhalachd.
maw-worm, *s.* cnuimh goile.
maxim, *s.* fìrinn - shuidhichte, gnàth-fhacal, seanfhacal.
may, *v. auxil.* faod, faodaidh, feudaidh.
May, *s.* a Mhàigh, an céitean.
May-day, *s.* latha Bealltainn.
mayor, *s.* àrd-bhàillidh baile-mhóir (an Sasuinn).
mayoralty, *s.* ceannardachd bailemhòir.
mayoress, *s.* bana-bhàillidh.
maze, *s.* cuairt-shloc ; tuaineal, im-acheist, ioma-chomhairle.

mazy, *adj.* cuairteach, troimh chéile.
mazzard, *s.* cnàimh a' pheirceill.
me, *pron.* mi, mise.
mead, *s.* leann-meala.
mead, meadow, *s.* lòn, àilean, cluan, miadan, miadair, faiche, innis.
meadow-sweet, *s.* Cneas-Cuchulainn, lus-Chuchulainn.
meagre, *adj.* caol, bochd, tana, lom, gun fheòil ; acrach, gortach, gann.
meagerness, *s.* caoile, tainead, luime.
meal, *s.* tràth bìdh ; min.
mealman, *s.* ceannaiche mine.
mealy, *adj.* tioram, mar mhin.
mealy-mouthed, *adj.* tlàth-bheulach, sod alach, brosgalach, mìnbhriathrach, cealgach.
mean, *adj.* ìosal, suarach, mìodhoir, tàireil ; dìblidh, dìmeasach.
mean, *s.* meadhonachd, cuibheasachd tomhas, riaghailt.
mean, *v. a.* rùnaich, cuir romhad, togair ; ciallaich ; biodh a mhiann ort.
meander, *s.* cuairtchar, luibean aibhne-rathad camacach.
meander, *v. n.* lùb, fiar, crom.
meaning, *s.* rùn-suidhichte ; ciall, seadh, brìgh bladh ; tuigse.
meanness, *s.* ìsleachd, bochdainn, suar-achas ; tàirealachd ; spìocaireachd, mosaiche.
meant, *part. pass.* of to mean, ciallaichte, rùnaichte.
measles, *s.* a' ghriuthach, a' ghriùthrach, a' ghriobhach.
measurable, *adj.* a ghabhas tomhas.
measure, *s.* tomhas, cuimse, riaghailt, inneal-tomhais ; gu leòir, ni's leòir ; cuibhrionn, cuid, roinn, earrann ; measarrachd.
measure, *v. a.* tomhais.
measureless, *adj.* do-thomhas.
measurement, *s.* tomhas.
measurer, *s.* fear-tomhais.
meat, *s.* feòil ; biadh, teachd an-tìr.
mechanic, *s.* fear-céirde.
mechanic, mechanical, *adj.* cèirdeil, inn-leachdach, saoithreachail, ionnsaichte an cèird ; oibreachail.
mechanician, mechanist, *s.* fear-cèirde, fear-eulain.
mechanics, *s.* ealain-chèirde.
medal, *s.* seana - chùinneadh, bonn - cuimhne, duais sgoileireachd, no gaisga.
meddle, *v.* buin ri, bean ri ; dèan ead-raiginn, cuir làmh ann ; biodh làmh agad ann.
meddler, *s.* beadagan, meachranaiche.
mediate, *v.* slthich, réitich, dèan rèidh ; rach an eadraiginn.
mediation, *s.* eadraiginn, réite, réiteach-adh, sìtheachadh, eadar-ghuidhe.

mediator, s. eadar-mheadhonair.

mediatorship, s. eadar - mheadhonaire - achd.

mediatory, adj. eadar-mheadhonach.

medicable, adj. a bhuineas do chung-aidhean-leighis.

medical, s. léigh.

medicament, s. cungaidh-leighis.

medicate, v. a. measgaich le iocshlaint, glan.

medicinal, adj. iocshlainteach.

medicine, s. eòlas-leighis, iocshlaint.

mediocre, adj. meadhonach, an eatorras, cùibheasach.

mediocrity, s. eatorras, cùibheas.

meditate, v. tionnsgain, deilbh ; smuain-ich, cnuasaich, beachdsmaointich.

meditation, s. smaointean, breithneach-adh, beachd-smaointean.

meditative, adj. smaointeachail.

Mediterranean, adj. meadhon - thìreach, eadarra-thìr.

medium, s. inneal ; meadhon.

medley, s. coimeasgadh, treamsgal.

medullar, medullary, adj. smiorach, beo-smiorach.

meed, s. duais ; tiodhlac, tabhartas.

meek, adj. macanta, ciùin, màlda, soith-eamh, mìn, sèimh, iriosal.

meekness, s. macantas, irioslachd.

meet, adj. iomchuidh, freagarrach.

meet, v. n. còmhlaich, coinnich, tachair ; cùm còdhail ; cruinnich.

meeting, s. cruinneachadh, coimhthional, còdhail, coinneachadh.

meetness, s. iomchuidheachd.

megrim, s. galar-cinn, ceannghalar, luairean.

melancholic, adj. dubhach, fo leann-dubh, trom ; brònach ; muladach, tiamhaidh.

melancholy, s. leann - dubh, mulad ; truime-inntinn, dù-bhròn ; dubhachas, cianalas, tùrsa.

meliorate, v. a. leasaich, càirich.

melioration, meliority, s. leasachadh, càradh, feabhas.

mellifluous, adj. mealach, milshruthach, air bhlas meala, binn-bhriathrach.

mellow, adj. tlàth-fhuaimneach ; làn-abaich ; miadh ; fo bhláthachadh deoch.

mellowness, s. làn-abachd ; tlàthghuth-achd, buigead.

melodious, adj. leudarra, fonnmhor, binn, ceileireach, ceòl-bhinn.

melody, s. ceòl-bhinneas, binneas.

melon, s. meal-bhucan.

melt, v. leagh, taisich, bogaich, caith as.

melter, s. leaghadair.

member, s. ball, ball-cuirp.

membrane, s. féith-lianan, cochull.

membraneous, adj. féith-liananach.

memento, s. cuimhneachan, sanas.

memoir, s. mion-eachdraidh.

memorable, adj. ainmeil, cliùiteach.

memorandum, s. cuimhneachan.

memorial, s. cuimhneachan-duaise, car-ragh-cuimhne.

memorialist, s. fear - cuir - an - cuimhne, fear-athchuinge.

memory, s. cuimhne, meadhair.

men, plural of man, daoine, fir.

menace, v. a. bagair, maoidh.

menace, s. bagradh, maoidheadh.

menage, menagerie, s. co-chruinneach-adh fhiadh-bheathaichean.

mend, v. a. càirich, dèan suas ; leasaich ; cuidich ; rach am feabhas, cinn na's fearr.

mendacity, s. breugaireachd.

mender, s. fear-càradh.

mendicant, s. déirceach, deòraidh.

menial, s. seirbheiseach.

menology, s. féilire na h-eaglais Ghreug-aich.

menstrual, adj. mìosach.

mensurate, v. a. tomhais.

mensuration, s. tomhas.

mental, adj. inntinneach, inntinneil.

mention, s. ainmeachadh, iomradh.

mention, v. a. ainmich, aithris.

mephitical, adj. lobhte, grod, breun-bholtrach.

mercantile, adj. malairteach, margail.

mercenary, adj. gionach, sanntach.

mercenary, s. seirbhiseach-duaise, saighd-ear tuarasdail.

mercer, s. ceannaiche sìoda.

mercery, s. ceannachd shìoda.

merchandise, s. ceannachd ; bathar.

merchant, s. ceannaiche.

merchantman, s. long cheannachd.

merciful, adj. tròcaireach, iochdmhor, bàigheil.

merciless, adj. an-tròcaireach, an-iochd-mhor, cruaidh-chridheach.

mercurial, adj. mar airgiod beò.

mercury, s. airgiod-beò ; sunnt.

mercy, s. tròcair, iochd, mathanas.

mercy-seat, s. cathair-na-tròcair.

mere, s. loch ; crìoch.

mere, adj. a mhàin.

merely, adv. a mhàin, dìreach.

meretricious, adj. macnusach, fallsail.

meridian, s. meadhon - latha, àird' an latha ; cridhe na h-airde-deas.

meridional, adj. deiseal, mu dheas.

merit, s. fiùghantas, fiùghalach, òirdheir-ceas.

meritorious, adj. airidh, cliùiteach.

merle, s. an lon-dubh.

merlin, s. seòrsa seabhaic.

mermaid, s. maighdeann-mhara.

merriment, s. aighear, subhachas, meogh-ail, mire, sùgradh, aiteas, sùigeart, fonn.

merry, *adj.* aoibhinn, àit ; mear, mireagach, aighearach, subhach, geanail, suigeartach.

merry-andrew, *s.* baoth-chleasaiche.

merrythought, *s.* an cnàimh-pòsaidh, cnàimh-uchd no uga eòin.

mesh, *s.* mogull-lìn.

mess, *s.* mias ; comaith ; biadh cuideachd.

mess, *v. n.* ith ; rach an comaith.

message, *s.* teachdaireachd.

messenger, *s.* teachdaire, gille - ruith ; maor, earraid.

Messiah, *s.* Mesiah, an Slànaighear.

messmate, *s.* fear-comaith.

messuage, *s.* tigh-còmhnaidh.

met, *pret.* and *part.* of to meet, choinnich, chòmhlaich ; coinnichte, còmhlaichte.

metal, *s.* miotailt.

metallic, *adj.* miotailteach.

metalline, *adj.* làn miotailt.

metallurgy, *s.* obair-mheatailtean.

metamorphosis, *s.* cruth-chaochla, cruthatharachadh.

metaphor, *s.* briathar-samhla, samhla.

metaphorical, *adj.* samhlachail.

metaphrase, *s.* eadar-theangachadh.

metaphysical, *adj.* domhain, diomhair, àrd-fhiosrach.

metaphysics, *s.* àrd-fheallsanachd.

metathesis, *s.* atharrachadh, iomlaid (àite), litir cas mu sheach.

mete, *v. a.* tomhais, cothromaich.

meteor, *s.* driug, dreag.

meteorological, *adj.* driugach.

meteorologist, *s.* speuradair.

meteorology, *s.* speuradaireachd.

meter, *s.* fear-tomhais, inneal-tomhais.

metewand, meteyard, *s.* slat-thonhais.

methinks, *v. imp.* ar leam.

method, *s.* dòigh, seòl, rian, modh.

methodical, *adj.* dòigheil, òrdail, seòlta, rianail.

methodically, *adv.* gu dòigheil, gu riaghailteach.

methodise, *v. a.* cuir air dòigh.

methought, *pret.* of methinks, shaoil mi, shaoil leam, ar leam.

metonymy, *s.* samhla, modh-samhla.

metre, *s.* rannachd, dàn.

metrical, *adj.* rannach, rann-réidh.

metropolis, *s.* àrd-bhaile-mór.

metropolitan, *s.* àrd-easbuig.

mettle, *s.* smioralachd ; stuth.

mettled, mettlesome, *adj.* smiorail, misneachail, duineil, fearail, cruadalach.

mew, *s.* eunlann ; fang ; faoileag.

mew, *v.* druid suas, dèan prìosanaich ; tilg na h-itean ; dèan miamhail, mar chat.

mewl, *v. n.* ràn, mar naoidhean.

mice, *plural* of mouse, luchan, luchainn.

Michaelmas, *s.* An Fhéill-Mìcheil.

mickery, *s.* siolcaireachd, frith-ghoid.

microcosm, *s.* an saoghal beag ; corp an duine.

microscope, *s.* glaine mheudachaidh.

mid, midst, *adj.* eadar-mheadhonach.

midday, *s.* meadhon-latha.

middle, *adj.* meadhon.

middle, *s.* meadhon, buillsgean.

middlemost, midmost, *adj.* 'sa' mheadhon, sa' bhuillsgean, sa' chridhe, 's an fhìor-mheadhon, teis-meadhon.

middling, *adj.* meadhonach, an eatorras, cùibheasach.

midge, *s.* meanbh-chuileag.

mid-heaven, *s.* meadhon nan speur.

mid-leg, *s.* leth a' chalpa.

midnight, *s.* meadhon oidhche.

midriff, *s.* an sgairt.

midshipman, *s.* òg-oifigeach luinge.

midstream, *s.* coilleach-an-t-srutha.

Midsummer, *s.* An Fhéill-Eoin.

midway, *s.* leth an rathaid, leitheach slighe.

midway, *adv.* 'sa mheadhon.

midwife, *s.* bean-ghlùine.

midwifery, *s.* banas-glùine.

Midwinter, *s.* An Fhéill-Shlinnein.

mien, *s.* snuadh, dreach, aogas, tuar, gnùis, coltas, cruth.

might, *pret.* of may, dh' fhaodadh.

might, *s.* cumhachd, neart, spionnadh.

mightiness, *s.* mór-chumhachd.

mighty, *adj.* cumhachdach, neartmhor, treun euchdach ; smachdail, uachdranach, ùghdarrach ; làidir, foghainteach.

migrate, *v. n.* rach air imrich, falbh.

migration, *s.* imrich, dol air imrich.

milch, *adj.* bainneach, bainnear.

mild, *adj.* bàigheil ; mìn, ciùin, sèimh ; neo-gheur, milis, blasda.

mildew, *s.* crithreothadh, cithreodhadh, liathreodhadh, fuardhealt, millcheò ; liathtas.

mildness, *s.* bàighealachd ; ciùine.

mile, *s.* mìle, 1760 slat.

milestone, *s.* clach-mhìle.

milfoil, *s.* earr-thalmhuinn.

miliary, *adj.* caol, meanbh.

militant, *adj.* cogach, cathach.

military, *adj.* cathachail, cogail.

militate, *v. n.* cuir an aghaidh, cathaich.

militia, *adj.* feachd-dùthcha.

milk, *s.* bainne ; sùgh-luibhean.

milk, *v. a.* bleodhainn, bligh, leig.

milken, *adj.* bainneach, bliochdach.

milkiness, *s.* bainneachas.

milkmaid, *s.* banarach, banachaig.

milkpail, *s.* currasan, cuman.

milksop, *s.* boganach ; gealtaire, claghaire ; fear-cailleachail.

milk-teeth, *s.* ceud fhiaclan searraich.

milk-white, *adj.* geal mar bhainne.

milky, *adj.* bainneach ; maoth, ciùin.

milky-way, s. geal-shruth nan speur.
mill, s. mùileann, meiligir.
mill, v. a. bleith, meil, pronn.
mill-dam, s. linne-muilinn.
millenary, s. mìle-bliadhna.
millennium, s. ùine mìle bliadhna tha cuid a' saoilsinn, anns an riaghail Criosd fathast air thalamh maille ris na naoimh, an deigh na h-aiseirigh.
millepede, s. corra-chòsag.
miller, s. mùilnear.
millesimal, adj. mìlteamh, mìleamh.
milliner, s. bean ghrinneis.
millinery, s. grinneas bhan, ceann-aodach bhoireannach.
million, s.. deich ceud mìle.
millstone, s. clach-mhuilinn.
milt, s. mealag éisg; meilg; an dubh-liath.
milter, s. iasg mealagach or meilgeach.
mimic, s. fear-atharrais.
mimic, mimical, adj. atharraiseach, fochaideach, fanaideach.
mimicry, s. atharrais, sgeigireachd.
mince, v. a. mìn-ghearr; falbh le meanbh cheum, imich gu mùirneach.
mind, s. inntinn, tuigse; tùr; toil, déidh, togradh; smuaintean; beachd.
mind, v. a. thoir an aire, thoir fainear, beachdaich; cuir an cuimhne.
minded, adj. togarrach, deònach.
mindful, adj. faicilleach, cùramach, cuimhneachail.
mindless, adj. neo-aireil, neo-chùramach, neo-fhaicilleach.
mine, pron. poss. mo, leamsa.
mine, s. sloc-mèinne, àite mèinne; sloc-séisdidh.
mine, v. a. cladhaich fodha; mill gun fhios, mill gu dìomhair.
miner, s. fear-cladhaich mèinne.
mineral, s. mèinn.
mineral, adj. mèinneach.
mineralist, s. mèinneadair.
mineralogist, s. fear mèinn-eòlais.
mineralogy, s. mèinn-eòlas.
mingle, v. a. measgaich, coimeasg, cuir an ceann a chéile; truaill; cuir troimh chéile.
mingle, s. measgadh, coimeasgadh.
miniature, s. meanbh-dhealbh.
minikin, adj. beag, crìon, meanbh.
minim, minum, s. duairce; punc-chiùil àraid.
minimum, s. a' chuid as lugha.
minimus, s. an creutair as lugha.
minion, s. peasan, beadagan-millte.
minion, adj. mùirneach, greannar.
minister, s. ministear; fear-riaghlaidh, fear-comhairle; teachdaire.
minister, v. fritheil; tabhair, builich, bairig, thoir seachad.
ministerial, adj. ministearach, fritheilteach.

ministration, s. ministrealachd.
ministry, s. dreuchd, seirbheis; ministrealachd; meadhonachd, luchd-riaghlaidh, luchd-comhairle.
minnow, s. am bior-deamhnaidh.
minor, s. neach nach do ràinig làn-aois.
minorate, v. a. lùghdaich, beagaich.
minority, s. òg-aois; a' chuid as lugha.
minster, s. cill-mhanach.
minstrel, s. cruitear, clàrsair.
minstrelsy, s. cruitearachd, ceòl, coisir-chiùil.
mint, s. mionnt, meannt; tigh-cùinnidh.
minute, adj. meanbh, beag, mion.
minute, s. mionaid, trì ficheadamh earrann na h-uarach; gearr-chunntas, sgrìobhadh.
minute, v. a. sgrìobh gearr-chunntas.
minute-book, s. leabhar chuimhne.
minutely, adv. gu meanbh, gu mion, gu mionaideach.
minuteness, s. meanbhachd, bige.
minutiae, s. meanbh-phoncan.
minx, s. gaorsach, caile bheag-narach, aigeannach.
miracle, s. mìorbhuil.
miraculous, adj. mìorbhuileach.
miraculously, adv. gu mìorbhuileach, gu h-iongantach.
mirador, s. àradh, lobhta.
mire, s. poll, làthach, eabar, clàbar.
mire, v. a. salaich, eabraich.
mirror, s. sgàthan.
mirth, s. mire, sùgradh, aighear.
mirthful, adj. aighearach, cridheil, sùgach; aoibhneach.
miry, adj. clàbarach, eabarach.
misadventure, s. mìshealbh, donas, amlisg.
misadvise, v. a. mi-chomhairlich.
misadvised, adj. mi-chomhairlichte.
misaimed, adj. mi-chuimsichte.
misanthrope, s. fear-fuathachaidh dhaoine, fuathadair dhaoine.
misanthropy, s. fuath do dhaoine.
misapplication, s. mì-bhuileachadh, mì-fheum.
misapply, v. a. mì-bhuilich.
misapprehend, v. n. mì-bhreithnich.
misapprehension, s. mì-bhreithneachadh, mì-thuigsinn.
misbecome, v. n. bi mì-chiatach.
misbegotten, adj. dìolain.
misbehave, v. n. cleachd mì-bheus.
misbehaviour, s. droch-giùlan, droch oilean.
misbelief, s. saobh-chreideamh.
misbeliever, s. saobh-chreideach.
miscalculation, s. mear-chunntadh, barail mheallta.
miscalculate, v. a. dèan mear-chunntadh, dèan mì-chunntadh.
miscarriage, s. aisead-anabaich.

miscarry, *v. n.* beir anabaich ; rach am mearachd, mì-ghiùlain.

miscellaneous, *adj.* measgaichte.

miscellany, *s.* co-measgadh.

mischance, *s.* tubaist, droch-dhàn.

mischief, *s.* aimhleas, cron, lochd.

mischievous, *adj.* aimhleasach, cronail, do-bheairteach.

miscible, *adj.* so-mheasgadh.

mis-citation, *s.* mì-aithris.

misclaim, *s.* tagradh gun chòir.

misconception, *s.* barail mhearachdach, mì-bharail.

misconduct, *s.* mì-riaghladh ; droch ghiulan, mì-bheus.

misconjecture, *s.* beachd mearachdach, mì-bheachd.

misconstruction, *s.* mì-mhìneachadh, mì-sheadh, togail chearr.

misconstrue, *v. a.* mì-mhìnich, tog cearr.

miscreance, *s.* as-creideamh.

miscreant, *s.* as-creideach, saobh-chreideach, anspiorad, baobh.

misdeed, *s.* dòbheart, droch-bheart.

misdeem, *v. a.* thoir mì-bhreth air.

misdemeanour, *s.* droch-ghnìomh, coire.

misdoubt, *v. a.* cuir an teagamh.

misemploy, *v. a.* mì-bhuilich, dèan mì-fheum.

misemployment, *s.* mì-bhuileachadh.

miser, *s.* spìocaire, fineag.

miserable, *adj.* truagh, neo-shona, ainnis ; gortach, gann, cruaidh.

miserableness, *s.* truaighe, gainne.

misery, *s.* truaighe, bochdainn, dòruinn ; mi-shealbh.

misfashion, *v. a.* mì-dhealbhaich, mì-chùm, cuir an droch riochd.

misfortune, *s.* mìshealbh, tubaist.

misgive, *v. a.* cuir am mì-earbsa.

misgiving, *s.* teagamh ; an earbsa.

misgovern, *v. a.* mì-riaghail.

misguidance, *s.* iomrall, seacharan.

misguide, *v. a.* cuir iomrall, cuir air seacharan.

mishap, *s.* mìathapadh, droch thuiteamas, sgiorradh, tubaist.

misinfer, *v. a.* mì-mheasraich.

misinform, *v. a.* thoir fios meallta.

misinterpret, *v. a.* mì-bhreithnich, tog cearr.

misjudge, *v. a.* thoir breith chearbach.

mislay, *v. a.* cuir air chall.

mislead, *v. a.* meall.

mislike, *v. a.* bi mì-thoilichte le.

mislike, *s.* mì-thoileachadh, gràin.

misly, *adj.* ciurach, braonach.

mismanage, *v. a.* dèan droch riaghladh.

mismanagement, *s.* droch riaghladh.

misname, *v. a.* thoir frith-ainm.

misnomer, *s.* ainn mì-cheart.

misobserve, *v. a.* mì-bheachdaich.

misogamist, *s.* fuathadair pòsaidh.

misogyny, *s.* fuath bhan.

misorder, *v. a.* mì-stiùr, cuir á òrdugh.

mispersuasion, *s.* droch-iompaidh.

misplace, *v. a.* mì-shuidhich, cuir an àite cearr.

misprint, *s.* mearachd clò-bhualaidh.

misprision, *s.* tàire dearmad, dio-chuimhne, ceiltinn ; mearachd.

misproportion, *s.* mì-chuimse.

misreckon, *v. a.* dèan droch cunntadh.

misrelate, misreport, *v. a.* dèan aithris mhì-cheart.

misrepresent, *v. a.* thoir iomradh mì-cheart.

misrule, *s.* buaireas, droch riaghladh.

miss, *s.* òigh, maighdeann.

miss, *v.* mearachdaich, rach iomrall ; mi-amais ; thig gearr, caill ; ion-drainn ; leig seachad.

missal, *s.* leabhar-aifrionn.

missile, *adj.* tilgte leis an làimh.

mission, *s.* teachdaireachd.

missionary, *s.* teachdaire, searmonaiche, ministear-siubhail.

missive, *s.* litir-chumhachan, litir.

mist, *s.* ceò, citheach, ceathach, braon.

mistake, *v.* rach iomrall, mi-thuig.

mistake, *s.* mearachd, iomrall.

mistime, *v. a.* mì-thràthaich.

mistiness, *s.* ceòthachd, neulachd.

mistletoe, *s.* an t-uil-ìoc.

mistress, *s.* bana-mhaighstear ; bann-seilbheadair, bean-theagaisg, coimh-leapach.

mistrust, *s.* an-earbsa, teagamh.

mistrustful, *adj.* mì-earbsach.

mistrustfully, *adv.* gu h-an-earbsach, gu neo-dhòchasach.

misty, *adj.* ceòthach, ceòthar, citheach ; dorcha, doilleir, neulach.

misunderstand, *v. a.* mì-thuig.

misunderstanding, *s.* mì-thuigse, mear-achd, mì-bhreithneachadh, aimhreit, mì-chòrdadh.

misusage, misuse, *s.* droch bhuileachadh, mì-bhuileachadh, drochcàramh ; ni-ghnàthachadh.

mite, *s.* fineag ; dadmunn ; tùrn, an dara cuid deug do sgillinn.

mithridate, *s.* deoch-nimh-chasg.

mitigate, *v. a.* lughdaich, aotromaich ; lasaich, sàmhaich, ciùinich ; bogaich, maothaich.

mitigation, *s.* lùghdachadh, aotromach-adh ; lasachadh, sèimheachadh ; bog-achadh, maothachadh.

mitre, *s.* crùn-easbuig ; coron.

mitred, *adj.* crùnte mar easbuig.

mittens, *s.* meatagan, làmhainean.

mittimus, *s.* òrdugh prìosanachaidh.

mix, *v. a.* measgaich.

mixture, *s.* measgachadh, measgadh.

mizen-mast, *s.* an crann-deiridh.

moan, *v.* caoidh, guil, gearain, caoin, dèan cumha, dèan tuireadh.
moan, *s.* caoidh, gearan, acan, iargain, caoineadh, tuireadh.
moat, *s.* dìg, ruith uisge mar dhìdean.
mob, *s.* prasgan-buairidh, gràisg, corra-mhargaidh.
mob, *v. a.* tionail gràisg.
mobby, *v.* leann-buntàta.
mobility, *s.* gluasadachd ; gràisg.
moble, *v. a.* sgeadaich gu cearbach.
mock, *v. a.* mag, dèan fanaid.
mock, *adj.* meallta, feallsa, breugach.
mockable, *adj.* ion-fhochaideach.
mockery, *s.* sgeigeireachd, fanaid.
mode, *s.* modh, dòigh, gnè ; seòl, cumadh ; rian, gnàths.
model, *s.* cumadh ; riaghailt, tomhas.
model, *v. a.* dealbh, cùm, dèan coltach.
moderate, *adj.* ciùin, stuama, sèimh ; measarra, cuimseach ; meadhonach, cùibheasach.
moderate, *v. a.* ciùinich, ceannsaich, dèan measarra ; riaghail.
moderately, *adv.* gu fòil.
moderation, *s.* ciùineachd, stuaim.
moderator, *s.* fear-riaghlaidh.
modern, *adj.* ùr, neo-shean.
modernise, *v. a.* dèan ùr, ùraich.
modest, *adj.* nàrach, màlda, stuama ; banail, beusach, bìth.
modesty, *s.* beusachd, màldachd, stuamachd, measarrachd.
modicum, *s.* cuibhrionn bheag.
modification, *s.* atharrachadh.
modify, *v. a.* atharraich, cùm, ciùinich, taisich ; lagaich.
modish, *adj.* fasanta, nòsach.
modishness, *s.* fasantachd, nòsachd.
modulate, *v. a.* cuir fonn-ciùil air.
modulation, *s.* binneas ; gleus.
modulator, *s.* fear-gleusaidh, aibidil-ciùil.
modus, *s.* dìoladh deachaimh.
moiety, *s.* leth, leth-earrann, tuaram.
moil, *v.* eabraich, salaich, làbanaich ; sgìthich, sàraich ; oibrich 's an làth-aich, luidrich.
moist, *adj.* àitidh, bog, tais.
moisten, *v. a.* taisich, bogaich.
moistness, *s.* àitidheachd, buige.
moisture, *s.* taiseachd, fliche, buige.
mole, *s.* ball-dòrain, miun ; famh, ùir-readhadh.
mole-catcher, *s.* famhair.
molehill, *s.* famh-thòrr.
molest, *v. a.* cuir dragh air, buair.
molestation, *s.* aimheal, dragh.
molewarp, mouldwarp, *s.* famh.
mollient, *adj.* maoth, taiseachail.
mollification, *s.* maothachadh.
mollify, *v. a.* bogaich, taisich, maothaich ; ceannsaich, ciùinich ; lasaich.

molosses, molasses, *s.* druaip an t-siùcair.
molten, *part. pass.* from to melt, leaghte.
molting, moulting, *part. a.* a' cur nan itean, a' tilgeadh a' bhreunfhionnaidh, a' tilgeadh nan cabar, etc.
moly, *s.* creamh fhiadhaich.
mome, *s.* burraidh, amhlar ; post.
moment, *s.* toirt, brìgh, toradh, luach, tiota.
momentary, *adj.* gradùineach, goirid.
momentous, *adj.* cudthromach, toirteil, feumail.
monachal, *adj.* manachail.
monachism, *s.* beatha-manaich.
monarch, *s.* àrdrigh, righ.
monarchial, *adj.* àrd rìoghail.
monarchical, *adj.* riaghladh rìgheachail.
monarchy, *s.* rìoghachd.
monastery, *s.* manachainn.
monastic, *adj.* manachail.
Monday, *s.* Di-luain.
money, *s.* airgead.
moneyed, *adj.* airgeadach, beartach.
moneyless, *adj.* gun airgead, bochd.
monger, *s.* fear reic is ceannaich.
mongrel, *adj.* truaillidh, anuasal.
mongrel, *s.* cù de fhuil anuasal, plannt anuasal.
monition, *s.* earail.
monitive, *adj.* comhairleach.
monitor, *s.* comhairleach.
monitory, *adj.* comhairleach.
monitory, *s.* comhairle.
monk, *s.* manach.
monkey, *s.* ap, apa, amadan gòrach.
monkish, *adj.* manachail, aonarach.
monocular, monoculous, *adj.* lethshùil-each, aonsùileach.
monody, *s.* òran air a ghabhail le aon neach ; cumha.
monogamy, *s.* pòsadh aon bhean.
monologue, *s.* còmhradh aig fear 's e leis fhéin.
monopetalous, *adj.* aon-duilleagach.
monopolist, *s.* ceannaiche aig a bheil, a chothrom air aon bhadhar ('s gun e aig duine eile).
monosyllable, *s.* facal aon lididh.
monotony, *s.* aonfhuaim.
monotonous, *adj.* duanach, neo-bhinn.
monster, *s.* uilebheist ; ni mì-nàdurrach, ni gràineil ; cuis-uabhais.
monstrous, *adj.* mì-nàdurra ; fuathasach, uabhasach, oillteil, sgreataidh, gairs-inneach.
month, *s.* mìos, mì.
monthly, *adj.* mìosach, mìosail.
monument, *s.* barpa, càrn-cuimhne ; carragh, leac.
monumental, *adj.* barpail, càrnach.
mood, *s.* suidheachadh ; seòl, gleus dòigh, corraich, fraoch, friodh.

moody, *adj.* feargach, corrach ; gruamach, greannach, frionasach, cas, bras, tiamhaidh ; trom, muladach, brònach, dubhach.
moon, *s.* gealach, ré, mìos.
moonbeam, *s.* gath-gealaich.
moon-calf, *s.* uilebheist, burraidh.
moon-eyed, *adj.* ròspshuileach.
moonlight, *s.* solus-gealaich.
moonstruck, *adj.* mearanach.
moor, *s.* sliabh mhonadh ; càthair, mòinteach ; duine-dubh.
moor, *v.* tilg acair ; bi acraichte.
moorhen, *s.* cearc-fhraoich.
mooring, *s.* cala, acarsaid.
moorish, moory, *adj.* sliabhach ; mòinteachail, mònadail ; mar dhaoinedubha.
moorland, *s.* sliabh, cathair.
moose, *s.* an lon Americanach.
moot, *v. a.* tagair, connspaidich.
moot case or point, *s.* cùis - thagraidh theagamhach.
mooted, *adj.* spìont á bun.
mop, *s.* moibeal, maban, sguab-làir.
mope, *v. n.* bi trom, bi neo-shunntach, bi tùrsach, bi turra-chadalach.
mope, mopus, *s.* rongaire ; aisliniche.
moppet, mopsey, *s.* fear-brèige ; duinemaide ; liùbhag.
moral, *adj.* modhannail, beusach, beustheagasgail.
moral, *s.* modh, modhalachd, beus ; dheagh bheus.
moralise, *v.* dèan deagh-bheusach ; teagaisg deagh-bheusan.
moraliser, *s.* fear-dheanamh dheagh bheus, fear-teagaisg bheus.
moralist, *s.* fear-teagaisg dheagh bheus, fear-beusach.
morality, *s.* deagh beusachd, modhalachd, subhailcean.
morals, *s.* deagh-bheusan, modhannan, subhailcean.
morass, *s.* boglach, mòinteach.
morbid, *adj.* euslainteach, galarach, dubhach.
morbidness, *s.* euslainteachd, dubhachas.
morbific, *adj.* galarach, mì-fhallain.
morbose, *adj.* euslan, galarach.
mordacious, *adj.* beumach ; sgobach.
more, *adv.* ni's mò, ni bu mhò ; tuilleadh, barrachd, fòs.
more, *s.* tuilleadh, barrachd.
moreover, *adv.* os bàrr, a' bharr a thuilleadh, air so.
morion, *s.* clogaid, ceannbheairt.
morn, morning, *s.* madainn.
morose, *adj.* gruamach, mùgach.
moroseness, *s.* gruamaiche, mùgaiche, doirbhe, dùire.
morphew, *s.* leus-mùire, luibhre.
Morris-dance, *s.* Dàmhs-nan-clag.

morrow, *s.* am màireach.
morse, *s.* an t-each-mara.
morsel, *s.* gréim, criomag, crioman, mìr, bideag, rud beag.
mort, *s.* iolach séilge.
mortal, *adj.* bàsmhor ; bàsdhualach, marbhtach, sgriosail ; daonna, talmhaidh.
mortal, *s.* duine, bith-bàsmhor creutairtalmhaidh.
mortality, *s.* bàsmhorachd ; marbhtachd ; nàdur-daonna.
mortar, *s.* aol-tàthaidh ; soitheach pronnaidh, clach-chnotain ; gunna-thoirmshligean.
mortgage, *v. a.* thoir fearann no tighean seachad an geall airgeid.
mortgagee, *s.* fear a leigeas a mach airgiod air urras fearainn, no togalaichean.
mortification, *s.* grodadh, breothadh ; claoidh, doilghios.
mortify, *v.* claoidh, marbh, thoir bàs ; ceannsaich, smachdaich ; ìslich, cuir doilghios air ; breò, grod.
mortise, *s.* toll-alpaidh.
mortmain, *s.* seilbh-beatha.
mortuary, *s.* dìleab do 'n eaglais.
mosaic, mosaical, *adj.* a bhuineas do lagh agus do fhrithealadh Mhaois ; bhreacdhualadh air clachan, etc.
mosque, *s.* àit-aoraidh Mohamedanach.
mosquito, *s.* creathlag Innseanach.
moss, *s.* mòinteach, mòine ; còinneach, coinnteach, liath-sgrath.
mossy, *adj.* mòinteachail, còinneachail, coinnteachail, liathsgrathach.
most, *adj.* as mò, a' chuid as mò.
most, *s.* a' chuid as mò, a' chuid mhór, a' mhórchuid.
mostly, *adv.* mar is trice, cha mhór nach, 's beag nach.
mote, *s.* dùradan, smùirnean.
moth, *s.* leòman, raodan, cnuimh.
mother, *s.* màthair ; deasgann.
motherless, *adj.* gun mhàthair.
motherly, *adj.* màithreil ; caomh.
mothery, *adj.* deasgainneach.
mothy, *adj.* leòmanach, raodanach.
motion, *s.* gluasad, car ; deò, beatha ; siubhal, ceum ; tairgse, iarrtas, comhairle.
motionless, *adj.* neo-ghluasadach.
motive, *s.* cuspair-gluasaid, aobharbrosnachaidh.
motley, *adj.* iomdhathach, iomghnèitheach, measgaichte.
motto, *s.* facal-suaicheantais.
mould, *s.* liathtas ; ùir, talamh ; molltair, cumadair ; dealbh, cruth, cumachd.
mould, *v. a.* dealbh, riochdaich, cùm ; lobh, fàs liath.

moulder, *v.* crìon, tionndaidh gu luaithre ; fàs 'na d' luaithre.

mouldering, *part. adj.* a' tionndadh gu ùir, a' tionndadh gu smùir.

mouldiness, *s.* liathfas, cloimh-liath.

moulding, *s.* stìom-oire.

mouldy, *adj.* air liathadh, liath.

moult, *v. a.* tilg na h-itean.

mound, *s.* tòrr, tom, tolm, bruach-dhìona, fàl-sgéithe.

mount, *s.* sliabh, beinn, cnoc.

mount, *v.* dìrich, streap ; cuir air muin eich ; sgeadaich, grinnich ; éirich suas ; leum air muin eich ; rach air freiceadan.

mountain, *s.* sliabh, beinn, monadh, cruach, meall, màm, tòrr, àrd, aonach, fireach.

mountaineer, *s.* fear - sléibhe, fear-monaidh.

mountainous, *adj.* sléibhteach, beanntach, monadail, garbh.

mountebank, *s.* baothchleasaiche, lighichebréige.

mounting, *s.* spàngan-sgeadachaidh.

mourn, *v.* caoidh, caoin, guil ; bi fo bhròn, dean caoidh, bi tùrsach.

mourner, *s.* fear-bròin, fear-caoidh.

mournful, *adj.* brònach, tùrsach, muladach, dubhach, tiamhaidh.

mourning, *s.* bròn, mulad, caoidh, tuireadh, tùrsa, caoineadh, cumha ; éideadh-bròin.

mouse, *s.* luch.

mouse-ear, *s.* lus-nam-mial.

mouser, *s.* sealgair-luch.

mouth, *s.* beul, craos ; clab.

mouth, *v.* labhair àrd, glaodh, gabh làn beòil ; glac 'n ad chraos.

mouthful, *s.* lan-beòil ; balgum.

mouthless, *adj.* gun bheul.

move, *v.* gluais, atharraich, caraich ; cuir air ghluasad ; cuir iompaidh air, aom gu ; feargaich, brosnaich ; buair, luaisg ; imich, siubhail, triall, bi beò, bi gluasadach.

moveable, *adj.* so-ghluasad.

moveables, *s.* earnais, treathlaich.

moveless, *adj.* gun ghluasad.

movement, *s.* gluasad, carachadh.

moving, *part. adj.* drùidhteach, brònach.

mow, *v.* gearr, buain le fàladair ; speal, sgud, gearr sìos.

mow, *s.* cruach, tudan.

mow-burn, *s.* brachadh-dearg.

mower, *s.* spealadair.

moxa, or **moxo,** *s.* coinnteach Innseann-ach.

much, *adv.* móran, iomadh, ioma.

much, *s.* móran ; cus, ro, glé.

mucid, *adj.* sleamhainn, slìobach, ceòth-ach, àitidh, air liathadh.

mucidness, *s.* sleamhnachd, liathtachd, àiteachd.

mucilage, *s.* slamban, sleamhnachd, glaodh tana.

mucilaginous, *adj.* slambanach, slamb-ach ; barragach ; sleamhainn.

muck, *s.* inneir, mathachadh ; aolach, salchar, buachar.

muck, *v. a.* mathaich, innearaich.

muckhill, *s.* òtrach, dùnan, sitig.

muckiness, *s.* òtrach, salachar, anabas, mosaiche.

muck-worm, *s.* a' chnuimheag-bhuachair, a' chnuimh-aolaich, priompollan.

mucky, *adj.* otrachail, salach.

mucous, muculent, *adj.* ronnach, sglong-ach, smugach, slamach.

mucronated, *adj.* barra-chaol.

mucus, *s.* ronn, sglong, sglongaid.

mud, *s.* eabar, làthach, poll, clàbar.

muddiness, *s.* sal, druaipealachd.

muddle, *v. a.* cuir troimh chéile, salaich, truaill ; cuir air leth-dhaoraich, dèan froganach, dèan soganach.

muddy, *adj.* salach, drabastach ; eabar-ach ; gruamach, dorcha.

muff, *s.* mùtan, làmh-bhian.

muffle, *v.* ceil, cuir sgàil air, còmhdaich ; paisg, trus, mùch (fuam).

muffler, *s.* crabhat.

mufti, *s.* àrd-shagart Turcach, deise ghnàthaichte.

mug, *s.* soitheach òil, cuach, noigean.

muggish, muggy, *adj.* tais, fliuch, àitidh ; doilleir, mùgach.

mug-house, *s.* tigh leanna, taigh-òil.

mugwort, *s.* an liath-lus, gròban.

mulatto, *s.* neach-lachdunn, leth-bhriod.

mulberry, *s.* smeur, maol-dhearc.

mulct, *s.* ùbhladh, peanas, caidheann.

mule, *s.* muileid, muilead.

muller, *s.* bràth dhathan.

mullet, *s.* an cearbanach.

mulligrubs, *s.* an gréim-mionaich.

mullock, *s.* anabas, mosaiche.

multangular, *adj.* iomchearnach.

multifarious, *adj.* iomghneitheach, iom-chùiseach.

multifidous, *adj.* iomearrainneach.

multiform, *adj.* iomchruthach.

multiformity, *s.* iomchruthachd.

multilateral, *adj.* iomshliosach.

multilineal, *adj.* iomshreathach.

multiparous, *adj.* iomghinteach.

multipede, *s.* iomchasach.

multiplication, *s.* meudachadh.

multiplicator, *s.* am meudachair.

multiplicity, *s.* iomadachd, lìonmhorachd.

multiplier, *s.* fear-meudachaidh.

multiply, *v. a.* siolaich, lìonmhoraich ; meudaich.

multipotent, *adj.* ioma-chumhachdach, iombhuadhach.

multisonous, *adj.* iomghuthach.
multitude, *s.* mór-shluagh ; cruinneach-adh, dòmhlachadh.
multitudinous, *adj.* iom-fhillteach, lion-mhor.
multocular, *adj.* iomshùileach.
multure, *s.* meilteir, cìs, molltair.
mum ! *interj.* tosd ! éisd !
mum, *s.* seòrsa leanna.
mumble, *v.* dèan prondal bruidhne, brolaich, leth labhair.
mumbler, *s.* glugaire, fear manndach, fear-liodach.
mumm, *v. a.* dèan cluich-chidhis.
mummer, *s.* fear-cidhis, chleasaiche.
mummery, *s.* balbh-chleasachd.
mummy, *s.* corp-spìosraichte.
mump, *v. a.* cagainn ; abair gu mann-tach ; iarr déirc.
mumper, *s.* fear-iarraidh dhéirc.
mumps, *s.* gruaim, tosdfhearg, stùrd ; stuirt ; an tinneas-plocach, glòigeach.
mundane, *adj.* saoghalta, talmhaidh.
mundanity, *s.* saoghalachd.
mundation, *s.* glanadh, sgùradh.
munerary, *adj.* tìodhlacail.
municipal, *adj.* comunnach ; a bhuineas do bhaile mór.
munificence, *s.* toirbheartas.
munificent, *adj.* toirbheartach.
muniment, *s.* daingneach, dìdean ; dìon, tèarmann ; daingneachd-sgrìobhaidh, còraichean, ranntanan bann-sgrìobhte.
munition, *s.* daingneach, dìon, gach seorsa armachd.
mural, *adj.* a bhuineas do bhalla.
murder, *s.* mort.
murder, *v. a.* mort, dèan mort.
murderer, *s.* mortair.
murderous, *adj.* mortach, fuilteach.
muriatic, *adj.* saillte.
murk, *s.* moignean mheas, dorchadas.
murky, *adj.* dorcha, doilleir, dubh.
murmur, *s.* borbhan, torman, dùrdan, crònan ; monmhur, gearan, talach, cànran.
murmur, *v. a.* dèan borbhan, dèan crònan, dèan torman, dèan monmhur.
murmurer, *s.* gearanaiche, fear-talaich, fear-cànrain.
murrain, *s.* tinneas-dubh na spréidhe.
murrey, *adj.* dùbhdhearg, dùbhruadh.
muscle, *s.* féith, feith-lùthaidh.
muscoseness, muscosity, *s.* coinnteach, coinneach.
muscular, *adj.* fèitheach, neartmhor, stairbeanta, laidir.
muse, *v.* beachd-smuainich, cnuasaich, trom-smuainich.
muse, *s.* buaidh na bàrdachd ; the muses, a' cheòlraidh.
mushroom, *s.* ballag-bhuachair.
music, *s.* ceòl, binneas, fonn.

musical, *adj.* ceòlmhor, bìnn.
musician, *s.* fear-ciùil.
musing, *s.* beachd-smuainteachadh.
musk, *s.* seòrsa deagh boltraich.
musket, *s.* musg, gunna-saoighdear.
musketeer, musqueteer, *s.* saighdear-musgaide.
musketoon, *s.* gearrghunna.
musky, *adj.* cùbhraidh, boltrachail.
muslin, *s.* anart-grinn, péarluinn.
musrol, *s.* iall-sròine sréine.
mussel, *s.* feusgan, clab-dubh.
Mussulman, *s.* Mahomatanach.
must, *verb imperf.* feumaidh, feumar, 's éigin, b' éigin, 's fheudar, b' fheudar, etc.
mustaches, mustachioes, *s.* caisean-feusaig, feusag beil-àrd.
mustard, *s.* sgeallan, cas na tonnaig.
muster, *v. n.* cruinnich, co-chruinnich, truis, tionail.
muster, *s.* sealladh airm, feachdsheall-adh ; cruinneachadh, feachdthional, buidheann.
muster-master, *s.* fear-cruinneachaidh shaighdearan.
muster-roll, *s.* ainmchlàr feachd.
mustiness, *s.* liathtas, àiteachd.
musty, *adj.* àitidh, mùsgach, dongaidh, liath ; trom, lunndach.
mutability, *s.* caochlaidheachd.
mutable, *adj.* caochlaidheach.
mutation, *s.* atharrachadh.
mute, *adj.* balbh, tosdach, bìth.
mute, *s.* balbhan, balbh.
mutely, *adv.* gu tosdach.
muteness, *s.* tosdachd, balbhachd.
mutilate, *v. a.* ciurramaich, gearr dheth, sguid deth.
mutilation, *s.* ciurramachadh.
mutineer, *s.* fear-ceannairc, fear-àr-a-mach.
mutinous, *adj.* ceannairceach.
mutiny, *v. n.* dèan àr-a-mach, dèan ceannairc.
mutiny, *s.* ar-a-mach, ceannairc.
mutter, *v.* dèan dranndan, dèan dùrdan, dèan gearain, talaich.
mutton, *s.* muilt-fheoil ; caora.
mutton-fist, *s.* garbh-dhòrn-dearg.
mutual, *adj.* a réir a' chéile, aontachail, mu seach, a bhuineas do dhithis.
mutuality, *s.* co-iasad, coingheall.
muzzle, *s.* beul ; bus-iall, glas-ghuib.
muzzle, *v.* bus-iallaich, cuir glas-ghuib, glomharaich.
my, *pron. poss.* mo.
myography, *s.* féith-eòlas.
myology, *s.* féith-theagasg.
myotomy, *s.* féith-shnasadh.
myriad, *s.* àireamh dheich mìle.
myrrh, *s.* mir, spiosraidh chùraidh.

myrtle, s. miortal, lus cùbhraidh.
myself, pron. mi-féin, mise féin.
mysterious, adj. domhain, dìomhair.
mysteriously, adv. gu diamhair.
mysteriousness, s. dìomhaireachd.
mysterise, v. a. diamhairich, dorchnaich,
doileirich.

mystery, s. dìomhaireachd.
mystic, mystical, adj. dìomhair, dorcha,
do-thuigsinn.
mythological, adj. faoinsgeulach.
mythologist, s. faoinsgeulaiche.
mythology, s. faoin sgeulachd ; eachdraidh nan dia bréige.

N

nab, v. a. grad-ghlac, foill-ghlac.
nadir, s. am bad as isle do'n chruinne.
nag, v. tr. bi ghnàth a faotainn coire.
nag, s. each beag ; each òg.
nail, s. ionga ; tarung ; tomhas dhà
òirleich is cairteal.
nailer, s. gobha thàirngnean.
naïve, a. sìmplidh, leanabail.
naked, adj. lomnochd ; rùisgte, nochdaidh, gun arm ; soilleir, fosgailte, lom.
nakedness, s. nochdachd, luime, lomnochd.
name, s. ainm ; iomradh ; cliù, alla.
name, v. a. ainmich ; goir air ainm.
nameless, adj. nach faodar ainmeachadh,
gun ainm.
namely, adv. gu sònràichte.
namesake, s. fear-cinnidh, co-ainm.
nankeen, s. seòrsa do dh' aodach canaich.
nap, s. dùsal, pràmh ; cnap, caitean.
nape, s. alt a' mhuineil, alt na h-amhach.
napkin, s. neapuig, nèapaigin.
napless, adj. gun chaitean, lom.
nappy, adj. cobharach, ròmach.
narcissus, s. lus-a'-chroma-chinn.
narcotic, adj. cadalach, tuainealach,
breisleachail.
narrable, adj. so-aithris.
narrate, v. a. innis, aithris.
narration, s. aithris, sgeul, iomradh,
tuaireasgeul.
narrative, adj. aithriseach, innseach.
narrator, s. fear-aithris, fear-innsidh,
fear-eachdraidh, seanachaidh.
narrow, adj. cumhann, àimhleathan,
caol, sanntach ; spìocach, mosach.
narrowly, adv. gu cumhann.
narrow-minded, adj. sanntach, spìocach,
beag-aigneach, cumhang ; air bheag
eòlais. neo-charthannach.
narrowness, s. cuingead, bochdainn,
spìocaireachd.
nasal, adj. glòmach, bhuineas do'n
t-sròin, smotach.
nascent, a. aig ire breth ; anabaich ; air
tì tòischeachadh.
nastily, adv. gu salach, gu truaillidh,
gu drabasta.
nastiness, s. trustaireachd ; drabastachd,
draosdachd, salachar.

nasty, adj. salach, mosach, truaillidh.
natal, adj. bhuineas do là-breith.
nation, s. fine, cinneadh, cinneach,
sluagh, muinntir, dùthaich, rìoghachd.
national, adj. dùthchasach, dùthchail
cinneadail.
native, adj. nàdurrach, gnèitheil ; dùthchasach, dualach.
native, s. dùthchasaiche ; pl. natives,
gnà-mhuinntir.
nativity, s. breith ; tìr-bhreith.
natural, adj. nàdurrach, nàdurra ; gnèitheil ; dàimheil, caoimhneil ; tlàth,
dìolain.
natural, s. amadan, staid nàduir.
naturalisation, s. dèanamh dùthchasach
de choigreach.
naturalise, v. a. thoir sochairean dùthchasach.
naturalist, s. fear-eòlais nàdurra.
naturally, adv. gu nàdurrach.
naturalness, s. nàdurrachd.
nature, s. nàdur, gnè, seòrsa ; càil ;
mèinn ; an domhan, an cruthachadh ;
dàimh, nàdurrachd.
naught, s. neoni, beag luach, beag
maith.
naughtiness, s. drochmheinn, olcas.
naughty, adj. olc, aingidh, dona, truaillidh, crosda, droch.
nausea, s. togradh gu dìobhairt, gòmadh.
nauseate, v. gre ataich ; cuir sgreat air,
gabh sgreat roimh.
nauseous, adj. sgreataidh, sgreamhail,
déisinneach, gràineil.
nauseousness, s. sgreamhalachd, deis-
inneachd, sgreatachd, gràin.
nautical, adj. fairgeach, cuanach.
naval, adj. longach, cabhlachail.
nave, s. cìoch, cuibhle ; meadhon
eaglais.
navel, s. imleag ; meadhon.
navigable, adj. so-sheòladh, domhainn.
navigableness, s. doimhneachd-uisge.
navigate, v. a. seòl long.
navigation, s. maraireachd, sgoil-mhara.
navigator, s. maraiche, sgoilear-mara.
navy, s. cabhlach, luingeas-chogaidh.
navvy, s. fear-oibreach, fear-cladhach aig
rathad, etc.

nay, *adv.* ni h-eadh.
neaf, *s.* dòrn.
neal, *v. a.* dèan tais no cruaidh le blàthas teine ; adhairt.
neap-tide, *s.* conntraigh.
near, nearly, *adv.* fagus, faisg, aig làimh, dlùth ; an dàimh, an cleamhnas.
near, *adj.* faisg, dlùth, fagus, teann ; dàimheil ; gann, spìocach.
nearness, *s.* fagusachd, dlùthachd, faisgeachd ; dàimh, dìlseachd ; gainne, spìocaireachd, gortachd.
neat, *adj.* snasmhor, grinn, cuimir.
neatly, *adv.* gu snasmhor.
neatness, *s.* snasmhorachd, grinneas, sgiultachd.
neb, *s.* gob eòin, beul.
nebulous, *adj.* neulach, ceòthach.
necessaries, *s.* feumalachdan, goireasan.
necessary, *adj.* feumail, goireasach ; dualach, neo-sheachanta.
necessary, *s.* tigh-fuagairt.
necessitate, *v. a.* éignich.
necessitous, *adj.* àimbeartach, feumach, bochd.
necessitude, *s.* aimbeart, gainne.
necessity, *s.* airc, éigin, aimbeart, do-sheachnaidheachd ; dàn.
neck, *s.* muineal, amhach.
neckcloth, *s.* éideadh muineil.
necked, *adj.* muinealach, sgòrnanach.
necklace, *s.* usgar-bràgaid, seud-muineil ; paidearan.
necromancer, *s.* taracadair, fiosaiche, fàidh draoidh.
necromancy, *s.* taracandachd, drùidheachd, fiosachd.
necromantic, *adj.* fiosachdail.
nectar, *s.* deoch mhilis nan dia bréige, deoch fìor bhlasda.
nectareous, nectarine, *adj.* milis, mar dheoch nan diathan bréige.
nectarine, *s.* seòrsa plùmbais.
nectary, *s.* cuach-mhile nam flùran.
need, neediness, *s.* dìth, feum, easbhuidh, airc.
need, *v.* feum ; bi a dhìth, bi feumach.
needful, *adj.* feumach, bochd, truagh, ainniseach.
needle, *s.* snàthad ; bior-gréisidh, dealg na cairt-iùil.
needlemaker, *s.* gobha-shnàthad.
needless, *adj.* gun fheum, dìomhain.
needlework, *s.* obair-ghréis.
needs, *adv.* feumaidh, 's éigin.
needy, *adj.* bochd, ainniseach, feumach, dòghlum.
nefarious, *adj.* ro-aingidh, mallaichte, uamhar, gràineil, fuathasach.
negation, *s.* diùltadh, àicheadh.
negative, *adj.* diùltach, àicheanach.
negative, *s.* am facal-àicheadh, (*mar.* neo-, ni-cha),

negatively, *adv.* gu h-àicheadhach.
neglect, *v. a.* dèan dearmad ; cuir suarach, dèan tàir, cuir an neo-shùim.
neglect, *s.* dearmad ; dìmeas, tàir, neo-shùim, mì-chùram.
neglectful, *adj.* dearmadach, neo-chùramach ; dìmeasach, neo-shuimeil.
negligence, *s.* dearmad.
negligent, *adj.* dearmadach, neo-aireil, mì-chùramach.
negotiate, *v. n.* dèan gnothach, thoir gu buil, thoir gu h-ìre.
negotiation, *s.* co-ghnothach, cùmhnant, socrachadh, conaltradh gnothuich.
negro, *s.* duine-dubh.
neigh, *s.* sitir.
neigh, *v. n.* dèan sitir, dèan sitrich.
neighbour, *s.* coimhearsnach, nàbaidh.
neighbour, *adj.* coimhearsnachail, nàbaidheach, dlùth.
neighbourhood, *s.* nàbaidheachd, nàbachd, coimhearsnachd ; luchd - coimhears-nachd.
neighbourly, *adj.* coingheallach, càirdeil.
neither, *conj.* cha, cha mhò, chan e, ni mò, ni h-è, etc.
nemoral, *adj.* badanach, doireach.
neoteric, *adj.* ùr, nodha, nuadh.
nepenthe, *s.* iocshlaint leigheis nan uile phian, etc.
nephew, *s.* mac peathar no bràthar.
nephritic, *adj.* àirneach ; leigheasach air a' ghalar-fhuail.
nerve, *s.* féith-mhothachaidh.
nerve, *v. a.* neartaich, lùghaich, spionntaich.
nerveless, *adj.* gun lùth, gun bhrìgh, gun seadh, gun bhladh.
nervous, nervy, *adj.* mion-mhothachail, féitheach ; neartmhor, lùghmhor, critheanach, iomnuidheach.
nervousness, *s.* féith-laigseachd, crith-miapadh.
nescience, *s.* ain-fhios, aineolas.
nest, *s.* nead ; còs, còmhnaidh.
nest-egg, *s.* ubh-nid.
nestle, *v. n.* neadaich, crùb sìos, gabh fasgadh, laigh clùth ; cuir an nead, cuir an còs ; eiridnich.
nestling, *s.* isean, eun òg 's an nead.
net, *s.* lìon, eangach, ribe.
nether, *adj.* ìochdrach.
nethermost, *adj.* as ìochdraiche.
netting, *s.* obair-lìn, lìon-obair.
nettle, *s.* feanntag, deanntag.
nettle, *v. a.* brosnaich, feargaich.
neurotomy, *s.* gearradh-fhéithean.
neuter, neutral, *adj.* neo-phàirteach, nach buin do thaobh seach taobh ; eadarra-cheathairn.
neutrality, *s.* neo-phàirteachd.
never, *adv.* gu bràth, gu suthainn, gu dìlinn, a chaoidh ; riamh, am feasd.

nevertheless, *conj.* gidheadh.
new, *adj.* ùr, nuadh ; annasach.
newfangled, *adj.* mùirneach mu annasaibh, no fasanan ùra.
newish, *adj.* breac-ùr, a leth-char ùr.
newly, *adv.* gu h-ùr, gu h-ùrail.
newness, *s.* ùrachd, nuadhachd.
news, *s.* naidheachd, ursgeul.
newsmonger, *s.* fear-naidheachd.
newspaper, *s.* pàipear-naidheachd.
newt, *s.* arc-luachrach bheag.
next, *adj.* as faisge, dlùithe.
next, *adv.* anns an ath àite ; a rithist, an déigh sin.
nib, *s.* gob eòin, rinn snàthaid, peann.
nibbed, *adj.* gobach, srònach.
nibble, *v.* spiol, créim, teum, tiolp.
nice, *adj.* poncail, faicilleach, eagnaidh ; eagallach, fiamhach, amharusach ; grinn, innealta ; duilich, deacair ; aralach, blasda ; àluinn, taitneach.
niceness, *s.* eagnaidheachd, poncalachd, aralachd.
nicety, *s.* poncalachd ; grinneas, innealtachd ; cùram, faicilleachd ; mùirn, mùirnealachd.
niche, *s.* oisinn, cùil, fròg.
nick, *s.* eag.
nick, *v. a.* amais, buail dìreach ; eagaich ; thoir an car, meall.
nickname, *s.* frithainm, farainm, leasainm, aithnisg.
nickname, *v.* thoir frithainm.
niece, *s.* nighean bràthar no peathar.
niggard, *s.* spìocaire, fineag.
niggard, niggardly, *adj.* spìocach, mosach, cruaidh, gann, gortach, sanntach, lom.
niggardish, *adj.* a lethchar spìocach, rud eigin cruaidh.
niggardliness, *s.* spìocaireachd.
nigh, nighly, *adv.* fagus do, goirid o, làimh ri, dlùth, an taice.
night, *s.* oidhche, dorchadas.
nightcap, *s.* currac-oidhche.
nightdew, *s.* braon-oidhche.
nightdress, *s.* eideadh-oidhche.
nightfire, *s.* teine-fionn, teine-sionnachain, teine-bianain.
nightingale, *s.* an spìdeag.
nightly, *adv.* gach oidhche.
night-man, *s.* fear-cartaidh.
nightmare, *s.* an trom-lighe.
nightshade, *s.* lus-na-h-oidhche.
night-warbling, *s.* ceilleireachd-oidhche, canntaireachd-oidhche.
night-watch, *s.* faire na h-oidhche.
nigrescent, *adj.* a' fàs dorcha, dorganta, dubh.
nimble, *adj.* luath, lùthmhor, clis.
nimble-footed, *adj.* lùthchasach.
nimbleness, *s.* luaths, clise.
nine, *adj.* naodh, naoidh, naoi.

ninefold, *s.* naoidh-fillte.
nineteen, *adj.* naoidh-deug.
ninety, *adj.* ceithir fichead 's a deich.
ninny, ninny-hammer, *s.* lethchiallach, baothbhallan, amadan.
ninth, *adj.* an naodhamh.
ninthly, *adv.* anns an naodhamh àite.
nip, *v. a.* spiol, pioc, teum, thoir greim á.
nip, *s.* bìd, bìdeag, gòmag ; osag, onfhadh ; beum.
nippers, *s.* turcais ; greimiche.
nipple, *s.* sine ; ceann na cìche.
nit, *s.* sneagha, sneamh.
nitid, *adj.* soilleir, boillsgeach, dèarsach, soillseach.
nitre, *s.* mearshalunn.
nitrous, *adj.* mearshailt.
nitty, *adj.* sneaghach.
nival, *adj.* sneachdach, làn sneachda.
niveous, *adj.* sneachdaidh, sneachdagheal ; geal mar shneachda.
nizy, *s.* guarraiceach, tamhasg.
no, *adv.* ni, cha, chan e ; chan'ann, chan'eil, ni h-eadh, etc.
no, *adj.* air bith, neach sam bith, aon, sam bith.
nobility, *s.* àrd-uaisleachd, àrd-uaislean ; maithean, mór-uaislean ; àrd-urram, mórachd.
noble, *adj.* uasal, flathail ; mór, àrd, allail, urramach ; fiùghantach, fial.
noble, *s.* àrd-uasal, morair, flath.
nobleman, *s.* àrd-dhuin-uasal, morair, maith ; *plur.* maithean.
nobleness, *s.* àrd-uaisleachd, flathalachd, fiallach.
noblesse, *s.* uaislean tìr chéin.
nobly, *adv.* gu mórdha, gu h-allail.
nocent, nocive, *adj.* ciontach, coireach ; cronail, àimhleasach, dochannach, ciùrrail.
noctambulist, *s.* coisiche-cadail, fear a bhios a' coiseachd 'na chadal.
noctuary, *s.* cunntas-oidhche.
nocturn, *s.* cràbhadh-oidhche.
nocturnal, *adj.* oidhcheach.
nod, *v.* aom, claon ; crith, crithich, lùb, crom, dean cromadh cinn ; dèan turrachadal.
noddle, *s.* claigeann gun chiall.
noddy, noodle, *s.* buamasdair, burraidh, bàirisg, ùmaidh.
node, *s.* meall, cnap, snaim.
nodous, *adj.* cnapanach, meallanach.
noggin, *s.* noigean, gogan.
noise, *s.* fuaim, farum, tartar, toirm, torman ; glaodh, gleadhar, sgread, iolach, gàir ; buaireas.
noiseless, *adj.* neo-fhuaimneach.
noisiness, *s.* fuaimneachd, farumachd, gleadhrachd, tartarachd, bruidhneachd.

noisome, *adj.* cronail, ciurrail, aimh-leasach ; neo-fhallain ; sgreataidh, sgreamhail, déisinneach.

noisy, *adj.* fuaimneach, farumach, tar-tarach, gleadhrach, buaireasach.

nolition, *s.* aindeonachd, aindeoin.

nombles, *s.* grealach féidh.

nomenclature, *s.* facalair-ainm.

nominal, *adj.* ainmeach, an ainm a mhàin.

nominate, *v. a.* gairm air ainm.

nomination, *s.* còir ainmeachaidh.

nominee, *s.* neach-ainmichte.

nonage, *s.* ògaois, aois-leanabais.

non-appearance, *s.* neo-theachd-an-lath-air ; fuireach air falbh.

non-compliance, *s.* diùltadh.

nonconformist, *s.* fear-àicheadh eaglais stéidhichte.

nonconformity, *s.* neo-aontachd.

nondescript, *adj.* neo-shloinnte, creutar gun diù.

none, *adj.* chan . . . aon, neach, ni, neach sam bith, ni sam bith ; a' bheag.

nonentity, *s.* neo-bhith, creutar gun tùr — gun tulchuis.

nonesuch, *s.* òirdhearcas, ainm ubhail àraidh.

non-existence, *s.* neo-bhitheachd.

nonjuror, *s.* fear-diùltaidh dìlseachd do 'n rìgh dhligheach.

nonpareil, *s.* barrachd, òirdheirceas, meanbh-litir clò-bhualaidh.

nonplus, *s.* imcheist.

nonplus, *v. a.* cuir an imcheist.

non-resident, *s.* fear á dhùthaich féin, fear o'n bhaile.

non-resident, *adj.* neo-chòmhnaidheach, air choigrich.

non-resistance, *s.* làn-ghéill.

non-resistant, *adj.* làn-ghéilleach.

nonsense, *s.* neo-sheadh, bòilich.

nonsensical, *adj.* neo-sheadhach.

nonsparing, *adj.* neo-thròcaireach.

nonsuit, *v. a.* cuir stad air cùis lagha.

nook, *s.* cùil, oisinn, cèarn.

noon, *s.* ard-mheadhon-latha.

noonday, noontide, *s.* nòin, meadhon-latha, àird' an làtha.

noose, *s.* lùb-ruith, snaim-ruith.

noose, *v. a.* snàim, rib, ceangal pòsaidh.

nor, *conj.* no, ni mò, ni's mò, na's mò, cha mhò.

normal, *adj.* riaghailteach, gnàthach.

north, *s.* an àirde-tuath ; tuath.

north-east, *s.* an àird' an ear-thuath.

northerly, northern, northward, *adj.* tuathach, tuath, á tuath.

north-star, *s.* reull na h-àirde tuath.

northward, *adv.* mu thuath.

north-west, *s.* an àird' an iar-thuath.

Norwegian, *s.* and *adj.* Lochlannach.

nose, *s.* sròn ; fàile, sicireachd.

nose, *v.* srònaisich, gabh, fàile.

nosegay, *s.* giobag bhlàth-luibhean.

nosology, *s.* eòlas ghalaran.

nostril, *s.* cuinnean, pollair.

nostrum, *s.* leigheas dìomhair.

not, *adv.* cha, ni, chan e, ni h-eadh.

notable, *adj.* ainmeil, sònraichte.

notableness, *s.* ainmealachd.

notary, *s.* nòtair, fear-lagha.

notation, *s.* pùngachadh, cur sìos.

notch, *s.* and *v. tr.* eag, gàg, peasg.

note, *s.* comharradh ; fios, aire ; inbhe, cliù, iomradh ; mìchliu, tàir ; pong-chiùil ; cuimhneachan ; litir bheag ; bann, bann-sgrìobhte ; mìneachadh.

note, *v. a.* comharraich, cuir sìos, thoir fainear, beachdaich.

noted, *part.* àinmeil, sònraichte.

notedness, *s.* ainmealachd.

noteless, *adj.* neo-ainmeil.

nothing, *s.* neoni.

nothingness, *s.* neonitheachd.

notice, *s.* aire, beachd ; fios, sanas.

notice, *v. a.* beachdaich, thoir fainear, thoir an aire.

notification, *s.* cur an céill, rabhadh, bàirligeadh.

notify, *v. a.* cuir an céill, foillsich, thoir fios.

notion, *s.* breithneachadh, smuain.

notional, *adj.* inntinneach, beachdach.

notoriety, *s.* fiosrachadh follaiseach, ainm gun tairbh.

notorious, *adj.* comharraichte ainmeil, suaicheanta, comharraichte 's an olc.

notus, *s.* a' ghaoth a deas.

notwithstanding, *conj.* gidheadh.

nought, *s.* neoni.

nourish, *v. a.* àraich, tog, eiridnich.

nourishable, *adj.* so-àraich, so-thogail, so-bheathachadh.

nourishment, *s.* beathachadh, àrach.

novel, *adj.* nuadh, annasach, ùr.

novelist, *s.* ùr-sgeulaiche.

novelty, *s.* ùrachd, annas.

November, *s.* ceud-mhìos a' gheamh-raidh.

novercal, *adj.* muimeach.

novice, *s.* neach neo-theòma, neach aìneolach, ùr-chreideach, iompachan òg.

now, *adv.* a nise, an dràsta, an ceartuair, 's an àm so, 'sa' cheart àm, air an uair.

nowadays, *adv.* anns na làithibh so.

nowhere, *adv.* an àite sam bith (with a preceding negative).

nowise, *adv.* idir, air dòigh sam bith : requiring a negative to precede.

noxious, *adj.* ciurrail, cronail, doch-annach ; neo-fhallain.

noxiousness, *s.* dochannachd, neo-fhall-aineachd.

nozzle, *s.* smeachan, bus, gnos.

nubble, v. a. cnadan, caoran.
nubiferous, adj. neulach.
nubilate, v. a. neulaich, dorchaich.
nubile, adj. aig aois pòsaidh.
nuciferous, adj. cnòdhach, cnùdhach.
nucleus, s. eitean, mathair-iongarach.
nudation, s. lomadh, rùsgadh.
nude, adj. lom, rùisgte, lomnochd.
nudity, s. lomnochdas, luime.
nugacity, nugality, s. gusgul, briot, pronna-ghlòir.
nugatory, adj. faoin, diamhain, baoth, gun fhiù.
nuisance, s. trusdaireachd, salachar, dragh.
null, adj. neo-stàthach, gun fheum.
nullity, s. neo-thairbhe; neo-bhìth.
numb, adj. fuar, rag, rag le fuachd.
numb, v. a. meilich, ragaich le fuachd.
number, v. a. cunnt, dean suas.
number, s. àireamh, cunntas, uimhir, iomadaidh fonn, rannachd.
numberer, s. fear-àireamh.
numberless, adj. gun-àireamh.
numbness, s. marbhfhuachd; leitheadh.
numerable, adj. so-àireamh.
numeral, adj. àireamhach.
numerary, adj. a bhuineas do àireamh.
numeration, s. àireamhachadh.
numerator, s. fear-àireamh.
numerical, adj. àireamhail.
numerous, adj. lìonmhor, iomadaidh, iomadach.
nummary, adj. a bhuineas do chuinneadh.
numskull, s. ploccheann, amadan.

nun, s. cailleach-dhubh, piuthar-bhochd.
nuncio, s. teachdaire o'n Phàpa.
nuncupative, nuncupatory, adj. a chuireas an céill gu follaiseach, le càinnt beòil.
nunnery, s. tigh chailleacha-dubha.
nuptial, adj. a bhuineas do phòsadh.
nuptials, s. pòsadh, banais.
nurse, s. banaltrum, bean-eiridnidh.
nurse, v. a. altrum, àraich, eiridnich.
nursery, s. gàradh-altrum; seòmar-altrum, seòmar cloinne.
nursing, s. banaltrumachd.
nursling, s. dalta, ban-dalta.
nurture, s. àrach, teachd-an-tìr, lòn, oilean; fòghlum.
nurture, v. a. àraich, tog suas, teagaisg, fòghlum, ionnsaich.
nustle, v. a. caidrich; cniadaich.
nut, s. cnò, cìoch cuibhle.
nutation, s. clisgeadh, oilt-chrith.
nutgall, s. am buicean-daraich.
nutmeg, s. a' chnò-mheannt.
nutrication, s. seòl-beathachaidh.
nutricious, nutritive, adj. beathachail, àrachail.
nutriment, s. beathachadh, lòn.
nutrimental, adj. beathachail, biadhar, àrachail.
nutrition, s. buaidh-àraich.
nutriture, s. biadhadh, beathachadh, àrach.
nut-tree, s. craobh-chnò.
nuzzle, v. a. falaich do cheann mar ni leanabh.
nymph, s. ban-dia nan coilltean, ainnir, rìbhinn, maighdean.

O

O! interj. O! a!
oaf, s. amadan, ùmaidh, ònaid.
oafish, adj. baoth, amadanach.
oafishness, s. baoghaltachd.
oak, s. darag, darach.
oak-apple, s. cnò-dharaich.
oaken, adj. daraich, de dharach.
oakling, s. ògdharach.
oakum, s. calcas.
oar, s. ràmh, suaibe.
oar, v. iomair, dean iomaradh.
oatcake, s. bonnach-coirce.
oaten, adj. corcach, coirceach, coirce.
oath, s. mòid, boid, mionnan.
oath-breaking, s. eitheach.
oatmalt, s. braich-choirce.
oatmeal, s. min choirce.
oats, s. corc, coirc, coirce.
obambulation, s. coiseachd mun cuairt, cuairtiomachd.
obcordate, adj. air cumadh cridhe.

obduce, v. a. còmhdaich thairis.
obduction, s. còmhdachadh.
obduracy, s. cruas-cridhe, neo-aithreachas, rag-mhuinealas.
obdurate, adj. cruaidh-chridheach, rag-mhuinealach, neo-aithreachail, reasgach.
obdurately, adv. gu neo-ghéilleach, gu neo-umhailte.
obduration, obdurateness, s. rag-mhuinealas, cruas-cridhe.
obedience, s. ùmhlachd, géill.
obedient, adj. ùmhail, so-riaghladh.
obediential, adj. ùmhlachdail.
obeisance, s. fàilte, ùmhlachd, beic.
obelisk, s. carragh-cuimhne àrd, biorach.
obese, adj. reamhar, meath, culach.
obey, v. a. strìochd, géill, freagair.
obiit, s. bhàsaich e'.
obituary, s. clàr-innsidh nam marbh, gearr iomradh air duine marbh.

object, s. cuspair, nì, cùis, crìoch.
object, v. a. cuir an aghaidh, diùlt.
objection, s. cur an aghaidh tagradh ; fàth-gearain, coire, talach.
objective, adj. cuspaireach, cùiseach.
objector, s. fear-diùltaidh.
objuration, s. bòid-cheangail.
objurgate, v. a. cronaich, trod.
objurgation, s. achmhasan, trod.
objurgatory, adj. achmhasanach.
oblation, s. tabhartas, ìobairt.
obligation, s. ceangal, còir, dleasanas ; cùmhnant ; comain.
obligatory, adj. ceangaltach, cùmhnantach, comaineach.
oblige, v. a. cuir mar fhiachaibh air, thoir air ; cuir fo chomain, cuir comain air.
obligee, s. neach fo chomain.
obliging, adj. coingheallach, suairce.
oblique, adj. neo-dhìreach, siar, fiar.
obliqueness, obliquity, s. fiaradh, siaradh, camadh, cromadh ; claonadh, cluaintearachd.
obliterate, v. a. dubh a mach, mill.
obliteration, s. dubhadh as, milleadh.
oblivion, s. diochuimhne ; mathanas.
oblivious, adj. dìochuimhneach.
obloquy, s. coire, cùlchainnt, masladh.
obmutescence, s. balbhachd reasgach.
obnoxious, adj. buailteach do, gràineil.
obol, s. bonn airgid Greugach, mu 1½d.
obscene, adj. draosda, drabasda, neoghlan truaillidh, salach ; déisinneach, sgreataidh.
obscenity, s. draosdachd, drabasdachd, neo-ghlaine.
obscuration, s. doilleireachd, duirche.
obscure, adj. dorcha, doilleir, dubharach ; uaigneach, falaichte ; deacair, dìomhair ; neo-ainmeil.
obscure, v. a. dorchaich, doilleirich, neulaich ; ceil, falaich ; sgàilich, dean deacair.
obscureness, obscurity, s. duirche, doilleireachd ; uaigneas ; deacaireachd, doirbheachd.
obsecration, s. achanaich.
obsequies, s. seirbhis-tiodhlaicidh.
obsequious, adj. ùmhail, strìochdail.
obsequiousness, s. strìochdalachd.
observable, adj. so-fhaicinn, comharraite ; soillir.
observably, adv. gu comharraite.
observance, s. modh, urram, ùmhlachadh ; aoradh, gnàth-aoradh ; aire, faicill, cùram ; riaghailt ; spéis, meas.
observant, adj. aireil, faicilleach, cùramach ; spéis-thabhartach.
observation, s. beachd, beachdachadh, dearcadh, aire, toirt-fainear ; sealladh,

amharc ; fiosrachadh ; deas-ghnàthachadh, frithealadh.
observator, observer, s. fear-amhairc, fear-aire, fear-coimheid, fear-beachdachaidh.
observatory, s. tigh-amharc na speur.
observe, v. beachdaich, seall, amhairc ; thoir fainear, fiosraich ; fritheil, faic ; bi air t' fhaicill.
obsession, s. séisd, séisdeadh.
obsolete, adj. á cleachdadh.
obstacle, s. grabadh, bacadh, cnapstarra ; ball-toirmisg.
obstinacy, s. rag-mhuinealas.
obstinate, adj. ceann-laidir, rag.
obstinately, adv. gu reasgach.
obstinateness, s. rag-mhuinealachd.
obstreperous, adj. gleadhrach, rag, ceannasach.
obstriction, s. daingneachadh, bann.
obstruct, v. a. bac, dùin suas.
obstruction, s. ceap-starra, bacadh ; ball-toirmisg.
obstructive, adj. grabach, amlach.
obstruent, adj. grabanta, éiseil.
obtain, v. a. buannaich, coisinn, faigh ; mair, buanaich ; bi seasmhach.
obtainable, adj. so-fhaotainn.
obtainment, s. buannachadh, cosnadh, faotainn.
obtemperate, v. a. strìochd, géill.
obtend, v. a. cuir an aghaidh, cum a mach.
obtenebration, s. dorchadas, duibhre, doillearachd.
obtention, s. cur an aghaidh.
obtest, v. aslaich, guidh, grìos.
obtestation, s. aslachadh, grìosad.
obtrectation, s. cùl-chàineadh.
obtrude, v. a. rach gun chuireadh.
obtruder, s. sgimilear.
obtrusion, s. sgimilearachd.
obtrusive, adj. sgimilearach.
obtund, v. a. maolaich ; lagaich.
obtuse, adj. maol, neo-gheur ; clodcheannach, marbhanta, tromcheannach.
obtusely, adv. gun rinn, maol.
obtuseness, s. maoile, neo-ghéire.
obtusion, s. maoladh.
obverse, adj. air a bheul-fodha.
obvert, v. a. tionndaidh chuige.
obviate, v. a. thig 'san rathad, bac, grab, coinnich.
obvious, adj. soilleir, furasda ; réidh.
obviousness, s. soilleireachd.
occasion, s. tuiteamas, tachartas, cothrom, fàth, àm ; aobhar ; feum.
occasion, v. a. aobharaich, tàrmaich ; thoir mu'n cuairt.
occasional, adj. tachartach, air uairibh, tuiteamach.

occasionally, *adv.* an dràsd 's a rithist, air uairibh.

occident, *s.* an iar, an airde 'n iar.

occidental, occiduous, *adj.* iar, siar, iarach.

occiput, *s.* cùl a' chinn.

occlude, *v. a.* dùin suas.

occult, *adj.* dìomhair, falaichte.

occultation, *s.* reullfhalach.

occultness, *s.* dìomhaireachd.

occupancy, *s.* séilbhghabhail.

occupant, *s.* fear-sealbhachaidh, fear-àiteachaidh.

occupate, *v. a.* gabh séilbh.

occupation, *s.* obair, dreuchd, ceaird, gnothach.

occupier, *s.* fear-séilbhe, sealbhadair.

occupy, *v.* gabh sealbh, séilbhich, gléidh ; saoithrich, gnàthaich, caith ; lean ; cuir gu buil.

occur, *v. n.* thig 's a chuimhne ; thig 's an rathad ; tachair.

occurrence, *s.* tachartas, tuiteamas.

ocean, *s.* cuan, lear, fairge, muir, aibheis.

ocellated, *adj.* sùileach, coltach ri sùil.

ochre, *s.* ruadhchailc, cailc-dhatha.

ochreous, *adj.* ruadh-chailceach.

octagon, *s.* ochdshlisneag.

octagonal, *adj.* ochdchearnach.

octangular, *adj.* ochd-oisinneach.

octavo, *adj.* ochd-dhuilleagach, tomhais leabhair.

octennial, *adj.* ochdbhliadhnach.

October, *s.* Mios deireannach an fhoghair.

octonocular, *adj.* ochdshùileach.

octopetalous, *adj.* ochdbhileach.

octuple, *adj.* ochd-fhillteach.

ocular, *adj.* fo shealladh sùl.

oculist, *s.* léigh-shùl, sùil-léigh.

odd, *adj.* còrr, gàbhaidh, neònach, ioghantach ; sònraichte.

oddity, *s.* neònachas, neach iongantach, annas.

oddness, *s.* còrr, neo-ghnàthachd.

odds, *s.* barrachdas ; lamh an uachdar ; tuasaid, sabaid, carraid.

ode, *s.* duanag, luinneag, rann.

odious, *adj.* fuathmhor, gràineil.

odiousness, *s.* fuathmhorachd.

odium, *s.* fuath, gamhlas, coire.

odoriferous, *adj.* cùbhraidh.

odorous, *adj.* boltrachail, cùbhraidh.

odour, *s.* cùbhraidheachd, bòladh.

œcumenical, *adj.* coitcheann.

o'er, *adv.* contracted from **over**, thall.

of, *prep.* de dhe, a ; o ; mu, mu dhéibh-inn ; á, as ; am measg.

off, *adv.* dheth ; as ; air cùl.

off, *interj.* air falbh ! teich as mo shealladh ! as m' fhianais !

off, *prep.* de, dhe ; o.

offal, *s.* spruilleach, fuighleach, dràib, blionach, mionach.

offence, *s.* cionta, coire, drochbheart ; oilbheum, tàmailt ; ionnsaidh, ruathar.

offenceful, *adj.* cronail, ciùrrail ; oil-bheumach, tàmailteach.

offenceless, *adj.* neo-oilbheumach.

offend, *v.* feargaich, brosnaich ; thoir ionnsaigh, buail ; dèan coire.

offender, *s.* ciontach, coireach.

offensive, *adj.* oilbheumach ; dochannach cronail ; ionnsaigheach ; mì-thait-neach, fuathmhor.

offensiveness, *s.* cron, dochair ; gràineal-achd, fuathmhorachd.

offer, *v.* tairg ; ìobair ; nochd, tòisich ; thig 's an làthair, bi am fagus ; thoir ionnsaigh.

offer, *s.* tairgse.

offering, *s.* tabhartas, ìobairt.

offertory, *s.* tabhartas ; ionad-tasgaidh iobairtean.

office, *s.* seirbhis, feum ; gnothach, obair ; seòmar-gnothaich.

officer, *s.* oifigeach.

official, *adj.* dreuchdail, le ùghdaras.

officiate, *v.* coimhlion ; fritheil.

officious, *adj.* draghail, a' tairgse comh-nadh gun iarraidh, bleideil.

officiousness, *s.* bleidealachd.

offing, *s.* bàgh ; mach o chladach.

offscouring, *s.* anabas, salchar.

offset, *s.* meangan, fiùran, ùr-fhàs.

offspring, *s.* iarmad, sliochd, sìol, àl, gineal, clann.

oft, often, oftentimes, ofttimes, *adv.* gu tric, gu minig.

often, *adj.* tric, minig, iomadh uair.

ogee, ogive, *s.* seòrsa do bhreac-dhualadh air clachan aitribh.

ogle, *v. n.* claon-amhairc, caog.

ogling, *s.* claonamharc, caogadh.

oh ! *interj.* o ! och ! mo thruaighe !

oil, *s.* ola, ùilleadh, eòlan.

oil, *v. a.* olaich, ùill, ùillich.

oiliness, *s.* olachd, ùillidheachd.

oily, *adj.* olach, ùilleach.

ointment, *s.* ola-ungaidh, ola-leighis, acuinn, sàbh.

old, olden, *adj.* sean, aosmhor aosda ; àrsaidh.

old-fashioned, *adj.* sean-ghnàthach.

oldish, *adj.* a lethchar sean, seanacharr.

oldness, *s.* seanachd, aosdachd.

oleaginous, oleose, oleous, *adj.* eòlanach, ùilleach.

olfactory, *adj.* fàileach, fàileanta.

oligarchy, *s.* dòigh-riaghlaidh stàta.

olivaster, *adj.* lachdunn, riabhach.

olive, *s.* crann-ola, dearcan-ola, meas a' chroinn ola.

ombre, *s.* cluich triùir air chairtean.

omega, *s.* an litir dheireannach do'n aibidil Ghreugaich, deireadh, crìoch.

omelet, *s.* sgreabhag, bonnach-uibhe.

omen, *s.* manadh, roimh-chomharradh.
omer, *s.* tomhas Eabhreach thrì pinnt.
ominate, *v.* fàisnich, roimh-innis.
ominous, *adj.* droch-thargrach, bagarach.
omission, omittance, *s.* dearmad, dì-chuimhn, neo-chùram, neo-aire.
omit, *v. a.* dearmaid, dìochuimhnich ; fàg as, fàg a mach.
omnific, *adj.* uile-dhèanadach.
omniform, *adj.* uile-chruthach.
omnigenous, *adj.* uile-ghnèitheach.
omnipotence, omnipotency, *s.* uilechumhachd, uile-chomas.
omnipotent, *adj.* uile-chumhachdach, uile-chomasachd.
omnipresence, *s.* uile-làthaireachd.
omnipresent, *adj.* uile-làthaireach.
omniscience, *s.* uil'-fhiosrachd.
omniscient, *adj.* uil'-fhiosrach.
omnivorous, *adj.* uile-shluigeach.
on, *prep.* and *adv.* air.
on ! *interj.* air adhart ! air t' adhart !
once, *adv.* aon uair ; uair, uair-eigin.
one, *adj.* aon, a h-aon.
one, *s.* neach, urra, aon fear, té.
one-eyed, *adj.* lethshuileach, cam.
onerary, *adj.* luchdail, lòdail, cudthromach.
onerate, *v. a.* luchdaich, sacaich.
onerous, *adj.* trom, sàrachail.
onion, *s.* uinnean.
only, *adv.* a mhàin.
onset, *s.* ionnsaigh, ruathar.
ontology, *s.* eòlas-bhithean.
onward, *adv.* air adhart, air aghaidh.
onyx, *s.* clach-onics, seud shoilleir.
ooze, *s.* dràib, làthach ; sileadh.
ooze, *v. n.* snith, sil, drùidh.
oozy, *adj.* dràibeach, silteach.
opacity, *s.* duirche, doilleireachd.
opacous, opaque, *adj.* dorcha.
opal, *s.* seud àraidh, clach-uasal.
open, *v.* fosgail ; mìnich ; tòisich.
open, *adj.* fosgailte ; soilleir, follaiseach ; fosgarra, réidh, saor.
open-eyed, *adj.* furachail, leirsinneach.
open-handed, *adj.* toirbheartach ; fialaidh, fiùghantach.
open-hearted, *adj.* saor-chridheach, còir, càirdeil.
open-heartedness, *s.* fiùghalachd ; bealach.
opening, *s.* fosgladh ; bealach.
openly, *adv.* gu fosgailt, gu follaiseach.
open-mouthed, *adj.* beul-fhosgailte, beul-fharsuing, geòcach ; gleadhrach.
openness, *s.* fosgailteachd, soilleireachd, soillseachd ; follaiseachd.
opera, *s.* ceòl-chluich, cluich-ciùil.
operate, *v. n.* gnìomhaich, oibrich.
operation, *s.* gnìomhachd, obair.
operative, *adj.* gnìomhach.
operator, *s.* gnìomharraiche.
operose, *adj.* saothrachail, draghail.

ophthalmia, *s.* galar-nan-sùl.
ophthalmic, *adj.* fradharcail.
opiate, *s.* cungaidh-chadail.
opinion, *s.* barail, beachd.
opinionative, *adj.* rag-bharalach.
opium, *s.* cungaidh-chadail.
opponent, *adj.* eascairdeach.
opponent, *s.* nàmhaid, eascaraid.
opportune, *adj.* tràthail, àmail.
opportunity, *s.* fàth, cothrom.
oppose, *v.* cuir an aghaidh, bac, grab ; dùbhlanaich ; taisbean, nochd ; coinnich.
opposite, *adj.* fa chomhair, mu choinnimh.
opposition, *s.* aghaidh-ri-aghaidh, comhstrì, neo-aonachd.
oppress, *v. a.* sàraich, claoidh.
oppression, *s.* sàrachadh, fòirneart, cruaidhchas, àmhghar, deuchainn, truaighe.
oppressive, *adj.* an-iochdmhor, cruaidh ; fòirneartach ; trom.
oppressor, *s.* fear-sàrachaidh, fear-fòirneirt, fear-foireignidh.
opprobrious, *adj.* sgainnealach.
opprobriousness, *s.* sgainnealachd.
opprobrium, *s.* masladh, mìchliù.
oppugn, *v. a.* cuir an aghaidh.
oppugnancy, *s.* cothachadh.
optative, *adj.* iarrtach, iarrtanach.
optic, *adj.* léirsinneach, fradharcach.
optic, *s.* sùil ; inneal-fradhairc.
optician, *s.* ceannaiche speuclairean.
optics, *s.* eòlas-fradhairc, eòlas air laghan soluis.
option, *s.* roghainn, comas taghaidh.
opulence, opulency, *s.* saibhreas, beartas, pailteas, maoin, toic.
opulent, *adj.* saoibhir, beartach.
or, *conj.* either, no, air neo.
oracle, *s.* facal, taisbean ; guth-àite ; fear ro-ghlic.
oracular, oraculous, *adj.* taisbeanach, briathrach, smachdail ; dorcha, diamhair.
oral, *adj.* beul-aithriseach.
orange, *s.* òrubhall, òrmheas.
oration, *s.* òraid, deaschainnt, duan.
orator, *s.* fear deaschainnteach, fear-labhairt.
oratorical, *adj.* deaschainnteach, ùr-labhrach, binnghloireach.
oratorio, *s.* naomhcheol.
oratory, *s.* deaschainnt, ùr-labhradh, òraideachd.
orb, *s.* cruinne, cuairt, cearcall, rath, roth, reull ; sùil, rosg.
orbate, *adj.* gun chuid, gun chàirdean, gun sliochd.
orbation, *s.* call-sliochda, bochdainn.
orbed, *adj.* cruinn, cuairteach.
orbicular, *adj.* cruinn.
orbit, *s.* reull-chuairt, reull-shlighe.

orchard, *adj.* ubhallghart, liosmheas, gàradh-abhaill.
orchestra, *s.* ionad-luchd-ciùil ; lobhta-ciùil ; luchd-ciùil.
ordain, *v. a.* sònraich, socraich, suidhich, cuir air leth, òrduich.
ordeal, *s.* cruaidh-dheuchainn.
order, *s.* òrdugh, suidheachadh, dòigh ; riaghailt, àinte ; ceannsal.
order, *v. a.* òrduich, ceartaich, riaghail ; cuir an òrdugh, suidhich, socraich ; àithn.
orderless, *adj.* mì-riaghailteach.
orderly, *adj.* riaghailteach, dòigheil.
ordinal, *adj.* riaghailteach.
ordinal, *s.* leabhar riaghailtean.
ordinance, *s.* reachd, riaghailt, lagh.
ordinary, *adj.* riaghailteach, dòigheil, suidhichte ; gnàthaichte ; cumanta, ìosal, suarach ; neo àluinn ; **Lord Ordinary,** britheamh Cuirt an t-Seision.
ordinate, *v. a.* sònraich, suidhich.
ordination, *s.* suidheachadh, cur air leth (gu dreuchd ministeir no éildeir).
ordnance, *s.* gunnachan móra.
ordure, *s.* gaorr, inneir, buachar.
ore, *s.* miotailt amh.
orgal, *s.* druaip fiona.
organ, *s.* ball ; inneal-ciùil àraidh.
organic, organical, *adj.* a bhuineas do bhuill a' chuirp.
organisation, *s.* cruth-shuidheachadh, dealbhadh, cur an òrdugh (air son obair).
organise, *v. a.* cruth-shuidhich, cuir (buidheann) an òrdugh.
organist, *s.* òraganaiche.
orgasm, *s.* fraoch-feirge, déine.
orgies, *s.* misg, ruidhtearachd.
orient, *adj.* camhanach, soills-bhristeach, loinnireach, deàrsach.
orient, *s.* an ear, an aird' an ear.
oriental, *adj.* earach, searach, soir.
orifice, *s.* beul, fosgladh, toll.
origin, *s.* tùs, toiseach, bun, ceud-aobhar, màthair-aobhar ; sinnsearachd.
original, *adj.* prìomh, tùsail.
originality, *s.* tùsalachd.
originate, *v. a.* tàrmaich, tòisich ; gin, thoir gu bith.
orison, oraison, *s.* ùrnaigh.
ornament, *s.* ball-maise, seud.
ornament, *v. a.* ball-mhaisich, maisich, sgeadaich.
ornamental, *adj.* ballmhaiseach.
ornate, *adj.* grinn, breagha.
ornithology, *s.* eun-eòlas.
orphan, *s.* dìlleachdan.
orpiment, *s.* seòrsa mèinn.
orpine, *s.* lus-nan-laogh.
orthodox, *adj.* ceart-chreideach.
orthodoxy, *s.* fallaineachd-teagaisg.
orthographer, *s.* ceart-sgrìobhair.

orthographical, *adj.* ceart-sgrìobhte.
orthography, *s.* ceart-sgrìobhadh.
orts, *s.* fuigheall, farstus, sprùilleach.
oscillation, *s.* luasgan, udal.
oscillatory, *adj.* luasganach.
oscitancy, oscitation, *s.* meunanaich.
oscitant, *adj.* meunanach, tromcheann-ach.
osier, *s.* craobh sheilich.
osprey, *s.* an iolair-uisge.
ossicle, *s.* meanbhchnàimh.
ossification, *s.* cnàimheachadh.
ossifrage, *s.* seors' iolaire.
ossify, *v. a.* dean 'na chnàimh.
ostensible, *adj.* nochdaidh.
ostensive, *adj.* taisbeanach, follaiseach.
ostentation, *s.* faoin-ghlòir, uaill.
ostentatious, *adj.* faoin-ghlòireach.
ostentatiousness, *s.* faoin-uaill.
ostler, *s.* gille-stàbaill.
ostrich, *s.* sruth, sruth-chàmhal.
other, *pron.* eile.
otherwise, *adv.* air mhodh eile, no.
otter, *s.* dòbhran, biast-dubh.
ought, or aught, *s.* ni, ni-eigin dad, rud, nì sam bith.
ought, *v. imp.* is còir, is cubhaidh.
ounce, *s.* ùnnsa.
our, *pron. poss.* ar.
ourselves, *pron. recip.* sinn-féin.
ousel, *s.* lon, fiagh mòr.
oust, *v. a.* falmhaich ; tilg a mach.
out, *adv.* a muigh, a mach ; o'n taigh ; ann am mearachd ; an ìomchomh-airle ; ás, air falbh.
out ! *interj.* gabh a mach ! a mach !
outbrave, *v. a.* cuir fo gheilt.
outbreak, *s.* briseadh a mach.
outcast, *s.* dìobarach, fògarrach.
outcraft, *v. a.* cuir a mach le seòltachd.
outcry, *s.* gaoir, gàir, iolach.
outdare, *v. a.* cuir a mach le dànadas.
outdo, *v. a.* buadhaich, coisinn (air).
outer, *adj.* a muigh, a mach.
outermost, *adj.* as fhaide mach.
outface, *v. a.* nàraich, cuir a mach.
outgrow, *v. a.* fàs thairis, fàs.
outguard, *s.* freiceadan-iomaill.
outknave, *v. a.* meall am mealltair.
outlandish, *adj.* allmhara.
outlast, *v. a.* mair na 's faide na.
outlaw, *s.* fear-cùirn, fògarrach, ceath-airneach-coille, coilltear.
outlaw, *v. a.* cuir air choilltearachd, cuir fo choill.
outlawry, *s.* binn-fhògraidh.
outline, *s.* dealbh ; crìoch, iomall.
outlive, *v. a.* fan beò na's fhaide na.
outlook, *s.* sealladh ; fradharc ; cothrom.
outmost, *adj.* iomallach.
outrage, *s.* sabaid, eucoir, ainneart.
outrage, *v.* càin, màb, maslaich, dèan àimhleas, dèan caonnag.

outrageous, *adj.* cuthachail, fiadhaich ; sabaideach, àimhleasach, àinneartach ; ana-measarra, mallaichte ; ro-aingidh.

outrageousness, *s.* cuthach, fearg.

outright, *adv.* gu buileach, gu h-iomlan, gu tur ; gu h-ealamh, gun dàil.

outrun, *v. a.* ruith seachad air, ruith na's luaithe (na neach eile).

outscorn, *v. a.* dèan dìmeas air.

outshine, *v. a.* deàrrs a mach (na's dearrsaiche na fear eile).

outshoot, *v. a.* tilg seachad air (na's fhaide).

outside, *s.* an taobh a muigh.

outskirt, *s.* iomall a muigh.

outspread, *v. a.* sgaoil a mach.

outstrip, *v. a.* fàg air deireadh.

outvie, *v. a.* faigh barrachd.

outward, *adj.* air an taobh muigh ; faicsinneach ; corporra ; céin.

outward, *adv.* gu tìr chéin.

outwardly, *adv.* do réir coltais, o'n taobh a muigh.

outwards, *adv.* a chum an taobh a muigh, an leth a muigh.

outwit, *v. a.* meall, thoir an car á.

outwork, *s.* balla muigh-daingnich.

oval, *adj.* air chumadh uibhe.

ovarious, *adj.* ubhach, uibheach.

ovary, *s.* machlag, uibheagan.

ovation, *s.* mion-chaithream.

oven, *s.* àmhuinn.

over, *prep.* and *adv.* os-cionn ; thar ; thairis ; tarsainn, air a tharsainn ; null ; thall, a' nall ; seachad, seach ; a rithist ; tuilleadh agus, a bharrachd, a bharr air, os-barr.

overact, *v. a.* dèan tuilleadh 's a' chòir, rach thar a' chòir.

over-anxious, *adj.* ro-chùramach.

overarch, *v. a.* drochaitich.

overawe, *v. a.* sgàthaich, eagalaich.

overbalance, *v. a.* taobh-thromaich, cuir thairis.

overbalance, *s.* taobh-trom.

overbear, *v. a.* cùm fo smachd, claoidh.

overbid, *v. a.* tairg barrachd.

overboard, *adv.* a mach thar stoc.

overboil, *v. a.* mill le bruich.

overburden, *v. a.* an-luchdaich.

overbuy, *v. a.* ceannaich ro dhaor, ceannaich cus.

overcast, *v. a.* dorchaich, neulaich.

overcharge, *v. a.* iarr tuilleadh 'sa' chòir ; dèan tuilleadh is làn.

overcloud, *v. a.* neulaich ; dubharaich, gruamaich.

overcome, *v. a.* buadhaich, ceannsaich, faigh buaidh.

overdo, *v. a.* dèan tuilleadh 's a' chòir.

overdrive, *v. a.* iomain ro luath.

over-eager, *adj.* ro-dhian, ro-bhras.

overflow, *v.* cuir thairis, sruth thairis, lion thairis.

overflowing, *s.* ro-làn ; cur thairis.

overforwardness, *s.* ro-dhéine, tuilleadh is dàn.

overgrow, *v. a.* fàs ro-mhòr, laom.

overgrowth, *s.* ro-fhàs, ro-chinneas, laomadh.

overhaul, *v. a.* ath-sgrùd, mion-rannsaich.

overhead, *adv.* gu h-àrd ; os cionn.

overhear, *v.* dèan farchluais.

overjoy, *v. a.* dèan ùr-ghàirdeachas.

overjoy, *s.* ùr-ghàirdeachas.

overlay, *v. a.* mùch ; còmhdaich thairis.

overload, *v. a.* an-luchdaich.

overlook, *v. a.* amhairc sios air ; dèan dìmeas air ; seall thairis air.

overmatch, *v. a.* fairtlich air.

overmuch, *adj.* tuille 's a' chòir.

overpay, *v. a.* dìol tuille 's a' chòir.

overplus, *s.* barrachd, an còrr.

overpower, *v. a.* faigh làmh-an-uachdar, ceannsaich.

overprize, *v. a.* meas thar a luach.

overreach, *v. a.* faigh os cionn, meall, thoir an car.

overrule, *v. a.* cùm fo smachd ; cuir fo smachd, diùlt.

overrun, *v. a.* sàraich, mill, claoidh, spùinn ; rach thairis air ; ioma-sgaoil, sgaoil thairis ; cuir thairis, ruith thairis.

oversee, *v. a.* amhairc thairis.

overseer, *s.* fear-coimhid.

overset, *v. a.* tilg bun os ceann.

overshade, *v. a.* dùibhrich, neulaich, sgàilich.

overshadow, *v. a.* cuir sgàil air.

oversight, *s.* mearachd, dearmad ; coimhead, cùram.

oversoon, *adv.* ro thràth.

overspent, *adj.* sàraichte, claoidhte.

overspread, *v. a.* sgaoil thairis.

overstock, *v. a.* dòmhlaich, an-lìon.

overstrain, *v.* thoir dian-ionnsaigh.

overt, *adj.* fosgailte, soilleir.

overtake, *v. a.* beir, glac, thig suas.

overthrow, *v. a.* tilg bun os cionn ; ceannsaich ; mill, sgrios, cuir ás da.

overthwart, *adj.* mu choinneamh, mu chomhair, tarsainn, trasd.

overtire, *v. a.* dù-sgìthich, sàraich.

overtop, *v. a.* éirich os cionn.

overture, *s.* fosgladh ; foillseachadh, soillseachadh, tòiseachadh.

overturn, *v. a.* tilg sios, mill, sgrios.

overvalue, *v. a.* meas thar a luach.

overween, *v. n.* bi féin-bheachdail.

overwhelm, *v. a.* mùch, brùth.

overwork, *v. a.* sgìthich le obair.

overworn, *part.* air caitheamh as.

overwrought, *part.* claoidhte le obair, sàraichte.

oviform, *adj.* air cumadh uighe.

OWE—PALL-MALL

520

owe, *v. a.* bi fo fiachaibh do.
owl, owlet, *s.* a' chomhachag, a' chailleach oidhche.
own, *pron.* féin ; my own share, mo chuid féin.
own, *v. a.* gabh ri, gabh le ; aidich.
owner, *s.* sealbhadair, fear-seilbhe.
ownership, *s.* sealbh, maoin, còir.
ox, *s.* damh ; *pl.* daimh.

oxeye, *s.* am bréinean-brothach.
oxgang, *s.* damh-imir, tomhas fearainn fhichead acair.
oxlip, *s.* bròg-na-cuthaig.
oxtongue, *s.* am bog-lus.
oxycrate, *s.* fion-geur agus uisge.
O yes ! *interj.* eisdibh ! thugaibh aire ! thugaibh fainear !
oyster, *s.* eisir, eisear.

P

pabular, pabulous, *adj.* biadhar, innlinneach, feurach, ionaltrach.
pacated, *adj.* siochail, sìtheil.
pace, *s.* ceum, gàmag ; imeachd, gluasad ; tomhas chòig troighean.
pace, *v.* cèimnich, gluais ; tomhais le gàmagan.
pacer, *s.* ceumaiche, falaire.
pacific, *adj.* sìothchail, ciùin, sèimh.
pacification, *s.* sìtheachadh.
pacificator, *s.* fear dèanamh sìthe.
pacificatory, *adj.* sìth-dhèanadach.
pacifier, *s.* fear-ciùineachaidh.
pacify, *v. a.* sìthich, ciùinich.
pack, *s.* eallach, uallach, cuallach, trusachan ; sac, luchd ; lothainn chon ; droch comunn, gràisg.
pack, *v.* trus, ceangail suas, paisg.
packer, *s.* fear-trusaidh, fear-ceangail, fear-pacaidh.
packet, *s.* ceanglachan, sac, sacan ; long-aisig, bàt-aisig.
packhorse, *s.* each saic.
packsaddle, *s.* srathair.
packthread, *s.* sgeinnidh.
pact, paction, *s.* cùmhnant.
pad, *v. n.* coisich gu fòill ; dèan reubainn rathaid mhóir.
padar, *s.* garbhan, garbhmhin.
paddle, *v. a.* iomair ; luidrich.
paddle, *s.* ràmh beag ; pleadhan.
paddock, *s.* mial-mhàg, cràigean.
padlock, *s.* glas-chrochaidh.
pæan, *s.* dàn buaidh-chaithream.
pagan, *s.* pàganach, ana-criosdaidh.
paganism, *s.* pàganachd.
page, *s.* taobh-duilleig ; gille-freasdail, gille-bùird.
pageant, *s.* greadhnachas.
pageant, *adj.* greadhnach, faicheil.
pageantry, *s.* greadhnachd, faichealachd, mòralachd.
paginal, *adj.* duilleagach.
paid, *pret.* and *part. pass.* of to pay, pàighte, dìolte.
pail, *s.* cuinneag, cuman, miodar.
pain, *s.* cràdh, pian ; péin, goimh, guin, dòrainn.

pain, *v. a.* cràidh, pian, claoidh.
painful, *adj.* cràiteach, piantach.
painfulness, *s.* àmhghar, cràdh.
painless, *adj.* neo - chràiteach, gun phian.
painstaker, *s.* fear-saoithreachail, fear-dìchiollach.
painstaking, *adj.* saoithreachail.
paint, *v. a.* tarruing dealbh.
paint, *s.* peant.
painting, *s.* dealbh.
pair, *s.* càraid ; lànan ; dithis.
pair, *v. a.* càraidich, aonaich.
palace, *s.* lùchairt, mùr-rìoghail.
palatable, *adj.* blasda, milis.
palate, *s.* mullach beòil, coguis.
pale, *adj.* bàn, glaisneulach.
pale, *v. a.* dèan bàn ; bànaich ; iomdhruid.
pale, *s.* cliath-mhaide, buaile ; lann, post ; dùthaich, cearn.
palefaced, *adj.* glas-ghnùiseach, glasneulach.
palender, *s.* long-chòrsaireachd.
paleness, *s.* glaisneulachd, bànachd.
palfrey, *s.* each - marcachd bain - tighearna.
paling, *s.* cliath-dhìdinn, ataigin.
palisade, palisado, *s.* callaid, bann iomdhruididh.
palisade, *v. a.* druid le callaid, cuir callaid mu thimchioll.
palish, *adj.* glasaidh, bànaidh.
pall, *s.* brat-mairbh ; falluing àird-easbuig.
pall, *v.* fàs mì-bhlasda, dèan mì-bhlasda ; lagaich ; sàsaich, fàs lag.
pallet, *s.* seid, leabaidh-làir.
palliate, *v. a.* falluingich, còmhdaich ; gabh leisgeul, thoir leisgeul, lùghdaich coire no cionta ; lasaich.
palliation, *s.* leisgeulachadh, lùghdachadh coire no cionta ; faothachadh, fuasgladh, lasachadh.
palliative, *adj.* leisgeulach, lùghdachail ; lasachail, fuasglach.
pallid, *adj.* bàn, glasdaidh.
pall-mall, *s.* seòrsa cluiche.

palm, s. craobh-phailm ; buaidh ; bois, bas, dèarna ; tomhas trì òirlich.

palm, v. a. falaich 's a bhois ; meall ; slìob, cnìadaich.

palmipede, adj. (eun) aig a bheil spòg-shnàmh.

palmister, s. dèarnadair.

palmistry, s. dèarnadaireachd.

palmy, adj. pailmeach ; buadhach.

palpable, adj. so-bheanailteach, a ghabas làimhseachadh.

palpation, s. mothachadh, làimhseachadh.

palpitate, v. n. plosg, buail.

palpitation, s. plosgartaich.

palsied, adj. pairiliseach.

palsy, s. pairilis, criththinneas.

paltriness, s. fagharsachd.

paltry, adj. fagharsach, suarrach.

pamper, v. a. sàthaich, sàsaich, peataich.

pamphlet, s. duilleachan, leabhran.

pan, s. aghann ; falman na glùine.

panacea, s. uil'-ic, uil-ioc.

panada, panado, s. aran air a bhogadh an uisge goileach agus bainne leis.

pancake, s. loireag, foileag.

pancreas, s. am brisgean-milis.

pandemic, adj. and s. (galar) gabhaltach, sgaoilteach.

pander, s. fear-cuideachaidh an ana-miann.

pane, s. ceàrnag ghloine ; lòsan.

panegyric, s. moladh, dàn-molaidh.

panegyrist, s. bàrd-molaidh.

panel, s. ceàrnag ; ainmchlàr luchd-breith (jury).

pang, s. guin, goimh, cràdh, pian.

pang, v. a. gon, cràidh, pian.

panic, s. clisgeadh, maoim ; he was panic-struck, thuit a thud 's a thad as.

pannel, s. srathair, sumag, plàt.

pannier, s. curran, cliabh.

panoply, s. làn-armachd ; lànfhasair, lànuidheam.

pant, v. n. plosg ; miannaich, bi 'n ro gheall air.

pant, s. plosgadh, àinich.

pantaloon, s. triubhas ; cleasaiche.

pantheon, s. teampull nan uile dhia bréige.

panther, s. fiadhbheathach ballach.

pantile, pentile, s. crom-shlige-chrè.

pantler, s. fear-gleidhidh arain.

pantomime, s. baoth-chleasachd.

pantry, s. seomar-shoithichean, àite-gleidhidh bidh.

pap, s. ceann-cìche ; biadh-leanaibh.

papa, s. athair, facal cloinne.

papacy, s. pàpanachd.

papal, adj. pàpanach.

paper, s. pàipeir, pàpair.

paper, v. a. paisg am pàipeir, pàipeirich.

paper-maker, s. fear dèanamh phàipeir.

papermill, s. muileann 's an dèanar pàipeir.

paper-stainer, s. dathadair phàipeirean.

papillary, papillous, adj. cìochach.

papist, s. pàpanach.

papistical, adj. pàpanach.

pappus, s. clòimhteach ghìogan.

pappy, adj. bog, sùghmhor.

par, s. co-ionannachd.

parable, s. cosamhlachd.

parabolical, adj. co-shamhlachail.

paraclete, s. an comhfhurtair.

parade, s. feachd-riaghailt ; uaill, bòilich.

paradise, s. pàrras, nèamh.

paradox, s. dubh-fhacal, frith-bharail.

paradoxical, adj. baoth-bharaileach, air dhreach na bréige.

paragon, s. eisimpleir coimhlionta, ni no neach ro-òirdheirc ; companach.

paragraph, s. earrann no rann.

parallel, adj. co-shìnte ; co-ionann, caspanach.

parallel, s. ionannachd ; samhailt, leth-bhreac.

parallel, v. a. co-shìn ; coimeas, samh-laich.

parallelism, s. co-shìnteachd, co-samhla.

paralyse, v. a. buaill e pairilis.

paralysis, s. pairilis.

paralytic, adj. pairiliseach, critheanach.

paramount, s. am priomh, an t-àrd.

paramour, s. leannan, suiridheach.

parapet, s. obair-àrd, uchd-bhalla.

paraphrase, s. eadar-mhìneachadh.

paraphrast, s. fear-mìneachaidh.

parasite, s. fear-sodail, bleidire.

parasitical, adj. sodalach, miodalach, sgimeileireach, bleideil.

parasol, s. grian-sgàilean.

parboil, v. a. leth-bhruich, slaop.

parcel, s. trusachan, achlasan.

parcel, v. a. roinn 'na earrannan.

parch, v. tiormaich le teas, déasg.

parchedness, s. déasgachd, sgreadhadh, tiormachd.

parchment, s. craicionn - sgrìobhaidh, meambran.

pard, pardale, s. liobard.

pardon, v. a. math, thoir mathanas.

pardon, s. mathanas, loghadh.

pardonable, adj. so-mhathadh.

pardonableness, s. so-mhathachd.

pare, v. a. sgrathaich, gèarr, bearr, rùisg.

parent, s. pàrant, athair no màthair.

parentage, s. breith, sìnnsearachd.

parental, adj. athaireil, no màithreil.

parenthesis, s. mìneachadh am meadhon sgrìobhaidh.

parenticide, s. mort athar, no màthar.

parer, s. inneal-bearraidh no rùsgaidh.

parhelion, s. grian-bréige.

paring, s. rusg, sliseag, sgrath.

parish, *s.* sgrìeachd, sgìre.
parishioner, *s.* fear-sgìreachd.
parity, *s.* co-ionannachd.
park, *s.* pàirce, frìth, lann.
parley, parle, *s.* còmhradh.
parley, *v. n.* dèan gnothach le còmhradh beoil.
parliament, *s.* pàrlamaid, àrd-chomhairle, rìoghachd.
parliamentary, *adj.* pàrlamaideach.
parlour, *s.* seòmar-suidhe.
parlous, *adj.* geur, beòthail, peasanach.
parochial, *adj.* sgìreachdail.
parody, *s.* atharrais dàin.
parole, *s.* gealltannas beòil.
paroxysm, *s.* ruathar, tinnis.
parricidal, *adj.* athair-mhortach.
parricide, *s.* mortair athar.
parrot, *s.* parraid, pitheid.
parry, *v. n.* dìon o bhuille, cum dhiot (buille).
parsimonious, *adj.* gléidhteach, spìocach, cruaidh, gann.
parsimony, *s.* spìocaireachd.
parsley, *s.* fionnas-gàraidh.
parsnip, parsnep, *s.* an curran-geal.
parson, *s.* pears-eaglais, ministear.
parsonage, *s.* tigh ministeir, mansa.
part, *s.* cuid, earrann, roinn, cuibhrionn; gnothach, obair.
part, *v. a.* roinn; sgar; eadar-dhealaich; dealaich; gabh cead o; thoir seachad.
partake, *v.* compàirtich, roinn ri.
partaker, *s.* compàirtiche.
partial, *adj.* claonbhreitheach, leth-bhreitheach; bàigheil ri, aon taobh.
partiality, *s.* claonbhreitheachd.
participable, *adj.* so-phàirteachadh.
participant, *adj.* co-roinnteach.
participate, *v.* compàirtich.
participation, *s.* co-roinn, compàirt.
particle, *s.* dad, mionfhacal, smùir-nean.
particular, *adj.* àraidh, sònraichte; pon-cail; còrr, cùramach.
particularise, *v. a.* sònraich.
parting, *s.* dealachadh, siubhal.
partisan, *s.* fear-leanmhainn.
partisan, *s.* sleagh le làmhcharan fada.
partition, *v. a.* roinn; eadar-sgar.
partition, *s.* roinn, cailbhe, talan.
partlet, *s.* cearc, stìm.
partly, *adv.* ann an cuid.
partner, *s.* còmpanach, fear-pàirt.
partnership, *s.* còmpanas, co-roinn.
partook, *pret.* of to partake, chompairtich.
partridge, *s.* cearc-thomain; seòrsa fiodh'a.
parts, *s.* buadhan nàdurrach, buadhan-inntinn, ceudfathan; earrannan-dùth-cha; pàirtean.
parturition, *s.* breith, aisead.
party, *s.* dream, cuideachd, buidheann; bannal; neach air leth; freiceadan.

party-coloured, *adj.* iomdhathach.
party-man, *s.* fear-aon-taoibh.
parvitude, parvity, *s.* mionaideachd; eagarachd, pungalachd.
paschal, *adj.* càisgeach, càisgeil.
pass, *v.* rach thairis, gabh seachad, rach thar; rach troimh; buadhaich, dearmaid, dìochuimhnich; leig le, òrduich; leig seachad, math; thoir binn a mach.
pass, *s.* glac, bealach, slighe, rathad; leitir, cead siubhail; cor, inbhe.
passable, *adj.* so-imeachd; an eatarais, cuibheasach.
passade, passado, *s.* uspag.
passage, *s.* turas, aisir; slighe; trannsa; earrann, ceann.
passenger, *s.* fear-turais, fear-aisig.
passible, *adj.* so-athailteachadh.
passing, *part. adj.* anabarrach.
passing-bell, *s.* clag-bàis.
passion, *s.* boile; fearg, corraich, buaireas; déigh, miann, gràdh; fulangas Chriosd.
passionate, *adj.* cas, crosda, feargach, lasanta, grad.
passionateness, *s.* lasantachd, caise.
passion-week, *s.* seachdain-na ceusda.
passive, *adj.* fulangach, ciùin.
passiveness, passivity, *s.* fulangachd, foighidneachd, ciùineachd.
passover, *s.* a chàisg; an t-uan càisge.
passport, *s.* litir cead-siubhail.
past, *part.* seachad, a thréig.
past, *s.* an ùine a chaidh, an t-àm a dh' fhalbh, an linn a thréig.
paste, *s.* glaodh flùir.
pasteboard, *s.* bòrd paipeir.
pastern, *s.* rùdan eich, glùn eich.
pastime, *s.* fearas-chuideachd.
pastor, *s.* aoghair, pears'-eaglais.
pastoral, *adj.* aogharachail.
pastoral, *s.* òran-dùthcha.
pastorship, *s.* aogharachd.
pastry, *s.* biadh fuinte, pitheannan.
pasturable, *adj.* so-ionaltradh.
pasturage, *s.* feurach, ionaltradh, innis.
pasture, *s.* ionaltradh, feurachas.
pasture, *v.* ionaltair, feuraich, inilt.
pasty, *s.* pithean.
pat, *adj.* iomchuidh, freagarrach.
pat, *s.* coilleag; boiseag.
pat, *v. a.* slìob, buail aotrom.
patch, *s.* breaban, bréid, tùthag.
patch, *v. a.* clùd, càirich, tùthagaich, bréideich, cnòdaich.
patcher, *s.* clùdaire, cnòdaire.
pate, *s.* claigeann, ceann.
patent, *adj.* fosgailte, follaiseach.
patent, *s.* sgrìobhadh còrach o'n rìgh.
patentee, *s.* fear-còrach.
paternal, *adj.* athaireil.
paternity, *s.* athaireachd.
paternoster, *s.* a' phaidir.

path, pathway, s. ceum, slighe, rathad, aisridh, cascheum, casan, bealach.
pathetic, pathetical, adj. drùighteach, tiamhaidh, cianail.
pathless, adj. gun rathad, gun slighe.
pathology, s. eòlas-ghalar.
pathos, s. déine, dian-labhairt, drùighteachd.
pathway, s. frithrathad, ceum, lonaig.
patience, s. foighidinn, fulangas.
patient, adj. foighidneach, fulangach, foisneach.
patient, s. neach tinn, neach euslan.
patly, adv. gu freagarrach, iomchuidh.
patriarch, s. prìomhathair.
patriarchal, adj. prìomh athaireil.
patrician, adj. uasal, àrd, flathail.
patrician, s. àrd-uasal, àrd-fhlath.
patrimonial, adj. dligheach, sinnsearrach, dualach.
patrimony, s. oighreachd-sinnsearachd, dualachas.
patriot, s. fear-gràidh d'a dhùthaich, tìr-ghràdhaiche.
patriotism, s. gràdh dùthcha.
patrol, s. freiceadan sràide, freacadan mara.
patron, s. fear comaraidh, fear-taic.
patronage, s. comaradh, dìon, taic.
patroness, s. ban-chomaraidh.
patronise, v. a. dìon, cùm suas, seas, thoir comaradh.
patronymic, s. ainm sìnnsearachd.
patten, s. bròg fhiodha agus iaruinn.
patter, v. a. dèan stairirich.
pattern, s. ball-sampuill ; cumadh, eis-impleir.
paucity, s. ainneamhachd, gainne.
paunch, s. brù, maodal.
pauper, s. dìol-déirce, bochd.
pauperism, s. déirceachd.
pause, s. stad, anail, grabadh, tosd.
pause, v. n. fuirich, smuainich, thoir fainear ; stad, clos ; bi aig fois.
pave, v. a. ùrlaraich, leag ùrlar.
pavement, s. ùrlar-cloiche, càbhsair.
paver, paviour, s. càbhsairiche.
pavilion, s. pàilliun, bùth.
paw, s. spòg, spàg, màg, cràg, cròg.
paw, v. a. crògairich, bùraich, sgrìob, dean miodal.
pawn, v. a. thoir an geall.
pawnbroker, s. malairtear-gìll.
pay, v. a. dìol, pàidh, ìoc.
pay, s. tuarasdal, luach-saoithreach.
payable, adj. ri dhìoladh.
payment, s. dìoladh, pàidheadh.
pea, s. peasair, gràinne peasarach.
peace, s. sìth ; sìothchaint ; fois, tamh, réite, socair-inntinn.
peace ! interj. tosd ! clos !
peaceable, adj. soitheamh, sìothchail ; foistinneach ; sàmhach.

peaceableness, s. sìthealachd.
peaceful, adj. sìochail, ciùin.
peacefulness, s. siochainnt.
peacemaker, s. fear-réite, fear-sìtheachaidh.
peace-offering, s. sìth-thabhartas.
peachick, s. isean na peucaig.
peacock, s. coileach-peucag.
peahen, s. peucag, eucag, feucag.
peak, s. stùc, scòrr, binnein, bàrr.
peal, s. stàiririch, toirm, torrunn.
pear, s. peur, meas àraidh.
pearl, s. neamhnaid ; leus-sùl.
pearly, adj. neamhnaideach.
peasant, s. fear dubh-chosnaidh, fear de'n tuath.
peasantry, s. tuath-cheathairn.
peasecod, s. balg peasrach.
peat, s. mòine ; fàd no fòid mònach.
pebble, pebble - stone, s. éideag, clach-muil.
pebbly, adj. éideagach.
peccability, s. buailteachd do'n pheacadh.
peccadillo, s. meanbhchoire.
peccancy, s. drochmheinn.
peccant, adj. ciontach, peacach ; droch-mhèinneach, aingidh.
peccavi, pret. v. pheacaich mi, chaidh mi cearr.
peck, s. peic, ceithreamh.
peck, v. a. pioc, gobhaich ; spiol.
pectoral, adj. uchdail, broileachail.
pectoral, s. uchd-éideadh.
peculate, v. n. dèan gadaidheachd.
peculation, s. mèirle, goid.
peculiar, adj. àraidh, sònraichte.
peculiarity, s. buaidh-air-leth.
pecuniary, adj. airgeadach.
pedagogue, s. maighistir-sgoile (facal tamailteach).
pedal, adj. casach, luirgneach.
pedant, s. beadagan fòghluim.
pedantic, adj. uailleil á beagan-fòghluim.
pedantry, pedanticness, s. moit ionnsachaidh.
pedestal, s. buncarragh.
pedestrial, pedestrious, adj. air chois, a' coiseachd.
pedestrian, s. coisiche.
pedicle, s. cuiseag, lurga duilleig.
pedicular, pediculous, adj. mialach.
pedigree, s. sìnnsearrachd, sloinntearachd.
pedler, s. ceannaiche-màileid, ceannaiche-siubhail.
pedlery, s. frithcheannachd.
pedling, s. frithcheannach.
pedobaptism, s. naoidh-bhaisteadh.
pedobaptist, s. naoidh-bhaisteach.
peel, v. a. rùisg, plaoisg, creach.
peel, s. rùsg, plaosg ; greidilein.
peep, v. n. thoir caog shealladh, amhairc troimh tholl, gabh sealladh bradach, dèan dìdeagaich.

peep, s. grad shealladh ; caogadh, seall-adh, bradach, dìdeag.
peer, s. flath, morair, còmpanach.
peer, v. seall gu geur, nochd a mach.
peerage, peerdom, s. flathachd, morair-eachd.
peeress, s. banmhorair.
peerless, adj. gun choimeas, gun leth-bhreac.
peerlessness, s. neo-choimeasachd.
peevish, adj. dreamach, dranndanach, frionasach, cas, corrach, feargach, crosda.
peevishness, s. dranndanachd, caise.
peg, s. cnag stéill, ealachag.
pelf, s. maoin, saoibhreas, beartas.
pelican, s. pelican, eun mór fàsaich.
pellet, s. peileir, ruagaire.
pellicle, s. sgrath, sgannan.
pellitory, s. lus-a'-bhalla.
pell-mell, adv. troimh chéile, air muin a cheile, muin air mhuin.
pellucid, adj. trìd-shoilleir, soilleir.
pelt, s. peleid, craicionn, bian, seiche ; buille, cnap, sgailc.
pelt, v. a. tilg air, buail, caith air.
pelting, part. tilgeadh chlach.
peltmonger, s. ceannaiche-chraicionn, boicionnaich.
pen, s. peann ; crò, buaile, fang.
penal, adj. peanasach, dioghaltach.
penality, s. buailteachd do pheanas.
penalty, s. peanas, pian, ùbhladh.
penance, s. aithridh, peanas air son peacadh, ceusadh na feòla.
pence, s. pl. of penny, sgillinnean.
pencil, s. bioran luaidhe ; gath soluis.
pendant, s. fàinne-cluaise ; grinneas crochte ; bratach-bheag.
pendency, s. dàil, teagamh.
pendent, adj. an crochadh ; thairis air.
pending, adj. an crochadh, a' teagamh-ach, an geall.
pendulous, adj. an crochadh, crochte.
pendulum, s. cudthrom-siùdain, teanga uaireadair.
penetrable, adj. drùidhteach.
penetrant, adj. drùidhteach, geur.
penetrate, v. drùidh ; toll ; faigh troimhe, breathnaich.
penetration, s. tolladh, deargadh, drùigh-eadh ; breithneachadh ; geur-thuigse.
penetrative, adj. geur, drùidhteach ; geur-chuiseach.
peninsula, s. tairbeart, ros.
penitence, s. aithreachas.
penitent, adj. aithreachail.
penitent, s. iompachan.
penitential, adj. aithreachail.
penitentiary, s. prìoson, dubh-phrìoson.
penknife, s. sgian-pheann.
penman, s. ùghdar, sgrìobhair.
penmanship, s. sgrìobhaireachd.

pennant, s. ball-tàirnne ; bratach.
pennated, adj. sgiathach.
penniless, adj. gun pheighinn, ainnis.
pennon, s. bratach.
penny, s. peighinn, sgillinn.
pennyworth, s. luach peighinn.
pension, s. saor-dhuais bhliadhnach.
pensionary, adj. saor-dhuaiseach.
pensioner, s. fear-saor-dhuais.
pensive, adj. trom smaointeachail.
pensiveness, s. tron smaointinneachd.
pentacapsular, adj. cóigchlaiseach.
pentachord, s. cruit-nan-cóig-teud.
pentaedrous, adj. cóigshliseach.
pentagon, s. cóigchearnag.
pentangular, adj. cóigchearnach.
pentapetalous, adj. cóigdhuilleach.
pentateuch, s. cóig leabhraichean Mhaois.
Pentecost, s. a' chaingeis.
Pentecostal, adj. caingeiseach.
penthouse, s. tigh-sgàile.
penurious, adj. spìocach, crìon.
penuriousness, s. spìocaiche, crìne.
penury, s. bochduinn, ainniseachd.
people, s. pobull, sluagh, aiteam.
people, v. a. lìon le sluagh.
pepper, s. spìosraidh, peabar.
pepper, v. a. peabraich ; slac, spuaic.
peppercorn, s. smùirnein, dùradan.
peradventure, adv. theagamh.
perambulate, v. a. cuairtimich, sràid-imich.
perambulation, s. cuairtimeachd.
perceivable, adj. so-fhaicsinn.
perceive, v. a. beachdaich, tuig.
perceptibility, s. so-léirsinneachd.
perceptible, adj. so-léirsinneach.
perception, s. amharc, beachd ; eòlas, fiosrachadh ; mothachadh.
perceptive, adj. léirsinneach, beachdach.
perch, s. creagag, muc-locha, tomhas chóig slat gu leth ; spiris, spàrr.
perch, v. cuir air spiris ; rach air spàrdan ; suidh mar eun.
perchance, adv. a theagamh.
percipient, adj. geurbheachdach.
percolate, v. a. sìolaidh.
percolation, s. sìoladh.
percolator, s. sìolachan, sioltachan.
percuss, v. a. buail, thoir buille.
percussion, s. bualadh, buille, farum.
perdition, s. sgrios ; bàs sìorruidh.
perdu, adv. am falach ; am fagus.
perdulous, adj. caillte.
peregrinate, v. n. dèan turus céin.
peregrination, s. céin-thuras, sgrìob, cuairt (dùthcha).
peregrinator, s. taisdealach.
peregrine, adj. céinthireach.
peremptory, adj. smachdail, teann.
perennial, adj. a mhaireas ré bliadhna ; sìor-maireannach.

perennity, s. buan-mhaireannachd.
perfect, adj. iomlan, foirfe, coimhlionta ; làn-eòlach ; neochoireach, fìorghlan ; cinnteach, dearbhte.
perfect, v. a. dèan iomlan, dèan foirfe, dèan coimhlionta ; làn-chrìochnaich.
perfection, s. iomlanachd, foirfeachd, coimhliontachd, diongmhaltachd.
perfectness, s. iomlanachd, foirfeachd ; làn-mhathas.
perfidious, adj. cuilbheartach, meallta, foilleil, sligheach.
perfidiousness, s. cuilbheartachd.
perforate, v. a. toll, toll troimh.
perforation, s. tolladh.
perforator, s. sniomhaire, tora.
perforce, adv. a dh' aindeoin, air éigin.
perform, v. a. coimhlion, gniomhaich.
performance, s. coimhlionadh, gnìomh, deanadas, deananaich.
performer, s. fear-coimhlionaidh, fear-cluiche.
perfume, s. boltrach, cùbhraidhach.
perfume, v. a. dèan cùbhraidh.
perfumer, s. boltraiche, ceannaiche bholtraichean.
perfunctory, adj. dearmadach, neo-chùramach ; neo-choimhlionta.
perhaps, adv. math a dh' fheudte, theagamh, 's dòcha.
pericardium, s. cochull a' chridhe.
pericranium, s. cochull na h-eanchain.
peril, s. cunnart, baoghal, gàbhadh.
perilous, adj. cunnartach, gàbhaidh.
perimeter, s. cuairt-thomhas, oir a muigh cearcaill.
period, s. cuairt ; ùine, àm, ré ; crìoch, ceann, deireadh ; pong.
periodical, adj. riaghailteach, aig àmaibh suidhichte.
periphery, s. cuairt thomhas, tomhas air oir buaile.
periphrasis, s. cuairtlabhairt.
periphrastic, adj. cuairtlabhrach.
perish, v. rach a dhìth, faigh bàs, bàsaich ; rach am mugha.
perishable, adj. bàsmhor, claoidhteach, dìtheachail.
periwig, s. pìorbhuic, gruag.
periwinkle, s. gille-fionn, faochag.
perjure, v. a. thoir mionnan-eithich.
perjurer, s. fear-eithich.
perjury, s. eitheach, mionnan-eithich.
perk, v. n. bi guanach, bi gog-cheannach.
permanence, s. buanas, maireannachd, seasmhachd.
permanent, adj. buan, maireannach.
permissible, adj. ceadach, a dh' fhaodas tachart.
permission, s. cead, saorsa, comas.
permissive, adj. ceadachail.
permit, v. a. ceadaich ; fuiling, luthasaich, thoir suas.

permit, s. baranta-cuspuinn, ùghdaras, cothrom.
permutation, s. malairt, mùthadh.
pernicious, adj. millteach, callmhor, sgriosail.
perniciously, adv. gu sgriosail.
peroration, s. co-dhùnadh òraid.
perpend, v. a. gabh dlùth-bheachd.
perpendicular, adj. 'na sheasamh dìreach.
perpendicular, s. dìreachan.
perpension, s. smuaineachadh.
perpetrate, v. a. ciontaich.
perpetration, s. ciontachadh.
perpetual, adj. sìor-mhaireannach.
perpetuate, v. a. cùm an gnàth-chleachdadh.
perpetuity, s. sìor-mhaireannachd.
perplex, v. a. cuir an iomchomhairle, cuir an iomcheist.
perplexed, adj. iomcheisteach, deacair, duilich.
perplexity, s. iomchomhairle.
perquisite, s. frith-bhuannachd, tiodhlac.
perry, s. peur-leann.
persecute, v. a. geur-lean, ioma-ruag, dèan an-iochd.
persecution, s. geur-leanmhainn.
persecutor, s. fear-geur-leanmhainn.
perseverance, s. buan-leanaltas.
perseverant, adj. buan-leanailteach.
persevere, v. n. buanaich, lean.
persist, v. n. lean ri, bi seasmhach, cùm air.
persistance, s. seasmhachd.
persistive, adj. buanachail.
person, s. neach, urra ; pearsa.
personable, adj. cumair ; tlachdmhor.
personage, s. urra, neach fiùghail.
personal, adj. aonurrach, pearsanta.
personality, s. aon-urralachd, féinachd ; athais, innisg.
personally, adv. gu pearsanta.
personate, v. a. gabh coslas, neach eile, riochdaich.
personation, s. dol an rìochd neach eile.
personification, s. riochd-samhlachadh.
personify, v. a. riochd-shamhlaich, gabh àite fir eile, thoir buadhan pearsanta do nithean.
perspective, s. fradharc ; sealladh, suidh-eachadh nàdurach (an dealbh).
perspective, adj. fradharcach.
perspicacious, adj. geur-fhradharcach.
perspicacity, s. geurshùileachd, tulchuis, fìor-bhreithneachadh.
perspicuity, s. soilleireachd.
perspicuous, adj. soilleir, so-thuigsinn.
perspirable, adj. fallusach.
perspiration, s. fallus, cur falluis.
perspire, v. n. cuir fallus dhiot.
persuade, v. a. comhairlich ; earalaich, cuir iompaidh ; dèan deònach.
persuasible, adj. so-chomhairleach.

persuasion, s. comhairle, earalachadh ; barail, creideamh.

persuasive, persuasory, adj. comhairleach, earaileach, iompaidheach.

pert, adj. clis, beothail, ealamh, beadaidh, ladarna, goileamach.

pertain, v. a. buin do.

pertinacious, adj. danarra, rag.

pertinacity, s. danarrachd, raige, rag-mhuinealachd, déine.

pertinence, s. iomchuidheachd, freagarr-achd.

pertinent, adj. iomchuidh, cubhaidh.

pertly, adv. gu clis, gu beadaidh.

pertness, s. beadaidheachd.

perturbate, v. a. buair, àimhreitich.

perturbation, s. iomagain ; buaireas.

pertusion, s. tolladh ; toll.

peruke, s. gruag, faraghruag.

perusal, s. leughadh ; rannsachadh.

peruse, v. a. leugh ; rannsaich.

pervade, v. a. trìd-shiubhail, rach air feadh.

pervasion, s. trìdshiubhal, dol troimh.

perverse, adj. fiar, claon ; dian 's an eucoir, rag - mhuinealach, aingidh ; mallaichte, crosta.

perverseness, s. rag-mhuinealachd, ain-gealtas, dalmachd.

perversion, s. fiaradh, claonadh.

pervert, v. a. fiar, claon ; truaill.

pervertible, adj. so-chlaonadh.

pervicacious, adj. reasgach, dàna.

pervious, adj. neo-dhìonach.

pest, s. plàigh ; dragh, buaireas.

pester, v. a. cuir dragh, buair.

pesthouse, s. tigh-leighis na plàighe.

pestiferous, adj. plàigheach, marbhtach, gabhaltach.

pestilence, s. plàigh, sgrios-ghalar.

pestilent, adj. plàigheach, gabhaltach.

pestle, s. plocan-pronnaidh.

pet, s. dod, frionas ; uan-pheata, uilleagan.

petal, s. duilleag, bileag.

petalous, adj. duilleagach, bileagach.

petition, s. achanaich, iarrtas, guidhe, aslachadh.

petition, v. a. guidh, aslaich, iarr.

petitionary, adj. aslachail.

petitioner, s. fear-aslachaidh.

petrifaction, s. tionndadh gu cloich.

petrify, v. a. tionndaidh, gu cloich.

petticoat, s. còta-bàn.

pettifogger, s. fear-lagha gun fhiù, ball-donais ; luimeire, gearra-ghobaich.

pettifogging, adj. suarach.

pettiness, s. bige, crìne.

pettish, adj. dodach, frionasach.

petty, adj. beag, suarrach, crìon.

petulance, s. beadaidheachd.

petulant, adj. beadaidh, leamh, peasan-ach, bleideil ; goileamach, beag-narach, mì-mhodhail.

pew, s. suidheachan, àite-suidhe.

pewet, s. a' chrann-lach.

pewter, s. staoin, feòdar, flòdar.

pewterer, s. cèard-staoine.

phalanx, s. dlùth-fheachd.

phantasm, s. faoin-bharail.

phantom, s. taibhse, tannasg.

pharisaical, adj. cràbhach o'n leth a muigh ; cealgach.

pharmacy, s. eòlas chungaidhean.

pharos, s. tigh-soluis, taigh-faire.

phasis, s. aghaidh, cruth, dealbh.

pheasant, s. an easag.

phenomenon, s. sealladh iongantach, nì neo-àbhaiseach.

phial, s. searrag bheag.

philanthropy, s. gràdh-daonna ; caomhal-achd ; seirc.

philippic, s. màbaireachd, càineadh.

philologer, philologist, s. cànanaich ; cainntear.

philology, s. eòlas-chànan, eòlas slo-innteireachd fhacal.

philomel, s. an spìdeag.

philosopher, s. feallsanach, teallsanach, càileadair.

philosopher's-stone, s. clach-nam-buadh.

philosophical, adj. feallsanta, ionns-aichte, eagnaidh, fiosrach.

philosophy, s. feallsanachd, teallsanachd, eagnaidheachd, reusonachadh, àrd-fhoghlum.

philter, s. eòlas-gràidh.

phiz, s. aogas, aghaidh, aodann.

phlebotomise, v. a. tarruing fuil.

phlebotomist, s. fear tarruing fala.

phlebotomy, s. fuil-tharruing.

phlegm, s. ronn ; leanntan-cuirp.

phlegmatic, adj. ronnach ; trom, lunnd-ach.

phleme, s. tuadh-fhala.

phosphorus, s. reull na maidne, coinnle-pianain.

phraseology, s. modh-labhairt.

phthisis, s. tinneas-caithe, éiteach.

phthisical, adj. caithteach, éiteachail, searganach.

phylactery, s. crios air an robh sgrìobh-aidhean sònraicht' aig na h-Iudhaich.

physic, s. eòlas leighis ; cungaidhean-leighis ; feallsanachd-nàduir.

physical, adj. nàdurra, càileadarach, leigheasach.

physician, s. léigh, lighiche.

physiognomy, s. gnùis-fhiosachd ; aogas, aogasg.

physiologist, s. feallsanach ghnèithean is chàilean.

physiology, s. feallsanachd ghnèithean is chàilean, eòlas air buadhan a' chuirp.

pick, v. tagh, gabh roghadh is taghadh ; tog, tionail ; cuir air leth, glan ; fosgail glas ; tiolp ; spiol, criom.

pickaxe, s. piocaid.
picked, piked, adj. guineach, geur.
pickeer, v. spùinn, spùill.
pickle, s. picill ; staid, cor, càradh.
pickle, v. a. saill, dèan saillte.
picklock, s. glas-phiocaidh.
pickpocket, s. frithmheirleach, meirleach nam pòcaidean.
picktooth, s. bioran fhiacal.
picture, s. dealbh, dreach, coltas.
picturesque, adj. bòidheach, àillidh.
piddle, v. a. pioc, bi faoineasach, dèan féileaganaich.
pie, s. pithean ; pioghaid.
piece, s. mìr, roinn, earrann ; caob, bloigh ; gunna ; bonn, pìos (soitheach airgid, pàiper balla = 12 slat, anart grinn = 10 slat).
piece, v. cuir mìr ri ; ceangail, tàth, tuthagaich.
piecemeal, adv. mìr air mhìr, 'n a chaoban.
pied, adj. breac, ballach, balla-bhreac.
pier, s. seòlait, laimhrig ; carragh.
pierce, v. toll, sàth ; drùigh, gluais ; lot, gon, guin.
piercer, s. brodaiche, bior-tollaidh.
piety, s. cràbhadh ; diadhachd.
pig, s. uircean, muc gàta.
pigeon, s. calman, colm.
piggin, s. pigean, soitheachan.
pigment, s. dath, lìth.
pigmy, s. duairce, troich, luspardan.
pig-nut, s. cnò-thalmhuinn.
pike, s. geadas, crann-shleagh.
pikestaff, s. crann-sleagha.
pilaster, s. carragh ceithir-chearnach.
pilchard, pilcher, s. sgadan-sligeach.
pilcher, s. faluing air a lìnigeadh le bian.
pile, s. post ; cruach, dùn ; aitreabh.
pile, v. tòrr, cruach, càrn ; lìon.
pilewort, s. an searraiche.
pilfer, v. tiolp, dèan braide.
pilferer, s. frith-mheirleach.
pilgrim, s. eilthireach, fear-cuairt, taisd-ealach.
pilgrimage, s. eilthireachd.
pill, s. cungaidh leighis.
pillage, s. creach, spùinn, togail.
pillage, v. a. spùinn, spùill, creach.
pillar, s. carragh, colbh ; fear-cul-taic.
pillion, s. sumag, peallag, pilleag.
pillory, s. ballan-stiallach, brangas, nàire fhollaiseach.
pillow, s. adhartan, cluasag.
pillow-beer, s. còmhdach-cluasaig.
pilosity, s. ròmaiche, molaiche.
pilot, s. fear-iùil luinge.
pilot, v. a. treòraich ; stiùr.
pilotage, s. duais-threòraichidh, duais fear-iùil.
pilous, adj. ròmach, molach.
pimento, s. peabar-dubh.
pimp, s. maor-shiùrsaichean.

pimpernel, s. seamrag-muire.
pimping, adj. leibideach, crìon.
pimple, s. buicean, plucan, guirean.
pin, s. dealg, prìne ; cnag, dùl.
pincers, s. turcais, teanchor.
pinch, v. fàisg, gàmagaich ; teannaich ; brùth ; goirtich, ciùrr ; éignich, sàr-aich, pioc, claoidh ; caomhainn, bi gann.
pinch, s. gàmag ; teanntachd.
pinchbeck, s. seòrsa miotailte.
pincushion, s. prìneachan.
pine, s. craobh ghiuthais.
pine, v. caoidh, searg, caith as.
pinfold, s. punnd, fang.
pinion, s. cleite, ite-sgéithe ; glas-làmh.
pinion, v. a. ceangail na sgiathan, cuibhrich, ceangail na làmhan.
pink, s. luibh àraidh ; seòrs' éisg ; roghadh, taghadh ; dath bàndhearg.
pink, v. bior, toll ; sàth ; caog.
pin-money, s. airgead pòcaid bhan.
pinnace, s. geòla, sgoth luinge.
pinnacle, s. binnein, turraid.
pinner, s. ceannbharr.
pint, s. pinnt, lethchart.
pioneer, s. saoighdear-tochlaidh, ceud fhear-àiteachaidh.
pious, adj. diadhaidh, cràbhach.
pip, s. pìochan, galar-chearc.
pipe, s. pìob, feadan ; guth, anail.
pipe, v. dèan pìobaireachd.
piper, s. pìobaire.
piping, adj. lag, faoin, goileach.
pipkin, s. soitheachan creadha.
piquant, adj. beur, geur, goirt, teth.
pique, s. falachd, mìorun, gamhlas.
pique, v. a. feargaich ; farranaich.
piracy, s. muir-spùinneadh.
pirate, s. spùinneadair-mara.
piratical, adj. spùinneach.
piscary, s. cead-iasgaich.
piscation, s. iasgaireachd.
piscatory, adj. iasgach.
piscivorous, adj. iasg-itheach.
pish ! interj. fuith ! fuidh ! fuich !
pismire, s. seangan, sneaghan.
piss, s. mùn ; fual ; v. n. mùin.
pistol, s. daga, dag ; seòra cùinidh.
piston, s. slat-stealladair.
pit, s. toll, sloc ; aigein ; uaigh.
pitapat, s. plosgadh-cridhe ; luaths-analach ; plosgartaich.
pitch, s. bìgh, àirde, tomhas, cor.
pitch, v. suidhich ; òrduich ; tilg, tilg an coinneamh a chinn ; tuit an comhair do chinn ; tagh.
pitcher, s. pigidh-uisge, muga-mór.
pitchfork, s. gobhlag aolaich, gràp.
pitchy, adj. bìgheach ; doilleir, dubh.
pit-coal, s. ala-ghual.
piteous, adj. muladach, brònach, tùrsach, truagh ; truacanta.

pitfall, s. bùthach, ribe ; toll fo fhraoch, sloc-thuislidh.

pith, s. glaodhan ; spionnadh.

pithiness, s. spionnadh, treòir.

pithless, adj. gun spionnadh, fann.

pithy, adj. glaodhanach ; spìonntail, laidir, smiorail.

pitiable, adj. truagh, bochd.

pitiful, adj. truacanta, tròcaireach ; teò-chridheach, truagh; muladach, bròn-ach ; leibideach.

pitiless, adj. neo-thruacanta, an-iochd-mhor, cruaidh-chridheach, mì-thròcair-each ; gun truas.

pittance, s. cuibhrionn, rud beag truagh.

pity, s. truacantas, truas.

pity, v. gabh truas.

pivot, s. udalan ; cuairt-udalan, lùdagan.

pix, s. naomhchiste.

placable, adj. so-chìosnachadh, soirbh, ciùin.

placard, placart, s. fuagradh ; sanas-follaiseach.

place, s. àite, ionad; còmhnaidh; dreuchd.

place, v. a. suidhich, socraich.

placid, adj. ciùin, socrach, soirbh.

placidness, s. ciùineachd, soirbheachd.

plagiarism, s. mèirle-sgrìobhaidh.

plagiary, plagiarist, s. mèirleach-sgrìobh-aidh.

plague, s. plàigh ; claoidh ; dragh, buaireadh.

plague, v. a. pian, buair, leamhaich.

plaguy, adj. plàigheach ; draghail.

plaice, s. leòbag-mhór.

plaid, s. breacan ; suaineach.

plain, adj. réidh, còmhnard, mìn, lom ; fosgailte ; saor, soilleir, soirbh.

plain, s. còmhnard, réidhlean, réidhleach, faiche, blàr, lom.

plain-dealing, s. tréidhireachd.

plainness, s. còmhnardachd, réidheachd, mìneachd ; fosgailteachd, tréidhir-eachd ; neo-sgeamhalachd.

plaint, s. gearan, caoidh, acan, bròn.

plaintiff, s. fear-agairt.

plaintive, adj. tiamhaidh.

plait, s. filleadh, filleag, dual, pleat.

plan, s. innleachd ; dealbh, cumadh.

plan, v. a. dealbh, deilbh, suidhich.

planched, adj. déileach.

plancher, s. déile, bòrd.

plane, s. locair ; còmhnard.

plane, v. a. locair, locraich.

planet, s. reull, reull-shiùbhlach.

planetary, adj. reulltach.

plank, s. bòrd, clàr, déile.

plank, v. a. bòrdaich, clàraich.

planner, s. fear-tionnsgain.

plant, s. luibh, meacan ; fiùran.

plant, v. suidhich ; cuir, sìolaich, socraich, daingnich.

plantain, s. cuach-Phàdruig.

plantation, s. suidheachadh ; ùr-àiteach-adh ; toirt a steach.

planter, s. fear-suidheach, fear-àiteach-aidh.

planting, s. suidheachadh, curachd.

plash, s. lochan, pollag ; fiùran meanglan.

plash, v. a. luidrig ; figh air a' chéile.

plashy, adj. lodanach, uisgidh, fuarraidh.

plasm, s. molldair, ladhadair, cumadair.

plaster, s. sglàib ; plàsda-leighis.

plaster, v. a. sglàibrich ; glaodh, cuir plàsd' air.

plasterer, s. sglàibeadair.

plastic, adj. cruth-thabhairteach.

plat, s. mìr fearainn, goirtean.

plate, s. lann ; éideadh-màilleach, obair-airgeid ; truinnsear.

plate, v. a. lannaich ; airgeadaich.

platform, s. còmhnard ; dealbh, clàr-aghaidh; uchdan, ardadan, leubhann.

platoon, s. gunnairean, buidheann shaighdearan.

platter, s. mias-mhór; aiseid ; dualadair.

plaudit, s. caithream aoibhneis, lùth-ghair, iolach.

plausibility, s. dreach fìrinn.

plausible, adj. coltach, beulchar, carach.

play, v. cluich ; dèan fearas-chuideachd ; dèan mire, dèan àbhachd, dèan sùg-radh ; meall, mag, dèan fochaid ; oibrich, gluais.

play, s. cluiche, mire, sùgradh, aighear ; cleas ; macnus ; comas-gluasaid.

player, s. fear-cluiche, cleasaiche.

playfellow, s. companach-cluiche.

playful, adj. cleasanta, beadrach, mir-eagach, sùgrach, mear.

playhouse, s. tigh-cluiche, tigh-cleasachd.

playsome, adj. mireagach, sùgach.

plaything, s. ball-cluiche, ceann-réidh.

plea, s. cùis-thagraidh ; leisgeul.

plead, v. a. dìon, tagair ; agair, reusonaich.

pleader, s. fear-tagraidh.

pleading, s. tagradh, agairt.

pleasant, adj. taitneach, ciatach ; tlachd-mhor, sunntach, faoilidh, cridheil.

pleasantness, s. taitneachd, tlachd, ciat-achd, tlachdmhorachd ; sunnt, cridh-ealas.

pleasantry, s. cridhealas, aighear, àbh-acus, abhcaid.

please, v. toilich, riaraich, taitinn.

pleasurable, adj. taitneach, ciatach.

pleasure, s. taitneas, tlachd, toileachadh, toil-inntinn, ciataidh.

plebeian, s. duine cumanta, fear de 'n tuath.

plebeian, adj. cumanta, anuasal.

pledge, s. geall ; deoch-slàinte.

pledge, v. a. cuir an geall, òl air slàinte.

Pleiades, s. an grigleachan.

plenary, adj. làn, foirfe ; iomlan.

plenipotence, s. làn-chumhachd.

plenipotent, *adj.* làn-chumhachdach, le àrd-ùghdaras.
plenipotentiary, *s.* àrd-theachdair, teachdaire-rioghachd (aig a bheil làn-ùghdaras).
plenitude, *s.* lànachd ; pailteas.
plenteous, *adj.* pailt, tarbhach.
plentiful, *adj.* lìonmhor ; torach, pailt.
plenty, *s.* pailteas ; lànachd, saoibhreas.
plethora, plethory, *s.* làntachd cuirp, dòmhlachd cuirp.
plethoric, *adj.* làn, dòmhail.
pleurisy, *s.* an treaghaid.
pleuritic, *adj.* treaghaideach.
pliable, *adj.* sùbailte, maoth.
pliableness, *s.* sùbailteachd.
pliant, *adj.* so-lùbadh, leam-leat.
pliers, *s.* greimiche, turcais.
plight, *s.* cor, càradh, inbhe, cùis.
plight, *v. a.* thoir geall, thoir urras.
plinth, *s.* bunait carraigh, stéidh.
plod, *v. n.* saoithrich, oibrich, imich gu trom ; dian-chnuasaich.
plodder, *s.* fear-trom-shaoithreach, buan-oibriche.
plot, *s.* croit, goirtean ; innleachd ; feall-chomhairle ; cuilbheart, foill.
plot, *v.* tionnsgainn ; suidhich ; dèan foill ; dèan as-innleachd.
plough, *s.* crann, crann-àraidh.
plough, *v. a.* treabh, àr ; reub.
ploughman, *s.* treabhaiche.
ploughshare, *s.* soc croinn.
plover, *s.* feadag.
pluck, *v. a.* spìon, buain.
pluck, *s.* tarruing, spìonadh ; cridhe ; sgamhan agus grùthan beathaich.
plug, *s.* plucan, cnag, geinn, tùc.
plug, *v. a.* plucaich, geinnich, dùin.
plum, *s.* plumbas.
plumage, *s.* iteach.
plumb, *v. a.* feuch doimhneachd, feuch dìrichead.
plumb, *adv.* dìreach (mar balla).
plumber, *s.* ceard-luaidhe.
plume, *s.* ite, fàbhar, dos-mullaich, seòcan.
plume, *v.* tog itean ; cuir dos air, dosaich ; séid suas, àt.
plummet, *s.* sreang-thomhais doimhneachd ; luaidhe, inghar.
plump, *adj.* sultmhor, dòmhail, reamhar, reachmhor, taiceil, tiugh.
plump, *v. n.* plub, plum.
plumpness, *s.* sultmhorachd, somaltachd, domhladachd.
plum-pudding, *s.* marag phlumbais.
plumy, *adj.* còmhdaichte le itean.
plunder, *s.* cobhartach, creach.
plunder, *v. a.* spùinn ; tog creach.
plunderer, *s.* spùinneadair.
plunge, *v.* tùm, cuir fodha ; tilg ; sàth, leum ('s an uisge).

plunge, *s.* tumadh, bogadh ; àmhghar, airc, teinn.
plural, *adj.* iomarra.
pluralist, *s.* fear aig a bheil barrachd air aon dreuchd.
plurality, *s.* iomadachd.
plush, *s.* seòrsa aodaich molach.
pluvial, pluvious, *adj.* frasach, braonach, robach, fliuch.
ply, *v.* saoithrich, oibrich ri, iomair, dian-ghnàthaich, grìos, aslaich, guidh ; lùb.
ply, *s.* aomadh, car, laighe ; filleadh.
pneumatic, *adj.* gaothach.
pneumatics, *s.* eòlas gaoithe, eòlas air laghan na gaoithe.
pneumonia, *s.* teasach sgamhan.
pneumonics, *s.* leigheas sgamhain.
poach, *v.* slaop ; dèan goid frìthe.
poacher, *s.* mèirleach seilge.
poachy, *adj.* àitidh, bog.
pock, *s.* bòc, guirean brice ; pocan.
pocket, *s.* pòcaid, pòca, pùidse.
pocket, *v. a.* cuir 's a' phòcaid.
pocket-book, *s.* leabhar-pòcaid.
poculent, *adj.* a dh' fhaodair òl.
pod, *s.* cochull, plaosg, sgrath, rùsg.
poem, *s.* dàn, duan, laoidh.
poesy, *s.* bàrdachd, rannaighachd.
poet, *s.* bàrd, filidh, aos-dàna.
poetaster, *s.* sgonna-bhàrd.
poetess, poetress, *s.* ban-bhàrd.
poetic, poetical, *adj.* bàrdail.
poetry, *s.* bàrdachd, ranntachd.
poignancy, *s.* gairge, géire, seirbhe.
poignant, *adj.* garg, geur, searbh.
point, *s.* roinn, bior ; rudha, sròn ; neart, seadh, brìgh, tiota ; cor ; ponc, comharradh ; ball ; cuspair, an dearbh-nì.
point, *v. a.* geuraich, thoir roinn air, bioraich ; seòl, comharraich ; cuimsich ; poncaich ; feuch, nochd.
pointed, *adj.* and *part.* geur, biorach ; poncail, eagnaidh.
pointer, *s.* cù-eunach.
pointless, *adj.* maol ; gun roinn.
poise, *s.* co-chothrom, air mheidh.
poise, *v. a.* co-chothromaich.
poison, *s.* nimh, puinnsean.
poison, *v. a.* nimhich ; truaill, mill.
poisonous, *adj.* nimheach, nimheil.
poitrel, *s.* uchdbheairt eich, etc.
poke, *s.* poca, baig, màileid.
poke, *v. a.* smeuraich, rùraich.
poker, *s.* bioran-griosaich.
pole, *s.* crann, maide, cabar, cuaille ; cùig slat gu leth.
polecat, *s.* feòcullan, taghan.
polemic, *adj.* connspaideach.
polemic, *s.* connspaidiche.
pole-star, *s.* an reull-iùil thuath.
police, *s.* riaghladh baile.
policy, *s.* innleachd-riaghlaidh ; seòltachd, steòrnadh, crìontachd, gliocas.

polish, v. lìomh, liomhaich, sgéimhich ; oileanaich.
polish, s. lìomhadh, loinnireachd.
polisher, s. fear-lìomhaidh.
polite, adj. modhail, oileanach.
politeness, s. modhalachd.
politic, political, adj. eòlach, eagnaidh, seòlta, domhain, carach ; cuilbheartach ; a bhuineas do dh'eòlas-riaghlaidh.
politician, s. fear eòlach mu innleachdan riaghlaidh.
politics, s. feallsanachd riaghlaidh.
politure, s. liomharachd.
polity, s. modh riaghlaidh.
poll, s. ceann ; ainmchlar.
poll, v. a. sgud, bèarr, sgath dheth ; spùinn, creach, lom ; gabh ainmean, gearr falt
pollard, s. craobh bhearrte ; damh gun chròic ; garbhan, pronn.
pollenger, s. preaschoille.
pollute, v. a. truaill, salaich, measgaich le salchar.
polluted, part. and adj. truaillte.
pollution, s. truailleadh, salchar.
poltroon, s. gealtaire, cladhaire.
polyanthus, s. sòbhrach-gheamhraidh.
polygamy, s. iomphòsadh, barrachd air aon bhean còmhla.
polyglot, adj. iomchainnteach.
polygon, s. iomchearnag.
polypous, adj. iomchasach.
polypus, s. at-cuinnein.
polysyllable, s. iomshiola.
pomade, s. ola-cinn, ola-fuilt.
pomatum, s. ungadh fuilt.
pomegranate, s. grànubhall.
pommel, s. ubhal claidheimh.
pommel, v. a. slad, slacainn, pronn.
pomp, s. greadhnachas, uaill.
pomposity, s. mórchuis.
pompous, adj. mórchuiseach, uailleil.
pompousness, s. móralachd.
pond, s. linne, uisge-tàimh.
ponder, v. smuainich, beachdsmuainich, fidrich, cnuasaich.
ponderosity, s. cudthromachd ; cùramachd.
ponderous, adj. cudthromach, cùramach, laidir.
poniard, s. cuinnsear.
pontage, s. cìs-drochaid.
pontiff, s. àrd-shagart, am pàpa.
pontifical, adj. àrd-shagartach.
pontifical, s. leabhar nan deas-ghnàth.
pontificate, s. pàpanachd.
pontoon, s. drochaid-fhleodraidh.
pony, s. each beag.
poop, s. deireadh luinge, uisge-tàimh.
poor, adj. bochd, aimbeartach, dòlum, ainnis ; ìosal, suarrach, leibideach ; truagh, cruaidh ; caol, seang.

poorly, adj. euslainteach, tinn.
pop, s. sgailc, bragh, braghadh.
pope, s. am pàpa.
popedom, s. pàpachd.
popery, papistry, s. pàpanachd.
popgun, potgun, s. gunna-sgailc.
popinjay, s. an snagan-daraich.
popish, adj. pàpanach.
poplar, s. a' chritheann.
poppy, s. an cromlus.
populace, s. an sluagh, an cumanta.
popular, adj. taitneach do 'n t-sluagh ; cumanta ; so-thuigsinn.
popularity, s. sluagh-thaitneachd, meas, ùidh.
populate, v. n. fàs lìonmhor, sìolaich ; lion le sluagh.
population, s. sluagh tìre.
populous, adj. sluaghmhor.
porcelain, s. criadh fhìnealta.
porch, s. sgàilthigh, foirdhorus, fosgalan.
pore, s. pòr, tollan-falluis.
pore, v. n. geur-amhairc ; geur-sgrùd, geur-bheachdaich.
pore-blind, adj. dalladh-eunain.
pork, s. muicfheòil ùr.
porker, porkling, s. uircean.
porosity, s. tolltachd, còsachd.
porous, pory, adj. tolltach, pòrach.
porpoise, porpus, s. péileag, cana.
porridge, pottage, s. lite, brochan.
porringer, s. soitheach beag creadha.
port, s. port ; cala, acarsaid, dorus, geata ; iomchar, giùlan ; fion-dearg.
portable, adj. so-ghiùlan, aotrom.
portal, s. dorus-àrd, geata mór.
portcullis, s. drochaid-thogalach.
portend, v. a. fàisnich, fiosaich.
portent, s. droch comharradh.
portentous, adj. droch-thargrach.
porter, s. dorsair ; gille-teachdaireachd ; dubh-lionn.
porterage, s. duais iomchair.
portglaive, portglave, s. fear-iomchair claidheimh, gille-claidheimh.
porthole, s. toll gunna mhóir, uinneag (an cliathach luinge).
portico, s. sràid chòmhdaichte.
portion, s. earrann, roinn, cuid.
portion, v. a. roinn ; thoir dlighe no tochradh do.
portliness, s. stàtalachd, foghainteachd, riochdalachd.
portly, adj. stàtail, foghainteach, domhail.
portmanteau, s. màileid-turais.
portrait, s. dealbh duine, sàmhla.
portray, v. a. tarruing dealbh.
portress, s. bandorsair.
pose, v. a. cuir 'na thosd, cuir an iomacheist ; ceasnaich.
position, s. suidheachadh.
positional, adj. ionadach.

positive, *adj.* fìor, fìrinneach ; dearbh-chinnteach, dearbhte ; dìreach, sòn-raichte, soilleir ; féin - bharalach ; suidhichte, stéidhichte, socraichte, ùghdarrach.
positiveness, *s.* cinnteachd, dearbh tachd ; féin-bharalachd.
posse, *s.* buidheann, feachd.
possess, *v. a.* sealbhaich, gabh seilbh.
possession, *s.* sealbhachadh, seilbh.
possessive, possessory, *adj.* seilbheach seilbheachail.
possessor, *s.* sealbhadair.
posset, *s.* bainne air a bhinndeachadh le fìon, etc.
possibility, *s.* comas, comasachd.
possible, *adj.* comasach, a ghabhas deanamh.
post, *s.* gille-litrichean ; post ; turas-cabhagach ; ionad-freiceadain ; dreuchd ; àite ; gnothach.
post, *v. n.* dèan turas cabhagach.
postage, *s.* prìs-giùlain litreach.
post-boy, *s.* fear carbaid-rathaid.
post-chaise, *s.* carbad-duaise.
posterior, *adj.* deireannach.
posteriors, *s.* leth-deiridh, màsan.
posterity, *s.* na linntean ri teachd, sliochd.
postern, *s.* dorus beag, frith-gheata.
post-haste, *s.* cabhag, grad-shiubhal.
posthumous, *adj.* an déigh bàis.
postillion, *s.* gille-carbaid.
postman, *s.* gille-litrichean.
postmaster, *s.* ceannard tigh-litrichean.
post-office, *s.* tigh-litrichean.
postpone, *v. a.* cuir dàil.
postscript, *s.* fath-sgrìobhadh.
postulate, *s.* beachd no fìrinn gun dearbhadh, bonn a dh'aidichear air sgàth argumaid.
posture, *s.* suidheachadh, laighe, dòigh suidhe no seasamh no laighe ; staid, seòl.
posy, *s.* blàth-dhos, blàth-bhad.
pot, *s.* poit, prais, praiseach.
pot, *v. a.* cuir am poit.
potash, *s.* luath luibhean.
potation, *s.* pòit, pòitearachd, deoch.
potato, *s.* buntàta.
pot-bellied, *adj.* bronnach.
potch, *v. a.* dèan goid, dèan mèirle.
pot companion, *s.* companach òil.
potency, *s.* neart, cumhachd.
potent, *adj.* cumhachdach, treun.
potentate, *s.* righ, àrd-uachdaran.
potential, *adj.* comasach ; buadhach, neartmhor.
potentiality, *s.* comasachd.
pother, *s.* gleadhraich, buaireas.
potion, *s.* deoch.
potsherd, *s.* spreadhan, pigean, slige-chreadha.

potter, *s.* criadhadair.
pottery, *s.* criadhadaireachd.
pottle, *s.* tomhas cheithir pinnt.
pouch, *s.* pòcaid, pòca, brù mhór.
poult, *s.* isean-eòin, pùda.
poulterer, *s.* fear-reic eun, fear - togail eun.
poultice, *s.* fuarlite, fuarag.
poultry, *s.* cearcan, eòin-tighe.
pounce, *s.* spòg, cràg ; ìnean eòin.
pound, *s.* pund ; pund-Sasunnach ; punnd spréidhe.
pound, *v. a.* pronn, brùth, bleith ; cuir am punnd.
poundage, *s.* airgead-puinnd.
pour, *v. a.* dòirt, taom, brùchd.
pout, *s.* bodach-ruadh, pollach.
pout, *v. n.* cuir gnoig ort, cuir spliug ort, cuir spreill ort.
poverty, *s.* bochdainn, ainnis.
powder, *s.* fùdar, dus, smùr, sad.
powder, *v. a.* mìn-phronn, dèan 'na smùr ; crath smùr air ; fùdaraich, crath salann air.
powder-horn, *s.* adharc-fhùdair.
powdery, *adj.* mìn, pronn.
power, *s.* cumhachd, comas.
powerful, *adj.* cumhachdach.
powerfulness, *s.* neartmhorachd.
powerless, *adj.* lagchuiseach, fann.
pox, *s.* breac ; a' bhreac-Fhràngach.
practic, *adj.* cleachdach ; teòma.
practicable, *adj.* so-dhèanta, a dh'fhaodar a dhèanamh, a ghabhas dèanamh.
practical, *adj.* cleachdail, cleachdte.
practice, *s.* cleachdadh, àbhais ; gnàth, innleachd, dòigh.
practise, *v.* cleachd, gnàthaich.
practitioner, *s.* fear-cleachdaidh, fear-lagha, leighiche.
pragmatical, *adj.* beadaidh, leamh.
praise, *s.* cliù, moladh.
praise, *v. a.* mol, cliùthaich.
praiseworthiness, *s.* ion-mholtachd.
praiseworthy, *adj.* ion-mholta.
prame, *s.* bàta-leathann, coite.
prance, *v. n.* leum, geàrr sùrdag, sùrdag-aich ; céimnich gu h-uallach.
prancing, *adj.* leumnach, sùrdagach, beiceiseach, meamnach.
prank, *s.* cleas, cleasachd, meamna, àbhcaid, mire ; droch-cleas.
prate, *v. n.* dèan goileam, dèan lonais, dèan beulais.
prate, *s.* faoinchainnt, lonais.
prater, *s.* glagaire, gobaire.
prating, *s.* glagaireachd, goileam.
pratingly, *adv.* gu goileamach.
prattle, *s.* faoin-chainnt, gobaireachd, briotas, briot, còmhradh clainn bhig.
prattle, *v. n.* déan gobaireachd.
prattler, *s.* goileamaiche.
pravity, *s.* truaillidheachd.

prawn, *s.* am muasgan-caol.
pray, *v.* dèan ùrnaigh, guidh.
prayer, *s.* ùrnaigh, guidhe, iarrtas, athchuinge.
prayer-book, *s.* leabhar-ùrnaigh.
preach, *v.* searmonaich.
preacher, *s.* searmonaiche.
preaching, *s.* searmonachadh.
preamble, *s.* roimh-ràdh.
precarious, *adj.* neo-chinnteach, cunnartach.
precariously, *adv.* gu teagmhach, gu baoghalach.
precariousness, *s.* neo-chinnteachd.
precaution, *s.* faicill, roimh-chùram.
precaution, *v. a.* roimh-earalaich, cuir air fhaiceall.
precede, *v. a.* roimh-imich, rach roimhe.
precedence, *s.* roimh-imeachd, toiseach, tùs ; urram toisich.
precedent, *adj.* roimhe, tùsach.
precedent, *s.* eiseamplair.
precedently, *adv.* roimh-làimh.
precentor, *s.* fear-togail-fuinn.
precept, *s.* reachd, riaghailt, àithne.
preceptive, *adj.* reachdach, àithnteil.
preceptor, *s.* oid-ionnsachaidh.
precinct, *s.* comharradh-crìche, àruinn.
precious, *adj.* luachmhor, prìseil.
preciousness, *s.* luachmhorachd.
precipice, *s.* sgòrr, caschreag.
precipitance, *s.* caise, braise, cabhag, deifir, braisead, déine.
precipitant, *adj.* cas, bras, dian.
precipitate, *v.* tilg sìos, tilg an comhair a' chinn, cabhagaich, deifirich ; tuit sìos, sìolaidh gu grunnd.
precipitate, *adj.* chabhagach, deifireach, neo-fhaicilleach.
precipitately, *adv.* an comhair a' chinn.
precipitation, *s.* caise, braise ; tuiteam sìos ; sioladh gu grunnd.
precipitous, *adj.* cas, corrach, sgorrach, creagach ; bras.
precipitousness, *s.* caise, braise.
precise, *adj.* poncail, eagarrach, fuirmeil.
precision, preciseness, *s.* poncalachd, eagarrachd.
preclude, *v. a.* dùin a mach, grab, bac, cuir bacadh air.
preclusive, *adj.* toirmeasgach.
precocious, *adj.* seanacharra.
precociousness, precocity, *s.* seanacharrachd.
precognition, *s.* roimh fhiosrachadh, ceud cheasnachadh (air fianuisean).
preconceit, *s.* roimh-bheachd.
preconceive, *v. a.* roimh-bheachdaich.
preconception, *s.* roimh-bheachd.
preconcert, *v.* roimh-shuidhich.
precontract, *s.* roimh-chùmhnant.
precontract, *v.* roimh-chùmhnantaich.
precurse, *s.* roimh-ruith.

precursor, *s.* roimh-ruithear.
precursory, *adj.* roimh-ruitheach.
predaceous, *adj.* creachach.
predatory, *adj.* reubainneach.
predecessor, *s.* roimh-shealbhadair, fear mu dheireadh a bha 's an dreuchd.
predestinate, *v. a.* roimh-òrduich.
predestination, *s.* roimh-òrduchadh Dhé, roimh-thaghadh Dhé.
predestine, *v. a.* roimh-òrduich.
predetermination, *s.* roimh-òrduchadh, roimh-shònrachadh.
predetermine, *v. a.* roimh-òrduich, roimh-shònraich, roimh-rùnaich.
predicament, *s.* cor, ìre, gne, càs.
predicate, *s.* tuairisgeul, aithris.
predicate, *v.* abair, innis, aithris, cuir an céill.
predication, *s.* innse ; iomradh.
predict, *v. a.* roimh-innis, roimh-aithris.
prediction, *s.* fàisneachd.
predictive, *adj.* roimh-innseach.
predictor, *s.* fiosaiche, fàidh.
predigestion, *s.* roimh-mheirbheadh.
predilection, *s.* roimh-thlachd.
predispose, *v. a.* roimh-uidheamaich.
predisposition, *s.* roimh-uidheamachadh, roimh-ullachadh.
predominance, predominancy, *s.* barrachd, uachdranachd, làmh-an-uachdar, buaidh, ceannas.
predominant, *adj.* uachdranach, ceannasach, buadhach.
predominate, *v. n.* buadhaich.
pre-elect, *v. a.* roimh-thagh.
pre-eminence, *s.* àrd-bhuaidh, àrd-urram.
pre-eminent, *adj.* àrd-bhuadhach.
pre-engage, *v. a.* roimh-cheangail, gabh roimh-làimh.
pre-engagement, *s.* roimh-cheangal, roimh-ghealladh, roimh-chumhnant.
pre-establishment, *s.* roimh-shuidheachadh, roimh-shocrachadh.
pre-exist, *v. n.* bi ann roimh-làimh.
pre-existence, *s.* roimh-bhith.
pre-existent, *adj.* roimh-bhitheach.
preface, *s.* roimh-ràdh.
preface, *v. n.* roimh-abair.
prefatory, *adj.* roimh-ràdhach.
prefect, *s.* ceannard, fear-dìona.
prefer, *v. a.* roghnaich, àrdaich.
preferable, *adj.* na's feàrr.
preference, *s.* roghainn.
preferment, *s.* àrdachadh.
prefiguration, *s.* roimh-shamhlachadh.
prefix, *v. a.* roimh-shuidhich.
prefix, *s.* roimh-fhacal.
pregnable, *adj.* ghabhas glacadh.
pregnancy, *s.* lethtromachd.
pregnant, *adj.* torrach, leth-tromach, làn, trom, air chloinn, tarbhach, sìolmhor.
pregustation, *s.* roimh-bhlasad.

prejudge, *v. a.* roimh-bhreithnich, thoir beachd roimh-làimh.

prejudgment, *s.* roimh-bhreith, claon-bhreith.

prejudice, *s.* claon-bhàigh ; cron, beachd air blaigh eòlais.

prejudice, *v.* cuir an droch bheachd, cuir an claon-bharail ; dochainn le claon bhreith ; ciùrr, lochdaich.

prejudicial, *adj.* claon-bhreitheach ; cron-ail, aimhleasach.

prelacy, *s.* easbuigeachd.

prelate, *s.* easbuig.

prelatical, *adj.* easbuigeach.

prelection, *s.* searmonachadh, lectorachd.

preliminary, *adj.* tòiseachail, 's an dol a mach.

preliminary, *s.* ceudthus, toiseach.

prelude, *s.* deuchainn-ghleusta ; toiseach, roimh-ghnothach, roimh-chùis.

prelude, *v. a.* roimh-thaisbean.

prelusive, *adj.* roimh-làimheach.

premature, *adj.* roimh 'n mhithich, roimh'n àm, roimh-abaich.

prematurely, *adv.* gu h-an-tràthail, roimh 'n mhithich.

premeditate, *v. a.* roimh-thionnsgain, roimh-bheachdaich, roimh-chnuasaich.

premeditation, *s.* roimh-thionnsgnadh, roimh-bheachdachadh, roimh-chnuasachadh.

premerit, *v. a.* roimh-thoill.

premier, *adj.* prìomh, as àirde.

premier, *s.* àrd-chomhairliche (rìgh).

premise, *v. a.* roimh-mhìnich.

premises, *s.* roimh-fhìrinnean ; tighean, aitreabh, fearann.

premium, *s.* duais-barrachd.

premonish, *v. a.* roimh-earalaich.

premonition, *s.* roimh-fhiosrachadh.

premonstrate, *v. a.* roimh-thaisbean.

prenominate, *v. a.* roimh-ainmich.

prenomination, *s.* roimh-ainmeachadh.

preoccupation, *s.* roimh-ghabhail ; claon-bhàigh.

preoccupy, *v. a.* roimh-shealbhaich.

preominate, *v. a.* roimh-innis.

preopinion, *s.* roimh-bharail.

preordain, *v. a.* roimh-òrduich.

preordination, *s.* roimh-òrduchadh.

preparation, *s.* uidheamachadh.

preparative, *s.* gleusadh.

preparatory, *adj.* ullachail.

prepare, *v. a.* ullaich, uidheamaich, deasaich, dèan réidh.

preparedness, *s.* ullamhachd.

prepense, *adj.* roimh-smuaintichte, roimh-bheachdaichte, suidhichte, socraichte, rùnaichte.

preponderance, *s.* barrachd cudthrom, barrachd cothrom.

prepose, *v. a.* roimh-chuir.

preposition, *s.* roimh-bhriathar.

prepossess, *v. a.* roimh-shealbhaich.

prepossession, *s.* roimh-sheilbh.

prepossessor, *s.* roimh-shealbhadair.

preposterous, *adj.* docharach.

preposterously, *adv.* gu docharach, gu h-eu-céillidh.

prerequisite, *adj.* roimh-fheumail.

preresolve, *v. a.* roimh-shuidhich.

prerogative, *s.* còir-dhlighe.

prerogatived, *adj.* còir-dhligheach.

presage, presagement, manadh, fàisneachd, sanus.

presage, *v. a.* roimh-innis, roimh-thaisbean, targair, dèan fiosachd.

presbyter, *s.* fear-cléire, cléireach, pears'-eaglais ; sagart.

presbyterial, *adj.* cléireachail.

presbytery, *s.* cléir, ionad-naomh (an eaglais easbuigeach), tigh sagairt.

prescience, *s.* roimh-fhios.

prescient, *adj.* roimh-fhiosrach.

prescribe, *v.* thoir seòladh.

prescript, prescription, *s.* seòladh, òrdugh, riaghailt, òrdugh-cungaidh.

presence, *s.* làthaireachd, làthair ; dreach, tuar, aogas, dealbh, cruth ; tapachd, teòmachd.

present, *adj.* a làthair, dlùth, làthaireach, aig làimh ; 's an àm, 's a' cheart àm ; an cuimhne ; fo bheachd.

present, *s.* tìodhlac, tabhartas.

present, *v. a.* thoir an làthair, cuir 's an làthair, nochd, taisbean ; tairg, tabhair ; thoir seachad, thoir do, builich, air, thoir còir do.

presentable, *adj.* dreachmhor ; snasail ; as fhiach a thairgse.

presentation, *s.* tairgsinn, buileachadh, tabhairt, taisbeanadh, nochdadh, cur 's an làthair.

presentation, presention, *s.* roimh-fhaireachadh, roimh-fhiosrachd, roimh-bheachd. *See* present.

presentee, *s.* neach a fhuair còir air beathachadh eaglais.

presently, *adv.* 's a cheart àm, an ceart uair, air an uair, gu grad, gu clis, gu luath.

presentiment, *s.* roimh-bheachd, fios mothachail (roimh-làimh).

presentment, *s.* tabhairt.

presentness, *s.* cliseachd.

preservable, *adj.* so-ghléidhteach.

preservation, *s.* saoradh, tèarnadh, gleidh-eadh, tasgaidh, dìon.

preservative, *s.* cungaidh-leighis, inneal-gleidhidh (sam bith = salann, etc.).

preserve, *v. a.* saor, teasraig, dìon gléidh ; gréidh, dèan suas le cungaidh.

preserve, *s.* meas gréidhte.

preserver, *s.* fear teasraiginn.

preside, *v. n.* riaghail, riaghailtich.

presidency, *s.* riaghlaireachd.

president, s. fear-riaghlaidh; ceann-suidhe.
presignification, s. roimh-sheadh.
presignify, v. a. roimh-sheadhaich, innis roimh-laimh.
press, v. fàisg, brùth ; claoidh, sàraich ; éignich, co-éignich ; sparr, cuir iompadh ; fòirn.
press, s. bruthadair, fàsgadair ; clò-chlàr ; dòmhlachd, mùchadh ; déine, braise ; còrnchlar.
press-gang, s. luchd-ghlacaidh.
pression, s. bruthadh, fàsgadh.
pressman, s. fear clò-bhualaidh.
press-money, s. airgead-glacaidh.
pressure, s. bruthadh, fàsgadh, teannach-adh ; éigin, ainneart.
prest, adj. grad, clis, luath.
presumable, adj. coltach ri fìrinn.
presume, v. a. roimh-chreid, roimh-bheachdaich, gabh mar fhìrinn ; abair gun dearbhadh ; gabh ort, gabh mar dhànadas ; thoir ionnsaigh ladarna, thoir dàn-ionnsaigh.
presumption, s. roimh-bheachd ; faoin-dhànadas ; coltas cudthromach ; dànadas, ladarnas ; dall-earbsa.
presumptive, adj. roimh-smuainichte ; a réir coltais, coltach ; dàna, ladarna.
presumptuous, adj. àrdanach, dalma ; aindiadhaidh, neo-urramach, dàna ('s gun chòir).
presumptuousness, s. uaimhreachas, ladornas, dalmachd.
presupposal, s. roimh-bharail.
presuppose, v. a. roimh-bharalaich.
pretence, s. leithsgeul, sgàth, faoinsgeul ; cur an ìre, gabhail air féin.
pretend, v. leig ort, gabh ort ; dèan mealladh, gabh feall-choltas ; agair, tagair.
pretender, s. fear-agairt còrach air ni nach bun da.
pretensions, s. agartas, còire ; faoin-choltas.
preternatural, adj. mì-nàdurra.
pretext, s. còmhdach, falach, leisgeul.
priory, s. comunn mhanach, abaid.
prism, s. gloine-sgaraidh ghathan soluis.
prison, s. gainntir, prìosan.
prisoned, part. prìosanaichte.
prisoner, s. prìosanach, ciomach.
prisonment, s. prìosanachd.
pristine, adj. priomh, sean, àrsaidh.
privacy, s. uaigneachd, a o n a r a c h d, dìomhaireachd, falach, cleith.
private, adj. uaigneach, dìomhair, fal-aichte, neo-fhollaiseach, neo-choit-cheann ; saighdear-cumanta.
privateer, s. long-spùinnidh.
privateness, s. dìomhaireachd.
privately, adv. gu dìomhair.
privation, s. toirt air falbh, dìobhail, call, uireasbhuidh, dìth.

privative, adj. a' toirt air falbh, dosgain-neach.
privilege, s. sochair, dlighe, còir.
privilege, v. a. builich sochair, thoir sochair do, saor o chìs.
privity, s. rabhadh dìomhair.
privy, adj. uaigneach ; fiosrach air.
privy, s. tigh-fuagairt, tigh-beag.
prize, s. duais, geall ; creach.
prize, v. a. meas, cuir mòr mheas air, cuir luach air.
pro, prep. air son, as leth.
probability, s. coltachd, coltas.
probable, adj. coslach, coltachail.
probat, probate, s. dearbhadh, còmh-dach, deanamh a mach.
probation, s. dearbhadh, feuchainn.
probationary, adj. deuchainneach.
probationer, s. deuchainniche, searmon-aiche (a' feitheamh ri gairm).
probe, s. bior-rannsachaidh lotan.
probe, v. a. sir, iarr, rannsaich.
probity, s. fìrinn, tréidhireas.
problem, s. ceist.
problematical, adj. ceisteach, teagm-hach.
proboscis, s. gnos, soc fada.
procedure, s. dòigh, stiùradh.
proceed, v. n. imich, gluais, rach air t' aghaidh ; rach a mach ; sruth, tarm-aich, éirich o ; thig air aghaidh ; cuir air aghaidh.
proceeding, s. dol, imeachd, siubhal, teachd air aghaidh.
proceeds, s. toradh, teachd a mach.
procerity, s. àirde.
process, s. dol air aghaidh, siubhal, gluasad ; sruth, sruthadh ; seòl, dòigh, innleachd ; cùis-lagha.
procession, s. mòr-chuideachd, mòr-bhuidheann air siubhal, treud.
proclaim, v. a. glaodh, foillsich, éigh.
proclamation, s. glaodhaich.
proclivity, s. aomadh, claonadh, togradh, déidh, miann, ealamhachd.
procrastinate, v. dean moille, cuir dàil, bi màirnealach.
procrastination, s. dàil, màirneal.
procreant, adj. torrach, sìolmhor.
procreate, v. a. gin, sìolaich, dèan.
procreation, s. gineamhuinn.
procreative, adj. gineamhuinneach.
procreator, s. gineadair.
proctor, s. fear-gnothaich.
proctorship, s. dreuchd fir gnothaich.
procurable, adj. so-fhaotainn.
procurator, s. procadair.
procure, v. a. faigh, coisinn.
procurer, s. fear-solair.
procuress, s. bean-sholar strìopach.
prodigal, adj. struidheil, caithteach.
prodigal, s. struidhear.
prodigality, s. stròdhalachd.

prodigious, *adj.* uabhasach, anabarrach, còrr, eagalach.
prodigy, *s.* mìorbhuill, iongantas, neònachas, uamhas.
produce, *v. a.* thoir 'san làthair, nochd, taisbean ; thoir mar fhianais.
produce, *s.* toradh, cinneas.
produce, *s.* toradh, suim, tomad, fàs, cinntinn, àireamh, obair.
producible, *adj.* a dh'fhaodar a nochdadh.
production, *s.* dèanamh, obair, toirt a mach, toirt am fianais ; toradh.
productive, *adj.* tarbhach, torach, sìolmhor, lìonmhor, pailt, gineadach.
proem, *s.* roimh-ràdh.
profanation, *s.* mì-naomhachadh.
profane, *adj.* mì-naomha.
profane, *v. a.* mì-naomhaich.
profaneness, *s.* mì-naomhachd.
profaner, *s.* fear mì-naomhachaidh.
profess, *v.* aidich, cuir an céill, nochd, taisbean, dèan aideachadh.
profession, *s.* cèaird, obair, dreuchd, ealain ; aideachadh.
professional, *adj.* ealainneach.
professor, *s.* fear-aidmheil, ard-fholumaiche, ollamh.
professorship, *s.* dreuchd an ard-fhoghlum.
proffer, *v. a.* tairg, thoir tairgse, thoir ionnsaidh.
proffer, *s.* tairgse ; deuchainn, oidhirp, ionnsaidh.
proficience, proficiency, *s.* teachd air aghart, aghartachd.
proficient, *a.* fear-ionnsaichte.
profit, *s.* buannachd, tairbhe, feum.
profit, *v.* buannaich, tarbhaich, dèan math do, buidhinn ; coisinn.
profitable, *adj.* buannachdach, buannachdail ; tarbhach, feumail.
profitableness, *s.* buannachd.
profitless, *adj.* neo-tharbhach.
profligacy, *s.* mì-stuamachd.
profligate, *adj.* mì-stuama.
profligate, *s.* struidhear.
profound, *adj.* domhain ; tulchuiseach, tùrail ; iriosal, ùmhal ; ro-ionnsaichte, foghlumte.
profundity, *s.* doimhneachd.
profuse, *adj.* pailt, sgaoilteach.
profuseness, *s.* pailteachd ; anameasarrachd, anacaitheamh.
profusion, *s.* pailteas ; sgapadh, anacaitheamh, struidheas.
progeneration, *s.* sìolachadh.
progenitor, *s.* gineadair, athair.
progeny, *s.* sìol, gineal, sliochd, clann, iarmad, teaghlach, àl.
prognostic, *s.* fiosachd, targradh.
prognosticate, *v. a.* roimh-innis, targair, dèan fiosachd, dèan-fàisneachd.
prognostication, *s.* fiosachd, fàisneachd, targandachd, roimh-innse.

prognosticator, *s.* fiosaiche.
progress, progression, *s.* cùrsa, siubhal, imeachd ; dol air aghart, teachd air aghart ; triall, turas, astar.
progressional, progressive, *adj.* siùbhlach, a dol air aghart, aghartach.
prohibit, *v. a.* bac, toirmisg, diùlt.
prohibition, *s.* bacadh, toirmeasg.
prohibitory, *adj.* toirmeasgach.
project, *v.* tilg ; tionnsgainn, cnuasaich ; sìn a mach.
project, *s.* tionnsgnadh, dealbh, cnuasachd, innleachd, seòl.
projectile, *adj.* gluasadach, urchair, peileir.
projection, *s.* tilgeadh, caitheamh air adhart, crochadh thar ; dealbh, tionnsgnadh.
projector, *s.* fear tionnsgnaidh.
projecture, *s.* stùc, sròn.
prolific, *adj.* clannmhor, sìolmhor, torrach ; lìonmhor.
prolification, *s.* sìolmhorachd.
prolix, *adj.* draolainneach, seamsanach, màirnealach, fadalach.
prolixity, *s.* draolainneachd, fadalachd, athaiseachd, maidheanachd.
prolong, *v. a.* sìn a mach, cuir dàil, cuir seachad.
prolongation, *s.* sìneadh a mach ; dàil, cur seachad.
promenade, *s.* sràid, sràidimeachd.
prominence, *s.* sròn, gob, roinn.
prominent, *adj.* soilleir, follaiseach, faicsinneach.
promiscuous, *adj.* coimeasgte, troimhe chéile.
promise, *v.* geall, thoir gealladh.
promiser, *s.* fear geallaidh.
promissory, *adj.* gealltannach.
promontory, *s.* roinn, rudha, maoil, ceanntìre.
promote, *v. a.* tog gu inbhe, àrdaich, cuir air adhart.
promoter, *s.* fear àrdachaidh, feargnothuich.
promotion, *s.* àrdachadh.
prompt, *adj.* deas, ealamh, ullamh, èasgaidh, clis, tapaidh.
prompt, *v. a.* cuidich, thoir còmhnadh do ; deachdaich, innis ; brosnaich, cuir thuige, stuig ; cuir an cuimhne.
prompter, *s.* fear-sanais, fear-cuimhne ; fear-earalachaidh, comhairliche.
promptitude, promptness, *s.* graide, tapachd.
promulgate, promulge, *v. a.* craobhsgaoil, foillsich.
promulgation, *s.* craobh-sgaoileadh, foillseachadh.
promulgator, *s.* fear foillseachaidh, fearnochdaidh.

prone, *adj.* crom, a' cromadh ; air a bhroinn, an coinneamh a' chinn ; air bhlian, a bhial 's a shròn fodha ; claon, ag aomadh corrach, càs.

proneness, *s.* cromadh, lùbadh sìos ; laighe air bolg ; leathad ; aomadh, claonadh, lùbadh, miann, toil, togradh.

pronoun, *s.* riochd-fhacal.

pronounce, *v. a.* abair, labhair, cuir a mach gu poncail, aithris, fuaimnich (facal).

pronunciation, *s.* fuamfhacal.

proof, *s.* dearbhadh, fianais, daingneachadh, còmhdach ; deuchainn, feuchainn ; dearbhadh clò-bhualaidh.

proof, *adj.* daingeann, làidir, a sheasas an aghaidh, dìonach.

proofless, *adj.* neo-dhearbte.

prop, *v. a.* cum suas, cuir tac, cum tac.

prop, *s.* taic, cul-taic, colbh, gobhal, cumail suas.

propagate, *v.* sìolaich, tàrmaich ; craobhsgaoil, leudaich, meudaich ; cuir air adhart ; gin ; bi sìolmhor.

propagation, *s.* sìolachadh, craobhsgaoileadh, leudachadh.

propagator, *s.* fear-sgaoilidh, fear craobhsgaoilidh, fear leudachaidh.

propel, *v. a.* cuir air adhart, spàrr.

propend, *v. n.* aom, claon, fiar.

propensity, *s.* aomadh, claonadh, lùbadh, toil, dèidh.

proper, *adj.* àraidh, àraid, sònraichte ; iomchuidh, cubhaidh, freagarrach ; ceart, cothromach ; fìor, neo-shamhlachail ; eireachdail.

properly, *adv.* gu cubhaidh.

property, *s.* buaidh, càil, nàdur, gnè ; seilbh, maoin, cuid, còir ; earras eudail.

prophecy, *s.* fàisneachd, targradh.

prophesy, *v.* fàisnich, targair.

prophet, *s.* fàidh, fiosaiche.

prophetess, *s.* ban-fhàidh.

prophetic, *adj.* fàisneachail.

propinquity, *s.* fagusachd ; dàimh.

propitiate, *v. a.* réitich, ciùinich.

propitiation, *s.* réiteachadh ; ìobairt-réitich, dìoladh, éirig.

propitiatory, *adj.* réiteachail.

propitious, *adj.* fàbharrach, gràsmhor, tròcaireach, caoimhneil.

propitiously, *adv.* fàbharach.

proponent, *s.* fear-tairgse.

proportion, *s.* co-ionannachd ; co-fhreagarrachd ; coimeas ; cumadh, dealbh, meudachd.

proportion, *v. n.* cuimsich, coimeas ; dèan co-fhreagarrach, cùm.

proportionable, *adj.* co - fhreagarrach, dealbhach, cumadail.

proportional, *adj.* co-ionann.

proportionate, *adj.* co-fhreagarrach.

proposal, *s.* tionnsgnadh, comhairl'-inntinn ; tairgse.

propose, *v. a.* tairg, thoir tairgse.

proposer, *s.* fear-tairgse.

proposition, *s.* ciall-ràdh ; tairgse.

propound, *v. a.* tairg, nochd, taisbein.

proprietor, *s.* sealbhadair.

propriety, *s.* iomchuidheachd, freagarrachd, ceartas ; seilbh-chòir.

prorogue, *v. a.* sìn a mach ; cuir dàil, cuir seachad, sgaoil (Parlamaid).

prosaic, *adj.* rosgach, sgìtheach, air bheig sgoinn.

proscribe, *v. a.* dìt gu bàs, thoir binn.

proscription, *s.* dìteadh gu bàs.

prose, *s.* rosg.

prosecute, *v. a.* lean, dlùth-lean ; giùlain air adhart ; tagair, thoir suas (gu cuirt), thoir do'n lagh.

prosecution, *s.* leantainn, cur air adhart ; agairt, tagradh.

proselyte, *s.* ùr-chreideach.

prosodian, prosodist, *s.* duanaire.

prosody, *s.* ranntachd.

prospect, *s.* sealladh, fradharc ; àite-fradhairc ionad-seallaidh ; dùil, beachd.

prospective, *adj.* a' sealltainn roimhe, a' beachdachadh fad' as ; glic, sicir, fad-sheallach, an dùil, a' tighinn.

prosper, *v.* soirbhich, dèan sona, cuidich le ; buadhaich ; cinn, fàs, thig air t' adhart.

prosperity, *s.* soirbheachadh, sonas, sealbh, rath, piseach.

prosperous, *adj.* sealbhach, sona, àdhmhor, rathail.

prostitute, *v. a.* truaill, mill, mì-bhuilich.

prostitute, *s.* strìopach, siùrsach.

prostitution, *s.* truailleadh, mì-bhuileachadh ; strìopachas.

prostrate, *adj.* sìnte, 'na laighe air a bhlian ; strìochdte ; sleuchdte.

prostrate, *v. a.* tilg sìos, sleuchd.

prostration, *s.* sleuchdadh tuiteam sìos, cromadh sìos ; lagachadh.

protect, *v. a.* dìon, teasraig, sàbhail.

protection, *s.* dìon, tèarmunn.

protective, *adj.* tèarmunnach.

protector, *s.* fear-tèarmuinn.

protend, *v. a.* cùm a mach, sìn a mach.

protest, *v.* tog fianais an aghaidh, gairm fianais, cuir fianais air.

protest, *s.* cur an agaidh, fianais-thogte.

protestant, *adj.* ath-leasaichte.

protestant, *s.* protastanach, pròstanach.

protestation, *s.* briathran bòid.

prothonotary, *s.* àrd-nòtair.

prototype, *s.* roimh-shamhla.

protract, *v. a.* sìn a mach, cuir dàil.

protraction, *s.* dàil, fadal.

protractive, *adj.* seamsanach.

protrude, *v.* pùc, spàrr ; dinn.

protrusion, *s* pùcadh, sparradh.

protuberance, s. pluc, meall, at.
protuberant, adj. plucach, meallach.
proud, adj. bòsdail, beachdail; uaibh-reach, àrdanach, mórchuiseach; mór, àrd, stàtail; basdalach, spleaghach, uallach, leòmach; ain-fheoileach, at-mhor.
provable, adj. so-dhearbhadh.
prove, v. dearbh, còmhdaich; feuch, cuir gu deuchainn; fàs, tionndaidh a mach.
proveditor, provedore, s. fear-solair bidh do luchd-feachda.
provender, s. innlinn, biadh spréidhe, fodar, feur; feur-saoidh.
proverb, s. gnàth-fhacal, sean-fhacal.
proverbial, adj. gnàth-fhaclach.
provide, v. a. ullaich, solair, solaraich; tionail; cùmhnantaich.
providence, s. freasdal; crìonnachd, faicill, faicilleachd; caomhantachd.
provident, adj. solarach, cùramach, faicil-leach, freasdalach.
providential, adj. freasdalach.
provider, s. solaraiche.
providing, s. cnuasachadh.
province, s. mórroinn; dùthaich, tìr; siorrachd; gnothach, dreuchd.
provincial, adj. dùthchail, neo-choit-cheann.
provision, s. deasachadh, ullachadh, uidheam, solar, cnuasachadh; biadh, lòn; cùmhnant, bann.
provisional, adj. air chois car ùine; a réir cùmhnanta.
proviso, s. bann, cùmhnant, cumha.
provocation, s. brosnachadh, buaireadh, cùis-chorraich, farran.
provoke, v. a. buair, brosnaich, feargaich, farranaich, cuir corraich.
provoker, s. fear-brosnachaidh.
provoking, adj. farranach, buaireasach, brosnachail.
provost, s. prothaist.
prow, s. toiseach luinge.
prowess, s. gaisge, treuntas.
prowl, v. èalaidh air son cobhartaich, siap.
prowler, s. èaladair; sèapaire.
proximate, proxime, adj. fagus, dlùth, faisg, am fagus.
proximity, s. fasgusachd, dlùthachd, nàbaidheachd, coimhearsnachd.
proxy, s. fear-ionaid.
prude, s. uailleag, leòmag.
prudence, s. gliocas, crìonnachd.
prudent, adj. glic, crìonna, sicir.
prudential, adj. faicilleach, cùram.
prudery, s. moitealachd.
prudish, adj. moiteil, pròiseil, nàrach (ma 's fhìor).
prune, v. sgath, bèarr, meang.
prune, s. plumbas tiormaichte.

prunello, s. seòrsa aodaich sìoda.
pruner, s. sgathadair, bearradair.
pruning-knife, s. sgian-bhearraidh, sgian-sgathaidh.
prurience, pruriency, s. tachas; mór-dhéidh, fileadh.
prurient, adj. tachasach.
psalm, s. sàlm, laoidh naomha.
psalmist, s. sàlmaire, salmadair.
psalmody, s. sàlmadaireachd.
psalter, s. leabhar shalm.
pseudo, adj. feallsa, baoth, faoin.
pshaw! interj. fuigh! fuigh ort!
puberty, pubescence, s. aois-leannanachd, inbhidheachd.
pubescent, adj. inbheach.
public, adj. follaiseach, fosgailte, aith-nichte, sgaoilte; coitcheann.
public, s. sluagh, am mór-shluagh.
publican, s. cis-mhaor; òsdair.
publication, s. foillseachadh, sgaoileadh, craobh-sgaoileadh, cur-a-mach leabhar (ge b'e seòrsa).
publicly, adv. gu follaiseach.
publicness, s. follaiseachd.
publish, v. a. foillsich, dèan aithnichte; gairm, glaodh, cuir a mach (leabhar).
publisher, s. fear chuir a mach leabh-raichean.
pucelage, s. maighdeannas.
puck, s. tuath; siochair.
pucker, v. a. liorcaich, cas, preas.
pudding, s. marag.
puddle, s. poll, eabar, làthach, làib.
puddle, v. a. làbanaich, salaich.
puddly, adj. làibeach, ruaimleach.
pudency, pudicity, s. màldachd, nàrachd, beusachd.
puerile, adj. leanabaidh, leanabail.
puerility, s. leanabachd, leanabantas.
puff, s. osag, oiteag, séideag, feochan, tòth, moladh-bréige.
puff, v. a. séid suas, bòchd, at, bi 'g àinich.
puffin, s. seòrsa eòin; am buthaide; seòrsa éisg, am bolgan-beiceach.
puffy, adj. gaothar, osagach, oiteagach, àtmhor; falamh, bolgach.
pug, s. cù beag, ap, apag.
pugh! interj. ab! ab!
pugilism, s. dòrnaireachd.
pugilist, s. dòrnair.
puisne, adj. òg, beag, crìon, meanbh, ìochdarach, suarrach.
puissance, s. cumhachd; neart.
puissant, adj. cumhachdach, treun.
puke, puker, s. deoch dìobhairt.
puke, v. a. sgeith, tilg, dìobhair.
pulchritude, s. bòidhche, maise.
pule, v. n. dèan bìogail; guil, caoin.
pull, v. a. tarruinn, slaod, spìon.
pull, s. tarruing, spioladh, slaod.
pullet, s. eireag.
pulley, s. ulag, fulag.

pulmonary, pulmonic, *adj.* sgamhanach, a bhuineas do'n sgamhan.

pulp, *s.* laoghan, glaodhan ; taois.

pulpit, *s.* cùbaid, crannag.

pulpous, *adj.* bogar laoghanach, sùghmhor, brìoghmhor ; feòlmhor.

pulpousness, *s.* bogarachd, sùghmhorachd, laoghanachd.

pulpy, *adj.* bog, bogar, sùghmhor.

pulsation, *s.* bualadh cuisle.

pulse, *s.* cuisle, gluasad na fala ; peasair ; pònair, no pòr mogulach sam bith.

pulverisation, *s.* mìn-phronnadh.

pulverise, *v. a.* mìn-phronn.

pulvil, *s.* fàileadh cùbhraidh.

pumice, *s.* sligeart, mìn-chlach.

pump, *s.* taosgair ; bròg-dhamhsa.

pump, *v. n.* taoisg, taom ; tarruinn.

pun, *s.* gearrfhacal, beum abhcaid.

pun, *v. n.* beum, gearr ; dèan abhcaid.

punch, *s.* tolladair, farraiche ; deoch làidir ; dù-chleasaiche ; amadan ; fear beag, staigean ; bun, cnapanach.

punch, *v. a.* toll, brodaich.

puncheon, *s.* togsaid gu leth.

punctilio, *s.* modh, modhalachd.

punctilious, *adj.* modhail, moiteil, cùramach mu uair.

punctual, *adj.* poncail, cinnteach.

punctuality, *s.* poncalachd.

punctuation, *s.* poncadh, pungadh.

puncture, *s.* toll stuib, peasgadh, toll-stainge.

pungency, *s.* géiread, gairgead.

pungent, *adj.* geur, goirt, garg ; guineach, biorach, dealgach ; teumnach, beumnach.

puniness, *s.* crìne, suarraichead.

punish, *v. a.* peanasaich, pian, cràidh, smachdaich.

punishable, *adj.* toilltinneach air peanas no air pian ; buailteach do pheanas, airidh air peanas.

punishment, *s.* dìoghaltas.

punition, *s.* peanas.

punk, *s.* siùrsach, strìopach.

punster, *s.* beumadair.

puny, *adj.* òg ; crìon, beag ; suarrach, leibideach ; fann, lag, truagh.

pup, *v. n.* beir cuileanan.

pupil, *s.* clach na sùl ; sgoilear.

pupilage, *adj.* leanabantachd, òige.

puppet, *s.* fear-bréige.

puppy, *s.* cuilean ; balach bòsdail gun iùl gun mhodh.

purblind, *adj.* gearrsheallach.

purchasable, *adj.* ghabhas ceannach.

purchase, *v. a.* ceannaich.

purchase, *s.* ceannach ; cùnradh.

purchaser, *s.* fear ceannaich.

pure, *adj.* fìorghlan ; soilleir ; neothruaillichte, slàn, fallain ; geanmnaidh, màlda, macanta ; neochoireach.

purely, *adv.* gu fiorghlan, gu'n druaip ; gun choire ; gun ghò, gu glan, a mhàin.

pureness, *s.* fìor-ghloine ; soilleireachd ; teistealachd, geanmnaidheachd ; neochiontas.

purgation, *s.* glanadh, sgùradh, clìostradh.

purgative, *adj.* purgaideach, sgùrach, glanadach.

purgative, *s.* pùrgaid.

purgatory, *s.* purgadair, ionad-glanaidh.

purge, *v.* glan, sgùr, purgaidich, nigh, ionnlaid ; cairt ; soilleirich.

purge, *s.* sgùradh-cuim.

purification, *s.* glanadh, sìoladh.

purifier, *s.* fear-glanaidh.

purify, *v. a.* tur-ghlan ; sìolaidh.

puritan, *s.* fear rò-chràbhach, duine eudmhor (air son lagh Dhé), seann diadhaire.

puritanical, *adj.* ro-chràbhach, cràbhach, eudmhor.

purity, *s.* glaine, gloine, gloinead, fìor-ghloine ; neo-chiontas ; geanmnaidheachd, macantas, teistealachd.

purl, *s.* leann luibheanach.

purl, *v. n.* dèan torman, dèan crònan.

purlieu, *s.* iomall, buaile.

purling, *part. adj.* tormanach.

purloin, *v. a.* goid, siolp.

purple, *adj.* cròidhearg, flannach, purpur.

purplish, *adj.* gòrmdhearg.

purport, *s.* ciall, brìgh, rùn, seadh.

purport, *v. n.* bi los, cuir romhad.

purpose, *v. a.* rùnaich, miannaich, cuir romhad, sònraich, bi 'm brath.

purpose, *s.* gnothach ; cùis ; rùn, miann, togradh, smuain ; deòin.

purposely, *adv.* a dh' aon obair, a dh' aon ghnothach ; le deòin.

purr, *v. n.* dèan crònan, dèan dùrdan.

purse, *s.* sporan ; ionmhas.

purser, *s.* gille-sporain, ionmhasair.

pursuable, *adj.* so-leantainn.

pursuance, *s.* leantainn.

pursuant, *adj.* a réir, do réir.

pursue, *v.* lean, tòraich ; mair.

pursuer, *s.* fear-tòire, fear-agairt.

pursuit, *s.* ruaig, ruagadh, tòir ; leantainn, geur-leanmhainn, etc.

pursuivant, *s.* maor ; teachdaire.

pursy, *adj.* bronnach, pocanach.

purtenance, *s.* grealach, mionach.

purulence, purulency, *s.* iongar.

purulent, *adj.* làn iongrach.

purvey, *v.* solair, cnuasaich, cruinnich, teachd-an-tìr.

purveyance, *s.* solar bìdh.

purveyor, *s.* fear solaraidh bìdh.

pus, *s.* iongar, salchar lota.

push, *v. a.* pùc, purr, starr, sàth, stailc ; put, putagaich, utagaich.

push, s. pùcadh, purradh, utag, putadh, starradh, sàthadh, stailceadh ; urchair ; càs, deuchainn, teanntachd.
pushing, adj. adhartach, teòma, beothail ; dìchiollach, oidhirpeach.
pusillanimity, s. cladhaireachd.
pusillanimous, adj. gealtach.
puss, s. stìoda, stìdidh, ainm cait.
pustule, s. guirean, bucaid ; at, bristeadh a mach, plucan.
pustulous, adj. guireanach, bucaideach, plucanach, builgeineach.
put, v. cuir ; socraich ; suidhich, etc.
put, s. dubhbhalach.
putative, adj. smuainichte.
putid, adj. crìon, ìosal, dìblidh, suarrach, faoin, fagharsach.
putrefaction, s. bréine, breuntas.
putrefy, v. grod, lobh, malc, breun.
putrid, adj. loibht ; grod, malcte.
putridness, s. breuntas, loibhteachd.

putting-stone, s. clach-neart.
puttoc, s. am beilbhean-ruadh.
putty, s. taois-cailce.
puzzle, v. a. cuir an imcheist.
puzzle, s. imcheist, toimhseachan.
pygmean, adj. beag, duairceach.
pygmy, pigmy, s. duairce, arrachd, troich, gircean, luch-armunn.
pyramid, s. biorramaid, biorcharragh, biorstuc, carragh barrachaol.
pyramidal, pyramidical, adj. barrachaol, biorach, binneineach.
pyre, s. cairbh-theine.
pyretics, s. ùr-chasg-fhiabhras.
pyrites, s. clach-theine.
pyromancy, s. teine-fiosachd.
pyrotechnics, s. obair-theine.
pyrotechny, s. eòlas obair-theine.
pyrrhonism, s. teagamhachd.
pyx, s. bocsa nan abhlan coisrighte.

Q

quack, v. n. ràc mar thunnaig ; dèan gàgail, gabh ort (eòlas leighis).
quack, s. sgoitich, feall-léigh.
quackery, s. sgoiteachd.
quadragesimal, adj. carghusach.
quadrangle, s. ceithirchearnag.
quadrangular, adj. ceithirchearnach, ceithir-oisinneach.
quadrant, s. ceithreamh, seòrsa inneal tomhais, carst-cearcaill.
quadrantal, adj. ceithirthaobhach.
quadrate, s. ceithir shlisneag.
quadrate, adj. ceithir shliosach.
quadrature, s. ceithirchearnadh.
quadrennial, adj. ceithir-bhliadhnachail.
quadrifid, adj. ceithir-earrannach.
quadrilateral, adj. ceithirshlisneach, ceithirshliseach.
quadrille, s. seòrsa dannsa ; gnè de chluich air chairtean.
quadripartite, adj. ceithreannaichte.
quadruped, s. ceithirchasach.
quadruple, adj. ceithir fillte.
quaff, v. a. òl, sguab as e.
quaggy, adj. bog, ruaimleach, féithech.
quagmire, s. suil-chritheach, boglach.
quail, s. gearra-goirt.
quaint, adj. cuimir ; snasmhor, greannar, fìnealta, freagarrach, bòidheach.
quaintness, s. fìnealtachd ; cuimireachd ; freagarrachd, bòichead.
quake, v. n. crith, criothnaich.
quake, s. crith, criothnachadh.
qualification, s. deasachadh, uidheamachadh ; taiseachadh ; lughdachadh ; feart, buaidh, càil, gné.

qualify, v. a. deasaich, ullaich, dèan freagarrach, taisich.
quality, s. inbhe, uaillse, àirde ; gnè, buaidh, càil, feart ; uaillsean.
qualm, s. òrrais, sleogadh, giorrag coguis, cuairt, gòmadh.
qualmish, adj. òrraiseach, sleogach.
quandary, s. teagamh.
quantity, s. meud, uibhir, tomad ; cudthrom ; na h-urrad.
quantum, s. an t-iomlan.
quarantine, s. ùine as éigin do luingeas a thig o chéin fuireach, mu 'm faod iad tighinn gu cala.
quarrel, s. còmhstrì, connsachadh, droch còrdadh, iorghuill, tuasaid, sabaid, àimhreite, cur a mach ; trod.
quarrel, v. n. troid, connsaich.
quarrelsome, adj. sabaideach, tuasaideach, brionglaideach, carraideach, connspaideach, crosda, àimhreiteach, trodach.
quarrelsomeness, s. tuasaideachd, brionglaideachd, strangalachd.
quarry, s. gairbheal ; seòrsa saighde, cairbh, sealg.
quarry, v. n. tochail, cladhaich ; bùraich ; thig beò air.
quart, s. càrt, ceathramh.
quartanague, s. am fiabhrais-critheanach.
quarter, s. ceathramh ; cairteal, àite, cearn, ionad, tìr, dùthaich, earrann baile no dùthcha, àirde ; ràidhe ; cairtealan, bàigh, tròcair, iochd.
quarter, v. a. roinn 'na cheithir earrannan, gabh còmhnaidh, cùir suas, fan, fuirich.

quarterage, s. cuid ràithe, luathasachadh ràithe.

quarter-deck, s. clàr-uachdair deiridh luinge.

quarterly, adj. and adv. ràitheil, gach ràithe ; uair 'san ràithe.

quartermaster, s. oifigear airm.

quartern, s. cairteal, ceithreamh.

quarters, s. cairtealan

quarter-session, s. mòd-ràithe.

quarter-staff, s. ursann-chatha.

quarto, adj. ceathramh (tomhas pàipear ; tomhas leabhair).

quash, v. a. mùch, caisg, cum sìos, cum sàmhach ; cuir air chùl, ceannsaich.

quashing, s. mùchadh, casgadh.

quaternary, quaternion, quaternity, s. ceithrear.

quatrain, s. rann cheithir-sreath.

quaver, v. n. crith, crath ; bog, ceileirich.

quay, s. làimhrig.

quean, s. dubhchaile, strìopach.

queasy, adj. tinn, sleogach.

queen, s. bànrigh, bànrighinn.

queer, adj. neònach, iongantach.

queerness, s. neònachas.

quell, v. mùch, cum fodha ; smachdaich, caisg, closnaich ; ceannsaich.

quench, v. cuir as, mùch, bàth.

quenchable, adj. ghabhas mùchadh.

quenchless, adj. nach gabh mùchadh.

querist, s. ceasnaiche, sgrùdaire.

quern, s. bràth, muilleann-làimhe.

querpo, s. seacaid, deacaid.

querulous, adj. gearanach, casaideach, dranndanach, sraonaiseach.

querulousness, s. dranndanachd.

query, s. ceisd, faighneachd.

quest, s. sireadh, rannsachadh, faighneachd, sgrùdadh, tòir, iarrtas, iarraidh, deidh.

question, s. ceist, teagamh ; amharus, connspaid, deasbaireachd ; faighneachd.

question, v. feòraich, faighneachd, ceasnaich, sgrùd, farraid, cuir an teagamh.

questionable, adj. teagmhach.

questionary, adj. ceasnachail, rannsachail, sgrùdach.

quib, s. geurfhacal, carfhacal.

quibble, v. n. thoir beum, cluich air facal.

quibbler, s. carfhaclaiche.

quick, adj. grad, ealamh ; beò, beothail, smiorail, tapaidh, ullamh, deas, luath, clis, èasgaidh ; cabhagach.

quick, s. beò ; beò-fheòil.

quickbeam, s. an Gall-uinnsean.

quicken, v. beothaich, ath-bheothaich, brosnaich, greas, deifirich ; geuraich.

quickener, s. brosnachair ; beothachair ; greasadair.

quicklime, s. aol-teth, aol-beò.

quickly, adv. gu luath, gu grad, gu clis.

quickness, s. luathas, graide, beothalachd, deifir, cabhag, tapadh, tapachd, smioralas ; géire.

quicksand, s. beò-ghainneamh, suilchruthaich.

quick-set, s. planntan sgithich.

quick-sighted, adj. biorshuileach, gradsheallach, gradshuileach.

quicksilver, s. airgead beò.

quiddity, s. carcheist, carfhacal.

quiescence, s. sàmhchair, suaimhneas, fois, tàmh, sèimhe, socair, bailbhe.

quiescent, adj. sàmhach, féitheil, socrach, balbh, tosdach, ciùin.

quiet, adj. sàmhach, tosdach, ciùin ; màlta, macanta, suairce, socrach ; suaimhneach ; soitheamh ; aig fois.

quiet, s. fois, sàmhchair, sèimhe, ciùineas, tàmh, sìth, suaimhneas ; tosdachd, tosd.

quiet, v. a. caisg, cuir sàmhach, ciùinich, sìothaich, foisnich, socraich.

quietly, adv. gu ciùin ; aig fois.

quietness, s. sàmhchair, ciùineachd, ciùineas, sìth ; sèimhe, fois, féith.

quietude, s. sìth, fois, socair, tàmh.

quill, s. cléite, ite, sgeithe.

quilt, s. cùibhrig, brat-leapa.

quince, s. cuinnse, craobh-chuinnse.

quinquangular, adj. cóigchearnach.

quinquefoliated, adj. cóigbhileach.

quinquennial, adj. an ceann gach còigeamh bliadhna.

quinsy, s. at sgòrnain, at slugain.

quint, s. cóignear, cóig.

quintal, s. ceud punnt.

quintessence, s. làn-bhrìgh, bladh, feart.

quintuple, adj. cóig-fillte, a chóig uiread, air aithris, cóig uairean.

quip, s. fochaid, sgeig, beum.

quire, s. ceithir clair fichead pàipeir.

quire, v. n. co-sheinn, co-sheirm.

quirister, s. fear-co-sheirm.

quirk, s. car, cuilbheart ; slighe ; cleas ; beum.

quit, v. a. fàg ; tréig, cuidhtich, cuir cùl ri ; dealaich ; pàigh, dìol.

quit, adj. saor, ionann, cuidhte.

quitch-grass, s. feur-nan-con.

quite, adv. gu tur, gu léir.

quittance, s. cuidhteas ; saorsa, seachnadh.

quiver, s. dòrnlach, balg-shaighead.

quiver, v. n. crith, ball-chrith.

quodlibet, s. car, carfhacal.

quoif, quoiffure, s. ceannabharr.

quoit, s. peileastair.

quotation, s. còmhdachadh le earrann o sgrìobhadh neach eile.

quote, v. a. ainmich ùghdar, thoir mar ùghdar, thoir mar ùghdarras.

quoth, v. imperf. arsa, ars'.

quotidian, adj. lathail, gach latha.

quotient, s. a' cho liugha uair.

R

rabbet, s. tàthadh, gleusadh, gròbadh.
Rabbi, Rabbin, s. Ollamh Iùdhach.
rabbit, s. coinean.
rabble, s. gràisg, pràbar.
rabid, adj. cuthaich, borb, garg.
race, s. réis, ruith, steud, co-ruith ; coimhliong ; blàr-réis ; gineal, ginealach ; sliochd, sìol, clann, fine, cinneadh, teaghlach.
racer, s. falaire, steudeach.
racemiferous, adj. bagaideach.
raciness, s. searbhas, goirteas.
rack, s. inneal pianaidh, cuidhle-sgaraidh; prasach.
rack, v. a. sàraich, claoidh, pian.
racket, s. callaid ; gleadhraich, straoidhlich, sabaid.
rack-rent, s. màl-mór; màl-sàrachaidh ; àrd-mhàl.
racoon, s. broc Americanach.
racy, adj. làidir, beothail.
radiance, s. lannair, soillse, boillsgealachd, loinnreachas ; dealradh, dearsadh ; glòir.
radiant, adj. lannaireach, soillseach, boillsgeil, boillsgeach, dealrach, dearrsach ; glan, soilleir.
radiate, v. n. dealraich, soillsich.
radiation, s. dealrachd, lannaireachd, boillsgealachd.
radical, adj. nàdurra ; gnéitheil, tur.
radicate, v. a. freumhaich.
radish, s. meacan, curran-dearg.
radius, s. ladag, spòg rotha, an fhad 's a tha eadar teis-meadhon buaileig agus a cearcul.
raffle, v. n. disnich, tilg dìsnean.
raffle, s. crannchur-gìll.
raft, s. ràth, slaod-uisge, ràmhach.
rafter, s. taobhan, tarsunnan.
rag, s. giobal, luideag, clùd, cearb, broineag, giobag.
ragamuffin, s. sgonnbhalach, balach piullach, balach crosd na sràide.
rage, s. boile, bàinidh, fearg, cuthach, fraoch, corraich, buaireadh.
ragged, adj. luideagach, luideach, clùdach ; broineagach ; giobalach, giobagach.
raging, adj. buaireasach, feargach, fraochail, air a' chuthach, air bhoil.
ragout, s. feòil air a deasachadh a réir seòl nam Fràngach.
ragwort, s. am buaghallan.
rail, s. cliath, iadhlann, iarunn (rathad iaruinn).
rail, v. druid, cuir fàl suas ; càin.
railing, s. iadhlann ; callaid.
raillery, s. sgallais, sglàmhradh.

raiment, s. aodach, earradh.
rain, v. a. sil ; fras ; dòirt.
rain, s. frasachd, fearrshion, uisge.
rainbow, s. bogha-frois.
rain-goose, s. an learg.
rainy, adj. frasach, fliuch, silteach.
raise, v. a. tog suas ; àrdaich ; dùisg.
raisin, s. fìondhearc chaoinichte.
rake, s. ràsdal, ràcan ; trusdar.
rake, v. ràsdalaich, ràc, cruinnich, trus, tionail r'a chéile ; sgrùd.
rake-hell, s. drùisear, trustar.
rakish, adj. ana-measarra, stròdhail.
rally, v. ath-bhrosnaich, ath-chruinnich feachd.
ram, s. reithe, rùd.
ram, v. spàrr, starr, stailc.
ramble, s. iomrall, spaidsearachd.
ramble, v. a. iomrallaich.
rambler, s. fear-fàrsain.
rambling, adj. seacharanach, luaineach, fàrsanach.
ramification, s. craobh-sgaoileadh ; sgaoileadh, meurachadh, iomsgaoileadh, craobhadh.
ramify, v. a. meuraich, sgaoil.
rammer, s. farraiche ; slat gunna.
ramous, adj. meanglanach, meurach.
ramp, s. leum, sùrdag.
ramp, v. n. leum, sùrdagaich.
rampant, adj. ruith-leumnach, ruideiseach, sùrdagach, àrd - leumnach ; macnusach, a' seasamh air na casan deiridh.
rampart, rampire, s. bàdhun, balladionaidh, baideal.
ran, pret. of to run, ruith.
rancid, adj. trom-fhàileach, breun.
rancorous, adj. mìorunach, gamhlasach ; fuathach, tnùthar.
rancour, s. mìorun, gamhlas.
random, s. tubaist, tuaram.
random, adj. tubaisteach, tuaireamach ; air thuaram.
rang, pret. of to ring, shéirm, bheum.
range, s. òrdugh, sreud, sreath, breath ; cuairt, creadhal-theine.
range, v. a. cuir an òrdugh, marasglaich ; cuir am breathan, riaghailtich ; cuairtich ; siubhail, rach sìos is suas.
ranger, s. fear-rannsaichidh ; fidriche ; peathair ; forsair, maor coille.
rank, adj. làidir, àrd, garbh mar fheur ; breun, faileach.
rank, v. rangaich, sreathaich, cuir an òrdugh, cuir taobh ri taobh, inbhich ; àitich, gabh àite no inbhe.
rank, s. sreath, sreud ; inbhe ; staid.
rankle, v. n. feargaich.

ranny, *s.* an dallag.
ransack, *v. a.* rannsaich, creach.
ransom, *s.* éirig, dìol, pàigheadh, fuasgladh ; saorsa.
ransom, *v. a.* fuasgail, saor.
rant, *v. n.* dèan stairirich.
rant, *s.* gleadhraich, beucail, duan gun ghleus.
ranter, *s.* fear-bòilich ; ranntair.
rantipole, *adj.* mì-gheamnaidh.
ranunculus, *s.* lus-an-ròcais.
rap, *v. n.* buail, grad-bhuail.
rap, *s.* buille, sgailleag, pailleart.
rapacious, *adj.* fòirneartach, gionach, lonach, craosach.
rapacity, *s.* creachadaireachd, sannt.
rape, *s.* cùis-éigin, truailleadh.
rapid, *a.* cas, bras, dian, grad, luath, ealamh, ullamh, clis.
rapidity, *s.* braise, déine, graide.
rapier, *s.* claidheamh-bruididh.
rapine, *s.* creachadh.
rapture, *s.* aoibhneas, mór-aoibhneas ; àrd-thoileachadh.
raptured, *adj.* aoibhinn.
rapturous, *adj.* aoibhneach.
rare, *adj.* ainminig, tearc, gann ; annasach ; ainneamh, sàrmhath.
raree-show, *s.* faoin-shealladh ; neònachas, iongantas-féille.
rarefaction, *s.* tanachadh ; meudachadh, sgaoileadh.
rarefy, *v. a.* tanaich ; leudaich.
rarely, *adv.* gu h-ainminig, gu tearc, gu h-ainneamh, gu gann.
rareness, rarity, *s.* ainminigead, teirce, annas, ganntachd.
rascal, *s.* slaoightire, crochaire.
rascality, *s.* pràbar, gràisg.
rascallion, *s.* dùbhalach.
rascally, *adj.* dìblidh, suarrach, crosda, deamhnaidh.
rase, *v. a.* spion á bun ; mill.
rash, *adj.* dàna, ceann-làidir, bras, cas, grad, obann, dian ; cabhagach.
rash, *s.* briseadh a mach, broth.
rasher, *s.* sliseag mhuicfheoil.
rashness, *s.* dànadas, braisead.
rasp, *s.* suidheag, sùghag ; eighe.
rasp, *v. a.* eighich.
raspberry, *s.* sugh-craobh, suibheag.
rasure, *s.* sgrìobadh-as.
rat, *s.* radan, rodan.
ratafia, *s.* seòrsa dibhe làidir.
rate, *s.* prìs, luach, fiach.
rate, *v. a.* meas ; prìsich ; troid.
rateable, *adj.* luachail, prìseil.
rather, *adv.* docha, fearr ; an àite, an àite sin, na's ro thoiliche.
ratification, *s.* daingneachadh.
ratify, *v. a.* daingnich, socraich.
ratiocinate, *v. a.* reusonaich.
ratiocination, *s.* reusonachadh.

rational, *adj.* reusonta, tuigseach.
rationality, *s.* reusonachd.
ratsbane, *s.* puinnsein nan radan.
rattle, *v. n.* dèan gleadhraich, glagan.
rattle, *s.* faoinchainnt, glag ; clachbhalg ; gleadhraich stairearaich, stàirn, braoidhlich.
rattling, *adj.* gleadhrach.
rattlesnake, *s.* an nathair-ghlagain.
rattoon, *s.* sionnach-Innseanach.
raucity, *s.* tùchanachd.
ravage, *v. a.* sgrios, dèan fàs, fàsaich, creach, spùill, léir-sgrios.
ravage, *s.* sgrios, fàsachadh, creachadh, spùilleadh, léir-sgrios.
rave, *v. n.* bi air bhoil, bi 'm breislich.
ravel, *v. a.* rib ; cuir air àimhreidh ; buair ; cuir an imcheist ; fuasgail, thoir as·a chéile, sgeith (aodaich).
raven, *s.* fitheach, coirbidh.
ravenous, *adj.* cìocrach, slugach, glamhach, geòcach, craosach.
ravenousness, *s.* miann-creich.
ravish, *v. a.* thoir air éigin ; éignich ; thoir cùis a dh' aindeoin ; truaill, mill ; toilich, dèan aoibhinn.
ravisher, *s.* fear-éigneachaidh, fear fòirneirt ; fear-truaillidh.
ravishment, *s.* éigneachadh, éigin, truailleadh ; làn-éibhneas.
raw, *adj.* amh, amhaidh ; glas, ùr ; fuar ; neo-abaich ; neo-mhèirbhte ; neo-theòma.
rawboned, *adj.* cnàmhach, cnàmhalach.
rawness, *s.* amhachd ; aineolas.
ray, *s.* gath-soluis ; leus.
raze, *v. a.* tilg sìos, leag ; lom-sgrios, fàsaich ; dubh a mach.
razor, *s.* ealtainn, bearrsgian.
razure, *s.* dubhadh a mach.
reach, *v. n.* ruig ; sìn ; faigh.
reach, *s.* cumhachd ; comas urrainn, ruigsinn, ruigheachd ; comas ruigsinn, ruigheachd ; sìneadh.
reaction, *s.* athghluasad, aththhilleadh.
read, *v.* leugh, tuig ; rannsaich.
reader, *s.* leughair, leughadair, fear-leughaidh.
readily, *adv.* gu réith, gu toileach, gu h-ullamh.
readiness, *s.* ullamhachd, deise.
reading, *s.* leughadh.
readmission, *s.* athleigeil a steach.
readmit, *v. a.* athghabh a steach.
ready, *adj.* ullamh, réidh, deas, deasaichte ; ealamh, toileach ; furas.
reaffirm, *v. a.* athchomhdaich.
reaffirmance, *s.* ath-chòmhbdachadh.
real, *adj.* fìor ; cinnteach.
reality, *s.* fìrinn, cinnteachd.
realise, *v. a.* thoir gu buil, tionndaidh gu airgead.

really, *adv.* gu fìor ; a rìreadh.
realm, *s.* rìoghachd, dùthaich.
ream, *s.* buinnseal paipeir.
reanimate, *v. a.* ath-bheothaich.
reannex, *v. a.* athcheangail.
reap, *v. a.* buain ; buannaich.
reaper, *s.* buanaiche, inneal buana.
rear, *s.* deireadh feachd ; deireadh.
rear, *v. a.* tog, àraich ; éirich.
rearmouse, raremouse, *s.* ialtag.
reascend, *v.* ath-dhìrich.
reason, *s.* reuson, toinisg, tuigse ; ciall ; aobhar, fàth, ceannfàth.
reason, *v. a.* reusonaich, deasbairich.
reasonable, *adj.* reusonta, ciallach ; measarra, meadhonach, cuimseach ; ceart, cothromach.
reasoning, *s.* deasbaireachd, reusonachadh ; argamaid.
reassemble, *v. a.* athchruinnich.
reassert, *v. a.* athdhearbh, abair a rìs.
reassume, *v. a.* athghabh.
reassure, *v. a.* thoir athchinnte.
reave, *v. a.* thoir leat le ainneart.
rebaptize, *v. a.* ath-bhaist.
rebate, *v. a.* math ; lùghdaich, leig sìos (prìs).
rebel, *s.* fear ar-a-mach, ceannairceach.
rebel, *v. a.* dèan ar-a-mach, dèan ceannairc.
rebellion, *s.* ar-a-mach, ceannairc.
rebellious, *adj.* ceannairceach.
rebound, *v.* leum air ais, leum-làir.
rebuff, *s.* athbhualadh ; diùltadh.
rebuff, *v. a.* buail air ais ; diùlt.
rebuild, *v. a.* ath-thog.
rebuke, *v. a.* thoir achmhasan.
rebuke, *s.* achmhasan, cronachadh.
rebus, *s.* dealbhfhacal, seòrsa tòimhseachain.
recall, *v. a.* gairm air ais.
recall, *s.* athghairm, aisghairm.
recant, *v. a.* seun, àicheadh.
recantation, *s.* seunadh, àicheadh.
recapitulate, *v. a.* ath-innis.
recapitulation, *s.* ath-innseadh.
recaption, *s.* athghlacadh.
recede, *v. n.* rach air ais.
receipt, *s.* gabhail ri ; bann - cuidhteachaidh, cuidhteas.
receivable, *adj.* as urrainnear a ghabhail.
receive, *v. a.* gabh, gabh ri, faigh.
receiver, *s.* fear-gabhail.
recent, *adj.* ùr, o cheann ghoirid.
recentness, *s.* nuadhachd.
receptacle, *s.* ionad-tasgaidh.
reception, *s.* furmailt, fàilte ; di-beatha, gabhail, gabhail ri.
receptive, *adj.* so-ghabhail.
recess, *s.* uaigneas, dìomhaireachd, sàmhchair ; fàgail, sgur, tàmh, clos, fosadh, fòis.
recession, *s.* pilltinn, dol air ais.

rechange, *v. a.* ath-mhùth.
recipe, *s.* riaghailt còcaireachd, dòigh deasachaidh.
recipient, *s.* gabhadair.
reciprocal, *adj.* malairteach, air gach taobh, o gach taobh, a réir a chéile ; mu seach.
reciprocate, *v. a.* malairtich, dèan a réir a chéile.
reciprocation, *s.* co-mhùthadh.
recital, recitation, *s.* aithris ; innseadh, sgeulachd.
recitative, recitativo, *s.* fonn, séis, canntaireachd.
recite, *v. a.* ath-aithris ; ath-innis, gabh (rann no rosg).
reckless, *adj.* neo-chùramach, coma.
reckon, *v.* cunnt ; meas, saoil.
reckoning, *s.* cunntadh, meas.
reclaim, *v. a.* leasaich, ath-leasaich, iompaich, aisghairm ; ceannsaich, smachdaich, thoir a steach (talamh).
recline, *v. n.* sìn, leth-shuidhe, laigh air do lethtaobh ; claon sìos ; crom sìos, leig taice.
reclose, *v. a.* ath-dhùin.
recluse, *adj.* aonaranach, uaigneach ; *s.* neach aig nach 'eil déidh air cuideachd.
recoagulation, *s.* ath-bhinndeachadh.
recognisance, *s.* gealladh, bann.
recognise, *v. a.* aidich ; aithnich.
recognition, *s.* aideachadh, cuimhneachadh ; aithneachadh.
recoil, *v. n.* leum no clisg air t' ais.
recoinage, *s.* athchuinneadh.
recollect, *v. a.* cuimhnich ; ath-chruinnich, ath-thionail.
recollection, *s.* cuimhne.
recommence, *v. a.* ath-thòisich.
recommend, *v. a.* mol ; cliùthaich.
recommendation, *s.* moladh, cliù.
recommendatory, *adj.* moladach.
recompense, *v. a.* ath-dhiol, dèan suas.
recompense, *s.* ath-dhìoladh.
reconcile, *v. a.* dèan réidh, réitich.
reconcilable, *adj.* so-réiteachadh.
reconcilement, *s.* réite, sìth.
reconciliation, *s.* réite.
recondite, *adj.* dìomhair, dorcha, domhain, do-thuigsinn.
reconduct, *v. a.* ath-threòraich.
reconnoitre, *v. a.* beachdaich, rannsaich.
reconquer, *v. a.* ath-cheannsaich.
reconsecrate, *v. a.* ath-choisrig.
reconvene, *v. n.* ath-chruinnich.
record, *v. a.* sgrìobh, cùm air chuimhne.
record, *s.* leabhar-cuimhne.
recorder, *s.* seanachaidh, eachdraiche.
recount, *v. a.* innis, cuir an céill.
recourse, *s.* dòigh, oidhirp, innleachd.
recover, *v.* faigh air ais ; thig uaithe ; fàs gu math.

recoverable, *adj.* so-leigheas.
recovery, *s.* faotainn air ais ; dol am feabhas, leigheas, fàs gu math.
recreant, *adj.* gealtach, neo-dhuineil, *s.* gealtaire, duine gun diù.
recreate, *v. a.* ath-bheothaich, ath-ùraich ; toilich, sòlasaich, aotromaich.
recreation, *s.* cur-seachad, culaidh-shùgraidh, lasachadh.
recreative, *adj.* ùrachail ; lasachail.
recrement, *s.* dràbhag ; salachar.
recremental, recrementitious, *adj.* dràbhagach, deasgannach.
recriminate, *v. a.* cuir fo choire.
recrimination, *s.* coireachadh.
recruit, *v. a.* ath-neartaich, ath-leasaich ; tog saighdearan.
recruit, *s.* saighdear ùr.
rectangle, *s.* ceartchearnag.
rectangular, *adj.* ceartchearnach.
rectifiable, *adj.* ghabhas ceartachadh.
rectification, *s.* ceartachadh.
rectifier, *s.* fear ceartachaidh.
rectify, *v. a.* ceartaich, leasaich, cuir air dòigh ; ath-tharruing.
rectilinear, *adj.* dìreach.
rectitude, *s.* dìrichead ; ionracas.
rector, *s.* ministear sgìreachd Shasunnach ; ceann sgoile ; ceannard, riaghladair.
rectory, *s.* aitreabh agus glìob ministear sgìreachd easbuigeach, etc.
recubation, recumbency, *s.* leth-laighe ; sìneadh, aomadh.
recumbent, *adj.* 'n a leth-shuidhe.
recur, *v.* thig an aire, thig an cuimhne.
recurrence, recursion, *s.* pilltinn, athphilltinn, aththachairt.
recurrent, *adj.* ath-phìlltinneach.
recurvation, *s.* cùl-aomadh, cromadh an comhair a chùil.
recusant, *s.* fear a dhiùltas caidreamh a' mhórchomuinn.
recuse, *v. a.* diùlt, àicheadh.
red, *adj.* dearg, ruadh, flannach.
redbreast, *s.* am brùdhearg.
redden, *v.* deargaich ; dèan dearg ; fàs dearg, cinn dearg.
reddishness, *s.* deirgeachd, ruadhan.
rede, *s.* comhairle, sanus.
redeem, *v. a.* saor ; ath-cheannaich.
redeemable, *adj.* ghabhas saoradh.
redeemer, *s.* fear-saoraidh, Slànaighear an-t-saoghail.
redeliver, *v. a.* ath-shaor, liubhair ; thoir air ais.
redemption, *s.* éirig ; saorsa, saorsainn, sàbhaladh, athfhuasgladh.
redemptory, *adj.* éirigeil.
red lead, *s.* basgluaidhe, basguir.
redness, *s.* deirge, ruaidhe.
redolence, redolency, *s.* cùbhraidheachd, boltrachas.

redolent, *adj.* cùbhraidh, deagh-bholtrachail.
redouble, *v. a.* dùblaich.
redoubt, *s.* dùn beag, dùn catha.
redoubtable, *adj.* eagalach, fuathasach, uabhasach.
redound, *v. n.* pill air, thig air ais air ; tuit air.
redress, *v. a.* cuir ceart, ceartaich, leasaich ; furtaich ; dìol ; dèan suas.
redress, *s.* leasachadh, dìoladh, dìol, fuasgladh, furtachd ; dèanamh suas.
reduce, *v. a.* lùghdaich, dèan na's lugha ; cuir an lughad ; ìslich, irioslaich ; ceannsaich, smachdaich ; leasaich.
reducement, *s.* lùghdachadh, ceannsachadh, smachdachadh.
reducible, *adj.* ghabhas leasachadh.
reduction, *s.* lùghdachadh, cur an lughad, beagachadh ; sàrachadh.
redundance, redundancy, *s.* anabharra, lìonmhorachd, làine.
redundant, *adj.* làn-phailt, a chorr, tuilleadh 's a' chùis.
reduplicate, *v. a.* ath-dhùblaich.
reduplication, *s.* ath-dhùblachadh.
reduplicative, *adj.* dùbailte.
ree, *v. a.* criathair, ridilich.
reed, *s.* cuilc ; ribheid ; slinn.
re-edify, *v. a.* ath-thog.
reedy, *adj.* cuilceach.
reek, *s.* deathach, smùid, toit.
reek, *v. n.* cuir smùid dhiot.
reeky, *adj.* smùideach, toiteach.
reel, *s.* ceangaldair, crois-thachrais.
reel, *v. n.* tachrais, siùganaich.
re-election, *s.* aththaghadh.
re-embark, *v. a.* ath-chuir air bòrd.
re-enforce, *v. a.* ath-neartaich.
re-enforcement, *s.* ath-neartachadh.
re-enjoy, *v. a.* ath-shealbhaich.
re-enter, *v. a.* ath-inntrinn.
re-establish, *v. a.* ath-shocraich.
reeve, reve, *s.* stiùbhard.
re-examine, *v. a.* ath-cheasnaich.
refectory, *s.* pronnlios ; proinnlios.
refer, *v.* leig gu breth neach eile.
reference, *s.* leigeil gu breth.
refine, *v. a.* tur-ghlan.
refined, *adj.* tur-ghlan, fìorghlan.
refinement, *s.* fìor-ghlanadh ; snas, glaine ; grinneas, fineáltachd.
refiner, *s.* leaghadair.
refit, *v. a.* ath-chàirich, tog a rithist.
reflect, *v. a.* smaointich, ath-smaointich.
reflection, *s.* smaoin ; ath-smaointeachadh ; beachd ; seadh, sùim ; cronachadh coire ; aisthilgeadh ; aisthilgeadh coire ; aisthilgeadh.
reflective, *adj.* smaoienteachail, smuaireanach ; a thilgeas faileas ; sgàthanach.
reflector, *s.* fear-smaointeachaidh.
reflex, *adj.* athbhuailte.

reflexible, *adj.* leumas air ais, a lùbas ; a dh' aomas.

reflourish, *v. n.* ath-chinn, ath-fhàs.

reflow, *v. n.* ath lìon ; athshruth.

refluent, *adj.* a' tràghadh.

reflux, *s.* tràghadh, traoghadh.

reform, *v.* leasaich, ath-leasaich ; ath-dhealbh, ath-chruth ; ceartaich.

reform, *s.* leasachadh ; feabhas ; ceartachadh.

reformation, *s.* ath-leasachadh, leasachadh ; atharrachadh, ceartachadh.

reformer, *s.* fear-leasachaidh.

refract, *v. a.* tionndaidh, cuir gu taobh ; claon gathan soluis.

refraction, *s.* tionndadh ; claonadh.

refractive, *adj.* so-thionndadh.

refragable, *adj.* bristeach ; neo-sheasmhach.

refrain, *v.* cum air ais, smachdaich, ceannsaich ; cum ort, na dèan ; caomhain.

refrangible, *adj.* a chlaonas (mar ghath soluis), a sgaras.

refresh, *v. a.* ùraich, neartaich, beothaich, ath-bheothaich.

refreshment, *s.* ùrachadh, fois, tàmh, lasachadh ; lòn, biadh.

refrigerant, *adj.* fionnar, fallain.

refrigerate, *v. a.* fionnaraich.

refrigeration, *s.* fionnarachadh.

refrigerative, *adj.* fionnar.

refuge, *s.* tèarmann, dìon, dìdean, fasgath ; sgàth, sgàile.

refugee, *s.* fògarrach.

refulgence, *s.* lainnireachd.

refulgent, *adj.* lainnireach.

refund, *v. a.* dòirt air ais ; dìol, ath-dhìol, dèan suas, aisig.

refusal, *s.* diùltadh, àicheadh ; obadh, seunadh.

refuse, *v.* diùlt, àicheidh ; ob, seun.

refuse, *s.* fuigheall, fuighleach, sprùileach, deireadh, diù, fartas, fòtus, deasgann, drabh.

refuser, *s.* fear-diùltaidh.

refutal, *s.* cur a mach ; tosdadh.

refutation, *s.* cur a mach, tosdadh ; dìteadh, breugnachadh.

refute, *v. a.* cuir a mach, cuir sàmhach, cuir an aghaidh ; dìt, breugnaich.

regain, *v. a.* ath-choisinn.

regal, *adj.* rìoghail.

regale, *v. a.* ath-bheothaich ; thoir cuirm, dèan fleaghachas.

regalement, *s.* cuirm, ròic, fleagh.

regalia, *s.* suaicheantais rìoghail.

regality, *s.* rìoghalachd.

regard, *v. a.* gabh suim, gabh beachd, thoir suim, thoir fainear, thoir an aire ; gabh seadh, gabh cùram, gabh meas, thoir urram.

regard, *s.* suim, beachd, seadh, aire, cùram, meas, urram.

regardful, *adj.* furachair, faicilleach, cùramach, suimeil, aireachail.

regardless, *adj.* neo-chùramach, neo-fhaicilleach, dearmadach, coma.

regardlessness, *s.* mi-chùramachd.

regency, *s.* tàinistearachd.

regenerate, *v. a.* ath-ghin, ath-bhreith, ath-nuadhaich.

regenerate, *adj.* ath-ghinte, ath-bhreithte, ath-nuadhaichte.

regeneration, *s.* ath-ghineamhuinn, ath-bhreith, ath-nuadhachadh.

regent, *s.* tàinistear ; riaghlair.

regicide, *s.* rìghmhort.

regimen, *s.* lòn-riaghladh.

regiment, *s.* feachd-mìle, réiseamaid.

regimental, *adj.* feachdach.

region, *s.* tìr, dùthaich, fearann, fonn, cearn, àirde ; talamh, roinn, ceithreamh.

register, *s.* clàr-cuimhne.

register, *v. a.* sgrìobh, cuir sìos.

regorge, *v. a.* tilg ; sgeith ; ath-shluig.

regrade, *v. n.* rach air t' ais, fàs na's mion.

regrant, *v. a.* ath-bhuilich.

regrate, *v. n.* ceannaich roimh-làimh.

regress, *s.* pilltinn, dol air ais.

regression, *s.* pilleadh, teachd air ais.

regret, *s.* duilichinn, farran, aithreachas.

regret, *v. a.* bi duilich, bi farranach.

regular, *adj.* riaghailteach.

regularity, *s.* riaghailteachd.

regulate, *v. a.* riaghlaich ; seòl.

regulation, *s.* riaghailt ; reachd.

regulator, *s.* conn-riaghlaidh ; treòraiche, fear-seòlaidh ; conn.

regurgitate, *v.* dòirt air ais.

regurgitation, *s.* dòrtadh air ais.

rehear, *v. a.* ath-chluinn.

rehearsal, *s.* athinnseadh.

rehearse, *v. a.* ath-aithris.

reign, *v. n.* rìoghaich, riaghlaich.

reign, *s.* rìoghachadh, riaghlachadh.

reimburse, *v. a.* ath-dhìol.

reimbursement, *s.* athdhioladh.

rein, *s.* srian.

rein, *v. a.* ceannsaich, smachdaich.

reinforce, *v. a.* ath-neartaich.

reinforcement, *s.* ath-neartachadh, cuideachadh, feachd-còmhnaidh.

reins, *s.* na h-àirnean, caol an droma.

reinsert, *v. a.* ath-chuir sìos.

reinspire, *v. a.* ath-bheothaich.

reinstate, *v.* cuir an seilbh as ùr.

reinvest, *v. a.* cuir an seilbh a rithist ; cuir ath-shéisd ri baile.

reiterate, *v. a.* aithris a rithisd 'sa rithisd.

reiteration, *s.* ath-aithris.

reject, *v. a.* diùlt, tilg air falbh.

rejection, *s.* diùltadh ; dìmeas.

rejoice, *v.* dèan gàirdeachas, dèan aoibhneas, dèan luath-ghàir, dèan mire, bi ait, bi sùgach.

rejoin, v. aon ri chéile rithisd ; ath-choinnich ; ath-fhreagair.
rejoinder, s. athfhreagairt.
rejudge, v. a. ath-sgrùd, ath-cheasnaich, ath-rannsaich.
rekindle, v. a. ath-bheothaich.
relapse, v. n. tuislich, tuit air ais, gabh aththinneas, cùl-sleamhnaich.
relapse, s. tuiteam air ais, fàs na's miosa, athphilleadh tinneis.
relate, v. innis, aithris, cuir an céill ; buin do, buin ri.
related, part. and adj. inniste, air innseadh, aithriste, air aithris ; càirdeach, dìleas.
relation, s. innseadh, aithris, cur an céill ; sgeula, naidheachd ; caraid.
relative, s. caraid, bancharaid, fearcinnidh, dàimheach.
relative, adj. dàimheil ; dìleas, a thaobh.
relax, v. lasaich ; fuasgail ; dearmadaich cuir air dìochuimhne ; dèan socair.
relaxation, s. lasachadh, fuasgladh, socair, athais, fois ; dearmadachd.
relay, s. mùthadh each (air slighe rofhada).
release, v. a. fuasgail, cuir fa sgaoil.
relegate, v. a. fuadaich, fògair.
relegation, s. fuadach, fògradh.
relent, v. a. maothaich ; taisich, bogaich, ciùinich, gabh truas.
relentless, adj. neo-thruacanta.
reliance, s. earbsa, muinghinn.
relic, s. fuigheall, fuighleach, fàgail, iarmad ; cuimhneachan.
relict, s. banntrach.
relief, s. lasachadh, còmhnadh, furtachd, faothachadh, cobhair, fuasgladh, cuideachadh ; sòlas.
relievable, adj. so-lasachail ; ghabhas còmhnadh, ghabhas cuideachadh.
relieve, v. a. lasaich, cobhair, cuidich ; thoir còmhnadh ; mùth, atharraich.
relievo, s. dealbh grabhailte.
religion, s. diadhachd, cràbhadh, creideamh, aidmheil.
religionist, s. baoth-chreideach.
religious, adj. diadhaidh, cràbhach, cneasta, naomha, creideach.
relinquish, v. a. tréig, cuir cùl, thoir thairis.
relish, s. blas taitneach ; déidh, miann, sòlas, toil, tlachd.
relish, v. fàilich ; dèan blasta, blastaich, gabh tlachd do ni ; bi blasta.
relucent, adj. deàrsach, soilleir.
reluctance, s. aindeonachd.
reluctant, adj. aindeonach.
relume, v. a. ath-las.
rely, v. a. earb, cuir dòchas, cuir muinghinn, dèan bun.
remain, v. n. fuirich, fan.

remainder, s. fuigheall, fuighleach.
remains, s. duslach ; corp marbh.
remand, v. a. cuir air ais, gairm air ais, cuir fios air ais.
remark, s. beachd, ràdh.
remark, v. a. beachdaich, thoir fainear ; comharraich a mach.
remarkable, adj. comharraichte, sònraichte ; suaicheanta.
remedy, s. leigheas, ìocshlaint, cungaidh leigheis ; comas, còmhnadh.
remedy, v. a. leighis, slànaich.
remember, v. a. cuimhnich.
remembrance, s. cuimhneachan.
remembrancer, s. meòraiche.
remigration, s. ath-imrich, pilleadh.
remind, v. a. cuimhnich, cuir an cuimhne.
reminiscence, s. cuimhneachadh.
remiss, adj. tais, mì-thapaidh ; neochùramach, dearmadach, leisg, neo-aireachail, neo-shuimeil, mall, màirnealach.
remissible, adj. so-mhathadh.
remission, s. mathanas ; saorsa.
remissness, s. màirneal, neo-aire, dearmad, neo-chùram, neo-shuim.
remit, v. lasaich ; math, lùghdaich, thoir suas ; dàilich, cuir dàil ; cuir air ais.
remittance, s. sùim airgid, a chuireas neach gu neach eile ; pàigheadh.
remnant, s. fuigheall, fuighleach, iarmad ; an còrr.
remonstrance, s. cur an aghaidh.
remonstrate, v. a. connsaich, reusonaich, thoir reuson, cuir an aghaidh, earalaich.
remorse, s. agartas-cogais ; truacantachd, iochdmhorachd.
remorseful, adj. truacanta, maoth.
remorseless, adj. an-iochdmhor.
remote, adj. iomallach, cian, an céin, air astar, fad as, fad air falbh.
remoteness, s. céin, iomallachd.
remotion, s. carachadh, gluasad.
remount, v. a. ath-dhìrich.
removable, adj. so-ghluasadach.
removal, s. gluasad, imrich.
remove, v. cuir as àite, cuir air falbh, cuir air imrich ; falbh, gluais rach air imrich.
remove, s. falbh ; imeachd, gluasad, carachadh, mùthadh.
remunerable, adj. ghabhas dìoladh.
remunerate, v. a. ath-dhìol, pàigh.
remuneration, s. dìol, ath-dhìoladh.
renard, s. ruairidh, ainm a' mhadaidh-ruaidh ; cealgaire.
renascent, adj. ath-ghineach.
renavigate, v. a. ath-sheòl.
rencounter, s. còmhrag, co-strì.
rencounter, v. coinnich, buail ; rach an dàil, thoir ionnsaigh, dèan còmhrag, thoir coinneamh ; còmhlaich, tachair air.

rend, v. a. srac, reub ; beubanaich.

render, v. a. ìoc, dìol, ath-dhìol ; builich, thoir, tabhair ; bàirig eadar-theangaich, mìnich ; thoir thairis, liobhair ; tiomain.

rendezvous, s. ionad-còmhlachaidh.

rendition, s. liobhairt, toirt suas.

renegade, renegado, s. naomh-thréigeach ; fear ceannairceach.

renew, v. a. ath-nuadhaich.

renewal, s. ath-nuadhachadh.

rennet, s. binid ; deasgainn.

renounce, v. a. diùlt, ob, tréig.

renovate, v. a. nuadhaich, ùraich.

renovation, s. nuadhachadh.

renown, s. cliù, alla, iomradh.

renowned, adj. cliùiteach, allail, iomraiteach, ainmeil.

rent, s. sracadh, reub ; bèarn ; gearradh ; màl, tighinn a steach ; cìs.

rent, v. gabh no thoir air son màil ; srac, reub, stroic, sgoilt.

rent, part. sracte, reubte.

rental, s. màl oighreachd.

renter, s. màladair ; tuathanach.

renumerate, v. a. ath-dhìol, ath-chunnt.

renunciation, s. cùlachadh, àicheadh, toirt thairis.

reordain, v. a. ath-òrduich.

reordination, s. ath-òrduchadh.

repaid, part. pàighte, ath-dhìolte.

repair, v. càirich, leasaich, imich, falbh, siubhail ; tog ort, rach.

repair, s. càradh ; leasachadh.

repairable, reparable, adj. ghabhas leasachadh, ghabhas càradh.

reparation, s. càradh, dìoladh.

repartee, s. freagairt-geur, beum, freagairt ealamh.

repass, v. n. ath-shiubhail.

repast, s. biadh, lòn, teachd-an-tìr.

repay, v. a. ath-dhìol, pàigh, ìoc.

repeal, v. a. cuir sìos, cuir air chùl, thoir gu neo-ni.

repeal, s. cur air chùl, cur sìos.

repeat, v. a. aithris ; abair a rìthist ; gabh (rann, etc.).

repeatedly, adv. gu minig, gu tric.

repeater, s. fear-aithris ; uaireadear.

repel, v. a. tilg air ais, diùlt.

repent, v. n. gabh aithreachas.

repentance, s. aithreachas.

repentant, adj. aithreachail.

repercuss, v. a. buail air.

repercussion, s. cur air ais.

repertory, s. ionad-tasgaidh.

repetition, s. athaithris ; athchantain ; athdhanamh ; athiarrtas.

repine, v. n. dèan talach, dèan frionas, dèan gearan.

repiner, s. fear talaich.

replace, v. a. cuir 'na àite, dèan suas (an call).

replant, v. a. ath-shuidhich.

replenish, v. a. lion ; àirneisich.

replete, adj. làn, iomlan.

repletion, s. làine, lìontachd.

replication, s. freagairt.

reply, v. n. freagair, thoir freagairt.

reply, s. freagairt.

repolish, v. a. ath-lìobhaich.

report, v. a. innis, aithris ; abair, dèan sgeula ; dèan iomradh.

report, s. fathunn, biùthas ; iomradh, sgeul ; fuaim, bragh, làmhach.

reporter, s. fear-naidheachd.

reposal, s. foisneachadh.

repose, v. foisnich, gabh tàmh.

repose, s. fois, tàmh ; cadal.

reposit, v. a. taisg ; cuir seachad.

reposition, s. tasgaidh, cur suas.

repository, s. ionad-tasgaidh.

repossess, v. a. ath-shealbhaich.

repossession, s. ath-shealbhachadh.

reprehend, v. a. cronaich, coirich.

reprehender, s. fear-cronachaidh.

reprehensible, adj. ion - choireachail ; airidh air achmhasan.

reprehension, s. achmhasan.

reprehensive, adj. achmhasanach.

reprehensory, adj. achmhasanach.

represent, v. a. feuch ; nochd ; foillsich, taisbean, cuir an céill ; dealbh ; riochdaich.

representation, s. nochdadh, foillseachadh, taisbeanadh, coltas ; riochd, dealbh, ìomhaigh, aogas.

representative, s. fear-ionaid.

representment, s. iomhaigh ; samhla.

repress, v. a. caisg ; sàraich ; ceannsaich, cìosnaich, smachdaich ; mùch ; cùm fodha.

repress, repression, s. casg, sàrachadh, ceannsachadh, cìosnachadh, mùchadh, cumail fodha.

repressive, adj. smachdail.

reprieve, v. a. cuir dàil am peanas, thoir maitheanas.

reprieve, s. mathadh, dàil peanais.

reprimand, v. a. achmhasanaich.

reprimand, s. achmhasan, trod.

reprint, v. a. clò-bhuail as ùr.

reprisal, s. éirig ; dìoladh.

reproach, v. a. cronaich ; maslaich ; cuir as leth, tilg suas.

reproach, s. cronachadh, maslachadh ; mì-chliù, masladh, sgainneal, tàmailt, aithis ; tailceas, innisg, ilisg.

reproachable, adj. maslachail.

reproachful, adj. maslach, nàr, gràineil, tàmailteach ; tailceasach, beumach, toibheumach.

reprobate, s. daoidhear.

reprobate, adj. olc, aingidh, baoth.

reprobate, v. a. mì-cheadaich ; diùlt ; cuir cùl ; dìt.

reprobation, *s.* dìteadh ; dìmeas.
reproduce, *v. a.* ath-thoir a mach; dèan as ùr.
reproduction, *s.* ath-thoirt a mach.
reproof, *s.* sglamhradh, trod.
reprovable, *adj.* airidh air cronachadh.
reprove, *v. a.* sglàmhraich ; coirich.
re-prune, *v. a.* ath-sgath, ath-bhearr.
reptile, *s.* biast-snàigeach ; trudar.
reptile, *adj.* snàgach, snàigeach.
republic, *s.* co-fhlaitheachd.
republican, *adj.* co-fhlaitheachdach.
republican, *s.* fear-co-fhlaitheachd.
repudiate, *v. a.* dealaich, àicheadh.
repudiation, *s.* dealachadh.
repugnant, *adj.* mì-thoileach, gràineil.
repulse, *v. a.* cùm air ais.
repulse, *s.* aisbhualadh, pilleadh.
repulsive, repulsory, *adj.* aisbhuailteach, doirbh, oillteil.
repurchase, *v. a.* ath-cheannaich.
reputable, *adj.* cliùiteach.
reputation, *s.* cliù, meas, alla.
repute, *v. a.* meas ; creid ; saoil.
repute, *s.* cliù, meas, iomradh.
request, *s.* iarrtas, achanaich.
request, *v. a.* iarr, sir, guidh.
requiem, *s.* laoidh-guidhe, air son nam marbh, tuireadh.
require, *v. a.* iarr ; sir.
requisite, *adj.* feumail, iomchuidh.
requisite, *s.* nì feumail.
requital, *s.* dìol, pàigheadh, éirig.
requite, *v. a.* ath-dhìol, ath-phàigh.
rereward, *s.* feachd-deiridh, cul-taic.
resale, *s.* athreic.
resalute, *v. a.* ath-fhàiltich.
rescind, *v. a.* gearr, cuir as lagh.
rescission, *s.* sgathadh, gearradh.
rescribe, *v. a.* ath-sgrìobh.
rescript, *s.* reachd rìgh.
rescue, *s.* saoradh, fuasgladh, tiorcadh, sàbhaladh.
rescue, *v. a.* saor, sgaoil ; tèarainn.
research, *s.* rannsachadh, ceasnachadh, sgrùdadh, athshireadh.
research, *v. a.* rannsaich, ceasnaich, lorgaich.
resemblance, *s.* samhla, coltas.
resemble, *v. a.* bi coltach, coimeas.
resent, *v. a.* gabh gu dona, gabh gu h-olc, gabh mar thàmailt ; dìoghail.
resentful, *adj.* feargach.
resentment, *s.* fearg, dìoghaltas.
reservation, *s.* cùl-earalas, falach.
reserve, *v. a.* taisg, caomhain.
reserve, *s.* tasgadh, gleidhteanas, cùl-earalas ; stuaim, nàire, macantas.
reserved, *adj.* màlda, stuama, macanta ; dùinte ; fada thall, mùgach ; neo-shaor ; caomhainte, taisgte.
reservedness, *s.* fiatachd, mùig.
reservoir, *s.* màthair-uisge baile.

resettlement, *s.* ath-shocrachadh.
reside, *v. n.* fuirich, gabh còmhnaidh, cuir suas ; traogh, sìolaidh.
residence, resiance, *s.* ionad-còmhnaidh, fàrdoch, tàimheach.
resident, resiant, *adj.* a' fuireach, a' tàmh, a chòmhnaidh.
resident, *s.* fear-còmhnaidh.
residue, *s.* fuigheall, iarmad.
resign, *v. a.* thoir suas ; géill.
resignation, *s.* toirt-seachad ; ùmhlachd, strìochdadh, géilleadh.
resignment, *s.* toirt suas.
resilience, *s.* leum air ais.
resin, rosin, *s.* ròiseid.
resinous, *adj.* ròiseideach, bìtheach.
resist, *v. a.* cuir an aghaidh.
resistance, *s.* strì, cur an aghaidh.
resistible, *adj.* so-bhacadh.
resistless, *adj.* do-bhacadh, dian.
resoluble, *adj.* so-leaghadh.
resolute, *adj.* suidhichte, sònraichte, dàn, danarra, misneachail, gramail, bunailteach, seasmhach.
resolution, *s.* rùin-seasmhach, inntinn, misneach ; sònrachadh ; bunailteachd, bunaiteachd ; fuasgladh, mìneachadh.
resolvable, *adj.* so-sgrùdadh, so-thuigsinn.
resolve, *v.* sònraich ; cuir romhad ; fuasgail, sgrùd ; leagh.
resolve, *s.* rùn-suidhichte.
resolved, *adj.* sònraichte, suidhichte.
resolvedly, *adv.* gu suidhichte.
resolvent, *adj.* leaghach.
resonant, *adj.* ath-fhuaimneach, fuamnach.
resort, *v. n.* taghaich ; rach.
resort, *s.* tional, co-thional, cruinneachadh ; coinneamh, còdhail.
resound, *v. a.* ath-fhuaimnich, fuamnach.
resource, *s.* cùl-earalas, tèarmann ; saoibhreas, seòl, dòigh, rathad.
respect, *v. a.* urramaich, thoir meas.
respect, *s.* urram, meas, spéis.
respectable, *adj.* measail.
respectful, *adj.* modhail, beusach.
respective, *adj.* sònraichte ; àraid.
respectively, *adv.* fa leth.
respersion, *s.* spultadh, spairteadh.
respiration, *s.* analachadh, fois.
respire, *v. n.* analaich, leig t' anail.
respite, *s.* fois, anail, tàmh ; fosadh.
respite, *v. a.* thoir fois ; cuir dàil.
resplendence, *s.* deàlrachd deàlradh, loinnireachd, dearrsadh, soillse.
resplendent, *adj.* dealrach, lonnrach, dearrsach, boillsgeil.
respond, *v. a.* freagair.
respondent, *s.* fear freagairt.
response, *s.* freagairt.
responsible, *adj.* freagarrach, cunntachail.
responsion, *s.* an ceud cheasnachadh air son, B.A. (Oxford).

responsive, responsory, *adj.* freagairteach ; ath-fhuaimneach.

rest, *s.* fois, tàmh, cadal, sìth, sàmhchair, socair, suaimhneas, ciùineas, clos ; fosadh, sgur ; fèith ; taic, prop, stad ; a' chuid eile ; càch.

rest, *v. n.* gabh fois ; caidil, leig t' anail, sguir, dèan tàmh, gabh gu clos ; fuirich, fan ; earb ri, earb á.

restauration, *s.* nuadhachadh.

restful, *adj.* sàmhach, ciùin.

restiff, restive, resty, *adj.* ceannlaidir, reasgach, stadach, rag.

restitution, *s.* toirt air ais, dìoladh.

restiveness, *s.* reasgachd, an-fhois.

restless, *adj.* mì-fhoisneach, mi-fhoighidneachd ; mì-shuaimhneach ; luaineach, neo-shuidhichte, iomairteach, àimhreiteach, buaireasach.

restlessness, *s.* mì-fhoisneachd, neo-fhoisneachd, mì - fhoighidinn, mì - shuaimhneas, dìth foise.

restorable, *adj.* so-aiseag.

restoration, *s.* athaiseag, toirt air ais.

restorative, *adj.* leigheasail.

restorative, *s.* leigheas - beothachaidh, iocshlaint-neartachaidh.

restore, *v. a.* thoir air ais ; leighis, ath-bheothaich.

restrain, *v. a.* bac ; caisg ; cùm air ais, toirmisg, ceannsaich, cùm fodha, smachdaich, cùm fo cheannsal.

restraint, *s.* bacadh, maille, toirmeasg, grabadh, ceannsachd.

restrict, *v. a.* bac, ceannsaich, grab, cùm a steach ; ceangail.

restriction, *s.* bacadh ; grabadh, cuibhreachadh, ceangal.

restrictive, *adj.* ceanglach, cuingealach.

restringent, *adj.* ceanglach.

result, *s.* buil, crìoch ; deireadh.

resume, *v. a.* ath-thionnsgain.

resumption, *s.* ath-thionnsgnadh.

resurrection, *s.* aiseirigh.

re-survey, *v. a.* ath-bheachdaich.

resuscitate, *v. a.* ath-dhùisg, ath-bheothaich.

resuscitation, *s.* ath-dhùsgadh.

retail, *v. a.* reic (beag is mòr).

retailer, *s.* frith-cheannaiche.

retain, *v. a.* cùm, gléidh, coimhid.

retake, *v. a.* athghlac, athghabh.

retaliate, *v. a.* ath-dhìol, dìol air ais ; thoir buille air son buille.

retaliation, *s.* dìoladh.

retard, *v.* bac, grab, cùm air ais, cuir maill' air, cuir éis air.

retardation, *s.* bacadh, grabadh.

retch, *v. n.* sgeith, sgeath, tilg.

retention, *s.* cumail ; cuimhneachadh ; cuimhne ; dùnadh.

retentive, *adj.* dìonach ; cuimhneachail, cumailteach.

reticular, retiform, *adj.* lìonanach ; mar lìon ; sùileagach, sgannanach.

retinue, *s.* coigleachd.

retire, *v.* rach gu taobh ; falbh, teich.

retired, *adj.* uaigneach ; aonaranach, air toirt thairis (dreuchd).

retirement, *s.* uaigneas, dol an comhair a' chùil.

retort, *v. a.* aisthilg, tilg air ais.

retort, *s.* geur-fhreagairt ; seòrsa do shoitheach glainne.

retouch, *v. a.* ath-bhean ri ; leasaich.

retrace, *v. a.* ath-lòrgaich.

retract, *v. a.* tarruing air ais, thoir a steach, thoir air ais (cainnt).

retractation, *s.* athbharail.

retraction, *s.* aistarruing.

retreat, *s.* ionad dìomhair ; tèarmann, dìdean, àite teichidh, fasgadh ; teicheadh-airm, ruaig, airseap.

retreat, *v. n.* teich ; gabh dion.

retrench, *v. a.* gearr dheth, sgath, lughdaich (cosgais).

retrenchment, *s.* lùghdachadh.

retribute, *v. a.* ath-dhìol, phàigh.

retribution, *s.* athdhìoladh.

retributive, *adj.* dioghalt.

retrieve, *v. a.* faigh air ais, aisig, ath-bhuidhinn ; athghairm, coisinn air ais.

retrievable, *adj.* a dh' fhaodair fhaighinn air ais.

retrocession, *s.* dol air ais.

retrospect, *s.* sealltainn air ais.

retrospection, *s.* sealladh air ais.

return, *v.* thig air ais, pìll ; dìol, pàigh, ìoc ; thoir air ais, cuir air ais.

return, *s.* pilleadh ; teachd air ais ; dìoladh, pàidheadh, freagairt ; tairbhe ; buannachd.

reunion, *s.* athaonadh.

reveal, *v. a.* nochd, foillsich, taisbean, leig ris ; innis, aithris.

revel, *s.* cuirm ; ruidhtearachd.

revel, *v. n.* dèan pòit, dèan ròic ; dèan ruidhtearachd.

revelation, *s.* taisbeanadh.

reveller, *s.* craosaire, pòitear.

revel-rout, *s.* gràisg-phrasgan.

revelry, *s.* ruidhtearachd, pòitearachd, baoisleachd.

revenge, *v. a.* gabh dìoghaltas, thoir aichbheil, thoir dìoladh.

revenge, *s.* dìoghaltas, dìoladh.

revengeful, *adj.* dìoghaltach.

revenger, *s.* fear-dìoghaltais.

revenue, *s.* teachd a steach, màl ; cìs.

reverberate, *v. a.* dèan ath-ghairm.

reverberation, *s.* ath-ghairm, mac talla.

reverberatory, *adj.* ath - fhuaimneach ; ath-phillteach.

revere, *v. a.* thoir àrd urram, thoir àrd meas, urramaich.

reverence, s. urram ; ùmhlachd.
reverence, v. a. urramaich.
reverend, adj. urramach, measail.
reverent, adj. iriosal, ùmhal, ùmhlachdail, strìochdail.
reverently, adv. le urram.
reversal, s. atharrachadh breitheanais, tionndadh air ais.
reverse, v. a. cuir bun os ceann ; atharraich, mùth, caochail.
reverse, s. atharrachadh, caochladh.
reversible, adj. atharrachail.
reversion, s. ath-shealbhachadh ; còir-sealbhachaidh.
revert, v. mùth, atharraich ; pill.
revertible, adj. so-thiondadh.
revery, reverie, s. smaoin, trom-smaoin ; beachd-smaoin.
revest, v. a. ath-sgeudaich.
review, v. a. ath-bheachdaich ; rann-saich ; sgrùd.
review, s. ath-bheachdachadh ; rann-sachadh ; sgrùdadh, beachdachadh.
reviewer, s. fear-rannsachaidh.
revile, v. a. càin, maslaich.
reviler, s. fear-càinidh, fear-tarcuis.
revisal, revision, s. ath-leughadh ; ath-sgrùdadh, mion-sgrùdadh.
revise, v. a. ath-leugh ; ath-sgrùd.
revise, s. ath-leughadh ; ath-sgrùdadh, ath-cheartachadh.
reviser, s. sgrùdaire, fear sgrùdaidh.
revisit, v. a. ath-thaghail.
revival, s. ath-bheothachadh.
revive, v. ath-bheothaich ; ùraich ; thig beò a rithisd ; thig thuige ; dùisg, brosnaich ; glac misneach.
revocable, adj. so-atharrachadh.
revocate, v. a. gairm air ais.
revocation, s. aisghairm.
revoke, v. a. tarruing air ais.
revolt, v. n. dèan ar-a-mach ; éirich.
revolt, s. ar-a-mach ; éirigh.
revolution, s. cuairt ; iom-chuartachadh, atharrachadh ; ceannairc ; iomsgaradh (air tigh rioghail).
revolve, v. iom-chuairtich ; cnuasaich, beachd-smuainich.
revulsion, s. gràin obann.
revulsive, adj. gràineachail.
reward, v. a. gràineachail, dìol, pàigh.
reward, s. dìol, dìoladh, pàigheadh, duais, luach-saoithreach.
rhapsodist, s. àrd-ghlòraiche.
rhapsody, s. àrd-ghlòir, seòrsa canntair-eachd.
rhetoric, s. ùr-labhradh.
rhetorical, adj. ùr-labhrach.
rhetorician, s. ùr-labhartaiche.
rheum, s. ronnan, tias, mùsgan.
rheumatic, adj. lòinidheach.
rheumatism, s. lòinidh ; altghalar.
rheuminess, s. mùsganachd.

rheumy, adj. mùsgach, ronnach.
rhinoceros, s. an sròn-adharcach.
rhomb, s. ceithir-shlisneach.
rhomboid, s. am bradan-leathan.
rhubarb, s. luibh-na-pùrgaid.
rhyme, s. rann ; dàn ; duan.
rhyme, v. n. rannaich, dean rann.
rhymer, s. rannair, duanair.
rhythmical, adj. duanach, binn.
rib, s. aisinn ; reang, tarsannan.
ribald, s. baobh, trusdar drabasda.
ribaldry, s. draosdachd.
riband, ribbon, s. stìom, ribean.
rib-wort, s. slànlus.
rice, s. gràn Innseanach.
rich, adj. beairteach, saoibhir, toiceil ; cosgail, luachmhor, prìseil, pailt, tor-ach ; tarbhach, reamhar.
riches, s. beairteas, saibhreas, maoin, stòras, earras, pailteas, toic.
richly, adv. gu saoibhir pailt.
richness, s. reamhrachd, saoibhreachd, toraichead, beairtichead.
rick, s. cruach, rucan ; cuidhleag, mulan, tudan.
rickets, s. an teannadh.
rickety, adj. teannadach.
rid, v. a. cuir fa-sgaoil, saor, fuasgail ; cuir air falbh ; dìobair, fuadaich.
riddance, s. fuasgladh ; saoradh.
riddle, s. tòimhseachan ; ruideal ; cria-thar-garbh.
riddle, v. ruidealaich, ruidil.
ride, v. marcaich ; smachdaich.
rider, s. marcaiche, marc-neach.
ridge, s. druim, croit, mullach ; fireach, creachann, aonach ; magh, gead, imire.
ridgel, ridgeling, s. rùda, roige.
ridgy, adj. druimeanach.
ridicule, s. fanaid, sgeig ; ceòl-gàire ; fearas-chuideachd.
ridicule, v. a. dèan sgeig.
ridiculous, adj. ceòl-ghaireach, aighear-ach, neònach.
riding, s. marcachd, earrann, dùthcha.
riding-hood, s. deise-mharcachd.
rife, adj. pailt, lìonmhor.
rifle, v. a. spùinn, creach, slad.
rifle, s. gunna.
rift, s. sgoltadh, gàg ; brùchd.
rift, v. sgoilt, sgag, sgàin ; brùchd.
rig, v. a. uidheamaich ; sgeadaich.
rigadoon, s. dannsa Fràngach.
rigation, s. fliuchadh, uisgeachadh.
rigging, s. buill agus acainn luinge.
riggish, adj. drùiseil, neo-gheimnidh.
right, adj. ceart ; cubhaidh ; freagarr-ach ; dìreach ; tréidhireach, còir.
right, s. ceartas ; còir, dlighe.
right, v. a. thoir ceartas, cuir ceart.
righteous, adj. fìreanach, tréidhireach, còir, math, ionraic, cothromach ; subh-ailceach.

righteousness, s. fìreantachd tréidhireas, ionracas.
rightful, adj. dligheach, ceart.
rightly, adv. gu ceart.
rigid, adj. rag ; forganta, geurtheann, doirbh ; dùr, cruaidh, fuar, leacanta.
rigidity, s. raige ; dùiread, cruas.
rigorous, adj. cruaidh, cruadalach, gàbhaidh ; min-phongail.
rigour, s. cruas, fuachd ; déine.
rill, rillet, s. caochan, sruthan, alltan, srùlag.
rim, s. oir, iomall, bile.
rime, s. liathreothadh, crithreothadh, cithreothadh.
rimple, v. a. preas, luirc, cas.
rimy, adj. ceòthar ; liath le reothadh.
rind, s. cairt, rùsg, cochull.
rind, v. a. rùisg, plaoisg, cairt.
rindle, s. guitear, claiseag.
ring, s. fàinne ; ailbheag, cearcall, cuairteag, beum cluig.
ring, v. a. beum, seirm, buail.
ringdove, s. an smùdan.
ringer, s. fear-cluig.
ringleader, s. ceann-gràisge.
ringlet, s. dualag, bachlag, ciabhag, fainneag, cuachag, cleachdag.
ringtail, s. bréid-air-tòin.
ringworm, s. buaileag-thimchill.
rinse, v. a. sruthall, nigh, rusail.
rinser, s. sruthlair, nigheadair.
riot, s. tuaireap, àimhreite ; ruidhteireachd.
riot, v. n. tog tuaireap.
rioter, s. fear-tuaireap.
riotous, adj. tuaireapach ; gràineil.
rip, v. a. srac, reub, srac suas, srac as a chéile, sgoilt ; nochd, innis, foillsich, taisbean, leig ris.
ripe, adj. abaich ; foire ; inbheach.
ripe, ripen, v. n. abaich.
ripeness, s. abaichead ; foirfeachd.
ripple, v. n. faochanaich, crith.
rise, v. n. éirich ; dìrich ; bris a mach, dèan ceannairc, dèan àr-a-mach, dèan tuaireap.
rise, s. éiridh, dìreadh ; tùs.
risen, part. air éiridh.
risible, adj. gàireachail.
risk, s. cunnart, gàbhadh.
risk, v. a. cuir an cunnart.
rite, s. deas-ghnàth.
ritual, adj. deas-ghnàthach.
ritual, s. leabhar dheas-ghnàth.
rival, s. co-dheuchainniche, fear-còmhstrith ; co-shuirdhiche.
rival, adj. co-strìtheach.
rivalry, s. comh-dheuchainn, co-dheuchainneachd, còmhstrith.
rive, v. reub, srac, sgàin, sgoilt.
rivel, v. a. cas, preas, liurc.
riven, part. reubte, sracte, sgàinte.

river, s. abhainn.
river-dragon, s. an croghall-mór.
river-horse, s. an t-each-uisge.
rivet, s. sparrag, teannachan.
rivet, v. a. sparr, teannaich.
rivulet, s. sruthan, caochan, srùlag.
rix-dollar, s. bonn cheithir tastain is sia sgillinn.
roach, s. seòrs' éisg.
road, s. rathad, ròd, slighe, aisridh, acarsaid; bàdh, bàdhan, poll, òban, calladh.
roam, v. seabhaid ; rach air seachran, rach gu taobh, bi 'san athamanaich, rach air fàrsan.
roan, adj. grìsfhionn, riabhach.
roar, v. n. beuc, geum, éigh, glaodh, sgairtich, ràn ; roic ; dèan burral.
roar, s. beuc, geum, roic, éigh, glaodh, ràn, sgairt, burral, ulfhart.
roast, s. ròsta ; v. a. ròist.
rob, v. a. spùill, creach, slad.
robber, s. creachadair, spùilleadair, fear-reubainn, fear-slaide.
robbery, s. reubainn, creach.
robe, v. a. sgeadaich, còmhdaich.
robe, s. falluinn, trusgan.
robin-redbreast, s. am brùdhearg.
robust, adj. garbh, làidir, calma, neartmhor, comasach, lùthor, féitheach, gramail, garg.
robustness, s. neart, spionnadh.
rocambole, s. creamh-nan-creag.
rochealum, s. an t-alm-fìorghlan.
rochet, s. léine-aifrionn ; seòrs' éisg.
rock, s. carraig, creag, sgòrrbheann ; cuigeal ; tèarmunn, dìdean.
rock, v. luaisg, tulg, siudanaich ; fuluaisg, cuir a chadal ; bi air udal.
rocky, adj. creagach, carraigeach, garbh ; clachach, cruaidh.
rod, s. slat ; sgiùrsair.
rode, pret. of to ride, mharcaich.
roe, s. earba, ruadhag ; iuchair éisg.
roebuck, s. boc-earba.
rogation, s. seadhan, aslachadh.
rogation-week, s. seachduin bhogadhnan-gad, an seachdamh latha roimh 'n chàingis.
rogue, s. slaightear, cealgair.
roguery, s. slaightearachd.
roguish, adj. slaighteil, carach.
roist, v. n. dèan gleadhraich.
roll, v. fill ; cuir car air char ; tonnluaisg, cuairsg, cuairtich, cuir mu chuairt, rach mu chuairt.
roll, s. rola, ruileag.
roller, s. lunn.
Roman, adj. Ròmanach.
romance, s. ròlaist, spleaghraich.
romancer, s. ròlaistiche, spleaghaire.
Romanist, s. pàpanach.
romantic, adj. ròlaisteach, spleaghach, spleighreach.

Rome, s. An Ròimh.
Romish, adj. Ròimheach, pàpanach.
romp, s. dubhchaile ; garbh-chluich.
romp, v. n. dèan garbh-chleasachd.
romping, s. garbh-chleasachd.
rondeau, s. iorram, ùilean.
ronion, s. umarlaid, bronnag.
rood, s. ròd, an ceathramh cuid de acair fearainn ; a' chrois naomha.
roof, s. mullach tighe, fraigh, tughadh ; uachdar a' chàirein.
roof, v. a. cuir mullach air tigh.
rook, s. ròcas ; cealgair.
rook, v. n. thoir an car as ; meall, creach, spuinn, spuill, slad.
rookery, s. ionad-ròcas.
room, s. seòmar, rùm ; àite ; ionad.
roomy, adj. farsuing, leathan.
roost, s. spàrr, spiris, iris, faradh.
roost, v. n. rach air spiris.
root, s. freumh ; stoc, bun ; meacan, tùs, mathair-aobhair, aobhar.
root, v. freumhaich, gabh freumh ; suidhich, daingnich ; sgrios ; spìon as a' bhun ; mill.
rooted, adj. freumhaichte.
rootedly, adv. gu domhainn, gu daingeann, gu teann.
rope, s. togha, ròp, ball.
rope, v. n. righnich, fàs tiugh.
rope-maker, s. fear deanamh ròp.
ropiness, s. rìghneachd.
ropy, adj. rìghinn, bìtheanach.
roquelaure, s. cleòca fireannaich ; faluinn-uachdair.
rosary, s. a' chonair, paidirean.
roscid, adj. drùchdach.
rose, s. an ròs, an dris-bhil.
rose, pret. of to rise, dh' éirich.
roseate, adj. ròsach, ruiteach.
Rosemary, s. Ròs-Muire.
roset, s. gnè do dhath dearg.
rosin, s. ròsaid.
rostrum, s. gob ; claigeann toisich luinge, ciannag, sgàlan.
rosy, adj. ruiteach, mar ròs.
rot, v. grod, lobh, breò, malc.
rot, s. an tòchd ; malcadh-tioram, grodadh, lobhadh.
rotary, rotatory, adj. cuairteach, rothach, cuairsgeach.
rotation, s. dol mun cuairt, dol ceann sreath.
rote, v. a. ionnsaich air do theangaidh.
rote, s. sriut, facail air teangaidh.
rotten, adj. grod, lobhte, malcte, breun, breoite, cnàmhte.
rotund, adj. cruinn.
rotunda, s. togail chruinn.
rotundity, s. cruinnead ; cruinne.
rouge, s. dearg, dath dearg.
rough, adj. garbh ; molach, ròmach, ròinneach ; gruamach, gnò ; dòbh-

aidh, gailbheach, garbh, gàbhaidh, doinionnach, stuadh - ghreannach ; garg, searbh, geur, goirt ; dealgach ; creagach, clachach.
rough-cast, s. dealbh gun lìobhadh.
rough-draught, s. ceud-dhealbh.
roughen, v. dèan garbh, fàs garbh ; fàs gruamach, sgaiteach no coimheach ; fàs gailbheach.
roughly, adv. gu garbh, gu garg.
roughness, s. gairbhead, molaichead, romaiche, gairge, comheachas ; seirbhe ; gailbhichead, fiadhaichead.
round, adj. cruinn, cearclach ; slàn ; glan, cuimir, riochdail ; pongail, luath ; sgairteil ; mór.
round, s. cuairt, cearcall ; car.
round, adv. mun cuairt ; air gach taobh ; timchioll, mu thimchioll.
roundelay, s. luinneag, coilleag.
roundhouse, s. prìosan, gainntir.
roundish, adj. a lethchar cruinn.
roundness, s. cruinnead.
rouse, v. dùisg ; caraich ; brosnaich ; mosgail, brosgail ; brod.
rousing, adj. brosnachail, mosglach.
rout, s. pràbar, cumasg ; ruaig.
rout, v. ruag, sgiùrs, sgap.
route, s. rathad, slighe.
rove, v. bi air fàrsan, rach air iomrall, siubhail gu luaineach.
rover, s. fear-fàrsain, allmharach ; fear luaineach ; creachadair mara.
roving, adj. fàrsanach, seachranach ; iomrallach, neo-shuidhichte.
row, s. sréad, sreath, breath, sabaid.
row, v. a. iomair, dèan iomaradh.
rowel, s. spuir, silteach eich.
rower, s. iomaraiche, ràmhaiche.
royal, adj. rìoghail.
royalist, s. fear tha dìleas do rìgh.
royalty, s. rìoghalachd, teaghlach rìoghail.
rub, v. suath ; tachais ; sgrìob ; teannaich ; glan, sgùr.
rub, s. suathadh ; bacadh, moille ; cruadal.
rubber, s. sgrìobadair ; inneal suathaidh ; seòrsa eighe.
rubbish, s. salachar, trusdaireachd, trealaich.
rubify, v. a. dearg, deargaich.
rubric, v. s. an sgrìobhadh dearg.
ruby, s. ruiteachan, rùban ; deargsheud ; guirean no plucan dearg.
ructation, s. brùc, brùcail.
rudder, s. stiùir.
ruddiness, s. deirge, ruthadh.
ruddle, s. céir dhearg, clach-dhearg.
ruddy, adj. ruiteach, dearg.
rude, adj. borb ; doirbh, mì-mhodhail ; brùideil, aineolach, neo-fhoghluimte, neo - shnasmhor ; neo - ghrinn, neo-ealanta ; neo-sgileil, neo-theòma.

rudeness, *s.* buirbe; mìomhodh; brùidealachd ; aineolas ; déine.
rudiment, *s.* tionnsgnadh, ceud thoiseach, ceud-fhoghlum.
rudimental, *adj.* tionnsgnach.
rue, *v. a.* crean, gabh aithreachas.
rue, *s.* an rùdh, an ruadhlus.
rueful, *adj.* muladach, brònach, dubhach, trom creanachail.
ruefulness, *s.* mulad, doilghios.
ruff, *s.* gibeag-muineil ; seòrsa éisg.
ruffian, *s.* fear-brùideil.
ruffian, *adj.* bruideil, olc.
ruffle, *v. a.* cuir á òrdugh ; buair ; tog greann mar ni gaoth air uisge.
ruffle, *s.* frilleag, gibeag ; sabaid.
rug, *s.* brat-teallaich.
rugged, *adj.* garbh, creagach, sturrach ; bacach, bacanach, stacach ; drochmhuinte, doirbh, borb, brùideil ; mìmhodhail ; gailbheach.
ruggedness, *s.* gairbhe ; buirbe.
rugose, *adj.* caisreagach, preasach.
ruin, *s.* léirsgrios ; lomsgrios ; dol sìos ; mìshealbh ; làrach, seann tobhta.
ruin, *v. a.* léir-sgrios ; dith-mhill, dèan truagh, tilg sìos, leag ; creach.
ruinate, *v. a.* thoir gu bochdainn.
ruination, *s.* léirchreach.
ruinous, *adj.* sgriosal, millteach.
rule, *s.* riaghailt ; àithne ; òrdugh ; riaghladh ; smachd, ceannas ; nòs, gnàth, àbhaist ; lagh, reachd.
rule, *v. a.* riaghail ; stiùr ; smachdaich ; cuir gu dòigh.
ruler, *s.* uachdaran, riaghladair.
rum, *s.* deoch làidir air a tarruing of chuilc an t-siùcair.
rumble, *v. n.* dèan rùchdail.
ruminant, *adj.* a chnàmhas cìr.
ruminate, *v.* cnàmh cìr ; cnuasaich.
rumination, *s.* cnàmhadh cìre, athchagnadh, cnuasachadh.
rummage, *v.* rannsaich ; sgrùd, sir, dèan sporghail.
rummer, *s.* glaine-òil ; còrn, cuach.
rumour, *s.* fathunn, iomradh, sgeul.
rumour, *v. a.* sgaoil, innis, aithris.
rump, *s.* an dronn, an rumpull, am feaman, bun an earbaill, mìr-urram nam bàrd.
rumple, *s.* preasag ; cas, lorc.
rumple, *v. a.* preas, cas, liurc.

run, *v.* ruith, greas, steud ; teich ; sruth ; leagh ; troimh-lot, bior, sàth.
run, *s.* ruith, steud ; gluasad, slighe.
runagate, *s.* dìobarach, cladhaire.
rundlet, runlet, *s.* buideal.
rung, *s.* rong, rongas.
runnel, *s.* sruthan, srùlag, caochan.
runner, *s.* steudair ; gill-ruithe, teachdaire ; clach-mhuilinn.
runnet, *s.* binid ; deasgainn.
running, *adj.* steudach ; siùbhlach.
runnion, *s.* sgonnbhalach, ùmaidh.
runt, *s.* mart beag ; arrach.
rupee, *s.* bonn Innseannach (=2s. 3d.).
ruption, *s.* briseadh, sgaoileadh.
rupture, *s.* mam-sic ; sgàineadh ; àimhreit, eas-còrdadh.
rupture, *v. a.* bris, sgàin, sgaoil.
rural, *adj.* dùthchail, tìreil.
rush, *s.* luachair, buigneach ; nì suarrach sam bith ; dian-ruith.
rush, *v. n.* brùchd, ruith, pùc, buail air adhart ; stiall ; thoir ionnsaigh làidir, thoir garbh-ionnsaigh.
rush-light, *s.* coinneal-buaic, sitheag.
rushy, *adj.* luachrach ; luachaireach.
rusk, *s.* seòrsa de aran-ròsta.
russet, *adj.* donn, dùbh-ruadh.
russet, *s.* drògaid, éideadh dùthcha.
rust, *s.* meirg, ruadhsmal.
rust, *v.* meirg ; meirgich.
rustic, *adj.* dùthchail ; neo-shnasmhor aineolach ; sìmplidh.
rustic, *s.* gallbhodach, fear-dùthcha.
rusticate, *v.* tuinich 'san dùthaich ; fuadaich do 'n dùthaich.
rusticity, *s.* sìmplidheachd, neo-sheòltachd, neo-chealgachd.
rustle, *v. n.* dèan starbhanaich.
rustling, *s.* starbhanaich.
rusty, *adj.* meirgeach.
rut, *s.* clais-cas-cùirn, dàmhair no dàradh nam fiadh, cullachd nan torc-coille, daimsear.
ruth, *s.* truas, truacantas, bàigh.
ruthful, *adj.* muladach, brònach, truagh ; caomh, bàigheil, truacanta.
ruthless, *adj.* cruaidh, borb, cruadalach, neo-thruacanta.
ruttish, *adj.* coineanach ; drùisel, macnusach ; teth, air dàradh.
rye, *s.* seagal, siogal.
rye-grass, *s.* feur-seagail.

S

sabaoth, *s.* feachd, armailt, sluagh.
sabbath, *s.* sàbaid ; dòmhnach.
sabbatical, *adj.* sàbaideach.
sable, *s.* dubhradan, bian dubh.

sable, *adj.* dubh, dorcha, ciar.
sabre, *s.* claidheamh crom.
sabulous, *adj.* grinnealach.
saccharine, *adj.* siùcarach, milis.

554 SACERDOTAL—SALVO

sacerdotal, *adj.* sagartach.
sachel, *s.* pocan ; sacan, balgan.
sack, *s.* sac, poca ; balg, soire, creach, reubainn ; seòrsa fìona.
sack, *v. a.* sacaich, cuir an sac ; creach ; sgrios baile.
sackbut, *s.* seòrsa pìob-chiùil.
sackcloth, *s.* sacaodach.
sack-posset, *s.* bainne agus fìon.
sacrament, *s.* sàcramaid ; bòid.
sacramental, *adj.* sàcramaideach.
sacred, *adj.* naomha, seunta, coisrigte, diadhaidh.
sacredness, *s.* naomhachd.
sacrific, *adj.* ìobairteach.
sacrifice, *s.* ìobairt, tabhartas.
sacrifice, *v. a.* ìobair, thoir suas, ìoc, marbh ; thoir thairis.
sacrificial, *adj.* ìobairteach.
sacrilege, *s.* ceall-shlad, ceall-ghoid, goid nithe naomha, aircheall.
sacrilegious, *adj.* ceall-shladach ; a' truailleadh nithean naomha.
sacring-bell, *s.* an clagan-coisrigidh.
sacristan, *s.* cléireach sagairt ; maor-eaglais ; fear-gleidhidh nan nithe coisrigte.
sacristy, *s.* ionad tasgaidh nithe naomha no coisrigte.
sad, *adj.* brònach, dubhach, muladach, tùrsach, trom, dòlasach, doilghiosach, neo-éibhinn ; dorcha ; nàr, maslach ; olc, aingidh.
sadden, *v. a.* dèan brònach, dèan dubhach, dèan muladach, dèan tùrsach no trom ; dèan doilghiosach, cuir fo sproc ; fàs muladach.
saddle, *s.* dìollaid, pillean.
saddle, *v. a.* dìollaidich ; cuir mar uallach.
saddler, *s.* dìolladair.
sadness, *s.* bròn, dubhachas, mulad, truime, sproc, doilghios.
safe, *adj.* tèaruinte, slàn, sàbhailte.
safeguard, *s.* dìon, dìdean, tèarmunn, tèaruinteachd, coimheadachd.
safety, *s.* tèaruinteachd.
saffron, *s.* an cròch.
saffron, *adj.* buidhe ; cròchach.
sag, *v.* luchdaich, tromaich ; sacaich, flagaich.
sagacious, *adj.* geurchùiseach, glic, tuigseach, toinisgeil, fadsheallach, sicir, crìonna.
sagacity, *s.* geurchuis, tuigse, toinisg, gliocas, crìonnachd.
sage, *s.* slànlus ; duine glic.
sage, *adj.* glic, foghluimte ; sicir.
sago, *s.* seòrsa gràin Innseanach.
said, *pret.* and *part.* of say, thubhairt ; mar a thùbhradh.
sail, *s.* seòl ; brat-siùil.
sail, *v.* seòl, bi seòladh.
sail-fish, *s.* an cearban.

sailor, *s.* seòladair, maraiche.
sail-yard, *s.* slat-shiùil.
sainfoin, *s.* an saoidhdhearg.
saint, *s.* naomh.
saint, *v.* naomhaich, àireamh am measg nan naomh.
sainted, *adj.* naomha, cràbhach.
saintly, saint-like, *adj.* naomha, diadhaidh, beannaichte, cneasta.
sake, *s.* for the s——, air sgàth, air son.
saker, *s.* seòrsa de ghunna mór.
salacious, *adj.* macnusach, drùiseil, neo-gheimnidh, baoiseach.
salacity, *s.* macnus, drùis.
salad, *s.* biadh lus, biadh luibhean.
salamander, *s.* a' chorra-chagailt.
salary, *s.* tuarasdal bliadhna.
sale, *s.* reic, màrgadh.
saleable, *adj.* so-reic, margail, a ghabhas reic.
salesman, *s.* fear-reic, ceannaiche.
salient, *adj.* leumnach, sùrdagach ; stìn-leagach ; plosgartach.
saline, salinous, *adj.* saillte.
saliva, *s.* smugaid, seile, ronn
salivate, *v. a.* ronnaich.
salivation, *s.* sileadh ronn.
sallow, *s.* gealsheileach.
sallow, *adj.* bànaidh, glasdaidh, glas-neulach.
sally, *s.* brùchd ; ionnsaigh.
sally, *v. n.* brùc, bris a mach, thoir ionnsaigh.
salmagundi, *s.* iomchumasg (mios air a dhèanamh suas le feòil phronn, sgadan, ola, fion-geur, peabar is uinneinean).
salmon, *s.* bradan, iasg geal.
salmon-trout, *s.* bànag, gealbhreac.
saloon, *s.* àrd-thalla, seòmar-suidhe.
salt, *s.* salann ; *adj.* saillte.
saltcellar, *s.* saillear.
salter, *s.* ceannaiche-salainn.
saltern, *s.* obair-shalainn.
saltish, *adj.* a lethchar saillte.
saltness, *s.* saillteachd.
saltpetre, *s.* mearshalann.
salubrity, *s.* slàinte, fallaineachd.
salutary, *adj.* slàinteil, slàn.
salutation, *s.* fàilte ; furan.
salute, *v. a.* cuir fàilte, cuir furan, dèan beatha, fàiltich, furanaich, pòg.
salute, *s.* fàilte, furan, pòg.
salvable, *adj.* ion-shàbhaladh, a ghabhas sàbhaladh.
salvation, *s.* saoradh, saorsainn, sàbhaladh ; slàinte ; slànachadh.
salve, *s.* sàbh-leigheis, ìoc, ùngadh.
salver, *s.* mias, aisead.
salvo, *s.* leithsgeul, cur-seachad, cumha (air còrdadh), seòrsa cungaidh cogais.
salvo, *s.* làdach, urchraichean ghunnachan móra (gu léir comhla).

SAME—SAUCY 555

same, *adj.* ionann, ceudna ; ceart.
sameness, *s.* co-ionannachd.
samlet, *s.* glasbhreac, bradan òg.
samphire, *s.* lus-nan-cnàmh.
sample, *s.* samhla, eisimpleir.
sampler, *s.* foir-theagaisg fuaigheil.
sanable, *adj.* so-leigheas.
sanative, *adj.* leigheasach.
sanctification, *s.* naomhachadh.
sanctifier, *s.* fear naomhachaidh.
sanctify, *v. a.* naomhaich ; coisrig.
sanctimonious, *adj.* cràbhach (an cainnt 's an gnùis).
sanctimony, *s.* naomhachd.
sanction, *s.* aontachadh ; ùghdarras ; rùn ; toil ; comas, cead ; reachd ; òrdugh.
sanctitude, **sanctity,** *s.* naomhachd ; diadhachd, glaine, mathas.
sanctuary, *s.* ionad-naomha ; tèarmunn, dìdean, comaraich.
sand, *s.* gainmheach, grinneal.
sandal, *s.* bonn-bhròg ; cuaran.
sand-blind, *adj.* gearrsheallach.
sandstone, *s.* clach ghainmheich, goireal.
sandy, *adj.* gaineamheach.
sane, *adj.* glic, ciallach ; fallain.
sang, *pret.* of to sing, shéinn.
sanguinary, *adj.* fuilteach, fuileach, fuileachdach, garg, borb, marbhtach.
sanguine, *adj.* flann-dearg ; teth, blàth, dian, deòthasach, earbsach. diandhòchasach, toileil.
sanguineous, *adj.* fuilteach, fuileach.
sanhedrim, *s.* àrd - chomhairle nan Iudhach.
sanicle, *s.* seòrsa luibhe (the **Yorkshire** sanicle), am bodan dubh.
sanious, *adj.* iongarach.
sanity, *s.* gliocas, toinisg, ciall, tuigse, slàinte, càil-inntinn.
sank, *pret.* of to sink, air siothladh, air dol fodha, air dol gu grunnd.
sap, *s.* brìgh, sùgh, snothach.
sap, *v.* fo-chladhaich, mill.
sapid, *adj.* sùghmhor, blasda, milis.
sapidity, *s.* blasdachd, mìlseachd.
sapience, *s.* gliocas, tuigse, tùr.
sapient, *adj.* glic, tuigseach, tùrail.
sapless, *adj.* gun sùgh, gun bhrìgh.
sapling, *s.* faillean, fiùran, ògan.
saponaceous, **saponary,** *adj.* siabunnach, mar shiabunn.
sapor, *s.* blas.
sapphire, *adj.* sapir, lèig ghorm.
sappiness, *s.* sùgharachd ; ùraireachd.
sappy, *adj.* sùghar, brìghmhor.
saraband, *s.* dannsa Spàinteach.
sarcasm, *s.* gearradh, beum ; tearrachd, geurmhagadh.
sarcastic, **sarcastical,** *adj.* beumnach, geur, tearrachdail, sgeigeil.
sarcenet, *s.* sìoda, fìnealta.

sarcle, *v. a.* dèan gartghlanadh.
sarcophagus, *s.* tuamh, tunga, cistelaighe claich.
sardine, **sardonyx,** *s.* seòrsa do chloich luachmhoir.
sarsaparilla, *s.* seòrsa do luibh iocshlainteach a tha tighinn a Jamaica.
sash, *s.* crios ; bann ; stiom sròl ; uinneag-thogalach.
sassafras, *s.* luibh ioc-shlainteach a tha tighinn á America.
Satan, *s.* Sàtan, an diabhol, an-t-aibhistear, an t-àbharsair, an riabhachmòr, an donus, an dòlas, am buaireadair, am fear as miosa, am fear ud.
Satanic, **Satanical,** *adj.* Diabhlaidh, deamhnaidh, aingidh, ifrinneach.
satchel, *s.* pocan-màileid.
sate, **satiate,** *v. a.* sàth, lìon gu sàth, sàthaich ; làn-thoilich.
satellite, *s.* planad a bhios a' ruith timchioll fir eile ; fear a chuideachd duine mhòir.
satiate, *adj.* sàthach, sàsaichte, lìonta, làn, toilichte, buidheach.
satiety, *s.* teannadh, teann-shàth, sàth, leòir.
satin, *s.* sròl, seòrsa sìoda.
satire, *s.* aoir, tearrachd.
satiric, **satirical,** *adj.* aoireil, beumach, sgaiteach, tearrachdail.
satirise, *v. a.* dèan aoireadh ; càin.
satirist, *s.* eisg, beithir-bheuma, aoireadair, tearracadair.
satisfaction, *s.* taitneas, sàsachadh ; lantoileachadh ; dìoladh, éirig.
satisfactory, *adj.* taitneach.
satisfied, *adj.* toilichte ; sàsaichte ; sàthach ; buidheach.
satisfy, *v.* toilich, sàsaich ; dìol ; dèan cinnteach ; thoir toileachas inntinn, taitinn ri, thig ri, dèan buidheach, riaraich.
saturable, *adj.* so-shàsachadh.
saturant, *adj.* sàsachail, lìontach.
saturate, *v. a.* sàsaich, lìon, bog.
Saturday, *s.* Di-sathuirne.
saturity, *s.* sàth, làn, leòir.
Saturn, *s.* (am planad) Sathurn.
saturnian, *adj.* sona ; òrdha.
saturnine, *adj.* dorcha, gruamach ; dubhach, brònach, tròm.
satyr, *s.* seòrsa apa ; dia-coille.
sauce, *s.* leannra ; sùgh.
sauce-box, *s.* peasan, fear lonach.
saucepan, *s.* sgeileid, àghann.
saucer, *s.* flat, truinnsear beag (air am bi copan 'n a shuidhe).
sauciness, *s.* beadaidheachd, peasanachd, gobaireachd, mìomhodh.
saucy, *adj.* gobach, lonach, mì-mhodhail, làsdach, stràiceil, beadaidh ; peasanach.

saunter, *v. n.* spaidseirich.
sausage, *s.* ìsbean, marag.
savage, *adj.* allmharra, fiadhaich, borb, allaidh ; brùideil ; an - iochdmhor ; neo-thruacanta, cruaidh-chridheach.
savage, *s.* borbanach, duine fiadhaich.
savageness, *s.* buirbe, fiadhaichead, an-iochdmhorachd, brùidealachd, allmharrachd, neo-thruacantachd.
savanna, *s.* magh fada réidh.
save, *v. a.* saor, teasairg, sàbhail, tèaruinn dìon, gléidh, coimhid ; caomhain.
save, *adv.* ach ; saor o.
saved, *part.* saorte, sàbhailte, tèaruinte, gléidhte ; caomhainte.
savin, *s.* seòrsa luibhe ; samhan.
saving, *adj.* caontach, grunndail, gléidhteach, spìocach, crìon.
saving, *adv.* ach, saor o.
savingness, *s.* caontachd ; grunndalachd, spiocaireachd.
saviour, *s.* slànuighear.
savory, *adj.* garbhag-ghàraidh.
savour, *s.* fàile, boltrach, blas.
savour, *v.* cuir fàileadh, amhairc coltach ri ; seall mar.
savouriness, *s.* boltrachd, mìlse.
savoury, *adj.* boltrachail, cùbhraidh, fàileach, milis ; blasta.
savoy, *s.* seòrsa càil.
saw, *pret.* of see, chunna, chunnaic, bheachdaich, dhearc.
saw, *s.* sàbh, tuireasg ; seanfhacal.
saw, *v. a.* sàbh, dèan sàbhadh.
sawdust, *s.* min-sàibh, sadach shàbhaidh, garbhan tuirisg.
saw-fish, *s.* am fiaclachan.
sawpit, *s.* sloc sàbhaidh.
sawyer, *s.* sàbhadair.
saxifrage, *s.* lus-nan-cluas.
say, *v. a.* abair, innis, labhair, aithris.
saying, *s.* ràdh, facal, briathar.
scab, *s.* créim, sgreab, sgab, càrr ; cloimh, broth, tachas, sgrìobach, guirean.
scabbard, *s.* truaill, duille.
scabby, *adj.* creimeach, sgreabach, sgabach, carrach, cloimheach, clomhach, clamhrach, brothach ; truagh, dìblidh, mosach.
scabrous, *adj.* garbh, molach, robach, neobhinn.
scaffold, *s.* sgàlan ; lobhta.
scaffolding, *s.* lobhtachan, sgàlain.
scalade, scalado, *s.* fàrachadh, toirt a mach baile le streap.
scald, *v. a.* sgailt, loisg, plod.
scald, *s.* càrr, sgreab ; losgadh, sgalltadh, plodadh.
scale, *s.* slige chothrom, lann éisg ; fàradh, dreimire ; sgreab, sgrath, sgròilleag ; aon de chomharran na gréinchrios ; an aibidil chiùil.
scale, *v. a.* streap, streap le fàradh,

cothromaich ; lannaich, sgrath, sgròillich.
scaled, *adj.* lannach, sligeach.
scaliness, *s.* lannachd.
scall, *s.* luibhre, càrr, mùir.
scallion, *s.* creamh gàraidh.
scallop, *s.* slige-chreachainn ; eagachadh, fiaclachadh.
scalp, *s.* mullach a' chinn, craicionn a chinn (leis an fhalt), mullach lom cnuic.
scalpel, *s.* sgian ghearraidh léigh.
scaly, *adj.* lannach ; sligeach.
scamble, *v.* sgròbaich ; bi tuasaideach, beubanaich, reub, stròic.
scamble, *s.* tuasaid ; streapaid.
scammony, *s.* seòrsa pùrgaid.
scamper, *v. n.* thoir na buinn as.
scan, *v. a.* tomhais ; ceasnaich, sgrùd.
scandal, *s.* sgainneal, tuaileas, toibheum, droch-alla, oilbheum, cùlchaineadh, dìmeas.
scandalise, *v. a.* sgainnealaich, maslaich, tuaileasaich, dèan tàir, nàraich.
scandalous, *adj.* maslach, tàmailteach, sgainnealach, nàr.
scandalously, *adv.* gu maslach.
scanning, *s.* tomhas-rann.
scant, *adj.* gann, tearc ; gortach.
scantiness, *s.* gainnead, crìne.
scantlet, *s.* beagan, criomag ; roinn.
scanty, *adj.* gann ; cumhang, crìon, gearr, beag, bochd, spìocach.
scape, *v. a.* teich, tàr as, seachainn.
scapula, *s.* cnàimh an t-slinnein.
scapular, *adj.* slinneineach.
scar, *s.* aile, athailt ; leòn, sgòrr, eàrra.
scar, *v. a.* comharraich, leòn.
scarab, *s.* daol, daolag dhubh.
scarce, *adj.* gann ; tearc ; teirc, ainmig ; ana-minig ; ainneamh.
scarce, scarcely, *adv.* air éigin, ach gann, is gann.
scarceness, scarcity, *s.* gainnead, gainne, teirce, tearcad, ainmigead ; daorsa.
scare, *v. a.* fuadaich, fògair saodaich, cuir eagal air.
scarecrow, *s.* bodach-ròcais ; buachaillbréige, fear-bréige, bòchdan.
scarf, *s.* tonnag, guailleachan.
scarf-skin, *s.* craicionn ; sgannan.
scarification, *s.* sgròilleachadh.
scarify, *v. a.* sgor ; sgrìob, feann, càineadh piantail.
scarlet, *s.* and *adj.* sgàrlaid.
scatches, *s.* casan-corrach.
scate, *s.* sgait, sòrnan ; bròg-spéidhilidh, speidhleachan.
scate, *v. n.* speidhil.
scathe, *v. a.* sgath, mill, caith.
scathing, *adj.* sgaithteach.
scatter, *v.* sgap, sgaoil, sgainnir ; bi sgaoilte, bi sgaipte.

scattering, s. sgapadh, sgaoileadh.
scavenger, s. clàbadair, fear-sguabadh sràide.
scelerat, s. daoidhear, daoidh.
scene, s. coltas ; taisbeanadh, roinn-cluiche ; sgàilbhrat, no brat-croch-aidh tigh-cluiche.
scenery, s. riochd-àite ; dealbh-choltas.
scent, s. fàileadh, bòladh, lòrg.
scent, v. n. cuir a mach fàileadh.
scented, adj. boltrach.
sceptic, s. fear as-creideach.
sceptical, adj. neo-chreideach.
scepticism, s. mì-chreideamh, teagamh.
sceptre, s. colbh, slat-rìoghail.
scheme, s. dòigh, modh, innleachd.
schemer, s. fear-innleachd.
schism, s. eas-aontachd eaglais.
schismatic, s. fear brisidh eaglais.
schismatical, adj. eas-aontach.
scholar, s. sgoilear, foghlumach.
scholarship, s. sgoilearachd, ionnsachadh, foghlum, oilean.
scholastic, scholastical, adj. sgoilearach, ionnsaichte, foghlumte.
scholiast, s. fear-mìneachaidh.
scholium, s. mìneachadh.
school, s. sgoil ; tigh-fòghluim.
schoolfellow, s. co-sgoilear.
schoolmaster, s. maighstear-sgoile.
schoolmistress, s. banmhaighstir sgoile, ban-oid-fhoghluim, bansgolair.
sciatic, s. lòinidh.
sciatical, adj. gu h-olc leis an loinidh.
science, s. ealain ; ceirdeolas.
scientific, adj. ealanta ; ionnsaichte.
scimitar, s. claidheamh-crom.
scintillate, v. n. sradagaich.
scintillating, adj. sradagach.
scintillation, s. sradadh, caoireadh.
scion, s. faillean, maothan, fiùran.
scirrhosity, s. cruadhachadh fàireig.
scirrhous, adj. cruaidh mar fhàireig.
scirrhus, s. at fàireig, beum-sice.
scissible, scissile, adj. ghabhas sgoltadh, ghabhas gearradh, ghabhas sgaradh.
scissors, s. siosar ; deimheas bheag.
scissure, s. sgoltadh, sgàineadh, gàgadh, sgadadh, peasgadh, sgreadhadh.
sclerotic, adj. cruaidh, greannach.
scoff, v. n. mag, dèan fanaid.
scoffer, v. sgeigear ; fear fochaid.
scoffingly, adv. gu fanaideach.
scold, v. a. troid ; cronaich.
scolding, adj. sglàmhrach, eallsgail.
scollop, s. an creachann.
sconce, s. sgàthdhun ; dìon ; ùbhladh ; ceann ; coinnlear-meurach.
scoop, s. liagh, ladar, taoman.
scoop, v. a. sluaisdich, cladhaich.
scope, s. rùn, ciall, miann ; rùm, àite, comas ; fuasgladh.
scopulous, adj. creagach, garbh.

scorbutic, adj. carrach, tachasach.
scorch, v. loisg, dàth ; gread.
score, s. sgrioch ; sgrìob ; sreath ; sgàth ; fiachan, cunntas ; fichead.
scorious, adj. salach ; stùrach.
scorn, v. dèan dìmeas, dèan tàir.
scorn, s. dìmeas, tarcuis, fanaid.
scorner, s. fear-fanaid, sgeigire.
scornful, adj. dìmeasach, fanaideach, sgeigeil, tàireil, tarcuiseach.
scorpion, s. nathair-nimhe, aon do chomharran a' ghréinchrios.
scotch, v. a. gearr, peasg, sgoch.
scotch, s. gearradh, peasg, sgoch.
scot-free, adj. saor ; dol as o chìs.
scotomy, s. tuainealaich.
Scotticism, s. A' Bheurla Albannach.
scoundrel, s. slaoightire.
scour, v. a. glan, soilleirich ; nigh sgànraich ; teich, ruith.
scourer, s. glanadair.
scourge, s. sgiùrsair, sgiùrsadh.
scourge, v. a. sgiùrs, peanasaich.
scout, s. fear-coimheid, beachdair.
scout, v. n. faigh eòlas (gun fhios) air gluasad nàmhaid.
scovel, s. moibeall, meaban.
scowl, v. a. bi fo ghruaim, cuir mùig ort.
scrag, s. blianach, feòil bhochd.
scraggy, adj. blian, bochd ; creagach.
scramble, v. n. smearaich, streap.
scramble, s. streapais, streap.
scrap, s. crioman, crimeag, pronnan, mìr, pioc ; fuigheall ; bruanag.
scrape, s. cruaidh-chàs, teanntachd ; dragh ; sgrìob.
scrape, v. sgrìob ; sgròb ; cnuasaich, teanail, trus ; bi sgrìobadh.
scraper, s. sgrìobachan ; sgrìoban ; sgrìobadair ; droch-fhìdhleir ; spìo-caire.
scratch, v. a. sgrìob, sgrùb ; tachais.
scratch, s. sgrìob, sgròb ; sgrìoch.
scratches, s. galar each.
scraw, s. sgrath, rùsg.
scrawl, s. sgròbaireachd, sgròblaich.
screak, v. n. sgread, sgreuch, sgiamh.
scream, v. n. sgread, sgreuch, sgriach, sgairt, glaodh, ràn, sian.
screech, v. n. sgreuch, sgread.
screech-owl, s. a' chailleach-oidhche.
screen, v. a. dìon, sgàilich, falaich.
screen, s. dìon, sgàilean, fasgadh.
screw, s. bidhis.
scribble, v. a. dèan sgròbail sgrìobhaidh.
scribble, s. sgròbail, droch sgrìobhadh.
scribbler, s. ùghdar suarach, droch sgrìobhaiche.
scribe, s. sgrìobhaiche.
scrine, s. tasgaidh sgrìobhaidhean.
scrip, s. màla, màileid, pocan, balg, sporan ; duilleag-sgrìobhaidh.
scriptory, adj. sgrìobte, sgrìobhach.

scriptural, *adj.* sgriobturail.
scripture, *s.* sgriobtur.
scrivener, *s.* sgrìobhadair.
scrofula, *s.* tinneas-an-rìgh, silteach.
scrofulous, *adj.* guireanach, silteach, leanntach.
scroll, *s.* ròla, ròl.
scrotum, *s.* clachbhalg, am poca.
scrub, *s.* spìocaire, sgrubaire, sgruimbean ; seann sguabach.
scrub, *v. a.* glan, nigh, suath, sgùr.
scrubbed, scrubby, *adj.* suarrach, spìocach, crìon, gun fhiù.
scruple, *s.* amharus, teagamh, iomacheist, iomchomhairle ; tomhas léigh, fichead gràinne air chudthrom.
scruple, *v. n.* cuir amharus, sòr, bi 'n teagamh, bi 'n iomchomhairle.
scrupulosity, *s.* amharus, teagamh, amharusachd, teagamhachd.
scrupulous, *adj.* teagamhach.
scrupulousness, *s.* teagamhachd, faicilleachd.
scrutable, *adj.* so-sgrùdadh, so-rannsachadh.
scrutinise, *v. a.* sgrùd, rànnsaich, ceasnaich, mion-cheasnaich.
scrutiny, *s.* sgrùdadh, rannsachadh.
scrutoire, *s.* clàr-sgrìobhaidh.
scud, *v. n.* ruith roimh 'n ghaoith, teich.
scuffle, *s.* brionglaid, tuasaid, collaid, caonnag, sabaid, àimhreit.
sculk, *v. n.* dèan cùiltearachd.
sculker, *s.* cùiltear, fògaraiche.
scull, *s.* claigeann ; pleadhan.
sculler, *s.* eithear-pleadhain.
scullery, *s.* seòmar sguideileireachd.
sculling, *s.* pleadhanachd.
scullion, *s.* sguidleir ; dubhchaile.
sculptor, *s.* grabhaltaiche.
sculpture, *s.* gràbhaladh.
scum, *v. a.* sgùm, thoir cobhar dheth.
scum, *s.* barrag, uachdar, cobhar.
scurf, *s.* sgrath ; créim, càrr, sgreab.
scurfy, *adj.* sgrathach, creimeach, carrach, sgreabach.
scurrility, *s.* sglàmhrainn.
scurrilous, *adj.* sglàmhrainneach, sgainnealach, ana-cainnteach.
scurrilousness, *s.* sglamhrainneachd.
scurvy, *s.* an tachas-tioram. *M.Ir.* clam.
scurvy, *adj.* sgabach, carrach, suarrach, diblidh.
scurvy-grass, *s.* lus-nam-mial.
scut, *s.* feaman maigheich.
scutcheon, *s.* suaicheantas.
scuttle, *s.* sgùile ; dian-choiseachd.
scythe, *s.* speal, fàladair.
sea, *s.* muir, cuan, fairge, garbhthonn, sùmainn, sùmaid.
sea-beach, *s.* tràigh, cladach, mol.
sea-beaten, *s.* tonn-bhuailte.
sea-boy, *s.* giullan maraiche.

sea-breach, *s.* briseadh mara.
sea - breeze, *s.* learghaoth, soirbheas seòlaidh.
sea-calf, *s.* ròn ; codrum.
sea-coast, *s.* taobh na mara, cladach.
seafarer, *s.* maraiche, seòladair.
sea-fight, *s.* cath mara.
sea-fowl, *s.* eun-mara.
sea-girt, *adj.* lear-chuartaichte.
sea-green, *adj.* liathghorm.
sea-gull, *s.* farspag, farspach, faoileag.
seal, *s.* ròn ; seula ; comharradh.
seal, *v. a.* seulaich ; seul ; daingnich, naisg ; dùin.
sealing-wax, *s.* céir-sheulachaidh.
seam, *s.* sgar ; fuaigheal ; tàthadh, aonadh.
seam, *v. a.* tàth ; fuaigh, fàitheim.
sea-maid, *s.* maighdean-mhara.
seaman, *s.* seòladair, maraiche.
sea-mew, *s.* faoilinn, faoileag.
seamless, *adj.* gun tàth ; gun fhàitheam ; gun sgar.
sea-moss, *s.* coireall, lìnean.
seamstress, *s.* ban-fhuaghlaiche.
sea-piece, *s.* dealbh mara.
sea-pink, *s.* neòinean cladaich.
seaport, *s.* port, caladh.
sear, *v. a.* loisg ; crannaich.
searce, *s.* criathar ; siolachan.
searce, *v. a.* criathair ; dràbh.
searcer, *s.* criathradair.
search, *v. a.* rannsaich ; sgrùd.
search, *s.* sireadh, rannsachadh ; sgrùdadh ; iarraidh ; tòir.
searching, *s.* sireadh, rannsachadh.
sear-cloth, *s.* bréid-céire.
sea-sickness, *s.* tinneas na mara, cur na mara.
season, *s.* am, aimsir, tràth ; cothrom, àm iomchuidh, mithich.
season, *v. a.* gréidh, leasaich, dèan blasta ; dèan ri, cleachd ri.
seasonable, *adj.* amail ; tràthail, iomchuidh, freagarrach.
seat, *s.* suidheachan, cathair, àite-suidhe ; àros, àite-còmhnaidh.
seat, *v. a.* suidh ; dèan suidhe, socraich, daingnich.
secede, *v. n.* teich, rach a thaobh.
seceder, *s.* fear-tréigsinn.
secern, *v. a.* sgar ; criathair.
secession, *s.* tréigsinn, fàgail, dealachadh.
seclude, *v. a.* dùin a mach, dealaich, cuir air leth.
seclusion, *s.* uaigneas, aonaranachd, dùnadh a mach.
second, *s.* tiota ; fear-còmhnaidh.
second, *adj.* dara ; faisge, faigse.
second, *v. a.* cuidich ; cobhair.
secondary, *adj.* ìochdrach, dara, na 's ìsle, air bheag spéis.
secondary, *s.* fear-ionaid.

second-hand, *adj.* ath-ghnàthach, air bloigh caitheamh.

secondly, *adv.* anns an dara h-àite.

secrecy, *s.* uaighneas, cleith.

secret, *adj.* dìomhair, uaigneach ; falaichte ; falachaidh, ceilte.

secret, *s.* rùn-dìomhair, cogar, cagar.

secretary, *s.* rùn-chléireach.

secrete, *v. a.* falaich, ceil, cleith ; dealaich, sgar ; sìolaidh ; fàisg.

secretion, *s.* fàsgadh, sìoladh ; dealachadh.

secretness, *s.* dìomhaireachd.

sect, *s.* dream, luchd-co-bharail.

sectary, *s.* fear dealachaidh o'n Eaglais choitcheann.

section, *s.* roinn ; earrann, cuibhrionn, gearradh.

sector, *s.* roinneadair.

secular, *adj.* saoghalta, talmhaidh.

secularity, *s.* saoghaltachd.

secure, *adj.* tèaruinte ; seasgair, neochunnartach, gun chùram, cinnteach, muinghinneach, misneachail.

secure, *v. a.* tèaruinn ; dèan cinnteach, gabh aig ; dìon, dèan diongmhalta ; glac.

security, *s.* dìon, dìonadh, fasgadh ; tèaruinteachd, cinnte, urras ; seasgaireachd, mi-chùram, cion-aire, neoshùim.

sedan, *s.* cathair-iomchair.

sedate, *adj.* ciùin, sàmhach, bith, socrach soimeach, màlda, suidhichte, stéidheil, stòlda.

sedateness, *s.* ciùineachd, socair.

sedentary, *adj.* suidheach.

sedge, *s.* seileasdair.

sedgy, *s.* seileasdaireach.

sediment, *s.* grunnd, grùid, dràbhag, deasgann, druaip.

sedition, *s.* ceannairc, àr-a-mach, éirigh, buaireas.

seditious, *adj.* ceannairceach, buaireasach, buaireante.

seditiously, *adv.* gu ceannairceach.

seduce, *v. a.* thoir a thaobh ; buair ; meall ; truaill.

seducement, *s.* buaireadh, mealladh.

seducible, *adj.* ghabhas mealladh.

seduction, *s.* mealladh, buaireadh, truailleadh, mealltaireachd.

sedulity, *s.* dìchioll, dìchiollachd, dùrachd, tulchuiseachd.

sedulous, *adj.* dìchiollach, dùrachdach, adhartach, saoithreachail.

sedulously, *adv.* gu dìchiollach.

see, *s.* cathair-easbuig.

see, *v. a.* faic, seall, amhairc ; dearc feuch.

see ! *interj.* faic ! seall ! feuch ! amhairc !

seed, *s.* sìol, iarmad, fras ; fros, pòr ; gineal, clann, sliochd.

seed, *v. n.* sìolaich ; cuir fras dhìot.

seedling, *s.* faillean, fiùran, ògan.

seedsman, *s.* fear cura.

seedtime, *s.* àm cuir an t-sìl.

seedy, *adj.* sìolach, pòrach.

seeing, *s.* fradharc ; léirsinn ; faicinn.

seeing, *adv.* a chionn, do brìgh.

seek, *v. a.* iarr, rannsaich ; sir, feòraich, fiosraich, lean, bi air tòir.

seem, *v. a.* gabh ort, leig ort.

seeming, *s.* aogas, coltas ; beachd.

seemliness, *s.* eireachdas, bòidhchead, maise.

seemly, *adj.* eireachdail, ceanalta, bòidheach, eugasach, maiseach, grinn, ciatach ; freagarrach, iomchuidh, cubhaidh.

seen, *adj.* eòlach, fiosrach.

seer, *s.* fear seallaidh, tàisear, fear da-shealladh ; fiosaiche, fàidh.

see-saw, *s.* udalanachd.

seethe, *v.* bruich, earrabhruich ; goil, bi air ghoil.

segment, *s.* gearradh-cuairteig.

segregate, *v. a.* dealaich ; sgar, cuir a thaobh.

segregation, *s.* dealachadh, sgaradh, sgarachdainn.

seine, *s.* seòrsa lin-iasgaich.

seize, *v. a.* glac, greimich, dèan gréim air, cuir làmh air, gabh.

seizin, *s.* gabhail seilbh.

seizure, *s.* glacadh ; gréim ; fasdadh.

seldom, *adv.* gu h-ainmig, gu tearc ; ainmig, tearc, teirc.

select, *v. a.* tagh, raghnaich.

select, *adj.* taghte, raghnaichte.

selection, *s.* taghadh, ròghnachadh.

self, *pron.* féin, e-féin, fhéin.

self-conceit, *s.* féin-spéis.

self-conceited, *adj.* fein-spéiseil.

self-denial, *s.* féin-àicheadh.

self-evident, *adj.* làn-shoilleir.

self-existence, *s.* féin-bhith.

self-interest, *s.* féin-bhuannachd.

selfish, *adj.* féineil, féinchuiseach.

selfishness, *s.* féineileachd.

self-same, *adj.* ceart, ionann, an dearbh.

self-will, *s.* féin-thoil ; reasgachd.

sell, *v. a.* reic.

sellander, *s.* sgab glùin eich.

seller, *s.* reiceadair, fear-reic.

selvage, *s.* oir aodaich, balt.

selves, *s. plur.* of self, sinne, sinn-féin.

semblance, *s.* samhla, coltas, aogas, dreach, riochd ; suaip.

semi, *s.* leth.

semi-annular, *adj.* leth-chruinn.

semi-circle, *s.* lethchearcall.

semi-circular, *adj.* leth-chearclach.

semicolon, *s.* pong stada mar so (;).

semi-lunar, *adj.* air chumadh na gealaich ùire.

seminal, *adj.* siolach, pòrach.
seminary, *s.* sgoil ; lios froise.
semination, *s.* sìolchur, cur.
semiquaver, *s.* pong ciùil.
semitone, *s.* leth-phung.
semivowel, *s.* leth-fhoghair.
sempiternal, *adj.* sìorruidh.
sempiternity, *s.* siorruidheachd.
senary, *adj.* sèathnar, seiseir.
senate, *s.* ard-chomhairle.
senator, *s.* comhairleach.
send, *v. a.* cuir, cuir fios, cuir air ghnothach ; cuir a mach, sgaoil.
seneschal, *adj.* àrd-stiùbhard.
senile, *adj.* sean ; seantaidh, aosda.
senior, *s.* am fear as sine.
senior, *adj.* as sine, na's sine.
seniority, *s.* aois, sinead.
senna, *s.* seòrsa pùrgaid.
senocular, *adj.* siashuileach.
sensation, *s.* mothachadh ; càil, beachd, faireachadh ; faireachdainn.
sense, *s.* mothachadh ; càil, beachd ; brìgh ; barail, sęadh ; ciall ; tuigse, toinisg, geur-mhothachadh.
senseless, *adj.* neo-mhothachail, gun mhothachadh ; gun chàil ; neo-thuigseach ; baoghalta, amaideach, gun tuigse, gun toinisg ; gun chiall.
sensibility, *s.* mothachadh, mothachalachd ; càil.
sensible, *adj.* mothachail ; so-fhaireachail ; tùrail ; tuigseach.
sensitive, *adj.* mothachail.
sensorium, sensory, *s.* ionad a' mhothachaidh, ball a' mhothachaidh.
sensual, *adj.* feòlmhor, collaidh ; sòghmhor, nàdurra ; mì-gheimnidh, macnusach.
sensualise, *v. a.* dèan feòlmhor, dèan macnusach ; truaill.
sensualist, *s.* fear mì-gheimnidh ; fear macnusach ; drùisear, trusdar.
sensuality, *s.* feòlmhorachd, collaidheachd, macnus, macnusachd, mì-gheimnidheachd.
sentence, *s.* binn, breth.
sentence, *v. a.* thoir breth, dìt, thoir binn, thoir a mach binn.
sententious, *adj.* brìoghmhor ; drùighteach, goirid, gearr.
sententiousness, *s.* giorrad cainnte, brìoghmhorachd, brìgh.
sentient, *adj.* mothachail.
sentiment, *s.* smuain, barail, beachd, rùn, miann, dùrachd.
sentinel, sentry, *s.* fear-faire, fear-freiceadain, freiceadan.
sentry-box, *s.* bothan-faire.
separable, *adj.* so-dhealachadh.
separate, *v. a.* dealaich, sgar, tearb, roinn, cuir as a chéile ; cuir air leth, rach a thaobh, rach air leth.

separate, *adj.* dealaichte, roinnte, as a chéile, o chéile, air leth ; leis féin.
separation, *s.* dealachadh, sgaradh, tearbadh ; sgaoileadh.
seposition, *s.* cur air leth.
sepoy, *s.* saighdear-Innseanach.
sept, *s.* cinneach, gineal, fine.
septangular, *adj.* seachd oisinneach.
September, *s.* mìos meadhonach an fhoghair, an seachdmhios.
septenary, *adj.* seachdnar.
septennial, *adj.* an ceann gach seachdamh bliadhna.
septentrion, *s.* an àirde tuath.
septentrional, *adj.* tuathach.
septilateral, *adj.* seachd-shlisneach.
Septuagint, *s.* an seann Tiomnadh 's a' Ghreugais.
septuple, *adj.* seachd-fillte.
sepulchral, *adj.* tuamach, uaigheach.
sepulchre, *s.* tuam, uaigh.
sepulchre, *v. a.* adhlaic, tìodhlaic.
sepulture, *s.* adhlacadh, tiodhlacadh.
sequacity, *s.* rìghneachd.
sequel, *s.* an ni a leanas, crìoch, deireadh, ceann-thall.
sequence, *s.* leanmhainn.
sequent, *adj.* leanmhainneach.
sequester, *v. a.* cuir gu taobh, cuir air leth, cuir sàradh.
sequestered, *adj.* air leth, diomhair, uaigneach.
sequestration, *s.* dealachadh ; tabhairt air falbh buannachd seilbhe.
sequestrator, *s.* fear-sàraidh.
seraglio, *s.* tigh-bhan Mhahomat.
seraph, *s.* àrd-aingeal.
seraphic, *adj.* ainglidh, fìorghlan.
seraphim, *s.* aingeal.
sere, *adj.* tioram, seacte, seargte.
serenade, *s.* ceòl-leannanachd.
serene, *adj.* soineannta ; fèitheil, ciùin, foisneach ; soilleir, sàmhach, maiseach, farasda.
serenely, *adv.* gu soineanta, ciùin.
sereneness, serenity, *s.* soineanntachd, ciùineas, fèith, sàmhchair, fois, sèimheachd.
serenitude, *s.* soineanntas, ciùine.
serge, *s.* cùrainn.
sergeant, *s.* ceannard air dà shaighdear dheug ; àrd-fhear-lagha.
series, *s.* sreath, srèad, òrdugh.
serious, *adj.* suidhichte, dùrachdach ; stòlda, smuaireanach, foisneach ; diadhaidh ; cudthromach, trom.
seriousness, *s.* stòldachd ; farasdachd ; aire dhùrachdach.
sermon, *s.* searmoin, teagasg.
sermonise, *v. n.* sgrìobh searmon.
serosity, *s.* uisgealachd.
serous, *adj.* uisgidh, uisgeil, tana.
serpent, *s.* nathair, beithir.

serpentine, *adj.* lùbach, carach.
serrate, serrated, *adj.* gròbach, fiaclach, cabach ; eagach.
serum, *s.* meug fala.
servant, *s.* seirbheiseach, gille, òglach, sgalag, banoglach, bean - mhuinntir, searbhanta.
serve, *v.* dèan seirbheis ; thoir ùmhlachd ; cuidich, foghainn ; toilich ; riaraich.
service, *s.* seirbheis ; muinntearas, dreuchd, obair ; dleasnas, còmhnadh, feum, stà, deagh thùrn ; aoradh ; cùrsa, riarachadh, saighdearachd.
serviceable, *adj.* feumail ; iomchuidh ; stàthmhor ; èasgaidh, dìchiollach.
servile, *adj.* tràilleil ; dìblidh, suarrach ; truaillidh, eisimeileach.
servility, servileness, *s.* dìblidheachd, tràillealachd ; suarrachas.
servitor, *s.* seirbhiseach.
servitude, *s.* daorsa, tràillealachd ; seirbheis ; muinntearas.
sess, *s.* cìs, càin.
session, *s.* àm suidhe mòid, suidhe mòid.
set, *v.* suidhich, socraich, àitich, planntaich ; sònraich, òrduich ; cuir cnàimh 'n a àite, cuir spealt.
set, *part.* suidhichte, socraichte, sònraichte ; riaghailteach ; àitichte, gnàthach.
set, *s.* srèud, dòrlach de ni sam bith ; càraid, lethbhreacan ; bannal, buidheann, cuideachd ; planntan.
seton, *s.* silteach.
settee, *s.* làmhsaid ; beinc.
setter, *s.* fear-suidheachaidh, cù-eunaich, cù-luirg.
setting, *s.* suidheachadh ; dol fodha.
settle, *s.* cathair, suidheagan, séis.
settle, *v.* socraich, suidhich ; àitich, tuinich ; sìolaidh ; traogh, ciùinich, caisg.
settlement, *s.* socrachadh, suidheachadh ; còrdadh, sònrachadh, bann ; àiteachas ; tuineachas.
seven, *adj.* seachd, seachdnar, mór-sheisear.
sevenfold, *adj.* seachd-fillte.
seventeen, *adj.* seachd-deug.
seventeenth, *adj.* seachdamh fear deug.
seventh, *adj.* seachdamh.
seventhly, *adv.* anns an t-seachdamh àite.
seventy, *adj.* tri-fichead 's a deich.
sever, *v.* sgàr, thoir as a chéile, dealaich; tearb, cuir air leth.
several, *adj.* iomadh, iomadaidh.
several, *s.* iomadh, leth-fa-leth.
severance, *s.* dealachadh, sgaradh.
severe, *adj.* geur, cruaidh, teann, doirbh ; gruamach ; an-iochdmhor, borb, neo-thruacanta, garg, geur-theann ; gàbhaidh, gaillionnach.
severity, *s.* cruadhas, cruas, géire ;

teinne, teinnead ; doirbhe, ain-iochd, buirbe ; neo - thruacantas ; docair, gairge, gàbhadh ; truime.
sew, *v. a.* fuaigh, fuaighil.
sewer, *s.* fuaghalaiche ; gille cuirme ; guitear, clais uisge.
sex, *s.* gineal, cineal, gnè, firionn no boirionn.
sexagenary, *adj.* tri fichead bliadhna dh' aois.
sexagonal, *adj.* sèshlisneach.
sextant, *s.* an sèathamh cuid do chearcall, inneal tomhais speuradaireachd.
sexton, *s.* fear-cluig ; maor-eaglais.
sextuple, *adj.* sè-fillte ; a shè uiread.
shabbiness, *s.* suarraichead, crìne, leibideachd, spìocaireachd.
shabby, *adj.* suarrach, crìon, leibideach, dìblidh, air dhroch éideadh.
shackle, *v. a.* geimhlich, cùingich.
shackles, *s.* ceanglaichean.
shade, *s.* sgàil, dubhar, duibhre, doirche, duirche ; dìon, fasgadh ; sgàil, sgàilean ; taibhse, tannasg.
shade, *v. a.* sgàil, duibhrich, dorchaich ; dìon, cuir sgàil air.
shadiness, *s.* duibhre, duirche.
shadow, *s.* faileas ; dubhar, dùbhradh ; dìon, fasgadh, fàbhar, tèarmann ; comharradh, lorg ; samhla.
shadow, *v. a.* duibhrich, dorchaich, dubharaich, sgàilich ; cuir faileas.
shadowy, *adj.* faileasach, sgàileach ; dubharach, dorcha, samhlachail.
shady, *adj.* dubharach, sgàileach, ceal-gach.
shaft, *s.* saighead ; cas, samhach.
shag, *s.* fionnadh, calg ; seòrsa eudaich, seòrsa eoin.
shaggy, *adj.* molach, ròmach, roinneach, robach, rònach, caiteanach, peallagach, giobach.
shagreen, *s.* craicionn-mùrlaich.
shake, *v.* crath ; cuir air chrith ; luaisg ; crith, criothnaich ; tribhuail.
shake, *s.* crathadh ; bogadh, luasgadh ; crith, tribhualadh.
shaker, *s.* crathadair ; bogadair.
shall, *v.* ; we shall go, théid sinn.
shalloon, *s.* clò-greòsgach.
shallop, shalloop, *s.* sgoth, curach.
shallow, *adj.* tana, eudomhain ; fàs, faoin ; lag.
shallow, *s.* tanalach ; àthan, oitir.
shallowness, *s.* tainead ; eudoimhn, tanalachd ; baoghaltachd.
sham, *v. a.* meall, thoir an car á.
sham, *s.* mealladh ; leithsgeul ; cur dheth ; cur seachad ; cleas, car.
sham, *adj.* fallsail, mealltach.
shambles, *s.* margadh feòla, tigh-bùidsearachd.
shambling, *adj.* luidseach.

shame, s. nàire, masladh ; mìchliu, tàir, tàmailt, eas-onair.

shame, v. nàraich, cuir gu nàire, maslaich, gabh nàire.

shamefaced, adj. gnùis-nàrach.

shameful, adj. nàr, nàrach, maslach, tàmailteach, tàireil, sgainnealach.

shameless, adj. beag-nàrach, mì-nàrach dàna ; beadaidh, ladarna.

shamois, or chamois, s. fiadh-ghobhar, gobhar-allaidh.

shamrock, s. seamrag, seamair.

shank, s. lurga ; cas, samhach.

shanky, adj. luirgneach.

shape, v. a. cùm, dealbh, cruth.

shape, s. cumadh, cumachd, dealbh.

shapeless, adj. neo-chuimir, neo-chumadail, mì-dhealbhach, neo-eireachdail, gun chumadh, á cumadh.

shapeliness, s. cumadalachd, cuimireachd, deagh chumadh, eireachdas.

shapely, adj. cuimir, cumadail cùmte dealbhach, eireachdail, dreachmhor.

shard, s. bloigh, bloighd, sgealb spreaghan, pigean, plaosg, lus àraidh ; seòrsa éisg.

share, v. a. roinn, pàirtich, riaraich ; gabh pàirt, faigh cuibhrionn.

share, s. roinn, earrann, cuid, cuibhrionn ; crannchur ; comaidh ; soc.

sharer, s. fear-roinn, fear-comaidh.

shark, s. iasg fuilteach craosach ; fear cuilbheartach gionach.

sharp, adj. geur ; smiorail, sgairteil, tapaidh, ealamh, dealasach, deas ; faobharach, biorach, guineach, lotar ; beur ; geur, goirt, garg ; sgreadanach, cruaidh.

sharpen, v. geuraich, roinnich ; bioraich, faobharaich, thoir roinn ; thoir faobhar.

sharper, s. beuraiche, cealgair, mealltair, caraiche ; gadaiche, meirleach.

sharpness, s. beurachd, géire, géiread ; guineachas ; faobhar.

sharp-set, adj. acrach, cìocrach.

sharp-sighted, adj. geurshuileach, biorshuileach, biorach.

sharp-witted, adj. geur, beumach.

shatter, v. a. bris, bruan, bloidich, dèan 'na mhìreannan.

shave, v. a. bearr, lom, lomair.

shave-grass, s. a' bhiorag.

shaver, s. bearradair.

shaving, vbl. n. bearradh ; sliseag.

shawl, s. guailleachan.

she, pron. i, ise, si.

sheaf, s. sguab ; dòrlach, beum (eòrna) ; bad (coirc).

shear, v. a. buain ; bearr, lom, lomair.

shearer, s. buanaiche.

shearing, s. buain.

shears, s. siosar, deamhais.

sheath, s. truaill, duille.

sheathe, seath, v. a. truaill, cuir an truaill, cuir an duille.

shed, v. a. dòirt, taom, sil ; cuir.

shed, s. bùth, sgàil ; bothan.

sheen, adj. loinnreach ; glan, soilleir.

sheen, s. boillsgeadh, deàrsadh.

sheep, s. sing. and pl. caora, othaisg, òisg ; caoirich, meanbhchrobh.

sheepcot, sheepfold, s. crò-chaorach, bothan-chaorach, fang, mainnir.

sheep-hook, s. cromag cìobair, bachall buachailleachd.

sheepish, adj. baoghalta ; nàrach, air bheag sgoinn, liugach.

sheepishness, s. baoghaltachd, faiteachas, gnuis-nàire, diùideachd.

sheep's-eye, s. gràdh-shealladh.

sheep-shearing, s. lomairt ; àm rùsgadh nan caorach.

sheep-walk, s. ionaltradh chaorach.

sheer, adj. glan, fiorghlan.

sheer off, v. n. goid air falbh ; teich as an rathad, seup.

sheet, s. clàr paipeir ; braithlin, lianbhrat, lìonaodach, lionanart ; pill ; seòl, bréid, sgòd-siùil.

sheet, v. a. còmhdaich, paisg.

sheet-anchor, s. acair-bhàis.

shekel, s. bonn airgeid Iùdhach.

shelf, s. sgeilp ; còrnchlar, sgeir.

shell, s. slige, sgrath, plaosg.

shell, v. a. plaoisg, sgrath, fosgail.

shell-fish, s. maorach, faoch.

shelly, adj. sligeach ; faochagach.

shelter, s. fasgadh, dìon, tèarmann, dìdean, sgàil.

shelter, v. dìon, tèarmainn.

shelving, adj. claon, aomta, corrach.

s h e l v y, adj. eudomhain ; sgeireach, creagach.

shepherd, s. aoghair, cìbeir.

shepherdess, s. bana-chìbeir.

sherbet, s. seòrsa dibhe.

sherd, s. slige-chreadha, pigean.

sheriff, s. siorraidh, siorram.

sheriffalty, s. siorraidheachd.

sherry, s. fìon Spàinteach.

shew, v. a. feuch, nochd, foillsich, dearbh ; cuir an céill, mìnich, leig, ris, taisbean, dèan aithnichte.

shield, s. sgiath, targaid ; dìon, dìdean, tèarmann.

shield, v. a. dìon, gléidh, tèaruinn, coimhead, còmhdaich.

shift, v. caraich, glidich, mùth, rach á h-àite ; tionndaidh, solair, rach as.

shift, s. seòl, modh, dòigh ; innleachd ; cleas ; laoim, car, cuilbheart ; mùthadh, atharrachadh.

shifter, s. cealgair, duine carach.

shifting, s. caràchadh, imrich.

shifting, adj. cealgach, carach.

shiftless, *adj.* neo-innleachdach, neo-sholarach, lethoireach.

shilling, *s.* tastan, sgillinn-Shasunnach.

shin, *s.* faobhar na lurgann.

shine, *v. n.* dealraich, dèarrs, soillsich, loinnir ; bi sònraichte, bi suaicheant ; bi urramach.

shine, *s.* aimsir ghrianach ; dealradh.

shingles, *s.* seòrsa de theine dé; deir ; deilginneach ; clachan muil.

shiny, *adj.* deàlrach, dèarrsach.

ship, *s.* long, soitheach, bàrc.

ship, *v. a.* cuir air bòrd luinge.

shipboard, *s.* bòrd-luinge.

shipman, *s.* maraiche, seòladair.

shipping, *s.* cabhlach, luingeas.

shipwreck, *s.* long-bhriseadh.

shipwright, *s.* saor luingeis, saor dubh.

shire, *s.* siorrachd, siorramachd.

shirt, *s.* léine, cneas-lìn.

shittim, *s.* seòrsa fiodha Arabach.

shive, *s.* sliseag ; sgealb, bloigh ; mìr arain, sliseag arain.

shiver, *v.* crith ; brùan ; bris ; spealg.

shiver, *s.* sgealb, spealg, bruan.

shivering, *s.* ballchrith crith-fhuachd, crith ; briseadh, sgealbadh, sgoltadh, spealgadh.

shoal, *s.* oitir ; tanalach ; cailcean, sgeir ; sgaoth, sgann.

shoaly, *adj.* tana, eudomhain, oitireach, sgeireachd, cailceanach.

shock, *s.* crith, criothnachadh ; oilbheum ; oillt ; gràin, déisinn ; ionnsaidh ; ruathar ; adag, rucan, mulan, cù molach.

shock, *v.* adagaich ; rucanaich ; crith, crath, criothnaich ; thoir oilbheum, cuir déisinn, cuir gràin air, cuir gairisinn air, thoir ionnsaigh.

shocking, *adj.* oillteil, eagalach, gràineil ; gairisineach déisinneach.

shoe, *s.* bròg, crudha.

shoe, *v. a.* brògaich, crùdhaich.

shoe-boy, *s.* gille-bhròg.

shoemaker, *s.* greusaiche.

shoot, *v.* tilg ; cuir a mach, fàs.

shoot, *s.* meangan, meanglan, failiean, maothan, ùr-fhas, fiùran, ògan.

shooter, *s.* fear tilgidh.

shop, *s.* bùth ; bathair, bùth-oibre.

shop-board, *s.* bòrd-oibreach.

shopkeeper, *s.* fear-bùth.

shore, *s.* tràigh, cladach, tìr, taobh mara.

shore, *s.* taic, prop, sgòrradh.

shoreless, *adj.* gun tràigh.

shorn, *part.* and *part.* of to shear, lomairte, lomte, bearrte, buainte.

short, *adj.* goirid ; gearr ; beag ; crìon ; cutach ; gann ; aithghearr ; crosda, dreamach, càs.

shorten, *v. a.* giorraich.

short-lived, *adj.* gearr-shaoghalach.

shortness, *s.* giorrad, giorradas.

short-sighted, *adj.* gearrsheallach.

shot, *pret.* and *p. part.* of to shoot, thilg ; tilgte.

shot, *s.* urchair, braidhe, spraidhe, làmhach, peileirean ; lach.

shot-free, *adj.* lach-shaor, saor.

shoulder, *s.* gualainn, slinnean.

shoulder-belt, *s.* crios-guaille.

shoulder-blade, *s.* cnàimh-slinnein.

shout, *s.* caithream, glaodh, iolach.

shout, *v. n.* glaodh, tog iolach.

shove, *v. a.* pùc, fùc, put, dinn.

shove, *s.* pùcadh, putadh, ùpag.

shovel, *s.* sluasaid.

show, *s.* iongantas-féille ; sealladh-iongantais ; ball-amhairc ; greadhnachas, mòrchuis ; spaglainn.

show, *v. a.* feuch, nochd, leig ris, foillsich, taisbean.

showbread, shewbread, *s.* aran-taisbeanta, aran-coisrigte.

shower, *s.* fras, sileadh.

shower, *v. a.* fras, dòirt, sil, taom, sgap, sgaoil ; bi frasach.

showery, *adj.* frasach, silteach.

showy, *adj.* briagha, grinn ; greadhnach, rìomhach, basdalach, faicheil.

shred, *s.* mìr, bìdeag, cearb.

shrew, *s.* té ladarna ; bancheard.

shrewd, *adj.* sicir, glic, ciallach ; dùbailte, cealgach, seòlta, geur ; olc.

shrieft, *s.* faoisid peacaidh.

shriek, *v.* sgread, sgreuch, sgairt, glaodh, ràn, sian, thoir sgal.

shrift, *s.* aideachadh.

shrill, *adj.* sgreadach, cruaidh, sgalanta, sgalach, binn, geur.

shrimp, *s.* carran ; duairce.

shrine, *s.* naomh-chiste.

shrink, *v. n.* crup ; geiltich, ath.

shrink, *s.* crupadh, crìonadh, seargadh, seacadh, preasadh.

shrive, *v. a.* éisd ri faoisid.

shrivel, *v. a.* crup, preas, preasagaich, searg, liurc ; sgreag.

shrivelled, *adj.* preasach.

shroud, *s.* marbhphaisg, aisleine, linnseach, aodach-mairbh ; còmhdach.

shroud, *v.* còmhdaich, dìon, thoir fasgadh ; gabh fasgadh.

Shrovetide, *s.* Di-mairt-inid.

shrub, *s.* preas.

shrub, *s.* deoch mhilis.

shrubby, *adj.* preasach.

shrug, *v. a.* crup, crùb, clòimhdich.

shrug, *s.* clòimhteachadh ; giùig.

shudder, *v. n.* criothnaich, oilltich.

shudder, *s.* ballchrith, oillt, allsgath.

shuffle, *v.* cuir thar a chéile, cuir troimh chéile ; coimeasg.

shuffle, *s.* coimeasgadh ; cleas, cuilbheart, seamaguad.

shun, *v. a.* seachain.
shut, *v. a.* dùin, druid.
shut, *adj.* dùinte, druidte.
shutter, *s.* comhla uinneige.
shuttle, *s.* spàl, spàl fìgheadair.
shy, *adj.* fiata, coimheach, taghanta, fiadhaich ; moiteil ; faicilleach ; amharusach, socharach, ailleanach.
shyness, *s.* fiatachd, mòitealachd.
sibilation, *s.* feadail, fead.
sicamore, sycamore, *s.* crann-sice.
sick, *adj.* tinn, euslainteach.
sicken, *v.* fàs tinn ; gabh tinneas ; dèan tinn, cuir galar air.
sickle, *s.* corran, corran-buana.
sickly, *adj.* tinn, euslainteach.
sickness, *s.* tinneas, euslainte, eucail.
side, *s.* taobh, slios ; oir, cliathach, mòrchuis.
side, *v.* aom ; cùm taobh ri, cuidich, cuir le ; gabh taobh.
sidelong, *adj.* lethtaobhach.
side-saddle, *s.* dìollaid-boireannaich.
sideways, sidewise, *adv.* an comhair a thaoibh, a lethtaobh.
siege, *s.* séisd, iomdhruideadh.
sieve, *s.* criathar.
sift, *v. a.* criathair, criathraich.
sifter, *s.* criathradair, criathraiche.
sigh, *s.* osann, acain, osna.
sigh, *v. a.* osnaich, dèan osann.
sighing, *s.* osnaich ; acain.
sight, *s.* sealladh ; fradharc, léirsinn.
sightless, *adj.* gun fradharc, dall.
sightly, *adj.* taitneach, maiseach.
sign, *s.* comharradh, mìorbhuil, iongantas ; àile, lòrg ; bratach, meirghe ; samhla ; smèid ; dealbh, sop-reic, comharradh-ceannaich.
sign, *v. a.* cuir do làmh ri, cuir t' ainm ri ; comharraich ; ciallaich.
signal, *s.* sanus, fios, comharradh.
signal, *adj.* sònraichte, ion-chomharraichte, mór, àraidh.
signalise, *v. a.* dèan ainmeil.
signature, *s.* ainm-sgrìobhte, comharradh, suaicheantas ; fo-sgrìobhadh, litir-chomharrachaidh.
signet, *s.* seula ; saoil ; seula rìgh.
significancy, *s.* ciall ; seadh, sùim, meas, urram, brìgh, bladh ; cothrom, cudthrom.
significant, *adj.* ciallachail, ciallaidheach, cudthromach.
signification, *s.* ciall, brìgh ; seadh.
significative, *adj.* seadhach.
signify, *v.* feuch, innis, dèan aithnichte, cuir an céill, thoir sanas, thoir fios ; ciallaich.
signpost, *s.* colbh-seòlaidh.
silence, *s.* sàmhchair, ciùineas, sèimhe, fèith, tàmh, fois.
silence, *interj.* tost ! bi sàmhach !

silence, *v. a.* cuir sàmhach, cuir 'na thosd.
silent, *adj.* sàmhach, tosdach, balbh, ciùin, bìth.
silicious, *adj.* ròinneach, ròmach ; clachach, sgorach, sporach.
silk, *s.* sìoda ; *adj.* sìoda.
silken, *adj.* sìoda, sìodail ; mìn.
silk-mercer, *s.* marsanta-sìoda.
silk-weaver, *s.* breabadair-sìoda.
silkworm, *s.* cnuimh-shìoda.
silky, *adj.* sìodach, sìodail ; mìn.
sill, *s.* clach an doruis ; bonn uinneig.
silliness, *s.* faoineachd ; baoghaltachd, amaideachd, gòraich.
silly, *adj.* faoin, baoghalta, fachanta, neo-thùrail, amaideach, gòrach, simplidh ; socharach.
silvan, sylvan, *adj.* coillteach, coilltidh, coillteachail.
silver, *s.* airgead.
silver, *adj.* airgeadach ; airgid.
silversmith, *s.* ceàrd airgid.
simar, *s.* earrasaid.
similar, *adj.* coltach, co-ionann.
similarity, *s.* co-ionannachd, coltas.
simile, *s.* samhla, coimeas.
similitude, *s.* cosmhalachd.
simmer, *v. n.* bruich, earrabhruich.
simony, *s.* ceall-shlad, goid no reic nithe naomha, no ni a bhuineas do dh' eaglais.
simper, *s.* fàite, fèith-ghàire.
simper, *v. n.* dèan snodha gàire.
simple, *adj.* glan, neo-thruaillte ; aon-fhillte ; simplidh, neo-chiontach, neo-chronail ; còir, onarach ; iriosal ; amaideach, baoghalta, socharach, aineolach, neo-theòma.
simple, *s.* ni aon-ghneitheach ; ni leis féin, lus, luibh.
simpler, simplest, *s.* lighiche-lus.
simpleton, *s.* baothalan, baothaire.
simplicity, *s.* sìmplidheachd, aon-fhillteachd, ionracas ; socharachd ; baogh-altachd.
simplify, *v. a.* dèan so-thuigsinn.
simply, *adv.* gu h-amaideach.
simulation, *s.* cealgaireachd.
simultaneous, *adj.* còmhla, maraon, cuideachd.
sin, *s.* peacadh ; cionta, lochd.
sin, *v. n.* peacaich ; ciontaich.
since, *adv.* a chionn ; o chionn, o'n.
since, *prep.* o, bho ; o 'n àm sin.
sincere, *adj.* treibhdhireach, ionraic, onorach, fìrinneach, neo-chealgach.
sincerity, *s.* ionracas, treibhdhireas.
sinecure, *s.* oifigeach diamhain.
sinew, *s.* féith ; féith-lùghaidh.
sinful, *adj.* peacach, mì-naomh, olc.
sing, *v.* séinn, gabh òran ; mol.
singe, *v. a.* dath, doth.

singer, s. fear-séinn, òranaiche.

single, adj. aon-fhillte ; gun bhi phòsta, àraidh ; aonaranach ; glan, iomlan, foirfe.

singleness, s. aon-fhillteachd ; foirfeachd, ionracas.

singular, adj. sònraichte ; àraid, àraidh, air leth, neònach, iongantach ; còrr, aineamh.

singularise, v. a. dèan sònraichte.

singularity, s. sònraichead, neònachas.

sinister, adj. cèarr, clì ; olc, eas-ionraic ; neo-cheart, neo-chothromach ; mì-shealbhar, mì-shona.

sink, v. cuir fodha ; bàth, tùm, ceil, sàraich, ìslich ; rach fodha ; rach air chùl, rach gu neo-ni ; traogh.

sink, s. clais ; guitear ; sloc.

sinless, adj. neo-lochdach, neochiontach, neo-thruaillidh.

sinner, s. peacach, peacair.

sin-offering, s. ìobairt pheacaidh.

sinuate, v. a. lùb, crom, fiar.

sinuous, adj. lùbach, carach.

sinus, s. camas, geotha, bàdh.

sip, v. òl, srùbagaich.

sip, s. balgam, srùbag.

sir, s. a shàir, a mhaighstir, le 'r cead.

sire, s. athair ; a rìgh !

siren, syren, s. bandia ; bean tàlaidh gu sgrios.

siren, adj. mealltach ; a' tàladh.

Sirius, s. Reull a' choin.

sirocco, s. gaoth thòitidh.

sirrah, s. facal dìmeas.

sister, s. piuthar.

sisterhood, s. piuthrachas.

sisterly, adj. piutharail.

sit, v. suidh, dèan suidhe.

site, s. suidheachadh, àite, làrach.

sitter, s. suidhear ; eun-guir.

sitting, s. suidhe ; gur.

situate, situated, adj. suidhichte.

situation, s. àite ; inbhe, cor ; staid, suidheachadh.

six, adj. sè ; sianar.

sixfold, adj. sè fillte ; a shè uiread.

sixpence, s. sè-sgillinn.

sixscore, s. sè fichead.

sixteen, adj. sè deug.

sixteenth, adj. seathamh deug.

sixth, adj. sèathamh.

sixth, s. an sèathamh cuid.

sixtieth, adj. trì ficheadamh.

sixty, adj. trì fichead.

size, s. meud, meudachd, tomad.

size, v. a. tomhais ; sònraich.

sizy, adj. righinn, glaodhar.

skate, s. sgait ; bròg-spéilidh.

skean, s. cuinnsear, sgian.

skein, s. sgeinn, sgeinnidh.

skeleton, s. cnàimhneach, taisean.

skeptic, s. fear teagamhach.

skeptical, adj. teagamhach.

sketch, s. ceud tharruing air dealbh.

sketch, v. a. dealbh, tarruinn.

skewer, s. bior-feòla ; dealg.

skiff, s. sgoth, curach, eather.

skilful, adj. sgileil, eòlach, teòma.

skilfulness, s. sgil, teòmachd.

skill, s. sgil, eòlas, teòmachd.

skilled, adj. sgileil, seòlta, eòlach.

skillet, s. sgeileid.

skim, v. a. sgiob, siab ; sgùm, thoir uachdar dheth, tog barrag dheth.

skim milk, s. bainne-lom, boinne togalach.

skin, s. craicionn, bian, seiche ; rùsg.

skin, v. fionn, feann, faobhaich, thoir an craicionn de, rùisg ; còmhdaich le craicionn.

skinker, s. gille-copain.

skinner, s. craicionnaiche.

skinny, adj. tana, caol, cruaidh.

skip, v. leum ; sùrdagaich ; rach thairis, rach seach.

skip, s. leum, sùrdag, frithleum.

skipper, s. sgiobair.

skirmish, s. arabhaig ; beag-chath.

skirt, s. sgòd ; oir, cearb ; sgioball ; iomall, fraidhe, taobh.

skit, s. aoir ; slios-bhualadh.

skittish, adj. fiadhta, gealtach, sgeunach ; luaineach, aotrom, guanach, mear, sgaomach.

skreen, s. criathar-garbh ; fasgath.

skull, s. claigeann.

skulk, v. n. falaich, bi cùiltearachd, bi 'n ad bhuanna.

sky, s. speur, iarmailt, adhar.

skylark, s. riabhag, uiseag, topag.

skylight, s. adharleus, uinneag-tughaidh.

slab, s. leac, cùl-déile.

slabber, v. n. sil ronn ; smugaich, ronnaich, fliuch, salaich.

slabby, s. ronnach ; smugaideach.

slack, adj. las, lasach, fuasgailte, neo-dhaingeann, neo-dhiongmhalta ; tais, mall, màirnealach, athaiseach ; neo-chùramach ; fann, lag, flagach.

slack, slacken, v. lasaich, dèan lasach, fuasgail, failnich, fannaich ; dèan moille, flagaich.

slack, s. gual mìn, gual pronn.

slackness, s. lasaiche, lasaichead, fuasg-ailteachd ; màirnealachd, athaiseachd, mi-chùram.

slag, s. luaithre no sal iaruinn.

slain, part. pass. of to slay, mharbhadh, chaidh as.

slain, s. slinn (breabadair).

slake, v. a. mùch, caisg, bàth.

slander, s. tuaileas, sgainneal.

slander, v. a. cul-chàin, maslaich.

slanderer, s. fear-tuaileis.

slanderous, s. tuaileasach.

slant, v. claon, fiar, aom.
slant, slanting, adj. claon, fiar, aomte, aomadh, neo-dhìreach.
slap, s. sgailc, boiseag, pailleart, sgealp, déiseag, sgailleag.
slap, v. a. sgailc, déiseagaich.
slapdash, adv. muin air mhuin.
slash, v. a. gearr, sgath ; beum.
slash, s. gearradh, leòn, beum.
slate, s. sglèat, leac.
slate, v. a. sgleat, sglèataich.
slater, s. sglèatair.
slattern, s. straille, dràic sgliùrach, trusdar caile, sgumrag.
slaughter, s. àr, marbhadh, casgradh, spadadh.
slaughter, v. a. casgair, marbh.
slaughterhouse, s. tigh-spadaidh, tigh-casgraidh, broth-thigh.
slaughterman, s. fear-spadaidh.
slave, s. tràill, bruid, braighde, ciomach, tàrlaid.
slaver, v. n. sil ronnan.
slaver, s. ronnan, staonag.
slavery, s. braighdeanas, daorsa, tràill-ealachd.
slavish, adj. tràilleil.
slavishness, s. tràillealachd.
slay, v. a. marbh, casgair.
slayer, s. mortair ; marbhaiche.
sled, sledge, s. càrn-slaoid ; òrd mór gobha.
sleek, sleeky, adj. mìn, slìogach, slìom, sliobach, sleamhainn.
sleekness, s. mìnead, slìobachd.
sleep, s. pràmh, suain ; cadal.
sleepiness, s. cadalachd ; truime.
sleepless, adj. gun chadal.
sleepy, adj. cadalach, cadaltach.
sleet, s. clàmhainn, glìob.
sleet, v. n. cuir clàmhainn.
sleety, adj. clàmhainneach.
sleeve, s. muilicheann, muinichill.
sleight, s. cleas, seòl, car.
slender, adj. tana, caol, seang, bochd, meuranta ; beag, crìon, gann.
slenderness, s. caoile, caoilead, tainead ; dìth tomaid ; gainne.
slice, s. sliseag ; mìr tana.
slice, v. a. sliseagaich, snaidh.
slide, v. n. sleamhnaich, spéidhil.
slide, v. sleamhnachadh, spéileadh.
slight, s. dearmad, dìmeas, tàir.
slight, adj. tana ; neo-ghramail ; faoin, beag, suarrach, aotrom.
slight, v. a. dearmaid, dearmadaich, cuir air dìmeas, no air bheag sùim.
slightness, s. caoilead, tainead, an-fhannachd ; eu-treòir ; fadharsachd.
slim, adj. seang, caol, maoth.
slime, s. làthach ; clàbar.
sliminess, s. bìtheantachd ; rìghneachd, sleamhneachd,

slimy, adj. bìtheanta, rìghinn, sleamhainn, tiugh.
sling, s. crann-tabhaill, bann, longag.
sling, v. a. tilg le crann-tabhaill.
slink, v. n. sèap, siap, snàg air falbh, goid air falbh.
slip, s. tuisleadh ; mearachd ; car ; crioman, stiall ; cuiseag, maothan.
slip, v. sleamhnaich, spéil, tuislich ; snàg ; dèan mearachd.
slip-knot, s. lùb-ruithe, snàim-ruith.
slipper, s. bròg-sheòmair.
slipperiness, s. sleamhnachd.
slippery, slippy, adj. sleamhainn ; mùghtach.
slit, v. a. sgoilt, sgoch, gearr.
slit, s. sgoltadh, sgoch, gearradh.
sliver, v. a. sgoilt, sgath.
sliver, s. spealtag, spithag.
slobber, v. fliuch le smugaidean, splàn-graich, roillich.
sloe, s. áirneag ; draighneag.
sloop, s. soitheach aon chroinn.
slop, v. a. òl gu gionach ; spliut, spairt, sguab as.
slope, s. leathad, claon-bhruthach ; fiar-adh, claonadh, slios (cnuic).
slope, adj. claon, aom, fiar cam.
sloppy, adj. eabarach, fliuch.
slot, s. lorg féidh ; beul-maothain.
sloth, s. leisg, dìomhanas.
sloth, s. a' chorra-leisg, lunndaireachd.
slothful, adj. leisg, slaodach.
slouch, s. cromadh, slaodaire cuacaire, sealladh dìblidh.
slough, s. rumach, làthach ; càthar ; cochull, mogunn.
sloughy, adj. féitheach, clàbarach.
sloven, s. straille draic ; tàsan, liobasdair ; slaodaire.
slovenly, adj. dràichdeil, slaodach, liobasda, salach, rapach.
slow, adj. mall, màirnealach, athaiseach, tàsanach, slaodach ; leisg.
slowness, s. maille ; màirnealachd, athaiseachd, slaodachd.
slow-worm, s. an dall-chnuimh.
slubber, v. a. dèan air dòigh sam bith, pat thairis.
slubberdegullion, s. trusdar.
sludge, s. poll, eabar, làthach.
slug, s. leisgean, slaod ; rong ; seilcheag ; peileir-greannach.
sluggard, s. leisgean, lunndaire.
sluggish, adj. leisg, lunndach, cadalach ; trom, marbhanta, mall.
sluice, s. tuildhorus.
slumber, v. n. caidil, gabh pràmh.
slumber, s. clò-chadal, dùsal, pràmh.
slumberous, adj. cadalach, trom.
slur, v. a. salaich, mill, truaill ; meall.
slur, s. tàir, athais, dìmeas.
slut, s. botramaid, bréineag.

sluttish, *adj.* salach, breun, mosach.
sluttishness, *s.* mosaiche.
sly, *adj.* carach, sligheach, mealltach.
smack, *s.* blas, deagh-bhlas ; sgleog pòige ; long aon chrannach.
small, *adj.* beag, crìon, cutach ; caol ; meanbh ; mìn, pronn.
small-coal, *s.* gual-caoranach.
smallness, *s.* bigead, crine, lughad, caoile, caoilead ; laigead, di-neart.
smallpox, *s.* a' Ghall-bholgach ; a' bhreac ; a' bhàn-ghucach ; a' bheanmhath ; buaicneach.
smalt, *s.* guirmean, dath gorm.
smart, *adj.* sgairteil, tapaidh, beothail ; sgealparra, smiorail, geur, sgiobalta.
smart, *s.* pian, guin, goimh, cràdh.
smart, *v. n.* pian, goirtich, crean.
smartness, *s.* sgairtealachd, tapadh, beothalachd, smioralas, géire, sgiobalt- achd.
smatch, *s.* blas ; fàileadh.
smattering, *s.* letheolas.
smear, *v. a.* smiùr, buaichd.
smell, *v.* snòtaich, srònaisich ; biodh fàileadh dhìot.
smell, *s.* fàileadh, bòladh.
smelt, *s.* am mòrgadair.
smelt, *v. a.* leagh.
smelter, *s.* leaghadair.
smerk, *v. n.* amhairc gu tlàth ; gràdh- iach, etc.
smerk, smirk, *adj.* cridheil ; sunntach.
smicket, *s.* còta-bàn boireannaich.
smile, *v. n.* dean fàite ; dèan snodha gàire ; bi mìogshuileach.
smile, *s.* fàite, fèith-ghàire, fiamh-ghàire, snodha-gàire ; mìogshealladh.
smite, smitten, *part. pass.* of to smite, buailte, marbh, millte.
smite, *v. a.* buail, marbh, mill.
smith, *s.* gobha, *gen.* gobhann.
smithery, smithy, *s.* cèardach.
smock, *s.* léine boirionnaich.
smockfaced, *adj.* smigeideach, lom.
smoke, *s.* smùid, ceò, deatach.
smoke, *v.* tilg smùid, no toit ; gabh pìob thombaca, faigh air fhàileadh ; lòrg- aich a mach.
smoke-dry, *v. a.* tiormaich 'san toit, réisg.
smoky, *adj.* toiteach, ceòthach.
smooth, *adj.* mìn, sleamhainn réidh, còmhnard ; tlàth, ciùin ; dèimh ; lom.
smooth, *v. a.* mìnich ; dèan réidh ; dèan còmhnard, slìob, lìomh ; sleamhnaich, ciùinich.
smoothness, *s.* mìnead ; lìomhachas ; sleamhnad, ciùinead.
smote, *pret.* of to smite, bhuail, mharbh, mhill.
smother, *v. a.* mùch, tachd, caisg.
smother, *s.* toitearlach, casg.

smug, *adj.* deas, sgeinmeil, sgeilmeil, spailpeanta ; cuimir, sgiult.
smuggle, *v. a.* dèan cùiltearachd.
smuggler, *s.* cùiltear.
smuggling, *s.* cùiltearachd.
smugness, *s.* sgeinmealachd.
smut, *s.* salachar, draosdachd.
smutty, *adj.* salach ; draosda.
snack, *s.* roinn, cuid, cuibhrionn, gréim (bidh).
snaffle, *s.* srian-sròine.
snail, *s.* seilicheag, seilcheag.
snake, *s.* rìghinn, nathair.
snake-root, *s.* seòrsa luibh.
snaky, *adj.* nathaireil ; lùbach.
snap, *v.* cnac, bris, teum, beum, gearr, tiolam ; glac gu grad.
snap, *s.* cnac, teum, beum, tiolam.
snapper, *s.* tiolpadair, beumaire.
snappish, *adj.* tiolamach ; beumach ; dranndanach, dreamach, crosda.
snap-sack, *s.* àbarsgaig saighdear.
snare, *s.* ribe, painntir, lion, eangach, ceap-tuislidh, goisid.
snare, *v. a.* rib, glac, painntirich.
snarl, *v. n.* dèan dranndan, dèan gruns- gul ; labhair gu cas.
snarler, *s.* dranndanaich ; diorrasan.
snatch, *v.* glac, beir air ; tiolp, teum, thoir tiolam, thoir sitheadh.
snatch, *s.* greis ; tiolp, làn-beòil.
sneak, *v. n.* fèathlaidh, snàig, crùb.
sneaking, *adj.* snàgach, dìblidh.
sneer, *v. a.* seall gu tarcuiseach, dèan gàire, dèan fanaid, mag.
sneer, *s.* sealladh-magaidh, sealladh, fanaideach, facal tàireil ; beum.
sneeze, *v. n.* dèan sreothart.
sneeze, *s.* sreothart, sreothartaich.
sneezewort, *s.* am meacan-ragaim.
snicer, *v. n.* dèan faoin-ghàire.
snick and snee, *s.* biodagraich.
snipe, *s.* an meannan-adhair.
snivel, *v. n.* dèan smùchanaich.
snore, *s.* srannchadal.
snort, *s.* srannartaich, séidrich.
snout, *s.* soc ; gnos, sòrn, sròn.
snow, *s.* sneachda.
snowdrop, *s.* a' ghealag-làir.
snowy, *adj.* sneachdach ; sneachdaidh.
snub, *s.* cruaidhshnaimh, gath, athais.
snuff, *s.* smàl coinnle ; snaoisean.
snuff, *v.* sròineisch ; snòtaich, gabh snòitean ; smàl.
snuffbox, *s.* bocsa-snaoisein.
snuffers, *s.* smàladair.
snuffle, *v. n.* labhair gu glòmach.
snug, *adj.* clùmhar, blàth, comhfhurtail.
snuggle, *v. n.* laigh gu clùmhar.
so, *adv.* mar sin, mar so, mar sud, air an dòigh so, air an dòigh sin, air an dòigh ud, air an t-seòl so, air an t-seòl sin, air an t-seòl ud.

soak, v. bog, sùgh ; fliuch ; sùigh, òl.

soap, s. siabunn.

soar, v. n. itealaich gu h-àrd ; éirich (air sgéith).

sob, s. osann, osna, ospag, plosg.

sob, v. n. dèan osann, dèan osnaich.

sober, adj. measarra, stuama, geimnidh, ciùin ; riaghailteach.

sober, v. a. dèan measarra ; dèan cùim, thoir gu céill.

soberness, sobriety, s. measarrachd ; stuamachd, geimnidheachd, ciùineas.

sociable, adj. caidreach, caideara, cuideachdail, càirdeil ; còmpanta, conaltrach.

sociableness, s. caireamhachd ; caidearachd ; còmpantachd.

social, adj. caidreamhach, comunnach, daonnach.

society, s. comunn, cuideachd ; aonachd ; cinneadh-daonna ; còisir.

socinian, s. fear cumail a mach nach co-ionann Criosd ri Dia, fear-leanmhainn Socinus.

sock, s. stocainn ; bréid-bròige, osan goirid.

socket, s. ceal ; lag na sùl.

sod, s. fàl, fàilean, tobhta.

sodality, s. còmpanas, comunn.

sodden, part. leth-bhruich.

sofa, s. langsaid, làmhsaid, séis.

soft, adj. bog, bogar ; tais ; maoth, tlà ; mìn, ciùin, sèimh ; farasda, fòil, caomh, baoghalta.

soft, interj. socair ! air do shocair !

soften, v. bogaich, taislich, maothaich, ciùinich.

softly, adv. gu fòil, gu ciùin.

softness, s. buige, taise ; coibhneas, ciùineas, maothalachd ; taisealachd.

soil, v. a. salaich, dubh, truaill ; mathaich, innearaich.

soil, s. ùir, talamh ; fearann ; inneir, aolach, salchar ; sal.

sojourn, v. n. còmhnaich, gabh còmhnaidh ; tuinich, fan, fuirich.

sojourn, s. còmhnaidh, cuairt.

sojourner, s. fear-cuairt, aoigh.

sojourning, s. and part. cuairt ; eilthire, turas.

solace, s. sòlas ; co-ghàirdeachas.

solace, v. a. thoir sòlas, furtaich.

solan-goose, s. sùlaire ; guga.

solar, solary, adj. gréine ; grianach.

sold, pret. part. of to sell, reicte.

soldier, s. saighdear, mìlidh.

soldiership, s. saighdearachd.

soldiery, s. saighdearan.

sole, s. bonn coise no bròige ; lèabag.

sole, v. a. cuir bonn air.

sole, adj. a mhain, aon-fhillte.

solecism, s. baoth-labhradh.

solely, adv. a mhàin ; gu sònraichte.

solemn, adj. sòlaimte, greadhnach ; foirmeil ; tiamhaidh, trom.

solemnise, v. a. urramaich ; coimhid gu deas-ghnàthach.

solemnity, s. sòlaimteachd ; deas-ghnàth bliadhnail ; greadhnachas.

solicit, v. a. aslaich, guidh, grìos.

solicitation, s. aslachadh, guidhe, grìosadh ; sireadh ; mosgladh, dùsgadh, brosnachadh.

solicitor, s. fear-tagairt.

solicitous, adj. iomaguineach, cùramach ; déidheil.

solicitude, s. iomaguin, ro-chùram.

solid, adj. teann, daingeann, tiugh, deanta, trom, tarbhach ; neò-fhàs, làidir ; fior ; glic, suidhichte.

solid, s. tiugh, a' chuid theann do'n chorp ; ni sam bith aig am beil fad, leud, agus tiuighead.

solidity, s. tairbhe, tiuighead, taicealachd ; gramalas ; ciall, toinisg.

solidness, s. tiuighead ; ciall.

soliloquise, v. a. labhair riut-féin.

soliloquist, s. féin-labhairtiche.

soliloquy, s. féin-labhairt.

solitary, adj. aonaranach ; uaigneach, fàs ; tiamhaidh ; ùdlaidh.

solitude, s. uaigneas ; fàsach.

solo, s. òran aon neach.

solstice, s. an uair is àirde ghrian.

soluble, adj. leaghtach, fuasglach.

solution, s. dealachadh ; leaghadh ; nì leaghte ; fuasgladh, mìneachadh.

solutive, adj. purgaideach.

solve, v. a. fuasgail, mìnich.

solvency, s. comasachd air ìocadh.

solvent, adj. comasach air ìocadh.

somatology, s. corp-theagasg, eòlas air a' chorp.

sombre, sombrous, adj. dorcha, neulach, gruamach, dubh.

some, adj. cuid, roinn, feadhainn.

somebody, s. neacheigin, cuideigin.

somehow, adv. air choreigin.

somersault, sumerset, s. car-a'-mhuiltean.

something, s. rudeigin, nieigin.

something, adv. a lethchar.

sometime, adv. uaireigin.

sometimes, adv. air uairibh.

somewhat, s. beagan, rudeigin.

somewhat, adv. a lethchar.

somewhere, adv. an àit'eigin.

somniferous, somnific, adj. cadalach, cadaltach, dùsalach.

somnolency, s. cadaldachd.

son, s. mac.

song, s. àmhran, òran ; dàn.

songster, s. òranaiche.

songstress, s. ban-òranaiche.

soniferous, sonorific, sonoriferous, adj. fuaimneach.

son-in-law, s. cliamhuinn.
sonnet, s. luinneag, duanag.
sonorous, adj. fuaimneach.
soon, adv. a chlisge, gu luath, an ùin ghearr, gu tràthail, luath, grad.
soot, s. sùithe.
sooted, adj. sùidhte, làn sùithe.
sooth, s. fìrinn ; dearbh-fhìrinn.
soothe, v. a. breug, tàlaidh ; ciùinich, comhfhurtaich.
soothsay, v. a. fàisnich.
soothsayer, s. fiosaiche, fàidh.
soothsaying, s. fiosachd, fàisneachd.
sooty, adj. sùitheach, dorcha.
sop, s. ròmag, stapag.
sop, v. a. tùm.
soph, s. stuidear òg Sasunnach.
sophism, s. cealg-ràdh.
sophist, sophister, s. breug-reusonaiche, feallsanach carach.
sophistical, adj. fallsa, cealgach.
sophisticate, v. a. truaill, mill.
sophistication, s. truailleadh.
sophistry, s. reusonachd mheallta.
soporiferous, soporific, adj. cadalach, cadaltach, pràmhail.
sorcerer, s. fiosaiche, drùidh.
sorceress, s. ban-drùidh, baobh.
sorcery, s. drùidheachd, fiosachd.
sord, s. àilean, lianan.
sordes, s. mosaiche ; anabas, draib.
sordid, adj. salach, mosach, crìon, mìodhur, biastail, spìocach.
sore, s. creuchd, lot, cneadh.
sore, adj. goirt, cràiteach, piantail.
sorel, s. tribhliadhnach buic.
sorrel, s. sealbhag ; biadh-eunain.
sorrow, s. mulad, bròn.
sorrowful, adj. muladach, brònach.
sorry, adj. duilich, muladach, brònach ; suarrach, dìblidh, truagh.
sort, s. seòrsa, gnè ; modh, dòigh.
sort, v. cuir air dòigh, cuir an òrdugh ; seòrsaich ; roinn ; riaghailtich.
sortance, s. freagarrachd.
sortment, s. cur an òrdugh.
sot, s. burraidh, ùmaidh, misgear.
sottish, adj. misgeach, ùmadail.
soul, s. anam ; deò, spiorad.
sound, adj. slàn, fallain ; glic.
sound, s. caolas ; tanalach mara ; fuaim.
sound, v. dèan fuaim, dèan toirm ; gleang; tomhais doimhneachd; sgrùd, rannsaich ; séinn, mol, séirm.
sounding, adj. fuaimneach.
soundness, s. fallaineachd, slàinte fìrinn, tréidhireas.
soup, s. eanaraich, eun-bhrith.
sour, adj. goirt, geur, garg, searbh, doirbh, crosda, dùr, gruamach.
source, s. tobar ; ceud-aobhar mathair-aobhair, bun, freumh.

sourish, adj. a lethchar goirt.
sous, s. bonn-Fràngach.
souse, adv. le splad ; le sic.
south, s. an àirde deas, deas.
south, adj. deas, deasach.
south-east, s. an earra-dheas.
southerly, adj. deas, á deas, mu dheas ; deiseal.
south-west, s. an iar-dheas, an iarras.
sovereign, s. rìgh ; òr-fhichead-tastan.
sovereign, adj. rioghail ; còrr.
sovereignty, s. uachdaranachd.
sow, s. muc, crain, orc, banbh.
sow, v. cuir, sìol-chuir ; sgaoil.
sowens, s. làghan, càbhraich.
space, s. uidhe, rùm ; farsuinneachd ; ùin ; àm, tìm ; astar, greis.
spacious, adj. farsuinn, mòr.
spaciousness, s. farsuinneachd.
spaddle, s. pleadhan, pleadhag.
spade, s. spaid ; caibe, sluasaid.
spall, s. a' ghualainn.
span, s. réis, naoi òirlich.
span, v. a. tomhais le réis.
spangle, s. spangan.
spangle, v. a. loinnrich, boillsg.
spaniel, s. cù-eunaich ; sgimileir.
Spanish, adj. Spàinteach.
spanner, s. gleus - gunna, glamaradh làimhe.
spar, s. tarsannan, crann, glas.
spar, v. dùin, glais ; dòrn, cath.
sparable, s. mion-tharung.
spare, v. caomhain, sàbhail, bi bàigheil ri ; seachainn, bi caonntach.
spare, adj. gann, truagh ; caonntach.
spare-rib, s. lomasunn.
sparing, adj. gann, spìocach.
spark, s. srad, sradag ; dril ; lasgaire, gasganach, òganach spairiseach.
sparkle, s. tuireann ; lannair, dealradh, sradagraich.
sparkle, v. lannair, dealraich ; srad-agaich ; deàrrs, boillsg, soillsich.
sparkling, adj. loinnreach, dealrach ; sradagach ; drìlseach, soillseach.
sparrow, s. gealbhonn, glaiseun.
sparrow-grass, s. creamh-mac-féigh.
sparrow-hawk, s. an speireag.
spasm, spasmodical, s. féith-chrupadh, orc, ìonga, gréim (analach).
spasmodic, adj. féith-chrupach, orcach ; iodhach, ìneach.
spat, s. maoirneag.
spatter, v. spult, salaich ; tilg smugaid, cùl-chàin.
spatterdashes, s. casa-gearra.
spatula, s. spaideal, maide-poite.
spaw, s. tobar-mheine.
spawl, s. smugaid, splangaid.
spawn, v. cladh ; sìolaich.
spawn, s. iuchair (éisg) ; sìol.
spawner, s. iasg-iochrach.

spawning, s. cladh, mealagachadh.

spay, v. a. spoth ainmhidhean boireann.

speak, v. labhair, bruidhinn, abair, can, bruidhnich ; innis, luaidh, aithris.

speakable, adj. labhairteach ; còmhraideach, conaltrach.

speaker, s. fear-labhairt, ceann-suidhe (Parlamaid).

speaking, s. bruidheann, labhairt.

spear, s. sleagh, craosach, mòrghath.

spearmint, s. mionntainn.

spearwort, s. glaisleun.

special, adj. àraidh, sònraichte ; òirdheirc, prìomh ; neo-choitcheann.

species, s. gné, seòrsa, dream.

specific, adj. àraid, àraidh, sònraichte.

specific, s. ùrchasg ; iocshlaint.

specify, v. a. comharraich, ainmich.

specimen, s. samhla ; sampull.

specious, adj. greadhnach ; dealbhach, aogasach, coltach.

speck, s. smal, sal, ball.

speck, v. a. salaich, ballaich.

speckle, s. spotag, ball beag.

speckle, v. a. ballaich, breacaich.

speckled, adj. ballach, ballbhreac.

spectable, s. sealladh, ball-amhairc.

spectacles, s. speuclairean.

spectator, s. fear-amhairc.

spectre, s. tannasg, bòcan.

speculate, v. smaointich, beachdaich, cnuasaich ; cunnartaich.

speculation, s. beachdachadh, smaointeachadh, rannsachadh, deuchainn, dealbhadh.

speculative, adj. beachdail, smuainteachail, tionnsgnach.

speculator, s. dealbhadair, tionnsgnaiche ; fear-beachdachaidh.

speculum, s. sgàthair.

speech, s. cainnt, cànan, bruidheann ; labhairt, seanachas, òraid, uirghioll.

speechless, adj. balbh, gun chainnt.

speed, v. greas, luathaich, deifirich.

speed, s. luaths, deifir, cabhag ; good speed, deagh shoirbheachadh.

speedy, adj. luath, cabhagach.

spell, s. òradh, giseag, seun ; greis.

spell, v. n. litirich.

spelter, s. seòrsa miotailt.

spend, v. caith, builich, caisg ; claoidh.

spendthrift, s. struidhear.

sperm, s. siol-sìolachaidh.

spermaceti, s. blonag muice mara.

spermatic, adj. sìolach.

spew, v. tilg, sgeith, dìobhair.

sphacelus, s. cnàmhuinn.

sphere, s. cuairt cruinne, cruinne-cé ; ball cruinn ; inbhe, àite.

spheric, spherical, adj. cruinn, cuairteach, guairneach, guairsgeach.

sphericalness, sphericty, s. cruinnead, cuairteachd, guairsgeachd.

spherics, s. eòlas cruinne.

spherule, s. cruinne beag.

spice, s. spìosraidh.

spicery, s. spìosraidh, peabar.

spick and span, adv. ùr nogha, gu snasail.

spicy, adj. spìosrach ; cùbhraidh.

spider, s. damhan-allaidh, breabadair ladhrach, cuideag.

spigot, s. spiocaid, leigeadair.

spike, s. dias arbhair ; bior iaruinn.

spike, v. a. tàirng, spàrr bior iaruinn.

spikenard, s. boltrachan ; spiocnard.

spill, v. dòirt ; taom, caill, mill.

spilth, s. ni taomte sam bith.

spin, v. snìomh, toinn, cuir dàil.

spinage, or spinach, s. bloinigean-gàraidh.

spindle, s. dealgan, fearsaid.

spindle-shanked, adj. caolchasach.

spine, s. cnàimh an droma, gob biorach.

spinet, s. seòrsa inneal-ciùil.

spiniferous, adj. deilgneach.

spink, s. an lasair-choille.

spinster, s. bana-chalanaich, ban-sniomhaich, maighdeann, seann mhaighdeann.

spiny, adj. deilgneach, driseach.

spiracle, s. toll gaoithe, toll caol.

spiral, adj. snìomhanach.

spire, s. stìopull ; binein.

spirit, s. spiorad ; tannasg, anam ; misneach, smior, smioralas, smearalas, beothalas ; nàdur, gné, càil ; deò, beatha ; uisge-beatha, deoch làidir.

spirit, v. a. misnich, brosnaich ; meall ; tàlaidh, goid air falbh.

spirited, adj. misneachail, smiorail, duineil, beò, sgairteil.

spiritedness, s. misneach, smioralas.

spiritless, adj. neo-mhisneachail, neo-smiorail, neo-dhuineil, neo-bheothail, neo-sgairteil ; gealtach, tròm, marbh, neo-shunntach.

spiritual, adj. spioradail, neo-chorporra, nèamhaidh ; naomha, diadhaidh, inntinneach.

spiritualise, v. a. naomhaich, glan.

spirituality, s. spioradalachd, neo-chorporrachd, cràbhadh.

spirituous, adj. làidir mar dheoch.

spirt, v. sgiùrd, spùt, steall.

spiry, adj. barrachaol ; spiriseach.

spit, s. bior feòla, bior-ròstaidh.

spit, v. cuir air bior ; tilg smugaid.

spitchcock, s. easgann ròiste.

spite, s. gamhlas, mìorun falachd, miosgainn, fuath.

spite, v. a. farranaich, feargaich.

spiteful, adj. gamhlasach.

spitefulness, s. gamhlasachd.

spittle, s. smugaid, seile.

splash, v. a. spairt, spliut, steall.

splashy, adj. salach, làthachail.

splay, v. a. cuir as an alt.

splayfoot, adj. spliathach, pliutach.

spleen, s. an dubh-liath, fearg ; farmad, gamhlas ; beum-corraich ; airsneal.
spleenful, adj. farmadach, gamhlasach, feargach, crosda.
splendent, adj. loinnreach, dearsach, dealrach, boillsgeil, soillseach.
splendid, adj. dealrach, loinnreach ; òirdhearc ; greadhnach, basdalach.
splendour, s. dealradh, dearrsadh, lainnir, boillsgeadh ; greadnachas.
splenetic, adj. frionasach, crosta.
splenetive, adj. teinntidh, dian.
splice, v. a. tàth, teum, leig.
splint, s. bloigh ; pl. bloighdean.
splinter, s. sgealban, spealg.
split, v. a. sgoilt, sgealb ; bris, bruan ; crac ; srac, sgàin.
splutter, s. tuasaid, sabaid, caonnag, aimhreite, connsachadh, ùprait.
spoil, v. spùinn, spùill, creach, mill, truaill, cuir a dholaidh.
spoil, s. cobhartach, creach.
spoiler, s. spùilleadair, fear reubainn, milltear ; fear truaillidh.
spoke, s. tarsunnan ratha, asann.
spokesman, s. fear-labhairt.
spoliation, s. spùilleadh, milleadh.
sponsal, adj. maraisteach, pòsaidh.
sponsor, s. goistidh, urras.
spontaneous, adj. saor, deònach, de làn thoil, as a ghuth-thàmh.
spontaneously, adv. a dheòin.
spontaneousness, s. deònachd.
spool, s. iteachan ; piurna.
spoon, s. spàin.
spoonful, s. làn spàine.
sport, s. cluich spòrs ; fala-dhà, fearaschuideachd ; àbhachd, sealg.
sport, v. cluich, dèan mire, dèan sùgradh, dèan spòrs, dèan meoghail.
sportful, adj. cridheil, sunntach, aighearach, mireagach, sùgach.
sportfulness, s. cridhealas, mire.
sportive, adj. mear, cridheil, aighearach, sùgach, suigeartach.
sportsman, s. gìomanach, sealgair.
spot, s. smal, ball, bail ; ionaid ; tàmailt.
spot, v. a. salaich ; ballaich, truaill.
spotless, adj. gun smal, gun bhall, gun ghaoid, gun ghò, gun choire.
spotted, adj. ballach, bhreac, salach, truaillidh.
spousal, s. pòsadh, maraiste.
spouse, s. céile, céile-pòsta.
spout, s. steall, pìoban ; srùlag, srùp.
spout, v. a. spùt, steall, doirt.
spout-fish, s. muirsgian.
sprain, s. snìomh, siachadh, sguch.
sprat, s. gearrasgadan, sàrdail.
sprawl, v. n. smogaich, snàig.
spray, s. cathadh mara ; barr-géige.
spread, v. sgaoil ; sgap ; còmhdaich ; sìn a mach, foillsich.

sprig, s. faillean, maothan, fiùran.
spright, s. tannasg.
sprightliness, s. beothalas.
sprightly, adj. beò, meamnach, mear, smiorail, cridheil, sunntach, suilbhear ; aotrom.
spring, v. fàs, cinn ; sruth a mach ; spùt ; leum, thoir leum.
spring, s. earrach ; leum, cruinnleum, sùrdag ; fuaran, sùbailteachd.
springe, s. ribe, gòisid.
springhalt, s. ceum-crùbaich.
springle, s. dul, lub-ruithe.
spring-tide, s. reothairt ; aislear.
sprinkle, v. crath, sgap ; sgaoil.
sprinkling, s. crathadh, sgapadh, sgaoileadh, maoth-fhliuchadh.
sprit, s. ogan, maothfhailean.
sprite, s. spiorad, tannasg, màileachan.
spritsail, s. seòl-spreòid.
sprout, v. n. cuir a mach faillean.
sprout, s. faillean, fiùran, maothan, buinneag, ùr-fhàs, gineag.
spruce, adj. sgeilmeil, sgiolta ; snasmhor ; spailpeanta ; deas.
spruce, s. seòrsa giubhais.
spruceness, s. sgilmeileachd.
sprunt, s. maide garbh cutach.
spud, s. duirceall, buntàta.
spume, s. cobhar, cop.
spumous, spumy, adj. cobharach.
spun, pret. and p. part. of to spin, shnìomh ; snìomhte.
spung, s. spong, fàisgean.
spungy, adj. spongach, còsagach.
spunk, s. brathadair, lasadan.
spur, s. spor ; spuir ; brosnachadh.
spur, v. a. spor, greas, stuig, brod.
spurious, adj. mealltach, truaillidh.
spurling, s. spéirleag.
spurn, v. breab ; cuir dimeas air ; diùlt le tàir ; dèan tarcuis air.
spurn, s. breab, dimeas, tarcuis.
spurt, s. briosgadh, ruid.
sputter, v. dèan bladaireachd.
spy, s. beachdair, fear-brathaidh, farchluais.
spy, v. beachdaich, faigh a mach ; brath, rannsaich ; dearc leis an t-sùil, dèan farchluais.
spy-boat, s. bàta brathaidh.
spy-glass, s. glaine-amhairc.
squab, adj. neo-chlòimhichte, goirid, cutach, bunach, dòmhail ; tiugh ; reamhar, pocanach.
squab, s. sasag, suidheachan.
squabbish, squabby, adj. feòlmhor, dòmhail, trom, somalta.
squabble, v. n. connsaich, dean strìth.
squabble, s. tuasaid, sabaid, connsachadh, brionglaid, buaireas.
squabbler, s. buaireadair.
squadron, s. earrann cabhlaich no feachd.

squalid, *adj.* salach ; mosach, déisneach, sgreamhail.
squall, squeal, *v. n.* sgread, sgiamh.
squall, *s.* sgal gaoithe, sgread, sgiamh, sgrèach.
squally, *adj.* oibeagach, gaòthar.
squamose, squamous, *adj.* lannach.
squander, *v. a.* caith, strùidh, sgap, cosg, mill.
squanderer, *s.* strùidhear.
square, *adj.* ceithir - chèarnach ; co-thromach ; ceart, ionraic.
square, *s.* ceithirchearnag.
square, *v.* dèan ceithir chèarnach ; socraich, dèan cothromach ; riagh-ailtich, cuir an òrdugh.
squash, *s.* splad, splaitseadh, scing.
squat, *v. n.* crùb, liùg, laigh sìos.
squat, *s.* crùban, gurraban.
squat, *adj.* saigeanta, cutach, bunach.
squeak, *v. n.* sgiamh ; sgread, sian.
squeak, *s.* sgiamh chabhagach.
squeamish, *adj.* òrraiseach, gratharra, àilleasach, faralach.
squeeze, *v. a.* teannaich, mùch ; brùth fàisg ; sàraich, claoidh.
squelch, *s.* splad, plaidse.
squib, *s.* paipeir sradagach.
squint, *adj.* claon, fiar-shuileach.
squint, *v.* seall claon no fiar.
squint-eyed, *adj.* fiarshuileach.
squire, *s.* ridire beag.
squire, *v. a.* comhaidich, treòraich.
squirrel, *s.* an fheòrag.
squirt, *v. a.* sgiort, steall, taosg.
squirt, *s.* stealladair, gunna-spùt.
stab, *v. a.* troimh-lot, sàth.
stab, *s.* sàthadh, lot, leòn.
stability, *s.* bunailteachd, buansheasamh, maireannachd ; cinnteachd.
stable, *adj.* daingeann, buan, bunailteach, seasmhach, maireannach, diongmhalta.
stable, *s.* stàbull, marclann, eachlann.
stack, *s.* cruach, mulan, ruc, tudan.
stack, *v. a.* cruach, cruinnich, càrn.
staddle, *s.* lorg, trostan ; òg-chrann.
staff, *s.* bata, lorg ; bachall ; cuaille ; samhach, cas ; suaicheantas ; cùl-taic.
stag, *s.* damh cabrach féidh.
stage, *s.* ionad-cluiche, ceann-uidhe.
stage-coach, *s.* càrbad-réidh.
staggard, *s.* damh féidh 'n a cheithir-bhliadhnach.
stagger, *v.* breathlaich, bi dabhdail, tuainealaich, tuislich, bi gu tuiteam ; bi 'n ioma-cheist ; oilltich, cuir am breathal, cuir air boile.
staggers, *s.* galair each.
stagnant, *adj.* neo-ghluasadach, cadalach, mar bhreun-loch.
stagnate, *v. n.* bi mar bhreunloch.
stagnation, *s.* lodachadh, stad.
staid, *adj.* stòlda, suidhichte, glic.

stain, *s.* ball, sal, spot, coire, truailleadh ; lochd, gaoid ; dath, lì tàmailt, nàire, mìchliu.
stain, *v. a.* salaich, ballaich ; truaill ; nàraich ; maslaich.
stair, *s.* staidhre.
staircase, *s.* staidhreach.
stake, *s.* post, maolanach ; carragh, colbh ; geall ; cipein, bacan.
stake, *v. a.* gramaich, daighnich, gabh aige ; cuir geall.
stalactite, *s.* caisean-snidhe.
stale, *adj.* sean ; goirt ; searbh, malcaidh.
stale, *v. n.* mùin, dèan uisge.
staleness, *s.* seanndachd, goirteas.
stalk, *v. n.* ceumnaich ; spaisdeirich, imich gu stàtail ; eulaidh, sealg.
stalk, *s.* ceum uallach ; calp cuiseige, cuinnlein, cuiseag, gas, galan.
stalking-horse, *s.* each-séilge.
stalky, *adj.* cuiseagach, cuinnleineach, gasach, galanach.
stall, *s.* prasach, buaigheal, bualaidh, ionad-biathaidh mhart no each.
stall, *v. a.* biath, cuir am bàthaich.
stallion, *s.* òigeach, àigeach, greigheach, greigheire.
stamina, *s.* brìgh, stuth ; smior, bun.
stammer, *v. n.* bi manndach, liodach, dèan gagaireachd.
stammerer, *s.* fear manndach, liodach, gagaire, glugaire.
stamp, *v.* stailc ; pronn, brùth ; comhar-raich.
stamp, *s.* àile ; dealbh, comharradh-uidheam comharrachaidh, seòrsa, sliochd.
stanch, *v.* caisg.
stanch, *adj.* dian ; diongmhalta, daing-eann, làidir, bunaiteach, fìrinneach, fior, dìleas.
stanchion, *s.* cul-taic, gobhal, gàd.
stand, *s.* seasamh, àite-seasaimh ; stad, teagamh ; imcheist ; bùth.
stand, *v.* seas, seasamh ; dèan seasamh, fuirich, fan, stad ; mair ; fuilig, giùlain ; buanaich.
standard, *s.* suaicheantas, bratach, meirghe ; craobh ; riaghailt-shuidh-ichte, modh-seasmhach.
standel, *s.* seann chraobh.
standing, *s.* seasamh ; buanachadh ; mairsinn ; cor ; inbhe.
standing, *part. adj.* suidhichte, socraichte, seasmhach, buan.
standish, *s.* copan inc.
stang, *s.* cùig slat gu leth.
stannary, *s.* méinn staoine.
stanza, *s.* rann, ceithreamh.
staple, *s.* margadh shuidhichte ; stìnleag, stapall.
staple, *adj.* socraichte, margail.
star, *s.* rionnag, reull.

starboard, s. taobh deas luinge.
starch, s. stalcair, stalc, stuthaigeadh.
starch, v. a. stalcaich, stalc.
starched, adj. stalcanta.
stare, v. n. spleuc, geur-bheachdaich.
stare, s. spleuc, geur-amharc.
stargazer, s. reuladair, speuradair.
stark, adj. fìor, iomlan ; rag, làidir ;
teann, dearrasach.
starkly, adv. gu rag, gu làidir.
starlight, s. reull-sholus.
starlike, adj. rionnagach, reannagach,
drilinneach.
starling, s. druid, druid-dubh.
starred, adj. rionnagach, reulltach.
starry, adj. rionnagach, reulltach.
starshoot, s. sgeith-rionnaige, rionnag-
earbaill.
start, v. clisg, grad - leum, criothnaich,
grad-éirich, falbh, siubhail ; cuir clisg-
adh air ; cuir as an alt ; cuir as àite ;
cuir san rathad.
start, s. clisgeadh ; briosgadh, gradleum ;
teannadh air falbh ; toiseach.
starting, s. clisgeadh, briosgadh, leum.
startish, startlish, adj. gealtach, eagalach,
maoimeach.
startle, v. clisg, cuir clisgeadh air ;
oilltich, cuir eagal air, cuir maoim air ;
crup, crùb.
starve, v. cuir gu bàs le gort no fuachd ;
traod ; meillich.
starveling, s. fear-caoile, creutar truagh,
gortach.
statary, adj. ceangailte, suidhichte.
state, s. staid, inbhe, cor, gné ; rìoghachd,
dùthaich ; mórchuis, greadhnachas,
móralachd, luchd-riaghlaidh, stàta.
state, v. a. cuir an céill, aithris gu
puncail, thoir cunntas.
stateliness, s. stàidealachd, greadhnachas, mòralachd, uaill.
stately, adj. stàideil, greadhnach, flathail,
rìmheach, uallach, allail.
statement, s. cunntas, iomradh.
statesman, s. fear-stàta, comhairleach-
rìoghachd.
station, s. seasamh ; àite, ionad ;
dreuchd, post, oifig, inbhe.
station, v. a. socraich ; suidhich.
stationary, adj. socraichte, aitichte.
stationer, s. reiceadair phàipeirean.
stationery, s. bathar phàipeirean.
statuary, s. gràbhalaiche.
statue, s. ìomhaigh ; riochd.
stature, s. àirde, àirdead.
statute, s. lagh, reachd, òrdugh
stave, v. cuir 'na chlàraibh.
stave, s. clàr ; plur. clàir.
stay, v. fuirich, fan, feith, stad, seas ;
buanaich ; còmhnaich, tuinich ; cùm,
bac, caisg, gabh roimh ; cùm suas ;
cum taic ri.

stay, s. fanachd, fantainn, fuireach,
feitheamh, buanachd, stad ; dàil ;
bacadh ; taic, cùl-taic ; dìon, tèarmann ; stadh ; cliabh.
stayed, adj. suidhichte, socraichte, stòlta,
socrach ; bacte, grabte ; ciùin, ciùinichte.
stays, s. stadhannan ; seacaid bheag
(boirionnaich).
stead, s. ionad, riochd ; stà, feum.
steadfast, adj. bunaiteach, suidhichte,
daingeann, seasmhach, buan.
steadfastness, s. bunailteas.
steadiness, s. bunailt ; seasmhachd.
steady, adj. bunailteach, gramail ; daingeann ; socrach, suidhichte, cinnteach ;
a steady hand, làmh chinnteach.
steady, v. a. socraich, daingnich, cum
suas.
steak, s. staoig, toitean ; fillean.
steal, v. goid ; dèan mèirle.
stealth, s. goid, mèirle, braide, gadachd.
steam, s. toit, smùid.
steed, s. steud ; steudeach ; fàlaire.
steel, s. stàilinn, cruaidh.
steel, v. a. cruadhaich, stàilinnich.
steel, adj. stàilinneach, cruaidh.
steely, adj. cruaidh mar stàilinn.
steelyard, s. biorsamaid.
steep, adj. corrach, cas.
steep, s. bruach, uchdach, bruthach.
steep, v. a. bogaich, tùm, taisich.
steeple, s. stìopall, binean.
steepness, s. caisead, corraichead.
steepy, adj. corrach, cas, creagach.
steer, s. damh òg ; tarbh òg.
steer, v. stiùr, seòl ; treòraich.
steerage, s. stiùradh, seòladh, riaghladh,
steòrnadh ; seòmar-mór luinge, am
faradh as saoire.
steersman, s. stiùradair.
stellar, stellary, adj. rionnagach.
stellation, s. drillinn.
stellion, s. arc-luachrach bhallach.
stem, s. lorg, cas, cuiseag ; bun, stoc ;
sliochd, clann, gineal, teaghlach ;
toiseach luinge.
stem, v. a. gabh roimh, cum roimh, bac,
caisg, cuir stad air.
stench, s. droch thòchd, bréine.
stenography, s. gearr-sgrìobhadh.
stentorian, adj. àrd-labhrach.
stentorophonic, adj. àrd-ghlòireach.
step, v. n. thoir ceum, imich, ceumnaich,
coisich, gluais, rach, falbh.
step, s. ceum ; gluasad, imeachd.
stepdame, stepmother, s. muime.
stepdaughter, s. dalta nighinn.
stepfather, s. oide.
stercoraceous, adj. inneireach.
stercoration, s. mathachadh.
sterility, s. fàsalachd ; seasgad.
sterling, adj. fìor, firinneach.

sterling, s. airgead Sasunnach.
stern, adj. gruamach, duairceach, gnù, gnò, cruaidh ; neo-thruacanta.
stern, s. deireadh luinge.
sternness, s. gruaim, gruamaiche ; cruathas, duairceas ; an-iochd.
sternon, sternum, s. cnàimh a' bhroilich, cnàimh-uchda.
stew, v. a. stòbh ; earrbhruich.
stew, s. stòbh ; taigh-teth.
steward, s. stiùbhard.
stewardship, s. stiùbhardachd.
stick, s. bioran, maide, bata, lorg.
stick, v. sàth ; lot ; lean, coimhlean ; dlùthaich ri ; lean ri ; stad ; cùm ri.
stickle, v. n. connsaich ; seas ri.
stickler, s. fear-cuidichidh, fear a chumas taobh ri neach ; fear a chumas a mach gu dian ; duine ro-phoncail.
sticky, adj. righinn, leanailteach.
stiff, adj. rag, do-lùbadh ; reasgach, dùr ; teann, cruaidh, deacair.
stiffen, v. dèan rag, ragaich.
stiff-necked, adj. rag-mhuinealach.
stiffness, s. reasgachd, raige.
stifle, v. mùch, tachd ; cùm fodha, caisg, falaich, ceil ; cuir as.
stigma, s. comharradh-maslaidh, lorg, tàmailt, sgainneal, mìchliu.
stigmatise, v. a. comharraich le tàire ; cuir fo thàmailt.
stile, s. staidhir, ceum bealaich ; meur uaireadair gréine.
stiletto, s. cuinnsear, biodag.
still, adj. sàmhach, ciùin, sèimh.
still, s. poit-dubh, poit-thogalach ; sàmhchair, tosd.
still, v. a. ciùinich, cuir sàmhach, caisg, sìthich.
stillness, s. ciùineas, tost, fèith.
stilts, s. trosdain ; casan-corrach ; casan gòrrach.
stimulate, v. a. spor, brod, stuig, brosnaich, cuir thuige, buair.
stimulus, s. sporadh, brodadh, brosnachadh, buaireadh.
sting, s. gath ; guin, goimh.
sting, v. a. gath, cuir gath, gathaich, guin. leòn, lot, cràidh.
stinginess, s. spìocaireachd.
stingo, s. seann lionn.
stingy, adj. cruaidh ; sanntach.
stink, s. bòladh breun ; tòchd ; tùt.
stinkard, s. spìocaire ; bréinean.
stint, v. a. socraich ; cùm a stigh.
stint, s. crìoch, ceann, bacadh ; earrann, cuibhrionn, cuid.
stipend, s. stìopain ; tuarasdal, pàidheadh suidhichte.
stipendiary, s. fear-tuarasdail.
stipulate, v. a. cùmhnantaich, socraich, sònraich, suidhich.
stipulation, s. cùmhnant.

stipulative, adj. cùmhnantach.
stipulator, s. cùmhnantaiche.
stir, v. gluais, caraich, glidich ; brosnaich ; beothaich ; stuig, cuir thuige ; tog.
stir, s. buaireas, othail, ùinich, àimhreit, strìth, iomairt.
stirrer, s. buaireadair, brosnaiche, fear moch-éirigh.
stirrup, s. cas-dul, stiorap.
stitch, v. a. fuaigh ; tàth.
stitch, s. gréim snàthaid, gréim fuaigheil ; guin, goimh, treathaid.
stithy, s. innein.
stive, v. a. dòmhlaich, dèan teth.
stock, s. stoc ; post, bun ; baothaire ; gurraiceach, ùmaidh ; sìol, sliochd, clann, gineal, pòr, teaghlach ; stòr, stòras, maoin ; pac.
stock, v. a. lìon, stocaich ; cruach, càrn, cruinnich.
stock-dove, s. smùdan.
stock-fish, s. trosg tioram.
stocking, s. stocainn, osan.
stocklock, s. glas-chip.
stocks, s. ceap-peanais, glas-chas.
stoic, s. teallsanach a ta leanmhainn Sèno.
stole, s. còta fada ; rìoghail ; brat.
stolid, a. neo-ghluasadach, amh.
stolidity, s. baothaireachd, amhalachd.
stomach, s. goile, stamac, maodal ; sannt bìdh, acras, àrdan, misneach, toil, togradh, déidh.
stomach, v. gabh gu dona, gabh corraich ; gabh fearg.
stomacher, s. uchdchrios.
stomachic, s. leigheas goile.
stone, s. clach, ail.
stone, adj. cloiche, de chloich.
stone, v. a. clach, tilg clachan.
stonecast, s. urchair cloiche.
stone-fruit, s. clach-mheas, gach meas anns a bheil clach.
stone-horse, s. òigeach, àigeach.
stone-pit, s. clach-thochailt.
stony, adj. clachach, làn chlach, sgàirneach ; cruaidh ; an-iochdmhor.
stool, s. stòl, suidheachan ; ionad-suidhe ; tom, fuasgladh cuirp.
stoop, v. n. crom, lùb, aom, géill, strìochd, crùb, ìslich.
stoop, s. cromadh, lùbadh, aomadh, tuiteam ; crùbadh.
stop, v. a. stad, cuir stad, bac, toirmisg, cùm, grab, caisg, cuir dheth, cuir dàil ; sguir, leig dhìot, fan, fuirich.
stop, s. stad, grabadh, toirmeasg ; fanachd, fuireach ; dàil.
stoppage, s. aobhar stad, bacadh ; stad, sgur, dàil, maille, grabadh.
stopple, stopper, s. àrcan, ceann (botuil).

store, s. maoin, stòras, beairteas, pailteas, stoc, ionmhas ; faodail, feudail ; tasg-thaigh.

store, v. uidheamaich, lìon, stòr, stocaich, taisg, càrn suas, cuir seachad.

storehouse, s. tigh-stòir, tigh-tasgaidh.

stork, s. a chorra-bhàn, corra-ghritheach.

storm, s. ànradh, doireann, gaillionn, doinionn, stoirm, toirm, an-uair ; ionnsaidh air baile-dìona.

storm, v. thoir ionnsaigh làidir, tog gaillionn no doinionn ; bi fo chorraich ; cuir séisd.

stormy, adj. ànradhach, gaillionnach, doinionnach, gaothar ; crosta.

story, s. naidheachd, sgeul, sgeulachd ; uirsgeul, eachdraidh ; breug, ùrlar, lobhta.

stot, s. damh.

stout, adj. làidir, treun, foghainteach, calma, comasach, toirteil, gramail, garbh, tiugh ; tùrail ; dàna, danarra, misneachail.

stoutness, s. treise, spionnadh, tréine, gramalas, dànadas ; reasgachd, misneach.

stove, s. tigh-teth ; àmhuinn, seòrsa fùirneis.

stow, v. a. taisg, càrn suas.

stowage, s. àite-tasgaidh.

strabism, s. caogadh.

straddle, v. n. imich gu góbhlach ; (theirig) casan-góbhlach.

straggle, v. n. rach air iomrall, rach air seacharan, rach air faontradh.

straggler, s. fear-fuadain, slaodaire.

straight, adj. dìreach ; deas.

straight, straightways, adv. gu grad, gu h-ealamh, air ball, gu luath, gun stad, gun dàil.

straighten, v. a. dìrich.

strain, v. fàisg ; sìolaidh ; teannaich, dlùthaich ; sìach, snìomh, cumhannaich, dèan spàirn.

strain, s. fonn ; sìachadh, snìomh, spàirn.

strainer, s. sìoltachan.

strait, adj. teann, cumhann, àimhleathan ; dlùth ; cruaidh, duilich, docair, deacair.

strait, s. caolas, cuan ; cunglach, àirleag ; càs, teinn, teanntachd ; bochdainn, sàrachadh, uireasbhuidh.

straiten, v. a. teannaich, dèan àimhleathan ; sàraich, claoidh.

straitness, s. cuingead, cuinge, cruadhas, teanntachd.

strand, s. tràigh, cladach ; bruach.

strand, v. cuir air, rach air ; cuir no rach air cladach.

strange, adj. iongantach, neònach, miorbhuileach ; coimheach, coigreach, allmharra, gallda ; fiadhaich, ainneamh, annasach ; anabarrach.

strange, interj. iongantach !

stranger, s. coigreach, allmharrach.

strangle, v. a. tachd, mùch, croch, tachd.

strangles, s. an galar-greidh.

strangury, s. an galar-fuail.

strap, s. crios, iall, stìom, giort.

strappado, s. sgiùrsadh.

strapping, adj. mór, calma, deas, foghainteach, tlachdmhor.

strata, s. leapaichean, sreathan.

stratagem, s. cuilbheart (cogaidh).

stratum, s. leabaidh, breath, sreath.

straw, s. connlach ; fodar.

strawberry, s. sùbh-làir.

stray, v. n. rach air seacharan, rach air iomrall ; rach am mearachd.

stray, s. ainmhidh seacharain, conadal.

streak, s. stiall, stìom, srìan, ball.

streak, v. a. stiall, stiallaich.

streaky, adj. stiallach, srìanach, ballach.

stream, s. sruth ; buinne.

stream, v. sruth, ruith, dòirt.

streamer, s. bratach, sròl, meirghe.

streamlet, s. caochan, sruthan.

streamy, adj. sruthanach.

street, s. sràid.

strength, s. neart, spionnadh, tréine, treise ; marsainn, lùgh, treòir ; cumhachd ; gramalas ; dìon ; tèarmann ; dùn, daighneach ; armailt.

strengthen, v. neartaich ; beothaich ; daingnich ; socraich.

strengthener, s. neartachair.

strenuous, adj. dàna ; gaisgeil, misneachail ; dùrachdach ; curanta, dian, dealasach.

streperous, adj. àrd-fhuaimneach.

stress, s. cudthrom ; cothrom ; strìth ; spàirn ; eallach ; éigin.

stretch, v. a. sìn, sgaoil ; ragaich ; sìn a mach ; leudaich.

stretch, s. sìneadh ; ionnsaigh.

stretcher, s. ragadair ; sìneadair ; lunnchas luchd-iomaraidh.

strew, v. n. sgaoil, sgap, crath.

striæ, s. claisean slige-chreachainn no slige-coilleige.

striate, striated, adj. claiseach.

stricken, part. buailte.

strickle, s. stràcadair.

strict, adj. teann, cruaidh, geur ; doirbh ; leacanta ; poncail, dìreach.

stricture, s. crupadh, teannachadh ; buille ; beantainn, bacadh.

stride, v. n. thoir sìnteag, thoir sùrdag, rach gòbhlach, thoir ceum fada.

stride, s. sìnteag, sùrdag, fad-cheum.

strife, s. strìth, còmhstrith, connsachadh, caonnag, buaireas, ùtag, sabaid, tuasaid, aimhreit.

strike, v. buail, dòrnaich ; géill.

striker, s. fear bualaidh.

striking, *part. adj.* drùidhteach, iongantach, neònach.

string, *s.* sreang, sreangan, toinntean, còrd ; teud-chiùil.

string, *v. a.* sreangaich, teudaich.

stringed, *adj.* teudaichte.

stringent, *adj.* ceangaltach, geur (blas).

stringy, *adj.* sreangach, teudach.

strip, *v. a.* rùisg, lom, nochd, faobhaich, sgath ; cairt, sgrath, plaoisg.

strip, *s.* stìall, stìom.

stripe, *v. a.* stìall, stìallaich ; buail ; sgiùrs, sgiuts ; *s.* ball (an aodach).

stripling, *s.* òganach, balachan.

strive, *v. n.* dèan spàirn, dèan strìth.

striving, *s.* còmhstrith, gleachd.

stroke, *s.* buille, gleadhar, stràc, strioch.

stroke, *v. a.* mìnich, slìog, slìob.

stroking, *s.* slìobadh, suathadh.

stroll, *v. n.* sràid-imich, seabhaid.

stroller, *s.* sabhdaire, spaisdear.

strong, *adj.* làidir, neartmhor, treun, lùthmhor, calma, foghainteach, gramail ; fallain, slàinteil ; dian, deòthasach ; diongmhalta ; daingeann ; teann.

strow, *v. a.* sgaoil ; sgap ; crath.

structure, *s.* togail ; aitreabh.

struggle, *v. n.* gleachd ; dèan spàirn, dèan strìth ; streap, dèan iomairt ; saoithrich.

struggle, *s.* gleachd, spàirn, strìth.

strumpet, *s.* siùrsach, strìopach.

strut, *v. n.* imich gu stràiceil ; bòc.

strut, *s.* ceum uallach, ceum coilich.

stub, *s.* bun, òrda, durc.

stub, *v. a.* spion as a bhun.

stubbed, *adj.* bunach, stumpach, gearr, goirid, geinneach, cutach.

stubble, *s.* asbhuain, stailcneach.

stubborn, *adj.* rag, rag-mhuinealach, reasgach, eas-ùmhal.

stubbornness, *s.* ragaireachd, reasgachd, danarrachd, eas-ùmhlachd.

stubby, *adj.* cutach, stobanach, bunach, bunanta, goirid.

stuckle, *s.* stùcan, adag, sgrùdhan.

stud, *s.* tarag, tacaid ; greigh.

student, *s.* sgoilear, stuidear.

studied, *adj.* ionnsaichte.

studious, *adj.* déidheil air foghlum ; smuainteachail ; meòrach.

study, *s.* smuainteachadh ; cnuasachd, seòmar meòraich, meòrachadh.

study, *v.* smuainich, smaointich ; cnuasaich, meòraich, beachdaich, thoir fainear, breithnich, ionnsaich.

stuff, *s.* stuth ; cùngaidh ; seòrsa clò.

stuff, *v.* lìon, lìon gu sàth ; spàrr, dinn ; bòc ; at, ith séid.

stuffing, *s.* lìonadh, dinneadh, sparradh, mìlsean am feòil.

stultiloquence, *s.* glòireamas ; baois.

stum, *s.* fion ùr ; braileis.

stumble, *v.* tuislich, sleamhnaich.

stumble, *s.* tuisleadh, sleamhnachadh, cliobadh, mearachd, sgiorradh.

stumbler, *s.* fear-tuislidh.

stumbling, *s.* tuisleadh, sleamhnachadh, spéidhleadh, clibeadh.

stumbling-block, *s.* ceap-tuislidh.

stump, *s.* bun ; stoc, ceapan.

stumpy, *adj.* bunach, cutach.

stun, *v. a.* cuir tuaineal, cuir tàineal.

stunt, *v. a.* cum o fhàs.

stupefaction, *s.* neo-mhothachadh.

stupefy, *v. a.* cuir tuaineal.

stupendous, *adj.* fuathasach, uabhasach, iongantach, anabarrach.

stupid, *adj.* dùr ; baoghalta.

stupidity, *s.* baoghaltachd.

stupor, *s.* tuaineal ; tàineal.

sturdiness, *s.* neart, spionnadh, gramalas, duinealas, bunantachd.

sturdy, *adj.* làidir, neartmhor, bunanta, gramail, calma, garbh.

sturgeon, *s.* an stirean.

stutter, *v. n.* bi manndach, bi liodach, bi gagach, bi glugach.

stutterer, *s.* fear manndach, fear liodach, gagaire, glugaire.

sty, *s.* fail mhuc.

stygian, *adj.* ifrinneach.

style, *s.* modh-labhairt ; dòigh-labhairt ; modh-sgrìobhaidh ; dòigh-sgrìobhaidh ; tiodal, ainm ; seòl, modh, dòigh.

style, *v. a.* ainmich, goir.

styptic, *adj.* casgach air fuil.

styptic, *s.* casg-fala.

suasible, *adj.* so-earalachadh.

suavity, *s.* mìlse ; taitneachd, caomhalachd.

subacid, *adj.* a lethchar goirt ; rudeigin searbh.

subacrid, *adj.* a lethchar geur.

subaltern, *s.* ìochdaran, fo-oifigeach.

subdue, *v. a.* ceannsaich, ciùinich, sàraich, cuir fodha, cìosnaich.

subduer, *s.* fear-ceannsachaidh.

subject, *v. a.* cuir fo smachd, smachdaich, ceannsaich, sàraich, cuir fo cheannsal ; dèan buailteach do.

subject, *adj.* ùmhal ; fo smachd, ceannsaichte, fo chìs ; buailteach.

subject, *s.* ìochdaran ; ceann-eagair, ceann-teagaisg, stéidh-theagaisg.

subjection, *s.* ceannsachadh, ceannsal, ceannasachd, smachd.

subjoin, *v. a.* cuir ri ; fàth-sgrìobh.

subjugate, *v. a.* ceannsaich, cìosnaich, cuir fo cheannas.

subjugation, *s.* ceannsachadh.

subjunction, *s.* leasachadh.

sublimation, *s.* togail le neart teine.

sublime, *v. a.* tog le neart teine.

sublime, *adj.* àrd ; òirdheirc ; mór ; uaibhreach, greadhnach ; urramach.

sublimity, *s.* àirde ; òirdheirceas.

sublunar, sublunary, *adj.* talmhaidh, saoghalta ; tìmeil.

submarine, *adj.* fo 'n mhuir.

submerge, *v. a.* cuir fo 'n uisge.

submersion, *s.* cur fo 'n uisge.

submission, *s.* ùmhlachd, géilleadh.

submissive, *adj.* ùmhal, iriosal.

submissively, *adv.* gu h-ùmhal.

submissiveness, *s.* ùmhlachd.

submit, *v.* géill, strìochd, lùb.

subordinacy, *s.* ìochdranachd.

subordinate, *adj.* ìochdarach.

subordination, *s.* ìochdaranachd.

suborn, *v. a.* solair os iosal ; brìob.

subornation, *s.* foill-cheannach

suborner, *s.* fear-foille.

subpœna, *s.* rabhadh laghail.

subscribe, *v. n.* fo-sgrìobh.

subscriber, *s.* fo-sgrìobhair.

subscription, *s.* fo-sgrìobhadh ; còmhnadh, cuideachadh, aontachadh.

subsequence, *s.* leantainn.

subsequent, *adj.* a leanas.

subserve, *v. a.* fritheil ; cuidich.

subservience, *s.* frithealadh.

subservient, *adj.* fritheilteach, cuideachail, còmhnachail ; feumail.

subside, *v. n.* traogh, tràigh, tuit sìos ; ciùinich, ìslich, sìolaidh.

subsidency, *s.* traoghadh, tràghadh, sìoladh, tuiteam sìos.

subsidiary, *adj.* cuideachail.

subsidy, *s.* cuideachadh, còmhnadh.

subsign, *v. a.* cuir ainm ri.

subsist, *v. n.* buanaich, thig beò, thig suas, bi beò, beathaich.

subsistence, *s.* bith ; beatha ; buanachadh, tighinn beò, beathachadh, teachd-an-tìr, lòn.

subsistent, *adj.* beò, maireann.

substance, *s.* bith ; corp ; brìgh, bladh, stuth, tairbhe ; maoin, saoibhreas, beairteas.

substantial, *adj.* fìor ; beò ; corporra ; làidir ; gramail ; socrach, tàbhachdach, tarbhach ; beairteach reachdmhor, biadhchar, brìoghmhor.

substantiality, *s.* corporrachd.

substantiate, *v. a.* fìrinnich.

substantive, *s.* rud, nì aig a bheil bith.

substitute, *v. a.* cuir an àite.

substitute, *s.* fear-ionaid.

subsultive, *adj.* leumnach, clisgeach.

subtend, *v. n.* sìn mu choinneamh.

subtense, *s.* sreang bogha.

subterfuge, *s.* leithsgeul, cleas.

subterranean, subterraneous, *adj.* fo-thìreach, iochdrach, fo 'n talamh.

subtile, *adj.* tana, caol ; seang ; fìnealta, sligheach ; geur, carach, cealgach,

cuilbheartach, eòlach, seòlta, innleachdach.

subtileness, *s.* taine, caoile, fìnealtachd ; géire, cuilbheartachd.

subtiliate, *v. a.* tanaich, dèan tana.

subtiliation, *s.* tanachadh.

subtilty, *s.* taine, tainead, fìnealtachd ; car, cuilbheart, innleachd.

subtle, *adj.* carach, cuilbheartach, seòlta, eòlach, sligheach.

subtract, *v. a.* thoir uaithe.

subtraction, *s.* toirt uaithe.

suburb, *s.* iomall baile, fo-bhaile.

subversion, *s.* tilgeadh sìos, sgrios.

subversive, *adj.* millteach, sgriosail.

subvert, *v.* tilg bun os ceann.

succedaneous, *adj.* an àite ni eile.

succedaneum, *s.* ni an àite ni eile.

succeed, *v.* lean, thig an déidh, thig an lòrg, thig an àite ; soirbhich.

success, *s.* soirbheachadh, àgh ; buaidh ; sealbh, rath, sonas, sèamhas.

successful, *adj.* soirbheasach, àghmhor, buadhach, sealbhach.

succession, *s.* leantainn, leanachd ; lorg slighe ; còir-sheilbh.

successive, *adj.* leantainneach ; a leanas ; an òrdugh, an riaghailt.

successor, *s.* fear-ionaid, fear a thig an àite fir eile.

succinct, *adj.* cuimir, truiste ; deas, gearr, aithghearr.

succory, *s.* lus-an-t-siùcair.

succour, *v. a.* cuidich, cobhair, furtaich, thoir furtachd.

succour, *s.* còmhnadh, cuideachadh, cobhair, furtachd.

succulent, *adj.* brìoghmhor, sùghmhor, sultmhor.

succumb, *v. n.* géill, strìochd, lùb.

succussion, *s.* crathadh, bogadanaich.

such, *pron.* a leithid ; mar.

suck, *v.* sùigh, deoghail ; srùb.

suck, *s.* sùgadh, sùghadh, deoghal, srùbadh, bainne-cìche.

sucker, *s.* deoghladair ; sùghair, srùbair ; faillean, fiùran, maothan.

sucket, *s.* mìlsean.

suckle, *v. a.* thoir cìoch, àraich.

suckling, *s.* cìochran, naoidhean.

suction, *s.* sùghadh ; deoghal.

sudden, *adj.* grad, obann, cas, ealamh, cabhagach ; disgir.

suddenly, *adv.* gu h-obann.

sudorific, *adj.* fallusach.

suds, *s.* cobhar shiabuinn, bùrn siabuinn.

sue, *v.* cuir thuige, lean, tagair, agair, guidh, aslaich, sir, iarr.

suet, *s.* geir, ìgh, blonag.

suety, *adj.* reamhar, blonagach.

suffer, *v. a.* fuiling, giùlain, iomchair ; leig le ; ceadaich.

sufferable, *adj.* so-fhulang.

sufferance, s. fulangas, foighidinn, giùlan; cead, comas.

sufferer, s. fulangaiche.

suffering, s. fulangas, foighidinn, pian, cràdh.

suffice, v. foghainn ; sàsaich.

sufficiency, s. diongmhaltas ; foghainteachd ; éifeachd ; pailteas ; foghnadh ; leòir, na 's leòir, sàsachadh.

sufficient, adj. diongmhalta, foghainteach, comasach, iomchuidh, freagarrach, leòir, na 's leòir.

suffocate, v. a. tachd, mùch.

suffocation, s. tachdadh, mùchach.

suffocative, adj. tachdach, mùchach.

suffragan, s. easbuig-cuideachaidh.

suffragant, s. comh-oibriche.

suffrage, s. còir-taghaidh (buill Parlamaid) ; co-aontachadh, còmhnadh, bhòt.

suffuse, v. a. còmhdaich, sgaoil air.

suffusion, s. còmhdachadh.

sugar, s. siùcar.

sugary, adj. siùcarach, milis.

suggest, v. a. thoir sanas ; cuir an ceann, cuir an cuimhne, cuir an aire ; cagair.

suggestion, s. sanas, rabhadh, cagar.

suicide, s. féin-mhortair ; féin-mhort.

suit, s. iarrtas, iarraidh ; sireadh ; cùis, cùis-lagha, cùis-tagraidh ; culaidh, deise, trusgan ; suiridhe.

suit, v. freagarraich, freagair ; uidheamaich ; deasaich ; éid ; còird.

suitable, adj. freagarrach, iomchuidh, cumhaidh.

suitableness, s. freagarrachd.

suiter, suitor, s. suirdhiche ; leannan ; fear-aslachaidh.

sulkiness, s. gruaim, mùig.

sulky, adj. gruamach, iargalta, mùgach, coimheach, neo-aoigheil.

sullen, adj. doirbh, doichiollach ; gnò, gnù ; dùr, reasgach, cianail.

sullenness, s. doirbheas, doireanntachd, gruamaichead ; mùgalachd, dùiread, reasgachd.

sully, v. a. salaich, truaill ; mill.

sulphur, s. pronnasg, rif, riof.

sulphureous, adj. pronnasgach.

sulphury, adj. pronnasgach.

Sultan, s. Impire nan Turcach.

Sultana, s. Ban-Impire nan Turcach.

sultry, adj. bruthainneach, blàth.

sum, s. àireamh, sùim, brìgh.

sum, v. a. àireamh, sùim, cunnt.

sumless, adj. do-àireamh.

summary, adj. aithghearr, gearr.

summary, s. giorrachadh.

summer, s. sàmhradh ; sail-ùrlair.

summer-house, s. tigh-sàmhraidh.

summerset, s. car-a'-mhuiltein.

summit, s. mullach, binnein, barr,

summon, v. a. gairm, òrduich.

summoner, s. maor gairme.

summons, s. gairm gu mòd, bàirlinn.

sumpter, s. each-saic.

sumptuary, adj. a riaghladh cosgais.

sumptuous, adj. cosgail ; sòghail.

sumptuousness, s. cosgalachd.

sun, s. grian, lò-chrann.

sunbeam, s. gath-gréine, deò-gréine.

sunburnt, adj. grian-loisgte.

Sunday, s. Di-dòmhnaich.

sunder, v. a. dealaich, sgar.

sundew, s. lus-na-fearna-guirme.

sundial, s. uaireadair-gréine.

sundries, s. pl. cruinneachadh de gach seòrsa.

sundry, s. iomadaidh.

sunflower, s. neòinean-gréine.

sunk, part. of sink, air dol fodha.

sunless, adj. gun ghrian, gun teas.

sunny, adj. grianach ; deisearach.

sunrise, s. èirigh na gréine.

sunset, s. laighe na gréine, dol fodha na gréine.

sunshine, s. dèarsadh na gréine.

sunshiny, adj. grianach dèarsach.

sup, v. òl ; gabh suipeir.

sup, s. balgum, làn-beòil.

superable, adj. sò-cheannsachail.

superabound, v. n. bi lìonmhor.

superabundance, s. tuille 's a chòir, làn phailteas.

superabundant, adj. anabarra pailt.

superadd, v. a. cuir ri.

superaddition, s. cuir ris.

superannuate, v. a. cuir air duais—air painsean.

superb, adj. rìmheach, greadhnach.

supercargo, s. fear-cùram luchda.

supercilious, adj. àrdanach, uallach.

superciliousness, s. àrdan, uaill.

supereminence, s. barrachd.

supereminent, adj. barrachdach.

supererogation, s. bàrra-ghnìomh, airidheachd a chorr.

superexcellent, adj. barraichte.

superfice, s. uachdar.

superficial, adj. uachdrach ; suarrach, faoin ; neo-dhiongmhalta, neo-ghramail; neo-ionnsaichte ; eu-domhain ; air bheag eòlais.

superficialness, s. suarraichead ; eu-doimhneachd, beag-eòlas.

superficies, s. an taobh a muigh, an t-uachdar, am barr.

superfine, adj. tur-finealta.

superfluity, s. anabharra.

superfluous, adj. neo-fheumail.

superflux, s. anacuimse.

superhuman, adj. thar nàdur-daonna.

superincumbent, adj. air muin.

superintend, v. a. amhairc thairis.

superintendency, s. riaghladh.

superintendent, s. riaghladair.

superior, *adj.* as àirde, as fearr.
superiority, *s.* barrachd ; ceannas.
superlative, *adj.* as airde, còrr.
superlatively, *adv.* gu barrachdail.
supernal, *adj.* nèamhaidh.
supernatural, *adj.* os cionn nàduir.
supernumerary, *adj.* còrr, a chorr.
superscribe, *v. a.* sgrìobh air taobh muigh no air cùl litreach.
superscription, *s.* cùl-sgrìobhadh.
supersede, *v.* cuir air chùl.
superstition, *s.* saobh-chràbhadh.
superstitious, *adj.* saobh-chràbhach.
superstruct, *v. a.* tog, tog air.
superstruction, *s.* togail.
superstructure, *s.* togail, aitreabh.
supervise, *v. a.* seall thairis.
supervisor, *s.* fear-rannsachaidh.
supine, *adj.* air druim - dìreach, leisg, màirnealach, coma.
supineness, *s.* leisg, tromasanachd.
supper, *s.* suipeir.
supperless, *adj.* gun suipeir.
supplant, *v. a.* cuir á àite le foill.
supple, *adj.* sùbailte, so-lùbadh, maoth ; carach, miodalach, brosgalach, sodalach, goileamach.
supplement, *s.* leasachadh.
supplemental, supplementary, *adj.* leasachail, ath-leasachail.
suppleness, *s.* sùbailteachd.
suppliant, *adj.* aslachail.
suppliant, supplicant, *s.* fear-aslachaidh, achanaiche.
supplicate, *v. a.* aslaich, guidh.
supplication, *s.* aslachadh, guidhe, grìosadh, ùrnaigh, achanaich.
supply, *v. a.* dèan suas ; cum ri, seas air son, dèan àite.
supply, *s.* còmhnadh, cobhair ; furtachd, dèanamh suas, co-leasachadh.
support, *v. a.* cùm suas, cùm taic ri, dèan cùl-taic, cùm taobh ri, dèan còmhnadh le, cuidich, cobhair ; beathaich, dìon.
support, *s.* taic, cul-taic ; sorchan, còmhnadh, cobhair, cuideachadh.
supportable, *adj.* so-ghiùlan, so-iomchar, so-fhulang.
supporter, *s.* fear cumail suas, dionadair ; cul-taic.
supposable, *adj.* so-shaoilsinn.
suppose, *v. a.* saoil, smaointich, baralaich, beachdach.
supposition, *s.* saoilsinn, barail, smuain, beachd.
supposititious, *adj.* air sgath argumaid.
suppress, *v. a.* ceannsaich, lùb, cùm fodha, sàraich, falaich, ceil, mùch, cùm sàmhach ; cùm a stigh.
suppression, *s.* ceannsachadh, cumail fodha, lùbadh, falach, ceiltinn, mùchadh, cleith.

suppressor, *s.* ceileadair, mùchadair.
suppurate, *v. a.* iongraich.
suppuration, *s.* iongrachadh.
suppurative, *adj.* iongarach.
supramundane, *adj.* os cionn-an-t-saoghail, uachdrach.
supravulgar, *adj.* os cionn a chumanta, barraichte, barrail.
supremacy, *s.* ard-cheannas, ceannasachd, àrd-uachdranachd.
supreme, *adj.* ard, is àirde.
sural, *adj.* calpach ; luirgneach.
surcease, *v.* sguir, stad, cuir stad air, cuir crìoch air.
surcease, *s.* sgur ; stad, fosadh.
surcharge, *v. a.* an-luchdaich.
surcharge, *s.* an luchd, antruime.
surcingle, *s.* crios-tarra, giort.
surcoat, *s.* còta-uachdair.
surd, *adj.* bodhar, balbh.
surdity, *s.* buidhre.
sure, *adj.* cinnteach, neo-thuisleach, neo - mhearachdach, fìor, fiosrach ; daingeann ; tèaruinte.
sure, surely, *adv.* air chinnte, gun teagamh ; gu dearbh, gu deimhin, gu fior, gu firinneach.
surface, *s.* uachdar, aghaidh, taobh a muigh, leith a muigh.
surfeit, *v.* sàsaich, lìon, gu sàth ; ith gu sàth.
surfeit, *s.* sàsachadh ; sàth ; tarbhas, teann-shàth, séid, gràin le ithe.
surge, *s.* sumainn, bòcthonn.
surge, *v. n.* at ; éirich, bòc.
surgeon, *s.* leighiche.
surgery, *s.* dreuchd leighiche, oifis leighiche.
surgy, *adj.* sùmainneach, stuadhach.
surliness, *s.* iargaltachd.
surly, *adj.* iargalta, doirbh, gruamach, nuarranta, mì - mhodhail ; neo-shìobhalta, gnò, gnù, gnùtha.
surmise, *s.* barail, umhaill, saoilsinn.
surmount, *v. a.* rach os cionn, rach thairis, buadhaich, thoir buaidh, faigh lamh-an-uachdar.
surmountable, *adj.* so-cheannsachadh.
surname, *s.* sloinneadh.
surname, *v. a.* sloinn.
surpass, *v. a.* thoir bàrr, fairtlich, buadhaich ; bi os cionn.
surpassing, *adj.* òirdheirc ; barrail.
surplice, *s.* leine-aifrionn.
surplus, *s.* còrr, barrachd, barrachdas, còrrlach, fuigheall, fuighleach.
surprise, *s.* ioghnadh, iongantas ; fuathas ; clisgeadh, uabhas ; teachd gun fhios ; glacadh gun fhios.
surprise, *v. a.* thig gun fhios, cuir ioghnadh, clisg, glac gun fhios ; thig gun fhaireachdadh.
surprising, *part. adj.* iongantach, neònach, mìorbhuileach.

surrender, v. strìochd, géill ; thoir suas ; thoir air ais.
surrender, s. strìochdadh, géilleachdainn ; toirt thairis, toirt suas.
surreptitious, adj. meallta, bradach.
surrogation, s. cur an àite neach.
surround, v. a. cuartaìch, iomdhruid, iadh mu thimchioll.
surtout, s. cota caol, faluinn.
survey, v. a. gabh beachd, amhairc, gabh sealladh ; tomhais fearann.
survey, s. sealladh, beachd, sealltuinn thairis ; tomhas.
surveyor, s. fear tomhais ; fear riagh-laidh, fear-beachdachaidh.
survive, v. mair beò, bi làthair, mair an déidh, bi beò an déidh.
surviver, survivor, s. an t-aon a bhios a làthair an déigh bàs neach eile.
susceptibility, s. faireachdainn.
susceptible, susceptive, adj. mothachail, beothail ; a' faireachadh.
susception, s. gabhail.
suscipient, s. fear-gabhail.
suscitate, v. a. dùisg, brosnaich.
suspect, v. cuir an amharus, cuir umhaill ; bi amharasach, cùm an teagamh ; baralaich ; saoil ciontach, smaoinich ciontach.
suspected, adj. fo amharus.
suspend, v. a. croch, cuir an crochadh, dàilich, cuir dàil ; cuir á dreuchd car ùine, cùm an imcheist.
suspense, s. teagamh, eadarra-bharail.
suspension, s. crochadh ; bacadh, cur dheth, dàileachadh, grabadh ; cumail air ais.
suspicion, s. amharus, an-amharus, umh-aill ; teagamh.
suspicious, adj. amharusach ; eu-cinn-teach ; fo amharus.
suspiration, s. osann, osnaich.
suspire, v. n. tarruing anail ; tarruing osann, osnaich.
sustain, v. a. cùm suas, giùlain ; cùm taic ri ; cuidich ; fuiling, cùm beò.
sustenance, s. biadh, lòn, beathachadh, teachd-an-tìr.
susurrate, v. n. dèan cagarsnaich.
susurration, s. cagar, torman.
sutler, s. ceannaiche.
suture, s. tàthadh, ceangal-chnàmh, fuaigheal.
swab, s. moibean, sguab-làir.
swab, v. a. glan le moibean.
swaddle, v. a. paisg, sgaoil.
swaddle, s. aodach suainidh.
swag, v. n. croch gu tròm ; bi trom-sanaich.
swagger, v. n. dèan spaglainn ; dèan buamasdaireachd, bi spaillichdeil, dèan bòsd, dèan ràiteachas.
swaggerer, s. buamasdair, bladhastair,

fear spagluinneach, fear spaillichdeil ; fear bòsdail.
swaggy, adj. trom, liobasta, lòdail.
swain, s. òganach, òigear, fleasgach ; tuathanach, buachaille.
swallow, s. gòbhlan-gaoithe.
swallow, v. a. sluig.
swamp, s. boglach, féith, càthar.
swampy, adj. bog, càtharach.
swan, s. eala.
sward, s. fàilean ; fòd, sgrath, feur, rùsg ; craicionn muice.
swarm, s. sgaoth, sgann.
swarm, v. n. cruinnich mar sgaoth.
swarthy, adj. ciar, odhar, lachdunn.
swash, s. pluinnse, plubartaich.
swash, v. a. dèan plubartaich ; dèan gleadhraich, dèan fuaim.
swathe, v. a. paisg, spaoil.
sway, v. riaghail, òrduich ; seòl, stiùr ; aom ; bi cumhachdach.
sway, s. iomairt, truime ; cumhachd ; seòladh, riaghladh ; smachd.
sweal, swale, v. n. caith as.
swear, v. mionnaich, thoir mionnan ; cuir air mhionnan, gabh mionnan.
swearer, s. mionntair.
swearing, s. mionnachadh.
sweat, s. fallus.
sweat, v. cuir fallus dhìot, cuir am fallus ; saoithrich.
sweaty, adj. fallusach ; goirt.
sweep, v. sguab, glan ; sguids.
sweep, s. sguabadh ; deannadh.
sweepings, s. trusdaireachd, fòtus.
sweepnet, s. lìon-sgrìobaidh.
sweepstakes, s. cosnadh nan geall gu léir còmhladh le aon fhear.
sweet, adj. milis, blasda, ùr ; cùbhraidh ; coibhneil, caoin, caomh, beulchar, tlà ; taitneach, sòlasach, sèimh, ciùin ; binn, ceòlmhor ; ciatach, laoghach, bòidheach, lurach, grinn, greannar, màlda.
sweet, s. mìls, milseachd.
sweetbread, s. aran-milis.
sweetbrier, s. feara-dhris.
sweeten, v. a. mìlsich ; dèan milis.
sweetheart, s. leannan.
sweetish, adj. a lethchar milis.
sweetmeat, s. mìlsean, biadh-milis.
sweetness, s. mìlseachd, mìlsead.
swell, v. at, séid, bòc ; séid suas, bolg a mach ; meudaich, fàs dòmhail.
swell, s. at, séid, dòmhladas ; tonn, sumainn, sùmaid ; spailpire.
swelling, s. at, iongrachadh, éirigh, cnap, meall ; séideadh, bòcadh.
swelter, v. tiormach, crion, sgreag.
sweltry, adj. bruthainneach.
swerve, v. n. claon, fiar, aom ; lùb, rach a thaobh.
swift, adj. luath, siùbhlach, luainneach,

lùthmhor, grad, ealamh ; clis ; deas, èasgaidh.
swift, s. gobhlan-gainmhich.
swiftness, s. luathas, luas.
swig, v. òl gu lonach ; gabh balgam mór.
swill, v. òl gu lonach ; bogaich, fliuch ; cuir air mhisg, cuir thairis (le òl).
swill, s. sos, biadh mhuc.
swim, v. snàmh ; gluais gu fòil.
swim, s. balg-snàmha.
swimmer, s. snàmhaiche.
swimming, s. snàmh ; tuaineal.
swindle, v. a. meall, thoir an car á.
swindler, s. mealltair, cealgair.
swindling, s. mealltaireachd.
swine, s. muc ; mucan.
swineherd, s. mucair, buachaille mhuc.
swing, v. seòg, seòganaich, luaisg, tulg, udail, siùdain, siùd.
swing, s. greallag ; siùdan, tulgadh, seògan, luasgan, luasgadh ; ceadféin.
swinge, v. a. sgiùrs, buail, gabh air.
swinging, adj. air udal ; le sùrd ; an crochadh.
swingle, v. n. luaisg, seòg, siùd.
swinish, adj. mucanta ; salach.
switch, s. slat-chaoil, slatag.
switch, v. a. buail le slait, sgiùrs, tionndaidh dheth.
swivel, s. udalan, seòrsa gunna.
swobber, s. sguabadair.
swoon, v. n. rach an neul, rach am plathadh, rach am preathal, tiomtàisean, tioma-tàisean.
sword, s. claidheamh, slacan.
sword-fish, s. an brod-iasg.
sword-man, s. fear-claidheimh.
sword-player, s. basbair.
sycophant, s. sodalaiche.
sycophantic, adj. sodalach.

syllabic, syllabical, adj. lideachail, dùrdach, smideachail.
syllable, s. lideadh, dùrd, smid, siol.
syllabus, s. ceann-eagair.
syllogism, s. argamaid, molltair reusonachaidh.
sylph, s. sìthiche ; màileachan.
sylvan, adj. coillteach ; dubharach.
sylvan, s. dia-coille.
symbol, s. samhla, coltas, cruth.
symbolical, adj. samhlachail.
symbolise, v. samhlaich, riochdaich.
symmetrical, symmetral, adj. co-fhreagarrach, dealbhach, cumadail.
symmetry, s. co-fhreagarrachd ; cumadh, cumadalachd, cumaireachd.
sympathetic, adj. co-mhothachail ; truacanta, co-fhulangach, bàigheil.
sympathise, v. a. co-mhothaich, co-fhuiling, comh-fhairich.
sympathy, s. co-mhothachadh, co-fhulangas, truacantas, bàigh.
symphonious, adj. co-shéirmeach.
symphony, s. co-shéirm.
symptom, s. comharradh, coltas.
symptomic, adj. a' tachairt air uairibh.
synagogue, s. sinagog, tigh - aoraidh Iudhach.
syncope, s. neul ; giorrachadh facail.
synod, s. sionadh.
synodical, adj. a bhuineas do shionadh.
synonymous, adj. co-chiallach.
synonymy, s. co-fhacal.
synopsis, s. giorrachadh, suim.
syntax, s. cur ri chéile fhacal, riaghailtean sgrìobhaidh no labhairt canain.
synthesis, s. co-thàthadh.
syringe, s. steallaire, gunna-spùt.
system, s. riaghailt ; dòigh, seòl.
systematical, adj. riaghailteach.
systole, s. crìonadh cridhe ; giorrachadh air lideadh fada.

T

tabby, s. seòrsa sìoda.
tabby, adj. slatach ; stiallach.
tabefy, v. n. caith, searg, meath.
tabernacle, s. pàilliun, bùth.
tabernacle, v. n. pàilliunaich.
tabid, adj. éiteachail, gaoideil.
tablature, s. grinneas-balla.
table, s. bòrd ; clàr ; clàr-innseadh.
tablecloth, s. anart-bùird.
tableman, s. fear-feòirne.
tablet, s. bòrdan, clàran.
tabour, s. druma-bheag.
tabourine, s. druma-meòir.
tabular, adj. cèarnach, leacach.
tabulated, adj. còmhnard, leacach.

tache, s. cromag, lùb, dul.
tacit, adj. sàmhach, tosdach, balbh.
taciturnity, s. sàmhchair, tost.
tack, v. tàth, fuaigh ; tionndaidh.
tack, s. tacaid ; aonta ; siubhal luinge an aghaidh na gaoithe, gualainn seòlaidh.
tackle, s. acuinn, cungaidh, uidheam ; buill ; saighead.
tackling, s. acuinn-luinge, uidheam.
tactic, adj. a bhuineas do dh' òrdugh catha.
tactics, s. feachdoilean, cath - gbleus, rian-arm.
tadpole, s. ceann-phollag, ceann-simid.
taffeta, taffety, s. seòrsa sìoda.
tag, s. othaisg ; aigilean.

tag, *v. a.* tàth, ceangail, fuaigh.
tail, *s.* earball, earr, feaman, breaman, runnsan, rùmpull, ruinns, dronn.
tailor, *s.* tàillear.
taint, *v.* salaich, truaill, mill ; bi salach no truaillidh.
taint, *s.* ball, sal, salchar ; gaoid ; galar ; coire, truailleadh.
tainture, *s.* ball-dubh, salachadh.
take, *v.* gabh, glac, beir air, cuir làmh air ; cuir an làimh.
taking, *s.* glacadh, gabhail, trioblaid.
talbot, *s.* gaothar-ballach.
tale, *s.* sgeulachd, sgeul, ursgeul ; faoin-sgeul ; spleadh.
talebearer, *s.* fear-tuaileis ; breugaire, fear-geòlaim, gobaire.
talent, *s.* tàlann, suim àraidh airgid ; càil, ceud-fàth, comas, feart.
talisman, *s.* dealbh druidheachd.
talk, *v. n.* labhair, bruidhnich.
talk, *s.* labhairt, bruidheann, cainnt, brosgal, seanachas ; conaltradh ; iom-radh, falthunn ; gobais, goileam.
talkative, *adj.* bruidhneach, gobach, goileamach, còmhraiteach, beulach, beulchar ; brosgalach.
talkativeness, *s.* goileam, lonais, gobaire-achd, gobais, gusgul.
talker, *s.* goileamaiche, gobaire.
talking, *s.* còmhradh, cainnt, labhairt, bruidheann, conaltradh.
tall, *adj.* àrd, mór, fada.
tallage, *s.* càin, cìs.
tallness, *s.* àirde.
tallow, *s.* geir, ìgh, blonag.
tally, *v.* dèan freagarrach.
tally, *s.* cunntas-eag.
Talmud, Thalmud, *s.* leabhar beul-aithris nan Iùdhach.
talon, *s.* ionga, pliut, spuir, spor.
tamarind, *s.* meas Innseanach.
tambourine, *s.* druma bheag.
tame, *adj.* callda, callaidh ; ciùin ; soirbh ; soitheamh ; socrach ; soirbh ; ceannsaichte, solt.
tame, *v. a.* callaich, ciùinich ; ceannsaich, dèan soirbh, dèan soimeach.
tameness, *s.* callaidheachd, ciùine ; socair ; séimheachd, soirbhe.
tammy, taminy, *s.* stuth-cùrainn.
tamper, *v. a.* bean ri, bean do, meach-ranaich, cleachd ìnnleachdan.
tan, *v.* cairt ; cairtich.
tang, *s.* blas làidir, fuaim, guth.
tangible, *adj.* so-làimhseachail.
tangle, *v. a.* rib, cuir an sàs, cuir air aimhreidh, amhlaich.
tangle, *s.* slat-mhara, barr-staimh, liadhag.
tank, *s.* amar-uisge.
tankard, *s.* curraighean, soitheach-òil.
tanner, *s.* fear deasachaidh leathair.

tanpit, *s.* sloc-cartaidh.
tansy, *s.* lus-na-Fràing.
tantalise, *v. a.* sàraich miann, claoidh ; leamhaich.
tantamount, *adj.* co-ionann.
tantivy, *s., a., v.*, glaodh seilg, grad, ealamh, ruid, ruathar.
tap, *v. a.* maoth-bhuail, bean ; cnag ; bris air, fosgail, leig, tarruinn á.
tap, *s.* maothbhuille ; goc, pìoban-taosgaidh, pìob-tharruinn.
tape, *s.* stìom, crios caol, stiall.
taper, *adj.* barra-chaol.
taper, *v. n.* dèan bìorach ; fàs barra-chaol.
taper, *s.* dreòs, coinneal-chéire.
tapestry, *s.* obair-ghréis.
tapster, *s.* buidileir.
tar, *s.* bìth, teàrr ; seòladair.
tarantula, *s.* damhan-allaidh.
tardiness, *s.* athaiseachd.
tardy, *adj.* athaiseach, mall, màirnealach, slaodach, socrach, leisg.
tare, *s.* cogull, dìthean.
target, *s.* targaid, sgiath.
tariff, *s.* cuspunn ; cìs air ceannachd.
tarnish, *v.* salaich, mill ; fàs dubh.
tarpaulin, *s.* cainb-thearra, aodach can-bhais air a thearradh.
tarry, *v.* fuirich, stad, dèan moille.
tart, *adj.* garg, searbh, geur, goirt.
tart, *s.* pithean-meas.
tartan, *s.* breacan ; càdadh, catas.
tartar, *s.* tart-thìreach, Tartair ; sgrisleach, cruaidh-sgrath.
Tartary, *s.* an Tart-thìr.
tartness, *s.* gairgead, seirbhe.
task, *s.* obair r'a dèanamh ; gnìomh, dleasdanas.
tassel, *s.* cluigein, babaid, babag ; froin-ich ; lus-na-màighdinn.
taste, *v.* blais, gabh blas ; feuch.
taste, *s.* blas ; feuchainn, aithne.
tastefulness, *s.* blasdachd.
tasteless, *adj.* neo-bhlasta.
tastelessness, *s.* neo-bhlastachd.
taster, *s.* fear-blasaid ; còrn.
tatter, *v. a.* reub, srac, stròic.
tatter, *s.* luideag, stròic, cearb.
tatterdemalion, *s.* luinnsear, ruibealtaich, fear-luideagach.
tattle, *v. n.* dèan goileam, labhair gu gobach ; dèan briot, bi cabach.
tattle, *s.* goileam, briot, gobair, cabaich.
tattler, *s.* goileamaiche, gobaire.
tattoo, *s.* drumadh shaighdeirean dhach-aigh.
taunt, *v. a.* beum, sgeig, mag, dèan fochaid air ; maslaich.
taunt, *s.* beum, geur-fhacal, beurr-fhacal ; magadh, sgeig fanaid.
taunter, *s.* beumadair.
tavern, *s.* tigh-òsda.

taw, v. dèan leathar (le alm an àite cairt).

taw, s. cluiche air bhulagan.

tawdry, adj. fàoin-bhreagh.

tawny, adj. odhar, lachdunn, ciar.

tax, s. cìs-rìgh, càin.

tax, v. a. cìs, càin, leag cìs, cuir càin ; cronaich, coirich, cuir as leth.

taxable, adj. buailteach do chìs.

taxation, s. cìs-leagadh.

tea, s. tì.

teach, v. teagaisg, ionnsaich, oileanaich, foghluim, innis.

teachable, adj. so-theagasg.

teacher, s. oid-ionnsaich, fear-teagaisg, maighistear-sgoile.

Teague, s. Eireannach.

teal, s. crann-lach.

team, s. feun ; greigh, graidh.

tear, s. deur, boinne ; sracadh, reubadh, stroiceadh.

tear, v. srac, stròic, reub ; spìon, thoir as a chéile ; bi air bhoil.

tearful, adj. deurach, caointeach.

tease, v. a. cìr, spiol ; tlàm ; buair, faranaich, cuir dragh air.

teasel, s. lus-an fhùcadair.

teat, s. sine, deala.

technical, adj. ealanta.

techy, tetchy, adj. frionasach, dreamach, dodach, crosda, dìorrasach, gèarr, cas, cabhagach.

ted, v. a. sgaoil feur-saoidh.

tedious, adj. mall, màirnealach, maidheanach, seamsanach ; buan, sarachail.

teem, v. beir, thoir a mach ; bi torrach, bi làn, cuir thairis.

teemful, adj. torrach, sìolmhor.

teens, s. deugan ; eadar dà bliadhna dheug is fichead bliadhna.

tegument, s. rùsg, sgrath, cochull.

teint, s. dath, lì, neul.

telegraph, s. céin-chagair, fios dealain.

telescope, s. gloine-amhairc.

tell, v. innis, aithris, nochd, cuir an céill, foillsich ; abair, cunnt, àireamh ; thoir fios, cuir fios.

teller, s. fear-innsidh, cunntair airgid (am banca).

tell-tale, s. gobaire ; fear-aithris ; fear-tuaileis.

temerarious, adj. bras, dàna, cas.

temerity, s. braise, dànadas.

temper, v. a. ciùinich ; measarraich ; measgaich, coimeasg ; thoir gu staid fhreagarrach.

temper, s. nàdur, gné, càil-aignidh ; gean ; measarrachd, stuaim ; ciall ; faobhar ; fadhairt.

temperament, s. càil, càileachd, staid, nàdur.

temperance, s. measarrachd, stuamachd, foighidinn, ciùineas.

temperate, adj. measarra, stuama, foighidneach, ciùin ; macanta.

temperature, s. tomhas teas no fuachd.

tempest, s. doireann, doinionn, stoirm, ànradh, anuair, gailionn.

tempestuous, adj. ànrach, stoirmeil, gailbheach, doinionnach.

templar, s. stuidear-san-lagh.

temple, s. teampull ; leth-cheann.

temporal, adj. aimsireil ; talmhaidh.

temporality, s. séilbh-thalmhaidh.

temporals, s. pl. nithe saoghalta.

temporalty, s. an sluagh (eadar-dhealaichte o'n chléir).

temporary, adj. neo-mhaireann, neo-bhuan, car ùine, ré seal.

temporise, v. n. cuir dàil, maillich ; aontaich ; géill do na h-amannaibh, imich a réir na h-aimsir, bi seòlta, bi carach.

tempt, v. buair, meall ; brosnaich, feuch ri, thoir ionnsaigh ; tàlaidh.

temptation, s. buaireadh, mealladh ; cathachadh ; brosnachadh.

tempter, s. buaireadair ; mealltair ; an t-aibhisdear, an diabhol.

ten, s. deich, deichnear.

tenable, adj. so-ghleidheadh.

tenacious, adj. féin-bharaileach, dòchasach ; cumailteach, leanailteach, righinn ; spìocach, iongach, sporach, crìon, gann ; greimeil.

tenacity, s. leanailteachd, rìghneachd, cumailteachd, greimealtachd.

tenant, s. tuathanach ; fear-aonta.

tenantable, adj. so-àitichte.

tenantless, adj. neo-àitichte.

tenantry, s. tuathcheatharn, tuath (dùthcha).

tench, s. seòrsa éisg àibhne.

tend, v. gléidh, thoir an aire air, cum sùil air, fair, lean, treòraich ; aom ; siubhail a dh' ionnsaigh.

tendence, tendency, s. aomadh ; rùn, miann, seòladh, cùrsa.

tender, adj. maoth, anfhann, lag, fann, tais, bog ; caomh, suairce, còir, caoimhneil, tlusail, truacanta ; caoin, mìn, òg, fiùranta.

tender, v. a. tairg, nochd.

tender, s. tairgse ; long-fhreacadain.

tender-hearted, adj. teòchridheach, tiomchridheach, blàthchridheach, tlusail, truacanta.

tenderling, s. maoth-chabar, maoth-chreutar.

tenderness, s. anfhainneachd ; maoth-alachd ; ùiread ; caomhalachd, tlus, caoimhneas, bàigh, truacantas ; gràdh, gaol ; cùram.

tendinous, adj. féitheach.

tendon, s. féith-lùghaidh, rùdan.

tendril, s. maotharan, faillean.

tenebrious, *adj.* dorcha, guamach.
tenement, *s.* aitreabh, gabhail, etc.
tenet, *s.* barail-shuidhichte, beachd ; punc-chreidimh.
tennis, *s.* cluich-cneutaig.
tenon, *s.* làmh.
tenor, tenour, *s.* brìgh, bladh, ciall, seadh ; rùn ; staid, inbhe ; modh ; aomadh, claonadh, cùrsa ; fuaim ; guth cruaidh (seinn).
tense, *adj.* teann, rag, tarruinnte.
tenseness, *s.* teinnead, raigead.
tension, *s.* teannachadh, sìneadh, ragachadh, tarruinn.
tent, *s.* bùth, pubull, pàilliun.
tentation, *s.* deuchainn, buaireadh.
tented, *adj.* bùthach, pàilliunach.
tenter, *s.* cromag, dubhan.
tenth, *adj.* deicheamh.
tenth, *s.* deicheamh, deachamh.
tenthly, *adv.* 'san deicheamh àite.
tenuity, *s.* tainead ; caoile.
tenuous, *adj.* tana, caol, meanbh.
tenure, *s.* còir-fearainn, gabhaltas.
tepefaction, *s.* blàthachadh.
tepid, *adj.* meagh-bhlàth, flodach.
tepidity, *s.* meagh-bhlàthas.
tergeminous, *adj.* trì-fillte.
tergiversation, *s.* dol air ais ; cùl-cheumnachadh, cur dheth ; car ; caochlaideachd, luaineachas.
term, *s.* crìoch, iomall, ceann, ceann-criche ; facal, briathar ; ainm ; cùmhnant ; ùine, tìm ; àm suidhe mòid.
term, *v. a.* ainmich, gairm, goir.
termagant, *adj.* buaireasach.
termagant, *s.* ban-sglàmhrainn.
terminable, *adj.* so-chrìochnachadh.
terminate, *v.* crìochnaich.
termination, *s.* crìochnachadh.
termless, *adj.* neo-chrìochnach.
terrace, *s.* barrabhalla.
terraqueous, *adj.* bog, fliuch, le tighinn fodha (talamh).
terrene, terrestrial, *adj.* saoghalta.
terrestrial, terrestrious, *adj.* talmhaidh, saoghalach.
terrible, *adj.* eagalach, uabhasach, uabharra, fuathasach, oillteil.
terrier, *s.* abhac.
terrific, *adj.* eagalach, uabhasach, uabharra, fuathasach, oillteil.
terrify, *v. a.* cuir eagal no oillt air, geiltich.
territory, *s.* tìr, fearann, fonn, dùthaich, talamh.
terror, *s.* eagal, oillt, uabhas ; culaidh-eagail, cùis-eagail.
terse, *adj.* glan, cuimir, grinn, sgiobalta (cainnt).
tertian, *s.* fiabhras-critheanach.
test, *s.* deuchainn ; ceasnachadh.
testaceous, *adj.* sligeach.

testament, *s.* tiomnadh.
testamentary, *adj.* a réir tiomnaidh.
testator, *s.* fear-tiomnaidh, tiomnaidhear.
testatrix, *s.* bean-tiomnaidh.
tester, *s.* sè-sgillinn ; brat-leapa.
testicle, *s.* magairle, clach.
testify, *v.* thoir fianuis, dearbh.
testimonial, *s.* teisteanas.
testimony, *s.* fianais, dearbhadh.
testiness, *s.* frionasachd, frithearachd, crosdachd, caise.
testy, *adj.* frionasach, crosda, snoigeasach, dranndanach, feargach, cas.
tête-à-tête, *s.* còmhradh càirdeil, conaltradh uaigneach.
tether, *s.* teaghair, aghastar, taod.
tetter, *s.* frìd, miol-chrìon.
tewtaw, towtow, *v. a.* buail, bris.
text, *s.* ceann-teagaisg, bonn-teagasg.
textile, *adj.* mar aodach stuth air fhighe.
textuary, *adj.* a réir ceann-teagaisg.
texture, *s.* figheadaireachd, fighe.
than, *adv.* na.
thane, *s.* morair, iarla.
thank, *v. a.* thoir taing, thoir buidheachas.
thankful, *adj.* taingeil, buidheach.
thankfulness, *s.* taingealachd.
thankless, *adj.* mì-thaingeil.
thankoffering, *s.* iobairt-bhuidheachais, iobairt-thaingealachd.
thanks, *s.* buidheachas, taing.
thanksgiving, *s.* breith-buidheachas.
that, *dem. pron.* sin, ud ; *rel. pron.* a ; *conj.* gu, gum, gun, gur, chum ; *adv.* a chionn, do bhrìgh, a thaobh.
thatch, *s.* tugha.
thatch, *v. a.* tugh, dèan tughadh.
thatcher, *s.* tughadair.
thaw, *s.* aiteamh ; leaghadh.
thaw, *v.* leagh ; dèan aiteamh.
the, *article, definite,* an.
theatre, *s.* tigh-cluiche, tigh-cleasachd.
theatric, theatrical, *adj.* cluicheil.
thee, *pron. s.* thu, thusa.
theft, *s.* mèirle, goid, braide.
their, *pron. poss.* an, am.
theist, *s.* fear tha creidsinn gu bheil Dia ann.
them, *pron.* iad, iadsan.
theme, *s.* stéidh, cùis, aobhar.
themselves, *pron.* iad-féin.
then, *adv.* air sin, air an àm sin, an déigh sin ; uime sin, mata.
thence, *adv.* as an, as an àite sin, o 'n àm sin ; o sin ; air son sin.
thenceforth, *adv.* o 'n àm sin.
thenceforward, *adv.* o sin suas.
theocracy, *s.* Dia-riaghladh, riaghladh Dia mar rìgh (aimsireil).
theodolite, *s.* inneal tomhais (sapper).
theologian, *s.* diadhaire.
theological, *adj.* diadhaireach.

theologist, theologue, s. diadhaire.

theology, s. diadhaireachd.

theoretic, theoretical, adj. smuainteachail, beachdail, tionnsgalach.

theorist, s. beachdair.

theory, s. smuainteachadh, beachd ; dealbh-inntinn, tionnsgnadh.

there, adv. an sin, an sud, san àite sin ; do 'n àite sin.

thereabout, adv. air feadh sin, mun àite sin, mu sin ; mun tuairmeis sin, mu thimchioll.

thereafter, adv. an déidh sin.

thereat, adv. an sin, aige sin ; air son sin ; 'san àite sin.

thereby, adv. le sin, leis a' sin, teann air a sin, dlùth, am fagus.

therefore, adv. uime sin, air an aobhar sin, le sin, air son sin.

therefrom, adv. o sin, o sud, o so, uaithe sin, uaithe so.

therein, adv. an sin, ann, a stigh an sin.

thereinto, adv. a steach ann, ann.

thereof, adv. de sin, de so.

thereon, adv. air a sin, air so.

thereout, adv. á sin, a mach, as.

thereto, thereunto, adv. thuige sin, a chum sin, gu sin.

therewith, adv. leis a sin, air ball.

therewithal, adv. a bharr, a thuileadh, a thuileadh air sin.

thermometer, s. teasmheidh, inneal tomhais teas, no fuachd.

these, pron. pl. iad, iad so.

thesis, s. argumaid, argainn.

they, pron. iad, iadsan.

thick, adj. tiugh, garbh ; reamhar.

thick, s. tiuighead, tiughalachd.

thick, adv. gu tric, gu minig ; gu dlùth.

thicken, v. tiughaich ; dòmhlaich ; neartaich ; binndich, rìghnich ; fàs tiugh, fàs dòmhail.

thicket, s. doire, dlùthchoille, badan.

thickness, s. tiughad, tiuighead, dòmhlachd, gairbhe ; maoilead.

thickset, adj. dlùth air a chéile, dèanta ; tapaidh.

thief, s. mèirleach, gadaiche.

thief-catcher, s. maor-mhèirleach.

thieve, v. n. goid, dèan mèirle.

thievery, s. mèirle, braide, goid.

thievish, adj. bradach, tiolpach.

thigh, s. sliasaid, leis.

thill, s. cas-chùirn ; cas-charbaid.

thimble, s. meuran.

thin, adj. tana, caol ; fìnealta ; seang ; gann, tearc ; bochd.

thin, v. a. caolaich, tanaich.

thine, pron. do, d', leat-sa.

thing, s. ni, rud, cùis ; gnothach.

think, v. smaointich, saoil, baralaich, meòraich, measraich, meas, cuir an suim ; cuimhnich, thoir fainear.

thinking, s. smaointeachadh ; baralachadh ; saoilsinn.

thinness, s. tainead ; tearcad, teirce, teircead, ainmigead ; caoilead.

third, adj. an treas.

third, s. an trian, treas cuid.

thirdly, adv. anns an treas àite.

thirst, s. pathadh, tart ; iotadh ; tiormachd ; ro-mhiann, ro-dhéidh, rogheall, dian-thogradh.

thirst, v. bi pàiteach, bi tartmhor.

thirstiness, s. pàiteachd, tartmhorachd, iotmhorachd ; tiormachd.

thirsty, adj. pàiteach, tartmhor, iotmhor, tioram, déidheil.

thirteen, adj. trì-deug.

thirteenth, adj. an treasamh aon deug.

thirty, adj. deich ar fhichead.

this, pron. dem. so, an ni so.

thistle, s. cluaran, fòthannan.

thistly, adj. cluaranach.

thither, adv. thun a sin, an sin, gu ruig a sin, do 'n àite sin.

thitherto, adv. chum na crìche sin.

thitherward, adv. gu ruig a sin.

thong, s. iall, stiall, balt.

thoracic, adj. maothanach.

thorax, s. uchd, maothan, broilleach.

thorn, s. dris, droigheann.

thornback, thornbut, s. sgait.

thorny, adj. driseach, droighneach ; stobach ; deacair, draghail.

thorough, adj. iomlan, foirfe.

thorough, prep. trìd, tre, troimh.

thoroughfare, s. rathad, slighe.

thorough-paced, adj. coimhlionta.

those, pron. plural of that, iad sud, iad sin ; sud, sin, ud.

thou, the second pers. pron. tu, thu.

though, conj. ged ; gidheadh.

thought, s. smaoin, smuain, aire, beachd, barail, saoilsinn, seadh, suim, cùram ; dùil, dòchas, iomagain.

thoughtful, adj. smaointeachail, smuaireanach ; iomaguineach, cùramach, cumhneach, dìomhair.

thoughtless, adj. neo-smaointeachail, neo-chùramach, neo-fhaicilleach ; mishuimeil, faoin, baoth, gòrach.

thought-sick, adj. iargaineach.

thousand, adj. mìle, deich ceud.

thowl, s. urracag, cnag ; bac.

thraldom, s. tràillealachd, daorsa.

thrall, s. tràill ; tràilleachd, daorsa.

thrash, v. buail ; slacainn ; gréidh ; boicnich, dòrnaich, oibrich, saothraich ; sùist, buail arbhar.

thrasher, s. buailtear.

thrasonical, adj. ràiteachail ; bòsdal.

thread, s. snàthainn, toinntean.

thread, v. a. cuir snàthainn troimh.

threadbare, adj. lom, caithte.

threat, s. bagairt, maoidheadh.

threaten, *v. a.* bagair, maoidh.
threatening, *s.* bagradh, mùiseag.
threatful, *adj.* bagarrach.
three, *adj.* and *s.* trì, triùir.
threefold, *adj.* trì fillte.
threnody, *s.* cumha, dàn bròin.
threshold, *s.* stairseach.
thrice, *adv.* trì uairean.
thrift, *s.* deagh bhuil, sùrd.
thriftiness, *s.* fearas-tighe, dìchioll, cùram.
thriftless, *adj.* neo-shùrdail, neo-dhèan-adach ; stròdhail.
thrifty, *adj.* sùrdail ; gnìomhach, dèanad-ach, cùramach, gléidhteach.
thrill, *v.* cuir gaoir ann (le aoibhneas no uamhas), dean fuaim geur ; clisg, crith.
thrive, *v. n.* soirbhich ; cinn, fàs.
throat, *s.* sgòrnan, sgòrnach.
throb, *s.* plosg, plosgart, ospag.
throb, *v. n.* dèan plosgartaich, ploisg.
throe, *s.* ospag, uspag, éigin, gréim ; pian, saothair, frith-bhualadh, iodh (*pl.* iodhannan).
throne, *s.* cathair, rìgh-chathair.
throng, *s.* dòmhladas, mór-shluagh.
throng, *v. n.* dòmhlaich, teannaich ; mùch ; brùth, trus, cruinnich.
throstle, *s.* smeòrach.
throttle, *s.* sealbhan, sealghan.
throttle, *v. a.* tachd, mùch.
through, *prep.* troimh, tre, trìd.
throughout, *adv.* troimh ; o cheann gu ceann ; gu crìch, gu deireadh, anns gach àite, feagh gach àite.
throughly, *adv.* gu tur, gu h-uile.
throw, *v.* tilg ; thoir urchair, tilg sìos, leag ; tilg air falbh.
throwster, *s.* fear-tachrais sìoda.
thrum, *s.* fuidheag.
thrum, *v. a.* dèan dreangail chluiche.
thrush, *s.* smeòrach, céirseach, ciarsach.
thrust, *v.* sàth ; spàrr ; put, pùc, purr, dinn, fuadaich, thoir ionnsaigh ; tor-chuir, troimh-lot.
thrust, *s.* sàthadh, sparradh, pucadh, purradh, ionnsaigh ghuineach.
thumb, *s.* òrdag làimhe.
thumb, *v. a.* meuraich, làimhsich.
thump, *s.* buille, gleadhar, stràc.
thump, *v.* buail ; slacainn, dòrnaich.
thunder, *s.* tàirneanach.
thunder, *v.* tàirneanaich ; maoidh le briathraibh bòrb, dèan tàirnthoirm, no stairirich.
thunderbolt, *s.* beithir.
thunderclap, *s.* bradh torrainn.
thunderer, *s.* tàirneanaiche.
thunderous, *adj.* torrannach.
thunderstruck, *adj.* buailte le dealanach ; fo amhluadh ; air grad chlisgeadh ; fo oillt.
Thursday, *s.* Diar-daoin.
thus, *adv.* mar so, air an dòigh so.

thwack, *v. a.* buail, spuac, cnap.
thwack, *s.* buille, gleadhar, dòrn.
thwart, *adj.* crosgach, tarsainn ; trasta, crosta, reasgach, draghail.
thwart, *v.* cuir an aghaidh ; cuir tarsuing, thig tarsuing ; bi 'n aghaidh, seas an aghaidh.
thy, *pron.* of thee, do.
thyme, *s.* mionnt.
thyself, *pron. recip.* tu-féin, thu-féin, thu-fhéin, thusa-féin.
tiar, tiara, *s.* crùn, coron, fleasg.
tick, *s.* creideas ; earbsa ; feursanan, mial, mial - chon ; aodach - adhairt ; buille uaireadair.
ticket, *s.* diocaid.
tickle, *v.* diogail, ciogail ; taitinn.
ticklish, *adj.* ciogailteach ; deacair.
tiddle, *v. a.* dèan mùirn, dèan beadradh ; mùirnich, breug, tàlaidh.
tide, *s.* seòl-mara, làn-mara, sruth, buinne-shruth, àm, ùin, tràth.
tidewaiter, *s.* maor-cuspainn.
tidiness, *s.* sgioltachd, sgiobaltachd.
tidings, *s.* naidheachd ; sgeul.
tidy, *adj.* sgiolta, sgiobalta, cuimir.
tie, *v. a.* ceangail, snàim.
tie, *s.* ceangal, snàim, bann.
tier, *s.* sreath, breath, sreud.
tierce, *s.* togsaid ; trian.
tiff, *s.* deoch ; dod, snoigeas.
tiger, *s.* tìgeir, fiadhbheathach mór céin-thireach air chumadh cait.
tight, *adj.* teann ; gramail, cuimir.
tighten, *v. a.* teannaich, daingnich, dìonaich, dlùthaich.
tightness, *s.* teinnead, daingneachd.
tigress, *s.* tìgeir (boìrionn).
tile, *s.* criadhleac (air son tugha).
tiler, *s.* tughadair (chriadhleac).
tiling, *s.* tughadh chriadhleac.
till, *s.* cobhan airgid.
till, *prep.* gu, gus, gu ruig, thun.
till, *v. a.* àitich, treabh, ruamhair, oibrich, saothraich, saoithrich.
tillable, *adj.* so-àiteach.
tillage, *s.* treabhadh, àr.
tiller, *s.* treabhaiche ; ailm.
tilt, *s.* armchleas, bùth, sgàilean ; còmh-dach ; aomadh.
tilt, *v.* rach an dàil, ruith an aghaidh ; aom, còmhdaich, cathaich le cuinns-earaibh.
timber, *s.* fiodh ; maide.
timbered, *adj.* fiodha.
timbrel, *s.* tìompan.
time, *s.* ùin, àm, aimsir, uair, tràth, tìm.
time, *v. a.* cùm tìm, tràthaich.
timeful, *adj.* tìmeil, tràthail.
timekeeper, timepiece, *s.* uaireadair.
timeless, *adj.* neo-thìmeil.
timely, *adj.* an deagh àm ; ann an deagh thràth, tràthail.

time-serving, *adj.* leam-leat, gluasad réir barail dhaoine, déigheil air meas dhaoine.

timid, *adj.* gealtach, clisgeach.

timidity, timorousness, *s.* gealtachd, sgàthachd, cladhaireachd, meath-chridheachd, athadh.

timorous, *adj.* eagalach, sgàthach.

tin, *s.* staoin, iarunn-geal.

tincture, *s.* dath, lìth ; sùgh.

tincture, *v. a.* dath, cuir lìth air.

tinder, *s.* fadadh-spùinge, clach spor.

tine, *v. a.* fadaich, las, cuir ri theine.

tine, *s.* fiacail cléithe ; fiacail gràp.

tinge, *v. a.* dath, lìth ; salaich.

tingle, *v. n.* gliong, dèan gaoir, cluinn gaoir, cluinn fuaim, fairich crith-ghluasad.

tinker, *s.* cèard, dubhcheard.

tinkle, *v.* gliong, dèan gliongarsaich ; thoir gliong air.

tinman, *s.* cèard-staoine.

tinsel, *s.* faoin-bhreaghas.

tinsel, *adj.* basdalach, soillseach.

tint, *s.* dath, lìth, neul, tuar.

tiny, *adj.* crìon, meanbh, beag.

tip, *s.* bàrr, binnein, biod.

tip, *v. a.* cuir air ; rinn faom, cuir thairis.

tippet, *s.* éididh-muineil.

tipple, *v.* bi déidheil air òl, dèan pòit.

tippler, *s.* misgear, pòitear.

tipsy, *adj.* air mhisg, soganach, froganach, froidhleach.

tiptoe, *s.* corra-biod ; corra-cnàmh.

tire, *s.* sréad, sreath, breath ; aodach-cinn, àirneis, acuinn.

tire, *v.* sgìthich, sàraich, dèan sgìth ; fàs sgìth ; éid, sgeadaich.

tired, *adj.* sgìth, sgìthichte.

tiresome, *adj.* sgìtheachail, sàrachail.

tiring-room, *s.* seòmar-sgeadachaidh.

tissue, *s.* òrneileis.

tit, *s.* each beag ; eun beag ; leanabh bochd, nighean bheag.

tithe, *s.* deicheamh, deachamh ; cléir-chàin.

titheable, *adj.* buailteach do chàin.

tither, *s.* fear-trusaidh deachaimh.

titillation, *s.* giogal, ciogailt, diogladh, druideadh, drunnsail.

title, *s.* tiodal, ainm ; còir, dlighe.

title, *v. a.* ainmich, goir, tiodalaich.

title-page, *s.* clàr-ainme.

titmouse, tit, *s.* am mionnaran.

titter, *v. n.* dèan fa-ghàire.

tittle, *s.* pong, pung ; lideadh.

tittle-tattle, *s.* goileam ; lonais.

titubation, *s.* tuisleachadh.

titular, *adj.* ainmichte.

to, *prep.* do, a dh' ionnsaigh ; ri, ris ; gu ; gus ; chum, gu ruig ; thun ; sign of the *infinitive*, ag.

toad, *s.* a mhial-mhàgach, màgach.

toadstool, *s.* balg-losgainn.

toast, *s.* deoch-slàinte ; aran-ròsta.

toast, *v.* òl deoch-slàinte ; thoir deoch-slàinte ; caoinich.

tobacco, *s.* tombaca.

tobacconist, *s.* fear reic tombaca.

tod, *s.* ochd puint fhichead ollainn, tiùrr duillich.

toes, *s. pl.* òrdagan nan cas.

together, *adv.* le chéile, còmhla, còmh-luath, le chéile, cuideachd ; maraon ; gu léir.

toil, *v.* saoithrich, oibrich ; gabh saoth-air ; sgìthich, sàraich.

toil, *s.* saothair, obair ghoirt.

toilet, *s.* bòrd-sgeadachaidh.

toilsome, *adj.* saoithreachail, goirt.

toilsomeness, *s.* sgìos.

token, *s.* cuimhneachan, tabhartas, comh-arradh ; comhar.

told, *part.* dh' innis, thubhairt ; dh' aithris ; chùnnt.

tolerable, *adj.* so-ghiùlan ; meadhonach, an eatorras, cùibheasach ; mar sin fhéin ; mun làimh.

tolerance, *s.* fulangas.

tolerate, *v. a.* fuiling, ceadaich.

toleration, *s.* fulang, comas.

toll, *s.* càin, cìs ; buille cluig.

toll, *v. a.* buail clag.

tollbooth, *s.* toll-bùth, toll-dubh.

tomb, *s.* tuam, tùnga, tùngais, uaigh.

tombless, *adj.* gun uàigh ; gun leac.

tomboy, *s.* cailebhalach.

tombstone, *s.* tuamleac, leac-laighe, leac-lighidh, leac-uaghach.

tome, *s.* earrann-leabhair, leabhar.

ton, *s.* tunna, cuthrom dà mhìle punt ; nòs, àird' an fhasain.

tone, *s.* fonn, fuaim ; gleus.

tong, *s.* crambaid, teanga bucail.

tongs, *s.* clobha, teanchair.

tongue, *s.* teanga ; cainnt, cànan.

tongue, *v.* troid ; tachair ri.

tongue-tied, *adj.* manntach, gagach, glas-ghuib.

tonic, *adj.* gleusach, guthach.

tonnage, *s.* tunna-chìs.

tonsure, *s.* bearradh, lomairt.

too, *adv.* cuideachd, fòs, mar an ceudna ; tuilleadh 's a' chòir.

took, *pret.* of take, ghabh.

tool, *s.* ball-acfhuinn, inneal.

tooth, *s.* fiacail.

toothache, *s.* déideadh a' chnuimh.

toothless, *adj.* gun fhiaclan, bèarnach.

toothpick, *s.* bior-fhiacal.

toothsome, *adj.* deagh-bhlasda.

top, *s.* mullach, bàrr, binnein, bidein, uachdar, druim, bràighe, roinn, gille-mirean.

top, v. barraich; thoir barrachd, bearraich, còmhdaich mullach; thoir barrachd, thoir bàrr, smàl.

topaz, s. clach-bhuidhe phrìseil.

tope, v. n. pòit, bi air mhisg.

topee, s. pòitear, misgear.

topful, adj. lom-làn, dearr-làn.

topgallant, s. baideal.

tophet, s. ifrinn, an dùbhshloc.

topic, s. ceann-còmhraidh, stéidh labhairt.

top-knot, s. dos-cinn, dos mullaich.

topmost, adj. uachdrach, as àirde.

topography, s. tìr-chunntas, sgrìobhadh mu dhéidhinn àiteachan.

topsail, s. seòl-àrd, rò-sheòl, seòl mullaich.

top-stone, s. clach-mhullaich.

topsy-turvy, s. bun-os-cionn, trumach air thearrach.

tor, s. binnein, cruach.

torch, s. leus, dòrnleus.

torment, v. a. cràidh, pian, claoidh.

torment, s. cràdh, pian, pianadh, claoidh, àmhghar, dòrainn.

tormentil, s. cara-mhil-a'-choin, leanartach, cairt-bhlàir.

tormentor, s. claoidheadair, fear pianaidh fear-léiridh.

tornado, s. iomghaoth, gaoth-sgrios.

torpedo, s. orciasg, peilear spreadhaidh.

torpent, adj. marbh, marbhanach.

torpid, adj. gun chlì, gun chàil.

torpidness, s. marbhantachd.

torpor, s. marbhantachd, cion lùis.

torrent, s. beum-sléibhe, brasshruth, tuil, abhainn 'n a leum.

torrid, adj. teth, tioram, loisgeach.

tort, s. beud, dochan, cron.

tortile, tortive, adj. snìomhanach, dualach, faineach, cuairteagach.

tortoise, s. sligeanach.

tortuous, adj. snìomhach, lùbach, camacach.

torture, s. cràdh, pian, claoidh.

torture, v. a. cràidh, pian, claoidh, sàraich, léir, cuir gu cràdh.

Tory, s. tòrachd.

toss, v. luaisg, gluais, tilg, thoir urchair; tilg sios agus suas; tilg a null 's a nall; siùdain, seòganaich.

toss-pot, s. pòitear, misgear.

total, a., s., v. t., iomlan, uile; làn; àireamh.

totally, adv. gu léir.

totter, v. n. crithich, crith, turamanaich, bi corrach.

touch, s. beantainn; buntuinn; mothachadh, feuchainn, deuchainn; car; speal, greadan; suaip; buille; beagan, rudeigin; làimhseachadh.

touch, v. bean do, buin do, buin ri, cuir meur air, cuir corrag air, laimhsich; drùigh air.

touch-hole, s. toll-cluaise (gunna).

touching, adj. drùidhteach.

touchstone, s. clach-dearbhaidh.

touchwood, s. caisleach spuinge.

touchy, adj. crosda, frithearra, cas.

tough, adj. righinn; buan; teann.

toughen, v. n. rìghnich, dèan righinn.

toughness, s. rìghneachd, righnead.

tour, s. turas, cuairt, astar.

tourist, s. fear-turais, fear-cuairt.

tournament, s. cath-chleasachd, féill chluiche.

tourniquet, s. inneal air son casgadh fala.

touse, v. slaoid, tarruing; reub, spion.

tow, s. asgart, pab; barrach.

tow, v. a. slaoid (tre uisge).

toward, adj. ullamh, aontachail.

toward, adv. fagus, air aghaidh, deas.

towards, prep. chum; mu thimchioll.

towel, s. tubhailte, searadair.

tower, s. tùr, tòr, dùn, turaid; caisteal; daingneach; currac-àrd.

tower, v. n. itealaich gu h-àrd.

towery, adj. tùrach, turaideach.

town, s. baile-mór; baile-margaidh.

town-clerk, s. cléireach baile.

townsman, s. fear a mhuinntir baile.

toxic, adj. nimheach, puinnseanta.

toy, s. àilleagan, déideag.

toy, v. n. cluich; dèan mire, dèan sùgradh, dèan beadradh.

trace, v. a. lorgaich; rach air tòir; comharraich a mach.

tracer, s. lorgair, cù-luirg.

traces, s. beairtiall, beairt-dhreollaig, beairt-tharuing, beairt-shlaoid.

track, s. lorg, aile, frithrathad, casan.

trackless, adj. gun slighe, gun cheum.

tract, s. dùthaich; cùrsa; leabhran.

tractable, adj. soitheamh, soirbh; sotheagasg; aontachail, ciùin.

tractableness, s. soimeachas; socair.

tractile, adj. a ghabhas bualadh a mach, so-bhualadh a mach.

trade, s. cèaird; ealain; co-cheannachd, malairt; cleachdadh, gnàths.

trade, v. dèan ceannachd; malartaich.

trader, s. fear-malairt.

tradesman, s. fear-ceirde, fear-bùth.

tradition, s. beul-aithris, beul-oideas.

traditional, traditionary, adj. beul-aithriseach, beul-iomraidheach.

traduce, v. a. cul-chàin; dèan tarcuis.

traducement, s. cùl-chaineadh, tàir.

traducer, s. fear cùl-chàinidh.

traduction, s. tarruing; aithris.

traffic, s. ceannachd, bathar, othail sràide, dol is tighinn (treang).

trafficker, s. fear-malairt.

tragedian, s. sgrìobhadair bròin-chluich, cleasaiche bròin-chluich.

tragedy, s. bròn-chluich.

tragic, tragical, adj. brònach.

tragi-comedy, s. cluich bròin is aoibhneis, cluich bròin is aighir.

trail, v. slaoid, tarruing ; lorgaich.

trail, s. lorg ; sguain, slaod, earball (rionnaig), rathad (troimh shneachda).

train, v. a. tarruinn ; meall ; tog, àraich ; teagaisg, ionnsaich ; cleachd.

train, s. mealladh ; cuideach, buidheann ; slaod, earball, iomall ; òrdugh, cùrsa ; luchd-leanmhainn.

train-bands, s. dìon-fheachd.

train-oil, s. ola muice-mara.

trait, s. buille ; tuar, suaip, cliù, buadh (an cliù neach).

traitor, s. fear-brathaidh.

traitorly, traitorous, adj. brathach ; feall-tach, slaoighteil.

traitress, s. ban-bhrathadair.

trammel, s. lìon ; ribe ; cuibhreach.

trammel, v. a. glac, rib ; grab, stad.

trample, v. a. saltair, breab.

trance, transe, s. neul, plathadh.

tranced, adj. ann an neul.

tranquil, adj. sàmhach, sìochail, ciùin, fèitheil, sèimh, stòlta.

tranquillise, v. sìthich, ciùinich.

tranquillity, s. sàmhchair, ciùineas.

transact, v. a. dèan gnothach ; cuir air adhart, cuir gu dòigh.

transaction, s. gnothach, gnìomh.

transcend, v. a. rach thairis, thoir barrachd, thoir barr.

transcendence, transcendency, s. barrachd, barrachas, barrmhaise.

transcendent, adj. barrachdail.

transcribe, v. a. ath-sgrìobh.

transcriber, s. ath-sgrìobhair.

transcript, s. ath-sgrìobhadh.

transcription, s. athsgrìobhadh.

transfer, v. a. thoir thairis ; reic.

transfer, s. malairt ; toirt thairis.

transferable, adj. so-thoirt thairis.

transfiguration, s. cruth - chaochladh, cruth-atharrachadh.

transfigure, v. a. cruth-atharraich.

transfix, v. a. troimh-lot, sàth.

transform, v. a. cruth-atharraich.

transformation, s. cruth-atharrachadh, cruth-chaochladh.

transfuse, v. a. coimeasg, dòirt a steach.

transgress, v. rach thairis ; ciontaich.

transgression, s. cionta, easantas.

transgressive, adj. ciontach.

transgressor, s. ciontach, peacach.

transient, adj. diombuan, neo-mhaireann, caochlaideach.

transientness, s. diombuanas.

transit, s. dol thairis, dol tarsuing.

transition, s. imeachd, caochla.

transitory, adj. diombuan, caochlaideach, neo-mhaireann.

translate, v. a. eadar-theangaich ; athar-raich, tionndaidh.

translation, s. eadar-theangachadh.

translator, s. eadar-theangair.

translucency, s. trìd-shoillseachd.

translucid, translucent, s. trìdshoilleir, tre-shoillseach, glan.

transmarine, adj. thall thar chuan.

transmigrate, v. a. rach o thìr gu tìr.

transmigration, s. cian-imrich.

transmission, s. cur o àite gu àite.

transmissive, adj. air a chur sios o neach gu neach.

transmit, v. a. cuir o àite gu àite.

transmutable, adj. mùthach.

transmutation, s. tur-chaochladh.

transmute, v. a. tur-chaochail.

transom, s. tarsannan, rùngas.

transparency, s. trìd-shoillse, glaine.

transparent, adj. trìd-shoilleir, glan.

transpierce, v. a. troimh-shàth.

transpire, v. bris a mach, thig am follais, tachair.

transplace, v. a. atharraich, cuir as àite, cuir do àite eile.

transplant, v. a. ath-shuidhich, suidhich an àite eile.

transport, v. a. thoir o àite gu àite ; giùlain, iomchair, fògair, sgiùrs.

transport, s. long-ghiùlan ; iomchar, buaireadh ; aoibhneas, fògarach.

transportation, s. fògradh.

transposal, s. atharrachadh.

transpose, v. a. atharraich.

transposition, s. atharrachadh.

transubstantiate, v. a. brìgh-atharraich, brìgh-mhùth.

transubstantiation, s. brìgh-atharrachadh ; an teagasg gu bheil fìor chorp Chriosd anns an t-sàcramaid.

transude, v. n. rach seachad an ceò.

transverse, v. a. mùth ; caochail.

transverse, adj. crasgach, trasta.

transversely, adv. gu crasgach.

trap, s. ribe, painntear.

trap, v. a. rib, glac ; cuir an sàs.

trap-door, s. dorus-dìomhair.

trappings, s. rìmheadh ; briaghas, àirneis eich.

trash, s. ni gun fhiù ; trusdaireachd.

trashy, adj. suarach, gun fhiù.

travail, v. sàraich, claoidh, pian, sgìthich ; bi ri saothair chloinne.

travail, s. saothair, éigin, obair, sgìtheach-adh ; saothair chloinne.

travel, v. rach air thuras, triall, siubhail thairis air ; falbh, gluais, imich ; saothraich, saoithrich.

travel, s. turas, taisdeal, siubhal.

traveller, s. fear turais, fear-astair, fear-siubhail, coisiche, taisdealaiche, fear gabhail an rathaid.

travelling, s. siubhal, imeachd.

traverse, adj. tarsainn, fiar.

traverse, *v.* seòl tarsaing, siubhail, triall ; coisich, imich ; grab, bac ; cuir crasgach, rannsaich.
travesty, *adj.* neònach ; baoth, atharrais.
tray, *s.* sgàl, sgùil ; losaid.
treacherous, *adj.* mealltach.
treachery, *s.* ceilg, brath, foill.
treacle, *s.* dràbhag siùcair.
tread, *v.* saltair, ceumnaich ; cliath.
tread, *s.* ceum ; slighe, rathad.
treadles, *s.* casan-beaga beart breabadair, sgimileirean.
treason, *s.* ar-a-mach, ceannairc.
treasonable, *adj.* foilleil, brath rìoghachd.
treasure, *s.* ionmhas, maoin.
treasure, *v. a.* taisg, cuir seachad.
treasurer, *s.* fear-coimheid ionmhais.
treasury, *s.* ionad an ionmhais.
treat, *v.* socraich, cuir gu dòigh ; labhair air ; làimhsich ; gnàthaich ; gabh ri ; cùmhnantaich ; thoir cuirm.
treat, *s.* fleagh, cuirm, féisd.
treatise, *s.* seanachas, sgrìobhte.
treatment, *s.* gnàthachadh.
treaty, *s.* bann, cùmhnant ; còrdadh (eadar rìoghachdan).
treble, *adj.* trì-fillte ; binn, cruaidh.
tree, *s.* craobh, crann, dos.
trefoil, *s.* an trì-bhileach.
trellis, *s.* obair-chliath.
tremble, *v. n.* crith-criothnaich.
trembling, *adj.* critheanach.
trembling, *s.* criothnachadh.
tremendous, *adj.* fuathasach, uamhasach, eagalach, uamharra, oillteil.
tremor, *s.* ballchrith.
tremulous, *adj.* critheanach, eagalach.
tren, *s.* morghath éisg.
trench, *v. a.* cladhaich, claisich.
trench, *s.* clais-bhlàir, sloc, dìg.
trencher, *s.* trinnsear, ceannbheart (oileanaich).
trepan, *v. a.* rib, glac, meall.
trepan, *s.* boireal ; ribe, painntear.
trepidation, *s.* geilt-chrith.
trespass, *v. n.* ciontaich, peacaich.
trespass, *s.* cionta, peacadh, aingaidheachd, coire, easantas, briseadh-riaghailte, aindlighe.
tress, *s.* caisreag, ciabhag, bachlag, camag, dual, flann.
tressy, *adj.* bachlagach, camagach, caisreagach, ciabhagach, dualach.
trestle, tressel, *s.* sorachan.
tret, *s.* ludhaigeadh ; leigeadh leis (an tomhais badhair).
trevet, *s.* trìchasach.
trey, *s.* an treas ball do chairtean no do dhìsnean.
triad, *s.* triùir ; triear.
trial, *s.* deuchainn ; dearbhadh ; spàirn, strìth ; buaireadh ; cùis-lagha.
triangle, trigon, *s.* trìchearnag.

triangular, *adj.* trì-chearneach.
tribe, *s.* treubh, fine, cinneadh, clann, teaghlach, sliochd, sìol ; seòrsa, pòr.
tribulation, *s.* trioblaid, àmhghar, teinn, teanntachd, anshocair, éigin.
tribunal, *s.* cathair-breitheanais cùirt-lagha, mòd-ceartais.
tribune, *s.* ceann-feadhna Ròmanach.
tributary, *adj.* fo cheannsal, fo chìs ; *s.* fo-abhainn, allt a' ruith a dh'abhainn.
tribute, *s.* cìs, càin ; ùmhlachd.
trice, *s.* tiota ; sealan ; gradag.
trick, *s.* car, cleas, cuilbheart.
trick, *v.* meall, thoir an car á ; sgeadaich, uidheamaich.
tricking, *s.* sgeadachadh, caradh.
trickle, *v. n.* sil, sruth, ruith.
trident, *s.* muirghe ; coron-meurach.
triduan, *adj.* gach treas latha.
triennial, *adj.* gach treas bliadhna.
trifle, *v. n.* dèan bàbhdaireachd, caith aimsir gu diomhain.
trifle, *s.* faoineas ; rud beag, ni gun fhiù, ni suarach.
trifler, *s.* bàbhdaire.
trifling, *adj.* bàbhdach, gun fhiù ; féileaganaich, beag, crion, suarach.
trifoliate, *adj.* trì-dhuilleach.
trigger, *s.* iarunn-leigidh, òrd gunna.
trigon, *s.* trì-shlisneag.
trigonal, *adj.* trì-oisneach.
trilateral, *adj.* trì-shlisneach.
trill, *s.* caireall, crith, crithcheol.
trim, *v.* uidheamaich, gleus, deasaich, cuir gu dòigh ; cuir an òrdugh ; càirich, snas, ceartaich.
trim, *s.* uidheam, gleus, òrdugh.
trim, *adj.* glan, sgiobalta, speisealta, sgeinmeil ; cuimir, cuanta.
trimmer, *s.* fear leam-leat ; geinn.
trimming, *s.* sgiamh, breaghas.
Trinity, *s.* An Trianaid.
trinket, *s.* àilleagan, seud.
trio, *s.* ceòl-triùir, triùir.
trip, *v.* cuir camacag ; cuir bacag, tuislich, sleamhnaich ; gabh ceum ; rach am mearachd.
trip, *s.* bacag ; cas - bhacaig ; tuisleadh, mearachd ; turas beag, astaran.
tripartite, *adj.* an trì earrannaibh.
tripe, *s.* maodal ; grealach.
triphthong, *s.* trifhoghair.
triple, *adj.* trì-fillte.
triplet, *s.* trì de aon seòrsa.
triplicate, *adj.* trìoblaichte.
tripod, *s.* stòl trìchasach.
tripoli, *s.* pronnsgal chlach.
tripping, *adj.* iullagach, luath.
trisyllable, *s.* trìshiola.
trite, *adj.* as an fhasan ; caithte.
tritheism, *s.* aoradh trì diathan.
triturable, *adj.* so-phronnadh.
trituration, *s.* pronnadh.

triumph, s. buaidh-chaithream ; glòir ; buaidh ; gàirdeachas.

triumph, v. dèan buaidh-chaithream, dèan luathghàir ; faigh buaidh ; giùlain buaidh gu tarcuiseach.

triumphal, triumphant, adj. buadhach, buadhmhor ; caithreamach.

triumvirate, s. riaghladh triùir.

triune, adj. tri-aon, mar an trionaid.

trivet, s. trìchasach.

trivial, adj. faoin ; suarrach ; gun fhiù, gun seadh, gun suim, coitcheann.

trod, trodden, part. pass. of to tread, saltairt fo chasaibh.

troll, v. ruidhil ; ruith mun cuairt ; dèan iasgach gheadas ; cuir air falbh gu siùbhlach.

trollop, s. draip, sgliùrach, botrumaid, dubhchaile, trusdar caile.

troop, v. n. ruith am buidheann ; triall le cabhaig.

troop, s. buidheann, bannal, cuideachd ; trùp, marc-shluagh.

trooper, s. trùpair, saighdear-eich.

trope, s. mùthadh seadh facail.

trophied, adj. cosgarra ; sgeadaichte le buaidh-shuaicheantais.

trophy, s. craobh-chosgair, creach buadha.

tropic, s. an crios as fhaisge air crios-meadhoin na talmhainn (tuath is deas).

tropical, adj. samhlachail.

trot, v. trot ; cuir na throtan.

trot, s. trot, trotail, trotan.

troth, s. creideas ; fìrinn, briathar.

trotter, s. cas caorach.

trouble, s. buaireas, àimhreite ; dragh, saothair ; farran ; éigin, airc, cruaidh-chas, teanntachd, teinn ; anshocair, àmhghar, truaighe, trioblaid.

trouble, v. a. buair ; cuir dragh air, farranaich, cuir gu trioblaid, cuir thar a chéile, pian.

troublesome, adj. draghail ; buaireasach, àimhreiteach, trioblaideach.

troublesomeness, s. draghalachd.

trough, s. amar, clàr.

trounce, v. a. cuir gu taic ; peanasaich ; lunndrainn, buail, dòrnaich.

trousers, s. triubhas, briogais.

trout, s. breac, brican, dubhbreac.

trow, v. n. saoil, smuainich.

trowel, s. sgreadhal, trùghan, spainn-aoil.

truant, v. lùrdan ; sgoilear a sheachnas an sgoil.

truant, adj. màirnealach.

truce, s. fosadh-còmhraig ; anail.

trucidation, s. marbhadh, milleadh.

truck, v. n. dèan malairt, iomlaidich.

truckle, v. n. strìochd, lùb, crùb.

truculent, adj. borb, garg, fiadhaich, gruamach ; fuilteach.

trudge, v. n. triall air éigin.

true, adj. fìrinneach, fìor, dìleas, tréidhireach ; ceart, dligheach, còir ; deimhinn, cinnteach, seasmhach.

true-bred, adj. de 'n fhìor bhrid.

true-hearted, adj. ionraic, dìleas.

trueness, s. fìrinn, ionracas.

true-penny, s. fear-cinnteach, ceart.

trull, s. strìopach bhochd.

truly, adv. gu fìrinneach, gu dearbh, gu deimhinn ; a cheart da-rìreadh.

trump, s. trompaid ; buadhchairt.

trumpery, s. faoineas ; faoinchainnt.

trumpet, s. tròmbaid, triùmpaid, buabhall, stoc.

trumpet, v. a. gairm, foillsich, dèan aithnichte ; séid le tròmbaid.

trumpeter, s. tròmbaidear.

truncheon, s. siolpan ; bata.

trundle, s. ruithlean, roilean.

trundle, v. n. ruithil, roill ; theirig car mu char, car air char.

trunk, s. stoc, bun-craoibhe ; cobhan, ciste, gnos, sròn ; corp, còm.

trunnion, s. deilg-taoibh gunna-móir.

truss, s. crios trusaidh, braghairt, buinn-seal ; muillean.

truss, v. a. trus, ceangail.

trust, s. earbsa, dòchas, creideas.

trust, v. earb, cuir dòchas ann, cuir muinghinn ann, creid, thoir creideas do, bi earbsach, bi cinnteach ; bi 'n dòchas, bi 'n dùil.

trustee, s. ceileadair, fear-cùraim, fear-urrais.

trusty, adj. dìleas, earbsach, ionraic, fìrinneach, fìor, diongmhalta, daingeann, seasmhach, làidir.

truth, s. fìrinn ; ionracas.

try, v. feuch, feuch ri ; thoir ionnsaigh, cuir deuchainn air ; dearbh, cuir gu deuchainn, ceasnaich, rannsaich, sgrùd fidir.

tub, s. ballan, cùdainn, tuba.

tube, s. pìob, feadan.

tubercle, s. plucan, guirean, buicean, a' chaitheamh.

tuberous, adj. plucanach, buiceanach.

tubular, tubulated, tubulous, adj. pìobach, pìobanach, feadanach.

tuck, s. claidheamh-caol ; eangach.

tuck, v. a. trus, criosraich.

tucker, s. eideadh-uchd mnà.

Tuesday, s. Di-Màirt.

tuft, s. dos, dosan, babag, toipean, tolman, toman, bad, gasan, gasgan, badan, doire, garan.

tufty, adj. dosach, dosrach ; topanach, badanach ; gasganach ; tolmanach, tomanach, doireach.

tug, v. spiol, spìon, tarruing, dragh, slaoid ; gleachd, dèan strìth.

tug, s. spioladh, spionadh, spiodadh,

draghadh, tarruing, slaodadh, dubadh, long-shlaodaidh.

tuition, *s.* ionnsachadh, teagasg.

tumble, *v.* tuit, tuislich ; tilg sios, cuir car.

tumble, *s.* tuiteam, leagadh.

tumbler, *s.* cleasaiche-car ; còrn.

tumbrel, *s.* cairt-innearach.

tumefaction, *s.* at, bòcadh.

tumefy, *v. n.* at, bòc, séid suas.

tumid, *adj.* atmhor ; làn, bòsdail, mórchuiseach, spagluinneach.

tumorous, *adj.* bòcach ; spaideil, spagluinneach, mórchùiseach.

tumour, *s.* at ; iongrachadh, màm, meall ; spagluinn ; mórchuis.

tumult, *s.* iorghuill, sabaid, aimhreite, buaireas, mi-riaghailt.

tumultuary, *adj.* iorghuilleach, àimhreiteach, sabaideach, mì - riaghailteach, troimh-chéile.

tumultuous, *adj.* iorghuilleach, sabaideach, àimhreiteach, buaireasach, mìriaghailteach.

tun, *s.* tunna.

tune, *s.* port, fonn, séis.

tune, *v. a.* gleus, cuir am fonn.

tuneful, *adj.* fonnmhor, binn.

tuneless, *adj.* neo-fhonnmhor, neo-bhinn, neo-ghleusta.

tuner, *s.* fear-gleusaidh.

tunic, *s.* casag.

tunnage, *s.* tunna-chìs ; tomhas.

tunnel, *s.* luidheir ; lìonadair, rathad fo thalamh, toll (fo thalamh).

tup, *s.* reithe ; *v.* put (mar ni reithe).

turban, *s.* ceann-éideadh Turcach.

turbary, *s.* còir moinntich.

turbid, *adj.* tiugh, ruaimleach, neoshoilleir, thar a chéile.

turbidness, *s.* ruaimleachd.

turbinated, *adj.* toinnte, snìomhte.

turbot, *s.* am bradan-leathann, turbaid.

turbulence, *s.* buaireas ; mì-riaghailt, àimhreite, troimh-chéile.

turbulent, *adj.* buaireasach.

turd, *s.* cac, inneir, aolach, salachar.

turf, *s.* sgroth, sgràth ; tota, fàl, fòd.

turfy, *adv.* fàileanach, gòrm.

turgent, *adj.* làn, atmhor ; gaothar.

turgid, *adj.* gaothar ; atmhor.

Turk, *s.* Turcach ; *adj.* Turcach.

turkey, *s.* eun-Fràngach.

turmeric, *s.* dath-buidhe.

turmoil, *v. tr.* bi cruaidh shaothair ; bi sgìth, bi sàraichte ; *s.* ùparaid, triomh, chéile.

turn, *s.* tionndadh ; lùb, car ; cuairt ; atharrachadh ; pilleadh, pilltinn ; grathunn, tacan ; gnothach cùis ; tùrn, gniomh ; faothachadh ; aomadh, claonadh.

turn, *v.* pill, tionndaidh ; iompaich ; lùb ; cuir mun cuairt, cuir a cheann

fodha, fàs, cinn ; dealbh, cùm ; mùth, atharraich, thig air t' ais.

turncoat, *s.* fear-leam-leat.

turner, *s.* tuairnear.

turning, *s.* tionndadh, car, lùb.

turnip, *s.* snèap, nèap, nèip.

turnpike, *s.* chachaileith-cìse.

turnsole, *s.* an grain-ròs.

turpentine, *s.* bàn-bhìth giubhais.

turpitude, *s.* gràinealachd, olcas.

turret, *s.* turait ; binnein ; baideal.

turtle, *s.* calman, turtur.

tush ! *interj.* bi d' thosd ! uist ! eist !

tusk, *s.* tosg, sgor-fhiacail.

tut ! *interj.* tut ! h-ud !

tutelage, *s.* oideas ; togail suas.

tutelar, tutelary, *adj.* dìonach.

tutor, *s.* oide-ionnsaich ; tùitear.

tutorage, *s.* uachdranachd fir-foghluim, ionnsachadh ; foghlum.

tuz, tuzz, *s.* ciabhag, badan fuilt.

twain, *adj.* dithis, càraid.

twang, *s.* srann ; fuaim gheur.

twang, *v. n.* dèan srann.

twattle, *v. n.* dèan gobaireachd.

tweak, *v. a.* gòmagaich, teannaich.

tweedle, *v. a.* meuraich gu tlà.

tweezers, *s.* greimiche.

twelfth, *adj.* an dara deug.

twelve, *adj. and s.* a dhà dheug.

twentieth, *adj.* am ficheadamh.

twenty, *adj. and s.* fichead.

twice, *adv.* dà uair ; dà chuairt.

twig, *s.* faillean, maothan, gineag.

twilight, *s.* eadarra-sholus, camhanaich, camhanach, chamh-fhàir.

twilight, *adj.* dorcha, dubharach.

twin, *s.* lethaon.

twine, *v. a.* toinn, dual, figh, suainn.

twine, *s.* sgéinnidh ; toinntean ; toinneamh, sniamh.

twinge, *v. a.* fàisg, toinn, cràidh.

twinkle, *v. n.* priob ; boillsg.

twinkling, *s.* priobadh ; crith-bhoillsge, dealradh, plathadh ; gliosgardaich.

twinling, *s.* lethaon.

twirl, *v. a.* ruidhil mun cuairt.

twirl, *s.* ruidhle, cuartalan.

twist, *v. n.* toinn, toinneamh, snìomh, figh, dualaich, cuir an amladh a chéile, bi sniomhte, bi toinnte.

twist, *s.* toinneamh, snìomh, car ; toinntean, sreang, snàthain.

twister, *s.* fear-toinneimh, sniomhaire, sniomhadair ; corra-shiamain.

twisting, *s.* toinneamh, sniomh.

twit, *v. a.* beum ; maoidh, sgeig, mag, fochaidich, dèan fanaid.

twitch, *s.* spioladh ; spìonadh ; guin.

twitch, *v. a.* spiol, spion, pioc ; biorg.

twitter, *v. n.* dèan diorrasan ; sitrich, truitrich, crith ; sgeig, mag, dèan fàite, dèan snodha.

twitter, *s.* diorrasan ; ceilearadh.
two, *adj.* a dhà, dà, dithis ; càraid.
two-fold, *adj.* dà-fhillte.
two-handed, *adj.* dà-làmhach.
twopence, *s.* dà-sgilling.
tympanum, *s.* druma (na cluaise).
type, *s.* samhla, comhar ; clò-litir.
typical, *adj.* samhlachail.
typify, *v. a.* samhlaich.

typographer, *s.* clò-bhuailtear.
typographical, *adj.* samhlachail.
typography, *s.* clò-bhualadh.
tyrannic, tyrannical, *adj.* àintighearnail ; smachdail, ceannasach ; ainneartach, sàrachail ; borb.
tyrannise, *v. a.* bi aintighearnail.
tyranny, *s.* àintighearnas.
tyro, *s.* foghlumaiche.

U

uberty, *s.* pailteas, tairbhe.
ubiquitary, *adj.* uile-làthaireach.
ubiquity, *s.* uile-làthaireachd.
udder, *s.* ùgh, ùgh mairt.
ugliness, *s.* duaichneachd.
ugly, *adj.* grannda, duaichnidh.
ulcer, *s.* neasgaid, leannachadh ; iongrachadh ; bolg, leus, bucaid, spucaid, guirean, creuchd.
ulcerate, *v.* iongraich, leannaich.
ulceration, *s.* iongrachadh, creuchd.
ulcerous, *adj.* neasgaideach ; leannachail, siteach, creuchdach.
uliginous, *adj.* féitheach, fliuch, bog, làthachail, làbanach, clàbarach.
ultimate, *adj.* deireannach.
ultramarine, *adj.* allmharrach.
ultramarine, *s.* dath gorm maiseach.
umber, *s.* dath buidhe ; seòrs éisg.
umbles, *s.* grealach féidh.
umbo, *s.* cop, cnap-sgéithe.
umbrage, *s.* sgàile, dubhar, dùbhradh, duibhre ; leithsgeul ; amharus, umh-aill ; corraich, fearg ; mìothlachd.
umbrageous, umbrose, *adj.* sgaileach, dubharach, dorch.
umbrella, *s.* sgàilean.
umpire, *s.* breitheamh ; fear-breithe.
un, *neg. part.* neo ; mi, eu, as, an, ana, do.
unabashed, *adj.* neo-nàraichte.
unable, *adj.* neo-chomasach.
unacceptable, *adj.* neo-thaitneach.
unaccompanied, *adj.* aonarach.
unaccomplished, *adj.* neo-chrìochnaichte, neo-oileanaichte, neo-ionnsaichte.
unaccountable, *adj.* do-aithriseach, do-luaidh ; iongantach, neònach, neo-fhreagarrach.
unaccustomed, *adj.* neo-chleachdte.
unacquainted, *adj.* aineolach.
unactive, *adj.* neo-theòma.
unadmired, *adj.* neo-urramaichte.
unadorned, *adj.* neo-sgeadaichte.
unadvised, *adj.* neo-chomhairlichte.
unaffected, *adj.* fìor, ionraic, neo-chealgach ; còir ; sìmplidh.
unaffecting, *adj.* neo-dhrùidhteach.
unaided, *adj.* neo-chuidichte.

unalienable, *adj.* neo-bhuileachail, nach gabh sgaradh.
unallied, *adj.* neo-chàirdeach.
unalterable, *adj.* neo-chaochlaideach ; diongalta, maireann.
unaltered, *adj.* neo-atharraichte.
unamendable, *adj.* do-leasachail.
unamiable, *adj.* neo - chiatach, mì-thlachdmhor.
unanimity, *s.* aon-inntinn.
unanimous, *adj.* aon-inntinneach, aon-sgeulach.
unanswerable, *adj.* do-fhreagairteach.
unappalled, *adj.* neo-sgàthach.
unappeasable, *adj.* nach gabh riarachadh.
unapprehensive, *adj.* gun amharus.
unapproached, *adj.* do-ruigheachdach.
unapt, *adj.* neo-fhreagarrach.
unaptness, *s.* neo-fhreagarrachd.
unargued, *adj.* neo-chonnsaichte.
unarmed, *adj.* neo-armaichte.
unartful, *adj.* neo-ealanta, simplidh.
unasked, *adj.* gun iarraidh.
unaspiring, *adj.* neo-mhiannach.
unassailable, *adj.* air nach ruig buille ; fìor sheasmhach, air nach 'eil maith ionnsaigh a thoirt.
unassisted, *adj.* neo-chuidichte, gun chòmhnadh.
unassuming, *adj.* neo-stràiceil.
unattainable, *adj.* air nach ruigear.
unattempted, *adj.* gun deuchainn.
unattended, *adj.* gun chuideachd.
unauthorised, *adj.* gun ùghdarras.
unavailable, unavailing, *adj.* gun stà, gun mhath, faoin gun fheum.
unavoidable, *adj.* do-sheachanta.
unawakened, *adj.* neo-dhùisgte.
unaware, unawares, *adv.* gun fhios, gun fhaireachadh, gun aire, gun aithne ; gu h-obann, gu grad.
unawed, *adj.* gun fhìamh, gun athadh.
unbar, *v. a.* thoir an crann deth, fosgail.
unbeaten, *adj.* neo-bhuailte.
unbecoming, *adj.* mi-chiatach.
unbefitting, *adj.* neo-fhreagarrach.
unbelief, *s.* ana-creideamh, as-creidimh ; mi-chreidimh.

unbeliever, s. ana-creideach.
unbent, adj. do-lùbadh.
unbeseeming, adj. neo-chiatach.
unbewailed, adj. neo-chaoidhte.
unbidden, adj. gun iarraidh, gun sireadh, gun chuireadh.
unbind, v. a. fuasgail, tuasgail.
unblamable, adj. neochoireach.
unblest, adj. neo-bheannaichte.
unbodied, adj. neo-chorparra.
unbolt, v. a. thoir an crann deth, fosgail.
unbosom, v. a. leig ris ; nochd.
unbottomed, adj. gun ghrunnd.
unbought, adj. neo-cheannaichte.
unbounded, adj. neo-chrìochnach.
unbreeched, adj. gun bhriogais.
unbroken, adj. neo - cheannsaichte, neo-bhrisde.
unbrotherly, adj. neo-bhràthaireil.
unburden, v. a. aotromaich.
unburied, adj. neo-adhlaicte.
unbutton, v. a. fosgail putan.
uncalcined, adj. neo-loisgte.
uncalled, adj. gun chuireadh.
uncaught, adj. neo-ghlacte.
uncautious, adj. neo-aireachail.
unceasing, adj. gun sgur.
uncertain, adj. neo-chinnteach.
uncertainty, s. neo-chinnteachd.
unchangeable, adj. neo-chaochlaideach, maireannach, buan.
uncharitable, adj. neo-sheirceil.
uncharitableness, s. mi-sheircealachd, mi-charthannachd.
unchaste, adj. neo-gheimnidh.
unchristian, adj. ana-crìosdail.
uncircumcised, adj. neo-thimchioll-ghearrta, gun timchioll-ghearradh.
uncivil, adj. mì-shuairce, borb.
uncivilised, adj. borb, fiadhaich.
uncle, s. brathair-athar no màthar.
unclean, adj. neò-ghlan, peacach.
uncleanliness, s. neòghloine.
unclerical, adj. neo-chléireachail.
unclouded, adj. neo-ghruamach.
uncock, v. a. cuir gunna bharr lagh.
uncollected, adj. neo-chruinnichte.
uncoloured, adj. neo-dhathte.
uncombed, adj. neo-chìrte.
uncomeliness, s. mì-chiatachd.
uncomely, adj. mì-chiatach.
uncomfortable, a. anshocrach.
uncommon, adj. neo-ghnàthach.
uncommunicated, adj. neo-bhuilichte.
uncomplaisant, adj. mì-shuairce.
uncompounded, adj. neo-mheasgte.
uncompressed, adj. neo-theannaichte.
unconcern, s. neo-chùram.
unconcerned, adj. neo-chùramach, coma.
unconditional, adj. neo-chùmhnantach, gun chùmhnanta, aig làn shaorsa.
unconfinable, adj. neo-iomallach.
unconfirmed, adj. neo-dhaingnichte.

unconformity, s. neo-fhreagarrachd.
uncongealed, adj. neo-reòta.
unconjugal, adj. neo-mharaisteach.
unconquerable, adj. nach gabh ceann-sachadh ; do-chìosnach.
unconscionable, adj. neo - chogaiseach, mì-chogaiseach.
unconscious, adj. neo-fhiosrach.
uncourteous, adj. mì-shuairce.
uncouth, adj. neònach, neo-mhìn.
uncreate, v. a. cuir gu neo-bhith.
uncreated, adj. neo-chruthaichte.
uncrown, v. a. dì-chrùnaich.
unction, s. ungadh ; taiseachadh.
unctuous, adj. reamhar, sailleil.
unculled, adj. neo-thaghte.
uncultivated, adj. fiadhaich, neo-àitichte ; neo-foghluimte.
uncumbered, adj. saor o dhragh.
uncurtailed, adj. neo-ghiorraichte.
uncut, adj. neo-ghearrte.
undaunted, adj. neo-ghealtach.
undebauched, adj. neo-thruaillichte.
undeceive, v. a. cuir ceart.
undeceived, adj. neo-mheallta.
undecided, adj. neo-chinnteach, eadarra-bharail.
undecisive, adj. neo-chinnteach.
undecked, adj. neo-sgeadaichte.
undefeasible, adj. seasmhach.
undefiled, adj. neo-thruaillidh.
undefined, adj. neo-mhìnichte ; gun chrìoch, neo-shònraichte.
undeniable, adj. do-àicheadh.
undeplored, adj. neo-chaoidhte.
undepraved, adj. neo-thruaillte.
under, adv. and prep. fo ; an-ìochdar.
underbid, v. a. tairg na's lugha.
undergo, v. a. fuiling, giùlain.
underground, s. fo 'n talamh.
underhand, adj. dìomhair ; cealgach, fo làimh.
underling, s. iochdaran.
undermine, v. a. cladhaich fodha ; fo-chladhaich ; cuir neach as àite gun fhios, no le foill.
undermost, adj. as ìsle, ìochdrach.
underneath, prep. fo, fodha.
underplot, s. fo-chluich.
underprize, v. a. dì-mheas.
underrate, v. a. dì-mheas.
undersell, v. a. reic fo luach, reic na's saoire na fear eile.
understand, v. tuig ; thoir fainear.
understanding, s. tuigse ; ciall.
understanding, adj. tuigseach, sgileil.
understrapper, s. ìochdaran.
undertake, v. gabh os làimh.
undertaker, s. fear-gnothaich ; fear a ghabhas adhlac os laimh.
undertaking, s. gnothach, obair.
undervalue, v. a. dì-mheas.
underwood, s. preasarnach, crìonach.

underwrite, *v. a.* fo-sgrìobh.
underwriter, *s.* urrasaiche.
underwritten, *adj.* fo-sgrìobhte.
undescried, *adj.* neo-fhaicinte.
undeserved, *adj.* neo-thoillteannach.
undeserving, *adj.* neo-airidh.
undesigning, *adj.* neo-chealgach.
undestroyed, *adj.* neo-sgrioste.
undetermined, *adj.* neo-shònraichte.
undigested, *adj.* neo-mheirbhte.
undiminished, *adj.* neo-lughdaichte.
undiscerned, *adj.* no-fhaicsinn.
undiscernible, *adj.* neo-fhaicsinneach.
undiscerning, *adj.* neo-thuigseach.
undisciplined, *adj.* neo-ionnsaichte.
undiscovered, *adj.* neo-aithnichte.
undiscreet, *adj.* gòrach, eu-crìonna, mì-chiallach, mì-shuairce.
undisguised, *adj.* nochdte; fìor.
undisputed, *adj.* neo-chonnsachail.
undisturbed, *adj.* neo-bhuairte.
undivided, *adj.* neo phàirtichte.
undo, *v. a.* mill; sgrios; fuasgail.
undone, *adj.* caillte, neo-chrìochnaichte; neo-dhèante, sgrioste.
undoubted, *adj.* cinnteach; fìor.
undoubtedly, *adv.* gu cinnteach, air chinnte, gun teagamh, gun amharus.
undress, *v. a.* lom; rùisg.
undressed, *adj.* neo-sgeadaichte.
undulate, *v. a.* udail mar thonn.
undulation, *s.* tonn-luasgadh.
undulatory, *adj.* tonn-luasgach.
undutiful, *adj.* mì-dhleasanach.
uneasiness, *s.* anshocair; imcheist; cùram; ro-chùram, aimheal.
uneasy, *adj.* anshocrach; neo-shocrach, aimhealach.
uneligible, *adj.* neo-roghnachail.
unemployed, *adj.* gun obair, 'na thàmh, dìomhanach.
unenjoyed, *adj.* neo-shealbhaichte.
unenlightened, *adj.* neo-shoillsichte.
unentertaining, *adj.* neo-aighearach.
unequal, *adj.* neo-ionann.
unequitable, *adj.* neo-cheart.
unequivocal, *adj.* soilleir.
unerring, *adj.* neo-mhearachdach.
uneven, *adj.* neo-chòmhnard.
unevenness, *s.* neo-chòmhnardachd.
unexampled, *adj.* neo-choimeiseil.
unexceptionable, *adj.* gun choire.
unexecuted, *adj.* neo-choimhlionta.
unexercised, *adj.* neo-chleachdte.
unexhausted, *adj.* neo-thràighte.
unexpected, *adj.* gun dùil.
unexperienced, *adj.* neo-chleachdte, neo-eolach.
unexplored, *adj.* neo-rannsaichte.
unexpressible, *adj.* do-labhairt.
unextinguishable, *adj.* do-mhùchadh, nach gabh cuir ás.
unfading, *adj.* neo-sheargte, buan.

unfailing, *adj.* neo-fhàillinneach.
unfair, *adj.* mì-cheart, claon.
unfaithful, *adj.* neo-dhìleas.
unfashionable, *adj.* neo-fhasanta.
unfashioned, *adj.* neo-chùmte.
unfathomable, *adj.* do-thomhas.
unfathomed, *adj.* neo-ghrùnndaichte.
unfatigued, *adj.* neo-sgìth.
unfavourable, *adj.* neo-fhàbharrach.
unfed, *adj.* neo-bhiadhta.
unfeeling, *adj.* neo-thlusail.
unfeigned, *adj.* neo-chealgach, fìor.
unfelt, *adj.* neo-mhothaichte.
unfermented, *adj.* gun bheirm.
unfertile, *adj.* neo-thorrach.
unfettered, *adj.* neo-chuibhrichte.
unfinished, *adj.* neo-chrìochnaichte.
unfirm, *adj.* neo-sheasmhach, lag.
unfit, *adj.* neo-iomchuidh.
unfit, *v. a.* dèan neo-iomchuidh.
unfitness, *s.* neo-iomchuidhead.
unfixed, *adj.* neo-shuidhichte.
unfledged, *adj.* gun itean.
unfold, *v. a.* fosgail; nochd, foillsich.
unforeseen, *adj.* neo-fhairichte.
unforgiving, *adj.* neo-mhathach.
unformed, *adj.* neo-chumadail.
unforsaken, *adj.* neo-thréigte.
unfortified, *adj.* neo-dhaingnichte.
unfortunate, *adj.* mì-shealbhach.
unfrequent, *adj.* ainmig, tearc.
unfrequented, *adj.* neo-àitichte; fàs.
unfriended, *adj.* gun charaid.
unfriendly, *adj.* neo-chàirdeil.
unfrozen, *adj.* neo-reòta.
unfruitful, *adj.* neo-tharbhach.
unfurl, *v. a.* sgaoil siùil, no brat.
unfurnished, *adj.* gun àirneis; neo-uidheamaichte, neo-dheasaichte.
ungain, ungainly, *adj.* neo-chiatach; neo-eireachdail, mì-chuannta.
ungenerative, *adj.* neo-thorrach.
ungenerous, *adj.* mì-shuairce, neo-fhialaidh, spìocach, crìon.
ungenial, *adj.* neo-bhaigheil.
ungenteel, *adj.* neo-eireachdail.
ungentle, *adj.* neo-shuairce.
ungentlemanlike, *adj.* neo-uasal; mìodhoir, neo-mhodhail.
ungirt, *adj.* neo-chrioslaichte.
ungodliness, *s.* mì-dhiadhachd.
ungodly, *adj.* mì-dhiadhaidh.
ungorged, *adj.* neo-lìonta.
ungovernable, *adj.* nach gabh ceann-sachadh, nach gabh riaghladh, borb.
ungoverned, *adj.* neo-cheannsaichte.
ungraceful, *adj.* neo-ghrinn.
ungracious, *adj.* neo-thaitneach, neo-chàirdeil.
ungrateful, *adj.* mì-thaingeil; neo-thaingeil; neo-thaitneach.
ungrounded, *adj.* gun stéidh.
unguarded, *adj.* neo-dhìonta.

unguent, *s.* ungadh ; ola.
unhandsome, *adj.* neo-thlachdmhor, mì-mhaiseach.
unhandy, *adj.* neo-làmhchair.
unhappy, *adj.* mì-shona, truagh.
unharmed, *adj.* neo-dhochannaichte.
unharmonious, *adj.* neo-fhonnmhor, mì-chòrdte.
unharness, *v. a.* neo-bheairtich.
unhealthful, unhealthy, *adj.* euslainteach, eucaileach, tinn.
unheard, *adj.* neo-iomraiteach.
unheeded, *adj.* gun mheas, gun sùim.
unholy, *adj.* mì-naomha.
unhonoured, *adj.* neo-onoraichte, gun urram.
unhopeful, *adj.* neo-dhòchasach.
unhorse, *v. a.* tilg bhàrr eich, leag (marcaiche).
unhospitable, *adj.* neo-aoigheil.
unhurt, *adj.* neo-chiùrrte, gun dochann, gun bheud.
unhusk, *v. a.* plaoisg, faoisg.
unicorn, *s.* aon-adharcach, buabhall.
uniform, *adj.* aon-dealbhach, fo'n aon fhuam.
uniformity, *s.* riaghailteachd, co-ionannachd, aon-fhuirm.
unimaginable, *adj.* do - smuainteachail. air nach ruig smuain.
unimpairable, *adj.* nach gabh milleadh.
unimpaired, *adj.* neo-mhillte.
unimportant, *adj.* fadharsach.
unimprovable, *adj.* do-leasachadh.
unimproved, *adj.* neo-leasaichte.
uninclosed, *adj.* neo-dhìonte.
unindifferent, *adj.* neo-choidheis.
uninformed, *adj.* neo-ionnsaichte.
uningenuous, *adj.* neo-ionraic.
uninhabitable, *adj.* do-àiteachail.
uninhabited, *adj.* neo-àitichte.
uninjured, *adj.* gun chiorram.
uninspired, *adj.* neo-dheachdte.
uninstructed, *adj.* neo-theagaisgte.
uninstructive, *adj.* neo-ionnsachail.
unintelligent, *adj.* aineolach.
unintelligible, *adj.* do-thuigsinneach.
unintentional, *adj.* neo-rùnaichte.
uninterested, *adj.* gun seadh, coma.
uninterrupted, *adj.* neo-bhacte.
uninvestigable, *adj.* nach gabh sgrùdadh.
uninvited, *adj.* neo-chuirte.
union, *s.* aonachd ; co-bhann.
uniparous, *adj.* aon-bhreitheach.
unison, *adj.* aon-ghuthach.
unison, *s.* aon-ghuth ; gleus.
unit, *s.* aon, a h-aon.
unitarian, *s.* fear-àicheadh Chriosd.
unite, *v.* ceangail ; dlùthaich, aontaich, tàth, cuir ri chéile ; gabh tàthadh, fàs mar aon.
unition, *s.* aontachas ; aontachadh.
unity, *s.* aonachd, co-chòrdadh.

universal, *adj.* coitcheann.
universe, *s.* an domhan.
university, *s.* àrd-thigh-foghlum.
univocal, *adj.* aon-ghuthach.
unjust, *adj.* eucorach, mì-cheart.
unjustifiable, *adj.* nach gabh fìrean-achadh, nach measar cothromach.
unkennel, *v. a.* cuir á saobhaidh.
unkept, *adj.* neo-ghléidhte.
unkind, *adj.* neo-chaoimhneil.
unkindness, *s.* neo-chaoimhneas.
unknightly, *adj.* neo-fhlathail.
unknit, *v. a.* sgar, sgaoil, fosgail.
unknowing, *adj.* aineolach.
unknown, *adj.* neo-aithnichte.
unlaboured, *adj.* neo-shaothairichte.
unlace, *v. a.* fuasgail, sgaoil.
unlade, *v. a.* aotromaich.
unladen, *adj.* neo-luchdaichte.
unlaid, *adj.* neo-leagte.
unlamented, *adj.* neo-chaoidhte.
unlawful, *adj.* mì-laghail.
unlearned, *adj.* neo-fhoghluimte.
unleavened, *adj.* neo-ghoirtichte.
unless, *conj.* saor o ; mur, mu's.
unlettered, *adj.* neo-ionnsaichte.
unlevelled, *adj.* neo-chòmhnard.
unlibidinous, *adj.* neo-chonnanach.
unlicensed, *adj.* neo-cheadaichte.
unlicked, *adj.* neo-imlichte ; neo-chùmte, neo-sheamhsar.
unlike, *adj.* neo-choltach.
unlikelihood, unlikeliness, *s.* eu-cosalachd; eucoltas.
unlikely, *adj.* eu-coltach.
unlimited, *adj.* neo-chrìochnach.
unload, *v. a.* aotromaich.
unlock, *v. a.* fosgail glas.
unlooked-for, *adj.* gun dùil ris.
unloose, *v. a.* fuasgail.
unlovely, *adj.* neo-ionmhuinn.
unloving, *adj.* neo-ghaolach.
unlucky, *adj.* mì-shealbhar.
unmade, *adj.* neo-dhèante.
unmaimed, *adj.* neo-chiorramach.
unman, *v.* dèan tais, dèan mì-fhearail, mì-mhisnich, spoth.
unmanageable, *adj.* do-cheannsachadh, do-riaghladh ; trom.
unmanly, *adj.* neo-fhearail, meata.
unmannered, *adj.* mì-mhodhail.
unmannerly, *adj.* neo-shìobhalta.
unmarked, *adj.* neo-chomharraichte.
unmarried, *adj.* neo-phòsta.
unmask, *v. a.* leig ris ; rùisg.
unmasked, *adj.* leigte ris ; rùisgte.
unmastered, *adj.* neo-cheannsaichte.
unmatchable, *adj.* gun choimeas.
unmatched, *adj.* gun lethbhreac.
unmeaning, *adj.* gun seadh.
unmeant, *adj.* neo-rùnaichte.
unmeasurable, *adj.* nach gabh tomhais.
unmeasured, *adj.* neo-thomhaiste.

unmeet, *adj.* neo-airidh, neo-iomchuidh, neo-fheagarrach.
unmelted, *adj.* neo-leaghte.
unmerciful, *adj.* neo-thròcaireach.
unmeritable, *adj.* neo-airidh.
unminded, *adj.* neo-chuimhnichte.
unmindful, *adj.* dìochuimhneach.
unmingled, *adj.* neo-choimeasgta.
unmixed, *adj.* neo-mheasgta, glan.
unmolested, *adj.* gun dragh.
unmourned, *adj.* neo-chaoidhte.
unmovable, *adj.* neo-ghluasadach.
unmoved, *adj.* neo-ghluaiste.
unmusical, *adj.* neo-cheòlmhor.
unnamed, *adj.* neo-ainmichte.
unnatural, *adj.* mi nàdurra.
unnavigable, *adj.* do-sheòladh.
unnecessary, *adj.* neo-fheumail.
unneighbourly, *adj.* neo-choimhearsnach-ail, neo-nàbachail; neo-chòir, neo-chaoimhneil, neo-choingheallach; neo-chòmpanta.
unnervate, *adj.* anfhannaichte.
unnerve, *v. a.* anfhannaich.
unnerved, *adj.* anfhann; tais.
unnumbered, *adj.* do-àireamh.
unobservable, *adj.* nach 'eil ri fhaicinn.
unobservant, *adj.* neo-shuimeil.
unobserved, *adj.* neo-bheachdaichte.
unobstructed, *adj.* neo-bhacte.
unobtainable, *adj.* nach 'eil ri fhaotainn.
unoccupied, *adj.* neo-shealbhaichte.
unoffending, *adj.* neochoireach.
unoperative, *adj.* neo-éifeachdach.
unopposed, *adj.* neo-bhacte.
unorderly, *adj.* mì-riaghailteach.
unorthodox, *adj.* neo-fhallain.
unpack, *v. a.* fuasgail, fosgail.
unpaid, *adj.* neo-phàighte.
unpalatable, *adj.* neo-bhlasda.
unparalleled, *adj.* gun choimeas.
unpardonable, *adj.* gun leithsgeul, nach mathar; nach fhaodar a mhathadh, nach faigh mathanas.
unpardoned, *adj.* neo-mhathte.
unparliamentary, *adj.* an aghaidh achd suidhichte na pàrlamaid, mì-mhodhail.
unparted, *adj.* neo-dhealaichte.
unpartial, *adj.* dìreach, neo-chlaon, co-thromach, neo-leth-bhreitheach.
unpassable, *adj.* air nach fhaighear seachad.
unpawned, *adj.* neo-ghealltainte.
unpeaceable, *adj.* buaireasach.
unpensioned, *adj.* neo-dhuaisichte.
unpeople, *v. a.* dèan fàs; cuir fàs.
unperceivable, *adj.* do-mhothachail; do-fhaireachail.
unperceived, *adj.* gun fhios.
unperfect, *adj.* neo-iomlan.
unperformed, *adj.* neo-dhèanta.
unperishable, *adj.* maireannach.
unperplexed, *adj.* gun amhluadh.

unpetrified, *adj.* neo-cruadhaichte.
unphilosophical, *adj.* neo-fheallsanta.
unpillowed, *adj.* gun chluasag.
unpin, *v. a.* fuasgail dealg.
unpitied, *adj.* gun truas ri.
unpitying, *adj.* neo-thruacanta.
unpleasant, *adj.* mì-thaitneach.
unpleased, *adj.* mì-thoilichte.
unpleasing, *adj.* mì-thaitneach.
unpliant, *adj.* do-lùbadh, rag.
unploughed, *adj.* neo-threabhta.
unpoetical, *adj.* neo-fhileanta.
unpolished, *adj.* neo-liobhta; borb.
unpolite, *adj.* mì-mhodhail.
unpolluted, *adj.* neo-thruaillte.
unpopular, *adj.* neo-ionmhainn.
unpractised, *adj.* neo-chleachdte.
unpraised, *adj.* gun iomradh.
unprecedented, *adj.* gun choimeas.
unpreferred, *adj.* neo-àrdaichte.
unpregnant, *adj.* neo-thorrach.
unprejudicate, *adj.* neo-chlaon.
unprejudiced, *adj.* neo-leth-bhretheach, neo-chlaon-bhretheach.
unpremeditated, *adj.* neo-smuaintichte roimh-làimh, neo-shònraichte.
unprepared, *adj.* neo-ullamh.
unprepossessed, *adj.* gun taobh ri.
unpretending, *adj.* neo-dhàna.
unprevented, *adj.* neo-bhacte.
unprincely, *adj.* mì-fhlathail.
unprincipled, *adj.* neo-chogaiseach.
unprinted, *adj.* neo-chlò-bhuailte.
unprized, *adj.* neo-mheaste.
unproclaimed, *adj.* neo-ghairmte.
unprofaned, *adj.* neo-thruailhte.
unprofitable, *adj.* neo-tharbhach.
unprolific, *adj.* seasg, aimrid.
unpropitious, *adj.* mì-ghealltanach.
unproportioned, *adj.* neo-chumadail.
unpropped, *adj.* gun chùl-taic.
unprosperous, *adj.* mì-shealbhar.
unprotected, *adj.* gun dìon.
unprovided, *adj.* neo-sholaraichte.
unprovoked, *adj.* neo-bhrosnaichte.
unpruned, *adj.* neo-ghearrta.
unpublished, *adj.* neo-fhoillsichte.
unqualified, *adj.* neo-fhreagarrach.
unqualify, *v. a.* dèan neo-fhreagarrach.
unquenchable, *adj.* nach gabh mùchadh.
unquenched, *adj.* neo-mhùchte.
unquestionable, *adj.* gun cheist.
unquestionably, *adv.* air chinnt.
unquestioned, *adj.* neo-cheasnaichte.
unquiet, *adj.* neo-fhoisneach.
unracked, *adj.* neo-shìolaidhte.
unravel, *v. a.* fuasgail, réitich.
unread, *adj.* neo-leughte.
unready, *adj.* neo-dheas.
unreal, *adj.* neo-fhìor, faoin.
unreasonable, *adj.* mì-reusonta.
unreclaimed, *adj.* neo-chìosnaichte.
unreconciled, *adj.* neo-réidh.

unrecorded, *adj.* neo-sgrìobhte.
unrecounted, *adj.* neo-aithriste.
unreduced, *adj.* neo-lughdaichte.
unreformable, *adj.* do-leasachail.
unreformed, *adj.* neo-leasaichte.
unrefreshed, *adj.* neo-ùraichte.
unregarded, *adj.* gun sùim.
unregenerate, *adj.* neo-ath-ghinte.
unregistered, *adj.* neo-sgrìobhte.
unrelenting, *adj.* neo-thruacanta.
unrelievable, *adj.* do-chòmhnachail.
unremediable, *adj.* do-leigheas.
unrepented, *adj.* neo-aithreachail.
unrepining, *adj.* neo-aithreach.
unreplenished, *adj.* neo-lìonta.
unreproached, *adj.* neo-chronaichte.
unreproved, *adj.* neo-achmhasanaichte.
unrequested, *adj.* gun iarraidh.
unrequitable, *adj.* neo-dhìolta.
unreserved, *adj.* fosgarra.
unresisted, *adj.* gun bhacadh.
unresolved, *adj.* neo-shònraichte.
unrestored, *adj.* neo-aisigte.
unrestrained, *adj.* neo-smachdaichte.
unrevealed, *adj.* ceilte.
unrevenged, *adj.* neo-dhìolta.
unrevoked, *adj.* seasmhach.
unrewarded, *adj.* neo-dhuaisichte.
unriddle, *v. a.* tomhais ; fuasgail.
unrig, *v. a.* rùisg dheth.
unrighteous, *adj.* eas-ionraic.
unrightful, *adj.* neo-dhligheach.
unripe, *adj.* anabaich, glas.
unrivalled, *adj.* gun choimeas.
unroll, *v. a.* fosgail, fuasgail.
unroof, *v. a.* thoir mullach dheth.
unroot, *v. a.* spìon á bhun.
unrounded, *adj.* neo-chruinn.
unruffle, *v. n.* bi ciùin.
unruly, *adj.* àimhreiteach.
unsafe, *adj.* neo-thèaruinte.
unsaid, *adj.* neo-ainmichte.
unsalted, *adj.* neo-shaillte.
unsaluted, *adj.* neo-fhàiltichte.
unsanctified, *adj.* neò-naomhaichte.
unsatiable, *adj.* do-shàsachadh.
unsatisfactory, *adj.* neo-thaitneach.
unsatisfied, *adj.* neo-thoilichte.
unsavoury, *adj.* mì-bhlasda ; breun.
unsay, *v. a.* thoir air ais facal.
unscholastic, *adj.* neo-ionnsaichte.
unschooled, *adj.* gun sgoil.
unscreened, *adj.* neo-sgàilichte.
unseal, *v. a.* fosgail seula.
unsealed, *adj.* neo-sheulaichte.
unseasonable, *adj.* neo-thràthail.
unseasonableness, *s.* mì-thràth.
unseasoned, *adj.* neo-shaillt ; neo-thràth-ail ; neo-thiormaichte.
unseconded, *adj.* neo-chuidichte.
unsecure, *adj.* neo-thèaruinte.
unseemly, *adj.* mì-chiatach.
unseen, *adj.* as an t-sealladh.

unserviceable, *adj.* gun stà.
unsettle, *v. a.* dean mì-chinnteach.
unsettled, *adj.* neo-shocrach, neo-shuidh-ichte, neo-shònraichte ; luaineach, siùbhlach ; caochlaideach ; neo-àit-ichte ; guanach, aotrom.
unsevered, *adj.* neo-sgarte.
unshackle, *v. a.* mì-chuibhrich.
unshaken, *adj.* neo-charaichte, neo-ghluasadach ; daingeann.
unshapen, *adj.* neo-chumadail.
unsheath, *v. a.* rùisg, tarruing.
unsheltered, *adj.* gun fhasgadh.
unship, *v. a.* thoir á long.
unshod, *adj.* gun bhrògan.
unshorn, *adj.* neo-bhuainte.
unsifted, *adj.* neo-chriathairte.
unsightliness, *s.* duaichneachd.
unsightly, *adj.* duaichnidh.
unskilful, *adj.* mì-theòma.
unskilfulness, *s.* aineolas.
unskilled, *adj.* aineolach.
unslaked, *adj.* neo-mhùchta.
unsociable, *adj.* neo-chaidreach.
unsoiled, *adj.* neo-shalaichte.
unsold, *adj.* gun bhi air a reic.
unsolid, *adj.* fàs ; neo-ghramail.
unsophisticated, *adj.* ionraic ; fìor.
unsorted, *adj.* neo-dhòigheil.
unsought, *adj.* gun iarraidh.
unsound, *adj.* mì-fhallain ; grod.
unspeakable, *adj.* do-labhairt.
unspecified, *adj.* neo-ainmichte.
unspoiled, *adj.* neo-chreachta, neo-mhillte ; neo-thruaillichte.
unspotted, *adj.* gun bhall ; gun smal.
unstable, *adj.* neo-sheasmhach.
unstained, *adj.* gun sal ; gun smal.
unstaunched, *adj.* neo-chaisgte.
unsteadfast, *adj.* mì-stéidheil.
unsteady, *adj.* neo-sheasmhach.
unstinted, *adj.* neo-ghann, fial, pailt.
unstrained, *adj.* neo-éignichte.
unstring, *v. a.* lasaich, fuasgail.
unsubstantial, *adj.* gun bhrìgh.
unsuccessful, *adj.* mì-shealbhar.
unsugared, *adj.* gun siùcar.
unsuitable, *adj.* neo-iomchuidh.
unsuiting, *adj.* neo-fhreagarrach.
unsullied, *adj.* gun truailleadh.
unsung, *adj.* neo-iomraiteach.
unsunned, *adj.* neo-ghrianaichte.
unsupported, *adj.* neo-chuidichte.
unsuspected, *adj.* saor o amharus.
unsuspecting, *adj.* neo-amharusach.
unsuspicious, *adj.* gun umhaill.
unsustained, *adj.* neo-thaicichte.
unswayed, *adj.* neo-cheannsaichte.
unswear, *v. a.* thoir mionnan air ais.
untainted, *adj.* neo-thruaillichte.
untamed, *adj.* neo-chàllaichte.
untasted, *adj.* gun blasad (air).
untaught, *adj.* neo-ionnsaichte.

untempered, *adj.* neo-chruadhaichte.
untenable, *adj.* neo-sheasmhach ; nach gabh dearbhadh.
untenanted, *adj.* neo-àitichte.
untented, *adj.* neo-fhritheilte.
unterrified, *adj.* gun sgàth.
unthanked, *adj.* gun taing, nach d' fhuair taing.
unthankful, *adj.* mì-thaingeil.
unthawed, *adj.* gun aiteamh.
unthinking, *adj.* neo-smaointeachail.
unthought-of, *adj.* gun spéis.
unthreatened, *adj.* neo-bhagairte.
unthrift, *s.* struidhear.
unthrifty, *adj.* stròdhail, sgapach.
unthriving, *adj.* mì-shoirbheasach.
untie, *v. a.* fuasgail, lasaich.
untied, *adj.* fuasgailte, las.
until, *adv.* gu ruig, gu, gus.
untilled, *adj.* neo-àitichte.
untimely, *adj.* neo-thràthail, an an-am.
untimely, *adv.* roimh 'n àm.
untinged, *adj.* neo-dhàthte.
untired, *adj.* neo-sgìth.
untitled, *adj.* neo-thiodalaichte.
unto, *prep.* do, gu, chum, thun', a dh' ionnsaigh, gu ruig.
untold, *adj.* neo-aithriste.
untouched, *adj.* neo-làmhaichte.
untoward, *adj.* rag, reasgach, fiar.
untraceable, *adj.* do-lòrgachadh.
untraced, *adj.* neo-lòrgaichte.
untrained, *adj.* neo-ionnsaichte.
untransparent, *adj.* dorcha.
untravelled, *adj.* neo-choisichte.
untried, *adj.* neo-dheuchainte.
untrod, *adj.* neo-lòrgaichte.
untroubled, *adj.* neo-bhuairte.
untrue, *adj.* neo-dhìleas.
untruly, *adv.* gu neo-dhìleas, gu fallsa, gu mealltach.
untruth, *s.* breug ; sgleò.
untunable, *adj.* nach gabh gleusadh.
unturned, *adj.* neo-thionndaidhte.
untutored, *adj.* neo-ionnsaichte.
untwine, untwist, *v. a.* thoir as a chéile, thoir as an fhighe, sgaoil.
unusual, *adj.* neo-àbhaisteach.
unvalued, *adj.* dì-measte.
unvanquished, *adj.* neo-cheannsaichte, neo-chlaoidhte.
unvaried, *adj.* gun atharrachadh.
unvarnished, *adj.* neo-lìtheach, gun chòmhdach.
unveil, *v. a.* leig, ris, nochd.
unveritable, *adj.* fallsa, breugach.
unversed, *adj.* neo-eòlach.
unviolated, *adj.* neo-bhriste, slàn.
unvisited, *adj.* gun bhi air a thadhal.
unwarlike, *adj.* neo-churanta.
unwarned, *adj.* gun sanas.
unwarrantable, *adj.* neo-cheadaichte, neo-laghal.

unwarranted, *adj.* neo-chinnteach.
unwary, *adj.* neo-fhaiceallach ; obann.
unwashed, *adj.* neo-nighte ; salach.
unwasted, *adj.* neo-chaithte.
unwearied, *adj.* neo-sgìth.
unwed, *adj.* nach 'eil pòsda.
unwelcome, *adj.* neo-thaitneach.
unwholesome, *adj.* neo-fhallain.
unwieldy, *adj.* trom, liobasda.
unwind, *v. a.* thoir as a chéile, fuasgail.
unwise, *adj.* neo-ghlic, gòrach.
unwonted, *adj.* ainneamh, tearc.
unworthy, *adj.* neo-airidh.
unwreathe, *v. a.* thoir as an dual.
unwritten, *adj.* neo-sgrìobhte.
unwrought, *adj.* neo-oibrichte.
unwrung, *adj.* neo-fhàisgte.
unyielded, *adj.* neo-strìochdte.
unyoke, *v. a.* neo-bheartaich.
up, *adv.* shuas ; gu h-àrd.
up, *prep.* suas ri bruthach.
upbraid, *v. a.* maoidh ; troid.
upheld, *part.* air a chumail suas.
uphill, *adj.* ri bruthach, duilich.
uphold, *v. a.* cum suas, tog.
upholder, *s.* fear taice.
upholsterer, *s.* fear àirneisiche.
upland, *s.* airde aonach ; mullach.
uplay, *v. a.* càrn suas, cnuasaich.
uplift, *v. a.* tog suas, àrdaich.
upmost, *adj.* as àirde.
upon, *prep.* air, air muin.
upper, *adj.* uachdrach.
uppermost, *adj.* as uachdraiche.
upraise, *v. a.* tog suas, àrdaich.
upright, *adj.* treibhdhireach ; ionraic ; dìreach 'na sheasamh, onarach, sìmplidh, ceart, cothromach, fior.
uprightness, *s.* treibhdhireas, fìreantachd ; seasamh dìreach.
uprise, *v. n.* éirich suas.
uproar, *s.* gàire ; buaireas.
uproot, *v. a.* spìon á bun.
upshot, *s.* co-dhùnadh, crìoch ; deireadh, ceann mu dheireadh.
upside, *adv.* an t-uachdar.
upstart, *s.* ùranach, peasan moiteil.
upstart, *v. a.* leum suas.
upward, *adj.* suas, gu h-àrd.
urbanity, *s.* furmailt, suairceas.
urchin, *s.* cràineag ; isean, gàrlach.
urethra, *s.* fual-chuisle.
urge, *v. a.* earalaich ; spàrr ; aslaich ; brosnaich stuig ; cuir thuige ; teannaich ; fàisg, pùc, brùth.
urgency, *s.* cabhag ; earailteachd, feumalachd, fòghnadh, déine.
urgent, *adj.* dian, earailteach, cabhagach, feumail
urger, *s.* fear-earaich ; earalaiche.
urinal, *s.* soitheach-fuail.
urinary, *adj.* fualach, mùnach.

urine, s. maighistir, fual, mùn.
urn, s. poit tasgaidh luaithre nam marbh ; soigheach uisge.
us, pron. sinn, sinne.
usage, s. àbhaist, nòs, gnàth ; càradh.
usance, s. riadh, ùin-réidh.
use, s. stà, math, feum ; dìol, gnàthachadh ; cleachdadh, nòs, àbhaist ; coghnàth ; riadh.
use, v. gnàthaich ; buin ri, dèan feum ; cleachd ; bi cleachdte, giùlain, iomchair.
used, adj. gnàthaichte, cleachdte.
useful, adj. feumail, iomchuidh, freagarrach, stàmhor, tarbhach, math.
usefulness, s. feumalachd.
useless, adj. neo-fheumail, gun stà.
usher, s. fo-mhaighstir ; gille-doruis.
usher, v. a. thoir a steach, feuch a steach.
usquebaugh, s. uisge-beatha.
usual, adj. coitcheann, tric, minig, gnàthach, gnàthaichte.
usually, adv. gu minig, a réir àbhaist, mar is trice.
usurer, s. fear-riadh, fear-ocair.

usurious, adj. riadhach ; ocarach.
usurp, v. a. gléidh gun chòir, glac le àinneart.
usurpation, s. glacadh gun chòir.
usurper, s. rìgh neo-dhligheach.
usury, s. airgead, riadh.
utensil, s. ball-acfhuinn, beart ; goireas, ball-àirneis, uidheam.
uterine, adj. machlagach.
uterus, s. machlag, machlach.
utility, s. feum ; math, stà.
utmost, adj. iomallach, deireannach, is deireannaiche, is mò, is àirde.
utmost, s. meud, làn-oidhirp.
utter, v. a. labhair, abair, innis, nochd, cuir an céill ; reic ; sgaoil.
utterable, adj. so-labhairt.
utterance, s. labhairt ; guth.
utterly, adv. gu tur, gu léir.
uttermost, s. a' chuid as mò.
uttermost, adj. as iomallaiche, is fhaide mach, is faid air fàlbh.
uvula, s. cioch-shlugain.
uxorious, adj. mùirneach mu mhnaoi.
uxoriousness, s. céile-mhùirn.

V

vacancy, s. fàslach ; àite falamh, àite fàs ; anail, clos, tàmh ; còs, bèarn ; neo-thoirt.
vacant, adj. fàs, falamh ; faoin.
vacate, v. a. falmhaich ; fàg ; dèan faoin, cuir air chùl ; tréig.
vacation, s. uine shaor ; sgaoileadh ; tàmh, anail.
vaccination, s. cur breac a' chruidh.
vaccine, adj. cruidh.
vacuation, s. falmhachadh.
vacuity, s. failmhe.
vacuous, adj. falamh, fàs, faoin.
vacuum, s. falamhachd.
vade-mecum, s. leabhar-pòcaid.
vagabond, s. fear-fuadain.
vagary, s. faoin-dhòchas.
vagrant, s. fear-seacharain, diol-déirce, déirceach.
vagrant, adj. siùbhlach ; seachranach, iomrallach.
vague, adj. sgaoilte, faontrach, neoshoilleir.
vail, v. leig sìos · ìslich ; géill.
vails, s. airgead doruis, sineas, brìob.
vain, adj. faoin ; diomhain ; neoéifeachdach, neo-tharbhach ; falamh ; fàs ; uallach, stràiceil ; suarrach ; sgàileanta ; bòsdail, spaglainneach.
vain-glorious, adj. ràiteachail.
vain-glory, s. ràiteachas.
vale, s. gleann, srath.

valentine, s. leannan ; dealbh-gaoil.
valerian, s. an trì-bhileach.
valet, s. gille-coise.
valetudinarian, s. neach tinn, neach tuilleadh is iomnach mu shlàinte.
valiant, adj. treun, foghainteach, calma, làidir neartmhor, misneachail.
valiantness, s. gaisge, tréine.
valid, adj. tàbhachdach ; éifeachdach, comasach ; cumhachdach, foghainteach, làidir ; tarbhach.
validity, s. tàbhachd ; éifeachd.
valley, s. gleann ; glac, lag.
valorous, adj. gaisgeanta, curanta.
valour, s. gaisge, tréine, cruadal.
valuable, adj. luachmhor, priseil.
valuation, s. meas, luach ; fiach, sgoradh.
value, s. prìs, luach, fiach ; toirt.
value, v. a. meas, prìsich, cuir meas.
valve, s. pìob-chòmhla ; duilleag-doruis.
vamp, s. leathar-uachdair.
vamp, v. a. càirich, clùd, clùdaich.
van, s. toiseach-feachda ; tùs ; inneal-giùlan.
vane, s. coileach-gaoithe.
vanguard, s. tùs-feachd.
vanilla, s. faoineag ; seòrsa luibh.
vanish, v. n. rach as an t-sealladh, falbh mar sgàile ; siolaidh air falbh.
vanity, s. dìomhanas, faoineas ; uaill.
vanquish, v. a. buadhaich, ceannsaich, cìosnaich, thoir buaidh ; claoidh ;

faigh làmh-an-uachdar, cuir fo smachd; cuir fo cheannsal.

vanquisher, *s.* buadhaire.

vantage, *s.* tairbhe, làmh-an-uachdar, cosnadh, cothrom.

vapid, *adj.* neo-bhrìgheil, marbhanta, air dol eug ; air bàsachadh mar leann.

vaporous, *adj.* smùideach, ceòthar.

vapour, *s.* deatach ; ceò-gréine.

vapours, *s.* leanntras, liunntras.

variable, *adj.* caochlaideach.

variableness, *s.* caochlaideachd.

variance, *s.* àimhreite, cur a mach.

variation, *s.* caochla, dealachadh.

variegate, *v. a.* breac, breacaich, ballaich, balla-bhreacaich, stiallaich.

variegated, *adj.* breac, ballach.

variety, *s.* atharrachadh, caochla.

various, *adj.* eugsamhail, iomadach, iomadh, móran ; ioma-ghnèitheach.

varlet, *s.* crochaire ; gàrlach.

varnish, *s.* slìob-ola, falaid.

varnish, *v. a.* slìobaich, falaidich.

varnisher, *s.* slìobaiche, falaidiche.

vary, *v.* caochail, eugsamhlaich, atharraich ; breacaich, ballaich ; rach a thaobh, claon.

vase, *s.* soire, soitheach.

vassal, *s.* ìochdaran ; coitear.

vassalage, *s.* ìochdranachd.

vast, *s.* fàsach, ionad fàsail.

vast, vasty, *adj.* mór, ro-mhór, ana-measarra, fuathasach ; anabharrach, ana-cuimseach, aibhseach.

vastness, *s.* ana-cuimseachd, anmhorachd, anabharrachd.

vat, *s.* dabhach.

vaticide, *s.* mortair-bhàrd.

vaticinate, *v. n.* fàisnich.

vault, *s.* bogha ; seileir ; uamh, tuam.

vault, *v.* leum, gearr sùrdag ; dèan ruideis, tog bogha.

vaulted, vaulty, *adj.* boghata.

vaunt, *s.* bòsd ; spaglainn.

vaunt, *v.* dèan bòsd, dèan uaill.

veal, *s.* laoigh-fheoil.

vecture, *s.* giùlan, iomchar.

veer, *v.* tionndaidh, atharraich ; rach mu'n cuairt ; cuir mu'n cuairt cuir timchioll ; cuir tiomall.

vegetable, *s.* luibh, lus.

vegetate, *v. n.* fàs mar lus.

vegetation, *s.* fàs, luibhean.

vegetative, *adj.* a' fàs mar luibh.

vegete, *adj.* làidir, lùghar, beò.

vehemence, *s.* déineas, déine, gairgead, deòthas, dealas, braisead.

vehement, *adj.* dìan ; déineachdach, borb, garg, deòthasach, loisgeanta, bras, dealasach, da-rìreadh.

vehicle, *s.* càrn, carbad, cairt, inneal giùlain, inneal-iomchair.

veil, *s.* gnùisbhrat, sgàile.

veil, *v. a.* còmhdaich, falaich, ceil.

vein, *s.* cuisle, féith ; gnè ; slighe ; stiall ; nàdur, inntinn, càil, sannt.

veined, *adj.* cuisleach, féitheach stiallach, snìomh-chuisleach, breac.

vellicate, *v. a.* spìon, spiol.

vellication, *s.* spìonadh, spioladh.

vellum, *s.* craicionn-sgrìobhaidh.

velocity, *s.* luathas, clise.

velvet, *s.* sìoda molach, melbheid.

venal, *adj.* so-cheannach, an geall air duais, sanntach ; cuisleach, féitheach.

venality, *s.* brìobachd, sannt duaise.

venatic, *adj.* sealgach.

venation, *s.* sealg, faoghaid.

vend, *v. a.* reic, noch ri reic.

vender, *s.* reiceadair, fear-reic.

vendible, *adj.* reiceadach, so-reic.

veneer, *v. a.* còmhdaich le fiodh tana.

veneficial, *adj.* nìmhneach, nimhe.

venenate, *v. a.* puinnseanaich.

venerable, *adj.* urramach, measail.

venerate, *v. a.* urramaich.

veneration, *s.* àrd-urram.

venereal, *adj.* drùiseil, macnusach.

venery, *s.* drùis ; macnusachd.

venesection, *s.* leagail-fala.

vengeance, *s.* dìoghaltas ; peanas.

vengeful, *adj.* dìoghaltach.

veniable, venial, *adj.* so-mhathadh, so-lughadh, ceadaichte.

venison, *s.* sithionn ; fiaghach.

venom, *s.* nimhe, puinnsean.

venomous, *adj.* nimheil, mì-runach.

venomousness, *s.* nimhealachd.

vent, *s.* luidhear ; fosgladh ; toll-gaoithe, leigeil a mach.

vent, *v. a.* leig a mach ; abair, labhair ; dòirt a mach, thoir gaoth, foillsich; leig ruith le.

ventilate, *v. a.* leig gaoth, fidrich.

ventilation, *s.* troimh sheòmar, fionnarachadh, cur ris a' ghaoith ; fidreachadh, rannsachadh, sgrùdadh.

ventricle, *s.* goile, bronnag ; bolgan.

ventriloquist, *s.* brù-chainntear.

venture, *s.* tuaiream ; cunnart.

venture, *v.* cuir an cunnart, cunnartaich ; dùraig ; gabh cuid cunnairt, rach an cunnart, thoir ionnsaigh.

venturesome, venturous, *adj.* misneachail, dàna, neo-ghealtach.

veracity, *s.* fìrinnichead, fìrinn.

verb, *s.* facal, briathar.

verbal, *adj.* faclach ; beòil.

verbatim, *adv.* facal air an fhacal.

verberate, *v. a.* fri-bhuail ; sgiùrs.

verberation, *s.* straoidhleireachd.

verbose, *adj.* briathrach, ràiteach.

verbosity, *s.* briathrachas.

verdant, *adj.* gorm ; feurach, uaine.

verdict, *s.* breth-bharail.

verdigris, *s.* meirg umha.
verdure, *s.* feur-uaine ; glasradh.
verge, *s.* slat-shuaicheantais ; oir.
verge, *v. n.* aom, claon ; teann ri.
verification, *s.* fìrinneachadh.
verifier, *s.* dearbhair, fear-dearbhaidh (cùis).
verify, *v. a.* dearbh ; fìrinnich ; daighnich, còmhdaich.
verily, *adv.* gu deimhinn, gu fìor, gu fìrinneach, gu cinnteach, gu dearbha.
verisimilar, *adj.* coltach, coslach.
verisimilitude, verisimility, *s.* cosmhalachd, cosamhlachd.
veritable, *adj.* fìor, cinnteach.
verity, *s.* fìrinn dhearbhte.
verjuice, *s.* sùgh goirt ubhall.
vermiculation, *s.* snìomhanachd.
vermicule, *s.* cnuimh, durrag.
vermiculous, *adj.* cnuimheagach.
vermifuge, *s.* fùdar-nam-biast.
vermilion, *s.* seòrsa deirg.
vermin, *s.* meanbhbhéistean, mialan.
verminous, *adj.* béisteagach.
vernacular, *adj.* dùthchasach.
vernal, *adj.* earrachail, céitein.
vernility, *s.* tràillealachd.
versatile, *adj.* so-thionndadh ; caochlaideach, luaineach ; luasganach, coimhdheis.
versatility, *s.* caochlaideachd.
verse, *s.* rann ; dàn ; duan ; ceithreamh ; earrann ; rannachd.
versed, *adj.* teòma, sgileil, eòlach, fiosrach foghluimte, ionnsaichte.
versification, *s.* ranndachd.
versifier, *s.* bàrd, duanaire.
versify, *v.* cuir an dàn, rannaich.
version, *s.* atharrachadh ; eadar-theangachadh ; tionndadh, caochla.
vert, *s.* gorm-choille.
vertebra, *s.* alt droma.
vertebral, *adj.* druim-altach.
vertex, *s.* mullach ; bior ; binnein.
vertical, *adj.* dìreach os cionn.
vertiginous, *adj.* cuairteach, tuainealach cuairsgach, timchiollach.
vertigo, *s.* tuaineal ; stùird.
vervain, *s.* crubh-an-leòghain.
very, *adj.* fìor, ceart ; *adv.* ro ; glé.
vesicle, *s.* leus, builgein, guirein.
vesicular, *adj.* fàs, tolltach, còsach.
vesper, *s.* rionnag-an-fheasgair.
vespers, *s.* feasgarain.
vessel, *s.* soitheach, long.
vest, *s.* siostacot, peiteag.
vest, *v. a.* sgeadaich, éid ; gabh.
vestal, *s.* maighdeann-fhìorghlan.
vestal, *adj.* glan-maighdeannail.
vestibule, *s.* fordhorus, fosgalan.
vestige, *s.* lòrg ; comharradh.
vestment, *s.* aodach, éideadh, earradh, trusgan ; culaidh.

vestry, *s.* seòmar-ministeir ; coinneamh fhoirfeach.
vesture, *s.* aodach, éideadh, earradh, trusgan, culaidh.
vetch, *s.* peasair-nan-each.
veteran, *s.* seann-saighdear.
veterinarian, *s.* spréidh-lighich.
vex, *v. a.* buair, cràidh, claoidh, sàraich, farranaich.
vexation, *s.* buaireadh, campar, aimheal, farran, àmhghar.
vexatious, *adj.* buaireasach, càmparach, farranach, aimhealach, draghalach, àmhgharach.
vexatiousness, *s.* aimhealachd.
vial, *s.* searrag ghlaine.
viand, *s.* biadh, lòn.
viaticum, *s.* biadh - siùbhail, biadh-mòintich.
vibrate, *v.* triobhuail ; crath, crith.
vibration, *s.* triobhualadh, crith.
vibratory, *adj.* triobhualach.
vicar, *s.* biocair, co-arbha.
vicarage, *s.* co-arbachd.
vicarious, *adj.* ionadach, an riochd.
vice, *s.* dubhailc ; aingidheachd ; droch-bheart ; glamaire.
vicegerent, *s.* fear-ionaid.
viceroy, *s.* fear ionaid rìgh.
vicinage, *s.* nàbachd ; dlùthas.
vicinal, vicine, *adj.* fagus, dlùth air.
vicinity, *s.* coimhearsnachd.
vicious, *adj.* dubhailceach, aingidh.
vicissitude, *s.* caochla, tionnda.
victim, *s.* iobairt ; neach air a sgrios.
victor, *s.* buadhair, curaidh.
victorious, *adj.* buadhach, gaisgeil.
victoriously, *adv.* buadhach.
victory, *s.* buaidh ; làmh an uachdar.
victual, *s.* lòn, biadh, beatha.
victualler, *s.* biotailliche.
victuals, *s.* biotailt, biadh.
videlicet, *adv.* is e sin ri ràdh.
viduity, *s.* bantrachas.
vie, *v. n.* dèan strìth, dèan spàirn.
view, *v. a.* beachdaich, amhairc air, dearc, feuch, gabh fradharc, gabh beachd, gabh sealladh.
view, *s.* beachd, sealladh, fradharc ; léirsinn, faicinn ; dùil.
vigil, *s.* faire ; trasg, ùrnaigh-fheasgair ; aoradh-oidhche.
vigilance, *s.* faiceallachd, furachras ; beachdalachd, faire, caithris.
vigilant, *adj.* faiceallach, furachail, aireachail, cùramach ; caithriseach.
vigorous, *adj.* treun, làidir, calma, neartmhor, gramail, lùghor, beò.
vigour, *s.* tréine, spionnadh, treòir, neart, lùgh, comas, cumhachd.
vile, *adj.* salach, grannda, gràineil ; truaillidh, dìblidh, suarrach, fo dhìmeas ; aingidh, dubhailceach.

vileness, *s.* truaillidheachd, suarrachas, gràinealachd, trustaireachd, dìblidheachd, tàirealachd.

vilify, *v. a.* maslaich ; ìslich, dèan tàir, salaich, truaill ; màb, càin ; dimheas, dèan suarrach.

vill, villa, *s.* taigh - dùthcha, taigh sàmhraidh, baile duin' uasail.

village, *s.* frith-bhaile, baile-beag.

villager, *s.* fear frith-bhaile.

villain, *s.* slaoightire, crochaire.

villainous, *adj.* slaoighteil ; dìblidh.

villainy, *s.* slaightearachd, aingidheachd ; cionta, coire ; lochd, do-bheart.

villous, *adj.* molach, ròmach, ròinneach, giobach, cléiteagach.

vimineous, *adj.* maothranach, slatagach, fiùranach, caolach, gadanach.

vincible, *a.* ceannsachail.

vindicate, *v. a.* fìreanaich, dìol ; dearbh, dìon, cùm suas.

vindication, *s.* fìreanachadh.

vindicative, *adj.* dìoghaltach.

vindicator, *s.* fear-dìonaidh.

vindictive, *adj.* dìoghaltach.

vine, *s.* fìonan, crann-fìona.

vinegar, *s.* fìon-geur.

vine-press, *s.* fìon-amar.

vineyard, *s.* fìon-lios, gàradh-fìona.

vinous, *adj.* fìonach.

vintage, *s.* fìon-fhoghar.

vintager, *s.* fìon-fhogharaiche.

vintner, *s.* fìon-òsdair.

vintry, *s.* fìon-mhargadh.

viol, *s.* fidheall.

violable, *adj.* so-chiùrradh.

violate, *v. a.* ciùrr, mill, bris, dochainn ; truaill, éignich.

violation, *s.* milleadh, briseadh-éigneachadh ; truailleadh.

violence, *s.* àinneart, fòirneart, éigin, droch - ionnsaigh ; déine ; braise, deòthas, ciurram ; cron, éigneachadh, truailleadh.

violent, *adj.* dìan ; àinneartach ; ceann-làidir ; garg, fòirneartach, borb, deòthasach.

violet, *s.* fail-chuaich, dail-chuach.

violin, *s.* fidheall.

violist, *s.* fìdhleir.

violoncello, *s.* fidheall mhór.

viper, *s.* nathair-nimhe, baobh.

virago, *s.* aigeannach.

virent, *adj.* uaine, gorm, glas.

virgin, *s.* maighdeann, òigh, ainnir.

virgin, *adj.* maighdeannail, òigheil.

virginal, *s.* òigh-cheòl.

virginal, *adj.* òigheil, banail, màlda.

virginity, *s.* maighdeannas.

viridity, *s.* guirme, uainead.

virile, *adj.* fearail ; duineil.

virility, *s.* fearachas.

virtual, *adj.* éifeachdach, feartach, buadhach ; nàdurail ; brìgheil.

virtuality, *s.* éifeachd.

virtuate, *v. a.* dèan éifeachdach.

virtue, *s.* subhailc; deagh-bheus; buaidh ; neart, comas ; èifeachd.

virtuoso, *s.* fear-ionnsaichte.

virtuous, *adj.* subhailceach ; beusach, geimnidh ; éifeachdach, cumhachdach, comasach, slàinteil, math.

virulence, *s.* nimhe ; géire, gairge, falachd, gamhlas, mìorun, miosgainn.

virulent, *adj.* nimhneach ; cnàmhtach, geur, garg, gamhlasach, mìorunach, miosgainneach.

virus, *s.* speach, nimh, ionghair.

visage, *s.* aghaidh, aodann, gnùis, sealladh, tuar, dreach.

viscerate, *v. a.* thoir am mionach á.

viscid, *adj.* righinn, sticeach.

viscidity, *s.* leanailteachd.

viscosity, *s.* rìghneachd.

viscount, *s.* biocas, morair.

viscountess, *s.* bana-bhiocas.

viscous, *adj.* glaodhanta, bìthanach.

visibility, visibleness, *s.* faicsinneachd, leirsinneachd, soilleireachd.

visible, *adj.* faicsinneach ; soilleir.

vision, *s.* fradharc ; sealladh, taisbean, foillseachadh ; taibhs, tannasg ; sgàile ; bruadar, aisling.

visionary, *adj.* faoin, meallta, taisbeanach, baralach, dòchasach.

visionary, *s.* taibhsear, aisliche.

visit, *s.* céilidh ; coimhead.

visit, *v.* fiosraich ; taghail, dèan céilidh, rach, a choimhead.

visitant, *s.* fear-céilidh.

visitation, *s.* fiosrachadh, breitheanas ; cuairt-rannsachaidh.

visiter, visitor, *s.* aoigh ; dàimh.

visor, *s.* cidhis, sgàile, cleith.

vista, *s.* caol-shealladh, aisir, fad-shealladh.

visual, *adj.* fradharcach, léirsinneach.

vital, *adj.* beathail, beò.

vitality, *s.* beathalachd.

vitals, *s.* buill na beatha, neart.

vitiate, *v. a.* mill ; truaill, salaich.

vitiation, *s.* truailleadh ; milleadh.

vitious, *adj.* dubhailceach, truaillidh.

vitreous, *adj.* glaineach, glaine.

vitrify, *v.* tionndaidh gu glaine.

vitriol, *s.* uisge-loisgeach.

vitriolic, *adj.* mar uisge-loisgeach.

vituperate, *v. a.* coirich, cronaich.

vituperation, *s.* cronachadh, trod.

vivacious, *adj.* maireann, buan, beò ; mear, sgairteil, sùnntach.

vivacity, *s.* beothalas, meanmnachd.

vivid, *adj.* beò ; boillsgeanta, grad.

vividness, *s.* beothalachd, boillsge.

vivific, *adj.* beothachaidh.
vivify, *v. a.* thoir beò ; beothaich.
viviparous, *adj.* beò-bhreitheach.
vixen, *s.* sionnach boireann.
viz., *adj.* is e sin ri ràdh.
vizard, *s.* cidhis, sgàil.
vizier, *s.* àrd-fhear-comhairle an Turcaich, prìomh-chomhairleach Turcach.
vocabulary, *s.* facalair.
vocal, *adj.* gathach, fonnar.
vocality, *s.* labhairt, cainnt.
vocation, *s.* gairm, cèaird ; rabhail.
vociferate, *v.* glaodh, sgairt ; beuc.
vociferation, *s.* glaodh, sgairt, beucail, sgairteachd ; gàir, iolach.
vociferous, *adj.* beucach, sgairteach ; stàirneach, glaodhach, guthach.
vogue, *s.* fasan, gnàths, nòs.
voice, *s.* guth, glaodh ; guth-taghaidh ; facal, sgairt, éigh, labhairt.
void, *adj.* falamh, fàs, faoin.
void, *s.* fàsalachd, falaimhe.
void, *v. a.* falmhaich ; tilg a mach.
voidable, *adj.* seachnachail ; seachnach.
volatile, *adj.* itealach, leumnach, gradshiùbhlach ; beò, beothail, spioradail, mear ; caochlaideach ; mùiteach ; gradthioram, lasanta.
volatileness, volatility, *s.* grad-thiormachd ; luaineachd, caochlaideachd ; beothalachd, iomaluaths.
volcano, *s.* beinn-theine.
vole, *s.* buaidh-iomlan.
volery, volary, *s.* sgaoth eun.
volitation, *s.* comas-itealaich.
volition, *s.* toil, rùn, deònachadh.
volley, *s.* làdach ; *v.* tilg a mach.
volubility, *s.* deas-labhairteachd, caochlaideachd ; lonais, beulais.
voluble, *adj.* deas-chainnteach ; luaineach, caochlaideach ; siùbhlach.
volume, *s.* rola, leabhar, pasgan.
voluminous, *adj.* ioma-rolach.
voluntary, *adj.* toileach, a dheòin.
volunteer, *s.* saighdear saor-thoile.

voluptuary, *s.* ròicear, sòganiche.
voluptuous, *adj.* sòghmhor, sòghail.
voluptuousness, *s.* mì-stuamachd.
vomit, *v. a.* tilg, sgeith, dìobhair, tilg a mach, cuir a mach.
vomit, *s.* tilgeadh, sgeith ; dìobhart purgaid-thilgidh.
voracious, *adj.* cìocrach, gionach ; craosach, glutach, lonach.
voraciousness, voracity, *s.* cìocras, craosaireachd, glamaireachd, gionaichead lon, glutaireachd.
vortex, *s.* cuairt-shlugan ; coire-cuairteig, faochag, cuairteag, cuinneag-thuaitheil, ioma-ghaoth.
vortical, *adj.* tuathallach.
votaress, *s.* ban-bhòidiche.
votary, *s.* fear-bòide.
vote, *s.* guth-taghaidh, bhòt.
vote, *v. a.* thoir guth-taghaidh.
voter, *s.* fear guth-taghaidh.
votive, *adj.* bòideach.
vouch, *v. a.* dearbh, còmhdaich, thoir fianais, tog fianais.
vouch, *s.* fianais ; dearbhadh ; teisteannas, briathar.
voucher, *s.* fear dearbhaidh, fianuis, teisteanas, dearbhadh.
vow, *s.* bòid, mòid, mionnan, guidhe, gealladh, mionnan-cùmhnainte.
vow, *v.* bòidich, mionnaich.
vowel, *s.* foghair, guth.
voyage, *s.* taisdeal, turas-mara.
voyager, *s.* taisdealaich.
vulgar, *adj.* coitcheann ; gràisgeil ; ìosal, suarrach ; balachail ; neo-shuairce, mì-mhodhail.
vulgar, *s.* gràisg, pràbar.
vulgarism, *s.* trustaireachd.
vulgarity, *s.* gràisgealachd.
vulgate, *s.* Bìobull Laidinn.
vulnerable, *adj.* so-leònte.
vulnerate, *v. a.* leòn ; dochainn.
vulture, *s.* fang, preachan.
vulturine, *adj.* preachanach.

W

wabble, *v. n.* gluais o thaobh gu taobh, dèan luaghainn.
wad, *s.* cuifein ; muillean.
wadding, *s.* garbh-lìnig, cuifein.
waddle, *v. n.* imich 's an turraman ; (dèan) ceum tonnaig.
wade, *v. n.* rach troimh uisge.
wafer, *s.* abhlan, dèarnagan ; breacag.
waft, *v.* giùlain ; iomchair troimh 'n adhar, snàmh.
waft, *s.* crathadh brataich ri gaoith.
wag, *v.* crath, gluais ; crith, bog, seòg, siubhail.

wag, *s.* fear ancheardach.
wage, *v. a.* feuch ri ; naisg geall ; thoir ionnsaigh, dèan.
wager, *s.* geall ; tairgse bòide.
wager, *v. a.* cuir geall, cuir an geall.
wages, *s.* tuarasdal, duais.
waggery, *s.* fala-dhà, aincheard.
waggish, *adj.* aincheardach, leasanta ; sgeigeil, sgeigeach, magail, àbhcaideach.
waggle, *v. n.* dèan turramanaich.
waggon, *s.* cairt-mhór.
waggoner, *s.* cairtear.

wagtail, s. breachd-an-t-sìl, an glaisean-seilich.

waif, s. faotail : ulaidh.

wail, wailing, s. caoidh, caoineadh, bròn, tuireadh, gul, gal.

wail, v. dèan-tuireadh, dèan bron, dèan gal, caoidh, caoin, guil.

wailful, adj. tùrsach, brònach, muladach, dubhach, deurach.

wain, s. feun, fèanaidh, lòpan.

wainscot, s. cailbhe-fhiodh ; talainte ; darach-buidhe.

waist, s. meadhon, cneas, crios.

waistcoat, s. siostacota, peiteag.

wait, v. feith, fuirich, fritheil ; stad.

wait, s. laighe, plaid-laighe.

waiter, s. gille-frithealaidh.

waits, s. ceòl-òidhche.

waive, v. a. cuir gu taobh ; tréig.

wake, v. dùisg, mosgail, fairich ; bros-nach cuir chuige, bruidich ; dèan caithris, dèan faire.

wake, s. féill coisrigidh eaglais ; rotal luinge ; lòrg.

wakeful, adj. furachair, faicilleach ; aireachail, caithriseach.

waken, v. dùisg, mosgail, fairich.

walk, s. sràid ; rathad, slighe, imeach ; ceum sràide ; coiseachd, sràidimeachd.

walk, v. coisich, imich, ceum, sràideas-aich, sraidimich ; spaidsearaich ; falbh, siubhail, triall.

walker, s. coisiche ; oifigeach.

walking-stick, s. lorg, bata-làimhe.

walkmill, s. mullinn-luaidh.

wall, v. a. cuartaich le balla ; dìon, druid, callaidich, tog balla.

wall, s. balla ; callaid.

wallet, s. màileid, balg ; poca.

wall-eyed, adj. gealshuileach.

wallop, v. n. teas, goil, bruich.

wallow, v. n. luidir, aornagaich, aoineag-aich, aoineagraich, loirc.

walnut, s. geinmchno.

waltron, s. an t-each-uisge.

wan, adj. glasneulach ; glasdaidh.

wand, s. slat, slatag, maothan.

wander, v. seachranaich, iomrallaich, rach air seachran, rach air iomrall ; rach am mearachd, rach air àimhreidh, rach air faontradh.

wanderer, s. seachranaiche, iomrallaiche, fògaraiche ; deòiridh, fear - allabain, fear-fuadain.

wandering, s. seachran, iomralladh, iom-rall, faontradh, allaban.

wane, v. n. beagaich, lughdaich ; searg, rach air ais, caith air falbh, crìon, fas sean.

wane, s. (of the moon), earrdhubh ; eàrradh, crìonadh, lughdachadh.

want, s. uireasbhuidh, dìth, gainne, bochdainn, easbhuidh ; cion.

want, v. n. bi dh' easbhuidh ; bi an uireasbhuidh, bi am feum, bi as eugmhais ; bi an dìth ; sir, iarr ; bi as aonais ; fàilnich, thig gearr.

wanton, s. strìopach, siùrsach, gaorsach ; drùisear, trurstar.

wanton, adj. macnusach, feòlmhor, mear meamnach ; aotrom.

wanton, v. n. dèan mire.

wanty, s. giort ; crios-tarra.

war, s. còmhrag, cogadh ; cath.

war, v. còmhraig, cog ; cathaich.

warble, v. canntairich ; ceileirich.

warbler, s. ceileiriche ; canntairiche.

ward, s. daingneach, àite-dìon, faire ; freiceadan ; leanabh fo oid-fhoghlum ; earrann, cearn glaise.

ward, v. dìon ; cùm freiceadan ; cùm air falbh.

warden, s. fear-gleidhidh.

warder, s. maor-coimhid.

wardrobe, s. seòmar-aodaich, deiseach-ean.

wardship, s. tuitearachd.

wareful, adj. furachair, fàicilleach.

warehouse, s. tigh-taisg.

wares, s. bathar, marsantachd.

warfare, s. cogadh, cath.

warily, adv. gu faicilleach.

warlike, adj. curanta, cogach ; coganta, cathach, gaisgeil.

warlock, s. druidh, draoidh.

warm, adj. blàth ; teth ; teinnteach ; feargach ; dian, cas, lasanta ; teò-chridheach ; coibhneil.

warm, v. a. blàthaich, teò, teòthaich, teasaich, brosnaich, las.

warming-pan, s. aghann-blàthachaidh.

warmth, s. blàthas, blàs, déine, teas-inntinn, deothas, dealas.

warn, v. a. thoir sanas, thoir rabhadh, thoir bàirlinn ; thoir faireachadh.

warning, s. sanas, rabhadh, comhairle, faireachadh, bàirlinn ; fios.

warp, v. tionndaidh a thaobh ; rach gu taobh, atharraich, claon ; crup ; seac, lùb ; trus.

warp, s. dlùth ; snàth-deilbhe.

warrant, s. barantas ; comas.

warrant, v. a. urrasaich, barandaich, dèan cinnteach, thoir barantas, rach an urras, deimhinnich.

warrantable, adj. barantach ; laghail ; dligheach, ceadaichte.

warranty, s. barantas, urras.

warren, s. broclach ; faiche.

warrior, s. mìlidh, curaidh, gaisgeach, laoch ; cathach, fear-feachd, fear-cogaidh, saighdear.

wart, s. foinne.

warty, adj. foinneamhach.

wary, adj. faicilleach, cùramach.

was, pret. bu, bha.

wash, *v. a.* nigh, glan, ionnlaid.

wash, *s.* bog, boglach, féith ; uisge siabuinn ; spùt ; sos, biadh-mhuc ; sluisrich ; nigheadaireachd.

washer, *s.* nìgheadair ; sgùradair.

washerwoman, *s.* bean-nigheadaireachd, bean-nighe.

washy, *adj.* fliuch, àitidh, uisgidh bog, tais, lag, spùtach, steallach.

wasp, *s.* connspeach, connsbeach.

waspish, *adj.* speachanta ; speacharra, dreamach, dranndanach, crosda.

wassail, *s.* deoch, phòit.

wassailer, *s.* pòitear, misgear.

waste, *v.* caith, sgrios, struidh, cosg, mill ; caith air falbh, lùghdaich, searg ; rach an lughad.

waste, *adj.* fàs ; uaigneach, dìthreabhach, sgriosta, mìllte ; suarrach, gun stà ; anabarrach, ro mhor.

waste, *s.* caitheamh, ana-caitheamh, struidheadh, stròdh, diombuil ; sgrios ; fàsach, milleadh, lùghdachadh, fartas, asgart, dìthreabh.

wasteful, *adj.* caithteach ; sgriosail mill-teach ; cosgail, strùidheil, stròdhail ; uaigneach, fàs.

waster, *s.* strùidhear, milltear.

watch, *s.* faire, faireachadh ; caithris ; beachd, sùil ; uaireadair ; luchd-faire ; freiceadan ; forair.

watch, *v.* dèan faire, cùm faire ; suidh ; cùm sùil, dèan freiceadan, dìon, gléidh, coimhead, cùm ; bi cùramach, bi faicilleach.

watchful, *adj.* cairiseach, furachair, faicilleach, faireil, aireach.

watch-house, *s.* tigh-aire, tigh-faire ; tigh-caithris, tigh-freiceadain, gainn-tir.

watching, *s.* caithris, faire.

watchmaker, *s.* òr-cheard.

watchman, *s.* fear-faire, fear-caithris, gocmunn, gocuman.

watchword, *s.* ciall-chagar ; diùbhras an airm, facal-faire.

water, *s.* uisge ; bùrn ; muir, mùn.

water, *v.* uisgich, fliuch ; sil, fras.

watercresses, *s.* biolaire an fhuarain ; an dobhar-lus.

water-dog, *s.* cù-uisge.

waterfall, *s.* eas, leum-uisge.

water-fowl, *s.* eun-uisge.

water-gruel, *s.* brochan - uisge, dubh-bhrochan, stiùireag, easach.

water-lily, *s.* bileag-bhàite ; bioras ; cuirinnein.

waterman, *s.* portair, fear-aisig.

water-mark, *s.* àird' an làin-mhara, tiùrr an làin, ainm an deanamh pàipeir.

water-mill, *s.* muileann-uisge.

waterwork, *s.* obair-uisge.

watery, *adj.* fliuch, uisgidh, bog.

wattle, *s.* slat-chaoil ; sprogan coilich.

wattle, *v. a.* figh le caol.

wave, *s.* tonn, sùmainn, sùmaid, stuadh, lunn, bàrc.

wave, *v.* tog tonn ; crath, luaisg ; cuir dheth, fàg, tréig ; cuir gu taobh, seachainn ; giùlain ; séid suas.

waver, *v. n.* bi 'n iomchomhairle, bi air udal, bi eadar da chomhairle, bi an teagamh, bi neo-shuidhichte.

waverer, *s.* fear - iomluath, fear neo-sheasmhach ('n a bheachd).

wavy, *adj.* tonnach, stuadhach.

wax, *s.* céir, céir-sheillean.

wax, *v.* céirich ; fas mór, cinn.

waxed, waxen, *adj.* céireach.

way, *s.* rathad, slighe, ròd ; car, bealach ; aisrdh, ceum ; modh, seòl, dòigh, meadhon ; astar.

wayfarer, *s.* fear-turais, fear-astair, fear-gabhail an rathaid.

waylay, *v. a.* dèan plaid-laighe, dèan feall-fhalach, dèan fàth-fheitheamh.

way-mark, *s.* post-seòlaidh rathaid.

wayward, *adj.* bras, cabhagach, frith-earra, dian, obann, reasgach, dream-luinneach, crosda, corrach.

we, *pron.* sinn, sinne.

weak, *adj.* lag, fann ; gun dìon.

weaken, *v. a.* lagaich, fannaich.

weakling, *s.* spreòchan.

weakly, *adj.* lag ; fann, anfhann.

weakness, *s.* laigse, anfhannachd.

weal, *s.* math ; sonas, soirbheachadh.

wealth, *s.* beartas, saibhreas.

wealthy, *adj.* beairteach, saoibhir.

wean, *v. a.* cuir bhàrr na cìche ; caisg.

weapon, *s.* ball-airm, inneal-cogaidh.

wear, *v.* caith ; lughadaich, claoidh, sàraich ; cosg, cuir umad ; cuir timchioll searg as.

wear, *s.* caitheamh ; tuil-dhorus ; àbh-ias-gaich, cabhall, tàbhan.

wearer, *s.* fear-caitheamh.

wearied, *adj.* sgìth ; air toirt thairis.

weariness, *s.* sgìos, fannachadh ; fadal, fadachd.

wearing, *adj.* aodach, earradh.

wearisome, *adj.* sgìtheil ; fadalach.

weary, *adj.* sgith ; claoidhte.

weary, *v. a.* sgìthich ; fannaich ; thoir thairis ; sàraich ; oibrich ; caith ; lèir, claoidh.

weasand, weason, *s.* stéic-bhràghaid ; it-igheach.

weasel, *s.* neas, nios.

weather, *s.* aimsir, àm, uair ; sìde.

weather, *v. a.* seas ri ; cùm ri, rach air fuaradh ; cùm ri fuaradh, cuir fodha ; cuir ri gaoith.

weather-beaten, *adj.* sàraichte ; cruadh-aichte ; cleachdte ri droch shìde.

weather-board, s. taobh-an-fhuaraidh, toabh na gaoithe.

weathercock, s. coileach-gaoithe.

weather-gage, s. adharmheidh.

weather-wise, adj. sgileil mun aimsir.

weave, v. figh, dual, dlùthaich, amlaich, pleat ; dèan fighe.

weaver, s. breabadair ; figheadair.

web, s. cathan-aodaich, còrn (aodaich).

webbed, adj. ceangailte le lìon.

web-foot, s. spòg-shnàmha.

wed, v. a. pòs, ceangail am pòsadh.

wedded, adj. pòsta.

wedding, s. pòsadh ; banais.

wedge, s. geinn, deinn ; faraich (f.).

wedge, v. a. teannaich le geinn.

wedlock, s. pòsadh, ceangal-pòsaidh.

Wednesday, s. Dì-ciadain.

weed, s. luibh, éideadh-bròin.

weed, v. a. gart-ghlan.

weeder, s. gart-ghlanaiche.

weedy, adj. lusanch ; fiadhain.

week, s. seachdain.

weekly, adj. gach seachdain.

weel, s. poll-cuairteig ; cabhall.

ween, v. n. saoil, smuainich.

weep, v. dèan gul, dèan caoidh, guil, caoin, dèan tuireadh, dèan bròn.

weeper, s. fear-bròin ; geala-bhréid-bròin, bàn-shròl-bròin.

weeping, s. gul, caoineadh, caoidh.

weeping, adj. deurach ; snitheach.

weevil, s. leòmann, reudan.

weft, s. inneach, snàth-cura.

weftage, s. fighe, pleatadh.

weigh, v. cothromaich ; beachd-smuaintich, breathnaich.

weighed, adj. cothromaichte.

weigher, s. fear-cothromachaidh.

weight, s. cothrom ; cudthrom, uallach, eallach, eire.

weightiness, s. truime, truimead, cud-thromachd, chothromachd.

weightless, adj. aotrom ; faoin, neo-throm ; gun chothrom.

weighty, adj. tròm, cudthromach.

welcome, adj. taitneach ; faoilteach, fàilteach, furanach, furmailteach.

welcome, s. fàilte, faoilte, furan.

welcome ! interj. fàilte ! 's e do bheatha ! 's e bhur beatha !

welcome, v. a. fàiltich ; faoiltich, furanaich altaich beatha, cuir fàilt' air ; cuir furan air.

welcomer, s. fear-fàilte.

weld, v. a. buail 'na chéile, tàth.

weld, would, s. am buidh-fhliodh.

welding, s. tàth, tàthadh.

welfare, s. sonas, àdh, slàinte.

welkin, s. na speuran.

well, s. tobar, fuaran, tiobairt.

well, adj. math ; ceart, gasta slàn, fallain, tarbhach, sona.

well, adv. gu math, gu ceart ; gu slàn, gu fallain ; gu gleusda, gu gasda.

welladay ! interj. mo chreach ! mo thruaighe ! mo dhunaidh ! mo sgaradh ! mo léireadh !

well-being, s. soirbheas ; sonas, leas.

well-born, adj. uasal, inbheach, àrd.

well-bred, adj. modhail ; beusach, air dheagh oilean.

well done ! interj. math thu féin ! 's math a fhuaradh tu, sin a lochain !

well-favoured, adj. sgiamhach, ciatach, maiseach, eireachdail, bòidheach, tlachdmhor cuanda.

well-nigh, adv. am fagus ; ach beag, cha mhór nach.

well-set, adj. fuirbineach.

well-spring, s. tobar fhìoruisg.

well-wish, s. deagh-rùn.

well-wisher, s. fear deagh-rùin.

welt, s. balt ; oir, fàitheam.

welt, v. a. fàithem.

welter, v. n. aoirneagaich ; luidir.

wen, s. futh ; fliodh.

wench, s. siùrsach.

wench, v. n. bì ri siùrsachd.

wencher, s. fear strìopachais.

wend, v. n. rach, imich, falbh.

wenny, adj. fluthach ; fliodhach.

went, pret. and part. of go, chaidh.

wept, part. ghuil, chaoin ; caointe.

were, pret. of to be, bhà, bu.

west, s. an iar, an àirde an iar, àirde laighe na gréine, an taobh siar.

west, adj. suas, shuas, siar.

west, adv. an iar, iar.

westering, adj. siar, gus an iar.

westerly, western, adj. as an airde an iar, o 'n iar ; chum na h-airde an iar.

westward, adj. gu 's an airde an iar.

wet, s. fliuiche, uisge, fliuchadh.

wet, adj. fliuch, àitidh ; bog, tais.

wet, v. a. fliuch, uisgich.

wether, s. mult, reithe spoite.

wetness, s. fliuichead, fliuchalachd.

wettish, adj. a lethchar fliuch.

wex, v. a. cinn, fàs mòr.

whale, s. muc-mhara ; orc.

wharf, s. làimhrig.

wharfage, s. cìs-làimhrig.

wharfinger, s. fear-làimhrig.

what, pron. ciod ; creud.

whatever, whatsoever, pron. ciod air bith, ciod sam bith, ge b'e air bith.

wheal, s. guirean, spucaid, plucan.

wheat, s. cruithneachd.

wheaten, adj. de chruithneachd.

wheedle, v. a. meall le briodal.

wheedling, adj. briodalach.

wheel, s. cuidhle, cuidheall, roth.

wheel, v. cuidhil, ruidhil, rol ; cuir mun cuairt, tionndaidh mu 'n cuairt, rach mu 'n cuairt.

wheel-barrow, *s.* bara-rotha, breamhainn.
wheelwright, *s.* saor-chuidhleachan, tuair-near.
wheely, *adj.* cruinn ; rothach, ruidh-leanach, cearclach, cuairsgeach.
wheeze, *v. n.* bi pìochanaich.
wheezing, *adj.* pìochanach.
whelk, *s.* màighdealag ; guirean, bocaid.
whelm, *v. a.* còmhdaich, cuibhrig.
whelp, *s.* cuilein.
when, *adv.* c'uin ? *i.e.* cia ùine ? ciod an t-àm ? 'nuair, air an àm.
whence, *adv.* cia as ? cò as ? ciod as ? cò uaithe ? c' arson ? ciod uime ?
whencesoever, *adv.* ciod air bith an t-aite as, ge b' e air bith cò as.
whenever, *adv.* cho luath agus ceart cho luath 's, ge b' e uair.
where, *adv.* c' àite ? far.
whereabout, *adv.* cia mu thimchioll ?
whereas, *adv.* a chionn gu, air a mheud 's gu, air a mheud 's gum, a chionn gum, do bhrìgh gun, a thaobh gur, do bhrìgh gur ; a chionn gur ; 'nuair ; an àite sin.
whereat, *adv.* aige, aige sin ; cò aige ? ciod aige ?
whereby, *adv.* leis ; cò leis ? leis an do.
wherever, *adv.* cia b' e air bith àite, c' àite sam bith, ge b' e àite.
wherefore, *adv.* c' arson ? ciod uime ? air an aobhar sin, uime sin.
wherein, *adv.* far, anns an, anns am ; c' àite ? ciod ann ? cò ann ?
whereinto, *adv.* a dh' ionnsaigh.
whereof, *adv.* do, cò dheth ? cò leis ?
whereon, *adv.* air, air an do ; ciod air ?
wheresoever, *adv.* ge b' e air bith àite.
whereunto, *adv.* ciod fàth ? ciod do ? ciod is crìoch do ? c' arson ? a dh' ionnsaigh.
whereupon, *adv.* air a sin.
wherewithal, *adv.* cò leis ? ciod leis ? leis, le, leis an do.
wherret, *v. a.* cuir dragh air.
wherry, *s.* bàta dà chroinn.
whet, *v. a.* geuraich ; faobharaich.
whet, *s.* geurachadh ; faobharachadh.
whether, *pron.* cò aca ? cò dhiù.
whether, *adv.* co dhiù, ge b' e.
whetstone, *s.* clach-fhaobhair, clach-ghleusaidh.
whetter, *s.* fear-geurachaidh.
whey, *s.* meòg, meug.
wheyey, wheyish, *adj.* meògach, meogar, meugaidh.
which, *pron. inter.* cia ? ciod ?
which, *pron. rel.* a ; nach, ni.
whichever, whichsoever, *pron.* cia air bith, ciod air bith, ciod sam bith.
whiff, *s.* toth ; oiteag, séideag, osag.
whiffle, *v. a.* bi an iomchomhairle ; crath, crith ; sgap, sgaoil.

whiffler, *s.* gaoithean.
Whig, *s.* Cuigse.
Whiggish, *adj.* Cuigseach.
Whiggism, *s.* Cuigseachd.
while, *v.* cuir dheth aimsir ; sìn ùine.
while, *s.* grathunn, tacan ; greis.
while, whiles, whilst, *adv.* am feadh, 'nuair, an àm, fhad 's ; am fad 's, ré na h-ùine.
whim, whimsey, *s.* faoineachd ; faoin-dhòchas, amaideachd ; neònachas, faoineas, saobh-smuain.
whimper, *v. n.* dèan sgiùganaich.
whimsical, *adj.* faoin, neònach, iongant-ach, breisleachail.
whin, *s.* conasg, conusg.
whine, *v. n.* dèan caoidhearan ; guil.
whine, *s.* caoidhearan.
whinny, *v. n.* dèan sitrich.
whip, *v.* sgiùrsair, slat, cuip.
whip, *v.* sgiùrs, tilip.
whipcord, *s.* còrd-sgiùrsaidh.
whip-hand, *s.* làmh-an-uachdar.
whip-saw, *s.* tuireasg, sàbh-mór.
whirl, *v.* cuairtich, cuibhlich, ruidhil ; ruith mun cuairt.
whirl, *s.* cuairt, cuibhle, ruidhil ; dol mun cuairt, cuartag.
whirligig, *s.* gille-mirean.
whirlpool, *s.* cuairt-shlugan, faochag, cuairt-shruth, coire-tuaicheal.
whirlwind, *s.* iomghaoth.
whirring, *s.* sgiath fharum.
whisk, *s.* sguab, sguabag.
whisk, *v.* sguab, sguab seachad.
whisker, *s.* ciabhag.
whisky, *s.* uisge-beatha.
whisper, *v. n.* cogair, cagair.
whisper, *s.* cogar, cagar, sanas.
whisperer, *s.* fear-cagarsaich.
whist ! *interj.* uist ! éisd ! bi do thosd ! tòst, bi sàmhach !
whist, *s.* seòrsa cluiche air chairtean.
whistle, *v.* dèan fead, gearr fead.
whistle, *s.* feadag, feadan ; fead.
whistler, *s.* fear-feadaireachd.
whit, *s.* mìr, dad ; smod, dadum.
white, *adj.* geal ; bàn, fionn.
white, *s.* gile, geal ; baine, gealagan.
white, *v. a.* gealaich, bànaich.
whiten, *v.* gealaich, bànaich.
whiteness, *s.* gile, gilead, bàinead.
whitewash, *s.* uisge aoil.
whither, *adv.* c' àite ? cia 'n taobh ? ciod an car, ciod an rathad ? far, a dh' ionnsaigh.
whithersoever, *adv.* ge b'e air bith àite ; c' àit air bith.
whiting, *s.* cùiteag, phronn-chailc.
whitish, *adj.* a lethchar geal.
whitlow, *s.* anabhiorach.
whitster, *s.* fear-gealachaidh.
Whitsuntide, *s.* Caingis, Bealltuinn.

whittle, s. sgian, corc.
whiz, v. n. srann.
whizzing, s. srannail.
who, pron. interrog. cò ?
who, rel. pron. a ; nach.
whoever, pron. cò air bith.
whole, adj. slàn, fallain ; iomlan ; uile, gu léir, uile gu léir.
whole, s. an t-iomlan.
wholesale, s. mórbhathar ; prìs àraidh.
wholesome, adj. slàn, fallain.
wholly, adv. gu slàn ; gu tur ; gu h-iomlan, gu léir, gu buileach.
whom, accus. sing. and pl. of who, a.
whomsoever, pron. cò air bith ; aon air bith, neach sam bith.
whoop, s. coileach-oidhche ; glaodh, gàir, iolach ; gàir-chatha.
whore, s. siùrsach, strìopach.
whoredom, s. strìopachas.
whoremaster, whoremonger, s. drùisear, fear-strìopachais.
whoreson, s. mac-dìolain.
whorish, adj. strìopachail.
whortleberry, whurt, s. braoileag.
whose, pron. interrog. cò ? cò leis ?
whose, pron. poss. of who and which, aig am beil.
whosoever, pron. cò air bith.
why, adv. c'arson ? ciod uime ? cia fàth ? c' uige ? c' uime ?
wick, s. buaic, siobhag.
wicked, adj. olc, aingidh ; mallaichte, ciontach, peacach, dubhailceach.
wickedness, s. aingidheachd ; olc, droch-bheart, peacadh, cionta.
wicker, adj. and s. slatach, gadach.
wicket, s. caoldhorus, dorus cumhang, fadhorus.
wide, adj. farsuing, leathann, mór, leòbhar.
widen, v. leudaich, farsuinnich ; leathannaich ; fàs farsuing.
widgeon, s. an t-amadan-mòintich.
widow, s. bantrach.
widower, s. aonrachdan.
widowhood, s. bantrachas.
width, s. farsuingeachd ; leud.
wield, v. a. làimhsich ; stiùr.
wieldy, adj. so-làimhseachadh.
wife, s. bean-phòsta, céile.
wig, s. pìorbhuic ; fara-ghruag.
wight, s. neach ; bith, urra.
wight, adj. uallach ; iullagach.
wightly, adv. gu luath.
wild, adj. fiadhaich ; borb ; allaidh ; allta ; allmharra ; fiadhain ; fàs, garbh, neo-àitichte ; mì-riaghailteach ; mac-meanmnach, faoin.
wild, s. dìthreabh, fàstalamh.
wilder, v. a. cuir air seachran.
wilderness, s. fàsach.
wild-fire, s. teine-gradaig.

wild-goose, s. cadhan.
wilding, s. ubhal-fiadhain.
wildness, s. fiadhaichead, buirbe.
wile, s. car, cleas, cealg, cuilbheart.
wilful, adj. rag, reasgach, ceannlaidir, danarra ; dùr, doirbh ; an-srìanta, dearrasach.
wilfulness, s. an-toilealachd, reasgachd, rag-mhuinealachd.
will, s. toil, rùn, àill, gean, miann, togradh ; deòin, roghainn ; tiomnadh.
will, v. a. iarr ; toilich ; miannaich ; rùnaich, sanntaich ; togair, òrduich.
willing, adj. toileach, deònach, togarrach ; miannach.
willow, s. seileach.
will-with-a-wisp, s. sionnachan.
wily, adj. eòlach, seòlta, culbheartach, sligheach, innleachdach.
wimble, s. tora, boireal.
win, v. coisinn ; buidhinn, faigh.
wince, winch, v. n. breab ; tilg.
winch, s. beart-shnìomhain.
wind, s. gaoth ; soirbheas ; anail.
wind, v. tionndaidh, toinn, lùb, trus, tachrais ; fàilich ; rothainn ; atharraich ; rach mun cuairt.
wind-egg, s. ugh-maothaig.
winder, s. toinneadair, toinntear, fear-tachrais ; cuidhle-thachrais.
wind-flower, s. lus-na-gaoithe.
wind-gun, s. gunna-gaoithe.
windiness, s. gaotharachd.
winding, s. lùbadh ; fiaradh, car.
winding-sheet, s. lìonaodach, aodach mairbh.
windlass, s. ailig-ghuairneach, unndais ; tachrasan.
windle, s. dealgan, fearsaid.
windmill, s. muileann-gaoithe.
window, v. a. uinneagaich.
window, s. uinneag.
windpipe, s. det-igheach, stéic-bràghad.
windward, adv. air fuaradh.
windy, adj. gaothar ; stoirmeil, doinionnach ; gaothach, aotrom.
wine, s. fìon.
wine-press, s. fìon-amar.
wing, s. sgiath ; cùl-tigh.
wing, v. a. cuir sgiathan air ; falbh air iteig ; leòn 's an sgéith.
winged, adj. sgiathach, luath.
wink, s. priobadh, caogadh, smèideadh.
wink, v. n. caog ; priob, smèid ; ceadaich aontaich ; leig seachad.
winner, s. fear-buanachadh.
winning, adj. tàirngeach, dlùth-thairngeach mealltach, ionmhuinn ; maiseach ; taitneach, ciatach ; gaolach.
winning, s. cosnadh ; buidhinn.
winnow, v. fasgain ; glan, gréidh rannsaich ; feuch ; dealaich, sgar.

winter, *s.* geamhradh ; dùbhlachd.
winter, *v.* geamhraich ; cuir thairis nò caith an geamhradh.
winterly, wintry, *adj.* geamhradail, geamhrail, geamhrach.
winy, *adj.* fìonach.
wipe, *v. a.* siab, sguab, glan.
wipe, *s.* siabadh, suathadh, glanadh ; beum ; buille, gleadhar.
wire, *s.* cruaidh-theud.
wisdom, *s.* gliocas, tuigse, eòlas, ciall, tùr, eagnaidheachd ; crìonnachd.
wise, *adj.* glic, eòlach, sicir, crìonna, ciallach, fiosrach, stòlda.
wiseacre, *s.* baothaire, burraidh.
wish, *v.* mìannaich, guidh, togair ; sanntaich, iarr, rùnaich, bi deònach.
wish, *s.* mìann, àill, togradh ; guidhe ; toil, dùrachd, déidh ; iarrtas.
wisher, *s.* fear-mìannachaidh.
wishful, *adj.* togarrach, mìannach, sanntach, déidheil, cionail.
wisket, whisket, *s.* sgùile, sgùlan.
wisp, *s.* mùillean, boitein, sop.
wistful, *adj.* dùrachdach, smuainteach, aireach, cùramach.
wit (to), is e sin ri ràdh.
wit, *s.* aigneadh, ciall, inntinn, tuigse, tùr, toinisg, meamna, mac-meamna, mac-meanmain ; geur-labhairt ; fear geurchuiseach, fear geurchainnteach, bearradair ; fear tulchuiseach, fear mór-thuigse ; innleachd, tionnsgnadh.
witch, *s.* bana-bhuidseach, ban-druidh, briosag.
witchcraft, *s.* buidseachd, rosachd, druidheachd ; geasan, dolbh.
with, *prep.* le, leis, maille ri ; mar ri, cuide ris, am fochar ; with me, thee, her, him, leam, leat, leatha, leis ; with us, you, them, leinn, leibh, leo.
withal, *adv.* leis, mar ri.
withdraw, *v.* falbh, thoir air ais, thoir air falbh, rach a thaobh ; cuir a thaobh ; ais-chéimnich.
withdrawing-room, *s.* seòmar suidhe.
withe, *s.* slat-chaoil ; cual-chaoil.
wither, *v.* searg, seac, crìon, caith air falbh, sgreag, meath.
withering, *s.* seargadh, seacadh, crìonadh, sgreagadh.
withers, *s. pl.* slinneanan eich.
withhold, *v. a.* cùm air ais, bac.
within, *adv.* and *prep.* a stigh.
withinside, *adv.* an leth a stigh.
without, *prep.* gun ; as eugmhais ; a mach, a muigh, an taobh a muigh.
without, *conj.* mur, saor ; mur dèan, mur bi, mur tachair.
without, *adv.* am muigh, a mach.
withstand, *v. a.* cùm ris, cùm an aghaidh, cùm roimh, seas ri.
withy, *s.* gad.

witless, *s.* gòrach ; amaideach, eu-céillidh, faoin, neo-thùrail.
witling, *adj.* fear leth-gheur ; *s.* leth-chiallach.
witness, *s.* fianais.
witness, *v.* thoir fianais, dèan fianuis, dearbh le fianuis, tog fianuis.
witted, *adj.* geur, tùrail.
witticism, *s.* maol-abhachd.
witty, *adj.* geur, beumnach, aigneach, bearradach, tuigseach, tulchuiseach, geur-chuiseach, macmeamnach, geurfhaclach ; sgaiteach.
wive, *v. a.* pòs, gabh bean.
wives, *s. pl.* of **wife,** mnathan.
wizard, *s.* baobh ; fiosaiche ; drùidh.
woe, *s.* an-aoibhneas ; truaighe.
woad, *s.* seòrsa guirmein.
woful, *adj.* truagh, dubhach, brònach, muladach, tùrsach, cumhach, doil-ghiosach, an-aoibhneach.
wolf, *s.* madadh-allaidh ; mac-tìre ; faol.
wolf-dog, *s.* faol-chù.
wolf's-bane, *s.* fuath-a-mhadaidh.
woman, *s.* bean ; boireannach.
woman-hater, *s.* fear-fuathachaidh bhan, bean-fhuathaiche.
womanish, *adj.* banail, màlda.
womankind, *s.* an cinneadh banail.
womanly, *adj.* banail ; mar mhnaoi.
womb, *s.* machlag, bolg ; brù.
womb, *v. a.* dùin ; gin an uaigneas.
women, *s. pl.* of **woman,** mnài.
wonder, *s.* iongantas, neònachas.
wonder, *v. n.* gabh iongantas.
wonderful, *adj.* iongantach.
wonderstruck, *adj.* fo amhluadh.
wondrous, *adj.* neònach.
wont, *v. n.* gnàthaich, cleachd.
wonted, *part. adj.* gnàthaichte ; coitcheann, cumanta, cleachdte.
woo, *v.* dèan suiridhe, dèan mire no beadradh ; iarr ; sir.
wood, *s.* coill, coille ; fiodh, fiùdhaidh ; iùdh, and iuch.
woodbine, *s.* eidheann-mu-chrann ; iadh-shlat ; deòthlag.
woodcock, *s.* coileach-coille, cromnan-duileag, creòthar.
wooded, *adj.* coillteach.
wooden, *adj.* fiodha, de fhiodh.
woodhole, *s.* toll-connaidh.
woodland, *s.* fearann-coilleach.
woodland, *adj.* coillteachail.
woodlark, *s.* an riabhag-choille.
woodlouse, *s.* reudan, mial-fhiodha.
woodman, woodsman, *s.* gìomanach ; eunadair, sealgair ; maor-coille.
woodmonger, *s.* fear-reic-fiodha, ceann-aiche-fiodha.
wood-nymph, *s.* annir-choille.
woodpecker, *s.* an lasair-choille, an snagan-daraich.

woodsare, *s.* smugaid-na-cuthaige.
wood-sorrel, *s.* biadh-an-eòin, biadh-eunain, glaodhran, feada-coille.
woody, *adj.* coillteach, doireach.
wooer, *s.* suiridheach, suiridhche.
woof, *s.* inneach, snath-cur.
wool, *s.* clòimh, olunn.
woollen, *adj.* olla, do chlòimh.
woolly, *adj.* ollach, clòimheach.
woolpack, *s.* poca cloimhe.
wool-stapler, *s.* ceannaiche-clòimhe.
word, *s.* facal, briathar ; gealladh.
word, *v.* faclaich, deachd.
wordy, *adj.* briathrach ; faclach.
wore, *pret.* of **to wear,** chaith.
work, *s.* obair, saothair, gnìomh, gnothach, cùis ; dragh.
work, *v.* oibrich, saoithrich.
worker, *s.* oibriche.
workhouse, *s.* tigh-nam-bochd.
working-day, *s.* latha-oibre.
workman, *s.* fear-cèairde ; fear-oibre.
workmanlike, *adj.* ealanta.
workmanship, *s.* obair, ealain.
workshop, *s.* bùth-oibre.
workwoman, *s.* ban-fhuaighealaich.
world, *s.* saoghal, domhan, an cruinne ; an cinne-daonna.
worldling, *s.* duine saoghalta.
worldly, *adj.* talmhaidh ; saoghaltach, saoghalta, sanntach, spìocach, teannchruaidh.
worm, *v.* snìomh, toinn troimhe.
worm, *s.* cnuimh, cnuimheag, durrag ; cliath-thogalach.
wormwood, *s.* burmaid ; burban.
wormy, *adj.* cnuimheach.
worn, *part. pass.* of **to wear,** caithte.
worril, *s.* feursanan.
worry, *v. a.* reub ; stròic, beubanaich.
worse, *adj.* na's miosa.
worship, *s.* onoir, spéis ; aoradh ; urram.
worship, *v.* dèan aoradh.
worshipful, *adj.* urramach.
worst, *adj.* as miosa.
worsted, *s.* abhras.
wort, *s.* brailis, seòrsa càil.
worth, *s.* fiach, luach, prìs ; luach-mhorachd, fiachalachd.
worth, *adj.* fiù, airidh, fiach.
worthiness, *s.* toillteannas ; òirdheirceas ; subhailc ; mathas.
worthless, *adj.* suarrach, gun fhiù.
worthlessness, *s.* neo-fhiùghalachd.
worthy, *adj.* fiachail, fiùghail airidh, cubhaidh, toillteannach, cliù-thoillteannach, òirdheirc.
wot, *v. n.* bi fiosrach.
would, *pret.* of **to will,** b' àill.
wound, *s.* lot, cneadh, creuchd, dochann, leòn, gearradh.

wound, *v. a.* leòn, creuchd, reub, lot, dochainn, cràidh, ciùrr.
wound, *pret.* of **to wind,** tachraiste.
wove, *pret. and part.* of **to weave,** dh' fhigh air fhige.
woven, *part.* fighte.
wrack, *s.* bristeadh, sgrios, call.
wrangle, *v. n.* connsaich, deasbairich ; cuir a mach, troid.
wrangle, *s.* connsachadh, trod.
wrangler, *s.* fear-connsachaidh.
wrap, *v. a.* paisg, trus ; fill, cuairsg.
wrapper, *s.* filleag, còmhdach.
wrath, *s.* fraoch ; corraich ; fearg.
wrathful, *adj.* fraochanta, feargach, corrach, cas, frithearra.
wreak, *v. a.* dèan dìoghaltas.
wreak, *s.* dìoghaltas.
wreakful, *adj.* dìoghaltach.
wreath, *s.* blàthfhleasg, coron, fleasg, figheachan ; clàideag, lùbag, dual, camag ; cuidhe.
wreathe, *v. a.* toinn, pleat, dual, cas, snìomh, cuairsg.
wreathy, *adj.* snìomhanach, cuairsgeach, leadanach, dualach.
wreck, *s.* longbhriseadh ; léirsgrios, bàthadh.
wreck, *v.* sgrios le ànradh cuain ; bris, mill ; bi air do bhriseadh.
wren, *s.* dreadhan donn.
wrench, *v. a.* toinn, snìomh ; spìon.
wrench, *s.* toinneamh ; snìomh, spìonadh, siachadh, sguchadh.
wrest, *v. a.* spìon ; toinn, toinneamh, snìomh ; éignich.
wrest, *s.* toinneamh ; éigin.
wrestle, *v. n.* gleachd, dèan strì.
wrestler, *s.* gleachadair.
wretch, *s.* truaghan ; crochaire.
wretched, *adj.* truagh, dòlum, bochd ; dona, mi-shealbhar, dòruinneach, truaillidh, crìon, suarrach ; dòlasach, doilghiosach, àmhgharach ; leibideach, tàireil.
wretchedness, *s.* truaighe, donas.
wriggle, *v.* frìth-oibrich ; siùd, seòg.
wriggling, *s.* seòganaich, crathail.
wright, *s.* saor-dubh ; tuairnear.
wring, *v.* fàisg ; toinn, snìomh ; sàraich, claoidh ; gabh a dh' aindeoin, dèan ainneart.
wrinkle, *s.* preas, preasadh, crupag, criopag, lorc, caisreag.
wrinkle, *v. n.* preas, preasagaich, crup, cas, liurc, sream.
wrinkled, *adj.* preasagach ; preasagaichte casach, liurcach.
wrist, *s.* caol an dùirn.
wristband, *s.* bann-dùirn.
writ, *s.* sgrìobtur ; reachd.
write, *v.* sgrìobh ; gràbhail, geàrr.

writer, s. sgrìobhadair, ùghdar.
writhe, v. toinn, toinneamh, snìomh, cas ; cam, siach, fiar.
writing, vbl. n. sgrìobhadh.
written, pass. part. of **to write,** sgrìobhte, air a sgrìobhadh.
wrizzled, adj. preasach, sreamach ; seacte, seargte.
wrong, s. eucoir, euceart, mearachd ; dochair, coire.
wrong, wrongly, adv. air àimhreit.
wrong, adj. eucorach, docharach, mearachdach, olc ; coireach, cearr, air àimhreit, neo - chothromach, neo-chubhaidh.

wrong, v. a. dèan eucoir air, dochannaich, bhalaich, ciùrr.
wrongful, adj. eucorach, euceartach, mearachdach, lochdach, ciontach, cronail, coireach.
wrongfully, adv. gu neo-dhligheach, gu cronail, gu mìcheart.
wrong-headed, adj. caoch-cheannach, gòrach, amaideach, baoghalta, eu-céillidh, mearachdach.
wrote, pret. part. of **to write,** sgrìobh.
wroth, adj. feargach, an corraich.
wrought, part. oibrichte ; dèante.
wrung, part. of **to wring,** fàisgte.
wry, adj. cam, fiar, claon, crotach.

X

xebeck, s. bìrlinn.
xenodochy, s. aoigheachd.
xerif, s. flath barbarianach.
xerocollyrium, s. sàbh-shùl.

xerophagy, s. biadh-tioram.
xiphoides, s. maothan.
xylography, s. gràbhaladh air fiodh.
xystus, s. rathad spaidsearachd.

Y

yacht, s. long toileachais.
yard, s. gàradh ; iodhlann, lios, cùirt, slat ; slat-thomhais, slat-shiùil.
yardward, s. tomhas-slaite.
yarn, s. snàth ; snàth-ollainn, abhras.
yarrow, s. eàrr-thalmhuinn.
yawl, s. geòla, bàta luinge.
yawn, s. meunan, mianan.
yawn, v. n. dèan meunanaich.
yawning, s. meunanaich.
yawning, adj. meunanach, cadaltach.
ycleped, part. ainmichte.
ye, nominative plur. of **thou,** sibhse.
yea, adv. 's eadh ; air chinnt.
yean, v. n. beir uan.
yeanling, s. uan, uanan, uainein.
year, s. bliadhna.
yearling, s. bliadhnach.
yearly, adv. gach bliadhna.
yearn, v. n. gabh truas, mothaich truas ; fàisg, léir, cràidh, togair.
yearning, s. truacantas, bàigh, togradh.
yelk, yolk, s. buidheagan uighe.
yell, s. sgrèach, sgriàch, sgal, glaodh, sgairt, ulfhart, ràn, burral.
yell, v. n. sgrèach, sgriàch, sgal, glaodh, sgairt, ulfhart, ràn, burral.
yellow, adj. buidhe.
yellow, s. dath-buidhe.
yellow-hammer, s. buidheag-bhuachair.
yellowish, adj. a lethchar buidhe.
yellowness, s. buidhead.

yelp, s. tathunn, tathunnaich, comhartaich, deithleann.
yelp, v. n. dèan tathunn, tathunnaich.
yeoman, s. tuathanach, fear gabhalach ; leth dhuin'-uasal.
yeomanry, s. tuath-mheasail.
yerk, s. sgailleag, frithbhuille, gleog, gleadhar ; sitheadh.
yerk, v. buail gu grad, frithbhuail ; thoir sitheadh, sgiùrs, gabh air ; thoir grad leum.
yes, adv. There is no single word corresponding to the English " yes." The verb of the question suggests the proper word to be used in replying : a bheil e fuar ? is it cold ?—thà = it is ; chan éil = it is not. An robh e fliuch ? was it wet ?—bhà = it was : cha robh = it was not.
yest, yeast, s. beirm, cop.
yesterday, adv. an dé.
yesternight, adv. an raoir.
yesty, yeasty, adj. beirmeach.
yet, conj. gidheadh, fòs, fathast.
yet, adv. fathast, fhathast ; osbarr, tuilleadh fòs ; as yet, gus a nise.
yew, s. iubhar.
yewen, adj. iubhair.
yield, v. géill ; strìoc ; lub, feac ; thoir a mach ; thoir suas, aontaich.
yoke, s. cuing, ceangal, slàbhraidh ; càraid, dithis ; daorsa, tràilleachd.

yoke, *v. a.* beartaich ; cuir cuing (air —)
cuir fodha (an t-each) ; sàraich,
claoidh, ceannsuich, tràillich, cìosnaich.
yoke-fellow, *s.* comh-oibriche.
yon, yonder, *adv.* ud, an sud.
yore, *adv.* o shean, o chian.
you, *pron. oblique case* of ye, thu, thusa,
tu ; sibh, sibhse.
young, *adj.* òg ; aineolach, lag.
young, *s.* òigridh ; àl-òg.
younger, *adj.* na's òige.
youngest, *adj.* as òige.
youngish, *adj.* a lethchar òg.

youngling, *s.* ogan, maotharan.
youngster, younker, *s.* òganach.
your, *pron. sing.* do.
your, *pron. pl.* bhur.
yours, *pron. sing.* leat, leatsa.
yours, *pron. pl.* leibh, leibhse.
yourself, *pron.* thu-féin.
yourselves, *pron.* sibh-féin.
youth, *s.* oigear ; òige, pàiste, òigeachd ;
òigridh, òganaich.
youthful, *adj.* òg, ògail, òigeil.
youthly, youthy, *adj.* òg, ògail.
Yule, *s.* An Nollaig.

Z

zeal, *s.* mìann, eud ; dian-dheòthas ;
dealas, deagh-dhùrachd.
zealot, *s.* fear-leanmhainn, fear-dealaidh,
duine eudmhor.
zealous, *adj.* eudmhor, miannmhor,
dealasach, deòthasach, dùrachdach,
dian ; teth, bras, togarrach.
zealousness, *s.* dealasachd, dùrachd.
zebra, *s.* an asal-stìallach.
zenana, *s.* seòmar nam mnathan (an
tigh Innseanach).
zenith, *s.* am bad dhe'n adhar dìreach
os cionn neach, fior-mhullach (soirbheachaidh, no sonais), an inbhe as àirde.
zephyr, zephyrus, *s.* tlàthghaoth ; seàmh-
ghaoth ; gaoth an iar.
zest, *s.* blas ; blas taitneach.

zest, *v. a.* dèan blasda, cuir cridhe
('s an obair), bi sunntach.
zigzag, *adj.* carach ; lùbach, cam, null
's a nall.
zinc, *s.* seòrsa miotailt.
zodiac, *s.* grianchrios.
zodiacal, *adj.* grianchriosach.
zone, *s.* crios ; cearcall, cuairt ; bann ;
crios mu'n talamh.
zoographer, *s.* fear-sgrìobhaidh mu thim-
choll ainmhidhean.
zoography, *s.* cunntas mu thimchioll
cumadh agus nàduir ainmhidhean.
zoology, *s.* cunntas mu ainmhidhibh.
zoophyte, *s.* beòluibh.
zootomist, *s.* cairbh-sgathaich.
zootomy, *s.* cairbh-sgathadh.